GABRIEL MANTZ

YEARBOOK OF EUROPEAN FOOTBALL

2019-2020

A selection of our other statistical books, available from the address below or via www.soccer-books.co.uk:

The Complete European Football Championships 1958-2000 (ISBN 9781862233430)
The Complete European Football Championships 2002-2016 (ISBN 9781862233423)
The Complete World Cup 1930-1974 (ISBN 9781862232624) • The Complete World Cup 1976-1986 (ISBN 9781862232860)
The Complete World Cup 1988-1998 (ISBN 9781862231528) • The Complete World Cup 2000-2006 (ISBN 9781862231542)
The Complete World Cup 2007-2010 (ISBN 9781862232112) • The Complete World Cup 2011-2014 (ISBN 9781862233034)
The Complete World Cup 2015-2018 (ISBN 9781862233874)
The Complete Results & Line-ups of the Copa America 1916-2019 (ISBN 9781862234154)
The Africa Cup of Nations 1957-2019 (ISBN 9781862234123)
The Complete Results & Line-ups of the UEFA Cup 1971-1991 (ISBN 9781862231092)
The Complete Results & Line-ups of the UEFA Cup 1991-2004 (ISBN 9781862231153)
The Complete Results & Line-ups of the UEFA Cup 2004-2009 (ISBN 9781862231870)
The Complete Results & Line-ups of the UEFA Europa League 2009-2012 (ISBN 9781862232471)
The Complete Results & Line-ups of the UEFA Europa League 2012-2015 (ISBN 9781862233133)
The Complete Results & Line-ups of the UEFA Europa League 2015-2018 (ISBN 9781862233867)
The Complete Results & Line-ups of the European Fairs Cup 1955-1971 (ISBN 9781862230859)
The Complete Results & Line-ups of the European Cup 1955-1991 (ISBN 9781862230897)
The Complete Results & Line-ups of the European Champions League 1991-2004 (ISBN 9781862231146)
The Complete Results & Line-ups of the European Champions League 2004-2009 (ISBN 9781862231863)
The Complete Results & Line-ups of the UEFA Champions League 2009-2012 (ISBN 9781862232488)
The Complete Results & Line-ups of the UEFA Champions League 2012-2015 (ISBN 9781862233126)
The Complete Results & Line-ups of the UEFA Champions League 2015-2018 (ISBN 9781862233850)
The Complete Results & Line-ups of the European Cup-Winners' Cup 1960-1999 (ISBN 9781862230873)
The Mitropa Cup – A Statistical Record 1927-1992 (ISBN 9781862233201)
The Complete Results & Line-ups of the Copa Libertadores 1960-1990 (ISBN 9781862232327)
The Complete Results & Line-ups of the Copa Libertadores 1991-2005 (ISBN 9781862232334)
The Complete Results & Line-ups of the Copa Libertadores 2006-2011 (ISBN 9781862232297)
The Complete Results & Line-ups of the Copa Libertadores 2012-2015 (ISBN 9781862233225)
The FIFA Women's World Cup 1991-2019 – A Statistical Record (ISBN 9781862234116)
The Complete Women's Euro Finals Tournaments 1984-2017 (ISBN 9781862233935)
The England Women's FC 1972-2018 The Lionesses – A Statistical Record (ISBN 9781862233911)
A Decade of English League & Cup Football 2008-2018 (ISBN 9781862233904)
English Football League & FA Premier League Tables 1888-2019 (ISBN 9781862234031)
Scottish Football Tables 1890-2019 (ISBN 9781862234055)
Scottish F.A. Cup 1873-2019 – The Complete Results (ISBN 9781862234185)
Welsh Football Tables 1893-2019 (ISBN 9781862234048) • Welsh Cup 1877-2019 – The Complete Results (ISBN 9781862234161)
Non-League Football Tables 1889-2019 (ISBN 9781862234024) • The National League 1979-2019 (ISBN 9781862234017)
Non-League Football Tables of South West England 1889-2015 (ISBN 9781862233249)
Non-League Football Tables of North West England 1889-2016 (ISBN 9781862233409)
Non-League Football Tables of South East England 1894-2017 (ISBN 9781862233676)
Non-League Football Tables of North East England 1889-2018 (ISBN 9781862233881)
Non-League Football Tables of the West Midlands of England 1889-2019 (ISBN 9781862234147)
South American Football International Line-Ups & Statistics Volume 1 (ISBN 9781862232877)
South American Football International Line-Ups & Statistics Volume 2 (ISBN 9781862232884)
South American Football International Line-Ups & Statistics Volume 3 (ISBN 9781862232891)
European Football International Line-Ups & Statistics Volume 1 (ISBN 9781862233294)
European Football International Line-Ups & Statistics Volume 2 (ISBN 9781862233300)
European Football International Line-Ups & Statistics Volume 3 (ISBN 9781862233386)
European Football International Line-Ups & Statistics Volume 4 (ISBN 9781862233485)
European Football International Line-Ups & Statistics Volume 5 (ISBN 9781862233492)
European Football International Line-Ups & Statistics Volume 6 (ISBN 9781862233690)
European Football International Line-Ups & Statistics Volume 7 (ISBN 9781862233713)
European Football International Line-Ups & Statistics Volume 8 (ISBN 9781862233843)
European Football International Line-Ups & Statistics Volume 9 (ISBN 9781862233973)

British Library Cataloguing in Publication Data
A catalogue record for this book is available from the British Library

ISBN 978-1-86223-413-0

Copyright © 2019, SOCCER BOOKS LIMITED (01472 696226)
72 St. Peter's Avenue, Cleethorpes, N.E. Lincolnshire, DN35 8HU, England

Web site www.soccer-books.co.uk • e-mail info@soccer-books.co.uk

All rights are reserved. No part of this publication may be reproduced, stored in a retrieval system or transmitted, in any form or by any means, electronic, mechanical, photocopying, recording, or otherwise, without the prior written permission of Soccer Books Limited.

Printed in the UK by Short Run Press.

Dear Readers

The 2018/2019 football season in Europe was dominated by the UEFA Nations League, a new international competition which commenced during the autumn of 2018, followed by the start of the qualification process for the 2020 UEFA European Championship.

All 55 UEFA members were involved in the 2018/2019 inaugural season of the UEFA Nations League, the national teams being seeded into four Leagues, A to D. Each of these Leagues were then split into four Groups containing either 3 or 4 teams. It is important to note that results in the league phase of this competition were used to seed teams for the qualifying group stage of UEFA Euro 2020 and will also be used to award berths in the play-offs to decide four of the twenty-four final tournament slots. Teams also competed for promotion and relegation to a higher or lower league. As with all tournaments, there were some notable surprises in these Nations League games. League A – Group 1: Netherlands (who had failed to qualify for both the 2018 World Cup and Euro 2016) won the group ahead of World Champions France and Germany who failed to win a game, losing both of their away matches. Group 2: Switzerland comprehensively defeated Belgium 5-2 in the home tie to secure top place in the group. Group 4: Croatia – runners-up of the last World Cup – lost 0-6 in Spain, but England finished as group winners after defeating Spain 3-2 in Sevilla (despite losing 2-1 in their home tie at Wembley).
League B – the results were generally as expected, but Bosnia and Herzegovina's group win ahead of Austria surprised many, as did the fact that a usually obdurate Northern Ireland team lost all four of their matches. League C – Cyprus obtained five points in Group 3 including a 2-1 victory over Slovenia who finished bottom of the group. League D – Andorra obtained four points (all their home matches ended draws as did the game in Latvia) and Luxembourg surprisingly won promotion to League C after winning 10 points with performances including a 4-0 victory over Moldova and two victories over San Marino. Also notable was two wins for Gibraltar in Group 4 against Liechtenstein at home and Armenia away.

The winners of the four Groups in League A, England, Netherlands, Portugal and Switzerland played the Final Tournament of the new competition in June 2019. All the games were played in Portugal and the host team duly won their second title after the Euro 2016, defeating Switzerland 3-1 in the semi-finals and the Netherlands 1-0 in the final game played at Estádio do Dragão in Porto.

Initially, it was planned that four teams (the last team in each group: Germany, Croatia, Poland and Iceland) should be relegated from League A to League B. However, to maintain the level of League A and also to avoid the absence of some famous names, UEFA decided to change their previous relegations and instead increased all groups to four teams instead of three for the next edition to be played in 2020/2021. This rule was also applied for Leagues B and C and, as a result, there will only be 7 teams in League D for the next edition.

Despite some scepticism before the start of the new competition, the UEFA Nations League proved to be a success, especially given that it offers serious competitive matches as an alternative to friendlies with no great interest or excitement for players and spectators alike. On the other hand, the "small nations" can now potentially manage – through playing opponents of similar stature – to earn results which were just not possible in the past against stronger teams.

Spring 2019 was dominated by the qualifying matches for the 2020 UEFA European Championship. As noted above, this competition is linked with the 2018–19 edition of the UEFA Nations League which provides countries a secondary route to qualify for the finals tournament. The 55 participating teams were drawn into 10 groups containing either five or six teams and Kosovo entered the competition for the first time. Ukraine, England, Spain, Poland, the Republic of Ireland, Italy and Turkey (with a surprising 2-0 win over France at home) started the qualifiers strongly and there were also notable wins for Hungary over Croatia (2-1) and Wales (1-0), both on home ground. Germany obtained a big win in Amsterdam to get some revenge for the defeat suffered there in the Nations League. On the other hand, Portugal, the title holders, didn't have the strongest of starts with two draws at home against Ukraine and Serbia. The decisive qualifying group matches are played during the autumn of 2019 and the play-offs will then take place in March 2020.

Some notes about competitions at club level. In the summer of 2018, two Spanish teams played the final of the European Super Cup (Atletico Madrid defeating fierce rivals Real Madrid 4-2 in Tallinn). By the end of the 2018-2019 season, the strength of English football was on show, as all four finalists of the two European competitions came from England. In Bakı, Azerbaijan, Chelsea FC defeated their London rivals Arsenal FC in the UEFA Europa League final by a comprehensive 4-1 scoreline to secure the club's second title in this competition.
The UEFA Champions League final, played in the Metropolitano Stadium of Madrid, brought a deserved 2-0 victory of Liverpool FC against another London team, Tottenham Hotspur FC. This marked the sixth title for the Anfield club in the most prestigious European club competition and the first for German manager Jürgen Klopp who had lost two previous finals with Borussia Dortmund and Liverpool FC.

This second edition of the Yearbook of European Football contains complete statistics for the national championships of all European countries with league tables and national cup competition finals. Player appearances (including substitute appearances) and goals scored are presented for all top division clubs from Europe with the unfortunate exception of those in Kosovo where it has only proved possible to obtain club squads. You will also find detailed National Cup matches for each European country and there are also complete statistics for national teams and the international players for each country and their clubs.

Great thanks to Mr. Dirk Karsdorp, who once again provided full line-ups and complete statistics for both of the major European Club competitions during 2018/2019.

Please enjoy the read!

The Author

FIFA COUNTRY CODES

EUROPE

ALB	Albania
AND	Andorra
ARM	Armenia
AUT	Austria
AZE	Azerbaijan
BLR	Belarus
BEL	Belgium
BIH	Bosnia-Herzegovina
BUL	Bulgaria
CRO	Croatia
CYP	Cyprus
CZE	Czech Republic
DEN	Denmark
ENG	England
EST	Estonia
FRO	Faroe Islands
FIN	Finland
FRA	France
GEO	Georgia
GER	Germany
GIB	Gibraltar
GRE	Greece
HUN	Hungary
ISL	Iceland
ISR	Israel
ITA	Italy
KAZ	Kazakhstan
KVX	Kosovo
LVA	Latvia
LIE	Liechtenstein
LTU	Lithuania
LUX	Luxembourg
MKD	Macedonia
MLT	Malta
MDA	Moldova
MNE	Montenegro
NED	Netherlands
NIR	Northern Ireland
NOR	Norway
POL	Poland
POR	Portugal
IRL	Republic of Ireland
ROU	Romania
RUS	Russia
SMR	San Marino
SCO	Scotland
SRB	Serbia
SVK	Slovakia
SVN	Slovenia
ESP	Spain
SWE	Sweden
SUI	Switzerland
TUR	Turkey
UKR	Ukraine
WAL	Wales

Former countries:

TCH	Czechoslovakia
YUG	Yugoslavia

ASIA

AFG	Afghanistan
AUS	Australia
BHR	Bahrain
BAN	Bangladesh
CHN	China P.R.
TPE	Chinese Taipei
IDN	Indonesia
IRN	Iran
IRQ	Iraq
JPN	Japan
JOR	Jordan
PRK	Korea D.P.R.
KOR	Korea Republic
KGZ	Kyrgyzstan
LIB	Lebanon
OMA	Oman
PAL	Palestine
PHI	Philippines
QAT	Qatar
KSA	Saudi Arabia
TJK	Tajikistan
THA	Thailand
TLS	Timor-Leste
TKM	Turkmenistan
UAE	United Arab Emirates
UZB	Uzbekistan

OCEANIA

NZL	New Zealand

OTHER ABBREVIATIONS

DOB Date of birth
M Matches played
G Goals
(F) International friendly matches
(ECQ) 2020 Euro Championship Qualifiers
(UNL) 2018-2019 UEFA Nations League

AFRICA

ALG	Algeria
ANG	Angola
BEN	Benin
BOT	Botswana
BFA	Burkina Faso
BDI	Burundi
CMR	Cameroon
CPV	Cape Verde Islands
CTA	Central African Republic
CHA	Chad
COM	Comoros Islands
CGO	Congo
COD	D.R. Congo
EGY	Egypt
EQG	Equatorial Guinea
ERI	Eritrea
ETH	Ethiopia
GAB	Gabon
GAM	Gambia
GHA	Ghana
GUI	Guinea
GNB	Guinea-Bissau
CIV	Ivory Coast
KEN	Kenya
LBR	Liberia
LBY	Libya
MAD	Madagascar
MWI	Malawi
MLI	Mali
MTN	Mauritania
MRI	Mauritius
MAR	Morocco
MOZ	Mozambique
NAM	Namibia
NIG	Niger
NGA	Nigeria
RWA	Rwanda
STP	São Tome e Principe
SEN	Senegal
SLE	Sierra Leone
RSA	South Africa
TAN	Tanzania
TOG	Togo
TUN	Tunisia
UGA	Uganda
ZAM	Zambia
ZIM	Zimbabwe

NORTH AND CENTRAL AMERICA

BER	Bermuda
CAN	Canada
CRC	Costa Rica
CUB	Cuba
CUW	Curaçao
DOM	Dominican Republic
SLV	El Salvador
GYF	French Guiana
GRE	Grenada
GLP	Guadeloupe
GUA	Guatemala
HAI	Haiti
HON	Honduras
JAM	Jamaica
MTQ	Martinique
MEX	Mexico
MSR	Montserrat
NCA	Nicaragua
PAN	Panama
SUR	Suriname
TRI	Trinidad and Tobago
USA	United States

SOUTH AMERICA

ARG	Argentina
BOL	Bolivia
BRA	Brazil
CHI	Chile
COL	Colombia
ECU	Ecuador
PAR	Paraguay
PER	Peru
URU	Uruguay
VEN	Venezuela

SUMMARY

COMPETITIONS FOR NATIONAL TEAMS

EUROPEAN CLUB COMPETITIONS

NATIONAL ASSOCIATIONS

COMPETITIONS FOR NATIONAL TEAMS

2018 - 2019 UEFA NATIONS LEAGUE

The 55 UEFA national teams would be divided into the four "Leagues": 12 teams in League A, 12 teams in League B, 15 teams in League C, and 16 teams in League D, according to their UEFA national team coefficients after the conclusion of the 2018 FIFA World Cup qualifiers, with the highest-ranked teams playing in League A. The seeding pots were as follows:

LEAGUE A	
Germany	40,747
Portugal	38,655
Belgium	38,123
Spain	37,311
France	36,617
England	36,231
Switzerland	34,986
Italy	34,426
Poland	32,982
Iceland	31,155
Croatia	31,139
Netherlands	29,866

LEAGUE B	
Austria	29,418
Wales	29,269
Russia	29,258
Slovakia	28,555
Sweden	28,487
Ukraine	28,286
Republic of Ireland	28,249
Bosnia and Herzegovina	28,200
Northern Ireland	27,127
Denmark	27,052
Czech Republic	27,028
Turkey	26,538

LEAGUE C	
Hungary	26,486
Romania	26,057
Scotland	25,662
Slovenia	25,148
Greece	24,931
Serbia	24,847
Albania	24,430
Norway	24,208
Montenegro	23,912
Israel	22,792
Bulgaria	22,091
Finland	20,501
Cyprus	19,491
Estonia	19,441
Lithuania	18,101

LEAGUE D	
Azerbaijan	17,761
Macedonia	17,071
Belarus	16,868
Georgia	16,523
Armenia	15,846
Latvia	15,821
Faroe Islands	15,490
Luxembourg	14,231
Kazakhstan	13,431
Moldova	13,130
Liechtenstein	10,950
Malta	10,870
Andorra	10,240
Kosovo	9,950
San Marino	8,190
Gibraltar	7,550

The draw for the league phase took place at the SwissTech Convention Center in Lausanne (Switzerland) on 24.01.2018.

LEAGUE A

GROUP 1

Results

06.09.2018	München	Germany - France	0-0
09.09.2018	Paris	France - Netherlands	2-1(1-0)
13.10.2018	Amsterdam	Netherlands - Germany	3-0(1-0)
16.10.2018	Paris	France - Germany	2-1(0-1)
16.11.2018	Rotterdam	Netherlands - France	2-0(1-0)
19.11.2018	Gelsenkirchen	Germany - Netherlands	2-2(2-0)

Final Standings

1.	**Netherlands**	4	2	1	1	8	-	4	7
2.	France	4	2	1	1	4	-	4	7
3.	Germany	4	0	2	2	3	-	7	2

Netherlands qualified for the Final Tournament

GROUP 2

Results

08.09.2018	St. Gallen	Switzerland - Iceland	6-0(2-0)
11.09.2018	Reykjavík	Iceland - Belgium	0-3(0-2)
12.10.2018	Bruxelles	Belgium - Switzerland	2-1(0-0)
15.10.2018	Reykjavík	Iceland - Switzerland	1-2(0-0)
15.11.2018	Bruxelles	Belgium - Iceland	2-0(0-0)
18.11.2018	Luzern	Switzerland - Belgium	5-2(3-2)

Final Standings

1.	**Switzerland**	4	3	0	1	14	-	5	9
2.	Belgium	4	3	0	1	9	-	6	9
3.	Iceland	4	0	0	4	1	-	13	0

Switzerland qualified for the Final Tournament

GROUP 3

Results

07.09.2018	Bologna	Italy - Poland	1-1(0-1)
10.09.2018	Lisboa	Portugal - Italy	1-0(0-0)
11.10.2018	Chorzów	Poland - Portugal	2-3(1-2)
14.10.2018	Chorzów	Poland - Italy	0-1(0-0)
17.11.2018	Milano	Italy - Portugal	0-0
20.11.2018	Guimarães	Portugal - Poland	1-1(1-0)

Final Standings

1.	**Portugal**	4	2	2	0	5	-	3	8
2.	Italy	4	1	2	1	2	-	2	5
3.	Poland	4	0	2	2	4	-	6	2

Portugal qualified for the Final Tournament

GROUP 4

Results

08.09.2018	London	England - Spain	1-2(1-2)
11.09.2018	Elche	Spain - Croatia	6-0(3-0)
12.10.2018	Rijeka	Croatia - England	0-0
15.10.2018	Sevilla	Spain - England	2-3(0-3)
15.11.2018	Zagreb	Croatia - Spain	3-2(0-0)
18.11.2018	London	England - Croatia	2-1(0-0)

Final Standings

1.	**England**	4	2	1	1	6	-	5	7
2.	Spain	4	2	0	2	12	-	7	6
3.	Croatia	4	1	1	2	4	-	10	4

England qualified for the Final Tournament

FINAL TOURNAMENT

SEMI-FINALS

05.06.2019	Porto	Portugal - Switzerland	3-1(1-0)
06.06.2019	Guimarães	Netherlands - England	3-1(0-1,1-1)

THIRD PLACE PLAY-OFF

09.06.2019	Guimarães	Switzerland - England	0-0; 5-6 on penalties

FINAL

09.06.2019; Estádio do Dragão, Porto; Referee: Alberto Undiano Mallenco (Spain); Attendance: 43,199

PORTUGAL - NETHERLANDS 1-0(0-0)

POR: Rui Patrício, Nélson Semedo, José Fonte, Raphaël Guerreiro, Danilo Pereira, Rúben Dias, William Carvalho (90+3.Rúben Neves), Bruno Fernandes (81.João Moutinho), Bernardo Silva, Gonçalo Guedes (75.Rafa Silva), Cristiano Ronaldo (Cap). Trainer: Fernando Manuel Fernandes da Costa Santos.

NED: Jacobus Antonius Peter Cillessen, Denzel Dumfries, Virgil van Dijk (Cap), Matthijs de Ligt, Daley Blind, Marten Elco de Roon (81.Luuk de Jong), Frenkie de Jong, Georginio Gregion Emile Wijnaldum, Ryan Guno Babel (46.Quincy Anton Promes), Memphis Depay, Steven Charles Bergwijn (60.Donny van de Beek). Trainer: Ronald Koeman.

Goal: 1-0 Gonçalo Guedes (60).

LEAGUE B

GROUP 1

Results

06.09.2018	Uh. Hradiště	Czech Republic - Ukraine	1-2(1-1)
09.09.2018	Lviv	Ukraine - Slovakia	1-0(0-0)
13.10.2018	Trnava	Slovakia - Czech Republic	1-2(0-0)
16.10.2018	Kharkiv	Ukraine - Czech Republic	1-0(1-0)
16.11.2018	Trnava	Slovakia - Ukraine	4-1(2-0)
19.11.2018	Praha	Czech Republic - Slovakia	1-0(1-0)

Final Standings

1.	**Ukraine**	4	3	0	1	5	-	5	9
2.	Czech Repub.	4	2	0	2	4	-	4	6
3.	Slovakia	4	1	0	3	5	-	5	3

Ukraine promoted to League A

GROUP 2

Results

07.09.2018	Trabzon	Turkey - Russia	1-2(1-1)
10.09.2018	Stockholm	Sweden - Turkey	2-3(1-0)
11.10.2018	Kaliningrad	Russia - Sweden	0-0
14.10.2018	Sochi	Russia - Turkey	2-0(1-0)
17.11.2018	Konya	Turkey - Sweden	0-1(0-0)
20.11.2018	Stockholm	Sweden - Russia	2-0(1-0)

Final Standings

1.	**Sweden**	4	2	1	1	5	-	3	7
2.	Russia	4	2	1	1	4	-	3	7
3.	Turkey	4	1	0	3	4	-	7	3

Sweden promoted to League A

GROUP 3

Results

08.09.2018	Belfast	N. Ireland - Bosnia and Herzeg.	1-2(0-1)
11.09.2018	Zenica	Bosnia and Herzeg. - Austria	1-0(0-0)
12.10.2018	Wien	Austria - Northern Ireland	1-0(0-0)
15.10.2018	Sarajevo	Bosnia and Herzeg. - N. Ireland	2-0(1-0)
15.11.2018	Wien	Austria – Bosnia and Herzeg.	0-0
18.11.2018	Belfast	Northern Ireland - Austria	1-2(0-0)

Final Standings

1.	**Bosnia-Herz.**	4	3	1	0	5	-	1	10
2.	Austria	4	2	1	1	3	-	2	7
3.	Nor. Ireland	4	0	0	4	2	-	7	0

Bosnia and Herzegovina promoted to League A

GROUP 4

Results

06.09.2018	Cardiff	Wales - Republic of Ireland	4-1(3-0)
09.09.2018	Aarhus	Denmark - Wales	2-0(1-0)
13.10.2018	Dublin	Rep. of Ireland - Denmark	0-0
16.10.2018	Dublin	Republic of Ireland - Wales	0-1(0-0)
16.11.2018	Cardiff	Wales - Denmark	1-2(0-1)
19.11.2018	Aarhus	Denmark - Rep. of Ireland	0-0

Final Standings

1.	**Denmark**	4	2	2	0	4	-	1	8
2.	Wales	4	2	0	2	6	-	5	6
3.	R. of Ireland	4	0	2	2	1	-	5	2

Denmark promoted to League A

LEAGUE C

GROUP 1

Results

07.09.2018	Elbasan	Albania - Israel	1-0(0-0)
10.09.2018	Glasgow	Scotland - Albania	2-0(0-0)
11.10.2018	Haifa	Israel - Scotland	2-1(0-1)
14.10.2018	Beer Sheba	Israel - Albania	2-0(1-0)
17.11.2018	Shkodër	Albania - Scotland	0-4(0-2)
20.11.2018	Glasgow	Scotland - Israel	3-2(2-1)

Final Standings

1.	**Scotland**	4	3	0	1	10	-	4	9
2.	**Israel**	4	2	0	2	6	-	5	6
3.	Albania	4	1	0	3	1	-	8	3

Scotland and Israel promoted to League B

GROUP 2

Results

08.09.2018	Tampere	Finland - Hungary	1-0(1-0)
08.09.2018	Tallinn	Estonia - Greece	0-1(0-1)
11.09.2018	Turku	Finland - Estonia	1-0(1-0)
11.09.2018	Budapest	Hungary - Greece	2-1(2-1)
12.10.2018	Tallinn	Estonia - Finland	0-1(0-0)
12.10.2018	Athína	Greece - Hungary	1-0(0-0)
15.10.2018	Tallinn	Estonia - Hungary	3-3(1-1)
15.10.2018	Tampere	Finland - Greece	2-0(0-0)
15.11.2018	Budapest	Hungary - Estonia	2-0(1-0)
15.11.2018	Athína	Greece - Finland	1-0(1-0)
18.11.2018	Budapest	Greece - Estonia	0-1(0-1)
18.11.2018	Athína	Hungary - Finland	2-0(2-0)

Final Standings

1.	**Finland**	6	4	0	2	5	-	3	12
2.	**Hungary**	6	3	1	2	9	-	6	10
3.	Greece	6	3	0	3	4	-	5	9
4.	Estonia	6	1	1	4	4	-	8	4

Finland and Hungary promoted to League B

GROUP 3

Results

06.09.2018	Ljubljana	Slovenia - Bulgaria	1-2(1-1)
06.09.2018	Oslo	Norway - Cyprus	2-0(2-0)
09.09.2018	Sofia	Bulgaria - Norway	1-0(0-0)
09.09.2018	Nicosia	Cyprus - Slovenia	2-1(0-0)
13.10.2018	Oslo	Norway - Slovenia	1-0(1-0)
13.10.2018	Sofia	Bulgaria - Cyprus	2-1(0-1)
16.10.2018	Oslo	Norway - Bulgaria	1-0(1-0)
16.10.2018	Ljubljana	Slovenia - Cyprus	1-1(0-1)
16.11.2018	Nicosia	Cyprus - Bulgaria	1-1(1-0)
16.11.2018	Ljubljana	Slovenia - Norway	1-1(1-0)
19.11.2018	Sofia	Bulgaria - Slovenia	1-1(0-0)
19.11.2018	Nicosia	Cyprus - Norway	0-2(0-1)

Final Standings

1.	**Norway**	6	4	1	1	7	-	2	13
2.	**Bulgaria**	6	3	2	1	7	-	5	11
3.	Cyprus	6	1	2	3	5	-	9	5
4.	Slovenia	6	0	3	3	5	-	8	3

Norway and Bulgaria promoted to League B

GROUP 4

Results

07.09.2018	Vilnius	Lithuania - Serbia	0-1(0-1)
07.09.2018	Ploieşti	Romania - Montenegro	0-0
10.09.2018	Podgorica	Montenegro - Lithuania	2-0(2-0)
10.09.2018	Beograd	Serbia - Romania	2-2(1-0)
11.10.2018	Vilnius	Lithuania - Romania	1-2(0-1)
11.10.2018	Podgorica	Montenegro - Serbia	0-2(0-1)
14.10.2018	Bucureşti	Romania - Serbia	0-0
14.10.2018	Vilnius	Lithuania - Montenegro	1-4(0-3)
17.11.2018	Beograd	Serbia - Montenegro	2-1(2-0)
17.11.2018	Ploieşti	Romania - Lithuania	3-0(1-0)
20.11.2018	Beograd	Serbia - Lithuania	4-1(0-0)
20.11.2018	Podgorica	Montenegro - Romania	0-1(0-1)

Final Standings

1.	**Serbia**	6	4	2	0	11	-	4	14
2.	**Romania**	6	3	3	0	8	-	3	12
3.	Montenegro	6	2	1	3	7	-	6	7
4.	Lithuania	6	0	0	6	3	-	16	0

Serbia and Romania promoted to League B

LEAGUE D

GROUP 1

Results

06.09.2018	Astana	Kazakhstan - Georgia	0-2(0-0)
06.09.2018	Rīga	Latvia - Andorra	0-0
09.09.2018	Tbilisi	Georgia - Latvia	1-0(0-0)
10.09.2018	Andorra la V.	Andorra - Kazakhstan	1-1(0-0)
13.10.2018	Tbilisi	Georgia - Andorra	3-0(1-0)
13.10.2018	Rīga	Latvia - Kazakhstan	1-1(1-1)
16.10.2018	Astana	Kazakhstan - Andorra	4-0(2-0)
16.10.2018	Rīga	Latvia - Georgia	0-3(0-2)
15.11.2018	Astana	Kazakhstan - Latvia	1-1(1-0)
15.11.2018	Andorra la V.	Andorra - Georgia	1-1(0-1)
19.11.2018	Tbilisi	Georgia - Kazakhstan	2-1(0-0)
19.11.2018	Andorra la V.	Andorra - Latvia	0-0

Final Standings

1.	**Georgia**	6	5	1	0	12	-	2	16
2.	**Kazakhstan**	6	1	3	2	8	-	7	6
3.	Latvia	6	0	4	2	2	-	6	4
4.	Andorra	6	0	4	2	2	-	9	4

Georgia and Kazakhstan promoted to League C

GROUP 2

Results

08.09.2018	Minsk	Belarus - San Marino	5-0(2-0)
08.09.2018	Lëtzebuerg	Luxembourg - Moldova	4-0(1-0)
11.09.2018	Chişinău	Moldova - Belarus	0-0
11.09.2018	Serravalle	San Marino - Luxembourg	0-3(0-2)
12.10.2018	Minsk	Belarus - Luxembourg	1-0(1-0)
12.10.2018	Chişinău	Moldova - San Marino	2-0(1-0)
15.10.2018	Minsk	Belarus - Moldova	0-0
15.10.2018	Lëtzebuerg	Luxembourg - San Marino	3-0(1-0)
15.11.2018	Lëtzebuerg	Luxembourg - Belarus	0-2(0-1)
15.11.2018	Serravalle	San Marino - Moldova	0-1(0-0)
18.11.2018	Serravalle	San Marino - Belarus	0-2(0-1)
18.11.2018	Chişinău	Moldova - Luxembourg	1-1(0-0)

Final Standings

1.	**Belarus**	6	4	2	0	10	-	0	14
2.	**Luxembourg**	6	3	1	2	11	-	4	10
3.	Moldova	6	2	3	1	4	-	5	9
4.	San Marino	6	0	0	6	0	-	16	0

Belarus, Luxembourg and Moldova promoted to League C

GROUP 3

Results

07.09.2018	Bakı	Azerbaijan - Kosovo	0-0
07.09.2018	Tórshavn	Faroe Islands - Malta	3-1(2-1)
10.09.2018	Attard	Malta - Azerbaijan	1-1(1-1)
10.09.2018	Prishtinë	Kosovo - Faroe Islands	2-0(0-0)
11.10.2018	Tórshavn	Faroe Islands - Azerbaijan	0-3(0-1)
11.10.2018	Prishtinë	Kosovo - Malta	3-1(1-0)
14.10.2018	Bakı	Azerbaijan - Malta	1-1(0-1)
14.10.2018	Tórshavn	Faroe Islands - Kosovo	1-1(0-1)
17.11.2018	Bakı	Azerbaijan - Faroe Islands	2-0(2-0)
17.11.2018	Attard	Malta - Kosovo	0-5(0-1)
20.11.2018	Prishtinë	Kosovo - Azerbaijan	4-0(1-0)
20.11.2018	Attard	Malta - Faroe Islands	1-1(1-1)

Final Standings

1.	**Kosovo**	6	4	2	0	15	-	2	14
2.	**Azerbaijan**	6	2	3	1	7	-	6	9
3.	Faroe Islands	6	1	2	3	5	-	10	5
4.	Malta	6	0	3	3	5	-	14	3

Kosovo and Azerbaijan promoted to League C

GROUP 4

Results

06.09.2018	Yerevan	Armenia - Liechtenstein	2-1(1-1)
06.09.2018	Gibraltar	Gibraltar - North Macedonia	0-2(0-2)
09.09.2018	Skopje	North Macedonia - Armenia	2-0(1-0)
09.09.2018	Vaduz	Liechtenstein - Gibraltar	2-0(1-0)
13.10.2018	Yerevan	Armenia - Gibraltar	0-1(0-0)
13.10.2018	Skopje	N. Macedonia - Liechtenstein	4-1(3-1)
16.10.2018	Yerevan	Armenia - North Macedonia	4-0(1-0)
16.10.2018	Gibraltar	Gibraltar - Liechtenstein	2-1(0-1)
16.11.2018	Vaduz	Liechtenstein – N. Macedonia	0-2(0-0)
16.11.2018	Gibraltar	Gibraltar - Armenia	2-6(1-1)
19.11.2018	Skopje	North Macedonia - Gibraltar	4-0(1-0)
19.11.2018	Vaduz	Liechtenstein - Armenia	2-2(1-1)

Final Standings

1.	**N.Macedonia**	6	5	0	1	14	-	5	15
2.	**Armenia**	6	3	1	2	14	-	8	10
3.	Gibraltar	6	2	0	4	5	-	15	6
4.	Liechtenstein	6	1	1	4	7	-	12	4

North Macedonia and Armenia promoted to League C

RANKING OF THIRD PLACED TEAMS

1.	**Moldova**	6	2	3	1	4	-	5	9
2.	Gibraltar	6	2	0	4	5	-	15	6
3.	Faroe Islands	6	1	2	3	5	-	10	5
4.	Latvia	6	0	4	2	2	-	6	4

UEFA EUROPEAN CHAMPIONSHIP 2020

The qualifying group stage draw was held on 02.12.2018 in Dublin (Republic of Ireland). The 55 paricipating teams were drawn into 10 groups: five groups of five teams (Groups A–E) and five groups of six teams (Groups F–J). The teams were seeded based on the November 2018 UEFA Nations League overall rankings.

UNL Pot: Switzerland, Portugal (title holders 2016), Netherlands, England;
Pot 1: Belgium, France, Spain, Italy, Croatia, Poland;
Pot 2: Germany, Iceland, Bosnia and Herzegovina, Ukraine, Denmark, Sweden, Russia, Austria, Wales, Czech Republic;
Pot 3: Slovakia, Turkey, Republic of Ireland, Northern Ireland, Scotland, Norway, Serbia, Finland, Bulgaria, Israel;
Pot 4: Hungary, Romania, Greece, Albania, Montenegro, Cyprus, Estonia, Slovenia, Lithuania, Georgia;
Pot 5: Macedonia, Kosovo, Belarus, Luxembourg, Armenia, Azerbaijan, Kazakhstan, Moldova, Gibraltar, Faroe Islands;
Pot 6: Latvia, Liechtenstein, Andorra, Malta, San Marino.

QUALIFIERS
(Matches from March to June 2019]

GROUP A

Results

22.03.2019	Sofia	Bulgaria - Montenegro	1-1(0-0)
22.03.2019	London	England - Czech Republic	5-0(2-0)
25.03.2019	Prishtinë	Kosovo - Bulgaria	1-1(0-1)
25.03.2019	Podgorica	Montenegro - England	1-5(1-2)
07.06.2019	Praha	Czech Republic - Bulgaria	2-1(1-1)
07.06.2019	Podgorica	Montenegro - Kosovo	1-1(0-1)
10.06.2019	Sofia	Bulgaria - Kosovo	2-3(1-1)
10.06.2019	Olomouc	Czech Rep. - Montenegro	3-0(1-0)

Standings

1.	England	2	2	0	0	10	-	1	6
2.	Czech Rep.	3	2	0	1	5	-	6	6
3.	Kosovo	3	1	2	0	5	-	4	5
4.	Bulgaria	4	0	2	2	5	-	7	2
5.	Montenegro	4	0	2	2	3	-	10	2

Next matches:

07.09.2019:	Kosovo - Czech Republic; England - Bulgaria
11.10.2019:	Montenegro - Bulgaria; Czech Republic - England
14.11.2019:	England - Montenegro; Czech Republic - Kosovo
10.09.2019:	England - Kosovo; Montenegro - Czech Republic
14.10.2019:	Bulgaria - England; Kosovo - Montenegro
17.11.2019:	Bulgaria - Czech Republic; Kosovo - England

GROUP B

Results

22.03.2019	Lëtzebuerg	Luxembourg - Lithuania	2-1(1-1)
22.03.2019	Lisboa	Portugal - Ukraine	0-0
25.03.2019	Lëtzebuerg	Luxembourg - Ukraine	1-2(1-1)
25.03.2019	Lisboa	Portugal - Serbia	1-1(1-1)
07.06.2019	Vilnius	Lithuania - Luxembourg	1-1(0-1)
07.06.2019	Lviv	Ukraine - Serbia	5-0(2-0)
10.06.2019	Beograd	Serbia - Lithuania	4-1(3-0)
10.06.2019	Lviv	Ukraine - Luxembourg	1-0(1-0)

Standings

1.	Ukraine	4	3	1	0	8	-	1	10
2.	Luxembourg	4	1	1	2	4	-	5	4
3.	Serbia	3	1	1	1	5	-	7	4
4.	Portugal	2	0	2	0	1	-	1	2
5.	Lithuania	3	0	1	2	3	-	7	1

Next matches:

07.09.2019:	Lithuania - Ukraine; Serbia - Portugal
11.10.2019:	Ukraine - Lithuania; Portugal - Luxembourg
14.11.2019:	Portugal - Lithuania; Serbia - Luxembourg
10.09.2019:	Lithuania - Portugal; Luxembourg - Serbia
14.10.2019:	Lithuania - Serbia; Ukraine - Portugal
17.11.2019:	Luxembourg - Portugal; Serbia - Ukraine

GROUP C

Results

21.03.2019	Rotterdam	Netherlands - Belarus	4-0(2-0)
21.03.2019	Belfast	Northern Ireland - Estonia	2-0(0-0)
24.03.2019	Belfast	Northern Ireland - Belarus	2-1(1-1)
24.03.2019	Amsterdam	Netherlands - Germany	2-3(0-2)
08.06.2019	Tallinn	Estonia - Northern Ireland	1-2(1-0)
08.06.2019	Borisov	Belarus - Germany	0-2(0-1)
11.06.2019	Borisov	Belarus - Northern Ireland	0-1(0-0)
11.06.2019	Mainz	Germany - Estonia	8-0(5-0)

Standings

1.	No. Ireland	4	4	0	0	7	-	2	12
2.	Germany	3	3	0	0	13	-	2	9
3.	Netherlands	2	1	0	1	6	-	3	3
4.	Belarus	4	0	0	4	1	-	9	0
5.	Estonia	3	0	0	3	1	-	12	0

Next matches:

06.09.2019:	Estonia - Belarus; Germany - Netherlands
10.10.2019:	Belarus - Estonia; Netherlands - Northern Ireland
16.11.2019:	Germany - Belarus; Northern Ireland - Netherlands
09.09.2019:	Northern Ireland - Germany; Estonia - Netherlands
13.10.2019:	Belarus - Netherlands; Estonia - Germany
19.11.2019:	Germany - Northern Ireland; Netherlands - Estonia

GROUP D

Results

23.03.2019	Tbilisi	Georgia - Switzerland	0-2(0-0)
23.03.2019	Gibraltar	Gibraltar – Rep. of Ireland	0-1(0-0)
26.03.2019	Basel	Switzerland - Denmark	3-3(1-0)
26.03.2019	Dublin	Rep. of Ireland - Georgia	1-0(1-0)
07.06.2019	Tbilisi	Georgia - Gibraltar	3-0(1-0)
07.06.2019	København	Denmark - Rep. of Ireland	1-1(0-0)
10.06.2019	København	Denmark - Georgia	5-1(2-1)
10.06.2019	Dublin	Rep. of Ireland - Gibraltar	2-0(1-0)

Standings

1.	R. of Ireland	4	3	1	0	5	-	1	10
2.	Denmark	3	1	2	0	9	-	5	5
3.	Switzerland	2	1	1	0	5	-	3	4
4.	Georgia	4	1	0	3	4	-	8	3
5.	Gibraltar	3	0	0	3	0	-	6	0

Next matches:

05.09.2019:	Gibraltar - Denmark; Republic of Ireland - Switzerland
12.10.2019:	Georgia - Republic of Ireland; Denmark - Switzerland
15.11.2019:	Denmark - Gibraltar; Switzerland - Georgia

08.09.2019:	Georgia - Denmark; Switzerland - Gibraltar
15.10.2019:	Gibraltar - Georgia; Switzerland - Republic of Ireland
18.11.2019:	Republic of Ireland - Denmark; Gibraltar - Switzerland

GROUP E

Results

21.03.2019	Zagreb	Croatia - Azerbaijan	2-1(1-1)
21.03.2019	Trnava	Slovakia - Hungary	2-0(1-0)
24.03.2019	Cardiff	Wales - Slovakia	1-0(1-0)
24.03.2019	Budapest	Hungary - Croatia	2-1(1-1)
08.06.2019	Osijek	Croatia - Wales	2-1(1-0)
08.06.2019	Bakı	Azerbaijan - Hungary	1-3(0-1)
11.06.2019	Bakı	Azerbaijan - Slovakia	1-5(1-3)
11.06.2019	Budapest	Hungary - Wales	1-0(0-0)

Standings

1.	Hungary	4	3	0	1	6	-	4	9
2.	Slovakia	3	2	0	1	7	-	2	6
3.	Croatia	3	2	0	1	5	-	4	6
4.	Wales	3	1	0	2	2	-	3	3
5.	Azerbaijan	3	0	0	3	3	-	10	0

Next matches:

06.09.2019:	Wales - Azerbaijan; Slovakia - Croatia
10.10.2019:	Croatia - Hungary; Slovakia - Wales
16.11.2019:	Azerbaijan - Wales; Croatia - Slovakia

09.09.2019:	Azerbaijan - Croatia; Hungary - Slovakia
13.10.2019:	Hungary - Azerbaijan; Wales - Croatia
19.11.2019:	Slovakia - Azerbaijan; Wales - Hungary

GROUP F

Results

23.03.2019	Attard	Malta - Faroe Islands	2-1(1-0)
23.03.2019	Stockholm	Sweden - Romania	2-1(2-0)
23.03.2019	Valencia	Spain - Norway	2-1(1-0)
26.03.2019	Cluj-Napoca	Romania - Faroe Islands	4-1(3-1)
26.03.2019	Attard	Malta - Spain	0-2(0-1)
26.03.2019	Oslo	Norway - Sweden	3-3(1-0)
07.06.2019	Tórshavn	Faroe Islands - Spain	1-4(1-3)
07.06.2019	Stockholm	Sweden - Malta	3-0(1-0)
07.06.2019	Oslo	Norway - Romania	2-2(0-0)
10.06.2019	Tórshavn	Faroe Islands - Norway	0-2(0-0)
10.06.2019	Attard	Malta - Romania	0-4(0-3)
10.06.2019	Madrid	Spain - Sweden	3-0(0-0)

Standings

1.	Spain	4	4	0	0	11	-	2	12
2.	Romania	4	2	1	1	11	-	5	7
3.	Sweden	4	2	1	1	8	-	7	7
4.	Norway	4	1	2	1	8	-	7	5
5.	Malta	4	1	0	3	2	-	10	3
6.	Faroe Islands	4	0	0	4	3	-	12	0

Next matches:

05.09.2019:	Faroe Islands - Sweden; Norway - Malta; Romania - Spain
08.09.2019:	Romania - Malta; Spain - Faroe Islands; Sweden - Norway
12.10.2019:	Faroe Islands - Romania; Malta - Sweden; Norway - Spain
15.10.2019:	Faroe Islands - Malta; Romania - Norway; Sweden - Spain
15.11.2019:	Norway - Faroe Islands; Spain - Malta; Romania - Sweden
18.11.2019:	Sweden - Faroe Islands; Malta - Norway; Spain - Romania

GROUP G

Results

21.03.2019	Haifa	Israel - Slovenia	1-1(0-0)
21.03.2019	Skopje	North Macedonia - Latvia	3-1(2-0)
21.03.2019	Wien	Austria - Poland	0-1(0-0)
24.03.2019	Haifa	Israel - Austria	4-2(2-1)
24.03.2019	Warszawa	Poland - Latvia	2-0(0-0)
24.03.2019	Ljubljana	Slovenia - North Macedonia	1-1(1-0)
07.06.2019	Rīga	Latvia - Israel	0-3(0-1)
07.06.2019	Skopje	North Macedonia - Poland	0-1(0-0)
07.06.2019	Klagenfurt	Austria - Slovenia	1-0(0-0)
10.06.2019	Warszawa	Poland - Israel	4-0(1-0)
10.06.2019	Rīga	Latvia - Slovenia	0-5(0-4)
10.06.2019	Skopje	North Macedonia - Austria	1-4(1-1)

Standings

1.	Poland	4	4	0	0	8	-	0	12
2.	Israel	4	2	1	1	8	-	7	7
3.	Austria	4	2	0	2	7	-	6	6
4.	Slovenia	4	1	2	1	7	-	3	5
5.	N. Macedonia	4	1	1	2	5	-	7	4
6.	Latvia	4	0	0	4	1	-	13	0

Next matches:		
	06.09.2019:	Israel - North Macedonia [05.09.]; Austria - Latvia; Slovenia - Poland
	09.09.2019:	Slovenia - Israel; Latvia - North Macedonia; Poland - Austria
	10.10.2019:	Austria - Israel; Latvia - Poland; North Macedonia - Slovenia
	13.10.2019:	Poland - North Macedonia; Slovenia - Austria; Israel - Latvia [15.10.]
	16.11.2019:	Slovenia - Latvia; Israel - Poland; Austria - North Macedonia
	19.11.2019:	North Macedonia - Israel; Latvia - Austria; Poland - Slovenia

GROUP H

Results

22.03.2019	Shkodër	Albania - Turkey	0-2(0-1)
22.03.2019	Andorra la V.	Andorra - Iceland	0-2(0-1)
22.03.2019	Chişinău	Moldova - France	1-4(0-3)
25.03.2019	Eskişehir	Turkey - Moldova	4-0(2-0)
25.03.2019	Andorra la V.	Andorra - Albania	0-3(0-1)
25.03.2019	Paris	France - Iceland	4-0(1-0)
08.06.2019	Reykjavík	Iceland - Albania	1-0(1-0)
08.06.2019	Chişinău	Moldova - Andorra	1-0(1-0)
08.06.2019	Konya	Turkey - France	2-0(2-0)
11.06.2019	Elbasan	Albania - Moldova	2-0(0-0)
11.06.2019	Andorra la V.	Andorra - France	0-4(0-3)
11.06.2019	Reykjavík	Iceland - Turkey	2-1(2-1)

Standings

1.	France	4	3	0	1	12	-	3	9
2.	Turkey	4	3	0	1	9	-	2	9
3.	Iceland	4	3	0	1	5	-	5	9
4.	Albania	4	2	0	2	5	-	3	6
5.	Moldova	4	1	0	3	2	-	10	3
6.	Andorra	4	0	0	4	0	-	10	0

Next matches:		
	07.09.2019:	Iceland - Moldova; France - Albania; Turkey - Andorra
	10.09.2019:	Albania - Iceland; France - Andorra; Moldova - Turkey
	11.10.2019:	Turkey - Albania; Andorra - Moldova; Iceland - France
	14.10.2019:	Moldova - Albania; Iceland - Andorra; France - Turkey
	14.11.2019:	Turkey - Iceland; Albania - Andorra; France - Moldova
	17.11.2019:	Albania - France; Andorra - Turkey; Moldova - Iceland

GROUP I

Results

21.03.2019	Astana	Kazakhstan - Scotland	3-0(2-0)
21.03.2019	Nicosia	Cyprus - San Marino	5-0(4-0)
21.03.2019	Bruxelles	Belgium - Russia	3-1(2-1)
24.03.2019	Nur-Sultan	Kazakhstan - Russia	0-4(0-2)
24.03.2019	Serravalle	San Marino - Scotland	0-2(0-1)
24.03.2019	Nicosia	Cyprus - Belgium	0-2(0-2)
08.06.2019	Saransk	Russia - San Marino	9-0(4-0)
08.06.2019	Bruxelles	Belgium - Kazakhstan	3-0(2-0)
08.06.2019	Glasgow	Scotland - Cyprus	2-1(0-0)
11.06.2019	Nur-Sultan	Kazakhstan - San Marino	4-0(1-0)
11.06.2019	Bruxelles	Belgium - Scotland	3-0(1-0)
11.06.2019	Nizhny Novg.	Russia - Cyprus	1-0(1-0)

Standings

1.	Belgium	4	4	0	0	11	-	1	12
2.	Russia	4	3	0	1	15	-	3	9
3.	Kazakhstan	4	2	0	2	7	-	7	6
4.	Scotland	4	2	0	2	4	-	7	6
5.	Cyprus	4	1	0	3	6	-	5	3
6.	San Marino	4	0	0	4	0	-	20	0

Next matches:		
	06.09.2019:	Cyprus - Kazakhstan; San Marino - Belgium; Scotland - Russia
	09.09.2019:	Scotland - Belgium; Russia - Kazakhstan; San Marino - Cyprus
	10.10.2019:	Kazakhstan - Cyprus; Belgium - San Marino; Russia - Scotland
	13.10.2019:	Kazakhstan - Belgium; Cyprus - Russia; Scotland - San Marino
	16.11.2019:	Cyprus - Scotland; Russia - Belgium; San Marino - Kazakhstan
	19.11.2019:	Belgium - Cyprus; Scotland - Kazakhstan; San Marino - Russia

GROUP J

Results

23.03.2019	Sarajevo	Bosnia and Herz. - Armenia	2-1(1-0)
23.03.2019	Udine	Italy - Finland	2-0(1-0)
23.03.2019	Vaduz	Liechtenstein - Greece	0-2(0-1)
26.03.2019	Yerevan	Armenia - Finland	0-2(0-1)
26.03.2019	Zenica	Bosnia and Herz. - Greece	2-2(2-0)
26.03.2019	Parma	Italy - Liechtenstein	6-0(4-0)
08.06.2019	Yerevan	Armenia - Liechtenstein	3-0(2-0)
08.06.2019	Tampere	Finland - Bosnia and Herz.	2-0(0-0)
08.06.2019	Athína	Greece - Italy	0-3(0-3)
11.06.2019	Athína	Greece - Armenia	2-3(0-2)
1106.2019	Torino	Italy - Bosnia and Herz.	2-1(0-1)
11.06.2019	Vaduz	Liechtenstein - Finland	0-2(0-1)

Standings

1.	Italy	4	4	0	0	13	-	1	12
2.	Finland	4	2	0	2	4	-	4	9
3.	Armenia	4	2	0	2	7	-	6	6
4.	Greece	4	1	1	2	6	-	8	4
5.	Bosnia and H.	4	1	1	2	5	-	7	4
6.	Liechtenstein	4	0	0	4	0	-	13	0

Next matches:		
	05.09.2019:	Armenia - Italy; Bosnia and Herzegovina - Liechtenstein; Finland - Greece
	08.09.2019:	Armenia - Bosnia and Herzegovina; Finland - Italy; Greece - Liechtenstein
	12.10.2019:	Bosnia and Herzegovina - Finland; Liechtenstein - Armenia; Italy - Greece
	15.10.2019:	Finland - Armenia; Greece - Bosnia and Herzegovina; Liechtenstein - Italy
	15.11.2019:	Armenia - Greece; Finland - Liechtenstein; Bosnia and Herzegovina - Italy
	18.11.2019:	Italy - Armenia; Liechtenstein - Bosnia and Herzegovina; Greece - Finland

EUROPEAN CLUB COMPETITIONS

UEFA CHAMPIONS LEAGUE 2018/2019

PRELIMINARY ROUND – SEMI-FINALS

6.06.2018; Victoria Stadium, Gibraltar: Referee: Paul McLaughlin (Republic of Ireland); Attendance: 288

FC Santa Coloma – FC Drita **0-2(0-0,0-0)**

FC Santa Coloma: Eloy Casals, Ildefons Lima, Marc Rebés, Andreu Ramos, Víctor Rodríguez (86.Albert Mercadé), Moisés San Nicolás, Yago Pérez, Loren Burón (105+1.Cédric Fauré), Aleix Cistero (84.Jaime Noguerol), Gabi Riera (62.Juli Sánchez), Juanma Torres. Trainer: Marc Rodriguez Rebull.

FC Drita: Leutrim Rexhepi, Liridon Leci, Fidan Gërbeshi, Viktor Kuka, Ardian Limani, Haxhi Neziraj (112.Denis Haliti), Drilon Musaj (98.Arbër Shala), Bujar Shabani, Xhevdet Shabani, Endrit Krasniqi, Leotrim Kryeziu (85.Përparim Livoreka). Trainer: Bekim Isufi.

Goals: 0-1 Xhevdet Shabani (99), 0-2 Fidan Gërbashi (105+3 penalty).

26.06.2018; Victoria Stadium, Gibraltar: Referee: Jørgen Burchardt (Denmark); Attendance: 840

SP La Fiorita – Lincoln Red Imps FC **0-2(0-1)**

SP La Fiorita: Gianluca Vivan, Samuele Olivi, Roberto Di Maio, Marco Gasperoni, Riccardo Mezzadri, Damiano Tommasi, Simone Loiodice (69.Luca Righini), Ivan Buonocunto (89.Alessandro Cattelan), Armando Amati, Danilo Rinaldi (75.Andy Selva), Emiliano Olcese. Trainer: Gianluca Procopio.

Lincoln Red Imps FC: Lolo Soler, Joseph Chipolina, Oliver "Oli" (74.Sykes Garro), Bernardo Lopes, Jean Garcia, Calderón, Diego Gámiz, "Álex" Moreno (69.Ryan Casciaro), Juan Montesinos, Juanma Ortiz (61.Lee Casciaro), Anthony Hernandez. Trainer: Diego Perez Jimenez "Yiyi".

Goals: 0-1 Anthony Hernandez (2), 0-2 "Álex" Moreno (51).

PRELIMINARY ROUND – FINALS

29.06.2018; Victoria Stadium, Gibraltar: Referee: Manfredas Lukjancukas (Lithuania); Attendance: 468

Lincoln Red Imps FC – FC Drita **1-4 (0-1,1-1)**

Lincoln Red Imps FC: Lolo Soler, Joseph Chipolina (105.Jean Garcia), Oliver "Oli", Bernardo Lopes [*sent off 105+2*], Calderón (46.Pedro Corral), Diego Gámiz, "Álex" Moreno, Juan Montesinos (46.André dos Santos), Juanma Ortiz (72.Falu Aranda), Anthony Hernandez, Lee Casciaro. Trainer: Diego Perez Jimenez "Yiyi".

FC Drita: Leutrim Rexhepi, Liridon Leci, Fidan Gërbeshi [*sent off 101*], Viktor Kuka, Ardian Limani, Haxhi Neziraj, Drilon Musaj (68.Arbër Shala), Bujar Shabani, Xhevdet Shabani (120+3.Adonis Ruhani), Endrit Krasniqi (120+2.Denis Haliti), Leotrim Kryeziu (73.Përparim Livoreka). Trainer: Bekim Isufi.

Goals: 0-1 Liridon Leci (2), 1-1 Pedro Corral (61), 1-2 Liridon Leci (105+3 penalty), 1-3 Xhevdet Shabani (120), 1-4 Haxhi Neziraj (120+4).

FIRST QUALIFYING ROUND

10.07.2018; "Ramaz Shengelia" Stadioni, Kutaisi; Referee: Aleksandrs Golubevs (Latvia); Attendance: 7,251

Torpedo Kutaisi – FC Sheriff Tiraspol **2-1(1-1)**

Torpedo Kutaisi: Roin Kvaskhvadze, Manuka Kobakhidze (82.Davit Khurtsilava), Giorgi Kimadze (77.Beka Tughushi), Levan Gegetchkori, Oleksandr Azatskyi, Lazar Marin, Grigol Dolidze (62.Arfang Daffé), Levan Kutalia, Giorgi Kukhianidze, Marek Hlinka, Mate Tsintsadze. Trainer: Kakhaber Chkhetiani.

Sheriff Tiraspol: Zvonimir Mikulic, Ante Kulusic, Mateo Susic, Vladimir Kovacevic, Cristiano, Antun Palic, Yuri Kendysh, Rifet Kapic (66.Joálisson), Ziguy Badibanga, Al-Hadji Kamara, Gerson Rodrigues (78.Alexandru Boiciuc). Trainer: Goran Sablic.

Goals: 0-1 Ziguy Badibanga (14), 1-1 Giorgi Kimadze (24), 2-1 Giorgi Kukhianidze (64 penalty).

18.07.2018; Bolshaya Sportivnaya Arena, Tiraspol; Referee: Peter Kjærsgaard-Andersen (Denmark); Attendance: 5,740

FC Sheriff Tiraspol – Torpedo Kutaisi **3-0(2-0)**

Sheriff Tiraspol: Zvonimir Mikulic, Ante Kulusic, Mateo Susic, Veaceslav Posmac, Cristiano, Antun Palic, Yuri Kendysh (75.Gheorghe Anton), Rifet Kapic (73.Gerson Rodrigues), Ziguy Badibanga, Joálisson (89.Vladimir Kovacevic), Al-Hadji Kamara. Trainer: Goran Sablic.

Torpedo Kutaisi: Roin Kvaskhvadze, Davit Khurtsilava, Manuka Kobakhidze, Giorgi Kimadze, Levan Gegetchkori (46.Arfang Daffé), Oleksandr Azatskyi, Lazar Marin, Levan Kutalia (68.Tornike Kapanadze), Giorgi Kukhianidze (57.Beka Tugushi), Marek Hlinka, Mate Tsintsadze. Trainer: Kakhaber Chkhetiani.

Goals: 1-0 Ziguy Badibanga (9), 2-0, 3-0 Joálisson (40, 55).

[FC Sheriff Tiraspol won 4-2 on aggregate]

10.07.2018; A. Le Coq Arena, Tallinn; Referee: Erik Lambrechts (Belgium); Attendance: 1,106

FC Flora Tallinn – Hapoel Be'er Sheva FC **1-4(0-2)**

Flora Tallinn: Mait Toom, Gert Kams, Joseph Saliste (57.Kevin Aloe), Jürgen Lorenz, Madis Vihmann, Aleksandr Dmitrijev, Zakaria Beglarishvili (71.Markus Poom), Mihkel Ainsalu, Rauno Alliku, Rauno Sappinen, Frank Liivak (66.Maksim Gussev). Trainer: Arno Pijpers.

Hapoel Be'er Sheva: David Goresh, Ben Bitton, Loai Taha, Shir Tzedek, Oren Bitton, Hen Ezra, Maor Melikson, Hanan Maman (61.Niv Zrihan), Daniel Einbinder, Marwan Kabha (48.Vladimir Brown), Ben Sahar (79.Tomás Pekhart). Trainer: Bachar Bakhar.

Goals: 0-1 Ben Sahar (18), 0-2 Shir Tzedek (36 penalty), 0-3 Hanan Maman (53), 1-3 Rauno Sappinen (73 penalty), 1-4 Hen Ezra (85).

17.07.2018; Yaakov Turner Toto Stadium, Beersheba; Referee: Tomasz Musial (Poland); Attendance: 11,850

Hapoel Be'er Sheva FC – FC Flora Tallinn **3-1(2-0)**

Hapoel Be'er Sheva: Giannis Anestis, Julien Cétout, Ben Bitton, Loai Taha, Shir Tzedek (74.Amit Bitton), Oren Bitton, John Ogu (57.Daniel Einbinder), Hen Ezra, Maor Melikson, Hanan Maman (67.Niv Zrihan), Ben Sahar. Trainer: Bachar Bakhar.

Flora Tallinn: Mait Toom, Gert Kams, Kevin Aloe, Jürgen Lorenz, Madis Vihmann, Aleksandr Dmitrijev, Mihkel Ainsalu (57.German Slein), Markus Poom, Rauno Alliku, Rauno Sappinen, Frank Liivak (46.Maksim Gussev). Trainer: Arno Pijpers.

Goals: 1-0 Hen Ezra (15), 2-0 Hanan Maman (27), 3-0 Maor Melikson (48), 3-1 Rauno Alliku (86).

[Hapoel Be'er Sheva FC won 7-2 on aggregate]

10.07.2018; Stade "Jos Nosbaum", Dudelange; Referee: Zaven Hovhannisyan (Armenia); Attendance: 1,057

F91 Dudelange – MOL Vidi FC Székesfehérvár **1-1(0-1)**

F91 Dudelange: Jonathan Joubert, Tom Schnell, Jerry Prempeh, Bryan Mélisse, Marc-André Kruska, Stélvio (46.Patrick Stumpf, 74.Jordann Yéyé), Dominik Stolz (90.Sanel Ibrahimovic), Edisson Jordanov, Clément Couturier, Danel Sinani, David Turpel. Trainer: Dino Toppmöller.

MOL Vidi FC: Ádam Kovácsik, Attila Fiola, Loïc Négo, Paulo Vinícius, Stopira, Szabolcs Huszti (79.Stefan Scepovic), Anel Hadzic, Máté Pátkai, István Kovács (69.Boban Nikolov), Danko Lazovic, Marko Scepovic. Trainer: Marko Nikolic.

Goals: 0-1 Szabolcs Huszti (42), 1-1 Bryan Mélisse (58).

17.07.2018; Pancho Aréna, Felcsút; Referee: Donald Robertson (Scotland); Attendance: 2,514

MOL Vidi FC Székesfehérvár – F91 Dudelange **2-1(1-0)**

MOL Vidi FC: Ádam Kovácsik, Roland Juhász, Attila Fiola, Loïc Négo, Paulo Vinícius, Stopira, Szabolcs Huszti (63.Boban Nikolov), Anel Hadzic, Máté Pátkai, Danko Lazovic (84.József Varga), Marko Scepovic (89.István Kovács). Trainer: Marko Nikolic.

F91 Dudelange: Jonathan Joubert, Tom Schnell, Jerry Prempeh, Bryan Mélisse [*sent off 90+4*], Marc-André Kruska (83.Nicolas Perez), Stélvio, Dominik Stolz (70.Sanel Ibrahimovic), Edisson Jordanov, Clément Couturier, Danel Sinani (76.Jordann Yéyé), David Turpel. Trainer: Dino Toppmöller.

Goals: 1-0 Danko Lazovic (18), 1-1 Clément Couturier (54), 2-1 Marko Scepovic (58).

[MOL Vidi FC Székesfehérvár won 3-2 on aggregate]

10.07.2018; "Vazgen Sargsyan" Hanrapetakan Stadium, Yerevan; Referee: Danilo Grujic (Serbia); Attendance: 4,948

FC Alashkert – Celtic FC Glasgow Glasgow **0-3(0-1)**

FC Alashkert: Ognjen Cancarevic, Gagik Daghbashyan, Artak Yedigaryan, Oliver Práznovsky, Taron Voskanyan, Artur Yedigaryan (82.Mihran Manasyan), Artak Dashyan, Danilo Sekulic, Jefferson (85.Artem Simonyan), Artak Grigoryan, Uros Nenadovic (55.César Romero). Trainer: Varuzhan Sukiasyan.

Celtic: Craig Gordon, Jozo Simunovic, Kieran Tierney, Kristoffer Ajer, Jack Hendry, Scott Brown, James Forrest, Callum McGregor, Olivier Ntcham (68.Kouassi Eboue), Moussa Dembélé (68.Scott Sinclair), Odsonne Édouard (77.Lewis Morgan). Trainer: Brendan Rodgers.

Goals: 0-1 Odsonne Édouard (45+2), 0-2 James Forrest (81), 0-3 Callum McGregor (90).

18.07.2018; Celtic Park, Glasgow; Referee: Horatiu Fesnic (Romania); Attendance: 59,047.

Celtic FC Glasgow – FC Alashkert **3-0(3-0)**

Celtic: Craig Gordon, Jozo Simunovic [*sent off 11*], Kieran Tierney, Kristoffer Ajer, Jack Hendry, Scott Brown, James Forrest (76.Michael Johnson), Callum McGregor, Olivier Ntcham, Moussa Dembélé (66.Ryan Christie), Odsonne Édouard (64.Scott Sinclair). Trainer: Brendan Rodgers.

FC Alashkert: Ognjen Cancarevic, Gagik Dagbashyan, Artak Yedigaryan, Oliver Práznovsky, Taron Voskanyan, Artur Yedigaryan, Artak Dashyan, Danilo Sekulic (64.Artem Simonyan), Jefferson (86.César Romero), Artak Grigoryan, Uros Nenadovic (46.Mihran Manasyan). Trainer: Varuzhan Sukiasyan.

Goals: 1-0, 2-0 Moussa Dembélé (8, 19 penalty), 3-0 James Forrest (35).

[Celtic FC Glasgow won 6-0 on aggregate]

10.07.2018; Svangaskard, Toftir; Referee: Robert Hennessy (Republic of Ireland); Attendance: 300

Víkingur Gøta – HJK Helsinki **1-2(0-2)**

Víkingur Gøta: Elias Rasmussen, Atli Gregersen, Hans Djurhuus (59.Dennis Nieblas), Hanus Jacobsen, Adrian Cascaval, Gunnar Vatnhamar (89.Hans Jákup Lervig), Elias Jóhannesson Lervig, Sølvi Vatnhamar, Hedin Hansen (74.Karl Løkin), Filip Djordjevic, Adeshina Lawal. Trainer: Sigfrídur Clementsen.

HJK Helsinki: Maksim Rudakov, Rafinha, Hannu Patronen, Faith Obilor, Roni Peiponen (46.Valtteri Vesiaho), Anthony Annan, Moshtagh Yaghoubi, Sebastian Dahlström, Riku Riski (80.Eetu Vertainen), Evans Mensah, Klauss. Trainer: Mika Lehkosuo.

Goals: 0-1 Sebastian Dahlström (9), 0-2 Atli Gregersen (29 own goal), 1-2 Gunnar Vatnhamar (51).

17.07.2018; Telia 5G-areena, Helsinki; Referee: Duje Strukan (Croatia); Attendance: 5,125

HJK Helsinki – Víkingur Gøta **3-1(3-1)**

HJK Helsinki: Maksim Rudakov, Rafinha, Hannu Patronen, Daniel O'Shaughnessy, Faith Obilor, Anthony Annan, Moshtagh Yaghoubi, Sebastian Dahlström (84.Otto Ollikainen), Riku Riski, Evans Mensah (71.Enoch Banza), Klauss (67.Filip Valencic). Trainer: Mika Lehkosuo.

Víkingur Gøta: Elias Rasmussen, Atli Gregersen, Hans Djurhuus (59.Karl Løkin), Hanus Jacobsen, Adrian Cascaval (67.Hedin Hansen), Dennis Nieblas, Gunnar Vatnhamar, Elias Jóhannesson Lervig, Sølvi Vatnhamar, Filip Djordjevic, Adeshina Lawal (72.Andreas Olsen). Trainer: Sigfrídur Clementsen.

Goals: 1-0 Klauss (1), 2-0 Evans Mensah (10), 3-0 Moshtagh Yaghoubi (19), 3-1 Gunnar Vatnhamar (21).

[HJK Helsinki won 5-2 on aggregate]

10.07.2018; Telekom Arena, Skopje; Referee: Timotheos Christofi (Cyprus); Attendance: 2,700

KF Shkëndija 79 – The New Saints **5-0(2-0)**

KF Shkëndija: Kostadin Zahov, Mevlan Murati, Visar Musliu, Egzon Bejtulai, Mevlan Adili, Armend Alimi, Sciprim Taipi (80.Arbin Zejnulai), Besart Ibraimi (75.Shefit Shefiti), Izair Emini (83.Remzi Selmani), Stênio Júnior, Marjan Radeski. Trainer: Qatip Osmani.

The New Saints: Paul Harrison, Simon Spender (73.Kane Lewis), Christopher Marriott, Blaine Hudson, Benjamin Cabango, Jamie Mullan, Jonathan Routledge, Daniel Redmond (67.Aeron Edwards), Ryan Brobbel, Thomas Holland, Dean Ebbe (64.Kurtis Byrne). Trainer: Scott Ruscoe.

Goals: 1-0 Izair Emini (16), 2-0, 3-0, 4-0, 5-0 Besart Ibraimi (38, 53, 60, 66).

17.07.2018; Park Hall Stadium, Oswestry; Referee: Pavel Orel (Czech Republic); Attendance: 756

The New Saints – KF Shkëndija 79 **4-0(3-0)**

The New Saints: Paul Harrison, Christopher Marriott, Blaine Hudson, Kane Lewis, Benjamin Cabango, Jamie Mullan, Aeron Edwards, Jonathan Routledge, Daniel Redmond (83.Adrian Cieslewicz), Thomas Holland (89.Kurtis Byrne), Dean Ebbe (56.Greg Draper). Trainer: Scott Ruscoe.

KF Shkëndija: Kostadin Zahov, Visar Musliu, Egzon Bejtulai, Mevlan Adili, Alma Wakili, Armend Alimi, Blagoja Todorovski (46.Marjan Radeski), Shefit Shefiti (46.Besart Ibraimi), Arbin Zejnulai (89.Konstantin Cheshmedzhiev), Izair Emini, Stênio Júnior. Trainer: Qatip Osmani.

Goals: 1-0 Dean Ebbe (15), 2-0 Daniel Redmond (30), 3-0 Benjamin Cabango (35), 4-0 Kurtis Byrne (90+6).

[KF Shkëndija 79 won 5-4 on aggregate]

10.07.2018; Stadiumi Olimpik "Adem Jashari", Mitrovica; Referee: Boris Marhefka (Slovakia); Attendance: 9,780

FC Drita – Malmö FF **0-3(0-2)**

FC Drita: Leutrim Rexhepi, Liridon Leci (83.Denis Haliti), Viktor Kuka, Ardian Limani, Arbër Shala, Haxhi Neziraj, Drilon Musaj (76.Leotrim Kryeziu), Bujar Shabani, Xhevdet Shabani, Betim Haxhimusa (54.Përparim Livoreka), Endrit Krasniqi. Trainer: Bekim Isufi.

Malmö FF: Johan Dahlin, Behrang Safari (64.Franz Brorsson), Rasmus Bengtsson, Eric Larsson, Lasse Nielsen, Søren Rieks, Fouad Bachirou, Arnór Ingvi Traustason, Oscar Lewicki, Markus Rosenberg (84.Bonke Innocent), Carlos Strandberg (61.Alexander Jeremejeff). Trainer: Uwe Rösler.

Goals: 0-1 Carlos Strandberg (13), 0-2 Arnór Ingvi Traustason (49), 0-3 Markus Rosenberg (82).

17.07.2018; Swedbank Stadion, Malmö; Referee: Laurent Kopriwa (Luxermbourg); Attendance: 10,623

Malmö FF – FC Drita **2-0(0-0)**

Malmö FF: Johan Dahlin, Rasmus Bengtsson (64.Behrang Safari), Eric Larsson, Lasse Nielsen, Franz Brorsson, Søren Rieks (58.Egzon Binaku), Fouad Bachirou (71.Bonke Innocent), Oscar Lewicki, Samuel Adrian, Alexander Jeremejeff, Carlos Strandberg. Trainer: Uwe Rösler.

FC Drita: Edvan Bakaj, Liridon Leci, Viktor Kuka, Ardian Limani, Arbër Shala, Haxhi Neziraj, Drilon Musaj (88.Përparim Livoreka), Bujar Shabani, Xhevdet Shabani, Endrit Krasniqi (62.Betim Haxhimusa), Leotrim Kryeziu (72.Zgjim Mustafa). Trainer: Bekim Isufi.

Goals: 1-0 Carlos Strandberg (55), 2-0 Eric Larsson (60).

[Malmö FF won 5-0 on aggregate]

10.07.2018; Turner's Cross, Cork; Referee: Radu Petrescu (Romania); Attendance: 5,795

Cork City – Legia Warszawa **0-1(0-0)**

Cork City: Peter Cherrie, Damien Delaney, Shane Griffin, Conor McCarthy (61.Steven Beattie), Sean McLoughlin, Jimmy Keohane, Conor McCormack, Gearóid Morrissey (52.Graham Cummins), Barry McNamee (82.Kieran Sadlier), Garry Buckley, Karl Sheppard. Trainer: John Caulfield.

Legia Warszawa: Arkadiusz Malarz, Iñaki Astiz, William Rémy, Marko Vesovic, Mateusz Wieteska, Kasper Hämäläinen (82.Sandro Kulenovic), Krzysztof Maczynski, Michal Kucharczyk, Cafú, Sebastian Szymanski (76.Dominik Nagy), José Kanté (76.Adam Hlousek). Trainer: Dean Klafuric.

Goal: 0-1 Michal Kucharczyk (79).

17.07.2018; Stadion "Marszalka Józefa Pilsudskiego", Warszawa; Referee: Kai Erik Steen (Norway); Attendance: 14,576

Legia Warszawa – Cork City FC **3-0(1-0)**

Legia Warszawa: Arkadiusz Malarz, Iñaki Astiz, William Rémy, Dominik Nagy, Mateusz Wieteska (69.Domagoj Antolic), Miroslav Radovic, Krzysztof Maczynski, Marko Vesovic, Michal Kucharczyk (46.Adam Hlousek), Cafú, José Kanté (64.Carlitos López). Trainer: Dean Klafuric.

Cork City: Peter Cherrie, Damien Delaney, Steven Beattie (79.Danny Kane), Shane Griffin, Sean McLoughlin, Jimmy Keohane, Conor McCormack, Barry McNamee, Garry Buckley (79.Kieran Sadlier), Graham Cummins (78.Josh O'Hanlon), Karl Sheppard. Trainer: John Caulfield.

Goals: 1-0 José Kanté (27), 2-0 Miroslav Radovic (73 penalty), 3-0 Carlitos López (89).

[Legia Warszawa won 4-0 on aggregate]

11.07.2018; Astana Arena, Astana; Referee: Ferenc Karakó (Hungary); Attendance: 20,500

Astana FC – FK Sutjeska Nikšić 1-0(1-0)

Astana FC: Nenad Eric, Antonio Rukavina, Marin Anicic, Dmitriy Shomko, Evgeni Postnikov, Marin Tomasov, Ivan Maevski, Serikzhan Muzhikov (90+2.Baktiyor Zaynutdinov), László Kleinheisler, Djordje Despotovic (73.Aleksey Shchetkin), Roman Murtazaev (86.Marko Stanojevic). Trainer: Roman Grygorchuk.

FK Sutjeska Nikšić: Vladan Giljen, Darko Bulatovic, Stefan Cicmil, Marko Cetkovic (78.Veljko Vukovic), Stefan Stefanovic, Milos Vucic, Stefan Loncar, Marko Vucic (90+3.Dragan Grivic), Nemanja Nedic, Luka Merdovic, Saleta Kordic (85.Bojan Bozovic). Trainer: Nikola Rakojevic.

Goal: 1-0 Roman Murtazaev (29 penalty).

18.07.2018; Stadion kraj Bistrice, Nikšić; Referee: João Pedro Pinheiro (Portugal); Attendance: 3,200

FK Sutjeska Nikšić – Astana FC 0-2(0-1)

Sutjeska Nikšić: Vladan Giljen, Darko Bulatovic, Stefan Cicmil, Marko Cetkovic, Stefan Stefanovic (61.Vladan Bubanja), Milos Vucic, Stefan Loncar, Marko Vucic (54.Stefan Denkovic), Nemanja Nedic, Luka Merdovic, Saleta Kordic (71.Zarko Grbovic). Trainer: Nikola Rakojevic.

Astana FC: Nenad Eric, Antonio Rukavina, Marin Anicic, Dmitriy Shomko, Evgeni Postnikov, Marin Tomasov, Ivan Maevski, Serikzhan Muzhikov, László Kleinheisler (81.Richard Almeyda), Djordje Despotovic (79.Aleksey Shchetkin), Roman Murtazaev (85.Baktiyor Zaynutdinov). Trainer: Roman Grygorchuk.

Goals: 0-1 Djordje Despotovic (38), 0-2 Serikzhan Muzhikov (65).

[Astana FC won 3-0 on aggregate]

11.07.2018; Marijamolés sporto centro stadione, Marijampolé; Referee: Fedayi San (Switzerland); Attendance: 3,378

FK Sūduva Marijampolé – APOEL FC Nicosia 3-1(3-0)

Sūduva Marijampolé: Ivan Kardum, Vaidas Slavickas, Algis Jankauskas, Andro Svrljuga, Aleksandar Zivanovic, Povilas Leimonas, Gerson Acevedo (59.Gui Finkler), Ovidijus Verbickas (83.Bruno Dybal), Giedrius Matulevicius, Mihret Topcagic (30.Robertas Vézevicius), Rigino Cicilia. Trainer: Vladimir Cheburin.

APOEL: Boy Waterman, Zhivko Milanov (63.Leonardo Natel), Giorgios Merkis, Yohan Tavares, Caju, Nuno Morais, Tomás De Vincenti (46.Mickaël Poté), Lucas Souza, Roland Sallai (46.Efstathios Aloneftis), Dellatorre, Musa Al-Taamari. Trainer: Bruno Baltazar.

Goals: 1-0, 2-0, 3-0 Rigino Cicilia (9, 13, 19), 3-1 Caju (90+4).

17.07.2018; Stádio Neo GSP, Nicosia; Referee: Glenn Nyberg (Sweden); Attendance: 12,149

APOEL FC Nicosia – FK Sūduva Marijampolé 1-0(1-0)

APOEL: Boy Waterman, Zhivko Milanov, Carlão, Yohan Tavares, Nicolas Ioannou (77.Leonardo Natel), Nuno Morais, Giorgos Efrem (77.Efstathios Aloneftis), Lucas Souza, Mickaël Poté, Dellatorre, Musa Al-Taamari (65.Roland Sallai). Trainer: Bruno Baltazar.

Sūduva Marijampolé: Ivan Kardum, Vaidas Slavickas, Algis Jankauskas, Andro Svrljuga, Aleksandar Zivanovic, Povilas Leimonas, Gerson Acevedo (76.Robertas Vézevicius), Ovidijus Verbickas, Giedrius Matulevicius, Mihret Topcagic (53.Julius Kasparavicius), Rigino Cicilia (90+5.Gui Finkler). Trainer: Vladimir Cheburin.

Goal: 1-0 Mickaël Poté (20).

[FK Sūduva Marijampolé won 3-2 on aggregate]

11.07.2018; Stadions Skonto, Riga; Referee: Mykola Balakin (Ukraine); Attendance: 2,068

FK Spartaks Jūrmala – FK Crvena Zvezda Beograd 0-0

Spartaks Jūrmala: Jevgēnijs Nerugals, Gints Freimanis, Aleksandar Kosoric, Mārcis Oss, Ingus Slampe, Aleksejs Visnakovs, Artemiy Maleev, Oleg Dmitriev (77.Pāvels Mihadjuks), Evgeni Kobzar (60.Denis Davydov), Kaspars Svārups (66.Diego Aguirre), Vitor Faísca. Trainer: Aleksandr Grishin.

Crvena Zvezda: Milan Borjan, Vujadin Savic, Milan Rodic, Filip Stojkovic, Srdjan Babic, Nenad Krsticic, Branko Jovicic, Nemanja Milic (46.Lorenzo Ebecilio), Nikola Stojiljkovic (18.Milan Pavkov), Mohamed Ben Nabouhane, Nemanja Radonjic (82.Milan Jevtovic). Trainer: Vladan Milojevic.

17.07.2018; Stadion „Rajko Mitić", Beograd; Referee: Alper Ulusoy (Turkey); Attendance: 23,390

FK Crvena Zvezda Beograd – FK Spartaks Jūrmala 2-0(0-0)

Crvena Zvezda: Milan Borjan, Vujadin Savic, Milan Rodic, Milos Degenek, Filip Stojkovic, Nenad Krsticic, Branko Jovicic, Nemanja Milic (60.Milan Pavkov), Lorenzo Ebecilio (72.Dejan Meleg), Mohamed Ben Nabouhane, Nemanja Radonjic (85.Dusan Jovancic). Trainer: Vladan Milojevic.

Spartaks Jūrmala: Jevgēnijs Nerugals, Gints Freimanis, Aleksandar Kosoric, Mārcis Oss, Ingus Slampe, Aleksejs Visnakovs (49.Denis Davydov), Artemiy Maleev, Oleg Dmitriev (83.Ariagner Smith), Evgeni Kobzar, Kaspars Svārups (56.Diego Aguirre), Vitor Faísca. Trainer: Aleksandr Grishin.

Goals: 1-0 Mohamed Ben Nabouhane (78), 2-0 Nenad Krsticic (81).

[FK Crvena Zvezda Beograd won 2-0 on aggregate]

11.07.2018; Stadión "Antona Malatinského", Trnava; Referee: Denis Scherbakov (Belarus); Attendance: *played behind closed doors*

FC Spartak Trnava – HŠK Zrinjski Mostar 1-0(0-0)

Spartak Trnava: Martin Chudy, Matús Conka, Ivan Hladík, Boris Godál, Andrej Kadlec, Erik Grendel (78.Senad Jarovic), Jakub Rada, Lukás Gressák, Vakhtang Chanturishvili [*sent off 89*], Erik Jirka, Marvin Egho (87.Fabian Miesenböck). Trainer: Radoslav Látal.

Zrinjski Mostar: Ivan Brkic, Pero Stojkic, Slobodan Jakovljevic, Ognjen Todorovic (73.Semir Pezer), Milos Filipovic (89.Marko Bencun), Hrvoje Barisic, Frane Cirjak [*sent off 70*], Edin Rustemovic, Marin Galic, Nemanja Bilbija, Milos Acimovic (68.Toni Jovic). Trainer: Ante Mise.

Goal: 1-0 Erik Jirka (79).

18.07.2018; Stadion pod Bijelim Brijegom, Mostar; Referee: Julian Weinberger (Austria); Attendance: 5,100

HŠK Zrinjski Mostar – FC Spartak Trnava 1-1(0-1)

Zrinjski Mostar: Ivan Brkic, Pero Stojkic, Slobodan Jakovljevic, Ognjen Todorovic, Milos Filipovic, Hrvoje Barisic, Edin Rustemovic (54.Marko Bencun), Ismar Hairlahovic (81.Semir Pezer), Marin Galic, Nemanja Bilbija, Milos Acimovic (75.Toni Jovic). Trainer: Ante Mise.

Spartak Trnava: Martin Chudy, Martin Tóth (17.Fabian Miesenböck), Matús Conka, Ivan Hladík, Boris Godál, Andrej Kadlec, Erik Grendel (79.Matej Oravec), Jakub Rada, Lukás Gressák, Erik Jirka, Marvin Egho (81.Senad Jarovic). Trainer: Radoslav Látal.

Goals: 0-1 Boris Godál (15), 1-1 Ognjen Todorovic (58).

[FC Spartak Trnava won 2-1 on aggregate]

11.07.2018; Ludogorets Arena, Razgrad; Referee: Dumitri Muntean (Moldova); Attendance: 4,597

PFC Ludogorets Razgrad – Crusaders FC Belfast 7-0(2-0)

PFC Ludogorets Razgrad: Renan, Cosmin Moti, Cicinho, Rafael Forster, Svetoslav Dyakov, Gustavo Campanharo (64.Lucas Sasha), Wanderson (77.Jody Lukoki), Natanael Pimienta, Claudiu Keserü (68.Jakub Swierczok), Marcelinho, Virgil Misidjan. Trainer: Paulo Autuori.

Crusaders FC: Sean O'Neill, Billy Joe Burns, Howard Beverland, Rodney Brown, Declan Caddell (59.Kyle Owens), Philip Lowry, Jordan Forsythe, Paul Heatley (75.Jamie Glackin), Matthew Snoddy, Michael Carvill (76.Ross Clarke), Jordan Owens. Trainer: Stephen Baxter.

Goals: 1-0 Marcelinho (25), 2-0 Rodney Brown (40 own goal), 3-0 Claudiu Keserü (53), 4-0 Marcelinho (66), 5-0, 6-0, 7-0 Jakub Swierczok (73, 78, 80).

17.07.2018; Seaview, Belfast; Referee: Roomer Tarajev (Estonia); Attendance: 1,116

Crusaders FC Belfast– PFC Ludogorets Razgrad 0-2(0-1)

Crusaders FC: Sean O'Neill, Billy Joe Burns, Howard Beverland, Kyle Owens, Rodney Brown, Philip Lowry (67.Declan Caddell), Jordan Forsythe, Matthew Snoddy, Ross Clarke (81.Jamie Glackin), Michael Carvill, Jordan Owens (32.David Cushley). Trainer: Stephen Baxter.

Ludogorets Razgrad: Jorge Broun, Cosmin Moti, Cicinho (61.Tsvetomir Panov), Georgi Terziev, Svetoslav Dyakov, Lucas Sasha, Natanael Pimienta (70.Anton Nedyalkov), João Paulo, Marcelinho, Jody Lukoki, Jakub Swierczok (79.Dimo Balakov). Trainer: Paulo Autuori.

Goals: 0-1 Rodney Brown (11 own goal), 0-2 Jakub Swierczok (65).

[PFC Ludogorets Razgrad won 9-0 on aggregate]

11.07.2018; "Loro Boriçi" Stadiumi, Shkodër; Referee: Thóroddur Hjaltalín (Iceland); Attendance: 350

FK Kukësi – Valletta FC 0-0

FK Kukësi: Stivi Frashëri, Ylli Shameti, Willian Cordeiro, Simon Rrumbullaku, Vangjel Zguro (58.Valon Ethemi), Harallamb Qaqi, Irakli Dzaria, Donjet Shkodra (80.Dino Spehar), Arber Çyrbja, Besar Musolli, Sebino Plaku (75.Haris Harba). Trainer: Peter Pacult.

Valetta FC: Henry Bonello, Joseph Zerafa, Ryan Camilleri, Steve Borg, Rowen Muscat (70.Juan Gill), Raed Ibrahim Al Mukhaini (90+1.Jean Borg), Enmy Peña, Santiago Malano, Miguel Alba (76.Kyrian Nwoko), Matteo Piciollo, Mario Fontanella. Trainer: Gilbert Agius.

17.07.2018; MFA Centenary Stadium, Ta'Qali; Referee: Igor Pajac (Croatia); Attendance: 1,307

Valletta FC – FK Kukësi 1-1(0-0)

Valetta FC: Henry Bonello, Joseph Zerafa (88.Kyrian Nwoko), Ryan Camilleri, Steve Borg, Rowen Muscat, Raed Ibrahim Al Mukhaini (83.Juan Gill), Enmy Peña, Santiago Malano, Miguel Alba (90.Bogdan Gavrila), Matteo Piciollo, Mario Fontanella. Trainer: Gilbert Agius.

FK Kukësi: Stivi Frashëri, Ylli Shameti, Willian Cordeiro, Simon Rrumbullaku, Vangjel Zguro [*sent off 87 on the bench*] (57.Dino Spehar), Albi Alla, Irakli Dzaria, Donjet Shkodra (57.Haris Harba), Arber Çyrbja (65.Valon Ethemi), Besar Musolli, Sebino Plaku. Trainer: Armando Cungu.

Goals: 1-0 Santiago Malano (67), 1-1 Irakli Dzaria (84).

[FK Kukësi won on away goals rule (1-1 on aggregate)]

Stadion Stozice, Ljubljana; Referee: Lawrence Visser (Belgium); Attendance: 5,248

NK Olimpija Ljubljana – Qarabag FK Bakı 0-1(0-0)

Olimpija Ljubljana: Aljaz Ivacic, Aris Zarifovic, Dino Stiglec, Macky Bagnack, Marko Gajic, Rok Kronaveter (81.Goran Brkic), Marko Putincanin, Stefan Savic (71.Matic Crnic), Daniel Avramovski (88.Kingsley Boateng), Tomislav Tomic, Issah Abass [*sent off 85*]. Trainer: Ilija Stolica.

Qarabag FK: Vagner, Jakub Rzezniczak, Maksim Medvedev, Badavi Hüseynov, Míchel, Gara Garayev[*sent off 90+1*], Filip Ozobic (63.Dani Quintana), Wilde Guerrier, Joshgun Diniyev (46.Simeon Slavchev), Abdellah Zoubir (90+3.Rashad Sadygov), Mahir Madatov. Trainer: Gurban Gurbanov.

Goal: 0-1 Wilde Guerrier (79).

18.07.2018; "Tofiq Bahramov" adina Respublika stadionu, Bakı; Referee: Erez Papir (Israel); Attendance: 21,520

Qarabag FK Bakı – NK Olimpija Ljubljana 0-0

Qarabag FK: Vagner, Jakub Rzezniczak, Maksim Medvedev, Badavi Hüseynov, Míchel, Dani Quintana (42.Filip Ozobic), Simeon Slavchev, Wilde Guerrier, Joshgun Diniyev, Abdellah Zoubir, Mahir Madatov (90+4.Ansi Agolli). Trainer: Gurban Gurbanov.

Olimpija Ljubljana: Aljaz Ivacic, Aris Zarifovic, Dino Stiglec, Macky Bagnack (74.Branko Ilic), Marko Gajic [*sent off 90+6*], Rok Kronaveter (72.Danijel Miskic), Marko Putincanin, Stefan Savic (46.Matic Crnic), Daniel Avramovski, Tomislav Tomic, Kingsley Boateng. Trainer: Ilija Stolica.

[Qarabag FK Bakı won 1-0 on aggregate]

11.07.2018; Vodafonevöllurinn, Reykjavík; Referee: Rade Obrenovic (Slovenia); Attendance: 1,088

Knattspyrnufélagið Valur Reykjavík – Rosenborg BK Trondheim 1-0(0-0)

Valur: Anton Ari Einarsson, Birkir Sævarsson, Bjarni Eiríksson, Eidur Sigurbjörnsson, Arnar Geirsson, Haukur Sigurdsson, Kristinn Sigurdsson, Sigurdur Lárusson, Ólafur Finsen (74.Gudjon Lydsson), Patrick Pedersen, Tobias Thomsen (85.Kristinn Halldórsson). Trainer: Ólafur Jóhannesson.

Rosenborg: André Hansen, Tore Reginiussen, Even Hovland, Vegar Hedenstad (41.Marius Lundemo), Birger Meling, Erlend Reitan, Mike Jensen, Anders Trondsen, Nicklas Bendtner, Erik Botheim (64.Alexander Søderlund), Jonathan Levi. Trainer: Kåre Ingebrigtsen.

Goal: 1-0 Eidur Sigurbjörnsson (84).

18.07.2018; Lerkendal Stadion, Trondheim; Referee: Stefan Apostolov (Bulgaria); Attendance: 10,604

Rosenborg BK Trondheim – Valur Reykjavík 3-1(0-0)

Rosenborg: André Hansen, Tore Reginiussen, Even Hovland, Vegar Hedenstad, Birger Meling, Mike Jensen, Anders Trondsen, Marius Lundemo (86.Matthías Vilhjálmsson), Nicklas Bendtner, Pål Helland, Jonathan Levi (81.Alexander Søderlund). Trainer: Kåre Ingebrigtsen.

Valur Reykjavík: Anton Ari Einarsson, Birkir Sævarsson, Bjarni Eiríksson, Eidur Sigurbjörnsson, Arnar Geirsson, Haukur Sigurdsson (74.Gudjón Lydsson), Kristinn Sigurdsson, Sigurdur Lárusson, Ólafur Finsen (75.Einar Karl Ingvarsson), Patrick Pedersen [*sent off 90+3 on the bench*] (89.Ívar Jónsson), Tobias Thomsen. Trainer: Ólafur Jóhannesson.

Goals: 1-0 Nicklas Bendtner (55 penalty), 2-0 Anders Trondsen (72), 2-1 Kristinn Sigurdsson (85 penalty), 3-1 Nicklas Bendtner (90+4 penalty).

[Rosenborg BK Trondheim won 3-2 on aggregate]

SECOND QUALIFYING ROUND

CHAMPIONS ROUTE

24.07.2018; Astana Arena, Astana; Referee: Radu Petrescu (Romania); Attendance: 23,010

Astana FC – FC Midtjylland Herning 2-1(1-0)

Astana FC: Nenad Eric, Antonio Rukavina, Marin Anicic, Dmitriy Shomko, Evgeni Postnikov, Marin Tomasov, Ivan Maevski, Serikzhan Muzhikov (76.Richard Almeyda), László Kleinheisler, Pedro Henrique (85.Rangelo Janga), Roman Murtazaev (46.Aleksey Shchetkin). Trainer: Roman Grygorchuk.

FC Midtjylland: Jesper Hansen, Kian Hansen (77.Zsolt Korcsmár), Erik Sviatchenko, Marc Hende, Bubacarr Sanneh, Alexander Munksgaard, Jakob Poulsen, Tim Sparv, Gustav Wikheim (85.Mayron George), Ayo Simon Okosun (68.Franck Ogochukwu), Ebere Paul Onuachu. Trainer: Jess Thorup.

Goals: 1-0 László Kleinheisler (31), 1-1 Gustav Wikheim (51), 2-1 László Kleinheisler (90+4).

01.08.2018; MCH Arena, Herning; Referee: Juan Martínez Munuera (Spain); Attendance: 8,731

FC Midtjylland Herning – Astana FC 0-0

FC Midtjylland: Jesper Hansen, Kian Hansen, Erik Sviatchenko (76.Ayo Simon Okosun), Marc Hende, Bubacarr Sanneh, Alexander Munksgaard, Jakob Poulsen, Tim Sparv (59.Awer Mabil), Gustav Wikheim, Franck Ogochukwu (71.Mikkel Duelund), Ebere Paul Onuachu. Trainer: Jess Thorup.

Astana FC: Nenad Eric, Antonio Rukavina, Marin Anicic, Dmitriy Shomko, Evgeni Postnikov, Marin Tomasov, Ivan Maevski, Serikzhan Muzhikov, László Kleinheisler (90+2.Yuriy Logvinenko), Pedro Henrique (78.Roman Murtazaev), Junior Kabananga (62.Aleksey Shchetkin). Trainer: Roman Grygorchuk.

[Astana FC won 2-1 on aggregate]

24.07.2018; Stadionul "Dr. Constantin Radulescu", Cluj-Napoca; Referee: Nikoa Dabanovic (Montenegro); Attendance: 6,950

FC CFR 1907 Cluj – Malmö FF 0-1(0-1)

CFR Cluj: Giedrius Arlauskis, Andrei Muresan, Paulo Vinícius, Camora, Cristian Manea, Emmanuel Culio, Ciprian Deac (79.Alexandru Paun), Ovidiu Hoban (60.Mate Males), Damjan Djokovic (46.Alexandru Ionita (II)), George Tucudean, Billel Omrani. Trainer: Eduard Iordanescu.

Malmö FF: Johan Dahlin, Behrang Safari, Rasmus Bengtsson, Eric Larsson (89.Andreas Vindheim), Lasse Nielsen, Søren Rieks, Anders Christiansen, Arnór Ingvi Traustason (89.Samuel Adrian), Oscar Lewicki, Markus Rosenberg, Carlos Strandberg (86.Marcus Antonsson). Trainer: Uwe Rösler.

Goal: 0-1 Carlos Strandberg (45).

01.08.2018; Swedbank Stadion, Malmö; Referee: Andrew Dallas (Scotland); Attendance: 18,153

Malmö FF – FC CFR 1907 Cluj 1-1(0-1)

Malmö FF: Johan Dahlin, Behrang Safari, Rasmus Bengtsson, Eric Larsson (81.Andreas Vindheim), Lasse Nielsen, Søren Rieks, Anders Christiansen, Fouad Bachirou, Arnór Ingvi Traustason (73.Oscar Lewicki), Markus Rosenberg, Carlos Strandberg (61.Marcus Antonsson). Trainer: Uwe Rösler.

CFR Cluj: Giedrius Arlauskis, Andrei Muresan, Paulo Vinícius, Camora, Cristian Manea, Emmanuel Culio [*sent off 77*], Ciprian Deac (43.Sebastian Mailat), Ovidiu Hoban (64.Giuseppe De Luca), Damjan Djokovic (58.Mihai Bordeianu), George Tucudean, Billel Omrani. Trainer: Toni.

Goals: 0-1 Damjan Djokovic (36), 1-1 Arnór Ingvi Traustason (55).

[Malmö FF won 2-1 on aggregate]

24.07.2018; Stadion Makdimir, Zagreb; Referee: Ali Palabiyik (Turkey); Attendance: 9,056

GNK Dinamo Zagreb – Hapoel Be'er Sheva FC 5-0(2-0)

Dinamo Zagreb: Daniel Zagorac, Marin Leovac, Kévin Théophile-Catherine, Emir Dilaver, Arijan Ademi, Izet Hajrovic (86.Ivan Fiolic), Petar Stojanovic, Amer Gojak, Daniel Olmo, Mario Budimir (70.Armin Hodzic), Mislav Orsic (74.Mario Situm). Trainer: Nenad Bjelica.

Hapoel Be'er Sheva: Giannis Anestis, Julien Cétout (46.Hanan Maman), Ben Bitton, Loai Taha, Shir Tzedek, Oren Bitton, John Ogu, Hen Ezra (54.Anthony Nwakaeme), Maor Melikson, Daniel Einbinder (74.Eden Ben Basat), Ben Sahar. Trainer: Bachar Bakhar.

Goals: 1-0 Izet Hajrovic (22), 2-0 Mislav Orsic (28), 3-0, 4-0 Arijan Ademi (51, 62), 5-0 Armin Hodzic (82).

31.07.2018; Yaakov Turner Toto Stadium, Beersheva; Referee: François Letexier (France); Attendance: 10,181

Hapoel Be'er Sheva FC – GNK Dinamo Zagreb 2-2(2-0)

Hapoel Be'er Sheva: David Goresh, Matan Ohayon, Ben Bitton, Shir Tzedek, Oren Bitton, John Ogu, Maor Melikson (84.Niv Zrihan), Hanan Maman (72.Hen Ezra), Daniel Einbinder, Eden Ben Basat (76.Ben Sahar), Anthony Nwakaeme. Trainer: Bachar Bakhar.

Dinamo Zagreb: Daniel Zagorac, Marin Leovac, Kévin Théophile-Catherine, Emir Dilaver, Arijan Ademi, Izet Hajrovic (82.Ivan Fiolic), Petar Stojanovic, Amer Gojak, Daniel Olmo (77.Ivan Sunjic), Mario Budimir (56.Mario Gavranovic), Mislav Orsic. Trainer: Nenad Bjelica.

Goals: 1-0 John Ogu (14), 2-0 Petar Stojanovic (34 own goal), 2-1 Mario Budimir (49), 2-2 Izet Hajrovic (54).

[GNK Dinamo Zagreb won 7-2 on aggregate]

24.07.2018; Telekom Arena, Skopje; Referee: Mads-Kristoffer Kristoffersen (Denmark); Attendance: 3,696

KF Shkëndija 79 – FC Sheriff Tiraspol 1-0(1-0)

KF Shkëndija: Kostadin Zahov, Mevlan Murati, Visar Musliu, Egzon Bejtulai, Mevlan Adili, Armend Alimi, Ennur Totre (75.Sciprim Taipi), Besart Ibraimi, Izair Emini (86.Konstantin Cheshmedzhiev), Stênio Júnior, Remzi Selmani (66.Shefit Shefiti). Trainer: Qatip Osmani.

Sheriff Tiraspol: Zvonimir Mikulic, Ante Kulusic, Mateo Susic, Veaceslav Posmac, Vladimir Kovacevic, Cristiano, Antun Palic, Yuri Kendysh, Rifet Kapic (80.Gerson Rodrigues), Ziguy Badibanga, Joálisson (88.Evgheni Oancea), Al-Hadji Kamara (73.Alexandru Boiciuc). Trainer: Goran Sablic

Goal: 1-0 Besart Ibraimi (24).

31.07.2018; Bolshaya Sportivnaya Arena, Tiraspol; Referee: Ville Nevalainen (Finland); Attendance: 6,319

FC Sheriff Tiraspol – KF Shkëndija 79 0-0

Sheriff Tiraspol: Sergei Pascenco, Mateo Susic, Veaceslav Posmac, Vladimir Kovacevic, Cristiano, Antun Palic, Yuri Kendysh, Rifet Kapic (78.Alexandru Boiciuc), Ziguy Badibanga (56.Gerson Rodrigues), Joálisson (69.Wilfred Balima), Al-Hadji Kamara. Trainer: Goran Sablic.

KF Shkëndija: Kostadin Zahov, Mevlan Murati, Visar Musliu, Egzon Bejtulai, Mevlan Adili, Armend Alimi, Ennur Totre (84.Sciprim Taipi), Besart Ibraimi, Izair Emini (67.Valmir Nafiu), Stênio Júnior, Remzi Selmani (90+3.Konstantin Cheshmedzhiev). Trainer: Qatip Osmani.

[KF Shkëndija 79 won 1-0 on aggregate]

24.07.2018; Stadion „Rajko Mitić", Beograd; Referee: Bastian Dankert (Germany); Attendance: 23,218

FK Crvena Zvezda Beograd – FK Sūduva Marijampolė 3-0(2-0)

Crvena Zvezda: Milan Borjan, Vujadin Savic, Milan Rodic, Milos Degenek, Filip Stojkovic, Nenad Krsticic (37.Dusan Jovancic), Branko Jovicic, Nemanja Milic, Lorenzo Ebecilio (64.Milan Jevtovic), Mohamed Ben Nabouhane, Nemanja Radonjic (78.Marko Gobeljic). Trainer: Vladan Milojevic.

Sūduva Marijampolė: Ivan Kardum, Vaidas Slavickas, Algis Jankauskas, Andro Svrljuga, Aleksandar Zivanovic, Povilas Leimonas, Gerson Acevedo, Ovidijus Verbickas, Giedrius Matulevicius (80.Vitaly Gayduchik), Mihret Topcagic (8.Robertas Vézevicius), Rigino Cicilia. Trainer: Vladimir Cheburin.

Goals: 1-0 Lorenzo Ebecilio (23), 2-0, 3-0 Nemanja Radonjic (35, 58).

01.08.2018; Marijampolės sporto centro stadione, Marijampolė; Referee: Tiago Martins (Portugal); Attendance: 4,020

FK Sūduva Marijampolė – FK Crvena Zvezda Beograd 0-2(0-2)

FK Sūduva Marijampolė: Ivan Kardum, Vaidas Slavickas, Algis Jankauskas, Andro Svrljuga, Aleksandar Zivanovic (68.Vitaly Gayduchik), Guilherme, Povilas Leimonas, Robertas Vézevicius (60.Julius Kasparavicius), Ovidijus Verbickas, Giedrius Matulevicius (77.Gerson Acevedo), Rigino Cicilia. Trainer: Vladimir Cheburin.

Crvena Zvezda: Milan Borjan, Vujadin Savic, Milan Rodic (66.Marko Gobeljic), Milos Degenek, Filip Stojkovic, Nenad Krsticic, Slavoljub Srnic (76.Lorenzo Ebecilio), Branko Jovicic, Nemanja Milic (60.Nikola Stojiljkovic), Mohamed Ben Nabouhane, Nemanja Radonjic. Trainer: Vladan Milojevic.

Goals: 0-1 Mohamed Ben Nabouhane (8), 0-2 Nemanja Radonjic (38).

[FK Crvena Zvezda Beograd won 5-0 on aggregate]

24.07.2018; Stadion "Marszalka Józefa Pilsudskiego", Warszawa; Referee: Ádám Farkas (Hungary); Attendance: 15,527

Legia Warszawa – FC Spartak Trnava 0-2(0-1)

Legia Warszawa: Arkadiusz Malarz, Iñaki Astiz, Adam Hlousek, Krzysztof Maczynski (17.Mateusz Wieteska), Marko Vesovic, Domagoj Antolic, Chris Philipps (69.Kasper Hämäläinen), Cafú, Sebastian Szymanski (63.Miroslav Radovic), José Kanté, Carlitos López. Trainer: Dean Klafuric.

Spartak Trnava: Martin Chudy, Martin Tóth, Matús Conka, Boris Godál, Andrej Kadlec, Erik Grendel (64.Fabian Miesenböck), Jakub Rada, Anton Sloboda (86.Ivan Hladík), Lukás Gressák, Erik Jirka, Marvin Egho (90+1.Ján Vlasko). Trainer: Radoslav Látal.

Goals: 0-1 Erik Grendel (16), 0-2 Ján Vlasko (90+3).

31.07.2018; City Arena, Trnava; Referee: Roi Reinshreiber (Israel); Attendance: 17,204

FC Spartak Trnava – Legia Warszawa 0-1(0-0)

Spartak Trnava: Martin Chudy, Martin Tóth, Matús Conka, Boris Godál, Andrej Kadlec, Erik Grendel (70.Fabian Miesenböck), Jakub Rada, Anton Sloboda (76.Ján Vlasko), Lukás Gressák, Erik Jirka, Marvin Egho (90+1.Ivan Hladík). Trainer: Radoslav Látal.

Legia Warszawa: Arkadiusz Malarz, Michal Pazdan (53.Carlitos López), Iñaki Astiz, Adam Hlousek, Mateusz Wieteska, Miroslav Radovic (46.Cafú), Krzysztof Maczynski (80.Kasper Hämäläinen), Marko Vesovic [*sent off 37*], Domagoj Antolic [*sent off 85*], Michal Kucharczyk, José Kanté. Trainer: Dean Klafuric.

Goal: 0-1 Iñaki Astiz (63).

[FC Spartak Trnava won 2-1 on aggregate]

25.07.2018; Ludogorets Arena, Razgrad; Referee: Bojan Pandzic (Sweden); Attendance: 5,327

PFC Ludogorets Razgrad – MOL Vidi FC Székesfehérvár 0-0

Ludogorets Razgrad: Renan, Cosmin Moti, Cicinho, Rafael Forster, Svetoslav Dyakov, Lucas Sasha (61.Gustavo Campanharo), Wanderson, Natanael Pimienta, Claudiu Keserü (60.Jakub Swierczok), Marcelinho, Virgil Misidjan (84.Jody Lukoki). Trainer: Paulo Autuori.

MOL Vidi FC: Ádam Kovácsik, Roland Juhász, Attila Fiola, Loïc Négo, Paulo Vinícius, Stopira, Szabolcs Huszti, József Varga, István Kovács (68.Máté Pátkai), Boban Nikolov (71.Danko Lazovic), Marko Scepovic (80.Stefan Scepovic). Trainer: Marko Nikolic.

01.08.2018; Pancho Aréna, Felcsút; Referee: Manuel Schüttengruber (Austria); Attendance: 2,878

MOL Vidi FC Székesfehérvár – PFC Ludogorets Razgrad 1-0(1-0)

MOL Vidi FC: Ádam Kovácsik, Roland Juhász, Attila Fiola, Loïc Négo, Paulo Vinícius, Stopira, Szabolcs Huszti, Anel Hadzic (89.Boban Nikolov), József Varga, István Kovács (90.Máté Pátkai), Marko Scepovic (75.Stefan Scepovic). Trainer: Marko Nikolic.

Ludogorets Razgrad: Renan, Cosmin Moti, Cicinho, Georgi Terziev, Svetoslav Dyakov, Gustavo Campanharo (46.Jacek Góralski), Wanderson (74.João Paulo), Natanael Pimienta, Marcelinho, Virgil Misidjan [*sent off 39*], Jakub Swierczok (67.Claudiu Keserü). Trainer: Paulo Autuori.

Goal: 1-0 Anel Hadzic (45).

[MOL Vidi FC Székesfehérvár won 1-0 on aggregate]

25.07.2018; Stadiumi Loro Boriçi, Shkodër; Referee: Ola Hobber Nilsen (Norway); Attendance: 700

FK Kukësi – Qarabag FK Bakı **0-0**

FK Kukësi: Stivi Frashëri, Ylli Shameti, Willian Cordeiro, Simon Rrumbullaku, Edis Maliki, Albi Alla, Harallamb Qaqi, Irakli Dzaria, Arber Çyrbja (90+2.Valon Ethemi), Besar Musolli, Sebino Plaku (76.Haris Harba). Trainer: Armando Cungu.

Qarabag FK: Vagner, Rashad Sadygov, Ansi Agolli, Maksim Medvedev, Badavi Hüseynov, Míchel, Gara Garayev, Filip Ozobic, Simeon Slavchev, Wilde Guerrier (89.Abbas Hüseynov), Mahir Madatov. Trainer: Gurban Gurbanov.

01.08.2018; "Tofiq Bahramov" adina Respublika stadionu, Bakı; Referee: Peter Královic (Slovakia); Attendance: 25,030

Qarabag FK Bakı – FK Kukësi **3-0(1-0)**

Qarabag FK: Vagner, Rashad Sadygov (77.Jakup Rzezniczak), Maksim Medvedev, Badavi Hüseynov, Míchel, Dani Quintana (60.Dzon Delarge), Gara Garayev, Simeon Slavchev, Wilde Guerrier, Abdellah Zoubir, Innocent Emeghara (66.Mahir Madatov). Trainer: Gurban Gurbanov.

FK Kukësi: Stivi Frashëri, Ylli Shameti, Willian Cordeiro, Simon Rrumbullaku, Edis Maliki, Albi Alla [*sent off 52*], Harallamb Qaqi, Irakli Dzaria, Arber Çyrbja (46.Dino Spehar), Besar Musolli (84.Donjet Shkodra), Sebino Plaku (46.Reginaldo). Trainer: Armando Cungu

Goals: 1-0, 2-0 Dani Quintana (24 penalty, 57 penalty), 3-0 Dzon Delarge (89).

[Qarabag FK Bakı won 3-0 on aggregate]

25.07.2018; Borisov Arena, Borisov; Referee: Marco Di Bello (Italy); Attendance: 11,567

FC BATE Borisov – HJK Helsinki **0-0**

BATE Borisov: Denis Scherbitski, Egor Filipenko, Maksim Volodko, Aleksandar Filipovic, Alexei Rios, Igor Stasevich, Dmitri Baga, Stanislav Dragun, Mirko Ivanic, Maksim Skavysh (65.Aliaksandr Hleb), Nikolay Signevich. Trainer: Alexey Baga.

HJK Helsinki: Maksim Rudakov, Rafinha, Hannu Patronen, Daniel O'Shaughnessy, Faith Obilor, Anthony Annan, Moshtagh Yaghoubi, Sebastian Dahlström, Riku Riski (70.Nikolai Alho), Evans Mensah (89.Mikko Sumusalo), Klauss (85.Macauley Chrisantus). Trainer: Mika Lehkosuo.

01.08.2018; Telia 5G-areena, Helsinki; Referee: Jonathan Lardot (Belgium); Attendance: 10,210

HJK Helsinki – FC BATE Borisov **1-2(1-2)**

HJK Helsinki: Maksim Rudakov, Rafinha, Hannu Patronen, Mikko Sumusalo, Faith Obilor, Anthony Annan, Moshtagh Yaghoubi, Sebastian Dahlström (74.Eetu Vertainen), Riku Riski (69.Nikolai Alho), Evans Mensah, Klauss. Trainer: Mika Lehkosuo.

BATE Borisov: Denis Scherbitski, Egor Filipenko, Maksim Volodko, Aleksandar Filipovic, Alexei Rios, Igor Stasevich (86.Jasse Tuominen), Dmitri Baga (77.Yevgeniy Berezkin), Stanislav Dragun, Mirko Ivanic (67.Maksim Skavysh), Evgeni Yablonski, Nikolay Signevich. Trainer: Alexey Baga.

Goals: 0-1 Rafinha (20 own goal), 0-2 Igor Stasevich (24), 1-2 Moshtagh Yaghoubi (28).

[FC BATE Borisov won 2-1 on aggregate]

25.07.2018; Celtic Park, Glasgow; Referee: Bart Vertenten (Belgium); Attendance: 51,184

Celtic FC Glasgow – Rosenborg BK Trondheim **3-1(1-1)**

Celtic: Craig Gordon, Cristian Gamboa, Kieran Tierney, Kristoffer Ajer, Jack Hendry, Scott Brown, Scott Sinclair, James Forrest, Callum McGregor, Olivier Ntcham (76.Tom Rogic), Odsonne Édouard. Trainer: Brendan Rodgers.

Rosenborg: André Hansen, Tore Reginiussen, Even Hovland, Vegar Hedenstad, Birger Meling, Mike Jensen, Anders Trondsen, Marius Lundemo (61.Alexander Søderlund), Nicklas Bendtner, Pål Helland (72.Alexander Gersbach), Jonathan Levi. Trainer: Rini Coolen.

Goals: 0-1 Birger Meling (16), 1-1 Odsonne Édouard (43), 2-1 Olivier Ntcham (46), 3-1 Odsonne Édouard (75).

01.08.2018; Lerkendal Stadion, Trondheim; Referee: Sandro Schärer (Switzerland); Attendance: 14,263

Rosenborg BK Trondheim – Celtic FC Glasgow **0-0**

Rosenborg: André Hansen, Tore Reginiussen, Even Hovland, Vegar Hedenstad, Birger Meling, Mike Jensen, Anders Trondsen (75.Matthías Vilhjálmsson), Marius Lundemo (90+2.Erik Botheim), Nicklas Bendtner, Pål Helland (58.Jonathan Levi), Alexander Søderlund. Trainer: Rini Coolen.

Celtic: Craig Gordon, Cristian Gamboa, Kieran Tierney (85.Mikael Lustig), Kristoffer Ajer, Jack Hendry, Scott Brown, Scott Sinclair, James Forrest (63.Tom Rogic), Callum McGregor, Olivier Ntcham, Odsonne Édouard (72.Ryan Christie). Trainer: Brendan Rodgers.

[Celtic FC Glasgow won 3-1 on aggregate]

LEAGUE ROUTE

24.07.2018; Stádio Toumbas, Thessaloniki; Referee: Bobby Madley (England); Attendance: 24,670

PAOK Thessaloníki – FC Basel **2-1(1-0)**

PAOK: Alexandros Paschalakis, Léo Matos, José Ángel Crespo, Fernando Varela, Vieirinha, Maurício, Cañas, Dimitris Pelkas, Aleksandar Prijovic (83.Amr Warda), Dimitris Limnios (90+3.Yevhen Shakhov), Léo Jabá (72.Omar El Kaddouri). Trainer: Razvan Lucescu.

FC Basel: Jonas Omlin, Marek Suchy, Éder Álvarez Balanta, Blas Riveros, Valentin Stocker, Serey Dié, Luca Zuffi, Fabian Frei, Raoul Petretta (44.Yves Kaiser), Albian Ajeti (90+4.Kevin Bua), Dimitri Oberlin (62.Aldo Kalulu). Trainer: Raphaël Wicky.

Goals: 1-0 Cañas (32), 2-0 Aleksandar Prijovic (80), 2-1 Albian Ajeti (82).

01.08.2018; St. Jakob-Park, Basel; Referee: Paolo Valeri (Italy); Attendance: 14,328

FC Basel – PAOK Thessaloníki **0-3(0-1)**

FC Basel: Jonas Omlin, Marek Suchy, Silvan Widmer, Éder Álvarez Balanta, Eray Cümart, Valentin Stocker (46.Samuele Campo), Serey Dié, Luca Zuffi, Aldo Kalulu (84.Dimitri Oberlin), Kevin Bua, Albian Ajeti (73.Ricky van Wolfswinkel). Trainer: Alexander Frei.

PAOK: Alexandros Paschalakis, Léo Matos, José Ángel Crespo, Fernando Varela, Evgen Khacheridi, Omar El Kaddouri (74.Léo Jabá), Maurício, Cañas (81.Yevhen Shakhov), Dimitris Pelkas (85.Amr Warda), Aleksandar Prijovic, Dimitris Limnios. Trainer: Razvan Lucescu.

Goals: 0-1 Fernando Varela (7), 0-2 Aleksandar Prijovic (52), 0-3 Omar El Kaddouri 60).

[PAOK Thessaloníki won 5-1 on aggregate]

25.07.2018; „Johan Cruijff" Arena, Amsterdam; Referee: Alejandro Hernández Hernández (Spain); Attendance: 53,106

AFC Ajax Amsterdam – SK Sturm Graz **2-0(1-0)**

Ajax Amsterdam: André Onana, Nicolás Tagliafico, Matthijs de Ligt, Lasse Schöne (66.Dusan Tadic), Hakim Ziyech, Donny van de Beek, Carel Eiting (84.Daley Blind), Noussair Mazraoui, Frenkie de Jong, Klaas-Jan Huntelaar (87.Kaj Sierhuis), David Neres. Trainer: Erik ten Hag.

Sturm Graz: Jörg Siebenhandl, Fabian Koch, Anastasios Avlonitis, Filipe Ferreira (46.Sandi Lovric), Lukas Spendlhofer, Dario Maresic, Stefan Hierländer, Markus Lackner, Peter Zulj, Lukas Grozurek (76.Philipp Huspek), Emeka Eze (58.Philipp Hosiner). Trainer: Heiko Vogel.

Goals: 1-0 Hakim Ziyech (15), 2-0 Lasse Schöne (57).

01.08.2018; Merkur Arena, Graz; Referee: Bartosz Frankowski (Poland); Attendance: 15,172

SK Sturm Graz – AFC Ajax Amsterdam **1-3(0-1)**

Sturm Graz: Jörg Siebenhandl, Fabian Koch, Filipe Ferreira, Lukas Spendlhofer, Dario Maresic, Stefan Hierländer, Markus Lackner (59.Raphael Obermair), Peter Zulj, Sandi Lovric, Philipp Hosiner (46.Markus Pink), Emeka Eze (66.Philipp Huspek). Trainer: Heiko Vogel.

Ajax Amsterdam: André Onana, Nicolás Tagliafico (55.Daley Blind), Matthijs de Ligt, Lasse Schöne, Dusan Tadic (67.Donny van de Beek), Hakim Ziyech, Carel Eiting (75.Maximilian Wöber), Noussair Mazraoui, Frenkie de Jong, Klaas-Jan Huntelaar, David Neres. Trainer: Erik ten Hag.

Goals: 0-1 Klaas-Jan Huntelaar (39), 0-2 Dusan Tadic (48), 0-3 Klaas-Jan Huntelaar (77), 1-3 André Onana (89 own goal).

[AFC Ajax Amsterdam won 5-1 on aggregate]

THIRD QUALIFYING ROUND

CHAMPIONS ROUTE

07.08.2018; Astana Arena, Astana; Referee: John Beaton (Scotland); Attendance: 26,500

Astana FC – GNK Dinamo Zagreb 0-2(0-1)

Astana FC: Nenad Eric, Antonio Rukavina, Marin Anicic, Dmitriy Shomko, Evgeni Postnikov, Marin Tomasov (80.Roman Murtazaev), Ivan Maevski, Serikzhan Muzhikov (46.Richard Almeyda), László Kleinheisler, Pedro Henrique, Junior Kabananga (63.Rangelo Janga). Trainer: Roman Grygorchuk.
Dinamo Zagreb: Daniel Zagorac, Marin Leovac, Kévin Théophile-Catherine, Emir Dilaver, Arijan Ademi (63.Ivan Sunjic), Izet Hajrovic (82.Damian Kadzior), Petar Stojanovic, Amer Gojak, Daniel Olmo, Mario Budimir (46.Mario Gavranovic), Mislav Orsic. Trainer: Nenad Bjelica.
Goals: 0-1 Mario Budimir (39), 0-2 Daniel Olmo (84).

14.08.2018; Stadion Maksimir, Zagreb; Referee: Gediminas Mazeika (Lithuania); Attendance: 11,903

GNK Dinamo Zagreb – Astana FC) 1-0(0-0

Dinamo Zagreb: Daniel Zagorac, Marin Leovac, Kévin Théophile-Catherine, Emir Dilaver, Arijan Ademi, Izet Hajrovic, Petar Stojanovic, Amer Gojak (70.Ivan Sunjic), Daniel Olmo, Mario Budimir (56.Mario Gavranovic), Mislav Orsic (82.Dino Peric). Trainer: Nenad Bjelica.
Astana FC: Nenad Eric, Antonio Rukavina, Dmitriy Shomko, Sergiy Maliy, Evgeni Postnikov, Marin Tomasov, Ivan Maevski, Richard Almeyda (78.Serikzhan Muzhikov), László Kleinheisler (78.Aleksey Shchetkin), Rangelo Janga (78.Junior Kabananga), Pedro Henrique. Trainer: Roman Grygorchuk.
Goal: 1-0 Mario Gavranovic (74).
[GNK Dinamo Zagreb won 3-0 on aggregate]

07.08.2018; "Tofiq Bahramov" adina Respublika stadionu, Bakı; Referee: Andreas Ekberg (Sweden); Attendance: 29,000

Qarabag FK Bakı – FC BATE Borisov 0-1(0-1)

Qarabag FK: Hannes Halldórsson, Rashad Sadygov, Maksim Medvedev, Badavi Hüseynov, Míchel, Gara Garayev, Simeon Slavchev (80.Filip Ozobic), Wilde Guerrier, Abdellah Zoubir, Innocent Emeghara, Dzon Delarge (67.Mahir Madatov). Trainer: Gurban Gurbanov.
BATE Borisov: Denis Scherbitski, Egor Filipenko, Maksim Volodko, Aleksandar Filipovic, Alexei Rios, Igor Stasevich (85.Aliaksandr Hleb), Dmitri Baga, Stanislav Dragun (75.Yevgeniy Berezkin), Mirko Ivanic (62.Maksim Skavysh), Evgeni Yablonski, Nikolay Signevich. Trainer: Alexey Baga
Goal: 0-1 Stanislav Dragun (36).

14.08.2018; Borisov Arena, Borisov; Referee: Andris Treimanis (Latvia); Attendance: 12,489

FC BATE Borisov – Qarabag FK Bakı 1-1(1-0)

BATE Borisov: Denis Scherbitski, Egor Filipenko, Maksim Volodko, Aleksandar Filipovic, Alexei Rios, Igor Stasevich, Dmitri Baga (70.Aliaksandr Hleb), Stanislav Dragun, Mirko Ivanic (78.Maksim Skavysh), Evgeni Yablonski, Nikolay Signevich. Trainer: Alexey Baga.
Qarabag FK: Hannes Halldórsson, Rashad Sadygov, Maksim Medvedev (85.Dzon Delarge), Badavi Hüseynov, Míchel, Gara Garayev, Simeon Slavchev (77.Filip Ozobic), Wilde Guerrier, Abdellah Zoubir, Innocent Emeghara [*sent off 77*], Mahir Madatov. Trainer: Gurban Gurbanov.
Goals: 1-0 Mirko Ivanic (20), 1-1 Míchel (54).
[FC BATE Borisov won 2-1 on aggregate]

07.08.2018; Swedbank Stadion, Malmö; Referee: Matej Jug (Slovenia); Attendance: 17,209

Malmö FF – MOL Vidi FC Székesfehérvár 1-1(0-0)

Malmö FF: Johan Dahlin, Behrang Safari, Rasmus Bengtsson (31.Franz Brorsson), Eric Larsson, Lasse Nielsen, Søren Rieks, Anders Christiansen, Fouad Bachirou, Arnór Ingvi Traustason (46.Oscar Lewicki), Markus Rosenberg, Marcus Antonsson (80.Romain Gall). Trainer: Uwe Rösler.
MOL Vidi FC: Ádam Kovácsik, Roland Juhász, Attila Fiola, Loïc Négo, Paulo Vinícius, Stopira, Anel Hadzic, István Kovács (78.Máté Pátkai), Boban Nikolov, Danko Lazovic (89.Stefan Scepovic), Marko Scepovic (82.József Varga). Trainer: Marko Nikolic.
Goals: 1-0 Anders Christiansen (62), 1-1 Loïc Négo (71).

14.08.2018; Pancho Aréna, Felcsút; Referee: Xavier Estrada Fernández (Spain); Attendance: 3,432

MOL Vidi FC Székesfehérvár – Malmö FF 0-0

MOL Vidi FC: Ádam Kovácsik, Roland Juhász, Attila Fiola, Loïc Négo, Paulo Vinícius, Stopira, Anel Hadzic, István Kovács (89.Szabolcs Huszti), Boban Nikolov (85.Máté Pátkai), Danko Lazovic (90+5.Krisztián Tamás), Marko Scepovic. Trainer: Marko Nikolic.
Malmö FF: Johan Dahlin, Eric Larsson (75.Andreas Vindheim), Lasse Nielsen, Franz Brorsson, Søren Rieks, Anders Christiansen, Fouad Bachirou, Oscar Lewicki, Bonke Innocent (79.Romain Gall), Markus Rosenberg, Carlos Strandberg (70.Marcus Antonsson). Trainer: Uwe Rösler.
[MOL Vidi FC Székesfehérvár won on away goals rule (1-1 on aggregate)]

07.08.2018; Stadion „Rajko Mitić", Beograd; Referee: Carlos del Cerro Grande (Spain); Attendance: 37,112

FK Crvena Zvezda Beograd – FC Spartak Trnava 1-1(1-1)

Crvena Zvezda: Milan Borjan, Vujadin Savic, Milan Rodic, Milos Degenek, Filip Stojkovic, Nenad Krsticic, Branko Jovicic, Nikola Stojiljkovic (53.Nemanja Milic, 73.Slavoljub Srnic), Lorenzo Ebecilio (79.Veljko Simic), Mohamed Ben Nabouhane, Nemanja Radonjic. Trainer: Vladan Milojevic.
Spartak Trnava: Martin Chudy, Martin Tóth, Matús Conka, Boris Godál, Andrej Kadlec, Erik Grendel (89.Fabian Miesenböck), Jakub Rada (90+5.Ivan Hladík), Anton Sloboda, Lukás Gressák, Erik Jirka, Marek Bakos (75.Marvin Egho). Trainer: Radoslav Látal.
Goals: 1-0 Mohamed Ben Nabouhane (23 penalty), 1-1 Erik Grendel (25).

14.08.2018; City Arena, Trnava; Referee: Serdar Gözübüyük (Netherlands); Attendance: 18,032

FC Spartak Trnava – FK Crvena Zvezda Beograd 1-2(1-1,1-1)

Spartak Trnava: Martin Chudy, Martin Tóth, Matús Conka (106.Ivan Hladík), Boris Godál, Andrej Kadlec, Erik Grendel, Jakub Rada (100.Filip Dangubic), Anton Sloboda, Lukás Gressák, Erik Jirka, Marek Bakos. Trainer: Radoslav Látal.
Crvena Zvezda: Milan Borjan, Vujadin Savic, Milan Rodic, Milos Degenek, Filip Stojkovic, Nenad Krsticic, Veljko Simic (85.Branko Jovicic), Dusan Jovancic (101.Marko Gobeljic), Nikola Stojiljkovic (75.Milan Pavkov), Mohamed Ben Nabouhane, Nemanja Radonjic (108.Srdan Babic). Trainer: Vladan Milojevic.
Goals: 1-0 Marek Bakos (6), 1-1 Mohamed Ben Nabouhane (7), 1-2 Nemanja Radonjic (98).
[FK Crvena Zvezda Beograd won 3-2 on aggregate]

08.08.2018; Red Bull Arena, Wals-Siezenheim; Referee: Äliyar Agayev (Azerbaijan); Attendance: 10,050

FC Red Bull Salzburg – KF Shkëndija 79 3-0(2-0)

Red Bull Salzburg: Cican Stankovic, Andreas Ulmer, Stefan Lainer, André Ramalho, Marin Pongracic, Zlatko Junuzovic [*sent off 83*], Reinhold Yabo (73.Takumi Minamino), Xaver Schlager (83 Enock Mwepu), Diadié Samassékou, Moanes Dabour (90+1.Patson Daka), Hannes Wolf. Trainer: Marco Rose.
KF Shkëndija: Kostadin Zahov, Mevlan Murati (75.Gledi Mici), Visar Musliu, Egzon Bejtulai, Mevlan Adili, Armend Alimi, Ennur Totre, Besart Ibraimi, Valmir Nafiu, Stênio Júnior (90+5.Shefit Shefiti), Remzi Selmani (62.Izair Emini). Trainer: Qatip Osmani.
Goals: 1-0, 2-0 Moanas Dabour (16 penalty, 45+3), 3-0 Diadié Samassékou (81 penalty).

14.08.2018; Telekom Arena, Skopje (North Macedonia); Referee: Tamás Bognár (Hungary); Attendance: 3,213

KF Shkëndija 79 – FC Red Bull Salzburg 0-1(0-0)

KF Shkëndija: Kostadin Zahov, Gledi Mici, Visar Musliu, Egzon Bejtulai, Mevlan Adili (71.Remzi Selmani), Armend Alimi, Ennur Totre, Besart Ibraimi, Izair Emini (86.Shefit Shefiti), Valmir Nafiu (46.Besmir Bojku), Stênio Júnior. Trainer: Qatip Osmani.
Red Bull Salzburg: Cican Stankovic, Andreas Ulmer, Stefan Lainer, André Ramalho, Marin Pongracic, Reinhold Yabo (68.Takumi Minamino), Xaver Schlager (89.Christoph Leitgeb), Diadié Samassékou, Amadou Haïdara, Moanes Dabour (76.Patson Daka), Hannes Wolf. Trainer: Marco Rose.

Goal: 0-1 Takumi Minamino (90+2).
[FC Red Bull Salzburg won 4-0 on aggregate]

08.08.2018; Celtic Park, Glasgow; Referee: Luca Banti (Italy); Attendance: 54,370

Celtic FC Glasgow – AEK Athína 1-1(1-1)

Celtic: Craig Gordon, Mikael Lustig (77.Scott Sinclair), Kieran Tierney, Kristoffer Ajer, Jack Hendry, Scott Brown, James Forrest, Callum McGregor, Tom Rogic (63.Leigh Griffiths), Olivier Ntcham, Odsonne Édouard. Trainer: Brendan Rodgers.
AEK Athína: Vassilis Barkas, Niklas Hult, Konstantinos-Vassilios Lambropoulos, Hélder Lopes, Marios Oikonomou, Michalis Bakakis, André Simões, Konstantinos Galanopoulos [*sent off 57*], Marko Livaja (77.Ezequiel Ponce), Anastasios Bakasetas (66.Alef), Viktor Klonaridis (80.Rodrigo Galo). Trainer: Marinos Ouzounidis.
Goals: 1-0 Callum McGregor (17), 1-1 Viktor Klonaridis (44).

14.08.2018; Stádio Olympiako „Spiros Louis", Athína; Referee: Vladislav Bezborodov (Russia); Attendance: 32,300

AEK Athína – Celtic FC Glasgow 2-1(1-0)

AEK Athína: Vassilis Barkas, Niklas Hult, Rodrigo Galo (82.Christos Albanis), Konstantinos-Vassilios Lambropoulos, Marios Oikonomou, Michalis Bakakis, André Simões, Alef, Marko Livaja, Anastasios Bakasetas (90+1.Uros Cosic), Viktor Klonaridis (73.Petros Mandalos). Trainer: Marinos Ouzounidis.
Celtic: Craig Gordon, Mikael Lustig (60.Moussa Dembélé), Jozo Simunovic, Kieran Tierney, Jack Hendry, Scott Brown, James Forrest, Callum McGregor, Tom Rogic (76.Scott Sinclair), Olivier Ntcham, Leigh Griffiths. Trainer: Brendan Rodgers.
Goals: 1-0 Rodrigo Galo (6), 2-0 Marko Livaja (50), 2-1 Scott Sinclair (78).
[AEK Athína won 3-2 on aggregate]

LEAGUE ROUTE

07.08.2018; Eden Aréna, Praha; Referee: Craig Pawson (England); Attendance: 19,370

SK Slavia Praha – FK Dinamo Kyiv 1-1(0-0)

Slavia Praha: Ondrej Kolár, Jan Boril, Vladimír Coufal, Simon Deli, Josef Husbauer, Miroslav Stoch, Jan Sykora (Peter Olayinka), Michael Ngadeu-Ngadjui, Jaromír Zmrhal (80.Alexandru Baluta), Tomás Soucek, Milan Skoda (60.Stanislav Teci). Trainer: Jindrich Trpisovsky.
Dinamo Kyiv: Denis Boyko, Mikola Morozyuk, Tamás Kádár, Tomasz Kedziora, Mykyta Burda, Sergiy Sydorchuk, Denys Garmash, Vitaliy Buyalskiy (68.Volodymyr Shepelev), Benjamin Verbic, Viktor Tsygankov (90+1.Oleksandr Andrievsky), Artem Besedin. Trainer: Aleksandr Khatskevich.
Goals: 0-1 Benjamin Verbic (82), 1-1 Josef Husbauer (90+5 penalty).

14.08.2018; Olimpijskyj Stadium, Kyiv; Referee: Daniel Stefanski (Poland); Attendance: 39,318

FK Dinamo Kyiv – SK Slavia Praha 2-0(1-0)

Dinamo Kyiv: Denis Boyko, Josip Pivaric, Tamás Kádár, Tomasz Kedziora, Mykyta Burda (75.Artem Shabanov), Sergiy Sydorchuk, Denys Garmash, Benjamin Verbic, Viktor Tsygankov (90+2.Mikola Morozyuk), Volodymyr Shepelev (88.Vitaliy Buyalskiy), Artem Besedin. Trainer: Aleksandr Khatskevich.
Slavia Praha: Ondrej Kolár, Jan Boril, Vladimír Coufal, Simon Deli, Josef Husbauer (85.Michal Frydrych), Miroslav Stoch, Jan Sykora, Michael Ngadeu-Ngadjui, Jaromír Zmrhal (68.Alexandru Baluta), Tomás Soucek, Stanislav Teci (75.Milan Skoda). Trainer: Jindrich Trpisovsky.
Goals: 1-0 Benjamin Verbic (11), 2-0 Artem Besedin (74).
[FK Dinamo Kyiv won 3-1 on aggregate]

07.08.2018; Stade "Maurice Dufrasne", Liège; Referee: Tobias Stieler (Germany); Attendance: 20,355

R Standard Liège – AFC Ajax Amsterdam 2-2(0-2)

Standard Liège: Guillermo Ochoa, Luis Cavanda, Kostas Laifis, Collins Fai, Christian Luyindama Nekadio, Mehdi Carcela-González, Paul M'Poku (85.Moussa Djenepo), Razvan Marin, Uche Agbo, Samuel Bastien (76.Gojko Cimirot), Orlando Sá (66.Renaud Emond). Trainer: Michel Preud'homme.
Ajax Amsterdam: André Onana, Daley Blind, Nicolás Tagliafico, Matthijs de Ligt, Lasse Schöne (89.Carel Eiting), Hakim Ziyech (73.Zakaria Labyad), Noussair Mazraoui, Frenkie de Jong (79.Donny van de Beek), Klaas-Jan Huntelaar, Dusan Tadic, David Neres. Trainer: Erik ten Hag.
Goals: 0-1 Klaas-Jan Huntelaar (19), 0-2 Dusan Tadic (34), 1-2 Mehdi Carcela-González (67), 2-2 Renaud Emond (90+4 penalty).

14.08.2018; „Johan Cruijff" Arena, Amsterdam; Referee: Ivan Kruzliak (Slovakia); Attendance: 51,841

AFC Ajax Amsterdam – R Standard Liège 3-0(2-0)

Ajax Amsterdam: André Onana, Daley Blind, Nicolás Tagliafico, Matthijs de Ligt, Lasse Schöne, Hakim Ziyech (90.Zakaria Labyad), Noussair Mazraoui (76.Rasmus Kristensen), Frenkie de Jong, Klaas-Jan Huntelaar, Dusan Tadic, David Neres (82.Donny van de Beek). Trainer: Erik ten Hag.
Standard Liège: Guillermo Ochoa, Luis Cavanda (Sébastien Pocognoli), Kostas Laifis, Collins Fai, Christian Luyindama Nekadio, Mehdi Carcela-González, Paul M'Poku, Razvan Marin, Uche Agbo, Samuel Bastien (53.Gojko Cimirot), Renaud Emond (78.Orlando Sá). Trainer: Michel Preud'homme.
Goals: 1-0 Klaas-Jan Huntelaar (30), 2-0 Matthijs de Ligt (34), 3-0 David Neres (46)
[AFC Ajax Amsterdam won 5-2 on aggregate]

07.08.2018; Estádio da Luz, Lisboa; Referee: Aleksei Kulbakov (Belarus); Attendance: 57,878

Sport Lisboa e Benfica – SK Fenerbahçe İstanbul 1-0(0-0)

Benfica: Odisseas Vlachodimos, André Almeida, Jardel, Álex Grimaldo, Rúben Dias, Ljubomir Fejsa, Pizzi, Eduardo Salvio (75.Andrija Zivkovic), Franco Cervi, Gedson Fernandes, Facundo Ferreyra (63.Nicolás Castillo). Trainer: Rui Vitória.
Fenerbahçe: Volkan Demirel, Martin Skrtel, Mauricio Isla, Roman Neustädter, Hasan-Ali Kaldirim, Mathieu Valbuena (61.Mehmet Ekici), Mehmet Topal, Nabil Dirar (87.Baris Alici), Giuliano, Alper Potuk (74.Soldado), Eljif Elmas. Trainer: Phillip Cocu.
Goal: 1-0 Franco Cervi (69).

14.08.2018; „Sükrü Saraçoglu" Stadyumu, İstanbul; Referee: Slavko Vincic (Slovenia); Attendance: 42,245

SK Fenerbahçe İstanbul – Sport Lisboa e Benfica 1-1(1-1)

Fenerbahçe: Volkan Demirel, Martin Skrtel, Mauricio Isla (80 Sener Özbayrakli), Roman Neustädter, Hasan-Ali Kaldirim, Mathieu Valbuena (65.Soldado), Mehmet Topal (65.Baris Alici), Giuliano, Alper Potuk, Eljif Elmas, André Ayew. Trainer: Phillip Cocu.
Benfica: Odisseas Vlachodimos, André Almeida, Jardel, Álex Grimaldo, Rúben Dias, Ljubomir Fejsa, Pizzi, Eduardo Salvio (72.Alfa Semedo), Franco Cervi, Gedson Fernandes, Nicolás Castillo (34.Facundo Ferreyra). Trainer: Rui Vitória.
Goals: 0-1 Gedson Fernandes (26), 1-1 Alper Potuk (45+1).
[Sport Lisboa e Benfica won 2-1 on aggregate]

08.08.2018; Stádio Toumbas, Thessaloniki; Referee: Orel Grinfeld (Israel); Attendance: 24,463

PAOK Thessaloníki – FK Spartak Moskva 3-2(3-2)

PAOK: Alexandros Paschalakis, Léo Matos, José Ángel Crespo, Fernando Varela, Evgen Khacheridi, Omar El Kaddouri (61.Amr Warda), Maurício (84.Yevhen Shakhov), Cañas, Dimitris Pelkas, Aleksandar Prijovic, Dimitris Limnios (79.Léo Jabá). Trainer: Razvan Lucescu.
Spartak Moskva: Aleksandr Maksimenko, Salvatore Bocchetti (90+4.Nikolai Rasskazov), Andrey Eshchenko, Samuel Gigot, Dmitriy Kombarov, Ivelin Popov (64.Artiom Timofeev), Fernando, Roman Zobnin, Quincy Promes, Aleksandr Lomovitski, Luiz Adriano (77.Zé Luís). Trainer: Massimo Carrera.
Goals: 0-1 Ivelin Popov (7), 0-2 Quincy Promes (17), 1-2 Aleksandar Prijovic (29 penalty), 2-2 Dimitris Limnios (37), 3-2 Dimitris Pelkas (44).

14.08.2018; Otkrytiye Arena, Moskva; Referee: Ruddy Buquet (France); Attendance: 40,385

FK Spartak Moskva – PAOK Thessaloníki 0-0

Spartak Moskva: Aleksandr Maksimenko, Andrey Eshchenko, Georgi Dzhikiya, Samuel Gigot, Dmitriy Kombarov (76.Lorenzo Melgarejo), Denis Glushakov, Fernando (63.Aleksandr Samedov), Roman Zobnin, Quincy Promes, Aleksandr Tashaev (46.Zé Luís), Luiz Adriano [*sent off 33*]. Trainer: Massimo Carrera.

PAOK: Alexandros Paschalakis, Léo Matos, José Ángel Crespo, Fernando Varela, Vieirinha (65.Evgen Khacheridi), Omar El Kaddouri (46.Amr Warda), Maurício, Cañas, Dimitris Pelkas (79.Yevhen Shakhov), Aleksandar Prijovic, Dimitris Limnios. Trainer: Razvan Lucescu.

[PAOK Thessaloníki won 3-2 on aggregate]

PLAY-OFFS

CHAMPIONS ROUTE

21.08.2018; Stadion „Rajko Mitić", Beograd; Referee: Daniele Orsato (Italy); Attendance: *played behind closed doors*

FK Crvena Zvezda Beograd – FC Red Bull Salzburg 0-0

Crvena Zvezda: Milan Borjan, Vujadin Savic (46.Srdan Babic), Milan Rodic, Milos Degenek, Filip Stojkovic, Nenad Krsticic, Branko Jovicic, Nikola Stojiljkovic (79.Dusan Jovancic), Mohamed Ben Nabouhane, Jonathan Cafú (60.Veljko Simic), Nemanja Radonjic. Trainer: Vladan Milojevic.

Red Bull Salzburg: Cican Stankovic, Andreas Ulmer, Stefan Lainer, André Ramalho, Marin Pongracic, Zlatko Junuzovic (46.Xaver Schlager), Reinhold Yabo (79.Patson Daka), Diadié Samassékou, Amadou Haïdara, Moanes Dabour, Hannes Wolf (87.Takumi Minamino). Trainer: Marco Rose.

29.08.2018; Red Bull Arena, Wals-Siezenheim; Referee: Cüneyt Çakir (Turkey); Attendance: 26,500

FC Red Bull Salzburg – FK Crvena Zvezda Beograd 2-2(1-0)

Red Bull Salzburg: Cican Stankovic, Andreas Ulmer, Stefan Lainer, André Ramalho, Marin Pongracic, Xaver Schlager (83.Smail Prevljak), Diadié Samassékou, Amadou Haïdara, Moanes Dabour, Patson Daka (69.Reinhold Yabo), Hannes Wolf. Trainer: Marco Rose.

Crvena Zvezda: Milan Borjan, Vujadin Savic, Milan Rodic, Milos Degenek, Filip Stojkovic, Nenad Krsticic, Veljko Simic (37.Dusan Jovancic), Branko Jovicic, Nemanja Milic (50.Milan Pavkov), Mohamed Ben Nabouhane, Nemanja Radonjic (82.Marko Gobeljic). Trainer: Vladan Milojevic.

Goals: 1-0, 2- 0 Moanes Dabour (45 penalty, 48), 2-1, 2-2 Mohamed Ben Nabouhane (65, 66).

[FK Crvena Zvezda Beograd won on away goals rule (2-2 on aggregate)]

21.08.2018; Borisov Arena, Borisov; Referee: Felix Zwayer (Germany); Attendance: 9,284

FC BATE Borisov – PSV Eindhoven 2-3(1-1)

BATE Borisov: Denis Scherbitski, Egor Filipenko, Nemanja Milunovic, Aleksandar Filipovic, Alexei Rios, Igor Stasevich, Dmitri Baga, Stanislav Dragun (65.Aliaksandr Hleb), Mirko Ivanic (81.Maksim Volodko), Jasse Tuominen (60.Maksim Skavysh), Evgeni Yablonski. Trainer: Alexey Baga.

PSV Eindhoven: Jeroen Zoet, Daniel Schwaab, Nick Viergever, José Angeliño, Denzel Dumfries, Jorrit Hendrix, Gastón Pereiro (82.Mauro Júnior), Pablo Rosario (90+4.Nicolas Isimat-Mirin), Luuk de Jong, Steven Bergwijn, Hirving Lozano (87.Donyell Malen). Trainer: Mark van Bommel.

Goals: 1-0 Jasse Tuominen (9), 1-1 Gastón Pereiro (35 penalty), 1-2 Hirving Lozano (61), 2-2 Aliaksandr Hleb (88), 2-3 Donyell Malen (89).

29.08.2018; Philips Stadion, Eindhoven; Referee: Anthony Taylor (England); Attendance: 34,200

PSV Eindhoven – FC BATE Borisov 3-0(2-0)

PSV Eindhoven: Jeroen Zoet, Daniel Schwaab, Nick Viergever (71.Nicolas Isimat-Mirin), José Angeliño, Denzel Dumfries, Jorrit Hendrix, Gastón Pereiro, Pablo Rosario (74.Bart Ramselaar), Luuk de Jong, Steven Bergwijn (79.Donyell Malen), Hirving Lozano. Trainer: Mark van Bommel.

BATE Borisov: Denis Scherbitski, Egor Filipenko, Nemanja Milunovic, Maksim Volodko, Aleksandar Filipovic, Aliaksandr Hleb (30.Mirko Ivanic), Alexei Rios, Igor Stasevich, Dmitri Baga, Stanislav Dragun (76.Yevgeniy Berezkin), Jasse Tuominen (51.Nilolay Signevich). Trainer: Alexey Baga.

Goals: 1-0 Steven Bergwijn (14), 2-0 Luuk de Jong (36), 3-0 Hirving Lozano (62).

[PSV Eindhoven won 6-2 on aggregate]

22.08.2018; Stade de Suise, Bern; Referee: Alberto Undiano Mallenco (Spain); Attendance: 21,463

BSC Young Boys Bern – GNK Dinamo Zagreb 1-1(1-1)

Young Boys: David von Ballmoos, Steve von Bergen, Loris Benito, Kevin Mbabu, Gregory Wüthrich, Miralem Sulejmani, Sékou Junior Sanogo, Nicolas Moumi Ngamaleu (81.Jean Pierre Nsamé), Djibril Sow, Christian Fassnacht (70.Michel Aebischer), Guillaume Hoarau. Trainer: Gerardo Seoane.

Dinamo Zagreb: Daniel Zagorac, Marin Leovac, Kévin Théophile-Catherine, Emir Dilaver, Petar Stojanovic, Arijan Ademi, Amer Gojak, Daniel Olmo (86.Ivan Sunjic), Mario Gavranovic (74.Mario Budimir), Mislav Orsic, Izet Hajrovic (83.Damian Kadzior). Trainer: Nenad Bjelica.

Goals: 1-0 Kevin Mbabu (2), 1-1 Mislav Orsic (40).

28.08.2018; Stadion Maksimir, Zagreb; Referee: Björn Kuipers (Netherlands); Attendance: 28,137

GNK Dinamo Zagreb – BSC Young Boys Bern 1-2(1-0)

Dinamo Zagreb: Daniel Zagorac, Marin Leovac (74.Mario Budimir), Kévin Théophile-Catherine, Emir Dilaver, Petar Stojanovic, Arijan Ademi (32.Ivan Sunjic), Amer Gojak, Daniel Olmo, Mario Gavranovic, Mislav Orsic (83.Damian Kadzior), Izet Hajrovic. Trainer: Nenad Bjelica.

Young Boys: David von Ballmoos, Steve von Bergen, Loris Benito, Kevin Mbabu, Gregory Wüthrich, Miralem Sulejmani (55.Roger Assalé), Sékou Junior Sanogo, Nicolas Moumi Ngamaleu (90+3.Michel Aebischer), Djibril Sow, Christian Fassnacht (84.Leonardo Bertone), Guillaume Hoarau. Trainer: Gerardo Seoane.

Goals: 1-0 Izet Hajrovic (7), 1-1, 1-2 Guillaume Hoarau (64 penalty, 66).

[BSC Young Boys Bern won 3-2 on aggregate]

22.08.2018; Groupama Aréna, Budapest; Referee: Gianluca Rocchi (Italy); Attendance: 10,681

MOL Vidi FC Székesfehérvár – AEK Athína 1-2(0-1)

MOL Vidi FC: Ádam Kovácsik, Roland Juhász, Attila Fiola, Loïc Négo, Paulo Vinícius, Stopira, Szabolcs Huszti [*sent off 22*], Anel Hadzic, István Kovács, Boban Nikolov (54.Marko Scepovic), Danko Lazovic. Trainer: Marko Nikolic.

AEK Athína: Vassilis Barkas, Niklas Hult, Konstantinos-Vassilios Lambropoulos, Marios Oikonomou, Petros Mandalos, Michalis Bakakis, André Simões, Konstantinos Galanopoulos (66.Alef), Marko Livaja (86.Ezequiel Ponce), Anastasios Bakasetas [*sent off 53*], Viktor Klonaridis (82.Hélder Lopes). Trainer: Marinos Ouzounidis.

Goals: 0-1 Viktor Klonaridis (34), 0-2 Anastasios Bakasetas (49), 1-2 Danko Lazovic (67).

28.08.2018; Stádio Olympiako „Spiros Louis", Athína; Referee: Szymon Marciniak (Poland); Attendance: 29,774

AEK Athína – MOL Vidi FC Székesfehérvár 1-1(0-0)

AEK Athína: Vassilis Barkas, Niklas Hult, Konstantinos-Vassilios Lambropoulos, Hélder Lopes [*sent off 80*], Marios Oikonomou, Petros Mandalos (90.Uros Cosic), Michalis Bakakis, André Simões, Konstantinos Galanopoulos, Marko Livaja (84.Alef), Viktor Klonaridis (62.Ezequiel Ponce). Trainer: Marinos Ouzounidis.

MOL Vidi FC: Ádam Kovácsik, Roland Juhász, Attila Fiola, Loïc Négo, Paulo Vinícius, Stopira, Anel Hadzic, István Kovács, Boban Nikolov (46.Máté Pátkai), Danko Lazovic, Marko Scepovic. Trainer: Marko Nikolic.

Goals: 1-0 Petros Mandalos (48 penalty), 1-1 Loïc Négo (57).

[AEK Athína won 3-2 on aggregate]

LEAGUE ROUTE

21.08.2018; Estádio da Luz, Lisboa; Referee: Milorad Mazic (Serbia); Attendance: 44,084

Sport Lisboa e Benfica – PAOK Thessaloníki 1-1(1-0)

Benfica: Odisseas Vlachodimos, André Almeida, Jardel, Álex Grimaldo, Rúben Dias, Ljubomir Fejsa, Pizzi (80.João Félix), Andrija Zickovic (65.Rafa Silva), Franco Cervi (79.Haris Seferovic), Gedson Fernandes, Facundo Ferreyra. Trainer: Rui Vitória.
PAOK: Alexandros Paschalakis, Léo Matos, José Ángel Crespo, Fernando Varela, Vieirinha, Maurício, Cañas, Dimitris Pelkas, Aleksandar Prijovic (87.Chuba Akpom), Dimitris Limnios (53.Amr Warda), Léo Jabá (81.Yevhen Shakhov). Trainer: Razvan Lucescu.
Goals: 1-0 Pizzi (45+1 penalty), 1-1 Amr Warda (76).

29.08.2018; Stádio Toumbas, Thessaloniki; Referee: Dr. Felix Brych (Germany); Attendance: 26,725

PAOK Thessaloníki – Sport Lisboa e Benfica 1-4(1-3)

PAOK: Alexandros Paschalakis, Léo Matos [*sent off 76*], José Ángel Crespo, Fernando Varela, Vieirinha, Omar El Kaddouri (76.Chuba Akpom), Maurício, Cañas (64.Yevhen Shakhov), Dimitris Pelkas, Aleksandar Prijovic, Dimitris Limnios (46.Amr Warda). Trainer: Razvan Lucescu.
Benfica: Odisseas Vlachodimos, André Almeida, Jardel, Álex Grimaldo, Rúben Dias, Ljubomir Fejsa, Pizzi (76.Andrija Zickovic), Eduardo Salvio (63.Alfa Semedo), Franco Cervi, Gedson Fernandes, Haris Seferovic (85.João Félix). Trainer: Rui Vitória
Goals: 1-0 Aleksandar Prijovic (13), 1-1 Jardel (20), 1-2 Eduardo Salvio (26 penalty), 1-3 Pizzi (39), 1-4 Eduardo Salvio (50 penalty).
[Sport Lisboa e Benfica won 5-2 on aggregate]

22.08.2018; „Johan Cruijff" Arena, Amsterdam; Referee: Clément Turpin (France); Attendance: 52,706

AFC Ajax Amsterdam – FK Dinamo Kyiv 3-1(3-1)

Ajax Amsterdam: André Onana, Daley Blind, Nicolás Tagliafico, Matthijs de Ligt, Lasse Schöne, Hakim Ziyech, Donny van de Beek (87.Dani de Wit), Noussair Mazraoui, Frenkie de Jong, Klaas-Jan Huntelaar, Dusan Tadic. Trainer: Erik ten Hag.
Dinamo Kyiv: Denis Boyko, Josip Pivaric, Tamás Kádár, Tomasz Kedziora, Mykyta Burda, Sergiy Sydorchuk (77.Tchê Tchê), Denys Garmash (46.Volodymyr Shepelev), Vitaliy Buyalskiy, Benjamin Verbic, Viktor Tsygankov, Artem Besedin. Trainer: Aleksandr Khatskevich.
Goals: 1-0 Donny van de Beek (2), 1-1 Tomasz Kedziora (16), 2-1 Hakim Ziyech (35), 3-1 Dusan Tadic (43).

28.08.2018; Olimpijskyj Stadium, Kyiv; Referee: Damir Skomina (Slovenia); Attendance: 40,131

FK Dinamo Kyiv – AFC Ajax Amsterdam 0-0

Dinamo Kyiv: Denis Boyko, Josip Pivaric, Tamás Kádár, Tomasz Kedziora, Mykyta Burda, Sergiy Sydorchuk (64.Mykola Shaparenko), Vitaliy Buyalskiy (85.Nazariy Rusyn), Benjamin Verbic, Viktor Tsygankov, Volodymyr Shepelev (46.Denys Garmash), Vladyslav Supriaha. Trainer: Aleksandr Khatskevich.
Ajax Amsterdam: André Onana, Daley Blind, Matthijs de Ligt, Maximilian Wöber (79.Carel Eiting), Lasse Schöne, Hakim Ziyech, Donny van de Beek (85.Dani de Wit), Noussair Mazraoui, Frenkie de Jong, Klaas-Jan Huntelaar, Dusan Tadic. Trainer: Erik ten Hag.
[AFC Ajax Amsterdam won 3-1 on aggregate]

GROUP STAGE

Please note: Winners and runners-up of each group were qualified for the Round of 16. Teams ranked third were qualified for the UEFA Europa League.

GROUP A

1.	**BV Borussia 09 Dortmund**	6	4	1	1	10	-	2	13
2.	**Club Atlético de Madrid**	6	4	1	1	9	-	6	13
3.	Club Brugge KV	6	1	3	2	6	-	5	6
4.	AS Monaco FC	6	0	1	5	2	-	14	1

18.09.2018; „Jan Breydel" Stadion, Brugge; Referee: Danny Desmond Makkelie (Netherlands); Attendance: 25,181

Club Brugge KV – BV Borussia 09 Dortmund 0-1(0-0)

Club Brugge: Karlo Letica, Benoît Poulain, Stefano Denswil, Matej Mitrovic, Thibault Vlietinck (56.Dion Cools), Ruud Vormer, Mats Rits, Hans Vanaken, Jelle Vossen (82.Loïs Openda), Wesley, Arnaut Danjuma Groeneveld (76.Emmanuel Dennis). Trainer: Ivan Leko.
Borussia Dortmund: Roman Bürki, Lukasz Piszczek, Marcel Schmelzer, Abdou Diallo, Manuel Akanji, Axel Witsel, Mario Götze (62.Shinji Kagawa), Julian Weigl (84.Mahmoud Dahoud), Jadon Sancho (69.Christian Pulisic), Marco Reus, Marius Wolf. Trainer: Lucien Favre.
Goal: 0-1 Christian Pulisic (85).

18.09.2018; Stade „Louis II", Monaco; Referee: William Collum (Scotland); Attendance: 10,575

AS Monaco FC – Club Atlético de Madrid 1-2(1-2)

AS Monaco: Diego Benaglio, Kamil Glik, Djibril Sidibé, Benjamin Henrichs, Jemerson, Nacer Chadli (58.Jordi Mboula), Jean-Eudes Aholou (69.Adama Traoré (II)), Youri Tielemans, Kévin N'Doram, Radamel Falcao, Samuel Grandsir (77.Moussa Sylla). Trainer: Leonardo Jardim.
Atlético Madrid: Jan Oblak, Juanfran, Diego Godín, José Giménez, Lucas Hernández, Saúl, Koke, Rodri Hernández, Diego Costa, Antoine Griezmann, Ángel Correa (70.Thomas Lemar). Trainer: Diego Simeone.
Goals: 1-0 Samuel Grandsir (18), 1-1 Diego Costa (31), 1-2 José Giménez (45+1).

03.10.2018; Estadio Wanda Metropolitano, Madrid; Referee: Ivan Kruzliak (Slovakia); Attendance: 55,742

Club Atlético de Madrid – Club Brugge KV 3-1(1-1)

Atlético Madrid: Jan Oblak, Diego Godín, Santiago Arias, José Giménez (46.Filipe Luís), Lucas Hernández, Saúl, Koke, Thomas Lemar, Thomas Partey (63.Ángel Correa), Diego Costa (69.Rodri Hernández), Antoine Griezmann. Trainer: Diego Simeone.
Club Brugge: Karlo Letica, Benoît Poulain, Stefano Denswil, Brandon Mechele, Thibault Vlietinck (56.Clinton Mata), Ruud Vormer, Mats Rits (75.Loïs Openda), Hans Vanaken, Siebe Schrijvers (56.Marvelous Nakamba), Wesley, Arnaut Danjuma Groeneveld. Trainer: Ivan Leko.
Goals: 1-0 Antoine Griezmann (28), 1-1 Arnaut Danjuma Groeneveld (39), 2-1 Antoine Griezmann (67), 3-1 Koke (90+4).

03.10.2018; Signal-Iduna-Park, Dortmund; Referee: Aleksei Kulbakov (Belarus); Attendance: 66,099

BV Borussia 09 Dortmund – AS Monaco FC 3-0(0-0)

Borussia Dortmund: Roman Bürki, Lukasz Piszczek, Abdou Diallo, Manuel Akanji, Dan-Axel Zagadou, Axel Witsel, Thomas Delaney (65.Julian Weigl), Jadon Sancho (84.Maximilian Philipp), Marco Reus, Paco Alcácer, Marius Wolf (46.Jacob Bruun Larsen). Trainer: Lucien Favre.
AS Monaco: Diego Benaglio (45.Danijel Subasic), Andrea Raggi, Kamil Glik, Djibril Sidibé, Benjamin Henrichs, Jemerson, Jean-Eudes Aholou, Aleksandr Golovin (77.Nacer Chadli), Youri Tielemans, Moussa Sylla (70.Samuel Grandsir), Radamel Falcao. Trainer: Leonardo Jardim.
Goals: 1-0 Jacob Bruun Larsen (51), 2-0 Paco Alcácer (72), 3-0 Marco Reus (90+2).

24.10.2018; „Jan Breydel" Stadion, Brugge; Referee: Michael Oliver (England); Attendance: 23,957

Club Brugge KV – AS Monaco FC 1-1(1-1)

Club Brugge: Karlo Letica, Benoît Poulain, Stefano Denswil, Brandon Mechele, Thibault Vlietinck (83.Clinton Mata), Ruud Vormer, Hans Vanaken, Marvelous Nakamba, Kaveh Rezaei (79.Loïs Openda), Wesley, Emmanuel Dennis Bonaventure (90.Krépin Diatta). Trainer: Ivan Leko.
AS Monaco: Loïc Badiashile, Andrea Raggi, Kamil Glik, Djibril Sidibé (64.Benjamin Henrichs), Jemerson, Nacer Chadli, Aleksandr Golovin, Youri Tielemans, Youssef Aït Bennasser, Moussa Sylla, Stevan Jovetic (12.Sofiane Diop, 73.Jean-Eudes Aholou). Trainer: Thierry Henry.
Goals: 0-1 Moussa Sylla (31), 1-1 Wesley (39)

24.10.2018; Signal-Iduna-Park, Dortmund; Referee: Anthony Taylor (England); Attendance: 66,099

BV Borussia 09 Dortmund – Club Atlético de Madrid 4-0(1-0)

Borussia Dortmund: Roman Bürki, Lukasz Piszczek, Abdou Diallo, Achraf Hakimi, Dan-Axel Zagadou, Axel Witsel, Thomas Delaney (35.Mahmoud Dahoud), Mario Götze, Christian Pulisic (79.Jadon Sancho), Marco Reus, Jacob Bruun Larsen (63.Raphaël Guerreiro). Trainer: Lucien Favre.

Atlético Madrid: Jan Oblak, Juanfran, Filipe Luís, Diego Godín, Lucas Hernández, Saúl (70.Ángel Correa), Koke, Thomas Lemar, Thomas Partey (46.Rodri Hernández), Diego Costa, Antoine Griezmann. Trainer: Diego Simeone.

Goals: 1-0 Axel Witsel (38), 2-0 Raphaël Guerreiro (73), 3-0 Jadon Sancho (83), 4-0 Raphaël Guerreiro (89).

06.11.2018; Stade „Louis II", Monaco; Referee: Artur Soares Dias (Portugal); Attendance: 8,347

AS Monaco FC – Club Brugge KV 0-4(0-3)

AS Monaco: Diego Benaglio, Kamil Glik (76.Almamy Touré), Djibril Sidibé, Jemerson, Antonio Barreca, Nacer Chadli, Youri Tielemans, Youssef Aït Bennasser (68.Han-Noah Massengo), Moussa Sylla, Sofiane Diop, Radamel Falcao (61.Gobe Gouano). Trainer: Thierry Henry.

Club Brugge: Ethan Horvath, Benoît Poulain, Stefano Denswil, Clinton Mata (77.Thibault Vlietinck), Brandon Mechele, Ruud Vormer, Mats Rits, Hans Vanaken, Marvelous Nakamba, Wesley (72.Kaveh Rezaei), Krépin Diatta (6.Dion Cools). Trainer: Ivan Leko.

Goals: 0-1, 0-2 Hans Vanaken (12, 17 penalty), 0-3 Wesley (24), 0-4 Ruud Vormer (85)

06.11.2018; Estadio Wanda Metropolitano, Madrid; Referee: Daniele Orsato (Italy); Attendance: 61,023

Club Atlético de Madrid – BV Borussia 09 Dortmund 2-0(1-0)

Atlético Madrid: Jan Oblak, Juanfran, Filipe Luís, José Giménez (46.Francisco Montero), Lucas Hernández, Saúl, Thomas Partey, Rodri Hernández, Nikola Kalinic (62.Gelson Martins), Antoine Griezmann, Ángel Correa (81.Vitolo). Trainer: Diego Simeone.

Borussia Dortmund: Roman Bürki, Lukasz Piszczek, Ömer Toprak, Manuel Akanji, Achraf Hakimi, Axel Witsel, Thomas Delaney, Christian Pulisic (59.Raphaël Guerreiro), Jadon Sancho (79.Jacob Bruun Larsen), Marco Reus, Paco Alcácer (75.Mario Götze). Trainer: Lucien Favre.

Goals: 1-0 Saúl (33), 2-0 Antoine Griezmann (80).

28.11.2018; Estadio Wanda Metropolitano, Madrid; Referee: Mattias Gestranius (Finland); Attendance: 56,314

Club Atlético de Madrid – AS Monaco FC 2-0(2-0)

Atlético Madrid: Jan Oblak, Filipe Luís, Santiago Arias, Stefan Savic [*sent off 82*], Lucas Hernández, Koke (46.Vitolo), Thomas Lemar (63.Nikola Kalinic), Thomas Partey, Rodri Hernández, Antoine Griezmann, Ángel Correa (69.Saúl). Trainer: Diego Simeone.

AS Monaco: Diego Benaglio, Andrea Raggi, Jemerson, Benoît Badiashile, Giulian Biancone, Nacer Chadli (63.Sofiane Diop), Aleksandre Golovin (63.Khéphren Thuram-Ulien), Youri Tielemans, Moussa Sylla (55.Radamel Falcao), Han-Noah Massengo, Samuel Grandsir. Trainer: Thierry Henry.

Goals: 1-0 Koke (2), 2-0 Antoine Griezmann (24).

28.11.2018; Signal-Iduna-Park, Dortmund; Referee: Gediminas Mazeika (Lithuania); Attendance: 66,099

BV Borussia 09 Dortmund – Club Brugge KV 0-0

Borussia Dortmund: Roman Bürki, Lukasz Piszczek, Raphaël Guerreiro (73.Jadon Sancho), Abdou Diallo (80.Achraf Hakimi), Manuel Akanji, Dan-Axel Zagadou, Axel Witsel (90.Thomas Delaney), Mahmoud Dahoud, Christian Pulisic, Marco Reus, Paco Alcácer. Trainer: Lucien Favre.

Club Brugge: Ethan Horvath, Benoît Poulain, Stefano Denswil, Clinton Mata, Brandon Mechele, Ruud Vormer (90+3.Saulo Decarli), Hans Vanaken, Marvelous Nakamba, Sofyan Amrabat, Wesley (90+2.Loïs Openda), Emmanuel Dennis (76.Mats Rits). Trainer: Ivan Leko.

11.12.2018; „Jan Breydel" Stadion, Brugge; Referee: Davide Massa (Italy); Attendance: 25,645

Club Brugge KV – Club Atlético de Madrid 0-0

Club Brugge: Ethan Horvath, Benoît Poulain, Stefano Denswil, Brandon Mechele, Ruud Vormer, Hans Vanaken (90+1.Mats Rits), Marvelous Nakamba, Sofyan Amrabat, Wesley, Loïs Openda (74.Siebe Schrijvers), Cyril Ngonge (69.Luan Peres). Trainer: Ivan Leko.

Atlético Madrid: Jan Oblak, Diego Godín, Santiago Arias, Francisco Montero, Saúl, Koke, Thomas Lemar (61.Vitolo), Thomas Partey (68.Nikola Kalinic), Rodri Hernández, Antoine Griezmann, Gelson Martins (60.Ángel Correa). Trainer: Diego Simeone.

11.12.2018; Stade „Louis II", Monaco; Referee: Craig Pawson (England); Attendance: 8,731

AS Monaco FC – BV Borussia 09 Dortmund 0-2(0-1)

AS Monaco: Diego Benaglio, Andrea Raggi, Kamil Glik, Benjamin Henrichs, Benoît Badiashile, Giulian Biancone (78.Julien Serrano), Youri Tielemans, Youssef Aït Bennasser, Han-Noah Massengo (69.Khéphren Thuram-Ulien), Sofiane Diop, Radamel Falcao (64.Moussa Sylla). Trainer: Thierry Henry.

Borussia Dortmund: Marwin Hitz, Marcel Schmelzer, Ömer Toprak, Raphaël Guerreiro (90+2.Sergio Gómez), Abdou Diallo, Achraf Hakimi, Mario Götze, Julian Weigl, Mahmoud Dahoud (76.Marius Wolf), Christian Pulisic, Maximilian Philipp (79.Paco Alcácer). Trainer: Lucien Favre.

Goals: 0-1, 0-2 Raphaël Guerreiro (15, 88).

GROUP B

1.	**FC Barcelona**	6	4	2	0	14	-	5	14
2.	**Tottenham Hotspur FC London**	6	2	2	2	9	-	10	8
3.	Internazionale FC Milano	6	2	2	2	6	-	7	8
4.	PSV Eindhoven	6	0	2	4	6	-	13	2

18.09.2018; Estadio Camp Nou, Barcelona; Referee: Anastasios Sidiropoulos (Greece); Attendance: 73,462

FC Barcelona – PSV Eindhoven 4-0(1-0)

FC Barcelona: Marc-André ter Stegen, Piqué, Jordi Alba, Sergi Roberto, Samuel Umtiti [*sent off 79*], Ivan Rakitic (85.Arturo Vidal), Sergio Busquets, Philippe Coutinho (81.Clément Lenglet), Lionel Messi, Luis Suárez, Ousmane Dembélé (83.Arthur). Trainer: Ernesto Valverde.

PSV Eindhoven: Jeroen Zoet, Daniel Schwaab, Nick Viergever (66.Nicolas Isimat-Mirin), José Angeliño, Denzel Dumfries, Jorrit Hendrix, Gastón Pereiro, Pablo Rosario (82.Érick Gutiérrez), Luuk de Jong, Steven Bergwijn (78.Donyell Malen), Hirving Lozano. Trainer: Mark van Bommel.

Goals: 1-0 Lionel Messi (32), 2-0 Ousmane Dembélé (75), 3-0 Lionel Messi (77), 4-0 Lionel Messi (87).

18.09.2018; Stadio „Giuseppe Meazza", Milano; Referee: Clément Turpin (France); Attendance: 64,123

Internazionale FC Milano – Tottenham Hotspur FC London 2-1(0-0)

Internazionale: Samir Handanovic, João Miranda, Stefan de Vrij, Milan Skriniar, Ivan Perisic (64.Antonio Candreva), Radja Nainggolan (89.Borja Valero), Kwadwo Asamoah, Matías Vecino, Marcelo Brozovic, Mauro Icardi, Matteo Politano (72.Keita Baldé Diao). Trainer: Luciano Spalletti.

Tottenham Hotspur: Michel Vorm, Jan Vertonghen, Serge Aurier, Benjamin Davies, Davinson Sánchez, Mousa Dembélé, Érik Lamela (72.Harry Winks), Christian Eriksen, Eric Dier, Son Heung-Min (64.Lucas Moura), Harry Kane (90.Danny Rose). Trainer: Mauricio Pochettino.

Goals: 0-1 Christian Eriksen (53), 1-1 Mauro Icardi (86), 2-1 Matías Vecino (90+2)

03.10.2018; Wembley Stadium, London; Referee: Felix Zwayer (Germany); Attendance: 82,137

Tottenham Hotspur FC London – FC Barcelona 2-4(0-2)

Tottenham Hotspur: Hugo Lloris, Toby Alderweireld, Kieran Trippier, Benjamin Davies, Davinson Sánchez, Victor Wanyama (57.Eric Dier), Érik Lamela (79.Llorente), Lucas Moura, Harry Winks, Son Heung-Min (66.Moussa Sissoko), Harry Kane. Trainer: Mauricio Pochettino.

FC Barcelona: Marc-André ter Stegen, Piqué, Jordi Alba, Clément Lenglet, Nélson Semedo, Ivan Rakitic, Sergio Busquets (90+1.Thomas Vermaelen), Philippe Coutinho (83.Rafinha), Arthur (87.Arturo Vidal), Lionel Messi, Luis Suárez. Trainer: Ernesto Valverde.

Goals: 0-1 Philippe Coutinho (2), 0-2 Ivan Rakitic (28), 1-2 Harry Kane (52), 1-3 Lionel Messi (56), 2-3 Érik Lamela (66), 2-4 Lionel Messi (90).

03.10.2018; Philips Stadion, Eindhoven; Referee: Milorad Mazic (Serbia); Attendance: 34,750

PSV Eindhoven – Internazionale FC Milano **1-2(1-1)**

PSV Eindhoven: Jeroen Zoet, Daniel Schwaab, Nick Viergever, José Angeliño, Denzel Dumfries, Jorrit Hendrix, Gastón Pereiro (75.Donyell Malen), Pablo Rosario, Luuk de Jong, Steven Bergwijn, Hirving Lozano. Trainer: Mark van Bommel.

Internazionale: Samir Handanovic, Stefan de Vrij, Danilo D'Ambrosio, Milan Skriniar, Ivan Perisic, Radja Nainggolan (86.Borja Valero), Kwadwo Asamoah, Matías Vecino, Marcelo Brozovic, Mauro Icardi, Matteo Politano (90+1.Antonio Candreva). Trainer: Luciano Spalletti.

Goals: 1-0 Pablo Rosario (27), 1-1 Radja Nainggolan (44), 1-2 Mauro Icardi (60).

24.10.2018; Philips Stadion, Eindhoven; Referee: Slavko Vincic (Slovenia); Attendance: 35,000

PSV Eindhoven – Tottenham Hotspur FC London **2-2(1-1)**

PSV Eindhoven: Jeroen Zoet, Daniel Schwaab, Nick Viergever, José Angeliño, Denzel Dumfries, Jorrit Hendrix, Gastón Pereiro (83.Cody Gakpo), Pablo Rosario, Luuk de Jong, Hirving Lozano, Donyell Malen. Trainer: Mark van Bommel.

Tottenham Hotspur: Hugo Lloris [*sent off 79*], Toby Alderweireld, Kieran Trippier, Benjamin Davies, Davinson Sánchez, Moussa Dembélé (74.Harry Winks), Christian Eriksen, Lucas Moura (64.Érik Lamela), Eric Dier, Son Heung-Min (81.Michel Vorm), Harry Kane. Trainer: Mauricio Pochettino.

Goals: 1-0 Hirving Lozano (30), 1-1 Lucas Moura (39), 1-2 Harry Kane (55), 2-2 Luuk de Jong (87).

24.10.2018; Estadio Camp Nou, Barcelona; Referee: Ovidiu Hategan (Romania); Attendance: 86,290

FC Barcelona – Internazionale FC Milano **2-0(1-0)**

FC Barcelona: Marc-André ter Stegen, Piqué, Jordi Alba, Sergi Roberto, Clément Lenglet, Ivan Rakitic, Sergio Busquets, Philippe Coutinho (88.Munir), Rafinha (72.Nélson Semedo), Arthur (78.Arturo Vidal), Luis Suárez. Trainer: Ernesto Valverde.

Internazionale: Samir Handanovic, João Miranda, Kwadwo Asamoah, Danilo D'Ambrosio, Milan Skriniar, Ivan Perisic (77.Keita Baldé), Antonio Candreva (46.Matteo Politano), Borja Valero (63.Lautaro Martínez), Matías Vecino, Marcelo Brozovic, Mauro Icardi. Trainer: Luciano Spalletti.

Goals: 1-0 Rafinha (32), 2-0 Jordi Alba (83).

06.11.2018; Wembley Stadium, London; Referee: Ivan Kruzliak (Slovakia); Attendance: 46,588

Tottenham Hotspur FC London – PSV Eindhoven **2-1(0-1)**

Tottenham Hotspur: Paulo Gazzaniga, Toby Alderweireld, Serge Aurier (75.Kieran Trippier), Benjamin Davies, Davinson Sánchez, Christian Eriksen, Lucas Moura (62.Érik Lamela), Dele Alli, Harry Winks, Son Heung-Min (75.Llorente), Harry Kane. Trainer: Mauricio Pochettino.

PSV Eindhoven: Jeroen Zoet, Daniel Schwaab, Nick Viergever, José Angeliño, Denzel Dumfries, Jorrit Hendrix, Gastón Pereiro (73.Donyell Malen), Pablo Rosario, Luuk de Jong (81.Trent Sainsbury), Steven Bergwijn (86.Érick Gutiérrez), Hirving Lozano. Trainer: Mark van Bommel.

Goals: 0-1 Luuk de Jong (2), 1-1, 2-1 Harry Kane (78, 89).

06.11.2018; Stadio „Giuseppe Meazza", Milano; Referee: Szymon Marciniak (Poland); Attendance: 70,915

Internazionale FC Milano – FC Barcelona **1-1(0-0)**

Internazionale: Samir Handanovic, Kwadwo Asamoah, Sime Vrsaljko, Stefan de Vrij, Milan Skriniar, Ivan Perisic, Radja Nainggolan (63.Borja Valero), Matías Vecino, Marcelo Brozovic (85.Lautaro Martínez), Mauro Icardi, Matteo Politano (81.Antonio Candreva). Trainer: Luciano Spalletti.

FC Barcelona: Marc-André ter Stegen, Piqué, Jordi Alba, Sergi Roberto, Clément Lenglet, Ivan Rakitic, Sergio Busquets, Philippe Coutinho, Arthur (74.Arturo Vidal), Luis Suárez, Ousmane Dembélé (81.Malcom). Trainer: Ernesto Valverde.

Goals: 0-1 Malcom (83), 1-1 Mauro Icardi (87).

28.11.2018; Philips Stadion, Eindhoven; Referee: Pavel Královec (Czech Republic); Attendance: 34,600

PSV Eindhoven – FC Barcelona **1-2(0-0)**

PSV Eindhoven: Jeroen Zoet, Daniel Schwaab, Nick Viergever, José Angeliño, Denzel Dumfries, Jorrit Hendrix (71.Érick Gutiérrez), Gastón Pereiro (71.Donyell Malen), Pablo Rosario, Luuk de Jong, Steven Bergwijn (79.Maximiliano Romero), Hirving Lozano. Trainer: Mark van Bommel.

FC Barcelona: Marc-André ter Stegen, Piqué, Jordi Alba, Clément Lenglet, Nélson Semedo, Ivan Rakitic, Arturo Vidal, Sergio Busquets, Philippe Coutinho (69.Malcom), Lionel Messi, Ousmane Dembélé (80.Denis Suárez). Trainer: Ernesto Valverde.

Goals: 0-1 Lionel Messi (61), 0-2 Piqué (70), 1-2 Luuk de Jong (83).

28.11.2018; Wembley Stadium, London; Referee: Cüneyt Çakir (Turkey); Attendance: 57,132

Tottenham Hotspur FC London – Internazionale FC Milano **1-0(0-0)**

Tottenham Hotspur: Hugo Lloris, Jan Vertonghen, Toby Alderweireld, Serge Aurier, Benjamin Davies, Moussa Sissoko, Érik Lamela (70.Christian Eriksen), Lucas Moura (62.Son Heung-Min), Dele Alli, Harry Winks (87.Eric Dier), Harry Kane. Trainer: Mauricio Pochettino.

Internazionale: Samir Handanovic, Kwadwo Asamoah, Stefan de Vrij (82.João Miranda), Danilo D'Ambrosio, Milan Skriniar, Ivan Perisic, Radja Nainggolan (44.Borja Valero), Matías Vecino, Marcelo Brozovic, Mauro Icardi, Matteo Politano (83.Keita Baldé). Trainer: Luciano Spalletti.

Goal: 1-0 Christian Eriksen (80).

11.12.2018; Estadio Camp Nou, Barcelona; Referee: Milorad Mazic (Serbia); Attendance: 69,961

FC Barcelona – Tottenham Hotspur FC London **1-1(1-0)**

FC Barcelona: Jasper Cillessen, Thomas Vermaelen, Clément Lenglet, Nélson Semedo, Juan Miranda, Ivan Rakitic (46.Sergio Busquets), Philippe Coutinho, Arthur, Carles Aleñá, Munir (63.Lionel Messi), Ousmane Dembélé (76.Denis Suárez). Trainer: Ernesto Valverde.

Tottenham Hotspur: Hugo Lloris, Jan Vertonghen, Danny Ross, Toby Alderweireld, Kyle Walker-Peters (61.Érik Lamela), Moussa Sissoko, Christian Eriksen, Dele Alli, Harry Winks (83.Llorente), Son Heung-Min (71.Lucas Moura), Harry Kane. Trainer: Mauricio Pochettino.

Goals: 1-0 Ousmane Dembélé (7), 1-1 Lucas Moura (85).

11.12.2018; Stadio „Giuseppe Meazza", Milano; Referee: Felix Zwayer (Germany); Attendance: 62,533

Internazionale FC Milano – PSV Eindhoven **1-1(0-1)**

Internazionale: Samir Handanovic, Kwadwo Asamoah (69.Lautaro Martínez), Stefan de Vrij, Danilo D'Ambrosio, Milan Skriniar, Ivan Perisic, Antonio Candreva (56.Keita Baldé), Borja Valero, Marcelo Brozovic, Mauro Icardi, Matteo Politano (83.Sime Vrsaljko). Trainer: Luciano Spalletti.

PSV Eindhoven: Jeroen Zoet, Nick Viergever, Trent Sainsbury, José Angeliño, Denzel Dumfries, Jorrit Hendrix, Érick Gutiérrez (65.Michal Sadílek), Pablo Rosario, Luuk de Jong, Steven Bergwijn (71.Donyell Malen), Hirving Lozano (90+5.Gastón Pereiro). Trainer: Mark van Bommel.

Goals: 0-1 Hirving Lozano (13), 1-1 Mauro Icardi (73).

GROUP C

1.	**Paris Saint-Germain FC**	6	3	2	1	17	-	9	11
2.	**Liverpool FC**	6	3	0	3	9	-	7	9
3.	SSC Napoli	6	2	3	1	7	-	5	9
4.	FK Crvena Zvezda Beograd	6	1	1	4	5	-	17	4

18.09.2018; Anfield Road, Liverpool; Referee: Cüneyt Çakir (Turkey); Attendance: 52,478

Liverpool FC – Paris Saint-Germain FC **3-2(2-1)**

Liverpool FC: Alisson, Virgil van Dijk, Andrew Robertson, Joseph Gomez, Trent Alexander-Arnold, James Milner, Georginio Wijnaldum, Jordan Henderson, Daniel Sturridge (72.Roberto Firmino), Mohamed Salah (85.Xherdan Shaqiri), Sadio Mané (90+3.Fabinho). Trainer: Jürgen Klopp.

Paris Saint-Germain: Alphonse Aréola, Thiago Silva, Thomas Meunier, Marquinhos, Juan Bernat, Presnel Kimpembe, Ángel Di María (80.Eric Maxim Choupo-Moting), Adrien Rabiot, Edinson Cavani (80.Julian Draxler), Neymar, Kylian Mbappé. Trainer: Thomas Tuchel.

Goals: 1-0 Daniel Sturridge (30), 2-0 James Milner (36 penalty), 2-1 Thomas Meunier (40), 2-2 Kylian Mbappé (83), 3-2 Roberto Firmino (90+2).

18.09.2018; Stadion „Rajko Mitić", Beograd; Referee: Szymon Marciniak (Poland) Attendance: 49,112

FK Crvena Zvezda Beograd – SSC Napoli 0-0

Crvena Zvezda: Milan Borjan, Vujadin Savic, Milan Rodic, Milos Degenek, Filip Stojkovic, Marko Marin (87.Veljko Simic), Nenad Krsticic, Goran Causic, Branko Jovicic (56.Dusan Jovancic), Richmond Boakye (81.Milan Pavkov), Mohamed Ben Nabouhane. Trainer: Vladan Milojevic.

SSC Napoli: David Ospina, Raúl Albiol, Mário Rui, Kalidou Koulibaly, Elseid Hysaj, Allan (61.Dries Mertens), Piotr Zielinski (75.Marek Hamsík), Fabián Ruiz, José Callejón (75.Adam Ounas), Lorenzo Insigne, Arkadiusz Milik. Trainer: Carlo Ancelotti.

03.10.2018; Parc des Princes, Paris; Referee: Artur Soares Dias (Portugal); Attendance: 39,979

Paris Saint-Germain FC – FK Crvena Zvezda Beograd 6-1(4-0)

Paris Saint-Germain: Alphonse Aréola, Thiago Silva (76.Thilo Kehrer), Thomas Meunier, Juan Bernat, Presnel Kimpembe, Ángel Di María, Marco Verratti, Adrien Rabiot, Edinson Cavani, Neymar (82.Julian Draxler), Kylian Mbappé (76.Eric Maxim Choupo-Moting). Trainer: Thomas Tuchel.

Crvena Zvezda: Milan Borjan, Vujadin Savic (46.Srdjan Babic), Milan Rodic, Milos Degenek, Filip Stojkovic, Marko Marin, Nenad Krsticic, Goran Causic, Veljko Simic (46.Milan Pavkov), Branko Jovicic, Mohamed Ben Nabouhane (73.Lorenzo Ebecilio). Trainer: Vladan Milojevic.

Goals: 1-0, 2-0 Neymar (20, 22), 3-0 Edinson Cavani (37), 4-0 Ángel Di María (42), 5-0 Kylian Mbappé (70), 5-1 Marko Marin (74), 6-1 Neymar (81).

03.10.2018; Stadio San Paolo, Napoli; Referee: Viktor Kassai (Hungary); Attendance: 37,057

SSC Napoli – Liverpool FC 1-0(0-0)

SSC Napoli: David Ospina, Raúl Albiol, Nikola Maksimovic, Mário Rui, Kalidou Koulibaly, Marek Hamsík (81.Piotr Zielinski), Allan, Fabián Ruiz (68.Simone Verdi), José Callejón, Lorenzo Insigne, Arkadiusz Milik (68.Dries Mertens). Trainer: Carlo Ancelotti.

Liverpool FC: Alisson, Virgil van Dijk, Andrew Robertson, Joseph Gomez, Trent Alexander-Arnold, James Milner (76.Fabinho), Georginio Wijnaldum, Naby Keïta (19.Jordan Henderson), Roberto Firmino, Mohamed Salah, Sadio Mané (89.Daniel Sturridge). Trainer: Jürgen Klopp.

Goal: 1-0 Lorenzo Insigne (90).

24.10.2018; Parc des Princes, Paris; Referee: Felix Zwayer (Germany); Attendance: 46,274

Paris Saint-Germain FC – SSC Napoli 2-2(0-1)

Paris Saint-Germain: Alphonse Aréola, Thomas Meunier, Marquinhos, Juan Bernat (46.Thilo Kehrer), Presnel Kimpembe, Ángel Di María, Marco Verratti (83.Moussa Diaby), Adrien Rabiot, Edinson Cavani (76.Julian Draxler), Neymar, Kylian Mbappé. Trainer: Thomas Tuchel.

SSC Napoli: David Ospina, Raúl Albiol, Nikola Maksimovic, Mário Rui, Kalidou Koulibaly, Marek Hamsík, Allan, Fabián Ruiz, Dries Mertens (84.Arkadiusz Milik), José Callejón (88.Marko Rog), Lorenzo Insigne (53.Piotr Zielinski). Trainer: Carlo Ancelotti.

Goals: 0-1 Lorenzo Insigne (29), 1-1 Mário Rui (61 own goal), 1-2 Dries Mertens (77), 2-2 Ángel Di María (90+3).

24.10.2018; Anfield Road, Liverpool; Referee: Daniel Siebert (Germany); Attendance: 53,024

Liverpool FC – FK Crvena Zvezda Beograd 4-0(2-0)

Liverpool FC: Alisson, Virgil van Dijk, Andrew Robertson (82.Alberto Moreno), Joseph Gomez, Trent Alexander-Arnold, Georginio Wijnaldum, Fabinho, Xherdan Shaqiri (68.Adam Lallana), Roberto Firmino, Mohamed Salah (73.Daniel Sturridge), Sadio Mané. Trainer: Jürgen Klopp.

Crvena Zvezda: Milan Borjan, Milos Degenek, Filip Stojkovic, Marko Gobeljic, Srdjan Babic, Nenad Krsticic, Lorenzo Ebecilio (65.Dusan Jovancic), Slavoljub Srnic, Branko Jovicic (75.Goran Causic), Richmond Boakye, Mohamed Ben Nabouhane (81.Veljko Simic). Trainer: Vladan Milojevic.

Goals: 1-0 Roberto Firmino (20), 2-0, 3-0 Mohamed Salah (45, 51 penalty), 4-0 Sadio Mané (80).

06.11.2018; Stadion „Rajko Mitić", Beograd; Referee: Antonio Mateu Lahoz (Spain); Attendance: 51,318

FK Crvena Zvezda Beograd – Liverpool FC 2-0(2-0)

Crvena Zvezda: Milan Borjan, Vujadin Savic, Milan Rodic, Milos Degenek, Filip Stojkovic (59.Marko Gobeljic), Marko Marin (64.Goran Causic), Nenad Krsticic (73.Branko Jovicic), Slavoljub Srnic, Dusan Jovancic, Mohamed Ben Nabouhane, Milan Pavkov. Trainer: Vladan Milojevic.

Liverpool FC: Alisson, Joel Matip, Virgil van Dijk, Andrew Robertson, Trent Alexander-Arnold (46.Joseph Gomez), James Milner, Georginio Wijnaldum, Adam Lallana (79.Divock Origi), Daniel Sturridge (46.Roberto Firmino), Mohamed Salah, Sadio Mané. Trainer: Jürgen Klopp.

Goals: 1-0, 2-0 Milan Pavkov (22, 29).

06.11.2018; Stadio San Paolo, Napoli; Referee: Björn Kuipers (Netherlands); Attendance: 55,489

SSC Napoli – Paris Saint-Germain FC 1-1(0-1)

SSC Napoli: David Ospina, Raúl Albiol, Nikola Maksimovic (76.Elseid Hysaj), Mário Rui, Kalidou Koulibaly, Marek Hamsík, Allan, Fabián Ruiz (71.Piotr Zielinski), Dries Mertens (83.Adam Ounas), José Callejón, Lorenzo Insigne. Trainer: Carlo Ancelotti.

Paris Saint-Germain: Gianluigi Buffon, Thiago Silva, Thomas Meunier (73.Presnel Kimpembe), Marquinhos, Juan Bernat, Thilo Kehrer (90+2.Eric Maxim Choupo-Moting), Ángel Di María (77.Edinson Cavani), Marco Verratti, Julian Draxler, Neymar, Kylian Mbappé. Trainer: Thomas Tuchel.

Goals: 0-1 Juan Bernat (45+2), 1-1 Lorenzo Insigne (63 penalty).

28.11.2018; Parc des Princes, Paris; Referee: Szymon Marciniak (Poland); Attendance: 46,880

Paris Saint-Germain FC – Liverpool FC 2-1(2-1)

Paris Saint-Germain: Gianluigi Buffon, Thiago Silva, Marquinhos, Juan Bernat, Presnel Kimpembe, Thilo Kehrer, Ángel Di María (65.Dani Alves), Marco Verratti, Edinson Cavani (65.Eric Maxim Choupo-Moting), Neymar, Kylian Mbappé (85.Adrien Rabiot). Trainer: Thomas Tuchel.

Liverpool FC: Alisson, Dejan Lovren, Virgil van Dijk, Andrew Robertson, Joseph Gomez, James Milner (77.Xherdan Shaqiri), Georginio Wijnaldum (66.Naby Keïta), Jordan Henderson, Roberto Firmino (71.Daniel Sturridge), Mohamed Salah, Sadio Mané. Trainer: Jürgen Klopp.

Goals: 1-0 Juan Bernat (13), 2-0 Neymar (37), 2-1 James Milner (45+1 penalty).

28.11.2018; Stadio San Paolo, Napoli; Referee: Jesús Gil Manzano (Spain); Attendance: 44,470

SSC Napoli – FK Crvena Zvezda Beograd 3-1(2-0)

SSC Napoli: David Ospina, Raúl Albiol (46.Elseid Hysaj), Nikola Maksimovic, Mário Rui, Kalidou Koulibaly, Marek Hamsík, Allan, Fabián Ruiz, Dries Mertens, José Callejón (86.Marko Rog), Lorenzo Insigne (77.Piotr Zielinski). Trainer: Carlo Ancelotti.

Crvena Zvezda: Milan Borjan, Milan Rodic, Milos Degenek, Marko Gobeljic, Srdjan Babic, Marko Marin, Nenad Krsticic, Slavoljub Srnic (64.Dusan Jovancic), Veljko Simic (77.Lorenzo Ebecilio), Nikola Stojiljkovic (46.Dejan Joveljic), Mohamed Ben Nabouhane. Trainer: Vladan Milojevic.

Goals: 1-0 Marek Hamsík (11), 2-0, 3-0 Dries Mertens (33, 52), 3-1 Mohamed Ben Nabouhane (57).

11.12.2018; Anfield Road, Liverpool; Referee: Damir Skomina (Slovenia); Attendance: 52,015

Liverpool FC – SSC Napoli 1-0(1-0)

Liverpool FC: Alisson, Joel Matip, Virgil van Dijk, Andrew Robertson, Trent Alexander-Arnold (90.Dejan Lovren), James Milner (85.Fabinho), Georginio Wijnaldum, Jordan Henderson, Roberto Firmino (79.Naby Keïta), Mohamed Salah, Sadio Mané. Trainer: Jürgen Klopp.

SSC Napoli: David Ospina, Raúl Albiol, Nikola Maksimovic, Mário Rui (70.Faouzi Ghoulam), Kalidou Koulibaly, Marek Hamsík, Allan, Fabián Ruiz (62.Piotr Zielinski), Dries Mertens (67.Arkadiusz Milik), José Callejón, Lorenzo Insigne. Trainer: Carlo Ancelotti.

Goal: 1-0 Mohamed Salah (34).

11.12.2018; Stadion „Rajko Mitić", Beograd; Referee: William Collum (Scotland); Attendance: 48,357

FK Crvena Zvezda Beograd – Paris Saint-Germain FC 1-4(0-2)

Crvena Zvezda: Milan Borjan, Milan Rodic, Milos Degenek, Filip Stojkovic, Marko Gobeljic, Marko Marin (86.Dejan Joveljic), Goran Causic, Veljko Simic (72.Lorenzo Ebecilio), Dusan Jovancic, Mohamed Ben Nabouhane, Milan Pavkov (72.Richmond Boakye). Trainer: Vladan Milojevic.

Paris Saint-Germain: Gianluigi Buffon, Thiago Silva, Marquinhos, Juan Bernat, Presnel Kimpembe, Thilo Kehrer, Ángel Di María (88.Julian Draxler), Marco Verratti (83.Adrien Rabiot), Edinson Cavani, Neymar, Kylian Mbappé. Trainer: Thomas Tuchel.

Goals: 0-1 Edinson Cavani (10), 0-2 Neymar (40), 1-2 Marko Gobeljic (56), 1-3 Marquinhos (74), 1-4 Kylian Mbappé (90+2).

GROUP D

1.	**FC Porto**	6	5	1	0	15 - 6	16
2.	**FC Schalke 04 Gelsenkirchen**	6	3	2	1	6 - 4	11
3.	Galatasaray SK İstanbul	6	1	1	4	5 - 8	4
4.	FK Lokomotiv Moskva	6	1	0	5	4 - 12	3

18.09.2018; Türk Telekom Stadyumu, İstanbul; Referee: Gianluca Rocchi (Italy); Attendance: 43,542

Galatasaray SK İstanbul – FK Lokomotiv Moskva 3-0(1-0)

Galatasaray: Fernando Muslera, Serdar Aziz, Yuto Nagatomo, Martin Linnes, Ryan Donk, Fernando, Younès Belhanda (73.Maicon), Papa Alioune "Badou" N'Diaye [*sent off 87*], Garry Rodrigues (90+1.Selçuk Inan), Emre Akbaba, Eren Derdiyok (82.Henry Onyekuru). Trainer: Fatih Terim.

Lokomotiv Moskva: Guilherme, Vedran Corluka, Benedikt Höwedes, Solomon Kverkvelia, Brian Idowu, Jefferson Farfán, Manuel Fernandes, Igor Denisov, Vladislav Ignatyev (69.Éder), Grzegorz Krychowiak, Aleksey Miranchuk (86.Anton Miranchuk). Trainer: Yuriy Semin.

Goals: 1-0 Garry Rodrigues (9), 2-0 Eren Derdiyok (67), 3-0 Selçuk Inan (90+4 penalty).

18.09.2018; VELTINS-Arena, Gelsenkirchen; Referee: Jesús Gil Manzano (Spain); Attendance: 45,755

FC Schalke 04 Gelsenkirchen – FC Porto 1-1(0-0)

Schalke 04: Ralf Fährmann, Naldo, Matija Nastasic, Salif Sané, Daniel Caligiuri, Nabil Bentaleb, Alessandro Schöpf, Suat Serdar (84.Amine Harit), Weston McKennie, Mark Uth (65.Yevhen Konoplyanka), Breel Embolo (72.Guido Burgstaller). Trainer: Domenico Tedesco.

FC Porto: Iker Casillas, Maxi Pereira, Alex Telles, Felipe Monteiro, Éder Militão, Héctor Herrera, Danilo Pereira, Otavinho (90.Hernâni), Yacine Brahimi (82.Sérgio Oliveira), Vincent Aboubakar (60.Jesús Corona), Moussa Marega. Trainer: Sérgio Conceição.

Goals: 1-0 Breel Embolo (64), 1-1 Otavinho (75 penalty).

03.10.2018; RZD Arena, Moskva; Referee: Anthony Taylor (England); Attendance: 21,471

FK Lokomotiv Moskva – FC Schalke 04 Gelsenkirchen 0-1(0-0)

Lokomotiv Moskva: Guilherme, Benedikt Höwedes, Solomon Kverkvelia, Brian Idowu, Manuel Fernandes, Vladislav Ignatyev, Grzegorz Krychowiak, Dmitry Barinov, Aleksey Miranchuk (83.Rifat Zhemaletdinov), Anton Miranchuk (72.Igor Denisov), Éder. Trainer: Yuriy Semin.

Schalke 04: Ralf Fährmann, Naldo, Salif Sané, Hamza Mendyl, Sebastian Rudy (55.Nabil Bentaleb), Daniel Caligiuri, Yevhen Konoplyanka, Omar Mascarell (46.Suat Serdar), Weston McKennie, Mark Uth, Breel Embolo (72.Guido Burgstaller). Trainer: Domenico Tedesco.

Goal: 0-1 Weston McKennie (88).

03.10.2018; Estádio do Dragão, Porto; Referee: Michael Oliver (England); Attendance: 42,711

FC Porto – Galatasaray SK İstanbul 1-0(0-0)

FC Porto: Iker Casillas, Maxi Pereira, Alex Telles, Felipe Monteiro, Éder Militão, Héctor Herrera (89.Sérgio Oliveira), Danilo Pereira, Otavinho (80.André Pereira), Yacine Brahimi, Jesús Corona (69.Óliver Torres), Moussa Marega. Trainer: Sérgio Conceição.

Galatasaray: Fernando Muslera, Serdar Aziz, Yuto Nagatomo, Maicon, Martin Linnes, Ryan Donk (68.Selçuk Inan), Fernando (86.Yunus Akgün), Younès Belhanda (74.Sofiane Féghouli), Garry Rodrigues, Sinan Gümüs, Henry Onyekuru. Trainer: Fatih Terim.

Goal: 1-0 Moussa Marega (49).

24.10.2018; RZD Arena, Moskva; Referee: Bobby Madden (Scotland); Attendance: 16,034

FK Lokomotiv Moskva – FC Porto 1-3(1-2)

Lokomotiv Moskva: Guilherme, Benedikt Höwedes, Solomon Kverkvelia [*sent off 76*], Manuel Fernandes (66.Rifat Zhemaletdinov), Igor Denisov, Vladislav Ignatyev, Grzegorz Krychowiak, Dmitry Barinov, Aleksey Miranchuk, Anton Miranchuk, Éder (81.Mikhail Lysov). Trainer: Yuriy Semin.

FC Porto: Iker Casillas, Maxi Pereira, Alex Telles, Felipe Monteiro, Éder Militão, Héctor Herrera, Danilo Pereira, Óliver Torres (83.Riechedly Bazoer), Yacine Brahimi (82.Adrián), Jesús Corona (69.André Pereira), Moussa Marega. Trainer: Sérgio Conceição.

Goals: 0-1 Moussa Marega (26 penalty), 0-2 Héctor Herrera (35), 1-2 Anton Miranchuk (38), 1-3 Jesús Corona (47).

24.10.2018; Türk Telekom Stadyumu, İstanbul; Referee: Benoît Bastien (France); Attendance: 46,667

Galatasaray SK İstanbul – FC Schalke 04 Gelsenkirchen 0-0

Galatasaray: Fernando Muslera, Yuto Nagatomo (81.Ömer Bayram), Maicon, Martin Linnes, Ozan Kabak, Ryan Donk, Younès Belhanda, Papa Alioune "Badou" N'Diaye, Garry Rodrigues, Eren Derdiyok (70.Mugdat Çelik), Sinan Gümüs (61.Selçuk Inan). Trainer: Fatih Terim.

Schalke 04: Alexander Nübel, Matija Nastasic, Benjamin Stambouli, Salif Sané, Hamza Mendyl, Sebastian Rudy, Daniel Caligiuri, Yevhen Konoplyanka (77.Steven Skrzybski), Suat Serdar, Mark Uth (90.Guido Burgstaller), Breel Embolo (82.Weston McKennie). Trainer: Domenico Tedesco.

06.11.2018; Estádio do Dragão, Porto; Referee: Davide Massa (Italy); Attendance: 34,616

FC Porto – FK Lokomotiv Moskva 4-1(2-0)

FC Porto: Iker Casillas, Maxi Pereira, Alex Telles, Felipe Monteiro, Éder Militão, Héctor Herrera, Danilo Pereira, Óliver Torres (85.Sérgio Oliveira), Yacine Brahimi (68.Otavinho), Jesús Corona (77.Hernâni), Moussa Marega. Trainer: Sérgio Conceição.

Lokomotiv Moskva: Guilherme, Verdan Corluka, Benedikt Höwedes, Brian Idowu, Manuel Fernandes (46.Jefferson Farfán), Igor Denisov, Vladislav Ignatyev, Grzegorz Krychowiak, Aleksey Miranchuk, Anton Miranchuk, Éder (71.Fyodor Smolov). Trainer: Yuriy Semin.

Goals: 1-0 Héctor Herrera (2), 2-0 Moussa Marega (42), 2-1 Jefferson Farfán (59), 3-1 Jesús Corona (67), 4-1 Otavinho (90+3).

06.11.2018; VELTINS-Arena, Gelsenkirchen; Referee: William Collum (Scotland); Attendance: 54,740

FC Schalke 04 Gelsenkirchen – Galatasaray SK İstanbul 2-0(1-0)

Schalke 04: Alexander Nübel, Matija Nastasic, Benjamin Stambouli, Salif Sané, Sebastian Rudy (76.Suat Serdar), Daniel Caligiuri, Alessandro Schöpf, Amine Harit (56.Weston McKennie), Guido Burgstaller, Mark Uth (63.Nabil Bentaleb), Breel Embolo. Trainer: Domenico Tedesco.

Galatasaray: Fernando Muslera, Serdar Aziz, Mariano, Martin Linnes (46.Ömer Bayram), Ozan Kabak, Ryan Donk, Younès Belhanda, Papa Alioune "Badou" N'Diaye, Garry Rodrigues (63.Selçuk Inan), Sinan Gümüs (72.Mugdat Çelik), Henry Onyekuru. Trainer: Fatih Terim.

Goals: 1-0 Guido Burgstaller (4), 2-0 Mark Uth (57).

28.11.2018; RZD Arena, Moskva; Referee: Antonio Mateu Lahoz (Spain); Attendance: 14,037

FK Lokomotiv Moskva – Galatasaray SK İstanbul 2-0(1-0)

Lokomotiv Moskva: Guilherme, Verdan Corluka, Solomon Kverkvelia, Jefferson Farfán (90.Boris Rotenberg), Igor Denisov, Maciej Rybus, Vladislav Ignatyev, Grzegorz Krychowiak, Aleksey Miranchuk (77.Dmitry Barinov), Anton Miranchuk, Fyodor Smolov (88.Éder). Trainer: Yuriy Semin.

Galatasaray: Fernando Muslera, Serdar Aziz, Yuto Nagatomo, Martin Linnes (89.Mariano), Ozan Kabak, Ryan Donk, Fernando (59.Sofiane Féghouli), Papa Alioune "Badou" N'Diaye (68.Selçuk Inan), Garry Rodrigues, Eren Derdiyok, Henry Onyekuru. Trainer: Fatih Terim.

Goals: 1-0 Ryan Donk (43 own goal), 2-0 Vladislav Ignatyev (54).

28.11.2018; Estádio do Dragão, Porto; Referee: Ovidiu Hategan (Romania); Attendance: 41,603

FC Porto – FC Schalke 04 Gelsenkirchen 3-1(0-0)

FC Porto: Iker Casillas, Maxi Pereira, Alex Telles, Felipe Monteiro, Éder Militão, Héctor Herrera (85.Hernâni), Danilo Pereira, Óliver Torres, Yacine Brahimi (74.Adrián), Jesús Corona (79.Otavinho), Moussa Marega. Trainer: Sérgio Conceição.

Schalke 04: Ralf Fährmann, Naldo, Matija Nastasic, Benjamin Stambouli (71.Sebastian Rudy), Hamza Mendyl, Daniel Caligiuri (62.Alessandro Schöpf), Yevhen Konoplyanka, Omar Mascarell, Nabil Bentaleb, Franco Di Santo, Steven Skrzybski (46.Amine Harit). Trainer: Domenico Tedesco.

Goals: 1-0 Éder Militão (52), 2-0 Jesús Corona (55), 2-1 Nabil Bentaleb (89 penalty), 3-1 Moussa Marega (90+4).

11.12.2018; Türk Telekom Stadyumu, İstanbul; Referee: Aleksei Kulbakov (Belarus); Attendance: 33,972

Galatasaray SK İstanbul – FC Porto 2-3(1-2)

Galatasaray: Fernando Muslera, Mariano, Yuto Nagatomo, Maicon, Ozan Kabak, Ryan Donk (46.Henry Onyekuru), Sofiane Féghouli (89.Mugdat Çelik), Fernando, Papa Alioune "Badou" N'Diaye, Garry Rodrigues, Eren Derdiyok. Trainer: Fatih Terim.

FC Porto: Iker Casillas, Maxi Pereira, Alex Telles, Felipe Monteiro, Diogo Leite, Héctor Herrera, Sérgio Oliveira (82.Chidozie Awaziem), Danilo Pereira, Adrián (73.André Pereira), Hernâni (73.Jorge), Moussa Marega. Trainer: Sérgio Conceição.

Goals: 0-1 Felipe Monteiro (17), 0-2 Moussa Marega (42 penalty), 1-2 Sofiane Féghouli (45+1 penalty), 1-3 Sérgio Oliveira (57), 2-3 Eren Derdiyok (65).

11.12.2018; VELTINS-Arena, Gelsenkirchen; Referee: Anastasios Sidiropoulos (Greece); Attendance: 48,883

FC Schalke 04 Gelsenkirchen – FK Lokomotiv Moskva 1-0(0-0)

Schalke 04: Ralf Fährmann, Naldo, Matija Nastasic, Benjamin Stambouli, Hamza Mendyl (16.Abdul Rahman Baba), Yevhen Konoplyanka, Omar Mascarell, Alessandro Schöpf, Suat Serdar, Benjamin Goller (59.Amine Harit), Cedric Teuchert (72.Ahmed Kutucu). Trainer: Domenico Tedesco.

Lokomotiv Moskva: Guilherme, Benedikt Höwedes, Solomon Kverkvelia, Jefferson Farfán (80.Fyodor Smolov), Igor Denisov, Maciej Rybus, Vladislav Ignatyev, Grzegorz Krychowiak, Dmitry Barinov, Aleksey Miranchuk, Éder (46.Anton Miranchuk). Trainer: Yuriy Semin.

Goal: 1-0 Alessandro Schöpf (90+1).

GROUP E

1.	**FC Bayern München**	6	4	2	0	15	-	5	14
2.	**AFC Ajax Amsterdam**	6	3	3	0	11	-	5	12
3.	Sport Lisboa e Benfica	6	2	1	3	6	-	11	7
4.	AEK Athína	6	0	0	6	2	-	13	0

19.09.2018; „Johan Cruijff" Arena, Amsterdam; Referee: Carlos del Cerro Grande (Spain); Attendance: 52,285

AFC Ajax Amsterdam – AEK Athína 3-0(0-0)

Ajax Amsterdam: André Onana, Daley Blind, Nicolás Tagliafico, Lasse Schöne, Hakim Ziyech, Carel Eiting, Noussair Mazraoui, Frenkie de Jong, Klaas Jan Huntelaar (62.Donny van de Beek), Dusan Tadic, David Neres (78.Kasper Dolberg). Trainer: Erik ten Hag.

AEK Athína: Vassilis Barkas, Niklas Hult, Konstantinos-Vassilios Lambropoulos, Uros Cosic, Marios Oikonomou, Petros Mandalos, Michalis Bakakis (70.Giannis Gianniotas), André Simões, Konstantinos Galanopoulos (61.Alef), Viktor Klonaridis, Ezequiel Ponce (81.Georgios Giakoumakis). Trainer: Marinos Ouzounidis.

Goals: 1-0 Nicolás Tagliafico (46), 2-0 Donny van de Beek (77), 3-0 Nicolás Tagliafico (90).

19.09.2018; Estádio da Luz, Lisboa; Referee: Antonio Mateu Lahoz (Spain); Attendance: 60,274

Sport Lisboa e Benfica – FC Bayern München 0-2(0-1)

Benfica: Odisseas Vlachodimos, André Almeida, Jardel, Álex Grimaldo, Rúben Dias, Ljubomir Fejsa, Pizzi (62.Rafa Silva), Eduardo Salvio (62.Gabriel), Franco Cervi, Gedson Fernandes (76.Andrija Zivkovic), Haris Seferovic. Trainer: Rui Vitória.

Bayern München: Manuel Neuer, Jérôme Boateng, Mats Hummels, David Alaba, Joshua Kimmich, Arjen Robben, Franck Ribéry (62.Serge Gnabry), Javi Martínez (88.Thomas Müller), James Rodríguez (79.Leon Goretzka), Renato Sanches, Robert Lewandowski. Trainer: Niko Kovac.

Goals: 0-1 Robert Lewandowski (10), 0-2 Renato Sanches (54).

02.10.2018; Allianz Arena, München; Referee: Pavel Královec (Czech Republic); Attendance: 70,000.

FC Bayern München – AFC Ajax Amsterdam 1-1(1-1)

Bayern München: Manuel Neuer, Jérôme Boateng, Mats Hummels (90+3.Niklas Süle), David Alaba, Joshua Kimmich, Arjen Robben (62.James Rodríguez), Franck Ribéry (74.Serge Gnabry), Javi Martínez, Thiago Alcântara, Thomas Müller, Robert Lewandowski. Trainer: Niko Kovac.

Ajax Amsterdam: André Onana, Daley Blind, Nicolás Tagliafico, Matthijs de Ligt, Max Wöber, Lasse Schöne, Hakim Ziyech, Donny van de Beek (75.Dani de Wit), Noussair Mazraoui, Dusan Tadic, David Neres (85.Kasper Dolberg). Trainer: Erik ten Hag.

Goals: 1-0 Mats Hummels (4), 1-1 Noussair Mazraoui (22).

02.10.2018; Stádio Olympiako „Spiros Louis", Athína; Referee: Orel Grinfeld (Israel); Attendance: 31,154

AEK Athína – Sport Lisboa e Benfica 2-3(0-2)

AEK Athína: Vassilis Barkas, Dmitro Chigrinskiy, Niklas Hult, Marios Oikonomou (68.Uros Cosic), Petros Mandalos, Michalis Bakakis, André Simões (79.Rodrigo Galo), Konstantinos Galanopoulos, Anastasios Bakasetas, Viktor Klonaridis, Ezequiel Ponce (60.Georgios Giakoumakis). Trainer: Marinos Ouzounidis.

Benfica: Odisseas Vlachodimos, André Almeida, Álex Grimaldo, Rúben Dias [*sent off 45+4*], Germán Conti, Ljubomir Fejsa, Pizzi (62.Alfa Semedo), Eduardo Salvio (46.Christian Lema), Rafa Silva (84.Franco Cervi), Gedson Fernandes, Haris Seferovic. Trainer: Rui Vitória.

Goals: 0-1 Haris Seferovic (6), 0-2 Álex Grimaldo (15), 1-2, 2-2 Viktor Klonaridis (53, 63), 2-3 Alfa Semedo (74).

23.10.2018; Stádio Olympiako „Spiros Louis", Athína; Referee: Aleksei Kulbakov (Belarus); Attendance: 61,221

AEK Athína – FC Bayern München 0-2(0-0)

AEK Athína: Vassilis Barkas, Dmitro Chigrinskiy, Niklas Hult, Konstantinos-Vassilios Lambropoulos, Petros Mandalos (76.Alef), Michalis Bakakis, André Simões, Konstantinos Galanopoulos (84.Rodrigo Galo), Anastasios Bakasetas, Viktor Klonaridis (64.Lucas Boyé), Ezequiel Ponce. Trainer: Marinos Ouzounidis.

Bayern München: Manuel Neuer, Rafinha, Mats Hummels, Niklas Süle, Joshua Kimmich, Arjen Robben, Javi Martínez, James Rodríguez (62.Leon Goretzka), Thiago Alcântara, Serge Gnabry (75.Thomas Müller), Robert Lewandowski (84.Sandro Wagner). Trainer: Niko Kovac.

Goals: 0-1 Javi Martínez (61), 0-2 Robert Lewandowski (63).

23.10.2018; „Johan Cruijff" Arena, Amsterdam; Referee: Ruddy Buquet (France); Attendance: 52,489

AFC Ajax Amsterdam – Sport Lisboa e Benfica 1-0(0-0)

Ajax Amsterdam: André Onana, Daley Blind, Nicolás Tagliafico, Matthijs de Ligt, Lasse Schöne, Hakim Ziyech, Donny van de Beek (88.David Neres), Noussair Mazraoui, Frenkie de Jong, Dusan Tadic, Kasper Dolberg. Trainer: Erik ten Hag.

Benfica: Odisseas Vlachodimos, André Almeida, Jardel, Álex Grimaldo, Germán Conti, Ljubomir Fejsa, Pizzi (79.Gabriel), Eduardo Salvio, Rafa Silva (90.Franco Cervi), Gedson Fernandes, Haris Seferovic. Trainer: Rui Vitória.

Goal: 1-0 Noussair Mazraoui (90+2).

07.11.2018; Allianz Arena, München; Referee: Matej Jug (Slovenia); Attendance: 70,000

FC Bayern München – AEK Athína 2-0(1-0)

Bayern München: Manuel Neuer, Jérôme Boateng, Mats Hummels, David Alaba, Joshua Kimmich, Franck Ribéry (84.Rafinha), Javi Martínez, Leon Goretzka, Serge Gnabry (87.Renato Sanches), Thomas Müller, Robert Lewandowski (90+1.Sandro Wagner). Trainer: Niko Kovac.

AEK Athína: Vassilis Barkas, Dmitro Chigrinskiy, Niklas Hult, Konstantinos-Vassilios Lambropoulos, Uros Cosic, Petros Mandalos (80.Lucas Boyé), Michalis Bakakis, André Simões, Alef (67.Erik Morán), Konstantinos Galanopoulos (78.Rodrigo Galo), Ezequiel Ponce. Trainer: Marinos Ouzounidis.

Goals: 1-0, 2-0 Robert Lewandowski (31 penalty, 71).

07.11.2018; Estádio da Luz, Lisboa; Referee: Gianluca Rocchi (Italy); Attendance: 51,328

Sport Lisboa e Benfica – AFC Ajax Amsterdam 1-1(1-0)

Benfica: Odisseas Vlachodimos, André Almeida, Jardel, Álex Grimaldo, Rúben Dias, Ljubomir Fejsa, Eduardo Salvio (48.Rafa Silva), Gabriel, Franco Cervi, Gedson Fernandes (75.Pizzi), Jonas (55.Haris Seferovic). Trainer: Rui Vitória.

Ajax Amsterdam: André Onana, Daley Blind, Nicolás Tagliafico, Matthijs de Ligt, Lasse Schöne, Hakim Ziyech, Donny van de Beek, Noussair Mazraoui, Frenkie de Jong (86.Max Wöber), Dusan Tadic, David Neres (74.Kasper Dolberg). Trainer: Erik ten Hag.

Goals: 1-0 Jonas (29), 1-1 Dusan Tadic (61).

27.11.2018; Stádio Olympiako „Spiros Louis", Athína; Referee: Michael Oliver (England); Attendance: 25,756

AEK Athína – AFC Ajax Amsterdam **0-2(0-0)**

AEK Athína: Vassilis Barkas, Dmitro Chigrinskiy, Niklas Hult, Rodrigo Galo (73.Lucas Boyé), Marios Oikonomou, Petros Mandalos (78.Viktor Klonaridis), Michalis Bakakis, Alef, Konstantinos Galanopoulos, Marko Livaja [*sent off 67*], Ezequiel Ponce (82.Georgios Giakoumakis). Trainer: Marinos Ouzounidis.

Ajax Amsterdam: André Onana, Daley Blind, Matthijs de Ligt, Max Wöber, Lasse Schöne, Donny van de Beek (86.Zakaria Labyad), Noussair Mazraoui (82.Rasmus Kristensen), Frenkie de Jong, Dusan Tadic, Kasper Dolberg (62.Klaas Jan Huntelaar), David Neres. Trainer: Erik ten Hag.

Goals: 0-1, 0-2 Dusan Tadic (68 penalty, 72).

27.11.2018; Allianz Arena, München; Referee: Daniele Orsato (Italy); Attendance: 70,000

FC Bayern München – Sport Lisboa e Benfica **5-1(3-0)**

Bayern München: Manuel Neuer, Rafinha, Jérôme Boateng, David Alaba, Niklas Süle, Joshua Kimmich, Arjen Robben (72.Renato Sanches), Franck Ribéry (78.Sandro Wagner), Leon Goretzka, Thomas Müller (81.Jeong Woo-Yeong), Robert Lewandowski. Trainer: Niko Kovac.

Benfica: Odisseas Vlachodimos, André Almeida, Álex Grimaldo, Rúben Dias, Germán Conti, Ljubomir Fejsa (76.Alfa Semedo), Pizzi (46.Gedson Fernandes), Gabriel, Rafa Silva, Franco Cervi, Jonas (59.Haris Seferovic). Trainer: Rui Vitória.

Goals: 1-0, 2-0 Arjen Robben (13, 30), 3-0 Robert Lewandowski (36), 3-1 Gedson Fernandes (46), 4-1 Robert Lewandowski (51), 5-1 Franck Ribéry (76).

12.12.2018; „Johan Cruijff" Arena, Amsterdam; Referee: Clément Turpin (France); Attendance: 52,244

AFC Ajax Amsterdam – FC Bayern München **3-3(0-1)**

Ajax Amsterdam: André Onana, Daley Blind, Nicolás Tagliafico, Matthijs de Ligt, Max Wöber [*sent off 67*], Hakim Ziyech, Donny van de Beek (78.Kasper Dolberg), Noussair Mazraoui, Frenkie de Jong, Dusan Tadic, David Neres (89.Klaas Jan Huntelaar). Trainer: Erik ten Hag.

Bayern München: Manuel Neuer, Rafinha, Jérôme Boateng, David Alaba, Niklas Süle, Joshua Kimmich, Franck Ribéry (71.Kingsley Coman), Leon Goretzka (89.Renato Sanches), Serge Gnabry (62.Thiago Alcântara), Thomas Müller [*sent off 75*], Robert Lewandowski. Trainer: Niko Kovac.

Goals: 0-1 Robert Lewandowski (13), 1-1, 2-1 Dusan Tadic (61, 82 penalty), 2-2 Robert Lewandowski (87 penalty), 2-3 Kingsley Coman (90), 3-3 Nicolás Tagliafico (90+5).

12.12.2018; Estádio da Luz, Lisboa; Referee: Bobby Madden (Scotland); Attendance: 33,633

Sport Lisboa e Benfica – AEK Athína **1-0(0-0)**

Benfica: Odisseas Vlachodimos, André Almeida, Jardel, Álex Grimaldo, Rúben Dias, Pizzi (59.Franco Cervi), Rafa Silva (35.Andrija Zivkovic), Gedson Fernandes, Alfa Semedo, Haris Seferovic, João Félix (77.Nicolás Castillo). Trainer: Rui Vitória.

AEK Athína: Vassilis Barkas, Dmitro Chigrinskiy, Niklas Hult, Uros Cosic, Marios Oikonomou, Erik Morán (77.Rodrigo Galo), Michalis Bakakis, Konstantinos Galanopoulos [*sent off 87*], Viktor Klonaridis (61.Giannis Gianniotas), Ezequiel Ponce, Lucas Boyé (68.Petros Mandalos). Trainer: Marinos Ouzounidis.

Goal: 1-0 Álex Grimaldo (88).

GROUP F

1.	**Manchester City FC**	6	4	1	1	16	-	6	13
2.	**Olympique Lyonnais**	6	1	5	0	12	-	11	8
3.	FK Shakhtar Donetsk	6	1	3	2	8	-	16	6
4.	TSG 1899 Hoffenheim	6	0	3	3	11	-	14	3

19.09.2018; Oblasny Sport Komplex Metalist, Kharkiv; Referee: Jakob Kehlet (Denmark); Attendance: 28,336

FK Shakhtar Donetsk – TSG 1899 Hoffenheim **2-2(1-2)**

Shakhtar Donetsk: Andriy Pyatov, Yaroslav Rakitskiy, Ismaily, Bogdan Butko, Davit Khotcholava, Marlos, Taras Stepanenko, Taison, Alan Patrick (76.Maycon), Sergiy Bolbat (57.Viktor Kovalenko), Júnior Moraes. Trainer: Paulo Fonseca.

Hoffenheim: Oliver Baumann, Håvard Nordtveit, Kevin Vogt, Pavel Kaderábek, Stefan Posch, Nico Schulz, Leonardo Bittencourt (64.Kerem Demirbay), Florian Grillitsch, Ádám Szalai (75.Steven Zuber), Andrej Kramaric (85.Reiss Nelson), Joelinton. Trainer: Julian Nagelsmann.

Goals: 0-1 Florian Grillitsch (6), 1-1 Ismaily (27), 1-2 Håvard Nordtveit (38), 2-2 Maycon (81).

19.09.2018; Etihad Stadium, Manchester; Referee: Daniele Orsato (Italy); Attendance: 40,111

Manchester City FC – Olympique Lyonnais **1-2(0-2)**

Manchester City: Ederson Moraes, Kyle Walker, Aymeric Laporte, John Stones, David Silva, Fernandinho, Fabian Delph, Ilkay Gündogan (55.Leroy Sané), Bernardo Silva, Raheem Sterling (76.Riyad Mahrez), Gabriel Jesus (63.Sergio "Kun" Agüero). Trainer: Pep Guardiola.

Olympique Lyonnais: Anthony Lopes, Marcelo, Rafael (76.Léo Dubois), Ferland Mendy, Jason Denayer, Tanguy Ndombélé, Pape Diop, Houssem Aouar, Memphis Depay, Nabil Fekir (79.Lucas Tousart), Maxwel Cornet (90+2.Bertrand Traoré). Trainer: Bruno Génésio.

Goals: 0-1 Maxwel Cornet (26), 0-2 Nabil Fekir (43), 1-2 Bernardo Silva (67).

02.10.2018; Rhein-Neckar-Arena, Sinsheim; Referee: Damir Skomina (Slovenia); Attendance: 24,851

TSG 1899 Hoffenheim – Manchester City FC **1-2(1-1)**

Hoffenheim: Oliver Baumann, Pavel Kaderábek, Kevin Akpoguma, Joshua Brenet, Stefan Posch, Justin Hoogma, Florian Grillitsch (82.Leonardo Bittencourt), Kerem Demirbay (89.Robin Hack), Ádám Szalai (54.Andrej Kramaric), Ishak Belfodil, Joelinton. Trainer: Julian Nagelsmann.

Manchester City: Ederson Moraes, Vincent Kompany, Nicolás Otamendi (64.John Stones), Kyle Walker, Aymeric Laporte, David Silva, Fernandinho, Ilkay Gündogan (68.Bernardo Silva), Sergio "Kun" Agüero, Raheem Sterling (75.Riyad Mahrez), Leroy Sané. Trainer: Pep Guardiola.

Goals: 1-0 Ishak Belfodil (1), 1-1 Sergio "Kun" Agüero (8), 1-2 David Silva (87).

02.10.2018; Groupama Stadium, Décines-Charpieu; Referee: Andris Treimanis (Latvia); Attendance: *played behind closed doors*

Olympique Lyonnais – FK Shakhtar Donetsk **2-2(0-1)**

Olympique Lyonnais: Anthony Lopes, Marcelo, Léo Dubois, Ferland Mendy, Jason Denayer, Tanguy Ndombélé (87.Pape Diop), Lucas Tousart, Houssem Aouar, Bertrand Traoré (63.Memphis Depay), Nabil Fekir, Moussa Dembélé (81.Maxwel Cornet). Trainer: Bruno Génésio.

Shakhtar Donetsk: Andriy Pyatov, Sergiy Krivtsov, Yaroslav Rakitskiy, Ismaily, Mykola Matvienko, Marlos (90+1.Fernando), Taras Stepanenko, Taison, Alan Patrick (75.Viktor Kovalenko), Maycon, Júnior Moraes (83.Olarenwaju Kayode). Trainer: Paulo Fonseca.

Goals: 0-1, 0-2 Júnior Moraes (44, 55), 1-2 Moussa Dembélé (70), 2-2 Léo Dubois (72).

23.10.2018; Rhein-Neckar-Arena, Sinsheim; Referee: Alberto Undiano Mallenco (Spain); Attendance: 24,144

TSG 1899 Hoffenheim – Olympique Lyonnais **3-3(1-1)**

Hoffenheim: Oliver Baumann, Kevin Vogt, Ermin Bicakcic (73.Reiss Nelson), Pavel Kaderábek, Kevin Akpoguma, Nico Schultz, Florian Grillitsch, Kerem Demirbay, Ádám Szalai (60.Joelinton), Andrej Kramaric, Ishak Belfodil (81.Steven Zuber). Trainer: Julian Nagelsmann.

Olympique Lyonnais: Anthony Lopes, Marcelo, Kenny Tete, Ferland Mendy, Jason Denayer, Tanguy Ndombélé, Lucas Tousart, Martin Terrier (82.Jordan Ferri), Houssem Aouar, Bertrand Traoré (90+1.Pape Diop), Memphis Depay (81.Moussa Dembélé). Trainer: Bruno Génésio.

Goals: 0-1 Bertrand Traoré (27), 1-1, 2-1 Andrej Kramaric (33, 47), 2-2 Tanguy Ndombélé (59), 2-3 Memphis Depay (67), 3-3 Joelinton (90+2).

23.10.2018; Oblasny Sport Komplex Metalist, Kharkiv; Referee: Carlos del Cerro Grande (Spain); Attendance: 37,106

FK Shakhtar Donetsk – Manchester City FC 0-3(0-2)

Shakhtar Donetsk: Andriy Pyatov, Sergiy Krivtsov, Yaroslav Rakitskiy, Ismaily, Mykola Matvienko, Taras Stepanenko, Viktor Kovalenko (62.Alan Patrick), Maycon, Júnior Moraes, Wellington Nem (69.Sergiy Bolbat), Fernando (84.Dentinho). Trainer: Paulo Fonseca.

Manchester City: Ederson Moraes, Nicolás Otamendi, Benjamin Mendy, Aymeric Laporte, John Stones (80.Kyle Walker), David Silva, Fernandinho, Kevin De Bruyne (69.Bernardo Silva), Riyad Mahrez, Raheem Sterling, Gabriel Jesus (87.Phil Foden). Trainer: Pep Guardiola.

Goals: 0-1 David Silva (30), 0-2 Aymeric Laporte (35), 0-3 Bernardo Silva (71).

07.11.2018; Groupama Stadium, Décines-Charpieu; Referee: Danny Desmond Makkelie (Netherlands); Attendance: 53,850

Olympique Lyonnais – TSG 1899 Hoffenheim 2-2(2-0)

Olympique Lyonnais: Anthony Lopes, Jérémy Morel, Marcelo, Rafael, Ferland Mendy, Jason Denayer, Tanguy Ndombélé (88.Pape Diop), Lucas Tousart, Houssem Aouar, Memphis Depay (87.Bertrand Traoré), Nabil Fekir (74.Moussa Dembélé). Trainer: Bruno Génésio.

Hoffenheim: Oliver Baumann, Kevin Vogt, Ermin Bicakcic, Pavel Kaderábek, Kasim Nuhu [*sent off 51*], Nico Schultz, Florian Grillitsch (57.Reiss Nelson), Kerem Demirbay (79.Håvard Nordtveit), Andrej Kramaric, Ishak Belfodil (67.Ádám Szalai), Joelinton. Trainer: Julian Nagelsmann.

Goals: 1-0 Nabil Fekir (19), 2-0 Tanguy Ndombélé (28), 2-1 Andrej Kramaric (65), 2-2 Pavel Kaderábek (90+2).

07.11.2018; Etihad Stadium, Manchester; Referee: Viktor Kassai (Hungary); Attendance: 52,286

Manchester City FC – FK Shakhtar Donetsk 6-0(2-0)

Manchester City: Ederson Moraes, Kyle Walker (61.Danilo), Aymeric Laporte, John Stones, David Silva (73.Ilkay Gündogan), Fernandinho (76.Fabian Delph), Riyad Mahrez, Oleksandr Zinchenko, Bernardo Silva, Raheem Sterling, Gabriel Jesus. Trainer: Pep Guardiola.

Shakhtar Donetsk: Andriy Pyatov, Sergiy Krivtsov, Yaroslav Rakitskiy, Ismaily, Mykola Matvienko, Taras Stepanenko, Taison (77.Wellington Nem), Sergiy Bolbat, Viktor Kovalenko, Maycon (77.Alan Patrick), Júnior Moraes (63.Olarenwaju Kayode). Trainer: Paulo Fonseca.

Goals: 1-0 David Silva (13), 2-0 Gabriel Jesus (24 penalty), 3-0 Raheem Sterling (49), 4-0 Gabriel Jesus (72 penalty), 5-0 Riyad Mahrez (84), 6-0 Gabriel Jesus (90+2).

27.11.2018; Rhein-Neckar-Arena, Sinsheim; Referee: Ivan Kruzliak (Slovakia); Attendance: 22,920

TSG 1899 Hoffenheim – FK Shakhtar Donetsk 2-3 (2-2)

Hoffenheim: Oliver Baumann, Håvard Nordtveit (84.Florian Grillitsch), Kevin Vogt, Ermin Bicakcic, Pavel Kaderábek, Steven Zuber (77.Reiss Nelson), Nico Schultz (84.Vincenzo Grifo), Kerem Demirbay, Ádám Szalai [*sent off 59*], Andrej Kramaric, Ishak Belfodil. Trainer: Julian Nagelsmann.

Shakhtar Donetsk: Andriy Pyatov, Sergiy Krivtsov, Ismaily, Davit Khotcholava, Mykola Matvienko, Taras Stepanenko (77.Alan Patrick), Taison, Viktor Kovalenko (85.Dentinho), Oleg Danchenko (90+4.Bogdan Butko), Maycon, Júnior Moraes. Trainer: Paulo Fonseca.

Goals: 0-1 Ismaily (14), 0-2 Taison (15), 1-2 Andrej Kramaric (17), 2-2 Steven Zuber (40), 2-3 Taison (90+2).

27.11.2018; Groupama Stadium, Décines-Charpieu; Referee: Gianluca Rocchi (Italy); Attendance: 56,039

Olympique Lyonnais – Manchester City FC 2-2(0-0)

Olympique Lyonnais: Anthony Lopes, Marcelo, Rafael (74.Kenny Tete), Fernando Marçal, Ferland Mendy, Jason Denayer, Tanguy Ndombélé, Houssem Aouar, Memphis Depay, Nabil Fekir (84.Bertrand Traoré), Maxwel Cornet (89.Martin Terrier). Trainer: Bruno Génésio.

Manchester City: Ederson Moraes, Kyle Walker, Aymeric Laporte, John Stones, David Silva, Fernandinho, Riyad Mahrez, Oleksandr Zinchenko, Sergio "Kun" Agüero (90+1.Phil Foden), Raheem Sterling, Leroy Sané (71.Fabian Delph). Trainer: Pep Guardiola.

Goals: 1-0 Maxwel Cornet (5), 1-1 Aymeric Laporte (62), 2-1 Maxwel Cornet (81), 2-2 Sergio "Kun" Agüero (83).

12.12.2018; Olimpiyskiy Stadium, Kyiv; Referee: Björn Kuipers (Netherlands); Attendance: 38,916

FK Shakhtar Donetsk – Olympique Lyonnais 1-1(1-0)

Shakhtar Donetsk: Andriy Pyatov, Sergiy Krivtsov, Ismaily, Davit Khotcholava (46.Bogdan Butko), Mykola Matvienko, Marlos (87.Sergiy Bolbat), Taras Stepanenko, Taison, Viktor Kovalenko (83.Olarenwaju Kayode), Maycon, Júnior Moraes. Trainer: Paulo Fonseca.

Olympique Lyonnais: Anthony Lopes, Marcelo, Fernando Marçal, Kenny Tete, Ferland Mendy, Jason Denayer, Lucas Tousart, Houssem Aouar, Bertrand Traoré (72.Tanguy Ndombélé), Memphis Depay (80.Moussa Dembélé), Nabil Fekir (89.Léo Dubois). Trainer: Bruno Génésio.

Goals: 1-0 Júnior Moraes (22), 1-1 Nabil Fekir (65).

12.12.2018; Etihad Stadium, Manchester; Referee: Andreas Ekberg (Sweden); Attendance: 50,411

Manchester City FC – TSG 1899 Hoffenheim 2-1(1-1)

Manchester City: Ederson Moraes, Nicolás Otamendi, Aymeric Laporte, John Stones (46.Kyle Walker), Ilkay Gündogan, Oleksandr Zinchenko (64.Fabian Delph), Bernardo Silva (85.Vincent Kompany), Phil Foden, Raheem Sterling, Leroy Sané, Gabriel Jesus. Trainer: Pep Guardiola.

Hoffenheim: Oliver Baumann, Benjamin Hübner, Pavel Kaderábek, Joshua Brenet (46.Reiss Nelson), Kasim Nuhu, Nico Schultz, Leonardo Bittencourt (70.Ishak Belfodil), Florian Grillitsch, Dennis Geiger (63.Nadiem Amiri), Andrej Kramaric, Joelinton. Trainer: Julian Nagelsmann.

Goals: 0-1 Andrej Kramaric (16), 1-1, 2-1 Leroy Sané (45+1, 61).

GROUP G

1.	**Real Madrid CF**	6	4	0	2	12	-	5	12
2.	**AS Roma**	6	3	0	3	11	-	8	9
3.	FC Viktoria Plzeň	6	2	1	3	7	-	16	7
4.	FK CSKA Moskva	6	2	1	3	8	-	9	7

19.09.2018; Estadio „Santiago Bernabéu", Madrid; Referee: Björn Kuipers (Netherlands); Attendance: 69,251

Real Madrid CF – AS Roma 3-0(1-0)

Real Madrid: Keylor Navas, Sergio Ramos, Marcelo, Daniel Carvajal, Raphaël Varane, Luka Modric (85.Dani Ceballos), Toni Kroos, Casemiro, Isco, Karim Benzema (62.Marco Asensio), Gareth Bale (73.Mariano Díaz). Trainer: Lopetegui.

AS Roma: Robin Olsen, Aleksandar Kolarov, Federico Fazio, Kostas Manolas, Alessandro Florenzi, Daniele De Rossi, Steven N'Zonzi (69.Patrik Schick), Cengiz Ünder, Nicolò Zaniolo (54.Lorenzo Pellegrini), Edin Dzeko, Stephan El Shaarawy (62.Diego Perotti). Trainer: Eusebio Di Francesco.

Goals: 1-0 Isco (45), 2-0 Gareth Bale (58), 3-0 Mariano Díaz (90+1).

19.09.2018; Doosan Aréna, Plzeň; Referee: Benoît Bastien (France); Attendance: 11,312

FC Viktoria Plzeň – FK CSKA Moskva 2-2(2-0)

Viktoria Plzeň: Matús Kozácik, Roman Hubník, Radim Rezník, David Limbersky, Ludek Pernica, Daniel Kolár (64.Ales Cermák), Tomás Horava (89.Lukás Hejda), Jan Kovarík, Jan Kopic, Patrik Hrosovsky, Michal Krmencík (74.Jakub Reznícek). Trainer: Pavel Vrba.

CSKA Moskva: Igor Akinfeev, Kirill Nababkin, Mário Fernandes, Nikita Chernov, Rodrigo Becão, Alan Dzagoev (74.Timur Zhamaletdinov), Dmitri Efremov (46.Ilzat Akhmetov), Nikola Vlasic, Ivan Oblyakov, Jaka Bijol, Fedor Chalov (81.Arnór Sigurdsson). Trainer: Goncharenko.

Goals: 1-0, 2-0 Michal Krmencík (29, 41), 2-1 Fedor Chalov (49), 2-2 Nikola Vlasic (90+5 penalty).

02.10.2018; Stadion Luzhniki, Moskva; Referee: Ovidiu Hategan (Romania); Attendance: 71,811

FK CSKA Moskva – Real Madrid CF 1-0(1-0)

CSKA Moskva: Igor Akinfeev [*sent off 90+5*], Kirill Nababkin, Mário Fernandes, Nikita Chernov, Rodrigo Becão, Alan Dzagoev (65.Dmitri Efremov), Nikola Vlasic, Ilzat Akhmetov, Ivan Oblyakov (90+8.Georgy Kyrnats), Jaka Bijol, Fedor Chalov (78.Arnór Sigurdsson). Trainer: Viktor Goncharenko.

Real Madrid: Keylor Navas, Nacho, Daniel Carvajal (43.Álvaro Odriozola), Raphaël Varane, Reguilón, Toni Kroos, Casemiro (58.Luka Modric), Lucas Vázquez (58.Mariano Díaz), Marco Asensio, Dani Ceballos, Karim Benzema. Trainer: Lopetegui.

Goal: 1-0 Nikola Vlasic (2).

02.10.2018; Stadio Olimpico, Roma; Referee: Pawel Raczkowski (Poland); Attendance: 41,243

AS Roma – FC Viktoria Plzeň 5-0(2-0)

AS Roma: Robin Olsen, Aleksandar Kolarov (74.Luca Pellegrini), Federico Fazio, Juan Jesus, Alessandro Florenzi, Steven N'Zonzi, Bryan Cristante, Lorenzo Pellegrini (74.Patrik Schick), Cengiz Ünder (74.Nicolò Zaniolo), Edin Dzeko, Justin Kluivert. Trainer: Eusebio Di Francesco.
Viktoria Plzeň: Matús Kozácik, Roman Hubník, Radim Rezník, David Limbersky, Lukás Hejda, Martin Zeman (71.Ubong Moses Ekpai), Tomás Horava (64.Daniel Kolár), Roman Procházka, Jan Kovarík, Patrik Hrosovsky, Michal Krmencík (78.Jakub Reznícek). Trainer: Pavel Vrba.
Goals: 1-0, 2-0 Edin Dzeko (3, 40), 3-0 Cengiz Ünder (64), 4-0 Justin Kluivert (73), 5-0 Edin Dzeko (90+2).

23.10.2018; Stadio Olimpico, Roma; Referee: Anastasios Sidiropoulos (Greece); Attendance: 46,005

AS Roma – FK CSKA Moskva 3-0(2-0)

AS Roma: Robin Olsen, Federico Fazio, Davide Santon, Kostas Manolas, Alessandro Florenzi, Daniele De Rossi (81.Patrik Schick), Steven N'Zonzi, Lorenzo Pellegrini (68.Bryan Cristante), Cengiz Ünder (73.Aleksandar Kolarov), Edin Dzeko, Stephan El Shaarawy. Trainer: Eusebio Di Francesco.
CSKA Moskva: Ilya Pomazun, Kirill Nababkin, Mário Fernandes, Hördur Magnússon, Nikita Chernov (57.Khetag Khosonov), Rodrigo Becão, Nikola Vlasic, Ilzat Akhmetov, Arnór Sigurdsson, Ivan Oblyakov (57.Alan Dzagoev), Fedor Chalov (89.Takuma Nishimura). Trainer: Viktor Goncharenko.
Goals: 1-0, 2-0 Edin Dzeko (30, 43), 3-0 Cengiz Ünder (50).

23.10.2018; Estadio „Santiago Bernabéu", Madrid; Referee: Orel Grinfeld (Israel); Attendance: 67,356

Real Madrid CF – FC Viktoria Plzeň 2-1(1-0)

Real Madrid: Keylor Navas, Sergio Ramos, Marcelo, Nacho, Luka Modric, Toni Kroos, Casemiro, Isco (54.Federico Valverde), Lucas Vázquez, Karim Benzema (88.Mariano Díaz), Gareth Bale (75.Marco Asensio). Trainer: Lopetegui.
Viktoria Plzeň: Ales Hruska, Roman Hubník, Radim Rezník, David Limbersky, Lukás Hejda, Milan Havel (76.Ubong Moses Ekpai), Milan Petrzela (86.Jakub Reznícek), Roman Procházka (65.Tomás Horava), Ales Cermák, Patrik Hrosovsky, Michal Krmencík. Trainer: Pavel Vrba.
Goals: 1-0 Karim Benzema (11), 2-0 Marcelo (55), 2-1 Patrik Hrosovsky (79).

07.11.2018; Stadion Luzhniki, Moskva; Referee: Cüneyt Çakir (Turkey); Attendance: 64,454

FK CSKA Moskva – AS Roma 1-2(0-1)

CSKA Moskva: Igor Akinfeev, Kirill Nababkin, Mário Fernandes (12.Georgiy Shchennikov), Hördur Magnússon [*sent off 56*], Rodrigo Becão, Nikola Vlasic, Ilzat Akhmetov (76.Khetag Khosonov), Arnór Sigurdsson (64.Nikita Chernov), Ivan Oblyakov, Jaka Bijol, Fedor Chalov. Trainer: Viktor Goncharenko.
AS Roma: Robin Olsen, Aleksandar Kolarov, Federico Fazio, Davide Santon, Kostas Manolas, Alessandro Florenzi (88.Juan Jesus), Steven N'Zonzi, Bryan Cristante, Lorenzo Pellegrini (82.Nicolò Zaniolo), Edin Dzeko, Justin Kluivert (70.Cengiz Ünder). Trainer: Eusebio Di Francesco.
Goals: 0-1 Kostas Manolas (4), 1-1 Arnór Sigurdsson (50), 1-2 Lorenzo Pellegrini (59).

07.11.2018; Doosan Aréna, Plzeň; Referee: Deniz Aytekin (Germany); Attendance: 11,483

FC Viktoria Plzeň – Real Madrid CF 0-5(0-4)

Viktoria Plzeň: Ales Hruska, Roman Hubník, Radim Rezník, David Limbersky, Lukás Hejda, Milan Havel (38.Milan Petrzela), Roman Procházka, Jan Kopic, Ales Cermák (61.Tomás Horava), Patrik Hrosovsky, Tomás Chory (80.Jakub Reznícek). Trainer: Pavel Vrba.
Real Madrid: Thibaut Courtois, Sergio Ramos (59.Javier Sánchez), Nacho, Álvaro Odriozola, Reguilón, Toni Kroos (73.Isco), Casemiro, Lucas Vázquez, Dani Ceballos, Karim Benzema (62.Vinícius Júnior), Gareth Bale. Trainer: Santiago Solari.
Goals: 0-1 Karim Benzema (21), 0-2 Casemiro (23), 0-3 Karim Benzema (37), 0-4 Gareth Bale (40), 0-5 Toni Kroos (67).

27.11.2018; Stadion Luzhniki, Moskva; Referee: Danny Desmond Makkelie (Netherlands); Attendance: 52,892

FK CSKA Moskva – FC Viktoria Plzeň 1-2(1-0)

CSKA Moskva: Igor Akinfeev, Kirill Nababkin, Georgiy Shchennikov (46.Dmitri Efremov), Mário Fernandes, Nikita Chernov, Rodrigo Becão, Nikola Vlasic, Kristijan Bistrovic, Arnór Sigurdsson, Ivan Oblyakov (72.Konstantin Kuchaev), Fedor Chalov (80.Timur Zhamaletdinov). Trainer: Viktor Goncharenko.
Viktoria Plzeň: Ales Hruska, Roman Hubník, Radim Rezník, David Limbersky (46.Jan Kopic), Lukás Hejda, Milan Petrzela (70.Milan Havel), Roman Procházka, Jan Kovarík, Ales Cermák, Patrik Hrosovsky, Tomás Chory (80.Jakub Reznícek). Trainer: Pavel Vrba.
Goals: 1-0 Nikola Vlasic (10 penalty), 1-1 Roman Procházka (56), 1-2 Lukás Hejda (81).

27.11.2018; Stadio Olimpico, Roma; Referee: Clément Turpin (France); Attendance: 59,124

AS Roma – Real Madrid CF 0-2(0-0)

AS Roma: Robin Olsen, Aleksandar Kolarov, Federico Fazio, Kostas Manolas, Alessandro Florenzi, Steven N'Zonzi (64.Ante Coric), Bryan Cristante, Cengiz Ünder, Nicolò Zaniolo (69.Rick Karsdorp), Stephan El Shaarawy (22.Justin Kluivert), Patrik Schick. Trainer: Eusebio Di Francesco.
Real Madrid: Thibaut Courtois, Sergio Ramos, Marcelo, Daniel Carvajal, Raphaël Varane, Luka Modric (80.Federico Valverde), Toni Kroos, Lucas Vázquez, Marcos Llorente, Karim Benzema (77.Mariano Díaz), Gareth Bale (84.Marco Asensio). Trainer: Santiago Solari.
Goals: 0-1 Gareth Bale (47), 0-2 Lucas Vázquez (59).

12.12.2018; Estadio „Santiago Bernabéu", Madrid; Referee: Artur Soares Dias (Portugal); Attendance: 51,636

Real Madrid CF – FK CSKA Moskva 0-3(0-2)

Real Madrid: Thibaut Courtois, Marcelo (74.Daniel Carvajal), Álvaro Odriozola, Jesús Vallejo, Javier Sánchez, Isco, Marcos Llorente (58.Toni Kroos), Marco Asensio, Federico Valverde, Karim Benzema (46.Gareth Bale), Vinícius Júnior. Trainer: Santiago Solari.
CSKA Moskva: Igor Akinfeev, Kirill Nababkin, Georgiy Shchennikov, Mário Fernandes, Hördur Magnússon, Rodrigo Becão, Nikola Vlasic, Kristijan Bistrovic, Arnór Sigurdsson (90+4.Takuma Nishimura), Ivan Oblyakov (89.Konstantin Kuchaev), Fedor Chalov (84.Abel Hernández). Trainer: Viktor Goncharenko.
Goals: 0-1 Fedor Chalov (37), 0-2 Georgiy Shchennikov (43), 0-3 Arnór Sigurdsson (73).

12.12.2018; Doosan Aréna, Plzeň; Referee: Anthony Taylor (England); Attendance: 11,217

FC Viktoria Plzeň – AS Roma 2-1(0-0)

Viktoria Plzeň: Ales Hruska, Roman Hubník, David Limbersky, Lukás Hejda, Milan Havel, Roman Procházka, Jan Kovarík, Jan Kopic (71.Milan Petrzela), Ales Cermák (82.Tomás Horava), Patrik Hrosovsky, Tomás Chory (87.Jakub Reznícek). Trainer: Pavel Vrba.
AS Roma: Antonio Mirante, Aleksandar Kolarov, Ivan Marcano, Davide Santon (75.Alessandro Florenzi), Kostas Manolas, Javier Pastore (59.Nicolò Zaniolo), Steven N'Zonzi (80.Luca Pellegrini [*sent off 90+2*]), Bryan Cristante, Cengiz Ünder, Patrik Schick, Justin Kluivert. Trainer: Eusebio Di Francesco.
Goals: 1-0 Jan Kovarík (62), 1-1 Cengiz Ünder (68), 2-1 Tomás Chory (72).

GROUP H

1.	**Juventus FC Torino**	6	4	0	2	9	-	4	12
2.	**Manchester United FC**	6	3	1	2	7	-	4	10
3.	Valencia CF	6	2	2	2	6	-	6	8
4.	BSC Young Boys Bern	6	1	1	4	4	-	12	4

19.09.2018; Stade de Suisse, Bern; Referee: Deniz Aytekin (Germany); Attendance: 31,120

BSC Young Boys Bern – Manchester United FC 0-3(0-2)

Young Boys: David von Ballmoos, Steve von Bergen, Loris Benito, Kevin Mbabu, Mohamed Aly Camara, Miralem Sulejmani, Sékou Junior Sanogo, Djibril Sow (59.Michel Aebischer), Christian Fassnacht (65.Nicolas Moumi Ngamaleu), Guillaume Hoarau (75.Jean Pierre Nsamé), Roger Assalé. Trainer: Gerardo Seoane.
Manchester United: David de Gea, Chris Smalling, Victor Lindelöf, Luke Shaw, Diogo Dalot, Nemanja Matic, Paul Pogba (75.Andreas Pereira), Fred (69.Marouane Fellaini), Romelu Lukaku, Anthony Martial, Marcus Rashford (69.Mata). Trainer: José Mourinho.
Goals: 0-1, 0-2 Paul Pogba (35, 44 penalty), 0-3 Anthony Martial (66).

19.09.2018; Estadio de Mestalla, Valencia; Referee: Dr. Felix Brych (Germany); Attendance: 46,067

Valencia CF – Juventus FC Torino 0-2(0-1)

Valencia CF: Neto, Jeison Murillo, Gabriel Paulista, José Gayà, Rúben Vezo (57.Denis Cheryshev), Daniel Wass, Dani Parejo, Gonçalo Guedes (70.Santi Mina), Carlos Soler, Rodrigo, Michy Batshuayi (70.Kevin Gameiro). Trainer: Marcelino.

Juventus: Wojciech Szczesny, Leonardo Bonucci, Giorgio Chiellini, Alex Sandro, João Cancelo, Blaise Matuidi, Sami Khedira (23.Emre Can), Miralem Pjanic (67.Douglas Costa, 89.Daniele Rugani), Cristiano Ronaldo [*sent off 29*], Mario Mandzukic, Federico Bernardeschi. Trainer: Massimiliano Allegri.

Goals: 0-1, 0-2 Miralem Pjanic (45 penalty, 51 penalty).

02.10.2018; Allianz Stadium, Torino; Referee: Sergei Karasev (Russia); Attendance: 40,961

Juventus FC Torino – BSC Young Boys Bern 3-0(2-0)

Juventus: Wojciech Szczesny, Andrea Barzagli, Leonardo Bonucci, Medhi Benatia, Alex Sandro, Blaise Matuidi (46.Emre Can), Miralem Pjanic (70.Sami Khedira), Juan Cuadrado, Mario Mandzukic (78.Moise Kean), Paulo Dybala, Federico Bernardeschi. Trainer: Massimiliano Allegri.

Young Boys: David von Ballmoos, Steve von Bergen, Loris Benito, Mohamed Aly Camara [*sent off 78*], Miralem Sulejmani (70.Nicolas Moumi Ngamaleu), Thorsten Schick, Sékou Junior Sanogo (46.Sandro Lauper), Leonardo Bertone, Djibril Sow, Christian Fassnacht (71.Roger Assalé), Guillaume Hoarau. Trainer: Gerardo Seoane.

Goals: 1-0, 2-0, 3-0 Paulo Dybala (5, 33, 69).

02.10.2018; Old Trafford, Manchester; Referee: Slavko Vincic (Slovenia); Attendance: 73,569

Manchester United FC – Valencia CF 0-0

Manchester United: David de Gea, Antonio Valencia, Chris Smalling, Luke Shaw, Eric Bailly, Marouane Fellaini, Nemanja Matic, Paul Pogba, Alexis Sánchez (76.Anthony Martial), Romelu Lukaku, Marcus Rashford. Trainer: José Mourinho.

Valencia CF: Neto, Ezequiel Garay, Gabriel Paulista, Cristiano Piccini, José Gayà, Dani Parejo, Francis Coquelin (78.Carlos Soler), Geoffrey Kondogbia, Gonçalo Guedes (83.Denis Cheryshev), Rodrigo, Michy Batshuayi (73.Kevin Gameiro). Trainer: Marcelino.

23.10.2018; Stade de Suisse, Bern; Referee: Andris Treimanis (Latvia); Attendance: 31,120

BSC Young Boys Bern – Valencia CF 1-1(0-1)

Young Boys: Marco Wölfli, Steve von Bergen, Loris Benito, Kevin Mbabu, Miralem Sulejmani (74.Nicolas Moumi Ngamaleu), Sékou Junior Sanogo, Djibril Sow, Christian Fassnacht (85.Leonardo Bertone), Sandro Lauper, Guillaume Hoarau (79.Jean Pierre Nsamé), Roger Assalé. Trainer: Gerardo Seoane.

Valencia CF: Neto, Gabriel Paulista, Cristiano Piccini, José Gayà, Mouctar Daikhaby, Dani Parejo, Geoffrey Kondogbia (70.Francis Coquelin), Carlos Soler, Ferrán Torres (67.Kevin Gameiro), Rodrigo, Michy Batshuayi. Trainer: Marcelino.

Goals: 0-1 Michy Batshuayi (26), 1-1 Guillaume Hoarau (55 penalty).

23.10.2018; Old Trafford, Manchester; Referee: Milorad Mazic (Serbia); Attendance: 73,946

Manchester United FC – Juventus FC Torino 0-1(0-1)

Manchester United: David de Gea, Ashley Young, Chris Smalling, Victor Lindelöf, Luke Shaw, Mata, Nemanja Matic, Paul Pogba, Romelu Lukaku, Anthony Martial, Marcus Rashford. Trainer: José Mourinho.

Juventus: Wojciech Szczesny, Leonardo Bonucci, Giorgio Chiellini, Alex Sandro, João Cancelo (87.Douglas Costa), Blaise Matuidi, Miralem Pjanic, Juan Cuadrado (81.Andrea Barzagli), Rodrigo Bentancur, Cristiano Ronaldo, Paulo Dybala (78.Federico Bernardeschi). Trainer: Massimiliano Allegri.

Goal: 0-1 Paulo Dybala (17).

07.11.2018; Estadio de Mestalla, Valencia; Referee: István Kovács (Romania); Attendance: 36,480

Valencia CF – BSC Young Boys Bern 3-1(2-1)

Valencia CF: Neto, Ezequiel Garay, Gabriel Paulista, José Gayà, Daniel Wass, Francis Coquelin, Geoffrey Kondogbia (87.Rúben Vezo), Gonçalo Guedes (75.Ferrán Torres), Carlos Soler, Rodrigo, Santi Mina (68.Kevin Gameiro). Trainer: Marcelino.

Young Boys: David von Ballmoos, Steve von Bergen, Loris Benito, Kevin Mbabu, Sékou Junior Sanogo [*sent off 77*], Nicolas Moumi Ngamaleu (46.Miralem Sulejmani), Djibril Sow, Christian Fassnacht (61.Jean Pierre Nsamé), Sandro Lauper, Guillaume Hoarau (75.Michel Aebischer), Roger Assalé. Trainer: Gerardo Seoane.

Goals: 1-0 Santi Mina (14), 1-1 Roger Assalé (37), 2-1 Santi Mina (42), 3-1 Carlos Soler (56).

07.11.2018; Allianz Stadium, Torino; Referee: Ovidiu Hategan (Romania); Attendance: 41,470

Juventus FC Torino – Manchester United FC 1-2(0-0)

Juventus: Wojciech Szczesny, Leonardo Bonucci, Giorgio Chiellini, Alex Sandro, Mattia De Sciglio (83.Andrea Barzagli), Sami Khedira (61.Blaise Matuidi), Miralem Pjanic, Juan Cuadrado (90+2.Mario Mandzukic), Rodrigo Bentancur, Cristiano Ronaldo, Paulo Dybala. Trainer: Massimiliano Allegri.

Manchester United: David de Gea, Ashley Young, Chris Smalling, Victor Lindelöf, Luke Shaw, Nemanja Matic, Ander Herrera (79.Mata), Paul Pogba, Jesse Lingard (70.Marcus Rashford), Alexis Sánchez (79.Marouane Fellaini), Anthony Martial. Trainer: José Mourinho.

Goals: 1-0 Cristiano Ronaldo (65), 1-1 Mata (86), 1-2 Leonardo Bonucci (90 own goal).

27.11.2018; Old Trafford, Manchester; Referee: Dr. Felix Brych (Germany); Attendance: 72,876

Manchester United FC – BSC Young Boys Bern 1-0(0-0)

Manchester United: David de Gea, Antonio Valencia (72.Mata), Chris Smalling, Phil Jones, Luke Shaw, Marouane Fellaini, Nemanja Matic, Fred (64.Paul Pogba), Jesse Lingard (64.Romelu Lukaku), Anthony Martial, Marcus Rashford. Trainer: José Mourinho.

Young Boys: David von Ballmoos, Steve von Bergen (46.Ulisses Garcia), Loris Benito, Kevin Mbabu, Mohamed Aly Camara, Miralem Sulejmani (66.Christian Fassnacht), Djibril Sow, Sandro Lauper, Michel Aebischer, Jean Pierre Nsamé (83.Nicolas Moumi Ngamaleu), Roger Assalé. Trainer: Gerardo Seoane.

Goal: 1-0 Marouane Fellaini (90+1).

27.11.2018; Allianz Stadium, Torino; Referee: William Collum (Scotland); Attendance: 39,070

Juventus FC Torino – Valencia CF 1-0(0-0)

Juventus: Wojciech Szczesny, Leonardo Bonucci, Giorgio Chiellini, Alex Sandro (46.Juan Cuadrado), João Cancelo, Blaise Matuidi, Miralem Pjanic, Rodrigo Bentancur, Cristiano Ronaldo, Mario Mandzukic, Paulo Dybala (79.Douglas Costa). Trainer: Massimiliano Allegri.

Valencia CF: Neto, Gabriel Paulista, José Gayà, Mouctar Daikhaby, Daniel Wass, Dani Parejo, Francis Coquelin, Geoffrey Kondogbia (72.Carlos Soler), Gonçalo Guedes, Rodrigo (46.Kevin Gameiro), Santi Mina (67.Michy Batshuayi). Trainer: Marcelino.

Goal: 1-0 Mario Mandzukic (59).

12.12.2018; Stade de Suisse, Bern; Referee: Tobias Stieler (Germany); Attendance: 30,114

BSC Young Boys Bern – Juventus FC Torino 2-1(1-0)

Young Boys: Marco Wölfli, Loris Benito, Kevin Mbabu, Ulisses Garcia, Mohamed Aly Camara, Nicolas Moumi Ngamaleu (85.Thorsten Schick), Djibril Sow (90+1.Gregory Wüthrich), Christian Fassnacht (80.Leonardo Bertone), Sandro Lauper, Michel Aebischer, Guillaume Hoarau. Trainer: Gerardo Seoane.

Juventus: Wojciech Szczesny, Leonardo Bonucci, Mattia De Sciglio (72.Paulo Dybala), Daniele Rugani, Miralem Pjanic (65.Emre Can), Juan Cuadrado (23.Alex Sandro), Douglas Costa, Rodrigo Bentancur, Cristiano Ronaldo, Mario Mandzukic, Federico Bernardeschi. Trainer: Massimiliano Allegri.

Goals: 1-0, 2-0 Guillaume Hoarau (30 penalty, 68), 2-1 Paulo Dybala (80).

12.12.2018; Estadio de Mestalla, Valencia; Referee: Georgi Kabakov (Bulgaria); Attendance: 36,544

Valencia CF – Manchester United FC **2-1(1-0)**

Valencia CF: Jaume Doménech, Cristiano Piccini, Rúben Vezo, Mouctar Daikhaby, Toni Lato (51.Ezequiel Garay), Dani Parejo, Denis Cheryshev (66.Ferrán Torres), Geoffrey Kondogbia, Carlos Soler, Michy Batshuayi, Santi Mina (68.Rodrigo). Trainer: Marcelino.

Manchester United: Sergio Romero, Antonio Valencia, Marcos Rojo (46.Ashley Young), Phil Jones, Eric Bailly, Marouane Fellaini, Mata, Paul Pogba, Fred (57.Marcus Rashford), Andreas Pereira, Romelu Lukaku (69.Jesse Lingard). Trainer: José Mourinho.

Goals: 1-0 Carlos Soler (17), 2-0 Phil Jones (47 own goal), 2-1 Marcus Rashford (87).

ROUND OF 16

12.02.2019; Old Trafford, Manchester; Referee: Daniele Orsato (Italy); Attendance: 74,054

Manchester United FC – Paris Saint-Germain FC **0-2(0-0)**

Manchester United: David de Gea, Ashley Young, Victor Lindelöf, Luke Shaw, Eric Bailly, Nemanja Matic, Ander Herrera, Paul Pogba [*sent off 89*], Jesse Lingard (45+4.Alexis Sánchez), Anthony Martial (46.Mata), Marcus Rashford (84.Romelu Lukaku). Trainer: Ole Gunnar Solskjær.

Paris Saint-Germain: Gianluigi Buffon, Dani Alves, Thiago Silva, Marquinhos, Juan Bernat, Presnel Kimpembe, Thilo Kehrer, Ángel Di María (81.Colin Dagba), Marco Verratti (75.Leandro Paredes), Julian Draxler, Kylian Mbappé. Trainer: Thomas Tuchel.

Goals: 0-1 Presnel Kimpembe (53), 0-2 Kylian Mbappé (60).

06.03.2019; Parc des Princes, Paris; Referee: Damir Skomina (Slovenia); Attendance: 47,441

Paris Saint-Germain FC – Manchester United FC **1-3(1-2)**

Paris Saint-Germain: Gianluigi Buffon, Dani Alves (90+5.Edinson Cavani), Thiago Silva, Marquinhos, Juan Bernat, Presnel Kimpembe, Thilo Kehrer (70.Leandro Paredes), Ángel Di María, Marco Verratti, Julian Draxler (70.Thomas Meunier), Kylian Mbappé. Trainer: Thomas Tuchel.

Manchester United: David de Gea, Ashley Young (87.Mason Greenwood), Chris Smalling, Victor Lindelöf, Luke Shaw, Eric Bailly (36.Diogo Dalot), Fred, Andreas Pereira (80.Tahith Chong), Scott McTominay, Romelu Lukaku, Marcus Rashford. Trainer: Ole Gunnar Solskjær.

Goals: 0-1 Romelu Lukaku (2), 1-1 Juan Bernat (12), 1-2 Romelu Lukaku (30), 1-3 Marcus Rashford (90+4 penalty).

[Manchester United FC won on away goals rule (3-3 on aggregate)]

12.02.2019; Stadio Olimpico, Roma; Referee: Danny Desmond Makkelie (Netherlands); Attendance: 51,727

AS Roma – FC Porto **2-1(0-0)**

AS Roma: Antonio Mirante, Aleksandar Kolarov, Federico Fazio, Kostas Manolas, Alessandro Florenzi, Daniele De Rossi, Bryan Cristante, Lorenzo Pellegrini (83.Steven N'Zonzi), Nicolò Zaniolo (87.Davide Santon), Edin Dzeko, Stephan El Shaarawy (90.Justin Kluivert). Trainer: Eusebio Di Francesco.

FC Porto: Iker Casillas, Pepe, Alex Telles, Felipe Monteiro, Éder Militão, Héctor Herrera, Danilo Pereira, Otávio (84.Hernâni), Yacine Brahimi (68.Adrián), Tiquinho Soares, Fernando Andrade (76.André Pereira). Trainer: Sérgio Conceição.

Goals: 1-0, 2-0 Nicolò Zaniolo (70, 76), 2-1 Adrián (79).

06.03.2019; Estádio do Dragão, Porto; Referee: Cüneyt Çakir (Turkey); Attendance: 49,029

FC Porto – AS Roma **3-1(1-1,2-1)**

FC Porto: Iker Casillas, Pepe, Alex Telles, Felipe Monteiro, Éder Militão (103.Maxi Pereira), Héctor Herrera, Danilo Pereira, Otávio (94.Hernâni), Tiquinho Soares (78.Fernando Andrade), Jesús Corona (69.Yacine Brahimi), Moussa Marega. Trainer: Sérgio Conceição.

AS Roma: Robin Olsen, Aleksandar Kolarov, Ivan Marcano (76.Bryan Cristante), Kostas Manolas, Juan Jesus, Rick Karsdorp (55.Alessandro Florenzi), Daniele De Rossi (45+4.Lorenzo Pellegrini, 96.Patrik Schick), Steven N'Zonzi, Nicolò Zaniolo, Edin Dzeko, Diego Perotti. Trainer: Eusebio Di Francesco.

Goals: 1-0 Tiquinho Soares (26), 1-1 Daniele De Rossi (37 penalty), 2-1 Moussa Marega (52), 3-1 Alex Telles (117 penalty).

[FC Porto won 4-3 on aggregate]

13.02.2019; Wembley Stadium, London; Referee: Antonio Mateu Lahoz (Spain); Attendance: 71,214

Tottenham Hotspur FC London – BV Borussia 09 Dortmund **3-0(0-0)**

Tottenham Hotspur: Hugo Lloris, Jan Vertonghen, Toby Alderweireld, Serge Aurier, Davinson Sánchez, Juan Foyth, Moussa Sissoko (90+1.Victor Wanyama), Christian Eriksen, Lucas Moura (84.Llorente), Harry Winks, Son Heung-Min (90.Érik Lamela). Trainer: Mauricio Pochettino.

Borussia Dortmund: Roman Bürki, Ömer Toprak, Abdou Diallo, Achraf Hakimi, Dan-Axel Zagadou (77.Marcel Schmelzer), Axel Witsel, Thomas Delaney, Mario Götze, Mahmoud Dahoud, Christian Pulisic (88.Jacob Bruun Larsen), Jadon Sancho (88.Raphaël Guerreiro). Trainer: Lucien Favre.

Goals: 1-0 Son Heung-Min (47), 2-0 Jan Vertonghen (83), 3-0 Llorente (86).

04.03.2019; Signal-Iduna-Park, Dortmund; Referee: Danny Desmond Makkelie (Netherlands); Attendance: 66,099

BV Borussia 09 Dortmund – Tottenham Hotspur FC London **0-1(0-0)**

Borussia Dortmund: Roman Bürki, Raphaël Guerreiro (62.Christian Pulisic), Abdou Diallo, Manuel Akanji, Axel Witsel, Mario Götze, Julian Weigl, Jadon Sancho, Marco Reus (74.Thomas Delaney), Paco Alcácer, Marius Wolf (62.Jacob Bruun Larsen). Trainer: Lucien Favre.

Tottenham Hotspur: Hugo Lloris, Jan Vertonghen, Toby Alderweireld, Serge Aurier, Ben Davies, Davinson Sánchez, Moussa Sissoko, Christian Eriksen (83.Danny Rose), Harry Winks (55.Eric Dier), Son Heung-Min (71.Érik Lamela), Harry Kane. Trainer: Mauricio Pochettino.

Goals: 0-1 Harry Kane (49).

[Tottenham Hotspur FC London won 4-0 on aggregate]

13.02.2019; „Johan Cruijff" Arena, Amsterdam; Referee: Damir Skomina (Slovenia); Attendance: 52,286

AFC Ajax Amsterdam – Real Madrid CF **1-2(0-0)**

Ajax Amsterdam: André Onana, Daley Blind, Nicolás Tagliafico, Matthijs de Ligt, Lasse Schöne (73.Kasper Dolberg), Hakim Ziyech, Donny van de Beek, Noussair Mazraoui, Frenkie de Jong, Dusan Tadic, David Neres. Trainer: Erik ten Hag.

Real Madrid: Thibaut Courtois, Sergio Ramos, Nacho, Daniel Carvajal, Reguilón, Luka Modric, Toni Kroos, Casemiro, Karim Benzema (73.Marco Asensio), Gareth Bale (61.Lucas Vázquez), Vinícius Júnior (81.Mariano). Trainer: Santiago Solari.

Goals: 0-1 Karim Benzema (60), 1-1 Hakim Ziyech (75), 1-2 Marco Asensio (87).

05.03.2019; Estadio „Santiago Bernabéu", Madrid; Referee: Dr. Felix Brych (Germany); Attendance: 77,013

Real Madrid CF – AFC Ajax Amsterdam **1-4(0-2)**

Real Madrid: Thibaut Courtois, Nacho [*sent off 90+3*], Daniel Carvajal, Raphaël Varane, Reguilón, Luka Modric, Toni Kroos, Casemiro (87.Federico Valverde), Lucas Vázquez (29.Gareth Bale), Karim Benzema, Vinícius Júnior (35.Marco Asensio). Trainer: Santiago Solari.

Ajax Amsterdam: André Onana, Daley Blind, Nicolás Tagliafico, Matthijs de Ligt, Lasse Schöne (73.Dani de Wit), Hakim Ziyech, Donny van de Beek, Noussair Mazraoui (81.Joël Veltman), Frenkie de Jong, Dusan Tadic, David Neres (74.Kasper Dolberg). Trainer: Erik ten Hag.

Goals: 0-1 Hakim Ziyech (7), 0-2 David Neres (18), 0-3 Dusan Tadic (62), 1-3 Marco Asensio (70), 1-4 Lasse Schöne (72).

[AFC Ajax Amsterdam won 5-3 on aggregate]

19.02.2019; Groupama Stadium, Décines-Charpieu; Referee: Cüneyt Çakir (Turkey); Attendance: 57,889

Olympique Lyonnais – FC Barcelona **0-0**

Olympique Lyonnais: Anthony Lopes, Marcelo, Léo Dubois, Ferland Mendy, Jason Denayer, Tanguy Ndombélé (84.Pape Diop), Martin Terrier (76.Maxwel Cornet), Houssem Aouar, Bertrand Traoré (69.Lucas Tousart), Memphis Depay, Moussa Dembélé. Trainer: Bruno Génésio.

FC Barcelona: Marc-André ter Stegen, Piqué, Jordi Alba, Sergi Roberto (81.Arturo Vidal), Clément Lenglet, Nélson Semedo, Ivan Rakitic, Sergio Busquets, Lionel Messi, Luis Suárez, Ousmane Dembélé (67.Philippe Coutinho). Trainer: Ernesto Valverde.

13.03.2019; Estadio Camp Nou, Barcelona; Referee: Szymon Marciniak (Poland); Attendance: 92,346

FC Barcelona – Olympique Lyonnais 5-1(2-0)

FC Barcelona: Marc-André ter Stegen, Piqué, Jordi Alba, Sergi Roberto (83.Nélson Semedo), Clément Lenglet, Ivan Rakitic, Sergio Busquets, Philippe Coutinho (70.Ousmane Dembélé), Arthur (74.Arturo Vidal), Lionel Messi, Luis Suárez. Trainer: Ernesto Valverde.

Olympique Lyonnais: Anthony Lopes (34.Mathieu Gorgelin), Marcelo, Fernando Marçal, Léo Dubois, Ferland Mendy (77.Maxwel Cornet), Jason Denayer, Tanguy Ndombélé, Lucas Tousart, Memphis Depay (73.Bertrand Traoré), Nabil Fekir, Moussa Dembélé. Trainer: Bruno Génésio.

Goals: 1-0 Lionel Messi (18 penalty), 2-0 Philippe Coutinho (31), 2-1 Lucas Tousart (58), 3-1 Lionel Messi (78), 4-1 Piqué (81), 5-1 Ousmane Dembélé (86).

[FC Barcelona won 5-1 on aggregate]

19.02.2019; Anfield Road, Liverpool; Referee: Gianluca Rocchi (Italy); Attendance: 52,250

Liverpool FC – FC Bayern München 0-0

Liverpool FC: Alisson, Joel Matip, Andrew Robertson, Trent Alexander-Arnold, Georginio Wijnaldum, Jordan Henderson, Fabinho, Naby Keïta (76.James Milner), Roberto Firmino (76.Divock Origi), Mohamed Salah, Sadio Mané. Trainer: Jürgen Klopp.

Bayern München: Manuel Neuer, Mats Hummels, David Alaba, Niklas Süle, Joshua Kimmich, Javi Martínez, James Rodríguez (88.Renato Sanches), Thiago Alcântara, Serge Gnabry (90+1.Rafinha), Kingsley Coman (81.Franck Ribéry), Robert Lewandowski. Trainer: Niko Kovac.

13.03.2019; Allianz Arena, München; Referee: Daniele Orsato (Italy) ; Attendance: 68,145

FC Bayern München – Liverpool FC 1-3(1-1)

Bayern München: Manuel Neuer, Rafinha, Mats Hummels, David Alaba, Niklas Süle, Franck Ribéry (61.Kingsley Coman), Javi Martínez (72.Leon Goretzka), James Rodríguez (79.Renato Sanches), Thiago Alcântara, Serge Gnabry, Robert Lewandowski. Trainer: Niko Kovac.

Liverpool FC: Alisson, Joel Matip, Virgil van Dijk, Andrew Robertson, Trent Alexander-Arnold, James Milner (87.Adam Lallana), Georginio Wijnaldum, Jordan Henderson (13.Fabinho), Roberto Firmino (83.Divock Origi), Mohamed Salah, Sadio Mané. Trainer: Jürgen Klopp.

Goals: 0-1 Sadio Mané (26), 1-1 Joel Matip (39 own goal), 1-2 Virgil van Dijk (69), 1-3 Sadio Mané (84).

[Liverpool FC won 3-1 on aggregate]

20.02.2019; VELTINS-Arena, Gelsenkirchen; Referee: Carlos del Cerro Grande (Spain); Attendance: 54,417

FC Schalke 04 Gelsenkirchen – Manchester City FC 2-3(2-1)

Schalke 04: Ralf Fährmann, Bastian Oczipka, Jeffrey Bruma, Matija Nastasic, Salif Sané, Hamza Mendyl (65.Guido Burgstaller), Daniel Caligiuri, Nabil Bentaleb, Suat Serdar, Weston McKennie (78.Steven Skrzybski), Mark Uth (87.Amine Harit). Trainer: Domenico Tedesco.

Manchester City: Ederson Moraes, Nicolás Otamendi [*sent off 68*], Kyle Walker, Aymeric Laporte, David Silva (70.Vincent Kompany), Fernandinho, Ilkay Gündogan, Kevin De Bruyne (87.Oleksandr Zinchenko), Bernardo Silva, Sergio "Kun" Agüero (78.Leroy Sané), Raheem Sterling. Trainer: Pep Guardiola.

Goals: 0-1 Sergio "Kun" Agüero (18), 1-1, 2-1 Nabil Bentaleb (38 penalty, 45 penalty), 2-2 Leroy Sané (85), 2-3 Raheem Sterling (90).

12.03.2019; Etihad Stadium, Manchester; Referee: Clément Turpin (France); Attendance: 51,518

Manchester City FC – FC Schalke 04 Gelsenkirchen 7-0(3-0)

Manchester City: Ederson Moraes, Kyle Walker, Danilo, Aymeric Laporte (72.Fabian Delph), David Silva (64.Phil Foden), Ilkay Gündogan, Oleksandr Zinchenko, Bernardo Silva, Sergio "Kun" Agüero (64.Gabriel Jesus), Raheem Sterling, Leroy Sané. Trainer: Pep Guardiola.

Schalke 04: Ralf Fährmann, Bastian Oczipka, Jeffrey Bruma, Benjamin Stambouli, Salif Sané, Yevhen Konoplyanka, Nabil Bentaleb, Suat Serdar, Weston McKennie (74.Hamza Mendyl), Guido Burgstaller (79.Cedric Teuchert), Breel Embolo (69.Steven Skrzybski). Trainer: Domenico Tedesco.

Goals: 1-0, 2-0 Sergio "Kun" Agüero (35 penalty, 38), 3-0 Leroy Sané (42), 4-0 Raheem Sterling (56), 5-0 Bernardo Silva (71), 6-0 Phil Foden (78), 7-0 Gabriel Jesus (84).

[Manchester City FC won 10-2 on aggregate]

20.02.2019; Estadio Wanda Metropolitano, Madrid; Referee: Felix Zwayer (Germany); Attendance: 67,193

Club Atlético de Madrid – Juventus FC Torino 2-0(0-0)

Atlético Madrid: Jan Oblak, Juanfran, Filipe Luís, Diego Godín, José Giménez, Saúl, Koke (67.Ángel Correa), Thomas Partey (61.Thomas Lemar), Rodri Hernández, Diego Costa (58.Álvaro Morata), Antoine Griezmann. Trainer: Diego Simeone.

Juventus: Wojciech Szczesny, Leonardo Bonucci, Giorgio Chiellini, Alex Sandro, Mattia De Sciglio, Blaise Matuidi (84.João Cancelo), Miralem Pjanic (73.Emre Can), Rodrigo Bentancur, Cristiano Ronaldo, Mario Mandzukic, Paulo Dybala (80.Federico Bernardeschi). Trainer: Massimiliano Allegri.

Goals: 1-0 José Giménez (78), 2-0 Diego Godín (83).

12.03.2019; Allianz Stadium, Torino; Referee: Björn Kuipers (Netherlands); Attendance: 40,884

Juventus FC Torino – Club Atlético de Madrid 3-0(1-0)

Juventus: Wojciech Szczesny, Leonardo Bonucci, Giorgio Chiellini, João Cancelo, Leonardo Spinazzola (67.Paulo Dybala), Blaise Matuidi, Miralem Pjanic, Emre Can, Cristiano Ronaldo, Mario Mandzukic (80.Moise Kean), Federico Bernardeschi. Trainer: Massimiliano Allegri.

Atlético Madrid: Jan Oblak, Juanfran, Diego Godín, Santiago Arias (77.Vitolo), José Giménez, Saúl, Koke, Thomas Lemar (57.Ángel Correa), Rodri Hernández, Antoine Griezmann, Álvaro Morata. Trainer: Diego Simeone.

Goals: 1-0, 2-0, 3-0 Cristiano Ronaldo (27, 48, 86 penalty)

[Juventus FC Torino won 3-2 on aggregate]

QUARTER-FINALS

09.04.2019; Anfield Road, Liverpool; Referee: Antonio Mateu Lahoz (Spain); Attendance: 52,465

Liverpool FC – FC Porto 2-0(2-0)

Liverpool FC: Alisson, Dejan Lovren, Virgil van Dijk, Trent Alexander-Arnold, James Milner, Jordan Henderson, Fabinho, Naby Keïta, Roberto Firmino (82.Daniel Sturridge), Mohamed Salah, Sadio Mané (73.Divock Origi). Trainer: Jürgen Klopp.

FC Porto: Iker Casillas, Maxi Pereira (77.Fernando Andrade), Alex Telles, Felipe Monteiro, Éder Militão, Danilo Pereira, Óliver Torres (73.Bruno Costa), Otávio, Tiquinho Soares (62.Yacine Brahimi), Jesús Corona, Moussa Marega. Trainer: Sérgio Conceição.

Goals: 1-0 Naby Keïta (5), 2-0 Roberto Firmino (26).

17.04.2019; Estádio do Dragão, Porto; Referee: Danny Desmond Makkelie (Netherlands); Attendance: 49,117

FC Porto – Liverpool FC 1-4(0-1)

FC Porto: Iker Casillas, Pepe, Alex Telles, Felipe Monteiro, Éder Militão, Héctor Herrera, Danilo Pereira, Otávio (46.Tiquinho Soares), Yacine Brahimi (81.Bruno Costa), Jesús Corona (78.Fernando Andrade), Moussa Marega. Trainer: Sérgio Conceição.

Liverpool FC: Alisson, Joel Matip, Virgil van Dijk, Andrew Robertson (71.Jordan Henderson), Trent Alexander-Arnold (66.Joseph Gomez), James Milner, Georginio Wijnaldum, Fabinho, Mohamed Salah, Sadio Mané, Divock Origi (46.Roberto Firmino). Trainer: Jürgen Klopp.

Goals: 0-1 Sadio Mané (26), 0-2 Mohamed Salah (65), 1-2 Éder Militão (69), 1-3 Roberto Firmino (77), 1-4 Virgil van Dijk (84).

[Liverpool FC won 6-1 on aggregate]

09.04.2019; Tottenham Hotspur Stadium, London; Referee: Björn Kuipers (Netherlands); Attendance: 60,044

Tottenham Hotspur FC London – Manchester City FC) 1-0(0-0)

Tottenham Hotspur: Hugo Lloris, Jan Vertonghen, Danny Rose, Toby Alderweireld, Kieran Trippier, Moussa Sissoko, Christian Eriksen, Dele Alli (87.Llorente), Harry Winks (81.Victor Wanyama), Son Heung-Min, Harry Kane (58.Lucas Moura). Trainer: Mauricio Pochettino.

Manchester City: Ederson Moraes, Nicolás Otamendi, Kyle Walker, Aymeric Laporte, David Silva (89.Kevin De Bruyne), Fernandinho, Fabian Delph, Ilkay Gündogan, Riyad Mahrez (89.Leroy Sané), Sergio "Kun" Agüero (71.Gabriel Jesus), Raheem Sterling. Trainer: Pep Guardiola.

Goal: 1-0 Son Heung-Min (78).

17.04.2019; Etihad Stadium, Manchester; Referee: Cüneyt Çakir (Turkey); Attendance: 53,348

Manchester City FC – Tottenham Hotspur FC London 4-3(3-2)

Manchester City: Ederson Moraes, Vincent Kompany, Kyle Walker, Benjamin Mendy (84.Leroy Sané), Aymeric Laporte, David Silva (63.Fernandinho), Ilkay Gündogan, Kevin De Bruyne, Bernardo Silva, Sergio "Kun" Agüero, Raheem Sterling. Trainer: Pep Guardiola.

Tottenham Hotspur: Hugo Lloris, Jan Vertonghen, Danny Rose (90+1.Davinson Sánchez), Toby Alderweireld, Kieran Trippier, Moussa Sissoko (41.Llorente), Victor Wanyama, Christian Eriksen, Lucas Moura (82.Benjamin Davies), Dele Alli, Son Heung-Min. Trainer: Mauricio Pochettino.

Goals: 1-0 Raheem Sterling (4), 1-1, 1-2 Son Heung-Min (7, 10), 2-2 Bernardo Silva (11), 3-2 Raheem Sterling (21), 4-2 Sergio "Kun" Agüero (59), 4-3 Llorente (73).

[Tottenham Hotspur FC London won on away goals rule (4-4 on aggregate)]

10.04.2019; „Johan Cruijff" Arena, Amsterdam; Referee: Carlos del Cerro Grande (Spain); Attendance: 50,390

AFC Ajax Amsterdam – Juventus FC Torino 1-1(0-1)

Ajax Amsterdam: André Onana, Daley Blind, Nicolás Tagliafico, Joël Veltman, Matthijs de Ligt, Lasse Schöne (75.Jurgen Ekkelenkamp), Hakim Ziyech, Donny van de Beek, Frenkie de Jong, Dusan Tadic, David Neres. Trainer: Erik ten Hag.

Juventus: Wojciech Szczesny, Leonardo Bonucci, Alex Sandro, João Cancelo, Daniele Rugani, Blaise Matuidi (75.Paulo Dybala), Miralem Pjanic, Rodrigo Bentancur, Cristiano Ronaldo, Mario Mandzukic (60.Douglas Costa), Federico Bernardeschi (90+3.Sami Khedira). Trainer: Massimiliano Allegri.

Goals: 0-1 Cristiano Ronaldo (45), 1-1 David Neres (46).

16.04.2019; Allianz Stadium, Torino; Referee: Clément Turpin (France); Attendance: 41,445

Juventus FC Torino – AFC Ajax Amsterdam 1-2(1-1)

Juventus: Wojciech Szczesny, Leonardo Bonucci, Alex Sandro, Mattia De Sciglio (64.João Cancelo), Daniele Rugani, Blaise Matuidi, Miralem Pjanic, Emre Can, Cristiano Ronaldo, Paulo Dybala (46.Moise Kean), Federico Bernardeschi (80.Rodrigo Bentancur). Trainer: Massimiliano Allegri.

Ajax Amsterdam: André Onana, Daley Blind, Joël Veltman, Matthijs de Ligt, Lasse Schöne, Hakim Ziyech (88.Klaas-Jan Huntelaar), Donny van de Beek, Noussair Mazraoui (11.Daley Sinkgraven, 82.Lisandro Magallán), Frenkie de Jong, Dusan Tadic, David Neres. Trainer: Erik ten Hag.

Goals: 1-0 Cristiano Ronaldo (28), 1-1 Donny van de Beek (34), 1-2 Matthijs de Ligt (67).

[AFC Ajax Amsterdam won 3-2 on aggregate]

10.04.2019; Old Trafford, Manchester; Referee: Gianluca Rocchi (Italy); Attendance: 74,093

Manchester United FC – FC Barcelona 0-1(0-1)

Manchester United: David de Gea, Ashley Young, Chris Smalling, Victor Lindelöf, Luke Shaw, Diogo Dalot (74.Jesse Lingard), Paul Pogba, Fred, Scott McTominay, Romelu Lukaku (68.Anthony Martial), Marcus Rashford (85.Andreas Pereira). Trainer: Ole Gunnar Solskjær.

FC Barcelona: Marc-André ter Stegen, Piqué, Jordi Alba, Clément Lenglet, Nélson Semedo, Ivan Rakitic, Sergio Busquets (90+3.Carles Aleñà), Philippe Coutinho (65.Arturo Vidal), Arthur (66.Sergi Roberto), Lionel Messi, Luis Suárez. Trainer: Ernesto Valverde.

Goal: 0-1 Luke Shaw (12 own goal).

16.04.2019; Estadio Camp Nou, Barcelona; Referee: Dr. Felix Brych (Germany); Attendance: 96,708

FC Barcelona – Manchester United FC 3-0(2-0)

FC Barcelona: Marc-André ter Stegen, Piqué, Jordi Alba, Sergi Roberto (71.Nélson Semedo), Clément Lenglet, Ivan Rakitic, Sergio Busquets, Philippe Coutinho (81.Ousmane Dembélé), Arthur (75.Arturo Vidal), Lionel Messi, Luis Suárez. Trainer: Ernesto Valverde.

Manchester United: David de Gea, Ashley Young, Chris Smalling, Phil Jones, Victor Lindelöf, Paul Pogba, Fred, Jesse Lingard (80.Alexis Sánchez), Scott McTominay, Anthony Martial (65.Diogo Dalot), Marcus Rashford (73.Romelu Lukaku). Trainer: Ole Gunnar Solskjær.

Goals: 1-0, 2-0 Lionel Messi (16, 20), 3-0 Philippe Coutinho (61).

[FC Barcelona won 4-0 on aggregate]

SEMI-FINALS

30.04.2019; Tottenham Hotspur Stadium, London; Referee: Antonio Mateu Lahoz (Spain); Attendance: 60,243

Tottenham Hotspur FC London – AFC Ajax Amsterdam 0-1(0-1)

Tottenham Hotspur: Hugo Lloris, Jan Vertonghen (39.Moussa Sissoko), Danny Rose (79.Benjamin Davies), Toby Alderweireld, Kieran Trippier (80.Juan Foyth), Davinson Sánchez, Victor Wanyama, Christian Eriksen, Lucas Moura, Dele Alli, Llorente. Trainer: Mauricio Pochettino.

Ajax Amsterdam: André Onana, Daley Blind, Nicolás Tagliafico, Joël Veltman, Matthijs de Ligt, Lasse Schöne (65.Noussair Mazraoui), Hakim Ziyech (87.Klaas-Jan Huntelaar), Donny van de Beek, Frenkie de Jong, Dusan Tadic, David Neres. Trainer: Erik ten Hag.

Goal: 0-1 Donny van de Beek (15).

08.05.2019; „Johan Cruijff" Arena, Amsterdam; Referee: Dr. Felix Brych (Germany); Attendance: 52,641

AFC Ajax Amsterdam – Tottenham Hotspur FC London 2-3(2-0)

Ajax Amsterdam: André Onana, Daley Blind, Nicolás Tagliafico, Matthijs de Ligt, Lasse Schöne (60.Joël Veltman), Hakim Ziyech, Donny van de Beek (90.Lisandro Magallán), Noussair Mazraoui, Frenkie de Jong, Dusan Tadic, Kasper Dolberg (67.Daley Sinkgraven). Trainer: Erik ten Hag.

Tottenham Hotspur: Hugo Lloris, Jan Vertonghen, Danny Rose (82.Benjamin Davies), Toby Alderweireld, Kieran Trippier (81.Érik Lamela), Moussa Sissoko, Victor Wanyama (46.Llorente), Christian Eriksen, Lucas Moura, Dele Alli, Son Heung-Min. Trainer: Mauricio Pochettino.

Goals: 1-0 Matthijs de Ligt (5), 2-0 Hakim Ziyech (35), 2-1, 2-2, 2-3 Lucas Moura (55, 59, 90+6).

[Tottenham Hotspur FC London won on away goals rule (3-3 on aggregate)]

01.05.2019; Estadio Camp Nou, Barcelona; Referee: Björn Kuipers (Netherlands); Attendance: 98,299

FC Barcelona – Liverpool FC 3-0(1-0)

FC Barcelona: Marc-André ter Stegen, Piqué, Jordi Alba, Sergi Roberto (90+3.Carles Aleñá), Clément Lenglet, Ivan Rakitic, Arturo Vidal, Sergio Busquets, Philippe Coutinho (60.Nélson Semedo), Lionel Messi, Luis Suárez (90+3.Ousmane Dembélé). Trainer: Ernesto Valverde.

Liverpool FC: Alisson, Joel Matip, Virgil van Dijk, Andrew Robertson, Joseph Gomez, James Milner (85.Divock Origi), Georginio Wijnaldum (79.Roberto Firmino), Fabinho, Naby Keïta (24.Jordan Henderson), Mohamed Salah, Sadio Mané. Trainer: Jürgen Klopp.

Goals: 1-0 Luis Suárez (26), 2-0, 3-0 Lionel Messi (75, 82).

07.05.2019; Anfield Road, Liverpool; Referee: Cüneyt Çakir (Turkey); Attendance: 55,212

Liverpool FC – FC Barcelona 4-0(1-0)

Liverpool FC: Alisson, Joel Matip, Virgil van Dijk, Andrew Robertson (46.Georginio Wijnaldum), Trent Alexander-Arnold, James Milner, Jordan Henderson, Fabinho, Xherdan Shaqiri (90.Daniel Sturridge), Sadio Mané, Divock Origi (85.Joseph Gomez). Trainer: Jürgen Klopp.

FC Barcelona: Marc-André ter Stegen, Piqué, Jordi Alba, Sergi Roberto, Clément Lenglet, Ivan Rakitic (80.Malcom), Arturo Vidal (75.Arthur), Sergio Busquets, Philippe Coutinho (60.Nélson Semedo), Lionel Messi, Luis Suárez. Trainer: Ernesto Valverde.

Goals: 1-0 Divock Origi (7), 2-0, 3-0 Georginio Wijnaldum (54, 56), 4-0 Divock Origi (79).

[Liverpool FC won 4-3 on aggregate]

FINAL

01.06.2019; Estadio Wanda Metropolitano, Madrid; Referee: Damir Skomina (Slovenia); Attendance: 63,272

Tottenham Hotspur FC London – Liverpool FC **0-2(0-1)**

Tottenham Hotspur: Hugo Lloris, Jan Vertonghen, Danny Rose, Toby Alderweireld, Kieran Trippier, Moussa Sissoko (74.Eric Dier), Christian Eriksen, Son Heung-Min, Dele Alli (82.Llorente), Harry Winks (66.Lucas Moura), Harry Kane. Trainer: Mauricio Pochettino.

Liverpool FC: Alisson, Joel Matip, Virgil van Dijk, Andrew Robertson, Trent Alexander-Arnold, Georginio Wijnaldum (62.James Milner), Jordan Henderson, Fabinho, Robert Firmino (58.Divock Origi), Mohamed Salah, Sadio Mané (90.Joseph Gomez). Trainer: Jürgen Klopp.

Goals: 0-1 Mohamed Salah (2 penalty), 0-2 Divock Origi (87).

UEFA Champions League Winner 2018/2019: **Liverpool FC** (England)
Best Goalscorer: Cristiano Ronaldo dos Santos Aveiro (POR, Real Madrid CF) – 15 goals

EUROPEAN CHAMPION CLUBS' CUP (1955 – 1992)
UEFA CHAMPIONS LEAGUE (1992 – 2019)
TABLE OF HONOURS

1955/1956	Real Madrid CF	*Spain*
1956/1957	Real Madrid CF	*Spain*
1957/1958	Real Madrid CF	*Spain*
1958/1959	Real Madrid CF	*Spain*
1959/1960	Real Madrid CF	*Spain*
1960/1961	Sport Lisboa e Benfica	*Portugal*
1961/1962	Sport Lisboa e Benfica	*Portugal*
1962/1963	AC Milan	*Italy*
1963/1964	FC Internazionale Milano	*Italy*
1964/1965	FC Internazionale Milano	*Italy*
1965/1966	Real Madrid CF	*Spain*
1966/1967	Celtic FC Glasgow	*Scotland*
1967/1968	Manchester United FC	*England*
1968/1969	AC Milan	*Italy*
1969/1970	SC Feijenoord Rotterdam	*Netherlands*
1970/1971	AFC Ajax Amsterdam	*Netherlands*
1971/1972	AFC Ajax Amsterdam	*Netherlands*
1972/1973	AFC Ajax Amsterdam	*Netherlands*
1973/1974	FC Bayern München	*Germany*
1974/1975	FC Bayern München	*Germany*
1975/1976	FC Bayern München	*Germany*
1976/1977	Liverpool FC	*England*
1977/1978	Liverpool FC	*England*
1978/1979	Nottingham Forest FC	*England*
1979/1980	Nottingham Forest FC	*England*
1980/1981	Liverpool FC	*England*
1981/1982	Aston Villa FC Birmingham	*England*
1982/1983	Hamburger SV	*Germany*
1983/1984	Liverpool FC	*England*
1984/1985	Juventus FC Torino	*Italy*
1985/1986	FC Steaua București	*Romania*
1986/1987	FC do Porto	*Portugal*
1987/1988	PSV Eindhoven	*Netherlands*
1988/1989	AC Milan	*Italy*
1989/1990	AC Milan	*Italy*
1990/1991	FK Crvena Zvezda Beograd	*Serbia*
1991/1992	FC Barcelona	*Spain*
1992/1993	Olympique de Marseille	*France*
1993/1994	AC Milan	*Italy*
1994/1995	AFC Ajax Amsterdam	*Netherlands*
1995/1996	Juventus FC Torino	*Italy*
1996/1997	BV Borussia 09 Dortmund	*Germany*
1997/1998	Real Madrid CF	*Spain*
1998/1999	Manchester United FC	*England*
1999/2000	Real Madrid CF	*Spain*
2000/2001	FC Bayern München	*Germany*
2001/2002	Real Madrid CF	*Spain*
2002/2003	AC Milan	*Italy*
2003/2004	FC do Porto	*Portugal*
2004/2005	Liverpool FC	*England*
2005/2006	FC Barcelona	*Spain*
2006/2007	AC Milan	*Italy*
2007/2008	Manchester United FC	*England*
2008/2009	FC Barcelona	*Spain*
2009/2010	FC Internazionale Milano	*Italy*
2010/2011	FC Barcelona	*Spain*
2011/2012	Chelsea FC London	*England*
2012/2013	FC Bayern München	*Germany*
2013/2014	Real Madrid CF	*Spain*
2014/2015	FC Barcelona	*Spain*
2015/2016	Real Madrid CF	*Spain*
2016/2017	Real Madrid CF	*Spain*
2017/2018	Real Madrid CF	*Spain*
2018/2019	Liverpool FC	*England*

UEFA EUROPA LEAGUE 2018/2019

PRELIMINARY ROUND

26.06.2018; Estadi Comunal, Andorra la Vella; Referee: Denys Shurman (Ukraine); Attendance: 380

UE Sant Julià – Gzira United FC **0-2(0-1)**

UE Sant Julià: Nico Ratti, Enric Pi, Nicolae Vasile, Pedro Muñoz, Jonny, Walter Balufo, Francisco Girau (69.Luis Blanco), José Aguilar Gómez (87.Daniel "Dani" Gonzalez), Alberto Molina, Vincent Ramaël, Joel Méndez (82.Diego Nájera). Trainer: Jesús Barón Tellez.

Gzira United: Justin Haber, Clifford Baldacchino, Rodolfo Soares, Thomas Veronese, Prince Mambouana, Nicky Muscat (62.Zachary Scerri), Andrew Cohen, Roderick Briffa, Édinson Bilbao Zarate, Amadou Samb (90+3.Luca Brincat), Emmanuel Okoye (70.Jorginho). Trainer: Darren Abdilla.

Goals: 0-1 Amadou Samb (20 penalty), 0-2 Jorginho (87).

05.07.2018; MFA Centenary Stadium, Ta'Qali; Referee: Juxhin Xhaja (Albania); Attendance: 649

Gzira United FC – UE Sant Julià **2-1(0-0)**

Gzira United: Justin Haber, Clifford Baldacchino, Rodolfo Soares, Thomas Veronese, Prince Mambouana, Andrew Cohen, Roderick Briffa, Édinson Bilbao Zarate, Zachary Scerri (89.Juan Corbalan), Amadou Samb (73.Jorginho), Emmanuel Okoye (70.Nicky Muscat). Trainer: Darren Abdilla.

UE Sant Julià: Nico Ratti, Enric Pi (57.Diego Nájera), Nicolae Vasile, Pedro Muñoz (76.Daniel "Dani" Gonzalez), Jonny, Walter Balufo, Jamal Zarioh Taouil, Luis Blanco [*sent off 90*], José Aguilar Gómez (48.Francisco Girau), Vincent Ramaël, Joel Méndez. Trainer: Jesús Barón Tellez.

Goals: 0-1 Joel Méndez (62), 1-1 Amadou Samb (65 penalty), 2-1 Édinson Bilbao Zarate (90+2).

[Gzira United FC won 4-1 on aggregate]

28.06.2018; Victoria Stadium, Gibraltar; Referee: João Carlos Santos Capela (Portugal); Attendance: 350

Europa FC Gibraltar – Prishtina KF **1-1(1-0)**

Europa FC: Javi Muñoz, Ibrahim Ayew, Iván Moya, Jesús Toscano, Guille Roldán, Toni García, Martín Belfortti, Liam Walker, Mustapha Yahaya, Enrique Carreño, Rubo Blanco (69.Joselinho). Trainer: Juan Gallardo Fernández.

Prishtina KF: Visar Bekaj, Armend Dallku, Arago Jamal, Ahmet Haliti, Përparim Osmani, Argjend Mustafa, Meriton Korenica, Gauthier Mankenda, Ergyn Ahmeti (82.Lorik Boshnjaku), Ahmed Januzi (87.Arbër Hoxha), Khalid Abdul Basit (65.Alen Jasharovski). Trainer: Mirel Josa.

Goals: 1-0 Enrique Carreño (45 penalty), 1-1 Meriton Korenica (50).

05.07.2018; Stadiumi Olimpik „Adem Jashari", Mitrovica; Referee: Ioannis Papadopoulos (Greece); Attendance: 1,140

Prishtina KF – Europa FC Gibraltar **5-0(3-0)**

Prishtina KF: Visar Bekaj, Armend Dallku, Arago Jamal, Ahmet Haliti, Përparim Osmani, Argjend Mustafa, Meriton Korenica (75.Mërgim Pefqeli), Gauthier Mankenda, Ergyn Ahmeti, Ahmed Januzi (66.Alen Jasharovski), Khalid Abdul Basit (69.Lorik Boshnjaku). Trainer: Mirel Josa.

Europa FC: Javi Muñoz, Alberto Merino (46.Rubo Blanco), Ibrahim Ayew, Iván Moya, Jesús Toscano, Guille Roldán (58.Joselinho), Toni García, Martín Belfortti, Liam Walker, Mustapha Yahaya, Enrique Carreño (71.Michael Yome). Trainer: Juan Gallardo Fernández.

Goals: 1-0 Armend Dallku (9 penalty), 2-0 Gauthier Mankenda (13), 3-0 Armend Dallku (35 penalty), 4-0 Ahmed Januzi (59), 5-0 Mërgim Pefqeli (86).

[Prishtina KF won 6-1 on aggregate]

28.06.2018; MFA Centenary Stadium, Ta'Qali; Referee: Besfort Kasumi (Kosovo); Attendance: 954

Birkirkara FC – KÍ Klaksvík **1-1(0-0)**

Birkirkara: Kristijan Naumovski, Edward Herrera, Cain Attard, Arian Mrsulja, Eduardo Mancha, Mislav Andjelkovic, Uchenna Umeh, Jake Grech, Fabiano, Michael Mifsud, Marcelinho (81.Stanimir Miloskovic). Trainer: Paul Zammit.

KÍ Klaksvík: Kristian Joensen, Marko Dusak (71.Steinbjørn Olsen), Deni Pavlovic, Ólafur Niclasen (87.Mikkjal á Bergi), Semir Hadzibulic, Boris Dosljak, Hørdur Askham, Jákub Andreasen, Jóannes Bjartalíd (82.Ronni Møller-Iversen), Jóannes Danielsen, Páll Klettskard. Trainer: Mikkjal Kjartansson Thomassen.

Goals: 1-0 Michael Mifsud (72), 1-1 Deni Pavlovic (88).

05.07.2018; Gundadalur, Tórshavn; Referee: Kristoffer Karlsson (Sweden); Attendance: 1,100

KÍ Klaksvík – Birkirkara FC **2-1(1-0)**

KÍ Klaksvík: Kristian Joensen, Ísak Simonsen, Deni Pavlovic, Ólafur Niclasen, Semir Hadzibulic (86.Steinbjørn Olsen, 90+3.Hjalgrím Elttør), Boris Dosljak, Hørdur Askham, Jákub Andreasen, Jóannes Danielsen, Ronni Møller-Iversen, Páll Klettskard. Trainer: Mikkjal Kjartansson Thomassen.

Birkirkara: Kristijan Naumovski, Cain Attard, Arian Mrsulja, Eduardo Mancha, Mislav Andjelkovic, Uchenna Umeh (79.Gianluca Zammit), Jake Grech (73.Stanimir Miloskovic), Neil Micallef (61.Edward Herrera), Fabiano, Michael Mifsud, Marcelinho. Trainer: Paul Zammit.

Goals: 1-0 Deni Pavlovic (45+2), 2-0 Páll Klettskard (59), 2-1 Marcelinho (90).

[KÍ Klaksvík won 3-2 on aggregate]

28.06.2018; Park Hall Stadium, Oswestry; Referee: Christopher Jäger (Austria); Attendance: 742

Cefn Druids AFC – FK Trakai Vilnius **1-1(0-0)**

Cefn Druids: Michael Jones, Neil Ashton, Nathan Peate, Aaron Simpson, Naim Arsan, Matty Owen, Alec Mudimu (76.Fisnik Hajdari), Ryan Kershaw (82.Iwan Cartwright), Arkadiusz Piskorski, James Davies, Jordan Evans. Trainer: Huw Griffiths.

FK Trakai: Tomas Svedkauskas, Valdemars Borovskis, Evgeniy Osipov, Justinas Janusevskis, Kevin Ntika Bondombe (71.Edvinas Baniulis), Vaidas Silėnas, Valentin Jeriomenko, Donatas Kazlauskas, Modestas Vorobjovas (56.Rokas Masenzovas), Svajūnas Cyzas (63.Etienne Mukanya), Dmitriy Otstavnov. Trainer: Jose Antonio Vicuña Ochandorena.

Goals: 1-0 James Davies (48), 1-1 Donatas Kazlauskas (86).

05.07.2018; Alytus Stadium, Alytus; Referee: Dejan Jakimovski (North Macedonia); Attendance: 850

FK Trakai Vilnius – Cefn Druids AFC **1-0(1-0)**

FK Trakai: Tomas Svedkauskas, Valdemars Borovskis, Evgeniy Osipov, Rokas Masenzovas, Kevin Ntika Bondombe, Diniyar Bilyaletdinov (73.Etienne Mukanya), Vaidas Silėnas, Valentin Jeriomenko, Donatas Kazlauskas, Justinas Marazas (83.Rokas Gedminas), Edvinas Baniulis (25.Svajūnas Cyzas). Trainer: Jose Antonio Vicuña Ochandorena.

Cefn Druids: Michael Jones, Neil Ashton, Nathan Peate, Aaron Simpson (86.Alun Morris), Naim Arsan, Matty Owen (69.Jonathan Taylor), Alec Mudimu, Ryan Kershaw, Arkadiusz Piskorski, James Davies, Jordan Evans. Trainer: Huw Griffiths.

Goal: 1-0 Diniyar Bilyaletdinov (29 penalty).

[FK Trakai Vilnius won 2-1 on aggregate]

28.06.2018; Estadi Comunal, Andorra la Vella; Referee: Kári Jóannesarson á Høvdanum (Faroe Islands); Attendance: 432

UE Engordany – SS Folgore/Falciano **2-1(1-0)**

UE Engordany: Jesús Coca, Christian Cellay, Walter Wagner (67.Fábio Serra Alves), Miguel Ruiz, Rafael Brito, Mateo Rodríguez Firpo, Mario Spano, Christopher Pousa, Larsen Touré, Luigi San Nicolas (83.Brian Figliamonte), Sebastián Gómez (87.Jorge Sebastian Varela). Trainer: José Luis Mengual Prades.

SS Folgore/Falciano: Filippo Giannelli, Manuel Muccini, Francesco Sartori, Nicola Marini, Fabio Sottile, Luca Bezzi, Stefano Sacco, Andrea Nucci, Lorenzo Dormi (66.Umberto Semeraro), Imre Badalassi (85.Alessandro Bianchi), Martin Lago Ramiro (75.Marco Bernardi). Trainer: Oscar Lasagni.

Goals: 1-0 Christian Cellay (39), 1-1 Umberto Semeraro (72), 2-1 Miguel Ruiz (86).

05.07.2018; Stadio „Tullo Morgagni", Forlì; Referee: Zbynek Proske (Czech Republic); Attendance: 349

SS Folgore/Falciano – UE Engordany 1-1(0-0)

SS Folgore/Falciano: Filippo Giannelli, Manuel Muccini, Francesco Sartori, Nicola Marini, Fabio Sottile, Luca Bezzi (39.Umberto Semeraro), Stefano Sacco, Andrea Nucci (65.Marco Domeniconi), Lorenzo Dormi, Imre Badalassi, Martin Lago Ramiro (57.Marco Bernardi). Trainer: Oscar Lasagni.

UE Engordany: Jesús Coca, Christian Cellay, Miguel Ruiz, Rafael Brito, Mateo Rodríguez Firpo, Edu Peppe (42.Christopher Pousa), Mario Spano, Hamza Bouharma (79.Jorge Sebastian Varela), Larsen Touré (70.Luigi San Nicolas), Sebastián Gómez, Fábio Serra Alves. Trainer: José Luis Mengual Prades.

Goals: 1-0 Stefano Sacco (86), 1-1 Francesco Sartori (90+6 own goal).

[UE Engordany won 3-2 on aggregate]

28.06.2018; Stadio „Tullo Morgagni", Forlì; Referee: Stanislav Todorov (Bulgaria); Attendance: 542

SP Tre Fiori Fiorentino – Bala Town FC 3-0(3-0)

SP Tre Fiori: Giorgio Pizzolato, Matteo Andreini, Guido Ghetti, Davide Bologna, Davide Succi, Luca Filippi, Giacomo Pracucci [*sent off 80*], Andrea Tamagnini, Danny Gasperoni (76.Davide Pasolini), Alessandro Teodorani (84.Nicola Della Valle), Mirco Vassallo (87.Sossio Aruta). Trainer: Matteo Cecchetti.

Bala Town: Ashley Morris, Stuart Jones Jr., Andrew Burns, Anthony Miley (79.Mike Hayes), Sean Smith, Chris Venables, Robert Pearson, Nathan Burke, Andrew Mangan, Steven Tames (54.Ian Sheridan), Kieran Smith (69.Evan Horwood). Trainer: Colin Caton.

Goals: 1-0 Anthony Miley (7 own goal), 2-0 Giacomo Pracucci (32), 3-0 Mirco Vassallo (36).

05.07.2018; Corbett Sports Stadium, Rhyl; Referee: Kristoffer Hagenes (Norway); Attendance: 610

Bala Town FC – SP Tre Fiori Fiorentino 1-0(0-0)

Bala Town: Ashley Morris, Stuart Jones Jr., Andrew Burns (88.Joshua Jones), Anthony Miley, Sean Smith (67.Evan Horwood), Chris Venables, Robert Pearson, Nathan Burke, Andrew Mangan (54.Steven Tames), Ian Sheridan, Kieran Smith. Trainer: Colin Caton.

SP Tre Fiori: Giorgio Pizzolato, Matteo Andreini, Guido Ghetti, Davide Bologna, Davide Succi (71.Enrico Magnani), Luca Filippi (82.Alessandro Caforio), Davide Pasolini, Andrea Tamagnini, Alessandro Teodorani (90+6.Simone Matteoni), Acquarelli Miacol, Mirco Vassallo. Trainer: Matteo Cecchetti.

Goal: 1-0 Nathan Burke (77).

[SP Tre Fiori Fiorentino won 3-1 on aggregate]

28.06.2018; Gundadalur, Tórshavn; Referee: Jari Järvinen (Finland); Attendance: 200

B36 Tórshavn – St. Joseph's FC 1-1(1-1)

B36 Tórshavn: Rói Hentze, Odmar Færø, Alex Mellemgaard, Erlendur Magnusson, Eli Nielsen, Meinhard Olsen (70.Hannes Agnarsson), Benjamin Heinesen, Andrias Eriksen (23.Magnus Holm Jacobsen), Robert Hedin Brockie, Kaimar Saag, Lukasz Cieslewicz. Trainer: Jákup á Borg.

St. Joseph's: Jamie Robba, Mauri Torres, Iván Lobato, Samuel Fernández, José Otero, Daniel Guerrero, Domingo Ferrer (81.Carlos Pomares), Pedrito, Pedro Muñoz, Ernesto Cornejo (73.Joselu), Boro (80.Dexter Panzavechia). Trainer: Raúl Procopio.

Goals: 1-0 Lukasz Cieslewicz (33 penalty), 1-1 Boro (41 penalty).

05.07.2018; Victoria Stadium, Gibraltar; Referee: Christophe Pires Martins (Luxembourg); Attendance: 536

St. Joseph's FC – B36 Tórshavn 1-1(0-1,1-1)

St. Joseph's: Félix Romero, Pecci, Mauri Torres, Iván Lobato (74.José Otero), Samuel "Samu" Fernández, Daniel Guerrero, Domingo Ferrer (94.Dexter Panzavechia), Pedrito, Pedro Muñoz, Ernesto Cornejo (54.John-Paul Duarte), Boro (67.Joselu). Trainer: Raúl Procopio.

B36 Tórshavn: Rói Hentze, Odmar Færø, Alex Mellemgaard, Erlendur Magnusson, Eli Nielsen, Meinhard Olsen, Benjamin Heinesen (76.Magnus Holm Jacobsen), Andrias Eriksen (49.Bjarni Petersen), Robert Hedin Brockie, Kaimar Saag (61.Hannes Agnarsson; 98.Hugin Samuelsen), Lukasz Cieslewicz. Trainer: Jákup á Borg.

Goals: 0-1 Lukasz Cieslewicz (14 penalty), 1-1 José Otero (88).

Penalties: John-Paul Duarte 1-0; Magnus Holm Jacobsen 1-1; Pedro Muñoz 2-1; Alex Mellemgaard 2-2; Pedrito (missed); Meinhard Olsen 2-3, Samuel "Samu" Fernández (missed); Odmar Færø 2-4.

[B36 Tórshavn won 4-2 on penalties (after 2-2 on aggregate)]

FIRST QUALIFYING ROUND

10.07.2018; „Mikheil Meskhi" Stadioni, Tbilisi; Referee: Timothy Marshall (Northern Ireland); Attendance: 778

FC Samtredia – FC Tobol Kostanay 0-1(0-0)

FC Samtredia: Sergey Pogorily, Ivan Fatic, Giorgi Guruli, Jemal Gogiashvili, Oleg Mamasakhlisi, Visako Bachiashvili, Roman Chachua (86.Shota Kerdzevadze), Avto Endeladze (76.Giorgi Akhaladze), Giorgi Pantsulaia (72.Lasha Kutchukhidze), Iinters Gui, Tamaz Makatsaria. Trainer: Giorgi Tsetsadze.

Tobol Kostanay: Dmytro Nepogodov, Viktor Dmitrenko, Fernander Kassaï, Dmitry Miroshnichenko, Jaba Kankava, Azat Nurgaliev, Artūras Zulpa, Nika Kvekveskiri, Tanat Nuserbayev (87.Samat Zharynbetov), Bayurzhan Turysbek (79.Zhasulan Moldakaraev), Maxim Fedin. Trainer: Vladimir Nikitenko.

Goal: 0-1 Maxim Fedin (90+5).

19.07.2018; Ortaliq Stadion, Kostanay; Referee: Tihomir Pejin (Croatia); Attendance: 8,012

FC Tobol Kostanay – FC Samtredia 2-0(1-0)

Tobol Kostanay: Dmytro Nepogodov, Viktor Dmitrenko, Fernander Kassaï, Dmitry Miroshnichenko (75.Aslan Darabaev), Marat Bystrov (69.Samat Zharynbetov), Jaba Kankava, Azat Nurgaliev, Artūras Zulpa, Nika Kvekveskiri, Bayurzhan Turysbek (63.Tanat Nuserbaev), Maxim Fedin. Trainer: Vladimir Nikitenko.

FC Samtredia: Sergey Pogorily, Ivan Fatic, Giorgi Guruli, Jemal Gogiashvili, Oleg Mamasakhlisi (67.Michael Olaitan), Visako Bachiashvili, Giorgi Akhaladze (77.Anatoli Mesiachenko), Jaba Lipartia, Avto Endeladze, Iinters Gui, Tamaz Makatsaria (71.Zaur Khabeishvili). Trainer: Giorgi Tsetsadze.

Goals: 1-0 Bayurzhan Turysbek (12), 2-0 Aslan Darabaev (83).

[FC Tobol Kostanay won 3-0 on aggregate]

11.07.2018; Banants Stadium, Yerevan; Referee: Rohit Saggi (Norway); Attendance: 3,000

FC Banants Yerevan – FK Sarajevo 1-2(1-2)

Banants Yerevan: Aram Ayrapetyan, Vahagn Ayvazyan, Borislav Jovanovic, Edward Kpodo, Narek Petrosyan, Ognjen Krasic (67.Karen Melkonyan), Aram Bareghamyan, Igor Stanojevic (85.Wal), Solomon Udo, Kwasi Sibo, Lester Peltier (89.Fagner). Trainer: Aram Voskanyan.

FK Sarajevo: Bojan Pavlovic, Dusan Hodzic (73.Halid Sabanovic), Nihad Mujakic, Emir Halilovic, Amar Rahmanovic, Anel Hebibovic, Milos Stanojevic (78.Alen Mustafic), Joachim Adukor, Mersudin Ahmetovic, Krste Velkoski, Aladin Sisic (82.Haris Handzic). Trainer: Husref Musemic.

Goals: 0-1 Mersudin Ahmetovic (16), 0-2 Emir Halilovic (21), 1-2 Vahagn Ayvazyan (34).

19.07.2018; Stadion "Asim Ferhatović Hase", Sarajevo; Referee: Lionel Tschudi (Switzerland); Attendance: 8,125

FK Sarajevo – FC Banants Yerevan 3-0(2-0)

FK Sarajevo: Bojan Pavlovic, Nihad Mujakic, Selmir Pidro (81.Milos Stanojevic), Emir Halilovic, Amar Rahmanovic, Anel Hebibovic, Joachim Adukor, Alen Mustafic, Mersudin Ahmetovic (74.Haris Handzic), Krste Velkoski, Aladin Sisic (68.Sevkija Resic). Trainer: Husref Musemic

Banants Yerevan: Anatoliy Ayvazov, Vahagn Ayvazyan, Borislav Jovanovic, Edward Kpodo, Narek Petrosyan, Aram Bareghamyan, Igor Stanojevic (66.Karen Melkonyan), Solomon Udo (75.Aram Loretsyan), Kwasi Sibo, Lester Peltier, Wal (46.Ognjen Krasic). Trainer: Aram Voskanyan.

Goals: 1-0 Nihad Mujakic (31), 2-0 Mersudin Ahmetovic (38), 3-0 Sevkija Resic (72).

[FK Sarajevo won 5-1 on aggregate]

11.07.2018; FFM Training Centre „Petar Milosevski", Skopje; Referee: Kristo Tohver (Estonia); Attendance: 730

FK Rabotnicki Skopje – Budapest Honvéd FC 2-1(1-1)

Rabotnicki Skopje: Daniel Bozinovski, Dejan Mitrev, Leon Najdovski, Dusan Stevic, Sebastián Herrera, Ljubomir Stevanovic (88.Nehar Sadiki), Ostoja Stjepanovic, Oliver Peev, Petar Petkovski (79.Geoffrey Charles Chinedu), Joel Bopesu, Nikolce Sarkoski (70.Filip Petkovski). Trainer: Djordje Jovanovski.

Budapest Honvéd: Dávid Gróf, Dino Skvorc, Bence Batik, Krisztián Vadócz, Eke Uzoma (72.Tonci Kukoc), Djordje Kamber, Gergö Nagy, Filip Holender (86.Fousseni Bamba), Dániel Gazdag, Danilo, Dániel Lukàcs (66.Milán Májer). Trainer: Attila Supka.

Goals: 1-0 Petar Petkovski (34), 1-1 Gergö Nagy (45+1), 2-1 Nikolce Sarkoski (60).

Bozsik József" Stadion, Budapest; Referee: Marius Avram (Romania), replaced by Iulian Călin (Romania) after 29 mins; Attendance: 64

Budapest Honvéd FC – FK Rabotnicki Skopje 4-0(2-0)

Budapest Honvéd: Dávid Gróf, Eke Uzoma (68.Tonci Kukoc), Tibor Heffler, Dino Skvorc, Bence Batik, Krisztián Vadócz, Djordje Kamber, Gergö Nagy (86.Nikolasz Kovács), Dániel Gazdag, Filip Holender (83.Dániel Lukàcs), Danilo. Trainer: Attila Supka.

Rabotnicki Skopje: Daniel Bozinovski, Dejan Mitrev, Leon Najdovski, Dusan Stevic, Sebastián Herrera [*sent off 62*], Ljubomir Stevanovic, Ostoja Stjepanovic, Oliver Peev, Petar Petkovski (70.Filip Petkovski), Joel Bopesu, Nikolce Sarkoski (70.Geoffrey Charles Chinedu). Trainer: Djordje Jovanovski.

Goals: 1-0, 2-0 Filip Holender (6, 16), 3-0,4-0 Danilo (63 penalty, 84).

[Budapest Honvéd FC won 5-2 on aggregate]

11.07.2018; Rheinpark Stadion, Vaduz; Referee: Fran Jović (Croatia); Attendance: 1,243

FC Vaduz – PFC Levski Sofia 1-0(1-0)

FC Vaduz: Andreas Hirzel, Maximilian Göppel, Nils von Niederhäusern, Philipp Muntwiler, Milan Gajic, Marco Mathys, Christopher Drazan (69.Gabriel Lüchinger), Sandro Wieser, Jodel Dossou (63.Maurice Brunner), Mohamed Coulibaly (86.Boris Babic), Igor Tadic. Trainer: Roland Vrabec.

Levski Sofia: Bozhidar Mitrev, Aymen Belaïd, David Jablonsky, Milos Cvetkovic, Ivan Goranov, Jordi Gómez, Gabriel Obertan, Davide Mariani (79.Stanislav Kostov), Anthony Belmonte, Jerson Cabral (59.Stanislav Ivanov), Sergiu Bus (74.Iliya Dimitrov). Trainer: Delio Rossi.

Goal: 1-0 Mohamed Coulibaly (14).

17.07.2018; Vivacom Arena – „Georgi Asparuhov" stadion, Sofia; Referee: Rob Harvey (Republic of Ireland); Attendance: 6,100

PFC Levski Sofia – FC Vaduz 3-2(1-1)

Levski Sofia: Bozhidar Mitrev (46.Martin Polacek), Aymen Belaïd, David Jablonsky, Milos Cvetkovic, Ivan Goranov, Jordi Gómez, Gabriel Obertan, Davide Mariani, Anthony Belmonte (65.Stanislav Kostov [*sent off 90+4*]), Jerson Cabral, Sergiu Bus (83.Iliya Dimitrov). Trainer: Delio Rossi.

FC Vaduz: Andreas Hirzel, Maximilian Göppel, Nils von Niederhäusern, Philipp Muntwiler, Milan Gajic, Marco Mathys, Christopher Drazan (46.Gabriel Lüchinger), Sandro Wieser, Jodel Dossou (76.Maurice Brunner), Mohamed Coulibaly (87.Mario Bühler), Igor Tadic. Trainer: Roland Vrabec.

Goals: 0-1 Mohamed Coulibaly (25), 1-1 Sergiu Bus (35), 2-1 Aymen Belaïd (53), 2-2 Igor Tadic (55), 3-2 Jerson Cabral (85).

[FC Vaduz won on away goals rule (3-3 on aggregate)]

11.07.2018; Gundadalur, Tórshavn; Referee: Alain Durieux (Luxembourg); Attendance: 487

KÍ Klaksvík – FK Žalgiris Vilnius 1-2(0-1)

KÍ Klaksvík: Kristian Joensen, Ísak Simonsen, Deni Pavlovic (53.Jóannes Bjartalíd, 87.Kristoffur Jakobsen), Ólavur Niclasen, Semir Hadzibulic, Boris Dosljak, Hørdur Askham, Jákup Andreasen, Jóannes Danielsen, Ronny Møller-Iversen (80.Steinbjørn Olsen), Páll Klettskard. Trainer: Mikkjal Kjartansson Thomassen.

Žalgiris Vilnius: Dziugas Bartkus, Venelin Filipov (82.Marquinhos Carioca), Rolandas Baravykas, Mamadou Mbodj, Saulius Mikoliūnas, Donovan Slijngard, Liviu Antal, Slavko Blagojevic, Jérémy Manzorro (64.Serge Nyuiadzi), Marko Tomic, Louis Ogana (74.Tomás Malec). Trainer: Valdas Urbonas.

Goals: 0-1 Liviu Antal (40), 1-1 Jóannes Bjartalíd (60 penalty), 1-2 Mamadou Mbodj (90+2).

19.07.2018; LFF stadionas, Vilnius; Referee: Milovan Milačić (Montenegro); Attendance: 2,500

FK Žalgiris Vilnius – KÍ Klaksvík 1-1(1-0)

Žalgiris Vilnius: Dziugas Bartkus, Rolandas Baravykas, Mamadou Mbodj, Saulius Mikoliūnas, Donovan Slijngard, Tomas Simkovic, Liviu Antal (36.Serge Nyuiadzi), Slavko Blagojevic, Marquinhos Carioca (46.Venelin Filipov), Jérémy Manzorro (66.Louis Ogana), Marko Tomic. Trainer: Valdas Urbonas.

KÍ Klaksvík: Kristian Joensen, Ísak Simonsen (90+2.Óli Poulsen), Deni Pavlovic, Ólavur Niclasen, Semir Hadzibulic, Boris Dosljak (75.Jóannes Bjartalíd), Hørdur Askham, Jákup Andreasen, Jóannes Danielsen, Ronny Møller-Iversen (87.Kristoffur Jakobsen), Páll Klettskard. Trainer: Mikkjal Kjartansson Thomassen.

Goals: 1-0 Liviu Antal (6), 1-1 Ronny Møller-Iversen (66).

[FK Žalgiris Vilnius won 3-2 on aggregate]

11.07.2018; Stade „Émile Mayrisch", Esch-sur-Alzette; Referee: Ívar Orri Kristjánsson (Iceland); Attendance: 1,007

CS Fola Esch – Prishtina KF 0-0

Fola Esch: Thomas Hym, Rodrigue Dikaba, Billy Bernard, Tom Laterza, Peter Chrappan, Mehdi Kirch (46.Enis Saiti), Veldin Muharemovic, Ryan Klapp, Corentin Koçur (69.Ken Corral), Samir Hadji, Moussa Seydi (46.Cédric Sacras). Trainer: Thomas Klasen.

Prishtina KF: Visar Bekaj, Armend Dallku, Arago Jamal, Ahmet Haliti, Armend Thaçi, Argjend Mustafa, Meriton Korenica (90+2.Abdul Bashiru), Gauthier Mankenda (80.Mërgim Pefqeli), Ergyn Ahmeti, Ahmed Januzi (84.Lorik Boshnjaku), Khalid Abdul Basit. Trainer: Mirel Josa.

19.07.2018; Stadiumi Olimpik „Adem Jashari", Mitrovica; Referee: Urs Schnyder (Switzerland); Attendance: 2,300

Prishtina KF – CS Fola Esch 0-0; 5-4 on penalties

Prishtina KF: Visar Bekaj, Armend Dallku, Arago Jamal, Ahmet Haliti, Armend Thaçi, Argjend Mustafa, Meriton Korenica, Gauthier Mankenda (76.Mërgim Pefqeli), Ergyn Ahmeti (98.Lorik Boshnjaku), Alen Jasharovski (93.Arbër Hoxha), Khalid Abdul Basit. Trainer: Mirel Josa.

Fola Esch: Thomas Hym, Rodrigue Dikaba, Billy Bernard (46.Julien Klein), Tom Laterza (66.Gérard Mersch), Peter Chrappan, Mehdi Kirch (105.Cédric Sacras), Veldin Muharemovic, Enis Saiti (72.Stefano Bensi), Ryan Klapp, Samir Hadji, Ken Corral. Trainer: Thomas Klasen.

Penalties: Stefano Bensi 1-0; Armend Dallku 1-1; Cédric Sacras (missed); Meriton Korenica 1-2; Samir Hadji 2-2; Armend Thaçi 2-3; Peter Chrappan 3-3; Mërgim Pefqeli (missed); Veldin Muharemovic (missed); Arbër Hoxha (missed); Rodrigue Dikaba (missed); Lorik Boshnjaku (missed); Ryan Klapp 4-3; Ahmet Haliti 4-4; Gérard Mersch 5-4; Arago Jamal (missed).

[Prishtina KF won 5-4 on penalties (after 0-0 on aggregate)]

11.07.2018; Mourneview Park, Lurgan; Referee: Mads-Kristoffer Kristoffersen (Denmark); Attendance: 631

Glenavon FC Lurgan – Molde FK 2-1(1-1)

Glenavon: Jonny Tuffey, Rhys Marshall, Andrew Doyle, Caolan Marron, Gary Muir, Andrew Hall, Stephen Murray (90+2.Dylan King), Mark Sykes, Joshua Daniels (90+5.Jordan Jenkins), Niall Grace, Stephen Donnelly (72.Robbie Norton). Trainer: Gary Hamilton.

Molde FK: Andreas Linde, Vegard Forren, Ruben Gabrielsen, Kristoffer Haugen, Christoffer Remmer, Petter Strand (70.Fredrik Brustad), Etzaz Hussain (60.Daniel Chima Chukwu), Babacar Sarr, Eirik Hestad, Fredrik Aursnes, Erling Håland (82.Tobias Svendsen). Trainer: Ole Gunnar Solskjær.

Goals: 0-1 Eirik Hestad (36), 1-1 Rhys Marshall (37), 2-1 Joshua Daniels (59).

19.07.2018; Aker Stadion, Molde; Referee: Alexandru Tean (Moldova); Attendance: 5,150

Molde FK – Glenavon FC Lurgan 5-1(2-0)

Molde FK: Andreas Linde, Vegard Forren, Ruben Gabrielsen (46.Stian Gregersen), Kristoffer Haugen, Christoffer Remmer, Etzaz Hussain, Babacar Sarr, Eirik Hestad, Mattias Mostrøm (74.Fredrik Aursnes), Fredrik Brustad (61.Ibrahima Wadji), Daniel Chima Chukwu. Trainer: Ole Gunnar Solskjær.

Glenavon: James Taylor, Andrew Doyle, Dylan King, Caolan Marron, Gary Muir, Andrew Hall (84.Jordan Jenkins), Stephen Murray, Mark Sykes, Joshua Daniels (90+2.Jack O'Mahony), Niall Grace, Stephen Donnelly (46.Robbie Norton). Trainer: Gary Hamilton.

Goals: 1-0 Etzaz Hussain (28 penalty), 2-0, 3-0 Eirik Hestad (34, 59), 3-1 Vegard Forren (62 own goal), 4-1 Eirik Hestad (90), 5-1 Babacar Sarr (90+4).

[Molde FK won 6-3 on aggregate]

12.07.2018; „Vazgen Sargsyan" Hanrapetakan Stadium, Yerevan; Referee: Michal Ocenás (Slovakia); Attendance: 2,000

FC Pyunik Yerevan – FK Vardar Skopje 1-0(1-0)

Pyunik Yerevan: Evgeni Kobozev, Vyacheslav Dmitriev, Maksim Zhestokov, Serob Grigoryan, Maksim Trusevich, Denis Voynov (58.Robert Hakobyan), Didier Kadio, Alik Arakelyan (65.Robert Minasyan), Vahagn Hayrapetyan, Petros Avetisyan, Mohamed Konaté (75.Ruslan Koryan). Trainer: Andrey Talalaev.

Vardar Skopje: Filip Gacevski, Goran Popov, Evgen Novak, Tigran Barseghyan (75.Maksim Maksimov), Kosta Manev, Kristijan Tosevski, Darko Micevski, Clarence Bitang, Besar Iseni (67.Ali Adem), Matej Cvetanoski, Willian Lira (46.Jakub Berisha). Trainer: Boban Babunski.

Goal: 1-0 Mohamed Konaté (28).

19.07.2018; Telekom Arena, Skopje; Referee: Ian McNabb (Northern Ireland); Attendance: 5,823

FK Vardar Skopje – FC Pyunik Yerevan 0-2(0-0)

Vardar Skopje: Filip Gacevski, Evgen Novak, Vladica Brdarovski (86.Filip Najdovski), Tigran Barseghyan, Kosta Manev, Kristijan Tosevski, Jovan Popzlatanov (71.Besar Iseni), Darko Micevski, Clarence Bitang, Jakub Berisha (46.Willian Lira), Maksim Maksimov. Trainer: Boban Babunski.

Pyunik Yerevan: Evgeni Kobozev (46.Andrija Dragojevic), Vyacheslav Dmitriev, Maksim Zhestokov, Serob Grigoryan, Maksim Trusevich (61.Vitali Stezhko), Denis Voynov, Didier Kadio, Alik Arakelyan, Vahagn Hayrapetyan, Ruslan Koryan (70.Bacar Baldé), Mohamed Konaté. Trainer: Andrey Talalaev.

Goals: 0-1, 0-2 Bacar Baldé (85, 89).

[FC Pyunik Yerevan won 3-0 on aggregate]

12.07.2018; Olimpiskā centra Ventspils Stadionā, Ventspils; Referee: Vasilis Dimitriou (Cyprus); Attendance: 2,300

FK Ventspils – Luftëtari Gjirokastër FC 5-0(5-0)

FK Ventspils: Maksims Uvarenko, Abdoul Mamah, Vitālijs Jagodinskis, Medzit Neziri, Hélio Batista, Ritvars Rugins (89.Raens Tālbergs), Abdullahi Alfa, Giuly Mandzhgaladze, Tosin Aiyegun, Vasili Pavlov (63.Nikita Kolesovs), Adeleke Akinyemi. Trainer: Dejan Vukicevic.

Luftëtari Gjirokastër: Hrvoje Bukovski, Nemanja Janicic, Ledio Liçaj, Jackson, Oltion Rapa, Vladan Milosavljev (63.Maldin Ymeraj), Erjon Vuçaj, Behar Ramadani (82.Donald Rapo), Albano Aleksi, Dejvi Bregu, Vasil Shkurtaj. Trainer: Milos Kostic.

Goals: 1-0, 2-0, 3-0 Adeleke Akinyemi (8 penalty, 12, 24), 4-0 Tosin Aiyegun (37 penalty), 5-0 Adeleke Akinyemi (43).

19.07.2018; Elbasan Arena, Elbasan; Referee: Anders Poulsen (Denmark); Attendance: 270

Luftëtari Gjirokastër FC – FK Ventspils 3-3(1-2)

Luftëtari Gjirokastër: Shkelzen Ruçi (45+2.Hrvoje Bukovski), Nemanja Janicic, Lejdi Liçaj (46.Aurel Demo), Oltion Rapa, Donald Rapo (71.Donaldo Açka), Vladan Milosavljev, Erjon Vuçaj, Behar Ramadani, Maldin Ymeraj, Albano Aleksi, Vasil Shkurtaj. Trainer: Milos Kostic.

FK Ventspils: Maksims Uvarenko, Abdoul Mamah, Vitālijs Jagodinskis (64.Nikita Kolesovs), Medzit Neziri, Hélio Batista, Ritvars Rugins (46.Raens Tālbergs), Abdullahi Alfa, Giuly Mandzhgaladze, Tosin Aiyegun, Vasili Pavlov (46.Kaspars Kokins), Adeleke Akinyemi. Trainer: Dejan Vukicevic.

Goals: 1-0 Vasil Shkurtaj (44 penalty), 1-1, 1-2 Adeleke Akinyemi (45+4, 45+8), 2-2 Maldin Ymeraj (55), 3-2 Vladan Milosavljev (61), 3-3 Abdullahi Alfa (90+3).

[FK Ventspils won 8-3 on aggregate]

12.07.2018; „Mikheil Meskhi" Stadioni, Tbilisi; Referee: Kai Erik Steen (Norway); Attendance: 1,220

FC Chikhura Sachkhere – Beitar Jerusalem FC 0-0

Chikhura Sachkhere: Dino Hamzic, Davit Maisashvili, Lasha Chikvaidze, Bakari Mirtshkulava, Davit Megrelishvili, Revaz Chiteishvili, Denis Dobrovolski (62.Demur Chikhladze), Irakli Lekvtadze (79.Giorgi Bukhaidze), Teimurazi Markozashvili (57.Mikheil Sardalishvili), Irakli Bugridze, Giorgi Gabedava. Trainer: Samson Pruidze.

Beitar Jerusalem: Itamar Nitzan, Carlos Cuéllar (90.Michael Siroshtein), Tal Kachila, Matan Peleg, Or Zehavi, Erik Sabo, Ofir Kriaf, Ya'akov Berihon (58.Lior Inbrum), David Keltjens, Jakub Sylvestr (65.Gaëtan Varenne), Idan Vered. Trainer: Guy Luzon.

19.07.2018; „Teddi Malcha" Stadium, Jerusalem; Referee: Marco Di Bello (Italy); Attendance: 1,300

Beitar Jerusalem FC – FC Chikhura Sachkhere 1-2(0-0)

Beitar Jerusalem: Itamar Nitzan, Carlos Cuéllar, Michael Siroshtein (78.Ya'akov Berihon), Tal Kachila, Matan Peleg (58.Gaëtan Varenne), Or Zehavi, Erik Sabo, Ofir Kriaf, Lior Inbrum, Jakub Sylvestr, Idan Vered. Trainer: Guy Luzon.

Chikhura Sachkhere: Dino Hamzic, Davit Maisashvili, Lasha Chikvaidze, Bakari Mirtshkulava, Davit Megrelishvili, Revaz Chiteishvili, Denis Dobrovolski (71.Levan Kakubava), Irakli Lekvtadze (59.Mikheil Sardalishvili), Teimurazi Markozashvili, Irakli Bugridze (72.Kakha Kakhabrishvili), Giorgi Gabedava. Trainer: Samson Pruidze.

Goals: 1-0 Idan Vered (62), 1-1 Levan Kakubava (73), 1-2 Giorgi Gabedava (83 penalty).

[FC Chikhura Sachkhere won 2-1 on aggregate]

12.07.2018; Stadiumi „Selman Stërmasi", Tiranë; Referee: Jérôme Brisard (France); Attendance: 1,050

FK Partizani Tiranë – NK Maribor 0-1(0-0)

Partizani Tiranë: Alban Hoxha (I), Renaldo Kalari (57.Jurgen Bardhi), Egzon Belica, Renato Gojkovic, Libanot Ibrahimi, Gerhard Progni (64.Stefan Nikolic), Bruno Telushi, Ardit Hila, Lorenc Trashi, Jasir Asani, Esat Mala (74.Besart Abdurahimi). Trainer: Skënder Gega.

NK Maribor: Jasmin Handanovic, Marko Suler, Mitja Viler, Martin Milec, Sasa Ivkovic, Blaz Vrhovec, Amir Dervisevic, Martin Kramaric (64.Dino Hotic), Marcos Tavares (80.Jan Mlakar), Gregor Bajde (87.Dare Vrsic), Luka Zahovic. Trainer: Darko Milanic.

Goal: 0-1 Gregor Bajde (50).

19.07.2018; Ljudski vrt, Maribor; Referee: Paul Tierney (England); Attendance: 6,876

NK Maribor – FK Partizani Tiranë 2-0(1-0)

NK Maribor: Jasmin Handanovic, Marko Suler, Mitja Viler, Martin Milec, Sasa Ivkovic, Blaz Vrhovec, Amir Dervisevic, Dino Hotic (83.Aleks Pihler), Martin Kramaric (78.Dare Vrsic), Luka Zahovic, Jan Mlakar (78.Marcos Tavares). Trainer: Darko Milanic.

Partizani Tiranë: Alban Hoxha (I), Sodiq Atanda, Renato Gojkovic, Libanot Ibrahimi, Gerhard Progni (66.Renaldo Kalari), Bruno Telushi, Ardit Hila, Lorenc Trashi, Jasir Asani (76.Stefan Nikolic), Jurgen Bardhi (56.Besart Abdurahimi), Esat Mala. Trainer: Skënder Gega.

Goals: 1-0 Amir Dervisevic (31), 2-0 Marcos Tavares (90+3).

[NK Maribor won 3-0 on aggregate]

12.07.2018; Stadion Ob Jezeru, Velenje; Referee: Luís Miguel Branco Godinho (Portugal); Attendance: 923

NK Rudar Velenje – SP Tre Fiori Fiorentino 7-0(1-0)

Rudar Velenje: Marko Pridigar, Josip Tomasevic, Klemen Bolha, Robert Pusaver, Ivan Vasiljevic, Damjan Trifkovic (64.Ante Solomun), Domagoj Muic (57.Vlatko Simunac), Anze Pisek, Dominik Radic, Djair Parfitt-Williams, Milan Tucic (72.Tim Vodeb). Trainer: Marijan Pusnik.

SP Tre Fiori: Giorgio Pizzolato, Matteo Andreini, Guido Ghetti, Dario Merendino (52.Filippo Matteoni), Davide Bologna (72.Nicola Della Valle), Luca Filippi, Mattia Costantini, Davide Pasolini, Alessandro Teodorani, Marco De Angelis (81.Alessandro Caforio), Mirco Vassallo. Trainer: Matteo Cecchetti.

Goals: 1-0 Milan Tucic (33), 2-0 Dominik Radic (48), 3-0 Djair Parfitt-Williams (49), 4-0 Milan Tucic (59), 5-0 Nicola Della Valle (75 own goal), 6-0 Dominik Radic (78), 7-0 Ante Solomun (84).

19.07.2018; Stadio „Tullo Morgagni", Forlì; Referee: Fyodor Zammit (Malta); Attendance: 245

SP Tre Fiori Fiorentino – NK Rudar Velenje 0-3(0-1)

SP Tre Fiori: Giorgio Pizzolato, Matteo Andreini, Guido Ghetti, Davide Succi, Luca Filippi, Mattia Costantini (63.Davide Pasolini), Nicola Della Valle (72.Espedito Marinaro), Andrea Tamagnini (82.Simone Matteoni), Alessandro Teodorani, Acquarelli Miacol, Mirco Vassallo. Trainer: Matteo Cecchetti.

Rudar Velenje: Marko Pridigar, Josip Tomasevic, Klemen Bolha (67.Domagoj Muic), Robert Pusaver, Ivan Vasiljevic, Damjan Trifkovic (46.Djair Parfitt-Williams), Anze Pisek, Ante Solomun, Dominik Radic (46.Vlatko Simunac), Milan Tucic, Abu Kamara. Trainer: Marijan Pusnik.

Goals: 0-1 Klemen Bolha (43), 0-2 Vlatko Simunac (47), 0-3 Abu Kamara (71).

[NK Rudar Velenje won 10-0 on aggregate]

12.07.2018; Telia 5G-areena, Tampere; Referee: Krzysztof Jakubik (Poland); Attendance: 1,511

FC Ilves Tampere – PFC Slavia Sofia 0-1(0-0)

Ilves Tampere: Mika Hilander, Jani Tanska, Tuomas Rannankari, Felipe Aspegren, Tatu Miettunen, Eero Tamminen, Lauri Ala-Myllymäki (83.Niklas Jokelainen), Mame Thiaw, Tuure Siira (83.Alim Moundi), Iiro Järvinen (87.Matias Ojala), Marius Noubissi. Trainer: Jarkko Wiss.

Slavia Sofia: Georgi Petkov, Aleksandar Aleksandrov, Emil Martinov, Andrea Hristov, Momchil Tsvetanov (90+2.Ivailo Dimitrov), Galin Ivanov, Slavcho Shokolarov (69.Georgi Yomov), Milen Gamakov, Yanis Karabelyov, Dimitar Velkovski, Milcho Angelov (87.Tsvetelin Chunchukov). Trainer: Zlatomir Zagorcic.

Goal: 0-1 Momchil Tsvetanov (80).

19.07.2018; Nationalen Stadion "Vasil Levski", Sofia; Referee: Nenad Djokic (Serbia); Attendance: 3,400

PFC Slavia Sofia – FC Ilves Tampere 2-1(1-0)

Slavia Sofia: Antonis Stergiakis, Aleksandar Aleksandrov, Emil Martinov, Andrea Hristov, Momchil Tsvetanov (84.Vladislav Uzunov), Galin Ivanov (90+3.Filip Krastev), Milen Gamakov, Yanis Karabelyov, Dimitar Velkovski, Georgi Yomov (67.Slavcho Shokolarov), Milcho Angelov. Trainer: Zlatomir Zagorcic.

Ilves Tampere: Mika Hilander, Jani Tanska (76.Tariq Kazi), Felipe Aspegren, Tatu Miettunen (62.Iiro Järvinen), Diogo Tomas, Matias Ojala, Eero Tamminen (69.Santeri Haarala), Lauri Ala-Myllymäki, Mame Thiaw, Tuure Siira, Marius Noubissi. Trainer: Jarkko Wiss.

Goals: 1-0 Galin Ivanov (36), 1-1 Marius Noubissi (55), 2-1 Galin Ivanov (56).

[PFC Slavia Sofia won 3-1 on aggregate]

12.07.2018; Qabala City Stadium, Qabala; Referee: Veaceslav Banari (Moldova); Attendance: 1,600

Qəbələ FK – FC Progrès Niederkorn 0-2(0-0)

Qəbələ FK: Dmitro Bezotosniy, Ilgar Gurbanov, Vojislav Stankovic (72.Lalawelé Atakora), Urfan Abbasov, Bahlul Mustafazade, Asif Mammadov, Sabien Lilaj, Elvin Jamalov (56.Tamkim Khalilzade), Steeven Joseph-Monrose, Rauf Aliyev, Segun Adeniyi (76.Roman Huseynov). Trainer: Senan Gurbanov.

Progrès Niederkorn: Sebastian Flauss, Mario Mutsch, Adrien Ferino, Marvin da Graça, Jordan Gobron, Tim Hall, Emmanuel Françoise, Sébastien Thill, Yannick Bastos (84.Yann Matias Marques), Olivier Thill (80.Ben Vogel), Mayron De Almeida (89.Dino Ramdedovic). Trainer: Paolo Amodio.

Goals: 0-1 Mayron De Almeida (51), 0-2 Olivier Thill (61 penalty).

19.07.2018; Stade Parc des Sports, Differdange; Referee: Keith Kennedy (Northern Ireland); Attendance: 1,842

FC Progrès Niederkorn – Qəbələ FK 0-1(0-1)

Progrès Niederkorn: Sebastian Flauss, Mario Mutsch, Adrien Ferino, Marvin da Graça, Jordan Gobron, Tim Hall, Emmanuel Françoise (85.Yann Matias Marques), Sébastien Thill, Yannick Bastos (29.Alexander Karapetyan), Olivier Thill (90.Ben Vogel), Mayron De Almeida. Trainer: Paolo Amodio.

Qəbələ FK: Dmitro Bezotosniy, Ilgar Gurbanov, Rasim Ramaldanov, Urfan Abbasov, Javid Hüseynov, Asif Mammadov (55.Lalawelé Atakora), Sabien Lilaj, Tamkim Khalilzade [*sent off 79*], Steeven Joseph-Monrose, Rauf Aliyev, Segun Adeniyi. Trainer: Senan Gurbanov.

Goal: 0-1 Steeven Joseph-Monrose (28).

[FC Progrès Niederkorn won 2-1 on aggregate]

12.07.2018; Lahden Stadion, Lahti; Referee: Yaroslav Kozyk (Ukraine); Attendance: 3,178

FC Lahti – FH Hafnarfjördur 0-3(0-2)

FC Lahti: Damjan Siskovski, Mikko Hauhia, Kalle Taimi, Artem Vyatkin, Santeri Hostikka, Artjom Dmitrijev, Xhevdet Gela (73.Pavel Osipov), Loorents Hertsi, Aleksi Paananen, Teemu Jäntti (46.Stenio, 56.Ville Salmikivi), Henri Anier. Trainer: Toni Korkeakunnas.

FH Hafnarfjördur: Gunnar Nielsen, Pétur Vidarsson, Hjörtur Valgardsson, Vidar Ari Jónsson, Rennico Clarke (56.Edi Gomes), Davíd Vidarsson, Gudmundur Kristjánsson (77.Robbie Crawford), Halldór Björnsson (69.Jónatan Jónsson), Brandur Hendriksson Olsen, Atli Gudnason, Steven Lennon. Trainer: Ólafur Kristjánsson.

Goals: 0-1 Halldór Björnsson (4), 0-2 Steven Lennon (18), 0-3 Robbie Crawford (90+1).

19.07.2018; Kaplakrikavöllur, Hafnarfjördur; Referee: Espen Eskås (Norway); Attendance: 742

FH Hafnarfjördur – FC Lahti 0-0

FH Hafnarfjördur: Gunnar Nielsen, Hjörtur Valgardsson, Vidar Ari Jónsson, Edi Gomes, Rennico Clarke, Davíd Vidarsson, Gudmundur Kristjánsson, Kristinn Steindórsson, Brandur Hendriksson Olsen (86.Robbie Crawford), Atli Gudnason (65.Zeiko Lewis), Steven Lennon (76.Geoffrey Castillion). Trainer: Ólafur Kristjánsson.

FC Lahti: Oskari Forsman, Mikko Hauhia, Kalle Taimi, Pavel Osipov, Artem Vyatkin, Santeri Hostikka, Paavo Voutilainen (59.Fareed Sadat), Artjom Dmitrijev (87.Eemelie Virta), Loorents Hertsi, Aleksi Paananen (74.Xhevdet Gela), Henri Anier. Trainer: Toni Korkeakunnas.

[FH Hafnarfjördur won 3-0 on aggregate]

12.07.2018; A. Le Coq Arena, Tallinn; Referee: Daniyar Sakhi (Kazakhstan); Attendance: 263

JK Narva Trans – FK Željezničar Sarajevo 0-2(0-1)

Narva Trans: Artur Kotenko, Igor Ovsjannikov (78.Arbër Basha), Viktor Plotnikov (31.Eduard Golovljov), Tanel Tamberg, Dante Leverock, Irie Elysée (84.Matheus), Dmitri Proshin, Denis Polyakov, Artjom Skinjov, Aleksandr Zakarlyuka, Dmitriy Barkov. Trainer: Adyam Kuzyaev.

Željezničar: Vedran Kjosevski, Jadranko Bogicevic, Sinisa Stevanovic, Milos Bakrac, Ivan Curjuric (84.Semir Dacic), Antonio Pavic, Filip Arezina (75.Haris Hajdarevic), Jovan Blagojevic, Anel Sabanadzovic, Sulejman Krpic, Dzenan Zajmovic (71.Mladen Veselinovic). Trainer: Slobodan Krcmarevic.

Goals: 0-1 Artur Kotenko (15 own goal), 0-2 Anel Sabanadzovic (74).

18.07.2018; Stadion Grbavica, Sarajevo; Referee: Cătălin Găman (Romania); Attendance: 7,603

FK Željezničar Sarajevo – JK Narva Trans 3-1(2-1)

Željezničar: Vedran Kjosevski, Jadranko Bogicevic, Sinisa Stevanovic, Milos Bakrac, Ivan Curjuric (78.Haris Hajdarevic), Antonio Pavic, Filip Arezina, Jovan Blagojevic (84.Semir Dacic), Anel Sabanadzovic, Sulejman Krpic, Dzenan Zajmovic (74.Mladen Veselinovic). Trainer: Slobodan Krcmarevic.

Narva Trans: Artur Kotenko, Igor Ovsjannikov (75.Vadim Mihhailov), Viktor Plotnikov, Tanel Tamberg, Dante Leverock, Irie Elysée (36.Matheus), Dmitri Proshin, Denis Polyakov, Artjom Skinjov (62.Arbër Basha), Aleksandr Zakarlyuka, Dmitriy Barkov. Trainer: Adyam Kuzyaev.

Goals: 0-1 Viktor Plotnikov (5), 1-1 Dzenan Zajmovic (25), 2-1, 3-1 Sulejman Krpic (29, 82).

[FK Željezničar Sarajevo won 5-1 on aggregate]

12.07.2018; LFF stadionas, Vilnius; Referee: Fábio José Costa Veríssimo (Portugal); Attendance: 400

FK Trakai Vilnius – FC Irtysh Pavlodar 0-0

FK Trakai: Tomas Svedkauskas, Valdemars Borovskis, Evgeniy Osipov, Rokas Masenzovas (60.Justinas Janusevskis), Kevin Ntika Bondombe, Diniyar Bilyaletdinov, Vaidas Silėnas, Valentin Jeriomenko (40.Modestas Vorobjovas), Donatas Kazlauskas, Svajūnas Cyzas, Justinas Marazas (75.Etienne Mukanya). Trainer: Kibu Vicuña.

Irtysh Pavlodar: Nikita Kalmykov, Aleksandr Kislitsyn, Milos Stamenkovic, Adrian Avramia, Dimitriy Schmidt, Sergey Kislyak, Ilya Kalinin (90+3.Vladimir Vomenko), Adrián Gómez, Doru Popadiuc (79.Kirill Shestakov), Carlos Fonseca, Ruslan Esimov. Trainer: Oyrat Saduov.

19.07.2018; Ortaliq Stadion, Pavlodar; Referee: Luca Barbeno (San Marino); Attendance: 6,250

FC Irtysh Pavlodar – FK Trakai Vilnius 0-1(0-1)

Irtysh Pavlodar: Nikita Kalmykov, Aleksandr Kislitsyn, Milos Stamenkovic, Dimitriy Schmidt (75.Vladimir Vomenko), Ilya Kalinin, Kirill Shestakov, Adrián Gómez, Doru Popadiuc, Gbolahan Salami, Carlos Fonseca (65.Arman Smailov), Ruslan Esimov. Trainer: Oyrat Saduov.

FK Trakai: Tomas Svedkauskas, Valdemars Borovskis, Evgeniy Osipov, Justinas Janusevskis, Kevin Ntika Bondombe (70.Valentin Jeriomenko), Diniyar Bilyaletdinov, Vaidas Silėnas, Donatas Kazlauskas (85.Rokas Gedminas), Modestas Vorobjovas, Svajūnas Cyzas (73.Aleksandras Levsinas), Justinas Marazas. Trainer: Kibu Vicuña.

Goal: 0-1 Svajūnas Cyzas (19).

[FK Trakai Vilnius won 1-0 on aggregate]

12.07.2018; Kadriorg staadion, Tallinn; Referee: Bojan Nikolić (Serbia); Attendance: 1,343

FCI Levadia Tallinn – Dundalk FC 0-1(0-0)

FCI Levadia Tallinn: Sergei Lepmets, Markus Jürgenson, Dmitri Kruglov, Maksim Podholjuzin, Igor Dudarev, Evgeny Kharin (75.Mark Oliver Roosnupp), Yuriy Tkachuk, Rasmus Peetson (67.Muamer Svraka), Marcelin Gando (56.Pavel Marin), Nikita Andreev, Roman Debelko. Trainer: Aleksandar Rogic.

Dundalk FC: Gary Rogers, Brain Gartland, Dane Massey, Sean Gannon, Sean Hoare, Chris Shields, Robbie Benson, Dylan Connolly (88.John Mountney), Jamie McGrath (81.Krisztián Adorján), Patrick Hoban, Michael Duffy (90+4.Ronan Murray). Trainer: Stephen Kenny.

Goal: 0-1 Dylan Connolly (53).

19.07.2018; Oriel Park, Dundalk; Referee: Adrien Jaccottet (Switzerland); Attendance: 3,000

Dundalk FC – FCI Levadia Tallinn 2-1(2-1)

Dundalk FC: Gary Rogers, Brain Gartland, Dane Massey, Sean Gannon, Sean Hoare, Chris Shields, Robbie Benson, Dylan Connolly (62.Krisztián Adorján), Jamie McGrath, Patrick Hoban (90+2.Georgie Kelly), Michael Duffy (83.Karolis Chvedukas). Trainer: Stephen Kenny.

FCI Levadia Tallinn: Sergei Lepmets, Markus Jürgenson (88.Rasmus Peetson), Dmitri Kruglov, Maksim Podholjuzin, Igor Dudarev, Muamer Svraka, Evgeny Kharin (80.Kirill Nesterov), Yuriy Tkachuk, Marcelin Gando (64.Mark Oliver Roosnupp), Nikita Andreev, Roman Debelko. Trainer: Aleksandar Rogic.

Goals: 1-0 Patrick Hoban (31), 2-0 Michael Duffy (33), 2-1 Roman Debelko (42).

[Dundalk FC won 3-1 on aggregate]

12.07.2018; Savon Sanomat Areena, Kuopio; Referee: Kirill Levnikov (Russia); Attendance: 2,890

Kuopion Palloseura – FC København 0-1(0-0)

Kuopion PS: Otso Virtanen, Henri Toivomäki, Lum Rexhepi, Luis Murillo, Juho Pirttijoki, Petteri Pennanen, Joni Mäkelä (61.Saku Savolainen), Ville Saxman, Ilmari Niskanen, Rasmus Karjalainen (89.Eetu Pellikka), Ats Purje (78.Rangel). Trainer: Jani Honkavaara.

FC København: Stephan Andersen, Pierre Bengtsson (66.Nicolai Boilesen), Sotirios Papagiannopoulos, Peter Ankersen, Denis Vavro, Ján Gregus (63.Carlo Holse), Rasmus Falk, Zeca, Robert Skov, Dame N'Doye, Kenan Kodro (84.Mads Roerslev Rasmussen). Trainer: Ståle Solbakken.

Goal: 0-1 Robert Skov (75).

19.07.2018; Telia Parken, København; Referee: Vilhjálmur Thórarinsson (Iceland); Attendance: 7,145

FC København – Kuopion Palloseura 1-1(0-0)

FC København: Jesse Joronen, Sotirios Papagiannopoulos, Nicolai Boilesen, Denis Vavro, Mads Roerslev Rasmussen (71.Peter Ankersen), Ján Gregus, Rasmus Falk (90+4.Andreas Bjelland), Zeca, Viktor Fischer, Dame N'Doye, Kenan Kodro (70.Robert Skov). Trainer: Ståle Solbakken.

Kuopion PS: Otso Virtanen, Henri Toivomäki, Lum Rexhepi, Luis Murillo, Juho Pirttijoki, Petteri Pennanen, Joni Mäkelä (71.Ats Purje), Ville Saxman, Ilmari Niskanen, Saku Savolainen, Rangel (61.Rasmus Karjalainen). Trainer: Jani Honkavaara.

Goals: 0-1 Rasmus Karjalainen (75), 1-1 Denis Vavro (81 penalty).

[FC København won 2-1 on aggregate]

12.07.2018; Stadions Daugava, Liepāja; Referee: Marco Guida (Italy); Attendance: 2,234

FK Liepāja – BK Häcken Göteborg 0-3(0-0)

FK Liepāja: Arsen Beglaryan, Sady Guèye, Seydina Keita, Vladimir Kamess (64.Verners Apins), Igors Kozlovs, Dmitrijs Hmizs (76.Cristián Torres), Jānis Ikaunieks, Raivis Jurkovskis, Leonel Strumia, Kristers Tobers, Mārtins Kigurs (55.Girts Karlsons). Trainer: Tamaz Pertia.

BK Häcken: Peter Abrahamsson, Kari Arkivuo, Emil Wahlström, Johan Hammar, Gustav Berggren, Erik Friberg (72.Alexander Faltsetas), Adam Andersson, Viktor Lundberg (56.Daleho Irandust), Mervan Çelik, Paulinho Guerreiro (84.Alhassan Kamara), Nasiru Mohammed. Trainer: Andreas Alm.

Goals: 0-1 Daleho Irandust (74), 0-2 Paulinho Guerreiro (77), 0-3 Mervan Çelik (82).

19.07.2018; Bravida Arena, Göteborg; Referee: Sergey Ivanov (Russia); Attendance: 1,713

BK Häcken Göteborg – FK Liepāja 1-2(1-1)

BK Häcken: Peter Abrahamsson, Emil Wahlström, Alexander Angelin, Johan Hammar (90.Kari Arkivuo), Gustav Berggren, Rasmus Lindgren, Erik Friberg (69.Alexander Faltsetas), Adam Andersson (76.Karl Bohm), Viktor Lundberg, Alhassan Kamara, Nasiru Mohammed. Trainer: Andreas Alm.

FK Liepāja: Arsen Beglaryan, Deniss Ivanovs, Sady Guèye, Seydina Keita, Vladimir Kamess, Dmitrijs Hmizs (52.Cristián Torres), Raivis Jurkovskis, Leonel Strumia, Kristers Tobers (79.Kristaps Grebis), Mārtins Kigurs (63.Benjamin Teidi), Girts Karlsons. Trainer: Tamaz Pertia.

Goals: 0-1 Sady Guèye (11), 1-1 Nasiru Mohammed (42), 1-2 Girts Karlsons (86).

[BK Häcken Göteborg won 4-2 on aggregate]

12.07.2018; Alytaus Centrinis stadionas, Alytus; Referee: Georgi Vadachkoria (Georgia); Attendance: 800

FC Stumbras Kaunas – Apollon Limassol FC 1-0(0-0)

Stumbras Kaunas: Rodrigo Josviaki, Lukas Cerkauskas, Matheus Bissi, Rimvydas Sadauskas, Jardel Nazaré, André Almeida, Dominykas Galkevicius (82.Levan Matcharashvili), Agostinho Cá, Marcos Junior (86.Amran Al-Jassasi), Lucas Villela, Nasro Bouchareb (67.Liu Yuhao). Trainer: Mariano Barreto.

Apollon: Bruno Vale, Charis Kyriakou, Kévin Bru (76.Antreas Karo), André Schembri (68.Ioannis Pittas), Héctor Yuste, Giorgos Vasiliou, Sasa Markovic, Esteban Sachetti, João Pedro, Fotis Papoulis (88.Luca Polizzi), Adrián Sardinero. Trainer: Sofronis Avgousti.

Goal: 1-0 Levan Matcharashvili (90+1).

19.07.2018; Stádio Neo GSP, Nicosia; Referee: Eldorjan Hamiti (Albania); Attendance: 2,556

Apollon Limassol FC – FC Stumbras Kaunas 2-0(1-0)

Apollon: Bruno Vale, Valentin Roberge, Charis Kyriakou, André Schembri (83.Emilio Zelaya), Héctor Yuste, Giorgos Vasiliou, Esteban Sachetti, João Pedro, Fotis Papoulis (90.Ioannis Pittas), Anton Maglica, Adrián Sardinero (68.Sasa Markovic). Trainer: Sofronis Avgousti.

Stumbras Kaunas: Rodrigo Josviaki, Lukas Cerkauskas, Matheus Bissi, Rimvydas Sadauskas, Jardel Nazaré, André Almeida, Agostinho Cá, Marcos Junior (56.Dominykas Galkevicius), Levan Matcharashvili (74.Alsény Bah), Lucas Villela, Nasro Bouchareb (46.Liu Yuhao). Trainer: Mariano Barreto.

Goals: 1-0, 2-0 Héctor Yuste (7, 62).

[Apollon Limassol FC won 2-1 on aggregate]

12.07.2018; Dalga Arena, Bakı; Referee: Dennis Higler (Netherlands); Attendance: 4,000

Neftçi PFC Bakı – Újpest FC 3-1(1-1)

Neftçi Bakı: Sälahät Agayev, Ruslan Abisov, Anton Krivotsyuk, Sony Mustivar, Goran Paracki, Rahman Hajiyev (77.Slavko Bralic), Kyrylo Petrov, Magomed Mirzabekov, Namig Alasgarov (42.Emin Makhmudov), Bagaliy Dabo (90.Kwame Karikari), Dário Júnior da Silva. Trainer: Roberto Bordin.

Újpest FC: Filip Pajovic, Mijusko Bojovic, Branko Pauljevic, Róbert Litauszki, Dzenan Burekovic, Dániel Nagy (90.Viktor Angelov), Benjámin Balász, Bojan Sankovic, Donát Zsótér (74.Kristóf Szücs), Benjámin Cseke, Soma Novothny (82.Patrik Tischler). Trainer: Nebojsa Vignjevic.

Goals: 0-1 Dániel Nagy (9), 1-1, 2-1 Bagaliy Dabo (23), 72), 3-1 Emin Makhmudov (90+2).

19.07.2018; „Szusza Ferenc" Stadion, Budapest; Referee: Ioannis Papadopoulos (Greece); Attendance: 3,738

Újpest FC – Neftçi PFC Bakı 4-0(2-0)

Újpest FC: Filip Pajovic, Mijusko Bojovic, Branko Pauljevic, Róbert Litauszki, Dzenan Burekovic, Dániel Nagy (88.Benjámin Cseke), Bojan Sankovic, Donát Zsótér (81.Benjámin Balász), Alassane Diallo, Obinna Nwobodo, Soma Novothny (90+1.Patrik Tischler). Trainer: Nebojsa Vignjevic.

Neftçi Bakı: Sälahät Agayev, Ruslan Abisov (41.Tural Akhundov), Slavko Bralic, Anton Krivotsyuk (54.Kwame Karikari), Sony Mustivar, Goran Paracki, Rahman Hajiyev (78.Mirabdulla Abbasov), Kyrylo Petrov, Magomed Mirzabekov, Bagaliy Dabo, Dário Júnior da Silva. Trainer: Roberto Bordin.

Goals: 1-0 Róbert Litauszki (19), 2-0 Bojan Sankovic (21), 3-0 Donát Zsótér (49), 4-0 Obinna Nwobodo (65).

[Újpest FC won 5-3 on aggregate]

12.07.2018; Brandywell Stadium, Derry; Referee: Nikola Popov (Bulgaria); Attendance: 1,467

Derry City FC – FC Dinamo Minsk 0-2(0-1)

Derry City: Gerard Doherty, Daniel Seaborne, Darren Cole, Conor McDermott [*sent off 81*], Dean Shiels, Aaron McEneff, Jamie McDonagh, Ben Fisk (78.Gavin Peers), Rory Hale (6.Ronan Hale), Aaron Splaine, Alistair Roy (60.Rory Patterson). Trainer: Kenny Shiels.

Dinamo Minsk: Andrey Gorbunov, Yuriy Ostroukh (77.Roman Begunov), Nino Galovic, Maksim Shvetsov, Maksim Zhavnerchik, Seidu Yahaya, Uros Nikolic, Nikita Kaplenko (29.Filipp Ivanov), Artem Gurenko, Vladimir Khvashchinskiy (67.Artem Solovey), Anton Saroka. Trainer: Sergei Gurenko.

Goals: 0-1 Nino Galovic (2), 0-2 Vladimir Khvashchinskiy (64).

19.07.2018; Dinamo Stadium, Minsk; Referee: Jens Maae (Denmark); Attendance: 13,750

FC Dinamo Minsk – Derry City FC 1-2(1-1)

Dinamo Minsk: Sergey Ignatovich, Roman Begunov, Maksim Shvetsov, Maksim Zhavnerchik, Seidu Yahaya, Artem Solovey (6.Vladimir Khvashchinskiy), Aleksandr Sachivko, Artem Bykov, Uros Nikolic, Artem Gurenko (85.Yuriy Ostroukh), Anton Saroka (63.Filipp Ivanov). Trainer: Sergei Gurenko.

Derry City: Gerard Doherty, Gavin Peers, Daniel Seaborne, Darren Cole, Dean Shiels (72.Ronan Hale), Aaron McEneff, Jamie McDonagh, Ben Fisk (89.Ben Doherty), Rory Hale, Aaron Splaine, Alistair Roy. Trainer: Kenny Shiels.

Goals: 0-1 Alistair Roy (7), 1-1 Aleksandr Sachivko (28), 1-2 Ronan Hale (75).

[FC Dinamo Minsk won 3-2 on aggregate]

12.07.2018; Corbett Sports Stadium, Rhyl; Referee: Juri Frischer (Estonia); Attendance: 577

Connah's Quay Nomads FC – FC Shakhtyor Solihorsk 1-3(0-2)

Connah's Quay Nomads: John Danby, George Horan, Laurence Wilson, Danny Holmes, John Disney, Michael Parker (66.Declan Poole), James Owen (81.Noah Edwards), Michael Bakare, Callum Morris, Ryan Wignall (86.Nathan Woolfe), Andrew Owens. Trainer: Andrew Morrison.

Shakhtyor Solihorsk: Andrey Klimovich, Pavel Rybak, Igor Kuzmenok, Igor Burko, Mikhail Shibun, Roger Cañas (83.Luka Simunovic), Aleksandr Selyava, Yuri Kovalev (80.Pyry Soiri), Július Szöke, Max Ebong Ngome, Elis Bakaj (73.Denis Laptev). Trainer: Sergey Tashuev.

Goals: 0-1 Max Ebong Ngome (20), 0-2 Elis Bakaj (34), 0-3 Mikhail Shibun (75), 1-3 Callum Morris (89 penalty).

19.07.2018; „Budaunik Stroitel" Stadium, Soligorsk; Referee: Admir Sehovic (Bosnia and Herzegovina); Attendance: 2,700

FC Shakhtyor Solihorsk – Connah's Quay Nomads FC 2-0(1-0)

Shakhtyor Solihorsk: Andrey Klimovich, Pavel Rybak, Igor Kuzmenok (45+1.Maksim Bordachev), Siarhei Matveichyk, Mikhail Shibun, Roger Cañas, Aleksandr Selyava, Yuri Kovalev, Július Szöke, Max Ebong Ngome (83.Pyry Soiri), Elis Bakaj (65.Denis Laptev). Trainer: Sergey Tashuev.

Connah's Quay Nomads: John Danby, George Horan (46.Jonathan Spittle), Laurence Wilson, Danny Holmes, John Disney, Michael Parker (66.Declan Poole), James Owen (53.Noah Edwards), Michael Bakare, Callum Morris, Ryan Wignall, Andrew Owens [*sent off 62*]. Trainer: Andrew Morrison.

Goals: 1-0 Elis Bakaj (24 penalty), 2-0 Maksim Bordachev (82).

[FC Shakhtyor Solihorsk won 5-1 on aggregate]

12.07.2018; Stadionul Zimbru, Chişinău; Referee: Karim Abed (France); Attendance: 2,700

CS Petrocub Hînceşti – NK Osijek 1-1(0-0)

Petrocub Hînceşti: Dumitru Celeadnic, Maxim Potîrniche, Victor Mudrac, Vlad Slivca, Artur Patras (56.Maxim Cojocaru), Alexandru Vremea (71.Ion Sandu), Dan Taras, Vladimir Ambros, Jessie Guera Djou, Donalio Melachio Douanla, Vladislav Ivanov (59.Sergiu Matei). Trainer: Lilian Popescu.

NK Osijek: Marko Malenica, Borna Barisic, Stjepan Radeljic, Tomislav Sorsa, Mile Skoric, Gabrijel Boban (84.Marin Pilj), Haris Hajradinovic (55.Domagoj Pusic), Benedik Mioc, Petar Bockaj (71.Dmitriy Lepa), Danijel Loncar, Mirko Maric. Trainer: Zoran Zekic.

Goals: 0-1 Mirko Maric (52), 1-1 Vladimir Ambros (65).

19.07.2018; Stadion Gradski vrt, Osijek; Referee: Dimitrios Massias (Cyprus); Attendance: 2,233

NK Osijek – CS Petrocub Hînceşti 2-1(1-1)

NK Osijek: Marko Malenica, Borna Barisic, Stjepan Radeljic, Tomislav Sorsa, Gabrijel Boban (22.Dmitriy Lepa, 66.Domagoj Pusic), Benedik Mioc, Petar Bockaj (78.Haris Hajradinovic), Robert Mudrazija, Danijel Loncar, Mirko Maric, Ezekiel Henty. Trainer: Zoran Zekic.

Petrocub Hînceşti: Dumitru Celeadnic, Maxim Potîrniche, Ion Sandu, Victor Mudrac, Maxim Cojocaru, Vlad Slivca (70.Sergiu Matei), Dan Taras (60.Artur Patras), Vladimir Ambros, Jessie Guera Djou, Donalio Melachio Douanla, Vladislav Ivanov (54.Alexandru Vremea). Trainer: Lilian Popescu.

Goals: 1-0 Robert Mudrazija (15), 1-1 Vladimir Ambros (22 penalty), 2-1 Borna Barisic (61).

[NK Osijek won 3-2 on aggregate]

12.07.2018; Stádio „Andonis Papadopoulos", Larnaca; Referee: José María Sánchez Martínez (Spain); Attendance: n/a

Anorthosis Famagusta FC – KF Laçi 2-1(0-1)

Anorthosis: Mário Felgueiras, Gordon Schildenfeld, Konstantinos Sotiriou, Erwin Koffi, Danijel Pranjic, João Victor, Rayo, Nosa Igiebor (34.Giorgos Economides), Sekou Cissé, Michal Duris, Beka Mikeltadze (81.Nikos Englezou). Trainer: Roni Levy.

KF Laçi: Gentian Selmani, Taulant Sefgjinaj, Erion Hoxhallari, Eglentin Gjoni, Andi Hadroj (90.Redon Xhixha), Ndricim Shtubina, Nikola Eller, Fjoart Jonuzi, Regi Lushkja, Vice Kendes, Myrto Uzuni. Trainer: Besnik Prenga.

Goals: 0-1 Erion Hoxhallari (21), 1-1 Danijel Pranjic (52 penalty), 2-1 Sekou Cissé (59).

19.07.2018; Stadiumi Laçi, Laçi; Referee: Donatas Rumsas (Lithuania); Attendance: 1,950

KF Laçi – Anorthosis Famagusta FC 1-0(0-0)

KF Laçi: Gentian Selmani, Taulant Sefgjinaj, Erion Hoxhallari, Eglentin Gjoni, Andi Hadroj (64.Abdurraman Fangaj), Ndricim Shtubina (80.Ded Bushi), Nikola Eller, Fjoart Jonuzi (80.Redon Xhixha), Regi Lushkja, Vice Kendes, Myrto Uzuni. Trainer: Besnik Prenga.

Anorthosis: Mário Felgueiras, Gordon Schildenfeld, Konstantinos Sotiriou (90.Nikos Englezou), Erwin Koffi, Danijel Pranjic, João Victor, Rayo, Nosa Igiebor, Sekou Cissé, Michal Duris, Beka Mikeltadze (51.Nika Kacharava). Trainer: Roni Levy.

Goal: 1-0 Myrto Uzuni (88).

[KF Laçi won on away goals rule (2-2 on aggregate)]

12.07.2018; Groupama Aréna, Budapest; Referee: Ricardo De Burgos Bengoetxea (Spain); Attendance: 14,127

Ferencvárosi TC – Maccabi Tel Aviv FC 1-1(0-0)

Ferencvárosi TC: Dénes Dibusz, Endre Botka, Miha Blazic, Abraham Frimpong, Stefan Spirovski, Lukács Böle, Fernando Gorriarán, Davide Lanzafame (75.Leandro de Almeida), Kjartan Finnbogason (80.Dániel Böde), Roland Varga (76.Ivan Petryak), Gergö Lovrencsics. Trainer: Thomas Doll.

Maccabi Tel Aviv: Predrag Rajkovic, Eitan Tibi, Avi Rikan (85.Sheran Yeini), Saborit, Elazar Dasa, Jair Amador, Eyal Golasa (64.Eliran Atar), Dor Mikha, Dor Peretz, Vidar Kjartansson (79.Omer Atzili), Aaron Schoenfeld. Trainer: Vladimir Ivic.

Goals: 1-0 Stefan Spirovski 61), 1-1 Eliran Atar (90+1).

19.07.2018; Winner Stadium, Netanya; Referee: Hugo Filipe Ferreira de Campos Moreira Miguel (Portugal); Attendance: 8,256

Maccabi Tel Aviv FC – Ferencvárosi TC 1-0(1-0)

Maccabi Tel Aviv: Predrag Rajkovic, Eitan Tibi, Avi Rikan (89.Sheran Yeini), Saborit, Elazar Dasa, Jair Amador, Dor Mikha, Roslan Barski, Dor Peretz, Vidar Kjartansson (66.Aaron Schoenfeld), Eliran Atar (73.Omer Atzili). Trainer: Vladimir Ivic.

Ferencvárosi TC: Dénes Dibusz, Marcel Heister, Miha Blazic, Abraham Frimpong, Stefan Spirovski, Lukács Böle, Ivan Petryak (74.Dániel Böde), Fernando Gorriarán, Davide Lanzafame (63.Roland Varga), Kjartan Finnbogason, Gergö Lovrencsics. Trainer: Thomas Doll.

Goal: 1-0 Eliran Atar (45+1).

[Maccabi Tel Aviv FC won 2-1 on aggregate]

12.07.2018; MFA Centenary Stadium, Ta'Qali; Referee: Volen Chinkov (Bulgaria); Attendance: 504

Balzan FC – Keshla FK 4-1(3-1)

Balzan FC: Steve Sultana, Elkin Serrano, Steven Bezzina, Ivan Bozovic, Michael Johnson, Cadú, Nenad Sljivic (85.Ricardo Correa), Milos Lepovic, Alfred Effiong (63.Uros Ljubomirac), Lecão, Bojan Kaljevic (78.Andrija Majdevac). Trainer: Marko Micovic.

Keshla FK: Kamran Agayev, Dênis, Tarlan Guliyev, Azer Salahli, Slavik Alkhasov, Sertan Taskin (84.Hervé Tchami-Ngangoue), Ebrima Sohna, Fuad Bayramov (60.Milos Bosancic), Vagif Javadov (63.Mammad Guliev), Andre Clennon, César Meza Colli. Trainer: Yuriy Maksimov.

Goals: 1-0 Alfred Effiong (12), 2-0 Lecão (21), 2-1 César Meza Colli (29 penalty), 3-1 Bojan Kaljevic (34), 4-1 Cadú (55).

19.07.2018; Dalga Arena, Bakı; Referee: Mikhail Vilkov (Russia); Attendance: 2,215

Keshla FK – Balzan FC 2-1(1-0)

Keshla FK: Kamran Agayev, Adrian Scarlatache, Dênis, Tarlan Guliyev, Slavik Alkhasov, Sertan Taskin (85.Mammad Guliev), Ebrima Sohna, Milos Bosancic (74.Hervé Tchami-Ngangoue), Andre Clennon, Bakhodir Nasimov (64.Amit Yunanov), César Meza Colli. Trainer: Yuriy Maksimov.

Balzan FC: Steve Sultana, Elkin Serrano, Steven Bezzina, Ivan Bozovic, Uros Ljubomirac (59.Lecão), Michael Johnson, Cadú, Nenad Sljivic, Milos Lepovic, Alfred Effiong (69.Justin Grioli), Bojan Kaljevic (85.Andrija Majdevac [*sent off 90+7*]). Trainer: Marko Micovic.

Goals: 1-0 César Meza Colli (11 penalty), 2-0 Slavik Alkhasov (90+1), 2-1 Andrija Majdevac (90+6).

[Balzan FC won 5-3 on aggregate]

12.07.2018; Complexul Sportiv Raional, Orhei; Referee: Vitali Romanov (Ukraine); Attendance: 3,000

FC Milsami Orhei – ŠK Slovan Bratislava 2-4(0-3)

Milsami Orhei: Radu Mîtu, Vadim Bolohan, Constantin Bogdan, Artur Craciun, Alexandru Antoniuc, Andrei Cojocari, Gheorghe Andronic (58.Romeo Surdu), Mihai Platica, Maxim Antoniuc (46.Vasile Jardan), Igor Bugaev, Sergiu Platica. Trainer: Veaceslav Rusnac.

Slovan Bratislava: Michal Sulla, Mitch Apau, Vasil Bozhikov, Artem Sukhotsky, Dávid Holman (68.Vukan Savicevic), Joeri de Kamps, Nono Delgado, Kenan Bajric, "Moha" Mohammed Rharsalla, Aleksandar Cavric (81.Dejan Drazic), Andraz Sporar (87.Filip Holosko). Trainer: Martin Sevela.

Goals: 0-1 Mohammed Rharsalla (10), 0-2 Andraz Sporar (22), 0-3 Mohammed Rharsalla (41), 1-3 Igor Bugaev (59), 2-3 Romeo Surdu (75), 2-4 Artur Craciun (79 own goal).

19.07.2018; Stadión Pasienky, Bratislava; Referee: Nejc Kajtazovič (Slovenia); Attendance: 3,175

ŠK Slovan Bratislava – FC Milsami Orhei 5-0(3-0)

Slovan Bratislava: Michal Sulla, Mitch Apau, Vasil Bozhikov, Artem Sukhotsky, Ibrahim Rabiu, Dávid Holman, Nono Delgado (58.Vukan Savicevic), Kenan Bajric, "Moha" Mohammed Rharsalla, Aleksandar Cavric (48.Boris Cmiljanic), Andraz Sporar (74.Dejan Drazic). Trainer: Martin Sevela.

Milsami Orhei: Radu Mîtu, Vadim Bolohan, Constantin Bogdan (54.Sergiu Platica), Dinu Graur, Artur Craciun, Alexandru Antoniuc (81.Ion Ibrean), Andrei Cojocari, Mihai Platica, Vadim Rata, Andrei Rusmac, Romeo Surdu (34.Igor Bugaev). Trainer: Veaceslav Rusnac.

Goals: 1-0, 2-0 Andraz Sporar (15, 25), 3-0 "Moha" Mohammed Rharsalla (33), 4-0 Boris Cmiljanic (52), 5-0 "Moha" Mohammed Rharsalla (77).

[ŠK Slovan Bratislava won 9-2 on aggregate]

12.07.2018; Stadion Bâlgarska Armija, Sofia; Referee: Mario Zebec (Croatia); Attendance: 7,500

PFC CSKA Sofia – Rīga FC 1-0(0-0)

CSKA Sofia: Vytautas Cerniauskas, Nikolaj Bodurov, Kristiyan Malinov, Boris Sekulic, Bozhidar Chorbadzhiyski, Geferson, Valentin Antov, Rúben Pinto, Tiago Rodrigues, Jorginho (89.Tonislav Yordanov), Henrique (46.Edwin Gyasi). Trainer: Nestor El Maestro.

Rīga FC: Roberts Ozols, Vladislavs Gabovs, Antons Kurakins, Stefan Panic, Volodymyr Baenko, Antonijs Cernomordijs, Tomislav Saric, Ivan Enin, George Davies, Darko Lemajic, Milan Vusurovic (90+1.Kriss Kārklins). Trainer: Viktor Skripnik.

Goal: 1-0 Tiago Rodrigues (49).

19.07.2018; Skonto Stadions, Rīga; Referee: Furkat Atazhanov (Kazakhstan); Attendance: 3,100

Rīga FC – PFC CSKA Sofia 1-0(1-0,1-0); 3-5 on penalties

Rīga FC: Roberts Ozols, Vladislavs Gabovs (66.Kriss Kārklins), Antons Kurakins (119.Thiago Primão), Stefan Panic [*sent off 109*], Volodymyr Baenko [*sent off 120+10*], Antonijs Cernomordijs, Tomislav Saric, Bogdan Vastsuk [*sent off 120+10*], Ivan Enin (101.Armands Pētersons), George Davies (80.Milan Vusurovic), Darko Lemajic. Trainer: Viktor Skripnik.

CSKA Sofia: Vytautas Cerniauskas, Nikolaj Bodurov [*sent off 120+10*], Kristiyan Malinov [*sent off 120+10*], Boris Sekulic (91.Steven Pereira), Bozhidar Chorbadzhiyski, Geferson, Valentin Antov (60.Henrique, 105+1.Janio Bikel), Rúben Pinto, Tiago Rodrigues [*sent off 74*], Kiril Despodov, Jorginho (61.Edwin Gyasi). Trainer: Nestor El Maestro.

Goal: 1-0 Antonijs Cernomordijs (44).

Penalty: Kristiyan Malinov 0-1; Darko Lemajic (missed); Nikolaj Bodurov 0-2; Thiago Primão 1-2; Geferson 1-3; Kriss Kārklins 2-3; Edwin Gyasi 2-4; Volodymyr Baenko 3-4; Kiril Despodov 3-5.

[PFC CSKA Sofia won 5-3 on penalties (after 1-1 on aggregate)]

12.07.2018; Stadion Pecara, Široki Brijeg; Referee: Petr Ardeleánu (Czech Republic); Attendance: 2,500

NK Široki Brijeg – NK Domžale 2-2(0-2)

Široki Brijeg: Luka Bilobrk, Josip Kvesic (46.Dejan Cabraja), Josip Barisic, Stipo Markovic, Bernardo Matic, Dominik Kovacic, Luka Begonja, Josip Corluka, Mateo Maric (61.Boze Vukoja), Drazen Bagaric, Tomislav Turcin (85.Eliomar). Trainer: Boris Pavic.

NK Domžale: Dejan Milic, Matija Sirok, Gaber Dobrovoljc, Tilen Klemencic, Dario Melnjak, Senijad Ibricic, Zeni Husmani, Lovro Bizjak (90+1.Nermin Haljeta), Adam Gnezda Cerin, Agim Ibraimi (85.Zan Zuzek), Shamar Nicholson (76.Tonci Mujan). Trainer: Simon Rozman.

Goals: 0-1 Lovro Bizjak (12), 0-2 Dario Melnjak (26), 1-2 Tomislav Turcin (47), 2-2 Stipo Markovic (83).

19.07.2018; Sportni Park, Domžale; Referee: Antti Munukka (Finland); Attendance: 2,000

NK Domžale – NK Široki Brijeg 1-1(1-0)

NK Domžale: Dejan Milic, Matija Sirok, Gaber Dobrovoljc, Tilen Klemencic, Dario Melnjak, Senijad Ibricic, Zeni Husmani, Lovro Bizjak (90+2.Andraz Kirm), Adam Gnezda Cerin, Agim Ibraimi (80.Zan Zuzek), Shamar Nicholson (67.Tonci Mujan). Trainer: Simon Rozman.

Široki Brijeg: Luka Bilobrk, Josip Barisic, Stipo Markovic (83.Josip Kvesic), Bernardo Matic, Dominik Kovacic, Danijel Kozul (46.Mateo Maric), Luka Begonja, Eliomar (60.Dejan Cabraja), Josip Corluka, Drazen Bagaric, Tomislav Turcin. Trainer: Boris Pavic.

Goals: 1-0 Dario Melnjak (11), 1-1 Bernardo Matic (73).

[NK Domžale won on away goals rule (3-3 on aggregate)]

12.07.2018; Stade „Josy Barthel“, Lëtzebuerg; Referee: Alex Troleis (Faroe Islands); Attendance: 1,383

Racing FC Union Luxembourg – FC Viitorul Constanța 0-2(0-1)

Union Luxembourg: Romain Ruffier, Thomas Birk, Pit Simon, Pape Ibra M'Boup, Kevin Nakache, Tarek Nouidra (87.Julien Humbert), Benoît Nyssen, Daniël Alves da Mota (90.Benssad Sulejmani), Sebastian Szimayer (80.Florik Shala), Edis Osmanovic, Jonathan Hennetier. Trainer: Patrick Grettnich.

Viitorul Constanța: Valentin Cojocaru, Sebastian Mladen, Tudor Baluta, Bradley de Nooijer (78.Radu Boboc), Mailson Lima, Vlad Achim, Bogdan Tîru, Ianis Hagi (86.Alexi Pitu), Ionut Vîna, Alexandru Matan (58.Lyes Houri), Denis Dragus. Trainer: Gheorghe Hagi.

Goals: 0-1 Denis Dragus (23), 0-2 Ianis Hagi (82 penalty).

19.07.2018; Stadionul Central, Ovidiu; Referee: Alexandr Aliyev (Kazakhstan); Attendance: 2,130

FC Viitorul Constanța – Racing FC Union Luxembourg 0-0

Viitorul Constanța: Valentin Cojocaru, Sebastian Mladen, Tudor Baluta, Bradley de Nooijer, Vlad Achim, Bogdan Tîru, Lyes Houri (83.Alexi Pitu), Ianis Hagi (56.Mihai Vodut), Ionut Vîna, Denis Dragus (55.Alexandru Matan), Mailson Lima. Trainer: Gheorghe Hagi.

Union Luxembourg: Romain Ruffier, Thomas Birk, Henrique, Pape Ibra M'Boup (80.Benssad Sulejmani), Julien Humbert, Kevin Nakache, Tarek Nouidra, Florik Shala (75.Sebastian Szimayer), Daniël Alves da Mota, Edis Osmanovic, Jonathan Hennetier. Trainer: Patrick Grettnich.

[FC Viitorul Constanța won 2-0 on aggregate]

12.07.2018; Gundadalur, Tórshavn; Referee: Aleksandrs Anufrijevs (Latvia); Attendance: 611

B36 Tórshavn – OFK Titograd Podgorica 0-0

B36 Tórshavn: Rói Hentze, Odmar Færø, Alex Mellemgaard, Bjarni Petersen, Erlendur Magnusson (69.Benjamin Heinesen), Ragnar Samuelsen (83.Gilli Samuelsen), Eli Nielsen, Meinhard Olsen, Magnus Holm Jacobsen (76.Hugin Samuelsen), Kaimar Saag, Lukasz Cieslewicz. Trainer: Jákup á Borg.

OFK Titograd: Damir Ljuljanovic, Milos B.Radulovic, Ivan Novovic, Branko Ojdanic, Marko Roganovic, Jovan Nikolic, Vasko Kalezic, Marko Milickovic, Ivica Jovanovic (71.Mirko Raicevic), Pjeter Ljuljdjuraj, Zoran Petrovic (61.Vojin Pavlovic). Trainer: Aleksandar Miljenovic.

19.07.2018; Stadion Pod Goricom, Podgorica; Referee: Omar Pashayev (Azerbaijan); Attendance: 2,050

OFK Titograd Podgorica – B36 Tórshavn 1-2(1-0)

OFK Titograd: Damir Ljuljanovic, Milos B.Radulovic, Ivan Novovic, Branko Ojdanic (81.Mirko Raicevic), Marko Roganovic, Jovan Nikolic, Vasko Kalezic, Marko Milickovic (73.Ognjen Gasevic), Ivica Jovanovic, Pjeter Ljuljdjuraj, Zoran Petrovic (32.Vojin Pavlovic). Trainer: Aleksandar Miljenovic.

B36 Tórshavn: Rói Hentze, Odmar Færø, Alex Mellemgaard, Bjarni Petersen, Erlendur Magnusson, Eli Nielsen, Meinhard Olsen, Benjamin Heinesen (71.Hugin Samuelsen), Magnus Holm Jacobsen (80.Robert Hedin Brockie), Kaimar Saag (87.Gilli Samuelsen), Lukasz Cieslewicz. Trainer: Jákup á Borg.

Goals: 1-0 Zoran Petrovic (4), 1-1 Benjamin Heinesen (51), 1-2 Milos B. Radulovic (83 own goal).

[B36 Tórshavn won 2-1 on aggregate]

12.07.2018; Stadion „Ernest Pohl", Zabrze; Referee: Filip Glova (Slovakia); Attendance: 19,528

KS Górnik Zabrze – FC Zaria Bălți 1-0(0-0)

Górnik Zabrze: Tomasz Loska, Dani Suárez, Adrian Gryszkiewicz, Przemyslaw Wisniewski, Szymon Matuszek, Angulo, Adam Wolniewicz, Adam Ryczkowski (46.Marcin Urynowicz), Maciej Ambrosiewicz (81.Daniel Liszka), Szymon Zurkowski [*sent off 90+2*], Jesús Jiménez (75.Rafal Wolsztynski). Trainer: Marcin Brosz.

Zaria Bălți: Vladimir Livsit, Oleg Ermak, Ion Burlacu, Felipe Alves (70.Rodrigo Bostan), Lucas Silva, Daniel Dumbravanu, Rúben Gómez, Serghei Alexeev, Conrado (81.Guilherme), Vadim Gulceac, Jean Patric (61.Georgi Ovsyannikov). Trainer: Vlad Goian.

Goal: 1-0 Angulo (87).

19.07.2018; Stadionul Zimbru, Chişinău; Referee: Rahim Hasanov (Azerbaijan); Attendance: 1,300

FC Zaria Bălți – KS Górnik Zabrze 1-1(1-0)

Zaria Bălți: Vladimir Livsit, Oleg Ermak, Ion Burlacu, Lucas Silva, Daniel Dumbravanu, Rúben Gómez, Rodrigo Bostan (73.Cristian Dros), Georgi Ovsyannikov, Guilherme, Conrado, Vadim Gulceac (87.Serghei Alexeev). Trainer: Vlad Goian.

Górnik Zabrze: Tomasz Loska, Dani Suárez, Wiktor Biedrzycki (73.Michal Koj), Adrian Gryszkiewicz, Przemyslaw Wisniewski, Szymon Matuszek, Angulo, Adam Wolniewicz, Adam Ryczkowski (54.Daniel Smuga), Maciej Ambrosiewicz (59.Daniel Liszka), Jesús Jiménez. Trainer: Marcin Brosz.

Goals: 1-0 Guilherme (7), 1-1 Daniel Smuga (85).

[KS Górnik Zabrze won 2-1 on aggregate]

12.07.2018; Estadi Comunal, Andorra la Vella; Referee: Iwan Arwel Griffith (Wales); Attendance: 657

UE Engordany – FC Kairat Almaty 0-3(0-2)

UE Engordany: Jesús Coca, Christian Cellay, Walter Wagner (74.Luigi San Nicolas), Miguel Ruiz, Rafael Brito, Mateo Firpo, Mario Spano, Christopher Pousa, Larsen Touré (90.Rodrigo Guida), Sebastián Gómez, Fabio Serra (62.Brian Figliamonte). Trainer: José Prades.

FC Kairat: Vladimir Plotnikov, Sheldon Bateau, Gafurzhan Suyumbaev, Aleksandr Sokolenko, Ákos Elek, Isael (64.Vyacheslav Shvyrev), Bauyrzhan Islamkhan (73.Georgiy Zhukov), Nuraly Alip, Andrey Arshavin, Juan Felipe Alves, Aderinsola Eseola (58.Márton Eppel). Trainer: Carlos Alós Ferrer.

Goals: 0-1 Walter Wagner (5 own goal), 0-2 Bauyrzhan Islamkhan (25 penalty), 0-3 Márton Eppel (90).

19.07.2018; Ortaliq Stadion, Almaty; Referee: Jovan Kaluđerović (Montenegro); Attendance: 10,500

FC Kairat Almaty – UE Engordany 7-1(4-0)

FC Kairat: Vladimir Plotnikov, Gafurzhan Suyumbaev, Aibol Abiken, Ákos Elek (46.Sheldon Bateau), Magomed Paragulgov, Islambek Kuat, Bauyrzhan Islamkhan (57.Georgiy Zhukov), Yan Vorogovskiy, Márton Eppel, Juan Felipe Alves, Aderinsola Eseola (46.Vyacheslav Shvyrev). Trainer: Carlos Alós Ferrer.

UE Engordany: Jesús Coca, Christian Cellay, Walter Wagner, Miguel Ruiz, Rafael Brito (57.Mateo Firpo), Mario Spano, Christopher Pousa (71.Morgan Lafont), Hamza Bouharma, Luigi San Nicolas (62.Fábio Serra), Sebastián Gómez, Brian Figliamonte. Trainer: José Prades.

Goals: 1-0, 2-0 Márton Eppel (4, 11), 3-0 Aderinsola Eseola (42), 4-0 Márton Eppel (44), 5-0 Bauyrzhan Islamkhan (53), 5-1 Morgan Lafont (72), 6-1 Márton Eppel (75), 7-1 Yan Vorogovskiy (87).

[FC Kairat Almaty won 10-1 on aggregate]

12.07.2018; Hásteinsvöllur, Vestmannaeyjar; Referee: Nick Walsh (Scotland); Attendance: 673

ÍBV Vestmannaeyjar – Sarpsborg 08 FF 0-4(0-0)

ÍBV Vestmannaeyjar: Halldór Geirsson, Yvan Erichot (15.Sigurdur Arnar Magnússon), David Atkinson, Sindri Snær Magnússon, Kaj Leo í Bartalsstovu, Atli Arnarson (63.Jonathan Franks), Priestley Griffiths, Dagur Hilmarsson, Felix Örn Fridriksson, Gunnar Thorvaldsson (76.Ágúst Björnsson), Shahab Zahedi Tabar. Trainer: Kristján Gudmundsson.

Sarpsborg 08: Aslak Falch, Amin Askar, Joackim Jørgensen, Joachim Thomassen, Joonas Tamm, Matti Lund Nielsen (85.Muhammed Usman), Ole Halvorsen, Kristoffer Zachariassen, Tobias Heintz (76.Kristoffer Larsen), Patrick Mortensen, Rashad Muhammed (71.Harmeet Singh). Trainer: Geir Bakke.

Goals: 0-1 Rashad Muhammed (59), 0-2 Patrick Mortensen (66), 0-3 Ole Halvorsen (90+1), 0-4 Amin Askar (90+4).

19.07.2018; Sarpsborg Stadion, Sarpsborg; Referee: Genc Nuza (Kosovo); Attendance: 3,552

Sarpsborg 08 FF – ÍBV Vestmannaeyjar 2-0(1-0)

Sarpsborg 08: Aslak Falch, Joackim Jørgensen, Joachim Thomassen, Bjørn Utvik, Jon-Helge Tveita, Kristoffer Zachariassen (70.Ole Halvorsen), Tobias Heintz, Muhammed Usman, Patrick Mortensen (62.Rashad Muhammed), Mikkel Agger, Kristoffer Larsen (67.Harmeet Singh). Trainer: Geir Bakke.

ÍBV Vestmannaeyjar: Halldór Geirsson, David Atkinson, Sindri Snær Magnússon, Kaj Leo í Bartalsstovu (70.Ágúst Björnsson), Alfred Már Hjaltalín, Atli Arnarson (60.Jonathan Franks), Priestley Griffiths (80.Róbert Eysteinsson), Dagur Hilmarsson, Felix Örn Fridriksson, Sigurdur Arnar Magnússon, Shahab Zahedi Tabar. Trainer: Kristján Gudmundsson.

Goals: 1-0, 2-0 Mikkel Agger (13, 82).

[Sarpsborg 08 FF won 6-0 on aggregate]

12.07.2018; Tallaght Stadium, Dublin; Referee: Alexander Harkam (Austria); Attendance: 2,817

Shamrock Rovers FC – AIK Stockholm 0-1(0-0)

Shamrock Rovers: Gavin Bazunu, Joey O'Brien (83.Roberto Lopes), Sean Kavanagh, Lee Grace, Sam Bone, Ronan Finn, Greg Bolger (78.Aaron Bolger), Ethan Boyle, Dylan Watts, Daniel Carr (75.Aaron Green), Joel Coustrain. Trainer: Stephen Bradley.

AIK Stockholm: Oscar Linnér, Per Karlsson, Haukur Hauksson, Daniel Sundgren, Alexander Milosevic, Robin Jansson, Tarik Elyounoussi (90+2.Stefan Silva), Ahmed Yasin (79.Denni Avdic), Enoch Adu, Kristoffer Olsson, Henok Goitom. Trainer: Rikard Norling.

Goal: 0-1 Daniel Sundgren (74).

19.07.2018; Friends Arena, Stockholm; Referee: Nicolas Laforge (Belgium); Attendance: 8,115

AIK Stockholm – Shamrock Rovers FC 1-1(0-1,0-1)

AIK Stockholm: Oscar Linnér, Per Karlsson, Daniel Sundgren, Alexander Milosevic, Rasmus Lindkvist (83.Nicolás Stefanelli), Robin Jansson, Tarik Elyounoussi (109.Haukur Hauksson), Ahmed Yasin, Enoch Adu, Denni Avdic (63.Kristoffer Olsson), Stefan Silva (63.Henok Goitom). Trainer: Rikard Norling.

Shamrock Rovers: Gavin Bazunu, Joey O'Brien, Sean Kavanagh, Roberto Lopes, Lee Grace, Sam Bone (84.Greg Bolger), Ronan Finn, Ethan Boyle, Dylan Watts (93.David McAllister), Daniel Carr (67.Aaron Bolger), Joel Coustrain (68.Aaron Green). Trainer: Stephen Bradley.

Goals: 0-1 Daniel Carr (19), 1-1 Nicolás Stefanelli (94).

[AIK Stockholm won 2-1 on aggregate]

12.07.2018; Stadion Kraj Bistrice, Nikšić; Referee: Stuart Steven Attwell (England); Attendance: 3,150

FK Rudar Pljevlja – FK Partizan Beograd 0-3(0-1)

Rudar Pljevlja: Vuk Radovic, Radule Zivkovic, Filip Mitrovic, Alphonse Soppo, Armin Bosnjak, Nemanja Sekulic, Milija Golubovic (74.Aleksandar Macanovic), Perisa Pesukic, Milos Zecevic, Radomir Djalovic (74.Velizar Janketic), Edvin Kuc (60.Marko Vukovic). Trainer: Vuko Bogavac.

Partizan Beograd: Vladimir Stojkovic, Marc Valiente (77.Nemanja Miletic (I)), Sasa Zdjelar, Zlatan Sehovic, Svetozar Markovic, Gabriel Enache, Marko Jevtovic (71.Marko Jankovic), Seydouba Soumah, Danilo Pantic, Nemanja Nikolic (64.Nebojsa Kosovic), Ricardo Gomes. Trainer: Miroslav Djukic.

Goals: 0-1 Marko Jevtovic (44 penalty), 0-2 Seydouba Soumah (50), 0-3 Ricardo Gomes (57).

19.07.2018; Stadion Partizan, Beograd; Referee: Daniele Doveri (Italy); Attendance: 5,869

FK Partizan Beograd – FK Rudar Pljevlja 3-0(2-0)

Partizan Beograd: Filip Kljajic, Marc Valiente (57.Svetozar Markovic), Nemanja Miletic (I), Sasa Zdjelar, Gabriel Enache, Seydouba Soumah (57.Zoran Tosic), Danilo Pantic, Nemanja Miletic (II), Ognjen Ozegovic (63.Ricardo Gomes), Djordje Ivanovic, Armin Djerlek. Trainer: Miroslav Djukic.

Rudar Pljevlja: Vuk Radovic, Zeljko Tomasevic (61.Radule Zivkovic), Filip Mitrovic, Alphonse Soppo, Armin Bosnjak, Aleksandar Macanovic (46.Velizar Janketic), Dejan Kotorac (68.Edvin Kuc), Nemanja Sekulic, Milija Golubovic, Radomir Djalovic, Marko Vukovic. Trainer: Vuko Bogavac.

Goals: 1-0 Danilo Pantic (11), 2-0 Ognjen Ozegovic (44), 3-0 Ricardo Gomes (83).

[FK Partizan Beograd won 6-0 on aggregate]

12.07.2018; Stadion Pod Goricom, Podgorica; Referee: Mete Kalkavan (Turkey); Attendance: 2,000

FK Buducnost Podgorica – AS Trenčín 0-2(0-2)

Buducnost Podgorica: Milan Mijatovic, Vladan Adzic, Luka Mirkovic, Ilija Tucevic, Stefan Milic, Miljan Vlaisavljevic, Milos Mijic (87.Dusan Bakic), Petar Vukcevic (48.Bojan Roganovic), Milan Djurisic, Igor Ivanovic, Balsa Sekulic (79.Mihailo Perovic). Trainer: Zoran Govedarica.

AS Trenčín: Igor Semrinec, Jamie Lawrence, Martin Sulek, Keston Julien, Reuben Yem, Ashraf El Mahdioui, Abdul Zubairu, Joey Sleegers, Antonio Mance (59.Emeka Umeh), Hamza Catakovic, Philip Azango (84.Philippe van Arnhem). Trainer: Ricardo Moniz.

Goals: 0-1 Hamza Catakovic (27), 0-2 Antonio Mance (30).

19.07.2018; Futbalový stadión Spartak Myjava, Myjava; Referee: Sergey Lapochkin (Russia); Attendance: 1,520

AS Trenčín – FK Buducnost Podgorica 1-1(0-0)

AS Trenčín: Igor Semrinec, Jamie Lawrence, Martin Sulek, Keston Julien, Reuben Yem, Ashraf El Mahdioui, Abdul Zubairu, Joey Sleegers, Antonio Mance (90+3.Emeka Umeh), Hamza Catakovic, Philip Azango. Trainer: Ricardo Moniz.

Buducnost Podgorica: Milan Mijatovic, Vladan Adzic, Luka Mirkovic, Ilija Tucevic (77.Dusan Bakic), Dominique Correa, Bojan Roganovic, Stefan Milic, Miljan Vlaisavljevic, Milos Mijic, Balsa Boricic (73.Balsa Sekulic), Igor Ivanovic (89.Mihailo Perovic). Trainer: Zoran Govedarica.

Goals: 1-0 Antonio Mance (70), 1-1 Mihailo Perovic (90).

[AS Trenčín won 3-1 on aggregate]

12.07.2018; Ibrox Stadium, Glasgow; Referee: Christian Dingert (Germany); Attendance: 49,309

Rangers FC Glasgow – KF Shkupi 2-0(1-0)

Rangers: Allan McGregor, James Tavernier, Connor Goldson, Jon Flanagan, Ross McCrorie, Nikola Katic, Jamie Murphy, Scott Arfield (67.Oviemuno Ejaria), Josh Windass (79.Glenn Middleton), Candeias (56.Ryan Jack), Alfredo Morelos. Trainer: Steven Gerrard.

KF Shkupi: Suat Zendeli, Muharem Bajrami (46.Amir Bilali), Blagojce Ljamcevski (61.Bunjamin Shabani), Toni Tipuric, Muarem Muarem, Ermadin Adem, Stephan Vujcic, Ron Broja, Basilio Nchama (90+2.Besart Krivanjeva), Blaze Ilijoski, Kristijan Stojkovski. Trainer: Zekirija Ramadani.

Goals: 1-0 Jamie Murphy (23), 2-0 James Tavernier (90+2 penalty).

17.07.2018; Telekom Arena, Skopje; Referee: Halil Umut Meler (Turkey); Attendance: 4,750

KF Shkupi – Rangers FC Glasgow 0-0

KF Shkupi: Suat Zendeli, Toni Tipuric, Amir Bilali, Besart Krivanjeva, Muarem Muarem (90+2.Fatih Ismaili), Ermadin Adem, Stephan Vujcic (76.Suhejlj Muharem), Ron Broja, Basilio Nchama (37.Bunjamin Shabani), Blaze Ilijoski, Kristijan Stojkovski. Trainer: Zekirija Ramadani.

Rangers: Allan McGregor, James Tavernier, Connor Goldson, Jon Flanagan, Ross McCrorie, Nikola Katic, Jamie Murphy (90+1.Andrew Halliday), Ryan Jack, Josh Windass (64.Glenn Middleton), Candeias (72.Oviemuno Ejaria), Alfredo Morelos. Trainer: Steven Gerrard.

[Rangers FC Glasgow won 2-0 on aggregate]

12.07.2018; Stadion Karađorđe, Novi Sad; Referee: Aleksei Matyunin (Russia); Attendance: 976

FK Spartak Subotica – Coleraine FC 1-1(0-1)

Spartak Subotica: Nikola Peric, Stefan Milosevic (75.Vladimir Torbica), Andrija Vukcevic, Noboru Shimura, Dejan Kerkez, Nemanja Calasan, Mile Savkovic, Bojan Cecaric (46.Ognjen Djuricin), Nemanja Glavcic, Milan Marcic, Dejan Djenic (35.Samuel Afum). Trainer: Vladimir Gacinovic.

Coleraine FC: Christopher Johns, Aaron Traynor, Gareth McConaghie, Adam Mullan, Stephen O'Donnell, Stephen Lowry, Darren McCauley (81.Ciaron Harkin), Aaron Burns, Ian Parkhill, Bradley Lyons (90+2.Matthew Kirk), Eoin Bradley (65.Jamie McGonigle). Trainer: Oran Kearney.

Goals: 0-1 Darren McCauley (23), 1-1 Mile Savkovic (90+4 penalty).

19.07.2018; The Showgrounds, Coleraine; Referee: Trustin Farrugia Cann (Malta); Attendance: 1,602

Coleraine FC – FK Spartak Subotica 0-2(0-1)

Coleraine FC: Christopher Johns, Aaron Traynor, Gareth McConaghie, Adam Mullan (85.James McLaughlin), Stephen O'Donnell, Stephen Lowry, Darren McCauley, Aaron Burns (60.Jamie McGonigle), Ian Parkhill (60.Ciaron Harkin), Bradley Lyons, Eoin Bradley. Trainer: Oran Kearney.

Spartak Subotica: Nikola Peric, Andrija Vukcevic, Branimir Jocic, Noboru Shimura (66.Vladimir Torbica), Dejan Kerkez, Nemanja Calasan, Mile Savkovic, Nemanja Glavcic (75.Milan Marcic), David Dundjerski, Samuel Afum (83.Bojan Cecaric), Ognjen Djuricin. Trainer: Vladimir Gacinovic.

Goals: 0-1 Mile Savkovic (33), 0-2 Bojan Cecaric (90+2).

[FK Spartak Subotica won 3-1 on aggregate]

12.07.2018; Solitude Stadium, Belfast; Referee: Sándor Andó-Szabó (Hungary); Attendance: 1,170

Cliftonville FC – FC Nordsjælland Farum 0-1(0-1)

Cliftonville FC: Brian Neeson, Jamie McGovern (62.Ryan Catney), Garry Breen, Liam Bagnall, Jamie Harney, Levi Ives, Christopher Curran, Conor McMenamin (74.Stephen Garrett), Rory Donnelly, Ryan Curran, Joe Gormley. Trainer: Barry Gray.

FC Nordsjælland: Nicolai Larsen, Karlo Bartolec, Mads Pedersen, Andreas Skovgaard, Mathias Jensen, Victor Nelsson, Andreas Skov Olsen (57.Matias Rasmussen), Mikkel Damsgaard, Mikkel Rygaard Jensen (87.Nicklas Strunck Jakobsen), Godsway Donyoh (71.Martin Frese), Benjamin Hansen. Trainer: Kasper Hjulmand.

Goal: 0-1 Andreas Skov Olsen (19).

19.07.2018; Right to Dream Park, Farum; Referee: Eitan Shemeulevitch (Israel); Attendance: 1,592

FC Nordsjælland Farum – Cliftonville FC 2-1(0-1)

FC Nordsjælland: Nicolai Larsen, Mads Aaquist (66.Andreas Skov Olsen), Viktor Tranberg (46.Mikkel Rygaard Jensen), Clinton Antwi, Ulrik Jenssen, Nicklas Strunck Jakobsen, Victor Nelsson, Ibrahim Sadiq (46.Godsway Donyoh), Jacob Christensen, Mikkel Damsgaard, Nikolai Baden Frederiksen. Trainer: Kasper Hjulmand.

Cliftonville FC: Brian Neeson, Jamie McGovern, Garry Breen, Liam Bagnall, Jamie Harney, Levi Ives, Christopher Curran (84.Stephen Garrett), Rory Donnelly, Ryan Curran (64.Conor McDonald), Joe Gormley, Jay Donnelly (73.Conor McMenamin). Trainer: Barry Gray.

Goals: 0-1 Joe Gormley (6 penalty), 1-1 Godsway Donyoh (58), 2-1 Jamie Harney (83 own goal).

[FC Nordsjælland Farum won 3-1 on aggregate]

12.07.2018; Stadion INEA, Poznań; Referee: Yigal Frid (Israel); Attendance: *played behind closed doors*

KKS Lech Poznań – FC Gandzasar Kapan 2-0(2-0)

Lech Poznań: Jasmin Buric, Thomas Rogne, Rafal Janicki, Volodymyr Kostevych, Vernon, Tomasz Cywka, Mihai Radut (58.Pedro Tiba), Maciej Makuszewski, Maciej Gajos, Darko Jevtic (69.Niklas Bärkroth), Christian Gytkjær (86.Pawel Tomczyk). Trainer: Ivan Djurdjevic.

Gandzasar Kapan: Gevorg Kasparov, Ara Khachatryan (82.Vardan Pogosyan), Vukasin Tomic, Hayk Ishkhanyan, Aleksandr Sverchinski, Gegham Harutyunyan, Christian Alex Júnior, Artur Yuspashyan (59.Gevorg Ohanyan), Wbeymar Angulo, Lubambo Musonda, Gevorg Nranyan (90+4.Davit Minasyan). Trainer: Ashot Barseghyan.

Goals: 1-0, 2-0 Christian Gytkjær (10, 15 penalty).

19.07.2018; „Vazgen Sargsyan" Hanrapetakan Stadium, Yerevan; Referee: Mohammed Al-Hakim (Sweden); Attendance: 1,645

FC Gandzasar Kapan – KKS Lech Poznań 2-1(0-0)

Gandzasar Kapan: Grigor Meliksetyan, Ara Khachatryan, Vukasin Tomic, Hayk Ishkhanyan, Aleksandr Sverchinski, Gegham Harutyunyan, Christian Alex Júnior, Artur Yuspashyan (64.Gevorg Ohanyan), Wbeymar Angulo, Lubambo Musonda, Gevorg Nranyan (83.Vardan Pogosyan). Trainer: Ashot Barseghyan.

Lech Poznań: Matús Putnocky, Nikola Vujadinovic, Piotr Tomasik, Rafal Janicki, Vernon, Tomasz Cywka, Lukasz Tralka, Maciej Makuszewski, Maciej Gajos (60.Mihai Radut), Pedro Tiba (60.Darko Jevtic), Christian Gytkjær. Trainer: Ivan Djurdjevic.

Goals: 1-0 Lubambo Musonda (50), 2-0 Gegham Harutyunyan (67), 2-1 Lukasz Tralka (90+5).

[KKS Lech Poznań won 3-2 on aggregate]

12.07.2018; Easter Road Stadium, Edinburgh; Referee: Manfredas Lukjančukas (Lithuania); Attendance: 12,501

Hibernian FC Edinburgh – NSÍ Runavík 6-1(4-0)

Hibernian FC: Ádám Bogdán, Steven Whittaker, Lewis Stevenson, Paul Hanlon, Darren McGregor (60.Danny Swanson), Efe Ambrose, Vykintas Slivka, Stephen Mallan, Martin Boyle, Florian Kamberi (51.Simon Murray), Oliver Shaw (82.Marvin Bartley). Trainer: Neil Lennon.

NSÍ Runavík: Tordhur Thomsen, Einar Tróndargjógv Hansen [*sent off 33*], Pól Justinussen, Jóhan Davidsen (46.Per Langgaard), Jens Joensen, Fródi Benjaminsen, Bárdur Jögvansson-Hansen, Árni Frederiksberg (46.Jann Benjaminsen), Betuel Hansen (40.Magnus Olsen), Petur Knudsen, Klæmint Andrasson Olsen. Trainer: Sámal Hentze.

Goals: 1-0, 2-0 Florian Kamberi (3 penalty, 21), 3-0 Oliver Shaw (29), 4-0 Stephen Mallan (43), 5-0 Florian Kamberi (48), 5-1 Petur Knudsen (53), 6-1 Stephen Mallan (84).

19.07.2018; Svangaskard, Toftir; Referee: Luis Miguel do Nascimento Teixeira (Portugal); Attendance: 587

NSÍ Runavík – Hibernian FC Edinburgh 4-6(3-3)

NSÍ Runavík: Eli Joensen, Pól Justinussen, Jens Joensen, Per Langgaard, Pætur Hentze, Fródi Benjaminsen, Bárdur Jögvansson-Hansen, Petur Knudsen, Jann Benjaminsen (88.Mórits Heini Mortensen), Magnus Olsen (71.Betuel Hansen), Klæmint Andrasson Olsen (74.Jann Mortensen). Trainer: Sámal Hentze.

Hibernian FC: Ádám Bogdán, Steven Whittaker (77.Vykintas Slivka), Lewis Stevenson, Efe Ambrose, David Gray, Ryan Porteous, Marvin Bartley (88.James Gullan), John McGinn, Stephen Mallan, Florian Kamberi, Oliver Shaw (78.Danny Swanson). Trainer: Neil Lennon.

Goals: 1-0 Efe Ambrose (1 own goal), 2-0 Klæmint Andrasson Olsen (6), 2-1 John McGinn (10), 2-2 Lewis Stevenson (16), 3-2 Klæmint Andrasson Olsen (35), 3-3 David Gray (45+1), 3-4 Efe Ambrose (50), 4-4 Klæmint Andrasson Olsen (57), 4-5, 4-6 Stephen Mallan (70, 77).

[Hibernian FC Edinburgh won 12-5 on aggregate]

12.07.2018; MOL Aréna, Dunajská Streda; Referee: Irfan Peljto (Bosnia and Herzegovina); Attendance: 8,759

FK DAC Dunajská Streda – FC Dinamo Tbilisi 1-1(1-1)

DAC Dunajská Streda: Patrik Macej, Lubomír Satka, Milan Simcák (46.Zsolt Kalmár), Timotej Záhumensky, Marin Ljubicic, Erik Pacinda (79.Marko Divkovic), Tomás Huk, Kristián Kostrna, Krisztopher Vida (67.Maksym Tretyakov), Christián Herc, Vakoun Issouf Bayo. Trainer: Marco Rossi.

Dinamo Tbilisi: Demetre Buliskeria, Gudzha Rukhaia, Luka Lochoshvili, Davit Kobouri, Nika Ninua, Levan Kharabadze, Dmitriy Ivanisenya, Akaki Shulaia (80.Bakar Kardava), Otari Kiteishvili, George Ivanishvili (46.Mikheil Ergemlidze), Budu Zivzivadze (73.Mate Vatsadze). Trainer: Kakhaber Katcharava.

Goals: 0-1 Budu Zivzivadze (15), 1-1 Vakoun Issouf Bayo (30).

19.07.2018; „Boris Paichadze" Dinamo Arena, Tbilisi; Referee: Dimitar Meckarovski (North Macedonia); Attendance: 6,111

FC Dinamo Tbilisi – FK DAC Dunajská Streda 1-2(1-0)

Dinamo Tbilisi: Demetre Buliskeria, Gudzha Rukhaia, Luka Lochoshvili, Davit Kobouri, Nika Ninua, Levan Kharabadze, Dmitriy Ivanisenya, Akaki Shulaia, Otari Kiteishvili, Budu Zivzivadze (74.Mate Vatsadze), Mikheil Ergemlidze (88.George Ivanishvili). Trainer: Kakhaber Katcharava.

DAC Dunajská Streda: Patrik Macej, Éric Davis (57.Zsolt Kalmár), Lubomír Satka, Timotej Záhumensky, Marin Ljubicic (72.Máté Vida), Erik Pacinda, Tomás Huk, Kristián Kostrna, Krisztopher Vida (80.Maksym Tretyakov), Christián Herc, Vakoun Issouf Bayo. Trainers: Marco Rossi & Peter Hyballa.

Goals: 1-0 Budu Zivzivadze (41), 1-1, 1-2 Vakoun Issouf Bayo (86, 90+4).

[FK DAC Dunajská Streda won 3-2 on aggregate]

12.07.2018; Stadion Čair, Niš; Referee: Jason Lee Barcelo (Gibraltar); Attendance: 8,500

FK Radnički Niš – Gzira United FC 4-0(1-0)

Radnički Niš: Mladen Zivkovic, Aleksandar Todorovski, Radovan Pankov, Djordje Crnomarkovic, Aleksandar Stanisavljevic (69.Sasa Stojanovic), Petar Grbic (83.Aleksandar Jovanovic (I)), Dusan Micic, Nikola Stankovic, Ryota Noma, Sladan Nikodijevic (46.Marko Mrkic), Nermin Haskic. Trainer: Nenad Lalatovic.

Gzira United: Justin Haber, Clifford Baldacchino, Rodolfo Soares, Thomas Veronese, Destin Prince Mambouana (81.Sacha Borg), Roderick Briffa (79.Luca Brincat), Édison Bilbao Zárate, Juan Corbalan, Zachary Scerri (63.Nikolai Muscat), Amadou Samb, Jorginho. Trainer: Darren Abdilla.

Goals: 1-0 Radovan Pankov (14), 2-0 Nermin Haskic (53), 3-0 Marko Mrkic (55), 4-0 Nermin Haskic (85).

19.07.2018; MFA Centenary Stadium, Ta'Qali; Referee: Suren Baliyan (Armenia); Attendance: 509

Gzira United FC – FK Radnički Niš 0-1(0-1)

Gzira United: Anthony Curmi, Clifford Baldacchino, Rodolfo Soares, Sacha Borg, Thomas Veronese, Andrew Cohen (65.Emmanuel Okoye), Roderick Briffa, Édison Bilbao Zárate, Juan Corbalan (82.Christian Sammut), Zachary Scerri, Jorginho (75.Luca Brincat). Trainer: Darren Abdilla.

Radnički Niš: Mladen Zivkovic, Aleksandar Todorovski, Radovan Pankov, Djordje Crnomarkovic (35.Taras Bondarenko), Aleksandar Stanisavljevic, Petar Grbic (46.Aleksa Jovanovic (II)), Dusan Micic, Nikola Stankovic, Ryota Noma, Nermin Haskic (63.Sladan Nikodijevic), Marko Mrkic. Trainer: Nenad Lalatovic.

Goal: 0-1 Radovan Pankov (7).

[FK Radnički Niš won 5-0 on aggregate]

12.07.2018; Samsung völlurinn, Gardabær; Referee: Radek Příhoda (Czech Republic); Attendance: 980

Stjarnan Garðabær – JK Nõmme Kalju 3-0(1-0)

Stjarnan Garðabær: Haraldur Björnsson, Baldur Sigurdsson, Brynjar Gudjónsson, Daníel Laxdal, Thorsteinn Már Ragnarsson (58.Jóhann Laxdal), Heidar Ægisson, Alex Thór Hauksson (74.Sölvi Fodilsson), Gudmundur Hafsteinsson (56.Eyjólfur Hédinsson), Gunjón Baldvinsson, Thórarinn Valdimarsson, Hilmar Árni Halldórsson. Trainer: Rúnar Sigmundsson.

Nõmme Kalju: Vitali Teles, Maximiliano Uggè, Trevor Elhi, William Gustavo, Andriy Markovych, Igor Subbotin, Réginald Mbu-Alidor, Aleksandr Volkov (70.Kasper Paur), Marko Brtan, Liliu, Rimo Hunt (46.Deniss Tjapkin). Trainer: Sergey Frantsev.

Goals: 1-0 Hilmar Árni Halldórsson (19 penalty), 2-0 Baldur Sigurdsson (49), 3-0 Gunjón Baldvinsson (70).

19.07.2018; Kadriorg staadion, Tallinn; Referee: Giorgi Kruashvili (Georgia); Attendance: 1,455

JK Nõmme Kalju – Stjarnan Garðabær 1-0(0-0)

Nõmme Kalju: Pavel Londak, Maximiliano Uggè, Trevor Elhi, Deniss Tjapkin (80.Alex Tamm), William Gustavo, Andriy Markovych, Igor Subbotin, Réginald Mbu-Alidor, Aleksandr Volkov (24.Kasper Paur), Liliu (71.Marko Brtan), Rimo Hunt. Trainer: Sergey Frantsev.

Stjarnan Garðabær: Haraldur Björnsson, Baldur Sigurdsson, Brynjar Gudjónsson, Daníel Laxdal, Eyjólfur Hédinsson (58.Gudmundur Hafsteinsson), Thorsteinn Már Ragnarsson (60.Jóhann Laxdal), Heidar Ægisson, Alex Thór Hauksson, Gunjón Baldvinsson, Thórarinn Valdimarsson, Hilmar Árni Halldórsson (81.Jósef Kristinn Jósefsson). Trainer: Rúnar Sigmundsson.

Goal: 1-0 Alex Tamm (88).

[Stjarnan Garðabær won 3-1 on aggregate]

SECOND QUALIFYING ROUND

CHAMPIONS PATH

Bye: Cork City FC.

26.07.2018; Slokas Stadionā, Jūrmala; Referee: Vitaliy Meshkov (Russia); Attendance: 648

FK Spartaks Jūrmala – SP La Fiorita 6-0(3-0)

Spartaks Jūrmala: Jevgenijs Nerugals, Gints Freimanis, Aleksandar Kosoric, Mārcis Oss, Ingus Slampe, Artemiy Maleev (71.Ingars Stuglis), Oleg Dmitriev, Evgeni Kobzar, Denis Davydov (17.Ariagner Smith), Diego Aguirre (53.Ricards Korzāns), Vitor Faísca. Trainer: Aleksandr Grishin.

SP La Fiorita: Gianluca Vivan, Samuele Olivi, Roberto Di Maio, Marco Gasperoni, Riccardo Mezzadri (68.Alessandro D'Addario), Damiano Tommasi (70.Simone Loiodice), Luca Righini, Adolfo José Hirsch, Armando Amati, Andy Selva (78.Fabrizio Castellazzi), Danilo Rinaldi. Trainer: Gianluca Procopio.

Goals: 1-0 Evgeni Kobzar (6), 2-0 Artemiy Maleev (20), 3-0 Evgeni Kobzar (26), 4-0 Ingus Slampe (64), 5-0 Ariagner Smith (66), 6-0 Ingars Stuglis (73).

02.08.2018; Stadio Tullo Morgagni, Forli (Italy); Referee: Alan Mario Sant (Malta); Attendance: 224

SP La Fiorita – FK Spartaks Jūrmala 0-3(0-2)

SP La Fiorita: Gianluca Vivan, Samuele Olivi, Roberto Di Maio, Marco Gasperoni, Riccardo Mezzadri, Damiano Tommasi (87.Alessandro Guidi), Luca Righini [*sent off 32*], Adolfo José Hirsch (54.Samuel Pancotti), Simone Loiodice (72.Tiziano Mottola), Armando Amati, Danilo Rinaldi. Trainer: Gianluca Procopio.

Spartaks Jūrmala: Mārcis Melecis, Gints Freimanis (51.Ioan Calin Revenco), Pāvels Mihadjuks, Mārcis Oss, Aleksejs Visnakovs (46.Kaspars Svārups), Ingars Stuglis, Oleg Dmitriev, Diego Aguirre, Ricards Korzāns, Vitor Faísca (61.Edgars Vardanjans), Ariagner Smith. Trainer: Aleksandr Grishin.

Goals: 0-1 Ariagner Smith (26), 0-2 Diego Aguirre (45+2), 0-3 Ariagner Smith (65).

[FK Spartaks Jūrmala won 9-0 on aggregate]

26.07.2018; „Ramaz Shengelia" Stadioni, Kutaisi; Referee: Artyom Kuchin (Kazakhstan); Attendance: 4,585

FC Torpedo Kutaisi – Víkingur Gøta 3-0(1-0)

Torpedo Kutaisi: Rion Kvaskhvadze, Mamuka Kobakhidze, Giorgi Kimadze, Levan Gegetchkori, Oleksandr Azatsky, Lazar Marin (46.Milos Lacny), Levan Kutalia, Marek Hlinka (70.Giorgi Kukhianidze), Arfang Daffé (59.Grigol Dolidze), Mate Tsintsadze, Tornike Kapanadze. Trainer: Kakhaber Chkhetiani.

Víkingur Gøta: Elias Rasmussen, Atli Gregersen, Hanus Jacobsen, Dennis Nieblas, Gunnar Vatnhamar, Elias Jóhannesson Lervig (90.Tonni Thomsen), Sølvi Vatnhamar, Karl Løkin, Hedin Hansen (59.Hans Jákup Lervig), Filip Djordjevic, Adeshina Lawal (80.Andreas Olsen). Trainer: Sigfrídur Clementsen.

Goals: 1-0 Tornike Kapanadze (27), 2-0 Giorgi Kimadze (73), 3-0 Levan Kutalia (84).

02.08.2018; Svangaskard, Toftir; Referee: Simon Lee Evans (Wales); Attendance: 300

Víkingur Gøta – FC Torpedo Kutaisi 0-4(0-2)

Víkingur Gøta: Elias Rasmussen, Atli Gregersen, Hanus Jacobsen, Gunnar Vatnhamar (70.Hedin Hansen), Elias Jóhannesson Lervig, Sølvi Vatnhamar (69.Adrian Cascaval), Karl Løkin, Filip Djordjevic, Hjalti Strømsten, Andreas Olsen (70.Dennis Nieblas), Adeshina Lawal. Trainer: Sigfrídur Clementsen.

Torpedo Kutaisi: Rion Kvaskhvadze, Davit Khurtsilava, Mamuka Kobakhidze, Giorgi Kimadze, Levan Gegetchkori, Oleksandr Azatsky, Grigol Dolidze (75.Anri Chichinadze), Marek Hlinka, Merab Gigauri (46.Giorgi Kukhianidze), Mate Tsintsadze, Milos Lacny (60.Tornike Kapanadze). Trainer: Kakhaber Chkhetiani.

Goals: 0-1 Milos Lacny (11), 0-2 Mamuka Kobakhidze (24), 0-3 Oleksandr Azatsky (59), 0-4 Tornike Kapanadze (81).

[FC Torpedo Kutaisi won 7-0 on aggregate]

26.07.2018; Stade „Jos Nusbaum", Dudelange; Referee: Leontios Trattou (Cyprus); Attendance: 737

F91 Dudelange – FC Drita Gjilan 2-1(0-1)

F91 Dudelange: Jonathan Joubert, Tom Schnell, Jerry Prempeh, Aniss El Hriti, Marc-André Kruska, Jordann Yéyé (54.Dominik Stolz), Edisson Jordanov, Clément Couturier (59.Mario Pokar), Danel Sinani, Nicolas Perez (74.Patrick Stumpf), David Turpel. Trainer: Dino Toppmöller.

Drita Gjilan: Edvan Bakaj, Liridon Leci, Viktor Kuka, Ardian Limani, Arbër Shala, Haxhi Neziraj (80.Eri Lamçja), Drilon Musaj (74.Përparim Livoreka), Bujar Shabani, Xhevdet Shabani, Betim Haxhimusa (89.Zgjim Mustafa), Endrit Krasniqi [*sent off 81*]. Trainer: Bekim Isufi.

Goals: 0-1 Xhevdet Shabani (45+2), 1-1 Nicolas Perez (66), 2-1 David Turpel (81 penalty).

02.08.2018; Stadiumi Olimpik „Adem Jashari", Mitrovica; Referee: Michael Tykgaard (Denmark); Attendance: 2,200

FC Drita Gjilan – F91 Dudelange 1-1(1-0)

Drita Gjilan: Edvan Bakaj, Liridon Leci, Fidan Gërbeshi, Ardian Limani, Arbër Shala (63.Albin Krasniqi), Haxhi Neziraj (76.Eri Lamçja), Drilon Musaj, Bujar Shabani, Xhevdet Shabani, Betim Haxhimusa, Përparim Livoreka (79.Zgjim Mustafa [*sent off 87*]). Trainer: Bekim Isufi.

F91 Dudelange: Jonathan Joubert, Tom Schnell, Jerry Prempeh, Aniss El Hriti (81.Kevin Malget), Marc-André Kruska, Dominik Stolz, Edisson Jordanov, Clément Couturier, Danel Sinani, David Turpel (90.Stélvio), Edis Agovic (34.Patrick Stumpf). Trainer: Dino Toppmöller.

Goals: 1-0 Ardian Limani (26), 1-1 Patrick Stumpf (46).

[F91 Dudelange won 3-2 on aggregate]

26.07.2018; Stadion pod Bijelim Brijegom, Mostar; Referee: Neil Doyle (Republic of Ireland); Attendance: 3,100

HŠK Zrinjski Mostar – FC Valletta 1-1(0-0)

Zrinjski Mostar: Ivan Brkic (45.Antonio Soldo), Pero Stojkic, Slobodan Jakovljevic, Ognjen Todorovic, Milos Filipovic (64.Marko Bencun), Hrvoje Barisic, Frane Cirjak, Marin Galic, Nemanja Bilbija, Amer Bekic (70.Milos Acimovic), Semir Pezer. Trainer: Ante Mise.

FC Valletta: Henry Bonello, Joseph Zerafa, Ryan Camilleri, Steve Borg (49.Juan Gill), Rowen Muscat, Raed Ibrahim Saleh Al Mukhaini, Kyrian Nwoko (65.Bogdan Gavrila), Santiago Malano, Miguel Alba (86.Jean Borg), Matteo Piciollo, Mario Fontanella. Trainer: Danilo Doncic.

Goals: 1-0 Nemanja Bilbija (51), 1-1 Mario Fontanella (90).

02.08.2018; MFA Centenary Stadium, Ta'Qali; Referee: Rade Obrenović (Slovenia); Attendance: 1,310

FC Valletta – HŠK Zrinjski Mostar 1-2(0-1)

FC Valletta: Henry Bonello, Joseph Zerafa, Ryan Camilleri, Steve Borg (81.Juan Gill), Rowen Muscat, Bogdan Gavrila (71.Kyrian Nwoko), Raed Ibrahim Saleh Al Mukhaini, Santiago Malano (88.Jean Borg), Miguel Alba, Matteo Piciollo, Mario Fontanella. Trainer: Danilo Doncic.

Zrinjski Mostar: Antonio Soldo, Pero Stojkic (46.Advan Kadusic), Slobodan Jakovljevic, Ognjen Todorovic, Milos Filipovic (90.Toni Jovic), Hrvoje Barisic, Edin Rustemovic, Marin Galic [*sent off 50*], Nemanja Bilbija, Marko Perisic (53.Neven Lastro), Semir Pezer. Trainer: Ante Mise.

Goals: 0-1 Hrvoje Barisic (31), 1-1 Steve Borg (56), 1-2 Milos Filipovic (66).

[HŠK Zrinjski Mostar won 3-2 on aggregate]

26.07.2018; Stádio Neo GSP, Nicosia; Referee: Marco Fritz (Germany); Attendance: 9,836

APOEL FC Nicosia – FC Flora Tallinn 5-0(2-0)

APOEL Nicosia: Boy Waterman, Zhivko Milanov, Carlão, Yohan Tavares, Nicolas Ioannou (81.Nektarios Alexandrou), Nuno Morais, Giorgos Efrem (76.Moussa Al Taamari), Lucas Souza, Ghayas Zahid, Roland Sallai, Mickaël Poté (66.Dellatorre). Trainer: Bruno Baltazar.

FC Flora Tallinn: Mait Toom, Gert Kams, Kevin Aloe, Jürgen Lorenz, Madis Vihmann, Aleksandr Dmitrijev, Maksim Gussev (76.Frank Liivak), German Slein, Mihkel Ainsalu (70.Markus Poom), Rauno Alliku, Rauno Sappinen. Traineres: Jürgen Henn & Arno Pijpers.

Goals: 1-0 Yohan Tavares (25), 2-0 Lucas Souza (44), 3-0 Nuno Morais (47 penalty), 4-0 Roland Sallai (73), 5-0 Dellatorre (78).

02.08.2018; A. Le Coq Arena, Tallinn; Referee: Amaury Delerue (France); Attendance: 801

FC Flora Tallinn – APOEL FC Nicosia 2-0(2-0)

FC Flora Tallinn: Mait Toom, Gert Kams, Kevin Aloe (81.Erik Sorga), Henrik Pürg, Madis Vihmann, Aleksandr Dmitrijev, Zakaria Beglarishvili, Maksim Gussev (67.Joseph Saliste), Markus Poom, Rauno Alliku, Frank Liivak (70.Mark Anders Lepik). Traineres: Jürgen Henn & Arno Pijpers.

APOEL Nicosia: Boy Waterman, Zhivko Milanov, Carlão (46.Praxitelis Vouros), Yohan Tavares, Nicolas Ioannou, Nuno Morais, Giorgos Efrem (46.Reza Ghoochannejhad), Lucas Souza, Ghayas Zahid (59.Savvas Gentsoglou), Moussa Al Taamari, Dellatorre. Trainer: Bruno Baltazar.

Goals: 1-0 Gert Kams (32), 2-0 Markus Poom (37).

[APOEL FC Nicosia won 5-2 on aggregate]

26.07.2018; Park Hall Stadium, Oswestry; Referee: Thorvaldur Árnason (Iceland); Attendance: 632

The New Saints FC – Lincoln Red Imps FC 2-1(1-1)

The New Saints: Paul Harrison, Christopher Marriott, Blaine Hudson, Kane Lewis, Benjamin Cabango, Aeron Edwards, Jon Routledge, Daniel Redmond (88.Adrian Cieslewicz), Tom Holland, Jamie Mullan, Dean Ebbe (40.Greg Draper). Trainer: Scott Ruscoe.

Lincoln Red Imps: Lolo Soler, Joseph Chipolina (84.André dos Santos), Oli (65.Louie Annesley), Ryan Casciaro, Jean Garcia, Diego Gámiz, Álex Moreno, Juan Montesinos, Falu Aranda (64.Juanma Ortiz), Anthony Hernandez, Sykes Garro, Trainer: Yiyi.

Goals: 1-0 Dean Ebbe (6), 1-1 Joseph Chipolina (31), 2-1 Blaine Hudson (83).

02.08.2018; Victoria Stadium, Gibraltar; Referee: Petri Viljanen (Finland); Attendance: 546

Lincoln Red Imps FC – The New Saints FC 1-1(1-0)

Lincoln Red Imps: Lolo Soler, Joseph Chipolina, Bernardo Lopes, Ryan Casciaro, Diego Gámiz, André dos Santos, Montesinos Romero (81.Jack Sergeant), Juanma Ortiz (75.Calderón), Anthony Hernandez, Lee Casciaro, Sykes Garro (46.Pedro Corral). Trainer: Yiyi.

The New Saints: Paul Harrison, Christopher Marriott, Blaine Hudson, Kane Lewis, Benjamin Cabango, Aeron Edwards, Jon Routledge, Daniel Redmond (68.Adrian Cieslewicz), Tom Holland (79.Greg Draper), Jamie Mullan, Kurtis Byrne (46.Dean Ebbe). Trainer: Scott Ruscoe.

Goals: 1-0 Montesinos Romero (41), 1-1 Dean Ebbe (82).

[The New Saints FC won 3-2 on aggregate]

26.07.2018; Estadi Comunal, Andorra la Vella; Referee: Sebastian Colţescu (Romania); Attendance: 385

FC Santa Coloma – Valur Reykjavík 1-0(0-0)

FC Santa Coloma: Eloy Casals, Ildefons Lima, Marc Rebés, Albert Mercadé (61.André Azevedo), Andreu Ramos, Jaime Noguerol, Moisés San Nicolás, Yago Pérez (87.Víctor Rodríguez), Loren Burón (72.Ibán Parra), Aleix Cistero, Juanma Torres. Trainer: Marc Rodríguez Rebull.

Valur Reykjavík: Anton Ari Einarsson, Birkir Sævarsson, Bjarni Eiríksson, Eidur Sigurbjörnsson, Sebastian Hedlund, Haukur Sigurdsson (86.Kristinn Halldórsson), Kristinn Sigurdsson, Sigurdur Lárusson (74.Andri Adolphsson), Einar Karl Ingvarsson (74.Gudjón Lydsson), Tobias Thomsen, Dion Jeremy Acoff. Trainer: Ólafur Jóhannesson.

Goal: 1-0 Bjarni Eiríksson (72.own goal).

02.08.2018; Völlurin, Reykjavík; Referee: Irfan Peljto (Bosnia and Herzegovina); Attendance: 825

Valur Reykjavík – FC Santa Coloma 3-0(0-0)

Valur Reykjavík: Anton Ari Einarsson, Birkir Sævarsson, Bjarni Eiríksson, Eidur Sigurbjörnsson, Sebastian Hedlund, Gudjón Lydsson (67.Einar Karl Ingvarsson), Haukur Sigurdsson, Kristinn Sigurdsson, Sigurdur Lárusson (79.Andri Adolphsson), Patrick Pedersen (90.Tobias Thomsen), Dion Jeremy Acoff. Trainer: Ólafur Jóhannesson.

FC Santa Coloma: Eloy Casals, Ildefons Lima, Marc Rebés, Albert Mercadé (54.André Azevedo), Andreu Ramos, Jaime Noguerol (66.Chus Sosa), Moisés San Nicolás, Yago Pérez, Loren Burón, Aleix Cistero (80.Ibán Parra), Juanma Torres. Trainer: Marc Rodríguez Rebull.

Goals: 1-0 Sigurdur Lárusson (53), 2-0 Bjarni Eiríksson (63), 3-0 Andri Adolphsson (90+4).

[Valur Reykjavík won 3-1 on aggregate]

26.07.2018; Stadion Kraj Bistrice, Nikšić; Referee: Alain Bieri (Switzerland); Attendance: 2,000

FK Sutjeska Nikšić – FC Alashkert 0-1(0-1)

Sutjeska Nikšić: Vladan Giljen, Darko Bulatovic, Stefan Cicmil, Dragan Grivic, Marko Cetkovic (83.Milutin Osmajic), Stefan Stefanovic (77.Vladan Bubanja), Stefan Loncar (46.Saleta Kordic), Nemanja Nedic, Luka Merdovic, Stefan Denkovic, Veljko Vukovic. Trainer: Nikola Rakojevic.

FC Alashkert: Ognjen Cancarevic, Gagik Daghbashyan, Oliver Práznovsky, Taron Voskanyan, Goran Antonic, Mladen Zeljkovic, Artur Yedigaryan, Jefferson (67.Danilo Sekulic), Mihran Manasyan (56.Artak Yedigaryan), Artak Grigoryan, Uros Nenadovic (84.Gustavo Marmentini dos Santos). Trainer: Varuzhan Sukiasyan.

Goal: 0-1 Mladen Zeljkovic (11).

02.08.2018; „Vazgen Sargsyan" Hanrapetakan Stadium, Yerevan; Referee: Ivaylo Stoyanov (Bulgaria); Attendance: 6,735

FC Alashkert – FK Sutjeska Nikšić 0-0

FC Alashkert: Ognjen Cancarevic, Artak Yedigaryan, Oliver Práznovsky, Taron Voskanyan, Goran Antonic, Mladen Zeljkovic (87.Artem Simonyan), Artur Yedigaryan (66.Danijel Stojkovic), Danilo Sekulic, Jefferson, Artak Grigoryan, Uros Nenadovic (79.Edgar Manucharyan). Trainer: Varuzhan Sukiasyan.

Sutjeska Nikšić: Vladan Giljen, Darko Bulatovic, Stefan Cicmil, Dragan Grivic, Marko Cetkovic (55.Vladan Bubanja), Stefan Stefanovic, Nemanja Nedic (85.Saleta Kordic), Bojan Bozovic, Luka Merdovic, Stefan Denkovic, Veljko Vukovic (65.Zarko Grbovic). Trainer: Nikola Rakojevic.

[FC Alashkert won 1-0 on aggregate]

26.07.2018; Stadion Stožice, Ljubljana; Referee: Enea Jorgji (Albania); Attendance: 2,980

NK Olimpija Ljubljana – Crusaders FC Belfast 5-1(1-0)

Olimpija Ljubljana: Aljaz Ivacic, Branko Ilic, Aris Zarifovic, Dino Stiglec, Macky Frank Bagnack, Matic Crnic, Daniel Avramovski (79.Stefan Savic), Tomislav Tomic (64.Asmir Suljic), Danijel Miskic, Nik Kapun, Kingsley Boateng (86.Haris Kadric). Trainer: Ilija Stolica.

Crusaders: Sean O'Neill, Sean Ward, Billy Joe Burns, Howard Beverland, Colin Coates, David Cushley (59.Paul Heatley), Declan Caddell (82.Rodney Brown), Philip Lowry (73.Ross Clarke), Jordan Forsythe, Matthew Snoddy, Michael Carvill. Trainer: Stephen Baxter.

Goals: 1-0 Kingsley Boateng (30), 2-0 Matic Crnic (56), 3-0 Kingsley Boateng (68), 3-1 Branko Ilic (73 own goal), 4-1 Matic Crnic (75), 5-1 Haris Kadric (90+2).

02.08.2018; Seaview Stadium, Belfast; Referee: Oliver Drachta (Austria); Attendance: 1,080

Crusaders FC Belfast – NK Olimpija Ljubljana 1-1(1-1)

Crusaders: Sean O'Neill, Sean Ward, Billy Joe Burns, Colin Coates, Kyle Owens (61.David Cushley), Rodney Brown, Declan Caddell, Jordan Forsythe, Paul Heatley (73.Ross Clarke), Matthew Snoddy, Michael Carvill (90+5.Philip Lowry). Trainer: Stephen Baxter.

Olimpija Ljubljana: Nejc Vidmar, Branko Ilic, Aris Zarifovic, Dino Stiglec, Vitalijs Maksimenko, Rok Kronaveter, Matic Crnic (90)+3 Matevz Turkus), Stefan Savic (76.Asmir Suljic), Tomislav Tomic, Nik Kapun, Haris Kadric (46.Kingsley Boateng). Trainer: Aleksandar Linta.

Goals: 0-1 Nik Kapun (15), 1-1 Paul Heatley (41).

[NK Olimpija Ljubljana won 6-2 on aggregate]

LEAGUE PATH

26.07.2018; Stadion Neftyanik, Ufa; Referee: Donatas Rumsas (Lithuania); Attendance: 11,210

FK Ufa – NK Domžale 0-0

FK Ufa: Aleksandr Belenov, Bojan Jokic, Denis Tumasyan, Ionut Nedelcearu, Jemal Tabidze, Veroljub Salatic, Ivan Paurevic, Dmitri Zhivoglyadov, Ivan Oblyakov (76.Catalin Carp), Sylvester Igboun, Vyacheslav Krotov (46.Kehinde Fatai). Trainer: Sergei Tomarov.

NK Domžale: Dejan Milic, Matija Sirok, Gaber Dobrovoljc, Tilen Klemencic, Dario Melnjak, Senijad Ibricic, Zeni Husmani, Lovro Bizjak (90+1.Zan Zuzek), Adam Gnezda Cerin, Agim Ibraimi (83.Shamar Nicholson), Andraz Kirm. Trainer: Simon Rozman.

02.08.2018; Sportni Park, Domžale; Referee: Arnold Hunter (Northern Ireland); Attendance: 2,500

NK Domžale – FK Ufa 1-1(0-0)

NK Domžale: Dejan Milic, Matija Sirok, Gaber Dobrovoljc, Tilen Klemencic, Dario Melnjak, Senijad Ibricic, Zeni Husmani, Lovro Bizjak, Adam Gnezda Cerin (90.Zan Zuzek), Agim Ibraimi, Tonci Mujan (76.Shamar Nicholson). Trainer: Simon Rozman.

FK Ufa: Aleksandr Belenov, Bojan Jokic, Denis Tumasyan, Ionut Nedelcearu, Jemal Tabidze, Veroljub Salatic, Ivan Paurevic, Dmitri Zhivoglyadov (56.Aleksandr Sukhov), Ivan Oblyakov (73.Catalin Carp), Kehinde Fatai (69.Azamat Zaseev), Sylvester Igboun. Trainer: Sergei Tomarov.

Goals: 1-0 Lovro Bizjak (50), 1-1 Bojan Jokic (87).

[FK Ufa won on away goals rule (1-1 on aggregate)]

26.07.2018; Olimpiskā centra Ventspils Stadionā, Ventspils; Referee: Sergey Lapochkin (Russia); Attendance: 3,055

FK Ventspils – FC Girondins de Bordeaux 0-1(0-1)

FK Ventspils: Maksims Uvarenko, Abdoul Mamah, Vitālijs Jagodinskis (55.Nauris Bulvītis), Medzit Neziri, Hélio Batista, Ritvars Rugins (46.Pedro Mendes), Abdullahi Alfa, Giuly Mandzhgaladze, Tosin Aiyegun, Vasili Pavlov (89.Raens Tālbergs), Adeleke Akinyemi. Trainer: Dejan Vukicevic.

Girondins de Bordeaux: Benoît Costil, Igor Lewczuk, Pablo Castro, Maxime Poundjé, Jules Koundé, Jaroslav Plasil, Younousse Sankharé, Lukas Lerager, Aurélien Tchouaméni (89.Otávio), Zaydou Youssouf (64.Nicolas de Préville), François Kamano (77.Gaëtan Laborde). Trainer: Gustavo Poyet.

Goal: 0-1 Zaydou Youssouf (3).

02.08.2018; Stade Matmut-Atlantique, Bordeaux; Referee: Hugo Filipe Ferreira de Campos Moreira Miguel (Portugal); Attendance: 15,863

FC Girondins de Bordeaux – FK Ventspils 2-1(1-0)

Girondins de Bordeaux: Benoît Costil, Igor Lewczuk, Pablo Castro, Maxime Poundjé, Jules Koundé, Jaroslav Plasil, Younousse Sankharé, Aurélien Tchouaméni (68.Valentín Vada), Zaydou Youssouf (83.Otávio), Nicolas de Préville, François Kamano (68.Gaëtan Laborde). Trainer: Gustavo Poyet.

FK Ventspils: Maksims Uvarenko, Abdoul Mamah, Vitālijs Jagodinskis (68.Nauris Bulvītis), Medzit Neziri, Hélio Batista, Pedro Mendes, Abdullahi Alfa (74.Raens Tālbergs), Giuly Mandzhgaladze, Tosin Aiyegun, Vasili Pavlov (46.Ritvars Rugins), Adeleke Akinyemi. Trainer: Dejan Vukicevic.

Goals: 1-0 François Kamano (9), 2-0 Jules Koundé (48), 2-1 Adeleke Akinyemi (66).

[FC Girondins de Bordeaux won 3-1 on aggregate]

26.07.2018; Ortaliq Stadion, Almaty; Referee: Aliyar Aghayev (Azerbaijan); Attendance: 20,000

FC Kairat Almaty – AZ Alkmaar 2-0(1-0)

FC Kairat: Vladimir Plotnikov, Sergey Politevich, Sheldon Bateau, Gafurzhan Suyumbaev, Isael, Islambek Kuat (85.Magomed Paragulgov), Bauyrzhan Islamkhan, Yan Vorogovskiy, Andrei Arshavin (90+1.Georgiy Zhukov), Juan Felipe Alves, Aderinsola Eseola (78.Márton Eppel). Trainer: Carlos Alós Ferrer.

AZ Alkmaar: Marco Bizot, Ron Vlaar, Jonas Svensson, Pantelis Hatzidiakos, Thomas Ouwejan, Fredrik Midtsjø, Mats Seuntjens, Guus Til, Oussama Idrissi, Fred Friday, Myron Boadu (72.Iliass Bel Hassani). Trainer: John van den Brom.

Goals: 1-0, 2-0 Aderinsola Eseola (12, 50).

02.08.18 AFAS Stadion, Alkmaar; Referee: Dimitar Meckarovski (North Macedonia); Attendance: 9,437

AZ Alkmaar – FC Kairat Almaty 2-1(1-1)

AZ Alkmaar: Marco Bizot, Ron Vlaar (57.Myron Boadu), Jonas Svensson, Pantelis Hatzidiakos, Thomas Ouwejan, Fredrik Midtsjø, Teun Koopmeiners, Guus Til, Oussama Idrissi, Dorin Rotariu (53.Iliass Bel Hassani), Fred Friday. Trainer: John van den Brom.

FC Kairat: Vladimir Plotnikov, Sergey Politevich, Sheldon Bateau, Gafurzhan Suyumbaev, Isael, Islambek Kuat, Bauyrzhan Islamkhan (61.Ákos Elek), Yan Vorogovskiy, Andrei Arshavin (70.Stanislav Lunin), Juan Felipe Alves, Aderinsola Eseola (75.Márton Eppel). Trainer: Carlos Alós Ferrer.

Goals: 0-1 Bauyrzhan Islamkhan (28 penalty), 1-1 Guus Til (41), 2-1 Teun Koopmeiners (90+4 penalty).

[FC Kairat Almaty won 3-2 on aggregate]

26.07.2018; Ortaliq Stadion, Kostanay; Referee: Juri Frischer (Estonia); Attendance: 7,700

FC Tobol Kostanay – FC Pyunik Yerevan 2-1(0-0)

Tobol Kostanay: Dmytro Nepogodov, Viktor Dmitrenko, Fernander Kassaï, Dmitry Miroshnichenko, Marat Bystrov (68.Tanat Nuserbaev), Jaba Kankava, Azat Nurgaliev (90+1.Samat Zharynbetov), Artūras Zulpa, Nika Kvekveskiri, Maxim Fedin, Juan Lescano (72.Bayurzhan Turysbek). Trainer: Vladimir Nikitenko.

Pyunik Yerevan: Evgeni Kobozev, Vyacheslav Dmitriev, Maksim Zhestokov, Serob Grigoryan, Maksim Trusevich, Denis Voynov (81.Albert Bogatyrev), Didier Kadio, Alik Arakelyan (62.Rumyan Hovsepyan), Vahagn Hayrapetyan, Petros Avetisyan, Mohamed Konaté (69.Ruslan Koryan). Trainer: Andrey Talalaev.

Goals: 1-0 Maxim Fedin (49), 2-0 Azat Nurgaliev (80), 2-1 Ruslan Koryan (90).

31.07.2018; „Vazgen Sargsyan" Hanrapetakan Stadium, Yerevan; Referee: Petr Ardeleánu (Czech Republic); Attendance: 8,000

FC Pyunik Yerevan – FC Tobol Kostanay 1-0(0-0)

Pyunik Yerevan: Andrija Dragojevic, Vyacheslav Dmitriev, Maksim Zhestokov, Serob Grigoryan, Maksim Trusevich, Denis Voynov (46.Mohamed Konaté), Didier Kadio, Rumyan Hovsepyan (46.Alik Arakelyan), Vahagn Hayrapetyan, Petros Avetisyan [*sent off 89*], Ruslan Koryan (76.Albert Bogatyrev). Trainer: Andrey Talalaev.

Tobol Kostanay: Dmytro Nepogodov, Viktor Dmitrenko (89.Aslan Darabaev), Fernander Kassaï, Dmitry Miroshnichenko, Marat Bystrov (79.Juan Lescano), Jaba Kankava, Azat Nurgaliev, Artūras Zulpa, Nika Kvekveskiri, Tanat Nuserbaev, Maxim Fedin (90+2.Bayurzhan Turysbek). Trainer: Vladimir Nikitenko.

Goal: 1-0 Mohamed Konaté (82).

[FC Pyunik Yerevan won on away goals rule (2-2 on aggregate)]

26.07.2018; Stadionul Central, Ovidiu; Referee: Davide Massa (Italy); Attendance: 2,543

FC Viitorul Constanța – SBV Vitesse Arnhem 2-2(1-0)

Viitorul Constanța: Valentin Cojocaru, Sebastian Mladen, Tudor Baluta, Bradley de Nooijer, Vlad Achim, Bogdan Tîru, Ianis Hagi, Ionut Vîna, Alexandru Matan (30.Lyes Houri), Denis Dragus (73.Andrei Artean [*sent off 79*]), Mailson Lima (73.Srdjan Luchin). Trainer: Gheorghe Hagi.

Vitesse Arnhem: Eduardo, Alexander Büttner, Rasmus Thelander, Vyacheslav Karavaev, Jake Clarke-Salter, Roy Beerens, Thulani Serero, Navarone Foor (84.Matús Bero), Thomas Bruns (69.Hilary Gong), Tim Matavz, Bryan Linssen. Trainer: Leonid Slutsky.

Goals: 1-0, 2-0 Denis Dragus (44, 49), 2-1 Tim Matavz (54), 2-2 Bryan Linssen (72).

02.08.2018; GelreDome, Arnhem; Referee: Kevin Clancy (Scotland); Attendance: 9,876

SBV Vitesse Arnhem – FC Viitorul Constanța 3-1(1-0)

Vitesse Arnhem: Eduardo, Alexander Büttner, Rasmus Thelander, Vyacheslav Karavaev, Jake Clarke-Salter (57.Maikel van der Werff), Thulani Serero, Navarone Foor, Matús Bero (57.Thomas Bruns), Roy Beerens, Tim Matavz, Bryan Linssen (90+2.Hilary Gong). Trainer: Leonid Slutsky.

Viitorul Constanța: Valentin Cojocaru, Sebastian Mladen, Tudor Baluta (71.Robert Hodorogea), Bradley de Nooijer, Vlad Achim, Bogdan Tîru, Lyes Houri (46.Andrei Ciobanu), Ianis Hagi, Ionut Vîna, Denis Dragus (77.Alexandru Matan), Mailson Lima. Trainer: Gheorghe Hagi.

Goals: 1-0 Tim Matavz (23), 2-0 Bryan Linssen (48), 2-1 Denis Dragus (50), 3-1 Roy Beerens (77).

[SBV Vitesse Arnhem won 5-3 on aggregate]

26.07.2018; Stadion Ob Jezeru, Velenje; Referee: Hüseyin Göçek (Turkey); Attendance: 450

NK Rudar Velenje – FCSB București 0-2(0-1)

Rudar Velenje: Marko Pridigar, Josip Tomasevic, Klemen Bolha, Robert Pusaver, Ivan Vasiljevic, Damjan Trifkovic (73.Tim Vodeb), Domagoj Muic, Anze Pisek, Dominik Radic, Djair Parfitt-Williams (56.Abu Kamara), Milan Tucic (69.Vlatko Simunac). Trainer: Marijan Pusnik.

FCSB București: Cristian Balgradean, Marko Momcilovic, Junior Maranhão, Daniel Benzar, Bogdan Planic, Filipe Teixeira (82.Lucian Filip), Mihai Pintilii, Kamer Qaka, Olimpiu Morutan (68.Antonio Jakolis), Harlem Gnohéré (46.Florin Tanase), Dennis Man. Trainer: Nicolae Dica.

Goals: 0-1 Dennis Man (5), 0-2 Filipe Teixeira (74).

02.08.18 Arena Națională, București; Referee: Sergey Ivanov (Russia); Attendance: 7,030

FCSB București – NK Rudar Velenje 4-0(1-0)

FCSB București: Cristian Balgradean, Junior Maranhão, Bogdan Planic, Mihai Balasa, Mihai Pintilii (59.Kamer Qaka), Antonio Jakolis, Ovidiu Popescu, Dragos Nedelcu, Olimpiu Morutan, Florin Tanase (46.Harlem Gnohéré), Florinel Coman (74.Daniel Benzar). Trainer: Nicolae Dica.

Rudar Velenje: Anze Malnar, David Kasnik, Josip Tomasevic, Klemen Bolha, Robert Pusaver, Ivan Vasiljevic, Domagoj Muic, Anze Pisek, Matej Santek (51.Djair Parfitt-Williams), Ante Solomun (62.Damjan Trifkovic), Vlatko Simunac (56.Abu Kamara). Trainer: Marijan Pusnik.

Goals: 1-0 Florin Tanase (22 penalty), 2-0 Olimpiu Morutan (49), 3-0 Florinel Coman (68), 4-0 Daniel Benzar (90+3).

[FCSB București won 6-0 on aggregate]

26.07.2018; MFA Centrenary Stadium, Ta'Qali; Referee: Jens Maae (Denmark); Attendance: 558

Balzan FC – ŠK Slovan Bratislava 2-1(1-0)

Balzan FC: Steve Sultana, Elkin Serrano, Steven Bezzina, Ivan Bozovic, Uros Ljubomirac, Michael Johnson, Cadú (82.Dale Camilleri), Nenad Sljivic, Milos Lepovic, Lecão (76.Ricardo Correa), Bojan Kaljevic (63.Alfred Effiong). Trainer: Marko Micovic.

Slovan Bratislava: Michal Sulla, Mitch Apau, Vasil Bozhikov, Artem Sukhotsky, Ibrahim Rabiu (72.Dejan Drazic), Dávid Holman (46.Vukan Savicevic), Nono Delgado, Kenan Bajric, "Moha" Mohammed Rharsalla, Aleksandar Cavric (72.Boris Cmiljanic), Andraz Sporar. Trainer: Martin Sevela.

Goals: 1-0 Bojan Kaljevic (17), 2-0 Uros Ljubomirac (67), 2-1 Vukan Savicevic (74).

02.08.2018; Štadion Pasienky, Bratislava; Referee: Alexandre Boucaut (Belgium); Attendance: 4,176

ŠK Slovan Bratislava – Balzan FC 3-1(1-0)

Slovan Bratislava: Michal Sulla, Kornel Saláta, Mitch Apau, Vasil Bozhikov, Nono Delgado, Kenan Bajric, Vukan Savicevic (82.Joeri de Kamps), "Moha" Mohammed Rharsalla, Aleksandar Cavric (75.Boris Cmiljanic), Andraz Sporar, Dejan Drazic (87.Filip Holosko). Trainer: Martin Sevela.

Balzan FC: Steve Sultana, Elkin Serrano, Steven Bezzina (83.Andrija Majdevac), Ivan Bozovic, Uros Ljubomirac, Michael Johnson, Cadú, Nenad Sljivic, Milos Lepovic (76.Ricardo Correa), Lecão (62.Alfred Effiong), Bojan Kaljevic. Trainer: Marko Micovic.

Goals: 1-0 Aleksandar Cavric (7), 2-0, 3-0 Andraz Sporar (70, 71), 3-1 Cadú (77).

[ŠK Slovan Bratislava won 4-3 on aggregate]

26.07.2018; „Sammy Ofer" Stadium, Haifa; Referee: Srđan Jovanović (Serbia); Attendance: 3,950

Hapoel Haifa FC – FH Hafnarfjördur 1-1(0-0)

Hapoel Haifa: Ernestas Setkus, Nisso Kapiloto, Dor Malul, Risto Mitrevski, Hen Dilmoni, Rasmus Sjöstedt (58.Ness Zamir), Gil Vermouth, Radu Gînsari (84.Guy Hadida), Gal Arel, Eli Elbaz (64.Thanasis Papazoglou), Maxim Plakushchenko. Trainer: Nir Klinger.

FH Hafnarfjördur: Gunnar Nielsen, Hjörtur Valgardsson, Vidar Ari Jónsson, Edi Gomes, Rennico Clarke, Davíd Vidarsson, Gudmundur Kristjánsson, Brandur Hendriksson Olsen (60.Robbie Crawford), Atli Gudnason (75.Pétur Vidarsson), Steven Lennon, Jákup Thomsen (82.Kristinn Steindórsson). Trainer: Ólafur Kristjánsson.

Goals: 0-1 Edi Gomes (53), 1-1 Thanasis Papazoglou (65).

02.08.2018; Kaplakrikavöllur, Hafnarfjördur; Referee: Sergey Tsinkevich (Belarus); Attendance: 1,136

FH Hafnarfjördur – Hapoel Haifa FC 0-1(0-0)

FH Hafnarfjördur: Gunnar Nielsen, Pétur Vidarsson (79.Atli Gudnason), Hjörtur Valgardsson, Vidar Ari Jónsson, Edi Gomes, Rennico Clarke, Davíd Vidarsson, Gudmundur Kristjánsson, Brandur Hendriksson Olsen, Robbie Crawford (80.Jákup Thomsen), Steven Lennon. Trainer: Ólafur Kristjánsson.

Hapoel Haifa: Ernestas Setkus, Gabriel Tamas, Nisso Kapiloto, Dor Malul, Hen Dilmoni, Rasmus Sjöstedt, Gil Vermouth, Radu Gînsari, Gal Arel (58.Guy Hadida), Thanasis Papazoglou (90+1.Risto Mitrevski), Maxim Plakushchenko (64.Eli Elbaz). Trainer: Nir Klinger.

Goals: 0-1 Eli Elbaz (68).

[Hapoel Haifa FC won 2-1 on aggregate]

26.07.2018; „Mikheil Meskhi" Stadioni, Tbilisi; Referee: Kevin Blom (Netherlands); Attendance: 3,500

FC Chikhura Sachkhere – NK Maribor 0-0

Chikhura Sachkhere: Dino Hamzic, Davit Maisashvili (88.Davit Megrelishvili), Lasha Chikvaidze, Bakari Mirtshkulava, Revaz Chiteishvili, Levan Kakubava, Irakli Lekvtadze (49.Kakha Kakhabrishvili), Teimurazi Markozashvili, Irakli Bugridze, Giorgi Gabedava, Mikheil Sardalishvili (78.Denis Dobrovolski). Trainer: Samson Pruidze.

NK Maribor: Jasmin Handanovic, Marko Suler, Mitja Viler, Sasa Ivkovic, Blaz Vrhovec, Amir Dervisevic (60.Alexandru Cretu), Aleks Pihler, Dino Hotic, Marcos Tavares, Gregor Bajde (81.Jasmin Mesanovic), Luka Zahovic (63.Dare Vrsic). Trainer: Darko Milanic.

02.08.2018; Ljudski vrt, Maribor; Referee: Halil Umut Meler (Turkey); Attendance: 7,166

NK Maribor – FC Chikhura Sachkhere 2-0(0-0)

NK Maribor: Jasmin Handanovic, Marko Suler, Mitja Viler, Sasa Ivkovic, Blaz Vrhovec, Amir Dervisevic, Aleks Pihler, Dino Hotic (89.Dare Vrsic), Marcos Tavares, Gregor Bajde (75.Jasmin Mesanovic), Luka Zahovic (86.Alexandru Cretu). Trainer: Darko Milanic.

Chikhura Sachkhere: Dino Hamzic, Davit Maisashvili, Lasha Chikvaidze (81.Demur Chikhladze), Bakari Mirtshkulava, Revaz Chiteishvili, Levan Kakubava (86.Giorgi Bukhaidze), Teimurazi Markozashvili, Irakli Bugridze, Giorgi Gabedava, Mikheil Sardalishvili, Kakha Kakhabrishvili (67.Davit Megrelishvili). Trainer: Samson Pruidze.

Goals: 1-0 Luka Zahovic (70), 2-0 Marcos Tavares (90+6).

[NK Maribor won 2-0 on aggregate]

26.07.2018; Red Bull Arena, Leipzig; Referee: Aleksandar Stavrev (North Macedonia); Attendance: 18,126

RasenBallsport Leipzig – BK Häcken Göteborg 4-0(2-0)

RB Leipzig: Péter Gulácsi, Willi Orban, Lukas Klostermann, Ibrahima Konaté, Stefan Ilsanker [*sent off 81*], Kevin Kampl, Diego Demme, Bruma (85.Niclas Stierlin), Marcelo Saracchi (68.Nordi Mukiele), Jean-Kévin Augustin, Matheus Cunha (89.Fabrice Hartmann). Trainer: Ralf Rangnick.

BK Häcken: Peter Abrahamsson, Kari Arkivuo, Johan Hammar, Rasmus Lindgren, Erik Friberg, Alexander Faltsetas (83.Gustav Berggren), Adam Andersson, Daleho Irandust (46.Nasiru Mohammed), Mervan Çelik (71.Viktor Lundberg), Paulinho Guerreiro, Alhassan Kamara. Trainer: Andreas Alm.

Goals: 1-0 Bruma (35), 2-0 Matheus Cunha (39), 3-0 Kevin Kampl (50), 4-0 Jean-Kévin Augustin (84).

02.08.2018; Bravida Arena, Göteborg, Referee: Mete Kalkavan (Turkey); Attendance: 2,968

BK Häcken Göteborg – RasenBallsport Leipzig 1-1(0-0)

BK Häcken: Jonathan Rasheed, Kari Arkivuo (81.Elohor Ekpolo), Johan Hammar, Gustav Berggren, Rasmus Lindgren, Erik Friberg (64.Kevin Ackermann), Adam Andersson, Viktor Lundberg, Mervan Çelik, Alhassan Kamara, Nasiru Mohammed (64.Daleho Irandust). Trainer: Andreas Alm.

RB Leipzig: Marius Müller, Willi Orban, Lukas Klostermann, Ibrahima Konaté (64.Oliver Bias), Emil Forsberg (63.Erik Majetschak), Diego Demme, Massimo Bruno, Marcelo Saracchi, Niclas Stierlin, Jean-Kévin Augustin, Matheus Cunha (70.Lukas Krüger). Trainer: Ralf Rangnick.

Goals: 0-1 Massimo Bruno (47), 1-1 Daleho Irandust (85).

[RasenBallsport Leipzig won 5-1 on aggregate]

26.07.2018; Aker Stadion, Molde; Referee: Adrien Jaccottet (Switzerland); Attendance: 4,179

Molde FK – KF Laçi 3-0(2-0)

Molde FK: Andreas Linde, Vegard Forren, Ruben Gabrielsen, Kristoffer Haugen, Christoffer Remmer, Etzaz Hussain (68.Leke James), Babacar Sarr, Eirik Hestad, Fredrik Aursnes, Pawel Cibicki (65.Magnus Eikrem), Erling Håland (74.Petter Strand). Trainer: Ole Gunnar Solskjær.

KF Laçi: Gentian Selmani, Marko Radas, Taulant Sefgjinaj, Erion Hoxhallari, Eglentin Gjoni, Ndricim Shtubina (48.Abdurraman Fangaj), Nikola Eller, Fjoart Jonuzi, Regi Lushkja (90+1.Serxho Ujka), Vice Kendes, Myrto Uzuni. Trainer: Besnik Prenga.

Goals: 1-0 Erling Håland (6 penalty), 2-0 Eirik Hestad (24), 3-0 Leke James (79).

02.08.2018; Stadiumi Laçi, Laçi; Referee: Kristo Tohver (Estonia); Attendance: 420

KF Laçi – Molde FK 0-2(0-2)

KF Laçi: Gentian Selmani, Marko Radas (73.Ndricim Shtubina), Taulant Sefgjinaj, Erion Hoxhallari, Eglentin Gjoni, Abdurraman Fangaj (76.Ded Bushi), Nikola Eller, Fjoart Jonuzi, Regi Lushkja, Vice Kendes (82.Serxho Ujka), Myrto Uzuni. Trainer: Besnik Prenga.

Molde FK: Andreas Linde, Vegard Forren, Ruben Gabrielsen, Kristoffer Haugen, Petter Strand, Magnus Eikrem (60.Pawel Cibicki), Babacar Sarr (46.Isak Ssewankambo), Fredrik Aursnes, Stian Gregersen, Mattias Mostrøm, Daniel Chima Chukwu (60.Leke James). Trainer: Ole Gunnar Solskjær.

Goals: 0-1 Fredrik Aursnes (41 penalty), 0-2 Petter Strand (45+1).

[Molde FK won 5-0 on aggregate]

26.07.2018; LFF stadionas, Vilnius; Referee: István Vad II (Hungary); Attendance: 3,000

FK Žalgiris Vilnius – FC Vaduz 1-0(0-0)

Žalgiris Vilnius: Dziugas Bartkus, Rolandas Baravykas, Mamadou Mbodj, Saulius Mikoliūnas, Donovan Slijngard, Tomas Simkovic (63.Serge Nyuiadzi), Liviu Antal, Slavko Blagojevic, Jérémy Manzorro (77.Domantas Simkus), Marko Tomic, Louis Ogana (84.Tomás Malec). Trainer: Valdas Urbonas.

FC Vaduz: Andreas Hirzel, Maximilian Göppel, Sadik Vitija, Philipp Muntwiler, Milan Gajic, Marco Mathys (46.Gabriel Lüchinger), Christopher Drazan, Sandro Wieser, Maurice Brunner (74.Jodel Dossou), Mohamed Coulibaly, Igor Tadic (90+1.Boris Babic). Trainer: Roland Vrabec.

Goal: 1-0 Liviu Antal (86).

02.08.2018; Rheinpark Stadion, Vaduz; Referee: Anastasios Papapetrou (Greece); Attendance: 853

FC Vaduz – FK Žalgiris Vilnius 1-1(1-0)

FC Vaduz: Andreas Hirzel, Mario Bühler, Maximilian Göppel, Sadik Vitija, Philipp Muntwiler, Marco Mathys (85.Noah Blasucci), Christopher Drazan (74.Boris Babic), Sandro Wieser, Jodel Dossou (72.Maurice Brunner), Mohamed Coulibaly, Igor Tadic. Trainer: Roland Vrabec.

Žalgiris Vilnius: Dziugas Bartkus, Rolandas Baravykas, Mamadou Mbodj, Saulius Mikoliūnas, Donovan Slijngard, Tomas Simkovic, Liviu Antal (90+3.Serge Nyuiadzi), Slavko Blagojevic, Jérémy Manzorro (65.Domantas Simkus), Marko Tomic, Louis Ogana (90+2.Tomás Malec). Trainer: Valdas Urbonas.

Goals: 1-0 Jodel Dossou (34), 1-1 Tomas Simkovic (66).

[FK Žalgiris Vilnius won 2-1 on aggregate]

26.07.2018; Winner Stadium, Netanya; Referee: Paolo Mazzoleni (Italy); Attendance: 8,161

Maccabi Tel Aviv FC – FK Radnički Niš 2-0(0-0)

Maccabi Tel Aviv: Predrag Rajkovic, Eitan Tibi, Avi Rikan (46.Eyal Golasa), Saborit, Elazar Dasa, Jair Amador, Dor Mikha (85.Roslan Barski), Dor Peretz, Vidar Kjartansson, Eliran Atar (66.Matan Hozez), Omer Atzili [*sent off 79*]. Trainer: Vladimir Ivic.

Radnički Niš: Mladen Zivkovic, Aleksandar Todorovski, Andrija Mijailovic (74.Sladan Nikodijevic), Radovan Pankov, Taras Bondarenko, Aleksandar Stanisavljevic (62.Aleksandar Jovanovic (I)), Petar Grbic, Dusan Micic, Nikola Stankovic, Ryota Noma, Marko Mrkic (46.Aleksa Jovanovic (II)). Trainer: Nenad Lalatovic.

Goals: 1-0, 2-0 Vidar Kjartansson (51, 69 penalty).

02.08.2018; Stadion Čair, Niš; Referee: Radu Petrescu (Romania); Attendance: 7,588

FK Radnički Niš – Maccabi Tel Aviv FC 2-2(1-2)

Radnički Niš: Mladen Zivkovic, Nikola Aksentijevic, Radovan Pankov, Djordje Crnomarkovic, Aleksandar Stanisavljevic, Petar Grbic, Dusan Micic, Nikola Stankovic, Ryota Noma (55.Sasa Stojanovic), Nermin Haskic (82.Sladjan Nikodijevic), Lazar Randjelovic (73.Marko Mrkic). Trainer: Nenad Lalatovic.

Maccabi Tel Aviv: Predrag Rajkovic, Eitan Tibi, Saborit (55.Sheran Yeini), Elazar Dasa, Jair Amador, Eyal Golasa, Dor Mikha, Dor Peretz, Vidar Kjartansson (83.Chikeluba Ofoedu), Eliran Atar (63.Roslan Barski), Aaron Schoenfeld. Trainer: Vladimir Ivic.

Goals: 0-1 Radovan Pankov (33 own goal), 0-2 Eliran Atar (38), 1-2, 2-2 Aleksandar Stanisavljevic (44, 58).

[Maccabi Tel Aviv FC won 4-2 on aggregate]

26.07.2018; Stadion Bâlgarska Armija, Sofia; Referee: John Beaton (Scotland); Attendance: 6,200

PFC CSKA Sofia – FC Admira Wacker Mödling 3-0(3-0)

CSKA Sofia: Vytautas Cerniauskas, Boris Sekulic, Bozhidar Chorbadzhiyski, Steven Pereira, Geferson, Rúben Pinto, Edwin Gyasi (81.Tonislav Yordanov), Janio Bikel, Kiril Despodov, Maurides (72.Valentin Antov), Jorginho (90.Angel Lyaskov). Trainer: Nestor El Maestro.

FC Admira Wacker Mödling: Andreas Leitner, Stephan Zwierschitz, Bjarne Thoelke, Sebastian Bauer, Milos Spasic, Wilhelm Vorsager, Morten Hjulmand (46.Daniel Toth), Marco Kadlec (83.Marcus Maier), Dominik Starkl, Sinan Bakis, Marin Jakolis (70.Patrick Schmidt). Trainer: Ernst Baumeister.

Goals: 1-0, 2-0 Kiril Despodov (29, 34), 3-0 Maurides (38 penalty).

02.08.2018; BSFZ-Arena, Maria Enzersdorf; Referee: Pol van Boekel (Netherlands); Attendance: 2,400

FC Admira Wacker Mödling – PFC CSKA Sofia 1-3(0-1)

FC Admira Wacker Mödling: Manuel Kuttin, Stephan Zwierschitz (84.Wilhelm Vorsager), Sebastian Bauer, Milos Spasic, Emanuel Aiwu (46.Bjarne Thoelke), Marcus Maier, Morten Hjulmand, Dominik Starkl (71.Marco Kadlec), Sinan Bakis, Marin Jakolis, Patrick Schmidt. Trainer: Ernst Baumeister.

CSKA Sofia: Vytautas Cerniauskas, Boris Sekulic (75.Aleksandar Dyulgerov), Bozhidar Chorbadzhiyski, Steven Pereira, Geferson, Rúben Pinto, Tiago Rodrigues, Janio Bikel, Kiril Despodov (46.Valentin Antov), Maurides (74.Edwin Gyasi), Jorginho. Trainer: Nestor El Maestro.

Goals: 0-1, 0-2 Maurides (14, 53), 1-2 Sinan Bakis (55), 1-3 Jorginho (80).

[PFC CSKA Sofia won 6-1 on aggregate]

26.07.2018; „Bozsik József" Stadion, Budapest; Referee: Mohammed Al-Hakim (Sweden); Attendance: 2,447

Budapest Honvéd FC – FC Progrès Niederkorn 1-0(0-0)

Budapest Honvéd: Dávid Gróf, Eke Uzoma, Tibor Heffler, Dino Skvorc, Bence Batik, Krisztián Vadócz, Djordje Kamber, Gergö Nagy (88.Zsolt Pölöskei), Dániel Gazdag, Filip Holender (74.Botond Baráth), Dániel Lukàcs (51.Dominik Cipf). Trainer: Attila Supka.

Progrès Niederkorn: Sebastian Flauss, Mario Mutsch (79.Ben Vogel), Adrien Ferino, Marvin da Graça, Jordan Gobron, Tim Hall, Yann Matias Marques, Emmanuel Françoise (69.Alexander Karapetyan), Sébastien Thill, Olivier Thill, Mayron De Almeida (90+4.Romeu Torres). Trainer: Paolo Amodio.

Goal: 1-0 Botond Baráth (82).

02.08.2018; Stade Parc des Sports, Differdange; Referee: Karim Abed (France); Attendance: 1,852

FC Progrès Niederkorn – Budapest Honvéd FC 2-0(1-0)

Progrès Niederkorn: Sebastian Flauss, Mario Mutsch, Marvin da Graça, Jordan Gobron, Tim Hall, Yann Matias Marques, Emmanuel Françoise (73.Yannick Bastos), Sébastien Thill (65.Metin Karayer), Olivier Thill, Alexander Karapetyan, Mayron De Almeida (88.Adrien Ferino). Trainer: Paolo Amodio.

Budapest Honvéd: Dávid Gróf, Eke Uzoma (87.Tonci Kukoc), Tibor Heffler, Dino Skvorc, Bence Batik, Krisztián Vadócz, Djordje Kamber, Gergö Nagy, Filip Holender (72.Dániel Lukàcs), Bence Banó-Szabó (33.Botond Baráth), Danilo. Trainer: Attila Supka.

Goals: 1-0 Mayron De Almeida (21), 2-0 Yann Matias Marques (84).

[FC Progrès Niederkorn won 2-1 on aggregate]

26.07.2018; Tele2 Arena, Stockholm; Referee: Miroslav Zelinka (Czech Republic); Attendance: 11,200

Djurgårdens IF Stockholm – FK Mariupol 1-1(0-1)

Djurgårdens IF: Andreas Isaksson, Erik Johansson, Marcus Danielsson, Niklas Gunnarsson (65.Jacob Une-Larsson), Jonathan Augustinsson, Haris Radetinac (77.Jonas Olsson), Jonathan Ring, Fredrik Ulvestad, Kerim Mrabti, Jesper Karlström (73.Kevin Walker), Aliou Badji. Trainer: Özcan Melkemichel.

FK Mariupol: Rustam Khudzhamov, Sergey Yavorskiy, Maksym Bilyi, Igor Kyryukhantsev (87.Pavel Polegenko), Besir Demiri, Oleksiy Bykov, Igor Tyshchenko, Vyacheslav Churko (76.Sergiy Gorbunov), Dmytro Myshnov (82.Sergiy Chobotenko), Oleksandr Pikhalyonok, Ruslan Fomin. Trainer: Oleksandr Babych.

Goals: 0-1 Sergey Yavorskiy (37), 1-1 Aliou Badji (90+4).

02.08.2018; Chornomorets Stadium, Odessa; Referee: Rob Harvey (Republic of Ireland); Attendance: 5,077

FK Mariupol – Djurgårdens IF Stockholm 2-1(0-0,1-1)

FK Mariupol: Rustam Khudzhamov, Sergey Yavorskiy, Maksym Bilyi (105.Sergiy Chobotenko), Pavel Polegenko, Besir Demiri (116.Joyskim Dawa), Oleksiy Bykov, Igor Tyshchenko (110.Igor Kyryukhantsev), Vyacheslav Churko (73.Vladislav Vakula), Dmytro Myshnov, Oleksandr Pikhalyonok, Ruslan Fomin. Trainer: Oleksandr Babych.

Djurgårdens IF: Andreas Isaksson, Jonas Olsson, Erik Johansson, Jacob Une-Larsson (105.Johan Andersson), Jonathan Augustinsson, Haris Radetinac (89.Dzenis Kozica), Jonathan Ring (101.Marcus Danielsson), Fredrik Ulvestad, Kerim Mrabti, Jesper Karlström (99.Kevin Walker), Aliou Badji. Trainer: Özcan Melkemichel.

Goals: 1-0 Oleksandr Pikhalyonok (63), 1-1 Aliou Badji (77), 2-1 Ruslan Fomin (97 penalty).

[FK Mariupol won 3-2 on aggregate]

26.07.2018; Stadion Miejski, Białystok; Referee: Ricardo de Burgos Bengoetxea (Spain); Attendance: 13,725

Jagiellonia Białystok – Rio Ave FC 1-0(1-0)

Jagiellonia Białystok: Marián Kelemen, Lukasz Burliga, Nemanja Mitrovic, Guilherme, Ivan Runje, Mateusz Machaj (71.Martin Pospísil), Arvydas Novikovas (83.Patryk Klimala), Przemyslaw Frankowski, Bartosz Kwiecien (75.Rafal Grzyb), Taras Romanczuk, Cillian Sheridan. Trainer: Ireneusz Mamrot.

Rio Ave: Giorgi Makaridze, Jonathan Buatu, Nélson Monte, Matheus Reis, Toni Borevkovic, Tarantini (76.João Schmidt), Leandrinho, Diego Lopes (18.Bruno Moreira), Gabrielzinho, Galeno (81.Damien Furtado), Gelson Dala. Trainer: José Gomes.

Goal: 1-0 Mateusz Machaj (9).

02.08.2018; Estádio dos Arcos, Vila do Conde; Referee: Marco Di Bello (Italy); Attendance: 5,930

Rio Ave FC – Jagiellonia Białystok 4-4(2-1)

Rio Ave: Giorgi Makaridze, Jonathan Buatu, Nadjack, Nélson Monte, Matheus Reis, Tarantini (70.Nikola Jambor), Leandrinho (89.Ricardo Schutte), Bruno Moreira, Gabrielzinho (80.Damien Furtado), Galeno, Gelson Dala. Trainer: José Gomes.

Jagiellonia Białystok: Marián Kelemen, Lukasz Burliga, Nemanja Mitrovic, Guilherme, Ivan Runje, Mateusz Machaj (61.Martin Pospísil), Arvydas Novikovas (87.Rafal Grzyb), Przemyslaw Frankowski, Bartosz Kwiecien (75.Karol Swiderski), Taras Romanczuk, Cillian Sheridan. Trainer: Ireneusz Mamrot.

Goals: 0-1 Cillian Sheridan (6), 1-1, 2-1 Galeno (27, 45+2), 2-2 Taras Romanczuk (56), 3-2 Gelson Dala (63), 3-3 Martin Pospísil (72), 3-4 Taras Romanczuk (79), 4-4 Damien Furtado (84).

[Jagiellonia Białystok won 5-4 on aggregate]

26.07.2018; „Budaunik Stroitel" Stadium, Soligorsk; Referee: Svein Oddvar Moen (Norway); Attendance: 3,700

FC Shakhtyor Solihorsk – KKS Lech Poznań 1-1(0-0)

Shakhtyor Solihorsk: Andrey Klimovich, Maksim Bordachev, Pavel Rybak, Siarhei Matveichyk, Igor Burko, Roger Cañas, Aleksandr Selyava, Yuri Kovalev, Július Szöke, Max Ebong Ngome (46.Sergey Balanovich), Elis Bakaj (73.Denis Laptev). Trainer: Sergey Tashuev.

Lech Poznań: Jasmin Buric, Thomas Rogne, Rafal Janicki, Volodymyr Kostevych, Vernon, Tomasz Cywka (90+3.Lukasz Tralka), Mihai Radut (77.Maciej Gajos), Maciej Makuszewski, Pedro Tiba, Darko Jevtic (70.João Amaral), Christian Gytkjær. Trainer: Ivan Djurdjevic.

Goals: 1-0 Elis Bakaj (53), 1-1 João Amaral (89).

02.08.2018; Stadion INEA, Poznań; Referee: Christian Dingert (Germany); Attendance: 16,507

KKS Lech Poznań – Shakthtyor Soligorsk 3-1(1-0,1-1)

Lech Poznań: Jasmin Buric, Thomas Rogne, Rafal Janicki (46.Maciej Orlowski), Volodymyr Kostevych, Vernon, Tomasz Cywka, Maciej Makuszewski, Maciej Gajos (89.Mihai Radut), Pedro Tiba (97.Lukasz Tralka), Darko Jevtic (66.João Amaral), Christian Gytkjær. Trainer: Ivan Djurdjevic.

Shakhtyor Solihorsk: Andrey Klimovich, Maksim Bordachev, Pavel Rybak [*sent off 120+1*], Siarhei Matveichyk, Igor Burko, Roger Cañas (73.Vitaly Lisakovich), Aleksandr Selyava, Yuri Kovalev, Július Szöke (91.Mikhail Shibun), Max Ebong Ngome (46.Sergey Balanovich [*sent off 117*]), Elis Bakaj (64.Denis Laptev [*sent off 120*]). Trainer: Sergey Tashuev.

Goals: 1-0 Christian Gytkjær (15), 1-1 Denis Laptev (79), 2-1, 3-1 Christian Gytkjær (94, 118).

[KKS Lech Poznań won 4-2 on aggregate]

26.07.2018; Right to Dream Park, Farum; Referee: Sébastien Delferière (Belgium); Attendance: 3,474

FC Nordsjælland Farum – AIK Stockholm 1-0(1-0)

FC Nordsjælland: Nicolai Larsen, Karlo Bartolec, Mads Pedersen, Andreas Skovgaard, Ulrik Jenssen, Victor Nelsson, Magnus Andersen (72.Nicklas Strunck Jakobsen), Andreas Skov Olsen (85.Mathias Rasmussen), Jacob Christensen, Mikkel Damsgaard (90+1.Benjamin Hansen), Mikkel Rygaard Jensen. Trainer: Kasper Hjulmand.

AIK Stockholm: Oscar Linnér, Per Karlsson, Daniel Sundgren, Alexander Milosevic, Rasmus Lindkvist (46.Heradi Rashidi), Robin Jansson, Tarik Elyounoussi (80.Henok Goitom), Sebastian Larsson, Enoch Adu, Kristoffer Olsson, Nicolás Stefanelli. Trainer: Rikard Norling.

Goal: 1-0 Magnus Andersen (11).

02.08.2018; Tele2 Arena, Stockholm; Referee: Jérôme Brisard (France); Attendance: 10,946

AIK Stockholm – FC Nordsjælland Farum 0-1(0-1)

AIK Stockholm: Oscar Linnér, Per Karlsson, Daniel Sundgren, Alexander Milosevic, Tarik Elyounoussi (82.Denni Avdic), Sebastian Larsson, Panajotis Dimitriadis (46.Enoch Adu), Kristoffer Olsson, Heradi Rashidi, Henok Goitom (71.Stefan Silva), Nicolás Stefanelli. Trainer: Rikard Norling.

FC Nordsjælland: Nicolai Larsen, Ulrik Jenssen, Karlo Bartolec (89.Mads Aaquist), Mads Pedersen, Andreas Skovgaard, Victor Nelsson, Magnus Andersen, Jacob Christensen, Mikkel Damsgaard, Mikkel Rygaard Jensen (67.Mathias Rasmussen), Andreas Skov Olsen (83.Nicklas Strunck Jakobsen). Trainer: Kasper Hjulmand.

Goal: 0-1 Andreas Skov Olsen (29).

[FC Nordsjælland Farum won 2-0 on aggregate]

26.07.2018; Linzer Stadion, Linz; Referee: Aleksei Eskov (Russia); Attendance: 8,304

LASK Linz – Lillestrøm SK 4-0(2-0)

LASK Linz: Alexander Schlager, Emanuel Pogatetz, Christian Ramsebner, Gernot Trauner, Reinhold Ranftl (84.Dominik Frieser), Maximilian Ullmann, James Holland, Thomas Goiginger, Peter Michorl, Yusuf Otubanjo (68.Samuel Tetteh), João Victor Santos Sá (77.Florian Jamnig). Trainer: Oliver Glasner.

Lillestrøm SK: Marko Maric, Frode Kippe, Marius Amundsen, Mats Haakenstad, Simen Rafn, Aleksander Melgalvis (87.Stefan Antonijevic), Fredrik Krogstad, Ifeanyi Matthew, Erling Knudtzon, Thomas Olsen (82.Moses Ebiye), Gary Martin (76.Simen Mikalsen). Trainer: Jörgen Lennartsson.

Goals: 1-0 Thomas Goiginger (6), 2-0 James Holland (45+1), 3-0 Thomas Goiginger (70), 4-0 Dominik Frieser (90+1).

02.08.2018; Åråsen Stadion, Lillestrøm; Referee: Vilhjálmur Thórarinsson (Iceland); Attendance: 1,975

Lillestrøm SK – LASK Linz 1-2(0-1)

Lillestrøm SK: Matvei Igonen, Frode Kippe (62.Stefan Antonijevic), Marius Amundsen, Simen Mikalsen, Mats Haakenstad, Simen Rafn, Erik Brenden, Fredrik Krogstad, Ifeanyi Matthew, Erling Knudtzon (62.Thomas Olsen), Gary Martin (73.Kristoffer Ødemarksbakken). Trainer: Jörgen Lennartsson.

LASK Linz: Alexander Schlager, Christian Ramsebner, Gernot Trauner, Reinhold Ranftl, Markus Wostry, Maximilian Ullmann, Florian Jamnig, James Holland (57.Fabian Benko), Thomas Goiginger (46.Dominik Frieser), Peter Michorl, Samuel Tetteh (73.Yusuf Otubanjo). Trainer: Oliver Glasner.

Goals: 0-1 Thomas Goiginger (35), 0-2 Samuel Tetteh (65), 1-2 Thomas Olsen (79).

[LASK Linz won 6-1 on aggregate]

26.07.2018; DASK Brestski Stadium, Brest; Referee: José María Sánchez Martínez (Spain); Attendance: 9,530

FK Dynamo Brest – APS Atromitos Athína 4-3(2-0)

Dynamo Brest: Pavel Pavlyuchenko, Oleg Veretilo, Giannis Kargas, Zeljko Filipovic (45.Pavel Nekhaychik), Oleksandr Noyok, Pavel Savitskiy, Chidi Osuchukwu (63.Andrey Zaleski), Roman Yuzepchuk (76.Maksim Vitus), Gaby Kiki, Oleksiy Khoblenko, Joel Fameyeh. Trainer: Aleksey Shpilevski.

Atromitos Athína: Nikola Mirkovic, Madson, Dimitrios Chatziisaias, Dimitris Giannoulis, Spyros Risvanis, Theodoros Vasilakakis (46.Iraklis Garoufalias), Azer Busuladzic, Spyridon Natsos, Georgios Manousos (76.Armin Mujakic), Efthymios Koulouris, Bruno Souza (46.Clarck N'Sikulu). Trainer: Damir Canadi.

Goals: 1-0 Zeljko Filipovic (5), 2-0, 3-0, 4-0 Pavel Savitskiy (13 penalty, 61, 70), 4-1 Georgios Manousos (74), 4-2 Oleg Veretilo (80 own goal), 4-3 Efthymios Koulouris (88).

02.08.2018; Stádio Peristeriou, Athína; Referee: Eitan Shemeulevitch (Israel); Attendance: 2,420

APS Atromitos Athína – FK Dynamo Brest 1-1(0-0)

Atromitos Athína: Nikola Mirkovic, Madson, Emanuel Sakic (75.Georgios Manousos), Dimitrios Chatziisaias, Dimitris Giannoulis, Spyros Risvanis, Javier Umbides, Kyriakos Kivrakidis, Armin Mujakic [*sent off 63 on the bench*] (60.Theodoros Vasilakakis), Kostas Kotsopoulos (60.Clarck N'Sikulu), Efthymios Koulouris. Trainer: Damir Canadi.

Dynamo Brest: Aleksandr Gutor, Maksim Vitus, Oleg Veretilo, Giannis Kargas, Zeljko Filipovic (82.Saliw Babawo), Oleksandr Noyok, Pavel Savitskiy, Chidi Osuchukwu, Roman Yuzepchuk, Oleksiy Khoblenko (69.Pavel Nekhaychik), Joel Fameyeh (46.Nivaldo). Trainer: Aleksey Shpilevski.

Goals: 1-0 Georgios Manousos (80), 1-1 Pavel Nekhaychik (90+5).

[FK Dynamo Brest won 5-4 on aggregate]

26.07.2018; Arena Zabrze, Zabrze; Referee: Mattias Gestranius (Finland); Attendance: 12,859

KS Górnik Zabrze – AS Trenčín 0-1(0-1)

Górnik Zabrze: Tomasz Loska, Dani Suárez, Adrian Gryszkiewicz, Daniel Liszka (79.Wiktor Biedrzycki), Przemyslaw Wisniewski, Szymon Matuszek, Angulo, Adam Wolniewicz, Daniel Smuga (61.Marcin Urynowicz), Szymon Zurkowski, Jesús Jiménez. Trainer: Marcin Brosz.

AS Trenčín: Igor Semrinec, Jamie Lawrence, Martin Sulek, Keston Julien (89.Lukás Skovajsa), Reuben Yem, Ashraf El Mahdioui, Abdul Zubairu, Joey Sleegers (73.Osman Bukari), Antonio Mance, Hamza Catakovic (83.Desley Ubbink), Philip Azango. Trainer: Ricardo Moniz.

Goal: 0-1 Philip Azango (39).

02.08.2018; Futbalovy stadión Spartak Myjava, Myjava; Referee: Ole Hobber Nilsen (Norway); Attendance: 1,897

AS Trenčín – KS Górnik Zabrze 4-1(2-0)

AS Trenčín: Igor Semrinec, Jamie Lawrence, Lukás Skovajsa, Martin Sulek, Reuben Yem, Ashraf El Mahdioui (90+1.Philippe van Arnhem), Abdul Zubairu, Joey Sleegers, Antonio Mance (90+1.Emeka Umeh), Hamza Catakovic, Philip Azango (86.Osman Bukari). Trainer: Ricardo Moniz.

Górnik Zabrze: Tomasz Loska, Dani Suárez, Adrian Gryszkiewicz, Daniel Liszka (46.Daniel Smuga), Przemyslaw Wisniewski, Szymon Matuszek, Angulo, Adam Wolniewicz, Marcin Urynowicz (46.Konrad Nowak), Szymon Zurkowski, Jesús Jiménez (73.Adam Ryczkowski). Trainer: Marcin Brosz.

Goals: 1-0 Angulo (10 own goal), 2-0 Hamza Catakovic (20), 3-0 Philip Azango (59), 3-1 Daniel Smuga (60), 4-0 Hamza Catakovic (90).

[AS Trenčín won 5-1 on aggregate]

26.07.2018; Gundadalur, Tórshavn; Referee: Evgen Aranovskiy (Ukraine); Attendance: 1,634

B36 Tórshavn – Beşiktaş JK İstanbul 0-2(0-2)

B36 Tórshavn: Rói Hentze, Odmar Færø, Alex Mellemgaard (41.Benjamin Heinesen), Bjarni Petersen, Erlendur Magnusson, Meinhard Olsen, Andrias Eriksen, Robert Hedin Brockie, Magnus Holm Jacobsen (79.Hugin Samuelsen), Kaimar Saag (60.Michal Przybylski), Lukasz Cieslewicz. Trainer: Jákup á Borg.

Beşiktaş: Tolga Zengin, Adriano, Caner Erkin, Gökhan Gönül, Gary Medel, Fatih Aksoy, Ryan Babel, Jeremain Lens (85.Vágner Love), Necip Uysal, Tolgay Arslan (78.Dorukhan Toköz), Cyle Larin (74.Mustafa Pektemek). Trainer: Senol Günes.

Goals: 0-1 Jeremain Lens (8), 0-2 Gökhan Gönül (26).

02.08.2018; Vodafone Stadyumu, İstanbul; Referee: Carlos Miguel Taborda Xistra (Portugal); Attendance: 23,929

Beşiktaş JK İstanbul – B36 Tórshavn 6-0(2-0)

Beşiktaş: Tolga Zengin, Adriano, Caner Erkin, Gökhan Gönül, Gary Medel, Fatih Aksoy (46.Oguzhan Özyakup), Ryan Babel (77.Vágner Love), Jeremain Lens (62.Gökhan Töre), Necip Uysal, Tolgay Arslan, Cyle Larin. Trainer: Senol Günes.

B36 Tórshavn: Trygvi Ashkam, Odmar Færø, Bjarni Petersen, Erlendur Magnusson, Eli Nielsen, Meinhard Olsen, Benjamin Heinesen, Andrias Eriksen, Robert Hedin Brockie, Michal Przybylski (62.Hugin Samuelsen), Lukasz Cieslewicz (20.Kaimar Saag, 71.Magnus Holm Jacobsen). Trainer: Jákup á Borg.

Goals: 1-0 Cyle Larin (31), 2-0 Caner Erkin (43), 3-0 Cyle Larin (61), 4-0 Oguzhan Özyakup (74), 5-0 Cyle Larin (79), 6-0 Vágner Love (90+3 penalty).

[Beşiktaş JK İstanbul won 8-0 on aggregate]

26.07.2018; Luminus Arena, Genk; Referee: Martin Strömbergsson (Sweden); Attendance: 10,300

KRC Genk – CS Fola Esch 5-0(4-0)

KRC Genk: Nordin Jackers, Sebastien Dewaest, Bojan Nastic, Jhon Lucumí, Pozuelo (63.Zinho Gano), Ruslan Malinovskiy (46.Ibrahima Seck), Sander Berge, Joakim Mæhle, Leandro Trossard, Mbwana Samatta (75.Jakub Piotrowski), Edon Zhegrova. Trainer: Philippe Clement.

Fola Esch: Thomas Hym, Rodrigue Dikaba, Peter Chrappan, Julien Klein, Mehdi Kirch, Cédric Sacras, Veldin Muharemovic, Ryan Klapp (80.Moussa Seydi), Gérard Mersch, Samir Hadji (84.Dejvid Sinani), Ken Corral (66.Stefano Bensi). Trainer: Thomas Klasen.

Goals: 1-0 Ruslan Malinovskiy (4), 2-0 Pozuelo (19), 3-0 Leandro Trossard (25), 4-0 Sebastien Dewaest (28), 5-0 Leandro Trossard (73 penalty).

01.08.2018; Stade „Émile Mayrisch", Esch-sur-Alzette; Referee: Filip Glova (Slovakia); Attendance: 1,550

CS Fola Esch – KRC Genk 1-4(0-2)

Fola Esch: Emanuel Cabral, Rodrigue Dikaba, Peter Chrappan, Julien Klein (77.Guillaume Mura), Mehdi Kirch (66.Corentin Koçur), Dejvid Sinani, Bruno Freire, Stefano Bensi (83.Lucas Raposo), Samir Hadji, Ken Corral, Roman Pierrard. Trainer: Thomas Klasen.

KRC Genk: Nordin Jackers, Bojan Nastic, Dries Wouters, Jhon Lucumí, Rubin Seigers, Ibrahima Seck, Manuel Benson, Bryan Heynen (66.Nikolaos Karelis), Jakub Piotrowski, Zinho Gano, Edon Zhegrova. Trainer: Philippe Clement.

Goals: 0-1 Edon Zhegrova (13), 0-2 Bryan Heynen (16), 0-3 Zinho Gano (59), 1-3 Stefano Bensi (61), 1-4 Edon Zhegrova (63).

[KRC Genk won 9-1 on aggregate]

26.07.2018; Stadion Poljud, Split; Referee: István Kovács (Romania); Attendance: 26,103

HNK Hajduk Split – PFC Slavia Sofia 1-0(0-0)

Hajduk Split: Josip Posavec, André Fomitschow, Zoran Nizic, Borja López, Ádám Gyurcsó, Mijo Caktas, Hamza Barry, Josip Juranovic, Fran Tudor (46.Ahmed Said), Ante Palaversa (53.Toma Basic), Mirko Ivanovski (76.Ivan Delic). Trainer: Zeljko Kopic.

Slavia Sofia: Georgi Petkov, Aleksandar Aleksandrov [*sent off 84*], Emil Martinov, Aleksandar Stanisavljevic, Andrea Hristov, Momchil Tsvetanov (71.Slavcho Shokolarov), Galin Ivanov (90+4.Georgi Yomov), Yanis Karabelyov, Dimitar Velkovski, Vladislav Uzunov, Milcho Angelov (86.Tsvetelin Chunchukov). Trainer: Zlatomir Zagorcic.

Goal: 1-0 Ahmed Said (79).

02.08.2018; Nationalen Stadion "Vasil Levski", Sofia; Referee: Daniele Doveri (Italy); Attendance: 2,100

PFC Slavia Sofia – HNK Hajduk Split 2-3(1-1)

Slavia Sofia: Antonis Stergiakis, Emil Martinov, Aleksandar Stanisavljevic, Momchil Tsvetanov (58.Slavcho Shokolarov), Galin Ivanov (90+1.Filip Krastev), Milen Gamakov, Yanis Karabelyov, Dimitar Velkovski, Georgi Yomov, Vladislav Uzunov, Tsvetelin Chunchukov (71.Milcho Angelov). Trainer: Zlatomir Zagorcic.

Hajduk Split: Marin Ljubic, André Fomitschow, Borja López, Bozo Mikulic, Ádám Gyurcsó (66.Michele Sego), Mijo Caktas, Hamza Barry (77.Stipe Vucur), Dino Besirovic (7.Stanko Juric), Toma Basic, Josip Juranovic, Ahmed Said. Trainer: Zeljko Kopic.

Goals: 0-1 Stanko Juric (25), 1-1 Galin Ivanov (45 penalty), 1-2 Mijo Caktas (55 penalty), 2-2 Georgi Yomov (70), 2-3 Mijo Caktas (87).

[HNK Hajduk Split won 4-2 on aggregate]

26.07.2018; Kybunpark, St. Gallen; Referee: Fábio José Costa Veríssimo (Portugal); Attendance: 6,335

FC St. Gallen – Sarpsborg 08 FF 2-1(1-1)

FC St. Gallen: Dejan Stojanovic, Milan Vilotic [*sent off 4*], Andreas Wittwer, Nicolas Lüchinger (84.Leonel Mosevich), Silvan Hefti, Marco Aratore (75.Nassim Ben Khalifa), Jordi Quintillà, Dereck Kutesa (46.Yannis Tafer), Vincent Sierro, Majeed Ashimeru, Roman Buess. Trainer: Peter Zeidler.

Sarpsborg 08: Aslak Falch, Amin Askar, Joackim Jørgensen, Joonas Tamm, Matti Lund Nielsen, Ole Halvorsen, Jon-Helge Tveita, Kristoffer Zachariassen, Tobias Heintz (23.Kristoffer Larsen, 72.Harmeet Singh), Patrick Mortensen, Rashad Muhammed (66.Mikkel Agger). Trainer: Geir Bakke.

Goals: 0-1 Tobias Heintz (6), 1-1 Silvan Hefti (41), 2-1 Roman Buess (66).

02.08.2018; Sarpsborg Stadion, Sarpsborg; Referee: Frank Schneider (France); Attendance: 5,460

Sarpsborg 08 FF – FC St. Gallen 1-0(1-0)

Sarpsborg 08: Alexander Vasyutin, Amin Askar, Joackim Jørgensen, Joachim Thomassen, Joonas Tamm, Matti Lund Nielsen, Ole Halvorsen, Jon-Helge Tveita, Kristoffer Zachariassen, Patrick Mortensen, Rashad Muhammed (90+1.Harmeet Singh). Trainer: Geir Bakke.

FC St. Gallen: Dejan Stojanovic, Andreas Wittwer, Nicolas Lüchinger, Silvan Hefti, Leonel Mosevich (82.Dereck Kutesa), Yannis Tafer, Marco Aratore (46.Nassim Ben Khalifa), Jordi Quintillà, Vincent Sierro, Majeed Ashimeru, Roman Buess (73.Cedric Itten). Trainer: Peter Zeidler.

Goal: 1-0 Patrick Mortensen (31).

[Sarpsborg 08 FF won on away goals rule (2-2 on aggregate)]

26.07.2018; MAPEI Stadium – Città del Tricolore, Reggio Emilia; Referee: Tamás Bognár (Hungary); Attendance: 7,518

Atalanta Bergamasca Calcio – FK Sarajevo 2-2(2-0)

Atalanta: Etrit Berisha, Andrea Masiello, Rafael Tolói, Hans Hateboer, Robin Gosens (83.Marco Tumminello), Gianluca Mancini (75.José Palomino), Alejandro Gómez, Marco D'Alessandro (54.Duván Zapata), Marten de Roon, Matteo Pessina, Musa Barrow. Trainer: Gian Piero Gasperini.

FK Sarajevo: Bojan Pavlovic, Amer Dupovac, Nihad Mujakic, Selmir Pidro, Emir Halilovic (84.Milos Stanojevic), Amar Rahmanovic, Anel Hebibovic, Joachim Adukor, Mersudin Ahmetovic (60.Haris Handzic), Krste Velkoski, Aladin Sisic (85.Benjamin Tatar). Trainer: Husref Musemic.

Goals: 1-0 Rafael Tolói (11), 2-0 Gianluca Mancini (45+3), 2-1 Haris Handzic (67), 2-2 Aladin Sisic (72).

02.08.2018; Stadion "Asim Ferhatović Hase", Sarajevo; Referee: Stuart Attwell (England); Attendance: 23,820

FK Sarajevo – Atalanta Bergamasca Calcio 0-8(0-5)

FK Sarajevo: Bojan Pavlovic, Amer Dupovac, Nihad Mujakic, Selmir Pidro, Emir Halilovic, Amar Rahmanovic (75.Milos Stanojevic), Anel Hebibovic, Joachim Adukor, Mersudin Ahmetovic (69.Haris Handzic), Krste Velkoski, Aladin Sisic (83.Benjamin Tatar). Trainer: Husref Musemic.

Atalanta: Etrit Berisha, Andrea Masiello, Rafael Tolói (75.Timothy Castagne), José Palomino, Hans Hateboer, Robin Gosens, Alejandro Gómez, Marten de Roon (55.Duván Zapata), Remo Freuler (81.Luca Valzania), Matteo Pessina, Musa Barrow. Trainer: Gian Piero Gasperini.

Goals: 0-1 José Palomino (4), 0-2 Alejandro Gómez (15), 0-3 Andrea Masiello (18), 0-4 Alejandro Gómez (28), 0-5 Mersudin Ahmetovic (39 own goal), 0-6, 0-7, 0-8 Musa Barrow (51, 70, 87).

[Atalanta Bergamasca Calcio won 10-2 on aggregate]

26.07.2018; Stadion Partizan, Beograd; Referee: Georgi Kabakov (Bulgaria); Attendance: 6,210

FK Partizan Beograd – FK Trakai Vilnius 1-0(0-0)

Partizan Beograd: Vladimir Stojkovic, Marc Valiente, Sasa Zdjelar, Zlatan Sehovic, Svetozar Markovic, Gabriel Enache, Nebojsa Kosovic, Seydouba Soumah, Danilo Pantic (68.Marko Jankovic), Ricardo Gomes, Djordje Ivanovic (81.Sasa Ilic). Trainer: Miroslav Djukic.

FK Trakai: Tomas Svedkauskas, Valdemars Borovskis, Evgeniy Osipov, Justinas Janusevskis, Diniyar Bilyaletdinov, Vaidas Silénas, Valentin Jeriomenko, Donatas Kazlauskas (58.Kevin Ntika Bondombe), Modestas Vorobjovas [*sent off 53*], Svajūnas Cyzas (76.Aleksandras Levsinas), Justinas Marazas (88.Rokas Masenzovas). Trainer: Kibu Vicuña.

Goal: 1-0 Justinas Janusevskis (57 own goal).

02.08.2018; LFF stadionas, Vilnius; Referee: Stephan Klossner (Switzerland); Attendance: 1,980

FK Trakai Vilnius – FK Partizan Beograd 1-1(1-1)

FK Trakai: Tomas Svedkauskas, Valdemars Borovskis, Evgeniy Osipov, Justinas Janusevskis, Diniyar Bilyaletdinov, Vaidas Silénas, Valentin Jeriomenko, Donatas Kazlauskas, Lajo Traore (58.Etienne Mukanya), Svajūnas Cyzas, Justinas Marazas (86.Elvinas Alisauskas). Trainer: Kibu Vicuña.

Partizan Beograd: Vladimir Stojkovic, Marc Valiente, Nemanja Miletic (I), Sasa Zdjelar, Gabriel Enache, Nebojsa Kosovic, Seydouba Soumah [*sent off 53*], Marko Jankovic (88.Djordje Ivanovic), Danilo Pantic (75.Armin Djerlek), Nemanja Miletic (II), Ricardo Gomes (82.Ognjen Ozegovic). Trainer: Miroslav Djukic.

Goals: 1-0 Evgeniy Osipov (9), 1-1 Nemanja Miletic (I) (45+3).

[FK Partizan Beograd won 2-1 on aggregate]

26.07.2018; Stadion Grbavica, Sarajevo; Referee: Alexander Harkam (Austria); Attendance: 11,821

FK Željezničar Sarajevo – Apollon Limassol FC 1-2(0-1)

Željezničar: Vedran Kjosevski, Jadranko Bogicevic, Milos Bakrac, Matej Rodin, Ivan Curjuric, Stojan Vranjes (70.Jovan Blagojevic), Antonio Pavic, Filip Arezina (84.Mladen Veselinovic), Anel Sabanadzovic, Sulejman Krpic, Dzenan Zajmovic (46.Asim Zec). Trainer: Slobodan Krcmarevic.

Apollon: Bruno Vale, Valentin Roberge, Charis Kyriakou, Richard Soumah (46.Giorgos Vasiliou), Héctor Yuste, Sasa Markovic (67.Facundo Pereyra), Esteban Sachetti, João Pedro, Fotis Papoulis (84.André Schembri), Anton Maglica, Adrián Sardinero. Trainer: Sofronis Avgousti.

Goals: 0-1 Jadranko Bogicevic (23 own goal), 0-2 Esteban Sachetti (79), 1-2 Sulejman Krpic (90).

02.08.2018; Stádio Neo GSP, Nicosia; Referee: Nikola Popov (Bulgaria); Attendance: 3,400

Apollon Limassol FC – FK Željezničar Sarajevo 3-1(1-1)

Apollon: Bruno Vale, Valentin Roberge, Charis Kyriakou, André Schembri (46.Facundo Pereyra), Héctor Yuste, Giorgos Vasiliou, Esteban Sachetti, João Pedro, Fotis Papoulis, Anton Maglica (46.Emilio Zelaya), Adrián Sardinero (73.Kevin Bru). Trainer: Sofronis Avgousti.

Željezničar: Vedran Kjosevski, Jadranko Bogicevic, Milos Bakrac, Aldin Sehic (57.Sinia Stevanovic), Ivan Curjuric, Stojan Vranjes, Antonio Pavic, Mladen Veselinovic (46.Dzenan Zajmovic), Anel Sabanadzovic (64.Jovan Blagojevic), Sulejman Krpic, Asim Zec. Trainer: Milomir Odovic.

Goals: 1-0 Fotis Papoulis (2), 1-1 Asim Zec (43), 2-1, 3-1 Fotis Papoulis (57 penalty, 90).

[Apollon Limassol FC won 5-2 on aggregate]

26.07.2018; Pittodrie Stadium, Aberdeen; Referee: Daniel Siebert (Germany); Attendance: 20,313

Aberdeen FC – Burnley FC 1-1(1-0)

Aberdeen FC: Joe Lewis, Shay Logan, Graeme Shinnie, Thomas Hoban, Michael Devlin, Dominic Ball, Scott McKenna, Niall McGinn (79.Scott Wright), Gary Mackay-Steven, Lewis Ferguson (57.Stephen Gleeson), Sam Cosgrove (77.Stevie May). Trainer: Derek McInnes.

Burnley FC: Nick Pope (14.Anders Lindegaard), Stephen Ward, Matthew Lowton, Ben Mee, James Tarkowski, Aaron Lennon, Jack Cork, Jóhann Gudmundsson, Ashley Westwood, Jeffrey Hendrick (67.Samuel Vokes), Chris Wood. Trainer: Sean Dyche.

Goals: 1-0 Gary Mackay-Steven (19 penalty), 1-1 Samuel Vokes (80).

02.08.2018; Turf Moor, Burnley; Referee: Massimiliano Irrati (Italy); Attendance: 17,404

Burnley FC – Aberdeen FC 3-1(1-1,1-1)

Burnley FC: Anders Lindegaard, Stephen Ward (91.Charlie Taylor), Matthew Lowton, Ben Mee, James Tarkowski, Aaron Lennon (87.Dwight McNeil), Jack Cork, Jóhann Gudmundsson, Ashley Westwood (105.Jeffrey Hendrick), Samuel Vokes, Chris Wood (46.Ashley Barnes). Trainer: Sean Dyche.

Aberdeen FC: Joe Lewis, Andrew Considine, Shay Logan, Graeme Shinnie, Thomas Hoban (88.Dominic Ball), Michael Devlin, Scott McKenna, Niall McGinn (81.Scott Wright), Gary Mackay-Steven, Lewis Ferguson (105.Chris Forrester), Sam Cosgrove (100.Stevie May). Trainer: Derek McInnes.

Goals: 1-0 Chris Wood (6), 1-1 Lewis Ferguson (27), 2-1 Jack Cork (102), 3-1 Ashley Barnes (114 penalty).

[Burnley FC won 4-2 on aggregate]

26.07.2018; Oriel Park, Dundalk; Referee: Harald Lechner (Austria); Attendance: 3,000

Dundalk FC – AEK Larnaca FC 0-0

Dundalk FC: Gary Rogers, Brain Gartland, Dane Massey (81.Dean Jarvis), Sean Hoare, Daniel Cleary, Chris Shields, Robbie Benson, Dylan Connolly (84.Ronan Murray), Jamie McGrath (67.Patrick McEleney), Patrick Hoban, Michael Duffy. Trainer: Stephen Kenny.

AEK Larnaca: Toño, Mikel González, Truyols, Thomas Ioannou, Igor Carioca, Ivan Trickovski, Jorge Larena (83.Nacho Cases), Acorán, Joan Tomás (62.Tete), Hector Hevel, Apostolos Giannou (90.Onisiforos Roushias). Trainer: Andoni Iraola.

02.08.2018; AEK Arena, Larnaca; Referee: Fran Jović (Croatia); Attendance: 3,991

AEK Larnaca FC – Dundalk FC 4-0(3-0)

AEK Larnaca: Toño, Mikel González, Truyols, Thomas Ioannou, Igor Carioca, Ivan Trickovski, Jorge Larena (70.Nacho Cases), Acorán (86.Joan Tomás), Hector Hevel, Apostolos Giannou, Tete (81.Konstantinos Konstantinou). Trainer: Andoni Iraola.

Dundalk FC: Gary Rogers, Brain Gartland, Dean Jarvis, Sean Hoare (65.Dane Massey), Daniel Cleary (46.Sean Gannon), Chris Shields, Robbie Benson, Dylan Connolly (46.Patrick McEleney), Jamie McGrath, Patrick Hoban, Michael Duffy. Trainer: Stephen Kenny.

Goals: 1-0 Ivan Trickovski (13), 2-0 Tete (21), 3-0 Ivan Trickovski (38), 4-0 Joan Tomás (87).

[AEK Larnaca FC won 4-0 on aggregate]

26.07.2018; Stadion Karađorđe, Novi Sad; Referee: Pawel Raczkowski (Poland); Attendance: 4,000

FK Spartak Subotica – AC Sparta Praha 2-0(1-0)

Spartak Subotica: Nikola Peric, Andrija Vukcevic (74.Samuel Afum), Branimir Jocic, Noboru Shimura, Dejan Kerkez, Nemanja Calasan, Nemanja Tekijaski, Mile Savkovic, Bojan Cecaric (86.Milan Marcic), Nemanja Glavcic, Ognjen Djuricin (75.Stefan Milosevic). Trainer: Vladimir Gacinovic.

AC Sparta Praha: Florin Nita, Semih Kaya, Uros Radakovic, Alexandru Chipciu, Tal Ben Chaim (61.Vukadin Vukadinovic), Nicolae Stanciu, Martin Frydek, Guélor Kanga, Srdjan Plavsic (46.Josef Sural), Jirí Kulhánek, Benjamin Tetteh (84.Mihailo Ristic). Trainer: Pavel Hapal.

Goals: 1-0 Nemanja Calasan (8), 2-0 Ognjen Djuricin (57).

02.08.2018; Generali Arena, Praha; Referee: Sebastian Colţescu (Romania); Attendance: 12,068

AC Sparta Praha – FK Spartak Subotica 2-1(1-0)

AC Sparta Praha: Florin Nita, Semih Kaya, Costa Nhamoinesu (85.Bogdan Vatajelu), Uros Radakovic, Alexandru Chipciu (90+6.Lukas Stetina), Josef Sural [*sent off 90+8*], Nicolae Stanciu, Martin Frydek, Guélor Kanga, Srdjan Plavsic, Benjamin Tetteh. Trainer: Zdenek Scasny.

Spartak Subotica: Nikola Peric, Andrija Vukcevic, Branimir Jocic, Noboru Shimura, Dejan Kerkez, Nemanja Calasan (36.Milan Marcic [*sent off 82*]), Nemanja Tekijaski, Mile Savkovic, Bojan Cecaric (90+4.Vladimir Torbica), Nemanja Glavcic, Ognjen Djuricin (56.Dejan Djenic). Trainer: Vladimir Gacinovic.

Goals: 1-0 Josef Sural (28), 2-0 Srdjan Plavsic (66), 2-1 Bojan Cecaric (75 penalty).

[FK Spartak Subotica won 3-2 on aggregate]

26.07.2018; Stadion Gradski vrt, Osijek; Referee: Paweł Gil (Poland); Attendance: 7,112

NK Osijek – Rangers FC Glasgow 0-1(0-1)

NK Osijek: Marko Malenica, Borna Barisic, Tomislav Sorsa (46.Petar Bockaj), Domagoj Pusic (80.Haris Hajradinovic), Mile Skoric, Benedik Mioc (62.Dmitriy Lepa), Alen Grgic, Robert Mudrazija, Danijel Loncar, Mirko Maric, Ezekiel Henty. Trainer: Zoran Zekic.

Rangers: Allan McGregor, James Tavernier, Connor Goldson, Jon Flanagan, Nikola Katic, Jamie Murphy (68.Josh Windass), Ryan Jack, Ryan Kent, Oviemuno Ejaria (78.Ross McCrorie), Lassana Coulibaly, Alfredo Morelos (90+4.Glenn Middleton). Trainer: Steven Gerrard.

Goal: 0-1 Alfredo Morelos (18).

02.08.2018; Ibrox Stadium, Glasgow; Referee: Dennis Higler (Netherlands); Attendance: 48,202

Rangers FC Glasgow – NK Osijek 1-1(0-0)

Rangers: Allan McGregor, James Tavernier, Connor Goldson, Jon Flanagan, Nikola Katic, Ryan Jack, Ryan Kent, Oviemuno Ejaria (90+3.Andrew Halliday), Lassana Coulibaly (75.Scott Arfield), Candeias (85.Josh Windass), Alfredo Morelos. Trainer: Steven Gerrard.

NK Osijek: Marko Malenica, Guti, Borna Barisic, Mile Skoric, Haris Hajradinovic, Benedik Mioc (80.Marin Pilj), Alen Grgic, Petar Bockaj (66.Tomislav Sorsa), Robert Mudrazija, Mirko Maric (66.Tomislav Strkalj), Ezekiel Henty. Trainer: Zoran Zekic.

Goals: 1-0 Nikola Katic (53), 1-1 Connor Goldson (89 own goal).

[Rangers FC Glasgow won 2-1 on aggregate]

26.07.2018; Easter Road Stadium, Edinburgh; Referee: Andreas Ekberg (Sweden); Attendance: 14,148

Hibernian FC Edinburgh – Asteras Tripolis FC 3-2(0-2)

Hibernian FC: Ádám Bogdán, Steven Whittaker (46.David Gray), Lewis Stevenson, Paul Hanlon (90+4.Ryan Porteous), Darren McGregor, Efe Ambrose, Vykintas Slivka, John McGinn, Stephen Mallan, Martin Boyle, Florian Kamberi. Trainer: Neil Lennon.

Asteras Tripolis: Georgios Athanasiadis, Konstantinos Triantafyllopoulos, Giorgos Kyriakopoulos, Triantafyllos Pasalidis [*sent off 84*], Matías Iglesias, Juan Munafo, Franco Bellocq (55.Martín Rolle), Nikolaos Kaltsas (77.Ángel Martínez), Michalis Manias, Kosmas Tsilianidis (86.Ioannis Christopoulos), Giannis Kotsiras. Trainer: Savvas Pantelidis.

Goals: 0-1, 0-2 Giorgos Kyriakopoulos (12, 35), 1-2 Efe Ambrose (64), 2-2 David Gray (77), 3-2 Florian Kamberi (90+3).

02.08.2018; Stádio „Theororos Kolokotronis", Tripoli; Referee: Benoît Millot (France); Attendance: 3,870

Asteras Tripolis FC – Hibernian FC Edinburgh 1-1(0-1)

Asteras Tripolis: Georgios Athanasiadis, Konstantinos Triantafyllopoulos, Giorgos Kyriakopoulos, Matías Iglesias, Juan Munafo, Franco Bellocq (57.Anastasios Douvikas), José Luis Valiente (90+1.Lucas Salas), Nikolaos Kaltsas (78.Martín Rolle), Michalis Manias [*sent off 48*], Kosmas Tsilianidis, Giannis Kotsiras. Trainer: Savvas Pantelidis.

Hibernian FC: Ádám Bogdán, Lewis Stevenson, Paul Hanlon, Darren McGregor (78.Steven Whittaker), Efe Ambrose, David Gray, Vykintas Slivka (89.Marvin Bartley), John McGinn, Stephen Mallan (90+2.Ryan Porteous), Martin Boyle, Florian Kamberi. Trainer: Neil Lennon.

Goals: 0-1 John McGinn (44), 1-1 Kosmas Tsilianidis (56).

[Hibernian FC Edinburgh won 4-3 on aggregate]

26.07.2018; Samsung völlurinn, Gardabær; Referee: Robert Schörgenhofer (Austria); Attendance: 1,050

Stjarnan Garðabær – FC København 0-2(0-0)

Stjarnan Garðabær: Haraldur Björnsson, Baldur Sigurdsson, Jósef Kristinn Jósefsson, Óttar Bjarni Gudmundsson, Daníel Laxdal, Jóhann Laxdal, Eyjólfur Hédinsson (67.Alex Thór Hauksson), Thorsteinn Már Ragnarsson (85.Sölvi Fodilsson), Gunjón Baldvinsson, Thórarinn Valdimarsson (62.Gudmundur Hafsteinsson), Hilmar Árni Halldórsson. Trainer: Rúnar Sigmundsson.

FC København: Stephan Andersen, Pierre Bengtsson, Sotirios Papagiannopoulos, Denis Vavro, Mads Roerslev Rasmussen, Ján Gregus, Rasmus Falk (46.Viktor Fischer), Zeca (46.Robert Skov), Nicolaj Thomsen, Dame N'Doye (64.Carlo Holse), Kenan Kodro. Trainer: Ståle Solbakken.

Goals: 0-1 Kenan Kodro (52), 0-2 Viktor Fischer (58).

02.08.2018; Telia Parken, København; Referee: Paul Tierney (England); Attendance: 8,726

FC København – Stjarnan Garðabær 5-0(3-0)

FC København: Stephan Andersen, Pierre Bengtsson (46.Denis Vavro), Sotirios Papagiannopoulos, Michael Lüftner, Mads Roerslev Rasmussen, William Kvist, Ján Gregus, Rasmus Falk (46.Nicolaj Thomsen), Viktor Fischer (53.Bashkim Kadrii), Kenan Kodro, Carlo Holse. Trainer: Ståle Solbakken.

Stjarnan Garðabær: Haraldur Björnsson, Baldur Sigurdsson (62.Thorri Geir Rúnarsson), Jósef Kristinn Jósefsson (52.Thórarinn Valdimarsson), Brynjar Gudjónsson, Daníel Laxdal, Jóhann Laxdal, Eyjólfur Hédinsson, Thorsteinn Már Ragnarsson (70.Sölvi Fodilsson), Alex Thór Hauksson, Gunjón Baldvinsson, Hilmar Árni Halldórsson. Trainer: Rúnar Sigmundsson.

Goals: 1-0 Viktor Fischer (4), 2-0 Carlo Holse (24), 3-0, 4-0, 5-0 Kenan Kodro (39, 47, 74).

[FC København won 7-0 on aggregate]

26.07.2018; MOL Aréna, Dunajská Streda; Referee: Sergiy Boyko (Ukraine); Attendance: 9,227

FK DAC Dunajská Streda – FC Dinamo Minsk 1-3(1-1)

DAC Dunajská Streda: Patrik Macej, Lubomír Satka, Milan Simcák [*sent off 39*], Marin Ljubicic, Erik Pacinda, Tomás Huk, Zsolt Kalmár (74.Máté Vida), Kristián Kostrna, Krisztopher Vida (87.Maksym Tretyakov), Christián Herc (42.Éric Davis), Vakoun Issouf Bayo. Trainer: Peter Hyballa.

Dinamo Minsk: Andrey Gorbunov, Igor Shitov, Luis Rocha, Roman Begunov, Nino Galovic, Maksim Zhavnerchik, Seidu Yahaya, Filipp Ivanov (72.Aleksandr Makas), Nikita Korzun (81.Dinko Trebotic), Uros Nikolic, Vladimir Khvashchinskiy (61.Artem Gurenko). Trainer: Sergei Gurenko.

Goals: 0-1 Roman Begunov (24), 1-1 Erik Pacinda (45 penalty), 1-2 Aleksandr Makas (77), 1-3 Uros Nikolic (90+4).

02.08.2018; Dinamo Stadium, Minsk; Referee: Antti Munukka (Finland); Attendance: 9,450

FC Dinamo Minsk – FK DAC Dunajská Streda 4-1(1-0)

Dinamo Minsk: Andrey Gorbunov, Igor Shitov, Luis Rocha, Roman Begunov, Nino Galovic, Maksim Shvetsov, Seidu Yahaya, Filipp Ivanov (61.Aleksandr Makas), Nikita Korzun, Uros Nikolic (70.Dinko Trebotic), Vladimir Khvashchinskiy (57.Artem Gurenko). Trainer: Sergei Gurenko.

DAC Dunajská Streda: Patrik Macej, Éric Davis, Souleymane Koné (18.Lubomír Satka), Marin Ljubicic, Tomás Huk, Zsolt Kalmár, Kristián Kostrna (79.Dominik Spiriak), Krisztopher Vida, Máté Vida, Christián Herc, Vakoun Issouf Bayo (41.Marko Divkovic). Trainer: Peter Hyballa.

Goals: 1-0 Uros Nikolic (19), 2-0 Vladimir Khvashchinskiy (47), 3-0 Filipp Ivanov (51 penalty), 4-0 Uros Nikolic (58), 4-1 Krisztopher Vida (73).

[FC Dinamo Minsk won 7-2 on aggregate]

26.07.2018; Estadio „Ramón Sánchez Pizjuán", Sevilla; Referee: Andris Treimanis (Latvia); Attendance: 29,671

Sevilla FC – Újpest FC 4-0(3-0)

Sevilla FC: Tomás Vaclík, Nicolás Pareja, Daniel Carriço, Sergio Escudero, Guilherme Arana (77.Borja Lasso), Jesús Navas (58.Sébastien Corchia), Franco Vázquez, Pablo Sarabia (70.Pejiño), Roque Mesa, Nolito, Wissam Ben Yedder. Trainer: Pablo Machín.

Újpest FC: Filip Pajovic, Mijusko Bojovic, Branko Pauljevic [*sent off 31*], Róbert Litauszki, Dzenan Burekovic, Dániel Nagy (33.Benjámin Balász), Bojan Sankovic, Donát Zsótér (64.Razvan Horj), Alassane Diallo, Obinna Nwobodo, Soma Novothny. Trainer: Nebojsa Vignjevic.

Goals: 1-0 Jesús Navas (7), 2-0 Wissam Ben Yedder (32 penalty), 3-0 Pablo Sarabia (43), 4-0 Franco Vázquez (90+2).

02.08.2018; „Szusza Ferenc" Stadion, Budapest; Referee: Kirill Levnikov (Russia); Attendance: 9,785

Újpest FC – Sevilla FC 1-3(0-1)

Újpest FC: Filip Pajovic, Mijusko Bojovic, Róbert Litauszki (89.Razvan Horj), Dzenan Burekovic, Dániel Nagy (67.Kristóf Szücs), Benjámin Balász, Bojan Sankovic, Donát Zsótér, Alassane Diallo, Obinna Nwobodo, Soma Novothny (66.Patrik Tischler). Trainer: Nebojsa Vignjevic.

Sevilla FC: Sergio Rico, Gabriel Mercado, Daniel Carriço, Sergio Escudero, Sébastien Corchia, Sergi Gómez, Éver Banega (72.Roque Mesa), Franco Vázquez, Pablo Sarabia (65.Nolito), Pejiño, Wissam Ben Yedder (66.Luis Muriel). Trainer: Pablo Machín.

Goals: 0-1, 0-2 Pablo Sarabia (36, 50), 1-2 Donát Zsótér 77), 1-3 Luis Muriel (83).

[Sevilla FC won 7-1 on aggregate]

THIRD QUALIFYING ROUND

CHAMPIONS PATH

09.08.2018; „Vazgen Sargsyan" Hanrapetakan Stadium, Yerevan; Referee: Sergey Boyko (Ukraine); Attendance: 9,000

FC Alashkert – FC CFR 1907 Cluj-Napoca 0-2(0-1)

FC Alashkert: Ognjen Cancarevic, Gagik Dagbashyan, Artak Yedigaryan, Oliver Práznovsky, Taron Voskanyan, Danijel Stojkovic, Artur Yedigaryan (52.Danilo Sekulic), Gustavo Marmentini dos Santos (53.Edgar Manucharyan), Jefferson (65.César Romero), Artak Grigoryan, Uros Nenadovic. Trainer: Varuzhan Sukiasyan.

CFR 1907: Giedrius Arlauskis, Andrei Muresan, Paulo Vinícius, Camora, Cristian Manea, Ovidiu Hoban, Damjan Djokovic, Mihai Bordeianu (82.Alexandru Ionita (II)), Alexandru Paun, Sebastian Mailat (63.Valentin Costache), George Tucudean (68.Robert Tambe).
Trainer: Toni Conceição.

Goals: 0-1, 0-2 George Tucudean (5, 49 penalty).

16.08.2018; Stadionul "Dr. Constantin Rădulescu", Cluj-Napoca; Referee: Vilhjálmur Alvar Thórarinsson (Iceland); Attendance: 5,500

FC CFR 1907 Cluj-Napoca – FC Alashkert 5-0(2-0)

CFR 1907: Cosmin Vatca, Andrei Muresan, Paulo Vinícius, Camora, Andrei Peteleu, Emmanuel Culio (64.Alexandru Ionita (II)), Ovidiu Hoban, Damjan Djokovic (56.Mihai Bordeianu), Alexandru Paun, George Tucudean, Billel Omrani (69.Sebastian Mailat). Trainer: Toni Conceição.

FC Alashkert: Ognjen Cancarevic, Gagik Dagbashyan, Artak Yedigaryan, Oliver Práznovsky, Mladen Zeljkovic, Danijel Stojkovic, Artur Yedigaryan, Danilo Sekulic (58.César Romero), Edgar Manucharyan (63.Artem Simonyan), Artak Grigoryan, Uros Nenadovic (58.Artak Dashyan). Trainer: Varuzhan Sukiasyan.

Goals: 1-0 Emmanuel Culio (19 penalty), 2-0 Billel Omrani (45+1), 3-0 Ovidiu Hoban (58), 4-0 Billel Omrani (62), 5-0 Sebastian Mailat (90+2).

[FC CFR 1907 Cluj-Napoca won 7-0 on aggregate]

09.08.2018; Skonto Stadions, Rīga; Referee: Thorvaldur Árnason (Iceland); Attendance: 1,435

FK Spartaks Jūrmala – FK Sūduva Marijampolė 0-1(0-0)

Spartaks Jūrmala: Jevgenijs Nerugals, Gints Freimanis, Aleksandar Kosoric, Mārcis Oss, Ingus Slampe, Aleksejs Visnakovs, Artemiy Maleev, Evgeni Kobzar (82.Ricards Korzāns), Kaspars Svārups (76.Diego Aguirre), Vitor Faísca, Ariagner Smith. Trainer: Aleksandr Grishin.

FK Sūduva Marijampolė: Ivan Kardum, Vaidas Slavickas, Algis Jankauskas, Vitaly Gayduchik, Andro Svrljuga, Aleksandar Zivanovic, Guilherme Finkler (90+1.Povilas Leimonas), Robertas Vézevicius (73.Julius Kasparavicius), Jovan Cadenovic, Ovidijus Verbickas (88.Daniel Offenbacher), Rigino Cicilia. Trainer: Vladimir Cheburin.

Goal: 0-1 Guilherme Finkler (52).

16.08.2018; Marijampoles sporto centro stadione, Marijampolė; Referee: Ola Hobber Nilsen (Norway); Attendance: 2,417

FK Sūduva Marijampolė – FK Spartaks Jūrmala 0-0

FK Sūduva Marijampolė: Ivan Kardum, Vaidas Slavickas, Algis Jankauskas, Vitaly Gayduchik, Andro Svrljuga, Guilherme Finkler (87.Julius Kasparavicius), Povilas Leimonas, Robertas Vézevicius (90+5.Marius Cinikas), Jovan Cadenovic, Ovidijus Verbickas (71.Daniel Offenbacher), Rigino Cicilia. Trainer: Vladimir Cheburin.

Spartaks Jūrmala: Jevgenijs Nerugals, Gints Freimanis, Aleksandar Kosoric, Mārcis Oss, Ingus Slampe, Aleksejs Visnakovs, Artemiy Maleev, Evgeni Kobzar (83.Ricards Korzāns), Kaspars Svārups (46.Diego Aguirre), Vitor Faísca, Ariagner Smith. Trainer: Tomas Razanauskas.

[FK Sūduva Marijampolė won 1-0 on aggregate]

09.08.2018; Ludogorets Arena, Razgrad; Referee: Vitaliy Meshkov (Russia); Attendance: 3,574

PFC Ludogorets Razgrad – HŠK Zrinjski Mostar 1-0(1-0)

Ludogorets Razgrad: Renan, Cosmin Moti, Cicinho, Rafael Forster, Svetoslav Dyakov (68.Jacek Góralski), Lucas Sasha (78.Gustavo Campanharo), Wanderson (82.João Paulo), Natanael Pimienta, Claudiu Keserü, Marcelinho, Jody Lukoki. Trainer: Paulo Autuori.

Zrinjski Mostar: Antonio Soldo, Slobodan Jakovljevic, Neven Lastro, Advan Kadusic, Ante Vrljicak (78.Marko Perisic), Ognjen Todorovic (75.Nemanja Bilbija), Samir Bekric, Milos Filipovic, Toni Jovic (85.Kristijan Stanic), Frane Cirjak, Semir Pezer. Trainer: Ante Mise.

Goal: 1-0 Cosmin Moti (16).

16.08.2018; Stadion Pecara, Sikori Brijeg; Referee: Hendrikus Sebastiaan Hermanus „Bas" Nijhuis (Netherlands); Attendance: 3,500

HŠK Zrinjski Mostar – PFC Ludogorets Razgrad 1-1(0-1)

Zrinjski Mostar: Antonio Soldo, Pero Stojkic (78.Semir Pezer), Slobodan Jakovljevic, Advan Kadusic, Ognjen Todorovic, Damir Sovsic (46.Toni Jovic), Hrvoje Barisic, Frane Cirjak, Edin Rustemovic, Nemanja Bilbija, Kristijan Stanic (61.Milos Filipovic). Trainer: Blaz Sliskovic.

Ludogorets Razgrad: Jorge Broun, Cosmin Moti, Cicinho, Rafael Forster, Svetoslav Dyakov, Gustavo Campanharo (90.Anton Nedyalkov), Wanderson, Natanael Pimienta, Claudiu Keserü (86.Jacek Góralski), Marcelinho, Virgil Misidjan (73.Jody Lukoki). Trainer: Paulo Autuori.

Goals: 0-1 Claudiu Keserü (24), 1-1 Nemanja Bilbija (90+2).

[PFC Ludogorets Razgrad won 2-1 on aggregate]

09.08.2018; Bolshaya Sportivnaya Arena, Tiraspol; Referee: Arnold Hunter (Northern Ireland); Attendance: 4,803

FC Sheriff Tiraspol – Valur Reykjavík 1-0(0-0)

FC Sheriff Tiraspol: Serghei Pascenco, Petru Racu, Ante Kulusic, Mateo Susic, Veaceslav Posmac, Cristiano, Antun Palic (46."Jô" Joálisson), Yuri Kendysh, Ziguy Badibanga, Al-Haji Kamara (81.Wilfried Balima), Gerson Rodrigues (59.Rifet Kapic). Trainer: Goran Sablic.

Valur Reykjavík: Anton Ari Einarsson, Bjarni Eiríksson, Eidur Sigurbjörnsson, Arnar Geirsson, Sebastian Hedlund, Kristinn Sigurdsson, Sindri Björnsson (68.Einar Karl Ingvarsson), Ólafur Finsen, Ívar Jónsson (78.Sigurdur Lárusson), Patrick Pedersen, Dion Jeremy Acoff (90+2.Kristinn Halldórsson). Trainer: Ólafur Jóhannesson.

Goals: 1-0 Ziguy Badibanga (85).

16.08.2018; Vodafone-Völlurin, Reykjavík; Referee: Marco Fritz (Germany); Attendance: 1,224

Valur Reykjavík – FC Sheriff Tiraspol 2-1(1-0)

Valur Reykjavík: Anton Ari Einarsson, Birkir Sævarsson, Bjarni Eiríksson, Eidur Sigurbjörnsson, Sebastian Hedlund, Haukur Sigurdsson, Kristinn Sigurdsson, Andri Adolphsson (69.Kristinn Halldórsson), Einar Karl Ingvarsson (81.Ólafur Finsen), Patrick Pedersen, Dion Jeremy Acoff. Trainer: Ólafur Jóhannesson.

FC Sheriff Tiraspol: Serghei Pascenco, Ante Kulusic, Mateo Susic, Veaceslav Posmac, Cristiano (66.Wilfried Balima), Yuri Kendysh, Gheorghe Anton, Evgheni Oancea (46."Jô" Joálisson), Ziguy Badibanga, Al-Haji Kamara, Gerson Rodrigues (46.Rifet Kapic). Trainer: Goran Sablic.

Goals: 1-0 Haukur Sigurdsson (40), 1-1 Ziguy Badibanga (68), 2-1 Kristinn Halldórsson (90+1).

[FC Sheriff Tiraspol won on away goals rule (2-2 on aggregate)]

09.08.2018; „Yaakov Turner Toto" Stadium, Beer Sheva; Referee: Aleksey Eskov (Russia); Attendance: 9,311

Hapoel Be'er Sheva FC – APOEL FC Nicosia 2-2(1-2)

Hapoel Be'er Sheva: David Goresh, Ben Bitton, Loai Taha, Shir Tzedek, Oren Biton, John Ogu, Maor Melikson (65.Hen Ezra), Hanan Maman (83.Ben Sahar), Daniel Einbinder, Eden Ben Basat (59.Tomás Pekhart), Anthony Nwakaeme. Trainer: Barak Bakhar.

APOEL Nicosia: Boy Waterman, Carlão, Emilio N'Sue (90+2.Zhivko Milanov), Praxitelis Vouros, Caju, Nuno Morais, Tomás De Vincenti (60.Savvas Gentsoglou), Lucas Souza, Roland Sallai, Moussa Al Taamari (72.Nicolas Ioannou), Dellatorre [*sent off 79*]. Trainer: Bruno Baltazar.

Goals: 0-1 Nuno Morais (13 penalty), 0-2 Dellatorre (28), 1-2 John Ogu (42), 2-2 Anthony Nwakaeme (70).

16.08.2018; Stádio Neo GSP, Nicosia; Referee: Mattias Gestranius (Finland); Attendance: 10,891

APOEL FC Nicosia – Hapoel Be'er Sheva FC 3-1(0-1)

APOEL Nicosia: Boy Waterman, Carlão, Emilio N'Sue, Praxitelis Vouros, Caju, Nuno Morais, Tomás De Vincenti, Lucas Souza, Ghayas Zahid (75.Savvas Gentsoglou), Roland Sallai (89.Nicolas Ioannou), Moussa Al Taamari (83.Zhivko Milanov). Trainer: Bruno Baltazar.

Hapoel Be'er Sheva: David Goresh, Samuel Scheimann, Matan Ohayon, Ben Bitton, Loai Taha, John Ogu, Hen Ezra (76.Ben Sahar), Daniel Einbinder (67.Hanan Maman), Marwan Kabha (82.Maor Melikson), Eden Ben Basat, Anthony Nwakaeme. Trainer: Barak Bakhar.

Goals: 0-1 Eden Ben Basat (19), 1-1 Anthony Nwakaeme (64 own goal), 2-1, 3-1 Lucas Souza (79, 90+3).

[APOEL FC Nicosia won 5-3 on aggregate]

09.08.2018; „Mikheil Meskhi" Stadioni, Tbilisi; Referee: Alan Mario Sant (Malta); Attendance: 4,521

FC Torpedo Kutaisi – FK Kukësi 5-2(4-1)

Torpedo Kutaisi: Rion Kvaskhvadze, Mamuka Kobakhidze (79.Davit Khurtsilava), Giorgi Kimadze, Levan Gegetchkori, Oleksandr Azatsky, Lazar Marin, Grigol Dolidze (72.Arfang Daffé), Giorgi Kukhianidze, Marek Hlinka, Mate Tsintsadze, Milos Lacny (67.Tornike Kapanadze). Trainer: Kakhaber Chkhetiani.

FK Kukësi: Stivi Frashëri, Ylli Shameti, Rustem Hoxha, William Cordeiro (74.Vangjel Zguro), Simon Rrumbullaku, Harallamb Qaqi, Irakli Dzaria (63.Donjet Shkodra), Arbër Çyrbja (63.Sebino Plaku), Besar Musolli, Haris Harba, Reginaldo. Trainer: Armando Cungu.

Goals: 1-0, 2-0 Giorgi Kukhianidze (3, 15), 2-1 Haris Harba (22), 3-1 Lazar Marin (28), 4-1 Giorgi Kimadze (31), 5-1 Tornike Kapanadze (86), 5-2 Sebino Plaku (88 penalty).

16.08.2018; Elbasan Arena, Elbasan; Referee: Alain Bieri (Switzerland); Attendance: 200

FK Kukësi – FC Torpedo Kutaisi 2-0(1-0)

FK Kukësi: Faton Maloku, Ylli Shameti, William Cordeiro, Simon Rrumbullaku, Edis Malikji, Albi Alla, Irakli Dzaria (68.Donjet Shkodra), Besar Musolli (83.Sebino Plaku), Valon Ethemi (52.Arbër Çyrbja), Haris Harba, Reginaldo. Trainer: Armando Cungu.

Torpedo Kutaisi: Rion Kvaskhvadze, Davit Khurtsilava, Mamuka Kobakhidze, Giorgi Kimadze (83.Levan Gegetchkori), Oleksandr Azatsky, Lazar Marin, Grigol Dolidze (62.Levan Kutalia), Giorgi Kukhianidze, Marek Hlinka (69.Merab Gigauri), Mate Tsintsadze, Milos Lacny. Trainer: Kakhaber Chkhetiani.

Goals: 1-0, 2-0 Reginaldo (29 penalty, 76 penalty).

[FC Torpedo Kutaisi won 5-4 on aggregate]

09.08.2018; Stadion Stožice, Ljubljana; Referee: Benoît Millot (France); Attendance: 4,900

NK Olimpija Ljubljana – HJK Helsinki 3-0(1-0)

Olimpija Ljubljana: Aljaz Ivacic, Branko Ilic, Aris Zarifovic, Dino Stiglec, Rok Kronaveter (78.Marko Gajic), Marko Putincanin, Matic Crnic [*sent off 83*], Daniel Avramovski (84.Stefan Savic), Tomislav Tomic, Nik Kapun, Issah Abass (70.Asmir Suljic). Trainer: Aleksandar Linta.

HJK Helsinki: Maksim Rudakov, Rafinha (89.Macauley Chrisantus), Hannu Patronen, Mikko Sumusalo, Faith Obilor, Anthony Annan, Moshtagh Yaghoubi, Sebastian Dahlström (63.Jordan Domínguez), Riku Riski, Evans Mensah (80.Nikolai Alho), Klauss. Trainer: Mika Lehkosuo.

Goals: 1-0 Issah Abass (38), 2-0 Rok Kronaveter (50 penalty), 3-0 Issah Abass (59).

16.08.2018; Telia 5G-areena, Helsinki; Referee: Evgen Aranovskiy (Ukraine); Attendance: 4,127

HJK Helsinki – NK Olimpija Ljubljana 1-4(0-1)

HJK Helsinki: Maksim Rudakov, Rafinha, Mikko Sumusalo, Faith Obilor, Roni Peiponen, Anthony Annan, Jordan Domínguez (64.Macauley Chrisantus), Riku Riski, Nikolai Alho (46.Sebastian Dahlström), Evans Mensah, Klauss (73.Eetu Vertainen). Trainer: Mika Lehkosuo.

Olimpija Ljubljana: Aljaz Ivacic, Branko Ilic, Aris Zarifovic, Dino Stiglec, Rok Kronaveter (65.Asmir Suljic), Marko Putincanin, Stefan Savic, Daniel Avramovski, Tomislav Tomic (62.Macky Frank Bagnack), Nik Kapun, Issah Abass (76.Goran Brkic). Trainer: Aleksandar Linta.

Goals: 0-1 Issah Abass (20), 0-2 Daniel Avramovski (72), 0-3 Rafinha (75 own goal), 1-3 Macauley Chrisantus (85), 1-4 Goran Brkic (90+2 penalty).

[NK Olimpija Ljubljana won 7-1 on aggregate]

09.08.2018; Turner's Cross, Cork; Referee: Petr Ardeleánu (Czech Republic); Attendance: 5,488

Cork City FC – Rosenborg BK Trondheim 0-2(0-2)

Cork City FC: Mark McNulty, Damien Delaney, Steven Beattie, Shane Griffin, Sean McLoughlin, Jimmy Keohane, Conor McCormack (61.Gearóid Morrissey), Barry McNamee (46.Kieran Sadlier), Garry Buckley, Graham Cummins, Karl Sheppard (72.Ronan Coughlin). Trainer: John Caulfield.

Rosenborg: André Hansen, Tore Reginiussen, Even Hovland, Vegar Hedenstad, Birger Meling, Mike Jensen, Anders Trondsen (87.Olaus Skarsem), Marius Lundemo, Nicklas Bendtner, Alexander Søderlund (78.Erik Botheim), Jonathan Levi. Trainer: Rini Coolen.

Goals: 0-1, 0-2 Jonathan Levi (22, 44).

16.08.2018; Lerkendal Stadion, Trondheim; Referee: Mads-Kristoffer Kristoffersen (Denmark); Attendance: 8,028

Rosenborg BK Trondheim – Cork City FC 3-0(2-0)

Rosenborg: André Hansen, Tore Reginiussen, Vegar Hedenstad (74.Erlend Reitan), Birger Meling, Besim Serbecic, Mike Jensen, Anders Trondsen (60.Anders Konradsen), Marius Lundemo, Nicklas Bendtner, Alexander Søderlund, Jonathan Levi (61.Pål Helland). Trainer: Rini Coolen.

Cork City FC: Mark McNulty, Damien Delaney, Steven Beattie, Shane Griffin, Sean McLoughlin, Jimmy Keohane, Conor McCormack, Gearóid Morrissey (46.Barry McNamee), Kieran Sadlier, Garry Buckley (75.John Dunleavy), Karl Sheppard (72.Ronan Coughlin). Trainer: John Caulfield.

Goals: 1-0 Besim Serbecic (26), 2-0 Alexander Søderlund (34), 3-0 Anders Trondsen (58).

[Rosenborg BK Trondheim won 5-0 on aggregate]

09.08.2018; Cardiff City Stadium, Cardiff; Referee: Peter Královic (Slovakia); Attendance: 863

The New Saints FC – FC Midtjylland 0-2(0-2)

The New Saints: Paul Harrison, Simon Spender, Christopher Marriott, Blaine Hudson, Benjamin Cabango, Aeron Edwards, Jon Routledge, Daniel Redmond (84.Joash Nembhard), Tom Holland (79.Kurtis Byrne), Jamie Mullan, Dean Ebbe (69.Adrian Cieslewicz). Trainer: Scott Ruscoe.

FC Midtjylland: Jesper Hansen, Kian Hansen, Marc Hende (61.Joel Andersson), Bubacarr Sanneh, Alexander Munksgaard, Rasmus Nicolaisen, Jakob Poulsen, Gustav Wikheim, Mikkel Duelund, Paul Ebere Onuachu (79.Mayron George), Awer Mabil (62.Ayo Simon Okosun). Trainer: Jess Thorup.

Goals: 0-1, 0-2 Paul Ebere Onuachu (9, 27).

16.08.2018; MCH Arena, Herning; Referee: Irfan Peljto (Bosnia and Herzegovina); Attendance: 4,368

FC Midtjylland – The New Saints FC 3-1(1-1)

FC Midtjylland: Jesper Hansen, Zsolt Korcsmár, Kian Hansen, Joel Andersson, Rasmus Nicolaisen, Jakob Poulsen, Mads Thychosen, Frank Onyeka (61.Ayo Simon Okosun), Mayron George, Paul Ebere Onuachu (84.Michael Baidoo), Awer Mabil (73.Bozhidar Kraev). Trainer: Jess Thorup.

The New Saints: Paul Harrison, Simon Spender, Christopher Marriott, Blaine Hudson, Benjamin Cabango, Aeron Edwards, Jon Routledge, Daniel Redmond (70.Adrian Cieslewicz), Tom Holland (79.Kurtis Byrne), Jamie Mullan, Dean Ebbe (74.Greg Draper). Trainer: Scott Ruscoe.

Goals: 1-0 Mayron George (16), 1-1 Dean Ebbe (22), 2-1, 3-1 Ayo Simon Okosun (62, 80).

[FC Midtjylland won 5-1 on aggregate]

09.08.2018; Stadion „Marszalka Józefa Pilsudskiego", Warszawa; Referee: Halis Özkahya (Turkey); Attendance: 9,923

Legia Warszawa – F91 Dudelange 1-2(1-1)

Legia Warszawa: Arkadiusz Malarz, Michal Pazdan, Iñaki Astiz [*sent off 44*], Dominik Nagy, Mateusz Wieteska, Krzysztof Maczynski, Michal Kucharczyk, Chris Philipps, Cafú (46.José Kanté), Sebastian Szymanski (65.Mateusz Zyro), Carlitos López (82.Mateusz Holownia). Trainer: Aleksandar Vukovic.

F91 Dudelange: Jonathan Joubert, Tom Schnell, Jerry Prempeh, Aniss El Hriti, Marc-André Kruska, Stélvio (73.Mario Pokar), Dominik Stolz, Edisson Jordanov, Clément Couturier (80.Nicolas Perez), Danel Sinani, Patrick Stumpf (58.David Turpel). Trainer: Dino Toppmöller.

Goals: 0-1 Clément Couturier (24), 1-1 Carlitos López (27), 1-2 David Turpel (62 penalty).

16.08.2018; Stade „Josy Barthel“, Lëtzebuerg; Referee: Ivaylo Stoyanov (Bulgaria); Attendance: 2,000

F91 Dudelange – Legia Warszawa **2-2(2-1)**

F91 Dudelange: Jonathan Joubert, Jerry Prempeh, Kevin Malget, Aniss El Hriti, Marc-André Kruska (79.Bryan Mélisse), Stélvio, Dominik Stolz (90.Danel Sinani), Edisson Jordanov, Clément Couturier, David Turpel, Patrick Stumpf (74.Milan Bisevac). Trainer: Dino Toppmöller.

Legia Warszawa: Arkadiusz Malarz, Michal Pazdan, Adam Hlousek, Dominik Nagy (69.Kasper Hämäläinen), Mateusz Wieteska, Krzysztof Maczynski (77.Eduardo da Silva), Michal Kucharczyk [*sent off 90+5*], Chris Philipps (46.Sebastian Szymanski), Cafú, José Kanté, Carlitos López. Trainer: Sá Pinto.

Goals: 1-0 Patrick Stumpf (7), 2-0 Stélvio (17), 2-1, 2-2 José Kanté (33, 86).

[F91 Dudelange won 4-3 on aggregate]

LEAGUE PATH

07.08.2018; „Vazgen Sargsyan" Hanrapetakan Stadium, Yerevan; Referee: Pol van Boekel (Netherlands); Attendance: 12,500

FC Pyunik Yerevan – Maccabi Tel Aviv FC **0-0**

Pyunik Yerevan: Andrija Dragojevic, Vyacheslav Dmitriev, Maksim Zhestokov, Serob Grigoryan (68.Sergey Kolychev), Maksim Trusevich, Denis Voynov, Didier Kadio, Rumyan Hovsepyan, Alik Arakelyan, Vahagn Hayrapetyan (43.Albert Bogatyrev), Mohamed Konaté (66.Ruslan Koryan). Trainer: Andrey Talalaev.

Maccabi Tel Aviv: Predrag Rajkovic, Eitan Tibi, Saborit, Elazar Dasa, Jair Amador, Eyal Golasa (60.Roslan Barski), Dor Mikha, Dan Glazer, Eliran Atar (67.Chikeluba Ofoedu), Aaron Schoenfeld (88.Vidar Kjartansson), Omer Atzili. Trainer: Vladimir Ivic.

16.08.2018; Winner Stadium, Netanya; Referee: Ville Nevalainen (Finland); Attendance: 8,932

Maccabi Tel Aviv FC – FC Pyunik Yerevan **2-1(0-1)**

Maccabi Tel Aviv: Predrag Rajkovic, Eitan Tibi, Saborit, Elazar Dasa, Jair Amador, Dor Mikha, Roslan Barski, Dor Peretz (79.Dan Glazer), Vidar Kjartansson (46.Itay Shechter), Eliran Atar, Omer Atzili (87.Matan Hozez). Trainer: Vladimir Ivic.

Pyunik Yerevan: Andrija Dragojevic, Vyacheslav Dmitriev, Maksim Zhestokov, Serob Grigoryan (45.Sergey Kolychev), Vitali Stezhko, Maksim Trusevich, Denis Voynov (68.Karlen Mkrtchyan), Rumyan Hovsepyan, Alik Arakelyan, Vahagn Hayrapetyan, Mohamed Konaté (59.Ruslan Koryan). Trainer: Andrey Talalaev.

Goals: 0-1 Denis Voynov (11), 1-1 Dor Mikha (55), 2-1 Eliran Atar (68).

[Maccabi Tel Aviv FC won 2-1 on aggregate]

09.08.2018; Stadion Neftyanik, Ufa; Referee: Stephan Klossner (Switzerland); Attendance: 6,794

FK Ufa – FC Progrès Niederkorn **2-1(1-0)**

FK Ufa: Aleksandr Belenov, Bojan Jokic, Denis Tumasyan, Catalin Carp, Ionut Nedelcearu, Jemal Tabidze, Veroljub Salatic, Ondrej Vanek (56.Azamat Zaseev), Dmitri Zhivoglyadov, Ivan Oblyakov (83.Kehinde Fatai), Sylvester Igboun. Trainer: Sergei Tomarov.

Progrès Niederkorn: Sebastian Flauss, Mario Mutsch, Marvin da Graça, Jordan Gobron, Metin Karayer (79.Romeu Torres), Tim Hall, Yann Matias Marques (66.Adrien Ferino), Emmanuel Françoise (71.Yannick Bastos), Olivier Thill, Alexander Karapetyan, Mayron De Almeida. Trainer: Paolo Amodio.

Goals: 1-0 Sylvester Igboun (38), 2-0 Ivan Oblyakov (63), 2-1 Olivier Thill (80).

16.08.2018; Stade Parc des Sports, Differdange; Referee: Manuel Schüttengruber (Austria); Attendance: 1,736

FC Progrès Niederkorn – FK Ufa **2-2(1-0)**

Progrès Niederkorn: Sebastian Flauss, Adrien Ferino, Marvin da Graça (70.Romeu Torres), Jordan Gobron, Metin Karayer, Tim Hall, Sébastien Thill, Yannick Bastos, Olivier Thill (86.Ben Vogel), Alexander Karapetyan, Mayron De Almeida. Trainer: Paolo Amodio.

FK Ufa: Aleksandr Belenov, Bojan Jokic, Pavel Alikin, Catalin Carp (46.Ondrej Vanek), Ionut Nedelcearu (82.Denis Tumasyan), Jemal Tabidze, Veroljub Salatic, Ivan Paurevic, Dmitri Zhivoglyadov, Ivan Oblyakov, Sylvester Igboun (80.Vyacheslav Krotov). Trainer: Sergei Tomarov.

Goals: 1-0 Pavel Alikin (2 own goal), 1-1 Ivan Paurevic (51), 2-1 Mayron De Almeida (72), 2-2 Ivan Paurevic (90+3).

[FK Ufa won 4-3 on aggregate]

09.08.2018; „Sammy Ofer“ Stadium, Haifa; Referee: Harald Lechner (Austria); Attendance: 6,412

Hapoel Haifa FC – Atalanta Bergamasca Calcio **1-4(1-2)**

Hapoel Haifa: Ernestas Setkus, Gabriel Tamas, Nisso Kapiloto, Dor Malul, Hen Dilmoni, Rasmus Sjöstedt, Gil Vermouth (59.Guy Hadida), Radu Gînsari (59.Eli Elbaz), Almog Buzaglo, Thanasis Papazoglou (69.Gal Arel), Maxim Plakushchenko. Trainer: Nir Klinger.

Atalanta: Pierluigi Gollini, Andrea Masiello, Rafael Tolói, José Palomino, Hans Hateboer, Robin Gosens, Alejandro Gómez (83.Andreas Cornelius), Marten de Roon, Remo Freuler, Matteo Pessina (60.Mario Pasalic), Duván Zapata (63.Musa Barrow). Trainer: Gian Piero Gasperini.

Goals: 1-0 Almog Buzaglo (7), 1-1 Hans Hateboer (18), 1-2 Duván Zapata (20), 1-3 Mario Pasalic (65), 1-4 Musa Barrow (86).

16.08.2018; MAPEI Stadium – Città del Tricolore, Reggio Emilia; Referee: Frank Schneider (France); Attendance: 6,546

Atalanta Bergamasca Calcio – Hapoel Haifa FC **2-0(0-0)**

Atalanta: Pierluigi Gollini, Andrea Masiello, Berat Djimsiti, Timothy Castagne, Gianluca Mancini, Alejandro Gómez (83.Musa Barrow), Remo Freuler (77.Luca Valzania), Mario Pasalic, Arkadiusz Reca, Matteo Pessina, Duván Zapata (86.Andreas Cornelius). Trainer: Gian Piero Gasperini.

Hapoel Haifa: Ernestas Setkus, Gabriel Tamas, Nisso Kapiloto, Dor Malul, Risto Mitrevski, Hen Dilmoni (76.Gal Arel), Rasmus Sjöstedt (67.Gil Vermouth), Radu Gînsari, Almog Buzaglo (30.Maxim Plakushchenko), Guy Hadida, Thanasis Papazoglou. Trainer: Nir Klinger.

Goals: 1-0 Duván Zapata (71), 2-0 Andreas Cornelius (90+2).

[Atalanta Bergamasca Calcio won 6-1 on aggregate]

09.08.2018; Red Bull Arena, Leipzig; Referee: Paweł Gil (Poland); Attendance: 16,648

RasenBallsport Leipzig – CS Universitatea Craiova **3-1(1-0)**

RB Leipzig: Yvon Mvogo, Willi Orban (61.Emil Forsberg), Lukas Klostermann, Ibrahima Konaté, Stefan Ilsanker, Kevin Kampl, Diego Demme, Bruma (62.Marcel Sabitzer), Marcelo Saracchi, Jean-Kévin Augustin (75.Yussuf Poulsen), Matheus Cunha. Trainer: Ralf Rangnick.

CS Universitatea Craiova: Mirko Pigliacelli, Renato Kelic, Ivan Martic, Marius Briceag, Tiago Ferreira (79.Matteo Fedele), Nicusor Bancu, Isaac Donkor, Alexandru Mateiu, Alexandru Mitrita (85.Jovan Markovic), Alexandru Cicaldau, Valentin Mihaila (27.Raoul Baicu). Trainer: Devis Mangia.

Goals: 1-0 Ibrahima Konaté (25), 2-0 Matheus Cunha (77), 3-0 Yussuf Poulsen (87), 3-1 Ivan Martic (90+3).

16.08.2018; Stadionul „Ion Oblemenco“, Craiova; Referee: Miroslav Zelinka (Czech Republic); Attendance: 12,050

CS Universitatea Craiova – RasenBallsport Leipzig **1-1(0-1)**

CS Universitatea Craiova: Mirko Pigliacelli, Renato Kelic, Ivan Martic (73.Tiago Ferreira), Marius Briceag, Nicusor Bancu, Isaac Donkor, Alexandru Mateiu, Alexandru Mitrita (51.Andrei Burlacu), Matteo Fedele (80.Jovan Markovic), Alexandru Cicaldau, Raoul Baicu. Trainer: Devis Mangia.

RB Leipzig: Yvon Mvogo, Willi Orban, Nordi Mukiele, Ibrahima Konaté, Emil Forsberg, Kevin Kampl, Diego Demme (72.Stefan Ilsanker), Marcel Sabitzer (64.Bruma), Marcelo Saracchi, Yussuf Poulsen, Matheus Cunha (46.Jean-Kévin Augustin). Trainer: Ralf Rangnick.

Goals: 0-1 Marcel Sabitzer (39), 1-1 Raoul Baicu (85).

[RasenBallsport Leipzig won 4-2 on aggregate]

09.08.2018; Dinamo Stadium, Minsk; Referee: Anastasios Papapetrou (Greece); Attendance: 21,750

FC Dinamo Minsk – FK Zenit Saint Petersburg **4-0(3-0)**

Dinamo Minsk: Andrey Gorbunov, Igor Shitov, Luís Rocha, Roman Begunov, Nino Galovic, Maksim Shvetsov, Seidu Yahaya, Filipp Ivanov (82.Artem Gurenko), Nikita Korzun, Uros Nikolic (79.Aleksandr Makas), Vladimir Khvashchinskiy (61.Nikita Kaplenko). Trainer: Sergei Gurenko.

Zenit Saint Petersburg: Yuriy Lodygin, Branislav Ivanovic, Aleksandr Anyukov, Miha Mevlja, Oleg Shatov, Hernani, Elmir Nabiullin, Matías Kranevitter (83.Magomed Ozdoev), Daler Kuzyaev, Emiliano Rigoni (46.Aleksandr Erokhin), Sebastián Driussi (46.Anton Zabolotny). Trainer: Sergey Semak.

Goals: 1-0 Uros Nikolic (12), 2-0 Vladimir Khvashchinskiy (32), 3-0 Nino Galovic (41), 4-0 Uros Nikolic (67).

16.08.2018; Stadion Petrovskiy, St. Petersburg; Referee: Sébastien Delferière (Belgium); Attendance: n/a

FK Zenit Saint Petersburg – FC Dinamo Minsk 8-1(1-0,4-0)

Zenit Saint Petersburg: Andrei Lunev, Branislav Ivanovic, Aleksandr Anyukov, Miha Mevlja, Christian Noboa (103.Igor Smolnikov), Aleksandr Erokhin (102.Róbert Mak), Leandro Paredes [*sent off 72*], Hernani (61.Sebastián Driussi), Elmir Nabiullin (59.Anton Zabolotny), Daler Kuzyaev, Artem Dzyuba. Trainer: Sergey Semak.

Dinamo Minsk: Andrey Gorbunov, Igor Shitov, Luís Rocha (92.Aleksey Gavrilovich), Roman Begunov, Nino Galovic, Maksim Shvetsov [*sent off 120+1*], Seidu Yahaya, Dinko Trebotic (72.Giorgi Navalovski), Filipp Ivanov (65.Aleksandr Makas), Nikita Korzun, Vladimir Khvashchinskiy (55.Nikita Kaplenko). Trainer: Sergei Gurenko.

Goals: 1-0 Leandro Paredes (22), 2-0 Christian Noboa (66), 3-0, 4-0 Artem Dzyuba (75, 78), 4-1 Seidu Yahaya (99), 5-1 Sebastián Driussi (109), 6-1 Artem Dzyuba (115 penalty), 7-1, 8-1 Róbert Mak (120+2 penalty, 120+3).

[FK Zenit Saint Petersburg won 8-5 on aggregate]

09.08.2018; Merkur Arena, Graz; Referee: Mohammed Al-Hakim (Sweden); Attendance: 7,612

SK Sturm Graz – AEK Larnaca FC 0-2(0-0)

SK Sturm Graz: Jörg Siebenhandl, Fabian Koch, Anastasios Avlonitis, Lukas Spendlhofer, Dario Maresic, Stefan Hierländer [*sent off 90+4*], Peter Zulj, Sandi Lovric (64.Markus Lackner), Philipp Hosiner (57.Emeka Eza), Markus Pink, Lukas Grozurek (46.Philipp Huspek). Trainer: Heiko Vogel.

AEK Larnaca: Toño, Mikel González, Truyols (80.Tete), Thomas Ioannou (59.Daniel Mojsov), Igor Carioca, Ivan Trickovski (77.Joan Tomás), Jorge Larena, Acorán, Nacho Cases, Hector Hevel, Apostolos Giannou. Trainer: Andoni Iraola.

Goals: 0-1 Truyols (46), 0-2 Ivan Trickovski (74).

16.08.2018; AEK Arena, Larnaca; Referee: Paolo Valeri (Italy); Attendance: 4,145

AEK Larnaca FC – SK Sturm Graz 5-0(1-0)

AEK Larnaca: Toño, Mikel González, Daniel Mojsov, Truyols, Igor Carioca, Ivan Trickovski, Jorge Larena (78.Jean Luc Assoubre), Acorán, Hector Hevel, Apostolos Giannou (81.Florian Taulemesse), Tete (69.Nacho Cases). Trainer: Andoni Iraola.

SK Sturm Graz: Tobias Schützenauer, Thomas Schrammel, Fabian Koch, Lukas Spendlhofer, Dario Maresic (46.Philipp Huspek), Markus Lackner, Peter Zulj, Sandi Lovric [*sent off 59*], Raphael Obermair, Philipp Hosiner (73.Emeka Eza), Markus Pink (63.Anastasios Avlonitis). Trainer: Heiko Vogel.

Goals: 1-0 Ivan Trickovski (8), 2-0 Jorge Larena (65 penalty), 3-0, 4-0 Ivan Trickovski (67, 80), 5-0 Florian Taulemesse (86).

[AEK Larnaca FC won 7-0 on aggregate]

09.08.2018; Andrův stadion, Olomouc; Referee: Massimiliano Irrati (Italy); Attendance: 6,118

SK Sigma Olomouc – FC Kairat Almaty 2-0(1-0)

SK Sigma Olomouc: Milos Buchta, Michal Veprek [*sent off 68*], Jan Sterba, Václav Jemelka, Václav Pilar (64.Martin Hála), Martin Sladky, Jakub Plsek (85.Jakub Yunis), David Houska, Simon Falta, Lukás Kalvach, Martin Nespor (75.Tomás Zahradnícek). Trainer: Václav Jílek.

FC Kairat: Vladimir Plotnikov, Sergey Politevich, Sheldon Bateau, Gafurzhan Suyumbaev [*sent off 38*], Ákos Elek, Isael, Bauyrzhan Islamkhan (79.Ivo Ilicevic), Stanislav Lunin, Andrei Arshavin (53.Islambek Kuat), Juan Felipe Alves, Aderinsola Eseola (57.Márton Eppel). Trainer: Carlos Alós Ferrer.

Goals: 1-0 Martin Sladky (21), 2-0 Václav Pilar (50).

16.08.2018; Ortaliq Stadion, Almaty; Referee: Sandro Schärer (Switzerland); Attendance: 20,000

FC Kairat Almaty – SK Sigma Olomouc 1-2(0-1)

FC Kairat: Stas Pokatilov, Sergey Politevich, Ákos Elek, Isael [*sent off 90+4*], Islambek Kuat, Bauyrzhan Islamkhan, Stanislav Lunin (57.Aleksandr Sokolenko), Nuraly Alip (34.Márton Eppel), Andrei Arshavin (74.Georgiy Zhukov), Juan Felipe Alves [*sent off 75*], Aderinsola Eseola. Trainer: Carlos Alós Ferrer.

SK Sigma Olomouc: Milos Buchta, Jan Sterba, Martin Hála, Václav Jemelka, Martin Sladky, Jakub Plsek (80.Jakub Yunis), David Houska, Tomás Zahradnícek (67.Budge Manzia), Simon Falta, Lukás Kalvach, Martin Nespor (63.Jirí Texl). Trainer: Václav Jílek.

Goals: 0-1 Martin Nespor (19), 0-2 David Houska (51), 1-2 Márton Eppel (61).

[SK Sigma Olomouc won 4-1 on aggregate]

09.08.2018; Chornomorets Stadium, Odessa; Referee: Ivan Bebek (Croatia); Attendance: 6,587

FK Mariupol – FC Girondins de Bordeaux 1-3(1-2)

FK Mariupol: Rustam Khudzhamov, Sergey Yavorskiy, Pavel Polegenko, Besir Demiri, Oleksiy Bykov, Joyskim Dawa (66.Vladislav Vakula), Igor Tyshchenko (82.Sergiy Gorbunov), Vyacheslav Churko (46.Andriy Boryachuk), Dmytro Myshnov, Oleksandr Pikhalyonok, Ruslan Fomin. Trainer: Oleksandr Babych.

Girondins de Bordeaux: Benoît Costil, Pablo Castro, Maxime Poundjé, Milan Gajic (78.Igor Lewczuk), Jules Koundé, Jaroslav Plasil, Younousse Sankharé (87.Valentín Vada), Aurélien Tchouaméni, Zaydou Youssouf (78.Lukas Lerager), Gaëtan Laborde, François Kamano. Trainer: Gustavo Poyet.

Goals: 1-0 Dmytro Myshnov (7), 1-1, 1-2 Gaëtan Laborde (33, 37), 1-3 Aurélien Tchouaméni (49).

16.08.2018; Stade Matmut-Atlantique, Bordeaux; Referee: Andrew Dallas (Scotland); Attendance: 11,375

FC Girondins de Bordeaux – FK Mariupol 2-1(0-0)

Girondins de Bordeaux: Benoît Costil, Igor Lewczuk, Pablo Castro, Maxime Poundjé, Otávio (89.Jaroslav Plasil), Jules Koundé, Younousse Sankharé, Lukas Lerager (62.Aurélien Tchouaméni), Zaydou Youssouf, Nicolas de Préville, François Kamano (63.Valentín Vada). Trainer: Gustavo Poyet.

FK Mariupol: Evgen Galchuk, Maksim Biliy, Igor Kyryukhantsev (46.Pavel Polegenko), Besir Demiri, Joyskim Dawa (46.Sergey Yavorskiy), Igor Tyshchenko (62.Vladislav Vakula), Vyacheslav Churko, Dmytro Myshnov, Oleksandr Pikhalyonok, Ruslan Fomin, Andriy Boryachuk. Trainer: Oleksandr Babych.

Goals: 1-0 Maxime Poundjé (54), 2-0 Younousse Sankharé (56), 2-1 Ruslan Fomin (66).

[FC Girondins de Bordeaux won 5-2 on aggregate]

09.08.2018; Stadión pod Dubnom, Zilina; Referee: Robert Schörgenhofer (Austria); Attendance: 6,817

AS Trenčín – Feyenoord Rotterdam 4-0(3-0)

AS Trenčín: Igor Semrinec, Jamie Lawrence, Lukás Skovajsa, Martin Sulek, Reuben Yem, Ashraf El Mahdioui, Abdul Zubairu (83.Desley Ubbink), Joey Sleegers (85.Osman Bukari), Antonio Mance, Hamza Catakovic, Philip Azango. Trainer: Ricardo Moniz.

Feyenoord Rotterdam: Justin Bijlow, Jan-Arie van der Heijden, Bart Nieuwkoop (90.Lutsharel Geertruida), Sven van Beek, Calvin Verdonk, Jens Toornstra, Jordy Clasie, Sofyan Amrabat, Steven Berghuis, Sam Larsson (61.Jean-Paul Boëtius), Dylan Vente. Trainer: Giovanni van Bronckhorst.

Goals: 1-0, 2-0 Antonio Mance (6, 37), 3-0 Philip Azango (44), 4-0 Antonio Mance (63).

16.08.2018; Stadion Feyenoord, Rotterdam; Referee: Jakob Kehlet (Denmark); Attendance: 31,500

Feyenoord Rotterdam – AS Trenčín 1-1(1-1)

Feyenoord Rotterdam: Kenneth Vermeer, Jan-Arie van der Heijden, Eric Botteghin, Bart Nieuwkoop (67.Lutsharel Geertruida), Tyrell Malacia (83.Wouter Burger), Jens Toornstra, Jordy Clasie, Tonny Vilhena, Robin van Persie (71.Dylan Vente), Steven Berghuis, Sam Larsson. Trainer: Giovanni van Bronckhorst.

AS Trenčín: Igor Semrinec, Jamie Lawrence, Lukás Skovajsa, Martin Sulek, Reuben Yem, Ashraf El Mahdioui, Abdul Zubairu (90+2.Desley Ubbink), Joey Sleegers, Antonio Mance (86.Emeka Umeh), Hamza Catakovic, Philip Azango. Trainer: Ricardo Moniz.

Goals: 1-0 Eric Botteghin (8), 1-1 Antonio Mance (9).

[AS Trenčín won 5-1 on aggregate]

09.08.2018; Stádio Neo GSP, Nicosia; Referee: Carlos Miguel Taborda Xistra (Portugal); Attendance: 3,590

Apollon Limassol FC – FK Dynamo Brest 4-0(0-0)

Apollon: Bruno Vale, Valentin Roberge, Charis Kyriakou, Facundo Pereyra, Héctor Yuste, Giorgos Vasiliou, Esteban Sachetti (77.Kévin Bru), Emilio Zelaya (73.Anton Maglica), João Pedro, Fotis Papoulis, Adrián Sardinero (83.Sasa Markovic). Trainer: Sofronis Avgousti.

Dynamo Brest: Aleksandr Gutor, Oleg Veretilo, Andrei Zaleski [*sent off 66*], Pavel Nekhaychik, Zeljko Filipovic (59.Pavel Savitskiy), Oleksandr Noyok, Chidi Osuchukwu (46.Oleksiy Khoblenko), Roman Yuzepchuk, Gaby Kiki, Nivaldo, Joel Fameyeh (83.Sergey Krivets). Trainer: Aleksey Shpilevski.

Goals: 1-0, 2-0 Emilio Zelaya (46, 58), 3-0 Sasa Markovic (87), 4-0 Oleg Veretilo (90+2 own goal).

16.08.2018; DASK Brestski Stadium, Brest; Referee: Martin Strömbergsson (Sweden); Attendance: 8,800

FK Dynamo Brest – Apollon Limassol FC 1-0(0-0)

Dynamo Brest: Aleksandr Gutor, Maksim Vitus, Oleg Veretilo, Giannis Kargas, Pavel Nekhaychik, Zeljko Filipovic (76.Sergey Krivets), Oleksandr Noyok, Pavel Savitskiy (84.Pavel Sedko), Chidi Osuchukwu, Gaby Kiki, Nivaldo (64.Oleksiy Khoblenko). Trainer: Marcel Licka.

Apollon: Bruno Vale, Valentin Roberge, Kévin Bru, Facundo Pereyra, Héctor Yuste, Giorgos Vasiliou, Esteban Sachetti (70.Mustapha Carayol), Emilio Zelaya (63.Anton Maglica), João Pedro, Fotis Papoulis (59.Sasa Markovic), Adrián Sardinero. Trainer: Sofronis Avgousti.

Goal: 1-0 Pavel Nekhaychik (86).

[Apollon Limassol FC won 4-1 on aggregate]

09.08.2018; Stadion Miejski, Białystok; Referee: Ali Palabiyik (Turkey); Attendance: 15,591

Jagiellonia Białystok – KAA Gent 0-1(0-0)

Jagiellonia Białystok: Marián Kelemen, Jakub Wójcicki, Nemanja Mitrovic, Guilherme, Ivan Runje, Arvydas Novikovas (80.Karol Swiderski), Martin Pospísil (84.Mateusz Machaj), Przemyslaw Frankowski, Bartosz Kwiecien, Taras Romanczuk, Cillian Sheridan (72.Roman Bezjak). Trainer: Ireneusz Mamrot.

KAA Gent: Colin Coosemans, Nana Asare, Igor Plastun, Sigurd Rosted, Thomas Foket, Vadis Odjidja-Ofoe (89.Brecht Dejaegere), Franko Andrijasevic, Birger Verstraete, Jean-Luc Dompé, Giorgi Chakvetadze (67.Roman Yaremchuk), Taiwo Awoniyi (69.Jonathan David). Trainer: Yves Vanderhaeghe.

Goal: 0-1 Jonathan David (85).

16.08.2018; GHELAMCO-arena, Gent; Referee: Bastian Dankert (Germany); Attendance: 16,000

KAA Gent – Jagiellonia Białystok 3-1(1-0)

KAA Gent: Lovre Kalinic, Nana Asare, Igor Plastun, Sigurd Rosted, Thomas Foket, Vadis Odjidja-Ofoe, Franko Andrijasevic (67.Roman Yaremchuk), Birger Verstraete, Jean-Luc Dompé (79.Stallone Limbombe), Giorgi Chakvetadze, Taiwo Awoniyi (77.Jonathan David). Trainer: Yves Vanderhaeghe.

Jagiellonia Białystok: Marián Kelemen, Lukasz Burliga, Nemanja Mitrovic, Guilherme, Ivan Runje, Arvydas Novikovas (81.Karol Swiderski), Martin Pospísil, Przemyslaw Frankowski (85.Jakub Wójcicki), Bartosz Kwiecien (43.Cillian Sheridan), Taras Romanczuk, Roman Bezjak. Trainer: Ireneusz Mamrot.

Goals: 1-0 Taiwo Awoniyi (13), 1-1 Martin Pospísil (58), 2-1 Roman Yaremchuk (84), 3-1 Jonathan David (89).

[KAA Gent won 4-1 on aggregate]

09.08.2018; Right to Dream Park, Farum; Referee: Alejandro Hernández Hernández (Spain); Attendance: 6,079

FC Nordsjælland Farum – FK Partizan Beograd 1-2(0-1)

FC Nordsjælland: Nicolai Larsen, Benjamin Hansen (65.Mathias Rasmussen), Karlo Bartolec, Mads Pedersen, Andreas Skovgaard, Victor Nelsson, Magnus Andersen, Jacob Christensen (78.Nicklas Strunck Jakobsen), Mikkel Damsgaard, Mikkel Rygaard Jensen (65.Mohammed Kudus), Andreas Skov Olsen. Trainer: Kasper Hjulmand.

Partizan Beograd: Vladimir Stojkovic, Marc Valiente, Nemanja Miletic (I), Sasa Zdjelar, Svetozar Markovic, Goran Zakaric (70.Milan Smiljanic), Nebojsa Kosovic (78.Nemanja Nikolic), Marko Jankovic (90+1.Gabriel Enache), Danilo Pantic, Nemanja Miletic (II), Ricardo Gomes. Trainer: Zoran Mirkovic.

Goals: 0-1 Ricardo Gomes (10), 0-2 Goran Zakaric (64), 1-2 Mathias Rasmussen (71).

16.08.2018; Stadion Partizan, Beograd; Referee: Kristo Tohver (Estonia); Attendance: 9,372

FK Partizan Beograd – FC Nordsjælland Farum 3-2(3-1)

Partizan Beograd: Vladimir Stojkovic, Marc Valiente, Nemanja Miletic (I), Sasa Zdjelar, Svetozar Markovic, Goran Zakaric (80.Milan Smiljanic), Nebojsa Kosovic, Marko Jankovic (70.Atmin Djerlek), Danilo Pantic (82.Gabriel Enache), Nemanja Miletic (II), Ricardo Gomes. Trainer: Zoran Mirkovic.

FC Nordsjælland: Nicolai Larsen, Karlo Bartolec, Mads Pedersen, Andreas Skovgaard, Abdel Mumin, Magnus Andersen (58.Mikkel Rygaard Jensen), Mohammed Kudus (68.Nicklas Strunck Jakobsen), Jacob Christensen, Mikkel Damsgaard, Godsway Donyoh (58.Jonathan Amon), Andreas Skov Olsen. Trainer: Kasper Hjulmand.

Goals: 0-1 Andreas Skov Olsen (9), 1-1 Nemanja Miletic (I) (11), 2-1 Marko Jankovic (30), 3-1 Svetozar Markovic (35), 3-2 Jonathan Amon (76).

[FK Partizan Beograd won 5-3 on aggregate]

09.08.2018; Nationalen Stadion "Vasil Levski", Sofia; Referee: Bart Vertenten (Belgium); Attendance: 18,100

PFC CSKA Sofia – FC København 1-2(1-0)

CSKA Sofia: Vytautas Cerniauskas, Boris Sekulic, Bozhidar Chorbadzhiyski [*sent off 41*], Steven Pereira, Rúben Pinto, Edwin Gyasi (37.Jorginho), Tiago Rodrigues (44.Aleksandar Dyulgerov), Janio Bikel, Angel Lyaskov, Kiril Despodov (78.Valentin Antov), Maurides. Trainer: Nestor El Maestro.

FC København: Jesse Joronen, Andreas Bjelland (45+2.Denis Vavro), Sotirios Papagiannopoulos, Peter Ankersen, Nicolai Boilesen, Rasmus Falk (76.Ján Gregus), Zeca, Viktor Fischer, Nicolaj Thomsen (62.Robert Skov), Dame N'Doye, Kenan Kodro. Trainer: Ståle Solbakken.

Goals: 1-0 Maurides (15), 1-1 Denis Vavro (64), 1-2 Kenan Kodro (74 penalty).

16.08.2018; Telia Parken, København; Referee: Halil Umut Meler (Turkey); Attendance: 10,078

FC København – PFC CSKA Sofia 2-1(1-0)

FC København: Jesse Joronen, Andreas Bjelland, Peter Ankersen, Nicolai Boilesen, Denis Vavro, Ján Gregus (60.William Kvist), Zeca, Viktor Fischer, Nicolaj Thomsen, Robert Skov (86.Kenan Kodro), Dame N'Doye (90+1.Pieros Sotiriou). Trainer: Ståle Solbakken.

CSKA Sofia: Vytautas Cerniauskas, Nikolaj Bodurov, Kristiyan Malinov (72.Janio Bikel), Boris Sekulic, Steven Pereira, Rúben Pinto, Edwin Gyasi (46.Evandro), Tiago Rodrigues, Angel Lyaskov, Kiril Despodov (79.Stanislav Manolev), Maurides. Trainer: Nestor El Maestro.

Goals: 1-0 Dame N'Doye (23), 1-1 Evandro (58), 2-1 Dame N'Doye (64).

[FC København won 4-2 on aggregate]

09.08.2018; Basaksehir „Fatih Terim" Stadyumu, İstanbul; Referee: Srđan Jovanović (Serbia); Attendance: 4,503

İstanbul Başakşehir FK – Burnley FC 0-0

İstanbul Başakşehir: Mert Günok, Manuel da Costa, Gaël Clichy, Alexandru Epureanu, Júnior Caiçara, Eljero Elia (84.Kerim Frei), Emre Belözoglu, Mahmut Tekdemir, Edin Visca, Irfan Kahveci (58.Milos Jojic), Rijad Bajic (89.Stefano Napoleoni). Trainer: Abdullah Avci.

Burnley FC: Joe Hart, Phil Bardsley, Ben Mee, James Tarkowski, Charlie Taylor, Jack Cork, Jóhann Gudmundsson (62.Samuel Vokes), Ashley Westwood, Jeffrey Hendrick, Jon Walters, Ashley Barnes (78.Aaron Lennon). Trainer: Sean Dyche.

16.08.2018; Turf Moor, Burnley; Referee: István Kovács (Romania); Attendance: 16,583

Burnley FC – İstanbul Başakşehir FK 1-0(0-0, 0-0)

Burnley FC: Joe Hart, Phil Bardsley, Stephen Ward, Kevin Long, Ben Gibson, Charlie Taylor, Aaron Lennon (58.Jóhann Gudmundsson), Ashley Westwood (82.Jack Cork), Jeffrey Hendrick, Ashley Barnes (120+2.James Tarkowski), Samuel Vokes (82.Chris Wood). Trainer: Sean Dyche.

İstanbul Başakşehir: Mert Günok, Manuel da Costa, Gaël Clichy, Alexandru Epureanu, Júnior Caiçara, Emre Belözoglu, Mahmut Tekdemir (92.Gökhan Inler), Edin Visca, Kerim Frei (102.Stefano Napoleoni), Irfan Kahveci (109.Milos Jojic), Rijad Bajic (66.Emmanuel Adebayor). Trainer: Abdullah Avci.

Goals: 1-0 Jack Cork (97).

[Burnley FC won 1-0 on aggregate]

09.08.2018; Luminus Arena, Genk; Referee: Marius Avram (Romania); Attendance: 13,540

KRC Genk – KKS Lech Poznań 2-0(1-0)

KRC Genk: Danny Vukovic, Sebastien Dewaest, Jere Uronen, Jhon Lucumí, Joakim Mæhle, Pozuelo, Ruslan Malinovskiy, Sander Berge, Leandro Trossard (82.Edon Zhegrova), Mbwana Samatta (65.Zinho Gano), Dieumerci N'Dongala. Trainer: Philippe Clement.

Lech Poznań: Jasmin Buric, Thomas Rogne (68.Nikola Vujadinovic), Volodymyr Kostevych, Vernon, Maciej Orlowski, Tomasz Cywka, Lukasz Tralka, Maciej Makuszewski (54.Kamil Józwiak), Maciej Gajos, Darko Jevtic (74.Pawel Tomczyk), Christian Gytkjær. Trainer: Ivan Djurdjevic.

Goals: 1-0 Ruslan Malinovskiy (44), 2-0 Mbwana Samatta (56).

16.08.2018; Stadion INEA, Poznań; Referee: Marco Guida (Italy); Attendance: 20,765

KKS Lech Poznań – KRC Genk 1-2(0-2)

Lech Poznań: Jasmin Buric, Thomas Rogne (29.Maciej Orlowski), Nikola Vujadinovic, Rafal Janicki, Vernon, Tomasz Cywka, Maciej Gajos (77.Darko Jevtic), Petro Tiba, Kamil Józwiak, Christian Gytkjær (73.Pawel Tomczyk), João Amaral. Trainer: Ivan Djurdjevic.

KRC Genk: Danny Vukovic, Sebastien Dewaest, Jere Uronen, Joseph Aidoo, Joakim Mæhle, Pozuelo (60.Jakub Piotrowski), Ruslan Malinovskiy (74.Ibrahima Seck), Sander Berge, Leandro Trossard (60.Edon Zhegrova), Mbwana Samatta, Dieumerci N'Dongala. Trainer: Philippe Clement.

Goals: 0-1 Mbwana Samatta (19), 0-2 Leandro Trossard (45+1 penalty), 1-2 Tomasz Cywka (50).

[KRC Genk won 4-1 on aggregate]

09.08.2018; GelreDome, Arnhem; Referee: Georgi Kabakov (Bulgaria); Attendance: 11,532

SBV Vitesse Arnhem – FC Basel 0-1(0-0)

Vitesse Arnhem: Eduardo, Alexander Büttner (87.Max Clark), Maikel van der Werff, Vyacheslav Karavaev, Jake Clarke-Salter, Thulani Serero, Navarone Foor, Thomas Bruns (70.Hilary Gong), Roy Beerens, Tim Matavz, Bryan Linssen. Trainer: Leonid Slutsky.

FC Basel: Jonas Omlin, Marek Suchy, Silvan Widmer, Éder Álvarez Balanta, Eray Cümart, Valentin Stocker (79.Kevin Bua), Luca Zuffi, Fabian Frei, Raoul Petretta, Ricky van Wolfswinkel, Albian Ajeti (90+2.Dimitri Oberlin). Trainer: Marcel Koller.

Goal: 0-1 Ricky van Wolfswinkel (90+3).

16.08.2018; St. Jakob-Park, Basel; Referee: Daniel Siebert (Germany); Attendance: 12,334

FC Basel – SBV Vitesse Arnhem 1-0(1-0)

FC Basel: Jonas Omlin, Silvan Widmer, Éder Álvarez Balanta, Eray Cümart, Valentin Stocker, Serey Dié, Luca Zuffi, Fabian Frei, Raoul Petretta, Ricky van Wolfswinkel (90+3.Kevin Bua), Albian Ajeti (46.Dimitri Oberlin). Trainer: Marcel Koller.

Vitesse Arnhem: Eduardo, Alexander Büttner, Maikel van der Werff, Vyacheslav Karavaev, Jake Clarke-Salter [*sent off 26*], Thulani Serero, Navarone Foor, Matús Bero (28.Rasmus Thelander), Roy Beerens (82.Mitchell van Bergen), Tim Matavz (71.Oussama Darfalou), Bryan Linssen. Trainer: Leonid Slutsky.

Goal: 1-0 Albian Ajeti (30).

[FC Basel won 2-0 on aggregate]

09.08.2018; Stádio „Giórgos Karaïskáki", Peiraiás; Referee: François Letexier (France); Attendance: 19,208

Olympiacos SFP Peiraiás – FC Luzern 4-0(3-0)

Olympiacos Peiraiás: Andreas Gianniotis, Jagos Vukovic, Omar Elabdellaoui, Roderick Miranda, Kostas Tsimikas, Lazaros Christodoulopoulos (78.Marius Vrousai), Kostas Fortounis (86.Ioannis Fetfatzidis), Andreas Bouchalakis, Daniel Podence, Mohamed Camara (90.Vasilios Torosidis), Guerrero. Trainer: Pedro Martins.

FC Luzern: Mirko Salvi, Christian Schwegler (58.Ruben Vargas), Simon Grether, Lucão, Yannick Schmid, Silvan Sidler, Idriz Voca, Christian Schneuwly (58.Marvin Schulz), Pascal Schürpf, Valeriane Gvilia, Blessing Eleke (74.Shkelqim Demhasaj). Trainer: René Weiler.

Goals: 1-0, 2-0 Lazaros Christodoulopoulos (10, 33), 3-0, 4-0 Guerrero (36, 84).

16.08.2018; Swissporarena, Luzern; Referee: Kirill Levnikov (Russia); Attendance: 6,258

FC Luzern – Olympiacos SFP Peiraiás 1-3(0-1)

FC Luzern: Mirko Salvi, Simon Grether, Lucão, Marvin Schulz, Silvan Sidler, Idriz Voca, Christian Schneuwly (66.Ruben Vargas), Pascal Schürpf, Valeriane Gvilia (81.Shkelqim Demhasaj), Filip Ugrinic (67.Stefan Wolf), Blessing Eleke. Trainer: René Weiler.

Olympiacos Peiraiás: Andreas Gianniotis, Jagos Vukovic, Omar Elabdellaoui, Roderick Miranda, Kostas Tsimikas, Lazaros Christodoulopoulos, Kostas Fortounis (63.Ioannis Fetfatzidis), Andreas Bouchalakis, Daniel Podence, Mohamed Camara (71.Vasilios Torosidis), Guerrero (70.Karim Ansarifard). Trainer: Pedro Martins.

Goals: 0-1, 0-2 Lazaros Christodoulopoulos (23, 59), 0-3 Guerrero (68), 1-3 Shkelqim Demhasaj (82).

[Olympiacos SFP Peiraiás won 7-1 on aggregate]

09.08.2018; Vodafone Stadyumu, İstanbul; Referee: Bartosz Frankowski (Poland); Attendance: 24,476

Beşiktaş JK İstanbul – LASK Linz 1-0(1-0)

Beşiktaş: Tolga Zengin, Pepe, Caner Erkin, Gökhan Gönül, Gary Medel, Ryan Babel, Jeremain Lens (71.Ricardo Quaresma), Necip Uysal, Tolgay Arslan, Oguzhan Özyakup (80.Vágner Love), Cyle Larin (88.Álvaro Negredo). Trainer: Senol Günes.

LASK Linz: Alexander Schlager, Emanuel Pogatetz, Christian Ramsebner, Gernot Trauner, Reinhold Ranftl, Maximilian Ullmann, James Holland, Thomas Goiginger, Peter Michorl (90+2.Dogan Erdogan), Dominik Frieser (67.Florian Jamnig), Samuel Tetteh (78.Yusuf Otubanjo). Trainer: Oliver Glasner.

Goal: 1-0 Ryan Babel (6).

16.08.2018; Linzer Stadion, Linz; Referee: Nikola Dabanović (Montenegro); Attendance: 13,739

LASK Linz – Beşiktaş JK İstanbul 2-1(1-0)

LASK Linz: Alexander Schlager, Emanuel Pogatetz, Christian Ramsebner, Gernot Trauner, Reinhold Ranftl, Maximilian Ullmann, James Holland, Thomas Goiginger (87.Yusuf Otubanjo), Peter Michorl, João Victor Santos Sá (66.Dominik Frieser), Samuel Tetteh (79.Florian Jamnig). Trainer: Oliver Glasner.

Beşiktaş: Tolga Zengin, Adriano, Pepe, Caner Erkin, Gary Medel, Enzo Roco, Ryan Babel, Jeremain Lens, Tolgay Arslan (72.Gökhan Gönül), Oguzhan Özyakup (46.Ricardo Quaresma), Cyle Larin (72.Álvaro Negredo [*sent off 90+2*]). Trainer: Senol Günes.

Goals: 1-0 João Victor Santos Sá (42), 2-0 Dominik Frieser (69), 2-1 Álvaro Negredo (90).

[Beşiktaş JK İstanbul won on away goals rule (2-2 on aggregate)]

09.08.2018; Slavutych-Arena, Zaporizhya; Referee: Tobias Welz (Germany); Attendance: 5,365

FK Zorya Luhansk – Sporting Clube de Braga 1-1(0-0)

Zorya Luhansk: Luis Felipe, Vitaliy Vernidub, Oleksandr Svatok, Oleksandr Tymchyk, Bogdan Mykhaylychenko, Dmytro Khomchenovsky, Igor Kharatin, Oleksandr Karavayev, Silas (66.Artem Gordienko), Bohdan Lednev (71.Vladyslav Kochergin), Rafael Ratão (74.Vladyslav Kabayev). Trainer: Yuriy Vernydub.

Sporting Clube de Braga: Matheus Magalhães, Raúl Silva, Ricardo Esgaio, Marcelo Goiano, Nuno Sequeira, Bruno Viana, Claudemir, Fransérgio, João Novais (89.Ricardo Ryller), Ricardo Horta (89.Fábio Martins), Wilson Eduardo (78.Dyego Sousa). Trainer: Abel Ferreira.

Goals: 0-1 Ricardo Horta (69), 1-1 Oleksandr Karavayev (72).

16.08.2018; Estádio Municipal de Braga, Braga; Referee: Aleksandar Stavrev (North Macedonia); Attendance: 12,224

Sporting Clube de Braga – FK Zorya Luhansk 2-2(0-0)

Sporting Clube de Braga: Matheus Magalhães, Raúl Silva (38.Pablo Santos), Ricardo Esgaio, Diogo Figueiras (85.Bruno Xadas), Nuno Sequeira, Bruno Viana, Fransérgio, João Novais (79.Ricardo Ryller), Ricardo Horta, Wilson Eduardo, Dyego Sousa. Trainer: Abel Ferreira.

Zorya Luhansk: Luis Felipe (68.Zauri Makharadze), Vitaliy Vernidub, Oleksandr Svatok, Oleksandr Tymchyk, Bogdan Mykhaylychenko, Dmytro Khomchenovsky, Igor Kharatin, Oleksandr Karavayev, Silas, Bohdan Lednev (46.Vladyslav Kochergin), Rafael Ratão (76.Vladyslav Kabayev). Trainer: Yuriy Vernydub.

Goals: 1-0 João Novais (65), 1-1 Rafael Ratão (70), 2-1 Ricardo Horta (73), 2-2 Oleksandr Karavayev (83).

[FK Zorya Luhansk won on away goals rule (3-3 on aggregate)]

09.08.2018; Sarpsborg Stadion, Sarpsborg; Referee: Kevin Clancy (Scotland); Attendance: 5,944

Sarpsborg 08 FF – HNK Rijeka 1-1(0-0)

Sarpsborg 08: Alexander Vasyutin, Amin Askar (84.Tobias Heintz), Joackim Jørgensen, Joachim Thomassen, Joonas Tamm, Matti Lund Nielsen (83.Harmeet Singh), Ole Halvorsen, Jon-Helge Tveita, Kristoffer Zachariassen, Patrick Mortensen, Rashad Muhammed (86.Jørgen Larsen). Trainer: Geir Bakke.

HNK Rijeka: Simon Sluga, Roberto Puncec, Dario Zuparic, Mario Pavelic, Leonard Zuta, Srdan Grahovac, Domagoj Pavicic (82.Antonio Colak), Dario Canadija, Alexander Gorgon, Héber (66.Zoran Kvrzic), Boadu Maxwell Acosty (90+1.Luka Capan). Trainer: Matjaz Kek.

Goals: 1-0 Kristoffer Zachariassen (72), 1-1 Alexander Gorgon (83).

16.08.2018; Stadion Rujevica, Rijeka; Referee: Donatas Rumsas (Lithuania); Attendance: 5,351

HNK Rijeka – Sarpsborg 08 FF 0-1(0-0)

HNK Rijeka: Simon Sluga, Roberto Puncec, Dario Zuparic, Mario Pavelic (87.Antonio Colak), Leonard Zuta, Srdan Grahovac, Domagoj Pavicic (67.Jakov Puljic), Dario Canadija, Alexander Gorgon, Héber (77.Zoran Kvrzic), Boadu Maxwell Acosty. Trainer: Matjaz Kek.

Sarpsborg 08: Alexander Vasyutin, Amin Askar (75.Tobias Heintz), Joackim Jørgensen (59.Bjørn Utvik), Joachim Thomassen, Joonas Tamm, Matti Lund Nielsen, Ole Halvorsen, Jon-Helge Tveita (82.Kristoffer Larsen), Kristoffer Zachariassen, Patrick Mortensen, Rashad Muhammed. Trainer: Geir Bakke.

Goal: 0-1 Patrick Mortensen (83).

[Sarpsborg 08 FF won 2-1 on aggregate]

09.08.2018; Easter Road Stadium, Edinburgh; Referee: Ádám Farkas (Hungary); Attendance: 16,339

Hibernian FC Edinburgh – Molde FK 0-0

Hibernian FC: Ross Laidlaw, Lewis Stevenson, Paul Hanlon, Efe Ambrose, David Gray, Ryan Porteous, Marvin Bartley (81.Emerson Hyndman), Vykintas Slivka, Stephen Mallan, Martin Boyle (90+4.Jamie MacLaren), Florian Kamberi (81.Oliver Shaw). Trainer: Neil Lennon.

Molde FK: Andreas Linde, Vegard Forren, Ruben Gabrielsen, Kristoffer Haugen, Petter Strand, Magnus Eikrem (62.Leke James), Etzaz Hussain, Babacar Sarr, Eirik Hestad (90+1.Pawel Cibicki), Stian Gregersen, Daniel Chima Chukwu (72.Mattias Mostrøm). Trainer: Ole Gunnar Solskjær.

16.08.2018; Aker Stadion, Molde; Referee: Dennis Higler (Netherlands); Attendance: 4,368

Molde FK – Hibernian FC Edinburgh 3-0(1-0)

Molde FK: Andreas Linde, Vegard Forren, Ruben Gabrielsen, Kristoffer Haugen, Christoffer Remmer, Etzaz Hussain, Eirik Hestad, Fredrik Aursnes, Stian Gregersen (71.Petter Strand), Pawel Cibicki (58.Magnus Eikrem), Erling Håland (83.Leke James). Trainer: Ole Gunnar Solskjær.

Hibernian FC: Ádám Bogdán, Lewis Stevenson (88.David Gray), Paul Hanlon, Efe Ambrose, Ryan Porteous, Marvin Bartley (40.Emerson Hyndman), Vykintas Slivka, Stephen Mallan, Martin Boyle, Jamie MacLaren (76.Oliver Shaw), Florian Kamberi. Trainer: Neil Lennon.

Goals: 1-0 Erling Håland (35), 2-0 Fredrik Aursnes (66), 3-0 Erling Håland (82).

[Molde FK won 3-0 on aggregate]

09.08.2018; Stadion Poljud, Split; Referee: Tiago Bruno Lopes Martins (Portugal); Attendance: 25,764

HNK Hajduk Split – FCSB București 0-0

Hajduk Split: Josip Posavec, André Fomitschow, Stipe Vucur, Borja López, Bozo Mikulic, Ádám Gyurcsó (56.Michele Sego), Mijo Caktas, Hamza Barry (76.Márkó Futács), Josip Juranovic, Stanko Juric, Mirko Ivanovski (64.Ahmed Said). Trainer: Zeljko Kopic.

FCSB București: Cristian Balgradean, Marko Momcilovic (45.Junior Maranhão), Romario Sandu Benzar, Bogdan Planic, Mihai Balasa, Filipe Teixeira, Mihai Pintilii, Lucian Filip, Harlem Gnohéré, Florin Tanase (87.Olimpiu Morutan), Dennis Man (47.Antonio Jakolis). Trainer: Nicolae Dica.

16.08.2018; Arena Națională, București; Referee: Juan Martínez Munuera (Spain); Attendance: 27,410

FCSB București – HNK Hajduk Split 2-1(0-0)

FCSB București: Cristian Balgradean, Junior Maranhão, Romario Sandu Benzar, Bogdan Planic, Mihai Balasa, Filipe Teixeira, Mihai Pintilii (83.Raul Rusescu), Lucian Filip (15.Dragos Nedelcu), Harlem Gnohéré, Florin Tanase (46.Olimpiu Morutan), Dennis Man. Trainer: Nicolae Dica.

Hajduk Split: Josip Posavec, André Fomitschow, Stipe Vucur, Borja López (65.Ádám Gyurcsó), Bozo Mikulic, Mijo Caktas, Hamza Barry, Josip Juranovic, Stanko Juric (56.Jairo), Mirko Ivanovski (73.Michele Sego), Ahmed Said. Trainer: Zeljko Kopic.

Goals: 1-0 Harlem Gnohéré (55 penalty), 1-1 Ahmed Said (82), 2-1 Harlem Gnohéré (90+3).

[FCSB București won 2-1 on aggregate]

09.08.2018; Ibrox Stadium, Glasgow; Referee: Roi Reinshreiber (Israel); Attendance: 48,001

Rangers FC Glasgow – NK Maribor 3-1(1-1)

Rangers: Allan McGregor, James Tavernier, Connor Goldson, Jon Flanagan, Nikola Katic, Scott Arfield, Ryan Kent (87.Ross McCrorie), Oviemuno Ejaria (78.Jamie Murphy), Lassana Coulibaly, Candeias, Alfredo Morelos (88.Umar Sadiq). Trainer: Steven Gerrard.

NK Maribor: Jasmin Handanovic, Marko Suler, Mitja Viler, Sasa Ivkovic, Denis Klinar, Blaz Vrhovec, Amir Dervisevic, Aleks Pihler, Marcos Tavares (79.Dare Vrsic), Gregor Bajde (61.Jasmin Mesanovic), Luka Zahovic. Trainer: Darko Milanic.

Goals: 1-0 Alfredo Morelos (6), 1-1 Mitja Viler (40), 2-1 James Tavernier (50 penalty), 3-1 Lassana Coulibaly (86).

16.08.2018; Ljudski vrt, Maribor; Referee: Jonathan Lardot (Belgium); Attendance: 11,166

NK Maribor – Rangers FC Glasgow 0-0

NK Maribor: Jasmin Handanovic, Marko Suler, Mitja Viler, Sasa Ivkovic, Denis Klinar (52.Aleks Pihler), Blaz Vrhovec, Amir Dervisevic (73.Dare Vrsic), Dino Hotic, Marcos Tavares, Jasmin Mesanovic (80.Jan Mlakar), Luka Zahovic. Trainer: Darko Milanic.

Rangers: Allan McGregor, James Tavernier, Connor Goldson, Nikola Katic, Scott Arfield, Ryan Jack, Andy Halliday, Oviemuno Ejaria (68.Ryan Kent), Jamie Murphy (76.Ross McCrorie), Candeias, Alfredo Morelos. Trainer: Steven Gerrard.

[Rangers FC Glasgow won 3-1 on aggregate]

09.08.2018; Stadion „Rajko Mitić“, Beograd; Referee: Kevin Blom (Netherlands); Attendance: 4,000

FK Spartak Subotica – Brøndby IF 0-2(0-1)

Spartak Subotica: Nikola Peric, Stefan Milosevic, Andrija Vukcevic (69.Vladimir Torbica), Noboru Shimura, Nemanja Calasan, Nemanja Tekijaski, Bojan Cecaric, Nemanja Glavcic, David Dundjerski (89.Tim Chow), Dejan Djenic, Ognjen Djuricin (69.Samuel Afum). Trainer: Vladimir Gacinovic.

Brøndby IF: Marvin Schwäbe, Benedikt Röcker, Johan Larsson, Anthony Jung, Hjörtur Hermannsson, Kasper Fisker (67.Lasse Vigen Christensen), Dominik Kaiser, Josip Radosevic, Simon Tibbling (46.Hany Mukhtar), Kamil Wilczek (84.Mikkel Uhre), Ante Erceg. Trainer: Alexander Zorniger.

Goals: 0-1 Dominik Kaiser (29), 0-2 Hany Mukhtar (47).

16.08.2018; Brøndby Stadion, Brøndby; Referee: Hüseyin Göçek (Turkey); Attendance: 10,142

Brøndby IF – FK Spartak Subotica 2-1(0-0)

Brøndby IF: Marvin Schwäbe, Paulus Arajuuri (66.Johan Larsson), Anthony Jung, Jens Gammelby, Joël Kabongo [*sent off 11*], Dominik Kaiser, Lasse Vigen Christensen, Josip Radosevic, Hany Mukhtar, Ante Erceg (14.Hjörtur Hermannsson), Mikkel Uhre (59.Kamil Wilczek). Trainer: Alexander Zorniger.

Spartak Subotica: Nikola Peric, Stefan Milosevic, Andrija Vukcevic, Noboru Shimura, Nemanja Tekijaski, Bojan Cecaric, Nemanja Glavcic, Milan Marcic (77.Tim Chow), David Dundjerski, Dejan Djenic, Ognjen Djuricin (68.Vladimir Torbica). Trainer: Vladimir Gacinovic.

Goals: 1-0 Dominik Kaiser (69), 1-1 Dejan Djenic (80), 2-1 Kamil Wilczek (90+3).

[Brøndby IF won 4-1 on aggregate]

09.08.2018; Stadión Pasienky, Bratislava; Referee: Pawel Raczkowski (Poland); Attendance: 9,563

ŠK Slovan Bratislava – SK Rapid Wien 2-1(1-1)

Slovan Bratislava: Dominik Greif, Kornel Saláta, Mitch Apau, Vasil Bozhikov, Dávid Holman (46.Vukan Savicevic), Nono Delgado (87.Ibrahim Rabiu), Kenan Bajric, "Moha" Mohammed Rharsalla, Aleksandar Cavric, Andraz Sporar, Dejan Drazic (90+1.Adam Laczkó). Trainer: Martin Sevela.

SK Rapid Wien: Richard Strebinger, Mario Sonnleitner, Marvin Potzmann, Boli Bolingoli-Mbombo, Mateo Barac, Christoph Knasmüllner (68.Andrei Ivan), Stefan Schwab, Thomas Murg (78.Jérémy Guillemenot), Dejan Ljubicic, Deni Alar, Veton Berisha. Trainer: Goran Djuricin.

Goals: 0-1 Stefan Schwab (12), 1-1 Vasil Bozhikov (29), 2-1 Mateo Barac (49 own goal).

16.08.2018; Allianz Stadion, Wien; Referee: Davide Massa (Italy); Attendance: 17,800

SK Rapid Wien – ŠK Slovan Bratislava 4-0(1-0)

SK Rapid Wien: Richard Strebinger, Mario Sonnleitner, Marvin Potzmann, Boli Bolingoli-Mbombo, Mateo Barac, Christoph Knasmüllner, Stefan Schwab (87.Mert Müldür), Thomas Murg (90.Aleksandar Kostic), Dejan Ljubicic, Deni Alar (78.Andrei Ivan), Veton Berisha. Trainer: Goran Djuricin.

Slovan Bratislava: Dominik Greif, Kornel Saláta, Mitch Apau (80.Boris Cmiljanic), Vasil Bozhikov, Ibrahim Rabiu (67.Vukan Savicevic), Nono Delgado, Kenan Bajric, "Moha" Mohammed Rharsalla, Aleksandar Cavric, Andraz Sporar, Dejan Drazic (81.Filip Holosko). Trainer: Martin Sevela.

Goals: 1-0, 2-0 Christoph Knasmüllner (3, 79), 3-0 Thomas Murg (84), 4-0 Christoph Knasmüllner (90+4).

[SK Rapid Wien won 5-2 on aggregate]

09.08.2018; Estadio „Ramón Sánchez Pizjuán“, Sevilla; Referee: Bojan Pandzic (Sweden); Attendance: 26,189

Sevilla FC – FK Žalgiris Vilnius 1-0(1-0)

Sevilla FC: Tomás Vaclík, Daniel Carriço, Aleix Vidal, Guilherme Arana, Joris Gnagnon, Juan Berrocal, Éver Banega (74.Ganso), Ibrahim Amadou, Pejiño (59.Luis Muriel), Nolito (74.Pablo Sarabia), Wissam Ben Yedder. Trainer: Pablo Machín.

Žalgiris Vilnius: Dziugas Bartkus, Rolandas Baravykas, Mamadou Mbodj, Saulius Mikoliūnas (74.Serge Nyuiadzi), Donovan Slijngard, Tomas Simkovic, Liviu Antal (90.Venelin Filipov), Slavko Blagojevic, Jérémy Manzorro (77.Domantas Simkus), Marko Tomic, Louis Ogana. Trainer: Valdas Urbonas.

Goal: 1-0 Éver Banega (34).

16.08.2018; LFF stadionas, Vilnius; Referee: Enea Jorgji (Albania); Attendance: 5,000

FK Žalgiris Vilnius – Sevilla FC 0-5(0-3)

Žalgiris Vilnius: Dziugas Bartkus, Rolandas Baravykas, Mamadou Mbodj, Saulius Mikoliūnas (46.Serge Nyuiadzi), Donovan Slijngard, Tomas Simkovic, Liviu Antal, Slavko Blagojevic, Jérémy Manzorro (54.Domantas Simkus), Marko Tomic, Louis Ogana (65.Tomás Malec). Trainer: Valdas Urbonas.

Sevilla FC: Tomás Vaclík, Daniel Carriço, Sergio Escudero (46.Guilherme Arana), Aleix Vidal, Sergi Gómez, Joris Gnagnon, Éver Banega (55.Juan Berrocal), Pablo Sarabia (46.Luis Muriel), Ibrahim Amadou, Nolito, Wissam Ben Yedder. Trainer: Pablo Machín.

Goals: 0-1 Nolito (6), 0-2, 0-3 Pablo Sarabia (7, 44), 0-4 Guilherme Arana (80), 0-5 Nolito (83).

[Sevilla FC won 6-0 on aggregate]

PLAY-OFFS

CHAMPIONS PATH

23.08.2018; „Mikheil Meskhi“ Stadioni, Tbilisi; Referee: Hüseyin Göçek (Turkey); Attendance: 17,869

FC Torpedo Kutaisi – PFC Ludogorets Razgrad 0-1(0-1)

Torpedo Kutaisi: Rion Kvaskhvadze, Mamuka Kobakhidze, Giorgi Kimadze (69.Arfang Daffé), Levan Gegetchkori, Oleksandr Azatsky, Lazar Marin, Grigol Dolidze, Giorgi Kukhianidze (83.Levan Kutalia), Marek Hlinka, Mate Tsintsadze, Milos Lacny (61.Tornike Kapanadze). Trainer: Kakhaber Chkhetiani.

Ludogorets Razgrad: Jorge Broun, Cosmin Moti, Cicinho, Anton Nedyalkov, Svetoslav Dyakov, Gustavo Campanharo (66.Jacek Góralski), Wanderson, Natanael Pimienta, Claudiu Keserü (80.Jody Lukoki), Marcelinho (90+4.Georgi Terziev), Virgil Misidjan. Trainer: Paulo Autuori.

Goal: 0-1 Wanderson (45+2).

30.08.2018; Ludogorets Arena, Razgrad; Referee: Mattias Gestranius (Finland); Attendance: 5,340

PFC Ludogorets Razgrad – FC Torpedo Kutaisi 4-0(2-0)

Ludogorets Razgrad: Renan, Cosmin Moti, Cicinho, Anton Nedyalkov, Svetoslav Dyakov (72.Jacek Góralski), Gustavo Campanharo, Wanderson (87.Dimo Bakalov), Natanael Pimienta, Claudiu Keserü, Marcelinho, Virgil Misidjan (70.Jody Lukoki). Trainer: Paulo Autuori.

Torpedo Kutaisi: Rion Kvaskhvadze, Mamuka Kobakhidze, Levan Gegetchkori, Oleksandr Azatsky, Lazar Marin, Grigol Dolidze (77.Giorgi Kimadze), Levan Kutalia (46.Arfang Daffé), Marek Hlinka, Mate Tsintsadze, Milos Lacny (58.Giorgi Kukhianidze), Tornike Kapanadze. Trainer: Kakhaber Chkhetiani.

Goals: 1-0 Virgil Misidjan (6), 2-0, 3-0 Gustavo Campanharo (38, 59), 4-0 Wanderson (62).

[PFC Ludogorets Razgrad won 5-0 on aggregate]

23.08.2018; Stádio Neo GSP, Nicosia; Referee: Daniel Siebert (Germany); Attendance: 12,855

APOEL FC Nicosia – Astana FC 1-0(0-0)

APOEL Nicosia: Boy Waterman, Carlão, Emilio N'Sue, Praxitelis Vouros, Caju, Nuno Morais, Lucas Souza, Ghayas Zahid (88.Savvas Gentsoglou), Roland Sallai, Moussa Al Taamari (74.Giorgos Efrem), Dellatorre (62.Reza Ghoochannejhad). Trainer: Bruno Baltazar.

Astana FC: Nenad Eric, Antonio Rukavina, Dmitriy Shomko, Sergiy Maliy, Evgeni Postnikov, Marin Tomasov (90+1 Abzal Beysebekov), Ivan Maevski, Serikzhan Muzhikov, László Kleinheisler, Pedro Henrique (72.Baktiyor Zaynutdinov), Junior Kabananga (85.Rangelo Janga). Trainer: Roman Grygorchuk.

Goal: 1-0 Caju (79).

30.08.2018; Astana Arena, Astana; Referee: Jakob Kehlet (Denmark); Attendance: 26,000

Astana FC – APOEL FC Nicosia 1-0(1-0,1-0,1-0); 2-1 on penalties

Astana FC: Nenad Eric, Antonio Rukavina, Marin Anicic, Dmitriy Shomko, Evgeni Postnikov, Marin Tomasov, Ivan Maevski (120+2.Yuriy Logvinenko), Serikzhan Muzhikov (53.Richard Almeyda), László Kleinheisler (99.Abzal Beysebekov), Pedro Henrique, Junior Kabananga (84.Rangelo Janga). Trainer: Roman Grygorchuk.

APOEL Nicosia: Boy Waterman, Carlão, Emilio N'Sue, Praxitelis Vouros (120+1.Savvas Gentsoglou), Caju, Nuno Morais, Lucas Souza, Ghayas Zahid (64.Tomás De Vincenti), Roland Sallai, Moussa Al Taamari (84.Giorgos Efrem), Reza Ghoochannejhad (94.Dellatorre). Trainer: Bruno Baltazar.

Goal: 1-0 Pedro Henrique (16 penalty).

Penalties: Nuno Morais 0-1; Richard Almeyda 1-1; Tomás De Vincenti (missed); Marin Anicic (missed); Giorgos Efrem (missed); Pedro Henrique 2-1; Dellatorre (missed); Abzal Beysebekov (missed); Lucas Souza (missed).

[Astana FC won 2-1 on penalties (after 1-1 on aggregate)]

23.08.2018; Marijampoles sporto centro stadione, Marijampolė; Referee: Ivan Bebek (Croatia); Attendance: 5,100

FK Sūduva Marijampolė – Celtic FC Glasgow 1-1(1-1)

FK Sūduva Marijampolė: Ivan Kardum, Vaidas Slavickas, Algis Jankauskas, Vitaly Gayduchik, Andro Svrljuga, Guilherme Finkler (46.Daniel Offenbacher), Povilas Leimonas, Robertas Vézevicius (60.Julius Kasparavicius), Jovan Cadenovic, Ovidijus Verbickas (90.Giedrius Matulevicius), Rigino Cicilia. Trainer: Vladimir Cheburin.

Celtic: Craig Gordon, Cristian Gamboa (66.Emilio Izaguirre), Jozo Simunovic (52.Mikael Lustig), Kieran Tierney, Kristoffer Ajer, Scott Brown, James Forrest, Callum McGregor, Olivier Ntcham, Moussa Dembélé, Michael Johnston (66.Leigh Griffiths). Trainer: Brendan Rodgers.

Goals: 0-1 Olivier Ntcham (3), 1-1 Ovidijus Verbickas (13).

30.08.2018; Celtic Park, Glasgow; Referee: Georgi Kabakov (Bulgaria); Attendance: 44,639

Celtic FC Glasgow – FK Sūduva Marijampolė 3-0(1-0)

Celtic: Craig Gordon, Mikael Lustig, Dedryck Boyata, Kieran Tierney (69.Emilio Izaguirre), Kristoffer Ajer, Scott Brown, Scott Sinclair, Callum McGregor, Olivier Ntcham, Leigh Griffiths (65.Ryan Christie), Michael Johnston (78.Jonny Hayes). Trainer: Brendan Rodgers.

FK Sūduva Marijampolė: Ivan Kardum, Vaidas Slavickas, Algis Jankauskas, Vitaly Gayduchik, Andro Svrljuga, Aleksandar Zivanovic, Gerson Acevedo, Daniel Offenbacher (79.Ovidijus Verbickas), Jovan Cadenovic (56.Povilas Leimonas), Sandro Gotal (73.Julius Kasparavicius), Rigino Cicilia. Trainer: Vladimir Cheburin.

Goals: 1-0 Leigh Griffiths (27), 2-0 Callum McGregor (53), 3-0 Kristoffer Ajer (61).

[Celtic FC Glasgow won 4-1 on aggregate]

23.08.2018; Bolshaya Sportivnaya Arena, Tiraspol; Referee: Harald Lechner (Austria); Attendance: 5,073

FC Sheriff Tiraspol – Qarabağ FK 1-0(1-0)

FC Sheriff Tiraspol: Serghei Pascenco, Mateo Susic, Veaceslav Posmac, Vladimir Kovacevic, Cristiano, Yuri Kendysh (88.Petru Racu), Gheorghe Anton, Rifet Kapic, Ziguy Badibanga, "Jô" Joálisson (72.Wilfried Balima), Alexandru Boiciuc (68.Al-Haji Kamara). Trainer: Goran Sablic.

Qarabağ FK: Vagner, Rashad Sadygov, Maksim Medvedev, Badavi Hüseynov, Míchel, Qara Qarayev, Filip Ozobic, Simeon Slavchev (73.Ansi Agolli), Wilde Guerrier, Dzon Delarge (46.Abdellah Zoubir), Mahir Madatov. Trainer: Gurban Gurbanov.

Goal: 1-0 Rifet Kapic (8).

30.08.2018; „Tofiq Bahramov“ adina Respublika stadionu, Bakı; Referee: Aleksandar Stavrev (North Macedonia); Attendance: 21,350

Qarabağ FK – FC Sheriff Tiraspol 3-0(2-0)

Qarabağ FK: Vagner, Rashad Sadygov, Maksim Medvedev, Badavi Hüseynov, Qara Qarayev, Filip Ozobic (82.Joshgun Diniyev), Simeon Slavchev, Wilde Guerrier, Abdellah Zoubir (80.Dzon Delarge), Innocent Emeghara, Mahir Madatov (88.Abbas Hüseynov). Trainer: Gurban Gurbanov.

FC Sheriff Tiraspol: Serghei Pascenco, Petru Racu (55.Antun Palic), Mateo Susic, Veaceslav Posmac, Vladimir Kovacevic, Cristiano, Gheorghe Anton, Rifet Kapic, Ziguy Badibanga, "Jô" Joálisson (68.Gerson Rodrigues), Alexandru Boiciuc (26.Al-Haji Kamara). Trainer: Goran Sablic.

Goals: 1-0 Maksim Medvedev (9), 2-0 Wilde Guerrier (42), 3-0 Filip Ozobic (55).

[Qarabağ FK won 3-1 on aggregate]

23.08.2018; Swedbank Stadion, Malmö; Referee: Srđan Jovanović (Serbia); Attendance: 11,487

Malmö FF – FC Midtjylland 2-2(2-0)

Malmö FF: Johan Dahlin, Behrang Safari (64.Franz Brorsson), Rasmus Bengtsson, Lasse Nielsen, Andreas Vindheim (78.Eric Larsson), Søren Rieks, Anders Christiansen, Fouad Bachirou, Oscar Lewicki (71.Arnór Ingvi Traustason), Markus Rosenberg, Marcus Antonsson. Trainer: Uwe Rösler.

FC Midtjylland: Jesper Hansen, Kian Hansen, Marc Hende, Alexander Scholz, Joel Andersson, Bubacarr Sanneh, Jakob Poulsen, Tim Sparv, Gustav Wikheim (78.Awer Mabil), Frank Onyeka (90+2.Mads Thychosen), Paul Ebere Onuachu (64.Ayo Simon Okosun). Trainer: Jess Thorup.

Goals: 1-0 Markus Rosenberg (12), 2-0 Marcus Antonsson (24), 2-1 Gustav Wikheim (60), 2-2 Ayo Simon Okosun (77).

30.08.2018; MCH Arena, Herning; Referee: Serdar Gözübüyük (Netherlands); Attendance: 9,175

FC Midtjylland – Malmö FF 0-2(0-1)

FC Midtjylland: Jesper Hansen, Kian Hansen, Marc Hende, Alexander Scholz, Joel Andersson (75.Awer Mabil), Bubacarr Sanneh, Jakob Poulsen, Tim Sparv, Gustav Wikheim, Ayo Simon Okosun (56.Paul Ebere Onuachu), Frank Onyeka (56.Mayron George). Trainer: Jess Thorup.

Malmö FF: Johan Dahlin, Behrang Safari (90.Franz Brorsson), Rasmus Bengtsson, Lasse Nielsen, Andreas Vindheim (80.Eric Larsson), Søren Rieks, Anders Christiansen, Fouad Bachirou, Oscar Lewicki, Markus Rosenberg, Marcus Antonsson (84.Arnór Ingvi Traustason). Trainer: Uwe Rösler.

Goals: 0-1 Marcus Antonsson (32), 0-2 Markus Rosenberg (79).

[Malmö FF won 4-2 on aggregate]

23.08.2018; Stade „Josy Barthel“, Lëtzebuerg; Referee: Andreas Ekberg (Sweden); Attendance: 2,556

F91 Luxembourg – FC CFR 1907 Cluj-Napoca 2-0(0-0)

F91 Dudelange: Jonathan Joubert (53.Joé Frising), Tom Schnell, Jerry Prempeh, Kevin Malget, Aniss El Hriti, Marc-André Kruska, Stélvio, Dominik Stolz, Clément Couturier (88.Bryan Mélisse), David Turpel, Patrick Stumpf (65.Danel Sinani). Trainer: Dino Toppmöller.

CFR 1907: Giedrius Arlauskas, Andrei Muresan, Paulo Vinícius, Camora, Cristian Manea, Emmanuel Culio (10.Mate Males), Ovidiu Hoban, Mihai Bordeianu (71.Giuseppe De Luca), Alexandru Paun (61.Sebastian Mailat), George Tucudean, Billel Omrani. Trainer: Toni Conceição.

Goals: 1-0 David Turpel (67), 2-0 Danel Sinani (80).

30.08.2018; Stadionul "Dr. Constantin Rădulescu", Cluj-Napoca; Referee: Davide Massa (Italy); Attendance: 12,000

FC CFR 1907 Cluj-Napoca – F91 Dudelange 2-3(0-0)

CFR 1907: Jesús Fernández, Paulo Vinícius, Camora, Ádám Lang, Cristian Manea, Mate Males, Alexandru Ionita (II), Mihai Bordeianu (54.Alexandru Paun), Sebastian Mailat (46.Robert Tambe), George Tucudean (68.Júlio Baptista), Billel Omrani. Trainer: Toni Conceição.

F91 Dudelange: Joé Frising, Tom Schnell, Jerry Prempeh, Bryan Mélisse, Kevin Malget (79.Edisson Jordanov), Aniss El Hriti, Stélvio, Dominik Stolz, Clément Couturier, Danel Sinani (87.Sanel Ibrahimovic), David Turpel (90+2.Mario Pokar). Trainer: Dino Toppmöller.

Goals: 0-1, 0-2 Danel Sinani (51, 54), 0-3 David Turpel (78), 1-3 Robert Tambe (85), 2-3 Billel Omrani (88).

[F91 Dudelange won 5-2 on aggregate]

23.08.2018; Stadion Stožice, Ljubljana; Referee: Craig Pawson (England); Attendance: 7,500

NK Olimpija Ljubljana – FC Spartak Trnava 0-2(0-2)

Olimpija Ljubljana: Aljaz Ivacic, Branko Ilic (82.Goran Brkic), Dino Stiglec, Vitalijs Maksimenko, Rok Kronaveter, Marko Putincanin, Stefan Savic, Daniel Avramovski (62.Asmir Suljic), Tomislav Tomic, Nik Kapun (62.Kingsley Boateng), Issah Abass. Trainer: Aleksandar Linta.

FC Spartak Trnava: Martin Chudy, Martin Tóth [*sent off 29*], Matús Conka, Ivan Hladík, Andrej Kadlec, Erik Grendel, Jakub Rada (71.Matej Oravec), Anton Sloboda, Lukás Gressák, Erik Jirka (86.Lukás Lupták), Marek Bakos (80.Oliver Janso). Trainer: Radoslav Látal.

Goals: 0-1 Marek Bakos (23 penalty), 0-2 Branko Ilic (35 own goal).

30.08.2018; Stadión „Antona Malatinského“, Trnava; Referee: Luca Banti (Italy); Attendance: 15,642

FC Spartak Trnava – NK Olimpija Ljubljana 1-1(1-1)

FC Spartak Trnava: Martin Chudy, Matús Conka, Ivan Hladík, Boris Godál, Andrej Kadlec, Matej Oravec, Erik Grendel (72.Oliver Janso), Jakub Rada, Vakhtang Chanturishvili (89.Lukás Lupták), Erik Jirka (90+2.Stefan Pekár), Marek Bakos. Trainer: Radoslav Látal.

Olimpija Ljubljana: Aljaz Ivacic, Branko Ilic, Dino Stiglec, Vitalijs Maksimenko, Macky Frank Bagnack, Rok Kronaveter, Matic Crnic, Tomislav Tomic, Nik Kapun (74.Goran Brkic), Kingsley Boateng (69.Stefan Savic), Issah Abass (82.Asmir Suljic). Trainer: Safet Hadzic.

Goals: 1-0 Boris Godál (12), 1-1 Nik Kapun (42).

[FC Spartak Trnava won 3-1 on aggregate]

23.08.2018; Lerkendal Stadion, Trondheim; Referee: Orel Grinfeld (Israel); Attendance: 8,767

Rosenborg BK Trondheim – KF Shkëndija 79 3-1(3-0)

Rosenborg: André Hansen, Tore Reginiussen, Even Hovland, Vegar Hedenstad (78.Erlend Reitan), Birger Meling, Mike Jensen, Anders Konradsen, Marius Lundemo (74.Djordje Denic), Nicklas Bendtner, Issam Jebali, Jonathan Levi (68.Pål Helland). Trainer: Rini Coolen.

KF Shkëndija 79: Kostadin Zahov, Gledi Mici, Mevlan Murati, Visar Musliu, Mevlan Adili, Armend Alimi, Ennur Totre, Besart Ibraimi, Izair Emini (78.Besmir Bojku), Valmir Nafiu (63.Remzi Selmani), Stênio Júnior. Trainer: Qatip Osmani.

Goals: 1-0 Issam Jebali (11), 2-0 Nicklas Bendtner (15), 3-0 Jonathan Levi (44), 3-1 Stênio Júnior (76).

30.08.2018; Telekom Arena, Skopje; Referee: Aleksey Kulbakov (Belarus); Attendance: 10,950

KF Shkëndija 79 – Rosenborg BK Trondheim 0-2(0-0)

KF Shkëndija 79: Kostadin Zahov, Gledi Mici (86.Shefit Shefiti), Mevlan Murati, Visar Musliu, Egzon Bejtulai, Armend Alimi, Ennur Totre (76.Besmir Bojku), Besart Ibraimi, Izair Emini, Valmir Nafiu (64.Remzi Selmani), Stênio Júnior. Trainer: Qatip Osmani.

Rosenborg: André Hansen, Tore Reginiussen (87.Besim Serbecic), Even Hovland, Vegar Hedenstad, Birger Meling, Mike Jensen, Anders Konradsen, Marius Lundemo, Nicklas Bendtner (74.Alexander Søderlund), Issam Jebali, Jonathan Levi (62.Djordje Denic). Trainer: Rini Coolen.

Goals: 0-1 Even Hovland (67), 0-2 Tore Reginiussen (84).

[Rosenborg BK Trondheim won 5-1 on aggregate]

LEAGUE PATH

23.08.2018; Krestovsky Stadium, St. Petersburg; Referee: Deniz Aytekin (Germany); Attendance: 40,677

FK Zenit Saint Petersburg – Molde FK 3-1(0-1)

Zenit Saint Petersburg: Andrei Lunev, Branislav Ivanovic, Aleksandr Anyukov, Igor Smolnikov (68.Anton Zabolotny), Miha Mevlja, Róbert Mak, Hernani (88.Magomed Ozdoev), Matías Kranevitter (59.Aleksandr Erokhin), Daler Kuzyaev, Artem Dzyuba, Sebastián Driussi. Trainer: Sergey Semak.

Molde FK: Andreas Linde, Vegard Forren, Ruben Gabrielsen, Kristoffer Haugen, Christoffer Remmer, Petter Strand (74.Fredrik Brustad), Etzaz Hussain, Babacar Sarr, Eirik Hestad (86.Magnus Eikrem), Fredrik Aursnes, Erling Håland (78.Stian Gregersen). Trainer: Ole Gunnar Solskjær.

Goals: 0-1 Eirik Hestad (42), 1-1 Artem Dzyuba (71), 2-1 Anton Zabolotny (80), 3-1 Miha Mevlja (90).

30.08.2018; Aker Stadion, Molde; Referee: Carlos del Cerro Grande (Spain); Attendance: 5,414

Molde – FK Zenit Saint Petersburg 2-1(0-1)

Molde FK: Andreas Linde, Vegard Forren, Ruben Gabrielsen, Kristoffer Haugen, Christoffer Remmer (90.Leke James), Petter Strand (61.Magnus Eikrem), Etzaz Hussain, Babacar Sarr, Eirik Hestad, Fredrik Aursnes (71.Pawel Cibicki), Erling Håland. Trainer: Ole Gunnar Solskjær.

Zenit Saint Petersburg: Andrei Lunev, Branislav Ivanovic, Aleksandr Anyukov (86.Neto), Igor Smolnikov, Miha Mevlja, Aleksandr Erokhin, Leandro Paredes, Hernani, Daler Kuzyaev (76.Matías Kranevitter), Anton Zabolotny, Sebastián Driussi (67.Róbert Mak). Trainer: Sergey Semak.

Goals: 0-1 Daler Kuzyaev (21), 1-1 Eirik Hestad (65), 2-1 Erling Håland (77).

[FK Zenit Saint Petersburg won 4-3 on aggregate]

23.08.2018; Stadión pod Dubnom, Zilina; Referee: Antonio Mateu Lahoz (Spain); Attendance: 6,107

AS Trenčín – AEK Larnaca FC 1-1(0-0)

AS Trenčín: Igor Semrinec, Lukás Skovajsa, Martin Sulek (86.Erhan Masovic), Keston Julien, Reuben Yem, Ashraf El Mahdioui, Abdul Zubairu (84.Desley Ubbink), Joey Sleegers (80.Osman Bukari), Antonio Mance, Hamza Catakovic, Philip Azango. Trainer: Ricardo Moniz.

AEK Larnaca: Toño, Mikel González, Daniel Mojsov, Truyols, Igor Carioca, Ivan Trickovski, Jorge Larena (78.Nacho Cases), Acorán, Hector Hevel, Apostolos Giannou (83.Florian Taulemesse), Tete (65.Jean Luc Assoubre). Trainer: Andoni Iraola.

Goals: 1-0 Joey Sleegers (55), 1-1 Acorán (60).

30.08.2018; AEK Arena, Larnaca; Referee: Sergei Karasev (Russia); Attendance: 4,777

AEK Larnaca FC – AS Trenčín 3-0(2-0)

AEK Larnaca: Toño, Mikel González, Daniel Mojsov, Truyols, Igor Carioca, Ivan Trickovski, Jorge Larena (84.Facundo García), Acorán, Hector Hevel, Apostolos Giannou (74.Florian Taulemesse), Tete (62.Nacho Cases). Trainer: Andoni Iraola.

AS Trenčín: Igor Semrinec, Martin Sulek, Keston Julien, Reuben Yem, Jakub Paur, Desley Ubbink (73.Peter Klescík), Ashraf El Mahdioui, Joey Sleegers (62.Osman Bukari), Antonio Mance (73.Emeka Umeh), Hamza Catakovic, Philip Azango. Trainer: Ricardo Moniz.

Goals: 1-0 Apostolos Giannou (1), 2-0 Acorán (36), 3-0 Apostolos Giannou (65).

[AEK Larnaca FC won 4-1 on aggregate]

23.08.2018; Andrův stadion, Olomouc; Referee: Bobby Madden (Scotland); Attendance: 11,709

SK Sigma Olomouc – Sevilla FC 0-1(0-0)

SK Sigma Olomouc: Milos Buchta, Michal Veprek, Jan Sterba, Václav Jemelka, Martin Sladky, Jakub Plsek (85.Pavel Dvorák), David Houska, Tomás Zahradnícek (87.Martin Hála), Simon Falta, Lukás Kalvach, Martin Nespor (79.Jirí Texl). Trainer: Václav Jílek.

Sevilla FC: Tomás Vaclík, Aleix Vidal (71.Jesús Navas), Guilherme Arana, Joris Gnagnon, Juan Berrocal, Éver Banega, Maxime Gonalons, Pablo Sarabia, Ibrahim Amadou (71.Sergi Gómez), Nolito (66.André Silva), Luis Muriel. Trainer: Pablo Machín.

Goal: 0-1 Pablo Sarabia (84).

30.08.2018; Estadio „Ramón Sánchez Pizjuán", Sevilla; Referee: István Kovács (Romania); Attendance: 30,311

Sevilla FC – SK Sigma Olomouc 3-0(2-0)

Sevilla FC: Tomás Vaclík, Daniel Carriço, Aleix Vidal, Sergi Gómez, Guilherme Arana, Joris Gnagnon, Éver Banega (68.Roque Mesa), Franco Vázquez (79.Luis Muriel), Maxime Gonalons, Nolito, André Silva (65.Wissam Ben Yedder). Trainer: Pablo Machín.

SK Sigma Olomouc: Milos Buchta, Michal Veprek, Roman Polom, Jan Kotouc, Martin Sladky, Jakub Plsek (58.Jirí Texl), David Houska, Tomás Zahradnícek, Simon Falta (70.Pavel Dvorák), Lukás Kalvach (60.Martin Hála), Martin Nespor. Trainer: Václav Jílek.

Goals: 1-0 Maxime Gonalons (21), 2-0 Martin Nespor (26 own goal), 3-0 Wissam Ben Yedder (75).

[Sevilla FC won 4-0 on aggregate]

23.08.2018; Sarpsborg Stadion, Sarpsborg; Referee: Vladislav Bezborodov (Russia); Attendance: 6,363

Sarpsborg 08 FF – Maccabi Tel Aviv FC 3-1(2-1)

Sarpsborg 08: Alexander Vasyutin, Amin Askar, Joackim Jørgensen, Joachim Thomassen, Joonas Tamm, Matti Lund Nielsen, Jon-Helge Tveita, Kristoffer Zachariassen, Tobias Heintz (88.Kristoffer Larsen), Patrick Mortensen, Rashad Muhammed (80.Jørgen Larsen). Trainer: Geir Bakke.

Maccabi Tel Aviv: Predrag Rajkovic, Eitan Tibi, Saborit, Elazar Dasa, Jair Amador, Dor Mikha, Roslan Barski (88.Eyal Golasa), Dan Glazer, Vidar Kjartansson (76.Itay Shechter), Aaron Schoenfeld, Omer Atzili (67.Chikeluba Ofoedu). Trainer: Vladimir Ivic.

Goals: 1-0 Tobias Heintz (2), 2-0 Matti Lund Nielsen (7 penalty), 2-1 Vidar Kjartansson (13 penalty), 3-1 Patrick Mortensen (56 penalty).

30.08.2018; Winner Stadium, Netanya; Referee: Artur Manuel Ribeiro Soares Dias (Portugal); Attendance: 10,673

Maccabi Tel Aviv FC – Sarpsborg 08 FF 2-1(0-0)

Maccabi Tel Aviv: Predrag Rajkovic, Sheran Yeini, Eitan Tibi, Saborit, Elazar Dasa, Dor Mikha, Roslan Barski (87.Aaron Schoenfeld), Dan Glazer, Vidar Kjartansson (46.Itay Shechter), Eliran Atar (71.Yonatan Cohen), Omer Atzili. Trainer: Vladimir Ivic.

Sarpsborg 08: Alexander Vasyutin, Amin Askar (86.Harmeet Singh), Joackim Jørgensen (89.Jørgen Horn), Joachim Thomassen, Bjørn Utvik, Matti Lund Nielsen, Ole Halvorsen, Jon-Helge Tveita, Kristoffer Zachariassen, Patrick Mortensen, Rashad Muhammed (64.Tobias Heintz). Trainer: Geir Bakke.

Goals: 1-0 Omer Atzili (52 penalty), 2-0 Eliran Atar (60), 2-1 Ole Halvorsen (81 penalty).

[Sarpsborg 08 FF won 4-3 on aggregate]

23.08.2018; St. Jakob-Park, Basel; Referee: Matej Jug (Slovenia); Attendance: 10,743

FC Basel – Apollon Limassol FC 3-2(1-0)

FC Basel: Martin Hansen, Silvan Widmer, Éder Álvarez Balanta (66.Taulant Xhaka), Raoul Petretta, Eray Cümart, Serey Dié, Luca Zuffi, Fabian Frei, Aldo Kalulu (59.Kevin Bua), Ricky van Wolfswinkel, Albian Ajeti (87.Samuele Campo). Trainer: Marcel Koller.

Apollon: Bruno Vale, Valentin Roberge, Charis Kyriakou, Kévin Bru (39.Mustapha Carayol), Héctor Yuste, Giorgos Vasiliou, Esteban Sachetti, João Pedro, Fotis Papoulis (79.Sasa Markovic), Anton Maglica (72.Emilio Zelaya), Adrián Sardinero. Trainer: Sofronis Avgousti.

Goals: 1-0 Ricky van Wolfswinkel (6), 1-1 Anton Maglica (49), 1-2 Fotis Papoulis (53), 2-2 Ricky van Wolfswinkel (69), 3-2 Eray Cümart (84).

30.08.2018; Stádio Neo GSP, Nicosia; Referee: Ruddy Buquet (France); Attendance: 4,005

Apollon Limassol FC – FC Basel 1-0(0-0)

Apollon: Bruno Vale, Valentin Roberge, Charis Kyriakou, André Schembri (63.Adrián Sardinero), Facundo Pereyra (78.Sasa Markovic), Héctor Yuste, Giorgos Vasiliou, Esteban Sachetti, João Pedro (73.Marios Stylianou), Fotis Papoulis, Anton Maglica. Trainer: Sofronis Avgousti.

FC Basel: Martin Hansen, Silvan Widmer, Éder Álvarez Balanta, Raoul Petretta, Eray Cümart, Serey Dié, Luca Zuffi (76.Afimico Pululu), Fabian Frei, Samuele Campo (46.Albian Ajeti), Ricky van Wolfswinkel, Noah Okafor (80.Kevin Bua). Trainer: Marcel Koller.

Goal: 1-0 Charis Kyriakou (53).

[Apollon Limassol FC won on away goals rule (3-3 on aggregate)]

23.08.2018; MAPEI Stadium – Città del Tricolore, Reggio Emilia; Referee: Pavel Královec (Czech Republic); Attendance: 7,680

Atalanta Bergamasca Calcio – FC København 0-0

Atalanta: Pierluigi Gollini, Andrea Masiello, Rafael Tolói, Hans Hateboer (90+2.Timothy Castagne), Robin Gosens, Gianluca Mancini, Alejandro Gómez, Marten de Roon, Remo Freuler, Mario Pasalic (46.Duván Zapata), Musa Barrow (80.Andreas Cornelius). Trainer: Gian Piero Gasperini.

FC København: Jesse Joronen, Andreas Bjelland, Peter Ankersen, Nicolai Boilesen, Denis Vavro, Zeca (46.William Kvist), Viktor Fischer (80.Kenan Kodro), Nicolaj Thomsen, Robert Skov, Dame N'Doye, Pieros Sotiriou (77.Ján Gregus). Trainer: Ståle Solbakken.

30.08.2018; Telia Parken, København; Referee: Anastasios Sidiropoulos (Greece); Attendance: 18,378

FC København – Atalanta Bergamasca Calcio 0-0; 4-3 on penalties

FC København: Jesse Joronen, Andreas Bjelland, Peter Ankersen, Nicolai Boilesen (109.William Kvist), Denis Vavro, Rasmus Falk (66.Pieros Sotiriou), Zeca, Viktor Fischer (109.Pierre Bengtsson), Nicolaj Thomsen (79.Ján Gregus), Robert Skov, Dame N'Doye. Trainer: Ståle Solbakken.

Atalanta: Pierluigi Gollini, Andrea Masiello, Rafael Tolói, José Palomino, Timothy Castagne, Robin Gosens (95.Ali Adnan), Alejandro Gómez, Marten de Roon, Remo Freuler (90.Matteo Pessina), Mario Pasalic (57.Musa Barrow), Duván Zapata (54.Andreas Cornelius). Trainer: Gian Piero Gasperini.

Penalties: Marten de Roon 0-1; Pieros Sotiriou 1-1; Ali Adnan 1-2; Ján Gregus 2-2; Alejandro Gómez (missed); Robert Skov 3-2; Andrea Masiello 3-3; Dame N'Doye (missed); Andreas Cornelius (missed); Denis Vavro 4-3.

[FC København won 4-3 on penalties (after 0-0 on aggregate)]

23.08.2018; Stádio „Giórgos Karaïskáki", Peiraiás; Referee: Slavko Vinčić (Slovenia); Attendance: 26,010

Olympiacos SFP Peiraiás – Burnley FC 3-1(1-1)

Olympiacos Peiraiás: Andreas Gianniotis, Jagos Vukovic, Omar Elabdellaoui, Roderick Miranda, Kostas Tsimikas, Lazaros Christodoulopoulos (84.Karim Ansarifard), Kostas Fortounis (89.Ioannis Fetfatzidis), Andreas Bouchalakis, Daniel Podence, Mohamed Camara, Guerrero. Trainer: Pedro Martins.

Burnley FC: Tom Heaton, Phil Bardsley, Stephen Ward (66.Aaron Lennon), Kevin Long, Ben Gibson [*sent off 59*], Charlie Taylor, Jack Cork, Jóhann Gudmundsson (76.Samuel Vokes), Jeffrey Hendrick, Ashley Barnes, Chris Wood (62.James Tarkowski). Trainer: Sean Dyche.

Goals: 1-0 Kostas Fortounis (19), 1-1 Chris Wood (33 penalty), 2-1 Andreas Bouchalakis (49), 3-1 Kostas Fortounis (60 penalty).

30.08.2018; Turf Moor, Burnley; Referee: Viktor Kassai (Hungary); Attendance: 15,234

Burnley FC – Olympiacos SFP Peiraiás 1-1(0-0)

Burnley FC: Tom Heaton, Phil Bardsley, Kevin Long, Ben Mee, Charlie Taylor, Aaron Lennon (75.Jack Cork), Ashley Westwood, Jeffrey Hendrick, Ashley Barnes (65.Matej Vydra), Samuel Vokes, Dwight McNeil (75.Chris Wood). Trainer: Sean Dyche.

Olympiacos Peiraiás: Andreas Gianniotis, Jagos Vukovic, Omar Elabdellaoui, Roderick Miranda, Kostas Tsimikas, Lazaros Christodoulopoulos, Kostas Fortounis (88.Vasilios Torosidis), Andreas Bouchalakis, Daniel Podence (90+4.Pape Cissé), Mohamed Camara, Guerrero (72.Ahmed Hassan „Koka"). Trainer: Pedro Martins.

Goals: 0-1 Daniel Podence (83), 1-1 Matej Vydra (86).

[Olympiacos SFP Peiraiás won 4-2 on aggregate]

23.08.2018; Stadion Partizan, Beograd; Referee: Ivan Kružliak (Slovakia); Attendance: 16,240

FK Partizan Beograd – Beşiktaş JK İstanbul 1-1(1-1)

Partizan Beograd: Vladimir Stojkovic, Marc Valiente, Nemanja Miletic (I), Sasa Zdjelar, Svetozar Markovic, Goran Zakaric, Nebojsa Kosovic (66.Aleksandar Scekic), Marko Jankovic (35.Djordje Ivanovic), Danilo Pantic, Nemanja Miletic (II), Ricardo Gomes (74.Nemanja Nikolic). Trainer: Zoran Mirkovic.

Beşiktaş: Tolga Zengin, Adriano, Pepe (76.Enzo Roco), Caner Erkin, Gökhan Gönül, Gary Medel, Domagoj Vida, Ricardo Quaresma (79.Gökhan Töre), Necip Uysal, Tolgay Arslan (89.Güven Yalçin), Cyle Larin. Trainer: Senol Günes.

Goals: 1-0 Ricardo Gomes (14), 1-1 Tolgay Arslan (15).

30.08.2018; Vodafone Stadyumu, İstanbul; Referee: Ovidiu Alin Haţegan (Romania); Attendance: 33,658

Beşiktaş JK İstanbul – FK Partizan Beograd 3-0(2-0)

Beşiktaş: Utku Yuvakuran, Adriano, Pepe, Caner Erkin (87.Gökhan Töre), Gökhan Gönül, Gary Medel (77.Dorukhan Toköz), Domagoj Vida, Ricardo Quaresma, Necip Uysal (27.Oguzhan Özyakup), Tolgay Arslan, Cyle Larin. Trainer: Senol Günes.

Partizan Beograd: Vladimir Stojkovic, Marc Valiente, Nemanja Miletic (I), Sasa Zdjelar, Svetozar Markovic (46.Nemanja Nikolic), Aleksandar Scekic (57.Gabriel Enache), Goran Zakaric, Danilo Pantic, Nemanja Miletic (II), Ricardo Gomes, Djordje Ivanovic (62.Seydouba Soumah). Trainer: Zoran Mirkovic.

Goals: 1-0 Pepe (37), 2-0 Oguzhan Özyakup (45+1), 3-0 Pepe (68).

[Beşiktaş JK İstanbul won 4-1 on aggregate]

23.08.2018; Allianz Stadion, Wien; Referee: William Collum (Scotland); Attendance: 19,300

SK Rapid Wien – FCSB Bucureşti 3-1(2-0)

SK Rapid Wien: Richard Strebinger, Mario Sonnleitner, Marvin Potzmann, Boli Bolingoli-Mbombo, Mateo Barac, Christoph Knasmüllner (86.Aleksandar Kostic), Stefan Schwab, Thomas Murg (89.Mert Müldür), Dejan Ljubicic, Deni Alar (68.Andrei Ivan), Veton Berisha [*sent off 84*]. Trainer: Goran Djuricin.

FCSB Bucureşti: Cristian Balgradean, Alexandru Stan, Romario Sandu Benzar, Bogdan Planic, Mihai Balasa, Filipe Teixeira, Mihai Roman (I) (58.Raul Rusescu), Mihai Pintilii, Ovidiu Popescu (46.Florinel Coman), Olimpiu Morutan (46.Dennis Man), Harlem Gnohéré. Trainer: Nicolae Dica.

Goals: 1-0 Christoph Knasmüllner (4), 2-0 Mario Sonnleitner (40), 2-1 Harlem Gnohéré (47), 3-1 Stefan Schwab (49).

30.08.2018; Arena Naţională, Bucureşti; Referee: Michael Oliver (England); Attendance: 31,274

FCSB Bucureşti – SK Rapid Wien 2-1(2-0)

FCSB Bucureşti: Andrei Vlad, Alexandru Stan, Romario Sandu Benzar, Bogdan Planic, Mihai Balasa [*sent off 90+1*], Filipe Teixeira, Mihai Roman (I) (74.Florinel Coman), Mihai Pintilii, Lucian Filip (85.Dennis Man), Harlem Gnohéré, Florin Tanase (45.Raul Rusescu). Trainer: Nicolae Dica.

SK Rapid Wien: Richard Strebinger, Mario Sonnleitner, Marvin Potzmann, Mateo Barac, Mert Müldür (65.Stephan Auer), Christoph Knasmüllner (76.Maximilian Hofmann), Stefan Schwab, Thomas Murg (90.Manuel Martic), Dejan Ljubicic, Deni Alar, Andrei Ivan. Trainer: Goran Djuricin.

Goals: 1-0 Harlem Gnohéré (12), 2-0 Mihai Roman (45+2), 2-1 Mario Sonnleitner (63).

[SK Rapid Wien won 4-3 on aggregate]

23.08.2018; Luminus Arena, Genk; Referee: Andris Treimanis (Latvia); Attendance: 12,110

KRC Genk – Brøndby IF 5-2(2-0)

KRC Genk: Danny Vukovic, Sebastien Dewaest, Jere Uronen, Jhon Lucumí, Joakim Mæhle, Pozuelo, Ruslan Malinovskiy, Sander Berge, Leandro Trossard, Mbwana Samatta, Dieumerci N'Dongala (74.Joseph Paintsil). Trainer: Philippe Clement.

Brøndby IF: Marvin Schwäbe, Paulus Arajuuri, Johan Larsson, Anthony Jung, Hjörtur Hermannsson, Dominik Kaiser (79.Simon Tibbling), Lasse Vigen Christensen (89.Kasper Fisker), Josip Radosevic, Hany Mukhtar, Kamil Wilczek, Ante Erceg (72.Mikkel Uhre). Trainer: Alexander Zorniger.

Goals: 1-0 Mbwana Samatta (36), 2-0 Leandro Trossard (45+1 penalty), 2-1 Hjörtur Hermannsson (47), 2-2 Kamil Wilczek (51), 3-2, 4-2 Mbwana Samatta (55, 70), 5-2 Leandro Trossard (90+1).

30.08.2018; Brøndby Stadion, Brøndby; Referee: Gediminas Mažeika (Lithuania); Attendance: 8,636

Brøndby IF – KRC Genk 2-4(1-2)

Brøndby IF: Marvin Schwäbe, Paulus Arajuuri, Johan Larsson, Anthony Jung, Joël Kabongo, Dominik Kaiser, Lasse Vigen Christensen (79.Jens Gammelby), Josip Radosevic (46.Simon Tibbling), Hany Mukhtar, Kamil Wilczek (79.Nikolai Laursen), Ante Erceg. Trainer: Alexander Zorniger.

KRC Genk: Danny Vukovic, Sebastien Dewaest, Jere Uronen, Jhon Lucumí, Joakim Mæhle (80.Rubin Seigers), Pozuelo (70.Jakub Piotrowski), Ruslan Malinovskiy, Sander Berge, Leandro Trossard (62.Joseph Paintsil), Mbwana Samatta, Dieumerci N'Dongala. Trainer: Philippe Clement.

Goals: 0-1 Ruslan Malinovskiy (15), 0-2 Dieumerci N'Dongala (33), 1-2 Kamil Wilczek (34), 2-2 Johan Larsson (58), 2-3 Sebastien Dewaest (66), 2-4 Mbwana Samatta (87).

[KRC Genk won 9-4 on aggregate]

23.08.2018; Slavutych-Arena, Zaporizhya; Referee: Benoît Bastien (France); Attendance: 5,127

FK Zorya Luhansk – RasenBallsport Leipzig 0-0

Zorya Luhansk: Luis Felipe, Vitaliy Vernidub, Oleksandr Svatok, Oleksandr Tymchyk, Bogdan Mykhaylychenko, Dmytro Khomchenovsky (59.Vladyslav Kabayev), Igor Kharatin, Oleksandr Karavayev (83.Artem Gordienko), Silas, Bohdan Lednev *[sent off 16]*, Rafael Ratão (57.Vladyslav Kochergin). Trainer: Yuriy Vernydub.

RB Leipzig: Yvon Mvogo, Willi Orban, Nordi Mukiele (62.Emil Forsberg), Ibrahima Konaté, Stefan Ilsanker, Diego Demme, Bruma, Konrad Laimer (80.Lukas Klostermann), Marcelo Saracchi, Timo Werner, Matheus Cunha (72.Yussuf Poulsen). Trainer: Ralf Rangnick.

30.08.2018; Red Bull Arena, Leipzig; Referee: Danny Desmond Makkelie (Netherlands); Attendance: 17,644

RasenBallsport Leipzig – FK Zorya Luhansk 3-2(1-1)

RB Leipzig: Yvon Mvogo, Willi Orban, Lukas Klostermann, Ibrahima Konaté (59.Emil Forsberg), Stefan Ilsanker, Kevin Kampl, Marcel Sabitzer, Konrad Laimer (79.Bruma), Yussuf Poulsen (59.Jean-Kévin Augustin), Timo Werner, Matheus Cunha. Trainer: Ralf Rangnick.

Zorya Luhansk: Luis Felipe, Vitaliy Vernidub, Artem Gordienko (68.Vladyslav Kochergin), Oleksandr Svatok, Oleksandr Tymchyk, Bogdan Mykhaylychenko, Igor Kharatin, Oleksandr Karavayev, Silas, Rafael Ratão (80.Vasiliy Prijma), Vladyslav Kabayev (69.Yevgen Cheberko). Trainer: Yuriy Vernydub.

Goals: 1-0 Matheus Cunha (7), 1-1 Rafael Ratão (35), 1-2 Artem Gordienko (48), 2-2 Jean-Kévin Augustin (69), 3-2 Emil Forsberg (90 penalty).

[RasenBallsport Leipzig won 3-2 on aggregate]

23.08.2018; GHELAMCO-arena, Gent; Referee: Aliyar Aghayev (Azerbaijan); Attendance: 13,239

KAA Gent – FC Girondins de Bordeaux 0-0

KAA Gent: Lovre Kalinic, Nana Asare, Igor Plastun, Sigurd Rosted, Thomas Foket, Vadis Odjidja-Ofoe, Birger Verstraete, Jean-Luc Dompé (79.Stallone Limbombe), Giorgi Chakvetadze (87.Brecht Dejaegere), Roman Yaremchuk, Taiwo Awoniyi (75.Jonathan David). Trainer: Yves Vanderhaeghe.

Girondins de Bordeaux: Benoît Costil, Igor Lewczuk, Pablo Castro, Maxime Poundjé, Jules Koundé *[sent off 90+2]*, Jaroslav Plasil, Younousse Sankharé, Lukas Lerager, Zaydou Youssouf (75.Samuel Kalu), Jimmy Briand, Nicolas de Préville (86.François Kamano). Trainer: Gustavo Poyet.

30.08.2018; Stade Matmut-Atlantique, Bordeaux; Referee: Jesús Gil Manzano (Spain); Attendance: 35,039

FC Girondins de Bordeaux – KAA Gent 2-0(1-0)

Girondins de Bordeaux: Benoît Costil, Igor Lewczuk, Pablo Castro, Maxime Poundjé, Sergi Palencia, Jaroslav Plasil, Lukas Lerager, Aurélien Tchouaméni, Jimmy Briand (68.Nicolas de Préville), François Kamano, Samuel Kalu (83.Zaydou Youssouf). Trainer: Gustavo Poyet.

KAA Gent: Lovre Kalinic, Nana Asare, Igor Plastun, Sigurd Rosted, Thomas Foket, Vadis Odjidja-Ofoe (46.Brecht Dejaegere), Birger Verstraete, Jean-Luc Dompé (69.Giorgi Kvilitaia), Giorgi Chakvetadze, Roman Yaremchuk, Taiwo Awoniyi (63.Jonathan David). Trainer: Yves Vanderhaeghe.

Goals: 1-0 François Kamano (10), 2-0 Jimmy Briand (64 penalty).

[FC Girondins de Bordeaux won 2-0 on aggregate]

23.08.2018; Ibrox Stadium, Glasgow; Referee: Daniel Stefanski (Poland); Attendance: 49,338

Rangers FC Glasgow – FK Ufa 1-0(1-0)

Rangers: Allan McGregor, James Tavernier, Connor Goldson, Jon Flanagan, Nikola Katic, Scott Arfield, Ryan Jack, Ryan Kent (77.Glenn Middleton), Oviemuno Ejaria, Candeias (69.Kyle Lafferty), Alfredo Morelos. Trainer: Steven Gerrard.

FK Ufa: Aleksandr Belenov, Bojan Jokic, Pavel Alikin, Ionut Nedelcearu, Jemal Tabidze, Azamat Zaseev (85.Ondrej Vanek), Veroljub Salatic, Ivan Paurevic, Dmitri Zhivoglyadov, Ivan Oblyakov (83.Catalin Carp), Sylvester Igboun (90+2.Vyacheslav Krotov). Trainer: Sergei Tomarov.

Goal: 1-0 Connor Goldson (41).

30.08.2018; Stadion Neftyanik, Ufa; Referee: Tobias Stieler (Germany); Attendance: 13,186

FK Ufa – Rangers FC Glasgow 1-1(1-1)

FK Ufa: Aleksandr Belenov, Bojan Jokic, Pavel Alikin (52.Ivan Oblyakov), Ionut Nedelcearu, Jemal Tabidze, Veroljub Salatic (76.Vyacheslav Krotov), Dmitry Sysuyev, Ivan Paurevic, Ondrej Vanek, Dmitri Zhivoglyadov, Sylvester Igboun. Trainer: Sergei Tomarov.

Rangers: Allan McGregor, James Tavernier, Connor Goldson, Jon Flanagan *[sent off 66]*, Nikola Katic, Scott Arfield (69.Andrew Halliday), Ryan Jack, Ryan Kent, Oviemuno Ejaria, Candeias (46.Kyle Lafferty), Alfredo Morelos *[sent off 38]*. Trainer: Steven Gerrard.

Goals: 0-1 Oviemuno Ejaria (9), 1-1 Dmitry Sysuyev (32).

[Rangers FC Glasgow won 2-1 on aggregate]

GROUP STAGE

GROUP A

1.	**TSV Bayer 04 Leverkusen**	6	4	1	1	16	- 9	13
2.	**FC Zürich**	6	3	1	2	7	- 6	10
3.	AEK Larnaca FC	6	1	2	3	6	- 12	5
4.	PFC Ludogorets Razgrad	6	0	4	2	5	- 7	4

20.09.2018; Ludogorets Arena, Razgrad; Referee: Paolo Mazzoleni (Italy); Attendance: 8,240

PFC Ludogorets Razgrad – TSV Bayer 04 Leverkusen 2-3(2-1)

Ludogorets Razgrad: Renan, Cosmin Moti, Cicinho, Anton Nedyalkov, Svetoslav Dyakov (76.Jacek Góralski), Gustavo Campanharo, Wanderson, Natanael Pimienta, Claudiu Keserü, Marcelinho (82.Juninho Brandão), Jody Lukoki. Trainer: Paulo Autuori

Bayer Leverkusen: Lukás Hrádecky, Aleksandar Dragovic, Mitchell Weiser, Wendell, Jonathan Tah, Lars Bender (72.Leon Bailey), Dominik Kohr, Kai Havertz, Isaac Kiese Thelin (90+1.Lucas Alario), Julian Brandt, Paulinho (46.Kevin Volland). Trainer: Heiko Herrlich.

Goals: 1-0 Claudiu Keserü (8), 2-0 Marcelinho (31), 2-1 Kai Havertz (38), 2-2 Isaac Kiese Thelin (63), 2-3 Kai Havertz (69).

20.09.2018; Stádio Neo GSP, Nicosia; Referee: Jonathan Lardot (Belgium); Attendance: 3,173

AEK Larnaca FC – FC Zürich 0-1(0-0)

AEK Larnaca: Toño, Mikel González, Daniel Mojsov, Thomas Ioannou, Igor Carioca (79.Jean Luc Assoubre), Ivan Trickovski, Jorge Larena (83.Facundo García), Acorán, Hector Hevel, Apostolos Giannou, Tete (64.Florian Taulemesse). Trainer: Andoni Iraola.

FC Zürich: Yanick Brecher, Umaru Bangura, Pa Modou Jagne [*sent off 84*], Andreas Maxsø, Victor Pálsson, Antonio Marchesano (86.Alain Nef), Salim Khelifi (90+2.Adrian Winter), Hekuran Kryeziu, Benjamin Kololli, Kevin Rüegg, Stephen Odey (75.Assan Ceesay). Trainer: Ludovic Magnin.

Goal: 0-1 Benjamin Kololli (61 penalty).

04.10.2018; Stadion Letzigrund, Zürich; Referee: Juan Martínez Munuera (Spain); Attendance: 7,092

FC Zürich – PFC Ludogorets Razgrad 1-0(0-0)

FC Zürich: Yanick Brecher, Alain Nef, Umaru Bangura, Andreas Maxsø, Marco Schönbächler (71.Roberto Rodríguez), Victor Pálsson, Hekuran Kryeziu, Benjamin Kololli, Kevin Rüegg, Toni Domgjoni, Stephen Odey (82.Assan Ceesay). Trainer: Ludovic Magnin.

Ludogorets Razgrad: Renan, Cosmin Moti, Cicinho, Anton Nedyalkov, Svetoslav Dyakov (70.Jacek Góralski), Gustavo Campanharo, Wanderson, Natanael Pimienta, Marcelinho (79.May Mahlangu), Jody Lukoki, Juninho Brandão (71.Jakub Swierczok). Trainer: Paulo Autuori.

Goal: 1-0 Victor Pálsson (84).

04.10.2018; BayArena, Leverkusen; Referee: Evgen Aranovskiy (Ukraine); Attendance: 23,354

TSV Bayer 04 Leverkusen – AEK Larnaca FC 4-2(1-1)

Bayer Leverkusen: Lukás Hrádecky, Sven Bender, Aleksandar Dragovic, Mitchell Weiser, Wendell, Lars Bender, Karim Bellarabi, Dominik Kohr (83.Tin Jedvaj), Kai Havertz (70.Julian Brandt), Kevin Volland, Leon Bailey (46.Lucas Alario). Trainer: Heiko Herrlich.

AEK Larnaca: Toño, Mikel González, Daniel Mojsov, Truyols, Igor Carioca, Ivan Trickovski, Acorán, Nacho Cases (82.Jean Luc Assoubre), Joan Tomás (67.Tete), Hector Hevel, Apostolos Giannou (89.Dimitris Raspas). Trainer: Andoni Iraola.

Goals: 0-1 Ivan Trickovski (25), 1-1 Kai Havertz (44), 2-1, 3-1 Lucas Alario (49, 88), 3-2 Dimitris Raspas (90+1), 4-2 Julian Brandt (90+2).

25.10.2018; Stadion Letzigrund, Zürich; Referee: Äliyar Agayev (Azerbaijan); Attendance: 12,427

FC Zürich – TSV Bayer 04 Leverkusen 3-2(1-0)

FC Zürich: Yanick Brecher, Umaru Bangura, Pa Modou Jagne, Andreas Maxsø, Adrian Winter (58.Salim Khelifi), Antonio Marchesano (89.Alain Nef), Hekuran Kryeziu, Benjamin Kololli (79.Roberto Rodríguez), Kevin Rüegg, Toni Domgjoni, Stephen Odey. Trainer: Ludovic Magnin.

Bayer Leverkusen: Lukás Hrádecky, Sven Bender, Aleksandar Dragovic (46.Mitchell Weiser), Wendell, Tin Jedvaj, Lars Bender, Karim Bellarabi, Dominik Kohr, Kai Havertz, Isaac Kiese Thelin (46.Kevin Volland), Leon Bailey (79.Julian Brandt). Trainer: Heiko Herrlich.

Goals: 1-0 Antonio Marchesano (44), 1-1, 1-2 Karim Bellarabi (50, 54), 2-2 Toni Domgjoni (59), 3-2 Stephen Odey (78).

25.10.2018; Stádio Neo GSP, Nicosia; Referee: Enea Jorgji (Albania); Attendance: 2,631

AEK Larnaca FC – PFC Ludogorets Razgrad 1-1(1-1)

AEK Larnaca: Toño, Mikel González, Catalá, Truyols (72.Acorán), Thomas Ioannou, Igor Carioca, Ivan Trickovski, Jorge Larena, Hector Hevel, Apostolos Giannou (63.Florian Taulemesse), Tete (83.Jean Luc Assoubre). Trainer: Andoni Iraola.

Ludogorets Razgrad: Renan, Cosmin Moti, Cicinho, Anton Nedyalkov, Svetoslav Dyakov (81.May Mahlangu), Gustavo Campanharo (62.Jacek Góralski), Wanderson, Natanael Pimienta, Claudiu Keserü (84.Jakub Swierczok), Marcelinho, Jody Lukoki. Trainer: Antoni Zdravkov.

Goals: 0- 1 Jody Lukoki (7), 1-1 Jorge Larena (25 penalty).

08.11.2018; BayArena, Leverkusen; Referee: Paweł Gil (Poland); Attendance: 16,179

TSV Bayer 04 Leverkusen – FC Zürich 1-0(0-0)

Bayer Leverkusen: Lukás Hrádecky, Aleksandar Dragovic, Mitchell Weiser, Wendell (74.Lars Bender), Tin Jedvaj, Charles Aránguiz (62.Paulinho), Julian Baumgartlinger, Dominik Kohr, Lucas Alario, Julian Brandt (62.Isaac Kiese Thelin), Leon Bailey. Trainer: Heiko Herrlich.

FC Zürich: Yanick Brecher, Alain Nef, Umaru Bangura, Andreas Maxsø, Antonio Marchesano (69.Assan Ceesay), Salim Khelifi (55.Victor Pálsson), Hekuran Kryeziu, Benjamin Kololli, Kevin Rüegg, Toni Domgjoni, Stephen Odey. Trainer: Ludovic Magnin.

Goal: 1-0 Tin Jedvaj (60).

08.11.2018; Ludogorets Arena, Razgrad; Referee: Ola Hobber Nilsen (Norway); Attendance: 4,520

PFC Ludogorets Razgrad – AEK Larnaca FC 0-0

Ludogorets Razgrad: Renan, Cosmin Moti, Cicinho, Anton Nedyalkov, Svetoslav Dyakov (66.Lucas Sasha), Gustavo Campanharo, Wanderson, Natanael Pimienta, Claudiu Keserü (76.Jakub Swierczok), Marcelinho, Jody Lukoki (86.João Paulo). Trainer: Antoni Zdravkov.

AEK Larnaca: Toño, Mikel González, Catalá, Thomas Ioannou, Igor Carioca, Ivan Trickovski (87.Konstantinos Konstantinou), Acorán (81.Florian Taulemesse), Hector Hevel, Facundo García, Apostolos Giannou, Jean Luc Assoubre (71.Tete). Trainer: Andoni Iraola.

29.11.2018; Stadion Letzigrund, Zürich; Referee: Aleksey Eskov (Russia); Attendance: 6,107

FC Zürich – AEK Larnaca FC 1-2(0-1)

FC Zürich: Yanick Brecher, Alain Nef, Umaru Bangura, Mirlind Kryeziu, Roberto Rodríguez (73.Adrian Winter), Victor Pálsson, Antonio Marchesano (46.Bledian Krasniqi), Salim Khelifi, Fabio Dixon, Toni Domgjoni (88.Simon Sohm), Stephen Odey. Trainer: Ludovic Magnin.

AEK Larnaca: Toño, Mikel González, Truyols, Thomas Ioannou, Igor Carioca, Jorge Larena (84.Joan Tomás), Acorán (77.Jean Luc Assoubre), Hector Hevel, Facundo García, Apostolos Giannou, Florian Taulemesse (65.Ivan Trickovski). Trainer: Andoni Iraola.

Goals: 0-1 Apostolos Giannou (38), 1-1 Salim Khelifi (74), 1-2 Ivan Trickovski (85).

29.11.2018; BayArena, Leverkusen; Referee: Dennis Higler (Netherlands); Attendance: 16,066

TSV Bayer 04 Leverkusen – PFC Ludogorets Razgrad 1-1(0-0)

Bayer Leverkusen: Ramazan Özcan, Aleksandar Dragovic, Mitchell Weiser, Wendell, Panagiotis Retsos (34.Julian Baumgartlinger), Charles Aránguiz (63.Lars Bender), Sam Schreck (73.Kai Havertz), Isaac Kiese Thelin, Lucas Alario, Leon Bailey, Paulinho. Trainer: Heiko Herrlich.

Ludogorets Razgrad: Renan, Cosmin Moti, Cicinho, Georgi Terziev, Rafael Forster, Svetoslav Dyakov, Lucas Sasha (89.Dimo Bakalov), Wanderson, Jacek Góralski, João Paulo (63.Marcelinho), Jakub Swierczok (82.Anton Nedyalkov). Trainer: Antoni Zdravkov.

Goals: 0-1 Marcelinho (69), 1-1 Mitchell Weiser (85).

13.12.2018; Stádio Neo GSP, Nicosia; Referee: François Letexier (France); Attendance: 1,584

AEK Larnaca FC – TSV Bayer 04 Leverkusen 1-5(1-2)

AEK Larnaca: Andreas Christodoulou, Català, Truyols, Thomas Ioannou, Igor Carioca, Acorán, Nacho Cases (46.Hector Hevel), Joan Tomás, Facundo García, Apostolos Giannou (84.Konstantinos Konstantinou), Tete (58.Ivan Trickovski). Trainer: Andoni Iraola.

Bayer Leverkusen: Thorsten Kirschbaum, Aleksandar Dragovic, Mitchell Weiser, Wendell (82.Jakub Bednarczyk), Julian Baumgartlinger, Dominik Kohr, Sam Schreck, Isaac Kiese Thelin, Lucas Alario (88.Adrian Stanilewicz), Julian Brandt (46.Leon Bailey), Paulinho. Trainer: Heiko Herrlich.

Goals: 1-0 Català (26), 1-1 Dominik Kohr (28), 1-2 Lucas Alario (41 penalty), 1-3 Dominik Kohr (68), 1-4 Paulinho (78), 1-5 Lucas Alario (86).

13.12.2018; Ludogorets Arena, Razgrad; Referee: Kirill Levnikov (Russia); Attendance: 2,150

PFC Ludogorets Razgrad – FC Zürich 1-1(1-1)

Ludogorets Razgrad: Jorge Broun, Cicinho, Georgi Terziev, Rafael Forster, Anton Nedyalkov, Svetoslav Dyakov (82.Lucas Sasha), Wanderson (87.Dimo Bakalov), Natanael Pimienta, Jacek Góralski, Marcelinho, Jakub Swierczok (72.Claudiu Keserü). Trainer: Antoni Zdravkov.

FC Zürich: Andris Vanins, Umaru Bangura, Mirlind Kryeziu, Hakim Guenouche, Adrian Winter, Victor Pálsson, Salim Khelifi, Benjamin Kololli (76.Roberto Rodríguez), Fabio Dixon (46.Bledian Krasniqi), Toni Domgjoni, Stephen Odey (90.Alain Nef). Trainer: Ludovic Magnin.

Goals: 0-1 Rafael Forster (21 own goal), 1-1 Jakub Swierczok (45+1).

GROUP B

1.	**FC Red Bull Salzburg**	6	6	0	0	17	-	6	18
2.	**Celtic FC Glasgow**	6	3	0	3	6	-	8	9
3.	RasenBallsport Leipzig	6	2	1	3	9	-	8	7
4.	Rosenborg BK Trondheim	6	0	1	5	4	-	14	1

20.09.2018; Red Bull Arena, Leipzig; Referee: Andreas Ekberg (Sweden); Attendance: 24,057

RasenBallsport Leipzig – FC Red Bull Salzburg 2-3(0-2)

RB Leipzig: Yvon Mvogo, Nordi Mukiele (46.Marcel Halstenberg), Dayot Upamecano, Ibrahima Konaté, Stefan Ilsanker, Kevin Kampl, Marcel Sabitzer, Bruma (46.Diego Demme), Konrad Laimer, Jean-Kévin Augustin (46.Yussuf Poulsen), Matheus Cunha. Trainer: Ralf Rangnick.

Red Bull Salzburg: Alexander Walke, Andreas Ulmer, Stefan Lainer, André Ramalho, Marin Pongracic, Reinhold Yabo (71.Takumi Minamino), Xaver Schlager (86.Zlatko Junuzovic), Diadié Samassékou, Amadou Haïdara, Munas Dabour (84.Fredrik Gulbrandsen), Hannes Wolf. Trainer: Marco Rose.

Goals: 0-1 Munas Dabour (20), 0-2 Amadou Haïdara (22), 1-2 Konrad Laimer (70), 2-2 Yussuf Poulsen (82), 2-3 Fredrik Gulbrandsen (89).

20.09.2018; Celtic Park, Glasgow; Referee: Paweł Gil (Poland); Attendance: 47,287

Celtic FC Glasgow – Rosenborg BK Trondheim 1-0(0-0)

Celtic: Craig Gordon, Mikael Lustig, Dedryck Boyata, Filip Benkovic, Kieran Tierney, Scott Brown, James Forrest (58.Michael Johnston), Callum McGregor, Tom Rogic (58.Scott Sinclair), Olivier Ntcham, Odsonne Édouard (76.Leigh Griffiths). Trainer: Brendan Rodgers.

Rosenborg: André Hansen, Tore Reginiussen, Even Hovland, Vegar Hedenstad, Birger Meling, Mike Jensen, Anders Konradsen (45+1.Marius Lundemo), Djordje Denic, Alexander Søderlund (78.Jonathan Levi), Issam Jebali, Yann-Erik de Lanlay (69.Anders Trondsen). Trainer: Rini Coolen.

Goal: 1-0 Leigh Griffiths (87).

04.10.2018; Lerkendal Stadion, Trondheim; Referee: Marco Guida (Italy); Attendance: 11,484

Rosenborg BK Trondheim – RasenBallsport Leipzig 1-3(0-1)

Rosenborg: André Hansen, Tore Reginiussen, Even Hovland, Vegar Hedenstad (62.Erlend Reitan), Alex Gersbach, Mike Jensen, Anders Konradsen, Djordje Denic (77.Matthías Vilhjálmsson), Alexander Søderlund, Yann-Erik de Lanlay (68.Issam Jebali), Jonathan Levi. Trainer: Rini Coolen.

RB Leipzig: Yvon Mvogo, Marcel Halstenberg (74.Marcelo Saracchi), Willi Orban, Nordi Mukiele (80.Marcel Sabitzer), Ibrahima Konaté, Stefan Ilsanker, Diego Demme (64.Lukas Klostermann), Bruma, Konrad Laimer, Jean-Kévin Augustin, Matheus Cunha. Trainer: Ralf Rangnick.

Goals: 0-1 Jean-Kévin Augustin (12), 0-2 Ibrahima Konaté (54), 0-3 Matheus Cunha (61), 1-3 Issam Jebali (79).

04.10.2018; Red Bull Arena, Salzburg; Referee: Sergey Boyko (Ukraine); Attendance: 24,085

FC Red Bull Salzburg – Celtic FC Glasgow 3-1(0-1)

Red Bull Salzburg: Alexander Walke, Andreas Ulmer, Stefan Lainer, André Ramalho, Marin Pongracic, Xaver Schlager, Diadié Samassékou, Amadou Haïdara, Munas Dabour (85.Reinhold Yabo), Takumi Minamino (71.Zlatko Junuzovic), Hannes Wolf (79.Fredrik Gulbrandsen). Trainer: Marco Rose.

Celtic: Craig Gordon, Mikael Lustig, Dedryck Boyata, Kieran Tierney, Jack Hendry, Youssuf Mulumbu (78.Ryan Christie), James Forrest [*sent off 72*], Callum McGregor, Olivier Ntcham, Leigh Griffiths (60.Scott Sinclair), Odsonne Édouard (82.Lewis Morgan). Trainer: Brendan Rodgers.

Goals: 0-1 Odsonne Édouard (2), 1-1 Munas Dabour (55), 2-1 Takumi Minamino (61), 3-1 Munas Dabour (73 penalty).

25.10.2018; Red Bull Arena, Salzburg; Referee: Irfan Peljto (Bosnia and Herzegovina); Attendance: 20,639

FC Red Bull Salzburg – Rosenborg BK Trondheim 3-0(1-0)

Red Bull Salzburg: Alexander Walke, Andreas Ulmer, Stefan Lainer, André Ramalho, Marin Pongracic, Zlatko Junuzovic, Diadié Samassékou (75.Xaver Schlager), Amadou Haïdara, Fredrik Gulbrandsen, Munas Dabour (72.Smail Prevljak), Hannes Wolf (82.Takumi Minamino). Trainer: Marco Rose.

Rosenborg: André Hansen, Even Hovland, Vegar Hedenstad, Alex Gersbach, Besim Serbecic, Mike Jensen (71.Djordje Denic), Anders Konradsen, Marius Lundemo, Nicklas Bendtner (56.Matthías Vilhjálmsson), Yann-Erik de Lanlay (66.Samuel Adegbenro), Jonathan Levi. Trainer: Rini Coolen.

Goals: 1-0 Munas Dabour (34), 2-0 Hannes Wolf (53), 3-0 Munas Dabour (59 penalty).

25.10.2018; Red Bull Arena, Leipzig; Referee: Pavel Královec (Czech Republic); Attendance: 38,126

RasenBallsport Leipzig – Celtic FC Glasgow 2-0(2-0)

RB Leipzig: Yvon Mvogo, Willi Orban, Lukas Klostermann, Dayot Upamecano, Kevin Kampl (84.Erik Majetschak), Marcel Sabitzer (61.Stefan Ilsanker), Bruma, Konrad Laimer, Marcelo Saracchi, Jean-Kévin Augustin (90+1.Yussuf Poulsen), Matheus Cunha. Trainer: Ralf Rangnick.

Celtic: Craig Gordon, Cristian Gamboa (46.Mikael Lustig), Dedryck Boyata, Jozo Simunovic (75.Jack Hendry), Kieran Tierney, Callum McGregor, Olivier Ntcham, Ryan Christie, Lewis Morgan (71.Scott Sinclair), Kouassi Eboue, Odsonne Édouard. Trainer: Brendan Rodgers.

Goals: 1-0 Matheus Cunha (31), 2-0 Bruma (35).

08.11.2018; Lerkendal Stadion, Trondheim; Referee: Aleksey Eskov (Russia); Attendance: 12,386

Rosenborg BK Trondheim – FC Red Bull Salzburg 2-5(0-4)

Rosenborg: André Hansen, Even Hovland, Birger Meling, Besim Serbecic, Erlend Reitan, Mike Jensen, Anders Konradsen, Djordje Denic (85.Matthías Vilhjálmsson), Nicklas Bendtner, Alexander Søderlund (46.Marius Lundemo), Samuel Adegbenro (75.Jonathan Levi). Trainer: Rini Coolen.

Red Bull Salzburg: Alexander Walke, Andreas Ulmer, Stefan Lainer, André Ramalho, Jérôme Onguéné, Xaver Schlager (89.Christoph Leitgeb), Diadié Samassékou, Amadou Haïdara, Fredrik Gulbrandsen (85.Smail Prevljak), Munas Dabour, Takumi Minamino (78.Hannes Wolf). Trainer: Marco Rose.

Goals: 0-1, 0-2 Takumi Minamino (6, 19), 0-3 Fredrik Gulbrandsen (37), 0-4 Takumi Minamino (45), 1-4 Samuel Adegbenro (52), 1-5 Even Hovland (57 own goal), 2-5 Mike Jensen (62).

08.11.2018; Celtic Park, Glasgow; Referee: Xavier Estrada Fernández (Spain); Attendance: 56,027

Celtic FC Glasgow – RasenBallsport Leipzig 2-1(1-0)

Celtic: Craig Gordon, Mikael Lustig, Dedryck Boyata, Filip Benkovic, Kieran Tierney, Scott Sinclair (90.Kristoffer Ajer), James Forrest (83.Youssuf Mulumbu), Callum McGregor, Tom Rogic, Ryan Christie, Odsonne Édouard. Trainer: Brendan Rodgers.

RB Leipzig: Yvon Mvogo, Willi Orban, Nordi Mukiele (70.Diego Demme), Dayot Upamecano, Stefan Ilsanker (46.Kevin Kampl), Marcel Sabitzer, Bruma, Konrad Laimer, Marcelo Saracchi (16.Marcel Halstenberg), Jean-Kévin Augustin, Matheus Cunha. Trainer: Ralf Rangnick.

Goals: 1-0 Kieran Tierney (11), 1-1 Jean-Kévin Augustin (78), 2-1 Odsonne Édouard (79).

29.11.2018; Red Bull Arena, Salzburg; Referee: Orel Grinfeld (Israel); Attendance: 29,520

FC Red Bull Salzburg – RasenBallsport Leipzig 1-0(0-0)

Red Bull Salzburg: Alexander Walke, Andreas Ulmer, Stefan Lainer, André Ramalho, Marin Pongracic, Zlatko Junuzovic, Xaver Schlager, Diadié Samassékou, Fredrik Gulbrandsen (76.Takumi Minamino), Munas Dabour (90+2.Smail Prevljak), Hannes Wolf (87.Patson Daka). Trainer: Marco Rose.

RB Leipzig: Yvon Mvogo, Willi Orban, Nordi Mukiele (70.Lukas Klostermann), Dayot Upamecano, Stefan Ilsanker, Bruma, Konrad Laimer, Marcelo Saracchi (78.Marcel Halstenberg), Timo Werner, Jean-Kévin Augustin (62.Yussuf Poulsen), Matheus Cunha. Trainer: Ralf Rangnick.

Goal: 1-0 Fredrik Gulbrandsen (74).

29.11.2018; Lerkendal Stadion, Trondheim; Referee: Halis Özkahya (Turkey); Attendance: 14,061

Rosenborg BK Trondheim – Celtic FC Glasgow 0-1(0-1)

Rosenborg: André Hansen, Tore Reginiussen, Even Hovland, Vegar Hedenstad, Birger Meling, Mike Jensen, Anders Konradsen (45+1.Djordje Denic), Anders Trondsen (66.Matthías Vilhjálmsson), Nicklas Bendtner, Yann-Erik de Lanlay, Samuel Adegbenro (78.Jonathan Levi). Trainer: Rini Coolen.

Celtic: Craig Gordon, Mikael Lustig (66.Cristian Gamboa), Dedryck Boyata, Filip Benkovic, Kieran Tierney, Scott Sinclair, James Forrest (77.Scott Brown), Callum McGregor, Tom Rogic, Ryan Christie, Odsonne Édouard (66.Leigh Griffiths). Trainer: Brendan Rodgers.

Goal: 0-1 Scott Sinclair (42).

13.12.2018; Red Bull Arena, Leipzig; Referee: Sergey Boyko (Ukraine); Attendance: 16,957

RasenBallsport Leipzig – Rosenborg BK Trondheim 1-1(0-0)

RB Leipzig: Yvon Mvogo, Willi Orban, Nordi Mukiele (81.Lukas Klostermann), Ibrahima Konaté, Stefan Ilsanker, Kevin Kampl (69.Marcel Sabitzer), Bruma, Konrad Laimer, Marcelo Saracchi, Jean-Kévin Augustin (46.Yussuf Poulsen), Matheus Cunha. Trainer: Ralf Rangnick.

Rosenborg: André Hansen, Tore Reginiussen, Even Hovland, Birger Meling, Erlend Reitan, Mike Jensen, Anders Konradsen, Anders Trondsen (75.Djordje Denic), Matthías Vilhjálmsson (83.Erik Botheim), Issam Jebali (68.Pål Helland), Samuel Adegbenro. Trainer: Rini Coolen.

Goals: 1-0 Matheus Cunha (47), 1-1 Tore Reginiussen (86).

13.12.2018; Celtic Park, Glasgow; Referee: Ruddy Buquet (France); Attendance: 57,578

Celtic FC Glasgow – FC Red Bull Salzburg 1-2(0-0)

Celtic: Craig Gordon, Mikael Lustig (21.Kristoffer Ajer), Jozo Simunovic, Filip Benkovic, Kieran Tierney, Scott Sinclair (46.Scott Brown), James Forrest, Callum McGregor, Tom Rogic, Ryan Christie (58.Olivier Ntcham), Odsonne Édouard. Trainer: Brendan Rodgers.

Red Bull Salzburg: Alexander Walke, Andreas Ulmer, Stefan Lainer, André Ramalho, Jérôme Onguéné, Zlatko Junuzovic, Diadié Samassékou, Enock Mwepu (80.Christoph Leitgeb), Munas Dabour (90+1.Smail Prevljak), Takumi Minamino (74.Fredrik Gulbrandsen), Hannes Wolf. Trainer: Marco Rose.

Goals: 0-1 Munas Dabour (67), 0-2 Fredrik Gulbrandsen (78), 1-2 Olivier Ntcham (90+5).

GROUP C

1.	**FK Zenit Saint Petersburg**	6	3	2	1	6	-	5	11
2.	**SK Slavia Praha**	6	3	1	2	4	-	3	10
3.	FC Girondins de Bordeaux	6	2	1	3	6	-	6	7
4.	FC København	6	1	2	3	3	-	5	5

20.09.2018; Telia Parken, København; Referee: Georgi Kabakov (Bulgaria); Attendance: 19,005

FC København – FK Zenit Saint Petersburg 1-1(0-1)

FC København: Jesse Joronen, Andreas Bjelland, Peter Ankersen, Nicolai Boilesen, Denis Vavro, Zeca, Viktor Fischer (90+3.Sotirios Papagiannopoulos), Nicolaj Thomsen (61.Rasmus Falk), Robert Skov, Dame N'Doye, Pieros Sotiriou (77.Ján Gregus). Trainer: Ståle Solbakken.

Zenit Saint Petersburg: Andrei Lunev, Branislav Ivanovic, Aleksandr Anyukov, Igor Smolnikov, Neto, Aleksandr Erokhin, Róbert Mak (58.Claudio Marchisio), Leandro Paredes, Daler Kuzyaev (89.Anton Zabolotny), Artem Dzyuba, Sebastián Driussi (79.Oleg Shatov). Trainer: Sergey Semak.

Goals: 0-1 Róbert Mak (44), 1-1 Pieros Sotiriou (63).

20.09.2018; Sinobo Stadium, Praha; Referee: Hendrikus Sebastiaan Hermanus „Bas" Nijhuis (Netherlands); Attendance: 16,548

SK Slavia Praha – FC Girondins de Bordeaux 1-0(1-0)

Slavia Praha: Ondrej Kolár, Ondrej Kúdela, Jan Boril, Vladimír Coufal, Jaromír Husbauer, Miroslav Stoch (79.Alexandru Baluta), Michael Ngadeu-Ngadjui, Jaromír Zmrhal (83.Michal Frydrych), Tomás Soucek, Ibrahim Traoré (90+3.Jan Matousek), Stanislav Tecl. Trainer: Jindrich Trpisovsky.

Girondins de Bordeaux: Benoît Costil, Pablo Castro, Youssouf Sabaly, Sergi Palencia, Jules Koundé, Jaroslav Plasil (85.Otávio), Younousse Sankharé (70.Andreas Cornelius), Aurélien Tchouaméni, Jimmy Briand, François Kamano (60.Yann Karamoh), Samuel Kalu. Trainer: Éric Bedouet.

Goal: 1-0 Jaromír Zmrhal (35).

04.10.2018; Stade Matmut-Atlantique, Bordeaux; Referee: Roi Reinshreiber (Israel); Attendance: 11,860

FC Girondins de Bordeaux – FC København 1-2(0-1)

Girondins de Bordeaux: Benoît Costil, Pablo Castro, Maxime Poundjé, Sergi Palencia, Otávio, Jules Koundé, Younousse Sankharé, Lukas Lerager (78.Aurélien Tchouaméni), Jimmy Briand (62.Andreas Cornelius), François Kamano (63.Yann Karamoh), Samuel Kalu. Trainer: Éric Bedouet.

FC København: Stephan Andersen, Andreas Bjelland, Sotirios Papagiannopoulos (86.Denis Vavro), Peter Ankersen, Nicolai Boilesen, William Kvist (58.Robert Skov), Ján Gregus, Zeca [*sent off 90+3*], Nicolaj Thomsen (70.Rasmus Falk), Dame N'Doye, Pieros Sotiriou. Trainer: Ståle Solbakken.

Goals: 0-1 Pieros Sotiriou (42), 1-1 Younousse Sankharé (84), 1-2 Robert Skov (90+2).

04.10.2018; Krestovsky Stadium, St. Petersburg; Referee: Hüseyin Göçek (Turkey); Attendance: 45,408

FK Zenit Saint Petersburg – SK Slavia Praha 1-0(0-0)

Zenit Saint Petersburg: Andrei Lunev, Branislav Ivanovic, Aleksandr Anyukov, Neto, Elmir Nabiullin (90+3.Anton Zabolotny), Aleksandr Erokhin, Róbert Mak (64.Daler Kuzyaev), Leandro Paredes, Matías Kranevitter, Artem Dzyuba, Sebastián Driussi (63.Aleksandr Kokorin). Trainer: Sergey Semak.

Slavia Praha: Ondrej Kolár, Ondrej Kúdela, Jan Boril, Vladimír Coufal (83.Michal Frydrych), Josef Husbauer, Miroslav Stoch, Michael Ngadeu-Ngadjui, Jaromír Zmrhal, Tomás Soucek, Ibrahim Traoré (90.Simon Deli), Jan Matousek (53.Alexandru Baluta). Trainer: Jindrich Trpisovsky.

Goal: 1-0 Aleksandr Kokorin (80).

25.10.2018; Krestovsky Stadium, St. Petersburg; Referee: Dr. Felix Brych (Germany); Attendance: 45,723

FK Zenit Saint Petersburg – FC Girondins de Bordeaux 2-1(1-1)

Zenit Saint Petersburg: Andrei Lunev, Branislav Ivanovic, Neto, Elmir Nabiullin, Emanuel Mammana, Aleksandr Erokhin, Róbert Mak (76.Oleg Shatov), Leandro Paredes, Daler Kuzyaev, Artem Dzyuba (86.Anton Zabolotny), Sebastián Driussi (88.Magomed Ozdoev). Trainer: Sergey Semak.

Girondins de Bordeaux: Benoît Costil, Igor Lewczuk, Pablo Castro, Maxime Poundjé, Otávio, Jules Koundé, Younousse Sankharé, Aurélien Tchouaméni, Jimmy Briand (79.Nicolas de Préville), Yann Karamoh (67.Zaydou Youssouf), Samuel Kalu. Trainer: Éric Bedouet.

Goals: 0-1 Jimmy Briand (26), 1-1 Artem Dzyuba (41), 2-1 Daler Kuzyaev (85).

25.10.2018; Telia Parken, København; Referee: Luca Banti (Italy); Attendance: 20,672

FC København – SK Slavia Praha 0-1(0-0)

FC København: Stephan Andersen, Pierre Bengtsson, Andreas Bjelland, Sotirios Papagiannopoulos, Peter Ankersen, Ján Gregus, Rasmus Falk (84.Denis Vavro), Viktor Fischer (71.Carlo Holse), Robert Skov (84.Kenan Kodro), Dame N'Doye, Pieros Sotiriou. Trainer: Ståle Solbakken.

Slavia Praha: Ondrej Kolár, Ondrej Kúdela, Jan Boril, Vladimír Coufal, Josef Husbauer (90+1.Simon Deli), Miroslav Stoch (86.Michal Frydrych), Michael Ngadeu-Ngadjui, Jaromír Zmrhal, Tomás Soucek, Ibrahim Traoré, Jan Matousek (72.Stanislav Tecl). Trainer: Jindrich Trpisovsky.

Goal: 0-1 Jan Matousek (46).

08.11.2018; Stade Matmut-Atlantique, Bordeaux; Referee: Harald Lechner (Austria); Attendance: 8,907

FC Girondins de Bordeaux – FK Zenit Saint Petersburg 1-1(1-0)

Girondins de Bordeaux: Benoît Costil, Pablo Castro, Youssouf Sabaly, Maxime Poundjé, Vukasin Jovanovic, Jaroslav Plasil (84.Nicolas de Préville), Younousse Sankharé, Lukas Lerager, Andreas Cornelius (46.Jimmy Briand), François Kamano (67.Yann Karamoh), Samuel Kalu. Trainer: Éric Bedouet.

Zenit Saint Petersburg: Andrei Lunev, Aleksandr Anyukov (60.Róbert Mak), Neto, Miha Mevlja, Elmir Nabiullin, Emanuel Mammana, Claudio Marchisio, Aleksandr Erokhin (65.Daler Kuzyaev), Leandro Paredes, Anton Zabolotny, Sebastián Driussi (78.Oleg Shatov). Trainer: Sergey Semak.

Goals: 1-0 François Kamano (35 penalty), 1-1 Anton Zabolotny (72).

08.11.2018; Sinobo Stadium, Praha; Referee: Mattias Gestranius (Finland); Attendance: 18,702

SK Slavia Praha – FC København 0-0

Slavia Praha: Ondrej Kolár, Michal Frydrych, Jan Boril, Simon Deli, Miroslav Stoch, Jan Sykora (79.Alexandru Baluta), Michael Ngadeu-Ngadjui, Jaromír Zmrhal (79.Milan Skoda), Tomás Soucek, Ibrahim Traoré, Peter Olayinka. Trainer: Jindrich Trpisovsky.

FC København: Stephan Andersen, Andreas Bjelland, Peter Ankersen, Nicolai Boilesen (35.Pierre Bengtsson), Denis Vavro, Ján Gregus, Rasmus Falk (79.Jonas Wind), Zeca, Robert Skov (64.Nicolaj Thomsen), Dame N'Doye, Pieros Sotiriou. Trainer: Ståle Solbakken.

29.11.2018; Krestovsky Stadium, St. Petersburg; Referee: Slavko Vinčić (Slovenia); Attendance: 45,199

FK Zenit Saint Petersburg – FC København 1-0(0-0)

Zenit Saint Petersburg: Andrei Lunev, Branislav Ivanovic, Aleksandr Anyukov, Miha Mevlja, Aleksandr Erokhin (74.Claudio Marchisio), Róbert Mak, Leandro Paredes, Hernani (88.Magomed Ozdoev), Daler Kuzyaev, Artem Dzyuba, Sebastián Driussi (60.Anton Zabolotny). Trainer: Sergey Semak.

FC København: Stephan Andersen, Pierre Bengtsson, Andreas Bjelland, Peter Ankersen, Denis Vavro (54.Sotirios Papagiannopoulos), Ján Gregus, Zeca, Robert Skov (78.Jonas Wind), Dame N'Doye, Pieros Sotiriou, Carlo Holse (60.Rasmus Falk). Trainer: Ståle Solbakken.

Goal: 1-0 Róbert Mak (59).

29.11.2018; Stade Matmut-Atlantique, Bordeaux; Referee: Fábio José Costa Veríssimo (Portugal); Attendance: 6,311

FC Girondins de Bordeaux – SK Slavia Praha 2-0(0-0)

Girondins de Bordeaux: Benoît Costil, Pablo Castro, Youssouf Sabaly, Sergi Palencia, Jules Koundé, Lukas Lerager, Aurélien Tchouaméni, Zaydou Youssouf (76.Younousse Sankharé), Nicolas de Préville (71.François Kamano), Andreas Cornelius, Samuel Kalu (81.Yann Karamoh). Trainer: Éric Bedouet.

Slavia Praha: Ondrej Kolár, Jan Boril, Vladimír Coufal, Simon Deli, Josef Husbauer, Miroslav Stoch (77.Milan Skoda), Michael Ngadeu-Ngadjui, Jaromír Zmrhal, Tomás Soucek, Ibrahim Traoré (46.Jan Sykora), Jan Matousek (51.Peter Olayinka). Trainer: Jindrich Trpisovsky.

Goals: 1-0 Nicolas de Préville (49), 2-0 Jules Koundé (90+5).

13.12.2018; Telia Parken, København; Referee: Hüseyin Göçek (Turkey); Attendance: 18,209

FC København – FC Girondins de Bordeaux 0-1(0-0)

FC København: Stephan Andersen, Andreas Bjelland (9.Sotirios Papagiannopoulos), Peter Ankersen, Nicolai Boilesen (62.Pierre Bengtsson), Denis Vavro, Rasmus Falk (73.Ján Gregus), Zeca, Nicolaj Thomsen, Robert Skov, Dame N'Doye, Pieros Sotiriou. Trainer: Ståle Solbakken.

Girondins de Bordeaux: Benoît Costil, Pablo Castro, Youssouf Sabaly, Maxime Poundjé, Otávio, Jules Koundé, Jaroslav Plasil, Lukas Lerager, Jimmy Briand, Nicolas de Préville (61.François Kamano), Andreas Cornelius (60.Yann Karamoh). Trainer: Éric Bedouet.

Goal: 0-1 Jimmy Briand (73).

13.12.2018; Sinobo Stadium, Praha; Referee: Andrew Dallas (Scotland); Attendance: 17,748

SK Slavia Praha – FK Zenit Saint Petersburg 2-0(2-0)

Slavia Praha: Ondrej Kolár, Ondrej Kúdela, Jaroslav Zeleny (90+2.Alexandru Baluta), Vladimír Coufal, Josef Husbauer, Miroslav Stoch (90.Michal Frydrych), Michael Ngadeu-Ngadjui, Jaromír Zmrhal, Tomás Soucek, Milan Skoda (85.Ibrahim Traoré), Peter Olayinka. Trainer: Jindrich Trpisovsky.

Zenit Saint Petersburg: Mikhail Kerzhakov, Igor Smolnikov, Neto, Miha Mevlja, Elmir Nabiullin (46.Róbert Mak), Emanuel Mammana, Claudio Marchisio, Oleg Shatov (73.Daler Kuzyaev), Hernani, Matías Kranevitter, Anton Zabolotny (46.Sebastián Driussi). Trainer: Sergey Semak.

Goals: 1-0 Jaromír Zmrhal (32), 2-0 Miroslav Stoch (41).

GROUP D

1.	**GNK Dinamo Zagreb**	6	4	2	0	11	-	3	14
2.	**Fenerbahçe SK İstanbul**	6	2	2	2	7	-	7	8
3.	FC Spartak Trnava	6	2	1	3	4	-	7	7
4.	RSC Anderlecht Bruxelles	6	0	3	3	2	-	7	3

20.09.2018; Stadión „Antona Malatinského“, Trnava; Referee: Kevin Clancy (Scotland); Attendance: 17,114

FC Spartak Trnava – RSC Anderlecht Bruxelles 1-0(0-0)

FC Spartak Trnava: Martin Chudy, Martin Tóth, Matús Conka (51.Jirí Kulhánek), Boris Godál, Andrej Kadlec, Matej Oravec, Erik Grendel, Jakub Rada, Vakhtang Chanturishvili, Erik Jirka (64.Patryk Malecki), Marek Bakos (87.Oliver Janso). Trainer: Radoslav Látal.

Anderlecht: Thomas Didillon, Ognjen Vranjes, Andy Najar (65.Kenny Saief), Antonio Milic, Bubacarr Sanneh, Sven Kums, Knowlegde Musona (83.Evgen Makarenko), Adrien Trebel, Ivan Santini, Landry Nany Dimata (83.Pieter Gerkens), Francis Amuzu. Trainer: Hein Vanhaezebrouck.

Goal: 1-0 Matej Oravec (79).

20.09.2018; Stadion Maksimir, Zagreb; Referee: Craig Pawson (England); Attendance: 17,303

GNK Dinamo Zagreb – Fenerbahçe SK İstanbul 4-1(2-0)

Dinamo Zagreb: Dominik Livakovic, Kévin Théophile-Catherine, Emir Dilaver, Petar Stojanovic, Amir Rrahmani, Ivan Sunjic, Amer Gojak, Daniel Olmo, Mario Gavranovic (85.Mario Budimir), Mislav Orsic (76.Damian Kadzior), Izet Hajrovic (82.Tongo Doumbia). Trainer: Nenad Bjelica.

Fenerbahçe: Harun Tekin, Roman Neustädter, Ismail Köybasi, Diego Reyes, Sener Özbayrakli, Mehmet Topal, Alper Potuk (80.Islam Slimani), Aatif Chahechouhe (65.Baris Ailici), Eljif Elmas, Michael Frey, Yassine Benzia (65.Jaílson). Trainer: Phillip Cocu.

Goals: 1-0 Ivan Sunjic (16), 2-0 Izet Hajrovic (25), 2-1 Roman Neustädter (47), 3-1 Izet Hajrovic (57), 4-1 Daniel Olmo (60).

04.10.2018; "Sükrü Saraçoglu" Stadyumu, İstanbul; Referee: Tobias Welz (Germany); Attendance: 29,622.

Fenerbahçe SK İstanbul – FC Spartak Trnava 2-0(0-0)

Fenerbahçe: Harun Tekin, Martin Skrtel, Mauricio Isla, Roman Neustädter, Hasan-Ali Kaldirim, Diego Reyes (76.Ismail Köybasi), Jaílson, Eljif Elmas, André Ayew (76.Mathieu Valbuena), Islam Slimani (88.Mehmet Topal), Michael Frey. Trainer: Phillip Cocu.

FC Spartak Trnava: Martin Chudy, Martin Tóth (66.Ivan Hladík), Boris Godál, Andrej Kadlec, Matej Oravec, Erik Grendel (68.Ali Ghorbani), Jakub Rada, Lukás Gressák, Vakhtang Chanturishvili, Erik Jirka (82.Fabian Miesenböck), Marek Bakos. Trainer: Radoslav Látal.

Goals: 1-0, 2-0 Islam Slimani (52, 69).

04.10.2018; Stade „Constant Vanden Stock“, Bruxelles; Referee: Vladislav Bezborodov (Russia); Attendance: 12,137

RSC Anderlecht Bruxelles – GNK Dinamo Zagreb 0-2(0-1)

Anderlecht: Thomas Didillon, Ognjen Vranjes [*sent off 46*], Andy Najar (66.Kenny Saief), Antonio Milic, Bubacarr Sanneh, Evgen Makarenko, Adrien Trebel, Zakaria Bakkali (89.Ryota Morioka), Ivan Santini, Landry Nany Dimata (85.Jamie Lawrence), Francis Amuzu. Trainer: Hein Vanhaezebrouck.

Dinamo Zagreb: Dominik Livakovic, Kévin Théophile-Catherine [*sent off 90+3*], Emir Dilaver (46.Dino Peric), Petar Stojanovic, Amir Rrahmani, Arijan Ademi, Amer Gojak, Daniel Olmo, Mislav Orsic (90.Mario Gavranovic), Izet Hajrovic (76.Ivan Sunjic), Bruno Petkovic. Trainer: Nenad Bjelica.

Goals: 0-1 Izet Hajrovic (19 penalty), 0-2 Amer Gojak (68).

25.10.2018; Stade „Constant Vanden Stock", Bruxelles; Referee: Georgi Kabakov (Bulgaria); Attendance: 13,292.

RSC Anderlecht Bruxelles – Fenerbahçe SK İstanbul 2-2(1-0)

Anderlecht: Thomas Didillon, Jamie Lawrence, Bubacarr Sanneh, Sebastiaan Bornauw, Alexis Saelemaekers (86.Andy Najar), Sven Kums, Adrien Trebel, Kenny Saief, Pieter Gerkens (86.Dauda Mohammed), Zakaria Bakkali, Ivan Santini. Trainer: Hein Vanhaezebrouck.

Fenerbahçe: Harun Tekin, Martin Skrtel, Mauricio Isla, Roman Neustädter, Hasan-Ali Kaldirim, Diego Reyes, Jaílson, Eljif Elmas (86.Alper Potuk), Islam Slimani (74.André Ayew), Michael Frey, Yassine Benzia (74.Oguz Güçtekin). Trainer: Phillip Cocu.

Goals: 1-0, 2-0 Zakaria Bakkali (35, 50), 2-1 Michael Frey (53), 2-2 Hasan-Ali Kaldirim (57).

25.10.2018; Stadión „Antona Malatinského", Trnava; Referee: Jakob Kehlet (Denmark); Attendance: *played behind closed doors*

FC Spartak Trnava – GNK Dinamo Zagreb 1-2(1-0)

FC Spartak Trnava: Martin Chudy, Martin Tóth, Matús Conka, Boris Godál, Matej Oravec, Erik Grendel, Jakub Rada (82.Davit Skhirtladze), Lukás Gressák, Vakhtang Chanturishvili, Erik Jirka (70.Patryk Malecki), Ali Ghorbani. Trainer: Radoslav Látal.

Dinamo Zagreb: Dominik Livakovic, Marko Leskovic, Petar Stojanovic, Amir Rrahmani, Dino Peric, Arijan Ademi, Amer Gojak, Daniel Olmo (86.Ivan Sunjic), Mario Gavranovic (88.Bruno Petkovic), Mislav Orsic, Izet Hajrovic (74.Damian Kadzior). Trainer: Nenad Bjelica.

Goals: 1-0 Ali Ghorbani (32), 1-1 Mario Gavranovic (64), 1-2 Mislav Orsic (77).

08.11.2018; "Sükrü Saraçoglu" Stadyumu, İstanbul; Referee: Andreas Ekberg (Sweden); Attendance: 32,789

Fenerbahçe SK İstanbul – RSC Anderlecht Bruxelles 2-0(0-0)

Fenerbahçe: Harun Tekin, Martin Skrtel, Roman Neustädter, Hasan-Ali Kaldirim, Sener Özbayrakli, Mathieu Valbuena (82.Ismail Köybasi), Jaílson (88.Mauricio Isla), Eljif Elmas, André Ayew, Islam Slimani, Michael Frey. Trainer: Erwin Koeman.

Anderlecht: Thomas Didillon, Ognjen Vranjes, Antonio Milic, Sebastiaan Bornauw (46.Bubacarr Sanneh), Alexis Saelemaekers (77.Andy Najar), Sven Kums, Evgen Makarenko, Adrien Trebel (77.Albert-Mboyo Sambi Lokonga), Pieter Gerkens, Zakaria Bakkali [*sent off 79*], Landry Nany Dimata. Trainer: Hein Vanhaezebrouck.

Goals: 1-0 Mathieu Valbuena (71), 2-0 Michael Frey (74).

08.11.2018; Stadion Maksimir, Zagreb; Referee: Sergey Boyko (Ukraine); Attendance: 18,154

GNK Dinamo Zagreb – FC Spartak Trnava 3-1(2-0)

Dinamo Zagreb: Dominik Livakovic, Kévin Théophile-Catherine, Petar Stojanovic, Amir Rrahmani, Dino Peric, Arijan Ademi, Amer Gojak, Daniel Olmo (90.Mario Budimir), Mario Gavranovic (77.Bruno Petkovic), Mislav Orsic (82.Ivan Sunjic), Izet Hajrovic. Trainer: Nenad Bjelica.

FC Spartak Trnava: Martin Chudy, Martin Tóth, Matús Conka, Boris Godál, Andrej Kadlec (86.Filip Dangubic), Jakub Rada, Lukás Gressák, Davit Skhirtladze (83.Jirí Kulhánek), Vakhtang Chanturishvili, Erik Jirka, Ali Ghorbani (71.Patryk Malecki). Trainer: Radoslav Látal.

Goals: 1-0 Amer Gojak (22), 2-0 Andrej Kadlec (36 own goal), 2-1 Vakhtang Chanturishvili (63), 3-1 Mislav Orsic (79).

29.11.2018; Stade „Constant Vanden Stock", Bruxelles; Referee: Anastasios Papapetrou (Greece); Attendance: 8,063

RSC Anderlecht Bruxelles – FC Spartak Trnava 0-0

Anderlecht: Thomas Didillon, Dennis Appiah, Jamie Lawrence, Bubacarr Sanneh, Sebastiaan Bornauw, Knowlegde Musona (81.Francis Amuzu), Ryota Morioka (81.Yari Verschaeren), Evgen Makarenko (81.Albert-Mboyo Sambi Lokonga), Kenny Saief, Edo Kayembe, Dauda Mohammed. Trainer: Hein Vanhaezebrouck.

FC Spartak Trnava: Martin Chudy, Martin Tóth, Matej Oravec, Patryk Malecki (90+3.Oliver Janso), Erik Grendel (90.Fabian Miesenböck), Lukás Gressák, Davit Skhirtladze, Vakhtang Chanturishvili, Erik Jirka, Jirí Kulhánek, Marek Bakos (60.Ali Ghorbani). Trainer: Radoslav Látal.

29.11.2018; "Sükrü Saraçoglu" Stadyumu, İstanbul; Referee: Robert Schörgenhofer (Austria); Attendance: 24,776

Fenerbahçe SK İstanbul – GNK Dinamo Zagreb 0-0

Fenerbahçe: Harun Tekin, Martin Skrtel, Mauricio Isla, Roman Neustädter, Hasan-Ali Kaldirim, Mathieu Valbuena, Baris Alici, Jaílson, Eljif Elmas, Michael Frey, Yassine Benzia. Trainer: Erwin Koeman.

Dinamo Zagreb: Dominik Livakovic, Kévin Théophile-Catherine, Emir Dilaver, Petar Stojanovic, Amir Rrahmani, Arijan Ademi, Amer Gojak, Daniel Olmo, Mario Gavranovic (62.Bruno Petkovic), Mislav Orsic (64.Ivan Sunjic), Izet Hajrovic (90+1.Damian Kadzior). Trainer: Nenad Bjelica.

13.12.2018; Stadión „Antona Malatinského", Trnava; Referee: José María Sánchez Martínez (Spain); Attendance: 11,413

FC Spartak Trnava – Fenerbahçe SK İstanbul 1-0(1-0)

FC Spartak Trnava: Martin Chudy, Martin Tóth (64.Jirí Kulhánek), Boris Godál, Matej Oravec, Erik Grendel (81.Fabian Miesenböck), Lukás Gressák, Davit Skhirtladze, Vakhtang Chanturishvili, Erik Jirka, Marek Bakos (75.Ali Ghorbani), Kubilay Yilmaz. Trainer: Radoslav Látal.

Fenerbahçe: Harun Tekin, Martin Skrtel, Mauricio Isla, Ismail Köybasi, Diego Reyes, Sener Özbayrakli, Yigithan Güveli (82.Deniz Yilmaz), Baris Alici, Jaílson, Mahsun Çapkan (73.Muhammet Çaki), Islam Slimani. Trainer: Erwin Koeman.

Goal: 1-0 Kubilay Yilmaz (41).

13.12.2018; Stadion Maksimir, Zagreb; Referee: Sandro Schärer (Switzerland); Attendance: 12,170

GNK Dinamo Zagreb – RSC Anderlecht Bruxelles 0-0

Dinamo Zagreb: Dominik Livakovic, Marin Leovac (46.Amir Rrahmani), Kévin Théophile-Catherine, Emir Dilaver, Petar Stojanovic, Ivan Sunjic, Amer Gojak, Daniel Olmo, Mario Gavranovic (65.Bruno Petkovic), Mislav Orsic (89.Mario Situm), Izet Hajrovic. Trainer: Nenad Bjelica.

Anderlecht: Frank Boeckx, Dennis Appiah, Antonio Milic (71.Alexis Saelemaeckers), Bubacarr Sanneh, Sebastiaan Bornauw (63.Hannes Delcroix), Ryota Morioka, Kenny Saief (69.Francis Amuzu), Pieter Gerkens, Zakaria Bakkali, Edo Kayembe, Ivan Santini. Trainer: Hein Vanhaezebrouck.

GROUP E

1.	**Arsenal FC London**	6	5	1	0	12	-	2	16
2.	**Sporting Clube de Portugal Lisboa**	6	4	1	1	13	-	3	13
3.	FK Vorskla Poltava	6	1	0	5	4	-	13	3
4.	Qarabağ FK	6	1	0	5	2	-	13	3

20.09.2018; Estádio „José Alvalade", Lisboa; Referee: François Letexier (France); Attendance: 30,098

Sporting Clube de Portugal Lisboa – Qarabağ FK 2-0(0-0)

Sporting: Romain Salin, Jérémy Mathieu (75.André Pinto), Sebastián Coates, Stefan Ristovski, Nemanja Gudelj, Rodrigo Battaglia, Bruno Fernandes, Nani (87.Jovane Cabral), Fredy Montero (90+2.Abdoulay Diaby), Marcos Acuña, Raphinha. Trainer: José Peseiro.

Qarabağ FK: Vagner, Jakub Rzezniczak, Maksim Medvedev (62.Abbas Hüseynov), Badavi Hüseynov, Qara Qarayev, Filip Ozobic, Wilde Guerrier, Joshgun Diniyev (58.Míchel), Abdellah Zoubir (68.Araz Abdullayev), Innocent Emeghara, Mahir Madatov. Trainer: Gurban Gurbanov.

Goals: 1-0 Raphinha (54), 2-0 Jovane Cabral (88).

20.09.2018; Emirates Stadium, London; Referee: Bart Vertenten (Belgium); Attendance: 59,039

Arsenal FC London – FK Vorskla Poltava 4-2(1-0)

Arsenal FC: Bernd Leno, Stephan Lichtsteiner, Nacho Monreal, Sokratis Papastathopoulos, Rob Holding, Henrikh Mkhitaryan, Mohamed El Neny, Alex Iwobi (70.Emile Smith Rowe), Lucas Torreira (57.Mattéo Guendouzi), Pierre-Emerick Aubameyang (57.Mesut Özil), Danny Welbeck. Trainer: Unai Emery.

Vorskla Poltava: Bogdan Shust, Volodimir Chesnakov, Igor Perduta, Artur, Ardin Dallku, Aleksandr Kobakhidze (77.Mykhaylo Sergiychuk), Pavlo Rebenok, Vyacheslav Sharpar, Dmitro Kravchenko (70.Aleksandr Sklyar), Vladislav Kulach (75.Nicolas Careca), Yuriy Kolomoyets. Trainer: Vasil Sachko.

Goals: 1-0 Pierre-Emerick Aubameyang (32), 2-0 Danny Welbeck (48), 3-0 Pierre-Emerick Aubameyang (56), 4-0 Mesut Özil (74), 4-1 Volodimir Chesnakov (77), 4-2 Vyacheslav Sharpar (90+3).

04.10.2018; Stadion Vorskla, Poltava; Referee: Nikola Dabanovic (Montenegro); Attendance: 10,082

FK Vorskla Poltava – Sporting Clube de Portugal Lisboa 1-2(1-0)

Vorskla Poltava: Bogdan Shust, Volodimir Chesnakov, Igor Perduta, Artur, Ardin Dallku, Pavlo Rebenok, Aleksandr Sklyar, Vyacheslav Sharpar, Dmitro Kravchenko (84.Artem Gabelyuk), Vladislav Kulach (62.Mykhaylo Sergiychuk), Yuriy Kolomoyets. Trainer: Vasil Sachko.

Sporting: Romain Salin, Jefferson, André Pinto, Sebastián Coates, Bruno Gaspar, Radosav Petrovic (70.Jovane Cabral), Bruno Fernandes, Nani, Abdoulay Diaby (70.Raphinha), Carlos Mané (58.Fredy Montero), Marcos Acuña. Trainer: José Peseiro.

Goals: 1-0 Vladislav Kulach (10), 1-1 Fredy Montero (90+1), 1-2 Jovane Cabral (90+3).

04.10.2018; Bakı Olimpiya Stadionu, Bakı; Referee: Davide Massa (Italy); Attendance: 63,412

Qarabağ FK – Arsenal FC London 0-3(0-1)

Qarabağ FK: Vagner, Ansi Agolli, Jakub Rzezniczak, Maksim Medvedev, Badavi Hüseynov, Míchel, Qara Qarayev (84.Simeon Slavchev), Filip Ozobic (67.Araz Abdullayev), Abdellah Zoubir, Innocent Emeghara, Mahir Madatov (61.Dzon Delarge). Trainer: Gurban Gurbanov.

Arsenal FC: Bernd Leno, Stephan Lichtsteiner, Nacho Monreal (46.Lucas Torreira), Sokratis Papastathopoulos, Sead Kolasinac, Rob Holding, Mohamed El Neny, Alex Iwobi (71.Alexandre Lacazette), Mattéo Guendouzi, Emile Smith Rowe (65.Mesut Özil), Danny Welbeck. Trainer: Unai Emery.

Goals: 0-1 Sokratis Papastathopoulos (4), 0-2 Emile Smith Rowe (53), 0-3 Mattéo Guendouzi (80).

25.10.2018; Bakı Olimpiya Stadionu, Bakı; Referee: Roi Reinshreiber (Israel); Attendance: 22,450

Qarabağ FK – FK Vorskla Poltava 0-1(0-0)

Qarabağ FK: Vagner, Rashad Sadygov, Jakub Rzezniczak, Maksim Medvedev, Míchel, Araz Abdullayev (69.Dzon Delarge), Qara Qarayev, Simeon Slavchev (58.Filip Ozobic), Wilde Guerrier, Abdellah Zoubir, Innocent Emeghara (58.Mahir Madatov). Trainer: Gurban Gurbanov.

Vorskla Poltava: Bogdan Shust, Vadim Sapay, Volodimir Chesnakov, Igor Perduta, Ardin Dallku, Najeeb Yakubu (46.Nicolas Careca), Pavlo Rebenok, Aleksandr Sklyar, Vyacheslav Sharpar, Vladislav Kulach (77.Mykhaylo Sergiychuk, 90+2.Oleksandr Chizhov), Yuriy Kolomoyets. Trainer: Vasil Sachko.

Goal: 0-1 Vladislav Kulach (48).

25.10.2018; Estádio „José Alvalade“, Lisboa; Referee: Damir Skomina (Slovenia); Attendance: 40,784

Sporting Clube de Portugal Lisboa – Arsenal FC London 0-1(0-0)

Sporting: Renan Ribeiro, André Pinto, Sebastián Coates, Stefan Ristovski (46.Bruno Gaspar), Radosav Petrovic, Nemanja Gudelj (71.Jovane Cabral), Rodrigo Battaglia, Bruno Fernandes, Nani (87.Abdoulay Diaby), Fredy Montero, Marcos Acuña. Trainer: José Peseiro.

Arsenal FC: Bernd Leno, Stephan Lichtsteiner, Sokratis Papastathopoulos, Rob Holding, Henrikh Mkhitaryan, Aaron Ramsey, Granit Xhaka, Mohamed El Neny (58.Lucas Torreira), Mattéo Guendouzi, Pierre-Emerick Aubameyang (86.Alex Iwobi), Danny Welbeck (81.Alexandre Lacazette). Trainer: Unai Emery.

Goal: 0-1 Danny Welbeck (78).

08.11.2018; Stadion Vorskla, Poltava; Referee: Sandro Schärer (Switzerland); Attendance: 5,479

FK Vorskla Poltava – Qarabağ FK 0-1(0-1)

Vorskla Poltava: Bogdan Shust, Volodimir Chesnakov, Oleksandr Chizhov, Igor Perduta, Artur, Najeeb Yakubu (55.Nicolas Careca), Pavlo Rebenok, Aleksandr Sklyar, Vyacheslav Sharpar, Vladislav Kulach, Yuriy Kolomoyets. Trainer: Vasil Sachko.

Qarabağ FK: Hannes Halldórsson, Rashad Sadygov, Jakub Rzezniczak, Maksim Medvedev, Míchel, Araz Abdullayev, Qara Qarayev, Simeon Slavchev, Wilde Guerrier, Abdellah Zoubir (81.Mahir Madatov), Dzon Delarge (88.Filip Ozobic). Trainer: Gurban Gurbanov.

Goal: 0-1 Araz Abdullayev (13 penalty).

08.11.2018; Emirates Stadium, London; Referee: Gediminas Mažeika (Lithuania); Attendance: 59,758

Arsenal FC London – Sporting Clube de Portugal Lisboa 0-0

Arsenal FC: Petr Cech, Stephan Lichtsteiner (74.Ainsley Maitland-Niles), Sokratis Papastathopoulos, Carl Jenkinson (60.Sead Kolasinac), Rob Holding, Henrikh Mkhitaryan, Aaron Ramsey, Alex Iwobi, Mattéo Guendouzi, Emile Smith-Rowe, Danny Welbeck (30.Pierre-Emerick Aubameyang). Trainer: Unai Emery.

Sporting: Renan Ribeiro, Jérémy Mathieu [*sent off 87*], Sebastián Coates, Bruno Gaspar, Nemanja Gudelj, Bruno Fernandes, Miguel Luís (85.Radosav Petrovic), Nani, Fredy Montero (69.Bas Dost), Abdoulay Diaby (83.Jovane Cabral), Marcos Acuña. Trainer: Tiago Fernandes.

29.11.2018; Bakı Olimpiya Stadionu, Bakı; Referee: Petr Ardeleánu (Czech Republic); Attendance: 5,416

Qarabağ FK – Sporting Clube de Portugal Lisboa 1-6(1-3)

Qarabağ FK: Hannes Halldórsson, Rashad Sadygov, Jakub Rzezniczak, Maksim Medvedev, Míchel, Araz Abdullayev (82.Dzon Delarge), Qara Qarayev, Simeon Slavchev (70.Filip Ozobic), Wilde Guerrier, Abdellah Zoubir, Mahir Madatov. Trainer: Gurban Gurbanov.

Sporting: Renan Ribeiro, Jefferson, André Pinto, Sebastián Coates, Bruno Gaspar (74.Thierry Correia), Nemanja Gudelj, Bruno Fernandes, Wendel, Nani (79.Carlos Mané), Bas Dost (71.Jovane Cabral), Abdoulay Diaby. Trainer: Marcel Keizer.

Goals: 0-1 Bas Dost (5 penalty), 1-1 Abdellah Zoubir (14), 1-2 Bruno Fernandes (20), 1-3 Nani (33), 1-4 Abdoulay Diaby (65), 1-5 Bruno Fernandes (75), 1-6 Abdoulay Diaby (82).

29.11.2018; NSK Olimpijskyj Stadium, Kyiv; Referee: Bartosz Frankowski (Poland); Attendance: 7,751

FK Vorskla Poltava – Arsenal FC London 0-3(0-3)

Vorskla Poltava: Bogdan Shust, Vadim Sapay (36.Nicolas Careca), Volodimir Chesnakov, Igor Perduta, Artur, Ardin Dallku, Pavlo Rebenok (85.Taras Sakiv), Aleksandr Sklyar, Vyacheslav Sharpar, Vladislav Kulach (71.Ibrahiim Kane), Yuriy Kolomoyets. Trainer: Vasil Sachko.

Arsenal FC: Petr Cech, Stephan Lichtsteiner, Carl Jenkinson, Rob Holding (60.Zech Medley), Aaron Ramsey (68.Bukayo Saka), Mohamed El Neny, Ainsley Maitland-Niles, Joseph Willock, Mattéo Guendouzi (76.Charlie Gilmour), Emile Smith-Rowe, Edward Nketiah. Trainer: Unai Emery.

Goals: 0-1 Emile Smith-Rowe (11), 0-2 Aaron Ramsey (27 penalty), 0-3 Joseph Willock (41).

13.12.2018; Estádio „José Alvalade“, Lisboa; Referee: Manuel Schüttengruber (Austria); Attendance: 25,504

Sporting Clube de Portugal Lisboa – FK Vorskla Poltava 3-0(3-0)

Sporting: Romain Salin, André Pinto, Sebastián Coates, Stefan Ristovski (64.Thierry Correia), Radosav Petrovic, Bruno Fernandes (73.Bruno Paz), Miguel Luís, Fredy Montero (59.Pedro Marques), Carlos Mané, Marcos Acuña, Jovane Cabral. Trainer: Marcel Keizer.

Vorskla Poltava: Oleksandr Tkachenko, Volodimir Chesnakov, Oleksandr Chizhov, Igor Perduta, Artur (77.Ibrahiim Kane), Ardin Dallku (46.Yuriy Kolomoyets), Taras Sakiv, Pavlo Rebenok, Aleksandr Sklyar, Artem Gabelyuk, Nicolas Careca (67.Mykhaylo Sergiychuk). Trainer: Vasil Sachko.

Goals: 1-0 Fredy Montero (17), 2-0 Miguel Luís (35), 3-0 Ardin Dallku (44 own goal).

13.12.2018; Emirates Stadium, London; Referee: Jens Maae (Denmark); Attendance: 58,101

Arsenal FC London – Qarabağ FK 1-0(1-0)

Arsenal FC: Emiliano Martínez, Sokratis Papastathopoulos, Laurent Koscielny (72.Nacho Monreal), Carl Jenkinson, Mesut Özil (83.Charlie Gilmour), Mohamed El Neny, Ainsley Maitland-Niles, Joseph Willock, Bukayo Saka, Alexandre Lacazette (63.Zech Medley), Edward Nketiah. Trainer: Unai Emery.

Qarabağ FK: Vagner, Rashad Sadygov, Jakub Rzezniczak (85.Filip Ozobic), Maksim Medvedev, Badavi Hüseynov, Míchel (61.Araz Abdullayev), Qara Qarayev, Simeon Slavchev, Wilde Guerrier, Abdellah Zoubir, Mahir Madatov (75.Dani Quintana). Trainer: Gurban Gurbanov.

Goal: 1-0 Alexandre Lacazette (17).

GROUP F

1.	**Real Betis Balompié Sevilla**	6	3	3	0	7 - 2	12
2.	**Olympiacos SFP Peiraiás**	6	3	1	2	11 - 6	10
3.	AC Milan	6	3	1	2	12 - 9	10
4.	F91 Dudelange	6	0	1	5	3 - 16	1

20.09.2018; Stade „Josy Barthel", Lëtzebuerg; Referee: Srđan Jovanović (Serbia); Attendance: 7,983

F91 Dudelange – AC Milan 0-1(0-0)

F91 Dudelange: Joé Frising, Tom Schnell, Jerry Prempeh, Kevin Malget (84.Edisson Jordanov), Aniss El Hriti (80.Bryan Mélisse), Marc-André Kruska, Stélvio (75.Patrick Stumpf), Dominik Stolz, Clément Couturier, Danel Sinani, David Turpel. Trainer: Dino Toppmöller.
AC Milan: Pepe Reina, Ignazio Abate, Alessio Romagnoli, Mattia Caldara, Andrea Bertolacci (70.Franck Kessié), Tiemoué Bakayoko, Samu Castillejo, Diego Laxalt, José Mauri (80.Hakan Çalhanoglu), Gonzalo Higuaín, Fabio Borini (88.Alen Halilovic). Trainer: Gennaro Gattuso.
Goal: 0-1 Gonzalo Higuaín (59).

20.09.2018; Stádio „Giórgos Karaïskáki", Peiraiás; Referee: Daniel Stefanski (Poland); Attendance: 28,650

Olympiacos SFP Peiraiás – Real Betis Balompié Sevilla 0-0

Olympiacos Peiraiás: Andreas Gianniotis, Jagos Vukovic, Omar Elabdellaoui, Yassine Meryah, Kostas Tsimikas [*sent off 73*], Ionnias Fetfatzidis (71.Lazaros Christodoulopoulos), Kostas Fortounis, Andreas Bouchalakis (35.Bibras Natcho), Daniel Podence (80.Vasilios Torosidis), Mohamed Camara, Ahmed Hassan „Koka". Trainer: Pedro Martins.
Betis Sevilla: Joel Robles, Barragán, Sidnei, Aïssa Mandi, Joaquín (80.Antonio Sanabria), Andrés Guardado, Javi García, Giovani Lo Celso (83.Takashi Inui), Sergio León (72.Canales), Cristian Tello, Loren Morón. Trainer: Quique Setién.

04.10.2018; Estadio „Benito Villamarín", Sevilla; Referee: Andrew Dallas (Scotland); Attendance: 40,133

Real Betis Balompié Sevilla – F91 Dudelange 3-0(0-0)

Betis Sevilla: Joel Robles, Barragán, Sidnei, Bartra, Andrés Guardado (61.Giovani Lo Celso), Javi García, Takashi Inui (72.Joaquín), William Carvalho, Sergio León (82.Wilfrid Kaptoum), Cristian Tello, Antonio Sanabria. Trainer: Quique Setién.
F91 Dudelange: Joé Frising, Tom Schnell, Jerry Prempeh, Bryan Mélisse (66.Patrick Stumpf), Aniss El Hriti, Marc-André Kruska, Dominik Stolz (76.Levan Kenia), Edisson Jordanov, Clément Couturier, Danel Sinani (82.Mario Pokar), David Turpel. Trainer: Dino Toppmöller.
Goals: 1-0 Antonio Sanabria (56), 2-0 Giovani Lo Celso (80), 3-0 Cristian Tello (88).

04.10.2018; Stadio „Giuseppe Meazza", Milano; Referee: Bobby Madden (Scotland); Attendance: 22,294

AC Milan – Olympiacos SFP Peiraiás 3-1(0-1)

AC Milan: Pepe Reina, Cristián Zapata, Ricardo Rodríguez, Alessio Romagnoli, Davide Calabria, Lucas Biglia, Giacomo Bonaventura (54.Hakan Çalhanoglu), Tiemoué Bakayoko, Samu Castillejo (54.Patrick Cutrone), Gonzalo Higuaín, Suso (80.Fabio Borini). Trainer: Gennaro Gattuso.
Olympiacos Peiraiás: José Sá, Vasilios Torosidis (77.Yassine Meryah), Roderick Miranda, Leonardo Koutris, Pape Cissé, Yaya Touré (83.Kostas Fortounis), Bibras Natcho, Guilherme, Ionnias Fetfatzidis, Matías Nahuel (72.Daniel Podence), Guerrero. Trainer: Pedro Martins.
Goals: 0-1 Guerrero (14), 1-1 Patrick Cutrone (70), 2-1 Gonzalo Higuaín (76), 3-1 Patrick Cutrone (79).

25.10.2018; Stadio „Giuseppe Meazza", Milano; Referee: Hendrikus Sebastiaan Hermanus „Bas" Nijhuis (Netherlands); Attendance: 22,405

AC Milan – Real Betis Balompié Sevilla 1-2(0-1)

AC Milan: Pepe Reina, Cristián Zapata, Alessio Romagnoli, Davide Calabria, Lucas Biglia (80.Andrea Bertolacci), Giacomo Bonaventura, Tiemoué Bakayoko (46.Suso), Samu Castillejo [*sent off 90+4*], Diego Laxalt, Gonzalo Higuaín, Fabio Borini (46.Patrick Cutrone). Trainer: Gennaro Gattuso.
Betis Sevilla: Pau López, Barragán, Sidnei, Aïssa Mandi, Bartra, Junior Firpo, Canales, William Carvalho (90+2.Zouhair Feddal), Giovani Lo Celso, Sergio León (67.Cristian Tello), Antonio Sanabria (79.Loren Morón). Trainer: Quique Setién.
Goals: 0-1 Antonio Sanabria (30), 0-2 Giovani Lo Celso (55), 1-2 Patrick Cutrone (83).

25.10.2018; Stade „Josy Barthel", Lëtzebuerg; Referee: Hüseyin Göçek (Turkey); Attendance: 7,500

F91 Dudelange – Olympiacos SFP Peiraiás 0-2(0-0)

F91 Dudelange: Landry Bonnefoi, Milan Bisevac, Tom Schnell, Jerry Prempeh, Aniss El Hriti (74.Levan Kenia), Marc-André Kruska, Stélvio (51.Danel Sinani), Dominik Stolz (65.Bryan Mélisse), Edisson Jordanov, Clément Couturier, David Turpel. Trainer: Dino Toppmöller.
Olympiacos Peiraiás: José Sá, Vasilios Torosidis (69.Omar Elabdellaoui), Jagos Vukovic, Leonardo Koutris, Pape Cissé, Kostas Fortounis, Andreas Bouchalakis, Daniel Podence, Matías Nahuel (78.Bibras Natcho), Mohamed Camara, Guerrero (18.Lazaros Christodoulopoulos). Trainer: Pedro Martins.
Goals: 0-1 Vasilios Torosidis (66), 0-2 Edisson Jordanov (81 own goal).

08.11.2018; Estadio „Benito Villamarín", Sevilla; Referee: Craig Pawson (England); Attendance: 45,647

Real Betis Balompié Sevilla – AC Milan 1-1(1-0)

Betis Sevilla: Pau López, Aïssa Mandi, Bartra, Zouhair Feddal, Junior Firpo, Joaquín (67.Andrés Guardado), Canales, William Carvalho, Giovani Lo Celso, Cristian Tello, Antonio Sanabria (74.Loren Morón). Trainer: Quique Setién.
AC Milan: Pepe Reina, Cristián Zapata, Mateo Musacchio (83.Alessio Romagnoli), Ricardo Rodríguez, Hakan Çalhanoglu (89.Andrea Bertolacci), Tiemoué Bakayoko, Diego Laxalt (76.Ignazio Abate), Franck Kessié, Fabio Borini, Suso, Patrick Cutrone. Trainer: Gennaro Gattuso.
Goals: 1-0 Giovani Lo Celso (12), 1-1 Suso (62).

08.11.2018; Stádio „Giórgos Karaïskáki", Peiraiás; Referee: Petr Ardeleánu (Czech Republic); Attendance: 24,032

Olympiacos SFP Peiraiás – F91 Dudelange 5-1(4-0)

Olympiacos Peiraiás: José Sá, Vasilios Torosidis, Roderick Miranda, Kostas Tsimikas, Pape Cissé, Lazaros Christodoulopoulos, Bibras Natcho (62.Yaya Touré), Kostas Fortounis (57.Ahmed Hassan „Koka"), Daniel Podence, Matías Nahuel (34.Ioannis Fetfatzidis), Mohamed Camara. Trainer: Pedro Martins.
F91 Dudelange: Landry Bonnefoi, Milan Bisevac, Tom Schnell, Jerry Prempeh, Bryan Mélisse, Marc-André Kruska (60.Leon Jensen), Dominik Stolz (85.Patrick Stumpf), Edisson Jordanov, Clément Couturier, Danel Sinani, David Turpel (74.Nicolas Perez). Trainer: Dino Toppmöller.
Goals: 1-0 Vasilios Torosidis (6), 2-0 Kostas Fortounis (15), 3-0 Lazaros Christodoulopoulos (26), 4-0 Kostas Fortounis (36), 4-1 Danel Sinani (69), 5-1 Ahmed Hassan „Koka" (71).

29.11.2018; Stadio „Giuseppe Meazza", Milano; Referee: Vladislav Bezborodov (Russia); Attendance: 15,521

AC Milan – F91 Dudelange 5-2(1-1)

AC Milan: Pepe Reina, Cristián Zapata, Stefan Simic, Davide Calabria, Andrea Bertolacci (58.José Mauri), Hakan Çalhanoglu, Tiemoué Bakayoko, Diego Laxalt, Alen Halilovic (52.Suso), Gonzalo Higuaín, Patrick Cutrone (80.Fabio Borini). Trainer: Gennaro Gattuso.
F91 Dudelange: Landry Bonnefoi, Tom Schnell, Jerry Prempeh, Bryan Mélisse, Marc-André Kruska, Stélvio (75.Mario Pokar), Dominik Stolz (80.Levan Kenia), Edisson Jordanov, Clément Couturier, Danel Sinani (87.Nicolas Perez), David Turpel. Trainer: Dino Toppmöller.
Goals: 1-0 Patrick Cutrone (21), 1-1 Dominik Stolz (39), 1-2 David Turpel (49), 2-2 Stélvio (66 own goal), 3-2 Hakan Çalhanoglu (70), 4-2 Tom Schnell (77 own goal), 5-2 Fabio Borini (80).

29.11.2018; Estadio „Benito Villamarín", Sevilla; Referee: Sergey Karasev (Russia); Attendance: 37,722

Real Betis Balompié Sevilla – Olympiacos SFP Peiraiás 1-0(1-0)

Betis Sevilla: Joel Robles, Sidnei, Aïssa Mandi, Bartra (74.Javi García), Junior Firpo, Canales, William Carvalho, Giovani Lo Celso, Sergio León (63.Takashi Inui), Cristian Tello (83.Barragán), Antonio Sanabria. Trainer: Quique Setién.

Olympiacos Peiraiás: José Sá, Jagos Vukovic, Omar Elabdellaoui, Kostas Tsimikas, Pape Cissé, Guilherme (81.Bibras Natcho), Kostas Fortounis, Andreas Bouchalakis (58.Guerrero), Daniel Podence, Matías Nahuel (72.Marius Vrushaj), Mohamed Camara. Trainer: Pedro Martins.

Goal: 1-0 Canales (39).

13.12.2018; Stade „Josy Barthel", Lëtzebuerg; Referee: Peter Královec (Czech Republic); Attendance: 4,931

F91 Dudelange – Real Betis Balompié Sevilla 0-0

F91 Dudelange: Landry Bonnefoi, Tom Schnell, Jerry Prempeh, Aniss El Hriti, Stélvio, Levan Kenia (71.Kevin Malget), Dominik Stolz, Edisson Jordanov, Clément Couturier (82.Bryan Mélisse), Danel Sinani (89.Leon Jensen), David Turpel. Trainer: Dino Toppmöller.

Betis Sevilla: Joel Robles, Sidnei, Zouhair Feddal, Joaquín (75.Ryad Boudebouz), Javi García, Takashi Inui, William Carvalho (74.Bartra), Wilfrid Kaptoum, Francis Guerrero, Cristian Tello, Loren Morón (70.Sergio León). Trainer: Quique Setién.

13.12.2018; Stádio „Giórgos Karaïskáki", Peiraiás; Referee: Benoît Bastien (France); Attendance: 31,010

Olympiacos SFP Peiraiás – AC Milan 3-1(0-0)

Olympiacos Peiraiás: José Sá, Jagos Vukovic, Omar Elabdellaoui, Leonardo Koutris, Pape Cissé, Guilherme, Ioannis Fetfatzidis (69.Bibras Natcho), Kostas Fortounis, Daniel Podence (85.Andreas Bouchalakis), Mohamed Camara (79.Vasilios Torosidis), Guerrero. Trainer: Pedro Martins.

AC Milan: Pepe Reina, Cristián Zapata, Ignazio Abate, Ricardo Rodríguez (85.Alen Halilovic), Davide Calabria, Hakan Çalhanoglu, Tiemoué Bakayoko, Samu Castillejo, Franck Kessié, Gonzalo Higuaín, Patrick Cutrone (78.Diego Laxalt). Trainer: Gennaro Gattuso.

Goals: 1-0 Pape Cissé (60), 2-0 Cristián Zapata (70 own goal), 2-1 Cristián Zapata (72), 3-1 Kostas Fortounis (81 penalty).

GROUP G

1.	**Villarreal CF**	6	2	4	0	12	-	5	10
2.	**SK Rapid Wien**	6	3	1	2	6	-	9	10
3.	Rangers FC Glasgow	6	1	3	2	8	-	8	6
4.	FK Spartak Moskva	6	1	2	3	8	-	12	5

20.09.2018; Estadio de la Cerámica, Villarreal; Referee: István Kovács (Romania); Attendance: 15,982

Villarreal CF – Glasgow Rangers 2-2(1-0)

Villarreal CF: Andrés Fernández, Daniele Bonera, Víctor Ruíz, Ramiro Funes Mori (67.Gerard Moreno), Miguelón Llambrich, Santi Cazorla, Alfonso Pedraza, Pablo Fornals, Carlos Bacca, Nicola Sansone (79.Samuel Chukwueze), Karl Toko Ekambi (60.Trigueros). Trainer: Javi Calleja.

Rangers: Allan McGregor, James Tavernier, Connor Goldson, Borna Barisic (85.Graham Dorrans), Joe Worrall, Scott Arfield, Andrew Halliday, Ryan Kent, Lassana Coulibaly (70.Glenn Middleton), Kyle Lafferty, Candeias (77.Ross McCrorie). Trainer: Steven Gerrard.

Goals: 1-0 Carlos Bacca (1), 1-1 Scott Arfield (67), 2-1 Gerard Moreno (69), 2-2 Kyle Lafferty (76).

20.09.2018; Allianz Stadion, Wien; Referee: Alain Bieri (Switzerland); Attendance: 21,400

SK Rapid Wien – FK Spartak Moskva 2-0(0-0)

SK Rapid Wien: Richard Strebinger, Mario Sonnleitner, Marvin Potzmann, Mateo Barac, Mert Müldür, Christoph Knasmüllner (86.Manuel Martic), Stefan Schwab, Thomas Murg, Dejan Ljubicic, Deni Alar (71.Andrija Pavlovic), Andrei Ivan (76.Veton Berisha). Trainer: Goran Djuricin.

Spartak Moskva: Aleksandr Maksimenko, Salvatore Bocchetti, Georgi Dzhikiya, Nikolai Rasskazov, Lorenzo Melgarejo, Fernando, Roman Zobnin, Artiom Timofeev (82.Mikhail Ignatov), Aleksandr Lomovitski (73.Aleksandr Samedov), Zé Luís, Pedro Rocha (73.Ivelin Popov). Trainer: Massimo Carrera.

Goals: 1-0 Artiom Timofeev (50 own goal), 2-0 Thomas Murg (68).

04.10.2018; Otkrytiye Arena, Moskva; Referee: Daniel Siebert (Germany); Attendance: 21,264

FK Spartak Moskva – Villarreal CF 3-3(1-1)

Spartak Moskva: Aleksandr Maksimenko, Salvatore Bocchetti, Georgi Dzhikiya, Nikolai Rasskazov, Dmitriy Kombarov (90.Artiom Timofeev), Lorenzo Melgarejo, Fernando, Roman Zobnin, Aleksandr Lomovitski (80.Aleksandr Tashaev), Mikhail Ignatov (69.Sofiane Hanni), Zé Luís. Trainer: Massimo Carrera.

Villarreal CF: Andrés Fernández, Daniele Bonera, Mario Gaspar, Víctor Ruíz, Ramiro Funes Mori, Trigueros, Alfonso Pedraza, Pablo Fornals, Samuel Chukwueze (71.Santi Cazorla), Nicola Sansone (61.Gerard Moreno), Karl Toko Ekambi (77.Miguel Layún). Trainer: Javi Calleja.

Goals: 0-1 Karl Toko Ekambi (13), 1-1 Zé Luís (34 penalty), 1-2 Pablo Fornals (49), 2-2 Zé Luís (82), 3-2 Lorenzo Melgarejo (85), 3-3 Santi Cazorla (90+6 penalty).

04.10.2018; Ibrox Stadium, Glasgow; Referee: Ruddy Buquet (France); Attendance: 47,534

Rangers FC Glasgow – SK Rapid Wien 3-1(1-1)

Rangers: Allan McGregor, James Tavernier, Connor Goldson, Jon Flanagan, Joe Worrall, Scott Arfield, Ryan Kent (90.Andrew Halliday), Ovie Ejaria, Lassana Coulibaly, Candeias, Alfredo Morelos (90+5.Glenn Middleton). Trainer: Steven Gerrard.

SK Rapid Wien: Richard Strebinger, Mario Sonnleitner, Marvin Potzmann, Mateo Barac (33.Christopher Dibon), Mert Müldür, Stefan Schwab, Thomas Murg, Dejan Ljubicic, Veton Berisha (72.Boli Bolingoli-Mbombo), Andrija Pavlovic, Andrei Ivan (58.Deni Alar). Trainer: Dietmar Kühbauer.

Goals: 0-1 Veton Berisha (42), 1-1 Alfredo Morelos (44), 2-1 James Tavernier (84 penalty), 3-1 Alfredo Morelos (90+4).

25.10.2018; Ibrox Stadium, Glasgow; Referee: Kevin Blom (Netherlands); Attendance: 49,068

Rangers FC Glasgow – FK Spartak Moskva 0-0

Rangers: Allan McGregor, James Tavernier, Connor Goldson, Jon Flanagan, Joe Worrall, Ryan Jack (68.Eros Grezda), Ryan Kent, Ovie Ejaria, Lassana Coulibaly, Candeias (86.Glenn Middleton), Alfredo Morelos. Trainer: Steven Gerrard.

Spartak Moskva: Aleksandr Maksimenko, Salvatore Bocchetti, Georgi Dzhikiya, Nikolai Rasskazov, Lorenzo Melgarejo, Fernando, Roman Zobnin, Aleksandr Tashaev (46.Sofiane Hanni), Aleksandr Lomovitski (46.Roman Eremenko), Mikhail Ignatov (84.Ivelin Popov), Zé Luís. Trainer: Raúl Riancho.

25.10.2018; Estadio de la Cerámica, Villarreal; Referee: Halis Özkahya (Turkey); Attendance: 14,158

Villarreal CF – SK Rapid Wien 5-0(3-0)

Villarreal CF: Andrés Fernández, Jaume Costa [*sent off 79*], Miguel Layún, Ramiro Funes Mori, Álvaro González, Miguelón Llambrich, Trigueros, Pablo Fornals (65.Samuel Chukwueze), Santiago Cáseres (78.Santi Cazorla), Karl Toko Ekambi, Dani Raba (70.Gerard Moreno). Trainer: Javi Calleja.

SK Rapid Wien: Richard Strebinger, Mario Sonnleitner, Marvin Potzmann (46.Andrei Ivan), Boli Bolingoli-Mbombo, Mateo Barac, Mert Müldür, Stefan Schwab, Thomas Murg (77.Christoph Knasmüllner), Dejan Ljubicic, Deni Alar, Veton Berisha (60.Manuel Thurnwald). Trainer: Dietmar Kühbauer.

Goals: 1-0 Pablo Fornals (26), 2-0 Karl Toko Ekambi (30), 3-0 Mateo Barac (45 own goal), 4-0 Dani Raba (63), 5-0 Gerard Moreno (85).

08.11.2018; Otkrytiye Arena, Moskva; Referee: Ivan Bebek (Croatia); Attendance: 22,296

FK Spartak Moskva – Rangers FC Glasgow 4-3(2-3)

Spartak Moskva: Aleksandr Maksimenko, Salvatore Bocchetti, Ilya Kutepov, Nikolai Rasskazov, Roman Eremenko (60.Denis Glushakov), Ivelin Popov (71.Artiom Timofeev), Lorenzo Melgarejo, Fernando, Roman Zobnin, Sofiane Hanni, Luiz Adriano (82.Zé Luís). Trainer: Raúl Riancho.

Rangers: Allan McGregor, James Tavernier, Connor Goldson, Jon Flanagan (82.Andy Halliday), Nikola Katic, Scott Arfield, Ovie Ejaria (90+4.Gareth McAuley), Lassana Coulibaly (82.Eros Grezda), Candeias, Alfredo Morelos, Glenn Middleton. Trainer: Steven Gerrard.

Goals: 0-1 Roman Eremenko (5 own goal), 1-1 Lorenzo Melgarejo (22), 1-2 Candeias (27), 2-2 Connor Goldson (35), 2-3 Glenn Middleton (41), 3-3 Luiz Adriano (58), 4-3 Sofiane Hanni (59).

08.11.2018; Allianz Stadion, Wien; Referee: Srđan Jovanović (Serbia); Attendance: 22,100

SK Rapid Wien – Villarreal CF **0-0**

SK Rapid Wien: Richard Strebinger, Mario Sonnleitner, Christopher Dibon (75.Boli Bolingoli-Mbombo), Marvin Potzmann, Mert Müldür, Stefan Schwab, Thomas Murg (46.Christoph Knasmüllner), Dejan Ljubicic, Veton Berisha, Andrija Pavlovic (90+2.Manuel Martic), Andrei Ivan. Trainer: Dietmar Kühbauer.

Villarreal CF: Andrés Fernández, Daniele Bonera (46.Ramiro Funes Mori), Mario Gaspar, Víctor Ruíz, Miguel Layún (61.Karl Toko Ekambi), Santi Cazorla, Alfonso Pedraza, Santiago Cáseres, Nicola Sansone, Gerard Moreno, Dani Raba (76.Pablo Fornals). Trainer: Javi Calleja.

29.11.2018; Otkrytiye Arena, Moskva; Referee: Paweł Gil (Poland); Attendance: 20,739

FK Spartak Moskva – SK Rapid Wien **1-2(1-0)**

Spartak Moskva: Artem Rebrov, Andrey Eshchenko, Ilya Kutepov, Georgi Dzhikiya, Dmitriy Kombarov, Denis Glushakov, Lorenzo Melgarejo (81.Ivelin Popov), Sofiane Hanni (72.Aleksandr Samedov), Artiom Timofeev, Luiz Adriano, Zé Luís. Trainer: Oleg Kononov.

SK Rapid Wien: Richard Strebinger, Marvin Potzmann, Maximilian Hofmann, Boli Bolingoli-Mbombo, Mateo Barac, Mert Müldür, Christoph Knasmüllner, Manuel Martic, Dejan Ljubicic (64.Stefan Schwab), Deni Alar (64.Philipp Schobesberger), Veton Berisha (81.Manuel Thurnwald). Trainer: Dietmar Kühbauer.

Goals: 1-0 Zé Luís (20), 1-1 Mert Müldür (80), 1-2 Philipp Schobesberger (90+1).

29.11.2018; Ibrox Stadium, Glasgow; Referee: Matej Jug (Slovenia); Attendance: 50,171

Rangers FC Glasgow – Villarreal CF **0-0**

Rangers: Allan McGregor, James Tavernier, Connor Goldson, Jon Flanagan, Joe Worrall, Scott Arfield, Ryan Jack, Lassana Coulibaly (90+2.Ross McCrorie), Candeias [*sent off 44*], Alfredo Morelos (79.Kyle Lafferty), Glenn Middleton. Trainer: Steven Gerrard.

Villarreal CF: Andrés Fernández, Mario Gaspar, Jaume Costa, Ramiro Funes Mori, Álvaro González, Trigueros (62.Santi Cazorla), Manu Morlanes, Pablo Fornals (74.Samuel Chukwueze), Santiago Cáseres, Carlos Bacca (63.Gerard Moreno), Karl Toko Ekambi. Trainer: Javi Calleja.

13.12.2018; Estadio de la Cerámica, Villarreal; Referee: Andris Treimanis (Latvia); Attendance: 12,903

Villarreal CF – FK Spartak Moskva **2-0(1-0)**

Villarreal CF: Andrés Fernández, Mario Gaspar, Jaume Costa [*sent off 90*], Víctor Ruíz, Álvaro González, Javi Fuego, Pablo Fornals, Samuel Chukwueze (80.Santi Cazorla), Santiago Cáseres, Gerard Moreno (77.Alfonso Pedraza), Karl Toko Ekambi (72.Carlos Bacca). Trainer: Luis García.

Spartak Moskva: Aleksandr Maksimenko, Ilya Kutepov, Georgi Dzhikiya, Nikolai Rasskazov, Denis Glushakov, Ivelin Popov, Lorenzo Melgarejo, Sofiane Hanni (67.Pedro Rocha), Aleksandr Lomovitski (55.Aleksandr Tashaev), Luiz Adriano (74.Jano Ananidze), Zé Luís. Trainer: Oleg Kononov.

Goals: 1-0 Samuel Chukwueze (11), 2-0 Karl Toko Ekambi (48).

13.12.2018; Allianz Stadion, Wien; Referee: Paolo Mazzoleni (Italy); Attendance: 23,850

SK Rapid Wien – Rangers FC Glasgow **1-0(0-0)**

SK Rapid Wien: Richard Strebinger, Stephan Auer, Maximilian Hofmann, Boli Bolingoli-Mbombo, Mateo Barac, Mert Müldür, Stefan Schwab, Thomas Murg (46.Christoph Knasmüllner), Manuel Martic (78.Dejan Ljubicic), Veton Berisha, Andrei Ivan (62.Philipp Schobesberger). Trainer: Dietmar Kühbauer.

Rangers: Allan McGregor, Gareth McAuley, James Tavernier, Connor Goldson, Borna Barisic, Ross McCrorie, Scott Arfield, Ryan Jack (79.Kyle Lafferty), Lassana Coulibaly (71.Eros Grezda), Alfredo Morelos, Glenn Middleton. Trainer: Steven Gerrard.

Goal: 1-0 Dejan Ljubicic (84).

GROUP H

1.	**Eintracht Frankfurt**	6	6	0	0	17	-	5	18
2.	**SS Lazio Roma**	6	3	0	3	9	-	11	9
3.	Apollon Limassol FC	6	2	1	3	10	-	10	7
4.	Olympique de Marseille	6	0	1	5	6	-	16	1

20.09.2018; Stade Vélodrome, Marseille; Referee: Matej Jug (Slovenia); Attendance: n/a

Olympique de Marseille – Eintracht Frankfurt **1-2(1-0)**

Olympique de Marseille: Yohann Pelé, Adil Rami (7.Luiz Gustavo), Duje Caleta-Car, Boubacar Kamara, Dimitri Payet, Kevin Strootman, Bouna Sarr, Lucas Ocampos (72.Nemanja Radonjic), Maxime Lopez, Valère Germain, Florian Thauvin (84.Kostas Mitroglou). Trainer: Rudi García.

Eintracht Frankfurt: Kevin Trapp, David Abraham, Jetro Willems [*sent off 59*], Danny da Costa, Evan Obite N'Dicka, Jonathan de Guzmán (62.Simon Falette), Makoto Hasebe, Filip Kostic, Lucas Torró, Mijat Gacinovic (46.Nicolai Müller), Sébastien Haller (75.Luka Jovic). Trainer: Adi Hütter.

Goals: 1-0 Lucas Ocampos (3), 1-1 Lucas Torró (52), 1-2 Luka Jovic (89).

20.09.2018; Stadio Olimpico, Roma; Referee: Aliyar Agayev (Azerbaijan); Attendance: 11,898

SS Lazio Roma – Apollon Limassol FC **2-1(1-0)**

Lazio Roma: Silvio Proto, Dusan Basta, Martín Cáceres, Francesco Acerbi, Riza Durmisi, Bastos, Milan Badelj (61.Lucas Leiva), Luis Alberto (62.Ciro Immobile), Sergej Milinkovic-Savic (73.Senad Lulic), Alessandro Murgia, Felipe Caicedo. Trainer: Simone Inzaghi.

Apollon: Bruno Vale, Valentin Roberge, Charis Kyriakou (46.Sasa Markovic), André Schembri, Facundo Pereyra (69.Emilio Zelaya), Héctor Yuste, Giorgos Vasiliou, Esteban Sachetti, João Pedro, Fotis Papoulis, Anton Maglica (46.Mustapha Carayol). Trainer: Sofronis Avgousti.

Goals: 1-0 Luis Alberto (14), 2-0 Ciro Immobile (84 penalty), 2-1 Emilio Zelaya (87).

04.10.2018; Stádio Neo GSP, Nicosia; Referee: Harald Lechner (Austria); Attendance: 3,031

Apollon Limassol FC – Olympique de Marseille **2-2(0-0)**

Apollon: Bruno Vale, Valentin Roberge, Kévin Bru, Richard Soumah, Facundo Pereyra, Héctor Yuste (11.Sasa Markovic), Mustapha Carayol (65.Anton Maglica), Esteban Sachetti, Emilio Zelaya, João Pedro, Adrián Sardinero (54.Fotis Papoulis). Trainer: Sofronis Avgousti.

Olympique de Marseille: Yohann Pelé, Hiroki Sakai (46.Bouna Sarr), Jordan Amavi, Duje Caleta-Car, Boubacar Kamara, Dimitri Payet, Luiz Gustavo (75.Grégory Sertic), Kevin Strootman, Maxime Lopez, Kostas Mitroglou (46.Valère Germain), Nemanja Radonjic. Trainer: Rudi García.

Goals: 0-1 Dimitri Payet (50), 0-2 Luiz Gustavo (67), 1-2 Sasa Markovic (74), 2-2 Emilio Zelaya (90).

04.10.2018; Commerzbank-Arena, Frankfurt am Main; Referee: Serdar Gözübüyük (Netherlands); Attendance: 47,000

Eintracht Frankfurt – SS Lazio Roma **4-1(2-1)**

Eintracht Frankfurt: Kevin Trapp, Marco Russ, Simon Falette, Danny da Costa, Jonathan de Guzmán (87.Marc Stendera), Makoto Hasebe, Filip Kostic (78.Taleb Tawatha), Lucas Torró, Mijat Gacinovic, Sébastien Haller, Luka Jovic (67.Ante Rebic). Trainer: Adi Hütter.

Lazio Roma: Silvio Proto, Dusan Basta [*sent off 45+3*], Francesco Acerbi, Riza Durmisi (18.Senad Lulic), Wallace, Luiz Felipe, Lucas Leiva (76.Luis Alberto), Marco Parolo, Joaquín Correa [*sent off 58*], Sergej Milinkovic-Savic (84.Valon Berisha), Ciro Immobile. Trainer: Simone Inzaghi.

Goals: 1-0 Danny da Costa (4), 1-1 Marco Parolo (23), 2-1 Filip Kostic (28), 3-1 Luka Jovic (52), 4-1 Danny da Costa (90+4).

25.10.2018; Commerzbank-Arena, Frankfurt am Main; Referee: Sergey Ivanov (Russia); Attendance: 47,000

Eintracht Frankfurt – Apollon Limassol FC **2-0(2-0)**

Eintracht Frankfurt: Frederik Rønnow, David Abraham (68.Marco Russ), Danny da Costa (57.Jetro Willems), Evan Obite N'Dicka, Jonathan de Guzmán, Makoto Hasebe, Gelson Fernandes, Filip Kostic, Mijat Gacinovic, Sébastien Haller, Ante Rebic (82.Luka Jovic). Trainer: Adi Hütter.

Apollon: Bruno Vale, Valentin Roberge, Chambos Kyriakou, Facundo Pereyra (46.Emilio Zelaya), Mustapha Carayol (46.André Schembri), Giorgos Vasiliou, Sasa Markovic, Esteban Sachetti, João Pedro, Fotis Papoulis, Anton Maglica (67.Marios Stylianou). Trainer: Sofronis Avgousti.

Goals: 1-0 Filip Kostic (13), 2-0 Sébastien Haller (32).

25.10.2018; Stade Vélodrome, Marseille; Referee: Jesús Gil Manzano (Spain); Attendance: 31,930

Olympique de Marseille – SS Lazio Roma 1-3(0-1)

Olympique de Marseille: Steve Mandanda, Adil Rami, Hiroki Sakai, Jordan Amavi (80.Bouna Sarr), Boubacar Kamara, Dimitri Payet, Luiz Gustavo, Kevin Strootman, Lucas Ocampos, Morgan Sanson (66.Clinton N'Jie), Kostas Mitroglou (66.Valère Germain). Trainer: Rudi García.

Lazio Roma: Thomas Strakosha, Stefan Radu, Martín Cáceres, Francesco Acerbi, Wallace, Lucas Leiva (48.Adam Marusic), Senad Lulic (62.Valon Berisha), Marco Parolo, Sergej Milinkovic-Savic, Felipe Caicedo (74.Danilo Cataldi), Ciro Immobile. Trainer: Simone Inzaghi.

Goals: 0-1 Wallace (10), 0-2 Felipe Caicedo (59), 1-2 Dimitri Payet (86), 1-3 Adam Marusic (90)

08.11.2018; Stádio Neo GSP, Nicosia; Referee: Tiago Bruno Lopes Martins (Portugal); Attendance: 6,888

Apollon Limassol FC – Eintracht Frankfurt 2-3(0-1)

Apollon: Tasos Kissas, Valentin Roberge, Chambos Kyriakou, Dylan Ouédraogo, André Schembri (68.David Faupala), Giorgos Vasiliou (61.João Pedro), Sasa Markovic, Marios Stylianou, Esteban Sachetti, Anton Maglica (46.Emilio Zelaya), Adrián Sardinero. Trainer: Sofronis Avgousti.

Eintracht Frankfurt: Kevin Trapp, David Abraham, Jetro Willems, Danny da Costa, Evan Obite N'Dicka, Makoto Hasebe, Gelson Fernandes (77.Jonathan de Guzmán), Mijat Gacinovic, Marc Stendera [*sent off 81*], Sébastien Haller (66.Ante Rebic), Luka Jovic (85.Nicolai Müller). Trainer: Adi Hütter.

Goals: 0-1 Luka Jovic (17), 0-2 Sébastien Haller (55), 0-3 Mijat Gacinovic (58), 1-3, 2-3 Emilio Zelaya (71, 90+4 penalty).

08.11.2018; Stadio Olimpico, Roma; Referee: Vladislav Bezborodov (Russia); Attendance: 14,705

SS Lazio Roma – Olympique de Marseille 2-1(1-0)

Lazio Roma: Thomas Strakosha, Francesco Acerbi, Riza Durmisi, Adam Marusic, Wallace (57.Bastos), Luiz Felipe, Marco Parolo, Valon Berisha (70.Sergej Milinkovic-Savic), Joaquín Correa (82.Luis Alberto), Danilo Cataldi, Ciro Immobile. Trainer: Simone Inzaghi.

Olympique de Marseille: Yohann Pelé, Adil Rami (79.Bouna Sarr), Hiroki Sakai, Duje Caleta-Car, Luiz Gustavo, Kevin Strootman, Lucas Ocampos, Morgan Sanson (69.Dimitri Payet), Maxime Lopez, Florian Thauvin (82.Kostas Mitroglou), Clinton N'Jie. Trainer: Rudi García.

Goals: 1-0 Marco Parolo (45+1), 2-0 Joaquín Correa (55), 2-1 Florian Thauvin (60).

29.11.2018; Commerzbank-Arena, Frankfurt am Main; Referee: John Beaton (Scotland); Attendance: 47,000

Eintracht Frankfurt – Olympique de Marseille 4-0(2-0)

Eintracht Frankfurt: Kevin Trapp, Marco Russ, Taleb Tawatha (64.Filip Kostic), Jetro Willems, Simon Falette, Danny da Costa, Makoto Hasebe, Gelson Fernandes, Mijat Gacinovic, Sébastien Haller (73.Ante Rebic), Luka Jovic (80.Nicolai Müller). Trainer: Adi Hütter.

Olympique de Marseille: Yohann Pelé, Tomás Hubocan, Jordan Amavi, Duje Caleta-Car, Boubacar Kamara, Luiz Gustavo, Bouna Sarr (80.Christopher Rocchia), Maxime Lopez (61.Rolando), Kostas Mitroglou, Valère Germain (64.Florian Chabrolle), Nemanja Radonjic. Trainer: Rudi García.

Goals: 1-0 Luka Jovic (2), 2-0 Luiz Gustavo (17 own goal), 3-0 Bouna Sarr (62 own goal), 4-0 Luka Jovic (67).

29.11.2018; Stádio Neo GSP, Nicosia; Referee: Roi Reinshreiber (Israel); Attendance: 1,131

Apollon Limassol FC – SS Lazio Roma 2-0(1-0)

Apollon: Bruno Vale, Valentin Roberge, Dylan Ouédraogo, Richard Soumah, André Schembri (66.Fotis Papoulis), Sasa Markovic, Esteban Sachetti, Danilo Spoljaric, João Pedro, Adrián Sardinero (78.Emilio Zelaya), David Faupala (66.Anton Maglica). Trainer: Sofronis Avgousti.

Lazio Roma: Silvio Proto, Martín Cáceres, Francesco Acerbi, Riza Durmisi, Bastos (60.Senad Lulic), Luiz Felipe, Valon Berisha, Joaquín Correa, Danilo Cataldi, Alessandro Murgia (60.Alessandro Rossi), Felipe Caicedo (85.Nicolò Armini). Trainer: Simone Inzaghi.

Goals: 1-0 David Faupala (31), 2-0 Sasa Markovic (82).

13.12.2018; Stade Vélodrome, Marseille; Referee: Radu Petrescu (Romania); Attendance: 9,274

Olympique de Marseille – Apollon Limassol FC 1-3(1-2)

Olympique de Marseille: Florian Escales, Adil Rami, Hiroki Sakai, Duje Caleta-Car, Boubacar Kamara [*sent off 7*], Dimitri Payet (76.Clinton N'Jie), Luiz Gustavo, Kevin Strootman (59.Bouna Sarr), Lucas Ocampos [*sent off 90+3*], Maxime Lopez, Florian Thauvin (62.Nemanja Radonjic). Trainer: Rudi García.

Apollon: Bruno Vale, Valentin Roberge, Chambos Kyriakou, Dylan Ouédraogo, Kévin Bru (46.Fotis Papoulis), André Schembri (59.David Faupala), Giorgos Vasiliou, Sasa Markovic, Marios Stylianou, Anton Maglica (71.Richard Soumah), Adrián Sardinero. Trainer: Sofronis Avgousti.

Goals: 0-1 Anton Maglica (8 penalty), 1-1 Florian Thauvin (11), 1-2 Anton Maglica (30), 1-3 Marios Stylianou (56).

13.12.2018; Stadio Olimpico, Roma; Referee: Halil Umut Meler (Turkey); Attendance: 18,252

SS Lazio Roma – Eintracht Frankfurt 1-2(0-0)

Lazio Roma: Silvio Proto, Martín Cáceres (75.Senad Lulic), Francesco Acerbi, Riza Durmisi, Bastos, Luiz Felipe, Valon Berisha (75.Alessandro Rossi), Luis Alberto, Joaquín Correa, Danilo Cataldi, Alessandro Murgia. Trainer: Simone Inzaghi.

Eintracht Frankfurt: Frederik Rønnow, Marco Russ, Taleb Tawatha, Jetro Willems, Simon Falette, Danny da Costa, Makoto Hasebe (32.Evan Obite N'Dicka), Gelson Fernandes, Nicolai Müller (79.Luka Jovic), Mijat Gacinovic (88.Marc Stendera), Sébastien Haller. Trainer: Adi Hütter.

Goals: 1-0 Joaquín Correa (56), 1-1 Mijat Gacinovic (65), 1-2 Sébastien Haller (71).

GROUP I

1.	**KRC Genk**	6	3	2	1	14	-	8	11
2.	**Malmö FF**	6	2	3	1	7	-	6	9
3.	Beşiktaş JK İstanbul	6	2	1	3	9	-	11	7
4.	Sarpsborg 08 FF	6	1	2	3	8	-	13	5

20.09.2018; Vodafone Stadyumu, İstanbul; Referee: Tamás Bognár (Hungary); Attendance: 24,955

Beşiktaş JK İstanbul – Sarpsborg 08 FF 3-1(0-0)

Beşiktaş: Loris Karius, Pepe, Caner Erkin, Gökhan Gönül (85.Necip Uysal), Gary Medel, Enzo Roco, Jeremain Lens, Gökhan Töre (46.Ryan Babel), Oguzhan Özyakup, Adem Ljajic (78.Tolgay Arslan), Cyle Larin. Trainer: Senol Günes.

Sarpsborg 08: Alexander Vasyutin, Jørgen Horn, Amin Askar, Joachim Thomassen, Joonas Tamm, Matti Lund Nielsen (86.Gaute Vetti), Ole Halvorsen (70.Harmeet Singh), Kristoffer Zachariassen, Tobias Heintz, Patrick Mortensen, Rashad Muhammed (81.Jørgen Larsen). Trainer: Geir Bakke.

Goals: 1-0 Ryan Babel (51), 2-0 Enzo Roco (69), 3-0 Jeremain Lens (82), 3-1 Kristoffer Zachariassen (90+4).

20.09.2018; Luminus Arena, Genk; Referee: Aleksey Eskov (Russia); Attendance: 11,590

KRC Genk – Malmö FF 2-0(1-0)

KRC Genk: Danny Vukovic, Sebastien Dewaest, Jere Uronen, Joseph Aidoo, Joakim Mæhle, Pozuelo (76.Ibrahima Seck), Ruslan Malinovskiy, Sander Berge, Leandro Trossard, Mbwana Samatta (86.Marcus Ingvartsen), Dieumerci N'Dongala (72.Joseph Paintsil). Trainer: Philippe Clement.

Malmö FF: Johan Dahlin, Behrang Safari (80.Egzon Binaku), Rasmus Bengtsson, Lasse Nielsen, Andreas Vindheim, Søren Rieks, Anders Christiansen (86.Romain Gall), Fouad Bachirou, Oscar Lewicki, Markus Rosenberg, Marcus Antonsson (55.Arnór Ingvi Traustason). Trainer: Uwe Rösler.

Goals: 1-0 Leandro Trossard (37), 2-0 Mbwana Samatta (71).

04.10.2018; Swedbank Stadion, Malmö; Referee: Aleksandar Stavrev (North Macedonia); Attendance: 17,174

Malmö FF – Beşiktaş JK İstanbul 2-0(0-0)

Malmö FF: Johan Dahlin, Behrang Safari, Rasmus Bengtsson, Lasse Nielsen (90+2.Franz Brorsson), Andreas Vindheim, Søren Rieks, Anders Christiansen (72.Bonke Innocent), Fouad Bachirou, Arnór Ingvi Traustason (85.Marcus Antonsson), Oscar Lewicki, Markus Rosenberg. Trainer: Uwe Rösler.

Beşiktaş: Loris Karius, Pepe, Caner Erkin, Gökhan Gönül (82.Oguzhan Özyakup), Gary Medel, Domagoj Vida, Jeremain Lens, Necip Uysal, Gökhan Töre (59.Ryan Babel), Vágner Love, Adem Ljajic (70.Ricardo Quaresma). Trainer: Senol Günes.

Goals: 1-0 Caner Erkin (53 own goal), 2-0 Markus Rosenberg (76 penalty).

04.10.2018; Sarpsborg Stadion, Sarpsborg; Referee: Ivan Bebek (Croatia); Attendance: 7,885

Sarpsborg 08 FF – KRC Genk 3-1(1-0)

Sarpsborg 08: Alexander Vasyutin, Amin Askar, Joackim Jørgensen, Joachim Thomassen, Joonas Tamm, Matti Lund Nielsen, Ole Halvorsen (73.Tobias Heintz), Jon-Helge Tveita, Kristoffer Zachariassen, Patrick Mortensen, Rashad Muhammed (82.Harmeet Singh). Trainer: Geir Bakke.

KRC Genk: Danny Vukovic, Sebastien Dewaest, Bojan Nastic (46.Jere Uronen), Jhon Lucumí, Joakim Mæhle, Pozuelo, Ruslan Malinovskiy (66.Bryan Heynen), Sander Berge, Leandro Trossard, Mbwana Samatta, Dieumerci N'Dongala (46.Joseph Paintsil). Trainer: Philippe Clement.

Goals: 1-0 Patrick Mortensen (6), 1-1 Leandro Trossard (49), 2-1 Kristoffer Zachariassen (54), 3-1 Patrick Mortensen (63).

25.10.2018; Sarpsborg Stadion, Sarpsborg; Referee: Pawel Raczkowski (Poland); Attendance: 8,022

Sarpsborg 08 FF – Malmö FF 1-1(0-0)

Sarpsborg 08: Alexander Vasyutin, Jørgen Horn, Amin Askar (85.Jørgen Larsen), Joachim Thomassen, Joonas Tamm, Matti Lund Nielsen (87.Harmeet Singh), Ole Halvorsen, Jon-Helge Tveita, Kristoffer Zachariassen, Patrick Mortensen, Rashad Muhammed (77.Tobias Heintz). Trainer: Geir Bakke.

Malmö FF: Johan Dahlin, Behrang Safari, Rasmus Bengtsson (57.Franz Brorsson), Lasse Nielsen, Andreas Vindheim, Søren Rieks, Anders Christiansen (83.Bonke Innocent), Fouad Bachirou, Arnór Ingvi Traustason, Oscar Lewicki (65.Marcus Antonsson), Markus Rosenberg. Trainer: Uwe Rösler.

Goals: 0-1 Andreas Vindheim (79), 1-1 Ole Halvorsen (87)-

25.10.2018; Vodafone Stadyumu, İstanbul; Referee: Daniel Stefanski (Poland); Attendance: 25,209

Beşiktaş JK İstanbul – KRC Genk 2-4(0-1)

Beşiktaş: Loris Karius, Caner Erkin (85.Mustafa Pektemek), Gökhan Gönül, Gary Medel, Domagoj Vida, Jeremain Lens, Ricardo Quaresma, Necip Uysal, Tolgay Arslan (27.Enzo Roco), Oguzhan Özyakup, Cyle Larin (46.Vágner Love). Trainer: Senol Günes.

KRC Genk: Danny Vukovic, Sebastien Dewaest, Jere Uronen, Jhon Lucumí, Joakim Mæhle, Pozuelo (80.Ibrahima Seck), Ruslan Malinovskiy, Bryan Heynen, Mbwana Samatta (87.Zinho Gano), Dieumerci N'Dongala, Joseph Paintsil (75.Jakub Piotrowski). Trainer: Philippe Clement.

Goals: 0-1, 0-2 Mbwana Samatta (23, 70), 1-2 Vágner Love (74), 1-3 Dieumerci N'Dongala (81), 1-4 Jakub Piotrowski (83), 2-4 Vágner Love (86).

08.11.2018; Swedbank Stadion, Malmö; Referee: Miroslav Zelinka (Czech Republic); Attendance: 17,601

Malmö FF – Sarpsborg 08 FF 1-1(0-0)

Malmö FF: Johan Dahlin, Behrang Safari (86.Romain Gall), Rasmus Bengtsson, Lasse Nielsen, Andreas Vindheim (61.Eric Larsson), Søren Rieks, Anders Christiansen, Fouad Bachirou, Arnór Ingvi Traustason, Markus Rosenberg, Marcus Antonsson (79.Carlos Strandberg). Trainer: Uwe Rösler.

Sarpsborg 08: Alexander Vasyutin, Jørgen Horn, Amin Askar, Joachim Thomassen, Joonas Tamm, Matti Lund Nielsen, Ole Halvorsen, Jon-Helge Tveita, Gaute Vetti (90+1.Joackim Jørgensen), Patrick Mortensen, Rashad Muhammed (73.Tobias Heintz). Trainer: Geir Bakke.

Goals: 0-1 Patrick Mortensen (63), 1-1 Marcus Antonsson (67).

08.11.2018; Luminus Arena, Genk; Referee: Tobias Stieler (Germany); Attendance: 14,292

KRC Genk – Beşiktaş JK İstanbul 1-1(0-1)

KRC Genk: Danny Vukovic, Sebastien Dewaest, Jere Uronen, Joseph Aidoo, Joakim Mæhle, Pozuelo, Ruslan Malinovskiy (60.Sander Berge), Bryan Heynen, Mbwana Samatta, Dieumerci N'Dongala (89.Marcus Ingvartsen), Joseph Paintsil (66.Ivan Fiolic). Trainer: Philippe Clement.

Beşiktaş: Tolga Zengin, Pepe, Caner Erkin, Gary Medel, Domagoj Vida, Dorukhan Toköz (73.Adem Ljajic), Jeremain Lens (12.Mustafa Pektemek), Ricardo Quaresma, Necip Uysal, Oguzhan Özyakup (90.Vágner Love), Ryan Babel. Trainer: Senol Günes.

Goals: 0-1 Ricardo Quaresma (16), 1-1 Sander Berge (87).

29.11.2018; Sarpsborg Stadion, Sarpsborg; Referee: Harald Lechner (Austria); Attendance: 8,022

Sarpsborg 08 FF – Beşiktaş JK İstanbul 2-3(2-0)

Sarpsborg 08: Alexander Vasyutin, Jørgen Horn, Joachim Thomassen, Joonas Tamm (50.Joackim Jørgensen), Matti Lund Nielsen, Ole Halvorsen, Jon-Helge Tveita, Kristoffer Zachariassen, Tobias Heintz (68.Amin Askar), Patrick Mortensen, Rashad Muhammed (85.Jørgen Larsen). Trainer: Geir Bakke.

Beşiktaş: Loris Karius, Adriano (78.Fatih Aksoy), Caner Erkin, Domagoj Vida, Dorukhan Toköz, Jeremain Lens (90+2.Erdem Seçgin), Necip Uysal, Oguzhan Özyakup, Adem Ljajic, Mustafa Pektemek, Cyle Larin (58.Vágner Love). Trainer: Senol Günes.

Goals: 1-0 Rashad Muhammed (1), 2-0 Tobias Heintz (6), 2-1 Jeremain Lens (62), 2-2 Vágner Love (66), 2-3 Jeremain Lens (90).

29.11.2018; Swedbank Stadion, Malmö; Referee: Srđan Jovanović (Serbia); Attendance: 16,117

Malmö FF – KRC Genk 2-2(0-1)

Malmö FF: Johan Dahlin, Behrang Safari (81.Franz Brorsson), Rasmus Bengtsson, Lasse Nielsen, Andreas Vindheim, Søren Rieks, Anders Christiansen (82.Romain Gall), Fouad Bachirou, Arnór Ingvi Traustason (54.Marcus Antonsson), Oscar Lewicki, Markus Rosenberg. Trainer: Uwe Rösler.

KRC Genk: Danny Vukovic, Sebastien Dewaest, Jere Uronen, Joseph Aidoo, Joakim Mæhle, Pozuelo (86.Bryan Heynen), Ruslan Malinovskiy, Sander Berge, Leandro Trossard, Mbwana Samatta (73.Zinho Gano), Joseph Paintsil (54.Dieumerci N'Dongala). Trainer: Philippe Clement.

Goals: 0-1 Pozuelo (42), 0-2 Joseph Paintsil (53), 1-2 Oscar Lewicki (65), 2-2 Marcus Antonsson (67).

13.12.2018; Vodafone Stadyumu, İstanbul; Referee: Luca Banti (Italy); Attendance: 24,955

Beşiktaş JK İstanbul – Malmö FF 0-1(0-0)

Beşiktaş: Loris Karius, Adriano, Gary Medel, Domagoj Vida, Dorukhan Toköz, Ricardo Quaresma [*sent off 65*], Necip Uysal, Oguzhan Özyakup (60.Gökhan Töre), Vágner Love (72.Cyle Larin), Adem Ljajic, Mustafa Pektemek (78.Fatih Aksoy). Trainer: Senol Günes.

Malmö FF: Johan Dahlin, Behrang Safari (55.Franz Brorsson), Rasmus Bengtsson, Lasse Nielsen, Andreas Vindheim, Søren Rieks (80.Eric Larsson), Fouad Bachirou, Arnór Ingvi Traustason (75.Anders Christiansen), Oscar Lewicki, Markus Rosenberg, Marcus Antonsson. Trainer: Uwe Rösler.

Goal: 0-1 Marcus Antonsson (51).

13.12.2018; Luminus Arena, Genk; Referee: István Kovács (Romania); Attendance: 12,240

KRC Genk – Sarpsborg 08 FF 4-0(2-0)

KRC Genk: Danny Vukovic, Sebastien Dewaest, Jere Uronen (75.Bojan Nastic), Joseph Aidoo, Joakim Mæhle, Pozuelo (65.Ruslan Malinovskiy), Ibrahima Seck, Sander Berge, Leandro Trossard (80.Dieumerci N'Dongala), Zinho Gano, Joseph Paintsil. Trainer: Philippe Clement.

Sarpsborg 08: Alexander Vasyutin, Jørgen Horn, Joachim Thomassen (56.Amin Askar), Joonas Tamm, Matti Lund Nielsen, Ole Halvorsen (82.Kristoffer Larsen), Jon-Helge Tveita, Kristoffer Zachariassen, Tobias Heintz, Patrick Mortensen, Rashad Muhammed (62.Jørgen Larsen). Trainer: Geir Bakke.

Goals: 1-0 Zinho Gano (3), 2-0 Joseph Paintsil (5), 3-0 Sander Berge (64), 4-0 Joseph Aidoo (67).

GROUP J

1.	**Sevilla FC**	6	4	0	2	18	-	6	12
2.	**FK Krasnodar**	6	4	0	2	8	-	8	12
3.	R Standard Liège	6	3	1	2	7	-	9	10
4.	Akhisar Belediye Gençlik ve Spor Kulübü	6	0	1	5	4	-	14	1

20.09.2018; Estadio „Ramón Sánchez Pizjuán", Sevilla; Referee: Gediminas Mažeika (Lithuania); Attendance: 30,003

Sevilla FC – R Standard Liège 5-1(2-1)

Sevilla FC: Tomás Vaclík, Simon Kjær, Daniel Carriço, Sergi Gómez, Guilherme Arana, Jesús Navas (80.Nolito), Éver Banega, Franco Vázquez (76.Pablo Sarabia), Ibrahim Amadou (15.Roque Mesa), Wissam Ben Yedder, Quincy Promes. Trainer: Pablo Machín.

Standard Liège: Guillermo Ochoa, Luis Cavanda, Kostas Laifis, Collins Fai, Zinho Vanheusden, Christian Luyindama Nekadio, Mehdi Carcela-González (78.Uche Agbo), Gojko Cimirot, Razvan Marin, Moussa Djenepo (62.Maxime Lestienne), Orlando Sá (62.Renaud Emond). Trainer: Michel Preud'homme.

Goals: 1-0 Éver Banega (8), 1-1 Moussa Djenepo (39), 2-1 Franco Vázquez (41), 3-1, 4-1 Wissam Ben Yedder (49, 70), 5-1 Éver Banega (74 penalty).

20.09.2018; Spor Toto Akhisar Belediye Stadı, Akhisar; Referee: Ville Nevalainen (Finland); Attendance: 6,555

Akhisar Belediye Gençlik ve Spor Kulübü – FK Krasnodar 0-1(0-1)

Akhisar Belediye: Fatih Öztürk, Avdija Vrsajevic, Kadir Keles (81.Onur Ayik), Mustafa Yumlu, Caner Osmanpasa, Serginho, Güray Vural, Abdoulwhaid Sissoko, Josué (60.Bilal Kisa), Adrien Regattin (60.Elvis Manu), Evgen Seleznyov. Trainer: Cem Kavcak.

FK Krasnodar: Stanislav Kritsyuk, Aleksandr Martynovich, Uros Spajic, Cristian Ramírez, Pavel Mamaev (69.Mauricio Pereyra), Charles Kaboré, Dmitriy Stotskiy, Yuri Gazinskiy, Victor Claesson, Ari (84.Sergey Petrov), Wamberto (79.Christian Cueva). Trainer: Murad Musaev.

Goal: 0-1 Victor Claesson (26).

04.10.2018; Stadion FK Krasnodar, Krasnodar; Referee: Martin Strömbergsson (Sweden); Attendance: 31,346

FK Krasnodar – Sevilla FC 2-1(0-1)

FK Krasnodar: Stanislav Kritsyuk, Aleksandr Martynovich, Uros Spajic, Cristian Ramírez, Pavel Mamaev (74.Magomed Suleymanov), Charles Kaboré (69.Mauricio Pereyra), Christian Cueva, Yuri Gazinskiy, Sergey Petrov, Victor Claesson, Wamberto (84.Tornike Okriashvili). Trainer: Murad Musaev.

Sevilla FC: Tomás Vaclík, Simon Kjær, Sergi Gómez, Guilherme Arana, Joris Gnagnon, Jesús Navas, Éver Banega, Roque Mesa, Nolito (76.Franco Vázquez), Luis Muriel (61.André Silva), Quincy Promes (77.Wissam Ben Yedder). Trainer: Pablo Machín.

Goals: 0-1 Charles Kaboré (43 own goal), 1-1 Mauricio Pereyra (72), 2-1 Tornike Okriashvili (88).

04.10.2018; Stade „Maurice Dufrasne“, Liège; Referee: Manuel Schüttengruber (Austria); Attendance: 8,233

R Standard Liège – Akhisar Belediye Gençlik ve Spor Kulübü 2-1(2-1)

Standard Liège: Guillermo Ochoa, Sébastien Pocognoli, Luis Cavanda, Kostas Laifis, Christian Luyindama Nekadio, Mehdi Carcela-González, Gojko Cimirot, Razvan Marin, Uche Agbo (76.Paul M'Poku), Moussa Djenepo, Renaud Emond (83.Orlando Sá). Trainer: Michel Preud'homme.

Akhisar Belediye: Fatih Öztürk, Miguel Lopes, Mustafa Yumlu [*sent off 82*], Caner Osmanpasa, Bilal Kisa (40.Abdoulwhaid Sissoko), Güray Vural, Josué, Aykut Çeviker, Hélder Barbosa, Evgen Seleznyov (80.Elvis Manu), Onur Ayik (72.Adrien Regattin). Trainer: Cihat Arslan.

Goals: 1-0 Renaud Emond (17), 1-1 Onur Ayik (32), 2-1 Moussa Djenepo (40).

25.10.2018; Stade „Maurice Dufrasne“, Liège; Referee: Marco Guida (Italy); Attendance: 8,393

R Standard Liège – FK Krasnodar 2-1(0-1)

Standard Liège: Guillermo Ochoa, Sébastien Pocognoli, Luis Cavanda, Kostas Laifis, Collins Fai (78.Maxime Lestienne), Christian Luyindama Nekadio, Mehdi Carcela-González, Gojko Cimirot, Razvan Marin, Uche Agbo (46.Moussa Djenepo), Renaud Emond (84.Samuel Bastien). Trainer: Michel Preud'homme.

FK Krasnodar: Andrey Sinitsyn, Aleksandr Martynovich, Uros Spajic, Cristian Ramírez, Charles Kaboré, Mauricio Pereyra (77.Christian Cueva), Yuri Gazinskiy, Sergey Petrov, Victor Claesson, Ari (76.Ivan Ignatyev), Wamberto (80.Magomed Suleymanov). Trainer: Murad Musaev.

Goals: 0-1 Ari (39), 1-1 Renaud Emond (47), 2-1 Kostas Laifis (90+3).

25.10.2018; Estadio „Ramón Sánchez Pizjuán“, Sevilla; Referee: Kevin Clancy (Scotland); Attendance: 29,720

Sevilla FC – Akhisar Belediye Gençlik ve Spor Kulübü 6-0(3-0)

Sevilla FC: Tomás Vaclík, Gabriel Mercado, Daniel Carriço (59.Ibrahim Amadou), Aleix Vidal, Sergi Gómez, Jesús Navas (54.Nolito), Franco Vázquez, Pablo Sarabia (54.Guilherme Arana), Roque Mesa, Luis Muriel, Quincy Promes. Trainer: Pablo Machín.

Akhisar Belediye: Milan Lukac, Miguel Lopes, Kadir Keles (46.Hélder Barbosa), Dany Nounkeu, Caner Osmanpasa, Güray Vural, Abdoulwhaid Sissoko, Josué (77.Eray Ataseven), Adrien Regattin, Aykut Çeviker, Evgen Seleznyov (63.Onur Ayik). Trainer: Cihat Arslan.

Goals: 1-0 Roque Mesa (7), 2-0 Pablo Sarabia (9 penalty), 3-0 Milan Lukac (35 own goal), 4-0 Luis Muriel (50), 5-0 Quincy Promes (60), 6-0 Gabriel Mercado (67).

08.11.2018; Stadion FK Krasnodar, Krasnodar; Referee: Aleksandar Stavrev (North Macedonia); Attendance: 21,526

FK Krasnodar – R Standard Liège 2-1(0-1)

FK Krasnodar: Matvei Safonov, Aleksandr Martynovich, Uros Spajic, Charles Kaboré (73.Magomed Suleymanov), Christian Cueva (46.Mauricio Pereyra), Dmitriy Stotskiy, Yuri Gazinskiy, Sergey Petrov, Victor Claesson (66.Ivan Ignatyev), Ari, Wamberto. Trainer: Murad Musaev.

Standard Liège: Guillermo Ochoa, Kostas Laifis, Collins Fai, Zinho Vanheusden, Christian Luyindama Nekadio, Mehdi Carcela-González, Maxime Lestienne (83.Samuel Bastien), Gojko Cimirot, Razvan Marin (89.Paul M'Poku), Moussa Djenepo (89.Orlando Sá), Renaud Emond. Trainer: Michel Preud'homme.

Goals: 0-1 Mehdi Carcela-González (19), 1-1 Magomed Suleymanov (79), 2-1 Wamberto (82).

08.11.2018; Spor Toto Akhisar Belediye Stadı, Akhisar; Referee: Benoît Millot (France); Attendance: 6,430

Akhisar Belediye Gençlik ve Spor Kulübü – Sevilla FC 2-3(0-2)

Akhisar Belediye: Milan Lukac, Avdija Vrsajevic, Miguel Lopes, Caner Osmanpasa (46.Kadir Keles), Güray Vural, Abdoulwhaid Sissoko, Josué, Aykut Çeviker, Eray Ataseven (72.Onur Ayik), Hélder Barbosa (88.Bilal Kisa), Elvis Manu. Trainer: Cihat Arslan.

Sevilla FC: Tomás Vaclík, Sergio Escudero, Aleix Vidal, Sergi Gómez [*sent off 56*], Joris Gnagnon, Éver Banega, Franco Vázquez, Ibrahim Amadou, Nolito (64.Roque Mesa), Luis Muriel (74.Pablo Sarabia), Quincy Promes (88.Daniel Carriço). Trainer: Pablo Machín.

Goals: 0-1 Nolito (12), 0-2 Luis Muriel (38), 1-2 Elvis Manu (52), 2-2 Onur Ayik (78), 2-3 Éver Banega (87 penalty).

29.11.2018; Stadion FK Krasnodar, Krasnodar; Referee: Ivaylo Stoyanov (Bulgaria); Attendance: 11,008

FK Krasnodar – Akhisar Belediye Gençlik ve Spor Kulübü 2-1(0-1)

FK Krasnodar: Matvei Safonov, Aleksandr Martynovich, Uros Spajic, Cristian Ramírez, Charles Kaboré, Christian Cueva (70.Magomed Suleymanov), Dmitriy Stotskiy (46.Ivan Ignatyev), Yuri Gazinskiy, Sergey Petrov, Ari (72.Mauricio Pereyra), Wamberto. Trainer: Murad Musaev.

Akhisar Belediye: Milan Lukac, Avdija Vrsajevic, Miguel Lopes, Caner Osmanpasa, Serginho (84.Kadir Keles), Güray Vural, Abdoulwhaid Sissoko, Adrien Regattin, Aykut Çeviker (72.Eray Ataseven), Hélder Barbosa, Elvis Manu (42.Onur Ayik). Trainer: Cihat Arslan.

Goals: 0-1 Serginho (24), 1-1 Yuri Gazinskiy (49), 2-1 Ari (57).

29.11.2018; Stade „Maurice Dufrasne“, Liège; Referee: Daniel Siebert (Germany); Attendance: 12,882

R Standard Liège – Sevilla FC 1-0(0-0)

Standard Liège: Guillermo Ochoa, Kostas Laifis, Collins Fai, Zinho Vanheusden, Christian Luyindama Nekadio, Mehdi Carcela-González (85.Maxime Lestienne), Gojko Cimirot, Paul M'Poku (43.Razvan Marin), Samuel Bastien, Moussa Djenepo, Renaud Emond (65.Orlando Sá). Trainer: Michel Preud'homme.

Sevilla FC: Tomás Vaclík, Simon Kjær, Gabriel Mercado, Daniel Carriço, Aleix Vidal (52.Pablo Sarabia [*sent off 68*]), Guilherme Arana (85.Luis Muriel), Éver Banega, Franco Vázquez (76.André Silva), Roque Mesa, Wissam Ben Yedder, Quincy Promes. Trainer: Pablo Machín.

Goals: 1-0 Moussa Djenepo (62).

13.12.2018; Estadio „Ramón Sánchez Pizjuán“, Sevilla; Referee: Daniel Stefanski (Poland); Attendance: 34,114

Sevilla FC – FK Krasnodar 3-0(2-0)

Sevilla FC: Tomás Vaclík, Gabriel Mercado, Daniel Carriço, Sergio Escudero, Sergi Gómez, Éver Banega (70.Ibrahim Amadou), Franco Vázquez, Roque Mesa, Wissam Ben Yedder (72.Jesús Navas), Quincy Promes, André Silva (77.Luis Muriel). Trainer: Pablo Machín.

FK Krasnodar: Stanislav Kritsyuk, Jón Fjóluson, Aleksandr Martynovich, Cristian Ramírez [*sent off 48*], Charles Kaboré, Mauricio Pereyra (51.Dmitriy Stotskiy), Yuri Gazinskiy, Sergey Petrov, Victor Claesson, Wamberto (77.Roman Shishkin), Ivan Ignatyev (61.Christian Cueva). Trainer: Murad Musaev.

Goals: 1-0, 2-0 Wissam Ben Yedder (5, 10), 3-0 Éver Banega (49 penalty).

13.12.2018; Spor Toto Akhisar Belediye Stadı, Akhisar; Referee: Ádám Farkas (Hungary); Attendance: 2,674

Akhisar Belediye Gençlik ve Spor Kulübü – R Standard Liège 0-0

Akhisar Belediye: Milan Lukac, Avdija Vrsajevic, Kadir Keles, Caner Osmanpasa, Serginho (17.Eray Ataseven), Abdoulwhaid Sissoko, Josué, Adrien Regattin (71.Onur Ayik), Aykut Çeviker, Hélder Barbosa (90+2.Bilal Kisa), Elvis Manu. Trainer: Cihat Arslan.

Standard Liège: Guillermo Ochoa, Milos Kosanovic, Collins Fai, Zinho Vanheusden, Christian Luyindama Nekadio, Mehdi Carcela-González, Maxime Lestienne, Razvan Marin, Uche Agbo (60.Paul M'Poku), Samuel Bastien (83.Renaud Emond), Orlando Sá (83.Obbi Oularé). Trainer: Michel Preud'homme.

GROUP K

1.	**FK Dinamo Kyiv**	6	3	2	1	10 - 7	11
2.	**Stade Rennais FC**	6	3	0	3	7 - 8	9
3.	Astana FC	6	2	2	2	7 - 7	8
4.	FK Jablonec	6	1	2	3	6 - 8	5

20.09.2018; Roazhon Park, Rennes; Referee: Ole Hobber Nilsen (Norway); Attendance: 20,628

Stade Rennais FC – FK Jablonec 2-1(1-0)

Stade Rennais: Tomás Koubek, Damien Da Silva, Mexer, Hamari Traoré, Jérémy Gelin (65.Hatem Ben Arfa), Ramy Bensebaini, Clément Grenier, Benjamin André, Theoson Siebatcheu, Romain Del Castillo (61.M'Baye Niang), Ismaïli Sarr (75.Benjamin Bourigeaud). Trainer: Sabri Lamouchi.
FK Jablonec: Vlastimil Hrubý, Tomás Holes, Matej Hanousek, David Hovorka, David Lischka, Tomás Hübschman, Jakub Povazanec, Michal Trávník, Lukás Masopust (77.Vojtech Kubista), Martin Dolezal (46.Jan Chramosta), Vladimir Jovovic (88.Tomás Brecka). Trainer: Petr Rada.
Goals: 1-0 Ismaïli Sarr (31), 1-1 Michal Trávník (54), 2-1 Hatem Ben Arfa (90+1 penalty).

20.09.2018; NSK Olimpijskyj Stadium, Kyiv; Referee: Halis Özkahya (Turkey); Attendance: 21,783

FK Dinamo Kyiv – Astana FC 2-2(2-1)

Dinamo Kyiv: Denis Boyko, Josip Pivaric, Tamás Kádár, Tomasz Kedziora, Mykyta Burda, Sergiy Sydorchuk, Denys Garmash (79.Mikkel Duelund), Vitaliy Buyalskiy (90+3.Volodymyr Shepeliev), Benjamin Verbic, Viktor Tsygankov (90+1.Mikola Morozyuk), Nazariy Rusyn. Trainer: Aleksandr Khatskevich.
Astana FC: Nenad Eric, Antonio Rukavina, Marin Anicic, Dmitriy Shomko, Evgeni Postnikov, Marin Tomasov (88.Roman Murtazaev), Ivan Maevski, Richard Almeyda (80.Serikzhan Muzhikov), László Kleinheisler, Pedro Henrique, Junior Kabananga (82.Rangelo Janga). Trainer: Roman Grygorchuk.
Goals: 1-0 Viktor Tsygankov (11), 1-1 Marin Anicic (21), 2-1 Denys Garmash (45+1), 2-2 Roman Murtazaev (90+5).

04.10.2018; Astana Arena, Astana; Referee: Mattias Gestranius (Finland); Attendance: 25,302

Astana FC – Stade Rennais FC 2-0(0-0)

Astana FC: Nenad Eric, Antonio Rukavina, Marin Anicic, Dmitriy Shomko, Evgeni Postnikov, Marin Tomasov, Ivan Maevski, Richard Almeyda (63.Serikzhan Muzhikov), Pedro Henrique, Junior Kabananga (72.Rangelo Janga), Baktiyor Zaynutdinov (75.Yuriy Logvinenko). Trainer: Roman Grygorchuk.
Stade Rennais: Abdoulaye Diallo, Ludovic Baal (28.Ramy Bensebaini), Damien Da Silva, Medhi Zeffane, Jérémy Gelin, Clément Grenier, Benjamin André, Benjamin Bourigeaud, Denis Poha (77.Jakob Johansson), James Lea Siliki (69.Romain Del Castillo), M'Baye Niang. Trainer: Sabri Lamouchi.
Goals: 1-0 Baktiyor Zaynutdinov (64), 2-0 Marin Tomasov (90+1).

04.10.2018; Stadion Strelnice, Jablonec nad Nisou; Referee: Sébastien Delferière (Belgium); Attendance: 5,077

FK Jablonec – FK Dinamo Kyiv 2-2(1-2)

FK Jablonec: Vlastimil Hrubý, Tomás Holes, Matej Hanousek, David Hovorka, David Lischka, Tomás Hübschman, Jakub Povazanec, Michal Trávník, Lukás Masopust (86.Vojtech Kubista), Jan Chramosta (78.Davis Ikaunieks), Vladimir Jovovic (90+2.Eduard Sobol). Trainer: Petr Rada.
Dinamo Kyiv: Denis Boyko, Mikola Morozyuk, Josip Pivaric, Tamás Kádár, Tomasz Kedziora, Mykyta Burda, Sergiy Sydorchuk, Denys Garmash, Vitaliy Buyalskiy (79.Volodymyr Shepeliev), Viktor Tsygankov, Artem Besedin. Trainer: Aleksandr Khatskevich.
Goals: 0-1 Viktor Tsygankov (8), 0-2 Denys Garmash (14), 1-2 David Hovorka (33), 2-2 Michal Trávník (81).

25.10.2018; Stadion Strelnice, Jablonec nad Nisou; Referee: Robert Schörgenhofer (Austria); Attendance: 4,909

FK Jablonec – Astana FC 1-1(1-1)

FK Jablonec: Vlastimil Hrubý, Tomás Holes, Matej Hanousek, David Hovorka, David Lischka, Tomás Hübschman, Jakub Povazanec, Michal Trávník (90+1.Vojtech Kubista), Lukás Masopust, Jan Chramosta (57.Davis Ikaunieks), Vladimir Jovovic (87.Rafael Acosta). Trainer: Petr Rada.
Astana FC: Nenad Eric, Antonio Rukavina, Marin Anicic, Evgeni Postnikov, Marin Tomasov, Ivan Maevski, Richard Almeyda (90.Roman Murtazaev), László Kleinheisler, Pedro Henrique (46.Serikzhan Muzhikov), Junior Kabananga (74.Rangelo Janga), Baktiyor Zaynutdinov. Trainer: Roman Grygorchuk.
Goals: 1-0 Jakub Povazanec (4), 1-1 Pedro Henrique (11).

25.10.2018; Roazhon Park, Rennes; Referee: Tamás Bognár (Hungary); Attendance: 28,001

Stade Rennais FC – FK Dinamo Kyiv 1-2(1-1)

Stade Rennais: Abdoulaye Diallo, Damien Da Silva, Hamari Traoré, Jérémy Gelin, Ramy Bensebaini, Jakob Johansson (90.James Lea Siliki), Clément Grenier, Benjamin André, M'Baye Niang (74.Hatem Ben Arfa), Romain Del Castillo (61.Benjamin Bourigeaud), Ismaïla Sarr. Trainer: Sabri Lamouchi.
Dinamo Kyiv: Denis Boyko, Mikola Morozyuk (80.Tchê Tchê), Tamás Kádár, Tomasz Kedziora, Mykyta Burda, Sidcley, Vitali Mykolenko, Denys Garmash (68.Sergiy Sydorchuk), Vitaliy Buyalskiy, Benjamin Verbic (74.Vladyslav Supriaha), Volodymyr Shepeliev [*sent off 90+4*]. Trainer: Aleksandr Khatskevich.
Goals: 0-1 Tomasz Kedziora (21), 1-1 Clément Grenier (41), 1-2 Vitaliy Buyalskiy (89).

08.11.2018; Astana Arena, Astana; Referee: István Vad II (Hungary); Attendance: 20,092

Astana FC – FK Jablonec 2-1(1-1)

Astana FC: Nenad Eric, Antonio Rukavina, Marin Anicic, Evgeni Postnikov, Marin Tomasov, Ivan Maevski, Richard Almeyda (71.Serikzhan Muzhikov), László Kleinheisler, Pedro Henrique (80.Roman Murtazaev), Junior Kabananga (61.Rangelo Janga), Baktiyor Zaynutdinov. Trainer: Roman Grygorchuk.
FK Jablonec: Vlastimil Hrubý, Eduard Sobol (72.Milos Kratochvíl), Tomás Holes, Matej Hanousek, David Hovorka, David Lischka, Tomás Hübschman, Jakub Povazanec, Michal Trávník, Martin Dolezal, Vladimir Jovovic (89.Vojtech Kubista). Trainer: Petr Rada.
Goals: 1-0 Pedro Henrique (18), 1-1 Baktiyor Zaynutdinov (41 own goal), 2-1 Evgeni Postnikov (88).

08.11.2018; NSK Olimpijskyj Stadium, Kyiv; Referee: John Beaton (Scotland); Attendance: 24,402

FK Dinamo Kyiv – Stade Rennais FC 3-1(1-0)

Dinamo Kyiv: Denis Boyko, Tamás Kádár, Tomasz Kedziora, Mykyta Burda, Sidcley, Vitali Mykolenko, Vitaliy Buyalskiy, Tchê Tchê (83.Sergiy Sydorchuk), Benjamin Verbic (90.Vladyslav Supriaha), Viktor Tsygankov, Mykola Shaparenko (90+2.Mikkel Duelund). Trainer: Aleksandr Khatskevich.
Stade Rennais: Tomás Koubek, Damien Da Silva, Medhi Zeffane, Hamari Traoré (46.M'Baye Niang), Ramy Bensebaini, Gerzino Nyamsi (74.Jérémy Gelin), Hatem Ben Arfa, Benjamin Bourigeaud, Denis Poha, James Lea Siliki, Ismaïla Sarr (71.Theoson Siebatcheu). Trainer: Sabri Lamouchi.
Goals: 1-0 Benjamin Verbic (13), 2-0 Vitali Mykolenko (68), 3-0 Mykola Shaparenko (72), 3-1 Theoson Siebatcheu (89).

29.11.2018; Astana Arena, Astana; Referee: Ivan Bebek (Croatia); Attendance: 26,508

Astana FC – FK Dinamo Kyiv 0-1(0-1)

Astana FC: Nenad Eric, Antonio Rukavina, Marin Anicic, Evgeni Postnikov, Marin Tomasov, Ivan Maevski, Richard Almeyda (58.Serikzhan Muzhikov), László Kleinheisler, Junior Kabananga (62.Rangelo Janga), Roman Murtazaev, Baktiyor Zaynutdinov (76.Dmitriy Shomko). Trainer: Roman Grygorchuk.
Dinamo Kyiv: Denis Boyko, Tamás Kádár, Tomasz Kedziora, Mykyta Burda, Sidcley, Vitali Mykolenko, Tchê Tchê, Benjamin Verbic (76.Sergiy Sydorchuk), Viktor Tsygankov (84.Mikola Morozyuk), Mykola Shaparenko (64.Denys Garmash), Volodymyr Shepeliev. Trainer: Aleksandr Khatskevich.
Goal: 0-1 Benjamin Verbic (29).

29.11.2018; Stadion Strelnice, Jablonec nad Nisou; Referee: Tiago Bruno Lopes Martins (Portugal); Attendance: 4,712

FK Jablonec – Stade Rennais FC 0-1(0-0)

FK Jablonec: Vlastimil Hrubý, Eduard Sobol (63.Milos Kratochvíl), Tomás Holes, Vojtech Kubista, Matej Hanousek, David Hovorka, David Lischka, Tomás Hübschman (82.Jan Chramosta), Jakub Povazanec, Michal Trávník, Martin Dolezal. Trainer: Petr Rada.
Stade Rennais: Tomás Koubek, Damien Da Silva, Mexer, Medhi Zeffane, Hamari Traoré, Jakob Johansson, Clément Grenier (77.Hatem Ben Arfa), Benjamin André, Benjamin Bourigeaud (63.M'Baye Niang), James Lea Siliki, Ismaïla Sarr (89.Adrien Hunou). Trainer: Sabri Lamouchi.
Goal: 0-1 Clément Grenier (55).

13.12.2018; Roazhon Park, Rennes; Referee: Serdar Gözübüyük (Netherlands); Attendance: 24,535

Stade Rennais FC – Astana FC 2-0(0-0)

Stade Rennais: Abdoulaye Diallo, Damien Da Silva, Mexer, Hamari Traoré, Ramy Bensebaini, Hatem Ben Arfa (90+2.Adrien Hunou), Clément Grenier, Benjamin André, Benjamin Bourigeaud (82.M'Baye Niang), Theoson Siebatcheu (75.Jakob Johansson), Ismaïla Sarr. Trainer: Julien Stephane.

Astana FC: Nenad Eric, Antonio Rukavina, Marin Anicic, Evgeni Postnikov, Marin Tomasov, Ivan Maevski, Richard Almeyda (46.Abzal Beysebekov), László Kleinheisler (86.Dmitriy Shomko), Pedro Henrique (81.Roman Murtazaev), Junior Kabananga, Baktiyor Zaynutdinov. Trainer: Roman Grygorchuk.

Goals: 1-0, 2-0 Ismaïla Sarr (68), 73).

13.12.2018; NSK Olimpijskyj Stadium, Kyiv; Referee: Vilhjálmur Alvar Thórarinsson (Iceland); Attendance: 11,300

FK Dinamo Kyiv – FK Jablonec 0-1(0-1)

Dinamo Kyiv: Georgiy Bushchan, Tamás Kádár, Tomasz Kedziora, Mykyta Burda, Vitali Mykolenko, Sergiy Sydorchuk, Benjamin Verbic, Viktor Tsygankov, Mykola Shaparenko (60.Heorhii Tsitaishvili), Volodymyr Shepeliev, Artem Besedin (66.Mikkel Duelund, 76.Oleksandr Andrievsky). Trainer: Aleksandr Khatskevich.

FK Jablonec: Vlastimil Hrubý, Tomás Holes, Matej Hanousek, David Hovorka, David Lischka, Tomás Hübschman, Michal Trávník, Milos Kratochvíl (89.Tomás Brecka), Martin Dolezal, Jan Chramosta (70 Rafael Acosta), Vladimir Jovovic (79.Eduard Sobol). Trainer: Petr Rada.

Goal: 0-1 Martin Dolezal (10).

GROUP L

1.	**Chelsea FC London**	6	5	1	0	12	-	3	16
2.	**FC BATE Borisov**	6	3	0	3	9	-	9	9
3.	MOL Vidi FC Székesfehérvár	6	2	1	3	5	-	7	7
4.	PAOK Thessaloníki	6	1	0	5	5	-	12	3

20.09.2018; Stádio Toumba, Thessaloníki; Referee: Alberto Undiano Mallenco (Spain); Attendance: 24,310

PAOK Thessaloníki – Chelsea FC London 0-1(0-1)

PAOK: Alexandros Paschalakis, Fernando Varela, Evgen Khacheridi, Alin Tosca, Pontus Wernbloom, Vieirinha, Omar El Kaddouri, Maurício, Evgen Shakhov (69.Aleksandar Prijovic), Dimitrios Pelkas (62.Amr Warda), Léo Jabá (82.Diego Biseswar). Trainer: Razvan Lucescu.

Chelsea FC: Kepa, Marcos Alonso (66.Azpilicueta), Antonio Rüdiger, Davide Zappacosta, Andreas Christensen, Ross Barkley, Jorginho (65.Cesc Fàbregas), N'Golo Kanté, Willian, Pedro, Álvaro Morata (81.Olivier Giroud). Trainer: Maurizio Sarri.

Goal: 0-1 Willian (7).

20.09.2018; Groupama Aréna, Budapest; Referee: Mads-Kristoffer Kristoffersen (Denmark); Attendance: 14,726

MOL Vidi FC Székesfehérvár – FC BATE Borisov 0-2(0-1)

MOL Vidi FC: Tomás Tujvel, Roland Juhász, Attila Fiola (64.Armin Hodzic), Loïc Négo, Paulo Vinícius, Stopira, Anel Hadzic, Georgi Milanov (76.Szilveszter Hangya), István Kovács, Boban Nikolov (78.Zsombor Berecz), Marko Scepovic. Trainer: Marko Nikolic.

BATE Borisov: Denis Scherbitski, Egor Filipenko, Denis Polyakov, Nemanja Milunovic, Aleksander Filipovic [*sent off 90+5*], Igor Stasevich (88.Maksim Volodko), Dmitriy Baga, Stanislav Dragun, Mirko Ivanic (67.Mikhail Gordeychuk), Jasse Tuominen (61.Maksim Skavysh), Evgeni Yablonski. Trainer: Aleksei Baga.

Goals: 0-1 Jasse Tuominen (27), 0-2 Egor Filipenka (85).

04.10.2018; Borisov Arena, Borisov; Referee: Robert Schörgenhofer (Austria); Attendance: 10,527

FC BATE Borisov – PAOK Thessaloníki 1-4(0-3)

BATE Borisov: Denis Scherbitski, Egor Filipenko, Denis Polyakov, Maksim Volodko, Aleksey Rios, Igor Stasevich (77.Mikhail Gordeychuk), Dmitriy Baga, Stanislav Dragun (71.Aliaksandr Hleb), Mirko Ivanic, Jasse Tuominen (59.Maksim Skavysh), Evgeni Yablonski. Trainer: Aleksei Baga.

PAOK: Alexandros Paschalakis, Léo Matos, José Ángel Crespo, Fernando Varela, Alin Tosca, Maurício, Cañas, Dimitrios Pelkas, Aleksandar Prijovic (76.Chuba Akpom), Dimitris Limnios (70.Diego Biseswar), Léo Jabá (86.Vieirinha). Trainer: Razvan Lucescu.

Goals: 0-1 Aleksandar Prijovic (6), 0-2, 0-3 Léo Jabá (11, 17), 1-3 José Ángel Crespo (61 own goal), 1-4 Dimitrios Pelkas (73).

04.10.2018; Stamford Bridge, London; Referee: Miroslav Zelinka (Czech Republic); Attendance: 39,925

Chelsea FC London – MOL Vidi FC Székesfehérvár 1-0(0-0)

Chelsea FC: Kepa, Gary Cahill, Emerson, Davide Zappacosta, Andreas Christensen, Cesc Fàbregas, Mateo Kovacic, Ruben Loftus-Cheek (66.Ross Barkley), Willian (74.Victor Moses), Pedro (54.Eden Hazard), Álvaro Morata. Trainer: Maurizio Sarri.

MOL Vidi FC: Tomás Tujvel, Roland Juhász, Attila Fiola, Loïc Négo, Paulo Vinícius, Stopira, Szabolcs Huszti (77.István Kovács), Anel Hadzic (83.Máté Pátkai), Georgi Milanov (83.Armin Hodzic), Boban Nikolov, Marko Scepovic. Trainer: Marko Nikolic.

Goal: 1-0 Álvaro Morata (70).

25.10.2018; Stamford Bridge, London; Referee: Paolo Mazzoleni (Italy); Attendance: 39,799

Chelsea FC London – FC BATE Borisov 3-1(2-0)

Chelsea FC: Kepa, Gary Cahill, Emerson, Davide Zappacosta, Andreas Christensen, Cesc Fàbregas, Mateo Kovacic (77.N'Golo Kanté), Ruben Loftus-Cheek, Willian (57.Victor Moses), Olivier Giroud, Pedro (60.Callum Hudson-Odoi). Trainer: Maurizio Sarri.

BATE Borisov: Denis Scherbitski, Egor Filipenko, Maksim Volodko, Aleksander Filipovic, Aliaksandr Hleb (59.Mirko Ivanic), Aleksey Rios, Igor Stasevich, Dmitriy Baga (76.Evgeni Yablonski), Stanislav Dragun, Maksim Skavysh, Nikolay Signevich (71.Jasse Tuominen). Trainer: Aleksei Baga.

Goals: 1-0, 2-0, 3-0 Ruben Loftus-Cheek (2, 8, 54), 3-1 Aleksey Rios (80).

25.10.2018; Stádio Toumba, Thessaloníki; Referee: Yevhen Aranovskyi (Ukraine); Attendance: 15,118

PAOK Thessaloníki – MOL Vidi FC Székesfehérvár 0-2(0-2)

PAOK: Alexandros Paschalakis, Léo Matos, José Ángel Crespo, Fernando Varela, Alin Tosca, Omar El Kaddouri, Evgen Shakhov (52.Aleksandar Prijovic), Cañas, Dimitrios Pelkas, Nikolaos Karelis (66.Diego Biseswar), Dimitris Limnios (46.Amr Warda). Trainer: Razvan Lucescu.

MOL Vidi FC: Ádám Kovácsik, Roland Juhász, Attila Fiola, Loïc Négo, Paulo Vinícius, Stopira, Szabolcs Huszti (73.István Kovács), Anel Hadzic, Máté Pátkai, Georgi Milanov (79.Boban Nikolov), Marko Scepovic (65.Armin Hodzic). Trainer: Marko Nikolic.

Goals: 0-1 Szabolcs Huszti (12), 0-2 Stopira (45).

08.11.2018; Borisov Arena, Borisov; Referee: Nikola Dabanovic (Montenegro); Attendance: 13,141

FC BATE Borisov – Chelsea FC London 0-1(0-0)

BATE Borisov: Denis Scherbitski, Egor Filipenko, Aleksander Filipovic, Aliaksandr Hleb (81.Evgeniy Berezkin), Aleksey Rios, Igor Stasevich, Dmitriy Baga, Stanislav Dragun, Zakhar Volkov, Maksim Skavysh (76.Hervaine Moukam), Nikolay Signevich (73.Jasse Tuominen). Trainer: Aleksei Baga.

Chelsea FC: Kepa, Gary Cahill, Emerson, Davide Zappacosta, Andreas Christensen, Ross Barkley, Jorginho, Ruben Loftus-Cheek (64.Mateo Kovacic), Eden Hazard (62.Willian), Olivier Giroud, Pedro (85.Callum Hudson-Odoi). Trainer: Maurizio Sarri.

Goal: 0-1 Olivier Giroud (53).

08.11.2018; Groupama Aréna, Budapest; Referee: Ali Palabiyik (Turkey); Attendance: 17,208

MOL Vidi FC Székesfehérvár – PAOK Thessaloníki 1-0(0-0)

MOL Vidi FC: Ádam Kovácsik, Roland Juhász, Attila Fiola, Loïc Négo, Paulo Vinícius, Stopira, Szabolcs Huszti (66.István Kovács), Anel Hadzic, Máté Pátkai, Georgi Milanov (58.Boban Nikolov), Marko Scepovic (77.Armin Hodzic). Trainer: Marko Nikolic.

PAOK: Alexandros Paschalakis, Léo Matos, José Ángel Crespo, Fernando Varela, Alin Tosca, Pontus Wernbloom, Omar El Kaddouri (63.Chuba Akpom), Evgen Shakhov, Aleksandar Prijovic, Dimitris Limnios (60.Diego Biseswar), Léo Jabá (71.Amr Warda). Trainer: Razvan Lucescu.

Goal: 1-0 Georgi Milanov (50).

29.11.2018; Borisov Arena, Borisov; Referee: Carlos del Cerro Grande (Spain); Attendance: 8,963

FC BATE Borisov – MOL Vidi FC Székesfehérvár 2-0(1-0)

BATE Borisov: Denis Scherbitski, Egor Filipenko (46.Denis Polyakov), Aleksander Filipovic, Aliaksandr Hleb (66.Maksim Skavysh), Aleksey Rios, Igor Stasevich (90.Mikhail Gordeychuk), Dmitriy Baga, Stanislav Dragun, Mirko Ivanic, Zakhar Volkov, Nikolay Signevich. Trainer: Aleksei Baga.

MOL Vidi FC: Ádam Kovácsik, Roland Juhász, Attila Fiola, Loïc Négo (67.István Kovács), Paulo Vinícius, Stopira, Szabolcs Huszti (74.Boban Nikolov), Anel Hadzic, Máté Pátkai (64.Armin Hodzic), Georgi Milanov, Marko Scepovic. Trainer: Marko Nikolic.

Goals: 1-0 Nikolay Signevich (22), 2-0 Mirko Ivanic (85).

29.11.2018; Stamford Bridge, London; Referee: Kristo Tohver (Estonia); Attendance: 33,933

Chelsea FC London – PAOK Thessaloníki 4-0(2-0)

Chelsea FC: Kepa, Gary Cahill, Emerson, Davide Zappacosta (63.Ethan Ampadu), Andreas Christensen, Cesc Fàbregas, Ross Barkley, Ruben Loftus-Cheek, Olivier Giroud (75.Álvaro Morata), Pedro (66.Willian), Callum Hudson-Odoi. Trainer: Maurizio Sarri.

PAOK: Alexandros Paschalakis, Léo Matos, José Ángel Crespo, Evgen Khacheridi [*sent off 7*], Pontus Wernbloom, Vieirinha, Omar El Kaddouri (76.Fernando Varela), Maurício (78.Dimitrios Pelkas), Evgen Shakhov, Aleksandar Prijovic (46.Amr Warda), Léo Jabá. Trainer: Razvan Lucescu.

Goals: 1-0, 2-0 Olivier Giroud (27, 37), 3-0 Callum Hudson-Odoi (60), 4-0 Álvaro Morata (78).

13.12.2018; Stádio Toumba, Thessaloníki; Referee: Tobias Welz (Germany); Attendance: 13,483

PAOK Thessaloníki – FC BATE Borisov 1-3(0-3)

PAOK: Alexandros Paschalakis, Léo Matos, José Ángel Crespo, Fernando Varela, Vieirinha (46.Alin Tosca), Maurício, Cañas, Dimitrios Pelkas (55.Chuba Akpom), Aleksandar Prijovic, Dimitris Limnios (46.Amr Warda), Léo Jabá. Trainer: Razvan Lucescu.

BATE Borisov: Denis Scherbitski, Denis Polyakov, Aleksander Filipovic, Aleksey Rios, Igor Stasevich, Dmitriy Baga, Stanislav Dragun (88.Evgeni Yablonski), Mirko Ivanic, Zakhar Volkov, Maksim Skavysh (83.Mikhail Gordeychuk), Nikolay Signevich [*sent off 61*]. Trainer: Aleksei Baga.

Goals: 0-1 Maksim Skavysh (18), 0-2, 0-3 Nikolay Signevich (42, 45+1 penalty), 1-3 Aleksandar Prijovic (59).

13.12.2018; Groupama Aréna, Budapest; Referee: Aleksandar Stavrev (North Macedonia); Attendance: 19,242

MOL Vidi FC Székesfehérvár – Chelsea FC London 2-2(1-1)

MOL Vidi FC: Ádam Kovácsik, Roland Juhász, Attila Fiola, Loïc Négo, Paulo Vinícius, Stopira, Szabolcs Huszti (81.Armin Hodzic), Anel Hadzic (85.Máté Pátkai), Georgi Milanov (81.István Kovács), Boban Nikolov, Marko Scepovic. Trainer: Marko Nikolic.

Chelsea FC: Willy Caballero, Emerson, Davide Zappacosta, Andreas Christensen, Ethan Ampadu, Cesc Fàbregas, Ross Barkley, Ruben Loftus-Cheek, Willian (56.Pedro), Álvaro Morata (45+1.Olivier Giroud), Callum Hudson-Odoi. Trainer: Maurizio Sarri.

Goals: 0-1 Willian (30), 1-1 Ethan Ampadu (32 own goal), 2-1 Loïc Négo (56), 2-2 Olivier Giroud (75).

ROUND OF 32

Please note: SSC Napoli, Valencia CF, FC Internazionale Milano, Sport Lisboa e Benfica, FC Viktoria Plzeň, Club Brugge KV, FK Shakhtar Donetsk and Galatasaray SK İstanbul entered the UEFA Europa League as the group stage third-placed teams from the UEFA Champions League..

12.02.2019; "Sükrü Saraçoglu" Stadyumu, İstanbul; Referee: Ruddy Buquet (France); Attendance: 36,572

Fenerbahçe SK İstanbul – FK Zenit Saint Petersburg 1-0(1-0)

Fenerbahçe: Harun Tekin, Martin Skrtel, Mauricio Isla, Victor Moses (84.Alper Potuk), Hasan-Ali Kaldirim, Sadik Çiftpinar, Mathieu Valbuena (90+2.Roman Neustädter), Mehmet Topal, Jaílson, Eljif Elmas (72.André Ayew), Islam Slimani. Trainer: Ersun Yanal.

Zenit Saint Petersburg: Andrei Lunev, Branislav Ivanovic, Aleksandr Anyukov, Yaroslav Rakitskiy, Elmir Nabiullin (61.Igor Smolnikov), Róbert Mak (85.Claudio Marchisio), Hernani, Wilmar Barrios, Matías Kranevitter, Artem Dzyuba, Sebastián Driussi (74.Sardar Azmoun). Trainer: Sergey Semak.

Goal: 1-0 Islam Slimani (21).

21.02.2019; Gazprom Arena, Saint Petersburg; Referee: Michael Oliver (England); Attendance: 50,448

FK Zenit Saint Petersburg – Fenerbahçe SK İstanbul 3-1(2-1)

Zenit Saint Petersburg: Andrei Lunev, Branislav Ivanovic, Aleksandr Anyukov, Igor Smolnikov, Yaroslav Rakitskiy, Magomed Ozdoev, Hernani (56.Róbert Mak), Wilmar Barrios, Artem Dzyuba (88.Leon Musaev), Sardar Azmoun (80.Anton Zabolotny), Sebastián Driussi. Trainer: Sergey Semak.

Fenerbahçe: Harun Tekin, Martin Skrtel, Victor Moses, Hasan-Ali Kaldirim (67.Ismail Köybasi), Sener Özbayrakli, Sadik Çiftpinar, Mehmet Topal, Alper Potuk (46.Tolgay Arslan), Jaílson (80.Islam Slimani), Eljif Elmas, André Ayew. Trainer: Ersun Yanal.

Goals: 1-0 Magomed Ozdoev (4), 2-0 Sardar Azmoun (37), 2-1 Mehmet Topal (43), 3-1 Sardar Azmoun (76).

[FK Zenit Saint Petersburg won 3-2 on aggregate]

14.02.2019; Allianz Stadion, Wien; Referee: Tobias Stieler (Germany); Attendance: 23,850

SK Rapid Wien – FC Internazionale Milano 0-1(0-1)

SK Rapid Wien: Richard Strebinger, Mario Sonnleitner, Marvin Potzmann, Maximilian Hofmann, Boli Bolingoli-Mbombo, Manuel Thurnwald (53.Philipp Schobesberger), Stefan Schwab, Srdan Grahovac (64.Christoph Knasmüllner), Dejan Ljubicic, Veton Berisha (82.Thomas Murg), Andrei Ivan. Trainer: Dietmar Kühbauer.

Internazionale: Samir Handanovic, João Miranda, Kwadwo Asamoah, Stefan de Vrij, Cédric Soares, Ivan Perisic, Radja Nainggolan (83.Danilo D'Ambrosio), Borja Valero, Matías Vecino, Matteo Politano (78.Antonio Candreva), Lautaro Martínez. Trainer: Luciano Spalletti.

Goals: 0-1 Lautaro Martínez (39 penalty).

21.02.2019; Stadio „Giuseppe Meazza", Milano; Referee: Artur Manuel Ribeiro Soares Dias (Portugal); Attendance: 32,158

FC Internazionale Milano – SK Rapid Wien 4-0(2-0)

Internazionale: Samir Handanovic, Kwadwo Asamoah, Andrea Ranocchia, Cédric Soares, Milan Skriniar (77.João Miranda), Ivan Perisic, Antonio Candreva, Radja Nainggolan, Matías Vecino, Marcelo Brozovic (62.Borja Valero), Lautaro Martínez (66.Matteo Politano). Trainer: Luciano Spalletti.

SK Rapid Wien: Richard Strebinger, Mario Sonnleitner, Marvin Potzmann, Maximilian Hofmann, Boli Bolingoli-Mbombo (75.Philipp Schobesberger), Christoph Knasmüllner (64.Stefan Schwab), Srdan Grahovac, Thomas Murg, Dejan Ljubicic, Andrija Pavlovic, Andrei Ivan (64.Mert Müldür). Trainer: Dietmar Kühbauer.

Goals: 1-0 Matías Vecino (11), 2-0 Andrea Ranocchia (18), 3-0 Ivan Perisic (80), 4-0 Matteo Politano (87).

[FC Internazionale Milano won 5-0 on aggregate]

14.02.2019; Sinobo Stadium, Praha; Referee: Andris Treimanis (Latvia); Attendance: 18,125

SK Slavia Praha – KRC Genk 0-0

Slavia Praha: Ondrej Kolár, Ondrej Kúdela, Jan Boril, Vladimír Coufal, Josef Husbauer (77.Alex Král), Miroslav Stoch, Michael Ngadeu-Ngadjui, Jaromír Zmrhal (60.Peter Olayinka), Petr Sevcík, Tomás Soucek, Milan Skoda (76.Mick van Buren). Trainer: Jindrich Trpisovsky.

KRC Genk: Danny Vukovic, Sebastien Dewaest, Joseph Aidoo, Joakim Mæhle, Ruslan Malinovskiy, Ivan Fiolic (57.Pozuelo), Casper De Norre, Bryan Heynen, Leandro Trossard (87.Jakub Piotrowski), Mbwane Samatta, Dieumerci N'Dongala (69.Joseph Paintsil). Trainer: Philippe Clement.

21.02.2019; Luminus Arena, Genk; Referee: Bobby Madden (Scotland); Attendance: 13,688

KRC Genk – SK Slavia Praha 1-4(1-1)

KRC Genk: Danny Vukovic (58.Nordin Jackers), Sebastien Dewaest, Jhon Lucumí, Joakim Mæhle, Pozuelo, Ruslan Malinovskiy, Casper De Norre (56.Jere Uronen), Bryan Heynen (29.Dries Wouters), Leandro Trossard, Mbwane Samatta, Junya Ito. Trainer: Philippe Clement.

Slavia Praha: Ondrej Kolár, Ondrej Kúdela, Jan Boril, Vladimír Coufal, Simon Deli, Alex Král, Jaromír Zmrhal, Lukás Masopust (65.Peter Olayinka), Tomás Soucek, Ibrahim Traoré (63.Miroslav Stoch), Milan Skoda (75.Mick van Buren). Trainer: Jindrich Trpisovsky.

Goals: 1-0 Leandro Trossard (10), 1-1 Vladimír Coufal (23), 1-2 Ibrahim Traoré (54), 1-3, 1-4 Milan Skoda (64, 69).

[SK Slavia Praha won 4-1 on aggregate]

14.02.2019; Stadion FK Krasnodar, Krasnodar; Referee: Davide Massa (Italy); Attendance: 34,827

FK Krasnodar – TSV Bayer 04 Leverkusen 0-0

FK Krasnodar: Stanislav Kritsyuk, Aleksandr Martynovich, Sergey Petrov, Uros Spajic, Charles Kaboré, Mauricio Pereyra (80.Artem Golubev), Dmitriy Stotskiy, Victor Claesson, Kristoffer Olsson (71.Magomed Suleymanov), Wamberto, Ivan Ignatyev. Trainer: Murad Musaev.

Bayer Leverkusen: Lukás Hradecky, Sven Bender (83.Aleksandar Dragovic), Mitchell Weiser, Wendell, Jonathan Tah, Charles Aránguiz, Karim Bellarabi, Kai Havertz, Kevin Volland, Julian Brandt, Leon Bailey (80.Lucas Alario). Trainer: Peter Bosz.

21.02.2019; BayArena, Leverkusen; Referee: Gedimanas Mazeika (Lithuania); Attendance: 16,084

TSV Bayer 04 Leverkusen – FK Krasnodar 1-1(0-0)

Bayer Leverkusen: Lukás Hradecky, Aleksandar Dragovic (86.Isaac Kiese Thelin), Mitchell Weiser, Wendell, Jonathan Tah, Charles Aránguiz, Kai Havertz (66.Julian Baumgartlinger), Kevin Volland, Lucas Alario, Julian Brandt, Leon Bailey. Trainer: Peter Bosz.

FK Krasnodar: Matvei Safonov, Aleksandr Martynovich, Sergey Petrov, Uros Spajic, Cristian Ramírez, Charles Kaboré, Mauricio Pereyra, Victor Claesson (78.Dmitriy Stotskiy), Kristoffer Olsson (61.Yuri Gazinskiy), Wamberto, Ivan Ignatyev (70.Magomed Suleymanov). Trainer: Murad Musaev.

Goals: 0-1 Magomed Suleymanov (84), 1-1 Charles Aránguiz (87).

[FK Krasnodar won on away goals rule (1-1 on aggregate)]

14.02.2019; Roazhon Park, Rennes; Referee: Anastasios Sidiropoulos (Greece); Attendance: 28,656

Stade Rennais FC – Real Betis Balompié Sevilla 3-3(3-1)

Stade Rennais: Tomás Koubek, Damien Da Silva, Mexer, Medhi Zeffane, Hamari Traoré, Hatem Ben Arfa, Clément Grenier (69.Jérémy Gelin), Benjamin André, Adrien Hunou (80.Ramy Bensebaini), M'Baye Niang, Ismaïla Sarr (49.Benjamin Bourigeaud). Trainer: Julien Stéphane.

Betis Sevilla: Joel Robles, Sidnei, Aïssa Mandi, Junior Firpo (27.Diego Lainez), Joaquín (84.Barragán), Andrés Guardado, Javi García, Canales, William Carvalho, Giovani Lo Celso, Loren Morón (72.Jesé). Trainer: Quique Setién.

Goals: 1-0 Adrien Hunou (2), 2-0 Javi García (10 own goal), 2-1 Giovani Lo Celso (32), 3-1 Hatem Ben Arfa (45+3 penalty), 3-2 Sidnei (62), 3-3 Diego Lainez (90).

21.02.2019; Estadio „Benito Villamarín", Sevilla; Referee: Viktor Kassai (Hungary); Attendance: 43,623

Real Betis Balompié Sevilla – Stade Rennais FC 1-3(1-2)

Betis Sevilla: Joel Robles, Sidnei, Aïssa Mandi, Bartra, Joaquín (89.Emerson), Andrés Guardado (78.Diego Lainez), Canales, William Carvalho, Giovani Lo Celso, Jesé (69.Sergio León), Loren Morón. Trainer: Quique Setién.

Stade Rennais: Tomás Koubek, Damien Da Silva, Mexer, Hamari Traoré, Ramy Bensebaini (78.Medhi Zeffane), Hatem Ben Arfa, Clément Grenier, Benjamin Bourigeaud (75.Jérémy Gelin), Adrien Hunou (84.Romain Del Castillo), M'Baye Niang, Ismaïla Sarr. Trainer: Julien Stéphane.

Goals: 0-1 Ramy Bensebaini (22), 1-1 Adrien Hunou (30), 1-2 Giovani Lo Celso (41), 1-3 M'Baye Niang (90+4).

[Stade Rennais FC won 6-4 on aggregate]

14.02.2019; Stádio „Giórgos Karaïskáki", Peiraiás; Referee: Craig Pawson (England); Attendance: 31,020

Olympiacos SFP Peiraiás – FK Dynamo Kyiv 2-2(2-1)

Olympiacos Peiraiás: José Sá, Jagos Vukovic, Yassine Meryah, KostasTsimikas, Pape Cissé, Guilherme, Kostas Fortounis (69.Bibras Natcho), Daniel Podence (81.Lazaros Christodoulopoulos), Mohamed Camara, Koka Ahmed Hassan, Gil Dias (86.Georgios Masouras). Trainer: Pedro Martins.

Dynamo Kyiv: Denis Boyko, Tomasz Kedziora, Mykyta Burda, Artem Shabanov, Vitali Mykolenko, Vitaliy Buyalskiy, Benjamin Verbic, Viktor Tsygankov, Mykola Shaparenko (82.Denys Garmash), Volodymyr Shepelev, Fran Sol (82.Nazariy Rusyn). Trainer: Aleksandr Khatskevich.

Goals: 1-0 Koka Ahmed Hassan (9), 1-1 Vitaliy Buyalskiy (27), 2-1 Gil Dias (40), 2-2 Benjamin Verbic (89).

21.02.2019; NSK Olimpiyskiy Stadium, Kyiv; Referee: Ivan Kružliak (Slovakia); Attendance: 48,902

FK Dynamo Kyiv – Olympiacos SFP Peiraiás 1-0(1-0)

Dynamo Kyiv: Denis Boyko, Tomasz Kedziora, Mykyta Burda, Artem Shabanov, Vitali Mykolenko, Vitaliy Buyalskiy, Benjamin Verbic (90+2.Yevhenii Smyrnyi), Viktor Tsygankov, Mykola Shaparenko (76.Denys Garmash), Volodymyr Shepelev, Fran Sol (90+2.Nazariy Rusyn). Trainer: Aleksandr Khatskevich.

Olympiacos Peiraiás: José Sá, Vasilios Torosidis, Yassine Meryah, KostasTsimikas, Pape Cissé, Guilherme, Kostas Fortounis (65.Guerrero), Andreas Bouchalakis (65.Bibras Natcho), Daniel Podence, Koka Ahmed Hassan, Gil Dias (46.Georgios Masouras). Trainer: Pedro Martins.

Goal: 1-0 Fran Sol (32).

[FK Dynamo Kyiv won 3-2 on aggregate]

14.02.2019; Stadio Olimpico, Roma; Referee: Slavko Vinčić (Slovenia); Attendance: 19,766

SS Lazio Roma – Sevilla FC 0-1(0-1)

Lazio Roma: Thomas Strakosha, Stefan Radu, Francesco Acerbi, Bastos (57.Luiz Felipe), Adam Marusic, Lucas Leiva, Senad Lulic, Marco Parolo (46.Danilo Cataldi), Luis Alberto (44.Riza Durmisi), Joaquín Correa, Felipe Caicedo. Trainer: Simone Inzaghi.

Sevilla FC: Tomás Vaclík, Simon Kjær, Gabriel Mercado, Sergio Escudero (75.Quincy Promes), Sergi Gómez, Jesús Navas, Éver Banega, Franco Vázquez, Pablo Sarabia (83.Ibrahim Amadou), Wissam Ben Yedder (72.Munir), André Silva. Trainer: Pablo Machín.

Goal: 0-1 Wissam Ben Yedder (22).

20.02.2019; Estadio „Ramón Sánchez Pizjuán", Sevilla; Referee: Anthony Taylor (England); Attendance: 34,521

Sevilla FC – SS Lazio Roma 2-0(1-0)

Sevilla FC: Tomás Vaclík, Simon Kjær, Gabriel Mercado, Sergio Escudero (6.Quincy Promes), Sergi Gómez, Jesús Navas, Franco Vázquez [*sent off 60*], Pablo Sarabia, Roque Mesa (82.Marko Rog), Wissam Ben Yedder, André Silva (64.Ibrahim Amadou). Trainer: Pablo Machín.

Lazio Roma: Thomas Strakosha, Stefan Radu, Francesco Acerbi, Patric (49.Joaquín Correa), Adam Marusic [*sent off 71*], Senad Lulic, Milan Badelj (76.Riza Durmisi), Danilo Cataldi, Sergej Milinkovic-Savic (56.Rômulo), Felipe Caicedo, Ciro Immobile. Trainer: Simone Inzaghi.

Goals: 1-0 Wissam Ben Yedder (20), 2-0 Pablo Sarabia (78).

[Sevilla FC won 3-0 on aggregate]

14.02.2019; Borisov Arena, Borisov; Referee: Srđan Jovanović (Serbia); Attendance: 12,527

FC BATE Borisov – Arsenal FC London 1-0(1-0)

BATE Borisov: Denis Scherbitski, Egor Filipenko, Aleksander Filipovic, Aliaksandr Hleb (58.Evgeniy Berezkin), Aleksey Rios, Igor Stasevich, Dmitriy Baga, Stanislav Dragun, Zakhar Volkov, Nemanja Milic (69.Bojan Dubajic), Maksim Skavysh (80.Hervaine Moukam). Trainer: Aleksei Baga.

Arsenal FC: Petr Cech, Nacho Monreal, Laurent Koscielny, Shkodran Mustafi, Sead Kolasinac (74.Denis Suárez), Henrikh Mkhitaryan, Granit Xhaka (69.Lucas Torreira), Alex Iwobi, Ainsley Maitland-Niles (68.Pierre-Emerick Aubameyang), Mattéo Guendouzi, Alexandre Lacazette [*sent off 85*]. Trainer: Unai Emery.

Goal: 1-0 Stanislav Dragun (45).

21.02.2019; Emirates Stadium, London; Referee: Alberto Undiano Mallenco (Spain); Attendance: 58,812

Arsenal FC London – FC BATE Borisov 3-0(2-0)

Arsenal FC: Petr Cech, Stephan Lichtsteiner, Nacho Monreal, Laurent Koscielny (56.Sokratis Papastathopoulos), Shkodran Mustafi, Mesut Özil, Henrikh Mkhitaryan (78.Denis Suárez), Granit Xhaka, Alex Iwobi, Mattéo Guendouzi (64.Lucas Torreira), Pierre-Emerick Aubameyang. Trainer: Unai Emery.

BATE Borisov: Denis Scherbitski, Egor Filipenko, Aleksander Filipovic, Aleksey Rios, Igor Stasevich, Dmitriy Baga (58.Aliaksandr Hleb), Stanislav Dragun (64.Evgeniy Berezkin), Slobodan Simovic, Zakhar Volkov, Nemanja Milic, Maksim Skavysh (72.Bojan Dubajic). Trainer: Aleksei Baga.

Goals: 1-0 Zakhar Volkov (4 own goal), 2-0 Shkodran Mustafi (39), 3-0 Sokratis Papastathopoulos (60).

[Arsenal FC London won 3-1 on aggregate]

14.02.2019; Türk Telekom Stadyumu, İstanbul; Referee: Jesús Gil Manzano (Spain); Attendance: 42,722

Galatasaray SK İstanbul – Sport Lisboa e Benfica 1-2(0-1)

Galatasaray: Fernando Muslera, Yuto Nagatomo, Martin Linnes (73.Mariano), Marcão Teixeira, Christian Luyindama Nekadio, Sofiane Féghouli, Fernando, Younès Belhanda, Papa Alioune "Badou" N'Diaye (73.Sinan Gümüs), Mbaye Diagne, Henry Onyekuru. Trainer: Fatih Terim.

Benfica: Odisseas Vlachodimos, Sébastien Corchia, Rúben Dias, Yuri Ribeiro, Francisco Ferreira "Ferro", Eduardo Salvio (48.Gabriel), Franco Cervi (81.Filip Krovinovic), Gedson Fernandes (87.Andreas Samaris), Florentino Luís, Haris Seferovic, João Félix. Trainer: Bruno Lage.

Goals: 0-1 Eduardo Salvio (27 penalty), 1-1 Christian Luyindama Nekadio (54), 1-2 Haris Seferovic (64).

21.02.2019; Estádio da Luz, Lisboa; Referee: Ovidiu Alin Hațegan (Romania); Attendance: 49,545

Sport Lisboa e Benfica – Galatasaray SK İstanbul 0-0

Benfica: Odisseas Vlachodimos, André Almeida, Álex Grimaldo, Rúben Dias, Francisco Ferreira "Ferro", Pizzi (83.Gabriel), Franco Cervi (59.Rafa Silva), Gedson Fernandes, Florentino Luís, Haris Seferovic, João Félix (76.Jonas). Trainer: Bruno Lage.

Galatasaray: Fernando Muslera, Mariano, Yuto Nagatomo, Marcão Teixeira, Christian Luyindama Nekadio, Ryan Donk (78.Sinan Gümüs), Sofiane Féghouli (84.Emre Akbaba), Younès Belhanda, Papa Alioune "Badou" N'Diaye, Mbaye Diagne, Henry Onyekuru (83.Yunus Akgün). Trainer: Fatih Terim.

Goals:

[Sport Lisboa e Benfica won 2-1 on aggregate]

14.02.2019; Doosan Aréna, Plzeň; Referee: Serdar Gözübüyük (Netherlands); Attendance: 9,731

FC Viktoria Plzeň – GNK Dinamo Zagreb 2-1(0-1)

Viktoria Plzeň: Matús Kozácik, Roman Hubník, Ludek Pernica, Milan Havel, Tomás Horava, Jan Kovarík, Ales Cermák (46.Roman Procházka), Patrik Hrosovsky, Joel Kayamba, Ubong Moses Ekpai (70.Milan Petrzela), Jean-David Beauguel (81.Tomás Chory). Trainer: Pavel Vrba.

Dinamo Zagreb: Dominik Livakovic, Marin Leovac, Kévin Théophile-Catherine, Emir Dilaver, Petar Stojanovic, Arijan Ademi, Amer Gojak, Daniel Olmo, Mislav Orsic (76.Iyayi Atiemwen), Mario Situm (64.Nikola Moro), Bruno Petkovic. Trainer: Nenad Bjelica.

Goals: 0-1 Daniel Olmo (41), 1-1, 2-1 Ludek Pernica (54, 83).

21.02.2019; Stadion Maksimir, Zagreb; Referee: István Kovács (Romania); Attendance: 25,860

GNK Dinamo Zagreb – FC Viktoria Plzeň 3-0(2-0)

Dinamo Zagreb: Dominik Livakovic, Marin Leovac, Kévin Théophile-Catherine, Emir Dilaver, Sadegh Moharrami, Arijan Ademi, Ivan Sunjic, Daniel Olmo, Mislav Orsic (88.Amer Gojak), Izet Hajrovic (68.Nikola Moro), Bruno Petkovic (90+2.Komnen Andric). Trainer: Nenad Bjelica.

Viktoria Plzeň: Matús Kozácik, David Limbersky [*sent off 86*], Ludek Pernica, Milan Havel (74.Radim Rezník), Milan Petrzela, Tomás Horava (57.Marek Bakos), Roman Procházka, Jan Kovarík, Patrik Hrosovsky, Joel Kayamba, Jean-David Beauguel (67.Tomás Chory). Trainer: Pavel Vrba.

Goals: 1-0 Mislav Orsic (15), 2-0 Emir Dilaver (34), 3-0 Bruno Petkovic (73).

[GNK Dinamo Zagreb won 4-2 on aggregate]

14.02.2019; "Jan Breydel" Stadium, Brugge; Referee: Georgi Kabakov (Bulgaria); Attendance: 16,457

Club Brugge KV – FC Red Bull Salzburg 2-1(0-1)

Club Brugge KV: Ethan Horvath, Stefano Denswil, Brandon Mechele, Dion Cools (46.Krépin Diatta), Ruud Vormer, Mats Rits, Hans Vanaken, Sofyan Amrabat (46.Benoît Poulain), Siebe Schrijvers (79.Loïs Openda), Wesley, Emmanuel Dennis Bonaventure. Trainer: Ivan Leko.

Red Bull Salzburg: Alexander Walke, Andreas Ulmer, Stefan Lainer, André Ramalho, Marin Pongracic, Zlatko Junuzovic, Xaver Schlager (76.Enock Mwepu), Diadié Samassékou, Fredrik Gulbrandsen (85.Takumi Minamino), Munas Dabour, Hannes Wolf (89.Patson Daka). Trainer: Marco Rose.

Goals: 0-1 Zlatko Junuzovic (17), 1-1 Stefano Denswil (64), 2-1 Wesley (81).

21.02.2019; Red Bull Arena, Wals-Siezenheim; Referee: Daniel Siebert (Germany); Attendance: 24,717

FC Red Bull Salzburg – Club Brugge KV 4-0(3-0)

Red Bull Salzburg: Alexander Walke, Andreas Ulmer, Stefan Lainer, Jérôme Onguéné, Marin Pongracic (77.Albert Vallci), Zlatko Junuzovic (71.Enock Mwepu), Xaver Schlager, Diadié Samassékou, Munas Dabour, Patson Daka, Hannes Wolf (63.Takumi Minamino). Trainer: Marco Rose.

Club Brugge KV: Ethan Horvath, Benoît Poulain, Stefano Denswil, Brandon Mechele, Ruud Vormer, Mats Rits, Hans Vanaken, Sofyan Amrabat (63.Krépin Diatta), Siebe Schrijvers (69.Loïs Openda), Wesley (84.Jelle Vossen), Emmanuel Dennis Bonaventure. Trainer: Ivan Leko.

Goals: 1-0 Xaver Schlager (17), 2-0, 3-0 Patson Daka (29, 43), 4-0 Munas Dabour (90+4).

[FC Red Bull Salzburg won 5-2 on aggregate]

14.02.2019; Stadion Letzigrund, Zürich; Referee: Milorad Mazic (Serbia); Attendance: 24,000

FC Zürich – SSC Napoli 1-3(0-2)

FC Zürich: Yanick Brecher, Alain Nef, Umaru Bangura, Joel Untersee, Andreas Maxsø, Levan Kharabadze, Adrian Winter (67.Assan Ceesay), Hekuran Kryeziu, Benjamin Kololli, Toni Domgjoni (46.Antonio Marchesano), Stephen Odey (80.Salim Khelifi). Trainer: Ludovic Magnin.

SSC Napoli: Alex Meret, Nikola Maksimovic, Kalidou Koulibaly, Kévin Malcuit, Faouzi Ghoulam (76.Sebastiano Luperto), Allan (59.Amadou Diawara), Piotr Zielinski, Fabián Ruiz, José Callejón, Lorenzo Insigne (68.Adam Ounas), Arkadiusz Milik. Trainer: Carlo Ancelotti.

Goals: 0-1 Lorenzo Insigne (12), 0-2 José Callejón (21), 0-3 Piotr Zielinski (77), 1-3 Benjamin Kololli (83 penalty).

21.02.2019; Stadio San Paolo, Napoli; Referee: Anastasios Sidiropoulos (Greece); Attendance: 17,579

SSC Napoli – FC Zürich 2-0(1-0)

SSC Napoli: Alex Meret, Vlad Chiriches (56.Sebastiano Luperto), Kalidou Koulibaly, Elseid Hysaj, Faouzi Ghoulam, Piotr Zielinski (66.Allan), Adam Ounas (77.Arkadiusz Milik), Amadou Diawara, Dries Mertens, Simone Verdi, Lorenzo Insigne. Trainer: Carlo Ancelotti.

FC Zürich: Yanick Brecher, Umaru Bangura, Mirlind Kryeziu, Marco Schönbächler (65.Bledian Krasniqi), Adrian Winter, Salim Khelifi, Benjamin Kololli (82.Levan Kharabadze), Toni Domgjoni, Simon Sohm, Assan Ceesay, Stephen Odey (60.Lavdim Zumberi). Trainer: Ludovic Magnin.

Goals: 1-0 Simone Verdi (43), 2-0 Adam Ounas (75).

[SSC Napoli won 5-1 on aggregate]

14.02.2019; Swedbank Stadion, Malmö; Referee: Aleksei Kulbakov (Belarus); Attendance: 20,312

Malmö FF – Chelsea FC London **1-2(0-1)**

Malmö FF: Johan Dahlin, Behrang Safari, Rasmus Bengtsson, Lasse Nielsen, Andreas Vindheim, Søren Rieks, Anders Christiansen (82.Romain Gall), Fouad Bachirou, Arnór Ingvi Traustason (70.Oscar Lewicki), Markus Rosenberg, Marcus Antonsson (70.Carlos Strandberg). Trainer: Uwe Rösler.

Chelsea FC: Kepa, David Luiz, Azpilicueta, Emerson, Andreas Christensen, Ross Barkley, Mateo Kovacic, Jorginho (74.N'Golo Kanté), Willian (71.Eden Hazard), Olivier Giroud, Pedro (84.Callum Hudson-Odoi). Trainer: Maurizio Sarri.

Goals: 0-1 Ross Barkley (30), 0-2 Olivier Giroud (58), 1-2 Anders Christiansen (80).

21.02.2019; Stamford Bridge, London; Referee: Orel Grinfeld (Israel); Attendance: 39,813

Chelsea FC London – Malmö FF **3-0(0-0)**

Chelsea FC: Willy Caballero, Azpilicueta (79.Ethan Ampadu), Emerson, Antonio Rüdiger, Andreas Christensen, Ross Barkley (76.Jorginho), Mateo Kovacic, N'Golo Kanté (76.Ruben Loftus-Cheek), Willian, Olivier Giroud, Callum Hudson-Odoi. Trainer: Maurizio Sarri.

Malmö FF: Johan Dahlin, Behrang Safari, Rasmus Bengtsson [*sent off 73*], Lasse Nielsen, Andreas Vindheim, Søren Rieks, Anders Christiansen (72.Oscar Lewicki), Fouad Bachirou, Arnór Ingvi Traustason (72.Romain Gall), Markus Rosenberg (62.Carlos Strandberg), Marcus Antonsson. Trainer: Uwe Rösler.

Goals: 1-0 Olivier Giroud (55), 2-0 Ross Barkley (74), 3-0 Callum Hudson-Odoi (84).

[Chelsea FC London won 5-1 on aggregate]

14.02.2019; Oblasny Sport Komplex Metalist, Kharkiv; Referee: Anthony Taylor (England); Attendance: 13,059

FK Shakhtar Donetsk – Eintracht Frankfurt **2-2(1-1)**

Shakhtar Donetsk: Andriy Pyatov, Sergiy Krivtsov, Ismaily, Bogdan Butko, Davit Khotcholava, Marlos (69.Manor Solomon), Taras Stepanenko [*sent off 11*], Taison, Alan Patrick, Viktor Kovalenko (81.Maksym Malyshev), Júnior Moraes (90.Sergiy Bolbat). Trainer: Paulo Fonseca.

Eintracht Frankfurt: Kevin Trapp, Martin Hinteregger, Danny da Costa, Evan Obite N'Dicka, Makoto Hasebe, Gelson Fernandes (82.Jonathan de Guzmán), Sebastian Rode (46.Jetro Willems), Filip Kostic, Mijat Gacinovic, Ante Rebic, Luka Jovic. Trainer: Adi Hütter.

Goals: 0-1 Martin Hinteregger (7), 1-1 Marlos (10 penalty), 1-2 Filip Kostic (50), 2-2 Taison (67).

21.02.2019; Commerzbank-Arena, Frankfurt am Main; Referee: Antonio Mateu Lahoz (Spain); Attendance: 47,000

Eintracht Frankfurt – FK Shakhtar Donetsk **4-1(2-0)**

Eintracht Frankfurt: Kevin Trapp, David Abraham, Martin Hinteregger, Danny da Costa, Evan Obite N'Dicka, Makoto Hasebe, Sebastian Rode (74.Jetro Willems), Filip Kostic, Mijat Gacinovic (90+1.Jonathan de Guzmán), Sébastien Haller, Luka Jovic (71.Ante Rebic). Trainer: Adi Hütter.

Shakhtar Donetsk: Andriy Pyatov, Ismaily, Bogdan Butko (66.Sergiy Bolbat), Davit Khotcholava, Mykola Matviyenko, Marlos, Taison, Alan Patrick, Viktor Kovalenko (80.Olarenwaju Kayode), Manor Solomon (46.Maycon), Júnior Moraes. Trainer: Paulo Fonseca.

Goals: 1-0 Luka Jovic (23), 2-0 Sébastien Haller (27 penalty), 2-1 Júnior Moraes (64), 3-1 Sébastien Haller (80), 4-2 Ante Rebic (88).

[Eintracht Frankfurt won 6-3 on aggregate]

14.02.2019; Celtic Park, Glasgow; Referee: Ovidiu Alin Haţegan (Romania); Attendance: 57,430

Celtic FC Glasgow – Valencia CF **0-2(0-1)**

Celtic: Scott Bain, Emilio Izaguirre, Dedryck Boyata, Jozo Simunovic, Jeremy Toljan, Scott Brown, Scott Sinclair (59.Timothy Weah), James Forrest, Callum McGregor, Ryan Christie (59.Odsonne Édouard), Oliver Burke. Trainer: Brendan Rodgers.

Valencia CF: Neto, Ezequiel Garay, Cristiano Piccini (78.Kevin Gamiero), Mouctar Daikhaby, Toni Lato, Daniel Wass, Dani Parejo (46.Francis Coquelin), Denis Cheryshev (64.Gonçalo Guedes), Geoffrey Kondogbia, Carlos Soler, Rubén Sobrino. Trainer: Marcelino.

Goals: 0-1 Denis Cheryshev (42), 0-2 Rubén Sobrino (49).

21.02.2019; Estadio de Mestalla, Valencia; Referee: Deniz Aytekin (Germany); Attendance: 36,619

Valencia CF – Celtic FC Glasgow **1-0(0-0)**

Valencia CF: Neto, Ezequiel Garay (23.Francis Coquelin), Mouctar Daikhaby, Toni Lato, Daniel Wass (76.Lee Kang-In), Dani Parejo, Gonçalo Guedes, Carlos Soler, Ferrán Torres, Rubén Sobrino (68.Kevin Gamiero), Santi Mina. Trainer: Marcelino.

Celtic: Scott Bain, Dedryck Boyata, Jozo Simunovic, Jeremy Toljan [*sent off 37*], Kristoffer Ajer, Scott Brown, Jonny Hayes, James Forrest (63.Odsonne Édouard), Callum McGregor, Ryan Christie, Oliver Burke (73.Michael Johnston). Trainer: Brendan Rodgers.

Goal: 1-0 Kevin Gamiero (70).

[Valencia CF won 3-0 on aggregate]

14.02.2019; Estádio „José Alvalade", Lisboa; Referee: Clément Turpin (France); Attendance: 27,134

Sporting Clube de Portugal Lisboa – Villarreal CF **0-1(0-1)**

Sporting: Romain Salin, André Pinto, Sebastián Coates, Bruno Gaspar (27.Stefan Ristovski), Radosav Petrovic (69.Wendel), Bruno Fernandes, Miguel Luís, Bas Dost, Marcos Acuña [*sent off 76*], Raphinha, Jovane Cabral (69.Luiz Phellype). Trainer: Marcel Keizer.

Villarreal CF: Andrés Fernández, Mario Gaspar, Víctor Ruíz, Ramiro Funes Mori, Álvaro González, Javi Fuego, Trigueros (63.Santiago Cáseres), Alfonso Pedraza, Pablo Fornals (80.Vicente Iborra), Samuel Chukwueze (74.Dani Raba), Carlos Bacca. Trainer: Javi Calleja.

Goal: 0-1 Alfonso Pedraza (3).

21.02.2019; Estadio de la Cerámica, Villarreal; Referee: Pavel Královec (Czech Republic); Attendance: 14,098

Villarreal CF – Sporting Clube de Portugal Lisboa **1-1(0-1)**

Villarreal CF: Andrés Fernández, Mario Gaspar, Víctor Ruíz, Ramiro Funes Mori, Miguelón Llambrich (71.Santi Cazorla), Javi Fuego (63.Vicente Iborra), Trigueros, Alfonso Pedraza, Pablo Fornals, Gerard Moreno, Dani Raba (57.Karl Toko Ekambi). Trainer: Javi Calleja.

Sporting: Romain Salin, Jefferson [*sent off 50*], Sebastián Coates, Stefan Ristovski (83.Luiz Phellype), Tiago Ilori, Cristian Borja, Nemanja Gudelj, Bruno Fernandes, Wendel, Bas Dost, Abdoulay Diaby (77.Raphinha). Trainer: Marcel Keizer.

Goals: 0-1 Bruno Fernandes (45+1), 1-1 Pablo Fornals (80).

[Villarreal CF won 2-1 on aggregate]

ROUND OF 16

07.03.2019; Commerzbank-Arena, Frankfurt am Main; Referee: William Collum (Scotland); Attendance: 48,000

Eintracht Frankfurt – FC Internazionale Milano **0-0**

Eintracht Frankfurt: Kevin Trapp, Martin Hinteregger, Danny da Costa, Evan Obite N'Dicka, Makoto Hasebe, Gelson Fernandes, Sebastian Rode (77.Jetro Willems), Filip Kostic, Mijat Gacinovic, Sébastien Haller (80.Gonçalo Paciência), Luka Jovic. Trainer: Adi Hütter.

Internazionale: Samir Handanovic, Kwadwo Asamoah, Stefan de Vrij, Danilo D'Ambrosio, Milan Skriniar, Ivan Perisic (59.Antonio Candreva), Borja Valero (80.Cédric Soares), Matías Vecino, Marcelo Brozovic, Matteo Politano, Lautaro Martínez. Trainer: Luciano Spalletti.

14.03.2019; Stadio „Giuseppe Meazza", Milano; Referee: Ovidiu Alin Haţegan (Romania); Attendance: 49,866

FC Internazionale Milano – Eintracht Frankfurt **0-1(0-1)**

Internazionale: Samir Handanovic, Stefan de Vrij, Danilo D'Ambrosio, Cédric Soares (62.Andrea Ranocchia), Milan Skriniar, Ivan Perisic, Antonio Candreva, Borja Valero (73.Sebastiano Esposito), Matías Vecino, Matteo Politano (80.Davide Merola), Keita Baldé. Trainer: Luciano Spalletti.

Eintracht Frankfurt: Kevin Trapp, Martin Hinteregger, Jetro Willems (73.Marc Stendera), Danny da Costa, Evan Obite N'Dicka, Makoto Hasebe, Sebastian Rode (89.Gonçalo Paciência), Filip Kostic, Mijat Gacinovic (59.Jonathan de Guzmán), Sébastien Haller, Luka Jovic. Trainer: Adi Hütter.

Goal: 0-1 Luka Jovic (6).

[Eintracht Frankfurt won 1-0 on aggregate]

07.03.2019; Stadion Maksimir, Zagreb; Referee: Michael Oliver (England); Attendance: 29,704

GNK Dinamo Zagreb – Sport Lisboa e Benfica 1-0(1-0)

Dinamo Zagreb: Dominik Livakovic, Marin Leovac, Kévin Théophile-Catherine, Emir Dilaver, Petar Stojanovic, Ivan Sunjic, Amer Gojak (78.Nikola Moro), Daniel Olmo, Mislav Orsic, Damian Kadzior (84.Mario Situm), Bruno Petkovic (89.Mario Gavranovic). Trainer: Nenad Bjelica.

Benfica: Odisseas Vlachodimos, Sébastien Corchia, Álex Grimaldo, Rúben Dias, Francisco Ferreira "Ferro", Gabriel, Filip Krovinovic, Gedson Fernandes (71.Andrija Zivkovic), Florentino Luís (58.Rafa Silva), Haris Seferovic (35.Franco Cervi), João Félix. Trainer: Bruno Lage.

Goal: 1-0 Bruno Petkovic (38 penalty).

14.03.2019; Estádio da Luz, Lisboa; Referee: Deniz Aytekin (Germany); Attendance: 47,808

Sport Lisboa e Benfica – GNK Dinamo Zagreb 3-0(0-0,1-0)

Benfica: Odisseas Vlachodimos, André Almeida, Rúben Dias, Yuri Ribeiro (46.Álex Grimaldo), Francisco Ferreira "Ferro", Ljubomir Fejsa, Pizzi (119.Gedson Fernandes), Gabriel, Andrija Zivkovic (46.Jonas), Rafa Silva, João Filipe "Jota" (62.João Félix). Trainer: Bruno Lage.

Dinamo Zagreb: Dominik Livakovic, Kévin Théophile-Catherine, Emir Dilaver, Petar Stojanovic [*sent off 104*], Amir Rrahmani, Amer Gojak (98.Iyayi Atiemwen), Nikola Moro, Daniel Olmo, Mislav Orsic (109.Dino Peric), Damian Kadzior (75.Mario Situm), Bruno Petkovic (86.Mario Gavranovic). Trainer: Nenad Bjelica.

Goals: 1-0 Jonas (71), 2-0 Francisco Ferreira "Ferro" (94), 3-0 Álex Grimaldo (105).

[Sport Lisboa e Benfica won 3-1 on aggregate]

07.03.2019; Estadio „Ramón Sánchez Pizjuán", Sevilla; Referee: Ruddy Buquet (France); Attendance: 30,698

Sevilla FC – SK Slavia Praha 2-2(2-2)

Sevilla FC: Tomás Vaclík (45+1.Juan Soriano), Simon Kjær, Gabriel Mercado, Sergi Gómez, Max Wöber (46.Roque Mesa), Jesús Navas, Éver Banega (76.Quincy Promes), Pablo Sarabia, Marko Rog, Wissam Ben Yedder, Munir. Trainer: Pablo Machín.

Slavia Praha: Ondrej Kolár, Ondrej Kúdela, Jan Boril, Vladimír Coufal, Simon Deli, Alex Král (79.Michael Ngadeu-Ngadjui), Miroslav Stoch, Jaromír Zmrhal (73.Milan Skoda), Lukás Masopust (60.Peter Olayinka), Tomás Soucek, Ibrahim Traoré. Trainer: Jindrich Trpisovsky.

Goals: 1-0 Wissam Ben Yedder (1), 1-1 Miroslav Stoch (25), 2-1 Munir (28), 2-2 Alex Král (39).

14.03.2019; Sinobo Stadium, Praha; Referee: Aleksei Kulbakov (Belarus); Attendance: 19,020

SK Slavia Praha – Sevilla FC 4-3(1-1,2-2)

Slavia Praha: Ondrej Kolár, Ondrej Kúdela, Jan Boril, Simon Deli, Alex Král (105 Michal Frydrych), Miroslav Stoch (93.Mick van Buren), Michael Ngadeu-Ngadjui, Lukás Masopust (90+2.Jaromír Zmrhal), Tomás Soucek, Ibrahim Traoré, Milan Skoda (77.Peter Olayinka). Trainer: Jindrich Trpisovsky.

Sevilla FC: Tomás Vaclík, Simon Kjær, Daniel Carriço, Sergi Gómez, Jesús Navas, Éver Banega, Pablo Sarabia (80.André Silva), Roque Mesa (74.Maxime Gonalons), Wissam Ben Yedder (104.Marko Rog), Quincy Promes, Munir (90.Franco Vázquez). Trainer: Pablo Machín.

Goals: 1-0 Michael Ngadeu-Ngadjui (15), 1-1 Wissam Ben Yedder (44 penalty), 2-1 Tomás Soucek (47 penalty), 2-2 Munir (54), 2-3 Franco Vázquez (98), 3-3 Mick van Buren (102), 4-3 Ibrahim Traoré (119).

[SK Slavia Praha won 6-5 on aggregate]

07.03.2019; Roazhon Park, Rennes; Referee: Ivan Kružliak (Slovakia); Attendance: 29,771

Stade Rennais FC – Arsenal FC London 3-1(1-1)

Stade Rennais: Tomás Koubek, Damien Da Silva, Mexer, Medhi Zeffane, Ramy Bensebaini, Hatem Ben Arfa, Clément Grenier (90+1.Jérémy Gelin), Benjamin André, Benjamin Bourigeaud (73.James Lea Siliki), Adrien Hunou, Ismaïla Sarr. Trainer: Julien Stéphane.

Arsenal FC: Petr Cech, Nacho Monreal, Sokratis Papastathopoulos [*sent off 41*], Laurent Koscielny, Shkodran Mustafi, Mesut Özil (70.Aaron Ramsey), Henrikh Mkhitaryan, Granit Xhaka, Alex Iwobi (53.Mattéo Guendouzi), Lucas Torreira, Pierre-Emerick Aubameyang (79.Sead Kolasinac). Trainer: Unai Emery.

Goals: 0-1 Alex Iwobi (4), 1-1 Benjamin Bourigeaud (42), 2-1 Nacho Monreal (65 own goal), 3-1 Ismaïla Sarr (88).

14.03.2019; Emirates Stadium, London; Referee: Andris Treimanis (Latvia); Attendance: 59,453

Arsenal FC London – Stade Rennais FC 3-0(2-0)

Arsenal FC: Petr Cech, Nacho Monreal, Laurent Koscielny, Shkodran Mustafi, Sead Kolasinac, Mesut Özil (70.Henrikh Mkhitaryan), Aaron Ramsey (87.Lucas Torreira), Granit Xhaka, Ainsley Maitland-Niles, Pierre-Emerick Aubameyang, Alexandre Lacazette (70.Alex Iwobi). Trainer: Unai Emery.

Stade Rennais: Tomás Koubek, Damien Da Silva, Mexer, Hamari Traoré, Ramy Bensebaini, Hatem Ben Arfa, Clément Grenier (70.Adrien Hunou), Benjamin André (79.James Lea Siliki), Benjamin Bourigeaud, M'Baye Niang, Ismaïla Sarr. Trainer: Julien Stéphane.

Goals: 1-0 Pierre-Emerick Aubameyang (5), 2-0 Ainsley Maitland-Niles (15), 3-0 Pierre-Emerick Aubameyang (72).

[Arsenal FC London won 4-3 on aggregate]

07.03.2019; Gazprom Arena, Saint Petersburg; Referee: Gianluca Rocchi (Italy); Attendance: 51,826

FK Zenit Saint Petersburg – Villarreal CF 1-3(1-1)

Zenit Saint Petersburg: Andrei Lunev, Branislav Ivanovic, Igor Smolnikov, Yaroslav Rakitskiy, Róbert Mak (72.Oleg Shatov), Magomed Ozdoev (88.Anton Zabolotny), Wilmar Barrios, Daler Kuzyaev, Artem Dzyuba, Sardar Azmoun (75.Hernani), Sebastián Driussi. Trainer: Sergey Semak.

Villarreal CF: Andrés Fernández, Jaume Costa, Víctor Ruíz, Ramiro Funes Mori, Álvaro González, Miguelón Llambrich, Vicente Iborra, Manu Morlanes (72.Santiago Cáseres), Pablo Fornals (78.Santi Cazorla), Samuel Chukwueze, Gerard Moreno (85.Carlos Bacca). Trainer: Javi Calleja.

Goals: 0-1 Vicente Iborra (33), 1-1 Sardar Azmoun (35), 1-2 Gerard Moreno (64), 1-3 Manu Morlanes (71).

14.03.2019; Estadio de la Cerámica, Villarreal; Referee: Artur Manuel Ribeiro Soares Dias (Portugal); Attendance: 14,027

Villarreal CF – FK Zenit Saint Petersburg 2-1(1-0)

Villarreal CF: Andrés Fernández, Mario Gaspar, Jaume Costa, Víctor Ruíz, Ramiro Funes Mori (77.Miguelón Llambrich), Álvaro González, Vicente Iborra (70.Santi Cazorla), Pablo Fornals, Santiago Cáseres (46.Manu Morlanes), Carlos Bacca, Gerard Moreno. Trainer: Javi Calleja.

Zenit Saint Petersburg: Andrei Lunev (64.Mikhail Kerzhakov), Branislav Ivanovic, Igor Smolnikov, Yaroslav Rakitskiy, Emanuel Mammana, Oleg Shatov, Magomed Ozdoev, Hernani, Wilmar Barrios (46.Matías Kranevitter), Sardar Azmoun (71.Róbert Mak), Sebastián Driussi. Trainer: Sergey Semak.

Goals: 1-0 Gerard Moreno (29), 2-0 Carlos Bacca (47), 2-1 Branislav Ivanovic (90+1).

[Villarreal CF won 5-2 on aggregate]

07.03.2019; Stamford Bridge, London; Referee: Slavko Vinčić (Slovenia); Attendance: 37,280

Chelsea FC London – FK Dynamo Kyiv 3-0(1-0)

Chelsea FC: Kepa, David Luiz, Marcos Alonso, Davide Zappacosta, Andreas Christensen, Ross Barkley (62.Ruben Loftus-Cheek), Mateo Kovacic, Jorginho (62.N'Golo Kanté), Willian (78.Callum Hudson-Odoi), Olivier Giroud, Pedro. Trainer: Maurizio Sarri.

Dynamo Kyiv: Denis Boyko, Tomasz Kedziora, Mykyta Burda, Artem Shabanov, Vitali Mykolenko, Sergiy Sydorchuk, Vitaliy Buyalskiy (71.Sidcley), Viktor Tsygankov, Mykola Shaparenko, Volodymyr Shepelev, Nazariy Rusyn (66.Denys Garmash). Trainer: Aleksandr Khatskevich.

Goals: 1-0 Pedro (17), 2-0 Willian (65), 3-0 Callum Hudson-Odoi (90).

14.03.2019; NSK Olimpiyskiy Stadium, Kyiv; Referee: Tobias Stieler (Germany); Attendance: 64,830

FK Dynamo Kyiv – Chelsea FC London 0-5(0-3)

Dynamo Kyiv: Denis Boyko, Tamás Kádár, Tomasz Kedziora, Mykyta Burda, Sidcley (81.Yevhenii Smyrnyi), Vitali Mykolenko, Sergiy Sydorchuk (65.Tchê Tchê), Denys Garmash, Viktor Tsygankov, Mykola Shaparenko, Volodymyr Shepelev (87.Oleksandr Andrievsky). Trainer: Aleksandr Khatskevich.

Chelsea FC: Kepa, Marcos Alonso, Antonio Rüdiger, Davide Zappacosta (69.Azpilicueta), Andreas Christensen, Mateo Kovacic, N'Golo Kanté (65.Jorginho), Ruben Loftus-Cheek, Willian (74.Pedro), Olivier Giroud, Callum Hudson-Odoi. Trainer: Maurizio Sarri.

Goals: 0-1, 0-2 Olivier Giroud (5, 33), 0-3 Marcos Alonso (45+1), 0-4 Olivier Giroud (59), 0-5 Callum Hudson-Odoi (78).

[Chelsea FC London won 8-0 on aggregate]

07.03.2019; Stadio San Paolo, Napoli; Referee: Aleksei Kulbakov (Belarus); Attendance: 32,579

SSC Napoli – FC Red Bull Salzburg 3-0(2-0)

SSC Napoli: Alex Meret, Nikola Maksimovic, Mário Rui, Kalidou Koulibaly, Elseid Hysaj, Allan, Piotr Zielinski (66.Amadou Diawara), Fabián Ruiz, Dries Mertens (72.Lorenzo Insigne), José Callejón, Arkadiusz Milik (81.Adam Ounas). Trainer: Carlo Ancelotti.

Red Bull Salzburg: Alexander Walke, Andreas Ulmer, Stefan Lainer, André Ramalho, Jérôme Onguéné, Zlatko Junuzovic (62.Enock Mwepu), Xaver Schlager, Diadié Samassékou, Munas Dabour (76.Takumi Minamino), Patson Daka (62.Fredrik Gulbrandsen), Hannes Wolf. Trainer: Marco Rose.

Goals: 1-0 Arkadiusz Milik (10), 2-0 Fabián Ruiz (18), 3-0 Jérôme Onguéné (58 own goal).

14.03.2019; Red Bull Arena, Wals-Siezenheim; Referee: Carlos del Cerro Grande (Spain); Attendance: 29,520

FC Red Bull Salzburg – SSC Napoli 3-1(1-1)

Red Bull Salzburg: Alexander Walke, Andreas Ulmer, Stefan Lainer, André Ramalho, Jérôme Onguéné, Diadié Samassékou, Dominik Szoboszlai (74.Christoph Leitgeb), Enock Mwepu (59.Fredrik Gulbrandsen), Munas Dabour, Takumi Minamino (86.Erling Håland), Hannes Wolf. Trainer: Marco Rose.

SSC Napoli: Alex Meret, Vlad Chiriches (78.Kévin Malcuit), Mário Rui, Elseid Hysaj, Sebastiano Luperto, Allan, Piotr Zielinski (74.Amadou Diawara), Fabián Ruiz, Dries Mertens (88.Amin Younes), José Callejón, Arkadiusz Milik. Trainer: Carlo Ancelotti.

Goals: 0-1 Arkadiusz Milik (14), 1-1 Munas Dabour (25), 2-1 Fredrik Gulbrandsen (65), 3-1 Christoph Leitgeb (90+2).

[SSC Napoli won 4-3 on aggregate]

07.03.2019; Estadio de Mestalla, Valencia; Referee: Orel Grinfeld (Israel); Attendance: 36,274

Valencia CF – FK Krasnodar 2-1(2-0)

Valencia CF: Neto, Gabriel Paulista, Cristiano Piccini, Mouctar Daikhaby, Toni Lato, Dani Parejo, Francis Coquelin, Gonçalo Guedes (70.Denis Cheryshev), Carlos Soler, Kevin Gamiero (79.Rubén Sobrino), Rodrigo (63.Santi Mina). Trainer: Marcelino.

FK Krasnodar: Matvei Safonov, Aleksandr Martynovich, Sergey Petrov, Uros Spajic, Cristian Ramírez, Charles Kaboré, Dmitriy Stotskiy (55.Ari), Yuri Gazinskiy (89.Artem Golubev), Victor Claesson, Kristoffer Olsson, Wamberto (80.Magomed Suleymanov). Trainer: Murad Musaev.

Goals: 1-0, 2-0 Rodrigo (12, 24), 2-1 Victor Claesson (63).

14.03.2019; Stadion FK Krasnodar, Krasnodar; Referee: Anthony Taylor (England); Attendance: 35,074

FK Krasnodar – Valencia CF 1-1(0-0)

FK Krasnodar: Matvei Safonov, Jón Fjóluson, Sergey Petrov (75.Magomed Suleymanov), Uros Spajic, Cristian Ramírez, Mauricio Pereyra (90+1.Ivan Taranov), Yuri Gazinskiy, Victor Claesson, Kristoffer Olsson, Wamberto, Ari (30.Dmitriy Stotskiy). Trainer: Murad Musaev.

Valencia CF: Neto, Gabriel Paulista, José Gayà, Mouctar Daikhaby, Daniel Wass, Francis Coquelin, Denis Cheryshev, Geoffrey Kondogbia, Carlos Soler (88.Kevin Gamiero), Rubén Sobrino (58.Rodrigo), Santi Mina (70.Gonçalo Guedes). Trainer: Marcelino.

Goals: 1-0 Magomed Suleymanov (85), 1-1 Gonçalo Guedes (90+3).

[Valencia CF won 3-2 on aggregate]

QUARTER-FINALS

11.04.2019; Emirates Stadium, London; Referee: Alberto Undiano Mallenco (Spain); Attendance: 59,738

Arsenal FC London – SSC Napoli 2-0(2-0)

Arsenal FC: Petr Cech, Nacho Monreal, Sokratis Papastathopoulos, Laurent Koscielny, Sead Kolasinac, Mesut Özil (67.Henrikh Mkhitaryan), Aaron Ramsey, Ainsley Maitland-Niles, Lucas Torreira (77.Mohamed El Neny), Pierre-Emerick Aubameyang, Alexandre Lacazette (67.Alex Iwobi). Trainer: Unai Emery.

SSC Napoli: Alex Meret, Nikola Maksimovic, Mário Rui, Kalidou Koulibaly, Elseid Hysaj, Allan, Piotr Zielinski, Fabián Ruiz (82.Adam Ounas), Dries Mertens (66.Arkadiusz Milik), José Callejón, Lorenzo Insigne (82.Amin Younes). Trainer: Carlo Ancelotti.

Goals: 1-0 Aaron Ramsey (14), 2-0 Kalidou Koulibaly (25 own goal).

18.04.2019; Stadio San Paolo, Napoli; Referee: Ovidiu Alin Haţegan (Romania); Attendance: 39,438

SSC Napoli – Arsenal FC London 0-1(0-1)

SSC Napoli: Alex Meret, Vlad Chiriches, Nikola Maksimovic (46.Dries Mertens), Kalidou Koulibaly, Faouzi Ghoulam (71.Mário Rui), Allan, Piotr Zielinski, Fabián Ruiz, José Callejón, Lorenzo Insigne (61.Amin Younes), Arkadiusz Milik. Trainer: Carlo Ancelotti.

Arsenal FC: Petr Cech, Nacho Monreal, Sokratis Papastathopoulos, Laurent Koscielny, Sead Kolasinac, Aaron Ramsey (34.Henrikh Mkhitaryan), Granit Xhaka (61.Mohamed El Neny), Ainsley Maitland-Niles, Lucas Torreira, Pierre-Emerick Aubameyang, Alexandre Lacazette (68.Alex Iwobi). Trainer: Unai Emery.

Goal: 0-1 Alexandre Lacazette (36).

[Arsenal FC London won 3-0 on aggregate]

11.04.2019; Estadio de la Cerámica, Villarreal; Referee: Michael Oliver (England); Attendance: 17,605

Villarreal CF – Valencia CF 1-3(1-1)

Villarreal CF: Andrés Fernández, Mario Gaspar (80.Alfonso Pedraza), Víctor Ruíz, Álvaro González, Xavi Quintillà, Santi Cazorla, Vicente Iborra (67.Carlos Bacca), Pablo Fornals, Samuel Chukwueze, Santiago Cáseres (72.Manu Morlanes), Gerard Moreno. Trainer: Javi Calleja.

Valencia CF: Neto, Ezequiel Garay, Facundo Roncaglia (58.Cristiano Piccini), Gabriel Paulista, José Gayà, Daniel Wass, Dani Parejo, Gonçalo Guedes, Ferrán Torres (61.Francis Coquelin), Kevin Gamiero (69.Denis Cheryshev), Rodrigo. Trainer: Marcelino.

Goals: 0-1 Gonçalo Guedes (6), 1-1 Santi Cazorla (36 penalty), 1-2 Daniel Wass (90), 1-3 Gonçalo Guedes (90+3).

18.04.2019; Estadio de Mestalla, Valencia; Referee: William Collum (Scotland); Attendance: 26,403

Valencia CF – Villarreal CF 2-0(1-0)

Valencia CF: Neto, Facundo Roncaglia, Mouctar Diakhaby, Toni Lato, Daniel Wass, Dani Parejo (62.Francis Coquelin), Gonçalo Guedes (68.Lee Kang-In), Carlos Soler (46.Gabriel Paulista), Ferrán Torres, Kevin Gameiro, Santi Mina. Trainer: Marcelino.

Villarreal CF: Andrés Fernández, Jaume Costa, Víctor Ruíz, Ramiro Funes Mori, Trigueros (74.Javi Fuego), Manu Morlanes, Alfonso Pedraza, Santiago Cáseres (64.Pablo Fornals), Andrei Ratiu, Gerard Moreno, Dani Raba (46.Samuel Chukwueze). Trainer: Javi Calleja.

Goals: 1-0 Toni Lato (13), 2-0 Dani Parejo (54).

[Valencia CF won 5-1 on aggregate]

11.04.2019; Estádio do Sport Lisboa e Befica, Lisboa; Referee: Anthony Taylor (England); Attendance: 54,175

Sport Lisboa e Benfica – Eintracht Frankfurt 4-2(2-1)

Benfica: Odisseas Vlachodimos, Sébastien Corchia (66.Pizzi), Jardel, Álex Grimaldo, Rúben Dias, Ljubomir Fejsa, Andreas Samaris (85.Andrija Zivkovic), Rafa Silva (60.Haris Seferovic), Franco Cervi, Gedson Fernandes, João Félix. Trainer: Bruno Lage.

Eintracht Frankfurt: Kevin Trapp, David Abraham, Martin Hinteregger, Danny da Costa, Evan Obite N'Dicka [*sent off 20*], Makoto Hasebe, Gelson Fernandes, Sebastian Rode (85.Mijat Gacinovic), Filip Kostic, Ante Rebic (68.Gonçalo Paciência), Luka Jovic (60.Jonathan de Guzmán). Trainer: Adi Hütter.

Goals: 1-0 João Félix (21 penalty), 1-1 Luka Jovic (40), 2-1 João Félix (43), 3-1 Rúben Dias (50), 4-1 João Félix (54), 4-2 Gonçalo Paciência (72).

18.04.2019; Commerzbank-Arena, Frankfurt am Main; Referee: Daniele Orsato (Italy); Attendance: 48,000

Eintracht Frankfurt – Sport Lisboa e Benfica 2-0(1-0)

Eintracht Frankfurt: Kevin Trapp, David Abraham, Simon Falette (90+2.Jetro Willems), Danny da Costa, Makoto Hasebe, Gelson Fernandes, Sebastian Rode (86.Lucas Torró), Filip Kostic, Mijat Gacinovic, Ante Rebic, Luka Jovic (76.Gonçalo Paciência). Trainer: Adi Hütter.

Benfica: Odisseas Vlachodimos, André Almeida (79.Jonas), Jardel, Álex Grimaldo, Rúben Dias, Ljubomir Fejsa, Andreas Samaris (70.Pizzi), Rafa Silva (72.Eduardo Salvio), Gedson Fernandes, Haris Seferovic, João Félix. Trainer: Bruno Lage.

Goals: 1-0 Filip Kostic (37), 2-0 Sebastian Rode (67).

[Eintracht Frankfurt won on away goals rule (4-4 on aggregate)]

11.04.2019; Sinobo Stadium, Praha; Referee: Felix Zwayer (Germany); Attendance: 17,484

SK Slavia Praha – Chelsea FC London 0-1(0-0)

Slavia Praha: Ondrej Kolár, Jan Boril, Vladimír Coufal, Simon Deli, Alex Král, Miroslav Stoch (64.Jaromír Zmrhal), Michael Ngadeu-Ngadjui, Lukás Masopust (74.Josef Husbauer), Petr Sevcík, Ibrahim Traoré, Peter Olayinka (82.Mick van Buren). Trainer: Jindrich Trpisovsky.

Chelsea FC: Kepa, Azpilicueta, Marcos Alonso, Antonio Rüdiger, Andreas Christensen, Ross Barkley (75.Ruben Loftus-Cheek), Mateo Kovacic (68.N'Golo Kanté), Jorginho, Willian, Olivier Giroud, Pedro (59.Eden Hazard). Trainer: Maurizio Sarri.

Goal: 0-1 Marcos Alonso (86).

18.04.2019; Stamford Bridge, London; Referee: Damir Skomina (Slovenia); Attendance: 38,326

Chelsea FC London – SK Slavia Praha 4-3(4-1)

Chelsea FC: Kepa, David Luiz, Azpilicueta, Emerson, Andreas Christensen, Ross Barkley (70.Jorginho), Mateo Kovacic, N'Golo Kanté, Eden Hazard (65.Willian), Olivier Giroud, Pedro (87.Callum Hudson-Odoi). Trainer: Maurizio Sarri.

Slavia Praha: Ondrej Kolár, Ondrej Kúdela, Jan Boril, Simon Deli, Alex Král, Michael Ngadeu-Ngadjui, Jaromír Zmrhal (85.Milan Skoda), Lukás Masopust (52.Peter Olayinka), Petr Sevcík (78.Miroslav Stoch), Tomás Soucek, Ibrahim Traoré. Trainer: Jindrich Trpisovsky.

Goals: 1-0 Pedro (5), 2-0 Simon Deli (9 own goal), 3-0 Olivier Giroud (17), 3-1 Tomás Soucek (25), 4-1 Pedro (27), 4-2, 4-3 Petr Sevcík (51, 54).

[Chelsea FC London won 5-3 on aggregate]

SEMI-FINALS

02.05.2019; Emirates Stadium, London; Referee: Clément Turpin (France); Attendance: 58,969

Arsenal FC London – Valencia CF 3-1(2-1)

Arsenal FC: Petr Cech, Sokratis Papastathopoulos, Laurent Koscielny (82.Nacho Monreal), Shkodran Mustafi, Sead Kolasinac, Mesut Özil (75.Henrikh Mkhitaryan), Granit Xhaka, Ainsley Maitland-Niles, Mattéo Guendouzi (58.Lucas Torreira), Pierre-Emerick Aubameyang, Alexandre Lacazette. Trainer: Unai Emery.

Valencia CF: Neto, Ezequiel Garay, Facundo Roncaglia, Gabriel Paulista, Cristiano Piccini, José Gayá, Mouctar Diakhaby, Dani Parejo, Gonçalo Guedes (71.Kevin Gameiro), Carlos Soler (71.Daniel Wass), Rodrigo (88.Santi Mina). Trainer: Marcelino.

Goals: 0-1 Mouctar Diakhaby (11), 1-1, 2-1 Alexandre Lacazette (18, 26), 3-1 Pierre-Emerick Aubameyang (90+1).

09.05.2019; Estadio de Mestalla, Valencia; Referee: Danny Desmond Makkelie (Netherlands); Attendance: 44,481

Valencia CF – Arsenal FC London 2-4(1-1)

Valencia CF: Neto, Ezequiel Garay, Gabriel Paulista, Cristiano Piccini (56.Carlos Soler), José Gayá, Daniel Wass, Dani Parejo, Francis Coquelin, Gonçalo Guedes (71.Ferrán Torres), Kevin Gameiro, Rodrigo (72.Santi Mina). Trainer: Marcelino.

Arsenal FC: Petr Cech, Nacho Monreal, Sokratis Papastathopoulos, Laurent Koscielny, Sead Kolasinac (71.Shkodran Mustafi), Mesut Özil (62.Henrikh Mkhitaryan), Granit Xhaka, Ainsley Maitland-Niles, Lucas Torreira (80.Mattéo Guendouzi), Pierre-Emerick Aubameyang, Alexandre Lacazette. Trainer: Unai Emery.

Goals: 1-0 Kevin Gameiro (11), 1-1 Pierre-Emerick Aubameyang (17), 1-2 Alexandre Lacazette (50), 2-2 Kevin Gameiro (58), 2-3, 2-4 Pierre-Emerick Aubameyang (69, 88).

[Arsenal FC London won 7-3 on aggregate]

02.05.2019; Commerzbank-Arena, Frankfurt am Main; Referee: Carlos del Cerro Grande (Spain); Attendance: 48,000

Eintracht Frankfurt – Chelsea FC London 1-1(1-1)

Eintracht Frankfurt: Kevin Trapp, David Abraham, Martin Hinteregger, Simon Falette, Danny da Costa, Makoto Hasebe, Gelson Fernandes (73.Gonçalo Paciência), Sebastian Rode, Filip Kostic, Mijat Gacinovic (90+2.Jetro Willems), Luka Jovic. Trainer: Adi Hütter.

Chelsea FC: Kepa, David Luiz, Azpilicueta, Emerson, Andreas Christensen, Jorginho, N'Golo Kanté, Ruben Loftus-Cheek (83.Mateo Kovacic), Willian (61.Eden Hazard), Olivier Giroud, Pedro. Trainer: Maurizio Sarri.

Goals: 1-0 Luka Jovic (23), 1-1 Pedro (45).

09.05.2019; Stamford Bridge, London; Referee: Ovidiu Alin Haţegan (Romania); Attendance: 36,070

Chelsea FC London – Eintracht Frankfurt 1-1(1-0,1-1)

Chelsea FC: Kepa, David Luiz, Azpilicueta, Emerson, Andreas Christensen (74.Davide Zappacosta), Mateo Kovacic, Jorginho, Ruben Loftus-Cheek (86.Ross Barkley), Willian (62.Pedro), Eden Hazard, Olivier Giroud (96.Gonzalo Higuaín). Trainer: Maurizio Sarri.

Eintracht Frankfurt: Kevin Trapp, David Abraham, Martin Hinteregger, Simon Falette, Danny da Costa, Makoto Hasebe, Sebastian Rode (70.Jonathan de Guzmán), Filip Kostic, Mijat Gacinovic (118.Gonçalo Paciência), Ante Rebic (90+3.Sébastien Haller), Luka Jovic. Trainer: Adi Hütter.

Goals: 1-0 Ruben Loftus-Cheek (28), 1-1 Luka Jovic (49).

Penalties: Sébastien Haller 0-1; Ross Barkley 1-1; Luka Jovic 1-2, Azpilicueta (missed); Jonathan de Guzmán 1-3; Jorginho 2-3; Martin Hinteregger (missed); David Luiz 3-3; Gonçalo Paciência (missed); Eden Hazard 4-3.

[Chelsea FC London won 4-3 on penalties (after 2-2 on aggregate)]

FINAL

29.05.2019; Bakı Olimpiya Stadionu, Bakı; Referee: Gianluca Rocchi (Italy); Attendance: 51,370

Chelsea FC London – Arsenal FC London 4-1(0-0)

Chelsea FC: Kepa, David Luiz, Azpilicueta, Emerson, Andreas Christensen, Mateo Kovacic (76.Ross Barkley), Jorginho, N'Golo Kanté, Eden Hazard (89.Davide Zappacosta), Olivier Giroud, Pedro (71.Willian). Trainer: Maurizio Sarri.

Arsenal FC: Petr Cech, Nacho Monreal (66.Mattéo Guendouzi), Sokratis Papastathopoulos, Laurent Koscielny, Sead Kolasinac, Mesut Özil (77.Joseph Willock), Granit Xhaka, Ainsley Maitland-Niles, Lucas Torreira (67.Alex Iwobi), Pierre-Emerick Aubameyang, Alexandre Lacazette. Trainer: Unai Emery.

Goals: 1-0 Olivier Giroud (49), 2-0 Pedro (60), 3-0 Eden Hazard (65 penalty), 3-1 Alex Iwobi (69), 4-1 Eden Hazard (72).

UEFA Champions League Winner 2018/2019: **Chelsea FC London** (England)

Best Goalscorers: Olivier Jonathan Giroud (Chelsea FC London) – 11 goals

FAIRS CUP (1958-1971)
UEFA CUP (1972-2009)
UEFA EUROPA LEAGUE (2010-2019)
TABLE OF HONOURS

1955/1958	FC Barcelona	*Spain*
1958/1960	FC Barcelona	*Spain*
1960/1961	AS Roma	*Italy*
1961/1962	Valencia CF	*Spain*
1962/1963	Valencia CF	*Spain*
1963/1964	Real Zaragoza	*Spain*
1964/1965	Ferencvárosi TC	*Hungary*
1965/1966	FC Barcelona	*Spain*
1966/1967	GNK Dinamo Zagreb	*Croatia*
1967/1968	Leeds United FC	*England*
1968/1969	Newcastle United FC	*England*
1969/1970	Arsenal FC London	*England*
1970/1971	Leeds United FC	*England*
1971/1972	Tottenham Hotspur FC London	*England*
1972/1973	Liverpool FC	*England*
1973/1974	Feyenoord Rotterdam	*Netherlands*
1974/1975	Borussia VfL Mönchengladbach	*Germany*
1975/1976	Liverpool FC	*England*
1976/1977	Juventus FC Torino	*Italy*
1977/1978	PSV Eindhoven	*Netherlands*
1978/1979	Borussia VfL Mönchengladbach	*Germany*
1979/1980	Eintracht Frankfurt	*Germany*
1980/1981	Ipswich Town FC	*England*
1981/1982	IFK Göteborg	*Sweden*
1982/1983	RSC Anderlecht Bruxelles	*Belgium*
1983/1984	Tottenham Hotspur FC London	*England*
1984/1985	Real Madrid CF	*Spain*
1985/1986	Real Madrid CF	*Spain*
1986/1987	IFK Göteborg	*Sweden*
1987/1988	TSV Bayer 04 Leverkusen	*Germany*
1988/1989	SSC Napoli	*Italy*
1989/1990	Juventus FC Torino	*Italy*
1990/1991	FC Internazionale Milano	*Italy*
1991/1992	AFC Ajax Amsterdam	*Netherlands*
1992/1993	Juventus FC Torino	*Italy*
1993/1994	FC Internazionale Milano	*Italy*
1994/1995	Parma AC	*Italy*
1995/1996	FC Bayern München	*Germany*
1996/1997	FC Schalke 04 Gelsenkirchen	*Germany*
1997/1998	FC Internazionale Milano	*Italy*
1998/1999	Parma AC	*Italy*
1999/2000	Galatasaray SK İstanbul	*Turkey*
2000/2001	Liverpool FC	*England*
2001/2002	Feyenoord Rotterdam	*Netherlands*
2002/2003	FC do Porto	*Portugal*
2003/2004	Valencia CF	*Spain*
2004/2005	FK CSKA Moskva	*Russia*
2005/2006	Sevilla FC	*Spain*
2006/2007	Sevilla FC	*Spain*
2007/2008	FK Zenit Saint Petersburg	*Russia*
2008/2009	FK Shakhtar Donetsk	*Ukraine*
2009/2010	Club Atlético de Madrid	*Spain*
2010/2011	FC do Porto	*Portugal*
2011/2012	Club Atlético de Madrid	*Spain*
2012/2013	Chelsea FC London	*England*
2013/2014	Sevilla FC	*Spain*
2014/2015	Sevilla FC	*Spain*
2015/2016	Sevilla FC	*Spain*
2016/2017	Manchester United FC	*England*
2017/2018	Club Atlético de Madrid	*Spain*
2018/2019	Chelsea FC London	*England*

UEFA SUPERCUP 2018

The 2018 UEFA Super Cup was the 43rd edition of the UEFA Super Cup, an annual football match organised by UEFA and contested by the winners of the two main European club competitions, the UEFA Champions League and the UEFA Europa League. The 2018 final match featured Spanish clubs Real Madrid CF (the title holders and winners of the 2017/2018 UEFA Champions League) and Club Atlético de Madrid (the winners of the 2017/2018 UEFA Europa League).

15.08.2018; A. Le Coq Arena, Tallinn; Referee: Szymon Marciniak (Poland); Attendance: 12, 424

Club Atlético de Madrid – Real Madrid CF 4-2(1-1,2-2)

Atlético Madrid: Jan Oblak, Juanfran, Stefan Savić, Diego Godín (Cap), Lucas Hernández, Thomas Lemar (90+1.Thomas Partey), Rodri (71.Vitolo), Saúl Ñíguez, Koke, Diego Costa (109.José Giménez), Antoine Griezmann (57.Ángel Correa). Trainer: Germán Adrián Ramón Burgos (Argentina).

Real Madrid: Keylor Navas, Dani Carvajal, Sergio Ramos (Cap), Raphaël Varane, Marcelo, Casemiro (76.Dani Ceballos), Toni Kroos (102.Borja Mayoral), Isco (83.Lucas Vázquez), Marco Asensio (57.Luka Modrić), Karim Benzema. Trainer: Julen Lopetegui Argote.

Goals: 1-0 Diego Costa (1), 1-1 Karim Benzema (27), 1-2 Sergio Ramos (63 penalty), 2-2 Diego Costa (79), 3-2 Saúl Ñíguez (98), 4-2 Koke (104).

UEFA Supercup Winner 2018: **Club Atlético de Madrid** (Spain)

UEFA SUPER CUP (SINCE 1972)
TABLE OF HONOURS

1972	AFC Ajax Amsterdam (not official)	*Netherlands*
1973	AFC Ajax Amsterdam	*Netherlands*
1974	*Not played*	
1975	FK Dinamo Kyiv	*Soviet Union*
1976	RSC Anderlecht Bruxelles	*Belgium*
1977	Liverpool FC	*England*
1978	RSC Anderlecht Bruxelles	*Belgium*
1979	Nottingham Forest FC	*England*
1980	CF Valencia	*Spain*
1981	*Not played*	
1982	Aston Villa FC Birmingham	*England*
1983	Aberdeen FC	*Scotland*
1984	Juventus FC Torino	*Italy*
1985	*Not played*	
1986	FC Steaua București	*Romania*
1987	FC do Porto	*Portugal*
1988	KV Mechelen	*Belgium*
1989	AC Milan	*Italy*
1990	AC Milan	*Italy*
1991	Manchester United FC	*England*
1992	FC Barcelona	*Spain*
1993	Parma AC	*Italy*
1994	AC Milan	*Italy*
1995	AFC Ajax Amsterdam	*Netherlands*
1996	Juventus FC Torino	*Italy*
1997	FC Barcelona	*Spain*
1998	Chelsea FC London	*England*
1999	SS Lazio Roma	*Italy*
2000	Galatasaray SK İstanbul	*Turkey*
2001	Liverpool FC	*England*
2002	Real Madrid CF	*Spain*
2003	AC Milan	*Italy*
2004	Valencia CF	*Spain*
2005	Liverpool FC	*England*
2006	Sevilla FC	*Spain*
2007	AC Milan	*Italy*
2008	FK Zenit Saint Petersburg	*Russia*
2009	FC Barcelona	*Spain*
2010	Club Atlético de Madrid	*Spain*
2011	FC Barcelona	*Spain*
2012	Club Atlético de Madrid	*Spain*
2013	FC Bayern München	*Germany*
2014	Real Madrid CF	*Spain*
2015	FC Barcelona	*Spain*
2016	Real Madrid CF	*Spain*
2017	Real Madrid CF	*Spain*
2018	Club Atlético de Madrid	*Spain*

ALBANIA

The Country:

Republic of Albania (Republika e Shqipërisë)
Capital: Tiranë
Surface: 28,748 km²
Inhabitants: 2,876,591 [2017]
Time: UTC+1

The FA:

Federata Shqiptare e Futbollit
Rruga e Elbasanit 1000 Tiranë
Tel: +355 42 346605
Foundation date: 06.06.1930
Member of FIFA since: 12.06.1932
Member of UEFA since: 1954
Website: www.fshf.org

NATIONAL TEAM RECORDS

First international match:	07.10.1946, Tiranë:	Albania – Yugoslavia 2-3
Most international caps:	Lorik Cana	- 93 caps (2003-2016)
Most international goals:	Erjon Bogdani	- 18 goal / 74 caps (1996-2013)

UEFA EUROPEAN CHAMPIONSHIP	
1960	Qualifiers
1964	Qualifiers
1968	Qualifiers
1972	Qualifiers
1976	*Did not enter*
1980	*Did not enter*
1984	Qualifiers
1988	Qualifiers
1992	Qualifiers
1996	Qualifiers
2000	Qualifiers
2004	Qualifiers
2008	Qualifiers
2012	Qualifiers
2016	Final Tournament (Group Stage)

FIFA WORLD CUP	
1930	*Did not enter*
1934	*Did not enter*
1938	*Did not enter*
1950	*Did not enter*
1954	*Did not enter*
1958	*Did not enter*
1962	*Did not enter*
1966	Qualifiers
1970	*Entry not accepted by FIFA*
1974	Qualifiers
1978	*Did not enter*
1982	Qualifiers
1986	Qualifiers
1990	Qualifiers
1994	Qualifiers
1998	Qualifiers
2002	Qualifiers
2006	Qualifiers
2010	Qualifiers
2014	Qualifiers
2018	Qualifiers

UEFA NATIONS LEAGUE
2018/2019 – League C

OLYMPIC FOOTBALL TOURNAMENTS 1908-2016							
1908	-	**1948**	-	**1972**	-	**1996**	-
1912	-	**1952**	-	**1976**	-	**2000**	Qualifiers
1920	-	**1956**	-	**1980**	-	**2004**	Qualifiers
1924	-	**1960**	-	**1984**	*Withdrew*	**2008**	Qualifiers
1928	-	**1964**	-	**1988**	-	**2012**	Qualifiers
1936	-	**1968**	-	**1992**	*Withdrew*	**2016**	Qualifiers

FIFA CONFEDERATIONS CUP 1992-2017
None

ALBANIAN CLUB HONOURS IN EUROPEAN CLUB COMPETITIONS:

European Champion Clubs' Cup (1956-1992) / UEFA Champions League (1993-2019)
None
Fairs Cup (1858-1971) / UEFA Cup (1972-2009) / UEFA Europa League (2010-2019)
None
UEFA Super Cup (1972-2019)
None
European Cup Winners' Cup 1961-1999*
None

**defunct competition*

NATIONAL COMPETITIONS
TABLE OF HONOURS

	CHAMPIONS	CUP WINNERS	BEST GOALSCORERS	
1930	SK Tiranë	-	-	
1931	SK Tiranë	-	Teli Samsuri (Skënderbeu Korçë)	9
1932	SK Tiranë	-	-	
1933	Skënderbeu Korçë	-	Servet Tefik Agai (Skënderbeu Korçë)	7
1934	SK Tiranë	-	Mark Gurashi (SK Tiranë)	12
1935	*No Competition*	-	*No Competition*	
1936	SK Tiranë	-	Riza Lushta (SK Tiranë)	11
1937	SK Tiranë	-	Riza Lushta (SK Tiranë)	25
1938	*No Competition*	-	*No Competition*	
1939	SK Tiranë *(unofficial)*	SK Tiranë	-	
1940	Vllaznia Shkodër *(unofficial)*	*No Competition*	-	
1941	*No Competition*	*No Competition*	*No Competition*	
1942	SK Tiranë *(unofficial)*	*No Competition*	-	
1943	*No Competition*	*No Competition*	*No Competition*	
1944	*No Competition*	*No Competition*	*No Competition*	
1945	Vllaznia Shkodër	*No Competition*	Loro Boriçi (Vllaznia Shkodër)	11
1946	Vllaznia Shkodër	*No Competition*	Xhevdet Shaqiri (Vllaznia Shkodër)	11
1947	Partizani Tiranë	*No Competition*	Hamdi Bakalli (Partizani Tiranë)	7
1948	Partizani Tiranë	Partizani Tiranë	Tish Daija (Flamurtari Vlorë) Zihni Gjinali (Partizani Tiranë)	11
1949	Partizani Tiranë	Partizani Tiranë	Zihni Gjinali (Partizani Tiranë)	14
1950	Dinamo Tiranë	Dinamo Tiranë	Refik Resmja (Partizani Tiranë)	?
1951	Dinamo Tiranë	Dinamo Tiranë	Refik Resmja (Partizani Tiranë)	59
1952	Dinamo Tiranë	Dinamo Tiranë	Refik Resmja (Partizani Tiranë)	17
1953	Dinamo Tiranë	Dinamo Tiranë	Refik Resmja (Partizani Tiranë)	9
1954	Partizani Tiranë	Dinamo Tiranë	Refik Resmja (Partizani Tiranë)	13
1955	Dinamo Tiranë	*No Competition*	Refik Resmja (Partizani Tiranë) Skënder Jareci (Dinamo Tiranë)	23
1956	Dinamo Tiranë	*No Competition*	Refik Resmja (Partizani Tiranë)	17
1957	Partizani Tiranë	Partizani Tiranë	Niko Bespalla (Teuta)	15
1958	Partizani Tiranë	Partizani Tiranë	Skënder Jareci (Dinamo Tiranë)	14
1959	Partizani Tiranë	*No Competition*	Stavri Lubonja (Dinamo Tiranë)	11
1960	Dinamo Tiranë	Dinamo Tiranë	Skënder Jareci (Dinamo Tiranë)	16
1961	Partizani Tiranë	Partizani Tiranë	Panajot Pano (Partizani Tiranë)	17
1962/1963	Partizani Tiranë	*No Competition*	Robert Jashari (Partizani Tiranë)	18
1963/1964	Partizani Tiranë	17 Nëntori Tiranë	Robert Jashari (Partizani Tiranë)	9
1964/1965	17 Nëntori Tiranë	Partizani Tiranë	Robert Jashari (Partizani Tiranë)	14
1965/1966	17 Nëntori Tiranë	Vllaznia Shkodër	Sajmir Dauti (Dinamo Tiranë)	13
1966/1967	Dinamo Tiranë	Partizani Tiranë	Medin Zhega (Dinamo Tiranë)	19
1968	17 Nëntori Tiranë	Partizani Tiranë	Skënder Hyka (17 Nëntori Tiranë)	19
1969/1970	17 Nëntori Tiranë	Partizani Tiranë	Panajot Pano (Partizani Tiranë)	17
1970/1971	Partizani Tiranë	Dinamo Tiranë	Ilir Përnaska (Dinamo Tiranë)	19
1971/1972	Vllaznia Shkodër	Vllaznia Shkodër	Ilir Përnaska (Dinamo Tiranë)	17
1972/1973	Dinamo Tiranë	Partizani Tiranë	Ilir Përnaska (Dinamo Tiranë)	12
1973/1974	Vllaznia Shkodër	Dinamo Tiranë	Ilir Përnaska (Dinamo Tiranë)	19
1974/1975	Dinamo Tiranë	Elbasani	Ilir Përnaska (Dinamo Tiranë)	17
1975/1976	Dinamo Tiranë	17 Nëntori Tiranë	Ilir Përnaska (Dinamo Tiranë)	18
1976/1977	Dinamo Tiranë	17 Nëntori Tiranë	Agim Murati (Partizani Tiranë)	12
1977/1978	Vllaznia Shkodër	Dinamo Tiranë	Agim Murati (Partizani Tiranë)	14
1978/1979	Partizani Tiranë	Vllaznia Shkodër	Agim Murati (Partizani Tiranë) Petrit Dibra (17 Nëntori Tiranë)	14
1979/1980	Dinamo Tiranë	Partizani Tiranë	Përparim Kovaçi (Tomori Berat)	18
1980/1981	Partizani Tiranë	Vllaznia Shkodër	Dashnor Bajaziti (Besa Kavajë)	12
1981/1982	KF Tiranë	Dinamo Tiranë	Vasil Ruci (Flamurtari Vlorë)	12
1982/1983	Vllaznia Shkodër	17 Nëntori Tiranë	Dashnor Bajaziti (Besa Kavajë)	16
1983/1984	Elbasani	17 Nëntori Tiranë	Vasil Ruci (Flamurtari Vlorë)	12
1984/1985	17 Nëntori Tiranë	Flamurtari Vlorë	Faslli Fakja (Vllaznia Shkodër) Arben Minga (17 Nëntori Tiranë)	13
1985/1986	Dinamo Tiranë	17 Nëntori Tiranë	Kujtim Majaci (Apolonia Fier)	20
1986/1987	Partizani Tiranë	Vllaznia Shkodër	Arben Arbëri (Tomori Berat)	14
1987/1988	17 Nëntori Tiranë	Flamurtari Vlorë	Agustin Kola (17 Nëntori Tiranë)	18
1988/1989	17 Nëntori Tiranë	Dinamo Tiranë	Agustin Kola (17 Nëntori Tiranë)	19
1989/1990	Dinamo Tiranë	Dinamo Tiranë	Kujtim Majaci (Apolonia Fier)	19
1990/1991	KS Flamurtari Vlorë	FK Partizani Tiranë	Kliton Bozgo (FK Tomori Berat)	29
1991/1992	KF Vllaznia Shkodër	KF Elbasani	Edmir Bilali (KF Vllaznia Shkodër)	21
1992/1993	FK Partizani Tiranë	Partizani Tiranë	Edmond Dosti (FK Partizani Tiranë)	20
1993/1994	KF Teuta Durrës	KF Tiranë	Edi Martini (KF Vllaznia Shkodër)	14
1994/1995	KF Tiranë	KF Teuta Durrës	Arben Shehu (Luftëtari Gjirokastër FC)	21
1995/1996	KF Tiranë	KF Tiranë	Altin Çuko (FK Tomori Berat & KF Laçi)	21
1996/1997	KF Tiranë	FK Partizani Tiranë	Viktor Paço (KS Flamurtari Vlorë)	14
1997/1998	KF Vllaznia Shkodër	KF Apolonia Fier	Dorian Bubeqi (KS Shkumbini Peqin)	26

1998/1999	KF Tiranë	KF Tiranë	Artan Bano (KS Lushnja)	22
1999/2000	KF Tiranë	KF Teuta Durrës	Klodian Arbëri (FK Tomori Berat)	18
2000/2001	KF Vllaznia Shkodër	KF Tiranë	Indrit Fortuzi (KF Tiranë)	31
2001/2002	FK Dinamo Tiranë	KF Tiranë	Indrit Fortuzi (KF Tiranë)	24
2002/2003	KF Tiranë	FK Dinamo Tiranë	Mahir Halili (KF Tiranë)	20
2003/2004	KF Tiranë	FK Partizani Tiranë	Vioresin Sinani (KF Vllaznia Shkodër)	36
2004/2005	KF Tiranë	KF Teuta Durrës	Dorian Bylykbashi (FK Partizani Tiranë)	24
2005/2006	KF Elbasani	KF Tiranë	Hamdi Salihi (KF Tiranë)	29
2006/2007	KF Tiranë	KS Besa Kavajë	Vioresin Sinani (KF Tiranë)	23
2007/2008	FK Dinamo Tiranë	KF Vllaznia Shkodër	Vioresin Sinani (KF Vllaznia Shkodër)	20
2008/2009	KF Tiranë	KS Flamurtari Vlorë	Migen Memelli (KF Tiranë)	23
2009/2010	FK Dinamo Tiranë	KS Besa Kavajë	Daniel Xhafa (KS Besa Kavajë)	18
2010/2011	KF Skënderbeu Korçë	KF Tiranë	Daniel Xhafa (KS Flamurtari Vlorë)	19
2011/2012	KF Skënderbeu Korçë	KF Tiranë	Roland Dervishi (KS Shkumbini Peqin)	20
2012/2013	KF Skënderbeu Korçë	KF Laçi	Migen Memelli (KS Flamurtari Vlorë)	19
2013/2014	KF Skënderbeu Korçë	KS Flamurtari Vlorë	Pero Pejić (CRO, KF Skënderbeu Korçë)	20
2014/2015	KF Skënderbeu Korçë	KF Laçi	Pero Pejić (CRO, FK Kukësi)	31
2015/2016	KF Skënderbeu Korçë	FK Kukësi	Hamdi Salihi (KF Skënderbeu Korçë)	27
2016/2017	FK Kukësi	KF Tiranë	Pero Pejić (CRO, FK Kukësi)	28
2017/2018	KF Skënderbeu Korçë	KF Skënderbeu Korçë	Ali Sowe (GAM, KF Skënderbeu Korçë)	21
2018/2019	FK Partizani Tiranë	FK Kukësi	Reginaldo Artur Faife (MOZ, FK Kukësi)	13

NATIONAL CHAMPIONSHIP

Albanian Superliga / Kategoria Superiore 2018/2019

(17.08.2018 – 30.05.2019)

Results

Round 1 [17-19.08.2018]
Skënderbeu Korçë - FK Partizani 1-0(0-0)
Luftëtari Gjirokastër - KS Kastrioti 0-1(0-0)
KF Tiranë - FC Kamza 0-1(0-0)
FK Kukësi - KF Laçi 1-1(1-0)
Teuta Durrës - Flamurtari Vlorë 0-0

Round 2 [24-26.08.2018]
KF Tiranë - Teuta Durrës 0-0
FC Kamza - FK Partizani 0-1(0-0)
KF Laçi - Luftëtari Gjirokastër 2-1(0-1)
KS Kastrioti - Skënderbeu Korçë 0-3(0-2)
Flamurtari Vlorë - FK Kukësi 1-0(1-0)

Round 3 [31.08.-02.09.2018]
Skënderbeu Korçë - KF Laçi 1-1(1-1)
Luftëtari Gjirokastër - Flamurtari Vl. 0-1(0-1)
FK Partizani - KS Kastrioti 1-0(1-0)
FK Kukësi - KF Tiranë 3-1(2-0)
Teuta Durrës - FC Kamza 1-0(0-0)

Round 4 [15-17.09.2018]
FC Kamza - KS Kastrioti 2-0(2-0)
Teuta Durrës - FK Kukësi 0-1(0-1)
KF Laçi - FK Partizani 0-0
KF Tiranë - Luftëtari Gjirokastër 3-1(2-1)
Flamurtari Vlorë - Skënderbeu Korçë 0-2(0-0)

Round 5 [21-23.09.2018]
FK Partizani - Flamurtari Vlorë 2-0(1-0)
Luftëtari Gjirokastër - Teuta Durrës 3-1(0-0)
Skënderbeu Korçë - KF Tiranë 1-1(0-1)
KS Kastrioti - KF Laçi 1-1(0-0)
FK Kukësi - FC Kamza 1-0(1-0)

Round 6 [28-29.09.2018]
KF Tiranë - FK Partizani 0-1(0-1)
FK Kukësi - Luftëtari Gjirokastër 1-0(0-0)
FC Kamza - KF Laçi 0-1(0-0)
Flamurtari Vlorë - KS Kastrioti 4-0(2-0)
Teuta Durrës - Skënderbeu Korçë 2-0(1-0)

Round 7 [03-04.10.2018]
KS Kastrioti - KF Tiranë 2-3(1-2)
KF Laçi - Flamurtari Vlorë 1-0(0-0)
Luftëtari Gjirokastër - FC Kamza 1-0(0-0)
FK Partizani - Teuta Durrës 3-0(2-0)
Skënderbeu Korçë - FK Kukësi 1-0(1-0)

Round 8 [07-08.10.2018]
FC Kamza - Flamurtari Vlorë 2-2(1-1)
Luftëtari Gjirokastër - Skënderbeu K. 0-2(0-0)
KF Tiranë - KF Laçi 0-1(0-0)
Teuta Durrës - KS Kastrioti 2-0(1-0)
FK Kukësi - FK Partizani 0-1(0-1)

Round 9 [20-22.10.2018]
KS Kastrioti - FK Kukësi 1-2(1-0)
KF Laçi - Teuta Durrës 0-3(0-2)
Skënderbeu Korçë - FC Kamza 2-0(1-0)
FK Partizani - Luftëtari Gjirokastër 2-1(1-1)
Flamurtari Vlorë - KF Tiranë 1-0(0-0)

Round 10 [27-29.10.2018]
FC Kamza - KF Tiranë 1-1(0-0)
Flamurtari Vlorë - Teuta Durrës 1-1(1-1)
KS Kastrioti - Luftëtari Gjirokastër 0-2(0-0)
KF Laçi - FK Kukësi 0-1(0-0)
FK Partizani - Skënderbeu Korçë 0-2(0-0)

Round 11 [02-03.11.2018]
FK Kukësi - Flamurtari Vlorë 1-2(0-2)
Teuta Durrës - KF Tiranë 2-1(0-1)
Luftëtari Gjirokastër - KF Laçi 0-1(0-0)
FK Partizani - FC Kamza 1-0(0-0)
Skënderbeu Korçë - KS Kastrioti 1-0(1-0)

Round 12 [06-07.11.2018]
KF Tiranë - FK Kukësi 0-0
FC Kamza - Teuta Durrës 1-3(1-0)
KS Kastrioti - FK Partizani 1-2(1-2)
KF Laçi - Skënderbeu Korçë 2-0(1-0)
Flamurtari Vlorë - Luftëtari Gjirokastër 0-0

Round 13 [11-12.11.2018]
KS Kastrioti - FC Kamza 3-0(2-0)
Luftëtari Gjirokastër - KF Tiranë 2-1(0-1)
FK Partizani - KF Laçi 1-0(0-0)
Skënderbeu Korçë - Flamurtari Vlorë 1-0(0-0)
FK Kukësi - Teuta Durrës 1-1(0-1)

Round 14 [23-25.11.2018]
Flamurtari Vlorë - FK Partizani 1-0(1-0)
KF Tiranë - Skënderbeu Korçë 1-1(1-1)
Teuta Durrës - Luftëtari Gjirokastër 1-0(1-0)
FC Kamza - FK Kukësi 0-2(0-2)
KF Laçi - KS Kastrioti 2-1(0-0)

Round 15 [30.11.-02.12.2018]
FK Partizani - KF Tiranë 2-1(0-0)
Luftëtari Gjirokastër - FK Kukësi 0-1(0-0)
Skënderbeu Korçë - Teuta Durrës 0-1(0-1)
KS Kastrioti - Flamurtari Vlorë 1-0(1-0)
KF Laçi - FC Kamza 0-0

Round 16 [07-09.12.2018]
FK Kukësi - Skënderbeu Korçë 1-0(0-0)
KF Tiranë - KS Kastrioti 4-0(2-0)
Teuta Durrës - FK Partizani 1-1(1-0)
FC Kamza - Luftëtari Gjirokastër 1-0(1-0)
Flamurtari Vlorë - KF Laçi 1-0(1-0)

Round 17 [14-16.12.2018]
FK Partizani - FK Kukësi 0-0
KF Laçi - KF Tiranë 2-1(2-0)
Flamurtari Vlorë - FC Kamza 1-0(0-0)
KS Kastrioti - Teuta Durrës 0-4(0-1)
Skënderbeu Korçë - Luftëtari Gjirok. 2-3(2-2)

Round 18 [21-23.12.2018]
FC Kamza - Skënderbeu Korçë 1-0(1-0)
KF Tiranë - Flamurtari Vlorë 1-0(0-0)
Teuta Durrës - KF Laçi 1-1(0-1)
FK Kukësi - KS Kastrioti 2-0(2-0)
Luftëtari Gjirokastër - FK Partizani 1-1(0-1)

Round 19 [25-27.01.2019]
Skënderbeu Korçë - FK Partizani 0-1(0-1)
FK Kukësi - KF Laçi 0-0
Luftëtari Gjirokastër - KS Kastrioti 1-5(0-2)
KF Tiranë - FC Kamza 4-1(0-1)
Teuta Durrës - Flamurtari Vlorë 1-1(1-1)

Round 20 [01-03.02.2019]
KF Tiranë - Teuta Durrës 1-1(1-1)
KS Kastrioti - Skënderbeu Korçë 2-1(0-0)
Flamurtari Vlorë - FK Kukësi 1-2(1-2)
FC Kamza - FK Partizani 0-1(0-0)
KF Laçi - Luftëtari Gjirokastër 0-2(0-2)

Round 21 [09-11.02.2019]
FK Partizani - KS Kastrioti 2-0(0-0)
FK Kukësi - KF Tiranë 0-1(0-0)
Luftëtari Gjirokastër - Flamurtari Vlorë 0-0
Teuta Durrës - FC Kamza 0-0
Skënderbeu Korçë - KF Laçi 2-1(0-0)

Round 22 [15-17.02.2019]
Teuta Durrës - FK Kukësi 2-1(0-1)
FC Kamza - KS Kastrioti 0-1(0-0)
KF Laçi - FK Partizani 1-0(1-0)
Flamurtari Vlorë - Skënderbeu Korçë 2-0(0-0)
KF Tiranë - Luftëtari Gjirokastër 1-1(0-1)

Round 23 [22-24.02.2019]
Skënderbeu Korçë - KF Tiranë 1-2(1-1)
Luftëtari Gjirokastër - Teuta Durrës 1-0(1-0)
FK Partizani - Flamurtari Vlorë 3-1(1-1)
FK Kukësi - FC Kamza 3-2(1-1)
KS Kastrioti - KF Laçi 1-1(0-1)

Round 24 [01-03.03.2019]
KF Tiranë - FK Partizani 0-0
FK Kukësi - Luftëtari Gjirokastër 3-0(2-0)
Teuta Durrës - Skënderbeu Korçë 2-2(1-0)
FC Kamza - KF Laçi 1-1(0-0)
Flamurtari Vlorë - KS Kastrioti 1-1(1-0)

Round 25 [16-17.03.2019]
Luftëtari Gjirokastër - FC Kamza 3-0*
Skënderbeu Korçë - FK Kukësi 1-0(1-0)
KS Kastrioti - KF Tiranë 1-0(1-0)
KF Laçi - Flamurtari Vlorë 0-0
FK Partizani - Teuta Durrës 3-0(2-0)

Round 26 [29-30.03.2019]
FK Kukësi - FK Partizani 1-1(0-0)
FC Kamza - Flamurtari Vlorë 0-3*
Luftëtari Gjirokastër - Skënderbeu K. 1-0(0-0)
KF Tiranë - KF Laçi 1-1(1-0)
Teuta Durrës - KS Kastrioti 1-0(1-0)

Round 27 [06.04.2019]
Skënderbeu Korçë - FC Kamza 3-0*
KS Kastrioti - FK Kukësi 2-1(0-1)
KF Laçi - Teuta Durrës 5-0(2-0)
Flamurtari Vlorë - KF Tiranë 1-0(1-0)
FK Partizani - Luftëtari Gjirokastër 1-3(1-2)

Round 28 [10.04.2019]
FC Kamza - KF Tiranë 0-3*
KS Kastrioti - Luftëtari Gjirokastër 1-0(1-0)
KF Laçi - FK Kukësi 0-1(0-0)
Flamurtari Vlorë - Teuta Durrës 3-1(1-0)
FK Partizani - Skënderbeu Korçë 2-0(1-0)

Round 29 [13-14.04.2019]
FK Partizani - FC Kamza 3-0*
FK Kukësi - Flamurtari Vlorë 1-2(0-1)
Luftëtari Gjirokastër - KF Laçi 1-0(0-0)
Skënderbeu Korçë - KS Kastrioti 4-0(3-0)
Teuta Durrës - KF Tiranë 1-3(0-1)

Round 30 [20.04.2019]
FC Kamza - Teuta Durrës 0-3*
KS Kastrioti - FK Partizani 1-1(0-0)
KF Laçi - Skënderbeu Korçë 1-0(1-0)
Flamurtari Vlorë - Luftëtari Gjirok. 1-1(0-0)
KF Tiranë - FK Kukësi 0-2(0-1)

Round 31 [27-28.04.2019]
KS Kastrioti - FC Kamza 3-0*
FK Partizani - KF Laçi 1-1(0-1)
FK Kukësi - Teuta Durrës 0-0
Luftëtari Gjirokastër - KF Tiranë 1-1(0-1)
Skënderbeu Korçë - Flamurtari Vlorë 2-0(1-0)

Round 32 [04.05.2019]
FC Kamza - FK Kukësi 0-3*
Flamurtari Vlorë - FK Partizani 0-3(0-1)
KF Laçi - KS Kastrioti 1-1(0-0)
KF Tiranë - Skënderbeu Korçë 1-0(0-0)
Teuta Durrës - Luftëtari Gjirokastër 0-0

Round 33 [12.05.2019]
KF Laçi - FC Kamza 3-0*
KS Kastrioti - Flamurtari Vlorë 2-0(1-0)
Luftëtari Gjirokastër - FK Kukësi 3-2(1-0)
FK Partizani - KF Tiranë 2-1(1-1)
Skënderbeu Korçë - Teuta Durrës 1-2(0-1)

Round 34 [18.05.2019]
FK Kukësi - Skënderbeu Korçë 0-3(0-2)
Flamurtari Vlorë - KF Laçi 1-0(1-0)
KF Tiranë - KS Kastrioti 0-0
Teuta Durrës - FK Partizani 2-0(1-0)
FC Kamza - Luftëtari Gjirokastër 0-3*

Round 35 [26.05.2019]
Flamurtari Vlorë - FC Kamza 3-0*
KS Kastrioti - Teuta Durrës 2-1(0-0)
KF Laçi - KF Tiranë 1-3(0-2)
FK Partizani - FK Kukësi 1-1(0-0)
Skënderbeu Korçë - Luftëtari Gjirok. 2-0(1-0)

Round 36 [30.05.2019]
FC Kamza - Skënderbeu Korçë 0-3*
FK Kukësi - KS Kastrioti 3-1(0-1)
KF Tiranë - Flamurtari Vlorë 3-0(0-0)
Luftëtari Gjirokastër - FK Partizani 1-1(1-0)
Teuta Durrës - KF Laçi 2-0(0-0)

*Result awarded.
Please note: FC Kamza were excluded from the league and relegated to the Second Division after violent incidents during the match against KF Laçi (Round 24). All following matches were annulled and awarded as 3-0 wins for the opponents.

Final Standings

1.	**FK Partizani Tiranë**	36	20	10	6	45	-	22		70
2.	FK Kukësi	36	17	8	11	42	-	29		59
3.	KF Teuta Durrës	36	15	12	9	43	-	36		57
4.	KF Skënderbeu Korçë	36	17	4	15	45	-	30		55
5.	KS Flamurtari Vlorë	36	15	9	12	35	-	32		54
6.	KF Laçi	36	12	13	11	33	-	30		49
7.	KF Tiranë	36	12	11	13	44	-	35		47
8.	Luftëtari Gjirokastër FC	36	13	8	15	37	-	39		47
9.	KS Kastrioti Krujë (*Relegated*)	36	12	6	18	35	-	53		42
10.	FC Kamza (*Relegated*)	36	4	5	27	13	-	66		17

Top goalscorers:

13 **Reginaldo Artur Faife (MOZ)**
FK Kukësi

12 Edon Hasani
KF Tiranë

12 Vasil Shkurtaj
Luftëtari Gjirokastër FC / FK Kukësi

NATIONAL CUP
Kupa e Shqipërisë 2018/2019

First Round [12-26.09.2018]

KF Veleçiku Koplik - KF Skënderbeu Korçë	0-3 / 0-4	KS Pogradeci - KF Apolonia Fier	0-1 / 2-3
FK Vora - Luftëtari Gjirokastër FC	0-4 / 0-1	FK Tomori Berat - KF Bylis Ballsh	2-1 / 1-4
KF Tërbuni Pukë - FK Partizani Tiranë	0-1 / 0-4	KS Iliria Fushë-Krujë - KF Tiranë	1-4 / 0-4
KS Besa Kavajë - FC Kamza	0-2 / 2-2	FK Shënkolli - KF Lushnja	1-2 / 2-2
KS Burreli - KF Vllaznia Shkodër	1-1 / 0-1	KF Turbina Cërrik - KF Teuta Durrës	0-3 / 2-4
KS Korabi Peshkopi - KS Kastrioti Krujë	1-1 / 0-1	KS Shkumbini - KS Flamurtari Vlorë	0-1 0-1
FK Dinamo Tiranë - KF Egnatia Rrogozhine	0-1 / 0-0	KF Naftëtari Kuçovë - KF Laçi	0-5 / 0-9
KS Besëlidhja Lezhë - KF Erzeni Shijak	2-0 / 1-3	KF Oriku - FK Kukësi	1-2 / 1-4

Second Round [22.01.-06.02.2019]

KS Besëlidhja Lezhë - KF Skënderbeu Korçë	1-2 / 0-3	KF Apolonia Fier - FK Kukësi	2-1 / 0-2
KS Kastrioti Krujë - FK Partizani Tiranë	2-4 / 0-3	KF Bylis Ballsh - KF Laçi	2-0 / 0-3
KF Egnatia Rrogozhine - Luftëtari Gjirokastër FC	0-3 / 0-0	KF Lushnja - KF Teuta Durrës	1-3 / 0-4
KF Vllaznia Shkodër - FC Kamza	2-1 / 0-1	KF Tiranë - KS Flamurtari Vlorë	2-0 / 0-1

Quarter-Finals [12.03.-03.04.2019]

FK Partizani Tiranë - Luftëtari Gjirokastër FC	1-2 / 0-1	FC Kamza - KF Skënderbeu Korçë	*not played*
KF Teuta Durrës - FK Kukësi	2-2 / 0-1	KF Tiranë - KF Laçi	3-0 / 0-2

Semi-Finals [24.04.-08.05.2019]

Luftëtari Gjirokastër FC - KF Tiranë	0-0 / 3-5	FK Kukësi - KF Skënderbeu Korçë	2-1 / 3-1

Final

02.06.2019; Elbasan Arena, Elbasan; Referee: Enea Jorgji; Attendance: 1,500
FK Kukësi - KF Tiranë **2-1(1-0)**

FK Kukësi: Stivi Frashëri, Ardijan Cuculi, Olsi Teqja, Simon Rrumbullaku, Valdet Rama (90.Arbër Çyrbja), William Cordeiro Melo, Eduart Rroca (46.Vesel Limaj), Besar Musolli, Valon Ethemi, Reginaldo Artur Faife (80.Irakli Dzaria), Vasil Shkurtaj. Trainer: Ernest Gjoka.

KF Tiranë: Ilion Lika, Eni Imami, Erion Hoxhallari (83.Marsel Ismajlgeci), Jurgen Goxha (43.Marvin Turtulli), Albi Doka, Tony Mawejje (46.Jurgen Çelhaka), Edon Hasani, Bedri Greca, Dorian Kërçiku, Winful Cobbinah, Michael Ngoo. Trainer: Ardian Mema.

Goals: 1-0 Vasil Shkurtaj (4), 1-1 Michael Ngoo (66), 2-1 Reginaldo Artur Faife (78).

THE CLUBS 2018/2019

Klubi Sportiv Flamurtari Vlorë

Founded: 23.03.1923 (*as Shoqeria Sportive Vlorë*)
Stadium: Stadiumi Flamurtari, Vlorë (8,500)

Goalkeepers:	**DOB**	**M**	**(s)**	**G**
Enea Kolici	13.02.1986	32		
Pano Qirko	16.06.1999	2		
Defenders:	**DOB**	**M**	**(s)**	**G**
Arbër Beqaj	29.09.1998	7	(10)	
Blerim Kotobelli	10.08.1992	27	(3)	
Arinaldo Rrapaj	09.08.2001	14	(4)	
Goran Siljanovski	01.07.1990	17		
Cristian Sîrghi (ROU)	23.11.1986	3		
Franc Veliu	11.11.1988	19	(1)	1
Sokol Ymeraj	13.03.1999	2	(14)	
Midfielders:	**DOB**	**M**	**(s)**	**G**
Albi Alla (GRE)	01.02.1993	10	(2)	1
Idriz Batha	28.03.1992	30		4
Fjoralb Deliaj	04.04.1997	21	(1)	
Shaqir Haruni	27.05.1999	2	(3)	
Alessio Hyseni	04.01.1997	8	(6)	
Kenviol Kreshpa	14.10.2000		(4)	
Emiljano Musta	31.01.1992	27	(6)	3
Argjend Mustafa (KVX)	30.08.1992	17	(14)	
Artim Položani (MKD)	25.06.1982	31	(1)	1
Muhamed Useini	21.11.1988	15	(2)	
Forwards:	**DOB**	**M**	**(s)**	**G**
Tomislav Bušić (CRO)	02.02.1986	17		5
Élton Pereira Gomes „Calé“ (BRA)	12.07.1988	19		
Danilo Almeida Alves (BRA)	11.04.1991	8	(2)	4
Gersi Diamanti	15.10.1999		(3)	
Lejdi Liçaj	19.01.1987	3	(1)	
Mateo Qarri	05.05.1999		(1)	
Andi Ribaj	21.11.1989	15	(6)	4
Xhevair Sukaj	05.10.1987	8	(2)	4
Agustin Gonzalo Torassa (ARG)	20.10.1988	19		2
Ardit Ziaj	08.03.2000	1	(7)	
Trainer:	**DOB**	**M**		
Ilir Daja	20.10.1966	35		

Football Club Kamza

Founded: 10.09.1936
Stadium: Stadiumi Kamëz, Kamëz (5,500)

Goalkeepers:	DOB	M	(s)	G
Ilir Avdyli (KVX)	20.05.1990	22		
Mario Kirev (BUL)	15.08.1989	1		
Elidon Selaci	03.05.1990	1		
Defenders:	**DOB**	**M**	**(s)**	**G**
Orjand Beqiri	21.02.1985	10		
Eneo Bitri	26.08.1996	4		
Claudio Bonanni (ITA)	05.03.1997	13	(2)	1
Mikel Brahilika	05.08.1999		(1)	
Harallamb Qaqi	17.09.1993	4		
Armando Rami	24.07.1997		(1)	
Arbër Shala	23.12.1991	4	(1)	
Olsi Teqja	27.07.1988	14		
Xhuljan Turhani	07.02.1996		(1)	
Midfielders:	**DOB**	**M**	**(s)**	**G**
Bruno Arrabal Passamani (BRA)	22.02.1992	20	(1)	
Plarent Fejzaj	05.07.1997		(1)	
Hektor Idrizaj	15.04.1989	18		
Argjend Malaj	16.10.1993	20		
Xhuljo Mehmeti	29.12.1993	18	(4)	
Anxhelo Mumajesi	28.03.1997	5	(12)	
Nurudeen Orelesi (NGA)	10.04.1989	8	(5)	
Niko Zisi	24.08.1995	11	(9)	
Forwards:	**DOB**	**M**	**(s)**	**G**
Erlis Frashëri	19.05.1988	17		
Masato Fukui (JPN)	14.11.1988	16	(2)	5
Jeton Krasniqi	16.01.2001	2	(1)	
Néstor Martinena (ARG)	22.01.1987	14	(6)	1
Majkel Peci	29.08.1996	3	(5)	
Sebino Plaku	20.05.1985	20	(1)	4
Ermir Rezi	12.05.1994	8	(11)	
Ognjen Rolović (MNE)	25.08.1993	11	(5)	2
Trainer:	**DOB**	**M**		
Bledar Devolli	15.01.1978	3		
Klodian Duro [04.09.2018]	21.12.1977	10		
Ernest Gjoka [15.11.2018]	25.01.1970	9		
Gentian Stojku [19.02.2019]	27.07.1974	2		

Klubi Sportiv Kastrioti Krujë

Founded: 1926
Stadium: Stadiumi „Redi Maloku“, Krujë (3,000)

Goalkeepers:	DOB	M	(s)	G
Amarildo Çekrezi	11.08.1993	15		
Klajdi Kuka	29.03.1990	14		
Bruno Puja	20.01.2000	6	(2)	
Defenders:	**DOB**	**M**	**(s)**	**G**
Johan Beçka	20.06.1997		(1)	
Emiliano Çela	21.07.1985	31		
David Domgjoni	21.05.1997	12	(2)	
Lukman Hussein (NGA)	28.08.1996	30	(1)	
Vilson Lila	06.10.1989	7	(1)	
Edward Nicolas M'Boyom (CMR)	12.12.1988	11	(1)	
Sokol Neziri	30.06.1996	2	(6)	
Armando Rami	24.07.1997		(2)	1
Adolf Selmani	26.06.2000		(7)	
Dajan Shehi	19.03.1997	14	(4)	
Midfielders:	**DOB**	**M**	**(s)**	**G**
Albert Caca	23.02.1992	1	(4)	
Xhynejt Çutra	23.11.1988	6	(4)	
Herald Marku	18.05.1996	20	(2)	5
Erblind Mulaj (KVX)	25.09.1995		(1)	
Sokol Mziu	21.07.1987	10		1
Edison Ndreca	05.07.1994	15		1
Henry Chimuchem Okebugwu (NGA)	19.06.1998	18	(7)	2
Pablo Gállego Lardiés (ESP)	01.10.1993	2	(1)	
Roger Junio Rodrigues Ferreira (BRA)	01.03.1996	31	(2)	10
Juljan Shehu	06.09.1998	30		4
Nikola Stijepović (MNE)	02.11.1993	17		
Ersil Ymeraj	06.07.1994	25	(3)	4
Forwards:	**DOB**	**M**	**(s)**	**G**
Alexandros Abdel Rahim (GRE)	23.02.1993	3		
Osinachi Kingsley Agbodike (NGA)	15.01.1999		(2)	
Charles Atsina (GHA)	24.03.1989	4	(5)	
Patrik Bardhi	21.05.1998	29	(5)	1
Kleo Fejzaj	23.06.1996		(2)	
Arlind Kalaja	27.12.1995	11	(1)	
Taulant Marku	14.06.1994	14	(13)	2
Brunild Pepa	22.11.1990		(5)	
Preston Tabortetaka Obiarrah (CMR)	10.06.1998		(3)	
Jurgen Vatnikaj	08.08.1995	7	(12)	1
Trainer:	**DOB**	**M**		
Elvis Plori	05.08.1978	9		
Stavri Nica [22.10.2018]	08.07.1954	9		
Gentian Stojku [07.01.2019]	27.70.1974	17		

Futboll Klub Kukësi

Founded: 04.03.1930
Stadium: Stadiumi Kamëz, Kukës (5,500)

Goalkeepers:	DOB	M	(s)	G
Stivi Frashëri	29.08.1990	32		
Maurice Gomis (ITA)	10.11.1997	1		
Faton Maloku (KVX)	14.06.1991	2		
Defenders:	**DOB**	**M**	**(s)**	**G**
Ardijan Cuculi (MKD)	19.07.1987	30	(1)	
Faton Džemaili	15.11.1998	1	(6)	
Gëzim Krasniqi	05.01.1990	12	(1)	
Simon Rrumbullaku	30.12.1991	18	(4)	
Ylli Shameti	07.06.1984	20	(1)	2
Olsi Teqja	27.07.1988	13	(1)	
William Cordeiro Melo (BRA)	15.07.1993	32		5
Vangjel Zguro	04.03.1993	10	(1)	
Midfielders:	**DOB**	**M**	**(s)**	**G**
Arbër Çyrbja	18.09.1993	21	(12)	
Irakli Dzaria (GEO)	01.12.1988	19	(7)	1
Valon Ethemi	03.10.1997	26	(5)	2
Kristi Joti	15.01.1998	1	(4)	
Edis Malikji (MKD)	04.05.1995	24		
Besar Musolli (KVX)	28.02.1989	9	(2)	
Harallamb Qaqi	17.09.1993	5	(3)	
Valdet Rama	20.11.1987	4	(6)	2
Reginaldo Artur Faife (MOZ)	04.06.1990	30	(3)	13
Eduart Rroca	28.07.1993	11	(3)	3
Toni Selimi	11.06.2000		(2)	
Donjet Shkodra	30.04.1989	14	(1)	
Chafik Tigroudja (FRA)	16.01.1992	10		
Forwards:	**DOB**	**M**	**(s)**	**G**
Haris Harba (BIH)	14.07.1988	2	(2)	
Arlind Kalaja	27.12.1995	1	(11)	
Vesel Limaj (GER)	01.12.1996	21	(9)	3
Vasil Shkurtaj	27.04.1992	14	(2)	5
Dino Špehar (CRO)	08.02.1994	2	(12)	1
Trainer:	**DOB**	**M**		
Armando Cungu	23.04.1973	25		
Ramadan Ndreu [19.03.2019]	30.03.1966	1		
Ernest Gjoka [06.04.2019]	25.01.1970	9		

Klubi i Futbollit Laçi

Founded: 1960
Stadium: Stadiumi Laçi, Laçi (2,300)

Goalkeepers:	**DOB**	**M**	**(s)**	**G**
Gentian Selmani	09.03.1998	35		1
Defenders:	**DOB**	**M**	**(s)**	**G**
Ded Bushi	02.10.1998	1	(3)	
David Domgjoni	21.05.1997	4	(6)	1
Nikola Eller (CRO)	17.01.1994	27	(4)	
Abdurraman Fangaj	12.10.1997	27	(1)	3
Eglentin Gjoni	02.12.1992	35		3
Andi Hadroj	22.02.1999	2	(4)	
Jon Mersinaj	08.02.1999	22	(3)	
Denis Pjeshka	28.05.1995		(1)	
Taulant Sefgjini	21.07.1986	29		
Sebastián Patricio Toro Hormazábal (CHI)	02.02.1990	21	(2)	
Midfielders:	**DOB**	**M**	**(s)**	**G**
Elvi Berisha	02.03.1999	7	(8)	
Enis Çokaj	23.02.1999	14	(1)	
Ardit Deliu	26.10.1997	1	(7)	
Regi Lushkja	17.05.1996	32		3
Bojan Najdenov (MKD)	27.08.1991	13	(5)	1
Erisildo Smaçi	15.07.1998		(11)	
Forwards:	**DOB**	**M**	**(s)**	**G**
Marijan Altiparmakovski (MKD)	18.07.1991	8	(6)	1
Erjon Dragoj	06.09.1999	1		
Fjoart Jonuzi	09.07.1996	23	(8)	
Malick Mané (SEN)	14.10.1988	7	(6)	
Anthony Okpotu (NGA)	05.03.1994	8	(2)	1
Fatmir Prengaj	01.05.2001	1	(3)	
Ndricim Shtubina	18.03.1987	32	(2)	10
Xhevair Sukaj	05.10.1987		(2)	
Redon Xhixha	14.07.1998	32	(1)	5
Myrto Artan Uzuni	31.05.1995	3		1
Trainer:	**DOB**	**M**		
Artan Mërgjyshi	06.05.1968	10		
Migen Memelli [31.10.2018]	25.04.1980	6		
Besnik Prenga [14.12.2018]	05.06.1969	8		
Sulejman Starova [15.03.2019]	12.12.1955	11		

Luftëtari Gjirokastër Football Club

Founded: 1929 *(as Shqiponja Gjirokastër)*
Stadium: Stadiumi Gjirokastra, Gjirokastër (8,400)

Goalkeepers:	**DOB**	**M**	**(s)**	**G**
Edvan Bakaj	20.07.1987	3		
Shkelzen Ruci	01.07.1992	31		
Defenders:	**DOB**	**M**	**(s)**	**G**
Aurel Demo	20.10.1996	19	(9)	1
Rustem Hoxha	04.07.1991	24		
Riste Ilijovski (MKD)	27.09.1994		(1)	
Jackson Ferreira Silvério (BRA)	12.04.1991	29		
Nemanja Janičić (SRB)	13.07.1986	14		
Dimitrios Kotsonis (GRE)	25.01.1989	14		1
Armenis Kukaj	11.08.1997	3	(1)	
Oltion Rapa	30.09.1989	27	(1)	
Donald Rapo	04.10.1990	23	(5)	5
Midfielders:	**DOB**	**M**	**(s)**	**G**
Donaldo Acka	17.09.1997	8	(9)	
Alvi Ahmetaj	12.07.1998	1	(1)	
Albano Aleksi	10.10.1992	21	(3)	2
Angelos Abdel Chanti (JOR)	07.09.1989	4	(5)	2
Erald Hyseni	12.11.1999	4	(9)	
Mergim Neziri (KVX)	30.04.1993	8	(4)	
Aldrit Oshafi	26.03.2000	2	(8)	
Mario Qerimi			(2)	
Balša Radović (MNE)	04.01.1991	8	(4)	
Behar Ramadani	06.04.1990	23		
Eduart Rroca	28.07.1993	9	(1)	
Maldin Ymeraj	06.03.1995	21	(6)	1
Forwards:	**DOB**	**M**	**(s)**	**G**
Romario Çekaj	03.05.1998	1	(3)	
Elian Çelaj	03.02.1999	1	(7)	
Ismael Salim Dunga (KEN)	24.02.1993	14	(10)	7
Realdo Fili	14.05.1996	14	(2)	2
Lejdi Liçaj	19.01.1987	11		
Vladan Milosavljev (SRB)	01.02.1987	18		1
Vasil Shkurtaj	27.04.1992	18		7
Eric Warden (GHA)	13.12.1992	1	(2)	
Trainer:	**DOB**	**M**		
Miloš Kostić (SVN)	23.11.1971	4		
Gentian Mezani [20.09.2018]	13.10.1979	15		
Julian Ahmataj [29.01.2019]	24.05.1979	15		

Futboll Klub Partizani Tiranë

Founded: 04.02.1946
Stadium: Stadiumi"Selman Stërmasi", Tiranë (9,600)

Goalkeepers:	**DOB**	**M**	**(s)**	**G**
Alban Hoxha	23.11.1987	31		
Dashamir Xhika	23.05.1989	4	(1)	
Defenders:	**DOB**	**M**	**(s)**	**G**
Sodiq Atanda (NGA)	26.08.1993	30		
Egzon Belica (MKD)	03.09.1990	33		1
Eneo Bitri	26.08.1996		(4)	
Ilirian Dushaj	16.07.2000	1		
Renato Gojković (BIH)	10.09.1995	2	(2)	
Labinot Ibrahimi	25.06.1986	31		
Hektor Idrizaj	15.04.1989	3		
Renaldo Kalari	25.06.1984	7	(9)	
Ded Noka	08.03.2000	1		
Lum Rexhepi (KVX)	03.08.1992	10	(1)	
Lorenc Trashi	19.05.1992	30	(1)	
Midfielders:	**DOB**	**M**	**(s)**	**G**
Jurgen Bardhi	06.11.1997	27	(3)	5
Dilaver Duka (USA)	15.09.1989	10	(3)	1
Besnik Ferati (MKD)	19.04.2000	2		
Ardit Hila	06.01.1993	25	(2)	1
Tijan Jaiteh (GAM)	31.12.1988	3		
Eneid Kodra	04.11.1999	1	(2)	
Alesio Kolonja	25.04.2001		(1)	
Kristi Kote	26.09.1998	8	(16)	
Esat Mala	18.10.1998	32		4
So Hyon-uk (PRK)	17.04.1992		(4)	
Bruno Telushi	14.11.1990	25	(1)	7
Forwards:	**DOB**	**M**	**(s)**	**G**
Jasir Asani	19.05.1995	31	(2)	8
Eraldo Cinari	11.10.1996	5	(16)	6
Rubin Hebaj	30.07.1998	7	(14)	4
Lucas Ferreira Cardoso (BRA)	07.04.1994	4	(8)	
Emmanuel Mensah (GHA)	30.06.1994	21	(9)	5
Gerhard Progni	06.11.1986	1	(1)	
Trainer:	**DOB**	**M**		
Skënder Gega	14.11.1963	35		

Klubi Futbollistik Skënderbeu Korçë

Founded: 1925
Stadium: Stadiumi Skënderbeu, Korçë (12,343)

Goalkeepers:	**DOB**	**M**	**(s)**	**G**
Mario Dajsinani	23.12.1998	11		
Aldo Teqja	04.05.1995	23		
Defenders:	**DOB**	**M**	**(s)**	**G**
Fidan Aliti (KVX)	03.10.1993	19		
Bruno Lulaj	02.04.1995	5	(7)	
Marko Radaš (CRO)	26.10.1983	25		
Kaba Sambou (GAM)	20.04.1996	17	(4)	
Kristi Vangjeli	05.09.1985	33		1
Midfielders:	**DOB**	**M**	**(s)**	**G**
Leonit Abazi	05.07.1993	29	(1)	
Alamir Ajzeraj (KVX)	05.10.1997		(1)	
Elmir Asani (SRB)	15.09.1995		(2)	
Beneyam Belye Demte (ETH)	18.07.1998	12	(3)	1
Bruno Dita	18.02.1993	30		3
Nazmi Gripshi	05.07.1997	27	(7)	2
Arnaud Guedj (FRA)	19.07.1997	7	(5)	
Zani Kurti	06.12.1993	1	(3)	
Uerdi Mara	30.01.1999		(3)	
Gjergj Muzaka	26.09.1984	28	(2)	8
Jorgo Pëllumbi	15.07.2000	11	(4)	
Marko Pervan (CRO)	04.04.1996	11	(3)	4
Aldo Qoshku (GRE)	20.10.2000		(1)	
Kwasi Sibo (GHA)	24.06.1998	13		1
Ščiprim Taipi	19.02.1997	6	(1)	
Idriz Toskic (MNE)	12.10.1995	1	(6)	
Forwards:	**DOB**	**M**	**(s)**	**G**
Dejvi Bregu	24.10.1995	25	(2)	8
Flavio Demollari	27.04.2000		(1)	
Realdo Fili	14.05.1996	3	(7)	
Saliou Guindo (MLI)	12.09.1996	2	(3)	
Ardit Hoxhaj	20.07.1994	2	(6)	1
Otto John (NGA)	25.01.1998	9	(19)	4
Blerim Krasniqi	05.07.1996	24	(5)	6
Trainer:	**DOB**	**M**		
Orges Shehi	25.09.1977	34		

Klubi Futbollit Teuta Durrës

Founded: 1920
Stadium: Stadiumi"Niko Dovana", Durrës (13,000)

Goalkeepers:	**DOB**	**M**	**(s)**	**G**
Bobi Celeski (MKD)	10.06.1997	2		
Isli Hidi	15.10.1980	33		
Defenders:	**DOB**	**M**	**(s)**	**G**
Renato Arapi	28.08.1986	15		1
Ditmar Bicaj	26.02.1989	21	(5)	3
Bojan Gjorgievski (MKD)	25.01.1992	16	(2)	
Ersin Hakaj	06.12.1996	24	(2)	
Tefik Osmani	08.06.1985	29		
Silvester Shkalla	10.08.1995	14	(5)	
Midfielders:	**DOB**	**M**	**(s)**	**G**
Florent Avdyli (KVX)	10.07.1993	22	(3)	
Fabjan Beqja	15.02.1994	11	(13)	1
Ledjo Beqja	18.06.2001	1		
Roni Gashi (KVX)	04.06.1998	15	(10)	1
Sherif Kallaku	01.03.1998	28	(5)	7
Arsid Kruja	08.06.1993	3	(5)	
Edison Ndreca	05.07.1994	2	(2)	
Klinti Qato	23.12.1997		(1)	
Lancinet Sidibé (GUI)	01.01.1997	31		1
Forwards:	**DOB**	**M**	**(s)**	**G**
Latif Amadu (GHA)	20.08.1993	20	(7)	9
Tomislav Bušić (CRO)	02.02.1986	10	(2)	1
Sekou Camara	20.07.1997	19	(6)	4
Erlis Frashëri	19.05.1988	12		
Gerhard Progni	06.11.1986	28	(2)	7
Boubacar Traoré (SEN)	26.07.1997	18	(5)	3
Armando Vajushi	03.12.1991	4	(5)	
Uendi Veçaj	18.02.1997	5	(12)	1
Lorenco Vila	14.12.1998	2	(10)	
Trainer:	**DOB**	**M**		
Bledi Shkëmbi	13.08.1979	35		

Klubi i Futbollit Tirana

Founded: 15.08.1920 *(as Shoqata Sportive Agimi)*
Stadium: Stadiumi"Selman Stërmasi", Tiranë (9,600)

Goalkeepers:	**DOB**	**M**	**(s)**	**G**
Alessio Abibi	04.12.1996	23		
Ilion Lika	17.05.1980	12		
Defenders:	**DOB**	**M**	**(s)**	**G**
Vincent Attingah (GHA)	30.10.1993	15	(1)	
Sedat Berisha (MKD)	23.09.1989	2	(1)	
Klisman Cake	02.05.1999	2	(2)	
Albi Doka	26.06.1997	26	(5)	4
Jurgen Goxha	29.12.1992	6	(6)	
Erion Hoxhallari	15.10.1995	31	(1)	
Eni Imami	19.12.1992	29	(1)	
Marsel Ismajlgeci	14.03.2000		(1)	
Gentian Muça	13.05.1987		(3)	
Marvin Turtulli	17.10.1994	21	(2)	1
Midfielders:	**DOB**	**M**	**(s)**	**G**
Dejan Blaževski (MKD)	06.12.1985	8	(2)	3
Jurgen Çelhaka	06.12.2000		(1)	
Winful Cobbinah (GHA)	06.09.1991	26	(5)	3
Asion Daja	14.03.1990	20	(4)	
Bedri Greca	23.10.1990	24	(7)	4
Edon Hasani	09.01.1992	31	(2)	12
Erando Karabeci	06.09.1988	24	(1)	1
Tony Mawejje (UGA)	15.11.1986	25	(6)	
Nnamdi Oduamadi (NGA)	17.10.1990	7	(4)	1
Forwards:	**DOB**	**M**	**(s)**	**G**
Grent Halili	24.05.1998	11	(7)	1
Dorian Kërçiku	30.08.1993	11	(6)	
Ernest Muci	19.03.2001	1	(7)	1
Michael Ngoo (ENG)	23.10.1992	15	(7)	4
Gideon Ofori Offei (GHA)	11.01.1999		(1)	
Yunus Sentamu (UGA)	13.08.1994	15	(7)	5
Trainer:	**DOB**	**M**		
José Marcelo Ferreira „Zé Maria" (BRA)	25.07.1973	8		
Ardian Mema [12.10.2018]	16.11.1971	27		

SECOND LEVEL
Albanian First Division 2018/2019

First Phase

Group A

1.	KF Vllaznia Shkodër	18	14	2	2	32 - 8	44
2.	KF Erzeni Shijak	18	10	2	6	24 - 15	32
3.	KS Besëlidhja Lezhë	18	9	3	6	22 - 16	30
4.	FK Dinamo Tiranë	18	8	3	7	15 - 11	27
5.	KF Korabi Peshkopi	18	8	3	7	18 - 19	27
6.	KF Veleçiku Koplik	18	8	1	9	18 - 23	25
7.	KS Burreli	18	8	0	10	18 - 23	24
8.	FK Shënkolli	18	6	2	10	14 - 23	20
9.	KS Iliria Fushë-Krujë	18	5	4	9	17 - 19	19
10.	FK Vorë	18	2	4	12	11 - 32	10

Group B

1.	KF Bylis Ballsh	18	13	3	2	30 - 7	42
2.	KS Besa Kavajë	18	10	5	3	22 - 11	35
3.	KF Egnatia Rrogozhinë	18	10	1	7	23 - 21	31
4.	KS Lushnja	18	7	6	5	19 - 14	27
5.	KF Oriku	18	7	6	5	17 - 14	27
6.	KS Pogradeci	18	8	2	8	24 - 19	26
7.	KF Apolonia Fier	18	6	5	7	13 - 11	23
8.	FK Tomori Berat*	18	5	5	8	17 - 25	17
9.	KF Elbasani	18	3	3	12	14 - 32	12
10.	KF Turbina Cërrik	18	2	2	14	11 - 36	8

**3 points deducted*

Top-5 qualified for the Promotion Round, while teams ranked 6-10 qualified for the Relegation Round.

Relegation Round

Group A

1.	KS Burreli	8	4	1	3	25 - 29	25
2.	KS Iliria Fushë-Krujë	8	4	2	2	27 - 29	24
3.	FK Shënkolli	8	4	1	3	29 - 36	23
4.	KF Veleçiku Koplik (*Relegation Play-off*)	8	3	1	4	26 - 32	23
5.	FK Vorë (*Relegated*)	8	2	1	5	21 - 44	12

Group B

1.	KS Pogradeci	8	5	0	3	36 - 29	28
2.	KF Apolonia Fier	8	4	1	3	26 - 18	25
3.	KF Turbina Cërrik	8	5	0	3	25 - 43	19
4.	KF Elbasani (*Relegation Play-off*)	8	4	1	3	23 - 44	19
5.	FK Tomori Berat (*Relegated*)	8	0	2	6	22 - 42	11

Relegation Play-off [23-30.05.2019]

KF Veleçiku Koplik – KS Shkumbini Peqin	1-0(0-0,0-0)
KF Elbasani – Luzi United Kavajë	3-0(1-0)
KS Shkumbini Peqin - Luzi United Kavajë	1-0(1-0)**

KF Veleçiku Koplik and KF Elbasani both remain at second level.

**KS Shkumbini Peqin won an Extra Play-off to replace FC Kamza (relegated directly to the Albanian Second Division / Third Level).

Promotion Round

Group A

1.	KF Vllaznia Shkodër (*Promoted*)	8	6	1	1	44 - 11	41
2.	FK Dinamo Tiranë	8	4	2	2	26 - 17	28
3.	KS Besëlidhja Lezhë	8	3	4	1	31 - 25	28
4.	KF Korabi Peshkopi	8	1	2	5	23 - 28	19
5.	KF Erzeni Shijak	8	0	3	5	27 - 28	19

Group B

1.	KF Bylis Ballsh (*Promoted*)	8	8	0	0	52 - 10	45
2.	KS Besa Kavajë	8	4	1	3	34 - 25	31
3.	KF Oriku	8	3	2	3	29 - 27	25
4.	KS Lushnja	8	1	4	3	27 - 28	21
5.	KF Egnatia Rrogozhinë	8	0	1	7	34 - 42	17

First Division Final [23.05.2019, Durrës]

KF Vllaznia Shkodër - KF Bylis Ballsh	1-3(1-0)

First Division Champions 2018/2019: **KF Bylis Ballsh**

NATIONAL TEAM

INTERNATIONAL MATCHES
(16.07.2018 – 15.07.2019)

07.09.2018	Elbasan	Albania - Israel	1-0(0-0)	(UNL)
10.09.2018	Glasgow	Scotland - Albania	2-0(0-0)	(UNL)
10.10.2018	Elbasan	Albania - Jordan	0-0	(F)
14.10.2018	Beer Sheva	Israel - Albania	2-0(1-0)	(UNL)
17.11.2018	Shkodër	Albania - Scotland	0-4(0-2)	(UNL)
20.11.2018	Elbasan	Albania - Wales	1-0(0-0)	(F)
22.03.2019	Shkodër	Albania - Turkey	0-2(0-1)	(ECQ)
25.03.2019	Andorra la Vella	Andorra - Albania	0-3(0-1)	(ECQ)
08.06.2019	Rekjavík	Iceland - Albania	1-0(1-0)	(ECQ)
11.06.2019	Elbasan	Albania - Moldova	2-0(0-0)	(ECQ)

07.09.2018 ALBANIA - ISRAEL 1-0(0-0) UEFA Nations League C, Group 1
Elbasan Arena, Elbasan; Referee: Viktor Kassai (Hungary); Attendance: 4,126
ALB: Thomas Strakosha, Frédéric Veseli (84.Mërgim Mavraj), Elseid Hysaj, Berat Ridvan Gjimshiti, Egzon Binaku, Jahmir Hyka (Cap), Migjen Xhevat Basha, Ledian Memushaj, Taulant Xhaka, Enis Gavazaj (72.Herdi Prenga), Sindrit Guri (46.Bekim Abdyl Balaj). Trainer: Christian Panucci (Italy).
Goal: Taulant Xhaka (55).

10.09.2018 SCOTLAND - ALBANIA 2-0(0-0) UEFA Nations League C, Group 1
Hampden Park, Glasgow; Referee: Matej Jug (Slovenia); Attendance: 17,455
ALB: Thomas Strakosha, Frédéric Veseli (90+1.Enea Mihaj), Elseid Hysaj (Cap), Berat Ridvan Gjimshiti, Egzon Binaku, Sabien Lilaj, Ledian Memushaj, Taulant Xhaka, Enis Gavazaj (46.Herdi Prenga), Emanuele Ndoj (66.Rey Aldo Manaj), Bekim Abdyl Balaj. Trainer: Christian Panucci (Italy).

10.10.2018 ALBANIA - JORDAN 0-0 Friendly International
Elbasan Arena, Elbasan; Referee: Genc Nuza (Kosovo); Attendance: n/a
ALB: Etrit Berisha, Mërgim Mavraj (Cap) (56.Kastriot Luan Dermaku), Berat Ridvan Gjimshiti, Egzon Binaku (61.Ermir Limon Lenjani), Enea Mihaj (9.Frédéric Veseli), Andi Lila, Taulant Xhaka (46.Emanuele Ndoj), Enis Gavazaj, Ylber Ramadani (46.Myrto Artan Uzuni), Eros Genc Grezda (46.Bekim Abdyl Balaj), Rey Aldo Manaj. Trainer: Christian Panucci (Italy).

14.10.2018 ISRAEL - ALBANIA 2-0(1-0) UEFA Nations League C, Group 1
"Yaakov Turner Toto" Stadium, Beer Sheva; Referee: Paolo Mazzoleni (Italy); Attendance: 14,950
ALB: Thomas Strakosha, Mërgim Mavraj (Cap), Elseid Hysaj, Berat Ridvan Gjimshiti, Egzon Binaku, Migjen Xhevat Basha (46.Sabien Lilaj), Ledian Memushaj, Taulant Xhaka, Eros Genc Grezda, Bekim Abdyl Balaj (73.Giacomo Vrioni), Myrto Artan Uzuni. Trainer: Christian Panucci (Italy).

17.11.2018 ALBANIA - SCOTLAND 0-4(0-2) UEFA Nations League C, Group 1
Stadiumi "Loro Boriçi", Shkodër; Referee: Vladislav Bezborodov (Russia); Attendance: 8,632
ALB: Etrit Berisha, Mërgim Mavraj (Cap) [*sent off 21*], Frédéric Veseli, Berat Ridvan Gjimshiti (52.Kastriot Luan Dermaku), Egzon Binaku, Ledian Memushaj, Taulant Xhaka, Ergys Kaçe (27.Ardian Ilmi Ismajli), Eros Genc Grezda, Myrto Artan Uzuni, Rey Aldo Manaj (62.Bekim Abdyl Balaj). Trainer: Christian Panucci (Italy).

20.11.2018 ALBANIA - WALES 1-0(0-0) Friendly International
Elbasan Arena, Elbasan; Referee: Dejan Jakimovski (North Macedonia); Attendance: 3,000
ALB: Etrit Berisha, Mërgim Mavraj (Cap), Frédéric Veseli, Elseid Hysaj, Ardian Ilmi Ismajli, Andi Lila (59.Ledian Memushaj), Migjen Xhevat Basha, Taulant Xhaka, Eros Genc Grezda (69.Sabien Lilaj), Myrto Artan Uzuni, Bekim Abdyl Balaj. Trainer: Christian Panucci (Italy).
Goal: Bekim Abdyl Balaj (58 penalty).

22.03.2019 ALBANIA - TURKEY 0-2(0-1) 16th EC. Qualifiers
Stadiumi "Loro Boriçi", Shkodër; Referee: Tobias Stieler (Germany); Attendance: 11,730
ALB: Etrit Berisha, Frédéric Veseli, Elseid Hysaj (Cap), Berat Ridvan Gjimshiti, Iván Balliu Campeny (58.Armando Sadiku), Ardian Ilmi Ismajli, Amir Malush Abrashi, Ledian Memushaj, Taulant Xhaka, Myrto Artan Uzuni, Bekim Abdyl Balaj (58.Eros Genc Grezda). Trainer: Christian Panucci (Italy).

25.03.2019 ANDORRA - ALBANIA 0-3(0-1) 16th EC. Qualifiers
Estadi Nacional, Andorra la Vella; Referee: Filip Glova (Slovakia); Attendance: 1,373
ALB: Etrit Berisha, Elseid Hysaj (Cap), Berat Ridvan Gjimshiti, Naser Ismail Aliji, Ardian Ilmi Ismajli, Migjen Xhevat Basha (87.Ledian Memushaj), Taulant Xhaka (67.Amir Malush Abrashi), Ergys Kaçe, Armando Sadiku, Eros Genc Grezda (70.Bekim Abdyl Balaj), Myrto Artan Uzuni. Trainer: Ervin Bulku.
Goals: Armando Sadiku (21), Bekim Abdyl Balaj (87), Amir Malush Abrashi (90+6).

08.06.2019 ICELAND - ALBANIA 1-0(1-0) 16th EC. Qualifiers
Laugardalsvöllur, Reykjavík; Referee: Robert Madden (Scotland); Attendance: 8,968
ALB: Etrit Berisha, Ermir Limon Lenjani, Frédéric Veseli, Elseid Hysaj (Cap), Kastriot Luan Dermaku, Ardian Ilmi Ismajli, Amir Malush Abrashi, Migjen Xhevat Basha (68.Ergys Kaçe), Taulant Xhaka (72.Emanuele Ndoj), Sokol Cikalleshi (80.Armando Sadiku), Bekim Abdyl Balaj. Trainer: Edoardo Reja (Italy).

11.06.2019 ALBANIA - MOLDOVA 2-0(0-0) 16th EC. Qualifiers
Elbasan Arena, Elbasan; Referee: Ville Nevalainen (Finland); Attendance: 5,004
ALB: Etrit Berisha, Mërgim Mavraj (Cap), Ermir Limon Lenjani (57.Odise Roshi), Frédéric Veseli, Elseid Hysaj, Ardian Ilmi Ismajli, Amir Malush Abrashi, Ergys Kaçe (84.Kristi Qose), Ylber Ramadani, Armando Sadiku (57.Sokol Cikalleshi), Myrto Artan Uzuni. Trainer: Edoardo Reja (Italy).
Goals: Sokol Cikalleshi (66), Ylber Ramadani (90+3).

NATIONAL TEAM PLAYERS
(16.07.2018 – 15.07.2019)

Name	DOB	Caps	Goals	2018/2019:	*Club*
Goalkeepers					
Etrit BERISHA	10.03.1989	**57**	**0**	2018/2019:	*Atalanta Bergamasca Calcio (ITA)*
Thomas STRAKOSHA	19.03.1995	**8**	**0**	2018/2019:	*SS Lazio Roma (ITA)*
Defenders					
Naser Ismail ALIJI	27.12.1993	**13**	**0**	2019:	*FC Dinamo Bucureşti (ROU)*
Iván BALLIU Campeny	01.01.1992	**1**	**0**	2019:	*FC Metz (FRA)*
Egzon BINAKU	27.08.1995	**5**	**0**	2018:	*Malmö FF (SWE)*
Kastriot Luan DERMAKU	15.01.1992	**3**	**0**	2018/2019:	*Cosenza Calcio (ITA)*
Berat Ridvan GJIMSHITI	19.02.1993	**23**	**1**	2018/2019:	*Atalanta Bergamasca Calcio (ITA)*
Elseid HYSAJ	02.02.1994	**48**	**0**	2018/2019:	*SSC Napoli (ITA)*
Ardian Ilmi ISMAJLI	30.09.1996	**6**	**0**	2018/2019:	*HNK Hajduk Split (CRO)*
Ermir Limon LENJANI	05.08.1989	**30**	**3**	2018/2019:	*FC Sion (SUI)*
Mërgim MAVRAJ	09.06.1986	**49**	**3**	2018: 03.01.2019->	*Aris Thessaloníki (GRE)* *FC Ingolstadt 04 (GER)*
Enea MIHAJ	05.06.1998	**2**	**0**	2018:	*Panetolikos GPS Agrinio (GRE)*
Herdi PRENGA	31.08.1994	**2**	**0**	2018:	*NK Intnter Zaprešić (CRO)*
Frédéric VESELI	20.11.1992	**21**	**0**	2018/2019:	*Empoli FC (ITA)*
Midfielders					
Amir Malush ABRASHI	27.03.1990	**31**	**1**	2019:	*SC Freiburg (GER)*
Migjen Xhevat BASHA	05.01.1987	**34**	**3**	2018/2019:	*Aris Thessaloníki (GRE)*
Enis GAVAZAJ	21.03.1995	**3**	**0**	2018:	*FK Yenisey Krasnoyarsk (RUS)*
Eros Genc GREZDA	15.04.1995	**13**	**1**	2018/2019:	*Rangers FC Glasgow (SCO)*
Jahmir HYKA	08.03.1988	**47**	**2**	2018:	*San Jose Earthquakes (USA)*
Ergys KAÇE	08.07.1993	**25**	**2**	2018/2019:	*PAE Panathinaïkos Athína (GRE)*
Andi LILA	12.02.1986	**70**	**0**	2018/2019:	*PAS Giannina (GRE)*
Sabien LILAJ	18.02.1989	**19**	**0**	2018:	*Qəbələ FK (AZE)*
Ledian MEMUSHAJ	07.12.1986	**36**	**1**	2018/2019:	*Delfino Pescara 1936 (ITA)*
Emanuele NDOJ	20.11.1996	**5**	**1**	2018/2019:	*Brescia Calcio (ITA)*
Kristi QOSE	10.06.1995	**2**	**0**	2019:	*MFK Ružomberok (SVK)*
Ylber RAMADANI	12.04.1996	**5**	**1**	2018/2019:	*Vejle BK (DEN)*
Odise ROSHI	22.05.1991	**51**	**4**	2019:	*FK Akhmat Grozny (RUS)*
Taulant XHAKA	28.03.1991	**30**	**1**	2018/2019:	*FC Basel (SUI)*
Forwards					
Bekim Abdyl BALAJ	11.01.1991	**33**	**6**	2018/2019:	*FK Akhmat Grozny (RUS)*
Sokol CIKALLESHI	27.07.1990	**30**	**3**	2019:	*Akhisar Belediye Gençlik ve Spor Kulübü (TUR)*
Sindrit GURI	23.10.1993	**2**	**0**	2018:	*KV Oostende (BEL)*
Rey Aldo MANAJ	24.02.1997	**8**	**1**	2018:	*Albacete Balompié (ESP)*
Armando SADIKU	27.05.1991	**37**	**12**	2019:	*FC Lugano (SUI)*
Myrto Artan UZUNI	31.05.1995	**7**	**0**	2018/2019:	*NK Lokomotiva Zagreb (CRO)*
Giacomo VRIONI	15.10.1998	**1**	**0**	2018:	*Venezia FC (ITA)*

National team coach

Christian PANUCCI (Italy) [19.07.2017 – 23.03.2019; Sacked]	12.04.1973	15 M; 4 W; 2 D; 9 L; 9-25
Ervin BULKU [23.03. – 17.04.2019; Interim]	03.03.1981	1 M; 1 W; 0 D; 0 L; 3-0
Edoardo REJA (Italy) [from 17.04.2019]	10.10.1945	2 M; 1 W; 0 D; 1 L; 2-1

ANDORRA

The Country:

Principality of Andorra (Principat d'Andorra)
Capital: Andorra la Vella
Surface: 467,63 km²
Inhabitants: 76,177 [2019]
Time: UTC+1

The FA:

Federació Andorrana de Futbol
c/ Batlle Tomàs, 4 Baixos, AD700 Escaldes-Engordany
Tel: +376 805 830
Foundation date: 1994
Member of FIFA since: 1996
Member of UEFA since: 1996
Website: www.faf.ad

NATIONAL TEAM RECORDS

First international match:	13.11.1996, Andorra la Vella:	Andorra – Estonia 1-6
Most international caps:	Ildefons Lima Solà	- 123 caps (1997-2019)
Most international goals:	Ildefons Lima Solà	- 11 goal / 123 caps (1997-2019)

UEFA EUROPEAN CHAMPIONSHIP	
1960	-
1964	-
1968	-
1972	-
1976	-
1980	-
1984	-
1988	-
1992	-
1996	*Did not enter*
2000	Qualifiers
2004	Qualifiers
2008	Qualifiers
2012	Qualifiers
2016	Qualifiers

FIFA WORLD CUP	
1930	-
1934	-
1938	-
1950	-
1954	-
1958	-
1962	-
1966	-
1970	-
1974	-
1978	-
1982	-
1986	-
1990	-
1994	*Did not enter*
1998	*Did not enter*
2002	Qualifiers
2006	Qualifiers
2010	Qualifiers
2014	Qualifiers
2018	Qualifiers

UEFA NATIONS LEAGUE
2018/2019 – League D

OLYMPIC FOOTBALL TOURNAMENTS 1908-2016							
1908	-	**1948**	-	**1972**	-	**1996**	-
1912	-	**1952**	-	**1976**	-	**2000**	Qualifiers
1920	-	**1956**	-	**1980**	-	**2004**	Qualifiers
1924	-	**1960**	-	**1984**	*Withdrew*	**2008**	-
1928	-	**1964**	-	**1988**	-	**2012**	Qualifiers
1936	-	**1968**	-	**1992**	*Withdrew*	**2016**	Qualifiers

FIFA CONFEDERATIONS CUP 1992-2017
None

ANDORRAN CLUB HONOURS IN EUROPEAN CLUB COMPETITIONS:

European Champion Clubs.Cup (1956-1992) / UEFA Champions League (1993-2019)
None
Fairs Cup (1858-1971) / UEFA Cup (1972-2009) / UEFA Europa League (2010-2019)
None
UEFA Super Cup (1972-2019)
None
European Cup Winners.Cup 1961-1999*
None

**defunct competition*

NATIONAL COMPETITIONS
TABLE OF HONOURS

	CHAMPIONS	CUP WINNERS	BEST GOALSCORERS	
1990/1991	-	FC Santa Coloma	-	
1991/1992	-	*No competition*	-	
1992/1993	-	*No competition*	-	
1993/1994	-	CE Principat Andorra La Vella	-	
1994/1995	FC Santa Colomaa	CE Principat Andorra La Vella	-	
1995/1996	FC Encamp	CE Principat Andorra La Vella	-	
1996/1997	CE Principat Andorra La Vella	CE Principat Andorra La Vella	Patricio González Fernández (CE Principat Andorra La Vella)	25
1997/1998	CE Principat Andorra La Vella	CE Principat Andorra La Vella	Rafael Sánchez Pedrosa (ESP, FC Santa Coloma)	36
1998/1999	CE Principat Andorra La Vella	CE Principat Andorra La Vella	-	
1999/2000	Constel·lació Esportiva Andorra La Vella	Constel·lació Esportiva Andorra La Vella	-	
2000/2001	FC Santa Coloma	FC Santa Coloma	-	
2001/2002	FC Encamp	FC Lusitanos Andorra La Vella	-	
2002/2003	FC Santa Coloma	FC Santa Coloma	-	
2003/2004	FC Santa Coloma	FC Santa Coloma	Jorge Filipe Sa Silva Carneiro (POR, UE Sant Julià)	16
2004/2005	UE Sant Julià	FC Santa Coloma	-	
2005/2006	FC Rànger's Andorra La Vella	FC Santa Coloma	-	
2006/2007	FC Rànger's Andorra La Vella	FC Santa Coloma	Norberto Urbani (ARG, FC Rànger's Andorra La Vella) Joan Carles Toscano Beltrán (FC Santa Coloma)	14
2007/2008	FC Santa Coloma	UE Sant Julià	-	-
2008/2009	UE Sant Julià	FC Santa Coloma	Norberto Urbani (ARG, FC Rànger's Andorra La Vella)	22
2009/2010	FC Santa Coloma	UE Sant Julià	Gabriel Riera Lancha (UE Sant Julià)	19
2010/2011	FC Santa Coloma	UE Sant Julià	Victor Bernat Cuadros (ESP, UE Santa Coloma)	16
2011/2012	FC Lusitanos Andorra La Vella	FC Santa Coloma	Victor Bernat Cuadros (ESP, UE Santa Coloma)	14
2012/2013	FC Lusitanos Andorra La Vella	UE Santa Coloma	Bruno Filipe Raposo Fernandes "Bruninho" (POR, FC Lusitanos Andorra La Vella)	17
2013/2014	FC Santa Coloma	UE Sant Julià	Luis Miguel dos Reis (POR, FC Lusitanos Andorra La Vella)	13
2014/2015	FC Santa Coloma	UE Sant Julià	Cristian Martínez Alejo (FC Santa Coloma)	22
2015/2016	FC Santa Coloma	UE Santa Coloma	Victor Bernat Cuadros (ESP, UE Santa Coloma)	12
2016/2017	FC Santa Coloma	UE Santa Coloma	Victor Bernat Cuadros (ESP, UE Santa Coloma)	18
2017/2018	FC Santa Coloma	FC Santa Coloma	Jesús David Sosa Sebastiá "Chus Sosa" (ESP, FC Santa Coloma)	14
2018/2019	FC Santa Coloma	UE Engordany	Nicolás Estebán Medina Ríos (CHI, FC Lusitanos Andorra La Vella) Joel Méndez del Río (ESP, UE Sant Julià) Enric Pi Solá (ESP, UE Sant Julià) Genís Soldevila Solduga (ESP, Inter Club d'Escaldes)	10

NATIONAL CHAMPIONSHIP
Primera Divisió 2018/2019
(16.09.2018 – 19.05.2019)

Regular Season - Results

Round 1 [16.09.2018]
FC Ordino - Inter Club d'Escaldes 1-2
FC Encamp - UE Santa Coloma 0-1
UE Engordany - UE Sant Julià 1-4
FC Santa Coloma - FC Lusitanos 0-0

Round 2 [23.09.2018]
UE Santa Coloma - UE Engordany 0-0
Inter Club d'Escaldes - FC Santa Coloma 1-0
UE Sant Julià - FC Ordino 1-1
FC Lusitanos - FC Encamp 1-1

Round 3 [30.09.2018]
FC Santa Coloma - FC Encamp 3-0
FC Ordino - UE Santa Coloma 2-1
UE Engordany - FC Lusitanos 1-1
Inter Club d'Escaldes - UE Sant Julià 0-1

Round 4 [07.10.2018]
UE Sant Julià - FC Santa Coloma 1-1
UE Santa Coloma - Inter Club d'Escaldes 1-1
FC Lusitanos - FC Ordino 1-0
FC Encamp - UE Engordany 0-1 [25.10.]

Round 5 [21.10.2018]
Inter Club d'Escaldes - FC Lusitanos 2-1
FC Ordino - FC Encamp 3-1
FC Santa Coloma - UE Engordany 0-0
UE Sant Julià - UE Santa Coloma 1-1

Round 6 [28.10.2018]
FC Encamp - Inter Club d'Escaldes 0-2
FC Lusitanos - UE Sant Julià 0-1
FC Santa Coloma - UE Santa Coloma 1-2
UE Engordany - FC Ordino 1-0

Round 7 [04.11.2018]
UE Santa Coloma - FC Lusitanos 0-2
UE Sant Julià - FC Encamp 4-2
FC Ordino - FC Santa Coloma 0-2
Inter Club d'Escaldes - UE Engordany 0-2

Round 8 [11.11.2018]
Inter Club d'Escaldes - FC Ordino 2-1
UE Sant Julià - UE Engordany 1-1
FC Lusitanos - FC Santa Coloma 1-4
UE Santa Coloma - FC Encamp 5-0

Round 9 [25.11.2018]
FC Encamp - FC Lusitanos 0-3
UE Engordany - UE Santa Coloma 2-1
FC Ordino - UE Sant Julià 0-0
FC Santa Coloma - Inter Club d'Escaldes 3-1

Round 10 [02.12.2018]
FC Encamp - FC Santa Coloma 1-3
FC Lusitanos - UE Engordany 4-0
UE Sant Julià - Inter Club d'Escaldes 3-0
UE Santa Coloma - FC Ordino 2-3

Round 11 [09.12.2018]
UE Engordany - FC Encamp 3-0
Inter Club d'Escaldes - UE Santa Coloma 1-0
FC Ordino - FC Lusitanos 1-3
FC Santa Coloma - UE Sant Julià 0-0

Round 12 [15-16.12.2018]
UE Santa Coloma - UE Sant Julià 1-3
FC Encamp - FC Ordino 2-0
UE Engordany - FC Santa Coloma 0-2
FC Lusitanos - Inter Club d'Escaldes 0-3

Round 13 [03.02.2019]
FC Ordino - UE Engordany 2-1
UE Sant Julià - FC Lusitanos 5-0
Inter Club d'Escaldes - FC Encamp 3-1
UE Santa Coloma - FC Santa Coloma 0-0

Round 14 [10.02.2019]
FC Encamp - UE Sant Julià 1-2
FC Santa Coloma - FC Ordino 1-0
FC Lusitanos - UE Santa Coloma 1-2
UE Engordany - Inter Club d'Escaldes 1-0

Round 15 [17.02.2019]
FC Encamp - UE Santa Coloma 1-1
FC Ordino - Inter Club d'Escaldes 1-3
UE Engordany - UE Sant Julià 0-2
FC Santa Coloma - FC Lusitanos 2-0

Round 16 [24.02.2019]
Inter Club d'Escaldes - FC Santa Coloma 1-1
UE Santa Coloma - UE Engordany 2-3
FC Lusitanos - FC Encamp 0-1
UE Sant Julià - FC Ordino 1-0

Round 17 [03.03.2019]
UE Engordany - FC Lusitanos 5-0
FC Santa Coloma - FC Encamp 1-0
FC Ordino - UE Santa Coloma 0-1
Inter Club d'Escaldes - UE Sant Julià 2-1

Round 18 [10.03.2019]
FC Encamp - UE Engordany 2-2
UE Sant Julià - FC Santa Coloma 0-2
UE Santa Coloma - Inter Club d'Escaldes 1-3
FC Lusitanos - FC Ordino 1-5

Round 19 [17.03.2019]
FC Ordino - FC Encamp 4-0
UE Sant Julià - UE Santa Coloma 2-1
FC Santa Coloma - UE Engordany 1-1
Inter Club d'Escaldes - FC Lusitanos 2-1

Round 20 [31.03.2019]
FC Encamp - Inter Club d'Escaldes 1-1
FC Lusitanos - UE Sant Julià 0-3
UE Engordany - FC Ordino 1-2
FC Santa Coloma - UE Santa Coloma 2-1

Round 21 [07.04.2019]
UE Santa Coloma - FC Lusitanos 0-0
Inter Club d'Escaldes - UE Engordany 0-0
UE Sant Julià - FC Encamp 4-2
FC Ordino - FC Santa Coloma 1-2

Regular Season - League table

1.	UE Sant Julià	21	13	6	2	42	-	16	45
2.	FC Santa Coloma	21	12	7	2	32	-	12	43
3.	Inter Club d'Escaldes	21	12	4	5	30	-	21	40
4.	UE Engordany	21	8	7	6	26	-	24	31
5.	FC Ordino	21	7	2	12	27	-	32	23
6.	UE Santa Coloma	21	5	6	10	25	-	29	21
7.	FC Lusitanos Andorra La Vella	21	5	4	12	21	-	38	19
8.	FC Encamp	21	2	4	15	16	-	47	10

Top-4 teams qualified for the Championship Play-offs, while teams ranked 5-8 were qualified for the Relegation Play-offs.

Relegation Play-offs - Results

Round 1 [14.04.2019]
FC Lusitanos - FC Ordino 0-1
UE Santa Coloma - FC Encamp 1-2

Round 2 [28.04.2019]
UE Santa Coloma - FC Lusitanos 2-0
FC Ordino - FC Encamp 1-0

Round 3 [01.05.2019]
FC Ordino - UE Santa Coloma 0-0
FC Lusitanos - FC Encamp 1-1

Round 4 [05.05.2019]
FC Ordino - FC Lusitanos 3-0
FC Encamp - UE Santa Coloma 0-2

Round 5 [11.05.2019]
FC Encamp - FC Ordino 4-1
FC Lusitanos - UE Santa Coloma 0-0

Round 6 [19.05.2019]
UE Santa Coloma - FC Ordino 3-1
FC Encamp - FC Lusitanos 1-0

Championship Play-offs - Results

Round 1 [14.04.2019]
Inter Club d'Escaldes - UE Sant Julià 2-0
FC Santa Coloma - UE Engordany 2-1

Round 2 [27-28.04.2019]
FC Santa Coloma - Inter Club d'Escaldes 1-1
UE Engordany - UE Sant Julià 2-2

Round 3 [01.05.2019]
Inter Club d'Escaldes - UE Engordany 1-0
UE Sant Julià - FC Santa Coloma 1-1

Round 4 [04-05.05.2019]
UE Engordany - FC Santa Coloma 0-1
UE Sant Julià - Inter Club d'Escaldes 3-2

Round 5 [12.05.2019]
UE Sant Julià - UE Engordany 3-0
Inter Club d'Escaldes - FC Santa Coloma 2-1

Round 6 [19.05.2019]
FC Santa Coloma - UE Sant Julià 3-1
UE Engordany - Inter Club d'Escaldes 1-1

Final Standings

Relegation Play-offs

5.	FC Ordino	27	10	3	14	34	-	39	33
6.	UE Santa Coloma	27	8	8	11	33	-	32	32
7.	FC Lusitanos Andorra La Vella *(Relegation Play-offs)*	27	5	6	16	22	-	46	21
8.	*(Relegated)*	27	5	5	17	24	-	53	20

Championship Play-offs

1.	**FC Santa Coloma**	27	15	9	3	41	-	18	54
2.	UE Sant Julià	27	15	8	4	52	-	26	53
3.	Inter Club d'Escaldes	27	15	6	6	39	-	27	51
4.	UE Engordany	27	8	9	10	30	-	34	33

Top goalscorers:

10 Nicolás Estebán Medina Ríos (CHI)
FC Lusitanos Andorra La Vella

10 Joel Méndez del Río (ESP)
UE Sant Julià

10 Enric Pi Solá (ESP)
UE Sant Julià

10 Genís Soldevila Solduga
Inter Club d'Escaldes

Relegation Play-offs [17-24.05.2018]

CE Carroi - FC Lusitanos Andorra La Vella 1-0(0-0) 0-1(0-0,0-1,0-1); 4-2 pen

CE Carroi promoted to Primera Divisió 2019/2020.

NATIONAL CUP
Copa Constitució 2018/2019

First Round [20.01.2019]

CE Carroi - UE Santa Coloma	1-3	Atlètic Club d'Escaldes - FC Ordino	2-1
Penya Encarnada d'Andorra - FC Encamp	1-1; 11-10 pen	FS La Massana - FC Lusitanos Andorra La Vella	0-3

Quarter-Finals [14.03.2019]

Inter Club d'Escaldes - UE Santa Coloma	0-1 aet	UE Sant Julià - Atlètic Club d'Escaldes	3-0
UE Engordany - Penya Encarnada d'Andorra	2-1	FC Santa Coloma - FC Lusitanos Andorra La Vella	6-0

Semi-Finals [03.04.2019]

UE Santa Coloma - UE Engordany	0-0; 3-5 pen	UE Sant Julià - FC Santa Coloma	1-2

Final

26.05.2019; Estadi Nacional, Andorra la Vella; Referee: Pedro Filipe Carvalho Da Costa; Attendance: n/a
UE Engordany - FC Santa Coloma **2-0(0-0)**

UE Engordany: Jesús Coca Noguerol, Deivis Hilario de Jesús Soares, Miguel Ruiz Enamorado, Jorge Sebastián Varela Delisa, Sébastien Jacques Aguero, Hamza Ryahi Bouharma (90.Rodrigo Gabriel Guida Darsaut), Miguel Ángel Laborda Gil (82.Cristopher Pousa Braganza), Mario Valentín Spano, Nikola Zugić, Sebastián Gómez Pérez, Joël Fabrice Goho Bah Thomas (68.Omar Camara). Trainer: Filipe Busto (Portugal).

FC Santa Coloma: Eloy Casals Rubio, Aleix Cístero Serna, Andreu Ramos Isus, Moisés San Nicolás Schellens, Francisco José Girau Rodríguez (66.Jesús David Sosa Sebastiá „Chus Sosa"), Pedro Santos Escolano, André Filipe Teixeira Azevedo, Diego Alejandro Nájera Quintero (80.Pablo Romero Díaz), Gabriel Riera Lancha (58.Lorenzo Burón Aranda), Víctor Rodríguez Soria, Julià Sánchez Soto. Trainer: Marc Rodríguez Rebull.

Goals: 1-0 Hamza Ryahi Bouharma (66), 2-0 Sebastián Gómez Pérez (88).

THE CLUBS 2018/2019

Please note: matches and goals includes statistics of both regular season and Play-offs (Championship & Relegation Play-offs).

Fútbol Club Encamp

Founded: 1950
Stadium: Camp de Futbol d'Encamp (550)

Goalkeepers:	**DOB**	**M**	**(s)**	**G**
Ángel De La Fuente Fernández (ESP)	29.12.1997	4		
Gerardo José Rubio Ortuna (ESP)	17.05.1987	20		
Andreas Matthias Werner (GER)	13.06.1996	3	(1)	
Defenders:	**DOB**	**M**	**(s)**	**G**
Christhian Barreto		3	(1)	
Sergi Gómez Calvo	29.12.1996	1	(1)	
Renzo Alejandro Dezotti (ARG)	17.11.1990	2	(1)	
Derrick Pachou Dibotti (CMR)	12.12.1992	13	(1)	
Gabriel Alejandro Fernández Otero	14.02.1997	5		
Jonathan Ferreira Silva	17.06.1993	6	(2)	
Tiago Paolo Flores (ESP)	07.05.1995	4	(3)	
Walter Eduardo Gómez (ARG)	28.08.1981	17	(2)	
André Manuel Marinho Teixeira	26.03.1993	23		
Brian Harald Mengual Maneiro	30.06.1994	2	(4)	
Rafael Moro Cervos		10	(1)	
Isaac Parramona Pedros		16	(3)	
Jorge Miquel Pinto Pedro	15.05.1994	18		1
Midfielders:	**DOB**	**M**	**(s)**	**G**
John Harry Cull (ENG)		1		
Gerard Escoda Amadeo			(1)	
Leonel Fernando Gancedo (ARG)	23.01.1971		(3)	
Joel Tomas Gancelo (ARG)		5	(2)	
Marc Gil Cardona			(1)	
Tomás Lanzini (ARG)	25.11.1991	16		1
João Pedro Lopes Leita	09.10.1991	3	(2)	
Antonio José Marinho Teixeira (POR)	30.05.1994	20	(2)	
Nicolas Mariano Minutella (ARG)	23.03.1995	10	(2)	1
Ferran Montobbio Borrell	10.03.1994	8	(8)	1
Diego Rafael Marinho Leite	16.06.1992	5	(4)	
Quim Altes Pascuet		2	(2)	
Diego Omar Sánchez Paredes (ARG)	22.04.1991	15	(1)	3
Brian Andre Teixeira Filipe	26.06.1995	3	(3)	
Alberto López Medel "Tete" (ESP)	21.11.1998	8	(2)	4
Forwards:	**DOB**	**M**	**(s)**	**G**
Helder Alves Lopes	25.01.1994	1		
Jaime Bauza Adrover (ESP)	15.05.1985	2	(1)	
José Ángel Belanche Goenaga (ESP)	28.03.1994	1	(3)	
Andreu Matos Muñoz	01.12.1995	10	(6)	1
Eric Pelfort Fuster	07.10.1999	7	(10)	
Eugenio Else Peralta Cabrera (PAR)	16.12.1977	18	(3)	5
Josep Maria Tizón Fernández	03.10.1997	2	(9)	
Gonzalo Ignacio Ucha Fernández (ARG)	07.02.1984	12	(2)	3
Trainer:	**DOB**	**M**		
Leonel Fernando Gancedo (ARG)	23.01.1971	27		

Unió Esportiva Engordany

Founded: 1980
Stadium: Estadi Comunal d'Andorra la Vella (1,300)

Goalkeepers:	DOB	M	(s)	G
Jesús Coca Noguerol (ESP)	22.05.1989	27		
Jonathan Lizcano Montenegro	27.05.2001		(1)	
Defenders:	**DOB**	**M**	**(s)**	**G**
Christian Ariel Cellay (ARG)	05.09.1981	12		
Deivis Hilario de Jesús Soares (ESP)	19.09.1991	13	(1)	2
Tiago Paolo Flores (ESP)	07.05.1995	4	(3)	
Jose Luis Marrufo Gil (ESP)	01.01.1997	4	(5)	1
Brian Harald Mengual Maneiro	30.06.1994	2	(4)	
Rafael Amaral Santos Brito (POR)	06.07.1986	12		
Mateo Rodríguez Firpo (ESP)	25.05.1993	18	(4)	4
Miguel Ruiz Enamorado (ESP)	16.07.1982	27		1
Jorge Sebastián Varela Delisa (URU)	23.09.1980	12	(3)	1
David Villanueva Cervera (ESP)	30.11.1995		(1)	
Walter Esteban Wagner (ARG)	12.01.1981	8		
Midfielders:	**DOB**	**M**	**(s)**	**G**
Sébastien Jacques Aguero (FRA)	17.08.1993	21	(5)	1
Hamza Ryahi Bouharma (ESP)	11.03.1993	19	(5)	1
Carlos Eduardo Peppe Britos "Edu Peppe"	28.01.1983	24	(1)	
Sebastián Gómez Pérez	01.11.1983	25		5
Miguel Ángel Laborda Gil (ESP)	18.02.1995	20	(3)	2
Cristopher Pousa Braganza	29.06.1992	14	(2)	
Mario Valentín Spano (URU)	07.02.1986	14		2
Nikola Zugić (SRB)	30.01.1990	7	(3)	1
Forwards:	**DOB**	**M**	**(s)**	**G**
Omar Camara (GAM)	1995	8	(3)	
Rodrigo Gabriel Guida Darsaut (ARG)	24.08.1982	2	(9)	1
Morgan Lafont (FRA)	22.11.1996		(4)	
Sergio William Leal González (URU)	25.09.1982	2	(2)	
Víctor Hugo Moreira Teixeira	05.10.1982	2	(15)	2
Luigi San Nicolas Schellens	28.06.1992	16	(2)	3
Fábio Filipe Serra Alves (POR)	24.08.1984	7	(3)	5
Joël Fabrice Goho Bah Thomas (FRA)	30.06.1987	9		1
Larsen Touré (GUI)	20.07.1984	3	(1)	
Trainer:	**DOB**	**M**		
Filipe Busto (POR)	27.12.1983	27		

Inter Club d'Escaldes

Founded: 1991
Stadium: Estadi Comunal d'Andorra la Vella (1,300)

Goalkeepers:	DOB	M	(s)	G
Joan Bayona Gallardo (ESP)	16.09.1979	27		
Defenders:	**DOB**	**M**	**(s)**	**G**
Josep Maria Cabanes Foix	02.04.1996	8	(2)	
Ildefons Lima Solà	10.12.1979	14	(1)	
Lucas Maciel Sousa (POR)	06.03.1991	11	(1)	
Xavier Moreno Marín	03.12.1990	9		
Óscar Reyes Sánchez (ESP)	12.03.1988	25		1
Eric Rodríguez Barcelo	02.04.1993	14	(1)	1
Mateo Rodríguez Firpo (URU)	25.05.1993	18	(4)	4
Iván Vigo Babot	07.09.1986	23		2
Midfielders:	**DOB**	**M**	**(s)**	**G**
Josep Manel Ayala Díaz	08.04.1980	5		
Roger Nazzaro Àlvarez	07.04.1997	6	(7)	1
Luis Filipe Pinto Escaleira	05.03.1987	16	(4)	
Albert Reyes Roig	24.03.1996	6	(1)	
Xavier Enes Rodrigues	15.06.2000		(1)	
Forwards:	**DOB**	**M**	**(s)**	**G**
Xavier Andorra Julià	07.06.1985	1	(5)	
Bruno Filipe Raposo Fernandes "Bruninho" (POR)	11.01.1986	20	(5)	1
Xavier Gallart Ayala	11.11.1980	4	(7)	2
Carlos Manuel Gomes Do Nascimento	18.10.1993	8	(7)	3
Maicon Dos Santos Venâncio (BRA)	28.05.1983	10	(6)	
Sergio Moreno Marín	25.11.1987	25		6
Alejandro Puga Caetano	30.11.2000		(3)	
Genís Soldevila Solduga (ESP)	03.03.1987	25	(1)	10
Santiago Triguero Blanch (ESP)	04.10.1976	8	(5)	4
Rodrigo Armando Vergara Brango (COL)	13.06.1995	10	(10)	4
Trainer:	**DOB**	**M**		
Adolfo Baines (ESP)	12.02.1972	27		

Futbol Club Lusitanos Andorra La Vella

Founded: 1999
Stadium: Centre d'Entrenaments, Andorra La Vella (300)

Goalkeepers:	DOB	M	(s)	G
Marcelo dos Santos Farias Valverde (BRA)	21.11.1989	22		
Alberto Usabiaga Guimera	06.11.1994	5	(2)	
Defenders:	**DOB**	**M**	**(s)**	**G**
Alexandre Correia Alfaiate (POR)	17.09.1995	8	(3)	1
Soualio Bakayoko (CIV)	18.05.1991	3		
Andrés Briñez Aranda (COL)		5	(1)	
Kemoko Doumbouya (FRA)	03.07.1993	4		
Fernando Tomás Lazcano Barros (CHI)	10.11.1988	4		1
Leonel Maciel Antunes (FRA)	02.07.1982		(4)	
Pedro Manuel Martins Araújo (POR)	10.01.1985	11	(1)	1
Artur Rafael Maques Almeida "Rafa" (POR)	14.02.1997		(1)	
Rafael Amaral Santos Brito (POR)	06.07.1986	12		
Adrián Rodrigues Gonçalves	14.08.1988	25		
Matias Nicolas Vaamonde (ARG)	30.11.1989	12		1
Mark Withers (USA)	10.11.1992	26		1
Midfielders:	**DOB**	**M**	**(s)**	**G**
Ismael Alfredo Canta Trujillo (PER)	07.03.1996	14		
David Sebastián Cortez		12		
Hugo Miguel Gonçalves da Costa (POR)	20.02.1990	2	(1)	
Sofiane Dridi (TUN)	30.11.1992	1	(1)	
Jean Andre Mbele Mavinga (FRA)	22.11.1993	12	(1)	
Bruno Gomes Mendonça (POR)	07.02.1994	10	(1)	
José Nuno Vilaça Campos (POR)	10.08.1998	12		
Iván García Pérez	01.04.1991	9	(3)	
Gemelson Nayry Fay Bill Vieira (GNB)	04.08.1992	7	(5)	
Xavier Vieira de Vasconcelos	14.01.1992	5		
Forwards:	**DOB**	**M**	**(s)**	**G**
David Astor		4	(4)	
Soumah Diafa Sadafi (BEL)	01.01.1999	3	(7)	
Maurizio Falzone (ITA)	27.01.1976	2	(3)	
Rashid Idris Saeffudeen (GHA)	30.09.1989	4	(2)	
Jefferson Martins Batista (BRA)	01.01.1995	6	(1)	1
Nicolás Esteban Medina Ríos (CHI)	28.03.1987	10	(1)	10
Luís Miguel dos Reis Rodrigues (POR)	22.03.1981	16	(6)	2
Rui André Gomes Amaral "Ruca" (POR)	15.06.1998	10	(2)	2
Sergio Urbano López (ESP)	08.12.1986	6	(4)	
Héctor Jesús Urrunaga Orellana (PER)	14.07.1995	11	(3)	
Manuel Veiga Machado	15.09.1986		(4)	1
Trainer:	**DOB**	**M**		
Joaquim Alberto Ferreira Machado (POR)	09.10.1971	27		

Futbol Club Ordino

Founded: 2010
Stadium: Centre Esportiu d'Ordino (200)

Goalkeepers:	**DOB**	**M**	**(s)**	**G**
Santiago Allan García Martínez (ESP)	01.01.1997	12		
Francisco José Domingo Gil	12.02.1999	2		
Ayoub Jilali (MAR)	02.01.1998	12		
Miquel Torres Vila*	07.10.1998	7	(6)	2
Defenders:	**DOB**	**M**	**(s)**	**G**
Joel Antonio			(1)	
Juan Felipe Carvajal Herrera (COL)	04.11.1994		(2)	
Miguel Del Castillo Somoza	30.09.1999	3	(2)	
Eric De Pablos Sola	08.03.1999	14		
Christian García González	04.02.1999	17	(1)	1
Thierno Kinty (FRA)	05.02.1992	10	(1)	
Levan Makharadze (UKR)	14.08.1993	26		
Rodrigo Varela		4	(13)	1
Midfielders:	**DOB**	**M**	**(s)**	**G**
Sebastià Bertrán Suárez	10.12.1992	22	(2)	5
Óscar Durán Millan	14.05.1987	2	(2)	
Juan Ezequiel García (ARG)	09.10.1991	3	(2)	
Lautaro Ezequiel García (ARG)		1	(3)	
Sandro Gutiérrez Merino	02.01.1996	6	(10)	
Jonathan Herrera Carvajal (COL)	30.07.1991	1	(1)	
Francesc Joel Martínez Vilar	31.12.1988	11	(1)	1
Dorian Nkashama (FRA)	12.02.1998	4		
Jorge Torres Martín (ARG)	11.04.1995	23	(1)	1
Forwards:	**DOB**	**M**	**(s)**	**G**
Lluis Martins Batista (BRA)	01.01.1998	16	(5)	6
Javier Isidro Charcopa Alegría (ECU)	02.09.1992	14	(3)	
Habibou Cissoko (FRA)		3	(6)	
Gabriel Gómez Román (ESP)	04.04.1985	11		2
Cristian Hidalgo González (ESP)	21.09.1983	23	(1)	7
Junior Gneprou Maxime Kobon (CIV)	21.12.1997	19	(4)	3
Pablo Navas Alors (ESP)	04.02.1992	12	(1)	1
Vinicius Frasnelli Maluf (BRA)	27.06.1996	22	(2)	3
Trainer:	**DOB**	**M**		
Joan Marmol Huguet (ESP)	07.10.1980	27		

*player used as goalkeeper and fielder!

Unió Esportiva Sant Julià de Lòria

Founded: 1982
Stadium: Estadi Comunal d'Andorra la Vella (1,300)

Goalkeepers:	**DOB**	**M**	**(s)**	**G**
Kévin Jacques Olimpa (MTQ)	10.03.1988	6		
Ferran Pol Pérez	28.02.1983	13		
Kevin Nicolás Ratti Fredes (ARG)	18.09.1993	8		
Defenders:	**DOB**	**M**	**(s)**	**G**
Fabrice Pierre Begeorgi Cabezas (FRA)	20.04.1987	9	(1)	
Mohamed Djitte Demba (CIV)		24	(2)	
Jhonattan Vinasco López „Jonny" (ESP)	31.01.1995	15	(4)	
Jean Pierre Valentin Miroux (FRA)	12.02.1998	7	(1)	1
Pedro Muñoz Fontalba	09.01.1988	19	(1)	
Nicolae Vasile (ROU)	29.12.1995	24	(1)	
Iván Vigo Babot (ESP)	07.09.1986	23		2
Midfielders:	**DOB**	**M**	**(s)**	**G**
José Antonio Aguilar Gómez (ESP)	11.10.1989	11	(5)	6
Luis Emilio Blanco Coto	15.01.1990	24	(2)	9
Francisco José Girau Rodríguez (ESP)	03.06.1985	4	(14)	
Antonio Lao Dona (ESP)	17.01.1984	25	(1)	
Miguel Ángel Luque Santiago (ESP)	23.07.1990	17	(4)	
Enric Pi Solá (ESP)	20.05.1983	25	(1)	10
Albert Reyes Roig	24.03.1996	6	(1)	
Jamal Zarioh Taouil	30.01.1989	5	(2)	
Forwards:	**DOB**	**M**	**(s)**	**G**
Fousseyni Cissé (FRA)	17.07.1989	14	(10)	6
Walter Fernández Balufo (ESP)	14.08.1989	17	(2)	2
Juan Manuel Hernández Sánchez "Juanma" (ESP)	22.07.1986	2	(8)	3
Adel Santana Mendy (FRA)	13.05.2000	3	(5)	2
Alberto Molina Rodríguez (ESP)	21.04.1988	14	(2)	1
Joel Méndez del Río (ESP)	01.05.1995	15	(3)	10
Diego Alejandro Nájera Quintero (MEX)	11.12.1994	16	(10)	6
Vincent Ramaël (FRA)	22.06.1988	5	(11)	2
Trainer:	**DOB**	**M**		
Jesús Barón Téllez (ESP)	09.09.1982	27		

Futbol Club Santa Coloma

Founded: 1986
Stadium: Estadi Comunal d'Andorra la Vella (1,300)

Goalkeepers:	**DOB**	**M**	**(s)**	**G**
Andrés Fabián Benítez Ruiz Díaz (PAR)	01.01.1983	5		
Eloy Casals Rubio (ESP)	22.10.1982	22		
Defenders:	**DOB**	**M**	**(s)**	**G**
Aleix Cístero Serna (ESP)	25.06.1994	23		4
Andreu Ramos Isus (ESP)	01.01.1989	25		4
Marc Rebés Ruíz	03.07.1994	24		1
Moisés San Nicolás Schellens	17.09.1993	23		
Midfielders:	**DOB**	**M**	**(s)**	**G**
Jesús David Sosa Sebastiá „Chus Sosa"(ESP)	05.01.1994	20	(2)	2
Francisco José Girau Rodríguez	03.06.1985	4	(14)	
Antonio Marinho (POR)	30.05.1994	2		
Yago Pérez Martínez	31.12.1987	15	(1)	1
Pedro Santos Escolano (ESP)	01.06.1993	24	(1)	2
Jamal Zarioh Taouil	30.01.1989	5	(2)	
Forwards:	**DOB**	**M**	**(s)**	**G**
André Filipe Teixeira Azevedo (POR)	19.07.1990	17	(8)	3
Lorenzo Burón Aranda (ESP)	06.10.1994	20	(3)	5
Joel Ferreira Sousa	03.12.2003		(1)	
Juan Manuel Torres Tena „Juanma" (ESP)	23.02.1990	21	(2)	1
Albert Mercadé Mellinas (ESP)	23.01.1985	3	(7)	
Diego Alejandro Nájera Quintero (MEX)	11.12.1994	24	(10)	6
Gabriel Riera Lancha	05.06.1985	4	(9)	4
Víctor Rodríguez Soria	07.09.1987	19	(5)	3
Julià Sánchez Soto	20.06.1978	1	(12)	4
Trainer:	**DOB**	**M**		
Marc Rodríguez Rebull		27		

Unió Esportiva Santa Coloma

Founded: 1986
Stadium: Estadi Comunal d'Andorra la Vella (1,300)

Goalkeepers:	**DOB**	**M**	**(s)**	**G**
José Eduardo Orestes Escobar Escalante	28.09.1994	1		
Josep Antoni Gomes Moreira	03.12.1985	24	(1)	
Ricard Fernández Lizarte (ESP)	26.05.1975	2		
Defenders:	**DOB**	**M**	**(s)**	**G**
Walid Bousenine Nafae (MAR)	07.04.1993	17	(1)	
Barthélémy Casanova (FRA)	02.03.1992	1	(1)	
Drissa Dao (FRA)	01.07.1996	9		
David Maneiro Ton	16.02.1989	21	(1)	2
Alexandre Martínez Gutiérrez	04.03.1987	13	(2)	1
Cristian Orosa Lodeiro (ESP)	12.12.1990	26		1
Jesús Rubio Gómez	09.09.1994	22	(1)	1
Jordi Rubio Gómez	01.11.1987	19	(2)	2
Midfielders:	**DOB**	**M**	**(s)**	**G**
Leonel Filipe Alves Alves	28.09.1993	3	(4)	
Marc Amat Mora	26.06.1993	3	(7)	
Paola Alberto da Costa	27.05.2000	3	(5)	
Alvaro Domingues Branco		3	(2)	
Abel Duarte Araujo	25.02.1994	14	(1)	1
Oriol Guillen García	18.10.1999		(1)	
Joel Malaga Ibarz	27.12.1997	8	(3)	
Freddy Merhawi Guillou (FRA)	27.12.1997	3		
Nourddin El Morabiti Talibe		4	(1)	
Brian Andre Teixeira Filipe	26.06.1995	2	(3)	
Forwards:	**DOB**	**M**	**(s)**	**G**
Gerard Aloy Soler	17.04.1989	16	(1)	
Boris Antón Codina	27.02.1987	12	(3)	
David Antunes da Silva	04.06.2000		(1)	
Victor Bernat Cuadros (ESP)	17.05.1987	11	(4)	3
Eric Carmona Bonache	19.06.2001		(2)	
Sergio Crespo Alonso	29.09.1992	24		3
Roberto Carlos Gomes Rebelo	21.10.1999	8	(4)	3
Adrián López Iglesias			(2)	
Luis Antonio Pajares González (PER)	14.10.1991	4	(7)	2
Aaron Sánchez Alburquerque	05.06.1990	15		9
Joan Salomó Téllez (ESP)	20.12.1983	7	(4)	5
Trainer:	**DOB**	**M**		
Albert Viladrich (ESP)	15.02.1983	27		

SECOND LEVEL
Segona Divisió 2018/2019

Regular Season - League table

1.	Atlètic Club d'Escaldes Escaldes-Engordany	18	15	1	2	82	-	15	46
2.	CE Carroi	18	15	0	3	62	-	22	45
3.	FS La Massana	18	13	1	4	79	-	24	40
4.	Penya Encarnada d'Andorra	18	12	2	4	53	-	21	38
5.	Inter Club d'Escaldes "B"	18	8	1	9	43	-	30	25
6.	UE Santa Coloma "B"	18	7	1	10	31	-	45	22
7.	FC Encamp "B"	18	6	2	10	23	-	43	20
8.	FC Rànger's Andorra la Vella	18	4	1	13	31	-	74	13
9.	UE Extremenya La Massana	18	3	3	12	30	-	60	12
10.	Sporting Club d'Escaldes	18	1	0	17	20	-	120	3
11.	CE Jenlai Escaldes-Engordany (*Retired*)								

Team ranked 1-4 and 8-9 were qualified for the Championship Play-offs. "B" teams are not allowed to promotion.

Championship Play-off – Final Standings

1.	Atlètic Club d'Escaldes Escaldes-Engordany (*Promoted*)	23	19	2	2	104	-	19	59
2.	CE Carroi (*Promotion Play-offs*)	23	17	2	4	75	-	29	53
3.	FS La Massana	23	16	2	5	104	-	33	50
4.	Penya Encarnada d'Andorra	23	15	2	6	70	-	31	47
5.	FC Rànger's Andorra la Vella	23	4	2	17	38	-	101	14
6.	UE Extremenya La Massana	23	3	4	16	35		92	13

NATIONAL TEAM

INTERNATIONAL MATCHES
(16.07.2018 – 15.07.2019)

18.08.2018	Grödig	Andorra - United Arab Emirates	0-0	(F)
06.09.2018	Rīga	Latvia - Andorra	0-0	(UNL)
10.09.2018	Andorra la Vella	Andorra - Kazakhstan	1-1(0-0)	(UNL)
13.10.2018	Tbilisi	Georgia - Andorra	3-0(1-0)	(UNL)
16.10.2018	Astana	Kazakhstan - Andorra	4-0(2-0)	(UNL)
15.11.2018	Andorra la Vella	Andorra - Georgia	1-1(0-1)	(UNL)
19.11.2018	Andorra la Vella	Andorra - Latvia	0-0	(UNL)
22.03.2019	Andorra la Vella	Andorra - Iceland	0-2(0-1)	(ECQ)
25.03.2019	Andorra la Vella	Andorra - Albania	0-3(0-1)	(ECQ)
08.06.2019	Chişinău	Moldova - Andorra	1-0(1-0)	(ECQ)
11.06.2019	Andorra la Vella	Andorra - France	0-4(0-3)	(ECQ)

18.08.2018 ANDORRA - UNITED ARAB EMIRATES 0-0 Friendly International
Das.Goldberg Stadion, Grödig (Austria); Referee: Christopher Jäger (Austria); Attendance: n/a
AND: Josep Antoni Gómes Moreira, Ildefons Lima Solà (Cap), Moisés San Nicolás Schellens, Marc Rebés Ruiz (89.Emili Josep García Miramontes), Jesús Rubio Gómez (68.Marc García Renom „Chiqui“), Max Llovera González-Adrio, Márcio Vieira de Vasconcelos, Cristian Martínez Alejo, Ludovic Clemente Garcés (80.Sebastiàn Gómez Pérez), Alexandre Martínez Palau (89.Sergio Moreno Marín), Ricard Fernández Betriu (68.Jordi Aláez Peña). Trainer: Jesús Luis Álvarez de Eulate Güergue "Koldo".

06.09.2018 LATVIA - ANDORRA 0-0 UEFA Nations League D, Group 1
Daugavas Stadions, Rīga; Referee: Keith Kennedy (Northern Ireland); Attendance: 4,803
AND: Josep Antoni Gómes Moreira, Ildefons Lima Solà (Cap), Marc Vales González, Moisés San Nicolás Schellens, Marc Rebés Ruiz, Jesús Rubio Gómez, Max Llovera González-Adrio, Joan Cervós Moro, Márcio Vieira de Vasconcelos (90+5.Emili Josep García Miramontes), Cristian Martínez Alejo (71.Jordi Aláez Peña), Ludovic Clemente Garcés (81.Víctor Rodríguez Soria). Trainer: Jesús Luis Álvarez de Eulate Güergue "Koldo".

10.09.2018 ANDORRA - KAZAKHSTAN 1-1(0-0) UEFA Nations League D, Group 1
Estadi Nacional, Andorra la Vella; Referee: Vilhjálmur Alvar Þórarinsson (Iceland); Attendance: 1,235
AND: Josep Antoni Gómes Moreira, Ildefons Lima Solà (Cap), Marc Vales González, Moisés San Nicolás Schellens (83.Jordi Rubio Gómez), Marc Rebés Ruiz, Jesús Rubio Gómez (79.Sebastiàn Gómez Pérez), Max Llovera González-Adrio, Joan Cervós Moro, Márcio Vieira de Vasconcelos, Cristian Martínez Alejo, Ludovic Clemente Garcés (70.Jordi Aláez Peña). Trainer: Jesús Luis Álvarez de Eulate Güergue "Koldo".
Goal: Jordi Aláez Peña (86).

13.10.2018 GEORGIA - ANDORRA 3-0(1-0) UEFA Nations League D, Group 1
“Boris Paichadze” Dinamo Arena, Tbilisi; Referee: Leontios Trattou (Cyprus); Attendance: 32,212
AND: Josep Antoni Gómes Moreira, Ildefons Lima Solà (Cap), Marc Vales González, Moisés San Nicolás Schellens, Marc Rebés Ruiz (78.Marc Pujol Pons), Jesús Rubio Gómez (88.Jordi Rubio Gómez), Max Llovera González-Adrio (45+1.Emili Josep García Miramontes), Joan Cervós Moro, Víctor Rodríguez Soria, Márcio Vieira de Vasconcelos [*sent off 90+2*], Cristian Martínez Alejo. Trainer: Jesús Luis Álvarez de Eulate Güergue "Koldo".

16.10.2018 KAZAKHSTAN - ANDORRA 4-0(2-0) UEFA Nations League D, Group 1
Astana Arena, Astana; Referee: Serhiy Boyko (Ukraine); Attendance: 19,854
AND: Josep Antoni Gómes Moreira, Ildefons Lima Solà (Cap), Marc Vales González (79.Sergio Moreno Marín), Moisés San Nicolás Schellens, Marc Rebés Ruiz, Jesús Rubio Gómez (84.Marc García Renom „Chiqui“), Max Llovera González-Adrio, Joan Cervós Moro, Víctor Rodríguez Soria, Marc Pujol Pons (90.Marc Ferré Nazzaro), Jordi Aláez Peña [*sent off 64*]. Trainer: Jesús Luis Álvarez de Eulate Güergue "Koldo".

15.11.2018 ANDORRA - GEORGIA 1-1(0-1) UEFA Nations League D, Group 1
Estadi Nacional, Andorra la Vella; Referee: Radu Petrescu (Romania); Attendance: 1,311
AND: Josep Antoni Gómes Moreira, Ildefons Lima Solà (Cap), Marc Vales González, Moisés San Nicolás Schellens, Marc Rebés Ruiz, Jesús Rubio Gómez, Max Llovera González-Adrio, Joan Cervós Moro (88.Jordi Rubio Gómez), Cristian Martínez Alejo (90+2.Emili Josep García Miramontes), Alexandre Martínez Palau, Ricard Fernández Betriu (81.Víctor Rodríguez Soria). Trainer: Jesús Luis Álvarez de Eulate Güergue "Koldo".
Goal: Cristian Martínez Alejo (63).

19.11.2018 ANDORRA - LATVIA 0-0 UEFA Nations League D, Group 1
Estadi Nacional, Andorra la Vella; Referee: Halil Umut Meler (Turkey); Attendance: 1,021
AND: Josep Antoni Gómes Moreira, Ildefons Lima Solà (Cap), Marc Vales González, Marc García Renom „Chiqui“ (79.Ricard Fernández Betriu), Moisés San Nicolás Schellens, Max Llovera González-Adrio, Joan Cervós Moro, Víctor Rodríguez Soria (73.Alexandre Martínez Palau), Sergio Moreno Marín (88.Julià Sánchez Soto), Cristian Martínez Alejo, Jordi Aláez Peña. Trainer: Jesús Luis Álvarez de Eulate Güergue "Koldo".

22.03.2019 ANDORRA - ICELAND 0-2(0-1) 16th EC. Qualifiers
Estadi Nacional, Andorra la Vella; Referee: Sandro Schärer (Switzerland); Attendance: 1,854
AND: Josep Antoni Gómes Moreira, Ildefons Lima Solà (Cap), Marc Vales González, Moisés San Nicolás Schellens, Marc Rebés Ruiz, Jesús Rubio Gómez (87.Julià Sánchez Soto), Max Llovera González-Adrio, Joan Cervós Moro, Márcio Vieira de Vasconcelos, Cristian Martínez Alejo (81.Ludovic Clemente Garcés), Alexandre Martínez Palau (71.Jordi Aláez Peña). Trainer: Jesús Luis Álvarez de Eulate Güergue "Koldo".

25.03.2019 ANDORRA - ALBANIA 0-3(0-1) 16th EC. Qualifiers
Estadi Nacional, Andorra la Vella; Referee: Filip Glova (Slovakia); Attendance: 1,373
AND: Josep Antoni Gómes Moreira, Ildefons Lima Solà (Cap), Marc Vales González (84.Marc Pujol Pons), Moisés San Nicolás Schellens, Marc Rebés Ruiz, Jesús Rubio Gómez, Max Llovera González-Adrio, Víctor Rodríguez Soria, Márcio Vieira de Vasconcelos, Cristian Martínez Alejo (74.Jordi Aláez Peña), Ludovic Clemente Garcés (67.Joan Cervós Moro). Trainer: Jesús Luis Álvarez de Eulate Güergue "Koldo".

08.06.2019 MOLDOVA - ANDORRA 1-0(1-0) 16th EC. Qualifiers
Zimbru Stadium, Chişinău; Referee: Bojan Pandžić (Sweden); Attendance: 5,000
AND: Josep Antoni Gómes Moreira, Ildefons Lima Solà (Cap), Marc Vales González, Moisés San Nicolás Schellens, Marc Rebés Ruiz (69.Sergio Moreno Marín), Jesús Rubio Gómez (72.Alexandre Martínez Palau), Max Llovera González-Adrio, Joan Cervós Moro, Márcio Vieira de Vasconcelos, Jordi Aláez Peña (82.Aaron Sánchez Alburquerque), Ludovic Clemente Garcés. Trainer: Jesús Luis Álvarez de Eulate Güergue "Koldo".

11.06.2019 ANDORRA - FRANCE **0-4(0-3)** 16th EC. Qualifiers

Estadi Nacional, Andorra la Vella; Referee: Fran Jović (Croatia); Attendance: 3,187

AND: Josep Antoni Gómes Moreira, Ildefons Lima Solà (Cap), Marc Vales González, Moisés San Nicolás Schellens, Marc Rebés Ruiz, Jesús Rubio Gómez, Max Llovera González-Adrio, Joan Cervós Moro (81.Víctor Rodríguez Soria), Márcio Vieira de Vasconcelos, Jordi Aláez Peña (85.Julià Sánchez Soto), Alexandre Martínez Palau (58.Jordi Rubio Gómez). Trainer: Jesús Luis Álvarez de Eulate Güergue "Koldo".

NATIONAL TEAM PLAYERS
(16.07.2018 – 15.07.2019)

Name	DOB	Caps	Goals	2018/2019:	*Club*
Goalkeepers					
Josep Antoni GÓMES Moreira	03.12.1985	**57**	**0**	2018/2019:	*UE Santa Coloma*
Defenders					
Joan CERVÓS Moro	24.02.1998	**11**	**0**	2018:	*FC Santboià Sant Boi de Llobregat (ESP)*
				02.01.2019->	*FC Andorra La Vella*
Emili Josep GARCÍA Miramontes	11.01.1989	**44**	**1**	2018:	*FC Andorra La Vella*
Ildefons LIMA Solà	10.12.1979	**123**	**11**	2018:	*FC Santa Coloma*
				23.08.2018->	*Inter Club d'Escaldes*
Max LLOVERA González-Adrio	08.01.1997	**30**	**0**	2018:	*UA Horta Barcelona (ESP)*
				01.01.2019->	*FC Santboià Sant Boi de Llobregat (ESP)*
Marc REBÉS Ruiz	03.07.1994	**25**	**2**	2018/2019:	*FC Santa Coloma*
Jesús RUBIO Gómez	09.09.1994	**22**	**0**	2018/2019:	*UE Santa Coloma*
Jordi RUBIO Gómez	01.11.1987	**44**	**0**	2018/2019:	*UE Santa Coloma*
Marc VALES González	04.04.1990	**61**	**0**	2018/2019:	*Sandefjord Fotball (NOR)*
Midfielders					
Jordi ALÁEZ Peña	23.01.1998	**21**	**1**	2018/2019:	*FC Andorra La Vella*
Marc García Renom „CHIQUI“	21.03.1988	**42**	**0**	2018:	*EC Granollers (ESP)*
Marc FERRÉ Nazzaro	11.01.1994	**1**	**0**	2018:	*FC Andorra La Vella*
Cristian MARTÍNEZ Alejo	16.10.1989	**54**	**3**	2018/2019:	*FC Andorra La Vella*
Marc PUJOL Pons	21.08.1982	**82**	**2**	2018/2019:	*FC Andorra La Vella*
Víctor RODRÍGUEZ Soria	07.09.1987	**25**	**0**	2018/2019:	*FC Santa Coloma*
Aaron SÁNCHEZ Alburquerque	05.06.1996	**12**	**0**	2019:	*UE Santa Coloma*
Moisés SAN NICOLÁS Schellens	17.09.1993	**42**	**0**	2018/2019:	*FC Santa Coloma*
Márcio VIEIRA de Vasconcelos	10.10.1984	**88**	**0**	2018/2019:	*CF Atlético de Monzón (ESP)*
Forwards					
Ludovic CLEMENTE Garcés	09.05.1986	**31**	**0**	2018/2019:	*FC Andorra La Vella*
Ricard FERNÁNDEZ Betriu	19.03.1999	**5**	**0**	2018:	*FC Andorra La Vella*
Sebastiàn GÓMEZ Pérez	01.11.1983	**31**	**0**	2018:	*UE Engordany*
Alexandre MARTÍNEZ Palau	10.10.1998	**19**	**1**	2018/2019:	*FC Andorra La Vella*
Sergio MORENO Marín	25.11.1987	**64**	**0**	2018/2019:	*Inter Club d'Escaldes*
Julià "JULI" SÁNCHEZ Soto	20.06.1978	**73**	**1**	2018/2019:	*FC Santa Coloma*

National team coach

Jesús Luis Alvarez de Eulate „KOLDO“ [from 02.02.2010]	04.09.1970	71 M; 3 W; 10 D; 58 L; 14-159

ARMENIA

The Country:

Republic of Armenia (Hayastani Hanrapetut'yun)
Capital: Yerevan
Surface: 29,743 km²
Inhabitants: 2,974,816
Time: UTC+4

The FA:

Football Federation of Armenia
Khanjyan Street 27 0010, Yerevan
Tel: +374 10 56 88 83
Foundation date: 18.01.1992
Member of FIFA since: 1992
Member of UEFA since: 1993
Website: www.ffa.am

NATIONAL TEAM RECORDS

First international match:	14.10.1992, Yerevan	Armenia – Moldova 0-0
Most international caps:	Sargis Hovsepyan	- 132 caps (1992-2012)
Most international goals:	Henrikh Mkhitaryan	- 27 goals / 84 caps (since 2007)

UEFA EUROPEAN CHAMPIONSHIP	
1960	-
1964	-
1968	-
1972	-
1976	-
1980	-
1984	-
1988	-
1992	*Did not enter*
1996	Qualifiers
2000	Qualifiers
2004	Qualifiers
2008	Qualifiers
2012	Qualifiers
2016	Qualifiers

FIFA WORLD CUP	
1930	-
1934	-
1938	-
1950	-
1954	-
1958	-
1962	-
1966	-
1970	-
1974	-
1978	-
1982	-
1986	-
1990	-
1994	*Did not enter*
1998	Qualifiers
2002	Qualifiers
2006	Qualifiers
2010	Qualifiers
2014	Qualifiers
2018	Qualifiers

UEFA NATIONS LEAGUE
2018/2019 – League D (promoted to League C)

OLYMPIC FOOTBALL TOURNAMENTS 1908-2016							
1908	-	**1948**	-	**1972**	-	**1996**	*Did not enter*
1912	-	**1952**	-	**1976**	-	**2000**	Qualifiers
1920	-	**1956**	-	**1980**	-	**2004**	Qualifiers
1924	-	**1960**	-	**1984**	-	**2008**	Qualifiers
1928	-	**1964**	-	**1988**	-	**2012**	Qualifiers
1936	-	**1968**	-	**1992**	*Did not enter*	**2016**	Qualifiers

FIFA CONFEDERATIONS CUP 1992-2017
None

ARMENIAN CLUB HONOURS IN EUROPEAN CLUB COMPETITIONS:

European Champion Clubs.Cup (1956-1992) / UEFA Champions League (1993-2019)
None
Fairs Cup (1858-1971) / UEFA Cup (1972-2009) / UEFA Europa League (2010-2019)
None
UEFA Super Cup (1972-2019)
None
European Cup Winners.Cup 1961-1999*
None

**defunct competition*

NATIONAL COMPETITIONS
TABLE OF HONOURS

ARMENIAN SSR (SOVIET ERA) CHAMPIONS

1936	Dinamo Yerevan
1937	Dinamo Yerevan
1938	Spartak Yerevan
1939	Spartak Yerevan
1940	Spartak Yerevan
1941-44	*No competition*
1945	Spartak Yerevan
1946	Dinamo Yerevan
1947	Dinamo Yerevan
1948	Dinamo Yerevan
1949	Dinamo Yerevan
1950	Urozhai Yerevan
1951	Shinarar Yerevan
1952	Spartak Yerevan
1953	Karmir Drosh Leninakan
1954	Spartak Yerevan

1955	Khimik Kirovakan
1956	FIMA Yerevan
1957	Karmir Drosh Leninakan
1958	FIMA Yerevan
1959	FIMA Yerevan
1960	Tekstilshchik Leninakan
1961	Tekstilshchik Leninakan
1962	Tekstilshchik Leninakan
1963	Lokomotiv Yerevan
1964	Khimik Kirovakan
1965	Araks Yerevan
1966	Elektrotekhnik Yerevan
1967	Kotayk Abovyan
1968	Araks Yerevan
1969	Araks Yerevan
1970	Motor Yerevan

1971	FIMA Yerevan
1972	Zvezda Yerevan
1973	Kotayk Abovyan
1974	FIMA Yerevan
1975	Kotayk Abovyan
1976	Kotayk Abovyan
1977	Araks Yerevan
1978	Kanaz Yerevan
1979	Aragats Leninakan
1980	Aragats Leninakan
1981–86	*No competition*
1987	Aragats Leninakan
1988	Elektrotekhnik Yerevan
1989	FC Kapan
1990	Ararat-2 Yerevan
1991	Syunik Kapan

	CHAMPIONS	CUP WINNERS	BEST GOALSCORERS	
1992	Shirak SC Gyumri Homenetmen Yerevan (shared)	FC Banants Yerevan	Vahe Yaghmuryan (FC Ararat Yerevan)	38
1993	FC Ararat Yerevan	FC Ararat Yerevan	Andranik Hovsepyan (Banants) Gegham Hovhannisyan (Homenetmen Yerevan)	26
1994	Shirak SC Gyumri	FC Ararat Yerevan	Arsen Avetisyan (Homenetmen Yerevan)	39
1995	*Transitional Season (No Winner)*	FC Ararat Yerevan	-	
1995/1996	FC Pyunik Yerevan	FC Pyunik Yerevan	Arayik Adamyan (Shirak SC Gyumri)	28
1996/1997	FC Pyunik Yerevan	FC Ararat Yerevan	Arsen Avetisyan (FC Pyunik Yerevan)	24
1997	FC Yerevan	-	Artur Petrosyan (Shirak SC Gyumri)	18
1998	FC Tsement Ararat	FC Tsement Ararat	Ara Hakobyan (Dvin Artashat)	20
1999	Shirak SC Gyumri	FC Tsement Ararat	Shirak SC Gyumri Sarikyan (FC Tsement Ararat)	21
2000	Araks Ararat FC	FC Mika Yerevan	Ara Hakobyan (Araks Ararat FC)	21
2001	FC Pyunik Yerevan	FC Mika Yerevan	Arman Karamyan (FC Pyunik Yerevan)	21
2002	FC Pyunik Yerevan	FC Pyunik Yerevan	Arman Karamyan (FC Pyunik Yerevan)	36
2003	FC Pyunik Yerevan	FC Mika Yerevan	Ara Hakobyan (FC Banants Yerevan)	45
2004	FC Pyunik Yerevan	FC Pyunik Yerevan	Edgar Manucharyan (FC Pyunik Yerevan) Galust Petrosyan (FC Pyunik Yerevan)	21
2005	FC Pyunik Yerevan	FC Mika Yerevan	Nshan Erzrumyan (Kilikia FC Yerevan)	18
2006	FC Pyunik Yerevan	FC Mika Yerevan	Aram Hakobyan (FC Banants Yerevan)	25
2007	FC Pyunik Yerevan	FC Banants Yerevan	Marcos Pinheiro Pizzelli (Ararat Yerevan)	22
2008	FC Pyunik Yerevan	FC Ararat Yerevan	Marcos Pinheiro Pizzelli (Ararat Yerevan)	17
2009	FC Pyunik Yerevan	FC Pyunik Yerevan	Artur Kocharyan (Ulisses FC Yerevan)	15
2010	FC Pyunik Yerevan	FC Pyunik Yerevan	Marcos Pinheiro Pizzelli (FC Pyunik Yerevan) Gevorg Ghazaryan (FC Pyunik Yerevan)	16
2011	Ulisses FC Yerevan	FC Mika Yerevan	Bruno César Correa (BRA, FC Banants Yerevan)	16
2011/2012	*Transitional Season (No winner)*	Shirak SC Gyumri	-	
2012/2013	Shirak SC Gyumri	FC Pyunik Yerevan	Norayr Gyozalyan (Impuls FC Dilijan)	21
2013/2014	FC Banants Yerevan	FC Pyunik Yerevan	Mihran Manasyan (FC Alashkert Yerevan)	17
2014/2015	FC Pyunik Yerevan	FC Pyunik Yerevan	César Romero Zamora (USA, FC Pyunik Yerevan) Jean-Jacques Bougouhi (CIV, Shirak SC Gyumri)	21
2015/2016	FC Alashkert Yerevan	FC Banants Yerevan	Héber Araujo dos Santos (BRA, FC Alashkert Yerevan); Mihran Manasyan (FC Alashkert Yerevan)	16
2016/2017	FC Alashkert Yerevan	Shirak SC Gyumri	Artak Yedigaryan (FC Alashkert Yerevan) Mihran Manasyan (FC Alashkert Yerevan)	13
2017/2018	FC Alashkert Yerevan	FC Gandzasar Kapan	Artak Yedigaryan (FC Alashkert Yerevan) Gegham Harutyunyan (FC Gandzasar Kapan)	12
2018/2019	FC Ararat-Armenia Yerevan	FC Alashkert Yerevan	Jonel Désiré (HAI, Lori FC Vanadzor)	17

Please note: Homenetmen Yerevan became FC Pyunik Yerevan (1995); Tsement Ararat changed its name to Araks Ararat FC (2000).

NATIONAL CHAMPIONSHIP

Armenian Premier League 2018/2019
(04.08.2018 – 30.05.2019)

Results

Round 1 [04-05.08.2018]
FC Banants - Shirak SC 0-0
Lori FC - FC Ararat-Armenia 0-2
FC Ararat - FC Alashkert 0-1
FC Pyunik - FC Gandzasar 0-1 [03.10.]

Round 2 [11-12.08.2018]
Artsakh FC - FC Banants 1-0
FC Ararat-Armenia - FC Ararat 1-2
Shirak SC - Lori FC 1-1
FC Alashkert - FC Pyunik 1-2 [19.09.]

Round 3 [18-19.08.2018]
Lori FC - Artsakh FC 3-2
FC Ararat - Shirak SC 0-0
FC Gandzasar - FC Alashkert 0-1
FC Pyunik - FC Ararat-Armenia 3-1

Round 4 [22.08.2018]
Artsakh FC - FC Ararat 1-1
FC Banants - Lori FC 1-3
Shirak SC - FC Pyunik 1-2
FC Ararat-Armenia - FC Gandzasar 0-0

Round 5 [25-26.08.2018]
FC Ararat - FC Banants 2-4
FC Gandzasar - Shirak SC 1-1
FC Alashkert - FC Ararat-Armenia 1-3
FC Pyunik - Artsakh FC 2-0

Round 6 [29.08.2018]
Shirak SC - FC Alashkert 0-0
Artsakh FC - FC Gandzasar 2-2
FC Banants - FC Pyunik 4-2
Lori FC - FC Ararat 1-0

Round 7 [01.09.2018]
FC Alashkert - Artsakh FC 6-0
FC Pyunik - Lori FC 0-3
FC Banants - FC Gandzasar 1-0
FC Ararat-Armenia - Shirak SC 3-1

Round 8 [15-16.09.2018]
Artsakh FC - FC Ararat-Armenia 1-1
Lori FC - FC Gandzasar 3-0
FC Ararat - FC Pyunik 1-3
FC Banants - FC Alashkert 1-0

Round 9 [22-23.09.2018]
FC Alashkert - Lori FC 2-1
FC Gandzasar - FC Ararat 4-0
Shirak SC - Artsakh FC 3-0
FC Ararat-Armenia - FC Banants 1-3

Round 10 [29-30.09.2018]
Shirak SC - FC Banants 0-0
FC Ararat-Armenia - Lori FC 0-0
FC Alashkert - FC Ararat 2-1
FC Gandzasar - FC Pyunik 1-2

Round 11 [06-07.10.2018]
FC Pyunik - FC Alashkert 0-1
Lori FC - Shirak SC 3-1
FC Ararat - FC Ararat-Armenia 0-1
FC Banants - Artsakh FC 2-1

Round 12 [20-21.10.2018]
Artsakh FC - Lori FC 2-3
Shirak SC - FC Ararat 1-0
FC Alashkert - FC Gandzasar 1-0
FC Ararat-Armenia - FC Pyunik 0-0

Round 13 [27-28.10.2018]
FC Ararat - Artsakh FC 0-0
FC Gandzasar - FC Ararat-Armenia 0-0
Lori FC - FC Banants 1-3
FC Pyunik - Shirak SC 1-1

Round 14 [31.10.2018]
Artsakh FC - FC Pyunik 0-0
FC Ararat - FC Banants 0-1
Shirak SC - FC Gandzasar 2-0
FC Ararat-Armenia - FC Alashkert 0-1

Round 15 [03-04.11.2018]
FC Alashkert - Shirak SC 1-0
FC Gandzasar - Artsakh FC 0-2
FC Pyunik - FC Banants 2-0
FC Ararat - Lori FC 2-2

Round 16 [11.11.2018]
Lori FC - FC Pyunik 0-1
Artsakh FC - FC Alashkert 0-0
Shirak SC - FC Ararat-Armenia 1-0
FC Gandzasar - FC Banants 3-0

Round 17 [24-25.11.2018]
FC Alashkert - FC Banants 1-0
FC Ararat-Armenia - Artsakh FC 3-1
FC Gandzasar - Lori FC 2-0
FC Pyunik - FC Ararat 0-1

Round 18 [28.11.2018]
FC Ararat - FC Gandzasar 0-2
Lori FC - FC Alashkert 1-1
FC Banants - FC Ararat-Armenia 0-3
Artsakh FC - Shirak SC 0-1

Round 19 [01-02.12.2018]
FC Banants - Shirak SC 4-0
Lori FC - FC Ararat-Armenia 0-1
FC Ararat - FC Alashkert 1-0
FC Pyunik - FC Gandzasar 1-3

Round 20 [02-03.03.2019]
FC Ararat-Armenia - FC Ararat 4-1
FC Alashkert - FC Pyunik 1-2
Artsakh FC - FC Banants 1-1
Shirak SC - Lori FC 0-0

Round 21 [06.03.2019]
FC Gandzasar - FC Alashkert 2-4
FC Pyunik - FC Ararat-Armenia 0-3
Lori FC - Artsakh FC 2-0
FC Ararat - Shirak SC 0-2

Round 22 [09-11.03.2019]
FC Ararat-Armenia - FC Gandzasar 2-0
Artsakh FC - FC Ararat 0-0
Shirak SC - FC Pyunik 0-2
FC Banants - Lori FC 0-0

Round 23 [15-17.03.2019]
FC Gandzasar - Shirak SC 0-0
FC Pyunik - Artsakh FC 1-0
FC Banants - FC Ararat 3-1
FC Alashkert - FC Ararat-Armenia 0-1

Round 24 [30.03.-01.04.2019]
Shirak SC - FC Alashkert 1-1
FC Banants - FC Pyunik 1-1
Lori FC - FC Ararat 2-2
Artsakh FC - FC Gandzasar 2-0

Round 25 [06-08.04.2019]
FC Gandzasar - FC Banants 1-2
FC Pyunik - Lori FC 1-2
FC Alashkert - Artsakh FC 1-0
FC Ararat-Armenia - Shirak SC 2-2

Round 26 [10-11.04.2019]
FC Banants - FC Alashkert 2-0
Lori FC - FC Gandzasar 0-0
Artsakh FC - FC Ararat-Armenia 1-3
FC Ararat - FC Pyunik 1-2

Round 27 [14-15.04.2019]
FC Alashkert - Lori FC 0-1
FC Gandzasar - FC Ararat 1-0
FC Ararat-Armenia - FC Banants 1-1
Shirak SC - Artsakh FC 0-0

Round 28 [19-20.04.2019]
FC Alashkert - FC Ararat 2-0
Shirak SC - FC Banants 0-0
FC Ararat-Armenia - Lori FC 3-0
FC Gandzasar - FC Pyunik 0-1

Round 29 [26-28.04.2019]
FC Ararat - FC Ararat-Armenia 2-6
FC Pyunik - FC Alashkert 1-0
FC Banants - Artsakh FC 3-0
Lori FC - Shirak SC 2-2

Round 30 [01-02.05.2019]
FC Alashkert - FC Gandzasar 2-0
FC Ararat-Armenia - FC Pyunik 1-4
Artsakh FC - Lori FC 2-1
Shirak SC - FC Ararat 3-0

Round 31 [04-06.05.2019]
FC Gandzasar - FC Ararat-Armenia 2-1
Lori FC - FC Banants 1-3
FC Pyunik - Shirak SC 2-0
FC Ararat - Artsakh FC 2-1

Round 32 [10-12.05.2019]
Artsakh FC - FC Pyunik 0-3
FC Banants - FC Ararat 1-1
Shirak SC - FC Gandzasar 0-0
FC Ararat-Armenia - FC Alashkert 2-1

Round 33 [14-15.05.2019]
FC Ararat - Lori FC 1-0
FC Gandzasar - Artsakh FC 0-1
FC Alashkert - Shirak SC 1-0
FC Pyunik - FC Banants 1-1

Round 34 [18-20.05.2019]
FC Banants - FC Gandzasar 0-5
Shirak SC - FC Ararat-Armenia 0-1
Artsakh FC - FC Alashkert 1-1
Lori FC - FC Pyunik 2-2

Round 35 [24-26.05.2019]
FC Alashkert - FC Banants 1-1
FC Ararat-Armenia - Artsakh FC 2-0
FC Gandzasar - Lori FC 1-1
FC Pyunik - FC Ararat 2-1

Round 36 [30.05.2019]
FC Ararat - FC Gandzasar 1-7
Lori FC - FC Alashkert 3-2
FC Banants - FC Ararat-Armenia 0-1
Artsakh FC - Shirak SC 3-2

Final Standings

1.	**FC Ararat-Armenia Yerevan**	32	18	7	7	53 - 28	61
2.	FC Pyunik Yerevan	32	18	6	8	46 - 32	60
3.	FC Banants Yerevan	32	14	10	8	43 - 35	52
4.	FC Alashkert Yerevan	32	15	6	11	37 - 27	51
5.	Lori FC Vanadzor	32	11	11	10	42 - 40	44
6.	FC Gandzasar Kapan	32	10	8	14	38 - 33	38
7.	Shirak SC Gyumri	32	7	15	10	26 - 30	36
8.	Artsakh FC Yerevan	32	6	10	16	25 - 49	28
9.	FC Ararat Yerevan	32	5	7	20	24 - 60	22

Top goalscorers:

17 Jonel Désiré (HAI)
Lori FC Vanadzor

15 Anton Kobyalko (RUS)
FC Ararat-Armenia Yerevan

10 Ivaylo Dimitrov (BUL)
FC Ararat-Armenia Yerevan

NATIONAL CUP
Armenian Cup 2018/2019

First Round [19.09.-04.10.2018]

FC Lokomotiv Yerevan - FC Ararat Yerevan	1-1 / 1-3
FC Junior Sevan Dzoraghbyur - Lori FC Vanadzor	2-3 / 2-2
FC Yerevan - FC Ararat-Armenia Yerevan	1-4 / 0-5
Artsakh FC Yerevan - Shirak SC-2 Gyumri	0-0 / 3-1

Quarter-Finals [24.10.-08.11.2018]

FC Banants Yerevan - FC Ararat Yerevan	3-1 / 1-0
Artsakh FC Yerevan - FC Alashkert Yerevan	1-2 / 0-1
FC Ararat-Armenia Yerevan - FC Gandzasar Kapan	1-1 / 1-0
Pyunik FC - Lori FC Vanadzor	0-2 / 1-1

Semi-Finals [ ]

FC Ararat-Armenia Yerevan - FC Alashkert Yerevan	2-2 / 0-0
FC Banants Yerevan - Lori FC Vanadzor	0-0 / 0-3 (awarded)

Final

08.05.2019; Banants Stadium, Yerevan; Referee: Alberto Undianco Mallenco (Spain); Attendance: 4,000
FC Alashkert Yerevan - Lori FC Vanadzor **1-0(0-0)**

FC Alashkert: Ognjen Cancarević, Denis Tumasyan, Gagik Dagbashyan, Joel Damahou, Taron Voskanyan, Goran Antonić, Danijel Stojković, Artur Yedigaryan (82.Hrayr Mkoyan), Artak Grigoryan, Aleksandr Prudnikov (90+2.Edgar Manucharyan), Uroš Nenadović (82.Artak Yedigaryan). Trainer: Abraham Khashmanyan.

Lori FC: Arsen Siukaev, Hayk Ishkhanyan, Alex Kakuba (79.Enock Darko), Arman Mkrtchyan (82.Nwani Williams Ikechukwu), Annan Mensah, Nana Antwi, Aram Kocharyan (12.John Ubong Friday), Sunday Umaru Inusa Ngbede, Isah Aliyu, Ugochukwu Iwu, Jonel Désiré. Trainer: Artur Petrosyan.

Goal: 1-0 John Ubong Friday (65 own goal).

THE CLUBS 2018/2019

Football Club Alashkert Yerevan

Founded: 1990
Stadium: Alashkert Stadium, Yerevan (6,850)

Goalkeepers:	**DOB**	**M**	**(s)**	**G**
Henri Avagyan	16.01.1996	5	(1)	
Ognjen Cancarević (SRB)	25.09.1989	27		
Defenders:	**DOB**	**M**	**(s)**	**G**
Goran Antonić (SRB)	03.11.1990	11	(2)	
Gagik Dagbashyan	19.10.1990	28	(1)	
Joel Damahou (CIV)	28.01.1987	7	(5)	1
Levon Hayrapetyan	17.04.1989	5	(5)	1
Oliver Praznovsky (SVK)	15.02.1991	2	(1)	
Danijel Stojković (SRB)	14.08.1990	24	(2)	1
Denis Tumasyan (RUS)	24.04.1985	9	(2)	1
Taron Voskanyan	22.02.1993	24	(1)	
Mladen Zeljković (SRB)	18.11.1987	19	(3)	2
Midfielders:	**DOB**	**M**	**(s)**	**G**
Gerson Elías Acevedo Rojas (CHI)	05.04.1988	1	(1)	
Artak Dashyan	20.11.1989	14		2
Artak Grigoryan	19.10.1987	27		
Benik Hovhannisyan	01.05.1993			
Jefferson Reis de Jesus (BRA)	08.11.1995	3	(6)	2
Haykaram Muradyan	21.04.2001		(1)	
Ghukas Poghosyan	06.02.1994	9	(6)	3
Danilo Sekulić (SRB)	18.04.1990	10	(7)	1
Sargis Shahinyan	10.09.1995	1	(3)	
Artem Simonyan	20.02.1995	5	(2)	
Artak Yedigaryan	18.03.1990	25	(7)	4
Artur Yedigaryan	26.06.1987	14	(8)	1
Forwards:	**DOB**	**M**	**(s)**	**G**
Gustavo Marmentini dos Santos (BRA)	08.03.1994	17	(5)	2
Razmik Hakobyan	09.02.1996		(1)	
Edgar Manucharyan	19.01.1987	15	(6)	3
Gláucio José de Araújo Silva (BRA)	03.02.1994	1	(2)	
Uroš Nenadović (SRB)	28.01.1994	20	(8)	6
Lester Peltier (TRI)	13.09.1988	1		
Aleksandr Prudnikov (RUS)	26.02.1989	10	(2)	3
César Romero (USA)	02.08.1989	1	(5)	
Nikita Tankov	29.09.1996	4	(3)	1
Trainer:	**DOB**	**M**		
Varuzhan Sukiasyan	05.08.1956	7		
Sergey Erzrumyan [22.09.2018]	22.11.1980	1		
Aram Voskanyan [30.09.2018]	26.08.1975	16		
Abraham Khashmanyan [19.04.2019]	11.11.1967	8		

Football Club Ararat Yerevan

Founded: 10.05.1935
Stadium: Alashkert Stadium, Yerevan (6,850)

Goalkeepers:	DOB	M	(s)	G
Poghos Ayvazyan	09.06.1995	5	(1)	
Vyacheslav Marikoda (RUS)	27.03.1991	7		
Mikhail Petrushchenkov (RUS)	28.06.1993	20		
Defenders:	**DOB**	**M**	**(s)**	**G**
Magomed Abidinov (RUS)	03.02.1989	5		
Vardan Arzoyan	30.04.1995	25	(1)	1
Vahe Chopuryan	01.12.1997	7		
Aboubacar Gassama (FRA)	27.04.1994	4		
Mykhailo Kaluhin (UKR)	20.11.1994	7		
Kevin Ntika Bondombe (BEL)	24.07.1995	8	(1)	
Gor Poghosyan	11.06.1988	24	(2)	2
Rafael Safaryan	30.01.1986	29	(1)	
Hayk Sargsyan	12.03.1998	1	(1)	
Maksim Starkov (RUS)	25.04.1996	4		
Alan Tataev (RUS)	03.08.1995	6	(2)	
Midfielders:	**DOB**	**M**	**(s)**	**G**
Ruslan Avagyan	24.06.1995	16	(4)	
David Azin (GER)	11.01.1990	7	(1)	
Zaven Badoyan	22.12.1989	23	(6)	4
Andrey Chukhley (BLR)	02.10.1987	2	(1)	
Pape Demba Dieye (SEN)	25.03.1998		(6)	
Matvey Guyganov (RUS)	28.07.1994	13		
Orbeli Hambardzumyan	26.03.1996	14	(5)	1
Stepan Harutyunyan	11.07.1997		(1)	
Garegin Kirakosyan	26.11.1995	12	(4)	
Dmitri Malyaka (RUS)	15.01.1990	8		1
Sergey Mkrtchyan	20.05.1995	2		
Dmitri Ostrovski (RUS)	15.04.1998	4	(8)	
Ronald Cezar Germano Filho "Roni" (BRA)	02.03.1997	2	(4)	
Sargis Shahinyan	10.09.1995	12		
Karen Shirkhanyan	06.04.2000	1		
Shim Woon-Seob (KOR)	24.02.1990	4	(2)	
Artem Simonyan	20.02.1995	12	(3)	6
Anthony Trajkoski (AUS)	28.04.1998	8	(2)	
Dejan Vukomanović (SRB)	31.10.1990	10	(3)	1
Andriy Yakovlev (UKR)	20.02.1989	7	(3)	
David Zakharyan (RUS)	08.08.1997	1	(4)	
Forwards:	**DOB**	**M**	**(s)**	**G**
Mikael Arustamyan	18.01.1996		(1)	
Razmik Hakobyan	09.02.1996	2	(9)	1
Andranik Kocharyan	29.01.1994	26	(5)	4
Sargis Metoyan	24.08.1997	11	(9)	2
Volodya Samsonyan	24.02.2001	2	(4)	
Mpumelelo Zwane (RSA)	28.07.1996	1		
Trainer:	**DOB**	**M**		
Armen Stepanyan	30.01.1974	9		
Abraham Khashmanyan [01.10.2018]	11.11.1967	15		
Tigran Yenayan [19.04.2018]	02.06.1972	8		

Football Club Ararat-Armenia Yerevan

Founded: 2017
Stadium: „Vazgen Sargsyan" Hanrapetakan Stadium, Yerevan (14,403)

Goalkeepers:	DOB	M	(s)	G
Dmitri Abakumov (RUS)	08.07.1989	28		
Stefan Čupić (SRB)	07.05.1994	3		
Arsen Siukaev (RUS)	07.03.1996	1	(1)	
Defenders:	**DOB**	**M**	**(s)**	**G**
Aleksandar Damčevski (MKD)	21.11.1992	16	(3)	
Artur Danielyan (UKR)	09.02.1998	9	(1)	1
Robert Darbinyan	04.10.1995	2		
Dmitri Guzj (RUS)	15.05.1988	24		1
Arman Hovhannisyan	07.07.1993	8		
Albert Khachumyan	23.06.1999	1		
Vladimir Khozin (RUS)	03.07.1989	24		3
Hrayr Mkoyan	02.09.1986	3		1
Georgi Pashov (BUL)	04.03.1990	23	(1)	2
Sergio González Testón „Sergi" (ESP)	26.05.1995	21	2()	
Midfielders:	**DOB**	**M**	**(s)**	**G**
Kódjo Kassé Alphonse (CIV)	28.05.1993	14		1
Armen Ambartsumyan	11.04.1994	14	(9)	
Artem Avanesyan (RUS)	17.07.1999	5	(5)	
Petros Avetisyan	07.01.1996	12	(2)	6
Alex Júnior Christian (HAI)	12.05.1993	9	(2)	
David Davidyan (RUS)	14.12.1997		(3)	
Maílson Lima Duarte Lopes (CPV)	29.05.1994	11	(4)	1
Gor Malakyan	12.06.1994	9	(12)	
Giovanny Martínez Cortés (COL)	07.07.1989	19	(6)	1
Armen Nahapetyan	24.07.1999	9	(2)	
Jerry Alberto Ortíz Cortés (COL)	07.11.1992	1		
Vladislav Oslonovskiy (RUS)	15.01.1995	7	(3)	1
Aleksey Pustozerov (RUS)	21.09.1988	24	(3)	
Liam Joseph Rose (AUS)	07.04.1997	4	(2)	
Danila Yashchuk (RUS)	13.03.1995		(2)	
Forwards:	**DOB**	**M**	**(s)**	**G**
Narek Alaverdyan	19.02.2002		(2)	
Jean-Jacques Bougouhi (CIV)	12.06.1992	7		3
Ivaylo Dimitrov (BUL)	26.03.1989	16	(1)	10
Kayron Batista Ramos (BRA)	03.04.1995	3	(11)	1
Anton Kobyalko (RUS)	14.05.1986	14	(12)	15
Charles Júnior Monsalvo Peralta (COL)	26.05.1990	9		1
Ogana Louis Ugochukwu (NGA)	29.12.1995	2	(8)	4
Zhirayr Shagoyan	10.04.2001		(10)	
Trainer:	**DOB**	**M**		
Vadim Skripchenko (BLR)	26.11.1975	8		
Artak Oseyan [26.09.2018]	16.05.1987	1		
Vardan Minasyan [01.10.2018]	05.01.1974	23		

Artsakh Football Club Yerevan

Founded: 2017
Stadium: Mika Stadium, Yerevan (7,250)

Goalkeepers:	DOB	M	(s)	G
Samur Agamagomedov (RUS)	30.11.1998	8		
Arman Meliksetyan	21.07.1995	18		
Erik Meliksetyan	26.08.2000	3		
Aleksey Solosin (RUS)	11.08.1987	3		
Defenders:	**DOB**	**M**	**(s)**	**G**
Robert Arzumanyan	24.07.1985	1		
Hamlet Asoyan	13.01.1995	7		1
Hakob Hambardzumyan	26.05.1997	13	(3)	
Vahagn Minasyan	25.04.1985	12	(1)	
Vardan Movsisyan	18.08.1991	11		
Erik Nazaryan	14.03.1996	3		
Hovhannes Nazaryan	11.03.1998	28		
Argishti Petrosyan	16.10.1992	28		1
Gevorg Poghosyan	26.08.1986	6	(1)	
Alan Tataev (RUS)	03.08.1995	8	(1)	
Midfielders:	**DOB**	**M**	**(s)**	**G**
Edvard Avagyan	21.03.1996	18	(7)	4
Vigen Avetisyan	12.01.1993	6	(3)	2
Irakli Bidzinashvili (GEO)	27.02.1997	2	(2)	
Marat Buraev (RUS)	22.10.1995	4	(3)	1
Geo Danny Ekra (CIV)	10.01.1999	3	(1)	
Maksim Ermakov	21.04.1995	1		
Yuri Gareginyan	03.02.1994	17	(4)	3
Artur Grigoryan	10.07.1993	31		
Narek Gyozalyan	10.07.1992	4	(3)	
Karen Harutyunyan	06.07.1995	13	(7)	
Benik Hovhannisyan	01.05.1993	11	(2)	
Dmytro Klimakov (UKR)	05.03.1989	6	(3)	1
Hovhannes Poghosyan	17.12.1997	9	(2)	1
Valter Poghosyan	16.05.1992	5		
Artur Stepanyan	17.11.1999	2	(2)	
Oleksandr Tupchiyenko (UKR)	10.12.1995	11		
Emil Yeghiazaryan	03.11.1997	17	(7)	1
Forwards:	**DOB**	**M**	**(s)**	**G**
Grigor Aghekyan	06.04.1996	9	(7)	3
Vardan Bakalyan	04.04.1995	8	(8)	2
Akmal Bakhtiyarov (KAZ)	02.06.1998	5	(3)	3
Sarkis Baloyan	24.08.1992	5	(4)	
Wilfried Eza (CIV)	28.12.1996	5	(6)	
Abdoul Gafar Sirima (BFA)	30.12.1998		(3)	
Norayr Gyozalyan	15.03.1990	7	(3)	
Edgar Movsisyan	09.09.1998	4	(5)	1
Trainer:	**DOB**	**M**		
Rafael Nazaryan	26.03.1975	16		
Sevada Arzumanyan [07.01.2019]	24.05.1969	16		

Football Club Banats Yerevan

Founded: 20.01.1992
Stadium: Banants Stadium, Yerevan (4,860)

Goalkeepers:	DOB	M	(s)	G
Anatoly Ayvazov	08.06.1996	5		
Stepan Ghazaryan	11.01.1985	2		
Aram Hayrapetyan	22.11.1986	25		
Defenders:	**DOB**	**M**	**(s)**	**G**
Artur Avagyan	04.07.1987	9	(2)	
Vahagn Ayvazyan	16.04.1992	25	(2)	5
Robert Darbinyan	04.10.1995	10	(1)	
Albert Gadzhibekov (RUS)	17.02.1988	14		1
Ilya Gultyaev (RUS)	05.09.1988	8	(1)	
Borislav Jovanović (SRB)	16.08.1986	11		
Edward Kpodo (GHA)	14.01.1990	27		3
Narek Petrosyan	25.01.1996	20	(3)	
Andranik Voskanyan	11.04.1990	3	(2)	
Midfielders:	**DOB**	**M**	**(s)**	**G**
Aram Bareghamyan	06.01.1988	29	(1)	4
Welat Cagro (BEL)	31.05.1999	4	(6)	
Pape Camara (SEN)	24.09.1991	10	(12)	1
Aleksandar Glišić (BIH)	03.09.1992	13		5
Narek Grigoryan	17.06.2001		(1)	
Hakob Hakobyan	29.03.1997	23	(2)	
Evgeni Kobzar (RUS)	09.08.1992	11	(1)	2
Ognjen Krasić (SRB)	09.04.1988	1	(1)	
Aram Loretsyan	07.03.1993	1	(2)	
Karen Melkonyan	25.03.1999	14	(8)	4
Kwasi Sibo (GHA)	24.06.1998	2		
Mikhail Solovyev (RUS)	07.04.1997	6	(9)	1
Igor Stanojević (SRB)	24.10.1991	15	(7)	3
Solomon Ime Udo (NGA)	15.07.1995	28		2
Forwards:	**DOB**	**M**	**(s)**	**G**
Adamu Abdullahi (NGA)	01.01.1994	4	(13)	1
Nathaniel Asamoah (GHA)	22.02.1990	13	(4)	2
Ilie Damaşcan (MDA)	12.10.1995	8	(3)	
Fagner Santos de Paíchao (BRA)	22.06.1998		(1)	
Lester Peltier (TRI)	13.09.1988	2		
Erik Petrosyan	19.02.1998	3	(5)	1
Vardan Pogosyan	08.03.1992		(2)	1
Walmerson Garcia Praia (BRA)	13.01.1994	11	(4)	5
Trainer:	**DOB**	**M**		
Aram Voskanyan	26.08.1975	2		
Ilshat Faizulin [12.08.2018]	05.03.1973	30		

Football Club Gandzasar Kapan

Founded: 2004
Stadium: „Vazgen Sargsyan" Hanrapetakan Stadium, Yerevan (14,403)

Goalkeepers:	**DOB**	**M**	**(s)**	**G**
Gevorg Kasparov	25.07.1980	16	(1)	
Grigor Meliksetyan	18.08.1986	16		
Defenders:	**DOB**	**M**	**(s)**	**G**
Hamlet Asoyan	13.01.1995	8	(1)	
Bacar Baldé (GNB)	15.01.1992	19		2
Arman Hovhannisyan	07.07.1993	5	(2)	
Hayk Ishkhanyan	24.06.1989	9	(2)	
Ashot Karapetyan	12.05.1993	5	(9)	
Ara Khachatryan	23.12.1984	4		
Álex Martín Magallanes Broggi (PER)	25.03.1997	4		
Hayk Sargsyan	12.03.1998		(1)	
Aleksandr Sverchinskiy (BLR)	16.09.1991	6		
David Terteryan	17.12.1997	16		
Vukasin Tomić (SRB)	08.04.1987	3		
Midfielders:	**DOB**	**M**	**(s)**	**G**
Adam Adamyan	22.04.1992	8	(8)	1
Wbeymar Angulo Mosquera (COL)	06.03.1992	28		1
Suren Arakelyan	12.07.1996		(3)	
Narek Aslanyan	04.06.1996	5	(4)	
Alex Júnior Christian (HAI)	12.05.1993	11	(3)	1
Alexander Hovhannisyan	20.07.1996	22	(1)	1
Hayk Mayilyan	21.06.2003		(1)	
Davit Minasyan	09.03.1993	10	(6)	2
Lubambo Musonda (ZAM)	01.03.1995	17		5
Gevorg Ohanyan	29.01.1992	11	(3)	3
Artur Yuspashyan	07.09.1989	6		
Forwards:	**DOB**	**M**	**(s)**	**G**
Jorge Miguel Feijoca Chula (POR)	13.02.1990	10	(2)	1
Drissa Diarrassouba (CIV)	15.11.1994	11	(1)	2
Martin Grigoryan	25.09.2000	3	(11)	
Gegham Harutyunyan	23.08.1990	12	(3)	8
Mihran Manasyan	13.01.1989	17	(12)	6
Gevorg Nranyan	09.03.1986	24	(4)	2
Vardan Pogosyan	08.03.1992	11	(4)	
Clive Junior Rupiya (ZIM)	20.12.1999	5	(3)	
Trainer:	**DOB**	**M**		
Ashot Barseghyan	05.05.1964	25		
Armen Petrosyan [01.05.2019]	26.09.1985	7		

Lori Football Club Vanadzor

Founded: 1936
Stadium: Vanadzor Football Academy Stadium, Vanadzot (1,000)

Goalkeepers:	**DOB**	**M**	**(s)**	**G**
Gor Elyazyan	01.06.1991	1		
Aleksandar Konov (BUL)	03.09.1993	14		
Danylo Ryabenko (UKR)	09.10.1998	2	(1)	
Arsen Siukaev (RUS)	07.03.1996	14		
Defenders:	**DOB**	**M**	**(s)**	**G**
Nana Antwi (GHA)	10.08.2000	27		1
Murad Asatryan	08.02.1996	3		
Richard Botchway (GHA)			(1)	
Deou Dosa (NGA)	29.07.1998	22	(8)	
Ekereuke Ekemini Ukoebe (NGA)	31.12.1998	2	(3)	
Hayk Ishkhanyan	24.06.1989	14		
Alex Kakuba (UGA)	12.06.1991	9	(1)	
Artyom Khachaturov	18.06.1992	19		1
Aram Kocharyan	05.03.1996	8	(1)	
Vardan Movsisyan	18.08.1991	4	(2)	
Annan Mensah (GHA)	06.07.1996	23	(1)	
Arman Mkrtchyan	09.07.1999	10	(4)	
Julius David Ufuoma (NGA)	14.02.2000	4	(2)	
Midfielders:	**DOB**	**M**	**(s)**	**G**
Aram Adamyan (BUL)	11.09.1997	2	(6)	
Isah Aliyu (NGA)	08.08.1999	29		7
Vigen Avetisyan	12.01.1993	14	(2)	2
Vladimir Babayan	06.05.1997	1		
David Udoh Etop (NGA)	11.11.1999	6	(9)	1
Ibrahim Fuseini (GHA)	10.01.2000	14	(3)	
Stepan Harutyunyan	11.07.1997		(2)	
Ugochukwu Iwu (NGA)	28.11.1999	29		2
Sunday Umaru Inusa Ngbede (NGA)	23.04.1998	16	(5)	7
Kirill Volchkov (RUS)	21.03.1996		(2)	
Forwards:	**DOB**	**M**	**(s)**	**G**
Areg Azatyan	29.06.1990	6	(7)	
Enock Darko (GHA)	09.09.2000	7	(6)	
Jonel Désiré (HAI)	12.02.1997	24	(1)	17
John Ubong Friday (NGA)	03.03.1998	6	(1)	
Nwani Williams Ikechukwu (NGA)	17.10.1998	1	(4)	2
Francis Uchenna Nwankwo (NGA)	14.12.1998	1	(6)	1
Alexandru Osipov (MDA)	30.07.2000	1	(7)	
Trainer:	**DOB**	**M**		
Armen Adamyan	14.10.1967	17		
Artur Petrosyan [25.12.2018]	17.12.1971	11		
Vahe Gevorgyan [12.05.2019]	21.09.1987	4		

Football Club Pyunik Yerevan

Founded: 1992 (*as Homenetmen Yerevan*)
Stadium: „Vazgen Sargsyan" Hanrapetakan Stadium, Yerevan (14,403)

Goalkeepers:	**DOB**	**M**	**(s)**	**G**
Andrija Dragojević (MNE)	25.12.1991	28		
Evgeni Kobozev (RUS)	11.01.1990	4		
Defenders:	**DOB**	**M**	**(s)**	**G**
Artak Asatryan	25.01.2001		(1)	
Vyacheslav Dmitriev (RUS)	28.05.1990	21	(2)	
Serob Grigoryan	04.02.1995	8	(1)	
Robert Hakobyan	22.10.1996	14	(3)	
Artur Kartashyan	08.01.1997	5	(4)	
Sergey Kolychev (RUS)	28.09.1988	12	(1)	
Armen Manucharyan	03.02.1995	16	(3)	
Kristi Marku (ALB)	13.04.1995	11		1
Edmon Movsisyan	01.06.1998	2		
Vahe Muradyan	28.01.1998		(1)	
Vitali Stezhko (RUS)	29.01.1997	19	(1)	1
Maksim Zhestokov (RUS)	19.06.1991	25		5
Midfielders:	**DOB**	**M**	**(s)**	**G**
Alik Arakelyan	21.05.1996	22	(1)	2
Petros Avetisyan	07.01.1996	7	(4)	2
Vigen Begoyan	08.09.1997		(2)	
Arsen Gyulambaryan	21.08.2001		(1)	
Vahagn Hayrapetyan	14.06.1997	7	(6)	
Rumyan Hovsepyan	13.11.1991	19	(8)	4
Hovhannes Ilangyozyan	14.01.1997	2	(2)	1
Karlen Mkrtchyan	25.11.1988	13	(9)	1
Artur Nadiryan	27.03.1998	2	(1)	
Serhiy Shevchuk (UKR)	18.06.1985	14	(1)	1
Denis Talalay (RUS)	10.02.1992	12	(2)	2
Maksym Trusevich (UKR)	01.08.1985	20	(2)	1
Erik Vardanyan	07.06.1998	10	(11)	8
Denis Voynov (RUS)	01.03.1990	8	(4)	1
Forwards:	**DOB**	**M**	**(s)**	**G**
Denis Dorozhkin (RUS)	08.06.1987	12	(6)	
Usman Mohammed Edu (NGA)	02.03.1994	10	(3)	2
Ashot Kocharyan	13.07.1999	1		
Mohamed Konaté (CIV)	12.12.1997	7	(8)	6
Ruslan Koryan	15.06.1988	2	(3)	1
Artur Miranyan	27.12.1995	15		5
Robert Minasyan	08.04.1997	4	(1)	
Grenik Petrosyan	05.12.2001		(7)	
Trainer:	**DOB**	**M**		
Andrey Talalaev (RUS)	05.10.1972	24		
Aleksandr Tarkhanov (RUS) [11.04.2019]	06.09.1954	8		

Shirak Sports Club Gyumri

Founded: 1958
Stadium: Gyumri City Stadium, Gyumri (2,844)

Goalkeepers:	**DOB**	**M**	**(s)**	**G**
Vsevolod Ermakov (RUS)	06.01.1996	31		
Sokrat Hovhannisyan	05.04.1996	1		
Defenders:	**DOB**	**M**	**(s)**	**G**
Artur Amiryan	06.07.1997	1		
Aghvan Davoyan	21.03.1990	30		
Zhirayr Margaryan	13.09.1997	32		
Artyom Mikaelyan	12.07.1991	26	(1)	2
Henri Ndong (GAB)	23.08.1992	2		1
Marko Prljević (SRB)	02.08.1988	15		
Aram Shakhnazaryan	21.04.1994	24		
Midfielders:	**DOB**	**M**	**(s)**	**G**
Arman Aslanyan	30.01.1994	13	(14)	
Pablo Cruz (USA)	30.12.1991	7	(3)	2
Moussa Diakité (MLI)	17.12.1998	8		
Georgi Gogichaev (RUS)	16.01.1991	5	(3)	1
Rafik Misakyan	02.01.2000	9	(8)	
Rudik Mkrtchyan	26.10.1998	19	(5)	1
Karen Muradyan	01.11.1992	24		1
Bunjamin Shabani (MKD)	30.01.1991	19	(5)	1
Khoren Veranyan	04.09.1986	14	(7)	
Forwards:	**DOB**	**M**	**(s)**	**G**
Éder Smith Arreola Díaz (USA)	13.11.1991	9	(1)	1
Moussa Bakayoko (CIV)	27.12.1996	18	(4)	4
Jean-Jacques Bougouhi (CIV)	12.06.1992	7	(3)	1
Artem Gevorkyan (RUS)	21.05.1993	7	(6)	1
David Ghandilyan	04.06.1993	10	(4)	1
Johns Kadima Kabangu (COD)	15.06.1993	6	(9)	2
Aram Muradyan	14.04.1995	13	(11)	4
Arlen Tsaturyan	05.01.1999	1	(7)	
Trainer:	**DOB**	**M**		
Vardan Bichakhchyan	09.10.1977	32		

SECOND LEVEL
Armenian First League 2018/2019

1.	FC Junior Sevan Dzoraghbyur	33	25	6	2	90	-	26	81
2.	FC Yerevan (*Promoted*)	33	22	4	7	112	-	46	70
3.	FC Banants-2 Yerevan	33	21	7	5	65	-	31	70
4.	FC Ararat-Armenia-2 Yerevan	33	18	7	8	70	-	40	61
5.	FC Alashkert-2 Yerevan	33	15	10	8	63	-	39	55
6.	FC Lokomotiv Yerevan	33	16	7	10	61	-	37	55
7.	FC Pyunik-2 Yerevan	33	11	7	15	47	-	56	40
8.	Shirak SC-2 Gyumri	33	11	4	18	38	-	56	37
9.	FC Banants-3 Yerevan	33	9	6	18	38	-	57	33
10.	FC Gandzasar-2 Kapan	33	7	6	20	43	-	94	27
11.	FC Ararat-2 Yerevan	33	6	7	20	40	-	94	25
12.	Erebuni SC Yerevan	33	1	1	31	12	-	103	4

Please note: Second teams of Premier League clubs are ineligible for promotion.

NATIONAL TEAM

INTERNATIONAL MATCHES
(16.07.2018 – 15.07.2019)

06.09.2018	Yerevan	Armenia - Liechtenstein	2-1(1-1)	(UNL)
09.09.2018	Skopje	North Macedonia - Armenia	2-0(1-0)	(UNL)
13.10.2018	Yerevan	Armenia - Gibraltar	0-1(0-0)	(UNL)
16.10.2018	Yerevan	Armenia - North Macedonia	4-0(1-0)	(UNL)
16.11.2018	Gibraltar	Gibraltar - Armenia	2-6(1-1)	(UNL)
19.11.2018	Vaduz	Liechtenstein - Armenia	2-2(1-1)	(UNL)
23.03.2019	Sarajevo	Bosnia and Herzegovina - Armenia	2-1(1-0)	(ECQ)
26.03.2019	Yerevan	Armenia - Finland	0-2(0-1)	(ECQ)
08.06.2019	Yerevan	Armenia - Liechtenstein	3-0(2-0)	(ECQ)
11.06.2019	Athína	Greece - Armenia	2-3(0-2)	(ECQ)

06.09.2018 ARMENIA - LIECHTENSTEIN 2-1(1-1) UEFA Nations League D, Group 4
„Vazgen Sargsyan" Hanrapetakan Stadium, Yerevan; Referee: Enea Jorgji (Albania); Attendance: 5,132
ARM: Aram Hayrapetyan, Hovhannes Hambartsumyan, André Jack Calisir, Varazdat Haroyan, Armen Manucharyan (42.Artak Yedigaryan), Henrikh Mkhitaryan (Cap), Karlen Mkrtchyan, Aras Özbiliz (83.Gevorg Ghazaryan), Edgar Malakyan, Marcos Pinheiro Pizzelli, Ivan Yagan (55.Tigran Barseghyan). Trainer: Vardan Minasyan.
Goals: Marcos Pinheiro Pizzelli (30), Tigran Barseghyan (76).

09.09.2018 NORTH MACEDONIA - ARMENIA 2-0(1-0) UEFA Nations League D, Group 4
"Toše Proeski" National Arena; Referee: Manuel Schüttengruber (Austria); Attendance: 4,730
ARM: Aram Hayrapetyan, Hovhannes Hambartsumyan, André Jack Calisir, Varazdat Haroyan, Ayk Ishkhanyan, Henrikh Mkhitaryan (Cap), Karlen Mkrtchyan, Gor Malakyan (68.Aras Özbiliz), Gevorg Ghazaryan, Tigran Barseghyan (77.Artur Sarkisov), Sargis Adamyan (46.Marcos Pinheiro Pizzelli). Trainer: Vardan Minasyan.

13.10.2018 ARMENIA - GIBRALTAR 0-1(0-0) UEFA Nations League D, Group 4
„Vazgen Sargsyan" Hanrapetakan Stadium, Yerevan; Referee: Fedayi San (Switzerland); Attendance: 11,000
ARM: Aram Hayrapetyan, Hrayr Mkoyan, Hovhannes Hambartsumyan, Varazdat Haroyan, Kamo Hovhannisyan, Henrikh Mkhitaryan (Cap), Artak Grigoryan, Gor Malakyan (46.Marcos Pinheiro Pizzelli), Yura Movsisyan (69.Sargis Adamyan), Gevorg Ghazaryan, Tigran Barseghyan (61.Artur Sarkisov). Trainer: Armen Gyulbudaghyants.

16.10.2018 ARMENIA - NORTH MACEDONIA 4-0(1-0) UEFA Nations League D, Group 4
„Vazgen Sargsyan" Hanrapetakan Stadium, Yerevan; Referee: Martin Strömbergsson (Sweden); Attendance: 8,300
ARM: Aram Hayrapetyan, Gagik Daghbashyan, Artyom Khachaturov, Varazdat Haroyan, Kamo Hovhannisyan, Henrikh Mkhitaryan (Cap), Rumyan Hovsepyan (83.Karlen Mkrtchyan), Yura Movsisyan (74.Tigran Barseghyan), Gevorg Ghazaryan, Marcos Pinheiro Pizzelli (22.Artak Grigoryan), Sargis Adamyan. Trainer: Armen Gyulbudaghyants.
Goals: Marcos Pinheiro Pizzelli (12), Yura Movsisyan (67), Gevorg Ghazaryan (81), Henrikh Mkhitaryan (90+4).

16.11.2018 GIBRALTAR - ARMENIA 2-6(1-1) UEFA Nations League D, Group 4
Victoria Stadium, Gibraltar; Referee: Kai Erik Steen (Norway); Attendance: 1,955
ARM: Aram Hayrapetyan, Gagik Daghbashyan, Varazdat Haroyan, Artur Kartashyan, Kamo Hovhannisyan, Henrikh Mkhitaryan (Cap), Artak Grigoryan, Rumyan Hovsepyan (62.Gor Malakyan), Yura Movsisyan (70.Aleksandr Karapetyan), Gevorg Ghazaryan, Sargis Adamyan (73.Edgar Malakyan). Trainer: Armen Gyulbudaghyants.
Goals: Yura Movsisyan (27, 48, 52, 54), Artur Kartashyan (66), Aleksandr Karapetyan (90+4).

19.11.2018 LIECHTENSTEIN - ARMENIA 2-2(1-1) UEFA Nations League D, Group 4
Rheinpark Stadion, Vaduz; Referee: Alain Durieux (Luxembourg); Attendance: 1,166
ARM: Henri Avagyan, Gagik Daghbashyan, Artyom Khachaturov, Hovhannes Hambartsumyan (88.Alik Arakelyan), Varazdat Haroyan, Henrikh Mkhitaryan (Cap), Artak Grigoryan, Rumyan Hovsepyan (72.Aleksandr Karapetyan), Yura Movsisyan, Gevorg Ghazaryan, Sargis Adamyan. Trainer: Armen Gyulbudaghyants.
Goals: Sargis Adamyan (9), Aleksandr Karapetyan (85).

23.03.2019 BOSNIA AND HERZEGOVINA - ARMENIA 2-1(1-0) 16th EC. Qualifiers
Stadion Grbavica, Sarajevo; Referee: Jakob Kehlet (Denmark); Attendance: 12,000
ARM: Aram Hayrapetyan, Gagik Daghbashyan, André Jack Calisir, Varazdat Haroyan, Kamo Hovhannisyan, Henrikh Mkhitaryan (Cap), Karlen Mkrtchyan, Artak Grigoryan, Gevorg Ghazaryan (81.Aras Özbiliz), Aleksandr Karapetyan (67.Norberto Briasco Balekian), Sargis Adamyan (67.Edgar Babayan). Trainer: Armen Gyulbudaghyants.
Goal: Henrikh Mkhitaryan (90+3 penalty).

26.03.2019 ARMENIA - FINLAND 0-2(0-1) 16th EC. Qualifiers
„Vazgen Sargsyan" Hanrapetakan Stadium, Yerevan; Referee: Nikola Dabanović (Montenegro); Attendance: 12,900
ARM: Aram Hayrapetyan, Gagik Daghbashyan, André Jack Calisir, Varazdat Haroyan, Kamo Hovhannisyan, Henrikh Mkhitaryan (Cap), Artak Grigoryan, Aras Özbiliz (67.Tigran Barseghyan), Gevorg Ghazaryan, Edgar Babayan (74.Petros Avetisyan), Norberto Briasco Balekian (59.Aleksandr Karapetyan). Trainer: Armen Gyulbudaghyants.

08.06.2019 ARMENIA - LIECHTENSTEIN 3-0(2-0) 16th EC. Qualifiers
„Vazgen Sargsyan" Hanrapetakan Stadium, Yerevan; Referee: Nikola Popov (Bulgaria); Attendance: 10,000
ARM: Aram Hayrapetyan, Hovhannes Hambartsumyan, Varazdat Haroyan, Taron Voskanyan, Kamo Hovhannisyan, Karlen Mkrtchyan (76.Artak Grigoryan), Henrikh Mkhitaryan (Cap), Petros Avetisyan (78.Rumyan Hovsepyan), Gevorg Ghazaryan, Aleksandr Karapetyan (73.Edgar Babayan), Tigran Barseghyan. Trainer: Armen Gyulbudaghyants.
Goals: Gevorg Ghazaryan (2), Aleksandr Karapetyan (18), Tigran Barseghyan (90+1).

11.06.2019 GREECE - ARMENIA 2-3(0-2) 16th EC. Qualifiers

Stádio Olympiako „Spiros Louis", Athína; Referee: Kristo Tohver (Estonia); Attendance: 7,011

ARM: Aram Hayrapetyan, Hovhannes Hambartsumyan, Varazdat Haroyan, Ayk Ishkhanyan, Kamo Hovhannisyan, Henrikh Mkhitaryan (Cap), Karlen Mkrtchyan (55.Rumyan Hovsepyan), Artak Grigoryan, Gevorg Ghazaryan (83.Petros Avetisyan), Aleksandr Karapetyan (70.Edgar Babayan), Tigran Barseghyan. Trainer: Armen Gyulbudaghyants.

Goals: Aleksandr Karapetyan (8), Gevorg Ghazaryan (33), Tigran Barseghyan (74).

NATIONAL TEAM PLAYERS
(16.07.2018 – 15.07.2019)

Name	DOB	Caps	Goals	2018/2019:	*Club*
Goalkeepers					
Henri AVAGYAN	16.01.1996	**1**	**0**	2018/2019:	*FC Alashkert Yerevan*
Aram AYRAPETYAN	22.11.1986	**11**	**0**	2018/2019:	*FC Banants Yerevan*
Defenders					
André Jack CALISIR	13.06.1990	**5**	**0**	2018/2019:	*IFK Göteborg (SWE)*
Gagik DAGHBASHYAN	19.10.1990	**14**	**0**	2018/2019:	*FC Alashkert Yerevan*
Hovhannes HAMBARTSUMYAN	04.10.1990	**29**	**2**	2018/2019:	*Enosis Neon Paralimni FC (CYP)*
Varazdat HAROYAN	24.08.1992	**45**	**2**	2018/2019:	*FK Ural Yekaterinburg (RUS)*
Kamo HOVHANNISYAN	05.10.1990	**46**	**0**	2018/2019:	*FC Zhetisu Taldiqorghan (KAZ)*
Ayk ISHKHANYAN	24.06.1989	**7**	**1**	2018: 08.02.2019->	*FC Gandzasar Kapan* *Lori FC Vanadzor*
Artur KARTASHYAN	08.01.1997	**1**	**1**	2018:	*FC Pyunik Yerevan*
Artyom KHACHATUROV	18.06.1992	**4**	**0**	2018:	*Lori FC Vanadzor*
Armen MANUCHARYAN	03.02.1995	**2**	**0**	2018:	*FC Pyunik Yerevan*
Hrayr MKOYAN	02.09.1986	**46**	**1**	2018:	*FC Alashkert Yerevan*
Taron VOSKANYAN	22.02.1993	**26**	**0**	2019:	*FC Alashkert Yerevan*
Artak YEDIGARYAN	18.03.1990	**30**	**1**	2018/2019:	*FC Alashkert Yerevan*
Midfielders					
Alik ARAKELYAN	21.05.1996	**1**	**0**	2018:	*FC Pyunik Yerevan*
Petros AVETISYAN	07.01.1986	**3**	**0**	2019:	*FC Ararat-Armenia Yerevan*
Edgar BABAYAN	28.10.1995	**5**	**0**	2019:	*Hobro IK (DEN)*
Gevorg GHAZARYAN	05.04.1988	**67**	**13**	2018/2019:	*GD Chaves (POR)*
Artak GRIGORYAN	19.10.1987	**21**	**1**	2018/2019:	*FC Alashkert Yerevan*
Rumyan HOVSEPYAN	13.11.1991	**17**	**2**	2018/2019:	*FC Pyunik Yerevan*
Edgar MALAKYAN	22.09.1990	**22**	**0**	2018:	*FC Zhetisu Taldiqorghan (KAZ)*
Gor MALAKYAN	12.06.1994	**14**	**0**	2018:	*FC Ararat-Armenia Yerevan*
Henrikh MKHITARYAN	21.01.1989	**84**	**27**	2018/2019:	*Arsenal FC London (ENG)*
Karlen MKRTCHYAN	25.11.1988	**54**	**2**	2018/2019:	*FC Pyunik Yerevan*
Aras ÖZBILIZ	09.03.1990	**39**	**6**	2018/2019:	*Willem II Tilburg (NED)*
Marcos Pinheiro PIZZELLI	03.10.1984	**66**	**11**	2018:	*FC Aktobe (KAZ)*
Ivan YAGAN	11.10.1989	**3**	**1**	2019:	*KAS Eupen (BEL)*
Forwards					
Sargis ADAMYAN	23.05.1993	**14**	**1**	2018/2019:	*SSV Jahn Regensburg (GER)*
Tigran BARSEGHYAN	22.09.1993	**22**	**4**	2018: 24.01.2019->	*FK Vardar Skopje (MKD)* *FC Kaysar Kyzylorda (KAZ)*
Norberto Alejandro BRIASCO Balekian	29.02.1996	**4**	**0**	2019:	*CA Huracán Buenos Aires (ARG)*
Aleksandr KARAPETYAN	23.12.1987	**8**	**4**	2018/2019:	*FC Progrès Niederkorn (LUX)*
Yura MOVSISYAN	02.08.1987	**38**	**14**	2018/2019:	*Chicago Fire SC (USA)*
Artur SARKISOV	19.01.1987	**40**	**6**	2018:	*FK Yenisey Krasnoyarsk (RUS)*

National team coach

Vardan MINASYAN [10.04. – 21.09.2018]	05.01.1974	4 M; 1 W; 2 D; 1 L; 3-5 Complete record as trainer of Armenia: 46 M; 16 W; 6 D; 24 L; 60-64 (28.03.2007) & (17.11.2007 – 21.11.2007) & (01.04.2009 – 15.10.2013) & (29.05.2018 – 04.06.2018)
Armen GYULBUDAGHYANTS [from 07.10.2018]	19.12.1966	8 M; 4 W; 1 D; 3 L; 19-11

AUSTRIA

The Country:

Republic of Austria (Republik Österreich)
Capital: Vienna
Surface: 83,879 km²
Inhabitants: 8,857,960 [2018]
Time: UTC+1

The FA:

Österreichischer Fußball-Bund
Ernst-Happel-Stadion - Sektor A/F, Meiereistrasse 7, 1021 Wien
Tel: +43 1 727 180
Foundation date: 1904
Member of FIFA since: 1905
Member of UEFA since: 1954
Website: www.oefb.at

NATIONAL TEAM RECORDS

First international match:	12.10.1902, Wien:	Austria – Hungary 5-0
Most international caps:	Andreas Herzog	- 103 caps (1988-2003)
Most international goals:	Anton Polster	- 44 goals / 95 caps (1982-2000)

UEFA EUROPEAN CHAMPIONSHIP

1960	Qualifiers
1964	Qualifiers
1968	Qualifiers
1972	Qualifiers
1976	Qualifiers
1980	Qualifiers
1984	Qualifiers
1988	Qualifiers
1992	Qualifiers
1996	Qualifiers
2000	Qualifiers
2004	Qualifiers
2008	Final Tournament (Group Stage)
2012	Qualifiers
2016	Final Tournament (Group Stage)

FIFA WORLD CUP

1930	*Did not enter*
1934	Final Tournament (4th Place)
1938	*Withdrew*
1950	*Withdrew*
1954	Final Tournament (3rd Place)
1958	Final Tournament (Group Stage)
1962	*Withdrew*
1966	Qualifiers
1970	Qualifiers
1974	Qualifiers
1978	Final Tournament (2nd Round)
1982	Final Tournament (2nd Round)
1986	Qualifiers
1990	Final Tournament (Group Stage)
1994	Qualifiers
1998	Final Tournament (Group Stage)
2002	Qualifiers
2006	Qualifiers
2010	Qualifiers
2014	Qualifiers
2018	Qualifiers

UEFA NATIONS LEAGUE

2018/2019 – League B

OLYMPIC FOOTBALL TOURNAMENTS 1908-2016

1908	-	**1948**	FT/ 1/8-Finals	**1972**	Qualifiers	**1996**	Qualifiers
1912	FT/ Quarter-Finals	**1952**	FT/ Quarter-Finals	**1976**	Qualifiers	**2000**	Qualifiers
1920	*Did not enter*	**1956**	*Did not enter*	**1980**	Qualifiers	**2004**	Qualifiers
1924	*Did not enter*	**1960**	Qualifiers	**1984**	*Did not enter*	**2008**	Qualifiers
1928	*Did not enter*	**1964**	Qualifiers	**1988**	Qualifiers	**2012**	Qualifiers
1936	FT/ Runners-up	**1968**	Qualifiers	**1992**	Qualifiers	**2016**	Qualifiers

FIFA CONFEDERATIONS CUP 1992-2017

None

AUSTRIAN CLUB HONOURS IN EUROPEAN CLUB COMPETITIONS:

European Champion Clubs.Cup (1956-1992) / UEFA Champions League (1993-2019)

None

Fairs Cup (1858-1971) / UEFA Cup (1972-2009) / UEFA Europa League (2010-2019)

None

UEFA Super Cup (1972-2019)

None

European Cup Winners.Cup 1961-1999*

None

**defunct competition*

NATIONAL COMPETITIONS
TABLE OF HONOURS

	CHAMPIONS	CUP WINNERS	BEST GOALSCORERS	
1911/1912	SK Rapid Wien	-	Johann Schwarz II (First Vienna FC 1894 Wien)	22
1912/1913	SK Rapid Wien	-	Richard Kuthan (SK Rapid Wien)	16
1913/1914	Wiener AF	-	Johann Neumann (Wiener AC)	25
1914/1915	Wiener AC	-	Leopold Deutsch (Floridsdorfer AC & Wiener AC)	12
1915/1916	SK Rapid Wien	-	Richard Kuthan (SK Rapid Wien)	24
1916/1917	SK Rapid Wien	-	Eduard Bauer (SK Rapid Wien) Leopold Neubauer (Wiener AF)	21
1917/1918	Floridsdorfer AC	-	Eduard Bauer (SK Rapid Wien)	21
1918/1919	SK Rapid Wien	SK Rapid Wien	Josef Uridil (SK Rapid Wien)	16
1919/1920	SK Rapid Wien	SK Rapid Wien	Josef Uridil (SK Rapid Wien) Ernst Winkler (SpC Rudolfshügel)	21
1920/1921	SK Rapid Wien	Wiener SV Amateure	Josef Uridil (SK Rapid Wien)	35
1921/1922	Wiener Sport-Club	Wiener AF	Richard Kuthan (SK Rapid Wien)	20
1922/1923	SK Rapid Wien	Wiener Sport-Club	Ferdinand Swatosch (Wiener SV Amateure)	22
1923/1924	Wiener SV Amateure	Wiener SV Amateure	Gustav Wieser (Wiener SV Amateure)	16
1924/1925	SC Hakoah Wien	Wiener SV Amateure	Gustav Wieser (Wiener SV Amateure)	19
1925/1926	Wiener SV Amateure	Wiener SV Amateure	Gustav Wieser (Wiener SV Amateure)	25
1926/1927	SK Admira Wien	SK Rapid Wien	Anton Schall (SK Admira Wien)	27
1927/1928	SK Admira Wien	SK Admira Wien	Anton Schall (SK Admira Wien)	36
1928/1929	SK Rapid Wien	First Vienna FC 1894 Wien	Anton Schall (SK Admira Wien)	21
1929/1930	SK Rapid Wien	First Vienna FC 1894 Wien	Franz Weselik (SK Rapid Wien)	24
1930/1931	First Vienna FC 1894 Wien	Wiener AC	Anton Schall (SK Admira Wien)	25
1931/1932	SK Admira Wien	SK Admira Wien	Anton Schall (SK Admira Wien)	22
1932/1933	First Vienna FC 1894 Wien	FK Austria Wien	Franz Binder (SK Rapid Wien)	25
1933/1934	SK Admira Wien	SK Admira Wien	Josef Bican (SK Rapid Wien)	29
1934/1935	SK Rapid Wien	FK Austria Wien	Matthias Kaburek (SK Rapid Wien)	29
1935/1936	SK Admira Wien	FK Austria Wien	Wilhelm Hahnemann (SK Admira Wien)	23
1936/1937	SK Admira Wien	First Vienna FC 1894 Wien	Franz Binder (SK Rapid Wien)	29
1937/1938	SK Rapid Wien	Wiener AC – Schwarz-Rot Wien	Franz Binder (SK Rapid Wien)	22
1938/1939	SK Admira Wien	-	Franz Binder (SK Rapid Wien)	27
1939/1940	SK Rapid Wien	-	Franz Binder (SK Rapid Wien)	18
1940/1941	SK Rapid Wien	-	Franz Binder (SK Rapid Wien)	27
1941/1942	Vienna FC Wien	-	Ernst Reitermaier (SC Wacker Wien)	20
1942/1943	Vienna FC Wien	-	Karl Kerbach (Floridsdorfer AC)	31
1943/1944	Vienna FC Wien	-	Karl Decker (First Vienna FC 1894 Wien)	32
1944/1945	SK Rapid Wien	-	Richard Fischer (First Vienna FC 1894 Wien)	15
1945/1946	SK Rapid Wien	SK Rapid Wien	Ernst Stojaspal I (FK Austria Wien)	34
1946/1947	SC Wacker Wien	SC Wacker Wien	Ernst Stojaspal I (FK Austria Wien)	18
1947/1948	SK Rapid Wien	FK Austria Wien	Ernst Stojaspal I (FK Austria Wien)	24
1948/1949	FK Austria Wien	FK Austria Wien	Erich Habitzl (SK Admira Wien)	23
1949/1950	FK Austria Wien	-	Karl Decker (First Vienna FC 1894 Wien)	23
1950/1951	SK Rapid Wien	-	Robert Dienst (SK Rapid Wien)	32
1951/1952	SK Rapid Wien	-	Ernst Stojaspal I (FK Austria Wien)	31
1952/1953	FK Austria Wien	-	Ernst Stojaspal I (FK Austria Wien) Robert Dienst (SK Rapid Wien)	30
1953/1954	SK Rapid Wien	-	Robert Dienst (SK Rapid Wien)	25
1954/1955	First Vienna FC 1894 Wien	-	Richard Brousek (SC Wacker Wien)	31
1955/1956	SK Rapid Wien	-	Johann Buzek (First Vienna FC 1894 Wien)	33
1956/1957	SK Rapid Wien	-	Robert Dienst (SK Rapid Wien)	32
1957/1958	Wiener Sport-Club	-	Walter Horak (Wiener Sport-Club)	33
1958/1959	Wiener Sport-Club	Wiener AC	Erich Hof (Wiener Sport-Club)	32
1959/1960	SK Rapid Wien	FK Austria Wien	Friedrich Cejka (Wiener Sport-Club)	28
1960/1961	FK Austria Wien	SK Rapid Wien	Horst Nemec (FK Austria Wien)	31
1961/1962	FK Austria Wien	FK Austria Wien	Horst Nemec (FK Austria Wien)	24
1962/1963	FK Austria Wien	FK Austria Wien	Erich Hof (Wiener Sport-Club)	21
1963/1964	SK Rapid Wien	ESV Admira Energie Wien	Horst Nemec (FK Austria Wien)	21
1964/1965	Linzer ASK	Linzer ASK	Wolfgang Gayer (Wiener Sport-Club)	18
1965/1966	ESV Admira Energie Wien	ESV Admira Energie Wien	Johann Buzek (FK Austria Wien)	18
1966/1967	SK Rapid Wien	FK Austria Wien	August Starek (SK Rapid Wien)	21
1967/1968	SK Rapid Wien	SK Rapid Wien	Jørn Bjerregaard (DEN, SK Rapid Wien)	23
1968/1969	FK Austria Wien	SK Rapid Wien	Helmut Köglberger (FK Austria Wien)	31
1969/1970	FK Austria Wien	FC Wacker Innsbruck	Günter Kaltenbrunner (Wiener Sport-Club)	22
1970/1971	FC Wacker Innsbruck	FK Austria Wien	Wilhelm Kreuz (ESV Admira Energie Wien)	26
1971/1972	SSW Innsbruck	Wiener Sport-Club	Alfred Riedl (FK Austria Wien)	16
1972/1973	SSW Innsbruck	SSW Innsbruck	Wolfgang Breuer (SSW Innsbruck)	22
1973/1974	SK VÖEST Linz	FK Austria Wien	Johann Krankl (SK Rapid Wien)	36
1974/1975	SSW Innsbruck	SSW Innsbruck	Helmut Köglberger (FK Austria/WAC Wien - Linzer ASK)	22
1975/1976	FK Austria/WAC Wien	SK Rapid Wien	Hans Pirkner (FK Austria/WAC Wien)	21
1976/1977	SSW Innsbruck	FK Austria Wien	Johann Krankl (SK Rapid Wien)	32
1977/1978	FK Austria Wien	SSW Innsbruck	Johann Krankl (SK Rapid Wien)	32

1978/1979	FK Austria Wien	SSW Innsbruck	Walter Schachner (FK Austria Wien)	24
1979/1980	FK Austria Wien	FK Austria Wien	Walter Schachner (FK Austria Wien)	34
1980/1981	FK Austria Wien	Grazer AK	Gernot Jurtin (SK Sturm Graz)	20
1981/1982	SK Rapid Wien	FK Austria Wien	Božo Bakota (YUG, SK Sturm Graz)	24
1982/1983	SK Rapid Wien	SK Rapid Wien	Johann Krankl (SK Rapid Wien)	23
1983/1984	FK Austria Wien	SK Rapid Wien	Tibor Nyilasi (HUN, FK Austria Wien)	26
1984/1985	FK Austria Wien	SK Rapid Wien	Anton Polster (FK Austria Wien)	24
1985/1986	FK Austria Wien	FK Austria Wien	Anton Polster (FK Austria Wien)	33
1986/1987	SK Rapid Wien	SK Rapid Wien	Anton Polster (FK Austria Wien)	39
1987/1988	SK Rapid Wien	Kremser SC	Zoran Stojadinović (YUG, SK Rapid Wien)	27
1988/1989	FC Swarovski Tirol Innsbruck	FC Swarovski Tirol Innsbruck	Peter Pacult (FC Swarovski Tirol)	26
1989/1990	FC Swarovski Tirol Innsbruck	FK Austria Wien	Gerhard Rodax (FC Admira/Wacker Wien)	35
1990/1991	FK Austria Wien	SV Stockerau	Václav Daněk (TCH, FC Swarovski Tirol)	29
1991/1992	FK Austria Wien	FK Austria Wien	Christoph Westerthaler (FC Swarovski Tirol)	17
1992/1993	FK Austria Wien	FC Wacker Innsbruck	Václav Daněk (TCH, FC Wacker Tirol)	24
1993/1994	SV Austria Salzburg	FK Austria Wien	Nikola Jurčević (CRO, SV Austria Salzburg) Heimo Pfeifenberger (SV Austria Salzburg)	14
1994/1995	SV Austria Salzburg	SK Rapid Wien	Souleyman Sané (SEN, FC Tirol Innsbruck)	20
1995/1996	SK Rapid Wien	SK Sturm Graz	Ivica Vastic (SK Sturm Graz)	20
1996/1997	SV Austria Salzburg	SK Sturm Graz	René Wagner (CZE, SK Rapid Wien)	28
1997/1998	SK Sturm Graz	SV Ried im Innkreis	Geir Frigård (NOR, LASK Linz)	23
1998/1999	SK Sturm Graz	SK Sturm Graz	Eduard Glieder (SV Austria Salzburg)	22
1999/2000	FC Tirol Innsbruck	Grazer AK	Ivica Vastic (SK Sturm Graz)	32
2000/2001	FC Tirol Innsbruck	FC Kärnten	Radosław Gilewicz (POL, FC Tirol Innsbruck)	22
2001/2002	FC Tirol Innsbruck	Grazer AK	Ronald Brunmayr (Grazer AK)	27
2002/2003	FK Austria Wien	FK Austria Wien	Axel Lawarée (BEL, SC Schwarz-Weiß Bregenz)	21
2003/2004	Grazer AK	Grazer AK	Roland Kollmann (Grazer AK)	24
2004/2005	SK Rapid Wien	FK Austria Wien	Christian Mayrleb (Grazer AK)	27
2005/2006	FK Austria Wien	FK Austria Wien	Sanel Kuljic (SV Ried) Roland Linz (FK Austria Wien)	15
2006/2007	FC Red Bull Salzburg	FK Austria Wien	Alexander Zickler (GER, FC Red Bull Salzburg)	22
2007/2008	SK Rapid Wien	-	Alexander Zickler (GER, FC Red Bull Salzburg)	16
2008/2009	FC Red Bull Salzburg	FK Austria Wien	Marc Janko (FC Red Bull Salzburg)	39
2009/2010	FC Red Bull Salzburg	SK Sturm Graz	Steffen Hofmann (GER, SK Rapid Wien)	20
2010/2011	SK Sturm Graz	SV Ried im Innkreis	Roland Linz (FK Austria Wien) Roman Kienast (SK Sturm Graz)	21
2011/2012	FC Red Bull Salzburg	FC Red Bull Salzburg	Jakob Jantscher (FC Red Bull Salzburg) Stefan Maierhofer (FC Red Bull Salzburg)	14
2012/2013	FK Austria Wien	FC Pasching	Philipp Hosiner (FK Austria Wien)	32
2013/2014	FC Red Bull Salzburg	FC Red Bull Salzburg	Jonathan Soriano Casas (ESP, FC Red Bull Salzburg)	31
2014/2015	FC Red Bull Salzburg	FC Red Bull Salzburg	Jonathan Soriano Casas (ESP, FC Red Bull Salzburg)	31
2015/2016	FC Red Bull Salzburg	FC Red Bull Salzburg	Jonathan Soriano Casas (ESP, FC Red Bull Salzburg)	21
2016/2017	FC Red Bull Salzburg	FC Red Bull Salzburg	Olarenwaju Ayobami Kayode (NGA, FK Austria Wien)	17
2017/2018	FC Red Bull Salzburg	SK Sturm Graz	Moanes Dabour (ISR, FC Red Bull Salzburg)	22
2018/2019	FC Red Bull Salzburg	FC Red Bull Salzburg	Moanes Dabour (ISR, FC Red Bull Salzburg)	20

NATIONAL CHAMPIONSHIP

Österreichische Fußballmeisterschaft – Bundesliga 2018/2019

(26.07.2018 – 26.05.2019)

Regular Season - Results

Round 1 [27-29.07.2018]
Austria Wien - Wacker Innsbruck 2-1(1-1)
Sturm Graz - TSV Hartberg 3-2(2-1)
SCR Altach - SV Mattersburg 2-3(1-1)
SKN St. Pölten - Wolfsberger AC 4-3(2-2)
FC Admira Wacker - Rapid Wien 0-3(0-3)
RB Salzburg - Linzer ASK 3-1(3-0)

Round 2 [04-05.08.2018]
Rapid Wien - SCR Altach 1-1(1-0)
SV Mattersburg - RB Salzburg 0-2(0-0)
Wacker Innsbruck - Sturm Graz 2-3(0-1)
TSV Hartberg - FC Admira Wacker 0-1(0-0)
Linzer ASK - SKN St. Pölten 0-0
Wolfsberger AC - Austria Wien 1-0(0-0)

Round 3 [11-12.08.2018]
RB Salzburg - Austria Wien 2-0(1-0)
SCR Altach - Wacker Innsbruck 1-2(1-2)
TSV Hartberg - SV Mattersburg 4-2(3-1)
SKN St. Pölten - Sturm Graz 2-0(1-0)
FC Admira Wacker - Linzer ASK 0-1(0-0)
Rapid Wien - Wolfsberger AC 0-0

Round 4 [18-19.08.2018]
RB Salzburg - TSV Hartberg 2-0(0-0)
SV Mattersburg - Wolfsberger AC 0-6(0-3)
Wacker Innsbruck - SKN St. Pölten 0-2(0-1)
Sturm Graz - SCR Altach 1-1(1-0)
Austria Wien - FC Admira Wacker 4-0(2-0)
Linzer ASK - Rapid Wien 2-1(0-0)

Round 5 [25-26.08.2018]
SCR Altach - RB Salzburg 2-3(1-2)
Wolfsberger AC - Sturm Graz 1-1(1-0)
SKN St. Pölten - Austria Wien 0-0
TSV Hartberg - Linzer ASK 0-1(0-1)
FC Admira Wacker - SV Mattersburg 0-0
Rapid Wien - Wacker Innsbruck 2-1(1-0)

Round 6 [01-02.09.2018]
Austria Wien - SV Mattersburg 2-1(0-1)
SCR Altach - SKN St. Pölten 1-2(0-1)
Wacker Innsbruck - TSV Hartberg 2-1(1-1)
Linzer ASK - Wolfsberger AC 2-0(1-0)
RB Salzburg - FC Admira Wacker 3-1(1-0)
Sturm Graz - Rapid Wien 1-1(1-0)

Round 7 [15-16.09.2018]
FC Admira Wacker - Sturm Graz 2-3(1-1)
SKN St. Pölten - RB Salzburg 1-3(1-1)
TSV Hartberg - SCR Altach 2-1(0-0)
Wolfsberger AC - Wacker Innsbruck 3-1(0-1)
SV Mattersburg - Linzer ASK 1-3(0-1)
Rapid Wien - Austria Wien 0-1(0-0)

Round 8 [22-23.09.2018]
Sturm Graz - SV Mattersburg 1-2(1-1)
SCR Altach - Wolfsberger AC 0-1(0-1)
SKN St. Pölten - TSV Hartberg 3-0(1-0)
Austria Wien - Linzer ASK 0-3(0-1)
Wacker Innsbruck - Admira Wacker 1-3(0-1)
RB Salzburg - Rapid Wien 2-1(1-0)

Round 9 [29-30.09.2018]
Rapid Wien - SKN St. Pölten 0-2(0-1)
FC Admira Wacker - SCR Altach 2-4(1-2)
Wolfsberger AC - RB Salzburg 1-4(0-0)
SV Mattersburg - Wacker Innsbruck 2-1(0-0)
TSV Hartberg - Austria Wien 0-1(0-0)
Linzer ASK - Sturm Graz 0-0

Round 10 [06-07.10.2018]
SCR Altach - Austria Wien 2-0(0-0)
Wolfsberger AC - TSV Hartberg 3-4(2-1)
SKN St. Pölten - FC Admira Wacker 0-0
Rapid Wien - SV Mattersburg 1-0(1-0)
Wacker Innsbruck - Linzer ASK 1-0(0-0)
Sturm Graz - RB Salzburg 1-2(1-1)

Round 11 [20-21.10.2018]
RB Salzburg - Wacker Innsbruck 1-1(0-0)
Linzer ASK - SCR Altach 1-1(0-0)
TSV Hartberg - Rapid Wien 3-0(2-0)
FC Admira Wacker - Wolfsberger AC 0-0
SV Mattersburg - SKN St. Pölten 2-0(0-0)
Austria Wien - Sturm Graz 1-1(0-1)

Round 12 [27-28.10.2018]
SV Mattersburg - SCR Altach 1-1(0-0)
Wacker Innsbruck - Austria Wien 0-0
TSV Hartberg - Sturm Graz 2-0(0-0)
Rapid Wien - FC Admira Wacker 2-0(1-0)
Wolfsberger AC - SKN St. Pölten 1-0(0-0)
Linzer ASK - RB Salzburg 3-3(2-2)

Round 13 [03-04.11.2018]
Sturm Graz - Wacker Innsbruck 1-1(0-0)
FC Admira Wacker - TSV Hartberg 2-3(0-1)
SKN St. Pölten - Linzer ASK 2-2(1-1)
RB Salzburg - SV Mattersburg 2-1(0-0)
Austria Wien - Wolfsberger AC 2-3(2-1)
SCR Altach - Rapid Wien 2-2(1-2)

Round 14 [10-11.11.2018]
Wacker Innsbruck - SCR Altach 1-0(1-0)
Sturm Graz - SKN St. Pölten 0-0
Linzer ASK - FC Admira Wacker 5-1(1-0)
SV Mattersburg - TSV Hartberg 1-2(0-0)
Wolfsberger AC - Rapid Wien 3-1(0-1)
Austria Wien - RB Salzburg 0-2(0-0)

Round 15 [24-25.11.2018]
TSV Hartberg - RB Salzburg 0-4(0-0)
Wolfsberger AC - SV Mattersburg 2-2(1-0)
FC Admira Wacker - Austria Wien 1-2(0-1)
SCR Altach - Sturm Graz 0-2(0-1)
SKN St. Pölten - Wacker Innsbruck 2-0(0-0)
Rapid Wien - Linzer ASK 0-1(0-0)

Round 16 [01-02.12.2018]
Austria Wien - SKN St. Pölten 2-0(2-0)
Linzer ASK - TSV Hartberg 3-3(2-2)
SV Mattersburg - FC Admira Wacker 2-2(0-1)
RB Salzburg - SCR Altach 1-0(1-0)
Wacker Innsbruck - Rapid Wien 0-1(0-0)
Sturm Graz - Wolfsberger AC 3-0(1-0)

Round 17 [08-09.12.2018]
SKN St. Pölten - SCR Altach 2-1(1-0)
Wolfsberger AC - Linzer ASK 1-1(1-1)
FC Admira Wacker - RB Salzburg 2-2(1-1)
SV Mattersburg - Austria Wien 2-1(0-1)
TSV Hartberg - Wacker Innsbruck 2-2(2-1)
Rapid Wien - Sturm Graz 0-0

Round 18 [15-16.12.2018]
Sturm Graz - FC Admira Wacker 3-0(0-0)
Wacker Innsbruck - Wolfsberger AC 0-0
Linzer ASK - SV Mattersburg 2-1(1-0)
RB Salzburg - SKN St. Pölten 5-1(5-0)
SCR Altach - TSV Hartberg 6-1(2-0)
Austria Wien - Rapid Wien 6-1(4-1)

Round 19 [22-24.02.2019]
Linzer ASK - Austria Wien 2-0(1-0)
Wolfsberger AC - SCR Altach 0-0
Admira Wacker - Wacker Innsbruck 3-0(2-0)
SV Mattersburg - Sturm Graz 1-1(1-0)
TSV Hartberg - SKN St. Pölten 1-1(0-0)
Rapid Wien - RB Salzburg 2-0(0-0)

Round 20 [02-03.03.2019]
SKN St. Pölten - Rapid Wien 0-4(0-2)
SCR Altach - FC Admira Wacker 0-1(0-0)
RB Salzburg - Wolfsberger AC 3-0(2-0)
Sturm Graz - Linzer ASK 0-3(0-1)
Austria Wien - TSV Hartberg 4-2(1-0)
Wacker Innsbruck - SV Mattersburg 0-1(0-0)

Round 21 [10.03.2019]
RB Salzburg - Sturm Graz 0-0
SV Mattersburg - Rapid Wien 2-1(1-1)
Austria Wien - SCR Altach 1-3(1-2)
TSV Hartberg - Wolfsberger AC 1-1(0-1)
FC Admira Wacker - SKN St. Pölten 3-2(1-1)
Linzer ASK - Wacker Innsbruck 2-0(1-0)

Round 22 [17.03.2019]
Wacker Innsbruck - RB Salzburg 0-2(0-1)
SCR Altach - Linzer ASK 1-2(1-0)
Wolfsberger AC - Admira Wacker 2-2(1-2)
SKN St. Pölten - SV Mattersburg 0-1(0-1)
Sturm Graz - Austria Wien 1-0(0-0)
Rapid Wien - TSV Hartberg 2-2(2-0)

Final Standings

1.	FC Red Bull Salzburg	22	17	4	1	51	-	18	55
2.	Linzer ASK	22	13	7	2	40	-	19	46
3.	SK Sturm Graz	22	7	10	5	26	-	23	31
4.	Wolfsberger AC	22	7	9	6	32	-	31	30
5.	FK Austria Wien	22	9	3	10	29	-	28	30
6.	SKN St. Pölten	22	8	6	8	26	-	29	30
7.	SV Mattersburg	22	8	5	9	28	-	36	29
8.	SK Rapid Wien	22	7	6	9	26	-	29	27
9.	TSV Hartberg	22	7	5	10	35	-	45	26
10.	FC Admira Wacker Mödling	22	5	6	11	26	-	42	21
11.	SC Rheindorf Altach	22	4	6	12	30	-	32	18
12.	FC Wacker Innsbruck	22	4	5	13	17	-	34	17

Teams ranked 1-6 were qualified for the Championship Round, while teams ranked 7-12 were qualified for the Relegation Round.

Championship Round

Results

Round 23 [31.03.2019]
Wolfsberger AC - Linzer ASK 0-3(0-3)
Sturm Graz - SKN St. Pölten 0-1(0-0)
RB Salzburg - Austria Wien 5-1(1-1)

Round 24 [07.04.2019]
Austria Wien - Sturm Graz 0-1(0-0)
SKN St. Pölten - Wolfsberger AC 1-3(0-1)
Linzer ASK - RB Salzburg 0-2(0-1)

Round 25 [14.04.2019]
Wolfsberger AC - Austria Wien 1-1(1-1)
Linzer ASK - SKN St. Pölten 0-0
RB Salzburg - Sturm Graz 3-1(0-1)

Round 26 [21.04.2019]
SKN St. Pölten - RB Salzburg 1-1(0-1)
Sturm Graz - Wolfsberger AC 1-2(1-0)
Austria Wien - Linzer ASK 2-2(1-1)

Round 27 [24.04.2019]
RB Salzburg - Wolfsberger AC 3-1(0-0)
Linzer ASK - Sturm Graz 1-2(0-0)
Austria Wien - SKN St. Pölten 2-2(0-0)

Round 28 [28.04.2019]
Wolfsberger AC - RB Salzburg 2-1(1-0)
SKN St. Pölten - Austria Wien 1-2(1-0)
Sturm Graz - Linzer ASK 2-3(2-1)

Round 29 [05.05.2019]
Linzer ASK - Wolfsberger AC 3-0(1-0)
SKN St. Pölten - Sturm Graz 0-1(0-1)
Austria Wien - RB Salzburg 1-2(0-0)

Round 30 [12.05.2019]
Sturm Graz - Austria Wien 1-3(1-1)
Wolfsberger AC - SKN St. Pölten 4-0(1-0)
RB Salzburg - Linzer ASK 2-1(2-0)

Round 31 [19.05.2019]
Austria Wien - Wolfsberger AC 2-0(0-0)
SKN St. Pölten - Linzer ASK 0-1(0-0)
Sturm Graz - RB Salzburg 1-2(1-1)

Round 32 [26.05.2019]
RB Salzburg - SKN St. Pölten 7-0(2-0)
Wolfsberger AC - Sturm Graz 2-1(0-1)
Linzer ASK - Austria Wien 5-2(0-1)

Final Standings

1.	**FC Red Bull Salzburg**	32	25	5	2	79	-	27	52
2.	Linzer ASK	32	18	9	5	59	-	31	40
3.	Wolfsberger AC	32	12	10	10	47	-	47	31
4.	FK Austria Wien	32	12	6	14	45	-	48	27
5.	SK Sturm Graz	32	10	10	12	37	-	40	24
6.	SKN St. Pölten	32	9	9	14	32	-	50	21

SK Sturm Graz were qualified for the Europa League Play-offs Final.

Top goalscorers:

20 Moanes Dabour (ISR)
FC Red Bull Salzburg

13 João Victor Santos Sá (BRA)
LASK Linz

11 Michael Liendl
Wolfsberger AC

Relegation Round

Results

Round 23 [30.03.2019]
Rapid Wien - FC Admira Wacker 3-0(1-0)
TSV Hartberg - Wacker Innsbruck 0-2(0-2)
SCR Altach - SV Mattersburg 2-1(1-1)

Round 24 [06.04.2019]
Wacker Innsbruck - Rapid Wien 0-2(0-1)
FC Admira Wacker - SCR Altach 1-1(1-0)
SV Mattersburg - TSV Hartberg 3-0(0-0)

Round 25 [13.04.2019]
Wacker Innsbruck - Admira Wacker 1-3(0-1)
TSV Hartberg - SCR Altach 0-1(0-0)
Rapid Wien - SV Mattersburg 2-1(0-0)

Round 26 [20.04.2019]
SCR Altach - Rapid Wien 2-2(0-0)
FC Admira Wacker - TSV Hartberg 2-1(1-1)
SV Mattersburg - Wacker Innsbruck 3-1(1-0)

Round 27 [23.04.2019]
Wacker Innsbruck - SCR Altach 0-4(0-0)
FC Admira Wacker - SV Mattersburg 0-2(0-0)
TSV Hartberg - Rapid Wien 2-4(1-1)

Round 28 [27.04.2019]
SCR Altach - Wacker Innsbruck 1-4(1-1)
SV Mattersburg - FC Admira Wacker 1-1(1-0)
Rapid Wien - TSV Hartberg 3-4(2-2)

Round 29 [04.05.2019]
FC Admira Wacker - Rapid Wien 3-4(0-3)
Wacker Innsbruck - TSV Hartberg 1-0(1-0)
SV Mattersburg - SCR Altach 0-0

Round 30 [11.05.2019]
SCR Altach - FC Admira Wacker 2-2(1-2)
TSV Hartberg - SV Mattersburg 2-1(0-0)
Rapid Wien - Wacker Innsbruck 1-0(0-0)

Round 31 [18.05.2019]
Admira Wacker - Wacker Innsbruck 3-2(2-0)
SCR Altach - TSV Hartberg 3-1(1-0)
SV Mattersburg - Rapid Wien 1-0(1-0)

Round 32 [25.05.2019]
Rapid Wien - SCR Altach 1-2(0-0)
TSV Hartberg - FC Admira Wacker 3-1(1-0)
Wacker Innsbruck - SV Mattersburg 4-0(2-0)

Final Standings

1.	SK Rapid Wien	32	13	7	12	48	-	44	32
2.	SV Mattersburg	32	12	7	13	41	-	48	28
3.	SC Rheindorf Altach	32	9	10	13	48	-	44	28
4.	FC Admira Wacker Mödling	32	8	9	15	42	-	62	22
5.	TSV Hartberg	32	10	5	17	48	-	66	22
6.	FC Wacker Innsbruck (*Relegated*)	32	8	5	19	32	-	51	20

Please note: Winners and runners-up were qualified for the Europa League Play-offs semi-finals.

Europa League Play-offs – Semi-Finals [26.05.2019]

SK Rapid Wien - SV Mattersburg 2-0(2-0)

Europa League Play-offs – Final [30.05.-02.06.2019]

SK Rapid Wien - SK Sturm Graz 1-2(0-0) 1-0(1-0)

NATIONAL CUP
ÖFB Cup 2018/2019

First Round [20-30.07.2018]

SV Leobendorf - SV Neuberg	2-0(0-0)	USK Anif - WSG Wattens	0-3(0-2)
SAK Klagenfurt - Völkermarkter ST 1868	1-0(0-0)	ASV Siegendorf - SK Sturm Graz	0-2(0-1)
SVG Reichenau - Kapfenberger SV	3-5(1-3)	FC Kitzbühel - SV Lafnitz	2-4(0-1,2-2)
SK Maria Saal - SKN St. Pölten	0-6(0-1)	SC Team Wiener Linien - FC Wacker Innsbruck	2-3(2-2)
SV Grödig - TSV Hartberg	1-3(0-1,1-1)	VfB Hohenems - Floridsdorfer AC	2-5(1-4)
SC Schwaz - FC Dornbirn	2-0(2-0)	ATSV Stadl-Paura - FC Blau Weiß Linz	1-1 aet; 4-3pen
WSC Hertha - Linzer ASK	0-3(0-2)	USV Scheiblingkirchen-Warth - SC Austria Lustenau	0-4(0-1)
USV Allerheiligen - SV Mattersburg	1-3(1-2)	Union Gurten - Wolfsberger AC	1-2(0-1)
ASK Ebreichsdorf - SK Vorwärts Steyr	1-2(0-1)	Grazer AK - FC Marchfeld Mannsdorf	6-0(3-0)
SC Neusiedl/See 1919 - FC Admira Wacker Mödling	1-0(0-0)	FCM Traiskirchen - SK Austria Klagenfurt	0-2(0-0)
Deutschlandsberger SC - SKU Amstetten	4-2(3-0)	FC Lendorf - ASK-BSC Bruck/Leitha	0-2(0-2)
FC Mauerwerk - SC Wiener Neustadt	0-2(0-1)	FC Pinzgau Saalfelden - SV Straßwalchen	4-0(2-0)
USV Mettersdorf - SV Horn	0-1(0-0)	FV Austria XIII - FK Austria Wien	0-4(0-1)
FC Kufstein - SK Rapid Wien	0-5(0-3)	SC/ESV Parndorf - SCR Altach	0-3(0-2)
Dornbirner SV - SV Ried im Innkreis	0-6(0-2)	ASKÖ Oedt - FC Red Bull Salzburg	0-6(0-2)
Union Vöcklamarkt - FC Alberschwende	4-0(3-0)	FC Stadlau - FC Gleisdorf 09	2-1(0-0,0-0)

Second Round [24-26.09.2018]

SAK Klagenfurt - Floridsdorfer AC	1-5(0-2)	Grazer AK - SK Vorwärts Steyr	0-0 aet; 4-2 pen
SV Leobendorf - SCR Altach	1-2(0-2)	FC Stadlau - Kapfenberger SV	0-4(0-2)
ASK-BSC Bruck/Leitha - SC Austria Lustenau	1-3(0-2)	SV Mattersburg - SK Rapid Wien	1-1 aet; 4-5 pen
Wolfsberger AC - SK Austria Klagenfurt	4-0(3-0)	FC Pinzgau Saalfelden - SKN St. Pölten	0-5(0-2)
Union Vöcklamarkt - SV Ried im Innkreis	0-1(0-1)	ATSV Stadl-Paura - Linzer ASK	0-8(0-3)
Deutschlandsberger SC - SC Wiener Neustadt	3-4(1-2,3-3)	SC Neusiedl/See 1919 - FC Wacker Innsbruck	1-3(1-3)
TSV Hartberg - WSG Wattens	3-0(3-0)	SC Schwaz - FC Red Bull Salzburg	0-6(0-2)
SV Horn - SV Lafnitz	0-2(0-1)	FK Austria Wien - SK Sturm Graz	2-0(0-0)

Third Round [30.10.-01.11.2018]

TSV Hartberg - FC Wacker Innsbruck	4-3(2-1)	SC Austria Lustenau - FC Red Bull Salzburg	0-1(0-0)
FK Austria Wien - Floridsdorfer AC	3-1(2-1)	SV Lafnitz - SKN St. Pölten	2-3(0-1)
Wolfsberger AC - SK Rapid Wien	0-3(0-2)	SV Ried im Innkreis - SC Wiener Neustadt	1-2(1-1)
SCR Altach - Linzer ASK	0-3(0-2)	Grazer AK - Kapfenberger SV	3-0(1-0)

Quarter-Finals [15-17.02.2019]

Grazer AK - FK Austria Wien	2-1(0-1)	SC Wiener Neustadt - FC Red Bull Salzburg	1-2(0-0)
Linzer ASK - SKN St. Pölten	6-0(4-0)	SK Rapid Wien - TSV Hartberg	5-2(1-0)

Semi-Finals [02.04.2019]

Grazer AK - FC Red Bull Salzburg	0-6(0-4)	Linzer ASK - SK Rapid Wien	1-1 aet; 3-4 pen

Final

01.05.2019; Wörthersee Stadion, Klagenfurt; Referee: Manuel Schüttengruber; Attendance: 24,200
FC Red Bull Salzburg - SK Rapid Wien **2-0(1-0)**

Red Bull: Alexander Walke, Patrick Farkas [*sent off 83*], Stefan Lainer, André Ramalho da Silva, Jérôme Onguéné, Zlatko Junuzović (72.Dominik Szoboszlai), Xaver Schlager, Diadié Samassékou, Fredrik Gulbrandsen (77.Patson Daka), Moanes Dabour, Hannes Wolf (67.Takumi Minamino). Trainer: Marco Rose (Germany).

Rapid: Richard Strebinger, Mario Sonnleitner (86.Andrei Virgil Ivan), Maximilian Hofmann, Boli Bolingoli-Mbombo, Mert Müldür, Stefan Schwab, Srđan Grahovac, Thomas Murg, Philipp Schobesberger, Dejan Ljubicic (64.Christoph Knasmüllner), Andrija Pavlović (70.Aliou Badji). Trainer: Dietmar Kühbauer.

Goals: 1-0 Patrick Farkas (37), 2-0 Moanes Dabour (39).

THE CLUBS 2018/2019

Fußballclub Admira Wacker Mödling

Founded: 1905
Stadium: BSFZ-Arena, Maria Enzersdorf – Südstadt (10,600)

Goalkeepers:	DOB	M	(s)	G
Andreas Leitner	25.03.1994	32		
Defenders:	**DOB**	**M**	**(s)**	**G**
Emanuel Aiwu	25.12.2000	16	(3)	3
Sebastian Bauer	07.11.1992	24		
Lukas Malicsek	06.06.1999	8	(3)	
Pascal Petlach	18.01.1999	3	(2)	
Christoph Schösswendter	16.07.1988	8		
Miloš Spasić (SRB)	29.01.1998	15	(2)	1
Fabio Strauss	06.08.1994		(1)	
Bjarne Thoelke (GER)	11.04.1992	16		
Stephan Zwierschitz	17.09.1990	27	(1)	4
Midfielders:	**DOB**	**M**	**(s)**	**G**
Morten Hjulmand (DEN)	25.06.1999	24	(5)	
Marco Kadlec	28.02.2000	1	(5)	
Marcus Maier	18.12.1995	15	(7)	1
Kolja Pusch (GER)	12.02.1993	9	(2)	2
Marco Sahanek	27.01.1990	10	(1)	1
Jonathan Scherzer	22.07.1995	11		
Daniel Toth	10.06.1987	27	(3)	
Wilhelm Vorsager	29.06.1997	26	(4)	2
Forwards:	**DOB**	**M**	**(s)**	**G**
Sinan Bakış (TUR)	22.04.1994	13	(14)	4
Marin Jakoliš (CRO)	26.12.1996	11	(12)	1
Sasa Kalajdzic	07.07.1997	10	(5)	8
Seth Paintsil (GHA)	20.05.1996	5	(6)	2
Patrick Schmidt	22.07.1998	19	(8)	8
Pyry Soiri (FIN)	22.09.1994	10	(2)	2
Dominik Starkl	06.11.1993	12	(6)	1
Trainer:	**DOB**	**M**		
Ernst Baumeister	22.01.1957	12		
Reiner Geyer (GER) [29.10.2018]	20.04.1964	20		

Fußballklub Austria Wien

Founded: 15.03.2011
Stadium: „Ernst Happel" Stadion / "Franz Horr" Stadion, Wien (50,000 / 17,565)

Goalkeepers:	DOB	M	(s)	G
Ivan Lučić	23.03.1995	5		
Patrick Pentz	02.01.1997	27		
Defenders:	**DOB**	**M**	**(s)**	**G**
Alexandar Borković	11.06.1999	4	(2)	1
Cristián Alejandro Cuevas Jara (CHI)	02.04.1995	15	(3)	
Igor Julio dos Santos de Paulo (BRA)	07.02.1998	27		
Florian Klein	17.11.1986	32		2
Michael Madl	21.03.1988	25	(1)	1
Christoph Martschinko	13.02.1994	10		
Christian Schoissengeyr	18.10.1994	20	(3)	1
Midfielders:	**DOB**	**M**	**(s)**	**G**
Vesel Demaku	05.02.2000	7	(8)	
Thomas Ebner	22.02.1992	17	(2)	
Dominik Fitz	16.06.1999		(2)	
Alexander Grünwald	01.05.1989	21	(1)	8
Niels Hahn	24.05.2001		(1)	
James Alexander Jeggo (AUS)	12.02.1992	17	(2)	1
Lucas Henrique Ferreira Venuto (BRA)	14.01.1995	2	(8)	1
Uroš Matić (SRB)	23.05.1990	29	(2)	5
Dominik Prokop	02.06.1997	19	(8)	1
Thomas Salamon	18.01.1989	3	(1)	
Manprit Sarkaria	26.08.1996	1	(6)	
Maximilian Sax	22.11.1992	15	(3)	2
Forwards:	**DOB**	**M**	**(s)**	**G**
Bright Osagie Edomwonyi (NGA)	24.07.1994	17	(7)	5
Ewandro Felipe de Lima Costa (BRA)	15.03.1996	2	(6)	1
Kevin Friesenbichler	06.05.1994	10	(3)	2
Christoph Monschein	22.10.1992	18	(10)	7
Alon Turgeman (ISR)	09.06.1991	8	(10)	6
Sterling Yateke (CTA)	15.09.1999	1	(1)	
Trainer:	**DOB**	**M**		
Thomas Letsch (GER)	26.08.1968	21		
Robert Ibertsberger [11.03.2019]	20.01.1977	11		

Linzer Athletik-Sport-Klub

Founded: 07.08.1908
Stadium: TGW Arena [Waldstadion], Pasching (7,870)

Goalkeepers:	DOB	M	(s)	G
Thomas Gebauer	30.06.1982	1		
Alexander Schlager	01.02.1996	31		
Defenders:	**DOB**	**M**	**(s)**	**G**
Emanuel Pogatetz	16.01.1983	8	(11)	
Christian Ramsebner	26.03.1989	26		2
Reinhold Ranftl	24.01.1992	30		2
Gernot Trauner	25.03.1992	28		4
Maximilian Ullmann	17.06.1996	32		4
Philipp Wiesinger	23.05.1994	28		3
Markus Wostry	19.07.1992	7	(1)	1
Midfielders:	**DOB**	**M**	**(s)**	**G**
Fabian Benko (GER)	05.06.1998	1	(2)	
Doğan Erdoğan (TUR)		1	(2)	
Dominik Frieser	09.09.1993	10	(21)	6
Thomas Goiginger	15.03.1993	30	(1)	6
Stefan Haudum	27.11.1994	2	(3)	1
James Robert Holland (AUS)	15.05.1989	28		3
Florian Jamnig	03.11.1990	2	(13)	1
João Victor Santos Sá (BRA)	27.03.1994	26	(1)	13
Peter Michorl	09.05.1995	30	(1)	3
Oh In-Pyo (KOR)	10.03.1997		(1)	
Forwards:	**DOB**	**M**	**(s)**	**G**
João Klauss de Mello (BRA)	01.03.1997	12	(2)	3
Yusuf Olaitan Otubanjo (NGA)	12.09.1992	11	(8)	2
Samuel Tetteh (GHA)	28.07.1996	8	(13)	4
Trainer:	**DOB**	**M**		
Oliver Glasner	28.08.1974	32		

Sportklub Rapid Wien

Founded: 1899
Stadium: Allianz Stadion, Wien (28,000)

Goalkeepers:	**DOB**	**M**	**(s)**	**G**
Tobias Knoflach	30.12.1993	3		
Richard Strebinger	14.02.1993	29		
Defenders:	**DOB**	**M**	**(s)**	**G**
Stephan Auer	11.01.1991	12	(5)	
Mateo Barać (CRO)	20.07.1994	10	(2)	
Boli Bolingoli-Mbombo (BEL)	01.07.1995	23	(2)	2
Christopher Dibon	02.11.1990	12		2
Maximilian Hofmann	07.08.1993	14		1
Mert Müldür	03.04.1999	17	(6)	
Patrick Obermüller	17.02.1999	1		
Marvin Potzmann	07.12.1993	18	(3)	1
Mario Sonnleitner	08.10.1986	22	(1)	5
Manuel Thurnwald	16.07.1998	3	(3)	
Midfielders:	**DOB**	**M**	**(s)**	**G**
Srđan Grahovac (BIH)	19.09.1992	7	(1)	
Andrei Virgil Ivan (ROU)	04.01.1997	14	(8)	1
Christoph Knasmüllner	30.04.1992	27	(2)	4
Aleksandar Kostić	12.10.1995	1	(4)	
Dejan Ljubicic	08.10.1997	18	(9)	1
Philipp Malicsek	03.06.1997	2	(1)	
Manuel Martic	15.08.1995	11	(4)	
Thomas Murg	14.11.1994	25	(4)	7
Stefan Schwab	27.09.1990	28	(1)	3
Nicholas Wunsch	05.10.2000		(1)	
Forwards:	**DOB**	**M**	**(s)**	**G**
Deni Alar	18.01.1990	12	(8)	4
Kelvin Arase	15.01.1999	1		
Aliou Badji (SEN)	10.10.1997	7	(6)	5
Veton Berisha (NOR)	13.04.1994	7	(10)	3
Jérémy Guillemenot (SUI)	06.01.1998	1	(2)	
Andrija Pavlović (SRB)	16.11.1993	14	(5)	4
Philipp Schobesberger	10.12.1993	13	(4)	2
Trainer:	**DOB**	**M**		
Goran Djuricin	16.10.1974	9		
Dietmar Kühbauer [29.09.2018]	04.04.1971	23		

Football Club Red Bull Salzburg

Founded: 13.09.1933 (*as SV Austria Salzburg*)
Stadium: Red Bull Arena, Wals-Siezenheim (31,895)

Goalkeepers:	**DOB**	**M**	**(s)**	**G**
Cican Stanković	04.11.1992	28		
Alexander Walke (GER)	06.06.1983	4		
Defenders:	**DOB**	**M**	**(s)**	**G**
André Ramalho da Silva (BRA)	16.02.1992	27		1
Patrick Farkas	09.09.1992	1	(2)	
Stefan Lainer	27.08.1992	25		1
Jérôme Onguéné (FRA)	22.12.1997	12	(1)	3
Marin Pongračić (CRO)	11.09.1997	13	(1)	
Darko Todorović (BIH)	05.05.1997	9	(3)	
Andreas Ulmer	30.10.1985	28		
Albert Vallci	02.07.1995	9	(1)	1
Jasper van der Werff (SUI)	09.12.1998	3	(1)	
Midfielders:	**DOB**	**M**	**(s)**	**G**
Antoine Bernède (FRA)	26.05.1999	1	(2)	
Amadou Haïdara (MLI)	31.01.1998	9	(3)	2
Zlatko Junuzović	26.09.1987	18	(3)	4
Christoph Leitgeb	14.04.1985	1	(4)	
Enock Mwepu (ZAM)	01.01.1998	9	(10)	1
Diadié Samassékou (MLI)	11.01.1996	26		1
Xaver Schlager	28.09.1997	24	(2)	5
Dominik Szoboszlai (HUN)	25.10.2000	7	(9)	3
Reinhold Yabo (GER)	10.02.1992	6	(3)	1
Forwards:	**DOB**	**M**	**(s)**	**G**
Moanes Dabour (ISR)	14.05.1992	23	(6)	20
Patson Daka (ZAM)	09.10.1998	9	(6)	3
Fredrik Gulbrandsen (NOR)	10.09.1992	14	(9)	7
Erling Håland (NOR)	21.07.2000	1	(1)	1
Takumi Minamino (JPN)	16.01.1995	19	(8)	6
Smail Prevljak (BIH)	10.05.1995	11	(12)	10
Hannes Wolf	16.04.1999	15	(7)	8
Trainer:	**DOB**	**M**		
Marco Rose (GER)	11.09.1976	32		

Sportclub Rheindorf Altach

Founded: 26.12.1929
Stadium: Stadion Schnabelholz, Altach (8,500)

Goalkeepers:	**DOB**	**M**	**(s)**	**G**
Reuf Duraković	21.03.1994		(1)	
Martin Kobras	19.06.1986	25		
Andreas Lukse	08.11.1987	7		
Defenders:	**DOB**	**M**	**(s)**	**G**
Anderson dos Santos Gomes (BRA)	03.01.1998	6		1
Emir Karic	09.06.1997	21	(4)	
Andreas Lienhart	28.01.1986	18	(1)	
Felix Luckeneder	21.03.1994	14	(2)	1
Philipp Netzer	02.10.1985	12		2
Emanuel Schreiner	02.02.1989	17	(2)	2
Benedikt Zech	03.11.1990	29		1
Jan Zwischenbrugger	16.06.1990	20	(1)	
Midfielders:	**DOB**	**M**	**(s)**	**G**
Kristijan Dobras	09.10.1992	10	(8)	3
Manfred Fischer	06.08.1995	24	(5)	7
Joshua Alexander Gatt (USA)	29.08.1991	9	(6)	1
Christian Gebauer	20.12.1993	28	(3)	4
Samuel Yves Oum Gouet (CMR)	14.12.1997	22	(3)	2
Marco Meilinger	03.08.1991	14	(5)	2
Valentino Müller	19.01.1999	9	(4)	
Louis Clement N'Gwat-Mahop (CMR)	16.09.1987	4	(3)	
Stefan Nutz	15.02.1992	18	(4)	3
Simon Piesinger	13.05.1992	15	(5)	2
Boris Prokopič	29.03.1988	1	(5)	
Forwards:	**DOB**	**M**	**(s)**	**G**
Hannes Aigner	16.03.1981	3	(5)	4
Mërgim Berisha (KVX)	11.05.1998	14		7
Adrian Grbić	04.08.1996	5	(11)	4
Sherko Karim Lateef Gubari (IRQ)	25.05.1996	3	(8)	
Brian Mwila (ZAM)	16.06.1994	4	(3)	2
Trainer:	**DOB**	**M**		
Werner Grabherr	08.09.1985	20		
Wolfgang Luisser [03.03.2019]	31.08.1979	2		
Alexander Anton Aiko Pastoor (NED) [18.03.2019]	26.10.1966	10		

Sportklub Niederösterreich St. Pölten

Founded: 2000
Stadium: NV Arena, Sankt Pölten (8,000)

Goalkeepers:	**DOB**	**M**	**(s)**	**G**
Christoph Riegler	30.03.1992	32		
Defenders:	**DOB**	**M**	**(s)**	**G**
Daniel Drescher	07.10.1989	22	(2)	
Manuel Haas	07.05.1996	23		
Sandro Ingolitsch	18.04.1997	26		
Luan Leite Da Silva (BRA)	31.05.1996	30		2
Luca Meisl	04.03.1999	22		1
Ahmet Muhamedbegovic	30.10.1998		(1)	
Danijel Petrović (SRB)	27.11.1992	8		
Patrick Puchegger	04.05.1995	1		
Midfielders:	**DOB**	**M**	**(s)**	**G**
Michael Ambichl	26.04.1991	14		1
Eldis Bajrami (MKD)	12.12.1992	6	(4)	1
Husein Balić (BIH)	15.02.1996	10	(19)	3
Nikola Despotović	11.01.2001		(1)	
Taxiarchis Fountas (GRE)	04.09.1995	13	(8)	4
Dominik Hofbauer	19.09.1990	4	(9)	
Robert Ljubicic (CRO)	14.07.1999	22	(4)	1
Daniel Luxbacher	13.03.1992	22	(8)	1
Roko Mišlov (CRO)	30.04.1988	26	(3)	
Martin Rasner	18.05.1995	13		
David Sauer	20.02.1998		(1)	
Daniel Schütz	19.06.1991	5	(10)	1
Forwards:	**DOB**	**M**	**(s)**	**G**
René Gartler	21.10.1985	30	(1)	9
Issiaka Ouédraogo (BFA)	19.08.1988	3	(8)	3
Pak Kwang-Ryong (PRK)	27.09.1992	20	(4)	4
Aleksandar Vucenovic	10.10.1997		(6)	
Trainer:	**DOB**	**M**		
Dietmar Kühbauer	04.04.1971	9		
Marcel Ketelaer (GER) [01.10.2018]	03.11.1977	1		
Ranko Popović (SRB) [10.10.2018]	26.06.1967	22		

Sportklub Sturm Graz

Founded: 1909
Stadium: Merkur-Arena, Graz (15,323)

Goalkeepers:	**DOB**	**M**	**(s)**	**G**
Tobias Schützenauer	19.05.1997	1		
Jörg Siebenhandl	18.01.1990	31		
Defenders:	**DOB**	**M**	**(s)**	**G**
Anastasios Avlonitis (GRE)	01.01.1990	19		
Filipe Miguel Neves Ferreira (POR)	27.09.1990	3		
Fabian Koch	24.06.1989	28	(2)	2
Dario Maresić	29.09.1999	28		
Gideon Mensah (GHA)	18.07.1998	12	(1)	
Thomas Schrammel	05.09.1987	10	(5)	
Lukas Spendlhofer	02.06.1993	31		2
Midfielders:	**DOB**	**M**	**(s)**	**G**
Stefan Hierländer	03.02.1991	25	(1)	2
Philipp Huspek	05.02.1991	11	(9)	
Jakob Jantscher	08.01.1989	6	(6)	1
Juan Domínguez Lamas (ESP)	08.01.1990	8	(2)	
Otar Kiteishvili (GEO)	26.03.1996	27	(2)	4
Tobias Koch	06.04.2001		(1)	
Markus Lackner	05.04.1991	13	(1)	1
Michael John Lema	13.09.1999	9	(7)	3
Ivan Ljubić	07.07.1996	11	(2)	
Sandi Lovrič	28.03.1998	15	(5)	1
Raphael Obermair (GER)	01.04.1996	3	(1)	
Peter Žulj	09.06.1993	17		5
Forwards:	**DOB**	**M**	**(s)**	**G**
Emeka Friday Eze (NGA)	26.09.1996	8	(15)	2
Lukas Grozurek	22.12.1991	16	(10)	5
Philipp Hosiner	15.05.1989	7	(7)	3
Arnel Jakupović	29.05.1998	2	(4)	
Markus Pink	24.02.1991	11	(12)	6
Trainer:	**DOB**	**M**		
Heiko Vogel (GER)	21.11.1975	13		
Günther Neukirchner [05.11.2018]	02.12.1971	1		
Roman Mählich [12.11.2018]	17.09.1971	18		

Sportverein Mattersburg

Founded: 1922
Stadium: Pappelstadion, Mattersburg (17,100)

Goalkeepers:	**DOB**	**M**	**(s)**	**G**
Tino Casali	14.11.1995	5		
Markus Kuster	22.02.1994	27		
Defenders:	**DOB**	**M**	**(s)**	**G**
César Ortiz Puentenueva (ESP)	30.01.1989	23		1
Philipp Erhardt	10.09.1993	21	(9)	
Francisco José Sánchez Rodríguez „Fran" (ESP)	08.02.1990	5	(3)	
Florian Hart	11.05.1990	15	(7)	
Alois Höller	15.03.1989	18	(7)	3
Daniel Kerschbaumer	11.06.1989	7	(2)	1
Michael Lercher	04.01.1996	2		
Thorsten Mahrer	22.01.1990	24	(3)	1
Nedeljko Malić (BIH)	15.05.1988	18	(3)	3
David Nemeth	18.03.2001	1		
Lukas Rath	18.01.1992	16	(1)	
Midfielders:	**DOB**	**M**	**(s)**	**G**
Julius Ertlthaler	25.04.1997	8	(9)	
Mario Grgic	10.09.1991		(2)	
Andreas Gruber	29.06.1995	30		6
Christoph Halper	21.05.1998	3	(4)	1
Alejandro Velasco Fariñas „Jano" (ESP)	23.12.1986	31		2
Andreas Kuen	24.03.1995	6	(4)	1
Michael Perlak	26.12.1985	3	(4)	
René Renner	29.11.1993	30		5
Patrick Salomon	10.06.1988	19		1
Forwards:	**DOB**	**M**	**(s)**	**G**
Patrick Bürger	27.06.1987	2	(8)	
Jefté Betancor Sánchez (ESP)	06.07.1993	1	(5)	1
Marko Kvasina	20.12.1996	15	(9)	6
Philipp Prosenik	03.03.1993	1	(8)	
Martin Pušić	24.10.1987	18	(6)	9
Barnabás Varga (HUN)	25.01.1994	3	(2)	
Trainer:	**DOB**	**M**		
Gerald Baumgartner	14.11.1964	4		
Markus Schmidt [21.08.2018]	12.10.1977	1		
Klaus Schmidt [28.08.2018]	21.10.1967	27		

Turn- und Sportverein Hartberg

Founded: 29.04.1946
Stadium: Profertil Arena, Hartberg (4,500)

Goalkeepers:	**DOB**	**M**	**(s)**	**G**
Florian Faist	10.04.1989	3		
Rene Swete	01.06.1990	29		
Defenders:	**DOB**	**M**	**(s)**	**G**
Michael Blauensteiner	11.02.1995	26		1
Michael Huber	14.01.1990	26		1
Tobias Kainz	31.10.1992	16	(7)	1
Siegfried Rasswalder	13.05.1987	26	(2)	1
Thomas Rotter	27.01.1992	13	(4)	2
Florian Sittsam	14.12.1994	14	(6)	1
Midfielders:	**DOB**	**M**	**(s)**	**G**
Reuben Acquah (GHA)	03.11.1996	1		
Mohamed Camara (MLI)	06.01.2000	5	(2)	
David Cancola	23.10.1996	8	(3)	2
Hamacire Youba Diarra (MLI)	24.03.1998	10		
Florian Flecker	29.10.1995	29	(3)	7
Jürgen Heil	04.04.1997	6	(2)	
Christian Ilić (CRO)	22.07.1996	6	(11)	2
Ivan Ljubić	07.07.1996	18		1
Philipp Siegl	16.12.1993	25		1
Peter Tschernegg	23.07.1992	5		
Forwards:	**DOB**	**M**	**(s)**	**G**
Marcel Holzer	06.10.1998		(5)	
Krešimir Kovačević (CRO)	07.08.1994	2	(5)	3
Christoph Kröpfl	04.05.1990	12	(13)	2
Rajko Rep (SVN)	20.06.1990	30		8
Zakaria Sanogo (BFA)	11.12.1996	16	(11)	4
Fabian Schubert	29.08.1994	3	(9)	
Meris Skenderović (GER)	28.03.1998	1	(4)	
Dario Tadić	11.05.1990	22	(6)	7
Trainer:	**DOB**	**M**		
Markus Schopp	22.02.1974	32		

Fußballclub Wacker Innsbruck

Founded: 21.06.2002
Stadium: Tivoli-Neu Stadion, Innsbruck (16,000)

Goalkeepers:	**DOB**	**M**	**(s)**	**G**
Hidajet Hankič	29.06.1994	2	(1)	
Christopher Knett	01.08.1990	30		
Defenders:	**DOB**	**M**	**(s)**	**G**
Dominik Baumgartner	20.07.1996	8	(4)	2
Florian Buchacher	28.09.1987	2	(3)	
Johannes Handl	07.05.1996	1		
Lukas Hupfauf	11.09.1996	15		
Christian Klem	21.04.1991	14		
Matthias Maak	12.05.1992	29	1	1
Manuel Maranda	09.07.1997	16		
Stefan Meusburger	28.10.1993	16	(7)	1
Stefan Perić	13.02.1997	7		
Michael Schimpelsberger	12.02.1991	17	(1)	
Albert Vallci	02.07.1995	16		
Midfielders:	**DOB**	**M**	**(s)**	**G**
Abdoul Conté (GUI)	25.08.1999	1		
Cheikhou Dieng (SEN)	23.11.1993	24	(2)	4
İlkay Durmuş (GER)	01.05.1994	11	(7)	1
Christoph Freitag	21.01.1990	10	(8)	1
Bryan Henning (GER)	16.03.1995	24	(3)	
Sascha Horvath	22.08.1996	12	(2)	
Roman Kerschbaum	19.07.1994	21		
Stefan Rakowitz	03.04.1990	7	(8)	1
Florian Rieder	16.05.1996		(4)	
Murat Satin	30.08.1996	9	(4)	1
Matthäus Taferner	30.01.2001	7		1
Forwards:	**DOB**	**M**	**(s)**	**G**
Zlatko Dedič (SVN)	05.10.1984	25	(3)	9
Patrik Eler (SVN)	13.06.1991	5	(8)	
Daniele Gabriele (GER)	16.12.1994	6	(11)	4
Alexander Gründler	24.07.1993	3	(4)	2
Martin Harrer	19.05.1992	15	(5)	4
Muhammed Kiprit (GER)	09.07.1999	2	(3)	
Trainer:	**DOB**	**M**		
Karl Daxbacher	15.04.1953	20		
Thomas Grumser [05.03.2019]	06.11.1979	12		

Wolfsberger Athletik Club

Founded: 1931
Stadium: Lavanttal-Arena, Wolfsberg (7,300)

Goalkeepers:	**DOB**	**M**	**(s)**	**G**
Christian Dobnik	10.07.1986	1	(1)	
Alexander Kofler	06.11.1986	30		
Marko Soldo	13.06.1996	1		
Defenders:	**DOB**	**M**	**(s)**	**G**
Stefan Gölles	04.10.1991	1	(3)	1
Manfred Gollner	22.12.1990	19	(3)	1
Ahogrenashinme Kigbu (ENG)	05.02.1999		(4)	
Michael Novak	30.12.1990	32		1
Nemanja Rnić (SRB)	30.09.1984	16	(4)	1
Lukas Schmitz (GER)	13.10.1988	30		2
Michael Sollbauer	15.05.1990	30		1
Midfielders:	**DOB**	**M**	**(s)**	**G**
Mario Leitgeb	30.06.1988	29	(1)	6
Michael Liendl	25.10.1985	32		11
Gerald Nutz	25.01.1994	2	(6)	
Marcel Ritzmaier	22.04.1993	29		1
Marc Andre Schmerböck	01.04.1994	16	(1)	6
Romano Schmid	27.01.2000	4	(8)	1
Lukas Schöfl	11.02.2001		(1)	
Sven Sprangler	27.03.1995	10	(9)	
Joshua Steiger	06.04.2001		(4)	
Christopher Wernitznig	24.02.1990	28	(3)	2
Forwards:	**DOB**	**M**	**(s)**	**G**
Kevin Friesenbichler	06.05.1994	11	(1)	2
Bernd Gschweidl	08.09.1995	3	(12)	
Amar Hodzic	12.07.1999		(4)	
Saša Jovanović (SRB)	30.08.1993	1	(16)	1
Sékou Koïta (MLI)	28.11.1999	13	(1)	5
Dever Akeem Orgill (JAM)	08.03.1990	14	(2)	4
Trainer:	**DOB**	**M**		
Christian Ilzer	21.10.1977	32		

SECOND LEVEL
Erste Liga 2018/2019

1.	WSG Wattens (*Promoted*)	30	19	8	3	59	-	26	65
2.	SV Ried im Innkreis	30	18	9	3	61	-	21	63
3.	SC Austria Lustenau	30	14	8	8	55	-	34	50
4.	Kapfenberger SV	30	13	7	10	44	-	40	46
5.	FC Blau-Weiß Linz	30	14	2	14	46	-	48	44
6.	FC Juniors OÖ Pasching	30	13	3	14	52	-	55	42
7.	SK Austria Klagenfurt	30	9	14	7	43	-	35	41
8.	Floridsdorfer AC Wien	30	11	8	11	35	-	41	41
9.	SKU Amstetten	30	10	6	14	45	-	43	36
10.	FC Liefering	30	10	5	15	50	-	54	35
11.	FK Austria Wien II	30	9	7	14	46	-	62	34
12.	SV Lafnitz	30	8	9	13	36	-	42	33
13.	SV Horn	30	6	7	17	33	-	62	25
14.	SK Vorwärts Steyr	30	5	6	19	32	-	68	21
15.	SC Wiener Neustadt (*Relegated*)	30	12	8	10	39	-	41	44
16.	FC Wacker Innsbruck II (*Relegated*)	30	10	11	9	40	-	44	41

NATIONAL TEAM

INTERNATIONAL MATCHES
(16.07.2018 – 15.07.2019)

06.09.2018	Wien	Austria - Sweden	2-0(1-0)	(F)
11.09.2018	Zenica	Bosnia and Herzegovina - Austria	1-0(0-0)	(UNL)
12.10.2018	Wien	Austria - Northern Ireland	1-0(0-0)	(UNL)
16.10.2018	Herning	Denmark - Austria	2-0(1-0)	(F)
15.11.2018	Wien	Austria - Bosnia and Herzegovina	0-0	(UNL)
18.11.2018	Belfast	Northern Ireland - Austria	1-2(0-0)	(UNL)
21.03.2019	Wien	Austria - Poland	0-1(0-0)	(ECQ)
24.03.2019	Haifa	Israel - Austria	4-2(2-1)	(ECQ)
07.06.2019	Klagenfurt am Wörthersee	Austria - Slovenia	1-0(0-0)	(ECQ)
10.06.2019	Skopje	North Macedonia - Austria	1-4(1-1)	(ECQ)

06.09.2018 AUSTRIA - SWEDEN 2-0(1-0) Friendly International
Generali Arena, Wien; Referee: Paweł Gil (Poland); Attendance: 11,000
AUT: Heinz Lindner, Sebastian Prödl (46.Aleksandar Dragović), David Olatukunbo Alaba (Cap) (65.Andreas Ulmer), Stefan Lainer, Martin Hinteregger, Stefan Ilsanker, Peter Žulj, Florian Grillitsch (81.Xaver Schlager), Alessandro Schöpf (59.Valentino Lando Lazaro), Marko Arnautovic (65.Marcel Sabitzer), Guido Burgstaller (59.Michael Gregoritsch). Trainer: Franco Foda (Germany).
Goals: Filip Helander (11 own goal), David Olatukunbo Alaba (64).

11.09.2018 BOSNIA AND HERZEGOVINA - AUSTRIA 1-0(0-0) UEFA Nations League B, Group 3
Stadion Bilino Polje, Zenica; Referee: Ruddy Buquet (France); Attendance: 9,100
AUT: Heinz Lindner, Sebastian Prödl, David Olatukunbo Alaba, Stefan Lainer, Martin Hinteregger, Stefan Ilsanker (86.Louis Schaub), Michael Gregoritsch (72.Marcel Sabitzer), Peter Žulj, Florian Grillitsch (81.Guido Burgstaller), Valentino Lando Lazaro, Marko Arnautovic (Cap). Trainer: Franco Foda (Germany).

12.10.2018 AUSTRIA - NORTHERN IRELAND 1-0(0-0) UEFA Nations League B, Group 3
"Ernst Happel" Stadion, Wien; Referee: Referee: Georgi Kabakov (Bulgaria); Attendance: 22,300
AUT: Heinz Lindner, Andreas Ulmer, Sebastian Prödl, Stefan Lainer, Martin Hinteregger, Stefan Ilsanker, Marcel Sabitzer (75.Alessandro Schöpf), Peter Žulj, Valentino Lando Lazaro (90+1.Aleksandar Dragović), Guido Burgstaller (83.Florian Kainz), Marko Arnautovic (Cap). Trainer: Franco Foda (Germany).
Goal: Marko Arnautovic (71).

16.10.2018 DENMARK - AUSTRIA 2-0(1-0) Friendly International
MCH Arena, Herning; Referee: Ola Hobber Nilsen (Norway); Attendance: 7,386
AUT: Richard Strebinger, Andreas Ulmer, Sebastian Prödl (Cap) (71.Marc Janko), Aleksandar Dragović, Martin Hinteregger (46.Kevin Wimmer), Marcel Sabitzer (46.Florian Kainz), Louis Schaub (78.Gernot Trauner), Alessandro Schöpf (71.Stefan Hierländer), Valentino Lando Lazaro, Xaver Schlager (37.Stefan Ilsanker), Guido Burgstaller. Trainer: Franco Foda (Germany).

15.11.2018 AUSTRIA - BOSNIA AND HERZEGOVINA 0-0 UEFA Nations League B, Group 3
"Ernst Happel" Stadion, Wien; Referee: Andrew Dallas (Scotland); Attendance: 37,200
AUT: Heinz Lindner, Aleksandar Dragović, David Olatukunbo Alaba, Stefan Lainer, Martin Hinteregger, Julian Baumgartlinger (Cap), Florian Kainz (46.Xaver Schlager), Peter Žulj (82.Marc Janko), Alessandro Schöpf (67.Michael Gregoritsch), Valentino Lando Lazaro, Marko Arnautovic. Trainer: Franco Foda (Germany).

18.11.2018 NORTHERN IRELAND - AUSTRIA 1-2(0-0) UEFA Nations League B, Group 3
Windsor Park, Belfast; Referee: Jonathan Lardot (Belgium); Attendance: 17,895
AUT: Heinz Lindner, Andreas Ulmer, Aleksandar Dragović, David Olatukunbo Alaba, Stefan Lainer, Martin Hinteregger, Julian Baumgartlinger (Cap), Stefan Ilsanker (46.Peter Žulj), Michael Gregoritsch (71.Marko Arnautovic), Valentino Lando Lazaro, Xaver Schlager. Trainer: Franco Foda (Germany).
Goals: Xaver Schlager (49), Valentino Lando Lazaro (90+3).

21.03.2019 AUSTRIA - POLAND 0-1(0-0) 16th EC. Qualifiers
"Ernst Happel" Stadion, Wien; Referee: Anastasios Sidiropoulos (Greece); Attendance: 40,400
AUT: Heinz Lindner, Aleksandar Dragović, David Olatukunbo Alaba, Stefan Lainer, Martin Hinteregger, Maximilian Wöber, Julian Baumgartlinger (Cap), Marcel Sabitzer, Florian Grillitsch (84.Karim Onisiwo), Valentino Lando Lazaro (81.Marc Janko), Marko Arnautovic. Trainer: Franco Foda (Germany).

24.03.2019 ISRAEL - AUSTRIA 4-2(2-1) 16th EC. Qualifiers

"Sammy Ofer" Stadium, Haifa; Referee: Yevhen Aranovskyi (Ukraine); Attendance: 16,180

AUT: Heinz Lindner, Andreas Ulmer, Aleksandar Dragović, Martin Hinteregger, Maximilian Wöber (60.Marc Janko), Julian Baumgartlinger (Cap), Marcel Sabitzer, Peter Žulj (85.Florian Kainz), Valentino Lando Lazaro, Xaver Schlager (61.Karim Onisiwo), Marko Arnautovic. Trainer: Franco Foda (Germany).

Goals: Marko Arnautovic (8, 75).

07.06.2019 AUSTRIA - SLOVENIA 1-0(0-0) 16th EC. Qualifiers

Wörthersee Stadion, Klagenfurt; Referee: Aleksei Kulbakov (Belarus); Attendance: 19,200

AUT: Heinz Lindner, Andreas Ulmer, Aleksandar Dragović, David Olatukunbo Alaba (Cap) (90.Florian Kainz), Stefan Lainer, Martin Hinteregger, Marcel Sabitzer (71.Guido Burgstaller), Valentino Lando Lazaro, Konrad Laimer (82.Stefan Ilsanker), Xaver Schlager, Marko Arnautovic. Trainer: Franco Foda (Germany).

Goal: Guido Burgstaller (74).

10.06.2019 NORTH MACEDONIA - AUSTRIA 1-4(1-1) 16th EC. Qualifiers

"Toše Proeski" Arena, Skopje; Referee: Aleksei Eskov (Russia); Attendance: 10,501

AUT: Heinz Lindner, Andreas Ulmer, Aleksandar Dragović (46.Stefan Posch), Stefan Lainer, Martin Hinteregger, Stefan Ilsanker, Marcel Sabitzer (90+2.Louis Schaub), Valentino Lando Lazaro, Konrad Laimer, Xaver Schlager, Marko Arnautovic (Cap) (88.Guido Burgstaller). Trainer: Franco Foda (Germany).

Goals: Valentino Lando Lazaro (39), Marko Arnautovic (62 penalty, 82), Egzon Bejtulai (86 own goal).

NATIONAL TEAM PLAYERS
(16.07.2018 – 15.07.2019)

Name	DOB	Caps	Goals	2018/2019:	*Club*
Goalkeepers					
Heinz LINDNER	17.07.1990	**28**	**0**	2018/2019:	*Grasshopper Club Zürich (SUI)*
Richard STREBINGER	14.02.1993	**1**	**0**	2018/2019:	*SK Rapid Wien*
Defenders					
Aleksandar DRAGOVIĆ	06.03.1991	**74**	**1**	2018/2019:	*TSV Bayer 04 Leverkusen (GER)*
Martin HINTEREGGER	07.09.1992	**41**	**3**	2018: 31.01.2019->	*FC Augsburg (GER)* *Eintracht Frankfurt (GER)*
Stefan LAINER	27.08.1992	**15**	**0**	2018/2019:	*FC Red Bull Salzburg*
Stefan POSCH	14.05.1997	**1**	**0**	2019:	*TSG 1899 Hoffenheim (GER)*
Sebastian PRÖDL	21.06.1987	**73**	**4**	2018/2019:	*Watford FC (ENG)*
Gernot TRAUNER	25.03.1992	**1**	**0**	2018/2019:	*Linzer ASK*
Andreas ULMER	30.10.1985	**12**	**0**	2018/2019:	*FC Red Bull Salzburg*
Kevin WIMMER	15.11.1992	**9**	**0**	2018:	*SV Hannover 96 (GER)*
Maximilian WÖBER	04.02.1998	**5**	**0**	2019:	*Sevilla FC (ESP)*
Midfielders					
David Olatukunbo ALABA	24.06.1992	**69**	**13**	2018/2019:	*FC Bayern München (GER)*
Julian BAUMGARTLINGER	02.01.1988	**68**	**1**	2018/2019:	*TSV Bayer 04 Leverkusen (GER)*
Florian GRILLITSCH	07.08.1995	**14**	**1**	2018/2019:	*TSG 1899 Hoffenheim (GER)*
Stefan HIERLÄNDER	03.02.1991	**3**	**0**	2018:	*SK Sturm Graz*
Stefan ILSANKER	18.05.1989	**36**	**0**	2018/2019:	*RasenBallsport Leipzig (GER)*
Florian KAINZ	24.10.1992	**15**	**0**	2018: 18.01.2019->	*SV Werder Bremen (GER)* *1.FC Köln (GER)*
Konrad LAIMER	27.05.1997	**2**	**0**	2018/2019:	*RasenBallsport Leipzig (GER)*
Valentino Lando LAZARO	24.03.1996	**23**	**2**	2018/2019:	*Hertha BSC Berlin (GER)*
Louis SCHAUB	29.12.1994	**12**	**5**	2018/2019:	*1.FC Köln (GER)*
Xaver SCHLAGER	28.09.1997	**11**	**1**	2018/2019:	*FC Red Bull Salzburg*
Alessandro SCHÖPF	07.02.1994	**22**	**4**	2018:	*FC Schalke 04 Gelsenkirchen (GER)*
Peter ŽULJ	09.06.1993	**10**	**0**	2018: 16.01.2019->	*SK Sturm Graz* *RSC Anderlecht Bruxelles (BEL)*
Forwards					
Marko ARNAUTOVIĆ	19.04.1989	**81**	**24**	2018/2019:	*West Ham United FC London (ENG)*
Guido BURGSTALLER	29.04.1989	**25**	**2**	2018/2019:	*FC Schalke 04 Gelsenkirchen*
Michael GREGORITSCH	18.04.1994	**11**	**1**	2018:	*FC Augsburg (GER)*
Marc JANKO	25.06.1983	**70**	**27**	2018/2019:	*FC Lugano (SUI)*
Karim ONISIWO	17.03.1992	**4**	**0**	2019:	*1.FSV Mainz 05 (GER)*
Marcel SABITZER	17.03.1994	**37**	**5**	2018/2019:	*RasenBallsport Leipzig (GER)*

National team coach

Franco FODA (Germany) [from 14.11.2017]	23.04.1966	16 M; 10 W; 1 D; 5 L; 24-15

AZERBAIJAN

The Country:
Republic of Azerbaijan (Azərbaycan Respublikası)
Capital: Bakı
Surface: 86,600 km²
Inhabitants: 10,000,000 [2019]
Time: UTC+4

The FA:
Azərbaycan Futbol Federasiyaları Assosiasiyası
2208 Nobel prospekti 1025, Bakı
Tel: +994 12 404 27 77
Foundation date: 1992
Member of FIFA since: 1994
Member of UEFA since: 1994
Website: www.affa.az

NATIONAL TEAM RECORDS

First international match:	17.09.1992, Gurdzhaani:	Georgia – Azerbaijan 6-3
Most international caps:	Rəşad Ferhad Sadıqov	- 111 caps (2001-2017)
Most international goals:	Qurban Osman Qurbanov	- 12 goals / 65 caps (1992-2005)

UEFA EUROPEAN CHAMPIONSHIP

1960	-
1964	-
1968	-
1972	-
1976	-
1980	-
1984	-
1988	-
1992	-
1996	Qualifiers
2000	Qualifiers
2004	Qualifiers
2008	Qualifiers
2012	Qualifiers
2016	Qualifiers

FIFA WORLD CUP

1930	-
1934	-
1938	-
1950	-
1954	-
1958	-
1962	-
1966	-
1970	-
1974	-
1978	-
1982	-
1986	-
1990	-
1994	*Did not enter*
1998	Qualifiers
2002	Qualifiers
2006	Qualifiers
2010	Qualifiers
2014	Qualifiers
2018	Qualifiers

UEFA NATIONS LEAGUE

2018/2019 – League D (promoted to League C)

OLYMPIC FOOTBALL TOURNAMENTS 1908-2016

1908	-	**1948**	-	**1972**	-	**1996**	Qualifiers
1912	-	**1952**	-	**1976**	-	**2000**	Qualifiers
1920	-	**1956**	-	**1980**	-	**2004**	Qualifiers
1924	-	**1960**	-	**1984**	-	**2008**	Qualifiers
1928	-	**1964**	-	**1988**	-	**2012**	Qualifiers
1936	-	**1968**	-	**1992**	-	**2016**	Qualifiers

FIFA CONFEDERATIONS CUP 1992-2017

None

AZERBAIJAN CLUB HONOURS IN EUROPEAN CLUB COMPETITIONS:

European Champion Clubs' Cup (1956-1992) / UEFA Champions League (1993-2019)

None

Fairs Cup (1858-1971) / UEFA Cup (1972-2009) / UEFA Europa League (2010-2019)

None

UEFA Super Cup (1972-2019)

None

European Cup Winners' Cup 1961-1999*

None

**defunct competition*

NATIONAL COMPETITIONS
TABLE OF HONOURS

AZERBAIJAN SSR (SOVIET ERA) CHAMPIONS

1928	Progress-2 Baku
1929–33	*Not known*
1934	Profsoyuz Baku
1935	Stroitel Yuga Baku
1936	Stroitel Yuga Baku
1937	Lokomotiv Baku
1938	Lokomotiv Baku
1939	Lokomotiv Baku
1940	Lokomotiv Baku
1941–43	*Not known*
1944	Dinamo Baku
1945	*No competition*
1946	Lokomotiv Baku
1947	Trudovye Rezervy Baku
1948	KKF Baku
1949	KKF Baku
1950	Iskra Baku
1951	Ordjonikidzeneft Baku
1952	Ordjonikidzeneft Baku
1953	Ordjonikidzeneft Baku
1954	Zavod S.M. Budennogo Baku
1955	Ordjonikidzeneft Baku
1956	NPU Ordgonikidzeneft Baku
1957	NPU Ordjonikidzeneft Baku
1958	NPU Ordjonikidzeneft Baku
1959	Baku Teams (Spartakiada)
1960	SKA Baku
1961	Spartak Guba
1962	SKA Baku
1963	Araz Baku
1964	Polad Sumgait
1965	Vostok Baku
1966	Vostok Baku
1967	Araz Baku
1968	SKA Baku
1969	Araz Baku
1970	SKA Baku
1971	Khimik Salyany
1972	Surahanets Baku
1973	Araz Baku
1974	Araz Baku
1975	Araz Baku
1976	Araz Baku
1977	Karabakh Khankendi
1978	SKIF Baku
1979	SKA Baku
1980	Energetik Ali-Bayramly
1981	Gandjlik Baku
1982	Tokhudju Baku
1983	Termist Baku
1984	Termist Baku
1985	Khazar Sumgayit
1986	Göyəzən
1987	Araz Naxçıvan
1988	Qarabağ Ağdam
1989	Stroitel Sabirabad
1990	Qarabağ Ağdam
1991	Khazar Sumgayit

	CHAMPIONS	CUP WINNERS	BEST GOALSCORERS	
1992	Neftçi PFK Bakı	İnşaatçı Bakı FK	Nazim Aliyev (FK Xəzər Lənkəran Sumqayit)	39
1993	Qarabağ FK Ağdam	Qarabağ FK Ağdam	Samir Alakbarov (Neftçi PFK Bakı)	16
1993/1994	FK Turan Tovuz	Kəpəz FK Gəncə	Musa Gurbanov (FK Turan Tovuz)	35
1994/1995	Kəpəz FK Gəncə	Neftçi PFK Bakı	Nazim Aliyev (Neftçi PFK Bakı)	26
1995/1996	Neftçi PFK Bakı	Neftçi PFK Bakı	Fazil Parvarov (Kəpəz FK Gəncə) Rovshan Ahmadov (Kəpəz FK Gəncə)	23
1996/1997	Neftçi PFK Bakı	Kəpəz FK Gəncə	Gurban Gurbanov (Neftçi PFK Bakı)	34
1997/1998	Kəpəz FK Gəncə	Kəpəz FK Gəncə	Nazim Aliyev (Bakı FK)	23
1998/1999	Kəpəz FK Gəncə	Neftçi PFK Bakı	Alay Bahramov (FK Viləş Masallı)	24
1999/2000	FK Şəmkir	Kəpəz FK Gəncə	Badri Kvaratskhelia (FK Şəmkir)	16
2000/2001	FK Şəmkir	Şəfa Bakı FK	Pasha Aliyev (Bakılı PFK Bakı)	12
2001/2002	*Championship abandoned*	Neftçi PFK Bakı	-	
2002/2003	*No competition*	*No competition*	-	
2003/2004	Neftçi PFK Bakı	Neftçi PFK Bakı	Samir Musayev (Qarabağ FK Ağdam)	20
2004/2005	Neftçi PFK Bakı	Bakı FK	Zaur Ramazanov (Karvan FK)	21
2005/2006	Bakı FK	Qarabağ FK Bakı	Yacouba Bamba (CIV, Karvan FK)	16
2006/2007	Xəzər Lənkəran FK	Xəzər Lənkəran FK	Zaur Ramazanov (Xəzər Lənkəran FK)	20
2007/2008	İnter PİK Bakı	Xəzər Lənkəran FK	Khagani Mammadov (İnter PİK Bakı)	19
2008/2009	Bakı FK	Qarabağ FK Bakı	Walter Guglielmone Gómez (URU, İnter PİK Bakı)	17
2009/2010	İnter PİK Bakı	Bakı FK	Farid Guliyev (Standard FK Sumqayit)	16
2010/2011	Neftçi PFK Bakı	Xəzər Lənkəran FK	Georgi Adamia (GEO, Qarabağ FK Bakı)	18
2011/2012	Neftçi PFK Bakı	Bakı FK	Bahodir Nasimov (UZB, Neftçi PFK Bakı)	16
2012/2013	Neftçi PFK Bakı	Neftçi PFK Bakı	Nicolás Sebastián Canales Calas (CHI, Neftçi PFK Bakı)	26
2013/2014	Qarabağ FK Bakı	Neftçi PFK Bakı	Reynaldo dos Santos Silva (Qarabağ FK Bakı)	22
2014/2015	Qarabağ FK Bakı	Qarabağ FK Bakı	Nurlan Novruzov (Bakı FK)	15
2015/2016	Qarabağ FK Bakı	Qarabağ FK Bakı	Daniel Quintana Sosa "Dani Quintana" (ESP, Qarabağ FK Bakı)	15
2016/2017	Qarabağ FK Bakı	Qarabağ FK Bakı	Filip Ozobić (CRO, Qəbələ FK) Rauf Aliyev (İnter PİK Bakı)	11
2017/2018	Qarabağ FK Bakı	Keşlə FK Bakı	Bagaliy Dabo (FRA, Qəbələ FK)	13
2018/2019	Qarabağ FK Bakı	Qəbələ FK	Mahir Anar Mədətov (Qarabağ FK Bakı)	16

Please note: Qarabağ FK moved 1993 from Ağdam to Bakı.

NATIONAL CHAMPIONSHIP

Azerbaijan Premier League – Azərbaycan Premyer Liqası 2018/2019
(11.08.2018 – 11.05.2019)

Results

Round 1 [11-12.08.2018]
Sumqayıt FK - Neftçi PFK Bakı 0-2(0-1)
Qəbələ FK - Səbail FK Bakı 3-0(1-0)
Keşlə FK Bakı - Sabah FC Bakı 0-1(0-1)
Qarabağ FK - Zirə FK Bakı 3-2(1-0) [26.09.]

Round 2 [18-19.08.2018]
Səbail FK Bakı - Qarabağ FK 0-2(0-1)
Zirə FK Bakı - Keşlə FK Bakı 2-2(2-0)
Neftçi PFK Bakı - Qəbələ FK 2-1(1-0)
Sabah FC Bakı - Sumqayıt FK 1-4(1-3)

Round 3 [25-26.08.2018]
Qəbələ FK - Sumqayıt FK 1-1(1-0)
Zirə FK Bakı - Sabah FC Bakı 0-2(0-2)
Keşlə FK Bakı - Səbail FK Bakı 1-2(0-1)
Qarabağ FK - Neftçi PFK Bakı 1-1(0-1)

Round 4 [14-16.09.2018]
Sumqayıt FK - Qarabağ FK 0-1(0-1)
Səbail FK Bakı - Zirə FK Bakı 3-0(awarded)
Sabah FC Bakı - Qəbələ FK 1-0(1-0)
Neftçi PFK Bakı - Keşlə FK Bakı 2-0(0-0)

Round 5 [22-23.09.2018]
Səbail FK Bakı - Sabah FC Bakı 0-0
Zirə FK Bakı - Neftçi PFK Bakı 1-2(1-1)
Keşlə FK Bakı - Sumqayıt FK 1-2(1-0)
Qarabağ FK - Qəbələ FK 4-1(2-0)

Round 6 [29-30.09.2018]
Neftçi PFK Bakı - Səbail FK Bakı 4-0(3-0)
Sabah FC Bakı - Qarabağ FK 0-2(0-0)
Qəbələ FK - Keşlə FK Bakı 1-1(0-1)
Sumqayıt FK - Zirə FK Bakı 1-0(1-0)

Round 7 [05.10.2018]
Zirə FK Bakı - Qəbələ FK 1-0(0-0)
Səbail FK Bakı - Sumqayıt FK 2-0(2-0)
Neftçi PFK Bakı - Sabah FC Bakı 2-0(1-0)
Keşlə FK Bakı - Qarabağ FK 1-1(0-0) [31.10.]

Round 8 [20-21.10.2018]
Qəbələ FK - Neftçi PFK Bakı 3-1(1-0)
Qarabağ FK - Səbail FK Bakı 0-3(awarded)
Sumqayıt FK - Sabah FC Bakı 0-1(0-1)
Keşlə FK Bakı - Zirə FK Bakı 1-0(1-0)

Round 9 [27-28.10.2018]
Sabah FC Bakı - Zirə FK Bakı 2-1(1-0)
Sumqayıt FK - Qəbələ FK 2-2(2-1)
Səbail FK Bakı - Keşlə FK Bakı 2-1(2-0)
Neftçi PFK Bakı - Qarabağ FK 3-1(2-0)

Round 10 [03-04.11.2018]
Keşlə FK Bakı - Neftçi PFK Bakı 0-1(0-1)
Qarabağ FK - Sumqayıt FK 2-0(1-0)
Qəbələ FK - Sabah FC Bakı 2-1(2-0)
Zirə FK Bakı - Səbail FK Bakı 0-0

Round 11 [10-11.11.2018]
Sabah FC Bakı - Səbail FK Bakı 0-4(0-2)
Neftçi PFK Bakı - Zirə FK Bakı 2-2(1-0)
Qəbələ FK - Qarabağ FK 1-3(1-0)
Sumqayıt FK - Keşlə FK Bakı 1-4(0-0)

Round 12 [24-25.11.2018]
Keşlə FK Bakı - Qəbələ FK 1-2(1-2)
Qarabağ FK - Sabah FC Bakı 1-1(1-1)
Səbail FK Bakı - Neftçi PFK Bakı 0-2(0-1)
Zirə FK Bakı - Sumqayıt FK 3-1(1-1)

Round 13 [01-03.12.2018]
Sabah FC Bakı - Neftçi PFK Bakı 1-2(0-2)
Sumqayıt FK - Səbail FK Bakı 1-0(0-0)
Qəbələ FK - Zirə FK Bakı 0-0
Qarabağ FK - Keşlə FK Bakı 5-1(1-1)

Round 14 [09.12.2018]
Sabah FC Bakı - Keşlə FK Bakı 1-2(0-1)
Zirə FK Bakı - Qarabağ FK 0-6(0-3)
Səbail FK Bakı - Qəbələ FK 0-0
Neftçi PFK Bakı - Sumqayıt FK 0-0

Round 15 [02-03.02.2019]
Zirə FK Bakı - Sabah FC Bakı 0-2(0-0)
Keşlə FK Bakı - Səbail FK Bakı 0-3(0-1)
Qəbələ FK - Sumqayıt FK 1-0(0-0)
Qarabağ FK - Neftçi PFK Bakı 1-1(1-1)

Round 16 [09-10.02.2019]
Sabah FC Bakı - Qəbələ FK 0-1(0-1)
Sumqayıt FK - Qarabağ FK 0-2(0-1)
Neftçi PFK Bakı - Keşlə FK Bakı 2-0(1-0)
Səbail FK Bakı - Zirə FK Bakı 0-2(0-1)

Round 17 [16-17.02.2019]
Keşlə FK Bakı - Sumqayıt FK 2-1(1-0)
Zirə FK Bakı - Neftçi PFK Bakı 0-0
Səbail FK Bakı - Sabah FC Bakı 1-0(0-0)
Qarabağ FK - Qəbələ FK 2-1(2-1)

Round 18 [23-24.02.2019]
Qəbələ FK - Keşlə FK Bakı 0-0
Sabah FC Bakı - Qarabağ FK 1-1(0-1)
Neftçi PFK Bakı - Səbail FK Bakı 1-2(0-2)
Sumqayıt FK - Zirə FK Bakı 0-1(0-1)

Round 19 [02-03.03.2019]
Səbail FK Bakı - Sumqayıt FK 0-0
Neftçi PFK Bakı - Sabah FC Bakı 3-0(2-0)
Zirə FK Bakı - Qəbələ FK 1-1(0-0)
Keşlə FK Bakı - Qarabağ FK 0-1(0-1)

Round 20 [09-10.03.2019]
Keşlə FK Bakı - Sabah FC Bakı 3-0(1-0)
Qarabağ FK - Zirə FK Bakı 0-0
Qəbələ FK - Səbail FK Bakı 2-1(0-0)
Sumqayıt FK - Neftçi PFK Bakı 1-2(1-0)

Round 21 [15.03.2019]
Sabah FC Bakı - Sumqayıt FK 1-1(0-1)
Zirə FK Bakı - Keşlə FK Bakı 2-0(0-0)
Səbail FK Bakı - Qarabağ FK 1-2(1-1)
Neftçi PFK Bakı - Qəbələ FK 1-1(0-0)

Round 22 [30.03.-01.04.2019]
Zirə FK Bakı - Səbail FK Bakı 1-2(0-1)
Keşlə FK Bakı - Neftçi PFK Bakı 0-1(0-0)
Qəbələ FK - Sabah FC Bakı 0-0
Sumqayıt FK - Qarabağ FK 0-6(0-3)

Round 23 [06-07.04.2019]
Sumqayıt FK - Keşlə FK Bakı 2-1(1-1)
Neftçi PFK Bakı - Zirə FK Bakı 4-2(2-0)
Qəbələ FK - Qarabağ FK 1-2(1-1)
Sabah FC Bakı - Səbail FK Bakı 3-1(1-1)

Round 24 [13-14.04.2019]
Zirə FK Bakı - Sumqayıt FK 2-0(1-0)
Qarabağ FK - Sabah FC Bakı 3-0(1-0)
Keşlə FK Bakı - Qəbələ FK 1-2(0-0)
Səbail FK Bakı - Neftçi PFK Bakı 2-2(0-0)

Round 25 [18-19.04.2019]
Sumqayıt FK - Səbail FK Bakı 1-2(1-0)
Qarabağ FK - Keşlə FK Bakı 3-0(1-0)
Qəbələ FK - Zirə FK Bakı 2-1(1-0)
Sabah FC Bakı - Neftçi PFK Bakı 0-2(0-0)

Round 26 [27.04.2019]
Zirə FK Bakı - Qarabağ FK 0-3(0-2)
Sabah FC Bakı - Keşlə FK Bakı 1-1(0-0)
Səbail FK Bakı - Qəbələ FK 2-1(2-1)
Neftçi PFK Bakı - Sumqayıt FK 2-3(1-2)

Round 27 [05.05.2019]
Keşlə FK Bakı - Zirə FK Bakı 1-3(1-1)
Qəbələ FK - Neftçi PFK Bakı 1-3(0-1)
Qarabağ FK - Səbail FK Bakı 4-0(2-0)
Sumqayıt FK - Sabah FC Bakı 1-0(0-0)

Round 28 [11.05.2019]
Səbail FK Bakı - Keşlə FK Bakı 1-4(0-3)
Sabah FC Bakı - Zirə FK Bakı 0-3(0-1)
Sumqayıt FK - Qəbələ FK 1-0(0-0)
Neftçi PFK Bakı - Qarabağ FK 2-3(2-1)

Final Standings

1.	**Qarabağ FK Bakı**	28	20	6	2	65	-	21	66
2.	Neftçi PFK Bakı	28	17	7	4	52	-	26	58
3.	Səbail FK Bakı	28	12	5	11	34	-	37	41
4.	Qəbələ FK	28	9	9	10	31	-	33	36
5.	Zirə FK Bakı	28	8	7	13	30	-	40	31
6.	Sumqayıt FK	28	8	5	15	24	-	42	29
7.	Sabah FC Bakı	28	7	6	15	20	-	41	27
8.	Keşlə FK Bakı (*Relegated*)	28	6	5	17	29	-	45	23

Please note: Keşlə FK Bakı remains at first level after MOIK Bakı failed to get license for promotion!

Top goalscorers:

16 Mahir Anar Mədətov
Qarabağ FK Bakı

14 Bagaliy Dabo (FRA)
Neftçi PFK Bakı

10 Segun James Adeniyi (NGA)
Qəbələ FK

NATIONAL CUP
Azərbaycan Kuboku 2018/2019

First Round [06.12.2018]

Ağsu FK - Sabah FC Bakı	0-3(0-2)	Kəpəz FK Gəncə - Səbail FK Bakı	0-4(0-2)
Qaradağ Lökbatan FK - Sumqayıt FK	0-4(0-2)	Şüvəlan FK Bakı - Keşlə FK Bakı	0-3(0-0)

Quarter-Finals [15-20.12.2018]

Zirə FK Bakı - Səbail FK Bakı	1-0(1-0) / 3-2(1-1)	Qəbələ FK - Sabah FC Bakı	1-0(1-0) / 1-0(0-0)
Neftçi PFK Bakı - Sumqayıt FK	0-2(0-2) / 1-0(1-0)	Qarabağ FK Bakı - Keşlə FK Bakı	1-0(1-0) / 1-1(0-1)

Semi-Finals [23.04.-01.05.2019]

Qəbələ FK - Qarabağ FK Bakı	1-0(0-0) / 1-2(0-1)	Sumqayıt FK - Zirə FK Bakı	0-0 / 3-3(3-0)

Final

19.05.2019; Naxçivan City Stadium, Naxçivan; Referee: İnqilab Məmmədov; Attendance: 10,000

Qəbələ FK - Sumqayıt FK **1-0(1-0)**

Qəbələ FK: Anar Nazirov, İlqar Bəhram Qurbanov, Vojislav Stanković, Ürfan Ağamehdi Abbasov, Bəhlul Mustafazadə, Çavid Şakir Hüseynov, Lalawélé Atakora (90+4.Asif Hüseyn Məmmədov), Elvin Çamalov, Steeven Joseph-Monrose, Rauf Sehraman Əliyev (90.Rövlan Muradov), Davit Volkovi. Trainer: Sənan Şamil Qurbanov.

Sumqayıt FK: Mehdi Cənnətov, Arif Nurəddin Daşdemirov (78.Nicat Samit Qurbanov), Vurğun Tofiq Hüseynov, Şəhriyar Əliyev (81.Cavid Qabil Tağıyev [*sent off 90+5*]), Adil Akif Nağıyev, Əli Babayev, Yusif Nəbiyev, Elvin Nəsrəddin Məmmədov, Əfran Amid İsmayılov (67.Ülvi Hümbət İsgəndərov), Amir Agayev, Peyman Babaei. Trainer: Ayxan Abbasov.

Goal: 1-0 Steeven Joseph-Monrose (3).

THE CLUBS 2018/2019

Keşlə Futbol Klubu Bakı

Founded: 1997
Stadium: ASK Arena, Keşlə (8,125)

Goalkeepers:	**DOB**	**M**	**(s)**	**G**
Kamran Ağayev	09.02.1986	19		
Davud Karimi	08.10.1984	7	(2)	
Shahin Zakiyev	11.06.1999	2		
Defenders:	**DOB**	**M**	**(s)**	**G**
Slavik Həsrət Alxasov	06.02.1993	27		3
Ruslan Ramiz Əmircanov	01.02.1985		(1)	
Cabir Əmirli	06.01.1997	15	(3)	1
Dênis Silva Cruz (BRA)	28.12.1985	26		3
Edvinas Girdvainis (LTU)	17.01.1993	17	(1)	1
Tərlan Şahmurad Quliyev	19.04.1992	19	(1)	
Azər Vəlhəd Salahlı	11.04.1994	17	(2)	
Adrian Manuel Scarlatache (ROU)	05.12.1986	1		
Sertan Taşkın	08.10.1997	13	(1)	2
Midfielders:	**DOB**	**M**	**(s)**	**G**
Seymur Nizami Əsədov	05.05.1994	6		
Miloš Bosančić (SRB)	22.05.1988	1	(1)	
Orkhan Faradzhov	07.01.2001		(1)	
Diallo Guidileye (MTN)	30.12.1989	7	(1)	
Vüsal Mahmud İsgəndərli	03.11.1995	13		
John Bankolé Kamara (SLE)	05.12.1988	13		1
Valeriy Kutsenko (UKR)	02.11.1986	6	(5)	
Nikola Mitrović (SRB)	02.01.1987	25		2
Louis Ángelo Peña Puentes (VEN)	25.12.1989	6	(2)	
Məmməd Bəkir Quliyev	20.08.1995		(3)	
Ebrima Sohna (GAM)	14.02.1988	7		
Forwards:	**DOB**	**M**	**(s)**	**G**
Jonathan Serge Folly Ayité (FRA)	22.07.1985	11	(6)	5
Vaqif Fizuli Cavadov	25.05.1989	4	(6)	
Elnur Cəfərov	28.03.1997	2	(1)	
Andre Anthony Clennon (JAM)	15.08.1989	9	(6)	2
Georgios Georgiadis (GRE)	14.11.1987	6	(1)	
Samir Məsimov	25.08.1995	13	(11)	2
Bakhodir Nasimov (UZB)	02.05.1987		(7)	
Nurlan Quliyev	16.02.1998		(1)	
Hervé Christian Tchami-Ngangoué (CMR)	20.02.1988	3	(1)	
Amil Yunanov	06.01.1993	13	(11)	5
Trainer:	**DOB**	**M**		
Mladen Milinković (SRB)	14.05.1968	8		
Tərlan Musa Əhmədov [30.10.2018]	17.11.1971	20		

Neftçi Peşəkar Futbol Klubu Bakı

Founded: 18.03.1937
Stadium: Bakcell Arena, Bakı (10,500)

Goalkeepers:	DOB	M	(s)	G
Səlahət Nüsrət Ağayev	04.01.1991	28		
Defenders:	**DOB**	**M**	**(s)**	**G**
Ruslan İbrahim Abışov	10.10.1987	2	(1)	1
Slavko Bralić (CRO)	15.12.1992	8	(2)	
Ömər Fuad Buludov	15.12.1998	20	(2)	1
Anton Viktor Krivotsyuk	20.08.1998	19	(4)	3
Pape Mamadou Mbodj (SEN)	12.03.1993	13		5
Magomed Mirzabekov	16.11.1990	10		
Kyrylo Petrov (UKR)	22.06.1990	20		
Petru Racu (MDA)	17.07.1987	1	(1)	
Elvin Kamran Sərkərov	24.02.1997		(5)	
Əli Şirinov	09.08.1998		(3)	
Midfielders:	**DOB**	**M**	**(s)**	**G**
Namiq Əvəz Ələsgərov	03.02.1995	10	(13)	3
Tural Möhsüm Axundov	01.08.1988	22	(3)	
Mamadou Kane (GUI)	22.01.1997	5	(4)	
Emin Cəbrayıl Mahmudov	27.04.1992	25	(1)	8
Soni Mustivar (HAI)	12.02.1990	23		
Goran Paracki (CRO)	21.01.1987	14	(8)	2
Turan Valizada	01.01.2001		(1)	
Forwards:	**DOB**	**M**	**(s)**	**G**
Mirabdulla Miryavər Abassov	27.04.1995	16	(12)	7
Bagaliy Dabo (FRA)	27.07.1988	26		14
Dário Frederico da Silva (BRA)	11.09.1991	13	(1)	3
Rəşad Elman Eyubov	03.12.1992	2	(3)	
Rəhman Xudayət Hacıyev	25.07.1993	7	(8)	
Kwame Amponsah Karikari (GHA)	21.01.1992	4	(4)	2
Vangelis Platellas (GRE)	01.12.1988	12	(1)	
Gianluca Sansone (ITA)	12.05.1987	8	(3)	2
Trainer:	**DOB**	**M**		
Roberto Bordin (ITA)	10.01.1965	28		

Qarabağ Futbol Klubu Bakı

Founded: 1951
Stadium: Azersun Arena, Bakı (5,800)

Goalkeepers:	DOB	M	(s)	G
Hannes Þór Halldórsson (ISL)	27.04.1984	4		
Şahrudin Maqomedaliyev	12.06.1994	9		
Vagner da Silva (BRA)	06.06.1986	15		
Defenders:	**DOB**	**M**	**(s)**	**G**
Ansi Agolli (ALB)	11.10.1982	7	(4)	
Abbas İsrafil Hüseynov	13.06.1995	11	(1)	1
Bədavi Ruslan Hüseynov	11.07.1991	18	(1)	1
Rahil Məmmədov	24.11.1995	13	(2)	
Maksim Medvedev	20.09.1989	21		
Jakub Rzeźniczak (POL)	26.10.1986	11		1
Rəşad Farhad Sadıqov	16.06.1982	15	(2)	
Midfielders:	**DOB**	**M**	**(s)**	**G**
Richard Almeida de Oliveira	20.03.1989	14		5
Daniel Quintana Sosa "Dani Quintana" (ESP)	08.03.1987	17	(1)	7
Coşqun Şahin Diniyev	13.09.1995	7		
Wilde-Donald Guerrier (HAI)	31.03.1989	16	(4)	1
Hacıağa Hacılı	30.01.1998	4		
İsmayıl İbrahimli	13.02.1998	2	(1)	
Miguel Marcos Madera "Míchel" (ESP)	08.11.1985	15	(5)	5
Filip Ozobić (CRO)	08.04.1991	24	(3)	9
Qara Elxan Qarayev	12.10.1992	13	(11)	
Simeon Slavchev (BUL)	25.09.1993	6	(10)	2
Forwards:	**DOB**	**M**	**(s)**	**G**
Araz Abdulla Abdullayev	18.04.1992	7	(11)	3
Dzon Delarge (CGO)	24.06.1990	6	(4)	2
Innocent Nkasiobi Emeghara (NGA)	27.05.1989	9	(2)	5
Mahir Anar Emreli (Mədətov)	01.07.1997	22	(5)	16
Reynaldo dos Santos Silva (BRA)	24.08.1989	2	(4)	1
Abdellah Zoubir (FRA)	05.12.1991	20	(4)	7
Trainer:	**DOB**	**M**		
Qurban Osman Qurbanov	13.04.1992	28		

Qəbələ Futbol Klubu

Founded: 01.09.1955
Stadium: Qabala City Stadium, Qabala (4,500)

Goalkeepers:	DOB	M	(s)	G
Dmytro Bezotosny (UKR)	15.11.1983	21		
Aqil Heydər Məmmədov	01.05.1989	4		
Anar Nazirov	08.09.1985	3	(1)	
Murad Popov	05.03.1999		(1)	
Defenders:	**DOB**	**M**	**(s)**	**G**
Ürfan Ağamehdi Abbasov	14.10.1992	24	(1)	1
Bəhlul Mustafazadə	27.02.1997	21	(2)	1
İlqar Bəhram Qurbanov	25.04.1986	13	(5)	
Rasim Əsədulla Ramaldanov	24.01.1986	9	(3)	1
Amin Seydiyev	15.11.1998	12		
Vojislav Stanković (SRB)	22.09.1987	24		1
Təmkin Şaiq Xəlilzadə	06.08.1993	11		1
Midfielders:	**DOB**	**M**	**(s)**	**G**
Qismat Aliyev	24.10.1996	9	(3)	
Elvin Çamalov	04.02.1995	21		1
Çavid Şakir Hüseynov	09.03.1988	21	(3)	
Roman Hüseynov	26.12.1997	1	(2)	
Sabien Lilaj (ALB)	10.02.1989	15	(8)	
Rövlan Muradov	28.03.1998	1		
Samir Davud Qurbanov	12.03.2001		(1)	
Forwards:	**DOB**	**M**	**(s)**	**G**
Segun James Adeniyi (NGA)	20.12.1992	24	(1)	10
Rauf Sehraman Əliyev	12.02.1989	16	(7)	4
Lalawélé Atakora (TOG)	09.11.1990	16	(7)	1
Steeven Joseph-Monrose (FRA)	20.07.1990	23	(2)	6
Asif Hüseyn Məmmədov	05.08.1986	8	(14)	1
Davit Volkovi (GEO)	03.06.1995	11	(2)	2
Trainer:	**DOB**	**M**		
Sənan Şamil Qurbanov	04.08.1980	28		

Sabah Football Club Bakı

Founded: 2016
Stadium: Alinja Arena, Masazır (13,000)

Goalkeepers:	DOB	M	(s)	G
Dmytro Bezruk (UKR)	30.03.1996	3		
Sasa Stamenković (SRB)	05.01.1985	25		
Defenders:	**DOB**	**M**	**(s)**	**G**
Kərim Şahin Diniyev	05.09.1993	23		
Filip Ivanović (SRB)	13.02.1992	22	(2)	1
Məqsəd İsayev	07.06.1994	19	(5)	1
Novruz Nasim Məmmədov	20.03.1991	13	(3)	
Zahid Mardanov	09.08.2000	1		
Wanderson Henrique do Nascimento Silva BRA)	13.09.1991	21	(4)	1
Təmkin Şaiq Xəlilzadə	06.08.1993	7	(1)	
Elvin Qərib Yunuszadə	22.08.1992	2		
Midfielders:	**DOB**	**M**	**(s)**	**G**
Elşən Mübariz Abdullayev	05.02.1994	8	(4)	1
Vadim Vaqif Abdullayev	17.12.1994	9	(8)	
Miloš Bosančić (SRB)	22.05.1988	8	(2)	1
Tərzin Elşən Cahangirov	17.01.1992	5	(11)	
Coşqun Şahin Diniyev	13.09.1995	12	(1)	
Kanan Hasanov	09.01.1999		(1)	
Cavid Əbdirəhman İmamverdiyev	08.01.1990	21	(3)	2
Éric Fabián Ramos Jara (PAR)	12.05.1987	24	(1)	
Eltun Turabov	18.02.1997	16	(5)	
Forwards:	**DOB**	**M**	**(s)**	**G**
Reza Biqdelo (IRN)	15.11.2000	1	(1)	
Marko Dević (UKR)	27.10.1983	20	(1)	8
Rəşad Elman Eyubov	03.12.1992	13		2
Vitaliy Kvashuk (UKR)	01.04.1993	9	(1)	
Elgün Nəbiyev	04.01.1996	17	(8)	1
Emil Qasımov	09.04.2000	1	(4)	
Tural Allahverən Qürbətov	01.03.1993		(3)	
Şakir Seyidov	31.12.2000	1	(7)	
Bəxtiyar İslam Soltanov	21.06.1989	7	(6)	1
Trainer:	**DOB**	**M**		
Elşad Əhmədov	11.09.1970	28		

Səbail Futbol Klubu Bakı

Founded: 2016
Stadium: Bayil Arena, Bakı (5,000)

Goalkeepers:	DOB	M	(s)	G
Emil Nazim Balayev	17.04.1994	14		
Elxan Əhmədov	02.07.1993	3	(1)	
Oleksandr Rybka (UKR)	10.04.1987	11		
Defenders:	**DOB**	**M**	**(s)**	**G**
Henrique Moura Perillo (BRA)	08.02.1991	14	(2)	1
Modou Lamine Jarjué (GNB)	30.09.1997	25		
Tome Kitanovski (MKD)	21.05.1992	17	(4)	
Ihor Korotetskyi (UKR)	13.09.1987	5	(1)	
Kamal Fizuli Qurbanov	06.05.1994	6	(5)	
Şəhriyar Ağali Rəhimov	06.04.1989	25		1
Eltun Sifik Yagublu	19.08.1991		(2)	
Elvin Qərib Yunuszadə	22.08.1992	12		2
Midfielders:	**DOB**	**M**	**(s)**	**G**
Murtuzali Abakarov	21.03.1998		(1)	
Rahid Ələkbər Əmirquliyev	01.09.1989	26		1
Vüqar Bəybala Bəybalayev	05.08.1993	10	(8)	
Eugeniu Cociuc (MDA)	11.05.1993	22	(2)	4
Michaël Kojo Essien (GHA)	03.12.1982	1	(3)	
Urfan İsmayılov	17.05.1996	1		
Emil Martinov (BUL)	18.03.1992	16	(5)	
Adilkhan Qarahmadov	05.06.2001	2	(2)	1
Aqşin Həsən Qurbanlı	15.07.1996	1	(15)	
Orxan Nizami Qurbanlı	12.07.1995		(3)	
Elchin Rahimli	17.06.1991		(3)	
Forwards:	**DOB**	**M**	**(s)**	**G**
Oke Akpoveta (NGA)	12.12.1991	5	(4)	2
Imanol Iriberri (ARG)	04.03.1987	2	(5)	
Kevin Koubemba (CGO)	23.03.1993	26	(2)	5
Fəhmin Muradbəyli	16.03.1996	25	(1)	3
Edgar Iván Pacheco Rodríguez (MEX)	22.01.1990	6	(2)	
Ruslan Qurbanov	12.09.1991	14	(7)	2
Ağabala Ramazanov	20.01.1993	19	(1)	7
Trainer:	**DOB**	**M**		
Aftandil Sabir Hacıyev	13.08.1981	28		

Sumqayıt Futbol Klubu

Founded: 1961 (*as Metallurg Sumqayit*)
Stadium: Kapital Bank Arena, Sumqayit (1,500)

Goalkeepers:	DOB	M	(s)	G
Rəşad Faiq Əzizli	01.01.1994	6	(1)	
Mehdi Cənnətov	26.01.1992	20	(1)	
Orxan Mehdi Sadıqlı	19.05.1993	2		
Defenders:	**DOB**	**M**	**(s)**	**G**
Elvin Bədəlov	14.06.1995	3	(1)	
Arif Nurəddin Daşdemirov	10.02.1987	21	(3)	
Bəxtiyar Bəyqulu Həsənalızadə	29.12.1992	13	(1)	
Vurğun Tofiq Hüseynov	25.04.1988	18	(3)	
Rail Nadiroğlu Məlikov	18.12.1985	23	(1)	
Yusif Nəbiyev	03.09.1997	19	(2)	1
Adil Akif Nağıyev	11.09.1995	12		
Qvanzav Maqomedov	08.06.1994		(2)	
Midfielders:	**DOB**	**M**	**(s)**	**G**
Şəhriyar Əliyev	25.12.1992	15	(3)	3
Əli Babayev	01.11.1990	24	(1)	
Bakhshali Bakhshaliyev	09.03.1998	1	(1)	
Aleksey Isaev	09.11.1995	26	(1)	
Murad Khachayev	14.04.1998	3	(4)	1
Turan Manafov	19.09.1998	1		
Xəyal Nazim Nəcəfov	19.12.1997	8	(5)	
Forwards:	**DOB**	**M**	**(s)**	**G**
Amir Agayev (ISR)	10.02.1992	3	(4)	2
Ibrahim Aliyev	17.07.1999		(2)	
Süleyman Vüqar Əhmədov	25.11.1999	7	(3)	
Peyman Babaei (IRN)	14.02.1994	10	(1)	3
Ülvi Hümbət İsgəndərov	17.04.1998	4	(8)	3
Əfran Amid İsmayılov	08.10.1988	16	(4)	3
Elvin Nəsrəddin Məmmədov	18.07.1988	10	(5)	2
Nicat Samit Qurbanov	17.02.1992	5	(12)	1
Ehtiram Etibar Şahverdiyev	01.07.1996	6	(2)	
Cavid Qabil Tağıyev	22.07.1992	21	(4)	2
Atilla Yıldırım	22.11.1990	11	(5)	3
Trainer:	**DOB**	**M**		
Nazim Süleymanov	17.02.1965	11		
Ayxan Abbasov [14.11.2018]	25.08.1981	17		

Zirə Futbol Klubu Bakı

Founded: 28.07.2014
Stadium: Zirə Olympic Spot Complex Stadium, Bakı (1,400)

Goalkeepers:	**DOB**	**M**	**(s)**	**G**
Kamal Bayramov	19.08.1985	10	(1)	
Anar Nazirov	08.09.1985	14		
Orxan Mehdi Sadıqlı	19.05.1993	2		
Abdulla Seyidəhmədov	04.06.1997	2		
Defenders:	**DOB**	**M**	**(s)**	**G**
İbrahim Aslanlı	01.12.1996	2		
Bəxtiyar Bəyqulu Həsənalızadə	29.12.1992	12		
Murad Musayev	13.06.1994	1		
Adil Akif Nağıyev	11.09.1995	13		
Sadiq Qəfər Quliyev	09.03.1995	6		
Ilkin Qyrtymov	04.11.1990	22	(1)	1
Miloš Radivojević (SRB)	05.04.1990	18	(1)	1
Adrian Manuel Scarlatache (ROU)	05.12.1986	19		
Midfielders:	**DOB**	**M**	**(s)**	**G**
Mirsahib Miryavər Abbasov	19.01.1993	7	(11)	3
Bilal Hamdi (ALG)	01.05.1991	16	(4)	1
Vüsal Mahmud İsgəndərli	03.11.1995	5	(6)	1
Rafael Maharramli	01.10.1999	1	(2)	
Kamal Nəsrullah Mirzəyev	14.09.1994	10	(3)	
İlkin Muradov	05.03.1996	20	(3)	
Vüqar Mustafayev	05.08.1994	12	(2)	
Tellur Mütəllimov	08.04.1995	22	(2)	2
Budaq Hikmət Nəsirov	15.07.1996	7	(5)	
Chafik Tigroudja (FRA)	16.01.1992	3	(2)	
Sadio Tounkara (MLI)	27.04.1992	13	(8)	2
Forwards:	**DOB**	**M**	**(s)**	**G**
Alexandru Dedov (MDA)	26.07.1989	17	(5)	2
Dylan Duventru (MTQ)	03.01.1989	19	(1)	1
Pərdis Fərcad-Azad	12.04.1988	13	(1)	2
Ismaël Béko Fofana (CIV)	08.09.1988	4	(7)	1
Rudolph Mpho Kgaswane (BOT)	13.06.1994	8	(3)	4
Robin Ngalande Junior (MWI)	02.11.1992	2	(4)	1
Julio César Rodríguez Giménez (PAR)	05.12.1990	8	(4)	8
Trainer:	**DOB**	**M**		
Ayxan Abbasov	25.08.1981	2		
Samir Abbasov [29.08.2018]	01.02.1978	26		

SECOND LEVEL
First Division - Azərbaycan Birinci Divizionu 2018/2019

1.	MOIK Bakı (*Promoted*)	26	21	2	3	51	-	21	65
2.	Sumqayıt FK-2	26	19	2	5	68	-	29	59
3.	Neftçi PFK-2 Bakı	26	16	4	6	51	-	28	52
4.	Zaqatala PFK	26	13	8	5	51	-	30	47
5.	Qarabağ FK-2 Bakı	26	14	3	9	51	-	35	45
6.	Keşla FK-2 Bakı	26	12	4	10	41	-	32	40
7.	Şüvəlan FK Bakı	26	11	7	8	31	-	25	40
8.	Sabah FC-2 Bakı	26	11	5	10	27	-	20	38
9.	Qaradağ Lökbatan FK	26	9	3	14	24	-	39	30
10.	Səbail FK-2 Bakı	26	8	3	15	37	-	57	27
11.	Kəpəz FK Gəncə	26	5	7	14	21	-	40	22
12.	Turan Tovuz IK	26	6	2	18	29	-	54	20
13.	Ağsu FK	26	4	5	17	24	-	62	17
14.	Zirə FK-2 Bakı	26	5	1	20	23	-	57	16

Please note: MOIK Bakı failed to get license for promotion!

NATIONAL TEAM

INTERNATIONAL MATCHES
(16.07.2018 – 15.07.2019)

07.09.2018	Bakı	Azerbaijan - Kosovo	0-0	(UNL)
10.09.2018	Attard	Malta - Azerbaijan	1-1(1-1)	(UNL)
11.10.2018	Tórshavn	Faroe Islands - Azerbaijan	0-3(0-1)	(UNL)
14.10.2018	Bakı	Azerbaijan - Malta	1-1(0-1)	(UNL)
17.11.2018	Bakı	Azerbaijan - Faroe Islands	2-0(2-0)	(UNL)
20.11.2018	Pristina	Kosovo - Azerbaijan	4-0(1-0)	(UNL)
21.03.2019	Zagreb	Croatia - Azerbaijan	2-1(1-1)	(ECQ)
25.03.2019	Bakı	Azerbaijan - Lithuania	0-0	(F)
08.06.2019	Bakı	Azerbaijan - Hungary	1-3(0-1)	(ECQ)
11.06.2019	Bakı	Azerbaijan - Slovakia	1-5(1-3)	(ECQ)

07.09.2018 AZERBAIJAN - KOSOVO 0-0 UEFA Nations League D, Group 3
Olimpiya Stadionu, Bakı; Referee: Ola Hobber Nilsen (Norway); Attendance: 19,500
AZE: Kamran Ağayev (Cap), Pavel Vaqif Paşayev, Maksim Medvedev, Ürfan Ağamehdi Abbasov, Badavi Ruslan Hüseynov, Qara Elxan Qarayev, Richard Almeida de Oliveira, Emin Cəbrayıl Mahmudov (61.Dmitriy Nazarov), Ruslan Qurbanov (66.Təmkin Şaiq Xəlilzadə), Ramil Teymur Şeydayev (74.Rauf Sehraman Əliyev), Mahir Anar Emreli. Trainer: Qurban Osman Qurbanov.

10.09.2018 MALTA - AZERBAIJAN 1-1(1-1) UEFA Nations League D, Group 3
Ta'Qali National Stadium, Attard; Referee: Referee: Nikola Dabanović (Montenegro); Attendance: 4,500
AZE: Kamran Ağayev (Cap), Pavel Vaqif Paşayev (34.Ürfan Ağamehdi Abbasov), Maksim Medvedev, Badavi Ruslan Hüseynov, Qara Elxan Qarayev, Richard Almeida de Oliveira, Emin Cəbrayıl Mahmudov (56.Cavid Əbdürəhman İmamverdiyev), Təmkin Şaiq Xəlilzadə, Rauf Sehraman Əliyev (68.Ramil Teymur Şeydayev), Dmitriy Nazarov, Mahir Anar Emreli. Trainer: Qurban Osman Qurbanov.
Goal: Təmkin Şaiq Xəlilzadə (26).

11.10.2018 FAROE ISLANDS - AZERBAIJAN 0-3(0-1) UEFA Nations League D, Group 3
Tórsvøllur, Tórshavn; Referee: Aleksei Eskov (Russia); Attendance: 2,820
AZE: Kamran Ağayev (Cap), Pavel Vaqif Paşayev, Maksim Medvedev, Badavi Ruslan Hüseynov, Rahil Məmmədov, Araz Abdulla Abdullayev (83.Ruslan Qurbanov), Qara Elxan Qarayev, Richard Almeida de Oliveira (87.Emin Cəbrayıl Mahmudov), Dmitriy Nazarov (88.Cavid Əbdürəhman İmamverdiyev), Rüfət Oleq Dadaşov, Mahir Anar Emreli. Trainer: Qurban Osman Qurbanov.
Goals: Richard Almeida de Oliveira (28), Dmitriy Nazarov (67), Richard Almeida de Oliveira (86 penalty).

14.10.2018 AZERBAIJAN - MALTA 1-1(0-1) UEFA Nations League D, Group 3
Olimpiya Stadionu, Bakı; Referee: Referee: Ivan Bebek (Croatia); Attendance: 16,200
AZE: Kamran Ağayev (Cap), Pavel Vaqif Paşayev, Maksim Medvedev, Badavi Ruslan Hüseynov, Rahil Məmmədov (46.Təmkin Şaiq Xəlilzadə), Araz Abdulla Abdullayev, Qara Elxan Qarayev, Richard Almeida de Oliveira, Dmitriy Nazarov, Rüfət Oleq Dadaşov, Mahir Anar Emreli (77.Cavid Əbdürəhman İmamverdiyev). Trainer: Qurban Osman Qurbanov.
Goal: Araz Abdulla Abdullayev (53).

17.11.2018 AZERBAIJAN - FAROE ISLANDS 2-0(2-0) UEFA Nations League D, Group 3
Olimpiya Stadionu, Bakı; Referee: Demetrios Masias (Cyprus); Attendance: 12,65
AZE: Kamran Ağayev (Cap) (46.Səlahət Ağayev), Pavel Vaqif Paşayev (72.Rahil Məmmədov), Badavi Ruslan Hüseynov, Maksim Medvedev, Araz Abdulla Abdullayev, Qara Elxan Qarayev, Richard Almeida de Oliveira, Təmkin Şaiq Xəlilzadə, Dmitriy Nazarov, Rüfət Oleq Dadaşov (78.Mirabdulla Abbasov), Mahir Anar Emreli. Trainer: Qurban Osman Qurbanov.
Goals: Dmitriy Nazarov (18), Mahir Anar Emreli (28).

20.11.2018 KOSOVO - AZERBAIJAN 4-0(1-0) UEFA Nations League D, Group 3
"Fadil Vokrri" Stadium, Pristina; Referee: Benoît Millot (France); Attendance: 12,532
AZE: Səlahət Ağayev, Pavel Vaqif Paşayev, Maksim Medvedev (Cap), Badavi Ruslan Hüseynov, Qara Elxan Qarayev, Araz Abdulla Abdullayev (71.Ruslan Qurbanov), Richard Almeida de Oliveira, Təmkin Şaiq Xəlilzadə, Dmitriy Nazarov, Rüfət Oleq Dadaşov (46.Əfran Amid İsmayılov), Mahir Anar Emreli (63.Mirabdulla Abbasov). Trainer: Qurban Osman Qurbanov.

21.03.2019 CROATIA - AZERBAIJAN 2-1(1-1) 16th EC. Qualifiers
Stadion Maksimir, Zagreb; Referee: Georgi Kabakov (Bulgaria); Attendance: 23,146
AZE: Səlahət Ağayev, Maksim Medvedev (Cap), Badavi Ruslan Hüseynov, Rahil Məmmədov, Şəhriyar Ağəli Rəhimov, Qara Elxan Qarayev (88.Rüfət Oleq Dadaşov), Richard Almeida de Oliveira (72.Emin Cəbrayıl Mahmudov), Eddy Silvestre Pascual İsrafilov, Dmitriy Nazarov (58.Araz Abdulla Abdullayev), Ramil Teymur Şeydayev, Mahir Anar Emreli. Trainer: Nikola Jurčević (Croatia).
Goal: Ramil Teymur Şeydayev (19).

25.03.2019 AZERBAIJAN - LITHUANIA 0-0 Friendly International
Bakcell Arena, Bakı; Referee: Horaţiu Fesnic (Romania); Attendance: 3,122
AZE: Səlahət Ağayev, Maksim Medvedev (Cap), Badavi Ruslan Hüseynov, Anton Viktor Krivotsyuk, Araz Abdulla Abdullayev (64.Mahir Anar Emreli), Qara Elxan Qarayev (85.Emin Cəbrayıl Mahmudov), Richard Almeida de Oliveira (46.Dmitriy Nazarov), Eddy Silvestre Pascual İsrafilov (75.Əli Babayev), Təmkin Şaiq Xəlilzadə (88.Mirabdulla Abbasov), Rüfət Oleq Dadaşov (65.Namik Əvəz Ələskərov), Ramil Teymur Şeydayev. Trainer: Nikola Jurčević (Croatia).

08.06.2019 AZERBAIJAN - HUNGARY 1-3(0-1) 16th EC. Qualifiers
Bakcell Arena, Bakı; Referee: Bernie "Kevin" Raymond Blom (Netherlands); Attendance: 11,000
AZE: Səlahət Ağayev, Maksim Medvedev (Cap), Badavi Ruslan Hüseynov, Rahil Məmmədov, Anton Viktor Krivotsyuk, Qara Elxan Qarayev, Richard Almeida de Oliveira, Ramil Teymur Şeydayev, Dmitriy Nazarov (86.Rüfət Oleq Dadaşov), Mahir Anar Emreli (74.Araz Abdulla Abdullayev), Renat Oleq Dadaşov (59.Ağabala Ramazanov). Trainer: Nikola Jurčević (Croatia).
Goal: Mahir Anar Emreli (69).

11.06.2019 AZERBAIJAN - SLOVAKIA 1-5(1-3) 16th EC. Qualifiers

Bakcell Arena, Bakı; Referee: John Beaton (Scotland); Attendance: 8,200

AZE: Sǝlahǝt Ağayev, Maksim Medvedev (Cap), Badavi Ruslan Hüseynov, Anton Viktor Krivotsyuk, Şǝhriyar Ağǝli Rǝhimov, Araz Abdulla Abdullayev (89.Renat Oleq Dadaşov), Qara Elxan Qarayev, Richard Almeida de Oliveira, Rǝşad Elman Eyyubov (80.Emin Cǝbrayıl Mahmudov), Ağabala Ramazanov (61.Mahir Emreli), Ramil Teymur Şeydayev. Trainer: Nikola Jurčević (Croatia).

Goal: Ramil Teymur Şeydayev (29).

NATIONAL TEAM PLAYERS
(16.07.2018 – 15.07.2019)

Name	DOB	Caps	Goals	2018/2019:	*Club*
Goalkeepers					
Kamran AĞAYEV	09.02.1986	**74**	**0**	2018/2019:	*Keşlǝ FK Bakı*
Sǝlahǝt AĞAYEV	04.01.1991	**18**	**0**	2018/2019:	*Neftçi PFK Bakı*
Defenders					
Ürfan Ağamehdi ABBASOV	14.10.1992	**10**	**1**	2018:	*Qǝbǝlǝ FK*
Bǝdavi Ruslan HÜSEYNOV	11.07.1991	**45**	**0**	2018/2019:	*Qarabağ FK Bakı*
Anton Viktor KRIVOTSYUK	20.08.1998	**3**	**0**	2019:	*Neftçi PFK Bakı*
Maksim MEDVEDEV	29.05.1989	**58**	**3**	2018/2019:	*Qarabağ FK Bakı*
Rahil Sǝrvǝr MƏMMƏDOV	24.11.1995	**7**	**0**	2018/2019:	*Qarabağ FK Bakı*
Pavel Vaqif PAŞAYEV	04.01.1988	**17**	**0**	2018:	*FK Oleksandriya (UKR)*
Şǝhriyar Ağǝli RƏHIMOV	06.04.1989	**3**	**0**	2019:	*Sǝbail FK Bakı*
Tǝmkin Şaiq XƏLILZADƏ	06.08.1993	**11**	**1**	2018:	*Qǝbǝlǝ FK*
Midfielders					
Araz Abdulla ABDULLAYEV	18.04.1992	**35**	**3**	2018/2019:	*Qarabağ FK Bakı*
Richard ALMEIDA de Oliveira	20.03.1989	**8**	**1**	2018: 12.01.2019->	*Astana FC (KAZ)* *Qarabağ FK Bakı*
Əli BABAYEV	01.11.1990	**1**	**0**	2019:	*Sumqayıt FK*
Rǝşad Elman EYYUBOV	03.12.1992	**4**	**0**	2018/2019:	*Sǝbail FK Bakı*
Emin Cǝbrayıl MAHMUDOV	27.04.1992	**12**	**1**	2018/2019:	*Neftçi PFK Bakı*
Qara Elxan QARAYEV	12.10.1992	**52**	**0**	2018/2019:	*Qarabağ FK Bakı*
Ağabala RAMAZANOV	20.01.1993	**14**	**1**	2019:	*Sǝbail FK Bakı*
Cavid Əbdürǝhman İMAMVERDIYEV	01.08.1990	**11**	**1**	2018:	*Sabah FC Bakı*
Eddy Silvestre Pascual İSRAFILOV	02.08.1992	**10**	**0**	2019:	*AD Alcorcón (ESP)*
Namik Əvǝz ƏLƏSKƏROV	03.02.1995	**16**	**0**	2019:	*Neftçi PFK Bakı*
Forwards					
Mirabdulla ABBASOV	27.04.1995	**3**	**0**	2018/2019:	*Neftçi PFK Bakı*
Renat Oleq DADAŞOV	17.05.1999	**3**	**0**	2019:	*GD Estoril Praia (POR)*
Rüfǝt Oleq DADAŞOV	29.09.1991	**23**	**4**	2018/2019:	*SC Preußen Münster (GER)*
Mahir Anar EMRELI (MƏDƏTOV)	01.07.1997	**17**	**3**	2017/2018:	*Qarabağ FK Bakı*
Dmitriy NAZAROV	04.04.1990	**40**	**8**	2018/2019:	*FC Erzgebirge Aue (GER)*
Ruslan Eldaroviç QURBANOV	12.09.1991	**26**	**1**	2018/2019:	*Sǝbail FK Bakı*
Əfran Amid İSMAYILOV	08.10.1988	**40**	**5**	2018/2019:	*Sumqayıt FK*
Ramil Teymur ŞEYDAYEV	15.03.1996	**20**	**3**	2018/2019:	*FK Krylia Sovetov Samara (RUS)*
Rauf Sehraman ƏLIYEV	12.02.1989	**47**	**7**	2018:	*Qǝbǝlǝ FK*

National team coach

Qurban Osman QURBANOV [01.01.-08.12.2018]	13.04.1972	12 M; 4 W; 5 D; 3 L; 14-12
Nikola JURČEVIĆ (CRO) [from 11.02.2019]	14.09.1966	4 M; 0 W; 1 D; 3 L; 3-10

BELARUS

The Country:
Рэспубліка Беларусь (Republic of Belarus)
Capital: Minsk
Surface: 207,595 km^2
Inhabitants: 9,491,800 [2018]
Time: UTC+3

The FA:
Belaruskaya Federatiya Futbola
Prospekt Pobeditelei, 20/3 220020, Minsk
Tel: +375 17 254 56 00
Foundation date: 1889
Member of FIFA since: 1992
Member of UEFA since: 1993
Website: www.bff.by

NATIONAL TEAM RECORDS

First international match:	28.10.1992, Minsk:	Belarus – Ukraine 1-1
Most international caps:	Alyaksandr Kulchy	- 102 caps (1996-2012)
Most international goals:	Maxym Romashchenko	- 20 goal / 64 caps (1998-2008)

UEFA EUROPEAN CHAMPIONSHIP	
1960	-
1964	-
1968	-
1972	-
1976	-
1980	-
1984	-
1988	-
1992	-
1996	Qualifiers
2000	Qualifiers
2004	Qualifiers
2008	Qualifiers
2012	Qualifiers
2016	Qualifiers

FIFA WORLD CUP	
1930	-
1934	-
1938	-
1950	-
1954	-
1958	-
1962	-
1966	-
1970	-
1974	-
1978	-
1982	-
1986	-
1990	-
1994	*Did not enter*
1998	Qualifiers
2002	Qualifiers
2006	Qualifiers
2010	Qualifiers
2014	Qualifiers
2018	Qualifiers

UEFA NATIONS LEAGUE
2018/2019 – League D (promoted to League C)

OLYMPIC FOOTBALL TOURNAMENTS 1908-2016							
1908	-	**1948**	-	**1972**	-	**1996**	Qualifiers
1912	-	**1952**	-	**1976**	-	**2000**	Qualifiers
1920	-	**1956**	-	**1980**	-	**2004**	Qualifiers
1924	-	**1960**	-	**1984**	-	**2008**	Qualifiers
1928	-	**1964**	-	**1988**	-	**2012**	FT / Group Stage
1936	-	**1968**	-	**1992**	-	**2016**	Qualifiers

FIFA CONFEDERATIONS CUP 1992-2017
None

BELARUSIAN CLUB HONOURS IN EUROPEAN CLUB COMPETITIONS:

European Champion Clubs.Cup (1956-1992) / UEFA Champions League (1993-2019)
None
Fairs Cup (1858-1971) / UEFA Cup (1972-2009) / UEFA Europa League (2010-2019)
None
UEFA Super Cup (1972-2019)
None
European Cup Winners.Cup 1961-1999*
None

**defunct competition*

NATIONAL COMPETITIONS
TABLE OF HONOURS

BELARUS SSR (SOVIET ERA) CHAMPIONS

1922	Minsk (city team)
1923	*Not known*
1924	Minsk (city team)
1925	*Not known*
1926	Bobruisk (city team)
1927	Unknown
1928	Gomel (city team)
1929–32	*Not known*
1933	Gomel (city team)
1934	BVO Minsk
1935	BVO Minsk
1936	BVO Minsk
1937	Dinamo Minsk
1938	Dinamo Minsk
1939	Dinamo Minsk
1940	DKA Minsk
1941–44	*Not known*
1945	Dinamo Minsk
1946	ODO Minsk
1947	Torpedo Minsk
1948	Traktor MTZ Minsk

1949	Traktor MTZ Minsk
1950	ODO Minsk
1951	Dinamo Minsk
1952	ODO Minsk
1953	Spartak Minsk
1954	ODO Minsk
1955	FSM Minsk
1956	Spartak Minsk
1957	Sputnik Minsk
1958	Spartak Bobruisk
1959	Minsk (city team)
1960	Sputnik Minsk
1961	Volna Pinsk
1962	Torpedo Minsk
1963	Naroch.Molodechno
1964	SKA Minsk
1965	SKA Minsk
1966	Torpedo Minsk
1967	Torpedo Minsk
1968	Sputnik Minsk
1969	Torpedo Minsk

1970	Torpedo Zhodino
1971	Torpedo Zhodino
1972	Stroitel.Bobruisk
1973	Stroitel.Bobruisk
1974	BATE Borisov
1975	Dinamo Minsk
1976	BATE Borisov
1977	Sputnik Minsk
1978	Shinnik Bobruisk
1979	BATE Borisov
1980	Torpedo Zhodino
1981	Torpedo Zhodino
1982	Torpedo Mogilev
1983	Obuvschik Lida
1984	Orbita Minsk
1985	Obuvschik Lida
1986	Obuvschik Lida
1987	Shinnik Bobruisk
1988	Sputnik Minsk
1989	Obuvschik Lida
1990	Sputnik Minsk
1991	Metallurg Molodechno

	CHAMPIONS	CUP WINNERS	BEST GOALSCORERS	
1992	FC Dinamo Minsk	FC Dinamo Minsk	Andrey Skorobogatko (FC Dnepr Mogilev)	11
1992/1993	FC Dinamo Minsk	FC Neman Grodno	Syarhey Baranovsky (FC Dinamo Minsk) Miroslav Romaschenko (FC Vedrich Rechitsa / FC Dnepr Mogilev)	19
1993/1994	FC Dinamo Minsk	FC Dinamo Minsk	Pyotr Kachuro (FC Dinamo-93 Minsk / FC Dinamo Minsk)	21
1994/1995	FC Dinamo Minsk	-	Pavel Shavrov (FC Dinamo-93 Minsk)	19
1995	FC Dinamo Minsk	FC Dinamo-93 Minsk	Syarhey Yaromko (MPKC Mozyr)	16
1996	MPKC Mozyr	MPKC Mozyr	Andrey Khlebasolaw (FC Belshina Bobruisk)	34
1997	FC Dinamo Minsk	FC Belshina Bobruisk	Andrey Khlebasolaw (FC Belshina Bobruisk)	19
1998	FC Dnepr Mogilev	FC Lokomotiv-96 Vitebsk	Syarhey Yaromko (FC Torpedo Minsk)	19
1999	FC BATE Borisov	FC Belshina Bobruisk	Valery Strypeykis (FC Slavia Mozyr)	21
2000	FC Slavia Mozyr	FC Slavia Mozyr	Raman Vasilyuk (FC Slavia Mozyr)	31
2001	FC Belshina Bobruisk	FC Belshina Bobruisk	Sergei Davydov (RUS, FC Neman Grodno)	25
2002	FC BATE Borisov	FC Gomel	Valery Strypeykis (FC Belshina Bobruisk)	18
2003	FC Gomel	FC Dinamo Minsk	Gennadi Bliznyuk (FC Gomel)	18
2004	FC Dinamo Minsk	FC Shakhtyor Solihorsk	Valery Strypeykis (Naftan Novopolotsk)	18
2005	FC Shakhtyor Solihorsk	MTZ-RIPO Minsk	Valery Strypeykis (Naftan Novopolotsk)	16
2006	FC BATE Borisov	FC BATE Borisov	Alyaksandr Klimenka (FC Shakhtyor Solihorsk)	17
2007	FC BATE Borisov	FC Dynamo Brest	Raman Vasilyuk (FC Gomel)	24
2008	FC BATE Borisov	MTZ-RIPO Minsk	Gennadi Bliznyuk (FC BATE Borisov) Vitali Rodionov (FC BATE Borisov)	16
2009	FC BATE Borisov	FC Naftan Novopolotsk	Maycon Rogério Silva Calijuri (BRA, FC Gomel)	15
2010	FC BATE Borisov	FC BATE Borisov	Renan Bardini Bressan (BRA, FC BATE Borisov)	15
2011	FC BATE Borisov	FC Gomel	Renan Bardini Bressan (BRA, FC BATE Borisov)	13
2012	FC BATE Borisov	FC Naftan Novopolotsk	Dzmitry Asipenka (FC Shakhtyor Solihorsk)	14
2013	FC BATE Borisov	FC Minsk	Vitali Rodionov (FC BATE Borisov)	14
2014	FC BATE Borisov	FC Shakhtyor Solihorsk	Mikalay Yanush (FC Shakhtyor Solihorsk)	15
2015	FC BATE Borisov	FC BATE Borisov	Mikalay Yanush (FC Shakhtyor Solihorsk)	15
2016	FC BATE Borisov	FC Torpedo-BelAZ Zhodino	Vitali Rodionov (FC BATE Borisov) Mikhayl Gordeichuk (FC BATE Borisov)	16
2017	FC BATE Borisov	FC Dinamo Brest	Mikhayl Gordeichuk (FC BATE Borisov)	18
2018	FC BATE Borisov	FC Dinamo Brest	Pavel Savitski (FC Dinamo Brest)	15

NATIONAL CHAMPIONSHIP
Belarusian Premier League 2018
(30.03.2018 – 02.12.2018)

Please note: FC Krumkachy Minsk were excluded from the Premier League before the start of 2018 season after failing to provide necessary licensing documents and pay off the salary debts to the players being replaced by FC Torpedo Minsk.

Results

Round 1 [30.03.-01.04.2018]
Luch Minsk - FC Minsk 0-0
Neman Grodno - FC Vitebsk 1-1(0-1)
FC Gomel - FC Slutsk 0-0
Shakhtyor Solihorsk - Dinamo Brest 0-0
Dinamo Minsk - Torpedo-BelAZ 2-1(1-0)
Isloch Minsk - Torpedo Minsk 1-1(1-0)
FC Gorodeya - Dnepr Mogilev 1-2(1-2)
BATE Borisov - FC Smolevichi 1-0(1-0)

Round 2 [05-07.04.2018]
Dinamo Brest - Luch Minsk 2-1(2-1)
FC Slutsk - Neman Grodno 1-1(1-1)
FC Minsk - BATE Borisov 0-2(0-2)
Torpedo-BelAZ - FC Smolevichi 1-0(0-0)
Dnepr Mogilev - FC Gomel 1-0(0-0)
Torpedo Minsk - FC Gorodeya 1-0(0-0)
FC Vitebsk - Shakhtyor Solihorsk 2-1(0-1)
Dinamo Minsk - Isloch Minsk 0-0

Round 3 [13-15.04.2018]
Luch Minsk - FC Vitebsk 0-2(0-0)
Shakhtyor Solihorsk - FC Slutsk 0-1(0-0)
Neman Grodno - Dnepr Mogilev 0-0
BATE Borisov - Dinamo Brest 2-0(0-0)
Isloch Minsk - Torpedo-BelAZ 0-0
FC Smolevichi - FC Minsk 1-1(1-1)
FC Gomel - Torpedo Minsk 0-0
FC Gorodeya - Dinamo Minsk 0-2(0-1)

Round 4 [21-23.04.2018]
Luch Minsk - FC Slutsk 0-3(0-2)
Dinamo Minsk - FC Gomel 2-1(1-1)
Torpedo-BelAZ - FC Minsk 2-1(1-0)
Torpedo Minsk - Neman Grodno 0-1(0-0)
Isloch Minsk - FC Gorodeya 0-0
Dinamo Brest - FC Smolevichi 2-2(1-0)
Dnepr Mogilev - Shakhtyor Solihorsk 1-1(1-0)
FC Vitebsk - BATE Borisov 0-1(0-1)

Round 5 [27-29.04.2018]
FC Minsk - Dinamo Brest 3-3(1-1)
FC Gomel - Isloch Minsk 1-2(1-1)
Shakhtyor Solihorsk - Torpedo Minsk 1-0(0-0)
BATE Borisov - FC Slutsk 3-1(2-1)
Neman Grodno - Dinamo Minsk 0-2(0-1)
Luch Minsk - Dnepr Mogilev 2-0(2-0)
FC Smolevichi - FC Vitebsk 1-1(0-0)
FC Gorodeya - Torpedo-BelAZ 1-1(1-0)

Round 6 [04-07.05.2018]
FC Slutsk - FC Smolevichi 1-0(0-0)
FC Vitebsk - FC Minsk 1-0(0-0)
Torpedo Minsk - Luch Minsk 0-1(0-1)
FC Gorodeya - FC Gomel 0-0
Dinamo Minsk - Shakhtyor Solihorsk 0-0
Torpedo-BelAZ - Dinamo Brest 2-0(0-0)
Isloch Minsk - Neman Grodno 1-2(0-1)
Dnepr Mogilev - BATE Borisov 0-1(0-1)

Round 7 [11-14.05.2018]
FC Minsk - FC Slutsk 0-2(0-0)
FC Smolevichi - Dnepr Mogilev 2-1(1-0)
FC Gomel - Torpedo-BelAZ 0-0
Dinamo Brest - FC Vitebsk 3-1(2-1)
Shakhtyor Solihorsk - Isloch Minsk 3-0(2-0)
Neman Grodno - FC Gorodeya 1-0(0-0)
BATE Borisov - Torpedo Minsk 2-0(0-0)
Luch Minsk - Dinamo Minsk 1-3(0-1)

Round 8 [20-23.05.2018]
Dnepr Mogilev - FC Minsk 0-0
Torpedo Minsk - FC Smolevichi 0-0
FC Vitebsk - Torpedo-BelAZ 2-0(1-0)
FC Gomel - Neman Grodno 0-2(0-0)
FC Gorodeya - Shakhtyor Solihorsk 0-1(0-0)
Isloch Minsk - Luch Minsk 1-1(0-0)
FC Slutsk - Dinamo Brest 1-1(1-0)
Dinamo Minsk - BATE Borisov 0-1(0-0)

Round 9 [26-29.05.2018]
FC Minsk - Torpedo Minsk 6-1(4-1)
FC Smolevichi - Dinamo Minsk 0-2(0-0)
Shakhtyor Solihorsk - FC Gomel 2-1(1-1)
Luch Minsk - FC Gorodeya 1-1(0-1)
BATE Borisov - Isloch Minsk 1-1(1-0)
Neman Grodno - Torpedo-BelAZ 1-0(1-0)
FC Vitebsk - FC Slutsk 2-0(0-0)
Dinamo Brest - Dnepr Mogilev 1-1(1-0)

Round 10 [01-03.06.2018]
Dinamo Minsk - FC Minsk 1-0(0-0)
Neman Grodno - Shakhtyor Solihorsk 0-1(0-1)
Torpedo Minsk - Dinamo Brest 1-1(0-1)
Dnepr Mogilev - FC Vitebsk 0-1(0-0)
FC Gomel - Luch Minsk 1-0(1-0)
FC Gorodeya - BATE Borisov 2-1(0-1)
Isloch Minsk - FC Smolevichi 1-0(0-0)
Torpedo-BelAZ - FC Slutsk 2-0(2-0)

Round 11 [11-13.06.2018]
FC Smolevichi - FC Gorodeya 2-0(0-0)
Luch Minsk - Neman Grodno 1-2(0-1)
FC Slutsk - Dnepr Mogilev 5-0(2-0)
FC Minsk - Isloch Minsk 0-1(0-0)
FC Vitebsk - Torpedo Minsk 2-0(1-0)
Shakhtyor Solih. - Torpedo-BelAZ 1-0(0-0)
BATE Borisov - FC Gomel 3-0(2-0)
Dinamo Brest - Dinamo Minsk 1-1(1-1)

Round 12 [16-18.06.2018]
Torpedo Minsk - FC Slutsk 0-1(0-1)
FC Gorodeya - FC Minsk 1-2(1-0)
Shakhtyor Solihorsk - Luch Minsk 4-0(1-0)
Torpedo-BelAZ - Dnepr Mogilev 1-0(1-0)
Neman Grodno - BATE Borisov 2-3(1-2)
Dinamo Minsk - FC Vitebsk 1-1(1-0)
FC Gomel - FC Smolevichi 0-2(0-1)
Isloch Minsk - Dinamo Brest 0-1(0-1)

Round 13 [22-25.06.2018]
Dnepr Mogilev - Torpedo Minsk 1-2(1-0)
FC Smolevichi - Neman Grodno 0-1(0-0)
FC Minsk - FC Gomel 0-2(0-2)
FC Slutsk - Dinamo Minsk 0-1(0-0)
BATE Borisov - Shakhtyor Solihorsk 0-0
Luch Minsk - Torpedo-BelAZ 1-3(0-3)
FC Vitebsk - Isloch Minsk 2-0(0-0)
Dinamo Brest - FC Gorodeya 5-2(1-0)

Round 14 [29.06.-01.07.2018]
Luch Minsk - BATE Borisov 1-2(0-2)
FC Gomel - Dinamo Brest 0-6(0-3)
Isloch Minsk - FC Slutsk 0-1(0-1)
Torpedo-BelAZ - Torpedo Minsk 1-0(1-0)
Neman Grodno - FC Minsk 2-2(1-0)
FC Gorodeya - FC Vitebsk 1-1(1-0)
Dinamo Minsk - Dnepr Mogilev 2-1(0-0)
Shakhtyor Solih. - FC Smolevichi 1-0(0-0)

Round 15 [06-09.07.2018]
BATE Borisov - Torpedo-BelAZ 2-1(0-1)
FC Minsk - Shakhtyor Solihorsk 0-0
Dinamo Minsk - Torpedo Minsk 1-0(0-0)
Dinamo Brest - Neman Grodno 1-0(0-0)
FC Vitebsk - FC Gomel 1-0(1-0)
FC Smolevichi - Luch Minsk 1-1(1-0)
FC Slutsk - FC Gorodeya 1-0(1-0)
Dnepr Mogilev - Isloch Minsk 0-0

Round 16 [13-16.07.2018]
FC Slutsk - FC Gomel 0-1(0-1)
FC Minsk - Luch Minsk 3-1(2-1)
FC Smolevichi - BATE Borisov 2-3(2-2)
FC Vitebsk - Neman Grodno 5-1(3-1)
Torpedo Minsk - Isloch Minsk 1-1(0-1)
Dnepr Mogilev - FC Gorodeya 1-2(0-1)
Dinamo Brest - Shakhtyor Solihorsk 1-3(1-1)
Torpedo-BelAZ - Dinamo Minsk 0-0 [31.10.]

Round 17 [20-23.07.2018]
Neman Grodno - FC Slutsk 0-3(0-1)
BATE Borisov - FC Minsk 2-0(0-0)
Luch Minsk - Dinamo Brest 1-1(1-1)
FC Gomel - Dnepr Mogilev 2-0(2-0)
FC Gorodeya - Torpedo Minsk 0-0
Isloch Minsk - Dinamo Minsk 0-1(0-0)
FC Smolevichi - Torpedo-BelAZ 1-2(0-1)
Shakhtyor Sol. - FC Vitebsk 2-1(1-0) [31.10.]

Round 18 [17-20.08.2018]
Dnepr Mogilev - Neman Grodno 0-0
FC Minsk - FC Smolevichi 0-0
Torpedo-BelAZ - Isloch Minsk 2-1(2-1)
FC Vitebsk - Luch Minsk 2-0(0-0)
FC Slutsk - Shakhtyor Solihorsk 1-3(0-3)
Dinamo Minsk - FC Gorodeya 0-2(0-1)
Torpedo Minsk - FC Gomel 1-2(0-0)
Dinamo Brest - BATE Boris. 1-3(1-0) [31.10.]

Round 19 [24-27.08.2018]
FC Minsk - Torpedo-BelAZ 0-0
FC Gorodeya - Isloch Minsk 2-0(0-0)
BATE Borisov - FC Vitebsk 1-1(0-0)
Neman Grodno - Torpedo Minsk 1-0(0-0)
FC Smolevichi - Dinamo Brest 1-0(1-0)
Shakhtyor Solihorsk - Dnepr Mogilev 3-1(2-1)
FC Gomel - Dinamo Minsk 0-0
FC Slutsk - Luch Minsk 1-0(0-0)

Round 20 [31.08.-02.09.2018]
Torpedo-BelAZ - FC Gorodeya 0-1(0-0)
FC Vitebsk - FC Smolevichi 4-0(1-0)
Dnepr Mogilev - Luch Minsk 0-0
Isloch Minsk - FC Gomel 0-1(0-1)
Dinamo Brest - FC Minsk 2-1(1-1)
Torpedo Minsk - Shakhtyor Solihorsk 2-3(1-2)
FC Slutsk - BATE Borisov 0-1(0-0)
Dinamo Minsk - Neman Grodno 1-0(0-0)

Round 21 [14-17.09.2018]
Luch Minsk - Torpedo Minsk 3-1(1-0)
FC Minsk - FC Vitebsk 1-3(0-1)
Shakhtyor Solihorsk - Dinamo Minsk 0-0
BATE Borisov - Dnepr Mogilev 3-1(2-0)
FC Smolevichi - FC Slutsk 1-2(1-1)
Neman Grodno - Isloch Minsk 6-0(3-0)
Dinamo Brest - Torpedo-BelAZ 2-0(2-0)
FC Gomel - FC Gorodeya 2-0(2-0)

Round 22 [21-26.09.2018]
Dnepr Mogilev - FC Smolevichi 0-1(0-0)
Isloch Minsk - Shakhtyor Solihorsk 1-0(1-0)
FC Slutsk - FC Minsk 0-1(0-0)
FC Vitebsk - Dinamo Brest 0-1(0-0)
Torpedo-BelAZ - FC Gomel 1-0(0-0)
Dinamo Minsk - Luch Minsk 3-2(1-0)
FC Gorodeya - Neman Grodno 0-2(0-0)
Torpedo Minsk - BATE Borisov 0-3(0-1)

Round 23 [28.09.-01.10.2018]
Luch Minsk - Isloch Minsk 1-1(0-0)
FC Minsk - Dnepr Mogilev 4-0(2-0)
Shakhtyor Solihorsk - FC Gorodeya 1-0(0-0)
FC Smolevichi - Torpedo Minsk 0-2(0-1)
Dinamo Brest - FC Slutsk 4-0(2-0)
Torpedo-BelAZ - FC Vitebsk 2-0(1-0)
BATE Borisov - Dinamo Minsk 2-1(0-1)
Neman Grodno - FC Gomel 2-0(1-0)

Round 24 [05-07.10.2018]
Torpedo Minsk - FC Minsk 1-0(1-0)
FC Gorodeya - Luch Minsk 1-1(1-1)
FC Slutsk - FC Vitebsk 0-2(0-2)
Dnepr Mogilev - Dinamo Brest 1-4(1-2)
FC Gomel - Shakhtyor Solihorsk 0-3(0-1)
Isloch Minsk - BATE Borisov 2-1(1-0)
Torpedo-BelAZ - Neman Grodno 3-0(0-0)
Dinamo Minsk - FC Smolevichi 2-0(1-0)

Round 25 [19-22.10.2018]
FC Vitebsk - Dnepr Mogilev 3-1(1-0)
FC Minsk - Dinamo Minsk 3-3(1-2)
BATE Borisov - FC Gorodeya 3-2(1-0)
Shakhtyor Solihorsk - Neman Grodno 1-0(1-0)
FC Slutsk - Torpedo-BelAZ 0-3(0-1)
FC Smolevichi - Isloch Minsk 0-1(0-0)
Dinamo Brest - Torpedo Minsk 2-0(2-0)
Luch Minsk - FC Gomel 1-0(0-0)

Round 26 [26-28.10.2018]
Isloch Minsk - FC Minsk 0-3(0-1)
Dnepr Mogilev - FC Slutsk 2-0(1-0)
Torpedo Minsk - FC Vitebsk 0-1(0-1)
FC Gorodeya - FC Smolevichi 4-1(1-1)
Neman Grodno - Luch Minsk 0-0
Torpedo-BelAZ - Shakhtyor Solih. 1-0(1-0)
Dinamo Minsk - Dinamo Brest 1-1(1-0)
FC Gomel - BATE Borisov 0-1(0-0)

Round 27 [02-05.11.2018]
FC Minsk - FC Gorodeya 0-5(0-2)
FC Vitebsk - Dinamo Minsk 0-1(0-1)
Dinamo Brest - Isloch Minsk 3-1(1-1)
FC Slutsk - Torpedo Minsk 1-3(1-3)
Dnepr Mogilev - Torpedo-BelAZ 0-3(0-2)
BATE Borisov - Neman Grodno 1-0(0-0)
Luch Minsk - Shakhtyor Solihorsk 1-1(0-1)
FC Smolevichi - FC Gomel 1-1(0-0)

Round 28 [09-11.11.2018]
FC Gorodeya - Dinamo Brest 1-0(0-0)
Dinamo Minsk - FC Slutsk 2-0(1-0)
Isloch Minsk - FC Vitebsk 0-1(0-1)
FC Gomel - FC Minsk 0-2(0-0)
Neman Grodno - FC Smolevichi 1-1(1-1)
Torpedo Minsk - Dnepr Mogilev 3-0(2-0)
Torpedo-BelAZ - Luch Minsk 0-0
Shakhtyor Solih. - BATE Bor 3-0(1-0)[21.11.]

Round 29 [24.11.2018]
Torpedo Minsk - Torpedo-BelAZ 0-2(0-1)
Dnepr Mogilev - Dinamo Minsk 0-3(0-1)
FC Slutsk - Isloch Minsk 0-1(0-0)
FC Vitebsk - FC Gorodeya 1-0(1-0)
Dinamo Brest - FC Gomel 0-0
FC Minsk - Neman Grodno 1-2(0-0)
FC Smolevichi - Shakhtyor Solih. 0-2(0-1)
BATE Borisov - Luch Minsk 4-1(0-1)

Round 30 [02.12.2018]
Torpedo-BelAZ - BATE Borisov 2-2(2-2)
Luch Minsk - FC Smolevichi 1-1(0-1)
Shakhtyor Solihorsk - FC Minsk 4-0(1-0)
Neman Grodno - Dinamo Brest 0-3(0-1)
FC Gomel - FC Vitebsk 1-3(1-1)
FC Gorodeya - FC Slutsk 2-0(1-0)
Isloch Minsk - Dnepr Mogilev 3-2(1-2)
Torpedo Minsk - Dinamo Minsk 0-3(0-1)

Final Standings

1.	**FC BATE Borisov**	30	23	4	3	55	-	24	73
2.	FC Shakhtyor Solihorsk	30	19	7	4	45	-	14	64
3.	FC Dinamo Minsk	30	18	9	3	41	-	17	63
4.	FC Vitebsk	30	19	5	6	47	-	20	62
5.	FC Torpedo-BelAZ Zhodino	30	16	7	7	36	-	18	55
6.	FC Dinamo Brest	30	14	10	6	52	-	30	52
7.	FC Neman Grodno	30	12	7	11	31	-	32	43
8.	FC Slutsk	30	11	3	16	26	-	36	36
9.	FC Gorodeya	30	9	7	14	31	-	33	34
10.	FC Isloch Minsk Raion	30	8	9	13	20	-	37	33
11.	FC Minsk	30	7	9	14	34	-	42	30
12.	FC Gomel	30	7	7	16	16	-	36	28
13.	FC Luch Minsk	30	4	12	14	24	-	44	24
14.	FC Torpedo Minsk	30	6	6	18	20	-	41	24
15.	FC Smolevichi (*Relegated*)	30	5	9	16	21	-	39	24
16.	FC Dnepr Mogilev (*Relegated*)	30	3	7	20	17	-	53	16

Top goalscorers:

15 Pavel Savitski
FC Dinamo Brest

12 Denis Laptev
FC Shakhtyor Solihorsk

11 Dmitriy Lebedev *FC Gorodeya*
11 Anton Matveenko *FC Vitebsk*
11 Yawhen Shikavka *FC Slutsk*
11 Maksim Skavysh *FC BATE Borisov*
11 Kirill Vergeychik *FC Vitebsk*

NATIONAL CUP
Kubak Belarusi 2017/2018

First Round [17.05.2017]

FC Livadiya Dzerzhinsk - FC Belita-Vitex Uzda	1-4	FC Senno - SMI Autotrans Smolevichi	0-1
Ivatsevichi - FC Kletsk	5-0	Batski Gomel – FC Victoria Maryina Gorka	1-2

Second Round [14.06.2017]

FC Sdiušor-MTZ-Siabar - FC Neman-Agro Stoŭbcy	0-1	Ivatsevichi - FC Torpedo Minsk	0-6
FGC Grodno - FC Smolevichi	1-5	UAS Zhitkovichi - FC Lida	2-1
FC SDYuShOR-3 Pinsk - FC Orsha	0-8	FC Energosbyt-BSATU - FC Baranovichi	1-4
FC SDYuShOR-8 Gomel - FC Osipovichi	1-0	FC Belita-Vitex Uzda - FC Granit Mikashevichi	1-2
FC Oshmyany FC - FC Luch Minsk	1-2	FC Sbornaya TF Gomel - FC Lokomotiv Gomel	0-2
FC Čisť - FC Khimik Svetlogorsk	1-0	FC Molodechno – FC Energetik-BGU Minsk	3-2
FC Sputnik Rechytsa - FC Volna Pinsk	0-3	FC Lyuban - FC Smorgon	1-2
FC Victoria Maryina Gorka - FC Belshina Bobruisk	1-2	SMI Autotrans Smolevichi - FC Slonim-2017	0-6

Third Round [05-09.07.2017]

FC SDYuShOR-8 Gomel - FC Neman Grodno	0-7(0-2)	FC Torpedo Minsk - FC Gomel	0-0; 2-3pen
FC Volna Pinsk - FC Minsk	0-1(0-1)	UAS Zhitkovichi - FC Slutsk	0-3 aet
FC Orsha - FC Slaviya Mozyr	1-1; 4-3pen	FC Molodechno - FC Krumkachy Minsk	0-3(0-2)
FC Smorgon - FC Dinamo Brest	1-4(0-3)	FC Granit Mikashevichi - FC Gorodeya	0-2(0-2)
FC Neman-Agro Stoŭbcy - FC BATE Borisov	1-5(1-2)	FC Slonim-2017 - FC Dnepr Mogilev	1-1; 3-4pen
FC Baranovichi - FC Naftan Novopolotsk	0-1(0-1)	FC Čisť - FC Dinamo Minsk	0-4(0-2)
FC Smolevichi - FC Torpedo-BelAZ Zhodino	0-2(0-1)	FC Belshina Bobruisk - FC Isloch Minsk	1-4(1-1)
FC Lokomotiv Gomel - FC Vitebsk	0-1(0-0)	FC Luch Minsk - FC Shakhtyor Solihorsk	1-5(0-3)

Fourth Round [22-23.07.2017; 12.11.2017*]			
FC Naftan Novopolotsk - FC Krumkachy Minsk	1-2(0-0)	FC Vitebsk - FC Slutsk	0-0; 2-4pen
FC Isloch Minsk - FC Gorodeya	2-1(0-0,1-1)	FC Dinamo Brest - FC Gomel	2-1(1-1)
FC Neman Grodno - FC Minsk	1-0(1-0)	FC Shakhtyor Solihorsk - FC Orsha	6-0(2-0)
FC Dinamo Minsk - FC Dnepr Mogilev	0-1(0-1)	FC BATE Borisov - FC Torpedo-BelAZ Zhodino*	2-1(0-0,1-1)

Quarter-Finals [11-18.03.2018]					
FC Neman Grodno - FC Krumkachy Minsk	3-0(w/o)	3-0(w/o)	FC Dinamo Brest - FC Slutsk	2-0(0-0)	2-1(1-0)
FC Shakhtyor Solihorsk - FC Dnepr Mogilev	3-1(0-1)	0-2(0-0)	FC Isloch Minsk - FC BATE Borisov	1-2(0-2)	1-2(1-0)

Semi-Finals [18.04.-22.05.2018]					
FC BATE Borisov - FC Neman Grodno	2-0(2-0)	0-0	FC Dinamo Brest - FC Dnepr Mogilev	2-0(1-0)	4-1(1-0)

Final

19.05.2018; Spartak Stadium, Mogiley; Referee: Syarhey Tsinkevich; Attendance: 7,200

FC Dinamo Brest - FC BATE Borisov **3-2(1-1)**

Dinamo Brest: Alyaksandr Hutor, Aleh Veretilo, Giannis Kargas, Alyaksey Gavrilovich (Cap), Maksim Vitus, Chidi Osuchukwu, Pavel Sedko (71.Željko Filipovič), Pavel Savitskiy, Pavel Nekhaychik, Artem Milevskiy, Sandro Gotal (71.Joel Fameyeh; 90+3.Roman Vasilyuk). Trainer: Syarhey Kovalchuk.

BATE Borisov: Denis Scherbitski, Aleksander Filipović, Zakhar Volkov, Maksim Valadzko, Dmitriy Baga, Stanislav Dragun, Ihar Stasevich (Cap), Evgeni Yablonski, Alyaksandr Hleb (79.Maksim Skavysh), Mirko Ivanić, Mikalay Signevich. Trainer: Aleh Dulub.

Goals: 0-1 Artem Milevskiy (13), 1-1 Mirko Ivanić (34), 1-2 Mirko Ivanić (49), 2-2 Joel Fameyeh (74), 3-2 Pavel Nekhaychik (89).

THE CLUBS 2018

Football Club BATE Borisov

Founded: 1996
Stadium: Borisov Arena, Borisov (13,126)

Goalkeepers:	**DOB**	**M**	**(s)**	**G**
Anton Chichkan	10.07.1995	4		
Denis Scherbitski	14.04.1996	26		
Defenders:	**DOB**	**M**	**(s)**	**G**
Aleksander Filipović (SRB)	20.12.1994	26	(1)	1
Uladislaw Malkevich	09.12.1999	2		
Nemanja Milunović (SRB)	31.05.1989	5		
Artyom Shkurdyuk	20.08.1998	1		
Nikola Vasiljević (SRB)	30.06.1991	4		
Zakhar Volkov	12.08.1997	17	(1)	1
Maksim Valadzko	10.11.1992	17	(5)	
Midfielders:	**DOB**	**M**	**(s)**	**G**
Dmitriy Baga	04.01.1990	24	(2)	3
Evgeniy Berezkin	05.07.1996	5	(8)	2
Stanislaw Drahun	04.06.1988	27	(1)	5
Alyaksandr Hleb	01.05.1981	5	(10)	
Mirko Ivanić (MNE)	13.09.1993	20	(5)	7
Alyaksey Ryas	14.05.1987	20		2
Slobodan Simović (SRB)	22.05.1989	4		
Ihar Stasevich	21.10.1985	28		8
Evgeni Yablonski	10.05.1995	22	(3)	1
Forwards:	**DOB**	**M**	**(s)**	**G**
Mihail Hardzeichuk	23.10.1989	6	(5)	4
Uladislaw Mukhamedov	04.01.1998		(8)	
Mikalay Signevich	20.02.1992	20	(3)	6
Maksim Skavysh	13.11.1989	12	(17)	11
Jasse Tuominen (FIN)	12.11.1995	8	(8)	
Trainer:	**DOB**	**M**		
Aleh Dulub [05.01.2018]	20.09.1965	10		
Aleksei Baga [04.06.2018]	04.02.1981	20		

Football Club Dinamo Brest

Founded: 1960
Stadium: Regional Sport Complex Brestsky (10,600)

Goalkeepers:	**DOB**	**M**	**(s)**	**G**
Alyaksandr Hutar	18.04.1989	24		
Pavel Pavlyuchenko	01.01.1998	6		
Defenders:	**DOB**	**M**	**(s)**	**G**
Dzmitry Borisov	08.01.1995	2		1
Dénis Paulo Duarte (POR)	04.05.1994	12		1
Alyaksey Gavrilovich	05.01.1990	13		1
Giannis Kargas (GRE)	09.12.1994	14	(3)	
Gaby Kiki (CMR)	15.02.1995	10		
Andrey Lebedev	01.02.1991	10	(2)	1
Aleh Veratsila	10.07.1988	25		
Maksim Vitus	11.02.1989	23	(1)	
Andrei Zaleski	20.01.1991	12	(4)	
Midfielders:	**DOB**	**M**	**(s)**	**G**
Artem Bykov	19.10.1992	12		2
Željko Filipovič (SVN)	03.10.1988	12	(5)	
Syarhey Kislyak	06.08.1987	4	(7)	
Syarhey Krivets	08.06.1986	10	(1)	1
Alyaksey Legchilin	11.04.1992	3	(3)	
Vladimir Medved	04.11.1999		(1)	
Pavel Nyakhaychyk	15.07.1988	15	(6)	3
Oleksandr Noyok (UKR)	15.05.1992	13	(1)	2
Chidi Osuchukwu (NGA)	16.02.1994	11	(1)	2
Kirill Premudrov	11.06.1992	3	(7)	
Pavel Sedko	03.04.1998	9	(7)	3
Roman Yuzepchuk	24.07.1997	12	(5)	2
Forwards:	**DOB**	**M**	**(s)**	**G**
Dickson Afoakwa (GHA)	26.04.1998		(1)	
Joel Fameyeh (GHA)	14.05.1997	20	(4)	7
Sandro Gotal (AUT)	09.09.1991	3	(3)	2
Oleksiy Khoblenko (UKR)	04.04.1994	9	(3)	4
Kirill Kirilenko	08.10.2000		(6)	
Artem Milevskiy (UKR)	12.01.1985	13	(1)	3
Nivaldo Rodriguez Ferreira (BRA)	22.06.1988	3	(5)	2
Marvin Ogunjimi (BEL)	12.10.1987	1	(2)	
Bogdan Sadovskiy	01.08.1999		(2)	
Pavel Savitski	12.07.1994	26	(3)	15
Roman Vasilyuk	23.11.1978		(2)	
Trainer:	**DOB**	**M**		
Radoslav Látal (CZE) [12.01.2018]	06.01.1970	6		
Syarhey Kovalchuk [11.05.2018]	16.12.1973	7		
Alyaksey Shpilevski [29.06.2018]	17.02.1988	4		
Marcel Lička (CZE) [11.08.2018]	17.07.1977	13		

Football Club Dinamo Minsk

Founded: 18.06.1927
Stadium: Traktor Stadium, Minsk (17,586)

Goalkeepers:	DOB	M	(s)	G
Andrey Harbunow	29.05.1983	28		
Syarhey Ignatovich	29.06.1992	2	(2)	
Defenders:	**DOB**	**M**	**(s)**	**G**
Roman Begunov	22.03.1993	13	(3)	
Alyaksandr Chizh	10.02.1997	5		
Nino Galović (CRO)	06.07.1992	27		4
Alyaksey Gavrilovich	05.01.1990	13		2
Giorgi Navalovski (GEO)	28.06.1986	7	(1)	
Yuriy Ostroukh	21.01.1988	7	(2)	
Luís Carlos Rocha (POR)	13.08.1986	4	(1)	1
Alyaksandr Sachivko	05.01.1986	7		
Ihar Shytaw	24.10.1986	9	(2)	
Maksim Shvetsov	02.04.1998	24	(1)	
Maksim Zhavnerchik	09.02.1985	9		
Midfielders:	**DOB**	**M**	**(s)**	**G**
Artem Bykov	19.10.1992	9	(6)	1
Artem Gurenko	18.06.1994	16	(4)	
Mikita Kaplenko	18.09.1995	15	(8)	
Mikita Korzun	06.03.1995	10	(2)	1
Uroš Nikolić (SRB)	14.12.1993	17	(3)	4
Oleksandr Noyok (UKR)	15.05.1992	10	(1)	2
Artem Solovey	01.11.1990	10	(13)	4
Dinko Trebotić (CRO)	30.07.1990	5	(5)	1
Seidu Yahaya (GHA)	31.12.1989	29		
Forwards:	**DOB**	**M**	**(s)**	**G**
Dmitri Antilevski	12.06.1997	1	(1)	
Kehinde Abdul Feyi Fatai (NGA)	19.02.1990	8	(1)	5
Filipp Ivanov	21.07.1990	12	(13)	4
Vladimir Khvashchinskiy	10.05.1990	16	(11)	6
Alyaksandr Makas	08.10.1991	6	(8)	2
Anton Saroka	05.03.1992	11		4
Trainer:	**DOB**	**M**		
Sergei Gurenko [02.05.2017]	30.09.1972	30		

Football Club Dnepr Mogilev

Founded: 04.01.1960
Stadium: Spartak Stadium, Mogilev (7,990)

Goalkeepers:	DOB	M	(s)	G
Maksim Belov	23.04.1999	2		
Aleksei Berezin (RUS)	16.04.1993	9		
Ihar Dovgyallo	17.07.1985	6		
Maksim Vysotsky	29.01.1995	13		
Defenders:	**DOB**	**M**	**(s)**	**G**
Ilya Boltrushevich	30.03.1999	5		
Maksim Chizh	08.10.1993	12	(2)	1
Aleh Chmyrikov	08.02.1996	13		
Vladyslav Gevlych (UKR)	23.09.1994	11	(2)	
Gaby Kiki (CMR)	15.02.1995	10		
Pavel Kirilchik	04.01.1981	7		
Danila Nechaev	30.10.1999	1	(1)	
Anton Shepelev	08.11.1989	18	(3)	2
Midfielders:	**DOB**	**M**	**(s)**	**G**
Pavel Bordukov	10.04.1993	18	(4)	
Evgen Chepurnenko (UKR)	06.09.1989	4	(2)	
Andrey Chukhley	02.10.1987	17		1
Andriy Derkach (UKR)	28.05.1985	10		
Denis Grechikho	22.05.1999	23	(3)	
Artyom Kontsevoi	26.08.1999	15	(4)	4
Daniil Kovalyov	25.03.2001		(2)	
Yawhen Krasnov	09.02.1998	5	(3)	
Pavel Lovgach	02.03.1995	11	(5)	1
Alyaksandr Pavlov	18.08.1984	23	(3)	2
Dmitri Podstrelov	06.09.1998	8	(2)	1
Sergiy Rudika (UKR)	14.06.1988	11	(1)	1
Yan Senkevich	18.02.1995	9	(14)	
Oleksandr Tsybulnyk (UKR)	09.01.1993	3	(1)	
Forwards:	**DOB**	**M**	**(s)**	**G**
Viulen Ayvazyan (ARM)	01.01.1995	1	(3)	
Vadim Demidovich	20.09.1985	7	(4)	
Kirill Gusev	06.04.1999		(1)	
Aleksey Kurzenev (RUS)	09.01.1995	6	(4)	1
Denis Levitskiy	05.02.1997	7	(3)	
Artem Radchenko (UKR)	02.01.1995	1	(6)	
Andrei Vshivtsev (RUS)	25.01.1994	1	(4)	
Trainer:	**DOB**	**M**		
Vyacheslav Levchuk [13.01.2018]	19.05.1971	13		
Evgeniy Kapov [29.06.2018]	30.01.1977	4		
Serhiy Litovchenko (UKR) [01.08.2018]	30.01.1979	10		
Yuriy Lukashov [07.11.2018]	29.12.1974	1		
Evgeniy Kapov [19.11.2018]	30.01.1977	2		

Football Club Gomel

Founded: 1959
Stadium: Central Stadium, Gomel (14,037)

Goalkeepers:	DOB	M	(s)	G
Dmitri Dudar	08.11.1991	22		
Aleh Kovalyov	24.05.1987	8		
Defenders:	**DOB**	**M**	**(s)**	**G**
Badri Akubardia (UKR)	11.01.1993	12		1
Dmitriy Aydov (RUS)	10.04.1982	12	(1)	
Gideon Baah (GHA)	01.10.1991	11		1
Otar Dzavashvili (GEO)	17.08.1993	6		
Valeri Karshakevich	15.02.1988	16		
Ruslan Yudenkov	28.04.1987	24		
Midfielders:	**DOB**	**M**	**(s)**	**G**
Maksim Andreev (RUS)	19.01.1988	10	(1)	
Oleksandr Batyshchev (UKR)	14.09.1991	30		1
Artem Filimonov (UKR)	21.02.1994	8	(1)	
Milovan Kapor (CAN)	05.08.1991	28	(1)	
Yawhen Milevskiy	14.01.1995		(3)	
Ihar Rozhkov	24.06.1981	13	(10)	1
Serhiy Shapoval (UKR)	07.02.1990	12		2
Andrey Shtygel	22.06.1994	4	(10)	1
Dmitriy Tereshchenko (UKR)	04.04.1987	29		
Ivan Zhestkin	08.05.1991	9	(17)	1
Forwards:	**DOB**	**M**	**(s)**	**G**
Lassina Dao (CIV)	20.12.1996	14	(11)	
Wilfried Kwassie Eza (CIV)	28.12.1996		(1)	
Christ Acel Fabrice Konan (CIV)	20.07.1997	7		
Mohamed Konaté (CIV)	12.12.1997	9	(2)	2
Anton Shramchenko	12.03.1993	28	(2)	3
Alyaksey Teslyuk	10.01.1994	1	(7)	
Roman Volkov	08.01.1987	17	(8)	2
Alyaksandr Yanchenko	14.02.1995		(6)	
Trainer:	**DOB**	**M**		
Vyacheslav Geraschenko	25.07.1972	8		
Alyaksey Merkulov [23.05.2018]	17.11.1972	22		

Football Club Gorodeya

Founded: 2004
Stadium: Gorodeya Stadium, Gorodeya (2,000)

Goalkeepers:	**DOB**	**M**	**(s)**	**G**
Ihar Dovgyallo	17.07.1985	12		
Nikolai Romanyuk	02.06.1984	16		
Uladislaw Vasilyuchek	28.03.1994	2		
Defenders:	**DOB**	**M**	**(s)**	**G**
Pavel Nazarenko	20.01.1995	27	(1)	1
Kirill Pavlyuchek	27.06.1984	28		
Pavel Plaskonny	29.01.1985	11	(3)	
Alexandr Pozniak	23.07.1994	22	(4)	1
Syarhey Pushnyakov	08.02.1993	19	(4)	3
Semen Shestilovski	30.05.1994	17	(3)	
Andrey Sorokin (RUS)	28.03.1996	4	(1)	
Syarhey Usenya	04.03.1988	19	(4)	1
Edgaras Žarskis (LTU)	04.05.1994	4		
Midfielders:	**DOB**	**M**	**(s)**	**G**
Martin Artyukh	06.05.1996		(5)	
Mikhail Bashilov (RUS)	12.01.1993	20		
Dmitriy Ignatenko	24.10.1988	28	(1)	1
Milan Jeremić (SRB)	22.09.1988		(1)	
Dmitriy Lebedev	13.05.1986	26	(1)	11
Ivan Petrović (SRB)	03.07.1993	14		
Syarhey Tikhonovskiy	26.06.1990	10	(1)	1
Yuri Volovik	19.06.1993	15	(5)	
Uladislaw Zavadski	04.02.1996	1	(3)	
Forwards:	**DOB**	**M**	**(s)**	**G**
Bojan Dubajić (SRB)	01.09.1990	19	(1)	10
Artem Kiyko	13.01.1996	4	(2)	
Andreja Lazović (SRB)	04.08.1994	1	(4)	1
Dmitriy Parkhachev	02.01.1985		(5)	
Ghukas Poghosyan (ARM)	06.02.1994	5	(6)	
Andrey Voronkov	08.02.1989	5	(6)	
Mikalay Zenko	11.03.1989	1	(4)	
Trainer:	**DOB**	**M**		
Syarhey Yaromko	07.04.1967	30		

Football Club Isloch Minsk Raion

Founded: 2007
Stadium: FC Minsk Stadium, Minsk (3,000)

Goalkeepers:	**DOB**	**M**	**(s)**	**G**
Egor Khatkevich	09.07.1988	13		
Syarhey Turanok	29.03.1986	17		
Defenders:	**DOB**	**M**	**(s)**	**G**
Dmitriy Aliseyko	28.08.1992	18	(3)	
Anton Bubnov	23.11.1988	13	(5)	
Weslie John (TRI)	29.07.1991	28		
Mikhail Kalugin (UKR)	20.11.1994	9		
Pavel Kirilchik	04.01.1981	3	(6)	
Dmitri Nekrashevich	26.08.2001		(1)	
Artem Rakhmanov	10.07.1990	12		
Artur Slabashevich	09.02.1989	25	(2)	2
Uladislaw Yasukevich	30.05.1994		(1)	
Ihar Zyulev	05.01.1984	10	(12)	1
Midfielders:	**DOB**	**M**	**(s)**	**G**
Mikita Bukatkin	07.03.1988	16	(5)	
Alyaksandr Bychenok	30.05.1985	18	(10)	
Aleh Patotskiy	24.06.1991	28		1
Vadim Pobudei	17.12.1994	9	(9)	
Alyaksandr Shagoyko	27.07.1980	26	(1)	
Maksim Taleyko	20.02.1993	8	(6)	1
Forwards:	**DOB**	**M**	**(s)**	**G**
Gennadiy Bliznyuk	30.07.1980	2	(7)	
Denis Firago	20.11.2000		(1)	
Alyaksandr Kholodinsky	16.10.1991	20	(7)	3
Dmitriy Komarovskiy	10.10.1986	30		8
Milo Mićunović (SRB)	25.06.1992	4	(5)	1
Dmitriy Osipenko	12.12.1982	4	(2)	1
Alyaksey Rudenok	25.02.1993	17	(7)	1
Trainer:	**DOB**	**M**		
Vitali Zhukovski	17.05.1984	30		

Football Club Luch Minsk

Founded: 2012
Stadium: SOK Olimpiysky Stadium, Minsk (1,530)

Goalkeepers:	**DOB**	**M**	**(s)**	**G**
Maksim Plotnikov	29.01.1998	8		
Denis Shelikhov (UKR)	23.06.1989	16		
Artem Soroko	01.04.1992	6	(1)	
Defenders:	**DOB**	**M**	**(s)**	**G**
Andrei Arkhipov	06.02.1995	9	(3)	
Arseni Bondarenko	09.10.1995	25		
Aleksei Ivanov	19.02.1997	21	(5)	1
Dmitri Kaplunov	21.01.1994	16	(6)	1
Artur Kats	26.12.1994	13	(7)	1
Dmitriy Yashin (RUS)	25.04.1993	11		1
Aleksei Zaleski	07.10.1994	9	(4)	
Midfielders:	**DOB**	**M**	**(s)**	**G**
Artyom Buloychik	16.06.1992	18	(2)	
Alyaksandr Dzhigero	15.04.1996	12	(2)	2
Maksim Grechikha	10.06.1993	1		
Yuri Kozlov	21.05.1991	23	(2)	3
Timofei Lukashevich	21.03.1997	11	(4)	
Valery Marov	17.11.1993	5	(6)	
Kirill Premudrov	11.06.1992	11	(2)	
Pavel Rassolko	29.04.1993		(1)	
Luka Rotković (MNE)	05.07.1988	1	(4)	1
Egor Semenov	06.01.1988	21	(3)	3
Valery Senko	07.04.1998	2	(6)	
Vitali Shepetovski	27.09.1983	4	(6)	
Maksim Shilo	17.04.1993	10	(2)	
Mikita Stepanov	06.04.1996	26	(1)	
Evgeni Veljko	23.02.1997	17	(3)	2
Forwards:	**DOB**	**M**	**(s)**	**G**
Roman Gribovski	17.07.1995	23	(3)	5
Leonid Khankevich	21.08.1995	6	(4)	1
Olabiran Blessing Muyiwa (NGA)	07.09.1998		(5)	
Dmitriy Osipenko	12.12.1982		(4)	1
Oleksij Shhebetun (UKR)	02.06.1997	5	(3)	
Trainer:	**DOB**	**M**		
Ivan Bionchik	07.10.1985	30		

Football Club Minsk

Founded: 2006
Stadium: FC Minsk Stadium, Minsk (3,000)

Goalkeepers:	**DOB**	**M**	**(s)**	**G**
Pavel Golovenko	12.01.1997	4		
Syarhey Veremko	16.10.1982	26		
Defenders:	**DOB**	**M**	**(s)**	**G**
Artem Dylevski	20.07.1997	2	(4)	
Petr Kazantsev	22.04.1998		(1)	
Oleksiy Kovtun (UKR)	05.02.1995	5		
Aleksei Lavrik	07.08.2000	2	(4)	
Illia Lukashevich	01.08.1998	19	(3)	
Dušan Matović (SRB)	08.07.1983	13		
Yuriy Ostroukh	21.01.1988	10		
Dzmitry Pryshchepa	21.06.2001		(1)	
Alyaksandr Sverchinski	16.09.1991	13		1
Egidijus Vaitkūnas (LTU)	08.08.1988	24	(1)	
Dmitri Zinovich	29.03.1995	15	(2)	
Midfielders:	**DOB**	**M**	**(s)**	**G**
Ivan Bakhar	10.07.1998	16	(9)	5
Dzmitry Bessmertny	03.01.1997	30		4
Aleh Evdokimov	25.02.1994	29		1
Arseny Kontsedaylov (RUS)	15.07.1997		(8)	
Vladislav Nasibulin (UKR)	06.07.1989	9	(1)	4
Mikita Nikolaevich	11.09.1997	14	(11)	2
Oleksandr Vasyliev (UKR)	27.04.1994	26		2
Forwards:	**DOB**	**M**	**(s)**	**G**
Dmitri Antilevski	12.06.1997	15	(1)	4
Evgen Bokhashvili (UKR)	05.01.1993	13		4
David Gatikoev (RUS)	14.09.1993	3	(7)	1
Pavel Gorbach	13.03.2000		(8)	
Andrey Shemruk	27.04.1994	4	(4)	
Evgeni Shevchenko	06.06.1996	29	(1)	5
Nikola Stojanović (SRB)	17.02.1995	7	(3)	
Artem Vasilyev	23.01.1997	2	(17)	1
Trainer:	**DOB**	**M**		
Alyaksandr Lukhvich	21.02.1970	30		

Football Club Neman Grodno

Founded: 1964
Stadium: Neman Stadium, Grodno (8,479)

Goalkeepers:	**DOB**	**M**	**(s)**	**G**
Syarhey Kurhanski	15.05.1986	16		
Uladislaw Vasilyuchek	28.03.1994	1		
Vladimir Zhurov	09.03.1991	13		
Defenders:	**DOB**	**M**	**(s)**	**G**
Jean-Patrick Abouna Ndzana Ndzana (CMR)	27.09.1990	23		2
Alyaksandr Anyukevich	10.04.1992	8	(1)	
Paul Rolland Bebey Kingué (CMR)	09.11.1986	28		
Andrey Gorbach	20.05.1985	7		
Mihailo Jovanovič (SRB)	14.02.1989	10		
Giorgi Kantaria (GEO)	27.04.1997	22		
Yegor Khvalko	18.02.1997	18	(1)	
Evgeni Leshko	24.06.1996	5		
Pavel Zabelin	30.06.1995	2	(6)	
Ruslan Zubkov (UKR)	24.11.1991	1	(1)	
Midfielders:	**DOB**	**M**	**(s)**	**G**
Vitalii Kvashuk (UKR)	01.04.1993	11	(1)	1
Alyaksey Legchilin	11.04.1992	13	(1)	3
Filipp Rudik	22.03.1987	5	(5)	
Evgeniy Savostyanov	30.01.1988	13	(6)	1
Pavel Tseslyukevich	11.05.1995	13	(8)	2
Maksim Yablonski	15.08.1996	16	(4)	2
Andrey Yakimov	17.11.1989	16	(9)	2
Valeriy Zhukovskiy	21.05.1984	23	(2)	7
Forwards:	**DOB**	**M**	**(s)**	**G**
Junior Atemengue (CMR)	01.07.1995	2	(2)	1
Vyatcheslav Hleb	12.02.1983		(3)	1
Artem Kontsevoy	20.05.1983	5	(4)	
Leonid Kovel	29.07.1986	4	(12)	1
Maksim Lukashevich	28.03.1992	11	(3)	
Hervaine Moukam (FRA)	24.05.1994	9	(6)	3
Joseph Yannick N'Djeng (CMR)	11.03.1990	4	(5)	
Gleb Rassadkin	05.04.1995	9	(4)	1
Nikolai Yanush	09.09.1984	22	(6)	4
Trainer:	**DOB**	**M**		
Ihar Kovalevich	03.02.1968	30		

Football Club Shakhtyor Solihorsk

Founded: 1961
Stadium: Stroitel Stadium, Solihorsk (4,200)

Goalkeepers:	**DOB**	**M**	**(s)**	**G**
Pavel Chesnovskiy	04.03.1986	1	(1)	
Andrey Klimovich	27.08.1988	29		
Defenders:	**DOB**	**M**	**(s)**	**G**
Maksim Bordachev	18.05.1986	11	(5)	
Ihar Burko	08.09.1988	22	(2)	1
Ihar Kuzmenok	06.07.1990	10	(4)	3
Syarhey Matvejchik	05.06.1988	29		
Nikola Raspopović (SRB)	18.10.1989			
Pavel Rybak	11.09.1983	27		4
Alyaksandr Sachivko	05.01.1986	8	(2)	
Alyaksey Yanushkevich	15.01.1986	7		1
Midfielders:	**DOB**	**M**	**(s)**	**G**
Elis Bakaj (ALB)	25.06.1987	27		9
Syarhey Balanovich	29.08.1987	12		3
Roger Cañas Henao (COL)	27.03.1990	15	(1)	
Max Ebong Ngome	26.08.1999	14	(2)	2
Valeryi Hramyka	23.01.1997	3	(6)	
Yury Kavalyow	27.01.1993	30		5
Ion Nicolăescu (MDA)	07.09.1998		(8)	
Alyaksandr Selyava	17.05.1992	16	(9)	
Mikhail Shibun	01.01.1996	6	(5)	1
Patrick Sibomana (RWA)	15.10.1996		(1)	
Luka Šimunović (CRO)	24.05.1997	10	(4)	1
Július Szőke (SVK)	01.08.1995	28		2
Forwards:	**DOB**	**M**	**(s)**	**G**
Christopher Jackson (LBR)	25.10.1996		(2)	
Tomislav Kiš (CRO)	04.04.1994	7	(3)	1
Evgeny Kozlov (RUS)	04.02.1995	1	(5)	
Dzyanis Laptsew	01.08.1991	17	(9)	12
Vitaly Lisakovich	08.02.1998		(2)	
Pyry Soiri (FIN)	22.09.1994		(4)	
Trainer:	**DOB**	**M**		
Marek Zub (POL)	24.08.1964	3		
Sergey Tashuev (RUS) [19.04.2018]	01.01.1959	27		

Football Club Slutsk

Founded: 1998
Stadium: City Stadium, Slutsk (2,150)

Goalkeepers:	**DOB**	**M**	**(s)**	**G**
Ilya Branovets	16.04.1990	3		
Boris Pankratov	30.12.1982	25		
Artem Soroko	01.04.1992	2		
Defenders:	**DOB**	**M**	**(s)**	**G**
Aliyu Audu Abubakar (NGA)	15.06.1996	10	(1)	
Pavel Kiiko	20.03.1996	1		
Miloš Nikolić (SRB)	03.10.1994	14	(3)	2
Denis Obrazov	24.06.1988	29		
Robert Primus (TRI)	10.11.1990	9	(2)	
Syarhey Shchegrikovich	19.12.1990	9	(8)	
Alyaksey Timoshenko	09.12.1986	22	(3)	
Vitaliy Trubilo	07.01.1985	22	(3)	1
Midfielders:	**DOB**	**M**	**(s)**	**G**
Konan Ahuie (CIV)	12.06.1994	14	(6)	1
Ihar Bobko	09.09.1985	20	(1)	1
Yawhen Elezarenko	04.07.1993	1	(2)	
Dmitriy German	12.06.1988	8		
Murat Khotov (RUS)	02.06.1987	20	(9)	2
Tchitchi Musa (COD)	12.08.1994	16	(8)	
Ihar Yasinsky	04.07.1990	7	(12)	
Uladislaw Zhuk		5	(3)	
Forwards:	**DOB**	**M**	**(s)**	**G**
Sékou Doumbia (CIV)	11.02.1994	24	(2)	1
Vitaliy Kibuk	07.01.1989	21	(3)	2
Cédric Kouadio (CIV)	25.07.1997		(3)	
Yawhen Shikavka	15.10.1992	29		11
Alyaksandr Yatskevich	04.01.1985	18	(7)	
Pavel Zuevich	12.07.1997	1	(9)	
Trainer:	**DOB**	**M**		
Vitaly Pavlov	21.08.1965	30		

Football Club Smolevichi

Founded: 2009
Stadium: Ozyorny Stadium, Smolevichi (1,600)

Goalkeepers:	**DOB**	**M**	**(s)**	**G**
Evgeni Abramovich	17.09.1995	7		
Anatolii Timofieiev (UKR)	19.04.1992	23		
Defenders:	**DOB**	**M**	**(s)**	**G**
Oleksandr Kaplienko (UKR)	07.03.1996	27	(1)	
Valeri Karshakevich	15.02.1988	12		3
Vyacheslav Lukhtanov (UKR)	12.02.1995	8	(1)	1
Terentiy Lutsevich	19.04.1991	16	(7)	1
Egor Potapov (RUS)	21.09.1993	18	(3)	
Stanislav Sazonovich	06.03.1992	19		1
Alyaksandr Skshinetskiy	28.02.1990	28	(1)	
Aleksa Vidić (SRB)	29.09.1994	24	(1)	
Midfielders:	**DOB**	**M**	**(s)**	**G**
Pavel Chikida	21.06.1995	12	(11)	
Artem Fedyanin	25.04.1994	16	(9)	4
Dmitri Kalineyko	09.04.1999		(1)	
Valeri Potorocha	16.04.1996	1	(3)	
Sergiy Rozhok (UKR)	25.04.1985	20	(2)	
Syarhey Rusetskiy	08.03.1989	6	(8)	
Maksim Shilo	17.04.1993	9	(6)	
Ivan Vasilyonok	17.05.1989	9	(3)	
Artiom Vaskov	21.10.1988	22	(1)	4
Yaroslav Yarotski	28.03.1996	8		
Uladislaw Zhuk	11.06.1994	11	(5)	
Forwards:	**DOB**	**M**	**(s)**	**G**
Dmitri Borodin	19.07.1999	10	(2)	
Roman Burets	28.01.1997	3	(8)	
Valery Gorbachik	19.01.1995	12	(4)	5
Alyaksandr Krasnov	14.02.1998	8	(4)	
Alyaksey Teslyuk	10.01.1994	1	(4)	1
Trainer:	**DOB**	**M**		
Alyaksandr Brazevich	01.06.1973	30		

Football Club Torpedo-BelAZ Zhodino

Founded: 1961
Stadium: Torpedo Stadium, Zhodino (6,524)

Goalkeepers:	**DOB**	**M**	**(s)**	**G**
Vladimir Bushma	24.11.1983	19		
Ivan Konovalov (RUS)	18.08.1994	7		
Maksim Plotnikov	29.01.1998	4		
Defenders:	**DOB**	**M**	**(s)**	**G**
Yann Emmanual Affi (CIV)	11.11.1995	9	(1)	
Inal Getigezhev (RUS)	23.05.1987	2		
Sergei Karpovich	29.03.1994	18		
Dzmitry Klimovich	09.02.1984	26		1
Syarhey Kontsevoy	21.06.1986	16	(2)	1
Alyaksandr Pavlovets	13.08.1996	28	(1)	2
Vladimir Shcherbo	01.04.1986	18	(4)	1
Midfielders:	**DOB**	**M**	**(s)**	**G**
Ilya Aleksievich	10.02.1991	13	(8)	
Mikhail Babichev	02.02.1995	11	(3)	
Andrey Khachaturyan	02.09.1987	10	(2)	2
Alyaksandr Kotlyarov	30.01.1993	23	(2)	3
Bogdan Myshenko (UKR)	29.12.1994	19	(7)	5
Edgar Olekhnovich	17.05.1987	26	(2)	1
Anton Postupalenko (UKR)	28.08.1988	6	(6)	1
Sergiy Shapoval (UKR)	07.02.1990	4	(8)	
Forwards:	**DOB**	**M**	**(s)**	**G**
Pavel Dolgov (RUS)	16.08.1996	7	(4)	2
Valery Gorbachik	19.01.1995	12	(2)	4
Uladislaw Klimovich	12.06.1996	24	(5)	5
Alyaksandr Krasnov	14.02.1998		(2)	
Denis Levitskiy	05.02.1997	2	(2)	
Jean-Morel Poé (CIV)	15.12.1996	10	(3)	2
Aleksandr Salugin (RUS)	23.10.1988	5	(3)	
Dmytro Yusov (UKR)	11.05.1993	11	(15)	5
Trainer:	**DOB**	**M**		
Aleh Kubarev	08.02.1966	30		

Football Club Torpedo Minsk

Founded: 1947
Stadium: SOK Olimpiysky Stadium, Minsk (1,530)

Goalkeepers:	**DOB**	**M**	**(s)**	**G**
Vladimir Pyatigorets	12.04.1990	1		
Konstantin Rudenok	15.12.1990	15		
Roman Stepanov	06.08.1991	14		
Defenders:	**DOB**	**M**	**(s)**	**G**
Roman Gaev	20.01.1989	28		
Uladislaw Glinski	29.05.2000	12	(4)	
Igor Gubanov (RUS)	04.02.1992	9	(1)	
Roman Krivulkin	18.02.1996	19		
Evgeni Morozov	17.04.1995	14	(4)	1
Ihar Shumilov	20.10.1993	16	(3)	1
Artem Sokol	30.03.1994	18		
Andrey Vasilyev (RUS)	11.02.1992	25		1
Midfielders:	**DOB**	**M**	**(s)**	**G**
Alyaksey Butarevich	12.01.1997	17	(3)	
Yawhen Elezarenko	04.07.1993	11	(1)	
Yuri Lovets	11.07.1996		(3)	
Mikita Patsko	23.02.1995	2	(11)	
Alyaksandr Perepechko	07.04.1989		(2)	
Syarhey Rusak	03.09.1993	18	(4)	2
Dmitri Tamelo	08.11.1992	16	(7)	3
Boris Tsygankov (RUS)	17.04.1998	12	(4)	1
Denis Yakubovich	31.03.1988	13	(3)	
Forwards:	**DOB**	**M**	**(s)**	**G**
Vadim Demidovich	20.09.1985	10	(1)	2
Alyaksandr Filanovich	01.12.1992	10	(7)	
Syarhey Glebko	23.08.1992	10	(2)	1
Pavel Klenyo	28.04.1999	2	(15)	2
Cédric Khaleb Kouadio (CIV)	25.07.1997	11		5
Syarhey Lynko	16.10.1989	18	(6)	1
Evgeni Nikitin	09.04.1993	4	(4)	
Maksim Sanets	04.04.1997		(1)	
Đorđe Šušnjar (SRB)	18.02.1992	5	(3)	
Trainer:	**DOB**	**M**		
Syarhey Kabelski	17.04.1973	12		
Leonid Lagun [18.06.2018]	22.06.1978	6		
Vladimir Nevinski [24.08.2018]	14.09.1973	12		

Football Club Vitebsk

Founded: 1960
Stadium: Vitebsky Central Sport Complex, Vitebsk (8,100)

Goalkeepers:	**DOB**	**M**	**(s)**	**G**
Dmitri Gushchenko	12.05.1988	9		
Andrey Shcherbakov	31.01.1991	21	(1)	
Defenders:	**DOB**	**M**	**(s)**	**G**
Aleh Karamushka (UKR)	30.04.1984	17	(3)	1
Evgeni Klopotskiy	12.08.1993	20	(4)	3
Mikita Naumov	15.11.1989	27	(1)	3
Kirill Pechenin	18.03.1997	12	(17)	3
Artem Skitov	21.01.1991	29		1
Aleksei Zaleski	07.10.1994	1	(12)	
Nikolai Zolotov	11.11.1994	29		
Midfielders:	**DOB**	**M**	**(s)**	**G**
Nenad Adamović (SRB)	12.01.1989	22	(2)	1
Alyaksandr Aleksandrovich	06.07.1997		(3)	
Ivan Berezun	19.08.1997		(1)	
Mikhail Kozlov	12.02.1990	24		2
Wanderson Cavalcante Melo „Maranhão" (BRA)	26.07.1994	28	(1)	
Anton Matveenko	03.09.1986	26	(4)	11
Rafael Pompeu Rodrigues Ledesma „Rafael Gaúcho" (BRA)	31.12.1982	12		2
Artem Stargorodskiy (UKR)	17.01.1982	14		
Sergei Volkov	27.01.1999		(2)	
Forwards:	**DOB**	**M**	**(s)**	**G**
Bruno de Oliveira Furlan (BRA)	09.07.1992	8	(10)	4
Ilya Shkurin	17.08.1999		(7)	
Ruslan Teverov	01.05.1994	3	(18)	3
Kirill Vergeychik	23.08.1991	28	(2)	11
Trainer:	**DOB**	**M**		
Syarhey Yasinsky	07.01.1965	30		

SECOND LEVEL
First League 2018

1.	FC Slavia Mozyr (*Promoted*)	28	21	7	0	69 - 13	70
2.	FC Energetik-BGU Minsk (*Promoted*)	28	21	4	3	69 - 23	67
3.	FC Belshina Bobruisk	28	18	5	5	59 - 23	59
4.	FC Lida	28	18	4	6	45 - 18	58
5.	FC Naftan Novopolotsk	28	10	11	7	28 - 24	41
6.	FC Lokomotiv Gomel	28	10	10	8	44 - 29	40
7.	FC Slonim-2017	28	9	9	10	37 - 37	36
8.	FC Granit Mikashevichi*	28	8	11	9	28 - 34	34
9.	FC Khimik Svetlogorsk	28	9	5	14	32 - 40	32
10.	FC AUS Zhitkovichi	28	6	10	12	23 - 38	28
11.	FC Smorgon	28	6	10	12	19 - 44	28
12.	FC Orsha	28	8	3	17	33 - 53	27
13.	FC Volna Pinsk	28	6	7	15	23 - 49	25
14.	FC Baranovichi	28	4	7	17	17 - 42	19
15.	FC Chist (*Relegated*)	28	1	7	20	30 - 89	10

* *1 point deducted* (due to delayed salary payment)

NATIONAL TEAM

INTERNATIONAL MATCHES
(16.07.2018 – 15.07.2019)

08.09.2018	Minsk	Belarus - San Marino	5-0(2-0)	(UNL)
11.09.2018	Chişinău	Moldova - Belarus	0-0	(UNL)
12.10.2018	Minsk	Belarus - Luxembourg	1-0(1-0)	(UNL)
15.10.2018	Minsk	Belarus - Moldova	0-0	(UNL)
15.11.2018	Letzëbuerg	Luxembourg - Belarus	0-2(0-1)	(UNL)
18.11.2018	Serravalle	San Marino - Belarus	0-2(0-1)	(UNL)
21.03.2019	Rotterdam	Netherlands - Belarus	4-0(2-0)	(ECQ)
24.03.2019	Belfast	Northern Ireland - Belarus	2-1(1-1)	(ECQ)
08.06.2019	Borisov	Belarus - Germany	0-2(0-1)	(ECQ)
11.06.2019	Borisov	Belarus - Northern Ireland	0-1(0-0)	(ECQ)

08.09.2018 BELARUS - SAN MARINO 5-0(2-0) UEFA Nations League D, Group 2
Stadion Dynama, Minsk; Referee: Sandro Schärer (Switzerland); Attendance: 13,634
BLR: Syarhey Chernik, Syarhey Palitsevich, Ihar Shytaw, Alyaksandr Martynovich (Cap), Maksim Valadzko, Pavel Nyakhaychyk (67.Syarhey Balanovich), Ihar Stasevich (75.Yury Kavalyow), Renan Bardini Bressan, Stanislaw Drahun, Ivan Maewski, Dzyanis Laptsew (56.Anton Saroka). Trainer: Ihar Kriushenko.
Goals: Ihar Stasevich (4), Stanislaw Drahun (26), Anton Saroka (67 penalty), Stanislaw Drahun (87), Yury Kavalyow (90+1).

11.09.2018 MOLDOVA - BELARUS 0-0 UEFA Nations League D, Group 2
Stadionul Zimbru, Chişinău; Referee: Mario Zebec (Croatia); Attendance: 4,942
BLR: Syarhey Chernik, Syarhey Palitsevich, Ihar Shytaw, Alyaksandr Martynovich (Cap), Maksim Valadzko, Pavel Nyakhaychyk (72.Syarhey Balanovich), Ihar Stasevich, Renan Bardini Bressan (77.Yury Kendysh), Stanislaw Drahun, Ivan Maewski, Dzyanis Laptsew (59.Anton Saroka). Trainer: Ihar Kriushenko.

12.10.2018 BELARUS - LUXEMBOURG 1-0(1-0) UEFA Nations League D, Group 2
Stadion Dynama, Minsk; Referee: Ali Palabıyık (Turkey); Attendance: 14,122
BLR: Andrey Harbunow, Dzyanis Palyakow, Mikhail Sivakov, Alyaksandr Martynovich (Cap), Maksim Valadzko, Anton Putsila (75.Yury Kendysh), Pavel Nyakhaychyk, Ihar Stasevich, Stanislaw Drahun (81.Mikita Korzun), Ivan Maewski, Anton Saroka (87.Dzyanis Laptsew). Trainer: Ihar Kriushenko.
Goal: Anton Saroka (43).

15.10.2018 BELARUS - MOLDOVA 0-0 UEFA Nations League D, Group 2
Stadion Dynama, Minsk; Referee: Kevin John Clancy (Scotland); Attendance: 10,870
BLR: Andrey Harbunow, Dzyanis Palyakow, Mikhail Sivakov, Alyaksandr Martynovich (Cap), Alyaksey Ryas, Ihar Stasevich, Syarhey Kislyak (69.Stanislaw Drahun), Ivan Maewski, Yury Kendysh (77.Anton Putsila), Yury Kavalyow, Anton Saroka (61.Mikalay Signevich). Trainer: Ihar Kriushenko.

15.11.2018 LUXEMBOURG - BELARUS 0-2(0-1) UEFA Nations League D, Group 2
Stade "Josy Barthel", Letzëbuerg; Referee: Serdar Gözübüyük (Netherlands); Attendance: 4,533
BLR: Andrey Harbunow, Mikhail Sivakov, Ihar Shytaw, Alyaksandr Martynovich (Cap), Maksim Valadzko, Alyaksandr Hleb (74.Anton Putsila), Ihar Stasevich, Stanislaw Drahun, Ivan Maewski, Pavel Savitski (72.Syarhey Balanovich), Anton Saroka (86.Mikalay Signevich). Trainer: Ihar Kriushenko.
Goals: Stanislaw Drahun (37, 54).

18.11.2018 SAN MARINO - BELARUS 0-2(0-1) UEFA Nations League D, Group 2
San Marino Stadium, Serravalle; Referee: Giorgi Kruashvili (Georgia); Attendance: 736
BLR: Syarhey Chernik, Syarhey Palitsevich, Dzyanis Palyakow, Ihar Shytaw, Alyaksandr Martynovich (Cap), Alyaksandr Hleb (70.Anton Putsila), Ihar Stasevich, Stanislaw Drahun, Ivan Maewski (80.Syarhey Kislyak), Pavel Savitski (66.Maksim Skavysh), Anton Saroka. Trainer: Ihar Kriushenko.
Goals: Stanislaw Drahun (8), Anton Saroka (53).

21.03.2019 NETHERLANDS - BELARUS 4-0(2-0) 16th EC. Qualifiers
Stadion Feijenoord, Rotterdam; Referee: Davide Massa (Italy); Attendance: 38,604
BLR: Andrey Harbunow, Dzyanis Palyakow, Mikhail Sivakov, Ihar Shytaw, Alyaksandr Martynovich (Cap), Anton Putsila, Ihar Stasevich, Ivan Maewski, Stanislaw Drahun (87.Dzyanis Laptsew), Yury Kavalyow (79.Pavel Savitski), Mikalay Signevich (63.Anton Saroka). Trainer: Ihar Kriushenko.

24.03.2019 NORTHERN IRELAND - BELARUS 2-1(1-1) 16th EC. Qualifiers
Windsor Park, Belfast; Referee: Paweł Raczkowski (Poland); Attendance: 18,188
BLR: Andrey Klimovich, Mikhail Sivakov, Ihar Shytaw (73.Dzyanis Palyakow), Alyaksandr Martynovich (Cap), Maksim Valadzko, Alyaksandr Hleb (66.Anton Putsila), Ihar Stasevich, Stanislaw Drahun, Ivan Maewski, Pavel Savitski (85.Pavel Nyakhaychyk), Dzyanis Laptsew. Trainer: Ihar Kriushenko.
Goal: Ihar Stasevich (33).

08.06.2019 BELARUS - GERMANY 0-2(0-1) 16th EC. Qualifiers
Borisov Arena, Borisov; Referee: Srđan Jovanović (Serbia); Attendance: 7,200
BLR: Alyaksandr Hutar, Dzyanis Palyakow, Ihar Shytaw, Alyaksandr Martynovich (Cap), Mikita Navumaw, Maksim Valadzko, Stanislaw Drahun, Ivan Maewski, Yury Kavalyow (69' Mihail Hardzeichuk), Valeryi Hramyka (57' Mikita Korzun), Dzyanis Laptsew (62' Maksim Skavysh). Trainer: Ihar Kriushenko.

11.06.2019 BELARUS - NORTHERN IRELAND 0-1(0-0) 16th EC. Qualifiers
Borisov Arena, Borisov; Referee: Harald Lechner (Austria); Attendance: 5,350
BLR: Alyaksandr Hutar, Dzyanis Palyakow, Ihar Shytaw (72.Aleh Veratsila), Alyaksandr Martynovich (Cap), Mikita Navumaw, Pavel Nyakhaychyk, Ihar Stasevich, Ivan Maewski, Mikita Korzun (46.Syarhey Kislyak), Yury Kavalyow, Yawhen Shikawka (58.Dzyanis Laptsew). Trainer: Ihar Kriushenko.

NATIONAL TEAM PLAYERS
(16.07.2018 – 15.07.2019)

Name	DOB	Caps	Goals	2018/2019:	Club
Goalkeepers					
Syarhey CHERNIK	20.07.1988	**18**	**0**	2018:	*AS Nancy-Lorraine (FRA)*
Andrey HARBUNOW	29.05.1983	**19**	**0**	2018:	*FC Dinamo Minsk*
				28.01.2019->	*FC Torpedo-BelAZ Zhodino*
Alyaksandr HUTAR	18.04.1989	**12**	**0**	2018/2019:	*FC Dinamo Brest*
Andrey KLIMOVICH	27.08.1988	**3**	**0**	2019:	*FC Shakhtyor Solihorsk*
Defenders					
Alyaksandr MARTYNOVICH	26.08.1987	**67**	**2**	2018/2019:	*FK Krasnodar (RUS)*
Mikita NAVUMAW	15.11.1989	**3**	**0**	2019:	*FC Zhetisu Taldiqorghan (KAZ)*
Syarhey PALITSEVICH	09.04.1990	**29**	**1**	2018:	*FC Kairat Almaty (KAZ)*
Dzyanis PALYAKOW	17.04.1991	**36**	**1**	2018:	*FC BATE Borisov*
				01.01.2019->	*FK Ural Yekaterinburg (RUS)*
Pavel SAVITSKI	12.07.1994	**18**	**4**	2018/2019:	*FC Dinamo Brest*
Ihar SHYTAW	24.10.1986	**66**	**1**	2018/2019:	*FC Dinamo Minsk*
Mikhail SIVAKOV	16.01.1988	**25**	**1**	2018/2019:	*FK Orenburg (RUS)*
Maksim VALADZKO	10.11.1992	**32**	**2**	2018:	*FC BATE Borisov*
				12.01.2019->	*FK Arsenal Tula (RUS)*
Aleh VERATSILA	10.07.1988	**18**	**0**	2019:	*FC Dinamo Brest*
Midfielders					
Syarhey BALANOVICH	29.08.1987	**33**	**2**	2018:	*FC Shakhtyor Solihorsk*
Renan Bardini BRESSAN	03.11.1988	**29**	**3**	2018:	*GD Chaves (POR)*
Stanislaw DRAHUN	04.06.1988	**59**	**10**	2018/2019:	*FC BATE Borisov*
Alyaksandr HLEB	01.05.1981	**80**	**6**	2018/2019:	*FC BATE Borisov*
Valeryi HRAMYKA	23.01.1997	**1**	**0**	2019:	*FC Shakhtyor Solihorsk*
Yury KAVALYOW	27.01.1993	**12**	**1**	2018/2019:	*FC Shakhtyor Solihorsk*
Yury KENDYSH	10.06.1990	**8**	**0**	2018/2019:	*FC Sheriff Tiraspol (MDA)*
Syarhey KISLYAK	06.08.1987	**70**	**9**	2018/2019:	*FC Dinamo Brest*
Mikita KORZUN	06.03.1995	**14**	**0**	2018:	*FC Dinamo Minsk*
				24.01.2019->	*Al-Fateh SC Al-Hasa (KSA)*
Ivan MAEWSKI	05.05.1988	**29**	**0**	2018/2019:	*FK Astana (KAZ)*
Pavel NYAKHAYCHYK	15.07.1988	**30**	**2**	2018/2019:	*FC Dinamo Brest*
Anton PUTSILA	10.06.1987	**56**	**6**	2018:	*MKE Ankaragücü SK Ankara (TUR)*
				10.01.2019->	*Altak SK İzmir (TUR)*
Alyaksey RYAS	14.05.1987	**10**	**1**	2018/2019:	*FC BATE Borisov*
Yawhen SHIKAWKA	15.10.1992	**2**	**0**	2019:	*AE Larissa (GRE)*
Ihar STASEVICH	21.10.1985	**47**	**5**	2018/2019:	*FC BATE Borisov*
Forwards					
Mihail HARDZEICHUK	23.10.1989	**26**	**4**	2019:	*FC Tobol Kostanay (KAZ)*
Dzyanis LAPTSEW	01.08.1991	**19**	**0**	2018:	*FC Shakhtyor Solihorsk*
				01.01.2019->	*FC Dinamo Brest*
Anton SAROKA	05.03.1992	**15**	**7**	2018/2019:	*KSC Lokeren (BEL)*
				19.03.2019->	*FC BATE Borisov*
Mikalay SIGNEVICH	20.02.1992	**16**	**1**	2018:	*FC BATE Borisov*
				30.01.2019->	*Ferencvárosi TC (HUN)*
Maksim SKAVYSH	13.11.1989	**13**	**1**	2018/2019:	*FC BATE Borisov*

National team coach

Ihar Nikolayevich KRIUSHENKO [from 01.03.2017]	10.02.1964	25 M; 8 W; 4 D; 13 L; 23-37

BELGIUM

The Country:

Royaume de Belgique / Koninkrijk België (Kingdom of Belgium)
Capital: Bruxelles
Surface: 30,528 km²
Inhabitants: 11,420,163 [2018]
Time: UTC+1

The FA:

Union royale belge des sociétés de football association / Koninklijke Belgische Voetbalbond
145, Avenue Houba de Strooper, 1020 Bruxelles
Tel: +32 2 477 1211
Foundation date: 1895
Member of FIFA since: 1904
Member of UEFA since: 1954
Website: www.belgianfootball.be

NATIONAL TEAM RECORDS

First international match:	01.05.1994, Bruxelles: Belgium – France 3-3	
Most international caps:	Jan Bert Lieve Vertonghen	- 114 caps (since 2007)
Most international goals:	Romelu Menama Lukaku Bolingoli	- 48 goals / 81 caps (since 2010)

UEFA EUROPEAN CHAMPIONSHIP	
1960	*Did not enter*
1964	Qualifiers
1968	Qualifiers
1972	Final Tournament (3rd Place)
1976	Qualifiers
1980	Final Tournament (Runners-up)
1984	Final Tournament (Group Stage)
1988	Qualifiers
1992	Qualifiers
1996	Qualifiers
2000	Final Tournament (Group Stage)
2004	Qualifiers
2008	Qualifiers
2012	Qualifiers
2016	Final Tournament (Quarter-Finals)

FIFA WORLD CUP	
1930	Final Tournament (Group Stage)
1934	Final Tournament (1st Round)
1938	Final Tournament (1st Round)
1950	*Withdrew*
1954	Final Tournament (Group Stage)
1958	Qualifiers
1962	Qualifiers
1966	Qualifiers
1970	Final Tournament (Group Stage)
1974	Qualifiers
1978	Qualifiers
1982	Final Tournament (2nd Round)
1986	Final Tournament (4th Place)
1990	Final Tournament (2nd Round of 16)
1994	Final Tournament (2nd Round of 16)
1998	Final Tournament (Group Stage)
2002	Final Tournament (2nd Round of 16)
2006	Qualifiers
2010	Qualifiers
2014	Final Tournament (Quarter-Finals)
2018	Final Tournament (3rd Place)

UEFA NATIONS LEAGUE
2018/2019 – League A

OLYMPIC FOOTBALL TOURNAMENTS 1908-2016							
1908	-	**1948**	*Did not enter*	**1972**	*Did not enter*	**1996**	Qualifiers
1912	-	**1952**	*Did not enter*	**1976**	*Did not enter*	**2000**	Qualifiers
1920	**Winners**	**1956**	*Did not enter*	**1980**	Qualifiers	**2004**	Qualifiers
1924	TF / 1/8-Finals	**1960**	*Did not enter*	**1984**	Qualifiers	**2008**	FT / 4th Place
1928	Quarter-Finals	**1964**	*Did not enter*	**1988**	Qualifiers	**2012**	Qualifiers
1936	*Did not enter*	**1968**	*Did not enter*	**1992**	Qualifiers	**2016**	Qualifiers

FIFA CONFEDERATIONS CUP 1992-2017
None

BELGIAN CLUB HONOURS IN EUROPEAN CLUB COMPETITIONS:

European Champion Clubs' Cup (1956-1992) / UEFA Champions League (1993-2019)		
None		
Fairs Cup (1858-1971) / UEFA Cup (1972-2009) / UEFA Europa League (2010-2019)		
RSC Anderlecht Bruxelles	**1**	1982/1983
UEFA Super Cup (1972-2019)		
RSC Anderlecht Bruxelles	**2**	1976, 1978
KV Mechelen	**1**	1988
European Cup Winners' Cup 1961-1999*		
RSC Anderlecht Bruxelles	**2**	1975/1976, 1977/1978
KV Mechelen	**1**	1987/1988

**defunct competition*

NATIONAL COMPETITIONS
TABLE OF HONOURS

	CHAMPIONS	CUP WINNERS	BEST GOALSCORERS	
1895/1896	FC Liégeois	-	Samuel Hickson (ENG, FC Liégeois)	?
1896/1897	Racing Club de Bruxelles	-	Samuel Hickson (ENG, FC Liégeois)	?
1897/1898	FC Liégeois	-	Franz König (SUI, Racing Club de Bruxelles)	?
1898/1899	FC Liégeois	-	Franz König (SUI, Racing Club de Bruxelles)	?
1899/1900	Racing Club de Bruxelles	-	Charles Richard Atkinson-Grimshaw (ENG, Racing Club de Bruxelles)	?
1900/1901	Racing Club de Bruxelles	-	Herbert Alfred Potts (ENG, K Beerschot VAC)	26
1901/1902	Racing Club de Bruxelles	-	Herbert Alfred Potts (ENG, K Beerschot VAC)	16
1902/1903	Racing Club de Bruxelles	-	Gustave Vanderstappen (Royale Union Saint-Gilloise)	?
1903/1904	Royale Union Saint-Gilloise	-	Gustave Vanderstappen (Royale Union Saint-Gilloise)	30
1904/1905	Royale Union Saint-Gilloise	-	Robert De Veen (FC Brugeois)	?
1905/1906	Royale Union Saint-Gilloise	-	Robert De Veen (FC Brugeois)	26
1906/1907	Royale Union Saint-Gilloise	-	Maurice Vertongen (Racing Club de Bruxelles)	29
1907/1908	Racing Club de Bruxelles	-	Maurice Vertongen (Racing Club de Bruxelles)	23
1908/1909	Royale Union Saint-Gilloise	-	Vahram Kevorkian (RUS, Racing Club de Bruxelles)	30
1909/1910	Royale Union Saint-Gilloise	-	Maurice Vertongen (Royale Union Saint-Gilloise)	36
1910/1911	CS Brugeois	-	Alphonse Six (CS Brugeois)	40
1911/1912	Daring Club de Bruxelles	Racing Club de Bruxelles	Maurice Taylor Bunyan (ENG, Racing Club de Bruxelles)	35
1912/1913	Royale Union Saint-Gilloise	Royale Union Saint-Gilloise	Sylva Brébart (Daring Club de Bruxelles)	31
1913/1914	Daring Club de Bruxelles	Royale Union Saint-Gilloise	Maurice Bunyan (ENG, Racing Club de Bruxelles)	28
1915-1919	*No competition*	*No competition*	-	
1919/1920	FC Brugeois	*No competition*	Honoré Vlamynck (Daring Club de Bruxelles)	26
1920/1921	Daring Club de Bruxelles	*No competition*	Ivan Thys (K Beerschot VAC)	23
1921/1922	K Beerschot VAC	*No competition*	Ivan Thys (K Beerschot VAC)	21
1922/1923	Royale Union Saint-Gilloise	*No competition*	Achille Meyskens (Royale Union Saint-Gilloise)	24
1923/1924	K Beerschot VAC	*No competition*	Charles Jooris (Racing Club de Bruxelles)	18
1924/1925	K Beerschot VAC	*No competition*	Joseph Taeymans (K Berchem Sport)	20
1925/1926	K Beerschot VAC	*No competition*	Laurent Grimmonprez (RC Gent)	28
1926/1927	RCS Brugeois	RCS Brugeois	Lucien Fabry (R Standard Liège)	28
1927/1928	K Beerschot VAC	*No competition*	Raymond Braine (K Beerschot VAC)	35
1928/1929	R Antwerp FC	*No competition*	Raymond Braine (K Beerschot VAC)	30
1929/1930	RCS Brugeois	*No competition*	Pierre De Vidts (Daring Club de Bruxelles)	26
1930/1931	R Antwerp FC	*No competition*	Jacques Secretin (RCFC Montegnée) Joseph Van Beeck (R Antwerp FC	21
1931/1932	K Lierse SK	*No competition*	Bernard Delmez (K Lierse SK)	26
1932/1933	Royale Union Saint-Gilloise	*No competition*	Willy Ulens (R Antwerp FC)	26
1933/1934	Royale Union Saint-Gilloise	*No competition*	Vital Van Landeghem (Royale Union Saint-Gilloise)	29
1934/1935	Royale Union Saint-Gilloise	Daring Club de Bruxelles	Marius Mondelé (Daring Club de Bruxelles)	28
1935/1936	Daring Club de Bruxelles SR	*No competition*	Flor Lambrechts (R Antwerp FC)	37
1936/1937	Daring Club de Bruxelles SR	*No competition*	Jean Collet (White Star WAC Bruxelles)	22
1937/1938	R Beerschot AC Antwerp	*No competition*	Marius Mondelé (Daring Club de Bruxelles)	32
1938/1939	R Beerschot AC Antwerp	*No competition*	Jozef Wagner (R Antwerp FC)	31
1939-1941	*No competition*	*No competition*	-	
1941/1942	K Liersche SK	*No competition*	Bert De Cleyn (R Antwerp FC)	34
1942/1943	RFC Malinois	*No competition*	Arthur Ceuleers (K Beerschot VAC) Jules Van Craen (K Lierse SK)	41
1943/1944	R Antwerp FC	*No competition*	Jan Goossens (ROC Charleroi)	34
1944/1945	*No competition*	*No competition*	-	
1945/1946	RFC Malinois	*No competition*	-	
1946/1947	RSC Anderlecht Bruxelles	*No competition*	Jef Mermans (RSC Anderlecht Bruxelles)	39
1947/1948	RFC Malinois	*No competition*	Jef Mermans (RSC Anderlecht Bruxelles)	23
1948/1949	RSC Anderlecht Bruxelles	*No competition*	René Thirifays (R Charleroi SC)	26
1949/1950	RSC Anderlecht Bruxelles	*No competition*	Jef Mermans (RSC Anderlecht Bruxelles)	37
1950/1951	RSC Anderlecht Bruxelles	*No competition*	Albert Dehert (K Berchem Sport)	27
1951/1952	RFC Liégeois	*No competition*	Jozef Mannaerts (KRC Mechelen)	25
1952/1953	RFC Liégeois	*No competition*	Rik Coppens (K Beerschot VAC)	35
1953/1954	RSC Anderlecht Bruxelles	R Standard Liège	Hippolyte Van Den Bosch (RSC Anderlecht Bruxelles)	29
1954/1955	RSC Anderlecht Bruxelles	R Antwerp FC	Rik Coppens (K Beerschot VAC)	35
1955/1956	RSC Anderlecht Bruxelles	RRC Tournaisien	Jean Mathonet (R Standard Liège)	26
1956/1957	R Antwerp FC	*No competition*	Maurice Willems (KAA Gent)	35
1957/1958	R Standard Liège	*No competition*	Jef Vliers (K Beerschot VAC)	25
1958/1959	RSC Anderlecht Bruxelles	*No competition*	Victor Wegria (RFC Liégeois)	26
1959/1960	K Lierse SK	*No competition*	Victor Wegria (RFC Liégeois)	21
1960/1961	R Standard Liège	*No competition*	Victor Wegria (RFC Liégeois)	23
1961/1962	RSC Anderlecht Bruxelles	*No competition*	Jacky Stockman (RSC Anderlecht Bruxelles)	29
1962/1963	R Standard Liège	*No competition*	Victor Wegria (RFC Liégeois)	29
1963/1964	RSC Anderlecht Bruxelles	ARA La Gantoise	Paul Van Himst (RSC Anderlecht Bruxelles)	26
1964/1965	RSC Anderlecht Bruxelles	RSC Anderlecht Bruxelles	Jean-Paul Colonval (RFC Tilleur Saint-Nicolas)	25

1965/1966	RSC Anderlecht Bruxelles	R Standard Liège	Paul Van Himst (RSC Anderlecht Bruxelles)	25
1966/1967	RSC Anderlecht Bruxelles	R Standard Liège	Johan Mulder (NED, RSC Anderlecht Bruxelles)	20
1967/1968	RSC Anderlecht Bruxelles	Club Brugge KV	Roger Claessen (R Standard Liège Liège) Paul Van Himst (RSC Anderlecht Bruxelles)	20
1968/1969	R Standard Liège	K Lierse SK	Antal Nagy (HUN, R Standard Liège Liège)	20
1969/1970	R Standard Liège	Club Brugge KV	Lothar Emmerich (GER, K Beerschot VAC)	29
1970/1971	R Standard Liège	K Beerschot VAV	Erwin Kostedde (GER, R Standard Liège Liège)	26
1971/1972	RSC Anderlecht Bruxelles	RSC Anderlecht Bruxelles	Raoul Lambert (Club Brugge KV)	17
1972/1973	Club Brugge KV	RSC Anderlecht Bruxelles	Pieter Robert Rensenbrink (NED, RSC Anderlecht Bruxelles) Alfred Riedl (AUT, K Sint-Truidense VV)	16
1973/1974	RSC Anderlecht Bruxelles	KSV Waregem	Attila Ladynski (HUN, RSC Anderlecht Bruxelles)	22
1974/1975	R White Daring Molenbeek	RSC Anderlecht Bruxelles	Alfred Riedl (AUT, R Antwerp FC)	28
1975/1976	Club Brugge KV	RSC Anderlecht Bruxelles	Hans Posthumus (K Lierse SK)	26
1976/1977	Club Brugge KV	Club Brugge KV	François Van Der Elst (RSC Anderlecht Bruxelles)	21
1977/1978	Club Brugge KV	KSK Beveren	Harald Nickel (R Standard Liège Liège)	22
1978/1979	KSK Beveren	K Beerschot VAV	Erwin Albert (KSK Beveren)	28
1979/1980	Club Brugge KV	K Waterschei SV Thor Genk	Erwin Vandenbergh (K Lierse SK)	39
1980/1981	RSC Anderlecht Bruxelles	R Standard Liège	Erwin Vandenbergh (K Lierse SK)	24
1981/1982	R Standard Liège	K Waterschei SV Thor Genk	Erwin Vandenbergh (K Lierse SK)	25
1982/1983	R Standard Liège	KSK Beveren	Erwin Vandenbergh (RSC Anderlecht Bruxelles)	20
1983/1984	KSK Beveren	KAA Gent	Nicolaas Pieter Claesen (RFC Seraing)	27
1984/1985	RSC Anderlecht Bruxelles	Cercle Brugge KSV	Ronny Martens (KAA Gent)	23
1985/1986	RSC Anderlecht Bruxelles	Club Brugge KV	Erwin Vandenbergh (RSC Anderlecht Bruxelles)	27
1986/1987	RSC Anderlecht Bruxelles	KV Mechelen	Arnór Guðjohnsen (ISL, RSC Anderlecht Bruxelles)	19
1987/1988	Club Brugge KV	RSC Anderlecht Bruxelles	Francis Severeyns (R Antwerp FC)	24
1988/1989	KV Mechelen	RSC Anderlecht Bruxelles	Edward Krncevic (AUS, RSC Anderlecht Bruxelles)	23
1989/1990	Club Brugge KV	RFC Liégeois	Frank Farina (AUS, Club Brugge KV)	24
1990/1991	RSC Anderlecht Bruxelles	Club Brugge KV	Erwin Vandenbergh (KAA Gent)	23
1991/1992	Club Brugge KV	Royal Antwerp F.C.	Josip Weber (CRO, Cercle Brugge KSV)	26
1992/1993	RSC Anderlecht Bruxelles	R Standard Liège	Josip Weber (CRO, Cercle Brugge KSV)	31
1993/1994	RSC Anderlecht Bruxelles	RSC Anderlecht Bruxelles	Josip Weber (Cercle Brugge KSV)	31
1994/1995	RSC Anderlecht Bruxelles	Club Brugge KV	Aurelio Vidmar (AUS, R Standard Liège Liège)	22
1995/1996	Club Brugge KV	Club Brugge KV	Mario Stanić (CRO, Club Brugge KV)	20
1996/1997	K Lierse SK	KFC Germinal Ekeren	Robert Špehar (CRO, Club Brugge KV)	26
1997/1998	Club Brugge KV	KRC Genk	Branko Strupar (KRC Genk)	22
1998/1999	KRC Genk	Lierse S.K.	Jan Koller (CZE, Lokeren)	24
1999/2000	RSC Anderlecht Bruxelles	KRC Genk	Ole Martin Årst (NOR, KAA Gent) Antonio Brogno (KVC Westerlo)	30
2000/2001	RSC Anderlecht Bruxelles	KVC Westerlo	Tomasz Radzinski (CAN, RSC Anderlecht Bruxelles)	23
2001/2002	KRC Genk	Club Brugge KV	Wesley Sonck (KRC Genk)	30
2002/2003	Club Brugge KV	RAA La Louvière	Cédric Roussel (RAEC Mons) Wesley Sonck (KRC Genk)	22
2003/2004	RSC Anderlecht Bruxelles	Club Brugge KV	Luigi Pieroni (Mouscron)	28
2004/2005	Club Brugge KV	KFC Germinal Beerschot	Nenad Jestrović (SRB, RSC Anderlecht Bruxelles)	18
2005/2006	RSC Anderlecht Bruxelles	SV Zulte-Waregem	Tosin Dosunmu (NGA, KFC Germinal Beerschot Antwerpen)	18
2006/2007	RSC Anderlecht Bruxelles	Club Brugge KV	François Sterchele (KFC Germinal Beerschot Antwerpen)	21
2007/2008	R Standard Liège	RSC Anderlecht Bruxelles	Joseph Eneojo Akpala (NGA, R Charleroi SC)	18
2008/2009	R Standard Liège	KRC Genk	Jaime Alfonso Ruiz (COL, KVC Westerlo)	18
2009/2010	RSC Anderlecht Bruxelles	KAA Gent	Romelu Menama Lukaku Bolingoli (RSC Anderlecht Bruxelles)	15
2010/2011	KRC Genk	R Standard Liège	Ivan Perišić (CRO, Club Brugge KV)	22
2011/2012	RSC Anderlecht Bruxelles	KSC Lokeren	Jérémy Perbet (FRA, RAEC Mons)	25
2012/2013	RSC Anderlecht Bruxelles	KRC Genk	Carlos Arturo Bacca Ahumada (COL, Club Brugge KV)	25
2013/2014	RSC Anderlecht Bruxelles	KSC Lokeren	Hamdi Harbaoui (TUN, KSC Lokeren Oost-Vlaanderen)	22
2014/2015	KAA Gent	Club Brugge KV	Aleksandar Mitrović (SRB, RSC Anderlecht Bruxelles)	20
2015/2016	Club Brugge KV	R Standard Liège	Jérémy Perbet (FRA, R Charleroi SC)	22
2016/2017	RSC Anderlecht Bruxelles	SV Zulte Waregem	Łukasz Teodorczyk (POL, RSC Anderlecht Bruxelles)	22
2017/2018	Club Brugge KV	R Standard Liège	Hamdi Harbaoui (TUN, SV Zulte Waregem)	22
2018/2019	KRC Genk	KV Mechelen	Hamdi Harbaoui (TUN, SV Zulte Waregem)	25

NATIONAL CHAMPIONSHIP

Eerste Divisie / Jupiler Pro League - 2018/2019

(27.07.2018 – 19.05.2019)

Regular Season - Results

Round 1 [27-29.07.2018]
Standard Liège - KAA Gent 3-2(1-1)
KV Kortrijk - RSC Anderlecht 1-4(0-2)
SV Zulte Waregem - Waasland-Bev. 2-2(1-0)
Sint-Truidense VV - Cercle Brugge 0-0
KV Oostende - Excel Mouscron 2-1(0-1)
Club Brugge KV - KAS Eupen 5-2(3-0)
R Charleroi SC - Antwerp FC 0-1(0-1)
KSC Lokeren - KRC Genk 0-4(0-2)

Round 2 [03-05.08.2018]
Waasland-Beveren - Standard Liège 0-0
KAS Eupen - R Charleroi SC 1-4(1-2)
Cercle Brugge - KSC Lokeren 3-2(2-1)
Antwerp FC - KV Kortrijk 0-0
KAA Gent - SV Zulte Waregem 1-1(0-0)
RSC Anderlecht - KV Oostende 5-2(0-0)
KRC Genk - Sint-Truidense VV 1-1(0-0)
Excel Mouscron - Club Brugge KV 0-1(0-0)

Round 3 [10-12.08.2018]
Club Brugge KV - KV Kortrijk 3-0(2-0)
Standard Liège - Cercle Brugge 0-0
SV Zulte Waregem - KAS Eupen 4-0(2-0)
Sint-Truidense VV - KSC Lokeren 1-1(0-0)
Excel Mouscron - Antwerp FC 0-1(0-0)
KV Oostende - KRC Genk 0-2(0-0)
R Charleroi SC - RSC Anderlecht 1-2(1-1)
KAA Gent - Waasland-Beveren 4-1(1-0)

Round 4 [17-19.08.2018]
RSC Anderlecht - Excel Mouscron 2-0(1-0)
KSC Lokeren - Standard Liège 0-3(0-0)
Cercle Brugge - SV Zulte Waregem 3-1(1-0)
Waasland-Bev. - Sint-Truidense VV 2-2(1-1)
KV Kortrijk - KV Oostende 1-2(0-1)
Antwerp FC - Club Brugge KV 1-1(0-0)
KRC Genk - R Charleroi SC 3-1(1-1)
KAS Eupen - KAA Gent 2-3(1-2)

Round 5 [24-26.08.2018]
KV Oostende - SV Zulte Waregem 3-1(1-1)
Standard Liège - Sint-Truidense VV 3-2(1-1)
Excel Mouscron - KAS Eupen 0-1(0-1)
Antwerp FC - Cercle Brugge 1-0(0-0)
R Charleroi SC - KV Kortrijk 0-2(0-1)
Club Brugge KV - RSC Anderlecht 2-1(2-1)
KAA Gent - KSC Lokeren 2-1(0-0)
KRC Genk - Waasland-Beveren 3-2(1-0)

Round 6 [31.08.-02.09.2018]
SV Zulte Waregem - Club Brugge 2-5(0-3)
KAS Eupen - Standard Liège 2-1(0-1)
KSC Lokeren - Waasland-Beveren 1-0(0-0)
Sint-Truidense VV - KV Oostende 1-0(0-0)
R Charleroi SC - Excel Mouscron 3-1(2-0)
RSC Anderlecht - Antwerp FC 1-1(1-0)
Cercle Brugge - KAA Gent 0-3(0-1)
KV Kortrijk - KRC Genk 3-3(0-0)

Round 7 [14-16.09.2018]
Club Brugge KV - KSC Lokeren 2-1(0-1)
Standard Liège - R Charleroi SC 0-0
KV Oostende - Cercle Brugge 1-1(0-0)
Waasland-Beveren - KAS Eupen 0-0
KRC Genk - RSC Anderlecht 1-0(0-0)
Excel Mouscron - KV Kortrijk 1-0(1-0)
Antwerp FC - SV Zulte Waregem 5-1(3-0)
KAA Gent - Sint-Truidense VV 1-2(0-1)

Round 8 [21-23.09.2018]
SV Zulte Waregem - KV Kortrijk 0-2(0-0)
Waasland-Beveren - R Charleroi SC 1-1(0-1)
KAS Eupen - KV Oostende 1-2(0-1)
KSC Lokeren - Excel Mouscron 0-0
Sint-Truidense VV - Antwerp FC 2-0(0-0)
KAA Gent - Club Brugge KV 0-4(0-1)
RSC Anderlecht - Standard Liège 2-1(0-1)
Cercle Brugge - KRC Genk 2-5(1-2)

Round 9 [28-30.09.2018]
KV Kortrijk - KAS Eupen 1-3(1-2)
KRC Genk - SV Zulte Waregem 4-0(2-0)
Excel Mouscron - Waasland-Beveren 0-3(0-2)
R Charleroi SC - KSC Lokeren 2-1(0-0)
Club Brugge KV - Cercle Brugge 4-0(2-0)
RSC Anderlecht - Sint-Truidense VV 0-0
KV Oostende - Standard Liège 1-3(0-1)
Antwerp FC - KAA Gent 2-2(1-2)

Round 10 [05-07.10.2018]
Cercle Brugge - R Charleroi SC 2-1(1-1)
KAS Eupen - Antwerp FC 1-2(1-0)
KSC Lokeren - KV Kortrijk 1-3(1-0)
Sint-Truidense VV - Excel Mouscron 3-1(1-1)
Waasland-Beveren - KV Oostende 1-1(0-0)
SV Zulte Waregem - RSC Anderlecht 1-2(0-1)
Standard Liège - Club Brugge KV 3-1(1-0)
KAA Gent - KRC Genk 1-5(1-3)

Round 11 [19-21.10.2018]
Club Brugge - Waasland-Beveren 1-1(0-0)
Excel Mouscron - Standard Liège 0-0
KV Kortrijk - Sint-Truidense VV 3-1(2-1)
Antwerp FC - KSC Lokeren 2-1(1-0)
KRC Genk - KAS Eupen 2-1(1-0)
RSC Anderlecht - Cercle Brugge 4-2(2-0)
KV Oostende - KAA Gent 0-4(0-2)
R Charleroi SC - SV Zulte Waregem 3-2(1-0)

Round 12 [26-28.10.2018]
KAA Gent - R Charleroi SC 2-1(1-1)
SV Zulte Waregem - Excel Mouscron 2-2(2-1)
Cercle Brugge - KV Kortrijk 1-1(0-1)
KSC Lokeren - KV Oostende 0-0
Sint-Truidense VV - Club Brugge 2-2(1-2)
Standard Liège - KRC Genk 1-1(0-0)
KAS Eupen - RSC Anderlecht 2-1(2-0)
Waasland-Beveren - Antwerp FC 0-1(0-0)

Round 13 [30.10.-01.11.2018]
Club Brugge KV - KV Oostende 4-0(3-0)
Excel Mouscron - KAA Gent 3-1(2-0)
R Charleroi SC - Sint-Truidense VV 1-0(0-0)
KV Kortrijk - Waasland-Beveren 2-2(2-0)
KAS Eupen - Cercle Brugge 2-0(0-0)
Antwerp FC - KRC Genk 2-4(2-0)
RSC Anderlecht - KSC Lokeren 1-1(0-0)
SV Zulte Waregem - Standard Liège 3-1(1-1)

Round 14 [02-04.11.2018]
KV Oostende - R Charleroi SC 2-1(1-0)
KRC Genk - Club Brugge KV 1-1(1-0)
Cercle Brugge - Excel Mouscron 2-1(0-1)
KAA Gent - KV Kortrijk 3-1(0-1)
Standard Liège - Antwerp FC 0-2(0-1)
Waasland-Beveren - RSC Anderlecht 1-2(0-1)
KSC Lokeren - KAS Eupen 2-0(2-0)
Sint-Truidense VV - Zulte Waregem 2-1(0-1)

Round 15 [09-11.11.2018]
Antwerp FC - KV Oostende 2-0(1-0)
R Charleroi SC - Club Brugge KV 2-1(1-1)
KAS Eupen - Sint-Truidense VV 1-4(0-2)
SV Zulte Waregem - KSC Lokeren 2-0(0-0)
Cercle Brugge - Waasland-Beveren 2-0(1-0)
RSC Anderlecht - KAA Gent 2-0(1-0)
KV Kortrijk - Standard Liège 0-2(0-1)
Excel Mouscron - KRC Genk 0-0

Round 16 [23-25.11.2018]
Club Brugge - SV Zulte Waregem 1-3(0-2)
Standard Liège - KAS Eupen 3-0(2-0)
KV Oostende - KV Kortrijk 1-2(1-1)
Waasland-Beveren - Excel Mouscron 1-2(0-1)
KRC Genk - Cercle Brugge 1-2(0-2)
KAA Gent - Antwerp FC 0-0
Sint-Truidense VV - RSC Anderlecht 4-2(1-1)
KSC Lokeren - R Charleroi SC 2-4(1-1)

Round 17 [30.11.-02.12.2018]
KSC Lokeren - KAA Gent 2-2(1-0)
R Charleroi SC - Cercle Brugge 3-1(1-0)
KV Kortrijk - Excel Mouscron 1-0(1-0)
SV Zulte Waregem - KV Oostende 1-1(1-0)
Antwerp FC - Sint-Truidense VV 1-3(1-2)
Club Brugge KV - Standard Liège 3-0(3-0)
RSC Anderlecht - KRC Genk 0-1(0-0)
KAS Eupen - Waasland-Beveren 1-0(1-0)

Round 18 [07-09.12.2018]
Waasland-Beveren - Club Brugge 2-1(0-0)
KRC Genk - KV Kortrijk 1-1(1-1)
Excel Mouscron - SV Zulte Waregem 0-0
KV Oostende - KSC Lokeren 1-0(0-0)
Sint-Truidense VV - Standard Liège 1-1(1-0)
Cercle Brugge - Antwerp FC 0-3(0-2)
RSC Anderlecht - R Charleroi SC 1-1(0-0)
KAA Gent - KAS Eupen 2-0(1-0)

Round 19 [14-16.12.2018]
R Charleroi SC - KAA Gent 2-0(0-0)
KV Kortrijk - Club Brugge KV 0-0
KAS Eupen - Excel Mouscron 1-0(0-0)
KSC Lokeren - Sint-Truidense VV 2-0(1-0)
Antwerp FC - Waasland-Beveren 0-2(0-0)
Cercle Brugge - RSC Anderlecht 2-1(1-1)
KRC Genk - KV Oostende 2-0(1-0)
Standard Liège - SV Zulte Waregem 4-1(2-0)

Round 20 [21-23.12.2018]
KAA Gent - Cercle Brugge 4-1(2-0)
Excel Mouscron - RSC Anderlecht 3-1(2-0)
Waasland-Beveren - KSC Lokeren 2-1(1-0)
Sint-Truidense VV - KV Kortrijk 0-0
Standard Liège - KV Oostende 3-1(3-0)
Club Brugge KV - Antwerp FC 5-1(2-0)
KAS Eupen - KRC Genk 0-2(0-2)
SV Zulte Waregem - R Charleroi SC 3-1(2-1)

Round 21 [26-27.12.2018]
KV Kortrijk - SV Zulte Waregem 4-2(0-1)
KV Oostende - Sint-Truidense VV 1-1(1-1)
Cercle Brugge - KAS Eupen 0-1(0-1)
Antwerp FC - Excel Mouscron 2-1(1-0)
R Charleroi SC - Standard Liège 0-1(0-1)
KRC Genk - KAA Gent 3-1(1-1)
KSC Lokeren - Club Brugge KV 0-1(0-0)
RSC Anderlecht - Waasland-Beveren 3-0(1-0)

Round 22 [18-20.01.2019]
Sint-Truidense VV - KRC Genk 2-3(1-1)
Standard Liège - KV Kortrijk 2-1(0-1)
KAS Eupen - KSC Lokeren 4-1(2-0)
Waasland-Beveren - Cercle Brugge 1-1(0-0)
SV Zulte Waregem - Antwerp FC 1-2(0-1)
Club Brugge KV - R Charleroi SC 0-1(0-1)
KAA Gent - RSC Anderlecht 1-0(0-0)
Excel Mouscron - KV Oostende 2-1(1-1)

Round 23 [25-27.01.2019]
Antwerp FC - Standard Liège 1-1(0-0)
R Charleroi SC - Waasland-Beveren 2-2(1-2)
Cercle Brugge - Sint-Truidense VV 1-2(1-1)
KSC Lokeren - SV Zulte Waregem 0-3(0-2)
KRC Genk - Excel Mouscron 1-2(0-1)
KV Oostende - Club Brugge KV 1-2(1-0)
RSC Anderlecht - KAS Eupen 2-1(0-1)
KV Kortrijk - KAA Gent 1-2(1-1)

Round 24 [01-03.02.2019]
Excel Mouscron - R Charleroi SC 3-0(1-0)
KV Oostende - Antwerp FC 0-2(0-1)
KV Kortrijk - KSC Lokeren 2-1(1-0)
SV Zulte Waregem - Cercle Brugge 3-2(2-1)
Waasland-Beveren - KRC Genk 1-2(1-0)
Club Brugge KV - KAA Gent 1-1(0-1)
Standard Liège - RSC Anderlecht 2-1(1-1)
Sint-Truidense VV - KAS Eupen 4-1(2-1)

Round 25 [08-10.02.2019]
KRC Genk - Standard Liège 2-0(0-0)
R Charleroi SC - KV Oostende 1-1(0-0)
KAS Eupen - KV Kortrijk 0-1(0-1)
Sint-Truidense - Waasland-Beveren 2-1(1-1)
KSC Lokeren - Antwerp FC 2-1(1-0)
Cercle Brugge - Club Brugge KV 2-2(1-2)
RSC Anderlecht - SV Zulte Waregem 0-0
KAA Gent - Excel Mouscron 1-2(0-1)

Round 26 [15-17.02.2019]
Standard Liège - KSC Lokeren 3-1(2-0)
KV Kortrijk - R Charleroi SC 1-2(0-0)
KV Oostende - KAS Eupen 1-1(1-0)
Zulte Waregem - Sint-Truidense VV 1-1(0-0)
Waasland-Beveren - KAA Gent 2-1(1-0)
Club Brugge KV - KRC Genk 3-1(2-0)
Antwerp FC - RSC Anderlecht 0-1(0-0)
Excel Mouscron - Cercle Brugge 3-0(0-0)

Round 27 [22-24.02.2019]
KAA Gent - Standard Liège 2-1(2-0)
KAS Eupen - SV Zulte Waregem 2-3(1-1)
Cercle Brugge - KV Oostende 2-2(0-0)
Waasland-Beveren - KV Kortrijk 2-6(0-2)
Excel Mouscron - KSC Lokeren 1-0(0-0)
RSC Anderlecht - Club Brugge KV 2-2(1-1)
KRC Genk - Antwerp FC 0-0
Sint-Truidense VV - R Charleroi SC 3-1(2-1)

Round 28 [01-03.03.2019]
Standard Liège - Excel Mouscron 1-1(0-0)
R Charleroi SC - KRC Genk 1-1(0-1)
KV Kortrijk - Cercle Brugge 2-1(0-1)
KV Oostende - Waasland-Beveren 1-1(0-0)
Club Brugge - Sint-Truidense VV 1-0(0-0)
SV Zulte Waregem - KAA Gent 1-3(1-1)
KSC Lokeren - RSC Anderlecht 1-2(0-1)
Antwerp FC - KAS Eupen 2-1(0-0)

Round 29 [10.03.2019]
RSC Anderlecht - KV Kortrijk 2-0(1-0)
KAA Gent - KV Oostende 2-1(1-1)
KRC Genk - KSC Lokeren 1-0(0-0)
Excel Mouscron - Sint-Truidense VV 1-1(1-1)
KAS Eupen - Club Brugge KV 0-4(0-3)
Cercle Brugge - Standard Liège 1-2(0-2)
Antwerp FC - R Charleroi SC 1-2(1-1)
Waasland-Beveren - Zulte Waregem 1-1(0-0)

Round 30 [17.03.2019]
Club Brugge KV - Excel Mouscron 1-2(0-1)
Standard Liège - Waasland-Beveren 4-3(0-2)
KV Kortrijk - Antwerp FC 2-0(0-0)
KV Oostende - RSC Anderlecht 0-2(0-0)
SV Zulte Waregem - KRC Genk 3-3(1-2)
KSC Lokeren - Cercle Brugge 3-1(3-0)
R Charleroi SC - KAS Eupen 1-2(1-1)
Sint-Truidense VV - KAA Gent 0-2(0-1)

Final Standings

1.	KRC Genk	30	18	9	3	63	-	31	63
2.	Club Brugge KV	30	16	8	6	64	-	32	56
3.	R Standard Liège	30	15	8	7	49	-	35	53
4.	RSC Anderlecht Bruxelles	30	15	6	9	49	-	34	51
5.	KAA Gent	30	15	5	10	53	-	45	50
6.	Antwerp FC	30	14	7	9	39	-	34	49
7.	Sint-Truidense VV	30	12	11	7	47	-	36	47
8.	KV Kortrijk	30	12	7	11	44	-	42	43
9.	R Charleroi SC	30	12	6	12	43	-	43	42
10.	Royal Excel Mouscron	30	11	7	12	33	-	33	40
11.	SV Zulte Waregem	30	8	9	13	49	-	60	33
12.	KAS Eupen	30	10	2	18	34	-	57	32
13.	Cercle Brugge KSV	30	7	7	16	35	-	59	28
14.	KV Oostende	30	6	9	15	29	-	52	27
15.	KVRS Waasland-Beveren	30	5	12	13	37	-	50	27
16.	KSC Lokeren (*Relegated*)	30	5	5	20	28	-	53	20

Teams ranked 1-6 were qualified for the Championship Play-offs (Playoff I), while teams ranked 7-15 and the three best teams from the 2018/2019 Belgian First Division B were qualified for the Europa League Play-offs (Playoff II).

Championship Play-offs

Results

Round 1 [29-31.03.2019]
Standard Liège - Antwerp FC 3-1(0-1)
KRC Genk - RSC Anderlecht 3-0(1-0)
Club Brugge KV - KAA Gent 3-0(2-0)

Round 2 [02-04.04.2019]
Antwerp FC - KRC Genk 1-0(1-0)
KAA Gent - Standard Liège 1-2(0-1)
RSC Anderlecht - Club Brugge KV 2-3(0-2)

Round 3 [06-08.04.2019]
KRC Genk - KAA Gent 2-1(2-0)
RSC Anderlecht - Antwerp FC 1-2(1-1)
Club Brugge KV - Standard Liège 4-0(3-0)

Round 4 [12-14.04.2019]
Standard Li. - RSC Anderlecht 5-0 (awarded)
KAA Gent - Antwerp FC 1-2(0-1)
KRC Genk - Club Brugge KV 3-1(1-1)

Round 5 [19-22.04.2019]
Standard Liège - KRC Genk 1-3(0-1)
RSC Anderlecht - KAA Gent 0-0
Antwerp FC - Club Brugge KV 0-0

Round 6 [26-28.04.2019]
Antwerp FC - Standard Liège 2-1(1-1)
KAA Gent - KRC Genk 0-1(0-0)
Club Brugge KV - RSC Anderlecht 1-0(0-0)

Round 7 [03-05.05.2019]
KRC Genk - Antwerp FC 4-0(1-0)
RSC Anderlecht - Standard Liège 2-1(1-0)
KAA Gent - Club Brugge KV 0-1(0-1)

Round 8 [10-12.05.2019]
Standard Liège - KAA Gent 2-3(1-1)
Antwerp FC - RSC Anderlecht 1-1(0-1)
Club Brugge KV - KRC Genk 3-2(0-1)

Round 9 [16.05.2019]
RSC Anderlecht - KRC Genk 1-1(0-1)
Standard Liège - Club Brugge KV 2-0(0-0)
Antwerp FC - KAA Gent 1-2(1-1)

Round 10 [19.05.2019]
Club Brugge KV - Antwerp FC 3-2(1-0)
KAA Gent - RSC Anderlecht 2-1(1-0)
KRC Genk - Standard Liège 0-0

Final Standings						
1. **KRC Genk**	10	6	2	2	19 - 8	52
2. Club Brugge KV	10	7	1	2	19 - 11	50
3. R Standard Liège	10	4	1	5	17 - 16	40
4. Antwerp FC	10	4	2	4	12 - 16	39
5. KAA Gent	10	3	1	6	10 - 15	35
6. RSC Anderlecht Bruxelles	10	1	3	6	8 - 19	32

KAA Gent were qualified for the Europa League Play-off Final.

Please note: The points obtained during the regular season were halved (and rounded up) before the start of the Play-offs. As a result, the teams started with the following points before the playoffs: KRC Genk - 32 points, Club Brugge KV - 28, R Standard Liège - 27, RSC Anderlecht - 26, KAA Gent - 25 and Antwerp FC - 25.

Top goalscorers:

25 Hamdi Harbaoui (TUN)
SV Zulte Waregem

23 Mbwana Ally Samatta (TAN)
KRC Genk

16 Victor James Osimhen (NGA)
R Charleroi SC

16 Ivan Santini (CRO)
RSC Anderlecht Bruxelles

Europa League Play-offs – Group A

Group A of the play-offs will consist of the teams finishing in positions 7, 9, 12 and 14 during the regular season and the first and third placed team in the qualifying positions in the 2018/2019 Belgian First Division B.

Results

Round 1 [30-31.03.2019]
KV Oostende - KAS Eupen 1-2(1-1)
Sint-Truidense VV - R Charleroi SC 3-1(1-1)
KVC Westerlo - K Beerschot VA 1-1(1-1)

Round 2 [03.04.2019]
R Charleroi SC - KV Oostende 1-2(1-1)
K Beerschot VA - Sint-Truidense VV 1-2(1-1)
KAS Eupen - KVC Westerlo 0-3(0-2)

Round 3 [06-07.04.2019]
KV Oostende - K Beerschot VA 2-1(1-1)
KVC Westerlo - Sint-Truidense VV 2-2(1-0)
KAS Eupen - R Charleroi SC 0-1(0-0)

Round 4 [13-14.04.2019]
K Beerschot VA - KAS Eupen 2-0(1-0)
Sint-Truidense VV - KV Oostende 1-0(0-0)
R Charleroi SC - KVC Westerlo 2-0(0-0)

Round 5 [20-22.04.2019]
KVC Westerlo - KV Oostende 0-0
KAS Eupen - Sint-Truidense VV 1-1(0-0)
R Charleroi SC - K Beerschot VA 4-0(1-0)

Round 6 [27-28.04.2019]
KV Oostende - R Charleroi SC 2-2(0-0)
KVC Westerlo - KAS Eupen 1-0(1-0)
Sint-Truidense VV - K Beerschot VA 2-2(0-1)

Round 7 [04.05.2019]
R Charleroi SC - Sint-Truidense VV 2-0(1-0)
KAS Eupen - KV Oostende 3-2(1-1)
K Beerschot VA - KVC Westerlo 3-2(2-0)

Round 8 [11-12.05.2019]
K Beerschot VA - R Charleroi SC 0-3(0-2)
KV Oostende - KVC Westerlo 0-3(0-1)
Sint-Truidense VV - KAS Eupen 2-2(0-1)

Round 9 [15.05.2019]
KV Oostende - Sint-Truidense VV 1-1(1-0)
KVC Westerlo - R Charleroi SC 0-2(0-1)
KAS Eupen - K Beerschot VA 1-0(0-0)

Round 10 [18.05.2019]
R Charleroi SC - KAS Eupen 2-0(0-0)
K Beerschot VA - KV Oostende 1-2(0-1)
Sint-Truidense VV - KVC Westerlo 2-1(0-1)

Final Standings						
1. *R Charleroi SC*	10	7	1	2	20 - 7	22
2. Sint-Truidense VV	10	4	5	1	16 - 13	17
3. KVC Westerlo	10	3	3	4	13 - 12	12
4. KV Oostende	10	3	3	4	12 - 15	12
5. KAS Eupen	10	3	2	5	9 - 15	11
6. K Beerschot VA	10	2	2	6	11 - 19	8

Please note: The points obtained during the regular season were halved (and rounded up) before the start of the Play-off.
R Charleroi SC were qualified for the Europa League Play-off Semi-Final.

Europa League Play-offs – Group B

Group B of the play-offs will consist of the teams finishing in positions 8, 10, 11, 13 and 15 during the regular season and the second placed qualifier from the 2017/2018 Belgian First Division B in group B.

Results

Round 1 [30-31.03.2019]
KV Kortrijk - Excel Mouscron 3-1(2-0)
Union St. Gilloise - Cercle Brugge 3-1(2-0)
SV Zulte Waregem - Waasland-Beveren 0-0

Round 2 [02.04.2019]
Cercle Brugge - SV Zulte Waregem 3-3(1-2)
Excel Mouscron - Union St. Gilloise 0-2(0-0)
Waasland-Beveren - KV Kortrijk 2-3(0-0)

Round 3 [05-06.04.2019]
KV Kortrijk - SV Zulte Waregem 4-2(2-2)
Union St. Gilloise - Waasland-Bever. 5-1(2-1)
Excel Mouscron - Cercle Brugge 2-3(0-0)

Round 4 [13.04.2019]
SV Zulte Waregem - Excel Mouscron 2-2(0-0)
Cercle Brugge - Waasland-Beveren 3-2(1-1)
KV Kortrijk - Union St. Gilloise 0-1(0-0)

Round 5 [20-21.04.2019]
Union St. Gilloise - Zulte Waregem 2-2(1-0)
Cercle Brugge - KV Kortrijk 1-2(0-0)
Waasland-Beveren - Excel Mouscron 2-1(1-1)

Round 6 [27.04.2019]
Excel Mouscron - KV Kortrijk 2-3(1-1)
Waasland-Bever. - Union St. Gilloise 3-2(1-1)
SV Zulte Waregem - Cercle Brugge 6-2(3-0)

Round 7 [04-05.05.2019]
Cercle Brugge - Union St. Gilloise 2-3(0-0)
KV Kortrijk - Waasland-Beveren 2-1(2-1)
Excel Mouscron - SV Zulte Waregem 3-0(2-0)

Round 8 [11.05.2019]
Waasland-Beveren - Cercle Brugge 2-1(0-1)
SV Zulte Waregem - KV Kortrijk 0-5(0-3)
Union St. Gilloise - Excel Mouscron 3-3(2-1)

Round 9 [14.05.2019]
Union St. Gilloise - KV Kortrijk 2-0(1-0)
Cercle Brugge - Excel Mouscron 0-3(0-0)
Waasland-Beveren - Zulte Waregem 0-5(0-1)

Round 10 [17.05.2019]
KV Kortrijk - Cercle Brugge 4-0(1-0)
Excel Mouscron - Waasland-Beveren 2-4(1-1)
Zulte Waregem - Union St. Gilloise 2-1(2-1)

Final Standings

1.	*KV Kortrijk*	10	8	0	2	26 - 12	24
2.	Royale Union Saint-Gilloise	10	6	2	2	24 - 14	20
3.	KVRS Waasland-Beveren	10	4	1	5	17 - 24	13
4.	SV Zulte Waregem	10	3	4	3	22 - 22	13
5.	Royal Excel Mouscron	10	2	2	6	19 - 22	8
6.	Cercle Brugge KSV	10	2	1	7	16 - 30	7

Please note: The points obtained during the regular season were halved (and rounded up) before the start of the Play-off.
KV Kortrijk were qualified for the Europa League Play-off Semi-Final.

Europa League Play-off Semi-Final

KV Kortrijk - R Charleroi SC	1-2(1-1)

Europa League Play-off Final

Antwerp FC - R Charleroi SC	3-2(2-2)

NATIONAL CUP
Coupe de Belgique / Beker van België 2018/2019

Fifth Round [24-27.08.2018]

KFC Dessel Sport - Oud-Heverlee Leuven	3-1	KFC Duffel - KVC Westerlo	3-0
SK Deinze - Racing White Brussels	6-0	Olsa Brakel - SC Eendracht Aalst	2-3 aet
Lierse SK - Lommel SK	2-3	KVK Westhoek - Excelsior Virton	0-4
AFC Tubize - Stade Braine	7-0	KSK Heist - KSC Menen	3-0
Hoogstraten VV - RE Acren Lessines	4-0	RUS Givry - Royal Knokke FC	3-5 pen
Sportkring Sint-Niklaas - KRC Harelbeke	0-1 aet	ASV Geel - K Beerschot Voetbalclub Antwerpen	0-2
Royale Union Saint-Gilloise - City Pirates Merksem	3-0	KFC Mandel United - KSV Temse	6-5 pen
ROC de Charleroi-Marchienne - KSV Roeselare	2-1	KV Mechelen - RUSG Quevy 89	2-0

Sixth Round [25-27.09.2018]

KAS Eupen - AFC Tubize	3-0(2-0)	Sint-Truidense VV - KFC Duffel	3-0(2-0)
KVRS Waasland-Beveren - KFC Mandel United	1-2(0-2)	KFC Dessel Sport - Royal Excel Mouscron	0-3(0-0)
KRC Harelbeke - KV Kortrijk	0-1(0-0)	Hoogstraten VV - KV Oostende	1-3(0-1)
KRC Genk - Lommel SK	4-0(2-0)	SC Eendracht Aalst - R Charleroi SC	0-2(0-0)
ROC de Charleroi-Marchienne - KSC Lokeren	2-5(1-3)	R Standard Liège - Royal Knokke FC	1-2(0-0)
Excelsior Virton - KAA Gent	2-4(1-1)	SK Deinze - Club Brugge KV	2-0(1-0)
Cercle Brugge KSV - K Beerschot VA	1-2(1-1)	KV Mechelen - Antwerp FC	3-1(1-1)
KSK Heist - SV Zulte Waregem	1-2(0-2)	RSC Anderlecht - Royale Union Saint-Gilloise	0-3(0-1)

1/8 Finals [04-06.12.2018]

KV Kortrijk - SV Zulte Waregem	1-0(1-0)	SK Deinze - KAS Eupen	1-3(1-2)
KAA Gent - K Beerschot Voetbalclub Antwerpen	3-0(2-0)	Sint-Truidense VV - KFC Mandel United	3-2(0-0)
Royal Excel Mouscron - KV Oostende	3-3 aet; 4-5 pen	R Charleroi SC - KRC Genk	1-3(1-0)
KV Mechelen - KSC Lokeren Oost-Vlaanderen	2-0(0-0)	Royale Union Saint-Gilloise - Royal Knokke FC	3-2(1-1)

Quarter-Finals [18-19.12.2018]

Sint-Truidense VV - KAA Gent	1-3(0-1)	KAS Eupen - KV Oostende	0-1(0-0)
KV Mechelen - KV Kortrijk	3-0(2-0)	Royale Union Saint-Gilloise - KRC Genk	2-2 aet; 4-3 pen

Semi-Finals [23/24.01.-29/30.01.2019]

KV Mechelen - Royale Union Saint-Gilloise	0-0	Royale Union Saint-Gilloise - KV Mechelen	1-2(0-1)
KAA Gent - KV Oostende	2-2(1-1)	KV Oostende - KAA Gent	2-2 aet; 3-4 pen

Final

01.05.2019; Stade "Roi Baudouin", Bruxelles; Referee: Erik Lambrechts; Attendance: 44,771

KV Mechelen - KAA Gent **2-1(1-1)**

KV Mechelen: Michael Verrips, Thibault Peyre (71.Gustav Per Fredrik Engvall), Arjan Swinkels, Germán Mera Cáceres, Lucas Bijker, Seth De Witte (Cap), Rob Schoofs (83.Tim Matthys), Joachim Van Damme, Nikola Storm (71.Alexander Corryn), Igor Albert Rinck de Diver Camargo, Clément Tainmont. Trainer: Wouter Vrancken.

KAA Gent: Thomas Kaminski, Arnaud Souquet (64.Brecht Dejaegere), Timothy Derijck, Nana Asare (Cap), Vadis Odjidja-Ofoe, Jonathan Christian David (68.Roman Bezus), Birger Verstraete, Alexander Sørloth, Jean-Luc Dompé, Giorgi Kvilitaia. Trainer: Jess Thorup (Denmark).

Goals: 0-1 Jean-Luc Dompé (32), 1-1 Nikola Storm (38), 2-1 Germán Mera Cáceres (62).

THE CLUBS 2018/2019

Please note: matches and goals includes statistics of both regular season and play-offs (Championship or Europa League).

Royal Sporting Club Anderlecht Bruxelles

Founded: 27.05.1908
Stadium: Stade "Constant Vanden Stock", Bruxelles (21,500)

Goalkeepers:	DOB	M	(s)	G
Thomas Didillon (FRA)	28.11.1995	40		
Defenders:	**DOB**	**M**	**(s)**	**G**
Dennis Appiah (FRA)	09.06.1992	15	(4)	
Sebastiaan Bornauw	22.03.1999	22	(1)	1
Elias Cobbaut	24.11.1997	10	(2)	
Hannes Delcroix	28.02.1999		(1)	
James Lawrence (WAL)	22.08.1992	22	(1)	
Serigne Mbodj (SEN)	11.11.1989	17		
Antonio Milić (CRO)	10.03.1994	16	(5)	
Ivan Obradović (SRB)	25.07.1988	9	(1)	
Alexis Saelemaekers	27.06.1999	22	(8)	
Bubacarr Sanneh (GAM)	14.11.1994	8	(4)	1
Ognjen Vranješ (BIH)	24.10.1989	10		
Midfielders:	**DOB**	**M**	**(s)**	**G**
Yannick Bolasie (COD)	24.05.1989	16	(1)	6
Pieter Gerkens	13.08.1995	22	(10)	7
Edo Kayembe (COD)	03.06.1998	6	(6)	
Sven Kums	26.02.1988	30	(1)	5
Evgen Makarenko (UKR)	21.05.1991	13	(2)	
Ryota Morioka (JPN)	12.04.1991	4	(2)	
Andy Aryel Najar Rodríguez (HON)	16.03.1993	21	(4)	
Kenny Saief (USA)	17.12.1993	2	(10)	
Albert-Mboyo Sambi Lokonga	22.10.1999	5	(1)	
Adrien Trebel (FRA)	03.03.1991	23	(2)	3
Yari Verschaeren	12.07.2001	19	(2)	2
Peter Žulj (AUT)	09.06.1993	8	(2)	
Forwards:	**DOB**	**M**	**(s)**	**G**
Kristal Abazaj (ALB)	06.07.1996		(1)	
Francis Amuzu	23.08.1999	19	(11)	1
Zakaria Bakkali	26.01.1996	13	(5)	1
Mohammed Dauda (GHA)	20.02.1998	1	(4)	
Nany Dimata	01.09.1997	17	(3)	13
Jérémy Doku	27.05.2002		(6)	
Knowledge Musona (ZIM)	21.06.1990	3	(5)	1
Ivan Santini (CRO)	21.05.1989	27	(7)	16
Trainer:	**DOB**	**M**		
Hein Vanhaezebrouck	16.02.1964	18		
Karim Belhocine (FRA) [16.12.2018]	02.04.1978	3		
Fred Rutten (NED) [06.01.2019]	05.12.1962	13		
Karim Belhocine (FRA) [16.04.2019]	02.04.1978	6		

Royal Antwerp Football Club

Founded: 1880
Stadium: Bosuilstadion, Antwerp (12,975)

Goalkeepers:	DOB	M	(s)	G
Sinan Bolat (TUR)	03.09.1988	41		
Defenders:	**DOB**	**M**	**(s)**	**G**
Dino Arslanagić	24.04.1993	36	(1)	1
Dylan Batubinsika (FRA)	15.02.1996	8	(3)	
Aurélio Gabriel Ulineia Buta (POR)	10.02.1997	19	(1)	
Gael Kakudji	06.07.1999		(1)	
Matheus Borges Nascimento (BRA)	22.01.1992	13	(1)	
Dan Opare (GHA)	18.10.1990	22	(1)	
Abdoulaye Seck (SEN)	04.06.1992	2		
Jelle Van Damme	10.10.1983	32	(2)	1
Midfielders:	**DOB**	**M**	**(s)**	**G**
David Martins Simão (POR)	15.05.1990	3	(9)	
Omar Nicolás Govea García (MEX)	18.01.1996	15		
Nader Ghandri (TUN)	18.02.1995		(1)	
Geoffry Hairemans	21.10.1991	10	(11)	1
Faris Haroun	22.09.1985	34		5
Simen Juklerød (NOR)	18.05.1994	39	(1)	1
Egor Nazaryna (UKR)	10.07.1997	7	(2)	
Sambou Yatabaré (MLI)	02.03.1989	19	(2)	1
Forwards:	**DOB**	**M**	**(s)**	**G**
Amara Baby (SEN)	23.02.1989	14	(10)	3
Jonathan Bolingi Mpangi Merikani (COD)	30.06.1994	22	(14)	2
Ivo Tiago dos Santos Rodrigues (POR)	30.03.1995	16	(12)	2
Reda Jaadi	14.02.1995		(1)	
Didier Lamkel Zé (CMR)	17.09.1996	19	(9)	4
Dieudonné Mbokani Bezua (COD)	22.11.1985	30	(2)	13
William Owusu (GHA)	13.09.1989	19	(14)	7
Zotsara Randriambololona (MAD)	22.04.1994		(1)	
Lior Refaelov (ISR)	26.04.1986	31	(4)	11
Trainer:	**DOB**	**M**		
Ladislau Bölöni (ROU)	11.03.1953	41		

Cercle Brugge Koninklijke Sportvereniging

Founded: 1899
Stadium: "Jan Breydel" Stadium, Brugge (29,042)

Goalkeepers:	DOB	M	(s)	G
Paul Nardi (FRA)	18.05.1994	38		
Miguel Van Damme	25.09.1993	2		
Defenders:	**DOB**	**M**	**(s)**	**G**
Zorhan Bassong	07.05.1999	1		
Benjamin Delacourt (FRA)	10.03.1985	14	(3)	3
Yoann Etienne (FRA)	19.05.1997	27	(4)	
Aboud Omar Khamis (KEN)	09.09.1992	8		
Isaac Koné (FRA)	03.01.1991	23	(4)	
Issa Marega (FRA)	20.04.1998	14	(1)	
Lloyd Palun (GAB)	28.11.1988	31	(1)	
Jérémy Taravel (FRA)	17.04.1987	25		2
Naomichi Ueda (JPN)	24.10.1994	22	(4)	1
Victor Alexander da Silva „Vitinho" (BRA)	23.07.1999	9	(3)	
Midfielders:	**DOB**	**M**	**(s)**	**G**
Kévin Appin (FRA)	20.01.1998	3	(4)	
Robbe Decostere	08.05.1998	2	(1)	
Olivier Deman	06.04.2000		(1)	
Kylian Hazard	05.08.1995	13	(8)	4
Kévin Hoggas (FRA)	16.11.1991	3	(3)	
Benjamin Lambot	02.05.1987	19	(2)	1
Arnaud Lusamba (FRA)	04.01.1997	24	(1)	
Xavier Mercier (FRA)	25.07.1989	35	(1)	4
Johanna Ochieng Omolo (KEN)	31.07.1989	13	(5)	2
Adama Traoré II (MLI)	28.06.1995	6	(2)	
Charles Vanhoutte	16.09.1998	1	(2)	
Forwards:	**DOB**	**M**	**(s)**	**G**
Nabil Alioui (FRA)	18.02.1999	2	(10)	1
Adrien Bongiovanni	20.09.1999	11	(10)	2
Gianni Bruno	19.08.1991	31	(3)	12
Irvin Cardona (FRA)	08.08.1997	14	(6)	6
Dylan De Belder	03.04.1992	13	(18)	3
Serge Gakpé (TOG)	07.05.1987	16	(10)	5
Anderson López (NED)	25.01.1999		(1)	
Guévin Tormin (FRA)	28.10.1997	20	(9)	2
Trainer:	**DOB**	**M**		
Laurent Guyot (FRA)	17.12.1969	36		
José Jeunechamps [02.05.2019]	02.05.1967	4		

Royal Charleroi Sporting Club

Founded: 01.01.1904
Stadium: Stade du Pays de Charleroi, Charleroi (14,000)

Goalkeepers:	**DOB**	**M**	**(s)**	**G**
Parfait Mandanda (COD)	10.11.1989	3		
Nicolas Penneteau (FRA)	20.02.1981	30		
Rémy Riou (FRA)	06.08.1987	9		
Defenders:	**DOB**	**M**	**(s)**	**G**
Gabriele Angella (ITA)	28.04.1989	20	(4)	2
Maxime Busi	14.10.1999	8	(1)	
Dorian Dervite (FRA)	25.07.1988		(1)	
Dorian Dessoleil	07.08.1992	35	(1)	2
Stergos Marinos (GRE)	17.09.1987	35	(2)	
Francisco Javier Martos Espigares (ESP)	04.01.1984	26	(2)	
Núrio Domingos Matias Fortuna (POR)	24.03.1995	31		1
Thomas Wildemeersch	18.01.2000	1	(2)	
Steeven Willems (FRA)	31.08.1990	17	(3)	
Gjoko Zajkov (MKD)	10.02.1995	11	(1)	
Midfielders:	**DOB**	**M**	**(s)**	**G**
Cristián Benavente Bristol (PER)	19.05.1994	22		9
Massimo Bruno	17.09.1993	26	(8)	4
Christophe Diandy	25.11.1990	20	(3)	
Romain Grange (FRA)	21.07.1988		(8)	
Gaëtan Hendrickx	30.03.1995	31	(2)	1
Marco Ilaimaharitra (MAD)	26.07.1995	33	(1)	1
Ryota Morioka (JPN)	12.04.1991	12	(3)	4
Ken Nkuba	21.01.2002		(2)	
Omid Noorafkan (IRN)	09.04.1997		(2)	
Nathan Rodes	11.12.1997		(1)	
Forwards:	**DOB**	**M**	**(s)**	**G**
Amara Baby (SEN)	23.02.1989	4		
Chris Bedia (CIV)	05.03.1996	1	(1)	
Younes Delfi (IRN)	02.10.2000	4	(2)	1
Mamadou Fall (SEN)	31.12.1991	1	(2)	
Ali Gholizadeh (IRN)	10.03.1996	13	(9)	1
David Henen	19.04.1996	10	(14)	2
Adama Niane (MLI)	16.06.1993	15	(16)	7
Victor James Osimhen (NGA)	29.12.1998	31	(3)	19
Jérémy Perbet (FRA)	12.12.1984	10	(27)	8
Kaveh Rezaei (IRN)	05.04.1992	3	(1)	3
Trainer:	**DOB**	**M**		
Felice Mazzù	12.03.1966	42		

Club Brugge Koninklijke Voetbalvereniging

Founded: 13.11.1891
Stadium: "Jan Breydel" Stadium, Brugge (29,042)

Goalkeepers:	**DOB**	**M**	**(s)**	**G**
Ethan Horvath (USA)	09.06.1995	28		
Karlo Letica (CRO)	11.02.1997	12		
Defenders:	**DOB**	**M**	**(s)**	**G**
Clinton Mata Pedro Lourenço (ANG)	07.11.1992	22	(2)	2
Dion Cools	04.06.1996	1	(14)	1
Saulo Decarli (SUI)	04.02.1992	5	(4)	
Stefano Denswil (NED)	07.05.1993	35		1
Luan Peres Petroni (BRA)	19.07.1994		(4)	
Brandon Mechele	28.01.1993	32		
Matej Mitrović (CRO)	10.11.1993	11	(1)	
Benoit Poulain (FRA)	27.07.1987	23	(1)	1
Alexander Scholz (DEN)	24.10.1992	1		
Ivan Tomečak (CRO)	07.12.1989	2	(1)	
Midfielders:	**DOB**	**M**	**(s)**	**G**
Sofyan Amrabat (MAR)	21.08.1996	10	(14)	1
Brandon Baiye	27.12.2000		(1)	
Marvelous Nakamba (ZIM)	19.01.1994	13	(5)	
Mats Rits	18.07.1993	35	(4)	3
Hans Vanaken	24.08.1992	40		14
Ruud Vormer (NED)	11.05.1988	36	(2)	6
Forwards:	**DOB**	**M**	**(s)**	**G**
Emmanuel Dennis Bonaventure (NGA)	15.11.1997	20	(6)	7
Arnaut Danjuma (NED)	31.01.1997	13	(7)	5
Krépin Diatta (SEN)	25.02.1999	21	(2)	2
Cyril Ngonge	26.05.2000	1	(3)	
Loïs Openda	16.02.2000	3	(17)	4
Kaveh Rezaei (IRN)	05.04.1992	4	(7)	1
Siebe Schrijvers	18.07.1996	25	(7)	12
Thibault Vlietinck	19.08.1997	6	(5)	1
Jelle Vossen	22.03.1989	4	(10)	5
Wesley Moraes Ferreira Da Silva (BRA)	26.11.1996	37	(1)	13
Trainer:	**DOB**	**M**		
Ivan Leko (CRO)	07.02.1978	40		

Königliche Allgemeine Sportvereinigung Eupen

Founded: 1945
Stadium: Kehrweg Stadion, Eupen (8,363)

Goalkeepers:	**DOB**	**M**	**(s)**	**G**
Babacar Niasse (SEN)	20.12.1996	3		
Hendrik Van Crombrugge	30.04.1993	37		
Defenders:	**DOB**	**M**	**(s)**	**G**
Siebe Blondelle	20.04.1986	35	(2)	2
Rocky Bushiri	30.11.1999	30	(1)	
Silas Gnaka (CIV)	18.12.1998	32	(1)	
Cheick Keita (MLI)	16.04.1996	19	(5)	2
Jordan Lotiès (FRA)	05.08.1984	5	(4)	1
Francesc Xavier "Xavi" Molina Arias (ESP)	19.07.1986	25		2
Julian Schauerte	02.04.1988	5		
Midfielders:	**DOB**	**M**	**(s)**	**G**
Alessio Castro-Montes	17.05.1997	20	(2)	2
Diawandou Diagné (SEN)	08.11.1994	1	(1)	
Mégan Laurent	24.03.1992	2	(8)	
Jean Thierry Lazare Amani (CIV)	07.03.1998	22	(5)	1
Luis García Fernández (ESP)	06.02.1981	35		8
Sulayman Marreh (GAM)	15.01.1996	29		1
Danijel Miličević (BIH)	05.01.1986	12	(8)	
Youssef Msakni (TUN)	28.10.1990	5	(8)	3
Rémi Mulumba (COD)	02.11.1992	15	(4)	
Konan N'Dri (CIV)		1	(8)	
Morteza Pouraliganji (IRN)	19.04.1992	6		2
Nils Schouterden	14.12.1988	3	(10)	1
Yuta Toyokawa (JPN)	09.09.1994	33	(5)	9
Forwards:	**DOB**	**M**	**(s)**	**G**
Samuel Essende (FRA)	23.01.1998		(16)	
Mamadou Fall (SEN)	31.12.1991	29	(1)	4
Sibiry Keita (MLI)	30.01.2001	2		
Eric Ocansey (GHA)	22.08.1997	23	(8)	2
David Pollet	12.08.1988	10	(9)	
Florian Raspentino (ALG)	06.09.1989		(4)	
Ivan Yagan (ARM)	11.10.1989	1	(4)	
Trainer:	**DOB**	**M**		
Claude Makélélé (FRA)	18.02.1973	40		

Koninklijke Racing Club Genk

Founded: 1988
Stadium: Luminus Arena, Genk (24,956)

Goalkeepers:	DOB	M	(s)	G
Nordin Jackers	05.09.1997	3		
Danny Vuković (AUS)	27.03.1985	37		
Defenders:	**DOB**	**M**	**(s)**	**G**
Joseph Aidoo (GHA)	29.09.1995	31	(2)	1
Sebastien Dewaest	27.05.1991	33	(1)	4
Jhon Janer Lucumi Bonilla (COL)	26.06.1998	16	(1)	
Joakim Mæhle (DEN)	20.05.1997	38	(1)	3
Vivaldo Borges dos Santos Neto „Netinho“ (BRA)	13.09.1996	1		
Jere Uronen (FIN)	13.07.1994	29	(2)	1
Dries Wouters	28.01.1997	2	(5)	
Midfielders:	**DOB**	**M**	**(s)**	**G**
Sander Berge (NOR)	14.02.1998	24	(4)	
Casper De Norre	07.02.1997	6	(5)	
Ivan Fiolić (CRO)	29.04.1996		(4)	
Bryan Heynen	06.02.1997	29	(6)	5
Ruslan Malinovskiy (UKR)	04.05.1993	34	(3)	13
Bojan Nastić (SRB)	06.07.1994	4	(3)	
Joseph Paintsil (GHA)	01.02.1998	10	(15)	3
Jakub Piotrowski (POL)	04.10.1997	2	(3)	
Alejandro Pozuelo Melero (ESP)	20.09.1991	27	(1)	5
Ibrahima Seck (SEN)	10.08.1989	2	(9)	
Rubin Seigers	11.01.1998	2	(2)	
Forwards:	**DOB**	**M**	**(s)**	**G**
Zinho Gano	13.10.1993	5	(16)	1
Marcus Ingvartsen (DEN)	04.01.1996	1	(7)	
Junya Ito (JPN)	09.03.1993	11	(2)	3
Dieumerci Ndongala (COD)	14.06.1991	21	(10)	4
Mbwana Samatta (TAN)	13.12.1992	36	(2)	23
Leandro Trossard	04.12.1994	32	(2)	14
Edon Zhegrova (KVX)	31.03.1999	4	(3)	1
Trainer:	**DOB**	**M**		
Philippe Clement	22.03.1974	40		

Koninklijke Atletiek Associatie Gent

Founded: 1900
Stadium: Ghelamco Arena, Gent (20,000)

Goalkeepers:	DOB	M	(s)	G
Colin Coosemans	03.08.1992	2		
Lovre Kalinić (CRO)	03.04.1990	14		
Thomas Kaminski	23.10.1992	19		
Yannick Thoelen	18.07.1990	5	(1)	
Defenders:	**DOB**	**M**	**(s)**	**G**
Nana Asare (GHA)	11.07.1986	37		
Dylan Bronn (TUN)	19.06.1995	26	(2)	7
Thibault De Smet	05.06.1998	3	(2)	1
Timothy Derijck	25.05.1987	16	(1)	1
Thomas Foket	25.09.1994	5		
Igor Plastun (UKR)	20.08.1990	17	(2)	
Sigurd Rosted (NOR)	22.07.1994	26	(3)	5
Arnaud Souquet (FRA)	12.02.1992	30	(1)	
Midfielders:	**DOB**	**M**	**(s)**	**G**
Franko Andrijašević (CRO)	22.06.1991	7	(3)	
Roman Bezus (UKR)	26.09.1990	4	(11)	
Giorgi Chakvetadze (GEO)	29.08.1999	20	(3)	5
Brecht Dejaegere	29.05.1991	22	(12)	2
Anderson Esiti (NGA)	24.05.1994	21	(5)	
Vadis Odjidja-Ofoe	21.02.1989	26	(2)	4
Renato Cardoso Porto Neto (BRA)	27.09.1991		(1)	
Eric Smith (SWE)	08.01.1997	1	(1)	
Birger Verstraete	16.04.1994	27	(7)	5
Forwards:	**DOB**	**M**	**(s)**	**G**
Taiwo Michael Awoniyi (NGA)	12.08.1997	5	(11)	
Philip Azongo Elayo (NGA)	21.05.1997		(1)	
Jonathan Christian David (CAN)	14.01.2000	21	(12)	12
Jean-Luc Dompé (FRA)	12.08.1995	14	(9)	1
Aboubakary Koita	20.09.1998	2	(4)	
Yūya Kubo (JPN)	24.12.1993	2		
Giorgi Kvilitaia (GEO)	01.10.1993	3	(8)	4
Stallone Limbombe	26.03.1991	14	(10)	4
Alexander Sørloth (NOR)	05.12.1995	18	(1)	4
Ahmed Mostafa Taher (EGY)	21.10.1997		(1)	
Roman Yaremchuk (UKR)	27.11.1995	33	(4)	8
Trainer:	**DOB**	**M**		
Yves Vanderhaeghe	30.01.1970	10		
Jess Thorup (DEN) [10.10.2018]	21.02.1970	30		

Koninklijke Voetbalclub Kortrijk

Founded: 1901
Stadium: Guldensporenstadion, Kortrijk (9,399)

Goalkeepers:	DOB	M	(s)	G
Sébastien Bruzzese	01.03.1989	18		
Joel Castro Dinis Pereira (POR)	28.06.1996	5		
Thomas Kaminski	23.10.1992	18		
Defenders:	**DOB**	**M**	**(s)**	**G**
Andriy Batsula (UKR)	06.02.1992	9	(7)	
Alloune Camara (SEN)	09.08.1997		(1)	
Petar Golubović (SRB)	13.07.1994	9	(3)	
Brendan Hines-Ike (USA)	07.04.1994	23	(2)	1
Gary Christofer Kagelmacher Pérez (URU)	21.04.1988	38		
Lucas Rougeaux (FRA)	10.03.1994	5	(1)	
Midfielders:	**DOB**	**M**	**(s)**	**G**
Abdul Jeleel Ajagun (NGA)	10.02.1993	4	(4)	
Larry Francis Abdel Azouni (FRA)	23.03.1994	23	(6)	
Charilaos Charisis (GRE)	12.01.1995	5	(13)	
Kristof D'Haene	06.06.1990	38		3
Julien De Sart	23.12.1994	30	(1)	5
Rubenilson dos Santos da Rocha „Kanu“ (BRA)	23.09.1987	6	(10)	1
Bennard Kumordzi (GHA)	21.03.1985	13	(5)	1
Christophe Lepoint	24.10.1984	28	(5)	3
Liam Prez	31.08.2000		(1)	
Elohim Rolland (FRA)	03.03.1989	17	(4)	2
Jovan Stojanović (SRB)	21.04.1992	23	(9)	11
Hannes Van der Bruggen	01.04.1993	34	(2)	2
Forwards:	**DOB**	**M**	**(s)**	**G**
Felipe Nicolás Avenatti Dovillabichus (URU)	26.04.1993	25	(4)	15
Teddy Chevalier	28.06.1987	31	(8)	8
Imoh Ezekiel (NGA)	24.10.1993	10	(14)	4
Aboubakary Koita	20.09.1998	6	(10)	2
Ilombe M'Boyo	22.04.1987	18	(2)	7
Idir Ouali (FRA)	21.05.1988	15	(7)	3
Jean Marco Toualy (CIV)	26.02.1999		(1)	
Trainer:	**DOB**	**M**		
Glen De Boeck	22.08.1971	15		
Yves Vanderhaeghe [15.11.12018]	30.01.1970	26		

Koninklijke Sporting Club Lokeren Oost-Vlaanderen

Founded: 22.01.1923
Stadium: Daknamstadion, Lokeren (12,136)

Goalkeepers:	DOB	M	(s)	G
Ortwin De Wolf	23.04.1997	19		
Davino Verhulst	25.11.1987	11		
Defenders:	**DOB**	**M**	**(s)**	**G**
Bambo Diaby (ESP)	17.12.1997	15	(3)	1
Omri Ben Harush (ISR)	07.03.1990	16	(4)	1
Olivier Deschacht	16.02.1981	24		2
Jakov Filipović (CRO)	17.10.1992	26		
Mijat Marić (SUI)	30.04.1984	4		1
Stefano Marzo	22.03.1991	1	(1)	
Arno Monsecour	19.01.1996	1		
Tracy Mpati Bibuangu	21.03.1992	2	(4)	
Ari Skúlason (ISL)	14.05.1987	17	(3)	1
Mario Tičinović (CRO)	20.08.1991	2	(3)	
Mickaël Tirpan	23.10.1993	23	(1)	1
Midfielders:	**DOB**	**M**	**(s)**	**G**
Amine Benchaib	18.06.1998	4	(6)	1
José Francisco Cevallos Enriquez (ECU)	18.01.1995	18	(5)	4
Steve De Ridder	25.02.1987	23	(1)	1
Lukáš Mareček (CZE)	17.04.1990	24	(1)	2
Killian Overmeire	06.12.1985	27		
Joher Rassoul (SEN)	31.12.1995	7	(5)	
Medhi Terki (FRA)	27.09.1991	10	(11)	3
Forwards:	**DOB**	**M**	**(s)**	**G**
Guus Hupperts (NED)	25.04.1992	18	(4)	2
Đorđe Jovanović (SRB)	15.02.1999	7	(3)	1
Yusuf Lawal (NGA)	23.03.1998		(2)	
Dylan Mbayo	11.10.2001	2		
Marko Mirić (SRB)	26.03.1987	14	(7)	4
Geoffrey Mujangi Bia	12.08.1989	1	(3)	
Knowledge Musona (ZIM)	21.06.1990	6		1
Jakub Řezníček (CZE)	26.05.1988	1	(3)	1
Anton Saroka (BLR)	05.03.1992	7	(10)	1
Bob Straetman	29.12.1997		(1)	
Laurens Symons	28.08.2001		(3)	
Trainer:	**DOB**	**M**		
Rúnar Kristinsson (ISL)	05.09.1969	2		
Peter Maes [09.08.2018]	01.06.1964	10		
Arnar Viðarsson (ISL) [27.10.2018]	15.03.1978	1		
Trond Johan Sollied (NOR) [02.11.2018]	29.04.1959	9		
Glen De Boeck [20.01.2019]	22.08.1971	8		

Royal Excel Mouscron

Founded: 1922 (*as RRC Péruwelz*)
Stadium: Stade Le Canonnier, Mouscron (10,571)

Goalkeepers:	DOB	M	(s)	G
Jean Butez (FRA)	08.06.1995	30		
Vaso Vasić (SRB)	26.04.1990	4		
Olivier Werner	16.04.1985	6		
Defenders:	**DOB**	**M**	**(s)**	**G**
Nemanja Antonov (SRB)	06.05.1995	9	(3)	1
Nathan De Medina	08.10.1997		(2)	
Christophe Diedhiou (SEN)	08.01.1988	3	(1)	
Noë Dussenne	07.04.1992	26		1
Georgios Galitsios (GRE)	06.07.1986	11	(4)	
Bruno Godeau	10.05.1992	32	(2)	1
Alexandros Katranis (GRE)	04.05.1998	7	(1)	
Rijad Sadiku (BIH)	18.01.2000	2	(1)	
Mergim Vojvoda (KVX)	01.02.1995	33	(4)	1
Midfielders:	**DOB**	**M**	**(s)**	**G**
Selim Amallah	15.11.1996	20	(3)	5
Marko Bakić (MNE)	01.11.1993	26		2
Manuel Benson	28.03.1997	17	(9)	4
Frank Thierry Boya (CMR)	01.07.1996	29	(1)	2
Bilal Chibani	15.10.1998	3	(4)	
Sidney Friede (GER)	12.04.1998	9	(1)	2
Nikola Gulan (SRB)	23.03.1989	26		
Alexandre Ippolito	05.01.1999		(1)	
Joel Kalonji-Kalonji	04.01.1998		(1)	
Luka Luković (SRB)	16.10.1996		(2)	
Dimitri Mohamed (FRA)	11.06.1989	24	(2)	2
Luca Napoleone	30.09.1993	3	(2)	
Andrés de Jesús Sarmiento Salas (COL)	15.01.1998	3	(1)	
Sebastjan Spahiu	30.10.1999		(2)	
Benjamin Van Durmen	20.03.1997	29	(4)	1
Forwards:	**DOB**	**M**	**(s)**	**G**
Taiwo Michael Awoniyi (NGA)	12.08.1997	14	(2)	11
Babacar Dione	22.03.1997	7	(3)	1
Mario Jelavić (CRO)	20.08.1993		(1)	
Mićo Kuzmanović (BIH)	18.03.1996	2	(11)	1
Mbaye Leye (SEN)	01.12.1982	18	(6)	6
Yanis Mbombo Lokwa	08.04.1994	4	(10)	1
Fabrice Olinga Essono (CMR)	12.05.1996	15	(5)	
Frantzdy Pierrot (HAI)	07.01.1997	22	(13)	8
Idrisa Sidi Sambú (POR)	27.03.1998	5	(2)	1
Mathéo Vroman (FRA)	19.11.2001	1	(2)	
Trainer:	**DOB**	**M**		
Frank Defays	23.02.1974	6		
Bernd Storck (GER) [02.09.2018]	25.01.1963	34		

Koninklijke Voetbalclub Oostende

Founded: 1904
Stadium: Versluys Arena, Ostend (8,432)

Goalkeepers:	DOB	M	(s)	G
William Dutoit (FRA)	18.09.1988	18		
Joseph Fabrice Ondoa Ebogo (CMR)	24.12.1995	22	(1)	
Defenders:	**DOB**	**M**	**(s)**	**G**
Jelle Bataille	20.05.1999	9	(9)	
Aleksandar Bjelica (SRB)	07.01.1994	7	(1)	1
Brecht Capon	24.04.1988	21	(4)	1
Laurens De Bock	07.11.1992	19	(1)	1
Wout Faes	03.04.1998	35		1
Nicolas Lombaerts	20.03.1985	21	(1)	
Goran Milović (CRO)	29.01.1989	37	(1)	2
Bojan Nastić (SRB)	06.07.1994	11	(1)	1
Logan Ndenbe	09.02.2000	1	(2)	
Amin Nouri (NOR)	10.01.1990	10	(2)	
Žarko Tomašević (MNE)	22.02.1990	19		1
Midfielders:	**DOB**	**M**	**(s)**	**G**
Emmanuel Junior Banda (ZAM)	29.09.1997	1	(4)	1
Indy Boonen	04.01.1999	10	(14)	3
Sander Coopman	12.03.1995	19	(4)	2
Robbie D'Haese	25.02.1999	6	(3)	2
Fernando Canesin Matos (BRA)	27.02.1992	26	(2)	6
Michiel Jonckheere	03.01.1990	1	(3)	
François Marquet	17.04.1995	9	(3)	
Aristote Nkaka	27.03.1996	19	(1)	
Kévin Vandendriessche (FRA)	07.08.1989	34	(1)	2
Jordi Vanlerberghe	27.06.1996	22	(9)	4
Forwards:	**DOB**	**M**	**(s)**	**G**
Tom De Sutter	03.07.1985	15	(1)	2
Sindri Guri (ALB)	23.10.1993	13	(17)	3
Nicolas Rajsel (FRA)	31.05.1993	2		
Fashion Sakala (ZAM)	14.03.1997	18	(15)	5
Richairo Živković (NED)	05.09.1996	15	(6)	3
Trainer:	**DOB**	**M**		
Gert Verheyen	20.09.1970	28		
Hugo Broos [06.03.2019]	10.04.1952	8		
Franky Van der Elst [29.04.2019]	30.04.1961	4		

Koninklijke Sint-Truidense Voetbalvereniging

Founded: 1924
Stadium: Stayen Stadium, Sint-Truiden (14,600)

Goalkeepers:	DOB	M	(s)	G
Lucas Pirard	10.03.1995	7	(1)	
Kenny Steppe	14.11.1988	33		
Defenders:	**DOB**	**M**	**(s)**	**G**
Wataru Endo (JPN)	09.02.1993	21	(5)	2
Pol García Tena (ESP)	18.02.1995	24		1
Avelino Jorge Filipe Teixeira (POR)	27.08.1986	32	(1)	
Sascha Kotysch (GER)	02.10.1988		(1)	
Samy Mmaee	08.09.1996	6	(1)	
Thallyson Augusto Tavares Dias (BRA)	01.12.1991		(1)	
Takehiro Tomiyasu (JPN)	05.11.1998	37		1
Midfielders:	**DOB**	**M**	**(s)**	**G**
Samuel Asamoah (GHA)	23.03.1994	34	(2)	
Jordan Botaka (COD)	24.06.1993	40		9
Alexandre De Bruyn	04.06.1994	3	(7)	
Casper De Norre	07.02.1997	18	(1)	2
Steven De Petter	22.11.1985	12	(5)	
Alexis De Sart	12.11.1996	36	(3)	6
Daichi Kamada (JPN)	05.08.1996	31	(3)	15
Jonathan Legear	13.04.1987	1	(8)	
Ibrahima Sankhon (GUI)	01.01.1996	16	(4)	
Takahiro Sekine (JPN)	19.04.1995	7	(4)	1
Rai Hendrikus Martinus Vloet (NED)	08.05.1995		(2)	
Forwards:	**DOB**	**M**	**(s)**	**G**
Elton Acolatse (NED)	25.07.1995	13	(14)	1
Roman Bezus (UKR)	26.09.1990	16		3
Yohan Boli (FRA)	17.11.1993	30	(4)	12
Mohamed Buya Turay (SLE)	10.01.1995	2	(4)	1
Cristian Ceballos Prieto (ESP)	03.12.1992	11	(12)	1
Paul Gladon (NED)	18.03.1992		(1)	
Wolke Janssens	01.08.1995		(8)	1
Kosuke Kinoshita (JPN)	03.10.1994	3	(4)	1
Duckens Moses Nazon (HAI)	07.04.1994	1	(4)	
Mamadou Sylla (SEN)	20.03.1994	6	(7)	4
Trainer:	**DOB**	**M**		
Marc Brys	10.05.1962	40		

Royal Standard de Liège

Founded: 1898
Stadium: Stade "Maurice Dufrasne", Liège (27,670)

Goalkeepers:	DOB	M	(s)	G
Francisco Guillermo Ochoa Magaña (MEX)	13.07.1985	40		
Defenders:	**DOB**	**M**	**(s)**	**G**
Luis Cavanda	02.01.1991	17	(3)	1
Collins Fai (CMR)	13.08.1992	30		1
Réginal Goreux (HAI)	31.12.1987	2	(3)	
Miloš Kosanović (SRB)	28.05.1990	15	(5)	1
Kostas Laifis (CYP)	19.05.1993	38	(1)	1
Christian Luyindama Nekadio (COD)	08.01.1994	20		3
Senna Miangue	05.02.1997	4	(2)	
Sébastien Pocognoli	01.08.1987	6	(2)	
Zinho Vanheusden	29.07.1999	22	(4)	2
Midfielders:	**DOB**	**M**	**(s)**	**G**
Uche Agbo (NGA)	04.12.1995	7	(3)	
William Balikwisha	12.05.1999		(5)	
Samuel Bastien	26.09.1996	14	(9)	2
Bopé Bokadi (COD)	21.05.1996	12	(1)	1
Joachim Carcela-González	16.12.1999		(1)	
Gojko Cimirot (BIH)	19.12.1992	36	(2)	
Alen Halilović (CRO)	18.06.1996	5	(9)	
Răzvan Marin (ROU)	23.05.1996	35	(3)	10
Forwards:	**DOB**	**M**	**(s)**	**G**
Mehdi Carcela-González (MAR)	01.07.1989	30	(6)	5
Carlos Vinicius Santos de Jesus „Carlinhos" (BRA)	22.06.1994		(2)	
Duje Čop (CRO)	01.02.1990		(2)	
Moussa Djénépo (MLI)	15.06.1998	24	(8)	8
Renaud Emond	05.12.1991	31	(3)	13
Maxime Lestienne	17.06.1992	18	(9)	5
Paul-José Mpoku Ebunge (COD)	19.04.1992	27	(3)	8
Orlando Carlos Braga de Sá (POR)	26.05.1988	3	(15)	1
Obbi Oularé	08.01.1996	4	(2)	1
Trainer:	**DOB**	**M**		
Michel Jean Georges Ghislain Preud'homme	24.01.1959	40		

Koninklijke Voetbalclub Red Star Waasland-Sportkring-Beveren

Founded: 2010 (*merged with KSK Beveren*)
Stadium: Freethiel Stadion, Beveren (8,190)

Goalkeepers:	DOB	M	(s)	G
Kevin Debaty	12.06.1989	8		
Davy Roef	06.02.1994	30		
Anthony Swolfs	25.11.1997	2		
Defenders:	**DOB**	**M**	**(s)**	**G**
Maximiliano Caufriez	16.02.1997	30	(1)	1
Daam Foulon	23.03.1999	14	(4)	
Alexis Yohaslin Gamboa Rojas (CRC)	20.03.1999	5	(1)	
Milan Massop (NED)	01.12.1993	27	(1)	1
Valtteri Moren (FIN)	15.06.1991	21		
Tobias Frank Salquist Nielsen (DEN)	18.05.1995	4	(1)	
Jur Schryvers	11.03.1997	26	(8)	1
Oscar Threlkeld (ENG)	15.12.1994	2		
Aleksandar Vukotić (SRB)	22.07.1995	38		1
Midfielders:	**DOB**	**M**	**(s)**	**G**
Anas Aalillou	10.01.2003			
Franko Andrijašević (CRO)	22.06.1991	14	(2)	3
Djihad Bizimana (RWA)	12.12.1996	21	(1)	
Daan Heymans	15.06.1999		(2)	
Denzel Jubitana	06.05.1999	6	(12)	2
Paul Keita (SEN)	23.06.1992	17	(4)	
Karlo Lulić (CRO)	10.05.1996	13	(9)	
Stefan Milošević (MNE)	23.06.1996	9	(5)	7
Joachim Van Damme	23.07.1991	4	(1)	1
Louis Verstraete	04.05.1999	27	(3)	2
Forwards:	**DOB**	**M**	**(s)**	**G**
Rafidine Abdullah (COM)	15.01.1994	8	(2)	
Nana Ampomah (GHA)	02.01.1996	26	(5)	8
Beni Badibanga	19.02.1996	11	(13)	2
Aleksandar Boljević (MNE)	12.12.1995	32	(1)	4
Tuur Dierckx	09.05.1995		(7)	
Francesco Forte (ITA)	01.05.1993	19	(12)	8
Lamine N'Dao	19.12.1994		(7)	
Cherif Ndiaye (SEN)	23.01.1996	1		
Din Sula (ALB)	02.03.1998		(2)	
Floriano Vanzo	22.04.1994	16	(6)	4
Apostolos Vellios (GRE)	08.01.1992	9	(8)	4
Trainer:	**DOB**	**M**		
Yannick Ferrera y Caro	24.09.1980	15		
Adnan Čustović (BIH) [17.11.2018]	16.04.1978	25		

Sportvereniging Zulte Waregem

Founded: 01.07.2001
Stadium: Regenboogstadion, Waregem (12,250)

Goalkeepers:	DOB	M	(s)	G
Eike Bansen (GER)	21.02.1998	5		
Sammy Bossut	11.08.1985	30		
Louis Bostyn	04.10.1993	5		
Defenders:	**DOB**	**M**	**(s)**	**G**
Marvin Baudry (CGO)	26.01.1990	28		
Johan Bjørdal (NOR)	05.05.1986	2	(1)	
Marco Bürki (SUI)	10.07.1993	23	(1)	1
Davy De fauw	08.07.1981	34	(3)	2
Erdin Demir (SWE)	27.03.1990	14	(1)	1
Timothy Derijck	25.05.1987	5		1
Michaël Heylen	03.01.1994	16	(1)	
Bryan Verboom	30.01.1992	1		
Sandy Walsh (NED)	14.03.1995	28	(3)	2
Midfielders:	**DOB**	**M**	**(s)**	**G**
Nill De Pauw	06.01.1990	30	(6)	4
Hicham Faik (NED)	19.03.1993	15	(4)	4
Onur Kaya	20.04.1986	1		
Damien Marcq (FRA)	08.12.1988	12	(3)	1
Urho Nissilä (FIN)	04.04.1996	3		1
Stef Peeters	09.02.1992	11	(2)	1
Ewoud Pletinckx	10.10.2000	16		1
Ibrahima Seck (SEN)	10.08.1989	16		
Florian Tardieu (FRA)	22.04.1992	18	(6)	
Jannes Van Hecke	15.01.2002		(2)	
Forwards:	**DOB**	**M**	**(s)**	**G**
Chris Bedia (CIV)	05.03.1996	5	(11)	
Henrik Bjørdal (NOR)	04.02.1997	17	(7)	2
Théo Bongonda	20.11.1995	33	(4)	14
Thomas Buffel	19.02.1981	13	(6)	4
Mathieu De Smet	27.04.2000	5	(1)	
Hamdi Harbaoui (TUN)	05.01.1985	33	(2)	25
Mikael Soisalo (FIN)	24.04.1998	5	(23)	1
Idrissa Sylla (GUI)	03.12.1990	9	(9)	3
Mamadou Sylla Diallo (SEN)	20.03.1994	7	(7)	1
Trainer:	**DOB**	**M**		
Francky Dury	11.10.1957	40		

SECOND LEVEL
First Division B 2018/2019

Opening Tournament

1.	KV Mechelen	14	9	3	2	29 - 9	30
2.	K Beerschot VA	14	7	3	4	23 - 14	24
3.	Royale Union Saint-Gilloise	14	7	3	4	19 - 19	24
4.	Lommel SK	14	6	4	4	21 - 20	22
5.	KVC Westerlo	14	6	1	7	16 - 20	19
6.	Oud-Heverle Leuven	14	4	3	7	19 - 24	15
7.	KSV Roeselare	14	3	4	7	14 - 24	13
8.	AFC Tubize	14	2	3	9	15 - 26	9

KV Mechelen were qualified for the Promotion Play-offs.

Closing Tournament

1.	K Beerschot VA	14	8	6	0	29 - 14	30
2.	KV Mechelen	14	8	5	1	26 - 16	29
3.	Royale Union Saint-Gilloise	14	6	3	5	18 - 15	21
4.	KSV Roeselare	14	5	5	4	19 - 17	20
5.	KVC Westerlo	14	3	6	5	12 - 17	15
6.	Oud-Heverle Leuven	14	4	2	8	21 - 24	14
7.	AFC Tubize	14	4	2	8	13 - 22	14
8.	Lommel SK	14	2	3	9	15 - 29	9

K Beerschot VA were qualified for the Promotion Play-offs.

Aggregate Table

1.	KV Mechelen	28	17	8	3	55 - 25	59
2.	K Beerschot VA	28	15	9	4	48 - 33	54
3.	Royale Union Saint-Gilloise	28	13	6	9	41 - 29	45
4.	KVC Westerlo	28	9	7	12	28 - 37	34
5.	KSV Roeselare	28	8	9	11	33 - 41	33
6.	Lommel SK	28	8	7	13	34 - 46	31
7.	Oud-Heverle Leuven	28	8	5	15	40 - 48	29
8.	AFC Tubize	28	6	5	17	28 - 48	23

Royale Union Saint-Gilloise and KVC Westerlo were qualified for the Europa League Play-offs.
Teams ranked 5-8 played in the Relegation Play-offs.

Relegation Play-offs

1.	Oud-Heverle Leuven	6	4	1	1	11 - 3	28
2.	KSV Roeselare	6	2	2	2	8 - 7	25
3.	Lommel SK	6	2	1	3	5 - 5	23
4.	AFC Tubize (*Relegated*)	6	1	2	3	3 - 12	17

Promotion Play-off [09-13.03.2019]

K Beerschot VA - KV Mechelen 0-0 1-2(0-0)

KV Mechelen promoted for the next season's Eerste Divisie, while K Beerschot VA were qualified for the Europa League Play-offs.

NATIONAL TEAM

INTERNATIONAL MATCHES
(16.07.2018 – 15.07.2019)

07.09.2018	Glasgow	Scotland - Belgium	0-4(0-1)	(F)
11.09.2018	Reykjavík	Iceland - Belgium	0-3(0-2)	(UNL)
12.10.2018	Bruxelles	Belgium - Switzerland	2-1(0-0)	(UNL)
16.10.2018	Bruxelles	Belgium - Netherlands	1-1(1-1)	(F)
15.11.2018	Bruxelles	Belgium - Iceland	2-0(0-0)	(UNL)
18.11.2018	Luzern	Switzerland - Belgium	5-2(3-2)	(UNL)
21.03.2019	Bruxelles	Belgium - Russia	3-1(2-1)	(ECQ)
24.03.2019	Nicosia	Cyprus - Belgium	0-2(0-2)	(ECQ)
08.06.2019	Bruxelles	Belgium - Kazakhstan	3-0(2-0)	(ECQ)
11.06.2019	Bruxelles	Belgium - Scotland	3-0(1-0)	(ECQ)

07.09.2018 SCOTLAND - BELGIUM 0-4(0-1) Friendly International
Hampden Park, Glasgow; Referee: Luca Banti (Italy); Attendance: 20,196
BEL: Thibaut Nicolas Marc Courtois, Vincent Jean Mpoy Kompany (46.Thomas Vermaelen), Jan Bert Lieve Vertonghen, Anga Dedryck Boyata, Timothy Castagne (46.Thomas Meunier), Moussa Sidi Yaya Dembélé (85.Birger Verstraete), Youri Tielemans, Eden Michael Hazard (Cap) (56.Hans Vanaken), Dries Mertens (46.Yannick Ferreira Carrasco), Thorgan Ganael Francis Hazard, Romelu Menama Lukaku Bolingoli (46.Michy Batshuayi-Atunga). Trainer: Roberto Martínez Montoliu (Spain).
Goals: Romelu Menama Lukaku Bolingoli (28), Eden Michael Hazard (46), Michy Batshuayi-Atunga (52, 60).

11.09.2018 ICELAND - BELGIUM 0-3(0-2) UEFA Nations League A, Group 2
Laugardalsvöllur, Reykjavík; Referee: Sergei Karasev (Russia); Attendance: 9,710
BEL: Thibaut Nicolas Marc Courtois, Vincent Jean Mpoy Kompany, Jan Bert Lieve Vertonghen, Tobias Albertine Maurits Alderweireld, Thomas Meunier, Axel Tomas Laurent Angel Lambert Witsel, Yannick Ferreira Carrasco (70.Nacer Chadli), Youri Tielemans (80.Moussa Sidi Yaya Dembélé), Eden Michael Hazard (Cap) (89.Thorgan Ganael Francis Hazard), Dries Mertens, Romelu Menama Lukaku Bolingoli. Trainer: Roberto Martínez Montoliu (Spain).
Goals: Eden Michael Hazard (29 penalty), Romelu Menama Lukaku Bolingoli (31, 81).

12.10.2018 BELGIUM - SWITZERLAND 2-1(0-0) UEFA Nations League A, Group 2
Stade "Roi Baudouin", Bruxelles; Referee: Antonio Miguel Mateu Lahoz (Spain); Attendance: 39,049
BEL: Thibaut Nicolas Marc Courtois, Vincent Jean Mpoy Kompany, Thomas Vermaelen (73.Anga Dedryck Boyata), Tobias Albertine Maurits Alderweireld, Thomas Meunier, Axel Tomas Laurent Angel Lambert Witsel, Yannick Ferreira Carrasco (76.Nacer Chadli), Youri Tielemans, Eden Michael Hazard (Cap), Dries Mertens (90+3.Thorgan Ganael Francis Hazard), Romelu Menama Lukaku Bolingoli. Trainer: Roberto Martínez Montoliu (Spain).
Goals: Romelu Menama Lukaku Bolingoli (58, 84).

16.10.2018 BELGIUM - NETHERLANDS 1-1(1-1) Friendly International
Stade "Roi Baudouin", Bruxelles; Referee: Artur Manuel Soares Dias (Portugal); Attendance: 34,747
BEL: Simon Luc Hildebert Mignolet, Tobias Albertine Maurits Alderweireld, Anga Dedryck Boyata, Timothy Castagne (73.Thomas Meunier), Jason Grégory Marianne Denayer, Axel Tomas Laurent Angel Lambert Witsel, Nacer Chadli, Youri Tielemans (83.Yannick Ferreira Carrasco), Eden Michael Hazard (Cap) (46.Thorgan Ganael Francis Hazard), Dries Mertens (46.Dennis Praet), Romelu Menama Lukaku Bolingoli (46.Michy Batshuayi-Atunga). Trainer: Roberto Martínez Montoliu (Spain).
Goal: Dries Mertens (5).

15.11.2018 BELGIUM - ICELAND 2-0(0-0) UEFA Nations League A, Group 2
Stade "Roi Baudouin", Bruxelles; Referee: Orel Grinfeld (Israel); Attendance: 28,891
BEL: Thibaut Nicolas Marc Courtois, Vincent Jean Mpoy Kompany (84.Jason Grégory Marianne Denayer), Thomas Meunier, Tobias Albertine Maurits Alderweireld, Anga Dedryck Boyata, Axel Tomas Laurent Angel Lambert Witsel, Youri Tielemans, Eden Michael Hazard (Cap) (75.Hans Vanaken), Dries Mertens (75.Adnan Januzaj), Thorgan Ganael Francis Hazard, Michy Batshuayi-Atunga. Trainer: Roberto Martínez Montoliu (Spain).
Goals: Michy Batshuayi-Atunga (65, 81).

18.11.2018 SWITZERLAND - BELGIUM 5-2(3-2) UEFA Nations League A, Group 2
Swissporarena, Luzern; Referee: Daniele Orsato (Italy); Attendance: 15,000
BEL: Thibaut Nicolas Marc Courtois, Vincent Jean Mpoy Kompany, Tobias Albertine Maurits Alderweireld, Anga Dedryck Boyata, Thomas Meunier (90.Divock Okoth Origi), Axel Tomas Laurent Angel Lambert Witsel, Nacer Chadli (65.Michy Batshuayi-Atunga), Youri Tielemans, Eden Michael Hazard (Cap), Dries Mertens, Thorgan Ganael Francis Hazard. Trainer: Roberto Martínez Montoliu (Spain).
Goals: Thorgan Ganael Francis Hazard (2, 17).

21.03.2019 BELGIUM - RUSSIA 3-1(2-1) 16th EC. Qualifiers
Stade "Roi Baudouin", Bruxelles; Referee: Ovidiu Alin Haţegan (Romania); Attendance: 34,245
BEL: Thibaut Nicolas Marc Courtois, Jan Bert Lieve Vertonghen, Tobias Albertine Maurits Alderweireld, Anga Dedryck Boyata, Timothy Castagne, Leander Dendoncker, Youri Tielemans, Eden Michael Hazard (Cap), Dries Mertens, Thorgan Ganael Francis Hazard (84.Nacer Chadli), Michy Batshuayi-Atunga. Trainer: Roberto Martínez Montoliu (Spain).
Goals: Youri Tielemans (14), Eden Michael Hazard (45 penalty, 88).

24.03.2019 CYPRUS - BELGIUM 0-2(0-2) 16th EC. Qualifiers
Stádio GSP, Nicosia; Referee: François Letexier (France); Attendance: 8,728
BEL: Thibaut Nicolas Marc Courtois, Thomas Vermaelen, Jan Bert Lieve Vertonghen, Tobias Albertine Maurits Alderweireld, Timothy Castagne, Leander Dendoncker, Youri Tielemans, Eden Michael Hazard (Cap), Dries Mertens (56.Adnan Januzaj), Thorgan Ganael Francis Hazard (68.Yannick Ferreira Carrasco), Michy Batshuayi-Atunga (89.Dennis Praet). Trainer: Roberto Martínez Montoliu (Spain).
Goals: Eden Michael Hazard (10), Michy Batshuayi-Atunga (18).

08.06.2019 BELGIUM - KAZAKHSTAN 3-0(2-0) 16th EC. Qualifiers

Stade "Roi Baudouin", Bruxelles; Referee: Irfan Peljto (Bosnia and Herzegovina); Attendance: 44,000

BEL: Thibaut Nicolas Marc Courtois, Vincent Jean Mpoy Kompany (78.Thomas Vermaelen), Jan Bert Lieve Vertonghen, Tobias Albertine Maurits Alderweireld, Timothy Castagne, Axel Tomas Laurent Angel Lambert Witsel, Kevin De Bruyne (67.Youri Tielemans), Eden Michael Hazard (Cap), Dries Mertens, Romelu Menama Lukaku Bolingoli (72.Michy Batshuayi-Atunga), Thorgan Ganael Francis Hazard. Trainer: Roberto Martínez Montoliu (Spain).

Goals: Dries Mertens (11), Timothy Castagne (14), Romelu Menama Lukaku Bolingoli (50).

11.06.2019 BELGIUM - SCOTLAND 3-0(1-0) 16th EC. Qualifiers

Stade "Roi Baudouin", Bruxelles; Referee: Petr Ardeleanu (Czech Republic); Attendance: 32,482

BEL: Thibaut Nicolas Marc Courtois, Vincent Jean Mpoy Kompany (90.Thomas Vermaelen), Jan Bert Lieve Vertonghen, Tobias Albertine Maurits Alderweireld, Thomas Meunier, Axel Tomas Laurent Angel Lambert Witsel, Kevin De Bruyne, Youri Tielemans (78.Dries Mertens), Eden Michael Hazard (Cap), Romelu Menama Lukaku Bolingoli, Thorgan Ganael Francis Hazard (90.Yannick Ferreira Carrasco). Trainer: Roberto Martínez Montoliu (Spain).

Goals: Romelu Menama Lukaku Bolingoli (45+1, 57), Kevin De Bruyne (90+2).

NATIONAL TEAM PLAYERS
(16.07.2018 – 15.07.2019)

Name	DOB	Caps	Goals	2018/2019:	*Club*
Goalkeepers					
Thibaut Nicolas Marc COURTOIS	11.05.1992	**74**	**0**	2018/2019:	*Real Madrid CF (ESP)*
Simon Luc Hildebert MIGNOLET	06.03.1988	**22**	**0**	2018/2019:	*Liverpool FC (ENG)*
Defenders					
Tobias Albertine Maurits ALDERWEIRELD	02.03.1989	**92**	**3**	2018/2019:	*Tottenham Hotspur FC London (ENG)*
Anga Dedryck BOYATA	28.11.1990	**16**	**0**	2018/2019:	*Celtic FC Glasgow (SCO)*
Timothy CASTAGNE	05.12.1995	**5**	**1**	2018/2019:	*Atalanta Bergamasca Calcio (ITA)*
Jason Grégory Marianne DENAYER	28.06.1995	**10**	**0**	2018:	*Olympique Lyonnais (FRA)*
Leander DENDONCKER	15.04.1995	**8**	**0**	2019:	*Wolverhampton Wanderers FC (ENG)*
Vincent Jean Mpoy KOMPANY	10.04.1986	**89**	**4**	2018/2019:	*Manchester City FC (ENG)*
Thomas MEUNIER	12.09.1991	**37**	**6**	2018/2019:	*Paris Saint-Germain FC (FRA)*
Thomas VERMAELEN	14.11.1985	**74**	**1**	2018/2019:	*FC Barcelona (ESP)*
Jan Bert Lieve VERTONGHEN	24.04.1987	**114**	**9**	2018/2019:	*Tottenham Hotspur FC London (ENG)*
Midfielders					
Yannick Ferreira CARRASCO	04.09.1993	**36**	**5**	2018/2019:	*Dalian Yifang FC (CHN)*
Nacer CHADLI	02.08.1989	**56**	**6**	2018/2019:	*AS Monaco FC (FRA)*
Kevin DE BRUYNE	28.06.1991	**70**	**16**	2018/2019:	*Manchester City FC (ENG)*
Moussa Sidi Yaya DEMBÉLÉ	16.07.1987	**82**	**5**	2018:	*Tottenham Hotspur FC London (ENG)*
Adnan JANUZAJ	05.02.1995	**11**	**1**	2018/2019:	*Real Sociedad San Sebastián (ESP)*
Dennis PRAET	14.05.1994	**3**	**0**	2018/2019:	*UC Sampdoria Genova (ITA)*
Youri TIELEMANS	07.05.1997	**23**	**1**	2018: 31.01.2019->	*AS Monaco FC (FRA)* *Leicester City FC (ENG)*
Hans VANAKEN	24.08.1992	**2**	**0**	2018:	*Club Brugge KV*
Birger VERSTRAETE	16.04.1994	**1**	**0**	2018:	*KAA Gent*
Axel Tomas Laurent Angel Lambert WITSEL	12.01.1989	**103**	**9**	2018/2019:	*BV Borussia Dortmund (GER)*
Forwards					
Michy BATSHUAYI-Atunga	02.10.1993	**26**	**13**	2018: 31.01.2019->	*Valencia CF (ESP)* *Crystal Palace FC London (ENG)*
Eden Michael HAZARD	07.01.1991	**102**	**30**	2018/2019:	*Chelsea FC London (ENG)*
Thorgan Ganael Francis HAZARD	29.03.1993	**23**	**3**	2018/2019:	*Borussia VfL Mönchengladbach (GER)*
Romelu Menama LUKAKU Bolingoli	13.05.1993	**81**	**48**	2018/2019:	*Manchester United FC (ENG)*
Dries MERTENS	06.05.1987	**85**	**17**	2018/2019:	*SSC Napoli (ITA)*
Divock Okoth ORIGI	18.04.1995	**25**	**3**	2018:	*Liverpool FC (ENG)*

National team coach

Roberto MARTÍNEZ Montoliu (Spain) [from 03.06.2016]	13.07.1973	37 M; 28 W; 6 D; 3 L; 105-31

BOSNIA AND HERZEGOVINA

The Country:

Bosnia and Herzegovina (Bosna i Hercegovina / Босна и Херцеговина)
Capital: Sarajevo
Surface: 51,197 km²
Inhabitants: 3,856,181 [2017]
Time: UTC+1

The FA:

Nogometni/Fudbalski Savez Bosne i Hercegovine
Bulevar Meše Selimovica 95 71000, Sarajevo
Tel: +387 33 276 660
Foundation date: 1920 / 1992
Member of FIFA since: 1996
Member of UEFA since: 1998
Website: www.nfsbih.ba

NATIONAL TEAM RECORDS

First international match:	30.11.1995, Tiranë	Albania - Bosnia and Herzegovina 2-0
Most international caps:	Edin Džeko	- 103 caps (since 2007)
Most international goals:	Edin Džeko	- 56 goals / 103 caps (since 2007)

UEFA EUROPEAN CHAMPIONSHIP	
1960	-
1964	-
1968	-
1972	-
1976	-
1980	-
1984	-
1988	-
1992	-
1996	*Did not enter*
2000	Qualifiers
2004	Qualifiers
2008	Qualifiers
2012	Qualifiers
2016	Qualifiers

FIFA WORLD CUP	
1930	-
1934	-
1938	-
1950	-
1954	-
1958	-
1962	-
1966	-
1970	-
1974	-
1978	-
1982	-
1986	-
1990	-
1994	-
1998	Qualifiers
2002	Qualifiers
2006	Qualifiers
2010	Qualifiers
2014	Final Tournament (Group Stage)
2018	Qualifiers

UEFA NATIONS LEAGUE
2018/2019 – League B (promoted to League A)

OLYMPIC FOOTBALL TOURNAMENTS 1908-2016							
1908	-	**1948**	-	**1972**	-	**1996**	-
1912	-	**1952**	-	**1976**	-	**2000**	Qualifiers
1920	-	**1956**	-	**1980**	-	**2004**	Qualifiers
1924	-	**1960**	-	**1984**	-	**2008**	-
1928	-	**1964**	-	**1988**	-	**2012**	Qualifiers
1936	-	**1968**	-	**1992**	-	**2016**	Qualifiers

FIFA CONFEDERATIONS CUP 1992-2017
None

BOSNIAN CLUB HONOURS IN EUROPEAN CLUB COMPETITIONS:

European Champion Clubs' Cup (1956-1992) / UEFA Champions League (1993-2019)
None
Fairs Cup (1858-1971) / UEFA Cup (1972-2009) / UEFA Europa League (2010-2019)
None
UEFA Super Cup (1972-2019)
None
European Cup Winners' Cup 1961-1999*
None

**defunct competition*

NATIONAL COMPETITIONS
TABLE OF HONOURS

FIRST LEAGUE OF BOSNIA AND HERZEGOVINA CHAMPIONS	
1994/1995	NK Čelik Zenica
1995/1996	NK Čelik Zenica
1996/1997	NK Čelik Zenica
1997/1998	NK Bosna Visoko
1998/1999	FK Sarajevo
1999/2000	NK Jedinstvo Bihać

FIRST LEAGUE OF HERZEG-BOSNIA CHAMPIONS	
1993/1994	NK Široki Brijeg
1994/1995	NK Široki Brijeg
1995/1996	NK Široki Brijeg
1996/1997	NK Široki Brijeg
1997/1998	NK Široki Brijeg
1998/1999	NK Posušje
1999/2000	NK Posušje

FIRST LEAGUE OF THE REPUBLIKA SRPSKA CHAMPIONS	
1995/1996	FK Boksit Milići
1996/1997	FK Rudar Ugljevik
1997/1998	FK Rudar Ugljevik
1998/1999	FK Radnik Bijeljina
1999/2000	FK Boksit Milići
2000/2001	FK Borac Banja Luka
2001/2002	FK Leotar Trebinje

BOSNIA AND HERZEGOVINA CUP WINNERS	
1994/1995	NK Čelik Zenica
1995/1996	NK Čelik Zenica
1996/1997	FK Sarajevo
1997/1998	FK Sarajevo
1998/1999	NK Bosna Visoko

HERZEG-BOSNIA CUP WINNERS	
1994/1995	NK Bigeste Ljubuški
1995/1996	NK Bigeste Ljubuški
1996/1997	NK Troglav 1918 Livno
1997/1998	HNK Orašje
1998/1999	NK Brotnjo
1999/2000	HNK Orašje

REPUBLIKA SRPSKA CUP WINNERS	
1993/1994	FK Kozara Gradiška
1994/1995	FK Borac Banja Luka
1995/1996	FK Borac Banja Luka
1996/1997	FK Sloga Trn
1997/1998	FK Rudar Ugljevik
1998/1999	FK Rudar Ugljevik
1999/2000	FK Kozara Gradiška

	PLAYOFF CHAMPIONS	CUP WINNERS	BEST GOALSCORERS	
1997/1998	FK Željezničar Sarajevo	FK Sarajevo	Stanko Bubalo (CRO, NK Široki Brijeg) Hadis Zubanović (FK Željezničar Sarajevo)	3
1998/1999	FK Sarajevo NK Posušje FK Radnik Bijeljina *(Regional winners shared)*	*No competition*	-	
1999/2000	NK Brotnjo	FK Željezničar Sarajevo	Zikret Kuljaninović (FK Budućnost Banovići) Alen Škoro (FK Sarajevo) Halim Stupac (NK Jedinstvo Bihać)	5
	PREMIER LEAGUE			
2000/2001	FK Željezničar Sarajevo	FK Željezničar Sarajevo	Dželaludin Muharemović (FK Željezničar Sarajevo)	31
2001/2002	FK Željezničar Sarajevo	FK Sarajevo	Ivica Huljev (FK Željezničar Sarajevo)	15
2002/2003	FK Leotar Trebinje	FK Željezničar Sarajevo	Emir Obuća (FK Sarajevo)	24
2003/2004	NK Široki Brijeg	FK Modriča	Alen Škoro (FK Sarajevo)	20
2004/2005	HŠK Zrinjski Mostar	FK Sarajevo	Zoran Rajović (SRB, HŠK Zrinjski Mostar)	17
2005/2006	NK Široki Brijeg	HNK Orašje	Petar Jelić (FK Modriča)	19
2006/2007	FK Sarajevo	NK Široki Brijeg	Stevo Nikolić (FK Modriča) Dragan Benić (FK Borac Banja Luka)	19
2007/2008	FK Modriča	HŠK Zrinjski Mostar	Darko Spalević (SRB, FK Slavija Sarajevo)	18
2008/2009	HŠK Zrinjski Mostar	FK Slavija Sarajevo	Darko Spalević (SRB, FK Slavija Sarajevo)	17
2009/2010	FK Željezničar Sarajevo	FK Borac Banja Luka	Feđa Dudić (NK Travnik)	16
2010/2011	FK Borac Banja Luka	FK Željezničar Sarajevo	Ivan Lendrić (CRO, HŠK Zrinjski Mostar)	16
2011/2012	FK Željezničar Sarajevo	FK Željezničar Sarajevo	Eldin Adilović (FK Željezničar Sarajevo)	19
2012/2013	FK Željezničar Sarajevo	NK Široki Brijeg	Emir Hadžić (FK Sarajevo)	20
2013/2014	HŠK Zrinjski Mostar	FK Sarajevo	Wagner Santos Lago (BRA, NK Široki Brijeg)	18
2014/2015	FK Sarajevo	FK Olimpik Sarajevo	Riad Bajić (FK Željezničar Sarajevo)	15
2015/2016	HŠK Zrinjski Mostar	FK Radnik Bijeljina	Leon Benko (CRO, FK Sarajevo)	17
2016/2017	HŠK Zrinjski Mostar	NK Široki Brijeg	Ivan Lendrić (CRO, FK Željezničar Sarajevo)	19
2017/2018	HŠK Zrinjski Mostar	FK Željezničar Sarajevo	Miloš Filipović (SRB, HŠK Zrinjski Mostar)	16
2018/2019	FK Sarajevo	FK Sarajevo	Sulejman Krpić (FK Sarajevo)	16

NATIONAL CHAMPIONSHIP
BH Telecom Premier League 2018/2019
(21.07.2018 – 25.05.2019)

Results

Round 1 [21-22.07.2018]
FK Krupa - Čelik Zenica 3-1(2-1)
FK Mladost - FK Zvijezda 09 0-0
GOŠK Gabela - FK Željezničar 0-1(0-0)
Sloboda Tuzla - Zrinjski Mostar 0-1(0-1)
Radnik Bijeljina - FK Sarajevo 2-1(1-0)
Široki Brijeg - FK Tuzla City 1-0(1-0)

Round 2 [28-29.07.2018]
FK Tuzla City - Radnik Bijeljina 0-0
FK Zvijezda 09 - Sloboda Tuzla 1-1(1-0)
FK Krupa - Široki Brijeg 2-2(2-1)
FK Sarajevo - FK Mladost 4-0(2-0)
Zrinjski Mostar - GOŠK Gabela 3-1(2-0)
Čelik Zenica - FK Željezničar 1-0(0-0)

Round 3 [04-05.08.2018]
Radnik Bijeljina - FK Krupa 2-2(1-2)
FK Mladost - FK Tuzla City 0-1(0-1)
GOŠK Gabela - FK Zvijezda 09 2-2(2-2)
Sloboda Tuzla - FK Sarajevo 0-1(0-1)
Široki Brijeg - Čelik Zenica 6-0(3-0)
FK Željezničar - Zrinjski Mostar 2-0(2-0)

Round 4 [11-12.08.2018]
FK Krupa - FK Mladost 2-2(2-0)
FK Sarajevo - GOŠK Gabela 1-1(1-0)
FK Tuzla City - Sloboda Tuzla 0-1(0-0)
FK Zvijezda 09 - FK Željezničar 1-3(0-1)
Čelik Zenica - Zrinjski Mostar 1-0(0-0)
Široki Brijeg - Radnik Bijeljina 0-0

Round 5 [15.08.2018]
FK Mladost - Široki Brijeg 0-1(0-0)
Radnik Bijeljina - Čelik Zenica 0-0
Sloboda Tuzla - FK Krupa 1-0(0-0)
GOŠK Gabela - FK Tuzla City 3-2(2-0)
FK Željezničar - FK Sarajevo 2-2(1-2)
Zrinjski Mostar - Zvijezda 09 5-2(2-0) [29.08.]

Round 6 [18-20.08.2018]
Čelik Zenica - FK Zvijezda 09 2-0(1-0)
FK Krupa - GOŠK Gabela 3-0(1-0)
Radnik Bijeljina - FK Mladost 3-1(2-1)
FK Tuzla City - FK Željezničar 0-2(0-0)
FK Sarajevo - Zrinjski Mostar 4-2(2-1)
Široki Brijeg - Sloboda Tuzla 0-0

Round 7 [25-26.08.2018]
FK Mladost - Čelik Zenica 1-1(0-0)
FK Zvijezda 09 - FK Sarajevo 0-4(0-3)
Sloboda Tuzla - Radnik Bijeljina 2-0(0-0)
Zrinjski Mostar - FK Tuzla City 1-0(0-0)
GOŠK Gabela - Široki Brijeg 0-0
FK Željezničar - FK Krupa 1-1(1-0)

Round 8 [01-02.09.2018]
FK Tuzla City - FK Zvijezda 09 3-1(2-0)
FK Krupa - Zrinjski Mostar 1-2(1-1)
Radnik Bijeljina - GOŠK Gabela 1-0(0-0)
FK Mladost - Sloboda Tuzla 1-0(1-0)
Čelik Zenica - FK Sarajevo 0-0
Široki Brijeg - FK Željezničar 0-3(0-1)

Round 9 [14-16.09.2018]
Sloboda Tuzla - Čelik Zenica 1-0(0-0)
FK Zvijezda 09 - FK Krupa 0-0
FK Sarajevo - FK Tuzla City 2-0(0-0)
Zrinjski Mostar - Široki Brijeg 0-0
GOŠK Gabela - FK Mladost 1-3(1-0)
FK Željezničar - Radnik Bijeljina 1-0(1-0)

Round 10 [22-23.09.2018]
FK Krupa - FK Sarajevo 1-4(0-2)
Radnik Bijeljina - Zrinjski Mostar 0-1(0-1)
Sloboda Tuzla - GOŠK Gabela 2-0(1-0)
FK Mladost - FK Željezničar 2-2(1-0)
Čelik Zenica - FK Tuzla City 1-1(0-0)
Široki Brijeg - FK Zvijezda 09 2-0(0-0)

Round 11 [26.09.2018]
GOŠK Gabela - Čelik Zenica 0-0
FK Zvijezda 09 - Radnik Bijeljina 0-0
FK Tuzla City - FK Krupa 2-1(1-0)
Zrinjski Mostar - FK Mladost 1-0(0-0)
FK Sarajevo - Široki Brijeg 1-0(1-0)
FK Željezničar - Sloboda Tuzla 0-0

Round 12 [29-30.09.2018]
Čelik Zenica - FK Krupa 3-1(1-0)
FK Tuzla City - Široki Brijeg 0-0
FK Zvijezda 09 - FK Mladost 0-2(0-2)
Zrinjski Mostar - Sloboda Tuzla 2-0(1-0)
FK Sarajevo - Radnik Bijeljina 2-1(1-1)
FK Željezničar - GOŠK Gabela 1-2(0-1)

Round 13 [05-06.10.2018]
FK Željezničar - Čelik Zenica 3-2(1-1)
Sloboda Tuzla - FK Zvijezda 09 0-3(0-1)
FK Mladost - FK Sarajevo 0-6(0-3)
Radnik Bijeljina - FK Tuzla City 3-1(2-0)
GOŠK Gabela - Zrinjski Mostar 0-4(0-2)
Široki Brijeg - FK Krupa 2-0(0-0)

Round 14 [20-21.10.2018]
FK Tuzla City - FK Mladost 0-1(0-1)
FK Zvijezda 09 - GOŠK Gabela 1-0(1-0)
Zrinjski Mostar - FK Željezničar 0-1(0-0)
FK Sarajevo - Sloboda Tuzla 1-0(0-0)
FK Krupa - Radnik Bijeljina 0-0
Čelik Zenica - Široki Brijeg 1-1(1-0)

Round 15 [27-28.10.2018]
FK Mladost - FK Krupa 2-1(0-0)
Radnik Bijeljina - Široki Brijeg 2-1(1-1)
Zrinjski Mostar - Čelik Zenica 3-0(2-0)
Sloboda Tuzla - FK Tuzla City 1-1(1-0)
GOŠK Gabela - FK Sarajevo 1-0(1-0)
FK Željezničar - FK Zvijezda 09 0-1(0-0)

Round 16 [03-04.11.2018]
Čelik Zenica - Radnik Bijeljina 1-0(1-0)
FK Krupa - Sloboda Tuzla 0-1(0-0)
FK Tuzla City - GOŠK Gabela 2-1(0-0)
FK Zvijezda 09 - Zrinjski Mostar 1-0(0-0)
FK Sarajevo - FK Željezničar 2-1(2-1)
Široki Brijeg - FK Mladost 1-1(0-1)

Round 17 [10-11.11.2018]
FK Zvijezda 09 - Čelik Zenica 2-0(1-0)
FK Mladost - Radnik Bijeljina 2-0(1-0)
Zrinjski Mostar - FK Sarajevo 2-2(1-0)
GOŠK Gabela - FK Krupa 1-0(1-0)
Sloboda Tuzla - Široki Brijeg 0-1(0-0)
FK Željezničar - FK Tuzla City 2-3(2-1)

Round 18 [24-25.11.2018]
FK Krupa - FK Željezničar 2-1(1-0)
FK Tuzla City - Zrinjski Mostar 1-2(0-1)
Čelik Zenica - FK Mladost 0-3(0-0)
Radnik Bijeljina - Sloboda Tuzla 0-1(0-0)
Široki Brijeg - GOŠK Gabela 1-1(0-0)
FK Sarajevo - FK Zvijezda 09 3-1(3-1)

Round 19 [30.11.-02.12.2018]
Zrinjski Mostar - FK Krupa 1-0(0-0)
FK Zvijezda 09 - FK Tuzla City 1-1(1-1)
Sloboda Tuzla - FK Mladost 2-1(1-0)
FK Sarajevo - Čelik Zenica 3-1(1-1)
FK Željezničar - Široki Brijeg 2-3(1-2)
GOŠK Gabela - Radnik Bijeljina 1-1(0-0)

Round 20 [23-24.02.2019]
FK Mladost - GOŠK Gabela 1-0(1-0)
FK Krupa - FK Zvijezda 09 1-1(1-1)
FK Tuzla City - FK Sarajevo 0-3(0-2)
Čelik Zenica - Sloboda Tuzla 2-1(2-0)
Radnik Bijeljina - FK Željezničar 1-0(1-0)
Široki Brijeg - Zrinjski Mostar 1-1(1-0)

Round 21 [02-03.03.2019]
FK Tuzla City - Čelik Zenica 1-1(1-0)
FK Sarajevo - FK Krupa 2-1(1-1)
FK Zvijezda 09 - Široki Brijeg 1-1(0-0)
Zrinjski Mostar - Radnik Bijeljina 0-0
GOŠK Gabela - Sloboda Tuzla 0-0
FK Željezničar - FK Mladost 2-1(0-1)

Round 22 [09-10.03.2019]
Čelik Zenica - GOŠK Gabela 3-1(1-0)
FK Mladost - Zrinjski Mostar 0-0
Radnik Bijeljina - FK Zvijezda 09 1-0(1-0)
FK Krupa - FK Tuzla City 0-2(0-2)
Sloboda Tuzla - FK Željezničar 0-0
Široki Brijeg - FK Sarajevo 0-3(0-0)

Round 23 [16-17.03.2019]
FK Mladost - Radnik Bijeljina 0-3(0-3)
Sloboda Tuzla - Čelik Zenica 0-1(0-1)
FK Sarajevo - FK Krupa 0-0
Zrinjski Mostar - GOŠK Gabela 1-0(0-0)
Široki Brijeg - FK Tuzla City 1-0(1-0)
FK Željezničar - FK Zvijezda 09 1-0(1-0)

Round 24 [30-31.03.2019]
FK Krupa - Radnik Bijeljina 2-2(0-1)
FK Tuzla City - Sloboda Tuzla 1-1(1-1)
FK Zvijezda 09 - Široki Brijeg 1-1(0-1)
FK Sarajevo - Zrinjski Mostar 0-1(0-0)
GOŠK Gabela - FK Željezničar 1-1(0-1)
Čelik Zenica - FK Mladost 1-0(1-0)

Round 25 [06-07.04.2019]
FK Mladost - FK Tuzla City 0-2(0-1)
Radnik Bijeljina - Čelik Zenica 0-0
Sloboda Tuzla - FK Zvijezda 09 2-1(0-1)
FK Željezničar - FK Sarajevo 0-3(0-2)
Široki Brijeg - GOŠK Gabela 1-0(1-0)
Zrinjski Mostar - FK Krupa 2-0(1-0)

Round 26 [13-14.04.2019]
FK Zvijezda 09 - FK Mladost 2-1(2-0)
FK Krupa - Čelik Zenica 5-2(3-1)
FK Tuzla City - Radnik Bijeljina 1-1(0-0)
Zrinjski Mostar - FK Željezničar 1-0(0-0)
GOŠK Gabela - Sloboda Tuzla 3-2(1-0)
FK Sarajevo - Široki Brijeg 0-0

Round 27 [20.04.2019]
Sloboda Tuzla - FK Sarajevo 2-1(0-1)
Čelik Zenica - FK Tuzla City 1-1(0-0)
FK Mladost - GOŠK Gabela 3-1(1-1)
Široki Brijeg - Zrinjski Mostar 1-0(0-0)
Radnik Bijeljina - FK Zvijezda 09 1-1(0-1)
FK Željezničar - FK Krupa 3-0(3-0)

Round 28 [24.04.2019]
FK Krupa - FK Tuzla City 1-0(0-0)
FK Sarajevo - FK Mladost 2-0(2-0)
GOŠK Gabela - Radnik Bijeljina 1-2(1-1)
Zrinjski Mostar - Sloboda Tuzla 1-0(1-0)
FK Zvijezda 09 - Čelik Zenica 4-0(2-0)
FK Željezničar - Široki Brijeg 0-0

Round 29 [27-29.04.2019]
Čelik Zenica - GOŠK Gabela 1-0(0-0)
FK Mladost - Zrinjski Mostar 2-2(1-1)
Široki Brijeg - FK Krupa 2-1(2-0)
Radnik Bijeljina - FK Sarajevo 0-0
Sloboda Tuzla - FK Željezničar 0-0
FK Tuzla City - FK Zvijezda 09 1-3(1-3)

Round 30 [03-05.05.2019]
FK Sarajevo - Čelik Zenica 5-0(3-0)
FK Krupa - FK Zvijezda 09 2-0(0-0)
Široki Brijeg - Sloboda Tuzla 4-0(1-0)
Zrinjski Mostar - Radnik Bijeljina 1-1(0-0)
GOŠK Gabela - FK Tuzla City 0-3(0-1)
FK Željezničar - FK Mladost 3-1(1-1)

Round 31 [11.05.2019]
Čelik Zenica - Zrinjski Mostar 0-1(0-0)
FK Mladost - Široki Brijeg 1-0(1-0)
Radnik Bijeljina - FK Željezničar 0-1(0-1)
Sloboda Tuzla - FK Krupa 1-2(1-1)
FK Tuzla City - FK Sarajevo 1-0(0-0)
FK Zvijezda 09 - GOŠK Gabela 2-1(0-0)

Round 32 [18.05.2019]
FK Krupa - GOŠK Gabela 4-0(0-0)
FK Sarajevo - FK Zvijezda 09 4-0(4-0)
Široki Brijeg - Radnik Bijeljina 2-1(2-0)
Sloboda Tuzla - FK Mladost 0-1(0-0)
FK Željezničar - Čelik Zenica 1-2(0-1)
Zrinjski Mostar - FK Tuzla City 5-1(4-0)

Round 33 [25.05.2019]
Čelik Zenica - Široki Brijeg 1-1(1-1)
GOŠK Gabela - FK Sarajevo 0-2(0-1)
FK Mladost - FK Krupa 3-1(1-0)
Radnik Bijeljina - Sloboda Tuzla 1-0(0-0)
FK Tuzla City - FK Željezničar 0-3(0-3)
FK Zvijezda 09 - Zrinjski Mostar 0-0

Final Standings

1.	**FK Sarajevo**	33	21	7	5	68	-	20	70
2.	HŠK Zrinjski Mostar	33	19	8	6	46	-	22	65
3.	NK Široki Brijeg	33	13	15	5	40	-	23	54
4.	FK Željezničar Sarajevo	33	14	8	11	43	-	32	50
5.	FK Radnik Bijeljina	33	10	14	9	29	-	25	44
6.	FK Mladost Doboj Kakanj	33	12	7	14	36	-	45	43
7.	NK Čelik Zenica	33	11	10	12	30	-	49	43
8.	FK Sloboda Tuzla	33	10	8	15	22	-	31	38
9.	FK Zvijezda 09 Bijeljina	33	9	11	13	33	-	45	38
10.	FK Tuzla City	33	9	9	15	32	-	44	36
11.	FK Krupa na Vrbasu (*Relegated**)	33	8	9	16	40	-	48	33
12.	NK GOŠK Gabela (*Relegated***)	33	5	8	20	23	-	54	23

* Relegation to the Prva Liga Republika Srpska
** Relegation to the Prva Liga Bosnia and Herzegovina

Top goalscorers:

16 Sulejman Krpić
FK Željezničar Sarajevo

14 Nemanja Bilbija
HŠK Zrinjski Mostar

14 Mersudin Ahmetović
FK Sarajevo

NATIONAL CUP
Kup Bosne i Hercegovine u nogometu 2018/2019

First Round [19.09.2018]

NK Igman Konjic - FK Rudar Prijedor	0-2(0-1)
FK Kozara - FK Radnik Bijeljina	1-4(0-2)
FK Velež Mostar - FK Sarajevo	0-1(0-0)
NK Moševac - FK Rudar Kakanj	1-1 aet; 3-4 pen
FK Tuzla City - HŠK Zrinjski Mostar	0-0 aet; 2-4 pen
NK Čelik Zenica - FK Krupa	1-2(0-1)
FK Zvijezda 09 Bijeljina - FK Mladost Doboj-Kakanj	1-0(1-0)
FK Modriča Maksima - FK Borac Banja Luka	1-3(0-0)
NK Metalleghe-BSI Jajce - FK Sloboda Tuzla	0-1(0-0)
FK Sloga Gornje Crnjelovo - FK Slavija Sarajevo	4-0(2-0)
NK Pobjeda Tešanjka - NK Zvijezda Gradačac	1-3(1-1)
NK TOSK Tesanj - FK Goražde	3-0(1-0)
NK Bosna Visoko - NK GOŠK Gabela	1-2(0-0)
FK Mladost Kikači - FK Leotar Trebinje	3-2(1-0)
NK Široki Brijeg - FK Željezničar Sarajevo	2-0(1-0)

Second Round [03.10.2018]

NK TOSK Tesanj - NK GOŠK Gabela	4-0
FK Rudar Kakanj - FK Sarajevo	0-0 aet; 2-4 pen
NK Zvijezda Gradačac - FK Zvijezda 09 Bijeljina	2-0(0-0)
FK Mladost Kikači - FK Sloga Gornje Crnjelovo	0-0 aet; 6-7 pen
FK Borac Banja Luka - FK Radnik Bijeljina	0-0 aet; 5-4 pen
FK Rudar Prijedor - FK Klis	2-2 aet; 2-3 pen
HŠK Zrinjski Mostar - FK Krupa	1-1 aet; 4-2 pen
FK Sloboda Tuzla - NK Široki Brijeg	1-1 aet; 4-5 pen

Quarter-Finals [27.02./05.03./13.03.2019]

NK Zvijezda Gradačac - NK TOSK Tesanj	0-2(0-1)
FK Sarajevo - HŠK Zrinjski Mostar	1-0(1-0)
NK Široki Brijeg - FK Borac Banja Luka	2-1(2-1)
FK Sloga Gornje Crnjelovo - FK Klis	1-1(0-1)
NK TOSK Tesanj - NK Zvijezda Gradačac	4-1(2-0)
FK Klis - FK Sloga Gornje Crnjelovo	2-2(1-2)
HŠK Zrinjski Mostar - FK Sarajevo	0-1(0-0)
FK Borac Banja Luka - NK Široki Brijeg	0-1(0-1)

Semi-Finals [03-10.04.2019]

FK Sloga Gornje Crnjelovo - FK Sarajevo	1-4(0-3)
NK Široki Brijeg - NK TOSK Tesanj	2-0(1-0)
NK TOSK Tesanj - NK Široki Brijeg	0-1(0-1)
FK Sarajevo - FK Sloga Gornje Crnjelovo	5-0(1-0)

Final

08.05.2018; Stadion "Asim Ferhatović Hase", Sarajevo; Referee: Dragan Petrović; Attendance: 7,500
FK Sarajevo - NK Široki Brijeg **3-0(2-0)**

FK Sarajevo: Vladan Kovačević, Darko Lazić, Nihad Mujakić, Emir Halilović (88.Amer Dupovac), Amar Rahmanović, Anel Hebibović, Ljuban Crepulja, Miloš Stanojević, Rifet Kapič (74.Krste Velkoski), Mersudin Ahmetović (80.Aladin Šišić), Benjamin Tatar. Trainer: Husref Musemić.

NK Široki Brijeg: Luka Bilobrk, Josip Barišić (46.Dino Ćorić), Ante Hrkać (46.Mateo Marić), Stipo Marković, Bernardo Matić, Dominik Kovačić, Mario Babić, Josip Čorluka, Ivan Enin, Dražen Bagarić (70.Mato Stanić), Stipe Jurić. Trainer: Goce Sedloski (North Macedonia).

Goals: 1-0 Amar Rahmanović (10), 2-0 Rifet Kapič (40), 3-0 Nihad Mujakić (90+3).

15.05.2018; Stadion Pecara, Široki Brijeg; Referee: Elvis Mujić; Attendance: 2,000

NK Široki Brijeg - FK Sarajevo **1-0(1-0)**

NK Široki Brijeg: Luka Bilobrk, Dino Ćorić (80.Marin Popović), Stipo Marković, Bernardo Matić, Dominik Kovačić, Mario Babić (28.Mato Stanić), Josip Čorluka, Ivan Enin, Mateo Marić (77.Zvonimir Vukoja), Dražen Bagarić, Stipe Jurić. Trainer: Goce Sedloski (North Macedonia).

FK Sarajevo: Vladan Kovačević, Darko Lazić, Nihad Mujakić, Numan Kurdić [*sent off* 72], Emir Halilović (65.Almir Bekić), Amar Rahmanović, Anel Hebibović (56.Halid Šabanović), Rifet Kapič (75.Aleksandar Šofranac), Mersudin Ahmetović, Krste Velkoski, Benjamin Tatar. Trainer: Husref Musemić.

Goals: 1-0 Dražen Bagarić (23).

Kup Bosne i Hercegovine Winner 2018/2019: **FK Sarajevo**

THE CLUBS 2018/2019

Nogometni klub Čelik Zenica

Founded: 16.06.1945
Stadium: Stadion Bilino Polje, Zenica (15,292)

Goalkeepers:	DOB	M	(s)	G
Ratko Dujković	16.03.1983	3	(1)	
Fikret Karajbić	15.05.1994	1		
Bojan Pavlović (SRB)	08.11.1986	13		
Branislav Ružić	02.04.1989	16		
Defenders:	**DOB**	**M**	**(s)**	**G**
Dino Bevab	13.01.1993	17		1
Almir Ćubara	21.11.1997	5	(4)	
Dušan Hodžić	31.10.1993	13		
Tin Karamatić (CRO)	01.03.1993	14	(1)	
Ivan Livaja	01.10.1987	20	(4)	1
Luka Miletić	04.10.1994	19		
Paschal Okoli (NGA)	17.10.1997	8	(3)	
Ljubiša Pecelj	29.09.1993	12	(1)	
Gabrijel Popović	16.09.1999	1		
Vedran Vrhovac	20.11.1998	24		1
Midfielders:	**DOB**	**M**	**(s)**	**G**
Tarik Adilović	31.07.1997	1	(1)	
Nikola Baban	29.09.1998	1	(5)	
Anel Dedić	02.05.1991	28		8
Senghor Faustin (SEN)	02.01.1994	6		
Vladimir Grahovac	12.01.1995	27	(4)	
Nermin Jamak	25.08.1986	27		2
Salko Jazvin	01.06.1993	3	(8)	
Sanjin Lelić	11.01.1997		(7)	
Adi Marković	19.12.1996		(1)	
Mahir Mehić	04.09.1997	5	(2)	
Fenan Salčinović	26.06.1987	6	(2)	
Aldin Šišić	29.09.1990	10	(5)	
Harun Vardo	04.10.1998		(5)	
Selim Zuna	02.08.2000	2	(2)	
Forwards:	**DOB**	**M**	**(s)**	**G**
Namir Alispahić	16.04.1995		(3)	
Ante Blažević (CRO)	05.05.1996	1	(5)	
Haris Dilaver	06.02.1990	24	(8)	10
Marin Jurina	26.11.1993	18	(5)	2
Moussa Marone (SEN)	17.12.1995	2	(2)	
Salko Mujanović	15.11.1996	2	(1)	
Stevo Nikolić	04.12.1984	4	(13)	
Ševko Okić	26.07.1988	30	(2)	5
Trainer:	**DOB**	**M**		
Adnan Örnek (TUR)	17.10.1965	20		
Cihat Arslan (TUR) [25.02.2019]	09.02.1970	13		

Nogometni klub Gabeoski Omladinski Športski Klub Gabela

Founded: 1919
Stadium: Stadion "Perica-Pero Pavlović", Gabela (5,000)

Goalkeepers:	DOB	M	(s)	G
Antonijo Brkić	23.09.1993	3		
Dalibor Kozić	10.02.1988	29		
Domagoj Lukač (CRO)	22.07.1998	1		
Defenders:	**DOB**	**M**	**(s)**	**G**
Boško Bošković	14.04.2001	2	(1)	
Darko Đajić	30.08.1992	28		1
Emrah Hasanhodžić	09.08.1993	26	(2)	1
Marin Karamarko (CRO)	14.04.1998	22	(3)	
Toni Nikić	27.03.1998	1	(1)	
Stjepan Vego (CRO)	09.07.1997	24	(1)	
Midfielders:	**DOB**	**M**	**(s)**	**G**
Elvedin Aletić	01.03.1995	16	(8)	
Elvir Čolić	17.07.1986	11	(8)	
Josip Ereiz	21.05.1994	25	(2)	1
Ernest Grvala (SVN)	11.10.1996	1	(2)	
Dino Hasanović	21.01.1996	29		
Miro Kovačić (CRO)	29.08.1994	19	(1)	
Duje Medak (CRO)	19.12.1993	5	(6)	
Safet Mujkić	26.09.1996	1	(5)	1
Antonio Raguž	24.08.1999		(1)	
Petar Raguž (CRO)	05.10.1996	25	(3)	1
Bože Vukoja	03.04.1998	7	(2)	1
Amir Zolj	24.11.1989	6	(9)	
Forwards:	**DOB**	**M**	**(s)**	**G**
Luka Anković	03.07.1996	6	(8)	1
Šime Gržan (CRO)	06.04.1994	12		1
Nermin Hajdarevič	10.02.1999	14	(3)	1
Anel Husić	12.12.1994	2	(2)	
Luka Knežević	14.03.1999	1	(7)	
Anđelo Kordić	06.02.1999		(1)	
Vedin Kulović	12.12.1995	26	(2)	5
Ivan Prskalo (CRO)	29.03.1995	4	(1)	
Mirsad Ramić	06.12.1992	16	(14)	8
Miha Vidmar (SVN)	16.06.1997	1	(3)	1
Trainer:	**DOB**	**M**		
Feđa Dudić	01.02.1983	11		
Mato Neretljak (CRO) [28.09.2018]	03.06.1979	12		
Stanko Mršić (CRO) [28.03.2019]	12.09.1955	10		

Fudbalski klub Krupa na Vrbasu

Founded: 1983
Stadium: Stadion NK Krupa, Krupa na Vrbasu (3,500)

Goalkeepers:	**DOB**	**M**	**(s)**	**G**
Jovan Kutić	19.05.1994	14		
Matej Marković	22.07.1996	19		
Defenders:	**DOB**	**M**	**(s)**	**G**
Vedran Dalić (CRO)	19.09.1995	2		
Ranko Dekić	21.11.1993	6	(1)	
Vladimir Ilić	20.07.1998	1	(1)	
Krešimir Jelić	28.04.1994	3		
Miloš Karišik (SRB)	07.10.1988	19	(1)	
Igor Makitan	12.10.1994	28	(1)	2
Stojan Maksimović (SRB)	06.01.1996	17	(1)	
Nemanja Marić	20.02.1995	5	(6)	
Saša Nikodijević (SRB)	16.07.1987	28	(1)	2
Bojan Puzigača	10.05.1985	21	(4)	1
Midfielders:	**DOB**	**M**	**(s)**	**G**
Siniša Babić (SRB)	13.02.1991	4	(6)	2
Marko Brtan (CRO)	07.04.1991	7	(2)	5
Ivan Crnov (CRO)	01.02.1990	10	(5)	2
Nikola Dujaković	27.06.1996	22	(1)	
Kenan Handžić	23.01.1991	7	(5)	
Lazar Marjanović (SRB)	08.09.1989	11	(5)	2
Josip Miketek	22.08.1997	7	(2)	
Andrej Modić	07.03.1996	2	(3)	
Lazar Nikolić	30.04.1999	7	(9)	2
Stefan Nikolić (SRB)	14.03.1994	13	(1)	
Kerim Palić	24.01.1997	15	(3)	
Ajdin Redžić	25.01.1997	12	(2)	
Stefan Savić	09.01.1995	6	(3)	
Đuro Zec (SRB)	06.03.1990	8	(2)	
Forwards:	**DOB**	**M**	**(s)**	**G**
Almir Aganspahić	12.09.1996	8	(15)	4
Bojan Golubović (SRB)	22.08.1983	1	(7)	1
Elvir Koljič	08.07.1995	7		8
Jovo Lukić	28.11.1998	8	(6)	
Nikola Mandić (CRO)	19.03.1995	12		3
Slobodan Milanović	27.08.1992	31		4
Mihael Modić	14.01.1998	2	(4)	1
Trainer:	**DOB**	**M**		
Branislav Krunić	28.01.1979	13		
Petar Kurčubić (SRB) [18.10.2018]	03.01.1963	9		
Slobodan Starčević [12.03.2019]	14.08.1971	11		

Fudbalski klub Mladost Doboj Kakanj

Founded: 25.05.1959
Stadium: MGM Farm Arena [Stadion Mladost Kakanj], Doboj (3,000)

Goalkeepers:	**DOB**	**M**	**(s)**	**G**
Semir Bukvić	21.05.1991	5		
Emil Velić (SVN)	06.02.1995	28		
Defenders:	**DOB**	**M**	**(s)**	**G**
Xhelil Asani (ALB)	12.09.1995	26	(1)	
Arnel Delić	13.02.1992	6	(12)	
Lamin Diallo (SVN)	07.12.1991	6	(4)	
Kenan Hreljic	01.12.1997	12	(10)	
Aladin Isaković	28.07.1985	30		2
Bojan Marković	12.11.1985	19	(3)	
Darko Mišić (CRO)	27.06.1991	11		1
Burak Yamaç (TUR)	29.03.1998		(1)	
Midfielders:	**DOB**	**M**	**(s)**	**G**
Emir Alihodžić	02.09.1993	3	(2)	
Nemanja Anđušić	17.10.1996	26		8
Filip Arežina	08.11.1992	9	(2)	3
Edin Biber	06.01.1999	2	(5)	
Petar Bojo	08.01.1998	26	(5)	3
Matthias Fanimo (ENG)	28.01.1994	8	(4)	1
Amer Hiroš	10.06.1996	11	(2)	
Kenan Horić	13.09.1990	10		
Anes Hrustanović	13.03.2002		(1)	
Nemanja Nikolić	21.02.2001	16	(3)	
Damir Sadiković	07.04.1995	12	(3)	
Anes Vehab	28.09.1996	2	(6)	
Nana Welbeck (GHA)	24.11.1994	20		1
Forwards:	**DOB**	**M**	**(s)**	**G**
Bahrudin Atajić	16.11.1993	22	(3)	5
Nemanja Dragutinović	09.04.1999		(4)	
Gedeon Guzina	26.12.1993	30		7
Abid Mujagič	05.08.1993	16	(2)	3
Ajdin Mujagić	03.01.1998		(6)	
Kenan Muslimović (AUT)	13.02.1997	1	(9)	
Dalibor Pandža	23.03.1991	1	(4)	
Maharafa Tandina (MLI)	18.08.1997	5	(6)	
Trainer:	**DOB**	**M**		
Nermin Šabić	21.12.1973	5		
Adnan Zildžović [17.08.2018]	28.10.1969	20		
Elvedin Beganović [08.04.2019]	07.11.1971	8		

Fudbalski klub Radnik Bijeljina

Founded: 14.06.1945
Stadium: Stadion Gradski, Bijeljina (6,000)

Goalkeepers:	**DOB**	**M**	**(s)**	**G**
Mladen Lučić	06.07.1985	32		
Igor Marković	16.03.1998	1		
Defenders:	**DOB**	**M**	**(s)**	**G**
Radoslav Aleksić (SRB)	06.03.1986	13	(2)	
Srđan Bečelić (SRB)	08.06.1992	9	(1)	
Domagoj Franić (CRO)	17.08.1993	15		
Tarik Isić	08.10.1994	9	(2)	
Alem Merajić	04.02.1994	7	(2)	
Slaviša Radović (SRB)	08.10.1993	26	(1)	
Miloš Simonović (SRB)	28.05.1990	14		
Ivan Šubert (SRB)	14.10.1993	13		
Midfielders:	**DOB**	**M**	**(s)**	**G**
Stefan Barić	17.02.1991	1	(3)	
Ognjen Đelmić	18.08.1988	13	(10)	1
Velibor Đurić	05.05.1982	29	(3)	4
Ismar Hairlahović	04.03.1996	11		
Dejan Maksimović	11.10.1995	13		2
Dušan Martinović (SRB)	22.12.1987	14		3
Nedim Mekić	15.04.1995	18	(10)	1
Demir Peco	31.07.1996	21	(1)	1
Nikola Popara	08.03.1992	17	(2)	
Nenad Srećković (SRB)	11.04.1988		(3)	
Pavle Sušić (SRB)	15.04.1988	11	(7)	
Josip Šantić	29.12.1993	3	(9)	
Aleksandar Vasić	04.01.1985	21	(6)	
Forwards:	**DOB**	**M**	**(s)**	**G**
Vladimir Bradonjić	11.12.1999	6	(10)	
Danijal Brković	03.06.1991		(9)	
Kenan Delić	02.05.1999		(3)	3
Aleksandar Glišić	03.09.1992	11	(6)	10
Irfan Hadžić	15.06.1993	31	(1)	
Jovan Motika	11.09.1998	4	(6)	
Trainer:	**DOB**	**M**		
Mladen Žižović	27.12.1980	33		

Fudbalski klub Sarajevo

Founded: 24.10.1946
Stadium: Stadion "Asim Ferhatović Hase", Sarajevo (35,630)

Goalkeepers:	DOB	M	(s)	G
Belmin Dizdarević	09.08.2001	1		
Vladan Kovačević	11.04.1998	30		
Bojan Pavlović (SRB)	08.11.1986	2		
Defenders:	**DOB**	**M**	**(s)**	**G**
Almir Bekić	01.06.1989	7	(3)	
Amer Dupovac	29.05.1991	18	(3)	
Dušan Hodžić	31.10.1993	2	(1)	
Numan Kurdić	01.07.1999	1	(4)	
Darko Lazić (SRB)	19.07.1994	13		1
Nihad Mujakić	15.04.1998	27		
Selmir Pidro	03.03.1998	17		1
Halid Šabanović	22.08.1999	10	(4)	1
Aleksandar Šofranac (MNE)	21.10.1990	4	(3)	
Midfielders:	**DOB**	**M**	**(s)**	**G**
Joachim Adukor (GHA)	02.05.1993	15		1
Ljuban Crepulja (CRO)	02.09.1993	16	(5)	
Andrej Đokanović	01.03.2001	1		
Emir Halilović	04.11.1989	14	(10)	2
Anel Hebibović	07.07.1990	26	(1)	5
Rifet Kapič	03.07.1995	6	(6)	
Alen Mustafić	05.07.1999	5	(4)	
Amar Rahmanović	13.05.1994	25	(3)	9
Đani Salčin	19.03.2000		(1)	
Aladin Šišić	28.09.1991	8	(6)	1
Miloš Stanojević (SRB)	20.11.1993	24	(1)	2
Forwards:	**DOB**	**M**	**(s)**	**G**
Mersudin Ahmetović	19.03.1985	26	(3)	14
Kenan Dervišagić	29.07.2000		(1)	1
Haris Handžić	20.06.1990	6	(18)	5
Nathan (BRA)	28.05.1999	1	(2)	
Ševkija Resić	04.12.1999	2	(6)	1
Benjamin Tatar	18.05.1994	27	(3)	12
Krste Velkoski (MKD)	20.02.1988	29	(2)	11
Trainer:	**DOB**	**M**		
Husref Musemić	04.07.1961	33		

Fudbalski Klub Sloboda Tuzla

Founded: 1919
Stadium: Stadion Tušanj, Tuzla (7,200)

Goalkeepers:	DOB	M	(s)	G
Goran Čokorilo (SRB)	29.12.1987	2	(1)	
Azir Muminović	18.04.1997	7		
Goran Vukliš	24.09.1987	24		
Defenders:	**DOB**	**M**	**(s)**	**G**
Muamer Adžem	01.11.1992	27	(1)	
Sabit Alispahić	03.09.1994	1	(1)	
Amar Beganović	25.11.1999	28	(1)	1
Muharem Čivić	04.01.1993	18	(7)	2
Aleksandar Ignjatović (SRB)	11.04.1988	29		
Perica Ivetić	28.11.1986	31		
Toni Livančić (CRO)	11.12.1994	4	(18)	1
Adnan Salihović	18.10.1992	7	(6)	
Borislav Terzić	01.11.1991	3	(1)	
Nikola Vasiljević	19.12.1983	4	(3)	
Midfielders:	**DOB**	**M**	**(s)**	**G**
Mehmed Alispahić	24.11.1987	21	(1)	1
Adis Hadžanović	02.01.1993	26	(3)	
Armin Hodžić	29.02.2000	1	(4)	
Dino Hodžić	06.07.1999		(3)	
Said Husejinović	17.05.1988	28	(1)	3
Semir Musić	20.07.1995		(5)	
Muris Pirić	27.12.1992		(9)	
Omar Pršeš	07.05.1995	19	(7)	
Antonio Vidović	25.07.1989	26	(4)	7
Forwards:	**DOB**	**M**	**(s)**	**G**
Ivan Baraban (CRO)	22.01.1988	30		5
Edis Smajič	10.09.1999	21	(2)	1
Andrej Todorović	18.09.1998		(1)	
Seid Zukić	09.04.1994	6	(20)	1
Trainer:	**DOB**	**M**		
Milenko Bošnjaković	04.03.1968	2		
Zlatan Nalić [31.07.2018]	23.01.1969	31		

Nogometni klub Široki Brijeg

Founded: 1948
Stadium: Stadion Pecara, Široki Brijeg (5,628)

Goalkeepers:	DOB	M	(s)	G
Krešimir Bandić	16.09.1995	3		
Luka Bilobrk	08.12.1985	27		
Martin Zlomislić	16.08.1998	3	(1)	
Defenders:	**DOB**	**M**	**(s)**	**G**
Josip Barišić	12.08.1983	21	(3)	1
Dino Ćorić	30.06.1990	17	(4)	1
Josip Kvesič	21.09.1990	7	(6)	1
Stipo Marković	03.12.1993	30	(2)	1
Domagoj Marušić	19.03.2000		(2)	
Marko Perković (CRO)	30.08.1991	12		
Midfielders:	**DOB**	**M**	**(s)**	**G**
Mario Babić (CRO)	03.07.1992	14	(6)	1
Dražen Bagarić (AUT)	12.11.1992	23	(4)	7
Luka Begonja (CRO)	23.05.1992	18	(3)	2
Josip Čorluka (CRO)	03.03.1995	24	(1)	
Eliomar Correia Silva (BRA)	16.03.1988	19	(1)	2
Ivan Enin (RUS)	06.02.1994	13		1
Petar Franjić (CRO)	21.08.1991	8	(3)	2
Ante Hrkać	11.03.1992	6		
Dominik Kovačić (CRO)	05.01.1994	28		
Danijel Kožul	01.08.1988	7	(5)	
Mateo Marić	18.03.1998	17	(9)	4
Bernardo Matić (CRO)	27.07.1994	23		2
Zvonko Pamić (CRO)	04.02.1991	3	(1)	
Marin Popović	28.08.1994	4	(13)	
Mato Stanić	11.01.1998	1	(8)	1
Bože Vukoja	03.04.1998	3	(5)	
Forwards:	**DOB**	**M**	**(s)**	**G**
Dejan Čabraja (CRO)	22.08.1993	11	(1)	2
Stipe Jurić	19.11.1998	11	(12)	7
Borna Petrović (CRO)	16.10.1997	5	(6)	
Tomislav Turčin (CRO)	31.05.1997	3	(2)	
Zvonimir Vukoja (CRO)	29.07.1997	2	(1)	1
Trainer:	**DOB**	**M**		
Boris Pavić (CRO)	04.12.1973	7		
Denis Ćorić (CRO) [27.08.2018]	10.12.1977	-		
Goce Sedloski (MKD) [31.08.2018]	10.04.1974	26		

Fudbalski klub Tuzla City

Founded: 1955 (*as FK Sloga Simin Han*)
Stadium: Stadion Tušanj, Tuzla (7,200)

Goalkeepers:	**DOB**	**M**	**(s)**	**G**
Benjamin Čalaković	31.10.2000	1		
Nevres Fejzić	04.11.1990	27	(1)	
Adis Nurković (KVX)	28.04.1984	5	(1)	
Defenders:	**DOB**	**M**	**(s)**	**G**
Dino Bevab	13.01.1993	10	(1)	
Slavko Brekalo	25.02.1990	9		
Denis Čomor	03.01.1990	19	(5)	
Jovo Kojić	08.04.1988	32		2
Ivan Kostić (SRB)	24.06.1989	18		3
Ermin Musić	28.05.1997	2	(1)	
Dejan Širanović	20.03.1991	8	(7)	1
Nemanja Zlatković (SRB)	21.08.1988	8	(3)	
Midfielders:	**DOB**	**M**	**(s)**	**G**
Samir Burić	08.06.1998	1	(2)	
Nermin Crnkić	31.08.1992	18	(7)	2
Samir Efendić	10.05.1991	28		
Ensar Hajrović (SUI)	17.03.1998	2	(3)	
Mirsad Hasanović (SUI)	03.07.1995	15	(1)	2
Huso Karjašević	10.07.1997	4	(3)	
Aleksandar Milaković	26.11.1992			
Nikola Mitrović (SRB)	14.12.1997	15	(7)	1
Suad Mujić	05.10.2001		(1)	
Ajdin Nukić	26.11.1997	18	(4)	2
Almir Omerović	30.08.1996		(1)	
Ivan Sesar	29.08.1989	6	(1)	
Nemanja Stjepanović (SRB)	07.02.1984	16	(2)	
Miloš Stojčev (MNE)	19.01.1987	20	(3)	1
Adnan Šećerović	01.12.1991	12	(2)	
Eldin Trumić	19.09.1989	3	(3)	
Stefan Vukmirović (SRB)	19.07.1991	9	(1)	1
Forwards:	**DOB**	**M**	**(s)**	**G**
Ajdin Mahmutović	06.04.1986	2	(1)	
Edin Murga	21.12.1994	8	(12)	1
Nedim Omeragic (SUI)	01.02.1999			
Husein Poturalić	29.06.1996		(11)	1
Jovica Stokić	07.04.1987	4	(3)	
Budimir Šarčević (SRB)	05.01.1996	14	(7)	1
Vojo Ubiparip (SRB)	10.05.1988	23		12
Almedin Dino Ziljkić (SRB)	25.02.1996	6	(3)	2
Trainer:	**DOB**	**M**		
Slobodan Starčević	14.08.1971	19		
Mirza Varesanović [07.02.2019]	31.05.1972	14		

Hrvatski športski klub Zrinjski Mostar

Founded: 1905
Stadium: Stadion pod Bijelim Brijegom, Mostar (20,000)

Goalkeepers:	**DOB**	**M**	**(s)**	**G**
Ivan Brkić (CRO)	29.06.1995	24		
Vasilije Kolak	08.03.1995	1		
Antonio Soldo	12.01.1988	8	(1)	
Bruno Šutalo (CRO)	23.05.1998		(1)	
Defenders:	**DOB**	**M**	**(s)**	**G**
Tomislav Barbarić (CRO)	29.03.1989	2		
Marin Galić	21.09.1995	20	(5)	1
Renato Gojković	10.09.1995	6		1
Slobodan Jakovljević (SRB)	26.05.1989	27		
Advan Kadušić	14.10.1996	21	(3)	
Neven Laštro (CRO)	01.10.1988	2	(3)	
Dario Rugašević (CRO)	29.01.1991	7		
Pero Stojkić	09.12.1986	16	(1)	
Midfielders:	**DOB**	**M**	**(s)**	**G**
Stefan Barić	17.02.1991	2		
Hrvoje Barišić (CRO)	03.02.1991	28		1
Frane Čirjak (CRO)	23.06.1995	21	(5)	1
Ivan Ćurjurić (CRO)	30.11.1988	11	(3)	1
Miloš Filipović (SRB)	09.05.1990	22	(1)	7
Ismar Hairlahović	04.03.1996	2	(6)	
Eman Marković (NOR)	08.05.1999	5	(8)	1
Josip Miketek	22.08.1997	3	(4)	
Marko Perišić	25.01.1991	12	(5)	
Semir Pezer	18.08.1992	14	(2)	1
Edin Rustemović	06.01.1993	19	(5)	3
Igor Savić	08.10.2000		(2)	
Srđan Stanić	06.07.1989	1		
Damir Šovšić (CRO)	05.02.1990	3	(2)	
Ognjen Todorović	24.03.1989	15	(2)	2
Forwards:	**DOB**	**M**	**(s)**	**G**
Milos Aćimovič	06.07.1997	1		1
Amer Bekić	05.08.1992	8	(6)	
Samir Bekrić	20.10.1984	10	(12)	2
Marko Bencun (CRO)	09.01.1992	1	(12)	1
Nemanja Bilbija	02.11.1990	16		14
Šime Gržan (CRO)	06.04.1994	1		
Nermin Hajdarevič	10.02.1999	3		
Toni Jović (CRO)	02.09.1992	11	(3)	1
Staniša Mandić (MNE)	27.01.1995	9	(1)	3
Abid Mujagič	05.08.1993	4	(1)	2
Kristijan Stanić	20.04.2001	4	(4)	
Dalibor Veselinović (SRB)	21.09.1987	4	(1)	
Trainer:	**DOB**	**M**		
Blaž Slišković	30.05.1959	33		

Fudbalski klub Zvijezda 09 Bijeljina

Founded: 2009
Stadium: Stadion u Ugljeviku, Ugljevik (5,000)

Goalkeepers:	DOB	M	(s)	G
Darko Dejanović (SRB)	17.03.1995	4		
Filip Erić (SRB)	10.10.1994	29		
Defenders:	**DOB**	**M**	**(s)**	**G**
Marko Andić (SRB)	14.12.1983	9	(1)	1
Dušan Babić (SRB)	07.01.1994	26		
Marko Bašanović (SRB)	26.09.1994	8		
Miladin Filipović	02.09.1995	19	(1)	
Dževad Hamzić	25.08.1998		(1)	
Luka Janković	20.08.2002		(1)	
Haris Mehmedagić (CRO)	29.03.1988	3		
Damir Memović (SRB)	19.01.1989	8		
Darko Mišić (CRO)	27.06.1991	12	(1)	
Miloš Nikolić (SRB)	22.02.1989	10		
Dejan Popara	10.03.2003		(1)	
Nemanja Vejnović	03.10.1991	2		
Aleksandar Vojinović	03.10.1996	27		
Miloš Zlatković (SRB)	01.01.1997	7	(1)	
Midfielders:	**DOB**	**M**	**(s)**	**G**
Igor Blagojević (SRB)	18.01.2000	4	(5)	
Marko Brkić	11.04.2000	20	(1)	
Saša Filipović (SRB)	30.04.1993	4	(1)	
Miljan Govedarica	26.05.1994	15	(6)	6
Ivan Jovanović (SRB)	18.10.1996		(2)	
Saša Jovović (SRB)	06.09.1986	8	(1)	3
Damjan Krajisnik	24.04.1997	11	(1)	1
Muhamed Omanović	10.10.1997		(1)	
Amer Osmanagić	07.05.1989	17	(5)	1
Nemanja Parmaković (SRB)	24.06.1999		(2)	
Fedor Predragović	08.04.1995	24	(2)	3
Nikola Stanisić	22.02.2001		(1)	
Slaven Stjepanović (MNE)	02.11.1987	7	(4)	1
Ibrahim Škahić	25.10.1993	8		
Kristijan Tojčić	06.12.1999	17	(4)	1
Stefan Tripković (SRB)	19.09.1994	1	(4)	
Predrag Zekanović	22.07.1997	12	(11)	2
Forwards:	**DOB**	**M**	**(s)**	**G**
Luka Asentić	15.03.1999	4	(2)	1
Danijel Ćulum	19.08.1989	5	(13)	1
Ermin Huseinbašić	11.07.1993	28	(1)	6
Anel Husić	12.12.1994	12	(2)	4
Selmir Mahmutović	10.11.1992	2	(17)	2
Trainer:	**DOB**	**M**		
Milan Đuričić (SRB)	31.10.1961	8		
Darko Nestorović [05.09.2018]	04.04.1965	15		
Milenko Bošnjaković [18.03.2019]	04.03.1968	10		

Fudbalski klub Željezničar Sarajevo

Founded: 19.09.1921
Stadium: Stadion Grbavica, Sarajevo (14,000)

Goalkeepers:	DOB	M	(s)	G
Irfan Fejzić	01.07.1986	10		
Vedran Kjosevski	22.05.1995	23		
Defenders:	**DOB**	**M**	**(s)**	**G**
Branko Bajić	04.06.1998	1		
Miloš Bakrač	25.02.1992	9	(1)	
Jadranko Bogičević	11.03.1983	19	(1)	
Mustafa Mujezinović	06.05.1993	9	(4)	
Kemal Osmanković	04.03.1997	7	(1)	
Antonio Pavić (CRO)	18.11.1994	26		
Matej Rodin (CRO)	13.02.1996	22	(2)	3
Siniša Stevanović (SRB)	12.01.1989	23		
Enes Šipović	11.09.1990	12		
Enio Zilić	12.07.2000	3		
Midfielders:	**DOB**	**M**	**(s)**	**G**
Jovan Blagojević (SRB)	15.03.1988	14		
Ivan Ćurjurić (CRO)	30.11.1988	18		1
Haris Hajdarević	07.10.1998	16	(5)	2
Filip Jazvić (CRO)	22.10.1990	4	(7)	2
Dzenan Osmanović	21.01.2000	2	(5)	
Sinan Ramović	13.10.1992	9	(3)	1
Damir Sadiković	07.04.1995	5	(7)	1
Srđan Stanić	06.07.1989	9	(1)	
Anel Šabanadžović	24.05.1999	25		
Eldar Šehić	28.04.2000	1	(3)	
Mladen Veselinović	04.01.1993	18	(7)	2
Stojan Vranješ	11.10.1986	3	(9)	1
Dženan Zajmović	11.11.1994	19	(4)	2
Forwards:	**DOB**	**M**	**(s)**	**G**
Filip Arežina	08.11.1992	1	(5)	1
Semir Dacić	10.04.1999		(10)	1
Mihael Klepač (CRO)	19.09.1997	1	(3)	
Sulejman Krpić	01.01.1991	32		16
Asim Zec	23.01.1994	19	(10)	6
Ermin Zec	18.02.1988	3	(3)	4
Faris Zubanović	12.06.2000		(1)	
Trainer:	**DOB**	**M**		
Slobodan Krčmarević (SRB)	12.06.1965	2		
Milomir Odović [30.07.2018]	26.03.1955	17		
Amar Osim [31.12.2018]	18.07.1967	14		

SECOND LEVEL
First League - Prva nogometna liga 2018/2019

First League of the Federation of Bosnia and Herzegovina

1.	FK Velež Mostar (*Promoted*)	30	24	4	2	78	-	18	76
2.	FK Olimpik Sarajevo	30	21	6	3	58	-	18	69
3.	NK TOŠK Tešanj	30	13	6	11	46	-	43	45
4.	FK Goražde	30	13	5	12	48	-	36	44
5.	NK Zvijezda Gradačac	30	13	5	12	44	-	43	44
6.	HNK Orašje	30	12	8	10	37	-	36	44
7.	FK Rudar Kakanj	30	13	4	13	51	-	49	43
8.	NK Jedinstvo Bihać	30	13	4	13	31	-	41	43
9.	NK Metalleghe-BSI Jajce	30	12	6	12	39	-	38	42
10.	NK Bratstvo Gračanica	30	13	3	14	31	-	37	42
11.	HNK Čapljina	30	13	3	14	39	-	51	42
12.	NK Slaven Živinice	30	13	2	15	41	-	41	41
13.	FK Igman Konjic	30	11	7	12	29	-	27	40
14.	NK Vitez (*Relegated*)	30	9	7	14	28	-	41	34
15.	NK Novi Travnik (*Relegated*)	30	4	7	19	20	-	55	19
16.	NK Bosna Visoko (*Relegated*)	30	3	3	24	16	-	68	12

First League of of the Republika Srpska

Regular Season

1.	FK Borac Banja Luka	22	17	4	1	36	-	6	55
2.	FK Sloga Gornje Crnjelovo	22	14	4	4	36	-	16	46
3.	FK Rudar Prijedor	22	11	6	5	23	-	16	39
4.	FK Željezničar Banja Luka	22	10	3	9	38	-	28	33
5.	FK Kozara Gradiška	22	8	5	9	23	-	25	29
6.	FK Podrinje Janja Bijeljina	22	8	5	9	25	-	30	29
7.	FK Tekstilac Derventa	22	6	7	9	15	-	23	25
8.	FK Alfa Modriča	22	5	9	8	19	-	27	24
9.	FK Slavija Sarajevo	22	6	6	10	22	-	34	24
10.	FK Drina Zvornik	22	5	7	10	21	-	28	22
11.	FK Sutjeska Foča	22	5	5	12	23	-	29	20
12.	FK Sloboda Mrkonjić Grad	22	4	5	13	15	-	34	17

Team ranked 1-6 were qualified for the Promotion Play-offs, while teams ranked 7-12 were qualified for the Relegation Play-offs.

Promotion Play-off

1.	FK Borac Banja Luka (*Promoted*)	32	25	5	2	60	-	14	80
2.	FK Sloga Gornje Crnjelovo	32	18	6	8	51	-	27	60
3.	FK Željezničar Banja Luka	32	16	3	13	55	-	42	51
4.	FK Rudar Prijedor	32	13	8	11	29	-	27	47
5.	FK Kozara Gradiška	32	12	9	11	36	-	40	45
6.	FK Podrinje Janja Bijeljina	32	9	6	17	30	-	51	33

Relegation Play-off

7.	FK Slavija Sarajevo	32	11	9	12	39	-	44	42
8.	FK Alfa Modriča	32	10	12	10	27	-	32	42
9.	FK Tekstilac Derventa	32	9	12	11	22	-	27	39
10.	FK Drina Zvornik (*Relegated*)	32	9	10	13	34	-	36	37
11.	FK Sutjeska Foča (*Relegated*)	32	9	7	16	37	-	41	34
12.	FK Sloboda Mrkonjić Grad (*Relegated*)	32	4	7	21	19	-	58	19

NATIONAL TEAM

INTERNATIONAL MATCHES
(16.07.2018 – 15.07.2019)

08.09.2018	Belfast	Northern Ireland - Bosnia and Herzegovina	1-2(0-1)	(UNL)
11.09.2018	Zenica	Bosnia and Herzegovina - Austria	1-0(0-0)	(UNL)
11.10.2018	Rize	Turkey - Bosnia and Herzegovina	0-0	(F)
15.10.2018	Sarajevo	Bosnia and Herzegovina - Northern Ireland	2-0(1-0)	(UNL)
15.11.2018	Wien	Austria - Bosnia and Herzegovina	0-0	(UNL)
18.11.2018	Las Palmas de Gran Canaria	Spain - Bosnia and Herzegovina	1-0(0-0)	(F)
23.03.2019	Sarajevo	Bosnia and Herzegovina - Armenia	2-1(1-0)	(ECQ)
26.03.2019	Zenica	Bosnia and Herzegovina - Greece	2-2(2-0)	(ECQ)
08.06.2019	Tampere	Finland - Bosnia and Herzegovina	2-0(0-0)	(ECQ)
11.06.2019	Torino	Italy - Bosnia and Herzegovina	2-1(0-1)	(ECQ)

08.09.2018 NORTHERN IRELAND - BOSNIA AND HERZEGOVINA 1-2(0-1) UEFA Nations League B, Group 3
Windsor Park, Belfast; Referee: Pavel Královec (Czech Republic); Attendance: 16,942
BIH: Ibrahim Šehić, Toni Šunjić, Ervin Zukanović, Eldar Čivić (76.Goran Zakarić), Miralem Pjanić (83.Riad Bajić), Edin Višća, Gojko Cimirot, Muhamed Bešić, Haris Duljević, Elvis Sarić (67.Rade Krunić), Edin Džeko (Cap). Trainer: Robert Prosinečki (Croatia).
Goals: Haris Duljević (36), Elvis Sarić (64).

11.09.2018 BOSNIA AND HERZEGOVINA - AUSTRIA 1-0(0-0) UEFA Nations League B, Group 3
Stadion Bilino Polje, Zenica; Referee: Ruddy Buquet (France); Attendance: 9,100
BIH: Ibrahim Šehić, Toni Šunjić, Ervin Zukanović, Eldar Čivić, Darko Todorović, Miralem Pjanić (89.Rade Krunić), Edin Višća (87.Goran Zakarić), Muhamed Bešić, Haris Duljević (90+3.Riad Bajić), Elvis Sarić, Edin Džeko (Cap). Trainer: Robert Prosinečki (Croatia).
Goal: Edin Džeko (78).

11.10.2018 TURKEY - BOSNIA AND HERZEGOVINA 0-0 Friendly International
"Yeni Rize Şehir" Stadyumu, Rize; Referee: Sergei Karasev (Russia); Attendance: 15,196
BIH: Ibrahim Šehić (46.Asmir Begović), Ervin Zukanović, Ognjen Vranješ, Bojan Nastić, Darko Todorović, Miralem Pjanić (46.Sanjin Prcić), Edin Višća (46.Deni Milošević), Gojko Cimirot, Goran Zakarić (69.Kenan Kodro-Maksumić), Rade Krunić (81.Elvis Sarić), Edin Džeko (Cap) (46.Riad Bajić). Trainer: Robert Prosinečki (Croatia).

15.10.2018 BOSNIA AND HERZEGOVINA - NORTHERN IRELAND 2-0(1-0) UEFA Nations League B, Group 3
Stadion Grbavica, Sarajevo; Referee: Mattias Gestranius (Finland); Attendance: 11,050
BIH: Ibrahim Šehić, Toni Šunjić, Ervin Zukanović, Ognjen Vranješ, Eldar Čivić, Miralem Pjanić, Edin Višća (88.Deni Milošević), Muhamed Bešić (90.Gojko Cimirot), Haris Duljević (75.Goran Zakarić), Elvis Sarić, Edin Džeko (Cap). Trainer: Robert Prosinečki (Croatia).
Goals: Edin Džeko (27, 73).

15.11.2018 AUSTRIA - BOSNIA AND HERZEGOVINA 0-0 UEFA Nations League B, Group 3
"Ernst Happel" Stadion, Wien; Referee: Andrew Dallas (Scotland); Attendance: 37,200
BIH: Ibrahim Šehić, Toni Šunjić, Ervin Zukanović, Ognjen Vranješ, Eldar Čivić, Miralem Pjanić (87.Amer Gojak), Edin Višća, Muhamed Bešić, Haris Duljević (79.Rade Krunić), Elvis Sarić, Edin Džeko (Cap). Trainer: Robert Prosinečki (Croatia).

18.11.2018 SPAIN - BOSNIA AND HERZEGOVINA 1-0(0-0) Friendly International
Estadio de Gran Canaria, Las Palmas; Referee: Carlos Miguel Taborda Xistra (Portugal); Attendance: 17,798
BIH: Ibrahim Šehić, Ervin Zukanović, Ermin Bičakčić, Bojan Nastić, Edin Višća (81.Riad Bajić), Gojko Cimirot, Muhamed Bešić, Elvis Sarić (79.Sanjin Prcić), Rade Krunić (62.Haris Duljević), Amer Gojak, Edin Džeko (Cap) (85.Kenan Kodro-Maksumić). Trainer: Robert Prosinečki (Croatia).

23.03.2019 BOSNIA AND HERZEGOVINA - ARMENIA 2-1(1-0) 16th EC. Qualifiers
Stadion Grbavica, Sarajevo; Referee: Jakob Kehlet (Denmark); Attendance: 12,000
BIH: Ibrahim Šehić, Ervin Zukanović, Ermin Bičakčić, Eldar Čivić, Darko Todorović, Miralem Pjanić, Edin Višća, Goran Zakarić (65.Deni Milošević), Muhamed Bešić, Rade Krunić (82.Amer Gojak), Edin Džeko (Cap) (87.Elvir Koljič). Trainer: Robert Prosinečki (Croatia).
Goals: Rade Krunić (33), Deni Milošević (80).

26.03.2019 BOSNIA AND HERZEGOVINA - GREECE 2-2(2-0) 16th EC. Qualifiers
Stadion Bilino Polje, Zenica; Referee: Danny Desmond Makkelie (Netherlands); Attendance: 10,500
BIH: Ibrahim Šehić, Toni Šunjić, Ervin Zukanović, Ermin Bičakčić, Sead Kolašinac, Miralem Pjanić [*sent off 65*], Edin Višća, Gojko Cimirot (90+3.Rade Krunić), Muhamed Bešić, Haris Duljević (80.Deni Milošević), Edin Džeko (Cap) (90.Amer Gojak). Trainer: Robert Prosinečki (Croatia).
Goals: Edin Višća (10), Miralem Pjanić (15).

09.06.2019 FINLAND - BOSNIA AND HERZEGOVINA 2-0(0-0) 16th EC. Qualifiers
Ratinan stadion, Tampere; Referee: Daniel Stefanski (Poland); Attendance: 16,103
BIH: Ibrahim Šehić, Toni Šunjić, Ervin Zukanović, Ermin Bičakčić, Eldar Čivić, Edin Višća, Gojko Cimirot, Muhamed Bešić (79.Amer Gojak), Haris Duljević (68.Riad Bajić), Elvis Sarić, Edin Džeko (Cap). Trainer: Robert Prosinečki (Croatia).

11.06.2019 ITALY - BOSNIA AND HERZEGOVINA 2-1(0-1) 16th EC. Qualifiers
Juventus Stadium, Torino; Referee: Xavier Estrada Fernández (Spain); Attendance: 29,100
BIH: Ibrahim Šehić, Ervin Zukanović, Ermin Bičakčić, Eldar Čivić (71.Bojan Nastić), Darko Todorović, Miralem Pjanić, Edin Višća, Muhamed Bešić, Elvis Sarić, Amer Gojak (80.Gojko Cimirot), Edin Džeko (Cap). Trainer: Robert Prosinečki (Croatia).
Goal: Edin Džeko (32).

NATIONAL TEAM PLAYERS
(16.07.2018 – 15.07.2019)

Name	DOB	Caps	Goals	2018/2019:	*Club*
Goalkeepers					
Asmir BEGOVIĆ	20.06.1987	**62**	**0**	2018:	*AFC Bournemouth (ENG)*
Ibrahim ŠEHIĆ	02.09.1988	**22**	**0**	2018/2019:	*Büyükşehir Belediye Erzurumspor (TUR)*
Defenders					
Ermin BIČAKČIĆ	24.01.1990	**29**	**3**	2018/2019:	*TSG 1899 Hoffenheim (GER)*
Eldar ĆIVIĆ	28.05.1996	**8**	**0**	2018/2019:	*AC Sparta Praha (CZE)*
Sead KOLAŠINAC	20.06.1993	**25**	**0**	2019:	*Arsenal FC London (GER)*
Bojan NASTIĆ	06.07.1994	**4**	**0**	2018:	*KRC Genk (BEL)*
				31.01.2019->	*KV Oostende (BEL)*
Toni ŠUNJIĆ	15.12.1988	**39**	**1**	2018/2019:	*FK Dinamo Moskva (RUS)*
Darko TODOROVIĆ	05.05.1997	**8**	**0**	2018/2019:	*FC Red Bull Salzburg (AUT)*
Ognjen VRANJEŠ	24.10.1989	**38**	**0**	2018:	*RSC Anderlecht Bruxelles (GRE)*
Ervin ZUKANOVIĆ	11.02.1987	**36**	**0**	2018/2019:	*Genoa CFC (ITA)*
Midfielders					
Muhamed BEŠIĆ	10.09.1992	**40**	**0**	2018/2019:	*Middlesbrough FC (ENG)*
Gojko CIMIROT	19.12.1992	**18**	**0**	2018/2019:	*R Standard Liège (BEL)*
Haris DULJEVIĆ	16.11.1993	**19**	**0**	2018/2019:	*SG Dynamo Dresden (GER)*
Amer GOJAK	13.02.1997	**6**	**0**	2018/2019:	*GNK Dinamo Zagreb (CRO)*
Rade KRUNIĆ	07.10.1993	**10**	**1**	2018/2019:	*Empoli FC (ITA)*
Deni MILOŠEVIĆ	09.03.1995	**6**	**1**	2018/2019:	*Konyaspor Kulübü (TUR)*
Miralem PJANIĆ	02.04.1990	**87**	**13**	2018/2019:	*Juventus FC Torino (ITA)*
Sanjin PRCIĆ	20.11.1993	**8**	**0**	2018:	*Levante UD Valencia (ESP)*
Elvis SARIĆ	21.07.1990	**14**	**1**	2018/2019:	*Suwon Samsung Bluewings FC (KOR)*
Edin VIŠĆA	17.02.1990	**46**	**9**	2018/2019:	*İstanbul Başakşehir FK (TUR)*
Goran ZAKARIĆ	07.11.1992	**11**	**0**	2018/2019:	*FK Partizan Beograd (SRB)*
Forwards					
Riad BAJIĆ	06.05.1994	**10**	**0**	2018/2019:	*İstanbul Başakşehir FK (TUR)*
Edin DŽEKO	17.03.1986	**103**	**56**	2018/2019:	*AS Roma (ITA)*
Kenan KODRO-MAKSUMIĆ	19.08.1993	**9**	**2**	2018:	*FC København (DEN)*
Elvir KOLJIĆ	08.07.1995	**3**	**0**	2019:	*CS Universitatea Craiova (ROU)*

National team coach

Robert PROSINEČKI (Croatia)	12.01.1969	16 M; 6 W; 6 D; 4 L; 14-11

BULGARIA

The Country:
Република България (Republic of Bulgaria)
Capital: Sofia
Surface: 110,994 km^2
Inhabitants: 7,050,034 [2017]
Time: UTC+2

The FA:
Български футболен съюз (Bulgarian Football Union)
18 Vitoshko lale Str. BG - 1616, Sofia
Tel: +359 2 9426 202
Foundation date: 1923
Member of FIFA since: 1924
Member of UEFA since: 1954
Website: www.bfunion.bg

NATIONAL TEAM RECORDS

First international match:	21.05.1924, Wien	Austria – Bulgaria 6-0
Most international caps:	Stilian Petrov	- 105 caps (1998-2011)
Most international goals:	Dimitar Berbatov	- 48 goals / 78 caps (1999-2010)

UEFA EUROPEAN CHAMPIONSHIP	
1960	Qualifiers
1964	Qualifiers
1968	Qualifiers
1972	Qualifiers
1976	Qualifiers
1980	Qualifiers
1984	Qualifiers
1988	Qualifiers
1992	Qualifiers
1996	Final Tournament (Group Stage)
2000	Qualifiers
2004	Final Tournament (Group Stage)
2008	Qualifiers
2012	Qualifiers
2016	Qualifiers

FIFA WORLD CUP	
1930	Did not enter
1934	Qualifiers
1938	Qualifiers
1950	Did not enter
1954	Qualifiers
1958	Qualifiers
1962	Final Tournament (Group Stage)
1966	Final Tournament (Group Stage)
1970	Final Tournament (Group Stage)
1974	Final Tournament (Group Stage)
1978	Qualifiers
1982	Qualifiers
1986	Final Tournament (2nd Round of 16)
1990	Qualifiers
1994	Final Tournament (4th Place)
1998	Final Tournament (Group Stage)
2002	Qualifiers
2006	Qualifiers
2010	Qualifiers
2014	Qualifiers
2018	Qualifiers

UEFA NATIONS LEAGUE
2018/2019 – League C (promoted to League B)

OLYMPIC FOOTBALL TOURNAMENTS 1908-2016							
1908	*Did not enter*	**1948**	*Did not enter*	**1972**	Qualifiers	**1996**	Qualifiers
1912	*Did not enter*	**1952**	1st Round	**1976**	Qualifiers	**2000**	Qualifiers
1920	*Did not enter*	**1956**	Semi-Finals	**1980**	Qualifiers	**2004**	Qualifiers
1924	1st Round	**1960**	Group Stage	**1984**	Qualifiers	**2008**	Qualifiers
1928	*Did not enter*	**1964**	Qualifiers	**1988**	Qualifiers	**2012**	Qualifiers
1936	*Did not enter*	**1968**	Runners-up	**1992**	Qualifiers	**2016**	Qualifiers

FIFA CONFEDERATIONS CUP 1992-2017
None

BULGARIAN CLUB HONOURS IN EUROPEAN CLUB COMPETITIONS:

European Champion Clubs' Cup (1956-1992) / UEFA Champions League (1993-2019)
None
Fairs Cup (1858-1971) / UEFA Cup (1972-2009) / UEFA Europa League (2010-2019)
None
UEFA Super Cup (1972-2019)
None
European Cup Winners' Cup 1961-1999*
None

**defunct competition*

NATIONAL COMPETITIONS
TABLE OF HONOURS

	STATE CHAMPIONSHIPS CHAMPIONS	CUP WINNERS*	BEST GOALSCORERS	
1924	*Not finished*	-	-	
1925	Vladislav Varna	-	-	
1926	Vladislav Varna	-	-	
1927	*No competition*	-	-	
1928	Slavia Sofia	-	-	
1929	Botev Plovdiv	-	-	
1930	SK Slavia Sofia	-	-	
1931	AS 23 Sofia	-	-	
1932	Spartak Varna	-	-	
1933	SK Levski Sofia	-	-	
1934	Vladislav Varna	-	-	
1935	Sportklub Sofia	-	-	
1936	SK Slavia Sofia	-	-	
1937	SK Levski Sofia	-	-	
1937/1938	Ticha Varna	FC 13 Sofia	Krum Milev (Slavia Sofia)	12
1938/1939	SK Slavia Sofia	Shipka Sofia	Georgi Pachedzhiev (AS 23 Sofia)	14
1939/1940	Lokomotiv Sofia	FC 13 Sofia	-	
1941	SK Slavia Sofia	AS 23 Sofia	-	
1942	SK Levski Sofia	Levski Sofia	-	
1943	Slavia Sofia	-	-	
1944	*Not finished*	-	-	

*called between 1938-1942 Tsar's Cup.

	REPUBLIC CHAMPIONSHIPS CHAMPIONS	CUP WINNERS**	BEST GOALSCORERS
1945	Lokomotiv Sofia	-	-
1946	SK Levski Sofia	SK Levski Sofia	-
1947	SK Levski Sofia	SK Levski Sofia	-
1948	CDNV Sofia	Lokomotiv Sofia	-

	„A" GROUP CHAMPIONS	CUP WINNERS**	BEST GOALSCORERS	
1948/1949	SK Levski Sofia	SK Levski Sofia	Dimitar Milanov (CSKA Sofia) Nedko Nedev (Cherno More Varna)	11
1950	SK Levski Sofia	SK Levski Sofia	Lyubomir Hranov (SK Levski Sofia)	13
1951	CDNA Sofia	CDNA Sofia	Dimitar Milanov (CDNA Sofia)	14
1952	CDNA Sofia	GUTP-DSO Udarnik Sofia	Dimitar Isakov (GUTP-DSO Udarnik Sofia) Dobromir Tashkov (Spartak Sofia)	10
1953	SK Levski Sofia	Lokomotiv Sofia	Dimitar Minchev (Spartak Pleven / VVS Sofia)	15
1954	CDNA Sofia	CDNA Sofia	Dobromir Tashkov (GUTP-DSO Udarnik Sofia)	25
1955	CDNA Sofia	CDNA Sofia	Todor Diev (Spartak Plovdiv)	13
1956	CDNA Sofia	SK Levski Sofia	Pavel Vladimirov (Minyor Pernik)	16
1957	CDNA Sofia	SK Levski Sofia	Hristo Iliev (SK Levski Sofia) Dimitar Milanov (CDNA Sofia)	14
1958	CDNA Sofia	Spartak Plovdiv	Dobromir Tashkov (FD Slavia Sofia) Georgi Arnaudov (Spartak Varna)	9
1958/1959	CDNA Sofia	SK Levski Sofia	Aleksandar Vasilev (FD Slavia Sofia)	13
1959/1960	CDNA Sofia	Septemvri Sofia	Dimitar Yordanov (SK Levski Sofia) Lyuben Kostov (Spartak Varna)	12
1960/1961	CDNA Sofia	CDNA Sofia	Ivan Sotirov (Botev Plovdiv)	20
1961/1962	CDNA Sofia	Botev Plovdiv	Nikola Yordanov (Dunav Ruse) Todor Diev (Spartak Plovdiv)	23
1962/1963	Spartak Plovdiv	FD Slavia Sofia	Todor Diev (Spartak Plovdiv)	26
1963/1964	Lokomotiv Sofia	FD Slavia Sofia	Nikola Tsanev (CDNA Sofia)	26
1964/1965	SK Levski Sofia	CSKA Cerveno Zname Sofia	Georgi Asparuhov (SK Levski Sofia)	27
1965/1966	CSKA Cerveno Zname Sofia	FD Slavia Sofia	Traycho Spasov (Marek Dupnitsa)	21
1966/1967	Botev Plovdiv	SK Levski Sofia	Petar Zhekov (Beroe Stara Zagora)	21
1967/1968	SK Levski Sofia	Spartak Sofia	Petar Zhekov (Beroe Stara Zagora)	31
1968/1969	CSKA Septemvrijsko Zname Sofia	CSKA Septemvrijsko Zname Sofia	Petar Zhekov (CSKA Septemvrijsko Zname Sofia)	36
1969/1970	DFS Levski-Spartak Sofia	DFS Levski-Spartak Sofia	Petar Zhekov (CSKA Septemvrijsko Zname Sofia)	31
1970/1971	CSKA Septemvrijsko Zname Sofia	DFS Levski-Spartak Sofia	Dimitar Yakimov (CSKA Septemvrijsko Zname Sofia)	26
1971/1972	CSKA Septemvrijsko Zname Sofia	CSKA Septemvrijsko Zname Sofia	Petar Zhekov (CSKA Septemvrijsko Zname Sofia)	27
1972/1973	CSKA Septemvrijsko Zname Sofia	CSKA Septemvrijsko Zname Sofia	Petar Zhekov (CSKA Septemvrijsko Zname Sofia)	29
1973/1974	DFS Levski-Spartak Sofia	CSKA Septemvrijsko Zname Sofia	Petko Petkov (Beroe Stara Zagora) Kiril Milanov (DFS Levski-Spartak Sofia)	19
1974/1975	CSKA Septemvrijsko Zname Sofia	DFS Slavia Sofia	Ivan Pritargov (Botev Plovdiv)	20
1975/1976	CSKA Septemvrijsko Zname Sofia	DFS Levski-Spartak Sofia	Petko Petkov (Beroe Stara Zagora) Pavel Panov (DFS Levski-Spartak Sofia)	18
1976/1977	DFS Levski-Spartak Sofia	DFS Levski-Spartak Sofia	Pavel Panov (DFS Levski-Spartak Sofia)	20
1977/1978	Lokomotiv Sofia	Marek Dupnitsa	Stoycho Mladenov (Beroe Stara Zagora)	21

1978/1979	DFS Levski-Spartak Sofia	DFS Levski-Spartak Sofia	Rusi Gochev (Chernomorets Burgas / DFS Levski-Spartak Sofia) 19
1979/1980	CSKA Septemvrijsko Zname Sofia	DFS Slavia Sofia	Spas Dzhevizov (CSKA Sofia) 23
1980/1981	CSKA Septemvrijsko Zname Sofia	Botev Plovdiv	Georgi Slavkov (Botev Plovdiv) 31
1981/1982	CSKA Septemvrijsko Zname Sofia	Lokomotiv Sofia	Mihail Valchev (DFS Levski-Spartak Sofia) 24
1982/1983	CSKA Septemvrijsko Zname Sofia	CSKA Septemvrijsko Zname Sofia	Antim Pehlivanov (Botev Plovdiv) 20
1983/1984	DFS Levski-Spartak Sofia	DFS Levski-Spartak Sofia	Eduard Eranosyan (Lokomotiv Plovdiv) Emil Spasov (DFS Levski-Spartak Sofia) 19
1984/1985	DFS Levski-Spartak Sofia	CSKA Septemvrijsko Zname Sofia	Plamen Getov (Spartak Pleven) 26
1985/1986	Beroe Stara Zagora	FK Vitosha Sofia	Atanas Pashev (Botev Plovdiv) 30
1986/1987	FK Sredets Sofia	FK Sredets Sofia	Nasko Sirakov (FK Vitosha Sofia) 36
1987/1988	FK Vitosha Sofia	FK Sredets Sofia	Nasko Sirakov (FK Vitosha Sofia) 28
1988/1989	CFKA Sredets Sofia	FK Sredets Sofia	Hristo Stoichkov (CFKA Sredets Sofia) 23
1989/1990	CFKA Sofia	FC Sliven	Hristo Stoichkov (CFKA Sofia) 38
1990/1991	FC Etar Veliko Tarnovo	PFC Levski Sofia	Ivaylo Yordanov (FC Lokomotiv Gorna Oryahovitsa) 21
1991/1992	PFC CSKA Sofia	PFC Levski Sofia	Nasko Sirakov (PFC Levski Sofia) 26
1992/1993	PFC Levski Sofia	PFC CSKA Sofia	Plamen Getov (PFC Levski Sofia) 26
1993/1994	PFC Levski Sofia	PFC Levski Sofia	Nasko Sirakov (PFC Levski Sofia) 30
1994/1995	PFC Levski Sofia	PFC Lokomotiv Sofia	Petar Mihtarski (PFC CSKA Sofia) 24
1995/1996	PFC Slavia Sofia	PFC Slavia Sofia	Ivo Georgiev (FC Spartak Varna) 21
1996/1997	PFC CSKA Sofia	PFC CSKA Sofia	Todor Pramatarov (PFC Slavia Sofia) 26
1997/1998	PFC Litex Lovech	PFC Levski Sofia	Anton Spasov (PFC Naftex Burgas) Bontcho Guentchev (PFC CSKA Sofia) 17
1998/1999	PFC Litex Lovech	PFC CSKA Sofia	Dimcho Belyakov (PFC Litex Lovech) 21
1999/2000	PFC Levski Sofia	PFC Levski Sofia	Mihail Mihaylov (FC Velbazhd Kyustendil) 20
2000/2001	PFC Levski Sofia	PFC Litex Lovech	Georgi Ivanov (PFC Levski Sofia) 22
2001/2002	PFC Levski Sofia	PFC Levski Sofia	Vladimir Manchev (PFC CSKA Sofia) 21
2002/2003	PFC CSKA Sofia	PFC Levski Sofia	Georgi Chilikov (PFC Levski Sofia) 23
2003/2004	PFC Lokomotiv Plovdiv	PFC Litex Lovech	Martin Kamburov (PFC Lokomotiv Plovdiv) 25
2004/2005	PFC CSKA Sofia	PFC Levski Sofia	Martin Kamburov (PFC Lokomotiv Plovdiv) 27
2005/2006	PFC Levski Sofia	PFC CSKA Sofia	Milivoje Novaković (SVN, Litex Lovech) José Emílio Robalo Furtado (CPV, OFC Vihren Sandanski / PFC CSKA Sofia) 16
2006/2007	PFC Levski Sofia	PFC Levski Sofia	Tsvetan Genkov (PFC Lokomotiv Sofia) 27
2007/2008	PFC CSKA Sofia	PFC Litex Lovech	Georgi Hristov (PFC Botev Plovdiv) 19
2008/2009	PFC Levski Sofia	PFC Litex Lovech	Martin Kamburov (PFC Lokomotiv Sofia) 17
2009/2010	PFC Litex Lovech	PFC Beroe Stara Zagora	Wilfried Niflore (FRA, PFC Litex Lovech) 19
2010/2011	PFC Litex Lovech	PFC CSKA Sofia	Garra Dembélé (MLI, PFC Levski Sofia) 26
2011/2012	PFC Ludogorets Razgrad	PFC Ludogorets Razgrad	Ivan Stoyanov (PFC Ludogorets Razgrad) Aluísio Chaves Ribeiro Moraes Júnior (BRA, PFC CSKA Sofia) 16
2012/2013	PFC Ludogorets Razgrad	PFC Beroe Stara Zagora	Basile Salomon Pereira de Carvalho (GNB, PFC Levski Sofia) 19
2013/2014	PFC Ludogorets Razgrad	PFC Ludogorets Razgrad	Wilmar Jordán Gil (COL, PFC Litex Lovech) Martin Kamburov (PFC Lokomotiv Plovdiv) 20
2014/2015	PFC Ludogorets Razgrad	PFC Cherno More Varna	Antonio Salas Quinta „Añete“ (ESP, PFC Levski Sofia) 14
2015/2016	PFC Ludogorets Razgrad	PFC CSKA Sofia	Martin Kamburov (PFC Lokomotiv Plovdiv) 18
2016/2017	PFC Ludogorets Razgrad	PFC Botev Plovdiv	Claudiu Andrei Keşerü (ROU, PFC Ludogorets Razgrad) 22
2017/2018	PFC Ludogorets Razgrad	PFC Slavia Sofia	Claudiu Andrei Keşerü (ROU, PFC Ludogorets Razgrad) 26
2018/2019	PFC Ludogorets Razgrad	PFC Lokomotiv Plovdiv	Stanislav Kostov (PFC Levski Sofia) 24

**called "Cup of the Soviet Army" (1945 - 1982) and Bulgarian Cup (from 1982 until today).

Please note:

FC CSKA Sofia changed several times its name as following: 1948 CDNV Sofia, 1949 NV Sofia, 1950 NA Sofia, 1951 CDNA Sofia, 1953 Sofijski Garnizon Sofia, 1953 CDNA Sofia, 1964 CSKA Cerveno Zname Sofia, 1968 CSKA Septemvrijsko Zname Sofia, 1985 FK Sredets Sofia, 1987 CFKA Sredets Sofia, November 1989 CFKA Sofia, 1st january 1990 PFC CSKA Sofia.

FC Levski Sofia changed several times its name as following: 1914 CS Levski Sofia, SK Levski Sofia, 1949 Dinamo Sofia, 1957 FD Levski Sofia, 1969 DFS Levski-Spartak Sofia, 1985 FK Vitosha Sofia, 1990 FK Levski-1914 Sofia, 1998 PFC Levski Sofia.

FC Slavia Sofia changed several times its name as following: 1913 Botev Sofia, 1915 SK Slavia Sofia, 1945 NFD Slavia Sofia, 1949 DSO Strojtel Sofia, 1951 USS-DSO Udarnik Sofia, 1952 GUTP-DSO Udarnik Sofia, 1957 FD Slavia Sofia, 1969 ZSK Slavia Sofia, 1971 DFS Slavia Sofia, 1986 FC Slavia Sofia; 1990 PFC Slavia Sofia.

NATIONAL CHAMPIONSHIP

First Professional Football League - Parwa liga 2018/2019

(20.07.2018 – 24.05.2019)

Regular Season - Results

Round 1 [20-23.07.2018]
Vitosha Bistritsa - Dunav Ruse 2-1(0-1)
Cherno More Varna - Botev Vratsa 2-1(1-1)
PFC Ludogorets - Etar Tarnovo 1-0(1-0)
Botev Plovdiv - Levski Sofia 0-1(0-0)
Slavia Sofia - Beroe Stara Zagora 1-1(0-1)
CSKA Sofia - Lokomotiv Plovdiv 2-0(0-0)
PFC Vereya - Septemvri Sofia 0-0

Round 2 [27-30.07.2018]
Etar Tarnovo - PFC Vereya 1-0(0-0)
Dunav Ruse - Botev Vratsa 3-1(2-0)
Septemvri Sofia - Botev Plovdiv 0-2(0-1)
Beroe Stara Zagora - PFC Ludogorets 1-1(0-0)
Lokomotiv Plovdiv - Slavia Sofia 2-4(1-2)
Vitosha Bistritsa - CSKA Sofia 0-2(0-2)
Levski Sofia - Cherno More Varna 2-2(0-1)

Round 3 [03-06.08.2018]
Botev Plovdiv - Etar Tarnovo 2-0(0-0)
PFC Vereya - Beroe Stara Zagora 0-2(0-1)
Cherno More Var. - Septemvri Sofia 1-5(0-2)
PFC Ludogorets - Lokomotiv Plovdiv 0-1(0-0)
Botev Vratsa - Levski Sofia 0-2(0-1)
CSKA Sofia - Dunav Ruse 3-0(2-0)
Slavia Sofia - Vitosha Bistritsa 0-2(0-2)

Round 4 [10-13.08.2018]
Etar Tarnovo - Cherno More Varna 1-1(1-0)
Lokomotiv Plovdiv - PFC Vereya 3-0(2-0)
Beroe Stara Zagora - Botev Plovdiv 2-1(0-0)
Dunav Ruse - Levski Sofia 1-2(0-0)
Vitosha Bistritsa - PFC Ludogorets 0-2(0-0)
CSKA Sofia - Slavia Sofia 2-1(1-0)
Septemvri Sofia - Botev Vratsa 1-2(0-1)

Round 5 [17-20.08.2018]
Slavia Sofia - Dunav Ruse 2-0(0-0)
Cherno More Varna - Beroe Stara Zagora 0-0
Botev Plovdiv - Lokomotiv Plovdiv 0-1(0-0)
Botev Vratsa - Etar Tarnovo 2-0(1-0)
Levski Sofia - Septemvri Sofia 2-0(2-0)
PFC Ludogorets - CSKA Sofia 1-0(1-0)
PFC Vereya - Vitosha Bistritsa 0-1(0-0)

Round 6 [24-27.08.2018]
Dunav Ruse - Septemvri Sofia 2-0(0-0)
Lokomotiv Plo. - Cherno More Varna 0-2(0-2)
Etar Tarnovo - Levski Sofia 1-2(0-2)
Vitosha Bistritsa - Botev Plovdiv 0-2(0-1)
Slavia Sofia - PFC Ludogorets 0-0
CSKA Sofia - PFC Vereya 4-0(1-0)
Beroe Stara Zagora - Botev Vratsa 4-0(2-0)

Round 7 [31.08.-01.09.2018]
PFC Vereya - Slavia Sofia 0-0
Cherno More Varna - Vitosha Bistrit. 1-0(1-0)
Septemvri Sofia - Etar Tarnovo 0-2(0-1)
Botev Plovdiv - CSKA Sofia 0-0
Levski Sofia - Beroe Stara Zagora 1-0(0-0)
Botev Vratsa - Lokomotiv Plovdiv 0-0
PFC Ludogorets - Dunav Ruse 3-1(1-0)

Round 8 [14-16.09.2018]
Vitosha Bistritsa - Botev Vratsa 1-1(1-1)
PFC Ludogorets - PFC Vereya 2-1(0-1)
Dunav Ruse - Etar Tarnovo 2-4(1-3)
Beroe Stara Zagora - Septemvri Sofia 1-0(0-0)
CSKA Sofia - Cherno More Varna 3-1(2-1)
Slavia Sofia - Botev Plovdiv 0-0
Lokomotiv Plovdiv - Levski Sofia 1-0(1-0)

Round 9 [21-23.09.2018]
Etar Tarnovo - Beroe Stara Zagora 1-1(1-0)
Levski Sofia - Vitosha Bistritsa 4-1(1-0)
Septemvri Sofia - Lokomotiv Plovdiv 1-3(1-1)
Botev Vratsa - CSKA Sofia 0-2(0-2)
PFC Vereya - Dunav Ruse 1-1(1-0)
Cherno More Varna - Slavia Sofia 1-2(1-1)
Botev Plovdiv - PFC Ludogorets 2-3(2-0)

Round 10 [28.09.-01.10.2018]
Vitosha Bistritsa - Septemvri Sofia 2-1(0-1)
CSKA Sofia - Levski Sofia 0-1(0-1)
PFC Ludogorets - Cherno More Var. 5-1(1-0)
Dunav Ruse - Beroe Stara Zagora 1-1(0-1)
PFC Vereya - Botev Plovdiv 1-2(0-2)
Lokomotiv Plovdiv - Etar Tarnovo 0-0
Slavia Sofia - Botev Vratsa 0-1(0-0)

Round 11 [05-07.10.2018]
Cherno More Varna - PFC Vereya 4-2(2-0)
Botev Plovdiv - Dunav Ruse 4-1(2-1)
Septemvri Sofia - CSKA Sofia 0-3(0-1)
Beroe Stara Zagora - Lokomotiv Plo. 1-0(0-0)
Etar Tarnovo - Vitosha Bistritsa 1-0(0-0)
Botev Vratsa - PFC Ludogorets 1-4(0-4)
Levski Sofia - Slavia Sofia 2-0(1-0)

Round 12 [19-22.10.2018]
PFC Vereya - Botev Vratsa 2-2(0-2)
Slavia Sofia - Septemvri Sofia 3-1(2-0)
Botev Plovdiv - Cherno More Varna 2-1(1-0)
PFC Ludogorets - Levski Sofia 2-1(2-0)
Dunav Ruse - Lokomotiv Plovdiv 1-0(0-0)
CSKA Sofia - Etar Tarnovo 3-0(1-0)
Vitosha Bistrit. - Beroe Stara Zagora 1-2(1-1)

Round 13 [26-28.10.2018]
Cherno More Varna - Dunav Ruse 3-2(2-1)
Levski Sofia - PFC Vereya 7-0(3-0)
Lokomotiv Plov. - Vitosha Bistritsa 2-1(2-0)
Beroe Stara Zagora - CSKA Sofia 1-1(1-1)
Botev Vratsa - Botev Plovdiv 0-1(0-0)
Etar Tarnovo - Slavia Sofia 3-0(1-0)
Septemvri Sofia - PFC Ludogorets 1-4(1-0)

Round 14 [03-05.11.2018]
Dunav Ruse - Vitosha Bistritsa 3-0(3-0)
Lokomotiv Plovdiv - CSKA Sofia 0-1(0-0)
Septemvri Sofia - PFC Vereya 1-0(1-0)
Botev Vratsa - Cherno More Varna 2-1(0-0)
Levski Sofia - Botev Plovdiv 4-1(1-1)
Etar Tarnovo - PFC Ludogorets 1-4(1-3)
Beroe Stara Zagora - Slavia Sofia 2-0(1-0)

Round 15 [09-11.11.2018]
CSKA Sofia - Vitosha Bistritsa 3-0(0-0)
Botev Plovdiv - Septemvri Sofia 2-0(0-0)
Cherno More Varna - Levski Sofia 1-0(1-0)
PFC Vereya - Etar Tarnovo 0-1(0-0)
Botev Vratsa - Dunav Ruse 1-0(0-0)
Slavia Sofia - Lokomotiv Plovdiv 1-1(0-1)
PFC Ludogorets - Beroe Stara Zagora 1-0(0-0)

Round 16 [23-25.11.2018]
Vitosha Bistritsa - Slavia Sofia 1-0(0-0)
Septemvri Sofia - Cherno More Var. 2-1(0-0)
Dunav Ruse - CSKA Sofia 0-2(0-1)
Lokomotiv Plovdiv - PFC Ludogorets 0-1(0-0)
Etar Tarnovo - Botev Plovdiv 1-0(1-0)
Beroe Stara Zagora - PFC Vereya 6-0(2-0)
Levski Sofia - Botev Vratsa 1-3(1-1)

Round 17 [30.11.-02.12.2018]
Cherno More Varna - Etar Tarnovo 1-0(0-0)
PFC Vereya - Lokomotiv Plovdiv 2-2(2-1)
Botev Plovdiv - Beroe Stara Zagora 4-1(2-1)
Levski Sofia - Dunav Ruse 3-0(3-0)
Botev Vratsa - Septemvri Sofia 4-1(2-1)
PFC Ludogorets - Vitosha Bistritsa 3-0(2-0)
Slavia Sofia - CSKA Sofia 1-0(0-0)

Round 18 [04-06.12.2018]
Beroe Stara Zagora - Cherno More V. 0-1(0-1)
Lokomotiv Plovdiv - Botev Plovdiv 0-2(0-0)
Etar Tarnovo - Botev Vratsa 2-1(2-0)
Septemvri Sofia - Levski Sofia 2-2(0-0)
Vitosha Bistritsa - PFC Vereya 2-0(1-0)
Dunav Ruse - Slavia Sofia 1-1(1-0)
CSKA Sofia - PFC Ludogorets 1-1(0-1)

Round 19 [08-10.12.2018]
Cherno More V. - Lokomotiv Plovdiv 2-0(2-0)
Botev Vratsa - Beroe Stara Zagora 0-1(0-1)
Levski Sofia - Etar Tarnovo 2-1(1-1)
Septemvri Sofia - Dunav Ruse 2-1(0-1)
PFC Vereya - CSKA Sofia 0-1(0-1)
PFC Ludogorets - Slavia Sofia 2-0(1-0)
Botev Plovdiv - Vitosha Bistritsa 3-0(3-0)

Round 20 [14-16.12.2018]
Slavia Sofia - PFC Vereya 4-0(2-0)
Vitosha Bistritsa - Cherno More Var. 1-1(0-1)
Lokomotiv Plovdiv - Botev Vratsa 4-0(0-0)
Beroe Stara Zagora - Levski Sofia 2-1(1-0)
Dunav Ruse - PFC Ludogorets 0-2(0-1)
Etar Tarnovo - Septemvri Sofia 2-0(1-0)
CSKA Sofia - Botev Plovdiv 2-1(2-0)

Round 21 [15-17.02.2019]
PFC Vereya - PFC Ludogorets 0-0
Botev Vratsa - Vitosha Bistritsa 1-0(0-0)
Cherno More Varna - CSKA Sofia 2-0(1-0)
Botev Plovdiv - Slavia Sofia 1-0(1-0)
Etar Tarnovo - Dunav Ruse 3-0(0-0)
Septemvri Sofia - Beroe Stara Zagora 1-0(1-0)
Levski Sofia - Lokomotiv Plovdiv 1-1(0-1)

Round 22 [19-21.02.2019]
Slavia Sofia - Cherno More Varna 3-2(1-2)
PFC Ludogorets - Botev Plovdiv 1-1(0-0)
CSKA Sofia - Botev Vratsa 2-1(0-0)
Dunav Ruse - PFC Vereya 1-0(0-0)
Lokomotiv Plovdiv - Septemvri Sofia 0-2(0-1)
Vitosha Bistritsa - Levski Sofia 0-2(0-2)
Beroe Stara Zagora - Etar Tarnovo 1-0(1-0)

Round 23 [23-25.02.2019]
Botev Vratsa - Slavia Sofia 1-3(1-1)
Cherno More Var. - PFC Ludogorets 1-0(1-0)
Botev Plovdiv - PFC Vereya 4-0(2-0)
Levski Sofia - CSKA Sofia 1-0(1-0)
Etar Tarnovo - Lokomotiv Plovdiv 2-0(1-0)
Beroe Stara Zagora - Dunav Ruse 1-0(1-0)
Septemvri Sofia - Vitosha Bistritsa 0-0

Round 24 [01-03.03.2019]
PFC Vereya - Cherno More Varna 0-2(0-1)
Dunav Ruse - Botev Plovdiv 1-1(1-0)
Lokomotiv Plo. - Beroe Stara Zagora 4-1(2-1)
CSKA Sofia - Septemvri Sofia 5-1(4-0)
Vitosha Bistritsa - Etar Tarnovo 1-1(1-0)
PFC Ludogorets - Botev Vratsa 2-0(2-0)
Slavia Sofia - Levski Sofia 0-3(0-2)

Round 25 [08-11.03.2019]
Botev Vratsa - PFC Vereya 3-0(1-0)
Lokomotiv Plovdiv - Dunav Ruse 4-1(3-1)
Etar Tarnovo - CSKA Sofia 1-3(0-0)
Septemvri Sofia - Slavia Sofia 1-2(0-1)
Cherno More Varna - Botev Plovdiv 0-0
Levski Sofia - PFC Ludogorets 0-2(0-1)
Beroe Stara Zagora - Vitosha Bistrit. 0-1(0-0)

Round 26 [15-17.03.2019]
Botev Plovdiv - Botev Vratsa 1-1(1-1)
PFC Vereya - Levski Sofia 3-4(1-3)
PFC Ludogorets - Septemvri Sofia 6-0(4-0)
CSKA Sofia - Beroe Stara Zagora 2-0(1-0)
Vitosha Bistritsa - Lokomotiv Plov. 0-3(0-0)
Dunav Ruse - Cherno More Varna 1-1(1-1)
Slavia Sofia - Etar Tarnovo 0-1(0-1)

Final Standings

1.	PFC Ludogorets Razgrad	26	19	5	2	53	-	14	62
2.	PFC CSKA Sofia	26	18	3	5	47	-	14	57
3.	PFC Levski Sofia	26	17	3	6	51	-	24	54
4.	PFC Botev Plovdiv	26	13	6	7	39	-	21	45
5.	PFC Cherno More Varna	26	12	6	8	36	-	34	42
6.	PFC Beroe Stara Zagora	26	12	6	8	32	-	23	42
7.	SFC Etar Veliko Tarnovo	26	12	4	10	30	-	27	40
8.	PFC Lokomotiv Plovdiv	26	10	5	11	32	-	28	35
9.	PFC Slavia Sofia	26	9	6	11	28	-	31	33
10.	POFC Botev Vratsa	26	9	4	13	29	-	40	31
11.	FC Vitosha Bistritsa	26	7	4	15	17	-	39	25
12.	PFC Septemvri Sofia	26	6	3	17	23	-	52	21
13.	FC Dunav Ruse 2010	26	5	5	16	25	-	47	20
14.	PFC Vereya Stara Zagora	26	0	6	20	12	-	60	6

Teams ranked 1-6 were qualified for the Championship Round, while teams ranked 7-14 were qualified for the Relegation Round.

Relegation Round

Results

Round 27 [29.03.-01.04.2019]
Etar Tarnovo - PFC Vereya 3-0(2-0)
Lokomotiv Plovdiv - Dunav Ruse 1-1(1-1)
Slavia Sofia - Septemvri Sofia 0-0
Botev Vratsa - Vitosha Bistritsa 3-0(1-0)

Round 28 [05-08.04.2019]
Etar Tarnovo - Botev Vratsa 0-0
Lokomotiv Plovdiv - Slavia Sofia 1-1(1-0)
PFC Vereya - Vitosha Bistritsa 0-2(0-1)
Dunav Ruse - Septemvri Sofia 2-2(2-1)

Round 29 [12-15.04.2019]
Slavia Sofia - Dunav Ruse 3-5(1-3)
Septemvri Sofia - Lokomotiv Plovdiv 1-0(1-0)
Botev Vratsa - PFC Vereya 5-0(2-0)
Vitosha Bistritsa - Etar Tarnovo 3-0(1-0)

Round 30 [19-22.04.2019]
Dunav Ruse - Lokomotiv Plovdiv 2-0(2-0)
Septemvri Sofia - Slavia Sofia 3-2(1-2)
PFC Vereya - Etar Tarnovo 0-3(0-2)
Vitosha Bistritsa - Botev Vratsa 2-5(1-4)

Round 31 [25-29.04.2019]
Vitosha Bistritsa - PFC Vereya 2-0(1-0)
Botev Vratsa - Etar Tarnovo 1-1(0-0)
Septemvri Sofia - Dunav Ruse 1-1(1-1)
Slavia Sofia - Lokomotiv Plovdiv 2-2(1-1)

Round 32 [01-03.05.2019]
PFC Vereya - Botev Vratsa 1-6(0-4)
Etar Tarnovo - Vitosha Bistritsa 2-0(2-0)
Lokomotiv Plovdiv - Septemvri Sofia 1-2(0-1)
Dunav Ruse - Slavia Sofia 0-1(0-0)

Final Standings

Group A									
1.	SFC Etar Veliko Tarnovo	32	15	6	11	39	-	31	51
2.	POFC Botev Vratsa	32	13	6	13	49	-	44	45
3.	FC Vitosha Bistritsa	32	10	4	18	26	-	49	34
4.	PFC Vereya Stara Zagora*	32	0	6	26	13	-	81	6

* PFC Vereya Stara Zagora were disqualified on 07.05.2019 for match fixing and relegated to the Second Division 2019/2020. All played matches were considered by Bulgarian FA as 3-0 wins for the opponents.

Group B									
1.	PFC Slavia Sofia	32	10	9	13	37	-	42	39
2.	PFC Lokomotiv Plovdiv	32	10	8	14	37	-	37	38
3.	PFC Septemvri Sofia	32	9	6	17	32	-	58	33
4.	FC Dunav Ruse 2010	32	7	8	17	36	-	55	29

Teams ranked 1-2 in both groups were qualified for the European play-offs, while teams ranked 3-4 in both groups were qualified for the Relegation Play-offs.

Championship Round

Results

Round 27 [30-31.03.2019]
PFC Ludogorets - Beroe Stara Zagora 0-0
CSKA Sofia - Cherno More Varna 1-0(0-0)
Levski Sofia - Botev Plovdiv 1-1(1-0)

Round 28 [06-07.04.2019]
PFC Ludogorets - CSKA Sofia 0-0
Cherno More Varna - Levski Sofia 0-1(0-1)
Beroe Stara Zagora - Botev Plovdiv 1-1(0-0)

Round 29 [13-14.04.2019]
Botev Plovdiv - Cherno More Varna 0-2(0-0)
CSKA Sofia - Beroe Stara Zagora 2-0(1-0)
Levski Sofia - PFC Ludogorets 0-2(0-1)

Round 30 [20-21.04.2019]
CSKA Sofia - Levski Sofia 0-0
PFC Ludogorets - Botev Plovdiv 3-0(2-0)
Beroe Stara Zagora - Cherno More V. 2-0(2-0)

Round 31 [26-29.04.2019]
Cherno More V. - PFC Ludogorets 2-1(1-1)
Levski Sofia - Beroe Stara Zagora 1-2(0-0)
Botev Plovdiv - CSKA Sofia 2-0(0-0)

Round 32 [03-04.05.2019]
Beroe Stara Zagora - PFC Ludogorets 1-1(0-0)
Cherno More Varna - CSKA Sofia 1-3(0-1)
Botev Plovdiv - Levski Sofia 1-3(0-1)

Round 33 [11-12.05.2019]
Botev Plovdiv - Beroe Stara Zagora 0-1(0-1)
CSKA Sofia - PFC Ludogorets 0-0
Levski Sofia - Cherno More Varna 5-1(3-0)

Round 34 [18.05.2019]
Cherno More Varna - Botev Plovdiv 1-0(1-0)
PFC Ludogorets - Levski Sofia 1-1(0-0)
Beroe Stara Zagora - CSKA Sofia 0-1(0-1)

Round 35 [21.05.2019]
Botev Plovdiv - PFC Ludogorets 0-2(0-2)
Levski Sofia - CSKA Sofia 0-2(0-0)
Cherno More Varna - Beroe Stara Zagora 0-0

Round 36 [24.05.2019]
Beroe Stara Zagora - Levski Sofia 3-1(1-0)
PFC Ludogorets - Cherno More V. 4-1(2-1)
CSKA Sofia - Botev Plovdiv 1-0(0-0)

Final Standings

1.	**PFC Ludogorets Razgrad**	36	23	10	3	67	-	19	79
2.	PFC CSKA Sofia	36	24	6	6	57	-	17	78
3.	PFC Levski Sofia	36	20	6	10	64	-	37	66
4.	PFC Beroe Stara Zagora	36	16	10	10	42	-	30	58
5.	PFC Cherno More Varna	36	15	7	14	44	-	51	52
6.	PFC Botev Plovdiv	36	14	8	14	44	-	36	50

PFC Levski Sofia were qualified for the European Play-off final.

Top goalscorers:

24 Stanislav Kostov
PFC Levski Sofia

20 Claudiu Andrei Keşerü (ROU)
PFC Ludogorets Razgrad

16 Martin Kamburov
PFC Beroe Stara Zagora

European Play-offs

07/10.05.2019, Quarter-Finals:
PFC Lokomotiv Plovdiv - SFC Etar Veliko Tarnovo 0-2, 0-1
POFC Botev Vratsa - PFC Slavia Sofia 0-0, 0-1 aet

20/23.05.2019, Semi-Finals:
PFC Slavia Sofia - SFC Etar Veliko Tarnovo 1-0, 0-2

28.05.2019, Final:
PFC Levski Sofia - SFC Etar Veliko Tarnovo 1-0

Relegation Play-offs

08/13-14.05.2019, First Round:
FC Dunav Ruse 2010 - FC Vitosha Bistritsa 0-0, 1-0
PFC Vereya Stara Zagora - PFC Septemvri Sofia 0-3, 0-3 (both awarded)

19/22.05.2019, Second Round:
FC Dunav Ruse 2010 - PFC Septemvri Sofia 0-1, 3-2
PFC Vereya Stara Zagora - FC Vitosha Bistritsa 0-3, 0-3 (both awarded)

29/30.05.2019, Third Round:
PFC Septemvri Sofia - FC Arda Kardzhali 0-1 aet
FC Vitosha Bistritsa - FC Montana 3-0

PFC Septemvri Sofia are relegated to the Second Division 2019/2020.

NATIONAL CUP
Bulgarian Cup 2018/2019

First Round [25-27.09.2018]

FC Botev Galabovo - FC Vitosha Bistritsa	0-0 aet; 8-9 aet	PFC Montana - PFC CSKA Sofia	0-2(0-0)
FC Dobrudzha Dobrich - FC Lokomotiv 1929 Sofia	0-1(0-0)	OFC Nesebar - PFC Ludogorets Razgrad	1-3(1-1)
FC Strumska Slava Radomir - FC Tsarsko Selo Sofia	2-1(1-0)	FC Arda Kardzhali - PFC Cherno More Varna	0-1(0-0)
FK Hebar Pazardzhik - PFC Beroe Stara Zagora	1-6(0-3)	FC Lokomotiv Gorna Oryahovitsa - FC Dunav Ruse	1-1 aet; 6-7 pen
FC Kariana Erden - PFC Septemvri Sofia	0-1(0-0)	FC Chernomorets Balchik - POFC Botev Vratsa	1-0(0-0)
OFC Pomorie - PFC Lokomotiv Plovdiv	0-1(0-0)	FC CSKA 1948 Sofia - PFC Botev Plovdiv	1-4(1-2)
FC Atletik Kuklen - PFC Levski Sofia	0-6(0-2)	OFC Pirin Blagoevgrad - PFC Slavia Sofia	0-2(0-1)
PFC Litex Lovech - SFC Etar Veliko Tarnovo	0-2(0-2)	FC Spartak Varna - PFC Vereya Stara Zagora	1-1 aet; 4-5pen

1/8-Finals [30.10.-01.11.2018]

FC Strumska Slava Rad. - FC Chernomorets Balchik	3-1(2-0)	PFC Cherno More Varna - PFC Levski Sofia	2-2 aet; 5-4 pen
FC Dunav Ruse 2010 - PFC Lokomotiv Plovdiv	1-2(0-0)	SFC Etar Veliko Tarnovo - PFC Vereya Stara Zagora	3-0(0-0)
PFC CSKA Sofia - FC Vitosha Bistritsa	3-1(1-0)	PFC Ludogorets Razgrad - PFC Slavia Sofia	2-2 aet; 4-3 pen
FC Lokomotiv 1929 Sofia - PFC Septemvri Sofia	2-3(1-0)	PFC Beroe Stara Zagora - PFC Botev Plovdiv	0-0 aet; 3-4 pen

Quarter-Finals [02-04.04.2019]

SFC Etar Veliko Tarnovo - PFC Lokomotiv Plovdiv	1-1 aet; 6-7 pen	FC Strumska Slava Radomir - PFC Septemvri Sofia	0-2(0-1)
PFC Ludogorets Razgrad - PFC CSKA Sofia	0-1(0-1)	PFC Botev Plovdiv - PFC Cherno More Varna	1-1 aet; 3-1 pen

Semi-Finals [16/17-23/24.04.2019]

PFC Lokomotiv Plovdiv - PFC Septemvri Sofia	4-0(3-0) / 0-0	PFC Botev Plovdiv - PFC CSKA Sofia	3-2(2-1) / 3-3(2-0)

Final

15.05.2019; Nationalen Stadion "Vasil Levski", Sofia; Referee: Nikolay Yordanov; Attendance: 20,500
PFC Lokomotiv Plovdiv - PFC Botev Plovdiv **1-0(0-0)**

Lokomotiv Plovdiv: Martin Lukov, Dimitar Vezalov, Stephen Eze, Josip Tomašević, Miloš Petrović (60.Yanko Angelov), Abdelhakim Bouhna, Igor Banović, Momchil Tsvetanov, Dimitar Iliev (Cap), Alen Ožbolt (78.Birsent Karagaren), Ante Aralica (89.Asen Georgiev). Trainer: Bruno Akrapović (Bosnia and Herzegovina).

Botev Plovdiv: Daniel Kajzer, Johnathan Carlos Pereira (46.Filip Filipov), Dimitar Pirgov, Kristian Dimitrov, Lazar Marin, Radoslav Terziev (77.Vasil Shopov), Ebert Cardoso da Silva (53.Férébory Doré), Lachezar Baltanov (Cap), Todor Nedelev, Aleksandar Tonev, Antonio Vutov. Trainer: Nikolai Kirov.

Goal: 1-0 Alen Ožbolt (73).

THE CLUBS 2018/2019

Please note: matches and goals includes statistics of regular season and play-offs (Championship Round and Relegation Round).

Professional Football Club Beroe Stara Zagora

Founded: 06.05.1916
Stadium: Stadion Beroe, Stara Zagora (12,128)

Goalkeepers:	DOB	M	(s)	G
Georgi Argilashki	13.06.1991		(1)	
Dušan Perniš (SVK)	28.11.1984	36		
Defenders:	**DOB**	**M**	**(s)**	**G**
Erol Alkan (TUR)	16.02.1994	19	(1)	
Nadim Angelov	26.01.1999		(1)	
Ivan Bandalovski	23.11.1986	32		1
Nikita Baranov (EST)	19.08.1992	13		
Pedro Miguel Pina Eugénio (POR)	26.06.1990	13	(2)	4
Kamen Hadzhiev	22.09.1991	18	(1)	
Valentin Ivanov	01.04.2000		(2)	
Martin Marinov	27.05.2001		(1)	
Matheus Izidorio Leoni (BRA)	20.09.1991	17	(8)	
Yaya Omnibes (CIV)	25.09.1997	8		
Aleksandar Vasilev	27.04.1995	22	(7)	1
Milen Zhelev	17.07.1993	16	(11)	
Midfielders:	**DOB**	**M**	**(s)**	**G**
Georgi Angelov	12.11.1990	12	(1)	
Plamen-Andrey Apostolov			(1)	
Ruben Luís Maurício Brígido (POR)	23.06.1991	25	(10)	4
Dragoş Petruţ Firtulescu (ROU)	15.05.1989		(2)	
Vladimir Gadzhev	18.07.1987	3	(6)	
Stoyan Ivanov	14.05.2001	1	(6)	
Ivan Minchev	28.05.1991	23	(6)	
Carlos Ohene (GHA)	21.07.1993	8	(2)	1
Martin Raynov	25.04.1992	13		2
Borislav Tsonev	29.04.1995	18		7
Aleksandar Tsvetkov	31.08.1990	33	(2)	
Forwards:	**DOB**	**M**	**(s)**	**G**
Alfredo Francisco Martins (BRA)	06.07.1992	3	(13)	
Martin Kamburov	13.10.1980	30	(5)	16
Nikola Marinov	30.07.2002		(2)	
Buomesca Tue Na Bangna „Mesca" (GNB)	06.05.1993	19	(13)	1
Wanderson Costa Viana (BRA)	07.02.1994	14	(4)	3
Trainer:	**DOB**	**M**		
Aleksandar Tomovski	02.09.1978	36		

Professional Football Club Botev Plovdiv

Founded: 12.03.1912
Stadium: Botev 1912 Football Complex, Plovdiv (4,000)

Goalkeepers:	DOB	M	(s)	G
Daniel Kajzer (POL)	23.02.1992	36		
Defenders:	**DOB**	**M**	**(s)**	**G**
Kristian Dimitrov	27.02.1997	31		4
Ebert Cardoso da Silva (BRA)	25.05.1993	13	(1)	
Filip Filipov	02.08.1988	21	(6)	
Johnathan Carlos Pereira (BRA)	04.04.1995	18	(3)	
Lazar Marin	09.02.1994	6	(3)	
Yordan Minev	14.10.1980	20		
Kostadin Nichev	22.07.1987	16	(1)	
Dimitar Pirgov	23.10.1989	22		
Radoslav Terziev	06.08.1994	20	(4)	
Midfielders:	**DOB**	**M**	**(s)**	**G**
Radoslav Apostolov	07.06.1997	4	(8)	
Lachezar Baltanov	11.07.1988	28	(5)	2
Milko Georgiev	03.08.1998		(1)	
Todor Nedelev	07.02.1993	35		14
Stevan Petkov	07.05.1995	13	(5)	6
Stanislav Shopov	23.02.2002		(4)	
Vasil Shopov	09.11.1991	19	(15)	3
Antonio Vutov	06.06.1996	20	(3)	6
Serkan Yusein	31.03.1996	12	(5)	2
Atanas Zehirov	13.02.1989	4	(1)	
Forwards:	**DOB**	**M**	**(s)**	**G**
Zapro Dinev	25.09.1999		(2)	
Diogo Campos Gomes (BRA)	31.12.1990	7	(5)	
Kristian Dobrev	27.04.2001	8	(17)	1
Férébory Doré (CGO)	21.01.1989	11	(5)	2
Gustavo Affonso Sauerbeck (BRA)	30.04.1993	18	(1)	2
Anton Karachanakov	17.01.1992	5	(6)	
Daudet N'Dongala (FRA)	16.09.1994	1		
Aleksandar Tonev	03.02.1990	8	(1)	
Ivan Vasilev	16.05.2001		(2)	1
Trainer:	**DOB**	**M**		
Nikolai Kirov	12.06.1975	36		

Professional Football Club Botev Vratsa

Founded: 1921
Stadium: Stadion "Hristo Botev", Vratsa (12,000)

Goalkeepers:	DOB	M	(s)	G
Hugo Cointard (FRA)	18.09.1995	1		
Krasimir Kostov	11.02.1995	27		
Nikolai Krastev	06.12.1996	2		
Hristo Mitov	24.01.1985	2		
Defenders:	**DOB**	**M**	**(s)**	**G**
Petar Alyoshev	11.05.1987			
Yordan Apostolov	30.11.1989	22	(1)	
Atanas Fidanin	09.08.1986	8		
Kostadin Gadzhalov	20.07.1989	4	(2)	
Mariyan Ivanov	10.07.1990	21		
Martin Kavdanski	13.02.1987	8		2
Ventsislav Kerchev	02.06.1997	28		1
Simeon Mechev	16.03.1990	9	(1)	1
Mihail Milchev	18.06.1988	3	(2)	
Iliya Milanov	19.02.1992	16	(1)	1
Ivailo Todorov	01.01.1994		(1)	
Midfielders:	**DOB**	**M**	**(s)**	**G**
Petar Atanasov	13.10.1990	23	(6)	7
Daniel Gadzhev	21.06.1985	16	(4)	
Daniel Genov	19.05.1989	18	(3)	4
Spas Georgiev	21.06.1992	7	(6)	
Ivaylo Mihaylov	18.01.1991	17	(9)	
Anton Ognyanov	30.06.1988	4	(3)	1
Emil Stoev	17.01.1996	24	(2)	6
Edgar Tur (EST)	28.12.1996	6	(2)	
Georgi Valchev	07.03.1991	12	(12)	1
Milan Vušurović (MNE)	18.04.1995	1	(5)	1
Forwards:	**DOB**	**M**	**(s)**	**G**
Valeri Bojinov	15.02.1986	11		7
Miroslav Budinov	23.01.1986	1	(7)	2
Valeri Domovchiyski	05.10.1986	19	(12)	8
Ivan Kolev	15.10.1995		(8)	
Yulian Nenov	17.11.1994	11	(8)	2
Denis Rusinov	08.08.2002		(1)	
Andreas Vasev	01.03.1991	31		
Trainer:	**DOB**	**M**		
Sasho Angelov	15.08.1969	32		

Professional Football Club Cherno More Varna

Founded: 03.03.1913
Stadium: Stadion Ticha, Varna (8,250)

Goalkeepers:	**DOB**	**M**	**(s)**	**G**
Ivan Dichevski	24.04.2001	1		
Ivan Dyulgerov	15.07.1999	11		
Georgi Kitanov	06.03.1995	10		
Blagoy Makendzhiev	11.07.1988	14		
Defenders:	**DOB**	**M**	**(s)**	**G**
Plamen Dimov	29.10.1990	24	(1)	1
Miroslav Enchev	08.08.1991	24	(2)	1
Victor Genev	27.10.1988	20		2
Ilias Hassani (FRA)	08.11.1995	14		
Hugo Konongo (CGO)	14.02.1992	25		
Martin Kostadinov	13.05.1996	10	(5)	
Tsvetomir Panov	17.04.1989	8		1
Viktor Popov	05.03.2000	2		
Stefan Stanchev	26.04.1989	13	(2)	
Midfielders:	**DOB**	**M**	**(s)**	**G**
Joakim Balmy (FRA)	17.09.1997		(1)	
Daniel Dimov	21.01.1989	3		
Aleksandar Georgiev	2002		(1)	
Georgi Iliev	05.09.1981	24	(8)	10
Dani Kiki	08.01.1988	12	(10)	4
Marian Ognyanov	30.07.1988		(2)	
Vasil Panayotov	16.07.1990	29	(2)	1
Patrick (CPV)	09.02.1993	15	(10)	4
Petar Vitanov	10.03.1995	27	(3)	
Petar Vutsov	07.08.2000		(1)	
Emil Yanchev	08.02.1999		(2)	
Lachezar Yordanov	31.05.2000		(1)	
Atanas Zehirov	13.02.1989	2	(4)	
Forwards:	**DOB**	**M**	**(s)**	**G**
Georgi Bozhilov	12.02.1987	3	(12)	4
Mehdi Fenouche (ALG)	20.02.1993	15	(7)	
Aristote N'Dongala Fundu (COD)	19.01.1994	27	(6)	2
Jorge Vinícius Oliveira Alves „Jorginho" (BRA)	03.05.1988	17	(8)	4
Martin Minchev	22.04.2001	22	(5)	2
Rodrigo Henrique Santana da Silva (BRA)	02.07.1993	6	(4)	
Radoslav Vasilev	12.10.1990	18	(9)	5
Valentin Yoskov	05.06.1998		(1)	
Trainer:	**DOB**	**M**		
Ilian Iliev	02.07.1968	36		

Professional Football Club Centralen Sporten Klub na Armiyata (CSKA) Sofia

Founded: 05.05.1948
Stadium: Balgarska Armiya Stadion, Sofia (18,495)

Goalkeepers:	**DOB**	**M**	**(s)**	**G**
Vytautas Černiauskas (LTU)	12.03.1989	34		
Dante Stipica (CRO)	30.05.1991	2		
Defenders:	**DOB**	**M**	**(s)**	**G**
Valentin Antov	09.11.2000	10	(8)	
Stoycho Atanasov	14.05.1997	6	(4)	
Nikolaj Bodurov	30.05.1986	29		
Bozhidar Chorbadzhiyski	10.11.1995	27	(2)	1
Alexander Dyulgerov	19.04.1990		(2)	
Geferson Cerqueira Teles (BRA)	13.05.1994	15	(1)	
Angel Lyaskov	18.03.1998	11	(3)	
Stanislav Manolev	16.12.1985	7	(4)	1
Nuno Miguel Adro Tomás (POR)	15.09.1995	12		
Steven Fernandes Pereira (CPV)	13.04.1994	7	(1)	
Boris Sekulić (SRB)	21.10.1991	11	(1)	
Ivan Turitsov	18.07.1999	13		
Midfielders:	**DOB**	**M**	**(s)**	**G**
Janio Bikel Figueiredo da Silva (POR)	28.06.1995	18	(12)	
Jorge Fernando Barbosa Intima „Jorghinho" (GNB)	21.09.1995	19	(13)	5
Kristiyan Malinov	16.07.1994	28	(3)	1
Rúben Rafael Melo Silva Pinto (POR)	24.04.1992	30	(3)	2
Tiago Filipe Sousa Nóbrega Rodrigues (POR)	29.01.1992	30	(3)	8
Andrey Yordanov	06.09.2001		(1)	
Forwards:	**DOB**	**M**	**(s)**	**G**
Borislav Budinov	01.01.2000		(1)	
Kiril Despodov	11.11.1996	14	(2)	8
Evandro da Silva (BRA)	14.01.1997	8	(12)	2
Edwin Gyasi (GHA)	01.07.1991	21	(9)	5
Henrique Roberto Rafael (BRA)	23.08.1993	9	(5)	1
Maurides Roque Junior (BRA)	10.03.1994	16	(5)	9
Martin Smolenski	08.03.2003		(2)	
Ali Sowe (GAM)	14.06.1994	19	(9)	11
Trainer:	**DOB**	**M**		
Nestor El Maestro (SRB)	25.03.1983	20		
Luboslav Penev [08.02.2019]	31.08.1966	11		
Dobromir Mitov [03.05.2019]	03.04.1972	5		

Football Club Dunav Ruse 2010

Founded: 16.02.1949
Stadium: Stadion Gradski, Ruse (12,400)

Goalkeepers:	**DOB**	**M**	**(s)**	**G**
Stanislav Antonov	21.03.1986	13		
Filip Dimitrov	13.04.1995	8		
Blagoy Makendzhiev	11.07.1988	11		
Defenders:	**DOB**	**M**	**(s)**	**G**
Emin Ahmed	10.03.1996	3		
Georgi Dinkov	20.05.1991	29		1
Eduardo Haas Gehlen „Duda" (BRA)	19.04.1994	1		
Samuel Inkoom (GHA)	22.08.1989	8		
Aleksandar Isaevski (MKD)	19.05.1995	8	(1)	
Martin Kovachev	12.03.1982	29		2
Iliya Munin	16.01.1993	4		1
Petar Patev	21.05.1993	23	(4)	
Preslav Petrov	01.05.1995	5	(1)	
Hristo Popadiyn	06.01.1994	24	(1)	
Midfielders:	**DOB**	**M**	**(s)**	**G**
Ahmed Ahmedov	04.03.1995	20	(11)	8
Borislav Baldzhiyski	12.10.1990	15	(3)	2
Ahmed Ben Aicha (FRA)	16.12.1994		(1)	
Diyan Dimov	27.09.1985	8	(3)	
Dragoş Petruţ Firtulescu (ROU)	15.05.1989	9	(2)	3
Ivan Kokonov	17.08.1991	18	(2)	1
Hristo Lemperov	22.04.1988	1		
Derrick Ediyaa Mensah (GHA)	28.05.1995		(3)	
Daniel Pehlivanov	01.07.1994		(4)	
Svilen Shterev	14.12.1992	5	(3)	
Martin Stankev	29.07.1989	2	(6)	
Krasimir Stanoev	14.09.1994	25	(4)	2
Kristian Varbanov			(1)	
Bozhidar Vasev	14.03.1993	25		4
Nassim Zitouni (ALG)	31.03.1994		(1)	
Forwards:	**DOB**	**M**	**(s)**	**G**
Aleksandar Aleksandrov	28.03.1994		(4)	
Gláucio José de Araujo Silva (BRA)	03.02.1994	2	(6)	
Ismail Isa Mustafa	26.06.1989	12	(9)	5
Branimir Kostadinov	04.03.1989	10	(7)	
Svetoslav Kovachev	14.03.1998	25	(2)	5
Mouhamadou N'Diaye (SEN)	24.08.1994	9	(14)	
Trainer:	**DOB**	**M**		
Malin Orachev	03.12.1972	8		
Tsvetomir Mladenov [17.09.2018]		2		
Ljudmil Kirov [01.10.2018]	16.02.1976	20		

Sports Football Club Etar Veliko Tarnovo

Founded: 17.07.2013
Stadium: Stadion Ivaylo, Veliko Tarnovo (18,000)

Goalkeepers:	DOB	M	(s)	G
Anatoliy Gospodinov	21.03.1994	2		
Hristo Ivanov	06.04.1982	30		
Defenders:	**DOB**	**M**	**(s)**	**G**
Artjom Artjunin (EST)	24.01.1990	15	(3)	
Plamen Galabov	02.11.1995	18	(1)	
Zdravko Iliev	19.10.1984	9	(2)	
Ivan Skerlev	28.01.1986	20	(1)	
Krum Stoyanov	01.08.1991	18	(5)	1
Ventsislav Vasilev	08.07.1988	22		1
Midfielders:	**DOB**	**M**	**(s)**	**G**
Dimo Atanasov	24.10.1985	17	(1)	
Veljko Batrović (MNE)	05.03.1994	24	(6)	7
Iliya Dzhamov	11.06.1998	1		
Aleksandar Georgiev	10.10.1997	4		
Chavdar Ivaylov	09.07.1996		(7)	
Nikola Kolev	06.06.1995	22	(5)	
Alasana Manneh (GAM)	08.04.1998	16	(4)	2
Dino Martinovič (SVN)	20.07.1990		(1)	
Daniel Mladenov	25.05.1987	22	(4)	10
Yani Pehlivanov	14.07.1988	3	(3)	
Erik Pochanski	05.04.1992	5	(10)	1
Rumen Rumenov	07.06.1993	24	(5)	3
Georgi Sarmov	07.09.1985	29		1
Kolyo Stanev	10.10.2001	1	(2)	
Ivan Valchanov	28.09.1991	1		
Forwards:	**DOB**	**M**	**(s)**	**G**
Milcho Angelov	02.01.1995	4	(7)	3
Florent Bojaj (ENG)	13.04.1996	25	(3)	5
Monteiro Varela da Silva „Gilson" (CPV)	12.05.1990	5	(3)	
Ivan Petkov	22.01.1982	4	(12)	4
Ivan Stoyanov	24.07.1983	11	(7)	
Trainer:	**DOB**	**M**		
Krassimir Balakov	29.03.1966	32		

Professional Football Club Levski Sofia

Founded: 24.05.1914
Stadium: Vivacom Arena – Stadion „Georgi Asparuhov", Sofia (25,000)

Goalkeepers:	DOB	M	(s)	G
Nikolai Krastev	06.12.1996	1		
Nikolay Mihaylov	28.06.1988	15		
Bozhidar Mitrev	31.03.1987	5		
Martin Polaček (SVK)	02.04.1990	15		
Defenders:	**DOB**	**M**	**(s)**	**G**
Aymen Belaïd (TUN)	02.01.1989	10	(1)	
Miloš Cvetković (SRB)	06.01.1990	27	(1)	
Hólmar Eyjólfsson (ISL)	06.08.1990	11	(1)	2
Ivan Goranov	10.06.1992	27	(1)	
Cédric Hountondji (BEN)	19.01.1994	3	(2)	
Diyan Ivanov	12.04.1996	5		
David Jablonský (CZE)	08.10.1991	20	(1)	1
Zhivko Milanov	15.07.1984	9	(1)	1
Louis Nganioni (FRA)	03.06.1995	7		
Nuno Miguel Pereira Reis (POR)	31.01.1991	22	(2)	1
Tomislav Papazov	24.08.2001		(1)	
Midfielders:	**DOB**	**M**	**(s)**	**G**
Anthony Belmonte (FRA)	16.10.1995	11	(5)	1
Filipe Guterres Nascimento (POR)	07.01.1995		(8)	
Jordi Gómez García-Penche (ESP)	24.05.1985	3	(1)	
Davide Mariani (SUI)	19.05.1991	32	(3)	11
Ivaylo Naydenov	22.03.1998	2	(5)	
Martin Petkov	15.01.2001	1	(7)	
Martin Raynov	25.04.1992	14	(2)	
Khaly Iyane Thiam (SEN)	07.01.1994	29		2
Bogdan Vaštšuk (EST)	04.10.1995	1	(9)	
Iliya Yurukov	22.09.1999	8	(6)	
Forwards:	**DOB**	**M**	**(s)**	**G**
Valeri Bojinov	15.02.1986	4	(6)	3
Sergiu Florin Buş (ROU)	02.11.1992	4	(14)	2
Jerson Cabral (CPV)	03.01.1991	25	(1)	8
Iliya Dimitrov	10.07.1996		(3)	1
Ivaylo Ivanov	11.01.2001		(1)	
Stanislav Ivanov	16.04.1999	10	(6)	2
Atanas Kabov	11.04.1999		(1)	
Stanislav Kostov	02.10.1991	31	(4)	24
Luan Viana Patrocínio (BRA)	14.01.1996		(1)	
Gabriel Obertan (FRA)	26.02.1989	20		1
Paulo Victor de Menezes Melo „Paulinho" (BRA)	29.05.1993	22	(4)	2
Martin Petkov	15.08.2002	1	(7)	
Rivaldo Vítor Borba Ferreira Júnior „Rivaldinho" (BRA)	29.04.1995		(4)	
Yerkebulan Seidakhmet (KAZ)	04.02.2000	2	(1)	
Trainer:	**DOB**	**M**		
Todor Simov	26.01.1985	2		
Slaviša Stojanovič (SVN) [31.07.2018]	06.12.1969	18		
Georgi Dermendjiev [21.01.2019]	04.01.1955	11		
Georgi Todorov [29.04.2019]	13.06.1956	5		

Professional Football Club Lokomotiv Plovdiv

Founded: 25.07.1926
Stadium: Stadion Lokomotiv, Plovdiv (13,000)

Goalkeepers:	DOB	M	(s)	G
Martin Lukov	05.07.1993	27		
Antoni Milina (CRO)	20.12.1989	1		
Ilko Pirgov	23.05.1986	4	(1)	
Defenders:	**DOB**	**M**	**(s)**	**G**
Mustapha Abdullahi (NGA)	18.01.1996	4	(2)	
Iskandar Dzhalilov (TJK)	01.06.1992	2		
Stephen Eze (NGA)	08.03.1994	25		
Asen Georgiev	09.07.1993	17	(2)	1
Lucas Gabriel Masoero Masi (ARG)	01.02.1995	5	(2)	
Martin Paskalev	25.12.2001		(1)	
Miloš Petrović (SRB)	05.05.1990	22	(1)	
Josip Tomašević (CRO)	04.03.1994	25	(1)	
Dimitar Vezalov	13.04.1987	19	(1)	1
Midfielders:	**DOB**	**M**	**(s)**	**G**
Yanko Angelov	29.06.1993	18	(6)	
Edin Bahtic (AUT)	14.07.1996	5	(2)	3
Igor Banović (CRO)	12.05.1987	24	(1)	1
Abdelhakim Bouhna (BEL)	24.05.1991	26	(1)	1
Eliton Pardinho Toreta Junior (BRA)	28.01.1998	6	(11)	1
Vilim Posinković (CRO)	10.01.1991	13	(7)	2
Ilia Tomov			(1)	
Parvizchon Umarbaev (TJK)	01.11.1994	19	(6)	1
Wiris Gustavo de Oliveira (BRA)	04.07.2000	3	(1)	
Oktay Yusein	15.04.2000	1	(1)	
Forwards:	**DOB**	**M**	**(s)**	**G**
Ante Aralica (CRO)	23.07.1996	18	(2)	4
Dimitar Iliev	25.09.1988	22	(6)	9
Zhelyazko Kalinov	04.07.2000		(1)	
Birsent Karagaren	06.12.1992	22	(8)	3
Filip Kolev			(1)	
Nikola Marić (CRO)	04.08.1997	4	(3)	
Filip Mihaljević (CRO)	09.03.1992	4	(1)	1
Alen Ožbolt (SVN)	24.06.1996	10	(11)	7
Simeon Raykov	11.11.1989	1	(5)	2
Petar Shopov			(1)	
Momchil Tsvetanov	03.12.1990	5	(4)	
Trainer:	**DOB**	**M**		
Bruno Akrapović (BIH)	26.09.1967	32		

Professional Football Club Ludogorets Razgrad

Founded: 1945
Stadium: Ludogorets Arena, Razgrad (10,442)

Goalkeepers:	DOB	M	(s)	G
Jorge Emanuel Broun (ARG)	26.05.1986	5		
Plamen Iliev	30.11.1991	12		
Renan dos Santos (BRA)	18.05.1989	19		
Defenders:	**DOB**	**M**	**(s)**	**G**
Neuciano de Jesus Gusmão „Cicinho" (BRA)	26.12.1988	27	(2)	
Dragoş Grigore (ROU)	07.09.1986	12		4
Stanislav Manolev	16.12.1985	2	(3)	
Cosmin Iosif Moţi (ROU)	03.12.1984	28		5
Natanael Batista Pimenta (BRA)	25.12.1990	13	(3)	1
Anton Nedyalkov	30.04.1993	34	(1)	1
Rafael Forster (BRA)	23.07.1990	11	(4)	
Tsvetomir Panov	17.04.1989	3		
Georgi Terziev	18.04.1992	10	(4)	
Midfielders:	**DOB**	**M**	**(s)**	**G**
Svetoslav Dyakov	31.05.1984	27	(3)	
Jacek Góralski (POL)	21.09.1992	21	(5)	
Gustavo Campanharo (BRA)	04.04.1992	13	(3)	
May Sphiwe Mahlangu (RSA)	01.05.1989	1	(3)	1
Marcelo Nascimento da Costa „Marcelinho"	24.08.1984	27	(2)	8
Adrian Dumitru Popa (ROU)	24.07.1988	6	(7)	
Lucas Pacheco Affini „Sasha" (BRA)	01.03.1990	9	(9)	1
Dominik Yankov	28.07.2000		(3)	
Serkan Yusein	31.03.1996	6	(2)	
Forwards:	**DOB**	**M**	**(s)**	**G**
Anicet Andrianantenaina Abel (MAD)	13.03.1990	6	(9)	
Dimo Bakalov	19.12.1988	8	(5)	2
David Ribeiro Pereira (BRA)	23.04.1998		(1)	
João Paulo da Silva Araujo (BRA)	02.06.1988	3	(8)	
Claudiu Andrei Keşerü (ROU)	02.12.1986	29	(6)	20
Jody Lukoki (COD)	15.11.1992	22	(6)	6
Virgil Misidjan (NED)	24.07.1993	5	(1)	1
Jakub Świerczok (POL)	28.12.1992	9	(16)	11
Wanderson Cristaldo Farias (BRA)	02.01.1988	28	(1)	6
Trainer:	**DOB**	**M**		
Paulo Autuori de Mello (BRA)	25.08.1956	11		
Antoni Zdravkov [09.10.2018]	20.08.1964	13		
Stoycho Stoev [06.03.2019]	15.07.1962	12		

Professional Football Club Septemvri Sofia

Founded: 05.11.1944 / 01.07.1988 (refounded)
Stadium: Nationalen Stadion "Vasil Levski", Sofia (43,230)

Goalkeepers:	DOB	M	(s)	G
Valentin Galev	01.01.1984	9	(1)	
Yanko Georgiev	22.10.1988	23		
Defenders:	**DOB**	**M**	**(s)**	**G**
Ivan Arsov	29.09.2000	1		
Aleksandar Bashliev	16.11.1989	4		
Alexandru Constantin Benga (ROU)	15.06.1989	24		
Sergio Castañeda Velásquez (COL)	05.11.1992	1		
Alassane Diaby (MLI)	06.10.1995	6		
Vasil Dobrev	05.01.1998	10	(1)	
Alexander Dyulgerov	19.04.1990	12		1
Fabiano Donato Alves (BRA)	01.12.1994	26	(2)	
Darko Glisić (MKD)	23.09.1991	13	(1)	
Stiliyan Nikolov	16.07.1991	15	(1)	2
Vladimir Nikolov	19.03.2001		(11)	
Mateo Stamatov	22.03.1999	1	(2)	
Ivan Stoyanov	26.08.2000	16	(6)	1
Midfielders:	**DOB**	**M**	**(s)**	**G**
Ishmael Baidu (GHA)	01.12.1998	17	(2)	3
Asen Chandarov	13.11.1998	31		4
Zdravko Dimitrov	24.08.1998	17	(9)	1
Boris Galchev	31.10.1983	24	(5)	4
Aleksandar Georgiev	10.10.1997	9		
Dimitar Kostadinov	14.08.1999	2	(4)	
Yaya Meledje Omnibes (CIV)	25.09.1997	9	(2)	
Suad Sahiti (KVX)	06.02.1995	5	(3)	1
Georgi Stoichkov	27.05.1994	22	(1)	
Ivan Tilev	05.01.1999	4	(19)	
Forwards:	**DOB**	**M**	**(s)**	**G**
Miroslav Budinov	23.01.1986	9	(10)	1
Iliya Dimitrov	10.07.1996	1	(6)	3
Chris Gadi N'Kiasala (FRA)	09.04.1992	16	(2)	5
Christopher Massamba Mandiangu (GER)	08.02.1992	12		5
Georgi Rusev	02.07.1998	13	(8)	
Trainer:	**DOB**	**M**		
Nikolai Mitov	18.03.1972	10		
Hristo Arangelov [28.09.2018]	25.02.1978	22		

Professional Football Club Slavia Sofia

Founded: 10.04.1913
Stadium: Stadion Slavia, Sofia (25,556) / Nationalen Stadion "Vasil Levski", Sofia (43,230)

Goalkeepers:	DOB	M	(s)	G
Georgi Georgiev	12.10.1988	4		
Emanuele Geria (ITA)	29.07.1995	2		
Georgi Petkov	14.03.1976	9	(1)	
Antonis Stergiakis (GRE)	16.03.1999	17		
Defenders:	**DOB**	**M**	**(s)**	**G**
Dimitar Burov	31.08.1997		(1)	
David Humanes Muñoz „David Bollo" (ESP)	14.11.1994	7		
Andrea Hristov	01.03.1999	12		
Nemanja Ivanov	06.10.1994	2	(1)	
Teynur Marem	23.09.1994	18	(1)	
Emil Martinov	18.03.1992	2	(1)	
Randy Onuoha (NED)	01.04.1994	3		
Preslav Petrov	01.05.1995	3	(3)	
Aleksandr Stanisavljević (SRB)	27.01.1998	11	(1)	
Ertan Tombak	30.05.1999	2		
Pavel Vidanov	01.08.1988		(1)	
Midfielders:	**DOB**	**M**	**(s)**	**G**
Sasho Aleksandrov	30.07.1986	14		
Aleks Borimirov	13.05.1998		(1)	
Milen Gamakov	12.04.1994	25		
Yanis Karabelyov	23.01.1996	30		3
Filip Krastev	15.10.2001	2	(11)	
Slavcho Shokolarov	20.08.1989	27	(2)	2
Luka Spoljarić (SRB)	13.09.1995	1	(1)	
Dimitar Stoyanov	14.04.2001	1		
Darko Tasevski (MKD)	20.05.1984	8	(1)	1
Vladislav Uzunov	24.05.1991	17	(12)	2
Denny Valentić-Bara (CRO)	02.07.1997		(3)	
Aleksandar Zlatkov	31.01.1999		(1)	
Forwards:	**DOB**	**M**	**(s)**	**G**
Milcho Angelov	02.01.1995	10	(6)	1
Stefan Aškovski (MKD)	24.02.1992	13	(3)	
Tsvetelin Chunchukov	26.12.1994	20	(8)	10
Galin Ivanov	15.04.1988	19		3
Hristo Ivanov	2000		(3)	
Radoslav Kirilov	29.06.1992	12		5
Ilian Micanski	20.12.1985	6	(8)	4
Kristiyan Peshov	16.06.1997	1	(11)	
Momchil Tsvetanov	03.12.1990	6	(8)	
Dimitar Velkovski	22.01.1995	24		1
Georgi Yomov	06.07.1997	24	(3)	3
Trainer:	**DOB**	**M**		
Zlatomir Zagorčić	15.06.1971	32		

Professional Football Club Vereya Stara Zagora

Founded: 15.07.2001
Stadium: Trace Arena, Stara Zagora (3,500)

Goalkeepers:	**DOB**	**M**	**(s)**	**G**
Gennady Ganev (UKR)	15.05.1990	6		
Georgi Georgiev	12.10.1988	16		
Kristiyan Katsarev	07.08.1995	6		
Bogomil Tsintsarski	14.05.1997	4	(1)	
Defenders:	**DOB**	**M**	**(s)**	**G**
Emin Ahmed	10.03.1996	4	(3)	
Midat Galbaev (KAZ)	14.03.1997	2	(2)	
Zdravko Iliev	19.10.1984	12	(3)	1
Denis Ivanov	18.10.2001	1		
Dmitriy Ivanov (RUS)	14.02.1987	5		
Ivo Ivanov	11.03.1985	24	(1)	
Emil Jørgensen (DEN)	14.11.1995	13	(2)	
Tomáš Košút (SVK)	13.01.1990	8		
Theofilos Kouroupis (GRE)	11.04.1990	24	(5)	1
Emilian Kurekov	22.06.2001		(1)	
Goderdzi Machaidze (GEO)	17.07.1992	15		
Simeon Mechev	16.03.1990	7	(2)	
Iliya Munin	16.01.1993	1	(1)	
Georgi Tanev	22.01.1998		(1)	
Veselin Veskov	28.01.2000	6		
Gabriel Zhelyazkov	24.07.2000	5	(1)	
Midfielders:	**DOB**	**M**	**(s)**	**G**
Stefan Alichkov	15.07.1997	1	(4)	
Andrei Ciofu (MDA)	31.05.1994		(2)	
Seydina Diarra (BEL)	01.04.1994	8	(1)	
Evgen Dobrovolskiy (UKR)	10.02.1995	6		
Elias Alves da Silva (BRA)	04.09.1981		(2)	
Velizar Ganev	05.04.2001		(1)	
Shota Gvazava (GEO)	26.10.1992	3		
Steliyan Kolev	07.07.2000	2	(5)	
Andrejs Kovaļjovs (LVA)	23.03.1989	6		
Aurélien Ngeyitala Lola (COD)	20.05.1994	2		1
Angel Maksimov	16.01.1997	4		
Bilel Ait Malek (FRA)	19.08.1996	12	(1)	
Dino Martinovič (SVN)	20.07.1990	6	(2)	1
Alexander N'Doumbou (GAB)	04.01.1992	13	(2)	
Josué Ulrich Ntoya (FRA)	18.05.1995	6		
Anton Ognyanov	30.06.1988	14	(1)	2
Hrvoje Rizvanović (CRO)	26.09.1997	5	(5)	
Timothée Rubin (FRA)	21.03.1994	6		
Sergiy Rudika (UKR)	14.06.1988	4		
Bedri Ryustemov	17.11.1995	9	(7)	
Plamen Stoyanov	17.03.2002	1	(2)	
Michael Tawiah (GHA)	01.12.1990	8		
Milen Tanev	04.03.1987	5	(3)	
Stilian Tenev	25.09.2000		(1)	
Dennis Vasilyev (UKR)	08.05.1987	15	(1)	
Branislav Vasiljević (SRB)	17.11.1989	7		
Milan Vušurović (MNE)	18.04.1995	17		2
Petar Yankov	22.06.2000		(1)	
Velin Zhelyazkov	08.04.2001	5		
Forwards:	**DOB**	**M**	**(s)**	**G**
Bojidar Atanasov Hristov	10.09.2001	5	(3)	
Stanislav Malamov	10.11.1989	9	(9)	2
Denislav Stanchev	28.03.2000	14	(6)	1
Trainer:	**DOB**	**M**		
Ivan Kolev	14.07.1957	4		
Nebojša Miličić Lekić (SRB) 19.08.2018]	16.09.1959	3		
Elias Alves da Silva (BRA) [11.09.2018]	04.09.1981	13		
Oleksandr Sevidov (UKR) [19.01.2019]	18.07.1969	7		
Ivan Vutsov [01.04.2019]	19.03.1944	5		

Football Club Vitosha Bistritsa

Founded: 1958
Stadium: Stadion Bistritsa, Bistritsa (2,500)

Goalkeepers:	**DOB**	**M**	**(s)**	**G**
Nikolaj Georgiev	06.09.1998	11		
Hristiyan Vasilev	05.12.1997	21		
Defenders:	**DOB**	**M**	**(s)**	**G**
Ventzislav Bonev	08.05.1980	6	(3)	
Todor Gochev	15.04.1993	24		
Rumen Gyonov	09.05.1992	17	(4)	
Georgi Kupenov	24.02.1997	25		1
Mihail Milchev	18.06.1988	21	(2)	
Radko Mutafchiyski	11.05.1989	10		
Julian Popev	07.07.1986	7	(2)	
Ivailo Todorov	01.01.1994	1		
Kristian Uzunov	04.02.1989	6	(6)	
Midfielders:	**DOB**	**M**	**(s)**	**G**
Georgi Amzin	18.04.1992	15	(10)	
Emil Gargorov	15.02.1981	5	(3)	2
Ivaylo Klimentov	03.02.1998	1	(2)	
Kristiyan Kochilov	03.04.1990	6	(11)	1
Lachezar Kotev	05.01.1998	29		
Ivaylo Lazarov	11.04.1992	28		3
Mihail Petrov	01.07.1986	1	(3)	
Chetin Sadula	16.06.1987	22	(6)	4
Angel Stoyanov	31.12.1986		(1)	
Petko Tsankov	19.12.1995	19	(3)	
Ivan Valchanov	28.09.1991	10	(4)	2
Forwards:	**DOB**	**M**	**(s)**	**G**
Grigor Dolapchiev	23.02.1994	9	(10)	5
Stefan Hristov	28.08.1989	24	(3)	4
Daniel Kutev	06.03.1991	12	(6)	2
Nasko Milev	18.07.1996	19	(4)	2
Anti Renia (ALB)	06.01.1993	3	(2)	
Trainer:	**DOB**	**M**		
Rosen Kirilov	04.01.1973	32		

SECOND LEVEL

Second Professional Football League 2018/2019

1.	FC Tsarsko Selo Sofia (*Promoted*)	30	24	4	2	68	-	27	76
2.	FC Montana (*Promotion Play-offs*)	30	18	9	3	49	-	22	63
3.	FC Arda Kardzhali (*Promotion Play-offs*)	30	19	5	6	44	-	18	62
4.	FC CSKA 1948 Sofia	30	16	11	3	39	-	18	59
5.	PFC Litex Lovech	30	12	9	9	43	-	26	45
6.	FC Strumska Slava Radomir	30	10	7	13	36	-	44	37
7.	FC Chernomorets Balchik	30	10	7	13	27	-	35	37
8.	FC Lokomotiv 1929 Sofia	30	9	9	12	25	-	28	36
9.	FC Lokomotiv Gorna Oryahovitsa	30	10	6	14	30	-	43	36
10.	OFC Pomorie	30	10	6	14	35	-	49	36
11.	PFC Ludogorets Razgrad II	30	9	5	16	31	-	43	32
12.	FC Kariana Erden	30	8	7	15	29	-	38	31
13.	OFC Pirin Blagoevgrad	30	9	4	17	29	-	49	31
14.	FC Botev Galabovo	30	7	10	13	32	-	38	31
15.	OFC Nesebar (*Relegated*)	30	6	9	15	33	-	51	27
16.	FC Dobrudzha Dobrich (*Relegated*)	30	4	10	16	17	-	38	22

NATIONAL TEAM

INTERNATIONAL MATCHES
(16.07.2018 – 15.07.2019)

06.09.2018	Ljubljana	Slovenia - Bulgaria	1-2(1-1)	(UNL)
09.09.2018	Sofia	Bulgaria - Norway	1-0(0-0)	(UNL)
13.10.2018	Sofia	Bulgaria - Cyprus	2-1(0-1)	(UNL)
16.10.2018	Oslo	Norway - Bulgaria	1-0(1-0)	(UNL)
16.11.2018	Nicosia	Cyprus - Bulgaria	1-1(1-0)	(UNL)
19.11.2018	Sofia	Bulgaria - Slovenia	1-1(0-0)	(UNL)
22.03.2019	Sofia	Bulgaria - Montenegro	1-1(0-0)	(ECQ)
25.03.2019	Pristina	Kosovo - Bulgaria	1-1(0-1)	(ECQ)
07.06.2019	Praha	Czech Republic - Bulgaria	2-1(1-1)	(ECQ)
10.06.2019	Sofia	Bulgaria - Kosovo	2-3(1-1)	(ECQ)

06.09.2018 SLOVENIA - BULGARIA 1-2(1-1) UEFA Nations League ABCD
Stadion Stožice, Ljubljana; Referee: Davide Massa (Italy); Attendance: 5,100
BUL: Plamen Iliev, Nikolay Bodurov, Ivan Bandalovski, Vasil Bozhikov (46.Angel Lyaskov), Bozhidar Chorbadzhiyski, Ivelin Popov (Cap), Georgi Kostadinov, Simeon Slavchev, Todor Nedelev (82.Ivan Goranov), Bozhidar Kraev (72.Martin Raynov), Kiril Despodov. Trainer: Petar Hubchev.
Goals: Bozhidar Kraev (3, 59).

09.09.2018 BULGARIA - NORWAY 1-0(0-0) UEFA Nations League ABCD
Nationalen Stadion "Vasil Levski", Sofia; Referee: Daniel Stefański (Poland); Attendance: 7,100
BUL: Plamen Iliev, Nikolay Bodurov, Ivan Bandalovski, Strahil Popov, Bozhidar Chorbadzhiyski, Ivelin Popov (Cap), Galin Ivanov, Georgi Kostadinov, Martin Raynov (50.Radoslav Vasilev), Bozhidar Kraev (83.Kristiyan Malinov), Kiril Despodov (74.Ivan Goranov). Trainer: Petar Hubchev.
Goal: Radoslav Vasilev (59).

13.10.2018 BULGARIA - CYPRUS 2-1(0-1) UEFA Nations League ABCD
Nationalen Stadion "Vasil Levski", Sofia; Referee: Srđan Jovanović (Serbia); Attendance: 6,700
BUL: Plamen Iliev, Nikolay Bodurov, Petar Zanev, Strahil Popov, Anton Nedyalkov, Ivelin Popov (Cap) (84.Radoslav Vasilev), Georgi Kostadinov, Simeon Slavchev, Todor Nedelev, Bozhidar Kraev (57.Georgi Milanov), Kiril Despodov (75.Vasil Bozhikov). Trainer: Petar Hubchev.
Goals: Kiril Despodov (59), Todor Nedelev (68).

16.10.2018 NORWAY - BULGARIA 1-0(1-0) UEFA Nations League ABCD
Ullevaal Stadion, Oslo; Referee: John Beaton (Scotland); Attendance: 9,523
BUL: Plamen Iliev, Nikolay Bodurov, Ivan Bandalovski, Petar Zanev, Vasil Bozhikov, Bozhidar Chorbadzhiyski (49.Radoslav Vasilev), Ivelin Popov (Cap), Georgi Kostadinov (78.Bozhidar Kraev), Simeon Slavchev (59.Kristiyan Malinov), Todor Nedelev, Kiril Despodov. Trainer: Petar Hubchev.

16.11.2018 CYPRUS - BULGARIA 1-1(1-0) UEFA Nations League ABCD
Stádio GSP, Nicosia; Referee: Mohammed Al Hakim (Sweden); Attendance: 3,844
BUL: Georgi Petkov, Nikolay Bodurov, Strahil Popov, Vasil Bozhikov, Anton Nedyalkov, Ivelin Popov (Cap), Galin Ivanov (56.Nikolay Dimitrov), Georgi Kostadinov, Simeon Slavchev (82.Stanislav Kostov), Todor Nedelev, Bozhidar Kraev (56.Spas Delev). Trainer: Petar Hubchev.
Goal: Nikolay Dimitrov (89 penalty).

19.11.2018 BULGARIA - SLOVENIA 1-1(0-0) UEFA Nations League ABCD
Nationalen Stadion "Vasil Levski", Sofia; Referee: Hüseyin Göçek (Turkey); Attendance: 3,092
BUL: Georgi Petkov, Nikolay Bodurov, Strahil Popov, Vasil Bozhikov, Anton Nedyalkov, Nikolay Dimitrov (64.Galin Ivanov), Ivelin Popov (Cap), Georgi Kostadinov, Simeon Slavchev, Spas Delev (73.Petar Zanev), Stanislav Kostov (59.Radoslav Vasilev). Trainer: Petar Hubchev.
Goal: Galin Ivanov (68).

22.03.2019 BULGARIA - MONTENEGRO 1-1(0-0) 16th EC. Qualifiers
Nationalen Stadion "Vasil Levski", Sofia; Referee: Ruddy Buquet (France); Attendance: 5,652
BUL: Nikolay Mihaylov, Nikolay Bodurov, Petar Zanev, Strahil Popov, Vasil Bozhikov, Ivelin Popov (Cap), Galin Ivanov (51.Stanislav Kostov), Georgi Kostadinov, Ivaylo Chochev (69.Simeon Slavchev), Todor Nedelev, Spas Delev (82.Martin Minchev). Trainer: Petar Hubchev.
Goal: Todor Nedelev (82 penalty).

25.03.2019 KOSOVO - BULGARIA 1-1(0-1) 16th EC. Qualifiers
Stadiumi "Fadil Vokrri", Pristina; Referee: Gediminas Mažeika (Lithuania); Attendance: 12,580
BUL: Nikolay Mihaylov, Nikolay Bodurov, Strahil Popov, Vasil Bozhikov, Kristiyan Malinov (76.Martin Minchev), Anton Nedyalkov, Ivelin Popov (Cap), Georgi Kostadinov (80.Valentin Antov), Simeon Slavchev, Todor Nedelev, Spas Delev (68.Petar Zanev). Trainer: Petar Hubchev.
Goal: Vasil Bozhikov (39).

07.06.2019 CZECH REPUBLIC - BULGARIA 2-1(1-1) 16th EC. Qualifiers
Generali Arena, Praha; Referee: Tamás Bognár (Hungary); Attendance: 13,482
BUL: Nikolay Mihaylov, Strahil Popov, Vasil Bozhikov, Kristiyan Malinov (64.Yanis Karabelyov), Anton Nedyalkov, Kristian Dimitrov, Georgi Sarmov, Ivelin Popov (Cap), Todor Nedelev (82.Tsvetelin Chunchukov), Martin Minchev (46.Kiril Despodov), Ismail Isa Mustafa. Trainer: Krasimir Balakov.
Goal: Ismail Isa Mustafa (3).

10.06.2019 BULGARIA - KOSOVO 2-3(1-1) 16th EC. Qualifiers
Nationalen Stadion "Vasil Levski", Sofia; Referee: Mads-Kristoffer Kristoffersen (Denmark); Attendance: 4,994
BUL: Nikolay Mihaylov, Strahil Popov, Vasil Bozhikov (46.Kristian Dimitrov), Ivan Goranov, Anton Nedyalkov, Ivelin Popov (Cap), Galin Ivanov, Georgi Kostadinov, Todor Nedelev (70.Georgi Iliev), Ismail Isa Mustafa (79.Tsvetelin Chunchukov), Kiril Despodov. Trainer: Krasimir Balakov.
Goals: Ivelin Popov (43), Kristian Dimitrov (55).

NATIONAL TEAM PLAYERS
(16.07.2018 – 15.07.2019)

Name	DOB	Caps	Goals	2018/2019:	*Club*
Goalkeepers					
Plamen ILIEV	30.11.1991	**13**	**0**	2018:	*AFC Astra Giurgiu (ROU)*
Nikolay MIHAYLOV	28.06.1988	**37**	**0**	2019:	*PFC Levski Sofia*
Georgi PETKOV	14.03.1976	**18**	**0**	2018:	*PFC Slavia Sofia*
Defenders					
Valentin ANTOV	09.11.2000	**1**	**0**	2019:	*PFC CSKA Sofia*
Ivan BANDALOVSKI	23.11.1986	**19**	**0**	2018:	*PFC Beroe Stara Zagora*
Nikolay BODUROV	30.05.1986	**41**	**2**	2018/2019:	*PFC CSKA Sofia*
Bozhidar CHORBADZHIYSKI	01.08.1995	**8**	**0**	2018:	*PFC CSKA Sofia*
Kristian DIMITROV	27.02.1997	**2**	**1**	2019:	*PFC Botev Plovdiv*
Ivan GORANOV	10.06.1992	**3**	**0**	2018/2019:	*PFC Levski Sofia*
Angel LYASKOV	18.03.1998	**1**	**0**	2018:	*PFC CSKA Sofia*
Anton NEDYALKOV	30.04.1993	**11**	**0**	2018/2019:	*PFC Ludogorets Razgrad*
Strahil POPOV	31.08.1990	**26**	**0**	2018/2019:	*Kasımpaşa SK Beyoğlu (TUR)*
Petar ZANEV	18.10.1985	**39**	**0**	2018/2019:	*FK Yenisey Krasnoyarsk (RUS)*
Midfielders					
Ivaylo CHOCHEV	18.02.1993	**18**	**3**	2019:	*US Città di Palermo (ITA)*
Kiril DESPODOV	11.08.1996	**7**	**1**	2018: 30.01.2019->	*PFC CSKA Sofia* *Cagliari Calcio (ITA)*
Nikolay DIMITROV	15.10.1987	**9**	**1**	2018:	*FK Ural Yekaterinburg (RUS)*
Georgi ILIEV	05.09.1981	**25**	**2**	2019:	*PFC Cherno More Varna*
Galin IVANOV	15.04.1988	**6**	**1**	2018: 13.02.2019->	*PFC Slavia Sofia* *Szombathelyi Haladás VSE (HUN)*
Yanis KARABELYOV	23.01.1996	**1**	**0**	2019:	*PFC Slavia Sofia*
Georgi KOSTADINOV	07.09.1990	**19**	**3**	2018/2019:	*FK Arsenal Tula (RUS)*
Bozhidar KRAEV	23.06.1997	**9**	**2**	2018/2019:	*FC Midtjylland Herning (DEN)*
Kristiyan MALINOV	30.03.1994	**5**	**0**	2018/2019:	*PFC CSKA Sofia*
Georgi MILANOV	19.02.1992	**41**	**2**	2018/2019:	*MOL Vidi FC Székesfehérvár (HUN)*
Todor NEDELEV	0702.1993	**25**	**2**	2018/2019:	*PFC Botev Plovdiv*
Martin RAYNOV	25.04.1992	**7**	**0**	2018/2019:	*PFC Beroe Stara Zagora*
Georgi SARMOV	07.09.1985	**13**	**0**	2019:	*SFC Etar Veliko Tarnovo*
Simeon SLAVCHEV	25.09.1993	**24**	**0**	2018/2019:	*Qarabağ FK Bakı (AZE)*
Forwards					
Tsvetelin CHUNCHUKOV	26.12.1994	**2**	**0**	2018/2019:	*PFC Slavia Sofia*
Spas DELEV	22.09.1989	**24**	**2**	2018/2019:	*MKS Pogoń Szczeczin (POL)*
Ismail ISA Mustafa	26.06.1989	**2**	**1**	2019:	*FC Dunav Ruse 2010*
Stanislav KOSTOV	02.10.1991	**3**	**0**	2018/2019:	*PFC Levski Sofia*
Martin MINCHEV	22.04.2001	**3**	**0**	2019:	*PFC Cherno More Varna*
Ivelin POPOV	26.10.1987	**84**	**15**	2018: 24.01.2019->	*FK Spartak Moskva (RUS)* *FK Rostov-na-Donu (RUS)*
Radoslav VASILEV	12.10.1990	**6**	**1**	2018/2019:	*PFC Cherno More Varna*

National team coach

Petar HUBCHEV [07.10.2016 – 14.05.2019]	26.02.1964	20 M; 8 W; 5 D; 7 L; 22-25
Krasimir BALAKOV [from 01.06.2019]	29.03.1966	2 M; 1 W; 0 D; 1 L; 4-4

CROATIA

The Country:
Republika Hrvatska (Republic of Croatia)
Capital: Zagreb
Surface: 56,594 km²
Inhabitants: 4,154,200 [2017]
Time: UTC+1

The FA:
Hrvatski nogometni savez
Vukovarska 269A, 10000 Zagreb
Tel: +385 1 2361 555
Foundation date: 16.07.1941 (as Independent State of Croatia); 03.07.1992 (as Croatia)
Member of FIFA since: 1992
Member of UEFA since: 1993
Website: www.hns-cff.hr

NATIONAL TEAM RECORDS

First international match:	02.04.1940, Zagreb:	Croatia – Switzerland 4-0
Most international caps:	Darijo Srna	- 134 caps (2002-2016)
Most international goals:	Davor Šuker	- 45 goals / 69 caps (1990-2002)

UEFA EUROPEAN CHAMPIONSHIP	
1960	-
1964	-
1968	-
1972	-
1976	-
1980	-
1984	-
1988	-
1992	-
1996	Final Tournament (Quarter-Finals)
2000	Qualifiers
2004	Final Tournament (Group Stage)
2008	Final Tournament (Quarter-Finals)
2012	Final Tournament (Group Stage)
2016	Final Tournament (Group Stage)

FIFA WORLD CUP	
1930	-
1934	-
1938	-
1950	-
1954	-
1958	-
1962	-
1966	-
1970	-
1974	-
1978	-
1982	-
1986	-
1990	-
1994	*Did not enter*
1998	Final Tournament (3rd Place)
2002	Final Tournament (Group Stage)
2006	Final Tournament (Group Stage)
2010	Qualifiers
2014	Final Tournament (Group Stage)
2018	Final Tournament (Runners-up)

UEFA NATIONS LEAGUE
2018/2019 – League A

OLYMPIC FOOTBALL TOURNAMENTS 1908-2016							
1908	-	**1948**	-	**1972**	-	**1996**	Qualifiers
1912	-	**1952**	-	**1976**	-	**2000**	Qualifiers
1920	-	**1956**	-	**1980**	-	**2004**	Qualifiers
1924	-	**1960**	-	**1984**	-	**2008**	Qualifiers
1928	-	**1964**	-	**1988**	-	**2012**	Qualifiers
1936	-	**1968**	-	**1992**	-	**2016**	Qualifiers

FIFA CONFEDERATIONS CUP 1992-2017
None

CROATIAN CLUB HONOURS IN EUROPEAN CLUB COMPETITIONS:

European Champion Clubs' Cup (1956-1992) / UEFA Champions League (1993-2019)		
None		
Fairs Cup (1858-1971) / UEFA Cup (1972-2009) / UEFA Europa League (2010-2019)		
GNK Dinamo Zagreb*	**1**	1966/1967
**represented Yugoslavia*		
UEFA Super Cup (1972-2019)		
None		
European Cup Winners' Cup 1961-1999*		
None		

**defunct competition*

NATIONAL COMPETITIONS
TABLE OF HONOURS

	CHAMPIONS	CUP WINNERS	BEST GOALSCORERS	
1992	HNK Hajduk Split	NK Inter Zaprešić	Ardian Kozniku (HNK Hajduk Split)	12
1992/1993	NK Croatia Zagreb	HNK Hajduk Split	Goran Vlaović (NK Croatia Zagreb)	23
1993/1994	HNK Hajduk Split	NK Croatia Zagreb	Goran Vlaović (NK Croatia Zagreb)	29
1994/1995	HNK Hajduk Split	HNK Hajduk Split	Robert Špehar (NK Osijek)	23
1995/1996	NK Croatia Zagreb	NK Croatia Zagreb	Igor Cvitanović (NK Croatia Zagreb)	19
1996/1997	NK Croatia Zagreb	NK Croatia Zagreb	Igor Cvitanović (NK Croatia Zagreb)	20
1997/1998	NK Croatia Zagreb	NK Croatia Zagreb	Mate Baturina (NK Zagreb)	18
1998/1999	NK Croatia Zagreb	NK Osijek	Joško Popović (HNK Šibenik)	21
1999/2000	GNK Dinamo Zagreb	HNK Hajduk Split	Tomo Šokota (GNK Dinamo Zagreb)	21
2000/2001	HNK Hajduk Split	GNK Dinamo Zagreb	Tomo Šokota (GNK Dinamo Zagreb)	20
2001/2002	NK Zagreb	GNK Dinamo Zagreb	Ivica Olić (NK Zagreb)	21
2002/2003	GNK Dinamo Zagreb	HNK Hajduk Split	Ivica Olić (GNK Dinamo Zagreb)	16
2003/2004	HNK Hajduk Split	GNK Dinamo Zagreb	Robert Špehar (NK Osijek)	18
2004/2005	HNK Hajduk Split	HNK Rijeka	Tomislav Erceg (HNK Rijeka)	17
2005/2006	GNK Dinamo Zagreb	HNK Rijeka	Ivan Bošnjak (GNK Dinamo Zagreb)	22
2006/2007	GNK Dinamo Zagreb	GNK Dinamo Zagreb	Eduardo (GNK Dinamo Zagreb)	34
2007/2008	GNK Dinamo Zagreb	GNK Dinamo Zagreb	Želimir Terkeš (BIH, NK Zadar)	21
2008/2009	GNK Dinamo Zagreb	GNK Dinamo Zagreb	Mario Mandžukić (GNK Dinamo Zagreb)	16
2009/2010	GNK Dinamo Zagreb	HNK Hajduk Split	Davor Vugrinec (NK Zagreb)	18
2010/2011	GNK Dinamo Zagreb	GNK Dinamo Zagreb	Ivan Krstanović (BIH, NK Zagreb)	19
2011/2012	GNK Dinamo Zagreb	GNK Dinamo Zagreb	Fatos Bećiraj (MNE, GNK Dinamo Zagreb)	15
2012/2013	GNK Dinamo Zagreb	HNK Hajduk Split	Leon Benko (HNK Rijeka)	19
2013/2014	GNK Dinamo Zagreb	HNK Rijeka	Duje Čop (GNK Dinamo Zagreb)	22
2014/2015	GNK Dinamo Zagreb	GNK Dinamo Zagreb	Andrej Kramarić (HNK Rijeka)	21
2015/2016	GNK Dinamo Zagreb	GNK Dinamo Zagreb	Ilija Nestorovski (MKD, NK Inter Zaprešić)	25
2016/2017	HNK Rijeka	HNK Rijeka	Márkó Futács (HUN, HNK Hajduk Split)	18
2017/2018	GNK Dinamo Zagreb	GNK Dinamo Zagreb	El Arabi Hillel Soudani (ALG, GNK Dinamo Zagreb)	17
2018/2019	GNK Dinamo Zagreb	HNK Rijeka	Mijo Caktaš (HNK Hajduk Split)	19

Please note: GNK Dinamo Zagreb were called NK Croatia Zagreb between 1993 and 2000.

NATIONAL CHAMPIONSHIP
Hrvatski Telekom Prva liga 2018/2019
(27.07.2018 – 26.05.2019)

Results

Round 1 [27-29.07.2018]
Dinamo Zagreb - NK Rudeš 1-1(0-1)
Lokomotiva Zagreb - Inter Zaprešić 4-0(3-0)
HNK Rijeka - HNK Gorica 2-0(2-0)
NK Istra 1961 - Slaven Belupo 1-1(0-0)
NK Osijek - Hajduk Split 4-1(2-1)

Round 2 [03-05.08.2018]
HNK Rijeka - Inter Zaprešić 4-0(1-0)
Dinamo Zagreb - NK Istra 1961 3-0(2-0)
HNK Gorica - Slaven Belupo 3-3(0-0)
NK Osijek - NK Rudeš 3-2(2-0)
Hajduk Split - Lokomotiva Zagreb 1-1(1-0)

Round 3 [10-12.08.2018]
Dinamo Zagreb - Slaven Belupo 2-1(2-0)
HNK Gorica - Inter Zaprešić 2-3(1-1)
Lokomotiva Zagreb - NK Rudeš 1-0(0-0)
NK Osijek - NK Istra 1961 3-0(0-0)
HNK Rijeka - Hajduk Split 1-1(0-0)

Round 4 [17-19.08.2018]
Dinamo Zagreb - NK Osijek 2-1(1-0)
NK Istra 1961 - Lokomotiva Zagreb 1-2(0-1)
NK Rudeš - HNK Rijeka 1-2(1-2)
Hajduk Split - HNK Gorica 0-2(0-2)
Slaven Bel. - Inter Zaprešić 2-1(1-0) [08.09.]

Round 5 [24-26.08.2018]
NK Osijek - Slaven Belupo 1-1(0-0)
HNK Gorica - NK Rudeš 2-0(1-0)
Dinamo Zagreb - Lokomotiva Zagreb 1-0(0-0)
Inter Zaprešić - Hajduk Split 2-2(1-0)
HNK Rijeka - NK Istra 1961 3-3(2-2)

Round 6 [31.08.-02.09.2018]
Inter Zaprešić - NK Rudeš 3-0(3-0)
Slaven Belupo - Hajduk Split 1-1(1-1)
NK Osijek - Lokomotiva Zagreb 2-1(1-0)
NK Istra 1961 - HNK Gorica 0-2(0-0)
Dinamo Zagreb - HNK Rijeka 1-1(1-1)

Round 7 [14-16.09.2018]
Inter Zaprešić - NK Istra 1961 1-2(0-1)
HNK Gorica - Dinamo Zagreb 0-1(0-0)
Hajduk Split - NK Rudeš 3-1(1-0)
Slaven Belupo - Lokomotiva Zagreb 2-5(0-2)
HNK Rijeka - NK Osijek 1-1(0-0)

Round 8 [21-23.09.2018]
Slaven Belupo - NK Rudeš 1-1(0-0)
NK Osijek - HNK Gorica 0-1(0-0)
Lokomotiva Zagreb - HNK Rijeka 2-0(1-0)
Dinamo Zagreb - Inter Zaprešić 5-3(1-0)
NK Istra 1961 - Hajduk Split 2-4(1-3)

Round 9 [29.09.-01.10.2018]
Hajduk Split - Dinamo Zagreb 0-0
Inter Zaprešić - NK Osijek 0-3(0-0)
HNK Gorica - Lokomotiva Zagreb 0-3(0-1)
HNK Rijeka - Slaven Belupo 0-0
NK Rudeš - NK Istra 1961 0-3(0-2)

Round 10 [05-07.10.2018]
Inter Zaprešić - Lokomotiva Zagreb 2-1(1-1)
HNK Gorica - HNK Rijeka 2-1(0-1)
Slaven Belupo - NK Istra 1961 3-1(1-0)
NK Rudeš - Dinamo Zagreb 0-3(0-2)
Hajduk Split - NK Osijek 0-2(0-1)

Round 11 [19-21.10.2018]
Inter Zaprešić - HNK Rijeka 1-2(0-1)
NK Rudeš - NK Osijek 1-4(1-0)
NK Istra 1961 - Dinamo Zagreb 1-4(1-1)
Slaven Belupo - HNK Gorica 0-1(0-0)
Lokomotiva Zagreb - Hajduk Split 2-0(1-0)

Round 12 [26-28.10.2018]
NK Rudeš - Lokomotiva Zagreb 0-4(0-0)
Inter Zaprešić - HNK Gorica 1-3(1-2)
NK Istra 1961 - NK Osijek 1-1(0-1)
Hajduk Split - HNK Rijeka 1-1(1-0)
Slaven Belupo - Dinamo Zagreb 0-2(0-0)

Round 13 [03-05.11.2018]
Lokomotiva Zagreb - NK Istra 1961 1-0(1-0)
HNK Gorica - Hajduk Split 1-1(1-1)
NK Osijek - Dinamo Zagreb 0-2(0-0)
Inter Zaprešić - Slaven Belupo 0-0
HNK Rijeka - NK Rudeš 5-1(2-1)

Round 14 [09-11.11.2018]
NK Rudeš - HNK Gorica 0-1(0-0)
Slaven Belupo - NK Osijek 0-2(0-0)
Hajduk Split - Inter Zaprešić 3-0(1-0)
NK Istra 1961 - HNK Rijeka 1-2(0-2)
Lokomotiva Zagreb - Dinamo Zagreb 0-1(0-1)

Round 15 [23-25.11.2018]
NK Rudeš - Inter Zaprešić 0-1(0-0)
HNK Rijeka - Dinamo Zagreb 1-0(0-0)
HNK Gorica - NK Istra 1961 0-2(0-0)
Hajduk Split - Slaven Belupo 2-2(1-1)
Lokomotiva Zagreb - NK Osijek 2-2(1-1)

Round 16 [30.11.-02.12.2018]
NK Istra 1961 - Inter Zaprešić 0-2(0-1)
Lokomotiva Zagreb - Slaven Belupo 1-1(0-0)
NK Osijek - HNK Rijeka 1-2(1-1)
NK Rudeš - Hajduk Split 1-4(0-2)
Dinamo Zagreb - HNK Gorica 1-0(0-0)

Round 17 [08-10.12.2018]
HNK Rijeka - Lokomotiva Zagreb 3-0(1-0)
Hajduk Split - NK Istra 1961 3-1(0-0)
Inter Zaprešić - Dinamo Zagreb 0-2(0-1)
HNK Gorica - NK Osijek 1-2(1-1)
NK Rudeš - Slaven Belupo 1-1(0-1)

Round 18 [14-16.12.2018]
Lokomotiva Zagreb - HNK Gorica 2-2(1-1)
NK Osijek - Inter Zaprešić 6-0(3-0)
Dinamo Zagreb - Hajduk Split 1-0(0-0)
NK Istra 1961 - NK Rudeš 1-0(0-0)
Slaven Bel. - NK Rijeka 1-1(0-0) [30.01.2019]

Round 19 [01-03.02.2019]
Lokomotiva Zagreb - Inter Zaprešić 2-0(0-0)
Dinamo Zagreb - NK Rudeš 7-2(4-1)
NK Istra 1961 - Slaven Belupo 1-1(0-0)
NK Osijek - Hajduk Split 0-1(0-0)
HNK Rijeka - HNK Gorica 1-3(1-1)

Round 20 [08-10.02.2019]
NK Rudeš - NK Osijek 0-1(0-0)
Slaven Belupo - HNK Gorica 2-0(2-0)
Dinamo Zagreb - NK Istra 1961 1-0(0-0)
Inter Zaprešić - HNK Rijeka 0-3(0-0)
Hajduk Split - Lokomotiva Zagreb 2-1(1-0)

Round 21 [15-17.02.2019]
Lokomotiva Zagreb - NK Rudeš 0-0
HNK Rijeka - Hajduk Split 0-0
HNK Gorica - Inter Zaprešić 2-2(1-2)
NK Osijek - NK Istra 1961 1-0(0-0)
Dinamo Zagreb - Slaven Belupo 3-0(0-0)

Round 22 [22-24.02.2019]
NK Rudeš - HNK Rijeka 2-4(1-2)
Slaven Belupo - Inter Zaprešić 0-1(0-0)
Hajduk Split - HNK Gorica 0-0
NK Istra 1961 - Lokomotiva Zagreb 0-0
Dinamo Zagreb - NK Osijek 3-0(2-0)

Round 23 [01-03.03.2019]
HNK Rijeka - NK Istra 1961 2-0(1-0)
HNK Gorica - NK Rudeš 3-1(3-0)
Lokomotiva Zagreb - Dinamo Zagreb 1-1(0-0)
Inter Zaprešić - Hajduk Split 1-3(0-2)
NK Osijek - Slaven Belupo 1-1(1-0)

Round 24 [08-10.03.2019]
NK Rudeš - Inter Zaprešić 2-0(0-0)
Slaven Belupo - Hajduk Split 1-2(0-0)
NK Istra 1961 - HNK Gorica 0-3(0-1)
NK Osijek - Lokomotiva Zagreb 1-1(0-1)
Dinamo Zagreb - HNK Rijeka 3-1(1-1)

Round 25 [15-17.03.2019]
Inter Zaprešić - NK Istra 1961 3-1(1-1)
Lokomotiva Zagreb - Slaven Belupo 3-1(1-1)
Hajduk Split - NK Rudeš 3-0(1-0)
HNK Gorica - Dinamo Zagreb 1-2(0-1)
HNK Rijeka - NK Osijek 3-1(2-0)

Round 26 [28-30.03.2019]
Slaven Belupo - NK Rudeš 2-1(2-1)
NK Osijek - HNK Gorica 2-2(0-1)
Lokomotiva Zagreb - HNK Rijeka 1-2(0-1)
Dinamo Zagreb - Inter Zaprešić 1-0(1-0)
NK Istra 1961 - Hajduk Split 0-2(0-1)

Round 27 [02-04.04.2019]
HNK Gorica - Lokomotiva Zagreb 0-2(0-1)
HNK Rijeka - Slaven Belupo 2-0(1-0)
Inter Zaprešić - NK Osijek 1-3(1-1)
Hajduk Split - Dinamo Zagreb 0-1(0-1)
NK Rudeš - NK Istra 1961 1-0(1-0)

Round 28 [06-08.04.2019]
Inter Zaprešić - Lokomotiva Zagreb 3-2(1-2)
HNK Gorica - HNK Rijeka 1-0(0-0)
NK Rudeš - Dinamo Zagreb 0-2(0-0)
Hajduk Split - NK Osijek 0-0
Slaven Belupo - NK Istra 1961 3-3(1-1)

Round 29 [12-14.04.2019]
NK Osijek - NK Rudeš 2-0(2-0)
NK Istra 1961 - Dinamo Zagreb 0-4(0-2)
HNK Rijeka - Inter Zaprešić 7-0(3-0)
HNK Gorica - Slaven Belupo 4-3(3-1)
Lokomotiva Zagreb - Hajduk Split 0-1(0-0)

Round 30 [19-20.04.2019]
NK Istra 1961 - NK Osijek 1-0(0-0)
Slaven Belupo - Dinamo Zagreb 0-1(0-0)
NK Rudeš - Lokomotiva Zagreb 1-2(1-1)
Inter Zaprešić - HNK Gorica 2-2(1-1)
Hajduk Split - HNK Rijeka 4-0(3-0)

Round 31 [26-28.04.2019]
Lokomotiva Zagreb - NK Istra 1961 1-1(1-0)
HNK Gorica - Hajduk Split 3-0(2-0)
NK Osijek - Dinamo Zagreb 2-1(1-1)
Inter Zaprešić - Slaven Belupo 1-3(0-1)
HNK Rijeka - NK Rudeš 3-1(2-1)

Round 32 [03-05.05.2019]
NK Rudeš - HNK Gorica 1-1(0-1)
Hajduk Split - Inter Zaprešić 3-2(2-1)
NK Istra 1961 - HNK Rijeka 0-7(0-2)
Slaven Belupo - NK Osijek 1-0(1-0)
Dinamo Zagreb - Lokomotiva Zagreb 3-0(0-0)

Round 33 [09-11.05.2019]
Inter Zaprešić - NK Rudeš 0-3(0-2)
HNK Gorica - NK Istra 1961 4-1(0-1)
Hajduk Split - Slaven Belupo 2-0(0-0)
Lokomotiva Zagreb - NK Osijek 0-4(0-1)
HNK Rijeka - Dinamo Zagreb 0-0

Round 34 [14-15.05.2019]
NK Istra 1961 - Inter Zaprešić 0-1(0-1)
NK Rudeš - Hajduk Split 1-4(0-1)
Slaven Belupo - Lokomotiva Zagreb 1-1(0-0)
Dinamo Zagreb - HNK Gorica 3-1(2-1)
NK Osijek - HNK Rijeka 2-1(1-1)

Round 35 [18-20.05.2019]
Inter Zaprešić - Dinamo Zagreb 2-3(2-2)
HNK Rijeka - Lokomotiva Zagreb 1-0(1-0)
Hajduk Split - NK Istra 1961 4-1(0-1)
HNK Gorica - NK Osijek 1-0(0-0)
NK Rudeš - Slaven Belupo 0-1(0-0)

Round 36 [24-26.05.2019]
NK Istra 1961 - NK Rudeš 2-0(0-0)
Slaven Belupo - HNK Rijeka 1-1(0-0)
Lokomotiva Zagreb - HNK Gorica 2-3(0-1)
NK Osijek - Inter Zaprešić 3-1(1-1)
Dinamo Zagreb - Hajduk Split 3-1(1-0)

Final Standings

1.	**GNK Dinamo Zagreb**	36	29	5	2	74	-	20	92
2.	HNK Rijeka	36	19	10	7	70	-	36	67
3.	NK Osijek	36	18	8	10	61	-	36	62
4.	HNK Hajduk Split	36	17	11	8	59	-	39	62
5.	HNK Gorica	36	17	8	11	57	-	46	59
6.	NK Lokomotiva Zagreb	36	13	10	13	51	-	43	49
7.	NK Slaven Belupo Koprivnica	36	7	16	13	41	-	53	37
8.	HNK Inter Zaprešić	36	9	4	23	40	-	84	31
9.	NK Istra 1961 Pula (*Relegation Play-offs*)	36	6	7	23	31	-	73	25
10.	NK Rudeš (*Relegated*)	36	3	5	28	26	-	80	14

Top goalscorers:

19 Mijo Caktaš
HNK Hajduk Split

18 Mirko Marić
NK Osijek

16 Jakov Puljić
HNK Rijeka

Relegation Play-offs [31.05.-03.06.2019]

HNK Šibenik - NK Istra 1961 Pula 1-1(1-1) 0-2(0.1)

NK Istra 1961 Pula remains at First Level.

NATIONAL CUP
Hrvatski nogometni kup 2018/2019

Preliminary Round [18/21/28/29.08.2018]

HNK Primorac Biograd na Moru - NK Zagora Unešić	3-1(0-1)	NK Križevci - NK Rovinj	2-0(0-0)
NK Rudar Labin - NK Krk	0-3(0-1)	NK Zagorec Krapina - NK Libertas Novska	9-0(4-0)
NK Nehaj Senj - NK Graničar Županja	4-1(2-1)	NK Višnjevac - NK Vrapce	1-2(0-1)
NK Hrvatski Dragovoljac - NK Varaždin ŠN	0-3(0-1)	NK BSK Bijelo Brdo - NK Vukovar 91	0-0 aet; 3-4 pen
NK Bednja Beletinec - NK Pitomača	2-0(2-0)	NK Jadran Luka Ploče - NK Bjelovar	1-0(0-0)
HNK Suhopolje - NK Kurilovec	2-3(0-1)	NK Međimurje - NK Sava Strmec	5-0(0-0)
NK Slavija Pleternica - HNK Segesta	1-0(0-0)	NK Nedelišće - NK Sloga Nova Gradiška	2-4(0-2)
NK Koprivnica - HNK Sloga Mravince	1-3(1-0)	NK Karlovac - NK Marsonia	1-2(1-0)

First Round [18/19/25/26.09.2018]

NK Bednja Beletinec - NK Inter Zaprešić	0-3(0-2)	HNK Primorac Biograd - NK Lokomotiva Zagreb	0-1(0-1)
NK Zagorec Krapina - NK Osijek	0-3(0-1)	NK Sloga Nova Gradiška - NK Istra 1961 Pula	2-4(0-0)
NK Kurilovec - NK Slaven Belupo Koprivnica	0-2(0-0)	NK Krk - HNK Cibalia Vinkovci	1-0(1-0)
NK Vukovar 91 - NK Zadar	3-5(2-3, 3-3)	NK Slavija Pleternica - NK Vinogradar	0-4(0-2)
HNK Sloga Mravince - GNK Dinamo Zagreb	0-1(0-0)	NK Marsonia - NK Zagreb	3-0(1-0)
NK Križevci - HNK Rijeka	0-9(0-5)	NK Nehaj Senj - HNK Šibenik	2-2 aet; 2-4 pen
NK Vrapce - HNK Hajduk Split	0-2(0-0)	NK Zelina - NK GOŠK Dubrovnik	2-0(0-0)
NK Jadran Luka Ploče - RNK Split	3-1(1-0)	NK Varaždin ŠN - NK Međimurje	2-0(2-0)

1/8-Finals [31.10.2018]

NK Zadar - NK Lokomotiva Zagreb	1-3(1-2)	NK Vinogradar - NK Jadran Luka Ploče	4-2(2-1)
NK Inter Zaprešić - NK Istra 1961 Pula	2-1(1-1)	NK Krk - NK Osijek	1-5(1-3)
NK Zelina - GNK Dinamo Zagreb	0-4(0-1)	HNK Šibenik - HNK Hajduk Split	1-2(1-0, 1-1)
NK Marsonia - NK Slaven Belupo Koprivnica	0-1(0-0)	NK Varaždin ŠN - HNK Rijeka	1-2(1-1)

Quarter-Finals [04-05.12.2018]

NK Inter Zaprešić - NK Vinogradar	3-0(2-0)	NK Osijek - HNK Hajduk Split	2-1(2-0)
NK Lokomotiva Zagreb - HNK Rijeka	1-2(1-0)	GNK Dinamo Zagreb - NK Slaven Belupo Koprivnica	1-0(1-0)

Semi-Finals [23-24.04.2019]

GNK Dinamo Zagreb - NK Osijek	2-0(1-0)	NK Inter Zaprešić - HNK Rijeka	1-2(0-1)

Final

22.05.2019; Stadion "Aldo Drosina", Pula; Referee: Damir Batinić; Attendance: 6,742
HNK Rijeka - GNK Dinamo Zagreb **3-1(2-0)**

HNK Rijeka: Simon Sluga, Roberto Punčec, Dario Župarić, João Rodrigo Pereira Escoval, Ivan Tomečak, Ivan Lepinjica (75.Stjepan Lončar), Tibor Halilović (80.Alexander Gorgon), Domagoj Pavičić, Luka Capan, Zoran Kvržić (Cap), Antonio Čolak (83.Jakov Puljić). Trainer: Igor Bišćan.

Dinamo Zagreb: Dominik Livaković, Kévin Théophile-Catherine (78.Izet Hajrović), Emir Dilaver, Petar Stojanović, Amir Rrahmani (46.Marin Leovac), Arijan Ademi (Cap), Ivan Šunjić, Daniel Olmo Carvajal „Dani Olmo",Iyayi Believe Atiemwen (46.Mario Gavranović), Mislav Oršić, Bruno Petković. Trainer: Nenad Bjelica.

Goals: 1-0 Antonio Čolak (13), 2-0 Tibor Halilović (39), 2-1 Mislav Oršić (63), 3-1 Zoran Kvržić (84).

Građanski nogometni klub Dinamo Zagreb

Founded: 09.06.1945
Stadium: Stadion Maksimir, Zagreb (35,123)

Goalkeepers:	**DOB**	**M**	**(s)**	**G**
Dominik Livaković	09.01.1995	21		
Adrian Šemper	12.01.1998	1		
Daniel Zagorac	07.02.1987	14		
Defenders:	**DOB**	**M**	**(s)**	**G**
Emir Dilaver (AUT)	07.05.1991	17	(1)	
Jan Lecjaks (CZE)	09.08.1990	1		
Marin Leovac	07.08.1988	12		2
Marko Lešković	27.04.1991	18		2
Mario Musa	06.07.1990	9	(3)	1
Dino Perić	12.07.1994	21	(1)	2
Amir Rrahmani (KVX)	24.02.1994	14	(1)	3
Petar Stojanović (SVN)	07.10.1995	17	(1)	
Kévin Théophile-Catherine (FRA)	28.10.1989	14		1
Midfielders:	**DOB**	**M**	**(s)**	**G**
Arijan Ademi (MKD)	29.05.1991	13	(2)	2
Daniel Olmo Carvajal „Dani Olmo" (ESP)	07.05.1998	16	(9)	8
Tongo Hamed Doumbia (MLI)	06.08.1989		(1)	
Marko Đira	05.05.1999		(2)	
Ivan Fiolić	29.04.1996	2		
Amer Gojak (BIH)	13.02.1997	19	(6)	2
Damian Kądzior (POL)	16.06.1992	19	(9)	6
Bojan Knežević	28.01.1997	3	(2)	
Lovro Majer	17.01.1998	8	(2)	1
Sadegh Moharrami (IRN)	01.03.1996	18	(1)	
Nikola Moro	12.03.1998	18	(1)	3
Mislav Oršić	29.12.1992	17	(7)	6
Ivan Šunjić	09.10.1996	22	(2)	
Forwards:	**DOB**	**M**	**(s)**	**G**
Komnen Andrić (SRB)	01.07.1995	7	(7)	4
Iyayi Believe Atiemwen (NGA)	24.01.1996	9	(2)	1
Mario Budimir	12.02.1986	4	(4)	5
Mario Gavranović (SUI)	24.11.1989	16	(8)	9
Izet Hajrović (BIH)	04.08.1991	12	(5)	4
Armin Hodžić (BIH)	17.11.1994	2		1
Antonio Marin	09.01.2001	2	(5)	
Luka Menalo (BIH)	22.07.1996	2	(8)	
Bruno Petković	16.09.1994	16	(9)	9
Mario Šitum	04.04.1992	12	(7)	2
Trainer:	**DOB**	**M**		
Nenad Bjelica	20.08.1971	36		

Hrvatski Nogometni Klub Gorica

Founded: 16.07.2009 (*as merger of NK Radnik Velika Gorica and NK Polet Buševec*)
Stadium: Stadion Gradski, Velika Gorica (5,000)

Goalkeepers:	**DOB**	**M**	**(s)**	**G**
Kristijan Kahlina (SVN)	24.07.1992	36		
Defenders:	**DOB**	**M**	**(s)**	**G**
Marijan Čabraja	25.02.1997	25	(1)	1
Igor Čagalj	08.10.1982	28		
Krešimir Krizmanić	03.07.2000		(1)	
Nemanja Ljubisavljević (SRB)	26.11.1996		(3)	
Giorgi Mchedlishvili (GEO)	18.01.1992	19	(3)	
Nasiru Moro (GHA)	24.09.1996	4	(1)	
Musa Muhammed Shehu (NGA)	31.10.1996	19	(7)	1
Godfrey Itama Oboabona (NGA)	16.08.1990	13	(1)	
Adrian Zenko	04.04.1998		(3)	
Damir Žutić	22.07.1993	2	(3)	
Midfielders:	**DOB**	**M**	**(s)**	**G**
Ronaldo Octavian Andrei Deaconu (ROU)	13.05.1997		(5)	
Aleksandar Jovičić (BIH)	18.07.1995	26	(1)	
Kristijan Lovrić	01.12.1995	23	(7)	10
Martin Maloča	21.03.1990	22	(5)	
Mario Marina (BIH)	03.08.1989	28	(2)	2
Michał Masłowski (POL)	19.12.1989	5	(5)	
Dinko Matošević	14.08.1997		(3)	
Farouk Miya (UGA)	26.11.1997	22	(8)	5
Matija Špičić	24.02.1988	12	(3)	
Martin Šroler (SVN)	20.06.1905	2	(11)	
Joey Suk (NED)	08.07.1989	25	(2)	5
Forwards:	**DOB**	**M**	**(s)**	**G**
David Arshakyan (ARM)	16.08.1994		(4)	
Iyayi Believe Atiemwen (NGA)	24.01.1996	17		7
Marko Dabro	28.03.1997		(3)	
Matija Dvorneković	01.01.1989	24	(9)	4
Justin Mathieu (NED)	12.04.1996	2	(7)	
Cherif Ndiaye (SEN)	23.01.1996	10	(7)	8
Łukasz Zwoliński (POL)	24.02.1993	32	(1)	14
Trainer:	**DOB**	**M**		
Sergej Jakirović (BIH)	23.12.1976			

Hrvatski nogometni klub Hajduk Split

Founded: 13.02.1911
Stadium: Stadion Poljud, Split (34,198)

Goalkeepers:	**DOB**	**M**	**(s)**	**G**
Goran Blažević	07.06.1986	4	(1)	
Tomislav Duka	07.09.1992	1		
Marin Ljubić	18.10.1997	2	(1)	
Josip Posavec	10.03.1996	29		
Defenders:	**DOB**	**M**	**(s)**	**G**
Borja López Menéndez (ESP)	02.02.1994	22	(1)	
Domagoj Bradarić	10.12.1999	21	(1)	
André Fomitschow (GER)	07.09.1990	11	(5)	
Ardian Ismajli (ALB)	30.09.1996	20		1
Josip Juranović	16.08.1995	22		
Zoran Nižić	11.10.1989	1		1
Oleksandr Svatok (UKR)	27.09.1994	10		
Stipe Vučur (AUT)	22.05.1992	14		1
Midfielders:	**DOB**	**M**	**(s)**	**G**
Hamza Barry (GAM)	15.10.1994	23	(3)	1
Toma Bašić	25.11.1996	1		
Dino Beširević (BIH)	31.01.1994	1	(2)	
Mijo Caktaš	08.05.1992	28		19
Steliano Filip (ROU)	15.05.1994	4	(2)	
Bassel Jradi (DEN)	06.07.1993	18	(7)	2
Stanko Jurić	16.08.1996	14	(10)	3
Anthony Kalik (AUS)	05.11.1997	3	(6)	
Darko Nejašmić	25.01.1999	20	(1)	1
Ante Palaversa	06.04.2000	21	(6)	2
Forwards:	**DOB**	**M**	**(s)**	**G**
Ivan Delić	29.09.1998	2	(6)	
Ádám Gyurcsó (HUN)	06.03.1991	21	(10)	4
Mirko Ivanovski (MKD)	31.10.1989	12	(8)	5
Jairo De Macedo Da Silva (BRA)	06.05.1992	33	(2)	13
Franko Kovačević	08.08.1999		(1)	
Božo Mikulić	29.01.1997	7	(1)	
Emir Sahiti (ALB)	29.11.1998		(4)	
Said Ahmed Said (GHA)	20.04.1993	7	(4)	3
Michele Šego	05.08.2000		(5)	
Edin Šehić (BIH)	03.02.1995	2	(1)	
Dario Špikić	22.03.1999		(1)	
Francesco Tahiraj (ALB)	21.09.1996	6	(5)	
Tonio Teklić	09.09.1999		(4)	
Fran Tudor	27.09.1995	16	(8)	1
Trainer:	**DOB**	**M**		
Željko Kopić	10.09.1977	6		
Zoran Vulić [09.09.2018]	04.10.1961	9		
Siniša Oreščanin [27.11.2018]	30.07.1972	21		

Nogometni Klub Inter Zaprešić

Founded: 25.06.1929 *(as NK Sava)*
Stadium: Stadion ŠRC Zaprešić, Zaprešić (5,228)

Goalkeepers:	**DOB**	**M**	**(s)**	**G**
Ivan Kelava	20.02.1988	14		
Mladen Matković	12.05.1989	22		
Defenders:	**DOB**	**M**	**(s)**	**G**
Antonio Bosec	28.08.1997	28	(2)	
Jurica Buljat	12.09.1986	7		
Ivan Čeliković	10.04.1989	19	(2)	
Vedran Dalić	19.09.1995	3		
Ivan Nekić	24.12.2000	1	(2)	
Herdi Prenga (ALB)	31.08.1994	13		
Andrej Šimunec	02.03.1995	24	(1)	2
Ivan Tatomirović (SRB)	11.01.1989	9		
Tomislav Valentić	04.06.1994	19	(2)	
Midfielders:	**DOB**	**M**	**(s)**	**G**
Mihael Benčić	25.06.2001		(2)	
Josip Brezovec	12.03.1986	16	(1)	
Marko Burzanović (MNE)	13.01.1998	7	(1)	1
Jasmin Čeliković (BIH)	07.01.1999	18	(4)	
Milan Čulum (SRB)	28.10.1984	5	(4)	
Tomislav Haramustek	17.07.1993	8	(4)	
Juraj Ljubić	26.05.2000		(5)	
Steven Luštica (AUS)	12.04.1991		(7)	
Robert Mišković (GER)	20.10.1999		(12)	
Karlo Muhar	17.01.1996	31	(3)	2
Igor Postonjski	04.02.1995	26	(4)	3
Borislav Tsonev (BUL)	29.04.1995	8	(5)	4
Forwards:	**DOB**	**M**	**(s)**	**G**
Goodness Ohiremen Ajayi (NGA)	06.10.1994	10	(6)	2
Komnen Andrić (SRB)	01.07.1995	15	(2)	10
Antonini Čulina	27.01.1992	9	(3)	
Andrija Kaluđerović (SRB)	05.07.1987	7	(1)	
Ivan Mamut	30.04.1997	10	(11)	4
Nikola Rak	29.08.1987	25	(5)	1
Serder Serderov (RUS)	10.03.1994	18		7
Theophilus Solomon (NGA)	18.01.1996	5	(2)	1
Matej Vuk	10.06.2000	5	(7)	
Marko Vukčević (MNE)	07.06.1993	12	(4)	1
Marin Žulim	26.10.1991	2	(3)	
Trainer:	**DOB**	**M**		
Samir Toplak	23.04.1970	36		

Nogometni Klub Istra 1961 Pula

Founded: 1948
Stadium: Stadion "Aldo Drosina", Pula (9,800)

Goalkeepers:	**DOB**	**M**	**(s)**	**G**
Josip Čondrić	27.08.1993	31		
Ioritz Landeta (ESP)	10.10.1995	5		
Defenders:	**DOB**	**M**	**(s)**	**G**
Petar Bosančić	19.04.1996	23		
Tomislav Čuljak	25.05.1987	6	(1)	
Einar Galilea Azaceta (ESP)	22.05.1995	10	(2)	
Martin Franić	13.01.1997	12	(2)	
Marin Grujević	23.12.1991	25	(2)	1
Julio César Rodríguez López (ESP)	07.12.1995	21	(1)	2
Maicon De Silva Moreira (BRA)	10.03.1993	4	(5)	
Daniel Arnaud N'Di (CMR)	18.08.1995	8	(3)	2
Tomás Alexis Oneto (ARG)	19.02.1998	10		
Markus Pavic (AUT)	26.03.1995	14	(1)	1
Hisa Ramadani (ALB)	13.04.1999	1	(1)	
Kévin Rimane (GYF)	23.02.1991	8	(1)	
Petar Rubić	03.07.1998	14	(4)	1
Agron Rufati (MKD)	06.04.1999	15	(1)	
Nicolas Senzemba (FRA)	25.03.1996	3		
Midfielders:	**DOB**	**M**	**(s)**	**G**
Agustín Ezequiel Cardozo (ARG)	30.05.1997	12	(1)	
Michel Espinosa (FRA)	15.09.1993	5	(3)	
Antonio Ivančić	25.05.1995	15	(2)	2
Kim Young-Gyu (KOR)	04.01.1995		(2)	
Stefan Lončar (MNE)	19.02.1996	11	(3)	
Madger Antonio Gomes Ajú (ESP)	01.02.1997	5		
Octavio Andrés Páez Gil (VEN)	28.02.2000	1	(2)	
Obeng Regan (GHA)	15.08.1994	26	(3)	4
José Luis Rodríguez Francis (PAN)	19.06.1998	8		
Forwards:	**DOB**	**M**	**(s)**	**G**
Adrián Fuentes González (ESP)	17.07.1996	8	(9)	4
Bruno Sávio da Silva (BRA)	01.08.1994	4	(5)	
Toni Burić	29.11.2000	5	(1)	
Jonathan Elias Caicedo Valencia (ECU)	25.12.1996	1	(5)	
Daniel Iglesias Gago (ESP)	18.08.1995	10	(10)	1
Karolis Laukžemis (LTU)	11.03.1992	5	(6)	1
Ramón Nazareno Miérez (ARG)	13.05.1997	19	(3)	9
Vice Miljanić	30.05.1998	2		
Arturo Segado Muñoz (ESP)	17.04.1997	9	(5)	
Michaël Jordan N'Kololo (COD)	09.11.1992	1	(1)	
Robert Perić-Komšić	30.03.1999	7	(9)	3
Goran Roce	12.04.1986	1	(1)	
Arona Sané (SEN)	21.06.1995	21	(2)	
Mohamady Traoré Diarra (ESP)	29.11.1994	10	(4)	
Luis Alfredo Vila (ARG)	06.03.1992		(6)	
Trainer:	**DOB**	**M**		
Manuel Márquez Roca (ESP)	07.09.1968	7		
Cristóbal Emilio "Curro" Torres Ruiz (ESP) [20.09.2018]	27.12.1976	5		
Krunoslav Rendulić [28.10.2018]	26.09.1973	11		
Igor Cvitanović [04.03.2019]	01.11.1970	13		

Nogometni klub Lokomotiva Zagreb

Founded: 01.05.1914 *(as ŽŠK Victoria Zagreb)*
Stadium: Stadion u Kranjčevićevoj ulici, Zagreb (8,850)

Goalkeepers:	**DOB**	**M**	**(s)**	**G**
Ivo Grbić	18.01.1996	36		
Krunoslav Hendija	19.03.1989		(1)	
Defenders:	**DOB**	**M**	**(s)**	**G**
Toni Datković	06.11.1993	25		2
Luka Hujber	16.06.1999	8	(6)	
Fran Karačić	12.05.1996	32		1
Denis Kolinger	14.01.1994	33		
Jan Lecjaks (CZE)	09.08.1990	29		2
Ante Majstorović	06.11.1993	32		2
Mario Musa	06.07.1990	2		1
Midfielders:	**DOB**	**M**	**(s)**	**G**
Mario Burić	25.10.1991	15	(7)	
Domagoj Drožđek	20.03.1996	13	(10)	2
Neven Đurasek	15.08.1998	10	(5)	
Dino Halilović	08.02.1998	1	(7)	1
Luka Ivanušec	26.11.1998	31		6
Kristijan Jakić	14.05.1997	22	(3)	1
Bojan Knežević	28.01.1997	3		
Frano Mlinar	30.03.1992	5	(7)	
Indrit Tuci (ALB)	23.06.1905		(1)	
Forwards:	**DOB**	**M**	**(s)**	**G**
Matko Babić	28.07.1998	3	(13)	2
Ivan Božić	08.06.1997		(5)	
Nikola Burić	01.10.1996	1	(1)	1
Lirim Kastrati (KVX)	16.01.1999	28	(4)	7
Nikola Krajinović	09.11.1999		(4)	
Ivan Krstanović (BIH)	05.01.1983	4	(11)	6
Loren Maružin	04.12.1997	2	(8)	
Dejan Radonjić	23.07.1990	31	(4)	8
Đorđe Rakić (SRB)	31.10.1985	2	(8)	2
Myrto Uzuni (ALB)	31.05.1995	28	(1)	7
Trainer:	**DOB**	**M**		
Goran Tomić	18.03.1977	36		

Nogometni klub Osijek

Founded: 27.02.1947
Stadium: Stadion Gradski vrt, Osijek (18,856)

Goalkeepers:	**DOB**	**M**	**(s)**	**G**
Marko Malenica	08.02.1994	36		
Defenders:	**DOB**	**M**	**(s)**	**G**
Borna Barišić	10.11.1992	1		
Petar Bočkaj	23.07.1996	16	(4)	4
Gutieri Tomelin „Guti“ (BRA)	29.06.1991	33		1
Erik Janža (SVN)	21.06.1993	18	(1)	
Luka Marin	16.03.1998	1		
Mile Škorić	19.06.1991	34		3
Boško Šutalo	01.01.2000	10	(2)	
Talys Alves Pereira Oliveira (BRA)	10.02.1999	8	(1)	1
Mihael Žaper	11.08.1998	10		2
Midfielders:	**DOB**	**M**	**(s)**	**G**
Marijan Ćavar (BIH)	02.02.1998	10	(3)	
Haris Hajradinović (BIH)	18.02.1994	16	(1)	7
Karlo Kamenar	15.03.1994	10	(6)	1
László Kleinheisler (HUN)	08.04.1994	10		1
Dmitriy Lepa (UKR)	23.11.1988	3	(12)	1
Danijel Lončar	26.06.1997	18	(6)	1
Benedik Mioč	06.10.1994	1	(3)	
Robert Mudražija	05.05.1997	11		1
Marko Pervan	04.04.1996		(5)	
Domagoj Pušić	24.10.1991	22	(5)	2
Forwards:	**DOB**	**M**	**(s)**	**G**
Kristal Abazaj (ALB)	06.07.1996	4	(5)	1
Gabrijel Boban	23.07.1989	17	(8)	3
Marko Dugandžić	07.04.1994		(3)	
Muzafer Ejupi (MKD)	16.09.1988		(9)	2
Alen Grgić	10.08.1994	28	(3)	1
Ezekiel Isoken Henty (NGA)	13.05.1993	16	(1)	4
Mirko Marić (BIH)	16.05.1995	35	(1)	18
Marin Pilj	03.12.1996	14	(12)	3
Tomislav Šorša	11.05.1989	9	(4)	1
Josip Špoljarić	05.01.1997	5	(6)	1
Tomislav Štrkalj	02.08.1996		(6)	
Trainer:	**DOB**	**M**		
Zoran Zekić	29.04.1974	25		
Dino Skender [29.03.2019]	10.12.1983	11		

Hrvatski Nogometni Klub Rijeka

Founded: 29.07.1946 (*as Sportsko Društvo Kvarner*)
Stadium: Stadion Rujevica, Rijeka (8,279)

Goalkeepers:	**DOB**	**M**	**(s)**	**G**
Andrej Prskalo	01.05.1987	1		
Simon Sluga	17.03.1993	35		
Defenders:	**DOB**	**M**	**(s)**	**G**
Filip Braut	05.06.2002	1		
Luka Capan	06.04.1995	6	(10)	1
João Rodrigo Pereira Escoval (POR)	08.05.1997	20	(3)	
Petar Mamić	06.03.1996	15	(3)	
Mario Pavelić (AUT)	19.09.1993	9		1
Roberto Punčec	27.10.1991	21	(1)	
Momčilo Raspopović (MNE)	18.03.1994	11		1
Hrvoje Smolčić	17.08.2000	5	(1)	
Ivan Smolčić	17.08.2000		(1)	
Darko Velkovski (MKD)	21.06.1995	4	(2)	
Leonard Zuta (MKD)	09.08.1992	13		
Dario Župarić	03.05.1992	29	(1)	1
Midfielders:	**DOB**	**M**	**(s)**	**G**
Denis Bušnja	14.04.2000	3	(9)	
Dario Čanađija	17.04.1994	12	(4)	
Srđan Grahovac (BIH)	19.09.1992	8	(4)	
Tibor Halilović	18.03.1995	13	(5)	2
Ivan Lepinjica	09.07.1999	10	(2)	1
Adrian Liber	09.01.2001		(1)	
Stjepan Lončar (BIH)	10.11.1996	24	(3)	2
Domagoj Pavičić	09.03.1994	29	(3)	4
Jakov Puljić	04.08.1993	19	(10)	16
Milan Ristovski (MKD)	08.04.1998	1	(2)	
Ivan Tomečak	07.12.1989	1	(1)	
Forwards:	**DOB**	**M**	**(s)**	**G**
Boadu Maxwell Acosty (GHA)	10.09.1991	18	(11)	7
Antonio Čolak	17.09.1993	16	(8)	12
Alexander Gorgon (AUT)	28.10.1988	23	(3)	8
Héber Araújo dos Santos (BRA)	10.08.1991	13	(2)	9
Zoran Kvržić (BIH)	07.08.1988	23	(6)	2
Robert Murić	12.03.1996	12	(4)	3
Matej Vuk	10.06.2000	1	(1)	
Trainer:	**DOB**	**M**		
Matjaž Kek (SVN)	09.09.1961	10		
Igor Bišćan [09.10.2018]	04.05.1978	26		

Nogometni Klub Rudeš

Founded: 1957
Stadium: Stadion u Kranjčevićevoj ulici, Zagreb (8,850)

Goalkeepers:	**DOB**	**M**	**(s)**	**G**
Ivan Banić	18.07.1994	26		
Dominik Picak	12.02.1992	10		
Defenders:	**DOB**	**M**	**(s)**	**G**
Gordan Barić	11.08.1994	10	(9)	
Antonio Borsic	19.09.1995	14	(5)	
Carlos Henrique Santos da Silva (BRA)	06.07.2000		(1)	
Josip Filipović	08.05.1996	22	(1)	
Erhun Obanor (NGA)	05.09.1995	21	(2)	
Maksim Oluić	20.05.1998	10		
Renato Pantalon	27.10.1997	16	(2)	1
Nikola Pejović (SRB)	22.09.1998	6		1
Siniša Rožman	16.10.1990	11		
Luka Smoljo	28.01.1996	12		
Vinko Soldo	15.02.1998	4	(1)	
Mate Šuto	02.10.1996	9		
Vilibald Vuco	15.07.1996	13		1
Midfielders:	**DOB**	**M**	**(s)**	**G**
Andrey Falinski Rodrigues (BRA)	18.03.1996	8	(4)	1
Dino Halilović	08.02.1998	13	(3)	
João Erick Marques da Silva (BRA)	15.05.1998	25	(1)	1
Matej Jukić	07.04.1997	9	(6)	
Dragan Juranović	10.02.1994	11		2
Anthony Kalik (AUS)	05.11.1997	15	(1)	
Toni Kovačević	15.05.2000		(1)	
David Lojber	29.11.1999		(3)	
Robert Mišković (GER)	20.10.1999	7	(6)	1
Luka Pasariček	12.03.1998	10	(2)	
Leon Sopić	28.10.2000		(1)	
Anes Vazda (BIH)	24.07.1997		(1)	
Forwards:	**DOB**	**M**	**(s)**	**G**
Ivan Božić	08.06.1997	7	(9)	
Mihael Klepač	19.09.1997	9	(6)	
Ivan Kovačec	27.06.1988	3	(2)	
Franko Kovačević	08.08.1999	10	(2)	
Nikola Krajinović	09.11.1999	2	(4)	
Vitaly Lisakovich (BLR)	08.02.1998	14		4
Tomislav Mrkonjić	22.02.1994	21	(5)	4
Borna Petrović	16.10.1997	8	(6)	1
Filip Soldo	12.03.1997		(4)	
Tomislav Štrkalj	02.08.1996	14	(1)	5
Ivan Tomičić	01.03.1993	3	(6)	1
Frane Vojković	20.12.1996	10	(1)	
Mario Vojković	20.12.1996	13	(3)	1
Wallace Lucas Aires da Silva (BRA)	17.07.1997		(5)	
Trainer:	**DOB**	**M**		
Ivan Matić	30.04.1971	9		
Marko Lozo [03.10.2018]	12.07.1988	7		
Darko Jozinović [05.12.2018]	15.08.1970	2		
Tomislav Ivković [24.12.2018]	11.08.1960	18		

Nogometni klub Slaven Belupo Koprivnica

Founded: 1907
Stadium: Gradski Stadion "Ivan Kušek Apaš", Koprivnica (3,205)

Goalkeepers:	**DOB**	**M**	**(s)**	**G**
Ivan Filipović	13.11.1994	24		
Antun Marković	04.07.1992	12		
Defenders:	**DOB**	**M**	**(s)**	**G**
Bruno Goda	17.04.1998	14	(2)	1
Marko Iharoš	23.06.1996	7	(1)	
Marko Martinaga	27.05.1998	2	(1)	
Vinko Međimorec	01.06.1996	26	(1)	
Božo Musa	15.09.1988	12	(1)	
Krystian Nowak (POL)	01.04.1994	16	(4)	1
Matko Zirdum	21.07.1998	2		
Midfielders:	**DOB**	**M**	**(s)**	**G**
Jorge Eduardo Aparicio Grijalva (GUA)	21.11.1992	5	(3)	
Stipe Bačelić-Grgić	16.02.1988	12	(7)	3
Dario Čanađija	17.04.1994	11		1
Ivan Dolček	24.04.2000	4	(6)	
Roei Gordana (ISR)	06.07.1990	12	(4)	3
Marko Karamarko	27.03.1993	16	(6)	
Mihael Mladen	28.09.1999	1	(10)	
Karlo Plantak	11.11.1997	8	(4)	1
David Puclin	17.06.1992	27	(2)	1
Zvonimir Šarlija	29.08.1996	31		
Miloš Vidović (SRB)	03.10.1989	31		2
Forwards:	**DOB**	**M**	**(s)**	**G**
Bruno Bogojević	29.06.1998	19	(5)	2
Rodrigue Bongongui (FRA)	07.02.1993	19	(3)	1
Mateas Delić	17.06.1988	24	(2)	3
Jan Doležal	12.02.1993	7	(10)	
Ivan Jajalo (AUT)	22.07.1993	5	(1)	
Matej Jelić	05.11.1990	15	(9)	5
Ivan Krstanović (BIH)	05.01.1983	9	(1)	7
Mateus Lima Cruz (BRA)	18.01.1993	10	(11)	5
Luka Menalo (BIH)	22.07.1996	9	(3)	
Jean-Philippe Mendy (FRA)	04.03.1987	6	(9)	4
Trainer:	**DOB**	**M**		
Tomislav Ivković	11.08.1960	14		
Ivica Sertić [13.11.2018]	14.05.1973	22		

SECOND LEVEL
FavBet Druga liga 2018/2019

1.	NK Varaždin (*Promoted*)	26	16	3	7	40	-	30	51
2.	HNK Šibenik (*Promotion Play-offs*)	26	13	7	6	38	-	25	46
3.	NK Osijek II*	26	13	5	8	37	-	26	44
4.	HNK Hajduk Split II*	26	12	7	7	36	-	29	43
5.	NK Dugopolje	26	13	4	9	29	-	26	43
6.	NK Sesvete	26	11	7	8	38	-	26	40
7.	GNK Dinamo Zagreb II*	26	10	7	9	31	-	26	37
8.	NK Zadar (*Relegated*)	26	9	7	10	36	-	40	34
9.	NK BSK Bijelo Brdo	26	6	10	10	31	-	37	28
10.	NK Solin	26	5	13	8	24	-	31	28
11.	NK Kustošija	26	7	7	12	20	-	28	28
12.	NK Hrvatski Dragovoljac Zagreb	26	7	6	13	23	-	29	27
13.	NK Međimurje Čakovec	26	6	7	13	26	-	42	25
14.	NK Lučko Zagreb (*Relegated*)	26	6	6	14	16	-	31	24

*Please note: reserve teams are ineligible for promotion to the Croatian First Football League!
NK Zadar were relegated due to revoked licence.

NATIONAL TEAM

INTERNATIONAL MATCHES
(16.07.2018 – 15.07.2019)

06.09.2018	Faro/Loulé	Portugal - Croatia	1-1(1-1)	(F)
11.09.2018	Elche	Spain - Croatia	6-0(3-0)	(UNL)
12.10.2018	Rijeka	Croatia - England	0-0	(UNL)
15.10.2018	Rijeka	Croatia - Jordan	2-1(1-0)	(F)
15.11.2018	Zagreb	Croatia - Spain	3-2(0-0)	(UNL)
18.11.2018	London	England - Croatia	2-1(0-0)	(UNL)
21.03.2019	Zagreb	Croatia - Azerbaijan	2-1(1-1)	(ECQ)
24.03.2019	Budapest	Hungary - Croatia	2-1(1-1)	(ECQ)
08.06.2019	Osijek	Croatia - Wales	2-1(1-0)	(ECQ)
11.06.2019	Varaždín	Croatia - Tunisia	1-2(0-1)	(F)

06.09.2018 PORTUGAL - CROATIA 1-1(1-1) Friendly International
Estádio Algarve, Faro/Loulé; Referee: Xavier Estrada Fernández (Spain); Attendance: 26,355
CRO: Lovre Kalinić, Šime Vrsaljko (46.Antonio Milić), Domagoj Vida (35.Tin Jedvaj), Matej Mitrović, Borna Barišić, Luka Modrić (Cap) (55.Mario Pašalić), Mateo Kovačić, Milan Badelj, Ivan Perišić (63.Duje Čop), Marko Livaja (57.Ivan Santini), Marko Pjaca (72.Marko Rog). Trainer: Zlatko Dalić.
Goal: Ivan Perišić (18).

11.09.2018 SPAIN - CROATIA 6-0(3-0) UEFA Nations League A, Group 4
Estadio "Manuel Martínez Valero", Elche; Referee: Benoît Bastien (France); Attendance: 26,900
CRO: Lovre Kalinić, Šime Vrsaljko (20.Marko Rog), Domagoj Vida, Matej Mitrović, Josip Pivarić, Luka Modrić (Cap), Ivan Rakitić, Ivan Perišić, Marcelo Brozović (62.Marko Pjaca), Mateo Kovačić, Ivan Santini (71.Marko Livaja). Trainer: Zlatko Dalić.

12.10.2018 CROATIA - ENGLAND 0-0 UEFA Nations League A, Group 4
Stadion Rujevica, Rijeka; Referee: Dr. Felix Brych (Germany); Attendance: *played behind closed doors*
CRO: Dominik Livaković, Domagoj Vida, Dejan Lovren, Josip Pivarić, Tin Jedvaj, Luka Modrić (Cap), Ivan Rakitić, Mateo Kovačić (73.Milan Badelj), Ivan Perišić (68.Marko Pjaca), Andrej Kramarić, Ante Rebić (80.Marko Livaja). Trainer: Zlatko Dalić.

15.10.2018 CROATIA - JORDAN 2-1(1-0) Friendly International
Stadion Rujevica, Rijeka; Referee: Andó-Szabó Sándor (Hungary); Attendance: 4,820
CRO: Dominik Livaković, Domagoj Vida (Cap), Dejan Lovren (46.Matej Mitrović), Antonio Milić (46.Josip Pivarić), Karlo Bartolec (64.Tin Jedvaj), Milan Badelj (46.Filip Bradarić), Mario Pašalić, Marko Rog, Andrej Kramarić (67.Ivan Santini), Marko Pjaca, Ante Rebić (64.Marko Livaja). Trainer: Zlatko Dalić.
Goals: Domagoj Vida (24), Matej Mitrović (63).

15.11.2018 CROATIA - SPAIN 3-2(0-0) UEFA Nations League A, Group 4
Stadion Maksimir, Zagreb; Referee: Aleksei Kulbakov (Belarus); Attendance: 33,018
CRO: Lovre Kalinić, Šime Vrsaljko, Domagoj Vida, Dejan Lovren, Tin Jedvaj, Luka Modrić (Cap), Ivan Rakitić (68.Nikola Vlašić), Marcelo Brozović, Ivan Perišić, Andrej Kramarić (89.Marko Pjaca), Ante Rebić (74.Josip Brekalo). Trainer: Zlatko Dalić.
Goals: Andrej Kramarić (54), Tin Jedvaj (69, 90+3).

18.11.2018 ENGLAND - CROATIA 2-1(0-0) UEFA Nations League A, Group 4
Wembley Stadium, London; Referee: Anastasios Sidiropoulos (Greece); Attendance: 78,221
CRO: Lovre Kalinić, Šime Vrsaljko (26.Antonio Milić), Domagoj Vida, Dejan Lovren, Tin Jedvaj, Luka Modrić (Cap), Ivan Perišić, Marcelo Brozović, Nikola Vlašić (79.Marko Rog), Andrej Kramarić, Ante Rebić (46.Josip Brekalo). Trainer: Zlatko Dalić.
Goal: Andrej Kramarić (57).

21.03.2019 CROATIA - AZERBAIJAN 2-1(1-1) 16th EC. Qualifiers
Stadion Maksimir, Zagreb; Referee: Georgi Kabakov (Bulgaria); Attendance: 23,146
CRO: Lovre Kalinić, Duje Ćaleta-Car, Domagoj Vida, Borna Barišić, Luka Modrić (Cap) (90+2.Milan Badelj), Ivan Rakitić, Ivan Perišić, Mateo Kovačić (73.Nikola Vlašić), Josip Brekalo, Andrej Kramarić, Bruno Petković (69.Ante Rebić). Trainer: Zlatko Dalić.
Goals: Borna Barišić (44), Andrej Kramarić (79).

24.03.2019 HUNGARY - CROATIA 2-1(1-1) 16th EC. Qualifiers
Groupama Arena, Budapest; Referee: Willie Collum (Scotland); Attendance: 19,400
CRO: Lovre Kalinić, Domagoj Vida, Dejan Lovren, Borna Barišić (30.Marin Leovac), Tin Jedvaj (77.Bruno Petković), Luka Modrić (Cap), Ivan Rakitić, Marcelo Brozović, Ivan Perišić, Andrej Kramarić, Ante Rebić (67.Josip Brekalo). Trainer: Zlatko Dalić.
Goal: Ante Rebić (13).

08.06.2019 CROATIA - WALES 2-1(1-0) 16th EC. Qualifiers
Stadion Gradski vrt, Osijek; Referee: István Kovács (Romania); Attendance: 17,061
CRO: Dominik Livaković, Domagoj Vida, Dejan Lovren, Tin Jedvaj, Marcelo Brozović, Luka Modrić (Cap), Borna Barišić, Mateo Kovačić (76.Milan Badelj), Ivan Perišić (90+3.Mile Škorić), Josip Brekalo (67.Mario Pašalić), Andrej Kramarić. Trainer: Zlatko Dalić.
Goals: James Alexander Lawrence (17 own goal), Ivan Perišić (48).

11.06.2019 CROATIA - TUNISIA 1-2(0-1) Friendly International
Stadion Gradski, Varaždín; Referee: Daniel Stefanski (Poland); Attendance: 8,036
CRO: Simon Sluga, Domagoj Vida (Cap), Dejan Lovren (46.Karlo Bartolec), Dario Melnjak, Filip Benković, Milan Badelj (55.Marcelo Brozović), Mateo Kovačić (55.Ivan Perišić), Mario Pašalić (70.Luka Modrić), Josip Brekalo (58.Alen Halilović), Andrej Kramarić (63.Mijo Caktaš), Bruno Petković. Trainer: Zlatko Dalić.
Goal: Bruno Petković (47).

NATIONAL TEAM PLAYERS
(16.07.2018 – 15.07.2019)

Name	DOB	Caps	Goals	2018/2019:	*Club*
Goalkeepers					
Lovre KALINIĆ	03.04.1990	**18**	**0**	2018:	*KAA Gent (BEL)*
				01.01.2019->	*Aston Villa FC Birmingham (ENG)*
Dominik LIVAKOVIĆ	09.01.1995	**4**	**0**	2018/2019:	*GNK Dinamo Zagreb*
Simon SLUGA	17.03.1993	**1**	**0**	2018/2019:	*HNK Rijeka*
Defenders					
Borna BARIŠIĆ	10.11.1992	**7**	**1**	2018/2019:	*Rangers FC Glasgow (SCO)*
Karlo BARTOLEC	20.04.1995	**2**	**0**	2018/2019:	*FC Nordsjælland Farum (DEN)*
Filip BENKOVIĆ	13.07.1997	**1**	**0**	2019:	*Celtic Glasgow FC (SCO)*
Duje ĆALETA-CAR	17.09.1996	**3**	**0**	2018/2019:	*Olympique de Marseille (FRA)*
Tin JEDVAJ	28.11.1995	**20**	**2**	2018/2019:	*TSV 04 Bayer Leverkusen (GER)*
Marin LEOVAC	07.08.1988	**5**	**0**	2019:	*GNK Dinamo Zagreb*
Dejan LOVREN	05.07.1989	**53**	**2**	2018/2019:	*Liverpool FC (ENG)*
Antonio MILIĆ	10.03.1994	**3**	**0**	2018:	*RSC Anderlecht Bruxelles (BEL)*
Matej MITROVIĆ	10.11.1993	**12**	**2**	2018/2019:	*Club Brugge KV (BEL)*
Josip PIVARIĆ	30.01.1989	**26**	**0**	2018/2019:	*FK Dynamo Kyiv (UKR)*
Mile ŠKORIĆ	19.06.1991	**2**	**0**	2018/2019:	*NK Osijek*
Domagoj VIDA	29.04.1989	**65**	**3**	2018/2019:	*Beşiktaş JK Istanbul (TUR)*
Šime VRSALJKO	10.01.1992	**45**	**0**	2018/2019:	*FC Internazionale Milano (ITA)*
Midfielders					
Milan BADELJ	25.02.1989	**47**	**2**	2018/2019:	*SS Lazio Roma (ITA)*
Filip BRADARIĆ	11.01.1992	**6**	**0**	2018/2019:	*Cagliari Calcio (ITA)*
Marcelo BROZOVIĆ	16.11.1992	**47**	**6**	2018/2019:	*FC Internazionale Milano (ITA)*
Mijo CAKTAŠ	08.05.1992	**1**	**0**	2019:	*HNK Hajduk Split*
Mateo KOVAČIĆ	06.05.1994	**46**	**1**	2018/2019:	*Chelsea FC London (ENG)*
Luka MODRIĆ	09.09.1985	**122**	**14**	2018/2019:	*Real Madrid CF (ESP)*
Mario PAŠALIĆ	09.02.1995	**10**	**0**	2018/2019:	*Atalanta Bergamasca Calcio (ITA)*
Ivan PERIŠIĆ	02.02.1989	**82**	**23**	2018/2019:	*FC Internazionale Milano (ITA)*
Ivan RAKITIĆ	10.03.1988	**104**	**15**	2018/2019:	*FC Barcelona (ESP)*
Marko ROG	19.07.1995	**16**	**0**	2018:	*SSC Napoli (ITA)*
Nikola VLAŠIĆ	04.10.1997	**5**	**0**	2018/2019:	*FK CSKA Moskva (RUS)*
Forwards					
Josip BREKALO	23.06.1998	**6**	**0**	2018/2019:	*VfL Wolfsburg (GER)*
Duje ČOP	01.02.1990	**14**	**2**	2018:	*Real Valladolid CF (ESP)*
Alen HALILOVIĆ	18.06.1996	**10**	**0**	2019:	*R Standard Liège (BEL)*
Andrej KRAMARIĆ	19.06.1991	**46**	**13**	2018/2019:	*TSG 1899 Hoffenheim (GER)*
Marko LIVAJA	26.08.1993	**4**	**0**	2018:	*AEK Athína (GRE)*
Dario MELNJAK	31.10.1992	**1**	**0**	2019:	*Çaykur Rizespor Kulübü (TUR)*
Bruno PETKOVIĆ	16.09.1994	**3**	**1**	2018/2019:	*GNK Dinamo Zagreb*
Marko PJACA	06.05.1995	**24**	**1**	2018/2019:	*ACF Fiorentina (ITA)*
Ante REBIĆ	21.09.1993	**28**	**3**	2018/2019:	*Eintracht Frankfurt (GER)*
Ivan SANTINI	21.05.1989	**5**	**0**	2018:	*RSC Anderlecht Bruxelles (BEL)*

National team coach

Zlatko DALIĆ [from 07.10.2017]	26.10.1966	24 M; 12 W; 5 D; 7 L; 36-33

CYPRUS

The Country:

Κυπριακή Δημοκρατία (Republic of Cyprus)
Capital: Nicosia
Surface: 9,251 km²
Inhabitants: 1,170,125 [2016]
Time: UTC+2

The FA:

Cyprus Football Association
10 Achaion Street 2413 Engomi, PO Box 25071 1306 Nicosia
Tel: +357 22 352 341
Foundation date: 23.09.1934
Member of FIFA since: 1948
Member of UEFA since: 1962
Website: www.cfa.com.cy

NATIONAL TEAM RECORDS

First international match:	13.11.1960, Nicosia:	Cyprus – Israel 1-1
Most international caps:	Yiannakis Okkas	- 103 caps (1997-2011)
Most international goals:	Michalis Konstantinou	- 32 goals / 84 caps (1997-2012)

UEFA EUROPEAN CHAMPIONSHIP	
1960	*Did not enter*
1964	*Did not enter*
1968	Qualifiers
1972	Qualifiers
1976	Qualifiers
1980	Qualifiers
1984	Qualifiers
1988	Qualifiers
1992	Qualifiers
1996	Qualifiers
2000	Qualifiers
2004	Qualifiers
2008	Qualifiers
2012	Qualifiers
2016	Qualifiers

FIFA WORLD CUP	
1930	*Did not enter*
1934	*Did not enter*
1938	*Did not enter*
1950	*Did not enter*
1954	*Did not enter*
1958	*Did not enter*
1962	Qualifiers
1966	Qualifiers
1970	Qualifiers
1974	Qualifiers
1978	Qualifiers
1982	Qualifiers
1986	Qualifiers
1990	Qualifiers
1994	Qualifiers
1998	Qualifiers
2002	Qualifiers
2006	Qualifiers
2010	Qualifiers
2014	Qualifiers
2018	Qualifiers

UEFA NATIONS LEAGUE
2018/2019 – League C

OLYMPIC FOOTBALL TOURNAMENTS 1908-2016							
1908	-	**1948**	-	**1972**	-	**1996**	Qualifiers
1912	-	**1952**	-	**1976**	-	**2000**	Qualifiers
1920	-	**1956**	-	**1980**	-	**2004**	Qualifiers
1924	-	**1960**	-	**1984**	-	**2008**	Qualifiers
1928	-	**1964**	-	**1988**	-	**2012**	Qualifiers
1936	-	**1968**	-	**1992**	Qualifiers	**2016**	Qualifiers

FIFA CONFEDERATIONS CUP 1992-2017
None

CYPRIOT CLUB HONOURS IN EUROPEAN CLUB COMPETITIONS:

European Champion Clubs' Cup (1956-1992) / UEFA Champions League (1993-2019)
None
Fairs Cup (1858-1971) / UEFA Cup (1972-2009) / UEFA Europa League (2010-2019)
None
UEFA Super Cup (1972-2019)
None
European Cup Winners' Cup 1961-1999*
None

**defunct competition*

NATIONAL COMPETITIONS
TABLE OF HONOURS

	CHAMPIONS	CUP WINNERS	BEST GOALSCORERS	
1934/1935	Enosis Neon Trust Nicosia	Enosis Neon Trust Nicosia	-	
1935/1936	APOEL FC Nicosia	Enosis Neon Trust Nicosia	-	
1936/1937	APOEL FC Nicosia	APOEL FC Nicosia	-	
1937/1938	APOEL FC Nicosia	Enosis Neon Trust Nicosia	-	
1938/1939	APOEL FC Nicosia	AEL Limassol	-	
1939/1940	APOEL FC Nicosia	AEL Limassol	-	
1940/1941	AEL Limassol	APOEL FC Nicosia	-	
1941-1944	*No competition*	*No competition*	-	
1944/1945	EPA Larnaca FC	EPA Larnaca FC	-	
1945/1946	EPA Larnaca FC	EPA Larnaca FC	-	
1946/1947	APOEL FC Nicosia	APOEL FC Nicosia	-	
1947/1948	APOEL FC Nicosia	AEL Limassol	-	
1948/1949	APOEL FC Nicosia	Anorthosis Famagusta FC	-	
1949/1950	Anorthosis Famagusta FC	EPA Larnaca FC	-	
1950/1951	Çetinkaya Türk Spor Kulübü	APOEL FC Nicosia	-	
1951/1952	APOEL FC Nicosia	Çetinkaya Türk Spor Kulübü	-	
1952/1953	AEL Limassol	EPA Larnaca FC	-	
1953/1954	Pezoporikos Larnaca FC	Çetinkaya Türk Spor Kulübü	-	
1954/1955	AEL Limassol	EPA Larnaca FC	-	
1955/1956	AEL Limassol	*No competition*	-	
1956/1957	Anorthosis Famagusta FC	*No competition*	-	
1957/1958	Anorthosis Famagusta FC	*No competition*	-	
1958/1959	*No competition*	Anorthosis Famagusta FC	-	
1959/1960	Anorthosis Famagusta FC	*No competition*	-	
1960/1961	AC Omonia Nicosia	*No competition*	Panikos Krystallis (Apollon Limassol FC)	26
1961/1962	Anorthosis Famagusta FC	Anorthosis Famagusta FC	Michalis Shialis (Anorthosis Famagusta FC)	22
1962/1963	Anorthosis Famagusta FC	APOEL FC Nicosia	Panikos Papadopoulos (AEL Limassol)	24
1963/1964	*Championship Abandoned*	Anorthosis Famagusta FC	*Championship abandoned*	
1964/1965	APOEL FC Nicosia	AC Omonia Nicosia	Kostakis Pieridis (Olympiakos Nicosia FC)	21
1965/1966	AC Omonia Nicosia	Apollon Limassol FC	Panikos Efthymiades (Olympiakos Nicosia FC)	20
1966/1967	Olympiakos Nicosia FC	Apollon Limassol FC	Andreas Stylianou (APOEL FC Nicosia)	29
1967/1968	AEL Limassol	APOEL FC Nicosia	Charalambos Papadopoulos (AEL Limassol)	31
1968/1969	Olympiakos Nicosia FC	APOEL FC Nicosia	Panikos Efthymiades (Olympiakos Nicosia FC)	17
1969/1970	EPA Larnaca FC	Pezoporikos Larnaca FC	Tasos Constantinou (EPA Larnaca FC)	24
1970/1971	Olympiakos Nicosia FC	Anorthosis Famagusta FC	Andreas Stylianou (APOEL FC Nicosia) Kostas Vasiliades (Apollon Limassol FC) Panikos Efthymiades (Olympiakos Nicosia FC)	11
1971/1972	AC Omonia Nicosia	AC Omonia Nicosia	Sotiris Kaiafas (AC Omonia Nicosia)	24
1972/1973	APOEL FC Nicosia	APOEL FC Nicosia	Lakis Theodorou (EPA Larnaca FC)	17
1973/1974	AC Omonia Nicosia	AC Omonia Nicosia	Sotiris Kaiafas (AC Omonia Nicosia)	20
1974/1975	AC Omonia Nicosia	Anorthosis Famagusta FC	Andros Savva (AC Omonia Nicosia)	21
1975/1976	AC Omonia Nicosia	APOEL FC Nicosia	Sotiris Kaiafas (AC Omonia Nicosia)	39
1976/1977	AC Omonia Nicosia	Olympiakos Nicosia FC	Sotiris Kaiafas (AC Omonia Nicosia)	44
1977/1978	AC Omonia Nicosia	APOEL FC Nicosia	Andreas Kanaris (AC Omonia Nicosia)	20
1978/1979	AC Omonia Nicosia	APOEL FC Nicosia	Sotiris Kaiafas (AC Omonia Nicosia)	28
1979/1980	APOEL FC Nicosia	AC Omonia Nicosia	Sotiris Kaiafas (AC Omonia Nicosia)	23
1980/1981	AC Omonia Nicosia	AC Omonia Nicosia	Sotiris Kaiafas (AC Omonia Nicosia)	14
1981/1982	AC Omonia Nicosia	AC Omonia Nicosia	Sotiris Kaiafas (AC Omonia Nicosia)	19
1982/1983	AC Omonia Nicosia	AC Omonia Nicosia	Panikos Hatziloizou (Aris Limassol FC)	17
1983/1984	AC Omonia Nicosia	APOEL FC Nicosia	Sylvester Vernon (Pezoporikos Larnaca FC) Lenos Kittos (Ermis Aradippou FC)	14
1984/1985	AC Omonia Nicosia	AEL Limassol	Giorgos Savvidis (AC Omonia Nicosia)	24
1985/1986	APOEL FC Nicosia	Apollon Limassol FC	Yiannos Ioannou (APOEL FC Nicosia)	22
1986/1987	AC Omonia Nicosia	AEL Limassol	Spas Dzhevizov (BUL, AC Omonia Nicosia)	32
1987/1988	Pezoporikos Larnaca FC	AC Omonia Nicosia	Tasos Zouvanis (Enosis Neon Paralimni FC)	23
1988/1989	AC Omonia Nicosia	AEL Limassol	Nigel McNeal (ENG, Nea Salamis Famagusta FC)	19
1989/1990	APOEL FC Nicosia	Nea Salamis Famagusta FC	Siniša Gogić (YUG, APOEL FC Nicosia)	19
1990/1991	Apollon Limassol FC	AC Omonia Nicosia	Suad Beširević (YUG, Apollon Limassol FC) Panikos Xiourouppas (AC Omonia Nicosia)	19
1991/1992	APOEL FC Nicosia	Apollon Limassol FC	József Dzurják (HUN, AC Omonia Nicosia)	21
1992/1993	AC Omonia Nicosia	APOEL FC Nicosia	Slađan Šćepović (YUG, Apollon Limassol FC)	25
1993/1994	Apollon Limassol FC	AC Omonia Nicosia	Siniša Gogić (YUG, Anorthosis Famagusta FC)	26
1994/1995	Anorthosis Famagusta FC	APOEL FC Nicosia	Pambis Andreou (Nea Salamis Famagusta FC)	25
1995/1996	APOEL FC Nicosia	APOEL FC Nicosia	József Kiprich (HUN, APOEL FC Nicosia)	25
1996/1997	Anorthosis Famagusta FC	APOEL FC Nicosia	Michalis Konstantinou (Enosis Neon Paralimni FC)	17
1997/1998	Anorthosis Famagusta FC	Anorthosis Famagusta FC	Rainer Rauffmann (GER, AC Omonia Nicosia)	42
1998/1999	Anorthosis Famagusta FC	APOEL FC Nicosia	Rainer Rauffmann (GER, AC Omonia Nicosia)	35
1999/2000	Anorthosis Famagusta FC	AC Omonia Nicosia	Rainer Rauffmann (GER, AC Omonia Nicosia)	34
2000/2001	AC Omonia Nicosia	Apollon Limassol FC	Rainer Rauffmann (GER, AC Omonia Nicosia)	30
2001/2002	APOEL FC Nicosia	Anorthosis Famagusta FC	Wojciech Kowalczyk (POL, Anorthosis Famagusta FC)	22
2002/2003	AC Omonia Nicosia	Anorthosis Famagusta FC	Marios Neophytou (Anorthosis Famagusta FC)	33

2003/2004	APOEL FC Nicosia	AEK Larnaca FC	Łukasz Sosin (POL, Apollon Limassol FC) Jozef Kožlej (SVK, AC Omonia Nicosia) 21
2004/2005	Anorthosis Famagusta FC	AC Omonia Nicosia	Łukasz Sosin (POL, Apollon Limassol FC) 21
2005/2006	Apollon Limassol FC	APOEL FC Nicosia	Łukasz Sosin (POL, Apollon Limassol FC) 28
2006/2007	APOEL FC Nicosia	Anorthosis Famagusta FC	Esteban Andrés Solari Poggio (ARG, APOEL FC Nicosia) 20
2007/2008	Anorthosis Famagusta FC	APOEL FC Nicosia	David Pereira da Costa (BRA, Doxa Katokopias FC) Łukasz Sosin (POL, Anorthosis Famagusta FC) 16
2008/2009	APOEL FC Nicosia	APOP Kinyras Peyias FC	Sérgio Luis Gardino da Silva "Serjão" (BRA, Doxa Katokopias FC) 24
2009/2010	AC Omonia Nicosia	Apollon Limassol FC	Joeano Pinto Chaves (BRA, Ermis Aradippou FC) José Filipe CorreiaSemedo (CPV, APOP Kinyras) 22
2010/2011	APOEL FC Nicosia	AC Omonia Nicosia	Miljan Mrdaković (SRB, Apollon Limassol FC) 21
2011/2012	AEL Limassol	AC Omonia Nicosia	Frederico Castro Roque dos Santos "Freddy" (ANG, AC Omonia Nicosia) 17
2012/2013	APOEL FC Nicosia	Apollon Limassol FC	Bernardo Lino Castro Paes Vasconcelos (POR, Alki Larnaca FC) 18
2013/2014	APOEL FC Nicosia	APOEL FC Nicosia	Gastón Maximiliano Sangoy (ARG, Apollon Limassol FC) Marco Tagbajumi (NGA, Ermis Aradippou FC) Jorge Filipe Monteiro dos Santos Lourenço (POR, AEL Limassol) 18
2014/2015	APOEL FC Nicosia	APOEL FC Nicosia	Mickaël Poté (BEN, AC Omonia Nicosia) 17
2015/2016	APOEL FC Nicosia	Apollon Limassol FC	Fernando Ezequiel Cavenaghi (ARG, APOEL FC Nicosia) André Alves dos Santos (BRA, AEK Larnaca FC) Dimitar Makriev (BUL, Nea Salamis Famagusta FC) 19
2016/2017	APOEL FC Nicosia	Apollon Limassol FC	Matthew Anthony Derbyshire (ENG, AC Omonia Nicosia) 24
2017/2018	APOEL FC Nicosia	AEK Larnaca FC	Matthew Anthony Derbyshire (ENG, AC Omonia Nicosia) 23
2018/2019	APOEL FC Nicosia	AEL Limassol	Adam Nemec (SVK, Pafos FC Paphos) 16

NATIONAL CHAMPIONSHIP
Cypriot First Division 2018/2019
(25.08.2018 – 19.05.2019)

Regular Season - Results

Round 1 [25-26.08.2018]
Ermis Aradippou - AEL Limassol 0-1(0-0)
AC Omonia - Alki Oroklini 1-0(1-0)
Doxa Katokopias - Anorthosis 0-1(0-0)
Nea Salamina - APOEL Nic. 2-3(0-2) [19.09.]
Apollon L. - Neon Paralimni 5-0(3-0) [28.09.]
AEK Larnaca - Paphos 3-0 (awarded)

Round 2 [01-02.09.2018]
AEL Limassol - Doxa Katokopias 2-0(1-0)
Paphos - Anorthosis 1-1(0-1)
Alki Oroklini - Ermis Aradippou 0-2(0-1)
Neon Paralimni - Nea Salamina 3-5(1-3)
APOEL Nic. - AC Omonia 2-0(1-0) [31.10.]
AEK Larnaca - Apollon Lim. 0-0 [09.01.2019]

Round 3 [15-17.09.2018]
Doxa Katokopias - Alki Oroklini 4-0(1-0)
Apollon Limassol - Paphos 5-1(3-0)
Nea Salamina - AEK Larnaca 1-1(0-1)
AC Omonia - Neon Paralimni 1-0(1-0)
Ermis Aradippou - APOEL Nicosia 0-1(0-1)
Anorthosis - AEL Limassol 0-1(0-1)

Round 4 [22-24.09.2018]
Neon Paralimni - Ermis Aradippou 2-0(0-0)
Paphos - AEL Limassol 0-2(0-0)
APOEL Nicosia - Doxa Katokopias 2-5(0-3)
Alki Oroklini - Anorthosis 0-0
AEK Larnaca - AC Omonia 1-0(0-0)
Apollon Limassol - Nea Salamina 1-0(0-0)

Round 5 [06-07.10.2018]
Nea Salamina - Paphos 3-0(3-0)
Doxa Katokopias - Neon Paralimni 2-1(0-0)
Anorthosis - APOEL Nicosia 2-3(2-2)
AEL Limassol - Alki Oroklini 5-1(4-0)
AC Omonia - Apollon Limassol 0-2(0-1)
Ermis Aradippou - AEK Larnaca 1-2(1-1)

Round 6 [20-22.10.2018]
Neon Paralimni - Anorthosis 1-1(1-0)
Apollon Limassol - Ermis Aradippou 5-0(4-0)
AEK Larnaca - Doxa Katokopias 3-0(0-0)
Nea Salamina - AC Omonia 1-0(1-0)
APOEL Nicosia - AEL Limassol 0-0
Paphos - Alki Oroklini 0-1(0-1)

Round 7 [27-29.10.2018]
AC Omonia - Paphos 2-4(1-0)
Alki Oroklini - APOEL Nicosia 2-4(0-1)
AEL Limassol - Neon Paralimni 4-1(0-1)
Ermis Aradippou - Nea Salamina 0-1(0-0)
Doxa Katokopias - Apollon Limassol 1-1(1-0)
Anorthosis - AEK Larnaca 1-2(0-1)

Round 8 [03-05.11.2018]
Apollon Limassol - Anorthosis 1-2(0-2)
Neon Paralimni - Alki Oroklini 2-0(0-0)
AEK Larnaca - AEL Limassol 0-1(0-0)
Paphos - APOEL Nicosia 0-0
AC Omonia - Ermis Aradippou 2-1(1-0)
Nea Salamina - Doxa Katokopias 1-0(1-0)

Round 9 [10-11.11.2018]
APOEL Nicosia - Neon Paralimni 3-0(2-0)
Ermis Aradippou - Paphos 3-0(3-0)
Anorthosis - Nea Salamina 1-0(0-0)
AEL Limassol - Apollon Limassol 0-3(0-2)
Doxa Katokopias - AC Omonia 1-2(1-0)
Alki Oroklini - AEK Larnaca 0-3(0-0)

Round 10 [24-26.11.2018]
AEK Larnaca - APOEL Nicosia 1-0(1-0)
Apollon Limassol - Alki Oroklini 3-0(2-0)
Paphos - Neon Paralimni 1-0(1-0)
AC Omonia - Anorthosis 1-1(1-1)
Nea Salamina - AEL Limassol 4-1(2-0)
Ermis Aradippou - Doxa Katokopias 1-1(0-0)

Round 11 [01-03.12.2018]
Alki Oroklini - Nea Salamina 2-0(1-0)
AEL Limassol - AC Omonia 2-1(0-1)
Doxa Katokopias - Paphos 3-2(1-1)
Anorthosis - Ermis Aradippou 2-1(1-0)
APOEL Nicosia - Apollon Limassol 5-1(3-1)
Neon Paralimni - AEK Larnaca 2-1(0-0)

Round 12 [08-10.12.2018]
Paphos - AEK Larnaca 1-0(1-0)
Alki Oroklini - AC Omonia 0-2(0-1)
Neon Paralimni - Apollon Limassol 0-2(0-2)
Anorthosis - Doxa Katokopias 3-1(1-1)
APOEL Nicosia - Nea Salamina 4-0(2-0)
AEL Limassol - Ermis Aradippou 3-2(2-2)

Round 13 [15-17.12.2018]
Doxa Katokopias - AEL Limassol 3-4(1-1)
Ermis Aradippou - Alki Oroklini 2-4(1-4)
Anorthosis - Paphos 2-2(1-1)
AC Omonia - APOEL Nicosia 1-2(1-0)
Nea Salamina - Neon Paralimni 0-0
Apollon Limassol - AEK Larnaca 3-3(2-1)

Round 14 [22-23.12.2018]
Paphos - Apollon Limassol 1-1(1-1)
APOEL Nicosia - Ermis Aradippou 2-0(1-0)
AEK Larnaca - Nea Salamina 0-1(0-1)
AEL Limassol - Anorthosis 0-3(0-1)
Alki Oroklini - Doxa Katokopias 2-1(1-1)
Neon Paralimni - AC Omonia 1-1(0-0)

Round 15 [05-07.01.2019]
AEL Limassol - Paphos 1-0(0-0)
Anorthosis - Alki Oroklini 0-0
Doxa Katokopias - APOEL Nicosia 1-2(0-0)
AC Omonia - AEK Larnaca 1-0(0-0)
Nea Salamina - Apollon Limassol 0-3(0-2)
Ermis Aradippou - Neon Paralimni 0-0

Round 16 [12-14.01.2019]
Paphos - Nea Salamina 1-3(0-1)
Neon Paralimni - Doxa Katokopias 0-1(0-1)
APOEL Nicosia - Anorthosis 4-0(1-0)
Apollon Limassol - AC Omonia 2-1(0-1)
AEK Larnaca - Ermis Aradippou 2-2(1-2)
Alki Oroklini - AEL Limassol 1-3(0-2)

Round 17 [19-21.01.2019]
AC Omonia - Nea Salamina 3-1(0-0)
Ermis Aradippou - Apollon Limassol 0-3(0-2)
AEL Limassol - APOEL Nicosia 0-1(0-0)
Alki Oroklini - Paphos 3-3(2-2)
Anorthosis - Neon Paralimni 2-0(1-0)
Doxa Katokopias - AEK Larnaca 0-5(0-3)

Round 18 [26-28.01.2019]
Nea Salamina - Ermis Aradippou 1-0(1-0)
Apollon Limassol - Doxa Katokopias 2-0(2-0)
Paphos - AC Omonia 1-0(1-0)
AEK Larnaca - Anorthosis 3-0(1-0)
Neon Paralimni - AEL Limassol 1-2(1-0)
APOEL Nicosia - Alki Oroklini 0-0

Round 19 [02-04.02.2019]
APOEL Nicosia - Paphos 1-2(1-1)
Anorthosis - Apollon Limassol 0-3 (awarded)
AEL Limassol - AEK Larnaca 0-0
Doxa Katokopias - Nea Salamina 1-1(0-1)
Alki Oroklini - Neon Paralimni 1-2(0-2)
Ermis Aradippou - AC Omonia 0-2(0-1)

Round 20 [09-11.02.2019]
Apollon Limassol - AEL Limassol 0-0
Nea Salamina - Anorthosis 0-2(0-2)
Neon Paralimni - APOEL Nicosia 0-2(0-1)
AC Omonia - Doxa Katokopias 2-2(0-1)
AEK Larnaca - Alki Oroklini 2-0(1-0)
Paphos - Ermis Aradippou 2-1(1-0)

Round 21 [16-17.02.2019]
APOEL Nicosia - AEK Larnaca 2-2(0-0)
Neon Paralimni - Paphos 1-1(1-0)
Alki Oroklini - Apollon Limassol 1-3(0-1)
Anorthosis - AC Omonia 0-0
AEL Limassol - Nea Salamina 3-2(2-2)
Doxa Katokopias - Ermis Aradippou 1-1(0-0)

Round 22 [23-24.02.2019]
Paphos - Doxa Katokopias 1-0(0-0)
Ermis Aradippou - Anorthosis 2-3(1-1)
AC Omonia - AEL Limassol 2-0(1-0)
Nea Salamina - Alki Oroklini 1-1(1-1)
Apollon Limassol - APOEL Nicosia 1-2(0-0)
AEK Larnaca - Neon Paralimni 3-0(0-0)

Final Standings

1.	APOEL FC Nicosia	22	15	4	3	45	-	20	49
2.	Apollon Limassol FC	22	14	5	3	50	-	17	47
3.	AEL Limassol	22	14	3	5	35	-	25	45
4.	AEK Larnaca FC	22	11	6	5	37	-	16	39
5.	AC Omonia Nicosia	22	9	4	9	25	-	24	31
6.	Nea Salamis Famagusta FC	22	9	4	9	28	-	30	31
7.	Anorthosis Famagusta FC*	22	9	7	6	27	-	26	28
8.	Pafos FC Paphos*	22	7	6	9	24	-	36	21
9.	Doxa Katokopias FC	22	5	5	12	28	-	39	20
10.	Enosis Neon Paralimni FC	22	4	5	13	17	-	38	17
11.	Alki Oroklini FC	22	4	5	13	19	-	43	17
12.	Ermis Aradippou FC	22	2	4	16	19	-	40	10

Teams ranked 1-6 were qualified for the Championship Round, while teams ranked 7-12 were qualified for the Relegation Round.
*6 points deducted for use of unregistered player.

Relegation Round

Results

Round 23 [03-04.03.2019]
Paphos - Alki Oroklini 0-3(0-2)
Ermis Aradippou - Anorthosis 2-1(1-0)
Neon Paralimni - Doxa Katokopias 1-0(1-0)

Round 24 [09-10.03.2019]
Doxa Katokopias - Paphos 0-0
Anorthosis - Neon Paralimni 1-1(1-1)
Alki Oroklini - Ermis Aradippou 2-1(0-1)

Round 25 [15-17.03.2019]
Ermis Aradippou - Neon Paralimni 1-2(0-1)
Paphos - Anorthosis 0-1(0-0)
Alki Oroklini - Doxa Katokopias 1-4(1-2)

Round 26 [30.03.-01.04.2019]
Neon Paralimni - Paphos 1-2(0-2)
Ermis Aradippou - Doxa Katokopias 0-4(0-1)
Anorthosis - Alki Oroklini 3-0(3-0)

Round 27 [06-07.04.2019]
Paphos - Ermis Aradippou 4-1(2-0)
Alki Oroklini - Neon Paralimni 2-0(1-0)
Doxa Katokopias - Anorthosis 3-3(3-1)

Round 28 [13-15.04.2019]
Doxa Katokopias - Neon Paralimni 2-2(1-1)
Alki Oroklini - Paphos 2-3(1-0)
Anorthosis - Ermis Aradippou 3-2(1-1)

Round 29 [20-21.04.2019]
Ermis Aradippou - Alki Oroklini 1-2(0-0)
Paphos - Doxa Katokopias 3-2(2-1)
Neon Paralimni - Anorthosis 2-2(1-1)

Round 30 [05.05.2019]
Neon Paralimni - Ermis Aradippou 4-1(2-1)
Anorthosis - Paphos 1-1(1-1)
Doxa Katokopias - Alki Oroklini 0-1(0-1)

Round 31 [12.05.2019]
Paphos - Neon Paralimni 0-2(0-0)
Doxa Katokopias - Ermis Aradippou 1-0(1-0)
Alki Oroklini - Anorthosis 1-0(0-0)

Round 32 [17-18.05.2019]
Ermis Aradippou - Paphos 1-2(1-1)
Anorthosis - Doxa Katokopias 0-3(0-1)
Neon Paralimni - Alki Oroklini 3-2(1-1)

7.	Anorthosis Famagusta FC	32	12	11	9	42	-	41	41
8.	Pafos FC Paphos	32	12	8	12	39	-	50	38
9.	Doxa Katokopias FC	32	9	8	15	47	-	50	35
10.	Enosis Neon Paralimni FC	32	9	8	15	35	-	51	35
11.	Alki Oroklini FC (*Relegated*)	32	10	5	17	35	-	58	35
12.	Ermis Aradippou FC (*Relegated*)	32	3	4	25	29	-	65	13

Championship Round

Results

Round 23 [02.03.2019]
AEK Larnaca - AEL Limassol 1-0(0-0)
Apollon Limassol - AC Omonia 3-1(2-0)
Nea Salamina - APOEL Nicosia 1-1(1-1)

Round 24 [09-10.03.2019]
AEL Limassol - Apollon Limassol 0-3(0-2)
AC Omonia - Nea Salamina 0-0
APOEL Nicosia - AEK Larnaca 0-0

Round 25 [16-17.03.2019]
Nea Salamina - AEK Larnaca 1-0(1-0)
AC Omonia - AEL Limassol 3-1(1-0)
Apollon Limassol - APOEL Nicosia 1-3(0-0)

Round 26 [30.03.2019]
AEK Larnaca - Apollon Limassol 2-1(1-1)
Nea Salamina - AEL Limassol 0-2(0-0)
APOEL Nicosia - AC Omonia 1-1(1-0)

Round 27 [06-07.04.2019]
AC Omonia - AEK Larnaca 0-2(0-0)
AEL Limassol - APOEL Nicosia 0-3(0-2)
Apollon Limassol - Nea Salamina 1-1(1-1)

Round 28 [13-14.04.2019]
APOEL Nicosia - Nea Salamina 4-0(2-0)
AEL Limassol - AEK Larnaca 2-3(1-1)
AC Omonia - Apollon Limassol 0-2(0-1)

Round 29 [21-22.04.2019]
Apollon Limassol - AEL Limassol 1-1(0-1)
AEK Larnaca - APOEL Nicosia 1-0(0-0)
Nea Salamina - AC Omonia 5-2(3-2)

Round 30 [04.05.2019]
AEK Larnaca - Nea Salamina 1-1(0-1)
APOEL Nicosia - Apollon Limassol 3-0(3-0)
AEL Limassol - AC Omonia 3-2(1-0)

Round 31 [11-12.05.2019]
AC Omonia - APOEL Nicosia 1-2(0-1)
AEL Limassol - Nea Salamina 5-2(1-2)
Apollon Limassol - AEK Larnaca 1-2(0-2)

Round 32 [18-19.05.2019]
APOEL Nicosia - AEL Limassol 4-0(1-0)
Nea Salamina - Apollon Limassol 2-1(1-0)
AEK Larnaca - AC Omonia 2-1(0-0)

Final Standings

1.	**APOEL FC Nicosia**	32	21	7	4	66	-	25	70
2.	AEK Larnaca FC	32	18	8	6	51	-	23	62
3.	Apollon Limassol FC	32	17	7	8	64	-	32	58
4.	AEL Limassol	32	17	4	11	49	-	47	55
5.	Nea Salamis Famagusta FC	32	12	8	12	41	-	47	44
6.	AC Omonia Nicosia	32	10	6	16	36	-	45	36

Top goalscorers:

16 Adam Nemec (SVK)
Pafos FC Paphos

15 Ivan Tričkovski (MKD)
AEK Larnaca FC

15 Rubén Jurado Fernández (ESP)
AEL Limassol

NATIONAL CUP
Kypello Kyprou 2018/2019

First Round [05/19.12.2018]

Aris Limassol FC - Alki Oroklini FC	4-1(1-1)
AC Omonia Nicosia - Onisilos Sotira 2014	3-0(2-0)
Akritas Chlorakas - Anorthosis Famagusta FC	0-7(0-3)
Olympiakos Nicosia FC - Pafos FC Paphos	0-5(0-3)
Omonia Aradippou FC - AEL Limassol	0-3(0-2)
Enosis Neon Paralimni FC - AC Digenis Oroklinis	5-1(4-0)
PAEE Kerynias - Nea Salamis Famagusta FC	0-4(0-2)
APOEL FC Nic. - Athlitikos Omilos Ayia Napa FC	5-0(1-0)

1/8-Finals [02.01./16.01./23.01./30.01./16.01./13.02./20.02.2019]

APOEL FC Nicosia - Doxa Katokopias FC	2-1(0-1) / 3-0(2-0)
Ermis Aradippou FC - ASIL Lysi	3-0(2-0) / 4-0(2-0)
Apollon Limassol FC - AC Omonia Nicosia	1-0(1-0) / 1-1(0-0)
Anorthosis Fam. FC - Enosis Neon Paralimni FC	2-3(2-1) / 0-0
Aris Limassol FC - Pafos FC Paphos	2-1(0-0) / 1-4(1-1)
Nea Salamis Famagusta FC - AEK Larnaca	1-2(1-1) / 0-2(0-1)
Karmiotissa Pano Polemidia - Ethnikos Achna FC	2-1(2-0) / 3-1(0-0)
AEL Limassol - Enosis Neon THOI Lakatamia	8-0(6-0) / 6-0(2-0)

Quarter-Finals [20.02./27.02./06.03.2019]

AEL Limassol - Ermis Aradippou FC	4-0(3-0) / 3-2(2-0)
Pafos FC Paphos - Enosis Neon Paralimni FC	2-2(1-1) / 1-1(1-0)
APOEL FC Nicosia - AEK Larnaca	1-1(1-1) / 3-3(1-1)
Karmiotissa Pano Polemidia - Apollon Limassol	1-5(1-4) / 1-2(0-2)

Semi-Finals [03/17.04.2019]

Apollon Limassol FC - AEL Limassol	1-2(0-1) / 0-0
APOEL FC Nicosia - Enosis Neon Paralimni FC	1-0(0-0) / 2-2(1-2)

Final

22.05.2019; Stádio GSP, Nicosia; Referee: Giorgos Nicolaou; Attendance: 8,980
AEL Limassol - APOEL FC Nicosia **2-0(1-0)**

AEL: Josimar Diaz Vózinha, Nils Teixeira, Kevin Pierre Lafrance, Dossa Momad Omar Hassamo Junior, André Ferreira Teixeira, Alexandre Afonso da Silva (49.Marko Adamović), Jon Gaztañaga Arrospide, Davor Zdravkovski, Rubén Jurado Fernández (88.Ivan Schranz), Andreas Avraam (60.Christos Wheeler), Andreas Makris. Trainer: Dušan Kerkez (Bosnia and Herzegovina).

APOEL: Boy Waterman, Giorgios Merkis, Praxitelis Vouros, Nicholas Ioannou, Wanderson de Jesus Martins „Caju", Nuno Miguel Barbosa Morais, Antonio Jakoliš (55.Roman Bezjak), Tomás Sebastián De Vincenti, Lucas Vieira de Souza (69.André Filipe Cunha Vidigal), Musa Suliman Al Taamari, Leonardo Natel Vieira „Léo Natel" (82.Efstathios Aloneftis). Trainer: Paolo Tramezzani (Italy).

Goals: 1-0 Dossa Momad Omar Hassamo Junior (10), 2-0 Marko Adamović (65).

THE CLUBS 2018/2019

Athletiki Enosi Kition Larnakas (AEK Larnaca)

Founded: 18.07.1994
Stadium: AEK Arena, Larnaca (7,400)

Goalkeepers:	DOB	M	(s)	G
Andreas Christodoulou	26.03.1997	1		
Antonio Ramírez Martínez „Toño" (ESP)	23.11.1986	31		
Defenders:	**DOB**	**M**	**(s)**	**G**
Marios Antoniades	14.05.1990	6	(2)	
David Catalá Jiménez (ESP)	03.05.1980	25	(2)	3
Igor Silva de Almeida „Igor Carioca" (BRA)	21.08.1996	19	(1)	1
Thomas Ioannou	19.07.1995	14	(2)	
Mikel González de Martín Martínez (ESP)	24.09.1985	21	(2)	2
Daniel Mojsov (MKD)	25.12.1987	11	(1)	
Joan Guillem Truyols Mascaró (ESP)	11.11.1989	20	(8)	4
Midfielders:	**DOB**	**M**	**(s)**	**G**
Konstantinos Anastasiou	05.07.1999	1	(5)	
Facundo García (ARG)	16.12.1999	15	(6)	
Jean Luc Gbayara Assoubre (CIV)	08.08.1992	3	(8)	
Hector Hevel (NED)	15.05.1996	22	(1)	2
Joan Tomás Campasol (ESP)	17.05.1985	2	(4)	
Jorge Larena Avellaneda Roig (ESP)	29.09.1981	25	(5)	3
Vincent Fabien Laban Bounayre	09.09.1984	1	(2)	
Ignacio Cases Mora „Nacho Cases" (ESP)	22.12.1987	15	(2)	1
Lluís Sastre Reus (ESP)	26.03.1986	9	(1)	
Alberto Sansimena Chamorro „Tete" (ESP)	26.05.1985	15	(6)	2
Forwards:	**DOB**	**M**	**(s)**	**G**
Acorán Barrera Reyes (ESP)	31.01.1983	18	(4)	3
Dani Aquino Pintos (ESP)	27.07.1990	8	(4)	2
Apostolos Giannou (AUS)	25.01.1990	19	(5)	4
Jeffrén Isaac Suárez Bermúdez (ESP)	20.01.1988	10	(4)	
Konstantinos Konstantinou	08.10.1999		(1)	
Onisiforos Roushias	15.07.1992		(11)	
Thierry Alain Florian Taulemesse (FRA)	31.01.1986	19	(5)	7
Ivan Tričkovski (MKD)	18.04.1987	22	(1)	15
Trainer:	**DOB**	**M**		
Andoni Iraola Sagarna (ESP)	22.06.1982	16		
Joseba Imanol Idiakez Barkaiztegui (ESP) [15.01.2019]	14.03.1972	16		

Athlitiki Enosi Lemesou (AEL Limassol)

Founded: 04.10.1930
Stadium: Stádio Tsirion, Limassol (13,331)

Goalkeepers:	DOB	M	(s)	G
Patryk Procek (POL)	01.03.1995	19		
Josimar Diaz Vózinha (CPV)	03.06.1986	13		
Defenders:	**DOB**	**M**	**(s)**	**G**
André Ferreira Teixeira (POR)	14.08.1993	23		
Omar Hassamo Júnior Dossa Momade	28.07.1986	18	(4)	1
Boris Godál (SVK)	27.05.1987	9		
Charalambos Kyriakou	15.10.1989	3	(2)	
Kevin Pierre Lafrance (HAI)	13.01.1990	21	(1)	3
Leandro Miguel Pereira Silva (POR)	04.05.1994	10	(8)	2
Konstantinos Michailidis	06.02.2000		(1)	
Nils Teixeira (GER)	10.07.1990	26	(2)	3
Christos Wheeler	29.06.1997	22	(4)	1
Midfielders:	**DOB**	**M**	**(s)**	**G**
Marko Adamović (SRB)	11.03.1991	18	(2)	2
Adnan Aganović (CRO)	03.10.1987	6	(6)	
Alexandre Afonso da Silva (BRA)	15.08.1983	19	(4)	5
Dani González Benítez (ESP)	07.04.1987	4	(3)	
Jon Gaztañaga Arrospide (ESP)	28.06.1991	20	(4)	1
Giannis Gerolemou	27.01.2000	1	(1)	
Fidelis Irhene (NGA)	20.01.1996	4	(6)	1
Manuel Torres Jiménez (ESP)	05.01.1991	12		3
Davor Zdravkovski (MKD)	20.03.1998	21	(2)	
Forwards:	**DOB**	**M**	**(s)**	**G**
Jarchinio Antonia (CUW)	27.12.1990	11	(2)	1
Andreas Avraam	06.06.1987	19	(4)	2
Joan Román Román i Ollè (ESP)	18.05.1993	1	(4)	2
Andreas Makris	27.11.1995	18	(6)	5
Kire Markoski (MKD)	20.02.1995	1	(6)	1
Nestoras Mitidis	01.06.1991	6	(13)	
Rubén Jurado Fernández (ESP)	25.04.1986	23	(8)	15
Ivan Schranz (SVK)	13.09.1993	4	(3)	
Trainer:	**DOB**	**M**		
Dušan Kerkez (BIH)	01.05.1976	32		

Alki Oroklini Football Club Larnaca

Founded: 1979 (*as Omonia Oroklini*)
Stadium: Stádio Ammochostos, Larnaca (5,500)

Goalkeepers:	DOB	M	(s)	G
Giorgos Panagi	16.07.1995	2		
Urko Rafael Pardo Goas	28.01.1983	30		
Defenders:	**DOB**	**M**	**(s)**	**G**
Costas Charalambous	12.08.1995	4	(10)	
Marios Chari	30.11.1994	6	(2)	
Sofyane Cherfa (ALG)	13.08.1984	20		
Martinos Christofi	26.07.1993	19	(1)	
Franco Valentín Flores (ARG)	28.05.1993	27	(1)	2
Stavrinos Konstantinou	19.03.1997	5	(12)	1
Panagiotis Loizides	28.02.1995	3		
Orlin Starokin (BUL)	08.01.1987	22	(2)	1
Alexis Theocharous	20.04.1992	2	(1)	
Midfielders:	**DOB**	**M**	**(s)**	**G**
Bai Andrew Antoniou (AUS)	04.06.1997		(1)	
Rafael Eduardo Acosta Cammarota (VEN)	13.02.1989	25	(3)	2
El Hedi Belameiri (ALG)	24.04.1991	27	(3)	4
Aikel Gadacha Charrad (FRA)	29.03.1993	18	(9)	
Dimitris Kyprianou	02.02.1993	27		
Matija Špoljarić (SRB)	02.04.1997	27	(3)	8
Duško Trajčevski (MKD)	01.11.1990	24	(2)	1
Yoann Tribeau (FRA)	26.02.1988	7	(10)	
Theo Lewis Weeks (LBR)	19.01.1990	1	(1)	
Forwards:	**DOB**	**M**	**(s)**	**G**
Alioun Badara (SEN)	01.10.1989		(8)	
Marios Elia	19.05.1996	9	(13)	2
Ivan Carlos França Coelho (BRA)	06.12.1989	24	(3)	10
Marlon da Silva de Moura	05.02.1990	2	(2)	
Andreas Stavrou	27.10.1988	21	(2)	3
Apollonas Vasiliou	29.03.1997		(5)	
Trainer:	**DOB**	**M**		
Costas Sakkas	22.05.1979	32		

Anorthosis Famagusta Football Club

Founded: 30.01.1911
Stadium: Stádio "Antonis Papadopoulos", Larnaca (10,230)

Goalkeepers:	**DOB**	**M**	**(s)**	**G**
Dimitris Dimitriou	15.01.1999	19	(1)	
Francis Odinaka Uzoho (NGA)	28.10.1998	3		
Ivan Vargić (CRO)	15.03.1987	10		
Defenders:	**DOB**	**M**	**(s)**	**G**
Panagiotis Artymatas	12.11.1998	10	(1)	
Douglas Ferreira „Douglão" (BRA)	18.05.1986	17	(1)	3
Erwin Koffi (FRA)	10.01.1995	22	(3)	1
Panayiotis Konstantinou	27.04.2000	1		
Gordon Schildenfeld (CRO)	18.03.1985	30		2
Andraž Struna (SVN)	23.04.1989	24	(2)	
Midfielders:	**DOB**	**M**	**(s)**	**G**
Vincent Bessat (FRA)	08.11.1985	21	(2)	2
Oliver Buff (SUI)	03.08.1992	3	(5)	1
Giorgos Economides	10.04.1990	3	(8)	
Nikos Englezou	11.07.1993	8	(9)	1
Konstantinos Georgallides	19.01.2002		(3)	
Emanuel Nosakhare Igiebor (NGA)	09.11.1990	7		
Michalis Ioannou	30.06.2000	12	(5)	
João Victor de Albuquerque Bruno (BRA)	07.11.1988	28		4
Gojko Kačar (SRB)	26.01.1987	4	(2)	
Neofytos Kyriakou	29.10.1997	3	(7)	
Chrysostomos Philippou	13.10.2000	1	(1)	
Danijel Pranjić (CRO)	02.12.1981	27	(1)	5
Rubén Rayo Serna (ESP)	21.06.1986	23	(2)	3
Nicolás Marcelo Stefanelli (ARG)	22.11.1994	12		2
Forwards:	**DOB**	**M**	**(s)**	**G**
Sekou Cissé (CIV)	23.05.1985	1	(7)	
Michal Ďuriš (SVK)	01.06.1988	28	(1)	11
Nika Kacharava (GEO)	13.01.1994	11	(12)	4
Ioannis Kosta	24.05.2000		(1)	
Ricardo Alexis Laborde León (COL)	16.02.1988	7	(6)	1
Beka Mikeltadze (GEO)	26.11.1997	15	(8)	2
Andreas Nikolaou	01.03.1999		(2)	
Nikos Panagiotou	12.05.2000	2	(1)	
Trainer:	**DOB**	**M**		
Ronny Levy (ISR)	14.11.1966	5		
Jurgen Streppel (NED) [11.10.2018]	25.06.1969	27		

Athletikos Podosferikos Omilos Ellinon Lefkosias (APOEL Football Club Nicosia)

Founded: 08.11.1926
Stadium: Stádio GSP, Nicosia (22,859)

Goalkeepers:	**DOB**	**M**	**(s)**	**G**
Rafael Enrique Romo Pérez (VEN)	25.02.1990	11	(1)	
Boy Waterman (NED)	24.01.1984	21		
Defenders:	**DOB**	**M**	**(s)**	**G**
Wanderson de Jesus Martins „Caju" (BRA)	17.07.1995	25		
Carlos Roberto da Cruz Júnior „Carlão" (BRA)	19.01.1986	21	(1)	1
Mickaël Facchinetti (SUI)	15.02.1991	3	(1)	
Nicholas Ioannou	10.11.1995	25		4
Jesús Rueda Ambrosio (ESP)	19.02.1987		(1)	
Giorgios Merkis	30.07.1984	23	(3)	
Emilio N'Sue López (EQG)	30.09.1989	9		3
Nuno Miguel Barbosa Morais (POR)	29.01.1984	26	(2)	13
Praxitelis Vouros (GRE)	05.05.1995	25	(3)	
Midfielders:	**DOB**	**M**	**(s)**	**G**
Musa Suliman Al Taamari (JOR)	10.06.1997	23	(1)	9
Kostakis Artymatas	15.04.1993	5	(7)	
Juan Bautista Cascini (ARG)	04.06.1997	1	(2)	
Tomás Sebastián De Vincenti (ARG)	09.02.1989	9	(3)	4
Giorgos Efrem	05.07.1989	4	(13)	1
Savvas Gentsoglou (GRE)	19.09.1990	8	(7)	
Antonio Jakoliš (CRO)	28.02.1992	12		2
Loukas Kalogirou	21.02.2002		(1)	
Lucas Vieira de Souza (BRA)	04.06.1990	21	(4)	5
Zhivko Milanov (BUL)	15.07.1984	3	(2)	
Paris Polikarpou	23.09.2000	1		
Forwards:	**DOB**	**M**	**(s)**	**G**
Efstathios Aloneftis	29.03.1983	4	(6)	2
André Filipe Cunha Vidigal (POR)	17.08.1998	1	(8)	1
Andreas Artemiou	03.02.1999		(1)	
Norbert Balogh (HUN)	21.02.1996	5	(7)	2
Roman Bezjak (SVN)	21.02.1989	7	(7)	4
Guilherme Augusto Alves Dellatorre (BRA)	01.05.1992	3	(5)	
Reza Ghoochannejhad Nournia (IRN)	20.09.1987	8	(2)	2
Leonardo Natel Vieira „Léo Natel" (BRA)	14.03.1997	24	(2)	8
Ghayas Zahid (NOR)	08.09.1994	24	(3)	3
Trainer:	**DOB**	**M**		
Bruno Miguel Nunes Baltazar (POR)	06.07.1977	1		
Giorgos Kostis (GRE) [18.09.2018]	07.10.1972	3		
Paolo Tramezzani (ITA) [10.10.2018]	30.07.1970	28		

Apollon Lemesou (Apollon Football Club Limassol)

Founded: 14.04.1954
Stadium: Stádio Tsirion, Limassol (13,331)

Goalkeepers:	**DOB**	**M**	**(s)**	**G**
Bruno Miguel Esteves do Vale (POR)	08.04.1983	30		
Tasos Kissas	18.01.1988	2	(1)	
Defenders:	**DOB**	**M**	**(s)**	**G**
Héctor Yuste Canton (ESP)	12.01.1988	11		4
Milan Kerbr	10.09.1989	2		
Antonis Mitas	09.02.2000	1	(1)	
Dylan Ouédraogo (FRA)	22.07.1998	12	(6)	
Konstantinos Papamichail	17.05.1999	2		
Valentin Sébastien Roger Roberge (FRA)	09.06.1987	25		2
Vahid Selimović (LUX)	03.04.1997	7	(1)	
Marios Stylianou	23.09.1993	5	(4)	
Midfielders:	**DOB**	**M**	**(s)**	**G**
Kévin Bru (MRI)	12.12.1988	15	(2)	4
Mustapha Carayol (GAM)	04.09.1988	3	(10)	2
Demetris Erodotou	20.04.2002		(1)	
Dimitris Flouris	12.11.2001		(1)	
João Pedro Guerra Cunha (POR)	04.05.1986	29		
Chambos Kyriakou	09.02.1995	20	(1)	
Saša Marković (SRB)	13.03.1991	20	(2)	2
Esteban Fernando Sachetti (ARG)	21.11.1985	22	(1)	1
Richard Soumah (GUI)	06.10.1986	5	(3)	
Danilo Spoljarić	14.07.1999	1	(7)	
Christoforos Tsolakis	30.10.2001	1		
Ionnis Vasileiadis	12.11.1999	1		
Giorgos Vasiliou	12.06.1984	20	(3)	1
Forwards:	**DOB**	**M**	**(s)**	**G**
Adrián Sardinero Corpa (ESP)	13.10.1990	22	(5)	3
Marios Andreou	07.11.2000		(1)	
David Faupala (FRA)	11.02.1997	1	(9)	1
Fotios Papoulis (GRE)	22.01.1985	17	(7)	6
Anton Maglica (CRO)	11.11.1991	14	(3)	7
Facundo Abel Pereyra (ARG)	03.09.1987	22	(3)	11
Petros Psychas	28.08.1998	3	(5)	1
André Schembri (MLT)	27.05.1986	16	(12)	5
Emilio José Zelaya (ARG)	30.07.1987	23	(3)	10
Trainer:	**DOB**	**M**		
Sofronis Avgousti	09.03.1977	32		

Doxa Katokopias Football Club

Founded: 1954
Stadium: Stádio "Makario", Nicosia (16,000)

Goalkeepers:	DOB	M	(s)	G
Armin Gremsl (AUT)	18.08.1994	31		
Giorgos Loizou	25.02.1992	1		
Defenders:	**DOB**	**M**	**(s)**	**G**
Zacharias Adoni	13.07.1999	5	(2)	
Alfonso Artabe Meca (ESP)	18.08.1988	4	(2)	1
Lamine Ba (FRA)	24.08.1997	4	(1)	
Yiannis Efstathiou	14.02.1992	6	(3)	
Joel Vieira Pereira (POR)	28.09.1996	29	(1)	
Bogdan Alexandru Mitrea (ROU)	29.09.1987	29		2
Stephanos Mouktaris	10.07.1994	19	(2)	1
Nélson Barbosa Conceição „Nelsinho" (BRA)	01.01.1988	19	(3)	
Konstantinos Sotiriou	21.06.1996	10	(1)	
Răzvan Tincu (ROU)	15.07.1987	21	(8)	
Midfielders:	**DOB**	**M**	**(s)**	**G**
Benjamin Akoto Asamoah (GHA)	04.01.1994	23	(2)	1
Vladimir Boljević (MNE)	17.01.1988	27	(2)	1
Jean-Charles Fernandez (GUI)	20.01.1998		(3)	
Luís Carlos Eneas da Conceição Lima (BRA)	15.06.1987	24	(3)	8
Andreas Pachipis	16.12.1994	1	(4)	
Vasilios Papafotis	10.08.1995	12	(14)	3
Nils Zatl (AUT)	03.04.1992	25	(7)	4
Forwards:	**DOB**	**M**	**(s)**	**G**
Nektarios Alexandrou	19.12.1983	15		
Paul Ştefan Batin (ROU)	29.06.1987	11	(2)	6
Ioannis Chatzivasilis	26.04.1990	16	(12)	4
Evgen Pavlov (UKR)	12.03.1991	9	(18)	4
Berat Sadik (FIN)	14.09.1986	11	(1)	12
Trainer:	**DOB**	**M**		
Loukas Hatziloukas	06.06.1967	32		

Enosi Neon Paralimniou (Enosis Neon Paralimni Football Club)

Founded: 1936
Stadium: Stádio "Tasos Markou", Paralimni (5,800)

Goalkeepers:	DOB	M	(s)	G
Boris Kleiman (ISR)	26.10.1990	26		
Konstantinos Petrou	23.09.1997	6	(2)	
Defenders:	**DOB**	**M**	**(s)**	**G**
Angelis Angeli	31.05.1989	18		
Borja Ekiza Imaz (ESP)	06.03.1988	1		
Sokratis Fitanidis (GRE)	25.05.1984	9	(3)	2
Riley Grant (USA)	27.01.1995	1		
Hovhannes Hambardzumyan (ARM)	04.10.1990	24		1
Antonis Koumis	11.02.1997	5	(8)	1
Andreas Kyriakou	05.02.1994	27		
Lefteris Mertakas	16.03.1985	5		
Demetris Moulazimis	15.01.1992	7	(6)	
Maximiliano Fernando Oliva (ARG)	16.03.1990	22	(3)	
Vasilios Vallianos (GRE)	11.09.1988	9	(3)	1
Midfielders:	**DOB**	**M**	**(s)**	**G**
Shaloze Chigozie Udoji (NGA)	16.07.1986	24	(5)	4
Rafail Eleftheriou	30.05.1999		(4)	
Eyong Tarkang Enoh (CMR)	23.03.1986	24		1
Andreas Frangos	19.01.1997	1	(3)	
Loizos Kosmas	25.01.1995	4	(9)	
Irakli Maisuradze (GEO)	22.08.1988	22	(7)	
Kyriakos Pavlou	04.09.1986	1		
Omar Reiss Rowe (ENG)	30.10.1994	1	(2)	1
Aleksandr Sherbakov (RUS)	26.06.1998	6	(5)	
Konstantinos Xiouros	10.08.2000		(1)	
Forwards:	**DOB**	**M**	**(s)**	**G**
Minas Antoniou	22.02.1994	13		5
Dominik Glavina (CRO)	06.12.1992	2	(1)	
Shoval Gozlan (ISR)	25.04.1994	8	(3)	3
Giorgos Kolokoudias	03.05.1989	5	(12)	
Theodoros Kolokoudias	06.07.1999		(2)	
Giorgos Nicolaou	24.06.2000	2		
Ioannis Pittas	10.07.1996	20	(8)	9
Morten Nicolas Rasmussen (DEN)	31.01.1985	12	(4)	2
Magatte Sarr (FRA)	02.09.1999	1		
Llorenc Riera Ortega „Sito Riera" (ESP)	05.01.1987	25		4
Gonzalo Eulogio Zárate (ARG)	06.08.1984	21	(3)	1
Trainer:	**DOB**	**M**		
André Paus (NED)	09.10.1965	10		
Carit Falch (DEN) [29.11.2018]	16.12.1976	22		

Ermis Aradippou Football Club

Founded: 1958
Stadium: Stádio GSZ, Larnaca (13,032)

Goalkeepers:	DOB	M	(s)	G
Giannis Arabatzis (GRE)	28.05.1984	16		
Giannis Firinidis (GRE)	01.07.1983	12		
Georgios Papadopoulos	24.04.1991	4	(1)	
Defenders:	**DOB**	**M**	**(s)**	**G**
Iván Malón Aragonés (ESP)	26.08.1986	16	(1)	
Marios Demetriou	25.12.1992	2	(3)	
David Sebastião Bondo Kuagika (ANG)	10.08.1990	26		2
Christos Mantovanis	18.12.1998		(4)	1
Francis N'Ganga (CGO)	16.06.1985	8		
Kostas Pileas	11.12.1998	14	(2)	
Paris Psaltis	12.11.1996	22	(4)	
Vladimir Volkov (MNE)	06.06.1986	3		
Midfielders:	**DOB**	**M**	**(s)**	**G**
Konstantinos Banousis (GRE)	23.01.1988	12	(5)	
Dídac Ángel Devesa Albis (ESP)	30.12.1990	20	(7)	1
Gerasimos Fylaktou	24.07.1991	23	(2)	1
Darryl Hérold Goulon (FRA)	12.06.1988	8	(1)	
Nikolai Kipiani (RUS)	25.01.1997	9	(3)	
Anastasios Lagos (GRE)	12.04.1992	10	(4)	
Loizos Pounnas	25.08.1999	1	(4)	
Marios Poutziouris	08.12.1993	15	(4)	
Giannis Taralidis (GRE)	17.05.1981	19	(3)	8
Forwards:	**DOB**	**M**	**(s)**	**G**
Sandro Sene Sakho Aníbal Embaló (POR)	01.05.1996	10		
Marcel Josué Essombé (CMR)	06.05.1988	3	(2)	
Ilias Georghiou	21.07.1997	6	(7)	
Widson Silva de Melo „Índio" (BRA)	20.05.1997	9	(8)	1
Georgios Katsiati	04.02.1996	17	(8)	4
Sekou Keita Souza (GUI)	12.12.1994	9		1
Enrique Boula Senobua „Kike Boula" (EQG)	17.07.1993	13		3
Savvas Lytras	16.01.2000	1	(7)	
Dimitar Makriev (BUL)	07.01.1984	10	(4)	
Yaroslav Martinyuk (UKR)	20.02.1989	23		2
Yiannis Mavrou	19.07.1994	11	(12)	4
Trainer:	**DOB**	**M**		
Costas Kaiafas	22.09.1974	6		
Demetris Daskalakis [21.10.2018]	18.11.1977	1		
João Carlos Pires de Deus (POR) [29.10.2018]	06.11.1976	6		
Stefano Cusin (ITA) [17.12.2018]	28.10.1968	4		
Chrysis Michael [28.01.2019]	26.05.1977	9		
Demetris Daskalakis [02.04.2019]	18.11.1977	6		

Nea Salamis Famagusta Football Club

Founded: 07.03.1948
Stadium: Stádio Ammochostos, Famagusta (5,500)

Goalkeepers:	DOB	M	(s)	G
John Alvbåge (SWE)	10.08.1982	1		
Goulielmos Lytras	28.07.1998	4		
Robert Veselovsky (SVK)	02.09.1985	27		
Defenders:	**DOB**	**M**	**(s)**	**G**
Agustín García Iñiguez „Agus" (ESP)	03.05.1985	4	(3)	
Anderson Correia de Barros (BRA)	06.05.1991	30	(1)	1
Kypros Christoforou	23.04.1993	24		1
Andreas Frageskou	26.07.1996		(2)	
Ivan Fuštar (CRO)	18.08.1989	25	(1)	2
Jaílson de Lima Araújo (BRA)	21.02.1991	9	(2)	
Thomas Nikolaou	22.10.2001	1	(2)	
Román Golobart Benet (ESP)	21.03.1992	20	(1)	1
Konstantinos Sergiou	02.10.2000	3	(1)	
Midfielders:	**DOB**	**M**	**(s)**	**G**
Lefteris Chatzikonstanti	24.05.2001	3	(2)	
Ioannis Costi	17.03.2000	10	(16)	1
Federico Domínguez	17.05.1991	5		
Charles Betrand Etoundi Eloundou (CMR)	04.12.1994	28	(2)	6
Andreas Lemesios	24.09.1997		(3)	
Renato João Inacio Margaça	17.07.1985	30		1
Konstantinos Mintikkis	14.07.1989	21	(1)	2
Farshad Noor (AFG)	02.10.1994	23	(6)	2
Timotheus Pavlou	08.09.1994	6		
Alasdair David Reynolds (SCO)	02.09.1996	8	(2)	
Tonia Tisdell (LBR)	20.03.1992	3	(3)	1
Forwards:	**DOB**	**M**	**(s)**	**G**
Stéphane Aziz Ki (BFA)	03.03.1996	1	(5)	
Demetris Chrysostomou	20.12.2002	1		1
Kingsley Onuegbu (NGA)	05.03.1986	32		11
Iasonas Pikis	11.11.2000		(4)	
Theodosis Siathas	16.12.1998	3	(11)	
Daniel Sikorski (AUT)	02.11.1987	3	(22)	
Thiago Ferreira Dos Santos (BRA)	12.07.1987	27	(1)	10
Trainer:	**DOB**	**M**		
Savvas Poursaitidis	23.06.1976	32		

Athlitikos Sillogos Omonia Lefkosias (Athletic Club Omonia Nicosia)

Founded: 04.06.1948
Stadium: Stádio GSP, Nicosia (22,859)

Goalkeepers:	DOB	M	(s)	G
Tomás Mejías Osorio (ESP)	30.01.1989	27	(1)	
Costas Panayi	08.10.1994	5		
Defenders:	**DOB**	**M**	**(s)**	**G**
Mickaël Gaffoor (FRA)	21.01.1987	8	(2)	
Michalis Gavriel	22.03.1999	1		
Jaílson de Lima Araújo (BRA)	21.02.1991	4	(2)	
Ioannis Kousoulos	14.06.1996	24	(4)	
Christian Manrique (ESP)	02.10.1998	17	(2)	
Marco Motta (ITA)	14.05.1986	7	(1)	
Franjo Prce (CRO)	07.01.1996	15	(2)	1
Loukas Vyntra (GRE)	05.02.1981	27		1
Midfielders:	**DOB**	**M**	**(s)**	**G**
Abdul Jeleel Ajagun (NGA)	10.02.1993	10	(1)	
Juan Ángel Albín Leites (URU)	17.07.1986		(2)	
Alexandre Miguel Barros Soares (POR)	01.03.1992	23	(4)	1
Christos Charalambous	20.06.1998	1	(3)	
Dimitris Christofi	28.09.1988	4	(2)	1
Cristian Montes López (ESP)	10.08.1997	9	(11)	2
Jordi Gómez García-Penche (ESP)	24.05.1985	30		8
Andronikos Kakouli	03.05.2001		(1)	
Fanos Katelaris	26.08.1996	13	(4)	1
Dimitrios Kolovos (GRE)	27.04.1993	14	(4)	4
Raoul Cédric Loé (CMR)	31.01.1989	4	(6)	
Loizos Loizou	18.07.2003		(2)	
Alberto Lora Ramos (ESP)	25.03.1987	14	(2)	
Charis Mavrias (GRE)	21.02.1994	15	(2)	2
Marinos Tzionis	16.07.2001	8	(3)	3
Forwards:	**DOB**	**M**	**(s)**	**G**
Jarchinio Antonia (CUW)	27.12.1990	5	(2)	
Matt Derbyshire (ENG)	14.04.1986	14	(11)	2
Jorge Enríquez García (MEX)	08.01.1991	3	(3)	
Jordan Neil Greenidge (ENG)	05.01.2000		(1)	
Juan Antonio Entrena Gálvez „Juanan" (ESP)	19.05.1996	2	(4)	
David Gerardo Ramírez Ruiz (CRC)	28.05.1993	27	(1)	8
Saša Živec (SVN)	02.04.1991	6	(6)	
Trainer:	**DOB**	**M**		
Juan Carlos Oliva Fornos (ESP)	04.01.1965	5		
Ángel Gómez Ruíz (ESP) [22.10.2018]	15.09.1976	2		
Yannis Anastasiou (GRE) [01.11.2018]	05.03.1973	25		

Pafos Football Club Paphos

Founded: 10.06.2014 (after the merger of AEK Kouklia and AEP Paphos)
Stadium: Stádio „Stelios Kyriakides", Paphos (9,394)

Goalkeepers:	DOB	M	(s)	G
Ioannis Angelopoulos (GRE)	03.04.1998	1		
Joël Mall (SUI)	05.04.1991	27		
Evgenios Petrou	06.09.1997	4		
Defenders:	**DOB**	**M**	**(s)**	**G**
Kyriakos Antoniou	03.05.2001	1	(1)	
Patrick Banggaard (DEN)	04.04.1994	29		
Radek Dejmek (TCH)	02.02.1988	2	(2)	
Aleksandr Dovbnya (RUS)	14.02.1996	8	(8)	1
Kevin Holt (SCO)	25.01.1993	26		
Jander Ribeiro Santana (BRA)	08.07.1988	16	(1)	
Andreas Karo	09.09.1996	16	(3)	2
Pavel Lelyukhin (RUS)	23.04.1998	6	(2)	
Lorran de Oliveira Quintanilha (BRA)	28.01.1996	4	(4)	
Andreas Panayiotou	31.05.1995	8	(13)	
Matija Širok (SVN)	31.05.1991	27	(3)	
Sotiris Zantis	24.01.2001		(2)	
Midfielders:	**DOB**	**M**	**(s)**	**G**
Brayan Angulo Mosquera (COL)	19.07.1993	25	(4)	9
Jens Cools (BEL)	16.10.1990	23	(2)	6
Zdeněk Folprecht (CZE)	01.07.1991	24	(5)	1
Konstantinos Nikolaos Giannoulis (GRE)	09.12.1987	1		
Abdisalam Abdulkadir Ibrahim (NOR)	01.05.1991	4	(3)	
Luis Marcelo Morais dos Reis „Lulinha" (BRA)	10.04.1990	2	(16)	
Luca Polizzi (BEL)	28.05.1996	3	(6)	
Ektoras Stefanou	12.04.2001		(1)	
Diego Živulić (CRO)	23.03.1992	24	(2)	
Forwards:	**DOB**	**M**	**(s)**	**G**
Kévin Bérigaud (FRA)	09.05.1988	3		
Mohamed Choukoud (NED)	01.01.1999		(2)	
Adam Nemec (SVK)	02.09.1985	27	(1)	16
Deniss Rakels (LVA)	20.08.1992	16	(1)	1
Federico Iván Rasic (ARG)	24.03.1992	18	(8)	3
Panyiotis Zachariou	26.02.1996	7	(6)	
Trainer:	**DOB**	**M**		
Steven John Pressley (SCO)	11.10.1973	1		
Željko Kopić (CRO) [10.09.2018]	10.09.1977	31		

SECOND LEVEL

Cypriot Second Division 2018/2019

1.	Ethnikos Achna FC (*Promoted*)	27	18	8	1	58	-	20	62
2.	Olympiakos Nicosia FC (*Promoted*)	27	19	3	5	63	-	27	60
3.	Aris Limassol FC	27	18	5	4	55	-	30	59
4.	Othellos Athienou FC	27	13	8	6	59	-	28	47
5.	Anagennisi Deryneia FC	27	12	5	10	38	-	28	41
6.	ASIL Lysi	27	11	6	10	32	-	33	39
7.	Omonia Aradippou FC	27	12	2	13	39	-	36	38
8.	Onisilos Sotira 2014	27	11	4	12	37	-	40	37
9.	Karmiotissa Pano Polemidia FC	27	11	4	12	42	-	53	37
10.	Athlitikos Omilos Ayia Napa FC	27	9	7	11	39	-	36	34
11.	Athletic Union of Zakaki	27	9	6	12	36	-	47	33
12.	Akritas Chlorakas FC	27	10	2	15	32	-	53	32
13.	MEAP Pera Choriou Nisou (*Relegated*)	27	7	6	14	38	-	48	27
14.	Enosis Neon THOI Lakatamia (*Relegated*)	27	6	8	13	22	-	49	26
15.	PAEE Kerynias (*Relegated*)	27	5	7	15	33	-	55	22
16.	AC Digenis Oroklinis (*Relegated*)	27	3	5	19	25	-	65	14

NATIONAL TEAM

INTERNATIONAL MATCHES
(16.07.2018 – 15.07.2019)

06.09.2018	Oslo	Norway - Cyprus	2-0(2-0)	(UNL)
09.09.2018	Nicosia	Cyprus - Slovenia	2-1(0-0)	(UNL)
13.10.2018	Sofia	Bulgaria - Cyprus	2-1(0-1)	(UNL)
16.10.2018	Ljubljana	Slovenia - Cyprus	1-1(0-1)	(UNL)
16.11.2018	Nicosia	Cyprus - Bulgaria	1-1(1-0)	(UNL)
19.11.2018	Nicosia	Cyprus - Norway	0-2(0-1)	(UNL)
21.03.2019	Nicosia	Cyprus - San Marino	5-0(4-0)	(ECQ)
24.03.2019	Nicosia	Cyprus - Belgium	0-2(0-2)	(ECQ)
08.06.2019	Glasgow	Scotland - Cyprus	2-1(0-0)	(ECQ)
11.06.2019	Nizhny Novgorod	Russia - Cyprus	1-0(1-0)	(ECQ)

06.09.2018 NORWAY - CYPRUS 2-0(2-0) UEFA Nations League C, Group 3
Ullevaal Stadion, Oslo; Referee: István Kovács (Romania); Attendance: 6,572
CYP: Urko Rafael Pardo Goas, Giorgos Merkis, Konstantinos Laifis, Charalambos Kyriakou (77.Grigoris Kastanos), Ioannis Kousoulos, Jason Demetriou (Cap), Renato João Inácio Margaça (82.Nicholas Ioannou), Giorgos Vasiliou (46.Georgios Efrem), Kostakis Artymatas, Fotios Papoulis, Pieros Sotiriou. Trainer: Ran Ben Shimon (Israel).

09.09.2018 CYPRUS - SLOVENIA 2-1(0-0) UEFA Nations League C, Group 3
Stádio GSP, Nicosia; Referee: Andris Treimanis (Latvia); Attendance: 1,115
CYP: Constantinos Panayi, Konstantinos Laifis, Charalambos Kyriakou, Nicholas Ioannou (67.Renato João Inácio Margaça), Ioannis Kousoulos, Georgios Efrem (90+2.Giorgos Merkis), Jason Demetriou (Cap), Kostakis Artymatas, Grigoris Kastanos (60.Onisiforos Roushias), Fotios Papoulis, Pieros Sotiriou. Trainer: Ran Ben Shimon (Israel).
Goals: Pieros Sotiriou (69), Petar Stojanović (89 own goal).

13.10.2018 BULGARIA - CYPRUS 2-1(0-1) UEFA Nations League C, Group 3
Nationalen Stadion "Vasil Levski", Sofia; Referee: Srđan Jovanović (Serbia); Attendance: 6,700
CYP: Constantinos Panayi, Giorgos Merkis, Konstantinos Laifis, Nicholas Ioannou (72.Demetris Christofi), Ioannis Kousoulos, Jason Demetriou (Cap), Andreas Avraam, Kostakis Artymatas, Grigoris Kastanos (65.Renato João Inácio Margaça), Fotios Papoulis (75.Onisiforos Roushias), Pieros Sotiriou. Trainer: Ran Ben Shimon (Israel).
Goal: Grigoris Kastanos (41).

16.10.2018 SLOVENIA - CYPRUS 1-1(0-1) UEFA Nations League C, Group 3
Stožice Stadium, Ljubljana; Referee: Mads-Kristoffer Kristoffersen (Denmark); Attendance: 5,318
CYP: Constantinos Panayi, Giorgos Merkis, Valentinos Sielis, Ioannis Kousoulos, Jason Demetriou (Cap), Renato João Inácio Margaça (86.Demetris Christofi), Giorgos Vasiliou (90+5.Nicholas Ioannou), Kostakis Artymatas, Grigoris Kastanos [*sent off 66*], Fotios Papoulis (73.Andreas Avraam), Pieros Sotiriou. Trainer: Ran Ben Shimon (Israel).
Goal: Fotios Papoulis (37).

16.11.2018 CYPRUS - BULGARIA 1-1(1-0) UEFA Nations League C, Group 3
Stádio GSP, Nicosia; Referee: Mohammed Al Hakim (Sweden); Attendance: 3,844
CYP: Constantinos Panayi, Giorgos Merkis (Cap), Konstantinos Laifis, Charalambos Kyriakou, Ioannis Kousoulos, Georgios Efrem (78.Vasilios Papafotis), Andreas Avraam (59.Nicholas Ioannou), Renato João Inácio Margaça, Kostakis Artymatas, Panayiotis Zachariou (67.Onisiforos Roushias), Andreas Makris. Trainer: Ran Ben Shimon (Israel).
Goal: Panayiotis Zachariou (24).

19.11.2018 CYPRUS - NORWAY 0-2(0-1) UEFA Nations League C, Group 3
Stádio GSP, Nicosia; Referee: István Vad (Hungary); Attendance: 1,513
CYP: Constantinos Panayi, Giorgos Merkis (Cap), Valentinos Sielis [*sent off 80*], Konstantinos Laifis, Nicholas Ioannou, Ioannis Kousoulos, Andreas Avraam (61.Georgios Efrem), Charalambos Kyriakou (78.Gerasimos Fylaktou), Kostakis Artymatas, Grigoris Kastanos, Panayiotis Zachariou (85.Andreas Makris). Trainer: Ran Ben Shimon (Israel).

21.03.2019 CYPRUS - SAN MARINO 5-0(4-0) 16th EC. Qualifiers

Stádio GSP, Nicosia; Referee: Juri Frischer (Estonia); Attendance: 3,175

CYP: Constantinos Panayi, Konstantinos Laifis, Nicholas Ioannou, Ioannis Kousoulos, Georgios Efrem, Jason Demetriou (Cap) (65.Giorgos Merkis), Kostakis Artymatas, Anthony Georgiou, Fotios Papoulis (54.Matija Špoljarić), Nestoras Mitidis, Pieros Sotiriou (37.Andreas Makris). Trainer: Ran Ben Shimon (Israel).

Goals: Pieros Sotiriou (19 penalty, 23 penalty), Ioannis Kousoulos (26), Georgios Efrem (31), Konstantinos Laifis (56).

24.03.2019 CYPRUS - BELGIUM 0-2(0-2) 16th EC. Qualifiers

Stádio GSP, Nicosia; Referee: François Letexier (France); Attendance: 8,728

CYP: Urko Rafael Pardo Goas, Giorgos Merkis (Cap), Dosa Júnior (46.Anthony Georgiou), Konstantinos Laifis, Nicholas Ioannou, Ioannis Kousoulos, Georgios Efrem (75.Matija Špoljarić), Renato João Inácio Margaça, Kostakis Artymatas, Fotios Papoulis, Minas Antoniou (81.Andreas Makris). Trainer: Ran Ben Shimon (Israel).

08.06.2019 SCOTLAND - CYPRUS 2-1(0-0) 16th EC. Qualifiers

Hampden Park, Glasgow; Referee: Ola Hobber Nilsen (Norway); Attendance: 31,277

CYP: Urko Rafael Pardo Goas, Konstantinos Laifis, Nicholas Ioannou, Ioannis Kousoulos, Georgios Efrem (Cap), Renato João Inácio Margaça, Kostakis Artymatas, Michalis Ioannou (66.Anthony Georgiou), Pieros Sotiriou, Andreas Makris (80.Ioannis Pittas), Matija Špoljarić (70.Ioannis Kosti). Trainer: Ran Ben Shimon (Israel).

Goal: Ioannis Kousoulos (87).

11.06.2019 RUSSIA - CYPRUS 1-0(1-0) 16th EC. Qualifiers

Nizhny Novgorod Stadium, Nizhny Novgorod; Referee: Marco Di Bello (Italy); Attendance: 42,228

CYP: Urko Rafael Pardo Goas, Konstantinos Laifis, Nicholas Ioannou, Ioannis Kousoulos, Ioannis Kosti, Andreas Avraam (Cap) (71.Ioannis Pittas), Renato João Inácio Margaça, Kostakis Artymatas, Anthony Georgiou (46.Georgios Efrem), Andreas Makris (81.Matija Špoljarić), Pieros Sotiriou. Trainer: Ran Ben Shimon (Israel).

NATIONAL TEAM PLAYERS
(16.07.2018 – 15.07.2019)

Name	DOB	Caps	Goals	2018/2019:	*Club*
Goalkeepers					
Constantinos PANAYI	08.10.1994	**18**	**0**	2018/2019:	*AC Omonia Nicosia*
Urko Rafael PARDO Goas	28.01.1983	**7**	**0**	2018/2019:	*Alki Oroklini FC*
Defenders					
Jason DEMETRIOU	18.11.1987	**50**	**1**	2018/2019:	*Southend United FC (ENG)*
Omar Hassamo Júnior Dossa Momade "DOSA JÚNIOR"	28.07.1986	**24**	**1**	2019:	*AEL Limassol*
Nicholas IOANNOU	10.11.1995	**13**	**0**	2018/2019:	*APOEL FC Nicosia*
Ioannis KOUSOULOS	14.06.1996	**12**	**2**	2018/2019:	*AC Omonia Nicosia*
Konstantinos LAIFIS	19.04.1993	**30**	**3**	2018/2019:	*R Standard Liège (BEL)*
Giorgos MERKIS	30.07.1984	**49**	**1**	2018/2019:	*APOEL FC Nicosia*
Valentinos SIELIS	01.03.1990	**32**	**1**	2018:	*Gangwon FC (KOR)*
Giorgos VASILIOU	12.06.1984	**11**	**0**	2018:	*Apollon Limassol FC*
Midfielders					
Kostakis ARTYMATAS	15.04.1993	**34**	**0**	2018/2019:	*APOEL FC Nicosia*
Andreas AVRAAM	06.06.1987	**41**	**5**	2018/2019:	*AEL Limassol*
Georgios EFREM	05.07.1989	**45**	**4**	2018/2019:	*APOEL FC Nicosia*
Gerasimos FYLAKTOU	24.07.1991	**4**	**0**	2018:	*Ermis Aradippou FC*
Anthony GEORGIOU	24.02.1997	**2**	**0**	2019:	*Levante UD Valencia (ESP)*
Grigoris KASTANOS	30.01.1998	**19**	**1**	2018/2019:	*Juventus FC Torino (ITA)*
Ioannis KOSTI	17.03.2000	**2**	**0**	2019:	*Nea Salamis Famagusta FC*
Charalambos KYRIAKOU	09.02.1995	**20**	**0**	2018/2019:	*Apollon Limassol FC*
Renato João Inácio MARGAÇA	17.07.1985	**19**	**0**	2018/2019:	*Nea Salamis Famagusta FC*
Vasilios PAPAFOTIS	10.08.1995	**2**	**0**	2018:	*Doxa Katokopias FC*
Fotios PAPOULIS	22.01.1985	**6**	**1**	2018/2019:	*Apollon Limassol FC*
Ioannis PITTAS	10.07.1996	**2**	**0**	2019:	*Enosis Neon Paralimni FC*
Matija ŠPOLJARIĆ	02.04.1997	**4**	**0**	2019:	*Alki Oroklini FC*
Forwards					
Minas ANTONIOU	22.02.1994	**2**	**0**	2019:	*Enosis Neon Paralimni FC*
Demetris CHRISTOFI	28.09.1988	**52**	**8**	2018/2019:	*AC Omonia Nicosia*
Michalis IOANNOU	30.06.2000	**1**	**0**	2019:	*Anorthosis Famagusta FC*
Andreas MAKRIS	27.09.1995	**23**	**0**	2018/2019:	*AEL Limassol*
Nestoras MITIDIS	01.06.1991	**33**	**5**	2018/2019:	*AEL Limassol*
Onisiforos ROUSHIAS	15.07.1992	**8**	**0**	2018:	*AEK Larnaca FC*
Pieros SOTIRIOU	13.01.1993	**35**	**8**	2018/2019:	*FC København (DEN)*
Panayiotis Zachariou	26.02.1996	**2**	**1**	2018:	*Pafos FC Paphos*
National team coach					
Ran BEN SHIMON (Israel) [from 05.07.2017]	28.11.1970	18 M; 3 W; 3 D; 12 L; 17-30			

CZECH REPUBLIC

The Country:

Česká republika (Czech Republic)
Capital: Praha
Surface: 78,866 km^2
Inhabitants: 10,649,800 [2019]
Time: UTC+1

The FA:

Fotbalová asociace České republiky
Atletická 2474/8 169 00, Praha
Tel: +420 233 029 111
Foundation date: 1901 (as Bohemia)
Member of FIFA since: 1907 (as Bohemia)
Member of UEFA since: 1954 (as Czechoslovakia)
Website: www.fotbal.cz

NATIONAL TEAM RECORDS

First international match:	28.08.1920, Antwerpen:	Czechoslovakia - Yugoslavia 7-0
Most international caps:	Petr Čech	- 124 caps (2002-2016)
Most international goals:	Jan Koller	- 55 goals / 91 caps (1999-2009)

UEFA EUROPEAN CHAMPIONSHIP	
1960	Final Tournament (3rd Place)
1964	Qualifiers
1968	Qualifiers
1972	Qualifiers
1976	**Final Tournament (Winners)**
1980	Final Tournament (3rd Place)
1984	Qualifiers
1988	Qualifiers
1992	Qualifiers
1996	Final Tournament (Runners-up)
2000	Final Tournament (Group Stage)
2004	Final Tournament (Semi-Finals)
2008	Final Tournament (Group Stage)
2012	Final Tournament (Quarter-Finals)
2016	Final Tournament (Qualified)

FIFA WORLD CUP	
1930	*Did not enter*
1934	Final Tournament (Runners-up)
1938	Final Tournament (Quarter-Finals)
1950	*Did not enter*
1954	Final Tournament (Group Stage)
1958	Final Tournament (Group Stage)
1962	Final Tournament (Runners-up)
1966	Qualifiers
1970	Final Tournament (Group Stage)
1974	Qualifiers
1978	Qualifiers
1982	Final Tournament (Group Stage)
1986	Qualifiers
1990	Final Tournament (Quarter-Finals)
1994	Qualifiers
1998	Qualifiers
2002	Qualifiers
2006	Final Tournament (Group Stage)
2010	Qualifiers
2014	Qualifiers
2018	Qualifiers

UEFA NATIONS LEAGUE
2018/2019 – League B

OLYMPIC FOOTBALL TOURNAMENTS 1908-2016							
1908	-	**1948**	*Did not enter*	**1972**	*Did not enter*	**1996**	Qualifiers
1912	-	**1952**	*Did not enter*	**1976**	Qualifiers	**2000**	Group Stage
1920	Runners-up	**1956**	*Did not enter*	**1980**	**Winners**	**2004**	Qualifiers
1924	1/8 Finals	**1960**	Qualifiers	**1984**	*Did not enter*	**2008**	Qualifiers
1928	*Did not enter*	**1964**	Runners-up	**1988**	Qualifiers	**2012**	Qualifiers
1936	*Did not enter*	**1968**	Group Stage	**1992**	Qualifiers	**2016**	Qualifiers

FIFA CONFEDERATIONS CUP 1992-2017
1997 (3rd Place)

CZECH CLUB HONOURS IN EUROPEAN CLUB COMPETITIONS:

European Champion Clubs' Cup (1956-1992) / UEFA Champions League (1993-2019)
None
Fairs Cup (1858-1971) / UEFA Cup (1972-2009) / UEFA Europa League (2010-2019)
None
UEFA Super Cup (1972-2019)
None
European Cup Winners' Cup 1961-1999*
None

**defunct competition*

NATIONAL COMPETITIONS
TABLE OF HONOURS

CZECHOSLOVAKIA 1925-1938 / BOHEMIA-MORAVIA 1938-1944 / CZECHOSLOVAKIA 1945-1993

	CHAMPIONS	CUP WINNERS	BEST GOALSCORERS	
1925	SK Slavia Praha	-	Jan Vaník (SK Slavia Praha)	13
1925/1926	AC Sparta Praha	-	Jan Dvořáček (AC Sparta Praha)	32
1927	AC Sparta Praha	-	Antonín Puč (SK Slavia Praha) Josef Šíma (AC Sparta Praha)	13
1927/1928	SK Viktoria Žižkov	-	Karel Meduna (SK Viktoria Žižkov)	12
1928/1929	SK Slavia Praha	-	Antonín Puč (SK Slavia Praha)	13
1929/1930	SK Slavia Praha	-	František Kloz (SK Kladno)	15
1930/1931	SK Slavia Praha	-	Josef Silný (AC Sparta Praha)	18
1931/1932	AC Sparta Praha	-	Raymond Braine (AC Sparta Praha)	16
1932/1933	SK Slavia Praha	-	Gejza Kocsis (Teplitzer FK / Bohemians AFK Vršovice)	23
1933/1934	SK Slavia Praha	-	Raymond Braine (AC Sparta Praha) Jiří Sobotka (SK Slavia Praha)	18
1934/1935	SK Slavia Praha	-	František Svoboda (SK Slavia Praha)	27
1935/1936	AC Sparta Praha	-	Vojtěch Bradáč (SK Slavia Praha)	42
1936/1937	SK Slavia Praha	-	František Kloz (SK Kladno)	28
1937/1938	AC Sparta Praha	-	Josef Bican (SK Slavia Praha)	22
1938/1939	AC Sparta Praha	-	Josef Bican (SK Slavia Praha)	29
1939/1940	SK Slavia Praha	-	Josef Bican (SK Slavia Praha)	50
1940/1941	SK Slavia Praha	-	Josef Bican (SK Slavia Praha)	38
1941/1942	SK Slavia Praha	-	Josef Bican (SK Slavia Praha)	45
1942/1943	SK Slavia Praha	-	Josef Bican (SK Slavia Praha)	39
1943/1944	AC Sparta Praha	-	Josef Bican (SK Slavia Praha)	57
1944/1945	*No competition*	-	-	
1945/1946	AC Sparta Praha	-	Josef Bican (SK Slavia Praha)	31
1946/1947	SK Slavia Praha	-	Josef Bican (SK Slavia Praha)	43
1947/1948	AC Sparta Praha	-	Jaroslav Cejp (AC Sparta Praha)	21
1948	*Championship abandoned*	-	Josef Bican (Sokol Slavia Praha)	21
1949	ŠK NV Bratislava	-	Ladislav Hlaváček (ZSJ Dynamo Slavia Praha)	28
1950	ŠK NV Bratislava	-	Josef Bican (Sokol Vítkovice Železárny)	22
1951	ŠK NV Bratislava	-	Alois Jaroš (ZSJ Vodotechna Teplice)	16
1952	Sparta ČKD Sokolovo	-	Miroslav Wiecek (OKD Ostrava)	20
1953	ÚDA Praha	-	Josef Majer (DSO Baník Kladno)	13
1954	TJ Spartak Praha Sokolovo	-	Jiří Pešek (TJ Spartak Praha Sokolovo)	13
1955	ŠK Slovan Bratislava	-	Emil Pažický (ÚNV Slovan Bratislava / Jiskra Slovena Žilina)	9
1956	AS Dukla Praha	-	Milan Dvořák (AS Dukla Praha) Miroslav Wiecek (DSO Baník Ostrava)	15
1957/1958	AS Dukla Praha	-	Miroslav Wiecek (DSO Baník Ostrava)	25
1958/1959	ČH Bratislava	-	Miroslav Wiecek (DSO Baník Ostrava)	20
1959/1960	DSO Spartak Hradec Králové	-	Michal Pucher (TJ Slovan Nitra)	18
1960/1961	AS Dukla Praha	AS Dukla Praha	Rudolf Kučera (AS Dukla Praha) Ladislav Pavlovič (TJ Tatran Prešov)	17
1961/1962	AS Dukla Praha	Slovan CHZJD Bratislava	Adolf Scherer (TJ Červená Hviezda Bratislava)	24
1962/1963	AS Dukla Praha	Slovan CHZJD Bratislava	Karel Petroš (TJ Tatran Prešov)	19
1963/1964	AS Dukla Praha	Spartak Praha Sokolovo	Ladislav Pavlovič (TJ Tatran Prešov)	21
1964/1965	TJ Spartak Praha Sokolovo	AS Dukla Praha	Pavol Bencz (Jednota Trenčín)	21
1965/1966	AS Dukla Praha	AS Dukla Praha	Ladislav Michalík (TJ Baník Ostrava)	15
1966/1967	TJ Sparta ČKD Praha	Spartak Trnava	Jozef Adamec (Spartak Trnava)	21
1967/1968	Spartak TAZ Trnava	Slovan CHZJD Bratislava	Jozef Adamec (Spartak TAZ Trnava)	18
1968/1969	Spartak TAZ Trnava	AS Dukla Praha	Ladislav Petráš (AS Dukla Banská Bystrica)	20
1969/1970	Slovan CHZJD Bratislava	TJ Gottwaldov	Jozef Adamec (Spartak TAZ Trnava)	18
1970/1971	Spartak TAZ Trnava	Spartak TAZ Trnava	Jozef Adamec (Spartak TAZ Trnava) Zdeněk Nehoda (TJ Gottwaldov)	16
1971/1972	Spartak TAZ Trnava	TJ Sparta ČKD Praha	Ján Čapkovič (Slovan CHZJD Bratislava)	19
1972/1973	Spartak TAZ Trnava	TJ Baník Ostrava OKD	Ladislav Józsa (TJ Lokomotíva Košice)	21
1973/1974	Slovan CHZJD Bratislava	Slovan CHZJD Bratislava	Ladislav Józsa (TJ Lokomotíva Košice) Přemysl Bičovský (TJ Sklo Union Teplice)	17
1974/1975	Slovan CHZJD Bratislava	Spartak TAZ Trnava	Ladislav Petráš (TJ Internacionál Slovnaft Bratislava)	20
1975/1976	TJ Baník Ostrava OKD	TJ Sparta ČKD Praha	Dušan Galis (TJ VSS Košice)	21
1976/1977	ASVS Dukla Praha	TJ Lokomotíva Košice	Ladislav Józsa (TJ Lokomotíva Košice)	18
1977/1978	Zbrojovka Brno	TJ Baník Ostrava OKD	Karel Kroupa (Zbrojovka Brno)	20
1978/1979	ASVS Dukla Praha	TJ Lokomotíva Košice	Karel Kroupa (Zbrojovka Brno) Zdeněk Nehoda (ASVS Dukla Praha)	17
1979/1980	TJ Baník Ostrava OKD	TJ Sparta ČKD Praha	Werner Lička (TJ Baník Ostrava OKD)	18
1980/1981	TJ Baník Ostrava OKD	ASVS Dukla Praha	Marián Masný (Slovan CHZJD Bratislava)	16
1981/1982	ASVS Dukla Praha	Slovan CHZJD Bratislava	Peter Herda (SK Slavia IPS Praha) Ladislav Vízek (ASVS Dukla Praha)	15
1982/1983	Bohemians ČKD Praha	ASVS Dukla Praha	Pavel Chaloupka (Bohemians ČKD Praha)	17

1983/1984	TJ Sparta ČKD Praha	AC Sparta Praha	Werner Lička (TJ Baník Ostrava OKD)	20
1984/1985	TJ Sparta ČKD Praha	ASVS Dukla Praha	Ivo Knoflíček (SK Slavia IPS Praha)	21
1985/1986	TJ Vítkovice	Spartak TAZ Trnava	Stanislav Griga (TJ Sparta ČKD Praha)	19
1986/1987	TJ Sparta ČKD Praha	DAC Dunajská Streda	Václav Daněk (TJ Baník Ostrava OKD)	24
1987/1988	TJ Sparta ČKD Praha	TJ Sparta ČKD Praha	Milan Luhový (ASVS Dukla Praha)	24
1988/1989	TJ Sparta ČKD Praha	TJ Sparta ČKD Praha	Milan Luhový (ASVS Dukla Praha)	25
1989/1990	TJ Sparta ČKD Praha	ASVS Dukla Praha	Ľubomír Luhový (TJ Internacionál Slovnaft ZŤS Bratislava)	20
1990/1991	TJ Sparta Praha	FC Baník Ostrava	Roman Kukleta (TJ Sparta Praha)	17
1991/1992	ŠK Slovan Bratislava	AC Sparta Praha	Peter Dubovský (ŠK Slovan Bratislava)	27
1992/1993	AC Sparta Praha	1. FC Košice	Peter Dubovský (ŠK Slovan Bratislava)	24

CZECH REPUBLIC (Since 1993)

1993/1994	AC Sparta Praha	FK Viktoria Žižkov	Horst Siegl (AC Sparta Praha)	20
1994/1995	AC Sparta Praha	SK Hradec Králové	Radek Drulák (FK Drnovice)	15
1995/1996	SK Slavia Praha	AC Sparta Praha	Radek Drulák (FK Drnovice)	22
1996/1997	AC Sparta Praha	SK Slavia Praha	Horst Siegl (AC Sparta Praha)	19
1997/1998	AC Sparta Praha	FK Jablonec 97	Horst Siegl (AC Sparta Praha)	13
1998/1999	AC Sparta Praha	SK Slavia Praha	Horst Siegl (AC Sparta Praha)	18
1999/2000	AC Sparta Praha	FC Slovan Liberec	Vratislav Lokvenc (AC Sparta Praha)	22
2000/2001	AC Sparta Praha	FK Viktoria Žižkov	Vítězslav Tuma (FK Drnovice)	15
2001/2002	FC Slovan Liberec	SK Slavia Praha	Jiří Štajner (FC Slovan Liberec)	15
2002/2003	AC Sparta Praha	FK Teplice	Jiří Kowalík (1. FC Synot Uherské Hradiště)	16
2003/2004	FC Baník Ostrava	AC Sparta Praha	Marek Heinz (FC Baník Ostrava)	19
2004/2005	AC Sparta Praha	FC Baník Ostrava	Tomáš Jun (AC Sparta Praha)	14
2005/2006	FC Slovan Liberec	AC Sparta Praha	Milan Ivana (FC Slovácko Uherské Hradiště)	11
2006/2007	AC Sparta Praha	AC Sparta Praha	Luboš Pecka (FK Mladá Boleslav)	16
2007/2008	SK Slavia Praha	AC Sparta Praha	Václav Svěrkoš (FC Baník Ostrava)	15
2008/2009	SK Slavia Praha	FK Teplice	Andrej Kerić (FC Slovan Liberec)	15
2009/2010	AC Sparta Praha	FC Viktoria Plzeň	Michal Ordoš (Sigma Olomouc)	12
2010/2011	FC Viktoria Plzeň	FK Mladá Boleslav	David Lafata (FK Baumit Jablonec)	19
2011/2012	FC Slovan Liberec	SK Sigma Olomouc	David Lafata (FK Baumit Jablonec)	25
2012/2013	FC Viktoria Plzeň	FK Baumit Jablonec	David Lafata (FK Baumit Jablonec / AC Sparta Praha)	20
2013/2014	AC Sparta Praha	AC Sparta Praha	Josef Hušbauer (AC Sparta Praha)	18
2014/2015	FC Viktoria Plzeň	FC Slovan Liberec	David Lafata (AC Sparta Praha)	20
2015/2016	FC Viktoria Plzeň	FK Mladá Boleslav	David Lafata (AC Sparta Praha)	20
2016/2017	SK Slavia Praha	FC Fastav Zlín	Milan Škoda (SK Slavia Praha) / David Lafata (AC Sparta Praha)	15
2017/2018	FC Viktoria Plzeň	SK Slavia Praha	Michael Krmenčík (FC Viktoria Plzeň)	16
2018/2019	SK Slavia Praha	SK Slavia Praha	Nikolay Komlichenko (RUS, FK Mladá Boleslav)	29

Name changements for most important Czech clubs:

AC Sparta Praha:
1893 - Athletic Club Královské Vinohrady; 1894 - Athletic Club Sparta Praha; 1948 - Athletic Club Sparta Bubeneč; 1949 - Sokol Bratrství Sparta Praha; 1951 - Sparta ČKD Sokolovo Praha; 1953 - TJ Spartak Praha Sokolovo; 1965 - TJ Sparta ČKD Praha; 1990 - TJ Sparta Praha; 1991 - AC Sparta Praha; 1993 - AC Sparta Praha fotbal, a.s.

SK Slavia Praha:
1892 - SK ACOS Praha (Sportovní klub Akademický cyklistický odbor Slavia Praha); 1893 - SK Slavia Praha (Sportovní klub Slavia Praha); 1948 - Sokol Slavia Praha; 1949 - ZSJ Dynamo Slavia Praha (Základní sportovní jednota Dynamo Slavia Praha); 1953 - DSO Dynamo Praha (Dobrovolná sportovní organizace Dynamo Praha); 1954 - TJ Dynamo Praha (Tělovýchovná jednota Dynamo Praha); 1965 - SK Slavia Praha (Sportovní klub Slavia Praha); 1973 - TJ Slavia Praha (Tělovýchovná jednota Slavia Praha); 1977 - TJ Slavia IPS Praha (Tělovýchovná jednota Slavia Inženýrské průmyslové stavby Praha); 1978 - SK Slavia IPS Praha (Sportovní klub Slavia Inženýrské průmyslové stavby Praha); 1991 - SK Slavia Praha (Sportovní klub Slavia Praha - fotbal, a.s.)

FK Viktoria Žižkov:
1903 - Sportovní kroužek Viktoria Žižkov; 1904 - SK Viktoria Žižkov; 1950 - Sokol Viktoria Žižkov; 1951 - Sokol ČSAD Žižkov; 1952 - TJ Slavoj Žižkov (after merger with Avia Čakovice); 1965 - TJ Viktoria Žižkov; 1973 - TJ Viktoria Žižkov Strojimport; 1982 - TJ Viktoria Žižkov PSO; 1992 - FK Viktoria Žižkov.

MFK Vítkovice:
1919 - SK Slavoj Vítkovice; 1922 - SK Vítkovice; 1923 - SSK Vítkovice; 1937 - SK Železárny Vítkovice; 1939 - ČSK Vítkovice; 1945 - SK Vítkovice Železárny; 1948 - Sokol Vítkovice Železárny; 1953 - Baník Vítkovice; 1957 - TJ VŽKG Ostrava; 1979 - TJ Vítkovice; 1993 - FC Vítkovice Kovkor; 1994 - FC Karviná-Vítkovice (after merger with Kovona Karviná); 1995 - FC Vítkovice (after spliting); 2012 - MFK Vítkovice.

FK Teplice:
1945 - SK Teplice-Šanov (Sportovní klub Teplice-Šanov); 1948 - Sokol Teplice; 1949 - ZSJ Technomat Teplice (Základní sportovní jednota Technomat Teplice); 1951 - ZSJ Vodotechna Teplice; 1952 - ZSJ Ingstav Teplice; 1953 - DSO Tatran Teplice (Dobrovolná sportovní organizace Tatran Teplice); 1960 - TJ Slovan Teplice (Tělovýchovná jednota Slovan Teplice); 1966 - TJ Sklo Union Teplice; 1991 - TFK VTJ Teplice (Tělovýchovný fotbalový klub Vojenská tělovýchovná jednota Teplice); 1993 - FK Frydrych Teplice (Fotbalový klub Frydrych Teplice); 1994 - FK Teplice (Fotbalový klub Teplice, a.s.).

FK Dukla Praha:
1948 - ATK Praha (Armádní tělovýchovný klub Praha); 1953 - ÚDA Praha (Ústřední dům armády Praha); 1956 - AS Dukla Praha (Armádní středisko Dukla Praha); 1976 - ASVS Dukla Praha (Armádní středisko vrcholového sportu Dukla Praha); 1991 - FC Dukla Praha (Football Club Dukla Praha); 1994 - FK Dukla Praha (Fotbalový klub Dukla Praha); 1996 - FK Marila Příbram (after merger between FC Příbram and FC Dukla Praha); 1998 - FK Dukla Praha, o.s. (Fotbalový klub Dukla Praha, občanské sdružení); 2007 - FK Dukla Praha, a.s. (Fotbalový klub Dukla Praha, akciová společnost).

FC Banik Ostrava:
1922 - SK Slezská Ostrava (Sportovní klub Slezská Ostrava); 1945 - SK Ostrava; 1948 - Sokol Trojice Ostrava; 1951 - Sokol OKD Ostrava (Sokol Ostravsko-karvinské doly Ostrava); 1952 - DSO Baník Ostrava (Dobrovolná sportovní organizace Baník Ostrava); 1961 - TJ Baník Ostrava (Tělovýchovná jednota Baník Ostrava); 1970 - TJ Baník Ostrava OKD; 1990 - FC Baník Ostrava (Football Club Baník Ostrava, a.s.).

FC Zbrojovka Brno:
1913 - SK Židenice; 1951 - Zbrojovka Brno; 1956 - Spartak ZJŠ Brno; 1968 - Zbrojovka Brno; 1992 - Boby Brno; 2000 - Stavo Artikel Brno; 2002 - 1.FC Brno; 2010 - FC Zbrojovka Brno.
Bohemians Praha 1905:
1905 - AFK Vršovice; 1927 - Bohemians AFK Vršovice; 1941 - Bohemia AFK Vršovice; 1945 - Bohemians AFK Vršovice; 1948 - Sokol Vršovice Bohemians; 1949 - Sokol Železničaři Bohemians Praha; 1950 - Sokol Železničaři Praha; 1951 - Sokol ČKD Stalingrad Praha; 1953 - Spartak Praha Stalingrad; 1962 - ČKD Praha; 1965 - Bohemians ČKD Praha; 1993 - Bohemians Praha; 1999 - CU Bohemians Praha; 2001 - FC Bohemians Praha; 2005 - Bohemians 1905; 2013 - Bohemians Praha 1905.

Name changements for most important Slovak clubs:

FK Inter Bratislava:
1940 - ŠK Apollo Bratislava; 1945 - TKNB Bratislava; 1948 - Sokol SNB Bratislava; 1952 - TJ Červená Hviezda Bratislava; 1962 - TJ Iskra Slovnaft Bratislava; 1965 - TJ Internacionál Slovnaft Bratislava; 1986 - TJ Internacionál Slovnaft ZŤS Bratislava (after merge with TJ ZŤS Petržalka); 1991 - AŠK Inter Slovnaft Bratislava; 2004 - FK Inter Bratislava; 2009 - Sold club license to FK Senica; 2009 - Inter Bratislava; 2014 - FK Inter Bratislava a.s.
ŠK Slovan Bratislava:
1919 - 1. ČsŠK Bratislava; 1939 - ŠK Bratislava; 1948 - Sokol ŠK NV Bratislava; 1953 - ÚNV Slovan Bratislava; 1961 - Slovan CHZJD Bratislava; 1990 - ŠK Slovan Bratislava.
FC Lokomotíva Košice:
1946 - ŠK Železničiari Košice; 1946 - ŠK Železničiari Sparta Košice (Merge with ŠK Sparta Košice); 1949 - ZSJ Dynamo ČSD Košice (Merge with Sokol Jednota Dynamo Košice); 1952 - TJ Lokomotíva Košice; 1965 - TJ Lokomotíva VSŽ Košice (Merge with TJ VSŽ Košice); 1967 - TJ Lokomotíva Košice (End of merge with TJ VSŽ Košice); 1990 - FK Lokomotíva Košice; 1994 - FK Lokomotíva Energogas Košice; 1999 - FK Lokomotíva PČSP Košice; 2003 - FC Lokomotíva Košice.
FC Spartak Trnava:
1923 - ŠK Rapid Trnava; 1939 - TSS Trnava; 1948 - Sokol NV Trnava; 1949 - ZTJ Kovosmalt Trnava; 1953 - Spartak Trnava; 1967 - Spartak TAZ Trnava; 1988 - Spartak ZTS Trnava; 1993 - FC Spartak Trnava.

NATIONAL CHAMPIONSHIP
Czech First League / Fortuna Liga 2018/2019
(20.07.2018 - 01.06.2019)

Regular Season - Results

Round 1 [20-23.07.2018]
Dukla Praha - Viktoria Plzeň 1-3(1-0)
FC Fastav Zlín - Mladá Boleslav 3-2(0-1)
Slovan Liberec - MFK Karviná 1-0(0-0)
1. FK Příbram - FK Teplice 1-1(1-0)
Sparta Praha - SFC Opava 2-0(0-0)
Bohemians 1905 - 1. FC Slovácko 2-1(2-0)
Sigma Olomouc - Slavia Praha 0-3(0-2)
Baník Ostrava - FK Jablonec 1-0(0-0)

Round 2 [27-30.07.2018]
Mladá Boleslav - Sigma Olomouc 0-4(0-1)
1. FK Příbram - Bohemians 1905 4-2(2-0)
SFC Opava - FC Fastav Zlín 1-2(1-1)
1. FC Slovácko - Baník Ostrava 2-1(1-1)
Slavia Praha - MFK Karviná 4-0(2-0)
FK Teplice - Dukla Praha 5-2(2-0)
FK Jablonec - Sparta Praha 1-2(0-0)
Viktoria Plzeň - Slovan Liberec 1-0(0-0)

Round 3 [03-06.08.2018]
Slavia Praha - SFC Opava 3-1(1-0)
Baník Ostrava - 1. FK Příbram 3-0(2-0)
FC Fastav Zlín - FK Jablonec 1-1(0-0)
Slovan Liberec - FK Teplice 2-2(1-1)
Sigma Olomouc - Viktoria Plzeň 0-1(0-0)
MFK Karviná - Mladá Boleslav 3-4(1-1)
Sparta Praha - 1. FC Slovácko 1-0(1-0)
Dukla Praha - Bohemians 1905 0-1(0-1)

Round 4 [10-13.08.2018]
Mladá Boleslav - Slavia Praha 0-1(0-1)
1. FK Příbram - Dukla Praha 4-0(0-0)
SFC Opava - Slovan Liberec 1-1(0-0)
FK Jablonec - MFK Karviná 4-1(2-0)
Viktoria Plzeň - FC Fastav Zlín 1-0(0-0)
1. FC Slovácko - Sigma Olomouc 3-1(1-0)
FK Teplice - Sparta Praha 0-4(0-4)
Bohemians 1905 - Baník Ostrava 0-1(0-0)

Round 5 [17-20.08.2018]
Dukla Praha - 1. FC Slovácko 1-2(1-1)
Slovan Liberec - Bohemians 1905 1-1(0-1)
FC Fastav Zlín - FK Teplice 1-0(0-0)
Mladá Boleslav - SFC Opava 6-1(3-1)
Slavia Praha - FK Jablonec 0-2(0-1)
MFK Karviná - Viktoria Plzeň 0-1(0-1)
Sparta Praha - 1. FK Příbram 2-2(1-1)
Sigma Olomouc - Baník Ostrava 1-4(0-2)

Round 6 [24-27.08.2018]
Bohemians 1905 - Sparta Praha 1-1(0-0)
1. FK Příbram - Slovan Liberec 1-3(0-1)
SFC Opava - MFK Karviná 1-3(0-1)
Baník Ostrava - Dukla Praha 2-0(2-0)
FK Teplice - Slavia Praha 0-3(0-2)
Viktoria Plzeň - Mladá Boleslav 6-1(2-1)
FK Jablonec - Sigma Olomouc 3-0(0-0)
1. FC Slovácko - FC Fastav Zlín 0-4(0-2)

Round 7 [31.08.-02.09.2018]
Sparta Praha - Dukla Praha 2-0(1-0)
Slovan Liberec - Baník Ostrava 0-0
FC Fastav Zlín - 1. FK Příbram 3-0(3-0)
Mladá Boleslav - FK Teplice 1-1(0-0)
SFC Opava - FK Jablonec 2-0(1-0)
Slavia Praha - Viktoria Plzeň 4-0(2-0)
MFK Karviná - 1. FC Slovácko 2-1(0-0)
Sigma Olomouc - Bohemians 1905 2-3(2-0)

Round 8 [14-17.09.2018]
Bohemians 1905 - FC Fastav Zlín 0-1(0-0)
1. FK Příbram - Sigma Olomouc 1-0(0-0)
Viktoria Plzeň - SFC Opava 1-0(0-0)
Dukla Praha - Slovan Liberec 2-0(0-0)
FK Jablonec - Mladá Boleslav 0-3(0-2)
FK Teplice - MFK Karviná 2-1(2-0)
1. FC Slovácko - Slavia Praha 1-3(0-2)
Baník Ostrava - Sparta Praha 0-1(0-0)

Round 9 [21-24.09.2018]
FC Fastav Zlín - Baník Ostrava 1-2(0-0)
Sigma Olomouc - Dukla Praha 1-0(1-0)
MFK Karviná - 1. FK Příbram 4-1(2-0)
Mladá Boleslav - 1. FC Slovácko 5-1(1-0)
SFC Opava - FK Teplice 2-0(1-0)
Sparta Praha - Slovan Liberec 4-1(3-0)
Slavia Praha - Bohemians 1905 1-0(1-0)
FK Jablonec - Viktoria Plzeň 3-0(2-0)

Round 10 [28-30.09.2018]
Bohemians 1905 - MFK Karviná 0-0
Viktoria Plzeň - Sparta Praha 1-0(0-0)
Dukla Praha - FC Fastav Zlín 1-1(1-0)
1. FK Příbram - Mladá Boleslav 3-0(1-0)
1. FC Slovácko - SFC Opava 0-2(0-1)
Slovan Liberec - Sigma Olomouc 3-0(1-0)
Baník Ostrava - Slavia Praha 2-1(2-1)
FK Teplice - FK Jablonec 1-2(1-1)

Round 11 [05-07.10.2018]
FC Fastav Zlín - Slovan Liberec 0-1(0-0)
Mladá Boleslav - Baník Ostrava 2-2(1-0)
Sigma Olomouc - Sparta Praha 1-0(1-0)
MFK Karviná - Dukla Praha 0-2(0-0)
SFC Opava - Bohemians 1905 0-1(0-0)
FK Jablonec - 1. FC Slovácko 2-0(2-0)
Viktoria Plzeň - FK Teplice 1-0(0-0)
Slavia Praha - 1. FK Příbram 4-1(3-1)

Round 12 [19-22.10.2018]
Bohemians 1905 - Viktoria Plzeň 2-2(1-1)
Sigma Olomouc - FC Fastav Zlín 1-1(0-0)
1. FK Příbram - FK Jablonec 0-6(0-2)
Baník Ostrava - MFK Karviná 1-1(0-1)
1. FC Slovácko - FK Teplice 0-2(0-2)
Dukla Praha - SFC Opava 1-0(0-0)
Slovan Liberec - Slavia Praha 0-1(0-1)
Sparta Praha - Mladá Boleslav 4-1(3-0)

Round 13 [26-29.10.2018]
FK Teplice - Baník Ostrava 0-1(0-1)
MFK Karviná - Sigma Olomouc 2-3(0-0)
Mladá Boleslav - Bohemians 1905 3-0(2-0)
SFC Opava - 1. FK Příbram 5-0(2-0)
FC Fastav Zlín - Sparta Praha 1-0(0-0)
Viktoria Plzeň - 1. FC Slovácko 2-1(1-0)
FK Jablonec - Slovan Liberec 0-0
Slavia Praha - Dukla Praha 4-1(2-0)

Round 14 [02-05.11.2018]
Bohemians 1905 - FK Teplice 2-3(2-1)
Baník Ostrava - Viktoria Plzeň 0-1(0-1)
1. FK Příbram - 1. FC Slovácko 0-3(0-0)
Dukla Praha - FK Jablonec 2-6(0-3)
Sigma Olomouc - SFC Opava 2-2(1-2)
FC Fastav Zlín - MFK Karviná 2-1(0-0)
Sparta Praha - Slavia Praha 2-2(2-1)
Slovan Liberec - Mladá Boleslav 1-0(0-0)

Round 15 [09-11.11.2018]
Mladá Boleslav - Dukla Praha 0-0
MFK Karviná - Sparta Praha 1-3(1-0)
1. FC Slovácko - Slovan Liberec 0-1(0-1)
SFC Opava - Baník Ostrava 2-1(1-0)
FK Jablonec - Bohemians 1905 3-1(1-1)
Viktoria Plzeň - 1. FK Příbram 1-1(1-1)
FK Teplice - Sigma Olomouc 0-0
Slavia Praha - FC Fastav Zlín 3-1(2-1)

Round 16 [23-25.11.2018]
Slovan Liberec - Viktoria Plzeň 1-1(0-0)
Dukla Praha - FK Teplice 1-0(1-0)
MFK Karviná - Slavia Praha 1-3(1-2)
Bohemians 1905 - 1. FK Příbram 2-2(1-0)
FC Fastav Zlín - SFC Opava 2-0(1-0)
Baník Ostrava - 1. FC Slovácko 0-3(0-1)
Sigma Olomouc - Mladá Boleslav 0-4(0-1)
Sparta Praha - FK Jablonec 0-0

Round 17 [30.11.-03.12.2018]
FK Teplice - Slovan Liberec 1-0(1-0)
Mladá Boleslav - MFK Karviná 1-1(1-0)
1. FC Slovácko - Sparta Praha 2-1(0-0)
Bohemians 1905 - Dukla Praha 0-0
1. FK Příbram - Baník Ostrava 0-2(0-1)
Viktoria Plzeň - Sigma Olomouc 2-0(2-0)
FK Jablonec - FC Fastav Zlín 4-0(2-0)
SFC Opava - Slavia Praha 2-3(1-1)

Round 18 [07-10.12.2018]
Dukla Praha - 1. FK Příbram 1-2(0-0)
FC Fastav Zlín - Viktoria Plzeň 0-2(0-2)
Baník Ostrava - Bohemians 1905 2-0(0-0)
Sigma Olomouc - 1. FC Slovácko 1-0(1-0)
MFK Karviná - FK Jablonec 2-1(1-1)
Slavia Praha - Mladá Boleslav 3-2(1-0)
Sparta Praha - FK Teplice 0-1(0-0)
Slovan Liberec - SFC Opava 1-2(1-1)

Round 19 [14-17.12.2018]
Baník Ostrava - Sigma Olomouc 0-0
1. FC Slovácko - Dukla Praha 1-0(1-0)
Bohemians 1905 - Slovan Liberec 0-0
FK Teplice - FC Fastav Zlín 2-1(1-1)
SFC Opava - Mladá Boleslav 2-1(1-0)
1. FK Příbram - Sparta Praha 1-1(1-1)
Viktoria Plzeň - MFK Karviná 2-1(2-0)
FK Jablonec - Slavia Praha 0-2(0-1)

Round 20 [08-10.02.2019]
Sigma Olomouc - FK Jablonec 1-2(0-0)
Dukla Praha - Baník Ostrava 1-1(1-1)
Slovan Liberec - 1. FK Příbram 4-0(3-0)
MFK Karviná - SFC Opava 1-1(1-1)
Mladá Boleslav - Viktoria Plzeň 1-1(0-1)
FC Fastav Zlín - 1. FC Slovácko 0-1(0-0)
Slavia Praha - FK Teplice 2-0(0-0)
Sparta Praha - Bohemians 1905 1-0(0-0)

Round 21 [15-18.02.2019]
FK Teplice - Mladá Boleslav 0-2(0-1)
Bohemians 1905 - Sigma Olomouc 0-1(0-1)
1. FK Příbram - FC Fastav Zlín 3-2(1-1)
1. FC Slovácko - MFK Karviná 2-0(1-0)
Baník Ostrava - Slovan Liberec 2-1(0-0)
FK Jablonec - SFC Opava 2-2(1-1)
Viktoria Plzeň - Slavia Praha 2-0(1-0)
Dukla Praha - Sparta Praha 2-3(1-1)

Round 22 [22-25.02.2019]
Slovan Liberec - Dukla Praha 2-0(0-0)
FC Fastav Zlín - Bohemians 1905 0-2(0-1)
Sigma Olomouc - 1. FK Příbram 2-0(1-0)
MFK Karviná - FK Teplice 1-1(1-0)
Mladá Boleslav - FK Jablonec 1-0(0-0)
Sparta Praha - Baník Ostrava 3-2(1-0)
SFC Opava - Viktoria Plzeň 1-2(0-1)
Slavia Praha - 1. FC Slovácko 4-0(2-0)

Round 23 [01-03.03.2019]
Baník Ostrava - FC Fastav Zlín 1-2(1-1)
Dukla Praha - Sigma Olomouc 0-4(0-2)
1. FK Příbram - MFK Karviná 2-1(1-0)
1. FC Slovácko - Mladá Boleslav 1-1(0-0)
Viktoria Plzeň - FK Jablonec 1-0(1-0)
Slovan Liberec - Sparta Praha 0-1(0-0)
Bohemians 1905 - Slavia Praha 0-3(0-2)
FK Teplice - SFC Opava 3-2(2-1)

Round 24 [08-11.03.2019]
FK Jablonec - FK Teplice 2-1(0-0)
MFK Karviná - Bohemians 1905 0-3(0-3)
Mladá Boleslav - 1. FK Příbram 2-0(0-0)
FC Fastav Zlín - Dukla Praha 2-1(1-1)
SFC Opava - 1. FC Slovácko 2-2(1-0)
Sparta Praha - Viktoria Plzeň 4-0(2-0)
Slavia Praha - Baník Ostrava 4-0(1-0)
Sigma Olomouc - Slovan Liberec 2-1(1-0)

Round 25 [15-17.03.2019]
Dukla Praha - MFK Karviná 2-1(2-1)
FK Teplice - Viktoria Plzeň 2-1(2-0)
Baník Ostrava - Mladá Boleslav 1-1(1-1)
Slovan Liberec - FC Fastav Zlín 1-0(1-0)
1. FC Slovácko - FK Jablonec 0-0
Sparta Praha - Sigma Olomouc 2-1(0-1)
Bohemians 1905 - SFC Opava 0-0
1. FK Příbram - Slavia Praha 0-2(0-1)

Round 26 [29-31.03.2019]
MFK Karviná - Baník Ostrava 2-0(0-0)
SFC Opava - Dukla Praha 2-0(1-0)
Mladá Boleslav - Sparta Praha 2-1(0-0)
FC Fastav Zlín - Sigma Olomouc 0-2(0-1)
FK Teplice - 1. FC Slovácko 2-0(2-0)
Slavia Praha - Slovan Liberec 1-1(0-0)
FK Jablonec - 1. FK Příbram 3-0(2-0)
Viktoria Plzeň - Bohemians 1905 3-2(2-0)

Round 27 [05-08.04.2019]
1. FK Příbram - SFC Opava 3-1(1-0)
Dukla Praha - Slavia Praha 1-5(0-3)
Sigma Olomouc - MFK Karviná 3-2(2-1)
Bohemians 1905 - Mladá Boleslav 0-0
Slovan Liberec - FK Jablonec 0-0
Baník Ostrava - FK Teplice 3-1(3-1)
1. FC Slovácko - Viktoria Plzeň 0-1(0-1)
Sparta Praha - FC Fastav Zlín 2-0(0-0)

Round 28 [12-15.04.2019]
FK Teplice - Bohemians 1905 1-2(0-0)
1. FC Slovácko - 1. FK Příbram 2-0(1-0)
SFC Opava - Sigma Olomouc 2-1(1-1)
MFK Karviná - FC Fastav Zlín 2-0(1-0)
Viktoria Plzeň - Baník Ostrava 2-1(1-1)
FK Jablonec - Dukla Praha 2-1(1-1)
Slavia Praha - Sparta Praha 1-1(1-0)
Mladá Boleslav - Slovan Liberec 1-2(0-0)

Round 29 [21.04.2019]
FC Fastav Zlín - Slavia Praha 1-0(0-0)
Sparta Praha - MFK Karviná 1-3(0-2)
Dukla Praha - Mladá Boleslav 2-2(0-1)
Baník Ostrava - SFC Opava 2-0(1-0)
Bohemians 1905 - FK Jablonec 1-0(1-0)
1. FK Příbram - Viktoria Plzeň 1-1(1-1)
Sigma Olomouc - FK Teplice 2-0(1-0)
Slovan Liberec - 1. FC Slovácko 3-2(1-0)

Round 30 [27.04.2019]
Mladá Boleslav - FC Fastav Zlín 3-0(3-0)
Slavia Praha - Sigma Olomouc 2-1(1-1)
SFC Opava - Sparta Praha 0-3(0-1)
MFK Karviná - Slovan Liberec 2-1(1-1)
Viktoria Plzeň - Dukla Praha 4-0(3-0)
FK Jablonec - Baník Ostrava 4-0(2-0)
FK Teplice - 1. FK Příbram 0-0
1. FC Slovácko - Bohemians 1905 1-1(0-1)

Final Standings

1.	SK Slavia Praha	30	23	3	4	72	-	23	72
2.	FC Viktoria Plzeň	30	21	5	4	47	-	27	68
3.	AC Sparta Praha	30	17	6	7	52	-	27	57
4.	FK Jablonec	30	15	6	9	53	-	26	51
5.	FC Baník Ostrava	30	13	6	11	38	-	36	45
6.	FC Slovan Liberec	30	11	9	10	33	-	28	42
7.	FK Mladá Boleslav	30	11	9	10	52	-	44	42
8.	SK Sigma Olomouc	30	12	4	14	37	-	43	40
9.	FC Fastav Zlín	30	12	3	15	32	-	40	39
10.	FK Teplice	30	10	6	14	32	-	42	36
11.	Bohemians Praha 1905	30	8	10	12	29	-	37	34
12.	1. FC Slovácko Uherské Hradiště	30	10	4	16	32	-	45	34
13.	Slezský FC Opava	30	9	6	15	39	-	49	33
14.	1. FK Příbram	30	8	7	15	33	-	63	31
15.	MFK Karviná	30	8	5	17	39	-	53	29
16.	FK Dukla Praha	30	5	5	20	25	-	62	20

Teams ranked 1-6 were qualified for the Championship Play-offs, teams ranked 7-10 were qualified for the Europa League Play-offs and teams ranked 11-16 were qualified for the Relegation Play-offs.

Relegation Play-offs

Results

Round 31 [03-05.05.2019]
Dukla Praha - Bohemians 1905 1-1(0-0)
1. FC Slovácko - 1. FK Příbram 5-1(3-1)
SFC Opava - MFK Karviná 1-0(0-0)

Round 32 [11.05.2019]
1. FK Příbram - MFK Karviná 1-0(0-0)
SFC Opava - Dukla Praha 3-2(1-0)
Bohemians 1905 - 1. FC Slovácko 0-0

Round 33 [14.05.2019]
MFK Karviná - Dukla Praha 3-0(2-0)
Bohemians 1905 - 1. FK Příbram 1-4(1-2)
1. FC Slovácko - SFC Opava 4-1(2-0)

Round 34 [18.05.2019]
MFK Karviná - Bohemians 1905 0-1(0-1)
Dukla Praha - 1. FC Slovácko 0-0
SFC Opava - 1. FK Příbram 2-1(1-0)

Round 35 [25.05.2019]
1. FC Slovácko - MFK Karviná 2-0(1-0)
Bohemians 1905 - SFC Opava 1-1(0-0)
1. FK Příbram - Dukla Praha 3-2(1-1)

Final Standings

1.	1. FC Slovácko Uherské Hradiště	35	13	6	16	43	-	47	45
2.	Slezský FC Opava	35	12	7	16	47	-	57	43
3.	Bohemians Praha 1905	35	9	13	13	33	-	43	40
4.	1. FK Příbram (*Relegation Play-offs*)	35	11	7	17	43	-	73	40
5.	MFK Karviná (*Relegation Play-offs*)	35	9	5	21	42	-	58	32
6.	FK Dukla Praha (*Relegated*)	35	5	7	23	30	-	72	22

Relegation Play-offs [28/29.05.-02.06.2019]

MFK Karviná - FC Vysočina Jihlava	2-1(2-0)	1-1(0-1)
FC Zbrojovka Brno - 1. FK Příbram	3-3(2-0)	0-0

Both 1. FK Příbram and MFK Karviná retained their places for the 2019–20 Czech First League.

Championship Play-offs

Results

Round 31 [04-05.05.2019]
Sparta Praha - Baník Ostrava 3-0(1-0)
Slovan Liberec - Slavia Praha 0-0
Viktoria Plzeň - FK Jablonec 2-1(0-1)

Round 32 [11-12.05.2019]
FK Jablonec - Baník Ostrava 2-0(0-0)
Sparta Praha - Slovan Liberec 1-0(1-0)
Slavia Praha - Viktoria Plzeň 3-1(0-0)

Round 33 [14-15.05.2019]
Baník Ostrava - Slovan Liberec 0-1(0-0)
Viktoria Plzeň - Sparta Praha 4-0(2-0)
Slavia Praha - FK Jablonec 2-1(1-1)

Round 34 [19.05.2019]
Baník Ostrava - Slavia Praha 0-0
Slovan Liberec - Viktoria Plzeň 0-2(0-1)
Sparta Praha - FK Jablonec 2-0(1-0)

Round 35 [26.05.2019]
Viktoria Plzeň - Baník Ostrava 1-1(1-0)
Slavia Praha - Sparta Praha 2-1(1-1)
FK Jablonec - Slovan Liberec 1-0(0-0)

Final Standings

1.	**SK Slavia Praha**	35	26	5	4	79	-	26	83
2.	FC Viktoria Plzeň	35	24	6	5	57	-	32	78
3.	AC Sparta Praha	35	20	6	9	59	-	33	66
4.	FK Jablonec	35	17	6	12	58	-	32	57
5.	FC Baník Ostrava	35	13	8	14	39	-	43	47
6.	FC Slovan Liberec	35	12	10	13	34	-	32	46

FC Baník Ostrava were qualified for the Europa League Play-offs final.

Top goalscorers:

29 Nikolay Komlichenko (RUS)
FK Mladá Boleslav

15 Martin Doležal
FK Jablonec

15 Jean-David Beauguel (FRA)
FC Fastav Zlín / FC Viktoria Plzeň

Europa League Play-offs [03/12/17/24.05.-01.06.2019]

First Round	FK Teplice - FK Mladá Boleslav	0-8(0-6)	1-1(0-1)
	FC Fastav Zlín - SK Sigma Olomouc	1-0(1-0)	2-3(2-1)
Second Round	FC Fastav Zlín - FK Mladá Boleslav	3-1(1-0)	0-3(0-0)
Europa League Play-off Final	FK Mladá Boleslav - FC Baník Ostrava	1-0(1-0)	

NATIONAL CUP

Pohár Českomoravského fotbalového svazu / MOL Cup 2018/2019

First Round [28.07./29.07./01.08./04.08./05.08.2018]

FK Luhačovice - FC Slavičín	1-1 aet; 4-5 pen
FK Přepeře - FK Zbuzany	2-0(2-0)
1. FC Olešnice u Bouzova - FK Šumperk	0-1
SK Hranice - TJ Sokol Ústí	5-4 aet
FK Blansko - SK Líšeň	1-3
1. BFK Frýdlant - FC Vsetín	2-0
TJ Nový Jičín - SK Spartak Hulín	3-1
FC Slovan Rosice - FC Dosta Bystrc-Kníničky	8-0
FK Nové Sady - TJ Jiskra Rýmařov	0-2
FC Heřmanice Slezská - FC Odra Petřkovice	3-5
FK Bospor Bohumín - FC Hlučín	3-1
FC ŽĎAS Žďár nad Sázavou - FC Slovan Havlíčkův Brod	3-0
AFC Humpolec - SK Tatran Ždírec nad Doubravou	2-1
FK Kozlovice - 1. FC Viktorie Přerov	2-0
TJ Sokol Lanžhot - TJ Slovan Bzenec	4-2
FSC Stará Říše - TJ Sokol Tasovice	0-2
FC Strání - FC Viktoria Otrokovice	1-5
SK Dětmarovice - MFK Havířov	0-1
SK Moravan Oldřišov - FC Slavoj Olympia Bruntál	3-4
FC Spartak Velká Bíteš - SFK Vrchovina	0-1
TJ Velký Beranov 1975 - Slavoj TKZ Polná	0-15
FK Vodňany - FK Spartak Soběslav	0-5
TJ Sokol Libiš - FK Čáslav	0-2
TJ Přeštice - FK Meteor Praha VIII	1-0
SK Aritma Praha - FK Neratovice-Byškovice	1-2
TJ Sokol Velké Hamry - SS Ostrá	0-2
FK Jindřichův Hradec - TJ Tatran Sedlčany	4-2
FK Tachov - FK Hořovicko	5-0
TJ Tatran Rakovník - FC Chomutov	2-1
FK Olympie Březová - FK Admira Praha	0-4
SK Libčany - FK Brandýs nad Labem	0-1
Mostecký FK - MFK Dobříš	4-2
SK Spartak Slatiňany - MFK Trutnov	2-1
FK Ostrov - SK Rakovník	0-2
FC Rokycany - SK Klatovy 1898	1-1
FK Náchod-Destné – FK Jiskra Mšeno	2-1
TJ Baník Nové Sedlo - SK Kladno	0-4
SK Vysoké Mýto - FK Kolín	3-2
FK Pěnčín-Turnov - SK Polaban Nymburk	2-0
TJ Dvůr Králové - SK Český Brod	2-0
Český lev-Union Beroun - SK Benátky nad Jizerou	1-4
FK Dukla Jižní Město - Sokol Hostouň	1-2
FC Jílové - FK Litoměřicko	0-4
FO Lanškroun - FC Hradec Králové	2-1
FC Horky nad Jizerou - SK Motorlet Praha	4-2
FK Baník Souš - FC Mariánské Lázně	2-3

Second Round [14.08./15.08./21.08./22.08.2018]

SK Klatovy 1898 - FK MAS Táborsko	1-2
SK Spartak Slatiňany - FC Hradec Králové	2-4
TJ Nový Jičín - MFK Vítkovice	1-4
TJ Jiskra Rýmařov - FK Fotbal Třinec	0-1
SFK Vrchovina - FC Vysočina Jihlava	1-3
FC Viktoria Otrokovice - MFK Vyškov	1-5
TJ Tatran Rakovník - FK Loko Vltavín	2-3
1. BFK Frýdlant - FK Frýdek-Místek	0-1 pen
TJ Sokol Tasovice - Velké Meziríčí	4-3 pen
FK Šumperk - SK Uničov	0-1
SK Líšeň - SK Prostějov	3-2 aet
Slavoj TKZ Polná - AFC Humpolec	6-1
FC Slavičín - Valašské Meziríčí	1-0
SK Rakovník - FK Baník Sokolov	0-4
FK Tachov - FK Olympia Radotín	0-1
FK Litoměřicko - FK Varnsdorf	2-0
Sokol Hostouň - FK Slavoj Vyšehrad	5-4
FK Čáslav - FC Sellier & Bellot Vlašim	1-2 pen
SS Ostrá - TJ Sokol Zápy	1-5
FK Admira Praha - FK Králův Dvůr	1-0
Benátky nad Jizerou - SK Benešov	2-1 aet
FC Horky nad Jizerou - FK Dobrovice	1-2
FK Pěnčín-Turnov - FK TJ Štěchovice	0-3
FK Neratovice-Byškovice - FC Slovan Velvary	1-4
FK Spartak Soběslav - FC Písek	0-3
TJ Přeštice - TJ Jiskra Domažlice	0-6
SK Kladno - FC Karlovy Vary	2-0
Mostecký FK - SK Sokol Brozany	0-2
FK Náchod-Destné - SK Převýšov	1-2
TJ Dvůr Králové - TJ Sokol Živanice	2-1 pen
SK Vysoké Mýto - TJ Jiskra Ústí nad Orlicí	0-2
SK Hranice - FK Bohumín	4-2 aet
MFK Havířov - FC Odra Petřkovice	1-3
TJ Sokol Lanžhot - SK Hanácká Slávia Kroměříž	0-2 aet
FC Slovan Rosice - FK Hodonín	3-1
FC Slavoj Olympia Bruntál - Dolní Benešov	0-1
FK Jindřichův Hradec - Dynamo České Budějovice	1-4
FC Mariánské Lázně - FK Ústí nad Labem	1-4
FO Lanškroun - FK Pardubice	0-1
FC ŽĎAS Žďár nad Sázavou - FC Zbrojovka Brno	0-2
FK Brandýs nad Labem - FK Viktoria Žižkov	1-4
FK Přepeře - MFK Chrudim	2-4
FK Kozlovice - 1. SC Znojmo	0-4

Third Round [28.08.-29.08./04.09./05.09.2018]

FK Frýdek-Místek - SFC Opava	0-5
Dolní Benešov - FC Vysočina Jihlava	2-5 aet
SK Uničov - FC Baník Ostrava	0-2
FC Slovan Velvary - FK Baník Sokolov	0-1
TJ Jiskra Domažlice - FK MAS Táborsko	1-2 aet
FK Admira Praha - FK Teplice	0-6
SK Sokol Brozany - MFK Chrudim	1-2
Benátky nad Jizerou - FK Pardubice	0-2
FK Dobrovice - Bohemians Praha 1905	0-3
TJ Dvůr Králové - FC Sellier & Bellot Vlašim	0-2
Sokol Hostouň - FK Loko Vltavín	1-5
FK Litoměřicko - SK Dynamo České Budějovice	0-2
SK Líšeň - MFK Karvina	0-4
FK Olympia Radotín - FC Hradec Králové	2-1
Slavoj TKZ Polná - SK Hranice	2-1
SK Převýšov - FK Mladá Boleslav	1-2
FC Slavičín - 1. SC Znojmo	3-3 aet; 5-4 pen
TJ Jiskra Ústí nad Orlicí - FK Viktoria Žižkov	0-1
MFK Vyškov - MFK Vítkovice	3-2 aet
SK Kladno - FK Ústí nad Labem	1-2
FC Odra Petřkovice - FK Fotbal Třinec	0-4
FC Písek - FK Dukla Praha	0-2
FC Slovan Rosice - FC Zbrojovka Brno	0-2
FK TJ Štěchovice - FC Slovan Liberec	1-5
TJ Sokol Tasovice - 1. FC Slovácko Uher. Hradiště	2-5
TJ Sokol Zápy - 1. FK Příbram	1-4
SK Hanácká Slávia Kroměříž - FC Fastav Zlín	0-5

Fourth Round [25.09./26.09./02.10./03.10./10.10./11.10./12.10./13.10.2018]

FC Slavičín - FC Fastav Zlín	3-9(1-6)
FK Baník Sokolov - FC Baník Ostrava	1-2(1-2)
MFK Chrudim - FK Mladá Boleslav	2-0(2-0)
FK Loko Vltavín - FK Teplice	1-2(1-1)
FK Olympia Radotín - 1. FC Slovácko Uher. Hradiště	0-5(0-1)
1. FK Příbram - FC Sellier & Bellot Vlašim	4-1(3-0)
SK Sigma Olomouc - FK Fotbal Třinec	7-0(3-0)
FC Zbrojovka Brno - FC Slovan Liberec	0-1(0-1)
SK Slavia Praha - FK Ústí nad Labem	2-0(1-0)
Slavoj TKZ Polná - AC Sparta Praha	1-4(0-1)
Bohemians Praha 1905 - Dynamo České Budějovice	1-0(0-0)
MFK Karvina - FK MAS Táborsko	2-0(0-0)
MFK Vyškov - FC Viktoria Plzeň	1-5(0-4)
SFC Opava - FC Vysočina Jihlava	1-0(0-0)
FK Viktoria Žižkov - FK Dukla Praha	0-1(0-0)
FK Pardubice - FK Jablonec	1-2(1-0)

1/8-Finals [31.10./07.11./15.11./16.11./28.11.2018]			
MFK Karvina - FK Jablonec	1-0(0-0)	FC Slovan Liberec - 1. FC Slovácko Uher. Hradiště	1-0(1-0)
FC Viktoria Plzeň - FC Baník Ostrava	2-3(1-0,2-2)	FK Dukla Praha - FK Teplice	1-3(0-2)
1. FK Příbram - Bohemians Praha 1905	1-2(0-1)	SK Slavia Praha - MFK Chrudim	3-1(2-0)
SK Sigma Olomouc - FC Fastav Zlín	2-1(0-0)	SFC Opava - AC Sparta Praha	0-0; 3-4 pen

Quarter-Finals [02-03.04.2019]			
FK Teplice - AC Sparta Praha	2-2 aet; 2-4 pen	FC Baník Ostrava - FC Slovan Liberec	2-1(1-1,1-1)
SK Slavia Praha - MFK Karvina	5-0(2-0)	Bohemians Praha 1905 - SK Sigma Olomouc	1-0(0-0)

Semi-Finals [24.04.2019]			
FC Baník Ostrava - Bohemians Praha 1905	1-0(1-0)	SK Slavia Praha - AC Sparta Praha	3-0(2-0)

Final

22.05.2018; Stadion Andrův, Olomouc; Referee: Petr Ardeleanu; Attendance: 11,661

SK Slavia Praha - FC Baník Ostrava **2-0(1-0)**

Slavia Praha: Ondřej Kolář, Michal Frydrych, Jan Bořil, Michael Ngadeu-Ngadjui, Simon Desiré Sylvanus Deli, Josef Hušbauer (74.Peter Oladeji Olayinka), Jaromír Zmrhal, Lukáš Masopust, Tomáš Souček, Ibrahim Traoré (55.Alex Král), Milan Škoda (84.Ondřej Kúdela). Trainer: Jindřich Trpišovský.

Baník Ostrava: Viktor Budinský, Václav Procházka, Lukáš Pazdera (46.Denis Granečný), Jiří Fleišman, Martin Šindelář (71.Dame Diop), Patrizio Stronati, Martin Fillo, Adam Jánoš, Robert Hrubý, Daniel Holzer, Nemanja Kuzmanović (81.Ondřej Šašinka). Trainer: Bohumil Páník.

Goals: 1-0 Tomáš Souček (36 penalty), 2-0 Lukáš Masopust (78).

THE CLUBS 2018/2019

Football Club Baník Ostrava

Founded: 1922 (*as SK Slezská Ostrava*)
Stadium: Městský stadion, Ostrava (15,123)

Goalkeepers:	DOB	M	(s)	G
Viktor Budinský (SVK)	09.05.1993	1		
Jan Laštůvka	07.07.1982	35		
Defenders:	**DOB**	**M**	**(s)**	**G**
Jiří Fleišman	02.10.1984	33		1
Denis Granečný	07.09.1998	8	(17)	
Artyom Meshaninov (RUS)	19.02.1996	10	(8)	
Lukáš Pazdera	06.03.1987	25	(2)	1
Jakub Pokorný	11.09.1996		(2)	
Václav Procházka	08.05.1984	19	(6)	2
Patrizio Stronati	17.11.1994	35		2
Martin Šindelář	22.01.1991	22	(3)	1
Midfielders:	**DOB**	**M**	**(s)**	**G**
Jakub Bolf	09.03.1998	1	(3)	
Martin Fillo	07.02.1986	32	(1)	3
Daniel Holzer	18.08.1995	32	(3)	2
Robert Hrubý	27.04.1994	29	(4)	2
Adam Jánoš	20.07.1992	28	(1)	1
Milan Jirásek	14.05.1992	16	(10)	
Bronislav Stáňa	12.11.1993		(4)	1
Forwards:	**DOB**	**M**	**(s)**	**G**
Milan Baroš	28.10.1981	15	(2)	6
Dame Diop (SEN)	15.02.1993	25	(4)	8
Nemanja Kuzmanović (SRB)	27.05.1989	13	(4)	4
Jakub Šašinka	02.10.1995	6	(11)	1
Ondřej Šašinka	21.03.1998	10	(18)	3
Trainer:	**DOB**	**M**		
Bohumil Páník	31.12.1956	36		

Bohemians Praha 1905

Founded: 1905
Stadium: Stadion Ďolíče, Praha (5,000)

Goalkeepers:	DOB	M	(s)	G
Tomáš Fryšták	18.08.1987	20		
Roman Valeš	06.03.1990	15	(1)	
Defenders:	**DOB**	**M**	**(s)**	**G**
Jiří Bederka	18.02.1995	12	(1)	
Martin Dostál	23.09.1989	33	(2)	2
Lukáš Hůlka	31.03.1995	16		3
Daniel Krch	20.03.1992	26		2
Lukáš Pokorný	05.07.1993	13		
Till Schumacher (GER)	10.12.1997	10		
Michal Šmíd	20.10.1986	20	(5)	
Michal Švec	19.03.1987	7	(4)	
Jan Vondra	13.09.1995		(1)	
Midfielders:	**DOB**	**M**	**(s)**	**G**
David Bartek	13.02.1988	28	(1)	2
Dominik Mašek	10.07.1995	9	(5)	1
Filip Hašek	20.03.1997	18	(5)	1
Martin Hašek	03.10.1995	12	(2)	2
Josef Jindřišek	14.02.1981	15	(4)	4
Vladislav Lyovin (RUS)	28.03.1995	10	(3)	
Mohamed Jasim Mohamed Ali Abdulla Marhoon (BHR)	12.02.1998		(1)	
Rudolf Reiter	28.09.1994	24	(7)	1
Kamil Vacek	18.05.1987	13	(1)	1
Antonín Vaníček	22.04.1998	23	(4)	1
Jan Vodháněl	25.04.1997	5	(11)	
Abdulla Yusuf Abdulrahim Mohamed Helal (BHR)	12.06.1993	11	(13)	5
Jan Záviška	21.08.1995	19	(8)	2
Forwards:	**DOB**	**M**	**(s)**	**G**
Lukáš Juliš	02.12.1994	5	(2)	1
Evgeni Kabaev (RUS)	28.02.1988		(1)	
Matěj Koubek	10.01.2000	3	(6)	1
Jakub Nečas	26.01.1995	9	(10)	4
Pavel Osmančík	26.02.2000			
David Puškáč	14.05.1993	9	(4)	
Denis Vala	11.10.2000			
Trainer:	**DOB**	**M**		
Martin Hašek	11.10.1969	35		

Fotbalový Klub Dukla Praha

Founded: 1958 (*as FK Dukla Dejvice*)
Stadium: Stadion Juliska, Praha (8,150)

Goalkeepers:	**DOB**	**M**	**(s)**	**G**
Matúš Hruška (SVK)	17.09.1994	5		
Filip Rada	05.09.1984	30		
Defenders:	**DOB**	**M**	**(s)**	**G**
Michal Bezpalec	19.08.1996	25	(1)	
Martin Chlumecký	11.01.1997	10	(1)	
David Douděra	31.05.1998	21	(9)	2
Ján Ďurica (SVK)	10.12.1981	17		2
Daniel Kozma	26.08.1995	4		
Branislav Milošević (SRB)	13.05.1988	30	(2)	3
Ivan Ostojić (SRB)	26.06.1989	23	(1)	
Jakub Podaný	15.06.1987	22	(4)	2
Dominik Preisler	20.09.1995	2		
Nikola Raspopović (SRB)	18.10.1989	13		
Daniel Souček	18.07.1998	21	(1)	
Midfielders:	**DOB**	**M**	**(s)**	**G**
David Breda	04.01.1996	5	(2)	
Frederik Bilovský (SVK)	03.03.1992	12	(4)	1
Samuel Dancák (SVK)	06.03.1998	1	(2)	
Mohamed Doumbia (CIV)	25.12.1998	13	(4)	
Marek Hanousek	06.08.1991	17	(2)	
Lukáš Holík	23.08.1992	14	(6)	2
Róbert Kovaľ (SVK)	16.01.1994	7	(2)	
Stepan Krunert	23.03.2000	4	(3)	1
Pablo González Juárez (ESP)	12.05.1993	9	(5)	
William Mackleyther Palacios Vera (COL)	26.12.2000		(1)	
Daniel Tetour	17.07.1994	27	(2)	3
Forwards:	**DOB**	**M**	**(s)**	**G**
David Bezdička	09.07.1996	1	(7)	
Patrik Brandner	04.01.1994	8	(8)	
Uroš Đjuranović (MNE)	01.02.1994	10	(19)	6
Vojtěch Hadaščok	08.01.1992	9	(4)	2
Jan Holenda	22.08.1985	13	(4)	1
Tomáš Kott	15.11.1999	1	(1)	
Ivan Schranz (SVK)	13.09.1993	9	(6)	4
Ondřej Štursa	17.06.2000	2	(1)	
Trainer:	**DOB**	**M**		
Pavel Drsek	22.09.1976	7		
Roman Skuhravý [06.09.2018]	06.01.1975	28		

Fotbalový Klub Jablonec

Founded: 1945
Stadium: Stadion Střelnice, Jablonec nad Nisou (6,108)

Goalkeepers:	**DOB**	**M**	**(s)**	**G**
Jan Hanuš	28.04.1988	2		
Vlastimil Hrubý	21.02.1985	33		
Defenders:	**DOB**	**M**	**(s)**	**G**
Tomáš Břečka	12.05.1994	20	(2)	
Matěj Hanousek	02.06.1993	19		
Tomáš Holeš	31.03.1993	35		6
David Hovorka	07.08.1993	29		1
Tomáš Hübschman	04.09.1981	29		1
Nikola Janković (SRB)	07.06.1993		(2)	
David Lischka	15.08.1997	18	(1)	2
Dominik Pleštil	09.08.1999		(6)	
Eduard Sobol (UKR)	20.04.1995	18	(3)	1
Bogdan Ilie Vătăjelu (ROU)	24.04.1993	12	(2)	2
Midfielders:	**DOB**	**M**	**(s)**	**G**
Alejandro Rafael Acosta Cabrera (URU)	02.10.1990	6	(19)	1
Andrej Fábry (SVK)	01.03.1997		(2)	
Miloš Kratochvíl	26.04.1996	9	(10)	1
Vojtěch Kubista	19.03.1993	12	(13)	1
Lukáš Masopust	12.02.1993	13		4
Jaroslav Peřina	19.01.2000		(1)	
Tomáš Pilík	20.12.1988		(7)	
Jakub Považanec (SVK)	31.01.1991	30	(4)	4
Michal Trávník	17.05.1994	33		10
Forwards:	**DOB**	**M**	**(s)**	**G**
Jan Chramosta	12.10.1990	9	(15)	5
Martin Doležal	03.05.1990	28	(1)	15
Dāvis Ikaunieks (LVA)	07.01.1994	2	(11)	
Vladimir Jovović (MNE)	26.10.1994	28	(3)	2
Trainer:	**DOB**	**M**		
Petr Rada	21.08.1958	35		

Městský fotbalový klub Karviná

Founded: 2003
Stadium: Stadion Městský, Karviná (4,833)

Goalkeepers:	**DOB**	**M**	**(s)**	**G**
Martin Berkovec	12.02.1989	32		
Martin Pastornický	18.03.1996	3		
Defenders:	**DOB**	**M**	**(s)**	**G**
Benjamin Čolić (BIH)	23.07.1991	27	(1)	
Soufiane Dramé (FRA)	27.02.1996	5	(7)	
Pavel Dreksa	17.09.1989	6		
Lazar Đorđević (SRB)	14.07.1992	7		
Jan Kalabiška	22.12.1986	1	(1)	
Gergő Kocsis (HUN)	07.03.1994	2		
Jan Krivak (SVK)	10.11.1993	19	(5)	
Bojan Letić (BIH)	21.12.1992	15	(3)	
Jiří Piroch	31.08.1995		(4)	
Oliver Putyera	21.08.1997	1		
Milan Rundić (SRB)	29.03.1992	15	(1)	
Luboš Tusjak	15.02.1992	8	(2)	
Timotej Zahumenský (SVK)	17.07.1995	12	(1)	
Midfielders:	**DOB**	**M**	**(s)**	**G**
Lukáš Budínský	27.03.1992	29	(2)	9
Martin Bukata (SVK)	02.10.1993	9	(7)	
Michal Faško (SVK)	24.08.1994	4	(5)	
Athanasios Fokaidis (GRE)	27.04.1999	1	(1)	
Ondřej Lingr	07.10.1998	23	(4)	1
Aleš Mertelj (SVN)	22.03.1987	10	(2)	
Jan Moravec	13.07.1987	26	(4)	1
Filip Panák	02.11.1995	13		1
Vojtěch Smrž	20.01.1997	19	(6)	2
Jan Suchan	18.01.1996	4	(7)	
Jan Šisler	24.04.1988		(2)	
Martin Vlachovsky	28.11.2000		(1)	
Vojtěch Wala	13.10.1999	1		
Tomáš Weber	26.05.1996		(1)	
Forwards:	**DOB**	**M**	**(s)**	**G**
Adriel D'Avila Ba Loua (CIV)	25.07.1996	18	(7)	2
Petr Galuška	08.07.1996	8	(5)	2
Dávid Guba (SVK)	29.06.1991	21	(8)	7
Christian Kouakou (CIV)	01.03.1991		(1)	
Eric Kleybel Ramírez Matheus (VEN)	20.11.1998	1	(12)	2
Tomáš Wágner	06.03.1990	26	(3)	13
Trainer:	**DOB**	**M**		
Roman Nádvorník	21.03.1973	15		
Norbert Hrnčár [19.11.2018]	09.06.1970	9		
František Straka [13.03.2019]	28.05.1958	11		

Fotbalový klub Mladá Boleslav

Founded: 1902
Stadium: Stadion Městský, Mladá Boleslav (5,000)

Goalkeepers:	DOB	M	(s)	G
Luboš Kamenár (SVK)	17.06.1987	2		
Jan Šeda	17.12.1985	32		
Jan Stejskal	14.02.1997	1		
Defenders:	**DOB**	**M**	**(s)**	**G**
Matěj Chaluš	02.02.1998	13	(2)	
Tomáš Fabián	10.09.1989	2		
Tomáš Hajek	01.12.1991	12		
Dominik Hašek	19.07.1998	2	(1)	
Jakub Jugas	05.05.1992	13		
Miroslav Keresteš (SVK)	30.07.1989	11		
Jakub Klíma	28.08.1998	2	(2)	
Jan Král	05.04.1999	7		
Antonín Křapka	22.01.1994	12	(2)	1
Marco Tulio De Paula Medeiros (BRA)	31.05.1998	3		
Petr Mareš	17.01.1991	13	(8)	2
Lukáš Pauschek (SVK)	09.12.1992	19		
Aleksandar Šušnjar (AUS)	19.08.1995	2		
Aleksey Tataev (RUS)	08.10.1998	6	(4)	
Midfielders:	**DOB**	**M**	**(s)**	**G**
Pavel Bucha	11.03.1998	11	(1)	1
Adnan Džafić (BIH)	10.05.1990	4	(6)	1
Ewerton Paixao da Silva (BRA)	28.12.1996		(3)	
Jakub Fulnek	26.04.1994	16		
Michal Hubínek	10.11.1994	24	(4)	
Jiří Kateřiňák	25.08.1995	1	(8)	
Tiémoko Konaté (CIV)	03.03.1990	14		1
Dominik Mašek	10.07.1995		(9)	1
Marek Matějovský	20.12.1981	13	(11)	3
Daniel Novák	28.04.1998		(6)	
Tomáš Přikrýl	04.07.1992	31	(2)	9
Laco Takács	15.07.1996	26	(6)	6
Jiří Valenta	14.02.1988		(4)	
Tomáš Wiesner	17.07.1997	7	(2)	
Forwards:	**DOB**	**M**	**(s)**	**G**
Jaroslav Diviš	09.07.1986	4	(8)	
Nikolay Komlichenko (RUS)	29.06.1995	32		29
Tomáš Ladra	24.04.1997	24	(6)	5
Muris Mešanović (BIH)	06.07.1990	7	(4)	5
Adam Provaznik	16.08.2000		(1)	
Trainer:	**DOB**	**M**		
Jozef Weber	25.12.1970	35		

Slezský fotbalový club Opava

Founded: 1907
Stadium: Stadion v Městských sadech, Opava (7,758)

Goalkeepers:	DOB	M	(s)	G
Vilém Fendrich	22.01.1991	12		
Vojtěch Šrom	03.05.1988	23		
Defenders:	**DOB**	**M**	**(s)**	**G**
Matěj Helebrand	19.06.1997	6	(3)	1
Matěj Hrabina	29.04.1993	26	(1)	
Marko Radić (SRB)	01.10.1985	3	(1)	
Dominik Simerský	29.09.1992	34		1
Jaroslav Svozil	09.09.1993	33		1
Jan Žídek	04.07.1985	21		1
Midfielders:	**DOB**	**M**	**(s)**	**G**
Jakub Janetzký	12.06.1997	16	(13)	3
Tomáš Jursa	09.03.1989	24	(4)	2
Jan Řezníček	22.11.1992	12	(6)	
Adam Rychlý	25.09.1998		(1)	
Jan Schaffartzik	15.12.1987	23	(7)	1
Filip Souček	18.09.2000		(2)	
Bronislav Stáňa	12.11.1993	6	(4)	2
Petr Zapalač	30.04.1987	32	(1)	2
Pavel Zavadil	30.04.1978	29		4
Forwards:	**DOB**	**M**	**(s)**	**G**
Tomáš Freit	04.03.1998		(1)	
Václav Jurečka	26.06.1994	13	(13)	2
Václav Juřena	02.02.1991	7	(22)	4
Joel Ngandu Kayamba (COD)	17.04.1992	11	(3)	3
Nemanja Kuzmanović (SRB)	27.05.1989	19		5
Budge Manzia (COD)	24.09.1994		(6)	
Endy Opoku Bernadina (NED)	03.05.1995		(8)	2
David Puškáč	14.05.1993	9	(2)	2
Tomáš Smola	19.01.1989	26	(5)	9
Trainer:	**DOB**	**M**		
Roman Skuhravý	06.01.1975	7		
Ivan Kopecký [05.09.2018]	10.06.1970	28		

1. Fotbalový Klub Příbram

Founded: 1928
Stadium: Stadion Na Litavce, Příbram (9,100)

Goalkeepers:	DOB	M	(s)	G
Ondřej Kočí	07.04.1995	23		
Milan Švenger	06.07.1986	12		
Defenders:	**DOB**	**M**	**(s)**	**G**
Matěj Chaluš	02.02.1998	8		
Tomáš Jablonský	21.06.1987	9	(5)	1
Juan Olivier Simo Kingue (CMR)	20.02.1996	9	(1)	1
Marek Kodr	17.08.1996	12	(5)	
Milan Nitrianský	13.12.1990	16	(5)	
Martin Nový	23.06.1993	29	(1)	
Matěj Polidar	20.12.1999	5	(3)	1
Karel Soldát	07.11.1993	19	(3)	1
Jaroslav Tregler	01.12.1995	32		
Midfielders:	**DOB**	**M**	**(s)**	**G**
Emmanuel Antwi (GHA)	05.05.1996	22	(7)	1
Antonín Fantiš	15.04.1992	30	(1)	7
Peter Grajciar (SVK)	17.09.1983		(1)	
Filip Hlúpik	30.04.1991	16	(2)	
Georgios Katidis (GRE)	12.02.1993	3	(4)	
David Kilián	07.12.1994	8	(5)	
Roman Květ	17.12.1997	27	(4)	2
Jan Matoušek	09.05.1998	20		10
Ruslan Mingazov (TKM)	23.11.1991	18	(3)	4
Michal Pecháček	14.04.1996	1		
Petr Průcha	30.10.1997	9	(8)	
Jan Rezek	05.05.1982	22	(4)	4
Rudi Skácel	17.07.1979	13	(3)	1
Egon Vůch	01.02.1991		(2)	
Forwards:	**DOB**	**M**	**(s)**	**G**
Rostislav Jandera	21.03.1998		(1)	
Ibrahim Div Keïta (FRA)	18.01.1996	5	(13)	2
Petr Pejša	13.08.1997	1	(6)	
Miroslav Slepička	10.11.1981	7	(2)	4
Radek Voltr	28.11.1991	9	(13)	2
Trainer:	**DOB**	**M**		
Josef Csaplár	29.10.1962	25		
Roman Nádvorník [18.03.2019]	21.03.1973	10		

Sportovní Klub Sigma Olomouc

Founded: 1919 (*as FK Hejčín Olomouc*)
Stadium: Stadion Andrův, Olomouc (12,483)

Goalkeepers:	DOB	M	(s)	G
Miloš Buchta	19.07.1980	30		
Aleš Mandous	01.04.1992	1		
Michal Reichl	14.09.1992	1		
Defenders:	**DOB**	**M**	**(s)**	**G**
Vít Beneš	12.08.1988	11		2
Juraj Chvátal (SVK)	13.07.1996	6	(3)	
Martin Hála	24.03.1992	3	(5)	
Václav Jemelka	23.06.1995	28		2
Jan Kotouč	01.10.1996	2		
Roman Polom	11.01.1992	5	(6)	
Jiří Sláma	08.01.1999		(1)	
Jan Štěrba	08.07.1994	15	(2)	
Michal Vepřek	17.06.1985	26		1
Midfielders:	**DOB**	**M**	**(s)**	**G**
Mojmír Chytil	29.04.1999		(4)	
Šimon Falta	24.03.1993	25	(4)	3
David Houska	29.06.1993	29		4
Lukáš Kalvach	19.07.1995	30		2
Milan Lalkovič (SVK)	09.12.1992	3	(14)	2
Václav Pilař	13.10.1988	7	(5)	
Jakub Plšek	13.12.1993	27	(3)	5
Martin Sladký	01.03.1992	23	(1)	2
Jiří Texl	03.01.1993	9	(9)	2
Tomáš Zahradníček	11.08.1993	29	(1)	2
Forwards:	**DOB**	**M**	**(s)**	**G**
Pavel Dvořák	19.02.1989	12	(12)	2
Budge Manzia (COD)	24.09.1994	1	(1)	
Martin Nešpor	05.06.1990	19	(7)	8
Jakub Yunis	25.03.1996	10	(17)	3
Trainer:	**DOB**	**M**		
Václav Jílek	16.05.1976	32		

Sportovní klub Slavia Praha

Founded: 02.11.1902 (*as Akademický cyklistický odbor Slavia*)
Stadium: Eden Arena, Praha (20,232)

Goalkeepers:	DOB	M	(s)	G
Ondřej Kolář	17.10.1994	33		
Přemysl Kovář	14.10.1985	2		
Defenders:	**DOB**	**M**	**(s)**	**G**
Jan Bořil	11.01.1991	27	(2)	2
Vladimír Coufal	22.08.1992	28		3
Simon Desiré Sylvanus Deli (CIV)	27.10.1991	19	(2)	
Michal Frydrych	27.02.1990	6	(13)	3
Ondřej Kúdela	26.03.1987	21	(1)	3
Michael Ngadeu-Ngadjui (CMR)	23.11.1990	29		
Lukáš Pokorný	05.07.1993	1	(1)	
Jaroslav Zelený	20.08.1992	9	(4)	
Midfielders:	**DOB**	**M**	**(s)**	**G**
Alexandru Mihail Băluţă (ROU)	13.09.1993	13	(9)	3
Jakub Hromada (SVK)	25.05.1996		(1)	
Josef Hušbauer	16.03.1990	32	(1)	9
Alex Král	19.05.1998	9	(3)	
Lukáš Masopust	12.02.1993	10	(2)	4
Jan Matoušek	09.05.1998	2	(5)	
Tomáš Souček	27.02.1995	34		13
Jan Sýkora	29.12.1993	8	(4)	1
Petr Ševčík	04.05.1994	4	(1)	
Ibrahim Traoré (CIV)	16.09.1988	9	(7)	2
Matej Valenta	09.02.2000		(1)	
Jaromír Zmrhal	02.08.1993	20	(3)	4
Forwards:	**DOB**	**M**	**(s)**	**G**
Muris Mešanović (BIH)	06.07.1990		(5)	
Peter Oladeji Olayinka (NGA)	16.11.1995	15	(9)	6
Miroslav Stoch (SVK)	19.10.1989	27	(6)	12
Milan Škoda	16.01.1986	17	(11)	8
Stanislav Tecl	01.09.1990	6	(4)	3
Mick van Buren (NED)	24.08.1992	4	(9)	3
Trainer:	**DOB**	**M**		
Jindřich Trpišovský	27.02.1976	35		

1. Fudbalový Klub Slovácko Uherské Hradiště

Founded: 1927 (*as SK Staré Město*)
Stadium: Městský fotbalový stadion "Miroslava Valenty", Uherské Hradiště (8,000)

Goalkeepers:	DOB	M	(s)	G
Michal Daněk	06.07.1983	12		
Matouš Trmal	02.10.1998	23		
Defenders:	**DOB**	**M**	**(s)**	**G**
Josef Divíšek	24.09.1990	14	(2)	
Domagoj Franić (CRO)	17.08.1993	2	(4)	
Stanislav Hofmann	17.06.1990	34		4
Michal Kadlec	13.12.1984	13	(1)	
Jiří Krejčí	22.03.1986	19		1
Petr Reinberk	23.05.1989	18	(5)	1
Patrik Šimko (SVK)	08.07.1991	9	(2)	
Filip Vecheta	15.02.2003		(1)	
Midfielders:	**DOB**	**M**	**(s)**	**G**
Vlastimil Daníček	15.07.1991	34		7
Marek Havlík	08.07.1995	28	(3)	3
Patrik Hellebrand	16.05.1999		(5)	
Dominik Janošek	13.06.1998	23	(1)	2
Jan Juroška	02.03.1993	31	(1)	
Jan Kalabiška	22.12.1986	20	(12)	3
David Machalík	21.06.1996	3	(4)	
Jan Navrátil	13.04.1990	30	(2)	1
Lukáš Sadílek	23.05.1996	15	(9)	5
Forwards:	**DOB**	**M**	**(s)**	**G**
Jaroslav Diviš	09.07.1986	8	(5)	1
Haris Harba (BIH)	14.07.1988		(4)	
Filip Hološko (SVK)	17.01.1984	3	(8)	1
Filip Kubala	02.09.1999	2	(9)	1
Jan Kuchta	08.01.1997	7	(7)	4
Jakub Petr	10.04.1990	10	(3)	
Jakub Rezek	29.05.1998	5	(9)	
Tomáš Zajíc	12.08.1996	22	(5)	6
Trainer:	**DOB**	**M**		
Michal Kordula	11.02.1978	11		
Petr Vlachovský [16.10.2018]	12.07.1983	4		
Martin Svědík [10.11.2018]	27.06.1974	20		

Football Club Slovan Liberec

Founded: 1958
Stadium: Stadion u Nisy, Liberec (9,900)

Goalkeepers:	**DOB**	**M**	**(s)**	**G**
Václav Hladký	14.11.1990	9		
Filip Nguyen	14.09.1992	26		
Defenders:	**DOB**	**M**	**(s)**	**G**
Michal Fukala	22.10.2000	7	(1)	
Matěj Hybš	03.01.1993	23	(2)	3
Taras Kacharaba (UKR)	07.01.1995	31		1
Ondřej Karafiát	01.12.1994	27	(2)	
Milan Kerbr	10.09.1989	7	(1)	
Ondřej Lehoczki	10.02.1998		(1)	
Jan Mikula	05.01.1992	20	(1)	
Damjan Vuklišević (SVN)	28.06.1995	7	(2)	
Midfielders:	**DOB**	**M**	**(s)**	**G**
Rolando Aarons (JAM)	16.11.1995	8	(4)	
Radim Breite	10.08.1989	34		1
Oscar Murphy Dorley (LBR)	19.07.1998	25		1
Martin Koscelník (SVK)	02.03.1995	12	(13)	1
Tomáš Malínský	25.08.1991	16	(9)	2
Kamso Mara (GUI)	24.12.1994	15	(4)	1
Erik Micovčák (SVK)	26.01.1996	1	(1)	
Aleš Nešický	01.06.1992	6	(10)	1
Jakub Pešek	24.06.1993	20	(7)	2
Jan Sýkora	29.12.1993	8		1
Petr Ševčík	04.05.1994	17		1
Forwards:	**DOB**	**M**	**(s)**	**G**
Libor Kozák	30.05.1989	13	(1)	7
Petar Musa (CRO)	04.03.1998	3	(7)	
Filip Oršula (SVK)	25.02.1993	6	(14)	2
Jan Pázler	10.01.1991	6	(14)	2
Roman Potočný	25.04.1991	32		6
Elvis Mashike Sukisa (COD)	06.06.1994	6	(7)	1
Trainer:	**DOB**	**M**		
Zsolt Hornyák (SVK)	01.05.1973	35		

Athletic Club Sparta Praha

Founded: 16.11.1893
Stadium: Generali Arena, Praha (18,887)

Goalkeepers:	**DOB**	**M**	**(s)**	**G**
Milan Heča	23.03.1991	9		
Florin Constantin Niţă (ROU)	03.07.1987	26		
Defenders:	**DOB**	**M**	**(s)**	**G**
Matěj Hanousek	02.06.1993	16		1
Semih Kaya (TUR)	24.02.1991	10		
Costa Nhamoinesu (ZIM)	06.01.1986	27	(1)	2
Dominik Plechatý	18.04.1999	4	(1)	
Uroš Radaković (SRB)	31.03.1994	24	(1)	1
Lukás Štetina (SVK)	28.07.1991	16	(1)	2
Bogdan Ilie Vătăjelu (ROU)	24.04.1993	4	(5)	
Tomáš Wiesner	17.07.1997	3	(2)	
Ondřej Zahustel	18.06.1991	13	(3)	2
Midfielders:	**DOB**	**M**	**(s)**	**G**
Alexandru Mihăiţă Chipciu (ROU)	18.05.1989	24	(3)	1
Eldar Čivić (BIH)	12.05.1996	8	(12)	
Bořek Dočkal	30.09.1988	3		
Martin Frýdek	24.03.1992	33		2
Pavel Hájek	03.08.2001		(1)	
Martin Hašek	03.10.1995	8	(6)	1
Guélor Kanga Kaku (GAB)	01.09.1990	22	(2)	12
Jiří Kulhánek	08.03.1996	1	(2)	
Srđan Plavšić (SRB)	03.12.1995	17	(2)	2
Mihailo Ristić (SRB)	31.10.1995		(1)	
Michal Sáček	19.09.1996	19	(6)	1
Lukáš Vácha	13.05.1989		(4)	
Vukadin Vukadinović (SRB)	14.12.1990	1	(9)	1
Forwards:	**DOB**	**M**	**(s)**	**G**
Tal Ben Haim (ISR)	05.08.1989	2		
Václav Drchal	25.07.1999	6	(4)	3
Adam Hložek	25.07.2002	14	(5)	3
Václav Kadlec	20.05.1992		(2)	
Golgol Mebrahtu (AUS)	28.08.1990	1	(6)	
David Moberg-Karlsson (SWE)	20.03.1994	12	(3)	3
Matěj Pulkrab	23.05.1997	9	(7)	3
Josef Šural (†**29.04.2019**)	30.05.1990	10	(5)	3
Benjamin Tetteh (GHA)	10.07.1997	26	(6)	11
Trainer:	**DOB**	**M**		
Pavel Hapal	27.07.1969	1		
Zdeněk Ščasný [28.07.2018]	09.08.1957	28		
Michal Horňák [25.04.2019]	28.04.1970	6		

Fotbalový klub Teplice

Founded: 1945
Stadium: Stadion Na Stínadlech, Teplice (18,221)

Goalkeepers:	**DOB**	**M**	**(s)**	**G**
Jakub Diviš	27.07.1986	14		
Tomáš Grigar	01.02.1983	18		
Defenders:	**DOB**	**M**	**(s)**	**G**
Pavel Čmovš	29.06.1990	12	(3)	
Jan Hošek	01.04.1989	7	(13)	1
Michal Jeřábek	10.09.1993	25	(1)	2
Jan Krob	27.04.1987	25	(1)	1
Matěj Radosta	10.05.2001	1	(3)	
Tomáš Vondrášek	26.10.1987	30		1
Midfielders:	**DOB**	**M**	**(s)**	**G**
Jakub Hora	23.02.1991	29	(2)	11
Alois Hyčka	22.07.1990	15	(8)	
Jan Knapík	11.12.2000		(1)	
Alex Král	19.05.1998	17		
Tomáš Kučera	20.07.1991	27	(1)	
Admir Ljevakovič (BIH)	07.08.1984	26	(1)	
Siim Luts (EST)	12.03.1989	2	(5)	
Jan Shejbal	20.04.1994	12	(8)	
Soune Daniel Soungole (CIV)	26.02.1995	4	(1)	
Daniel Trubač	17.07.1997	15	(9)	1
Patrik Žitný	21.01.1999	24	(5)	2
Forwards:	**DOB**	**M**	**(s)**	**G**
David Bezdička	09.07.1996		(5)	
Marek Červenka	17.12.1992	1	(5)	
Martin Jindráček	29.11.1989	14	(6)	
Jan Kuchta	08.01.1997	6	(2)	3
Pavel Moulis	07.04.1991	14	(7)	4
Benjamin Mustafik (MKD)	09.06.1998		(1)	
Patrik Ondrášek	13.02.1999		(1)	
Zdeněk Švejda	09.07.1998		(1)	
David Vaněček	09.03.1991	14	(2)	7
Jan Vošahlík	08.03.1989		(1)	
Trainer:	**DOB**	**M**		
Daniel Šmejkal	28.08.1970	9		
Stanislav Hejkal [25.09.2018]	03.01.1970	23		

Football Club Viktoria Plzeň

Founded: 11.06.1911
Stadium: Doosan Arena, Plzeň (11,700)

Goalkeepers:	**DOB**	**M**	**(s)**	**G**
Aleš Hruška	23.11.1985	24		
Matúš Kozáčik (SVK)	27.12.1983	11		
Defenders:	**DOB**	**M**	**(s)**	**G**
Jakub Brabec	06.08.1992	9	(1)	
Milan Havel	07.08.1994	8	(5)	1
Lukáš Hejda	09.03.1990	13	(2)	
Roman Hubník	06.06.1984	27		
David Limberský	06.10.1983	32		
Luděk Pernica	16.06.1990	21	(4)	1
Radim Řezník	20.01.1989	27		1
Midfielders:	**DOB**	**M**	**(s)**	**G**
Aleš Čermák	01.10.1994	19	(5)	1
Tomáš Hořava	29.05.1988	22	(8)	4
Patrik Hrošovský (SVK)	22.04.1992	35		5
Daniel Kolář	27.10.1985	2	(1)	
Jan Kopic	04.06.1990	23		5
Jan Kovařík	19.06.1988	18	(8)	5
Milan Petržela	19.06.1983	13	(9)	1
Roman Procházka (SVK)	14.03.1989	19	(4)	7
Martin Zeman	28.03.1989	4	(3)	
Forwards:	**DOB**	**M**	**(s)**	**G**
Marek Bakoš (SVK)	15.04.1983		(10)	
Jean-David Beauguel (FRA)	21.03.1992	9	(4)	6
Tomáš Chorý	26.01.1995	14	(12)	6
Joel Ngandu Kayamba (COD)	17.04.1992	12	(2)	
Michal Krmenčík	15.03.1993	13		7
Ubong Moses Ekpai (NGA)	17.10.1995	5	(7)	
Erik Pačinda (SVK)	09.05.1989	3	(8)	1
Jakub Řezníček	26.05.1988	2	(11)	2
Ondřej ŠturSa	17.06.2000		(1)	
Trainer:	**DOB**	**M**		
Pavel Vrba	06.12.1963	35		

Football Club Fastav Zlín

Founded: 1919
Stadium: Stadion Letná, Zlín (5,783)

Goalkeepers:	**DOB**	**M**	**(s)**	**G**
Stanislav Dostál	20.06.1991	22		
Matej Rakovan (SVK)	14.03.1990	12		
Defenders:	**DOB**	**M**	**(s)**	**G**
Ondřej Bačo	25.03.1996	20	(5)	
Lukáš Bartošák	03.07.1990	28	(2)	2
Petr Buchta	15.07.1992	31		
Zoran Gajić (SRB)	18.05.1990	29		1
Libor Holík	12.05.1998	21	(7)	1
Lukáš Holík	23.08.1992	3	(3)	
Robert Matejov (SVK)	05.07.1988	23	(4)	2
Midfielders:	**DOB**	**M**	**(s)**	**G**
Josip Balić (CRO)	08.07.1993		(1)	
Martin Cedidla	22.11.2001	1	(1)	
Vakhtang Chanturishvili (GEO)	05.08.1993	10	(2)	
Adnan Džafić (BIH)	10.05.1990	12	(6)	2
Marek Hlinka (SVK)	04.10.1990	12		1
Josef Hnaníček	28.12.1986	20	(2)	
Petr Hronek	04.07.1993	6	(17)	1
Petr Jiráček	02.03.1986	32		2
Tomáš Masař	22.10.1996		(1)	
Martin Nečas	04.09.1998	1		
Pablo Joaquín Podio (ARG)	07.08.1989	27	(1)	1
Ibrahim Benjamin Traoré (CIV)	16.09.1988	7		
Forwards:	**DOB**	**M**	**(s)**	**G**
Jean-David Beauguel (FRA)	21.03.1992	17	(1)	9
Alexander Jakubov	11.01.1991	2	(18)	1
Tomáš Poznar	27.08.1988	21	(1)	8
Patrik Slaměna	07.07.2000	2	(5)	
Pavel Vyhnal	25.05.1990	9	(8)	5
Lukáš Železník	18.06.1990	6	(14)	1
Trainer:	**DOB**	**M**		
Michal Bílek	13.04.1965	19		
Roman Pivarník (SVK) [17.01.2019]	17.02.1967	11		
Jan Kameník [30.04.2019]	25.01.1982	4		

SECOND LEVEL
Czech National Football League 2018/2019

1.	SK Dynamo České Budějovice (*Promoted*)	30	23	3	4	60	-	24	72
2.	FC Vysočina Jihlava (*Promotion Play-offs*)	30	17	7	6	50	-	33	58
3.	FC Zbrojovka Brno (*Promotion Play-offs*)	30	17	6	7	63	-	31	57
4.	FC Hradec Králové	30	15	8	7	36	-	18	53
5.	FK Ústí nad Labem	30	15	4	11	44	-	39	49
6.	FK Varnsdorf	30	13	9	8	33	-	26	48
7.	FK Pardubice	30	11	11	8	45	-	34	44
8.	MFK Vítkovice	30	11	7	12	32	-	44	40
9.	1. SK Prostějov	30	9	9	12	28	-	37	36
10.	FK Fotbal Třinec	30	10	6	14	36	-	42	36
11.	FK Baník Sokolov	30	9	6	15	28	-	40	33
12.	FC Sellier & Bellot Vlašim	30	7	11	12	30	-	38	32
13.	MFK Chrudim	30	8	5	17	39	-	56	29
14.	FK Viktoria Žižkov	30	7	6	17	33	-	59	27
15.	FC MAS Táborsko (*Relegated*)	30	6	7	17	37	-	53	25
16.	1. SC Znojmo FK (*Relegated*)	30	6	7	17	40	-	60	25

NATIONAL TEAM

INTERNATIONAL MATCHES
(16.07.2018 – 15.07.2019)

06.09.2018	Uherské Hradiště	Czech Republic - Ukraine	1-2(1-1)	(UNL)
10.09.2018	Rostov-na-Donu	Russia - Czech Republic	5-1(3-0)	(F)
13.10.2018	Trnava	Slovakia - Czech Republic	1-2(0-0)	(UNL)
16.10.2018	Kharkiv	Ukraine - Czech Republic	1-0(1-0)	(UNL)
15.11.2018	Gdańsk	Poland - Czech Republic	0-1(0-0)	(F)
19.11.2018	Praha	Czech Republic - Slovakia	1-0(1-0)	(UNL)
22.03.2019	London	England - Czech Republic	5-0(2-0)	(ECQ)
26.03.2019	Praha	Czech Republic - Brazil	1-3(1-0)	(F)
07.06.2019	Praha	Czech Republic - Bulgaria	2-1(1-1)	(ECQ)
10.06.2019	Olomouc	Czech Republic - Montenegro	3-0(1-0)	(ECQ)

06.09.2018 CZECH REPUBLIC - UKRAINE 1-2(1-1) UEFA Nations League B, Group 1
Městský fotbalový stadion "Miroslava Valenty", Uherské Hradiště; Referee: Anthony Taylor (England); Attendance: 7,974
CZE: Tomáš Vaclík, Theodor Gebre Selassie (Cap), Jakub Brabec, Jan Bořil, Pavel Kadeřábek, Tomáš Kalas, Josef Hušbauer, Jan Sýkora (90+2.Tomáš Hořava), Tomáš Souček, Michael Krmenčík (46.Jaromír Zmrhal), Patrik Schick (83.Stanislav Tecl). Trainer: Karel Jarolím.
Goal: Patrik Schick (4).

10.09.2018 RUSSIA - CZECH REPUBLIC 5-1(3-0) Friendly International
Rostov Arena, Rostov-na-Donu; Referee: Äliyar Ağhayev (Azerbaijan); Attendance: 45,000
CZE: Tomáš Koubek, Radim Řezník, Jan Bořil, Vladimír Coufal, Tomáš Kalas (46.Jakub Brabec), Tomáš Hořava (65.Jan Sýkora), Josef Hušbauer (Cap) (82.Michal Trávník), Tomáš Souček, Jaromír Zmrhal, Jakub Jankto, Stanislav Tecl (71.Michael Krmenčík). Trainer: Karel Jarolím.
Goal: Tomáš Souček (74).

13.10.2018 SLOVAKIA - CZECH REPUBLIC 1-2(0-0) UEFA Nations League B, Group 1
Štadión "Antona Malatinského", Trnava; Referee: Slavko Vinčić (Slovenia); Attendance: 17,251
CZE: Tomáš Vaclík, Ondřej Čelůstka, Theodor Gebre Selassie, Jakub Brabec, Pavel Kadeřábek (63.Filip Novák), Bořek Dočkal (Cap), David Pavelka, Jaromír Zmrhal, Tomáš Souček, Matěj Vydra (89.Jakub Jankto), Michael Krmenčík (73.Patrik Schick). Trainer: Jaroslav Šilhavý.
Goals: Michael Krmenčík (52), Patrik Schick (76).

16.10.2018 UKRAINE - CZECH REPUBLIC 1-0(1-0) UEFA Nations League B, Group 1
Metalist Stadium, Kharkiv; Referee: Gediminas Mažeika (Lithuania); Attendance: 38,100
CZE: Jiří Pavlenka, Ondřej Čelůstka, Theodor Gebre Selassie, Filip Novák, Jakub Brabec, Bořek Dočkal (Cap), David Pavelka, Antonín Barák, Jakub Jankto (81.Josef Šural), Matěj Vydra (67.Jaromír Zmrhal), Patrik Schick (73.Michael Krmenčík). Trainer: Jaroslav Šilhavý.

15.11.2018 POLAND - CZECH REPUBLIC 0-1(0-0) Friendly International
Stadion Energa, Gdańsk; Referee: Stephan Klossner (Switzerland); Attendance: 34,783
CZE: Jiří Pavlenka, Ondřej Čelůstka, Filip Novák, Jakub Brabec (46.Tomáš Kalas), Pavel Kadeřábek, Bořek Dočkal (Cap) (88.Michal Trávník), David Pavelka, Tomáš Souček (46.Vladimír Darida), Jakub Jankto (66.Jiří Skalák), Matěj Vydra (66.Theodor Gebre Selassie), Patrik Schick (77.Martin Doležal). Trainer: Jaroslav Šilhavý.
Goal: Jakub Jankto (52).

19.11.2018 CZECH REPUBLIC - SLOVAKIA 1-0(1-0) UEFA Nations League B, Group 1
Stadion Sinobo, Praha; Referee: Alejandro José Hernández Hernández (Spain); Attendance: 16,623
CZE: Tomáš Vaclík, Ondřej Čelůstka, Filip Novák, Pavel Kadeřábek, Tomáš Kalas, Bořek Dočkal (Cap), David Pavelka, Tomáš Souček, Jakub Jankto (76.Ladislav Krejčí), Matěj Vydra (64.Theodor Gebre Selassie), Patrik Schick (82.Martin Doležal). Trainer: Jaroslav Šilhavý.
Goal: Patrik Schick (32).

22.03.2019 ENGLAND - CZECH REPUBLIC 5-0(2-0) 16th EC. Qualifiers
Wembley Stadium, London; Referee: Artur Manuel Soares Dias (Portugal); Attendance: 82,575
CZE: Jiří Pavlenka, Ondřej Čelůstka, Theodor Gebre Selassie, Filip Novák, Pavel Kadeřábek, Tomáš Kalas, David Pavelka, Vladimír Darida (Cap) (67.Lukáš Masopust), Tomáš Souček, Jakub Jankto (46.Matěj Vydra), Patrik Schick(82.Milan Škoda). Trainer: Jaroslav Šilhavý.

26.03.2019 CZECH REPUBLIC - BRAZIL 1-3(1-0) Friendly International
Stadion Sinobo, Praha; Referee: Ovidiu Alin Haţegan (Romania); Attendance: 19,166
CZE: Jiří Pavlenka, Marek Suchý, Ondřej Čelůstka (59.Ondřej Kúdela), Filip Novák (46.Theodor Gebre Selassie), Vladimír Coufal, David Pavelka (69.Alex Král), Vladimír Darida (Cap) (56.Martin Frýdek), Jaromír Zmrhal (84.Jakub Jankto), Lukáš Masopust, Tomáš Souček, Patrik Schick (53.Matěj Vydra). Trainer: Jaroslav Šilhavý.
Goal: David Pavelka (37).

07.06.2019 CZECH REPUBLIC - BULGARIA 2-1(1-1) 16th EC. Qualifiers
Generali Arena, Praha; Referee: Tamás Bognár (Hungary); Attendance: 13,482
CZE: Tomáš Vaclík, Marek Suchý (Cap), Ondřej Čelůstka, Filip Novák, Pavel Kadeřábek, Alex Král, David Pavelka, Lukáš Masopust (66.Jan Kopic), Tomáš Souček, Jakub Jankto (82.Ladislav Krejčí), Patrik Schick (78.Martin Doležal). Trainer: Jaroslav Šilhavý.
Goals: Patrik Schick (20, 50).

10.06.2019 CZECH REPUBLIC - MONTENEGRO 3-0(1-0) 16th EC. Qualifiers
Stadion Andrův, Olomouc; Referee: Vladislav Bezborodov (Russia); Attendance: 11,565
CZE: Tomáš Vaclík, Marek Suchý (Cap), Ondřej Čelůstka, Filip Novák, Pavel Kadeřábek, Alex Král, David Pavelka, Lukáš Masopust (39.Jan Kopic), Tomáš Souček, Jakub Jankto (74.Ladislav Krejčí), Patrik Schick (88.Libor Kozák). Trainer: Jaroslav Šilhavý.
Goals: Jakub Jankto (18), Boris Kopitović (49 own goal), Patrik Schick (82 penalty).

NATIONAL TEAM PLAYERS
(16.07.2018 – 15.07.2019)

Name	DOB	Caps	Goals	2018/2019:	Club
Goalkeepers					
Tomáš KOUBEK	26.08.1992	**9**	**0**	2018:	*Stade Rennais FC (FRA)*
Jiří PAVLENKA	14.04.1992	**10**	**0**	2018/2019:	*SV Werder Bremen (GER)*
Tomáš VACLÍK	29.03.1989	**25**	**0**	2018/2019:	*Sevilla FC (ESP)*
Defenders					
Jan BOŘIL	11.01.1991	**9**	**0**	2018:	*SK Slavia Praha*
Jakub BRABEC	06.08.1992	**9**	**0**	2018:	*Çaykur Rizespor Kulübü (TUR)*
Vladimír COUFAL	22.08.1992	**4**	**0**	2018/2019:	*SK Slavia Praha*
Ondřej ČELŮSTKA	18.06.1989	**12**	**1**	2018/2019:	*Antalyaspor Kulübü (TUR)*
Theodor GEBRE SELASSIE	24.12.1986	**54**	**3**	2018/2019:	*SV Werder Bremen (GER)*
Pavel KADEŘÁBEK	25.04.1992	**39**	**3**	2018/2019:	*TSG 1899 Hoffenheim (GER)*
Tomáš KALAS	22.05.1993	**19**	**2**	2018/2019:	*Bristol City FC (ENG)*
Ondřej KÚDELA	26.03.1987	**1**	**0**	2019:	*SK Slavia Praha*
Filip NOVÁK	26.06.1990	**23**	**1**	2018/2019:	*Trabzonspor Kulübü (TUR)*
Radim ŘEZNÍK	20.01.1989	**2**	**0**	2018:	*FC Viktoria Plzeň*
Marek SUCHÝ	29.03.1988	**42**	**1**	2019:	*FC Basel (SUI)*
Midfielders					
Antonín BARÁK	03.12.1994	**12**	**5**	2018/2019:	*Udinese Calcio (ITA)*
Vladimír DARIDA	08.08.1990	**55**	**4**	2018/2019:	*Hertha BSC Berlin (GER)*
Bořek DOČKAL	30.09.1988	**39**	**6**	2018/2019:	*Philadelphia Union (USA)*
Martin FRÝDEK	24.03.1992	**7**	**0**	2019:	*AC Sparta Praha*
Tomáš HOŘAVA	29.05.1988	**14**	**3**	2018:	*FC Viktoria Plzeň*
Josef HUŠBAUER	16.03.1990	**18**	**1**	2018:	*SK Slavia Praha*
Jakub JANKTO	19.01.1996	**21**	**3**	2018/2019:	*UC Sampdoria Genova (ITA)*
Jan KOPIC	04.06.1990	**16**	**3**	2019:	*FC Viktoria Plzeň*
Alex KRÁL	19.05.1998	**3**	**0**	2019:	*SK Slavia Praha*
Ladislav KREJČÍ	05.07.1992	**40**	**5**	2018/2019:	*Bologna FC 1909 (ITA)*
Lukáš MASOPUST	12.02.1993	**5**	**0**	2019:	*SK Slavia Praha*
David PAVELKA	18.05.1991	**22**	**1**	2018/2019:	*Kasımpaşa SK İstanbul (TUR)*
Jiří SKALÁK	12.03.1992	**17**	**0**	2018:	*Millwall FC London (ENG)*
Tomáš SOUČEK	27.02.1995	**20**	**2**	2018/2019:	*SK Slavia Praha*
Jan SÝKORA	29.12.1993	**10**	**1**	2018:	*SK Slavia Praha*
Milan ŠKODA	16.01.1986	**19**	**4**	2019:	*SK Slavia Praha*
Michal TRÁVNÍK	17.05.1994	**5**	**0**	2018:	*FK Jablonec*
Jaromír ZMRHAL	02.08.1993	**13**	**1**	2018/2019:	*SK Slavia Praha*
Forwards					
Martin DOLEŽAL	03.05.1990	**3**	**0**	2018/2019:	*FK Jablonec*
Libor KOZÁK	30.05.1989	**9**	**2**	2019:	*FC Slovan Liberec*
Michael KRMENČÍK	15.03.1993	**19**	**8**	2018:	*FC Viktoria Plzeň*
Patrik SCHICK	24.01.1996	**18**	**8**	2018/2019:	*AS Roma (ITA)*
Josef ŠURAL (†**29.04.2019**)	30.05.1990	**20**	**1**	2018:	*AC Sparta Praha*
Stanislav TECL	01.09.1990	**5**	**0**	2018:	*SK Slavia Praha*
Matěj VYDRA	01.05.1992	**26**	**5**	2018/2019:	*Burnley FC (ENG)*

National team coach

Karel JAROLÍM [01.08.2016 – 11.09.2018]	23.08.1956	22 M; 10 W; 4 D; 8 L; 35-28
Jaroslav ŠILHAVÝ [from 18.09.2018]	03.11.1961	8 M; 5 W; 0 D; 3 L; 10-11

DENMARK

The Country:

Kongeriget Danmark (Kingdom of Denmark)
Capital: København
Surface: 42,925 km^2
Inhabitants: 5,814,461 [2019]
Time: UTC+1

The FA:

Dansk Boldspil-Union
House of Football, DBU Allé 1, 2605 Brøndby
Tel: +45 43 262 222
Foundation date: 18.05.1889
Member of FIFA since: 1904
Member of UEFA since: 1954
Website: www.dbu.dk

NATIONAL TEAM RECORDS

First international match:	19.10.1908, London:	France – Denmark 0-9 (5th OG. 1st Round)
Most international caps:	Peter Schmeichel	- 129 caps (1987-2001)
Most international goals:	Jon Dahl Tomasson	- 52 goals / 112 caps (1997-2008)
	Poul "Tist" Nielsen	- 52 goals / 38 caps (1910-1925)

UEFA EUROPEAN CHAMPIONSHIP	
1960	Qualifiers
1964	Final Tournament (4th Place)
1968	Qualifiers
1972	Qualifiers
1976	Qualifiers
1980	Qualifiers
1984	Final Tournament (Semi-Finals)
1988	Final Tournament (Group Stage)
1992	**Final Tournament (Winners)**
1996	Final Tournament (Group Stage)
2000	Final Tournament (Group Stage)
2004	Final Tournament (Quarter-Finals)
2008	Qualifiers
2012	Final Tournament (Group Stage)
2016	Qualifiers

FIFA WORLD CUP	
1930	*Did not enter*
1934	*Did not enter*
1938	*Did not enter*
1950	*Did not enter*
1954	*Did not enter*
1958	Qualifiers
1962	*Did not enter*
1966	Qualifiers
1970	Qualifiers
1974	Qualifiers
1978	Qualifiers
1982	Qualifiers
1986	Final Tournament (2nd Round of 16)
1990	Qualifiers
1994	Qualifiers
1998	Final Tournament (Quarter-Finals)
2002	Final Tournament (2nd Round of 16)
2006	Qualifiers
2010	Final Tournament (Group Stage)
2014	Qualifiers
2018	Final Tournament (2nd Round of 16)

UEFA NATIONS LEAGUE
2018/2019 – League B (promoted to League A)

OLYMPIC FOOTBALL TOURNAMENTS 1908-2016							
1908	Runners-up	**1948**	3rd Place	**1972**	Second Round	**1996**	Qualifiers
1912	Runners-up	**1952**	Quarter-Finals	**1976**	Qualifiers	**2000**	Qualifiers
1920	First Round	**1956**	*Did not enter*	**1980**	Qualifiers	**2004**	Qualifiers
1924	*Did not enter*	**1960**	Runners-up	**1984**	Qualifiers	**2008**	Qualifiers
1928	*Did not enter*	**1964**	Qualifiers	**1988**	Qualifiers	**2012**	Qualifiers
1936	*Did not enter*	**1968**	*Did not enter*	**1992**	Group Stage	**2016**	Quarter-Finals

FIFA CONFEDERATIONS CUP 1992-2017
1995 (Winners)

DANISH CLUB HONOURS IN EUROPEAN CLUB COMPETITIONS:

European Champion Clubs' Cup (1956-1992) / UEFA Champions League (1993-2019)
None
Fairs Cup (1858-1971) / UEFA Cup (1972-2009) / UEFA Europa League (2010-2019)
None
UEFA Super Cup (1972-2019)
None
European Cup Winners' Cup 1961-1999*
None

**defunct competition*

NATIONAL COMPETITIONS
TABLE OF HONOURS

	CHAMPIONS	CUP WINNERS*	BEST GOALSCORERS	
1912/1913	Kjøbenhavns Boldklub	-	-	
1913/1914	Kjøbenhavns Boldklub	-	-	
1914/1915	*No competition*	-	-	
1915/1916	B 93 København	-	-	
1916/1917	Kjøbenhavns Boldklub	-	-	
1917/1918	Kjøbenhavns Boldklub	-	-	
1918/1919	Akademisk BK København	-	-	
1919/1920	B 1903 København	-	-	
1920/1921	Akademisk BK København	-	-	
1921/1922	Kjøbenhavns Boldklub	-	-	
1922/1923	BK Frem København	-	-	
1923/1924	B 1903 København	-	-	
1924/1925	Kjøbenhavns Boldklub	-	-	
1925/1926	B 1903 København	-	-	
1926/1927	B 93 København	-	-	
1927/1928	*No competition*	-		
1928/1929	B 93 København	-	*Not available*	
1929/1930	B 93 København	-	*Not available*	
1930/1931	BK Frem København	-	*Not available*	
1931/1932	Kjøbenhavns Boldklub	-	*Not available*	
1932/1933	BK Frem København	-	*Not available*	
1933/1934	B 93 København	-	*Not available*	
1934/1935	B 93 København	-	*Not available*	
1935/1936	BK Frem København	-	*Not available*	
1936/1937	Akademisk BK København	-	Pauli Jørgensen (BK Frem København)	19
1937/1938	B 1903 København	-	Knud Andersen (B 1903 København)	23
1938/1939	B 93 København	-	Erik Petersen (B 93 København)	27
1939/1940	Kjøbenhavns Boldklub	-	Frede Jensen (Køge BK) Kaj Hansen (B 93 København)	12
1940/1941	BK Frem København	-	-	
1941/1942	B 93 København	-	-	
1942/1943	Akademisk BK København	-	-	
1943/1944	BK Frem København	-	-	
1944/1945	Akademisk BK København	-	-	
1945/1946	B 93 København	-	Jørgen Leschly Sørensen (B 93 København)	16
1946/1947	Akademisk BK København	-	Helge Broneé (Østerbros Boldklub)	21
1947/1948	Kjøbenhavns Boldklub	-	John Hansen (BK Frem København)	20
1948/1949	Kjøbenhavns Boldklub	-	Jørgen Leschly Sørensen (Odense Boldklub)	16
1949/1950	Kjøbenhavns Boldklub	-	James Rønvang (Akademisk BK København)	15
1950/1951	Akademisk BK København	-	James Rønvang (Akademisk BK København) Henning Bjerregaard (B 93 København) Jens Peter Hansen (Esbjerg fB)	11
1951/1952	Akademisk BK København	-	Valdemar Kendzior (Skovshoved IF) Poul Erik Petersen (Køge BK)	13
1952/1953	Kjøbenhavns Boldklub	-	Valdemar Kendzior (Skovshoved IF)	17
1953/1954	Køge BK	-	Jens-Carl Kristensen (Akademisk BK København)	12
1954/1955	AGF Aarhus	AGF Aarhus	Henning Jensen (BK Frem København)	17
1955/1956	AGF Aarhus	BK Frem København	Gunnar Kjeldberg (AGF Aarhus)	18
1956/1957	AGF Aarhus	AGF Aarhus	Søren Andersen (BK Frem København)	27
1958	Vejle Boldklub	Vejle Boldklub	Henning Enoksen (Vejle Boldklub)	27
1959	B 1909 Odense	Vejle Boldklub	Per Jensen (Kjøbenhavns Boldklub)	20
1960	AGF Aarhus	AGF Aarhus	Harald Nielsen (Frederikshavn fI)	19
1961	Esbjerg fB	AGF Aarhus	Jørgen Ravn (Kjøbenhavns Boldklub)	26
1962	Esbjerg fB	B 1909 Odense	Henning Enoksen (AGF Aarhus) Carl Emil Christiansen (Esbjerg fB)	24
1963	Esbjerg fB	B 1913 Odense	Mogens Haastrup (B 1909 Odense)	21
1964	B 1909 Odense	Esbjerg fB	Jørgen Ravn (Kjøbenhavns Boldklub)	21
1965	Esbjerg fB	AGF Aarhus	Per Petersen (B 1903 København)	18
1966	Hvidovre IF	Aalborg BK	Henning Enoksen (AGF Aarhus)	16
1967	Akademisk BK København	Randers Freja	Leif Nielsen (BK Frem København)	15
1968	Kjøbenhavns Boldklub	Randers Freja	Niels-Christian Holmstrøm (Kjøbenhavns Boldklub)	23
1969	B 1903 København	Kjøbenhavns Boldklub	Steen Rømer Larsen (B 1903 København)	15
1970	B 1903 København	Aalborg BK	Ole Forsing (B 1903 København)	18
1971	Vejle Boldklub	B 1909 Odense	Uffe Brage (Kjøbenhavns Boldklub) John Nielsen (B 1901 Nykøbing)	19
1972	Vejle Boldklub	Vejle Boldklub	Karsten Lund (Vejle Boldklub) John Nielsen (B 1901 Nykøbing)	16
1973	Hvidovre IF	Randers Freja	Hans Aabech (Hvidovre IF)	28
1974	Kjøbenhavns Boldklub	Vanløse IF	Niels-Christian Holmstrøm (Kjøbenhavns Boldklub)	24
1975	Køge BK	Vejle Boldklub	Bjarne Petersen (Kjøbenhavns Boldklub)	25
1976	B 1903 København	Esbjerg fB	Mogens Jespersen (Aalborg BK)	22
1977	Odense Boldklub	Vejle Boldklub	Allan Hansen (Odense Boldklub)	23

1978	Vejle Boldklub	BK Frem København	John Eriksen (Odense Boldklub)	22
1979	Esbjerg fB	B 1903 København	John Eriksen (Odense Boldklub)	20
1980	Kjøbenhavns Boldklub	Hvidovre IF	Hans Aabech (Kjøbenhavns Boldklub)	19
1981	Hvidovre IF	Vejle Boldklub	Allan Hansen (Odense Boldklub)	28
1982	Odense Boldklub	B 93 København	Ib Jacquet (Vejle Boldklub)	20
1983	Lyngby Boldklub	Odense Boldklub	Vilhelm Munk Nielsen (Odense Boldklub)	20
1984	Vejle Boldklub	Lyngby Boldklub	Steen Thychosen (Vejle Boldklub)	24
1985	Brøndby IF	Lyngby Boldklub	Lars Bastrup (Ikast FS)	20
1986	AGF Aarhus	B 1903 København	Claus Nielsen (Brøndby IF)	16
1987	Brøndby IF	AGF Aarhus	Claus Nielsen (Brøndby IF)	20
1988	Brøndby IF	AGF Aarhus	Bent Christensen (Brøndby IF)	21
1989	Odense Boldklub	Brøndby IF	Miklos Molnar (BK Frem København) Flemming Christensen (Lyngby Boldklub) Lars Jakobsen (Odense Boldklub)	14
1990	Brøndby IF	Lyngby Boldklub	Bent Christensen (Brøndby IF)	17
1991	Brøndby IF	Odense Boldklub	Bent Christensen (Brøndby IF)	11
1991/1992	Lyngby Boldklub	AGF Aarhus	Peter Møller (Aalborg BK)	17
1992/1993	FC København	Odense Boldklub	Peter Møller (Aalborg BK)	22
1993/1994	Silkeborg IF	Brøndby IF	Søren Frederiksen (Silkeborg IF)	18
1994/1995	Aalborg BK	FC København	Erik Bo Andersen (Aalborg BK)	24
1995/1996	Brøndby IF	AGF Aarhus	Thomas Thorninger (AGF Aarhus)	20
1996/1997	Brøndby IF	FC København	Miklos Molnar (Lyngby Boldklub)	26
1997/1998	Brøndby IF	Brøndby IF	Ebbe Sand (Brøndby IF)	28
1998/1999	Aalborg BK	Akademisk BK København	Heine Fernandez (Viborg FF)	23
1999/2000	Herfølge BK	Viborg FF	Peter Lassen (Silkeborg IF)	16
2000/2001	FC København	Silkeborg IF	Peter Graulund (Brøndby IF)	21
2001/2002	Brøndby IF	Odense Boldklub	Peter Madsen (Brøndby IF) Kaspar Dalgas (Odense Boldklub)	22
2002/2003	FC København	Brøndby IF	Søren Frederiksen (Viborg FF) Jan Kristiansen (Esbjerg fB)	18
2003/2004	FC København	FC København	Steffen Højer (Odense Boldklub) Mohamed Zidan (EGY, FC Midtjylland Herning) Tommy Bechmann (Esbjerg fB) Mwape Miti (ZAM, Odense Boldklub)	19
2004/2005	Brøndby IF	Brøndby IF	Steffen Højer (Odense Boldklub)	20
2005/2006	FC København	Randers FC	Steffen Højer (Viborg FF)	16
2006/2007	FC København	Odense Boldklub	Rade Prica (SWE, Aalborg BK)	19
2007/2008	Aalborg BK	Brøndby IF	Jeppe Lund Curth (Aalborg BK)	17
2008/2009	FC København	FC København	Morten Nordstrand (FC København) Marc Nygaard (Randers FC)	16
2009/2010	FC København	FC Nordsjælland Farum	Peter Maduabuchi Utaka (NGA, Odense Boldklub)	18
2010/2011	FC København	FC Nordsjælland Farum	Dame N'Doye (SEN, FC København)	25
2011/2012	FC Nordsjælland Farum	FC København	Dame N'Doye (SEN, FC København)	18
2012/2013	FC København	Esbjerg fB	Andreas Cornelius (FC København)	18
2013/2014	Aalborg BK	Aalborg BK	Thomas Dalgaard (Viborg FF)	18
2014/2015	FC Midtjylland Herning	FC København	Martin Pušić (AUT, Esbjerg fB / FC Midtjylland Herning)	17
2015/2016	FC København	FC København	Lukas Spalvis (LTU, Aalborg BK)	18
2016/2017	FC København	FC København	Marcus Ingvartsen (FC Nordsjælland Farum)	23
2017/2018	FC Midtjylland Herning	Brøndby IF	Pål Alexander Kirkevold (NOR, Hobro IK)	22
2018/2019	FC København	FC Midtjylland Herning	Robert Skov (FC København)	29

*Cup competition were called Landspokalturneringen (1954-1989), Giro Cup (1898-1996), Compaq Cup (1996-1999), DONG Cup (1999-2004), Landspokalturneringen (2004-2008), Ekstra Bladet Cup (2008-2011) and DBU Pokalen (since 2011).

NATIONAL CHAMPIONSHIP

Alka Superligaen 2018/2019

(13.07.2018 – 31.05.2019)

Regular Season - Results

Round 1 [13-16.07.2018]
Vejle BK - Hobro IK 3-1(0-0)
SønderjyskE - Aalborg BK 0-1(0-0)
FC Midtjylland - AGF Aarhus 0-0
FC Nordsjælland - Esbjerg fB 1-1(1-0)
Vendsyssel FF - Odense BK 3-2(0-0)
FC København - AC Horsens 1-2(0-0)
Randers FC - Brøndby IF 0-2(0-1)

Round 2 [20-23.07.2018]
Aalborg BK - FC Midtjylland 2-1(0-1)
Esbjerg fB - Vendsyssel FF 2-3(0-2)
AC Horsens - Randers FC 1-1(0-1)
Odense BK - SønderjyskE 2-2(0-2)
AGF Aarhus - FC Nordsjælland 1-1(0-1)
Brøndby IF - Vejle BK 1-1(1-1)
Hobro IK - FC København 0-3(0-1)

Round 3 [27-30.07.2018]
SønderjyskE - AC Horsens 2-0(0-0)
FC Midtjylland - Esbjerg fB 3-1(2-1)
FC Nordsjælland - Vendsyssel FF 3-0(1-0)
Randers FC - Odense BK 1-0(1-0)
Hobro IK - Brøndby IF 1-2(0-0)
FC København - Aalborg BK 4-0(3-0)
Vejle BK - AGF Aarhus 1-1(0-0)

Round 4 [03-06.08.2018]
AGF Aarhus - SønderjyskE 1-0(1-0)
Esbjerg fB - Randers FC 3-3(2-0)
Vejle BK - FC Midtjylland 1-3(1-0)
AC Horsens - Hobro IK 2-2(1-0)
Odense BK - FC København 0-1(0-0)
Brøndby IF - FC Nordsjælland 2-0(1-0)
Vendsyssel FF - Aalborg BK 0-1(0-0)

Round 5 [10-13.08.2018]
Vendsyssel FF - Vejle BK 1-1(1-0)
Hobro IK - Odense BK 3-2(3-0)
Aalborg BK - FC Nordsjælland 1-0(0-0)
FC København - Brøndby IF 3-1(1-0)
Randers FC - AGF Aarhus 0-0
FC Midtjylland - AC Horsens 3-0(1-0)
Esbjerg fB - SønderjyskE 1-0(0-0)

Round 6 [17-20.08.2018]
SønderjyskE - Vendsyssel FF 2-1(0-0)
FC Nordsjælland - Vejle BK 2-0(1-0)
Randers FC - Hobro IK 3-0(2-0)
AGF Aarhus - FC København 1-1(1-0)
Brøndby IF - Esbjerg fB 0-1(0-0)
Odense BK - FC Midtjylland 1-1(0-0)
AC Horsens - Aalborg BK 0-0

Round 7 [24-27.08.2018]
Hobro IK - AGF Aarhus 0-2(0-1)
FC Nordsjælland - AC Horsens 0-1(0-1)
Vejle BK - Odense BK 0-2(0-2)
Vendsyssel FF - Brøndby IF 1-2(0-1)
FC København - SønderjyskE 3-2(2-1)
FC Midtjylland - Randers FC 3-0(1-0)
Aalborg BK - Esbjerg fB 0-1(0-0)

Round 8 [31.08.-02.09.2018]
AC Horsens - Vejle BK 0-0
SønderjyskE - Hobro IK 1-1(1-0)
Odense BK - FC Nordsjælland 0-0
Randers FC - Aalborg BK 2-2(2-1)
Esbjerg fB - FC København 0-2(0-2)
AGF Aarhus - Vendsyssel FF 1-1(1-1)
Brøndby IF - FC Midtjylland 2-2(1-1)

Round 9 [14-17.09.2018]
Esbjerg fB - Odense BK 2-0(1-0)
FC Nordsjælland - Randers FC 4-1(2-0)
Vendsyssel FF - Hobro IK 1-1(1-1)
AC Horsens - AGF Aarhus 3-2(3-1)
Brøndby IF - SønderjyskE 2-4(2-2)
FC Midtjylland - FC København 3-1(1-0)
Aalborg BK - Vejle BK 1-1(1-0)

Round 10 [21-24.09.2018]
Vejle BK - Esbjerg fB 1-0(0-0)
Randers FC - Vendsyssel FF 2-0(0-0)
SønderjyskE - FC Midtjylland 0-0
Hobro IK - Aalborg BK 0-5(0-2)
FC København - FC Nordsjælland 2-1(1-0)
AGF Aarhus - Brøndby IF 3-2(2-1)
Odense BK - AC Horsens 4-0(1-0)

Round 11 [28.09.-01.10.2018]
Vejle BK - Randers FC 1-1(1-1)
FC Midtjylland - Hobro IK 5-2(4-0)
Vendsyssel FF - FC København 2-1(0-1)
Esbjerg fB - AGF Aarhus 0-0
Aalborg BK - Odense BK 0-1(0-1)
Brøndby IF - AC Horsens 1-2(1-0)
FC Nordsjælland - SønderjyskE 4-1(2-1)

Round 12 [05-07.10.2018]
SønderjyskE - Vejle BK 3-0(0-0)
Odense BK - AGF Aarhus 2-2(1-2)
Hobro IK - FC Nordsjælland 3-2(2-1)
AC Horsens - Esbjerg fB 1-2(0-1)
FC København - Randers FC 4-0(1-0)
Aalborg BK - Brøndby IF 1-3(0-1)
FC Midtjylland - Vendsyssel FF 3-0(2-0)

Round 13 [19-22.10.2018]
Esbjerg fB - Hobro IK 2-0(0-0)
FC Nordsjælland - FC Midtjylland 1-4(0-1)
Vendsyssel FF - AC Horsens 0-1(0-1)
Randers FC - SønderjyskE 1-1(1-0)
Vejle BK - FC København 1-3(1-0)
AGF Aarhus - Aalborg BK 2-2(1-0)
Brøndby IF - Odense BK 1-1(0-0)

Round 14 [26-29.10.2018]
SønderjyskE - Odense BK 0-0
AC Horsens - FC Nordsjælland 3-3(2-3)
Hobro IK - Vejle BK 1-0(1-0)
Randers FC - Esbjerg fB 0-2(0-2)
FC København - AGF Aarhus 4-2(1-1)
Aalborg BK - Vendsyssel FF 0-1(0-1)
FC Midtjylland - Brøndby IF 3-2(1-2)

Round 15 [02-05.11.2018]
Odense BK - Hobro IK 1-0(1-0)
Vendsyssel FF - SønderjyskE 2-3(1-0)
Brøndby IF - FC København 0-1(0-0)
FC Nordsjælland - Aalborg BK 1-1(0-1)
AGF Aarhus - Randers FC 0-2(0-2)
Esbjerg fB - FC Midtjylland 2-2(0-0)
Vejle BK - AC Horsens 3-1(2-0)

Round 16 [09-11.11.2018]
Brøndby IF - AGF Aarhus 2-0(0-0)
AC Horsens - SønderjyskE 1-1(1-1)
Hobro IK - Vendsyssel FF 1-0(0-0)
Randers FC - FC Nordsjælland 1-1(0-1)
Aalborg BK - FC København 1-1(0-0)
FC Midtjylland - Vejle BK 5-0(2-0)
Odense BK - Esbjerg fB 2-1(1-1)

Round 17 [23-26.11.2018]
Vejle BK - Aalborg BK 1-1(0-0)
Hobro IK - Randers FC 0-1(0-0)
Vendsyssel FF - Esbjerg fB 1-1(0-0)
FC Nordsjælland - Odense BK 1-3(1-1)
SønderjyskE - Brøndby IF 0-2(0-1)
FC København - FC Midtjylland 2-1(1-0)
AGF Aarhus - AC Horsens 1-2(0-2)

Round 18 [30.11.-03.12.2018]
Esbjerg fB - Aalborg BK 1-4(0-2)
Odense BK - Vendsyssel FF 2-0(1-0)
SønderjyskE - FC Nordsjælland 1-2(0-1)
Randers FC - FC Midtjylland 1-2(1-1)
AC Horsens - FC København 1-6(1-2)
Brøndby IF - Hobro IK 1-0(1-0)
AGF Aarhus - Vejle BK 2-1(1-1)

Round 19 [07-10.12.2018]
FC Midtjylland - Odense BK 3-0(2-0)
Hobro IK - SønderjyskE 0-0
Vendsyssel FF - Randers FC 0-1(0-1)
Aalborg BK - AC Horsens 2-4(2-2)
FC København - Esbjerg fB 3-0(2-0)
Vejle BK - Brøndby IF 1-2(1-0)
FC Nordsjælland - AGF Aarhus 1-0(0-0)

Round 20 [14-17.12.2018]
Odense BK - Aalborg BK 1-2(1-0)
Randers FC - Vejle BK 2-0(0-0)
Esbjerg fB - FC Nordsjælland 3-0(2-0)
AC Horsens - FC Midtjylland 1-3(1-1)
SønderjyskE - FC København 0-3(0-2)
Brøndby IF - Vendsyssel FF 2-3(1-0)
AGF Aarhus - Hobro IK 1-0(0-0)

Round 21 [08-11.02.2019]
AGF Aarhus - Esbjerg fB 2-0(1-0)
Vejle BK - SønderjyskE 2-0(2-0)
Hobro IK - AC Horsens 0-0
Aalborg BK - Randers FC 0-3(0-0)
FC Nordsjælland - Brøndby IF 3-3(1-1)
FC København - Odense BK 6-1(3-0)
Vendsyssel FF - FC Midtjylland 0-1(0-1)

Round 22 [15-18.02.2019]
SønderjyskE - AGF Aarhus 0-2(0-1)
FC Nordsjælland - Hobro IK 2-1(1-0)
AC Horsens - Vendsyssel FF 3-0(0-0)
Odense BK - Vejle BK 1-0(1-0)
Randers FC - FC København 0-2(0-1)
Esbjerg fB - Brøndby IF 2-1(1-0)
FC Midtjylland - Aalborg BK 2-1(1-0)

Round 23 [22-25.02.2019]
Aalborg BK - SønderjyskE 3-0(2-0)
Vejle BK - FC Nordsjælland 1-3(0-1)
Hobro IK - Esbjerg fB 2-0(1-0)
AC Horsens - Odense BK 1-2(1-1)
AGF Aarhus - FC Midtjylland 1-2(1-1)
Brøndby IF - Randers FC 2-1(1-0)
FC København - Vendsyssel FF 1-1(0-1)

Round 24 [01-04.03.2019]
Aalborg BK - Hobro IK 1-1(0-1)
Esbjerg fB - AC Horsens 1-0(0-0)
SønderjyskE - Randers FC 3-0(3-0)
Vendsyssel FF - AGF Aarhus 2-2(1-2)
FC København - Vejle BK 2-0(2-0)
Odense BK - Brøndby IF 2-0(1-0)
FC Midtjylland - FC Nordsjælland 3-3(1-2)

Round 25 [08-11.03.2019]
Hobro IK - FC Midtjylland 1-2(0-1)
Vejle BK - Vendsyssel FF 1-1(0-1)
Randers FC - AC Horsens 2-0(0-0)
SønderjyskE - Esbjerg fB 3-1(1-1)
FC Nordsjælland - FC København 2-2(0-1)
Brøndby IF - Aalborg BK 3-3(1-2)
AGF Aarhus - Odense BK 1-2(0-0)

Round 26 [17.03.2019]
Aalborg BK - AGF Aarhus 3-1(1-1)
Vendsyssel FF - FC Nordsjælland 0-1(0-0)
FC Midtjylland - SønderjyskE 2-1(1-1)
Odense BK - Randers FC 1-0(1-0)
Esbjerg fB - Vejle BK 2-1(0-0)
AC Horsens - Brøndby IF 1-3(1-2)
FC København - Hobro IK 3-1(1-1)

Final Standings

1.	FC København	26	19	4	3	65	-	23	61
2.	FC Midtjylland Herning	26	18	6	2	62	-	26	60
3.	Odense Boldklub	26	12	6	8	35	-	31	42
4.	Brøndby IF	26	11	5	10	44	-	40	38
5.	Esbjerg fB	26	11	5	10	32	-	35	38
6.	FC Nordsjælland Farum	26	9	9	8	42	-	39	36
7.	Aalborg BK	26	9	9	8	38	-	35	36
8.	Randers FC	26	9	7	10	29	-	34	34
9.	AGF Aarhus	26	7	10	9	31	-	34	31
10.	AC Horsens	26	8	7	11	31	-	45	31
11.	Sønderjysk Elitesport	26	7	7	12	30	-	37	28
12.	Vendsyssel FF Hjørring	26	5	7	14	24	-	41	22
13.	Hobro IK	26	5	6	15	22	-	45	21
14.	Vejle Boldklub	26	4	8	14	22	-	42	20

Teams ranked 1-6 were qualified for the Championship Round, while teams ranked 7-14 were qualified for the Relegation Round.

Championship Round

Results

Round 27 [29-31.03.2019]
Brøndby IF - Odense BK 2-2(1-1)
FC Midtjylland - FC Nordsjælland 0-0
FC København - Esbjerg fB 1-0(1-0)

Round 28 [07-08.04.2019]
Esbjerg fB - FC Midtjylland 2-2(0-0)
Odense BK - FC København 0-1(0-0)
FC Nordsjælland - Brøndby IF 1-1(1-0)

Round 29 [14.04.2019]
FC Nordsjælland - Esbjerg fB 1-2(1-1)
Brøndby IF - FC København 1-2(1-2)
FC Midtjylland - Odense BK 2-0(1-0)

Round 30 [18-19.04.2019]
Esbjerg fB - Brøndby IF 1-0(0-0)
FC København - FC Midtjylland 3-0(2-0)
Odense BK - FC Nordsjælland 2-2(0-0)

Round 31 [22-23.04.2019]
FC Nordsjælland - FC København 0-3(0-2)
FC Midtjylland - Brøndby IF 1-2(1-1)
Esbjerg fB - Odense BK 0-0

Round 32 [28-29.04.2019]
Brøndby IF - Esbjerg fB 0-1(0-0)
FC København - Odense BK 4-0(1-0)
FC Nordsjælland - FC Midtjylland 1-2(1-0)

Round 33 [05-06.05.2019]
FC København - Brøndby IF 3-2(2-1)
Odense BK - FC Midtjylland 3-1(1-0)
Esbjerg fB - FC Nordsjælland 0-0

Round 34 [10-13.05.2019]
Odense BK - Esbjerg fB 4-1(2-0)
FC Midtjylland - FC København 4-0(1-0)
Brøndby IF - FC Nordsjælland 2-0(2-0)

Round 35 [19-20.05.2019]
FC Nordsjælland - Odense BK 2-2(1-2)
Esbjerg fB - FC København 4-3(2-0)
Brøndby IF - FC Midtjylland 4-1(2-1)

Round 36 [25.05.2019]
FC København - FC Nordsjælland 1-3(0-1)
FC Midtjylland - Esbjerg fB 1-2(1-2)
Odense BK - Brøndby IF 0-2(0-1)

Final Standings

1.	**FC København**	36	26	4	6	86	-	37	82
2.	FC Midtjylland Herning	36	21	8	7	76	-	43	71
3.	Esbjerg fB	36	16	8	12	45	-	47	56
4.	Brøndby IF	36	15	7	14	60	-	52	52
5.	Odense Boldklub	36	14	10	12	48	-	48	52
6.	FC Nordsjælland Farum	36	10	14	12	52	-	54	44

Brøndby IF were qualified for the Europa League Play-off Final.

Top goalscorers:

29 Robert Skov
FC København

22 Dame N'Doye (SEN)
FC København

22 Andreas Skov Olsen
FC Nordsjælland Farum

Relegation Round

Group A - Results

Round 27 [31.03.-01.04.2019]
SønderjyskE - AC Horsens 0-0
AGF Aarhus - Vejle BK 2-2(0-0)

Round 28 [05-07.04.2019]
Randers FC - Vendsyssel FF 1-1(1-1)
Vejle BK - SønderjyskE 4-1(3-0)

Round 29 [12-15.04.2019]
Vejle BK - AC Horsens 3-0(0-0)
SønderjyskE - AGF Aarhus 0-1(0-1)

Round 30 [18.04.2019]
AGF Aarhus - SønderjyskE 2-1(1-1)
AC Horsens - Vejle BK 0-0

Round 31 [21.04.2019]
AC Horsens - SønderjyskE 0-1(0-0)
Vejle BK - AGF Aarhus 2-4(2-1)

Round 32 [28.04.2019]
AGF Aarhus - AC Horsens 3-1(3-0)
SønderjyskE - Vejle BK 4-1(1-1)

Group B - Results

Round 27 [31.03.2019]
Vendsyssel FF - Hobro IK 3-3(1-1)
Aalborg BK - Randers FC 1-2(1-0)

Round 28 [06-07.04.2019]
AC Horsens - AGF Aarhus 0-3(0-1)
Hobro IK - Aalborg BK 1-1(1-0)

Round 29 [13-14.04.2019]
Vendsyssel FF - Aalborg BK 1-0(1-0)
Hobro IK - Randers FC 1-2(0-1)

Round 30 [17-19.04.2019]
Aalborg BK - Vendsyssel FF 1-1(1-1)
Randers FC - Hobro IK 1-0(1-0)

Round 31 [22.04.2019]
Hobro IK - Vendsyssel FF 3-2(2-0)
Randers FC - Aalborg BK 0-2(0-1)

Round 32 [26.04.2019]
Aalborg BK - Hobro IK 1-1(0-0)
Vendsyssel FF - Randers FC 0-0

Final Standings

Group A

1.	AGF Aarhus	32	12	11	9	46	-	40	47
2.	Sønderjysk Elitesport	32	9	8	15	37	-	45	35
3.	AC Horsens	32	8	9	15	32	-	55	33
4.	Vejle Boldklub	32	6	10	16	34	-	53	28

Group B

1.	Randers FC	32	12	9	11	35	-	39	45
2.	Aalborg BK	32	10	12	10	44	-	41	42
3.	Vendsyssel FF Hjørring	32	6	11	15	32	-	49	29
4.	Hobro IK	32	6	9	17	31	-	55	27

Please note: Winners and runners-up of both groups were qualified for the European Play-offs. Teams ranked 3-4 of both groups were qualified for the Relegation Play-offs.

Europa League Play-offs [05-12.05/18-26.05./31.05.2019]

First Round	Aalborg BK - AGF Aarhus	0-1(0-1)	0-2(0-1)
	Sønderjysk Elitesport - Randers FC	1-1(1-0)	3-4(1-2)
Second Round	Randers FC - AGF Aarhus	2-1(2-1)	1-1(0-0)
Europa League Play-off Final	Brøndby IF - Randers FC	4-2(0-1)	

Relegation Play-offs [12-19.05./30.05.-02.06.2019]

First Round (Relegation)	Vendsyssel FF Hjørring - AC Horsens	0-1(0-0)	1-1(0-1)
	Hobro IK - Vejle Boldklub	0-1(0-1)	2-0(1-0,1-0)

Vendsyssel FF Hjørring and Vejle Boldklub relegated.

Second Round (Promotion)	Lyngby Boldklub - Vendsyssel FF Hjørring	2-1(2-1)	2-2(1-0)
	Hobro IK - Viborg FF	1-0(1-0)	2-0(2-0)

Lyngby Boldklub and **Hobro IK** promoted to 2019/2020 Danish Superliga.

NATIONAL CUP
DBU Pokalen / Sydbank Pokalen 2018/2019

Second Round [04/05/06/11/12.09.2018]

B 1908 Amager - BK Avarta	2-1(0-0)
Viby IF - Skive IK	2-1(2-1)
Silkeborg KFUM - Kolding IF	0-3(0-1)
Hedensted IF - Aarhus Fremad	1-2(1-0)
Herlev IF - BK Marienlyst	2-2 aet; 2-4 pen
Gentofte-Vangede IF - Sønderjysk Elitesport	0-3(0-2)
FC Djursland - Jammerbugt FC	1-3(0-2)
Bramdrupdam GIF - Dalum IF	0-11(0-1)
NB Bornholm - Hillerød GI	0-2(0-0)
BK Fremad Amager - FC Roskilde	2-5(0-3)
Brabrand IF - Silkeborg IF	2-3(0-0)
Kjellerup IF - Middelfart Fodbold	0-1(0-0)
Hørsholm-Usserød IK - Esbjerg fB	1-11(0-5)
IF Lyseng - Hobro IK	1-2(1-0,1-1)
Egen UI - Vendsyssel FF Hjørring	1-9(1-6)
FC Sydvest 05 - AGF Aarhus	0-2(0-0)
FC Helsingør - Næstved BK	1-1 aet; 4-5 pen
B93 København - HB Køge	1-3(0-2)
AB Gladsaxe - Odense Boldklub	0-4(0-3)
Hundested IK - Tårnby FF	4-1(2-1)
Næsby BK - Randers FC	1-1 aet; 2-4 pen
Frem Bjæverskov - Ledøje-Smørum	0-3(0-0)
BK Frem København - Vejle BK	3-4(1-1,2-2) aet
Tarup-Paarup IF - Thisted FC	0-1(0-0)
Hellerup IK - Nykøbing FC	2-3(1-2,2-2) aet
Viborg FF - FC Fredericia	2-2 aet; 4-5 pen

Third Round [25-27.09./03.10./10.10.2018]

Ledøje-Smørum - Hobro IK	1-2(1-0)
Kolding IF - Randers FC	2-1(0-1,1-1)
Hundested IK - Vendsyssel FF Hjørring	0-3(0-0)
Jammerbugt FC - Esbjerg fB	0-1(0-0)
B 1908 Amager - BK Marienlyst	2-4(1-2,2-2)
Dalum IF - FC Midtjylland Herning	1-2(1-0,1-1)
Næstved BK - Silkeborg IF	1-0(1-0)
Aarhus Fremad - AGF Aarhus	1-5(0-1)
FC Roskilde - Aalborg BK	0-5(0-2)
FC Fredericia - Sønderjysk Elitesport	0-2(0-1)
HB Køge - FC Nordsjælland	0-4(0-1)
Viby IF - FC København	0-3(0-1)
Hillerød GI - Brøndby IF	1-4(1-1)
Middelfart Fodbold - AC Horsens	0-3(0-2)
Thisted FC - Odense Boldklub	0-2(0-0)
Nykøbing FC - Vejle BK	1-2(0-2)

1/8-Finals [31.10./01.11./06.11./07.11./22.11./05.12.2018]			
Næstved BK - AGF Aarhus	2-1(2-1)	Hobro IK - Odense Boldklub	2-4(2-4)
Aalborg BK - AC Horsens	1-0(1-0)	Sønderjysk Elitesport - Esbjerg fB	1-2(1-2,1-1) aet
Kolding IF - Vejle BK	3-1(3-1,3-1) aet	BK Marienlyst - Brøndby IF	1-4(1-3)
FC Midtjylland Herning - FC København	2-0(2-0)	FC Nordsjælland - Vendsyssel FF Hjørring	0-1(0-1)

Quarter-Finals [27-28.02./13-14-03.2019]			
Odense Boldklub - Esbjerg fB	2-2 aet; 3-2 pen	Kolding IF - FC Midtjylland Herning	0-2(0-1)
Vendsyssel FF Hjørring - Brøndby IF	0-2(0-1)	Næstved BK - Aalborg BK	1-3(1-2)

Semi-Finals [03-04.04.2019]			
FC Midtjylland Herning - Odense Boldklub	4-0(1-0)	Brøndby IF - Aalborg BK	1-0(1-0)

Final

17.05.2019; Telia Parken, København; Referee: Peter Kjærsgaard-Andersen; Attendance: 31,349

FC Midtjylland Herning - Brøndby IF **1-1(1-1,1-1,1-1); 4-3 on penalties**

FC Midtjylland: Jesper Hansen, Kian Hansen (94.Rasmus Nicolaisen), Erik Sviatchenko, Marc Dal Hende, Alexander Scholz, Mads Døhr Thychosen, Jakob Poulsen (Cap), Tim Sparv, Gustav Wikheim (106.Awer Mabil), Evander Da Silva Ferreira (66.Frank Ogochukwu Onyeka), Ebere Paul Onuachu (100.Artem Dovbyk). Trainer: Kenneth Andersen.

Brøndby IF: Marvin Schwäbe, Paulus Arajuuri, Anthony Jung, Hjörtur Hermannsson, Dominik Kaiser, Josip Radošević, Kevin Mensah, Hany Mukhtar (115.Lasse Vigen), Kamil Wilczek (Cap), Simon Hedlund (74.Simon Tibbling), Mikkel Uhre (120.Besar Halimi). Trainer: Martin Retov.

Goals: 1-0 Kian Hansen (6), 1-1 Dominik Kaiser (21).

Penalties: Dominik Kaiser (saved); Jakob Poulsen 1-0; Anthony Jung 1-1; Mads Døhr Thychosen (saved); Kamil Wilczek 2-1; Marc Dal Hende 2-2; Josip Radošević (saved); Awer Mabil 3-2; Besar Halimi 3-3; Alexander Scholz 4-3.

THE CLUBS 2018/2019

Please note: matches and goals includes statistics of both regular season and play-offs (Championship Round, Relegation Round or European Play-offs).

Aalborg Boldspilklub

Founded: 13.05.1985
Stadium: Aalborg Portland Park (13,797)

Goalkeepers:	DOB	M	(s)	G
Jacob Rinne (SWE)	20.06.1993	34		
Defenders:	**DOB**	**M**	**(s)**	**G**
Jakob Ahlmann	18.01.1991	25		
Jakob Blåbjerg	11.01.1995	10	(4)	
Bardhec Bytyqi (ALB)	08.01.1997		(1)	
Lukas Klitten	01.05.2000	3		
Patrick Kristensen	28.04.1987	13	(1)	1
Jores Okore	11.08.1992	31		
Kristoffer Pallesen	30.04.1990	16	(2)	
Kasper Pedersen	13.01.1991	21	(1)	4
Mathias Ross	15.01.2001	7	(2)	
Midfielders:	**DOB**	**M**	**(s)**	**G**
Oliver Abildgaard	10.06.1996	24	(1)	1
Lucas Andersen	13.09.1994	21	(2)	10
Frederik Børsting	13.02.1995	16	(7)	1
Magnus Christensen	20.08.1997	24	(3)	1
Robert Kakeeto (UGA)	19.05.1995		(1)	
Kasper Kusk	10.11.1991	32	(1)	5
Filip Lesniak (SVK)	14.05.1996	5	(3)	
Philipp Ochs (GER)	17.04.1997	13	(7)	1
Kasper Risgård	04.01.1983	7	(22)	3
Rasmus Thellufsen	09.01.1997	19	(12)	4
Rasmus Würtz	18.09.1983	10	(8)	
Forwards:	**DOB**	**M**	**(s)**	**G**
Wessam Abou Ali	04.01.1999	11	(11)	1
Mikkel Kaufmann	03.01.2001	2	(6)	1
Oliver Klitten	01.05.2000		(2)	
Jannik Pohl	06.04.1996	6		1
Pavol Šafranko (SVK)	16.11.1994	1	(1)	
Tom van Weert (NED)	07.06.1990	23	(2)	8
Trainer:	**DOB**	**M**		
Morten Wieghorst	25.02.1971	17		
Jacob Friis [25.11.2018]	11.12.1976	17		

Aarhus Gymnastikforening

Founded: 1880
Stadium: Ceres Park, Aarhus (20,032)

Goalkeepers:	DOB	M	(s)	G
Kamil Grabara (POL)	08.01.1999	16		
Aleksandar Jovanović (SRB)	06.12.1992	7		
Kasper Kristensen	04.08.1999	3	(2)	
Óscar Alexander Whalley Guardado (ESP)	29.03.1994	10		
Defenders:	**DOB**	**M**	**(s)**	**G**
Magnus Anbo	18.09.2000	3		
Niklas Backman (SWE)	13.11.1988	12		
Sebastian Hausner	11.04.2000	6		
Casper Højer Nielsen	20.11.1994	31		4
Jesper Juelsgård	26.01.1989	29	(2)	
Pierre Kanstrup	21.02.1989	14	(1)	1
Dino Mikanović (CRO)	07.05.1994	20		
Alexander Munksgaard	13.12.1997	9	(1)	
Daniel Thøgersen	08.01.2000	4		
Frederik Tingager	22.02.1993	14		
Midfielders:	**DOB**	**M**	**(s)**	**G**
Mustafa Amini (AUS)	20.04.1993	27	(4)	2
Jakob Ankersen	22.09.1990	33	(1)	8
Bror Blume	22.01.1992	16	(3)	2
Adama Guira (BFA)	24.04.1988	22	(8)	
Benjamin Hvidt	12.03.2000	2	(4)	
Kasper Jakobsen	17.07.1999	8	(2)	2
Kasper Junker	05.03.1994	3	(4)	
Magnus Kaastrup	28.12.2000		(4)	
Tobias Sana (SWE)	11.07.1989	20	(12)	7
Martin Spelmann	21.03.1987	7	(8)	2
Jens Stage	08.11.1996	34		6
Björn Sverrisson (ISL)	29.05.1990	4	(3)	
Youssef Toutouh	06.10.1992	4	(11)	1
Forwards:	**DOB**	**M**	**(s)**	**G**
Alexander Ammitzbøll	17.02.1999	6	(3)	3
Mustapha Bundu (SLE)	27.02.1997	18	(13)	4
Ryan Mmaee (BEL)	01.11.1997	4	(5)	
Patrick Mortensen	13.07.1989	10	(2)	9
André Riel	21.10.1989		(1)	
Trainer:	**DOB**	**M**		
David Nielsen	01.12.1976	36		

Brøndbyernes Idrætsforening

Founded: 03.12.1964
Stadium: Brøndby Stadion, Brøndby (29,000)

Goalkeepers:	**DOB**	**M**	**(s)**	**G**
Benjamin Bellot (GER)	30.07.1990	1		
Marvin Schwäbe (GER)	25.04.1995	36	(1)	
Defenders:	**DOB**	**M**	**(s)**	**G**
Paulus Arajuuri (FIN)	15.06.1988	26	(1)	
Jens Gammelby	05.02.1995	15	(2)	1
Hjörtur Hermannsson (ISL)	08.02.1995	19	(2)	
Anthony Jung (GER)	03.11.1991	31	(1)	
Joël Kabongo	05.04.1998	12	(3)	
Björn Kopplin (GER)	07.01.1989	2	(1)	
Kevin Mensah	15.05.1991	7	(1)	
Benedikt Röcker (GER)	19.11.1989	18	(5)	1
Midfielders:	**DOB**	**M**	**(s)**	**G**
Kasper Fisker	22.05.1988	4	(6)	
Morten Frendrup	07.04.2001		(3)	
Besar Halimi (KVX)	12.12.1994	9	(12)	2
Simon Hedlund (SWE)	11.03.1993	15	(1)	4
Dominik Kaiser (GER)	16.09.1988	27	(6)	3
Hany Mukhtar (GER)	21.03.1995	27	(2)	6
Christian Nørgaard	10.03.1994	1		
Josip Radošević (CRO)	03.04.1994	29	(1)	2
Simon Tibbling (SWE)	07.09.1994	24	(12)	5
Lasse Vigen	15.08.1994	21	(4)	1
Forwards:	**DOB**	**M**	**(s)**	**G**
Uffe Manich Bech	13.01.1993	5	(3)	2
Ante Erceg (CRO)	12.12.1989	11	(11)	4
Nikolai Laursen	19.02.1998	5	(12)	1
Mikkel Uhre	30.09.1994	10	(18)	6
Kamil Wilczek (POL)	14.01.1988	33	(1)	22
Trainer:	**DOB**	**M**		
Alexander Zorniger (GER)	08.10.1967	22		
Martin Retov [19.02.2019]	05.05.1980	15		

Esbjerg forenede Boldklubber

Founded: 23.07.1924
Stadium: Blue Water Arena, Esbjerg (16,942)

Goalkeepers:	**DOB**	**M**	**(s)**	**G**
Jeppe Højbjerg	30.04.1995	36		
Lasse Mikkelsen	18.01.1998		(1)	
Defenders:	**DOB**	**M**	**(s)**	**G**
Agustín García Iñiguez „Agus“ (ESP)	03.05.1985	10		
Daniel Anyembe	22.07.1998	26	(2)	
Rodolph Austin (JAM)	01.06.1985	20	(1)	4
Jeppe Brinch	08.05.1995	20	(4)	
Nikolaj Hagelskjær	06.05.1990		(2)	
Markus Halsti (FIN)	19.03.1984	33		
Jesper Lauridsen	27.03.1991	35		
Jonas Mortensen	16.01.2001		(1)	
Kristian Riis	17.02.1997		(1)	
Midfielders:	**DOB**	**M**	**(s)**	**G**
Simon Bækgård	14.10.1999		(1)	
Mark Brink	15.03.1998	12	(18)	
Patrick Egelund	02.08.2000		(2)	
Joni Kauko (FIN)	12.07.1990	35		8
Matthias Kristensen	21.03.1997	27	(7)	4
Mads Larsen	20.09.2001		(3)	
Emmanuel Oti (GHA)	24.09.1996	11	(13)	
Lasha Parunashvili (GEO)	14.02.1993	32		2
Jacob Sørensen	03.03.1998	35	(1)	3
Rafael Ferdinand van der Vaart (NED)	11.02.1983		(3)	
Forwards:	**DOB**	**M**	**(s)**	**G**
Anders Laustrup Dreyer	02.05.1998	4		1
Carlo Holse	02.06.1999	13	(1)	3
Brent McGrath (AUS)	18.06.1991	1	(8)	
William Møller	10.03.1998		(6)	
Adrian Petre (ROU)	11.02.1998	24	(11)	8
Adnane Tighadouini (MAR)	30.10.1992	10	(7)	4
Yuri Yakovenko (UKR)	03.09.1993	12	(15)	7
Trainer:	**DOB**	**M**		
John Lammers (NED)	11.09.1973	36		

Football Club København

Founded: 01.07.1992
Stadium: Telia Parken, København (38,065)

Goalkeepers:	**DOB**	**M**	**(s)**	**G**
Stephan Andersen	26.11.1981	5	(1)	
Frederik Ibsen	28.03.1997	1		
Jesse Joronen (FIN)	21.03.1993	30	(1)	
Defenders:	**DOB**	**M**	**(s)**	**G**
Peter Ankersen	22.09.1990	34		1
Pierre Bengtsson (SWE)	12.04.1988	9	(6)	
Andreas Bjelland	11.07.1988	28	(2)	1
Nicolai Boilesen	16.02.1992	26	(1)	1
Michael Lüftner (CZE)	14.03.1994	1		
Sotirios Papagiannopoulos (SWE)	05.09.1990	11	(7)	
Guillermo Varela Olivera (URU)	24.03.1993	4	(3)	
Denis Vavro (SVK)	10.04.1996	33	(2)	
Midfielders:	**DOB**	**M**	**(s)**	**G**
Ahmed Daghim	07.04.2001		(3)	
Rasmus Falk	15.01.1992	33		4
Viktor Fischer	09.06.1994	24	(1)	9
Ján Greguš (SVK)	29.01.1991	7	(11)	2
William Kvist	24.02.1985	2	(14)	
Robert Mudražija (CRO)	05.05.1997	1	(1)	
Nicolaj Thomsen	08.05.1993	17	(12)	3
José Carlos Gonçalves Rodrigues „Zeca“ (GRE)	31.08.1988	32		1
Forwards:	**DOB**	**M**	**(s)**	**G**
Mohammed Daramy	07.01.2002	5	(6)	1
Carlo Holse	02.06.1999	2	(8)	1
Kenan Kodro (BIH)	19.08.1993	3	(5)	1
Dame N'Doye (SEN)	21.02.1985	33		22
Robert Skov	20.05.1996	31	(3)	29
Pieros Sotiriou (CYP)	13.01.1993	8	(12)	2
Jonas Wind	07.02.1999	16	(5)	6
Trainer:	**DOB**	**M**		
Ståle Solbakken (NOR)	27.02.1968	36		

Hobro Idræts Klub

Founded: 1913
Stadium: DS Arena, Hobro (10,700)

Goalkeepers:	**DOB**	**M**	**(s)**	**G**
Jesper Rask	18.07.1988	32		
Defenders:	**DOB**	**M**	**(s)**	**G**
Yaw Amankwah (NOR)	07.07.1988	20	(1)	
Jesper Bøge	22.02.1990	30		
Nicholas Gotfredsen	05.02.1989	10	(10)	1
Mathias Haarup	10.02.1996	25	(2)	1
Rasmus Minor Petersen	13.09.1988	32		
Frans Dhia Putros (IRQ)	14.07.1993	13	(5)	
Jacob Tjørnelund	31.12.1991	3	(6)	1
Midfielders:	**DOB**	**M**	**(s)**	**G**
Edgar Babayan	28.10.1995	19	(2)	5
Jonas Brix-Damborg	17.04.1986	28		
Christian Cappis (USA)	13.08.1999	1	(2)	
Vito Hammershøy-Mistrati	15.06.1992	31		3
Mikkel Mejlstrup Pedersen	07.01.1996	13	(12)	1
Martin Mikkelsen	29.04.1986	26	(2)	
Danny Olsen	11.06.1985	3	(3)	
Emmanuel Sabbi (USA)	24.12.1997	23	(4)	5
Mathies Skjellerup	23.05.1996		(6)	
Collins Tanor (GHA)	04.01.1998		(2)	
Forwards:	**DOB**	**M**	**(s)**	**G**
Quincy Antipas (ZIM)	20.04.1984	4	(4)	2
Alexander Baun	18.11.1995		(1)	
Baye Djiby Fall (SEN)	20.04.1985	3	(3)	
Sebastian Grønning	03.02.1997	5	(18)	
Pål Kirkevold (NOR)	10.11.1990	15	(4)	7
Julian Kristoffersen (NOR)	10.05.1997	16	(7)	4
Trainer:	**DOB**	**M**		
Allan Kuhn	02.03.1968	22		
Peter Sørensen [21.02.2019]	24.03.1973	10		

Alliance Club Horsens

Founded: 1994
Stadium: CASA Arena, Horsens (10,400)

Goalkeepers:	**DOB**	**M**	**(s)**	**G**
Matej Delač (CRO)	20.08.1992	27		
Kevin Ray Mendoza (PHI)	29.09.1994	5	(1)	
Defenders:	**DOB**	**M**	**(s)**	**G**
Mads Andersen	27.12.1997	19	(1)	3
Sebastian Avanzini (ITA)	01.04.1995	4	(7)	
Rune Frantsen	15.10.1991	23	(1)	
Thomas Kortegaard	02.07.1984	11	(2)	
Michael Lumb	09.01.1988	20	(2)	2
Sonni Ragnar Nattestad (FRO)	05.08.1994	3	(1)	
Mathias Nielsen	02.03.1991	21	(3)	
Peter Nymann	22.08.1982	30	(1)	2
Mikkel Qvist	22.04.1993	20	(8)	2
Søren Reese	29.07.1993	20		2
Midfielders:	**DOB**	**M**	**(s)**	**G**
Jonas Borring	04.01.1985	15	(3)	1
Hallur Hansson (FRO)	08.07.1992	26	(2)	7
Bjarke Jacobsen	21.08.1993	25	(4)	2
Lasse Kryger	03.11.1982		(5)	1
Frederik Mortensen	30.10.1998	1		
Sivert Nilsen (NOR)	02.10.1991	23	(4)	1
Louka Prip	29.06.1997	3	(7)	1
Sammy Skytte	20.02.1997	20	(5)	
Forwards:	**DOB**	**M**	**(s)**	**G**
Tobias Arndal	01.09.1997	3	(7)	
Nicolai Brock-Madsen	09.01.1993	3	(3)	
Oliver Drost	04.11.1995	11	(10)	3
Kasper Junker	05.03.1994	18	(4)	3
Mathias Kristensen	24.06.1993	1	(5)	1
Martin Pušić (AUT)	24.10.1987		(1)	
Trainer:	**DOB**	**M**		
Bo Henriksen	07.02.1975	32		

Football Club Midtjylland Herning

Founded: 02.02.1999
Stadium: MCH Arena, Herning (11,800)

Goalkeepers:	**DOB**	**M**	**(s)**	**G**
Mikkel Andersen	17.12.1988	2		
Jesper Hansen	31.03.1985	34		
Defenders:	**DOB**	**M**	**(s)**	**G**
Joel Andersson (SWE)	11.11.1996	29	(1)	1
Kian Hansen	03.03.1989	27		1
Marc Dal Hende	06.11.1990	24		7
Manjrekar James (CAN)	05.08.1993	5		
Zsolt Korcsmár (HUN)	09.01.1989	4		
Alexander Munksgaard	13.12.1997	3	(1)	
Rasmus Nicolaisen	16.03.1997	13	(4)	4
Oliver Olsen	13.08.2000		(1)	
Bubacarr Sanneh (GAM)	14.11.1994	4		
Alexander Scholz	24.10.1992	27		3
Erik Sviatchenko	04.10.1991	27		1
Mads Døhr Thychosen	27.06.1997	11	(2)	2
Midfielders:	**DOB**	**M**	**(s)**	**G**
Jens-Lys Cajuste (SWE)	10.08.1999	1	(1)	
Evander Da Silva Ferreira (BRA)	09.06.1998	20	(6)	9
Rilwan Olanrewaju Hassan (NGA)	09.02.1991	6	(12)	2
Bozhidar Kraev (BUL)	23.06.1997	2	(10)	
Awer Mabil (AUS)	15.09.1995	24	(6)	6
Ayo Simon Okosun	21.07.1993	5	(5)	
Frank Ogochukwu Onyeka (NGA)	01.01.1998	12	(9)	4
Jakob Poulsen	07.07.1983	33	(1)	7
Tim Sparv (FIN)	20.02.1987	19	(2)	2
Gustav Wikheim (NOR)	18.03.1993	17	(11)	3
Forwards:	**DOB**	**M**	**(s)**	**G**
Artem Dovbyk (UKR)	21.06.1997	2	(3)	
Mikkel Duelund Poulsen	29.06.1997	3	(2)	
Mayron George (CRC)	23.10.1993	7	(18)	4
José Francisco dos Santos Júnior "Júnior Brumado" (BRA)	15.05.1999	2	(2)	
Rafał Kurzawa (POL)	29.01.1993	5	(1)	1
Ebere Paul Onuachu (NGA)	28.05.1994	28	(2)	17
Trainer:	**DOB**	**M**		
Jess Thorup	21.02.1970	12		
Kenneth Andersen [10.10.2018]	23.10.1967	24		

Football Club Nordsjælland Farum

Founded: 01.07.2003
Stadium: Right to Dream Park, Farum (9,900)

Goalkeepers:	**DOB**	**M**	**(s)**	**G**
Nicolai Larsen	09.03.1991	30		
Peter Vindahl Jensen	16.02.1998	6		
Defenders:	**DOB**	**M**	**(s)**	**G**
Clinton Antwi (GHA)	06.11.1999	2	(1)	
Karlo Bartolec (CRO)	20.04.1995	34		2
Marcus Gudmann	27.02.2000		(1)	
Benjamin Hansen	07.02.1994	6	(4)	
Abdel Mumin (GHA)	06.06.1998	13	(1)	
Victor Nelsson	14.10.1998	34		
Mads Pedersen	01.09.1996	20	(2)	
Andreas Skovgaard	27.03.1997	12	(3)	
Viktor Tranberg	26.02.1997	1		
Ulrik Yttergård Jenssen (NOR)	17.07.1996	27	(4)	4
Midfielders:	**DOB**	**M**	**(s)**	**G**
Oliver Antman (FIN)	15.08.2001	1	(4)	
Mikkel Damsgaard	03.07.2000	27	(5)	1
Martin Frese	04.01.1998		(2)	
Magnus Kofod Andersen	10.05.1999	29	(2)	
Mohammed Kudus (GHA)	02.08.2000	19	(7)	3
Mathias Jensen	01.01.1996	1		
Mikkel Rygaard	25.12.1990	20	(7)	2
Jacob Steen Christensen	25.06.2001	14	(8)	
Nicklas Strunck Jakobsen	17.08.1999	10	(10)	2
Forwards:	**DOB**	**M**	**(s)**	**G**
Jonathan Amon (USA)	30.04.1999	15	(10)	4
Isaac Atanga (GHA)	29.07.2000		(2)	
Nikolai Baden Frederiksen	18.05.2000	1		
Godsway Donyoh (GHA)	14.10.1994	23	(5)	10
Mathias Rasmussen (NOR)	25.11.1997	16	(15)	
Joachim Rothmann	29.06.2000	1	(4)	
Ibrahim Sadiq (GHA)	07.05.2000	1	(7)	1
Andreas Skov Olsen	29.12.1999	33	(3)	22
Trainer:	**DOB**	**M**		
Kasper Hjulmand	09.04.1972	26		
Flemming Pedersen [25.03.2019]	30.06.1963	10		

Odense Boldklub

Founded: 12.07.1887
Stadium: Nature Energy Park, Odense (15,633)

Goalkeepers:	**DOB**	**M**	**(s)**	**G**
Oliver Christensen	22.03.1999	1		
Sten Grytebust (NOR)	25.10.1989	35		
Defenders:	**DOB**	**M**	**(s)**	**G**
Gustav Grubbe Madsen	27.01.2003		(1)	
Ryan Johnson Laursen	14.04.1992	30		2
Jacob Laursen	17.11.1994	29	(1)	5
Ramon Leeuwin (NED)	01.09.1987	23		2
Alexander Ludwig	30.06.1993	21	(5)	1
Marco Lund	30.06.1996	14	(3)	1
Oliver Lund	21.08.1990	12	(1)	2
Daniel Obbekjær	16.07.2002		(1)	
Kenneth Petersen	15.01.1985	5		
Mikkel Desler Puggard	19.02.1995	5	(7)	
Jeppe Tverskov	12.03.1993	35		1
Midfielders:	**DOB**	**M**	**(s)**	**G**
Yao Dieudonne (CIV)	14.02.1997		(2)	
Janus Drachmann	11.05.1988	30	(1)	1
Julius Eskesen	16.03.1999	10	(11)	
Mads Frøkjær-Jensen	29.07.1999		(4)	
Mathias Greve	11.02.1995	10	(11)	
Troels Kløve	23.10.1990	30	(2)	4
Casper Nielsen	29.04.1994	24	(5)	3
Jens Thomasen	25.06.1996	14	(6)	3
Kamil Vacek (CZE)	18.05.1987		(2)	
Forwards:	**DOB**	**M**	**(s)**	**G**
Rasmus Festersen	26.08.1986	1	(8)	2
Nicklas Helenius	08.05.1991	14	(13)	7
Anders Jacobsen	27.10.1989	22	(10)	2
Mathias Jørgensen	20.09.2000	4	(9)	2
Bashkim Kadrii	09.07.1991	27		10
Trainer:	**DOB**	**M**		
Jakob Michelsen	30.09.1980	36		

Randers Football Club

Founded: 01.01.2003
Stadium: BioNutria Park, Randers (12,000)

Goalkeepers:	**DOB**	**M**	**(s)**	**G**
Patrik Carlgren (SWE)	08.01.1992	37		
Defenders:	**DOB**	**M**	**(s)**	**G**
Jonas Bager	18.07.1996	35		1
Kevin Conboy	15.10.1987	30	(1)	3
Tobias Damsgaard	03.08.1998		(12)	
Kasper Enghardt	27.05.1992	12	(9)	
Simon Graves	22.03.1999	1	(3)	
Björn Kopplin (GER)	07.01.1989	8	(5)	2
Erik Marxen	02.12.1990	34		1
Johnny Thomsen	26.02.1982	35		
Midfielders:	**DOB**	**M**	**(s)**	**G**
Mads Aaquist	31.12.1994	11	(12)	2
Joel Allansson (SWE)	03.11.1992	4	(3)	1
Andreas Bruhn	17.02.1994		(3)	
Mikkel Kallesøe	20.04.1997	22	(2)	3
Tobias Klysner	03.07.2001		(1)	
Frederik Lauenborg	18.05.1997	8	(12)	
Saba Lobzhanidze (GEO)	18.12.1994	37		8
Nikolai Poulsen	15.08.1993	33		1
André Rømer	18.07.1993	33		5
Forwards:	**DOB**	**M**	**(s)**	**G**
Mikael Boman (SWE)	14.07.1988	2	(13)	
Marvin Egho (AUT)	09.05.1994	23	(6)	8
Kasper Høgh	06.12.2000		(2)	
Emil Riis Jakobsen	24.06.1998	13	(17)	4
Marcus Mølvadgaard	03.08.1999	2	(2)	
Benjamin Stokke (NOR)	20.08.1990	27	(7)	5
Trainer:	**DOB**	**M**		
Thomas Thomasberg	15.10.1974	37		

Sønderjysk Elitesport

Founded: 01.01.2004
Stadium: Sydbank Park, Haderslev (10,000)

Goalkeepers:	**DOB**	**M**	**(s)**	**G**
Sebastian Mielitz (GER)	18.07.1989	34		
Defenders:	**DOB**	**M**	**(s)**	**G**
Anders Egholm	15.05.1983		(5)	
Stefan Gartenmann	02.02.1997	33		4
João Duarte Vieira Pereira (POR)	10.05.1990	1	(1)	
Thomas Juel-Nielsen	18.06.1990	2	(1)	1
Kees Luijckx (NED)	11.02.1986	32		2
Nicholas Marfelt	15.09.1994	15	(2)	
Marc Pedersen	31.07.1989	28		
Simon Poulsen	07.10.1984	15	(1)	
Jeppe Simonsen	21.11.1995	8	(6)	
Midfielders:	**DOB**	**M**	**(s)**	**G**
Danny Amankwaa	30.01.1994	4	(9)	1
Alexander Bah	09.12.1997	19	(4)	2
Victor Sylvestre Mpindi Ekani (CMR)	27.02.1997	12	(2)	
Søren Frederiksen	07.08.1989	8	(13)	2
Christian Jakobsen	27.03.1993	24	(7)	6
Eggert Jónsson (ISL)	18.08.1988	24	(2)	2
Marco Rodrigo Rojas (NZL)	05.11.1991	6	(5)	1
Marcel Rømer	08.08.1991	27		1
Rasmus Vinderslev	12.08.1997	1	(10)	
Niki Zimling	19.04.1985	17	(2)	1
Forwards:	**DOB**	**M**	**(s)**	**G**
Johan Absalonsen	16.09.1985	21	(4)	5
Peter Christiansen	02.12.1999	6	(6)	2
Mads Hvilsom	23.08.1992	6	(10)	1
Senad Jarović (GER)	20.01.1998		(4)	
Mart Lieder (NED)	01.05.1990	31	(2)	7
William Joel Tchuameni Kouemo (CMR)	25.12.1996		(1)	
Trainer:	**DOB**	**M**		
Claus Nørgaard	17.12.1979	20		
Glen Riddersholm [01.02.2019]	24.04.1972	22		

Vejle Boldklub

Founded: 1891
Stadium: Vejle Stadium, Vejle (10,418)

Goalkeepers:	**DOB**	**M**	**(s)**	**G**
Pavol Bajza (SVK)	04.09.1991	24		
Thomas Hagelskjær	04.02.1995	8	(2)	
Defenders:	**DOB**	**M**	**(s)**	**G**
Malte Amundsen	11.02.1998	6	(4)	
Viljormur Davidsen (FRO)	19.07.1991	24	(2)	
Felix Örn Friðriksson (ISL)	16.03.1999		(1)	
Mads Greve	12.09.1989	31		4
Branko Ilič (SVN)	06.02.1983	5		
Vladis Emmerson Illoy Ayyet (CGO)	07.10.1995	8	(3)	
Mads Lauritsen	14.04.1993	18		
Rasmus Lauritsen	27.02.1996	16	(2)	2
Kerim Memija (BIH)	06.01.1996	15	(4)	
Midfielders:	**DOB**	**M**	**(s)**	**G**
Allan Gonçalves Sousa (BRA)	27.01.1997	27		10
Melker Hallberg (SWE)	20.10.1995	18	(7)	1
Tobias Mølgaard	22.07.1996	19	(2)	
Arbnor Mucolli	15.09.1999	18	(7)	1
Nicolaj Madsen	16.07.1988	2	(3)	
Sean Murray (IRL)	11.10.1993	3	(8)	
Ylber Ramadani (ALB)	12.04.1996	24	(2)	
Mathias Rasmussen	02.08.1995	2		
Jacob Schoop	23.12.1988	26	(2)	1
Vladlen Yurchenko (UKR)	22.01.1994	10	(6)	3
Forwards:	**DOB**	**M**	**(s)**	**G**
Jonas Andersen	29.08.1999		(4)	1
Kjartan Finnbogason (ISL)	09.07.1986	10	(1)	4
Sergiy Gryn (UKR)	06.06.1994	6	(1)	2
Adam Jakobsen	07.04.1999	8	(9)	1
Imed Louati (TUN)	11.10.1993	15	(6)	2
Thais Nielsen	23.03.2000		(1)	
Gustaf Nilsson (SWE)	23.05.1997	9	(10)	2
Kelade Nathan Oduwa (ENG)	05.03.1996		(3)	
Zhen'ao Wang (CHN)	10.08.1999		(2)	
Trainer:	**DOB**	**M**		
Adolfo Sormani (ITA)	11.08.1965	24		
Constantin Gâlcă (ROU) [06.03.2019]	08.03.1972	8		

Vendsyssel FF Hjørring

Founded: 1886
Stadium: Nord Energi Arena, Hjørring (7,500)

Goalkeepers:	**DOB**	**M**	**(s)**	**G**
Nicolai Flø	09.08.1995	26		
Michael Tørnes	08.01.1986	6		
Defenders:	**DOB**	**M**	**(s)**	**G**
Daniel Christensen	19.09.1988	10	(3)	
Sander Fischer (NED)	03.09.1988	27	(3)	1
Søren Henriksen	04.02.1992	23	(2)	1
Jakob Hjorth	19.09.1994	7	(1)	1
Alexander Juel Andersen	29.01.1991	31		
Andreas Kaltoft	22.05.1998	25	(2)	1
Benjamin Lund	12.03.1997	2	(1)	
Dylan John McGowan (AUS)	06.08.1991		(3)	1
Mads Roerslev Rasmussen	24.06.1999	2	(2)	
Jeppe Svenningsen	14.10.1994	6	(3)	
Midfielders:	**DOB**	**M**	**(s)**	**G**
Francisco Santos Silva Júnior (POR)	18.01.1992	9	(1)	
Mikkel Frankoch	14.01.1996	9	(1)	
Lucas Jensen	08.10.1994	15	(11)	1
Morten Knudsen	28.04.1995	21	(5)	1
Moses Opondo (UGA)	28.10.1997	21	(1)	4
Matti Steinmann (GER)	08.01.1995	8		1
Mikkel Wohlgemuth	04.06.1995	20	(6)	
Jón Dagur Þorsteinsson (ISL)	26.11.1998	20	(2)	3
Forwards:	**DOB**	**M**	**(s)**	**G**
Seyi Shinobu Adeyinka Adekoya (USA)	05.12.1995	5	(9)	1
Washington Brandão dos Santos (BRA)	18.08.1990	11	(5)	1
Sebastian Czajkowski	15.09.1996	8	(5)	2
Ninos Gouriye (NED)	14.01.1991	3	(2)	
Jeppe Illum	25.03.1992		(3)	
Benjamin Källman (FIN)	17.06.1998	5	(2)	2
Alhaji Kamara (SLE)	16.04.1994	6	(2)	4
Tiémoko Konaté (CIV)	03.03.1990	12		1
Marcus Solberg Mathiasen	17.02.1995		(1)	
Mads Mikkelsen	11.12.1999	2	(2)	1
Emmanuel Ifeanyi Ogude (NGA)	29.03.1994	10	(13)	3
Myroslav Slavov (UKR)	08.09.1990	2	(2)	
Trainer:	**DOB**	**M**		
Jens Berthel Askou	19.08.1982	32		

SECOND LEVEL
1. division - NordicBet Liga 2018/2019

1.	Silkeborg IF (*Promoted*)	33	18	7	8	60	-	41	61
2.	Viborg FF (*Promotion Play-offs*)	33	17	9	7	61	-	37	60
3.	Lyngby Boldklub (*Promotion Play-offs*)	33	15	7	11	51	-	47	52
4.	Næstved Boldklub	33	13	11	9	43	-	40	50
5.	BK Fremad Amager	33	13	11	9	42	-	45	50
6.	FC Fredericia	33	14	5	14	51	-	47	47
7.	HB Køge	33	12	9	12	51	-	47	45
8.	Nykøbing FC	33	12	9	12	44	-	47	45
9.	FC Roskilde	33	9	8	16	57	-	66	35
10.	Hvidovre IF	33	9	8	16	39	-	49	35
11.	FC Helsingør (*Relegated*)	33	6	13	14	35	-	43	31
12.	Thisted FC (*Relegated*)	33	7	9	17	35	-	61	30

NATIONAL TEAM

INTERNATIONAL MATCHES
(16.07.2018 – 15.07.2019)

05.09.2018	Trnava	Slovakia - Denmark	3-0(2-0)	(F)
09.09.2018	Aarhus	Denmark - Wales	2-0(1-0)	(UNL)
13.10.2018	Dublin	Republic of Ireland - Denmark	0-0	(UNL)
16.10.2018	Herning	Denmark - Austria	2-0(1-0)	(F)
16.11.2018	Cardiff	Wales - Denmark	1-2(0-1)	(UNL)
19.11.2018	Aarhus	Denmark - Republic of Ireland	0-0	(UNL)
21.03.2019	Pristina	Kosovo - Denmark	2-2(1-0)	(F)
26.03.2019	Basel	Switzerland - Denmark	3-3(1-0)	(ECQ)
07.06.2019	København	Denmark - Republic of Ireland	1-1(0-0)	(ECQ)
10.06.2019	København	Denmark - Georgia	5-1(2-1)	(ECQ)

05.09.2018 SLOVAKIA - DENMARK 3-0(2-0) Friendly International
Štadión "Antona Malatinského", Trnava; Referee: Julian Weinberger (Austria); Attendance: 6,432
DEN: Christoffer Haagh, Simon Møller Vollesen (77.Christopher Jakobsen), Mads Priisholm Bertelsen (61.Anders Fønss), Nicolai Vestergaard Johansen, Daniel Nielsen, Christian Bannis (46.Anders Hunsballe), Rasmus Gaudin, Oskar Georg Højbye (61.Adam Fogt), Rasmus Engel Johansson (84.Christian Bommelund Christensen), Christian Offenberg (Cap), Kasper Kempel (61.Daniel Holm Sørensen Sørensen). Trainer: John Jensen.

09.09.2018 DENMARK - WALES 2-0(1-0) UEFA Nations League B, Group 4
Ceres Park & Arena, Aarhus; Referee: Deniz Aytekin (Germany); Attendance: 17,506
DEN: Kasper Schmeichel, Simon Thorup Kjær (Cap), Mathias Jattah-Njie Jørgensen, Henrik Dalsgaard, Jens Stryger Larsen, Lasse Schøne, Thomas Joseph Delaney, Christian Dannemann Eriksen, Martin Braithwaite Christensen, Yussuf Yurary Poulsen (86.Andreas Cornelius), Pione Sisto Ifolo Emirmija (46.Viktor Fischer). Trainer: Åge Fridtjof Hareide (Norway).
Goals: Christian Dannemann Eriksen (32, 63 penalty).

13.10.2018 REPUBLIC OF IRELAND - DENMARK 0-0 UEFA Nations League B, Group 4
Aviva Stadium, Dublin; Referee: Xavier Estrada Fernández (Spain); Attendance: 41,220
DEN: Kasper Schmeichel, Simon Thorup Kjær (Cap), Mathias Jattah-Njie Jørgensen, Henrik Dalsgaard, Jens Stryger Larsen, Lasse Schøne, Thomas Joseph Delaney, Martin Braithwaite Christensen, Kasper Dolberg Rasmussen (79.Andreas Bødtker Christensen), Yussuf Yurary Poulsen, Pione Sisto Ifolo Emirmija. Trainer: Åge Fridtjof Hareide (Norway).

16.10.2018 DENMARK - AUSTRIA 2-0(1-0) Friendly International
MCH Arena, Herning; Referee: Ola Hobber Nilsen (Norway); Attendance: 7,386
DEN: Kasper Schmeichel, Simon Thorup Kjær (Cap) (61.Mathias Jattah-Njie Jørgensen), Jonas Hjort Knudsen (90.Jens Stryger Larsen), Peter Svarrer Ankersen, Jannik Vestergaard, Andreas Bødtker Christensen (62.Mike Lindemann Jensen), Pierre-Emile Kordt Højbjerg, Lukas Reiff Lerager, Kasper Dolberg Rasmussen (46.Christian Lund Gytkjær), Yussuf Yurary Poulsen (46.Martin Braithwaite Christensen), Pione Sisto Ifolo Emirmija. Trainer: Åge Fridtjof Hareide (Norway).
Goals: Lukas Reiff Lerager (29), Martin Braithwaite Christensen (90+3).

16.11.2018 WALES - DENMARK 1-2(0-1) UEFA Nations League B, Group 4
Cardiff City Stadium, Cardiff; Referee: Ivan Kružliak (Slovakia); Attendance: 32,354
DEN: Kasper Schmeichel, Mathias Jattah-Njie Jørgensen, Henrik Dalsgaard, Jens Stryger Larsen, Andreas Bødtker Christensen, Lasse Schøne (79.Lukas Reiff Lerager), Thomas Joseph Delaney, Christian Dannemann Eriksen (Cap), Nicolai Mick Jørgensen (70.Kasper Dolberg Rasmussen), Martin Braithwaite Christensen, Yussuf Yurary Poulsen. Trainer: Åge Fridtjof Hareide (Norway).
Goals: Nicolai Mick Jørgensen (42), Martin Braithwaite Christensen (88).

19.11.2018 DENMARK - REPUBLIC OF IRELAND 0-0 UEFA Nations League B, Group 4
Ceres Park & Arena, Aarhus; Referee: Aliyar Aghayev (Azerbaijan); Attendance: 11,130
DEN: Frederik Riis Rønnow, Mathias Jattah-Njie Jørgensen, Andreas Bjelland, Jonas Hjort Knudsen, Peter Svarrer Ankersen, Lasse Schøne, Pierre-Emile Kordt Højbjerg, Christian Dannemann Eriksen (Cap) (46.Lukas Reiff Lerager), Nicolai Mick Jørgensen, Martin Braithwaite Christensen (78.Andreas Cornelius), Yussuf Yurary Poulsen (46.Christian Lund Gytkjær). Trainer: Åge Fridtjof Hareide (Norway).

21.03.2019 KOSOVO - DENMARK 2-2(1-0) Friendly International

Stadiumi „Fadil Vokrri", Pristina; Referee: Ali Palabiyik (Turkey); Attendance: 13,000

DEN: Kasper Schmeichel (Cap), Mathias Jattah-Njie Jørgensen, Henrik Dalsgaard (46.Jens Stryger Larsen), Peter Svarrer Ankersen, Andreas Bødtker Christensen (60.Simon Thorup Kjær), Thomas Joseph Delaney, Pierre-Emile Kordt Højbjerg, Lukas Reiff Lerager (60.Christian Dannemann Eriksen), Nicolai Mick Jørgensen (60.Kasper Dolberg Rasmussen), Martin Braithwaite Christensen, Jacob Bruun Larsen (77.Christian Lund Gytkjær). Trainer: Åge Fridtjof Hareide (Norway).

Goals: Christian Dannemann Eriksen (63 penalty), Pierre-Emile Kordt Højbjerg (90+1).

26.03.2019 SWITZERLAND - DENMARK 3-3(1-0) 16th EC. Qualifiers

St. Jakob Park, Basel; Referee: Damir Skomina (Slovenia); Attendance: 18,352

DEN: Kasper Schmeichel, Simon Thorup Kjær (Cap), Mathias Jattah-Njie Jørgensen, Henrik Dalsgaard, Jens Stryger Larsen, Lasse Schøne (70.Pierre-Emile Kordt Højbjerg), Thomas Joseph Delaney, Christian Dannemann Eriksen, Nicolai Mick Jørgensen (70.Christian Lund Gytkjær), Martin Braithwaite Christensen, Yussuf Yurary Poulsen. Trainer: Åge Fridtjof Hareide (Norway).

Goals: Mathias Jattah-Njie Jørgensen (84), Christian Lund Gytkjær (88), Henrik Dalsgaard (90+3).

07.06.2019 DENMARK - REPUBLIC OF IRELAND 1-1(0-0) 16th EC. Qualifiers

Parken Stadium, København; Referee: Cüneyt Çakır (Turkey); Attendance: 34,610

DEN: Kasper Schmeichel, Simon Thorup Kjær (Cap), Henrik Dalsgaard, Jens Stryger Larsen, Andreas Bødtker Christensen, Lasse Schøne (72.Pierre-Emile Kordt Højbjerg), Thomas Joseph Delaney, Christian Dannemann Eriksen, Nicolai Mick Jørgensen, Martin Braithwaite Christensen (65.Kasper Dolberg Rasmussen), Yussuf Yurary Poulsen. Trainer: Åge Fridtjof Hareide (Norway).

Goal: Pierre-Emile Kordt Højbjerg (76).

10.06.2019 DENMARK - GEORGIA 5-1(2-1) 16th EC. Qualifiers

Parken Stadium, København; Referee: Robert Schörgenhofer (Austria); Attendance: 15,387

DEN: Kasper Schmeichel, Simon Thorup Kjær (Cap) (36.Mathias Jattah-Njie Jørgensen), Jens Stryger Larsen, Peter Svarrer Ankersen, Andreas Bødtker Christensen, Thomas Joseph Delaney, Pierre-Emile Kordt Højbjerg, Christian Dannemann Eriksen, Robert Skov (62.Daniel Wass), Kasper Dolberg Rasmussen, Yussuf Yurary Poulsen (75.Martin Braithwaite Christensen). Trainer: Åge Fridtjof Hareide (Norway).

Goals: Kasper Dolberg Rasmussen (14), Christian Dannemann Eriksen (30 penalty), Kasper Dolberg Rasmussen (63), Yussuf Yurary Poulsen (73), Martin Braithwaite Christensen (90+3).

NATIONAL TEAM PLAYERS
(16.07.2018 – 15.07.2019)

Name	DOB	Caps	Goals	2018/2019:	*Club*
Goalkeepers					
Christoffer HAAGH	17.02.1987	**1**	**0**	2018:	*Jægersborg Boldklub Gentofte*
Frederik Riis RØNNOW	04.08.1992	**7**	**0**	2018:	*Eintracht Frankfurt (GER)*
Kasper Peter SCHMEICHEL	05.11.1986	**47**	**0**	2018/2019:	*Leicester City FC (ENG)*
Defenders					
Peter Svarrer ANKERSEN	22.09.1990	**25**	**1**	2018/2019:	*FC København*
Christian BANNIS	04.01.1992	**1**	**0**	2018:	*Tarup-Paarup IF*
Mads Priisholm BERTELSEN	18.12.1994	**1**	**0**	2018:	*Tarup-Paarup IF*
Andreas BJELLAND	11.07.1988	**29**	**2**	2018:	*FC København*
Christian BOMMELUND Christensen	03.09.1989	**1**	**0**	2018:	*Jægersborg Boldklub Gentofte*
Andreas Bødtker CHRISTENSEN	10.04.1996	**26**	**1**	2018/2019:	*Chelsea FC London (ENG)*
Henrik DALSGAARD	27.07.1989	**21**	**1**	2018/2019:	*Brentford FC London (ENG)*
Nicolai Vestergaard JOHANSEN	24.02.1994	**1**	**0**	2018:	*Vanløse IF*
Mathias Jattah-Njie JØRGENSEN	23.04.1990	**23**	**2**	2018/2019:	*Huddersfield Town AFC (ENG)*
Simon Thorup KJÆR	26.03.1989	**89**	**3**	2018/2019:	*Sevilla FC (ESP)*
Jonas Hjort KNUDSEN	16.09.1992	**6**	**0**	2018:	*Ipswich Town FC (ENG)*
Daniel NIELSEN	01.05.1995	**1**	**0**	2018:	*Vanløse IF*
Jens Stryger LARSEN	21.02.1991	**24**	**1**	2018/2019:	*Udinese Calcio (ITA)*
Jannik VESTERGAARD	03.08.1992	**17**	**1**	2018:	*Southampton FC (ENG)*
Midfielders					
Thomas Joseph DELANEY	03.09.1991	**38**	**4**	2017/2018:	*BV Borussia 09 Dortmund (GER)*
Christian Dannemann ERIKSEN	14.02.1992	**89**	**27**	2018/2019:	*Tottenham Hotspur FC London (ENG)*
Viktor Gorridsen FISCHER	09.06.1994	**21**	**3**	2018:	*FC København*
Adam FOGT	04.09.1983	**1**	**0**	2018:	*Kastrup Boldklub*
Rasmus GAUDIN	19.08.1995	**1**	**0**	2018:	*Vanløse IF*
Pierre-Emile Kordt HØJBJERG	05.08.1995	**27**	**3**	2018/2019:	*Southampton FC (ENG)*
Oskar Georg HØJBYE	29.11.1996	**1**	**0**	2018:	*Vanløse IF*
Anders HUNSBALLE	12.09.1992	**1**	**0**	2018:	*Greve Fodbold*
Christopher JAKOBSEN	14.09.1994	**1**	**0**	2018:	*Hillerød Fodbold*
Mike Lindemann JENSEN	19.02.1988	**7**	**0**	2018:	*Rosenborg BK Trondheim (NOR)*
Rasmus Engel JOHANSSON	04.04.1995	**1**	**0**	2018:	*Hellerup IK*

Kasper KEMPEL	16.04.1994	**1**	**0**	2018:	*Skovshoved IF*
Lukas Reiff LERAGER	12.07.1993	**5**	**0**	2018: 29.01.2019->	*FC Girondins de Bordeaux (FRA)* *Genoa CFC (ITA)*
Lasse SCHØNE	27.05.1986	**45**	**3**	2018/2019:	*AFC Ajax Amsterdam (NED)*
Pione SISTO Ifolo Emirmija	04.02.1995	**21**	**1**	2018:	*RC Celta de Vigo (ESP)*
Simon Møller VOLLESEN	26.01.1998	**1**	**0**	2018:	*IF Skjold Birkerød*
Daniel WASS	31.05.1989	**17**	**0**	2019:	*Valencia CF (ESP)*

Forwards

Martin BRAITHWAITE Christensen	05.06.1991	**33**	**4**	2018: 03.01.2019->	*Middlesbrough FC (ENG)* *CD Leganés (ESP)*
Jacob BRUUN LARSEN	19.09.1998	**1**	**0**	2019:	*BV Borussia 09 Dortmund (GER)*
Andreas Evald CORNELIUS	16.03.1993	**23**	**4**	2018:	*FC Girondins de Bordeaux (FRA)*
Kasper DOLBERG Rasmussen	06.10.1997	**13**	**3**	2018/2019:	*AFC Ajax Amsterdam (NED)*
Anders FØNSS	20.06.1988	**1**	**0**	2018:	*Tarup-Paarup IF*
Christian Lund GYTKJÆR	06.05.1990	**5**	**1**	2018/2019:	*KKS Lech Poznań*
Daniel HOLM Sørensen	07.03.1995	**1**	**0**	2018:	*Skovshoved IF*
Nicolai Mick JØRGENSEN	15.01.1991	**39**	**9**	2018/2019:	*Feyenoord Rotterdam (NED)*
Christian OFFENBERG	30.11.1987	**1**	**0**	2018:	*BK Avarta Rødovre*
Yussuf Yurary POULSEN	15.06.1994	**39**	**6**	2018/2019:	*RasenBallsport Leipzig (GER)*
Robert SKOV	20.05.1996	**1**	**0**	2019:	*FC København*

National team coach

Åge Fridtjof HAREIDE (Norway) [from 01.03.2016]	23.09.1953	36 M; 17 W; 16 D; 3 L; 63-25
John JENSEN [caretaker, on 05.09.2018]	03.05.1965	1 M; 0 W; 0 D; 1 L; 0-3

ENGLAND

The Country:
England
Capital: London
Surface: 130,279 km^2
Inhabitants: 55,619,400 [2017]
Time: UTC

The FA:
The Football Association
Wembley Stadium, P.O. Box 1966, SWIP 9EQ, London
Tel: +44 844 980 8200
Foundation date: 1863
Member of FIFA: 1905-1918, 1924-1928, since 1946
Member of UEFA since: 1954
Website: www.thefa.com

NATIONAL TEAM RECORDS

First international match:	30.11.1872, Glasgow:	Scotland – England 0-0
Most international caps:	Peter Leslie Shilton	- 125 caps (1970-1990)
Most international goals:	Wayne Mark Rooney	- 53 goals / 120 caps (2003-2018)

UEFA EUROPEAN CHAMPIONSHIP	
1960	*Did not enter*
1964	Qualifiers
1968	Final Tournament (3rd Place)
1972	Qualifiers
1976	Qualifiers
1980	Final Tournament (Group Stage)
1984	Qualifiers
1988	Final Tournament (Group Stage)
1992	Final Tournament (Group Stage)
1996	Final Tournament (Semi-Finals)
2000	Final Tournament (Group Stage)
2004	Final Tournament (Quarter-Finals)
2008	Qualifiers
2012	Final Tournament (Quarter-Finals)
2016	Final Tournament (2nd Round of 16)

FIFA WORLD CUP	
1930	*Did not enter*
1934	*Did not enter*
1938	*Did not enter*
1950	Final Tournament (Group Stage)
1954	Final Tournament (Quarter-Finals)
1958	Final Tournament (Group Stage)
1962	Final Tournament (Quarter-Finals)
1966	**Final Tournament (Winners)**
1970	Final Tournament (Quarter-Finals)
1974	Qualifiers
1978	Qualifiers
1982	Final Tournament (2nd Round)
1986	Final Tournament (Quarter-Finals)
1990	Final Tournament (4th Place)
1994	Qualifiers
1998	Final Tournament (2nd Round of 16)
2002	Final Tournament (Quarter-Finals)
2006	Final Tournament (Quarter-Finals)
2010	Final Tournament (2nd Round of 16)
2014	Final Tournament (Group Stage)
2018	Final Tournament (4th Place)

UEFA NATIONS LEAGUE
2018/2019 – League A; Final Tournament – 3rd Place

FIFA CONFEDERATIONS CUP 1992-2017
None

ENGLISH CLUB HONOURS IN EUROPEAN CLUB COMPETITIONS:

European Champion Clubs' Cup (1956-1992) / UEFA Champions League (1993-2019)		
Liverpool FC	6	1976/1977, 1977/1978, 1980/1981, 1983/1984, 2004/2005, 2018/2019
Manchester United FC	3	1967/1968, 1998/1999, 2007/2008
Notthingam Forest FC	2	1978/1979, 1979/1980
Aston Villa FC Birmingham	1	1981/1982
Chelsea FC London	1	2011/2012
Fairs Cup (1858-1971) / UEFA Cup (1972-2009) / UEFA Europa League (2010-2019)		
Liverpool FC	3	1972/1973, 1975/1976, 2000/2001
Leeds United FC	2	1967/1968, 1970/1971
Tottenham Hotspur FC London	2	1971/1972, 1983/1984
Chelsea FC London	2	2012/2013, 2018/2019
Newcastle United FC	1	1968/1969
Arsenal FC London	1	1969/1970
Ipswich Town FC	1	1980/1981
Manchester United FC	1	2016/2017
UEFA Super Cup (1972-2019)		
Liverpool FC	4	1977, 2001, 2005, 2019
Notthingam Forest FC	1	1979

Aston Villa FC Birmingham	**1**	1982
Manchester United FC	**1**	1991
Chelsea FC London	**1**	1998
European Cup Winners' Cup 1961-1999*		
Chelsea FC London	**2**	1970/1971, 1997/1998
Tottenham Hotspur FC London	**1**	1962/1963
West Ham United FC London	**1**	1964/1965
Manchester City FC	**1**	1969/1970
Everton FC Liverpool	**1**	1984/1985
Manchester United FC	**1**	1990/1991
Arsenal FC London	**1**	1993/1994

**defunct competition*

NATIONAL COMPETITIONS TABLE OF HONOURS

	CHAMPIONS	CUP WINNERS	BEST GOALSCORERS	
1871/1872	-	Wanderers FC London	-	
1872/1873	-	Wanderers FC London	-	
1873/1874	-	Oxford University AFC	-	
1874/1875	-	Royal Engineers AFC	-	
1875/1876	-	Wanderers FC London	-	
1876/1877	-	Wanderers FC London	-	
1877/1878	-	Wanderers FC London	-	
1878/1879	-	Old Etonians AFC	-	
1879/1880	-	Clapham Rovers FC	-	
1880/1881	-	Old Carthusians FC	-	
1881/1882	-	Old Etonians AFC	-	
1882/1883	-	Blackburn Olympic FC	-	
1883/1884	-	Blackburn Rovers FC	-	
1884/1885	-	Blackburn Rovers FC	-	
1885/1886	-	Blackburn Rovers FC	-	
1886/1887	-	Aston Villa FC Birmingham	-	
1887/1888	-	West Bromwich Albion FC	-	
1888/1889	Preston North End FC	Preston North End FC	John Goodall (Preston North End FC)	21
1889/1890	Preston North End FC	Blackburn Rovers FC	Jimmy Ross (SCO, Preston North End FC)	24
1890/1891	Everton FC Liverpool	Blackburn Rovers FC	Jack Southworth (Blackburn Rovers FC)	26
1891/1892	Sunderland AFC	West Bromwich Albion FC	John Campbell (SCO, Sunderland AFC)	32
1892/1893	Sunderland AFC	Wolverhampton Wanderers FC	John Campbell (SCO, Sunderland AFC)	31
1893/1894	Aston Villa FC Birmingham	Notts County FC	Jack Southworth (Everton FC Liverpool)	27
1894/1895	Sunderland AFC	Aston Villa FC Birmingham	John Campbell (SCO, Sunderland AFC)	22
1895/1896	Aston Villa FC Birmingham	The Wednesday Sheffield FC	John James Campbell (SCO, Aston Villa FC Birmingham) Stephen Bloomer (Derby County FC)	20
1896/1897	Aston Villa FC Birmingham	Aston Villa FC Birmingham	Stephen Bloomer (Derby County FC)	22
1897/1898	Sheffield United FC	Nottingham Forest FC	Fred Wheldon (Aston Villa FC Birmingham)	21
1898/1899	Aston Villa FC Birmingham	Sheffield United FC	Stephen Bloomer (Derby County FC)	23
1899/1900	Aston Villa FC Birmingham	Bury FC	Billy Garraty (Aston Villa FC Birmingham)	27
1900/1901	Liverpool FC	Tottenham Hotspur FC London	Stephen Bloomer (Derby County FC)	23
1901/1902	Sunderland AFC	Sheffield United FC	Jimmy Settle (Everton FC Liverpool)	18
1902/1903	The Wednesday Sheffield FC	Bury FC	Sam Raybould (Liverpool FC)	31
1903/1904	The Wednesday Sheffield FC	Manchester City FC	Stephen Bloomer (Derby County FC)	20
1904/1905	Newcastle United FC	Aston Villa FC Birmingham	Arthur Brown (Sheffield United FC)	22
1905/1906	Liverpool FC	Everton FC Liverpool	Albert Shepherd (Bolton Wanderers FC)	26
1906/1907	Newcastle United FC	The Wednesday Sheffield FC	Alex Young (SCO, Everton FC Liverpool)	30
1907/1908	Manchester United FC	Wolverhampton Wanderers FC	Enoch West (Nottingham Forest FC)	27
1908/1909	Newcastle United FC	Manchester United FC	Bert Freeman (Everton FC Liverpool)	38
1909/1910	Aston Villa FC Birmingham	Newcastle United FC	Jack Parkinson (Liverpool FC)	30
1910/1911	Manchester United FC	Bradford City AFC	Albert Shepherd (Newcastle United FC)	25
1911/1912	Blackburn Rovers FC	Barnsley FC	Harry Hampton (Aston Villa FC Birmingham) George Holley (Sunderland AFC) David McLean (The Wednesday Sheffield FC)	25
1912/1913	Sunderland AFC	Aston Villa FC Birmingham	David McLean (SCO, The Wednesday Sheffield FC)	30
1913/1914	Blackburn Rovers FC	Burnley FC	George Elliot (Middlesbrough FC)	32
1914/1915	Everton FC Liverpool	Sheffield United FC	Bobby Parker (SCO, Everton FC Liverpool)	35
1915-1919	*No competition*	*No competition*	-	
1919/1920	West Bromwich Albion FC	Aston Villa FC Birmingham	Fred Morris (West Bromwich Albion FC)	37
1920/1921	Burnley FC	Tottenham Hotspur FC London	Joe Smith (Bolton Wanderers FC)	38
1921/1922	Liverpool FC	Huddersfield Town AFC	Andy Wilson (SCO, Middlesbrough FC)	31
1922/1923	Liverpool FC	Bolton Wanderers FC	Charles Murray Buchan (SCO, Sunderland AFC)	30
1923/1924	Huddersfield Town AFC	Newcastle United FC	Wilf Chadwick (Everton FC Liverpool)	28
1924/1925	Huddersfield Town AFC	Sheffield United FC	Frank Roberts (Manchester City FC)	31
1925/1926	Huddersfield Town AFC	Bolton Wanderers FC	Ted Harper (Blackburn Rovers FC)	43
1926/1927	Newcastle United FC	Cardiff City FC (WAL)	Jimmy Trotter (The Wednesday Sheffield FC)	37
1927/1928	Everton FC Liverpool	Blackburn Rovers FC	William Ralph Dean (Everton FC Liverpool)	60
1928/1929	The Wednesday Sheffield FC	Bolton Wanderers FC	Dave Halliday (SCO, Sunderland AFC)	43
1929/1930	Sheffield Wednesday FC	Arsenal FC London	Victor Martin Watson (West Ham United FC)	41

1930/1931	Arsenal FC London	West Bromwich Albion FC	Thomas Waring (Aston Villa FC Birmingham)	49
1931/1932	Everton FC Liverpool	Newcastle United FC	William Ralph Dean (Everton FC Liverpool)	44
1932/1933	Arsenal FC London	Everton FC Liverpool	John William Anslow Bowers (Derby County FC)	35
1933/1934	Arsenal FC London	Manchester City FC	John William Anslow Bowers (Derby County FC)	34
1934/1935	Arsenal FC London	Sheffield Wednesday FC	Edward Joseph Drake (Arsenal FC London)	42
1935/1936	Sunderland AFC	Arsenal FC London	William "Ginger" Richardson (West Bromwich Albion FC)	39
1936/1937	Manchester City FC	Sunderland AFC	Frederick Charles Steele (Stoke City FC)	33
1937/1938	Arsenal FC London	Preston North End FC	Thomas Lawton (Everton FC Liverpool)	28
1938/1939	Everton FC Liverpool	Portsmouth FC	Thomas Lawton (Everton FC Liverpool)	35
1939-1945	*No competition*	*No competition*	-	
1945/1946	*No competition*	Derby County FC	-	
1946/1947	Liverpool FC	Charlton Athletic FC	Dennis Westcott (Wolverhampton Wanderers FC)	37
1947/1948	Arsenal FC London	Manchester United FC	Ronald Leslie Rooke (Arsenal FC London)	33
1948/1949	Portsmouth FC	Wolverhampton Wanderers FC	William Moir (SCO, Bolton Wanderers FC)	25
1949/1950	Portsmouth FC	Arsenal FC London	Richard Daniel Davis (Sunderland AFC)	25
1950/1951	Tottenham Hotspur FC London	Newcastle United FC	Stanley Harding Mortensen (Blackpool FC)	30
1951/1952	Manchester United FC	Newcastle United FC	Jorge Robledo Oliver (CHI, Newcastle United FC)	33
1952/1953	Arsenal FC London	Blackpool FC	Charles Wayman (Preston North End FC)	24
1953/1954	Wolverhampton Wanderers FC	West Bromwich Albion FC	Jimmy Glazzard (Huddersfield Town AFC)	29
1954/1955	Chelsea FC London	Newcastle United FC	Ronald Allen (West Bromwich Albion FC)	27
1955/1956	Manchester United FC	Manchester City FC	Nathaniel Lofthouse (Bolton Wanderers FC)	33
1956/1957	Manchester United FC	Aston Villa FC Birmingham	William John Charles (WAL, Leeds United FC)	38
1957/1958	Wolverhampton Wanderers FC	Bolton Wanderers FC	Robert Alfred Smith (Tottenham Hotspur FC)	36
1958/1959	Wolverhampton Wanderers FC	Nottingham Forest FC	James Peter Greaves (Chelsea FC London)	33
1959/1960	Burnley FC	Wolverhampton Wanderers FC	Dennis Sydney Viollet (Manchester United FC)	32
1960/1961	Tottenham Hotspur FC London	Tottenham Hotspur FC London	James Peter Greaves (Chelsea FC London)	41
1961/1962	Ipswich Town FC	Tottenham Hotspur FC London	Raymond Crawford (Ipswich Town FC) Derek Tennyson Kevan (West Bromwich Albion FC)	33
1962/1963	Everton FC Liverpool	Manchester United FC	James Peter Greaves (Tottenham Hotspur FC)	37
1963/1964	Liverpool FC	West Ham United FC London	James Peter Greaves (Tottenham Hotspur FC)	35
1964/1965	Manchester United FC	Liverpool FC	Andrew McEvoy (IRL, Blackburn Rovers FC) James Peter Greaves (Tottenham Hotspur FC)	29
1965/1966	Liverpool FC	Everton FC Liverpool	William John Irvine (NIR, Burnley FC)	29
1966/1967	Manchester United FC	Tottenham Hotspur FC London	Ron Davies (WAL, Southampton FC)	37
1967/1968	Manchester City FC	West Bromwich Albion FC	George Best (NIR, Manchester United FC) Ronald Tudor Davies (WAL, Southampton FC)	28
1968/1969	Leeds United FC	Manchester City FC	James Peter Greaves (Tottenham Hotspur FC)	27
1969/1970	Everton FC Liverpool	Chelsea FC London	Jeffrey Astle (West Bromwich Albion FC)	25
1970/1971	Arsenal FC London	Arsenal FC London	Anthony Brown (West Bromwich Albion FC)	28
1971/1972	Derby County FC	Leeds United FC	Francis Henry Lee (Manchester City FC)	33
1972/1973	Liverpool FC	Sunderland AFC	Bryan Stanley Robson (West Ham United FC)	28
1973/1974	Leeds United FC	Liverpool FC	Michael Roger Channon (Southampton FC)	21
1974/1975	Derby County FC	West Ham United FC London	Malcolm Ian Macdonald (Newcastle United FC)	21
1975/1976	Liverpool FC	Southampton FC	Edward John MacDougall (SCO, Norwich City FC)	23
1976/1977	Liverpool FC	Manchester United FC	Malcolm Ian Macdonald (Arsenal FC London) Andrew Mullen Gray (SCO, Aston Villa FC)	25
1977/1978	Nottingham Forest FC	Ipswich Town FC	Robert Dennis Latchford (Everton FC Liverpool)	30
1978/1979	Liverpool FC	Arsenal FC London	Frank Stewart Worthington (Bolton Wanderers FC)	24
1979/1980	Liverpool FC	West Ham United FC London	Philip John Boyer (Southampton FC)	23
1980/1981	Aston Villa FC Birmingham	Tottenham Hotspur FC London	Peter Withe (Aston Villa FC Birmingham) Steven Archibald (SCO, Tottenham Hotspur FC)	20
1981/1982	Liverpool FC	Tottenham Hotspur FC London	Joseph Kevin Keegan (Southampton FC)	26
1982/1983	Liverpool FC	Manchester United FC	Luther Loide Blissett (Watford FC)	27
1983/1984	Liverpool FC	Everton FC Liverpool	Ian James Rush (WAL, Liverpool FC)	32
1984/1985	Everton FC Liverpool	Manchester United FC	Kerry Michael Dixon (Chelsea FC London) Gary Winston Lineker (Leicester City FC)	24
1985/1986	Liverpool FC	Liverpool FC	Gary Winston Lineker (Everton FC Liverpool)	30
1986/1987	Everton FC Liverpool	Coventry City FC	Clive Darren Allen (Tottenham Hotspur FC London)	33
1987/1988	Liverpool FC	Wimbledon	John William Aldridge (IRL, Liverpool FC)	26
1988/1989	Arsenal FC London	Liverpool FC	Alan Martin Smith (Arsenal FC London)	23
1989/1990	Liverpool FC	Manchester United FC	Gary Winston Lineker (Tottenham Hotspur FC)	24
1990/1991	Arsenal FC London	Tottenham Hotspur FC London	Alan Martin Smith (Arsenal FC London)	22
1991/1992	Leeds United FC	Liverpool FC	Ian Edward Wright (Crystal Palace FC London/Arsenal FC London)	29
1992/1993	Manchester United FC	Arsenal FC London	Edward Paul Sheringham (Nottingham Forest FC/Tottenham Hotspur FC London)	22
1993/1994	Manchester United FC	Manchester United FC	Andrew Alexander Cole (Newcastle United FC)	34
1994/1995	Blackburn Rovers FC	Everton FC Liverpool	Alan Shearer (Blackburn Rovers FC)	34
1995/1996	Manchester United FC	Manchester United FC	Alan Shearer (Blackburn Rovers FC)	31
1996/1997	Manchester United FC	Chelsea FC London	Alan Shearer (Newcastle United FC)	25
1997/1998	Arsenal FC London	Arsenal FC London	Christopher Roy Sutton (Blackburn Rovers FC) Dion Dublin (Coventry City FC) Michael James Owen (Liverpool FC)	18
1998/1999	Manchester United FC	Manchester United FC	Jimmy Floyd Hasselbaink (NED, Leeds United FC) Michael James Owen (Liverpool FC) Dwight Eversley Yorke (TRI, Manchester United)	18

1999/2000	Manchester United FC	Chelsea FC London	Kevin Mark Phillips (Sunderland AFC)	30
2000/2001	Manchester United FC	Liverpool FC	Jimmy Floyd Hasselbaink (NED, Chelsea FC London)	23
2001/2002	Arsenal FC London	Arsenal FC London	Thierry Daniel Henry (FRA, Arsenal FC London)	24
2002/2003	Manchester United FC	Arsenal FC London	Rutgerus Johannes Martinus "Ruud" van Nistelrooy (NED, Manchester United FC)	25
2003/2004	Arsenal FC London	Manchester United FC	Thierry Daniel Henry (FRA, Arsenal FC London)	30
2004/2005	Chelsea FC London	Arsenal FC London	Thierry Daniel Henry (FRA, Arsenal FC London)	25
2005/2006	Chelsea FC London	Liverpool FC	Thierry Daniel Henry (FRA, Arsenal FC London)	27
2006/2007	Manchester United FC	Chelsea FC London	Didier Yves Drogba Tébily (CIV, Chelsea FC London)	20
2007/2008	Manchester United FC	Portsmouth FC	Cristiano Ronaldo dos Santos Aveiro (POR, Manchester United FC)	31
2008/2009	Manchester United FC	Chelsea FC London	Nicolas Sébastien Anelka (FRA, Chelsea FC London)	19
2009/2010	Chelsea FC London	Chelsea FC London	Didier Yves Drogba Tébily (CIV, Chelsea FC London)	29
2010/2011	Manchester United FC	Manchester City FC	Dimitar Berbatov (BUL, Manchester United FC) Carlos Alberto Martínez Tevez (ARG, Manchester City FC)	20
2011/2012	Manchester City FC	Chelsea FC London	Robin van Persie (NED, Arsenal FC London)	30
2012/2013	Manchester United FC	Wigan Athletic FC	Robin van Persie (NED, Manchester United FC)	26
2013/2014	Manchester City FC	Arsenal FC London	Luis Alberto Suárez Díaz (URU, Liverpool FC)	31
2014/2015	Chelsea FC London	Arsenal FC London	Sergio Leonel Agüero del Castillo (ARG, Manchester City FC)	26
2015/2016	Leicester City FC	Manchester United FC	Harry Edward Kane (Tottenham Hotspur FC)	25
2016/2017	Chelsea FC London	Arsenal FC London	Harry Edward Kane (Tottenham Hotspur FC)	29
2017/2018	Manchester City FC	Chelsea FC London	Mohamed Salah Ghaly (EGY, Liverpool FC)	32
2018/2019	Manchester City FC	Manchester City FC	Pierre-Emerick Emiliano François Aubameyang (GAB, Arsenal FC London) Sadio Mané (SEN, Liverpool FC) Mohamed Salah Ghaly (EGY, Liverpool FC)	22

Please note: the championship was called Football League (1888–1892), Football League First Division (1892–1992) and Premier League (1992–present).

EFL (LEAGUE) CUP WINNERS

1960/1961	Aston Villa FC Birmingham
1961/1962	Norwich City FC
1962/1963	Birmingham City FC
1963/1964	Leicester City FC
1964/1965	Chelsea FC London
1965/1966	West Bromwich Albion FC
1966/1967	Queens Park Rangers FC
1967/1968	Leeds United FC
1968/1969	Swindon Town FC
1969/1970	Manchester City FC
1970/1971	Tottenham Hotspur FC London
1971/1972	Stoke City FC
1972/1973	Tottenham Hotspur FC London
1973/1974	Wolverhampton Wanderers FC
1974/1975	Aston Villa FC Birmingham
1975/1976	Manchester City FC
1976/1977	Aston Villa FC Birmingham
1977/1978	Nottingham Forest FC
1978/1979	Nottingham Forest FC
1979/1980	Wolverhampton Wanderers FC
1980/1981	Liverpool FC
1981/1982	Liverpool FC
1982/1983	Liverpool FC
1983/1984	Liverpool FC
1984/1985	Norwich City FC
1985/1986	Oxford United FC
1986/1987	Arsenal FC London
1987/1988	Luton Town FC
1988/1989	Nottingham Forest FC
1989/1990	Nottingham Forest FC
1990/1991	Sheffield Wednesday FC
1991/1992	Manchester United FC
1992/1993	Arsenal FC London
1993/1994	Aston Villa FC Birmingham
1994/1995	Liverpool FC
1995/1996	Aston Villa FC Birmingham
1996/1997	Leicester City FC
1997/1998	Chelsea FC London
1998/1999	Tottenham Hotspur FC London
1999/2000	Leicester City FC
2000/2001	Liverpool FC
2001/2002	Blackburn Rovers FC
2002/2003	Liverpool FC
2003/2004	Middlesbrough FC
2004/2005	Chelsea FC London
2005/2006	Manchester United FC
2006/2007	Chelsea FC London
2007/2008	Tottenham Hotspur FC London
2008/2009	Manchester United FC
2009/2010	Manchester United FC
2010/2011	Birmingham City FC
2011/2012	Liverpool FC
2012/2013	Swansea City AFC
2013/2014	Manchester City FC
2014/2015	Chelsea FC London
2015/2016	Manchester City FC
2016/2017	Manchester United FC
2017/2018	Manchester City FC
2018/2019	Manchester City FC

NATIONAL CHAMPIONSHIP

Premier League 2018/2019

(10.08.2018 – 12.05.2019)

Results

Round 1 [10-12.08.2018]
Manchester United - Leicester City 2-1(1-0)
Newcastle United - Tottenham Hotsp. 1-2(1-2)
AFC Bournemouth - Cardiff City 2-0(1-0)
Fulham - Crystal Palace 0-2(0-1)
Huddersfield Town - Chelsea 0-3(0-2)
Watford - Brighton & Hove 2-0(1-0)
Wolverhampton - Everton 2-2(1-1)
Southampton - Burnley 0-0
Liverpool FC - West Ham 4-0(2-0)
Arsenal - Manchester City 0-2(0-1)

Round 2 [18-20.08.2018]
Cardiff City - Newcastle United 0-0
Everton - Southampton 2-1(2-0)
Leicester City - Wolverhampton 2-0(2-0)
Tottenham Hotspur - Fulham 3-1(1-0)
West Ham - AFC Bournemouth 1-2(1-0)
Chelsea - Arsenal 3-2(2-2)
Burnley - Watford 1-3(1-1)
Manchester City - Huddersfield T. 6-1(3-1)
Brighton & Hove - Manchester Unit. 3-2(3-1)
Crystal Palace - Liverpool FC 0-2(0-1)

Round 3 [25-27.08.2018]
Wolverhampton - Manchester City 1-1(0-0)
Arsenal - West Ham 3-1(1-1)
AFC Bournemouth - Everton 2-2(0-0)
Huddersfield Town - Cardiff City 0-0
Southampton - Leicester City 1-2(0-0)
Liverpool FC - Brighton & Hove 1-0(1-0)
Watford - Crystal Palace 2-1(0-0)
Fulham - Burnley 4-2(3-2)
Newcastle United - Chelsea 1-2(0-0)
Manchester Unit. - Tottenham Hotsp. 0-3(0-0)

Round 4 [01-02.09.2018]
Leicester City - Liverpool FC 1-2(0-2)
Brighton & Hove - Fulham 2-2(0-1)
Chelsea - AFC Bournemouth 2-0(0-0)
Crystal Palace - Southampton 0-2(0-0)
Everton - Huddersfield Town 1-1(1-1)
West Ham - Wolverhampton 0-1(0-0)
Manchester City - Newcastle United 2-1(1-1)
Cardiff City - Arsenal 2-3(1-1)
Burnley - Manchester United 0-2(0-2)
Watford - Tottenham Hotspur 2-1(0-0)

Round 5 [15-17.09.2018]
Tottenham Hotspur - Liverpool FC 1-2(0-1)
AFC Bournemouth - Leicester City 4-2(3-0)
Chelsea - Cardiff City 4-1(2-1)
Huddersfield Town - Crystal Palace 0-1(0-1)
Manchester City - Fulham 3-0(2-0)
Newcastle United - Arsenal 1-2(0-0)
Watford - Manchester United 1-2(0-2)
Wolverhampton - Burnley 1-0(0-0)
Everton - West Ham 1-3(1-2)
Southampton - Brighton & Hove 2-2(1-0)

Round 6 [22-23.09.2018]
Fulham - Watford 1-1(0-1)
Burnley - AFC Bournemouth 4-0(2-0)
Cardiff City - Manchester City 0-5(0-3)
Crystal Palace - Newcastle United 0-0
Leicester City - Huddersfield Town 3-1(1-1)
Manchester United - Wolverhampton 1-1(1-0)
Liverpool FC - Southampton 3-0(3-0)
Brighton & Hove - Tottenham Hotsp. 1-2(0-1)
West Ham - Chelsea 0-0
Arsenal - Everton 2-0(0-0)

Round 7 [29.09.-01.10.2018]
West Ham - Manchester United 3-1(2-0)
Arsenal - Watford 2-0(0-0)
Everton - Fulham 3-0(0-0)
Huddersfield T. - Tottenham Hotspur 0-2(0-2)
Manchester City - Brighton & Hove 2-0(1-0)
Newcastle United - Leicester City 0-2(0-1)
Wolverhampton - Southampton 2-0(0-0)
Chelsea - Liverpool FC 1-1(1-0)
Cardiff City - Burnley 1-2(0-0)
AFC Bournemouth - Crystal Palace 2-1(1-0)

Round 8 [05-07.10.2018]
Brighton & Hove - West Ham 1-0(1-0)
Burnley - Huddersfield Town 1-1(1-0)
Crystal Palace - Wolverhampton 0-1(0-0)
Leicester City - Everton 1-2(1-1)
Tottenham Hotspur - Cardiff City 1-0(1-0)
Watford - AFC Bournemouth 0-4(0-3)
Manchester Unit. - Newcastle United 3-2(0-2)
Fulham - Arsenal 1-5(1-1)
Southampton - Chelsea 0-3(0-1)
Liverpool FC - Manchester City 0-0

Round 9 [20-22.10.2018]
Chelsea - Manchester United 2-2(1-0)
AFC Bournemouth - Southampton 0-0
Cardiff City - Fulham 4-2(2-2)
Manchester City - Burnley 5-0(1-0)
Newcastle United - Brighton & Hove 0-1(0-1)
West Ham - Tottenham Hotspur 0-1(0-1)
Wolverhampton - Watford 0-2(0-2)
Huddersfield Town - Liverpool FC 0-1(0-1)
Everton - Crystal Palace 2-0(0-0)
Arsenal - Leicester City 3-1(1-1)

Round 10 [27-29.10.2018]
Brighton & Hove - Wolverhampton 1-0(0-0)
Fulham - AFC Bournemouth 0-3(0-1)
Liverpool FC - Cardiff City 4-1(1-0)
Southampton - Newcastle United 0-0
Watford - Huddersfield Town 3-0(2-0)
Leicester City - West Ham 1-1(0-1)
Burnley - Chelsea 0-4(0-1)
Crystal Palace - Arsenal 2-2(1-0)
Manchester United - Everton 2-1(1-0)
Tottenham Hotsp. - Manchester City 0-1(0-1)

Round 11 [03-05.11.2018]
AFC Bournemouth - Manchester Unit 1-2(1-1)
Cardiff City - Leicester City 0-1(0-0)
Everton - Brighton & Hove 3-1(1-1)
Newcastle United - Watford 1-0(0-0)
West Ham - Burnley 4-2(1-1)
Arsenal - Liverpool FC 1-1(0-0)
Wolverhampton - Tottenham Hotspur 2-3(0-2)
Manchester City - Southampton 6-1(4-1)
Chelsea - Crystal Palace 3-1(1-0)
Huddersfield Town - Fulham 1-0(1-0)

Round 12 [10-11.11.2018]
Cardiff City - Brighton & Hove 2-1(1-1)
Huddersfield Town - West Ham 1-1(1-0)
Leicester City - Burnley 0-0
Newcastle Unit. - AFC Bournemouth 2-1(2-1)
Southampton - Watford 1-1(1-0)
Crystal Palace - Tottenham Hotspur 0-1(0-0)
Liverpool FC - Fulham 2-0(1-0)
Chelsea - Everton 0-0
Arsenal - Wolverhampton 1-1(0-1)
Manchester City - Manchester United 3-1(1-0)

Round 13 [24-26.11.2018]
Brighton & Hove - Leicester City 1-1(1-0)
Everton - Cardiff City 1-0(0-0)
Fulham - Southampton 3-2(2-1)
Manchester United - Crystal Palace 0-0
Watford - Liverpool FC 0-3(0-0)
West Ham - Manchester City 0-4(0-3)
Tottenham Hotspur - Chelsea 3-1(2-0)
AFC Bournemouth - Arsenal 1-2(1-1)
Wolverhampton - Huddersfield Town 0-2(0-1)
Burnley - Newcastle United 1-2(1-2)

Round 14 [30.11.-02.12.2018]
Cardiff City - Wolverhampton 2-1(0-1)
Crystal Palace - Burnley 2-0(1-0)
Huddersfield T. - Brighton & Hove 1-2(1-1)
Leicester City - Watford 2-0(2-0)
Manchester City - AFC Bournemouth 3-1(1-1)
Newcastle United - West Ham 0-3(0-1)
Southampton - Manchester United 2-2(2-2)
Chelsea - Fulham 2-0(1-0)
Arsenal - Tottenham Hotspur 4-2(1-2)
Liverpool FC - Everton 1-0(0-0)

Round 15 [04-05.12.2018]
AFC Bournemouth - Huddersfield T. 2-1(2-1)
Brighton & Hove - Crystal Palace 3-1(3-0)
West Ham - Cardiff City 3-1(0-0)
Watford - Manchester City 1-2(0-1)
Burnley - Liverpool FC 1-3(0-0)
Fulham - Leicester City 1-1(1-0)
Wolverhampton - Chelsea 2-1(0-1)
Everton - Newcastle United 1-1(1-1)
Manchester United - Arsenal 2-2(1-1)
Tottenham Hotspur - Southampton 3-1(1-0)

Round 16 [08-10.12.2018]
AFC Bournemouth - Liverpool FC 0-4(0-1)
Arsenal - Huddersfield Town 1-0(0-0)
Burnley - Brighton & Hove 1-0(1-0)
Cardiff City - Southampton 1-0(0-0)
Manchester United - Fulham 4-1(3-0)
West Ham - Crystal Palace 3-2(0-1)
Chelsea - Manchester City 2-0(1-0)
Leicester City - Tottenham Hotspur 0-2(0-1)
Newcastle United - Wolverhampton 1-2(1-1)
Everton - Watford 2-2(1-0)

Round 17 [15-16.12.2018]
Manchester City - Everton 3-1(1-0)
Crystal Palace - Leicester City 1-0(1-0)
Huddersfield T. - Newcastle United 0-1(0-0)
Tottenham Hotspur - Burnley 1-0(0-0)
Watford - Cardiff City 3-2(1-0)
Wolverhampton - AFC Bournemouth 2-0(1-0)
Fulham - West Ham 0-2(0-2)
Brighton & Hove - Chelsea 1-2(0-2)
Southampton - Arsenal 3-2(2-1)
Liverpool FC - Manchester United 3-1(1-1)

Round 18 [21-23.12.2018]
Wolverhampton - Liverpool FC 0-2(0-1)
Arsenal - Burnley 3-1(1-0)
AFC Bournemouth - Brighton & Ho. 2-0(1-0)
Chelsea - Leicester City 0-1(0-0)
Huddersfield Town - Southampton 1-3(0-2)
Manchester City - Crystal Palace 2-3(1-2)
Newcastle United - Fulham 0-0
West Ham - Watford 0-2(0-1)
Cardiff City - Manchester United 1-5(1-3)
Everton - Tottenham Hotspur 2-6(1-3)

Round 19 [26-27.12.2018]
Fulham - Wolverhampton 1-1(0-0)
Burnley - Everton 1-5(1-3)
Crystal Palace - Cardiff City 0-0
Leicester City - Manchester City 2-1(1-1)
Liverpool FC - Newcastle United 4-0(1-0)
Manchester United - Huddersfield T. 3-1(1-0)
Tottenham Hots. - AFC Bournemouth 5-0(3-0)
Brighton & Hove - Arsenal 1-1(1-1)
Watford - Chelsea 1-2(1-1)
Southampton - West Ham 1-2(0-0)

Round 20 [29-30.12.2018]
Brighton & Hove - Everton 1-0(0-0)
Fulham - Huddersfield Town 1-0(0-0)
Leicester City - Cardiff City 0-1(0-0)
Tottenham Hotspur - Wolverhampton 1-3(1-0)
Watford - Newcastle United 1-1(0-1)
Liverpool FC - Arsenal 5-1(4-1)
Crystal Palace - Chelsea 0-1(0-0)
Burnley - West Ham 2-0(2-0)
Southampton - Manchester City 1-3(1-3)
Manchester Unit - AFC Bournemouth 4-1(3-1)

Round 21 [01-03.01.2019]
Everton - Leicester City 0-1(0-0)
Arsenal - Fulham 4-1(1-0)
Cardiff City - Tottenham Hotspur 0-3(0-3)
AFC Bournemouth - Watford 3-3(3-3)
Chelsea - Southampton 0-0
Huddersfield Town - Burnley 1-2(1-1)
West Ham - Brighton & Hove 2-2(0-0)
Wolverhampton - Crystal Palace 0-2(0-0)
Newcastle Unit. - Manchester United 0-2(0-0)
Manchester City - Liverpool FC 2-1(1-0)

Round 22 [12-14.01.2019]
West Ham - Arsenal 1-0(0-0)
Brighton & Hove - Liverpool FC 0-1(0-0)
Burnley - Fulham 2-1(2-1)
Cardiff City - Huddersfield Town 0-0
Crystal Palace - Watford 1-2(1-0)
Leicester City - Southampton 1-2(0-2)
Chelsea - Newcastle United 2-1(1-1)
Everton - AFC Bournemouth 2-0(0-0)
Tottenham Hotsp. - Manchester Unit. 0-1(0-1)
Manchester City - Wolverhampton 3-0(2-0)

Round 23 [19-20.01.2019]
Wolverhampton - Leicester City 4-3(2-0)
AFC Bournemouth - West Ham 2-0(0-0)
Liverpool FC - Crystal Palace 4-3(0-1)
Manchester Unit. - Brighton & Hove 2-1(2-0)
Newcastle United - Cardiff City 3-0(1-0)
Southampton - Everton 2-1(0-0)
Watford - Burnley 0-0
Arsenal - Chelsea 2-0(2-0)
Huddersfield T. - Manchester City 0-3(0-1)
Fulham - Tottenham Hotspur 1-2(1-0)

Round 24 [29-30.01.2019]
Fulham - Brighton & Hove 4-2(0-2)
Arsenal - Cardiff City 2-1(0-0)
Huddersfield Town - Everton 0-1(0-1)
Wolverhampton - West Ham 3-0(0-0)
Manchester United - Burnley 2-2(0-0)
Newcastle United - Manchester City 2-1(0-1)
AFC Bournemouth - Chelsea 4-0(0-0)
Southampton - Crystal Palace 1-1(0-1)
Liverpool FC - Leicester City 1-1(1-1)
Tottenham Hotspur - Watford 2-1(0-1)

Round 25 [02-04.02.2019]
Tottenham Hotsp. - Newcastle United 1-0(0-0)
Crystal Palace - Fulham 2-0(1-0)
Burnley - Southampton 1-1(0-0)
Chelsea - Huddersfield Town 5-0(2-0)
Brighton & Hove - Watford 0-0
Everton - Wolverhampton 1-3(1-2)
Cardiff City - AFC Bournemouth 2-0(1-0)
Leicester City - Manchester United 0-1(0-1)
Manchester City - Arsenal 3-1(2-1)
West Ham - Liverpool FC 1-1(1-1)

Round 26 [09-11.02.2019]
Fulham - Manchester United 0-3(0-2)
Huddersfield Town - Arsenal 1-2(0-2)
Liverpool FC - AFC Bournemouth 3-0(2-0)
Southampton - Cardiff City 1-2(0-0)
Watford - Everton 1-0(0-0)
Crystal Palace - West Ham 1-1(0-1)
Brighton & Hove - Burnley 1-3(0-1)
Tottenham Hotspur - Leicester City 3-1(1-0)
Manchester City - Chelsea 6-0(4-0)
Wolverhampton - Newcastle United 1-1(0-0)

Round 27 [22-24.02.2019]
Everton - Manchester City 0-2(0-1) [06.02.]
West Ham - Fulham 3-1(2-1)
Cardiff City - Watford 1-5(0-1)
Burnley - Tottenham Hotspur 2-1(0-0)
Newcastle United - Huddersfield T. 2-0(0-0)
AFC Bournemouth - Wolverhampton 1-1(1-0)
Leicester City - Crystal Palace 1-4(0-1)
Manchester United - Liverpool FC 0-0
Arsenal - Southampton 2-0(2-0)
Chelsea - Brighton & Hove 3-0(1-0) [03.04.]

Round 28 [26-27.02.2019]
Leicester City - Brighton & Hove 2-1(1-0)
Cardiff City - Everton 0-3(0-1)
Huddersfield Town - Wolverhampton 1-0(0-0)
Newcastle United - Burnley 2-0(2-0)
Arsenal - AFC Bournemouth 5-1(2-1)
Southampton - Fulham 2-0(2-0)
Crystal Palace - Manchester United 1-3(0-1)
Chelsea - Tottenham Hotspur 2-0(0-0)
Liverpool FC - Watford 5-0(2-0)
Manchester City - West Ham 1-0(0-0)

Round 29 [02-03.03.2019]
Tottenham Hotspur - Arsenal 1-1(0-1)
Wolverhampton - Cardiff City 2-0(2-0)
Burnley - Crystal Palace 1-3(0-1)
Brighton & Hove - Huddersfield T. 1-0(0-0)
AFC Bournemouth - Manchester City 0-1(0-0)
Manchester United - Southampton 3-2(0-1)
West Ham - Newcastle United 2-0(2-0)
Watford - Leicester City 2-1(1-0)
Fulham - Chelsea 1-2(1-2)
Everton - Liverpool FC 0-0

Round 30 [09-10.03.2019]
Crystal Palace - Brighton & Hove 1-2(0-1)
Huddersfield T. - AFC Bournemouth 0-2(0-1)
Leicester City - Fulham 3-1(1-0)
Cardiff City - West Ham 2-0(1-0)
Newcastle United - Everton 3-2(0-2)
Southampton - Tottenham Hotspur 2-1(0-1)
Manchester City - Watford 3-1(0-0)
Liverpool FC - Burnley 4-2(2-1)
Chelsea - Wolverhampton 1-1(0-0)
Arsenal - Manchester United 2-0(1-0)

Round 31 [16-17.03.2019]
West Ham - Huddersfield Town 4-3(1-2)
Burnley - Leicester City 1-2(1-1)
AFC Bournemouth - Newcastle Unit. 2-2(0-1)
Fulham - Liverpool FC 1-2(0-1)
Everton - Chelsea 2-0(0-0)
Tottenham - Crystal Palace 2-0(0-0) [03.04.]
Brighton & Ho - Cardiff City 0-2(0-1) [16.04.]
Watford - Southampton 1-1(0-1) [23.04.]
Wolverhampton - Arsenal 3-1(3-0) [24.04.]
Manchester U.-Manchester C. 0-2(0-0)[24.04.]

Round 32 [30.03.-01.04.2019]
Fulham - Manchester City 0-2(0-2)
Leicester City - AFC Bournemouth 2-0(1-0)
Crystal Palace - Huddersfield Town 2-0(0-0)
Brighton & Hove - Southampton 0-1(0-0)
Manchester United - Watford 2-1(1-0)
Burnley - Wolverhampton 2-0(1-0)
West Ham - Everton 0-2(0-2)
Cardiff City - Chelsea 1-2(0-0)
Liverpool FC - Tottenham Hotspur 2-1(1-0)
Arsenal - Newcastle United 2-0(1-0)

Round 33 [02-08.04.2019]
Watford - Fulham 4-1(1-1)
Wolverhampton - Manchester United 2-1(1-1)
Manchester City - Cardiff City 2-0(2-0)
Southampton - Liverpool FC 1-3(1-1)
AFC Bournemouth - Burnley 1-3(1-2)
Newcastle United - Crystal Palace 0-1(0-0)
Huddersfield Town - Leicester City 1-4(0-1)
Everton - Arsenal 1-0(1-0)
Chelsea - West Ham 2-0(1-0)
Tottenham - Brighton & Ho. 1-0(0-0) [23.04.]

Round 34 [12-15.04.2019]
Leicester City - Newcastle United 0-1(0-1)
Tottenham Hotspur - Huddersfield T. 4-0(2-0)
Brighton & Ho. - AFC Bournemouth 0-5(0-1)
Burnley - Cardiff City 2-0(1-0)
Fulham - Everton 2-0(0-0)
Southampton - Wolverhampton 3-1(2-1)
Manchester United - West Ham 2-1(1-0)
Crystal Palace - Manchester City 1-3(0-1)
Liverpool FC - Chelsea 2-0(0-0)
Watford - Arsenal 0-1(0-1)

Round 35 [20-22.04.2019]
Manchester City - Tottenham Hotsp. 1-0(1-0)
AFC Bournemouth - Fulham 0-1(0-0)
Huddersfield Town - Watford 1-2(0-1)
West Ham - Leicester City 2-2(1-0)
Wolverhampton - Brighton & Hove 0-0
Newcastle United - Southampton 3-1(2-0)
Everton - Manchester United 4-0(2-0)
Arsenal - Crystal Palace 2-3(0-1)
Cardiff City - Liverpool FC 0-2(0-0)
Chelsea - Burnley 2-2(2-2)

Round 36 [26-28.04.2019]
Liverpool FC - Huddersfield Town 5-0(3-0)
Tottenham Hotspur - West Ham 0-1(0-0)
Crystal Palace - Everton 0-0
Fulham - Cardiff City 1-0(0-0)
Southampton - AFC Bournemouth 3-3(1-2)
Watford - Wolverhampton 1-2(0-1)
Brighton & Hove - Newcastle United 1-1(0-1)
Leicester City - Arsenal 3-0(0-0)
Burnley - Manchester City 0-1(0-0)
Manchester United - Chelsea 1-1(1-1)

Round 37 [03-06.05.2019]
Everton - Burnley 2-0(2-0)
AFC Bournemouth - Tottenham Hot. 1-0(0-0)
West Ham - Southampton 3-0(1-0)
Wolverhampton - Fulham 1-0(0-0)
Cardiff City - Crystal Palace 2-3(1-2)
Newcastle United - Liverpool FC 2-3(1-2)
Chelsea - Watford 3-0(0-0)
Huddersfield T. - Manchester United 1-1(0-1)
Arsenal - Brighton & Hove 1-1(1-0)
Manchester City - Leicester City 1-0(0-0)

Round 38 [12.05.2019]
Brighton & Hove - Manchester City 1-4(1-2)
Burnley - Arsenal 1-3(0-0)
Crystal Palace - AFC Bournemouth 5-3(3-1)
Fulham - Newcastle United 0-4(0-2)
Leicester City - Chelsea 0-0
Liverpool FC - Wolverhampton 2-0(1-0)
Manchester United - Cardiff City 0-2(0-1)
Southampton - Huddersfield Town 1-1(1-0)
Tottenham Hotspur - Everton 2-2(1-0)
Watford - West Ham 1-4(0-2)

Final Standings

1.	**Manchester City FC**	38	32	2	4	95	-	23	98
2.	Liverpool FC	38	30	7	1	89	-	22	97
3.	Chelsea FC London	38	21	9	8	63	-	39	72
4.	Tottenham Hotspur FC London	38	23	2	13	67	-	39	71
5.	Arsenal FC London	38	21	7	10	73	-	51	70
6.	Manchester United FC	38	19	9	10	65	-	54	66
7.	Wolverhampton Wanderers FC	38	16	9	13	47	-	46	57
8.	Everton FC Liverpool	38	15	9	14	54	-	46	54
9.	Leicester City FC	38	15	7	16	51	-	48	52
10.	West Ham United FC London	38	15	7	16	52	-	55	52
11.	Watford FC	38	14	8	16	52	-	59	50
12.	Crystal Palace FC London	38	14	7	17	51	-	53	49
13.	Newcastle United FC	38	12	9	17	42	-	48	45
14.	AFC Bournemouth	38	13	6	19	56	-	70	45
15.	Burnley FC	38	11	7	20	45	-	68	40
16.	Southampton FC	38	9	12	17	45	-	65	39
17.	Brighton & Hove Albion FC	38	9	9	20	35	-	60	36
18.	Cardiff City FC (*Relegated*)	38	10	4	24	34	-	69	34
19.	Fulham FC London (*Relegated*)	38	7	5	26	34	-	81	26
20.	Huddersfield Town AFC (*Relegated*)	38	3	7	28	22	-	76	16

Top goalscorers:

22 Pierre-Emerick Emiliano François Aubameyang (GAB) *Arsenal FC London*

22 Sadio Mané (SEN) *Liverpool FC*

22 Mohamed Salah Ghaly (EGY) *Liverpool FC*

21 Sergio Leonel Agüero del Castillo (ARG) *Manchester City FC*

18 Jamie Richard Vardy *Leicester City FC*

17 Harry Edward Kane *Tottenham Hotspur FC London*

17 Raheem Shaquille Sterling *Manchester City FC*

EFL (League) Cup Final 2018/2019

24.02.2019; Wembley Stadium, London; Referee: Jonathan Moss; Attendance: 81,775

Manchester City FC – Chelsea FC London **0-0; 4-3 on penalties**

Manchester City: Ederson Santana de Moraes, Kyle Andrew Walker, Nicolás Hernán Gonzalo Otamendi, Aymeric Jean Louis Gerard Alphonse Laporte (46.Vincent Jean Mpoy Kompany), Oleksandr Zinchenko, Kevin De Bruyne (86.Leroy Aziz Sané), Fernando Luiz Roza „Fernandinho" (91.Danilo Luiz da Silva), David Josué Jiménez Silva (Cap) (79.İlkay Gündoğan), Bernardo Mota Veiga de Carvalho e Silva, Sergio Leonel Agüero del Castillo, Raheem Shaquille Sterling. Trainer: Josep Guardiola Sala (Spain).

Chelsea: Kepa Arrizabalaga Revuelta, César Azpilicueta Tanco (Cap), Antonio Rüdiger, David Luiz Moreira Marinho, Emerson Palmieri dos Santos, Filho Jorge Luiz Frello „Jorginho",Ross Barkley (89.Ruben Ira Loftus-Cheek), Willian Borges da Silva (95.Gonzalo Gerardo Higuaín), Eden Michael Hazard, Pedro Eliezer Rodríguez Ledesma (79.Callum James Hudson-Odoi). Trainer: Maurizio Sarri (Italy).

Penalties: Filho Jorge Luiz Frello „Jorginho" (saved); İlkay Gündoğan 1-0; César Azpilicueta Tanco 1-1; Sergio Leonel Agüero del Castillo 2-1; Emerson Palmieri dos Santos 2-2; Leroy Aziz Sané (saved); David Luiz Moreira Marinho (missed); Bernardo Mota Veiga de Carvalho e Silva 3-2; Eden Michael Hazard 3-3; Raheem Shaquille Sterling 4-3.

NATIONAL CUP
FA Cup 2018/2019

Second Round [30.11./01.12./03.12./11.12./17.11./18.12.2018]

Solihull Moors FC - Blackpool FC	0-0 / 2-3 aet	Wrexham AFC - Newport County AFC	0-0 / 0-4(0-0)
FC Halifax Town - AFC Wimbledon	1-3(0-1)	Bury FC - Luton Town FC	0-1(0-1)
Southend United FC - Barnsley FC	2-4(1-1)	Tranmere Rovers FC - Southport FC	1-1(1-0) / 2-0(2-0)
Peterborough Un. FC - Bradford City AFC	2-2(2-0) / 4-4 aet; 3-2 pen	Shrewsbury Town FC - Scunthorpe United FC	1-0(1-0)
Maidstone United - Oldham Athletic AFC	0-2(0-1)	Chesterfield FC - Grimsby Town FC	0-2(0-1)
Lincoln City FC - Carlisle United FC	2-0(1-0)	Swindon Town FC - Woking FC	0-1(0-0)
Plymouth Argyle FC - Oxford United FC	1-2(0-0)	Barnet FC - Stockport County FC	1-0(1-0)
Walsall FC - Sunderland AFC	1-1(0-1) / 1-0(0-0)	Rochdale AFC - Portsmouth FC	0-1(0-0)
Accrington Stanley FC - Cheltenham Town FC	3-1(0-0)	Slough Town FC - Gillingham FC	0-1(0-0)
Charlton Athletic FC London - Doncaster Rovers FC	0-2(0-0)	Guiseley AFC - Fleetwood Town FC	1-2(1-2)

Third Round [04/05/06/07/15/16.01.2019]

Tranmere Rovers FC - Tottenham Hotspur FC	0-7(0-1)	Derby County FC - Southampton FC	2-2(0-1) / 2-2 aet; 5-3 pen
Sheffield Wednesday FC - Luton Town FC	0-0 /1-0(0-0)	Accrington Stanley FC - Ipswich Town FC	1-0(0-0)
Manchester United FC - Reading FC	2-0(2-0)	Newcastle United FC - Blackburn Rovers FC	1-1(0-0) / 4-2 aet
West Bromwich Albion FC - Wigan Athletic FC	1-0(1-0)	Crystal Palace FC London - Grimsby Town FC	1-0(0-0)
Shrewsbury Town FC - Stoke City FC	1-1(1-0) / 3-2(0-2)	Bristol City FC - Huddersfield Town AFC	1-0(0-0)
AFC Bournemouth - Brighton & Hove Albion FC	1-3(0-2)	Blackpool FC - Arsenal FC London	0-3(0-2)
West Ham United FC London - Birmingham City FC	2-0(1-0)	Norwich City FC - Portsmouth FC	0-1(0-0)
Burnley FC - Barnsley FC	1-0(0-0)	Millwall FC London - Hull City AFC	2-1(0-0)
Bolton Wanderers FC - Walsall FC	5-2(0-1)	Preston North End FC - Doncaster Rovers FC	1-3(0-1)
Brentford FC - Oxford United FC	1-0(0-0)	Fulham FC London - Oldham Athletic AFC	1-2(0-0)
Chelsea FC London - Nottingham Forest FC	2-0(0-0)	Manchester City FC - Rotherham United FC	7-0(3-0)
Fleetwood Town FC - AFC Wimbledon	2-3(0-1)	Woking FC - Watford FC	0-2(0-1)
Middlesbrough FC - Peterborough United FC	5-0(0-0)	Queens Park Rangers FC London - Leeds United FC	2-1(1-1)
Aston Villa FC Birmingham - Swansea City AFC	0-3(0-1)	Sheffield United FC - Barnet FC	0-1(0-1)
Gillingham FC - Cardiff City FC	1-0(0-0)	Newport County AFC - Leicester City FC	2-1(1-0)
Everton FC Liverpool - Lincoln City FC	2-1(2-1)	Wolverhampton Wanderers FC - Liverpool FC	2-1(1-0)

Fourth Round [25/26/27/28.01.-05-06.02.2019]

Bristol City FC - Bolton Wanderers FC	2-1(2-1)	Middlesbrough FC - Newport County AFC	1-1(0-0) / 0-2(0-0)
Arsenal FC London - Manchester United FC	1-3(1-2)	Manchester City FC - Burnley FC	5-0(1-0)
Accrington Stanley FC - Derby County FC	0-1(0-0)	Portsmouth FC - Queens Park Rangers FC	1-1(0-0) / 0-2(0-0)
Swansea City AFC - Gillingham FC	4-1(2-0)	Millwall FC London - Everton FC Liverpool	3-2(1-1)
Shrewsbury Town - Wolverhampton Wanderers	2-2(0-0) / 2-3(2-2)	AFC Wimbledon - West Ham United FC London	4-2(2-0)
Brighton & Hove Albion - West Bromwich Albion	0-0 / 3-1 aet	Crystal Palace FC London - Tottenham Hotspur FC	2-0(2-0)
Doncaster Rovers FC - Oldham Athletic AFC	2-1(0-0)	Chelsea FC London - Sheffield Wednesday FC	3-0(1-0)
Newcastle United FC - Watford FC	0-2(0-0)	Barnet FC - Brentford FC	3-3(0-1) / 1-2(0-2)

1/8-Finals [15-18.02.2019]

Queens Park Rangers FC London - Watford FC	0-1(0-1)	Bristol City FC - Wolverhampton Wanderers FC	0-1(0-1)
Brighton & Hove Albion FC - Derby County FC	2-1(2-0)	Doncaster Rovers FC - Crystal Palace FC London	0-2(0-2)
AFC Wimbledon - Millwall FC London	0-1(0-1)	Swansea City AFC - Brentford FC	4-1(0-1)
Newport County AFC - Manchester City FC	1-4(0-0)	Chelsea FC London - Manchester United FC	0-2(0-2)

Quarter-Finals [16-17.03.2019]

Watford FC - Crystal Palace FC London	2-1(1-0)	Wolverhampton Wanderers FC - Manchester United	2-1(0-0)
Swansea City AFC - Manchester City FC	2-3(2-0)	Millwall FC London - Brighton & Hove Albion FC	2-2 aet; 4-5 pen

Semi-Finals [06-07.04.2019]

Manchester City FC - Brighton & Hove Albion FC	1-0(1-0)	Watford FC - Wolverhampton Wanderers FC	3-2(0-1,2-2)

Final

18.05.2019; Wembley Stadium, London; Referee: Kevin Friend; Attendance: 85,854

Manchester City FC – Watford FC **6-0(1-0)**

Manchester City: Ederson Santana de Moraes, Kyle Andrew Walker, Vincent Jean Mpoy Kompany (Cap), Aymeric Jean Louis Gerard Alphonse Laporte, Oleksandr Zinchenko, Bernardo Mota Veiga de Carvalho e Silva, İlkay Gündoğan (73.Leroy Aziz Sané), David Josué Jiménez Silva (79.John Stones), Riyad Karim Mahrez (55.Kevin De Bruyne), Gabriel Fernando de Jesus, Raheem Shaquille Sterling. Trainer: Josep Guardiola Sala (Spain).

Watford: Heurelho da Silva Gomes, Adrian Joseph Mariappa, Craig George Cathcart, José Lloyd Holebas, Francisco Femenía Far "Kiko Femenía", William James Hughes (73.Thomas William Cleverley), Abdoulaye Doucouré, Étienne Capoue, Roberto Maximiliano Pereyra (66.Isaac Ajayi Success), Gerard Deulofeu Lázaro (66.Andre Anthony Gray), Troy Matthew Deeney (Cap). Trainer: Javier Gracia Carlos (Spain).

Goals: 1-0 David Josué Jiménez Silva (26), 2-0 Gabriel Fernando de Jesus (38), 3-0 Kevin De Bruyne (61), 4-0 Gabriel Fernando de Jesus (68), 5-0 Raheem Shaquille Sterling (81), 6-0 Raheem Shaquille Sterling (87).

Arsenal Football Club London

Founded: 1886
Stadium: Emirates Stadium, London (60,260)

Goalkeepers:	**DOB**	**M**	**(s)**	**G**
Petr Čech (CZE)	20.05.1982	7		
Bernd Leno (GER)	04.03.1992	31	(1)	
Defenders:	**DOB**	**M**	**(s)**	**G**
Héctor Bellerín Moruno (ESP)	19.03.1995	18	(1)	
Robert Samuel Holding	20.09.1995	9	(1)	
Carl Daniel Jenkinson	08.02.1992	2	(1)	
Sead Kolašinac (BIH)	20.06.1993	22	(2)	
Laurent Koscielny (FRA)	10.09.1985	13	(4)	3
Stephan Lichtsteiner (SUI)	16.01.1984	10	(4)	
Ainsley MaitlandNiles	29.08.1997	11	(5)	1
Konstantinos Mavropanos (GRE)	11.12.1997	3	(1)	
Shkodran Mustafi (GER)	17.04.1992	31		2
Ignacio Monreal Eraso „Nacho Monreal" (ESP)	26.02.1986	21	(1)	1
Sokratis Papastathopoulos (GRE)	09.06.1988	25		1
Bukayo Saka	05.09.2001		(1)	
Midfielders:	**DOB**	**M**	**(s)**	**G**
Mohamed Naser Elsayed Elneny (EGY)	11.07.1992	5	(3)	
Mattéo Guendouzi (FRA)	14.04.1999	23	(10)	
Henrikh Mkhitaryan (ARM)	21.01.1989	19	(6)	6
Mesut Özil (GER)	15.10.1988	20	(4)	5
Aaron Ramsey (WAL)	26.12.1990	14	(14)	4
Lucas Sebastián Torreira Di Pascua (URU)	11.02.1996	24	(10)	2
Denis Suárez Fernández (ESP)	06.01.1994		(4)	
Joseph George Willock	20.08.1999	1	(1)	
Granit Xhaka (SUI)	27.09.1992	29		4
Forwards:	**DOB**	**M**	**(s)**	**G**
Pierre Emerick François Aubameyang (GAB)	18.06.1989	30	(6)	22
Alexander Chuka Iwobi (NGA)	03.05.1996	22	(13)	3
Alexandre Lacazette (FRA)	28.05.1991	27	(8)	13
Edward Keddar Nketiah	30.05.1999		(5)	1
Daniel Nii Tackie Mensah Welbeck	26.11.1990	1	(7)	1
Trainer:	**DOB**	**M**		
Unai Emery Etxegoien (ESP)	03.11.1971	38		

Athletic Football Club Bournemouth

Founded: 1899
Stadium: Vitality Stadium, Bournemouth (11,329)

Goalkeepers:	**DOB**	**M**	**(s)**	**G**
Asmir Begović (BIH)	20.06.1987	24		
Artur Boruc (POL)	20.02.1980	12		
Mark Travers (IRL)	18.05.1999	2		
Defenders:	**DOB**	**M**	**(s)**	**G**
Nathan Benjamin Aké (NED)	18.02.1995	38		4
Nathaniel Clyne	05.04.1991	13	(1)	
Steve Cook	19.04.1991	31		1
Charlie Daniels	07.09.1986	17	(4)	1
Diego Rico (ESP)	23.02.1993	5	(7)	
Simon Francis	16.02.1985	13	(4)	
Christopher James Mepham (WAL)	05.11.1997	10	(3)	
Tyrone Deon Mings	13.03.1993	2	(3)	
Jack Benjamin Simpson	08.01.1997	4	(2)	
Adam James Smith	29.04.1991	25		1
Midfielders:	**DOB**	**M**	**(s)**	**G**
David Robert Brooks (WAL)	08.07.1997	29	(1)	7
Lewis John Cook	03.02.1997	8	(5)	
Ryan Fraser (SCO)	24.02.1994	35	(3)	7
Daniel Gosling	02.02.1990	19	(6)	2
Emerson Schellas Hyndman (USA)	07.04.1996		(1)	
Jefferson Andrés Lerma Solís (COL)	25.10.1994	29	(1)	2
Felix Junior Stanislas	26.11.1989	11	(12)	2
Andrew Ronald Edward Surman (RSA)	20.08.1986	16	(2)	
Sam Surridge	28.07.1998		(2)	
Forwards:	**DOB**	**M**	**(s)**	**G**
Jermain Colin Defoe	07.10.1982		(4)	
Jordon Femi Ashley Ibe	08.12.1995	9	(10)	1
Joshua Christian Kojo King (NOR)	15.01.1992	34	(1)	12
Lys Mousset (FRA)	08.02.1996	1	(23)	1
Dominic Solanke	14.09.1997	2	(8)	
Callum Eddie Graham Wilson	27.02.1992	29	(1)	14
Trainer:	**DOB**	**M**		
Edward Howe	29.11.1977	38		

Brighton & Hove Albion Football Club

Founded: 24.06.1901
Stadium: Falmer Stadium, Brighton and Hove (30,666)

Goalkeepers:	**DOB**	**M**	**(s)**	**G**
David Robert Edmund Button	27.02.1989	4		
Mathew David Ryan (AUS)	08.04.1992	34		
Defenders:	**DOB**	**M**	**(s)**	**G**
Leon-Aderemi Balogun (NGA)	28.06.1988	5	(3)	1
Bernardo Fernandes da Silva Junior (BRA)	14.05.1995	19	(3)	
Gaëtan Bong Songo (CMR)	25.04.1988	19	(3)	
Bruno Saltor Grau (ESP)	01.10.1980	14		
Shane Duffy (IRL)	01.01.1992	35		5
Lewis Dunk	21.11.1991	36		2
Martín Montoya Torralbo (ESP)	14.04.1991	24	(1)	
Midfielders:	**DOB**	**M**	**(s)**	**G**
Yves Bissouma (MLI)	30.08.1996	17	(11)	
Pascal Groß (GER)	15.06.1991	24	(1)	3
Biram Kayal (ISR)	02.05.1988	9	(9)	1
Anthony Knockaert (FRA)	20.11.1991	18	(12)	2
Solomon March	26.07.1994	30	(5)	1
Davy Pröpper (NED)	02.09.1991	30		1
Dale Stephens	12.12.1989	29	(1)	1
Forwards:	**DOB**	**M**	**(s)**	**G**
Florin Andone (ROU)	11.04.1993	8	(15)	3
José Heriberto Izquierdo Mena (COL)	07.07.1992	9	(6)	
Alireza Jahanbakhsh (IRN)	08.10.1993	12	(7)	
Jürgen Locadia (NED)	07.11.1993	12	(14)	2
Glenn Murray	25.09.1983	30	(8)	13
Trainer:	**DOB**	**M**		
Christopher William Gerard Hughton (IRL)	11.12.1958	38		

Burnley Football Club

Founded: 18.05.1882
Stadium: Turf Moor, Burnley (21,944)

Goalkeepers:	**DOB**	**M**	**(s)**	**G**
Charles Joseph John Hart	19.04.1987	19		
Thomas David Heaton	15.04.1986	19		
Defenders:	**DOB**	**M**	**(s)**	**G**
Phillip Anthony Bardsley (SCO)	28.06.1985	19		
Benjamin James Gibson	15.01.1993	1		1
Kevin Finbarr Long (IRL)	18.08.1990	5	(1)	
Matthew John Lowton	09.06.1989	19	(2)	
Benjamin Mee	21.09.1989	38		
James Alan Tarkowski	19.11.1992	35		3
Charles James Taylor	18.09.1993	35	(3)	
Stephen Robert Ward (IRL)	20.08.1985	3		
Midfielders:	**DOB**	**M**	**(s)**	**G**
Robert Brady (IRL)	14.01.1992	6	(10)	
Jack Frank Porteous Cork	25.06.1989	37		1
Steven Arnold Defour (BEL)	15.04.1988	6		
Jóhann Guðmundsson (ISL)	27.10.1990	19	(10)	3
Jeffrey Patrick Hendrick (IRL)	31.01.1992	25	(7)	3
Aaron Justin Lennon	16.04.1987	14	(2)	1
Ashley Roy Westwood	01.04.1990	31	(3)	2
Forwards:	**DOB**	**M**	**(s)**	**G**
Ashley Luke Barnes	30.10.1989	26	(11)	12
Peter James Crouch	30.01.1981		(6)	
Dwight James Matthew McNeil	22.11.1999	19	(2)	3
Samuel Michael Vokes (WAL)	21.10.1989	10	(10)	3
Matěj Vydra (CZE)	01.05.1992	3	(10)	1
Christopher Grant Wood (NZL)	07.12.1991	29	(9)	10
Trainer:	**DOB**	**M**		
Sean Mark Dyche	28.06.1971	38		

Cardiff City Football Club

Founded: 1899 (*as Riverside AFC*)
Stadium: Cardiff City Stadium, Cardiff (33,316)

Goalkeepers:	**DOB**	**M**	**(s)**	**G**
Neil Leonard Dula Etheridge (PHI)	07.02.1990	38		
Defenders:	**DOB**	**M**	**(s)**	**G**
Souleymane Bamba (CIV)	13.01.1985	28		4
Joseph Bennett	28.03.1990	30		
Gregory Richard Cunningham (IRL)	31.01.1991	7		
Bruno Écuélé Manga (GAB)	16.07.1988	37	(1)	
Sean Morrison	08.01.1991	34		1
Lee Peltier	11.12.1986	17	(3)	
Ashley Darel Jazz Richards (WAL)	12.04.1991		(4)	
Midfielders:	**DOB**	**M**	**(s)**	**G**
Harry Nicholas Arter (IRL)	28.12.1989	24	(1)	
Leandro Bacuna (CUW)	21.08.1991	4	(7)	
Víctor Camarasa Ferrando (ESP)	28.05.1994	31	(1)	5
Loïc Damour (FRA)	08.01.1991		(2)	
Aron Einar Malmquist Gunnarsson (ISL)	22.04.1989	27	(1)	1
Kadeem Harris	08.06.1993	3	(10)	1
David Wayne Hoilett (CAN)	05.06.1990	23	(9)	3
Nathaniel Otis MendezLaing	15.04.1992	11	(9)	4
Callum Paterson (SCO)	13.10.1994	21	(6)	4
Joseph Ralls	13.10.1993	22	(6)	
Forwards:	**DOB**	**M**	**(s)**	**G**
Rhys Healey	12.06.1994		(3)	
Gary Madine	24.08.1990		(5)	
Joshua Murphy	24.02.1995	22	(7)	3
Oumar Niasse (SEN)	18.04.1990	12	(1)	
Bobby Armani Reid	02.02.1993	16	(11)	5
Daniel Carl Ward	11.12.1991	4	(10)	1
Kenneth Dahrup Zohore (DEN)	31.01.1994	7	(12)	1
Trainer:	**DOB**	**M**		
Neil Warnock	01.12.1948	38		

Chelsea Football Club London

Founded: 10.03.1905
Stadium: Stamford Bridge, London (40,853)

Goalkeepers:	**DOB**	**M**	**(s)**	**G**
Wilfredo Daniel Caballero Lazcano (ARG)	28.09.1981	2		
Kepa Arrizabalaga Revuelta (ESP)	03.10.1994	36		
Defenders:	**DOB**	**M**	**(s)**	**G**
César Azpilicueta Tanco (ESP)	28.08.1989	38		1
Gary James Cahill	19.12.1985		(2)	
Andreas Bødtker Christensen (DEN)	10.04.1996	6	(2)	
David Luiz Moreira Marinho (BRA)	22.04.1987	36		3
Emerson Palmieri dos Santos (ITA)	03.08.1994	7	(3)	
Marcos Alonso Mendoza (ESP)	28.12.1990	31		2
Antonio Rüdiger (GER)	03.03.1993	33		1
Davide Zappacosta (ITA)	11.06.1992	1	(3)	
Midfielders:	**DOB**	**M**	**(s)**	**G**
Ross Barkley	05.12.1993	13	(14)	3
Francesc "Cesc" Fàbregas Soler (ESP)	04.05.1987	1	(5)	
Filho Jorge Luiz Frello „Jorginho" (ITA)	20.12.1991	37		2
N'Golo Kanté (FRA)	29.03.1991	36		4
Mateo Kovačić (CRO)	06.05.1994	21	(11)	
Ruben Ira Loftus-Cheek	23.01.1996	6	(18)	6
Victor Moses (NGA)	12.12.1990		(2)	
Forwards:	**DOB**	**M**	**(s)**	**G**
Olivier Giroud (FRA)	30.09.1986	7	(20)	2
Eden Michael Hazard (BEL)	07.01.1991	32	(5)	16
Gonzalo Gerardo Higuaín (ARG)	10.12.1987	13	(1)	5
Callum James Hudson-Odoi	07.11.2000	4	(6)	
Álvaro Borja Morata Martín (ESP)	23.10.1992	11	(5)	5
Pedro Eliezer Rodríguez Ledesma (ESP)	28.07.1987	21	(10)	8
Willian Borges da Silva (BRA)	09.08.1988	26	(6)	3
Trainer:	**DOB**	**M**		
Maurizio Sarri (ITA)	10.01.1959	38		

Crystal Palace Football Club London

Founded: 10.09.1905
Stadium: Selhurst Park, London (26,074)

Goalkeepers:	**DOB**	**M**	**(s)**	**G**
Vicente Guaita Panadero (ESP)	10.01.1987	20		
Wayne Robert Hennessey (WAL)	24.01.1987	17	(1)	
Julian Maria Speroni (ARG)	18.05.1979	1		
Defenders:	**DOB**	**M**	**(s)**	**G**
Scott Dann	14.02.1987	7	(3)	
Martin Ronald Kelly	27.04.1990	12	(1)	
Mamadou Sakho (FRA)	13.02.1990	27		
Pape N'Diaye Souaré (SEN)	06.06.1990		(1)	
James Oliver Charles Tomkins	29.03.1989	29		1
Patrick John Miguel van Aanholt (NED)	29.08.1990	36		3
Aaron WanBissaka	26.11.1997	35		
Joel Edward Philip Ward	29.10.1989	6	(1)	1
Midfielders:	**DOB**	**M**	**(s)**	**G**
Luke Dreher	27.11.1998		(1)	
Cheikhou Kouyaté (SEN)	21.12.1989	21	(10)	
James McFarlane McArthur (SCO)	07.10.1987	36	(2)	3
Max Meyer (GER)	18.09.1995	15	(14)	1
Luka Milivojević (SRB)	07.04.1991	38		12
Jason David Ian Puncheon	26.06.1986		(5)	
Bakary Sako (MLI)	26.04.1988		(4)	
Jeffrey Schlupp (GHA)	23.12.1992	18	(12)	4
Andros Darryl Townsend	16.07.1991	34	(4)	6
Forwards:	**DOB**	**M**	**(s)**	**G**
Jordan Pierre Ayew (GHA)	11.09.1991	14	(6)	1
Michy Batshuayi Atunga (BEL)	02.10.1993	9	(2)	5
Christian Benteke Liolo (BEL)	03.12.1990	9	(7)	1
Alexander Sørloth (NOR)	05.12.1995		(12)	
Connor Wickham	31.03.1993		(6)	
Dazet Wilfried Armel Zaha (CIV)	10.11.1992	34		10
Trainer:	**DOB**	**M**		
Roy Hodgson	09.08.1947	38		

Everton Football Club Liverpool

Founded: 1878
Stadium: Goodison Park, Liverpool (39,221)

Goalkeepers:	**DOB**	**M**	**(s)**	**G**
Jordan Lee Pickford	07.03.1994	38		
Defenders:	**DOB**	**M**	**(s)**	**G**
Leighton John Baines	11.12.1984	5	(1)	
Séamus Coleman (IRL)	11.08.1988	29		2
Lucas Digne (FRA)	20.07.1993	33	(2)	4
Mason Anthony Holgate	22.10.1996	4	(1)	
Philip Nikodem Jagielka	17.08.1982	4	(3)	1
Michael Vincent Keane	11.01.1993	33		1
Jonjoe Kenny	15.03.1997	8	(2)	
Yerry Fernando Mina González (COL)	23.09.1994	10	(3)	1
Kurt Zouma (FRA)	27.10.1994	29	(3)	2
Midfielders:	**DOB**	**M**	**(s)**	**G**
André Filipe Tavares Gomes (POR)	30.07.1993	24	(3)	1
Bernard Anício Caldeira Duarte (BRA)	08.09.1992	25	(9)	1
Thomas Davies	30.06.1998	10	(6)	
Idrissa Gana Gueye (SEN)	26.09.1989	32	(1)	
James Patrick McCarthy (IRL)	12.11.1990		(1)	
Morgan Schneiderlin (FRA)	08.11.1989	10	(4)	
Gylfi Sigurðsson (ISL)	08.09.1989	36	(2)	13
Forwards:	**DOB**	**M**	**(s)**	**G**
Dominic Calvert-Lewin	16.03.1997	19	(16)	6
Ademola Olajade Alade Aylola Lookman	20.10.1997	3	(18)	
El Hadji Baye Oumar Niasse (SEN)	18.04.1990		(5)	
Richarlison de Andrade (BRA)	10.05.1997	32	(3)	13
Cenk Tosun (TUR)	07.06.1991	10	(15)	3
Theo James Walcott	16.03.1989	24	(13)	5
Trainer:	**DOB**	**M**		
Marco Alexandre Saraiva da Silva (POR)	12.07.1977	38		

Fulham Football Club London

Founded: 1879 (*as St. Andrews Cricket & Football Club*)
Stadium: Craven Cottage, London (25,700)

Goalkeepers:	**DOB**	**M**	**(s)**	**G**
Marcus Bettinelli	24.05.1992	7		
Fabricio Agosto Ramírez (ESP)	31.12.1987	2		
Sergio Rico González (ESP)	01.09.1993	29		
Defenders:	**DOB**	**M**	**(s)**	**G**
Joseph Bryan	17.09.1993	27	(1)	
Calum Chambers	20.01.1995	29	(2)	2
Cyrus Sylvester Christie (IRL)	30.09.1992	19	(9)	
Timothy Evans Fosu Mensah (NED)	02.01.1998	10	(2)	
Maxime Le Marchand (FRA)	11.10.1989	25	(1)	
Alfie Robert John Mawson	19.01.1994	13	(2)	
Denis Odoi (BEL)	27.05.1988	29	(2)	
Timothy Ream (USA)	05.10.1987	25	(1)	
Midfielders:	**DOB**	**M**	**(s)**	**G**
Tom Cairney	20.01.1991	24	(7)	1
Ibrahima Cissé (BEL)	28.02.1994	1	(2)	
Stefan Marius Johansen (NOR)	08.01.1991	4	(8)	
Neeskens Kebano (COD)	10.03.1992		(7)	
Lazar Marković (SRB)	02.03.1994		(1)	
Kevin McDonald (SCO)	04.11.1988	10	(5)	
Håvard Nordtveit (NOR)	21.06.1990	4	(1)	
Jean Michaël Seri (CIV)	19.07.1991	27	(5)	1
André-Frank Zambo Anguissa (CMR)	16.11.1995	16	(6)	
Forwards:	**DOB**	**M**	**(s)**	**G**
Floyd Ayité (TOG)	15.12.1988	3	(13)	1
Ryan Guno Babel (NED)	19.12.1986	15	(1)	5
Harvey Elliott	04.04.2003		(2)	
Aboubakar Kamara (FRA)	07.03.1995	5	(8)	3
Aleksandar Mitrović (SRB)	16.09.1994	37		11
André Horst Schürrle (GER)	06.11.1990	21	(3)	6
Kouassi Ryan Sessegnon	18.05.2000	26	(9)	2
Luciano Darío Vietto (ARG)	05.12.1993	10	(10)	1
Trainer:	**DOB**	**M**		
Slaviša Jokanović (SRB)	16.08.1968	12		
Claudio Ranieri (ITA) [14.11.2018]	20.10.1951	16		
Scott Matthew Parker [01.03.2019]	13.10.1980	10		

Huddersfield Town Association Football Club

Founded: 15.08.1908
Stadium: Kirklees Stadium, Huddersfield (24,500)

Goalkeepers:	DOB	M	(s)	G
Joel Coleman	26.09.1995	1		
Benjamin John Hamer	20.11.1987	7		
Jonas Bybjerg Lössl (DEN)	01.02.1989	30	(1)	
Defenders:	**DOB**	**M**	**(s)**	**G**
Demeaco Duhaney	13.10.1998	1		
Erik Durm (GER)	12.05.1992	21	(7)	
Florent Hadergjonaj (SUI)	31.07.1994	19	(5)	
Mathias Jørgensen (DEN)	23.04.1990	24		3
Terence Kongolo (NED)	14.02.1994	32		1
Chris Jörg Löwe (GER)	16.04.1989	23	(6)	
Christopher Wolfgang Georg August Schindler (GER)	29.04.1990	37		1
Tom George Smith	14.04.1992	13	(2)	
Jon Gorenc Stankovič (SVN)	14.01.1996	9	(2)	1
Midfielders:	**DOB**	**M**	**(s)**	**G**
Juninho Bacuna (CUW)	07.08.1997	16	(5)	1
Philip Anyanwu Billing (DEN)	11.06.1996	25	(2)	2
Matthew Daly	10.03.2001		(2)	
Jonathan Lee Hogg	06.12.1988	29		
Aaron Frank Mooy (AUS)	15.09.1989	25	(4)	3
Alex David Pritchard	03.05.1993	26	(4)	2
Jason David Ian Puncheon	26.06.1986	5	(1)	
Aaron Rowe	07.09.2000	1	(1)	
Abdelhamid Sabiri (GER)	28.11.1996	1	(1)	
Ramadan Sobhi Ramadan Ahmed (EGY)	23.01.1997		(4)	
Rajiv Ramon van La Parra (NED)	04.06.1991	5		
Daniel Charles Williams (USA)	08.03.1989	1	(4)	
Forwards:	**DOB**	**M**	**(s)**	**G**
Karlan Ahearne Grant	18.09.1997	9	(4)	3
Laurent Depoitre (BEL)	07.12.1988	10	(13)	
Adama Diakhaby (FRA)	05.07.1996	6	(6)	
Elias Kachunga (COD)	22.04.1992	13	(7)	
Isaac Mbenza (BEL)	08.03.1996	10	(12)	1
Steve Mounié (BEN)	29.09.1994	19	(12)	2
Collin Quaner (GER)	18.06.1991		(2)	
Trainer:	**DOB**	**M**		
David Wagner (USA)	19.10.1971	22		
Mark Hudson [14.01.2019]	30.03.1982	1		
Jan Siewert (GER) [21.01.2019]	23.08.1982	15		

Leicester City Football Club

Founded: 1884
Stadium: King Power Stadium, Leicester (32,273)

Goalkeepers:	DOB	M	(s)	G
Kasper Peter Schmeichel (DEN)	05.11.1986	38		
Defenders:	**DOB**	**M**	**(s)**	**G**
Daniel Amartey (GHA)	21.12.1994	7	(2)	
Benjamin James Chilwell	21.12.1996	36		
Jonathan Grant Evans (NIR)	03.01.1988	21	(3)	1
Christian Fuchs (AUT)	07.04.1986	2	(1)	
Jacob Harry Maguire	05.03.1993	31		3
Westley Nathan Morgan (JAM)	21.01.1984	21	(1)	3
Daniel Peter Simpson	04.01.1987	3	(3)	
Çağlar Söyüncü (TUR)	23.05.1996	4	(2)	
Midfielders:	**DOB**	**M**	**(s)**	**G**
Adrien Sébastien Perruchet da Silva (POR)	15.03.1989	1	(1)	
Marc Kevin Albrighton	18.11.1989	18	(9)	2
Harvey Lewis Barnes	09.12.1997	11	(5)	1
Hamza Dewan Choudhury	01.10.1997	7	(2)	
Demarai Remelle Gray	28.06.1996	23	(11)	4
Vicente Iborra de la Fuente (ESP)	16.01.1988	3	(5)	
James Maddison	23.11.1996	35	(1)	7
Nampalys Mendy (FRA)	23.06.1992	23	(8)	
Onyinye Wilfred Ndidi (NGA)	16.12.1996	37	(1)	2
Ricardo Domingos Barbosa Pereira (POR)	06.10.1993	35		2
Youri Tielemans (BEL)	07.05.1997	13		3
Forwards:	**DOB**	**M**	**(s)**	**G**
Fousséni Diabaté (MLI)	18.10.1995	1		
Rachid Ghezzal (ALG)	09.05.1992	8	(11)	1
Kelechi Promise Iheanacho (NGA)	03.10.1996	9	(21)	1
Shinji Okazaki (JPN)	16.04.1986	1	(20)	
Jamie Richard Vardy	11.01.1987	30	(4)	18
Trainer:	**DOB**	**M**		
Claude Puel (FRA)	02.09.1961	27		
Michael Stowell [24.02.2019]	19.04.1965	1		
Brendan Rodgers (NIR) [27.02.2019]	26.01.1973	10		

Liverpool Football Club

Founded: 03.06.1892
Stadium: Anfield Road, Liverpool (54,074)

Goalkeepers:	DOB	M	(s)	G
Alisson Ramses Becker (BRA)	02.10.1992	38		
Defenders:	**DOB**	**M**	**(s)**	**G**
Nathaniel Edwin Clyne	05.04.1991	1	(3)	
Alberto Moreno Pérez (ESP)	05.07.1992	2		
Trent John Alexander-Arnold	07.10.1998	27	(2)	1
Joseph Dave Gomez	23.05.1997	12	(4)	
Ki-Jana Hoever (NED)	18.01.2002			
Dejan Lovren (CRO)	05.07.1989	11	(2)	1
Job Joël André Matip (CMR)	08.08.1991	17	(5)	1
Andrew Robertson (SCO)	11.03.1994	36		
Virgil van Dijk (NED)	08.07.1991	38		4
Midfielders:	**DOB**	**M**	**(s)**	**G**
Fabio Henrique Tavares "Fabinho" (BRA)	23.10.1993	21	(7)	1
Jordan Brian Henderson	17.06.1990	21	(11)	1
Naby Keïta (GUI)	10.02.1995	16	(9)	2
Adam David Lallana	10.05.1988	5	(8)	
James Philip Milner	04.01.1986	19	(12)	5
Alexander Mark David Oxlade-Chamberlain	15.08.1993		(2)	
Rafael Euclides Soares Camacho (POR)	22.05.2000		(1)	
Georginio Gregion Emile Wijnaldum (NED)	11.11.1990	32	(3)	3
Forwards:	**DOB**	**M**	**(s)**	**G**
Sadio Mané (SEN)	10.04.1992	35	(1)	22
Divock Okoth Origi (BEL)	18.04.1995	4	(8)	3
Roberto Firmino Barbosa de Oliveira (BRA)	02.10.1991	31	(3)	12
Mohamed Salah Ghaly (EGY)	15.06.1992	37	(1)	22
Xherdan Shaqiri (SUI)	10.10.1991	11	(13)	6
Daniel Andre Sturridge	01.09.1989	4	(14)	2
Trainer:	**DOB**	**M**		
Jürgen Norbert Klopp (GER)	16.06.1967	38		

Manchester City Football Club

Founded: 1880
Stadium: Etihad (City of Manchester) Stadium, Manchester (55,017)

Goalkeepers:	**DOB**	**M**	**(s)**	**G**
Ederson Santana de Moraes (BRA)	17.08.1993	38		
Defenders:	**DOB**	**M**	**(s)**	**G**
Danilo Luiz da Silva (BRA)	15.07.1991	9	(2)	1
Vincent Jean Mpoy Kompany (BEL)	10.04.1986	13	(4)	1
Aymeric Jean Louis Gerard Alphonse Laporte (FRA)	27.05.1994	34	(1)	3
Benjamin Mendy (FRA)	17.07.1994	10		
Nicolás Hernán Gonzalo Otamendi (ARG)	12.02.1988	14	(4)	
John Stones	28.05.1994	20	(4)	
Kyle Andrew Walker	28.05.1990	30	(3)	1
Oleksandr Zinchenko (UKR)	15.12.1996	14		
Midfielders:	**DOB**	**M**	**(s)**	**G**
David Josué Jiménez Silva (ESP)	08.01.1986	28	(5)	6
Kevin De Bruyne (BEL)	28.06.1991	11	(8)	2
Fabian Delph	21.11.1989	8	(3)	
Fernando Luiz Roza „Fernandinho“ (BRA)	04.05.1985	27	(2)	1
Philip Walter Foden	28.05.2000	3	(10)	1
İlkay Gündoğan (GER)	24.10.1990	23	(8)	6
Riyad Karim Mahrez (ALG)	21.02.1991	14	(13)	7
Forwards:	**DOB**	**M**	**(s)**	**G**
Sergio Leonel Agüero del Castillo (ARG)	02.06.1988	31	(2)	21
Bernardo Mota Veiga de Carvalho e Silva (POR)	10.08.1994	31	(5)	7
Gabriel Fernando de Jesus (BRA)	03.04.1997	8	(21)	7
Leroy Aziz Sané (GER)	11.01.1996	21	(10)	10
Raheem Shaquille Sterling	08.12.1994	31	(3)	17
Trainer:	**DOB**	**M**		
Josep "Pep" Guardiola Sala (ESP)	18.01.1971	38		

Manchester United Football Club

Founded: 1878
Stadium: Old Trafford, Manchester (74,879)

Goalkeepers:	**DOB**	**M**	**(s)**	**G**
David de Gea Quintana (ESP)	07.11.1990	38		
Defenders:	**DOB**	**M**	**(s)**	**G**
Eric Bertrand Bailly (CIV)	12.04.1994	8	(4)	
Matteo Darmian (ITA)	02.12.1989	5	(1)	
José Diogo Dalot Teixeira (POR)	18.03.1999	12	(4)	
Philip Anthony Jones	21.02.1992	15	(3)	
Victor Jörgen Nilsson Lindelöf (SWE)	17.07.1994	29	(1)	1
Faustino Marcos Alberto Rojo (ARG)	20.03.1990	2	(3)	
Luke Paul Hoare Shaw	12.07.1995	29		1
Christopher Lloyd Smalling	22.11.1989	24		1
Luis Antonio Valencia Mosquera (ECU)	04.08.1985	5	(1)	
Ashley Simon Young	09.07.1985	28	(2)	2
Midfielders:	**DOB**	**M**	**(s)**	**G**
Ander Herrera Agüera (ESP)	14.08.1989	16	(6)	2
Andreas Hugo Hoelgebaum Pereira (BRA)	01.01.1996	6	(9)	1
Marouane Fellaini-Bakkioui (BEL)	22.11.1987	6	(8)	
Frederico Rodrigues de Paula Santos "Fred" (BRA)	05.03.1993	13	(4)	1
James David Garner	13.03.2001		(1)	
Adilson Angel Abreu de Almeida Gomes	31.08.2000		(2)	
Jesse Ellis Lingard	15.12.1992	19	(8)	4
Juan Manuel Mata García (ESP)	28.04.1988	16	(6)	3
Nemanja Matić (SRB)	01.08.1988	28		1
Scott Francis McTominay (SCO)	08.12.1996	9	(7)	2
Paul Labile Pogba (FRA)	15.03.1993	34	(1)	13
Forwards:	**DOB**	**M**	**(s)**	**G**
Tahith Chong (NED)	04.12.1999		(2)	
Mason Greenwood	01.10.2001	1	(2)	
Romelu Menama Lukaku Bolingoli (BEL)	13.05.1993	22	(10)	12
Anthony Joran Martial (FRA)	05.12.1995	18	(9)	10
Marcus Rashford	31.10.1997	26	(7)	10
Alexis Alejandro Sánchez Sánchez (CHI)	19.12.1988	9	(11)	1
Trainer:	**DOB**	**M**		
José Mário dos Santos Mourinho Félix (POR)	26.01.1963	17		
Ole Gunnar Solskjær (NOR) [19.12.2018]	26.02.1973	21		

Newcastle United Football Club

Founded: 09.12.1892
Stadium: St James' Park, Newcastle upon Tyne (52,354)

Goalkeepers:	**DOB**	**M**	**(s)**	**G**
Martin Dúbravka (SVK)	15.01.1989	38		
Defenders:	**DOB**	**M**	**(s)**	**G**
Antonio Barreca (ITA)	18.03.1995		(1)	
Ciaran Clark (IRL)	26.09.1989	9	(2)	3
Paul Dummett (WAL)	26.09.1991	21	(5)	
Federico Fernández (ARG)	21.02.1989	17	(2)	
Jamaal Lascelles	11.11.1993	32		
Florian Gregoire Claude Lejeune (FRA)	20.05.1991	12		
Javier Manquillo Gaitán (ESP)	05.05.1994	12	(6)	
Fabian Schär (SUI)	20.12.1991	22	(2)	4
DeAndre Roselle Yedlin (USA)	09.07.1993	28	(1)	1
Midfielders:	**DOB**	**M**	**(s)**	**G**
Miguel Ángel Almiron Rejala (PAR)	10.02.1994	9	(1)	
Ayoze Pérez Gutiérrez (ESP)	23.07.1993	34	(3)	12
Mohamed Diamé (SEN)	14.06.1987	24	(5)	
Isaac Scot Hayden	22.03.1995	21	(4)	1
Robert Kenedy Nunes Nascimento (BRA)	08.02.1996	14	(11)	1
Ki Sung-Yueng (KOR)	24.01.1989	14	(4)	
Sean David Longstaff	30.10.1997	8	(1)	1
Matthew Thomas Ritchie (SCO)	10.09.1989	35	(1)	2
Jonjo Shelvey	27.02.1992	10	(6)	1
Forwards:	**DOB**	**M**	**(s)**	**G**
Christian Atsu Twasam (GHA)	10.01.1992	15	(13)	1
José Luis Mato Sanmartín „Joselu“ (ESP)	27.03.1990	5	(11)	2
Jacob Kai Murphy	24.02.1995	3	(6)	
Yoshinori Mutō (JPN)	15.07.1992	5	(12)	1
José Salomón Rondón Giménez (VEN)	16.09.1989	30	(2)	11
Trainer:	**DOB**	**M**		
Rafael Benítez Maudes (ESP)	16.04.1960			

Southampton Football Club

Founded: 21.11.1885
Stadium: St. Mary's Stadium, Southampton (32,384)

Goalkeepers:	DOB	M	(s)	G
Fraser Gerard Forster	17.03.1988	1		
Angus Fraser James Gunn	22.01.1996	12		
Alex Simon McCarthy	03.12.1989	25		
Defenders:	**DOB**	**M**	**(s)**	**G**
Jan Bednarek (POL)	12.04.1996	24	(1)	
Ryan Dominic Bertrand	05.08.1989	24		1
Cédric Ricardo Alves Soares (POR)	31.08.1991	16	(2)	1
Wesley Hoedt (NED)	06.03.1994	13		
Kayne Ramsay	10.10.2000	1		
Jack Stephens	27.01.1994	19	(5)	1
Matthew Robert Targett	18.09.1995	13	(3)	1
Yan Valery (FRA)	22.02.1999	20	(3)	2
Jannik Vestergaard (DEN)	03.08.1992	23		
Maya Yoshida (JPN)	24.08.1988	17		
Midfielders:	**DOB**	**M**	**(s)**	**G**
Stuart Armstrong (SCO)	30.03.1992	16	(13)	3
Steven Davis (NIR)	01.01.1985	1	(2)	
Pierre-Emile Højbjerg (DEN)	05.08.1995	31		4
Mario René Junior Lemina (GAB)	01.09.1993	18	(3)	1
Oriol Romeu Vidal (ESP)	24.09.1991	25	(6)	1
Nathan Daniel Jerome Redmond	06.03.1994	36	(2)	6
Callum Slattery	08.02.1999	1	(2)	
James Michael Edward Ward-Prowse	01.11.1994	21	(5)	7
Forwards:	**DOB**	**M**	**(s)**	**G**
Charlie Austin	05.07.1989	11	(14)	2
Mohamed Amine Elyounoussi (NOR)	04.08.1994	8	(8)	
Manolo Gabbiadini (ITA)	26.11.1991	4	(8)	1
Samuel James Gallagher	15.09.1995		(4)	
Daniel William John Ings	23.07.1992	23	(1)	7
Tyreke Martin Johnson	03.11.1998		(1)	
Shane Patrick Long (IRL)	22.01.1987	12	(14)	5
Michael Oluwadurotimi Obafemi (IRL)	06.07.2000	1	(5)	1
Joshua Samuel Sims	28.03.1997	2	(5)	
Trainer:	**DOB**	**M**		
Kelvin Davis	29.09.1976	15		
Ralph Hasenhüttl (AUT) [06.12.2018]	09.08.1967	23		

Tottenham Hotspur Football Club London

Founded: 05.09.1882
Stadium: Wembley Stadium / Tottenham Hotspur Stadium, London (90,000 / 62,062)

Goalkeepers:	DOB	M	(s)	G
Paulo Dino Gazzaniga (ARG)	02.01.1992	3		
Hugo Lloris (FRA)	26.12.1986	33		
Michel Armand Vorm (NED)	20.10.1983	2		
Defenders:	**DOB**	**M**	**(s)**	**G**
Tobias Albertine Maurits Alderweireld (BEL)	02.03.1989	33	(1)	
Serge Alain Stephane Aurier (CIV)	24.12.1992	6	(2)	
Benjamin Thomas Davies (WAL)	24.04.1993	20	(7)	
Juan Marcos Foyth (ARG)	12.01.1998	10	(2)	1
Daniel Lee Rose	02.07.1990	20	(6)	
Dávinson Sánchez Mina (COL)	12.06.1996	22	(1)	1
Kieran John Trippier	19.09.1990	26	(1)	1
Jan Bert Lieve Vertonghen (BEL)	24.04.1987	22		1
Kyle Leonardus Walker-Peters	13.04.1997	4	(2)	
Midfielders:	**DOB**	**M**	**(s)**	**G**
Bamidele Jermaine "Dele" Alli	11.04.1996	22	(3)	5
Luke Ayodele Amos	23.02.1997		(1)	
Mousa Sidi Yaya Dembélé (BEL)	16.07.1987	7	(3)	
Eric Jeremy Edgar Dier	15.01.1994	18	(2)	3
Christian Dannemann Eriksen (DEN)	14.02.1992	30	(5)	8
Érik Manuel Lamela (ARG)	04.03.1992	9	(10)	4
Lucas Rodrigues Moura da Silva (BRA)	13.08.1992	25	(7)	10
Moussa Sissoko (FRA)	16.08.1989	27	(2)	
Oliver Skipp	16.09.2000	2	(6)	
Victor Mugubi Wanyama (KEN)	25.06.1991	4	(9)	1
Harry Billy Winks	02.02.1996	17	(9)	1
Forwards:	**DOB**	**M**	**(s)**	**G**
Vincent Janssen (NED)	15.06.1994		(3)	
Harry Edward Kane	28.07.1993	27	(1)	17
Fernando Javier Llorente Torres (ESP)	26.02.1985	6	(14)	1
Georges-Kévin N'Koudou Mbida (FRA)	13.02.1995		(1)	
Son Heung-Min (KOR)	08.07.1992	23	(8)	12
Trainer:	**DOB**	**M**		
Mauricio Roberto Pochettino Trossero (ARG)	02.03.1972	38		

Watford Football Club

Founded: 1881
Stadium: Vicarage Road, Watford (20,400)

Goalkeepers:	DOB	M	(s)	G
Benjamin Anthony Foster	03.04.1983	38		
Defenders:	**DOB**	**M**	**(s)**	**G**
Miguel Ángel Britos Cabrera (URU)	17.07.1985	2	(1)	
Craig George Cathcart (NIR)	06.02.1989	35	(1)	3
José Lloyd Holebas (GRE)	27.06.1984	27	(1)	3
Daryl Janmaat (NED)	22.07.1989	17	(1)	
Christian Kabasele (BEL)	24.02.1991	19	(2)	
Adrian Joseph Mariappa (JAM)	03.10.1986	20	(6)	
Adam Masina (ITA)	02.01.1994	11	(3)	
Marc Navarro Ceciliano (ESP)	02.07.1995	1	(1)	
Sebastian Prödl (AUT)	21.06.1987		(1)	
Benjamin Lewis Wilmot	04.11.1999		(2)	
Midfielders:	**DOB**	**M**	**(s)**	**G**
Étienne Capoue (FRA)	11.07.1988	33		1
Nathaniel Chalobah	12.12.1994	3	(6)	
Thomas William Cleverley	12.08.1989	4	(9)	1
Domingos Quina (POR)	18.11.1999	3	(5)	1
Abdoulaye Doucouré (FRA)	01.01.1993	34	(1)	5
William James Hughes	07.04.1995	31	(1)	2
Francisco Femenía Far "Kiko Femenía" (ESP)	02.02.1991	22	(7)	1
Roberto Maximiliano Pereyra (ARG)	07.01.1991	33		6
Ken Nlata Sema (SWE)	30.09.1993	9	(8)	1
Forwards:	**DOB**	**M**	**(s)**	**G**
Troy Matthew Deeney	29.06.1988	28	(4)	9
Gerard Deulofeu Lázaro (ESP)	13.03.1994	26	(4)	10
Andre Anthony Gray	26.06.1991	13	(16)	7
Stefano Chuka Okaka (ITA)	09.08.1989		(2)	
Isaac Ajayi Success (NGA)	07.01.1996	9	(21)	1
Trainer:	**DOB**	**M**		
Javier Gracia Carlos (ESP)	01.05.1970	38		

West Ham United Football Club London

Founded: 29.06.1895
Stadium: London Stadium, London (60,000)

Goalkeepers:	**DOB**	**M**	**(s)**	**G**
Łukasz Fabiański (POL)	18.04.1985	38		
Defenders:	**DOB**	**M**	**(s)**	**G**
Fabián Cornelio Balbuena González (PAR)	23.08.1991	23		1
Aaron William Cresswell	15.12.1989	18	(2)	
Issa Diop (FRA)	09.01.1997	33		1
Ryan Marlow Fredericks	10.10.1992	12	(3)	1
Benjamin Anthony Johnson	24.01.2000	1		
Fuka-Arthur Masuaku Kawela (COD)	07.11.1993	19	(4)	
Obinze Angelo Ogbonna (ITA)	23.05.1988	20	(4)	1
Declan Rice	14.01.1999	34		2
Pablo Javier Zabaleta Girod (ARG)	16.01.1985	23	(3)	
Midfielders:	**DOB**	**M**	**(s)**	**G**
Michail Gregory Antonio	28.03.1990	22	(11)	6
Grady Diangana	19.04.1998	6	(11)	
Felipe Anderson Pereira Gomes (BRA)	15.04.1993	36		9
Manuel Lanzini (ARG)	15.02.1993	8	(2)	1
Samir Nasri (FRA)	26.06.1987	3	(2)	
Mark James Noble	08.05.1987	29	(2)	5
Pedro Mba Obiang Avomo (ESP)	27.03.1992	12	(12)	
Carlos Alberto Sánchez Moreno (COL)	06.02.1986	2	(5)	
Robert Snodgrass (SCO)	07.09.1987	25	(8)	2
Jack Andrew Garry Wilshere	01.01.1992	4	(4)	
Forwards:	**DOB**	**M**	**(s)**	**G**
Marko Arnautović (AUT)	19.04.1989	24	(4)	10
Andrew Thomas Carroll	06.01.1989	3	(9)	
Javier Hernández Balcázar (MEX)	01.06.1988	14	(11)	7
Lucas Pérez Martínez (ESP)	10.09.1988	4	(11)	3
Alexandre Nascimento Costa Silva „Xande Silva" (POR)	16.03.1997		(1)	
Andrey Yarmolenko (UKR)	23.10.1989	5	(4)	2
Trainer:	**DOB**	**M**		
Manuel Luis Pellegrini Ripamonti (CHI)	16.09.1953	38		

Wolverhampton Wanderers Football Club

Founded: 1877 (*as St. Luke's FC*)
Stadium: Molineux Stadium, Wolverhampton (32,050)

Goalkeepers:	**DOB**	**M**	**(s)**	**G**
William James Norris	12.08.1993		(1)	
John Thomas Gordon Ruddy	24.10.1986	1		
Rui Pedro dos Santos Patrício (POR)	15.02.1988	37		
Defenders:	**DOB**	**M**	**(s)**	**G**
Ryan Bennett	06.03.1990	34		1
Willy Arnaud Zobo Boly (FRA)	03.02.1991	36		4
Matthew Doherty (IRL)	16.01.1992	35	(3)	4
Jonathan Castro Otto "Jonny" (ESP)	03.03.1994	32	(1)	1
Max Kilman	23.05.1997		(1)	
Rúben Gonçalo Silva Nascimento Vinagre (POR)	09.04.1999	7	(10)	
Midfielders:	**DOB**	**M**	**(s)**	**G**
Conor Coady	25.02.1993	38		
Leander Dendoncker (BEL)	15.04.1995	17	(2)	2
Diogo José Teixeira da Silva „Diogo Jota" (POR)	04.12.1996	29	(4)	9
Morgan Gibbs White	27.01.2000	5	(21)	
João Filipe Iria Santos Moutinho (POR)	08.09.1986	35	(3)	1
Rúben Diogo da Silva Neves (POR)	13.03.1997	34	(1)	4
Romain Saïss (MAR)	26.03.1990	12	(7)	2
Forwards:	**DOB**	**M**	**(s)**	**G**
Hélder Wander Sousa de Azevedo "Hélder Costa" (ANG)	12.01.1994	16	(9)	1
Ivan Ricardo Neves Abreu Cavaleiro (POR)	18.10.1993	6	(17)	3
Raúl Alonso Jiménez Rodríguez (MEX)	05.05.1991	36	(2)	13
Leonardo Bonatini Lohner Maia "Léo Bonatini" (BRA)	28.03.1994		(7)	
Adama Traoré Diarra (MLI)	25.01.1996	8	(21)	1
Trainer:	**DOB**	**M**		
Nuno Herlander Simões do Espírito Santo (POR)	25.01.1974	38		

SECOND LEVEL
EFL Championship 2018/2019

1.	Norwich City FC (*Promoted*)	46	27	13	6	93	-	57	94
2.	Sheffield United FC (*Promoted*)	46	26	11	9	78	-	41	89
3.	Leeds United FC	46	25	8	13	73	-	50	83
4.	West Bromwich Albion FC	46	23	11	12	87	-	62	80
5.	Aston Villa FC Birmingham	46	20	16	10	82	-	61	76
6.	Derby County FC	46	20	14	12	69	-	54	74
7.	Middlesbrough FC	46	20	13	13	49	-	41	73
8.	Bristol City FC	46	19	13	14	59	-	53	70
9.	Nottingham Forest FC	46	17	15	14	61	-	54	66
10.	Swansea City AFC	46	18	11	17	65	-	62	65
11.	Brentford FC	46	17	13	16	73	-	59	64
12.	Sheffield Wednesday FC	46	16	16	14	60	-	62	64
13.	Hull City AFC	46	17	11	18	66	-	68	62
14.	Preston North End FC	46	16	13	17	67	-	67	61
15.	Blackburn Rovers FC	46	16	12	18	64	-	69	60
16.	Stoke City FC	46	11	22	13	45	-	52	55
17.	Birmingham City FC*	46	14	19	13	64	-	58	52
18.	Wigan Athletic FC	46	13	13	20	51	-	64	52
19.	Queens Park Rangers FC London	46	14	9	23	53	-	71	51
20.	Reading FC	46	10	17	19	49	-	66	47
21.	Millwall FC London	46	10	14	22	48	-	64	44
22.	Rotherham United FC (*Relegated*)	46	8	16	22	52	-	83	40
23.	Bolton Wanderers FC (*Relegated*)	46	8	8	30	29	-	78	32
24.	Ipswich Town FC (*Relegated*)	46	5	16	25	36	-	77	31

**9 points deducted*
Clubs ranked 3-6 were qualified for the Promotion Play-offs.

Promotion Play-offs [11-27.05.2019]

Aston Villa FC Birmingham - West Bromwich Albion FC	2-1(0-1)	0-1(0-1,0-1,0-1); 4-3 pen
Derby County FC - Leeds United FC	0-1(0-0)	4-2(1-1)
Aston Villa FC Birmingham - Derby County FC	2-1(1-0)	

Aston Villa FC Birmingham promoted to the 2019/2020 Premier League.

NATIONAL TEAM

INTERNATIONAL MATCHES
(16.07.2018 – 15.07.2019)

08.09.2018	London	England - Spain	1-2(1-2)	(UNL)
11.09.2018	Leicester	England - Switzerland	1-0(0-0)	(F)
12.10.2018	Rijeka	Croatia - England	0-0	(UNL)
15.10.2018	Seville	Spain - England	2-3(0-3)	(UNL)
15.11.2018	London	England - United States	3-0(2-0)	(F)
18.11.2018	London	England - Croatia	2-1(0-0)	(UNL)
22.03.2019	London	England - Czech Republic	5-0(2-0)	(ECQ)
25.03.2019	Podgorica	Montenegro - England	1-5(1-2)	(ECQ)
06.06.2019	Guimarães	Netherlands - England	3-1(0-1,1-1)	(UNL)
09.06.2019	Guimarães	Switzerland - England	0-0; 5-6 on penalties	(UNL)

08.09.2018 ENGLAND - SPAIN 1-2(1-2) UEFA Nations League A, Group 4
Wembley Stadium, London; Referee: Danny Desmond Makkelie (Netherlands); Attendance: 81,392
ENG: Jordan Lee Pickford, Kieran John Trippier, Jacob Harry Maguire, John Stones, Luke Paul Hoare Shaw (53.Daniel Lee Rose), Joseph Dave Gomez, Jordan Brian Henderson (64.Eric Jeremy Edgar Dier), Bamidele Jermaine Alli, Jesse Ellis Lingard, Harry Edward Kane (Cap), Marcus Rashford (90+4.Daniel Nii Tackie Mensah Welbeck). Trainer: Gareth Southgate.
Goal: Marcus Rashford (11).

11.09.2018 ENGLAND - SWITZERLAND 1-0(0-0) Friendly International
King Power Stadium, Leicester; Referee: Clément Turpin (France); Attendance: 30,256
ENG: Jack Butland, Daniel Lee Rose (79.Benjamin James Chilwell), Kyle Andrew Walker, James Alan Tarkowski (61.John Stones), Jacob Harry Maguire, Trent John Alexander-Arnold (78.Kieran John Trippier), Fabian Delph (68.Jordan Brian Henderson), Eric Jeremy Edgar Dier (Cap), Ruben Ira Loftus-Cheek (61.Jesse Ellis Lingard), Daniel Nii Tackie Mensah Welbeck (61.Harry Edward Kane), Marcus Rashford.Trainer: Gareth Southgate.
Goal: Marcus Rashford (54).

12.10.2018 CROATIA - ENGLAND 0-0 UEFA Nations League ABCD
Stadion Rujevica, Rijeka; Referee: Dr. Felix Brych (Germany); Attendance: *played behind closed doors*
ENG: Jordan Lee Pickford, Kyle Andrew Walker, Jacob Harry Maguire, John Stones, Benjamin James Chilwell, Jordan Brian Henderson, Ross Barkley, Eric Jeremy Edgar Dier, Harry Edward Kane (Cap), Raheem Shaquille Sterling (78.Jadon Malik Sancho), Marcus Rashford. Trainer: Gareth Southgate.

15.10.2018 SPAIN - ENGLAND 2-3(0-3) UEFA Nations League ABCD
Estadio "Benito Villamarín", Sevilla; Referee: Szymon Marciniak (Poland); Attendance: 50,355
ENG: Jordan Lee Pickford, Kieran John Trippier (85.Trent John Alexander-Arnold), Jacob Harry Maguire, Joseph Dave Gomez, Benjamin James Chilwell, Ross Barkley (76.Kyle Andrew Walker), Eric Jeremy Edgar Dier, Harry Billy Winks (90+1.Nathaniel Nyakie Chalobah) , Harry Edward Kane (Cap), Raheem Shaquille Sterling, Marcus Rashford. Trainer: Gareth Southgate.
Goals: Raheem Shaquille Sterling (16), Marcus Rashford (30), Raheem Shaquille Sterling (38).

15.11.2018 ENGLAND - UNITED STATES 3-0(2-0) Friendly International
Wembley Stadium, London; Referee: Jesús Gil Manzano (Spain); Attendance: 68,155
ENG: Jordan Lee Pickford (46.Alex Simon McCarthy), Trent John Alexander-Arnold, Lewis Carl Dunk, Michael Vincent Keane, Benjamin James Chilwell (58.Eric Jeremy Edgar Dier), Fabian Delph (Cap), Bamidele Jermaine Alli (58.Jordan Brian Henderson), Jesse Ellis Lingard (58.Wayne Mark Rooney), Harry Billy Winks (70.Ruben Ira Loftus-Cheek), Jadon Malik Sancho, Callum Eddie Graham Wilson (79.Marcus Rashford). Trainer: Gareth Southgate.
Goals: Jesse Ellis Lingard (25), Trent John Alexander-Arnold (27), Callum Eddie Graham Wilson (77).

18.11.2018 ENGLAND - CROATIA 2-1(0-0) UEFA Nations League ABCD
Wembley Stadium, London; Referee: Anastasios Sidiropoulos (Greece); Attendance: 78,221
ENG: Jordan Lee Pickford, Kyle Andrew Walker, John Stones, Joseph Dave Gomez, Benjamin James Chilwell, Fabian Delph (73.Jesse Ellis Lingard), Ross Barkley (63.Bamidele Jermaine Alli), Eric Jeremy Edgar Dier, Harry Edward Kane (Cap), Raheem Shaquille Sterling, Marcus Rashford (73.Jadon Malik Sancho). Trainer: Gareth Southgate.
Goals: Jesse Ellis Lingard (78), Harry Edward Kane (85).

22.03.2019 ENGLAND - CZECH REPUBLIC 5-0(2-0) 16th EC. Qualifiers
Wembley Stadium, London; Referee: Artur Manuel Soares Dias (Portugal); Attendance: 82,575
ENG: Jordan Lee Pickford, Kyle Andrew Walker, Jacob Harry Maguire, Michael Vincent Keane, Benjamin James Chilwell, Jordan Brian Henderson, Bamidele Jermaine Alli (63.Declan Rice), Eric Jeremy Edgar Dier (17.Ross Barkley), Jadon Malik Sancho, Harry Edward Kane (Cap), Raheem Shaquille Sterling (70.Callum James Hudson-Odoi). Trainer: Gareth Southgate.
Goals: Raheem Shaquille Sterling (24), Harry Edward Kane (45+2 penalty), Raheem Shaquille Sterling (62, 68), Tomáš Kalas (84 own goal).

25.03.2019 MONTENEGRO - ENGLAND 1-5(1-2) 16th EC. Qualifiers
Stadion pod Goricom, Podgorica; Referee: Aleksei Kulbakov (Belarus); Attendance: 8,329
ENG: Jordan Lee Pickford, Daniel Lee Rose, Kyle Andrew Walker, Jacob Harry Maguire, Michael Vincent Keane, Ross Barkley (81.James Michael Edward Ward-Prowse), Bamidele Jermaine Alli (64.Jordan Brian Henderson), Declan Rice, Harry Edward Kane (Cap) (83.Callum Eddie Graham Wilson), Raheem Shaquille Sterling, Callum James Hudson-Odoi. Trainer: Gareth Southgate.
Goals: Michael Vincent Keane (30), Ross Barkley (39, 59), Harry Edward Kane (71), Raheem Shaquille Sterling (81).

06.06.2019 NETHERLANDS - ENGLAND 3-1(0-1,1-1) UEFA Nations League, Semi-Finals
Estádio „D. Afonso Henriques", Guimarães (Portugal); Referee: Clément Turpin (France); Attendance: 25,711
ENG: Jordan Lee Pickford, Kyle Andrew Walker, Jacob Harry Maguire, John Stones, Benjamin James Chilwell, Ross Barkley, Fabian Delph (77.Jordan Brian Henderson), Declan Rice (105.Bamidele Jermaine Alli), Jadon Malik Sancho (61.Jesse Ellis Lingard), Raheem Shaquille Sterling (Cap), Marcus Rashford (46.Harry Edward Kane). Trainer: Gareth Southgate.
Goal: Marcus Rashford (32 penalty).

09.06.2019 SWITZERLAND - ENGLAND **0-0; 5-6 on penalties** UEFA Nations League, Third Place Play-off
Estádio „D. Afonso Henriques", Guimarães (Portugal); Referee: Ovidiu Alin Haţegan (Romania); Attendance: 15,742
ENG: Jordan Lee Pickford, Daniel Lee Rose (70.Kyle Andrew Walker), Jacob Harry Maguire, Joseph Dave Gomez, Trent John Alexander-Arnold, Eric Jeremy Edgar Dier, Fabian Delph (106.Ross Barkley), Bamidele Jermaine Alli, Jesse Ellis Lingard (106.Jadon Malik Sancho), Harry Edward Kane (Cap) (75.Callum Eddie Graham Wilson), Raheem Shaquille Sterling. Trainer: Gareth Southgate.
Penalties: Jacob Harry Maguire, Ross Barkley, Jadon Malik Sancho, Raheem Shaquille Sterling, Jordan Lee Pickford, Eric Jeremy Edgar Dier.

NATIONAL TEAM PLAYERS
(16.07.2018 – 15.07.2019)

Name	DOB	Caps	Goals	2018/2019:	*Club*
Goalkeepers					
Jack BUTLAND	10.03.1993	**9**	**0**	2018/2019:	*Stoke City FC*
Alex Simon McCARTHY	03.12.1989	**1**	**0**	2018:	*Southampton FC*
Jordan Lee PICKFORD	07.03.1994	**19**	**0**	2018/2019:	*Everton FC Liverpool*
Defenders					
Trent John ALEXANDER-ARNOLD	07.10.1998	**6**	**1**	2018/2019:	*Liverpool FC*
Benjamin James CHILWELL	21.12.1996	**7**	**0**	2018/2019:	*Leicester City FC*
Lewis Carl DUNK	21.11.1991	**1**	**0**	2018:	*Brighton & Hove Albion FC*
Joseph Dave GOMEZ	23.05.1997	**7**	**0**	2018/2019:	*Liverpool FC*
Michael Vincent KEANE	11.01.1993	**7**	**1**	2018/2019:	*Everton FC Liverpool*
Jacob Harry MAGUIRE	05.03.1993	**20**	**1**	2018/2019:	*Leicester City FC*
Daniel Lee ROSE	02.07.1990	**27**	**0**	2018/2019:	*Tottenham Hotspur FC London*
Luke Paul Hoare SHAW	12.07.1995	**8**	**0**	2018:	*Manchester United FC*
John STONES	28.05.1994	**38**	**2**	2018/2019:	*Manchester City FC*
James Alan TARKOWSKI	19.11.1992	**2**	**0**	2018:	*Burnley FC*
Kieran John TRIPPIER	19.09.1990	**16**	**1**	2018:	*Tottenham Hotspur FC London*
Kyle Andrew WALKER	28.05.1990	**48**	**0**	2018/2019:	*Manchester City FC*
Midfielders					
Bamidele Jermaine "Dele" ALLI	11.04.1996	**37**	**3**	2018/2019:	*Tottenham Hotspur FC London*
Ross BARKLEY	05.12.1993	**29**	**4**	2018/2019:	*Chelsea FC London*
Nathaniel Nyakie CHALOBAH	12.12.1994	**1**	**0**	2018:	*Watford FC*
Fabian DELPH	21.11.1989	**20**	**0**	2018/2019:	*Manchester City FC*
Eric Jeremy Edgar DIER	15.01.1994	**40**	**3**	2018/2019:	*Tottenham Hotspur FC London*
Jordan Brian HENDERSON	17.06.1990	**51**	**0**	2018/2019:	*Liverpool FC*
Jesse Ellis LINGARD	15.12.1992	**24**	**4**	2018/2019:	*Manchester United FC*
Ruben Ira LOFTUS-CHEEK	23.01.1996	**10**	**0**	2018:	*Chelsea FC London*
Declan RICE	14.01.1999	**3**	**0**	2019:	*West Ham United FC London*
James Michael Edward WARD-PROWSE	01.11.1994	**2**	**0**	2019:	*Southampton FC*
Harry Billy WINKS	02.02.1996	**3**	**0**	2018:	*Tottenham Hotspur FC London*
Forwards					
Callum James HUDSON-ODOI	07.11.2000	**2**	**0**	2019:	*Chelsea FC London*
Harry Edward KANE	28.07.1993	**39**	**22**	2018/2019:	*Tottenham Hotspur FC London*
Marcus RASHFORD	31.10.1997	**32**	**7**	2018/2019:	*Manchester United FC*
Wayne Mark ROONEY	24.10.1985	**120**	**53**	2018:	*Washington DC United (USA)*
Jadon Malik SANCHO	25.03.2000	**6**	**0**	2018/2019:	*BV Borussia 09 Dortmund (GER)*
Raheem Shaquille STERLING	08.12.1994	**51**	**8**	2018/2019:	*Manchester City FC*
Daniel Nii Tackie Mensah WELBECK	26.11.1990	**42**	**16**	2018:	*Arsenal FC London*
Callum Eddie Graham WILSON	27.02.1992	**3**	**1**	2018/2019:	*AFC Bournemouth*

National team coach

Gareth SOUTHGATE [from 30.11.2016]	03.09.1970	35 M; 19 W; 9 D; 7 L; 60-28

ESTONIA

The Country:

Eesti Vabariik (Republic of Estonia)
Capital: Tallinn
Surface: 45,339 km²
Inhabitants: 1,323,824 [2019]
Time: UTC+2

The FA:

Eesti Jalgpalli Liit
A. Le Coq Arena, Asula 4c, 11312 Tallinn
Tel: +372 627 9960
Foundation date: 14.12.1921
Member of FIFA since: 1923
Member of UEFA since: 1992
Website: www.jalgpall.ee

NATIONAL TEAM RECORDS

First international match:	20.10.1920, Helsinki:	Finland – Estonia 6-0
Most international caps:	Martin Reim	- 157 caps (1991-2009)
Most international goals:	Andres Oper	- 38 goals / 134 caps (1995-2014)

UEFA EUROPEAN CHAMPIONSHIP	
1960	-
1964	-
1968	-
1972	-
1976	-
1980	-
1984	-
1988	-
1992	-
1996	Qualifiers
2000	Qualifiers
2004	Qualifiers
2008	Qualifiers
2012	Qualifiers
2016	Qualifiers

FIFA WORLD CUP	
1930	-
1934	Qualifiers
1938	Qualifiers
1950	-
1954	-
1958	-
1962	-
1966	-
1970	-
1974	-
1978	-
1982	-
1986	-
1990	-
1994	Qualifiers
1998	Qualifiers
2002	Qualifiers
2006	Qualifiers
2010	Qualifiers
2014	Qualifiers
2018	Qualifiers

UEFA NATIONS LEAGUE
2018/2019 – League C

OLYMPIC FOOTBALL TOURNAMENTS 1908-2016							
1908	-	**1948**	-	**1972**	-	**1996**	Qualifiers
1912	-	**1952**	-	**1976**	-	**2000**	Qualifiers
1920	-	**1956**	-	**1980**	-	**2004**	Qualifiers
1924	-	**1960**	-	**1984**	-	**2008**	Qualifiers
1928	-	**1964**	-	**1988**	-	**2012**	Qualifiers
1936	-	**1968**	-	**1992**	-	**2016**	Qualifiers

FIFA CONFEDERATIONS CUP 1992-2017
None

ESTONIAN CLUB HONOURS IN EUROPEAN CLUB COMPETITIONS:

European Champion Clubs' Cup (1956-1992) / UEFA Champions League (1993-2019)
None
Fairs Cup (1858-1971) / UEFA Cup (1972-2009) / UEFA Europa League (2010-2019)
None
UEFA Super Cup (1972-2019)
None
European Cup Winners' Cup 1961-1999*
None

**defunct competition*

NATIONAL COMPETITIONS
TABLE OF HONOURS

ESTONIAN SSR (SOVIET ERA) CHAMPIONS

1945	Dünamo Tallinn
1946	BL Tallinn
1947	Dünamo Tallinn
1948	Balti Laevastik Tallinn
1949	Dünamo Tallinn
1950	Dünamo Tallinn
1951	Balti Laevastik Tallinn
1952	Balti Laevastik Tallinn
1953	Dünamo Tallinn
1954	Dünamo Tallinn
1955	Kalev Tallinn
1956	Balti Laevastik Tallinn
1957	Kalev Ülemiste
1958	Kalev Ülemiste
1959	Kalev Ülemiste
1960	Balti Laevastik Tallinn

1961	Kalev Kopli
1962	Kalev Ülemiste
1963	Tempo Tallinn
1964	Norma Tallinn
1965	Balti Laevastik Tallinn
1966	Balti Laevastik Tallinn
1967	Norma Tallinn
1968	Balti Laevastik Tallinn
1969	Dvigatel Tallinn
1970	Norma Tallinn
1971	Tempo Tallinn
1972	Balti Laevastik Tallinn
1973	Kreenholm Narva
1974	Baltika Narva
1975	Baltika Narva
1976	Dvigatel Tallinn

1977	Baltika Narva
1978	Dünamo Tallinn
1979	Norma Tallinn
1980	Dünamo Tallinn
1981	Dünamo Tallinn
1982	Tempo Tallinn
1983	Dünamo Tallinn
1984	Estonia Jõhvi
1985	Kalakombinaat/MEK Pärnu
1986	Zvezda Tallinn
1987	Tempo Tallinn
1988	Norma Tallinn
1989	Zvezda Tallinn
1990	Tallinna VMK
1991	Tallinna VMK

	CHAMPIONS	CUP WINNERS	BEST GOALSCORERS	
1921	Sport Tallinn	-	-	
1922	Sport Tallinn	-	-	
1923	Kalev Tallinn	-	-	
1924	Sport Tallinn	-	-	
1925	Sport Tallinn	-	-	
1926	Jalgpalliklubi Tallinn	-	-	
1927	Sport Tallinn	-	-	
1928	Jalgpalliklubi Tallinn	-	-	
1929	Sport Tallinn	-	-	
1930	Kalev Tallinn	-	-	
1931	Sport Tallinn	-	-	
1932	Sport Tallinn	-	-	
1933	Sport Tallinn	-	-	
1934	Tallinn	-	-	
1935	Tallinn	-	-	
1936	Tallinn	-	-	
1937/1938	Tallinn	SK Tallinna Sport	-	
1938/1939	Tallinn	Jalgpalliklubi Tallinn	-	
1939/1940	Olümpia Tartu	-	-	
1941	*Championship not finished*	-	-	
1942	PSR Tartu (*unofficial*)	-	-	
1943	Tallinn (*unofficial*)	-	-	
1944	*Championship not finished*	-	-	
1992	FC Norma Tallinn	-	Sergei Bragin (FC Norma Tallinn)	18
1992/1993	FC Norma Tallinn	FC Nikol Tallinn	Sergei Bragin (FC Norma Tallinn)	27
1993/1994	FC Flora Tallinn	FC Norma Tallinn	Maksim Gruznov (JK Narva Trans/Tevalte Tallinn)	21
1994/1995	FC Flora Tallinn	FC Flora Tallinn	Serhiy Morozov (UKR, FC Lantana Tallinn)	25
1995/1996	FC Lantana Tallinn	JK Tallinna Sadam	Lembit Rajala (FC Flora Tallinn)	16
1996/1997	FC Lantana Tallinn	JK Tallinna Sadam	Sergei Bragin (FC Lantana Tallinn)	18
1997/1998	FC Flora Tallinn	-	Konstantin Kolbassenko (JK Tallinna Sadam)	18
1998	FC Flora Tallinn	FC Flora Tallinn	Konstantin Kolbassenko (JK Tallinna Sadam)	13
1999	FC Levadia Maardu	FC Levadia Maardu	Toomas Krõm (FC Levadia Maardu)	19
2000	FC Levadia Maardu	FC Levadia Maardu	Egidijus Juška (LTU, FC Tallinna VMK) Toomas Krõm (FC Levadia Maardu)	24
2001	FC Flora Tallinn	JK Narva Trans	Maksim Gruznov (JK Narva Trans)	37
2002	FC Flora Tallinn	FC Levadia Maardu	Andrei Krõlov (FC Tallinna VMK)	37
2003	FC Flora Tallinn	FC Tallinna VMK	Tor Henning Hamre (NOR, FC Flora Tallinn)	39
2004	FC Levadia Maardu	FC Levadia Maardu	Vjatšeslav Zahovaiko (FC Flora Tallinn)	28
2005	FC Tallinna VMK	FC Levadia Tallinn	Tarmo Neemelo (FC Tallinna VMK)	41
2006	FC Levadia Tallinn	FC Tallinna VMK	Maksim Gruznov (JK Narva Trans)	31
2007	FC Levadia Tallinn	FC Levadia Tallinn	Russia Dmitri Lipartov (JK Narva Trans)	30
2008	FC Levadia Tallinn	FC Flora Tallinn	Ingemar Teever (Nõmme Kalju FC)	23
2009	FC Levadia Tallinn	FC Flora Tallinn	Vitali Gussev (FC Levadia Tallinn)	26
2010	FC Flora Tallinn	FC Levadia Tallinn	Sander Post (FC Flora Tallinn)	24
2011	FC Flora Tallinn	FC Flora Tallinn	Latvia Aleksandrs Čekulajevs (JK Narva Trans)	46
2012	Nõmme Kalju FC	FC Levadia Tallinn	Vladislav Ivanov (RUS, JK Sillamäe Kalev / JK Narva Trans)	23
2013	FC Levadia Tallinn	FC Flora Tallinn	Vladimir Voskoboinikov (Nõmme Kalju FC)	23
2014	FC Levadia Tallinn	FC Levadia Tallinn	Russia Yevgeni Kabaev (JK Sillamäe Kalev)	36
2015	FC Flora Tallinn	Nõmme Kalju FC	Ingemar Teever (FC Levadia Tallinn)	24

2016	FC Infonet Tallinn	FC Flora Tallinn	Russia Yevgeni Kabaev (JK Sillamäe Kalev)	25
2017	FC Flora Tallinn	FC Infonet Tallinn	Albert Prosa (FC Infonet Tallinn) Rauno Sappinen (FC Flora Tallinn)	27
2018	Nõmme Kalju FC	FCI Levadia Tallinn	Ellinton Antonio Costa Morais "Liliu" (BRA, Nõmme Kalju FC)	31

NATIONAL CHAMPIONSHIP
Meistriliiga 2018
(03.03.2018 – 10.11.2018)

Results

Round 1 [03-04.03.2018]
FC Kuressaare - Narva Trans 0-5(0-2)
FC Flora - Viljandi JK 1-0(1-0)
FCI Levadia - Paide Linnameeskond 1-1(1-0)
JK Tallinna - JK Tammeka 0-1(0-1)
JK Nõmme - Pärnu JK Vaprus 7-0(3-0)

Round 2 [09-11.03.2018]
FC Flora - Paide Linnameeskond 6-0(4-0)
Pärnu JK Vaprus - JK Tammeka 0-1(0-1)
Viljandi JK - JK Tallinna 1-0(1-0)
Narva Trans - JK Nõmme 2-2(1-0)
FCI Levadia - FC Kuressaare 4-0(3-0)

Round 3 [13-14.03.2018]
Paide Linnameeskond - Pärnu JK 2-2(0-0)
JK Tallinna - Narva Trans 1-2(1-1)
JK Tammeka - FCI Levadia 0-3(0-0)
FC Kuressaare - Viljandi JK 3-1(2-1)
JK Nõmme - FC Flora 2-0(1-0)

Round 4 [16-18.03.2018]
Narva Trans - Paide Linnameeskond 1-0(1-0)
JK Tallinna - FC Kuressaare 5-0(1-0)
FC Flora - Pärnu JK Vaprus 5-0(2-0)
Viljandi JK - FCI Levadia 0-7(0-1)
JK Nõmme - JK Tammeka 1-0(0-0)

Round 5 [30.03.-01.04.2018]
FC Kuressaare - JK Tammeka 0-4(0-3)
Paide Linnameeskond - JK Nõmme 1-4(0-1)
Pärnu JK Vaprus - Viljandi JK 1-1(1-0)
FCI Levadia - Narva Trans 5-0(2-0)
FC Flora - JK Tallinna 1-0(1-0)

Round 6 [03-04.04.2018]
JK Tammeka - Paide Linnameeskond 5-2(2-1)
Narva Trans - Viljandi JK 2-0(1-0)
FC Kuressaare - FC Flora 0-7(0-5)
JK Tallinna - Pärnu JK Vaprus 4-2(2-0)
FCI Levadia - JK Nõmme 2-2(0-1)

Round 7 [07-08.04.2018]
Pärnu JK Vaprus - FCI Levadia 0-5(0-2)
Paide Linnameesk. - FC Kuressaare 3-1(0-0)
FC Flora - Narva Trans 0-0
Viljandi JK - JK Tammeka 0-2(0-1)
JK Nõmme - JK Tallinna 3-0(2-0)

Round 8 [13-15.04.2018]
JK Tallinna - Paide Linnameeskond 2-3(0-0)
JK Tammeka - Narva Trans 1-1(0-1)
Viljandi JK - JK Nõmme 0-6(0-3)
FCI Levadia - FC Flora 2-1(1-0)
Pärnu JK Vaprus - FC Kuressaare 1-1(1-0)

Round 9 [20-22.04.2018]
JK Tammeka - Pärnu JK Vaprus 4-2(1-0)
Viljandi JK - FC Flora 0-6(0-0)
FC Kuressaare - JK Nõmme 0-3(0-1)
Narva Trans - JK Tallinna 2-2(2-1)
Paide Linnameeskond - FCI Levadia 1-3(0-3)

Round 10 [27-29.04.2018]
JK Nõmme - Narva Trans 5-2(2-1)
Paide Linnameeskond - FC Flora 0-2(0-1)
FC Kuressaare - JK Tallinna 1-0(1-0)
FCI Levadia - JK Tammeka 3-1(2-1)
Viljandi JK - Pärnu JK Vaprus 2-1(1-0)

Round 11 [01-02.05.2018]
JK Tammeka - FC Kuressaare 1-2(0-2)
Narva Trans - FCI Levadia 1-1(0-0)
Pärnu JK Vaprus - Paide Linnameesk.1-1(0-0)
JK Tallinna - Viljandi JK 1-2(0-0)
FC Flora - JK Nõmme 3-3(0-1)

Round 12 [04-06.05.2018]
Narva Trans - FC Kuressaare 3-0(2-0)
JK Tallinna - FC Flora 1-3(1-1)
FCI Levadia - Viljandi JK 5-0(3-0)
Pärnu JK Vaprus - JK Nõmme 0-6(0-1)
Paide Linnameeskond - JK Tammeka 3-3(2-2)

Round 13 [11-13.05.2018]
FCI Levadia - JK Tallinna 3-0(1-0)
JK Tammeka - JK Nõmme 1-1(0-0)
Pärnu JK Vaprus - FC Flora 1-8(1-4)
Viljandi JK - Narva Trans 0-6(0-5)
FC Kuressaare - Paide Linnameesk. 1-4(1-2)

Round 14 [15-20.05.2018]
Narva Trans - JK Tammeka 4-1(1-0)
JK Nõmme - FCI Levadia 2-1(0-0)
FC Flora - FC Kuressaare 2-1(1-0)
Viljandi JK - Paide Linnameeskond 1-1(0-0)
Pärnu JK Vaprus - JK Tallinna 0-4(0-1)

Round 15 [22-23.05.2018]
Paide Linnameeskond - Narva Trans 0-2(0-1)
JK Tammeka - Viljandi JK 0-0
JK Tallinna - JK Nõmme 2-2(1-1)
FC Kuressaare - Pärnu JK Vaprus 1-3(1-2)
FC Flora - FCI Levadia 2-2(1-1)

Round 16 [26-27.05.2018]
FCI Levadia - Pärnu JK Vaprus 6-1(2-0)
Viljandi JK - FC Kuressaare 1-3(0-1)
Narva Trans - FC Flora 2-4(1-1)
JK Nõmme - Paide Linnameeskond 3-2(1-1)
JK Tallinna - JK Tammeka 2-1(0-1)

Round 17 [05-06.06.2018]
Paide Linnameeskond - Viljandi JK 4-0(0-0)
JK Tallinna - FCI Levadia 0-4(0-3)
JK Nõmme - FC Kuressaare 8-3(4-2)
Narva Trans - Pärnu JK Vaprus 6-0(2-0)
FC Flora - JK Tammeka 3-1(1-0)

Round 18 [12-13.06.2018]
JK Nõmme - Viljandi JK 8-2(4-1)
Pärnu JK Vaprus - Narva Trans 0-4(0-2)
FC Kuressaare - FCI Levadia 1-1(0-0)
Paide Linnameeskond - JK Tallinna 2-0(1-0)
JK Tammeka - FC Flora 0-3(0-3)

Round 19 [20-22.07.2018]
FC Flora - Viljandi JK 4-0(1-0)
JK Tallinna - FC Kuressaare 3-0(2-0)
FCI Levadia - Paide Linnameeskond 4-0(3-0)
Pärnu JK Vaprus - JK Tammeka 1-1(1-0)
Narva Trans - JK Nõmme 0-3(0-2)

Round 20 [27-29.07.2018]
Viljandi JK - JK Tallinna 2-2(1-2)
JK Nõmme - FCI Levadia 1-0(0-0)
JK Tammeka - Narva Trans 2-1(2-1)
Paide Linnameesk. - FC Kuressaare 2-1(0-1)
Pärnu JK Vaprus - FC Flora 0-6(0-3) [23.10.]

Round 21 [03-05.08.2018]
Viljandi JK - Pärnu JK Vaprus 1-1(0-1)
Narva Trans - Paide Linnameeskond 1-2(1-1)
JK Nõmme - JK Tallinna 1-1(0-1)
FC Kuressaare - FC Flora 0-4(0-0)
FCI Levadia - JK Tammeka 0-1(0-0)

Round 22 [10-12.08.2018]
Paide Linnameeskond - FC Flora 3-3(0-2)
JK Nõmme - FC Kuressaare 4-0(2-0)
FCI Levadia - Narva Trans 6-1(1-1)
JK Tammeka - Viljandi JK 1-0(1-0)
Pärnu JK Vaprus - JK Tallinna 2-4(0-1)

Round 23 [17-19.08.2018]
Narva Trans - Viljandi JK 4-1(2-0)
FC Kuressaare - JK Tammeka 1-3(0-3)
Paide Linnameeskond - JK Nõmme 0-3(0-2)
Pärnu JK Vaprus - FCI Levadia 0-4(0-0)
FC Flora - JK Tallinna 3-1(0-0)

Round 24 [24-25.08.2018]
FC Flora - JK Tammeka 5-0(2-0)
Viljandi JK - Paide Linnameeskond 0-3(0-2)
JK Nõmme - Pärnu JK Vaprus 4-0(3-0)
FCI Levadia - FC Kuressaare 4-0(1-0)
JK Tallinna - Narva Trans 0-1(0-1)

Round 25 [28-29.08.2018]
Viljandi JK - JK Nõmme 2-5(0-2)
FC Kuressaare - Narva Trans 0-3(0-0)
Pärnu JK Vaprus - Paide Linnameesk.0-3(0-0)
JK Tammeka - JK Tallinna 1-0(0-0)
FC Flora - FCI Levadia 3-0(1-0)

Round 26 [31.08.-02.09.2018]
Narva Trans - Pärnu JK Vaprus 1-1(0-1)
FC Kuressaare - Viljandi JK 1-4(0-1)
Paide Linnameeskond - JK Tammeka 2-1(2-0)
FCI Levadia - JK Tallinna 3-2(3-1)
JK Nõmme - FC Flora 1-1(1-1)

Round 27 [14-16.09.2018]
JK Tammeka - JK Nõmme 0-1(0-0)
JK Tallinna - Paide Linnameeskond 1-2(0-0)
FC Flora - Narva Trans 2-2(1-0)
Pärnu JK Vaprus - FC Kuressaare 3-1(1-1)
Viljandi JK - FCI Levadia 0-4(0-1)

Round 28 [18-19.09.2018]
FC Kuressaare - JK Nõmme 2-4(2-1)
Narva Trans - JK Tammeka 2-1(1-1)
FCI Levadia - Pärnu JK Vaprus 4-0(2-0)
JK Tallinna - Viljandi JK 0-2(0-2)
FC Flora - Paide Linnameeskond 7-2(5-0)

Round 29 [22-23.09.2018]
Viljandi JK - JK Tammeka 3-2(1-1)
FC Kuressaare - FCI Levadia 0-5(0-3)
Paide Linnameeskond - Narva Trans 2-5(1-2)
FC Flora - Pärnu JK Vaprus 3-0(1-0)
JK Tallinna - JK Nõmme 0-2(0-1)

Round 30 [28-30.09.2018]
Narva Trans - FC Kuressaare 2-1(1-1)
Paide Linnameeskond - FCI Levadia 1-4(0-3)
JK Nõmme - Viljandi JK 4-0(2-0)
JK Tammeka - Pärnu JK Vaprus 5-0(3-0)
JK Tallinna - FC Flora 2-2(0-0)

Round 31 [02-03.10.2018]
FC Kuressaare - Paide Linnameesk. 1-3(0-2)
Pärnu JK Vaprus - Viljandi JK 0-3(0-0)
Narva Trans - JK Tallinna 3-2(1-0)
JK Tammeka - FC Flora 0-4(0-2)
FCI Levadia - JK Nõmme 0-0

Round 32 [06-07.10.2018]
Viljandi JK - FC Kuressaare 1-2(1-1)
Pärnu JK Vaprus - Narva Trans 0-1(0-0)
JK Tallinna - FCI Levadia 1-4(1-2)
JK Tammeka - Paide Linnameeskond 1-1(1-1)
FC Flora - JK Nõmme 2-2(2-2)

Round 33 [20-21.10.2018]
FC Kuressaare - JK Tallinna 3-3(1-2)
Paide Linnam. - Pärnu JK Vaprus 2-1(1-1)
Narva Trans - FC Flora 1-2(1-2)
FCI Levadia - Viljandi JK 2-1(0-0)
JK Nõmme - JK Tammeka 2-2(1-0)

Round 34 [26-28.10.2018]
JK Nõmme - Paide Linnameeskond 0-0
FC Flora - FC Kuressaare 4-0(1-0)
JK Tallinna - Pärnu JK Vaprus 5-0(3-0)
Viljandi JK - Narva Trans 4-1(0-0)
JK Tammeka - FCI Levadia 0-3(0-0)

Round 35 [02-04.11.2018]
Pärnu JK Vaprus - JK Nõmme 0-5(0-2)
Viljandi JK - FC Flora 1-3(0-2)
JK Tammeka - FC Kuressaare 6-1(2-1)
Narva Trans - FCI Levadia 1-2(0-0)
Paide Linnameeskond - JK Tallinna 2-2(2-2)

Round 36 [10.11.2018]
FCI Levadia - FC Flora 2-1(0-1)
JK Nõmme - Narva Trans 4-1(2-0)
JK Tammeka - JK Tallinna 2-1(0-0)
Paide Linnameeskond - Viljandi JK 4-1(3-0)
FC Kuressaare - Pärnu JK Vaprus 2-1(1-0)

Final Standings

1.	**Nõmme Kalju FC**	36	25	11	0	114	-	32	86
2.	FCI Levadia Tallinn	36	26	6	4	109	-	26	84
3.	FC Flora Tallinn	36	25	8	3	116	-	32	83
4.	JK Narva Trans	36	18	7	11	76	-	57	61
5.	Paide Linnameeskond	36	14	9	13	64	-	74	51
6.	JK Tammeka Tartu	36	14	7	15	56	-	58	49
7.	Viljandi JK Tulevik	36	8	5	23	37	-	100	29
8.	JK Tallinna Kalev	36	7	7	22	54	-	68	28
9.	FC Kuressaare *(Relegation Play-offs)*	36	6	3	27	34	-	115	21
10.	Pärnu JK Vaprus *(Relegated)*	36	2	7	27	25	-	123	13

Top goalscorers:

31 Ellinton Antonio Costa Morais "Liliu" (BRA) *Nõmme Kalju FC*

30 Zakaria Beglarishvili (GEO) *FC Flora Tallinn*

28 Roman Debelko (UKR) *FC Levadia Tallinn*

Relegation Play-offs [17-24.11.2018]

FC Elva - FC Kuressaare	0-1(0-0)	0-1(0-1)

FC Kuressaare remains at first level.

NATIONAL CUP
Eesti Karikas 2018

First Round [10-27.06.2017]

Viimsi JK II - Nõmme Kalju FC	0–13
JK Piraaja Tallinn - FC Maardu Aliens	1-2
Tallinna FC Soccernet - Kohtla-Nõmme	1-3
FC Jõgeva Wolves II - JK Õismäe Torm	3-2
Pirita JK Reliikvia - Rakvere JK Tarvas	1-5
FC Flora Tallinn U-21 - Rumori Calcio II	10-0
Anija JK - FC Puhkus Mehhikos	7-0
JK Väätsa Vald - SK Tääksi	0-1
Tallinna FC TransferWise - FC Tallinna Wolves	2-0
Raplamaa JK - Tartu JK Welco	0-1
FC Otepää - Tallinna JK Jalgpallihaigla	6-0
JK Kernu Kadakas - JK Raudteetöölised	7-2
Paide Linnameeskond - FC Hiiu United	27-0
Navi Vutiselts - Kuusalu JK Rada	2-2 aet; 2-4 pen
FC Kose - Raasiku FC Joker	1-10
FC Flora Tallinn U-19 - FC Vastseliina	5-0
Rakvere JK Tarvas II - Kohtla-Järve JK Järve	0-7
FC Tartu - Tallinna FC Eston Villa	3-1
Kadrina SK Moe - Põlva FC Lootos	4-1
FCP Pärnu - Türi Ganvix JK	1-4
NPM Silmet - Maarjamäe FC Igiliikur	2-0
Tartu Ülikool Fauna - Viimsi Lõvid	1-0
Saue JK Laagri - Rasmus Värki Jalgpallikool	10-2
Lihula JK - FC Elbato	7-1
Tartu JK Tammeka U-21 - Tallinna FC Olympic Olybet	6-1
Jõgeva SK Noorus-96 - SK Imavere	4-1 aet
FC Ararat Tallinn - Tallinna FC Zapoos	5-3 aet
Paide Linnameeskond III - Pärnu JK Poseidon II	12-1
FCI Tallinn - FCI Tallinn U-21	7-0
FC Levadia Tallinn - FC Nõmme United	3-0
JK Narva Trans - Maardu Linnameeskond	6-1
FC Jõgeva Wolves - FK Odratakkel	5-1
FC Järva-Jaani - JK 32.KK	18-2
FC Flora Tallinn - Tartu FC Helios	17-1

Byes:
Meistriliiga: JK Sillamäe Kalev, Tartu JK Tammeka, Pärnu JK Vaprus, Viljandi JK Tulevik
Esiliiga: FC Santos Tartu, JK Tallinna Kalev, FC Kuressaare, FC Elva
Esiliiga B: Viimsi JK
II Liiga: FCI Levadia Tallinn III, Tallinna JK Legion, Maardu United, Kohtla-Järve JK Järve II, Narva United FC
III Liiga: Põhja-Tallinna JK Volta, JK Tallinna Kalev III, Rumori Calcio Tallinn, Suure-Jaani United, Koeru JK, Ambla Vallameeskond, JK Loo, Pärnu JK Poseidon, Tallinna FC Castovanni Eagles, FC Zenit Tallinn, Läänemaa JK, FC Lelle
IV Liiga: Tallinna Depoo, Kohila Püsivus, FC Warrior Valga
Rahvaliiga: JK Rapla Lokomotiiv

Second Round [16.07.-02.08.2017]			
FC Kuressaare - Kadrina SK Moe	12-0	FC Järva-Jaani - Põhja-Tallinna JK Volta	1-4
Kohtla-Järve JK Järve II - FC Flora Tallinn U-21	0-8	FCI Levadia Tallinn III - Tallinna JK Legion	3-0
JK Tallinna Kalev - Rakvere JK Tarvas	0-0; 5-6 pen	FC Zenit Tallinn - FC Otepää	5-2
FC Flora Tallinn U19 - Tartu JK Welco	0-1	FC Elva - Tallinna FC Ararat TTÜ	8-0
FC Maardu Aliens - SK Tääksi	6-1	Paide Linnameeskond - Jõgeva SK Noorus-96	7-3
Maardu United - Valga FC Warrior	10-0	JK Tallinna Kalev III - FC Tartu	1-5
FC Jõgeva Wolves II - Kohila Püsivus	0-3	Narva United FC - Pärnu JK Vaprus	2-1
Tallinna FC TransferWise - Tartu Ülikool Fauna	3-2 aet	Pärnu JK Poseidon - Raasiku FC Joker	2-0
FC Lelle - Kohtla-Nõmme	2-2 aet; 4-2 pen	FC Santos Tartu - Paide Linnameeskond III	0-3
Tallinna FC Castovanni Eagles - FCI Tallinn	0-4	Ambla Vallameeskond - Läänemaa JK	1-4
JK Kernu Kadakas - JK Rapla Lokomotiv	2-1	Koeru JK - Nõmme Kalju FC	0-1
Kuusalu JK Rada - JK Loo	2-1 aet	Rumori Calcio Tallinn - NPM Silmet	6-0
Viimsi JK - FC Jõgeva Wolves	6-1	JK Narva Trans - Suure-Jaani United	8-0
Türi Ganvix JK - Tallinna Depoo	12-1	Kohtla-Järve JK Järve - Saue JK Laagri	w/o
JK Sillamäe Kalev - FC Levadia Tallinn	1-2 aet	Viljandi JK Tulevik - Tartu JK Tammeka	1-0
Anija JK - Lihula JK	5-1	Tartu JK Tammeka U-21 - FC Flora Tallinn	0-7

Third Round [06-30.08.2017]			
FC Kuressaare - Kuusalu JK Rada	9-1	Rakvere JK Tarvas - Pärnu JK Poseidon	4-0
FC Levadia Tallinn - Paide Linnameeskond	3-1	Nõmme Kalju FC - FC Lelle	8-0
Maardu United - Tallinna FC TransferWise	3-3 aet; 4-3 pen	Läänemaa JK - Türi Ganvix JK	2-1
JK Narva Trans - FCI Levadia Tallinn III	9-2	Põhja-Tallinna JK Volta - FC Zenit Tallinn	5-1
FCI Tallinn - Anija JK	16-0	Paide Linnameeskond III - FC Tartu	11-0
Narva United FC - FC Flora Tallinn	0-8	Rumori Calcio Tallinn - JK Kernu Kadakas	3-2
Kohila Püsivus - Viljandi JK Tulevik	0-8	Kohtla-Järve JK Järve - Tartu JK Welco	5-0
Viimsi JK - FC Flora Tallinn U-21	0-2	FC Maardu Aliens - FC Elva	0-3

Fourth Round [19-27.09.2017]			
Läänemaa JK - FCI Tallinn	1-7	Nõmme Kalju FC - Paide Linnameeskond III	1-1 aet; 5-4 pen
FC Flora Tallinn - FC Elva	2-0	Põhja-Tallinna JK Volta - FC Flora Tallinn U-21	0-3
FCI Levadia Tallinn - Kohtla-Järve JK Järve	7-0	Rumori Calcio Tallinn - FC Kuressaare	0-6
Viljandi JK Tulevik - Maardu United	w/o	JK Narva Trans - Rakvere JK Tarvas	2-0 aet

Quarter-Finals [17-18.04.2018]			
Nõmme Kalju FC - FCI Levadia Tallinn	0-1	FC Kuressaare - FC Flora Tallinn	0-7
JK Narva Trans - FCI Tallinn	6-0	FC Flora Tallinn U-21 - Viljandi JK Tulevik	7-3

Semi-Finals [08-09.05.2018]			
JK Narva Trans - FCI Levadia Tallinn	0-5	FC Flora Tallinn U-21- FC Flora Tallinn	3-9

Final

19.05.2018; A. Le Coq Arena, Tallinn; Referee: Kristo Tohver; Attendance: 2,369

FCI Levadia Tallinn - FC Flora Tallinn **1-0(0-0)**

Levadia: Sergei Lepmets, Dmitri Kruglov, Maksim Podholjuzin, Igor Dudarev, Markus Jürgenson, Muamer Svraka, Yuriy Tkachuk, Evgeny Kharin, Aimé Marcelin Gando Biala (89.Kirill Nesterov), Nikita Andreev (81.Rasmus Peetson), Roman Debelko. Trainer: Aleksandar Rogić (Serbia).

Flora: Mait Toom, Gert Kams, Madis Vihmann, Jürgen Lorenz, Kevin Aloe, Aleksandr Dmitrijev, Mihkel Ainsalu, Joseph Saliste (79.Henri Järvelaid), Zakaria Beglarishvili (75.Markus Poom), Rauno Alliku, Frank Liivak (56.Erik Sorga). Trainer: Jürgen Henn.

Goals: 1-0 Roman Debelko (67).

Football Club Flora Tallinn

Founded: 10.03.1990
Stadium: A. Le Coq Arena, Tallinn (10,340)

Goalkeepers:	**DOB**	**M**	**(s)**	**G**
Magnus Karofeld	20.08.1996	10		
Mait Toom	07.05.1990	26		
Defenders:	**DOB**	**M**	**(s)**	**G**
Kevin Aloe	07.05.1995	28		1
Gert Kams	25.05.1985	34		3
Märten Kuusk	05.04.1996	13	(4)	1
Jürgen Lorenz	11.05.1993	8	(1)	
Anselmi Nurmela	22.11.1996	8	(3)	
Henrik Pürg	03.06.1996	17		3
Joseph Saliste	10.04.1995	14	(6)	4
Madis Vihmann	05.10.1995	35		8
Midfielders:	**DOB**	**M**	**(s)**	**G**
Mihkel Ainsalu	08.03.1996	20	(2)	2
Zakaria Beglarishvili (GEO)	30.04.1990	36		30
Aleksandr Dmitrijev	18.02.1982	22	(3)	
Maksim Gussev	20.07.1994	10	(11)	6
Henri Järvelaid	11.12.1998	2	(7)	3
Vladislavs Kreida	25.09.1999		(5)	
Martin Miller	25.09.1997	5		2
Markus Poom	27.02.1999	29	(7)	4
Herol Riiberg	14.04.1997	3	(6)	
Vlasiy Sinyavskiy	27.11.1996		(7)	1
German Šlein	28.03.1996	1	(1)	
Forwards:	**DOB**	**M**	**(s)**	**G**
Rauno Alliku	02.03.1990	25	(3)	9
Mark Anders Lepik	10.09.2000	12	(3)	10
Frank Liivak	07.07.1996	31	(3)	16
Mattias Männilaan	08.09.2001		(2)	1
Rauno Sappinen	23.01.1996	1	(1)	
Erik Sorga	08.07.1999	6	(21)	9
Trainer:	**DOB**	**M**		
Jürgen Henn	02.06.1987	18		
Arnoldus Dick Pijpers (NED)[01.07.2018]	21.04.1959	18		

Football Club Infonet Levadia Tallinn

Founded: 22.10.1998
Stadium: Staadion Kadriorg, Tallinn (5,000)

Goalkeepers:	**DOB**	**M**	**(s)**	**G**
Sergei Lepmets	05.04.1987	36		
Defenders:	**DOB**	**M**	**(s)**	**G**
Igor Dudarev (RUS)	12.08.1993	28	(5)	1
Markus Jürgenson	09.09.1987	33	(1)	2
Martin Käos	18.06.1998		(1)	
Dmitri Kruglov	24.05.1984	35		5
Marko Lipp	19.03.1999	3	(4)	1
Igor Morozov	27.05.1989	9	(2)	1
Roman Nesterovski	09.06.1989		(1)	
Maksim Podholjuzin	13.11.1992	33	(1)	3
Midfielders:	**DOB**	**M**	**(s)**	**G**
Timur Bulavkin	13.03.1998		(2)	
Pavel Dõmov	31.12.1993	1	(3)	
Aimé Marcelin Gando Biala (CMR)	27.02.1997	26	(8)	15
Evgeny Kharin (RUS)	11.06.1995	19		4
Cristofer Kuusma	16.06.1998		(1)	
Pavel Marin	14.06.1995	1	(5)	
Kirill Nesterov (RUS)	21.07.1989	15	(15)	6
Rasmus Peetson	03.05.1995	6	(21)	3
Muamer Svraka (BIH)	14.02.1988	33		13
Yuriy Tkachuk (UKR)	18.04.1995	31		2
Igor Zhurakhovskyi (UKR)	19.09.1994	5	(1)	1
Forwards:	**DOB**	**M**	**(s)**	**G**
Nikita Andreev (RUS)	22.09.1988	17	(3)	7
Roman Debelko (UKR)	08.08.1993	34	(2)	27
Cem Fələk (GER)	12.05.1996	7	(7)	4
Anton Krutogolov	05.04.2001		(3)	
Karl Rudolf Õigus	05.11.1998		(5)	
Mark Roosnupp	12.05.1997	24	(8)	10
Markus Vaherna	27.01.1999		(1)	
Trainer:	**DOB**	**M**		
Aleksandar Rogić (SRB)	03.08.1981			

Football Club Kuressaare

Founded: 14.03.1997
Stadium: Kuressaare linnastaadion, Kuressaare (1,000)

Goalkeepers:	**DOB**	**M**	**(s)**	**G**
Roland Kütt	22.04.1987	4		
Ingmar Paplavskis	17.05.1999	32		
Defenders:	**DOB**	**M**	**(s)**	**G**
Ranon Kriisa	28.01.1996	11		
Mairo Miil	15.02.2000	30	(1)	
Mario Pruul	10.09.1990	26		
Renno Soosaar	03.09.1998	5	(1)	
Elari Valmas	02.07.1988	28	(1)	2
Sander Viira	29.08.1989	29	(1)	
Reivo Vinter	02.02.1997	8	(9)	
Midfielders:	**DOB**	**M**	**(s)**	**G**
Sander Laht	26.09.1991	32		15
Amor Luup	18.02.1992	8	(8)	
Karl Maar	26.02.1993	12	(7)	1
Kristjan Moorats	24.11.2000		(1)	
Märten Opp	15.09.1999	21	(9)	
Karmo Paju	12.09.1999	17	(12)	3
Eerik Poopuu	23.06.1998	4	(10)	1
Margus Rajaver	16.07.1989	12	(7)	2
Oliver Rass	25.05.2000	24	(7)	1
Alari Saar	28.03.1996	9	(2)	
Rasmus Saar	02.03.2000	21	(6)	2
Sander Seeman	12.09.1992	32		1
Georg Ander Sild	10.09.2001		(3)	
Danel Tiirats	11.02.1997		(1)	
Miikael Tuus	14.10.1998		(1)	
Forwards:	**DOB**	**M**	**(s)**	**G**
Aivar Jäns	13.03.2001		(1)	
Kristo Kallas	02.01.1995	1	(2)	
Tõnis Koppel	12.12.1982	1	(4)	1
Mario Stern	26.07.1997	7	(6)	3
Maarek Suursaar	16.07.1997	22	(7)	1
Trainer:	**DOB**	**M**		
Jan Važinski	10.08.1964	36		

Jalgpalliklubi Narva Trans

Founded: 1979
Stadium: Narva Kreenholm staadion, Narva (1,065)

Goalkeepers:	**DOB**	**M**	**(s)**	**G**
Betim Halimi (KVX)	28.02.1996	6	(1)	
Artur Kotenko	20.08.1981	30		
Defenders:	**DOB**	**M**	**(s)**	**G**
Artjom Davõdov	04.03.1999		(1)	
Sergei Kondrattsev	23.09.2001		(5)	
Dante Roger Leverock (BER)	11.04.1997	34		8
Matheus Junior de Nascimento Troche (BRA)	17.06.1996	1		
Igor Ovsjannikov	23.02.1992	20		1
Nikita Savenkov	28.07.1998	10	(8)	1
Tanel Tamberg	06.06.1992	24	(1)	
Maksim Tšerezov	26.03.2001	15	(7)	
Midfielders:	**DOB**	**M**	**(s)**	**G**
Arbër Basha (ALB)	13.01.1998	11		
Elysée Irié Bi Séhi (CIV)	13.09.1989	20	(5)	1
Svjatoslav Jakovlev	24.04.1996	7	(1)	1
Arseni Kovaltšuk	07.01.2001	7	(9)	2
Vadim Mihailov	06.06.1998	14	(11)	3
Denis Polyakov (RUS)	21.02.1992	30		3
Dmitri Proshin (RUS)	06.01.1984	29		7
Artjom Škinjov	30.01.1996	16	(1)	1
Aleksandr Zakarlyuka (RUS)	24.06.1995	33	(1)	3
Forwards:	**DOB**	**M**	**(s)**	**G**
Dmitriy Barkov (RUS)	19.06.1992	29		17
Eduard Golovljov	25.01.1997	21	(8)	11
Roman Grigorevski (RUS)	11.06.1997	4	(12)	2
Nikita Mihhailov	20.06.2002	2	(7)	
Viktor Plotnikov	14.07.1989	33		14
Aleksei Stepanov	13.02.2002		(3)	
Trainer:	**DOB**	**M**		
Adyam Kuzyaev (RUS)	06.01.1965	22		
Oleg Kurotskin [13.08.2018]	11.05.1971	-		
Cenk Özcan (TUR) [17.08.2018]	25.04.1974	14		

Nõmme Kalju Football Club

Founded: 1923 (Re-established in 1997)
Stadium: Hiiu staadion, Tallinn (650)

Goalkeepers:	**DOB**	**M**	**(s)**	**G**
Pavel Londak	14.05.1980	21		
Henri Perk	14.10.1999		(1)	
Vitali Teleš	17.10.1983	15	(1)	
Defenders:	**DOB**	**M**	**(s)**	**G**
Vladimir Avilov	10.03.1995	22	(6)	4
Trevor Elhi	11.04.1993	35		4
Martin Mägi	18.06.1996	1	(1)	
Andriy Markovych (UKR)	25.06.1995	32		1
Henrik Pürg	03.06.1996	10		1
Maximiliano Uggè (ITA)	24.09.1991	33		8
William Gustavo Constancio (BRA)	09.01.1992	11	(1)	
Midfielders:	**DOB**	**M**	**(s)**	**G**
Marko Brtan (CRO)	07.04.1991	21	(2)	10
Nikolai Mašitšev (RUS)	05.12.1988	8	(18)	1
Réginald Mbu-Alidor (FRA)	19.05.1993	32	(1)	1
Kaspar Paur	16.02.1995	11	(2)	1
Vlasiy Sinyavskiy	27.11.1996	5	(4)	2
Deniss Tjapkin	30.01.1991	15	(2)	2
Sergei Tumasyan (RUS)	31.01.1990	6		3
Forwards:	**DOB**	**M**	**(s)**	**G**
Jevgeni Demidov	11.02.2000		(3)	
Rimo Hunt	05.11.1985	21	(8)	14
Robert Kirss	03.09.1994	25	(10)	7
Peeter Klein	28.01.1997		(6)	
Ellinton Antonio Costa Morais „Liliu" (BRA)	30.03.1990	30		31
Igor Subbotin	26.06.1990	33	(3)	10
Alex Tamm	24.07.2001	1	(10)	1
Aleksandr Volkov	11.10.1994	8	(18)	10
Trainer:	**DOB**	**M**		
Sergey Frantsev (RUS)	17.03.1959	36		

Paide Linnameeskond

Founded: 2004
Stadium: Paide linnastaadion, Paide (268)

Goalkeepers:	**DOB**	**M**	**(s)**	**G**
Andrea Liotti (ITA)	20.02.1997	20		
Rene Merilo	23.08.2001	8		
Kaarel Rumberg	02.05.2000	2		
Kristjan Tamme	21.09.1995	6		
Defenders:	**DOB**	**M**	**(s)**	**G**
Sören Kaldma	03.07.1996	23	(2)	
Martin Kase	02.09.1993	25	(7)	3
Johannes Kukebal	19.07.1993	2		
Michael Lilander	10.06.1997	22	(1)	2
Tanel Neubauer	22.02.2000	3	(3)	1
Moussa Ouattara (CIV)	02.07.1988	10	(3)	
Märten Pajunurm	29.04.1993	11	(2)	1
Kristjan Pelt	12.07.2001	15		
Oleksandr Sukharov (UKR)	18.02.1994	12		1
Edgar Tur	28.12.1996	28	(3)	1
Midfielders:	**DOB**	**M**	**(s)**	**G**
Pavel Dõmov	31.12.1993	10	(2)	
Andre Frolov	18.04.1988	33	(2)	8
Joel Kokla	20.06.2001		(6)	
Sander Sinilaid	07.10.1990	31	(2)	3
Magnar Vainumäe	19.04.1998	12	(2)	2
Henri Välja	04.11.2001	6	(9)	4
Yann Michael Yao (CIV)	20.06.1997	28	(4)	4
Forwards:	**DOB**	**M**	**(s)**	**G**
Dejan Djermanovič (SVN)	17.06.1988	6	(3)	4
Henri Hanson	18.04.1995	14	(11)	4
Samson Iyede Onomigho (NGA)	28.01.1998	14	(3)	8
Tarmo Neemelo	10.02.1982	11	(19)	6
Kristofer Piht	24.04.2001	15	(9)	5
Randin Rande	28.07.1997	2	(7)	
Ander Ott Valge	20.10.1998	27	(3)	4
Trainer:	**DOB**	**M**		
Vjatšeslav Zahovaiko	29.12.1981	36		

Jalgpalliklubi Tallinna Kalev Tallinn

Founded: 1909 (*as Meteor Tallinn*); Re-established on 01.09.2002
Stadium: Kalev Keskstaadion, Tallinn (11,500)

Goalkeepers:	**DOB**	**M**	**(s)**	**G**
Daniil Koroljov	11.12.1999	17		
Sten-Marten Vahi	28.03.1997	1		
Karl Vallner	28.02.1998	18		
Defenders:	**DOB**	**M**	**(s)**	**G**
Sandro Sene Sakho Aníbal Embaló (POR)	01.05.1996	12	(2)	
Artjom Artjunin	24.01.1990	15	(1)	1
Hans-Kristjan Hansberg	06.05.1996	4	(2)	
Freddie Heinmaa	22.11.1999		(3)	
Steve Kingue (CMR)	23.01.2000	13	(1)	3
Kaspar Laur	08.04.2000	24	(1)	2
Marco Lukka	04.12.1996	10	(2)	
Denis Maksimenko	12.08.1998		(2)	
Karl Mööl	04.03.1992	18		2
Andreas Raudsepp	13.12.1993	31		
Daniil Sheviakov (RUS)	29.07.1999	6	(6)	
Hans Tammerik	30.09.1995	7	(2)	1
Midfielders:	**DOB**	**M**	**(s)**	**G**
Abdoul Karim Conte (GUI)	25.08.1999	17		
Alger Džumadil	29.07.1996	25	(4)	1
Mikk Kruusalu	06.12.2000		(3)	
Takuya Matsunaga (JPN)	10.06.1990	35		4
Innar Paal	30.06.1994		(2)	
Reinhard Reimaa	12.11.1998	10	(5)	1
Alex Sander Sepp	08.04.1995		(1)	
Gregor Wahl	08.11.1995	1	(7)	1
Hidetoshi Wakui (JPN)	12.02.1983	31		9
Ioan Yakovlev (RUS)	19.01.1998	30	(2)	3
Forwards:	**DOB**	**M**	**(s)**	**G**
Hannes Anier	16.01.1993	10	(4)	5
Brandon Bachmann	28.02.2000		(3)	
Andre Järva	21.11.1996	18	(12)	7
Kevin Rääbis	02.01.1994	14	(9)	8
Juhan Jograf Siim	22.04.1996		(2)	
Roman Sobtšenko	25.01.1994	29	(3)	4
Trainer:	**DOB**	**M**		
Argo Arbeiter	05.12.1973	36		

Jalgpallikool Tammeka Tartu

Founded: 13.06.1989
Stadium: Tartu Tamme staadion, Tartu (1,500)

Goalkeepers:	**DOB**	**M**	**(s)**	**G**
Karl Pechter	02.03.1996	35		
Karl Vaabel	25.08.1997	1		
Defenders:	**DOB**	**M**	**(s)**	**G**
Kevin Anderson	10.11.1993	26	(3)	2
Silver Grauberg	26.11.1996	32	(1)	
Kennet Jädal	08.05.1990		(1)	
Mikk Laas	30.09.1990	6	(8)	
Daaniel Maanas	05.01.2000	1	(5)	
Akim Sairinen (FIN)	22.05.1994	36		4
Mikhail Slashchyov (RUS)	21.06.1997	35		2
Midfielders:	**DOB**	**M**	**(s)**	**G**
Henri Järvelaid	11.12.1998	17		2
Reio Laabus	14.03.1990	34		1
Temari Nuuma	09.04.1996		(5)	
Andre Paju	05.01.1995	29	(4)	3
Tauno Tekko	14.12.1994	31	(1)	6
Artur Uljanov	25.03.1999		(9)	
Forwards:	**DOB**	**M**	**(s)**	**G**
Mikhel Järviste	28.05.2000	13	(14)	
Martin Jõgi	05.01.1995	9	(11)	1
Sander Kapper	08.12.1994	29	(4)	3
Tristan Koskor	28.11.1995	36		21
Rait Läll	31.12.1999		(3)	
Kaspar Paur	16.02.1995	16	(1)	4
Mart Preiman	01.05.1997	3	(15)	3
Sten Reinkort	29.04.1998	6	(14)	3
Rasmus Tauts	07.01.1997	1	(3)	
Patrik Genro Veelma	15.04.2002		(1)	
Trainer:	**DOB**	**M**		
Kaido Koppel	09.05.1988	36		

Viljandi Jalgpalliklubi Tulevik

Founded: 1912
Stadium: Viljandi linnastaadion, Viljandi (1,084)

Goalkeepers:	**DOB**	**M**	**(s)**	**G**
Ergo Hünerson	24.11.1999		(1)	
Andreas Kallaste	29.06.2000	13		
Karl-Romet Nõmm	04.01.1998	23		
Defenders:	**DOB**	**M**	**(s)**	**G**
Martin Allik	13.08.1994	19		1
Gerdo Juhkam	19.06.1994	24	(1)	1
Janar Õunap	09.09.1994	26		1
Sander Post	10.09.1984	15		3
Gustav-Hendrik Seeder	29.11.2000	23	(6)	1
Gunnar-Laur Sindi	15.05.2000	12	(2)	
Midfielders:	**DOB**	**M**	**(s)**	**G**
Arlet Hunt	23.04.2000	5	(10)	
Indrek Ilves	27.04.1990	33		
Tanel Lang	15.08.1995	15		
Illimar Loigo	14.08.1998	26	(8)	1
Kristjan Kask	05.07.1999	18		4
Eero Maling	06.05.1999		(1)	
Tauno Mõttus	27.06.1995	19	(1)	
Karl Rudolf Org	15.05.2001		(1)	
Andre Raik	30.05.2001		(2)	
Herol Riiberg	14.04.1997	11	(3)	4
Raido Roman	22.11.1987		(1)	
Alex Roosalu	04.05.1999	27	(2)	
Yosuke Saito (JPN)	07.04.1988	8	(1)	2
Robert Taar	24.03.1994	2	(1)	
Herbert Velleste	17.01.2001		(1)	
Forwards:	**DOB**	**M**	**(s)**	**G**
Lauri Elur	20.02.1999	8	(18)	4
Kristen Kähr	05.10.1989	25	(2)	7
Rainer Peips	11.08.1990	27	(5)	8
Rainer Rüütel	22.10.1998		(8)	
Roger Teor	11.05.1997	17	(16)	
Trainer:	**DOB**	**M**		
Marko Kristal	02.06.1973	8		
Sander Post [19.04.2018]	10.09.1984	28		

Pärnu Jalgpalliklubi Vaprus

Founded: 1922
Stadium: Pärnu Rannastaadion, Pärnu (1,501)

Goalkeepers:	**DOB**	**M**	**(s)**	**G**
Richard Aland	15.03.1994	36		
Defenders:	**DOB**	**M**	**(s)**	**G**
Georg Grahv	17.10.2001		(5)	
Uku Kõrre	19.04.2000	20	(2)	
Dmitri Kutsarev	13.01.1998	2	(5)	
Oskar Lepik	15.11.1999	16	(1)	1
Karl Palatu	05.12.1982	3		
Joosep Sarapuu	30.07.1994	21	(1)	
Kaspar Tilga	24.10.1998	10	(2)	
Magnus Villota	11.02.1998	30		
Midfielders:	**DOB**	**M**	**(s)**	**G**
Robyn Hallmere	10.06.1999	2	(10)	1
Rasmus Ilves	04.03.1999	33	(1)	
Juhan Jakobson	28.02.1993	14		
Gegi Kekua (GEO)	23.12.1995	17	(1)	3
Robin Limberg	10.10.2001	2	(6)	
Reno Mark	16.11.2000	28	(3)	1
Rocco Mõtt	24.04.2001	12	(9)	2
Rauno Tutk	10.04.1988	14	(6)	
Tõnis Vihmoja	15.01.1993	31	(2)	8
Forwards:	**DOB**	**M**	**(s)**	**G**
Kristofer Kaasik	21.10.1996	31	(1)	1
Kristian Lenk	20.05.1997		(5)	
David Moli (ENG)	08.01.1995	1		
Jaak-Peeter Oja	03.10.1995		(5)	
Rene Prans	26.11.1996	1	(4)	
Kristen Saarts	28.10.1994	1	(8)	1
Artur Šalda	11.08.2000		(2)	
Karl Sõerde	06.04.1996	15	(10)	2
Ronaldo Tiismaa	02.05.2001	24	(5)	
Enrico Veensalu	19.08.1999	32	(2)	
Trainer:	**DOB**	**M**		
Indrek Zelinski	13.11.1974	36		

SECOND LEVEL
Esiliiga 2018

1.	Maardu Linnameeskond (*Promoted*)	36	29	1	6	126	-	41	88
2.	FC Flora U-21 Tallinn*	36	21	8	7	115	-	31	71
3.	FC Levadia U-21 Tallinn*	36	18	7	11	67	-	56	61
4.	FC Elva (*Promoted*)	36	15	10	11	51	-	66	55
5.	Rakvere JK Tarvas	36	14	10	12	62	-	60	52
6.	Tartu Jalgpalliklubi Welco	36	12	6	18	44	-	78	42
7.	FC Santos Tartu** (*Relegated*)	36	11	8	17	47	-	68	41
8.	JK Tallinna Kalev U-21	36	10	9	17	37	-	52	39
9.	Keila JK (*Relegation Play-offs*)	36	10	5	21	41	-	88	35
10.	Nõmme Kalju FC U-21 (*Relegated*)	36	5	6	25	37	-	89	21

*as reserve team, not eligible for promotion.
** FC Santos Tartu took a voluntary relegation for the purpose of reorganization!

Relegation Play-offs (2nd/3rd Level) [17-24.11.2018]

Kothla-Järve JK - Keila JK	3-1(0-0)	0-1(0-0)

Kothla-Järve JK promoted for the 2019 Esiliiga.

NATIONAL TEAM

INTERNATIONAL MATCHES
(16.07.2018 – 15.07.2019)

08.09.2018	Tallinn	Estonia - Greece	0-1(0-1)	(UNL)
11.09.2018	Turku	Finland - Estonia	1-0(1-0)	(UNL)
12.10.2018	Tallinn	Estonia - Finland	0-1(0-0)	(UNL)
15.10.2018	Tallinn	Estonia - Hungary	3-3(1-1)	(UNL)
15.11.2018	Budapest	Hungary - Estonia	2-0(1-0)	(UNL)
18.11.2018	Athína	Greece - Estonia	0-1(0-1)	(UNL)
11.01.2019	Doha	Finland - Estonia	1-2(0-1)	(F)
15.01.2019	Doha	Iceland - Estonia	0-0	(F)
21.03.2019	Belfast	Northern Ireland - Estonia	2-0(0-0)	(ECQ)
26.03.2019	Gibraltar	Gibraltar - Estonia	0-1(0-0)	(F)
08.06.2019	Tallinn	Estonia - Northern Ireland	1-2(1-0)	(ECQ)
11.06.2019	Mainz	Germany - Estonia	8-0(5-0)	(ECQ)

08.09.2018 ESTONIA - GREECE 0-1(0-1) UEFA Nations League C, Group 2
A. Le Coq Arena, Tallinn; Referee: Serdar Gözübüyük (Netherlands); Attendance: 5,567
EST: Mihkel Aksalu, Gert Kams, Nikita Baranov, Karol Mets, Artur Pikk, Madis Vihmann, Artjom Dmitrijev, Konstantin Vassiljev (Cap), Siim Luts (85.Sander Puri), Henri Anier (63.Sergei Zenjov), Henrik Ojamaa (80.Joonas Tamm). Trainer: Martin Reim.

11.09.2018 FINLAND - ESTONIA 1-0(1-0) UEFA Nations League C, Group 2
Veritas Stadion, Turku; Referee: Orel Greenfield (Israel); Attendance: 4,632
EST: Mihkel Aksalu, Ragnar Klavan (Cap), Taijo Teniste, Ken Kallaste, Joonas Tamm, Karol Mets, Artjom Dmitrijev (77.Ilja Antonov), Konstantin Vassiljev, Siim Luts (77.Henri Anier), Sergei Zenjov (87.Ats Purje), Henrik Ojamaa. Trainer: Martin Reim.

12.10.2018 ESTONIA - FINLAND 0-1(0-0) UEFA Nations League C, Group 2
A. Le Coq Arena, Tallinn; Referee: Craig Pawson (England); Attendance: 8,087
EST: Mihkel Aksalu, Taijo Teniste, Ken Kallaste, Joonas Tamm, Nikita Baranov, Sander Puri, Artjom Dmitrijev, Konstantin Vassiljev (Cap) (88.Marek Kaljumäe), Sergei Zenjov (60.Siim Luts), Henrik Ojamaa, Rauno Sappinen (71.Ats Purje). Trainer: Martin Reim.

15.10.2018 ESTONIA - HUNGARY 3-3(1-1) UEFA Nations League C, Group 2
A. Le Coq Arena, Tallinn; Referee: Halis Özkahya (Turkey); Attendance: 3,043
EST: Mihkel Aksalu (43.Sergei Lepmets), Taijo Teniste, Joonas Tamm, Nikita Baranov, Karol Mets, Artur Pikk, Konstantin Vassiljev (Cap), Siim Luts, Ilja Antonov, Henri Anier (90.Ats Purje), Henrik Ojamaa. Trainer: Martin Reim.
Goals: Siim Luts (20), Máté Pátkai (70 own goal), Henri Anier (79).

15.11.2018 HUNGARY - ESTONIA 2-0(1-0) UEFA Nations League C, Group 2
Groupama Aréna, Budapest; Referee: Enea Jorgji (Albania); Attendance: 7,775
EST: Mihkel Aksalu, Taijo Teniste, Joonas Tamm, Artur Pikk, Madis Vihmann, Artjom Dmitrijev, Konstantin Vassiljev (Cap) (82.Ats Purje), Siim Luts (77.Sander Puri), Ilja Antonov, Henri Anier, Henrik Ojamaa (61.Sergei Zenjov). Trainer: Martin Reim.

18.11.2018 GREECE - ESTONIA 0-1(0-1) UEFA Nations League C, Group 2
Stádio Olympiako „Spiros Louis“, Athína; Referee: Yevhen Aranovskyi (Ukraine); Attendance: 5,179
EST: Sergei Lepmets, Gert Kams (Cap), Ken Kallaste, Joonas Tamm, Nikita Baranov, Madis Vihmann, Artjom Dmitrijev, Siim Luts, Brent Lepistu (68.Ilja Antonov), Sergei Zenjov (81.Artur Pikk), Rauno Sappinen (86.Henrik Ojamaa). Trainer: Martin Reim.
Goal: Vasilis Lambropoulos (44 own goal).

11.01.2019 FINLAND - ESTONIA 1-2(0-1) Friendly International
Khalifa International Stadium, Doha (Qatar); Referee: Khalid Marhoun Sulaiman Al Shaqsi (Oman); Attendance: 200
EST: Sergei Lepmets, Taijo Teniste, Gert Kams (Cap), Trevor Elhi, Henrik Pürg, Madis Vihmann, Brent Lepistu (46.Markus Poom), Rasmus Peetson (46.Artjom Dmitrijev), Henri Anier (74.Tristan Koskor), Robert Kirss (59.Sander Puri), Frank Liivak (46.Mark Oliver Roosnupp). Trainer: Martin Reim.
Goals: Gert Kams (35), Henri Anier (62).

15.01.2019 ICELAND - ESTONIA 0-0 Friendly International
„Sheikh Jassim Bin Hamad“ Stadium, Doha (Qatar); Referee: Abdulla Ali Al Athba Al Marri (Qatar); Attendance: 35
EST: Marko Meerits, Taijo Teniste (62.Trevor Elhi), Joonas Tamm (46.Henrik Pürg), Hindrek Ojamaa, Märten Kuusk, Madis Vihmann, Sander Puri, Artjom Dmitrijev (76.Rasmus Peetson), Konstantin Vassiljev (Cap) (46.Markus Poom), Mark Oliver Roosnupp (46.Frank Liivak), Tristan Koskor (46.Henri Anier). Trainer: Martin Reim.

21.03.2019 NORTHERN IRELAND - ESTONIA 2-0(0-0) 16th EC. Qualifiers
Windsor Park, Belfast; Referee: Ivan Bebek (Croatia); Attendance: 18,176
EST: Sergei Lepmets, Gert Kams, Joonas Tamm, Nikita Baranov, Karol Mets (Cap), Artur Pikk, Madis Vihmann, Artjom Dmitrijev (85.Rauno Sappinen), Mattias Käit, Henri Anier (76.Sergei Zenjov), Henrik Ojamaa (68.Konstantin Vassiljev). Trainer: Martin Reim.

26.03.2019 GIBRALTAR - ESTONIA 0-1(0-0) Friendly International
Victoria Stadium, Gibraltar; Referee: Nicholas Walsh (Scotland); Attendance: 1,900
EST: Mihkel Aksalu, Gert Kams (44.Nikita Baranov), Dmitri Kruglov, Karol Mets, Madis Vihmann, Brent Lepistu, Konstantin Vassiljev (Cap), Mark Oliver Roosnupp (58.Frank Liivak), Mattias Käit, Sergei Zenjov (78.Henrik Ojamaa), Rauno Sappinen (71.Henri Anier). Trainer: Martin Reim.
Goal: Konstantin Vassiljev (53).

08.06.2019 ESTONIA - NORTHERN IRELAND 1-2(1-0) 16th EC. Qualifiers
A. Le Coq Arena, Tallinn; Referee: Fabio Verissimo (Portugal); Attendance: 8,378
EST: Sergei Lepmets, Taijo Teniste (85.Gert Kams), Karol Mets, Artur Pikk, Madis Vihmann, Artjom Dmitrijev, Konstantin Vassiljev (Cap), Vlasiy Sinyavskiy, Mattias Käit (85.Joonas Tamm), Sergei Zenjov, Rauno Sappinen (61.Erik Sorga). Trainer: Martin Reim.
Goal: Konstantin Vassiljev (25).

11.06.2019 GERMANY - ESTONIA **8-0(5-0)** 16th EC. Qualifiers

Opel Arena, Mainz; Referee: Ali Palabıyık (Turkey); Attendance: 26,050

EST: Sergei Lepmets, Taijo Teniste, Gert Kams, Joonas Tamm, Karol Mets, Artur Pikk, Madis Vihmann, Sander Puri, Artjom Dmitrijev (59.Mattias Käit), Konstantin Vassiljev (Cap) (82.Vladislav Kreida), Sergei Zenjov (71.Henrik Ojamaa). Trainer: Martin Reim.

NATIONAL TEAM PLAYERS
(16.07.2018 – 15.07.2019)

Name	DOB	Caps	Goals	2018/2019:	Club
					Goalkeepers
Mihkel AKSALU	07.11.1984	**45**	**0**	2018/2019:	*Seinäjoen Jalkapallokerho (FIN)*
Sergei LEPMETS	05.04.1987	**7**	**0**	2018/2019:	*FCI Levadia Tallinn*
Marko MEERITS	26.04.1992	**12**	**0**	2019:	*Unattached*
					Defenders
Nikita BARANOV	19.08.1992	**34**	**0**	2018: 16.01.2019->	*Songndal Fotball (NOR)* *PFC Beroe Stara Zagora (BUL)*
Trevor ELHI	11.04.1993	**9**	**0**	2019:	*POFC Botev Vratsa (BUL)*
Marek KALJUMÄE	18.02.1991	**5**	**0**	2018:	*PS Kemi (FIN)*
Ken KALLASTE	31.08.1988	**41**	**0**	2018:	*Korona Kielce (POL)*
Gert KAMS	25.05.1985	**58**	**3**	2018/2019:	*FC Flora Tallinn*
Ragnar KLAVAN	30.10.1985	**125**	**3**	2018:	*Cagliari Calcio (ITA)*
Dmitri KRUGLOV	24.05.1984	**115**	**4**	2019:	*FCI Levadia Tallinn*
Märten KUUSK	05.04.1996	**1**	**0**	2019:	*FC Flora Tallinn*
Karol METS	16.05.1993	**56**	**0**	2018: 14.03.2019->	*NAC Breda (NED)* *AIK Stockholm (SWE)*
Hindrek OJAMAA	12.06.1995	**4**	**0**	2019:	*Vaasan Palloseura (FIN)*
Artur PIKK	05.03.1993	**33**	**1**	2018/2019:	*MKS Miedź Legnica (POL)*
Henrik PÜRG	03.06.1996	**2**	**0**	2019:	*FC Flora Tallinn*
Joonas TAMM	02.02.1992	**31**	**3**	2018: 31.12.2018-> 08.02.2019->	*Sarpsborg 08 FF (NOR)* *FC Flora Tallinn* *Korona Kielce (POL)*
Taijo TENISTE	31.01.1988	**72**	**0**	2018/2019:	*SK Brann Bergen (NOR)*
Madis VIHMANN	05.10.1995	**19**	**0**	2018/2019: 16.03.2019->	*FC Flora Tallinn* *Stabæk Fotball Bærum (NOR)*
					Midfielders
Ilja ANTONOV	05.12.1992	**47**	**2**	2018:	*FC Hermannstadt Sibiu (ROU)*
Artjom DMITRIJEV	14.11.1988	**22**	**0**	2018: 22.01.2019->	*FC Lahti (FIN); 01.01.2019-> Unattached* *FC Okzhetpes Kokshetau (KAZ)*
Vladislav KREIDA	25.09.1999	**1**	**0**	2019:	*FC Flora Tallinn*
Mattias KÄIT	29.06.1998	**20**	**5**	2019:	*Fulham FC London (ENG)*
Brent LEPISTU	26.03.1993	**13**	**0**	2018/2019:	*Kristiansund BK (NOR)*
Siim LUTS	12.03.1989	**41**	**4**	2018:	*FK Teplice (CZE)*
Rasmus PEETSON	03.05.1995	**2**	**0**	2019:	*FCI Levadia Tallinn*
Markus POOM	27.02.1999	**2**	**0**	2019:	*FC Flora Tallinn*
Sander PURI	07.05.1988	**77**	**4**	2018: 07.02.2019->	*Waterford FC (IRL)* *Nõmme Kalju FC*
Mark Oliver ROOSNUPP	12.05.1997	**7**	**0**	2018/2019:	*FCI Levadia Tallinn*
Konstantin VASSILJEV	16.08.1984	**114**	**25**	2018/2019: 27.02.2019->	*GKS Piast Gliwice (POL)* *FC Flora Tallinn*
					Forwards
Henri ANIER	17.12.1990	**60**	**13**	2018: 01.02.2019->	*FC Lahti (FIN); 01.01.2019-> Unattached* *Suwon FC (KOR)*
Robert KIRSS	03.09.1994	**1**	**0**	2019:	*Nõmme Kalju FC*
Tristan KOSKOR	28.11.1995	**2**	**0**	2018/2019:	*JK Tammeka Tartu*
Frank LIIVAK	07.07.1996	**12**	**2**	2019:	*FC Flora Tallinn*
Henrik OJAMAA	20.05.1991	**38**	**1**	2018/2019:	*MKS Miedź Legnica (POL)*
Ats PURJE	03.08.1985	**69**	**10**	2018:	*KuPS Kuopio (FIN)*
Rauno SAPPINEN	23.01.1996	**21**	**2**	2018/2019:	*FC Den Bosch (NED)*
Vlasiy SINYAVSKIY	27.11.1996	**1**	**0**	2019:	*FC Flora Tallinn*
Erik SORGA	08.07.1999	**1**	**0**	2019:	*FC Flora Tallinn*
Sergei ZENJOV	20.04.1989	**78**	**13**	2018: 16.02.2019->	*MKS Cracovia Kraków (POL)* *FC Shakhter Karagandy (KAZ)*

National team coach

Martin REIM [from 14.09.2016]	14.05.1971	36 M; 13 W; 8 D; 15 L; 39-48

FAROE ISLANDS

The Country:
Faroe Islands (Føroyar)
Capital: Tórshavn
Surface: 1,399 km²
Inhabitants: 51,540 [2018]
Time: UTC

The FA:
Fótbóltssamband Føroya
Gundadalur P.O. Box 3028, 110 Tórshavn
Tel: +298 351 979
Foundation date: 1979
Member of FIFA since: 1988
Member of UEFA since: 1990
Website: www.football.fo

NATIONAL TEAM RECORDS

First international match:	24.08.1988, Akranes:	Iceland – Faroe Islands 1-0
Most international caps:	Fróði Benjaminsen	- 95 caps (1999-2017)
Most international goals:	Rógvi Jacobsen	- 10 goals / 53 caps (1999-2009)

UEFA EUROPEAN CHAMPIONSHIP	
1960	-
1964	-
1968	-
1972	-
1976	-
1980	-
1984	-
1988	-
1992	Qualifiers
1996	Qualifiers
2000	Qualifiers
2004	Qualifiers
2008	Qualifiers
2012	Qualifiers
2016	Qualifiers

FIFA WORLD CUP	
1930	-
1934	-
1938	-
1950	-
1954	-
1958	-
1962	-
1966	-
1970	-
1974	-
1978	-
1982	*Did not enter*
1986	*Did not enter*
1990	*Did not enter*
1994	Qualifiers
1998	Qualifiers
2002	Qualifiers
2006	Qualifiers
2010	Qualifiers
2014	Qualifiers
2018	

UEFA NATIONS LEAGUE
2018/2019 – League D

OLYMPIC FOOTBALL TOURNAMENTS 1900-2016
2012 & 2016 (Qualifiers)

FIFA CONFEDERATIONS CUP 1992-2017
None

FAROE ISLANDS CLUB HONOURS IN EUROPEAN CLUB COMPETITIONS:

European Champion Clubs' Cup (1956-1992) / UEFA Champions League (1993-2019)
None
Fairs Cup (1858-1971) / UEFA Cup (1972-2009) / UEFA Europa League (2010-2019)
None
UEFA Super Cup (1972-2019)
None
European Cup Winners' Cup 1961-1999*
None

**defunct competition*

NATIONAL COMPETITIONS
TABLE OF HONOURS

	CHAMPIONS	CUP WINNERS	BEST GOALSCORERS	
1942	KÍ Klaksvík	-	-	
1943	TB Tvøroyri	-	-	
1944	*No competition*	-	-	
1945	KÍ Klaksvík	-	-	
1946	B36 Tórshavn	-	-	
1947	SÍ Sørvágur	-	-	
1948	B36 Tórshavn	-	-	
1949	TB Tvøroyri	-	-	
1950	B36 Tórshavn	-	-	
1951	TB Tvøroyri	-	-	
1952	KÍ Klaksvík	-	-	
1953	KÍ Klaksvík	-	-	
1954	KÍ Klaksvík	-	-	
1955	HB Tórshavn	HB Tórshavn	-	
1956	KÍ Klaksvík	TB Tvøroyri	-	
1957	KÍ Klaksvík	HB Tórshavn	-	
1958	KÍ Klaksvík	TB Tvøroyri	-	
1959	B36 Tórshavn	HB Tórshavn	-	
1960	HB Tórshavn	TB Tvøroyri	-	
1961	KÍ Klaksvík	TB Tvøroyri	-	
1962	B36 Tórshavn	HB Tórshavn	-	
1963	HB Tórshavn	HB Tórshavn	-	
1964	HB Tórshavn	HB Tórshavn	-	
1965	HB Tórshavn	B36 Tórshavn	-	
1966	KÍ Klaksvík	KÍ Klaksvík	-	
1967	KÍ Klaksvík	KÍ Klaksvík	-	
1968	KÍ Klaksvík	HB Tórshavn	-	
1969	KÍ Klaksvík	HB Tórshavn	-	
1970	KÍ Klaksvík	*Cup Final not played*	-	
1971	HB Tórshavn	HB Tórshavn	-	
1972	KÍ Klaksvík	HB Tórshavn	-	
1973	HB Tórshavn	HB Tórshavn	-	
1974	HB Tórshavn	VB Vágur	-	
1975	HB Tórshavn	HB Tórshavn	-	
1976	TB Tvøroyri	HB Tórshavn	-	
1977	TB Tvøroyri	TB Tvøroyri	-	
1978	HB Tórshavn	HB Tórshavn	-	
1979	ÍF Fuglafjørður	HB Tórshavn	-	
1980	TB Tvøroyri	HB Tórshavn	Jóan Petur Olgarsson (TB Tvøroyri)	18
1981	HB Tórshavn	HB Tórshavn	Jóannes Jakobsen (HB Tórshavn)	14
1982	HB Tórshavn	HB Tórshavn	Jóannes Jakobsen (HB Tórshavn)	9
1983	Gøtu Ítróttarfelag	Gøtu Ítróttarfelag	Petur Hans Hansen (B68 Toftir) Hans Leo í Bartalsstovu (Gøtu Ítróttarfelag)	10
1984	B68 Toftir	HB Tórshavn	Aksel Højgaard (B68 Toftir) Erling Jacobsen (HB Tórshavn)	10
1985	B68 Toftir	Gøtu Ítróttarfelag	Símun Petur Justinussen (Gøtu Ítróttarfelag)	10
1986	Gøtu Ítróttarfelag	NSÍ Runavík	Jesper Wiemer (DEN, B68 Toftir) Símun Petur Justinussen (Gøtu Ítróttarfelag)	13
1987	TB Tvøroyri	HB Tórshavn	Símun Petur Justinussen (Gøtu Ítróttarfelag)	10
1988	HB Tórshavn	HB Tórshavn	Jógvan Petersen (B68 Toftir)	9
1989	B71 Sandoy	HB Tórshavn	Egill Steinþórsson (ISL, VB Vágur)	16
1990	HB Tórshavn	KÍ Klaksvík	Gunnar Mohr (HB Tórshavn) Jens Erik Rasmussen (MB Miðvágur)	10
1991	Klaksvíkar Ítróttarfelag	B36 Tórshavn	Símun Petur Justinussen (Gøtu Ítróttarfelag)	15
1992	B68 Toftir	HB Tórshavn	Símun Petur Justinussen (Gøtu Ítróttarfelag)	14
1993	Gøtu Ítróttarfelag	B71 Sandur	Uni Arge (HB Tórshavn)	11
1994	Gøtu Ítróttarfelag	KÍ Klaksvík	John Petersen (Gøtu Ítróttarfelag)	21
1995	Gøtu Ítróttarfelag	HB Tórshavn	Súni Fríði Johannesen (B68 Toftir)	24
1996	Gøtu Ítróttarfelag	Gøtu Ítróttarfelag	Kurt Mørkøre (KÍ Klaksvík)	20
1997	B36 Tórshavn	Gøtu Ítróttarfelag	Uni Arge (HB Tórshavn)	24
1998	HB Tórshavn	HB Tórshavn	Jákup á Borg (B36 Tórshavn)	20
1999	Klaksvíkar Ítróttarfelag	KÍ Klaksvík	Jákup á Borg (B36 Tórshavn)	17
2000	VB Vágur	Gøtu Ítróttarfelag	Súni Fríði Johannesen (B36 Tórshavn)	16
2001	B36 Tórshavn	B36 Tórshavn	Helgi L. Petersen (Gøtu Ítróttarfelag)	19
2002	HB Tórshavn	NSÍ Runavík	Andrew av Fløtum (HB Tórshavn)	18
2003	HB Tórshavn	B36 Tórshavn	Hjalgrím Elttør (KÍ Klaksvík)	13
2004	HB Tórshavn	HB Tórshavn	Sonni L. Petersen (EB/Streymur)	13
2005	B36 Tórshavn	Gøtu Ítróttarfelag	Christian Høgni Jacobsen (NSÍ Runavík)	18
2006	HB Tórshavn	B36 Tórshavn	Christian Høgni Jacobsen (NSÍ Runavík)	18
2007	NSÍ Runavík	EB/Streymur	Amed Davy Sylla (FRA, B36 Tórshavn)	18
2008	EB/Streymur	EB/Streymur	Arnbjørn Hansen (EB/Streymur)	20
2009	HB Tórshavn	Víkingur Gøta	Finnur Justinussen (Víkingur Gøta)	19

2010	HB Tórshavn	EB/Streymur	Arnbjørn Hansen (EB/Streymur) Christian Høgni Jacobsen (NSÍ Runavík)	22
2011	B36 Tórshavn	EB/Streymur	Finnur Justinussen (Víkingur Gøta)	21
2012	EB/Streymur	Víkingur Gøta	Clayton Soares do Nascimento (BRA, ÍF Fuglafjørður) Páll Klettskarð (KÍ Klaksvík)	22
2013	HB Tórshavn	Víkingur Gøta	Klæmint Andrasson Olsen (NSÍ Runavík)	21
2014	B36 Tórshavn	Víkingur Gøta	Klæmint Andrasson Olsen (NSÍ Runavík)	22
2015	B36 Tórshavn	Víkingur Gøta	Klæmint Andrasson Olsen (NSÍ Runavík)	21
2016	Víkingur Gøta	KÍ Klaksvík	Klæmint Andrasson Olsen (NSÍ Runavík)	23
2017	Víkingur Gøta	NSÍ Runavík	Adeshina Abayomi Lawal (NGA, (Víkingur Gøta)	17
2018	HB Tórshavn	B36 Tórshavn	Adrian Justinussen (HB Tórshavn)	20

NATIONAL CHAMPIONSHIP
Faroe Islands Premier League - Effodeildin 2018
(11.03.2018 – 27.10.2018)

Results

Round 1 [11.03.2018]
AB Argir - 07 Vestur 1-1(0-1)
HB Tórshavn - KÍ Klaksvík 0-3(0-1)
EB/Streymur - B36 Tórshavn 3-2(0-1)
TB/FCS/Royn - NSÍ Runavík 0-4(0-2)
Víkingur Gøta - Skála ÍF 1-0(0-0)

Round 2 [17.03.2018]
HB Tórshavn - Víkingur Gøta 2-1(1-1)
07 Vestur - TB/FCS/Royn 1-2(1-1)
NSÍ Runavík - KÍ Klaksvík 0-1(0-1)
Skála ÍF - B36 Tórshavn 0-2(0-0)
EB/Streymur - AB Argir 0-0

Round 3 [02.04.2018]
07 Vestur - EB/Streymur 0-3(0-3)
B36 Tórshavn - HB Tórshavn 1-1(1-0)
TB/FCS/Royn - KÍ Klaksvík 0-1(0-1)
Víkingur Gøta - NSÍ Runavík 1-2(0-2)
AB Argir - Skála ÍF 0-2(0-2)

Round 4 [07-08.04.2018]
Skála ÍF - TB/FCS/Royn 3-0(1-0)
NSÍ Runavík - 07 Vestur 3-1(0-0)
Víkingur Gøta - B36 Tórshavn 2-1(1-1)
KÍ Klaksvík - AB Argir 3-1(2-0)
EB/Streymur - HB Tórshavn 0-1(0-0)

Round 5 [12.04.2018]
07 Vestur - KÍ Klaksvík 2-3(2-1)
AB Argir - Víkingur Gøta 1-2(1-0)
B36 Tórshavn - TB/FCS/Royn 1-0(0-0)
Skála ÍF - HB Tórshavn 0-3(0-1)
EB/Streymur - NSÍ Runavík 2-2(1-0)

Round 6 [15.04.2018]
07 Vestur - B36 Tórshavn 0-3(0-3)
NSÍ Runavík - HB Tórshavn 1-2(1-1)
Skála ÍF - KÍ Klaksvík 0-0
EB/Streymur - Víkingur Gøta 1-1(0-0)
TB/FCS/Royn - AB Argir 0-1(0-1)

Round 7 [22.04.2018]
B36 Tórshavn - AB Argir 2-1(0-0)
KÍ Klaksvík - EB/Streymur 2-0(1-0)
TB/FCS/Royn - HB Tórshavn 0-1(0-0)
NSÍ Runavík - Skála ÍF 1-0(1-0)
Víkingur Gøta - 07 Vestur 4-1(1-0)

Round 8 [29.04.2018]
B36 Tórshavn - KÍ Klaksvík 3-2(2-1)
EB/Streymur - Skála ÍF 0-0
Víkingur Gøta - TB/FCS/Royn 0-0
AB Argir - NSÍ Runavík 0-2(0-1)
HB Tórshavn - 07 Vestur 3-0(0-0)

Round 9 [06.05.2018]
HB Tórshavn - AB Argir 5-0(0-0)
KÍ Klaksvík - Víkingur Gøta 1-2(1-1)
NSÍ Runavík - B36 Tórshavn 0-2(0-1)
Skála ÍF - 07 Vestur 2-1(1-0)
TB/FCS/Royn - EB/Streymur 3-2(2-1)

Round 10 [13.05.2018]
07 Vestur - TB/FCS/Royn 0-3(0-2)
AB Argir - EB/Streymur 2-0(0-0)
KÍ Klaksvík - NSÍ Runavík 1-1(0-0)
Víkingur Gøta - HB Tórshavn 1-2(1-2)
B36 Tórshavn - Skála ÍF 5-1(3-0)

Round 11 [21.05.2018]
07 Vestur - NSÍ Runavík 0-5(0-2)
B36 Tórshavn - Víkingur Gøta 2-1(1-0)
Skála ÍF - TB/FCS/Royn 2-0(1-0)
AB Argir - KÍ Klaksvík 0-2(0-1)
HB Tórshavn - EB/Streymur 1-0(0-0)

Round 12 [27.05.2018]
07 Vestur - Skála ÍF 4-1(1-1)
B36 Tórshavn - NSÍ Runavík 2-3(2-1)
EB/Streymur - TB/FCS/Royn 2-2(0-1)
Víkingur Gøta - KÍ Klaksvík 0-3(0-2)
AB Argir - HB Tórshavn 0-1(0-0)

Round 13 [03.06.2018]
TB/FCS/Royn - Víkingur Gøta 1-4(0-2)
KÍ Klaksvík - B36 Tórshavn 3-1(2-0)
NSÍ Runavík - AB Argir 6-0(0-0)
Skála ÍF - EB/Streymur 0-2(0-2)
HB Tórshavn - 07 Vestur 3-1(1-0)

Round 14 [16-17.06.2018]
NSÍ Runavík - Víkingur Gøta 1-2(0-1)
TB/FCS/Royn - KÍ Klaksvík 0-1(0-1)
HB Tórshavn - B36 Tórshavn 2-1(1-1)
Skála ÍF - AB Argir 2-0(1-0)
EB/Streymur - 07 Vestur 2-1(1-0)

Round 15 [22-23.06.2018]
Skála ÍF - NSÍ Runavík 1-1(0-0)
AB Argir - B36 Tórshavn 1-4(0-4)
07 Vestur - Víkingur Gøta 0-1(0-0)
EB/Streymur - KÍ Klaksvík 0-1(0-0)
TB/FCS/Royn - HB Tórshavn 1-4(1-2)

Round 16 [27-28.07.2018]
Víkingur G. - EB/Streymur 3-1(0-0) [27.06.]
AB Argir - TB/FCS/Royn 0-4(0-1)
KÍ Klaksvík - Skála ÍF 3-1(2-0)
HB Tórshavn - NSÍ Runavík 0-2(0-0)
B36 Tórshavn - 07 Vestur 2-0(1-0) [26.09.]

Round 17 [05-06.08.2018]
HB Tórshavn - Skála ÍF 2-1(1-0)
KÍ Klaksvík - 07 Vestur 3-0(0-0)
NSÍ Runavík - EB/Streymur 5-0(2-0)
Víkingur Gøta - AB Argir 3-0(1-0)
TB/FCS/Royn - B36 Tórshavn 1-1(1-1)

Round 18 [10-12.08.2018]
B36 Tórshavn - EB/Streymur 2-2(1-1)
KÍ Klaksvík - HB Tórshavn 0-1(0-0)
NSÍ Runavík - TB/FCS/Royn 1-0(0-0)
Skála ÍF - Víkingur Gøta 0-2(0-2)
07 Vestur - AB Argir 1-0(0-0)

Round 19 [19.08.2018]
AB Argir - B36 Tórshavn 1-1(1-1)
HB Tórshavn - TB/FCS/Royn 4-0(3-0)
KÍ Klaksvík - EB/Streymur 3-0(1-0)
NSÍ Runavík - Skála ÍF 2-0(1-0)
Víkingur Gøta - 07 Vestur 1-4(0-1)

Round 20 [23.08.2018]
B36 Tórshavn - KÍ Klaksvík 2-1(0-0) [16.08.]
07 Vestur - HB Tórshavn 1-4(1-2) [16.08.]
Víkingur Gøta - TB/FCS/Royn 0-2(0-1)
AB Argir - NSÍ Runavík 0-2(0-1)
EB/Streymur - Skála ÍF 1-1(1-0)

Round 21 [31.08.-01.09.2018]
KÍ Klaksvík - Víkingur Gøta 1-1(1-1)
HB Tórshavn - AB Argir 3-0(2-0)
NSÍ Runavík - B36 Tórshavn 1-2(0-1)
TB/FCS/Royn - EB/Streymur 2-1(1-1)
Skála ÍF - 07 Vestur 5-0(3-0)

Round 22 [16.09.2018]
07 Vestur - B36 Tórshavn 1-3(0-0)
HB Tórshavn - NSÍ Runavík 2-1(2-0)
Skála ÍF - KÍ Klaksvík 1-0(1-0)
EB/Streymur - Víkingur Gøta 2-2(1-1)
TB/FCS/Royn - AB Argir 0-1(0-0)

Round 23 [23.09.2018]
AB Argir - 07 Vestur 1-2(0-1)
KÍ Klaksvík - HB Tórshavn 1-2(0-0)
TB/FCS/Royn - NSÍ Runavík 2-2(2-1)
Víkingur Gøta - Skála ÍF 2-2(0-1)
B36 Tórshavn - EB/Streymur 5-1(4-1)

Round 24 [30.09.2018]
KÍ Klaksvík - AB Argir 3-0(2-0)
NSÍ Runavík - 07 Vestur 7-1(4-0)
EB/Streymur - HB Tórshavn 0-3(0-1)
TB/FCS/Royn - Skála ÍF 2-1(1-1)
Víkingur Gøta - B36 Tórshavn 1-1(1-1)

Round 25 [06.10.2018]
07 Vestur - KÍ Klaksvík 4-2(2-2)
AB Argir - Víkingur Gøta 1-0(1-0)
B36 Tórshavn - TB/FCS/Royn 1-0(0-0)
Skála ÍF - HB Tórshavn 0-1(0-1)
EB/Streymur - NSÍ Runavík 2-4(1-1)

Round 26 [21-23.10.2018]
B36 Tórshavn - HB Tórshavn 1-3(0-1)
KÍ Klaksvík - TB/FCS/Royn 3-1(1-1)
Víkingur Gøta - NSÍ Runavík 0-3(0-2)
07 Vestur - EB/Streymur 3-3(1-2)
AB Argir - Skála ÍF 2-4(1-2)

Round 27 [27.10.2018]
HB Tórshavn - Víkingur Gøta 2-1(0-1)
NSÍ Runavík - KÍ Klaksvík 2-1(0-1)
Skála ÍF - B36 Tórshavn 1-5(1-3)
EB/Streymur - AB Argir 0-2(0-1)
TB/FCS/Royn - 07 Vestur 1-0(0-0)

Final Standings

1.	**HB Tórshavn**	27	24	1	2	58	-	18	73
2.	NSÍ Runavík	27	17	4	6	64	-	25	55
3.	B36 Tórshavn	27	16	5	6	58	-	33	53
4.	KÍ Klaksvík	27	16	3	8	48	-	25	51
5.	Víkingur Gøta	27	11	6	10	39	-	37	39
6.	Skála ÍF	27	8	5	14	31	-	42	29
7.	TB/FC Suðuroy/Royn	27	8	4	15	27	-	42	28
8.	EB/Streymur	27	4	9	14	30	-	53	21
9.	AB Argir	27	5	3	19	16	-	55	18
10.	07 Vestur Sørvágur (*Relegated*)	27	5	2	20	30	-	71	17

Top goalscorers:

20	Adrian Justinussen *HB Tórshavn*
13	Klæmint Andrasson Olsen *NSÍ Runavík*
13	Meinhard Egilsson Olsen *B36 Tórshavn*

NATIONAL CUP
Løgmanssteypid 2018

First Round

TB/FC Suðuroy/Royn - KÍ Klaksvík	2-1
ÍF Fuglafjarðar - B36 Tórshavn	0-3
NSÍ Runavík - AB Argir	0-1
B68 Toftir - HB Tórshavn	0-4
Undrið FF Tórshavn - EB/Streymur	0-3
B71 Sandoy - Giza Hoyvík	4-0
Skála ÍF - 07 Vestur Sørvágur	1-0
Víkingur Gøta (Bye)	

Quarter-Finals

AB Argir - EB/Streymur	2-2; 3-1pen
B36 Tórshavn - Skála ÍF	2-0
Víkingur Gøta - TB/FC Suðuroy/Royn	0-2
HB Tórshavn - B71 Sandoy	6-0

Semi-Finals

HB Tórshavn - AB Argir	2-0 / 4-1
B36 Tórshavn - TB/FC Suðuroy/Royn	4-2 / 4-0

Final

25.08.2018; Tórsvøllur, Tórshavn; Referee: Kári á Høvdanum; Attendance: 3,221
B36 Tórshavn - HB Tórshavn **2-2(0-0,2-2,2-2); 5-4 on penalties**

B36: Rói Hentze, Odmar Færø, Alex Mellemgaard, Bjarni Petersen (85.Robert Heðin Brockie [*sent off 86*]), Erlendur Magnussen, Eli Nielsen, Meinhard Egilsson Olsen, Benjamin Heinesen [*sent off 90+3*], Andrias Eriksen (80.Hannes Agnarsson), Michał Przybylski (73.Róaldur Jakobsen), Kaimar Saag. Trainer: Jákup á Borg.

HB: Teitur Matras Gestsson, Brynjar Hlöðversson (102.John Frederiksen), Jógvan Davidsen, Bartal Wardum, Lasse Andersen, Magnus Egilsson, Tróndur Jensen, Grétar Snær Gunnarsson, Adrian Justinussen, Símun Samuelsen (64.Dan í Soylu), Ari Mohr Olsen (78.Jógvan Andrias Nolsøe)., Trainer: Heimir Guðjónsson (Iceland).

Goals: 0-1 Tróndur Jensen (56), 1-1 Odmar Færø (60 penalty), 1-2 Adrian Justinussen (63), 2-2 Hannes Agnarsson (90+5).

Penalties: Lasse Andersen 0-1; Odmar Færø 1-1; Magnus Egilsson 1-2; Alex Mellemgaard 2-2; John Frederiksen (saved); Meinhard Egilsson Olsen 3-2; Adrian Justinussen 3-3; Erlendur Magnussen 4-3; Dan í Soylu 4-4; Róaldur Jakobsen 5-4.

THE CLUBS 2018

07 Vestur Sørvágur

Founded: 06.11.2007
Stadium: á Dungasandi, Sørvágur (500)

Goalkeepers:	**DOB**	**M**	**(s)**	**G**
Silas Eyðsteinsson	13.02.1998	18		
Ivan Stojković (SRB)	30.01.1977	9	(1)	
Defenders:	**DOB**	**M**	**(s)**	**G**
Jóannis á Steig	21.03.1997	9	(9)	
Petur Dalbø	15.03.1991	1	(1)	
Hørður Egilsson	11.09.1998	1	(5)	
Ásbjørn Héðinsson	19.12.2000	14	(8)	
Niels Mouritsen	25.11.1998	7	(2)	
Høgni Nielsen	29.04.1997	27		2
Oskar Weihe	27.03.1999		(3)	
Midfielders:	**DOB**	**M**	**(s)**	**G**
Tór-Ingar Akselsen	01.05.1981	8	(4)	
Martin Dam	30.03.1999		(1)	
Sølvi Egilsson	24.01.1995	15	(5)	3
Dann Fróðason	27.04.2000	22	(1)	
Ndende Guéye (SEN)	05.01.1983	19	(1)	1
Nikola Krčmarević (SRB)	18.12.1991	14		
Jákup Sveinbjørn Olsen	06.10.1994	10	(1)	
Teitur Olsen	11.07.1998	8	(9)	
Janus Samuelsen	27.09.1998	21	(5)	
Kyrylo Silich (UKR)	03.08.1990	18	(7)	2
Martin Tausen	04.05.1990	17	(1)	
Karl Weihe	22.11.1999		(1)	
Forwards:	**DOB**	**M**	**(s)**	**G**
Ken Fagerberg (SWE)	09.01.1989	23	(3)	3
Sonny Hansen Jakobsen (DEN)	14.11.1990	11	(1)	11
Charlie Machell (ENG)	25.10.1994	9		1
Gilli Samuelsen	12.02.1999	13	(1)	6
Jón Krosslá Poulsen	17.02.1988	3	(8)	
Trainer:	**DOB**	**M**		
Pauli Poulsen	21.09.1973	21		
Sigtór Petersen [18.09.2017]	06.04.1988	6		

Argja Bóltfelag Argir

Founded: 15.08.1973
Stadium: Skansi Arena, Argir (2,000)

Goalkeepers:	DOB	M	(s)	G
Áki Dahl	04.04.1993		(1)	
Mattias Lamhauge	02.08.1999	2		
Heðin Stenberg	14.01.1989	25		
Defenders:	**DOB**	**M**	**(s)**	**G**
Jákup Pauli Breckmann	16.04.1998	18	(2)	
Absalon Eliasen	30.05.1997		(1)	
Beinir Henriksen	16.02.1997	7	(5)	
Teitur Olsen	04.02.1992	2	(10)	
Sørin Samuelsen	29.04.1992	26		
Jónas Stenberg	07.04.1987	24	(1)	
Hørður Tórsson	29.08.1998	2	(2)	
Midfielders:	**DOB**	**M**	**(s)**	**G**
Tóki á Lofti	06.12.1993	19	(5)	4
Jobin Drangastein	01.11.1990	19	(3)	3
Mikkjal Hentze	08.12.1986	25		
Filip í Liða	06.11.2000	9	(15)	2
Jógvan Johannesson	02.06.1998		(2)	
Árni Olsen	13.09.1993	25		
Bárður Olsen	05.12.1985	26		2
Bartal Petersen	22.11.2000	1	(17)	
Bjarni Skála	14.11.1997	13	(5)	
Ragnar Skála	05.09.2000		(1)	
Rasmus Sørensen	27.05.1995	19		1
Forwards:	**DOB**	**M**	**(s)**	**G**
Hans Jákup Annfinsson	19.03.1999	9	(2)	
Bjarki Nielsen	02.11.1998	25		4
John Tordar Poulsen	17.09.1985	1		
Ragnar Rasmussen	13.07.2000		(1)	
Trainer:	**DOB**	**M**		
Sorin Vasile Anghel Olaru (ROU)	16.07.1979	27		

Bóltfelagið 1936 Tórshavn

Founded: 28.03.1936
Stadium: Gundadalur, Tórshavn (5,000)

Goalkeepers:	DOB	M	(s)	G
Trygvi Askham	28.03.1988	17		
Rói Hentze	22.09.1999	10	(1)	
Defenders:	**DOB**	**M**	**(s)**	**G**
Odmar Færø	01.11.1989	23		3
Erlendur Magnussen	02.07.1998	20	(3)	6
Alex Mellemgaard	27.11.1991	21	(2)	1
Jónas Næs	27.12.1986	4	(1)	
Bjarni Petersen	12.08.1998	12	(7)	
Jóhan Simonsen	10.09.1998		(1)	
Andreas Thomsen	04.10.2001	1		
Midfielders:	**DOB**	**M**	**(s)**	**G**
Hannes Agnarsson	26.02.1999	4	(11)	1
Robert Heðin Brockie	21.12.1992	6	(6)	1
Andrias Eriksen	22.02.1994	23	(2)	
Tórur Hardlei	20.11.2001		(2)	
Benjamin Heinesen	26.03.1996	20	(4)	3
Magnus Holm Jacobsen	23.05.2000	10	(3)	
Róaldur Jakobsen	23.01.1991	3	(4)	
Andrass Johansen	16.11.2001	1	(3)	
Eli Nielsen	23.09.1992	21	(2)	3
Michał Przybylski (POL)	29.12.1997	11	(1)	5
Ragnar Samuelsen	23.08.1999	7	(4)	1
Heini í Skorini	14.05.1983		(1)	
Forwards:	**DOB**	**M**	**(s)**	**G**
Łukasz Cieślewicz (POL)	15.11.1987	13	(2)	3
Christian Mouritsen	03.12.1988		(2)	
Meinhard Egilsson Olsen	10.04.1997	24	(1)	13
Kaimar Saag (EST)	05.08.1988	23	(4)	11
Gilli Samuelsen	12.02.1999	6	(1)	2
Hugin Samuelsen	12.02.1999	17	(7)	4
Trainer:	**DOB**	**M**		
Jákup á Borg	26.10.1979	27		

Eiðis Bóltfelag / Streymur

Founded: 1993
Stadium: Við Margáir, Streymnes (2,000)

Goalkeepers:	DOB	M	(s)	G
Jákup Højgaard	06.02.1994	1		
Rói Zachariasen	12.10.1998	26		
Defenders:	**DOB**	**M**	**(s)**	**G**
Gestur Dam	17.09.1994	26		3
Ragnar Danielsen	24.02.1992	21	(3)	2
Marni Djurhuus	06.09.1985	17	(6)	2
Mikkjal Hellisá	18.02.2002	1	(2)	
Oddur Højgaard	12.09.1989	20	(1)	1
Ári Kruse	02.01.1996		(2)	
Rógvi Nielsen	07.12.1992	26		2
Andras Olsen	24.10.1995	16	(3)	1
Rói Olsen	03.03.1997	5	(6)	
Petur Zachariassen	19.04.1995	25	(1)	2
Midfielders:	**DOB**	**M**	**(s)**	**G**
Gutti Dahl-Olsen	19.01.2002		(2)	
Aksel Bjartalíð Danielsen	03.04.1999	6		1
Ari Ellingsgaard	03.02.1993	10	(2)	
Tóki Johannesen	17.03.1997	6	(1)	
Fríði Johansen	17.05.2000		(10)	1
Jónstein Magnussen	21.05.1990	10	(8)	1
Pætur Petersen	29.03.1998	26		7
Forwards:	**DOB**	**M**	**(s)**	**G**
Arnar Dam	18.10.1991	18		
Silas Ejdesgaard	03.04.2000		(1)	
Arnbjørn Hansen	27.02.1986	2	(13)	3
Høgni Hummeland	14.07.1996	1		
Jens Michael Jensen	24.01.1991	2	(3)	2
Leif Niclasen	01.10.1986	15	(2)	1
Hans Pauli Samuelsen	18.10.1984	17	(3)	1
Trainer:	**DOB**	**M**		
Heðin Askham	03.07.1960	27		

Havnar Bóltfelag Tórshavn

Founded: 04.10.1904
Stadium: Gundadalur, Tórshavn (5,000)

Goalkeepers:	**DOB**	**M**	**(s)**	**G**
Teitur Matras Gestsson	19.08.1992	26		
Bjarti Vitalis Mørk	07.06.2001	1		
Defenders:	**DOB**	**M**	**(s)**	**G**
Lasse Andersen (DEN)	24.05.1995	23	(1)	
Jógvan Davidsen	09.10.1991	24		1
Brynjar Hlöðversson (ISL)	03.04.1989	20	(2)	
Bartal Wardum	03.05.1997	22	(1)	1
Midfielders:	**DOB**	**M**	**(s)**	**G**
Hjalti Djurhuus	14.07.1998	3	(3)	
Magnus Egilsson	19.03.1994	26		1
Grétar Snær Gunnarsson (ISL)	08.01.1997	11	(3)	1
Dan í Soylu	09.07.1996	22	(3)	4
Teit Jacobsen	16.03.1998	6		1
Tróndur Jensen	06.02.1993	23		1
Daniel Johansen	09.07.1998	9	(16)	
Villiam Emil Klein	21.11.2000		(1)	
Heri Mohr	13.05.1997		(1)	
Jógvan Andrias Nolsøe	20.05.1992	9	(11)	5
Tórmóður Petursson Djurhuus	02.09.2000		(1)	
Forwards:	**DOB**	**M**	**(s)**	**G**
John Frederiksen	10.01.1996	3	(13)	2
Adrian Justinussen	21.07.1998	25	(1)	20
Niklas Kruse	11.05.1999	1	(1)	2
Ari Olsen	16.12.1997	14	(7)	7
Sebastian Pingel (DEN)	11.05.1993	1	(2)	
Símun Samuelsen	21.05.1985	25		9
Aleksandar Stankov (MKD)	19.02.1991	3	(2)	
Trainer:	**DOB**	**M**		
Heimir Guðjónsson (ISL)	03.04.1969	27		

Klaksvíkar Ítróttarfelag

Founded: 24.08.1904
Stadium: Við Djúpumýrar, Klaksvík (4,000)

Goalkeepers:	**DOB**	**M**	**(s)**	**G**
Kristian Joensen	21.12.1992	16	(1)	
Meinhardt Joensen	27.11.1979	11		
Defenders:	**DOB**	**M**	**(s)**	**G**
Mikkjal á Bergi	03.02.1997	1		
Marko Dušak (CRO)	29.06.1989	12		
Jóhan Høgnesen	20.06.1998		(2)	
Ólavur Niclasen	07.07.1998	10	(5)	
Deni Pavlović (SRB)	01.09.1993	20		2
Børge Petersen	24.04.2002	1	(1)	
Predrag Pocuca (CRO)	24.01.1986	4		
Ísak Simonsen	12.10.1993	12	(3)	
Midfielders:	**DOB**	**M**	**(s)**	**G**
Jákup Andreasen	31.05.1998	20	(2)	1
Hørður Askham	22.09.1994	27		1
Aksel Danielsen	03.04.1999		(2)	1
Jóannes Danielsen	10.09.1997	27		1
Boris Došljak (MNE)	04.06.1989	24	(2)	5
Hjalgrím Elttør	03.03.1983	2	(9)	1
Semir Hadžibulić (SRB)	16.08.1986	25		3
Jonn Johannesen	30.12.2001		(3)	
Steinbjørn Olsen	11.09.1996	10	(13)	2
Óli Poulsen	30.05.2001	14	(10)	4
Forwards:	**DOB**	**M**	**(s)**	**G**
Jóannes Bjartalíð	10.07.1996	19	(7)	8
Kristoffur Jakobsen	07.11.1988	2	(7)	3
Páll Klettskarð	17.05.1990	27		9
Ronny Møller-Iversen (DEN)	17.07.1994	13	(6)	2
Trainer:	**DOB**	**M**		
Mikkjal Thomassen	12.01.1976	27		

Nes Sóknar Ítróttarfelag Runavík

Founded: 1957
Stadium: Við Løkin, Runavík (2,000)

Goalkeepers:	**DOB**	**M**	**(s)**	**G**
Tórður Thomsen	11.06.1986	27		
Defenders:	**DOB**	**M**	**(s)**	**G**
Jóhan Davidsen	31.01.1988	20	(2)	4
Pætur Hentze	06.11.1999	17	(3)	
Jens Joensen	17.05.1989	23		1
Pól Justinussen	13.01.1989	23	(2)	6
Per Langgaard	30.05.1991	17	(3)	
Sjúrður Pauli Chin Nielsen	18.04.2000		(2)	
Einar Tróndargjógv	02.04.1988	11	(2)	3
Midfielders:	**DOB**	**M**	**(s)**	**G**
Andri Benjaminsen	12.01.1999		(1)	
Fróði Benjaminsen	14.12.1977	26		4
Jann Benjaminsen	02.03.1997	7	(16)	1
Árni Frederiksberg	13.06.1992	26		11
Bárður Hansen	13.03.1992	19		
Betuel Hansen	14.03.1997	19	(5)	2
Petur Knudsen	21.04.1998	24	(2)	9
Jann Mortensen	18.07.1989	1	(3)	
Mórits Heini Mortensen	25.03.1999		(4)	
Magnus Olsen	26.10.1986	1	(10)	
Pætur Turiðarson Skipanes	20.10.2000		(1)	1
Forwards:	**DOB**	**M**	**(s)**	**G**
Øssur Dalbúð	28.03.1989	6	(9)	6
Klæmint Andrasson Olsen	17.07.1990	21	(1)	13
Trainer:	**DOB**	**M**		
Sámal Hentze	27.01.1972	27		

Skála Ítróttarfelag

Founded: 1965
Stadium: Undir Mýruhjalla, Skála (1,500)

Goalkeepers:	DOB	M	(s)	G
Karstin Hansen	05.10.1997	26		
Sonni Højgaard	02.02.1997	1		
Defenders:	**DOB**	**M**	**(s)**	**G**
Bárður Danielsen	28.07.1985	9	(3)	
Jákup Jakobsen	22.11.1992	25		
Ahmed Mujdragić (SRB)	13.03.1986	18	(1)	
Midfielders:	**DOB**	**M**	**(s)**	**G**
Andri Benjaminsen	12.01.1999	2	(7)	1
Niels Pauli Danielsen	18.01.1989	22	(2)	2
Haraldur Højgaard	21.03.1995	7	(9)	
Edvin Jacobsen	12.04.1991	21	(3)	1
Pætur Jacobsen	05.12.1982	27		1
Jákup Joensen	27.02.2000		(2)	
Teitur Joensen	10.11.1986	13	(5)	1
Dávid Johansen	08.02.1997		(4)	
Heðin Klakstein	30.04.1992	23	(1)	2
Ólavur Mikkelsen	11.01.1992	15	(10)	2
Ari Olsen	09.09.1998	27		1
Jannik Mathias Olsen	28.12.1998	8	(10)	
Leivur Zachariassen	07.02.1994	17	(4)	
Forwards:	**DOB**	**M**	**(s)**	**G**
Jónhard Frederiksberg	27.08.1980		(1)	
Andreas Jacobsen	25.11.1999		(6)	
Brian Jacobsen	04.11.1991	20	(3)	10
Jákup Johansen	27.04.1993	6	(6)	4
Søren Brøsted Nielsen (DEN)	03.11.1990	10	(1)	6
Trainer:	**DOB**	**M**		
Eyðun Klakstein	28.11.1972	27		

Tvøroyrar Bóltfelag / Football Club Suðuroy / Royn Hvalba

Founded: 2017
Stadium: Við Stórá Stadium, Trongisvágur (4,000)

Goalkeepers:	DOB	M	(s)	G
Miloš Budaković (SRB)	10.07.1991	23		
Rani Johannessen	25.02.1990	4		
Defenders:	**DOB**	**M**	**(s)**	**G**
Ibrahim Arifović (SRB)	24.02.1990	25		1
Eirikur Ellendersen	05.03.1994	24	(1)	2
Dánjal Godtfred	07.03.1996	24		3
Dennis Nielsen (DEN)	04.06.1991	27		1
Teitur Olsen	10.05.1995	25		
Midfielders:	**DOB**	**M**	**(s)**	**G**
Salmundur Bech	10.01.1996	25		3
Nikolei Johannesen	15.05.2001		(1)	
Rani Johansen	30.06.1997	3	(3)	
John Villi Leo	13.08.1997	20	(3)	
Teitur Mortensen	01.01.1996	3	(3)	
Ari Krosslá Poulsen	27.07.1997	1	(14)	
Stefan Radosavljević	08.09.2000	22	(3)	5
Isaac Shaze (GHA)	25.06.1989	13		1
Forwards:	**DOB**	**M**	**(s)**	**G**
Búi Egilsson	04.01.1996	22	(2)	4
Pape Mamadou Faye (ISL)	06.03.1991	11		5
Poul Ingason	28.09.1995	10	(1)	
Reidar Joensen	27.03.1991	1	(1)	1
Heri Kjærbo	01.06.1995	13	(6)	
Jón Krosslá Poulsen	17.02.1988	1	(7)	
Trainer:	**DOB**	**M**		
Glenn Leif Ståhl (SWE)	25.08.1971	27		

Víkingur Gøta

Founded: 14.01.2008 (*after the merger of GÍ Gøta and Leirvík ÍF*)
Stadium: Sarpugerði, Norðragøta (3,000)

Goalkeepers:	DOB	M	(s)	G
Bárður á Reynatrøð	08.01.2000	3		
Elias Rasmussen	13.05.1996	23		
Tamas Túri Géza (HUN)	11.03.1974	1		
Defenders:	**DOB**	**M**	**(s)**	**G**
Adrian Cașcaval (MDA)	10.06.1987	19	(4)	6
Hans Djurhuus	29.11.1978	11		
Atli Gregersen	15.06.1982	23		1
Pól Enok Hansen	18.06.1997	1	(2)	
Magnus Heinason	18.12.1999		(6)	1
Hanus Jacobsen	25.05.1985	26		2
Dennis Nieblas (ESP)	16.10.1990	15	(2)	
Gunnar Vatnhamar	29.03.1995	26		4
Midfielders:	**DOB**	**M**	**(s)**	**G**
Magnus Jarnskor	14.12.1995		(2)	
Sámal Jákup Joensen	07.04.1993	1		
Elias Jóhannesson Lervig	26.02.1997	17	(4)	
Hans Jákup Lervig	26.02.1997	12	(9)	
Karl Løkin	19.04.1991	10		
Hjalti Strømsten	21.01.1997	11	(3)	1
Arnbjørn Svensson	01.07.1999		(1)	
Sølvi Vatnhamar	05.05.1986	22		5
Forwards:	**DOB**	**M**	**(s)**	**G**
Filip Đorđević (SRB)	07.03.1994	19	(5)	3
Heðin Hansen	30.07.1993	17	(2)	4
Adeshina Lawal (NGA)	17.10.1984	25	(2)	8
Andreas Olsen	09.10.1987	13	(8)	4
Tonni Thomsen	05.02.1999	2	(4)	
Trainer:	**DOB**	**M**		
Maurice Ross (SCO)	03.02.1981	11		
Sigfríður Clementsen [25.05.2018]	27.01.1973	16		

SECOND LEVEL

1.deild 2018

1.	ÍF Fuglafjarðar (*Promoted*)	27	21	3	3	91	-	39	66
2.	NSÍ Runavík II	27	16	4	7	83	-	38	52
3.	KÍ Klaksvík II	27	16	4	7	68	-	34	52
4.	B68 Toftir	27	16	4	7	60	-	34	52
5.	Víkingur Gøta II	27	11	5	11	43	-	45	38
6.	HB Tórshavn II	27	9	5	13	48	-	46	32
7.	Skála ÍF II	27	9	5	13	46	-	59	32
8.	B71 Sandoy	27	9	1	17	45	-	67	28
9.	FF Giza / FC Hoyvík (*Relegated*)	27	7	5	15	36	-	49	26
10.	TB/FC Suðuroy/Royn II (*Relegated*)	27	1	4	22	20	-	129	7

NATIONAL TEAM

INTERNATIONAL MATCHES
(16.07.2018 – 15.07.2019)

07.09.2018	Tórshavn	Faroe Islands - Malta	3-1(2-1)	(UNL)
10.09.2018	Pristina	Kosovo - Faroe Islands	2-0(0-0)	(UNL)
11.10.2018	Tórshavn	Faroe Islands - Azerbaijan	0-3(0-1)	(UNL)
14.10.2018	Tórshavn	Faroe Islands - Kosovo	1-1(0-1)	(UNL)
17.11.2018	Bakı	Azerbaijan - Faroe Islands	2-0(2-0)	(UNL)
20.11.2018	Attard	Malta - Faroe Islands	1-1(1-1)	(UNL)
23.03.2019	Attard	Malta - Faroe Islands	2-1(1-0)	(ECQ)
26.03.2019	Cluj-Napoca	Romania - Faroe Islands	4-1(3-1)	(ECQ)
07.06.2019	Tórshavn	Faroe Islands - Spain	1-4(1-3)	(ECQ)
10.06.2019	Tórshavn	Faroe Islands - Norway	0-2(0-0)	(ECQ)

07.09.2018 FAROE ISLANDS - MALTA 3-1(2-1) UEFA Nations League D, Group 3
Tórsvøllur, Tórshavn; Referee: Ville Nevalainen (Finland); Attendance: 3,234
FRO: Gunnar Nielsen, Atli Gregersen (Cap), Viljormur í Heiðunum Davidsen, Sonni Ragnar Nattestad, Gunnar Vatnhamar, Jóan Símun Edmundsson, Sølvi Vatnhamar (90.Rógvi Asmundur Baldvinsson), Hallur Hansson, Brandur Hendriksson Olsen (86.Finnur Justinussen), René Joensen, Gilli Rólantsson Sørensen (81.Kaj Leo í Bartalsstovu). Trainer: Lars Christian Olsen (Denmark).
Goals: Jóan Símun Edmundsson (31), René Joensen (38), Hallur Hansson (51).

10.09.2018 KOSOVO - FAROE ISLANDS 2-0(0-0) UEFA Nations League D, Group 3
Stadiumi „Fadil Vokrri", Pristina; Referee: Bart Vertenten (Belgium); Attendance: 12,677
FRO: Gunnar Nielsen, Atli Gregersen (Cap), Viljormur í Heiðunum Davidsen, Sonni Ragnar Nattestad, Gunnar Vatnhamar, Jóan Símun Edmundsson, Kaj Leo í Bartalsstovu (80.Rógvi Asmundur Baldvinsson), Hallur Hansson, Brandur Hendriksson Olsen (63.Sølvi Vatnhamar), René Joensen, Gilli Rólantsson Sørensen (89.Klæmint Andrasson Olsen). Trainer: Lars Christian Olsen (Denmark).

11.10.2018 FAROE ISLANDS - AZERBAIJAN 0-3(0-1) UEFA Nations League D, Group 3
Tórsvøllur, Tórshavn; Referee: Aleksei Eskov (Russia); Attendance: 2,820
FRO: Gunnar Nielsen, Odmar Færø, Atli Gregersen (Cap), Viljormur í Heiðunum Davidsen, Jóan Símun Edmundsson, Kaj Leo í Bartalsstovu (74.Rógvi Asmundur Baldvinsson), Hallur Hansson (78.Heini Vatnsdal), Brandur Hendriksson Olsen, Finnur Justinussen (78.Klæmint Andrasson Olsen), René Joensen, Gilli Rólantsson Sørensen. Trainer: Lars Christian Olsen (Denmark).

14.10.2018 FAROE ISLANDS - KOSOVO 1-1(0-1) UEFA Nations League D, Group 3
Tórsvøllur, Tórshavn; Referee: Miroslav Zelinka (Czech Republic); Attendance: 2,300
FRO: Gunnar Nielsen, Odmar Færø, Atli Gregersen (Cap), Viljormur í Heiðunum Davidsen, Rógvi Asmundur Baldvinsson, Jóan Símun Edmundsson (68.Klæmint Andrasson Olsen), Sonni Ragnar Nattestad, Hallur Hansson, Brandur Hendriksson Olsen (83.Heini Vatnsdal), René Joensen, Gilli Rólantsson Sørensen. Trainer: Lars Christian Olsen (Denmark).
Goal: René Joensen (50).

17.11.2018 AZERBAIJAN - FAROE ISLANDS 2-0(2-0) UEFA Nations League D, Group 3
Olimpiya Stadionu, Bakı; Referee: Demetrios Masias (Cyprus); Attendance: 12,65
FRO: Gunnar Nielsen, Odmar Færø (73.Árni Frederiksberg), Atli Gregersen (Cap), Viljormur í Heiðunum Davidsen (46.Kaj Leo í Bartalsstovu), Rógvi Asmundur Baldvinsson, Sonni Ragnar Nattestad, Sølvi Vatnhamar, Hallur Hansson, Brandur Hendriksson Olsen, Klæmint Andrasson Olsen (63.Jákup Ludvig Thomsen), Gilli Rólantsson Sørensen. Trainer: Lars Christian Olsen (Denmark).

20.11.2018 MALTA - FAROE ISLANDS 1-1(1-1) UEFA Nations League D, Group 3
Ta'Qali National Stadium, Attard; Referee: Vitali Meshkov (Russia); Attendance: 2,152
FRO: Gunnar Nielsen, Atli Gregersen (Cap), Viljormur í Heiðunum Davidsen, Sonni Ragnar Nattestad (83.Odmar Færø), Heini Vatnsdal, Sølvi Vatnhamar (68.Kaj Leo í Bartalsstovu), Hallur Hansson, Brandur Hendriksson Olsen, René Joensen, Rógvi Asmundur Baldvinsson, Jákup Ludvig Thomsen (75.Klæmint Andrasson Olsen). Trainer: Lars Christian Olsen (Denmark).
Goal: René Joensen (3).

23.03.2019 MALTA - FAROE ISLANDS 2-1(1-0) 16th EC. Qualifiers
Ta'Qali National Stadium, Attard; Referee: Vilhjálmur Þórarinsson (Iceland); Attendance: 7,531
FRO: Gunnar Nielsen, Odmar Færø, Atli Gregersen (Cap), Viljormur í Heiðunum Davidsen, Rógvi Asmundur Baldvinsson (79.Árni Frederiksberg), Sølvi Vatnhamar (68.Kaj Leo í Bartalsstovu), Hallur Hansson, Brandur Hendriksson Olsen, René Joensen (72.Klæmint Andrasson Olsen), Gilli Rólantsson Sørensen, Jákup Ludvig Thomsen. Trainer: Lars Christian Olsen (Denmark).
Goal: Jákup Ludvig Thomsen (90+8).

26.03.2019 ROMANIA - FAROE ISLANDS 4-1(3-1) 16th EC. Qualifiers
Stadionul "Dr. Constantin Rădulescu", Cluj-Napoca; Referee: Halil Umut Meler (Turkey); Attendance: 10,502
FRO: Gunnar Nielsen, Odmar Færø, Atli Gregersen (Cap), Viljormur í Heiðunum Davidsen, Heini Vatnsdal (28.Rógvi Asmundur Baldvinsson), Kaj Leo í Bartalsstovu (67.Árni Frederiksberg), Hallur Hansson (77.Sølvi Vatnhamar), Klæmint Andrasson Olsen, Brandur Hendriksson Olsen, René Joensen, Gilli Rólantsson Sørensen. Trainer: Lars Christian Olsen (Denmark).
Goal: Viljormur í Heiðunum Davidsen (40 penalty).

07.06.2019 FAROE ISLANDS - SPAIN 1-4(1-3) 16th EC. Qualifiers
Tórsvøllur, Tórshavn; Referee: Enea Jorgji (Albania); Attendance: 4,800
FRO: Teitur Matras Gestsson, Odmar Færø, Atli Gregersen (Cap), Viljormur í Heiðunum Davidsen, Sølvi Vatnhamar, Heini Vatnsdal (74.Rógvi Asmundur Baldvinsson), Hallur Hansson, Árni Frederiksberg (86.Meinhard Egilsson Olsen), Brandur Hendriksson Olsen, Klæmint Andrasson Olsen (68.Patrik Johannesen), Gilli Rólantsson Sørensen. Trainer: Lars Christian Olsen (Denmark).
Goal: Klæmint Andrasson Olsen (30).

10.06.2019 FAROE ISLANDS - NORWAY 0-2(0-0) 16th EC. Qualifiers

Tórsvøllur, Tórshavn; Referee: Donatas Rumšas (Lithuania); Attendance: 3,083

FRO: Teitur Matras Gestsson, Odmar Færø, Atli Gregersen (Cap), Viljormur í Heiðunum Davidsen, Rógvi Asmundur Baldvinsson, Sølvi Vatnhamar (69.Árni Frederiksberg), Hallur Hansson, Brandur Hendriksson Olsen, René Joensen (84.Heini Vatnsdal), Klæmint Andrasson Olsen (89.Patrik Johannesen), Gilli Rólantsson Sørensen. Trainer: Lars Christian Olsen (Denmark).

NATIONAL TEAM PLAYERS
(16.07.2018 – 15.07.2019)

Name	DOB	Caps	Goals	2018/2019:	*Club*
Goalkeepers					
Teitur Matras GESTSSON	19.08.1992	**5**	**0**	2019:	*HB Tórshavn*
Gunnar NIELSEN	07.10.1986	**52**	**0**	2018/2019:	*FH Hafnarfjarðar (ISL)*
Defenders					
Rógvi Asmundur BALDVINSSON	06.12.1989	**40**	**3**	2018/2019:	*Bryne FK (NOR)*
Viljormur í Heiðunum DAVIDSEN	19.07.1991	**33**	**1**	2018/2019:	*Vejle BK (DEN)*
Odmar FÆRØ	01.11.1989	**28**	**0**	2018:	*B36 Tórshavn*
				23.01.2019->	*Hamarkameratene (NOR)*
Atli GREGERSEN	15.06.1982	**53**	**1**	2018/2019:	*Víkingur Gøta*
Sonni Ragnar NATTESTAD	05.08.1994	**25**	**2**	2018:	*Molde FK (NOR)*
Heini VATNSDAL	18.10.1991	**13**	**0**	2018/2019:	*BK Fremad Amager (DEN)*
Midfielders					
Kaj Leo í BARTALSSTOVU	23.06.1991	**24**	**1**	2018/2019:	*ÍB Vestmannaeyja (ISL)*
Hallur HANSSON	08.07.1992	**43**	**5**	2018/2019:	*AC Horsens (DEN)*
René Shaki JOENSEN	08.02.1993	**25**	**3**	2018/2019:	*UMF Grindavík (ISL)*
Patrik JOHANNESEN	07.09.1995	**5**	**0**	2019:	*KÍ Klaksvík*
Brandur Hendriksson OLSEN	19.12.1995	**26**	**3**	2018/2019:	*FH Hafnarfjörður (ISL)*
Gilli Rólantsson SØRENSEN	11.08.1992	**33**	**1**	2018/2019:	*SK Brann Bergen (NOR)*
Gunnar VATNHAMAR	29.03.1995	**4**	**0**	2018:	*Víkingur Gøta*
Sølvi VATNHAMAR	05.05.1986	**31**	**1**	2018/2019:	*Víkingur Gøta*
Forwards					
Jóan Símun EDMUNDSSON	26.07.1991	**52**	**7**	2018:	*DSC Arminia Bielefeld (GER)*
Árni FREDERIKSBERG	13.06.1992	**7**	**0**	2018:	*NSÍ Runavík*
				08.01.2019->	*B36 Tórshavn*
Finnur JUSTINUSSEN	30.03.1989	**6**	**0**	2018/2019:	*Næstved Boldklub (DEN)*
Klæmint Andrasson OLSEN	17.07.1990	**23**	**1**	2018/2019:	*NSÍ Runavík*
Meinhard Egilsson OLSEN	10.04.1997	**1**	**0**	2019:	*Kristiansund BK (NOR)*
Jákup Ludvig THOMSEN	23.11.1997	**3**	**1**	2018/2019:	*FH Hafnarfjarðar (ISL)*

National team coach

Lars Christian OLSEN (Denmark) [from 01.12.2011]	02.02.1961	49 M; 8 W; 7 D; 34 L; 31-90

FINLAND

The Country:

Suomen tasavalta (Republic of Finland)
Capital: Helsinki
Surface: 338,424 km^2
Inhabitants: 5,520,535 [2018]
Time: UTC+2

The FA:

Suomen Palloliitto
Urheilukatu 1 PO Box 191, 00251 Helsinki
Tel: +358 9 7421 51
Foundation date: 1907
Member of FIFA since: 1908
Member of UEFA since: 1954
Website: https://www.palloliitto.fi

NATIONAL TEAM RECORDS

First international match:	22.10.1911, Helsinki:	Finland – Sweden 2-5
Most international caps:	Jari Olavi Litmanen	- 137 caps (1989-2010)
Most international goals:	Jari Olavi Litmanen	- 32 goals / 137 caps (1989-2010)

UEFA EUROPEAN CHAMPIONSHIP	
1960	Did not enter
1964	Did not enter
1968	Qualifiers
1972	Qualifiers
1976	Qualifiers
1980	Qualifiers
1984	Qualifiers
1988	Qualifiers
1992	Qualifiers
1996	Qualifiers
2000	Qualifiers
2004	Qualifiers
2008	Qualifiers
2012	Qualifiers
2016	Qualifiers

FIFA WORLD CUP	
1930	*Did not enter*
1934	*Did not enter*
1938	Qualifiers
1950	*Withdrew*
1954	Qualifiers
1958	Qualifiers
1962	Qualifiers
1966	Qualifiers
1970	Qualifiers
1974	Qualifiers
1978	Qualifiers
1982	Qualifiers
1986	Qualifiers
1990	Qualifiers
1994	Qualifiers
1998	Qualifiers
2002	Qualifiers
2006	Qualifiers
2010	Qualifiers
2014	Qualifiers
2018	Qualifiers

UEFA NATIONS LEAGUE
2018/2019 – League C (promoted to League B)

OLYMPIC FOOTBALL TOURNAMENTS 1908-2016							
1908	-	**1948**	-	**1972**	*Withdrew*	**1996**	Qualifiers
1912	-	**1952**	Round 1	**1976**	Qualifiers	**2000**	Qualifiers
1920	-	**1956**	-	**1980**	Group Stage	**2004**	Qualifiers
1924	-	**1960**	Qualifiers	**1984**	Qualifiers	**2008**	Qualifiers
1928	-	**1964**	Qualifiers	**1988**	Qualifiers	**2012**	Qualifiers
1936	Qualifiers	**1968**	Qualifiers	**1992**	Qualifiers	**2016**	Qualifiers

FIFA CONFEDERATIONS CUP 1992-2017
None

FINNISH CLUB HONOURS IN EUROPEAN CLUB COMPETITIONS:

European Champion Clubs.Cup (1956-1992) / UEFA Champions League (1993-2019)
None
Fairs Cup (1858-1971) / UEFA Cup (1972-2009) / UEFA Europa League (2010-2019)
None
UEFA Super Cup (1972-2019)
None
European Cup Winners.Cup 1961-1999*
None

**defunct competition*

NATIONAL COMPETITIONS
TABLE OF HONOURS

	CHAMPIONS	CUP WINNERS	BEST GOALSCORERS	
1908	Unitas Helsinki	-	-	
1909	PUS Helsinki	-	-	
1910	Åbo IFK Turku	-	-	
1911	HJK Helsinki	-	-	
1912	HJK Helsinki	-	-	
1913	KIF Helsinki	-	-	
1914	*No competition*	-	-	
1915	KIF Helsinki	-	-	
1916	KIF Helsinki	-	-	
1917	HJK Helsinki	-	-	
1918	HJK Helsinki	-	-	
1919	HJK Helsinki	-	-	
1920	Åbo IFK Turku	-	-	
1921	Helsingin Palloseura	-	-	
1922	Helsingin Palloseura	-	-	
1923	HJK Helsinki	-	-	
1924	Åbo IFK Turku	-	-	
1925	HJK Helsinki	-	-	
1926	Helsingin Palloseura	-	-	
1927	Helsingin Palloseura	-	-	
1928	TPS Turku	-	-	
1929	Helsingin Palloseura	-	-	
1930	IFK Helsingfors	-	Holger Salin (IFK Helsingfors) Olof Strömsten (KIF Helsinki)	9
1931	IFK Helsingfors	-	Holger Salin (IFK Helsingfors)	11
1932	Helsingin Palloseura	-	Lauri Lehtinen (TPS Turku)	13
1933	IFK Helsingfors	-	Olof Strömsten (IFK Helsingfors)	18
1934	Helsingin Palloseura	-	Olof Strömsten (IFK Helsingfors)	15
1935	Helsingin Palloseura	-	Aatos Lehtonen (HJK Helsinki) Nuutti Lintamo (VPS Vaasa)	13
1936	HJK Helsinki	-	Aatos Lehtonen (HJK Helsinki)	14
1937	IFK Helsingfors	-	Aatos Lehtonen (HJK Helsinki)	25
1938	HJK Helsinki	-	Aatos Lehtonen (HJK Helsinki)	14
1939	TPS Turku	-	Aatos Lehtonen (HJK Helsinki)	15
1940	Sudet Viipuri	-	*Not known*	
1941	TPS Turku	-	Jussi Valtonen (TPS Turku)	14
1942	HT Helsinki	-	*Not known*	
1943	*No competition*	-	-	
1944	VIFK Vaasa	-	Urho Teräs (TPS Turku) Leo Turunen (Sudet Viipuri)	9
1945	VPS Vaasa	-	*Not known*	
1946	VIFK Vaasa	-	*Not known*	
1947	IFK Helsingfors	-	*Not known*	
1948	VPS Vaasa	-	Stig-Göran Myntti (VIFK Vaasa)	15
1949	TPS Turku	-	Yrjö Asikainen (Ilves-Kissat Tampere) Kaimo Lintamo (VPS Vaasa)	20
1950	Ilves-Kissat Tampere	-	Yrjö Asikainen (Ilves-Kissat Tampere) Jorma Saarinen (VPS Vaasa)	15
1951	KTP Kotka	-	Åke Forsberg (KIF Helsinki)	16
1952	KTP Kotka	-	Mauri Vanhanen (KTP Kotka)	16
1953	VIFK Vaasa	-	Rainer Forss (Pyrkivä Turku)	15
1954	Pyrkivä Turku	-	Eino Koskinen (TuTo Turku)	16
1955	KIF Helsinki	FC Haka Valkeakoski	Yrjö Asikainen (KIF Helsinki)	12
1956	KuPS Kuopio	PPojat Helsinki	Pentti Styck (HJK Helsinki)	20
1957	Helsingin Palloseura	Drott Pietarsaari	Matti Sundelin (TPS Turku)	21
1958	KuPS Kuopio	KTP Kotka	Kalevi Lehtovirta (TPS Turku) Kai Pahlman (Helsingin Palloseura)	17
1959	IFK Helsingfors	FC Haka Valkeakoski	Matti Sundelin (TPS Turku)	21
1960	FC Haka Valkeakoski	FC Haka Valkeakoski	Matti Sundelin (TPS Turku)	30
1961	IFK Helsingfors	KTP Kotka	Kai Pahlman (Helsingin Palloseura)	20
1962	FC Haka Valkeakoski	Helsingin Palloseura	Tor Österlund (HIK Hanko)	22
1963	Reipas Lahti	FC Haka Valkeakoski	Juha Lyytikäinen (IFK Helsingfors)	16
1964	HJK Helsinki	Reipas Lahti	Arto Tolsa (KTP Kotka)	26
1965	FC Haka Valkeakoski	Åbo IFK Turku	Kai Pahlman (HJK Helsinki)	22
1966	KuPS Kuopio	HJK Helsinki	Markku Hyvärinen (KuPS Kuopio)	16
1967	Reipas Lahti	KTP Kotka	Tommy Lindholm (TPS Turku)	22
1968	TPS Turku	KuPS Kuopio	Tommy Lindholm (TPS Turku)	23
1969	KPV Kokkola	FC Haka Valkeakoski	Hannu Lamberg (KPV Kokkola) Pekka Talaslahti (HJK Helsinki)	18
1970	Reipas Lahti	MP Mikkeli	Matti Paatelainen (IFK Helsingfors)	20
1971	TPS Turku	MP Mikkeli	Pentti Toivola (MP Mikkeli)	17

1972	TPS Turku	Reipas Lahti	Matti Paatelainen (IFK Helsingfors) Heikki Suhonen (TPS Turku)	16
1973	HJK Helsinki	Reipas Lahti	Hannu Lamberg (KPV Kokkola)	13
1974	KuPS Kuopio	Reipas Lahti	Erkki Salo (TPS Turku)	17
1975	TPS Turku	Reipas Lahti	Reijo Rantanen (MiPK Mikkeli)	16
1976	KuPS Kuopio	Reipas Lahti	Matti Paatelainen (FC Haka Valkeakoski)	17
1977	FC Haka Valkeakoski	FC Haka Valkeakoski	Matti Paatelainen (FC Haka Valkeakoski)	20
1978	HJK Helsinki	Reipas Lahti	Atik Ismail (HJK Helsinki)	20
1979	OPS Oulu	FC Ilves Tampere	Atik Ismail (HJK Helsinki) Heikki Suhonen (TPS Turku)	15
1980	OPS Oulu	KTP Kotka	Hannu Rajaniemi (Sepsi-78 Seinäjoki)	19
1981	HJK Helsinki	HJK Helsinki	Juhani Himanka (OPS Oulu)	22
1982	FC Kuusysi Lahti	FC Haka Valkeakoski	Atik Ismail (HJK Helsinki)	19
1983	FC Ilves Tampere	FC Kuusysi Lahti	Mika Lipponen (TPS Turku)	22
1984	FC Kuusysi Lahti	HJK Helsinki	Mika Lipponen (TPS Turku)	25
1985	HJK Helsinki	FC Haka Valkeakoski	Ismo Lius (FC Kuusysi Lahti)	19
1986	FC Kuusysi Lahti	RoPS Rovaniemi	Ismo Lius (FC Kuusysi Lahti) Jari Niinimäki (FC Ilves Tampere)	13
1987	HJK Helsinki	FC Kuusysi Lahti	Ari Hjelm (FC Ilves Tampere)	20
1988	HJK Helsinki	FC Haka Valkeakoski	Ismo Lius (FC Kuusysi Lahti)	22
1989	FC Kuusysi Lahti	KuPS Kuopio	Ismo Lius (FC Kuusysi Lahti)	15
1990	HJK Helsinki	FC Ilves Tampere	Marek Czakon (POL, FC Ilves Tampere) Kimmo Tarkkio (HJK Helsinki)	16
1991	FC Kuusysi Lahti	TPS Turku	Kimmo Tarkkio (FC Haka Valkeakoski)	23
1992	HJK Helsinki	MyPa Myllykoski	Luiz Antônio Moraes (BRA, FC Jazz Pori)	21
1993	FC Jazz Pori	HJK Helsinki	Antti Sumiala (FC Jazz Pori)	20
1994	TPV Tampere	TPS Turku	Dionísio Domingos Rangel (BRA, TPV Tampere)	17
1995	FC Haka Valkeakoski	MyPa Myllykoski	Valeri Popovitch (RUS, FC Haka Valkeakoski)	21
1996	FC Jazz Pori	HJK Helsinki	Luiz Antônio Moraes (BRA, FC Jazz Pori)	17
1997	HJK Helsinki	FC Haka Valkeakoski	Rafael Pires Vieira (BRA, HJK Helsinki)	11
1998	FC Haka Valkeakoski	HJK Helsinki	Matti Hiukka (RoPS Rovaniemi)	11
1999	FC Haka Valkeakoski	Jokerit Helsinki	Valeri Popovitch (FC Haka Valkeakoski)	23
2000	FC Haka Valkeakoski	HJK Helsinki	Shefki Kuqi (Jokerit Helsinki)	19
2001	TamU Tampere	Atlantis Helsinki	Paulus Roiha (HJK Helsinki)	22
2002	HJK Helsinki	FC Haka Valkeakoski	Mika Kottila (HJK Helsinki)	18
2003	HJK Helsinki	HJK Helsinki	Saku Puhakainen (MyPa Myllykoski)	14
2004	FC Haka Valkeakoski	MyPa Myllykoski	Antti Pohja (TamU Tampere)	16
2005	MyPa Myllykoski	FC Haka Valkeakoski	Juho Mäkelä (HJK Helsinki)	16
2006	TamU Tampere	HJK Helsinki	Hermanni Vuorinen (FC Honka Espoo)	16
2007	TamU Tampere	TamU Tampere	Rafael Pires Vieira (BRA, FC Lahti)	14
2008	FC Inter Turku	HJK Helsinki	Aleksandr Kokko (FC Honka Espoo) Henri Myntti (TamU Tampere)	13
2009	HJK Helsinki	FC Inter Turku	Hermanni Vuorinen (FC Honka Espoo)	16
2010	HJK Helsinki	TPS Turku	Juho Mäkelä (HJK Helsinki)	16
2011	HJK Helsinki	HJK Helsinki	Timo Furuholm (FC Inter Turku)	22
2012	HJK Helsinki	FC Honka Espoo	Irakli Sirbiladze (GEO, FC Inter Turku)	17
2013	HJK Helsinki	RoPS Rovaniemi	Tim Väyrynen (FC Honka Espoo)	17
2014	HJK Helsinki	HJK Helsinki	Jonas Emet (FF Jaro Pietarsaari) Luis Emilio Solignac (ARG, IFK Mariehamn)	14
2015	SJK Seinäjoki	IFK Mariehamn	Aleksandr Kokko (RoPS Rovaniemi)	17
2016	IFK Mariehamn	SJK Seinäjoki	Roope Riski (SJK Seinäjoki)	17
2017	HJK Helsinki	HJK Helsinki	Aleksei Kangaskolkka (IFK Mariehamn)	16
2018	HJK Helsinki	FC Inter Turku	João Klauss De Mello (BRA, HJK Helsinki)	21

NATIONAL CHAMPIONSHIP
Veikkausliiga 2018
(07.04.2018 – 27.10.2018)

Results

Round 1 [07-08.04.2018]
Vaasan PS - FC Inter Turku 2-0(1-0)
SJK Seinäjoki - PS Kemi 0-1(0-0)
FC Lahti - TPS Turku 3-2(0-0)
HJK Helsinki - FC Ilves Tampere 3-1(0-1)
Rovaniemi PS - IFK Mariehamn 2-0(0-0)
Kuopion PS - FC Honka 1-1(1-1)

Round 2 [14-15.04.2018]
IFK Mariehamn - HJK Helsinki 0-1(0-0)
Vaasan PS - Rovaniemi PS 0-1(0-1)
FC Ilves Tampere - Kuopion PS 2-1(1-1)
PS Kemi - FC Inter Turku 2-4(1-2)
TPS Turku - SJK Seinäjoki 0-2(0-0)
FC Honka - FC Lahti 0-0

Round 3 [21-22.04.2018]
SJK Seinäjoki - FC Honka 2-0(1-0)
FC Inter Turku - TPS Turku 1-2(0-2)
HJK Helsinki - Kuopion PS 1-2(1-1)
FC Lahti - FC Ilves Tampere 2-0(1-0)
IFK Mariehamn - Vaasan PS 2-2(1-1)
Rovaniemi PS - PS Kemi 3-0(2-0)

Round 4 [28-29.04.2018]
TPS Turku - Rovaniemi PS 0-0
FC Honka - FC Inter Turku 2-2(2-1)
Vaasan PS - HJK Helsinki 1-2(1-0)
Kuopion PS - FC Lahti 1-1(0-1)
FC Ilves Tampere - SJK Seinäjoki 1-1(1-0)
PS Kemi - IFK Mariehamn 2-3(1-1)

Round 5 [03.05.2018]
Rovaniemi PS - FC Honka 1-2(1-0)
Vaasan PS - PS Kemi 3-1(2-0)
SJK Seinäjoki - Kuopion PS 1-3(1-1)
FC Inter Turku - FC Ilves Tampere 0-1(0-1)
HJK Helsinki - FC Lahti 1-2(0-1)
IFK Mariehamn - TPS Turku 3-2(1-1)

Round 6 [07.05.2018]
PS Kemi - HJK Helsinki 1-2(1-1)
FC Ilves Tampere - Rovaniemi PS 1-0(1-0)
TPS Turku - Vaasan PS 0-1(0-0)
Kuopion PS - FC Inter Turku 5-1(2-0)
FC Lahti - SJK Seinäjoki 1-0(0-0)
FC Honka - IFK Mariehamn 1-1(1-0)

Round 7 [13-14.05.2018]
PS Kemi - TPS Turku 2-2(2-1)
Rovaniemi PS - Kuopion PS 2-0(1-0)
IFK Mariehamn - FC Ilves Tampere 2-0(1-0)
Vaasan PS - FC Honka 1-1(0-1)
HJK Helsinki - Seinäjoki 4-0(1-0) [29.05.]
FC Inter Turku - FC Lahti 2-0(0-0) [26.09.]

Round 8 [18.05.2018]
FC Ilves Tampere - Vaasan PS 0-0
TPS Turku - HJK Helsinki 0-1(0-1)
FC Honka - PS Kemi 2-1(0-0)
Kuopion PS - IFK Mariehamn 2-1(2-1)
FC Lahti - Rovaniemi PS 0-0
SJK Seinäjoki - FC Inter Turku 0-1(0-1)

Round 9 [22.05.2018]
Vaasan PS - Kuopion PS 0-2(0-1)
TPS Turku - FC Honka 0-0
PS Kemi - FC Ilves Tampere 0-2(0-1)
HJK Helsinki - FC Inter Turku 3-0(0-0)
IFK Mariehamn - FC Lahti 1-2(0-1)
SJK Seinäjoki - Rovaniemi 2-1(0-0) [09.07.]

Round 10 [26.05.2018]
FC Ilves Tampere - TPS Turku 2-0(0-0)
Kuopion PS - PS Kemi 2-3(0-2)
SJK Seinäjoki - IFK Mariehamn 1-1(1-0)
FC Inter Turku - Rovaniemi PS 3-3(1-2)
HJK Helsinki - FC Honka 3-2(0-1)
FC Lahti - Vaasan PS 1-1(0-0)

Round 11 [01-02.06.2018]
Rovaniemi PS - HJK Helsinki 1-2(0-0)
TPS Turku - Kuopion PS 0-0
Vaasan PS - SJK Seinäjoki 1-1(1-0)
PS Kemi - FC Lahti 0-0
FC Honka - FC Ilves Tampere 4-1(1-1)
IFK Mariehamn - FC Inter Turku 2-3(0-2)

Round 12 [12.06.2018]
Kuopion PS - FC Ilves Tampere 3-1(2-1)
HJK Helsinki - IFK Mariehamn 2-0(1-0)
Rovaniemi PS - Vaasan PS 1-0(0-0)
FC Inter Turku - PS Kemi 1-0(1-0)
SJK Seinäjoki - TPS Turku 4-0(2-0)
FC Lahti - FC Honka 1-1(1-0)

Round 13 [15-16.06.2018]
TPS Turku - FC Lahti 1-1(1-0)
FC Honka - Kuopion PS 2-1(2-0)
FC Inter Turku - Vaasan PS 1-3(0-1)
PS Kemi - SJK Seinäjoki 1-0(1-0)
FC Ilves Tampere - HJK Helsinki 0-0
IFK Mariehamn - Rovaniemi PS 1-3(1-1)

Round 14 [20-21.06.2018]
Vaasan PS - IFK Mariehamn 4-1(2-0)
FC Ilves Tampere - FC Lahti 0-0
FC Honka - SJK Seinäjoki 3-1(2-1)
TPS Turku - FC Inter Turku 1-1(1-0)
Kuopion PS - HJK Helsinki 2-2(1-1)
PS Kemi - Rovaniemi PS 0-1(0-0)

Round 15 [25-26.06.2018]
HJK Helsinki - Vaasan PS 5-0(2-0)
FC Lahti - Kuopion PS 1-0(0-0)
IFK Mariehamn - PS Kemi 2-1(0-1)
SJK Seinäjoki - FC Ilves Tampere 2-3(0-0)
FC Inter Turku - FC Honka 2-3(0-1)
Rovaniemi PS - TPS Turku 0-0

Round 16 [29-30.06.2018]
TPS Turku - IFK Mariehamn 2-0(0-0)
FC Lahti - HJK Helsinki 2-1(1-0)
FC Ilves Tampere - FC Inter Turku 1-1(0-0)
PS Kemi - Vaasan PS 0-1(0-1)
FC Honka - Rovaniemi PS 2-2(1-2)
Kuopion PS - SJK Seinäjoki 1-1(0-0)

Round 17 [04.07.2018]
Rovaniemi PS - FC Ilves Tampere 2-0(0-0)
FC Inter Turku - Kuopion PS 0-1(0-0)
HJK Helsinki - PS Kemi 2-0(0-0)
SJK Seinäjoki - FC Lahti 1-0(1-0)
Vaasan PS - TPS Turku 2-0(2-0)
IFK Mariehamn - FC Honka 1-2(0-2)

Round 18 [07-08.07.2018]
Seinäjoki - HJK Helsinki 0-1(0-1) [18.04.]
Kuopion PS - Rovaniemi PS 0-1(0-0) [18.04.]
TPS Turku - PS Kemi 3-2(1-0)
FC Lahti - FC Inter Turku 1-2(1-2)
FC Honka - Vaasan PS 0-1(0-0)
Ilves Tampere - Mariehamn 1-2(0-0) [29.08.]

Round 19 [14.07.2018]
Rovaniemi PS - FC Lahti 2-0(1-0) [25.04.]
Vaasan PS - Ilves Tampere 1-1(1-0) [25.04.]
Mariehamn - Kuopion PS 1-4(1-1) [25.04.]
FC Inter Turku - SJK Seinäjoki 2-0(2-0)
HJK Helsinki - TPS Turku 2-1(0-0)
PS Kemi - FC Honka 1-1(1-1)

Round 20 [21-22.07.2018]
FC Inter Turku - HJK Helsinki 0-0 [25.04.]
Rovaniemi PS - SJK Seinäjoki 1-0(0-0)
FC Honka - TPS Turku 2-0(1-0)
FC Ilves Tampere - PS Kemi 2-0(1-0)
Kuopion PS - Vaasan PS 1-2(1-2)
FC Lahti - IFK Mariehamn 2-0(0-0)

Round 21 [26-30.07.2018]
Rovaniemi PS - FC Inter Turku 0-1(0-0)
FC Honka - HJK Helsinki 1-2(0-1)
PS Kemi - Kuopion PS 3-2(3-2)
IFK Mariehamn - SJK Seinäjoki 1-0(0-0)
Vaasan PS - FC Lahti 2-2(2-1)
TPS Turku - FC Ilves Tampere 1-3(0-2)

Round 22 [03-05.08.2018]
SJK Seinäjoki - Vaasan PS 0-0
HJK Helsinki - Rovaniemi PS 2-2(1-0)
FC Inter Turku - IFK Mariehamn 3-0(1-0)
Kuopion PS - TPS Turku 3-2(2-2)
FC Ilves Tampere - FC Honka 3-3(1-2)
FC Lahti - PS Kemi 1-1(1-1)

Round 23 [11-12.08.2018]
FC Honka - TPS Turku 3-0(2-0)
Vaasan PS - SJK Seinäjoki 0-2(0-1)
FC Lahti - FC Inter Turku 0-0
Kuopion PS - PS Kemi 3-1(2-0)
Rovaniemi PS - IFK Mariehamn 1-0(0-0)
Ilves Tamp. - HJK Helsinki 1-2(1-2) [26.09.]

Round 24 [17-20.08.2018]
TPS Turku - Vaasan PS 4-1(2-0)
FC Inter Turku - Kuopion PS 0-1(0-1)
HJK Helsinki - PS Kemi 0-0
IFK Mariehamn - FC Honka 0-0
FC Lahti - Rovaniemi PS 1-2(0-1)
SJK Seinäjoki - FC Ilves Tampere 2-3(0-1)

Round 25 [24-26.08.2018]
Vaasan PS - IFK Mariehamn 1-1(1-1)
FC Inter Turku - Rovaniemi PS 0-0
PS Kemi - SJK Seinäjoki 0-0
FC Honka - FC Lahti 2-0(1-0)
FC Ilves Tampere - TPS Turku 2-0(1-0)
Kuopion PS - HJK Helsinki 0-1(0-0)

Round 26 [31.08.-02.09.2018]
FC Lahti - Vaasan PS 1-1(1-0)
TPS Turku - PS Kemi 4-1(2-1)
Rovaniemi PS - FC Honka 2-1(2-0)
SJK Seinäjoki - Kuopion PS 1-2(1-0)
HJK Helsinki - FC Inter Turku 3-0(2-0)
IFK Mariehamn - FC Ilves Tampere 3-6(1-0)

Round 27 [13-14.09.2018]
Kuopion PS - FC Lahti 2-1(0-0)
HJK Helsinki - IFK Mariehamn 2-0(1-0)
SJK Seinäjoki - TPS Turku 1-0(1-0)
FC Ilves Tampere - FC Honka 0-1(0-1)
FC Inter Turku - Vaasan PS 1-1(1-1)
PS Kemi - Rovaniemi PS 0-2(0-1)

Round 28 [17.09.2018]
FC Lahti - HJK Helsinki 0-2(0-1)
Rovaniemi PS - Kuopion PS 1-1(0-0)
FC Honka - PS Kemi 2-1(0-0)
Vaasan PS - FC Ilves Tampere 1-2(1-2)
TPS Turku - FC Inter Turku 1-0(0-0)
IFK Mariehamn - SJK Seinäjoki 1-0(1-0)

Round 29 [21-23.09.2018]
HJK Helsinki - Rovaniemi PS 3-0(1-0)
SJK Seinäjoki - FC Lahti 0-0
PS Kemi - Vaasan PS 0-2(0-0)
Kuopion PS - FC Honka 1-1(0-1)
FC Ilves Tampere - FC Inter Turku 1-0(0-0)
IFK Mariehamn - TPS Turku 2-2(1-2)

Round 30 [29-30.09.2018]
FC Honka - HJK Helsinki 0-0
Vaasan PS - Kuopion PS 0-3(0-1)
FC Ilves Tampere - PS Kemi 4-0(0-0)
FC Inter Turku - IFK Mariehamn 1-1(0-0)
Rovaniemi PS - SJK Seinäjoki 0-1(0-1)
FC Lahti - TPS Turku 2-5(1-4)

Round 31 [06-07.10.2018]
PS Kemi - FC Inter Turku 0-2(0-0)
TPS Turku - Rovaniemi PS 1-2(0-2)
SJK Seinäjoki - FC Honka 0-1(0-1)
IFK Mariehamn - FC Lahti 3-0(1-0)
HJK Helsinki - Vaasan PS 1-0(0-0)
Kuopion PS - FC Ilves Tampere 2-0(1-0)

Round 32 [21.10.2018]
Vaasan PS - Rovaniemi PS 1-2(0-0)
PS Kemi - IFK Mariehamn 2-0(1-0)
Kuopion PS - TPS Turku 2-1(0-1)
HJK Helsinki - SJK Seinäjoki 1-0(1-0)
FC Ilves Tampere - FC Lahti 0-1(0-0)
FC Inter Turku - FC Honka 0-2(0-1)

Round 33 [27.10.2018]
FC Lahti - PS Kemi 1-2(0-0)
Rovaniemi PS - FC Ilves Tampere 1-0(1-0)
FC Honka - Vaasan PS 3-1(2-0)
SJK Seinäjoki - FC Inter Turku 2-2(2-0)
TPS Turku - HJK Helsinki 0-4(0-2)
IFK Mariehamn - Kuopion PS 1-2(1-1)

Final Standings

1.	**HJK Helsinki**	33	24	6	3	61	-	19	78
2.	Rovaniemen Palloseura	33	18	8	7	42	-	25	62
3.	Kuopion Palloseura	33	17	7	9	56	-	37	58
4.	FC Honka Espoo	33	15	13	5	51	-	33	58
5.	FC Ilves Tampere	33	14	7	12	45	-	41	49
6.	Vaasan Palloseura	33	10	11	12	37	-	43	41
7.	FC Inter Turku	33	10	10	13	37	-	44	40
8.	FC Lahti	33	9	13	11	30	-	38	40
9.	SJK Seinäjoki	33	8	8	17	28	-	37	32
10.	IFK Mariehamn	33	8	7	18	37	-	59	31
11.	Turun Palloseura Turku (*Relegation Play-offs*)	33	7	8	18	37	-	55	29
12.	Palloseura Kemi Kings (*Relegated*)	33	6	6	21	29	-	59	24

Top goalscorers:

21 João Klauss De Mello (BRA) *HJK Helsinki*

17 Rasmus Karjalainen *Kuopion Palloseura*

16 Macoumba Kandji (SEN) *FC Honka Espoo*

Relegation Play-offs [31.10.-03.11.2018]

Kokkolan Palloveikot - Turun Palloseura Turku	0-0	1-1(1-1)

Kokkolan Palloveikot promoted for the 2019 Veikkausliiga.

NATIONAL CUP
Suomen cup 2018

Fourth Round [19.01.-10.03.2018]

Group A	
Kuopion Palloseura - Musan Salama	5-2(2-1)
PS Kemi Kings - AC Kajaani	0-2(0-0)
AC Kajaani - AC Oulu	3-4(2-2)
Musan Salama - Rovaniemen Palloseura	0-6(0-3)
PS Kemi Kings - Kuopion Palloseura	1-3(1-1)
Rovaniemen Palloseura - PS Kemi Kings	1-2(0-0)
Kuopion Palloseura - AC Kajaani	6-1(2-1)
AC Oulu - Rovaniemen Palloseura	1-1(0-1)
Musan Salama - PS Kemi Kings	2-2(2-0)
Rovaniemen Palloseura - AC Kajaani	4-2(3-1)
AC Oulu - Kuopion Palloseura	2-6(1-3)
AC Oulu - Musan Salama	4-1(2-1)
PS Kemi Kings - AC Oulu	1-2(1-0)
Kuopion Palloseura - Rovaniemen Palloseura	2-0(1-0)
AC Kajaani - Musan Salama	2-0(2-0)
Qualified: Kuopion Palloseura (Quarter-Finals), AC Oulu (Play-offs)	

Group B	
Kokkolan Palloveikot - TPV Tampere	0-0
SJK Seinäjoki - PK Keski-Uusimaa	4-0(1-0)
Vaasan Palloseura - FF Jaro Jakobstad	2-0(0-0)
Kokkolan Palloveikot - SJK Seinäjoki	1-2(0-2)
TPV Tampere - FF Jaro Jakobstad	2-6(1-3)
PK Keski-Uusimaa - Vaasan Palloseura	0-5(0-2)
FF Jaro Jakobstad - PK Keski-Uusimaa	4-0(2-0)
SJK Seinäjoki - TPV Tampere	4-0(1-0)
Vaasan Palloseura - Kokkolan Palloveikot	3-3(2-2)
Vaasan Palloseura - TPV Tampere	6-0(2-0)
FF Jaro Jakobstad - SJK Seinäjoki	1-1(0-0)
PK Keski-Uusimaa - Kokkolan Palloveikot	1-5(1-3)
SJK Seinäjoki - Vaasan Palloseura	1-0(1-0)
Kokkolan Palloveikot - FF Jaro Jakobstad	4-2(2-1)
TPV Tampere - PK Keski-Uusimaa	2-0(0-0)
Qualified: SJK Seinäjoki (Quarter-Finals), Vaasan Palloseura (Play-offs)	

Group C	
FC Lahti - FC Haka Valkeakoski	2-1(2-0)
JJK Jyväskylä - Grankulla IFK	2-0(1-0)
FC Ilves Tampere - FC Viikingit	3-0(1-0)
JJK Jyväskylä - FC Ilves Tampere	0-3(0-2)
Grankulla IFK - FC Haka Valkeakoski	2-3(2-1)
FC Viikingit - FC Lahti	2-2(0-1)
FC Lahti - JJK Jyväskylä	4-2(2-1)
FC Ilves Tampere - Grankulla IFK	3-1(3-0)
FC Haka Valkeakoski - FC Viikingit	5-1(2-0)
FC Ilves Tampere - FC Lahti	2-2(0-2)
FC Viikingit - JJK Jyväskylä	0-1(0-0)
FC Lahti - Grankulla IFK	2-1(2-1)
FC Haka Valkeakoski - FC Ilves Tampere	0-0
JJK Jyväskylä - FC Haka Valkeakoski	1-2(1-0)
Grankulla IFK - FC Viikingit	2-1(1-0)
Qualified: FC Ilves Tampere (Quarter-Finals), FC Lahti, FC Haka Valkeakoski (Play-offs)	

Group D	
IFK Helsingfors - IF Gnistan	1-1(1-0)
HJK Helsinki - PEPO Lappeenranta	4-1(2-1)
IF Gnistan - HJK Helsinki	0-8(0-3)
FC Honka Espoo - FC Kotkan Työväen Palloilijat	1-0(0-0)
FC Kotkan Työväen Palloilijat - IF Gnistan	2-0(2-0)
PEPO Lappeenranta - IFK Helsingfors	1-4(0-3)
IFK Helsingfors - FC Kotkan Työväen Palloilijat	3-1(1-1)
IF Gnistan - PEPO Lappeenranta	1-0(0-0)
IFK Helsingfors - FC Honka Espoo	2-3(2-1)
HJK Helsinki - FC Kotkan Työväen Palloilijat	5-1(3-0)
HJK Helsinki - IFK Helsingfors	1-0(0-0)
PEPO Lappeenranta - FC Honka Espoo	0-3(0-1)
FC Honka Espoo - IF Gnistan	6-0(1-0)
FC Kotkan Työväen Palloilijat - PEPO Lappeenranta	6-1(2-1)
FC Honka Espoo - HJK Helsinki	2-1(1-0)
Qualified: FC Honka Espoo (Quarter-Finals), HJK Helsinki (Play-offs)	

Group E	
FC Inter Turku - Ekenäs IF	3-0(0-0)
Turun Palloseura Turku - Klubi 04 Helsinki	1-1(0-0)
IFK Mariehamn - FC Honka Espoo II	4-0(2-0)
IFK Mariehamn - Klubi 04 Helsinki	4-2(3-2)
Turun Palloseura Turku - IFK Mariehamn	1-1(0-1)
Klubi 04 Helsinki - FC Honka Espoo II	4-0(1-0)
FC Inter Turku - Turun Palloseura Turku	0-0
Klubi 04 Helsinki - Ekenäs IF	2-3(1-2)
IFK Mariehamn - FC Inter Turku	2-4(1-3)
Ekenäs IF - IFK Mariehamn	1-0(0-0)
FC Honka Espoo II - Turun Palloseura Turku	0-1(0-1)
FC Inter Turku - Klubi 04 Helsinki	4-0(2-0)
Ekenäs IF - FC Honka Espoo II	3-0(0-0)
Turun Palloseura Turku - Ekenäs IF	0-0
FC Honka Espoo II - FC Inter Turku	0-7(0-2)
Qualified: FC Inter Turku (Quarter-Finals), Ekenäs IF (Play-offs)	

Play-offs [17-18.03.2018]	
Ekenäs IF - AC Oulu	1-0(0-0)
HJK Helsinki - Vaasan Palloseura	4-1(0-0)
FC Haka Valkeakoski - FC Lahti	3-1 aet

Quarter-Finals [29.03.2018]	
FC Inter Turku - FC Ilves Tampere	2-0(0-0)
Ekenäs IF - FC Haka Valkeakoski	2-1(1-0)
SJK Seinäjoki - FC Honka Espoo	1-2(0-2)
HJK Helsinki - Kuopion Palloseura	2-0(2-0)

Semi-Finals [02-03.04.2018]	
HJK Helsinki - FC Honka Espoo	2-1(1-0)
Ekenäs IF - FC Inter Turku	0-5(0-4)

Final

12.05.2018; Telia 5G Areena, Helsinki; Referee: Mikko Leino; Attendance: 3,540
HJK Helsinki - FC Inter Turku **0-1(0-0)**

HJK Helsinki: Maksim Rudakov, Rafinha Scapini de Almeida, Ville Jalasto, Hannu Patronen (85.Amr Gamal Sayed), Faith Obilor, Anthony Annan, Moshtagh Yaghoubi, Sebastian Dahlström, Filip Valenčič, Nikolai Alho (78.Eetu Vertainen), João Klauss de Mello. Trainer: Mika Lehkosuo.

FC Inter Turku: Henrik Moisander, Ari Nyman, Kenny Mansally, Tero Mäntylä, Teemu Penninkangas, Ivan Sesar (67.Mika Mäkitalo), Niilo Mäenpää, Timo Furuholm, Mika Ojala, Benjamin Källman (88.Lucas Gabriel López García), Albion Ademi (71.Mikko Kuningas). Trainer: Fabrizio Piccareta (Italy)

Goals: 0-1 Mikko Kuningas (82).

THE CLUBS 2018

Football Club Honska Espoo

Founded: 1957
Stadium: Tapiolan Urheilupuisto, Espoo (6,000)

Goalkeepers:	**DOB**	**M**	**(s)**	**G**
Tim Murray (USA)	30.07.1987	22		
Davor Taleski (MKD)	19.05.1995	11	(1)	
Defenders:	**DOB**	**M**	**(s)**	**G**
Henri Aalto	20.04.1989	11	(1)	
Ahmed El Amrani (NOR)	16.02.1992	11	(2)	
Robert Ivanov	21.07.1993	29	(1)	3
Jatuli Laevuo	19.05.1995	12		2
Tommi Saarinen	31.01.1995	13		
Željko Savić (SRB)	18.03.1988	2	(1)	
Midfielders:	**DOB**	**M**	**(s)**	**G**
Duarte Cartaxo-Tammilehto	15.02.1990	6	(2)	
Javier Hervás Salmoral „Javi Hervás“ (ESP)	09.06.1989	25	(1)	4
Jonas Levänen	12.01.1994	32		1
Armend Kabashi	04.12.1995	3	(3)	
Lucas Paz Kaufmann (BRA)	26.03.1991	27	(3)	6
Antti Mäkijärvi	08.12.1993	3	(15)	
Juho Ojanen	02.01.2002		(1)	
Joel Perovuo	11.08.1985	22	(1)	
Konsta Rasimus	15.12.1990	31	(1)	1
Forwards:	**DOB**	**M**	**(s)**	**G**
Mosawer Ahadi	08.03.2000		(1)	
Borja Martín González (ESP)	28.06.1987	30		12
Borjas Martín González (ESP)	28.11.1987	1		
Macoumba Kandji (SEN)	02.08.1985	22	(4)	16
Joni Korhonen	08.02.1987	4	(12)	
Kasperi Liikonen	09.09.1994	7	(10)	
Alex Nimely-Tchuimeni (ENG)	11.05.1991	6	(14)	
Nemanja Obradović (SRB)	29.05.1989	5	(3)	1
Masar Ömer	12.06.1993	2	(1)	
Youness Rahimi	13.02.1995	16	(11)	3
Demba Savage (GAM)	17.06.1988	10	(2)	1
Trainer:	**DOB**	**M**		
Vesa Vasara	16.08.1976	33		

Football Club International Turku

Founded: 1990
Stadium: Veritas Stadion, Turku (10,000)

Goalkeepers:	DOB	M	(s)	G
Jere Koponen	23.05.1992	16		
Henrik Moisander	29.09.1985	17		
Defenders:	**DOB**	**M**	**(s)**	**G**
Arttu Hoskonen	16.04.1997	22	(3)	1
Daniel Kamy (CMR)	08.03.1996	15	(1)	2
Kenny Mansally (GAM)	29.01.1989	17	(3)	2
Tero Mäntylä	18.04.1991	25	(1)	
Niko Markkula	27.06.1990	8	(4)	
Ari Nyman	07.02.1984	22	(5)	
Tatu Varmanen	09.07.1998	14	(3)	
Midfielders:	**DOB**	**M**	**(s)**	**G**
Sneyder Julián Guevara Muñoz (COL)	04.05.1992	6	(4)	
Kasper Kaan Kairinen	22.12.1998	6		
Lucas Gabriel López García (ARG)	13.01.1988	3	(5)	
Mikko Kuningas	30.07.1997	22	(6)	2
Matias Lahti	16.04.1999	6		
Niilo Mäenpää	14.01.1998	12	(5)	
Mika Mäkitalo	12.06.1985	19	(3)	1
Teemu Penninkangas	24.07.1992	28	(1)	1
Ivan Sesar (BIH)	29.08.1989	11	(2)	
Forwards:	**DOB**	**M**	**(s)**	**G**
Albion Ademi (ALB)	19.02.1999	15	(10)	4
Timo Furuholm	11.10.1987	25	(4)	9
Joona Järvistö	29.12.1996	8	(10)	2
Benjamin Källman	17.06.1998	17	(3)	8
Mika Ojala	21.06.1988	20	(7)	3
Ansu Sherrif	01.01.1999	1	(2)	
Lassi Viholainen	16.06.1999	8	(10)	1
Trainer:	**DOB**	**M**		
Fabrizio Piccareta (ITA)	04.03.1969	33		

Helsingin Jalkapalloklubi

Founded: 19.06.1907
Stadium: Telia 5G–areena, Helsinki (10,770)

Goalkeepers:	DOB	M	(s)	G
Maksim Rudakov (RUS)	22.01.1996	27		
Markus Uusitalo	15.05.1997	6		
Defenders:	**DOB**	**M**	**(s)**	**G**
Ville Jalasto	19.04.1986	11	(4)	1
Kalle Katz	04.01.2000	1		
Kevin Kouassivi-Benissan	25.01.1999	2		
Samu Laitinen	13.08.1999		(1)	
Daniel O'Shaughnessy	14.09.1994	15	(2)	2
Faith Obilor (NGA)	05.03.1991	29		1
Otto Ollikainen	22.01.2001		(1)	
Hannu Patronen	23.05.1984	16	(4)	1
Roni Peiponen	09.04.1997	7	(4)	1
Juha Pirinen	22.10.1991	16	(6)	1
Rafinha Scapini de Almeida (BRA)	29.06.1982	21	(3)	1
Mikko Sumusalo	12.03.1990	5	(2)	
Midfielders:	**DOB**	**M**	**(s)**	**G**
Anthony Annan (GHA)	21.07.1986	23	(4)	
Sebastian Dahlström	05.11.1996	29	(3)	2
Jordan Domínguez Rajó (ESP)	31.01.1995	10	(1)	1
Riku Riski	16.08.1989	16	(6)	6
Santeri Väänänen	01.01.2002		(1)	
Filip Valenčič (SVN)	07.01.1992	13	(5)	5
Eetu Vertainen	11.05.1999	10	(9)	4
Valtteri Vesiaho	10.02.1999	9	(3)	
Moshtagh Yaghoubi	08.11.1994	19	(3)	2
Forwards:	**DOB**	**M**	**(s)**	**G**
Nikolai Alho	12.03.1993	23	(4)	5
Enoch Banza	04.02.2000	3	(2)	
Macauley Chrisantus (NGA)	20.08.1990	3	(6)	
Amr Gamal Sayed (EGY)	03.08.1991	4	(8)	1
João Klauss de Mello (BRA)	01.03.1997	28	(5)	21
Evans Mensah (GHA)	09.02.1998	13	(7)	4
Akseli Pelvas	08.02.1989	4	(3)	1
Trainer:	**DOB**	**M**		
Mika Lehkosuo	08.01.1970	33		

Tampereen Ilves

Founded: 1931
Stadium: Tammelan Stadion, Tampere (5,040)

Goalkeepers:	DOB	M	(s)	G
Mika Hilander	17.08.1983	29		
Johannes Luukkanen	30.03.1999	4		
Defenders:	**DOB**	**M**	**(s)**	**G**
Mikael Almen	08.03.2000	9	(2)	
Felipe Aspegren	12.02.1994	20	(1)	
Samuel Dahan	13.05.1998		(1)	
Martti Mikael Haukioja	06.10.1999	5		
Roope Huhtala	21.06.2000	4	(1)	
Tariq Kazi	06.10.2000	10	(2)	
Tatu Miettunen	24.04.1995	24	(3)	2
Jani Tanska	29.07.1988	18	(4)	1
Diogo Tomas	31.07.1997	25	(2)	1
Midfielders:	**DOB**	**M**	**(s)**	**G**
Lauri Ala-Myllymäki	04.06.1997	26	(4)	6
Abdoulaye Bâ (SEN)	12.10.1993	1	(1)	
Eero Hyökyvirta	17.03.1999	4	(6)	
Iiro Järvinen	03.11.1996	25	(5)	4
Janne-Pekka Laine	25.01.2001		(1)	
Alim Moundi (CMR)	03.02.1995	4	(2)	
Matias Ojala	28.02.1995	18	(5)	
Gomo Richard Onduku (NGA)	17.11.1993	3	(2)	1
Tuomas Rannankari	21.05.1991	19		
Tuure Siira	25.10.1994	24	(5)	1
Naatan Skyttä	07.05.2002		(2)	
Issa Thiaw (SEN)	12.10.1992	23	(4)	7
Forwards:	**DOB**	**M**	**(s)**	**G**
Jusif Ali	04.05.2000	1	(2)	
Tiémoko Fofana (CIV)	22.10.1999	2		1
Santeri Haarala	17.12.1999	9	(10)	
Jesse Huhtala	21.06.2000	1		
Niklas Jokelainen	30.03.2000	5	(13)	2
Ilari Mettälä	26.04.1994	9	(10)	4
Marius Noubissi (CMR)	28.11.1996	17	(2)	9
Mauro Severino	05.06.1999	1	(3)	
Eero Tamminen	19.05.1995	23	(6)	4
Trainer:	**DOB**	**M**		
Jarkko Wiss	17.04.1972	33		

Football Club Lahti

Founded: 1996
Stadium: Lahden Stadion, Lahti (15,000)

Goalkeepers:	**DOB**	**M**	**(s)**	**G**
Oskari Forsman	28.01.1988	9		
Damjan Siskovski (MKD)	18.03.1995	15		
Aleksandr Vasyutin (RUS)	04.03.1995	9		
Defenders:	**DOB**	**M**	**(s)**	**G**
Mikko Hauhia	03.09.1984	33		
Josimar Do Sameiro Spencer Silva Lima (CPV)	02.08.1989	8	(1)	
Igor Jovanović (GER)	03.05.1989	11		1
Hassan Sesay (SLE)	22.10.1987	26	(3)	1
Kalle Taimi	27.01.1992	19		
Paavo Voutilainen	25.02.1999	9	(4)	
Timi Voutilainen	01.01.1998		(1)	
Artem Vyatkin (RUS)	05.03.1996	26		2
Midfielders:	**DOB**	**M**	**(s)**	**G**
Xhevdet Gela (KVX)	14.11.1989	14	(7)	
Loorents Hertsi	13.11.1992	18	(9)	
Teemu Jäntti	02.03.2000	14	(7)	2
Oskari Kekkonen	24.09.1999	1	(1)	
Nuutti Laaksonen	09.08.1999	1		
Pavel Osipov (RUS)	28.01.1996	22	(5)	4
Aleksi Paananen	25.01.1993	29		3
Eemeli Virta	28.09.2000	3	(2)	
Forwards:	**DOB**	**M**	**(s)**	**G**
Henri Anier (EST)	17.12.1990	22	(9)	5
Jasin-Amin Assehnoun	26.12.1998	6	(4)	
Artjom Dmitrijev (EST)	14.11.1988	19	(6)	3
Santeri Hostikka	30.09.1997	22	(6)	4
Tomi Kult	04.07.2000		(1)	
Fareed Sadat	10.11.1998	2	(7)	
Irfan Sadik	12.01.1999	3	(7)	
Ville Salmikivi	20.05.1992	8	(6)	
Stênio Garcia Dutra (BRA)	29.06.1994	14	(7)	4
Trainer:	**DOB**	**M**		
Toni Korkeakunnas	15.05.1968	30		
Sami Ristilä [01.10.2018]	15.08.1974	3		

Idrottsföreningen Kamraterna Mariehamn

Founded: 1919
Stadium: Wiklöf Holding Arena, Mariehamn (4,000)

Goalkeepers:	**DOB**	**M**	**(s)**	**G**
Anton Lepola	24.07.1996	7		
Igor Levchenko (UKR)	23.02.1991	15		
Marc Nordqvist	01.06.1997	11		
Defenders:	**DOB**	**M**	**(s)**	**G**
Hamed Coulibaly (CIV)	16.12.1996	11		
Petter Hemming	17.02.1999		(1)	
Kristian Kojola	12.09.1986	30		2
Aapo Mäenpää	14.01.1998	7	(4)	
Dylan Murnane (AUS)	18.01.1995	31		1
Philip Sparrdal Mantilla (SWE)	11.08.1993	15	(2)	
Ivan Tatomirović (SRB)	11.01.1989	26	(1)	1
Midfielders:	**DOB**	**M**	**(s)**	**G**
Pontus Åsbrink (SWE)	27.06.1992	18	(7)	2
Amos Ekhalie (KEN)	08.07.1988	15	(7)	1
Keaton Isaksson	21.04.1994	7	(6)	1
Joel Karlstrom	17.05.2001		(1)	
Thomas Mäkinen	30.01.1997	17	(12)	3
Nicklas Maripuu (SWE)	02.03.1992	19	(3)	
Amin Nazari (PHI)	26.04.1993	20	(4)	3
Gabriel Petrović (SWE)	25.05.1984	13	(2)	1
Robin Sid	21.09.1994	26	(2)	4
Simon Silverholt (SWE)	17.06.1993	24	(3)	6
Forwards:	**DOB**	**M**	**(s)**	**G**
Júlio César Fernandes (BRA)	09.11.1996	5	(12)	2
Aleksei Kangaskolkka	29.10.1988	28	(2)	10
Joel Mattsson	17.03.1999	18	(9)	
Trainer:	**DOB**	**M**		
Peter Lundberg	15.04.1981			

Palloseura Kemi Kings

Founded: 1999
Stadium: Sauvosaaren Urheilupuisto, Kemi (4,500)

Goalkeepers:	**DOB**	**M**	**(s)**	**G**
Matias Ahola	26.01.1988	1		
Oskari Forsman	28.01.1988	15		
Tatu Kujanpää	01.01.1995	2		
Mikko Vilmunen	23.08.1980	15	(1)	
Defenders:	**DOB**	**M**	**(s)**	**G**
Aliyu Abubakar (NGA)	15.06.1996	13		1
Jacob Esposito (AUS)	13.05.1995	16	(4)	
Kristian Heinolainen	11.05.1999	20	(4)	
Jorge Mesqueu Neto „Jorginho“ (BRA)	25.01.1991	8	(1)	
Kosta Manev	07.04.1993	14		
Jean-Felix Somay Moyengo Somy (FRA)	22.05.1997	12		1
Henrik Ölander	29.10.1997	11	(1)	
Midfielders:	**DOB**	**M**	**(s)**	**G**
Sneyder Julián Guevara Muñoz (COL)	04.05.1992	16		1
Keaton Isaksson	21.04.1994	17		4
Marek Kaljumäe (EST)	18.02.1991	29	(1)	2
Henri Korkeamäki	09.04.1997	2	(3)	
Luiyi Laguerre	22.02.2001	4	(8)	
Justus Lehto	06.04.1997	8	(6)	1
Kaapo Lepojärvi	23.12.1999		(2)	
Kevin Mombilo	06.05.1993	18		1
Sebastián Rusculleda (ARG)	28.04.1985	3	(4)	
Victor Sevcenco (MDA)	08.09.1991	22		4
Iiro Vanha	19.12.1994	13	(13)	1
Adam Vidjeskog	07.07.1998	12	(4)	
Forwards:	**DOB**	**M**	**(s)**	**G**
Hakeem Ayodeji Ayodele Craig Araba (ENG)	12.02.1991	5	(4)	1
Husein Demiri (MKD)	06.09.1995	10	(3)	
Demir Imeri (MKD)	27.10.1995	11	(1)	
Maksim Lipin (EST)	17.03.1992	12	(6)	1
Juho Mäkelä	23.06.1983	29	(3)	7
Ville Moilanen	27.04.1999	14	(15)	1
Ugur Özder (TUR)	19.01.2000		(1)	
Kevin Tano (NED)	17.04.1993	11	(2)	1
Trainer:	**DOB**	**M**		
Jari Åhman	14.08.1971	16		
David Hannah (SCO) [01.07.2018]	04.08.1973	17		

Kuopion Palloseura

Founded: 1923
Stadium: Savon Sanomat Areena, Kuopio (5,000)

Goalkeepers:	DOB	M	(s)	G
Miika Töyräs	05.06.1999	8		
Otso Virtanen	03.04.1994	25		
Defenders:	**DOB**	**M**	**(s)**	**G**
Hamed Coulibaly (CIV)	16.12.1996	14	(4)	1
Luc Landry Tabi Manga (CMR)	17.11.1994	11	(1)	2
Luis Carlos Murillo (COL)	16.10.1990	27		
Jiri Nissinen	30.05.1997	3	(2)	
Juho Janne Eemeli Pirttijoki	30.07.1996	10		
Mikko Pitkänen	02.01.1997	9	(1)	
Lum Rexhepi (KVX)	03.08.1992	15	(1)	
Henri Toivomäki	21.02.1991	30		
Nuutti Tykkyläinen	19.07.1999		(1)	
Midfielders:	**DOB**	**M**	**(s)**	**G**
Reuben Ayarna (GHA)	22.10.1985	11		1
Abdulla Mahmoud El Said Bekhit (EGY)	13.07.1985	6	(1)	
Reuben Shalu Gabriel (NGA)	25.09.1990	5	(2)	
Jere Hiltunen	11.06.1999	4	(5)	
Urho Nissilä	04.04.1996	11	(3)	2
Petteri Pennanen	19.09.1990	33		12
Ville Saxman	15.11.1989	32	(1)	3
Forwards:	**DOB**	**M**	**(s)**	**G**
Jhon Stiwar García Mena (COL)	06.09.1990		(4)	
Rasmus Karjalainen	04.04.1996	25	(6)	17
Joni Mäkelä	28.09.1993	4	(11)	1
Deivydas Matulevičius (LTU)	08.04.1989		(6)	
Ilmari Niskanen	27.10.1997	29	(4)	4
Eetu Pellikka	23.02.2000	1	(3)	
Ats Purje (EST)	03.08.1985	19	(12)	4
Lucas Rangel Nunes Gonvalves (BRA)	29.12.1994	12	(2)	4
Saku Savolainen	13.08.1996	19	(5)	2
Trainer:	**DOB**	**M**		
Jani Honkavaara	02.02.1976	33		

Rovaniemen Palloseura

Founded: 1950
Stadium: Rovaniemen keskuskenttä, Rovaniemi (4,000)

Goalkeepers:	DOB	M	(s)	G
Antonio Reguero Chapinal (ESP)	04.07.1982	33		
Defenders:	**DOB**	**M**	**(s)**	**G**
Jems Geffrard (CAN)	26.08.1994	9	(11)	
Juuso Hämäläinen	30.11.1992	26	(1)	
Juho Hyvärinen	27.03.2000	14	(3)	1
Lassi Järvenpää	28.10.1996	23	(4)	1
Fugo Segawa (JPN)	01.08.1997	2	(4)	
Taye Ismaila Taïwo (NGA)	16.04.1985	32		1
Leo Väisänen	23.07.1997	24		
Midfielders:	**DOB**	**M**	**(s)**	**G**
Agnaldo Pinto de Moraes Júnior (BRA)	11.03.1994	18	(3)	3
Rasmus Degerman	23.04.2001	2	(5)	
Giorgi Gorozia (GEO)	26.03.1995	7	(6)	1
Guirlain Désiré Wato Kuaté (CMR)	19.09.1995	17		1
Lucas Lingman	25.01.1998	30	(2)	5
Eetu Muinonen	05.04.1986	20	(2)	
Antti Okkonen	06.06.1982	20	(9)	1
Veka Pyyny	04.01.2000	2	(7)	
Erfan Zeneli (KVX)	28.12.1986	10	(1)	2
Forwards:	**DOB**	**M**	**(s)**	**G**
Vahid Hambo	03.02.1995	8	(3)	3
Aapo Heikkilä	13.04.1994	9	(7)	1
Filip Ivanovski (MKD)	01.05.1985	13	(3)	6
Aleksandr Kokko	04.06.1987	3	(5)	1
Lassi Lappalainen	24.08.1998	25	(1)	8
Jarkko Luiro	22.03.1998		(1)	
Simo Roiha	27.12.1990	16	(12)	4
Trainer:	**DOB**	**M**		
Toni Koskela	16.02.1983	33		

Seinäjoen Jalkapallokerho

Founded: 05.11.2007
Stadium: OmaSP Stadion, Seinäjoki (6,000)

Goalkeepers:	DOB	M	(s)	G
Mihkel Aksalu (EST)	07.11.1984	18		
Jesse Öst	20.10.1990	15	(1)	
Defenders:	**DOB**	**M**	**(s)**	**G**
Richard Dorman (WAL)	14.06.1988	15	(4)	
Dani Hatakka	12.03.1994	7	(3)	1
Jarkko Hurme	04.06.1986	16	(1)	
Didier Boris Kadio (CIV)	05.04.1990	10		
Joona Lautamaja	12.07.1995	9	(4)	
Joel Mero	07.02.1995	21	(4)	
Jordan David Mustoe (ENG)	28.01.1991	14	(7)	
Joonas Sundman	20.01.1998	22	(2)	
Ville Tikkanen	08.08.1999	11	(1)	
Midfielders:	**DOB**	**M**	**(s)**	**G**
Reuben Ayarna (GHA)	22.10.1985	16		1
Anders Bååth-Sjöblom (SWE)	13.04.1991	23	(6)	1
Mehmet Hetemaj	08.12.1987	20	(2)	3
Matti Klinga	10.12.1994	10	(7)	2
Johannes Laaksonen	13.12.1990	23	(5)	6
Marcus Vinicius Duarte (BRA)	09.04.1999	1		
Daniel William O'Brien (ENG)	12.03.1996	3	(6)	
Peter Opiyo Odhiambo (KEN)	15.11.1986	13		
Emile Paul Tendeng (SEN)	09.03.1992	19	(5)	2
Marc Vales González (AND)	04.04.1990	6		
Forwards:	**DOB**	**M**	**(s)**	**G**
Vahid Hambo	03.02.1995	6	(9)	2
William Greenwell Ions (ENG)	11.03.1994	5	(3)	
Aristote Mboma	30.06.1994	20	(7)	4
Denys Oliynyk (UKR)	16.06.1987	11	(2)	4
Jesse Sarajärvi	20.05.1995	12	(5)	1
Maximo Tolonen	04.03.2001	8	(6)	
Shahdon Shane Andre Winchester (TRI)	08.01.1992	9	(2)	1
Trainer:	**DOB**	**M**		
Tommi Kautonen	24.12.1971	8		
Alexey Eremenko [22.05.2018]	17.01.1964	25		

Turun Palloseura Turku

Founded: 1922
Stadium: Veritas Stadion, Turku (8,072)

Goalkeepers:	DOB	M	(s)	G
Miikka Mujunen	14.08.1996	1	(1)	
Jonathan Viscosi (CAN)	18.03.1991	32		
Defenders:	**DOB**	**M**	**(s)**	**G**
Niklas Friberg	14.03.1996	18	(4)	
Juri Kinnunen	09.03.1990	21	(5)	
Juho Montola	22.02.1999	4	(4)	
Sami Rähmönen	19.04.1987	20	(6)	1
Željko Savić (SRB)	18.03.1988	10		
Otto Schultz	01.06.1998	2		
Antto Tapaninen	16.06.1989	5	(2)	
Miro Tenho	02.04.1995	31		
Midfielders:	**DOB**	**M**	**(s)**	**G**
Niklas Blomqvist	08.02.1996	30	(1)	1
Rasmus Holma	13.09.1992	20	(3)	
Joakim Latonen	24.02.1998	6	(5)	
Ben Millar McKendry (CAN)	25.03.1993	26	(2)	
Jonni Peräaho	05.02.1994	14	(11)	1
Onni Valakari	18.08.1999	15	(1)	4
Jani Virtanen	06.05.1988	5	(7)	1
Forwards:	**DOB**	**M**	**(s)**	**G**
Mika Ääritalo	25.07.1985	29		8
Elias Ahde	06.03.1996	12	(9)	4
Oskari Jakonen	22.04.1997	21	(6)	4
Drago Milović (MNE)	23.05.1994	3	(9)	1
Albert Prosa (EST)	01.10.1990	3	(5)	1
Aleksi Ristola	06.11.1989	8	(6)	
Riku Sjöroos	10.03.1995	18	(7)	4
Sterling Yateke (CTA)	15.09.1999	9		7
Trainer:	**DOB**	**M**		
Mika Laurikainen	28.04.1963	33		

Vaasan Palloseura

Founded: 1924
Stadium: Elisa Stadion, Vaasa (6,000)

Goalkeepers:	DOB	M	(s)	G
Marko Meerits (EST)	26.04.1992	13		
Samu Volotinen	26.08.1998	20		
Defenders:	**DOB**	**M**	**(s)**	**G**
Eero-Matti Auvinen	05.03.1996	26	(2)	
Elhadji Ciss (SEN)	26.06.1994	11	(2)	2
Aubrey Robert David (TRI)	11.10.1990	20	(5)	1
Jesper Engström	24.04.1992	16		
Akseli Kalermo	17.03.1997		(1)	
Timi Lahti	28.06.1990	31		
Alexander Luke McQueen (GRN)	24.03.1995	8	(2)	
Hindrek Ojamaa (EST)	12.06.1995	13	(6)	
Midfielders:	**DOB**	**M**	**(s)**	**G**
Fabrice Gatambiye	19.01.2000	2	(7)	1
Berkant Güner (TUR)	19.02.1998	9	(4)	
Omar Jama	21.05.1998	18	(3)	1
Aatu Laatikainen	03.01.1997	22	(3)	
Juho Lähde	11.02.1991	17	(4)	3
Marco Privitera (ITA)	23.11.1994		(2)	
Sebastian Strandvall	16.09.1986	30	(1)	10
Joonas Vahtera	06.01.1996	9	(8)	3
Jerry Voutilainen	29.03.1995	26		
Forwards:	**DOB**	**M**	**(s)**	**G**
Samu Alanko	16.05.1998	4	5	
Douglas de Almeida Caé da Conceição (BRA)	24.10.1987	26	(6)	6
Ibrahima Gueye (SEN)	08.10.1996	11	(17)	3
Juha Hakola	27.10.1987	26	(4)	6
Steven Morrissey (JAM)	25.07.1986	4	(9)	
Momodou Sarr	31.03.2000	1	(2)	
Trainer:	**DOB**	**M**		
Petri Vuorinen	31.08.1972	33		

SECOND LEVEL

Ykkönen 2018

1.	IFK Helsingfors (*Promoted*)	27	16	6	5	47	-	22	54
2.	Kokkolan Palloveikot (*Promotion Play-offs*)	27	16	4	7	44	-	26	52
3.	Ekenäs IF	27	12	11	4	36	-	26	47
4.	AC Oulu	27	13	5	9	41	-	30	44
5.	FC Haka Valkeakoski	27	12	7	8	41	-	28	43
6.	FF Jaro Jakobstad	27	11	5	11	34	-	30	38
7.	FC Kotkan Työväen Palloilijat	27	7	8	12	29	-	40	29
8.	AC Kajaani	27	6	7	14	40	-	53	25
9.	JJK Jyväskylä (*Relegated*)	27	4	8	15	32	-	52	20
10.	Klubi 04 Helsinki (*Relegated*)	27	4	7	16	27	-	64	19

NATIONAL TEAM

INTERNATIONAL MATCHES
(16.07.2018 – 15.07.2019)

08.09.2018	Tampere	Finland - Hungary	1-0(1-0)	(UNL)
11.09.2018	Turku	Finland - Estonia	1-0(1-0)	(UNL)
12.10.2018	Tallinn	Estonia - Finland	0-1(0-0)	(UNL)
15.10.2018	Tampere	Finland - Greece	2-0(0-0)	(UNL)
15.11.2018	Athína	Greece - Finland	1-0(1-0)	(UNL)
18.11.2018	Budapest	Hungary - Finland	2-0(2-0)	(UNL)
08.01.2019	Doha	Sweden - Finland	0-1(0-1)	(F)
11.01.2019	Doha	Estonia - Finland	2-1(1-0)	(F)
23.03.2019	Udine	Italy - Finland	2-0(1-0)	(ECQ)
26.03.2019	Yerevan	Armenia - Finland	0-2(0-1)	(ECQ)
08.06.2019	Tampere	Finland - Bosnia and Herzegovina	2-0(0-0)	(ECQ)
11.06.2019	Vaduz	Liechtenstein - Finland	0-2(0-1)	(ECQ)

08.09.2018 FINLAND - HUNGARY 1-0(1-0) UEFA Nations League C, Group 2
Ratinan Stadion, Tampere; Referee: Gediminas Mažeika (Lithuania); Attendance: 10,220
FIN: Lukáš Hrádecký, Jukka Raitala, Paulus Arajuuri (Cap), Joona Marko Aleksi Toivio, Jere Uronen (45+1.Albin Granlund), Rasmus Schüller (63.Tim Sparv), Joni Kauko, Robin Lod, Jasse Tuominen, Teemu Eino Antero Pukki, Pyry Henri Hidipo Soiri (85.Robert Taylor). Trainer: Markku Kanerva.
Goal: Teemu Eino Antero Pukki (7).

11.09.2018 FINLAND - ESTONIA 1-0(1-0) UEFA Nations League C, Group 2
Veritas Stadion, Turku; Referee: Orel Grinfeld (Israel); Attendance: 4,632
FIN: Lukáš Hrádecký, Jukka Raitala, Paulus Arajuuri, Joona Marko Aleksi Toivio, Albin Granlund (76.Sauli Aapo Kasperi Väisänen), Tim Sparv (Cap), Rasmus Schüller, Robin Lod (87.Rasmus Karjalainen), Jasse Tuominen, Teemu Eino Antero Pukki (90+1.Joni Kauko), Pyry Henri Hidipo Soiri. Trainer: Markku Kanerva.
Goal: Teemu Eino Antero Pukki (12).

12.10.2018 ESTONIA - FINLAND 0-1(0-0) UEFA Nations League C, Group 2
A. Le Coq Arena, Tallinn; Referee: Craig Pawson (England); Attendance: 8,087
FIN: Lukáš Hrádecký, Jukka Raitala, Paulus Arajuuri, Joona Marko Aleksi Toivio, Jere Uronen, Tim Sparv (Cap), Rasmus Schüller (72.Glen Kamara), Robin Lod, Jasse Tuominen (87.Eero Pekka Sakari Markkanen), Teemu Eino Antero Pukki, Pyry Henri Hidipo Soiri (61.Jani Petteri Forsell). Trainer: Markku Kanerva.
Goal: Teemu Eino Antero Pukki (90+1).

15.10.2018 FINLAND - GREECE 2-0(0-0) UEFA Nations League C, Group 2
Ratinan Stadion, Tampere; Referee: Paweł Gil (Poland); Attendance: 10,107
FIN: Lukáš Hrádecký, Jukka Raitala, Paulus Arajuuri, Joona Marko Aleksi Toivio, Jere Uronen, Tim Sparv (Cap), Robin Lod, Glen Kamara, Jasse Tuominen (90+1.Rasmus Karjalainen), Teemu Eino Antero Pukki (12.Simon Skrabb), Pyry Henri Hidipo Soiri (86.Juha Pirinen). Trainer: Markku Kanerva.
Goals: Pyry Henri Hidipo Soiri (46), Glen Kamara (89).

15.11.2018 GREECE - FINLAND 1-0(1-0) UEFA Nations League C, Group 2
Stádio Olympiako „Spiros Louis", Athína; Referee: Luca Banti (Italy); Attendance: 6,376
FIN: Lukáš Hrádecký, Paulus Arajuuri (Cap), Joona Marko Aleksi Toivio, Albin Granlund, Jere Uronen, Joni Kauko, Robin Lod, Glen Kamara, Jasse Tuominen (83.Juha Pirinen), Teemu Eino Antero Pukki (90+3.Thomas Lam), Pyry Henri Hidipo Soiri (74.Fredrik Jensen). Trainer: Markku Kanerva.

18.11.2018 HUNGARY - FINLAND 2-0(2-0) UEFA Nations League C, Group 2
Groupama Aréna, Budapest; Referee: Slavko Vinčić (Slovenia); Attendance: 9,200
FIN: Jesse Joronen, Paulus Arajuuri (Cap), Albin Granlund (46.Joona Marko Aleksi Toivio), Jere Uronen, Thomas Lam (60.Joni Kauko), Sauli Aapo Kasperi Väisänen, Robert Taylor (74.Jani Petteri Forsell), Robin Lod, Glen Kamara, Jasse Tuominen, Teemu Eino Antero Pukki. Trainer: Markku Kanerva.

08.01.2019 SWEDEN - FINLAND 0-1(0-1) Friendly International
"Sheikh Jassim Bin Hamad" Stadium, Doha (Qatar); Referee: Abdulla Ali Al Athba Al Marri (Qatar); Attendance: 326
FIN: Jesse Joronen, Juha Pirinen, Joona Marko Aleksi Toivio, Juhani Lauri Henrik Ojala, Albin Granlund (85.Robert Ivanov), Tim Sparv (Cap) (46.Sebastian Dahlström), Rasmus Schüller (54.Kaan Kairinen), Lassi Lappalainen (68.Saku Ylätupa), Simon Skrabb (54.Robert Taylor), Eero Pekka Sakari Markkanen (68.Tim Väyrynen), Rasmus Karjalainen. Trainer: Markku Kanerva.
Goal: Eero Pekka Sakari Markkanen (22).

11.01.2019 ESTONIA - FINLAND 2-1(1-0) Friendly International
Khalifa International Stadium, Doha (Qatar); Referee: Khalid Marhoun Sulaiman Al Shaqsi (Qatar); Attendance: 200
FIN: Walter Viitala, Joona Marko Aleksi Toivio, Juhani Lauri Henrik Ojala (67.Albin Granlund), Robert Ivanov, Nicholas Antero Hämäläinen (84.Juha Pirinen), Tim Sparv (Cap) (60.Kaan Kairinen), Robert Taylor, Saku Ylätupa, Sebastian Dahlström (6.Eero Pekka Sakari Markkanen), Tim Väyrynen (60.Rasmus Karjalainen), Simon Skrabb (46.Lassi Lappalainen). Trainer: Markku Kanerva.
Goal: Rasmus Karjalainen (81).

23.03.2019 ITALY - FINLAND 2-0(1-0) 16th EC. Qualifiers
Stadio Friuli, Udine; Referee: Orel Grinfeld (Israel); Attendance: 24,000
FIN: Lukáš Hrádecký, Juha Pirinen, Paulus Arajuuri, Joona Marko Aleksi Toivio, Albin Granlund (90.Pyry Henri Hidipo Soiri), Sauli Aapo Kasperi Väisänen, Tim Sparv (Cap), Kasper Woldemar Hämäläinen (70.Lassi Lappalainen), Robin Lod, Glen Kamara, Teemu Eino Antero Pukki (83.Rasmus Karjalainen). Trainer: Markku Kanerva.

26.03.2019 ARMENIA - FINLAND 0-2(0-1) 16th EC. Qualifiers
Republican "Vazgen Sargsyan" Stadium, Yerevan; Referee: Nikola Dabanović (Montenegro); Attendance: 12,900
FIN: Lukáš Hrádecký, Juha Pirinen, Paulus Arajuuri, Joona Marko Aleksi Toivio, Albin Granlund, Tim Sparv (Cap), Kasper Woldemar Hämäläinen (57.Pyry Henri Hidipo Soiri), Robin Lod (87.Robert Taylor), Glen Kamara, Fredrik Jensen (69.Rasmus Schüller), Teemu Eino Antero Pukki. Trainer: Markku Kanerva.
Goals: Fredrik Jensen (14), Pyry Henri Hidipo Soiri (78).

08.06.2019 FINLAND - BOSNIA AND HERZEGOVINA 2-0(0-0) 16th EC. Qualifiers
Ratinan Stadion, Tampere; Referee: Daniel Stefański (Poland); Attendance: 16,103
FIN: Lukáš Hrádecký, Paulus Arajuuri, Joona Marko Aleksi Toivio, Albin Granlund [38.Jukka Raitala], Jere Uronen, Tim Sparv (Cap), Jani Petteri Forsell [63.Lassi Lappalainen], Robin Lod, Glen Kamara, Teemu Eino Antero Pukki, Simon Skrabb [84.Rasmus Schüller]. Trainer: Markku Kanerva.
Goals: Teemu Eino Antero Pukki (56, 68).

11.06.2019 LIECHTENSTEIN - FINLAND 0-2(0-1) 16th EC. Qualifiers
Rheinpark Stadion, Vaduz; Referee: Jens Maae (Denmark); Attendance: 2,160
FIN: Lukáš Hrádecký, Jukka Raitala [86.Leo Väisänen], Paulus Arajuuri, Joona Marko Aleksi Toivio, Jere Uronen, Tim Sparv (Cap) [61.Rasmus Schüller], Robin Lod, Glen Kamara, Lassi Lappalainen [74.Pyry Henri Hidipo Soiri], Teemu Eino Antero Pukki, Benjamin Källman. Trainer: Markku Kanerva.
Goals: Teemu Eino Antero Pukki (37), Benjamin Källman (57).

NATIONAL TEAM PLAYERS
(16.07.2018 – 15.07.2019)

Name	DOB	Caps	Goals	2018/2019:	Club
Goalkeepers					
Lukáš HRÁDECKÝ	24.11.1989	**53**	**0**	2018/2019:	*TSV Bayer 04 Leverkusen (GER)*
Jesse JORONEN	21.03.1993	**7**	**0**	2018/2019:	*FC København (DEN)*
Walter VIITALA	09.01.1992	**3**	**0**	2018/2019:	*Unattached*
Defenders					
Paulus ARAJUURI	15.06.1988	**39**	**3**	2018/2019:	*Brøndby IF (DEN)*
Albin GRANLUND	01.09.1989	**16**	**0**	2018/2019:	*Örebro SK (SWE)*
Nicholas Antero HÄMÄLÄINEN	05.03.1997	**1**	**0**	2019:	*Queens Park Rangers FC London (ENG)*
Robert IVANOV	21.07.1993	**2**	**0**	2019:	*FC Honka Espoo*
Juhani Lauri Henrik OJALA	19.06.1989	**26**	**1**	2019:	*BK Häcken Göteborg (SWE)*
Juha PIRINEN	22.10.1991	**17**	**0**	2018: 08.01.2019->	*HJK Helsinki* *Tromsø IL (NOR)*
Jukka RAITALA	15.09.1988	**46**	**0**	2018/2019:	*Montréal Impact FC (CAN)*
Joona Marko Aleksi TOIVIO	10.03.1988	**59**	**3**	2018/2019:	*BK Häcken Göteborg (SWE)*
Jere URONEN	13.07.1994	**36**	**1**	2018/2019:	*KRC Genk (BEL)*
Leo VÄISÄNEN	23.07.1997	**1**	**0**	2019:	*FC Den Bosch (NED)*
Sauli Aapo Kasperi VÄISÄNEN	05.06.1994	**15**	**0**	2018/2019:	*FC Crotone (ITA)*
Midfielders					
Sebastian DAHLSTRÖM	05.11.1996	**2**	**0**	2019:	*HJK Helsinki*
Jani Petteri FORSELL	16.10.1990	**12**	**1**	2018/2019:	*MKS Miedź Legnica (POL)*
Kasper Woldemar HÄMÄLÄINEN	08.08.1986	**63**	**9**	2019:	*Legia Warszawa (POL)*
Fredrik JENSEN	09.09.1997	**8**	**3**	2018/2019:	*FC Augsburg (GER)*
Kaan KAIRINEN	22.12.1998	**2**	**0**	2018/2019:	*HJK Helsinki*
Glen KAMARA	28.10.1995	**13**	**1**	2018: 31.01.2019->	*Dundee FC (SCO)* *Rangers FC Glasgow (CO)*
Joni KAUKO	12.07.1990	**13**	**0**	2018/2019:	*Esbjerg fB (DEN)*
Thomas LAM	18.12.1993	**21**	**0**	2018/2019:	*PEC Zwolle (NED)*
Robin LOD	17.04.1993	**33**	**3**	2018/2019:	*Real Sporting de Gijón (ESP)*
Rasmus SCHÜLLER	18.06.1991	**36**	**0**	2018/2019:	*Minnesota United (USA)*
Simon SKRABB	19.01.1995	**12**	**0**	2018/2019:	*IFK Norrköping (SWE)*
Pyry Henri Hidipo SOIRI	22.09.1994	**16**	**5**	2018/2019:	*FC Admira Wacker Mödling (AUT)*
Tim SPARV	20.02.1987	**71**	**1**	2018/2019:	*FC Midtjylland Herning (DEN)*
Robert TAYLOR	21.10.1994	**10**	**0**	2018/2019:	*Tromsø IL (NOR)*
Saku YLÄTUPA	04.08.1999	**2**	**0**	2018/2019:	*AFC Ajax Amsterdam (NED)*
Forwards					
Rasmus KARJALAINEN	04.04.1996	**7**	**1**	2018/2019:	*Kuopion Palloseura*
Benjamin KÄLLMAN	17.06.1998	**2**	**1**	2019:	*Vendsyssel FF Hjørring (DEN)*
Lassi LAPPALAINEN	24.08.1998	**5**	**0**	2018/2019:	*HJK Helsinki*
Eero Pekka Sakari MARKKANEN	03.07.1991	**17**	**1**	2018/2019:	*Dalkurd FF Uppsala (SWE)*
Teemu Eino Antero PUKKI	29.03.1990	**74**	**18**	2018/2019:	*Norwich City FC (ENG)*
Jasse TUOMINEN	12.11.1995	**11**	**0**	2018:	*FC BATE Borisov (BLR)*
Tim VÄYRYNEN	30.03.1993	**13**	**0**	2019:	*SV Roda JC Kerkrade (NED)*

National team coach

Markku KANERVA [from 12.12.2016]	24.05.1964	28 M; 15 W; 5 D; 8 L; 34-21 Complete record as trainer of Finland: 34 M; 17 W; 8 D; 9 L; 39-26 (09.02.2011 – 29.03.2011) & (04.09.2015 – 11.10.2015) & (09.01.2017 – 09.06.2018)

FRANCE

The Country:
French Republic (République française)
Capital: Paris
Surface: 643,801 km²
Inhabitants: 67,186,638 [2017]
Time: UTC+1

The FA:
Fédération Française de Football
87, Boulevard de Grenelle, 75738 Paris Cedex 15
Tel: +33 1 4431 7300
Foundation date: 07.04.1919
Member of FIFA since: 1907
Member of UEFA since: 1954
Website: www.fff.fr

NATIONAL TEAM RECORDS

First international match:	01.05.1994, Bruxelles:	Belgium – France 3-3
Most international caps:	Lilian Thuram	- 142 caps (1994-2008)
Most international goals:	Thierry Daniel Henry	- 51 goals / 123 caps (1997-2010)

UEFA EUROPEAN CHAMPIONSHIP	
1960	Final Tournament (4th Place)
1964	Qualifiers
1968	Qualifiers
1972	Qualifiers
1976	Qualifiers
1980	Qualifiers
1984	**Final Tournament (Winners)**
1988	Qualifiers
1992	Final Tournament (Group Stage)
1996	Final Tournament (Semi-Finals)
2000	**Final Tournament (Winners)**
2004	Final Tournament (Quarter-Finals)
2008	Final Tournament (Group Stage)
2012	Final Tournament (Quarter-Finals)
2016	Final Tournament (Runners-up)

FIFA WORLD CUP	
1930	Final Tournament (Group Stage)
1934	Final Tournament (1st Round)
1938	Final Tournament (Quarter-Finals)
1950	*Withdrew*
1954	Final Tournament (Group Stage)
1958	Final Tournament (3rd Place)
1962	Qualifiers
1966	Final Tournament (Group Stage)
1970	Qualifiers
1974	Qualifiers
1978	Final Tournament (Group Stage)
1982	Final Tournament (4th Place)
1986	Final Tournament (3rd Place)
1990	Qualifiers
1994	Qualifiers
1998	**Final Tournament (Winners)**
2002	Final Tournament (Group Stage)
2006	Final Tournament (Runners-up)
2010	Final Tournament (Group Stage)
2014	Final Tournament (Quarter-Finals)
2018	**Final Tournament (Winners)**

UEFA NATIONS LEAGUE
2018/2019 – League A

OLYMPIC FOOTBALL TOURNAMENTS 1908-2016							
1908	Final Tournament	**1948**	Quarter-Finals	**1972**	Qualifiers	**1996**	Quarter-Finals
1912	-	**1952**	Qualifiers	**1976**	Quarter-Finals	**2000**	Qualifiers
1920	Semi-Finals	**1956**	-	**1980**	Qualifiers	**2004**	Qualifiers
1924	Quarter-Finals	**1960**	Group Stage	**1984**	**Winners**	**2008**	Qualifiers
1928	1/8-Finals	**1964**	Qualifiers	**1988**	Qualifiers	**2012**	Qualifiers
1936	-	**1968**	Quarter-Finals	**1992**	Qualifiers	**2016**	Qualifiers

FIFA CONFEDERATIONS CUP 1992-2017
2001 (Winners), 2003 (Winners)

FRENCH CLUB HONOURS IN EUROPEAN CLUB COMPETITIONS:

European Champion Clubs' Cup (1956-1992) / UEFA Champions League (1993-2019)		
Olympique de Marseille	**1**	1992/1993
Fairs Cup (1858-1971) / UEFA Cup (1972-2009) / UEFA Europa League (2010-2019)		
None		
UEFA Super Cup (1972-2019)		
None		
European Cup Winners' Cup 1961-1999*		
Paris Saint-Germain FC	**1**	1995/1996

**defunct competition*

NATIONAL COMPETITIONS
TABLE OF HONOURS

	CHAMPIONS	CUP WINNERS	BEST GOALSCORERS	
1893/1894	Standard Athletic Club Paris	-	-	
1894/1895	Standard Athletic Club Paris	-	-	
1895/1896	Club Français Paris	-	-	
1896/1897	Standard Athletic Club Paris	-	-	
1897/1898	Standard Athletic Club Paris	-	-	
1898/1899	Le Havre AC	-	-	
1899/1900	Le Havre AC	-	-	
1900/1901	Standard Athletic Club Paris	-	-	
1901/1902	Racing Club de Roubaix	-	-	
1902/1903	Racing Club de Roubaix	-	-	
1903/1904	Racing Club de Roubaix	-	-	
1904/1905	Gallia Club Paris	-	-	
1905/1906	Racing Club de Roubaix	-	-	
1906/1907	Racing Club de France Paris	-	-	
1907/1908	Racing Club de Roubaix	-	-	
1908/1909	Stade Helvétique de Marseille	-	-	
1909/1910	US Tourcoing	-	-	
1910/1911	Stade Helvétique de Marseille	-	-	
1911/1912	Stade Saint-Raphaëlois	-	-	
1912/1913	Stade Helvétique de Marseille	-	-	
1913/1914	Olympique Lillois	-	-	
1914/1915	*No competition*	-	-	
1915/1916	*No competition*	-	-	
1916/1917	*No competition*	-	-	
1917/1918	*No competition*	Olympique de Pantin	-	
1918/1919	Le Havre AC	CASG Paris	-	
1919/1920	*No competition*	Cercle Athlétique de Paris	-	
1920/1921	*No competition*	Red Star FC Paris	-	
1921/1922	*No competition*	Red Star FC Paris	-	
1922/1923	*No competition*	Red Star FC Paris	-	
1923/1924	*No competition*	Olympique de Marseille	-	
1924/1925	*No competition*	CASG Paris	-	
1925/1926	*No competition*	Olympique de Marseille	-	
1926/1927	Cercle Athlétique de Paris	Olympique de Marseille	-	
1927/1928	Stade Français Paris	Red Star FC Paris	-	
1928/1929	Olympique de Marseille	Montpellier Hérault Sport Club	-	
1929/1930	*No competition*	FC Sète	-	
1930/1931	*No competition*	Club Français Paris	-	
1931/1932	*No competition*	AS Cannes	-	
1932/1933	Olympique Lillois	Excelsior Athlétic Club de Roubaix	Walter Kaiser (GER, Stade Rennais FC) Robert Mercier (Club Français Paris)	15
1933/1934	FC Sète	FC Sète	István Lukács (HUN, FC Sète)	28
1934/1935	Sochaux	Olympique de Marseille	André Abegglen (SUI, FC Sochaux-Montbéliard)	30
1935/1936	Racing Club de France Paris	RC Paris	Roger Courtois (FC Sochaux-Montbéliard)	34
1936/1937	Olympique de Marseille	FC FC Sochaux-Montbéliard	Oskar Rohr (GER, Racing Club de Strasbourg)	30
1937/1938	FC Sochaux-Montbéliard	Olympique de Marseille	Jean Nicolas (FC Rouen)	26
1938/1939	FC Sète	Racing Club de France Paris	Roger Courtois (FC Sochaux-Montbéliard) Désiré Koranyi (FC Sète)	27
1939/1940	*No competition*	Racing Club de France Paris	-	
1940/1941	*No competition*	FC Girondins de Bordeaux	-	
1941/1942	*No competition*	Red Star FC Paris	-	
1942/1943	*No competition*	Olympique de Marseille	-	
1943/1944	*No competition*	Équipe fédérale Nancy-Lorraine	-	
1944/1945	*No competition*	Racing Club de France Paris	-	
1945/1946	Lille OSC	Lille OSC	René Bihel (Lille OSC)	28
1946/1947	Racing Club de Roubaix–Tourcoing	Lille OSC	Pierre Sinibaldi (Stade de Reims)	33
1947/1948	Olympique de Marseille	Lille OSC	Jean Baratte (Lille OSC)	31
1948/1949	Stade de Reims	Racing Club de France Paris	Jean Baratte (Lille OSC) Josef Humpál (CZE, FC Sochaux-Montbéliard)	26
1949/1950	FC Girondins de Bordeaux	Stade de Reims	Jean Grumellon (Stade Rennais FC)	25
1950/1951	OGC Nice	Racing Club de Strasbourg	Roger Piantoni (AS Nancy-Lorraine) Jean Courteaux (OGC Nice)	27
1951/1952	OGC Nice	OGC Nice	Gunnar Andersson (SWE, Olympique de Marseille)	31
1952/1953	Stade de Reims	Lille OSC	Gunnar Andersson (SWE, Olympique de Marseille)	35
1953/1954	Lille OSC	OGC Nice	Édouard Kargu (FC Girondins de Bordeaux)	27
1954/1955	Stade de Reims	Lille OSC	René Bliard (Stade de Reims)	30
1955/1956	OGC Nice	CS Sedan	Thadée Cisowski (Racing Club de France Paris)	31
1956/1957	AS Saint-Étienne	Toulouse FC	Thadée Cisowski (Racing Club de France Paris)	33
1957/1958	Stade de Reims	Stade de Reims	Just Fontaine (Stade de Reims)	34
1958/1959	OGC Nice	Le Havre AC	Thadée Cisowski (Racing Club de France Paris)	30
1959/1960	Stade de Reims	AS Monaco FC	Just Fontaine (Stade de Reims)	28

1960/1961	AS Monaco FC	CS Sedan	Roger Piantoni (Stade de Reims)	28
1961/1962	Stade de Reims	AS Saint-Étienne	Sékou Touré (CIV, Montpellier Hérault Sport Club)	25
1962/1963	AS Monaco FC	AS Monaco FC	Serge Masnaghetti (USVA Valenciennes)	35
1963/1964	AS Saint-Étienne	Olympique Lyonnais	Ahmed Oudjani (ALG, Racing Club de Lens)	30
1964/1965	FC Nantes	Stade Rennais FC	Jacques Simon (FC Nantes)	24
1965/1966	FC Nantes	Racing Club de Strasbourg	Philippe Gondet (FC Nantes)	36
1966/1967	AS Saint-Étienne	Olympique Lyonnais	Hervé Revelli (AS Saint-Étienne)	31
1967/1968	AS Saint-Étienne	AS Saint-Étienne	Étienne Sansonetti (AC Ajaccio)	26
1968/1969	AS Saint-Étienne	Olympique de Marseille	André Guy (Olympique Lyonnais)	25
1969/1970	AS Saint-Étienne	AS Saint-Étienne	Hervé Revelli (AS Saint-Étienne)	28
1970/1971	Olympique de Marseille	Stade Rennais FC	Josip Skoblar (YUG, Olympique de Marseille)	44
1971/1972	Olympique de Marseille	Olympique de Marseille	Josip Skoblar (YUG, Olympique de Marseille)	30
1972/1973	FC Nantes	Olympique Lyonnais	Josip Skoblar (YUG, Olympique de Marseille)	26
1973/1974	AS Saint-Étienne	AS Saint-Étienne	Carlos Arcecio Bianchi (ARG, Stade de Reims)	30
1974/1975	AS Saint-Étienne	AS Saint-Étienne	Delio Onnis (ARG, AS Monaco FC)	30
1975/1976	AS Saint-Étienne	Olympique de Marseille	Carlos Arcecio Bianchi (ARG, Stade de Reims)	34
1976/1977	FC Nantes	AS Saint-Étienne	Carlos Arcecio Bianchi (ARG, Stade de Reims)	28
1977/1978	AS Monaco FC	AS Nancy-Lorraine	Carlos Arcecio Bianchi (ARG, Paris Saint-Germain FC)	37
1978/1979	Racing Club de Strasbourg	FC Nantes	Carlos Arcecio Bianchi (ARG, Paris Saint-Germain FC)	27
1979/1980	FC Nantes	AS Monaco FC	Erwin Kostedde (GER, Stade Lavallois) Delio Onnis (ARG, AS Monaco FC)	21
1980/1981	AS Saint-Étienne	SC Bastia	Delio Onnis (ARG, Tours FC)	24
1981/1982	AS Monaco FC	Paris Saint-Germain FC	Delio Onnis (ARG, Tours FC)	29
1982/1983	FC Nantes	Paris Saint-Germain FC	Vahid Halilhodžić (YUG, FC Nantes)	27
1983/1984	FC Girondins de Bordeaux	FC Metz	Patrice Garande (AJ Auxerre) Delio Onnis (ARG, Sporting Club Toulon)	21
1984/1985	FC Girondins de Bordeaux	AS Monaco FC	Vahid Halilhodžić (YUG, FC Nantes)	28
1985/1986	Paris Saint-Germain FC	FC Girondins de Bordeaux	Jules François Bocandé (SEN, FC Metz)	23
1986/1987	FC Girondins de Bordeaux	FC Girondins de Bordeaux	Bernard Zénier (FC Metz)	18
1987/1988	AS Monaco FC	FC Metz	Jean-Pierre Papin (Olympique de Marseille)	19
1988/1989	Olympique de Marseille	Olympique de Marseille	Jean-Pierre Papin (Olympique de Marseille)	22
1989/1990	Olympique de Marseille	Montpellier Hérault Sport Club	Jean-Pierre Papin (Olympique de Marseille)	30
1990/1991	Olympique de Marseille	AS Monaco FC	Jean-Pierre Papin (Olympique de Marseille)	23
1991/1992	Olympique de Marseille	*Not played to end*	Jean-Pierre Papin (Olympique de Marseille)	27
1992/1993	*No winner was declared by FFF*	Paris Saint-Germain FC	Alen Bokšić (CRO, Olympique de Marseille)	22
1993/1994	Paris Saint-Germain FC	AJ Auxerre	Roger Zokou Boli (Racing Club de Lens) Youri Djorkaeff (AS Monaco FC) Nicolas Pierre Ouédec (FC Nantes)	20
1994/1995	FC Nantes	Paris Saint-Germain FC	Patrice Loko (FC Nantes)	22
1995/1996	AJ Auxerre	AJ Auxerre	Anderson da Silva (BRA, AS Monaco FC)	21
1996/1997	AS Monaco FC	OGC Nice	Stéphane Pierre Yves Guivarc'h (Stade Rennais FC)	21
1997/1998	Racing Club de Lens	Paris Saint-Germain FC	Stéphane Pierre Yves Guivarc'h (AJ Auxerre)	21
1998/1999	FC Girondins de Bordeaux	FC Nantes	Sylvain Wiltord (FC Girondins de Bordeaux)	22
1999/2000	AS Monaco FC	FC Nantes	Anderson da Silva (BRA, Olympique Lyonnais)	23
2000/2001	FC Nantes	Racing Club de Strasbourg	Anderson da Silva (BRA, Olympique Lyonnais)	22
2001/2002	Olympique Lyonnais	FC Lorient	Djibril Cissé (AJ Auxerre) Pedro Miguel Carreiro Resendes "Pauleta" (POR, FC Girondins de Bordeaux)	22
2002/2003	Olympique Lyonnais	AJ Auxerre	Shabani Christophe Nonda (COD, AS Monaco FC)	26
2003/2004	Olympique Lyonnais	Paris Saint-Germain FC	Djibril Cissé (AJ Auxerre)	26
2004/2005	Olympique Lyonnais	AJ Auxerre	Alexander Frei (SUI, Stade Rennais FC)	20
2005/2006	Olympique Lyonnais	Paris Saint-Germain FC	Pedro Miguel Carreiro Resendes "Pauleta" (POR, Paris Saint-Germain FC)	21
2006/2007	Olympique Lyonnais	FC Sochaux-Montbéliard	Pedro Miguel Carreiro Resendes "Pauleta" (POR, Paris Saint-Germain FC)	15
2007/2008	Olympique Lyonnais	Olympique Lyonnais	Karim Mostafa Benzema (Olympique Lyonnais)	20
2008/2009	FC Girondins de Bordeaux	En Avant de Guingamp	André-Pierre Christian Gignac (Toulouse FC)	24
2009/2010	Olympique de Marseille	Paris Saint-Germain FC	Mamadou Hamidou Niang (SEN, Olympique de Marseille)	18
2010/2011	Lille OSC	Lille OSC	Moussa Sow (SEN, Lille OSC)	25
2011/2012	Montpellier Hérault Sport Club	Olympique Lyonnais	Olivier Giroud (Montpellier Hérault Sport Club) Anderson Luiz de Carvalho "Nenê" (BRA, Paris Saint-Germain FC)	21
2012/2013	Paris Saint-Germain FC	FC Girondins de Bordeaux	Zlatan Ibrahimović (SWE, Paris Saint-Germain FC)	30
2013/2014	Paris Saint-Germain FC	En Avant de Guingamp	Zlatan Ibrahimović (SWE, Paris Saint-Germain FC)	26
2014/2015	Paris Saint-Germain FC	Paris Saint-Germain FC	Alexandre Lacazette (Olympique Lyonnais)	27
2015/2016	Paris Saint-Germain FC	Paris Saint-Germain FC	Zlatan Ibrahimović (SWE, Paris Saint-Germain FC)	38
2016/2017	AS Monaco FC	Paris Saint-Germain FC	Edinson Roberto Cavani Gómez (URU, Paris Saint-Germain FC)	35
2017/2018	Paris Saint-Germain FC	Paris Saint-Germain FC	Edinson Roberto Cavani Gómez (URU, Paris Saint-Germain FC)	28
2018/2019	Paris Saint-Germain FC	Stade Rennais FC	Kylian Sanmi Mbappé Lottin (Paris Saint-Germain FC)	33

COUPE DE LA LIGUE* CUP WINNERS

1963/1964	Racing Club de Strasbourg
1964/1965	FC Nantes
1981/1982	Stade Lavallois
1983/1984	Stade Lavallois
1985/1986	FC Metz
1990/1991	Stade de Reims
1991/1992	Montpellier Hérault Sport Club
1993/1994	Racing Club de Lens
1994/1995	Paris Saint-Germain FC
1995/1996	FC Metz
1996/1997	Racing Club de Strasbourg
1997/1998	Paris Saint-Germain FC
1998/1999	Racing Club de Lens
1999/2000	FC Gueugnon
2000/2001	Olympique Lyonnais
2001/2002	FC Girondins de Bordeaux
2002/2003	AS Monaco FC
2003/2004	FC Sochaux-Montbéliard
2004/2005	Racing Club de Strasbourg
2005/2006	AS Nancy-Lorraine
2006/2007	FC Girondins de Bordeaux
2007/2008	Paris Saint-Germain FC
2008/2009	FC Girondins de Bordeaux
2009/2010	Olympique de Marseille
2010/2011	Olympique de Marseille
2011/2012	Olympique de Marseille
2012/2013	AS Saint-Étienne
2013/2014	Paris Saint-Germain FC
2014/2015	Paris Saint-Germain FC
2015/2016	Paris Saint-Germain FC
2016/2017	Paris Saint-Germain FC
2017/2018	Paris Saint-Germain FC
2018/2019	Racing Club de Strasbourg

*Competition called: Coupe de la Ligue (1963–1965), Coupe d'Été/Coupe de la Ligue (1982–1994) and Coupe de la Ligue (since 1994).

NATIONAL CHAMPIONSHIP

Ligue 1 2018/2019

(10.08.2018 – 24.05.2019)

Results

Round 1 [10-12.08.2018]
Olympique Marseille - Toulouse FC 4-0(1-0)
FC Nantes - AS Monaco 1-3(0-0)
Angers SCO - Nîmes Olympique 3-4(1-1)
Lille OSC - Stade Rennais 3-1(1-1)
Montpellier - Dijon FCO 1-2(1-0)
OGC Nice - Stade Reims 0-1(0-1)
AS Saint-Étienne - EA Guingamp 2-1(1-0)
Olympique Lyon - Amiens SC 2-0(1-0)
Girondins Bordeaux - RC Strasbourg 0-2(0-0)
Paris Saint-Germain - SM Caen 3-0(2-0)

Round 2 [17-19.08.2018]
Stade Reims - Olympique Lyon 1-0(1-0)
EA Guingamp - Paris Saint-Germain 1-3(1-0)
Amiens SC - Montpellier 1-2(0-0)
SM Caen - OGC Nice 1-1(0-0)
Dijon FCO - FC Nantes 2-0(1-0)
AS Monaco - Lille OSC 0-0
Stade Rennais - Angers SCO 1-0(0-0)
RC Strasbourg - AS Saint-Étienne 1-1(0-0)
Toulouse FC - Girondins Bordeaux 2-1(1-0)
Nîmes Olympique – Olymp Marseille 3-1(1-0)

Round 3 [24-26.08.2018]
Olympique Lyon - RC Strasbourg 2-0(1-0)
Paris Saint-Germain - Angers SCO 3-1(1-1)
Amiens SC - Stade Reims 4-1(1-0)
Montpellier - AS Saint-Étienne 0-0
FC Nantes - SM Caen 1-1(0-1)
OGC Nice - Dijon FCO 0-4(0-0)
Toulouse FC - Nîmes Olympique 1-0(0-0)
Lille OSC - EA Guingamp 3-0(2-0)
Girondins Bordeaux - AS Monaco 2-1(0-0)
Olympique Marseille - Stade Rennais 2-2(0-2)

Round 4 [31.08.-02.09.2018]
Olympique Lyon - OGC Nice 0-1(0-0)
Nîmes Olymp. - Paris Saint-Germain 2-4(0-2)
Angers SCO - Lille OSC 1-0(0-0)
Dijon FCO - SM Caen 0-2(0-1)
EA Guingamp - Toulouse FC 1-2(1-2)
Stade Reims - Montpellier 0-1(0-0)
RC Strasbourg - FC Nantes 2-3(1-2)
AS Saint-Étienne - Amiens SC 0-0
Stade Rennais - Girondins Bordeaux 2-0(2-0)
AS Monaco - Olympique Marseille 2-3(0-1)

Round 5 [14-16.09.2018]
OGC Nice - Stade Rennais 2-1(0-0)
Paris Saint-Germain - Saint-Étienne 4-0(1-0)
SM Caen - Olympique Lyon 2-2(0-1)
Amiens SC - Lille OSC 2-3(0-1)
Dijon FCO - Angers SCO 1-3(1-3)
Montpellier - RC Strasbourg 1-1(0-0)
Toulouse FC - AS Monaco 1-1(0-0)
FC Nantes - Stade Reims 0-0
Girondins Bordeaux - Nîmes Olymp. 3-3(1-2)
Olympique Marseille - EA Guingamp 4-0(0-0)

Round 6 [21-23.09.2018]
AS Monaco - Nîmes Olympique 1-1(1-1)
Lille OSC - FC Nantes 2-1(1-0)
Angers SCO - Toulouse FC 0-0
Montpellier - OGC Nice 1-0(1-0)
Stade Reims - Dijon FCO 0-0
AS Saint-Étienne - SM Caen 2-1(0-1)
RC Strasbourg - Amiens SC 3-1(0-1)
Stade Rennais - Paris Saint-Germain 1-3(1-1)
EA Guingamp - Girondins Bordeaux 1-3(0-0)
Olympique Lyon – Olymp. Marseille 4-2(1-1)

Round 7 [25-26.09.2018]
AS Monaco - Angers SCO 0-1(0-1)
FC Nantes - OGC Nice 1-2(0-1)
Toulouse FC - AS Saint-Étienne 2-3(0-1)
Amiens SC - Stade Rennais 2-1(0-0)
Girondins Bordeaux - Lille OSC 1-0(1-0)
SM Caen - Montpellier 2-2(1-1)
Dijon FCO - Olympique Lyon 0-3(0-3)
Olymp. Marseille - RC Strasbourg 3-2(2-1)
Nîmes Olympique - EA Guingamp 0-0
Paris Saint-Germain - Stade Reims 4-1(3-1)

Round 8 [28-30.09.2018]
AS Saint-Étienne - AS Monaco 2-0(1-0)
OGC Nice - Paris Saint-Germain 0-3(0-1)
Angers SCO - EA Guingamp 0-1(0-1)
SM Caen - Amiens SC 1-0(1-0)
Olympique Lyon - FC Nantes 1-1(1-0)
Stade Reims - Girondins Bordeaux 0-0
RC Strasbourg - Dijon FCO 3-0(1-0)
Stade Rennais - Toulouse FC 1-1(0-0)
Montpellier - Nîmes Olympique 3-0(2-0)
Lille OSC - Olympique Marseille 3-0(0-0)

Round 9 [05-07.10.2018]
Toulouse FC - OGC Nice 1-1(0-1)
Lille OSC - AS Saint-Étienne 3-1(1-1)
Amiens SC - Dijon FCO 1-0(1-0)
Angers SCO - RC Strasbourg 2-2(0-2)
EA Guingamp - Montpellier 1-1(0-1)
Nîmes Olympique - Stade Reims 0-0
Girondins Bordeaux - FC Nantes 3-0(3-0)
Olympique Marseille - SM Caen 2-0(2-0)
AS Monaco - Stade Rennais 1-2(0-1)
Paris Saint-Germain - Olymp. Lyon 5-0(1-0)

Round 10 [19-21.10.2018]
Olympique Lyon - Nîmes Olympique 2-0(1-0)
Paris Saint-Germain - Amiens SC 5-0(2-0)
SM Caen - EA Guingamp 0-0
Dijon FCO - Lille OSC 1-2(0-2)
FC Nantes - Toulouse FC 4-0(2-0)
Stade Reims - Angers SCO 1-1(0-1)
RC Strasbourg - AS Monaco 2-1(1-0)
Montpellier - Girondins Bordeaux 2-0(1-0)
AS Saint-Étienne - Stade Rennais 1-1(1-1)
OGC Nice - Olympique Marseille 0-1(0-1)

Round 11 [26-28.10.2018]
Nîmes Olympique - AS Saint-Étienne 1-1(0-1)
Angers SCO - Olympique Lyon 1-2(0-0)
Amiens SC - FC Nantes 1-2(0-1)
EA Guingamp - RC Strasbourg 1-1(1-0)
Lille OSC - SM Caen 1-0(0-0)
AS Monaco - Dijon FCO 2-2(1-1)
Toulouse FC - Montpellier 0-3(0-2)
Stade Rennais - Stade Reims 0-2(0-1)
Girondins Bordeaux - OGC Nice 0-1(0-0)
Oly. Marseille - Paris Saint-Germain 0-2(0-0)

Round 12 [02-04.11.2018]
Paris Saint-Germain - Lille OSC 2-1(0-0)
Olymp. Lyon - Girondins Bordeaux 1-1(1-0)
SM Caen - Stade Rennais 1-2(0-0)
Dijon FCO - Nîmes Olympique 0-4(0-2)
OGC Nice - Amiens SC 1-0(1-0)
Stade Reims - AS Monaco 1-0(1-0)
RC Strasbourg - Toulouse FC 1-1(0-0)
FC Nantes - EA Guingamp 5-0(1-0)
AS Saint-Étienne - Angers SCO 4-3(2-2)
Montpellier - Olympique Marseille 3-0(0-0)

Round 13 [09-11.11.2018]
Lille OSC - RC Strasbourg 0-0
EA Guingamp - Olympique Lyon 2-4(1-0)
Angers SCO - Montpellier 1-0(0-0)
Nîmes Olympique - OGC Nice 0-1(0-0)
AS Saint-Étienne - Stade Reims 2-0(2-0)
Toulouse FC - Amiens SC 0-1(0-1)
Girondins Bordeaux - SM Caen 0-0
Olympique Marseille - Dijon FCO 2-0(1-0)
Stade Rennais - FC Nantes 1-1(1-1)
AS Monaco - Paris Saint-Germain 0-4(0-2)

Round 14 [23-25.11.2018]
Olympique Lyon - AS Saint-Étienne 1-0(0-0)
Paris Saint-Germain - Toulouse FC 1-0(1-0)
SM Caen - AS Monaco 0-1(0-0)
Dijon FCO - Girondins Bordeaux 0-0
FC Nantes - Angers SCO 1-1(0-1)
Stade Reims - EA Guingamp 2-1(1-0)
RC Strasbourg - Nîmes Olympique 0-1(0-0)
Montpellier - Stade Rennais 2-2(1-1)
OGC Nice - Lille OSC 2-0(1-0)
Amiens SC - Olympique Marseille 1-3(1-1)

Round 15 [30.11.-02.12.2018]
AS Saint-Étienne - FC Nantes 3-0(0-0)
Lille OSC - Olympique Lyon 2-2(2-0)
Angers SCO - SM Caen 1-1(0-0)
EA Guingamp - OGC Nice 0-0
AS Monaco - Montpellier 1-2(1-0)
Nîmes Olympique - Amiens SC 3-0(1-0)
Toulouse FC - Dijon FCO 2-2(0-1)
Olympique Marseille - Stade Reims 0-0
Stade Rennais - RC Strasbourg 1-4(1-2)
Gir. Bordeaux - Paris Saint-Germain 2-2(0-1)

Round 16 [04-05.12.2018]
Amiens SC - AS Monaco 0-2(0-1)
OGC Nice - Angers SCO 0-0
Montpellier - Lille OSC 0-1(0-1)
Girondins Bordeaux - Saint-Étienne 3-2(1-1)
SM Caen - Nîmes Olympique 1-2(0-1)
Dijon FCO - EA Guingamp 2-1(1-0)
Olympique Lyon - Stade Rennais 0-2(0-2)
FC Nantes - Olympique Marseille 3-2(2-2)
Stade Reims - Toulouse FC 0-1(0-1)
RC Strasbourg - Paris Saint-Germain 1-1(1-0)

Round 17 [08-09.12.2018]
EA Guingamp - Amiens SC 1-2(0-0)
Stade Rennais - Dijon FCO 2-0(0-0)
RC Strasbourg - SM Caen 2-2(2-1)
Lille OSC - Stade Reims 1-1(0-0)
Angers SCO - Bordeaux 1-2(0-1) [15.01.19]
AS Monaco - OGC Nice 1-1(0-1) [16.01.19]
Nîmes Olymp - FC Nantes 1-0(0-0) [16.01.19]
Toulouse FC – Oly. Lyon 2-2(1-0) [16.01.19]
Saint-Étienne - Marseille 2-1(0-1) [16.01.19]
Paris SG - Montpellier 5-1(2-1) [20.02.19]

Round 18 [15-18.12.2018]
Stade Reims - RC Strasbourg 2-1(1-0)
Nîmes Olympique - Lille OSC 2-3(0-2)
OGC Nice - AS Saint-Étienne 1-1(0-0)
Olympique Lyon - AS Monaco 3-0(2-0)
SM Caen - Toulouse FC 2-1(1-1)
Amiens SC - Angers SCO 0-0 [08.01.19]
FC Nantes - Montpellier 2-0(0-0) [08.01.19]
Guingamp - Stade Rennais 2-1(1-0) [16.01.19]
Marseille - Gir. Bordeaux 1-0(1-0) [05.02.19]
Dijon FCO - Paris SG 0-4(0-2) [12.03.19]

Round 19 [22-23.12.2018]
Angers SCO - Olympique Marseille 1-1(1-0)
Lille OSC - Toulouse FC 1-2(1-0)
AS Monaco - EA Guingamp 0-2(0-0)
Montpellier - Olympique Lyon 1-1(0-0)
Paris Saint-Germain - FC Nantes 1-0(0-0)
Stade Reims - SM Caen 2-2(1-2)
Stade Rennais - Nîmes Olympique 4-0(2-0)
AS Saint-Étienne - Dijon FCO 3-0(1-0)
RC Strasbourg - OGC Nice 2-0(2-0)
Girondins Bordeaux - Amiens SC 1-1(1-0)

Round 20 [11-13.01.2019]
SM Caen - Lille OSC 1-3(0-2)
Olympique Lyon - Stade Reims 1-1(0-1)
Amiens SC - Paris Saint-Germain 0-3(0-0)
EA Guingamp - AS Saint-Étienne 0-1(0-1)
OGC Nice - Girondins Bordeaux 1-0(1-0)
FC Nantes - Stade Rennais 0-1(0-1)
Dijon FCO - Montpellier 1-1(0-0)
Toulouse FC - RC Strasbourg 1-2(1-1)
Olympique Marseille - AS Monaco 1-1(1-1)
Nîmes Olympique - Angers 3-1(2-0) [23.01.]

Round 21 [18-20.01.2019]
Lille OSC - Amiens SC 2-1(1-1)
Paris Saint-Germain - EA Guingamp 9-0(3-0)
AS Monaco - RC Strasbourg 1-5(1-2)
Nîmes Olympique - Toulouse FC 0-1(0-1)
Stade Reims - OGC Nice 1-1(1-0)
Stade Rennais - Montpellier 0-0
Angers SCO - FC Nantes 1-0(0-0)
SM Caen - Olympique Marseille 0-1(0-0)
Girondins Bordeaux - Dijon FCO 1-0(0-0)
AS Saint-Étienne - Olympique Lyon 1-2(1-0)

Round 22 [25-30.01.2019]
Olympique Marseille - Lille OSC 1-2(0-1)
Dijon FCO - AS Monaco 2-0(1-0)
EA Guingamp - Stade Reims 0-1(0-1)
OGC Nice - Nîmes Olympique 2-0(1-0)
RC Strasbourg - Girondins Bordeaux 1-0(0-0)
Montpellier - SM Caen 2-0(0-0)
Amiens SC - Olympique Lyon 0-1(0-0)
Toulouse FC - Angers SCO 0-0
Paris Saint-Germain - Stade Rennais 4-1(1-1)
FC Nantes - AS Saint-Étienne 1-1(0-0)

Round 23 [01-03.02.2019]
Lille OSC - OGC Nice 4-0(2-0)
Angers SCO - Dijon FCO 1-0(1-0)
AS Monaco - Toulouse FC 2-1(1-1)
Stade Rennais - Amiens SC 1-0(0-0)
Stade Reims - Olympique Marseille 2-1(1-0)
Nîmes Olympique - Montpellier 1-1(1-0)
Olympique Lyon - Paris SG 2-1(1-1)
Saint-Étienne - Strasbourg 2-1(2-0) [13.02.]
SM Caen - FC Nantes 0-1(0-0) [13.02.]
Girondins Bordeaux - Guingamp 0-0 [20.02.]

Round 24 [08-10.02.2019]
Dijon FCO - Olympique Marseille 1-2(1-0)
Paris SG - Girondins Bordeaux 1-0(1-0)
Amiens SC - SM Caen 1-0(0-0)
RC Strasbourg - Angers SCO 1-2(0-1)
Montpellier - AS Monaco 2-2(0-1)
FC Nantes - Nîmes Olympique 2-4(2-0)
Toulouse FC - Stade Reims 1-1(0-0)
EA Guingamp - Lille OSC 0-2(0-0)
Stade Rennais - AS Saint-Étienne 3-0(1-0)
OGC Nice - Olympique Lyon 1-0(0-0)

Round 25 [15-17.02.2019]
Nîmes Olympique - Dijon FCO 2-0(1-0)
Olympique Lyon - EA Guingamp 2-1(2-1)
Olympique Marseille - Amiens SC 2-0(2-0)
Angers SCO - OGC Nice 3-0(1-0)
AS Monaco - FC Nantes 1-0(1-0)
Girondins Bordeaux - Toulouse FC 2-1(1-0)
SM Caen - RC Strasbourg 0-0
Lille OSC - Montpellier 0-0
Stade Reims - Stade Rennais 2-0(1-0)
Saint-Étienne - Paris Saint-Germain 0-1(0-0)

Round 26 [22-24.02.2019]
Dijon FCO - AS Saint-Étienne 0-1(0-0)
RC Strasbourg - Lille OSC 1-1(0-1)
Paris Saint-Germain - Nîmes Olymp. 3-0(1-0)
Amiens SC - OGC Nice 1-0(1-0)
EA Guingamp - Angers SCO 1-0(0-0)
Montpellier - Stade Reims 2-4(1-1)
FC Nantes - Girondins Bordeaux 1-0(0-0)
Toulouse FC - SM Caen 1-1(0-1)
Stade Rennais - Olympique Marseille 1-1(1-0)
AS Monaco - Olympique Lyon 2-0(2-0)

Round 27 [02-05.03.2019]
SM Caen - Paris Saint-Germain 1-2(0-0)
Angers SCO - AS Monaco 2-2(2-0)
Stade Reims - Amiens SC 2-2(0-2)
EA Guingamp - FC Nantes 0-0
Lille OSC - Dijon FCO 1-0(0-0)
OGC Nice - RC Strasbourg 1-0(1-0)
Olympique Lyon - Toulouse FC 5-1(3-1)
Olympique Marseille - Saint-Étienne 2-0(2-0)
Girondins Bordeaux - Montpellier 1-2(1-1)
Nîmes Oly. - Stade Rennais 3-1(1-1) [09.04.]

Round 28 [09-10.03.2019]
RC Strasbourg - Olympique Lyon 2-2(0-1)
Amiens SC - Nîmes Olympique 2-1(0-0)
Dijon FCO - Stade Reims 1-1(1-1)
AS Monaco - Girondins Bordeaux 1-1(0-0)
Montpellier - Angers SCO 2-2(2-0)
AS Saint-Étienne - Lille OSC 0-1(0-0)
Toulouse FC - EA Guingamp 1-0(1-0)
Stade Rennais - SM Caen 3-1(1-1)
Olympique Marseille - OGC Nice 1-0(0-0)
FC Nantes - Paris SG 3-2(2-1) [17.04.]

Round 29 [15-17.03.2019]
OGC Nice - Toulouse FC 1-1(1-0)
Lille OSC - AS Monaco 0-1(0-0)
Angers SCO - Amiens SC 0-0
SM Caen - AS Saint-Étienne 0-5(0-3)
EA Guingamp - Dijon FCO 1-0(0-0)
Nîmes Olympique - RC Strasbourg 2-2(0-1)
Olympique Lyon - Montpellier 3-2(1-1)
Stade Reims - FC Nantes 1-0(0-0)
Girondins Bordeaux - Stade Rennais 1-1(0-0)
Paris Saint-Germain - Oly. Marseille 3-1(1-0)

Round 30 [29.03.-03.04.2019]
Stade Rennais - Olympique Lyon 0-1(0-0)
Olympique Marseille - Angers SCO 2-2(2-1)
Amiens SC - Girondins Bordeaux 0-0
Dijon FCO - OGC Nice 0-1(0-0)
AS Monaco - SM Caen 0-1(0-1)
FC Nantes - Lille OSC 2-3(0-0)
Toulouse FC - Paris Saint-Germain 0-1(0-0)
AS Saint-Étienne - Nîmes Olympique 2-1(1-1)
Montpellier - EA Guingamp 2-0(1-0)
RC Strasbourg - Stade Reims 4-0(1-0)

Round 31 [05-07.04.2019]
Girondins Bordeaux - Oly. Marseille 2-0(1-0)
Olympique Lyon - Dijon FCO 1-3(1-2)
Amiens SC - AS Saint-Étienne 2-2(1-1)
Angers SCO - Stade Rennais 3-3(0-1)
EA Guingamp - AS Monaco 1-1(1-0)
Nîmes Olympique - SM Caen 2-0(0-0)
Stade Reims - Lille OSC 1-1(0-0)
Toulouse FC - FC Nantes 1-0(0-0)
OGC Nice - Montpellier 1-0(1-0)
Paris Saint-Germain - RC Strasbourg 2-2(1-2)

Round 32 [12-14.04.2019]
Dijon FCO - Amiens SC 0-0
FC Nantes - Olympique Lyon 2-1(1-1)
Olymp. Marseille - Nîmes Olympique 2-1(0-0)
SM Caen - Angers SCO 0-1(0-0)
AS Monaco - Stade Reims 0-0
RC Strasbourg - EA Guingamp 3-3(1-1)
Montpellier - Toulouse FC 2-1(0-0)
Stade Rennais - OGC Nice 0-0
Saint-Étienne - Girondins Bordeaux 3-0(0-0)
Lille OSC - Paris Saint-Germain 5-1(1-1)

Round 33 [19-21.04.2019]
Dijon FCO - Stade Rennais 3-2(1-0)
Olympique Lyon - Angers SCO 2-1(2-0)
EA Guingamp - Olympique Marseille 1-3(0-2)
OGC Nice - SM Caen 0-1(0-0)
Nîmes Olymp. - Girondins Bordeaux 2-1(1-1)
RC Strasbourg - Montpellier 1-3(1-2)
FC Nantes - Amiens SC 3-2(0-0)
Toulouse FC - Lille OSC 0-0
Stade Reims - AS Saint-Étienne 0-2(0-1)
Paris Saint-Germain - AS Monaco 3-1(2-0)

Round 34 [26.04.-01.05.2019]
Girond. Bordeaux - Olympique Lyon 2-3(2-1)
Amiens SC - RC Strasbourg 0-0
Angers SCO - Stade Reims 1-1(0-0)
SM Caen - Dijon FCO 1-0(0-0)
Lille OSC - Nîmes Olympique 5-0(0-0)
OGC Nice - EA Guingamp 3-0(1-0)
AS Saint-Étienne - Toulouse FC 2-0(2-0)
Olympique Marseille - FC Nantes 1-2(1-1)
Montpellier - Paris Saint-Germain 3-2(1-1)
Stade Rennais - AS Monaco 2-2(2-0)

Round 35 [03-05.05.2019]
Strasbourg - Olympique Marseille 1-1(0-0)
Paris Saint-Germain - OGC Nice 1-1(0-0)
Girondins Bordeaux - Angers SCO 0-1(0-1)
EA Guingamp - SM Caen 0-0
Stade Reims - Nîmes Olympique 0-3(0-2)
Montpellier - Amiens SC 1-1(0-0)
FC Nantes - Dijon FCO 3-0(0-0)
Toulouse FC - Stade Rennais 2-2(1-1)
AS Monaco - AS Saint-Étienne 2-3(1-0)
Olympique Lyon - Lille OSC 2-2(1-0)

Round 36 [10-12.05.2019]
AS Saint-Étienne - Montpellier 0-1(0-0)
Angers SCO - Paris Saint-Germain 1-2(0-1)
Amiens SC - Toulouse FC 0-0
SM Caen - Stade Reims 3-2(3-1)
Dijon FCO - RC Strasbourg 2-1(1-0)
OGC Nice - FC Nantes 1-1(0-1)
Nîmes Olympique - AS Monaco 1-0(1-0)
Stade Rennais - EA Guingamp 1-1(1-0)
Lille OSC - Girondins Bordeaux 1-0(1-0)
Olymp. Marseille - Olympique Lyon 0-3(0-1)

Round 37 [18.05.2019]
Girondins Bordeaux - Stade Reims 0-1(0-1)
EA Guingamp - Nîmes Olympique 2-2(2-0)
Lille OSC - Angers SCO 5-0(2-0)
Olympique Lyon - SM Caen 4-0(0-0)
AS Monaco - Amiens SC 2-0(1-0)
Montpellier - FC Nantes 1-1(0-1)
Paris Saint-Germain - Dijon FCO 4-0(3-0)
AS Saint-Étienne - OGC Nice 3-0(1-0)
RC Strasbourg - Stade Rennais 0-2(0-1)
Toulouse FC - Olympique Marseille 2-5(1-1)

Round 38 [24.05.2019]
Amiens SC - EA Guingamp 2-1(1-0)
Angers SCO - AS Saint-Étienne 1-1(0-0)
SM Caen - Girondins Bordeaux 0-1(0-1)
Dijon FCO - Toulouse FC 2-1(0-1)
Olympique Marseille - Montpellier 1-0(0-0)
FC Nantes - RC Strasbourg 0-1(0-0)
OGC Nice - AS Monaco 2-0(1-0)
Nîmes Olympique - Olympique Lyon 2-3(2-1)
Stade Reims - Paris Saint-Germain 3-1(1-0)
Stade Rennais - Lille OSC 3-1(1-1)

Final Standings

1.	**Paris Saint-Germain FC**	38	29	4	5	105	-	35	91
2.	Lille OSC	38	22	9	7	68	-	33	75
3.	Olympique Lyonnais	38	21	9	8	70	-	47	72
4.	AS Saint-Étienne	38	19	9	10	59	-	41	66
5.	Olympique de Marseille	38	18	7	13	60	-	52	61
6.	Montpellier Hérault SC	38	15	14	9	53	-	42	59
7.	OGC Nice	38	15	11	12	30	-	35	56
8.	Stade de Reims	38	13	16	9	39	-	42	55
9.	Nîmes Olympique	38	15	8	15	57	-	58	53
10.	Stade Rennais FC	38	13	13	12	55	-	52	52
11.	Racing Club de Strasbourg	38	11	16	11	58	-	48	49
12.	FC Nantes	38	13	9	16	48	-	48	48
13.	Angers SCO	38	10	16	12	44	-	49	46
14.	Girondins de Bordeaux FC	38	10	11	17	34	-	42	41
15.	Amiens SC	38	9	11	18	31	-	52	38
16.	Toulouse FC	38	8	14	16	35	-	57	38
17.	AS Monaco FC	38	8	12	18	38	-	57	36
18.	Dijon FCO (*Relegation Play-offs*)	38	9	7	22	31	-	60	34
19.	Stade Malherbe Caen (*Relegated*)	38	7	12	19	29	-	54	33
20.	En Avant de Guingamp (*Relegated*)	38	5	12	21	28	-	68	27

Top goalscorers:

33 Kylian Sanmi Mbappé Lottin
Paris Saint-Germain FC

22 Nicolas Pépé (CIV)
Lille OSC

18 Edinson Roberto Cavani Gómez
Paris Saint-Germain FC

16 Florian Tristan Mariano Thauvin
Olympique de Marseille

15 Moussa Dembélé
Olympique Lyonnais

15 Radamel Falcao García Zárate
AS Monaco FC

15 Neymar da Silva Santos Júnior (BRA)
Paris Saint-Germain FC

Relegation Play-offs

Racing Club de Lens - Dijon FCO	1-1(0-0)	1-3(1-1)

Dijon FCO will remain in Ligue 1 for the next season.

NATIONAL CUP
Coupe de France 2018/2019

Round of 64 [04-07/16.01.2019]

FC Nantes - La Berrichonne de Châteauroux	4-1(2-1)	Olympique Saint-Quentin - FC Metz	1-2(0-1,1-1)
ES Viry-Chatillon - Angers SCO	1-0(0-0)	FC Sète 34 - FC Limonest	1-0(0-0)
Iris Club de Croix - US Raon-l'Etape	2-0(0-0)	Bourges Foot - Olympique Lyonnais	0-2(0-0)
Marignane Gignac FC - Clermont Foot 63	1-1 aet; 3-0 pen	Canet Roussillion FC - AS Monaco FC	0-1(0-1)
Tours FC - Les Herbiers Vendée Football	1-2(0-1)	AFS Andrézieux - Olympique de Marseille	2-0(1-0)
SC Bastia - US Concarneau	2-2 aet; 5-4 pen	Stade Rennais FC - Stade Brestois 29	2-2 aet; 5-4 pen
L'Entente San.Saint-Gratien - Montpellier Hérault SC	1-0(0-0)	Stade de Reims - Racing Club de Lens	2-0(2-0)
Bergerac Périgord FC - Chamois Niortais FC	2-1(2-1)	St-Pryvé St-Hilaire FC - FC Aurillac Arpajon CA	3-1(3-1)
US Orléans Loiret F. - L'Aiglon du Lamentin FC	3-2(1-0,1-1)	Olympique Strasbourg - AS Saint-Étienne	0-6(0-2)
Amiens SC - Valenciennes FC	1-0(0-0)	Noisy-Le-Grand FC - GFC Ajaccio	2-1(2-1)
AS Lyon-Duchère - Nîmes Olympique	3-0(1-0)	Toulouse FC - OGC Nice	4-1(2-0)
Le Puy Foot 43 Auvergne - AS Nancy-Lorraine	0-1(0-1)	ESC Longueau - AS Vitré	0-0 aet; 1-4 pen
Stade Pontivyen - En Avant de Guingamp	2-4(1-2)	Girondins Bordeaux - Le Havre AC	0-1(0-0)
Red Star FC Paris - Stade Malherbe Caen	0-1(0-0)	GSI Pontivy - Paris Saint-Germain FC	0-4(0-1)
US Gravelines Football - FC Villefranche-Beaujolais	0-3(0-0,0-0)	Lille OSC - FC Sochaux-Montbéliard	1-0(1-0)
SC de Schiltigheim - Dijon FCO	1-3(0-0)	Grenoble Foot 38 - Racing Club de Strasbourg	0-1(0-0,0-0)

Round of 32 [22-24.01/02.02.2019]

Toulouse FC - Stade de Reims	4-4 aet; 4-3 pen	Bergerac Périgord FC - US Orléans Loiret Football	2-3(0-0,2-2)
AS Nancy-Lorraine - En Avant de Guingamp	1-2(0-1,1-1)	ES Viry-Chatillon - Stade Malherbe Caen	0-6(0-3)
AFS Andrézieux - AS Lyon-Duchère	1-2(1-0)	Marignane Gignac FC - Iris Club de Croix	0-0 aet; 3-4 pen
FC Villefranche-Beaujolais - Les Herbiers Vendée F.	2-0(0-0)	Paris Saint-Germain FC - Racing Club de Strasbourg	2-0(1-0)
FC Sète 34 - Lille OSC	0-1(0-0)	SC Bastia - Noisy-Le-Grand FC	2-1(2-0)
AS Monaco FC - FC Metz	1-3(1-1)	AS Vitré - Le Havre AC	3-0(1-0)
AS Saint-Étienne - Dijon FCO	3-6(1-2)	Amiens SC - Olympique Lyonnais	0-2(0-2)
St-Pryvé St-Hilaire FC - Stade Rennais FC	0-2(0-1)	L'Entente Sannois Saint-Gratien - FC Nantes	0-1(0-0)

Round of 16 [05-07.02.2019]

Iris Club de Croix - Dijon FCO	0-3(0-2)	FC Villefranche-Beaujolais - Paris Saint-Germain FC	0-3(0-0,0-0)
FC Metz - US Orléans Loiret Football	0-1(0-1)	AS Vitré - AS Lyon-Duchère	3-2(2-2)
FC Nantes - Toulouse FC	2-0(2-0)	Stade Rennais FC - Lille OSC	2-1(0-0)
SC Bastia - Stade Malherbe Caen	2-2 aet; 3-5 pen	En Avant de Guingamp - Olympique Lyonnais	1-2(0-1)

Quarter-Finals [26-27.02/06.03.2019]

Paris Saint-Germain FC - Dijon FCO	3-0(2-0)	Olympique Lyonnais - Stade Malherbe Caen	3-1(1-0)
Stade Rennais FC - US Orléans Loiret Football	2-0(0-0)	AS Vitré - FC Nantes	0-2(0-2)

Semi-Finals [02-03.04.2019]

Olympique Lyonnais - Stade Rennais FC	2-3(0-1)	Paris Saint-Germain FC - FC Nantes	3-0(1-0)

Final

27.04.2019; Stade de France, Saint-Denis, Paris; Referee: Ruddy Buquet; Attendance: 75,000
Stade Rennais FC - Paris Saint-Germain FC **2-2(1-2,2-2,2-2); 6-5 on penalties**

Stade Rennais: Tomáš Koubek, Hamari Traoré, Damien Da Silva, Edson André Sitoe „Mexer", Ramy Bensebaini, Benjamin André (Cap), Clément Grenier, Ismaïla Sarr, Hatem Ben Arfa, Benjamin Bourigeaud (106.James Lea Siliki), M'Baye Niang. Trainer: Julien Stéphan.

Paris Saint-Germain: Alphonse Aréola, Colin Dagba (106.Moussa Diaby; 120+1.Christopher Nkunku), Marcos Aoás Corrêa „Marquinhos" (Cap), Presnel Kimpembe, Juan Bernat Velasco, Daniel Alves da Silva, Marco Verratti, Julian Draxler (91.Edinson Roberto Cavani Gómez), Ángel Fabián Di María Hernández (75.Leandro Daniel Paredes), Kylian Sanmi Mbappé Lottin [*sent off 118*], Neymar da Silva Santos Júnior. Trainer: Thomas Tuchel (Germany).

Goals: 0-1 Daniel Alves da Silva (13), 0-2 Neymar da Silva Santos Júnior (21), 1-2 Presnel Kimpembe (40 own goal), 2-2 Edson André Sitoe „Mexer" (66).

Penalties: M'Baye Niang 1-0; Edinson Roberto Cavani Gómez 1-1; Hatem Ben Arfa 2-1; Daniel Alves da Silva 2-2; Clément Grenier 3-2; Leandro Daniel Paredes 3-3; James Lea Siliki 4-3; Juan Bernat Velasco 4-4; Ramy Bensebaini 5-4; Neymar da Silva Santos Júnior 5-5; Ismaïla Sarr 6-5; Christopher Nkunku (missed).

Coupe de la Ligue Final 2018/2019

30.03.2019; Stade "Pierre Mauroy", Villeneuve-d'Ascq; Referee: Benoît Millot; Attendance: 49,161
Racing Club de Strasbourg - En Avant de Guingamp **0-0; 4-1 on penalties**

Racing Strasbourg: Bingourou Kamara, Lamine Koné (90.Lionel Carole), Stefan Mitrovič (Cap), Pablo Martinez, Kenny Lala, Anthony Caci, Ibrahima Sissoko (118.Dimitri Liénard), Sanjin Prcić, Adrien Thomasson, Lebogang Mothiba (81.Nuno Miguel da Costa Jóia), Ludovic Ajorque (105.Kévin Lucien Zohi). Trainer: Thierry Laurey.

EA Guingamp: Marc-Aurèle Caillard, Cheick Traoré, Jérémy Sorbon (Cap), Christophe Kerbrat, Pedro Miguel Braga Rebocho, Lebogang Phiri, Didier Ndong, Nicolas Benezet (86.Ronny Rodelin), Ludovic Blas (96.Étienne Didot), Marcus Thuram, Nolan Roux (67.Alexandre Mendy). Trainer: Jocelyn Gourvennec.

Penalties: Sanjin Prcić 1-0; Alexandre Mendy (missed); Adrien Thomasson 2-0; Étienne Didot 2-1; Dimitri Liénard 3-1; Ronny Rodelin (saved); Lionel Carole 4-1.

Amiens Sporting Club

Founded: 1901
Stadium: Stade de la Licorne, Amiens (12,097)

Goalkeepers:	DOB	M	(s)	G
Régis Gurtner	08.12.1986	38		
Defenders:	**DOB**	**M**	**(s)**	**G**
Abdoul Khaled Akiola Adénon (BEN)	28.07.1985	22	(1)	
Mathieu Bodmer	22.11.1982	10	(16)	1
Bakaye Dibassy (MLI)	11.08.1989	32	(2)	1
Oualid El Hajjam (MAR)	19.02.1991	6	(5)	
Prince Gouano	24.12.1993	30		1
Emil Henry Kristoffer Krafth (SWE)	02.08.1994	33	(2)	1
Jordan Lefort	09.08.1993	21	(2)	
Erik Pieters (NED)	07.08.1988	14	(1)	1
Sanasi Sy	04.12.1999		(1)	
Midfielders:	**DOB**	**M**	**(s)**	**G**
Alexis Blin	19.09.1996	25	(2)	1
Guessouma Fofana	17.12.1992	2	(1)	
Paulo Henrique Chagas de Lima "Ganso" (BRA)	12.10.1989	5	(7)	
Vhakka Eddy Stelh Gnahoré	14.11.1993	24	(10)	4
Thomas Monconduit	10.02.1991	32	(1)	
Cheick Timite (CIV)	20.11.1997	15	(12)	1
Gaoussou Traoré	04.12.1999	1	(2)	
Bongani Zungu (RSA)	09.10.1992	3	(2)	
Forwards:	**DOB**	**M**	**(s)**	**G**
Quentin Cornette	17.01.1994	3	(2)	
Saman Ghoddos (IRN)	06.09.1993	20	(7)	4
Serhou Guirassy	12.03.1996	13		3
Moussa Konaté (SEN)	03.04.1993	21	(6)	7
Rafał Kurzawa (POL)	29.01.1993	2	(9)	1
John Stiven Mendoza Valencia (COL)	27.06.1992	22	(3)	2
Juan Ferney Otero Tovar (COL)	26.05.1995	24	(9)	2
Stanley Segarel	04.03.1994		(3)	
Trainer:	**DOB**	**M**		
Christophe Pélissier	05.10.1965	38		

Angers Sporting Club de l'Ouest

Founded: 1919
Stadium: Stade "Raymond Kopa", Angers (17,835)

Goalkeepers:	DOB	M	(s)	G
Zacharie Boucher	07.03.1992	2		
Ludovic Butelle	13.04.1983	36		
Defenders:	**DOB**	**M**	**(s)**	**G**
Rayan Aït Nouri	06.06.2001		(3)	
Yoann Andreu	03.05.1989		(1)	
Abdoulaye Bamba (CIV)	25.04.1990	29	(1)	
Angelo Fulgini	20.08.1996	18	(13)	4
Vincent Manceau	10.07.1989	31		1
Elhadji Pape Diaw (SEN)	31.12.1994		(1)	
Mateo Pavlović (CRO)	09.06.1990	28	(2)	2
Théo Pellenard	04.03.1994	6		
Romain Thomas	12.06.1988	27	(1)	2
Midfielders:	**DOB**	**M**	**(s)**	**G**
Pierrick Capelle	15.04.1987	21	(5)	3
Thomas Mangani	29.04.1987	18	(11)	3
Harisson Manzala Tusumgama (COD)	06.03.1994		(8)	
Cheikh N'Doye (SEN)	29.03.1986	26	(1)	
Vincent Pajot	19.08.1990	10	(3)	
Jeff Reine-Adélaïde	17.01.1998	29	(6)	3
Baptiste Santamaría	09.03.1995	37	(1)	1
Flavien Tait	02.02.1993	34	(2)	5
Ismaël Traoré (CIV)	18.08.1986	29	(1)	3
Forwards:	**DOB**	**M**	**(s)**	**G**
Stéphane Bahoken	28.05.1992	31	(1)	11
Cristian (ESP)	24.07.1989	2	(17)	2
Farid El Melali (ALG)	05.05.1997		(18)	
Aka Kanga	21.02.1998	4	(14)	2
Trainer:	**DOB**	**M**		
Stéphane Moulin	04.08.1967	38		

Football Club des Girondins de Bordeaux

Founded: 1881
Stadium: Matmut Atlantique, Bordeaux (42,115)

Goalkeepers:	DOB	M	(s)	G
Benoît Costil	03.07.1987	37		
Gaëtan Poussin	13.01.1999	1		
Defenders:	**DOB**	**M**	**(s)**	**G**
Paul Baysse	18.05.1988		(1)	
Till Cissokho	08.02.2000	1		
Milan Gajić (SRB)	28.01.1996	1		
Vukašin Jovanović (SRB)	17.05.1996	15	(1)	
Jules Koundé	12.11.1998	37		
Alexandre Lauray	18.03.1997	3		
Igor Lewczuk (POL)	30.05.1985	3	(3)	
Pablo Nascimento Castro (BRA)	21.06.1991	25		1
Maxime Poundje	16.08.1992	28	(2)	
Youssouf Sabaly (SEN)	05.03.1993	21	(2)	
Sergi Palencia Hurtado (ESP)	23.03.1996	22	(3)	
Midfielders:	**DOB**	**M**	**(s)**	**G**
Yacine Adli	29.07.2000	2	(5)	
Toma Bašić (CRO)	25.11.1996	16	(7)	2
Yassine Benrahou	24.01.1999	1	(3)	
Lukas Reiff Lerager (DEN)	12.07.1993	15	(3)	
Albert Lottin	29.08.2001		(2)	
Otavio Henrique Passos Santos (BRA)	04.05.1994	33		
Jaroslav Plašil (CZE)	05.01.1982	16	(7)	
Younousse Sankharé (SEN)	10.09.1989	17	(5)	1
Aurélien Tchouaméni	27.01.2000	8	(2)	
Driss Trichard	27.03.1995	1		
Valentín Vada (ARG)	06.03.1996		(2)	
Forwards:	**DOB**	**M**	**(s)**	**G**
Jimmy Briand	02.08.1985	28	(7)	7
Andreas Evald Cornelius (DEN)	16.03.1993	6	(14)	3
Nicolas de Préville	08.01.1991	14	(9)	3
Samuel Kalu Ojim (NGA)	26.08.1997	14	(7)	3
François Kamano (GUI)	01.05.1996	29	(8)	10
Yann Karamoh	08.07.1998	13	(9)	3
Gaëtan Laborde	03.05.1994	1		
Joshua Erowoli Orisunmihare Oluwaseun Maja (ENG)	27.12.1998	3	(4)	1
Michaël Nilor	16.04.1998			
Zaydou Youssouf	11.07.1999	7	(4)	
Trainer:	**DOB**	**M**		
Gustavo Augusto Poyet Domínguez (URU)	15.11.1967	1		
Eric Bedouet [17.08.2018]	14.04.1954	3		
Ricardo Raymundo Gomes (BRA) [05.09.2018]	13.12.1964	23		
Paulo Manuel Carvalho Sousa (POR) [08.03.2019]	30.08.1970	11		

Stade Malherbe Caen

Founded: 17.11.1913
Stadium: Stade „Michel d'Ornano", Caen (20,453)

Goalkeepers:	DOB	M	(s)	G
Brice Samba	25.04.1994	38		
Defenders:	**DOB**	**M**	**(s)**	**G**
Yoël Armougom	05.06.1998	20	(9)	
Paul Baysse	18.05.1988	20		
Alexander Djiku	09.08.1994	31		1
Romain Genevois (HAI)	28.10.1987	5	(1)	
Jonathan Gradit	24.11.1992	23	(1)	
Frédéric Guilbert	24.12.1994	33	(1)	1
Emmanuel Imorou (BEN)	16.09.1988	12	(4)	
Adama Mbengue (SEN)	01.12.1993	8	(3)	
Younn Zahary	20.10.1998	7	(5)	
Midfielders:	**DOB**	**M**	**(s)**	**G**
Jessy Deminguet	07.01.1998	15	(5)	
Ismaël Diomandé (CIV)	28.08.1992	14	(4)	
Fayçal Fajr (MAR)	01.08.1988	36		5
Saîf-Eddine Khaoui (TUN)	27.04.1995	17	(8)	3
Aly Ndom	30.05.1996	1		
Prince Oniangué (CGO)	04.11.1988	26	(5)	2
Stef Peeters (BEL)	09.02.1992	5	(2)	
Baïssama Sankoh (GUI)	20.03.1992	6	(9)	
Forwards:	**DOB**	**M**	**(s)**	**G**
Yacine Bammou (MAR)	11.09.1991	9	(8)	2
Claudio Beauvue (GLP)	16.04.1988	16	(9)	3
Enzo Crivelli	06.02.1995	28	(5)	6
Evens Joseph	16.07.1999	2	(11)	
Herman Moussaki	10.02.1999	2	(4)	
Casimir Rodrigue Ninga (CHA)	17.05.1993	28	(5)	6
Timo Stavitski (FIN)	17.07.1999		(1)	
Malik Tchokounté	11.09.1988	16	(13)	
Trainer:	**DOB**	**M**		
Fabien Mercadal	29.02.1972	38		

Dijon Football Côte d'Or

Founded: 1998
Stadium: Stade „Gaston Gérard", Dijon (18,376)

Goalkeepers:	DOB	M	(s)	G
Bobby Allain	28.11.1991	13		
Rúnar Rúnarsson (ISL)	18.02.1995	25		
Defenders:	**DOB**	**M**	**(s)**	**G**
Nayef Aguerd (MAR)	30.03.1996	12	(1)	3
Mickaël Alphonse (GLP)	12.07.1989	6	(5)	1
Arnold Bouka Moutou (CGO)	28.11.1988		(3)	
Fouad Chafik (MAR)	16.10.1986	21		
Laurent Franco Ciman (BEL)	05.08.1985	7	(2)	
Senou Coulibaly	04.09.1994	6	(3)	1
Oussema Haddadi (TUN)	28.01.1992	30	(2)	2
Wesley Lautoa	25.08.1987	34		
Valentin Rosier	19.08.1996	16	(2)	
Cédric Yamberé	06.11.1990	30	(3)	
Midfielders:	**DOB**	**M**	**(s)**	**G**
Mehdi Abeid	06.08.1992	23	(3)	3
Romain Amalfitano	27.08.1989	30	(2)	
Florent Balmont	02.02.1980	15	(5)	
Yoann Miguel Gourcuff	11.07.1986		(8)	
Kwon Chang-Hoon (KOR)	30.06.1994	10	(9)	2
Enzo Loiodice	27.11.2000	10	(2)	
Jordan Marié	29.09.1991	20	(6)	1
Frédéric Sammaritano	23.03.1986	6	(8)	
Forwards:	**DOB**	**M**	**(s)**	**G**
Benjamin Jeannot	22.01.1992	19	(2)	2
Júlio Tavares (CPV)	19.11.1988	31	(5)	5
Sory Kaba (GUI)	28.07.1995	2	(7)	
Jules Keita (GUI)	20.07.1998	2	(15)	2
Wesley Saïd	19.04.1995	25	(9)	4
Naïm Sliti (TUN)	27.07.1992	25	(10)	3
Trainer:	**DOB**	**M**		
Olivier Dall'Oglio	16.05.1964	18		
Antoine Krilone Kombouaré [10.01.2019]	16.11.1963	20		

En Avant de Guingamp Côtes-d'Armor

Founded: 1912
Stadium: Stade du Roudourou, Guingamp (18,378)

Goalkeepers:	DOB	M	(s)	G
Marc-Aurèle Caillard	12.05.1994	21		
Karl-Johan Johnsson (SWE)	28.01.1990	17		
Defenders:	**DOB**	**M**	**(s)**	**G**
Papy Djilobodji (SEN)	01.12.1988	2	(2)	
Félix Eboa Eboa (CMR)	19.04.1997	27		3
Jordan Ikoko (COD)	03.02.1994	19	(1)	
Christophe Kerbrat	02.08.1986	25		
Djegui Koita	05.12.1999	1	(1)	
Johan Larsson (SWE)	05.05.1990	1		
Pedro Miguel Braga Rebocho (POR)	23.01.1995	36		
Jérémy Sorbon	05.08.1983	29	(4)	1
Cheick Traoré	31.03.1995	16	(4)	
Midfielders:	**DOB**	**M**	**(s)**	**G**
Nicolas Benezet	24.02.1991	18	(7)	3
Ludovic Blas	31.12.1997	27	(7)	1
Louis Carnot	25.02.2001		(1)	
Marcus Coco	24.06.1996	21	(12)	1
Lucas Deaux	26.12.1988	17	(1)	3
Étienne Didot	24.07.1983	23	(8)	1
Guessouma Fofana	17.12.1992	4	(6)	
Mehdi Merghem	19.07.1997	9		
Didier Ndong (GAB)	17.06.1994	8	(3)	
Lebogang Phiri (RSA)	09.11.1994	23	(1)	
Franck Tabanou	30.01.1989	2		
Forwards:	**DOB**	**M**	**(s)**	**G**
Nathaël Julan	19.07.1996	3	(7)	
Alexandre Mendy	20.03.1994	8	(8)	3
Yeni N'Gbakoto	23.01.1992	4	(11)	1
Matthias Phaeton	08.01.2000		(4)	
Ronny Rodelin	18.11.1989	8	(9)	
Nolan Roux	01.03.1988	17	(9)	2
Yannis Salibur	24.01.1991		(1)	
Marcus Thuram	06.08.1997	32		9
Trainer:	**DOB**	**M**		
Antoine Kombouaré	16.11.1963	12		
Sylvain Didot [07.11.2018]	08.10.1975	1		
Jocelyn Gourvennec [12.11.2018]	22.03.1972	25		

Lille Olympique Sporting Club

Founded: 23.09.1944
Stadium: Stade "Pierre Mauroy", Villeneuve-d'Ascq (50,157)

Goalkeepers:	**DOB**	**M**	**(s)**	**G**
Mike Maignan	03.07.1995	38		
Defenders:	**DOB**	**M**	**(s)**	**G**
Fodé Ballo-Touré	03.01.1997	18		
Mehmet Çelik (TUR)	17.02.1997	34		1
Kouadio-Yves Dabila (CIV)	01.01.1997	8	(4)	
Gabriel dos Santos Magalhaes (BRA)	19.12.1997	11	(3)	1
Edgar Miguel Ié (POR)	01.05.1994	1	(6)	
José Miguel da Rocha Fonte (POR)	22.12.1983	36		3
Youssouf Koné (MLI)	05.07.1995	19	(1)	
Jérémy Pied	23.02.1989	4	(7)	
Reinildo Isnard Mandava (MOZ)	21.01.1994	1	(2)	
Adama Soumaoro	18.06.1992	20		
Midfielders:	**DOB**	**M**	**(s)**	**G**
Jonathan Ikoné	02.05.1998	34	(4)	3
Boubakary Soumaré	27.02.1999	5	(13)	1
Thiago Maia Alencar (BRA)	23.03.1997	10	(14)	
Thiago Henrique Mendes Ribeiro (BRA)	15.03.1992	35		
Miguel Ângelo da Silva Rocha „Xeka" (POR)	10.11.1994	26	(1)	2
Arton Zekaj (SRB)	16.04.2000		(1)	
Forwards:	**DOB**	**M**	**(s)**	**G**
Jonathan Bamba	26.03.1996	35	(3)	13
Yassine Benzia (ALG)	08.09.1994	2		
Luiz Araujo Guimarães Neto (BRA)	02.06.1996	6	(19)	3
Lebogang Mothiba (RSA)	28.01.1996	3		1
Nicolas Pépé (CIV)	29.05.1995	37	(1)	22
Rafael Alexandre da Conceição Leão (POR)	10.06.1999	16	(8)	8
Loïc Rémy	02.01.1987	14	(12)	7
Rui Pedro da Rocha Fonte (POR)	23.04.1990	5	(13)	1
Trainer:	**DOB**	**M**		
Christophe Galtier	26.08.1966	38		

Olympique Lyonnais

Founded: 1950
Stadium: Groupama Stadium, Décines-Charpieu, Lyon (59,186)

Goalkeepers:	**DOB**	**M**	**(s)**	**G**
Anthony Lopes (POR)	01.10.1990	34		
Mathieu Gorgelin	05.08.1990	4		
Defenders:	**DOB**	**M**	**(s)**	**G**
Jason Denayer (BEL)	28.06.1995	31		2
Léo Dubois	14.09.1994	21	(4)	1
Fernando Marçal de Oliveira (BRA)	19.02.1989	12		
Marcelo Antônio Guedes Filho (BRA)	25.05.1987	33		
Ferland Mendy	08.06.1995	27	(3)	2
Jérémy Morel (MAD)	02.04.1984	12		
Rafael Pereira da Silva (BRA)	09.07.1990	11	(7)	
Oumar Solet	07.02.2000	1		
Kenny Joelle Tete (NED)	09.10.1995	12	(1)	
Midfielders:	**DOB**	**M**	**(s)**	**G**
Houssem Aouar	30.06.1998	35	(2)	7
Pape Cheik Diop Gueye (ESP)	08.08.1997	5	(7)	
Nabil Fekir	18.07.1993	24	(5)	9
Yassin Fékir	05.05.1997		(1)	
Jordan Ferri	12.03.1992	1	(3)	
Tanguy NDombèlé	28.12.1996	31	(3)	1
Lucas Tousart	29.04.1997	20	(10)	
Forwards:	**DOB**	**M**	**(s)**	**G**
Maxwel Cornet (CIV)	27.09.1996	12	(15)	7
Moussa Dembélé	12.07.1996	21	(12)	15
Memphis Depay (NED)	13.02.1994	29	(7)	10
Mariano Díaz Mejía (DOM)	01.08.1993	2	(1)	
Lenny Pintor	05.08.2000		(1)	
Martin Terrier	04.03.1997	16	(16)	9
Bertrand Traoré (BFA)	06.09.1995	24	(10)	7
Trainer:	**DOB**	**M**		
Bruno Génésio	01.09.1966	38		

Olympique de Marseille

Founded: 31.08.1899
Stadium: Stade Orange Vélodrome, Marseille (67,394)

Goalkeepers:	**DOB**	**M**	**(s)**	**G**
Steve Mandanda	28.03.1985	31		
Yohann Pelé	04.11.1982	7	(2)	
Defenders:	**DOB**	**M**	**(s)**	**G**
Jordan Amavi	09.03.1994	24	(4)	
Duje Ćaleta-Car (CRO)	17.09.1996	17	(3)	
Tomáš Hubočan (SVK)	17.09.1985		(2)	
Boubacar Kamara	23.11.1999	27	(4)	1
Adil Rami	27.12.1985	16		1
Christopher Rocchia	01.02.1998		(1)	
Rolando Jorge Pires da Fonseca (POR)	31.08.1985	9	(1)	
Hiroki Sakai (JPN)	12.04.1990	26	(1)	1
Bouna Sarr (GUI)	31.01.1992	25	(4)	1
Grégory Sertić	05.08.1989	1	(3)	
Midfielders:	**DOB**	**M**	**(s)**	**G**
Maxime Lopez	04.12.1997	25	(7)	1
Luiz Gustavo Dias (BRA)	23.07.1987	26	(4)	2
Lucas Ariel Ocampos (ARG)	11.07.1994	31	(3)	4
Florent Dimitri Payet	29.03.1987	23	(8)	4
Morgan Sanson	18.08.1994	27	(6)	5
Kevin Strootman (NED)	13.02.1990	21	(7)	1
Forwards:	**DOB**	**M**	**(s)**	**G**
Mario Balotelli (ITA)	12.08.1990	12	(3)	8
Valère Germain	17.04.1990	23	(13)	8
Kostas Mitroglou (GRE)	12.03.1988	7	(7)	3
Clinton Mua N'Jie (CMR)	15.08.1993	3	(14)	3
Nemanja Radonjić (SRB)	15.02.1996	7	(10)	
Florian Tristan Mariano Thauvin	26.01.1993	30	(3)	16
Trainer:	**DOB**	**M**		
Rudi García	20.02.1964	38		

Association Sportive de Monaco Football Club

Founded: 23.08.1924
Stadium: Stade „Louis II“, Monaco (18,523)

Goalkeepers:	DOB	M	(s)	G
Diego Benaglio (SUI)	08.09.1983	22	(1)	
Danijel Subašić (CRO)	27.10.1984	14		
Seydou Sy (SEN)	12.12.1995	2	(1)	
Defenders:	**DOB**	**M**	**(s)**	**G**
Benoît Badiashile	26.03.2001	20		1
Fodé Ballo-Touré	03.01.1997	18		
Antonio Barreca (ITA)	18.03.1995	7		
Giulian Biancone	31.03.2000	1		
Kamil Glik (POL)	03.02.1988	33		1
Benjamin Henrichs (GER)	23.02.1997	21	(1)	1
Jemerson de Jesus Nascimento (BRA)	24.08.1992	25		
Ronaldo Aparecido Rodrigues „Naldo“ (BRA)	10.09.1982	5	(2)	
Ronaël Pierre-Gabriel	13.06.1998	4		
Andrea Raggi (ITA)	24.06.1984	6		
Julien Serrano	13.02.1998	1	(2)	
Djibril Sidibé	29.07.1992	22	(4)	
Almamy Touré (MLI)	28.04.1996	4		
Midfielders:	**DOB**	**M**	**(s)**	**G**
Adrien Sebastian Perruchet Silva (POR)	15.03.1989	13	(2)	
Jean-Eudes Aholou (CIV)	20.03.1994	12	(5)	
Youssef Aït Bennasser (MAR)	07.07.1997	12	(1)	
Francesc „Cesc“ Fàbregas Soler (ESP)	04.05.1987	12	(1)	1
Sofiane Diop	09.06.2000	9	(4)	
Romain Faivre	14.07.1998	1		
Aleksandr Golovin (RUS)	30.05.1996	27	(3)	3
Han-Noah Massengo	07.07.2001		(3)	
Kévin N'Doram	22.01.1996	2	(2)	
Judilson Mamadú Tuncará Gomes „Pelé" (POR)	29.09.1991	4	(4)	
Marcos Paulo Mesquita Lopes „Rony Lopes“ (POR)	28.12.1995	22	(2)	2
Youri Tielemans (BEL)	07.05.1997	20		5
Adama Traoré (MLI)	28.06.1995	3	(3)	
William Vainqueur	19.11.1988	1	(2)	
Forwards:	**DOB**	**M**	**(s)**	**G**
Carlos Vinícius Alves Morais (BRA)	22.03.1995	3	(13)	2
Nacer Chadli (BEL)	02.09.1989	9	(7)	
Radamel Falcao García Zárate (COL)	10.02.1986	29	(4)	15
Gelson Dany Batalha Martins (POR)	11.05.1995	16		4
Willem Geubbels	16.08.2001		(1)	
Samuel Grandsir	14.08.1996	4	(8)	
Wilson Isidor	27.08.2000		(1)	
Jordi Mboula Queralt (ESP)	16.03.1999	3	(4)	
Stevan Jovetić (MNE)	02.11.1989	4	(4)	2
Georges-Kévin N'Koudou	13.02.1995		(3)	
Pietro Pellegri (ITA)	17.03.2001		(3)	1
Moussa Sylla	25.11.1999	7	(11)	
Trainer:	**DOB**	**M**		
José Leonardo Nunes Alves Sousa Jardim (POR)	01.08.1974	9		
Thierry Daniel Henry [13.10.2018]	17.08.1977	12		
José Leonardo Nunes Alves Sousa Jardim (POR) [25.01.2019]	01.08.1974	17		

Montpellier Hérault Sport Club

Founded: 1919
Stadium: Stade de la Mosson, Montpellier (32,939)

Goalkeepers:	DOB	M	(s)	G
Dimitry Bertaud	06.06.1998	1		
Benjamin Lecomte	26.04.1991	37		
Defenders:	**DOB**	**M**	**(s)**	**G**
Ruben Aguilar	26.04.1993	29		1
Daniel Congré	05.04.1985	37		2
Nicolas Cozza	08.01.1999	11	(1)	
Vitorino Hilton de Silva (BRA)	13.09.1977	36		
Damien Le Tallec	19.04.1990	31	(5)	3
Ambroise Oyongo Bitolo (CMR)	22.06.1991	25	(1)	2
Pedro Filipe Teodosio Mendes (POR)	01.10.1990	31		1
Morgan Poaty	15.07.1997	1		
Mihailo Ristić (SRB)	31.10.1995	3	(7)	1
Mathías Sebastián Suárez Suárez (URU)	24.06.1996	7	(3)	
Midfielders:	**DOB**	**M**	**(s)**	**G**
Bilal Boutobba	29.08.1998		(2)	
Keagan Larenzo Dolly (RSA)	22.01.1993	2	(1)	
Paul Lasne	16.01.1989	18	(17)	2
Florent Mollet	19.11.1991	31	(1)	6
Facundo Julián Píriz González (URU)	27.03.1990		(6)	
Junior Sambia	07.09.1996	7	(23)	
Ellyes Skhiri (TUN)	10.05.1995	35	(2)	3
Forwards:	**DOB**	**M**	**(s)**	**G**
Yannis Ammour	21.05.1999		(1)	
Souleymane Camara (SEN)	22.12.1982		(12)	3
Andy Delort (ALG)	09.10.1991	36		14
Gaëtan Laborde	03.05.1994	35	(1)	11
Giovanni-Guy Yann Sio (CIV)	31.03.1989	1		
Petar Škuletić (SRB)	29.06.1990	4	(24)	1
Trainer:	**DOB**	**M**		
Michel Der Zakarian	18.02.1963	38		

Football Club de Nantes

Founded: 1943
Stadium: Stade de la Beaujoire, Nantes (37,473)

Goalkeepers:	DOB	M	(s)	G
Maxime Dupé	04.03.1993	10	(1)	
Alexandre Olliero	15.02.1996	1		
Ciprian Anton Tătăruşanu (ROU)	09.02.1986	27		
Defenders:	**DOB**	**M**	**(s)**	**G**
Thomas Basila	30.04.1999	1	(1)	
Diego Carlos Santos Silva (BRA)	15.03.1993	35		1
Edgar Miguel Ié (POR)	01.05.1994	9		
Fábio Pereira da Silva (BRA)	09.07.1990	15	(5)	
Lévy Koffi Djidji (CIV)	30.11.1992	1		
Enock Kwateng	09.04.1997	22	(8)	
Lucas Pedro Alves de Lima (BRA)	10.10.1991	28	(3)	
Matthew Miazga (USA)	19.07.1995	8		
Serigne Modou Kara Mbodji (SEN)	11.11.1989	6		
Nicolas Pallois	19.09.1987	24		2
Charles Traoré (MLI)	01.01.1992	13		
Anthony Walongwa (COD)	15.10.1993	1		
Midfielders:	**DOB**	**M**	**(s)**	**G**
Alexis Alégué Elandi (CMR)	23.12.1996		(1)	
Andrei Girotto (BRA)	17.02.1992	18	(2)	2
Gabriel Boschilia (BRA)	05.03.1996	14	(15)	4
Abdoulaye Dabo	04.03.2001	2		
Valentin Eysseric	25.03.1992	3	(2)	1
Rene Krhin (SVN)	21.05.1990	12	(4)	
Imran Louza	01.05.1999	1		
Lucas Evangelista Santana de Oliveira (BRA)	06.05.1995	9	(5)	1
Samuel Moutoussamy	12.08.1996	19	(9)	2
Valentin Rongier	07.12.1994	36		4
Abdoulaye Touré	03.03.1994	30	(4)	3
Forwards:	**DOB**	**M**	**(s)**	**G**
Kalifa Coulibaly (MLI)	21.08.1991	19	(13)	8
Randal Kolo Muani (COD)	05.12.1998	1	(5)	
Anthony Limbombe (BEL)	15.07.1994	12	(17)	1
Antonio Mance (CRO)	07.08.1995		(5)	
Emiliano Sala (ARG)	31.10.1990	16	(3)	12
Majeed Waris (GHA)	19.09.1991	25	(8)	5
Thody Élie Youan	07.04.1999		(1)	
Trainer:	**DOB**	**M**		
José Miguel Azevedo Cardoso (POR)	28.05.1972	8		
Vahid Halilhodžić (BIH) [02.10.2018]	15.05.1952	30		

Olympique Gymnaste Club Nice Côte d'Azur

Founded: 09.07.1904 (*as Le Gymnaste Club de Nice*)
Stadium: Allianz Riviera, Nice (35,624)

Goalkeepers:	DOB	M	(s)	G
Walter Daniel Benítez (ARG)	19.01.1993	35		
Yoan Cardinale	27.03.1994	3		
Defenders:	**DOB**	**M**	**(s)**	**G**
Youcef Atal (ALG)	17.05.1996	25	(4)	6
Olivier Boscagli	18.11.1997	10	(4)	
Patrick Burner	11.04.1996	15	(2)	
Racine Coly (SEN)	08.12.1995	6	(3)	
Bonfim Costa Santos Dante (BRA)	18.10.1983	36		1
Christophe Hérelle	22.08.1992	33		
Christophe Jallet	31.10.1983	11	(3)	1
Andy Pelmard	12.03.2000	4		
Malang Sarr	23.01.1999	34	(1)	1
Paul Wade	17.04.2000		(1)	
Midfielders:	**DOB**	**M**	**(s)**	**G**
Wylan Cyprien	28.01.1995	27	(2)	4
Danilo Barbosa da Silva (BRA)	28.02.1996	18	(4)	
Assil Jaziri (TUN)	03.08.1999		(3)	
Pierre Lees-Melou	25.05.1993	26	(4)	2
Jean-Victor Makengo	12.06.1998	11	(14)	1
Pedro David Brazão Teixeira (POR)	30.12.2002		(1)	
Bassem Srarfi (TUN)	25.06.1997	8	(14)	1
Eddy Sylvestre	29.08.1999	3	(2)	
Adrien Tameze	04.02.1994	34	(3)	
Rémi Walter	26.04.1995	8	(11)	2
Forwards:	**DOB**	**M**	**(s)**	**G**
Mario Balotelli (ITA)	12.08.1990	9	(1)	
Mohamed Diaby	19.01.2001	2	(4)	
Ignatius Kpene Ganago (CMR)	16.02.1999	9	(11)	2
Mickaël Le Bihan	16.05.1990	2	(3)	1
Myziane Maolida	14.02.1999	10	(4)	
Maxime Pelican	12.05.1998	1	(1)	
Ihsan Sacko	19.07.1997	4	(9)	
Allan Saint-Maximin	12.03.1997	34		6
Trainer:	**DOB**	**M**		
Patrick Vieira	23.06.1976	38		

Nîmes Olympique

Founded: 10.04.1937 (*as Le Gymnaste Club de Nice*)
Stadium: Stade des Costières, Nîmes (18,482)

Goalkeepers:	DOB	M	(s)	G
Paul Bernardoni	18.04.1997	38		
Defenders:	**DOB**	**M**	**(s)**	**G**
Sofiane Alakouch	29.07.1998	23	(2)	1
Anthony Briançon	28.11.1994	33		2
Féthi Harek (ALG)	21.10.1982	2	(1)	
Loïck Landré	05.05.1992	19	(3)	3
Hervé Libohy	23.07.1983	15	(2)	2
Florian Miguel	01.09.1996	12	(1)	
Gaëtan Paquiez	15.02.1994	14	(6)	
Midfielders:	**DOB**	**M**	**(s)**	**G**
Antonin Bobichon	14.09.1995	24	(6)	7
Denis Bouanga (GAB)	11.11.1994	29	(6)	8
Moustapha Diallo (SEN)	14.05.1986	6	(1)	
Jordan Ferri	12.03.1992	21	(3)	2
Renaud Ripart	14.03.1993	34	(4)	8
Theo Sainte-Luce	20.10.1998		(1)	
Téji Savanier	22.12.1991	32		6
Pierrick Valdivia	18.04.1988		(2)	
Theo Valls	18.12.1995	20	(11)	
Forwards:	**DOB**	**M**	**(s)**	**G**
Rachid Alioui (MAR)	18.06.1992	11	(16)	5
Umut Bozok (TUR)	19.09.1996	14	(11)	2
Clement Depres	25.11.1994	4	(13)	4
Baptiste Guillaume (BEL)	16.06.1995	15	(9)	2
Faitout Maouassa	06.07.1998	25	(2)	
Sada Thioub	01.06.1995	27	(11)	3
Trainer:	**DOB**	**M**		
Bernard Blaquart	16.08.1957	38		

Paris Saint-Germain Football Club

Founded: 12.08.1970
Stadium: Stade Parc des Princes, Paris (48,583)

Goalkeepers:	DOB	M	(s)	G
Alphonse Aréola	27.02.1993	21		
Gianluigi Buffon (ITA)	28.01.1978	17		
Defenders:	**DOB**	**M**	**(s)**	**G**
Colin Dagba	09.09.1998	9	(8)	
Daniel Alves da Silva (BRA)	06.05.1983	19	(4)	1
Juan Bernat Velasco (ESP)	01.03.1993	21	(4)	1
Thilo Kehrer (GER)	21.09.1996	19	(8)	1
Presnel Kimpembe	13.08.1995	23	(1)	
Layvin Kurzawa	04.09.1992	11	(8)	1
Marcos Aoás Corrêa „Marquinhos" (BRA)	14.05.1994	30		3
Loïc Mbe Soh	13.06.2001	2		
Thomas Meunier (BEL)	12.09.1991	19	(3)	3
Kévin Rimane (GYF)	23.02.1991		(1)	
Thiago Emiliano Silva (BRA)	22.09.1984	24	(1)	
Midfielders:	**DOB**	**M**	**(s)**	**G**
Antoine Bernède	26.05.1999	2		
Lassana Diarra	10.03.1985	2	(1)	
Giovani Lo Celso (ARG)	09.04.1996		(1)	
Stanley N'Soki	09.04.1999	8	(4)	
Christopher Nkunku	14.11.1997	13	(9)	2
Leandro Daniel Paredes (ARG)	29.06.1994	14	(2)	
Adrien Rabiot-Provost	03.04.1995	12	(2)	2
Marco Verratti (ITA)	05.11.1992	23	(3)	
Forwards:	**DOB**	**M**	**(s)**	**G**
Edinson Roberto Cavani Gómez (URU)	14.02.1987	20	(1)	18
Eric Maxim Choupo-Moting (CMR)	23.03.1989	8	(14)	3
Ángel Fabián Di María Hernández (ARG)	14.02.1988	28	(2)	12
Moussa Diaby	07.07.1999	10	(15)	2
Julian Draxler (GER)	20.09.1993	22	(9)	3
Metehan Güçlü	02.04.1999		(1)	1
Kylian Sanmi Mbappé Lottin	20.12.1998	24	(5)	33
Neymar da Silva Santos Júnior (BRA)	05.02.1992	16	(1)	15
Timothy Tarpeh Weah (USA)	22.02.2000	1	(1)	1
Trainer:	**DOB**	**M**		
Thomas Tuchel (GER)	29.08.1973	38		

Stade de Reims

Founded: 1931 (*as Société Sportive du Parc Pommery*)
Stadium: Stade „Auguste Delaune“, Reims (21,684)

Goalkeepers:	**DOB**	**M**	**(s)**	**G**
Edouard Mendy	01.03.1992	38		
Defenders:	**DOB**	**M**	**(s)**	**G**
Yunis Abdelhamid	28.09.1987	38		
Abdul Rahman Baba (GHA)	02.07.1994	11		1
Axel Disasi	11.03.1998	1	(3)	
Björn Engels (BEL)	15.09.1994	33		1
Thomas Foket (BEL)	25.09.1994	32		
Thomas Fontaine (MAD)	08.05.1991	4	(3)	
Ghislain N'Clomandès Konan (CIV)	27.12.1995	20		
Romain Métanire	28.03.1990	4	(1)	
Midfielders:	**DOB**	**M**	**(s)**	**G**
Mathieu Cafaro	25.03.1997	24	(10)	7
Xavier Chavalerin	07.03.1991	36		2
Tristan Dingomé	17.02.1991	17	(3)	1
Moussa Doumbia (MLI)	15.08.1994	18	(10)	3
Hassane Kamara (GAM)	05.03.1994	9	(7)	
Marvin Martin	10.01.1988	8	(5)	
Nolan Mbemba	19.02.1995	4	(4)	
Moreto Moro Cassamá (POR)	16.02.1998	1		
Aly Ndom	30.05.1996	3	(8)	
Jacques Alaixys Romao (TOG)	18.01.1984	36		
Forwards:	**DOB**	**M**	**(s)**	**G**
Pablo Chavarría (ARG)	02.01.1988	23	(7)	5
Boulaye Dia	16.11.1996	8	(10)	3
Grejohn Kyei	12.08.1995		(1)	
Oluwaseyi Babajide Ojo (ENG)	19.06.1997	3	(12)	
Rémi Oudin	18.11.1996	32	(5)	10
Virgile Pinson	22.02.1996		(1)	
Suk Hyun-Jun (KOR)	29.06.1991	7	(15)	3
Arber Zeneli (KVX)	25.02.1995	8	(7)	3
Trainer:	**DOB**	**M**		
David Guion	30.09.1967	38		

Stade Rennais Football Club

Founded: 10.03.1901
Stadium: Roazhon Park, Rennes (29,778)

Goalkeepers:	**DOB**	**M**	**(s)**	**G**
Abdoulaye Diallo (SEN)	30.03.1992	6		
Tomáš Koubek (CZE)	26.08.1992	32	(1)	
Defenders:	**DOB**	**M**	**(s)**	**G**
Ludovic Baal (GYF)	24.05.1986	1	(1)	
Ramy Bensebaini (ALG)	16.04.1995	24	(1)	1
Sacha Boey	13.09.2000		(1)	
Damien Da Silva	17.05.1988	32	(1)	2
Souleyman Doumbia (CIV)	24.09.1996	7		
Jérémy Gelin	24.04.1997	12	(10)	
Edson André Sitoe „Mexer“ (MOZ)	08.09.1988	29		
Gerzino Nyamsi	22.01.1997	6	(2)	
Hamari Traoré (MLI)	27.01.1992	33	(1)	
Medhi Zeffane	19.05.1992	14	(6)	1
Midfielders:	**DOB**	**M**	**(s)**	**G**
Benjamin André	03.08.1990	28	(2)	3
Hatem Ben Arfa	07.03.1987	23	(3)	7
Benjamin Bourigeaud	14.01.1994	28	(6)	6
Eduardo Camavinga (ANG)	10.11.2002	4	(3)	
Romain Del Castillo	29.03.1996	15	(14)	
Clément Grenier	07.01.1991	29	(4)	2
Adrien Hunou	19.01.1994	14	(5)	7
Nicolas Janvier	11.08.1998		(1)	
Jakob Johansson (SWE)	21.06.1990	7	(9)	1
Denis Will Poha	28.05.1997		(2)	
James Lea Siliki	12.06.1996	14	(10)	
Forwards:	**DOB**	**M**	**(s)**	**G**
Armand Laurienté	04.12.1998		(1)	
M'Baye Niang (SEN)	19.12.1994	19	(10)	11
Diafra Sakho (SEN)	24.12.1989	32	(3)	8
Theoson Siebatcheu	26.04.1996	7	(8)	3
Trainer:	**DOB**	**M**		
Sabri Lamouchi	09.11.1971	15		
Julien Stéphane [03.12.2018]	18.09.1980	23		

Association Sportive de Saint-Étienne Loire

Founded: 1919
Stadium: Stade „Geoffroy Guichard“, Saint-Étienne (41,965)

Goalkeepers:	**DOB**	**M**	**(s)**	**G**
Jessy Moulin	13.01.1986	1		
Stéphane Ruffier	27.09.1986	37		
Defenders:	**DOB**	**M**	**(s)**	**G**
Mathieu Debuchy	28.07.1985	23	(1)	4
Gabriel Moisés Antunes da Silva (BRA)	13.05.1991	16	(3)	
Timothée Kolodziejczak	01.10.1991	35	(1)	3
Mickaël Panos	10.02.1997		(1)	
Loïc Perrin	07.08.1985	31		1
Pierre-Yves Polomat (MTQ)	27.12.1993	11	(7)	
William Saliba	24.03.2001	13	(3)	
Neven Subotić (SRB)	10.12.1988	26		1
Midfielders:	**DOB**	**M**	**(s)**	**G**
Youssef Aït Bennasser (MAR)	07.07.1996	11	(2)	
Rémy Cabella	08.03.1990	34		8
Mahdi Camara	30.06.1998		(1)	
Assane Dioussé El Hadji (SEN)	20.09.1997	2	(5)	
Wesley Fofana	17.12.2000	1	(1)	
Wahbi Khazri (TUN)	08.02.1991	32		13
Yann Gérard M'Vila	29.06.1990	37		
Kenny Rocha Santos (CPV)	03.01.2000		(1)	
Ole Kristian Selnæs (NOR)	07.07.1994	19	(1)	
Valentín Vada (ARG)	06.03.1996	3	(9)	1
Forwards:	**DOB**	**M**	**(s)**	**G**
Charles Abi	12.04.2000		(3)	
Robert Berić (SVN)	17.06.1991	12	(11)	9
Loïs Diony	20.12.1992	19	(11)	5
Lamine Ghezali	06.07.1999		(6)	1
Makhtar Gueye (SEN)	04.12.1997		(5)	1
Romain Hamouma	29.03.1987	19	(8)	4
Kévin Monnet-Paquet	19.08.1988	16	(7)	1
Arnaud Nordin	17.06.1998	11	(14)	3
Yannis Salibur	24.01.1991	9	(12)	1
Trainer:	**DOB**	**M**		
Jean-Louis Gasset	09.12.1953	38		

Racing Club de Strasbourg Alsace

Founded: 1906
Stadium: Stade de la Meinau, Strasbourg (29,230)

Goalkeepers:	DOB	M	(s)	G
Eiji Kawashima (JPN)	20.03.1983	1		
Matz Willy Sels (BEL)	26.02.1992	37		
Defenders:	**DOB**	**M**	**(s)**	**G**
Ismaël Aaneba	29.05.1999	3		
Lionel Carole	12.04.1991	20	(3)	
Lamine Koné (CIV)	01.02.1989	23	(4)	1
Kenny Lala	03.10.1991	34		5
Pablo Martinez	21.02.1989	32		3
Stefan Mitrovič (SRB)	22.05.1990	34		
Abdallah N'Dour (SEN)	20.12.1993	4		
Moataz Zemzemi (TUN)	07.08.1999		(2)	
Midfielders:	**DOB**	**M**	**(s)**	**G**
Anthony Caci	01.07.1997	26	(3)	
Benjamin Corgnet	06.04.1987	6	(11)	1
Youssouf Fofana	10.01.1999	10	(7)	2
Anthony Gonçalves	06.03.1986	12	(6)	5
Jérémy Grimm	27.03.1987	2	(3)	
Dimitri Liénard	13.02.1988	15	(7)	
Jonas Martin	09.04.1990	23		3
Sanjin Prcić (BIH)	20.11.1993	12	(1)	2
Ibrahima Sissoko	27.10.1997	30	(2)	3
Adrien Thomasson	10.12.1993	28	(6)	5
Forwards:	**DOB**	**M**	**(s)**	**G**
Ludovic Ajorque	25.02.1994	18	(7)	9
Samuel Grandsir	14.08.1996	2	(6)	
Lebogang Mothiba (RSA)	28.01.1996	18	(14)	9
Nuno Miguel da Costa Jóia (CPV)	10.02.1991	22	(12)	8
Idriss Saâdi (ALG)	08.02.1992		(1)	
Kévin Lucien Zohi (CIV)	19.12.1996	6	(14)	1
Trainer:	**DOB**	**M**		
Thierry Laurey	14.02.1964	38		

Toulouse Football Club

Founded: 1970
Stadium: Stadium Municipal, Toulouse (33,150)

Goalkeepers:	DOB	M	(s)	G
Mauro Daniel Goicoechea Furia (URU)	27.03.1988	7	(1)	
Baptiste Reynet	28.10.1990	31		
Defenders:	**DOB**	**M**	**(s)**	**G**
Kelvin Amian Adou	08.02.1998	32		
Bafodé Diakité	06.01.2001	7	(2)	1
Steven Fortès (CPV)	17.04.1992	1	(2)	
Christopher Jullien	22.03.1993	34		1
Clément Michelin	11.05.1997	1		
Steven Moreira	13.08.1994	10		
François Moubandje (SUI)	21.06.1990	21	(1)	
Gen Shōji (JPN)	11.12.1992	18		
Issiaga Sylla (GUI)	01.01.1994	23	(1)	2
Jean-Clair Todibo	30.12.1999	10		1
Midfielders:	**DOB**	**M**	**(s)**	**G**
Yann Bodiger	09.02.1995		(1)	
John Joseph Bostock (ENG)	15.01.1992	10	(6)	
Yannick Cahuzac	18.01.1985	15	(8)	1
Mathieu Dossevi (TOG)	12.02.1988	30	(5)	4
Hakim El Mokeddem	15.02.1999		(2)	
Kouadio Koné	17.05.2001	1		
Manuel „Manu" García Alonso (ESP)	02.01.1998	21	(10)	
Stéphane M'bia Etoundi (CMR)	20.05.1986	5		
Nathan Ngoumou	14.03.2000	1		
Ibrahim Sangaré (CIV)	02.12.1997	27	(1)	1
Kalidou Sidibé	28.01.1999	18	(2)	1
Forwards:	**DOB**	**M**	**(s)**	**G**
Jimmy Touma Durmaz (SWE)	22.03.1989	21	(15)	4
Max-Alain Gradel (CIV)	30.11.1987	36		11
Corentin Jean	15.07.1995	6	(13)	
Aaron Leya Iseka (BEL)	15.11.1997	15	(13)	4
Firmin Ndombe Mubele (COD)	17.04.1994	4	(11)	1
Yaya Sanogo	27.01.1993	13	(8)	3
Trainer:	**DOB**	**M**		
Alain Casanova	18.09.1961	38		

SECOND LEVEL
Ligue 2 2018/2019

1.	FC Metz (*Promoted*)	38	24	9	5	60	-	23	81
2.	Stade Brestois 29 (*Promoted*)	38	21	11	6	64	-	35	74
3.	ES Troyes Aube Champagne (*Promotion Play-offs*)	38	21	8	9	51	-	28	71
4.	Paris FC (*Promotion Play-offs*)	38	17	14	7	36	-	22	65
5.	Racing Club de Lens (*Promotion Play-offs*)	38	18	9	11	49	-	28	63
6.	FC Lorient-Bretagne Sud	38	17	12	9	51	-	41	63
7.	Le Havre AC	38	13	15	10	45	-	40	54
8.	US Orléans Loiret Football	38	15	7	16	51	-	53	52
9.	Grenoble Foot 38	38	13	11	14	43	-	47	50
10.	Clermont Foot 63	38	11	15	12	44	-	37	48
11.	La Berrichonne de Châteauroux	38	11	15	12	37	-	42	48
12.	Chamois Niortais FC	38	11	14	13	34	-	41	47
13.	Valenciennes FC	38	11	10	17	52	-	61	43
14.	AS Nancy-Lorraine	38	12	6	20	36	-	50	42
15.	AJ Auxerre	38	10	11	17	34	-	36	41
16.	FC Sochaux-Montbéliard	38	11	8	19	27	-	43	41
17.	AC Ajaccio	38	9	13	16	29	-	45	40
18.	Gazélec FC Ajaccio (*Relegation Play-offs*)	38	9	12	17	30	-	54	39
19.	Avenir Sportif Béziers (*Relegated*)	38	9	11	18	33	-	50	38
20.	Red Star FC Paris (*Relegated*)	38	7	9	22	28	-	58	30

Promotion Play-offs [21.05.-02.06.2019]

First Round	Paris FC - Racing Club de Lens	1-1(0-1,1-1,1-1); 4-5 pen
Second Round	ES Troyes Aube Champagne - **Racing Club de Lens**	1-2(1-1,1-1)

Relegation Play-offs [28.05.-02.06.2019]

Le Mans FC - Gazélec FC Ajaccio	1-2(0-1)	2-0(0-0)

Le Mans FC promoted for the 2019/2020 Ligue 2.

NATIONAL TEAM

INTERNATIONAL MATCHES
(16.07.2018 – 15.07.2019)

06.09.2018	München	Germany - France	0-0	(UNL)
09.09.2018	Paris	France - Netherlands	2-1(1-0)	(UNL)
11.10.2018	Guingamp	France - Iceland	2-2(0-1)	(F)
16.10.2018	Paris	France - Germany	2-1(0-1)	(UNL)
16.11.2018	Rotterdam	Netherlands - France	2-0(1-0)	(UNL)
20.11.2018	Paris	France - Uruguay	1-0(0-0)	(F)
22.03.2019	Chişinău	Moldova - France	1-4(0-2)	(ECQ)
25.03.2019	Paris	France - Iceland	4-0(1-0)	(ECQ)
02.06.2019	Nantes	France - Bolivia	2-0(2-0)	(F)
08.06.2019	Konya	Turkey - France	2-0(2-0)	(ECQ)
11.06.2019	Andorra la Vella	Andorra - France	0-4(0-3)	(ECQ)

06.09.2018 GERMANY - FRANCE 0-0 UEFA Nations League A, Group 1
Allianz Arena, München; Referee: Daniele Orsato (Italy); Attendance: 67,485
FRA: Alphonse Francis Areola, Benjamin Jacques Marcel Pavard, Raphaël Xavier Varane (Cap), Samuel Yves Umtiti, Lucas François Bernard Hernández, Blaise Matuidi (86.Corentin Tolisso), Paul Pogba, N'Golo Kanté, Kylian Sanmi Mbappé Lottin, Olivier Giroud (66.Ousmane Dembélé), Antoine Griezmann (80.Nabil Fekir). Trainer: Didier Claude Deschamps.

09.09.2018 FRANCE - NETHERLANDS 2-1(1-0) UEFA Nations League A, Group 1
Stade de France, Saint-Denis, Paris; Referee: Alberto Undiano Mallenco (Spain); Attendance: 76,452
FRA: Alphonse Francis Areola, Benjamin Jacques Marcel Pavard, Raphaël Xavier Varane (Cap), Samuel Yves Umtiti, Lucas François Bernard Hernández (62.Benjamin Mendy), Blaise Matuidi, Paul Pogba, N'Golo Kanté, Kylian Sanmi Mbappé Lottin, Olivier Giroud (89.Ousmane Dembélé), Antoine Griezmann (81.Steven N'Kemboanza Mike Christopher Nzonzi). Trainer: Didier Claude Deschamps.
Goals: Kylian Sanmi Mbappé Lottin (14), Olivier Giroud (75).

11.10.2018 FRANCE - ICELAND 2-2(0-1) Friendly International
Stade de Roudourou, Guingamp; Referee: Tiago Bruno Lopes Martins (Portugal); Attendance: 17,000
FRA: Hugo Lloris (Cap), Benjamin Jacques Marcel Pavard, Lucas Digne, Raphaël Xavier Varane (46.Kurt Happy Zouma), Presnel Kimpembe, Steven N'Kemboanza Mike Christopher Nzonzi, Paul Pogba (67.Tanguy Ndombele Alvaro), Florian Tristan Mariano Thauvin (59.Thomas Lemar), Ousmane Dembélé (67.Dimitri Payet), Olivier Giroud, Antoine Griezmann (60.Kylian Sanmi Mbappé Lottin). Trainer: Didier Claude Deschamps.
Goals: Hólmar Örn Eyjólfsson (86 own goal), Kylian Sanmi Mbappé Lottin (90 penalty).

16.10.2018 FRANCE - GERMANY 2-1(0-1) UEFA Nations League A, Group 1
Stade de France, Saint-Denis, Paris; Referee: Milorad Mažić (Serbia); Attendance: 77,300
FRA: Hugo Lloris (Cap), Benjamin Jacques Marcel Pavard, Raphaël Xavier Varane, Presnel Kimpembe, Lucas François Bernard Hernández, Blaise Matuidi, Paul Pogba, N'Golo Kanté (90+4.Steven N'Kemboanza Mike Christopher Nzonzi), Kylian Sanmi Mbappé Lottin (86.Ousmane Dembélé), Olivier Giroud, Antoine Griezmann (90+1.Tanguy Ndombele Alvaro). Trainer: Didier Claude Deschamps.
Goals: Antoine Griezmann (62, 80 penalty).

16.11.2018 NETHERLANDS - FRANCE 2-0(1-0) UEFA Nations League A, Group 1
Stadion Feijenoord, Rotterdam; Referee: Anthony Taylor (England); Attendance: 44,366
FRA: Hugo Lloris (Cap), Benjamin Jacques Marcel Pavard, Lucas Digne, Raphaël Xavier Varane, Presnel Kimpembe, Steven N'Kemboanza Mike Christopher Nzonzi (81.Tanguy Ndombele Alvaro), Blaise Matuidi (65.Moussa Sissoko), N'Golo Kanté, Kylian Sanmi Mbappé Lottin, Olivier Giroud (65.Ousmane Dembélé), Antoine Griezmann. Trainer: Didier Claude Deschamps.

20.11.2018 FRANCE - URUGUAY 1-0(0-0) Friendly International
Stade de France, Saint-Denis, Paris; Referee: Damir Skomina (Slovenia); Attendance: 70,000
FRA: Hugo Lloris (Cap), Benjamin Jacques Marcel Pavard, Mamadou Sakho (46.Presnel Kimpembe), Adil Rami, Ferland Mendy, Blaise Matuidi (62.Steven N'Kemboanza Mike Christopher Nzonzi), N'Golo Kanté, Tanguy Ndombele Alvaro (70.Nabil Fekir), Kylian Sanmi Mbappé Lottin (36.Florian Tristan Mariano Thauvin), Olivier Giroud (80.Alassane Pléa), Antoine Griezmann (90+3.Moussa Sissoko). Trainer: Didier Claude Deschamps.
Goal: Olivier Giroud (52 penalty).

22.03.2019 MOLDOVA - FRANCE 1-4(0-2) 16th EC. Qualifiers
Stadionul Zimbru, Chişinău; Referee: Aleksandar Stavrev (Macedonia); Attendance: 10,042
FRA: Hugo Lloris (Cap), Benjamin Jacques Marcel Pavard, Raphaël Xavier Varane, Samuel Yves Umtiti, Layvin Kurzawa, Paul Pogba, N'Golo Kanté, Blaise Matuidi (73.Florian Tristan Mariano Thauvin), Kylian Sanmi Mbappé Lottin, Olivier Giroud (81.Nabil Fekir), Antoine Griezmann (73.Thomas Lemar). Trainer: Didier Claude Deschamps.
Goals: Antoine Griezmann (24), Raphaël Xavier Varane (27), Olivier Giroud (36), Kylian Sanmi Mbappé Lottin (87).

25.03.2019 FRANCE - ICELAND 4-0(1-0) 16th EC. Qualifiers
Stade de France, Saint-Denis, Paris; Referee: István Kovács (Romania); Attendance: 64,538
FRA: Hugo Lloris (Cap), Benjamin Jacques Marcel Pavard, Raphaël Xavier Varane, Samuel Yves Umtiti, Layvin Kurzawa (85.Presnel Kimpembe), Blaise Matuidi, Paul Pogba, N'Golo Kanté (80.Thomas Lemar), Kylian Sanmi Mbappé Lottin, Olivier Giroud (90.Moussa Sissoko), Antoine Griezmann. Trainer: Didier Claude Deschamps.
Goals: Samuel Yves Umtiti (12), Olivier Giroud (68), Kylian Sanmi Mbappé Lottin (78), Antoine Griezmann (84).

02.06.2019 FRANCE - BOLIVIA 2-0(2-0) Friendly International
Stade de la Beaujoire, Nantes; Referee: Alberto Undiano Mallenco (Spain); Attendance: 35,228
FRA: Alphonse Francis Areola, Benjamin Jacques Marcel Pavard (46.Léo Dubois), Raphaël Xavier Varane (Cap), Samuel Yves Umtiti (89.Kurt Happy Zouma), Lucas Digne (79.Ferland Mendy), Paul Pogba, Thomas Lemar (66.Kingsley Coman), Tanguy Ndombele Alvaro (66.Blaise Matuidi), Florian Tristan Mariano Thauvin, Kylian Sanmi Mbappé Lottin (46.Wissam Ben Yedder), Antoine Griezmann. Trainer: Didier Claude Deschamps.
Goals: Thomas Lemar (5), Antoine Griezmann (43).

08.06.2019 **TURKEY - FRANCE** **2-0(2-0)** 16th EC. Qualifiers

Büyükşehir Stadium, Konya; Referee: Damir Skomina (Slovenia); Attendance: 36,783

FRA: Hugo Lloris (Cap), Benjamin Jacques Marcel Pavard, Raphaël Xavier Varane, Samuel Yves Umtiti, Lucas Digne (46.Ferland Mendy), Blaise Matuidi (46.Kingsley Coman), Moussa Sissoko, Paul Pogba, Kylian Sanmi Mbappé Lottin, Olivier Giroud (72.Wissam Ben Yedder), Antoine Griezmann. Trainer: Didier Claude Deschamps.

11.06.2019 **ANDORRA - FRANCE** **0-4(0-3)** 16th EC. Qualifiers

Estadi Nacional, Andorra la Vella; Referee: Fran Jović (Croatia); Attendance: 3,187

FRA: Hugo Lloris (Cap), Kurt Happy Zouma, Clément Nicolas Laurent Lenglet, Léo Dubois, Ferland Mendy, Paul Pogba, Tanguy Ndombele Alvaro (64.Moussa Sissoko), Wissam Ben Yedder (73.Olivier Giroud), Florian Tristan Mariano Thauvin (81.Thomas Lemar), Kylian Sanmi Mbappé Lottin, Antoine Griezmann. Trainer: Didier Claude Deschamps.

Goals: Kylian Sanmi Mbappé Lottin (11), Wissam Ben Yedder (30), Florian Tristan Mariano Thauvin (45+1), Kurt Happy Zouma (60).

NATIONAL TEAM PLAYERS
(16.07.2018 – 15.07.2019)

Name	DOB	Caps	Goals	2018/2019:	*Club*
Goalkeepers					
Alphonse Francis AREOLA	27.02.1993	**3**	**0**	2018/2019:	*Paris Saint-Germain FC*
Hugo LLORIS	26.12.1986	**112**	**0**	2018/2019:	*Tottenham Hotspur FC London (ENG)*
Defenders					
Lucas DIGNE	20.07.1993	**25**	**0**	2018/2019:	*Everton FC Liverpool (ENG)*
Léo DUBOIS	14.09.1994	**2**	**0**	2019:	*Olympique Lyonnais*
Lucas François Bernard HERNÁNDEZ	14.02.1996	**15**	**0**	2018:	*Club Atlético de Madrid (ESP)*
Presnel KIMPEMBE	13.08.1995	**8**	**0**	2018/2019:	*Paris Saint-Germain FC*
Layvin KURZAWA	04.09.1992	**13**	**1**	2019:	*Paris Saint-Germain FC*
Clément Nicolas Laurent LENGLET	17.06.1995	**1**	**0**	2019:	*FC Barcelona (ESP)*
Benjamin MENDY	17.07.1994	**9**	**0**	2018:	*Manchester City FC (ENG)*
Ferland Sinna MENDY	08.06.1995	**4**	**0**	2018/2019:	*Olympique Lyonnais*
Benjamin Jacques Marcel PAVARD	28.03.1996	**22**	**1**	2018/2019:	*VfB Stuttgart (GER)*
Adil RAMI	27.12.1985	**36**	**1**	2018:	*Olympique de Marseille*
Mamadou SAKHO	13.02.1990	**29**	**2**	2018:	*Crystal Palace FC London (ENG)*
Samuel Yves UMTITI	14.11.1993	**31**	**4**	2018/2019:	*FC Barcelona (ESP)*
Raphaël Xavier VARANE	25.04.1993	**58**	**4**	2018/2019:	*Real Madrid CF (ESP)*
Kurt Happy ZOUMA	27.10.1994	**5**	**1**	2018/2019:	*Everton FC Liverpool (ENG)*
Midfielders					
N'Golo KANTÉ	29.03.1991	**38**	**1**	2018/2019:	*Chelsea FC London (ENG)*
Blaise MATUIDI	09.04.1987	**81**	**9**	2018/2019:	*Juventus FC Torino (ITA)*
Steven N'Kemboanza Mike Christopher NZONZI	15.12.1988	**14**	**0**	2018:	*AS Roma (ITA)*
Tanguy NDOMBELE Alvaro	28.12.1996	**6**	**0**	2018/2019:	*Olympique Lyonnais*
Paul Labile POGBA	15.03.1993	**69**	**10**	2018/2019:	*Manchester United FC (ENG)*
Moussa SISSOKO	16.08.1989	**58**	**2**	2018/2019:	*Tottenham Hotspur FC London (ENG)*
Corentin TOLISSO	03.08.1994	**15**	**0**	2018:	*FC Bayern München (GER)*
Forwards					
Wissam BEN YEDDER	12.08.1990	**4**	**1**	2018/2019:	*Sevilla FC (ESP)*
Kingsley COMAN	13.06.1996	**18**	**1**	2019:	*FC Bayern München (GER)*
Ousmane DEMBÉLÉ	15.05.1997	**21**	**2**	2018:	*FC Barcelona (ESP)*
Nabil FEKIR	18.07.1993	**21**	**2**	2018/2019:	*Olympique Lyonnais*
Olivier GIROUD	30.09.1986	**91**	**35**	2018/2019:	*Chelsea FC London (ENG)*
Antoine GRIEZMANN	21.03.1991	**72**	**29**	2018/2019:	*Club Atlético de Madrid (ESP)*
Thomas LEMAR	12.11.1995	**18**	**4**	2018/2019:	*Club Atlético de Madrid (ESP)*
Kylian Sanmi MBAPPÉ Lottin	20.12.1998	**33**	**13**	2018/2019:	*Paris Saint-Germain FC*
Florent Dimitri PAYET	29.03.1987	**38**	**8**	2018:	*Olympique de Marseille*
Alassane PLÉA	10.03.1993	**1**	**0**	2018:	*Borussia VfL Mönchengladbach (GER)*
Florian Tristan Mariano THAUVIN	26.01.1993	**10**	**1**	2018/2019:	*Olympique de Marseille*

National team coach

Didier Claude DESCHAMPS [from 08.07.2012]	15.10.1968	94 M; 60 W; 17 D; 17 L; 183-80

GEORGIA

The Country:

Georgia (საქართველო)
Capital: Tbilisi
Surface: 69,700 km²
Inhabitants: 3,723,500 [2019]
Time: UTC+4

The FA:

Georgian Football Federation
76a Chavchavadze Avenue, 0162 Tbilisi
Tel: +995 32 912 680
Founded: 1936/re-founded 1990
Member of FIFA since: 1992
Member of UEFA since: 1992
Website: www.gff.ge

NATIONAL TEAM RECORDS

First international match:	27.05.1990, Tbilisi:	Georgia – Lithuania 2-2
Most international caps:	Levan Kobiashvili	- 100 caps (1996-2011)
Most international goals:	Shota Arveladze	- 26 goals / 61 caps (1992-2007)

UEFA EUROPEAN CHAMPIONSHIP	
1960	-
1964	-
1968	-
1972	-
1976	-
1980	-
1984	-
1988	-
1992	-
1996	Qualifiers
2000	Qualifiers
2004	Qualifiers
2008	Qualifiers
2012	Qualifiers
2016	Qualifiers

**was part of Soviet Union between 1930-1990*

FIFA WORLD CUP	
1930	-
1934	-
1938	-
1950	-
1954	-
1958	-
1962	-
1966	-
1970	-
1974	-
1978	-
1982	-
1986	-
1990	-
1994	Did not enter
1998	Qualifiers
2002	Qualifiers
2006	Qualifiers
2010	Qualifiers
2014	Qualifiers
2018	Qualifiers

UEFA NATIONS LEAGUE
2018/2019 – League D (promoted to League C)

OLYMPIC FOOTBALL TOURNAMENTS 1908-2016							
1908	-	**1948**	-	**1972**	-	**1996**	Qualifiers
1912	-	**1952**	-	**1976**	-	**2000**	Qualifiers
1920	-	**1956**	-	**1980**	-	**2004**	Qualifiers
1924	-	**1960**	-	**1984**	-	**2008**	Qualifiers
1928	-	**1964**	-	**1988**	-	**2012**	Qualifiers
1936	-	**1968**	-	**1992**	-	**2016**	Qualifiers

FIFA CONFEDERATIONS CUP 1992-2017
None

GEORGIAN CLUB HONOURS IN EUROPEAN CLUB COMPETITIONS:

European Champion Clubs.Cup (1956-1992) / UEFA Champions League (1993-2019)		
None		
Fairs Cup (1858-1971) / UEFA Cup (1972-2009) / UEFA Europa League (2010-2019)		
None		
UEFA Super Cup (1972-2019)		
None		
European Cup Winners.Cup 1961-1999*		
FC Dinamo Tbilisi*	**1**	1980/1981
**represented the Soviet Union*		

**defunct competition*

NATIONAL COMPETITIONS
TABLE OF HONOURS

GEORGIAN SSR (SOVIET ERA) CHAMPIONS

1927	Batumi XI
1928	Tbilisi XI
1929-1935	*No competition*
1936	ZII Tbilisi
1937	FC FC Lokomotivi Tbilisi
1938	FC FC Dinamo Batumi
1939	Nauka Tbilisi
1940	FC FC Dinamo Batumi
1941-1942	*No competition*
1943	ODKA Tbilisi
1944	*No competition*
1945	FC FC Lokomotivi Tbilisi
1946	Dinamo Kutaisi
1947	FC Dinamo Sokhumi
1948	FC Dinamo Sokhumi
1949	FC FC Torpedo Kutaisi
1950	TODO Tbilisi
1951	TODO Tbilisi
1952	TTU Tbilisi
1953	TTU Tbilisi
1954	TTU Tbilisi
1955	Dinamo Kutaisi
1956	FC FC Lokomotivi Tbilisi
1957	TTU Tbilisi
1958	TTU Tbilisi
1959	Metallurg Rustavi
1960	Imereti Kutaisi
1961	FC Guria Lanchkhuti
1962	Imereti Kutaisi
1963	Imereti Kutaisi
1964	IngurGES Zugdidi
1965	Tolia Tbilisi
1966	FC Guria Lanchkhuti
1967	Mertskhali Makharadze
1968	SKA Tbilisi
1969	Sulori Vani
1970	SKIF Tbilisi
1971	FC Guria Lanchkhuti
1972	Lokomotivi FC Samtredia
1973	Dinamo Zugdidi
1974	Metallurg Rustavi
1975	Magaroeli Chiatura
1976	SKIF Tbilisi
1977	Mziuri Gali
1978	Kolheti Poti
1979	Metallurg Rustavi
1980	Meshakhte Tkibuli
1981	Meshakhte Tkibuli
1982	Mertskhali Makharadze
1983	Samgulari Tskhaltubo
1984	Metallurg Rustavi
1985	Shadrevani-83 Tskhaltubo
1986	Shevardeni-1906 Tbilisi
1987	Mertskhali Makharadze
1988	Kolheti Poti
1989	Shadrevani-83 Tskhaltubo

	CHAMPIONS	CUP WINNERS	BEST GOALSCORERS	
1990	FC Iberia Tbilisi	FC Guria Lanchkhuti	Gia Guruli (FC Iberia Tbilisi) Mamuka Pantsulaia (FC Gorda Rustavi)	23
1991	FC Iberia Tbilisi	FC Dinamo Tbilisi	Otar Korgalidze (FC Guria Lanchkhuti)	14
1991/1992	FC Dinamo Tbilisi	FC Dinamo Tbilisi	Otar Korgalidze (FC Guria Lanchkhuti)	40
1992/1993	FC Dinamo Tbilisi	FC Dinamo Tbilisi	Merab Megreladze (Samgurali Tskhaltubo)	41
1993/1994	FC Dinamo Tbilisi	FC Dinamo Tbilisi	Merab Megreladze (FC Margveti Zestafoni)	31
1994/1995	FC Dinamo Tbilisi	FC Dinamo Tbilisi	Giorgi Daraselia (FC Kolkheti-1913 Poti)	26
1995/1996	FC Dinamo Tbilisi	FC Dinamo Tbilisi	Zviad Endeladze (FC Margveti Zestafoni)	40
1996/1997	FC Dinamo Tbilisi	FC Dinamo Batumi	Giorgi Demetradze (FC Dinamo Tbilisi) David Ujmajuridze (FC Dinamo Batumi)	26
1997/1998	FC Dinamo Tbilisi	FC Torpedo Kutaisi	Levan Khomeriki (FC Dinamo Tbilisi)	23
1998/1999	FC Dinamo Tbilisi	FC Lokomotivi Tbilisi	Mikheil Ashvetia (FC Dinamo Tbilisi)	26
1999/2000	FC Torpedo Kutaisi	FC Torpedo Kutaisi	Zurab Ionanidze (FC Torpedo Kutaisi)	24
2000/2001	FC Torpedo Kutaisi	FC Lokomotivi Tbilisi	Zaza Zirakishvili (FC Dinamo Tbilisi)	21
2001/2002	FC Torpedo Kutaisi	FC Dinamo Tbilisi	Suliko Davitashvili (FC Lokomotivi Tbilisi / FC Merani Tbilisi)	18
2002/2003	FC Dinamo Tbilisi	FC Dinamo Tbilisi	Zurab Ionanidze (FC Torpedo Kutaisi)	26
2003/2004	FC WIT Georgia Tbilisi	FC Lokomotivi Tbilisi	Suliko Davitashvili (FC Torpedo Kutaisi)	20
2004/2005	FC Dinamo Tbilisi	FC Ameri Tbilisi	Levani Melkadze (FC Dinamo Tbilisi)	27
2005/2006	FC Sioni Bolnisi	FC Ameri Tbilisi	Jaba Dvali (FC Dinamo Tbilisi)	21
2006/2007	FC Olimpi Rustavi	FC Zestafoni	Sandro Iashvili (FC Dinamo Tbilisi)	27
2007/2008	FC Dinamo Tbilisi	FC Dinamo Tbilisi	Mikheil Khutsishvili (FC Dinamo Tbilisi)	16
2008/2009	FC WIT Georgia Tbilisi	FC WIT Georgia Tbilisi	Nikoloz Gelashvili (FC Zestafoni)	20
2009/2010	FC Olimpi Rustavi	FC Gagra	Brazil Anderson Aquino (FC Metalurgi Rustavi)	26
2010/2011	FC Zestafoni	FC Dila Gori	Nikoloz Gelashvili (FC Zestafoni)	18
2011/2012	FC Zestafoni	FC Dinamo Tbilisi	Jaba Dvali (FC Zestafoni)	20
2012/2013	FC Dinamo Tbilisi	FC Dinamo Tbilisi	Spain Xisco (FC Dinamo Tbilisi)	24
2013/2014	FC Dinamo Tbilisi	FC Dinamo Tbilisi	Spain Xisco (FC Dinamo Tbilisi)	19
2014/2015	FC Dila Gori	FC Dinamo Tbilisi	Irakli Modebadze (FC Dila Gori)	16
2015/2016	FC Dinamo Tbilisi	FC Torpedo Kutaisi	Giorgi Kvilitaia (FC Dinamo Tbilisi)	24
2016	FC Samtredia	FC Chikhura Sachkhere	Budu Zivzivadze (FC Samtredia)	11
2017	FC Torpedo Kutaisi	FC Guria Lanchkhuti	Irakli Sikharulidze (FC Lokomotivi Tbilisi)	25
2018	FC Saburtalo Tbilisi	FC Torpedo Kutaisi	Giorgi Gabedava (FC Chikhura Sachkhere) Budu Zivzivadze (FC Dinamo Tbilisi)	22

Please note: FC Dinamo Tbilisi changed its name to FC Iberia Tbilisi between 1990-1992; FC Olimpi Rustavi became FC Metalurgi Rustavi (2011-2015) and later FC Rustavi (since 2011).

NATIONAL CHAMPIONSHIP
Erovnuli Liga 2018
(02.03.2018 – 08.12.2018)

Results

Round 1 [02-05.03.2018]
Torpedo Kutaisi - Dila Gori 2-3(1-1)
Chikhura Sachkhere - Kolkheti Poti 6-1(3-0)
Lokomotivi Tbilisi - FC Samtredia 1-2(0-1)
Dinamo Tbilisi - FC Rustavi 1-2(0-0)
FC Saburtalo - Sioni Bolnisi 3-1(0-1)

Round 2 [09-11.03.2018]
Dila Gori - Chikhura Sachkhere 1-1(0-0)
FC Rustavi - Torpedo Kutaisi 0-1(0-1)
Kolkheti Poti - FC Saburtalo 1-4(1-0)
Lokomotivi Tbilisi - Dinamo Tbilisi 1-4(1-2)
FC Samtredia - Sioni Bolnisi 0-1(0-0)

Round 3 [16-18.03.2018]
Dinamo Tbilisi - FC Samtredia 3-1(2-0)
Torpedo Kutaisi - Lokomotivi Tbilisi 4-0(2-0)
Chikhura Sachkhere - FC Rustavi 1-0(0-0)
Sioni Bolnisi - Kolkheti Poti 0-0
FC Saburtalo - Dila Gori 2-0(1-0)

Round 4 [31.03.-01.04.2018]
Lokomotivi Tbilisi - Chikhura Sach. 1-1(1-0)
FC Rustavi - FC Saburtalo 0-2(0-0)
Dila Gori - Sioni Bolnisi 3-2(3-0)
Dinamo Tbilisi - Torpedo Kutaisi 2-0(2-0)
FC Samtredia - Kolkheti Poti 0-2(0-0)

Round 5 [04-05.04.2018]
Sioni Bolnisi - FC Rustavi 0-2(0-1)
FC Saburtalo - Lokomotivi Tbilisi 1-2(0-0)
Chikhura Sachkhere - Dinamo Tbilisi 1-2(1-2)
Kolkheti Poti - Dila Gori 0-3(0-0)
Torpedo Kutaisi - FC Samtredia 1-0(0-0)

Round 6 [13-15.04.2018]
FC Rustavi - Kolkheti Poti 2-0(2-0)
Lokomotivi Tbilisi - Sioni Bolnisi 1-2(1-2)
Torpedo Kutaisi - Chikhura Sachk. 0-1(0-0)
FC Samtredia - Dila Gori 0-0
Dinamo Tbilisi - FC Saburtalo 0-1(0-0)

Round 7 [20-22.04.2018]
Kolkheti Poti - Lokomotivi Tbilisi 3-1(2-1)
Sioni Bolnisi - Dinamo Tbilisi 1-2(0-0)
Dila Gori - FC Rustavi 2-2(1-0)
Chikhura Sachkhere - FC Samtredia 0-0
FC Saburtalo - Torpedo Kutaisi 2-0(1-0)

Round 8 [26-27.04.2018]
Lokomotivi Tbilisi - Dila Gori 1-3(1-2)
FC Samtredia - FC Rustavi 0-0
Chikhura Sachkhere - FC Saburtalo 2-1(0-0)
Dinamo Tbilisi - Kolkheti Poti 4-1(2-0)
Torpedo Kutaisi - Sioni Bolnisi 3-0(1-0)

Round 9 [01-02.05.2018]
Sioni Bolnisi - Chikhura Sachkhere 0-2(0-2)
FC Saburtalo - FC Samtredia 1-0(0-0)
Kolkheti Poti - Torpedo Kutaisi 1-1(0-1)
FC Rustavi - Lokomotivi Tbilisi 1-0(1-0)
Dila Gori - Dinamo Tbilisi 1-1(1-1)

Round 10 [05-06.05.2018]
Sioni Bolnisi - FC Saburtalo 0-2(0-2)
Kolkheti Poti - Chikhura Sachkhere 2-2(1-0)
FC Samtredia - Lokomotivi Tbilisi 1-1(0-0)
FC Rustavi - Dinamo Tbilisi 0-2(0-0)
Dila Gori - Torpedo Kutaisi 1-1(0-1)

Round 11 [11-13.05.2018]
FC Saburtalo - Kolkheti Poti 5-0(2-0)
Sioni Bolnisi - FC Samtredia 1-1(1-1)
Chikhura Sachkhere - Dila Gori 0-3(0-1)
Torpedo Kutaisi - FC Rustavi 2-1(0-1)
Dinamo Tbilisi - Lokomotivi Tbilisi 0-1(0-1)

Round 12 [19-20.05.2018]
FC Samtredia - Dinamo Tbilisi 1-2(0-1)
Kolkheti Poti - Sioni Bolnisi 2-0(1-0)
Lokomotivi Tbilisi - Torpedo Kutaisi 1-0(0-0)
FC Rustavi - Chikhura Sachkhere 0-4(0-2)
Dila Gori - FC Saburtalo 4-1(1-0)

Round 13 [24-26.05.2018]
FC Saburtalo - FC Rustavi 2-1(1-1)
Sioni Bolnisi - Dila Gori 2-2(0-1)
Torpedo Kutaisi - Dinamo Tbilisi 1-1(1-1)
Chik. Sachkhere - Lokomotivi Tbilisi 1-3(1-1)
Kolkheti Poti - FC Samtredia 2-2(1-1)

Round 14 [09-10.06.2018]
FC Samtredia - Torpedo Kutaisi 1-4(1-2)
FC Rustavi - Sioni Bolnisi 2-2(1-1)
Dila Gori - Kolkheti Poti 2-0(0-0)
Lokomotivi Tbilisi - FC Saburtalo 1-1(0-0)
Dinamo Tbilisi - Chikhura Sachkhere 1-0(1-0)

Round 15 [16-18.06.2018]
Kolkheti Poti - FC Rustavi 0-0
Dila Gori - FC Samtredia 3-0(2-0)
Sioni Bolnisi - Lokomotivi Tbilisi 1-0(1-0)
FC Saburtalo - Dinamo Tbilisi 1-0(0-0)
Chikhura Sachk. - Torpedo Kutaisi 1-0(1-0)

Round 16 [22-23.06.2018]
Lokomotivi Tbilisi - Kolkheti Poti 2-1(2-1)
FC Rustavi - Dila Gori 2-2(1-1)
FC Samtredia - Chikhura Sachkhere 0-1(0-0)
Dinamo Tbilisi - Sioni Bolnisi 2-1(1-0)
Torpedo Kutaisi - FC Saburtalo 1-2(0-2)

Round 17 [27-29.06.2018]
Dila Gori - Lokomotivi Tbilisi 3-2(0-1)
FC Saburtalo - Chikhura Sachkhere 1-0(0-0)
Sioni Bolnisi - Torpedo Kutaisi 1-2(0-0)
Kolkheti Poti - Dinamo Tbilisi 3-6(1-1)
FC Rustavi - FC Samtredia 2-1(1-1)

Round 18 [04-05.07.2018]
FC Samtredia - FC Saburtalo 1-3(1-2)
Torpedo Kutaisi - Kolkheti Poti 3-0(1-0)
Chikhura Sachkhere - Sioni Bolnisi 4-0(2-0)
Lokomotivi Tbilisi - FC Rustavi 1-1(0-1)
Dinamo Tbilisi - Dila Gori 5-0(4-0)

Round 19 [03-06.08.2018]
Dinamo Tbilisi - FC Rustavi 2-1(2-0)
Lokomotivi Tbilisi - FC Samtredia 3-2(0-0)
FC Saburtalo - Sioni Bolnisi 3-0(1-0)
Chikhura Sachkhere - Kolkheti Poti 3-1(2-1)
Torpedo Kutaisi - Dila Gori 2-0(2-0) [03.10.]

Round 20 [10-12.08.2018]
FC Samtredia - Sioni Bolnisi 0-4(0-3)
Kolkheti Poti - FC Saburtalo 1-3(0-2)
Lokomotivi Tbilisi - Dinamo Tbilisi 2-4(0-3)
Dila Gori - Chikhura Sachkhere 1-3(0-2)
FC Rustavi - Torpedo Kutaisi 0-0 [12.09.]

Round 21 [17-19.08.2018]
Sioni Bolnisi - Kolkheti Poti 2-0(2-0)
Chikhura Sachkhere - FC Rustavi 0-0
Dinamo Tbilisi - FC Samtredia 0-0
FC Saburtalo - Dila Gori 0-0
Torpedo Kutaisi - Lok Tbilisi 3-1(3-0) [17.10.]

Round 22 [25-26.08.2018]
Lokomotivi Tbilisi - Chikhura Sachk. 3-2(1-1)
FC Rustavi - FC Saburtalo 0-2(0-1)
FC Samtredia - Kolkheti Poti 1-0(1-0)
Dila Gori - Sioni Bolnisi 0-0
Dinamo Tbilisi - Tor. Kutaisi 0-1(0-1) [31.10.]

Round 23 [31.08.-02.09.2018]
Chikhura Sachkhere - Dinamo Tbilisi 1-2(1-1)
FC Saburtalo - Lokomotivi Tbilisi 2-1(1-1)
Kolkheti Poti - Dila Gori 0-2(0-1)
Sioni Bolnisi - FC Rustavi 0-4(0-2)
Torpedo Kutaisi - FC Samtredia 5-2(1-2)

Round 24 [14-16.09.2018]
FC Samtredia - Dila Gori 3-5(0-1)
Lokomotivi Tbilisi - Sioni Bolnisi 1-0(0-0)
Dinamo Tbilisi - FC Saburtalo 2-1(0-1)
FC Rustavi - Kolkheti Poti 0-0
Torpedo Kutaisi - Chikhura Sachkh. 1-0(0-0)

Round 25 [21-24.09.2018]
Kolkheti Poti - Lokomotivi Tbilisi 1-0(0-0)
Sioni Bolnisi - Dinamo Tbilisi 0-0
FC Saburtalo - Torpedo Kutaisi 0-3(0-1)
Dila Gori - FC Rustavi 2-0(2-0)
Chikhura Sachkhere - FC Samtredia 2-0(0-0)

Round 26 [27-28.09.2018]
Lokomotivi Tbilisi - Dila Gori 2-1(0-0)
Dinamo Tbilisi - Kolkheti Poti 2-1(1-1)
Torpedo Kutaisi - Sioni Bolnisi 3-0(1-0)
Chikhura Sachkhere - FC Saburtalo 0-1(0-0)
FC Samtredia - FC Rustavi 1-1(1-1)

Round 27 [30.09.-02.10.2018]
Kolkheti Poti - Torpedo Kutaisi 0-0
Dila Gori - Dinamo Tbilisi 1-0(0-0)
Sioni Bolnisi - Chikhura Sachkhere 1-2(0-1)
FC Saburtalo - FC Samtredia 1-1(1-0)
FC Rustavi - Lokomotivi Tbilisi 1-1(0-1)

Round 28 [05-07.10.2018]
Kolkheti Poti - Chikhura Sachkhere 0-1(0-1)
Sioni Bolnisi - FC Saburtalo 2-3(2-2)
FC Samtredia - Lokomotivi Tbilisi 1-0(0-0)
FC Rustavi - Dinamo Tbilisi 0-3(0-2)
Dila Gori - Torpedo Kutaisi 0-0

Round 29 [19-21.10.2018]
Chikhura Sachkhere - Dila Gori 2-1(2-0)
Sioni Bolnisi - FC Samtredia 4-2(2-0)
Dinamo Tbilisi - Lokomotivi Tbilisi 0-0
Torpedo Kutaisi - FC Rustavi 2-2(0-0)
FC Saburtalo - Kolkheti Poti 4-1(2-0)

Round 30 [26-28.10.2018]
FC Rustavi - Chikhura Sachkhere 1-2(0-1)
Kolkheti Poti - Sioni Bolnisi 1-1(0-0)
FC Samtredia - Dinamo Tbilisi 1-8(1-3)
Dila Gori - FC Saburtalo 0-0
Lokomotivi Tbilisi - Torpedo Kutaisi 0-1(0-1)

Round 31 [02-04.11.2018]
Chikhura Sachkhere - Lokomotivi Tbilisi 0-0
Sioni Bolnisi - Dila Gori 3-1(2-0)
FC Saburtalo - FC Rustavi 2-1(2-1)
Kolkheti Poti - FC Samtredia 0-1(0-1)
Torpedo Kutaisi - Dinamo Tbilisi 2-2(0-0)

Round 32 [09-11.11.2018]
FC Rustavi - Sioni Bolnisi 0-3(0-1)
Lokomotivi Tbilisi - FC Saburtalo 1-1(0-1)
Dila Gori - Kolkheti Poti 1-0(0-0)
FC Samtredia - Torpedo Kutaisi 0-8(0-3)
Dinamo Tbilisi - Chikhura Sachkhere 1-4(0-1)

Round 33 [24-26.11.2018]
Chikhura S. - Torpedo Kut. 0-2(0-2) [21.11.]
Kolkheti Poti - FC Rustavi 0-1(0-1)
Dila Gori - FC Samtredia 3-0(0-0)
Sioni Bolnisi - Lokomotivi Tbilisi 1-2(0-0)
FC Saburtalo - Dinamo Tbilisi 2-1(2-1)

Round 34 [29-30.11.2018]
FC Samtredia - Chikhura Sachkhere 1-2(0-2)
FC Rustavi - Dila Gori 0-0
Lokomotivi Tbilisi - Kolkheti Poti 5-1(2-1)
Dinamo Tbilisi - Sioni Bolnisi 5-2(2-2)
Torpedo Kutaisi - FC Saburtalo 0-0

Round 35 [03-04.12.2018]
FC Rustavi - FC Samtredia 3-0(1-0)
Kolkheti Poti - Dinamo Tbilisi 0-2(0-1)
Sioni Bolnisi - Torpedo Kutaisi 0-3(0-1)
Dila Gori - Lokomotivi Tbilisi 4-0(1-0)
FC Saburtalo - Chikhura Sachkhere 0-0

Round 36 [08.12.2018]
Chikhura Sachkhere - Sioni Bolnisi 2-1(2-0)
FC Samtredia - FC Saburtalo 1-4(0-2)
Dinamo Tbilisi - Dila Gori 1-2(0-1)
Lokomotivi Tbilisi - FC Rustavi 1-0(1-0)
Torpedo Kutaisi - Kolkheti Poti 4-0(3-0)

Final Standings

1.	**FC Saburtalo Tbilisi**	36	24	7	5	64	-	29	79
2.	FC Dinamo Tbilisi	36	21	6	9	73	-	38	69
3.	FC Torpedo Kutaisi	36	20	9	7	66	-	25	69
4.	FC Chikhura Sachkhere	36	19	7	10	54	-	33	64
5.	FC Dila Gori	36	17	12	7	60	-	40	63
6.	FC Lokomotivi Tbilisi	36	12	8	16	43	-	55	44
7.	FC Rustavi	36	8	13	15	33	-	44	37
8.	FC Sioni Bolnisi (*Relegation Play-offs*)	36	8	7	21	39	-	65	31
9.	FC Samtredia (*Relegation Play-offs*)	36	4	9	23	28	-	81	21
10.	FC Kolkheti-1913 Poti (*Relegated*)	36	4	8	24	26	-	76	14

Top goalscorers:

22 Giorgi Gabedava
FC Chikhura Sachkhere

22 Budu Zivzivadze
FC Dinamo Tbilisi

21 Mykola Kovtalyuk (UKR)
FC Dila Gori

Relegation Play-offs [12-15.12.2018]

FC Gagra - **FC Sioni Bolnisi**	0-1(0-1)	0-3(0-1)
FC Samtredia - **FC WIT Georgia Tbilisi**	2-2(1-0)	0-4(0-2)

NATIONAL CUP
Georgian Cup - Sakartvelos tasi 2018

First Round [16-18.04.2018]

Dinamo Sokhumi - FC Meshakhte Tkibuli	2-6	Lazika Zugdidi - FC Kakheti Telavi	0-2
Sakartvelos Universiteti - Liakhvi Tskhinvali	3-5	Zana Abasha - Mark Stars Tbilisi	1-5
Tbilisi City - Racha Ambrolauri	7-0	FC Guria Lanchkhuti - FC Shevardeni-1906 Tbilisi	2-1
Kolkhi Gulripshi - FK Imereti Khoni II	4-0	Meta FC - Voyage Tbilisi	1-0
Chkherimela FC - Tbilisi 2016 FC	0-2	FC Rustavi II - Sulori Vani	1-3
FC Torpedo Kutaisi II - Iveria Khashuri	0-2	FC Meskheti Akhaltsikhe - Khikhani Khulo	0-1
Sairme Baghdati - Mertskhali Ozurgeti	3-2	Senakuri Senaki - Spaeri FC	3-0
Squri Tsalenjikha - FC Merani Martvili	4-5 aet	Lazika Zugdidi - FC Iberia Tbilisi	1-0
FC Zestafoni - FC Dinamo Batumi II	3-2	Betlemi Keda - Matchakhela Khelvachauri	3-1
FC Tbilisi - FC Samgurali Tskhaltubo II	4-5 pen	FK Borjomi - FC Khobi	1-2
Kojaeli Mtskheta - FC Tskhumi Sukhumi	2-0	Hereti Tchabukiani - FK Imereti Khoni	0-2
FC Gareji Sagarejo - FC Chiatura	1-0	FC Dusheti - FC Algeti Marneuli	3-4
FS 35 Sapekhburto Skola - Tori Borjomi	1-4	Bakhmaro Chokhatauri - FC Saburtalo II	0-1 aet
Sarti Sartitchala - FC Gardabani	0-1	FC Margveti - Spartaki Tskhinvali	1-0
Varketili FK - Gori FC	0-1 aet	Liakhvi Achabeti - Samegrelo Chkhorotsku	2-3 aet

Second Round [08-09.05.2018]

Tbilisi City - FC Samgurali Tskhaltubo II	5-3	Kojaeli Mtskheta - Sairme Baghdati	3-1
FC Merani Martvili - Liakhvi Tskhinvali	2-5	Tori Borjomi - Meta FC	2-4 pen
Iveria Khashuri - Gori FC	1-2	FC WIT Georgia Tbilisi II - Betlemi Keda	3-1
FC Khobi - FC Norchi Dinamoeli	1-2	FC Margveti - Kolkhi Gulripshi	3-0
Sulori Vani - FC Kakheti Telavi	3-4	Tbilisi 2016 FC - Samegrelo Chkhorotsku	5-3
Khikhani Khulo - FC Meshakhte Tkibuli	2-4	FC Guria Lanchkhuti - FC Saburtalo II	1-0
Senakuri Senaki - Mark Stars Tbilisi	0-1	FC Gareji Sagarejo - FC Algeti Marneuli	1-2
FC Zestafoni - FC Gardabani	1-3	Lazika Zugdidi - FK Imereti Khoni	0-2 aet

Third Round [12-14.06.2018]

Mark Stars Tbilisi - FC Merani Martvili	2-4	FC WIT Georgia Tbilisi II - FC Saburtalo	4-2 pen
Meta FC - Tbilisi City	3-2 pen	FC Gagra - FC Sioni Bolnisi	2-1 aet
Kojaeli Mtskheta - FC Dila Gori	0-8	FC Lokomotivi Tbilisi - FC Dinamo Tbilisi	3-5 pen
FC Meshakhte Tkibuli - FC Samtredia	2-3	FC WIT Georgia Tbilisi - FC Dinamo Batumi	1-0
FC Samgurali Tskhaltubo - FC Rustavi	5-6 pen	Liakhvi Tskhinvali - FC Algeti Marneuli	5-2
FC Guria Lanchkhuti - FC Kolkheti-1913 Poti	1-0	FC Gardabani - FK Imereti Khoni	3-1
Gori FC - FC Torpedo Kutaisi	0-2	FC Margveti - FC Kakheti Telavi	0-4
Tbilisi 2016 FC - FC Chikhura Sachkhere	0-6	FC Shukura Kobuleti - FC Norchi Dinamoeli	4-0

1/8 - Finals [19-20.09.2018]

FC Merani Martvili - FC Dinamo Tbilisi	1-2
FC Guria Lanchkhuti - FC Samtredia	3-1
FC WIT Georgia Tbilisi - FC Chikhura Sachkhere	3-0 pen
FC Kakheti Telavi - FC Dila Gori	1-0
FC Torpedo Kutaisi - FC Rustavi	2-0 aet
FC WIT Georgia Tbilisi II - FC Gagra	1-2
FC Gardabani - FC Shukura Kobuleti	0-3
Liakhvi Tskhinvali - Meta FC	2-5

Quarter-Finals [03.10.2018]

Meta FC - FC Gagra	0-1
FC Guria Lanchkhuti - FC Dinamo Tbilisi	0-5
FC WIT Georgia Tbilisi - FC Kakheti Telavi	0-3
FC Shukura Kobuleti - FC Torpedo Kutaisi[24.10.]	1-3

Semi-Finals [07.11.2018]

FC Gagra - FC Dinamo Tbilisi	1-0 aet
FC Kakheti Telavi - FC Torpedo Kutaisi	0-1

Final

25.11.2018; Stadioni Angisi, Batumi; Referee: Giorgi Vadatchkoria; Attendance: 2,000

FC Torpedo Kutaisi – FC Gagra **2-2(0-1,2-2,2-2); 4-2 on penalties**

Torpedo Kutaisi: Roin Kvaskhvadze, Davit Khurtsilava, Mamuka Kobakhidze, Giorgi Kimadze (54.Miloš Lačný), Levan Gegetchkori, Oleksandr Azatskyi, Grigol Dolidze, Levan Kutalia, Merab Gigauri (71.Tengiz Tsikaridze), Mate Tsintsadze (46.Arfang Daffé), Tornike Kapanadze (93.Giorgi Kukhianidze). Trainer: Kakhaber Shkhetiani.

FC Gagra: Vadim Shevchuk, Erekle Kiladze, Giga Samkharadze (110.Giorgi Ivaniadze), Tornike Gaprindashvili, Vasil Khositashvili, Erekle Sultanishvili, Rati Tsatskrialashvili (81.Jaba Kasrelishvili), Ivane Khabelashvili (87.Tamaz Lomsadze), Rati Kakiashvili, Giorgi Gaprindashvili, Nugzar Spanderashvili (65.Vazha Matiashvili). Trainer: Denis Khomutov (Ukraine).

Goals: 0-1 Nugzar Spanderashvili (37), 0-2 Ivane Khabelashvili (49), 1-2 Miloš Lačný (74), 2-2 Miloš Lačný (90+1).

Penalties: Mamuka Kobakhidze 1-0; Rati Kakiashvili 1-1; Tengiz Tsikaridze 2-1; Jaba Kasrelishvili (missed); Levan Gegetchkori 3-1; Giorgi Gaprindashvili 3-2; Miloš Lačný 4-2; Erekle Sultanishvili (saved).

THE CLUBS 2018

Football Club Chikhura Sachkhere

Founded: 1938
Stadium: Stadioni „Ramaz Shengelia", Kutaisi (19,400)

Goalkeepers:	DOB	M	(s)	G
Dino Hamzić (BIH)	22.01.1988	32		
Zurab Mtskerashvili	13.04.1986	4	(1)	
Defenders:	**DOB**	**M**	**(s)**	**G**
Lasha Chikvaidze	04.10.1989	32		
Revaz Chiteishvili	30.01.1994	25		
Shota Kashia	22.10.1984	5		
Davit Maisashvili	18.02.1989	34		
Davit Megrelishvili	25.09.1991	29	(1)	
Bakar Mirtskhulava	24.05.1992	33		1
Midfielders:	**DOB**	**M**	**(s)**	**G**
Irakli Bugridze	03.01.1998	33	(2)	8
Demur Chikhladze	23.09.1996	4	(22)	2
Denis Dobrovolski	10.10.1985	18	(10)	
Quaresma de Lima e Silva Pedro Vitor „Guga"	01.02.1994		(5)	
Levan Kakubava	15.10.1990	30		1
Irakli Lekvtadze	30.08.1991	15	(8)	4
Teimuraz Markozashvili	09.08.1994	31		2
Forwards:	**DOB**	**M**	**(s)**	**G**
Giorgi Bukhaidze	09.12.1991	6	(17)	4
Giorgi Gabedava	03.10.1989	35		22
Davit Ionanidze	05.08.1998		(11)	2
Kakhaber Kakhabrishvili	08.07.1993	15	(12)	3
Mikheil Sardalishvili	17.09.1992	15	(3)	4
Bachana Tskhadadze	23.10.1987		(5)	
Trainer:	**DOB**	**M**		
Samson Pruidze	06.10.1957	36		

Football Club Dila Gori

Founded: 1949
Stadium: Stadioni „Tengiz Burjanadze", Gori (8,230)

Goalkeepers:	DOB	M	(s)	G
Giorgi Begashvili	12.02.1991	19		
Luka Gugeshashvili	29.04.1999	17		
Defenders:	**DOB**	**M**	**(s)**	**G**
Gia Chaduneli	15.05.1994	31	(1)	
Eriks de Souza Santos Pereira(BRA)	23.02.1996	14		
Giorgi Gadrani	30.09.1994	9	(1)	1
Jemal Gogiashvili	06.05.1988	4	(2)	
Tornike Grigalashvili	28.01.1993	15		
Alexander Kvakhadze	17.08.1984	14		1
Goderdzi Machaidze	17.07.1992	9		
Anzor Sukhiashvili	28.01.1988	25	(1)	
Midfielders:	**DOB**	**M**	**(s)**	**G**
Gogita Gogua	04.10.1983	11	(3)	
Gaira Joof (GAM)	13.12.1998	4	(1)	1
Nodar Kavtaradze	02.01.1993	28	(3)	5
Zaur Kereleishvili	25.09.1998	6	(1)	
Giorgi Koripadze	03.10.1989	19	(9)	1
Issifu Lamptey	01.06.1995	17	(9)	3
Levan Nonikashvili	05.04.1995	3	(2)	5
Amos Nondi Obiero (KEN)	10.02.1999	9	(11)	
Davit Razhamashvili	28.10.1988	13	(14)	1
Luka Razmadze	30.12.1983	27	(3)	
Guram Samushia	05.09.1994	1	(9)	
Forwards:	**DOB**	**M**	**(s)**	**G**
Alvin Mateus Fortes (NED)	25.05.1994	8	(7)	4
Imeda Ashortia	01.01.1996	1	(4)	
Pa Omar Babou (GAM)	01.10.1998	2	(3)	
Mykola Kovtaliuk (UKR)	26.04.1995	24	(7)	21
Leandro Joaquim Ribeiro (BRA)	13.01.1995	32	(1)	14
Giorgi Pantsulaia	06.01.1994	7	(6)	2
Trainer:	**DOB**	**M**		
Georgi Daraselia (ISR) [01.07.2017]	17.09.1968	19		
Giorgi Shashiashvili [14.08.2018]	01.09.1979	17		

Football Club Dinamo Tbilisi

Founded: 1925
Stadium: „Boris Paichadze“ Dinamo Arena, Tbilisi (54,549)

Goalkeepers:	**DOB**	**M**	**(s)**	**G**
Demetre Buliskeria	09.01.2000	18		
Ştefan Sicaci (MDA)	08.09.1988	18		
Defenders:	**DOB**	**M**	**(s)**	**G**
Tornike Dzotsenidze	07.11.1999	3		
Luka Kapianidze	10.01.1999	3		
Levan Kharabadze	26.01.2000	27	(4)	4
Davit Kobouri	24.01.1998	34		
Luka Lochoshvili	29.05.1998	18	(3)	
Nika Ninua	22.06.1999	27	(2)	3
Guja Rukhaia	22.07.1987	34	(1)	1
Lasha Totadze	24.08.1988	31		3
Midfielders:	**DOB**	**M**	**(s)**	**G**
Beka Dartsmelia	21.03.2000	1	(2)	
Dmytro Ivanisenia (UKR)	11.01.1994	31	(2)	3
Bakar Kardava	04.10.1994	6	(1)	
Otar Kiteishvili	26.03.1996	18		11
Paata Kiteishvili	16.01.1999		(1)	
Lasha Kochladze	22.08.1995	4	(13)	
Giorgi Kutsia	27.10.1999	13	(6)	2
Akaki Shulaia	06.09.1996	32		1
Giorgi Tevzadze	25.08.1996		(1)	
Giorgi Zaria	14.07.1997	3	(6)	
Forwards:	**DOB**	**M**	**(s)**	**G**
Tamaz Babunadze	04.01.2000		(7)	
Nika Dzalamidze	06.01.1992	1	(8)	1
Mikheil Ergemlidze	28.09.1999	3	(18)	1
Giorgi Ivanishvili	18.10.1989	17	(9)	3
Levan Shengelia	27.10.1995	13	(3)	5
Mate Vatsadze	17.12.1988	7	(5)	2
Budu Zivzivadze	10.03.1994	34	(1)	22
Trainer:	**DOB**	**M**		
Kakhaber Katcharava	19.06.1966	31		
Zaur Svanadze [11.11.2018]	23.01.1958	5		

Football Club Kolkheti-1913 Poti

Founded: 1913
Stadium: Chele Arena, Kobuleti (6,000)

Goalkeepers:	**DOB**	**M**	**(s)**	**G**
Lasha-Giorgi Gurgenidze	25.02.1999	1		
Denis Kniga (RUS)	14.04.1992	13		
Bacho Mikava	12.01.1994	4		
Luka Nanava	19.09.2001	1	(1)	
Andriy Poltavtsev (UKR)	07.12.1991	15		
Aleksey Solosin (RUS)	11.08.1987	2		
Defenders:	**DOB**	**M**	**(s)**	**G**
Murad Apkhazava	02.02.1995	16	(1)	1
Temuri Dzadzamia	26.06.2000	5	(4)	
Giorgi Dumbadze	08.01.1996		(2)	
Lasha Gogonaia	24.01.1990	15		4
Tornike Jimsheleishvili	04.10.1992	8	(4)	
Patterson Kabore (BFA)	05.05.1990	25	(6)	
Zaur Kereleishvili	25.09.1998	15		
Lasha Khatiashvili	11.06.1997	8	(1)	
Giorgi Kilasonia	21.05.1986	13	(1)	1
Bachuki Kokaia	28.10.1999	1	(1)	
Boris Makharadze	08.11.1990	14		
Lasha Mtchedlishvili	07.02.1993		(2)	
Davit Mtivlishvili	26.10.1994	7	(3)	
Vladimir Ponomarev (RUS)	22.04.1987	15		
Giga Tcheishvili	17.09.1993	12	(3)	
Irakli Tsikolia (UKR)	26.05.1987	16	(1)	
Midfielders:	**DOB**	**M**	**(s)**	**G**
Zurab Arziani	19.10.1987	12	(3)	
Tornike Chubitidze	12.08.1995		(3)	
Sergey Danilov (RUS)	01.07.1989	15		
Kyrylo Doroshenko (UKR)	17.10.1989	14	(1)	2
Vladimir Gogberashvili (RUS)	16.04.1987	14	(3)	2
Levan Kakulia	28.05.1992	13	(9)	
Jemal Kanchashvili	01.09.1994		(1)	
Luka Khvichia	23.07.1999		(1)	
Luis Eduardo Mello"Luizinho" (BRA)	13.03.1993	2		
Luka Makharadze	25.12.1999	1	(7)	
Stanislav Prychynenko	26.06.1991	9	(1)	
Tamaz Shalikashvili	21.06.1999	2	(12)	
Tchiaber Tchetchelashvili	10.10.1995	8	(2)	
Valiko Tkemaladze	14.11.1987	24	(7)	
Forwards:	**DOB**	**M**	**(s)**	**G**
Giorgi Arkania	16.04.1993		(3)	
Imeda Ashortia	01.01.1996	14	(2)	1
Luka Gogidze	26.04.2000		(1)	
Luka Imnadze	26.08.1997	24	(3)	5
Giorgi Kakhelishvili	22.05.1987	8	(2)	1
Yaroslav Kvasov (UKR)	05.03.1992	6	(5)	2
Otar Kvernadze	10.09.1993	3	(3)	
Illia Mykhaliov (UKR)	31.07.1990	2		7
Irakli Penderava	04.09.1997	1	(4)	
Trainer:	**DOB**	**M**		
Konstantin Galkin (RUS) [01.01.2018]	19.01.2018	2		
Viktor Demidov (RUS) [15.03.2018]	08.11.1964	16		
Roberto Landi (ITA) [01.08.2018]	02.01.1956	18		

Football Club Lokomotivi Tbilisi

Founded: 1936
Stadium: Stadioni „Mikheil Meskhi“, Tbilisi (27,223)

Goalkeepers:	**DOB**	**M**	**(s)**	**G**
Luka Sherozia	11.08.1997	12		
Revaz Tevdoradze	14.02.1988	24		
Defenders:	**DOB**	**M**	**(s)**	**G**
Beqa Buighlishvili	27.09.2000	1		
Giorgi Gabadze	02.03.1995	32	(1)	
Teimuraz Ghonghadze	21.05.1985	5	(3)	
Giorgi Khidesheli	01.05.1988	1	(1)	
Levan Kurdadze	03.09.1990	15	(1)	
Ucha Lobjanidze	23.02.1987	17	(1)	1
Nika Tchanturia	19.01.1995	29		
Dachi Tsnobiladze	28.01.1994	4	(4)	
Davit Ubilava	27.01.1994	3		1
Midfielders:	**DOB**	**M**	**(s)**	**G**
Aleksandre Andronikashvili	09.04.1999	2		
Rati Ardazishvili	27.01.1998	1	(8)	1
Zurab Davitashvili	15.02.2001	17	(2)	3
Tornike Dzebniauri	27.11.1999	14	(6)	
Levan Grdzelidze	18.08.2000	2	(1)	
Lasha Gvalia	06.10.1991	21	(7)	
Luka Janashia	21.06.2000		(1)	
Levan Kenia	18.10.1990		(3	
Luka Kikabidze	21.01.1995	12	(7)	2
Giorgi Kiknadze	27.09.1997	1	(2)	
Irakli Komakhidze	26.03.1997	9	(7)	
Davit Samurkasovi	05.02.1998	24	(3)	
Temuri Shonia	28.05.1990	28	(2)	7
Forwards:	**DOB**	**M**	**(s)**	**G**
Vato Arveladze	04.03.1998	7	(2)	2
Mamia Gavashelishvili	08.01.1995	24	(5)	11
Revaz Injgia	31.12.2000	2	(15)	1
Davit Jikia	10.01.1995	2	(9)	5
John Oluremi William (USA)	13.06.1985	5	(4)	
Otar Kobakhidze	29.02.1996	23	(4)	6
Lasha Ozbetelashvili	20.01.1999	1	(4)	
Shota Shekiladze	14.02.2000		(1)	
Roman Tchanturia	09.02.1996	4	(3)	1
Trainer:	**DOB**	**M**		
Lasha Chagiashvili	17.02.1981	36		

Football Club Rustavi

Founded: 1948
Stadium: Stadioni Poladi, Rustavi (10,720)

Goalkeepers:	DOB	M	(s)	G
Soso Kardava	08.12.1997		(1)	
Omar Migineishvili	02.06.1984	5		
Nukri Revishvili	02.03.1987	16		1
Koka Sepiashvili	19.03.1986	15		
Defenders:	**DOB**	**M**	**(s)**	**G**
Luka Gadrani	12.04.1997	7	(1)	
Levan Gegetchkori	05.06.1994	13	(1)	
Teimuraz Ghonghadze	21.05.1985	7		
Tsotne Kapanadze	30.08.2001	1		
Akaki Khubutia	17.03.1986	3		
Varlam Kilasonia	09.01.1993	12		
Davit Kvirkvelia	27.06.1980	11	(2)	2
Mamuka Kobakhidze	23.08.1992	14	(1)	2
Giorgi Samadashvili	27.09.1977		(1)	
Taras Tsarikaev (RUS)	17.06.1989	1	(1)	
Albert Tskhovrebov (RUS)	02.05.1993	11		
Midfielders:	**DOB**	**M**	**(s)**	**G**
Georgi Bugulov (RUS)	17.03.1993	1		
Temur Chogadze	05.05.1998	6	(11)	
Ukwubile Chukwurah (NGA)	17.05.1992	11	(1)	
Avto Endeladze	17.09.1994	4	(4)	
Georgi Gabulov (RUS)	04.09.1988	11		1
Avtandil Gujabidze	06.07.1997	3	(5)	
Batraz Khadartsev (RUS)	23.05.1993	5	(2)	1
Tornike Kirkitadze	23.07.1996	19	(2)	
Irakli Klimiashvili	30.05.1988		(1)	
Khvicha Kvaratskhelia	12.02.2001	16	(2)	3
Mate Kvirkvia	14.06.1996	8	(7)	
Giorgi Papava	16.02.1993	34		1
Papuna Poniava	10.03.1994	24	(2)	1
Luka Silagadze	21.04.1999	9	(5)	
Data Sichinava	21.03.1989		(1)	
Tornike Tarkhnishvili	07.03.1990	8	(7)	
Mate Tsintsadze	07.01.1995	13	(2)	2
Luka Zviadadze	20.05.1999	1	(4)	
Forwards:	**DOB**	**M**	**(s)**	**G**
Revaz Barabadze	04.10.1988	1	(1)	
Mikheil Gorelishvili (RUS)	29.05.1993	1	(1)	
Beka Kavtaradze	15.06.1999	15	(12)	4
Elguja Lobjanidze	17.09.1992	11	(4)	2
Tamaz Makatsaria	03.10.1995	7	(3)	1
Otar Martsvaladze	14.07.1984	14	(9)	4
Beka Mikeltadze	26.11.1997	12	(1)	3
Zaza Tsitskishvili	04.07.1995	23	(3)	4
Trainer:	**DOB**	**M**		
Vladimir Gazzaev (RUS)	01.07.1980	12		
Varlam Kilasonia [23.05.2018]	13.08.1967	10		
Ucha Sosiashvili [01.09.2018]	26.07.1989	14		

Football Club Saburtalo Tbilisi

Founded: 20.08.1999
Stadium: Stadioni „Mikheil Meskhi“, Tbilisi (27,223)

Goalkeepers:	DOB	M	(s)	G
Beka Kurdadze	24.01.1997	1	(1)	
Lazare Kupatadze	01.01.1996	35		
Defenders:	**DOB**	**M**	**(s)**	**G**
Grigol Chabradze	20.04.1996	2	(5)	
Tedore Grigalashvili	12.05.1993	6		1
Nodar Iashvili	24.01.1993	14	(1)	
Jemali-Giorgi Jinjolava	28.01.2000	1		
Luka Lakvekheliani	20.10.1998	22	(5)	1
Gagi Margvelashvili	30.10.1996	36		3
Tsotne Nadaraia	21.02.1997	11	(3)	
Giorgi Rekhviashvili	01.02.1988	31	(1)	2
Dachi Tsnobiladze	28.01.1994		(1)	
Midfielders:	**DOB**	**M**	**(s)**	**G**
Sandro Altunashvili	19.05.1997	8	(13)	
Giorgi Diasamidze	08.05.1992	31	(2)	7
Tornike Gorgiashvili	27.04.1988	32	(2)	3
Beka Gvaradze	11.08.1997	9	(7)	2
Nikoloz Mali	27.01.1999	1	(2)	
Vladimer Mamuchashvili	28.08.1997	6	(1)	
Lasha Shindagoridze	30.01.1993		(1)	
David Targamadze	22.08.1989	1	(6)	1
Tornike Tarkhnishvili	07.03.1990	5	(2)	
Alwyn Tera (KEN)	18.01.1997	2	(6)	1
Forwards:	**DOB**	**M**	**(s)**	**G**
Vladimer Dvalishvili	20.04.1986	6	(4)	1
Vagner Gonçalves Nogueira de Souza (FRA)	27.04.1996	31	(1)	11
Guram Goshteliani	05.01.1997	12	(12)	2
Giorgi Kokhreidze	18.11.1998	27	(6)	1
Dimitri Tatanashvili	19.10.1983	6	(14)	6
Davit Volkovi	03.06.1995	16	(12)	8
Trainer:	**DOB**	**M**		
Giorgi Chiabrishvili	07.10.1979	36		

Football Club Sioni Bolnisi

Founded: 1936
Stadium: Stadioni „Tamaz Stephania“, Bolnisi (3,242)

Goalkeepers:	DOB	M	(s)	G
Giorgi Chochishvili	07.05.1998	2		
Mikheil Mujrishvili	30.04.1984	12	(1)	
Tornike Zarkua	01.09.1990	22		
Defenders:	**DOB**	**M**	**(s)**	**G**
Guram Giorbelidze	25.02.1996	33		
Aleksandre Gureshidze	23.04.1995	3	(1)	2
Givi Khetsuriani	02.07.1999	3		1
Guram Mindorashvili	16.02.1990	31	(2)	
Luka Nozadze	25.12.1996	28	(3)	1
Gulverd Tomashvili	13.10.1988	12	(2)	
Midfielders:	**DOB**	**M**	**(s)**	**G**
Giorgi Datunaishvili	09.02.1985	19	(2)	3
Giorgi Gaprindashvili	06.05.1995	17	(1)	
Levan Khmaladze	06.04.1985	26	(3)	2
Vazha Kikava	28.12.1995	23	(3)	
Aleksandre Koshkadze	04.12.1981	19	(9)	3
Lasha Managadze	11.11.1994	9	(13)	
Giorgi Mikaberidze	17.02.1988	13	(13)	3
Tsotne Samushia	24.10.1994	6	(2)	
Zviad Sikharulia	01.08.1992	15	(12)	2
Forwards:	**DOB**	**M**	**(s)**	**G**
Giorgi Beriashvili	10.09.1986	8	(4)	1
Jaba Dvali	08.02.1985	12	(1)	2
Vili Isiani	22.03.1991	11	(4)	3
Davit Kirkitadze	03.09.1992	17		6
Lasha Lezhava	11.01.1998	7	(13)	2
Bidzina Makharoblidze	10.10.1992	1	(4)	6
Giorgi Tcheishvili	16.01.1996	1		
Serhiy Tretiak (UKR)	28.11.1984	7	(1)	
Jaba Ugulava	08.04.1992	3	(13)	1
Trainer:	**DOB**	**M**		
Koba Zhorzhikashvili	03.01.1962	18		
Temur Shalamberidze [12.07.2018]	08.12.1969	18		

Football Club Samtredia

Founded: 1936 (*as Sanavardo Samtredia*)
Stadium: Stadioni „Erosi Manjgaladze", Samtredia (5,000)

Goalkeepers:	**DOB**	**M**	**(s)**	**G**
Davit Kupatadze	06.06.1991	9		
Omar Migineishvili	02.06.1984	12		
Serhii Pogorily	28.07.1986	6		
Otar Sturua	20.08.1997	9		
Defenders:	**DOB**	**M**	**(s)**	**G**
Giorgi Akhaladze	26.07.1997	16	(5)	1
Vasiko Bachiashvili	04.11.1992	17		1
Gigla Burkadze	05.12.1997	1	(4)	
Roman Chachua	01.11.1997	29	(1)	
Avto Endeladze	17.09.1994	16	(1)	1
Ivan Fatić (MNE)	01.08.1988	23	(3)	1
Jemal Gogiashvili	06.05.1988	16		
Giorgi Guruli	31.07.1988	15		
Giorgi Jgerenaia	28.12.1993	9		
Givi Karkuzashvili	20.09.1986	11		
Demur Kashibadze	01.07.1998		(2)	
Ucha Lobjanidze	23.02.1987	3		
Davit Manjgaladze	01.02.1998		(1)	
Henri Ndong (GAB)	23.08.1992	4		
Tornike Shalikashvili	24.10.1990		(2)	
Yehor Smirnov (UKR)	03.08.1996	1	(2)	
Dmytro Ulyanov (UKR)	01.12.1993	2		
Midfielders:	**DOB**	**M**	**(s)**	**G**
Murtaz Daushvili	01.05.1989	12		
Giorgi Eristavi	04.02.1994	11	(8)	4
George Ganugrava	21.02.1988	3		
Shota Kerdzevadze	20.03.1993	24	(4)	
Nikoloz Khachidze	06.07.1999		(4)	
Davit Kirkitadze	03.09.1992	15	(3)	
Ihor Koshman	07.03.1995	1	(7)	1
Jaba Lipartia	16.11.1987	15	(1)	2
Oleg Mamasakhlisi	25.11.1995	1	(5)	3
Anatoli Mesyachenko	21.04.1991	7	(9)	
Akaki Ninua	17.02.1999	1	(5)	1
Valeri Olkhovi	18.08.1998	7	(5)	
Sidy Sagna (SEN)	04.02.1990	7	(1)	
Beka Tugushi	24.01.1989	16		1
Vincent Weijl (FRA)	11.11.1990	2	(8)	1
Forwards:	**DOB**	**M**	**(s)**	**G**
Giorgi Giorbelidze	11.01.2000	3	(4)	
Mikheil Gorelishvili	29.05.1993	11		
Inters Gui (CIV)	08.08.1992	16	(1)	3
Zaur Khabeishvili	11.08.1998	12		2
Lasha Kuchukhidze	14.03.1992	4	(5)	1
Tamaz Makatsaria	03.10.1995	4	(5)	
Michael Olaitan (NGA)	01.01.1993	2		1
Giorgi Pantsulaia	06.01.1994	5	(3)	4
Trainer:	**DOB**	**M**		
Ucha Sosiashvili	26.07.1989	17		
Giorgi Tsetsadze [03.07.2018]	03.09.1974	6		
Giorgi Daraselia [05.09.2018]	16.09.1978	13		

Football Club Torpedo Kutaisi

Founded: 1946
Stadium: Stadioni „Ramaz Shengelia", Kutaisi (19,400)

Goalkeepers:	**DOB**	**M**	**(s)**	**G**
Roin Kvaskhvadze	31.05.1989	32		
Maksime Kvilitaia	17.09.1985	4	(1)	
Defenders:	**DOB**	**M**	**(s)**	**G**
Oleksandr Azatskyi (UKR)	13.01.1994	18		
Anri Chichinadze	05.10.1997	1	(2)	
Levan Gegetchkori	05.06.1994	13	(2)	
Tornike Grigalashvili	28.01.1993	7	(1)	
Giorgi Guruli	31.07.1988	13		
Davit Khurtsilava	09.03.1988	2	(2)	
Giorgi Kimadze	11.02.1992	35		7
Mamuka Kobakhidze	23.08.1992	17		1
Oleg Mamasakhlisi	25.11.1995	1	(4)	1
Lazar Marin (BUL)	09.02.1994	14	(2)	1
Vazha Tabatadze	01.02.1991	13	(3)	
Midfielders:	**DOB**	**M**	**(s)**	**G**
Grigol Dolidze	25.10.1982	24	(6)	7
Merab Gigauri	05.01.1993	29	(3)	2
Marek Hlinka (SVK)	04.10.1990	7	(5)	2
Giorgi Kukhianidze	01.07.1992	21	(11)	4
Levan Kutalia	19.07.1989	31	(3)	1
Jaba Lipartia	16.11.1987	5	(7)	
Mikheil Sardalishvili	17.09.1999	5	(6)	
Beka Tugushi	24.01.1989	3	(3)	1
Tengiz Tsikaridze	21.12.1995	1	(12)	6
Mate Tsintsadze	07.01.1995	13	(1)	1
Forwards:	**DOB**	**M**	**(s)**	**G**
Yevhen Bokhashvili (UKR)	05.01.1993	5	(5)	1
Arfang Daffé (SEN)	24.06.1991	11	(6)	2
Tornike Kapanadze	04.06.1992	19	(8)	14
Lasha Kuchukhidze	14.03.1992		(5)	
Miloš Lačný (SVK)	08.03.1988	6	(7)	2
Merab Megreladze	29.10.1999		(1)	
Gleofilo Hasselbaink (SUR)	17.09.1999	1	(2)	1
Trainer:	**DOB**	**M**		
Kakhaber Shkhetiani	24.02.1978	36		

SECOND LEVEL
Erovnuli Liga 2 2018

1.	FC Dinamo Batumi (*Promoted*)	36	26	5	5	72	-	25	83
2.	FC WIT Georgia Tbilisi (*Promotion Play-offs*)	36	24	8	4	67	-	16	80
3.	FC Gagra (*Promotion Play-offs*)	36	18	5	13	52	-	48	59
4.	FC Norchi Dinamo Tbilisi	36	16	5	15	46	-	46	53
5.	FC Telavi	36	16	5	15	46	-	38	53
6.	FC Shevardeni-1906 Tbilisi	36	14	10	12	42	-	40	52
7.	FC Shukura Kobuleti	36	11	7	18	62	-	75	40
8.	FC Samgurali Tskhaltubo (*Relegated*)	36	11	4	21	47	-	68	37
9.	FC Tskhinvali Gori (*Relegated*)	36	7	6	23	33	-	75	27
10.	FC Merani Martvili (*Relegated*)	36	6	7	23	32	-	68	25

Relegation Play-offs (2nd / 3rd Level)

FC Guria Lanchkhuti - FC Samgurali Tskhaltubo	1-0(1-0)	1-2(0-2)
FC Tskhinvali Gori - FC Bakhmaro Chokhatauri	2-1(2-0)	2-0(0-0)

NATIONAL TEAM

INTERNATIONAL MATCHES
(16.07.2018 – 15.07.2019)

06.09.2018	Astana	Kazakhstan - Georgia	0-2(0-0)	(UNL)
09.09.2018	Tbilisi	Georgia - Latvia	1-0(0-0)	(UNL)
13.10.2018	Tbilisi	Georgia - Andorra	3-0(1-0)	(UNL)
16.10.2018	Rīga	Latvia - Georgia	0-3(0-2)	(UNL)
15.11.2018	Andorra la Vella	Andorra - Georgia	1-1(0-1)	(UNL)
19.11.2018	Tbilisi	Georgia - Kazakhstan	2-1(0-0)	(UNL)
23.03.2019	Tbilisi	Georgia - Switzerland	0-2(0-0)	(ECQ)
26.03.2019	Dublin	Republic of Ireland - Georgia	1-0(1-0)	(ECQ)
07.06.2019	Tbilisi	Georgia - Gibraltar	3-0(1-0)	(ECQ)
10.06.2019	København	Denmark - Georgia	5-1(2-1)	(ECQ)

06.09.2018 KAZAKHSTAN - GEORGIA 0-2(0-0) UEFA Nations League D, Group 1
Astana Arena, Astana; Referee: Halil Umut Meler (Turkey); Attendance: 28,736
GEO: Giorgi Loria, Giorgi Navalovski, Guram Kashia, Solomon Kvirkvelia, Otar Kakabadze, Jaba Kankava (Cap), Giorgi Merebashvili, Nika Kvekveskiri, Valeri Qazaishvili (84.Davit Khocholava), Giorgi Chakvetadze (75.Tornike Okriashvili), Giorgi Kvilitaia (65.Valerian Gvilia). Trainer: Vladimír Weiss (Slovakia).
Goals: Giorgi Chakvetadze (69), Serhiy Malyi (74 own goal).

09.09.2018 GEORGIA - LATVIA 1-0(0-0) UEFA Nations League D, Group 1
"Boris Paichadze" Dinamo Arena, Tbilisi; Referee: Referee: Anastasios Papapetrou (Greece); Attendance: 45,716
GEO: Giorgi Loria, Giorgi Navalovski, Guram Kashia, Solomon Kvirkvelia, Otar Kakabadze, Jaba Kankava (Cap), Nika Kvekveskiri, Tornike Okriashvili (81.Valerian Gvilia), Valeri Qazaishvili (90.Davit Khocholava), Giorgi Chakvetadze (85.Giorgi Papunashvili), Nika Kacharava. Trainer: Vladimír Weiss (Slovakia).
Goal: Tornike Okriashvili (77 penalty).

13.10.2018 GEORGIA - ANDORRA 3-0(1-0) UEFA Nations League D, Group 1
"Boris Paichadze" Dinamo Arena, Tbilisi; Referee: Leontios Trattou (Cyprus); Attendance: 32,212
GEO: Giorgi Loria, Giorgi Navalovski, Guram Kashia, Solomon Kvirkvelia, Otar Kakabadze, Jaba Kankava (Cap), Nika Kvekveskiri, Valeri Qazaishvili, Otar Kiteishvili (68.Jano Ananidze), Giorgi Chakvetadze (90.Vakhtang Tchanturishvili), Nika Kacharava (81.Valerian Gvilia). Trainer: Vladimír Weiss (Slovakia).
Goals: Valeri Qazaishvili (33, 84), Jaba Kankava (90+5).

16.10.2018 LATVIA - GEORGIA 0-3(0-2) UEFA Nations League D, Group 1
Daugavas Stadions, Rīga; Referee: Petr Ardeleanu (Czech Republic); Attendance: 3,185
GEO: Giorgi Loria, Giorgi Navalovski, Davit Khocholava, Otar Kakabadze, Lasha Dvali, Jaba Kankava (Cap) (34.Giorgi Aburjania), Giorgi Merebashvili (80.Jambul Jighauri), Nika Kvekveskiri, Valeri Qazaishvili, Valerian Gvilia, Giorgi Chakvetadze (89.Luka Zarandia). Trainer: Vladimír Weiss (Slovakia).
Goals: Jaba Kankava (8), Valerian Gvilia (29), Giorgi Chakvetadze (61).

15.11.2018 ANDORRA - GEORGIA 1-1(0-1) UEFA Nations League D, Group 1
Estadi Nacional, Andorra la Vella; Referee: Radu Petrescu (Romania); Attendance: 1,311
GEO: Giorgi Loria, Giorgi Navalovski (Cap), Davit Khocholava, Otar Kakabadze, Jemal Tabidze, Nika Kvekveskiri, Valeri Qazaishvili, Otar Kiteishvili (78.Vakhtang Tchanturishvili), Valerian Gvilia (88.Luka Zarandia), Giorgi Chakvetadze, Bachana Arabuli (78.Nika Kacharava). Trainer: Vladimír Weiss (Slovakia).
Goal: Giorgi Chakvetadze (9).

19.11.2018 GEORGIA - KAZAKHSTAN 2-1(0-0) UEFA Nations League D, Group 1
"Boris Paichadze" Dinamo Arena, Tbilisi; Referee: Tiago Bruno Lopes Martins (Portugal); Attendance: 46,686
GEO: Giorgi Loria, Guram Kashia, Solomon Kvirkvelia, Otar Kakabadze (86.Davit Khocholava), Lasha Dvali, Jaba Kankava (Cap), Giorgi Merebashvili, Nika Kvekveskiri, Valeri Qazaishvili, Valerian Gvilia (75.Nika Kacharava), Giorgi Chakvetadze (90.Giorgi Aburjania). Trainer: Vladimír Weiss (Slovakia).
Goals: Giorgi Merebashvili (59), Giorgi Chakvetadze (84).

23.03.2019 GEORGIA - SWITZERLAND 0-2(0-0) 16th EC. Qualifiers
"Boris Paichadze" Dinamo Arena, Tbilisi; Referee: Craig Pawson (England); Attendance: 49,207
GEO: Giorgi Loria, Guram Kashia, Davit Khocholava, Otar Kakabadze, Jemal Tabidze (62.Solomon Kvirkvelia), Jaba Kankava (Cap), Jano Ananidze (84.Nika Kacharava), Nika Kvekveskiri, Valeri Qazaishvili, Valerian Gvilia, Giorgi Kvilitaia (73.Saba Lobjanidze). Trainer: Vladimír Weiss (Slovakia).

26.03.2019 REPUBLIC OF IRELAND - GEORGIA 1-0(1-0) 16th EC. Qualifiers
Aviva Stadium, Dublin; Referee: Serdar Gözübüyük (Netherlands); Attendance: 40,317
GEO: Giorgi Loria, Guram Kashia, Solomon Kvirkvelia, Davit Khocholava (65.Levan Kharabadze), Otar Kakabadze (85.Tornike Okriashvili), Jaba Kankava (Cap), Nika Kvekveskiri, Vato Arveladze (73.Valeri Qazaishvili), Otar Kiteishvili, Valerian Gvilia, Giorgi Kvilitaia. Trainer: Vladimír Weiss (Slovakia).

07.06.2019 GEORGIA - GIBRALTAR 3-0(1-0) 16th EC. Qualifiers
"Boris Paichadze" Dinamo Arena, Tbilisi; Referee: Antti Munukka (Finland); Attendance: 17,357
GEO: Giorgi Loria, Gia Grigalava, Guram Kashia, Otar Kakabadze, Levan Kharabadze, Jaba Kankava (Cap) (77.Levan Mchedlidze), Giorgi Merebashvili (72.Otar Kiteishvili), Nika Kvekveskiri, Vato Arveladze, Valerian Gvilia, Khvicha Kvaratskhelia (47.Giorgi Papunashvili). Trainer: Vladimír Weiss (Slovakia).
Goals: Valerian Gvilia (30), Giorgi Papunashvili (59), Vato Arveladze (76 penalty).

10.06.2019 DENMARK - GEORGIA 5-1(2-1) 16th EC. Qualifiers
Parken Stadium, København; Referee: Robert Schörgenhofer (Austria); Attendance: 15,387
GEO: Giorgi Loria, Giorgi Navalovski (79.Lasha Dvali), Gia Grigalava, Guram Kashia, Otar Kakabadze, Jaba Kankava (Cap), Nika Kvekveskiri, Lasha Parunashvili (58.Giorgi Papunashvili), Saba Lobjanidze, Otar Kiteishvili (73.Elguja Lobjanidze), Valerian Gvilia. Trainer: Vladimír Weiss (Slovakia).
Goal: Saba Lobjanidze (25).

NATIONAL TEAM PLAYERS
(16.07.2018 – 15.07.2019)

Name	DOB	Caps	Goals	2018/2019:	Club
Goalkeepers					
Giorgi LORIA	27.01.1986	**52**	**0**	2018: 18.01.2019->	*Unattached* *1.FC Magdeburg (GER)*
Defenders					
Lasha DVALI	14.05.1995	**13**	**1**	2018: 30.01.2019->	*MKS Pogoń Szczecin (POL)* *Ferencvárosi TC (HUN)*
Gia GRIGALAVA	05.08.1989	**26**	**0**	2019:	*FK Arsenal Tula (RUS)*
Otar KAKABADZE	27.06.1995	**27**	**0**	2018/2019:	*FC Luzern (SUI)*
Guram KASHIA	04.07.1987	**74**	**2**	2018/2019:	*San Jose Earthquakes (USA)*
Levan KHARABADZE	26.01.2000	**2**	**0**	2019:	*FC Zürich (SUI)*
Davit KHOCHOLAVA	08.02.1993	**18**	**0**	2018/2019:	*FK Shakhtar Donetsk (UKR)*
Solomon KVIRKVELIA	06.02.1992	**35**	**0**	2018/2019:	*FK Lokomotiv Moskva (RUS)*
Giorgi NAVALOVSKI	28.06.1986	**36**	**0**	2018: 03.03.2019->	*FC Dinamo Minsk (BLR)* *FC Dinamo Batumi*
Jemal TABIDZE	18.03.1996	**8**	**1**	2018/2019:	*FK Ufa (RUS)*
Midfielders					
Giorgi ABURJANIA	02.01.1995	**12**	**0**	2018/2019:	*CD Lugo (ESP)*
Jano ANANIDZE	10.10.1992	**41**	**6**	2018: 13.01.2019->	*FK Spartak Moskva (RUS)* *FK Krylia Sovetov Samara (RUS)*
Giorgi CHAKVETADZE	29.08.1999	**7**	**5**	2018:	*KAA Gent (BEL)*
Valerian GVILIA	24.05.1994	**23**	**3**	2018: 11.01.2019->	*FC Luzern (SUI)* *KS Górnik Zabrze (POL)*
Jambul „Jaba" JIGHAURI	08.07.1992	**13**	**0**	2018:	*Grenoble Foot 38 (FRA)*
Jaba KANKAVA	18.03.1986	**82**	**9**	2018/2019:	*FC Tobol Kostanay (KAZ)*
Otar KITEISHVILI	26.03.1996	**10**	**0**	2018/2019:	*SK Sturm Graz (SUI)*
Khvicha KVARATSKHELIA	12.02.2001	**1**	**0**	2019:	*FK Lokomotiv Moskva (RUS)*
Nika KVEKVESKIRI	29.05.1992	**25**	**0**	2018/2019:	*FC Tobol Kostanay (KAZ)*
Saba LOBJANIDZE	18.12.1994	**7**	**2**	2019:	*Randers FC (DEN)*
Levan MCHEDLIDZE	24.03.1990	**32**	**2**	2019:	*Empoli FC (ITA)*
Giorgi MEREBASHVILI	15.08.1986	**32**	**3**	2018/2019:	*Wisła Płock (POL)*
Tornike OKRIASHVILI	12.02.1992	**37**	**9**	2018: 01.01.2019->	*FK Krasnodar (RUS)* *Unattached*
Giorgi PAPUNASHVILI	02.09.1995	**11**	**2**	2018/2019:	*Real Zaragoza (ESP)*
Lasha PARUNASHVILI	14.02.1993	**2**	**0**	2019:	*Esbjerg fB (DEN)*
Valeri QAZAISHVILI	29.01.1993	**41**	**10**	2018/2019:	*San Jose Earthquakes (USA)*
Luka ZARANDIA	17.02.1996	**2**	**0**	2018:	*MZKS Arka Gdynia (POL)*
Vakhtang TCHANTURISHVILI	05.08.1993	**5**	**0**	2018/2019:	*FC Spartak Trnava (SVK)*
Forwards					
Bachana ARABULI	05.01.1994	**6**	**0**	2018:	*Puskás Ferenc Labdarugó Akadémia Felcsút (HUN)*
Vato ARVELADZE	04.03.1998	**2**	**1**	2019:	*Korona Kielce (POL)*
Nika KACHARAVA	13.01.1994	**17**	**1**	2018/2019:	*Anorthosis Famagusta FC (CYP)*
Giorgi KVILITAIA	01.10.1993	**17**	**4**	2018/2019:	*KAA Gent (BEL)*
Elguja LOBJANIDZE	17.09.1992	**2**	**0**	2018/2019:	*FC Taraz (KAZ)*

National team coach

Vladimír WEISS (Slovakia) [from 14.03.2016]	22.09.1964	34 M; 13 W; 9 D; 12 L; 48-39

GERMANY

The Country:

Bundesrepublik Deutschland (Federal Republic of Germany)
Capital: Berlin
Surface: 357,168 km²
Inhabitants: 83,019,200 [2018]
Time: UTC+1

The FA:

Deutscher Fußball-Bund
Otto-Fleck-Schneise 6, Postfach 710265, 60492 Frankfurt am Main
Tel: +49 69 678 80
Foundation date: 28.01.1900
Member of FIFA since: 1904
Member of UEFA since: 1954
Website: www.dfb.de

NATIONAL TEAM RECORDS

First international match:	05.04.1908, Basel:	Switzerland – Germany 5-3
Most international caps:	Lothar Herbert Matthäus	- 150 caps (1980-2000)
Most international goals:	Miroslav Klose	- 71 goals / 137 caps (2001-2014)

UEFA EUROPEAN CHAMPIONSHIP	
1960	Did not enter
1964	Did not enter
1968	Qualifiers
1972	**Final Tournament (Winners)**
1976	Final Tournament (Runners-up)
1980	**Final Tournament (Winners)**
1984	Final Tournament (Group Stage)
1988	Final Tournament (Semi-Finals)
1992	Final Tournament (Runners-up)
1996	**Final Tournament (Winners)**
2000	Final Tournament (Group Stage)
2004	Final Tournament (Group Stage)
2008	Final Tournament (Runners-up)
2012	Final Tournament (Semi-Finals)
2016	Final Tournament (Semi-Finals)

FIFA WORLD CUP	
1930	Did not enter
1934	Final Tournament (3rd Place)
1938	Final Tournament (1st Round)
1950	*Banned*
1954	**Final Tournament (Winners)**
1958	Final Tournament (3rd Place)
1962	Final Tournament (Quarter-Finals)
1966	Final Tournament (Runners-up)
1970	Final Tournament (3rd Place)
1974	**Final Tournament (Winners)**
1978	Final Tournament (Second Round)
1982	Final Tournament (Runners-up)
1986	Final Tournament (Runners-up)
1990	**Final Tournament (Winners)**
1994	Final Tournament (Quarter-Finals)
1998	Final Tournament (Quarter-Finals)
2002	Final Tournament (Runners-up)
2006	Final Tournament (3rd Place)
2010	Final Tournament (3rd Place)
2014	**Final Tournament (Winners)**
2018	Final Tournament (Group Stage)

UEFA NATIONS LEAGUE
2018/2019 – League A

OLYMPIC FOOTBALL TOURNAMENTS 1908-2016							
1908	-	**1948**	-	**1972**	Seconfd Round	**1996**	Qualifiers
1912	1st Round	**1952**	4th Place	**1976**	Qualifiers	**2000**	Qualifiers
1920	-	**1956**	1st Round	**1980**	Qualifiers	**2004**	Qualifiers
1924	-	**1960**	Qualifiers	**1984**	Quarter-Finals	**2008**	Qualifiers
1928	Quarter-Finals	**1964**	Qualifiers	**1988**	3rd Place	**2012**	Qualifiers
1936	Quarter-Finals	**1968**	-	**1992**	Qualifiers	**2016**	Runners-up

FIFA CONFEDERATIONS CUP 1992-2017
1999 (Group Stage), 2005 (3rd Place), **2017 (Winners)**

GERMAN CLUB HONOURS IN EUROPEAN CLUB COMPETITIONS:

European Champion Clubs' Cup (1956-1992) / UEFA Champions League (1993-2019)		
FC Bayern München	**5**	1973/1974, 1974/1975, 1975/1976, 2000/2001, 2012/2013
Hamburger SV	**1**	1982/1983
BV Borussia Dortmund	**1**	1996/1997
Fairs Cup (1858-1971) / UEFA Cup (1972-2009) / UEFA Europa League (2010-2019)		
Borussia VfL Mönchengladbach	**2**	1974/1975, 1978/1979
Eintracht Frankfurt	**1**	1979/1980
TSV Bayer 04 Leverkusen	**1**	1987/1988
FC Bayern München	**1**	1995/1996
FC Schalke 04 Gelsenkirchen	**1**	1996/1997

UEFA Super Cup (1972-2018)		
FC Bayern München	1	2013
European Cup Winners' Cup 1961-1999*		
BV Borussia Dortmund	1	1965/1966
Hamburger SV	1	1976/1977
FC Bayern München	1	1966/1967
SV Werder Bremen	1	1991/1992

**defunct competition*

NATIONAL COMPETITIONS
TABLE OF HONOURS

	CHAMPIONS	CUP WINNERS	BEST GOALSCORERS	
1902/1903	VfB Leipzig	-	-	
1903/1904	*No champions (final not played)*	-	-	
1904/1905	Berliner TuFC Union 1892	-	-	
1905/1906	VfB Leipzig	-	-	
1906/1907	Freiburger FC	-	-	
1907/1908	Berliner TuFC Viktoria 1889	-	-	
1908/1909	FC Phönix Karlsruhe	-	-	
1909/1910	Karlsruher FV	-	-	
1910/1911	Berliner TuFC Viktoria 1889	-	-	
1911/1912	Holstein Kiel	-	-	
1912/1913	VfB Leipzig	-	-	
1913/1914	SpVgg Fürth	-	-	
1914-1919	*No competition*	-	-	
1919/1920	1. FC Nürnberg	-	-	
1920/1921	1. FC Nürnberg	-	-	
1921/1922	*No champions (title declined by DFB)*	-	-	
1922/1923	Hamburger SV	-	-	
1923/1924	1. FC Nürnberg	-	-	
1924/1925	1. FC Nürnberg	-	-	
1925/1926	SpVgg Fürth	-	-	
1926/1927	1. FC Nürnberg	-	-	
1927/1928	Hamburger SV	-	-	
1928/1929	SpVgg Fürth	-	-	
1929/1930	Hertha BSC Berlin	-	-	
1930/1931	Hertha BSC Berlin	-	-	
1931/1932	FC Bayern München	-	-	
1932/1933	TSV Fortuna Düsseldorf	-	-	
1933/1934	FC Schalke 04 Gelsenkirchen	-	-	
1934/1935	FC Schalke 04 Gelsenkirchen	1. FC Nürnberg	-	
1935/1936	1. FC Nürnberg	VfB Leipzig	-	
1936/1937	FC Schalke 04 Gelsenkirchen	FC Schalke 04 Gelsenkirchen	-	
1937/1938	SV Hannover 96	SK Rapid Wien	-	
1938/1939	FC Schalke 04 Gelsenkirchen	1. FC Nürnberg	-	
1939/1940	FC Schalke 04 Gelsenkirchen	Dresdner SC	-	
1940/1941	SK Rapid Wien	Dresdner SC	-	
1941/1942	FC Schalke 04 Gelsenkirchen	TSV 1860 München	-	
1942/1943	Dresdner SC	1894 First Vienna FC	-	
1943/1944	Dresdner SC	*No competition*	-	
1944/1945	*No competition*	*No competition*	-	
1945/1946	VfB Stuttgart	*No competition*	-	
1946/1947	1. FC Nürnberg	*No competition*	-	
1947/1948	1. FC Nürnberg	*No competition*	-	
1948/1949	VfR Mannheim	*No competition*	-	
1949/1950	VfB Stuttgart	*No competition*	-	
1950/1951	1. FC Kaiserslautern	*No competition*	-	
1951/1952	VfB Stuttgart	*No competition*	-	
1952/1953	1. FC Kaiserslautern	Rot-Weiss Essen	-	
1953/1954	SV Hannover 96	VfB Stuttgart	-	
1954/1955	Rot-Weiss Essen	Karlsruher SC	-	
1955/1956	BV Borussia 09 Dortmund	Karlsruher SC	-	
1956/1957	BV Borussia 09 Dortmund	FC Bayern München	-	
1957/1958	FC Schalke 04 Gelsenkirchen	VfB Stuttgart	-	
1958/1959	Eintracht Frankfurt	TB Schwarz-Weiß Essen	-	
1959/1960	Hamburger SV	Borussia VfL Mönchengladbach	-	
1960/1961	1. FC Nürnberg	SV Werder Bremen	-	
1961/1962	1. FC Köln	1. FC Nürnberg	-	
1962/1963	BV Borussia 09 Dortmund	Hamburger SV	-	
1963/1964	1. FC Köln	TSV 1860 München	Uwe Seeler (Hamburger SV)	30
1964/1965	SV Werder Bremen	BV Borussia 09 Dortmund	Rudolf Brunnenmeier (TSV 1860 München)	24
1965/1966	TSV 1860 München	FC Bayern München	Lothar Emmerich (BV Borussia 09 Dortmund)	31
1966/1967	TSV Eintracht Braunschweig	FC Bayern München	Lothar Emmerich (BV Borussia 09 Dortmund) Gerhard Müller (FC Bayern München)	28
1967/1968	1. FC Nürnberg	1. FC Köln 1. FC Köln	Johannes Löhr (1. FC Köln)	27

1968/1969	FC Bayern München	FC Bayern München	Gerhard Müller (FC Bayern München)	30
1969/1970	Borussia VfL Mönchengladbach	Kickers Offenbach FC	Gerhard Müller (FC Bayern München)	38
1970/1971	Borussia VfL Mönchengladbach	FC Bayern München	Lothar Kobluhn (SC Rot-Weiß Oberhausen)	24
1971/1972	FC Bayern München	FC Schalke 04 Gelsenkirchen	Gerhard Müller (FC Bayern München)	40
1972/1973	FC Bayern München	Borussia VfL Mönchengladbach	Gerhard Müller (FC Bayern München)	36
1973/1974	FC Bayern München	Eintracht Frankfurt	Gerhard Müller (FC Bayern München) Josef Heynckes (Borussia VfL Mönchengladbach)	30
1974/1975	Borussia VfL Mönchengladbach	Eintracht Frankfurt	Josef Heynckes (Borussia VfL Mönchengladbach)	27
1975/1976	Borussia VfL Mönchengladbach	Hamburger SV	Klaus Fischer (FC Schalke 04 Gelsenkirchen)	29
1976/1977	Borussia VfL Mönchengladbach	1. FC Köln	Dieter Müller (1. FC Köln)	34
1977/1978	1. FC Köln	1. FC Köln	Dieter Müller (1. FC Köln) Gerhard Müller (FC Bayern München)	24
1978/1979	Hamburger SV	TSV Fortuna Düsseldorf	Klaus Allofs (TSV TSV Fortuna Düsseldorf)	22
1979/1980	FC Bayern München	TSV Fortuna Düsseldorf	Karl-Heinz Rummenigge (FC Bayern München)	26
1980/1981	FC Bayern München	Eintracht Frankfurt	Karl-Heinz Rummenigge (FC Bayern München)	29
1981/1982	Hamburger SV	FC Bayern München	Horst Hrubesch (Hamburger SV)	27
1982/1983	Hamburger SV	1. FC Köln	Rudolf Völler (SV Werder Bremen)	23
1983/1984	VfB Stuttgart	FC Bayern München	Karl-Heinz Rummenigge (FC Bayern München)	26
1984/1985	FC Bayern München	FC Bayer 05 Uerdingen	Klaus Allofs (1. FC Köln)	26
1985/1986	FC Bayern München	FC Bayern München	Stefan Kuntz (VfL Bochum)	22
1986/1987	FC Bayern München	Hamburger SV	Uwe Rahn (Borussia VfL Mönchengladbach)	24
1987/1988	SV Werder Bremen	Eintracht Frankfurt	Jürgen Klinsmann (VfB Stuttgart)	19
1988/1989	FC Bayern München	BV Borussia 09 Dortmund	Thomas Allofs (1. FC Köln) Roland Wohlfarth (FC Bayern München)	17
1989/1990	FC Bayern München	1. FC Kaiserslautern	Jørn Andersen (NOR, Eintracht Frankfurt)	18
1990/1991	1. FC Kaiserslautern	SV Werder Bremen	Roland Wohlfarth (FC Bayern München)	21
1991/1992	VfB Stuttgart	SV Hannover 96	Fritz Walter (VfB Stuttgart)	22
1992/1993	SV Werder Bremen	TSV Bayer 04 Leverkusen	Ulf Kirsten (TSV Bayer 04 Leverkusen) Anthony Yeboah (GHA, Eintracht Frankfurt)	20
1993/1994	FC Bayern München	SV Werder Bremen	Stefan Kuntz (1. FC Kaiserslautern) Anthony Yeboah (GHA, Eintracht Frankfurt)	18
1994/1995	BV Borussia 09 Dortmund	Borussia VfL Mönchengladbach	Mario Basler (SV Werder Bremen) Heiko Herrlich (Borussia VfL Mönchengladbach)	20
1995/1996	BV Borussia 09 Dortmund	1. FC Kaiserslautern	Fredi Bobič (VfB Stuttgart)	17
1996/1997	FC Bayern München	VfB Stuttgart	Ulf Kirsten (TSV Bayer 04 Leverkusen)	22
1997/1998	1. FC Kaiserslautern	FC Bayern München	Ulf Kirsten (TSV Bayer 04 Leverkusen)	22
1998/1999	FC Bayern München	SV Werder Bremen	Michael Preetz (Hertha BSC Berlin)	23
1999/2000	FC Bayern München	FC Bayern München	Martin Max (TSV 1860 München)	19
2000/2001	FC Bayern München	FC Schalke 04 Gelsenkirchen	Sergej Barbarez (BIH, Hamburger SV) Ebbe Sand (DEN, FC Schalke 04 Gelsenkirchen)	22
2001/2002	BV Borussia 09 Dortmund	FC Schalke 04 Gelsenkirchen	Márcio Amoroso dos Santos (BRA, BV Borussia 09 Dortmund) Martin Max (TSV 1860 München)	18
2002/2003	FC Bayern München	FC Bayern München	Thomas Christiansen Tarín (DEN, VfL Bochum) Giovane Élber de Souza (BRA, FC Bayern München)	21
2003/2004	SV Werder Bremen	SV Werder Bremen	Aílton Gonçalves da Silva (BRA, SV Werder Bremen)	28
2004/2005	FC Bayern München	FC Bayern München	Marek Mintál (SVK, 1. FC Nürnberg)	24
2005/2006	FC Bayern München	FC Bayern München	Miroslav Klose (SV Werder Bremen)	25
2006/2007	VfB Stuttgart	1. FC Nürnberg	Theofanis Gekas (GRE, VfL Bochum)	20
2007/2008	FC Bayern München	FC Bayern München	Luca Toni Varchetta (ITA, FC Bayern München)	24
2008/2009	VfL Wolfsburg	SV Werder Bremen	Edinaldo Batista Libânio "Grafite" (BRA, VfL Wolfsburg)	28
2009/2010	FC Bayern München	FC Bayern München	Edin Džeko (BIH, VfL Wolfsburg)	22
2010/2011	BV Borussia 09 Dortmund	FC Schalke 04 Gelsenkirchen	Mario Gómez García (FC Bayern München)	28
2011/2012	BV Borussia 09 Dortmund	BV Borussia 09 Dortmund	Dirk Jan Klaas Huntelaar (NED, FC Schalke 04 Gelsenkirchen)	29
2012/2013	FC Bayern München	FC Bayern München	Stefan Kießling (TSV Bayer 04 Leverkusen)	25
2013/2014	FC Bayern München	FC Bayern München	Robert Lewandowski (POL, BV Borussia 09 Dortmund)	20
2014/2015	FC Bayern München	VfL Wolfsburg	Alexander Meier (Eintracht Frankfurt)	19
2015/2016	FC Bayern München	FC Bayern München	Robert Lewandowski (POL, FC Bayern München)	30
2016/2017	FC Bayern München	BV Borussia 09 Dortmund	Pierre-Emerick Emiliano François Aubameyang (GAB, BV Borussia 09 Dortmund)	31
2017/2018	FC Bayern München	Eintracht Frankfurt	Robert Lewandowski (POL, FC Bayern München)	29
2018/2019	FC Bayern München	FC Bayern München	Robert Lewandowski (POL, FC Bayern München)	22

Please note: the Bundesliga was introduced at the start of the 1963/1964 season.

NATIONAL CHAMPIONSHIP
Bundesliga 2018/2019
(24.08.2018 – 18.05.2019)

Results

Round 1 [24-26.08.2018]
Bayern München - 1899 Hoffenheim 3-1(1-0)
Hertha BSC - 1. FC Nürnberg 1-0(1-0)
Werder Bremen - Hannover 96 1-1(0-0)
SC Freiburg - Eintracht Frankfurt 0-2(0-1)
VfL Wolfsburg - Schalke 04 2-1(1-0)
Fortuna Düsseldorf - FC Augsburg 1-2(1-0)
Mönchengladbach – Bay. Leverkusen 2-0(0-0)
1. FSV Mainz 05 - VfB Stuttgart 1-0(0-0)
Borussia Dortmund - RB Leipzig 4-1(3-1)

Round 2 [31.08.-02.09.2018]
Hannover 96 - Borussia Dortmund 0-0
1899 Hoffenheim - SC Freiburg 3-1(0-1)
Bayer Leverkusen - VfL Wolfsburg 1-3(1-1)
Eintracht Frankfurt - Werder Bremen 1-2(0-1)
FC Augsburg - Mönchengladbach 1-1(1-0)
1. FC Nürnberg - 1. FSV Mainz 05 1-1(0-1)
VfB Stuttgart - Bayern München 0-3(0-1)
RB Leipzig - Fortuna Düsseldorf 1-1(0-0)
Schalke 04 - Hertha BSC 0-2(0-1)

Round 3 [14-16.09.2018]
Bor. Dortmund - Eintracht Frankfurt 3-1(1-0)
RB Leipzig - Hannover 96 3-2(2-1)
1. FSV Mainz 05 - FC Augsburg 2-1(0-0)
VfL Wolfsburg - Hertha BSC 2-2(0-0)
Fortuna Düsseldorf - Hoffenheim 2-1(1-0)
Bayern München - Bayer Leverkusen 3-1(2-1)
Mönchengladbach - Schalke 04 2-1(1-0)
Werder Bremen - 1. FC Nürnberg 1-1(1-0)
SC Freiburg - VfB Stuttgart 3-3(1-1)

Round 4 [21-22.09.2018]
VfB Stuttgart - Fortuna Düsseldorf 0-0
1899 Hoffenheim - Bor. Dortmund 1-1(1-0)
Hertha BSC - Mönchengladbach 4-2(2-1)
FC Augsburg - Werder Bremen 2-3(1-2)
VfL Wolfsburg - SC Freiburg 1-3(0-2)
1. FC Nürnberg - Hannover 96 2-0(0-0)
Schalke 04 - Bayern München 0-2(0-1)
Bayer Leverkusen - 1. FSV Mainz 05 1-0(0-0)
Eintracht Frankfurt - RB Leipzig 1-1(1-0)

Round 5 [25-26.09.2018]
Werder Bremen - Hertha BSC 3-1(2-0)
Bayern München - FC Augsburg 1-1(0-0)
Hannover 96 - 1899 Hoffenheim 1-3(0-1)
SC Freiburg - Schalke 04 1-0(0-0)
Fortuna Düsseldorf - B. Leverkusen 1-2(0-0)
Borussia Dortmund - 1. FC Nürnberg 7-0(2-0)
RB Leipzig - VfB Stuttgart 2-0(1-0)
Mönchengladbach - Eintracht Frankf. 3-1(0-0)
1. FSV Mainz 05 - VfL Wolfsburg 0-0

Round 6 [28-30.09.2018]
Hertha BSC - Bayern München 2-0(2-0)
Schalke 04 - 1. FSV Mainz 05 1-0(1-0)
1899 Hoffenheim - RB Leipzig 1-2(0-0)
VfB Stuttgart - Werder Bremen 2-1(1-0)
VfL Wolfsburg - Mönchengladbach 2-2(1-1)
1. FC Nürnberg - Fortuna Düsseldorf 3-0(1-0)
Bayer Leverkusen - Bor. Dortmund 2-4(2-0)
Eintracht Frankfurt - Hannover 96 4-1(2-0)
FC Augsburg - SC Freiburg 4-1(2-0)

Round 7 [05-07.10.2018]
Werder Bremen - VfL Wolfsburg 2-0(1-0)
Borussia Dortmund - FC Augsburg 4-3(0-1)
Hannover 96 - VfB Stuttgart 3-1(2-0)
1. FSV Mainz 05 - Hertha BSC 0-0
Fortuna Düsseldorf - Schalke 04 0-2(0-0)
Bayern München - Mönchengladbach 0-3(0-2)
SC Freiburg - Bayer Leverkusen 0-0
Hoffenheim - Eintracht Frankfurt 1-2(0-1)
RB Leipzig - 1. FC Nürnberg 6-0(4-0)

Round 8 [19-21.10.2018]
Eintracht Frankfurt - Fortuna Düssel. 7-1(3-0)
Bayer Leverkusen - Hannover 96 2-2(1-1)
VfB Stuttgart - Borussia Dortmund 0-4(0-3)
FC Augsburg - RB Leipzig 0-0
VfL Wolfsburg - Bayern München 1-3(0-1)
1. FC Nürnberg - 1899 Hoffenheim 1-3(1-0)
Schalke 04 - Werder Bremen 0-2(0-1)
Hertha BSC - SC Freiburg 1-1(1-1)
Mönchengladbach - 1. FSV Mainz 05 4-0(1-0)

Round 9 [26-28.10.2018]
SC Freiburg - Mönchengladbach 3-1(1-1)
Borussia Dortmund - Hertha BSC 2-2(1-1)
Hannover 96 - FC Augsburg 1-2(0-1)
1. FSV Mainz 05 - Bayern München 1-2(0-1)
Fortuna Düsseldorf - VfL Wolfsburg 0-3(0-1)
1899 Hoffenheim - VfB Stuttgart 4-0(0-0)
1. FC Nürnberg - Eintracht Frankfurt 1-1(0-0)
RB Leipzig - Schalke 04 0-0
Werder Bremen - Bayer Leverkusen 2-6(0-3)

Round 10 [02-04.11.2018]
VfB Stuttgart - Eintracht Frankfurt 0-3(0-2)
Bayern München - SC Freiburg 1-1(0-0)
Schalke 04 - Hannover 96 3-1(0-0)
Bayer Leverkusen - 1899 Hoffenheim 1-4(1-2)
FC Augsburg - 1. FC Nürnberg 2-2(1-0)
VfL Wolfsburg - Borussia Dortmund 0-1(0-1)
Hertha BSC - RB Leipzig 0-3(0-1)
Mönchengladbach - Fortuna Düssel. 3-0(0-0)
1. FSV Mainz 05 - Werder Bremen 2-1(1-0)

Round 11 [09-11.11.2018]
Hannover 96 - VfL Wolfsburg 2-1(1-0)
1899 Hoffenheim - FC Augsburg 2-1(0-0)
Werder Bremen - Mönchengladbach 1-3(0-1)
SC Freiburg - 1. FSV Mainz 05 1-3(0-2)
Fortuna Düsseldorf - Hertha BSC 4-1(0-0)
1. FC Nürnberg - VfB Stuttgart 0-2(0-0)
Bor. Dortmund - Bayern München 3-2(0-1)
RB Leipzig - Bayer Leverkusen 3-0(1-0)
Eintracht Frankfurt - Schalke 04 3-0(0-0)

Round 12 [23-25.11.2018]
Bayer Leverkusen - VfB Stuttgart 2-0(0-0)
Bayern München - Fortuna Düsseld. 3-3(2-1)
Hertha BSC - 1899 Hoffenheim 3-3(1-2)
FC Augsburg - Eintracht Frankfurt 1-3(0-1)
1. FSV Mainz 05 - Bor. Dortmund 1-2(0-0)
VfL Wolfsburg - RB Leipzig 1-0(0-0)
Schalke 04 - 1. FC Nürnberg 5-2(2-1)
SC Freiburg - Werder Bremen 1-1(1-0)
Mönchengladbach - Hannover 96 4-1(2-1)

Round 13 [30.11.-03.12.2018]
Fortuna Düsseld. - 1. FSV Mainz 05 0-1(0-0)
Borussia Dortmund - SC Freiburg 2-0(1-0)
VfB Stuttgart - FC Augsburg 1-0(1-0)
Werder Bremen - Bayern München 1-2(1-1)
Hannover 96 - Hertha BSC 0-2(0-1)
1899 Hoffenheim - Schalke 04 1-1(0-0)
RB Leipzig - Mönchengladbach 2-0(2-0)
Eintracht Frankfurt - VfL Wolfsburg 1-2(0-1)
1. FC Nürnberg - Bayer Leverkusen 1-1(0-1)

Round 14 [07-09.12.2018]
Werder Bremen - Fortuna Düsseldorf 3-1(1-1)
Bayern München - 1. FC Nürnberg 3-0(2-0)
Schalke 04 - Borussia Dortmund 1-2(0-1)
Bayer Leverkusen - FC Augsburg 1-0(0-0)
SC Freiburg - RB Leipzig 3-0(2-0)
VfL Wolfsburg - 1899 Hoffenheim 2-2(2-1)
Hertha BSC - Eintracht Frankfurt 1-0(1-0)
1. FSV Mainz 05 - Hannover 96 1-1(0-1)
Mönchengladbach - VfB Stuttgart 3-0(0-0)

Round 15 [14-16.12.2018]
1. FC Nürnberg - VfL Wolfsburg 0-2(0-0)
1899 Hoffenheim - Mönchengladbach 0-0
VfB Stuttgart - Hertha BSC 2-1(0-1)
FC Augsburg - Schalke 04 1-1(0-0)
Hannover 96 - Bayern München 0-4(0-2)
Fortuna Düsseldorf - SC Freiburg 2-0(0-0)
Borussia Dortmund - Werder Bremen 2-1(2-1)
RB Leipzig - 1. FSV Mainz 05 4-1(2-1)
Eintracht Frankfurt - B. Leverkusen 2-1(1-0)

Round 16 [18-19.12.2018]
Mönchengladbach - 1. FC Nürnberg 2-0(0-0)
Hertha BSC - FC Augsburg 2-2(2-2)
VfL Wolfsburg - VfB Stuttgart 2-0(2-0)
Fortuna Düsseldorf - Bor. Dortmund 2-1(1-0)
Schalke 04 - Bayer Leverkusen 1-2(1-2)
Bayern München - RB Leipzig 1-0(0-0)
Werder Bremen - 1899 Hoffenheim 1-1(0-1)
SC Freiburg - Hannover 96 1-1(1-1)
1. FSV Mainz 05 - Eintracht Frankf. 2-2(2-2)

Round 17 [21-23.12.2018]
Bor. Dortmund - Mönchengladbach 2-1(1-1)
Bayer Leverkusen - Hertha BSC 3-1(2-1)
RB Leipzig - Werder Bremen 3-2(2-0)
VfB Stuttgart - Schalke 04 1-3(0-1)
Hannover 96 - Fortuna Düsseldorf 0-1(0-0)
1. FC Nürnberg - SC Freiburg 0-1(0-1)
Eintracht Frankf. - Bayern München 0-3(0-1)
FC Augsburg - VfL Wolfsburg 2-3(0-2)
1899 Hoffenheim - 1. FSV Mainz 05 1-1(1-1)

Round 18 [18-20.01.2019]
1899 Hoffenheim - Bayern München 1-3(0-2)
Bay. Leverkusen - Mönchengladbach 0-1(0-1)
Hannover 96 - Werder Bremen 0-1(0-1)
Eintracht Frankfurt - SC Freiburg 3-1(3-0)
VfB Stuttgart - 1. FSV Mainz 05 2-3(0-2)
FC Augsburg - Fortuna Düsseldorf 1-2(0-1)
RB Leipzig - Borussia Dortmund 0-1(0-1)
1. FC Nürnberg - Hertha BSC 1-3(1-1)
Schalke 04 - VfL Wolfsburg 2-1(1-1)

Round 19 [25-27.01.2019]
Hertha BSC - Schalke 04 2-2(2-2)
SC Freiburg - 1899 Hoffenheim 2-4(1-1)
VfL Wolfsburg - Bayer Leverkusen 0-3(0-1)
Mönchengladbach - FC Augsburg 2-0(0-0)
Borussia Dortmund - Hannover 96 5-1(1-0)
1. FSV Mainz 05 - 1. FC Nürnberg 2-1(1-1)
Werder Bremen - Eintracht Frankfurt 2-2(1-1)
Bayern München - VfB Stuttgart 4-1(1-1)
Fortuna Düsseldorf - RB Leipzig 0-4(0-3)

Round 20 [01-03.02.2019]
Hannover 96 - RB Leipzig 0-3(0-1)
Eintracht Frankfurt - Bor. Dortmund 1-1(1-1)
1. FC Nürnberg - Werder Bremen 1-1(0-0)
Hertha BSC - VfL Wolfsburg 0-1(0-0)
Hoffenheim - Fortuna Düsseldorf 1-1(1-0)
Bayer Leverkusen - Bayern München 3-1(0-1)
Schalke 04 - Mönchengladbach 0-2(0-0)
FC Augsburg - 1. FSV Mainz 05 3-0(2-0)
VfB Stuttgart - SC Freiburg 2-2(0-1)

Round 21 [08-10.02.2019]
1. FSV Mainz 05 - Bayer Leverkusen 1-5(1-4)
Borussia Dortmund - Hoffenheim 3-3(2-0)
RB Leipzig - Eintracht Frankfurt 0-0
Mönchengladbach - Hertha BSC 0-3(0-1)
SC Freiburg - VfL Wolfsburg 3-3(1-1)
Hannover 96 - 1. FC Nürnberg 2-0(1-0)
Bayern München - Schalke 04 3-1(2-1)
Werder Bremen - FC Augsburg 4-0(3-0)
Fortuna Düsseldorf - VfB Stuttgart 3-0(1-0)

Round 22 [15-18.02.2019]
FC Augsburg - Bayern München 2-3(2-2)
VfB Stuttgart - RB Leipzig 1-3(1-1)
1899 Hoffenheim - Hannover 96 3-0(2-0)
Schalke 04 - SC Freiburg 0-0
VfL Wolfsburg - 1. FSV Mainz 05 3-0(1-0)
Hertha BSC - Werder Bremen 1-1(1-0)
Eintracht Frankf. - Mönchengladbach 1-1(1-0)
B. Leverkusen - Fortuna Düsseldorf 2-0(1-0)
1. FC Nürnberg - Borussia Dortmund 0-0

Round 23 [22-25.02.2019]
Werder Bremen - VfB Stuttgart 1-1(1-1)
1. FSV Mainz 05 - Schalke 04 3-0(1-0)
Bayern München - Hertha BSC 1-0(0-0)
SC Freiburg - FC Augsburg 5-1(3-0)
Mönchengladbach - VfL Wolfsburg 0-3(0-1)
Fortuna Düsseldorf - 1. FC Nürnberg 2-1(0-1)
Hannover 96 - Eintracht Frankfurt 0-3(0-0)
Bor. Dortmund - Bayer Leverkusen 3-2(2-1)
RB Leipzig - 1899 Hoffenheim 1-1(0-1)

Round 24 [01-03.03.2019]
FC Augsburg - Borussia Dortmund 2-1(1-0)
Eintracht Frankfurt - Hoffenheim 3-2(1-1)
1. FC Nürnberg - RB Leipzig 0-1(0-1)
Bayer Leverkusen - SC Freiburg 2-0(1-0)
Hertha BSC - 1. FSV Mainz 05 2-1(0-0)
Schalke 04 - Fortuna Düsseldorf 0-4(0-1)
Mönchengladbach - Bayern München 1-5(1-2)
VfB Stuttgart - Hannover 96 5-1(3-0)
VfL Wolfsburg - Werder Bremen 1-1(0-0)

Round 25 [08-11.03.2019]
Werder Bremen - Schalke 04 4-2(1-1)
Borussia Dortmund - VfB Stuttgart 3-1(0-0)
SC Freiburg - Hertha BSC 2-1(1-0)
RB Leipzig - FC Augsburg 0-0
Bayern München - VfL Wolfsburg 6-0(2-0)
1. FSV Mainz 05 - Mönchengladbach 0-1(0-0)
1899 Hoffenheim - 1. FC Nürnberg 2-1(1-0)
Hannover 96 - Bayer Leverkusen 2-3(0-2)
Fortuna Düsseldorf - Eintracht Frank. 0-3(0-0)

Round 26 [15-17.03.2019]
Mönchengladbach - SC Freiburg 1-1(1-1)
VfB Stuttgart - 1899 Hoffenheim 1-1(0-1)
Schalke 04 - RB Leipzig 0-1(0-1)
FC Augsburg - Hannover 96 3-1(0-1)
VfL Wolfsburg - Fortuna Düsseldorf 5-2(1-1)
Hertha BSC - Borussia Dortmund 2-3(2-1)
Bayer Leverkusen - Werder Bremen 1-3(0-2)
Eintracht Frankfurt - 1. FC Nürnberg 1-0(1-0)
Bayern München - 1. FSV Mainz 05 6-0(3-0)

Round 27 [29-31.03.2019]
1899 Hoffenheim - Bayer Leverkusen 4-1(1-1)
SC Freiburg - Bayern München 1-1(1-1)
Fortuna Düsseld. - Mönchengladbach 3-1(3-0)
1. FC Nürnberg - FC Augsburg 3-0(0-0)
Werder Bremen - 1. FSV Mainz 05 3-1(2-0)
Borussia Dortmund - VfL Wolfsburg 2-0(0-0)
RB Leipzig - Hertha BSC 5-0(2-0)
Hannover 96 - Schalke 04 0-1(0-1)
Eintracht Frankfurt - VfB Stuttgart 3-0(1-0)

Round 28 [05-07.04.2019]
1. FSV Mainz 05 - SC Freiburg 5-0(3-0)
Bayer Leverkusen - RB Leipzig 2-4(2-1)
Schalke 04 - Eintracht Frankfurt 1-2(1-1)
VfL Wolfsburg - Hannover 96 3-1(1-1)
Hertha BSC - Fortuna Düsseldorf 1-2(1-1)
VfB Stuttgart - 1. FC Nürnberg 1-1(0-1)
Bayern München - Bor. Dortmund 5-0(4-0)
FC Augsburg - 1899 Hoffenheim 0-4(0-1)
Mönchengladbach - Werder Bremen 1-1(0-0)

Round 29 [12-14.04.2019]
1. FC Nürnberg - Schalke 04 1-1(0-0)
VfB Stuttgart - Bayer Leverkusen 0-1(0-0)
Hannover 96 - Mönchengladbach 0-1(0-0)
Werder Bremen - SC Freiburg 2-1(0-0)
RB Leipzig - VfL Wolfsburg 2-0(2-0)
Bor. Dortmund - 1. FSV Mainz 05 2-1(2-0)
1899 Hoffenheim - Hertha BSC 2-0(1-0)
Fortuna Düsseld. - Bayern München 1-4(0-2)
Eintracht Frankfurt - FC Augsburg 1-3(1-2)

Round 30 [20-22.04.2019]
FC Augsburg - VfB Stuttgart 6-0(3-0)
Bayern München - Werder Bremen 1-0(0-0)
1. FSV Mainz 05 - Fortuna Düsseld. 3-1(1-1)
Bayer Leverkusen - 1. FC Nürnberg 2-0(0-0)
Mönchengladbach - RB Leipzig 1-2(0-1)
Schalke 04 - 1899 Hoffenheim 2-5(0-2)
SC Freiburg - Borussia Dortmund 0-4(0-1)
Hertha BSC - Hannover 96 0-0
VfL Wolfsburg - Eintracht Frankfurt 1-1(0-0)

Round 31 [26-28.04.2019]
FC Augsburg - Bayer Leverkusen 1-4(1-1)
Borussia Dortmund - Schalke 04 2-4(1-2)
Eintracht Frankfurt - Hertha BSC 0-0
Fortuna Düsseldorf - Werder Bremen 4-1(2-1)
RB Leipzig - SC Freiburg 2-1(1-0)
Hannover 96 - 1. FSV Mainz 05 1-0(0-0)
VfB Stuttgart - Mönchengladbach 1-0(0-0)
1899 Hoffenheim - VfL Wolfsburg 1-4(1-1)
1. FC Nürnberg - Bayern München 1-1(0-0)

Round 32 [03-05.05.2019]
1. FSV Mainz 05 - RB Leipzig 3-3(1-2)
Mönchengladbach - Hoffenheim 2-2(0-1)
Hertha BSC - VfB Stuttgart 3-1(2-0)
Bayern München - Hannover 96 3-1(2-0)
VfL Wolfsburg - 1. FC Nürnberg 2-0(1-0)
Werder Bremen - Borussia Dortmund 2-2(0-2)
Schalke 04 - FC Augsburg 0-0
SC Freiburg - Fortuna Düsseldorf 1-1(1-1)
B. Leverkusen - Eintracht Frankfurt 6-1(6-1)

Round 33 [11-12.05.2019]
RB Leipzig - Bayern München 0-0
Bayer Leverkusen - Schalke 04 1-1(1-0)
1. FC Nürnberg - Mönchengladbach 0-4(0-0)
FC Augsburg - Hertha BSC 3-4(1-0)
1899 Hoffenheim - Werder Bremen 0-1(0-1)
Hannover 96 - SC Freiburg 3-0(1-0)
VfB Stuttgart - VfL Wolfsburg 3-0(1-0)
Bor. Dortmund - Fortuna Düsseldorf 3-2(1-0)
Eintracht Frankf. - 1. FSV Mainz 05 0-2(0-0)

Round 34 [18.05.2019]
1. FSV Mainz 05 - 1899 Hoffenheim 4-2(0-2)
Mönchengladbach - Bor. Dortmund 0-2(0-1)
Hertha BSC - Bayer Leverkusen 1-5(1-2)
Werder Bremen - RB Leipzig 2-1(1-0)
Schalke 04 - VfB Stuttgart 0-0
Bayern München - Eintracht Frankf. 5-1(1-0)
VfL Wolfsburg - FC Augsburg 8-1(3-0)
Fortuna Düsseldorf - Hannover 96 2-1(0-0)
SC Freiburg - 1. FC Nürnberg 5-1(2-0)

Final Standings							
1. **FC Bayern München**	34	24	6	4	88 - 32	78
2. BV Borussia 09 Dortmund	34	23	7	4	81 - 44	76
3. RasenBallsport Leipzig	34	19	9	6	63 - 29	66
4. TSV Bayer 04 Leverkusen	34	18	4	12	69 - 52	58
5. Borussia VfL Mönchengladbach	34	16	7	11	55 - 42	55
6. VfL Wolfsburg	34	16	7	11	62 - 50	55
7. Eintracht Frankfurt	34	15	9	10	60 - 48	54
8. SV Werder Bremen	34	14	11	9	58 - 49	53
9. TSG 1899 Hoffenheim	34	13	12	9	70 - 52	51
10. TSV Fortuna Düsseldorf	34	13	5	16	49 - 65	44
11. Hertha BSC Berlin	34	11	10	13	49 - 57	43
12. 1. FSV Mainz 05	34	12	7	15	46 - 57	43
13. SC Freiburg	34	8	12	14	46 - 61	36
14. FC Schalke 04 Gelsenkirchen	34	8	9	17	37 - 55	33
15. FC Augsburg	34	8	8	18	51 - 71	32
16. VfB Stuttgart (*Relegation Play-offs*)	34	7	7	20	32 - 70	28
17. SV Hannover 96 (*Relegated*)	34	5	6	23	31 - 71	21
18. 1. FC Nürnberg (*Relegated*)	34	3	10	21	26 - 68	19

Top goalscorers:

22 Robert Lewandowski (POL) *FC Bayern München*

18 Francisco "Paco" Alcácer García (ESP) *BV Borussia 09 Dortmund*

17 Kai Havertz *TSV Bayer 04 Leverkusen*

17 Luka Jović (SRB) *Eintracht Frankfurt*

17 Andrej Kramarić (CRO) *1899 Hoffenheim*

17 Marco Reus *BV Borussia 09 Dortmund*

17 Wout Weghorst (NED) *VfL Wolfsburg*

Relegation Play-offs

VfB Stuttgart – 1.FC Union Berlin	2-2(1-1)	0-0

1.FC Union Berlin promoted for the Bundesliga 2019/2020.

NATIONAL CUP
DFB Pokal Final 2018/2019

First Round [17-20.08.2018]

SV Wehen Wiesbaden - FC St. Pauli Hamburg	3-2(1-0,1-1)	1. FC Lok Stendal - DSC Arminia Bielefeld	0-5(0-1)
1. FC Magdeburg - SV Darmstadt 98	0-1(0-1)	TSV Steinbach Haiger - FC Augsburg	1-2(0-1)
1. FC Schweinfurt 05 - FC Schalke 04 Gelsenkirchen	0-2(0-1)	Rot-Weiß Koblenz - TSV Fortuna Düsseldorf	0-5(0-4)
SV Linx - 1. FC Nürnberg	1-2(1-1)	Weiche Flensburg 08 - VfL Bochum	1-0(1-0)
SV Rödinghausen - SG Dynamo Dresden	3-2(2-2,2-2)	BSG Chemie Leipzig – SSV Jahn Regensburg	2-1(0-1)
SV 07 Elversberg - VfL Wolfsburg	0-1(0-0)	Berliner FC Dynamo - 1. FC Köln	1-9(1-4)
TuS Dassendorf - MSV Duisburg	0-1(0-1)	SSV Jeddeloh - 1. FC Heidenheim 1846	2-5(0-3)
VfR Wormatia 08 Worms - SV Werder Bremen	1-6(1-5)	FC Viktoria Köln - RasenBallsport Leipzig	1-3(1-0)
SV Drochtersen/Assel - FC Bayern München	0-1(0-0)	Karlsruher SC - Hannover 96	0-6(0-3)
1. FC Kaiserslautern - TSG 1899 Hoffenheim	1-6(1-3)	TSV 1860 München - SV Holstein Kiel	1-3(1-0)
1. CfR Pforzheim - TSV Bayer 04 Leverkusen	0-1(0-1)	FC Carl Zeiss Jena - 1. FC Union Berlin	2-4(2-3)
SSV Ulm 1846 - Eintracht Frankfurt	2-1(0-0)	BSC Hastedt - Borussia VfL Mönchengladbach	1-11(0-6)
TuS Erndtebrück - Hamburger SV	3-5(1-2)	SC Paderborn 07 - FC Ingolstadt 04	2-1(2-0)
Rot-Weiß Oberhausen - SV Sandhausen	0-6(0-2)	FC Energie Cottbus - SC Freiburg	2-2 aet; 3-5 pen
Erzgebirge Aue - 1. FSV Mainz 05	1-3(0-1)	TSV Eintracht Braunschweig - Hertha BSC Berlin	1-2(0-1)
FC Hansa Rostock - VfB Stuttgart	2-0(1-0)	SpVgg Greuther Fürth - BV Borussia 09 Dortmund	1-2(0-0,1-1)

Second Round [30-31.10.2018]

BSG Chemie Leipzig - SC Paderborn 07	0-3(0-2)	FC Hansa Rostock - 1. FC Nürnberg	2-2 aet; 2-4 pen
SSV Ulm 1846 - TSV Fortuna Düsseldorf	1-5(1-4)	Weiche Flensburg 08 - SV Werder Bremen	1-5(1-3)
Hannover 96 - VfL Wolfsburg	0-2(0-1)	1. FC Köln - FC Schalke 04 Gelsenkirchen	1-1 aet; 5-6 pen
SV Darmstadt 98 - Hertha BSC Berlin	0-2(0-0)	BV Borussia 09 Dortmund - 1. FC Union Berlin	3-2(1-0,2-2)
SV Wehen Wiesbaden - Hamburger SV	0-3(0-1)	SV Holstein Kiel - SC Freiburg	2-1(1-1)
SV Rödinghausen - FC Bayern München	1-2(0-2)	DSC Arminia Bielefeld - MSV Duisburg	0-3(0-3)
1. FC Heidenheim 1846 - SV Sandhausen	3-0(2-0)	RasenBallsport Leipzig - TSG 1899 Hoffenheim	2-0(0-0)
FC Augsburg - 1. FSV Mainz 05	3-2(1-2,2-2)	Borussia Mönchengladbach - Bayer 04 Leverkusen	0-5(0-2)

Third Round [05-06.02.2019]

Hamburger SV - 1. FC Nürnberg	1-0(0-0)	SV Holstein Kiel - FC Augsburg	0-1(0-0)
1. FC Heidenheim 1846 - TSV Bayer 04 Leverkusen	2-1(0-1)	RasenBallsport Leipzig - VfL Wolfsburg	1-0(1-0)
MSV Duisburg - SC Paderborn 07	1-3(0-0)	Schalke 04 Gelsenkirchen - TSV Fortuna Düsseldorf	4-1(1-0)
BV Borussia 09 Dortmund - SV Werder Bremen	3-3 aet; 2-4 pen	Hertha BSC Berlin - FC Bayern München	2-3(1-1,2-2)

Quarter-Finals [02-03.04.2019]

SC Paderborn 07 - Hamburger SV	0-2(0-0)	FC Bayern München - 1. FC Heidenheim 1846	5-4(1-2)
FC Augsburg - RasenBallsport Leipzig	1-2(0-0,1-1)	FC Schalke 04 Gelsenkirchen - SV Werder Bremen	0-2(0-0)

Semi-Finals [23-24.04.2019]

Hamburger SV - RasenBallsport Leipzig	1-3(1-1)	SV Werder Bremen - FC Bayern München	2-3(0-1)

Final

25.05.2019; Olympiastadion, Berlin; Referee: FC Bayern München; Attendance: 74,322

FC Bayern München - RasenBallsport Leipzig **3-0(1-0)**

Bayern München: Manuel Peter Neuer (Cap), Joshua Walter Kimmich, Niklas Süle, Mats Julian Hummels, David Olatukunbo Alaba, Javier Martínez Aginaga „Javi Martínez" (65.Corentin Tolisso), Thiago Alcântara do Nascimento, Thomas Müller, Serge David Gnabry (73.Arjen Robben), Robert Lewandowski, Kingsley Coman (87.Franck Ribéry). Trainer: Niko Kovač (Croatia).

RB Leipzig: Péter Gulácsi, Lukas Manuel Klostermann, Ibrahima (82.Konaté Amadou Haïdara), Willi Orban (Cap) (70.Dayotchanculle Upamecano), Marcel Halstenberg, Tyler Shaan Adams (65.Konrad Laimer), Marcel Sabitzer, Kevin Kampl, Emil Forsberg, Yussuf Yurary Poulsen, Timo Werner. Trainer: Ralf Rangnick.

Goals: 1-0 Robert Lewandowski (29), 2-0 Kingsley Coman (78), 3-0 Robert Lewandowski (85).

THE CLUBS 2018/2019

Fußball-Club Augsburg 1907

Founded: 08.08.1907
Stadium: WWK Arena, Augsburg (30,660)

Goalkeepers:	DOB	M	(s)	G
Fabian Giefer	17.05.1990	4		
Gregor Kobel (SUI)	06.12.1997	16		
Andreas Luthe	10.03.1987	14	(1)	
Defenders:	**DOB**	**M**	**(s)**	**G**
Simon Asta	25.01.2001	1		
Jan-Ingwer Callsen-Bracker	23.09.1984		(1)	
Kevin Danso (AUT)	19.09.1998	13	(5)	1
Raphael Framberger	06.09.1995	6	(1)	
Jeffrey Gouweleeuw (NED)	10.07.1991	24	(1)	
Martin Hinteregger (AUT)	07.09.1992	18		2
Christoph Janker	14.02.1985	1	(3)	
Philipp Max	30.09.1993	30		4
Reece Joel Oxford (ENG)	16.12.1998	6	(2)	
Kostas Stafylidis (GRE)	02.12.1993	11	(1)	
Jozo Stanić	06.04.1999		(1)	
Midfielders:	**DOB**	**M**	**(s)**	**G**
Daniel Baier	18.05.1984	33		
Caiuby Francisco da Silva (BRA)	14.07.1988	10	(4)	1
Felix Götze	11.02.1998		(6)	1
André Hahn	13.08.1990	21	(7)	4
Fredrik Jensen (FIN)	09.09.1997	2	(4)	
Rani Khedira	27.01.1994	30		4
Koo Ja-Cheol (KOR)	27.02.1989	19	(7)	2
Jan Morávek (CZE)	01.11.1989	7	(6)	
Jonathan Schmid (FRA)	26.06.1990	28		3
Georg Teigl (AUT)	09.02.1991	2	(4)	
Forwards:	**DOB**	**M**	**(s)**	**G**
Sergio Duvan Cordóva Lezama (VEN)	09.07.1997	3	(17)	3
Alfreð Finnbogason (ISL)	01.02.1989	17	(1)	10
Michael Gregoritsch (AUT)	18.04.1994	28	(4)	6
Ji Dong-Won (KOR)	28.05.1991	10	(4)	4
Marco Richter	24.11.1997	17	(8)	5
Julian Schieber	13.02.1989	3	(6)	
Trainer:	**DOB**	**M**		
Manuel Baum	30.08.1979	28		
Martin Schmidt (SUI)	12.04.1967	6		

Bayer 04 Leverkusen Fußball GmbH

Founded: 01.07.1904
Stadium: BayArena, Leverkusen (30,210)

Goalkeepers:	DOB	M	(s)	G
Lukáš Hrádecký (FIN)	24.11.1989	32		
Ramazan Özcan (AUT)	28.06.1984	2		
Defenders:	**DOB**	**M**	**(s)**	**G**
Sven Bender	27.04.1989	25	(2)	
Aleksandar Dragović (AUT)	06.03.1991	13	(5)	2
Benjamin Henrichs	23.02.1997	1		
Tin Jedvaj (CRO)	28.11.1995	13	(3)	
Jonathan Glao Tah	11.02.1996	33		3
Wendell (BRA)	20.07.1993	25	(3)	2
Midfielders:	**DOB**	**M**	**(s)**	**G**
Charles Mariano Aránguiz Sandoval (CHI)	17.04.1989	22	(2)	2
Leon Bailey Butler (JAM)	09.08.1997	21	(8)	5
Julian Baumgartlinger (AUT)	02.01.1988	16	(5)	
Karim Bellarabi	08.04.1990	14	(5)	5
Lars Bender	27.04.1989	18	(2)	1
Julian Brandt	02.05.1996	30	(3)	7
Kai Havertz	11.06.1999	33	(1)	17
Dominik Kohr	31.01.1994	10	(8)	
Mitchell Weiser	21.04.1994	22	(8)	1
Forwards:	**DOB**	**M**	**(s)**	**G**
Lucas Nicolás Alario (ARG)	08.10.1992	11	(16)	9
Isaac Kiese Thelin (SWE)	24.06.1992	1	(5)	
Paulo Henrique Sampaio Filho „Paulinho" (BRA)	15.07.2000		(15)	
Kevin Volland	30.07.1992	32	(2)	14
Trainer:	**DOB**	**M**		
Heiko Herrlich	03.12.1971	17		
Peter Sylvester Bosz (NED) [23.12.2018]	21.11.1963	17		

Fußball-Club Bayern München

Founded: 27.02.1900
Stadium: Allianz Arena, München (75,000)

Goalkeepers:	**DOB**	**M**	**(s)**	**G**
Manuel Peter Neuer	27.03.1986	26		
Sven Ulreich	03.08.1988	8	(1)	
Defenders:	**DOB**	**M**	**(s)**	**G**
David Olatukunbo Alaba (AUT)	24.06.1992	29	(2)	3
Jérôme Agyenim Boateng	03.09.1988	19	(1)	
Mats Julian Hummels	16.12.1988	20	(1)	1
Javier Martínez Aginaga „Javi Martínez“ (ESP)	02.09.1988	16	(5)	3
Joshua Walter Kimmich	08.02.1995	34		2
Márcio Rafael Ferreira de Souza „Rafinha“ (BRA)	07.09.1985	9	(7)	1
Niklas Süle	03.09.1995	29	(2)	2
Midfielders:	**DOB**	**M**	**(s)**	**G**
Kingsley Coman (FRA)	13.06.1996	17	(4)	6
Leon Christoph Goretzka	06.02.1995	23	(7)	8
Renato Júnior Luz Sanches (POR)	18.08.1997	4	(13)	1
Franck Ribéry (FRA)	07.04.1983	10	(15)	6
James David Rodríguez Rubio (COL)	12.07.1991	13	(7)	7
Meritan Shabani	15.03.1999		(1)	
Thiago Alcântara do Nascimento (ESP)	11.04.1991	26	(4)	2
Corentin Tolisso (FRA)	03.08.1994	1	(1)	1
Forwards:	**DOB**	**M**	**(s)**	**G**
Alphonso Davies (CAN)	02.11.2000		(6)	1
Serge David Gnabry	14.07.1995	21	(9)	10
Jeong Woo-Yeong (KOR)	20.09.1999		(1)	
Robert Lewandowski (POL)	21.08.1988	33		22
Thomas Müller	13.09.1989	28	(4)	6
Arjen Robben (NED)	23.01.1984	7	(5)	4
Sandro Wagner	29.11.1987	1	(6)	
Trainer:	**DOB**	**M**		
Niko Kovač (CRO)	15.10.1971	34		

Ballspielverein Borussia 09 Dortmund

Founded: 19.12.1909
Stadium: Signal Iduna Park, Dortmund (81,360)

Goalkeepers:	**DOB**	**M**	**(s)**	**G**
Roman Bürki (SUI)	14.11.1990	32		
Marwin Hitz (SUI)	18.09.1987	2		
Defenders:	**DOB**	**M**	**(s)**	**G**
Manuel Akanji (SUI)	19.07.1995	25		1
Abdou Diallo (FRA)	04.05.1996	27	(1)	1
Achraf Hakimi (MAR)	04.11.1998	19	(2)	2
Łukasz Piszczek (POL)	03.06.1985	20		1
Marcel Schmelzer	22.01.1988	6	(3)	
Ömer Toprak (TUR)	21.07.1989	1	(8)	
Dan-Axel Zagadou (FRA)	03.06.1999	15	(2)	2
Midfielders:	**DOB**	**M**	**(s)**	**G**
Mahmoud Dahoud	01.01.1996	7	(7)	1
Thomas Joseph Delaney (DEN)	03.09.1991	27	(3)	3
Mario Götze	03.06.1992	19	(7)	7
Raphaël Adelino José Guerreiro (POR)	22.12.1993	17	(6)	2
Shinji Kagawa (JPN)	17.03.1989	1	(1)	
Julian Weigl	08.09.1995	16	(2)	1
Axel Laurent Angel Lambert Witsel (BEL)	12.01.1989	32	(1)	4
Forwards:	**DOB**	**M**	**(s)**	**G**
Jacob Bruun Larsen (DEN)	19.09.1998	16	(8)	2
Francisco „Paco“ Alcácer García (ESP)	30.08.1993	11	(15)	18
Maximilian Philipp	01.03.1994	9	(9)	1
Christian Pulisic (USA)	18.09.1998	9	(11)	4
Marco Reus	31.05.1989	27		17
Jadon Malik Sancho (ENG)	25.03.2000	26	(8)	12
Marius Wolf	27.05.1995	10	(6)	1
Trainer:	**DOB**	**M**		
Lucien Favre (SUI)	02.11.1957	34		

Borussia Verein für Leibesübungen 1900 Mönchengladbach

Founded: 01.08.1900
Stadium: Borussia-Park, Mönchengladbach (54,014)

Goalkeepers:	**DOB**	**M**	**(s)**	**G**
Yann Sommer (SUI)	17.12.1988	34		
Defenders:	**DOB**	**M**	**(s)**	**G**
Jordan Beyer	19.05.2000	8	(1)	
Nico Elvedi (SUI)	30.09.1996	30		2
Matthias Lukas Ginter	19.01.1994	27		2
Tony Jantschke	07.04.1990	10	(4)	
Michael Lang (SUI)	08.02.1991	15	(2)	1
Oscar Wendt (SWE)	24.10.1985	30	(2)	1
Midfielders:	**DOB**	**M**	**(s)**	**G**
László Bénes (SVK)	09.09.1997		(1)	
Mickaël Cuisance (FRA)	16.08.1999	1	(10)	
Patrick Herrmann	12.02.1991	10	(14)	3
Jonas Hofmann	14.07.1992	21	(6)	5
Fabian Marco Johnson (USA)	11.12.1987	11	(7)	1
Christoph Kramer	19.02.1991	13	(5)	2
Florian Neuhaus	16.03.1997	25	(7)	3
Tobias Strobl	12.05.1990	26	(3)	
Ibrahima Traoré (GUI)	21.04.1988	5	(11)	
Denis Zakaria (SUI)	20.11.1996	21	(10)	4
Forwards:	**DOB**	**M**	**(s)**	**G**
Josip Drmić (SUI)	08.08.1992	2	(3)	2
Thorgan Hazard (BEL)	29.03.1993	33		10
Alassane Pléa (FRA)	10.03.1993	28	(6)	12
Raffael Caetano de Araújo (BRA)	28.03.1985	5	(8)	2
Lars Stindl	26.08.1988	19	(2)	3
Trainer:	**DOB**	**M**		
Dieter Hecking	12.09.1964	34		

Eintracht Frankfurt

Founded: 08.03.1899
Stadium: Commerzbank-Arena, Frankfurt (51,500)

Goalkeepers:	DOB	M	(s)	G
Frederik Riis Rønnow (DEN)	04.08.1992	1	(1)	
Kevin Trapp	08.07.1990	33		
Defenders:	**DOB**	**M**	**(s)**	**G**
David Ángel Abraham (ARG)	15.07.1986	17		
Timothy Chandler (USA)	29.03.1990		(1)	
Danny da Costa	13.07.1993	34		2
Simon Falette (GUI)	19.02.1992	7		
Martin Hinteregger (AUT)	07.09.1992	14		1
Evan N'Dicka (FRA)	20.08.1999	24	(3)	1
Marco Russ	04.08.1985	3	(2)	
Carlos Joel Salcedo Hernández (MEX)	29.09.1993	6		
Taleb Tawatha (ISR)	21.06.1992	1	(2)	
Almamy Touré (FRA)	28.04.1996	6	(1)	
Jetro Willems (NED)	30.03.1994	7	(16)	
Midfielders:	**DOB**	**M**	**(s)**	**G**
Allan Rodrigues de Souza (BRA)	03.03.1997	2	(2)	
Danny Blum	07.01.1991		(1)	
Jonathan de Guzmán (NED)	13.09.1987	17	(11)	3
Marco Jhonfai Fabián de la Mora (MEX)	21.07.1989	1		
Gélson da Conceição Tavares Fernandes (SUI)	02.09.1986	28		1
Mijat Gaćinović (SRB)	08.02.1995	16	(13)	
Makoto Hasebe (JPN)	18.01.1984	28		
Filip Kostić (SRB)	01.11.1992	33	(1)	6
Lucas Torró Marset (ESP)	19.07.1994	6	(2)	
Nicolai Müller	25.09.1987	3	(4)	2
Sebastian Rode	11.10.1990	12		
Marc Stendera	10.12.1995		(7)	
Forwards:	**DOB**	**M**	**(s)**	**G**
Gonçalo Mendes Paciência (POR)	01.08.1994	4	(7)	3
Sébastien Haller (FRA)	22.06.1994	23	(6)	15
Branimir Hrgota (SWE)	12.01.1993		(1)	
Luka Jović (SRB)	23.12.1997	25	(7)	17
Ante Rebić (CRO)	21.09.1993	23	(5)	9
Trainer:	**DOB**	**M**		
Adolf Hütter (AUT)	11.02.1970	34		

Düsseldorfer Turn- und Sportverein Fortuna 1895

Founded: 05.05.1895
Stadium: Merkur Spiel-Arena, Düsseldorf (54,600)

Goalkeepers:	DOB	M	(s)	G
Jaroslav Drobný (CZE)	18.10.1979	2		
Michael Rensing	14.05.1984	32		
Defenders:	**DOB**	**M**	**(s)**	**G**
Kaan Ayhan (TUR)	10.11.1994	28		4
Robin Bormuth	19.09.1995	6	(4)	
Niko Gießelmann	26.09.1991	29	(1)	
Marcin Kamiński (POL)	15.01.1992	27		
Markus Suttner (AUT)	16.04.1987	6		1
Jean Zimmer	06.12.1993	17	(1)	1
Midfielders:	**DOB**	**M**	**(s)**	**G**
Aymane Barkok	21.05.1998	4	(8)	
Adam Bodzek	07.09.1985	20	(1)	
Oliver Fink	06.06.1982	13	(5)	3
André Hoffmann	28.02.1993	11	(2)	
Davor Lovren (CRO)	03.10.1998		(2)	
Alfredo Morales (USA)	12.05.1990	16	(7)	1
Marcel Sobottka	25.04.1994	11	(3)	
Kevin Stöger (AUT)	27.08.1993	24	(1)	1
Takashi Usami (JPN)	06.05.1992	10	(9)	1
Matthias Zimmermann	16.06.1992	34		1
Forwards:	**DOB**	**M**	**(s)**	**G**
Marvin Ducksch	07.03.1994	8	(8)	1
Rouwen Hennings	28.08.1987	19	(10)	7
Kenan Karaman (TUR)	05.03.1994	9	(12)	3
Dawid Kownacki (POL)	14.03.1997	7	(3)	4
Dodi Lukebakio Ngandoli (BEL)	24.09.1997	22	(9)	10
Benito Raman (BEL)	07.11.1994	19	(11)	10
Trainer:	**DOB**	**M**		
Friedhelm Funkel	10.12.1953	34		

Sport-Club Freiburg

Founded: 1904
Stadium: Schwarzwald-Stadion, Freiburg (24,000)

Goalkeepers:	DOB	M	(s)	G
Mark Flekken (NED)	13.06.1993	1		
Alexander Schwolow	02.06.1992	33		
Defenders:	**DOB**	**M**	**(s)**	**G**
Manuel Gulde	12.02.1991	20	(1)	1
Christian Günter	28.02.1993	32		
Dominique Heintz	15.08.1993	34		1
Robin Koch	17.07.1996	21	(3)	1
Lukas Kübler	30.08.1992	15	(1)	
Philipp Lienhart (AUT)	11.07.1996	7	(7)	
Chima Okoroji (ENG)	19.04.1997	1	(1)	
Keven Schlotterbeck	28.04.1997	8	(1)	
Nico Schlotterbeck	01.12.1999	2	(2)	
Pascal Stenzel	20.03.1996	16	(5)	
Midfielders:	**DOB**	**M**	**(s)**	**G**
Amir Abrashi (ALB)	27.03.1990	9	(1)	
Mike Frantz	14.10.1986	29	(2)	2
Jérôme Gondorf	26.06.1988	13	(12)	2
Vincenzo Grifo (ITA)	07.04.1993	16		6
Janik Haberer	02.04.1994	26	(1)	1
Nicolas Höfler	09.03.1990	18		
Patrick Kammerbauer	11.02.1997		(1)	
Yoric Ravet (FRA)	12.09.1989		(4)	
Roland Sallai (HUN)	22.05.1997	5	(5)	2
Marco Terrazzino	15.04.1991	7	(6)	1
Forwards:	**DOB**	**M**	**(s)**	**G**
Christoph Daferner	12.01.1998		(1)	
Lucas Höler	10.07.1994	11	(15)	4
Tim Kleindienst	31.08.1995	2	(2)	
Florian Niederlechner	24.10.1990	12	(12)	4
Nils Petersen	06.12.1988	20	(4)	10
Luca Waldschmidt	19.05.1996	16	(14)	9
Trainer:	**DOB**	**M**		
Christian Streich	11.06.1965	34		

Hannoverscher Sportverein von 1896

Founded: 12.04.1896
Stadium: HDI-Arena, Hannover (49,000)

Goalkeepers:	**DOB**	**M**	**(s)**	**G**
Michael Esser	22.11.1987	32		
Samuel Şahin-Radlinger (AUT)	07.11.1992	1		
Philipp Tschauner	03.11.1985	1		
Defenders:	**DOB**	**M**	**(s)**	**G**
Kevin Akpoguma	19.04.1995	4		
Miiko Martín Albornoz Inola (CHI)	30.11.1990	19	(3)	1
Waldemar Anton	20.07.1996	34		1
Josip Elez (CRO)	25.04.1994	7	(3)	
Felipe Trevizan Martins (BRA)	15.05.1987	14	(3)	2
Julian Korb	21.03.1992	11	(1)	
Matthias Ostrzolek	05.06.1990	16	(2)	
Oliver Sorg	29.05.1990	18	(1)	
Kevin Wimmer (AUT)	15.11.1992	17	(5)	
Midfielders:	**DOB**	**M**	**(s)**	**G**
Marvin Bakalorz	13.09.1989	16	(9)	1
Tim Dierßen	15.01.1996		(1)	
Iver Fossum (NOR)	15.07.1996	5	(4)	
Genki Haraguchi (JPN)	09.05.1991	22	(6)	
Linton Maina	23.06.1999	17	(3)	1
Nicolai Müller	25.09.1987	11	(3)	3
Florent Muslija (KVX)	06.07.1998	6	(11)	2
Edgar Prib	15.12.1989	2	(2)	
Noah Sarenren Bazee	21.08.1996	3		
Pirmin Schwegler (SUI)	09.03.1987	25	(2)	
Walace Souza Silva (BRA)	04.04.1995	23	(3)	1
Forwards:	**DOB**	**M**	**(s)**	**G**
Takuma Asano (JPN)	10.11.1994	9	(4)	
Ihlas Bebou (TOG)	23.04.1994	12		4
Uffe Manich Bech (DEN)	13.01.1993		(2)	
Niclas Füllkrug	09.02.1993	13	(1)	2
Benjamin Hadžić (BIH)	04.03.1999		(3)	
Jonathas Cristian de Jesus Maurício (BRA)	06.03.1989	6	(4)	3
Sebastian Guerra Soto (USA)	28.07.2000		(3)	
Hendrik Weydandt	16.07.1995	18	(10)	6
Bobby Shou Wood (USA)	15.11.1992	12	(8)	3
Trainer:	**DOB**	**M**		
André Breitenreiter	02.10.1973	19		
Thomas Jens Uwe Doll [27.01.2019]	09.04.1966	15		

Hertha Berliner Sport-Club

Founded: Olympiastadion, Berlin (74,475)
Stadium: 25.07.1892

Goalkeepers:	**DOB**	**M**	**(s)**	**G**
Rune Jarstein (NOR)	29.09.1984	31		
Thomas Kraft	22.07.1988	3	(1)	
Defenders:	**DOB**	**M**	**(s)**	**G**
Florian Baak	18.03.1999		(1)	
Lukas Klünter	26.05.1996	7	(3)	
Derrick Luckassen (NED)	03.07.1995	2	(2)	
Maximilian Mittelstädt	18.03.1997	20	(5)	1
Peter Pekarík (SVK)	30.10.1986	2	(1)	
Marvin Plattenhardt	26.01.1992	22		1
Karim Rekik (NED)	02.12.1994	24		
Niklas Stark	14.04.1995	22		1
Jordan Torunarigha	07.08.1997	13	(1)	2
Midfielders:	**DOB**	**M**	**(s)**	**G**
Vladimír Darida (CZE)	08.08.1990	3	(7)	
Ondrej Duda (SVK)	05.12.1994	30	(2)	11
Marko Grujić (SRB)	13.04.1996	20	(2)	5
Valentino Lazaro (AUT)	24.03.1996	31		3
Fabian Lustenberger (SUI)	02.05.1988	24	(5)	
Arne Maier	08.01.1999	23	(1)	
Per Skjelbred (NOR)	16.06.1987	12	(4)	
Forwards:	**DOB**	**M**	**(s)**	**G**
Palko Dárdai	24.04.1999	1	(6)	
Javairô Dilrosun (NED)	22.06.1998	7	(10)	2
Vedad Ibišević (BIH)	06.08.1984	24	(4)	10
Dennis Jastrzembski	20.02.2000		(5)	
Salomon Kalou (CIV)	05.08.1985	27	(3)	8
Pascal Köpke	03.09.1995		(7)	
Mathew Allan Leckie (AUS)	04.02.1991	10	(8)	2
Davie Selke	20.01.1995	16	(14)	3
Trainer:	**DOB**	**M**		
Pál Dárdai (HUN)	16.03.1976	34		

Turn- und Sportgemeinschaft 1899 Hoffenheim

Founded: 01.07.1899
Stadium: Wirsol Rhein-Neckar-Arena, Sinsheim (30,150)

Goalkeepers:	**DOB**	**M**	**(s)**	**G**
Oliver Baumann	02.06.1990	33		
Gregor Kobel (SUI)	06.12.1997	1		
Defenders:	**DOB**	**M**	**(s)**	**G**
Kasim Adams (GHA)	22.06.1995	11	(2)	
Kevin Akpoguma	19.04.1995	5	(3)	
Alfons Amade	12.11.1999		(1)	
Ermin Bičakčić (BIH)	24.01.1990	20	(5)	1
Joshua Brenet (NED)	20.03.1994	10	(4)	2
Justin Hoogma (NED)	11.06.1998	1	(1)	
Benjamin Hübner	04.07.1989	9	(1)	
Pavel Kadeřábek (CZE)	25.04.1992	28	(1)	3
Stefan Posch (AUT)	14.05.1997	16	(1)	
Nico Schulz	01.04.1993	29	(1)	1
Midfielders:	**DOB**	**M**	**(s)**	**G**
Nadiem Amiri	27.10.1996	10	(3)	3
Christoph Baumgartner (AUT)	01.08.1999	1	(1)	
Leonardo Jesus Loureiro Bittencourt	19.12.1993	13	(8)	1
Kerem Demirbay	03.07.1993	24	(2)	4
Dennis Geiger	10.06.1998	2	(2)	
Vincenzo Grifo (ITA)	07.04.1993	3	(4)	1
Florian Grillitsch (AUT)	07.08.1995	27	(3)	
Håvard Nordtveit (NOR)	21.06.1990	4	(4)	
Lukas Rupp	08.01.1991		(1)	
Steven Zuber (SUI)	17.08.1991	6	(3)	
Forwards:	**DOB**	**M**	**(s)**	**G**
Ishak Belfodil (ALG)	15.01.1992	20	(8)	16
Joelinton Cassio Apolinário de Lira (BRA)	14.08.1996	25	(3)	7
Andrej Kramarić (CRO)	19.06.1991	28	(2)	17
Reiss Luke Nelson (ENG)	10.12.1999	5	(18)	7
David Otto	03.03.1999		(3)	
Ádám Szalai (HUN)	09.12.1987	15	(15)	6
Trainer:	**DOB**	**M**		
Julian Nagelsmann	23.07.1987	34		

RasenBallsport Leipzig

Founded: 19.05.2009
Stadium: Red Bull Arena, Leipzig (42,558)

Goalkeepers:	DOB	M	(s)	G
Péter Gulácsi (HUN)	06.05.1990	33		
Yvon Mvogo (SUI)	06.06.1994	1	(1)	
Defenders:	**DOB**	**M**	**(s)**	**G**
Marcel Halstenberg	27.09.1991	27	(1)	3
Lukas Manuel Klostermann	03.06.1996	22	(4)	5
Ibrahima Konaté (FRA)	25.05.1999	27	(1)	1
Nordi Mukiele Mulere (FRA)	01.11.1997	14	(5)	1
Willi Orban (HUN)	03.11.1992	23	(1)	4
Marcelo Josemir Saracchi Pintos (URU)	23.04.1998	7	(2)	
Dayotchanculle Upamecano (FRA)	27.10.1998	14	(1)	
Midfielders:	**DOB**	**M**	**(s)**	**G**
Tyler Shaan Adams (USA)	14.02.1999	8	(2)	
Armindo Tué Na Bagna „Bruma“ (POR)	24.10.1994	6	(8)	1
Diego Demme	21.11.1991	24	(2)	
Emil Forsberg (SWE)	23.10.1991	14	(6)	4
Amadou Haïdara (MLI)	31.01.1998	4	(5)	1
Stefan Ilsanker (AUT)	18.05.1989	10	(9)	
Kevin Kampl (SVN)	09.10.1990	25	(2)	2
Konrad Laimer (AUT)	27.05.1997	20	(9)	1
Marcel Sabitzer (AUT)	17.03.1994	26	(4)	4
Emile Smith-Rowe (ENG)	28.07.2000		(3)	
Forwards:	**DOB**	**M**	**(s)**	**G**
Jean-Kévin Augustin (FRA)	16.06.1997	4	(13)	3
Matheus Santos Carneiro da Cunha (BRA)	27.05.1999	9	(16)	2
Yussuf Yurary Poulsen (DEN)	15.06.1994	27	(4)	15
Timo Werner	06.03.1996	29	(1)	16
Trainer:	**DOB**	**M**		
Ralf Rangnick	29.06.1958	34		

1. Fußball- und Sportverein Mainz 05

Founded: 16.03.1905
Stadium: Opel Arena, Mainz (34,000)

Goalkeepers:	DOB	M	(s)	G
Florian Müller	13.11.1997	24		
Robin Zentner	28.10.1994	10		
Defenders:	**DOB**	**M**	**(s)**	**G**
Aarón Martín Caricol (ESP)	22.04.1997	32	(1)	
Stefan Bell	24.08.1991	25		
Daniel Brosinski	17.07.1988	26		3
Niko Bungert	24.10.1986	3	(4)	
Gaëtan Bussmann (FRA)	02.02.1991	1		
Giulio Donati (ITA)	05.02.1990	6	(3)	
Ahmet Gürleyen	26.04.1999		(1)	
Alexander Hack	08.09.1993	11	(3)	1
Philipp Mwene (AUT)	29.01.1994	2	(4)	
Moussa Niakhaté (FRA)	08.03.1996	32	(1)	1
Midfielders:	**DOB**	**M**	**(s)**	**G**
Ridle Baku	08.04.1998	10	(5)	
Leandro Barreiro (LUX)	03.01.2000	1		
Pablo Ezequiel de Blasis (ARG)	04.02.1988	1		
Jean-Philippe Gbamin (CIV)	25.09.1995	30	(1)	2
Gerrit Holtmann	25.03.1995	1	(3)	
Danny Latza	07.12.1989	22	(2)	
Pierre Malong (CMR)	26.07.1995	23	(6)	
Alexandru Iulian Maxim (ROU)	08.07.1990	3	(19)	1
Levin Öztunali	15.03.1996	11	(4)	
Robin Kwamina Quaison (SWE)	09.10.1993	25	(3)	7
Forwards:	**DOB**	**M**	**(s)**	**G**
Issah Abass (GHA)	26.09.1998		(1)	
Jean-Paul Boëtius (NED)	22.03.1994	25	(5)	4
Jonathan Burkardt	11.07.2000	4		
Jean-Philippe Mateta (FRA)	28.06.1997	29	(5)	14
Karim Onisiwo (AUT)	17.03.1992	11	(15)	7
Anthony Ujah (NGA)	14.10.1990	6	(16)	4
Trainer:	**DOB**	**M**		
Sandro Schwarz	17.10.1978	34		

1. Fußball-Club Nürnberg Verein für Leibesübungen

Founded: 04.05.1900
Stadium: “Max Morlock“ Stadion, Nürnberg (49,923)

Goalkeepers:	DOB	M	(s)	G
Fabian Bredlow	02.03.1995	12	(1)	
Christian Mathenia	31.03.1992	22		
Defenders:	**DOB**	**M**	**(s)**	**G**
Robert Bauer	09.04.1995	19	(3)	
Ewerton José Almeida Santos (BRA)	23.03.1989	15	(3)	
Kevin Goden	22.02.1999	3	(2)	
Tim Leibold	30.11.1993	32		
Georg Margreitter (AUT)	07.11.1988	22	(5)	2
Lukas Mühl	27.01.1997	31		1
Enrico Valentini (ITA)	20.02.1989	15		
Midfielders:	**DOB**	**M**	**(s)**	**G**
Hanno Behrens	26.03.1990	30		4
Patrick Erras	21.01.1995	13	(6)	
Alexander Fuchs	05.01.1997	8	(1)	1
Ivo Iličević (CRO)	14.11.1986		(3)	
Lukas Jäger (AUT)	12.02.1994		(2)	
Sebastian Kerk	17.04.1994	17	(4)	
Eduard Löwen	28.01.1997	17	(5)	3
Matheus Fellipe Costa Pereira (BRA)	05.05.1996	16	(3)	3
Ondřej Petrák (CZE)	11.03.1992	18	(4)	
Simon Rhein	18.05.1998	7	(1)	
Timothy Tillman	04.01.1999	1	(5)	
Forwards:	**DOB**	**M**	**(s)**	**G**
Mikael Ishak (SWE)	31.03.1993	22	(7)	4
Törles Knöll	13.09.1997	2	(14)	1
Yūya Kubo (JPN)	24.12.1993	15	(7)	1
Virgil Misidjan (NED)	24.07.1993	17	(6)	1
Federico Palacios-Martínez	09.04.1995	9	(8)	2
Edgar Nicaise Constant Salli (CMR)	17.08.1992	1	(2)	
Adam Zreľák (SVK)	05.05.1994	10	(4)	2
Trainer:	**DOB**	**M**		
Michael Köllner	29.12.1969	21		
Boris Schommers [12.02.2019]	19.01.1979	13		

Fußballclub Gelsenkirchen-Schalke 04

Founded: 04.05.1904
Stadium: Veltins-Arena, Gelsenkirchen (62,271)

Goalkeepers:	**DOB**	**M**	**(s)**	**G**
Ralf Fährmann	27.09.1988	16	(1)	
Alexander Nübel	30.09.1996	18		
Defenders:	**DOB**	**M**	**(s)**	**G**
Abdul Rahman Baba (GHA)	02.07.1994	2		
Jeffrey Kevin van Homoet Bruma (NED)	13.11.1991	7	(2)	
Jonas Carls	25.03.1997	1		
Hamza Mendyl (MAR)	18.10.1997	7	(2)	
Ronaldo Aparecido Rodrigues „Naldo“ (BRA)	10.09.1982	7		
Matija Nastasić (SRB)	28.03.1993	28		1
Bastian Oczipka	12.01.1989	21		1
Sascha Riether	23.03.1983		(1)	
Salif Sané (SEN)	25.08.1990	29	(1)	2
Benjamin Stambouli (FRA)	13.08.1990	20	(1)	
George Timotheou (AUS)	29.07.1997	1		
Midfielders:	**DOB**	**M**	**(s)**	**G**
Nabil Bentaleb (ALG)	24.11.1994	19	(6)	3
Nassim Boujellab	20.06.1999	4	(3)	
Daniel Caligiuri	15.01.1988	31		7
Amine Harit (MAR)	18.06.1997	12	(6)	1
Yevhen Konoplyanka (UKR)	29.09.1989	7	(6)	1
Omar Mascarell González (ESP)	02.02.1993	11	(3)	
Weston McKennie (USA)	28.08.1998	19	(5)	1
Sebastian Rudy	28.02.1990	17	(4)	
Alessandro Schöpf (AUT)	07.02.1994	11	(4)	1
Suat Serdar	11.04.1997	20	(6)	2
Forwards:	**DOB**	**M**	**(s)**	**G**
Guido Burgstaller (AUT)	24.04.1989	17	(7)	4
Franco Matías Di Santo (ARG)	07.04.1989	3	(1)	
Breel-Donald Embolo (SUI)	14.02.1997	15	(5)	5
Ahmed Kutucu (TUR)	01.03.2000	3	(10)	2
Rabbi Matondo (WAL)	09.09.2000	1	(6)	
Steven Skrzybski	18.11.1992	8	(4)	3
Cedric Teuchert	14.01.1997	2	(3)	
Mark Alexander Uth	24.08.1991	15	(5)	2
Haji Wright (USA)	27.03.1998	2	(5)	1
Trainer:	**DOB**	**M**		
Domenico Tedesco	12.09.1985	25		
Hubertus Jozef Margaretha "Huub" Stevens (NED) [14.03.2019]	29.11.1953	9		

Verein für Bewegungsspiele Stuttgart 1893

Founded: 09.09.1893
Stadium: Mercedes-Benz Arena, Stuttgart (60,449)

Goalkeepers:	**DOB**	**M**	**(s)**	**G**
Ron-Robert Zieler	12.02.1989	34		
Defenders:	**DOB**	**M**	**(s)**	**G**
Antonis Aidonis	22.05.2001	1	(1)	
Dennis Aogo	14.01.1987	13	(2)	
Holger Badstuber	13.03.1989	5	(5)	
Timo Baumgartl	04.03.1996	18		1
Andreas Beck	13.03.1987	21	(3)	
Emiliano Adrián Insúa (ARG)	07.01.1989	24	(3)	2
Ozan Kabak (TUR)	25.03.2000	15		3
Marc Oliver Kempf	28.01.1995	23		2
Pablo Carmine Maffeo Becerra (ESP)	12.07.1997	8		
Benjamin Pavard (FRA)	28.03.1996	29		
Borna Sosa (CRO)	21.01.1998	7	(5)	
Midfielders:	**DOB**	**M**	**(s)**	**G**
Santiago Lionel Ascacíbar (ARG)	25.02.1997	27		
Gonzalo Castro	11.06.1987	19	(6)	2
Daniel Didavi	21.02.1990	8	(12)	2
Christian Gentner	14.08.1985	24	(5)	
Berkay Özcan (TUR)	15.02.1998		(3)	
Hans Nunoo Sarpei (GHA)	22.08.1998		(2)	
Erik Thommy	20.08.1994	6	(13)	1
Steven Zuber (SUI)	17.08.1991	13		5
Forwards:	**DOB**	**M**	**(s)**	**G**
Chadrac Akolo Ababa (COD)	01.04.1995	5	(11)	
Leon Dajaku	12.04.2001		(2)	
Anastasios Donis (GRE)	29.08.1996	11	(13)	5
Alexander Esswein	25.03.1990	15	(2)	
Mario Gomez García	10.07.1985	25	(6)	7
Nicolás Iván González (ARG)	06.04.1998	23	(7)	2
Trainer:	**DOB**	**M**		
Tayfun Korkut (TUR)	02.04.1974	7		
Markus Weinzierl [09.10.2018]	28.12.1974	22		
Nico Willig [20.04.2019]	11.12.1980	5		

Sportverein Werder Bremen von 1899

Founded: 04.02.1899
Stadium: Weser-Stadion, Bremen (42,100)

Goalkeepers:	**DOB**	**M**	**(s)**	**G**
Stefanos Kapino (GRE)	18.03.1994		(1)	
Jiří Pavlenka (CZE)	14.04.1992	34		
Luca Plogmann	10.03.2000		(1)	
Defenders:	**DOB**	**M**	**(s)**	**G**
Hans Carl Ludwig Augustinsson (SWE)	21.04.1994	34		1
Marco Friedl (AUT)	16.03.1998	5	(2)	
Theodor Gebre Selassie (CZE)	24.12.1986	32		3
Sebastian Langkamp	15.01.1988	15	(6)	
Niklas Moisander (FIN)	29.09.1985	30		
Miloš Veljković (SRB)	26.09.1995	21	(2)	1
Midfielders:	**DOB**	**M**	**(s)**	**G**
Philipp Bargfrede	03.03.1989	13	(2)	
Fin Bartels	07.02.1987		(2)	
Maximilian Eggestein	08.12.1996	34		5
Florian Kainz (AUT)	24.10.1992	5	(3)	
Davy Klaassen (NED)	21.02.1993	33		5
Kevin Möhwald	03.07.1993	7	(16)	3
Nuri Şahin (TUR)	05.09.1988	19	(1)	1
Forwards:	**DOB**	**M**	**(s)**	**G**
Johannes Eggestein	08.05.1998	12	(11)	4
Martin Harnik (AUT)	10.06.1987	10	(8)	4
Aron Jóhannsson (USA)	10.11.1990		(1)	
Max Kruse	19.03.1988	32		11
Yuya Osako (JPN)	18.05.1990	15	(6)	3
Claudio Miguel Pizarro Bossio (PER)	03.10.1978	3	(23)	5
Milot Rashica (KVX)	28.06.1996	19	(7)	9
Joshua Thomas Sargent (USA)	20.02.2000	1	(9)	2
Trainer:	**DOB**	**M**		
Florian Kohfeldt	05.10.1982	34		

Verein für Leibesübungen Wolfsburg

Founded: 12.09.1945
Stadium: Volkswagen Arena, Wolfsburg (30,000)

Goalkeepers:	**DOB**	**M**	**(s)**	**G**
Koen Casteels (BEL)	25.06.1992	26		
Pavao Pervan (AUT)	13.11.1987	8	(1)	
Defenders:	**DOB**	**M**	**(s)**	**G**
John Anthony Brooks (USA)	28.01.1993	29		3
Gian-Luca Itter	05.01.1999	1	(1)	
Sebastian Jung	22.06.1990	1		
Robin Knoche	22.05.1992	31		3
Jérôme Roussillon (FRA)	06.01.1993	28		3
Marcel Tisserand (COD)	10.01.1993	10		1
Felix Uduokhai	09.09.1997	2	(9)	
Paul Johannes Gerardus Verhaegh (NED)	01.09.1983	2		
William de Asevedo Furtado (BRA)	03.04.1995	30	(1)	2
Midfielders:	**DOB**	**M**	**(s)**	**G**
Maximilian Arnold	27.05.1994	33		2
Jakub Błaszczykowski (POL)	14.12.1985		(1)	
Josip Brekalo (CRO)	23.06.1998	15	(10)	3
Ignacio Camacho Barnola (ESP)	04.05.1990	6		
Yannick Gerhardt	13.03.1994	28	(2)	2
Josuha Guilavogui (FRA)	19.09.1990	18	(1)	2
Felix Klaus	13.09.1992	5	(10)	1
Yunus Mallı (TUR)	24.02.1992	5	(16)	1
Elvis Rexhbeçaj	01.11.1997	13	(11)	2
Renato Steffen (SUI)	03.11.1991	18	(13)	5
John Yeboah	23.06.2000		(2)	
Forwards:	**DOB**	**M**	**(s)**	**G**
Daniel Ginczek	13.04.1991	12	(12)	6
Admir Mehmedi (SUI)	16.03.1991	20	(6)	6
Wout Weghorst (NED)	07.08.1992	33	(1)	17
Trainer:	**DOB**	**M**		
Bruno Labbadia	08.02.1966	34		

SECOND LEVEL
2. Bundesliga 2018/2019

1.	1. FC Köln (*Promoted*)	34	19	6	9	84	-	47	63
2.	SC Paderborn 07 (*Promoted*)	34	16	9	9	76	-	50	57
3.	1. FC Union Berlin (*Promotion Play-offs*)	34	14	15	5	54	-	33	57
4.	Hamburger SV	34	16	8	10	45	-	42	56
5.	1. FC Heidenheim	34	15	10	9	55	-	45	55
6.	SV Holstein Kiel	34	13	10	11	60	-	51	49
7.	DSC Arminia Bielefeld	34	13	10	11	52	-	50	49
8.	SSV Jahn Regensburg	34	12	13	9	55	-	54	49
9.	FC St. Pauli Hamburg	34	14	7	13	46	-	53	49
10.	SV Darmstadt 98	34	13	7	14	45	-	53	46
11.	VfL Bochum	34	11	11	12	49	-	50	44
12.	SG Dynamo Dresden	34	11	9	14	41	-	48	42
13.	SpVgg Greuther Fürth	34	10	12	12	37	-	56	42
14.	FC Erzgebirge Aue	34	11	7	16	43	-	47	40
15.	SV Sandhausen	34	9	11	14	45	-	52	38
16.	FC Ingolstadt 04 (*Relegation Play-offs*)	34	9	8	17	43	-	55	35
17.	1. FC Magdeburg (*Relegated*)	34	6	13	15	35	-	53	31
18.	MSV Duisburg (*Relegated*)	34	6	10	18	39	-	65	28

Relegation Play-offs

SV Wehen Wiersbaden - FC Ingolstadt 04	1-2(0-1)	3-2(3-1)

SV Wehen Wiersbaden promoted for the 2. Bundesliga 2019/2020.

NATIONAL TEAM

INTERNATIONAL MATCHES
(16.07.2018 – 15.07.2019)

06.09.2018	München	Germany - France	0-0	(UNL)
09.09.2018	Sinsheim	Germany - Peru	2-1(1-1)	(F)
13.10.2018	Amsterdam	Netherlands - Germany	3-0(1-0)	(UNL)
16.10.2018	Paris	France - Germany	2-1(0-1)	(UNL)
15.11.2018	Leipzig	Germany - Russia	3-0(3-0)	(F)
19.11.2018	Gelsenkirchen	Germany - Netherlands	2-2(2-0)	(UNL)
20.03.2019	Wolfsburg	Germany - Serbia	1-1(0-1)	(F)
24.03.2019	Amsterdam	Netherlands - Germany	2-3(0-2)	(ECQ)
08.06.2019	Borisov	Belarus - Germany	0-2(0-1)	(ECQ)
11.06.2019	Mainz	Germany - Estonia	8-0(5-0)	(ECQ)

06.09.2018 GERMANY - FRANCE 0-0 UEFA Nations League A, Group 1
Allianz Arena, München; Referee: Daniele Orsato (Italy); Attendance: 67,485
GER: Manuel Peter Neuer (Cap), Jérôme Agyenim Boateng, Mats Julian Hummels, Antonio Rüdiger, Matthias Lukas Ginter, Joshua Walter Kimmich, Toni Kroos, Leon Christoph Goretzka (66.İlkay Gündoğan), Thomas Müller, Marco Reus (83.Leroy Aziz Sané), Timo Werner. Trainer: Joachim Löw.

09.09.2018 GERMANY - PERU 2-1(1-1) Friendly International
Wirsol Rhein-Neckar-Arena, Sinsheim; Referee: Robert Schörgenhofer (Austria); Attendance: 25,494
GER: Marc-André ter Stegen, Jérôme Agyenim Boateng (46.Antonio Rüdiger), Niklas Süle, Matthias Lukas Ginter (72.Jan Thilo Kehrer), Joshua Walter Kimmich, Toni Kroos (Cap), İlkay Gündoğan (84.Thomas Müller), Nico Schulz, Marco Reus (46.Julian Draxler), Julian Brandt (70.Nils Petersen), Timo Werner (88.Kai Havertz). Trainer: Joachim Löw.
Goals: Julian Brandt (25), Nico Schulz (85).

13.10.2018 NETHERLANDS - GERMANY 3-0(1-0) UEFA Nations League A, Group 1
"Johan Cruyff" Arena, Amsterdam; Referee: Cüneyt Çakır (Turkey); Attendance: 52,536
GER: Manuel Peter Neuer (Cap), Jérôme Agyenim Boateng, Mats Julian Hummels, Matthias Lukas Ginter, Joshua Walter Kimmich, Toni Kroos, Jonas Armin Hector, Emre Can (57.Julian Draxler), Mark Alexander Uth (68.Julian Brandt), Thomas Müller (57.Leroy Aziz Sané), Timo Werner. Trainer: Joachim Löw.

16.10.2018 FRANCE - GERMANY 2-1(0-1) UEFA Nations League A, Group 1
Stade de France, Saint-Denis, Paris; Referee: Milorad Mažić (Serbia); Attendance: 77,300
GER: Manuel Peter Neuer (Cap), Mats Julian Hummels, Niklas Süle, Matthias Lukas Ginter (83.Julian Brandt), Joshua Walter Kimmich, Jan Thilo Kehrer, Toni Kroos, Nico Schulz, Serge David Gnabry (88.Thomas Müller), Timo Werner, Leroy Aziz Sané (75.Julian Draxler). Trainer: Joachim Löw.
Goal: Toni Kroos (14 penalty).

15.11.2018 GERMANY - RUSSIA 3-0(3-0) Friendly International
Red Bull Arena, Leipzig; Referee: Sandro Schärer (Switzerland); Attendance: 35,288
GER: Manuel Peter Neuer (Cap), Antonio Rüdiger (61.Jonathan Glao Tah), Niklas Süle, Matthias Lukas Ginter, Joshua Walter Kimmich, Jan Thilo Kehrer, Jonas Armin Hector (70.Nico Schulz), Kai Havertz (65.Sebastian Rudy), Timo Werner (65.Julian Brandt), Serge David Gnabry (73.Thomas Müller), Leroy Aziz Sané (78.Leon Christoph Goretzka). Trainer: Joachim Löw.
Goals: Leroy Aziz Sané (8), Niklas Süle (25), Serge David Gnabry (40).

19.11.2018 GERMANY - NETHERLANDS 2-2(2-0) UEFA Nations League A, Group 1
Veltins-Arena, Gelsenkirchen; Referee: Ovidiu Alin Haţegan (Romania); Attendance: 42,186
GER: Manuel Peter Neuer (Cap), Mats Julian Hummels, Antonio Rüdiger, Niklas Süle, Joshua Walter Kimmich, Jan Thilo Kehrer, Toni Kroos, Nico Schulz, Serge David Gnabry (67.Thomas Müller), Timo Werner (63.Marco Reus), Leroy Aziz Sané (80.Leon Christoph Goretzka). Trainer: Joachim Löw.
Goals: Timo Werner (9), Leroy Aziz Sané (20).

20.03.2019 GERMANY - SERBIA 1-1(0-1) Friendly International
Volkswagen Arena, Wolfsburg; Referee: Robert Madden (Scotland); Attendance: 26,101
GER: Manuel Peter Neuer (Cap) (46.Marc-André ter Stegen), Marcel Halstenberg, Niklas Süle, Joshua Walter Kimmich, Jonathan Glao Tah, Lukas Manuel Klostermann (90.Jan Thilo Kehrer), İlkay Gündoğan, Kai Havertz (46.Marco Reus), Julian Brandt (56.Leon Christoph Goretzka), Timo Werner, Leroy Aziz Sané (90+6.Nico Schulz). Trainer: Joachim Löw.
Goal: Leon Christoph Goretzka (69).

24.03.2019 NETHERLANDS - GERMANY 2-3(0-2) 16th EC. Qualifiers
"Johan Cruyff" Arena, Amsterdam; Referee: Jesús Gil Manzano (Spain); Attendance: 51,694
GER: Manuel Peter Neuer (Cap), Antonio Rüdiger, Niklas Süle, Matthias Lukas Ginter, Joshua Walter Kimmich, Jan Thilo Kehrer, Toni Kroos, Nico Schulz, Leon Christoph Goretzka (70.İlkay Gündoğan), Serge David Gnabry (88.Marco Reus), Leroy Aziz Sané. Trainer: Joachim Löw.
Goals: Leroy Aziz Sané (15), Serge David Gnabry (34), Nico Schulz (90).

08.06.2019 BELARUS - GERMANY 0-2(0-1) 16th EC. Qualifiers
Borisov Arena, Borisov; Referee: Srđan Jovanović (Serbia); Attendance: 7,200
GER: Manuel Peter Neuer (Cap), Niklas Süle, Matthias Lukas Ginter, Joshua Walter Kimmich, Jonathan Glao Tah, Lukas Manuel Klostermann, İlkay Gündoğan (81.Leon Christoph Goretzka), Nico Schulz, Serge David Gnabry (71.Julian Draxler), Marco Reus (76.Julian Brandt), Leroy Aziz Sané. Trainer: Joachim Löw.
Goals: Leroy Aziz Sané (13), Marco Reus (62).

11.06.2019 GERMANY - ESTONIA 8-0(5-0) 16th EC. Qualifiers

Opel Arena, Mainz; Referee: Ali Palabıyık (Turkey); Attendance: 26,050

GER: Manuel Peter Neuer (Cap), Niklas Süle, Matthias Lukas Ginter, Joshua Walter Kimmich, Jan Thilo Kehrer, İlkay Gündoğan (53.Julian Draxler), Nico Schulz (46.Marcel Halstenberg), Leon Christoph Goretzka, Serge David Gnabry, Marco Reus (65.Timo Werner), Leroy Aziz Sané. Trainer: Joachim Löw.

Goals: Marco Reus (10), Serge David Gnabry (17), Leon Christoph Goretzka (20), İlkay Gündoğan (26 penalty), Marco Reus (37), Serge David Gnabry (62), Timo Werner (79), Leroy Aziz Sané (88).

NATIONAL TEAM PLAYERS
(16.07.2018 – 15.07.2019)

Name	DOB	Caps	Goals	2018/2019:	Club
Goalkeepers					
Manuel Peter NEUER	27.03.1986	**88**	**0**	2018/2019:	*FC Bayern München*
Marc-André TER STEGEN	30.04.1992	**22**	**0**	2018/2019:	*FC Barcelona (ESP)*
Defenders					
Jérôme Agyenim BOATENG	03.09.1988	**76**	**1**	2018:	*FC Bayern München*
Matthias Lukas GINTER	19.01.1994	**26**	**0**	2018/2019:	*Borussia VfL Mönchengladbach*
Marcel HALSTENBERG	27.09.1991	**3**	**0**	2019:	*RasenBallsport Leipzig*
Jonas Armin HECTOR	27.05.1990	**42**	**3**	2018:	*1. FC Köln*
Mats Julian HUMMELS	16.12.1988	**70**	**5**	2018:	*FC Bayern München*
Jan Thilo KEHRER	21.09.1996	**7**	**0**	2018/2019:	*Paris Saint-Germain FC (FRA)*
Joshua Walter KIMMICH	08.02.1995	**42**	**3**	2018/2019:	*FC Bayern München*
Lukas Manuel KLOSTERMANN	03.06.1996	**2**	**0**	2018/2019:	*RasenBallsport Leipzig*
Antonio RÜDIGER	03.03.1993	**30**	**1**	2018/2019:	*Chelsea FC London (ENG)*
Nico SCHULZ	01.04.1993	**8**	**2**	2018/2019:	*TSG 1899 Hoffenheim*
Niklas SÜLE	03.09.1995	**20**	**1**	2018/2019:	*FC Bayern München*
Jonathan Glao TAH	11.02.1996	**6**	**0**	2018/2019:	*TSV Bayer 04 Leverkusen*
Midfielders					
Julian BRANDT	02.05.1996	**25**	**2**	2018/2019:	*TSV Bayer 04 Leverkusen*
Emre CAN	12.01.1994	**21**	**1**	2018:	*Juventus FC Torino (ITA)*
Julian DRAXLER	20.09.1993	**51**	**6**	2018/2019:	*Paris Saint-Germain FC (FRA)*
Leon Christoph GORETZKA	06.02.1995	**23**	**8**	2018/2019:	*FC Bayern München*
İlkay GÜNDOĞAN	24.10.1990	**33**	**5**	2018/2019:	*Manchester City FC (ENG)*
Kai HAVERTZ	11.06.1999	**3**	**0**	2018/2019:	*TSV Bayer 04 Leverkusen*
Toni KROOS	04.01.1990	**92**	**14**	2018/2019:	*Real Madrid CF (ESP)*
Marco REUS	31.05.1989	**41**	**13**	2018/2019:	*BV Borussia 09 Dortmund*
Sebastian RUDY	28.02.1990	**27**	**1**	2018/2019:	*FC Schalke 04 Gelsenkirchen*
Leroy Aziz SANÉ	11.01.1996	**21**	**5**	2018/2019:	*Manchester City FC (ENG)*
Forwards					
Serge David GNABRY	14.07.1995	**8**	**7**	2018/2019:	*FC Bayern München*
Thomas MÜLLER	13.09.1989	**100**	**38**	2018:	*FC Bayern München*
Nils PETERSEN	06.12.1988	**2**	**0**	2018:	*SC Freiburg*
Mark Alexander UTH	24.08.1991	**1**	**0**	2018:	*FC Schalke 04 Gelsenkirchen*
Timo WERNER	06.03.1996	**25**	**10**	2018/2019:	*RasenBallsport Leipzig*

National team coach

Joachim LÖW [from 12.07.2006]	03.02.1960	175 M; 113 W; 33 D; 29 L; 415-166

GIBRALTAR

The Country:
Gibraltar [*British Overseas Territory*]
Capital: Gibraltar
Surface: 6,8 km²
Inhabitants: 32,194
Time: UTC+1

The FA:
Gibraltar Football Association
2nd Floor, 62-64 Irish town, P.O. Box 513 GX11, 1AA Gibraltar
Tel: +350 200 42 941
Foundation date: 1895
Member of FIFA since: 13.05.2016
Member of UEFA since: 24.05.2013
Website: www.gibraltarfa.com

NATIONAL TEAM RECORDS

First international match:	19.11.2013, Faro/Loulé (POR):	Gibraltar – Slovakia 0-0	
Most international caps:	Liam Walker		- 39 caps (since 2013)
Most international goals:	Lee Henry Casciaro		- 2 goals / 29 caps (since 2014)
	Joseph Louis Chipolina		- 2 goals / 36 caps (since 2014)
	Jake Gosling		- 2 goals / 11 caps (2014-2018)
	Liam Walker		- 2 goals / 39 caps (since 2013)

UEFA EUROPEAN CHAMPIONSHIP	
1960	Not a UEFA member
1964	Not a UEFA member
1968	Not a UEFA member
1972	Not a UEFA member
1976	Not a UEFA member
1980	Not a UEFA member
1984	Not a UEFA member
1988	Not a UEFA member
1992	Not a UEFA member
1996	Not a UEFA member
2000	Not a UEFA member
2004	Not a UEFA member
2008	Not a UEFA member
2012	Not a UEFA member
2016	Qualifiers

FIFA WORLD CUP	
1930	Not a FIFA member
1934	Not a FIFA member
1938	Not a FIFA member
1950	Not a FIFA member
1954	Not a FIFA member
1958	Not a FIFA member
1962	Not a FIFA member
1966	Not a FIFA member
1970	Not a FIFA member
1974	Not a FIFA member
1978	Not a FIFA member
1982	Not a FIFA member
1986	Not a FIFA member
1990	Not a FIFA member
1994	Not a FIFA member
1998	Not a FIFA member
2002	Not a FIFA member
2006	Not a FIFA member
2010	Not a FIFA member
2014	Not a FIFA member
2018	Qualifiers

UEFA NATIONS LEAGUE
2018/2019 – League D

OLYMPIC FOOTBALL TOURNAMENTS 1908-2016							
1908	-	**1948**	-	**1972**	-	**1996**	-
1912	-	**1952**	-	**1976**	-	**2000**	-
1920	-	**1956**	-	**1980**	-	**2004**	-
1924	-	**1960**	-	**1984**	-	**2008**	-
1928	-	**1964**	-	**1988**	-	**2012**	-
1936	-	**1968**	-	**1992**	-	**2016**	Did not enter

FIFA CONFEDERATIONS CUP 1992-2017
None

GIBRALTARIAN CLUB HONOURS IN EUROPEAN CLUB COMPETITIONS:

European Champion Clubs' Cup (1956-1992) / UEFA Champions League (1993-2019)
None
Fairs Cup (1858-1971) / UEFA Cup (1972-2009) / UEFA Europa League (2010-2019)
None
UEFA Super Cup (1972-2018)
None
European Cup Winners' Cup 1961-1999*
None

**defunct competition*

NATIONAL COMPETITIONS
TABLE OF HONOURS

	CHAMPIONS	CUP WINNERS
1894/1895	-	Gibraltar FC
1895/1896	Gibraltar FC	*Not known*
1896/1897	Jubilee FC	*Not known*
1897/1898	Jubilee FC	*Not known*
1898/1899	Albion FC	*Not known*
1899/1900	Exiles FC	*Not known*
1900/1901	Prince of Wales FC	*Not known*
1901/1902	Exiles FC	*Not known*
1902/1903	Prince of Wales FC	*Not known*
1903/1904	Prince of Wales FC	*Not known*
1904/1905	Athletic FC	*Not known*
1905/1906	Prince of Wales FC	*Not known*
1906/1907	*No competition*	*Not known*
1907/1908	FC Britannia XI	*Not known*
1908/1909	Prince of Wales FC	*Not known*
1909/1910	South United FC	*Not known*
1910/1911	South United FC	*Not known*
1911/1912	FC Britannia XI	*Not known*
1912/1913	FC Britannia XI	*Not known*
1913/1914	Prince of Wales FC	*Not known*
1914/1915	Royal Sovereign	*Not known*
1915/1916	*No competition*	*Not known*
1916/1917	Prince of Wales FC	*Not known*
1917/1918	FC Britannia XI	*Not known*
1918/1919	Prince of Wales FC	*Not known*
1919/1920	FC Britannia XI	*Not known*
1920/1921	Prince of Wales FC	*Not known*
1921/1922	Prince of Wales FC	*Not known*
1922/1923	Prince of Wales FC	*Not known*
1923/1924	Gibraltar FC	*Not known*
1924/1925	Prince of Wales FC	*Not known*
1925/1926	Prince of Wales FC	*Not known*
1926/1927	Prince of Wales FC	*Not known*
1927/1928	Prince of Wales FC	*Not known*
1928/1929	Europa FC	*Not known*
1929/1930	Europa FC	*Not known*
1930/1931	Prince of Wales FC	*Not known*
1931/1932	Europa FC	*Not known*
1932/1933	Europa FC	*Not known*
1933/1934	Commander of the Yard FC	*Not known*
1934/1935	Chief Construction FC	*Not known*
1935/1936	Chief Constructor FC	HMS Hood
1936/1937	FC Britannia XI	FC Britannia XI
1937/1938	Europa FC	Europa FC
1938/1939	Prince of Wales FC	2nd Battalion The King's Regiment
1939/1940	Prince of Wales FC	FC Britannia XI
1940/1941	FC Britannia XI	*No competition*
1941/1942	*No competition*	A.A.R.A.
1942/1943	*No competition*	Royal Air Force New Camp
1943/1944	*No competition*	4th Btallion Royal Scott
1944/1945	*No competition*	*No competition*
1945/1946	*No competition*	Europa FC
1946/1947	Gibraltar United FC	Gibraltar United FC
1947/1948	Gibraltar United FC	FC Britannia XI
1948/1949	Gibraltar United FC	Prince of Wales FC
1949/1950	Gibraltar United FC	Europa FC
1950/1951	Gibraltar United FC	Europa FC
1951/1952	Europa FC	Europa FC
1952/1953	Prince of Wales FC	*Not known*
1953/1954	Gibraltar United FC	*Not known*
1954/1955	FC Britannia XI	*Not known*
1955/1956	FC Britannia XI	*Not known*
1956/1957	FC Britannia XI	*Not known*
1957/1958	FC Britannia XI	*Not known*
1958/1959	FC Britannia XI	*Not known*
1959/1960	Gibraltar United FC	*Not known*
1960/1961	FC Britannia XI	*Not known*
1961/1962	Gibraltar United FC	*Not known*
1962/1963	FC Britannia XI	*Not known*
1963/1964	Gibraltar United FC	*Not known*
1964/1965	Gibraltar United FC	*Not known*
1965/1966	Glacis United FC	*Not known*

1966/1967	Glacis United FC	*Not known*
1967/1968	Glacis United FC	*Not known*
1968/1969	Glacis United FC	*Not known*
1969/1970	Glacis United FC	*Not known*
1970/1971	Glacis United FC	*Not known*
1971/1972	Glacis United FC	*Not known*
1972/1973	Glacis United FC	*Not known*
1973/1974	Glacis United FC	Manchester United FC
1974/1975	Manchester United FC	Glacis United FC
1975/1976	Glacis United FC	2nd Battalion Royal Green Jackets
1976/1977	Manchester United FC	Manchester United FC
1977/1978	*No competition*	*Not known*
1978/1979	Manchester United FC	St Joseph's FC
1979/1980	Manchester United FC	Manchester United FC
1980/1981	Glacis United FC	Glacis United FC
1981/1982	Glacis United FC	Glacis United FC
1982/1983	Glacis United FC	St Joseph's FC
1983/1984	Manchester United FC	St Joseph's FC
1984/1985	Glacis United FC & Lincoln Red Imps FC	St Joseph's FC
1985/1986	Lincoln Red Imps FC	Lincoln Red Imps FC
1986/1987	St Theresa's FC	St Joseph's FC
1987/1988	St Theresa's FC	Royal Air Force Gibraltar
1988/1989	Glacis United FC	Lincoln Red Imps FC
1989/1990	Lincoln Red Imps FC	Lincoln Red Imps FC
1990/1991	Lincoln Red Imps FC	*Not known*
1991/1992	Lincoln Red Imps FC	St Joseph's FC
1992/1993	Lincoln Red Imps FC	Lincoln Red Imps FC
1993/1994	Lincoln Red Imps FC	Lincoln Red Imps FC
1994/1995	Manchester United FC	St Theresa's FC
1995/1996	St Joseph's FC	St Joseph's FC
1996/1997	Glacis United FC	Manchester United FC
1997/1998	St Theresa's FC	Glacis United FC
1998/1999	Manchester United FC	Gibraltar United FC
1999/2000	Glacis United FC	Gibraltar United FC
2000/2001	Lincoln Red Imps FC	Gibraltar United FC
2001/2002	Gibraltar United FC	Lincoln Red Imps FC
2002/2003	Lincoln Red Imps FC	Manchester United FC
2003/2004	Lincoln Red Imps FC	Newcastle FC
2004/2005	Lincoln Red Imps FC	Newcastle FC
2005/2006	Lincoln Red Imps FC	Newcastle FC
2006/2007	Lincoln Red Imps FC	Newcastle FC
2007/2008	Lincoln Red Imps FC	Lincoln Red Imps FC
2008/2009	Lincoln Red Imps FC	Lincoln Red Imps FC
2009/2010	Lincoln Red Imps FC	Lincoln Red Imps FC
2010/2011	Lincoln Red Imps FC	Lincoln Red Imps FC
2011/2012	Lincoln Red Imps FC	St Joseph's FC
2012/2013	Lincoln Red Imps FC	St Joseph's FC
2013/2014	Lincoln Red Imps FC	Lincoln Red Imps FC
2014/2015	Lincoln Red Imps FC	Lincoln Red Imps FC
2015/2016	Lincoln Red Imps FC	Lincoln Red Imps FC
2016/2017	Europa FC	Europa FC
2017/2018	Lincoln Red Imps FC	Europa FC
2018/2019	Lincoln Red Imps FC	Europa FC

Please note: Manchester United FC changed its name to Manchester 62 FC (2013); Newcastle FC was a temporary name for Lincoln Red Imps FC.

NATIONAL CHAMPIONSHIP

Gibraltar Premier Division 2018/2019

(13.08.2018 – 20.05.2019)

Results

Round 1 [13-16.08.2018]
St. Joseph's FC - FC Boca Gibraltar 5-0
Gibraltar United FC - Lions Gibraltar FC 4-0
Lynx FC - Gibraltar Phoenix 0-0
Lincoln Red Imps FC - Glacis United FC 4-0
Europa FC - Mons Calpe SC 2-1

Round 2 [17-20.08.2018]
St. Joseph's FC - Gibraltar United FC 2-2
Lions Gibraltar FC - Lynx FC 0-3
FC Boca Gibraltar - Mons Calpe SC 0-3
Gibraltar Phoenix - Lincoln Red Imps FC 0-2
Glacis United FC - Europa FC 0-0

Round 3 [22-25.08.2018]
Gibraltar United FC - FC Boca Gibraltar 2-1
Lynx FC - St. Joseph's FC 2-3
Lincoln Red Imps FC - Lions Gibraltar FC 3-0
Europa FC - Gibraltar Phoenix 2-0
Mons Calpe SC - Glacis United FC 0-1

Round 4 [01-05.10.2018]
St. Joseph's FC - Lincoln Red Imps FC 0-5
FC Boca Gibraltar - Glacis United FC 0-2
Gibraltar Phoenix - Mons Calpe SC 1-0
Gibraltar United FC - Lynx FC 4-1
Lions Gibraltar FC - Europa FC 0-2

Round 5 [19-22.10.2018]
Lynx FC - FC Boca Gibraltar 0-1
Europa FC - St. Joseph's FC 2-3
Glacis United FC - Gibraltar Phoenix 1-3
Mons Calpe SC - Lions Gibraltar FC 3-0
Lincoln Red Imps FC - Gibraltar United 0-1

Round 6 [24-27.10.2018]
Gibraltar Phoenix - Europa FC 0-1
St. Joseph's FC - Mons Calpe SC 1-2
Lions Gibraltar FC - Glacis United FC 0-1
FC Boca Gibraltar - Gibraltar Phoenix 2-5
Lynx FC - Lincoln Red Imps FC 1-1

Round 7 [28.10.-03.11.2018]
Gibraltar United FC - Europa FC 1-3
Gibraltar Phoenix - Lions Gibraltar FC 1-0
Lincoln Red Imps FC - FC Boca Gibraltar 3-0
Europa FC - Lynx FC 4-0
Mons Calpe SC - Gibraltar United FC 1-1

Round 8 [22-24.11.2018]
Glacis United - St. Joseph's FC 0-2 [04.11.]
FC Boca Gibraltar - Lions Gibraltar FC 1-0
Gibraltar United FC - Glacis United FC 2-1
St. Joseph's FC - Gibraltar Phoenix 0-0
Lynx FC - Mons Calpe SC 0-3

Round 9 [25-30.11.2018]
Lincoln Red Imps FC - Europa FC 3-2
FC Boca Gibraltar - Gibraltar United FC 0-4
Glacis United FC - Lynx FC 0-0
Mons Calpe SC - Lincoln Red Imps FC 2-2
Lions Gibraltar - St. Joseph's FC 0-7 [01.12.]

Round 10 [02-07.12.2018]
Europa FC - FC Boca Gibraltar 3-0
Gibraltar Phoenix - Gibraltar United FC 2-1
Glacis United FC - Mons Calpe SC 2-3
FC Boca Gibraltar - St. Joseph's FC 1-1
Gibraltar Phoenix - Lynx FC 2-0

Round 11 [08-12.12.2018]
Glacis United FC - Lincoln Red Imps FC 1-2
Lions Gibraltar FC - Gibraltar United FC 1-0
Mons Calpe SC - Europa FC 1-2
St. Joseph's FC - Lynx FC 7-1
Lions Gibraltar FC - Lincoln Red Imps FC 0-2

Round 12 [15-18.12.2018]
Mons Calpe SC - FC Boca Gibraltar 3-0
Europa FC - Glacis United FC 1-0
Lynx FC - Lions Gibraltar FC 1-0
Gibraltar United FC - St. Joseph's FC 0-1
Lincoln Red Imps FC - Gibraltar Phoenix 4-0

Round 13 [03-08.01.2019]
Lincoln Red Imps FC - St. Joseph's FC 1-3
Lynx FC - Gibraltar United FC 2-2
Mons Calpe SC - Gibraltar Phoenix 3-0
Europa FC - Lions Gibraltar FC 5-1
Glacis United - FC Boca Gibraltar 6-1 [14.01.]

Round 14 [17-20.01.2019]
Gibraltar United - Lincoln Red Imps FC 1-5
Lions Gibraltar FC - Mons Calpe SC 0-4
Gibraltar Phoenix - Glacis United FC 6-0
St. Joseph's FC - Europa FC 0-1
FC Boca Gibraltar - Lynx FC 0-3 (awarded)

Round 15 [24-27.01.2019]
Glacis United FC - Lions Gibraltar FC 3-1
Mons Calpe SC - St. Joseph's FC 2-1
Europa FC - Gibraltar United FC 1-0
Lincoln Red Imps FC - Lynx FC 1-0
Gibraltar Phoenix - FC Boca Gibraltar 3-1

Round 16 [31.01.-03.02.2019]
Gibraltar United FC - Mons Calpe SC 2-1
Lions Gibraltar FC - Gibraltar Phoenix 1-3
FC Boca Gibraltar - Lincoln Red Imps 0-11
St. Joseph's FC - Glacis United FC 8-0
Lynx FC - Europa FC 1-1

Round 17 [15-18.02.2019]
Glacis United FC - Gibraltar United FC 0-2
Mons Calpe SC - Lynx FC 1-1
Europa FC - Lincoln Red Imps FC 1-1
Gibraltar Phoenix - St. Joseph's FC 1-2
Lions Gibraltar FC - FC Boca Gibraltar 2-1

Round 18 [21-24.02.2019]
Lynx FC - Glacis United FC 2-1
Gibraltar United FC - Gibraltar Phoenix 1-1
FC Boca Gibraltar - Europa FC 0-9
St. Joseph's FC - Lions Gibraltar FC 3-1
Lincoln Red Imps FC - Mons Calpe SC 3-1

Round 19 [28.02.-03.03.2019]
St. Joseph's FC - FC Boca Gibraltar 10-1
Europa FC - Mons Calpe SC 4-3
Lynx FC - Gibraltar Phoenix 1-2
Lincoln Red Imps FC - Glacis United FC 2-1
Gibraltar United FC - Lions Gibraltar FC 4-1

Round 20 [07-10.03.2019]
Glacis United FC - Europa FC 1-6
Gibraltar Phoenix - Lincoln Red Imps FC 0-3
FC Boca Gibraltar - Mons Calpe SC 0-5
St. Joseph's FC - Gibraltar United FC 2-1
Lions Gibraltar FC - Lynx FC 0-3

Round 21 [28-31.03.2019]
Mons Calpe SC - Glacis United FC 4-1
Europa FC - Gibraltar Phoenix 3-0
Gibraltar United FC - FC Boca Gibraltar 7-0
Lincoln Red Imps FC - Lions Gibraltar FC 5-1
Lynx FC - St. Joseph's FC 0-1

Round 22 [04-07.04.2019]
Lions Gibraltar FC - Europa FC 0-8
Gibraltar Phoenix - Mons Calpe SC 0-2
St. Joseph's FC - Lincoln Red Imps FC 1-3
Gibraltar United FC - Lynx FC 1-1
FC Boca Gibraltar - Glacis United FC 2-3

Round 23 [13-16.04.2019]
Europa FC - St. Joseph's FC 2-0
Lynx FC - FC Boca Gibraltar 1-0
Glacis United FC - Gibraltar Phoenix 1-1
Mons Calpe SC - Lions Gibraltar FC 6-0
Lincoln Red Imps FC - Gibraltar United 2-0

Round 24 [25-28.04.2019]
FC Boca Gibraltar - Gibraltar Phoenix 0-8
Lynx FC - Lincoln Red Imps FC 1-4
Lions Gibraltar FC - Glacis United FC 1-2
St. Joseph's FC - Mons Calpe SC 1-1
Gibraltar United FC - Europa FC 1-1

Round 25 [03-06.05.2019]
Glacis United FC - St. Joseph's FC 0-1
Europa FC - Lynx FC 5-0
Mons Calpe SC - Gibraltar United FC 5-2
Lincoln Red Imps - FC Boca Gibraltar 10-0
Gibraltar Phoenix - Lions Gibraltar FC 1-0

Round 26 [10-13.05.2019]
St. Joseph's FC - Gibraltar Phoenix 3-0
FC Boca Gibraltar - Lions Gibraltar FC 0-7
Lincoln Red Imps FC - Europa FC 2-0
Lynx FC - Mons Calpe SC 2-1
Gibraltar United FC - Glacis United FC 2-0

Round 27 [17.05.2019]
Lions Gibraltar FC - St. Joseph's FC 0-1
Mons Calpe SC - Lincoln Red Imps FC 2-0
Europa FC - FC Boca Gibraltar 13-1
Gibraltar Phoenix - Gibraltar United FC 2-0
Glacis United FC - Lynx FC 0-2

Final Standings						
1. **Lincoln Red Imps FC**	27	21	3	3	84 - 19	66
2. Europa FC	27	20	4	3	84 - 20	64
3. St. Joseph's FC	27	17	4	6	69 - 29	55
4. Mons Calpe SC	27	15	4	8	63 - 29	49
5. Gibraltar Phoenix FC	27	13	4	10	42 - 34	43
6. Gibraltar United FC	27	11	6	10	48 - 37	39
7. Lynx FC	27	8	7	12	29 - 45	31
8. Glacis United FC	27	7	3	17	28 - 58	24
9. Lions Gibraltar FC	27	3	0	24	17 - 77	9
10. FC Boca Gibraltar	27	2	1	24	13 - 129	7

Top goalscorers:

21 Salvador Manuel Alegre Delgado "Boro" (ESP) *St. Joseph's FC*

20 Juan Francisco García Peña "Juanfri" (ESP) *St. Joseph's FC*

18 Juan Pablo Pereira Sastre "Pibe" (ARG) *Mons Calpe SC*

16 Leonardo Ezequiel Carboni (ARG) *Mons Calpe SC*

NATIONAL CUP
Rock Cup 2018/2019

First Round [20.01.2019]

Leo FC - FC Bruno's Magpies	0-10

Second Round [06-10.02.2019]

St. Joseph's FC - FC Hound Dogs	12-0
Mons Calpe SC - College 1975 FC	14-0
Lincoln Red Imps FC - Europa FC	0-1
Manchester 62 FC - Gibraltar United FC	0-12
Lynx FC - Gibraltar Phoenix FC	1-3
Glacis United FC - Lions Gibraltar FC	1-1; 3-4 pen
Europa Point FC - FC Olympique 13	0-2
FC Boca Gibraltar - FC Bruno's Magpies	2-5

Quarter-Finals [12-13.03.2019]

Gibraltar United FC - FC Olympique 13	4-2
St. Joseph's FC - Mons Calpe SC	1-4
Gibraltar Phoenix FC - Lions Gibraltar FC	4-0
FC Bruno's Magpies - Europa FC	1-9

Semi-Finals [09-10.04.2019]

Gibraltar Phoenix FC - Europa FC	1-4
Gibraltar United FC - Mons Calpe SC	1-0

Final

26.05.2019; Victoria Stadium, Gibraltar; Referee: Herbert Warwick; Attendance: n/a
Europa FC - Gibraltar United FC **3-0(0-0)**

Europa FC: Dayle Edward Coleing, Ibrahim Ayew, Ethan Terence Jolley, Olmo González Casado, Emil Peter Jørgensen, Liam Walker (Cap), Alejandro Rodríguez Rivas "Álex Quillo", Mustapha Yahaya (70.José Domingo Utrera García), Urko Arroyo Rivas (73.Michael Thomas Yome), Manuel Jesús Arana Rodríguez, Manuel Dimas Suárez Arbelo (86.Razak Iddrisu). Trainer: Rafael Escobar (Spain).

Gibraltar United: Kyle Albert Goldwin (Cap), Erin Anthony Barnett, Aymen Mouelhi, Nicolás Márquez Olvera, Héctor Antona Granados, Francisco Álvarez Benito, David Gómez Prieto (62.Michael Lee Negrette), Carlos Carrasco Llorens, José Antonio Rubio Quirós „Chico" (55.Daniel Ponce De León García "Dani Ponce"), Nathan Albert Santos (74.Julio Gil Bado), Alberto Andrés Zapata Mico. Trainer: Francisco "Paco" Pascual Luna (Spain).

Goals: 1-0 Urko Arroyo Rivas (54), 2-0 Manuel Jesús Arana Rodríguez (62), 3-0 Liam Walker (65 penalty).

SECOND LEVEL
Gibraltar Second Division 2018/2019

1. FC Bruno's Magpies	18	15	2	1	91 - 19	47
2. Europa Point FC	18	13	0	5	50 - 26	39
3. FC Olympique 13	18	12	1	5	71 - 33	37
4. Manchester 62 FC	18	12	1	5	54 - 27	37
5. College 1975 FC	18	3	2	13	13 - 62	11
6. Leo FC	18	3	1	14	23 - 62	10
7. FC Hound Dogs	18	0	3	15	9 - 82	3

Football Club Boca Gibraltar

Founded: 2012
Stadium: Victoria Stadium, Gibraltar (2,800)

Goalkeepers:	DOB	M	(s)	G
Alejandro Arroyal Acris (ESP)	03.08.1998	7	(1)	
Francisco Javier Fernández Gómez (ESP)	01.06.1999	1		
Alonso García Palma (ESP)	18.06.1988	5		
John Machin (ENG)	28.02.1984	1		
Jamie Payas-Carlin	27.08.1992	7		
Álvaro Pérez Pichardo (ESP)	13.12.1996	6		
Francisco José Pérez (ESP)	04.01.1992	1		
Defenders:	**DOB**	**M**	**(s)**	**G**
Jared Buhagiar	20.10.1992	7	(2)	
Jaygan Chipol	24.10.1991	7	(3)	
Joseph Chipol	23.06.1981	10	(2)	
James Currer (ENG)	29.06.1992	2	(1)	
Jesus Glynn (ESP)	20.09.1989	3	(1)	
Oscar Moreno Núñez (ESP)	13.01.1986	21		2
Antony Moulds (ENG)	04.02.1988	10		1
Nicholas Pecino	08.07.1985	7		
Daniel Quiñones Campos (ESP)	10.04.1984	10	(2)	
Mario Ruesca Torres (ESP)	17.11.1993	8	(1)	
José María Sánchez (ESP)	12.12.1990	4	(1)	
Tomas Scaldafferro (ARG)	21.03.1997	11		
Midfielders:	**DOB**	**M**	**(s)**	**G**
Elijah Akin (USA)	30.11.1998	3	(1)	
Pedro Andrade Benito (ESP)	24.07.1990	7	(2)	
Julio Gil Bado	03.06.1983	8	(1)	
Javier Cantelmi (ARG)	14.02.1995	6	(2)	
Israel Castillo Rafoso (ESP)	31.07.1993	12		3
Federico Cataruozzolo (ARG)	08.09.1987	10		
Felix Formica-Corsi	25.01.1977	8	(1)	
Antonio González García (ESP)	06.05.1996	5	(2)	
Diego González Ruiz (USA)	2000	6		1
Unai Gutiérrez Albizu (ESP)	15.02.1991	3	(3)	
Daniel Herbert	19.12.1993	6	(2)	
Phil Macedo	09.04.1984	5		
José Luis Manzano Fernández (ESP)	07.03.1995	7		
Alfredo Medina (ESP)	25.08.1985	2		
Rafael Moreno Flores (ESP)	09.08.1994	2		
Romeo Natera (USA)	14.07.2000	1	(3)	
Francisco Ramírez Caravante "Paquito" (ESP)	30.03.1992	5	(1)	1
James Pecino	12.03.1979	10		
Daniel Pérez Barea (ESP)	04.06.1993	1		
Ivan Rodríguez García (ESP)	24.12.1990	7		
Tariq Turay-Aruna (ENG)	03.02.1997	6	(2)	
Forwards:	**DOB**	**M**	**(s)**	**G**
Max Bothen (SWE)	27.04.1991	4	(4)	
Álvaro Caravante (ESP)	10.03.1994	6	(3)	
Zayne Da Costa	15.11.2001	4	(5)	
Nathan Albert Santos	11.10.1988	10	(1)	2
Haitham Tarrak	20.05.2001	3		
José Alberto Mateos Valdivia (ESP)	18.01.1996	8	(3)	3
Trainer:	**DOB**	**M**		
Juan José Pomares García (ESP)	13.09.1986	12		
Allen Bula [19.12.2018]	04.01.1965	15		

Please note: Alejandro Arroyal Acris (ESP) was used both as goalkeeper and midfielder.

Europa Football Club

Founded: 1925
Stadium: Victoria Stadium, Gibraltar (2,800)

Goalkeepers:	DOB	M	(s)	G
Dayle Edward Coleing	23.10.1996	8		
Javier Muñoz Arévalo	27.01.1982	19		
Defenders:	**DOB**	**M**	**(s)**	**G**
Ibrahim Ayew (GHA)	16.04.1988	25		2
Martín Belforti Rodríguez (ARG)	04.07.1981	1		
Nalys Castro (FRA)	10.07.1999	3	(4)	
Thomas Hastings	23.09.1992	2	(1)	
Ethan Terence Jolley	29.03.1997	20	(2)	
Emil Peter Jørgensen (DEN)	14.11.1995	5	(1)	
Alberto Merino Sánchez (ESP)	02.05.1975	2		
Olmo González Casado (ESP)	15.06.1987	22		
Jesse Picardo Peralta	19.08.2001		(1)	
Jonathan Rodrigues (ESP)	18.03.1997		(1)	
Jesús Toscano Serrano (ESP)	13.12.1990	21		
Midfielders:	**DOB**	**M**	**(s)**	**G**
Alejandro Rodríguez Rivas "Álex Quillo" (ESP)	07.10.1986	22	(2)	10
José Domingo Utrera García	26.10.1988	1	(3)	
Sean Gilbert	14.11.1992		(1)	
Jemar Matto	19.01.2001		(1)	1
Iván Moya Tornay (ESP)	16.09.1987	1	(1)	
Aaron Payas	24.05.1985	2	(12)	1
Liam Walker	13.04.1988	26		12
Mustapha Yahaya (GHA)	09.01.1994	24	(1)	1
Forwards:	**DOB**	**M**	**(s)**	**G**
Manuel Jesús Arana Rodríguez (ESP)	03.12.1984	21		10
Urko Arroyo Rivas (ESP)	14.05.1987	18	(4)	12
Lance Cabezutto	03.03.1993		(1)	
Andre Tjay De Barr	13.03.2000	23	(2)	14
Manuel Dimas Suárez Arbelo	18.04.1992	10	(1)	6
Morris Figueras	04.01.1999		(1)	
Robert Alexandre Fischer (BRA)	15.02.1993	2	(6)	
Razak Iddrisu (GER)	12.02.1996	1	(7)	2
Lee Muscat	23.09.1988	1	(6)	1
Guillermo Roldán Méndez (ESP)	23.06.1981	2	(1)	1
Rubén Blanco Rodríguez "Rubo" (ESP)	15.06.1993	3		
Michael Thomas Yome	29.08.1994	12	(9)	7
Trainer:	**DOB**	**M**		
Juan José Gallardo Fernández (ESP)	21.05.1976	8		
Miguel Ángel Rodríguez (ESP) [23.11.2018]		8		
Rafael Escobar (ESP) [06.02.2019]	12.08.1969	11		

Gibraltar Phoenix Football Club

Founded: 2011
Stadium: Victoria Stadium, Gibraltar (2,800)

Goalkeepers:	DOB	M	(s)	G
Víctor Manuel Ayala Orrillo (ESP)	1999	1		
Matthew Cafer	27.09.1994	25		
Francisco José Fernández Morales (ESP)	28.08.1986	1		
Defenders:	**DOB**	**M**	**(s)**	**G**
Francisco José Cano Hernández (ESP)	01.03.1991	13		
Lee Coombes	20.06.1996		(2)	
Jean-Carlos Anthony Garcia	05.07.1992	13	(2)	2
Cristofer Miñano Leal (ESP)	04.01.1993	11	(1)	3
José Antonio Peralta Fernández (ESP)	28.12.1991	16		
Jason Pusey	18.02.1989	3	(3)	
Peter Sardeña	03.03.1996	1	(4)	
Carlos Trujillo García (ESP)	24.01.1987	10	(2)	1
Adrián Vera Tovar (ESP)	21.02.1990	18	(5)	
Midfielders:	**DOB**	**M**	**(s)**	**G**
Blas Álvarez Cortés (ESP)	19.07.1995	19		1
Scott Ballantine	12.04.1996	8	(1)	
Jayce Nicholas Consigliero	03.08.1997	19	(4)	2
Jeremy Joseph López	09.07.1989	9	(9)	
Francisco Javier Moreno (ESP)	18.09.1990	1	(4)	
Antonio Jiménez Ramos „Ñito" (ESP)	07.05.1996	17	(1)	1
Francisco David González García "Paquito" (ESP)	04.05.1986	7	(6)	
Tyson Paul Ruiz	10.03.1988	9		1
Carlos Sánchez Rodríguez (ESP)	28.12.1987	7	(5)	1
Raúl Segura Castaño (ESP)	11.04.1991	24	(1)	10
Forwards:	**DOB**	**M**	**(s)**	**G**
Salvador Argüez (ESP)	16.02.1986	1	(5)	1
Gabriel Lima Oliveira "Gabriel Pimba" (BRA)	04.07.1990	1	(1)	
Juan Manuel Labrador Aguilar "Labra" (ESP)	24.06.1995	25	(1)	11
Juan Manuel Llaves (ESP)	03.11.1984	14	(4)	7
Felício Silvano Intalte Quiaque (POR)	21.02.1997	2	(7)	1
Ezequiel Rojas Piñer (ESP)	22.06.1990	24		
Jordan Serna (FRA)	21.07.1997	3	(5)	
Trainer:	**DOB**	**M**		
Juan Maria Sánchez Fernández (ESP)	07.12.1971	27		

Gibraltar United Football Club

Founded: 1943
Stadium: Victoria Stadium, Gibraltar (2,800)

Goalkeepers:	DOB	M	(s)	G
Jorge Manuel Avellano	15.12.2000	2	(1)	
Kyle Albert Goldwin	24.04.1985	25		
Defenders:	**DOB**	**M**	**(s)**	**G**
Héctor Antona Granados (ESP)	25.10.1996	10		1
Erin Anthony Barnett	02.09.1996	14	(4)	
Steffan Cardona	03.03.1992	7		
David Gómez Prieto (ESP)	05.10.1993	24		
Gonzalo Guijarro Rodríguez (ESP)	01.01.1996	24	(2)	
Nicolás Márquez Olvera (URU)	13.06.1998	8	(1)	
Aymen Mouelhi (TUN)	14.09.1986	19	(1)	5
Moisés Suárez Burgos (ESP)	15.12.1999	3	(8)	
Xavier Carmona Velasco "Xavi" (ESP)	21.01.1993	12		1
Midfielders:	**DOB**	**M**	**(s)**	**G**
Rufat Abilov (AZE)	17.09.1997	3	(3)	
Julio Gil Bado	03.06.1983	5	(4)	
James Louis Bosio	24.09.1991	4		
Carlos Carrasco Llorens (ESP)	03.01.1993	20		
José Antonio Rubio Quirós „Chico" (ESP)	11.07.1996	13	(6)	6
Shaun Michael De Los Santos	26.01.1998		(1)	
Ernest De Torres	27.11.1997	2	(8)	
Michael Lee Negrette	14.09.1998	21	(1)	3
Guido Ratto Canziani (ARG)	08.06.1999	5	(7)	2
Forwards:	**DOB**	**M**	**(s)**	**G**
Francisco Álvarez Benito (ESP)	17.01.1997	25		2
Álvaro Castiella Sánchez Ortíz (ESP)	18.04.1991	9	(1)	3
Germán Cortés Narváez (ESP)	03.02.1994	10	(3)	8
Daniel Ponce De León García "Dani Ponce" (ESP)	16.05.1991	13	(6)	5
Achraf Nait Brahim (NED)	25.02.1997	8	(5)	1
Nathan Albert Santos	11.10.1988	7	(5)	2
Alberto Andrés Zapata Mico (ESP)	17.05.1989	10	(3)	8
Trainer:	**DOB**	**M**		
Lucas Cazorla Luque (ESP)	06.10.1962	13		
Francisco "Paco" Pascual Luna (ESP) [06.01.2019]	20.03.1964	14		

Glacis United Football Club

Founded: 1965
Stadium: Victoria Stadium, Gibraltar (2,800)

Goalkeepers:	DOB	M	(s)	G
Vlad Ignat-Kleemann	16.10.1996	1		
Victor Martin Fernández (ESP)		10		
Borja Valadés González (ESP)	30.06.1988	12		
Frank Warwick	15.03.1994	4		
Defenders:	**DOB**	**M**	**(s)**	**G**
Francisco José Cano Hernández (ESP)	01.03.1991	10		2
Jaydan Catania	06.03.1993	7		
Rayan Elamari (SUI)	17.09.1997	2	(3)	
Yassin El Melki	01.01.1998	5	(2)	
Juan Ferrer (ESP)	09.08.1988	14		2
Jarrett Flores	08.06.2000	1	(1)	
Courtney Lewis (ENG)	01.03.1996	10		1
Rhys Mason (ENG)	03.09.1997	6	(1)	1
Lucas Olmos (ARG)	17.03.1996	7		
Ashley Joseph Perez	23.02.1989	1		
Niall Serra	03.05.2001	12	(2)	
Samuel François Vermeeren (NED)	29.01.1998	2		
Midfielders:	**DOB**	**M**	**(s)**	**G**
Maxime Agnoly (FRA)	17.03.1991	7	(3)	2
Adrián Amado Mena (ESP)	21.12.1993	3	(1)	
Naoufal El Andaloussi	07.04.1991	13	(8)	
Luis Ignacio Fernández Ríos (ESP)	28.01.1988	24		1
Dylan Llufrio	20.04.1993	2	(1)	
Karim Dechraqui Piñero (ESP)	30.04.1992	10		
Iván Ruiz Pecino (ESP)	16.09.1990	12		
Tyson Paul Ruiz*	10.03.1988	5		
Aidan Serra	28.12.1994	17	(1)	4
Hatim Smith	25.12.2000		(1)	
Antonio Jesús Urenda Aranda (ESP)	27.12.1995	8	(8)	
Forwards:	**DOB**	**M**	**(s)**	**G**
Kivan Francharles Castle*	21.02.1990	18		
Antonio Cerezo Ramos (ESP)	20.08.1993	8	(3)	2
Yuri Ruh Dos Santos (POR)	07.02.1998	5	(5)	
Martin Gándara (ITA)	25.03.1996	2	(3)	
Daniel Hoyos Villalta (ESP)	15.08.1989	10	(3)	1
Nathan Luan Araujo da Silva (BRA)	25.02.1996	4	(6)	2
Gabriele Novello (ITA)	18.08.1998	13	(5)	5
Alan Parker	15.05.1996	19	(3)	2
Juan José Pérez Jiménez (ESP)	21.09.1990	8	(1)	
Daniel Pratts	06.06.1998		(2)	
Mariano Nicolás Pereira (ARG)	27.03.1990	10	(9)	
Rene Santillan Jr. (USA)	21.07.1998	3		1
Trainer:	**DOB**	**M**		
Alfonso Cortijo Cabrera (ESP)	14.09.1966	7		
Jesús Antonio Napolitano Rodríguez (ARG) [10.11.2018]	04.02.1988	20		

**number of matches played as substitute not known*

Lincoln Red Imps Football Club

Founded: 1976
Stadium: Victoria Stadium, Gibraltar (2,800)

Goalkeepers:	DOB	M	(s)	G
Jaylan Hankins	17.11.2000	7		
Lucio Francisco Hernando Cid (ARG)	05.10.1994	1		
Manuel Soler Ortuño (ESP)	17.09.1986	19		
Defenders:	**DOB**	**M**	**(s)**	**G**
André Luiz Dos Santos „Andrezinho“ (BRA)	19.02.1992	19		
Louie John Annesley	03.05.2000	3		
Bernardo Morgado Gaspar Lopes (POR)	30.07.1993	22		1
Joseph Luis Chipolina	14.12.1987	16	(1)	11
Roy Alan Chipolina	20.01.1983	9	(5)	2
Jean-Carlos Anthony García	05.07.1992	2	(1)	
Shaylon Hanglin	24.04.2000		(1)	
Álvaro Oliver París (ESP)	25.01.1992	17		3
Marcos Luis Pérez Trujillo (ESP)	30.09.1989	9		
Maximiliano Alejandro Rosales (ARG)	01.04.1996	5	(2)	
Ethan Thorne-Llambias	23.11.2000	1		
Midfielders:	**DOB**	**M**	**(s)**	**G**
Alejandro José Moreno Cerrillo “Álex Moreno” (ESP)	09.07.1992	3	(2)	
Anthony Michael Bardon	19.01.1993	2	(2)	
Evan De Haro	28.09.1992	1		
Craig Galliano	23.04.2002	1		
Diego Antonio Gámiz Maroto (ESP)	07.06.1992	10	(2)	4
Sykes Al Garro	26.02.1993	5	(3)	
Borja Gil Albarracín (ESP)	04.12.1990	10	(2)	
Andrew Albert Hernandez	10.01.1999	1	(2)	
Anthony Alland Hernandez	03.02.1995	18	(2)	6
Shay Jones	24.02.2002		(1)	
Sergio Molina Rivero (ESP)	14.11.1983	8	(8)	4
José Manuel Montesinos Romero (ESP)	19.03.1993	19	(3)	1
Alain Anthony Pons	16.09.1995	15	(2)	1
Forwards:	**DOB**	**M**	**(s)**	**G**
George Cabrera	14.12.1988	4	(4)	6
Kyle Casciaro	02.12.1987	7	(4)	
Lee Henry Casciaro	29.09.1981	17		4
Pedro Corral Valero (ESP)	22.10.1986	9	(3)	3
Julian Del Rio	15.02.2002	1	(3)	1
Rafael Aranda Vincueria “Falu Aranda” (ESP)	05.01.1994	8	(9)	8
Héctor Figueroa Cabrera (ESP)	30.10.1988	8	(2)	10
Enrique “Kike” Gómez Bernal (PHI)	04.05.1994	7		7
Adam Gracia	28.05.2001		(1)	
Juan Manuel Ortiz Jiménez “Juanma” (ESP)	28.05.1986	5	(1)	4
Dylan Peacock	24.08.2001	1	(8)	2
Giovanni Goran Rodríguez Rivero (ESP)	25.08.1998	8	(3)	5
Michael Ruiz	07.12.2000	1		
Trainer:	**DOB**	**M**		
Yiyi Pérez (ESP)		7		
Manolo Nuñez Sánchez (ESP) [08.11.2018]		4		
Víctor Manuel Afonso Mateos (ESP) [13.12.2018]	27.08.1971	16		

Lions Gibraltar Football Club

Founded: 1966
Stadium: Victoria Stadium, Gibraltar (2,800)

Goalkeepers:	DOB	M	(s)	G
John Paul Hernandez	08.03.2002	1	(1)	
Kayron Macedo	27.03.1984	6		
Juan Antonio Mateo (ESP)	24.12.1980	6		
Álvaro Pérez Pichardo (ESP)	13.12.1996	14		
Defenders:	**DOB**	**M**	**(s)**	**G**
Craig Bossano-Anes	22.10.2002	4	(5)	
Shea Kevin Luke Breakspear	22.11.1991	21		
Jared Buhagiar	20.10.1992	13		1
Manuel Jesús Cantizano Rodríguez (ESP)	1989	17		
Scott Kelly	15.10.1990	2		
Jorge Manrique Fernández (ESP)	25.12.1985	2		
David Moreno Gómez (ESP)	19.07.1988	2	(1)	
Jovan Ocaña	15.01.1991	2	(1)	
James Michael Parkinson	21.05.2000	17	(5)	
Kalian Perez „Ping“	22.08.1988	15		
José Utera (ESP)	21.12.1987	17		
Midfielders:	**DOB**	**M**	**(s)**	**G**
Rafael Jesús Bado Blanco	30.12.1984	5	(1)	1
James Bosio	27.03.1991	20	(1)	
Javier Cantelmi (ARG)	14.02.1995	14		2
Jordan Carnegie	24.09.2001	1	(5)	
Shaun Michael De Los Santos	26.01.1998	6	(7)	
Estivien Morente Vélez (ESP)	16.02.1991	20	(2)	1
Sacha Funes (ARG)	15.08.1984	12	(9)	1
Samuel Bobes-Gilroy	27.06.1993	2		
Borja Manuel Gómez Torres (ESP)	13.08.1992	7	(1)	
Julian Grech			(1)	
Hamza Gouicimhoussein (FRA)	14.01.2000		(2)	
Toufik Larouia (MAR)	27.08.1990	7	(1)	
Jonás Luque Gómez (ESP)	07.04.1996	12	(1)	1
Jamie Muir	08.04.2001		(4)	
Louis Parral	13.03.2002		(10)	1
Kaylan Alfred Rumbo	12.12.1990	14	(2)	
Antonio Cintas Sánchez (ESP)	11.01.1995	3		
Fernando Valdayo Cabrera (ESP)	09.08.1999	7	(2)	
Liam Yeo			(1)	
Forwards:	**DOB**	**M**	**(s)**	**G**
José Cano Rodríguez (ESP)		4	(5)	
Alberto Caravaca Castro (ESP)	23.03.1990	22		9
José Pablo Del Rio Corbacho (ESP)	02.02.1989		(2)	
Byron Manuel Espinosa	15.03.1999	1		
Raymond Gomez			(1)	
Jayce Marsh			(2)	
Brendan Ramagge	29.05.2002		(5)	
Kevin Ruiz Moreno (ESP)	06.06.1994	1		
Trainer:	**DOB**	**M**		
Albert Ferri Sola (ESP)	24.02.1970	27		

Lynx Football Club

Founded: 2007
Stadium: Victoria Stadium, Gibraltar (2,800)

Goalkeepers:	**DOB**	**M**	**(s)**	**G**
Bradley James Banda	20.01.1998	7	(1)	
Alex Caro Navarro (ESP)	15.12.1989	15		1
Sebastián Andrés Lallana (ARG)	19.07.1996	4	(1)	
Dean Penfold	16.03.1996	1	(1)	
Robert Copello Rae	30.05.1999		(1)	
Defenders:	**DOB**	**M**	**(s)**	**G**
Alfonso Aragón Herrera (ESP)	01.07.1989	1		
David Alberto Bautista Martos "Bati" (ESP)	27.02.1992	7	(3)	
Jonathan Breakwell Cámara (ESP)	31.03.1998	3		
Kenneth George Chipolina	08.04.1994	12	(2)	
Ryan John Dean	18.07.1998	4	(4)	
Raúl Fernández Ortega (ESP)	07.10.1998	8	(2)	
Gabriel González (ARG)	16.07.1991	19	(3)	1
Shaun Gonzalez	08.11.1993	4		
Aleksander Januszkiewicz (POL)	07.01.1994	4		1
Miguel Ángel Prieto (ESP)	08.05.1998	6		1
Brad Philip Power	29.10.1992	14	(1)	1
Mario Ruesca Torres (ESP)	17.11.1993	10		2
Midfielders:	**DOB**	**M**	**(s)**	**G**
Tyronne Avellano	01.05.2000		(1)	
Mohamed Badr Hassan (EGY)	25.11.1989	22	(1)	4
Yannis Bessaa (FRA)	28.04.1992	14		2
Federico Cataruozzolo (ARG)	08.09.1987	11	(1)	
Hamed Cheghannou Mehamed (MAR)	13.08.1992	8	(1)	
Leon Clinton	19.07.1998	9	(3)	1
Jefferson Duque (COL)	13.03.1997	4	(5)	1
Michael Felice	20.10.1975		(3)	
Ortiz Fernández (ESP)	06.12.1993	4	(5)	
Antonio González García (ESP)	06.05.1996	10	(2)	1
Jorge Junco Díaz (ESP)	14.04.1994	1	(1)	
Nicolás Márquez Barrios (COL)	14.01.1996	21		
Andrés Jesús Medina Cueto (ESP)	13.06.1993	16	(4)	
Dexter Panzavechia	30.12.1990	10	(2)	
Kaylan Villa	08.10.1999	1	(1)	
Forwards:	**DOB**	**M**	**(s)**	**G**
Sékou Oumar Cissoko (GUI)	08.01.1999	9	(1)	1
Eduardo Del Rio Ferreira (ESP)	27.10.1998		(1)	
Michael James Gracia	25.11.1992	4	(7)	
Matthias Alfonso Ramírez (FRA)	06.06.1997	3		
Leone Seatory	21.06.1997	4	(2)	2
Steven Michael Soussi	30.07.1992	13	(1)	
Kamran Ahmed Tariq (GER)	28.06.1993	2	(6)	
José Alberto Mateos Valdivia (ESP)	18.01.1996	11	(3)	8
Trainer:	**DOB**	**M**		
Albert Parody	30.08.1968	3		
Carlos Gobantes Chacón (ESP) [01.10.2018]	01.08.1978	24		

Mons Calpe Sports Club

Founded: 2013
Stadium: Victoria Stadium, Gibraltar (2,800)

Goalkeepers:	**DOB**	**M**	**(s)**	**G**
Christian Hernán Fraiz García (ARG)	22.02.1988	2		
Marcos Raúl Zappacosta (ARG)	17.04.1995	25		
Defenders:	**DOB**	**M**	**(s)**	**G**
Ethan Britto	30.11.2000	16	(1)	1
Leonardo Incorvaia (ARG)	26.06.1992	10	(1)	1
Karlo Kešinović (CRO)	12.12.1989	2	(1)	1
Juan Carlos Léon (ARG)	1998	2	(1)	
Miguel Londero (ARG)	03.01.1989	19	(1)	3
Edelmiro Martinich (ARG)	12.01.1987	2	(5)	
Scott Ritchie (SCO)	26.01.1993	2	(2)	
Ethan James Santos*	22.12.1998	5		
Leonardo Federico Vela (ARG)	05.12.1982	1		
Federico Martín Villar (ARG)	24.11.1985	25		
Francisco Javier Gil Zúñiga (MEX)	22.12.1990	14		3
Midfielders:	**DOB**	**M**	**(s)**	**G**
Rafael Jesús Bado Blanco	30.12.1984		(3)	
Diego Martínez Macarro "Dieguito" (ESP)	20.03.1989	14		1
Jonathan Rodolfo Di Toro (ARG)	22.12.1984	22	(1)	3
Ayoub El Hmidi*	30.09.2000	4		
Juan Sebastián Pegalajar Valero "Juanse" (ESP)*	19.04.1989	14		2
Jonathan Nahuel Pereyra (ARG)	18.12.1991	16	(4)	1
Kevagn Robba	20.09.1994	18		1
Juan Pablo Sosa (ESP)		1	(2)	
Graeme Lee Torrilla	03.09.1997	19	(3)	1
Isaac Vinet	20.04.2001	1	(1)	
Jaron Vinet*	12.12.1997	9		
Forwards:	**DOB**	**M**	**(s)**	**G**
Manuel Camacho Onega (ARG)	07.02.1993	2		
Leonardo Ezequiel Carboni (ARG)*	04.11.1984	21		16
Michele Di Piedi (ITA)	04.12.1980		(1)	
Lautaro Eloy Fernández Cipolla (ARG)	07.09.1993	8	(5)	1
Kelvin Morgan*	14.11.1997	8		3
Juan Pablo Pereira Sastre "Pibe" (ESP)	02.07.1987	22	(1)	18
Kevagn Ronco*	20.04.1998	18		
Néstor Nicolás Trecco (ARG)	30.11.1988	6	(5)	4
Trainer:	**DOB**	**M**		
Luis Manuel Blanco (ARG)	13.12.1953	27		

**number of matches played as substitute not known*

St. Joseph's Football Club

Founded: 1912
Stadium: Victoria Stadium, Gibraltar (2,800)

Goalkeepers:	**DOB**	**M**	**(s)**	**G**
Francisco Javier Mateo Vera (ESP)	14.08.1990	3		
Jaime Kevagn Robba	26.10.1991	24		
Defenders:	**DOB**	**M**	**(s)**	**G**
Javier Anaya Rojas (ESP)	12.07.1995	6	(1)	
Ryan Casciaro	11.05.1984	17	(2)	
Samuel Fernández Aragón (ESP)	08.04.1988	14	(3)	
Daniel Guerrero Heredia (ESP)	08.07.1983	12	(6)	
Iván Lobato González (ESP)	28.05.1991	8	(3)	
José Luis Otero Comino (ESP)	03.02.1996	2		
Abraham Paz Cruz (ESP)	29.06.1979	10	(1)	2
Brad Philip Power	29.10.1992	1		
Jaime Serra	30.10.1998	10	(1)	
Mauricio Torres Fernández	26.02.1988	23	(2)	1
Midfielders:	**DOB**	**M**	**(s)**	**G**
Antonio Calderón Vallejo (ESP)	31.03.1984	13	(8)	1
Domingo Jesús Ferrer López (ESP)	10.04.1989	22		3
Andrew Albert Hernandez	10.01.1999	11	(2)	
Dexter Panzavechia	30.12.1990		(1)	
Cristian Pecci Macías (ESP)	10.05.1988	22		
Pedro Jesús Fernández Martínez "Pedrito" (ESP)	28.11.1990	6	(15)	1
Forwards:	**DOB**	**M**	**(s)**	**G**
Salvador Manuel Alegre Delgado "Boro" (ESP)	04.05.1991	24	(2)	21
Ernesto Cornejo Sánchez (ESP)	25.03.1993	24	(3)	8
John-Paul Duarte	13.12.1986	12	(5)	5
Al Paul Hamilton Greene	05.05.1978	2	(2)	
Evan James Green	13.03.1993	4	(7)	1
Juan Francisco García Peña "Juanfri" (ESP)	01.10.1989	25	(2)	20
José Luís Reyes Verdejo (ESP)	05.10.1981	3	(11)	3
Trainer:	**DOB**	**M**		
Raúl Procopio Baizán (ESP)	10.07.1968	27		

NATIONAL TEAM

INTERNATIONAL MATCHES
(16.07.2018 – 15.07.2019)

06.09.2018	Gibraltar	Gibraltar - North Macedonia	0-2(0-2)	(UNL)
09.09.2018	Vaduz	Liechtenstein - Gibraltar	2-0(1-0)	(UNL)
13.10.2018	Yerevan	Armenia - Gibraltar	0-1(0-0)	(UNL)
16.10.2018	Gibraltar	Gibraltar - Liechtenstein	2-1(0-1)	(UNL)
16.11.2018	Gibraltar	Gibraltar - Armenia	2-6(1-1)	(UNL)
19.11.2018	Skopje	North Macedonia - Gibraltar	4-0(1-0)	(UNL)
23.03.2019	Gibraltar	Gibraltar - Republic of Ireland	0-1(0-0)	(ECQ)
26.03.2019	Gibraltar	Gibraltar - Estonia	0-1(0-0)	(F)
07.06.2019	Tbilisi	Georgia - Gibraltar	3-0(1-0)	(ECQ)
10.06.2019	Dublin	Republic of Ireland - Gibraltar	2-0(1-0)	(ECQ)

06.09.2018 GIBRALTAR - NORTH MACEDONIA 0-2(0-2) UEFA Nations League D, Group 4
Victoria Stadium, Gibraltar; Referee: Jens Maae (Denmark); Attendance: 1,850
GIB: Kyle Albert Goldwin, Joseph Luis Chipolina (Cap), Erin Anthony Barnett, Jayce Lee Mascarenhas-Olivero, Liam Walker, Alain Anthony Pons (75.Sykes Al Garro), John Iain Stephen Sergeant, Anthony Michael Bardon, Anthony Alland Hernandez, Lee Henry Casciaro (90+3.Jean-Carlos Anthony Garcia), Andre Tjay De Barr (80.Reece Styche). Trainer: Julio César Ribas Vlacovich (Uruguay).

09.09.2018 LIECHTENSTEIN - GIBRALTAR 2-0(1-0) UEFA Nations League D, Group 4
Rheinpark Stadion, Vaduz; Referee: Alan Mario Sant (Malta); Attendance: 1,110
GIB: Kyle Albert Goldwin, Joseph Luis Chipolina (Cap), Erin Anthony Barnett, Jayce Lee Mascarenhas-Olivero, Liam Walker, Alain Anthony Pons (46.Sykes Al Garro), John Iain Stephen Sergeant, Anthony Michael Bardon, Anthony Alland Hernandez, Lee Henry Casciaro, Andre Tjay De Barr (71.Reece Styche). Trainer: Julio César Ribas Vlacovich (Uruguay).

13.10.2018 ARMENIA - GIBRALTAR 0-1(0-0) UEFA Nations League D, Group 4
„Vazgen Sargsyan" Hanrapetakan Stadium, Yerevan; Referee: Fedayi San (Switzerland); Attendance: 11,000
GIB: Kyle Albert Goldwin, Joseph Luis Chipolina, Jayce Lee Mascarenhas-Olivero, Roy Alan Chipolina (Cap), Liam Walker, Alain Anthony Pons (90+6.Louie John Annesley), John Iain Stephen Sergeant, Andrew Albert Hernandez (85.Ethan Britto), Anthony Michael Bardon, James Timothy Barry Coombes (70.Reece Styche), Lee Henry Casciaro. Trainer: Julio César Ribas Vlacovich (Uruguay).
Goal: Joseph Luis Chipolina (50 penalty).

16.10.2018 GIBRALTAR - LIECHTENSTEIN 2-1(0-1) UEFA Nations League D, Group 4
Victoria Stadium, Gibraltar; Referee: Vasilis Dimitriou (Cyprus); Attendance: 2,000
GIB: Kyle Albert Goldwin, Joseph Luis Chipolina, Jayce Lee Mascarenhas-Olivero, Roy Alan Chipolina (Cap), Liam Walker, Alain Anthony Pons, John Iain Stephen Sergeant, Andrew Albert Hernandez (46.James Timothy Barry Coombes; 75.Kyle Casciaro), Anthony Michael Bardon, Lee Henry Casciaro, George Cabrera (90+6.Andre Tjay De Barr). Trainer: Julio César Ribas Vlacovich (Uruguay).
Goals: George Cabrera (61), Joseph Luis Chipolina (66).

16.11.2018 GIBRALTAR - ARMENIA 2-6(1-1) UEFA Nations League D, Group 4
Victoria Stadium, Gibraltar; Referee: Kai Erik Steen (Norway); Attendance: 1,955
GIB: Kyle Albert Goldwin, Joseph Luis Chipolina (84.Aymen Mouelhi), Jayce Lee Mascarenhas-Olivero, Roy Alan Chipolina (Cap), Liam Walker, Alain Anthony Pons (71.Adam Priestley), John Iain Stephen Sergeant, Anthony Michael Bardon, Anthony Alland Hernandez (72.Andrew Albert Hernandez), Lee Henry Casciaro, Andre Tjay De Barr. Trainer: Julio César Ribas Vlacovich (Uruguay).
Goals: Andre Tjay De Barr (10), Adam Priestley (78).

19.11.2018 NORTH MACEDONIA - GIBRALTAR 4-0(1-0) UEFA Nations League D, Group 4
"Toše Proeski" National Arena, Skopje; Referee: Daniyar Sakhi (Kazakhstan); Attendance: 2,152
GIB: Matthew Paul Cafer, Aymen Mouelhi, Jayce Lee Mascarenhas-Olivero, Roy Alan Chipolina (Cap), Louie John Annesley (88.Erin Anthony Barnett), Liam Walker, John Iain Stephen Sergeant, Andrew Albert Hernandez, Anthony Michael Bardon, Lee Henry Casciaro (79.Anthony Alland Hernandez), Andre Tjay De Barr (81.Adam Priestley). Trainer: Julio César Ribas Vlacovich (Uruguay).

23.03.2019 GIBRALTAR - REPUBLIC OF IRELAND 0-1(0-0) 16th EC. Qualifiers
Victoria Stadium, Gibraltar; Referee: Anastasios Papapetrou (Greece); Attendance: 2,000
GIB: Kyle Albert Goldwin, Joseph Luis Chipolina, Jayce Lee Mascarenhas-Olivero, Roy Alan Chipolina (Cap), Louie John Annesley (64.Adam Priestley), Liam Walker, John Iain Stephen Sergeant, Anthony Michael Bardon, Anthony Alland Hernandez (77.Alain Anthony Pons), Lee Henry Casciaro, Andre Tjay De Barr. Trainer: Julio César Ribas Vlacovich (Uruguay).

26.03.2019 GIBRALTAR - ESTONIA 0-1(0-0) Friendly International
Victoria Stadium, Gibraltar; Referee: Nicholas Walsh (Scotland); Attendance: 1,900
GIB: Kyle Albert Goldwin, Joseph Luis Chipolina (46.Aymen Mouelhi), Jayce Lee Mascarenhas-Olivero, Roy Alan Chipolina (Cap), Liam Walker, Alain Anthony Pons (46.Louie John Annesley), John Iain Stephen Sergeant, Anthony Michael Bardon (71.James Timothy Barry Coombes), Anthony Alland Hernandez (63.Adam Priestley), Lee Henry Casciaro (63.Reece Styche), Andre Tjay De Barr (90.Ethan Terence Jolley). Trainer: Julio César Ribas Vlacovich (Uruguay).

07.06.2019 GEORGIA - GIBRALTAR 3-0(1-0) 16th EC. Qualifiers
"Boris Paichadze" Dinamo Arena, Tbilisi; Referee: Antti Munukka (Finland); Attendance: 17,357
GIB: Kyle Albert Goldwin, Joseph Luis Chipolina, Jayce Lee Mascarenhas-Olivero, Roy Alan Chipolina (Cap), Louie John Annesley (86.Erin Anthony Barnett), Liam Walker, John Iain Stephen Sergeant, Anthony Michael Bardon (77.James Timothy Barry Coombes), Anthony Alland Hernandez, Lee Henry Casciaro (65.Alain Anthony Pons), Andre Tjay De Barr. Trainer: Julio César Ribas Vlacovich (Uruguay).

10.06.2019 REPUBLIC OF IRELAND - GIBRALTAR 2-0(1-0) 16th EC. Qualifiers
Aviva Stadium, Dublin; Referee: Radu Petrescu (Romania); Attendance: 36,281
GIB: Kyle Albert Goldwin, Joseph Luis Chipolina, Jayce Lee Mascarenhas-Olivero, Roy Alan Chipolina (Cap), Louie John Annesley, Liam Walker, Alain Anthony Pons (64.Ethan Britto), John Iain Stephen Sergeant, Andrew Albert Hernandez (76.Ethan Terence Jolley), Lee Henry Casciaro (9.Anthony Michael Bardon), Andre Tjay De Barr. Trainer: Julio César Ribas Vlacovich (Uruguay).

NATIONAL TEAM PLAYERS
(16.07.2018 – 15.07.2019)

Name	DOB	Caps	Goals	2018/2019:	*Club*
Goalkeepers					
Matthew Paul CAFER	27.09.1994	**1**	**0**	2018:	*Gibraltar Phoenix FC*
Kyle Albert GOLDWIN	24.04.1985	**10**	**0**	2018/2019:	*Gibraltar United FC*
Defenders					
Erin Anthony BARNETT	02.09.1996	**15**	**0**	2018/2019:	*Gibraltar United FC*
Ethan BRITTO	30.11.2000	**2**	**0**	2018/2019:	*Mons Calpe SC*
Joseph Luis CHIPOLINA	14.12.1987	**36**	**2**	2018/2019:	*Lincoln Red Imps FC*
Roy Alan CHIPOLINA	20.01.1983	**36**	**1**	2018/2019:	*Lincoln Red Imps FC*
Jean-Carlos Anthony GARCIA	05.07.1992	**26**	**0**	2018/2019:	*Lincoln Red Imps FC*
Ethan Terence JOLLEY	29.03.1997	**2**	**0**	2019:	*Europa FC*
Aymen MOUELHI	14.09.1986	**3**	**0**	2018/2019:	*Gibraltar United FC*
Jayce Lee MASCARENHAS-OLIVERO	02.07.1998	**22**	**0**	2018/2019:	*Abingdon United FC (ENG)*
John Iain Stephen SERGEANT	27.02.1995	**22**	**0**	2018/2019:	*West Didsbury & Chorlton AFC (ENG)*
Midfielders					
Louie John ANNESLEY	03.05.2000	**7**	**0**	2018: 30.01.2019->	*Lincoln Red Imps FC* *Blackburn Rovers FC (ENG)*
Anthony Michael BARDON	19.01.1993	**29**	**0**	2018: 2019->	*Lincoln Red Imps FC* *Unattached*
Kyle CASCIARO	12.03.1987	**24**	**1**	2018:	*Lincoln Red Imps FC*
Sykes Al GARRO	26.02.1993	**3**	**0**	2018:	*Lincoln Red Imps FC*
Andrew Albert HERNANDEZ	10.01.1999	**5**	**0**	2018: 02.01.2019->	*Lincoln Red Imps FC* *St. Joseph's FC*
Anthony Alland HERNANDEZ	03.02.1995	**20**	**1**	2018/2019:	*Lincoln Red Imps FC*
Alain Anthony PONS	16.09.1995	**13**	**0**	2018/2019:	*Lincoln Red Imps FC*
Liam WALKER	13.04.1988	**39**	**2**	2018/2019:	*Europa FC*
Forwards					
George CABRERA	14.12.1988	**8**	**1**	2018:	*Lincoln Red Imps FC*
Lee Henry CASCIARO	29.09.1981	**29**	**2**	2018/2019:	*Lincoln Red Imps FC*
James Timothy Barry COOMBES	27.05.1996	**13**	**0**	2018/2019:	*West Didsbury & Chorlton AFC (ENG)*
Andre Tjay DE BARR	13.03.2000	**10**	**1**	2018/2019:	*Europa FC*
Adam PRIESTLEY	14.08.1990	**17**	**1**	2018/2019:	*Ossett United FC (ENG)*
Reece STYCHE	03.05.1989	**5**	**0**	2018: 24.10.2018->	*Darlington FC (ENG)* *Alfreton Town FC (ENG)*

National team coach

Julio César RIBAS Vlacovich (Uruguay) [from 01.07.2018]	08.01.1957	10 M; 2 W; 0 D; 8 L; 5-22

GREECE

The Country:

Ελληνική Δημοκρατία (Hellenic Republic)
Capital: Athína
Surface: 131,957 km²
Inhabitants: 10,768,477 [2017]
Time: UTC+2

The FA:

Hellenic Football Federation
Goudi Park P.O. Box 14161, 11510 Athens
Tel: +30 21 0930 6000
Foundation date: 1926
Member of FIFA since: 1927
Member of UEFA since: 1954
Website: www.epo.gr

NATIONAL TEAM RECORDS

First international match:	07.04.1929, Athína:	Greece – Italy "B" 1-4
Most international caps:	Georgios Karagoúnis	- 139 caps (1999-2014)
Most international goals:	Nikolaos Anastopoulos	- 29 goals / 74 caps (1977-1988)

UEFA EUROPEAN CHAMPIONSHIP

1960	Qualifiers
1964	Did not enter
1968	Qualifiers
1972	Qualifiers
1976	Qualifiers
1980	Final Tournament (Group Stage)
1984	Qualifiers
1988	Qualifiers
1992	Qualifiers
1996	Qualifiers
2000	Qualifiers
2004	**Final Tournament (Winners)**
2008	Final Tournament (Group Stage)
2012	Final Tournament (Quarter-Finals)
2016	Qualifiers

FIFA WORLD CUP

1930	Did not enter
1934	Qualifiers
1938	Qualifiers
1950	Did not enter
1954	Qualifiers
1958	Qualifiers
1962	Qualifiers
1966	Qualifiers
1970	Qualifiers
1974	Qualifiers
1978	Qualifiers
1982	Qualifiers
1986	Qualifiers
1990	Qualifiers
1994	Final Tournament (Group Stage)
1998	Qualifiers
2002	Qualifiers
2006	Qualifiers
2010	Final Tournament (Group Stage)
2014	Final Tournament (2nd Round of 16)
2018	Qualifiers

UEFA NATIONS LEAGUE

2018/2019 – League C

OLYMPIC FOOTBALL TOURNAMENTS 1908-2016

1908	-	**1948**	-	**1972**	Qualifiers	**1996**	Qualifiers
1912	-	**1952**	Preliminary Round	**1976**	Qualifiers	**2000**	Qualifiers
1920	Quarter-Finals	**1956**	-	**1980**	Group Stage	**2004**	Group Stage
1924	-	**1960**	Qualifiers	**1984**	Qualifiers	**2008**	Qualifiers
1928	-	**1964**	Qualifiers	**1988**	Qualifiers	**2012**	Qualifiers
1936	-	**1968**	Qualifiers	**1992**	Qualifiers	**2016**	Qualifiers

FIFA CONFEDERATIONS CUP 1992-2017

2005 (Group Stage)

GREEK CLUB HONOURS IN EUROPEAN CLUB COMPETITIONS:

European Champion Clubs' Cup (1956-1992) / UEFA Champions League (1993-2019)

None

Fairs Cup (1858-1971) / UEFA Cup (1972-2009) / UEFA Europa League (2010-2019)

None

UEFA Super Cup (1972-2018)

None

European Cup Winners' Cup 1961-1999*

None

**defunct competition*

NATIONAL COMPETITIONS
TABLE OF HONOURS

	CHAMPIONS	CUP WINNERS	BEST GOALSCORERS	
1905/1906	Ethnikos GS Athína	-	-	
1906/1907	Ethnikos GS Athína	-	-	
1907/1908	FC Goudi Athína	-	-	
1908/1909	Peiraikos Syndesmos	-	-	
1909/1910	FC Goudi Athína	-	-	
1910/1911	Podosferikos Omilos Athinon	-	-	
1911/1912	FC Goudi Athína	-	-	
1912/1913	*No competition*	-	-	
1913/1914	*No competition*	-	-	
1914/1915	*No competition*	-	-	
1915/1916	*No competition*	-	-	
1916/1917	*Championship not finished*	-	-	
1917/1918	*No competition*	-	-	
1918/1919	*No competition*	-	-	
1919/1920	*No competition*	-	-	
1920/1921	*No competition*	-	-	
1921/1922	Panellinios Podosferikos Omilos	-	-	
1922/1923	Peiraikos Syndesmos	-	-	
1923/1924	Apollonas Athína (Athína champions) APS Peiraiás (Athína/Peiraiás champions) Aris Thessaloníki (Thessaloníki champions)	-	-	
1924/1925	PAE Panathinaïkos Athína (Athína champions) Olympiacos SFP Peiraiás (Athína/Peiraiás champions)	-	-	
1925/1926	PAE Panathinaïkos Athína (Athína champions) Olympiacos SFP Peiraiás (Athína/Peiraiás champions) Aris Thessaloníki (Thessaloníki champions)	-	-	
1926/1927	PAE Panathinaïkos Athína (Athína champions) Olympiacos SFP Peiraiás (Athína/Peiraiás champions) Iraklis Thessaloníki (Thessaloníki champions)	-	-	
1927/1928	Aris Thessaloníki	-	-	
1928/1929	*No competition*	-	-	
1929/1930	PAE Panathinaïkos Athína	-	-	
1930/1931	Olympiacos SFP Peiraiás	-	-	
1931/1932	Aris Thessaloníki	AEK Athína	-	
1932/1933	Olympiacos SFP Peiraiás	Ethnikos Peiraiás	-	
1933/1934	Olympiacos SFP Peiraiás	*No competition*	-	
1934/1935	*Championship not finished*	*No competition*	-	
1935/1936	Olympiacos SFP Peiraiás	*No competition*	-	
1936/1937	Olympiacos SFP Peiraiás	*No competition*	-	
1937/1938	Olympiacos SFP Peiraiás	*No competition*	-	
1938/1939	AEK Athína	AEK Athína	-	
1939/1940	AEK Athína	PAE Panathinaïkos Athína	-	
1940/1941	*Championship not finished*	*No competition*	-	
1941/1942	*No competition*	*No competition*	-	
1942/1943	*Championship not finished*	*No competition*	-	
1943/1944	*No competition*	*No competition*	-	
1944/1945	*No competition*	*No competition*	-	
1945/1946	Aris Thessaloníki	*No competition*	-	
1946/1947	Olympiacos SFP Peiraiás	Olympiacos SFP Peiraiás	-	
1947/1948	Olympiacos SFP Peiraiás	PAE Panathinaïkos Athína	-	
1948/1949	PAE Panathinaïkos Athína	AEK Athína	-	
1949/1950	*No competition*	AEK Athína	-	
1950/1951	Olympiacos SFP Peiraiás	Olympiacos SFP Peiraiás	-	
1951/1952	*No competition*	Olympiacos SFP Peiraiás	-	
1952/1953	PAE Panathinaïkos Athína	Olympiacos SFP Peiraiás	-	
1953/1954	Olympiacos SFP Peiraiás	Olympiacos SFP Peiraiás	-	
1954/1955	Olympiacos SFP Peiraiás	PAE Panathinaïkos Athína	-	
1955/1956	Olympiacos SFP Peiraiás	AEK Athína	-	
1956/1957	Olympiacos SFP Peiraiás	Olympiacos SFP Peiraiás	-	
1957/1958	Olympiacos SFP Peiraiás	Olympiacos SFP Peiraiás	-	
1958/1959	Olympiacos SFP Peiraiás	Olympiacos SFP Peiraiás	-	
1959/1960	PAE Panathinaïkos Athína	Olympiacos SFP Peiraiás	Konstantinos Nestoridis (AEK Athína)	30
1960/1961	PAE Panathinaïkos Athína	Olympiacos SFP Peiraiás	Konstantinos Nestoridis (AEK Athína)	27
1961/1962	PAE Panathinaïkos Athína	*Final abandoned, no winner*	Konstantinos Nestoridis (AEK Athína)	29
1962/1963	AEK Athína	Olympiacos SFP Peiraiás	Konstantinos Nestoridis (AEK Athína)	23
1963/1964	PAE Panathinaïkos Athína	AEK Athína	Dimitrios Papaioannou (AEK Athína)	29
1964/1965	PAE Panathinaïkos Athína	Olympiacos SFP Peiraiás	Giorgos Sideris (Olympiacos SFP Peiraiás)	29
1965/1966	Olympiacos SFP Peiraiás	AEK Athína	Dimitrios Papaioannou (AEK Athína)	23
1966/1967	Olympiacos SFP Peiraiás	PAE Panathinaïkos Athína	Giorgos Sideris (Olympiacos SFP Peiraiás)	24
1967/1968	AEK Athína	Olympiacos SFP Peiraiás	Thanasis Intzoglou (Panionios GSS Athína)	24
1968/1969	PAE Panathinaïkos Athína	PAE Panathinaïkos Athína	Giorgos Sideris (Olympiacos SFP Peiraiás)	35

1969/1970	PAE Panathinaïkos Athína	Aris Thessaloníki	Antonis Antoniadis (PAE Panathinaïkos Athína)	25
1970/1971	AEK Athína	Olympiacos SFP Peiraiás	Giorgos Dedes (Panionios GSS Athína)	28
1971/1972	PAE Panathinaïkos Athína	PAOK Thessaloníki	Antonis Antoniadis (PAE Panathinaïkos Athína)	39
1972/1973	Olympiacos SFP Peiraiás	Olympiacos SFP Peiraiás	Antonis Antoniadis (PAE Panathinaïkos Athína)	22
1973/1974	Olympiacos SFP Peiraiás	PAOK Thessaloníki	Antonis Antoniadis (PAE Panathinaïkos Athína)	26
1974/1975	Olympiacos SFP Peiraiás	Olympiacos SFP Peiraiás	Antonis Antoniadis (PAE Panathinaïkos Athína) Roberto Calcadera (URU, Ethnikos Peiraiás)	20
1975/1976	PAOK Thessaloníki	Iraklis Thessaloníki	Giorgos Dedes (AEK Athína)	15
1976/1977	PAE Panathinaïkos Athína	PAE Panathinaïkos Athína	Thanasis Intzoglou (Ethnikos Peiraiás) Dimitrios Papadopoulos (OFI Heraklion)	22
1977/1978	AEK Athína	AEK Athína	Thomas Mavros (AEK Athína)	22
1978/1979	AEK Athína	Panionios GSS Athína	Thomas Mavros (AEK Athína)	31
1979/1980	Olympiacos SFP Peiraiás	AGSK Kastoria	Dušan Bajević (YUG, AEK Athína)	25
1980/1981	Olympiacos SFP Peiraiás	Olympiacos SFP Peiraiás	Dinos Kouis (Aris Thessaloníki)	21
1981/1982	Olympiacos SFP Peiraiás	PAE Panathinaïkos Athína	Grigoris Charalampidis (PAE Panathinaïkos Athína)	21
1982/1983	Olympiacos SFP Peiraiás	AEK Athína	Nikolaos Anastopoulos (Olympiacos SFP Peiraiás)	29
1983/1984	PAE Panathinaïkos Athína	PAE Panathinaïkos Athína	Nikolaos Anastopoulos (Olympiacos SFP Peiraiás)	18
1984/1985	PAOK Thessaloníki	AE Larissa	Thomas Mavros (AEK Athína)	27
1985/1986	PAE Panathinaïkos Athína	PAE Panathinaïkos Athína	Nikolaos Anastopoulos (Olympiacos SFP Peiraiás)	19
1986/1987	Olympiacos SFP Peiraiás	OFI Heraklion	Nikolaos Anastopoulos (Olympiacos SFP Peiraiás)	16
1987/1988	AE Larissa	PAE Panathinaïkos Athína	Henrik Nielsen (DEN, AEK Athína)	20
1988/1989	AEK Athína	PAE Panathinaïkos Athína	Imre Boda (HUN, Olympiakos Volos)	20
1989/1990	PAE Panathinaïkos Athína	Olympiacos SFP Peiraiás	Thomas Mavros (Panionios GSS Athína)	22
1990/1991	PAE Panathinaïkos Athína	PAE Panathinaïkos Athína	Dimitrios Saravakos (PAE Panathinaïkos Athína)	23
1991/1992	AEK Athína	Olympiacos SFP Peiraiás	Vasilios Dimitriadis (AEK Athína)	28
1992/1993	AEK Athína	PAE Panathinaïkos Athína	Vasilios Dimitriadis (AEK Athína)	33
1993/1994	AEK Athína	PAE Panathinaïkos Athína	Alexandros Alexandris (AEK Athína) Krzysztof Warzycha (POL, PAE Panathinaïkos Athína)	24
1994/1995	PAE Panathinaïkos Athína	PAE Panathinaïkos Athína	Krzysztof Warzycha (POL, PAE Panathinaïkos Athína)	29
1995/1996	PAE Panathinaïkos Athína	AEK Athína	Vassilis Tsiartas (AEK Athína)	26
1996/1997	Olympiacos SFP Peiraiás	AEK Athína	Alexandros Alexandris (Olympiacos SFP Peiraiás)	23
1997/1998	Olympiacos SFP Peiraiás	Panionios GSS Athína	Krzysztof Warzycha (POL, PAE Panathinaïkos Athína)	32
1998/1999	Olympiacos SFP Peiraiás	Olympiacos SFP Peiraiás	Themistoklis Nikolaidis (AEK Athína)	22
1999/2000	Olympiacos SFP Peiraiás	AEK Athína	Dimitrios Nalitzis (Panionios, PAOK Thessaloníki)	24
2000/2001	Olympiacos SFP Peiraiás	PAOK Thessaloníki	Alexandros Alexandris (Olympiacos SFP Peiraiás)	19
2001/2002	Olympiacos SFP Peiraiás	AEK Athína	Alexandros Alexandris (Olympiacos SFP Peiraiás)	19
2002/2003	Olympiacos SFP Peiraiás	PAOK Thessaloníki	Nikolaos Liberopoulos (PAE Panathinaïkos Athína)	16
2003/2004	PAE Panathinaïkos Athína	PAE Panathinaïkos Athína	Giovanni Silva de Oliveira (BRA, Olympiacos SFP Peiraiás)	21
2004/2005	Olympiacos SFP Peiraiás	Olympiacos SFP Peiraiás	Theofanis Gekas (PAE Panathinaïkos Athína)	18
2005/2006	Olympiacos SFP Peiraiás	Olympiacos SFP Peiraiás	Dimitrios Salpingidis (PAOK Thessaloníki)	17
2006/2007	Olympiacos SFP Peiraiás	AE Larissa	Nikolaos Liberopoulos (AEK Athína)	18
2007/2008	Olympiacos SFP Peiraiás	Olympiacos SFP Peiraiás	Ismael Alfonso Blanco (ARG, AEK Athína)	19
2008/2009	Olympiacos SFP Peiraiás	Olympiacos SFP Peiraiás	Ismael Alfonso Blanco (ARG, AEK Athína) Luciano Martín Galletti (ARG, Olympiacos SFP Peiraiás)	14
2009/2010	PAE Panathinaïkos Athína	PAE Panathinaïkos Athína	Djibril Cissé (FRA, PAE Panathinaïkos Athína)	23
2010/2011	Olympiacos SFP Peiraiás	AEK Athína	Djibril Cissé (FRA, PAE Panathinaïkos Athína)	20
2011/2012	Olympiacos SFP Peiraiás	Olympiacos SFP Peiraiás	Kevin Antonio Joel Gislain Mirallas y Castillo (BEL, Olympiacos SFP Peiraiás)	22
2012/2013	Olympiacos SFP Peiraiás	Olympiacos SFP Peiraiás	Rafik Djebbour (ALG, Olympiacos SFP Peiraiás)	20
2013/2014	Olympiacos SFP Peiraiás	PAE Panathinaïkos Athína	Esteban Andrés Solari Poggio (ARG, Skoda Xanthi AC)	16
2014/2015	Olympiacos SFP Peiraiás	Olympiacos SFP Peiraiás	Jerónimo Barrales (ARG, AGS Asteras Tripoli)	17
2015/2016	Olympiacos SFP Peiraiás	AEK Athína	Konstantinos Fortounis (Olympiacos SFP Peiraiás)	18
2016/2017	Olympiacos SFP Peiraiás	PAOK Thessaloníki	Bengt Erik Markus Berg (SWE, PAE Panathinaïkos Athína)	22
2017/2018	AEK Athína	PAOK Thessaloníki	Aleksandar Prijović (SRB, PAOK Thessaloníki)	19
2018/2019	PAOK Thessaloníki	PAOK Thessaloníki	Efthymis Koulouris (APS Atromitos Athína)	19

NATIONAL CHAMPIONSHIP
Super League Souroti 2018/2019
(25.08.2018 – 05.05.2019)

Results

Round 1 [25-27.08.2018]
Panetolikos - Atromitos 1-2(1-1)
PAOK Thessaloníki - Asteras Trip. 1-0(0-0)
AEK Athína - PAS Giannina 2-0(1-0)
GS Apollon - AE Larissa 0-1(0-1)
AO Xanthi - Panathinaïkos 0-1(0-0)
Panionios - OFI Heraklion 2-2(2-2)
Olympiacos Peiraiás - Levadiakos 1-0(0-0)
PAS Lamia - Aris Thessaloníki 0-3(0-0)

Round 2 [01-03.09.2018]
Panathinaïkos - PAS Lamia 3-1(1-1)
Asteras Tripolis - AEK Athína 0-1(0-1)
Atromitos - AO Xanthi 0-0
Aris Thessaloníki - AE Larissa 2-0(0-0)
Panionios - PAOK Thessaloníki 0-1(0-0)
Olympiacos Peiraiás - PAS Giannina 5-0(2-0)
Levadiakos - GS Apollon 1-0(0-0)
Panetolikos - OFI Heraklion 2-1(1-0)

Round 3 [15-17.09.2018]
OFI Heraklion - PAOK Thessaloníki 1-3(1-2)
GS Apollon - PAS Giannina 1-2(0-1)
AEK Athína - Panionios 4-0(1-0)
AO Xanthi - Panetolikos 1-1(1-1)
AE Larissa - Panathinaïkos 1-3(0-1)
Atromitos - PAS Lamia 1-0(1-0)
Olympiacos Peiraiás - Asteras Trip. 2-1(1-0)
Aris Thessaloníki - Levadiakos 2-0(1-0)

Round 4 [22-24.09.2018]
Asteras Tripolis - GS Apollon 2-0(2-0)
Atromitos - AE Larissa 2-0(0-0)
PAS Giannina - Aris Thessaloníki 1-0(0-0)
AO Xanthi - OFI Heraklion 3-0(2-0)
Panathinaïkos - Levadiakos 3-0(2-0)
PAOK Thessaloníki - AEK Athína 2-0(1-0)
Panetolikos - PAS Lamia 2-2(1-0)
Panionios - Olympiacos Peiraiás 0-1(0-0)

Round 5 [29.09.-01.10.2018]
AE Larissa - Panetolikos 1-0(1-0)
Panathinaïkos - PAS Giannina 2-1(1-1)
OFI Heraklion - AEK Athína 0-3(0-2)
GS Apollon - Panionios 0-2(0-1)
Levadiakos - Atromitos 0-2(0-0)
Aris Thessaloníki - Asteras Tripolis 2-0(0-0)
Olympiacos Peiraiás - PAOK Thess. 0-1(0-0)
PAS Lamia - AO Xanthi 0-0

Round 6 [06-08.10.2018]
Panionios - Aris Thessaloníki 1-0(1-0)
Panetolikos - Levadiakos 2-1(0-0)
Asteras Tripolis - Panathinaïkos 1-1(0-0)
PAS Lamia - OFI Heraklion 1-1(0-0)
PAOK Thessaloníki - GS Apollon 2-0(1-0)
Atromitos - PAS Giannina 1-0(1-0)
AEK Athína - Olympiacos Peiraiás 1-1(0-0)
AO Xanthi - AE Larissa 1-0(0-0)

Round 7 [20-22.10.2018]
Panathinaïkos - Panionios 1-0(0-0)
PAS Giannina - Panetolikos 0-2(0-1)
GS Apollon - AEK Athína 0-2(0-1)
AE Larissa - PAS Lamia 1-2(1-0)
Levadiakos - AO Xanthi 1-2(0-1)
Aris Thessaloníki - PAOK Thessal. 1-2(1-1)
OFI Heraklion - Olympiacos Peiraiás 1-0(1-0)
Atromitos - Asteras Tripolis 3-2(1-0)

Round 8 [27-29.10.2018]
AE Larissa - OFI Heraklion 0-0
PAS Lamia - Levadiakos 3-2(2-0)
Panionios - Atromitos 2-2(1-1)
Panetolikos - Asteras Tripolis 1-1(0-0)
AEK Athína - Aris Thessaloníki 4-0(1-0)
AO Xanthi - PAS Giannina 2-1(0-1)
Olympiacos Peiraiás - GS Apollon 1-0(0-0)
PAOK Thessaloníki - Panathinaïkos 2-0(0-0)

Round 9 [03-05.11.2018]
Atromitos - PAOK Thessaloníki 1-1(0-1)
Panionios - Panetolikos 3-0(3-0)
Panathinaïkos - AEK Athína 0-0
Levadiakos - AE Larissa 1-1(0-1)
PAS Giannina - PAS Lamia 0-0
Aris Thessal. - Olympiacos Peiraiás 0-1(0-0)
OFI Heraklion - GS Apollon 0-0
Asteras Tripolis - AO Xanthi 0-1(0-0)

Round 10 [10-12.11.2018]
AE Larissa - PAS Giannina 2-0(0-0)
AO Xanthi - Panionios 0-1(0-1)
Levadiakos - OFI Heraklion 2-1(2-1)
AEK Athína - Atromitos 0-2(0-0)
PAOK Thessaloníki - Panetolikos 2-1(0-0)
PAS Lamia - Asteras Tripolis 0-0
Olympiacos Peiraiás - Panathinaïkos 1-1(0-0)
GS Apollon - Aris Thessaloníki 1-2(1-1)

Round 11 [24-26.11.2018]
Panathinaïkos - GS Apollon 5-1(2-0)
Asteras Tripolis - AE Larissa 2-0(0-0)
Panetolikos - AEK Athína 2-1(1-0)
PAOK Thessaloníki - AO Xanthi 2-0(0-0)
PAS Giannina - Levadiakos 2-0(1-0)
Atromitos - Olympiacos Peiraiás 1-2(1-0)
OFI Heraklion - Aris Thessaloníki 1-2(0-0)
Panionios - PAS Lamia 1-0(0-0)

Round 12 [01-03.12.2018]
AE Larissa - Panionios 4-2(1-1)
GS Apollon - Atromitos 1-1(1-1)
PAS Giannina - OFI Heraklion 1-1(0-0)
Levadiakos - Asteras Tripolis 0-2(0-0)
Aris Thessaloníki - Panathinaïkos 1-1(1-0)
AEK Athína - AO Xanthi 2-0(1-0)
PAS Lamia - PAOK Thessaloníki 0-1(0-0)
Olympiacos Peiraiás - Panetolikos 2-1(2-0)

Round 13 [08-10.12.2018]
Asteras Tripolis - PAS Giannina 1-0(0-0)
AEK Athína - PAS Lamia 2-0(1-0)
AO Xanthi - Olympiacos Peiraiás 1-1(0-0)
OFI Heraklion - Panathinaïkos 3-1(2-1)
Atromitos - Aris Thessaloníki 4-2(1-0)
PAOK Thessaloníki - AE Larissa 2-1(1-1)
Panetolikos - GS Apollon 2-1(2-0)
Panionios - Levadiakos 1-1(0-1)

Round 14 [15-17.12.2018]
PAS Giannina - Panionios 3-1(0-0)
Aris Thessaloníki - Panetolikos 1-2(0-0)
Asteras Tripolis - OFI Heraklion 2-1(0-1)
GS Apollon - AO Xanthi 1-0(0-0)
AE Larissa - AEK Athína 0-0
Panathinaïkos - Atromitos 1-0(1-0)
Olympiacos Peiraiás - PAS Lamia 3-0(1-0)
Levadiakos - PAOK Thessaloníki 1-2(0-1)

Round 15 [30-31.01.2019]
Panionios - Asteras Tripolis 1-0(1-0)
PAS Lamia - GS Apollon 2-1(2-1)
AEK Athína - Levadiakos 1-0(1-0)
PAOK Thessaloníki - PAS Giannina 2-1(1-0)
Panetolikos - Panathinaïkos 0-1(0-1)
Olympiacos Peiraiás - AE Larissa 4-0(3-0)
OFI Heraklion - Atromitos 1-1(1-1)
AO Xanthi - Aris Thessaloníki 0-1(0-1)

Round 16 [12-14.01.2019]
AE Larissa - GS Apollon 3-0(1-0)
Atromitos - Panetolikos 2-2(0-0)
OFI Heraklion - Panionios 1-1(1-0)
Levadiakos - Olympiacos Peiraiás 0-2(0-1)
Panathinaïkos - AO Xanthi 2-2(0-1)
Asteras Trip. - PAOK Thessaloníki 0-3(0-0)
Aris Thessaloníki - PAS Lamia 1-0(0-0)
PAS Giannina - AEK Athína 0-4(0-4)

Round 17 [19-21.01.2019]
PAS Giannina - Olympiacos Peiraiás 1-2(1-2)
GS Apollon - Levadiakos 0-0
PAOK Thessaloníki - Panionios 3-0(2-0)
OFI Heraklion - Panetolikos 3-0(1-0)
AE Larissa - Aris Thessaloníki 0-0
AO Xanthi - Atromitos 2-1(1-1)
AEK Athína - Asteras Tripolis 3-0(3-0)
PAS Lamia - Panathinaïkos 1-0(0-0)

Round 18 [26-27.01.2019]
PAS Giannina - GS Apollon 1-0(1-0)
Panetolikos - AO Xanthi 0-0
Panionios - AEK Athína 0-2(0-1)
Levadiakos - Aris Thessaloníki 1-0(1-0)
PAS Lamia - Atromitos 2-1(0-0)
PAOK Thessaloníki - OFI Heraklion 4-0(2-0)
Panathinaïkos - AE Larissa 1-1(1-0)
Asteras Trip. - Olympiacos Peiraiás 0-2(0-1)

Round 19 [02-03.02.2019]
PAS Lamia - Panetolikos 0-2(0-1)
Olympiacos Peiraiás - Panionios 4-0(0-0)
OFI Heraklion - AO Xanthi 0-0
GS Apollon - Asteras Tripolis 0-2(0-1)
AE Larissa - Atromitos 0-1(0-0)
Levadiakos - Panathinaïkos 0-0
Aris Thessaloníki - PAS Giannina 1-0(0-0)
AEK Athína - PAOK Thessaloníki 1-1(0-1)

Round 20 [09-11.02.2019]
Panionios - GS Apollon 0-1(0-0)
AO Xanthi - PAS Lamia 0-0
PAS Giannina - Panathinaïkos 1-0(0-0)
AEK Athína - OFI Heraklion 1-0(1-0)
Atromitos - Levadiakos 1-0(1-0)
PAOK Thess. - Olympiacos Peiraiás 3-1(2-0)
Panetolikos - AE Larissa 2-2(2-0)
Asteras Tripolis - Aris Thessaloníki 0-3(0-3)

Round 21 [16-18.02.2019]
Panathinaïkos - Asteras Tripolis 1-0(1-0)
PAS Giannina - Atromitos 0-2(0-1)
AE Larissa - AO Xanthi 1-1(1-1)
Levadiakos - Panetolikos 1-0(0-0)
Aris Thessaloníki - Panionios 1-1(0-0)
Olympiacos Peiraiás - AEK Athína 4-1(0-1)
GS Apollon - PAOK Thessaloníki 1-5(0-3)
OFI Heraklion - PAS Lamia 1-3(0-0)

Round 22 [23-25.02.2019]
Asteras Tripolis - Atromitos 1-1(1-0)
AEK Athína - GS Apollon 2-1(1-1)
Panionios - Panathinaïkos 2-0(1-0)
AO Xanthi - Levadiakos 0-1(0-0)
PAS Lamia - AE Larissa 2-1(1-1)
PAOK Thessaloníki - Aris Thessal. 1-1(1-0)
Olympiacos Peiraiás - OFI Heraklion 5-1(3-0)
Panetolikos - PAS Giannina 1-0(0-0)

Round 23 [02-04.03.2019]
Aris Thessaloníki - AEK Athína 2-0(1-0)
PAS Giannina - AO Xanthi 0-0
OFI Heraklion - AE Larissa 0-0
Atromitos - Panionios 3-0(2-0)
Levadiakos - PAS Lamia 1-1(1-1)
Panathinaïkos - PAOK Thessaloníki 0-2(0-1)
Asteras Tripolis - Panetolikos 3-0(2-0)
GS Apollon - Olympiacos Peiraiás 0-2(0-1)

Round 24 [09-11.03.2019]
AO Xanthi - Asteras Tripolis 0-0
AEK Athína - Panathinaïkos 0-0
AE Larissa - Levadiakos 2-0(0-0)
GS Apollon - OFI Heraklion 0-0
PAOK Thessaloníki - Atromitos 3-0(2-0)
PAS Lamia - PAS Giannina 1-1(0-0)
Olympiacos Peiraiás - Aris Thessal. 4-1(2-0)
Panetolikos - Panionios 5-0(3-0)

Round 25 [16-18.03.2019]
Asteras Tripolis - PAS Lamia 0-0
Panetolikos - PAOK Thessaloníki 1-2(0-0)
PAS Giannina - AE Larissa 0-0
OFI Heraklion - Levadiakos 2-0(1-0)
Atromitos - AEK Athína 0-1(0-0)
Panathinaïkos - Olympiacos P. 0-3 (awarded)
Panionios - AO Xanthi 1-0(0-0)
Aris Thessaloníki - GS Apollon 5-0(1-0)

Round 26 [30.03.-01.04.2019]
Levadiakos - PAS Giannina 0-2(0-0)
PAS Lamia - Panionios 1-0(1-0)
AE Larissa - Asteras Tripolis 2-1(1-1)
Aris Thessaloníki - OFI Heraklion 3-1(0-1)
AEK Athína - Panetolikos 4-0(1-0)
AO Xanthi - PAOK Thessaloníki 1-2(0-1)
Olympiacos Peiraiás - Atromitos 2-1(0-1)
GS Apollon - Panathinaïkos 1-3(0-1)

Round 27 [06-08.04.2019]
OFI Heraklion - PAS Giannina 1-0(1-0)
Panathinaïkos - Aris Thessaloníki 2-0(0-0)
Panionios - AE Larissa 1-0(1-0)
AO Xanthi - AEK Athína 1-3(1-0)
Asteras Tripolis - Levadiakos 0-0
Panetolikos - Olympiacos Peiraiás 0-5(0-1)
PAOK Thessaloníki - PAS Lamia 3-0(1-0)
Atromitos - GS Apollon 1-0(1-0)

Round 28 [14.04.2019]
AE Larissa - PAOK Thessaloníki 1-1(0-0)
GS Apollon - Panetolikos 0-1(0-1)
Aris Thessaloníki - Atromitos 0-2(0-2)
PAS Lamia - AEK Athína 2-2(1-1)
Levadiakos - Panionios 1-2(1-1)
Olympiacos Peiraiás - AO Xanthi 4-0(3-0)
Panathinaïkos - OFI Heraklion 1-3(1-0)
PAS Giannina - Asteras Tripolis 0-0

Round 29 [21.04.2019]
AEK Athína - AE Larissa 0-1(0-1)
AO Xanthi - GS Apollon 2-0(1-0)
Atromitos - Panathinaïkos 2-0(0-0)
PAS Lamia - Olympiacos Peiraiás 1-3(0-1)
OFI Heraklion - Asteras Tripolis 1-1(1-0)
PAOK Thessaloníki - Levadiakos 5-0(2-0)
Panetolikos - Aris Thessaloníki 1-2(0-1)
Panionios - PAS Giannina 2-1(1-0)

Round 30 [04-05.05.2019]
GS Apollon - PAS Lamia 0-3(0-0)
Panathinaïkos - Panetolikos 4-0(3-0)
AE Larissa - Olympiacos Peiraiás 0-3(0-1)
Aris Thessaloníki - AO Xanthi 7-2(2-1)
Asteras Tripolis - Panionios 3-0(1-0)
Atromitos - OFI Heraklion 0-2(0-1)
Levadiakos - AEK Athína 0-3(0-1)
PAS Giannina - PAOK Thessaloníki 0-2(0-0)

Final Standings

1.	**PAOK Thessaloníki**[1]	30	26	4	0	66	-	14	80
2.	Olympiacos SFP Peiraiás	30	24	3	3	71	-	17	75
3.	AEK Athína[2]	30	18	6	6	50	-	19	57
4.	APS Atromitos Athína	30	15	7	8	41	-	28	52
5.	Aris Thessaloníki	30	15	4	11	46	-	33	49
6.	Panionios GSS Athína	30	11	5	14	27	-	45	38
7.	PAS Lamia	30	9	10	11	28	-	37	37
8.	PAE Panathinaïkos Athína[3]	30	13	8	9	38	-	30	36
9.	Panetolikos GPS Agrinio	30	10	6	14	34	-	48	36
10.	AE Larissa	30	8	10	12	26	-	34	34
11.	AGS Asteras Tripolis	30	8	9	13	25	-	30	33
12.	AO Xanthi	30	7	11	12	22	-	34	32
13.	OFI Heraklion (*Relegation Play-offs*)	30	7	11	12	30	-	42	32
14.	PAS Giannina (*Relegated*)	30	7	6	17	19	-	38	27
15.	APO Levadiakos (*Relegated*)	30	5	6	19	15	-	45	21
16.	GS Apollon Smyrna (*Relegated*)	30	2	4	24	11	-	55	10

[1] *2 points deducted*;
[2] *3 points deducted*;
[4] *11 points deducted*;

Top goalscorers:

19 Efthymis Koulouris *APS Atromitos Athína*

16 Ezequiel Ponce Martínez (ARG) *AEK Athína*

12 Konstantinos Fortounis *Olympiacos SFP Peiraiás*

11 Ahmed Hassan Mahgoub Abdelmoneim (EGY) *Olympiacos SFP Peiraiás*

Relegation Play-offs [19-22.05.2019]

AO Platanias - OFI Heraklion	0-0	2-3(1-1)

NATIONAL CUP
Greek Football Cup - Kypello Elladas 2018/2019

Third Round [15-16.09.2018]

PAS Cithaeron Kaparelli - PASA Iródotos	1-3
Antimachos - PAE Volos	0-2
Thyella Kamari - Athlitiki Enosis Spartis	1-0
PAE AS Thesprotos - PAE Apollon Larissa	2-3
AO Kardia - PAE Apollon Pontou Kalamaria	1-5
Korinthos 2006 - Panachaiki 1891 FC Patras	0-2
OFI Ierapetra - AE Karaiskakis Arta	1-0
PS Apollon Paralimniou - Aiginiakos FC	5-4 pen
AE Ermionida - AO Chania Kissamikos PAE	3-7
Anagennisi Giannitsa - AO Trikala	2-3
AO Tilikratis - PAO Aittitos Spata	0-5
GS Ermis Amyntaio - GS Ergotelis Heraklion	0-3
Ethnikos Peiraiás 1923 - PAE Iraklis Thessaloníki	1-2 pen
AO Episkopi - AOK Kerkyra	0-1
AMPS Aris Avato - AO Platanias	2-1 pen
GS Niki Volos - GS Doxa Drama	1-0

Group Stage [25.09.-20.12.2018]	

Group A	
APS Atromitos Athína - PAS Giannina	1-2(0-2)
Thyella Kamari - PAE Iraklis Thessaloníki	0-3(0-0)
PAE Iraklis Thessaloníki - APS Atromitos Athína	1-6(0-1)
PAS Giannina - Thyella Kamari	5-0(3-0)
PAE Iraklis Thessaloníki - PAS Giannina	2-0(0-0)
Thyella Kamari - APS Atromitos Athína	0-8(0-5)
Qualified: APS Atromitos Athína, PAS Giannina	

Group B	
PAE Volos - PAE Apollon Larissa	5-1(1-0)
AEK Athína - PAS Lamia	2-1(0-0)
PAS Lamia - PAE Volos	1-1(1-1)
PAE Apollon Larissa - AEK Athína	0-4(0-2)
PAE Apollon Larissa - PAS Lamia	0-7(0-1)
PAE Volos - AEK Athína	1-3(1-1)
Qualified: AEK Athína, PAS Lamia	

Group C	
OFI Ierapetra - AO Chania Kissamikos PAE	0-2(0-0)
Panetolikos GPS Agrinio - PAE Panathinaïkos Athína	0-1(0-0)
AO Chania Kissamikos PAE - Panetolikos GPS Agrinio	0-0
PAE Panathinaïkos Athína - OFI Ierapetra	2-2(1-2)
OFI Ierapetra - Panetolikos GPS Agrinio	0-0
AO Chania Kissamikos PAE - PAE Panathinaïkos Athína	1-2(0-1)
Qualified: PAE Panathinaïkos Athína, AO Chania Kissamikos PAE	

Group D	
PAO Aittitos Spata - GS Ergotelis Heraklion	1-1(0-1)
PAOK Thessaloníki - Aris Thessaloníki	1-1(1-1)
Aris Thessaloníki - PAO Aittitos Spata	2-1(0-0)
GS Ergotelis Heraklion - PAOK Thessaloníki	1-2(0-1)
GS Ergotelis Heraklion - Aris Thessaloníki	3-2(1-0)
PAO Aittitos Spata - PAOK Thessaloníki	0-6(0-2)
Qualified: PAOK Thessaloníki, GS Ergotelis Heraklion	

Group E	
AMPS Aris Avato - Panachaiki 1891 FC Patras	0-1(0-0)
Olympiacos SFP Peiraiás - APO Levadiakos	1-0(0-0)
APO Levadiakos - AMPS Aris Avato	4-0(1-0)
Panachaiki 1891 FC Patras - Olympiacos SFP Peiraiás	0-2(0-1)
AMPS Aris Avato - Olympiacos SFP Peiraiás	1-2(1-2)
Panachaiki 1891 FC Patras - APO Levadiakos	2-1(1-0)
Qualified: Olympiacos SFP Peiraiás, Panachaiki 1891 FC Patras	

Group F	
PS Apollon Paralimniou - AO Trikala	1-1(1-1)
AGS Asteras Tripolis - GS Apollon Smyrna	2-1(0-0)
AO Trikala - AGS Asteras Tripolis	0-1(0-1)
GS Apollon Smyrna - PS Apollon Paralimniou	5-0(1-0)
PS Apollon Paralimniou - AGS Asteras Tripolis	0-4(0-2)
AO Trikala - GS Apollon Smyrna	1-1(0-0)
Qualified: AGS Asteras Tripolis, GS Apollon Smyrna	

Group G	
AO Xanthi - OFI Heraklion	0-0
GS Niki Volos - AOK Kerkyra	0-1(0-1)
OFI Heraklion - GS Niki Volos	3-0(2-0)
AOK Kerkyra - AO Xanthi	0-1(0-0)
AOK Kerkyra - OFI Heraklion	0-3(0-2)
GS Niki Volos - AO Xanthi	1-0(0-0)
Qualified: OFI Heraklion, AO Xanthi	

Group H	
PASA Iródotos - PAE Apollon Pontou Kalamaria	0-1(0-0)
Panionios GSS Athína - AE Larissa	2-0(1-0)
AE Larissa - PASA Iródotos	4-1(1-0)
PAE Apollon Pontou Kalamaria - Panionios GSS Athína	0-4(0-2)
PASA Iródotos - Panionios GSS Athína	1-2(0-1)
PAE Apollon Pontou Kalamaria - AE Larissa	0-4(0-2)
Qualified: Panionios GSS Athína, AE Larissa	

1/8-Finals [08-10/23-24.01.2019]			
PAS Giannina - Panionios GSS Athína	1-1 / 0-2	GS Apollon Smyrna - APS Atromitos Athína	0-3 / 1-2
Panachaiki 1891 FC Patras - PAOK Thessaloníki	2-1 / 0-5	AE Larissa - AGS Asteras Tripolis	3-2 / 3-5
AO Xanthi - Olympiacos SFP Peiraiás	0-0 / 1-3	AO Chania Kissamikos PAE - AEK Athína	1-1 / 0-5
GS Ergotelis Heraklion - OFI Heraklion	1-1 / 4-3 pen	PAS Lamia - PAE Panathinaïkos Athína	1-0 / 4-2 pen

Quarter-Finals [06-28.02.2019]			
PAS Lamia - Olympiacos SFP Peiraiás	3-3 / 0-1	GS Ergotelis Heraklion - AGS Asteras Tripolis	0-1 / 1-4
Panionios GSS Athína - PAOK Thessaloníki	2-1 / 2-4 aet	APS Atromitos Athína - AEK Athína	0-1 / 0-3

Semi-Finals [03-25.04.2019]			
PAOK Thessaloníki - AGS Asteras Tripolis	2-0 / 0-0	AEK Athína - PAS Lamia	2-0 / 4-0

Final

11.05.2019; Stádio Olympiako „Spiros Louis", Athína; Referee: Felix Zwayer (Germany); Attendance: *played behind closed doors*

PAOK Thessaloníki - AEK Athína **1-0(1-0)**

PAOK: Alexandros Paschalakis, Leonardo de Matos Cruz „Léo Matos", José Ángel Crespo Rincón, Fernando Lopes dos Santos Varela, Dimitrios Hristos Giannoulis, José Alberto Cañas Ruiz Herrera, Yevhen Shakhov, Diego Marvin Biseswar (90+3.Sverrir Ingi Ingason), Leonardo Rodrigues Lima „Léo Jabá" (66.Dimitrios Limnios), Dimitrios Pelkas (Cap) (80.Sérgio Miguel Relvas de Oliveira), Chuba Amechi Akpom. Trainer: Răzvan Lucescu (Romania).

AEK: Vassilis Barkas, Michalis Bakakis (80.Konstantinos Galanopoulos), Marios Oikonomou, Dmitro Chigrinskiy, Niklas Hult, Nenad Krstičić (76.Lucas Ariel Boyé), André Luis Gomes Simões, Petros Mantalos (Cap), Anastasios Bakasetas (71.Rodrigo Galo Brito), Marko Livaja, Ezequiel Ponce Martínez. Trainer: Manuel Enrique Jiménez (Spain).

Goal: 1-0 Chuba Amechi Akpom (45).

THE CLUBS 2018/2019

Athlitikí Énosis Konstantinoupóleos Athína

Founded: 1924
Stadium: Stádio Olympiako „Spiros Louis", Athína (69,618)

Goalkeepers:	DOB	M	(s)	G
Vassilis Barkas	30.09.1994	26		
Panagiotis Tsintotas	04.07.1993	4		
Defenders:	**DOB**	**M**	**(s)**	**G**
Michalis Bakakis	18.03.1991	24	(1)	
Dmitro Chigrinskiy (UKR)	07.11.1986	15		
Uroš Ćosić (SRB)	24.10.1992	13	(6)	
Giorgos Giannoutsos	16.07.1998		(1)	
Hélder Filipe Oliveira Lopes (POR)	04.01.1989	4	(2)	
Niklas Hult (SWE)	13.02.1990	20	(2)	
Vasilios Lambropoulos	31.03.1990	8		
Marios Oikonomou	06.10.1992	21		2
Rodrigo Galo Brito (BRA)	19.09.1986	20	(6)	1
Stratos Svarnas	11.11.1997	4	(1)	
Midfielders:	**DOB**	**M**	**(s)**	**G**
Alef dos Santos Saldanha (BRA)	28.01.1995	17	(5)	1
André Luis Gomes Simões (POR)	16.12.1989	14	(1)	1
Erik Morán Arribas (ESP)	25.05.1991	2	(2)	
Konstantinos Galanopoulos	28.12.1997	15	(2)	1
Christos Giousis	08.02.1999		(1)	
Viktor Klonaridis (BEL)	28.07.1992	13	(9)	2
Nenad Krstičić (SRB)	03.07.1990	7	(6)	
Petros Mantalos	31.08.1991	22	(3)	5
Forwards:	**DOB**	**M**	**(s)**	**G**
Christos Albanis	05.11.1994	1	(12)	1
Anastasios Bakasetas	28.06.1993	21	(1)	4
Lucas Ariel Boyé (ARG)	28.02.1996	12	(11)	6
Georgios Giakoumakis	09.12.1994		(6)	
Giannis Gianniotas	29.04.1993		(7)	
Marko Livaja (CRO)	26.08.1993	21	(4)	7
Ezequiel Ponce Martínez (ARG)	29.03.1997	26	(1)	16
Trainer:	**DOB**	**M**		
Marinos Ouzounidis	10.10.1968	19		
Manuel Enrique Jiménez (ESP) [from 06.02.2019]	26.01.1964	11		

Athlitiki Enosi Larissa

Founded: 17.05.1964
Stadium: AEL FC Arena, Larissa (16,118)

Goalkeepers:	DOB	M	(s)	G
Ögmundur Kristinsson (ISL)	19.06.1989	30		
Defenders:	**DOB**	**M**	**(s)**	**G**
Manolis Bertos	13.05.1989	8		1
Slavko Bralić (CRO)	15.12.1992	8		1
Aleksandar Gojković (SRB)	10.08.1988	16	(1)	
Nikos Golias	29.07.1993	13	(7)	1
Christos Gromitsaris	10.02.1991	7	(6)	
Hristofor Hubchev (BUL)	24.11.1995	10	(2)	
Nikos Karanikas	04.03.1992	18	(3)	
Vangelis Moras	26.08.1981	14	(2)	1
Stefan Živković (SRB)	01.06.1990	9	(2)	
Nikola Žižić (CRO)	23.01.1988	17	(5)	
Midfielders:	**DOB**	**M**	**(s)**	**G**
Fatjon Andoni (ALB)	19.06.1991	23		4
Panagiotis Ballas	06.09.1993	5	(1)	
Alexandre Coeff (FRA)	20.02.1992	5	(3)	1
Gertin Hoxhalli (ALB)	05.11.1996	1		
Nikola Jakimovski	26.02.1990	11	(4)	1
Leandro Sales de Santana „Leozinho" (BRA)	12.12.1985	4	(4)	
Radomir Milosavljević (SRB)	28.07.1992	26	(1)	2
Francisco Medina Luna "Piti" (ESP)	25.06.1981	9	(6)	
Noé Acosta Rivera (ESP)	10.12.1983	8	(5)	
Suad Sahiti (KVX)	06.02.1995	5	(3)	
Adnan Šećerović (BIH)	01.12.1991	10	(4)	
Forwards:	**DOB**	**M**	**(s)**	**G**
Kenan Bargan	25.10.1988	12	(7)	1
Miloš Deletić (SRB)	13.10.1993	23		5
Petar Kunić (BIH)	15.07.1993	7	(5)	
Basem Morsy Elkotb Abdalla (EGY)	01.01.1992	3	(2)	
Vangelis Nousios	06.07.1998	1	(3)	
Marko Nunič (SVN)	16.03.1993	19	(3)	6
Yevgeniy Shikavka (BLR)	15.10.1992	8	(7)	1
Trainer:	**DOB**	**M**		
Sotiris Antoniu	10.09.1975	4		
Gianluca Festa (ITA) [25.09.2018]	16.03.1969	26		

Gymnasticos Syllogos Apollon Smyrnis

Founded: 1891
Stadium: Stádio "Georgios Kamaras", Athína (14,856)

Goalkeepers:	DOB	M	(s)	G
Lefteris Astras	14.02.1997	4		
Huanderson Junio da Silva Santos (BRA)	03.08.1983	24		
Vaso Vasić (SRB)	26.04.1990	2		
Defenders:	**DOB**	**M**	**(s)**	**G**
Antonios Ikonomopoulos	09.05.1998		(3)	
Giannis Kontoes	24.05.1986	20		
Michalis Kyrgias	14.10.1989	19	(1)	
Andrej Lukić (CRO)	02.04.1994	12		
Leonidas Rossi (ALB)	19.04.1999	8	(3)	
Giannis Stathis	20.05.1987	22		
Adam Tzanetopoulos	10.02.1995	8	(2)	
Nikos Vafeas	21.02.1997	17	(1)	2
Midfielders:	**DOB**	**M**	**(s)**	**G**
Joel Gustavo Acosta (ARG)	16.01.1991	12	(8)	
Christos Agrodimos	16.03.1995	5	(2)	
Christian D'Urso (ITA)	26.07.1997	21	(7)	1
Matías Adrián Defederico (ARG)	23.08.1989	8	(6)	
David Nadales López „Fonsi" (ESP)	22.01.1986	15	(4)	
Iraklis Garoufalias	01.05.1993	6	(3)	
Klodian Gino (ALB)	13.02.1994	17	(3)	
Gonzalo Federico González Pereyra (URU)	07.10.1993	4	(1)	
João Pedro Almeida Machado (POR)	03.04.1993	4	(2)	
Emmanuel Koné (CIV)	31.12.1986	13	(1)	
Giannis Kontogiannopoulos	03.07.1999		(2)	
Matías Exequiel Orihuela Bonino (ARG)	17.02.1992	19	(1)	
Thomás Jaguaribe Bedinelli (BRA)	24.02.1993	22	(2)	2
Forwards:	**DOB**	**M**	**(s)**	**G**
Boris Garrós Torrent (ESP)	22.06.1988	1	(2)	
Justin Eilers (GER)	13.06.1988	1		
Hilal El Helwe (LIB)	24.11.1994	14	(7)	3
Evangelos Mantzios	22.04.1983	5	(1)	
Thomas Nazlidis	23.10.1987	7	(4)	
Germán Ariel Rivero (ARG)	17.03.1992	1	(3)	
Mahmoud Abdel Razek Fadlallah „Shikabala" (EGY)	05.03.1986	3	(7)	1
Panagiotis Triadis	09.09.1992	10	(4)	2
Giannis Varkas	27.03.1998	6	(9)	
Trainer:	**DOB**	**M**		
Valérien Ismaël (FRA)	28.09.1975	1		
Lefteris Velentzas [01.09.2018]	11.10.1969	1		
Alberto Jiménez Monteagudo (ESP) [12.09.2018]	27.09.1974	3		
Ioannis Matzourakis [03.10.2018]	06.06.1949	6		
Babis Tennes [26.11.2018]	17.11.1953	12		
Lefteris Velentzas [09.03.2019]	11.10.1969	7		

Aris Thessaloníki

Founded: 25.03.1914
Stadium: Stádio " Kleanthis Vikelidis", Thessaloníki (22,800)

Goalkeepers:	DOB	M	(s)	G
Alexandros Anagnostopoulos	18.08.1994		(1)	
Julián Cuesta Díaz (ESP)	28.03.1991	30		
Defenders:	**DOB**	**M**	**(s)**	**G**
Alejandro Menéndez Díez „Alex" (ESP)	15.07.1991	7	(4)	
Georgios Delizisis	01.12.1987	20		
Francisco Manuel Vélez Jiménez „Fran Vélez" (ESP)	23.06.1991	20	(3)	1
Hugo Filipe Gonçalves Martins de Sousa (POR)	04.06.1992	2	(5)	
Dimitrios Konstantinidis	02.06.1994	7	(2)	1
Mihály Korhut (HUN)	01.12.1988	13	(1)	1
Mërgim Mavraj (ALB)	09.06.1986	4	(1)	
Lindsay Rose (MRI)	08.02.1992	13		2
Manolis Tzanakakis	30.04.1992	19	(2)	
Georgios Valerianos	13.02.1992	14	(4)	
Midfielders:	**DOB**	**M**	**(s)**	**G**
Migjen Basha (ALB)	05.01.1987	19	(2)	
Nicolás Carlos Colazo (ARG)	08.07.1990	5	(3)	
Ioannis Fetfatzidis	21.12.1990	4	(6)	1
Mateo Ezequiel García (ARG)	10.09.1996	30		10
Lefteris Intzoglou	03.03.1987	1	(3)	
Javier Magro Matilla (ESP)	01.01.1988	20	(9)	3
Nicolás Martínez (ARG)	25.09.1987	7	(14)	3
Charalampos Pavlidis	06.05.1991		(3)	
Manolis Siopis	14.05.1994	22	(3)	1
Martín Tonso (ARG)	19.10.1989	4	(1)	1
Forwards:	**DOB**	**M**	**(s)**	**G**
Bruno Alexandre Vilela Gama (POR)	15.11.1987	14		2
Dimitrios Diamantopoulos	18.11.1988	2	(3)	1
Nicolas Diguiny (FRA)	31.05.1988	27		8
Daniel Larsson (SWE)	25.01.1987	11	(2)	2
Thomas Nazlidis	23.10.1987		(7)	
Hamza Younès (TUN)	16.04.1986	15	(9)	9
Trainer:	**DOB**	**M**		
Francisco „Paco" Herrera Lorenzo (ESP)	02.12.1953	10		
Savvas Pantelidis [14.11.2018]	07.04.1965	20		

Athletic Gymnastics Society Asteras Tripolis

Founded: 26.03.1931
Stadium: Stádio "Theodoros Kolokotronis", Tripolis (7,616)

Goalkeepers:	DOB	M	(s)	G
Georgios Athanasiadis	07.04.1993	8		
Nikolaos Papadopoulos	11.04.1990	22		
Defenders:	**DOB**	**M**	**(s)**	**G**
Ángel Martínez Ortega (ESP)	15.05.1991	15	(5)	
Giannis Christopoulos	22.07.2000	1	(1)	
Giannis Kotsiras	16.12.1992	24	(2)	
Giorgos Kyriakopoulos	05.02.1996	23	(1)	1
Patricio Matricardi (ARG)	07.01.1994	2	(1)	
Triantafyllos Pasalidis	19.07.1996	24		
Christos Tasoulis	03.05.1991	2	(4)	
Konstantinos Triantafyllopoulos	03.04.1993	25		
Valentinos Vlachos	14.02.1992	14	(4)	
Midfielders:	**DOB**	**M**	**(s)**	**G**
Franco Bellocq (ARG)	15.10.1993	8	(5)	
Walter Matías Iglesias (ARG)	18.04.1985	18	(2)	2
José Luis Valiente Giménez (ESP)	18.05.1991	21	(4)	2
Juan Manuel Munafo Horta (ARG)	20.03.1988	24		
Diego Martín Rolle (ARG)	02.02.1985	5	(8)	
Martín Tonso (ARG)	19.10.1989	11	(1)	4
Panagiotis Tzimas	12.03.2001		(1)	
Forwards:	**DOB**	**M**	**(s)**	**G**
Christos Aravidis	13.03.1987	4	(7)	
Giannis Bastianos	29.04.1998		(1)	
Anastasios Douvikas	02.08.1999	1	(17)	
Nikolaos Kaltsas	03.05.1990	25	(1)	5
Michalis Manias	20.02.1990	26	(2)	4
Marc Fernández Gràcia (ESP)	29.04.1990	14	(11)	5
Kosmas Tsilianidis	09.05.1994	13	(10)	1
Trainer:	**DOB**	**M**		
Savvas Pantelidis	07.04.1965	10		
Georgios Paraschos [12.11.2018]	23.08.1952	20		

PAE APS Atromitos Athinon

Founded: 30.04.1923
Stadium: Stádio Peristeri, Athína (10,005)

Goalkeepers:	DOB	M	(s)	G
Christos Mandas	17.09.2001	1		
Balázs Megyeri (HUN)	31.03.1990	26		
Christos Theodorakis	17.09.1996	3	(1)	
Defenders:	**DOB**	**M**	**(s)**	**G**
Dimitrios Chatziisaias	21.09.1992	28		
Dimitrios Hristos Giannoulis	17.10.1995	14	(1)	
Aristotelis Karasalidis	03.05.1991	14	(5)	
Alexandros Katranis	04.05.1998	8	(2)	
Kyriakos Kivrakidis	21.07.1992	15	(2)	1
Spyros Risvanis	03.01.1994	28		1
Emanuel Sakić (AUT)	25.01.1991	25		1
Stefanos Strougis	09.10.1997	2		
Midfielders:	**DOB**	**M**	**(s)**	**G**
Azer Bušuladžić (BIH)	12.11.1991	22	(5)	
Dawid Kort (POL)	29.04.1995		(3)	
Madson Henrique Nascimento Santos (BRA)	09.05.1991	24		
Spyros Natsos	09.06.1998	4	(5)	
Javier Horacio Umbides (ARG)	09.02.1982	11	(12)	
Theodoros Vasilakakis	20.07.1988	9	(3)	1
Forwards:	**DOB**	**M**	**(s)**	**G**
Bruno Felipe Souza da Silva (BRA)	26.05.1994	24	(3)	2
Konstantinos Kotsopoulos	17.02.1997	1	(13)	1
Efthimios Koulouris	06.03.1996	28		19
Georgios Manousos	03.12.1987	6	(9)	2
Armin Mujakić (AUT)	07.03.1995	3	(14)	1
Clarck N'Sikulu (COD)	10.07.1992	15	(8)	4
Roland Ugrai (HUN)	13.11.1992	9	(2)	3
Amr Warda (EGY)	17.09.1993	10	(2)	2
Trainer:	**DOB**	**M**		
Damir Canadi (AUT)	06.05.1970	30		

PAS Lamia 1964 Football Club

Founded: 01.06.1964
Stadium: Stádio Dimotiko, Lamia (6,000)

Goalkeepers:	**DOB**	**M**	**(s)**	**G**
Panagiotis Katsikas	10.03.1999	1		
Nikolaos Melissas	24.02.1993	10	(1)	
Bojan Šaranov (SRB)	22.10.1987	19		
Defenders:	**DOB**	**M**	**(s)**	**G**
Daniel Adejo (NGA)	07.08.1989	30		3
Anestis Anastasiadis	21.01.1983	6	(2)	
Mark Nyaaba Asigba (GHA)	07.07.1990	8	(5)	
Hristos Karypidis	02.12.1982	7	(3)	
Iordanis Papargyriou	15.05.1992		(1)	
Vasilios Pliatsikas	14.04.1988	17	(1)	
Giannis Skondras	21.02.1990	18	(4)	
Vanderson Scardovelli (BRA)	27.09.1984	25	(1)	
Stavros Vasilantonopoulos	28.01.1992	20	(5)	
Midfielders:	**DOB**	**M**	**(s)**	**G**
Jean Luc Assoubre (CIV)	08.08.1992	4	(2)	1
Danny Bryan Bejarano Yañez (BOL)	03.01.1994	11		
Facundo Daniel Bertoglio (ARG)	30.06.1990	26	(2)	5
Marko Blažić (SRB)	02.08.1985	16	(4)	
Konstantinos Bouloulis	07.12.1993	1	(8)	
Elini Dimoutsos	18.08.1988	26		
Joan Tomás Campasol (ESP)	17.05.1985	7	(7)	2
Hachim Mastour (MAR)	15.06.1998		(4)	
Abdul-Haq Seidu Osman (GHA)	27.02.1987		(6)	
Francisco Medina Luna „Piti“ (ESP)	26.05.1981	6	(4)	2
Forwards:	**DOB**	**M**	**(s)**	**G**
Jerónimo Barrales (ARG)	28.01.1986	26		9
Denis Epstein (GER)	02.07.1986	15	(9)	2
Thanasis Karagounis	25.09.1991	4	(6)	
Anastasios Karamanos	21.09.1990	24	(3)	3
Lazar Romanić (ITA)	23.03.1998	1	(6)	
Nikos Tsoukalos	23.03.1992	2	(6)	
Trainer:	**DOB**	**M**		
Ioakeim Chavos	05.09.1969	30		

APO Levadiakos Football Club

Founded: 01.12.1961
Stadium: Stádio Dimotiko, Levadia (6,500)

Goalkeepers:	**DOB**	**M**	**(s)**	**G**
Vladimir Bajić (SRB)	13.06.1987	21		
Devis Mboka (FRA)	02.02.1993	9		
Defenders:	**DOB**	**M**	**(s)**	**G**
Moïse Adilehou (BEN)	01.11.1995	20	(2)	1
Benjamin Angoua (CIV)	28.11.1986	6	(1)	
João Francisco Favaro Amaral (BRA)	22.04.1992	4	(1)	
Jovan Krneta (SRB)	04.05.1992	4	(1)	
Leonardo José Aparecido Moura (BRA)	09.03.1986	1		
Thanasis Panteliadis	06.09.1987	15	(3)	
Giorgi Rekhviashvili (GEO)	01.02.1988	9	(1)	
Savvas Tsabouris	16.07.1986	28	(1)	1
Georgios Zisopoulos	23.05.1984	26	(3)	1
Midfielders:	**DOB**	**M**	**(s)**	**G**
Stathis Chatzilampros	24.06.1997	5	(2)	
Marinaldo Cicero da Silva „Chumbinho“ (BRA)	21.09.1986	8		1
Jordão da Encarnação Tackey Diogo (STP)	12.11.1985	12	(2)	
Zisis Karachalios	10.01.1996	15	(5)	
Nikolaos Katharios	07.10.1994	2	(3)	
Emmanuel Koné (CIV)	31.12.1986	8		
David Henri Joel Manga Lembe (CTA)	03.02.1989	1	(5)	
Panagiotis Liagas	05.11.1999	7	(2)	
Dejan Meleg (SRB)	01.10.1994	4	(4)	
Pavlos Mitropoulos	04.04.1990	16	(4)	
Georgios Nikas	17.09.1999	4		
Suleiman Akeem Omolade (NGA)	15.12.1985	9	(6)	
Souleymane Sawadogo (BFA)	09.01.1993	17	(8)	1
Marko Stanojević (SRB)	22.06.1988	16	(5)	2
Panagiotis-Marios Vichos	14.01.2000		(2)	
Forwards:	**DOB**	**M**	**(s)**	**G**
Petros Giakoumakis	03.07.1992	14	(6)	1
Fotis Ioannidis	10.01.2000	6	(11)	2
Marko Markovski (SRB)	26.05.1986	23	(5)	3
Lenny Nangis (GLP)	24.03.1994	20	(6)	1
Trainer:	**DOB**	**M**		
Akis Mantzios	21.10.1969	7		
Giuseppe Sannino (ITA) [22.10.2018]	30.04.1957	9		
Nikos Karageorgiou [22.01.2019]	08.12.1962	14		

Ómilos Filáthlon Heraklíou

Founded: 1925
Stadium: Stádio „Theodoros Vardinogiannis“, Heraklion (9,088)

Goalkeepers:	**DOB**	**M**	**(s)**	**G**
Dimitrios Sotiriou	13.09.1987	10		
Georgios Strezos	06.07.1995	20	(1)	
Defenders:	**DOB**	**M**	**(s)**	**G**
Leonidas Argyropoulos	29.05.1990	6	(1)	
Manolis Bolakis	20.10.1994	3		
Christopher Braun (GER)	15.07.1991	13		
Konstantinos Giannoulis	09.12.1987	13		
Giannis Kiliaras	09.06.1988	2	(2)	
Dimitrios Komesidis	02.02.1988	4	(2)	
Marko Mihojević (BIH)	21.04.1996	19	(3)	
Anestis Nastos	28.04.1989	20	(3)	
Anastasios Papazoglou	24.09.1988	13	(3)	
Giannis Potouridis	27.02.1992	22	(1)	1
Midfielders:	**DOB**	**M**	**(s)**	**G**
Athanasios Dinas	12.11.1989	4	(13)	
Angelos Ikonomou	23.08.1995		(4)	
Nikos Korovesis	10.08.1991	25	(1)	1
Vasilios Koutsianikoulis	09.08.1988	11	(7)	
Pavlos Kyriakidis	03.09.1991	15	(4)	
Miguel Alberto Mellado (ARG)	18.03.1993	20		
Adil Nabi (ENG)	28.02.1994	7	(2)	3
Juan Ángel Neira (ARG)	21.02.1989	15	(5)	5
Manolis Papasterianos	15.08.1987	5	(7)	1
Vajebah Sakor (NOR)	14.04.1996	4	(4)	1
Ismaïl Sassi (TUN)	24.12.1991	10	(4)	3
Forwards:	**DOB**	**M**	**(s)**	**G**
Christos Aravidis	13.03.1987	5	(4)	1
Panagiotis Deligiannidis	29.08.1996	7	(2)	2
Felipe Souza Ferreyra (BRA)	21.05.1998	10	(1)	1
Georgios Giakoumakis	09.12.1994	6	(4)	2
Erik Pärsson (SWE)	07.04.1994	2	(3)	
Vangelis Platellas	01.12.1988	14	(1)	2
Ricardo Alvares Guedes Vaz (POR)	26.11.1994	11		3
Patrick Vouho (CIV)	25.06.1987	14	(6)	2
Trainer:	**DOB**	**M**		
Nikolaos Papadopoulos	05.10.1971	16		
Nikolaos Karabetakis [22.01.2019]	17.05.1971	1		
Jaime Andrés Vera Rodríguez (CHI) [25.01.2019]	25.03.1963	13		

Olympiakós Sýndesmos Filáthlon Peiraiós

Founded: 10.03.1925
Stadium: Stádio „Giórgos Karaïskáki", Peiraiás (32,115)

Goalkeepers:	**DOB**	**M**	**(s)**	**G**
Andreas Gianniotis	18.12.1992	7		
José Pedro Malheiro de Sá (POR)	17.01.1993	21		
Yuriy Lodygin (RUS)	26.05.1990	2		
Defenders:	**DOB**	**M**	**(s)**	**G**
Pape Cissé (SEN)	14.09.1995	19		1
Omar Elabdellaoui (NOR)	05.12.1991	23		5
Leonardo Koutris	23.07.1995	17		
Yassine Meryah (TUN)	02.07.1993	17	(1)	1
Avraam Papadopoulos	03.12.1984	1	(1)	
Roderick Jefferson Gonçalves Miranda (POR)	30.03.1991	7	(1)	
Vasilios Torosidis	10.06.1985	7	(6)	
Konstantinos Tsimikas	12.05.1996	13	(2)	
Jagoš Vuković (SRB)	10.06.1988	18		3
Midfielders:	**DOB**	**M**	**(s)**	**G**
Athanasios Androutsos	06.05.1997	2	(3)	
Andreas Bouchalakis	05.04.1993	15	(3)	1
Mady Camara (GUI)	28.02.1997	18	(6)	6
Ioannis Fetfatzidis	21.12.1990	3	(6)	1
Konstantinos Fortounis	16.10.1992	26	(2)	12
Gil Bastião Dias (POR)	28.09.1996	3	(4)	
Guilherme dos Santos Torres (BRA)	05.04.1991	22	(1)	4
Georgios Masouras	01.01.1994	7	(3)	4
Bibras Natcho (ISR)	18.02.1988	7	(14)	1
Edgar Felipe Pardo Castro (COL)	17.08.1990	1		
Gnégnéri Yaya Touré (CIV)	13.05.1983	1	(1)	
Forwards:	**DOB**	**M**	**(s)**	**G**
Lazaros Christodoulopoulos	19.12.1986	12	(5)	4
Daniel Castelo Podence (POR)	21.10.1995	26	(1)	5
Miguel Ángel Guerrero Martín (ESP)	12.07.1990	15	(8)	7
Ahmed Hassan Mahgoub Abdelmoneim „Kouka" (EGY)	05.03.1993	12	(10)	11
Dimitrios Manos	16.09.1994	1	(5)	1
Matías Nahuel Leiva Esquivel (ESP)	22.11.1996	4		
Franco Soldano (ARG)	14.09.1994	3	(3)	
Marius Vrushaj	02.07.1998		(1)	
Trainer:	**DOB**	**M**		
Pedro Rui da Mota Vieira Martins (POR)	17.07.1970	30		

Panathinaïkós Athlitikós Ómilos Athína

Founded: 03.02.1908
Stadium: Stádio "Apostolos Nikolaidis", Athína (16,003)

Goalkeepers:	**DOB**	**M**	**(s)**	**G**
Sokratis Dioudis	03.02.1993	26		
Konstantinos Kotsaris	25.07.1996	4	(1)	
Defenders:	**DOB**	**M**	**(s)**	**G**
Ilias Chatzitheodoridis	05.11.1997	8	(12)	3
Ousmane Coulibaly (MLI)	09.07.1989	16	(1)	
Vangelis Ikonomou	18.07.1987	9		
Emanuel Mariano Insúa Zapata (ARG)	10.04.1991	25		2
Mattias Johansson (SWE)	16.02.1992	18	(1)	4
Dimitrios Kolovetsios	16.10.1991	28		1
Theofanis Mavromatis	16.01.1997	20		
Epaminondas Pantelakis	10.02.1995	2	(2)	
Achilleas Poungouras	13.12.1995	10	(5)	
Midfielders:	**DOB**	**M**	**(s)**	**G**
Omri Altman (ISR)	23.03.1994	4	(7)	1
Konstantinos Apostolakis	28.05.1999	2		
Andreas Athanasakopoulos	27.11.2001	1	(1)	
Giannis Bouzoukis	27.03.1998	23	(1)	4
Christos Donis	09.10.1994	20	(5)	1
Ergys Kaçe (ALB)	08.07.1993	16	(4)	2
Dimitrios Kourbelis	02.11.1993	25		2
Anthony Mounier (FRA)	27.09.1987	5	(6)	
Paschalis Staikos	08.02.1996	6	(5)	
Vangelis Theocharis	06.07.1998	1		
Theofanis Tzandaris	13.06.1993	3	(4)	
Forwards:	**DOB**	**M**	**(s)**	**G**
Panagiotis Armenakas (AUS)	05.08.1998	1	(2)	
Anastasios Chatzigiovannis	31.05.1997	25	(2)	4
Dimitrios Emmanouilidis	24.10.2000	1	(10)	2
Anargyros Kampetsis	06.05.1999	6	(14)	2
Federico Macheda (ITA)	22.08.1991	25	(1)	10
Kristo Shehu	01.03.2000		(1)	
Nikolaos Vergos	13.01.1996		(4)	
Trainer:	**DOB**	**M**		
Georgios Donis	22.10.1969	30		

Panaetolikos Gymnastikos Philekpaideutikos Syllogos Agrinio

Founded: 09.03.1926
Stadium: Stádio Panetolikos, Agrinio (7,000)

Goalkeepers:	**DOB**	**M**	**(s)**	**G**
Nikos Giannakopoulos	19.02.1993	9	(2)	
Dimitrios Kyriakidis	24.09.1986	21		
Defenders:	**DOB**	**M**	**(s)**	**G**
Arghus Soares Bordignon (BRA)	19.01.1988	22		2
Dimitrios Chantakias	04.01.1995	3	(4)	
Luís Augusto Martins Rocha (POR)	27.06.1993	6	(2)	
Alexandros Malis	19.03.1997	16	(3)	1
Nikolaos Marinakis	12.09.1993	20	(3)	
Enea Mihaj (ALB)	05.07.1998	18	(1)	
Alexandros Parras	12.05.1998		(3)	
Pedro Miguel Gaspar Amaral (POR)	25.08.1997	11	(5)	
Anastasios Tsokanis	02.05.1991	14	(2)	
Midfielders:	**DOB**	**M**	**(s)**	**G**
Stathis Belevonis	06.02.1998		(3)	
Sebastian Anders Fredrik Eriksson (SWE)	31.01.1989	6		1
Frederico Fonseca Pires de Almeida Duarte (POR)	30.03.1999	3	(1)	1
Ilias Gianniotis	05.04.1997		(2)	
Gonçalo Rosa Gonçalves Pereira Rodrigues „Guga" (POR)	18.07.1997	6	(8)	
Georgios Liavas	12.02.2001	11	(8)	
Marcos Paulo Gelmini Gomes (BRA)	13.07.1988	11	(3)	
Franco Eduardo Mazurek (ARG)	24.09.1993	25	(2)	7
Angelos Tsigaras	24.07.1999	10	(5)	
Stathis Vasiloudis	23.02.1996		(3)	
Willyan Da Silva Barbosa (BRA)	17.02.1994	20	(2)	3
Forwards:	**DOB**	**M**	**(s)**	**G**
Admir Bajrović (SWE)	06.08.1995	10	(5)	5
Jorge Luis Díaz Gutiérrez (URU)	28.06.1989	25		
Alhassan Kamara (SLE)	16.03.1993	5	(6)	4
Óscar Adrián Lucero (ARG)	16.08.1985	22	(5)	1
Nicolás Andrés Maná (ARG)	25.03.1994	20	(7)	3
Vlad Călin Morar (ROU)	01.08.1993	16	(2)	6
Giorgos Vakrakos	18.10.1997		(2)	
Trainer:	**DOB**	**M**		
Traianos Dellas	31.01.1976	30		

Paniónios Gymnastikós Sýllogos Smýrnis Athína

Founded: 14.09.1890
Stadium: Stádio Nea Smyrni, Athína (11,700)

Goalkeepers:	DOB	M	(s)	G
Matic Kotnik (SVN)	23.07.1990	17	(1)	
Jérémy Malherbe (FRA)	15.03.1991	6	(1)	
Filip Manojlović (SRB)	25.04.1996	7	(1)	
Defenders:	**DOB**	**M**	**(s)**	**G**
Yaya Banana (CMR)	29.07.1991	18	(2)	
Luiz Gustavo Domingues (BRA)	28.09.1988	30		1
Milan Kocič (SVN)	16.02.1990	13		
Amiri Kurdi (KSA)	11.09.1991	18	(1)	
Antonio Mico (ALB)	27.01.2000	1	(2)	
Athanasios Papageorgiou	09.05.1987	20	(4)	
Giorgos Saramantas	29.01.1992	11	(2)	
Dimitrios Stavropoulos	01.05.1997	14	(3)	2
Midfielders:	**DOB**	**M**	**(s)**	**G**
Roland Romario Alberg (NED)	06.08.1990		(3)	1
Pedro Arce Latapí (MEX)	25.11.1991	4	(5)	
Olivier Boumal (CMR)	17.09.1989	8	(1)	
Abdoulaye Keita (MLI)	05.01.1994	14		
Panagiotis Korbos	11.09.1985	26		3
Peter Makrillos (AUS)	04.09.1995	3	(1)	
Novica Maksimović (SRB)	04.04.1988	6	(2)	2
Ioannis Maniatis	12.10.1986	7		
Georgios Manthatis	11.05.1997	4	(11)	
Georgios Masouras	30.11.1993	14		6
Giannis Masouras	24.08.1996	7		1
Giannis Oikonomidis	03.01.1998	10	(8)	
Sebastián Gerardo Píriz Ribas (URU)	04.03.1990	3	(3)	
Vasilios Rentzas	16.04.1992		(2)	
Gianni Seraf (ALG)	05.07.1994		(1)	
Srđan Spiridonović (AUT)	13.10.1993	14	(5)	2
Sotiris Tsiloulis	14.02.1995	17	(6)	2
Forwards:	**DOB**	**M**	**(s)**	**G**
Oumar Camara (FRA)	19.08.1992	4	(12)	1
Fiorin Durmishaj (ALB)	14.11.1996	26	(1)	6
Sofiane Sidi Ali (FRA)	14.07.1995	8	(6)	
Trainer:	**DOB**	**M**		
José Anigo (FRA)	15.04.1961	12		
Akis Mantzios [04.12.2018]	21.10.1969	18		

Panthessaloníkios Athlitikós Ómilos Konstantinoupolitón

Founded: 20.04.1926
Stadium: Stádio Toumba, Thessaloníki (28,703)

Goalkeepers:	DOB	M	(s)	G
Alexandros Paschalakis	28.07.1989	30		
Defenders:	**DOB**	**M**	**(s)**	**G**
José Ángel Crespo Rincón (ESP)	09.02.1987	30		2
Fernando Lopes dos Santos Varela (CPV)	26.11.1987	27		2
Dimitrios Hristos Giannoulis	17.10.1995	3	(5)	
Sverrir Ingi Ingason (ISL)	05.08.1993	1		
Evgen Khacheridi (UKR)	28.07.1987	2	(1)	
Stelios Kitsiou	28.09.1993	2		
Leonardo de Matos Cruz „Léo Matos" (BRA)	02.04.1986	27		3
Lefteris Lyratzis	22.02.2000		(1)	
Stelios Malezas	11.03.1985		(1)	
Alin Dorinel Toşca (ROU)	14.03.1992	4	(3)	
Adelino André Vieira de Freitas „Vieirinha" (POR)	24.01.1986	24	(2)	5
Midfielders:	**DOB**	**M**	**(s)**	**G**
Diego Marvin Biseswar (NED)	08.03.1988	26	(1)	8
José Alberto Cañas Ruiz Herrera (ESP)	27.05.1987	11	(3)	
Omar El Kaddouri (MAR)	21.08.1990	10	(7)	1
Maurício José Da Silveira Junior (BRA)	21.10.1988	19	(1)	5
Josip Mišić (CRO)	28.06.1994	1	(4)	
Dimitrios Pelkas	26.10.1993	17	(5)	3
Sérgio Miguel Relvas de Oliveira (POR)	02.06.1992	8	(3)	3
Yevhen Shakhov (UKR)	30.11.1990	16	(5)	5
Pontus Wernbloom (SWE)	25.06.1986	5	(6)	
Forwards:	**DOB**	**M**	**(s)**	**G**
Chuba Amechi Akpom (ENG)	09.10.1995	13	(7)	6
Nikolaos Karelis	24.02.1992	1	(4)	
Leonardo Rodrigues Lima „Léo Jabá" (BRA)	02.08.1998	16	(8)	3
Dimitrios Limnios	27.05.1998	14	(6)	1
Pedro Henrique Konzen Medina da Silva (BRA)	16.06.1990	3	(4)	3
Aleksandar Prijović (SRB)	21.04.1990	13		9
Karol Świderski (POL)	23.01.1997	3	(8)	4
Amr Warda (EGY)	17.09.1993	4	(5)	
Trainer:	**DOB**	**M**		
Răzvan Lucescu (ROU)	17.02.1969	30		

Panepirotikos Athlitikos Syllogos Giannina

Founded: 08.07.1966
Stadium: Stádio Zosimades, Ioannina (7,652)

Goalkeepers:	DOB	M	(s)	G
Neofytos Michail (CYP)	16.12.1993	9		
Markos Vellidis	04.04.1987	21		
Defenders:	**DOB**	**M**	**(s)**	**G**
Michalis Boukouvalas	14.01.1988	24		
Mite Cikarski (MKD)	06.01.1993	7		
Stefanos Evangelou	12.05.1998	1		
Alex Kakuba (UGA)	12.06.1991	4	(1)	
Giannis Kargas	09.12.1994	8		
Alexandros Michail	18.08.1986	26		
Lasha Shergelashvili (GEO)	17.01.1992	10		
Apostolos Skondras	29.12.1988	16	(3)	
Themistoklis Tzimopoulos (NZL)	20.11.1985	24	(2)	
Midfielders:	**DOB**	**M**	**(s)**	**G**
Alexandros Apostolopoulos	07.11.1991	12	(4)	
Edwin Fabry Castro Barros (COL)	21.02.1992	14	(2)	1
Higor Felipe Vidal (BRA)	26.09.1996	9	(6)	
Orest Kuzyk (UKR)	17.05.1995	2	(2)	
Andi Lila (ALB)	12.02.1986	19		
Vladyslav Naumets (UKR)	07.03.1999		(3)	
Alexandros Nikolias	23.07.1994	26	(2)	3
Dušan Pantelić (SRB)	15.04.1993	7	(4)	
Stefanos Siontis	04.09.1987	6	(6)	
Forwards:	**DOB**	**M**	**(s)**	**G**
Stefanos Athanasiadis	24.12.1988	13	(10)	2
Enes Dolovac (SRB)	01.02.1999	4		
Euripidis Giakos	09.04.1991	16	(5)	2
Sandi Križman (CRO)	17.08.1989	15	(5)	4
Jean-Baptiste Léo (FRA)	03.05.1996	6	(8)	1
Giannis Loukinas	20.09.1991	1		
Dimitrios Manos	16.09.1994	10	(4)	3
Ioannis Mystakidis	07.12.1994	5	(5)	1
Giorgos Pamlidis	13.11.1993	9	(6)	
Georgios Xydas	14.04.1997	6	(9)	
Trainer:	**DOB**	**M**		
Giannis Petrakis	20.05.1959	30		

Athlitikos Omilos Xanthi

Founded: 01.01.1967
Stadium: AO Xanthi Arena, Xanthi (7,422)

Goalkeepers:	**DOB**	**M**	**(s)**	**G**
Živko Živković (SRB)	14.04.1989	30		
Defenders:	**DOB**	**M**	**(s)**	**G**
Dimosthenis Baxevanidis	14.04.1988	25		1
Okan Chatziterzoglu	05.03.1996	3	(2)	
Dinis Costa Lima Almeida (POR)	28.05.1995	16	(5)	2
Mikael Dyrestam (GUI)	10.12.1991	6	(3)	
Konstantinos Fliskas	29.12.1980	2		
Jorge Casado Rodríguez (ESP)	26.06.1989	29		
Christos Lisgaras	12.02.1986	24		
Salimo Sylla (FRA)	25.01.1994	16	(3)	
Konstantinos Thymianis	28.02.2001	1	(1)	
Midfielders:	**DOB**	**M**	**(s)**	**G**
Jean Pierre Agustin Barrientos Díaz (URU)	16.09.1990	12	(2)	
Khassa Camara (MTN)	22.10.1992	21	(4)	
Pablo de Lucas Torres (ESP)	20.09.1986	5	(4)	
Petar Đuričković (SRB)	20.06.1991	16	(4)	2
Sofiane Khadda (FRA)	23.12.1991	22	(3)	
Aleksandar Kovačević (SRB)	09.01.1992	24	(3)	1
Dimitrios Meliopoulos	22.03.2000	5	(8)	
Petros Orfanidis	23.03.1996		(1)	
Forwards:	**DOB**	**M**	**(s)**	**G**
Armindo Rodrigues Mendes Furtado „Brito“ (POR)	16.11.1987	9	(10)	1
Matías Gastón Castro (ARG)	18.12.1991	11	(11)	5
Ioannis Fakis	14.04.2001	1	(3)	
Vasilios Fasidis	22.06.1996	1	(2)	
Erik Jendrišek (SVK)	26.10.1986	21	(2)	8
Enrique Boula Senobua „Kike“ (EQG)	17.07.1993	7	(1)	
Rafail Melissopoulos	19.02.1997	2	(2)	
Jeffrey Nana Darko Sarpong (NED)	03.08.1988	14	(7)	
Okan Suleiman	04.03.2000	2	(1)	
William Douglas De Amorim (BRA)	15.12.1991	5	(6)	
Trainer:	**DOB**	**M**		
Milan Rastavac (SRB)	01.11.1973	30		

SECOND LEVEL
Football League 2018/2019

1.	PAE Volos (*Promoted*)	30	18	6	6	61 - 27	60
2.	AO Platanias (*Promotion Play-offs*)	30	15	10	5	53 - 22	55
3.	PAE Apollon Larissa	30	16	9	5	44 - 27	54
4.	GS Ergotelis Heraklion	30	15	6	9	48 - 28	48
5.	Panachaiki 1891 FC Patras	30	12	12	6	32 - 25	48
6.	AO Chania Kissamikos PAE	30	13	7	10	40 - 24	46
7.	PAE Apollon Pontus Kalamaria	30	15	4	11	33 - 27	46
8.	GS Doxa Drama	30	12	9	9	41 - 28	45
9.	AOK Kerkyra	30	14	5	11	30 - 25	44
10.	AE Karaiskakis Arta	30	11	7	12	24 - 28	40
11.	PAE Iraklis Thessaloníki (*Relegated*)	30	11	9	10	29 - 24	39
12.	AO Trikala (*Relegated*)	30	9	8	13	27 - 30	35
13.	PASA Iródotos (*Relegated*)	30	9	4	17	24 - 50	28
14.	PAO Aittitos Spata (*Relegated*)	30	5	7	18	18 - 50	22
15.	PAE Aiginiakos (*Relegated*)	30	5	4	21	24 - 66	16
16.	Athlitiki Enosis Spartis (*Relegated*)	30	4	5	21	17 - 64	11

NATIONAL TEAM

INTERNATIONAL MATCHES
(16.07.2018 – 15.07.2019)

08.09.2018	Tallinn	Estonia - Greece	0-1(0-1)	(UNL)
11.09.2018	Budapest	Hungary - Greece	2-1(2-1)	(UNL)
12.10.2018	Athína	Greece - Hungary	1-0(0-0)	(UNL)
15.10.2018	Tampere	Finland - Greece	2-0(0-0)	(UNL)
15.11.2018	Athína	Greece - Finland	1-0(0-0)	(UNL)
18.11.2018	Athína	Greece - Estonia	0-1(0-1)	(UNL)
23.03.2019	Vaduz	Liechtenstein - Greece	0-2(0-1)	(ECQ)
26.03.2019	Zenica	Bosnia and Herzegovina - Greece	2-2(2-0)	(ECQ)
30.05.2019	Antalya	Turkey - Greece	2-1(2-0)	(F)
08.06.2019	Athína	Greece - Italy	0-3(0-3)	(ECQ)
11.06.2019	Athína	Greece - Armenia	2-3(0-2)	(ECQ)

08.09.2018 ESTONIA - GREECE 0-1(0-1) UEFA Nations League C, Group 2
A. Le Coq Arena, Tallinn; Referee: Serdar Gözübüyük (Netherlands); Attendance: 5,567
GRE: Vasilios Barkas, Vasilios Torosidis (Cap), Sokratis Papastathopoulos, Konstantinos Manolas, Haralambos Lykogiannis, Petros Mantalos, Konstantinos Fortounis, Andreas Bouchalakis (78.Alexandros Tziolis), Dimitrios Kourbelis, Dimitrios Pelkas (90+2.Efthimis Koulouris), Konstantinos Mitroglou (50.Anastasios Bakasetas). Trainer: Michael Heinz Skibbe (Germany).
Goal: Konstantinos Fortounis (14).

11.09.2018 HUNGARY - GREECE 2-1(2-1) UEFA Nations League C, Group 2
Groupama Aréna, Budapest; Referee: Aliaksei Kulbakov (Belarus); Attendance: *played behind closed doors*
GRE: Vasilios Barkas, Vasilios Torosidis (Cap), Sokratis Papastathopoulos, Giorgos Tzavelas (46.Haralambos Lykogiannis), Konstantinos Manolas (52.Marios Oikonomou), Lazaros Christodoulopoulos, Konstantinos Fortounis, Andreas Bouchalakis, Dimitrios Kourbelis, Dimitrios Pelkas, Anastasios Donis (46.Konstantinos Mitroglou). Trainer: Michael Heinz Skibbe (Germany).
Goal: Konstantinos Manolas (18).

12.10.2018 GREECE - HUNGARY 1-0(0-0) UEFA Nations League C, Group 2
Stádio Olympiako „Spiros Louis“, Athína; Referee: Tobias Stieler (Germany); Attendance: 9,040
GRE: Vasilios Barkas, Sokratis Papastathopoulos (Cap), Konstantinos Manolas, Michalis Bakakis, Konstantinos Tsimikas, Konstantinos Fortounis, José Carlos Gonçalves Rodrigues "Zeca", Dimitrios Kourbelis (46.Alexandros Tziolis), Dimitrios Pelkas (85.Lazaros Christodoulopoulos), Konstantinos Mitroglou (90+4.Andreas Bouchalakis), Anastasios Bakasetas. Trainer: Michael Heinz Skibbe (Germany).
Goal: Konstantinos Mitroglou (65).

15.10.2018 FINLAND - GREECE 2-0(0-0) UEFA Nations League C, Group 2
Ratinan Stadion, Tampere; Referee: Paweł Gil (Poland); Attendance: 10,107
GRE: Vasilios Barkas, Sokratis Papastathopoulos (Cap) (46.Giorgos Tzavelas), Konstantinos Manolas, Michalis Bakakis, Konstantinos Tsimikas, Alexandros Tziolis, Konstantinos Fortounis, José Carlos Gonçalves Rodrigues "Zeca", Dimitrios Pelkas (73.Efthimis Koulouris), Konstantinos Mitroglou, Anastasios Bakasetas (55.Lazaros Christodoulopoulos). Trainer: Michael Heinz Skibbe (Germany).

15.11.2018 GREECE - FINLAND 1-0(0-0) UEFA Nations League C, Group 2
Stádio Olympiako „Spiros Louis“, Athína; Referee: Luca Banti (Italy); Attendance: 6,376
GRE: Odisseas Vlachodimos, Vasilios Torosidis (Cap), Sokratis Papastathopoulos, Konstantinos Manolas (28.Dimitrios Siovas), Leonardo Koutris, Petros Mantalos, Konstantinos Fortounis, José Carlos Gonçalves Rodrigues "Zeca", Dimitrios Kourbelis, Dimitrios Pelkas (84.Anastasios Bakasetas), Konstantinos Mitroglou (69.Efthimis Koulouris). Trainer: Angelos Anastasiadis.
Goal: Albin Granlund (25 own goal).

18.11.2018 GREECE - ESTONIA 0-1(0-1) UEFA Nations League C, Group 2
Stádio Olympiako „Spiros Louis“, Athína; Referee: Yevhen Aranovskyi (Ukraine); Attendance: 5,179
GRE: Vasilios Barkas, Sokratis Papastathopoulos (Cap), Vasilios Konstantinos Lambropoulos, Michalis Bakakis (46.Vasilios Torosidis), Dimitrios Hristos Giannoulis, Andreas Samaris, José Carlos Gonçalves Rodrigues "Zeca", Andreas Bouchalakis (71.Petros Mantalos), Giorgos Masouras (57.Konstantinos Fortounis), Nikolaos Karelis, Anastasios Bakasetas. Trainer: Angelos Anastasiadis.

23.03.2019 LIECHTENSTEIN - GREECE 0-2(0-1) 16th EC. Qualifiers
Rheinpark Stadion, Vaduz; Referee: Alexandre Boucaut (Belgium); Attendance: 2,711
GRE: Odisseas Vlachodimos, Dimitrios Siovas, Michalis Bakakis, Leonardo Koutris, Andreas Samaris, Konstantinos Fortounis (83.Efthimis Koulouris), José Carlos Gonçalves Rodrigues "Zeca", Dimitrios Kourbelis, Giorgos Masouras, Konstantinos Mitroglou (Cap) (23.Anastasios Donis), Anastasios Bakasetas (71.Dimitrios Kolovos). Trainer: Angelos Anastasiadis.
Goals: Konstantinos Fortounis (45+1), Anastasios Donis (80).

26.03.2019 BOSNIA AND HERZEGOVINA - GREECE 2-2(2-0) 16th EC. Qualifiers
Stadion Bilino Polje, Zenica; Referee: Danny Desmond Makkelie (Netherlands); Attendance: 10,500
GRE: Odisseas Vlachodimos, Dimitrios Siovas, Sokratis Papastathopoulos (Cap), Michalis Bakakis (80.Efthimis Koulouris), Leonardo Koutris, Andreas Samaris, Konstantinos Fortounis, José Carlos Gonçalves Rodrigues "Zeca", Andreas Bouchalakis (46.Giorgos Masouras), Dimitrios Kourbelis (67.Dimitrios Kolovos), Anastasios Donis. Trainer: Angelos Anastasiadis.
Goals: (64 penalty), (85).

30.05.2019 TURKEY - GREECE 2-1(2-0) Friendly International
Antalya Stadyumu, Antalya; Referee: Radu Petrescu (Romania); Attendance: n/a
GRE: Alexandros Paschalakis, Giorgos Valerianos (54.Andreas Bouchalakis), Leonardo Koutris (46.Konstantinos Stafylidis), Andreas Samaris, Konstantinos Fortounis (Cap), Dimitrios Kourbelis, Emmanouil Siopis (75.Petros Mantalos), Haralampos Mavrias (73.Giannis Kotsiras), Dimitrios Pelkas (46.Dimitrios Kolovos), Giorgos Masouras (65.Fiorin Durmishaj), Efthimis Koulouris. Trainer: Angelos Anastasiadis.
Goal: (90+3).

08.06.2019 **GREECE - ITALY** **0-3(0-3)** 16th EC. Qualifiers

Stádio Olympiako „Spiros Louis", Athína; Referee: Anthony Taylor (England); Attendance: 19,828

GRE: Vasilios Barkas, Dimitrios Siovas, Sokratis Papastathopoulos (Cap), Konstantinos Manolas, Konstantinos Stafylidis, Andreas Samaris(77.Anastasios Bakasetas), Konstantinos Fortounis, José Carlos Gonçalves Rodrigues "Zeca", Dimitrios Kolovos (46.Haralampos Mavrias), Dimitrios Kourbelis (46.Emmanouil Siopis), Giorgos Masouras. Trainer: Angelos Anastasiadis.

11.06.2019 **GREECE - ARMENIA** **2-3(0-2)** 16th EC. Qualifiers

Stádio Olympiako „Spiros Louis", Athína; Referee: Kristo Tohver (Estonia); Attendance: 7,011

GRE: Odisseas Vlachodimos, Dimitrios Siovas, Sokratis Papastathopoulos (Cap), Leonardo Koutris, Andreas Samaris (75.Emmanouil Siopis), Konstantinos Fortounis, José Carlos Gonçalves Rodrigues "Zeca", Haralampos Mavrias (17.Giannis Kotsiras), Dimitrios Pelkas (68.Dimitrios Kolovos), Giorgos Masouras, Efthimis Koulouris. Trainer: Angelos Anastasiadis.

Goals: José Carlos Gonçalves Rodrigues "Zeca" (54), Konstantinos Fortounis (87).

NATIONAL TEAM PLAYERS
(16.07.2018 – 15.07.2019)

Name	DOB	Caps	Goals	2018/2019:	*Club*
Goalkeepers					
Vasilios BARKAS	30.05.1994	**8**	**0**	2018/2019:	*AEK Athína*
Alexandros PASCHALAKIS	28.07.1989	**1**	**0**	2019:	*PAOK Thessaloníki*
Odisseas VLACHODIMOS	26.04.1994	**4**	**0**	2018/2019:	*Sport Lisboa e Benfica (POR)*
Defenders					
Michalis BAKAKIS	18.04.1991	**9**	**0**	2018/2019:	*AEK Athína*
Dimitrios Hristos GIANNOULIS	17.10.1995	**2**	**0**	2018:	*APS Atromitos Athína*
Giannis KOTSIRAS	16.12.1992	**2**	**0**	2019:	*AGS Asteras Tripolis*
Leonardo KOUTRIS	23.07.1995	**5**	**0**	2018/2019:	*Olympiacos SFP Peiraiás*
Vasilios Konstantinos LAMBROPOULOS	03.03.1990	**2**	**0**	2018:	*AEK Athína*
Haralambos LYKOGIANNIS	22.03.1993	**4**	**0**	2018:	*Cagliari Calcio (ITA)*
Konstantinos MANOLAS	14.06.1991	**40**	**1**	2018/2019:	*AS Roma (ITA)*
Marios OIKONOMOU	06.10.1992	**6**	**0**	2018:	*AEK Athína*
Sokratis PAPASTATHOPOULOS	09.06.1988	**88**	**3**	2018/2019:	*Arsenal FC London (ENG)*
Dimitrios SIOVAS	16.09.1988	**17**	**0**	2018/2019:	*CD Leganés (ESP)*
Konstantinos STAFYLIDIS	02.12.1993	**26**	**2**	2019:	*FC Augsburg (GER)*
Vasilios TOROSIDIS	10.06.1985	**100**	**10**	2018:	*Olympiacos SFP Peiraiás*
Konstantinos TSIMIKAS	12.05.1996	**2**	**0**	2018:	*Olympiacos SFP Peiraiás*
Giorgos TZAVELAS	26.11.1987	**31**	**2**	2018:	*Alanyaspor (TUR)*
Giorgos VALERIANOS	13.02.1992	**1**	**0**	2019:	*Aris Thessaloníki*
Midfielders					
Andreas BOUCHALAKIS	05.04.1993	**6**	**0**	2018/2019:	*Olympiacos SFP Peiraiás*
Lazaros CHRISTODOULOPOULOS	19.12.1986	**35**	**1**	2018:	*Olympiacos SFP Peiraiás*
Konstantinos FORTOUNIS	16.10.1992	**44**	**7**	2018/2019:	*Olympiacos SFP Peiraiás*
Dimitrios KOLOVOS	27.04.1993	**8**	**1**	2019:	*AC Omonia Nicosia (CYP)*
Dimitrios KOURBELIS	02.11.1993	**11**	**1**	2018/2019:	*PAE Panathinaïkos Athína*
Petros MANTALOS	31.08.1991	**23**	**2**	2018/2019:	*AEK Athína*
Haralampos MAVRIAS	21.02.1994	**8**	**0**	2019:	*AC Omonia Nicosia (CYP)*
Dimitrios PELKAS	26.10.1993	**14**	**0**	2018/2019:	*PAOK Thessaloníki*
Andreas SAMARIS	13.06.1989	**38**	**1**	2018/2019:	*Sport Lisboa e Benfica (POR)*
Emmanouil SIOPIS	14.05.1994	**3**	**0**	2019:	*Aris Thessaloníki*
Alexandros TZIOLIS	13.02.1985	**75**	**2**	2018/2019:	*Al-Fayha FC al Majma'h (KSA)*
José Carlos Gonçalves Rodrigues "ZECA"	31.08.1988	**17**	**2**	2018/2019:	*FC København (DEN)*
Forwards					
Anastasios BAKASETAS	28.06.1993	**21**	**0**	2018/2019:	*AEK Athína*
Anastasios DONIS	29.08.1996	**9**	**1**	2018/2019:	*VfB Stuttgart*
Fiorin DURMISHAJ	14.11.1996	**1**	**0**	2019:	*Panionios GSS Athína*
Nikolaos KARELIS	24.02.1992	**19**	**3**	2018:	*PAOK Thessaloníki*
Efthimis KOULOURIS	06.03.1996	**9**	**0**	2018/2019:	*APS Atromitos Athína*
Giorgos MASOURAS	01.01.1994	**6**	**0**	2018: 01.01.2019->	*Panionios GSS Athína* *Olympiacos SFP Peiraiás*
Konstantinos MITROGLOU	12.03.1988	**65**	**17**	2018: 31.01.2019->	*Olympique de Marseille (FRA)* *Galatasaray SK İstanbul (TUR)*

National team coach

Michael Heinz SKIBBE (Germany) [30.10.2015 – 25.10.2018]	04.08.1965	27 M; 11 W; 6 D; 10 L; 30-26
Angelos ANASTASIADIS [08.11.2018 – 15.07.2019]	08.03.1953	7 M; 2 W; 1 D; 4 L; 8-11

HUNGARY

The Country:

Magyarország (Hungary)
Capital: Budapest
Surface: 93,030 km²
Inhabitants: 9,772,756 [2019]
Time: UTC+1

The FA:

Magyar Labdarúgó Szövetség
1112 Budapest, Kánai út 2.D
Tel: +36 1 577 9500
Foundation date: 00.00.1900
Member of FIFA since: 1901
Member of UEFA since: 1954
Website: www.mlsz.hu

NATIONAL TEAM RECORDS

First international match:	12.10.1902, Wien: Austria – Hungary 5-0	
Most international caps:	Gábor Király	- 108 caps (1998-2016)
Most international goals:	Ferenc Puskás	- 84 goals / 85 caps (1945-1956)

UEFA EUROPEAN CHAMPIONSHIP	
1960	Qualifiers
1964	Final Tournament (3rd Place)
1968	Qualifiers
1972	Final Tournament (4th Place)
1976	Qualifiers
1980	Qualifiers
1984	Qualifiers
1988	Qualifiers
1992	Qualifiers
1996	Qualifiers
2000	Qualifiers
2004	Qualifiers
2008	Qualifiers
2012	Qualifiers
2016	Final Tournament (2nd Round of 16)

FIFA WORLD CUP	
1930	Did not enter
1934	Final Tournament (Quarter-Finals)
1938	Final Tournament (Runners-up)
1950	Did not enter
1954	Final Tournament (Runners-up)
1958	Final Tournament (Group Stage)
1962	Final Tournament (Quarter-Finals)
1966	Final Tournament (Quarter-Finals)
1970	Qualifiers
1974	Qualifiers
1978	Final Tournament (Group Stage)
1982	Final Tournament (Group Stage)
1986	Final Tournament (Group Stage)
1990	Qualifiers
1994	Qualifiers
1998	Qualifiers
2002	Qualifiers
2006	Qualifiers
2010	Qualifiers
2014	Qualifiers
2018	Qualifiers

UEFA NATIONS LEAGUE
2018/2019 – League C (promoted to League B)

OLYMPIC FOOTBALL TOURNAMENTS 1908-2016							
1908	Did not enter	**1948**	Did not enter	**1972**	Runners-up	**1996**	Group Stage
1912	Quarter-Finals	**1952**	**Winners**	**1976**	Qualifiers	**2000**	Qualifiers
1920	Did not enter	**1956**	Did not enter	**1980**	Qualifiers	**2004**	Qualifiers
1924	1/8-Finals	**1960**	3rd Place	**1984**	Qualifiers	**2008**	Qualifiers
1928	Did not enter	**1964**	**Winners**	**1988**	Qualifiers	**2012**	Qualifiers
1936	1/8-Finals	**1968**	**Winners**	**1992**	Qualifiers	**2016**	Qualifiers

FIFA CONFEDERATIONS CUP 1992-2017
None

HUNGARIAN CLUB HONOURS IN EUROPEAN CLUB COMPETITIONS:

European Champion Clubs' Cup (1956-1992) / UEFA Champions League (1993-2019)		
None		
Fairs Cup (1858-1971) / UEFA Cup (1972-2009) / UEFA Europa League (2010-2019)		
Ferencvárosi FC	**1**	1964/1965
UEFA Super Cup (1972-2018)		
None		
European Cup Winners' Cup 1961-1999*		
None		

**defunct competition*

NATIONAL COMPETITIONS
TABLE OF HONOURS

	CHAMPIONS	CUP WINNERS	BEST GOALSCORERS	
1901	Budapesti Torna Club	-	Miltiades Manno (Budapesti Torna Club)	17
1902	Budapesti Torna Club	-	Miltiades Manno (Budapesti Torna Club)	10
1903	Ferencvárosi TC	-	Jenő Károly (MTK Budapest)	15
1904	MTK Budapest	-	József Pokorny (Ferencvárosi TC)	12
1905	Ferencvárosi TC	-	Jenő Károly (MTK Budapest)	13
1906/1907	Ferencvárosi TC	-	Béla Kelemen (Magyar Atlétikai Club)	21
1907/1908	MTK Budapest	-	Gyula Vangel (Magyar Atlétikai Club)	21
1908/1909	Ferencvárosi TC	-	Imre Schlosser (Ferencvárosi TC)	30
1909/1910	Ferencvárosi TC	MTK Budapest	Imre Schlosser (Ferencvárosi TC)	18
1910/1911	Ferencvárosi TC	MTK Budapest	Imre Schlosser (Ferencvárosi TC)	38
1911/1912	Ferencvárosi TC	MTK Budapest	Imre Schlosser (Ferencvárosi TC)	34
1912/1913	Ferencvárosi TC	Ferencvárosi TC	Imre Schlosser (Ferencvárosi TC)	33
1913/1914	MTK Budapest	MTK Budapest	Imre Schlosser (Ferencvárosi TC)	21
1914/1915	*No competition*	*No competition*	-	
1915/1916	*No competition*	*No competition*		
1916/1917	MTK Budapest	*No competition*	Imre Schlosser (MTK Budapest)	38
1917/1918	MTK Budapest	*No competition*	Alfréd Schaffer (MTK Budapest)	46
1918/1919	MTK Budapest	*No competition*	Alfréd Schaffer (MTK Budapest)	41
1919/1920	MTK Budapest	*No competition*	György Orth (MTK Budapest)	28
1920/1921	MTK Budapest	*No competition*	György Orth (MTK Budapest)	21
1921/1922	MTK Budapest	Ferencvárosi TC	György Orth (MTK Budapest)	26
1922/1923	MTK Budapest	MTK Budapest	István Priboj (Újpesti TE)	25
1923/1924	MTK Budapest	*No competition*	József Jeszmás (Újpesti TE)	15
1924/1925	MTK Budapest	MTK Budapest	György Molnár (MTK Budapest)	21
1925/1926	Ferencvárosi TC	Kispest AC	József Takács (Vasas SC Budapest)	29
1926/1927	Ferencvárosi TC	Ferencvárosi TC	László Horváth (Ferencvárosi TC)	14
1927/1928	Ferencvárosi TC	Ferencvárosi TC	József Takács (Ferencvárosi TC)	31
1928/1929	Hungária MTK FC Budapest	*No competition*	József Takács (Ferencvárosi TC)	41
1929/1930	Újpesti TE	Debreceni Bocskai FC	József Takács (Ferencvárosi TC)	40
1930/1931	Újpesti TE	III. Kerületi TVE	Jenő Vincze (Debreceni Bocskai FC)	20
1931/1932	Ferencvárosi TC	Hungária MTK FC Budapest	József Takács (Ferencvárosi TC)	42
1932/1933	Újpesti TE	Ferencvárosi TC	Pál Jávor (Újpesti TE)	31
1933/1934	Ferencvárosi TC	Soroksár FC	Géza Toldi (Ferencvárosi TC)	27
1934/1935	Újpesti TE	Ferencvárosi TC	László Cseh II (MTK Budapest)	23
1935/1936	Hungária MTK FC Budapest	*No competition*	György Sárosi dr. (Ferencvárosi TC)	36
1936/1937	Hungária MTK FC Budapest	*No competition*	László Cseh II (MTK Budapest)	36
1937/1938	Ferencvárosi TC	*No competition*	Gyula Zsengellér (Újpesti TE)	31
1938/1939	Újpesti TE	*No competition*	Gyula Zsengellér (Újpesti TE)	56
1939/1940	Ferencvárosi TC	*No competition*	György Sárosi dr. (Ferencvárosi TC)	23
1940/1941	Ferencvárosi TC	Szolnoki MÁV SE	György Sárosi dr. (Ferencvárosi TC)	29
1941/1942	Csepel SC Budapest	Ferencvárosi TC	György Kalmár (Szegedi AK)	35
1942/1943	Csepel SC Budapest	Ferencvárosi TC	Gyula Zsengellér (Újpesti TE) Jenő Jenőfi (Vasas SC Budapest)	26
1943/1944	Nagyváradi AC	Ferencvárosi TC	Gyula Zsengellér (Újpesti TE)	33
1945	Újpesti TE	*No competition*	Gyula Zsengellér (Újpesti TE)	36
1945/1946	Újpesti TE	*No competition*	Ferenc Deák (Szentlőrinci AC)	66
1946/1947	Újpesti TE	*No competition*	Ferenc Deák (Szentlőrinci AC)	48
1947/1948	Csepel SC Budapest	*No competition*	Ferenc Puskás (Budapest Honvéd SE)	50
1948/1949	Ferencvárosi TC	*No competition*	Ferenc Deák (Ferencvárosi TC)	59
1949/1950	Budapest Honvéd SE	*No competition*	Ferenc Puskás (Budapest Honvéd SE)	31
1950	Budapest Honvéd SE	*No competition*	Ferenc Puskás (Budapest Honvéd SE)	25
1951	Budapesti Textiles SE	*No competition*	Sándor Kocsis (Budapest Honvéd SE)	30
1952	Budapest Honvéd SE	Budapesti Bástya SE	Sándor Kocsis (Budapest Honvéd SE)	36
1953	Budapesti Vörös Lobogó SE	*No competition*	Ferenc Puskás (Budapest Honvéd SE)	27
1954	Budapest Honvéd SE	*No competition*	Sándor Kocsis (Budapest Honvéd SE)	33
1955	Budapest Honvéd SE	Vasas SC Budapest	Zoltán Czibor (Budapest Honvéd SE) Ferenc Machos (Budapest Honvéd SE)	20
1956	*No competition*	*No competition*	-	
1957	Vasas SC Budapest	*No competition*	Gyula Szilágyi (Vasas SC Budapest)	17
1957/1958	MTK Budapest	Ferencvárosi TC	Zoltán Friedmanszky (Ferencvárosi TC) János Molnár (MTK Budapest)	16
1958/1959	Csepel SC Budapest	*No competition*	Róbert Kisuczky (Csepel) Tivadar Monostori (Dorog) Lajos Tichy (Honvéd)	15
1959/1960	Újpesti Dózsa SC	*No competition*	Flórián Albert (Ferencvárosi TC)	27
1960/1961	Vasas SC Budapest	*No competition*	Flórián Albert (Ferencvárosi TC) Lajos Tichy (Budapest Honvéd SE)	21
1961/1962	Vasas SC Budapest	*No competition*	Lajos Tichy (Budapest Honvéd SE)	23
1962/1963	Ferencvárosi TC	*No competition*	Ferenc Bene (Újpesti Dózsa SC)	23
1963	Győri Vasas ETO	*No competition*	Lajos Tichy (Budapest Honvéd SE)	13
1964	Ferencvárosi TC	Budapest Honvéd SE	Lajos Tichy (Budapest Honvéd SE)	28

1965	Vasas SC Budapest	Rába Vasas ETO Győr	Flórián Albert (Ferencvárosi TC)	27
1966	Vasas SC Budapest	Rába Vasas ETO Győr	János Farkas (Vasas SC Budapest)	25
1967	Ferencvárosi TC	Rába Vasas ETO Győr	Antal Dunai II (Újpesti Dózsa SC)	36
1968	Ferencvárosi TC	MTK Budapest	Antal Dunai II (Újpesti Dózsa SC)	31
1969	Újpesti Dózsa SC	Újpesti Dózsa SC	Ferenc Bene (Újpesti Dózsa SC)	27
1970	Újpesti Dózsa SC	Újpesti Dózsa SC	Antal Dunai II (Újpesti Dózsa SC)	14
1970/1971	Újpesti Dózsa SC	*No competition*	Mihály Kozma (Budapest Honvéd SE)	25
1971/1972	Újpesti Dózsa SC	Ferencvárosi TC	Ferenc Bene (Újpesti Dózsa SC)	29
1972/1973	Újpesti Dózsa SC	Vasas Budapest SC	Ferenc Bene (Újpesti Dózsa SC)	23
1973/1974	Újpesti Dózsa SC	Ferencvárosi TC	Mihály Kozma (Budapest Honvéd SE)	27
1974/1975	Újpesti Dózsa SC	Újpesti Dózsa SC	Mihály Kozma (Budapest Honvéd SE) Ferenc Bene (Újpesti Dózsa SC)	20
1975/1976	Ferencvárosi TC	Ferencvárosi TC	László Fazekas (Újpesti Dózsa SC)	19
1976/1977	Vasas SC Budapest	Diósgyőri VTK	Béla Várady (Vasas SC Budapest)	36
1977/1978	Újpesti Dózsa SC	Ferencvárosi TC	László Fazekas (Újpesti Dózsa SC)	24
1978/1979	Újpesti Dózsa SC	Rába Vasas ETO Győr	László Fekete (Újpesti Dózsa SC)	31
1979/1980	Budapest Honvéd SE	Diósgyőri VTK	László Fekete (Újpesti Dózsa SC)	36
1980/1981	Ferencvárosi TC	Vasas Budapest SC	Tibor Nyilasi (Ferencvárosi TC)	30
1981/1982	Rába Vasas ETO Győr	Újpesti Dózsa SC	Péter Hannich (Rába Vasas ETO Győr)	22
1982/1983	Rába Vasas ETO Győr	Újpesti Dózsa SC	Lajos Dobány (Pécsi MSC / Szombathely)	23
1983/1984	Budapest Honvéd SE	Siófoki Bányász SK	József Szabó (Videoton SC Székesfehérvár)	19
1984/1985	Budapest Honvéd SE	Budapest Honvéd SE	Lajos Détári (Budapest Honvéd SE) József Kiprich (Tatabányai Bányász)	18
1985/1986	Budapest Honvéd SE	Vasas Budapest SC	Lajos Détári (Budapest Honvéd SE)	27
1986/1987	MTK-VM Budapest	Újpesti Dózsa SC	Lajos Détári (Budapest Honvéd SE)	19
1987/1988	Budapest Honvéd SE	Békéscsabai Előre SSC	Béla Melis (Debreceni VSC)	19
1988/1989	Budapest Honvéd SE	Budapest Honvéd SE	Tamás Petres (Videoton SC Székesfehérvár)	19
1989/1990	Újpesti TE	Pécsi MSC	József Dzurják (Ferencvárosi TC)	18
1990/1991	Budapest Honvéd SE	Ferencvárosi TC	József Gregor (Budapest Honvéd SE)	19
1991/1992	Ferencvárosi TC	Újpesti TE	Pál Fischer (Siófoki Bányász SK) Ferenc Orosz (Vác FC)	16
1992/1993	Kispest Honvéd FC	Ferencvárosi TC	László Répási (Vác FC)	16
1993/1994	Vác FC	Ferencvárosi TC	Béla Illés (Kispest Honvéd FC)	17
1994/1995	Ferencvárosi TC	Ferencvárosi TC	Sándor Preisinger (Zalaegerszeg)	21
1995/1996	Ferencvárosi TC	Kispest Honvéd FC	Ihor Nichenko (UKR, Stadler FC / Ferencvárosi TC)	18
1996/1997	MTK Budapest FC	MTK Budapest FC	Béla Illés (MTK Budapest FC)	23
1997/1998	Újpesti TE	MTK Budapest FC	Krisztián Tiber (Gázszer FC Gárdony)	20
1998/1999	MTK Hungária FC Budapest	Debreceni VSC	Béla Illés (MTK Hungária FC Budapest)	22
1999/2000	Dunaferr SE Dunaújváros	MTK Hungária FC Budapest	Attila Tököli (Dunaferr SE Dunaújváros)	22
2000/2001	Ferencvárosi TC	Debreceni VSC	Péter Kabát (Vasas SC Budapest)	24
2001/2002	Zalaegerszegi TE FC	Újpesti TE	Attila Tököli (Dunaferr SE Dunaújváros)	28
2002/2003	MTK Hungária FC Budapest	Ferencvárosi TC	Krisztián Kenesei (Zalaegerszegi TE FC)	23
2003/2004	Ferencvárosi TC	Ferencvárosi TC	Mihály Tóth (Soproni VSE)	17
2004/2005	Debreceni VSC	Sopron FC	Tomáš Medveď (SVK, Pápai FC)	18
2005/2006	Debreceni VSC	FC Fehérvár Székesfehérvár	Péter Rajczi (Újpest FC)	23
2006/2007	Debreceni VSC	Budapest Honvéd FC	Ibrahim Sidibe (SEN, Debreceni VSC) Péter Bajzát (Győri ETO FC)	18
2007/2008	MTK Budapest FC	Debreceni VSC	Róbert Waltner (Zalaegerszegi TE FC)	18
2008/2009	Debreceni VSC	Budapest Honvéd FC	Péter Bajzát (Győri ETO FC)	20
2009/2010	Debreceni VSC	Debreceni VSC	Nemanja Nikolić (SRB, Videoton FC Székesfehérvár)	18
2010/2011	Videoton FC Székesfehérvár	Kecskeméti TE	André Alves dos Santos (BRA, Videoton FC Székesfehérvár)	24
2011/2012	Debreceni VSC	Debreceni VSC	Adamo Coulibaly (FRA, Debreceni VSC)	20
2012/2013	Győri ETO FC	Debreceni VSC	Adamo Coulibaly (FRA, Debreceni VSC)	18
2013/2014	Debreceni VSC	Újpest FC	Nemanja Nikolić (Videoton FC Székesfehérvár) Attila Simon (Paksi FC)	21
2014/2015	Videoton FC Székesfehérvár	Ferencvárosi TC	Nemanja Nikolić (Videoton FC Székesfehérvár)	21
2015/2016	Ferencvárosi TC	Ferencvárosi TC	Dániel Böde (Ferencvárosi TC)	17
2016/2017	Budapest Honvéd FC	Ferencvárosi TC	Márton Eppel (Budapest Honvéd FC)	16
2017/2018	Videoton FC Székesfehérvár	Újpest FC	Davide Lanzafame (ITA, Budapest Honvéd FC)	18
2018/2019	Ferencvárosi TC	MOL Vidi FC Székesfehérvár	Davide Lanzafame (ITA, Budapest Honvéd FC) Filip Holender (Budapest Honvéd FC)	16

NATIONAL CHAMPIONSHIP

Nemzeti Bajnokság I 2018/2019

(21.07.2018 – 19.05.2019)

Results

Round 1 [21-22.07.2018]
Puskás Akadémia - Debreceni VSC 0-1(0-0)
Budapest Honvéd - Haladás 3-2(1-1)
MOL Vidi FC - Kisvárda FC 4-0(3-0)
Mezőkövesd - Paksi FC 3-1(2-1)
Ferencvárosi TC - Diósgyőri VTK 4-1(3-1)
Újpest FC - MTK Budapest 0-2(0-1)

Round 2 [28-29.07.2018]
Diósgyőri VTK - Puskás Akadémia 2-2(1-2)
MOL Vidi FC - Paksi FC 1-1(1-1)
Debreceni VSC - Mezőkövesd 1-1(0-0)
Budapest Honvéd - Kisvárda FC 4-0(1-0)
Haladás - Újpest FC 2-2(1-2)
MTK Budapest - Ferencvárosi TC 1-4(0-3)

Round 3 [04-05.08.2018]
Puskás Akadémia - MTK Budapest 1-2(0-1)
Debreceni VSC - Diósgyőri VTK 2-0(0-0)
Ferencvárosi TC - Haladás 3-1(1-0)
Újpest FC - Kisvárda FC 1-0(0-0)
Budapest Honvéd - Paksi FC 1-0(0-0)
MOL Vidi FC - Mezőkövesd 3-1(2-0) [26.09.]

Round 4 [10-12.08.2018]
MOL Vidi FC - Debreceni VSC 1-1(0-1)
Kisvárda FC - Ferencvárosi TC 0-2(0-0)
Haladás - Puskás Akadémia 2-1(0-0)
MTK Budapest - Diósgyőri VTK 1-0(0-0)
Paksi FC - Újpest FC 1-1(1-1)
Mezőkövesd - Budapest Honvéd 0-1(0-0)

Round 5 [17-18.08.2018]
Debreceni VSC - MTK Budapest 3-3(1-2)
Ferencvárosi TC - Paksi FC 1-1(1-1)
Puskás Akadémia - Kisvárda FC 1-1(0-0)
Újpest FC - Mezőkövesd 1-1(0-1)
Budapest Honvéd - MOL Vidi FC 0-3(0-2)
Diósgyőri VTK - Haladás 1-0(1-0)

Round 6 [25.08.2018]
Budapest Honvéd - Debreceni VSC 3-0(1-0)
Mezőkövesd - Ferencvárosi TC 0-1(0-0)
Paksi FC - Puskás Akadémia 3-2(1-0)
Kisvárda FC - Diósgyőri VTK 1-1(0-1)
Haladás - MTK Budapest 1-2(0-1)
MOL Vidi FC - Újpest FC 1-0(0-0) [21.11.]

Round 7 [01-02.09.2018]
Debreceni VSC - Haladás 1-1(1-1)
Mezőkövesd - Puskás Akadémia 2-0(1-0)
Újpest FC - Budapest Honvéd 0-0
MTK Budapest - Kisvárda FC 0-1(0-1)
Diósgyőri VTK - Paksi FC 0-0
Ferencvárosi TC - MOL Vidi FC 2-2(2-1)

Round 8 [15.09.2018]
Újpest FC - Debreceni VSC 1-0(1-0)
Puskás Akadémia - MOL Vidi FC 2-1(1-1)
Mezőkövesd - Diósgyőri VTK 4-2(3-0)
Paksi FC - MTK Budapest 3-0(1-0)
Kisvárda FC - Haladás 4-1(2-0)
Budapest Honvéd - Ferencvárosi TC 0-1(0-1)

Round 9 [29-30.09.2018]
Puskás Akadémia - Budapest Honvéd 1-0(1-0)
Haladás - Paksi FC 1-2(0-0)
MTK Budapest - Mezőkövesd 2-2(1-0)
Debreceni VSC - Kisvárda FC 3-1(0-1)
Ferencvárosi TC - Újpest FC 1-0(0-0)
Diósgyőri VTK - MOL Vidi FC 0-1(0-0)

Round 10 [06-07.10.2018]
Budapest Honvéd - Diósgyőri VTK 1-0(0-0)
Újpest FC - Puskás Akadémia 2-0(0-0)
Mezőkövesd - Haladás 2-0(1-0)
Paksi FC - Kisvárda FC 4-1(3-1)
Ferencvárosi TC - Debreceni VSC 2-2(0-1)
MOL Vidi FC - MTK Budapest 0-3(0-2)

Round 11 [20.10.2018]
Kisvárda FC - Mezőkövesd 1-2(1-0)
Haladás - MOL Vidi FC 0-2(0-0)
MTK Budapest - Budapest Honvéd 1-1(0-1)
Diósgyőri VTK - Újpest FC 1-2(0-0)
Debreceni VSC - Paksi FC 2-1(1-0)
Puskás Akadémia - Ferencvárosi TC 1-0(1-0)

Round 12 [27-28.10.2018]
MTK Budapest - Újpest FC 1-0(1-0)
Debreceni VSC - Puskás Akadémia 2-1(1-0)
Diósgyőri VTK - Ferencvárosi TC 1-4(0-3)
Haladás - Budapest Honvéd 0-1(0-0)
Paksi FC - Mezőkövesd 2-1(1-0)
Kisvárda FC - MOL Vidi FC 2-2(1-2)

Round 13 [03.11.2018]
Paksi FC - MOL Vidi FC 0-4(0-3)
Kisvárda FC - Budapest Honvéd 0-3(0-1)
Újpest FC - Haladás 2-0(0-0)
Puskás Akadémia - Diósgyőri VTK 2-1(0-0)
Mezőkövesd - Debreceni VSC 2-2(1-1)
Ferencvárosi TC - MTK Budapest 2-0(2-0)

Round 14 [10-11.11.2018]
Diósgyőri VTK - Debreceni VSC 1-0(1-0)
MTK Budapest - Puskás Akadémia 3-2(1-1)
Kisvárda FC - Újpest FC 1-4(1-1)
Paksi FC - Budapest Honvéd 0-0
Haladás - Ferencvárosi TC 1-0(0-0)
Mezőkövesd - MOL Vidi FC 1-0(0-0)

Round 15 [24-25.11.2018]
Budapest Honvéd - Mezőkövesd 1-1(0-0)
Újpest FC - Paksi FC 1-1(0-0)
Ferencvárosi TC - Kisvárda FC 2-0(2-0)
Puskás Akadémia - Haladás 2-0(2-0)
Diósgyőri VTK - MTK Budapest 3-2(2-0)
Debreceni VSC - MOL Vidi FC 0-1(0-1)

Round 16 [01-02.12.2018]
Kisvárda FC - Puskás Akadémia 1-0(1-0)
Mezőkövesd - Újpest FC 0-0
Haladás - Diósgyőri VTK 1-1(0-0)
MTK Budapest - Debreceni VSC 0-1(0-1)
Paksi FC - Ferencvárosi TC 0-3(0-2)
MOL Vidi FC - Budapest Honvéd 2-0(1-0)

Round 17 [08.12.2018]
Debreceni VSC - Budapest Honvéd 2-0(1-0)
Ferencvárosi TC - Mezőkövesd 3-2(1-0)
Puskás Akadémia - Paksi FC 1-1(0-1)
Diósgyőri VTK - Kisvárda FC 1-1(1-1)
MTK Budapest - Haladás 4-0(1-0)
Újpest FC - MOL Vidi FC 2-0(2-0)

Round 18 [15-16.12.2018]
Puskás Akadémia - Mezőkövesd 2-0(0-0)
Kisvárda FC - MTK Budapest 1-0(0-0)
Paksi FC - Diósgyőri VTK 1-2(1-1)
Haladás - Debreceni VSC 0-2(0-1)
Budapest Honvéd - Újpest FC 2-2(1-0)
MOL Vidi FC - Ferencvárosi TC 2-1(1-1)

Round 19 [02.02.2019]
MTK Budapest - Paksi FC 1-2(0-1)
Debreceni VSC - Újpest FC 0-0
MOL Vidi FC - Puskás Akadémia 0-3(0-1)
Diósgyőri VTK - Mezőkövesd 1-1(0-0)
Haladás - Kisvárda FC 0-1(0-0)
Ferencvárosi TC - Budapest Honvéd 1-0(0-0)

Round 20 [09.02.2019]
Budapest Honvéd - Puskás Akadémia 2-1(2-0)
Paksi FC - Haladás 1-1(1-0)
Mezőkövesd - MTK Budapest 2-3(1-1)
MOL Vidi FC - Diósgyőri VTK 1-2(1-2)
Kisvárda FC - Debreceni VSC 3-0(2-0)
Újpest FC - Ferencvárosi TC 1-1(0-1)

Round 21 [16.02.2019]
Debreceni VSC - Ferencvárosi TC 2-1(0-1)
Puskás Akadémia - Újpest FC 0-1(0-0)
Diósgyőri VTK - Budapest Honvéd 2-1(0-1)
Haladás - Mezőkövesd 1-2(1-2)
Kisvárda FC - Paksi FC 0-0
MTK Budapest - MOL Vidi FC 1-3(0-3)

Round 22 [23.02.2019]
Ferencvárosi TC - Puskás Akadémia 4-0(0-0)
Mezőkövesd - Kisvárda FC 2-2(1-2)
MOL Vidi FC - Haladás 1-0(0-0)
Újpest FC - Diósgyőri VTK 5-0(1-0)
Paksi FC - Debreceni VSC 2-1(0-0)
Budapest Honvéd - MTK Budapest 2-1(1-0)

Round 23 [02.03.2019]
Puskás Akadémia - Debreceni VSC 2-0(0-0)
Újpest FC - MTK Budapest 0-0
Budapest Honvéd - Haladás 1-3(0-1)
MOL Vidi FC - Kisvárda FC 2-1(0-1)
Mezőkövesd - Paksi FC 2-0(0-0)
Ferencvárosi TC - Diósgyőri VTK 7-0(3-0)

Round 24 [09.03.2019]
Paksi FC - MOL Vidi FC 2-2(2-1)
Kisvárda FC - Budapest Honvéd 1-1(1-1)
Haladás - Újpest FC 3-2(0-2)
Diósgyőri VTK - Puskás Akadémia 1-0(0-0)
Debreceni VSC - Mezőkövesd 1-0(1-0)
MTK Budapest - Ferencvárosi TC 1-3(0-3)

Round 25 [16.03.2019]
Puskás Akadémia - MTK Budapest 3-2(1-2)
Ferencvárosi TC - Haladás 2-0(0-0)
Újpest FC - Kisvárda FC 1-0(1-0)
Budapest Honvéd - Paksi FC 3-0(2-0)
MOL Vidi FC - Mezőkövesd 1-0(1-0)
Debreceni VSC - Diósgyőri VTK 1-0(1-0)

Round 26 [30.03.2019]
Mezőkövesd - Budapest Honvéd 3-1(0-0)
Paksi FC - Újpest FC 0-2(0-0)
Kisvárda FC - Ferencvárosi TC 0-1(0-0)
Haladás - Puskás Akadémia 3-0(2-0)
MTK Budapest - Diósgyőri VTK 2-1(2-1)
MOL Vidi FC - Debreceni VSC 2-1(0-0)

Round 27 [06.04.2019]
Puskás Akadémia - Kisvárda FC 0-4(0-2)
Ferencvárosi TC - Paksi FC 3-0(1-0)
Újpest FC - Mezőkövesd 2-1(0-1)
Diósgyőri VTK - Haladás 0-1(0-0)
Debreceni VSC - MTK Budapest 3-1(2-1)
Budapest Honvéd - MOL Vidi FC 0-1(0-0)

Round 28 [13.04.2019]
Budapest Honvéd - Debreceni VSC 1-1(1-1)
Mezõkövesd - Ferencvárosi TC 1-2(1-0)
Paksi FC - Puskás Akadémia 0-0
Kisvárda FC - Diósgyöri VTK 1-1(0-1)
Haladás - MTK Budapest 1-0(0-0)
MOL Vidi FC - Újpest FC 2-1(1-0)

Round 29 [20.04.2019]
Puskás Akadémia - Mezõkövesd 1-0(0-0)
Újpest FC - Budapest Honvéd 0-0
MTK Budapest - Kisvárda FC 0-1(0-1)
Diósgyöri VTK - Paksi FC 1-0(1-0)
Debreceni VSC - Haladás 2-1(1-0)
Ferencvárosi TC - MOL Vidi FC 4-1(1-1)

Round 30 [27.04.2019]
Újpest FC - Debreceni VSC 1-1(1-0)
MOL Vidi FC - Puskás Akadémia 1-1(0-0)
Mezõkövesd - Diósgyöri VTK 3-0(1-0)
Paksi FC - MTK Budapest 1-0(1-0)
Kisvárda FC - Haladás 1-2(1-2)
Budapest Honvéd - Ferencvárosi TC 3-2(1-0)

Round 31 [04.05.2019]
Puskás Akadémia - Budapest Honvéd 2-2(2-1)
Haladás - Paksi FC 1-1(0-0)
MTK Budapest - Mezõkövesd 0-1(0-0)
Diósgyöri VTK - MOL Vidi FC 2-1(1-0)
Debreceni VSC - Kisvárda FC 1-3(1-0)
Ferencvárosi TC - Újpest FC 2-1(1-1)

Round 32 [11.05.2019]
Újpest FC - Puskás Akadémia 0-1(0-0)
Budapest Honvéd - Diósgyöri VTK 4-4(2-1)
MOL Vidi FC - MTK Budapest 4-2(1-1)
Mezõkövesd - Haladás 1-0(0-0)
Paksi FC - Kisvárda FC 1-0(0-0)
Ferencvárosi TC - Debreceni VSC 2-1(1-1)

Round 33 [19.05.2019]
Puskás Akadémia - Ferencvárosi TC 1-1(0-0)
Kisvárda FC - Mezõkövesd 2-1(1-0)
Haladás - MOL Vidi FC 1-1(0-0)
MTK Budapest - Budapest Honvéd 1-4(1-1)
Diósgyöri VTK - Újpest FC 3-0(1-0)
Debreceni VSC - Paksi FC 4-1(3-1)

Final Standings

1.	**Ferencvárosi TC**	33	23	5	5	72	-	27	74
2.	MOL Vidi FC Székesfehérvár	33	18	7	8	53	-	37	61
3.	Debreceni VSC	33	14	9	10	44	-	39	51
4.	Budapest Honvéd FC	33	13	10	10	46	-	38	49
5.	Újpest FC	33	12	12	9	38	-	28	48
6.	Mezőkövesdi SE	33	12	8	13	45	-	40	44
7.	Puskás Ferenc Labdarugó Akadémia Felcsút	33	11	7	15	36	-	45	40
8.	Paksi FC	33	9	12	12	33	-	46	39
9.	Kisvárda FC	33	10	8	15	36	-	48	38
10.	Diósgyőri VTK	33	10	8	15	36	-	57	38
11.	MTK Budapest FC (*Relegated*)	33	10	4	19	42	-	56	34
12.	Szombathelyi Haladás (*Relegated*)	33	8	6	19	31	-	51	30

Please note: Videoton FC Székesfehérvár changed its name to MOL Vidi FC Székesfehérvár.

Top goalscorers:

16 Davide Lanzafame (ITA) *Ferencvárosi TC*

16 Filip Holender *Budapest Honvéd FC*

12 Josip Knežević (CRO) *Puskás Ferenc Labdarugó Akadémia*

12 Roland Varga *Ferencvárosi TC*

NATIONAL CUP
Magyar Kupa 2018/2019

Sixth Round [22-23.09.2018]

Nyírbátori FC - Nyíregyháza Spartacus FC	0-3
Nagyatádi FC - Pénzügyőr SE Pasarét	1-2
Nagykanizsai ULE - KSE Iváncsa	0-1
Fegyvernek VSE - Monori SE	0-6
1908 SZAC - Békéscsaba 1912 Előre SE	0-3
Hódmezővásárhely FC - Vác FC	1-3
Kecskeméti LC - Körmendi FC	0-1
Pécsi Tudományegyetem-PEAC - FC Ajka	1-4
Körösladány MSK - Budaörs SC	2-8
FC 1899 Szeged - Ferencvárosi TC	0-2
Bátaszék SE - Újpest FC	1-7
Király SZE - Kaposvári Rákóczi FC	0-3
Kozármisleny SE - Győri ETO FC	0-4
BKV Előre SC Budapest - Debreceni VSC	1-2
Szekszárdi UFC - Dorogi FC	4-3 pen
Berkenye SE - Tiszakécske FC	0-5
Komáromi VSE - Puskás Ferenc LA Felcsút	1-3
Sárrétudvari KSE - Zalaegerszegi TE	0-1
Tállya KSE - MTK Budapest	0-8
Fűzfői AK - Soroksár SC	0-5
Edelény FC - Sárvári FC	1-6
Gesztelyi FCE - Sajóbábony VSE	0-1
Tiszafuredi VSE - Dabas-Gyón FC	0-2
Úrkút SK - Balatonlelle SE	3-4 pen
KSE Csesztreg - Makó FC	0-4
Ikarus-Maroshegy - Taksony SE	0-2
Schott Lukácsháza SE - Balassagyarmati VSE	1-4
Tiszasziget SE - FC Tiszaújváros	1-3
Putnok VSE - Aqvital FC Csákvár	0-2
Szeged 2011 FC - Bodajk FC Siófok	0-1
Fővárosi Vízművek - Mezőkövesdi SE	0-5
Felsőtárkány SC - Ménfőcsanak ESK	1-3
Lipót Pékség SE - Kecskeméti TE	3-2
Biatorbágyi SE - Balatonfüredi FC	4-2
Dunaharaszti MTK - Szentlőrinci SE	0-1
Teskándi SE - Mezőfalvai MEDOSZ	3-0
Rákosmenti KSK - Tintahalak SE Szabadkikötő	6-7 pen
Thermál Spa Siklós - Paksi SE	0-5
Pécsi MFC - Kazincbarcikai SC	1-2
Tatabánya FC - Hajdúböszörményi TE	3-2
Budapesti Vasutas SC - Érdi Városi SE	0-1
Bőny SE - Budapest Honvéd FC	0-6
Cigánd SE - MOL Vidi FC Székesfehérvár	0-2
Balkanyi SE - Andráshida SC	1-3 aet
Öttevényi TC - Gyöngyösi AK-YTONG	0-1
Kalocsai FC - Ibrány SE	1-0
Bonyhád VLC - Budafoki LC	0-3
Gyöngyöshalász SE - Gyirmót SE	1-5
Szolnoki MÁV - Kisvárda FC	0-1
Csepel FC Budapest - Szombathelyi Haladás	0-2
Dabas FC - Salgotarjáni BTC	1-0
Jánossomorja SE - III. Kerületi TVE Budapest	0-4
ESMTK Budapest - Diósgyőri VTK	1-3 aet
Szegedi EOL SC – Balmazújvárosi FC	2-0
FC Hatvan - Ceglédi VSE	0-1
Jászberény FC - Mosonmagyaróvári TE	2-1
Jánoshalmi FC - Füzesgyarmati SK	2-3 aet
Egri FC - Dunaújvárosi Pálhalma SE	0-5
Szarvasi FC – Debreceni EAC	3-2 pen
Tordas SE - Sényő FC	5-6 pen
Oroszlányi SZE - Ózdi FC	1-0
Héviz FC - Pápai PFC	2-3
Sárisápi Bányász - Vecses FC	0-1
Nagykőrösi Kinizsi - Budapesti Vasas SC	1-4

Seventh Round [30-31.10.2018]			
Zalaegerszegi TE - Diósgyőri VTK	0-2	Balatonlelle SE - FC Tiszaújváros	0-2
III. Kerületi TVE Budapest - Gyirmót SE	2-1	Füzesgyarmati SK - Tintahalak SE Szabadkikötő	2-0
Szarvasi FC - Szombathelyi Haladás	1-3	Oroszlányi SZE - Sajóbábony VSE	2-6 aet
Sárvári FC - Ferencvárosi TC	0-4	Andráshida SC - Nyíregyháza Spartacus FC	1-0
Gyöngyösi AK-YTONG - Kisvárda FC	0-4	Körmendi FC - Soroksár SC	0-7
Vecses FC - MTK Budapest	0-5	Kalocsai FC - Bodajk FC Siófok	0-1
Teskándi SE - Debreceni VSC	0-3	Szegedi EOL SC - Kaposvári Rákóczi FC	1-2
Érdi Városi SE - Monori SE	2-1 aet	Kazincbarcikai SC - Budapesti Vasas SC	2-4
Lipót Pékség SE - FC Ajka	2-4	Dabas FC - Tiszakécske FC	0-1
Budaörs SC - Ceglédi VSE	5-0	Ménfőcsanak ESK - Mezőkövesdi SE	0-1
Sényő FC - Makó FC	2-1	Aqvital FC Csákvár - Paksi SE	1-2
Dabas-Gyón FC - Pénzügyőr SE Pasarét	0-1	Dunaújvárosi PSE - Puskás Ferenc LA Felcsút	0-2
Balassagyarmati VSE - Taksony SE	1-3	Tatabánya FC - Békéscsaba 1912 Előre SE	0-2
Szekszárdi UFC - Budafoki LC	1-3	Jászberény FC - Budapest Honvéd FC	0-1
KSE Iváncsa - Pápai PFC	1-0	Vác FC - MOL Vidi FC Székesfehérvár	1-3
Biatorbágyi SE - Szentlőrinci SE	0-4	Győri ETO FC - Újpest FC	2-3 aet

Eighth Round [04-05.12.2018]			
Pénzügyőr SE Pasarét - Puskás Ferenc LA Felcsút	0-6	KSE Iváncsa - Szombathelyi Haladás	2-4
Szentlőrinci SE - Kisvárda FC	1-4 aet	Érdi Városi SE - Andráshida SC	3-4 pen
III. Kerületi TVE - Mezőkövesdi SE	0-6	Füzesgyarmati SK - Tiszakécske FC	0-1
Sajóbábony VSE - Taksony SE	0-1	Soroksár SC - Békéscsaba 1912 Előre SE	2-0
Budapesti Vasas SC - Debreceni VSC	1-2	FC Ajka - MTK Budapest	2-1
Budaörs SC - Diósgyőri VTK	5-3	Budafoki LC - MOL Vidi FC Székesfehérvár	1-2
Sényő FC - Ferencvárosi TC	0-4	Bodajk FC Siófok - Paksi SE	2-3 pen
FC Tiszaújváros - Budapest Honvéd FC	0-4	Kaposvári Rákóczi FC - Újpest FC	1-0

1/8-Finals [19-20/26-27.02.2019]			
FC Ajka - Debreceni VSC	2-3 / 1-1	Tiszakécske FC - Budapest Honvéd FC	0-1 / 1-1
Budaörs SC - Kaposvári Rákóczi FC	2-1 / 0-0	Puskás Ferenc Labdarugó Akadémia - Paksi SE	1-2 / 3-1
Soroksár SC - Andráshida SC	3-2 / 1-0	Mezőkövesdi SE - Szombathelyi Haladás	0-0 / 1-0
Taksony SE - MOL Vidi FC Székesfehérvár	0-1 / 0-3	Ferencvárosi TC - Kisvárda FC	2-0 / 1-1

Quarter-Finals [12-13.03/02-03.04.2019]			
Debreceni VSC - Mezőkövesdi SE	1-0 / 2-1	Puskás Ferenc Labdarugó Akadémia - Soroksár SC	1-1 / 4-5 pen
Budaörs SC - Budapest Honvéd FC	1-2 / 2-4	Ferencvárosi TC - MOL Vidi FC Székesfehérvár	1-2 / 0-2

Semi-Finals [16-17.04/23-24.04.2019]			
MOL Vidi FC Székesfehérvár - Debreceni VSC	1-0 / 3-0	Budapest Honvéd FC - Soroksár SC	2-1 / 3-0

Final

25.05.2019; Groupama Aréna, Budapest; Referee: Zoltán Iványi; Attendance: 12,777

MOL Vidi FC Székesfehérvár - Budapest Honvéd FC 2-1(0-1)

MOL Vidi: Ádám Kovácsik, Attila Fiola (46.Anel Hadžić), Paulo Vinicius Souza Dos Santos, Loïc Négo, Roland Juhász, Ianique dos Santos Tavares „Stopira“, Ákos Elek (46.István Kovács), Szabolcs Huszti, Máté Pátkai (73.Márkó Futács), Boban Nikolov, Marko Šćepović. Trainer: Marko Nikolić (Serbia).

Budapest Honvéd: Dávid Gróf, Mohamed Mezghrani, Eke Uzoma (80.Tonči Kukoč), Bence Batik, Tibor Heffler, Ivan Lovrić, Dániel Gazdag (69.Änis Ben-Hatira), Đorđe Kamber, Gergő Nagy, Filip Holender, David N'Gog (76.Danilo Cirino de Oliveira). Trainer: Attila Supka.

Goals: 0-1 Filip Holender (14 penalty), 1-1 Marko Šćepović (79), 2-1 Anel Hadžić (90+1).

THE CLUBS 2018/2019

Debreceni Vasutas Sport Club

Founded: 12.03.1902
Stadium: Nagyerdei Stadion, Debrecen (20,340)

Goalkeepers:	**DOB**	**M**	**(s)**	**G**
Tomáš Košický (SVK)	11.03.1986	3	(1)	
Oleksandr Nad (UKR)	02.09.1985	30		
Defenders:	**DOB**	**M**	**(s)**	**G**
Szabolcs Barna	27.04.1996	11		1
Balázs Bényei	10.01.1990	9		
Erik Čikoš (SVK)	01.07.1988	6		
Ákos Kinyik	12.05.1993	23	(4)	2
Norbert Mészáros	19.08.1980	1	(1)	
Csaba Szatmári	14.06.1994	23	(1)	2
Midfielders:	**DOB**	**M**	**(s)**	**G**
Albion Avdijaj (ALB)	12.01.1994	11	(10)	1
Ádám Bódi	18.10.1990	31		7
Richárd Csősz	22.04.1997	7	(11)	1
Ezequiel Calvente Criado (ESP)	12.01.1991		(4)	1
János Ferenczi	03.04.1991	23	(2)	2
Attila Haris	23.01.1997	31		
Aleksandar Jovanović (BIH)	26.10.1984	4	(11)	
Erik Kusnyír	07.02.2000	18	(4)	
Krisztián Kuti	04.12.1992		(1)	
Bence Pávkovics	27.03.1997	24		2
Dániel Tőzsér	12.05.1985	27		5
Forwards:	**DOB**	**M**	**(s)**	**G**
Dániel Bereczki	02.06.1995	1	(5)	
Alex Damásdi	27.03.1997	3	(5)	
Norbert Könyves	10.06.1989	7	(4)	2
Kevin Nagy	11.09.1995		(1)	
Márk Szécsi	22.05.1994	23	(2)	8
Tamás Takács	20.02.1991	16	(16)	6
Kevin Varga	30.03.1996	28	(4)	3
Dániel Zsóri	14.10.2000	3	(10)	1
Trainer:	**DOB**	**M**		
András Herczeg	11.07.1956	33		

Diósgyőr-Vasgyári Testgyakorlók Köre

Founded: 06.02.1910
Stadium: Diósgyőri Stadion, Miskolc (15,325)

Goalkeepers:	**DOB**	**M**	**(s)**	**G**
Botond Antal	22.08.1991	21		
Erik Bukrán	06.12.1996	10		
Ivan Radoš (CRO)	21.02.1984	2		
Defenders:	**DOB**	**M**	**(s)**	**G**
Dušan Brković (SRB)	20.01.1989	31		1
Gábor Eperjesi	12.01.1994	4	(1)	
Dávid Forgács	29.09.1995	5	(3)	
Dejan Karan (SRB)	25.08.1988	23		1
Zoltán Lipták	10.12.1984	2	(1)	
Tibor Nagy	14.08.1991	1	(1)	
Yannick Ndzoumou (CMR)	18.05.1996		(2)	
Donát Orosz	28.07.2002		(1)	
Kristóf Polgár	28.11.1996	12		
Márk Tamás	28.10.1993	27		
Midfielders:	**DOB**	**M**	**(s)**	**G**
Bence Bárdos	05.02.1998	2	(5)	
Attila Busai	21.01.1989	3		
Támas Géringer	19.05.1999	1	(3)	
Florent Hasani (KVX)	30.03.1997	25	(6)	7
Kristof Korbely	26.05.2000		(3)	1
Dávid Márkvárt	20.09.1994	24		2
Tomislav Mazalović (CRO)	10.06.1990	8	(6)	
Branko Mihajlović (SRB)	20.02.1991	18	(9)	3
Ismaila Ousman (CMR)	17.06.1997		(1)	
Sergiy Shestakov (UKR)	12.04.1990	28	(1)	
Bence Szabó	16.01.1998	20	(2)	
Mátyás Tajti	02.06.1998	22	(7)	5
Barnabás Tóth	28.07.1994	9	(4)	1
Borisz Tóth	07.07.2002		(1)	
Forwards:	**DOB**	**M**	**(s)**	**G**
Patrik Bacsa	03.06.1992	9	(17)	1
Nikolaos Ioannidis (GRE)	26.04.1994	1	(4)	
Martin Juhár (SVK)	09.03.1988	23	(1)	1
Gábor Makrai	26.06.1996	5	(2)	1
Dániel Prosser	15.06.1994	9	(3)	3
Roland Ugrai	13.11.1992	1	(1)	
Richárd Vernes	24.02.1992	17	(11)	7
Trainer:	**DOB**	**M**		
Fernando Miguel Fernández Escribano (ESP)	02.06.1979	33		

Ferencvárosi Torna Club

Founded: 03.05.1899
Stadium: Groupama Aréna, Budapest (23,700)

Goalkeepers:	**DOB**	**M**	**(s)**	**G**
Dénes Dibusz	16.11.1990	32		
Ádám Holczer	28.03.1988	1		
Ádám Varga	12.02.1999		(1)	
Defenders:	**DOB**	**M**	**(s)**	**G**
Miha Blažič (SVN)	08.05.1993	29		2
Endre Botka	25.08.1994	7	(4)	
Lasha Dvali (GEO)	14.05.1995	12		2
Abraham Frimpong (GHA)	06.04.1993	9	(4)	1
Marcel Heister (GER)	29.07.1992	31		1
Julian Koch (GER)	11.11.1990	1	(1)	
Kenneth Otigba	29.08.1992	2	(1)	
Zsombor Takács	22.02.1999	1		
Midfielders:	**DOB**	**M**	**(s)**	**G**
Kornél Csernik	02.07.1998		(6)	
András Csonka	01.05.2000	2	(3)	
Fernando Gorriarán Fontes (URU)	27.11.1994	19	(5)	2
Igor Kharatin (UKR)	02.02.1995	13	(1)	2
Leandro Marcolini Pedroso de Almeida	19.03.1982	22	(7)	1
Tokmac Chol Nguen (NOR)	20.10.1993	7	(5)	4
Ivan Petryak (UKR)	13.03.1994	27	(1)	6
Matías Ezequiel Rodríguez (ARG)	29.03.1993		(4)	
Dávid Sigér	30.11.1990	20	(3)	2
Stefan Spirovski (MKD)	23.08.1990	13	(1)	2
Forwards:	**DOB**	**M**	**(s)**	**G**
Dániel Böde	24.10.1986	9	(13)	7
Lukács Bőle	27.03.1990	13	(12)	3
Kjartan Henry Finnbogason (ISL)	09.07.1986		(9)	
Isael da Silva Barbosa (BRA)	13.05.1988	8	(1)	1
Davide Lanzafame (ITA)	09.02.1987	24	(4)	16
Gergő Lovrencsics	01.09.1988	31		2
Rui Pedro Couto Ramalho (POR)	02.07.1988		(1)	
Nikolay Signevich (BLR)	20.02.1992	9	(2)	4
Krisztofer Szerető	10.01.2000		(1)	
Roland Varga	23.01.1990	21	(7)	12
Trainer:	**DOB**	**M**		
Thomas Doll (GER)	09.04.1966	5		
Serhiy Rebrov (UKR) [22.08.2018]	03.06.1974	28		

Szombathelyi Haladás

Founded: 1919
Stadium: Haladás Sportkomplexum, Szombathely (9,859)

Goalkeepers:	**DOB**	**M**	**(s)**	**G**
Gábor Király	01.04.1976	24		
Dániel Rózsa	24.11.1984	9	(3)	
Defenders:	**DOB**	**M**	**(s)**	**G**
Vít Beneš (CZE)	12.08.1988	12		
Predrag Bošnjak (SRB)	13.11.1985	13		
Márk Jagodics	12.04.1992	25		1
András Jancsó	22.04.1996	5	(2)	
Kristián Kolčák (SVK)	30.01.1990	14	(2)	
Dávid Mohl	22.04.1985	6	(1)	
Milán Németh	29.05.1988	19	(1)	
Kornél Saláta (SVK)	24.01.1985	7		
Szabolcs Schimmer	24.02.1984	8	(1)	
László Tamás	18.01.1988	18	(3)	
Midfielders:	**DOB**	**M**	**(s)**	**G**
Petró Balázs	07.07.1997	1		
Murtaz Daushvili (GEO)	01.05.1989	17	(1)	
Oleg Golodyuk (UKR)	02.01.1988	10		1
Yuriy Habovda (UKR)	06.05.1989	29	(1)	1
Péter Halmosi	25.09.1979	2	(8)	
Gergő Holdampf	31.07.1994	5	(3)	
Galin Ivanov (BUL)	15.04.1988	12	(1)	2
Lóránt Kovács (ROU)	06.06.1993	3	(1)	
Márió Németh	01.05.1995	6	(14)	1
Patrik Nyári	09.04.2001	2		
Barnabás Rácz	26.04.1996	7	(4)	
Forwards:	**DOB**	**M**	**(s)**	**G**
Funsho Ibrahim Bamgboye (NGA)	09.01.1999	14	(17)	4
Bálint Gaál	14.07.1991	14	(12)	5
Miroslav Grumić (SRB)	29.06.1984	7	(3)	
Emil Sigvardsen Lyng (DEN)	03.08.1989	2		
Karol Mészáros (SVK)	25.07.1993	17	(2)	2
Reagy Ofosu (GER)	20.09.1991	14	(9)	
Tamás Priskin	27.09.1986	17	(4)	7
Michael Rabušic (CZE)	17.09.1989	11	(4)	2
Rui Pedro Couto Ramalho (POR)	02.07.1988	13	(2)	5
Trainer:	**DOB**	**M**		
Michal Hipp (SVK)	13.03.1963	8		
Ferenc Horváth [27.09.2019]	06.05.1973	25		

Budapest Honvéd Football Club

Founded: 03.08.1909
Stadium: "Bozsik József" Stadion, Budapest (10,000)

Goalkeepers:	**DOB**	**M**	**(s)**	**G**
Dávid Gróf	17.04.1989	33		
Defenders:	**DOB**	**M**	**(s)**	**G**
Fousseni Bamba (GUI)	19.04.1990	7	(1)	
Botond Baráth	21.04.1992	16		
Bence Batik	08.11.1993	27	(1)	1
Tibor Heffler	17.05.1987	30	(1)	
Dávid Kálnoki	06.08.1991	8		
Tonči Kukoč (CRO)	25.09.1990	12	(12)	
Ivan Lovrić (CRO)	11.07.1985	11		2
Mohamed Mezghrani (BEL)	02.06.1994	10	(1)	
Dino Škvorc (CRO)	02.02.1990	10	(2)	
Eke Uzoma (NGA)	11.08.1989	13		1
Midfielders:	**DOB**	**M**	**(s)**	**G**
Bence Banó-Szabó	25.07.1999	3	(12)	
Änis Ben-Hatira (TUN)	18.07.1988	10	(2)	3
Dániel Gazdag	02.03.1996	25	(1)	1
Patrik Hidi	27.11.1990	10		
Gergő Holdampf	31.07.1994		(2)	
Đorđe Kamber (BIH)	20.11.1983	28	(2)	3
Gergő Nagy	07.01.1993	23	(2)	
Tomáš Pilík (CZE)	20.12.1988	6	(2)	
Zsolt Pölöskei	19.02.1991		(1)	
Krisztián Vadócz	03.05.1985	6		
Forwards:	**DOB**	**M**	**(s)**	**G**
Dominik Cipf	31.01.2001		(2)	
Danilo Cirino de Oliveira (BRA)	11.11.1986	25	(3)	9
Filip Holender	27.07.1994	33		16
Dániel Lukács	03.04.1996		(5)	2
Milán Májer	28.06.1999		(10)	
David N'Gog (FRA)	01.04.1989	11	(12)	6
Norbert Szendrei	27.03.2000	4	(2)	
Patrik Tischler	30.07.1991	2	(17)	1
Trainer:	**DOB**	**M**		
Attila Supka	19.09.1962	33		

Kisvárda Futball Club

Founded: 1911
Stadium: Várkerti Stadion, Kisvárda (2,850)

Goalkeepers:	**DOB**	**M**	**(s)**	**G**
Luiz Felipe Ventura dos Santos (BRA)	22.02.1984	32		
Mihai Adrian Mincă (ROU)	08.10.1984	1	(1)	
Defenders:	**DOB**	**M**	**(s)**	**G**
Anderson da Silveira Ribeiro „Anderson Pico" (BRA)	04.11.1988	9	(2)	
Theodoros Berios (GRE)	21.03.1989	20	(2)	
Cornel Ene (ROU)	21.07.1993	20	(1)	
Martin Izing	11.01.1992	4	(1)	
Gábor Jánvári	25.04.1990	1	(1)	
Pavlo Lukyanchuk (UKR)	19.05.1996	13		1
Temur Partsvaniya (UKR)	06.07.1991	4		
Radoš Protić (SRB)	31.01.1987	20	(4)	
Midfielders:	**DOB**	**M**	**(s)**	**G**
Gheorghe Teodor Grozav (ROU)	29.09.1990	14		5
Viktor Hei (UKR)	02.02.1996	2	(3)	
Hugo André Rodrigues Seco (POR)	17.06.1988	7	(6)	1
Roman Karasyuk (UKR)	27.03.1991	23	(7)	
Anton Kravchenko (UKR)	23.03.1991	14		1
Lucas Marcolini Dantas Bertucci (BRA)	06.05.1989	31		2
Bogdan Melnyk (UKR)	04.01.1997	19	(5)	1
Vuk Mitošević (SRB)	12.02.1991	4	(4)	
Sergiu Negruț (ROU)	01.04.1993	2	(9)	
Stavros Tsoukalas (GRE)	28.05.1988	15		4
Barnabás Vári	15.09.1987	22	(1)	3
Forwards:	**DOB**	**M**	**(s)**	**G**
András Gosztonyi	07.11.1990	20	(9)	1
Zoltán Horváth	30.07.1989	19	(11)	9
Brana Ilić (SRB)	16.02.1985	21	(9)	4
Artem Milevskiy (UKR)	12.01.1985	5	(3)	
Matija Mišić (CRO)	30.01.1992	10	(3)	1
Jefferson Gomes de Oliveira „Sassá" (BRA)	26.01.1988	9	(15)	2
Anton Shynder (UKR)	13.06.1987	2		
Trainer:	**DOB**	**M**		
Elemér Kondás	11.09.1963	4		
László Dajka [14.08.2018]	29.04.1959	29		

Mezőkövesdi Sport Egyesület

Founded: 31.01.1975
Stadium: Városi Stadion, Mezőkövesd (4,183)

Goalkeepers:	**DOB**	**M**	**(s)**	**G**
Dávid Dombó	26.02.1993	12		
Péter Szappanos	14.11.1990	21	(1)	
Defenders:	**DOB**	**M**	**(s)**	**G**
Alex Engel	11.08.1992	1		
Gábor Eperjesi	12.01.1994	6	(1)	
Danijel Farkaš (SRB)	13.01.1993	22		
Dávid Hudák (SVK)	21.03.1993	1	(2)	
Matija Katanec (CRO)	04.05.1990	14	(6)	
Róbert Pillár (SVK)	27.05.1991	32		1
Erik Silye	12.06.1996	14	(6)	
Attila Szalai	20.01.1998	21	(4)	2
Dániel Vadnai	19.02.1988	26		1
Midfielders:	**DOB**	**M**	**(s)**	**G**
Lajos Bertus	26.09.1990	11	(1)	
Bence Iszlai	29.05.1990	6	(2)	
Mykhailo Meskhi (UKR)	26.02.1997	17	(6)	
Patrick Mevoungou Mekoulou (CMR)	15.12.1986	10	(3)	
Amadou Moutari (NIG)	19.01.1994	4	(6)	3
László Pekár	20.01.1993	9	(1)	2
Dénes Szakály	15.03.1988	1	(9)	
Tamás Szeles	07.12.1993	23	(1)	1
Bence Tóth	27.07.1989	9	(1)	
Máté Tóth	20.06.1998		(2)	
Sándor Vajda	14.12.1991	19	(11)	5
Forwards:	**DOB**	**M**	**(s)**	**G**
André Alves dos Santos (BRA)	15.10.1983		(3)	
Tamás Cseri	15.01.1988	28	(1)	4
Filip Dragóner	12.03.1998		(2)	1
Stefan Dražić (SRB)	14.08.1992	28	(3)	10
Botond Földi	12.08.2001		(1)	
Márk Koszta	26.09.1996	10	(12)	4
Gábor Molnár	16.05.1994	18	(3)	8
László Varjas	17.05.2000		(1)	
Trainer:	**DOB**	**M**		
Attila Kuttor	29.05.1970	33		

MOL Vidi Football Club Székesfehérvár

Founded: 1941
Stadium: MOL Aréna Sóstó, Székesfehérvár (14,201) / Pancho Aréna, Felcsút (3,816)

Goalkeepers:	**DOB**	**M**	**(s)**	**G**
Ádám Kovácsik	04.04.1991	30		
Tomáš Tujvel (SVK)	19.09.1983	3	(1)	
Defenders:	**DOB**	**M**	**(s)**	**G**
Attila Fiola	17.02.1990	18	(1)	
Szilveszter Hangya	02.01.1994	1	(4)	
Roland Juhász	01.07.1983	29	(1)	4
Loïc Négo (FRA)	15.01.1991	32	(1)	5
Paulo Vinicius Souza Dos Santos	21.02.1990	24		
Ianique dos Santos Tavares „Stopira“ (CPV)	20.05.1988	27	(1)	3
Krisztián Tamás	18.04.1995	8	(3)	1
Midfielders:	**DOB**	**M**	**(s)**	**G**
Zsombor Berecz	13.12.1995	2	(8)	
Ákos Elek	21.07.1988	10	(2)	
Anel Hadžić (BIH)	16.08.1989	21	(5)	2
Szabolcs Huszti	18.04.1983	17	(10)	5
István Kovács	27.03.1992	27	(5)	4
Georgi Milanov (BUL)	19.02.1992	18	(6)	1
Boban Nikolov (MKD)	28.07.1994	17	(12)	2
Máté Pátkai	06.03.1988	26	(6)	5
Bence Sós	10.05.1994	1	(4)	
József Varga	06.06.1988	3		
Forwards:	**DOB**	**M**	**(s)**	**G**
Márkó Futács	22.02.1990	7	(6)	2
Elvir Hadzic (BIH)	18.01.1999		(1)	
Armin Hodžić (BIH)	17.11.1994	13	(13)	4
Danko Lazović (SRB)	17.05.1983	5	(1)	1
Marko Šćepović (SRB)	23.05.1991	23	(4)	10
Stefan Šćepović (SRB)	10.01.1990	1	(1)	1
Trainer:	**DOB**	**M**		
Marko Nikolić (SRB)	20.07.1979	33		

Magyar Testgyakorlók Köre Budapest Futball Club

Founded: 16.11.1888
Stadium: "Hidegkuti Nándor" Stadion, Budapest (5,322)

Goalkeepers:	**DOB**	**M**	**(s)**	**G**
László Horváth	23.02.1988	8		
Artem Kicsak (UKR)	16.05.1989	25		
Defenders:	**DOB**	**M**	**(s)**	**G**
Ákos Baki	24.08.1994	9	(1)	2
Béla Balogh	30.12.1984	21	(2)	
Nasiru Banahene	08.07.2000	1	(4)	
Bence Deutsch	04.08.1992	6	(1)	
Gergő Gengeliczki	08.06.1993	19		
Máté Katona	22.06.1997	22	(3)	1
Evgen Selin (UKR)	09.05.1988	26	(1)	1
Benedek Varju	21.05.2001	1		
Midfielders:	**DOB**	**M**	**(s)**	**G**
Anton Bidzilya (UKR)	07.06.2000	1	(1)	
István Bognár	05.05.1991	32	(1)	5
Patrick Ikenne-King (NGA)	29.10.1991	7		
József Kanta	24.03.1984	21	(6)	6
Tamás Kulcsár	13.10.1982	4	(9)	1
Slobodan Mihajlovic (AUT)	15.03.1997	1	(4)	
Ádám Pintér	12.06.1988	24		
András Schäfer	13.04.1999	12	(2)	1
Ronald Takács	26.01.1998		(1)	
Ádám Vass	09.09.1988	29		
Patrik Vass	17.01.1993	16	(6)	1
Bálint Vogyicska	27.02.1998	10	(8)	
Forwards:	**DOB**	**M**	**(s)**	**G**
Ulysse Diallo (MLI)	26.10.1992	2	(8)	1
Balázs Farkas	24.04.1988	3	(10)	2
Dániel Gera	29.08.1995	21	(4)	6
László Lencse	02.07.1988	22	(9)	6
Myke Bouard Ramos (BRA)	30.10.1992	4		1
Szabolcs Schön	27.09.2000	2	(3)	
Sándor Torghelle	05.05.1982	14	(15)	7
Trainer:	**DOB**	**M**		
Tamás Feczkó	08.09.1977	24		
Tamás Lucsánszky [11.03.2019]	01.05.1966	9		

Paksi Futball Club

Founded: 28.11.1952
Stadium: Fehérvári úti Stadion, Paks (6,150)

Goalkeepers:	**DOB**	**M**	**(s)**	**G**
Gergely Nagy	27.05.1994	26		
Gergő Rácz	20.11.1995	7		
Defenders:	**DOB**	**M**	**(s)**	**G**
Támas Báló	12.01.1984	10	(1)	
Dávid Bobál	31.08.1995	4	(1)	
András Fejes	26.08.1988	27		
Zsolt Gévay	19.11.1987	21	(1)	3
Dávid Kulcsár	25.02.1988	19		1
Bence Lenzsér	09.04.1996	18	(3)	
János Szabó	11.07.1989	17	(2)	1
András Vági	25.12.1988	2	(5)	
Péter Zachán	12.12.1997	1		
Midfielders:	**DOB**	**M**	**(s)**	**G**
Lajos Bertus	26.09.1990	18		1
Benjámin Cseke	22.07.1994	1	(4)	1
Tamás Egerszegi	02.08.1991	7	(13)	
Ádám Hajdú	16.01.1993	1		
Tamás Kecskés	15.01.1986	18	(5)	2
Barna Kesztyűs	04.09.1993	6	(3)	
Richárd Nagy	15.08.1995		(3)	
Kristóf Papp	14.05.1993	28		1
Mohamed Remili	31.05.1985	16	(7)	4
Ádám Simon	30.03.1990	3		
József Windecker	02.12.1992	10	(2)	
László Zsidai	16.07.1986	8		
Forwards:	**DOB**	**M**	**(s)**	**G**
László Bartha	09.02.1987	19	(10)	1
Áron Fejős	17.04.1997	1		
János Hahn	15.05.1995	27	(4)	9
Zsolt Haraszti	04.11.1991	15	(1)	
Péter Hórvath	12.02.1992		(6)	
Norbert Könyves	10.06.1989	8	(5)	2
Róbert Kővári	23.11.1995	11	(5)	
András Simon	30.03.1990	14	(15)	5
Trainer:	**DOB**	**M**		
Aurél Csertői	25.09.1965	33		

Puskás Ferenc Labdarugó Akadémia Felcsút

Founded: 2005
Stadium: Pancho Aréna, Felcsút (3,816)

Goalkeepers:	**DOB**	**M**	**(s)**	**G**
Branislav Danilović (SRB)	24.06.1988	15		
Lajos Hegedüs	19.12.1987	18		
Defenders:	**DOB**	**M**	**(s)**	**G**
Kamen Hadzhiev (BUL)	22.09.1991	15		
János Hegedűs	04.10.1996	22		2
Jonathan Heris (BEL)	03.09.1990	15	(6)	
Richard Križan (SVK)	23.09.1997		(1)	
Zsolt Nagy	25.05.1993	13	(1)	3
Attila Osváth	10.12.1995	12	(2)	
Patrik Poór	15.11.1993	19	(2)	
Csaba Spandler	07.03.1996	11	(1)	
Dejan Trajkovski (SVN)	14.04.1992	13		
Midfielders:	**DOB**	**M**	**(s)**	**G**
Balász Balogh	11.06.1990	13	(2)	
Szilárd Bokros	28.03.2000	5	(4)	
Josip Knežević (CRO)	03.10.1988	20	(4)	12
Nándor Kóródi	15.08.1999	1		
Liridon Latifi (ALB)	06.02.1994	7	(10)	1
Dávid Márkvárt	20.09.1994	3	(1)	
Benedik Mioč (CRO)	06.10.1994	20	(2)	
Bence Sós	10.05.1994	10	(1)	
Péter Szakály	17.08.1986	8	(8)	
Roland Szolnoki	21.01.1992	20		
Jozef Urblík (SVK)	22.08.1996	15	(4)	1
József Varga	06.06.1988	16	(1)	1
Diego Gonzalo Vega Martínez (URU)	29.06.1992	7	(3)	
Ján Vlasko (SVK)	11.01.1990	2	(2)	
László Zsidai	16.07.1986	4	(1)	
Forwards:	**DOB**	**M**	**(s)**	**G**
Bachana Arabuli (GEO)	05.01.1994	12	(10)	5
Bryan Alejandro de Jesús Pabón (ECU)	10.02.1995		(3)	1
Ulysse Diallo (MLI)	26.10.1992	4	(1)	1
Tamás Kiss	24.11.2000	20	(10)	3
Gábor Molnár	16.05.1994	3	(1)	1
András Radó	09.09.1993	17	(11)	3
Nándor Tamás (ROU)	24.10.2000	3	(4)	1
Trainer:	**DOB**	**M**		
Miklós Benczés	27.07.1969	17		
András Komjáti [08.12.2018]	20.11.1953	1		
János Radoki (GER) [29.12.2018]	07.03.1972	9		
András Komjáti [08.04.2019]	20.11.1953	6		

Újpest Football Club

Founded: 16.06.1885
Stadium: "Szusza Ferenc" Stadion, Budapest (13,501)

Goalkeepers:	**DOB**	**M**	**(s)**	**G**
Dávid Banai	09.05.1994	4		
Bence Gundel-Takács	06.04.1998	1		
Filip Pajović (SRB)	30.07.1993	28		
Defenders:	**DOB**	**M**	**(s)**	**G**
Mijuško Bojović (MNE)	09.08.1988	18	(1)	
Dženan Bureković (BIH)	29.05.1995	28		1
Răzvan Horj (ROU)	17.12.1995	2		1
Róbert Litauszki	15.03.1990	23		1
Branko Pauljević (SRB)	12.06.1989	26	(5)	
Kirce Ristevski (MKD)	22.10.1990	22		
Kristóf Szücs	03.01.1997	2	(1)	
Midfielders:	**DOB**	**M**	**(s)**	**G**
Benjámin Balázs	26.04.1990	14	(6)	1
Benjámin Cseke	22.07.1994	1		
Alassane Diallo (MLI)	19.02.1995	6	(9)	2
Lóránt Kovács (ROU)	06.06.1993	4	(1)	
Dávid Mohl	22.04.1985		(3)	
Dániel Nagy	15.03.1991	15	(9)	4
Obinna Nwobodo (NGA)	29.11.1996	26	(1)	4
Vincent Onovo (NGA)	10.12.1995	26	(3)	
Bence Pávkovics	27.03.1997	2		
Barnabás Rácz	26.04.1996	12	(1)	
Bojan Sanković (CRO)	21.11.1993	28	(2)	
Donát Zsótér	06.01.1996	23	(9)	4
Forwards:	**DOB**	**M**	**(s)**	**G**
Viktor Angelov (MKD)	27.03.1994		(3)	
Giorgi Beridze (GEO)	12.05.1997	19	(8)	4
Rossy Lubaki (COD)	10.02.1998		(1)	
Dániel Lukàcs	03.04.1996		(7)	
Soma Novothny	16.06.1994	21	(2)	9
Krisztián Simon	10.06.1991	2	(8)	1
Theophilus Solomon (NGA)	18.01.1996	1	(9)	
Patrik Tischler	30.07.1991	1	(4)	
Lacina Traoré (CIV)	20.08.1990	8	(1)	3
Trainer:	**DOB**	**M**		
Nebojša Vignjević (SRB)	15.04.1968	33		

SECOND LEVEL
Nemzeti Bajnokság II 2018/2019

1.	Zalaegerszegi TE FC (*Promoted*)	38	25	7	6	77	-	41	82
2.	Kaposvári Rákóczi FC (*Promoted*)	38	21	11	6	62	-	41	74
3.	Gyirmót FC Győr	38	20	5	13	75	-	50	65
4.	Vasas FC Budapest	38	18	11	9	73	-	64	65
5.	Budaörsi SC	38	20	4	14	65	-	46	64
6.	Békéscsaba 1912 Előre SE	38	17	9	12	56	-	49	60
7.	Soroksár SC	38	18	5	15	68	-	61	59
8.	Győri ETO FC	38	17	7	14	60	-	46	58
9.	Kazincbarcikai SC	38	16	8	14	59	-	50	56
10.	Nyíregyháza Spartacus FC	38	15	11	12	53	-	49	56
11.	Aqvital FC Csákvár	38	12	16	10	57	-	59	52
12.	Bodajk FC Siófok	38	12	11	15	49	-	53	47
13.	Vác FC	38	11	13	14	44	-	51	46
14.	Dorogi FC	38	10	13	15	54	-	59	43
15.	Tiszakécske FC	38	9	16	13	34	-	52	43
16.	Budafoki MTE	38	12	5	21	46	-	66	41
17.	Balmazújvárosi FC	38	10	10	18	33	-	48	40
18.	Cegléd VSE (*Relegated*)	38	8	8	22	35	-	68	32
19.	Mosonmagyaróvári TE (*Relegated*)	38	6	13	19	35	-	61	31
20.	Monori SE (*Relegated*)	38	7	9	22	49	-	70	30

NATIONAL TEAM

INTERNATIONAL MATCHES
(16.07.2018 – 15.07.2019)

08.09.2018	Tampere	Finland - Hungary	1-0(1-0)	(UNL)
11.09.2018	Budapest	Hungary - Greece	2-1(2-1)	(UNL)
12.10.2018	Athína	Greece - Hungary	1-0(0-0)	(UNL)
15.10.2018	Tallinn	Estonia - Hungary	3-3(1-1)	(UNL)
15.11.2018	Budapest	Hungary - Estonia	2-0(1-0)	(UNL)
18.11.2018	Budapest	Hungary - Finland	2-0(2-0)	(UNL)
21.03.2019	Trnava	Slovakia - Hungary	2-0(1-0)	(ECQ)
24.03.2019	Budapest	Hungary - Croatia	2-1(1-1)	(ECQ)
08.06.2019	Bakı	Azerbaijan - Hungary	1-3(0-1)	(ECQ)
11.06.2019	Budapest	Hungary - Wales	1-0(0-0)	(ECQ)

08.09.2018 FINLAND - HUNGARY 1-0(1-0) UEFA Nations League C, Group 2
Ratinan Stadion, Tampere; Referee: Gediminas Mažeika (Lithuania); Attendance: 10,220
HUN: Péter Gulácsi, Attila Fiola, Ádám Lang, Tamás Kádár, Gergő Lovrencsics, Máté Pátkai, Zoltán Stieber (54.Roland Varga), István Kovács (61.Zsolt Kalmár), László Kleinheisler, Ádám Csaba Szalai (Cap), Roland Sallai (73.Márton Eppel). Trainer: Marco Rossi (Italy).

11.09.2018 HUNGARY - GREECE 2-1(2-1) UEFA Nations League C, Group 2
Groupama Aréna, Budapest; Referee: Aliaksei Kulbakov (Belarus); Attendance: *played behind closed doors*
HUN: Péter Gulácsi, Attila Fiola, Barnabás Bese, Ádám Lang, Tamás Kádár, Ádám Nagy, István Kovács (81.Máté Pátkai), Roland Varga (62.Gergő Lovrencsics), László Kleinheisler, Roland Sallai, Ádám Csaba Szalai (Cap) (69.Márton Eppel). Trainer: Marco Rossi (Italy).
Goals: Roland Sallai (15), László Kleinheisler (42).

12.10.2018 GREECE - HUNGARY 1-0(0-0) UEFA Nations League C, Group 2
Stádio Olympiako „Spiros Louis", Athína; Referee: Tobias Stieler (Germany); Attendance: 9,040
HUN: Péter Gulácsi, Attila Fiola, Barnabás Bese (75.Krisztián Németh), Vilmos Tamás Orbán, Tamás Kádár, Ádám Nagy, László Kleinheisler, Zsolt Kalmár (55.István Kovács), Roland Varga (68.Dominik Nagy), Ádám Csaba Szalai (Cap), Roland Sallai. Trainer: Marco Rossi (Italy).

15.10.2018 ESTONIA - HUNGARY 3-3(1-1) UEFA Nations League C, Group 2
A. Le Coq Arena, Tallinn; Referee: Halis Özkahya (Turkey); Attendance: 3,043
HUN: Péter Gulácsi, Gergő Lovrencsics (81.Barnabás Bese), Botond Baráth, Vilmos Tamás Orbán, Tamás Kádár, Ádám Nagy, Dominik Nagy (75.Márton Eppel), István Kovács, László Kleinheisler (68.Máté Pátkai), Ádám Csaba Szalai (Cap), Roland Sallai. Trainer: Marco Rossi (Italy).
Goals: Dominik Nagy (24), Ádám Csaba Szalai (54, 81).

15.11.2018 HUNGARY - ESTONIA 2-0(1-0) UEFA Nations League C, Group 2
Groupama Aréna, Budapest; Referee: Enea Jorgji (Albania); Attendance: 7,775
HUN: Dénes Dibusz, Mihály Korhut, Botond Baráth, Vilmos Tamás Orbán, Tamás Kádár, Dominik Nagy (65.Balázs Dzsudzsák), Máté Pátkai, István Kovács, Zsolt Kalmár (84.László Kleinheisler), Ádám Nagy, Ádám Csaba Szalai (Cap) (76.Dániel Böde). Trainer: Marco Rossi (Italy).
Goals: Vilmos Tamás Orbán (8), Ádám Csaba Szalai (69).

18.11.2018 HUNGARY - FINLAND 2-0(2-0) UEFA Nations League C, Group 2
Groupama Aréna, Budapest; Referee: Slavko Vinčić (Slovenia); Attendance: 9,200
HUN: Péter Gulácsi, Mihály Korhut (54.Filip Holender), Botond Baráth (52.Ádám Lang), Vilmos Tamás Orbán, Tamás Kádár (46.Paulo Vinícius Souza dos Santos), Gergő Lovrencsics, Balázs Dzsudzsák (Cap), László Kleinheisler, Zsolt Kalmár, Ádám Nagy, Ádám Csaba Szalai. Trainer: Marco Rossi (Italy).
Goals: Ádám Csaba Szalai (29), Ádám Nagy (37).

21.03.2019 SLOVAKIA - HUNGARY 2-0(1-0) 16th EC. Qualifiers
Štadión "Antona Malatinského", Trnava; Referee: Vladislav Bezborodov (Russia); Attendance: 14,235
HUN: Péter Gulácsi, Mihály Korhut, Ádám Lang (81.Filip Holender), Vilmos Tamás Orbán, Tamás Kádár, Gergő Lovrencsics, László Kleinheisler (54.Dominik Szoboszlai), István Kovács, Zsolt Kalmár (61.Balázs Dzsudzsák), Ádám Nagy, Ádám Csaba Szalai (Cap). Trainer: Marco Rossi (Italy).

24.03.2019 HUNGARY - CROATIA 2-1(1-1) 16th EC. Qualifiers
Groupama Arena, Budapest; Referee: Willie Collum (Scotland); Attendance: 19,400
HUN: Péter Gulácsi, Botond Baráth, Vilmos Tamás Orbán, Tamás Kádár, Gergő Lovrencsics , Balázs Dzsudzsák (Cap) (85.Barnabás Bese), Máté Pátkai, Ádám Nagy, Dominik Nagy (40.Roland Varga), Dominik Szoboszlai (65.Zsolt Kalmár), Ádám Csaba Szalai. Trainer: Marco Rossi (Italy).
Goals: Ádám Csaba Szalai (34), Máté Pátkai (76).

08.06.2019 AZERBAIJAN - HUNGARY 1-3(0-1) 16th EC. Qualifiers
Bakcell Arena, Bakı; Referee: Bernie "Kevin" Raymond Blom (Netherlands); Attendance: 11,000
HUN: Péter Gulácsi, Botond Baráth, Vilmos Tamás Orbán, Mihály Korhut, Gergő Lovrencsics, Balázs Dzsudzsák (Cap) (86.Krisztián Németh), Dominik Nagy, László Kleinheisler (72.Máté Pátkai), Ádám Nagy, Dominik Szoboszlai (58.Dávid Holman), Ádám Csaba Szalai. Trainer: Marco Rossi (Italy).
Goals: Vilmos Tamás Orbán (18, 53), Dávid Holman (71).

11.06.2019 HUNGARY - WALES 1-0(0-0) 16th EC. Qualifiers
Groupama Arena, Budapest; Referee: Matej Jug (Slovenia); Attendance: 18,350
HUN: Péter Gulácsi, Botond Baráth, Vilmos Tamás Orbán, Mihály Korhut, Máté Pátkai, Gergő Lovrencsics, Balázs Dzsudzsák (Cap) (70.László Kleinheisler), Filip Holender (59.Roland Varga), Ádám Nagy, Dominik Szoboszlai (83.Barnabás Bese), Ádám Csaba Szalai. Trainer: Marco Rossi (Italy).
Goal: Máté Pátkai (80).

NATIONAL TEAM PLAYERS
(16.07.2018 – 15.07.2019)

Name	DOB	Caps	Goals	2018/2019:	Club
Goalkeepers					
Dénes DIBUSZ	16.11.1990	**7**	**0**	2018:	*Ferencvárosi TC*
Péter GULÁCSI	06.05.1990	**27**	**0**	2018/2019:	*RasenBallsport Leipzig (GER)*
Defenders					
Botond BARÁTH	21.04.1992	**6**	**0**	2018:	*Budapest Hovéd FC*
				01.01.2019->	*Sporting Kansas City (USA)*
Barnabás BESE	06.05.1994	**17**	**0**	2018/2019:	*AC Le Havre (FRA)*
Attila FIOLA	17.02.1990	**27**	**0**	2018/2019:	*MOL Vidi FC Székesfehérvár*
Tamás KÁDÁR	14.03.1990	**55**	**1**	2018/2019:	*FK Dynamo Kyiv (UKR)*
Mihály KORHUT	01.12.1988	**18**	**0**	2018:	*Hapoel Be'er Sheva FC (ISR)*
				14.01.2019->	*Aris Thessaloníki (GRE)*
Ádám LANG	17.01.1993	**26**	**1**	2018/2019:	*FC CFR 1907 Cluj-Napoca (ROU)*
Gergő LOVRENCSICS	01.09.1988	**32**	**1**	2018/2019:	*Ferencvárosi TC*
Vilmos Tamás „Willi" ORBÁN	03.11.1992	**8**	**3**	2018/2019:	*RasenBallsport Leipzig (GER)*
PAULO VINÍCIUS Souza dos Santos	12.02.1990	**7**	**0**	2018/2019:	*MOL Vidi FC Székesfehérvár*
Midfielders					
Balázs DZSUDZSÁK	23.12.1986	**102**	**21**	2018/2019:	*Al-Ittihad Kalba SC (UAE)*
Dávid HOLMAN	17.03.1993	**1**	**1**	2019:	*ŠK Slovan Bratislava (SVK)*
Zsolt KALMÁR	09.06.1995	**15**	**0**	2018:	*FC DAC 1904 Dunajská Streda (SVK)*
László KLEINHEISLER	08.04.1994	**26**	**2**	2018:	*Astana FC (KAZ)*
				15.02.2019->	*NK Osijek (CRO)*
István KOVÁCS	27.03.1992	**11**	**0**	2018/2019:	*MOL Vidi FC Székesfehérvár*
Dominik NAGY	08.05.1995	**7**	**1**	2018/2019:	*Legia Warszawa (POL)*
Ádám NAGY	17.06.1995	**33**	**1**	2018/2019:	*Bologna FC 1909 (ITA)*
Máté PÁTKAI	06.03.1988	**21**	**2**	2018/2019:	*MOL Vidi FC Székesfehérvár*
Zoltán STIEBER	16.10.1988	**26**	**3**	2018:	*Washington DC United (USA)*
Dominik SZOBOSZLAI	25.10.2000	**4**	**0**	2019:	*FC Red Bull Salzburg (AUT)*
Forwards					
Dániel BÖDE	21.10.1986	**25**	**5**	2018:	*Ferencvárosi TC*
Márton EPPEL	26.10.1991	**8**	**0**	2018/2019:	*FC Kairat Almaty (KAZ)*
Filip HOLENDER	27.07.1994	**3**	**0**	2018/2019:	*Budapest Honvéd FC*
Krisztián NÉMETH	05.01.1989	**36**	**4**	2018/2019:	*Sporting Kansas City (USA)*
Roland SALLAI	22.05.1997	**12**	**1**	2018:	*SC Freiburg (GER)*
Ádám Csaba SZALAI	09.12.1987	**56**	**20**	2018/2019:	*TSG 1899 Hoffenheim (GER)*
Roland VARGA	23.01.1990	**15**	**3**	2018/2019:	*Ferencvárosi TC*

National team coach

Marco ROSSI (Italy) [from 19.06.2018]	09.09.1964	10 M; 6 W; 1 D; 3 L; 15-10

ICELAND

The Country:
Ísland (Iceland)
Capital: Reykjavík
Surface: 102,775 km²
Inhabitants: 360,390 [2019]
Time: UTC

The FA:
Knattspyrnusamband Íslands
Laugardal 104, Reykjavík
Tel: +354 510 2900
Foundation date: 1947
Member of FIFA since: 1947
Member of UEFA since: 1954
Website: www.ksi.is

NATIONAL TEAM RECORDS

First international match:	17.07.1946, Reykjavík:	Iceland – Denmark 0-3
Most international caps:	Rúnar Kristinsson	- 104 caps (1987-2004)
Most international goals:	Eiður Smári Guðjohnsen	- 26 goals / 88 caps (1996-2016)

UEFA EUROPEAN CHAMPIONSHIP	
1960	Did not enter
1964	Qualifiers
1968	Did not enter
1972	Did not enter
1976	Qualifiers
1980	Qualifiers
1984	Qualifiers
1988	Qualifiers
1992	Qualifiers
1996	Qualifiers
2000	Qualifiers
2004	Qualifiers
2008	Qualifiers
2012	Qualifiers
2016	Final Tournament (Quarter-Finals)

FIFA WORLD CUP	
1930	Did not enter
1934	Did not enter
1938	Did not enter
1950	Did not enter
1954	*Entry not accepted by FIFA*
1958	Qualifiers
1962	Did not enter
1966	Did not enter
1970	Did not enter
1974	Qualifiers
1978	Qualifiers
1982	Qualifiers
1986	Qualifiers
1990	Qualifiers
1994	Qualifiers
1998	Qualifiers
2002	Qualifiers
2006	Qualifiers
2010	Qualifiers
2014	Qualifiers
2018	Final Tournament (Group Stage)

UEFA NATIONS LEAGUE
2018/2019 – League A

OLYMPIC FOOTBALL TOURNAMENTS 1908-2016							
1908	-	**1948**	-	**1972**	Qualifiers	**1996**	Qualifiers
1912	-	**1952**	-	**1976**	Did not enter	**2000**	Qualifiers
1920	-	**1956**	-	**1980**	Did not enter	**2004**	Qualifiers
1924	-	**1960**	Qualifiers	**1984**	Did not enter	**2008**	Qualifiers
1928	-	**1964**	Qualifiers	**1988**	Qualifiers	**2012**	Qualifiers
1936	-	**1968**	Qualifiers	**1992**	Qualifiers	**2016**	Qualifiers

FIFA CONFEDERATIONS CUP 1992-2017
None

ICELANDIAN CLUB HONOURS IN EUROPEAN CLUB COMPETITIONS:

European Champion Clubs' Cup (1956-1992) / UEFA Champions League (1993-2019)
None
Fairs Cup (1858-1971) / UEFA Cup (1972-2009) / UEFA Europa League (2010-2019)
None
UEFA Super Cup (1972-2018)
None
European Cup Winners' Cup 1961-1999*
None

**defunct competition*

NATIONAL COMPETITIONS
TABLE OF HONOURS

	CHAMPIONS	CUP WINNERS	BEST GOALSCORERS	
1912	KR Reykjavík	-	-	
1913	Fram Reykjavík	-	-	
1914	Fram Reykjavík	-	-	
1915	Fram Reykjavík	-	-	
1916	Fram Reykjavík	-	-	
1917	Fram Reykjavík	-	-	
1918	Fram Reykjavík	-	-	
1919	KR Reykjavík	-	-	
1920	Víkingur Reykjavík	-	-	
1921	Fram Reykjavík	-	-	
1922	Fram Reykjavík	-	-	
1923	Fram Reykjavík	-	-	
1924	Víkingur Reykjavík	-	-	
1925	Fram Reykjavík	-	-	
1926	KR Reykjavík	-	-	
1927	KR Reykjavík	-	-	
1928	KR Reykjavík	-	-	
1929	KR Reykjavík	-	-	
1930	Valur Reykjavík	-	-	
1931	KR Reykjavík	-	-	
1932	KR Reykjavík	-	-	
1933	Valur Reykjavík	-	-	
1934	KR Reykjavík	-	-	
1935	Valur Reykjavík	-	-	
1936	Valur Reykjavík	-	-	
1937	Valur Reykjavík	-	-	
1938	Valur Reykjavík	-	-	
1939	Fram Reykjavík	-	-	
1940	Valur Reykjavík	-	-	
1941	KR Reykjavík	-	-	
1942	Valur Reykjavík	-	-	
1943	Valur Reykjavík	-	-	
1944	Valur Reykjavík	-	-	
1945	Valur Reykjavík	-	-	
1946	Fram Reykjavík	-	-	
1947	Fram Reykjavík	-	-	
1948	KR Reykjavík	-	-	
1949	KR Reykjavík	-	-	
1950	KR Reykjavík	-	-	
1951	ÍA Akranes	-	-	
1952	KR Reykjavík	-	-	
1953	ÍA Akranes	-	-	
1954	ÍA Akranes	-	-	
1955	KR Reykjavík	-	-	
1956	Valur Reykjavík	-	-	
1957	ÍA Akranes	-	-	
1958	ÍA Akranes	-	-	
1959	KR Reykjavík	-	-	
1960	ÍA Akranes	KR Reykjavík	-	
1961	KR Reykjavík	KR Reykjavík	-	
1962	Fram Reykjavík	KR Reykjavík	-	
1963	KR Reykjavík	KR Reykjavík	-	
1964	Keflavík ÍF	KR Reykjavík	-	
1965	KR Reykjavík	Valur Reykjavík	-	
1966	Valur Reykjavík	KR Reykjavík	-	
1967	Valur Reykjavík	KR Reykjavík	-	
1968	KR Reykjavík	ÍBV Vestmannaeyjar	-	
1969	Keflavík ÍF	KA Akureyrar	-	
1970	ÍA Akranes	Fram Reykjavík	-	
1971	Keflavík ÍF	Víkingur Reykjavík	-	
1972	Fram Reykjavík	ÍBV Vestmannaeyjar	-	
1973	Keflavík ÍF	Fram Reykjavík	-	
1974	ÍA Akranes	Valur Reykjavík	-	
1975	ÍA Akranes	Keflavík ÍF	-	
1976	Valur Reykjavík	Valur Reykjavík	-	
1977	ÍA Akranes	Valur Reykjavík	-	
1978	Valur Reykjavík	ÍA Akranes	-	
1979	ÍBV Vestmannaeyjar	Fram Reykjavík	-	
1980	Valur Reykjavík	Fram Reykjavík	Matthias Hallgrimsson (Valur Reykjavík)	15
1981	Víkingur Reykjavík	ÍBV Vestmannaeyjar	Sigurlás Þorleifsson (ÍBV Vestmannaeyjar) Larus Gudmundsson (Víkingur Reykjavík)	12

1982	Víkingur Reykjavík	ÍA Akranes	Sigurlás Þorleifsson (ÍBV Vestmannaeyjar) Heimir Karlsson (Víkingur Reykjavík)	10
1983	ÍA Akranes	ÍA Akranes	Ingi Björn Albertsson (Valur Reykjavík)	14
1984	ÍA Akranes	ÍA Akranes	Guðmundur Steinsson (Fram Reykjavík)	10
1985	Valur Reykjavík	Fram Reykjavík	Ómar Torfason (Fram Reykjavík)	13
1986	Fram Reykjavík	ÍA Akranes	Gudmundur Torfason (Fram Reykjavík)	19
1987	Valur Reykjavík	Fram Reykjavík	Petur Ormslev (Fram Reykjavík)	12
1988	Fram Reykjavík	Valur Reykjavík	Sigurjón Kristjánsson (Valur Reykjavík)	13
1989	KA Akureyri	Fram Reykjavík	Hörður Magnússon (FH Hafnarfjörður)	12
1990	Fram Reykjavík	Valur Reykjavík	Hörður Magnússon (FH Hafnarfjörður)	13
1991	Víkingur Reykjavík	Valur Reykjavík	Hörður Magnússon (FH Hafnarfjörður) Guðmundur Steinsson (Víkingur Reykjavík)	13
1992	ÍA Akranes	Valur Reykjavík	Arnar Gunnlaugsson (ÍA Akranes)	15
1993	ÍA Akranes	ÍA Akranes	Þórður Guðjónsson (ÍA Akranes)	19
1994	ÍA Akranes	KR Reykjavík	Mihajlo Biberčić (SRB, ÍA Akranes)	14
1995	ÍA Akranes	KR Reykjavík	Arnar Gunnlaugsson (ÍA Akranes)	15
1996	ÍA Akranes	ÍA Akranes	Ríkharður Daðason (KR Reykjavík)	14
1997	ÍBV Vestmannaeyjar	Keflavík ÍF	Tryggvi Guðmundsson (ÍBV Vestmannaeyjar)	19
1998	ÍBV Vestmannaeyjar	ÍBV Vestmannaeyjar	Steingrímur Jóhannesson (ÍBV Vestmannaeyjar)	16
1999	KR Reykjavík	KR Reykjavík	Steingrímur Jóhannesson (ÍBV Vestmannaeyjar)	12
2000	KR Reykjavík	ÍA Akranes	Guðmundur Steinarsson (Keflavík ÍF) Andri Sigþórsson (KR Reykjavík)	14
2001	ÍA Akranes	Fylkir Reykjavík	Hjörtur Hjartarson (ÍA Akranes)	15
2002	KR Reykjavík	Fylkir Reykjavík	Grétar Hjartarson (UMF Grindavík)	13
2003	KR Reykjavík	ÍA Akranes	Björgólfur Takefusa (Þróttur Reykjavík)	10
2004	FH Hafnarfjörður	Keflavík ÍF	Gunnar Heiðar Þorvaldsson (ÍBV Vestmannaeyjar)	12
2005	FH Hafnarfjörður	Valur Reykjavík	Tryggvi Guðmundsson (FH Hafnarfjörður)	16
2006	FH Hafnarfjörður	Keflavík ÍF	Marel Baldvinsson (Breiðablik Kópavogur)	11
2007	Valur Reykjavík	FH Hafnarfjörður	Jónas Grani Garðarsson (Fram Reykjavík)	13
2008	FH Hafnarfjörður	KR Reykjavík	Guðmundur Steinarsson (Keflavík ÍF)	16
2009	FH Hafnarfjörður	Breiðablik Kópavogur	Björgólfur Takefusa (KR Reykjavík)	16
2010	Breiðablik Kópavogur	FH Hafnarfjörður	Gilles Mbang Ondo (GAB, UMF Grindavík)	14
2011	KR Reykjavík	KR Reykjavík	Garðar Jóhannsson (Stjarnan Garðabær)	15
2012	FH Hafnarfjörður	KR Reykjavík	Atli Guðnason (FH Hafnarfjörður)	12
2013	KR Reykjavík	Fram Reykjavík	Atli Viðar Björnsson (FH Hafnarfjörður) Viðar Örn Kjartansson (Fylkir Reykjavík) Gary Martin (ENG, KR Reykjavík)	13
2014	Stjarnan Garðabær	KR Reykjavík	Gary Martin (ENG, KR Reykjavík)	13
2015	FH Hafnarfjörður	Valur Reykjavík	Patrick Pedersen (DEN, Valur Reykjavík)	13
2016	FH Hafnarfjörður	Valur Reykjavík	Garðar Gunnlaugsson (ÍA Akranes)	14
2017	Valur Reykjavík	ÍBV Vestmannaeyjar	Andri Rúnar Bjarnason (UMF Grindavík)	19
2018	Valur Reykjavík	Stjarnan Garðabær	Patrick Pedersen (DEN, Valur Reykjavík)	17

NATIONAL CHAMPIONSHIP
Úrvalsdeild karla 2018
(27.04.2018 – 29.09.2018)

Results

Round 1 [27-28.04.2018]
Valur Reykjavík - KR Reykjavík 2-1(0-0)
Stjarnan - Keflavík 2-2(0-0)
Breiðablik - ÍBV Vestmannaeyjar 4-1(1-0)
Grindavík - FH Hafnarfjörður 0-1(0-1)
Fjölnir Reykjavík - KA Akureyri 2-2(2-2)
Víkingur Reykjavík - Fylkir Reykjav. 1-0(1-0)

Round 2 [06-07.05.2018]
Vestmannaeyjar - Fjölnir Reykjavík 1-1(0-0)
Fylkir Reykjavík - KA Akureyri 2-1(2-0)
Stjarnan - KR Reykjavík 2-3(1-2)
FH Hafnarfjörður - Breiðablik 1-3(0-1)
Keflavík - Grindavík 0-2(0-0)
Víkingur Reykjavík - Valur Reykjavík 0-0

Round 3 [12-14.05.2018]
Grindavík - KR Reykjavík 1-1(1-1)
KA Akureyri - ÍBV Vestmannaeyjar 2-0(1-0)
Breiðablik - Keflavík 1-0(1-0)
Fjölnir Reykjavík - FH Hafnarfjörður 2-3(1-0)
Valur Reykjavík - Fylkir Reykjavík 2-2(1-0)
Stjarnan - Víkingur Reykjavík 3-3(2-1)

Round 4 [17-18.05.2018]
FH Hafnarfjörður - KA Akureyri 3-1(0-0)
Fylkir Reykjavík - Vestmannaeyjar 2-1(1-0)
Keflavík - Fjölnir Reykjavík 1-2(0-1)
KR Reykjavík - Breiðablik 1-1(0-0)
Víkingur Reykjavík - Grindavík 0-1(0-1)
Valur Reykjavík - Stjarnan 2-2(1-1)

Round 5 [21-23.05.2018]
ÍBV Vestmannaeyjar - FH Hafnarfjörður 0-0
Fjölnir Reykjavík - KR Reykjavík 1-1(1-0)
KA Akureyri - Keflavík 0-0
Breiðablik - Víkingur Reykjavík 0-0
Grindavík - Valur Reykjavík 2-1(1-1)
Stjarnan - Fylkir Reykjavík 3-0(2-0)

Round 6 [27-28.05.2018]
Keflavík - ÍBV Vestmannaeyjar 1-3(0-1)
KR Reykjavík - KA Akureyri 2-0(1-0)
Víkingur Reykjavík - Fjölnir Reykj. 1-2(0-2)
Stjarnan - Grindavík 1-1(0-1)
Valur Reykjavík - Breiðablik 2-1(0-1)
FH Hafnarfjörður - Fylkir Reykjavík 1-1(0-1)

Round 7 [03-04.06.2018]
KA Akureyri - Víkingur Reykjavík 4-1(2-0)
ÍBV Vestmannaeyjar - KR Reykjavík 2-0(2-0)
Breiðablik - Stjarnan 0-1(0-0)
FH Hafnarfjörður - Keflavík 2-2(1-2)
Fjölnir Reykjavík - Valur Reykjavík 0-2(0-1)
Grindavík - Fylkir Reykjavík 2-1(0-1)

Round 8 [08-10.06.2018]
Fylkir Reykjavík - Keflavík 2-0(1-0)
Víkingur Reykjav. - Vestmannaeyjar 2-1(1-0)
Grindavík - Breiðablik 0-2(0-0)
Valur Reykjavík - KA Akureyri 3-1(2-1)
Stjarnan - Fjölnir Reykjavík 6-1(1-1)
KR Reykjavík - FH Hafnarfjörður 2-2(1-0)

Round 9 [13-14.06.2018]
Vestmannaeyjar - Valur Reykjavík 0-1(0-0)
Breiðablik - Fylkir Reykjavík 2-0(0-0)
KA Akureyri - Stjarnan 1-2(0-0)
FH Hafnarfjörður - Víkingur Reykj. 3-0(2-0)
Fjölnir Reykjavík - Grindavík 0-1(0-0)
Keflavík - KR Reykjavík 0-4(0-3)

Round 10 [19-20.06.2018]
Stjarnan - ÍBV Vestmannaeyjar 2-1(1-1)
Valur Reykjavík - FH Hafnarfjörður 2-1(2-1)
Grindavík - KA Akureyri 1-2(1-1) [12.07.]
Víkingur Reykj. - Keflavík 1-0(1-0) [13.07.]
Breiðablik - Fjölnir Reykj. 2-1(1-0) [16.07.]
Fylkir Reykj. - KR Reykj. 2-5(1-4) [16.07.]

Round 11 [01-02.07.2018]
ÍBV Vestmannaeyjar - Grindavík 3-0(1-0)
KA Akureyri - Breiðablik 0-0
Keflavík - Valur Reykjavík 0-2(0-2)
Fjölnir Reykjavík - Fylkir Reykjavík 2-1(0-0)
KR Reykjavík - Víkingur Reykjavík 0-1(0-0)
FH Hafnarfjörður - Stjarnan 2-3(1-1)

Round 12 [05-09.07.2018]
KA Akureyri - Fjölnir Reykjavík 2-0(2-0)
KR Reykjavík - Valur Reykjavík 1-1(1-1)
FH Hafnarfjörður - Grindavík 2-1(1-0)
ÍBV Vestmannaeyjar - Breiðablik 0-0
Keflavík - Stjarnan 0-2(0-2)
Fylkir Reykjavík - Víkingur Reykj. 2-3(0-3)

Round 13 [22-23.07.2018]
Fjölnir Reykjavík - Vestmannaeyjar 1-1(1-0)
Valur Reykjavík - Víkingur Reykj. 4-1(2-0)
KA Akureyri - Fylkir Reykjavík 5-1(2-0)
KR Reykjavík - Stjarnan 1-0(1-0)
Breiðablik - FH Hafnarfjörður 4-1(1-0)
Grindavík - Keflavík 3-0(2-0)

Round 14 [29-30.07.2018]
ÍBV Vestmannaeyjar - KA Akureyri 2-1(1-1)
Víkingur Reykjavík - Stjarnan 0-4(0-3)
FH Hafnarfjörður - Fjölnir Reykjavík 1-0(1-0)
Fylkir Reykjavík - Valur Reykjavík 0-0
Keflavík - Breiðablik 1-3(0-0)
KR Reykjavík - Grindavík 2-0(0-0)

Round 15 [04-08.08.2018]
Vestmannaeyjar - Fylkir Reykjavík 0-1(0-1)
Breiðablik - KR Reykjavík 1-0(0-0)
KA Akureyri - FH Hafnarfjörður 1-1(0-0)
Grindavík - Víkingur Reykjavík 2-1(2-1)
Fjölnir Reykjavík - Keflavík 0-0
Stjarnan - Valur Reykjavík 1-1(1-1) [29.08.]

Round 16 [12-13.08.2018]
FH Hafnarfjörður - Vestmannaeyjar 0-2(0-2)
Keflavík - KA Akureyri 0-3(0-2)
Fylkir Reykjavík - Stjarnan 0-2(0-0)
KR Reykjavík - Fjölnir Reykjavík 0-0
Víkingur Reykjavík - Breiðablik 2-3(1-2)
Valur Reykjavík - Grindavík 4-0(2-0)

Round 17 [18-20.08.2018]
ÍBV Vestmannaeyjar - Keflavík 1-0(1-0)
KA Akureyri - KR Reykjavík 0-1(0-0)
Fylkir Reykjavík - FH Hafnarfjörður 1-1(0-1)
Grindavík - Stjarnan 2-2(1-0)
Breiðablik - Valur Reykjavík 1-3(0-2)
Fjölnir Reykjavík - Víkingur Reykj. 2-2(1-0)

Round 18 [25-27.08.2018]
Víkingur Reykjavík - KA Akureyri 2-2(0-2)
Stjarnan - Breiðablik 2-1(2-1)
Valur Reykjavík - Fjölnir Reykjavík 5-3(1-0)
KR Reykjavík - ÍBV Vestmannaeyjar 4-1(3-0)
Keflavík - FH Hafnarfjörður 1-3(1-1)
Fylkir Reykjavík - Grindavík 3-1(0-0)

Round 19 [31.08.-02.09.2018]
Keflavík - Fylkir Reykjavík 1-2(0-0)
Fjölnir Reykjavík - Stjarnan 1-3(1-1)
Vestmannaeyjar - Víkingur Reykj. 1-1(1-1)
KA Akureyri - Valur Reykjavík 3-3(2-1)
Breiðablik - Grindavík 1-1(1-0)
FH Hafnarfjörður - KR Reykjavík 4-0(2-0)

Round 20 [16-19.09.2018]
KR Reykjavík - Keflavík 3-1(1-1)
Grindavík - Fjölnir Reykjavík 0-1(0-1)
Víkingur Reykj. - FH Hafnarfjörður 1-1(0-0)
Valur Reykjavík - Vestmannaeyjar 5-1(0-1)
Stjarnan - KA Akureyri 1-1(0-0)
Fylkir Reykjavík - Breiðablik 0-3(0-2)

Round 21 [23.09.2018]
FH Hafnarfjörður - Valur Reykjavík 2-1(0-0)
Fjölnir Reykjavík - Breiðablik 0-2(0-2)
ÍBV Vestmannaeyjar - Stjarnan 2-1(0-1)
KA Akureyri - Grindavík 4-3(4-2)
Keflavík - Víkingur Reykjavík 0-4(0-0)
KR Reykjavík - Fylkir Reykjavík 1-1(0-0)

Round 22 [29.09.2018]
Breiðablik - KA Akureyri 4-0(3-0)
Fylkir Reykjavík - Fjölnir Reykjavík 7-0(3-0)
Grindavík - ÍBV Vestmannaeyjar 2-5(1-2)
Stjarnan - FH Hafnarfjörður 0-1(0-1)
Valur Reykjavík - Keflavík 4-1(3-0)
Víkingur Reykjavík - KR Reykjavík 2-3(1-1)

Final Standings

1.	**Valur Reykjavík**	22	13	7	2	50	-	24	46
2.	Breiðablik Kópavogur	22	13	5	4	39	-	17	44
3.	Stjarnan Garðabær	22	11	7	4	45	-	26	40
4.	KR Reykjavík	22	10	7	5	36	-	25	37
5.	FH Hafnarfjörður	22	10	7	5	36	-	28	37
6.	ÍBV Vestmannaeyjar	22	8	5	9	29	-	31	29
7.	KA Akureyri	22	7	7	8	36	-	34	28
8.	Fylkir Reykjavík	22	7	5	10	31	-	37	26
9.	Víkingur Reykjavík	22	6	7	9	29	-	38	25
10.	UMF Grindavík	22	7	4	11	26	-	37	25
11.	Fjölnir Reykjavík (*Relegated*)	22	4	7	11	22	-	44	19
12.	Keflavík (*Relegated*)	22	0	4	18	11	-	49	4

Top goalscorers:

17 Patrick Pedersen (DEN)
Valur Reykjavík

16 Hilmar Árni Halldórsson
Stjarnan Garðabær

11 Pálmi Rafn Pálmason
KR Reykjavík

NATIONAL CUP
Borgunarbikar 2018

First Round [12-15.04.2018]

Ýmir - KV Vesturbæjar	2-5 aet	KFS Vestmannaeyjar - Víðir Garður	2-6
IF Grótta - Vatnaliljur	9-0	KF Garðabæjar - Afríka	5-0
Álftanes - Ísbjörninn	9-0	Stál-úlfur - UMF Skallagrímur	0-2
ÍR Reykjavík - Ægir	1-0	Sindri Höfn - UMF Einherji	2-5 aet
KF Berserkir - Reynir Sandgerði	1-5	Kórdrengir - Stokkseyri	18-2
Augnablik - Kormákur/Hvöt	17-0	Afturelding - KF Rangæinga	6-0
SR Reykjavík - Þróttur Vogar	0-4	IF Vestri - Kóngarnir	18-2
KH Hlídarendi - Kría	6-2	Fram Reykjavík - Ármann	6-0
Hvíti riddarinn - Vængir Júpiters	2-3	Nökkvi - KF Fjallabyggðar	10-1
IF Höttur - KF Fjarðabyggðar	1-0	Kári - Hörður ÍF	13-1
Léttir - Úlfarnir	1-0	UMF Njarðvík - KB Breiðholt	10-1
Árborg - Hamar Hveragerði	0-1	Álafoss - GG Grindavík	1-5
Mídas - Elliði	1-4	UMF Geisli/Aðaldal - Dalvík/Reynir	0-2
UMF Snæfell - ÍH Hafnarfjörður	2-7		

Second Round [19-23.04.2018]

ÍA Akranes - ÍH Hafnarfjörður	8-0	KH Hlídarendi - Leiknir Reykjavík	2-3
Afturelding - KV Vesturbæjar	8-2	Kórdrengir - UMF Njarðvík	0-2
Haukar Hafnarfjörður - IF Vestri	3-1	Þróttur Vogar - Víðir Garður	1-2
KF Garðabæjar - Víkingur Ólafsvík	0-5	UMF Skallagrímur - Reynir Sandgerði	0-9
Kári - Elliði	9-1	UMF Einherji - Leiknir Fáskrúðsfirði	1-0
UMF Selfoss - IF Grótta	3-2 pen	Fram Reykjavík - GG Grindavík	10-0
IF Höttur - Huginn	3-0	ÍF Magni - KF Fjallabyggðar	5-0
Léttir - Hamar Hveragerði	0-1	Þór Akureyri - Dalvík/Reynir	3-1
HK Kópavogur - Álftanes	5-0	ÍR Reykjavík - Augnablik	1-0
Vængir Júpiters - Þróttur Reykjavík	0-2	ÍF Völsungur - UMF Tindastóll	7-1

Third Round [30.04.-01.05.2018]

UMF Selfoss - ÍA Akranes	1-4	Hamar Hveragerði - Víkingur Ólafsvík	3-5
UMF Njarðvík - Þróttur Reykjavík	2-4	Víðir Garður - UMF Grindavík	2-4
ÍBV Vestmannaeyjar - UMF Einherji	4-2	ÍR Reykjavík - FH Hafnarfjörður	0-5
Reynir Sandgerði - Víkingur Reykjavík	0-2	Leiknir Reykjavík - Breiðablik Kópavogur	1-3
Afturelding - KR Reykjavík	1-7	Stjarnan Garðabær - Fylkir Reykjavík	2-1
Haukar Hafnarfjörður - KA Akureyri	1-2	ÍF Völsungur - Fram Reykjavík	1-2 aet
Kári - IF Höttur	5-2	ÍF Magni - Fjölnir Reykjavík	1-3
Þór Akureyri - HK Kópavogur	3-2	Valur Reykjavík - Keflavík	2-0

1/8-Finals [30-31.05.2018]

Valur Reykjavík - ÍBV Vestmannaeyjar	3-2 aet	Stjarnan Garðabær - Þróttur Reykjavík	5-0
Fjölnir Reykjavík - Þór Akureyri	1-1 aet; 3-4 pen	UMF Grindavík - ÍA Akranes	1-2
Fram Reykjavík - Víkingur Ólafsvík	0-1	FH Hafnarfjörður - KA Akureyri	1-0
Breiðablik Kópavogur - KR Reykjavík	1-0	Kári - Víkingur Reykjavík	3-4 aet

Quarter-Finals [25.06./18.07.2018]

ÍA Akranes - FH Hafnarfjörður	0-1	Valur Reykjavík - Breiðablik Kópavogur	1-2
Þór Akureyri - Stjarnan Garðabær	1-2 aet	Víkingur Reykjavík - Víkingur Ólafsvík	0-1

Semi-Finals [15-16.08.2018]

Stjarnan Garðabær - FH Hafnarfjörður	2-0	Breiðablik Kópavogur - Víkingur Ólafsvík	4-2 pen

Final

15.09.2018; Laugardalsvöllur, Reykjavík; Referee: Þóroddur Hjaltalín; Attendance: 3,814

Stjarnan Garðabær - Breiðablik Kópavogur **0-0; 4-1 on penalties**

Stjarnan: Haraldur Björnsson, Brynjar Guðjónsson, Jóhann Laxdal (118.Sölvi Guðbjargarson), Daníel Laxdal, Þórarinn Valdimarsson, Baldur Sigurðsson, Þorsteinn Már Ragnarsson (76.Ævar Jóhannesson), Eyjólfur Héðinsson, Alex Þór Hauksson (80.Guðmundur Hafsteinsson), Guðjón Baldvinsson, Hilmar Árni Halldórsson. Trainer: Rúnar Sigmundsson.

Breiðablik: Gunnleifur Gunnleifsson, Damir Muminović, Elfar Helgason (60.Kolbeinn Þórðarson), Jonathan Hendrickx (106.Arnór Gauti Ragnarsson), Viktor Örn Margeirsson (95.Guðmundur Guðjónsson), Oliver Sigurjónsson, Gísli Eyjólfsson, Davíð Kristján Ólafsson, Willum Þór Willumsson, Thomas Mikkelsen, Andri Yeoman (70.Arnþór Ari Atlason). Trainer: Ágúst Gylfason.

Penalties: Thomas Mikkelsen 0-1; Hilmar Árni Halldórsson 1-1; Baldur Sigurðsson 2-1; Oliver Sigurjónsson (missed); Arnór Gauti Ragnarsson (missed); Guðmundur Hafsteinsson 3-1; Eyjólfur Héðinsson 4-1.

THE CLUBS 2018

Breiðablik Kópavogur

Founded: 12.04.1950
Stadium: Kópavogsvöllur, Kópavogur (5,501)

Goalkeepers:	**DOB**	**M**	**(s)**	**G**
Gunnleifur Gunnleifsson	14.07.1975	21		
Ólafur Ólafsson	08.05.1995	1		
Defenders:	**DOB**	**M**	**(s)**	**G**
Guðmundur Guðjónsson	03.08.1989		(1)	
Elfar Helgason	27.07.1989	11	(4)	1
Jonathan Hendrickx (BEL)	25.12.1993	19	(1)	2
Viktor Örn Margeirsson	22.07.1994	15	(5)	2
Damir Muminović (SRB)	13.05.1990	22		
Midfielders:	**DOB**	**M**	**(s)**	**G**
Andri Baldursson	10.01.2002		(1)	
Gísli Eyjólfsson	31.05.1994	22		7
Davíð Kristján Ólafsson	15.05.1995	22		1
Oliver Sigurjónsson	05.05.1995	20		2
Brynjólfur Darri Willumsson	12.08.2000		(7)	
Willum Þór Willumsson	23.10.1998	16	(3)	6
Kolbeinn Þórðarson	12.03.2000	6	(6)	
Forwards:	**DOB**	**M**	**(s)**	**G**
Arnþór Ari Atlason	12.10.1993	15	(3)	
Aron Bjarnason	14.10.1995	14	(5)	2
Sveinn Guðjohnsen	12.05.1998	9	(3)	3
Karl Gunnarsson	06.07.2001		(1)	
Thomas Mikkelsen (DEN)	19.01.1990	11		10
Arnór Gauti Ragnarsson	04.02.1997		(16)	1
Alexander Helgi Sigurðarson	08.04.1996		(3)	1
Hrvoje Tokić (CRO)	17.06.1990	1	(4)	
Andri Yeoman	18.04.1992	17	(1)	1
Trainer:	**DOB**	**M**		
Ágúst Gylfason	01.08.1971	22		

Fimleikafélag Hafnarfjarðar

Founded: 15.10.1929
Stadium: Kaplakriki, Hafnarfjörður (6,738)

Goalkeepers:	**DOB**	**M**	**(s)**	**G**
Gunnar Nielsen (FRO)	07.10.1986	22		
Defenders:	**DOB**	**M**	**(s)**	**G**
Rennico Clarke (JAM)	26.08.1995	9		
Cédric D'Ulivo (FRA)	29.08.1989	7	(1)	1
Edi Gomes (DEN)	17.11.1988	13	(2)	1
Viðar Ari Jónsson	10.03.1994	15	(3)	
Egill Darri Makan	27.03.2001	3		
Hjörtur Valgarðsson	27.09.1988	19		
Pétur Viðarsson	25.11.1987	13		1
Midfielders:	**DOB**	**M**	**(s)**	**G**
Robbie Crawford (SCO)	19.03.1993	14	(4)	5
Þórir Jóhann Helgason	28.09.2000		(1)	1
Brandur Hendriksson (FRO)	19.12.1995	17	(3)	7
Guðmundur Kristjánsson	01.03.1989	19	(1)	
Zeiko Lewis (BER)	06.04.1994		(4)	
Kristinn Steindórsson	29.04.1990	13	(4)	
Jákup Ludvig Thomsen (FRO)	23.11.1997	9		3
Davíð Viðarsson	24.04.1984	21		
Forwards:	**DOB**	**M**	**(s)**	**G**
Atli Björnsson	04.01.1980		(12)	
Halldór Björnsson	02.03.1987	5	(9)	
Geoffrey Castillion (NED)	25.05.1991	7	(3)	1
Atli Guðnason	28.09.1984	8	(12)	2
Jónatan Jónsson	15.03.1999	8	(6)	2
Steven Lennon (SCO)	20.01.1988	20	(1)	9
Trainer:	**DOB**	**M**		
Ólafur Kristjánsson	20.05.1968	22		

Ungmennafélagið Fjölnir Reykjavík

Founded: 1988
Stadium: Extra völlurinn, Reykjavík (2,000)

Goalkeepers:	**DOB**	**M**	**(s)**	**G**
Hlynur Hlöðversson	12.05.1996		(1)	
Þórður Ingason	30.03.1988	22		
Defenders:	**DOB**	**M**	**(s)**	**G**
Arnór Breki Ásþórsson	08.02.1998	9	(1)	1
Birnir Snær Ingason	04.12.1996	20	(2)	5
Sigurpáll Melberg Pálsson	13.09.1996		(2)	
Mario Tadejević (CRO)	28.08.1989	19	(1)	
Midfielders:	**DOB**	**M**	**(s)**	**G**
Anton Freyr Ársælsson	11.05.1996	5		
Guðmundur Guðmundsson	30.03.1991	21	(1)	2
Hans Viktor Guðmundsson	09.09.1996	17	(1)	1
Jóhann Árni Gunnarsson	06.04.2001	1	(1)	
Torfi Gunnarsson	31.01.1999	18	(1)	1
Viktor Hafþórsson	16.08.2001		(4)	
Ísak Óli Helgason	02.06.1998	3	(5)	
Ægir Jónasson	08.03.1998	14	(1)	3
Igor Jugović (CRO)	23.01.1989	15	(6)	
Bergsveinn Ólafsson	09.09.1992	20		2
Almarr Ormarsson	25.02.1988	20		2
Ingimundur Óskarsson	04.02.1986		(5)	
Hallvarður Óskar Sigurðarson	13.01.1999		(8)	
Forwards:	**DOB**	**M**	**(s)**	**G**
Valmir Berisha (SWE)	06.06.1996	13	(5)	2
Valgeir Friðriksson	24.09.2001	8	(3)	
Þórir Guðjónsson	07.04.1991	17	(3)	3
Ingibergur Kort Sigurðsson	27.04.1998		(1)	
Trainer:	**DOB**	**M**		
Ólafur Snorrason	22.04.1982	22		

Íþróttafélagið Fylkir Reykjavík

Founded: 28.05.1967
Stadium: Floridana völlurinn, Reykjavík (5,000)

Goalkeepers:	DOB	M	(s)	G
Aron Snær Friðriksson	29.01.1997	22		
Defenders:	**DOB**	**M**	**(s)**	**G**
Ásgeir Eyþórsson	29.04.1993	13	(1)	1
Valdimar Þór Ingimundarson	28.04.1999	9	(6)	2
Andrés Jóhannesson	21.12.1988	11	(3)	
Hákon Ingi Jónsson	10.11.1995	11	(6)	4
Midfielders:	**DOB**	**M**	**(s)**	**G**
Davíð Þór Ásbjörnsson	24.02.1992	7	(2)	1
Ásgeir Ásgeirsson	16.04.1987	17	(3)	
Emil Ásmundsson	08.01.1995	19		4
Elís Rafn Björnsson	13.10.1992	5	(4)	
Helgi Daníelsson	13.07.1981	7	(6)	
Oddur Guðmundsson	28.01.1989	9	(7)	1
Ari Leifsson	19.04.1998	22		
Daði Ólafsson	05.01.1994	17	(1)	4
Ólafur Ingi Skúlason	01.04.1983	8		
Orri Sveinn Stefánsson	20.02.1996	15	(1)	1
Forwards:	**DOB**	**M**	**(s)**	**G**
Ásgeir Örn Arnþórsson	02.05.1990	6	(5)	
Arnar Björgvinsson	10.02.1990	1	(4)	
Jonathan Ricardo Glenn (TRI)	27.08.1987	7	(6)	6
Albert Ingason	16.01.1986	21	(1)	5
Andri Jónsson	24.02.1991	2	(1)	
Ragnar Sveinsson	18.12.1994	13	(5)	2
Trainer:	**DOB**	**M**		
Helgi Sigurðsson	17.09.1974	22		

Ungmennafélag Grindavíkur

Founded: 1935
Stadium: Grindavíkurvöllur, Grindavík (1,750)

Goalkeepers:	DOB	M	(s)	G
Kristijan Jajalo (BIH)	04.03.1993	20		
Maciej Majewski (POL)	24.01.1989	2		
Defenders:	**DOB**	**M**	**(s)**	**G**
Björn Bryde	08.07.1992	21		2
Matthías Friðriksson	09.06.1986	10	(6)	
Jóhann Hannesson	21.04.1990	5	(7)	
Jón Ingason	21.09.1995	6	(1)	
Sigurjón Rúnarsson	02.10.2000	11	(2)	
Elias Alexander Tamburini (FIN)	01.02.1995	10		
Midfielders:	**DOB**	**M**	**(s)**	**G**
Brynjar Ásgeir Guðmundsson	22.06.1992	11	(2)	
Marinó Axel Helgason	04.01.1997	10	(3)	
Sam Hewson (ENG)	28.11.1988	21		5
René Joensen (FRO)	08.02.1993	19	(1)	2
Aron Jóhannsson	11.01.1994	15	(5)	4
Juan Manuel Ortíz Jiménez „Juanma" (ESP)	28.05.1986		(3)	
Nemanja Latinovic	10.10.1995	9	(6)	1
Rodrigo Gomes Mateo „Rodri" (ESP)	09.02.1989	20		1
José Enrique Seoane Vergara (ESP)	16.03.1989	14	(4)	4
Simon Smidt (DEN)	26.10.1990		(1)	
Alexander Þórarinsson	14.12.1988	7	(9)	2
Gunnar Þorsteinsson	01.02.1994	19		
Forwards:	**DOB**	**M**	**(s)**	**G**
William Daniels (USA)	17.11.1990	12	(7)	5
Dagur Gunnarsson	02.07.2000		(4)	
Trainer:	**DOB**	**M**		
Óli Stefán Flóventsson	07.12.1975	22		

Íþróttabandalag Vestmannaeyja

Founded: 1903
Stadium: Hásteinsvöllur, Vestmannaeyjar (3,034)

Goalkeepers:	DOB	M	(s)	G
Derby Carrillo (USA)	19.09.1987	6		
Halldór Geirsson	21.07.1994	16		
Defenders:	**DOB**	**M**	**(s)**	**G**
David Atkinson (ENG)	27.04.1993	16		
Diogo Manuel Gonçalves Coelho (POR)	08.07.1992	7	(1)	
Yvan Erichot (FRA)	25.03.1990	17		
Felix Örn Friðriksson	16.03.1999	12		1
Alfreð Már Hjaltalín	26.06.1994	14	(2)	
Sigurður Arnar Magnússon	30.06.1999	16	(1)	2
Midfielders:	**DOB**	**M**	**(s)**	**G**
Ásgeir Elíasson	29.04.1998	1	(3)	
Róbert Eysteinsson	17.06.1999	1	(2)	
Priestley Griffiths (ENG)	11.06.1996	13	(4)	
Dagur Hilmarsson	02.06.1998	12	(2)	
Sindri Snær Magnússon	18.02.1992	22		6
Breki Ómarsson	10.08.1998	1	(7)	
Eyþór Orri Ómarsson	08.07.2003		(4)	
Forwards:	**DOB**	**M**	**(s)**	**G**
Atli Arnarson	29.11.1993	16	(3)	1
Sigurður Benónýsson	27.08.1996	4	(4)	1
Ágúst Björnsson	05.08.1997	1	(7)	1
Jonathan Franks (ENG)	06.04.1990	11	(6)	1
Guy Gnabouyou (FRA)	01.12.1989	3	(5)	
Devon Már Griffin	23.04.1997	2		
Kaj Leo í Bartalsstovu (FRO)	23.06.1991	22		2
Shahab Zahedi Tabar (IRN)	18.08.1995	9	(5)	4
Gunnar Þorvaldsson	01.04.1982	17	(1)	9
Víðir Þorvarðarson	07.07.1992	3	(4)	1
Trainer:	**DOB**	**M**		
Kristján Guðmundsson	03.02.1965	22		

Knattspyrnufélag Akureyrar

Founded: 1928
Stadium: Akureyrarvöllur, Akureyri (1,770)

Goalkeepers:	DOB	M	(s)	G
Aron Elí Gíslason	16.04.1998	10		
Cristian Martinez Liberato (ESP)	02.05.1989	12		
Defenders:	**DOB**	**M**	**(s)**	**G**
Bjarni Antonsson	27.12.1995	21	(1)	1
Birgir Baldvinsson	10.01.2001		(1)	
Milan Joksimović (SRB)	09.02.1990	16		
Hallgrímur Jónasson	04.05.1986	13	(1)	1
Hjörvar Sigurgeirsson	13.03.1998	2	(8)	
Hrannar Björn Steingrímsson	19.06.1992	21		
Guðmann Þórisson	30.01.1987	8	(1)	
Midfielders:	**DOB**	**M**	**(s)**	**G**
Frosti Brynjólfsson	16.04.2000	1	(4)	
Patrekur Hafliði Búason	04.04.1999		(1)	
Ýmir Már Geirsson	11.11.1997	1	(10)	1
Daníel Hafsteinsson	12.11.1999	18	(2)	3
Viktor Már Heiðarsson	27.06.1999		(1)	
Archange Nkumu (ENG)	05.11.1993	7	(10)	1
Ólafur Aron Pétursson	17.07.1995		(6)	
Hallgrímur Mar Steingrímsson	02.10.1990	22		5
Aleksandar Trninić (SRB)	27.03.1987	18	(1)	3
Callum Williams (ENG)	08.11.1994	17	(2)	3
Steinþór Þorsteinsson	29.07.1985	10	(4)	1
Forwards:	**DOB**	**M**	**(s)**	**G**
Elfar Aðalsteinsson	12.08.1990	19	(2)	5
Sæþór Olgeirsson	06.04.1998		(4)	
Ásgeir Sigurgeirsson	11.12.1996	19		10
Áki Sölvason	18.03.1999	1	(1)	
Vladimir Tufegdžić (SRB)	12.06.1991	6	(2)	
Trainer:	**DOB**	**M**		
Srdjan Tufegdzić (SRB)	06.04.1980	22		

Knattspyrnudeild Keflavík

Founded: 1929
Stadium: Keflavíkurvöllur, Keflavík (5,200)

Goalkeepers:	DOB	M	(s)	G
Jonathan Faerber (AUS)	15.03.1988	3		
Sindri Kristinn Ólafsson	19.01.1997	19		
Defenders:	**DOB**	**M**	**(s)**	**G**
Aron Kári Aðalsteinsson	09.07.1999	8		
Anton Freyr Guðlaugsson	17.02.1997	12	(2)	
Sindri Þór Guðmundsson	11.08.1997	20		1
Atli Geir Gunnarsson	22.06.2000	1	(1)	
Marc McAusland (SCO)	13.08.1988	19		1
Marko Nikolic (SRB)	09.01.1986	7		
Ísak Óli Olafsson	30.06.2000	22		1
Midfielders:	**DOB**	**M**	**(s)**	**G**
Ivan Aleksić (CRO)	06.03.1993	2	(3)	
Einar Einarsson	28.10.1989	9	(1)	
Sigurbergur Elísson	10.06.1992	4	(2)	
Frans Elvarsson	14.08.1990	21	(1)	2
Juraj Grizelj (CRO)	03.05.1986	4	(2)	
Ingimundur Aron Guðnason	29.03.1999	2	(4)	
Bojan Ljubicic	22.06.1992	2	(1)	
Aron Róbertsson	24.04.1996	4	(8)	
Hólmar Rúnarsson	10.12.1981	22		2
Rúnar Þór Sigurgeirsson	28.12.1999	1	(3)	
Leonard Sigurðsson	30.04.1996	9	(8)	
Dagur Þórhallsson	02.05.2000	12	(4)	1
Forwards:	**DOB**	**M**	**(s)**	**G**
Ágúst Leó Björnsson	05.08.1997	2	(1)	
Jeppe Løkkegaard Hansen (DEN)	10.02.1989	10		
Davíð Jóhannsson	15.06.2002	3	(7)	
Helgi Þór Jónsson	01.03.1994		(5)	1
Tómas Óskarsson	16.06.1998	2	(2)	
Lasse Rise (DEN)	09.06.1986	11	(4)	1
Adam Árni Róbertsson	12.01.1999	11	(4)	
Trainer:	**DOB**	**M**		
Guðlaugur Baldursson	08.07.1972	11		
Eysteinn Hauksson Kjerúlf [11.07.2018]	12.08.1974	11		

Knattspyrnufélag Reykjavíkur

Founded: 16.02.1899
Stadium: Alvogenvöllurinn, Reykjavík (3,333)

Goalkeepers:	DOB	M	(s)	G
Sindri Jensson	12.08.1986	1		
Beitir Ólafsson	02.07.1986	21		
Defenders:	**DOB**	**M**	**(s)**	**G**
Arnór Aðalsteinsson	26.01.1986	12	(1)	
Skúli Jón Friðgeirsson	30.07.1988	14		
Gunnar Gunnarsson	04.10.1985	9	(2)	
Kristinn Jónsson	04.08.1990	21		
Aron Jósepsson	21.11.1989	17	(2)	
Hjalti Sigurðsson	19.09.2000		(3)	
Albert Watson (NIR)	08.09.1985	13	(1)	
Midfielders:	**DOB**	**M**	**(s)**	**G**
Morten Beck (DEN)	06.12.1994	12		
Þorsteinn Örn Bernharðsson	19.08.1999		(1)	
Óskar Hauksson	22.08.1984	22		3
Finnur Margeirsson	08.03.1991	21		1
Adolf Mtasingwa Bitegeko (TAN)	26.12.1998		(2)	
Pálmi Pálmason	09.11.1984	22		11
Pablo Punyed (SLV)	18.04.1990	8	(12)	1
Atli Sigurjónsson	01.07.1991	4	(14)	3
Björgvin Stefánsson	20.12.1994	14	(5)	5
Forwards:	**DOB**	**M**	**(s)**	**G**
André Bjerregaard (DEN)	03.09.1991	12	(4)	4
Kennie Knak Chopart (DEN)	01.06.1990	19	(2)	7
Stefán Árni Geirsson	06.11.2000		(1)	
Tryggvi Snær Geirsson	11.06.2000		(1)	
Trainer:	**DOB**	**M**		
Rúnar Kristinsson	05.09.1969	22		

Ungmennafélagið Stjarnan Garðabær

Founded: 1960
Stadium: Samsung völlurinn, Garðabær (2,300)

Goalkeepers:	DOB	M	(s)	G
Haraldur Björnsson	11.01.1989	22		
Terrance Dieterich (USA)	30.03.1987		(1)	
Defenders:	**DOB**	**M**	**(s)**	**G**
Hörður Árnason	19.05.1989	1	(1)	
Heiðar Ægisson	10.08.1995	11		
Brynjar Guðjónsson	27.02.1992	21	(1)	1
Jósef Kristinn Jósefsson	12.09.1989	8	(2)	
Daníel Laxdal	22.09.1986	21		
Jóhann Laxdal	27.01.1990	7	(2)	
Þórarinn Valdimarsson	23.04.1990	18	(1)	1
Midfielders:	**DOB**	**M**	**(s)**	**G**
Sölvi Guðbjargarson	25.07.2001		(10)	1
Óttar Bjarni Guðmundsson	15.04.1990	4	(5)	
Guðmundur Hafsteinsson	14.06.1989	9	(8)	7
Alex Þór Hauksson	26.11.1999	17	(1)	
Eyjólfur Héðinsson	01.01.1985	15	(3)	2
Ævar Jóhannesson	31.01.1995	5	(9)	1
Þorsteinn Már Ragnarsson	19.04.1990	19	(2)	5
Þorri Geir Rúnarsson	24.04.1995	2	(8)	
Baldur Sigurðsson	24.04.1985	19	(1)	5
Forwards:	**DOB**	**M**	**(s)**	**G**
Guðjón Baldvinsson	15.02.1986	21		5
Hilmar Árni Halldórsson	14.02.1992	22		16
Trainer:	**DOB**	**M**		
Rúnar Sigmundsson	05.05.1974	22		

Knattspyrnufélagið Valur Reykjavík

Founded: 11.05.1911
Stadium: Valsvöllur, Reykjavík (2,465)

Goalkeepers:	DOB	M	(s)	G
Anton Ari Einarsson	25.08.1994	22		
Defenders:	**DOB**	**M**	**(s)**	**G**
Rasmus Christiansen (DEN)	06.10.1989	6	(2)	
Bjarni Eiríksson	28.03.1982	20		
Sebastian Starke Hedlund (SWE)	05.04.1995	10		
Sigurður Lárusson	22.01.1992	15	(3)	3
Birkir Sævarsson	11.11.1984	18		2
Eiður Sigurbjörnsson	26.02.1990	20		
Midfielders:	**DOB**	**M**	**(s)**	**G**
Sindri Björnsson	29.03.1995	3	(4)	
Ólafur Finsen	30.03.1992	3	(8)	2
Kristinn Halldórsson	08.04.1989	5	(11)	2
Einar Karl Ingvarsson	08.10.1993	14	(4)	2
Guðjón Lýðsson	28.12.1987	7	(10)	3
Haukur Sigurðsson	05.08.1987	19		3
Kristinn Sigurðsson	25.12.1991	20	(1)	6
Andri Stefánsson	22.04.1991		(2)	
Forwards:	**DOB**	**M**	**(s)**	**G**
Dion Jeremy Acoff (USA)	23.09.1991	12		4
Andri Adolphsson	01.12.1992	12	(2)	2
Arnar Geirsson	30.08.1991	4	(1)	
Ívar Jónsson	02.02.1994	7	(3)	1
Patrick Pedersen (DEN)	25.11.1991	21		17
Tobias Thomsen (DEN)	19.10.1992	4	(10)	1
Trainer:	**DOB**	**M**		
Ólafur Jóhannesson	30.06.1957	22		

Knattspyrnufélagið Víkingur Reykjavík

Founded: 21.04.1908
Stadium: Víkin, Reykjavík (1,613)

Goalkeepers:	DOB	M	(s)	G
Emil Andri Auðunsson	15.05.2000		(1)	
Andreas Larsen (DEN)	22.05.1990	20		
Aris Vaporakis (DEN)	06.01.1995	2		
Defenders:	**DOB**	**M**	**(s)**	**G**
Aron Brynjarsson	04.11.1998	4	(3)	
Gunnlaugur Guðmundsson	17.07.1994	11	(7)	1
Sölvi Ottesen	18.02.1984	12	(1)	
Jørgen Richardsen (NOR)	28.09.1988	16	(1)	
Sindri Scheving	19.11.1997	5	(6)	
Midfielders:	**DOB**	**M**	**(s)**	**G**
Erlingur Agnarsson	05.03.1998	7	(6)	1
Atli Hrafn Andrason	04.01.1999	5	(6)	
Alex Freyr Hilmarsson	26.07.1993	19	(1)	3
Arnþór Ingi Kristinsson	15.03.1990	18		4
Miloš Ozegovič (SRB)	11.05.1992	13	(1)	
Bjarni Páll Runólfsson	10.09.1996	11	(7)	2
Halldór Sigurðsson	04.10.1988	20		
Logi Tómasson	13.09.2000	1	(2)	
Forwards:	**DOB**	**M**	**(s)**	**G**
Viktor Örlygur Andrason	05.02.2000		(2)	
Davíð Atlason	18.08.1994	20		1
Gunnlaugur Birgisson	04.06.1995	5	(6)	
Geoffrey Castillion (NED)	25.05.1991	8		6
Örvar Eggertsson	28.02.1999	2	(12)	1
Nikolaj Andreas Hansen (DEN)	15.03.1993	18	(2)	6
Rick ten Voorde (NED)	20.06.1991	18		4
Vladimir Tufegdžić (SRB)	12.06.1991	7		
Trainer:	**DOB**	**M**		
Logi Ólafsson	14.11.1954	22		

SECOND LEVEL
1. deild karla 2018

1.	ÍA Akranes (*Promoted*)	22	14	6	2	42 - 16	48
2.	HK Kópavogur (*Promoted*)	22	14	6	2	38 - 13	48
3.	Þór Akureyri	22	13	4	5	46 - 37	43
4.	Víkingur Ólafsvík	22	12	6	4	38 - 22	42
5.	Þróttur Reykjavík	22	11	3	8	52 - 40	36
6.	UMF Njarðvík	22	7	6	9	24 - 34	27
7.	Leiknir Reykjavík	22	7	4	11	23 - 29	25
8.	Haukar Hafnarfjörður	22	7	4	11	33 - 45	25
9.	Fram Reykjavík	22	6	6	10	37 - 38	24
10.	IF Magni Grenivík	22	6	1	15	27 - 48	19
11.	ÍR Reykjavík (*Relegated*)	22	5	3	14	23 - 48	18
12.	UMF Selfoss (*Relegated*)	22	4	3	15	35 - 48	15

NATIONAL TEAM

INTERNATIONAL MATCHES
(16.07.2018 – 15.07.2019)

08.09.2018	St. Gallen	Switzerland - Iceland	6-0(2-0)	(UNL)
11.09.2018	Reykjavík	Iceland - Belgium	0-3(0-2)	(UNL)
11.10.2018	Guingamp	France - Iceland	2-2(0-1)	(F)
15.10.2018	Reykjavík	Iceland - Switzerland	1-2(0-1)	(UNL)
15.11.2018	Bruxelles	Belgium - Iceland	2-0(0-0)	(UNL)
19.11.2018	Eupen	Qatar - Iceland	2-2(1-1)	(F)
11.01.2019	Doha	Iceland - Sweden	2-2(1-1)	(F)
15.01.2019	Doha	Estonia - Iceland	0-0	(F)
22.03.2019	Andorra la Vella	Andorra - Iceland	0-2(0-1)	(ECQ)
25.03.2019	Paris	France - Iceland	4-0(1-0)	(ECQ)
08.06.2019	Reykjavík	Iceland - Albania	1-0(1-0)	(ECQ)
11.06.2019	Reykjavík	Iceland - Turkey	2-1(2-1)	(ECQ)

08.09.2018 SWITZERLAND - ICELAND 6-0(2-0) UEFA Nations League A, Group 2
Kybunpark, St. Gallen; Referee: Michael Oliver (England); Attendance: 14,912
ISL: Hannes Þór Halldórsson, Ragnar Sigurðsson, Birkir Már Sævarsson, Ari Skúlason, Sverrir Ingi Ingason, Birkir Bjarnason (65.Theódór Elmar Bjarnason), Gylfi Þór Sigurðsson (Cap), Guðlaugur Victor Pálsson, Rúrik Gíslason (74.Rúnar Sigurjónsson), Björn Bergmann Sigurðarson (60.Viðar Örn Kjartansson), Jón Daði Böðvarsson. Trainer: Erik Anders Hamrén (Sweden).

11.09.2018 ICELAND - BELGIUM 0-3(0-2) UEFA Nations League A, Group 2
Laugardalsvöllur, Reykjavík; Referee: Sergei Karasev (Russia); Attendance: 9,710
ISL: Hannes Þór Halldórsson, Ragnar Sigurðsson, Birkir Már Sævarsson, Ari Skúlason (80.Guðlaugur Victor Pálsson), Hörður Björgvin Magnússon, Sverrir Ingi Ingason, Birkir Bjarnason, Emil Hallfreðsson (84.Arnór Ingvi Traustason), Rúnar Sigurjónsson, Gylfi Þór Sigurðsson (Cap), Jón Daði Böðvarsson (71.Kolbeinn Sigþórsson). Trainer: Erik Anders Hamrén (Sweden).

11.10.2018 FRANCE - ICELAND 2-2(0-1) Friendly International
Stade de Roudourou, Guingamp; Referee: Tiago Bruno Lopes Martins (Portugal); Attendance: 17,000
ISL: Rúnar Alex Rúnarsson (46.Hannes Þór Halldórsson), Ragnar Sigurðsson, Birkir Már Sævarsson (81.Jón Guðni Fjóluson), Hólmar Örn Eyjólfsson, Birkir Bjarnason, Kári Árnason, Jóhann Berg Guðmundsson (71.Guðlaugur Victor Pálsson), Rúnar Sigurjónsson, Arnór Ingvi Traustason (59.Kolbeinn Sigþórsson), Alfreð Finnbogason (46.Albert Gudmundsson), Gylfi Þór Sigurðsson (Cap) (80.Rúrik Gíslason). Trainer: Erik Anders Hamrén (Sweden).
Goals: Birkir Bjarnason (30), Kári Árnason (58).

15.10.2018 ICELAND - SWITZERLAND 1-2(0-1) UEFA Nations League A, Group 2
Laugardalsvöllur, Reykjavík; Referee: Andreas Ekberg (Sweden); Attendance: 8,663
ISL: Hannes Þór Halldórsson, Ragnar Sigurðsson, Hólmar Örn Eyjólfsson, Hörður Björgvin Magnússon, Birkir Bjarnason, Kári Árnason, Jóhann Berg Guðmundsson, Rúnar Sigurjónsson (84.Albert Gudmundsson), Gylfi Þór Sigurðsson (Cap), Arnór Ingvi Traustason (68.Rúrik Gíslason), Alfreð Finnbogason. Trainer: Erik Anders Hamrén (Sweden).
Goal: Alfreð Finnbogason (81).

15.11.2018 BELGIUM - ICELAND 2-0(0-0) UEFA Nations League A, Group 2
Stade "Roi Baudouin", Bruxelles; Referee: Orel Grinfeld (Israel); Attendance: 28,891
ISL: Hannes Þór Halldórsson, Jón Guðni Fjóluson, Ari Skúlason, Hörður Björgvin Magnússon, Sverrir Ingi Ingason, Kári Árnason, Aron Einar Gunnarsson (Cap), Guðlaugur Victor Pálsson, Arnór Ingvi Traustason, Arnór Sigurðsson (64.Kolbeinn Sigþórsson), Albert Gudmundsson (87.Jón Dagur Thorsteinsson). Trainer: Erik Anders Hamrén (Sweden).

19.11.2018 QATAR - ICELAND 2-2(1-1) Friendly International
Kehrwegstadion, Eupen (Belgium); Referee: Paulus Hendrikus Martinus "Pol" van Boekel (Netherlands); Attendance: 2,830
ISL: Rúnar Alex Rúnarsson, Ari Skúlason, Hörður Björgvin Magnússon, Sverrir Ingi Ingason, Kári Árnason (Cap) (35.Hjörtur Hermannsson), Eggert Gunnþór Jónsson (62.Guðlaugur Victor Pálsson), Arnór Ingvi Traustason, Arnór Sigurðsson (74.Samúel Kári Friðjónsson), Rúrik Gíslason (75.Birkir Már Sævarsson), Kolbeinn Sigþórsson (62.Andri Rúnar Bjarnason), Albert Gudmundsson. Trainer: Erik Anders Hamrén (Sweden).
Goals: Saad Abdullah Al Sheeb (29 own goal), Kolbeinn Sigþórsson (56 penalty).

11.01.2019 ICELAND - SWEDEN 2-2(1-1) Friendly International
Khalifa International Stadium, Doha (Qatar); Referee: Mohammed Ahmed Al Shammari (Qatar); Attendance: 187
ISL: Frederik Schram, Birkir Már Sævarsson (Cap), Eiður Aron Sigurbjörnsson (70.Axel Óskar Andrésson), Hjörtur Hermannsson, Böðvar Böðvarsson, Eggert Gunnþór Jónsson (67.Aron Elís Þrándarson), Guðmundur Thórarinsson (78.Kolbeinn Birgir Finnsson), Samúel Kári Friðjónsson, Arnór Smárason (67.Hilmar Árni Halldórsson), Andri Rúnar Bjarnason (57.Jón Dagur Thorsteinsson), Óttar Magnús Karlsson. Trainer: Erik Anders Hamrén (Sweden).
Goals: Óttar Magnús Karlsson (6), Jón Dagur Thorsteinsson (90).

15.01.2019 ESTONIA - ICELAND 0-0 Friendly International
„Sheikh Jassim Bin Hamad" Stadium, Doha (Qatar); Referee: Abdulla Ali Al Athba Al Marri (Qatar); Attendance: 35
ISL: Ingvar Jónsson (80.Anton Ari Einarsson), Birkir Már Sævarsson (Cap), Hjörtur Hermannsson, Axel Óskar Andrésson, Davíð Kristján Ólafsson, Guðmundur Thórarinsson (46.Samúel Kári Friðjónsson), Aron Elís Þrándarson (69.Alex Þór Hauksson), Jón Dagur Thorsteinsson (69.Willum Þór Willumsson), Kolbeinn Birgir Finnsson, Hilmar Árni Halldórsson (46.Arnór Smárason), Óttar Magnús Karlsson (46.Andri Rúnar Bjarnason). Trainer: Erik Anders Hamrén (Sweden).

22.03.2019 ANDORRA - ICELAND 0-2(0-1) 16th EC. Qualifiers
Estadi Nacional, Andorra la Vella; Referee: Sandro Schärer (Switzerland); Attendance: 1,854
ISL: Hannes Þór Halldórsson, Ragnar Sigurðsson, Birkir Már Sævarsson, Ari Skúlason, Birkir Bjarnason, Kári Árnason, Aron Einar Gunnarsson (Cap) (63.Rúnar Sigurjónsson), Jóhann Berg Guðmundsson (83.Arnór Ingvi Traustason), Gylfi Þór Sigurðsson, Arnór Sigurðsson, Alfreð Finnbogason (70.Viðar Örn Kjartansson). Trainer: Erik Anders Hamrén (Sweden).
Goals: Birkir Bjarnason (22), Viðar Örn Kjartansson (80).

25.03.2019 **FRANCE - ICELAND** **4-0(1-0)** 16th EC. Qualifiers

Stade de France, Saint-Denis, Paris; Referee: István Kovács (Romania); Attendance: 64,538

ISL: Hannes Þór Halldórsson, Ragnar Sigurðsson, Birkir Már Sævarsson (84.Ari Skúlason), Hörður Björgvin Magnússon, Sverrir Ingi Ingason, Birkir Bjarnason, Kári Árnason, Aron Einar Gunnarsson (Cap), Rúnar Sigurjónsson (57.Arnór Ingvi Traustason), Gylfi Þór Sigurðsson, Albert Gudmundsson (62.Alfreð Finnbogason). Trainer: Erik Anders Hamrén (Sweden).

08.06.2019 **ICELAND - ALBANIA** **1-0(1-0)** 16th EC. Qualifiers

Laugardalsvöllur, Reykjavík; Referee: Robert Madden (Scotland); Attendance: 8,968

ISL: Hannes Þór Halldórsson, Ragnar Sigurðsson, Ari Skúlason, Hjörtur Hermannsson, Birkir Bjarnason, Kári Árnason, Aron Einar Gunnarsson (Cap), Jóhann Berg Guðmundsson (56.Arnór Ingvi Traustason), Rúnar Sigurjónsson (81.Arnór Sigurðsson), Gylfi Þór Sigurðsson, Viðar Örn Kjartansson (63.Kolbeinn Sigþórsson). Trainer: Erik Anders Hamrén (Sweden).

Goal: Jóhann Berg Guðmundsson (22).

11.06.2019 **ICELAND - TURKEY** **2-1(2-1)** 16th EC. Qualifiers

Laugardalsvöllur, Reykjavík; Referee: Szymon Marciniak (Poland); Attendance: 9,680

ISL: Hannes Þór Halldórsson, Ragnar Sigurðsson, Ari Skúlason 69.69.Hörður Björgvin Magnússon), Hjörtur Hermannsson, Birkir Bjarnason, Kári Árnason, Emil Hallfreðsson, Aron Einar Gunnarsson (Cap), Jóhann Berg Guðmundsson (80.Arnór Ingvi Traustason), Gylfi Þór Sigurðsson, Jón Daði Böðvarsson (64.Kolbeinn Sigþórsson). Trainer: Erik Anders Hamrén (Sweden).

Goals: Ragnar Sigurðsson (21, 32).

NATIONAL TEAM PLAYERS
(16.07.2018 – 15.07.2019)

Name	DOB	Caps	Goals	2018/2019:	*Club*
			Goalkeepers		
Anton Ari EINARSSON	25.08.1994	**2**	**0**	2019:	*Valur Reykjavík*
Hannes Þór HALLDÓRSSON	27.04.1984	**61**	**0**	2018/2019: 09.04.2019->	*Qarabağ FK Bakı (AZE)* *Valur Reykjavík*
Ingvar JÓNSSON	18.10.1989	**8**	**0**	2018/2019:	*Viborg FF (DEN)*
Rúnar Alex RÚNARSSON	18.02.1995	**5**	**0**	2018/2019:	*FC Nordsjælland Farum (DEN)*
Frederik August Albrecht SCHRAM	19.01.1995	**5**	**0**	2019:	*FC Roskilde (DEN)*
			Defenders		
Axel Óskar ANDRÉSSON	27.01.1998	**2**	**0**	2019:	*Viking FK Stavanger (NOR)*
Kári ÁRNASON	13.10.1982	**77**	**6**	2018/2019:	*Gençlerbirliği SK Ankara (TUR)*
Böðvar BÖÐVARSSON	09.04.1995	**5**	**0**	2019:	*Jagiellonia Białystok (POL)*
Hólmar Örn EYJÓLFSSON	06.08.1990	**12**	**1**	2018:	*PFC Levski Sofia (BUL)*
Jón Guðni FJÓLUSON	10.04.1989	**15**	**1**	2018/2019:	*FK Krasnodar (RUS)*
Samúel Kári FRIÐJÓNSSON	22.02.1996	**7**	**0**	2018/2019:	*Vålerenga Fotball Oslo (NOR)*
Hjörtur HERMANNSSON	08.02.1995	**12**	**1**	2018/2019:	*Brøndby IF (DEN)*
Sverrir Ingi INGASON	05.05.1993	**27**	**3**	2018: 31.01.2019->	*FK Rostov (RUS)* *PAOK Thessaloníki (GRE)*
Hörður Björgvin MAGNÚSSON	11.02.1993	**25**	**2**	2018/2019:	*FK CSKA Moskva (RUS)*
Davíð Kristján ÓLAFSSON	15.05.1995	**1**	**0**	2019:	*Breiðablik Kópavogur*
Eiður Aron SIGURBJÖRNSSON	26.02.1990	**1**	**0**	2019:	*Valur Reykjavík*
Ragnar SIGURÐSSON	19.06.1986	**88**	**5**	2018/2019:	*FK Rostov (RUS)*
Ari Freyr SKÚLASON	14.05.1987	**66**	**0**	2018/2019:	*KSC Lokeren (BEL)*
Birkir Már SÆVARSSON	11.11.1984	**90**	**1**	2018/2019:	*Valur Reykjavík*
			Midfielders		
Birkir BJARNASON	27.05.1988	**78**	**11**	2018/2019:	*Aston Villa FC Birmingham (ENG)*
Theódór Elmar BJARNASON	04.03.1987	**41**	**0**	2018:	*Sanica Boru Elazığspor (TUR)*
Kolbeinn Birgir FINNSSON	25.08.1999	**2**	**0**	2019:	*Brentford FC London (ENG)*
Rúrik GÍSLASON	25.02.1988	**53**	**3**	2018:	*SV Sandhausen (GER)*
Jóhann Berg GUÐMUNDSSON	27.10.1990	**74**	**7**	2018/2019:	*Burnley FC (ENG)*
Aron Einar GUNNARSSON	22.04.1989	**85**	**2**	2018/2019:	*Cardiff City FC (WAL)*
Hilmar Árni HALLDÓRSSON	14.02.1992	**4**	**0**	2019:	*Stjarnan Garðabær*
Emil HALLFREÐSSON	29.06.1984	**68**	**1**	2018: 03.01.2019->	*Frosinone Calcio (ITA);22.01.2019->unattached* *Udinese Calcio (ITA)*
Alex Þór HAUKSSON	26.11.1999	**1**	**0**	2019:	*Stjarnan Garðabær*
Eggert Gunnþór JÓNSSON	18.08.1988	**21**	**0**	2018/2019:	*Sønderjysk Elitesport (DEN)*
Guðlaugur Victor PÁLSSON	30.04.1991	**11**	**0**	2018:	*FC Zürich (SUI)*
Arnór SIGURÐSSON	15.05.1999	**4**	**0**	2018/2019:	*FK CSKA Moskva (RUS)*
Gylfi Þór SIGURÐSSON	08.09.1989	**68**	**20**	2018/2019:	*Everton FC Liverpool (ENG)*
Rúnar Már SIGURJÓNSSON	18.06.1990	**22**	**1**	2018/2019:	*Grasshopper Club Zürich (SUI)*
Arnór SMÁRASON	07.09.1988	**26**	**3**	2019:	*Lillestrøm SK (NOR)*

Jón Dagur THORSTEINSSON	26.11.1998	**3**	**1**	2018/2019:	*Vendsyssel FF Hjørring (DEN)*
Guðmundur THÓRARINSSON	15.04.1992	**5**	**0**	2019:	*IFK Nörrköping (SWE)*
Arnór Ingvi TRAUSTASON	30.04.1993	**28**	**5**	2018/2019:	*Malmö FF (SWE)*
Willum Þór WILLUMSSON	23.10.1998	**1**	**0**	2019:	*Breiðablik Kópavogur*
Aron Elís ÞRÁNDARSON	10.11.1994	**4**	**0**	2019:	*Aalesunds FK (NOR)*

Forwards

Andri Rúnar BJARNASON	12.11.1990	**5**	**1**	2018/2019:	*Helsingborgs IF*
Jón Daði BÖÐVARSSON	25.05.1992	**42**	**2**	2018/2019:	*Reading FC (ENG)*
Alfreð FINNBOGASON	01.02.1989	**54**	**14**	2018/2019:	*FC Augsburg (GER)*
Albert GUÐMUNDSSON	15.06.1997	**11**	**3**	2018/2019:	*AZ Alkmaar (NED)*
Óttar Magnús KARLSSON	21.02.1997	**7**	**2**	2019:	*Mjällby AIF Hällevik (SWE)*
Viðar Örn KJARTANSSON	11.03.1990	**18**	**2**	2018: 18.03.2019->	*FK Rostov (RUS)* *Hammarby IF Stockholm (SWE)*
Björn Bergmann SIGURÐARSON	26.02.1991	**17**	**1**	2018:	*FK Rostov (RUS)*
Kolbeinn SIGÞÓRSSON	14.03.1990	**50**	**23**	2018: 31.03.2019->	*FC Nantes (FRA)* *AIK Stockholm (SWE)*

National team coach

Erik Anders HAMRÉN (Sweden) [from 08.08.2018]	27.06.1957	12 M; 3 W; 4 D; 5 L; 12-24

ISRAEL

The Country:

מְדִינַת יִשְׂרָאֵל (State of Israel)
Capital: Jerusalem
Surface: 20,770–22,072 km²
Inhabitants: 9,085,970 [2019]
Time: UTC+2

The FA:

Israel Football Association
Ramat Gan Stadium 299, Aba Hilell Street, P.O. Box 3591, 52134 Ramat Gan, Tel Aviv
Tel: +972 3 617 1500
Foundation date: 18.07.1928
Member of FIFA since: 1929
Member of UEFA since: 1994
Website: www.football.org.il

NATIONAL TEAM RECORDS

First international match:	16.03.1934, Cairo: Egypt – Palestina 7-1	
Most international caps:	Yosef Shay Benayoun	- 102 caps (1998-2017)
Most international goals:	Mordechai Spiegler	- 83 goals / 32 caps (1963-1977)

UEFA EUROPEAN CHAMPIONSHIP	
1960	-
1964	-
1968	-
1972	-
1976	-
1980	-
1984	-
1988	-
1992	-
1996	Qualifiers
2000	Qualifiers
2004	Qualifiers
2008	Qualifiers
2012	Qualifiers
2016	Qualifiers

FIFA WORLD CUP	
1930	Did not enter
1934	Qualifiers
1938	Qualifiers
1950	Qualifiers
1954	Qualifiers
1958	Qualifiers
1962	Qualifiers
1966	Qualifiers
1970	Final Tournament (Group Stage)
1974	Qualifiers
1978	Qualifiers
1982	Qualifiers
1986	Qualifiers
1990	Qualifiers
1994	Qualifiers
1998	Qualifiers
2002	Qualifiers
2006	Qualifiers
2010	Qualifiers
2014	Qualifiers
2018	Qualifiers

UEFA NATIONS LEAGUE
2018/2019 – League C (promoted to League B)

OLYMPIC FOOTBALL TOURNAMENTS 1908-2016							
1908	-	**1948**	-	**1972**	Qualifiers	**1996**	Qualifiers
1912	-	**1952**	Qualifiers	**1976**	FT/Quarter-Finals	**2000**	Qualifiers
1920	-	**1956**	Qualifiers	**1980**	*Withdrew*	**2004**	Qualifiers
1924	-	**1960**	Qualifiers	**1984**	Qualifiers	**2008**	Qualifiers
1928	-	**1964**	Qualifiers	**1988**	Qualifiers	**2012**	Qualifiers
1936	-	**1968**	FT/Quarter-Finals	**1992**	Qualifiers	**2016**	Qualifiers

FIFA CONFEDERATIONS CUP 1992-2017
None

ISRAELI CLUB HONOURS IN EUROPEAN CLUB COMPETITIONS:

European Champion Clubs' Cup (1956-1992) / UEFA Champions League (1993-2019)
None
Fairs Cup (1858-1971) / UEFA Cup (1972-2009) / UEFA Europa League (2010-2019)
None
UEFA Super Cup (1972-2018)
None
European Cup Winners' Cup 1961-1999*
None

**defunct competition*

NATIONAL COMPETITIONS
TABLE OF HONOURS

	CHAMPIONS	CUP WINNERS	BEST GOALSCORERS	
1927/1928	–	Hapoel Tel Aviv FC Maccabi Hasmonean Jerusalem FC *(shared)*	–	
1928/1929	–	Maccabi Tel Aviv FC	–	
1929/1930	–	Maccabi Tel Aviv FC	–	
1930/1931	–	*No competition*	–	
1931/1932	United Kingdom British Police	United Kingdom British Police	–	
1932/1933	*No Championship*	Maccabi Tel Aviv FC	–	
1933/1934	Hapoel Tel Aviv FC	Hapoel Tel Aviv FC	–	
1934/1935	Hapoel Tel Aviv FC	Maccabi Petah Tikva FC	–	
1935/1936	Maccabi Tel Aviv FC	*No competition*	–	
1936/1937	Maccabi Tel Aviv FC	Hapoel Tel Aviv FC	–	
1937/1938	Hapoel Tel Aviv FC	Hapoel Tel Aviv FC	–	
1938/1939	*No Championship*	Hapoel Tel Aviv FC	–	
1939/1940	Hapoel Tel Aviv FC	Beitar Tel Aviv FC	–	
1940/1941	*No Championship*	Maccabi Tel Aviv FC	–	
1941/1942	Maccabi Tel Aviv FC	Beitar Tel Aviv FC	–	
1942/1943	*Championship not finished*	*No competition*	–	
1943/1944	Hapoel Tel Aviv FC	*No competition*	–	
1944/1945	Hapoel Tel Aviv FC Beitar Tel Aviv FC *(shared)*	*No competition*	–	
1945/1946	*No Championship*	Maccabi Tel Aviv FC	–	
1946/1947	Maccabi Tel Aviv FC	Maccabi Tel Aviv FC	–	
1947/1948	*Championship not finished*	*No competition*	–	
1948	*Championship not finished*	*No competition*	–	
1949/1950	Maccabi Tel Aviv FC	*No competition*	Yosef Merimovich (Maccabi Tel Aviv FC)	25
1950/1951	*No Championship*	*No competition*	–	–
1951/1952	Maccabi Tel Aviv FC	Maccabi Petah Tikva FC	Yehoshua Glazer (Maccabi Tel Aviv FC)	24
1952/1953	*No Championship*	*No competition*	–	–
1953/1954	Maccabi Tel Aviv FC	Maccabi Tel Aviv FC	Eliezer Spiegel (Maccabi Petah Tikva FC)	16
1954/1955	Hapoel Petah Tikva FC	Maccabi Tel Aviv FC	Nisim Elmaliah (Beitar Tel Aviv FC)	30
1955/1956	Maccabi Tel Aviv FC	*No competition*	Avraham Levi (Beitar Tel Aviv FC) Michael Michaelov (Beitar Tel Aviv FC)	16
1956/1957	Hapoel Tel Aviv FC	Hapoel Petah Tikva FC	Avraham Ginzburg (Hapoel Haifa FC)	16
1957/1958	Maccabi Tel Aviv FC	Maccabi Tel Aviv FC	Rafi Levi (Maccabi Tel Aviv FC)	14
1958/1959	Hapoel Petah Tikva FC	Maccabi Tel Aviv FC	Aharon Amar (Maccabi Haifa FC)	17
1959/1960	Hapoel Petah Tikva FC	*No competition*	Rafi Levi (Maccabi Tel Aviv FC)	19
1960/1961	Hapoel Petah Tikva FC	Hapoel Tel Aviv FC	Shlomo Levi (Hapoel Haifa FC) Zharia Ratzabi (Hapoel Petah Tikva FC)	15
1961/1962	Hapoel Petah Tikva FC	Maccabi Haifa FC	Shlomo Levi (Maccabi Haifa FC) Itzhak Nizri (Hapoel Tiberias)	16
1962/1963	Hapoel Petah Tikva FC	Hapoel Haifa FC	Zharia Ratzabi (Hapoel Petah Tikva FC)	12
1963/1964	Hapoel Haifa FC	Maccabi Tel Aviv FC	Israel Ashkenazi (Maccabi Jaffa FC)	21
1964/1965	Hakoah Ramat Gan FC	Maccabi Tel Aviv FC	Israel Ashkenazi (Maccabi Jaffa FC) Itzhak Mizrahi (Bnei Yehuda Tel Aviv FC)	18
1965/1966	Hapoel Tel Aviv FC	Hapoel Haifa FC	Moshe Romano (Shimshon Tel Aviv FC) Mordechai Spiegler (Maccabi Netanya FC)	17
1966/1967	-	Maccabi Tel Aviv FC		
1967/1968	Maccabi Tel Aviv FC [1966-1968]	Bnei Yehuda Tel Aviv FC	Mordechai Spiegler (Maccabi Netanya FC)	38
1968/1969	Hapoel Tel Aviv FC	Hakoah Ramat Gan FC	Mordechai Spiegler (Maccabi Netanya FC)	25
1969/1970	Maccabi Tel Aviv FC	Maccabi Tel Aviv FC	Moshe Romano (Shimshon Tel Aviv FC)	15
1970/1971	Maccabi Netanya FC	Hakoah Ramat Gan FC	Eli Ben Rimoz (Hapoel Jerusalem FC)	20
1971/1972	Maccabi Tel Aviv FC	Hapoel Tel Aviv FC	Yehouda Shaharabani (Hakoah Ramat Gan FC)	21
1972/1973	Hakoah Ramat Gan FC	Hapoel Jerusalem FC	Moshe Romano (Beitar Tel Aviv FC)	18
1973/1974	Maccabi Netanya FC	Hapoel Haifa FC	Benny Alon (Hapoel Haifa FC)	15
1974/1975	Hapoel Be'er Sheva FC	Hapoel Kfar Saba FC	Moshe Romano (Shimshon Tel Aviv FC)	17
1975/1976	Hapoel Be'er Sheva FC	Beitar Jerusalem FC	Oded Machnes (Maccabi Netanya FC)	21
1976/1977	Maccabi Tel Aviv FC	Maccabi Tel Aviv FC	Vicky Peretz (Maccabi Tel Aviv FC)	17
1977/1978	Maccabi Netanya FC	Maccabi Netanya FC	David Lavi (Maccabi Netanya FC)	16
1978/1979	Maccabi Tel Aviv FC	Beitar Jerusalem FC	Oded Machnes (Maccabi Netanya FC) Eli Miali (Beitar Jerusalem FC)	18
1979/1980	Maccabi Netanya FC	Hapoel Kfar Saba FC	David Lavi (Maccabi Netanya FC)	18
1980/1981	Hapoel Tel Aviv FC	Bnei Yehuda Tel Aviv FC	Hertzel Fitusi (Maccabi Petah Tikva FC)	22
1981/1982	Hapoel Kfar Saba FC	Hapoel Yehud	Oded Machnes (Maccabi Netanya FC)	26
1982/1983	Maccabi Netanya FC	Hapoel Tel Aviv FC	Oded Machnes (Maccabi Netanya FC)	22
1983/1984	Maccabi Haifa FC	Hapoel Lod	David Lavi (Maccabi Netanya FC)	16
1984/1985	Maccabi Haifa FC	Beitar Jerusalem FC	David Lavi (Maccabi Netanya FC)	18
1985/1986	Hapoel Tel Aviv FC	Beitar Jerusalem FC	Uri Malmilian (Beitar Jerusalem FC) Doron Rabinzon (Maccabi Petah Tikva FC)	14
1986/1987	Beitar Jerusalem FC	Maccabi Tel Aviv FC	Eli Yani (Hapoel Kfar Saba FC)	16
1987/1988	Hapoel Tel Aviv FC	Maccabi Tel Aviv FC	Zahi Armeli (Maccabi Haifa FC)	25

1988/1989	Maccabi Haifa FC	Beitar Jerusalem FC	Benny Tabak (Maccabi Tel Aviv FC)	18
1989/1990	Bnei Yehuda Tel Aviv FC	Hapoel Kfar Saba FC	Uri Malmilian (Maccabi Tel Aviv FC)	16
1990/1991	Maccabi Haifa FC	Maccabi Haifa FC	Nir Levine (Hapoel Petah Tikva FC)	20
1991/1992	Maccabi Tel Aviv FC	Hapoel Petah Tikva FC	Alon Mizrahi (Bnei Yehuda Tel Aviv FC)	20
1992/1993	Beitar Jerusalem FC	Maccabi Haifa FC	Alon Mizrahi (Bnei Yehuda Tel Aviv FC)	26
1993/1994	Maccabi Haifa FC	Maccabi Tel Aviv FC	Alon Mizrahi (Maccabi Haifa FC)	28
1994/1995	Maccabi Tel Aviv FC	Maccabi Haifa FC	Haim Revivo (Maccabi Haifa FC) Amir Turgeman (Maccabi Ironi Ashdod FC FC)	17
1995/1996	Maccabi Tel Aviv FC	Maccabi Tel Aviv FC	Haim Revivo (Maccabi Haifa FC)	26
1996/1997	Beitar Jerusalem FC	Hapoel Be'er Sheva FC	Motti Kakoun (Hapoel Petah Tikva FC)	21
1997/1998	Beitar Jerusalem FC	Maccabi Haifa FC	Alon Mizrahi (Maccabi Haifa FC)	18
1998/1999	Hapoel Haifa FC	Hapoel Tel Aviv FC	Andrzej Kubica (Maccabi Tel Aviv FC)	21
1999/2000	Hapoel Tel Aviv FC	Hapoel Tel Aviv FC	Assi Tubi (Maccabi Petah Tikva FC)	27
2000/2001	Maccabi Haifa FC	Maccabi Tel Aviv FC	Avi Nimni (Maccabi Tel Aviv FC)	25
2001/2002	Maccabi Haifa FC	Maccabi Tel Aviv FC	Kobi Refua (Maccabi Petah Tikva FC)	18
2002/2003	Maccabi Tel Aviv FC	Hapoel Haifa FC	Yaniv Abargil (Hapoel Kfar Saba FC) Shay Holtzman (Ironi Rishon LeZion FC / FC Ashdod)	18
2003/2004	Maccabi Haifa FC	Bnei Sakhnin FC	Ofir Haim (Hapoel Be'er Sheva FC) Shay Holtzman (FC Ashdod)	16
2004/2005	Maccabi Haifa FC	Maccabi Tel Aviv FC	Roberto Colautti (Maccabi Haifa FC)	19
2005/2006	Maccabi Haifa FC	Hapoel Tel Aviv FC	Shay Holtzman (FC Ashdod)	18
2006/2007	Beitar Jerusalem FC	Hapoel Tel Aviv FC	Yaniv Azran (FC Ashdod)	15
2007/2008	Beitar Jerusalem FC	Beitar Jerusalem FC	Samuel Yeboah (Hapoel Kfar Saba FC)	15
2008/2009	Maccabi Haifa FC	Beitar Jerusalem FC	Barak Yitzhaki (Beitar Jerusalem FC) Shimon Abuhatzira (Hapoel Petah Tikva FC) Eliran Atar (Bnei Yehuda Tel Aviv FC)	14
2009/2010	Hapoel Tel Aviv FC	Hapoel Tel Aviv FC	Shlomi Arbeitman (Maccabi Haifa FC)	28
2010/2011	Maccabi Haifa FC	Hapoel Tel Aviv FC	Toto Tamuz (Hapoel Tel Aviv FC)	21
2011/2012	Ironi Kiryat	Hapoel Tel Aviv FC	Achmad Saba'a (Maccabi Netanya FC)	20
2012/2013	Maccabi Tel Aviv FC	Hapoel Haifa FC	Eliran Atar (Maccabi Tel Aviv FC)	22
2013/2014	Maccabi Tel Aviv FC	Hapoel Ironi Kiryat Shmona FC	Eran Zahavi (Maccabi Tel Aviv FC)	29
2014/2015	Maccabi Tel Aviv FC	Maccabi Tel Aviv FC	Eran Zahavi (Maccabi Tel Aviv FC)	27
2015/2016	Hapoel Be'er Sheva FC	Maccabi Haifa FC	Eran Zahavi (Maccabi Tel Aviv FC)	35
2016/2017	Hapoel Be'er Sheva FC	Bnei Yehuda Tel Aviv FC	Viðar Örn Kjartansson (ISL, Maccabi Tel Aviv FC)	19
2017/2018	Hapoel Be'er Sheva FC	Hapoel Haifa FC	Dia Saba (Maccabi Netanya FC)	24
2018/2019	Maccabi Tel Aviv FC	Bnei Yehuda Tel Aviv FC	Ben Sahar (Hapoel Be'er Sheva FC)	15

NATIONAL CHAMPIONSHIP

Israeli Premier League (Ligat Winner) 2018/2019

(25.08.2018 – 25.05.2019)

Regular Season - Results

Round 1 [25-27.08.2018]
FC Ashdod - Bnei Yehuda 1-0(0-0)
Hapoel Hadera - Hapoel Tel Aviv 2-1(1-1)
Hapoel Haifa - Maccabi Netanya 5-0(3-0)
Hapoel Ironi - H. Be'er Sheva 1-1(0-1)
Bnei Sachnin - Hapoel Ra'anana 0-0
Maccabi Tel Aviv - Maccabi Haifa 2-0(0-0)
Maccabi Petach-Tikva - Beitar Jerus. 4-1(1-0)

Round 2 [01-03.09.2018]
Hapoel Ra'anana - Hapoel Ironi 2-1(1-1)
Maccabi Haifa - FC Ashdod 2-0(0-0)
Maccabi Netanya - Bnei Sachnin 1-1(1-1)
Hapoel Tel Aviv - Hapoel Haifa 1-0(0-0)
Bnei Yehuda - Maccabi Petach-Tikva 2-2(1-0)
Hapoel Be'er Sh. - Maccabi Tel Aviv 1-1(1-0)
Beitar Jerusalem - Hapoel Hadera 0-1(0-0)

Round 3 [15-17.09.2018]
Maccabi Tel Aviv - Hapoel Ra'anana 4-1(1-0)
Maccabi Petach-Tik. - Hapoel Hadera 1-1(0-0)
Bnei Sachnin - Hapoel Tel Aviv 1-1(0-0)
FC Ashdod - Hapoel Be'er Sheva 1-0(1-0)
Hapoel Ironi - Maccabi Netanya 1-0(0-0)
Bnei Yehuda - Maccabi Haifa 1-1(1-1)
Hapoel Haifa - Beitar Jerusalem 2-2(1-1)

Round 4 [22-24.09.2018]
Hapoel Tel Aviv - Hapoel Ironi 0-0
Hapoel Ra'anana - FC Ashdod 1-1(1-0)
Maccabi Haifa - Maccabi Petach-Tik. 1-2(1-0)
Maccabi Netanya - Maccabi Tel Aviv 1-2(0-1)
Hapoel Hadera - Hapoel Haifa 2-0(0-0)
Hapoel Be'er Sheva - Bnei Yehuda 0-0
Beitar Jerusalem - Bnei Sachnin 3-2(1-0)

Round 5 [29.09.-01.10.2018]
Maccabi Petach-Tikva - Hapoel Haifa 1-1(0-1)
Bnei Sachnin - Hapoel Hadera 1-2(1-1)
FC Ashdod - Maccabi Netanya 1-4(1-1)
Hapoel Ironi - Beitar Jerusalem 2-0(1-0)
Bnei Yehuda - Hapoel Ra'anana 3-0(1-0)
Maccabi Haifa - Hapoel Be'er Sheva 0-0
Maccabi Tel Aviv - Hapoel Tel Aviv 0-0

Round 6 [06-08.10.2018]
Hapoel Ra'anana - Maccabi Haifa 1-1(0-0)
Hapoel Haifa - Bnei Sachnin 0-3(0-1)
Maccabi Netanya - Bnei Yehuda 1-3(0-0)
Hapoel Be'er Sh. - Maccabi Petach-T. 4-1(3-1)
Hapoel Hadera - Hapoel Ironi 1-0(0-0)
Beitar Jerusalem - Maccabi Tel Aviv 0-2(0-1)
Hapoel Tel Aviv - FC Ashdod 0-0

Round 7 [20-22.10.2018]
Maccabi Tel Aviv - Hapoel Hadera 4-0(3-0)
Hapoel Ironi - Hapoel Haifa 1-1(0-1)
Bnei Yehuda - Hapoel Tel Aviv 0-0
Hapoel Be'er Sh. - Hapoel Ra'anana 2-0(0-0)
Maccabi Petach-Tikva - Bnei Sachnin 0-0
FC Ashdod - Beitar Jerusalem 1-1(1-0)
Maccabi Haifa - Maccabi Netanya 0-2(0-0)

Round 8 [27-29.10.2018]
Hapoel Ra'anana - Maccabi Petach-T. 1-0(0-0)
Bnei Sachnin - Hapoel Ironi 0-3(0-1)
Maccabi Netanya - Hapoel Be'er Sh. 1-0(0-0)
Beitar Jerusalem - Bnei Yehuda 1-5(0-2)
Hapoel Hadera - FC Ashdod 3-2(1-1)
Hapoel Haifa - Maccabi Tel Aviv 1-3(0-2)
Hapoel Tel Aviv - Maccabi Haifa 1-2(1-0)

Round 9 [03-05.11.2018]
Hapoel Ra'anana - Maccabi Netanya 1-2(0-0)
Maccabi Petach-T. - Hapoel Ironi 0-1(0-1)
FC Ashdod - Hapoel Haifa 0-3(0-0)
Maccabi Tel Aviv - Bnei Sachnin 3-0(1-0)
Bnei Yehuda - Hapoel Hadera 2-0(1-0)
Hap. Be'er Sheva - Hapoel Tel Aviv 2-1(0-0)
Maccabi Haifa - Beitar Jerusalem 1-2(1-0)

Round 10 [10-12.11.2018]
Maccabi Netanya - Maccabi Petach-T 0-1(0-0)
Hapoel Haifa - Bnei Yehuda 0-2(0-0)
Hapoel Tel Aviv - Hapoel Ra'anana 0-0
Hapoel Hadera - Maccabi Haifa 1-2(0-2)
Hapoel Ironi - Maccabi Tel Aviv 1-2(1-1)
Beitar Jerusalem - Hap. Be'er Sheva 2-3(0-0)
Bnei Sachnin - FC Ashdod 4-3(1-1)

Round 11 [01-02.12.2018]
Bnei Yehuda - Bnei Sachnin 0-1(0-1)
FC Ashdod - Hapoel Ironi 1-0(1-0)
Hapoel Be'er Sheva - Hapoel Hadera 2-2(2-1)
Maccabi Haifa - Hapoel Haifa 1-3(0-2)
M. Petach-Tikva - Maccabi Tel Aviv 1-1(0-1)
Hapoel Ra'anana - Beitar Jerusalem 2-1(0-0)
Maccabi Netanya - Hapoel Tel Aviv 1-1(0-1)

Round 12 [04-05.12.2018]
Hapoel Ironi - Bnei Yehuda 0-2(0-1)
Bnei Sachnin - Maccabi Haifa 0-2(0-0)
Maccabi Tel Aviv - FC Ashdod 4-0(2-0)
Hapoel Haifa - Hapoel Be'er Sheva 4-4(2-4)
Hapoel Hadera - Hapoel Ra'anana 0-0
Maccabi Petach-Tikva - Hapoel Tel Aviv 0-0
Beitar Jerusalem - Maccabi Netanya 1-1(0-0)

Round 13 [08-10.12.2018]
Maccabi Haifa - Hapoel Ironi 2-2(0-1)
FC Ashdod - Maccabi Petach-Tikva 1-1(1-0)
Hapoel Be'er Sheva - Bnei Sachnin 1-1(1-0)
Bnei Yehuda - Maccabi Tel Aviv 1-3(0-2)
Hapoel Ra'anana - Hapoel Haifa 0-3(0-1)
Maccabi Netanya - Hapoel Hadera 1-0(1-0)
Hapoel Tel Aviv - Beitar Jerusalem 0-3(0-1)

Round 14 [15-17.12.2018]
Hapoel Tel Aviv - Hapoel Hadera 1-1(0-0)
Hapoel Ra'anana - Bnei Sachnin 2-1(0-0)
Maccabi Netanya - Hapoel Haifa 1-2(1-0)
Hapoel Be'er Sheva - Hapoel Ironi 2-1(0-1)
Bnei Yehuda - FC Ashdod 2-0(2-0)
Beitar Jerusalem - Maccabi Petach-Tikva 0-0
Maccabi Haifa - Maccabi Tel Aviv 1-3(0-2)

Round 15 [25-27.12.2018]
Maccabi Petach-Tikva - Bnei Yehuda 1-1(1-0)
Bnei Sachnin - Maccabi Netanya 0-2(0-2)
Maccabi Tel Aviv - Hap. Be'er Sheva 3-0(1-0)
Hapoel Ironi - Hapoel Ra'anana 1-1(0-0)
Hapoel Haifa - Hapoel Tel Aviv 1-1(1-0)
FC Ashdod - Maccabi Haifa 0-1(0-1)
Hapoel Hadera - Beitar Jerusalem 0-3(0-2)

Round 16 [29-31.12.2018]
Hapoel Ra'anana - Maccabi Tel Aviv 0-2(0-1)
Maccabi Netanya - Hapoel Ironi 1-0(1-0)
Hapoel Be'er Sheva - FC Ashdod 1-0(0-0)
Maccabi Haifa - Bnei Yehuda 1-0(0-0)
Hapoel Hadera - Maccabi Petach-T. 3-0(2-0)
Hapoel Tel Aviv - Bnei Sachnin 2-0(1-0)
Beitar Jerusalem - Hapoel Haifa 1-1(0-0)

Round 17 [05-07.01.2019]
Hapoel Ironi - Hapoel Tel Aviv 1-0(0-0)
Hapoel Haifa - Hapoel Hadera 1-1(0-1)
Maccabi Petach-T. - Maccabi Haifa 1-2(0-0)
Bnei Sachnin - Beitar Jerusalem 0-0
FC Ashdod - Hapoel Ra'anana 1-1(1-1)
Bnei Yehuda - Hapoel Be'er Sheva 3-1(0-1)
Maccabi Tel Aviv - Maccabi Netanya 4-1(2-0)

Round 18 [12-14.01.2019]
Maccabi Netanya - FC Ashdod 1-0(0-0)
Hapoel Ra'anana - Bnei Yehuda 0-0
Hapoel Haifa - Maccabi Petach-Tikva 4-2(2-1)
Hapoel Hadera - Bnei Sachnin 2-1(0-0)
Hapoel Be'er Sheva - Maccabi Haifa 0-2(0-0)
Beitar Jerusalem - Hapoel Ironi 0-0
Hapoel Tel Aviv - Maccabi Tel Aviv 1-1(0-1)

Round 19 [19-21.01.2019]
Bnei Yehuda - Maccabi Netanya 0-0
Bnei Sachnin - Hapoel Haifa 0-4(0-2)
Maccabi Haifa - Hapoel Ra'anana 0-0
Maccabi Petach-Tikva - Be'er Sheva 1-3(0-2)
Hapoel Ironi - Hapoel Hadera 3-1(1-1)
FC Ashdod - Hapoel Tel Aviv 1-1(0-0)
Maccabi Tel Aviv - Beitar Jerusalem 1-0(0-0)

Round 20 [26-28.01.2019]
Hapoel Tel Aviv - Bnei Yehuda 3-2(2-1)
Hapoel Haifa - Hapoel Ironi 1-1(0-0)
Hapoel Ra'anana - Hap. Be'er Sheva 3-1(0-1)
Beitar Jerusalem - FC Ashdod 4-1(2-0)
Bnei Sachnin - Maccabi Petach-Tikva 0-1(0-0)
Maccabi Netanya - Maccabi Haifa 0-0
Hapoel Hadera - Maccabi Tel Aviv 0-2(0-2)

Round 21 [02-04.02.2019]
Maccabi Petach-T. - Hapoel Ra'anana 1-1(1-0)
FC Ashdod - Hapoel Hadera 2-3(1-2)
Hap. Be'er Sheva - Maccabi Netanya 1-1(1-1)
Bnei Yehuda - Beitar Jerusalem 0-2(0-1)
Hapoel Ironi - Bnei Sachnin 2-2(1-1)
Maccabi Tel Aviv - Hapoel Haifa 1-1(1-0)
Maccabi Haifa - Hapoel Tel Aviv 3-2(3-2)

Round 22 [09-11.02.2019]
Hapoel Haifa - FC Ashdod 0-1(0-0)
Hapoel Ironi - Maccabi Petach-Tikva 0-2(0-2)
Maccabi Netanya - Hapoel Ra'anana 1-0(1-0)
Hapoel Tel Aviv - Hap. Be'er Sheva 1-0(1-0)
Hapoel Hadera - Bnei Yehuda 0-4(0-3)
Beitar Jerusalem - Maccabi Haifa 1-1(1-1)
Bnei Sachnin - Maccabi Tel Aviv 0-0

Round 23 [16-18.02.2019]
Hapoel Ra'anana - Hapoel Tel Aviv 0-0
FC Ashdod - Bnei Sachnin 2-1(0-1)
Bnei Yehuda - Hapoel Haifa 4-2(2-1)
Maccabi Tel Aviv - Hapoel Ironi 3-0(2-0)
Maccabi Petach-T - Maccabi Netanya 1-4(1-2)
Maccabi Haifa - Hapoel Hadera 3-1(2-0)
Hap. Be'er Sheva - Beitar Jerusalem 3-1(1-1)

Round 24 [23-25.02.2019]
Maccabi Tel Aviv - M. Petach-Tikva 2-0(0-0)
Bnei Sachnin - Bnei Yehuda 2-1(1-1)
Hapoel Tel Aviv - Maccabi Netanya 1-2(0-1)
Beitar Jerusalem - Hapoel Ra'anana 2-0(1-0)
Hapoel Ironi - FC Ashdod 0-0
Hapoel Hadera - Hapoel Be'er Sheva 1-2(0-2)
Hapoel Haifa - Maccabi Haifa 0-0

Round 25 [02-04.03.2019]
Maccabi Haifa - Bnei Sachnin 2-0(1-0)
Bnei Yehuda - Hapoel Ironi 0-1(0-1)
FC Ashdod - Maccabi Tel Aviv 0-2(0-0)
Maccabi Netanya - Beitar Jerusalem 3-1(2-1)
Hapoel Ra'anana - Hapoel Hadera 1-0(1-0)
Hapoel Tel Aviv - Maccabi Petach-T. 6-0(2-0)
Hapoel Be'er Sheva - Hapoel Haifa 2-0(0-0)

Round 26 [09-11.03.2019]
Beitar Jerusalem - Hapoel Tel Aviv 0-1(0-0)
Hapoel Hadera - Maccabi Netanya 2-2(2-0)
Hapoel Haifa - Hapoel Ra'anana 2-2(1-1)
Hapoel Ironi - Maccabi Haifa 2-3(2-1)
Maccabi Petach-Tikva - FC Ashdod 2-0(1-0)
Bnei Sachnin - Hapoel Be'er Sheva 0-0
Maccabi Tel Aviv - Bnei Yehuda 2-1(0-1)

Final Standings

1.	Maccabi Tel Aviv FC	26	20	6	0	57	-	12	66
2.	Maccabi Haifa FC	26	12	8	6	34	-	27	44
3.	Maccabi Netanya FC	26	12	7	7	34	-	29	43
4.	Hapoel Be'er Sheva FC	26	10	9	7	36	-	32	39
5.	Bnei Yehuda Tel Aviv FC	26	10	7	9	39	-	25	37
6.	Hapoel Hadera–Giv'at Olga "Shulem Schwarz"	26	9	6	11	30	-	41	33
7.	Hapoel Haifa FC	26	7	11	8	42	-	37	32
8.	Hapoel Tel Aviv FC	26	6	13	7	26	-	23	31
9.	Hapoel Ironi Kiryat Shmona FC	26	7	9	10	25	-	28	30
10.	Hapoel Ra'anana AFC	26	6	12	8	20	-	30	30
11.	Beitar Jerusalem FC	26	7	8	11	32	-	37	29
12.	Maccabi Petah Tikva FC	26	6	10	10	26	-	40	28
13.	FC Ashdod	26	5	7	14	20	-	42	22
14.	Bnei Sakhnin FC	26	4	9	13	21	-	39	21

Teams ranked 1-6 were qualified for the Championship Round, while teams ranked 7-14 were qualified for the Relegation Round.

Championship Round

Results

Round 27 [16-17.03.2019]
Maccabi Tel Aviv - Hapoel Hadera 2-0(0-0)
Maccabi Haifa - Bnei Yehuda 0-2(0-2)
Maccabi Netanya - Hap. Be'er Sheva 0-1(0-0)

Round 28 [30.03.2019]
Hapoel Hadera - Hapoel Be'er Sheva 1-4(1-0)
Bnei Yehuda - Maccabi Netanya 1-1(0-1)
Maccabi Tel Aviv - Maccabi Haifa 1-0(0-0)

Round 29 [06-07.04.2019]
Hapoel Be'er Sheva - Bnei Yehuda 2-1(1-1)
Maccabi Haifa - Hapoel Hadera 1-3(0-0)
Maccabi Netanya - Maccabi Tel Aviv 1-4(1-1)

Round 30 [14-15.04.2019]
Hapoel Hadera - Bnei Yehuda 2-3(0-2)
Maccabi Haifa - Maccabi Netanya 2-1(2-1)
Maccabi Tel Aviv - Hapoel Be'er Sheva 0-0

Round 31 [22-23.04.2019]
Hapoel Be'er Sheva - Maccabi Haifa 0-1(0-0)
Maccabi Netanya - Hapoel Hadera 3-2(3-0)
Bnei Yehuda - Maccabi Tel Aviv 0-2(0-1)

Round 32 [27-29.04.2019]
Hapoel Hadera - Maccabi Tel Aviv 0-1(0-0)
Hap. Be'er Sheva - Maccabi Netanya 0-2(0-1)
Bnei Yehuda - Maccabi Haifa 2-2(2-2)

Round 33 [04-06.05.2019]
Hapoel Hadera - Maccabi Netanya 1-2(0-0)
Maccabi Tel Aviv - Bnei Yehuda 2-3(1-1)
Maccabi Haifa - Hapoel Be'er Sheva 3-1(2-1)

Round 34 [11-13.05.2019]
Maccabi Tel Aviv - Maccabi Netanya 3-0(1-0)
Bnei Yehuda - Hapoel Be'er Sheva 2-3(1-2)
Hapoel Hadera - Maccabi Haifa 2-0(1-0)

Round 35 [19.05.2019]
Hapoel Be'er Sheva - Hapoel Hadera 1-0(0-0)
Maccabi Netanya - Bnei Yehuda 0-2(0-2)
Maccabi Haifa - Maccabi Tel Aviv 1-1(0-1)

Round 36 [25.05.2019]
Bnei Yehuda - Hapoel Hadera 1-2(1-0)
Hap. Be'er Sheva - Maccabi Tel Aviv 0-4(0-2)
Maccabi Netanya - Maccabi Haifa 1-2(0-1)

Final Standings

1.	**Maccabi Tel Aviv FC**	36	27	8	1	77	-	17	89
2.	Maccabi Haifa FC	36	16	10	10	46	-	41	58
3.	Hapoel Be'er Sheva FC	36	15	10	11	48	-	46	55
4.	Maccabi Netanya FC	36	15	8	13	45	-	47	53
5.	Bnei Yehuda Tel Aviv FC	36	14	9	13	56	-	41	51
6.	Hapoel Hadera–Giv'at Olga "Shulem Schwarz"	36	12	6	18	43	-	59	42

Top goalscorers:

15 Ben Sahar *Hapoel Be'er Sheva FC*

13 Fatos Bećiraj (MNE) *Maccabi Netanya FC*

13 Lucielmo Palhano Soares "Lúcio Maranhão" (BRA) *Hapoel Hadera FC*

Relegation Round

Round 27 [16-17.03.2019]
Hapoel Ra'anana - Bnei Sachnin 2-2(1-0)
Hapoel Tel Aviv - FC Ashdod 5-1(1-0)
Hapoel Ironi - Maccabi Petach-Tikva 0-1(0-0)
Hapoel Haifa - Beitar Jerusalem 0-0

Round 28 [30.03.-01.04.2019]
FC Ashdod - Hapoel Ironi 3-2(2-2)
Maccabi Petach-T. - Hapoel Ra'anana 1-1(1-0)
Beitar Jerusalem - Bnei Sachnin 0-0
Hapoel Haifa - Hapoel Tel Aviv 0-0

Round 29 [06-08.04.2019]
Hapoel Ironi - Hapoel Haifa 3-0(0-0)
Bnei Sachnin - Maccabi Petach-Tikva 1-1(0-0)
Hapoel Ra'anana - FC Ashdod 1-2(1-0)
Hapoel Tel Aviv - Beitar Jerusalem 1-2(1-0)

Round 30 [13.04.2019]
Hapoel Haifa - Hapoel Ra'anana 0-2(0-1)
Hapoel Tel Aviv - Hapoel Ironi 2-2(1-0)
FC Ashdod - Bnei Sachnin 1-2(0-0)
Beitar Jerusalem - Maccabi Petach-T. 4-1(1-0)

Round 31 [27.04.2019]
Hapoel Ironi - Beitar Jerusalem 0-1(0-0)
Hapoel Ra'anana - Hapoel Tel Aviv 2-1(0-1)
Bnei Sachnin - Hapoel Haifa 1-2(0-1)
Maccabi Petach-Tikva - FC Ashdod 0-3(0-2)

Round 32 [04.05.2019]
Beitar Jerusalem - FC Ashdod 2-3(1-0)
Hapoel Haifa - Maccabi Petach-Tikva 0-3(0-2)
Hapoel Tel Aviv - Bnei Sachnin 3-0(1-0)
Hapoel Ironi - Hapoel Ra'anana 0-0

Round 33 [11-12.05.2019]
Hapoel Ra'anana - Beitar Jerusalem 1-2(0-0)
Bnei Sachnin - Hapoel Ironi 0-2(0-2)
Maccabi Petach-T. - Hapoel Tel Aviv 0-2(0-1)
FC Ashdod - Hapoel Haifa 1-0(1-0)

Final Standings

7.	Beitar Jerusalem FC	33	11	10	12	43	-	43	43
8.	Hapoel Tel Aviv FC	33	9	15	9	40	-	30	42
9.	Hapoel Ra'anana AFC	33	8	15	10	29	-	38	39
10.	Hapoel Ironi Kiryat Shmona FC	33	9	11	13	34	-	35	38
11.	Hapoel Haifa FC	33	8	13	12	44	-	47	37
12.	FC Ashdod	33	10	7	16	34	-	54	37
13.	Maccabi Petah Tikva FC (*Relegated*)	33	8	12	13	33	-	51	36
14.	Bnei Sakhnin FC (*Relegated*)	33	5	12	16	27	-	50	27

NATIONAL CUP
Israel State Cup (Gvia HaMedina) 2018/2019

Eighth Round [20-23.12.2018]

FC Ashdod - Hapoel Ramat Gan Givatayim FC	2-0(0-0)
Maccabi Netanya FC - FC Daburiyya	5-1(1-0)
Hapoel Afula FC - Hapoel Bnei Lod Rakevet FC	4-2(2-1)
Ironi Kiryat Shmona - Hapoel Migdal HaEmek FC	1-0(0-0)
AS Nordia Jerusalem - Bnei Yehuda Tel Aviv FC	1-3(1-0)
Hapoel Haifa FC - Hapoel Acre FC	0-1(0-0)
Maccabi Petah Tikva FC - Hapoel Kfar Saba FC	1-0(1-0)
Bnei Sakhnin FC - Maccabi Ahi Nazareth FC	1-0(1-0)
Hapoel Hadera FC - Sektzia Nes Tziona FC	1-0(1-0)
Hapoel Nazareth Illit FC - Hapoel Iksal FC	3-0(1-0)
Hapoel Ra'anana AFC - Hakoah Amidar Ramat Gan	0-0 aet; 4-5 pen
Hapoel Nir Ramat HaSharon FC - FC Kafr Qasim	0-1(0-0)
Maccabi Haifa FC - Hapoel Ironi Marmorek Rahevet	5-0(4-0)
Hapoel Be'er Sheva FC - Beitar Tel Aviv Bat Yam	1-0(0-0,0-0)
Beitar Jerusalem FC - Maccabi Tel Aviv FC	1-2(0-0)
Hapoel Katamon Jerusalem FC - Hapoel Tel Aviv FC	1-2(1-0)

1/8-Finals [15-17/22.01.2019]

Hapoel Afula FC - FC Ashdod	3-1(2-1)
Maccabi Petah Tikva - Hakoah Amidar Ramat Gan	4-1(1-0)
Maccabi Netanya FC - Hapoel Be'er Sheva FC	0-0 aet; 4-2 pen
Bnei Yehuda Tel Aviv FC - Hapoel Nazareth Illit FC	2-0(0-0)
FC Kafr Qasim - Hapoel Ironi Kiryat Shmona FC	1-0(1-0)
Maccabi Tel Aviv FC - Hapoel Acre FC	4-0(3-0)
Hapoel Tel Aviv FC - Hapoel Hadera FC	1-2(0-0)
Bnei Sakhnin FC - Maccabi Haifa FC	1-0(1-0)

Quarter-Finals [05-06/26-27.02.2019]

Hapoel Afula FC - Bnei Yehuda Tel Aviv FC	0-2 / 1-1
Maccabi Netanya FC - Maccabi Petah Tikva FC	1-0 / 1-1
FC Kafr Qasim - Hapoel Hadera FC	2-3 / 0-1
Bnei Sakhnin FC - Maccabi Tel Aviv FC	1-4 / 0-0

Semi-Finals [02-03.04.2019]

Maccabi Netanya FC - Hapoel Hadera FC	1-0
Bnei Yehuda Tel Aviv FC - Maccabi Tel Aviv FC	1-0

Final

15.05.2019; "Sammy Ofer" Stadium, Haifa; Referee: Idan Yarkoni; Attendance: 28,500
Bnei Yehuda Tel Aviv FC - Maccabi Netanya FC **1-1(0-1,1-1,1-1); 5-4 on penalties**

Bnei Yehuda: Emilijus Zubas, Dan Mori, Shay Konstantini, Itzhak Azuz (56.Amit Bitton), Matan Baltaxa, Carlos Javier Cuéllar Jiménez (75.Dor Jan), Dolev Haziza, Ismaila Wafougossani Soro (29.Sagas Tambi), Yuval Ashkenazi, Jakub Sylvestr (100.Amit Zenati), Mavis Tchibota Dufounou. Trainer: Yosef Abukasis.

Maccabi Netanya: Dani Amos, Muhammed Zubeidat (69.Dolev Azulai [*sent off 120*]), Branko Vrgoč, Jonathan Rey Bornstein, Tim Heubach, Jahmir Hyka (106.Moti Barshazky), Gavriel Kanichowsky, Ali Mohamed (51.Stav Finish), Nicolas Olsak, Guy Melamed (73.Aviv Avraham), Fatos Bećiraj. Trainer: Slobodan Drapić (Serbia).

Goals: 0-1 Guy Melamed (4), 1-1 Dor Jan (82).

Penalties: Stav Finish 0-1; Dor Jan 1-1; Moti Barshazky 1-2; Dolev Haziza 2-2; Tim Heubach 2-3; Sagas Tambi 3-3; Nicolas Olsak 3-4; Amit Zenati 4-4; Gavriel Kanichowsky (missed); Yuval Ashkenazi 5-4.

THE CLUBS 2018/2019

Please note: matches and goals includes statistics of both regular season and play-offs (Championship Round and Relegation Round).

Beitar Jerusalem Football Club

Founded: 1936
Stadium: Teddy Stadium, Jerusalem (31,733)

Goalkeepers:	**DOB**	**M**	**(s)**	**G**
David Goresh	01.02.1980	7		
Itamar Nitzan	23.06.1987	26		
Defenders:	**DOB**	**M**	**(s)**	**G**
Tal Ben Haim	31.03.1982	30		
Antoine Conte (FRA)	29.01.1994	5	(1)	
Tal Kahila	26.06.1992	13	(3)	2
Matan Peleg	11.11.1993	2	(1)	
Oz Raly	22.12.1987	4	(3)	
Samuel Scheimann	03.11.1987	23	(4)	
Michael Siroshtein	25.04.1989	16	(1)	1
Or Zahavi	23.04.1996	23		1
Midfielders:	**DOB**	**M**	**(s)**	**G**
Anthony Gildas Kofi Annan (GHA)	21.07.1986	2	(2)	
Afonso Miguel Castro Vilhena Taira (POR)	17.06.1992	16	(1)	1
Yacov Brihon	06.07.1993	1	(15)	2
Dan Einbinder	16.02.1989	26	(2)	4
Chibuzor Bruno Ibeh (NGA)	15.04.1995	1		
David Yair Keltjens	11.06.1995	25	(2)	1
Gadi Kinda	17.05.1994	10		1
Ofir Kriaf	17.03.1991	18	(4)	2
Eran Levi	04.08.1985	4	(10)	
Erik Sabo (SVK)	22.11.1991	2		
Liroy Zhairi	02.03.1989	1	(6)	
Forwards:	**DOB**	**M**	**(s)**	**G**
Yosef Shay Benayoun	05.05.1980	10	(5)	
Maor Buzaglo	14.01.1988	16	(8)	4
Roy Fadida	31.03.2000		(1)	
Lior Inbrum	12.01.1996	13	(4)	3
Aaron Samuel Olanare (NGA)	04.06.1994	4		1
Ange-Freddy Plumain (FRA)	02.03.1995	14	(1)	5
Jakub Sylvestr (SVK)	02.02.1989	12	(4)	1
Gaëtan Antony Varenne	24.06.1990	17	(7)	7
Idan Vered	01.01.1989	21	(6)	5
Mihai Voduț (ROU)	28.07.1994	1	(6)	
Trainer:	**DOB**	**M**		
Gay Luzon	07.08.1975	7		
David Martane [23.10.2018]	01.01.1989	1		
Nir Klinger [29.10.2018]	25.05.1966	25		

Bnei Sakhnin Football Club

Founded: 1991
Stadium: Doha Stadium, Sakhnin (8,500)

Goalkeepers:	**DOB**	**M**	**(s)**	**G**
Mahmoud Kannadil	11.08.1988	33		
Defenders:	**DOB**	**M**	**(s)**	**G**
Ali Abu Raia	13.09.1997	8		
Sari Falah	22.11.1991	23	(3)	
Marwan Gantos	15.06.1996	21	(3)	
Hassan Hilo	25.11.1999		(1)	
Obeida Khattab	14.07.1992	9	(4)	1
Emmanuel Mbola (ZAM)	10.05.1993	14	(1)	
Amir Nassar	24.11.1996	9	(1)	
Ali Ottman	08.02.1987	21	(2)	1
Alban Pnishi (KVX)	20.10.1990	31		
Ihab Shami	18.09.1993	8	(4)	
Oleksandr Stetsenko (UKR)	02.03.1990	2	(3)	
Midfielders:	**DOB**	**M**	**(s)**	**G**
Souhel Armeli	10.01.1996		(3)	
Bashir Bahjat	03.08.1998		(1)	
Claudemir Ferreira da Silva (BRA)	17.08.1984	7	(4)	
Ihab Ganayem	11.06.1996	20	(5)	2

Ataa Jaber	03.10.1994	11	(7)	1
Khaled Khalaila	16.12.1982	15	(5)	
Firas Mugrabi	24.07.1991	8	(2)	2
Maharan Radi	01.07.1982	29	(3)	2
Forwards:	**DOB**	**M**	**(s)**	**G**
George Akpabio (NGA)	16.11.1992	7	(3)	1
Shlomi Azulay	18.10.1989	27	(4)	9
Mohammad Ghadir	21.01.1991	18	(2)	5
Shuaibu Lalle Ibrahim (NGA)	19.12.1996	9	(2)	
Mohammed Kalibat	15.06.1990	15	(9)	3
Mohammad Khalaila	25.03.1999		(2)	
Osama Khalaila	06.04.1998	4	(10)	
Aleksandar Stanisavljević (SRB)	11.06.1989	4	(2)	
Israel Zaguri	29.01.1990	10	(11)	
Trainer:	**DOB**	**M**		
Benny Ben Zaken	18.10.1982	10		
Amir Turgeman [18.11.2018]	10.05.1972	9		
Giorgi Daraselia (GEO) [22.01.2019]	16.09.1968	8		
Eldad Shavit [25.03.2019]	09.07.1982	6		

Bnei Yehuda Football Club

Founded: 1936
Stadium: HaMoshava Stadium, Petah Tikva (11,500)

Goalkeepers:	**DOB**	**M**	**(s)**	**G**
Omer Niron	17.04.2001	1		
Yonathan Shabi	24.12.1996	6		
Emilijus Zubas (LTU)	10.07.1990	29		
Defenders:	**DOB**	**M**	**(s)**	**G**
Dean Akafi	07.06.1993	2		
Itzhak Azuz	30.10.1985	31		
Matan Baltaxa	20.09.1995	34	(1)	2
Amit Bitton	24.07.1996	10	(1)	
Carlos Javier Cuéllar Jiménez (ESP)	23.08.1981	23		1
Shay Konstantini	27.06.1996	31	(1)	7
Dan Mori	08.11.1988	30	(1)	
Daniel Pelshar	26.07.1997	11	(4)	
Ben Turgeman	09.01.1989	1	(3)	
Midfielders:	**DOB**	**M**	**(s)**	**G**
Souhel Armeli	10.01.1996		(3)	
Yuval Ashkenazi	13.02.1992	27	(4)	4

Dolev Haziza	05.07.1995	32	(3)	3
Sean Malka	27.04.1993	3	(11)	
Shay Mazor	14.06.1993	5	(8)	1
Ismaila Wafougossani Soro (CIV)	07.05.1998	31		
Sagas Tambi	21.10.1994	10	(2)	1
Forwards:	**DOB**	**M**	**(s)**	**G**
Roei Ben Shimon	04.12.2000		(1)	
Avishai Cohen	19.05.1995	4	(10)	
Dor Jan	16.12.1994	7	(26)	7
Fejsal Mulić (SRB)	03.10.1994	3	(7)	1
Yarden Shua	16.06.1999	17		9
Jakub Sylvestr (SVK)	02.02.1989	11	(2)	7
Mavis Tchibota Dufounou (CGO)	07.05.1996	29	(1)	11
Sagiv Yehezkel	21.03.1995	1	(10)	1
Amit Zenati	02.04.1997	7	(9)	1
Trainer:	**DOB**	**M**		
Yosef Abukasis	10.09.1970	36		

Football Club Ashdod

Founded: 1999
Stadium: Yud-Alef Stadium, Ashdod (8,200)

Goalkeepers:	**DOB**	**M**	**(s)**	**G**
Omer Aguzi	13.06.1997		(1)	
Yoav Gerafi	29.08.1993	28		
Roi Mishpati	23.11.1992	5		
Defenders:	**DOB**	**M**	**(s)**	**G**
Nir Bardea	25.01.1996	30	(1)	2
Tom Ben Zaken	29.10.1994	17		1
Amit Bitton	24.07.1996	15		1
Karlo Bručić (CRO)	17.04.1992	17		
Gil Cohen	08.11.2000	15		
Benel Edri	04.09.1997	1	(3)	
Obeida Khattab	14.07.1992	10		2
Aviv Solomon	10.01.1995	15	(2)	
Yuval Spungin	03.04.1987	6	(2)	
Midfielders:	**DOB**	**M**	**(s)**	**G**
Yitzhak Asefa	19.11.1998	8	(1)	
Dan Biton	20.07.1995	29	(3)	5
Yaniv Brik	28.05.1995	2	(1)	
Roei Gordana	06.07.1990	12	(1)	1
Yuval Jakobovich	09.11.1992	12	(4)	1
Mohamad Kanaan	14.01.2000		(2)	
Gadi Kinda	17.05.1994	7	(4)	2

Issoumaila Lingane (CIV)	15.03.1991	7	(7)	1
Leonard Owusu (GHA)	03.06.1997	25	(4)	
Ben Reichert	04.03.1994	7	(12)	1
Forwards:	**DOB**	**M**	**(s)**	**G**
Amran Alkrenawi	21.02.1996	3	(5)	
Hen Azriel	26.06.1988		(3)	
Dudu Biton	01.03.1988	4	(7)	2
Dean David	14.03.1996	12	(8)	5
Dor Galili	14.04.1997	6	(3)	
Romain Habran (FRA)	14.06.1994	17	(7)	2
Josip Ivančić (CRO)	29.03.1991	10	(1)	2
Filip Knežević (SRB)	08.11.1991	12	(7)	
Seybou Koita (NIG)	15.04.1994	4	(1)	
Benzion Moshal	31.07.1993	14	(6)	
Gal Tzroya	23.10.1989	5	(3)	1
Sagiv Yehezkel	21.03.1995	8	(1)	3
Trainer:	**DOB**	**M**		
Blagoja Milevski (MKD)	25.03.1971	10		
Yuval Naim [23.11.2018]	22.11.1967	10		
Moshe Ohayon [27.01.2019]	24.05.1983	3		
Avi Buchbut [19.02.2019]	18.05.1969	10		

Hapoel Be'er Sheva Football Club

Founded: 01.05.1949
Stadium: Turner Stadium, Be'er Sheva (16,126)

Goalkeepers:	**DOB**	**M**	**(s)**	**G**
Ariel Harush	08.02.1988	20		
Ohad Levita	17.02.1986	16		
Defenders:	**DOB**	**M**	**(s)**	**G**
Oren Biton	16.06.1994	16	(2)	
Ben Bitton	03.01.1991	24		
Julien Cétout (FRAU)	02.01.1988	2		
Hatem Abd Elhamed	18.03.1991	25	(1)	3
Dor Elo	26.09.1993	7	(1)	
Mihály Korhut (HUN)	01.12.1988	10		1
Miguel Ângelo Leonardo Vítor (POR)	30.06.1989	9		1
Matan Ohayon	25.02.1986	3	(4)	
Samuel Scheimann	03.11.1987	2		
Loai Taha	26.11.1989	27	(1)	
Ben Turgeman	09.01.1986	2		
Shir Tzedek	22.08.1989	14	(8)	
Midfielders:	**DOB**	**M**	**(s)**	**G**
Dan Einbinder	16.02.1989	1		
Hen Ezra	19.01.1989	4	(10)	
Marwan Kabha	23.02.1991	26	(6)	1
Hanan Maman	28.08.1989	20	(8)	5
Benny Natan	14.05.1998		(2)	
John Ugochukwu Ogu (NGA)	20.04.1988	23	(1)	1
Dia Saba	18.11.1992	14	(2)	5
Erik Sabo (SVK)	22.11.1991	22	(7)	1
Kevin Tapoko	13.04.1994	7		
Tomer Yosefi	02.02.1999	4	(5)	1
Forwards:	**DOB**	**M**	**(s)**	**G**
Eden Ben Basat	08.09.1986	6	(10)	1
Yonatan Elias	16.03.1998		(1)	
Mohammad Ghadir	21.01.1991		(1)	
Nigel Hasselbaink (NED)	21.11.1990	18	(14)	6
Guy Melamed	21.12.1992	1		1
Maor Melikson	30.10.1984	30	(3)	3
Michael Ohana	04.10.1995	2	(8)	
Ben Sahar	10.08.1989	29	(4)	14
Niv Zrihen	24.05.1994	12	(9)	3
Trainer:	**DOB**	**M**		
Barak Bakhar	21.09.1979	36		

Hapoel Hadera–Giv'at Olga "Shulem Schwarz" Football Club

Founded: 1936
Stadium: Netanya Stadium, Netanya (13,610)

Goalkeepers:	**DOB**	**M**	**(s)**	**G**
Adi Tabachnik	16.11.1998	2		
Augustine Amamchukwu Ejide (NGA)	08.04.1984	26		
Haviv Ohayon	17.08.1998	7		
Omer Hanin	14.05.1998	1	(2)	
Defenders:	**DOB**	**M**	**(s)**	**G**
Yakov Ababa	20.01.1992	1	(2)	
Gilad Avramov	30.03.2000	6	(2)	
Amit Cohen	21.11.1998	11	(8)	1
Maksim Grechkin	04.03.1996	18	(3)	1
Yahav Gurfinkel	27.06.1998	21	(1)	
Dia Lababidi	26.07.1992	23	(1)	
Yonatan Levi	02.01.1998	5	(1)	
David Mateos Ramajo (ESP)	22.04.1987	26		1
Yarin David Peretz	17.07.1998	20	(4)	1
Wassem Rabah	13.03.1994	21	(1)	
Roy Shohat	10.02.1999		(1)	
Elias Zana	30.12.1990	1	(3)	
Midfielders:	**DOB**	**M**	**(s)**	**G**
Mohammed Abu Fani	27.04.1998	15	(3)	1
Hassan Abu Zaid	04.02.1991	4	(7)	1
Salim Amash	05.07.1994	12	(6)	1
Ali El Khatib	18.03.1989	8	(3)	
Yonatan Elias	16.03.1998		(2)	
George Fochive (USA)	24.03.1992	15		2
Vitali Ganon	11.11.1991	8	(8)	2
Eden Karzev	11.04.2000	11	(2)	2
Eliel Peretz	18.11.1996	18	(11)	4
Kevin Tapoko	13.04.1994	18		1
Menashe Zalka	01.07.1990	17		
Forwards:	**DOB**	**M**	**(s)**	**G**
Eylon Almog	08.01.1999	14	(2)	2
Dovev Gabay	01.04.1987	7	(17)	3
Assi Guma	07.10.1989	1	(11)	2
Lucielmo Palhano Soares "Lúcio Maranhão" (BRA)	28.09.1988	33		13
Nathan Oduwa (ENG)	05.03.1996	9	(4)	1
Oz Peretz	19.04.1994	2	(2)	
Ange-Freddy Plumain (FRA)	02.03.1995	15	(1)	4
Trainer:	**DOB**	**M**		
Nisso Avitan	29.09.1971	34		
Ron Keller [15.05.2019]		2		

Hapoel Haifa Football Club

Founded: 24.04.1924
Stadium: „Sammy Ofer“ Stadium, Haifa (30,870)

Goalkeepers:	**DOB**	**M**	**(s)**	**G**
Ran Kadosh	04.10.1985	3		
Ernestas Šetkus (LTU)	25.05.1985	30		
Defenders:	**DOB**	**M**	**(s)**	**G**
Hen Dilmoni	07.05.1989	2	(2)	
Sean Goldberg	13.06.1995	26		
Nisso Kapiloto	10.01.1989	20	(1)	1
Dor Malul	30.04.1989	30	(1)	1
Guy Mishpati	21.06.1990	4	(5)	
Risto Mitrevski (MKD)	05.10.1991	27		1
Liran Serdal	02.07.1994	7	(6)	
Gabriel Sebastian Tamaș (ROU)	09.11.1983	22	(1)	2
Midfielders:	**DOB**	**M**	**(s)**	**G**
Gal Arel	09.07.1989	19	(11)	5
Shlomo Azulay	30.03.1990	4	(2)	
Radu Gînsari (MDA)	10.12.1991	29	(3)	5
Guy Hadida	23.07.1995	10	(17)	2
Maxim Plakushchenko	04.01.1996	15	(3)	2
Roei Shukrani	26.06.1990	1		
Rasmus Sjöstedt (SWE)	28.02.1992	24	(1)	1
Gil Vermouth	05.08.1985	19	(8)	2
Forwards:	**DOB**	**M**	**(s)**	**G**
Ben Azubel	19.09.1993	19	(9)	5
Dudu Biton	01.03.1988		(2)	
Almog Buzaglo	08.12.1992		(1)	
Eli Elbaz	21.01.1992	6	(6)	2
Matan Hozez	12.08.1996	13	(3)	5
Athanasios Papazoglou (GRE)	30.03.1988	2	(5)	
Idan Shemesh	06.08.1990	5	(5)	2
Ness Zamir	31.10.1990	26	(6)	6
Trainer:	**DOB**	**M**		
Nir Klinger	25.05.1966	6		
Sharon Mimer [31.10.2018]	06.09.1973	24		
Haim Silvas [17.04.2019]	21.11.1975	3		

Hapoel Ironi Kiryat Shmona Football Club

Founded: 2000
Stadium: Kiryat Shmona Municipal Stadium, Kiryat Shmona (5,300)

Goalkeepers:	**DOB**	**M**	**(s)**	**G**
Dziugas Bartkus (LTU)	07.11.1989	31		1
Mahdi Zoabi	15.07.1995	2		
Defenders:	**DOB**	**M**	**(s)**	**G**
Iyad Abu Abaid	31.12.1994	30		2
Hagai Goldenberg	15.09.1990	14	(2)	
Uri Magbo	12.09.1987	8	(6)	
Marcus Plínio Diniz Paixão (BRA)	01.08.1987	19	(1)	1
Jorge García Morcillo (ESP)	11.03.1986	17	(5)	2
Yaaquv Mor	07.01.1993	12	(1)	
Idan Nachmias	17.03.1997	31		3
Yuval Spungin	03.04.1987	6	(1)	
Midfielders:	**DOB**	**M**	**(s)**	**G**
Valon Ahmedi (ALB)	07.10.1994	17	(3)	1
Samuel Bar-On	03.03.1998	28	(2)	1
Vladimir Broun	06.05.1989	20	(6)	
Ido Davidov	23.11.1994		(3)	
Omer Lakau	27.02.1998	7	(9)	
Lucas Días do Nascimento Serafim (BRA)	06.03.1997		(4)	
Yadin Lugasi	04.04.1999	1	(2)	
Ismail Ryan	24.04.1994	21	(6)	4
Eden Shamir	25.06.1995	32		5
Forwards:	**DOB**	**M**	**(s)**	**G**
Shimon Abuhatzira	10.10.1986	8	(9)	1
Yoel Abuhatzira	12.07.1996	12	(5)	3
Hadji Barry (GUI)	08.12.1992	10	(4)	3
Alon Buzorgi	29.03.1990	1	(3)	
Levi Samuel García (TRI)	20.11.1997	18	(2)	3
Nigel Hasselbaink (NED)	21.11.1990	2		1
Rotem Hatuel	12.04.1998		(9)	1
Roy Ronen	17.01.1998		(3)	
Mohammed Shakar	14.11.1996	16	(10)	2
Trainer:	**DOB**	**M**		
Haim Silvas	21.11.1975	16		
Tomer Kashtan [30.12.2018]	25.12.1971	16		
Shimon Hadari [06.05.2019]	07.06.1962	1		

Hapoel Ra'anana Association Football Club

Founded: 1972
Stadium: National Stadium, Ramat Gan, Tel Aviv (41,583)

Goalkeepers:	**DOB**	**M**	**(s)**	**G**
Nîv Antman	02.08.1992	2		
Assaf Tsur	28.08.1998	31		
Defenders:	**DOB**	**M**	**(s)**	**G**
Yarden Cohen	26.03.1997	22	(2)	2
Maor Gerassi	03.10.1994	4	(5)	
Ido Levy	31.07.1990	33		1
Dean Maimoni	04.05.1990	3	(2)	
Emmanuel Mbola (ZAM)	10.05.1993	8		
Teddy Mézague (FRA)	27.05.1990	4		
Adi Nimni	27.08.1991	27		
Ben Vahaba	27.03.1992	29		
Omer Vered	25.01.1990	3	(1)	
Midfielders:	**DOB**	**M**	**(s)**	**G**
Diego Martín Alaníz Ávila (URU)	19.02.1993	6	(3)	1
Tal Ayala	25.05.1989	5	(7)	
Ben Binyamin	17.12.1985	22	(1)	
Ivo Davidov	23.11.1994	2	(5)	
Roy Levy	13.01.2000		(2)	
Nemanja Nikolić (MNE)	01.01.1988	12	(1)	
Mirko Oremuš (CRO)	06.09.1988	28	(2)	1
Ben Sabir	05.03.1998	13	(5)	
Snir Shoker	08.05.1989	3	(11)	
Avihai Yadin	26.10.1986	12	(4)	1
Martin Zeman (CZE)	28.03.1989	4	(6)	
Forwards:	**DOB**	**M**	**(s)**	**G**
Eugene Ansah (GHA)	16.12.1994	10	(1)	5
Karem Arshid	24.01.1995	22	(8)	2
Or Dasa	20.09.1998	15	(9)	3
Qays Ghanem	31.12.1997	22	(8)	7
Ariel Thierry Ngueukam (CMR)	15.11.1988	7	(8)	1
Yoav Tomer	17.01.1998	14	(8)	4
Trainer:	**DOB**	**M**		
Menahem Koretski	04.04.1974	33		

Hapoel Tel Aviv Football Club

Founded: 1923
Stadium: HaMoshava Stadium, Petah Tikva (11,500)

Goalkeepers:	**DOB**	**M**	**(s)**	**G**
Rubi Levkovich	31.08.1988	32		
Arik Yanko	21.12.1991	1		
Defenders:	**DOB**	**M**	**(s)**	**G**
Idan Cohen	06.01.1996	27	(1)	2
Orel Dgani	08.01.1989	27		
Abdi Farhat	03.06.1996	2	(2)	
Adi Gotlieb	16.08.1992	27		1
Marvin Peersman (BEL)	10.02.1991	29	(2)	
Amiran Shkalim	23.03.1988	3	(1)	
Raz Shlomo	13.08.1999	16	(8)	2
Midfielders:	**DOB**	**M**	**(s)**	**G**
Amir Agayev	10.02.1992	7	(6)	1
Emmanuel Boateng (GHA)	17.06.1997	12	(6)	1
Caio César Alves dos Santos (BRA)	29.05.1986	12	(10)	3
Claudemir Ferreira da Silva (BRA)	17.08.1984	16		4
Raz Cohen	11.11.1994	4	(8)	
Shay Elias	25.02.1999	13	(8)	
Nir Lax	10.08.1994	26		1
Roger de Oliveira Bernardo (BRA)	10.08.1985	4	(1)	
Ramzi Safouri	21.10.1995	25	(2)	8
Forwards:	**DOB**	**M**	**(s)**	**G**
Ahmed Abed	30.03.1990	25	(4)	4
Omer Damari	24.03.1989	11	(1)	2
Josef Ganda	10.03.1997	9	(14)	3
Shahar Hirsh	13.02.1993	4	(6)	4
Fejsal Mulić (SRB)	03.10.1994	4	(8)	
Nerijus Valskis (LTU)	04.08.1987	10		1
Roei Zikri	13.10.1992	17	(9)	1
Trainer:	**DOB**	**M**		
Kobi Refua	03.09.1974	10		
Ofir Haim [26.11.2918]	21.04.1975	7		
Kobi Refua [06.01.2019]	03.09.1974	16		

Maccabi Haifa Football Club

Founded: 1913
Stadium: "Sammy Ofer" Stadium, Haifa (30,870)

Goalkeepers:	DOB	M	(s)	G
Omri Glazer	11.03.1996	2	(1)	
Guy Haimov	09.03.1986	33		
Gil Ofek	09.01.1986	1		
Defenders:	**DOB**	**M**	**(s)**	**G**
Allyson Aires dos Santos (BRA)	23.10.1990	12	(3)	
Ofri Arad	11.09.1998	20	(1)	
Rami Gershon	12.08.1988	9	(3)	
Ayid Habshi	10.05.1995	30	(1)	
Ernest Mabouka (CMR)	16.06.1988	34		
Raz Meir	30.11.1996	20	(2)	2
Sun Menahem	07.09.1993	14	(8)	1
Etiënne Reijnen (NED)	05.04.1987	22	(3)	
Midfielders:	**DOB**	**M**	**(s)**	**G**
Mohammed Abu Fani	27.04.1998	4	(4)	1
Gal Alberman	17.04.1983		(2)	
Shlomi Azulay	30.03.1990	12	(5)	2
Kerim Frei (TUR)	19.11.1993	14	(2)	1
Manuel Rolando Iturra Urrutia (CHI)	23.06.1984	1	(1)	
Roi Kehat	12.05.1992	2	(6)	
Neta Lavi	25.08.1996	32	(2)	3
Georges Constant Mandjeck (CMR)	09.12.1988	31	(1)	5
Maxim Plakuschenko	04.01.1996	5	(11)	
Sintyahu Sallalich	01.01.1991	14	(5)	2
Seydouba Guinéenne Soumah (CMR)	11.06.1991	2	(4)	
Forwards:	**DOB**	**M**	**(s)**	**G**
Mohamad Awad	09.06.1997	20	(7)	7
Michiel Kramer (NED)	03.12.1988	4		
Ofir Mizrahi	04.12.1993	2	(5)	
Nikita Rukavytsya (AUS)	22.06.1987	32	(3)	9
Yarden Shua	16.06.1999	8	(7)	3
Shon Weissman	14.02.1996	16	(9)	8
Amit Zenati	02.04.1997		(10)	
Trainer:	**DOB**	**M**		
Fredericus Jacobus Rutten (NED)	05.12.1962	8		
Robertus Leonardus Adrianus Maas (NED) [01.11.2018]	17.12.1969	1		
Eli Guttman [08.11.2018]	24.02.1958	5		
Marco Balbul [19.12.2018]	13.07.1967	25		

Maccabi Netanya Football Club

Founded: 1934
Stadium: Netanya Stadium, Netanya (13,610)

Goalkeepers:	DOB	M	(s)	G
Dani Amos	02.02.1987	32		
Golan Elkaslasi	19.01.1994	4		
Defenders:	**DOB**	**M**	**(s)**	**G**
Dolev Azulai	09.10.1997	9	(4)	
Tim Heubach (GER)	12.04.1988	26	(1)	1
Viki Kahlon	15.01.1993	27	(1)	1
David Tiram	16.09.1993	18	(1)	3
Dudu Twito	06.02.1994	11	(1)	
Branko Vrgoč (CRO)	18.12.1989	19	(1)	
Muhammed Zubeidat	15.11.1991	9	(1)	
Midfielders:	**DOB**	**M**	**(s)**	**G**
Aviv Avraham	30.03.1996	19	(8)	2
Naftali Belay	28.03.1997		(4)	
Moti Barshazky	06.09.1996	13	(16)	4
Jonathan Rey Bornstein (USA)	07.11.1984	25		1
Yaniv Brik	28.05.1995	1		
Stav Finish	26.03.1992	16	(10)	1
Jahmir Hyka (ALB)	08.03.1988	9	(5)	3
Gavriel Kanichowsky	24.08.1997	24	(5)	3
Ali Mohamed	07.10.1995	32		
Nicolas Olsak	25.11.1991	26	(3)	1
Dia Saba	18.11.1992	2		
Elad Shahaf	13.01.1998	1	(1)	
Eylon Yerushalmi	10.03.1997	7	(3)	
Forwards:	**DOB**	**M**	**(s)**	**G**
Fatos Bećiraj (MNE)	05.05.1988	27	(3)	13
Shoval Gozlan	25.04.1994	4	(11)	1
Didier Kougbenya (TOG)	12.11.1995	3	(5)	
Yonas Maldeh	14.11.1999	6	(12)	1
Guy Melamed	21.12.1992	26	(4)	9
Trainer:	**DOB**	**M**		
Slobodan Drapić (SRB)	28.02.1965	36		

Maccabi Petah Tikva Football Club

Founded: 1912
Stadium: HaMoshava Stadium, Petah Tikva (11,500)

Goalkeepers:	DOB	M	(s)	G
Itzhak Gigi	01.12.1988	22		
Yossi Ginzburg	11.10.1991	11		
Defenders:	**DOB**	**M**	**(s)**	**G**
Idan Adneneny	01.04.1997	9	(4)	1
Anton Bratkov (UKR)	14.05.1993	1		
Issa Cissokho (SEN)	23.02.1985	22		1
Omer Danino	17.02.1995	22	(4)	1
Oded Elkayam	09.02.1988	5	(2)	
Johan Martial (MTQ)	30.05.1991	8		
Naor Peser	18.10.1985	9	(2)	
Gal Shish	28.01.1989	30		
Tomáš Sivok (CZE)	15.09.1983	31		3
Midfielders:	**DOB**	**M**	**(s)**	**G**
Franck Bambock (FRA)	07.04.1995	10	(1)	
Tomer Benbenishti	07.01.2000		(3)	
Jean-Charles Didier Kpéhi Brossou (CIV)	23.12.1989	12	(4)	
Armando Enrique Cooper Whitaker (PAN)	26.11.1987	12	(2)	5
Gidi Kanyuk	11.02.1993	31	(1)	5
Harisson Manzala Tusumgama (COD)	06.03.1994	7	(2)	
Romário Santos Pires (BRA)	16.01.1989	18		
Liran Rotman	07.06.1996	3	(10)	1
Muhamad Sarsur	26.04.1999	5	(9)	
Yuval Shabtai	18.12.1986	6	(5)	
Manor Solomon	24.07.1999	11	(1)	2
Itay Tako	23.04.1998	13	(4)	
Forwards:	**DOB**	**M**	**(s)**	**G**
Liel Avda	03.10.2001		(2)	
Tai Baribo	15.01.1998	15	(16)	7
Yosef Shay Benayoun	05.05.1980	10	(2)	3
Lidor Cohen	16.12.1992	21	(10)	2
Eli Elbaz	21.01.1992	5	(6)	1
Mouhamadou Habib Habibou (CTA)	16.04.1987	6	(2)	1
Ofir Mizrahi	04.12.1993	6	(5)	
Fadi Zidan (PLE)	02.06.1993	2		
Trainer:	**DOB**	**M**		
Elisha Levy	18.11.1957	20		
Guy Luzon [20.01.2019]	07.08.1975	13		

Maccabi Tel Aviv Football Club

Founded: 1906 (*as HaRishon LeZion-Yaffo*)
Stadium: Netanya Stadium, Netanya (13,610)

Goalkeepers:	**DOB**	**M**	**(s)**	**G**
Daniel Miller Tenenbaum (BRA)	19.04.1995	5		
Predrag Rajković (SRB)	31.10.1995	31		
Defenders:	**DOB**	**M**	**(s)**	**G**
Eli Dasa	03.12.1992	18	(5)	2
Ofir Davidzada	05.05.1991	7	(1)	
Jair Amador Silos (POR)	21.08.1989	18	(3)	
Maor Kandil	27.11.1993	17		2
Shahar Piven-Bachtiar	21.09.1995	22	(3)	
Enric Saborit Teixidor (ESP)	27.04.1992	29	(1)	3
Eitan Tibi	16.11.1987	7	(1)	
Midfielders:	**DOB**	**M**	**(s)**	**G**
Roslan Barsky	03.01.1992	9	(7)	
Bar Cohen	10.03.2001		(1)	
Dan Glazer	20.09.1996	27	(3)	1
Eyal Golasa	07.10.1991	9		2
Dor Micha	02.03.1992	24	(6)	4
Nadav Aviv Nidam	11.04.2001		(1)	
Dor Peretz	17.05.1995	29	(2)	8
Avi Rikan	10.09.1988	17	(14)	8
Sheran Yeini	08.12.1986	29		1
Forwards:	**DOB**	**M**	**(s)**	**G**
Eliran Atar	17.02.1987	19	(11)	12
Omer Atzili	27.07.1993	23	(6)	11
Yonatan Cohen	29.06.1996	13	(9)	6
Chikeluba Francis Ofoedu (NGA)	12.11.1992	15	(12)	5
Matan Hozez	12.08.1996		(1)	
Aaron Schoenfeld	17.04.1990	4	(10)	3
Itay Shechter	22.02.1987	24	(10)	8
Trainer:	**DOB**	**M**		
Vladimir Ivić (SRB)	07.05.1977	36		

SECOND LEVEL
Liga Leumit 2018/2019

Regular Season

1.	Hapoel Nazareth Illit FC	30	14	12	4	42 - 25	54
2.	Hapoel Katamon Jerusalem FC	30	13	9	8	40 - 33	48
3.	Sektzia Nes Tziona FC	30	14	5	11	48 - 35	47
4.	Hapoel Afula FC	30	12	11	7	38 - 28	47
5.	Hapoel Kfar Saba FC	30	12	8	10	41 - 35	44
6.	Hapoel Ashkelon FC	30	11	11	8	34 - 35	44
7.	Beitar Tel Aviv Ramla FC	30	12	7	11	40 - 37	43
8.	Hapoel Ramat Gan Givatayim FC	30	9	12	9	35 - 35	39
9.	Maccabi Ahi Nazareth FC	30	10	9	11	33 - 38	39
10.	Hapoel Acre FC	30	7	14	9	27 - 31	35
11.	Hapoel Petah Tikva FC	30	12	10	8	39 - 30	34
12.	Hapoel Rishon LeZion FC	30	8	10	12	34 - 43	34
13.	Hapoel Ironi Marmorek Rahevet FC	30	9	6	15	29 - 47	33
14.	Hapoel Bnei Lod Rakevet FC	30	8	8	14	31 - 40	32
15.	Hapoel Nir Ramat HaSharon FC	30	7	10	13	32 - 38	31
16.	Hapoel Iksal FC	30	7	8	15	31 - 44	29

Promotion Play-offs

1.	Hapoel Kfar Saba FC (*Promoted*)	37	18	9	10	53 - 38	63
2.	Sektzia Nes Tziona FC (*Promoted*)	37	18	8	11	57 - 38	62
3.	Hapoel Nazareth Illit FC	37	15	16	6	48 - 32	61
4.	Hapoel Katamon Jerusalem FC	37	15	11	11	44 - 42	56
5.	Hapoel Afula FC	37	14	13	10	43 - 36	55
6.	Hapoel Ashkelon FC	37	14	12	11	46 - 47	54
7.	Beitar Tel Aviv Ramla FC	37	14	8	15	47 - 44	50
8.	Hapoel Ramat Gan Givatayim FC	37	9	14	14	38 - 44	41

Relegation Play-offs

9.	Hapoel Bnei Lod Rakevet FC	37	12	11	14	45 - 48	47
10.	Hapoel Petah Tikva FC	37	15	13	9	50 - 36	46
11.	Maccabi Ahi Nazareth FC	37	12	10	15	43 - 49	46
12.	Hapoel Rishon LeZion FC	37	11	13	13	40 - 49	46
13.	Hapoel Nir Ramat HaSharon FC	37	11	12	14	41 - 42	45
14.	Hapoel Acre FC (*Relegation Play-off*)	37	10	15	12	37 - 38	45
15.	Hapoel Ironi Marmorek Rahevet FC (*Relegated*)	37	10	7	20	35 - 58	37
16.	Hapoel Iksal FC (*Relegated*)	37	7	10	20	35 - 61	31

Relegation Play-off: Hapoel Acre FC - Maccabi Herzliya FC 4-3(2-2) 3-1(1-1)

Hapoel Acre FC remains at second level.

NATIONAL TEAM

INTERNATIONAL MATCHES
(16.07.2018 – 15.07.2019)

07.09.2018	Elbasan	Albania - Israel	1-0(0-0)	(UNL)
11.09.2018	Belfast	Northern Ireland - Israel	3-0(2-0)	(F)
11.10.2018	Haifa	Israel - Scotland	2-1(0-1)	(UNL)
14.10.2018	Beer Sheva	Israel - Albania	2-0(1-0)	(UNL)
15.11.2018	Netanya	Israel - Guatemala	7-0(3-0)	(F)
20.11.2018	Glasgow	Scotland - Israel	3-2(2-1)	(UNL)
21.03.2019	Haifa	Israel - Slovenia	1-1(0-0)	(ECQ)
24.03.2019	Haifa	Israel - Austria	4-2(2-1)	(ECQ)
07.06.2019	Rīga	Latvia - Israel	0-3(0-1)	(ECQ)
10.06.2019	Warszawa	Poland - Israel	4-0(1-0)	(ECQ)

07.09.2018 ALBANIA - ISRAEL 1-0(0-0) UEFA Nations League C, Group 1
Elbasan Arena, Elbasan; Referee: Viktor Kassai (Hungary); Attendance: 4,126
ISR: Guy Haimov, Nissim Kapiloto (80.Dor Micha), Shiran Yeini, Taleb Tawatha, Elazar Dasa, Ayad Habashi, Bibras Natkho (Cap), Beram Kayal (72.Manor Solomon), Dor Peretz, Eran Zahavi (47.Tomer Hemed), Moanes Dabour. Trainer: Andreas Herzog (Austria).

11.09.2018 NORTHERN IRELAND - ISRAEL 3-0(2-0) Friendly International
Windsor Park, Belfast; Referee: Hendrikus Sebastiaan Hermanus "Bas" Nijhuis (Netherlands); Attendance: 12,913
ISR: Guy Haimov, Shiran Yeini, Taleb Tawatha (40.Samuel Scheimann), Eytan Tibi, Elazar Dasa (65.Ben Bitton), Ayad Habashi (46.Nissim Kapiloto), Bibras Natkho (Cap), Dor Micha (59.Alon Turgeman), Dor Peretz, Tomer Hemed (59.Dia Seba), Moanes Dabour (75.Dan Leon Glazer). Trainer: Andreas Herzog (Austria).

11.10.2018 ISRAEL - SCOTLAND 2-1(0-1) UEFA Nations League C, Group 1
"Sammy Ofer" Stadium, Haifa; Referee: Daniel Stefański (Poland); Attendance: 10,234
ISR: Ariel Harush, Shiran Yeini, Taleb Tawatha (76.Eliran Atar), Omri Ben Harush, Eytan Tibi, Elazar Dasa, Bibras Natkho (Cap), Beram Kayal (82.Dan Einbinder), Dor Peretz, Ben Sahar (46.Dia Seba), Moanes Dabour. Trainer: Andreas Herzog (Austria).
Goals: Dor Peretz (52), Kieran Tierney (75 own goal).

14.10.2018 ISRAEL - ALBANIA 2-0(1-0) UEFA Nations League C, Group 1
"Yaakov Turner Toto" Stadium, Beer Sheva; Referee: Paolo Mazzoleni (Italy); Attendance: 14,950
ISR: Ariel Harush, Shiran Yeini, Taleb Tawatha (77.Ayad Habashi), Omri Ben Harush, Eytan Tibi (46.Shir Tzedek), Elazar Dasa, Bibras Natkho (Cap), Beram Kayal, Dor Peretz, Tomer Hemed (66.Dia Seba), Moanes Dabour. Trainer: Andreas Herzog (Austria).
Goals: Tomer Hemed (8), Dia Seba (83).

15.11.2018 ISRAEL - GUATEMALA 7-0(3-0) Friendly International
Netanya Stadium, Netanya; Referee: Jérôme Brisard (France); Attendance: 5,900
ISR: Ariel Harush, Shiran Yeini, Taleb Tawatha (55.Dan Leon Glazer), Omri Ben Harush, Loai Taha (46.Shir Tzedek), Elazar Dasa, Bibras Natkho (Cap) (64.Dor Micha), Beram Kayal (55.Manor Solomon), Dor Peretz, Eran Zahavi (68.Ben Sahar), Moanes Dabour (55.Dia Seba). Trainer: Andreas Herzog (Austria).
Goals: Eran Zahavi (5), Taleb Tawatha (27), Moanes Dabour (37, 53), Dia Seba (62, 78), Ben Sahar (87).

20.11.2018 SCOTLAND - ISRAEL 3-2(2-1) UEFA Nations League C, Group 1
Hampden Park, Glasgow; Referee: Tobias Welz (Germany); Attendance: 21,281
ISR: Ariel Harush, Shiran Yeini, Taleb Tawatha (85.Tomer Hemed), Omri Ben Harush, Loai Taha (67.Almog Cohen), Elazar Dasa, Bibras Natkho (Cap), Beram Kayal, Dor Peretz(73.Dia Seba), Eran Zahavi, Moanes Dabour. Trainer: Andreas Herzog (Austria).
Goals: Beram Kayal (9), Eran Zahavi (75).

21.03.2019 ISRAEL - SLOVENIA 1-1(0-0) 16th EC. Qualifiers
"Sammy Ofer" Stadium, Haifa; Referee: Tiago Bruno Lopes Martins (Portugal); Attendance: 12,430
ISR: Ariel Harush, Shiran Yeini, Taleb Tawatha (77.Yonatan Cohen), Omri Ben Harush, Loai Taha, Elazar Dasa, Bibras Natkho (Cap) (79.Almog Cohen, Beram Kayal (63.Manor Solomon), Dor Peretz, Eran Zahavi, Moanes Dabour. Trainer: Andreas Herzog (Austria).
Goal: Eran Zahavi (55).

24.03.2019 ISRAEL - AUSTRIA 4-2(2-1) 16th EC. Qualifiers
"Sammy Ofer" Stadium, Haifa; Referee: Yevhen Aranovskyi (Ukraine); Attendance: 16,180
ISR: Ariel Harush, Shiran Yeini, Orel Dgani, Omri Ben Harush, Loai Taha (77.Ayad Habashi), Elazar Dasa, Bibras Natkho (Cap), Beram Kayal (72.Almog Cohen), Dor Peretz, Eran Zahavi, Moanes Dabour (80.Tomer Hemed). Trainer: Andreas Herzog (Austria).
Goals: Eran Zahavi (34, 45, 55), Moanes Dabour (66).

07.06.2019 LATVIA - ISRAEL 0-3(0-1) 16th EC. Qualifiers
Daugava Stadium, Rīga; Referee: Sergei Ivanov (Russia); Attendance: 5,508
ISR: Ariel Harush, Shiran Yeini, Omri Ben Harush (81.Yonatan Cohen), Loai Taha, Elazar Dasa, Bibras Natkho (Cap), Beram Kayal (73.Dan Leon Glazer), Nir Bitton, Dia Seba (66.Ben Sahar), Dor Peretz, Eran Zahavi. Trainer: Andreas Herzog (Austria).
Goals: Eran Zahavi (10, 60, 81).

10.06.2019 POLAND - ISRAEL 4-0(1-0) 16th EC. Qualifiers
Stadion Narodowy, Warszawa; Referee: Tobias Stieler (Germany); Attendance: 57,229
ISR: Ariel Harush, Shiran Yeini, Omri Ben Harush, Loai Taha, Elazar Dasa, Bibras Natkho (Cap), Beram Kayal (57.Yonatan Cohen), Nir Bitton (82.Hatem Abd Elhamed), Dor Peretz, Manor Solomon (72.Dia Seba), Eran Zahavi. Trainer: Andreas Herzog (Austria).

NATIONAL TEAM PLAYERS
(16.07.2018 – 15.07.2019)

Name	DOB	Caps	Goals	2018/2019:	*Club*
Goalkeepers					
Guy HAIMOV	09.03.1986	**3**	**0**	2018:	*Maccabi Haifa FC*
Ariel HARUSH	25.05.1988	**19**	**0**	2018/2019:	*Hapoel Be'er Sheva FC*
Defenders					
Omri BEN HARUSH	07.03.1990	**23**	**0**	2018/2019:	*KSC Lokeren (BEL)*
Ben BITTON	03.01.1991	**5**	**0**	2018:	*Hapoel Be'er Sheva FC*
Elazar DASA	03.12.1992	**19**	**0**	2018/2019:	*Maccabi Tel Aviv FC*
Orel DGANI	08.01.1989	**9**	**0**	2019:	*Hapoel Tel Aviv FC*
Hatem Abd ELHAMED	18.03.1991	**1**	**0**	2019:	*Hapoel Be'er Sheva FC*
Ayad HABASHI	10.05.1995	**4**	**0**	2018/2019:	*Maccabi Haifa FC*
Nissim KAPILOTO	01.10.1989	**2**	**0**	2018/2019:	*Hapoel Haifa FC*
Samuel SCHEIMANN	03.11.1987	**2**	**0**	2018:	*Hapoel Be'er Sheva FC*
Loai TAHA	26.11.1989	**7**	**0**	2018/2019:	*Hapoel Be'er Sheva FC*
Taleb TAWATHA	21.06.1992	**16**	**1**	2018/2019:	*Eintracht Frankfurt (GER)*
Eitan TIBI	16.11.1987	**38**	**1**	2018:	*Maccabi Tel Aviv FC*
Shir TZEDEK	22.08.1989	**16**	**0**	2018/2019:	*Hapoel Be'er Sheva FC*
Shiran YEINI	08.12.1986	**28**	**0**	2018/2019:	*Maccabi Tel Aviv FC*
Midfielders					
Nir BITTON	30.10.1991	**23**	**2**	2019:	*Celtic FC Glasgow (SCO)*
Almog COHEN	01.09.1988	**27**	**0**	2018/2019:	*FC Ingolstadt 04 (GER)*
Yonatan COHEN	29.06.1996	**3**	**0**	2019:	*Maccabi Tel Aviv FC*
Dan EINBINDER	16.02.1989	**8**	**1**	2018:	*Beitar Jerusalem FC*
Dan Leon GLAZER	20.09.1996	**3**	**0**	2018/2019:	*Maccabi Tel Aviv FC*
Beram KAYAL	02.05.1988	**43**	**2**	2018/2019:	*Brighton & Hove Albion FC (ENG)*
Dor MICHA	02.03.1992	**4**	**0**	2018:	*Maccabi Tel Aviv FC*
Bibras NATKHO	18.02.1988	**60**	**1**	2018/2019:	*Olympiacos SFP Peiraiás (GRE)*
Dor PERETZ	17.05.1995	**12**	**1**	2018/2019:	*Maccabi Tel Aviv FC*
Eran ZAHAVI	25.07.1987	**46**	**15**	2018/2019:	*Guangzhou R&F FC (CHN)*
Forwards					
Eliran ATAR	17.02.1987	**7**	**1**	2018:	*Maccabi Tel Aviv FC*
Moanes DABOUR	14.05.1992	**15**	**4**	2018/2019:	*FC Red Bull Salzburg (AUT)*
Tomer HEMED	02.05.1987	**36**	**17**	2018/2019:	*Queens Park Rangers FC London (ENG)*
Ben SAHAR	10.08.1989	**44**	**8**	2018/2019:	*Hapoel Be'er Sheva FC*
Dia SABA	18.11.1992	**8**	**3**	2018: 29.01.2019->	*Hapoel Be'er Sheva FC* *Guangzhou R&F FC (CHN)*
Manor SOLOMON	24.07.1999	**4**	**0**	2018: 11.01.2019->	*Maccabi Petah Tikva FC* *FK Shakhtar Donetsk (UKR)*
Alon TURGEMAN	09.06.1991	**2**	**0**	2018:	*FK Austria Wien (AUT)*

National team coach

Andreas HERZOG (Austria) [from 01.08.2018]	10.09.1968	10 M; 5 W; 1 D; 4 L; 21-15

ITALY

The Country:
Repubblica Italiana (Italian Republic)
Capital: Roma
Surface: 301,338 km²
Inhabitants: 60,483,973 [2017]
Time: UTC+1

The FA:
Federazione Italiana Giuoco Calcio
Via Gregorio Allegri 14, CP 2450 00198, Roma
Tel: +39 06 84 912553
Foundation date: 1898
Member of FIFA since: 1905
Member of UEFA since: 1954
Website: www.figc.it

NATIONAL TEAM RECORDS

First international match:	15.05.1910, Milano:	Italy – France 6-2
Most international caps:	Gianluigi Buffon	- 176 caps (1997-2018)
Most international goals:	Luigi Riva	- 35 goals / 42 caps (1965-1974)

UEFA EUROPEAN CHAMPIONSHIP	
1960	Did not enter
1964	Qualifiers
1968	**Final Tournament (Winners)**
1972	Qualifiers
1976	Qualifiers
1980	Final Tournament (4th Place)
1984	Qualifiers
1988	Final Tournament (Semi-Finals)
1992	Qualifiers
1996	Final Tournament (Group Stage)
2000	Final Tournament (Runners-up)
2004	Final Tournament (Group Stage)
2008	Final Tournament (Quarter-Finals)
2012	Final Tournament (Runners-up)
2016	Final Tournament (Quarter-Finals)

FIFA WORLD CUP	
1930	Did not enter
1934	**Final Tournament (Winners)**
1938	**Final Tournament (Winners)**
1950	Final Tournament (Group Stage)
1954	Final Tournament (Group Stage)
1958	Qualifiers
1962	Final Tournament (Group Stage)
1966	Final Tournament (Group Stage)
1970	Final Tournament (Runners-up)
1974	Final Tournament (Group Stage)
1978	Final Tournament (4th Place)
1982	**Final Tournament (Winners)**
1986	Final Tournament (Second Round of 16)
1990	Final Tournament (3rd Place)
1994	Final Tournament (Runners-up)
1998	Final Tournament (Quarter-Finals)
2002	Final Tournament (Second Round of 16)
2006	**Final Tournament (Winners)**
2010	Final Tournament (Group Stage)
2014	Final Tournament (Group Stage)
2018	Qualifiers

UEFA NATIONS LEAGUE
2018/2019 – League A

OLYMPIC FOOTBALL TOURNAMENTS 1908-2016							
1908	-	**1948**	Quarter-Finals	**1972**	Qualifiers	**1996**	Group Stage
1912	Round 1	**1952**	Round 1	**1976**	Did not enter	**2000**	Quarter-Finals
1920	Quarter-Finals	**1956**	Did not enter	**1980**	Group Stage	**2004**	3rd Place
1924	Quarter-Finals	**1960**	4th Place	**1984**	4th Place	**2008**	Quarter-Finals
1928	3rd Place	**1964**	Qualifiers	**1988**	4th Place	**2012**	Qualifiers
1936	**Winners**	**1968**	*Withdrew*	**1992**	Quarter-Finals	**2016**	Qualifiers

FIFA CONFEDERATIONS CUP 1992-2017
2009 (Group Stage), 2013 (3rd Place)

ITALIAN CLUB HONOURS IN EUROPEAN CLUB COMPETITIONS:

European Champion Clubs' Cup (1956-1992) / UEFA Champions League (1993-2019)		
AC Milan	7	1962/1963, 1968/1969, 1988/1989, 1989/1990, 1993/1994, 2002/2003, 2006/2007
FC Internazionale Milano	3	1963/1964, 1964/1965, 2009/2010
Juventus FC Torino	2	1984/1985, 1995/1996
Fairs Cup (1858-1971) / UEFA Cup (1972-2009) / UEFA Europa League (2010-2019)		
Juventus FC Torino	3	1976/1977, 1989/1990, 1992/1993
FC Internazionale Milano	3	1990/1991, 1993/1994, 1997/1998
AC Parma	2	1994/1995, 1998/1999
AS Roma	1	1960/1961
SSC Napoli	1	1988/1989

UEFA Super Cup (1972-2018)		
AC Milan	**5**	1989, 1990, 1994, 2003, 2007
Juventus FC Torino	**2**	1984, 1996
AC Parma	**1**	1993
SS Lazio Roma	**1**	1999
European Cup Winners' Cup 1961-1999*		
AC Milan	**2**	1967/1968, 1972/1973
AC Fiorentina	**1**	1960/1961
Juventus FC Torino	**1**	1983/1984
UC Sampdoria Genova	**1**	1989/1990
AC Parma	**1**	1992/1993

defunct competition

NATIONAL COMPETITIONS TABLE OF HONOURS

	CHAMPIONS	CUP WINNERS	BEST GOALSCORERS	
1898	Genoa CFC	-	-	
1899	Genoa CFC	-	-	
1900	Genoa CFC	-	-	
1901	AC Milan	-	-	
1902	Genoa CFC	-	-	
1903	Genoa CFC	-	-	
1904	Genoa CFC	-	-	
1905	Juventus FC Torino	-	-	
1906	AC Milan	-	-	
1907	AC Milan	-	-	
1908	FC Pro Vercelli	-	-	
1909	FC Pro Vercelli	-	-	
1909/1910	FC Internazionale Milano	-	-	
1910/1911	FC Pro Vercelli	-	-	
1911/1912	FC Pro Vercelli	-	-	
1912/1913	FC Pro Vercelli	-	-	
1913/1914	Casale FBC	-	-	
1914/1915	Genoa CFC	-	-	
1915/1916	*No competition*	-	-	
1916/1917	*No competition*	-	-	
1917/1918	*No competition*	-	-	
1918/1919	*No competition*	-	-	
1919/1920	FC Internazionale Milano	-	-	
1920/1921	FC Pro Vercelli	-	-	
1921/1922	USD Novese Novi Ligure (FIGC) FC Pro Vercelli (CCI)	FC Vado	-	
1922/1923	Genoa CFC	*No competition*	-	
1923/1924	Genoa CFC	*No competition*	Heinrich Schönfeld (AUT, FBC Torino)	22
1924/1925	Bologna SC	*No competition*	Mario Magnozzi (AS Livorno Calcio)	19
1925/1926	Juventus FC Torino	*No competition*	Ferenc Hirzer (HUN, Juventus FC Torino)	35
1926/1927	*Not awarded*	*No competition*	Anton Powolny (FC Internazionale Milano)	22
1927/1928	FBC Torino	*No competition*	Julio Libonatti (ARG, FBC Torino)	35
1928/1929	Bologna SC	*No competition*	Gino Rossetti (FBC Torino)	36
1929/1930	Ambrosiana-Inter Milano	*No competition*	Giuseppe Meazza (Ambrosiana-Inter Milano)	31
1930/1931	Juventus FC Torino	*No competition*	Rodolfo Volk (AS Roma)	29
1931/1932	Juventus FC Torino	*No competition*	Pedro Petrone Schiavione (URU, ACF Fiorentina) Angelo Schiavio (Bologna SC)	25
1932/1933	Juventus FC Torino	*No competition*	Felice Placido Borel (Juventus FC Torino)	29
1933/1934	Juventus FC Torino	*No competition*	Felice Placido Borel (Juventus FC Torino)	31
1934/1935	Juventus FC Torino	*No competition*	Enrico Guaita (ARG, AS Roma)	31
1935/1936	Bologna AGC	FBC Torino	Giuseppe Meazza (Ambrosiana-Inter Milano)	25
1936/1937	Bologna AGC	Genoa CFC	Silvio Piola (SS Lazio Roma)	21
1937/1938	Ambrosiana-Inter Milano	Juventus FC Torino	Giuseppe Meazza (Ambrosiana-Inter Milano)	20
1938/1939	Bologna AGC	FC Internazionale Milano	Aldo Boffi (AC Milan) Héctor Puricelli (URU, Bologna AGC)	19
1939/1940	Ambrosiana-Inter Milano	ACF Fiorentina	Aldo Boffi (AC Milan)	24
1940/1941	Bologna AGC	Venezia FBC	Héctor Puricelli (URU, Bologna AGC)	22
1941/1942	AS Roma	Juventus FC Torino	Aldo Boffi (AC Milan)	22
1942/1943	AC Torino	AC Torino	Silvio Piola (SS Lazio Roma)	21
1944	AC Spezia (*honorific title awarded in 2002*)	*No competition*	-	
1944/1945	*No competition*	*No competition*	-	
1945/1946	AC Torino	*No competition*	Guglielmo Gabetto (AC Torino)	22
1946/1947	AC Torino	*No competition*	Valentino Mazzola (AC Torino)	29
1947/1948	AC Torino	*No competition*	Giampiero Boniperti (Juventus FC Torino)	27
1948/1949	AC Torino	*No competition*	István Nyers (HUN, FC Internazionale Milano)	26

1949/1950	Juventus FC Torino	*No competition*	Gunnar Nordahl (SWE, AC Milan)	35
1950/1951	AC Milan	*No competition*	Gunnar Nordahl (SWE, AC Milan)	34
1951/1952	Juventus FC Torino	*No competition*	John Hansen (DEN, Juventus FC Torino)	30
1952/1953	FC Internazionale Milano	*No competition*	Gunnar Nordahl (SWE, AC Milan)	26
1953/1954	FC Internazionale Milano	*No competition*	Gunnar Nordahl (SWE, AC Milan)	23
1954/1955	AC Milan	*No competition*	Gunnar Nordahl (SWE, AC Milan)	26
1955/1956	ACF Fiorentina	*No competition*	Gino Pivatelli (Bologna FC)	29
1956/1957	AC Milan	*No competition*	Dino da Costa (BRA, AS Roma)	22
1957/1958	Juventus FC Torino	SS Lazio Roma	William John Charles (WAL, Juventus FC Torino)	28
1958/1959	AC Milan	Juventus FC Torino	Antonio Valentin Angelillo (ARG, FC Internazionale Milano)	33
1959/1960	Juventus FC Torino	Juventus FC Torino	Enrique Omar Sivori (ARG, Juventus FC Torino)	28
1960/1961	Juventus FC Torino	ACF Fiorentina	Sergio Brighenti (Sampdoria UC Genova)	27
1961/1962	AC Milan	SSC Napoli	José João Altafini "Mazzola" (BRA, AC Milan) Aurelio Milani (ACF Fiorentina)	22
1962/1963	FC Internazionale Milano	Atalanta Bergamasca Calcio	Harald Nielsen (DEN, Bologna FC) Pedro Waldemar Manfredini (ARG, AS Roma)	19
1963/1964	Bologna FC	AS Roma	Harald Nielsen (DEN, Bologna FC)	21
1964/1965	FC Internazionale Milano	Juventus FC Torino	Alessandro Mazzola (FC Internazionale Milano) Alberto Orlando (ACF Fiorentina)	17
1965/1966	FC Internazionale Milano	ACF Fiorentina	Luis Vinicio (Lanerossi Vicenza)	25
1966/1967	Juventus FC Torino	AC Milan	Luigi Riva (US Cagliari)	18
1967/1968	AC Milan	AC Torino	Pierino Prati (AC Milan)	15
1968/1969	ACF Fiorentina	AS Roma	Luigi Riva (US Cagliari)	21
1969/1970	US Cagliari	Bologna FC	Luigi Riva (US Cagliari)	21
1970/1971	FC Internazionale Milano	AC Torino	Roberto Boninsegna (FC Internazionale Milano)	24
1971/1972	Juventus FC Torino	AC Milan	Roberto Boninsegna (FC Internazionale Milano)	22
1972/1973	Juventus FC Torino	AC Milan	Giuseppe Savoldi (Bologna FC) Paolino Pulici (AC Torino) Gianni Rivera (AC Milan)	17
1973/1974	SS Lazio Roma	Bologna FC	Giorgio Chinaglia (SS Lazio Roma)	24
1974/1975	Juventus FC Torino	ACF Fiorentina	Paolino Pulici (AC Torino)	18
1975/1976	AC Torino	SSC Napoli	Paolino Pulici (AC Torino)	21
1976/1977	Juventus FC Torino	AC Milan	Francesco Graziani (AC Torino)	21
1977/1978	Juventus FC Torino	FC Internazionale Milano	Paolo Rossi (Lanerossi Vicenza)	24
1978/1979	AC Milan	Juventus FC Torino	Bruno Giordano (SS Lazio Roma)	19
1979/1980	FC Internazionale Milano	AS Roma	Roberto Bettega (Juventus FC Torino)	16
1980/1981	Juventus FC Torino	AS Roma	Roberto Pruzzo (AS Roma)	18
1981/1982	Juventus FC Torino	FC Internazionale Milano	Roberto Pruzzo (AS Roma)	15
1982/1983	AS Roma	Juventus FC Torino	Michel Platini (FRA, Juventus FC Torino)	16
1983/1984	Juventus FC Torino	AS Roma	Michel Platini (FRA, Juventus FC Torino)	20
1984/1985	AC Hellas Verona	Sampdoria UC Genova	Michel Platini (FRA, Juventus FC Torino)	18
1985/1986	Juventus FC Torino	AS Roma	Roberto Pruzzo (AS Roma)	19
1986/1987	SSC Napoli	SSC Napoli	Pietro Paolo Virdis (AC Milan)	17
1987/1988	AC Milan	Sampdoria UC Genova	Diego Armando Maradona (ARG, SSC Napoli)	15
1988/1989	FC Internazionale Milano	Sampdoria UC Genova	Aldo Serena (FC Internazionale Milano)	22
1989/1990	SSC Napoli	Juventus FC Torino	Marcel van Basten (NED, AC Milan)	19
1990/1991	Sampdoria UC Genova	AS Roma	Gianluca Vialli (Sampdoria UC Genova)	19
1991/1992	AC Milan	AC Parma	Marcel van Basten (NED, AC Milan)	25
1992/1993	AC Milan	Torino Calcio	Giuseppe Signori (SS Lazio Roma)	26
1993/1994	AC Milan	Sampdoria UC Genova	Giuseppe Signori (SS Lazio Roma)	23
1994/1995	Juventus FC Torino	Juventus FC Torino	Gabriel Omar Batistuta (ARG, ACF Fiorentina)	26
1995/1996	AC Milan	ACF Fiorentina	Igor Protti (AS Bari) Giuseppe Signori (SS Lazio Roma)	24
1996/1997	Juventus FC Torino	Vicenza Calcio	Filippo Inzaghi (Atalanta Bergamasca Calcio)	24
1997/1998	Juventus FC Torino	SS Lazio Roma	Oliver Bierhoff (GER, Udinese Calcio)	27
1998/1999	AC Milan	AC Parma	Márcio Amoroso dos Santos (BRA, Udinese Calcio)	22
1999/2000	SS Lazio Roma	SS Lazio Roma	Andriy Shevchenko (UKR, AC Milan)	24
2000/2001	AS Roma	ACF Fiorentina	Hernán Jorge Crespo (ARG, SS Lazio Roma)	26
2001/2002	Juventus FC Torino	AC Parma	David Sergio Trezeguet (FRA, Juventus FC Torino) Dario Hübner (Piacenza Calcio)	24
2002/2003	Juventus FC Torino	AC Milan	Christian Vieri (FC Internazionale Milano)	24
2003/2004	AC Milan	SS Lazio Roma	Andriy Shevchenko (UKR, AC Milan)	24
2004/2005	*Not awarded*	FC Internazionale Milano	Cristiano Lucarelli (AS Livorno Calcio)	24
2005/2006	FC Internazionale Milano	FC Internazionale Milano	Luca Toni (ACF Fiorentina)	31
2006/2007	FC Internazionale Milano	AS Roma	Francesco Totti (AS Roma)	26
2007/2008	FC Internazionale Milano	AS Roma	Alessandro Del Piero (Juventus FC Torino)	21
2008/2009	FC Internazionale Milano	SS Lazio Roma	Zlatan Ibrahimović (SWE, FC Internazionale Milano)	25
2009/2010	FC Internazionale Milano	FC Internazionale Milano	Antonio Di Natale (Udinese Calcio)	29
2010/2011	AC Milan	FC Internazionale Milano	Antonio Di Natale (Udinese Calcio)	28
2011/2012	Juventus FC Torino	SSC Napoli	Zlatan Ibrahimović (SWE, AC Milan)	28
2012/2013	Juventus FC Torino	SS Lazio Roma	Edinson Roberto Cavani Gómez (URU, SSC Napoli)	29
2013/2014	Juventus FC Torino	SSC Napoli	Ciro Immobile (Torino FC)	22
2014/2015	Juventus FC Torino	Juventus FC Torino	Mauro Emanuel Icardi (ARG, FC Internazionale Milano) Luca Toni (Hellas Verona FC)	22
2015/2016	Juventus FC Torino	Juventus FC Torino	Gonzalo Gerardo Higuaín (ARG, SSC Napoli)	36
2016/2017	Juventus FC Torino	Juventus FC Torino	Edin Džeko (BIH, AS Roma)	29

2017/2018	Juventus FC Torino	Juventus FC Torino	Mauro Emanuel Icardi (ARG, FC Internazionale Milano) Ciro Immobile (SS Lazio Roma)	29
2018/2019	Juventus FC Torino	SS Lazio Roma	Fabio Quagliarella (Sampdoria UC Genova)	26

NATIONAL CHAMPIONSHIP
Serie A 2018/2019
(18.08.2018 – 26.05.2019)

Results

Round 1 [18-20.08.2018]
Chievo Verona - Juventus 2-3(1-1)
Lazio Roma - SSC Napoli 1-2(1-1)
Torino FC - AS Roma 0-1(0-0)
Bologna FC - SPAL Ferrara 0-1(0-0)
Empoli FC - Cagliari 2-0(1-0)
Parma - Udinese 2-2(1-0)
US Sassuolo - Internazionale 1-0(1-0)
Atalanta - Frosinone 4-0(1-0)
Sampdoria - Fiorentina 1-1(0-1) [19.09.]
AC Milan - Genoa CFC 2-1(1-0) [31.10.]

Round 2 [25-27.08.2018]
Juventus - Lazio Roma 2-0(1-0)
SSC Napoli - AC Milan 3-2(0-1)
SPAL Ferrara - Parma 1-0(0-0)
Cagliari - US Sassuolo 2-2(1-0)
Fiorentina - Chievo Verona 6-1(2-0)
Frosinone - Bologna FC 0-0
Genoa CFC - Empoli FC 2-1(2-0)
Internazionale - Torino FC 2-2(2-0)
Udinese - Sampdoria 1-0(1-0)
AS Roma - Atalanta 3-3(1-3)

Round 3 [31.08.-02.09.2018]
AC Milan - AS Roma 2-1(1-0)
Bologna FC - Internazionale 0-3(0-0)
Parma - Juventus 1-2(1-1)
Fiorentina - Udinese 1-0(0-0)
Atalanta - Cagliari 0-1(0-1)
Chievo Verona - Empoli FC 0-0
Lazio Roma - Frosinone 1-0(0-0)
Sampdoria - SSC Napoli 3-0(2-0)
US Sassuolo - Genoa CFC 5-3(4-1)
Torino FC - SPAL Ferrara 1-0(0-0)

Round 4 [15-17.09.2018]
Internazionale - Parma 0-1(0-0)
SSC Napoli - Fiorentina 1-0(0-0)
Frosinone - Sampdoria 0-5(0-1)
AS Roma - Chievo Verona 2-2(2-0)
Genoa CFC - Bologna FC 1-0(0-0)
Juventus - US Sassuolo 2-1(0-0)
Udinese - Torino FC 1-1(1-0)
Empoli FC - Lazio Roma 0-1(0-0)
Cagliari - AC Milan 1-1(1-0)
SPAL Ferrara - Atalanta 2-0(0-0)

Round 5 [21-23.09.2018]
US Sassuolo - Empoli FC 3-1(1-1)
Parma - Cagliari 2-0(1-0)
Fiorentina - SPAL Ferrara 3-0(2-0)
Sampdoria - Internazionale 0-1(0-0)
Torino FC - SSC Napoli 1-3(0-2)
Bologna FC - AS Roma 2-0(1-0)
Chievo Verona - Udinese 0-2(0-0)
Lazio Roma - Genoa CFC 4-1(2-0)
AC Milan - Atalanta 2-2(1-0)
Frosinone - Juventus 0-2(0-0)

Round 6 [25-27.09.2018]
Internazionale - Fiorentina 2-1(1-0)
Udinese - Lazio Roma 1-2(0-0)
Atalanta - Torino FC 0-0
Cagliari - Sampdoria 0-0
Genoa CFC - Chievo Verona 2-0(1-0)
Juventus - Bologna FC 2-0(2-0)
SSC Napoli - Parma 3-0(1-0)
AS Roma - Frosinone 4-0(3-0)
SPAL Ferrara - US Sassuolo 0-2(0-0)
Empoli FC - AC Milan 1-1(0-1)

Round 7 [29.09.-01.10.2018]
AS Roma - Lazio Roma 3-1(1-0)
Juventus - SSC Napoli 3-1(1-1)
Internazionale - Cagliari 2-0(1-0)
Bologna FC - Udinese 2-1(1-1)
Chievo Verona - Torino FC 0-1(0-0)
Fiorentina - Atalanta 2-0(0-0)
Frosinone - Genoa CFC 1-2(1-2)
Parma - Empoli FC 1-0(1-0)
US Sassuolo - AC Milan 1-4(0-1)
Sampdoria - SPAL Ferrara 2-1(1-1)

Round 8 [05-07.10.2018]
Torino FC - Frosinone 3-2(1-0)
Cagliari - Bologna FC 2-0(1-0)
Udinese - Juventus 0-2(0-2)
Empoli FC - AS Roma 0-2(0-1)
Genoa CFC - Parma 1-3(1-3)
Atalanta - Sampdoria 0-1(0-0)
Lazio Roma - Fiorentina 1-0(1-0)
AC Milan - Chievo Verona 3-1(2-0)
SSC Napoli - US Sassuolo 2-0(1-0)
SPAL Ferrara - Internazionale 1-2(0-1)

Round 9 [20-22.10.2018]
AS Roma - SPAL Ferrara 0-2(0-1)
Juventus - Genoa CFC 1-1(1-0)
Udinese - SSC Napoli 0-3(0-1)
Frosinone - Empoli FC 3-3(1-1)
Bologna FC - Torino FC 2-2(0-1)
Chievo Verona - Atalanta 1-5(0-2)
Parma - Lazio Roma 0-2(0-0)
Fiorentina - Cagliari 1-1(0-0)
Internazionale - AC Milan 1-0(0-0)
Sampdoria - US Sassuolo 0-0

Round 10 [27-29.10.2018]
Atalanta - Parma 3-0(0-0)
Empoli FC - Juventus 1-2(1-0)
Torino FC - Fiorentina 1-1(1-1)
US Sassuolo - Bologna FC 2-2(1-1)
Cagliari - Chievo Verona 2-1(1-0)
Genoa CFC - Udinese 2-2(1-0)
SPAL Ferrara - Frosinone 0-3(0-1)
AC Milan - Sampdoria 3-2(2-2)
SSC Napoli - AS Roma 1-1(0-1)
Lazio Roma - Internazionale 0-3(0-2)

Round 11 [02-04.11.2018]
SSC Napoli - Empoli FC 5-1(2-0)
Internazionale - Genoa CFC 5-0(2-0)
Fiorentina - AS Roma 1-1(1-0)
Juventus - Cagliari 3-1(2-1)
Lazio Roma - SPAL Ferrara 4-1(2-1)
Chievo Verona - US Sassuolo 0-2(0-1)
Parma - Frosinone 0-0
Sampdoria - Torino FC 1-4(0-2)
Bologna FC - Atalanta 1-2(1-0)
Udinese - AC Milan 0-1(0-0)

Round 12 [09-11.11.2018]
Frosinone - Fiorentina 1-1(0-0)
Torino FC - Parma 1-2(1-2)
SPAL Ferrara - Cagliari 2-2(1-0)
Genoa CFC - SSC Napoli 1-2(1-0)
Atalanta - Internazionale 4-1(1-0)
Chievo Verona - Bologna FC 2-2(2-1)
Empoli FC - Udinese 2-1(1-0)
AS Roma - Sampdoria 4-1(1-0)
US Sassuolo - Lazio Roma 1-1(1-1)
AC Milan - Juventus 0-2(0-1)

Round 13 [24-26.11.2018]
Udinese - AS Roma 1-0(0-0)
Juventus - SPAL Ferrara 2-0(1-0)
Internazionale - Frosinone 3-0(1-0)
Parma - US Sassuolo 2-1(2-1)
Bologna FC - Fiorentina 0-0
Empoli FC - Atalanta 3-2(1-2)
SSC Napoli - Chievo Verona 0-0
Lazio Roma - AC Milan 1-1(0-0)
Genoa CFC - Sampdoria 1-1(1-1)
Cagliari - Torino FC 0-0

Round 14 [01-03.12.2018]
SPAL Ferrara - Empoli FC 2-2(1-2)
Fiorentina - Juventus 0-3(0-1)
Sampdoria - Bologna FC 4-1(3-1)
AC Milan - Parma 2-1(0-0)
Frosinone - Cagliari 1-1(1-0)
US Sassuolo - Udinese 0-0
Torino FC - Genoa CFC 2-1(2-1)
Chievo Verona - Lazio Roma 1-1(1-0)
AS Roma - Internazionale 2-2(0-1)
Atalanta - SSC Napoli 1-2(0-1)

Round 15 [07-09.12.2018]
Juventus - Internazionale 1-0(0-0)
SSC Napoli - Frosinone 4-0(2-0)
Cagliari - AS Roma 2-2(0-2)
Lazio Roma - Sampdoria 2-2(0-1)
US Sassuolo - Fiorentina 3-3(0-0)
Empoli FC - Bologna FC 2-1(1-1)
Parma - Chievo Verona 1-1(0-0)
Udinese - Atalanta 1-3(1-1)
Genoa CFC - SPAL Ferrara 1-1(1-1)
AC Milan - Torino FC 0-0

Round 16 [15-18.12.2018]
Internazionale - Udinese 1-0(0-0)
Torino FC - Juventus 0-1(0-0)
SPAL Ferrara - Chievo Verona 0-0
Fiorentina - Empoli FC 3-1(1-1)
Frosinone - US Sassuolo 0-2(0-1)
Sampdoria - Parma 2-0(0-0)
Cagliari - SSC Napoli 0-1(0-0)
AS Roma - Genoa CFC 3-2(2-2)
Atalanta - Lazio Roma 1-0(1-0)
Bologna FC - AC Milan 0-0

Round 17 [22.12.2018]
Lazio Roma - Cagliari 3-1(2-0)
Empoli FC - Sampdoria 2-4(1-1)
Genoa CFC - Atalanta 3-1(1-0)
AC Milan - Fiorentina 0-1(0-0)
SSC Napoli - SPAL Ferrara 1-0(1-0)
US Sassuolo - Torino FC 1-1(0-0)
Udinese - Frosinone 1-1(1-0)
Chievo Verona - Internazionale 1-1(0-1)
Parma - Bologna FC 0-0
Juventus - AS Roma 1-0(1-0)

Round 18 [26.12.2018]
Frosinone - AC Milan 0-0
Atalanta - Juventus 2-2(1-1)
Bologna FC - Lazio Roma 0-2(0-1)
Cagliari - Genoa CFC 1-0(1-0)
Fiorentina - Parma 0-1(0-1)
Sampdoria - Chievo Verona 2-0(0-0)
AS Roma - US Sassuolo 3-1(2-0)
SPAL Ferrara - Udinese 0-0
Torino FC - Empoli FC 3-0(1-0)
Internazionale - SSC Napoli 1-0(0-0)

Round 19 [29.12.2018]
Juventus - Sampdoria 2-1(1-1)
Chievo Verona - Frosinone 1-0(0-0)
Empoli FC - Internazionale 0-1(0-0)
Genoa CFC - Fiorentina 0-0
Lazio Roma - Torino FC 1-1(0-1)
Parma - AS Roma 0-2(0-0)
US Sassuolo - Atalanta 2-6(0-2)
Udinese - Cagliari 2-0(1-0)
SSC Napoli - Bologna FC 3-2(1-1)
AC Milan - SPAL Ferrara 2-1(1-1)

Round 20 [19-21.01.2019]
AS Roma - Torino FC 3-2(2-0)
Udinese - Parma 1-2(0-1)
Internazionale - US Sassuolo 0-0
Frosinone - Atalanta 0-5(0-2)
SPAL Ferrara - Bologna FC 1-1(0-1)
Fiorentina - Sampdoria 3-3(1-1)
Cagliari - Empoli FC 2-2(1-0)
SSC Napoli - Lazio Roma 2-1(2-0)
Genoa CFC - AC Milan 0-2(0-0)
Juventus - Chievo Verona 3-0(2-0)

Round 21 [26-28.01.2019]
US Sassuolo - Cagliari 3-0(2-0)
Sampdoria - Udinese 4-0(1-0)
AC Milan - SSC Napoli 0-0
Chievo Verona - Fiorentina 3-4(1-2)
Bologna FC - Frosinone 0-4(0-2)
Atalanta - AS Roma 3-3(1-3)
Parma - SPAL Ferrara 2-3(1-0)
Torino FC - Internazionale 1-0(1-0)
Lazio Roma - Juventus 1-2(0-0)
Empoli FC - Genoa CFC 1-3(0-1)

Round 22 [02-04.02.2019]
Empoli FC - Chievo Verona 2-2(1-2)
SSC Napoli - Sampdoria 3-0(2-0)
Juventus - Parma 3-3(1-0)
SPAL Ferrara - Torino FC 0-0
Udinese - Fiorentina 1-1(0-0)
Genoa CFC - US Sassuolo 1-1(1-1)
Internazionale - Bologna FC 0-1(0-1)
AS Roma - AC Milan 1-1(0-1)
Frosinone - Lazio Roma 0-1(0-1)
Cagliari - Atalanta 0-1(0-0)

Round 23 [07-10.02.2019]
Lazio Roma - Empoli FC 1-0(1-0)
Chievo Verona - AS Roma 0-3(0-2)
Fiorentina - SSC Napoli 0-0
Parma - Internazionale 0-1(0-0)
Bologna FC - Genoa CFC 1-1(1-1)
Sampdoria - Frosinone 0-1(0-1)
Atalanta - SPAL Ferrara 2-1(0-1)
Torino FC - Udinese 1-0(1-0)
US Sassuolo - Juventus 0-3(0-1)
AC Milan - Cagliari 3-0(2-0)

Round 24 [15-18.02.2019]
Juventus - Frosinone 3-0(2-0)
Cagliari - Parma 2-1(0-1)
Atalanta - AC Milan 1-3(1-1)
SPAL Ferrara - Fiorentina 1-4(1-1)
Udinese - Chievo Verona 1-0(0-0)
Genoa CFC - Lazio Roma 2-1(0-1)
Empoli FC - US Sassuolo 3-0(2-0)
Internazionale - Sampdoria 2-1(0-0)
SSC Napoli - Torino FC 0-0
AS Roma - Bologna FC 2-1(0-0)

Round 25 [22-24.02.2019]
AC Milan - Empoli FC 3-0(0-0)
Torino FC - Atalanta 2-0(1-0)
Frosinone - AS Roma 2-3(1-2)
Sampdoria - Cagliari 1-0(0-0)
Chievo Verona - Genoa CFC 0-0
Bologna FC - Juventus 0-1(0-0)
US Sassuolo - SPAL Ferrara 1-1(1-0)
Parma - SSC Napoli 0-4(0-2)
Fiorentina - Internazionale 3-3(1-2)
Lazio Roma - Udinese 2-0(2-0) [17.04.]

Round 26 [01-03.03.2019]
Cagliari - Internazionale 2-1(2-1)
Empoli FC - Parma 3-3(1-2)
AC Milan - US Sassuolo 1-0(1-0)
Lazio Roma - AS Roma 3-0(1-0)
Torino FC - Chievo Verona 3-0(0-0)
Udinese - Bologna FC 2-1(1-1)
Genoa CFC - Frosinone 0-0
SPAL Ferrara - Sampdoria 1-2(0-2)
Atalanta - Fiorentina 3-1(2-1)
SSC Napoli - Juventus 1-2(0-2)

Round 27 [08-11.03.2019]
Juventus - Udinese 4-1(2-0)
Parma - Genoa CFC 1-0(0-0)
Chievo Verona - AC Milan 1-2(1-1)
Bologna FC - Cagliari 2-0(1-0)
Sampdoria - Atalanta 1-2(0-0)
Internazionale - SPAL Ferrara 2-0(0-0)
Frosinone - Torino FC 1-2(1-0)
US Sassuolo - SSC Napoli 1-1(0-0)
Fiorentina - Lazio Roma 1-1(0-1)
AS Roma - Empoli FC 2-1(2-1)

Round 28 [15-17.03.2019]
Cagliari - Fiorentina 2-1(0-0)
US Sassuolo - Sampdoria 3-5(1-3)
SPAL Ferrara - AS Roma 2-1(1-0)
Torino FC - Bologna FC 2-3(1-2)
Genoa CFC - Juventus 2-0(0-0)
Atalanta - Chievo Verona 1-1(0-1)
Empoli FC - Frosinone 2-1(2-0)
Lazio Roma - Parma 4-1(4-0)
SSC Napoli - Udinese 4-2(2-2)
AC Milan - Internazionale 2-3(0-1)

Round 29 [29-31.03.2019]
Chievo Verona - Cagliari 0-3(0-3)
Udinese - Genoa CFC 2-0(1-0)
Juventus - Empoli FC 1-0(0-0)
Sampdoria - AC Milan 1-0(1-0)
Parma - Atalanta 1-3(1-1)
AS Roma - SSC Napoli 1-4(1-1)
Frosinone - SPAL Ferrara 0-1(0-1)
Fiorentina - Torino FC 1-1(1-1)
Bologna FC - US Sassuolo 2-1(0-0)
Internazionale - Lazio Roma 0-1(0-1)

Round 30 [02-04.04.2019]
AC Milan - Udinese 1-1(1-0)
Cagliari - Juventus 0-2(0-1)
Empoli FC - SSC Napoli 2-1(1-1)
AS Roma - Fiorentina 2-2(1-1)
Genoa CFC - Internazionale 0-4(0-2)
SPAL Ferrara - Lazio Roma 1-0(0-0)
Frosinone - Parma 3-2(2-1)
Torino FC - Sampdoria 2-1(2-0)
US Sassuolo - Chievo Verona 4-0(2-0)
Atalanta - Bologna FC 4-1(4-0)

Round 31 [06-08.04.2019]
Parma - Torino FC 0-0
Juventus - AC Milan 2-1(0-1)
Sampdoria - AS Roma 0-1(0-0)
Fiorentina - Frosinone 0-1(0-0)
Udinese - Empoli FC 3-2(3-2)
Cagliari - SPAL Ferrara 2-1(1-1)
Internazionale - Atalanta 0-0
Lazio Roma - US Sassuolo 2-2(0-0)
SSC Napoli - Genoa CFC 1-1(1-1)
Bologna FC - Chievo Verona 3-0(0-0)

Round 32 [13-15.04.2019]
SPAL Ferrara - Juventus 2-1(0-1)
AS Roma - Udinese 1-0(0-0)
AC Milan - Lazio Roma 1-0(0-0)
Torino FC - Cagliari 1-1(0-0)
Fiorentina - Bologna FC 0-0
Sampdoria - Genoa CFC 2-0(1-0)
US Sassuolo - Parma 0-0
Chievo Verona - SSC Napoli 1-3(0-1)
Frosinone - Internazionale 1-3(0-2)
Atalanta - Empoli FC 0-0

Round 33 [20-22.04.2019]
Parma - AC Milan 1-1(0-0)
Lazio Roma - Chievo Verona 1-2(0-0)
Cagliari - Frosinone 1-0(1-0)
Bologna FC - Sampdoria 3-0(0-0)
Udinese - US Sassuolo 1-1(0-1)
Empoli FC - SPAL Ferrara 2-4(1-2)
Genoa CFC - Torino FC 0-1(0-0)
Juventus - Fiorentina 2-1(1-1)
Internazionale - AS Roma 1-1(0-1)
SSC Napoli - Atalanta 1-2(1-0)

Round 34 [27-29.04.2019]
Bologna FC - Empoli FC 3-1(0-1)
AS Roma - Cagliari 3-0(2-0)
Internazionale - Juventus 1-1(1-0)
Frosinone - SSC Napoli 0-2(0-1)
SPAL Ferrara - Genoa CFC 1-1(1-0)
Chievo Verona - Parma 1-1(0-1)
Sampdoria - Lazio Roma 1-2(0-2)
Torino FC - AC Milan 2-0(0-0)
Atalanta - Udinese 2-0(0-0)
Fiorentina - US Sassuolo 0-1(0-1)

Round 35 [03-06.05.2019]
Juventus - Torino FC 1-1(0-1)
Chievo Verona - SPAL Ferrara 0-4(0-1)
Udinese - Internazionale 0-0
Empoli FC - Fiorentina 1-0(0-0)
Lazio Roma - Atalanta 1-3(1-1)
US Sassuolo - Frosinone 2-2(0-2)
Parma - Sampdoria 3-3(1-2)
Genoa CFC - AS Roma 1-1(0-0)
SSC Napoli - Cagliari 2-1(0-0)
AC Milan - Bologna FC 2-1(1-0)

Round 36 [11-13.05.2019]
Atalanta - Genoa CFC 2-1(0-0)
Cagliari - Lazio Roma 1-2(0-1)
Fiorentina - AC Milan 0-1(0-1)
Torino FC - US Sassuolo 3-2(0-1)
Sampdoria - Empoli FC 1-2(0-0)
Frosinone - Udinese 1-3(0-3)
SPAL Ferrara - SSC Napoli 1-2(0-0)
AS Roma - Juventus 2-0(0-0)
Bologna FC - Parma 4-1(0-0)
Internazionale - Chievo Verona 2-0(1-0)

Round 37 [18-20.05.2019]
Udinese - SPAL Ferrara 3-2(3-0)
Genoa CFC - Cagliari 1-1(0-1)
US Sassuolo - AS Roma 0-0
Chievo Verona - Sampdoria 0-0
Parma - Fiorentina 1-0(0-0)
Empoli FC - Torino FC 4-1(1-0)
AC Milan - Frosinone 2-0(0-0)
Juventus - Atalanta 1-1(0-1)
SSC Napoli - Internazionale 4-1(1-0)
Lazio Roma - Bologna FC 3-3(1-0)

Round 38 [25-26.05.2019]
Frosinone - Chievo Verona 0-0
Bologna FC - SSC Napoli 3-2(2-0)
Torino FC - Lazio Roma 3-1(0-0)
Sampdoria - Juventus 2-0(0-0)
Internazionale - Empoli FC 2-1(0-0)
Fiorentina - Genoa CFC 0-0
SPAL Ferrara - AC Milan 2-3(1-2)
AS Roma - Parma 2-1(1-0)
Atalanta - US Sassuolo 3-1(1-1)
Cagliari - Udinese 1-2(1-0)

Final Standings

1.	**Juventus FC Torino**	38	28	6	4	70	-	30	90
2.	SSC Napoli	38	24	7	7	74	-	36	79
3.	Atalanta Bergamasca Calcio	38	20	9	9	77	-	46	69
4.	FC Internazionale Milano	38	20	9	9	57	-	33	69
5.	AC Milan	38	19	11	8	55	-	36	68
6.	AS Roma	38	18	12	8	66	-	48	66
7.	Torino FC	38	16	15	7	52	-	37	63
8.	SS Lazio Roma	38	17	8	13	56	-	46	59
9.	Sampdoria UC Genova	38	15	8	15	60	-	51	53
10.	Bologna FC 1909	38	11	11	16	48	-	56	44
11.	US Sassuolo Calcio	38	9	16	13	53	-	60	43
12.	Udinese Calcio	38	11	10	17	39	-	53	43
13.	SPAL Ferrara	38	11	9	18	44	-	56	42
14.	Parma Calcio 1913	38	10	11	17	41	-	61	41
15.	Cagliari Calcio	38	10	11	17	36	-	54	41
16.	ACF Fiorentina	38	8	17	13	47	-	45	41
17.	Genoa CFC	38	8	14	16	39	-	57	38
18.	Empoli FC (*Relegated*)	38	10	8	20	51	-	70	38
19.	Frosinone Calcio (*Relegated*)	38	5	10	23	29	-	69	25
20.	AC Chievo Verona* (*Relegated*)	38	2	14	22	25	-	75	17

Top goalscorers:

26 Fabio Quagliarella
Sampdoria UC Genova

23 Duván Esteban Zapata Banguero (COL)
Atalanta Bergamasca Calcio

22 Krzysztof Piątek (POL)
Genoa CFC / AC Milan

21 Cristiano Ronaldo dos Santos Aveiro (POR) *Juventus FC Torino*

17 Arkadiusz Krystian Milik (POL)
SSC Napoli

**3 points deducted due to false accounting!*

NATIONAL CUP
Coppa Italia 2018/2019

First Round [28-29.07.2018]

Casertana FC - AZ Picerno	2-0(1-0)
US Alessandria Calcio 1912 - AS Giana Erminio	0-1(0-0)
AC Monza - SS Matelica Calcio	1-0(0-0)
FC Südtirol Bolzano - ASD Albalonga	2-1(0-0)
AS Viterbese Calcio - Rende Calcio 1968	1-0(0-0)
AC Renate - AC Rezzato	0-2(0-1)
SS Sambenedettese - SSD San Remo Calcio	1-0(0-0)
UC AlbinoLeffe - Pordenone Calcio	0-1(0-0)
LR Vicenza Virtus - ASD Calcio Chieri 1955	2-1(2-1)
Ternana Calcio - US Città de Pontedera	1-1 aet; 4-2 pen
Calcio Catania - Como 1907	3-0(2-0)
SS Juve Stabia - US Pistoiese 1921	1-0(0-0)
SS Monopoli 1966 - Piacenza Calcio 1919	1-1 aet; 5-3 pen
Carrarese Calcio 1908 - Imolese Calcio 1919	0-1(0-0)
Trapani Calcio - ASD Campodarsego	1-0(1-0)
FeralpiSalò - Virtus Francavilla Calcio	2-0(0-0)
Robur Siena - ASD Sicula Leonzio	2-0(0-0)
AC Pisa 1909 - US Triestina Calcio 1918	2-2 aet; 5-3 pen

Second Round [04-07.08.2018]

Ascoli Calcio 1898 FC - AS Viterbese Calcio	0-4(0-2)
Spezia Calcio - SS Sambenedettese	2-1(0-0)
Carpi FC 1909 - Ternana Calcio	0-2(0-2)
Trapani Calcio - Cosenza Calcio	1-2(0-0,1-1)
AS Cittadella - SS Monopoli 1966	1-0(0-0)
Benevento Calcio - Imolese Calcio 1919	3-1(3-0)
Venezia FC - FC Südtirol Bolzano	0-1(0-0)
Hellas Verona FC - SS Juve Stabia	4-1(2-0)
Brescia Calcio - FC Pro Vercelli 1892	1-1 aet; 4-1 pen
AC Perugia Calcio - Novara Calcio	1-3(0-2)
Virtus Entella - Robur Siena	3-0(2-0)
Calcio Padova - AC Monza	1-0(0-0)
AS Livorno Calcio - Casertana FC	1-1 aet; 7-6 pen
Pescara Calcio - Pordenone Calcio	2-2 aet; 4-3 pen
US Città di Palermo - LR Vicenza Virtus	2-2 aet; 6-5 pen
US Cremonese - AC Pisa 1909	3-3 aet; 2-4 pen
Foggia Calcio - Calcio Catania	1-3(0-1)
US Salernitana 1919 - AC Rezzato	6-1(1-0)
FC Crotone - AS Giana Erminio Gorgonzola	4-0(2-0)
US Lecce - FeralpiSalò	1-0(0-0,0-0)

Third Round [11-12.08.2018]

Udinese Calcio - Benevento Calcio	1-2(1-0,1-1)
Genoa CFC - US Lecce	4-0(4-0)
AC Chievo Verona - Pescara Calcio	1-0(0-0)
Spezia Calcio - SPAL 2013 Ferrara	0-1(0-0)
Calcio Catania - Hellas Verona FC	2-0(2-0)
Sampdoria UC Genova - AS Viterbese Calcio	1-0(0-0)
Sassuolo Calcio - Ternana Calcio	5-1(4-0)
AS Livorno Calcio - FC Crotone	0-1(0-0)
Parma Calcio 1913 - AC Pisa 1909	0-1(0-1)
Virtus Entella - US Salernitana 1919	2-0(2-0)
Empoli FC - AS Cittadella	0-3(0-1)
Frosinone Calcio - FC Südtirol Bolzano	0-2(0-1)
Brescia Calcio - Novara Calcio	2-2 aet; 4-5 pen
Cagliari Calcio - US Città di Palermo	2-1(1-0)
Torino FC - Cosenza Calcio	4-0(2-0)
Bologna FC - Calcio Padova	2-0(0-0)

Fourth Round [04-06.12.2018]

Benevento Calcio - AS Cittadella	1-0(0-0)
Bologna FC 1909- FC Crotone	3-0(1-0)
Sampdoria UC Genova - SPAL 2013 Ferrara	2-1(1-1)
Novara Calcio - AC Pisa 1909	3-2(1-1)
Sassuolo Calcio - Calcio Catania	2-1(1-1)
AC Chievo Verona - Cagliari Calcio	1-2(1-1)
Genoa CFC - Virtus Entella	3-3 aet; 6-7 pen
Torino FC - FC Südtirol Bolzano	2-0(1-0)

1/8-Finals [12-14.01.2019]

SS Lazio Roma - Novara Calcio	4-1(4-0)
Sampdoria UC Genova - AC Milan	0-2(0-0,0-0)
Bologna FC 1909 - Juventus FC Torino	0-2(0-1)
Torino FC - ACF Fiorentina	0-2(0-0)
FC Internazionale Milano - Benevento Calcio	6-2(3-0)
SSC Napoli - Sassuolo Calcio	2-0(1-0)
Cagliari Calcio - Atalanta	0-2(0-0)
AS Roma - Virtus Entella	4-0(2-0)

Quarter-Finals [29-31.01.2019]

AC Milan - SSC Napoli	2-0(2-0)
ACF Fiorentina - AS Roma	7-1(3-1)
Atalanta Bergamasca Calcio - Juventus FC Torino	3-0(2-0)
FC Internazionale Milano - SS Lazio Roma	1-1 aet; 3-4 pen

Semi-Finals [26-27.02/24-25.04.2019]

SS Lazio Roma - AC Milan	0-0
AC Milan - SS Lazio Roma	0-1(0-0)
ACF Fiorentina - Atalanta Bergamasca Calcio	3-3(2-2)
Atalanta Bergamasca Calcio - ACF Fiorentina	2-1(1-1)

Final

15.05.2019; Stadio Olimpico, Roma; Referee: Luca Banti; Attendance: 57,059

SS Lazio Roma - Atalanta Bergamasca Calcio **2-0(1-0)**

Lazio: Thomas Strakosha, Luiz Felipe Ramos Marchi, Francesco Acerbi, Bartolomeu Jacinto Quissanga "Bastos" (36.Stefan Daniel Radu), Adam Marušić, Marco Parolo, Lucas Pezzini Leiva, Luis Alberto Romero Alconchel (78.Sergej Milinković-Savić), Senad Lulić (Cap), Ciro Immobile (66.Felipe Salvador Caicedo Corozo), Carlos Joaquín Correa. Trainer: Simone Inzaghi.

Atalanta: Pierluigi Gollini, Andrea Masiello, José Luis Palomino, Berat Djimsiti, Hans Hateboer, Marten Elco de Roon (85.Mario Pašalić), Remo Freuler, Timothy Castagne (84.Robin Gosens), Alejandro Darío Gómez (Cap), Josip Iličič, Duván Esteban Zapata Banguero (84.Musa Barrow). Trainer: Gian Piero Gasperini.

Goals: 1-0 Sergej Milinković-Savić (82), 2-0 Carlos Joaquín Correa (90).

THE CLUBS 2018/2019

Atalanta Bergamasca Calcio

Founded: 17.10.1907
Stadium: Stadio Atleti Azzurri d'Italia, Bergamo (21,300)

Goalkeepers:	**DOB**	**M**	**(s)**	**G**
Etrit Berisha (ALB)	10.03.1989	18		
Pierluigi Gollini	18.03.1995	20		
Francesco Rossi	27.04.1991		(1)	
Defenders:	**DOB**	**M**	**(s)**	**G**
Ali Adnan Kadhim Al Tameemi (IRQ)	19.12.1993	2	(1)	
Timothy Castagne (BEL)	05.12.1995	21	(7)	4
Berat Djimsiti (SUI)	19.02.1993	20	(4)	1
Robin Gosens (GER)	05.07.1994	23	(5)	3
Hans Hateboer (NED)	09.01.1994	33	(2)	5
Roger Ibañez da Silva (BRA)	23.11.1998		(1)	
Gianluca Mancini	17.04.1996	25	(5)	5
Andrea Masiello	05.02.1986	22	(2)	
José Luis Palomino (ARG)	05.01.1990	25	(5)	1
Arkadiusz Reca (POL)	17.06.1995		(3)	
Rafael Tolói (BRA)	10.10.1990	20	(1)	1
Midfielders:	**DOB**	**M**	**(s)**	**G**
Marten Elco de Roon (NED)	29.03.1991	34	(1)	2
Remo Freuler (SUI)	15.04.1992	35		2
Dejan Kulusevski (SWE)	25.04.2000		(3)	
Mario Pašalić (CRO)	09.02.1995	17	(16)	5
Matteo Pessina	21.04.1997	1	(11)	
Emiliano Ariel Rigoni (ARG)	04.02.1993	6	(6)	3
Luca Valzania	05.03.1996	1	(1)	
Forwards:	**DOB**	**M**	**(s)**	**G**
Musa Barrow (GAM)	14.11.1998	6	(16)	1
Alejandro Darío Gómez (ARG)	15.02.1988	34	(1)	7
Josip Iličič (SVN)	29.01.1988	23	(8)	12
Roberto Piccoli	27.01.2001		(2)	
Marco Tumminello	06.11.1998		(2)	
Duván Esteban Zapata Banguero (COL)	01.04.1991	32	(5)	23
Trainer:	**DOB**	**M**		
Gian Piero Gasperini	26.01.1958	38		

Bologna Football Club 1909

Founded: 03.10.1909
Stadium: Stadio "Renato Dall'Ara", Bologna (38,279)

Goalkeepers:	**DOB**	**M**	**(s)**	**G**
Łukasz Skorupski (POL)	05.05.1991	38		
Defenders:	**DOB**	**M**	**(s)**	**G**
Arturo Calabresi	17.03.1996	16	(2)	1
Gabriele Corbo	11.01.2000		(1)	
Danilo Larangeira (BRA)	10.05.1984	35		1
Sebastien De Maio (FRA)	05.03.1987	6		
Mitchell Dijks (NED)	09.02.1993	23	(2)	1
Giancarlo González Castro (CRC)	08.02.1988	8	(4)	
Filip Helander (SWE)	22.04.1993	19	(1)	
Lyanco Evangelista Silveira Neves Vojnovic (SRB)	01.02.1997	13		1
Ibrahima M'Baye (SEN)	19.11.1994	22	(1)	2
Nehuén Mario Paz (ARG)	28.04.1993	1	(1)	
Midfielders:	**DOB**	**M**	**(s)**	**G**
Godfred Donsah (GHA)	07.06.1996	1	(5)	
Blerim Džemaili (SUI)	12.04.1986	20	(8)	1
Federico Mattiello	14.07.1995	16	(1)	1
Ádám Nagy (HUN)	17.06.1995	10	(4)	
Andrea Poli	29.09.1989	23	(7)	4
Erick Antonio Pulgar Farfán (CHI)	15.01.1994	27	(1)	6
Roberto Soriano	08.02.1991	17		2
Mattias Svanberg (SWE)	05.01.1999	13	(10)	
Juan Manuel Valencia Aponzá (COL)	20.06.1998		(1)	
Forwards:	**DOB**	**M**	**(s)**	**G**
Mattia Destro	20.03.1991	5	(12)	4
Simone Edera	09.01.1997	3	(1)	
Diego Falcinelli	26.06.1991	8	(8)	
Ladislav Krejčí (CZE)	05.07.1992	11	(7)	
Orji Okwonkwo (NGA)	19.01.1998	2	(6)	
Riccardo Orsolini	24.01.1997	19	(16)	8
Rodrigo Sebastián Palacio Alcalde (ARG)	05.02.1982	26	(2)	3
Nicola Sansone	10.09.1991	13	(2)	2
Federico Javier Santander Mereles (PAR)	04.06.1991	23	(9)	8
Trainer:	**DOB**	**M**		
Filippo Inzaghi	09.08.1973	21		
Siniša Mihajlović (SRB) [28.01.2019]	20.02.1969	17		

Cagliari Calcio

Founded: 30.05.1920
Stadium: Sardegna Arena, Cagliari (16,233)

Goalkeepers:	**DOB**	**M**	**(s)**	**G**
Alessio Cragno	28.06.1994	38		
Defenders:	**DOB**	**M**	**(s)**	**G**
Marco Andreolli	10.06.1986	1	(2)	
Fabrizio Cacciatore	08.10.1986	7		
Luca Ceppitelli	11.08.1989	24		1
Ragnar Klavan (EST)	30.10.1985	15		
Charalampos Lykogiannis (GRE)	22.10.1993	9	(2)	
Luca Pellegrini	07.03.1999	11	(1)	
Fabio Pisacane	28.01.1986	24	(3)	1
Filippo Romagna	26.05.1997	16	(2)	
Darijo Srna (CRO)	01.05.1982	24	(2)	
Midfielders:	**DOB**	**M**	**(s)**	**G**
Nicolò Barella	07.02.1997	35		1
Valter Birsa (SVN)	07.08.1986	4	(8)	
Filip Bradarić (CRO)	11.01.1992	17	(10)	
Lucas Nahuel Castro (ARG)	09.04.1989	10	(2)	1
Luca Cigarini	20.06.1986	20	(5)	
Alessandro Deiola	01.08.1995	5	(5)	
Daniele Dessena	10.05.1987	3	(8)	
Paolo Faragò	12.02.1993	17	(9)	1
Artur Ioniță (MDA)	17.08.1990	34	(3)	3
João Pedro Geraldino dos Santos Galvão (BRA)	09.03.1992	30	(4)	7
Simone Padoin	18.03.1984	22	(8)	
Marko Pajač (CRO)	11.05.1993		(3)	
Forwards:	**DOB**	**M**	**(s)**	**G**
Alberto Cerri	16.04.1996	7	(8)	
Kiril Despodov (BUL)	11.11.1996		(4)	
Diego Farias da Silva (BRA)	10.05.1990	7	(9)	3
Riccardo Doratiotto	07.06.1999	1		
Leonardo Pavoletti	26.11.1988	31	(1)	16
Marco Sau	03.12.1987	5	(9)	1
Cyril Théréau (FRA)	24.04.1983	1	(4)	
Francesco Verde	16.08.1999		(1)	
Trainer:	**DOB**	**M**		
Rolando Maran	14.07.1963			

Associazione Calcio ChievoVerona

Founded: 1929
Stadium: Stadio "Marc'Antonio Bentegodi", Verona (38,402)

Goalkeepers:	**DOB**	**M**	**(s)**	**G**
Andrea Seculin	14.07.1990	1	(1)	
Adrian Šemper (CRO)	12.01.1998	6		
Stefano Sorrentino	28.03.1979	31		
Defenders:	**DOB**	**M**	**(s)**	**G**
Marco Andreolli	10.06.1986	7	(1)	
Mattia Bani	10.12.1993	29	(1)	
Federico Barba	01.09.1993	29	(1)	
Fabrizio Cacciatore	08.10.1986	5	(2)	
Boštjan Cesar (SVN)	09.07.1982	11	(3)	1
Nicolas Frey (FRA)	06.03.1984	3	(2)	
Paweł Jaroszyński (POL)	02.10.1994	15	(4)	
Angelo Ndrecka (ALB)	24.09.2001	1		
Luca Rossettini	09.05.1985	20	(1)	
Strahinja Tanasijević (SRB)	12.06.1997		(1)	
Nenad Tomović (SRB)	30.08.1987	9	(1)	1
Midfielders:	**DOB**	**M**	**(s)**	**G**
Valter Birsa (SVN)	07.08.1986	12	(5)	2
Mauro Burruchaga (ARG)	27.06.1998		(1)	
Fabio Depaoli	24.04.1997	27	(6)	
Assane Dioussé (SEN)	20.09.1997	9	(5)	
Emanuele Giaccherini	05.05.1985	22	(4)	3
Përparim Hetemaj (FIN)	12.12.1986	25	(5)	2
Ibrahim Karamoko	23.07.2001		(2)	
Sofian Kiyine (BEL)	02.10.1997	9	(14)	
Mehdi Léris (FRA)	23.05.1998	18	(5)	
Joel Chukwuma Obi (NGA)	22.05.1991	9	(2)	1
Ivan Radovanović (SRB)	29.08.1988	19		
Nicola Rigoni	12.11.1990	23	(1)	
Ezequiel Schelotto	23.05.1989	2	(2)	
Emanuel Vignato	24.08.2000	8	(2)	1
Forwards:	**DOB**	**M**	**(s)**	**G**
Filip Đorđević (SRB)	28.09.1987	6	(7)	1
Sergej Grubač (MNE)	29.05.2000	2	(1)	
Musa Juwara (GAM)	26.12.2001		(1)	
Gustavo Lucas Domingues Piazón (BRA)	20.01.1994		(4)	
Riccardo Meggiorini	04.09.1985	18	(6)	3
Sergio Pellissier	12.04.1979	12	(7)	4
Manuel Pucciarelli	17.06.1991	3	(7)	
Mariusz Stępiński (POL)	12.05.1995	27	(8)	6
Trainer:	**DOB**	**M**		
Lorenzo D'Anna	29.01.1972	8		
Gian Piero Ventura [10.10.2018]	14.01.1948	4		
Domenico Di Carlo [13.11.2018]	23.03.1964	26		

Empoli Football Club

Founded: 1920
Stadium: Stadio "Carlo Castellani", Empoli (16,284)

Goalkeepers:	**DOB**	**M**	**(s)**	**G**
Bartłomiej Drągowski (POL)	19.08.1997	14		
Ivan Provedel	17.03.1994	16		
Pietro Terracciano	08.03.1990	8		
Defenders:	**DOB**	**M**	**(s)**	**G**
Luca Antonelli	11.02.1987	10	(3)	
Cristian Dell'Orco	10.02.1994	12		1
Giovanni Di Lorenzo	04.08.1993	37		5
Domenico Maietta	03.08.1982	21		
Dimitrios Nikolaou (GRE)	13.08.1998	4		
Manuel Pasqual	13.03.1982	13	(9)	1
Jacob Rasmussen (DEN)	28.05.1997	10	(4)	
Matías Agustín Silvestre (ARG)	25.09.1984	34		2
Joel Untersee (SUI)	11.02.1994	1	(2)	
Frédéric Veseli (SUI)	20.11.1992	28	(3)	
Midfielders:	**DOB**	**M**	**(s)**	**G**
Afriyie Acquah (GHA)	05.01.1992	19	(9)	2
Ismaël Bennacer (FRA)	01.12.1997	32	(5)	
Matteo Brighi	14.02.1981	1	(9)	1
Leonardo Capezzi	29.03.1995	9	(3)	
Rade Krunić (BIH)	07.10.1993	33		5
Marko Pajač (CRO)	11.05.1993	9	(1)	2
Hamed Traorè (CIV)	16.02.2000	26	(6)	2
Salih Uçan (TUR)	06.01.1994	1	(13)	1
Forwards:	**DOB**	**M**	**(s)**	**G**
Francesco Caputo	06.08.1987	38		16
Diego Farias da Silva (BRA)	10.05.1990	16		4
Antonino La Gumina	06.03.1996	12	(10)	2
Levan Mchedlidze (GEO)	23.03.1990		(11)	
Samuel Mráz (SVK)	13.05.1997	2	(4)	1
Dimitri Oberlin (SUI)	27.09.1997		(5)	
Alejandro Rodríguez de Miguel (ESP)	30.07.1991		(1)	
Trainer:	**DOB**	**M**		
Aurelio Andreazzoli	05.11.1953	11		
Giuseppe Iachini [06.11.2018]	07.05.1964	16		
Aurelio Andreazzoli [13.03.2019]	05.11.1953	11		

Associazione Calcio Fiorentina Firenze

Founded: 29.08.1926 (re-founded 01.08.2002)
Stadium: Stadio "Artemio Franchi", Firenze (43,147)

Goalkeepers:	**DOB**	**M**	**(s)**	**G**
Bartłomiej Drągowski (POL)	19.08.1997	2	(1)	
Alban Lafont (FRA)	23.01.1999	34		
Pietro Terracciano	08.03.1990	2		
Defenders:	**DOB**	**M**	**(s)**	**G**
Cristiano Biraghi	01.09.1992	36		1
Federico Ceccherini	11.05.1992	11	(4)	
Dávid Hancko (SVK)	13.12.1997	3	(2)	
Vincent Laurini (FRA)	10.06.1989	10	(5)	
Nikola Milenković (SRB)	12.10.1997	34		3
Germán Alejo Pezzella (ARG)	27.06.1991	32		2
Vitor Hugo Franchescoli de Souza (BRA)	20.05.1991	27	(3)	
Midfielders:	**DOB**	**M**	**(s)**	**G**
Marco Benassi	05.05.1994	29	(3)	7
Federico Chiesa	25.10.1997	34	(3)	6
Bryan Boulaye Kevin Dabo (FRA)	18.02.1992	6	(17)	1
Valentin Eysseric (FRA)	25.03.1992	4	(4)	
Edimilson Fernandes (SUI)	15.04.1996	23	(6)	2
Gerson Santos da Silva (BRA)	20.05.1997	27	(9)	3
Nicky Stéphane Medja Beloko (CMR)	16.02.2000		(1)	
Cristóbal Montiel Rodríguez „Tòfol Montiel" (ESP)	11.04.2000		(1)	
Christian Nørgaard (DEN)	10.03.1994	4	(2)	
Jordan Veretout (FRA)	01.03.1993	33		5
Forwards:	**DOB**	**M**	**(s)**	**G**
Kevin Antonio Joel Gislain Mirallas y Castillo (BEL)	05.10.1987	15	(12)	2
Luis Fernando Muriel Fruito (COL)	16.04.1991	16	(3)	6
Marko Pjaca (CRO)	06.05.1995	8	(11)	1
Giovanni Pablo Simeone Baldini (ARG)	05.07.1995	27	(9)	6
Riccardo Sottil	03.06.1999		(2)	
Cyril Théréau (FRA)	24.04.1983		(2)	
Dušan Vlahović (SRB)	28.01.2000	1	(9)	
Trainer:	**DOB**	**M**		
Stefano Pioli	20.10.1965	31		
Vincenzo Montella [10.04.2019]	18.06.1974	7		

Frosinone Calcio

Founded: 1912 (*as Unione Sportiva Frusinate*)
Stadium: Stadio „Benito Stirpe", Genova (16,227)

Goalkeepers:	**DOB**	**M**	**(s)**	**G**
Francesco Bardi	18.01.1992	3		
Marco Sportiello	10.05.1992	35		
Defenders:	**DOB**	**M**	**(s)**	**G**
Lorenzo Ariaudo	11.06.1989	19		
Nicolò Brighenti	01.08.1989	11		
Marco Capuano	14.10.1991	27		
Edoardo Goldaniga	02.11.1993	29		1
Luka Krajnc (SVN)	19.09.1994	9		
Cristian Molinaro	30.07.1983	13	(1)	
Bartosz Salamon (POL)	01.05.1991	19	(1)	
Francesco Zampano	30.09.1993	24	(3)	
Midfielders:	**DOB**	**M**	**(s)**	**G**
Joaquín Matías Ardaiz de los Santos (URU)	11.01.1999		(1)	
Andrea Beghetto	11.10.1994	25	(2)	
Francesco Cassata	16.07.1997	14	(5)	2
Raman Chibsah (GHA)	10.03.1993	30	(2)	1
Lorenzo Crisetig	20.01.1993	5	(3)	
Paolo Ghiglione	02.02.1997	6	(3)	1
Mirko Gori	04.02.1993	2	(8)	
Emil Hallfreðsson (ISL)	29.06.1984	5	(1)	
Raffaele Maiello	10.07.1991	22	(7)	
Luca Matarese	16.04.1998		(2)	
Luca Paganini	08.06.1993	12	(2)	2
Paolo Sammarco	17.03.1983	6	(2)	1
Luca Valzania	05.03.1996	11	(2)	2
Federico Viviani	24.03.1992	5		
Rai Hendrikus Martinus Vloet (NED)	08.05.1995	1	(4)	
Forwards:	**DOB**	**M**	**(s)**	**G**
Joel Nathaniel Campbell Samuels (CRC)	26.06.1992	11	(6)	
Camillo Ciano	22.02.1990	28	(5)	7
Daniel Ciofani	31.07.1985	17	(15)	5
Federico Dionisi	16.06.1987	1	(8)	1
Stipe Perica (CRO)	07.07.1995	6	(1)	
Andrea Pinamonti	19.05.1999	17	(10)	5
Danilo Soddimo	27.09.1987	1	(9)	
Marcello Trotta	29.09.1992	4	(8)	
Trainer:	**DOB**	**M**		
Moreno Longo	14.02.1976	16		
Marco Baroni [19.12.2018]	11.09.1963	22		

Genoa Cricket and Football Club

Founded: 07.09.1893
Stadium: Stadio „Luigi Ferraris“, Genova (36,685)

Goalkeepers:	DOB	M	(s)	G
Jandrei Chitolina Carniel (BRA)	01.03.1993	1		
Federico Marchetti	07.02.1983	4		
Ionuţ Andrei Radu (ROU)	28.05.1997	33		
Defenders:	**DOB**	**M**	**(s)**	**G**
Davide Biraschi	02.07.1994	32	(2)	
Domenico Criscito	30.12.1986	35		2
Koray Günter (GER)	16.08.1994	8	(6)	
Pedro Miguel Almeida Lopes Pereira (POR)	22.01.1998	15	(11)	
Giuseppe Pezzella	29.11.1997	1	(4)	
Cristian Gabriel Romero (ARG)	27.04.1998	27		2
Nicolás Federico Spolli (ARG)	20.02.1983	7		
Ervin Zukanović (BIH)	11.02.1987	22	(3)	
Midfielders:	**DOB**	**M**	**(s)**	**G**
Daniel Bessa	14.01.1993	25	(9)	1
Oscar Hiljemark (SWE)	28.06.1992	15	(2)	1
Iuri José Picanço Medeiros (POR)	10.07.1994	2		
Darko Lazović (SRB)	15.09.1990	30	(3)	3
Lukas Lerager (DEN)	12.07.1993	13	(1)	1
Luca Mazzitelli	15.11.1995	3	(7)	
Miguel Luís Pinto Veloso (POR)	11.05.1986	14	(7)	
Stéphane Oméonga (BEL)	27.03.1996		(3)	
Ivan Radovanović (SRB)	29.08.1988	15	(1)	
Esteban Leonardo Rolón (ARG)	25.09.1995	10	(9)	
Rômulo Souza Orestes Caldeira (BRA)	22.05.1987	17		1
Sandro Raniere Guimarães Cordeiro (BRA)	15.03.1989	9	(4)	
Stefano Sturaro	09.03.1993	4	(1)	1
Forwards:	**DOB**	**M**	**(s)**	**G**
Nicola Dalmonte	13.09.1997		(3)	
Andrea Favilli	17.05.1997		(6)	
Cristhian Kouamé (CIV)	06.12.1997	33	(5)	4
Gianluca Lapadula	07.02.1990	4	(4)	1
Goran Pandev (MKD)	27.07.1983	12	(14)	4
Antonio Sanabria (PAR)	04.03.1996	9	(6)	3
Trainer:	**DOB**	**M**		
Davide Ballardini	06.01.1964	7		
Ivan Jurić (CRO) [09.10.2018]	25.08.1975	7		
Cesare Claudio Prandelli [07.12.2018]	19.08.1957	24		

Football Club Internazionale Milano

Founded: 09.03.1908
Stadium: Stadio “Giuseppe Meazza”, Milano (80,018)

Goalkeepers:	DOB	M	(s)	G
Samir Handanovič (SVN)	14.07.1984	38		
Defenders:	**DOB**	**M**	**(s)**	**G**
Cédric Ricardo Alves Soares (POR)	31.08.1991	3	(1)	
Danilo D'Ambrosio	09.09.1988	29	(1)	2
Dalbert Henrique Chagas Estevão (BRA)	08.09.1993	9	(2)	
Stefan de Vrij (NED)	05.02.1992	28		2
João Miranda de Souza Filho (BRA)	07.09.1984	14		
Andrea Ranocchia	16.02.1988		(4)	
Milan Škriniar (SVK)	11.02.1995	35		
Šime Vrsaljko (CRO)	10.01.1992	8	(2)	
Midfielders:	**DOB**	**M**	**(s)**	**G**
Kwadwo Asamoah (GHA)	09.12.1988	30	(2)	
Borja Valero Iglesias (ESP)	12.01.1985	12	(15)	
Marcelo Brozović (CRO)	16.11.1992	31	(1)	2
Antonio Candreva	28.02.1987	5	(13)	1
Roberto Gagliardini	07.04.1994	13	(6)	5
João Mário Naval da Costa Eduardo (POR)	19.01.1993	12	(8)	1
Radja Nainggolan (BEL)	04.05.1988	22	(7)	6
Matías Vecino Falero (URU)	24.08.1991	23	(7)	3
Forwards:	**DOB**	**M**	**(s)**	**G**
Keita Baldé (SEN)	08.03.1995	8	(16)	5
Mauro Emanuel Icardi (ARG)	19.02.1993	24	(5)	11
Yann Karamoh (FRA)	08.07.1998		(1)	
Lautaro Javier Martínez (ARG)	22.08.1997	13	(14)	6
Ivan Perišić (CRO)	02.02.1989	30	(4)	8
Matteo Politano	03.08.1993	31	(5)	5
Trainer:	**DOB**	**M**		
Luciano Spalletti	07.03.1959	38		

Juventus Football Club Torino

Founded: 01.11.1897
Stadium: Allianz Stadium, Torino (41,507)

Goalkeepers:	DOB	M	(s)	G
Mattia Perin	10.11.1992	9		
Carlo Pinsoglio	16.03.1990	1		
Wojciech Szczęsny (POL)	18.04.1990	28		
Defenders:	**DOB**	**M**	**(s)**	**G**
Alex Sandro Lobo Silva (BRA)	26.01.1991	28	(3)	1
Andrea Barzagli	08.05.1981	4	(3)	
Medhi Benatia (ALG)	17.04.1987	5		
Leonardo Bonucci	01.05.1987	27	(2)	3
José Martín Cáceres Silva (URU)	07.04.1987	7	(2)	
Giorgio Chiellini	14.08.1984	22	(3)	1
Mattia De Sciglio	20.10.1992	19	(3)	
Paolo Gozzi Iweru	25.04.2001	1		
João Pedro Cavaco Cancelo (POR)	27.05.1994	22	(3)	1
Daniele Rugani	29.07.1994	15		2
Midfielders:	**DOB**	**M**	**(s)**	**G**
Rodrigo Bentancur Colmán (URU)	05.06.1997	21	(10)	2
Emre Can (GER)	12.01.1994	20	(9)	4
Grigoris Kastanos (CYP)	30.01.1998	1		
Sami Khedira (GER)	04.04.1987	8	(2)	2
Matheus Pereira da Silva (BRA)	25.02.1998	1	(2)	
Blaise Matuidi (FRA)	09.04.1987	29	(2)	3
Hans Nicolussi Caviglia	18.06.2000		(3)	
Miralem Pjanić (BIH)	02.04.1990	27	(4)	2
Manolo Portanova	02.06.2000		(1)	
Leonardo Spinazzola	25.03.1993	6	(4)	
Forwards:	**DOB**	**M**	**(s)**	**G**
Federico Bernardeschi	16.02.1994	14	(14)	2
Cristiano Ronaldo dos Santos Aveiro (POR)	05.02.1985	30	(1)	21
Juan Guillermo Cuadrado Bello (COL)	26.05.1988	14	(4)	1
Douglas Costa de Souza (BRA)	14.09.1990	7	(10)	1
Paulo Bruno Exequiel Dybala (ARG)	15.11.1993	24	(6)	5
Moise Bioty Kean	28.02.2000	5	(8)	6
Mario Mandžukić (CRO)	21.05.1986	23	(2)	9
Stephy Mavididi (ENG)	31.05.1998		(1)	
Trainer:	**DOB**	**M**		
Massimiliano Allegri	11.08.1967	38		

Società Sportiva Lazio Roma

Founded: 09.01.1900
Stadium: Stadio Olimpico, Roma (70,634)

Goalkeepers:	DOB	M	(s)	G
Guido Guerrieri	25.02.1996	1		
Silvio Proto (BEL)	23.05.1983	2		
Thomas Strakosha (ALB)	19.03.1995	35		
Defenders:	**DOB**	**M**	**(s)**	**G**
Francesco Acerbi	10.02.1988	37		3
Nicolò Armini	07.03.2001		(1)	
Bartolomeu Jacinto Quissanga „Bastos" (ANG)	23.11.1991	11	(7)	1
José Martín Cáceres Silva (URU)	07.04.1987	3	(1)	
Riza Durmisi (DEN)	08.01.1994	2	(8)	
Luiz Felipe Ramos Marchi (BRA)	22.03.1997	15	(2)	1
Jordan Zacharie Lukaku Menama Mokelenge (BEL)	25.07.1994	1	(6)	
Patricio Gabarrón Gil „Patric" (ESP)	17.04.1993	12	(3)	
Stefan Daniel Radu (ROU)	22.10.1986	28		
Wallace Fortuna dos Santos (BRA)	14.10.1994	14	(2)	
Midfielders:	**DOB**	**M**	**(s)**	**G**
Milan Badelj (CRO)	25.02.1989	14	(9)	1
Valon Berisha (KVX)	07.02.1993	1	(7)	
Bruno André Cavaco Jordão (POR)	12.10.1998	1	(2)	
Danilo Cataldi	06.08.1994	4	(8)	2
Carlos Joaquín Correa (ARG)	13.08.1994	18	(16)	5
Dias Luan David Capanni (BRA)	20.05.2000		(1)	
Lucas Pezzini Leiva (BRA)	09.01.1987	22	(5)	
Senad Lulić (BIH)	18.01.1986	34	(1)	4
Adam Marušić (MNE)	17.10.1992	24	(2)	1
Sergej Milinković-Savić (SRB)	27.02.1995	29	(2)	5
Alessandro Murgia	09.08.1996		(1)	
Marco Parolo	25.01.1985	28	(6)	4
Rômulo Souza Orestes Caldeira (BRA)	22.05.1987	9	(1)	
Forwards:	**DOB**	**M**	**(s)**	**G**
Felipe Salvador Caicedo Corozo (ECU)	05.09.1988	17	(11)	8
Ciro Immobile	20.02.1990	31	(5)	15
Luis Alberto Romero Alconchel (ESP)	28.11.1992	25	(2)	4
Pedro Lomba Neto (POR)	09.03.2000		(4)	
Trainer:	**DOB**	**M**		
Simone Inzaghi	05.04.1976	38		

Associazione Calcio Milan

Founded: 16.12.1899
Stadium: Stadio "Giuseppe Meazza", Milano (80,018)

Goalkeepers:	DOB	M	(s)	G
Gianluigi Donnarumma	25.02.1999	36		
José Manuel „Pepe" Reina Páez (ESP)	31.08.1982	2	(2)	
Defenders:	**DOB**	**M**	**(s)**	**G**
Ignazio Abate	12.11.1986	15	(4)	
Davide Calabria	06.12.1996	22	(4)	1
Andrea Conti	02.03.1994	4	(8)	
Diego Sebastián Laxalt Suárez (URU)	07.02.1993	6	(14)	
Mateo Pablo Musacchio (ARG)	26.08.1990	29		1
Ricardo Iván Rodríguez Araya (SUI)	25.08.1992	35		
Alessio Romagnoli	12.01.1995	32		2
Cristián Eduardo Zapata Valencia (COL)	30.09.1986	12	(1)	
Midfielders:	**DOB**	**M**	**(s)**	**G**
Tiemoué Bakayoko (FRA)	17.08.1994	26	(5)	1
Lucas Rodrigo Biglia (ARG)	30.01.1986	13	(3)	1
Giacomo Bonaventura	22.08.1989	8		3
Hakan Çalhanoğlu (TUR)	08.02.1994	34	(2)	3
Franck Yannick Kessié (CIV)	19.12.1996	34		7
Lucas Tolentino Coelho de Lima „Lucas Paquetá" (BRA)	27.08.1997	12	(1)	1
José Agustín Mauri	16.05.1996	2	(3)	
Forwards:	**DOB**	**M**	**(s)**	**G**
Fabio Borini	23.03.1991	10	(10)	2
Patrick Cutrone	03.01.1998	12	(22)	3
Gonzalo Gerardo Higuaín (ARG)	10.12.1987	15		6
Krzysztof Piątek (POL)	01.07.1995	16	(2)	9
Samuel Castillejo Azuaga (ESP)	18.01.1995	8	(23)	4
Jesús Joaquín Fernández Sáenz de la Torre „Suso" (ESP)	19.11.1993	35		7
Trainer:	**DOB**	**M**		
Gennaro Ivan Gattuso	09.01.1978	38		

Società Sportiva Calcio Napoli

Founded: 01.08.1926 (*as Associazione Calcio Napoli*)
Stadium: Stadio San Paolo, Napoli (60,240)

Goalkeepers:	DOB	M	(s)	G
Orestis Karnezis (GRE)	11.07.1985	9		
Alex Meret	22.03.1997	13	(1)	
David Ospina Ramírez (COL)	31.08.1988	16	(1)	
Defenders:	**DOB**	**M**	**(s)**	**G**
Vlad Iulian Chiricheș (ROU)	14.11.1989	3		
Faouzi Ghoulam (ALG)	01.02.1991	12	(4)	1
Elseid Hysaj (ALB)	02.02.1994	24	(3)	
Kalidou Koulibaly (SEN)	20.06.1991	35		2
Sebastiano Luperto	06.09.1996	6	(6)	
Nikola Maksimović (SRB)	25.11.1991	15	(2)	
Kévin Malcuit (FRA)	31.07.1991	20	(4)	
Mário Rui Silva Duarte (POR)	27.05.1991	17	(3)	1
Raúl Albiol Tortajada (ESP)	04.09.1985	19	(1)	1
Midfielders:	**DOB**	**M**	**(s)**	**G**
Allan Marques Loureiro (BRA)	08.01.1991	28	(5)	1
Amadou Diawara (GUI)	17.07.1997	8	(5)	
Fabián Ruiz Peña (ESP)	03.04.1996	20	(7)	5
Marek Hamšík (SVK)	27.07.1987	12	(1)	
Marko Rog (CRO)	19.07.1995	4	(5)	1
Piotr Zieliński (POL)	20.05.1994	33	(3)	6
Forwards:	**DOB**	**M**	**(s)**	**G**
Gianluca Gaetano	05.05.2000		(2)	
Lorenzo Insigne	04.06.1991	24	(4)	10
José María Callejón Bueno (ESP)	11.02.1987	29	(5)	3
Dries Mertens (BEL)	06.05.1987	23	(12)	16
Arkadiusz Krystian Milik (POL)	28.02.1994	27	(8)	17
Adam Ounas (ALG)	11.11.1996	6	(12)	3
Simone Verdi	12.07.1992	9	(13)	3
Amin Younes (GER)	06.08.1993	6	(6)	3
Trainer:	**DOB**	**M**		
Carlo Ancelotti	10.06.1959	38		

Parma Calcio 1913

Founded: 16.12.1913 (*as Parma Foot Ball Club*)
Stadium: Stadio Olimpico, Roma (70,634)

Goalkeepers:	DOB	M	(s)	G
Pierluigi Frattali	01.12.1985	1		
Luigi Sepe	08.05.1991	37		
Defenders:	**DOB**	**M**	**(s)**	**G**
Alessandro Bastoni	13.04.1999	18	(6)	1
Bruno Eduardo Regufe Alves (POR)	27.11.1981	33		4
Federico Dimarco	10.11.1997	10	(3)	1
Riccardo Gagliolo	28.04.1990	34		
Marcello Gazzola	03.04.1985	9	(11)	1
Massimo Gobbi	31.10.1980	13	(3)	
Simone Iacoponi	30.04.1987	38		
Francisco Andrés Sierralta Carvallo (CHI)	06.05.1997	2	(4)	
Midfielders:	**DOB**	**M**	**(s)**	**G**
Antonino Barillà	01.04.1988	30	(1)	3
Alessandro Deiola	01.08.1995	5	(5)	
Jacopo Dezi	10.02.1992	1		
Abdou Diakhate (SEN)	31.12.1998		(1)	
Alberto Grassi	07.03.1995	5	(2)	
Juraj Kucka (SVK)	26.02.1987	17	(1)	4
Gianni Munari	24.06.1983		(1)	
José Ndong Machín Dicombo „Pepín“ (EQG)	14.08.1996	1	(1)	
Luca Rigoni	07.12.1984	20	(3)	2
Matteo Scozzarella	05.06.1988	17	(5)	
Leo Štulac (SVN)	26.09.1994	17	(9)	
Forwards:	**DOB**	**M**	**(s)**	**G**
Jonathan Biabiany (FRA)	28.04.1988	12	(6)	
Fabio Ceravolo	05.03.1987	12	(13)	2
Amato Ciciretti	31.12.1993	1	(5)	
Alessio Sergio Fernando Da Cruz (NED)	18.01.1997	1	(2)	
Antonio Di Gaudio	16.08.1989	9	(3)	
Gervais Lombe Yao Kouassi „Gervinho“ (CIV)	27.05.1987	27	(3)	11
Roberto Inglese	12.11.1991	23	(2)	9
Nicolás Javier Schiappacasse Oliva (URU)	12.01.1999	1	(2)	
Luca Siligardi	26.01.1988	19	(10)	1
Mattia Sprocati	28.04.1993	5	(11)	1
Trainer:	**DOB**	**M**		
Roberto D'Aversa	12.08.1975	38		

Associazione Sportiva Roma

Founded: 07.06.1927
Stadium: Stadio Olimpico, Roma (70,634)

Goalkeepers:	DOB	M	(s)	G
Antonio Mirante	08.07.1983	11		
Robin Patrick Olsen (SWE)	08.01.1990	27		
Defenders:	**DOB**	**M**	**(s)**	**G**
Federico Julián Fazio (ARG)	17.03.1987	31	(3)	5
Juan Guilherme Nunes Jesus (BRA)	10.06.1991	15	(5)	1
Rick Karsdorp (NED)	11.02.1995	7	(4)	
Aleksandar Kolarov (SRB)	10.11.1985	32	(1)	8
Konstantinos Manolas (GRE)	14.06.1991	27		1
Iván Marcano Sierra (ESP)	23.06.1987	9	(1)	
Luca Pellegrini	07.03.1999	2	(2)	
Davide Santon	02.01.1991	11	(6)	
Midfielders:	**DOB**	**M**	**(s)**	**G**
Ante Ćorić (CRO)	14.04.1997		(2)	
Bryan Cristante	03.03.1995	26	(9)	4
Daniele De Rossi	24.07.1983	15	(3)	1
Alessandro Florenzi	11.03.1991	24	(5)	3
Steven N'Kemboanza Mike Christopher N'Zonzi (FRA)	15.12.1988	29	(1)	1
Javier Matías Pastore (ARG)	20.06.1989	7	(7)	3
Lorenzo Pellegrini	19.06.1996	21	(4)	3
Diego Perotti (ARG)	26.07.1988	6	(7)	5
Kevin Strootman (NED)	13.02.1990	1		
Cengiz Ünder (TUR)	14.07.1997	17	(9)	3
Nicolò Zaniolo	02.07.1999	20	(7)	4
Forwards:	**DOB**	**M**	**(s)**	**G**
Žan Celar (SVN)	14.03.1999		(1)	
Edin Džeko (BIH)	17.03.1986	28	(5)	9
Stephan El Shaarawy	27.10.1992	23	(5)	11
Justin Kluivert (NED)	05.05.1999	14	(15)	1
Patrik Schick (CZE)	24.01.1996	15	(9)	3
Trainer:	**DOB**	**M**		
Eusebio Di Francesco	08.09.1969	26		
Claudio Ranieri [08.03.2019]	20.10.1951	12		

Unione Calcio Sampdoria Genova

Founded: 12.08.1946
Stadium: Stadio "Luigi Ferraris", Genova (36,685)

Goalkeepers:	DOB	M	(s)	G
Emil Audero	18.01.1997	36		
Rafael Cabral Barbosa (BRA)	20.05.1990	2		
Defenders:	**DOB**	**M**	**(s)**	**G**
Joachim Andersen (DEN)	31.05.1996	32		
Bartosz Bereszyński (POL)	12.07.1992	24	(3)	
Omar Colley (GAM)	24.10.1992	21		
Alex Ferrari	01.07.1994	6		
Carlos Eugenio Júnior Tavares dos Santos (BRA)	07.08.1996	2	(1)	
Nicola Murru	16.12.1994	34	(1)	
Jacopo Sala	05.12.1991	16	(5)	
Lorenzo Tonelli	17.01.1990	17	(2)	1
Midfielders:	**DOB**	**M**	**(s)**	**G**
Edgar Osvaldo Barreto Cáceres (PAR)	15.07.1984	9	(3)	
Albin Ekdal (SWE)	28.07.1989	30	(2)	
Jakub Jankto (CZE)	19.01.1996	7	(18)	
Karol Linetty (POL)	02.02.1995	30	(2)	3
Dennis Praet (BEL)	14.05.1994	33	(1)	2
Gastón Exequiel Ramírez Pereyra (URU)	02.12.1990	19	(8)	4
Riccardo Saponara	21.12.1991	11	(11)	2
Ronaldo Vieira (ENG)	19.07.1998	6	(8)	
Forwards:	**DOB**	**M**	**(s)**	**G**
Gianluca Caprari	30.07.1993	12	(9)	6
Gregoire Defrel (FRA)	17.06.1991	26	(10)	11
Manolo Gabbiadini	26.11.1991	8	(10)	4
Dawid Kownacki (POL)	14.03.1997		(13)	1
Fabio Quagliarella	31.01.1983	37		26
Marco Sau	03.11.1987		(5)	
Trainer:	**DOB**	**M**		
Marco Giampaolo	02.08.1967	38		

Unione Sportiva Sassuolo Calcio

Founded: 17.07.1920
Stadium: Mapei Stadium – Città del Tricolore, Reggio Emilia (23,717)

Goalkeepers:	DOB	M	(s)	G
Andrea Consigli	27.01.1987	36		
Gianluca Pegolo	25.03.1981	2	(1)	
Defenders:	**DOB**	**M**	**(s)**	**G**
Claud Adjapong (GHA)	06.05.1998	3	(2)	1
Cristian Dell'Orco	10.02.1994	1	(2)	
Merih Demiral (TUR)	05.03.1998	14		2
Gianmarco Ferrari	15.02.1992	31		4
Paolo Mauricio Lemos Merladett (URU)	28.12.1995	3		
Pol Mikel Lirola Kosok (ESP)	13.08.1997	32	(3)	2
Giangiacomo Magnani	04.10.1995	17	(2)	
Marlon Santos da Silva Barbosa (BRA)	07.09.1995	18		1
Federico Peluso	20.01.1984	14	(2)	1
Rogério Oliveira da Silva (BRA)	13.01.1998	29	(4)	1
Leonardo Sernicola	30.03.1997		(1)	
Midfielders:	**DOB**	**M**	**(s)**	**G**
Kevin-Prince Boateng (GHA)	06.03.1987	11	(2)	4
Jérémie Boga (CIV)	03.01.1997	14	(11)	3
Mehdi Bourabia (FRA)	07.08.1991	21	(11)	1
Alfred Duncan (GHA)	10.03.1993	21	(5)	4
Filip Đuričić (SRB)	30.01.1992	16	(7)	2
Manuel Locatelli	08.01.1998	21	(8)	2
Francesco Magnanelli	12.11.1984	21	(5)	
Stefano Sensi	05.08.1995	23	(5)	2
Forwards:	**DOB**	**M**	**(s)**	**G**
Khouma Babacar (SEN)	17.03.1993	16	(13)	7
Domenico Berardi	01.08.1994	32	(3)	8
Enrico Brignola	08.07.1999	2	(5)	1
Federico Di Francesco	14.06.1994	14	(5)	2
Alessandro Matri	19.08.1984	6	(13)	2
Jens Odgaard (DEN)	31.03.1999		(1)	
Giacomo Raspadori	18.02.2000		(1)	
Marcello Trotta	29.09.1992		(1)	
Trainer:	**DOB**	**M**		
Roberto De Zerbi	06.06.1979	38		

Società Polisportiva Ars et Labor Ferrara

Founded: 1907 (re-founded 2005 and 2012)
Stadium: Stadio "Paolo Mazza", Ferrara (13,020)

Goalkeepers:	DOB	M	(s)	G
Alfred Gomis (SEN)	05.09.1993	19	(1)	
Vanja Milinković-Savić (SRB)	20.02.1997	2		
Giacomo Poluzzi	25.02.1988		(1)	
Emiliano Viviano	01.12.1985	17		
Defenders:	**DOB**	**M**	**(s)**	**G**
Kevin Bonifazi	19.05.1996	26	(1)	2
Thiago Rangel Cionek (POL)	21.04.1986	29	(2)	
Filippo Costa	21.05.1995	6	(3)	
Lorenzo Dickmann	24.09.1996	2	(4)	
Johan Djourou (SUI)	18.01.1987	3	(2)	
Felipe Dias da Silva dal Belo (BRA)	31.07.1984	27	(3)	3
Vasco Regini	09.09.1990	1	(3)	
Lorenco Šimić (CRO)	15.07.1996	2	(6)	
Francesco Vicari	03.08.1994	26	(2)	2
Midfielders:	**DOB**	**M**	**(s)**	**G**
Mohamed Fares (ALG)	15.02.1996	32	(3)	3
Jasmin Kurtić (SVN)	10.01.1989	29	(1)	6
Simone Missiroli	23.05.1986	33	(1)	
Alessandro Murgia	09.08.1996	11	(4)	
Pasquale Schiattarella	30.05.1987	20	(8)	
Mirko Valdifiori	21.04.1986	8	(7)	
Mattia Valoti	06.09.1993	14	(10)	2
Forwards:	**DOB**	**M**	**(s)**	**G**
Mirco Antenucci	08.09.1984	22	(13)	5
Sergio Floccari	12.11.1981	11	(9)	3
Marko Janković (MNE)	09.07.1995		(4)	
Gabriele Moncini	26.04.1996		(1)	
Alberto Paloschi	04.01.1990	8	(15)	2
Andrea Petagna	30.06.1995	35	(1)	16
Trainer:	**DOB**	**M**		
Leonardo Semplici	18.07.1967	38		

Torino Football Club

Founded: 03.12.1906
Stadium: Stadio Olimpico Grande Torino, Torino (27,994)

Goalkeepers:	DOB	M	(s)	G
Salvador Ichazo Fernández (URU)	26.01.1992	2	(1)	
Salvatore Sirigu	12.01.1987	36		
Defenders:	**DOB**	**M**	**(s)**	**G**
Temitayo Olufisayo Olaoluwa Aina (NGA)	08.10.1996	22	(8)	1
Cristian Daniel Ansaldi (ARG)	20.09.1986	23	(1)	3
Gleison Bremer Silva Nascimento (BRA)	18.03.1997	2	(3)	
Lorenzo De Silvestri	23.05.1988	30	(2)	2
Koffi Djidji (CIV)	30.11.1992	16	(1)	
Armando Izzo	02.03.1992	37		4
Lyanco Evangelista Silveira Neves Vojnović (SRB)	01.02.1997	1	(1)	
Emiliano Moretti	11.06.1981	22	(2)	
Nicolas Alexis Julio Nkoulou Ndoubena (CMR)	27.03.1990	36		2
Midfielders:	**DOB**	**M**	**(s)**	**G**
Daniele Baselli	12.03.1992	27	(7)	4
Saša Lukić (SRB)	13.08.1996	11	(13)	2
Soualiho Meïté (FRA)	17.03.1994	30	(5)	2
Tomás Eduardo Rincón Hernández (VEN)	13.01.1988	32	(2)	3
Roberto Soriano	08.02.1991	6	(5)	
Forwards:	**DOB**	**M**	**(s)**	**G**
Alejandro Berenguer Remiro „Álex“ (ESP)	04.07.1995	15	(16)	2
Andrea Belotti	20.12.1993	37		15
Vitalie Damaşcan (MDA)	24.01.1999		(1)	
Simone Edera	09.01.1997	1	(2)	
Iago Falqué Silva (ESP)	04.01.1990	19	(7)	6
Adem Ljajić (SRB)	29.09.1991		(1)	
Vincenzo Millico	12.08.2000		(1)	
Vittorio Parigini	25.03.1996	2	(15)	
Simone Zaza	25.06.1991	11	(18)	4
Trainer:	**DOB**	**M**		
Walter Mazzarri	01.10.1961	38		

Udinese Calcio

Founded: 1896
Stadium: Stadio Friuli, Udine (25,144)

Goalkeepers:	**DOB**	**M**	**(s)**	**G**
Juan Agustín Musso (ARG)	06.05.1994	29		
Simone Scuffet	31.05.1996	9		
Defenders:	**DOB**	**M**	**(s)**	**G**
Sebastien De Maio (FRA)	05.03.1987	13	(3)	1
Bram Nuytinck (NED)	04.05.1990	24	(3)	
Nicholas Opoku (GHA)	08.11.1997	9	(3)	
Samir Caetano de Souza Santos (BRA)	05.12.1994	21		2
Jens Stryger Larsen (DEN)	21.02.1991	36		1
Giuseppe Pezzella	29.11.1997	2	(2)	
Hidde ter Avest (NED)	20.05.1997	12	(1)	
William Troost-Ekong (NGA)	01.09.1993	35		
Molla Wagué (MLI)	21.02.1991	1	(1)	
Ben Wilmot (ENG)	04.11.1999	2	(3)	
Marvin Zeegelaar (NED)	12.08.1990	10	(2)	
Midfielders:	**DOB**	**M**	**(s)**	**G**
Emmanuel Agyemang-Badu (GHA)	02.12.1990	2	(2)	
Andrija Balić (CRO)	11.08.1997		(4)	
Antonín Barák (CZE)	03.12.1994	4	(4)	
Valon Behrami (SUI)	19.04.1985	17	(2)	1
Marco D'Alessandro	17.02.1991	16	(8)	
Rodrigo Javier de Paul (ARG)	24.05.1994	36		9
Seko Fofana (FRA)	07.05.1995	31		2
Emil Hallfreðsson (ISL)	29.06.1984	1	(2)	1
Rolando Mandragora	29.06.1997	33	(2)	3
Sandro Raniere Guimarães Cordeiro (BRA)	15.03.1989	7	(5)	
Forwards:	**DOB**	**M**	**(s)**	**G**
Felipe dos Reis Pereira Vizeu do Carmo (BRA)	12.03.1997		(5)	
Svante Ingelsson (SWE)	14.06.1998	1	(2)	
Kevin Lasagna	10.08.1992	26	(10)	6
Darwin Daniel Machís Marcano (VEN)	07.02.1993	4	(9)	
Petar Mićin (SRB)	29.09.1998		(1)	
Stefano Okaka	09.08.1989	11	(5)	6
Ignacio Pussetto (ARG)	21.12.1995	24	(11)	4
Łukasz Teodorczyk (POL)	03.06.1991	2	(14)	1
Trainer:	**DOB**	**M**		
Igor Tudor (CRO)	16.04.1978	38		

SECOND LEVEL
Serie B 2018/2019

1.	Brescia Calcio (*Promoted*)	36	18	13	5	69 - 42	67
2.	US Lecce (*Promoted*)	36	19	9	8	66 - 45	66
3.	Benevento Calcio (*Promotion Play-offs*)	36	17	9	10	61 - 45	60
4.	Delfino Pescara 1936 (*Promotion Play-offs*)	36	14	13	9	50 - 46	55
5.	Hellas Verona FC (*Promotion Play-offs*)	36	13	13	10	49 - 46	52
6.	Spezia Calcio (*Promotion Play-offs*)	36	14	9	13	53 - 46	51
7.	AS Cittadella (*Promotion Play-offs*)	36	12	15	9	49 - 38	51
8.	AC Perugia Calcio (*Promotion Play-offs*)	36	14	8	14	49 - 49	50
9.	US Cremonese	36	12	13	11	37 - 33	49
10.	Cosenza Calcio	36	11	13	12	34 - 42	46
11.	Unione Sportiva Città di Palermo (*Relegated*)	36	16	15	5	57 - 38	43
12.	FC Crotone	36	11	10	15	40 - 42	43
13.	Ascoli Calcio 1898 FC	36	10	13	13	40 - 56	43
14.	AS Livorno Calcio	36	9	12	15	38 - 51	39
15.	Venezia FC (*Relegation Play-out*)	36	8	14	14	35 - 46	38
16.	US Salernitana 1919 (*Relegation Play-out*)	36	10	8	18	41 - 57	38
17.	Foggia Calcio (*Relegated*)	36	10	13	13	44 - 49	37
18.	Calcio Padova (*Relegated*)	36	5	16	15	36 - 49	31
19.	Carpi FC 1909 (*Relegated*)	36	7	8	21	39 - 67	29

Please note: Both Unione Sportiva Città di Palermo (initially 20 points deducted for financial irregularities) and Foggia Calcio (initially 6 points deducted for administral irregularities) were excluded from the professional league, being relegated to Serie D.
On 29.05.2019 the Court of Appeal of the Italian Football Federation annulled the relegation of US Città di Palermo, which was sanctioned with 20 points of penalization instead, causing the immediate relegation of Foggia Calcio and the re-admission to the play-out of Venezia FC.

Relegation Play-out [05-09.06.2019]

US Salernitana 1919 - Venezia FC 2-1(2-0) 0-1(0-1,0-1,0-1); 4-2 on penalties.

On 12.07.2019 the FIGC retired the professional license to Unione Sportiva Città di Palermo. The relegation play-out was consequently considered null and void, both teams remained at second level.

Relegation Play-offs [17.05.-02.06.2019]

Preliminary Round	Spezia Calcio - AS Cittadella	1-2(0-1)	
	Hellas Verona FC - AC Perugia Calcio	4-1(2-0)	
Semi-Finals	AS Cittadella - Benevento Calcio	1-2(1-0)	3-0(2-0)
	Hellas Verona FC - Delfino Pescara 1936	0-0	1-0(0-0)
Finals	AS Cittadella - Hellas Verona FC	2-0(1-0)	0-3(0-1)

Hellas Verona FC promoted to 2019/2020 Serie A.

NATIONAL TEAM

INTERNATIONAL MATCHES
(16.07.2018 – 15.07.2019)

07.09.2018	Bologna	Italy - Poland	1-1(0-1)	(UNL)
10.09.2018	Lisboa	Portugal - Italy	1-0(0-0)	(UNL)
10.10.2018	Genoa	Italy - Ukraine	1-1(0-0)	(F)
14.10.2018	Chorzów	Poland - Italy	0-1(0-0)	(UNL)
17.11.2018	Milano	Italy - Portugal	0-0	(UNL)
20.11.2018	Genk	Italy - United States	1-0(0-0)	(F)
23.03.2019	Udine	Italy - Finland	2-0(1-0)	(ECQ)
26.03.2019	Parma	Italy - Liechtenstein	6-0(4-0)	(ECQ)
08.06.2019	Athína	Greece - Italy	0-3(0-3)	(ECQ)
11.06.2019	Torino	Italy - Bosnia and Herzegovina	2-1(0-1)	(ECQ)

07.09.2018 ITALY - POLAND 1-1(0-1) UEFA Nations League A, Group 3
Stadio "Renato Dall'Ara", Bologna; Referee: Felix Zwayer (Germany); Attendance: 24,000
ITA: Gianluigi Donnarumma, Leonardo Bonucci, Giorgio Chiellini (Cap), Cristiano Biraghi, Davide Zappacosta, Jorge Luiz Frello Filho "Jorginho", Roberto Gagliardini, Lorenzo Pellegrini (46.Giacomo Bonaventura), Mario Barwuah Balotelli (62.Andrea Belotti), Lorenzo Insigne (71.Federico Chiesa), Federico Bernardeschi. Trainer: Roberto Mancini.
Goal: Jorge Luiz Frello Filho "Jorginho" (78 penalty).

10.09.2018 PORTUGAL - ITALY 1-0(0-0) UEFA Nations League A, Group 3
Estádio da Luz, Lisboa; Referee: William Collum (Scotland); Attendance: 52,635
ITA: Gianluigi Donnarumma, Domenico Criscito (74.Emerson Palmieri dos Santos), Alessio Romagnoli, Mattia Caldara, Giacomo Bonaventura, Jorge Luiz Frello Filho "Jorginho", Bryan Cristante (79.Andrea Belotti), Manuel Lazzari, Ciro Immobile (Cap) (59.Domenico Berardi), Simone Zaza, Federico Chiesa. Trainer: Roberto Mancini.

10.10.2018 ITALY - UKRAINE 1-1(0-0) Friendly International
Stadio "Luigi Ferraris", Genova; Referee: Rade Obrenović (Slovenia); Attendance: 12,000
ITA: Gianluigi Donnarumma, Leonardo Bonucci, Giorgio Chiellini (Cap), Cristiano Biraghi (88.Domenico Criscito), Alessandro Florenzi (84.Cristiano Piccini), Marco Verratti (70.Giacomo Bonaventura), Jorge Luiz Frello Filho "Jorginho", Nicolò Barella (78.Lorenzo Pellegrini), Lorenzo Insigne (78.Domenico Berardi), Federico Bernardeschi (57.Ciro Immobile), Federico Chiesa. Trainer: Roberto Mancini.
Goal: Federico Bernardeschi (55).

14.10.2018 POLAND - ITALY 0-1(0-0) UEFA Nations League A, Group 3
Stadion Śląski, Chorzów; Referee: Damir Skomina (Slovenia); Attendance: 41,692
ITA: Gianluigi Donnarumma, Leonardo Bonucci, Giorgio Chiellini (Cap), Cristiano Biraghi, Alessandro Florenzi (84.Cristiano Piccini), Marco Verratti, Jorge Luiz Frello Filho "Jorginho", Nicolò Barella, Lorenzo Insigne, Federico Bernardeschi (81.Kevin Lasagna), Federico Chiesa. Trainer: Roberto Mancini.
Goal: Cristiano Biraghi (90+2).

17.11.2018 ITALY - PORTUGAL 0-0 UEFA Nations League A, Group 3
Stadio "Giuseppe Meazza", Milano; Referee: Danny Desmond Makkelie (Netherlands); Attendance: 73,000
ITA: Gianluigi Donnarumma, Leonardo Bonucci, Giorgio Chiellini (Cap), Cristiano Biraghi, Alessandro Florenzi, Marco Verratti (81.Lorenzo Pellegrini), Jorge Luiz Frello Filho "Jorginho", Nicolò Barella, Ciro Immobile (74.Kevin Lasagna), Lorenzo Insigne, Federico Chiesa (87.Domenico Berardi). Trainer: Roberto Mancini.

20.11.2018 ITALY - UNITED STATES 1-0(0-0) Friendly International
Luminus Arena, Genk (Belgium); Referee: Cüneyt Çakır (Turkey); Attendance: 13,500
ITA: Salvatore Sirigu, Leonardo Bonucci (Cap), Francesco Acerbi, Mattia De Sciglio, Emerson Palmieri dos Santos, Marco Verratti, Stefano Sensi, Nicolò Barella (76.Roberto Gagliardini), Domenico Berardi (62.Moise Bioty Kean), Kevin Lasagna (87.Matteo Politano), Federico Chiesa (46.Vincenzo Grifo). Trainer: Roberto Mancini.
Goal: Matteo Politano (90+4).

23.03.2019 ITALY - FINLAND 2-0(1-0) 16th EC. Qualifiers
Stadio Friuli, Udine; Referee: Orel Grinfeld (Israel); Attendance: 24,000
ITA: Gianluigi Donnarumma, Leonardo Bonucci, Giorgio Chiellini (Cap), Cristiano Biraghi (90+1.Leonardo Spinazzola), Cristiano Piccini, Marco Verratti (85.Nicolò Zaniolo), Jorge Luiz Frello Filho "Jorginho", Nicolò Barella, Ciro Immobile (80.Fabio Quagliarella), Federico Bernardeschi, Moise Bioty Kean. Trainer: Roberto Mancini.
Goals: Nicolò Barella (7), Moise Bioty Kean (74).

26.03.2019 ITALY - LIECHTENSTEIN 6-0(4-0) 16th EC. Qualifiers
Stadio "Ennio Tardini", Parma; Referee: Kirill Levnikov (Russia); Attendance: 19,834
ITA: Salvatore Sirigu, Leonardo Bonucci (Cap) (79.Armando Izzo), Leonardo Spinazzola, Alessio Romagnoli, Gianluca Mancini, Marco Verratti, Jorge Luiz Frello Filho "Jorginho" (57.Nicolò Zaniolo), Stefano Sensi, Fabio Quagliarella (72.Leonardo Pavoletti), Matteo Politano, Moise Bioty Kean. Trainer: Roberto Mancini.
Goals: Stefano Sensi (17), Marco Verratti (32), Fabio Quagliarella (35 penalty, 45+3 penalty), Moise Bioty Kean (69), Leonardo Pavoletti (76).

08.06.2019 GREECE - ITALY 0-3(0-3) 16th EC. Qualifiers
Stádio Olympiako „Spiros Louis", Athína; Referee: Anthony Taylor (England); Attendance: 19,828
ITA: Salvatore Sirigu, Leonardo Bonucci, Giorgio Chiellini (Cap), Alessandro Florenzi, Emerson Palmieri dos Santos (68.Mattia De Sciglio), Marco Verratti (81.Lorenzo Pellegrini), Jorge Luiz Frello Filho "Jorginho", Nicolò Barella, Lorenzo Insigne, Andrea Belotti (84.Federico Bernardeschi), Federico Chiesa. Trainer: Roberto Mancini.
Goals: Nicolò Barella (23), Lorenzo Insigne (30), Leonardo Bonucci (33).

11.06.2019 ITALY - BOSNIA AND HERZEGOVINA 2-1(0-1) 16th EC. Qualifiers

Juventus Stadium, Torino; Referee: Xavier Estrada Fernández (Spain); Attendance: 29,100

ITA: Salvatore Sirigu, Leonardo Bonucci, Giorgio Chiellini (Cap), Emerson Palmieri dos Santos, Gianluca Mancini (66.Mattia De Sciglio), Marco Verratti, Jorge Luiz Frello Filho "Jorginho", Nicolò Barella, Fabio Quagliarella (46.Federico Chiesa), Lorenzo Insigne, Federico Bernardeschi (80.Andrea Belotti). Trainer: Roberto Mancini.

Goals: Lorenzo Insigne (49), Marco Verratti (86).

NATIONAL TEAM PLAYERS
(16.07.2018 – 15.07.2019)

Name	DOB	Caps	Goals	2018/2019:	*Club*
Goalkeepers					
Gianluigi DONNARUMMA	25.02.1999	**12**	**0**	2018/2019:	*AC Milan*
Salvatore SIRIGU	12.01.1987	**22**	**0**	2018/2019:	*Torino FC*
Defenders					
Francesco ACERBI	10.08.1988	**3**	**0**	2018:	*SS Lazio Roma*
Cristiano BIRAGHI	01.09.1992	**5**	**1**	2018/2019:	*ACF Fiorentina*
Leonardo BONUCCI	01.05.1987	**89**	**7**	2018/2019:	*Juventus FC Torino*
Mattia CALDARA	05.05.1994	**2**	**0**	2018:	*AC Milan*
Giorgio CHIELLINI	14.08.1984	**103**	**8**	2018/2019:	*Juventus FC Torino*
Domenico CRISCITO	30.12.1986	**26**	**0**	2018:	*Genoa C&FC*
Mattia DE SCIGLIO	20.10.1992	**39**	**0**	2018/2019:	*Juventus FC Torino*
EMERSON Palmieri dos Santos	03.08.1994	**4**	**0**	2018/2019:	*Chelsea FC London (ENG)*
Alessandro FLORENZI	11.03.1991	**32**	**2**	2018/2019:	*AS Roma*
Armando IZZO	02.03.1992	**1**	**0**	2019:	*Torino FC*
Manuel LAZZARI	29.11.1993	**1**	**0**	2018:	*SPAL Ferrara*
Gianluca MANCINI	17.04.1996	**2**	**0**	2019:	*Atalanta Bergamasca Calcio*
Cristiano PICCINI	26.09.1992	**3**	**0**	2018/2019:	*Valencia CF (ESP)*
Alessio ROMAGNOLI	12.01.1995	**9**	**0**	2018/2019:	*AC Milan*
Leonardo SPINAZZOLA	25.03.1993	**7**	**0**	2018/2019:	*Juventus FC Torino*
Davide ZAPPACOSTA	11.06.1992	**13**	**0**	2018:	*Chelsea FC London (ENG)*
Midfielders					
Nicolò BARELLA	07.02.1997	**7**	**0**	2018/2019:	*Cagliari Calcio*
Giacomo BONAVENTURA	22.08.1989	**14**	**0**	2018:	*AC Milan*
Bryan CRISTANTE	03.03.1995	**6**	**0**	2018:	*AS Roma*
Roberto GAGLIARDINI	07.04.1994	**6**	**0**	2018:	*FC Internazionale Milano*
Jorge Luiz Frello Filho "JORGINHO"	20.12.1991	**17**	**1**	2018/2019:	*Chelsea FC London (ENG)*
Lorenzo PELLEGRINI	19.06.1996	**10**	**0**	2018/2019:	*AS Roma*
Stefano SENSI	05.08.1995	**2**	**0**	2018/2019:	*US Sassuolo Calcio*
Marco VERRATTI	05.11.1992	**33**	**3**	2018/2019:	*Paris Saint-Germain FC (FRA)*
Nicolò ZANIOLO	02.07.1999	**2**	**0**	2019:	*AS Roma*
Forwards					
Mario Barwuah BALOTELLI	12.08.1990	**35**	**14**	2018:	*OGC Nice (FRA)*
Andrea BELOTTI	20.12.1993	**22**	**5**	2018/2019:	*Torino FC*
Domenico BERARDI	01.08.1994	**5**	**0**	2018:	*US Sassuolo Calcio*
Federico BERNARDESCHI	16.02.1994	**19**	**2**	2018/2019:	*Juventus FC Torino*
Federico CHIESA	25.10.1997	**13**	**0**	2018/2019:	*ACF Fiorentina*
Vincenzo GRIFO	07.04.1993	**1**	**0**	2018:	*TSG 1899 Hoffenheim (GER)*
Ciro IMMOBILE	20.02.1990	**36**	**7**	2018/2019:	*SS Lazio Roma*
Lorenzo INSIGNE	04.06.1991	**32**	**6**	2018/2019:	*SSC Napoli*
Moise Bioty KEAN	28.02.2000	**3**	**2**	2018/2019:	*Juventus FC Torino*
Kevin LASAGNA	10.08.1992	**3**	**0**	2018:	*Udinese Calcio*
Leonardo PAVOLETTI	26.11.1988	**1**	**1**	2018/2019:	*Cagliari Calcio*
Matteo POLITANO	03.08.1993	**3**	**1**	2018/2019:	*FC Internazionale Milano*
Fabio QUAGLIARELLA	31.01.1983	**28**	**9**	2019:	*UC Sampdoria Genova*
Simone ZAZA	25.06.1991	**18**	**2**	2018:	*Torino FC*

National team coach

Roberto MANCINI [from 14.05.2018]	27.11.1964	13 M; 7 W; 4 D; 2 L; 21-9

KAZAKHSTAN

The Country:

Қазақстан Республикасы (Republic of Kazakhstan)
Capital: Nur-Sultan
Surface: 2,724,900 km²
Inhabitants: 18,448,600 [2019]
Time: UTC+5/+6

The FA:

Қазақстанның Футбол Федерациясы (Football Federation of Kazakhstan)
5a, Momyshuly Avenue, 010000 Nur-Sultan
Tel: +7 7172 790780
Foundation date: 1914
Member of FIFA since: 1994
Member of UEFA since: 2002
Website: www.kff.kz

NATIONAL TEAM RECORDS

First international match:	01.06.1992, Almaty:	Kazakhstan – Turkmenistan 1-0
Most international caps:	Samat Smakov	- 76 caps (2000-2016)
Most international goals:	Ruslan Baltiyev	- 13 goals / 73 caps (1997-2009)

UEFA EUROPEAN CHAMPIONSHIP	
1960	-
1964	-
1968	-
1972	-
1976	-
1980	-
1984	-
1988	-
1992	-
1996	-
2000	-
2004	-
2008	Qualifiers
2012	Qualifiers
2016	Qualifiers

FIFA WORLD CUP	
1930	-
1934	-
1938	-
1950	-
1954	-
1958	-
1962	-
1966	-
1970	-
1974	-
1978	-
1982	-
1986	-
1990	-
1994	Did not enter
1998	Qualifiers
2002	Qualifiers
2006	Qualifiers
2010	Qualifiers
2014	Qualifiers
2018	Qualifiers

UEFA NATIONS LEAGUE
2018/2019 – League D (promoted to League C)

OLYMPIC FOOTBALL TOURNAMENTS 1908-2016							
1908	-	**1948**	-	**1972**	-	**1996**	Qualifiers
1912	-	**1952**	-	**1976**	-	**2000**	Qualifiers
1920	-	**1956**	-	**1980**	-	**2004**	Did not enter
1924	-	**1960**	-	**1984**	-	**2008**	Qualifiers
1928	-	**1964**	-	**1988**	-	**2012**	Qualifiers
1936	-	**1968**	-	**1992**	-	**2016**	Qualifiers

FIFA CONFEDERATIONS CUP 1992-2017
None

KAZAKH CLUB HONOURS IN EUROPEAN CLUB COMPETITIONS:

European Champion Clubs' Cup (1956-1992) / UEFA Champions League (1993-2019)
None
Fairs Cup (1858-1971) / UEFA Cup (1972-2009) / UEFA Europa League (2010-2019)
None
UEFA Super Cup (1972-2018)
None
European Cup Winners' Cup 1961-1999*
None

**defunct competition*

NATIONAL COMPETITIONS
TABLE OF HONOURS

KAZAKH SSR (SOVIET ERA) CHAMPIONS

1936	Sbornaya Alma-Aty
1937	Dinamo Alma-Ata
1938	Dinamo Alma-Ata
1939/1945	*No Championship*
1946	Dinamo Alma-Ata
1947	Lokomotiv Jambul
1948	Trudovye Rezervy Alma-Ata
1949	Dinamo Karaganda
1950	Sbornaya Alma-Aty
1951	Meliorator Chimkent
1952	Meliorator Chimkent
1953	Meliorator Chimkent
1954	Dinamo Alma-Ata
1955	Dinamo Alma-Ata
1956	Sbornaya Alma-Aty
1957	Stroitel Alma-Ata
1958	Spartak Alma-Ata
1959	Spartak Alma-Ata

1960	Yenbek Guryev
1961	Avangard Petropavlovsk
1962	ADK Alma-Ata
1963	Tselinnik Semipalatinsk
1964	ADK Alma-Ata
1965	ADK Alma-Ata
1966	Aktyubinets Aktyubinsk
1967	Torpedo Kokchetav
1968	Gornyak Jezkangan
1969	Shakhtyor Saran'
1970	Stroitel Temir-Tau
1971	Yenbek Jezkangan
1972	Traktor Pavlodar
1973	Yenbek Jezkangan
1974	Gornyak Nikol'sky
1975	Meliorator Chimkent
1976	Khimik Stepnogorsk

1977	Khimik Stepnogorsk
1978	Trud Shevchenko
1979	Khimik Stepnogorsk
1980	Meliorator Chimkent
1981	Burevestnik Kustanay
1980	Traktor Pavlodar
1981	Aktyubinets Aktyubinsk
1982	Shakhtyor Karaganda
1983	Shakhtyor Karaganda
1984	Tselinnik Tselinograd
1985	Meliorator Chimkent
1986	Meliorator Chimkent
1987	Meliorator Chimkent
1988	Traktor Pavlodar
1989	Traktor Pavlodar
1990	Vostok Ust'-Kamenogorsk
1991	Aktyubinets Aktyubinsk

	CHAMPIONS	CUP WINNERS	BEST GOALSCORERS	
1992	FC Kairat Almaty	FC Kairat Almaty	Sergey Kogai (FC Kaysar Kyzylorda)	21
1993	FC Irtysh Pavlodar	FC Dostyk Almaty	Aleksandr Shmarikov (FC Taraz)	28
1994	FC Spartak Semey	FC Vostok Oskemen	Oleg Litvinenko (FC Taraz)	20
1995	FC Spartak Semey	FC Spartak Semey	Andrei Miroshnichenko (FC Spartak Semey)	23
1996	FC Taraz	-	Viktor Antonov (FC Irtysh Pavlodar)	21
1997	FC Irtysh Pavlodar	FC Kairat Almaty (1996/97)	Nurken Mazbaev (FC Taraz)	16
1998	FC Spartak Semey	FC Irtysh Pavlodar (1997/98)	Oleg Litvinenko (FC Spartak Semey)	14
1999	FC Irtysh Pavlodar	FC Kaysar Kyzylorda (1998/99)	Rejepmyrat Agabaýew (TKM, FC Kairat Almaty)	24
2000	FC Astana-64	FC Kairat Almaty (1999/2000)	Nilton Pereira Mendes (BRA, FC Irtysh Pavlodar)	21
#	-	FC Astana-64 (2000/2001)		
2001	FC Astana-64	FC Kairat Almaty	Arsen Tlekhugov (FC Astana-64)	30
2002	FC Irtysh Pavlodar	FC Astana-64	Evgeniy Lunev (FC Shakhter Karagandy)	16
2003	FC Irtysh Pavlodar	FC Kairat Almaty	Andrei Finonchenko (FC Shakhter Karagandy)	18
2004	FC Kairat Almaty	FC Taraz	Ulugbek Bakaev (UZB, FC Tobol Kostanay) Arsen Tlekhugov (FC Kairat Almaty)	22
2005	FC Aktobe	FC Astana-64	Murat Tleshev (FC Irtysh Pavlodar)	20
2006	FC Astana-64	FC Alma-Ata	Jafar Irismetov (UZB, FC Alma-Ata)	17
2007	FC Aktobe	FC Tobol Kostanay	Jafar Irismetov (UZB, FC Alma-Ata)	17
2008	FC Aktobe	FC Aktobe	Murat Tleshev (FC Irtysh Pavlodar)	13
2009	FC Aktobe	FC Atyrau	Murat Tleshev (FC Aktobe) Wladimir Baýramow (TKM, FC Tobol Kostanay)	20
2010	FC Tobol Kostanay	FC Lokomotiv Astana	Ulugbek Bakaev (UZB, FC Tobol Kostanay)	16
2011	FC Shakhter Karagandy	FC Ordabasy	Ulugbek Bakaev (UZB, FC Zhetysu Taldykorgan)	18
2012	FC Shakhter Karagandy	Astana FC	Ulugbek Bakaev (UZB, FC Irtysh Pavlodar)	14
2013	FC Aktobe	FC Shakhter Karagandy	Ihar Zenkovich (BLR, FC Shakhter Karagandy)	15
2014	Astana FC	FC Kairat Almaty	Foxi Kéthévoama (CTA, Astana FC)	16
2015	Astana FC	FC Kairat Almaty	Gerard Bi Goua Gohou (CIV, FC Kairat Almaty)	22
2016	Astana FC	Astana FC	Gerard Bi Goua Gohou (CIV, FC Kairat Almaty)	22
2017	Astana FC	FC Kairat Almaty	Gerard Bi Goua Gohou (CIV, FC Kairat Almaty)	24
2018	Astana FC	FC Kairat Almaty	Marcos Pinheiro Pizzelli (FC Aktobe)	18

Please note: FC Lokomotiv Astana changed its name to Astana FC in 2011.

NATIONAL CHAMPIONSHIP
Kazakhstan Premier League 2018
(11.03.2018 – 11.11.2018)

Results

Round 1 [11.03.2018]
Irtysh Pavlodar - FK Atyrau 2-1(2-0)
FC Kairat - FC Kyzylzhar 2-1(0-1)
Kaysar Kyzylorda - FC Aktobe 0-1(0-0)
FC Ordabasy - Shakhter Karagandy 2-1(1-0)
FC Zhetysu - Tobol Kostanay 0-1(0-1)
Astana FC - FC Akzhayik 3-0(1-0)

Round 2 [17.03.2018]
Irtysh Pavlodar - FC Aktobe 2-1(2-1)
FC Kairat - FK Atyrau 2-0(0-0)
Kaysar Kyzylorda - FC Akzhayik 1-1(0-0)
FC Ordabasy - FC Kyzylzhar 2-1(0-1)
Tobol Kostanay - Shakhter Karag. 0-1(0-0)
FC Zhetysu - Astana FC 0-2(0-2)

Round 3 [31.03.-01.04.2018]
FC Aktobe - FC Kairat 1-1(1-1)
FC Akzhayik - Irtysh Pavlodar 1-0(0-0)
FK Atyrau - FC Ordabasy 0-1(0-0)
Astana FC - Kaysar Kyzylorda 2-0(2-0)
FC Kyzylzhar - Tobol Kostanay 1-2(1-0)
Shakhter Karagandy - FC Zhetysu 1-1(1-0)

Round 4 [07.04.2018]
Irtysh Pavlodar - Astana FC 1-6(0-1)
Shakhter Karagandy - FC Kyzylzhar 2-1(2-0)
Tobol Kostanay - FK Atyrau 3-2(1-2)
FC Zhetysu - Kaysar Kyzylorda 1-0(1-0)
FC Kairat - FC Akzhayik 3-0(2-0)
FC Ordabasy - FC Aktobe 3-1(2-1)

Round 5 [14.04.2018]
Astana FC - FC Kairat 1-1(0-0)
FC Akzhayik - FC Ordabasy 4-1(3-1)
FC Kyzylzhar - FC Zhetysu 1-0(1-0)
Kaysar Kyzylorda - Irtysh Pavlodar 0-0
FC Aktobe - Tobol Kostanay 0-1(0-1)
FK Atyrau - Shakhter Karagandy 0-0

Round 6 [22.04.2018]
FC Kyzylzhar - FK Atyrau 1-1(1-0)
Tobol Kostanay - FC Akzhayik 1-1(0-1)
Shakhter Karagandy - FC Aktobe 1-1(0-1)
FC Zhetysu - Irtysh Pavlodar 2-1(0-1)
FC Kairat - Kaysar Kyzylorda 4-1(1-1)
FC Ordabasy - Astana FC 1-2(1-2)

Round 7 [28-29.04.2018]
FC Akzhayik - Shakhter Karagandy 1-1(1-0)
Kaysar Kyzylorda - FC Ordabasy 0-0
Irtysh Pavlodar - FC Kairat 1-2(1-1)
FK Atyrau - FC Zhetysu 1-0(0-0)
FC Aktobe - FC Kyzylzhar 2-0(1-0)
Astana FC - Tobol Kostanay 1-0(0-0)

Round 8 [05.05.2018]
FC Kyzylzhar - FC Akzhayik 2-1(2-0)
Shakhter Karagandy - Astana FC 1-0(0-0)
FC Zhetysu - FC Kairat 1-3(0-2)
FK Atyrau - FC Aktobe 1-1(0-1)
FC Ordabasy - Irtysh Pavlodar 1-0(0-0)
Tobol Kostanay - Kaysar Kyzylorda 0-3(0-1)

Round 9 [09.05.2018]
FC Akzhayik - FK Atyrau 1-1(0-1)
Irtysh Pavlodar - Tobol Kostanay 0-1(0-0)
FC Kairat - FC Ordabasy 2-0(1-0)
Kaysar Kyzylorda - Shakhter Karag. 3-0(1-0)
Astana FC - FC Kyzylzhar 2-0(0-0)
FC Aktobe - FC Zhetysu 1-1(1-0)

Round 10 [13-14.05.2018]
FC Kyzylzhar - Kaysar Kyzylorda 0-0
Shakhter Karagandy - Irtysh Pavlodar 0-1(0-0)
Tobol Kostanay - FC Kairat 1-0(0-0)
FK Atyrau - Astana FC 0-2(0-0)
FC Aktobe - FC Akzhayik 5-3(3-0)
FC Zhetysu - FC Ordabasy 4-2(2-0)

Round 11 [19.05.2018]
Irtysh Pavlodar - FC Kyzylzhar 5-0(3-0)
Astana FC - FC Aktobe 3-1(2-1)
Kaysar Kyzylorda - FK Atyrau 0-0
FC Akzhayik - FC Zhetysu 2-0(0-0)
FC Kairat - Shakhter Karagandy 2-0(1-0)
FC Ordabasy - Tobol Kostanay 0-1(0-1)

Round 12 [27.05.2018]
FC Kyzylzhar - FC Ordabasy 1-2(1-1)
Shakhter Karag. - Tobol Kostanay 0-1(0-0)
Astana FC - FC Zhetysu 3-0(1-0)
FC Akzhayik - Kaysar Kyzylorda 0-0
FK Atyrau - FC Kairat 1-3(0-2)
FC Aktobe - Irtysh Pavlodar 1-1(1-1)

Round 13 [31.05.2018]
FC Zhetysu - Shakhter Karagandy 1-0(1-0)
Kaysar Kyzylorda - Astana FC 0-2(0-1)
Irtysh Pavlodar - FC Akzhayik 2-0(2-0)
FC Kairat - FC Aktobe 3-2(1-2)
FC Ordabasy - FK Atyrau 0-2(0-1)
Tobol Kostanay - FC Kyzylzhar 0-1(0-1)

Round 14 [17-18.06.2018]
Astana FC - Irtysh Pavlodar 3-0(1-0)
FK Atyrau - Tobol Kostanay 0-2(0-0)
FC Akzhayik - FC Kairat 1-2(0-1)
Kaysar Kyzylorda - FC Zhetysu 0-0
FC Aktobe - FC Ordabasy 3-1(0-1)
FC Kyzylzhar - Shakhter Karagandy 1-0(0-0)

Round 15 [23-24.06.2018]
Shakhter Karagandy - FK Atyrau 3-0(1-0)
Tobol Kostanay - FC Aktobe 2-3(0-1)
FC Zhetysu - FC Kyzylzhar 2-1(1-0)
Irtysh Pavlodar - Kaysar Kyzylorda 0-1(0-0)
FC Ordabasy - FC Akzhayik 2-1(1-1)
FC Kairat - Astana FC 1-2(1-1)

Round 16 [30.06.-01.07.2018]
Astana FC - FC Ordabasy 5-3(3-1)
FC Akzhayik - Tobol Kostanay 1-3(0-0)
Irtysh Pavlodar - FC Zhetysu 0-2(0-0)
Kaysar Kyzylorda - FC Kairat 1-2(0-0)
FK Atyrau - FC Kyzylzhar 0-0
FC Aktobe - Shakhter Karagandy 2-0(1-0)

Round 17 [05-07.07.2018]
Tobol Kostanay - Astana FC 0-0
FC Ordabasy - Kaysar Kyzylorda 1-2(1-0)
FC Kairat - Irtysh Pavlodar 4-0(3-0)
FC Kyzylzhar - FC Aktobe 2-1(0-1)
FC Zhetysu - FK Atyrau 2-2(0-1)
Shakhter Karagandy - FC Akzhayik 1-2(0-1)

Round 18 [14-15.07.2018]
Kaysar Kyzylorda - Tobol Kostanay 2-2(0-1)
Astana FC - Shakhter Karagandy 2-0(1-0)
FC Akzhayik - FC Kyzylzhar 2-0(1-0)
FC Aktobe - FK Atyrau 5-1(1-0)
Irtysh Pavlodar - FC Ordabasy 1-2(0-1)
FC Kairat - FC Zhetysu 2-1(0-0)

Round 19 [21-22.07.2018]
FC Kyzylzhar - Astana FC 0-2(0-0) [25.04.]
FC Zhetysu - FC Aktobe 1-2(0-1)
Shakhter Karag. - Kaysar Kyzylorda 2-2(0-1)
FK Atyrau - FC Akzhayik 2-0(1-0)
Tobol Kostanay - Irtysh Pavlodar 1-1(0-0)
FC Ordabasy - FC Kairat 2-1(1-0)

Round 20 [28-29.07.2018]
Kaysar Kyzylorda - FC Kyzylzhar 2-1(2-0)
Astana FC - FK Atyrau 2-0(1-0)
FC Akzhayik - FC Aktobe 1-1(0-1)
FC Kairat - Tobol Kostanay 1-0(0-0)
Irtysh Pavlodar - Shakhter Karagandy 1-1(0-0)
FC Ordabasy - FC Zhetysu 1-2(0-2)

Round 21 [04-05.08.2018]
FC Zhetysu - FC Akzhayik 1-1(1-0)
FK Atyrau - Kaysar Kyzylorda 2-1(1-0)
FC Aktobe - Astana FC 1-1(0-1)
FC Kyzylzhar - Irtysh Pavlodar 1-0(1-0)
Tobol Kostanay - FC Ordabasy 1-1(0-0)
Shakhter Karagandy - FC Kairat 1-1(0-0)

Round 22 [11-12.08.2018]
FC Akzhayik - Astana FC 3-0(1-0) [23.05.]
Tobol Kostanay - FC Zhetysu 1-0(0-0)
FC Aktobe - Kaysar Kyzylorda 3-1(0-0)
FC Kyzylzhar - FC Kairat 1-3(1-1)
FK Atyrau - Irtysh Pavlodar 2-0(1-0)
Shakhter Karagandy - FC Ordabasy 0-0

Round 23 [18-19.08.2018]
FC Akzhayik - FC Aktobe 0-0
FK Atyrau - Tobol Kostanay 2-1(0-0)
FC Zhetysu - Irtysh Pavlodar 2-0(2-0)
Kaysar Kyzylorda - FC Ordabasy 2-1(0-0)
FC Kyzylzhar - FC Kairat 2-1(1-1) [31.10.]
Shakhter Karag. - Astana FC 3-1(3-0) [31.10.]

Round 24 [25-26.08.2018]
Irtysh Pavlodar - Shakhter Karagandy 1-1(1-0)
Tobol Kostanay - Kaysar Kyzylorda 0-0
FC Ordabasy - FC Akzhayik 1-0(1-0)
FC Aktobe - FC Zhetysu 2-3(0-1)
FC Kairat - FK Atyrau 4-2(1-0)
Astana FC - FC Kyzylzhar 3-0(2-0)

Round 25 [26.09.2018]
FC Kyzylzhar - Shakhter Karagandy 2-1(0-0)
Kaysar Kyzylorda - FC Kairat 1-2(0-2)
FC Zhetysu - FC Ordabasy 1-1(0-1)
FC Akzhayik - Tobol Kostanay 0-1(0-0)
FK Atyrau - Astana FC 0-1(0-0)
FC Aktobe - Irtysh Pavlodar 2-0(1-0)

Round 26 [16.09.2018]
Irtysh Pavlodar - FC Kyzylzhar 0-1(0-1)
Shakhter Karagandy - FK Atyrau 2-1(1-1)
Tobol Kostanay - FC Zhetysu 2-2(2-1)
Astana FC - Kaysar Kyzylorda 0-0
FC Kairat - FC Akzhayik 0-1(0-0)
FC Ordabasy - FC Aktobe 0-0

Round 27 [22-23.09.2018]
Kaysar Kyzylorda - Shakhter Karag. 2-1(0-1)
FC Zhetysu - FC Kairat 1-0(0-0)
FK Atyrau - FC Kyzylzhar 3-2(1-1)
FC Ordabasy - Irtysh Pavlodar 0-2(0-1)
FC Aktobe - Tobol Kostanay 3-1(0-0)
FC Akzhayik - Astana FC 1-2(1-2)

Round 28 [30.09.2018]
Irtysh Pavlodar - FK Atyrau 1-0(0-0)
FC Kyzylzhar - Kaysar Kyzylorda 1-0(1-0)
Shakhter Karagandy - FC Akzhayik 1-0(1-0)
FC Kairat - FC Aktobe 6-1(3-0)
Astana FC - FC Zhetysu 3-0(1-0)
Tobol Kostanay - FC Ordabasy 1-0(0-0)

Round 29 [06-07.10.2018]
Kaysar Kyzylorda - FK Atyrau 2-2(0-0)
FC Zhetysu - Shakhter Karagandy 1-1(0-1)
FC Akzhayik - FC Kyzylzhar 0-0
FC Ordabasy - FC Kairat 2-0(1-0)
Tobol Kostanay - Irtysh Pavlodar 1-2(0-0)
FC Aktobe - Astana FC 1-2(0-1)

Round 30 [20-21.10.2018]
Astana FC - FC Ordabasy 1-1(0-0)
FC Kairat - Tobol Kostanay 0-0
FC Kyzylzhar - FC Zhetysu 1-1(0-1)
Shakhter Karagandy - FC Aktobe 0-1(0-1)
FK Atyrau - FC Akzhayik 2-1(1-1)
Irtysh Pavlodar - Kaysar Kyzylorda 0-1(0-1)

Round 31 [27-28.10.2018]
FC Kairat - Irtysh Pavlodar 0-1(0-1)
FC Zhetysu - FK Atyrau 0-0
FC Ordabasy - Shakhter Karagandy 1-1(1-0)
FC Akzhayik - Kaysar Kyzylorda 0-4(0-1)
FC Aktobe - FC Kyzylzhar 1-0(1-0)
Tobol Kostanay - Astana FC 1-0(0-0)

Round 32 [03.11.2018]
FK Atyrau - FC Aktobe 3-1(1-1)
Irtysh Pavlodar - FC Akzhayik 2-0(0-0)
Kaysar Kyzylorda - FC Zhetysu 1-0(0-0)
FC Kyzylzhar - FC Ordabasy 1-2(0-0)
Shakhter Karag. - Tobol Kostanay 2-1(1-0)
Astana FC - FC Kairat 3-2(2-1)

Round 33 [11.11.2018]
FC Aktobe - Kaysar Kyzylorda 0-2(0-2)
Astana FC - Irtysh Pavlodar 4-0(1-0)
FC Kairat - Shakhter Karagandy 0-0
FC Ordabasy - FK Atyrau 1-0(1-0)
Tobol Kostanay - FC Kyzylzhar 3-0(1-0)
FC Zhetysu - FC Akzhayik 3-1(1-0)

Final Standings								
1.	**Astana FC**	33	24	5	4	66 - 22	77
2.	FC Kairat Almaty	33	19	5	9	60 - 33	62
3.	FC Tobol Kostanay	33	15	8	10	36 - 30	53
4.	FC Ordabasy Shymkent	33	13	7	13	38 - 44	46
5.	FC Kaysar Kyzylorda	33	11	12	10	35 - 31	45
6.	FC Zhetisu Taldiqorghan	33	11	10	12	36 - 40	43
7.	FC Aktobe*	33	13	9	11	51 - 47	42
8.	FC Shakhter Karagandy	33	8	12	13	29 - 36	36
9.	FC Atyrau	33	9	9	15	34 - 47	36
10.	FC Irtysh Pavlodar (*Relegation Play-offs*)	33	10	5	18	28 - 45	35
11.	FC Kyzylzhar SK Petropavlovsk (*Relegated*)	33	10	5	18	27 - 48	35
12.	FC Akzhayik Oral (*Relegated*)	33	7	9	17	31 - 48	30

**6 points deducted*

Top goalscorers:

18 Marcos Pinheiro Pizzelli
FC Aktobe

17 Aderinsola Habib Eseola (UKR)
FC Akzhayik Oral / FC Kairat Almaty

14 Marin Tomasov (CRO)
Astana FC

12 Isael da Silva Barbosa (BRA)
FC Kairat Almaty

Relegation Play-offs

FC Kyran Shimkent - FC Irtysh Pavlodar 0-3(0-2) 1-2(0-0)

FC Irtysh Pavlodar remains at first level.

NATIONAL CUP
Kazakhstan Kubok 2018

1/8 - Finals [18.04.2018]

FC Okzhetpes Kokshetau - FC Kairat Almaty	3-5
FC Kyran Shimkent - FC Ordabasy Shymkent	0-6
FC Shakhter Karag - FC Kyzylzhar SK Petropavlovsk	0-0 aet; 7-6 pen
FC Maqtaaral Jetisay - Astana FC	3-1
FC Kaysar Kyzylorda - FC Aktobe	2-0
FC Taraz - FC Irtysh Pavlodar	0-1
FC Akzhayik Oral - FC Atyrau	0-1
FC Tobol Kostanay - FC Zhetisu Taldiqorghan	1-0

Quarter-Finals [23.05.2018]

FC Shakhter Karagandy - FC Kaysar Kyzylorda	2-1 aet
FC Ordabasy Shymkent - FC Kairat Almaty	3-4 pen
FC Maqtaaral Jetisay - FC Irtysh Pavlodar	0-3
FC Atyrau - FC Tobol Kostanay	2-1

Semi-Finals [14/27.06.2018]

FC Shakhter Karagandy - FC Atyrau	0-0 / 1-3
FC Kairat Almaty - FC Irtysh Pavlodar	2-0 / 1-3

Final

24.11.2018; Astana Arena, Astana; Referee: Bakhyt Kyzylbaev; Attendance: 4,500

FC Kairat Almaty - FC Atyrau 1-0(1-0)

Kairat: Stanislav Pokatilov, Yeldos Akhmetov, Gafurzhan Suyumbayev (73.Rashid Lyukhay), Sergey Keiler, Nuray Alip, Aleksandr Sokolenko, Aybol Abiken, Magomed Paragulgov (88.Pavel Kriventsev), Bauyrzhan Islamkhan, Georgiy Zhukov, Samat Sarsenov (90+3.Vyacheslav Shvyrev). Trainer: Andrey Karpovich.

Atyrau: Vladimir Loginovskiy, Rizvan Ablitarov, Kuanysh Kalmuratov (44.Altynbek Saparov), Marat Khayrullin [*sent off 90+5*], Jure Obšivač, Eduard Sergienko, Joseph Nane Fils Eone, František Kubik, Predrag Sikimić (84.Aleksey Rodionov), Eldar Abdrakhmanov (63.Didar Zhalmukan), Babatunde Temitope Adeniji. Trainer: Viktor Kumykov.

Goal: 1-0 Aleksandr Sokolenko (16).

THE CLUBS 2018

Football Club Aktobe

Founded: 1967 (*as Aktyubinets*)
Stadium: Aktobe Central Stadium, Aktobe (15,000)

Goalkeepers:	**DOB**	**M**	**(s)**	**G**
Ramil Nurmukhametov	21.12.1987	18		
Igor Trofimets	20.08.1996	15		
Defenders:	**DOB**	**M**	**(s)**	**G**
Fabrício Silva Dornellas (BRA)	20.02.1990	8	(1)	
Bagdat Kairov	27.04.1993	31		2
Hrvoje Miličević (CRO)	20.04.1993	30	(1)	2
Aleksandar Simčević (SRB)	15.02.1987	28		2
Aybar Temirbayev	22.01.1997		(1)	
Rustam Temirkhan	10.08.1997	2	(1)	
Vitaliy Volkov (RUS)	22.03.1981	24		
Sayat Zhumagali	25.04.1995	15	(3)	1
Midfielders:	**DOB**	**M**	**(s)**	**G**
Syrym Adilzhanov	09.01.1997	2		
Aslanbek Kakimov	02.10.1993	11	(4)	3
Zhambyl Kukeyev	20.09.1988	17	(8)	2
Saša Marjanović (SRB)	13.11.1987	20	(3)	3
Milan Radin (SRB)	25.06.1991	26	(3)	4
Ardak Saulet	12.01.1997	6	(1)	
Anton Shurygin	03.12.1988	19	(8)	
Adilkhan Tanzharikov	25.11.1996	1	(1)	
Ruslan Valiullin	09.09.1994	21	(8)	1
Igor Yurin	03.07.1982	1	(4)	
Didar Zhalmukan	22.05.1996		(4)	
Forwards:	**DOB**	**M**	**(s)**	**G**
Abat Aimbetov	07.08.1995	12	(11)	2
Igor Boichuk	04.06.1997		(2)	
Ulan Konysbaev	28.05.1989	3	(9)	
Jean-Eudes Maurice (HAI)	21.06.1986	8	(6)	1
Marcos Pinheiro Pizzelli	03.10.1984	22	(2)	18
Reynaldo dos Santos Silva (BRA)	24.08.1989	22	(8)	7
Aleksandr Usachev	03.02.2000	1		
Adilkhan Zhumay	15.06.1997		(1)	
Trainer:	**DOB**	**M**		
Vladimir Mukhanov (RUS)	20.04.1954	33		

Football Club Akzhayik Oral

Founded: 1968
Stadium: „Petr Atoyan" Stadium, Oral (8,320)

Goalkeepers:	**DOB**	**M**	**(s)**	**G**
Yevhen Borovyk (UKR)	02.03.1985	22		
Sergey Tkachuk	15.02.1992	11	(1)	
Defenders:	**DOB**	**M**	**(s)**	**G**
Serhiy Basov (UKR)	19.01.1987	32		1
Azat Ersalimov	19.07.1988	32		1
Sergey Keiler	08.11.1994		(1)	
Yuriy Putrash	29.01.1990	3		
Bauyrzhan Omarov	03.08.1990	2	(7)	
Vladimir Pokatilov	08.12.1992	1	(12)	
Alibek Sakenov	30.07.1991		(2)	
Miram Sapanov	12.03.1986	31	(1)	2
Berik Shaikhov	20.02.1994	31	(2)	1
Oleksandr Volovyk (UKR)	28.10.1985	1		
Midfielders:	**DOB**	**M**	**(s)**	**G**
Ivan Antipov	14.01.1996	24	(6)	2
Adilet Bolatov	18.08.1998		(1)	
Ambrosiy Chachua (UKR)	02.04.1994	11		
Denis Glavina (CRO)	03.03.1986	10	(3)	
Ruslan Khairov	18.01.1990	17	(4)	
Ihor Khudobyak (UKR)	20.02.1985	22	(7)	1
Erkin Tapalov	03.09.1993	31	(1)	
Andriy Tkachuk (UKR)	18.11.1987	30	(1)	1
Forwards:	**DOB**	**M**	**(s)**	**G**
Aderinsola Habib Eseola (UKR)	28.06.1991	11	(2)	8
Arturs Karašausks (LVA)	29.01.1992	6	(8)	2
Idrissa Kouyaté (CIV)	27.04.1991		(3)	
Malick Mané (SEN)	14.10.1988	19	(8)	9
Yerkebulan Nurgaliyev	12.09.1993	15	(13)	3
Edige Oralbay	11.03.1997	1	(3)	
Trainer:	**DOB**	**M**		
Volodymyr Maziar (UKR)	28.09.1977	10		
Artur Avakyants [15.05.2018]	30.09.1972	10		
Serhiy Zaytsev (UKR) [25.07.2018]	13.04.1973	13		

Astana Football Club

Founded: 2009 (*as FC Lokomotiv Astana*)
Stadium: Astana Arena, Nur-Sultan (30,000)

Goalkeepers:	**DOB**	**M**	**(s)**	**G**
Nenad Erić	26.05.1982	20		
Aleksandr Mokin	19.06.1981	12	(1)	
Stanislav Pavlov	30.05.1994	1		
Defenders:	**DOB**	**M**	**(s)**	**G**
Marin Aničić (BIH)	17.08.1989	27		
Abzal Beysebekov	30.11.1992	24	(4)	
Adilzhan Duysembayev	24.02.2001		(1)	
Alim Ilyassov	22.04.2000	1		
Yuriy Logvinenko	22.07.1988	12	(4)	1
Sergey Malyi	05.06.1990	16	(1)	2
Samat Mazhit	24.03.2000	1		
Evgeni Postnikov (RUS)	16.04.1986	18	(1)	
Antonio Rukavina (SRB)	26.01.1984	3		
Igor Shitov (BLR)	24.10.1986	5		
Dmitriy Shomko	19.03.1990	22	(1)	2
Zhantore Zhumadilov	20.01.2000	1		
Midfielders:	**DOB**	**M**	**(s)**	**G**
Richard Almeida de Oliveira (AZE)	20.03.1989	5	(3)	1
Dauren Iskakov	25.04.1999	1		
Zhaslan Kairkenov	27.03.2000	1		
László Kleinheisler (HUN)	08.04.1994	16		
Ivan Maevskiy (BLR)	05.05.1988	21	(4)	
Ivan Maevski (BLR)	05.05.1988	15	(6)	3
Serikzhan Muzhikov	17.06.1989	5	(3)	
Yuriy Pertsukh	13.05.1996	3	(3)	1
Sultan Sagnayev	14.01.2000	5		
Lev Skvortsov	02.02.2000	1		
Marko Stanojević (SRB)	22.06.1988	4	(5)	
Marin Tomasov (CRO)	31.08.1987	26	(4)	14
Baktiyar Zainutdinov	02.04.1998	17	(10)	5
Madi Zhakipbayev	21.03.2000	1		
Forwards:	**DOB**	**M**	**(s)**	**G**
Stanislav Basmanov	24.06.2001		(1)	
Đorđe Despotović (SRB)	04.03.1992	11	(4)	5
Rangelo Maria Janga (CUW)	16.04.1992	8	(2)	4
Junior Kabananga Kalonji (COD)	04.04.1989	5	(1)	
Ramazan Karimov	05.07.1999	1		1
Roman Murtazayev	10.09.1993	22	(6)	8
Danil Pichkarev	10.09.2001		(1)	
Vladislav Prokopenko	01.07.2000	4	(2)	
Aleksey Shchetkin	21.05.1991	10	(16)	10
Patrick Twumasi (GHA)	09.05.1994	11	(4)	8
Trainer:	**DOB**	**M**		
Grigori Babayan	02.04.1980	15		
Roman Hryhorchuk (UKR) [01.06.2018]	22.03.1965	18		

Football Club Atyrau

Founded: 1980
Stadium: Munaishy Stadium, Atyrau (8,690)

Goalkeepers:	**DOB**	**M**	**(s)**	**G**
Vladimir Loginovskiy	08.10.1985	17		
Andrey Pasechenko	09.08.1987	16		
Defenders:	**DOB**	**M**	**(s)**	**G**
Rizvan Ablitarov (UKR)	18.04.1989	27	(1)	
Yerasyl Amanzhol	13.01.1999		(1)	
Rafkat Aslan	02.02.1994	9	(3)	
Tomislav Barbarić (CRO)	29.03.1989	21		1
Anton Chichulin	27.10.1984	10		
Joseph Nane Fils Eone (CMR)	03.12.1987	23	(1)	1
Ruslan Esatov	31.10.1984	3	(2)	
Kuanysh Kalmuratov	27.08.1996	24	(1)	1
Dauren Mazhitov	03.03.1996	2		
Jure Obšivač (CRO)	28.05.1990	9	(3)	2
Ruslan Zhanysbaev	04.11.1995		(1)	
Stefan Živković (SRB)	01.06.1990	8	(5)	
Midfielders:	**DOB**	**M**	**(s)**	**G**
Piraly Aliyev	13.01.1984	2		
Rinat Dzumatov	13.10.1997	12	(4)	
Dauren Kayralliev	15.05.1992	3	(9)	
Marat Khayrullin	26.04.1984	25		7
František Kubik (SVK)	14.03.1989	5	(3)	
Novica Maksimović (SRB)	04.04.1988	20	(3)	
Aibar Nurybekov	29.08.1992	11	(6)	
Yuriy Pertsukh	13.05.1996	9	(1)	1
Altynbek Saparov	26.04.1995	9	(5)	
Eduard Sergienko	18.02.1983	21	(4)	
Anton Zemlyanukhin (KGZ)	11.12.1988		(4)	
Didar Zhalmukan	22.05.1996	2	(8)	
Forwards:	**DOB**	**M**	**(s)**	**G**
Eldar Abdrakhmanov	16.01.1987	16	(2)	2
Babatunde Temitope Adeniji (NGA)	17.09.1995	25	(5)	8
Aleksey Rodionov	29.03.1994	1	(12)	2
Predrag Sikimić (CRO)	29.08.1982	23	(6)	5
Igor Zenkovich	17.09.1987	10	(5)	2
Trainer:	**DOB**	**M**		
Vakhid Masudov	10.10.1959	4		
Andrian Sosnovschi (MDA) [11.04.2018]	13.06.1977	12		
Viktor Kumykov [04.07.2018]	25.06.1963	17		

Football Club Irtysh Pavlodar

Founded: 1965
Stadium: Pavlodar Central Stadium, Pavlodar (15,000)

Goalkeepers:	**DOB**	**M**	**(s)**	**G**
Dzhurakhon Babakhanov	31.10.1991	2		
Almat Bekbaev	14.07.1984	1		
Nikita Kalmykov	24.08.1989	30		
Defenders:	**DOB**	**M**	**(s)**	**G**
Maksat Amirkhanov	10.02.1992	1	(1)	
Rafkat Aslan	02.02.1994	8		
Adrian Avrămia (MDA)	31.01.1992	8	(1)	
Berik Aytbaev	26.06.1991	1	(1)	
Aleksandr Kislitsyn	08.03.1986	30	(1)	
Miloš Stamenković (SRB)	01.06.1990	26		3
Dmitri Shmidt	17.11.1993	26	(2)	
Ruslan Yessimov	28.04.1990	31		
Sansyzbay Zhanturmysov	05.05.1999		(1)	
Midfielders:	**DOB**	**M**	**(s)**	**G**
Adrián Gómez Ramírez (ESP)	17.01.1994	28	(1)	
Carlos Manuel Costa Fernandes Fonseca (POR)	23.08.1987	25	(1)	3
Ilya Kalinin	03.02.1992	20	(9)	1
Arman Kenesov	04.09.2000	1	(1)	
Sergey Kislyak (BLR)	06.08.1987	14	(2)	
Doru Popadiuc (ROU)	18.02.1995	18	(8)	5
Artem Popov	17.01.1998	2	(2)	
Maydar Ramazanov	30.10.1997		(1)	
Rodrigo Antônio do Nascimento (BRA)	27.07.1987	14		1
Rakimzhan Rozybakiev	02.01.1991	4	(4)	
Pavel Shabalin	23.10.1988	14	(6)	6
Kiril Shestakov	19.06.1985	9	(10)	
Forwards:	**DOB**	**M**	**(s)**	**G**
Abel Issa Camará (GNB)	06.01.1990	12	(1)	1
John Chibuike (NGA)	10.10.1988	4	(8)	
Eddie Gabriel Hernández Padilla (HON)	27.02.1991	2	(6)	1
Hugo André Rodrigues Seco (POR)	17.06.1988	8	(3)	1
Fuad Gbolahan Salami (NGA)	15.04.1991	15	(2)	4
Arman Smailov	04.05.1997	1	(12)	
Vladimir Vomenko	22.05.1995	8	(8)	
Trainer:	**DOB**	**M**		
Gerard Nus Casanova (ESP)	31.01.1985	13		
Dmitri Kuznetsov (RUS) [16.06.2018]	28.08.1965	4		
Dimitar Dimitrov (BUL) [08.07.2018]	09.06.1959	16		

Football Club Kairat Almaty

Founded: 1954 *(as Lokomotiv Alma-Ata)*
Stadium: Almaty Central Stadium, Almaty (25,057)

Goalkeepers:	**DOB**	**M**	**(s)**	**G**
David Loria	31.10.1981	1		
Vladimir Plotnikov	03.04.1986	6		
Stanislav Pokatilov	08.12.1992	26		
Defenders:	**DOB**	**M**	**(s)**	**G**
Aybol Abiken	01.06.1996	5	(5)	
Yeldos Akhmetov	01.06.1990	11		
Nuray Alip	22.12.1999	15		
Sheldon Bateau (TRI)	29.01.1991	25		
Sergey Keiler	08.11.1994	2		
Stanislav Lunin	02.05.1993	13		2
Sergey Politsevich (BLR)	09.04.1990	6	(1)	
Aleksandr Sokolenko	23.11.1996	9	(6)	1
Gafurzhan Suyumbayev	19.08.1990	25	(2)	1
Midfielders:	**DOB**	**M**	**(s)**	**G**
Gai Assulin (ISR)	09.04.1991	1		
Ákos Elek (HUN)	21.07.1988	22		
Ivo Iličević (CRO)	14.11.1986	9	(5)	3
Bauyrzhan Islamkhan	23.02.1993	20	(9)	3
Islambek Kuat	12.01.1993	22	(3)	1
Rashid Lyukhay	30.07.1997	1		
Ramazan Orazov	30.01.1998	1		
Samat Sarsenov	19.08.1996	5		
Yan Vorogovskiy	07.08.1996	17	(5)	1
Georgiy Zhukov	19.11.1994	13	(7)	2
Forwards:	**DOB**	**M**	**(s)**	**G**
Juan Felipe Alves Ribeiro (BRA)	05.12.1987	22	(2)	
Chuma Emeka Uche Anene (NOR)	14.05.1993	3	(6)	4
Andrey Arshavin (RUS)	29.05.1981	18	(13)	9
Márton Eppel (HUN)	26.10.1991	6	(7)	3
Aderinsola Habib Eseola (UKR)	28.06.1991	9	(7)	9
Isael da Silva Barbosa (BRA)	13.05.1988	25	(3)	13
Magomed Paragulgov	26.03.1994	14	(3)	3
Vyacheslav Shvyrev	07.01.2001	1	(8)	
Hugo Gabriel Silveira Pereira (URU)	23.05.1993	10	(5)	4
Trainer:	**DOB**	**M**		
Carlos Alós Ferrer (ESP)	21.07.1975	28		
Andrey Karpovich [17.10.2018]	18.01.1981	5		

Football Club Kaysar Kyzylorda

Founded: 1968
Stadium: "Gany Muratbayev" Stadium, Kyzylorda (7,500)

Goalkeepers:	**DOB**	**M**	**(s)**	**G**
Aleksandr Grigorenko	06.02.1985	18		
Marsel Islamkulov	18.04.1994	15		
Defenders:	**DOB**	**M**	**(s)**	**G**
Ilyas Amirseitov	22.10.1989	28		
Aldan Baltaev	15.01.1989	1	(4)	
Valentin Chureyev	29.08.1986	15	(2)	
Mark Gorman	09.02.1989	12	(7)	1
Ivan Graf (CRO)	17.06.1987	31		
Abdel Lamanje (CMR)	27.07.1990	27		2
Aleksandr Marochkin	14.07.1990	19	(1)	1
Dmitriy Yevstigneyev	27.11.1986	9	(3)	
Midfielders:	**DOB**	**M**	**(s)**	**G**
Volodimir Arzhanov (UKR)	29.11.1985	24	(3)	3
Maksat Bayzhanov	06.08.1984	19	(3)	1
John Kamara (SLE)	12.05.1988	6	(17)	
Valeriy Korobkin	02.07.1984	19	(5)	
Duman Narzildaev	06.09.1993	26	(2)	2
Askhat Tagybergen	09.08.1990	20	(5)	5
Paul Were Ooko (KEN)	08.10.1993	9	(14)	
Aybol Zhakhayev	15.12.1996	1	(1)	
Forwards:	**DOB**	**M**	**(s)**	**G**
Yoann Axel Cyriac Arquin (MTQ)	15.04.1988	2	(5)	
Mathias Coureur (MTQ)	22.03.1988	27		7
Franck Dja Djédjé (CIV)	02.06.1986	6	(11)	2
Bratislav Punoševac (SRB)	09.07.1987	13		6
Darenbek Tazhimbetov	02.07.1985	1	(5)	
Igor Zenkovich	17.09.1987	4	(6)	3
Toktar Zhangylyshbay	25.05.1993	11	(4)	1
Trainer:	**DOB**	**M**		
Stoicho Mladenov (BUL)	12.04.1957	33		

Football Club Kyzylzhar Sport Club Petropavl

Founded: 1968
Stadium: Karasai Stadium, Petropavl (11,000)

Goalkeepers:	**DOB**	**M**	**(s)**	**G**
Anton Tsirin	10.08.1987	20		
Timurbek Zakirov	01.03.1996	13		
Defenders:	**DOB**	**M**	**(s)**	**G**
Olzhas Altaev	15.07.1989	8	(2)	
Viktor Gunchenko	25.08.1994	5	(13)	
Bakdaulet. Kozhabayev	19.06.1992	8	(1)	
Aleksey Muldarov	24.04.1984	6		
Giorgi Popkhadze (GEO)	25.09.1986	26	(2)	
Andrey Shabaev	15.02.1987	12	(4)	
Oleksandr Stetsenko (UKR)	02.03.1990	5	(4)	
Karam Sultanov	15.04.1996	20	(4)	
Mihail Venkov (BUL)	28.07.1983	14		
Midfielders:	**DOB**	**M**	**(s)**	**G**
Ildar Aitov	02.03.1990	28	(2)	
Ali Aliev	27.10.1980	4	(2)	
Alibek Ayaganov	13.01.1992	1	(1)	
Freddy Javier Coronel Ortíz (PAR)	22.07.1989	27	(2)	2
Uroš Delić (MNE)	10.08.1987	24	(2)	1
Maksym Drachenko (UKR)	28.01.1990	15	(1)	
Aslan Dzhanuzakov	06.01.1993	9	(12)	
Gogita Gogua (GEO)	04.09.1983	8	(3)	1
Shota Grigalashvili (GEO)	21.06.1986	27	(1)	5
Dmitriy Savchenko	09.06.2001		(2)	
Sergey Skorykh	25.05.1984	17	(4)	
Forwards:	**DOB**	**M**	**(s)**	**G**
Momodou Ceesay (GAM)	24.12.1988	12	(2)	3
Miroslav Lečić (SRB)	20.04.1985	6	(6)	2
Georgiy Makaev	12.08.1994	1	(1)	
Timur Muldinov	19.09.1993	24	(5)	8
Elmar Nabiev	23.12.1991		(5)	1
Bratislav Punoševac (SRB)	09.07.1987	14	(1)	4
Boško Stupić (BIH)	27.06.1984	9	(10)	
Trainer:	**DOB**	**M**		
Nikola Spasov (BUL)	15.12.1958	17		
Andrey Kucheryavykh [05.07.2018]	24.09.1970	16		

Football Club Ordabasy Shymkent

Founded: 2000
Stadium: "Kazhymukan Munaitpasov" Stadium, Shymkent (35,000)

Goalkeepers:	**DOB**	**M**	**(s)**	**G**
David Loria	31.10.1981	7		
Jasur Narzikulov (UZB)	13.04.1984	21	(1)	
Bekkhan Shayzada	28.02.1998	5		
Defenders:	**DOB**	**M**	**(s)**	**G**
Talgat Adyrbekov	26.01.1989	1	(1)	
Damir Dautov	03.03.1990	8	(2)	
Helton Dos Reis (FRAU)	01.05.1988	12		
Temirlan Erlanov	09.07.1993	17		4
Pablo Ezequiel Fontanello (ARG)	26.09.1984	31		
Hrvoje Spahija (CRO)	23.03.1988	14		
Mardan Tolebek	18.12.1990	29	(1)	
Ular Zhaksybayev	20.10.1994	10	(4)	
Midfielders:	**DOB**	**M**	**(s)**	**G**
Kayrat Ashirbekov	21.10.1982		(3)	
Facundo Daniel Bertoglio (ARG)	30.06.1990	11	(3)	1
Nikita Bocharov (RUS)	12.06.1992	27	(5)	2
Abdoulaye Diakhaté (SEN)	16.01.1988	28	(1)	7
Timur Dosmagambetov	01.05.1989	28	(2)	3
Jambuli Jigauri (GEO)	08.07.1992	2	(11)	3
Kyrylo Kovalchuk (UKR)	11.06.1986	29	(1)	
Mirzad Mehanovič (BIH)	05.01.1993	10	(3)	1
Luka Muženjak (CRO)	04.07.1993	3	(5)	
Samat Shamshi	05.12.1996	6	(9)	
Yerkebulan Tunggyshbayev	14.01.1995	31	(1)	5
Forwards:	**DOB**	**M**	**(s)**	**G**
Bekzhan Abdrakhman	10.02.1995		(1)	
Sergey Khizhnichenko	17.07.1991	2	(2)	
Nemanja Kojić (SRB)	03.02.1990	6	(7)	3
Vitali Li	13.03.1994	5	(15)	
Zhasulan Moldakaraev	07.05.1987	11	(3)	4
Ivan Nagaev (UZB)	03.07.1989	9	(6)	3
Alisher Suley	01.11.1995		(3)	
Trainer:	**DOB**	**M**		
Georgi Dermendjiev (BUL)	04.01.1955	13		
Kakhaber Tskhadadze (GEO) [15.06.2018]	07.09.1968	20		

Football Club Shakhter Karagandy

Founded: 1958
Stadium: Shakhter Stadium, Karaganda (20,000)

Goalkeepers:	**DOB**	**M**	**(s)**	**G**
Abylaykhan Duysen	03.06.1994	6	(1)	
Igor Shatskiy	11.05.1989	25		
Egor Tsuprikov	27.05.1997	2		
Defenders:	**DOB**	**M**	**(s)**	**G**
Ruslan Alimbayev	02.03.1997	5	(4)	
Anton Chichulin	27.10.1984	13	(1)	1
Mikhail Gabyshev	02.01.1990	17	(3)	
Birzhan Kulbekov	22.04.1994	10	(1)	
Mateo Mužek (CRO)	29.04.1995	29	(1)	
Kirill Pasichnik	24.05.1993	1	(3)	
Yevgeniy Tarasov	16.04.1985	16	(5)	2
Evhen Tkachuk (UKR)	27.06.1991	26		1
Midfielders:	**DOB**	**M**	**(s)**	**G**
Lukas Droppa (CZE)	22.04.1989	14		
Damir Kojašević (MNE)	03.06.1987	25	(1)	8
Ilnur Mangutkin	16.09.1986	3	(5)	
Oleksandr Migunov (UKR)	13.04.1994	15		1
Sergei Mošnikov (EST)	07.01.1988	6	(3)	
Gevorg Najaryan	06.01.1998	14	(11)	2
Igor Pikalkin	19.03.1992	19	(5)	
Milan Stojanović (SRB)	10.05.1988	11	(3)	
Aleksandr Volodko (BLR)	18.06.1986	20	(6)	1
Egon Vůch	01.02.1991	16	(7)	2
Igor Yurin	03.07.1982	4	(1)	
Madi Zhakipbayev	21.03.2000		(1)	
Forwards:	**DOB**	**M**	**(s)**	**G**
Gegham Harutyunyan (ARM)	23.08.1990	3	(4)	1
Oralkhan Omirtayev	16.07.1998	9	(14)	4
Sergey Shaff	15.04.1988	14	(9)	2
Marat Shakhmetov	06.02.1989	32		4
Danijel Subotić (SUI)	31.01.1989	6	(3)	
Aidos Tattybaev	26.04.1990	2	(3)	
Trainer:	**DOB**	**M**		
Vladimir Zhuravel (BLR)	09.06.1971	16		
Andrey Finonchenko [03.07.2018]	21.06.1982	2		
Nikolai Kostov (BUL) [18.07.2018]	02.07.1963	15		

Football Club Tobol Kostanay

Founded: 1967
Stadium: Kostanay Central Stadium, Kostanay (10,500)

Goalkeepers:	DOB	M	(s)	G
Sultan Busurmanov	10.05.1996	3		
Vyacheslav Kotlyar (UKR)	03.03.1982	3		
Dmytro Nepogodov (UKR)	17.02.1988	27	(1)	
Defenders:	**DOB**	**M**	**(s)**	**G**
Marat Bystrov	19.06.1992	8	(6)	1
Viktor Dmitrenko	04.04.1991	29		1
Fernander Kassaï (CTA)	01.07.1987	28	(1)	
Vasiliy Kobin	24.05.1985	4	(4)	
Ionuţ Larie (MDA)	16.01.1987	11	(1)	
Dmitry Miroshnichenko	26.02.1992	28	(2)	1
Grigori Sartakov	19.08.1994	2	(1)	
Vanče Šikov (MKD)	19.07.1985	11		
Timur Zhakupov	06.09.1995	1	(4)	
Midfielders:	**DOB**	**M**	**(s)**	**G**
Sultan Abilgazy	22.02.1997	5	(3)	
Aslan Darabaev	21.01.1989	21	(5)	2
Maxim Fedin	08.06.1996	25	(3)	2
Jaba Kankava (GEO)	18.03.1986	27	(1)	3
Nika Kvekveskiri (GEO)	29.05.1992	15	(8)	2
Azat Nurgaliev	30.06.1986	28		8
Samat Zharynbetov	04.01.1994	8	(6)	1
Aleksandr Zhukov	04.11.1997	1	(1)	
Nurbol Zhumaskaliyev	11.05.1981	1	(9)	1
Artūras Žulpa (LTU)	10.06.1990	30	(1)	
Forwards:	**DOB**	**M**	**(s)**	**G**
Temirlan Amyrgazi	25.07.1997	1		
Juan Eduardo Lescano (ARG)	29.10.1992	7	(2)	
Zhasulan Moldakaraev	07.05.1987	3	(9)	
Tanat Nuserbaev	01.01.1988	7	(18)	7
Anton Shynder	13.06.1987	5	(1)	3
Bauyrzhan Turysbek	15.10.1991	24	(6)	4
Trainer:	**DOB**	**M**		
Vladimir Nikitenko	08.01.1957	20		
Andrey Miroshnichenko [03.08.2018]	21.12.1968	1		
Marek Zub (POL) [06.08.2018]	24.08.1964	12		

Football Club Zhetysu Taldykorgan

Founded: 1981
Stadium: Zhetysu Stadium, Taldykorgan (4,000)

Goalkeepers:	DOB	M	(s)	G
Nurlybek Ayazbaev	24.01.1991	4	(1)	
Dzhurakhon Babakhanov	31.10.1991	2		
Almat Bekbaev	14.07.1984	13		
Andrey Shabanov	17.11.1986	14		
Defenders:	**DOB**	**M**	**(s)**	**G**
Lasha Kasradze (GEO)	28.07.1989	21		
Olzhas Kerymzhanov	16.05.1989	14	(2)	
Andrey Kharabara (RUS)	01.09.1985	10	(2)	
Ermek Kuantayev	13.10.1990	17	(2)	
Andrey Lebedev (BLR)	01.02.1991	14		
David Mawutor (GHA)	12.04.1992	30		2
Timur Rudoselskiy	21.12.1994	1	(1)	
Ivan Sadovnichiy (BLR)	11.05.1987	13	(2)	1
Midfielders:	**DOB**	**M**	**(s)**	**G**
Server Djeparov	03.10.1982	4	(1)	1
Raul Dzhalilov (KGZ)	20.07.1994	16	(7)	3
Denis Glavina (CRO)	03.03.1986	14		
Kamo Hovhannisyan (ARM)	05.10.1992	26	(5)	1
Sabyrkhan Ibraev	22.03.1988	23	(2)	1
Zhakyp Kozhamberdy	26.02.1992	9	(12)	1
Mantas Kuklys (LTU)	10.06.1987	28	(3)	5
Edgar Malakyan (ARM)	22.09.1990	22	(9)	2
Dino Martinovič (SVN)	20.07.1990	3	(1)	
Almir Mukhutdinov	09.06.1985	25	(2)	1
Forwards:	**DOB**	**M**	**(s)**	**G**
Elzhas Altynbekov	22.11.1993	10	(8)	2
Milan Bojović (SRB)	13.04.1987	10	(3)	4
Oleg Khromtsov (MDA)	30.05.1981	10	(16)	5
Rifat Nurmugamet	22.05.1996		(13)	1
Ruslan Stepanyuk (UKR)	16.01.1992	10	(2)	4
Trainer:	**DOB**	**M**		
Dmitrij Ogai	14.05.1960	33		

SECOND LEVEL
Kazakhstan First Division 2018

1.	FC Okzhetpes Kokshetau (*Promoted*)	33	23	5	5	61	-	27	74
2.	FC Taraz (*Promoted*)	33	19	10	4	61	-	27	67
3.	FC Kyran Shimkent (*Promotion Play-off*)	33	20	5	8	61	-	38	65
4.	FC Altay Semey	33	18	8	7	56	-	28	62
5.	FC Zhetisu II Taldiqorghan	33	18	3	12	45	-	26	57
6.	FC Ekibastuz	33	13	9	11	42	-	35	48
7.	FC Maqtaaral Jetisay	33	14	6	13	41	-	41	48
8.	Sport Academy Kayrat Almaty	33	12	8	13	50	-	51	44
9.	FC Baykonur Kyzylorda	33	10	8	15	36	-	47	38
10.	FC Shakhtar-Bulat Temirtau	33	6	3	24	28	-	65	21
11.	FC Kaspiy Aqtau	33	3	7	23	25	-	65	16
12.	FC Aktobe Jas	33	3	6	24	18	-	74	15

NATIONAL TEAM

INTERNATIONAL MATCHES
(16.07.2018 – 15.07.2019)

06.09.2018	Astana	Kazakhstan - Georgia	0-2(0-0)	(UNL)
10.09.2018	Andorra la Vella	Andorra - Kazakhstan	1-1(0-0)	(UNL)
13.10.2018	Rīga	Latvia - Kazakhstan	1-1(1-1)	(UNL)
16.10.2018	Astana	Kazakhstan - Andorra	4-0(2-0)	(UNL)
15.11.2018	Astana	Kazakhstan - Latvia	1-1(1-0)	(UNL)
19.11.2018	Tbilisi	Georgia - Kazakhstan	2-1(0-0)	(UNL)
21.02.2019	Kumköy	Kazakhstan - Moldova	1-0(0-0)	(F)
21.03.2019	Nur-Sultan	Kazakhstan - Scotland	3-0(2-0)	(ECQ)
24.03.2019	Nur-Sultan	Kazakhstan - Russia	0-4(0-2)	(ECQ)
08.06.2019	Bruxelles	Belgium - Kazakhstan	3-0(2-0)	(ECQ)
11.06.2019	Nur-Sultan	Kazakhstan - San Marino	4-0(1-0)	(ECQ)

06.09.2018 KAZAKHSTAN - GEORGIA 0-2(0-0) UEFA Nations League D, Group 1
Astana Arena, Astana; Referee: Halil Umut Meler (Turkey); Attendance: 28,736
KAZ: Nenad Erić, Dmitriy Shomko (Cap), Sergey Malyi, Abzal Beysebekov, Yevgeniy Postnikov, Serikzhan Muzhikov, Islambek Kuat (76.Bayurzhan Turysbek), Bauyrzhan Islamkhan (81.Baktiyor Zaynutdinov), Georgiy Zhukov, Aleksey Shchetkin, Roman Murtazayev (88.Yerkebulan Seidakhmet). Trainer: Stanimir Stoilov (Bulgaria).

10.09.2018 ANDORRA - KAZAKHSTAN 1-1(0-0) UEFA Nations League D, Group 1
Estadi Nacional, Andorra la Vella; Referee: Vilhjálmur Alvar Þórarinsson (Iceland); Attendance: 1,235
KAZ: Nenad Erić, Yuriy Logvinenko, Dmitriy Shomko (Cap), Abzal Beysebekov (90.Yerkebulan Seidakhmet), Yevgeniy Postnikov, Serikzhan Muzhikov [*sent off 76*], Islambek Kuat, Bauyrzhan Islamkhan, Yerkebulan Tungyshbayev (66.Baktiyor Zaynutdinov), Aleksey Shchetkin, Roman Murtazayev (59.Bayurzhan Turysbek). Trainer: Stanimir Stoilov (Bulgaria).
Goal: Yuriy Logvinenko (68).

13.10.2018 LATVIA - KAZAKHSTAN 1-1(1-1) UEFA Nations League D, Group 1
Daugava stadions, Rīga; Referee: Harald Lechner (Austria); Attendance: 4,878
KAZ: Nenad Erić, Dmitriy Shomko (Cap), Sergey Malyi, Abzal Beysebekov, Yevgeniy Postnikov, Islambek Kuat, Bauyrzhan Islamkhan (75.Maxim Fedin), Georgiy Zhukov, Baktiyor Zaynutdinov (65.Yerkebulan Seidakhmet), Aleksey Shchetkin, Roman Murtazayev (82.Bayurzhan Turysbek). Trainer: Stanimir Stoilov (Bulgaria).
Goal: Baktiyor Zaynutdinov (16).

16.10.2018 KAZAKHSTAN - ANDORRA 4-0(2-0) UEFA Nations League D, Group 1
Astana Arena, Astana; Referee: Serhiy Boyko (Ukraine); Attendance: 19,854
KAZ: Nenad Erić, Yuriy Logvinenko, Abzal Beysebekov, Yevgeniy Postnikov, Gafurzhan Suyumbayev (82.Yan Vorogovskiy), Serikzhan Muzhikov, Bauyrzhan Islamkhan (Cap), Georgiy Zhukov, Bayurzhan Turysbek, Baktiyor Zaynutdinov (71.Roman Murtazayev), Yerkebulan Seidakhmet (77.Maxim Fedin). Trainer: Stanimir Stoilov (Bulgaria).
Goals: Yerkebulan Seidakhmet (21), Bayurzhan Turysbek (39), Josep Antoni Gómes Moreira (61 own goal), Roman Murtazayev (74).

15.11.2018 KAZAKHSTAN - LATVIA 1-1(1-0) UEFA Nations League D, Group 1
Astana Arena, Astana; Referee: Jens Maae (Denmark); Attendance: 21,463
KAZ: Nenad Erić, Yuriy Logvinenko, Sergey Malyi, Abzal Beysebekov, Gafurzhan Suyumbayev, Serikzhan Muzhikov, Bauyrzhan Islamkhan (Cap), Georgiy Zhukov, Baktiyor Zaynutdinov (87.Yerkebulan Tungyshbayev), Bayurzhan Turysbek (74.Aleksey Shchetkin), Roman Murtazayev (80.Maxim Fedin). Trainer: Stanimir Stoilov (Bulgaria).
Goal: Gafurzhan Suyumbayev (37).

198.11.2018 GEORGIA - KAZAKHSTAN 2-1(0-0) UEFA Nations League D, Group 1
"Boris Paichadze" Dinamo Arena, Tbilisi; Referee: Tiago Bruno Lopes Martins (Portugal); Attendance: 46,686
KAZ: Dmytro Nepohodov, Yuriy Logvinenko (Cap), Sergey Malyi, Abzal Beysebekov, Gafurzhan Suyumbayev, Serikzhan Muzhikov, Islambek Kuat, Maxim Fedin (84.Bayurzhan Turysbek), Baktiyor Zaynutdinov, Aleksey Shchetkin (74.Yuriy Pertsukh), Roman Murtazayev (88.Oralkhan Omirtayev). Trainer: Stanimir Stoilov (Bulgaria).
Goal: Oralkhan Omirtayev (90).

21.02.2019 KAZAKHSTAN - MOLDOVA 1-0(0-0) Friendly International
Titanic Deluxe Belek Futbol Sahası, Kumköy; Referee: Manfredas Lukjančukas (Lithuania); Attendance: 500
KAZ: Dmytro Nepohodov (46.Igor Shatskiy), Dmitriy Shomko, Sergey Malyi, Dmitriy Miroshnichenko (46.Marat Bystrov), Temirlan Yerlanov (80.Rauan Orynbasar), Sagadat Tursynbay (66.Bekzat Shadmanov), Azat Nurgaliyev (Cap) (66.Yerkin Tapalov), Maxim Fedin (88.Rafkat Aslan), Yuriy Pertsukh, Roman Murtazayev (46.Oralkhan Omirtayev), Bayurzhan Turysbek (80.Gevorg Najaryan). Trainer: Michal Bílek (Czech Republic).
Goal: Oralkhan Omirtayev (61).

21.03.2019 KAZAKHSTAN - SCOTLAND 3-0(2-0) 16th EC. Qualifiers
Astana Arena, Nur-Sultan; Referee: Srđan Jovanović (Serbia); Attendance: 27,641
KAZ: Dmytro Nepohodov, Sergey Malyi, Yevgeniy Postnikov, Gafurzhan Suyumbayev, Temirlan Yerlanov (81.Yeldos Akhmetov), Islambek Kuat (Cap), Aleksandr Merkel, Yan Vorogovskiy, Baktiyor Zaynutdinov (84.Serikzhan Muzhikov), Yuriy Pertsukh, Roman Murtazayev (68.Bayurzhan Turysbek). Trainer: Michal Bílek (Czech Republic).
Goals: Yuriy Pertsukh (6), Yan Vorogovskiy (10), Baktiyor Zaynutdinov (51).

24.03.2019 KAZAKHSTAN - RUSSIA 0-4(0-2) 16th EC. Qualifiers
Astana Arena, Nur-Sultan; Referee: Slavko Vinčić (Slovenia); Attendance: 29,582
KAZ: Dmytro Nepohodov, Yuriy Logvinenko (30.Yan Vorogovskiy), Sergey Malyi, Yeldos Akhmetov, Abzal Beysebekov, Gafurzhan Suyumbayev, Islambek Kuat (Cap), Aleksandr Merkel, Baktiyor Zaynutdinov, Yuriy Pertsukh (85.Georgiy Zhukov), Roman Murtazayev (59.Bayurzhan Turysbek). Trainer: Michal Bílek (Czech Republic).

08.06.2019 BELGIUM - KAZAKHSTAN 3-0(2-0) 16th EC. Qualifiers

Stade "Roi Baudouin", Bruxelles; Referee: Irfan Peljto (Bosnia and Herzegovina); Attendance: 44,000

KAZ: Dmytro Nepohodov, Sergey Malyi, Abzal Beysebekov, Temirlan Yerlanov, Aleksandr Marochkin, Islambek Kuat (Cap)(78.Askat Tagybergen), Georgiy Zhukov, Maxim Fedin (66.Abat Aymbetov), Yan Vorogovskiy, Yuriy Pertsukh, Toktar Zhangylyshbay (46.Bauyrzhan Islamkhan). Trainer: Michal Bílek (Czech Republic).

11.06.2019 KAZAKHSTAN - SAN MARINO 4-0(1-0) 16th EC. Qualifiers

Astana Arena, Nur-Sultan; Referee: Bartosz Frankowski (Poland); Attendance: 18,652

KAZ: Dmytro Nepohodov, Dmitriy Shomko, Sergey Malyi, Gafurzhan Suyumbayev, Temirlan Yerlanov, Islambek Kuat (84.Yuriy Pertsukh), Bauyrzhan Islamkhan (Cap), Askat Tagybergen, Yan Vorogovskiy, Bayurzhan Turysbek (69.Toktar Zhangylyshbay), Abat Aymbetov (58.Maxim Fedin). Trainer: Michal Bílek (Czech Republic).

Goals: Islambek Kuat (45+1), Maxim Fedin (62), Gafurzhan Suyumbayev (65), Bauyrzhan Islamkhan (79).

NATIONAL TEAM PLAYERS
(16.07.2018 – 15.07.2019)

Name	DOB	Caps	Goals	2018/2019:	Club
Goalkeepers					
Nenad ERIĆ	26.05.1982	**8**	**0**	2018:	*Astana FC*
Dmytro NEPOHODOV	17.02.1988	**6**	**0**	2018: 14.01.2019->	*FC Tobol Kostanay* *FC Ordabasy Shymkent*
Igor SHATSKIY	11.05.1989	**1**	**0**	2019:	*FC Shakhter Karagandy*
Defenders					
Yeldos AKHMETOV	01.06.1990	**16**	**0**	2019:	*FC Kairat Almaty*
Rafkat ASLAN	02.02.1994	**1**	**0**	2019:	*FC Irtysh Pavlodar*
Abzal BEYSEBEKOV	30.11.1992	**26**	**0**	2018/2019:	*Astana FC*
Marat BYSTROV	19.06.1992	**1**	**0**	2019:	*FC Ordabasy Shymkent*
Yuriy LOGVINENKO	22.07.1988	**50**	**5**	2018/2019:	*Astana FC*
Sergey MALYI	05.06.1990	**35**	**0**	2018/2019:	*FC Ordabasy Shymkent*
Aleksandr MAROCHKIN	14.07.1990	**1**	**0**	2019:	*FC Kaysar Kyzylorda*
Dmitriy MIROSHNICHENKO	26.02.1992	**9**	**0**	2019:	*FC Tobol Kostanay*
Rauan ORYNBASAR	01.03.1998	**1**	**0**	2019:	*FC Zhetisu Taldiqorghan*
Yevgeniy POSTNIKOV	16.04.1986	**8**	**0**	2018/2019:	*Astana FC*
Bekzat SHADMANOV	12.08.1997	**1**	**0**	2019:	*FC Taraz*
Dmitriy SHOMKO	19.03.1990	**40**	**2**	2018/2019:	*Astana FC*
Gafurzhan SUYUMBAYEV	19.08.1990	**29**	**3**	2018/2019:	*FC Kairat Almaty*
Temirlan YERLANOV	09.07.1993	**4**	**0**	2019:	*FC Ordabasy Shymkent*
Midfielders					
Bauyrzhan ISLAMKHAN	23.02.1993	**38**	**3**	2018/2019:	*FC Kairat Almaty*
Islambek KUAT	12.01.1993	**27**	**4**	2018/2019:	*FC Kairat Almaty*
Aleksandr MERKEL	22.02.1992	**3**	**0**	2019:	*Heracles Almelo (NED)*
Serikzhan MUZHIKOV	07.08.1989	**22**	**1**	2018/2019:	*Astana FC*
Gevorg NAJARYAN	06.01.1998	**1**	**0**	2019:	*FC Shakhter Karagandy*
Azat NURGALIYEV	30.06.1986	**40**	**3**	2019:	*FC Tobol Kostanay*
Askat TAGYBERGEN	09.08.1990	**20**	**0**	2019:	*FC Kaysar Kyzylorda*
Yerkin TAPALOV	03.09.1993	**1**	**0**	2019:	*FC Zhetisu Taldiqorghan*
Sagadat TURSYNBAY	26.03.1999	**1**	**0**	2019:	*FC Ordabasy Shymkent*
Yan VOROGOVSKIY	07.08.1996	**7**	**1**	2018/2019:	*FC Kairat Almaty*
Baktiyar ZAYNUTDINOV	02.04.1998	**11**	**4**	2018: 12.01.2019->	*Astana FC* *FK Rostov-na-Donu (RUS)*
Toktar ZHANGYLYSHBAY	25.05.1993	**3**	**0**	2019:	*FC Ordabasy Shymkent*
Georgiy ZHUKOV	19.11.1994	**12**	**0**	2018/2019:	*FC Kairat Almaty*
Forwards					
Abat AYMBETOV	07.08.1995	**2**	**0**	2018/2019:	*FC Aktobe*
Maxim FEDIN	08.06.1996	**7**	**1**	2018/2019:	*FC Tobol Kostanay*
Roman MURTAZAYEV	10.09.1993	**22**	**3**	2018/2019:	*Astana FC*
Oralkhan OMIRTAYEV	16.07.1998	**2**	**2**	2018/2019:	*FC Shakhter Karagandy*
Yuriy PERTSUKH	13.05.1996	**8**	**1**	2018: 31.12.2018->	*FC Atyrau* *Astana FC*
Yerkebulan SEIDAKHMET	04.02.2000	**6**	**2**	2018:	*FK Ufa (RUS)*
Aleksey SHCHETKIN	21.05.1991	**27**	**1**	2018:	*FC Tobol Kostanay*
Yerkebulan TUNGYSHBAYEV	14.01.1995	**10**	**1**	2018/2019:	*FC Ordabasy Shymkent*
Bauyrzhan TURYSBEK	15.10.1991	**14**	**3**	2018/2019:	*FC Tobol Kostanay*

National team coach

Stanimir STOILOV (Bulgaria) [03.03.2018 – 17.01.2019]	13.02.1967	9 M; 3 W; 3 D; 3 L; 15-11
Michal BÍLEK (Czech Republic) [from 18.01.2019]	13.04.1965	5 M; 3 W; 0 D; 2 L; 8-7

KOSOVO

The Country:

Republika e Kosovës (Republic of Kosovo)
Capital: Prishtinë
Surface: 10,908 km²
Inhabitants: 1,809,280 [2019]
Time: UTC+1

The FA:

Federata e Futbollit e Kosovës
Rruga "28 Nëntori", nr. 171, Prishtinë / Kosovë 10000
Tel: +383 38 600 220
Foundation date: 1946
Member of FIFA since: 2016
Member of UEFA since: 2016
Website: www.ffk-kosova.com

NATIONAL TEAM RECORDS

First international match:	05.03.2014, Mitrovicë:	Kosovo – Haiti 0-0
Most international caps:	Samir Ujkani	- 25 caps (since 2014)
Most international goals:	Arbër Zeneli	- 7 goals / 18 caps (since 2016)

UEFA EUROPEAN CHAMPIONSHIP	
1960	-
1964	-
1968	-
1972	-
1976	-
1980	-
1984	-
1988	-
1992	-
1996	-
2000	-
2004	-
2008	-
2012	-
2016	-

FIFA WORLD CUP	
1930	-
1934	-
1938	-
1950	-
1954	-
1958	-
1962	-
1966	-
1970	-
1974	-
1978	-
1982	-
1986	-
1990	-
1994	-
1998	-
2002	-
2006	-
2010	-
2014	-
2018	Qualifiers

UEFA NATIONS LEAGUE
2018/2019 – League D (promoted to League C)

OLYMPIC FOOTBALL TOURNAMENTS 1908-2016
None

FIFA CONFEDERATIONS CUP 1992-2017
None

KOSOVO CLUB HONOURS IN EUROPEAN CLUB COMPETITIONS:

European Champion Clubs' Cup (1956-1992) / UEFA Champions League (1993-2019)
None
Fairs Cup (1858-1971) / UEFA Cup (1972-2009) / UEFA Europa League (2010-2019)
None
UEFA Super Cup (1972-2018)
None
European Cup Winners' Cup 1961-1999*
None

**defunct competition*

NATIONAL COMPETITIONS
TABLE OF HONOURS

Kosovo Province League (within F.R. Yugoslavia)

	CHAMPIONS	CUP WINNERS
1945	Jedinstvo Prishtinë	-
1946	Jedinstvo Prishtinë	-
1947	KF Trepça Mitrovicë	-
1947/1948	Proleteri Prishtinë	-
1948/1949	KF Trepça Mitrovicë	-
1950	KF Trepça Mitrovicë	-
1951	Kosova Prishtinë	-
1952	KF Trepça Mitrovicë	-
1953/1954	Kosova Prishtinë	-
1954/1955	KF Trepça Mitrovicë	-
1955/1956	Rudari Stantërg	-
1956/1957	Rudniku Hajvali	-
1957/1958	Rudari Stantërg	-
1958/1959	FC Prishtinë	-
1959/1960	Rudari Stantërg	-
1960/1961	FC Prishtinë	-
1961/1962	Buduqnosti Pejë	-
1962/1963	Crvena zvezda Gjilani	-
1963/1964	Slloga Lipyan	-
1964/1965	Slloga Lipyan	-
1965/1966	Buduqnosti Pejë	-
1966/1967	Obiliqi Kastriot	-
1967/1968	FC Vëllaznimi Gjakovë	-
1968/1969	FC Vëllaznimi Gjakovë	-
1969/1970	FC Vëllaznimi Gjakovë	-
1970/1971	FC Vëllaznimi Gjakovë	-
1971/1972	FC Obiliqi	-
1972/1973	KF Fushë Kosova	-
1973/1974	FC Vëllaznimi Gjakovë	-
1974/1975	KF Liria Prizreni	-
1975/1976	RHMK Obilić	-
1976/1977	FC Prishtinë	-
1977/1978	Buduqnosti Pejë	-
1978/1979	FC Prishtinë	-
1979/1980	FC Vëllaznimi Gjakovë	-
1980/1981	KF Liria Prizreni	-
1981/1982	FC Vëllaznimi Gjakovë	-
1982/1983	KNI Ramiz Sadiku	-
1983/1984	KF Liria Prizreni	-
1984/1985	Crvena zvezda Gjilani	FC Vëllaznimi Gjakovë
1985/1986	FC Vëllaznimi Gjakovë	FC Vëllaznimi Gjakovë
1986/1987	KF Liria Prizreni	FC Vëllaznimi Gjakovë
1987/1988	Crvena zvezda Gjilani	*No competition*
1988/1989	Buduqnosti Pejë	*No competition*
1989/1990	FC Vëllaznimi Gjakovë	*No competition*

Independent League of Kosovo

	CHAMPIONS	CUP WINNERS
1990/1991	KF Fushë-Kosova	*No competition*
1991/1992	FC Prishtinë	KF Trepça Mitrovicë
1992/1993	KF Trepça Mitrovicë	KF Flamurtari Prishtinë
1993/1994	KF Dukagjini Klinë	FC Prishtinë
1994/1995	KF Liria Prizreni	KF Liria Prizreni
1995/1996	FC Prishtinë	KF Flamurtari Prishtinë
1996/1997	FC Prishtinë	*Final not played*
1997/1998	*Tournament abandoned*	*No competition*
1998/1999	*No competition*	*No competition*

Establishment as top-league after UNMIK* take-over of Kosovo

	CHAMPIONS	CUP WINNERS
1999/2000	FC Prishtinë	SC Gjilani
2000/2001	FC Prishtinë	FC Drita Gjilani
2001/2002	KF Besiana Podujevë	KF Besiana Podujevo
2002/2003	FC Drita Gjilani	KF KEK-u Obilić
2003/2004	FC Prishtinë	KF Kosova Prishtinë
2004/2005	KF Besa Pejë Peć	KF Besa Pejë Peć
2005/2006	KF Besa Pejë Peć	FC Prishtinë
2006/2007	KF Besa Pejë Peć	KF Liria Prizreni
2007/2008	FC Prishtinë	FC Vëllaznimi Gjakovë

After proclamation of independence

	CHAMPIONS	CUP WINNERS
2008/2009	FC Prishtinë	KF Hysi Podujevo
2009/2010	KF Trepça Mitrovicë	KF Liria Prizreni
2010/2011	KF Hysi Milloshevë	FC Prishtinë
2011/2012	FC Prishtinë	KF Trepça'89 Mitrovicë
2012/2013	FC Prishtinë	FC Prishtinë
2013/2014	KF Vushtria	KF Hajvalia
2014/2015	KF Feronikeli Glogovac	KV Feronikeli Glogovac
2015/2016	KF Feronikeli Glogovac	FC Prishtinë

**United Nations Mission in Kosovo*

Please note: Jedinstvo Prishtinë changed its name to Proleteri Prishtinë, Kosova Prishtinë and finally to FC Prishtinë. Buduqnosti Pejë became KF Besa Pejë Peć; FC Obiliqi changed its name to RHMK Obilić and later KF KEK-u Obilić

After membership in UEFA and FIFA

	CHAMPIONS	CUP WINNERS	BEST GOALSCORERS	
2016/2017	KF Trepça'89 Mitrovicë	KF Llapi Podujevë	John Otto John (NGA, KF Trepça'89 Mitrovicë)	24
2017/2018	FC Drita Gjilan	FC Vëllaznimi Gjakovë	John Otto John (NGA, KF Trepça'89 Mitrovicë) Mirlind Daku (KF Llapi Podujevë)	17
2018/2019	KF Feronikeli Glogovac	KF Feronikeli Glogovac	Kastriot Rexha (KF Feronikeli Glogovac)	21

NATIONAL CHAMPIONSHIP

Football Superleague of Kosovo 2018/2019
(18.08.2018 – 19.05.2019)

Results

Round 1 [18-19.08.2018]
KF Feronikeli - KF Trepça'89 1-1
FC Drita Gjilan - KF KEK-u Obilić 5-0
KF Liria - KF Ballkani 0-1
KF Llapi - KF Drenica 0-1
KF Flamurtari - KF Ferizaj 1-0
FC Prishtinë - KF Gjilani 1-0 [19.09.]

Round 2 [25-26.08.2018]
KF KEK-u Obilić - KF Gjilani 2-3
KF Drenica - KF Feronikeli 0-0
KF Ballkani - KF Llapi 0-3
KF Trepça'89 - FC Prishtinë 0-2
KF Ferizaj - KF Liria 1-0
FC Drita Gjilan - KF Flamurtari 1-3

Round 3 [31.08.-02.09.2018]
KF Liria - FC Drita Gjilan 3-2
KF Llapi - KF Ferizaj 5-1
KF Feronikeli - KF Ballkani 1-0
KF Flamurtari - KF KEK-u Obilić 1-0
KF Gjilani - KF Trepça'89 1-0
FC Prishtinë - KF Drenica 1-0

Round 4 [11-12.09.2018]
KF Drenica - KF Gjilani 0-0
KF Ballkani - FC Prishtinë 1-1
KF KEK-u Obilić - KF Trepça'89 1-5
KF Ferizaj - KF Feronikeli 0-2
FC Drita Gjilan - KF Llapi 1-2
KF Flamurtari - KF Liria 3-1

Round 5 [15-16.09.2018]
KF Feronikeli - FC Drita Gjilan 4-0
FC Prishtinë - KF Ferizaj 0-0
KF Gjilani - KF Ballkani 1-3
KF Liria - KF KEK-u Obilić 6-2
KF Llapi - KF Flamurtari 0-0
KF Trepça'89 - KF Drenica 1-1

Round 6 [21-23.09.2018]
KF Ballkani - KF Trepça'89 0-0
KF KEK-u Obilić - KF Drenica 2-4
KF Flamurtari - KF Feronikeli 1-3
KF Liria - KF Llapi 2-3
KF Ferizaj - KF Gjilani 0-2
FC Drita Gjilan - FC Prishtinë 1-0

Round 7 [28-30.09.2018]
KF Trepça'89 - KF Ferizaj 1-0
KF Drenica - KF Ballkani 2-1
KF Llapi - KF KEK-u Obilić 2-0
KF Feronikeli - KF Liria 4-2
KF Gjilani - FC Drita Gjilan 1-0
FC Prishtinë - KF Flamurtari 1-1

Round 8 [02-04.10.2018]
KF Ferizaj - KF Drenica 2-0
KF KEK-u Obilić - KF Ballkani 2-2
FC Drita Gjilan - KF Trepça'89 1-1
KF Liria - FC Prishtinë 0-1
KF Llapi - KF Feronikeli 0-1
KF Flamurtari - KF Gjilani 1-1

Round 9 [06-07.10.2018]
KF Feronikeli - KF KEK-u Obilić 4-1
KF Drenica - FC Drita Gjilan 1-2
KF Ferizaj - KF Ballkani 1-0
FC Prishtinë - KF Llapi 2-1
KF Gjilani - KF Liria 0-1
KF Trepça'89 - KF Flamurtari 2-2

Round 10 [16-17.10.2018]
KF Flamurtari - KF Drenica 0-3
KF Liria - KF Trepça'89 0-4
FC Drita Gjilan - KF Ballkani 6-1
KF Llapi - KF Gjilani 3-1
KF KEK-u Obilić - KF Ferizaj 1-2 [07.11.]
KF Feronikeli - FC Prishtinë 0-1 [07.11.]

Round 11 [20-21.10.2018]
KF Drenica - KF Liria 1-0
KF Ballkani - KF Flamurtari 1-0
KF Ferizaj - FC Drita Gjilan 0-2
FC Prishtinë - KF KEK-u Obilić 3-0
KF Gjilani - KF Feronikeli 1-0
KF Trepça'89 - KF Llapi 1-1

Round 12 [26-27.10.2018]
KF Ballkani - KF Liria 1-0
KF Ferizaj - KF Flamurtari 2-3
KF KEK-u Obilić - FC Drita Gjilan 1-2
KF Trepça'89 - KF Feronikeli 0-1
KF Gjilani - FC Prishtinë 0-3
KF Drenica - KF Llapi 0-2

Round 13 [30-31.10.2018]
KF Flamurtari - FC Drita Gjilan 0-1
KF Liria - KF Ferizaj 0-0
KF Feronikeli - KF Drenica 2-1
KF Gjilani - KF KEK-u Obilić 2-0
KF Llapi - KF Ballkani 0-1
FC Prishtinë - KF Trepça'89 2-0

Round 14 [03-04.11.2018]
KF Ballkani - KF Feronikeli 0-1
KF Drenica - FC Prishtinë 0-1
KF KEK-u Obilić - KF Flamurtari 3-4
FC Drita Gjilan - KF Liria 0-1
KF Ferizaj - KF Llapi 0-1
KF Trepça'89 - KF Gjilani 1-1

Round 15 [10-12.11.2018]
KF Llapi - FC Drita Gjilan 1-0
KF Liria - KF Flamurtari 1-0
KF Gjilani - KF Drenica 1-0
FC Prishtinë - KF Ballkani 2-0
KF Trepça'89 - KF KEK-u Obilić 4-1
KF Feronikeli - KF Ferizaj 2-0

Round 16 [23-25.11.2018]
KF Drenica - KF Trepça'89 3-0
KF Ferizaj - FC Prishtinë 0-0
KF Ballkani - KF Gjilani 4-1
KF Flamurtari - KF Llapi 0-1
KF KEK-u Obilić - KF Liria 0-3
FC Drita Gjilan - KF Feronikeli 1-1

Round 17 [01-02.12.2018]
KF Drenica - KF KEK-u Obilić 5-1
KF Feronikeli - KF Flamurtari 2-0
KF Gjilani - KF Ferizaj 1-0
KF Llapi - KF Liria 1-0
KF Trepça'89 - KF Ballkani 1-0
FC Prishtinë - FC Drita Gjilan 2-0

Round 18 [15-18.02.2019]
KF KEK-u Obilić - KF Llapi 0-3
KF Ballkani - KF Drenica 2-0
FC Drita Gjilan - KF Gjilani 3-1
KF Ferizaj - KF Trepça'89 2-0
KF Flamurtari - FC Prishtinë 2-0
KF Liria - KF Feronikeli 0-2

Round 19 [23-24.02.2019]
KF Ballkani - KF KEK-u Obilić 3-0
KF Drenica - KF Ferizaj 3-1
KF Gjilani - KF Flamurtari 0-0
KF Feronikeli - KF Llapi 2-0
FC Prishtinë - KF Liria 4-0
KF Trepça'89 - FC Drita Gjilan 1-0

Round 20 [01-02.03.2019]
KF Ferizaj - KF Ballkani 1-0
FC Drita Gjilan - KF Drenica 2-0
KF Liria - KF Gjilani 1-1
KF KEK-u Obilić - KF Feronikeli 0-1
KF Llapi - FC Prishtinë 1-0
KF Flamurtari - KF Trepça'89 0-2

Round 21 [05-06.03.2019]
KF Ballkani - FC Drita Gjilan 1-2
KF Drenica - KF Flamurtari 1-1
KF Ferizaj - KF KEK-u Obilić 4-1
KF Gjilani - KF Llapi 0-1
KF Trepça'89 - KF Liria 1-2
FC Prishtinë - KF Feronikeli 1-1

Round 22 [09-10.03.2019]
FC Drita Gjilan - KF Ferizaj 1-0
KF Llapi - KF Trepça'89 3-1
KF Feronikeli - KF Gjilani 3-0
KF KEK-u Obilić - FC Prishtinë 1-2
KF Liria - KF Drenica 1-1
KF Flamurtari - KF Ballkani 0-0

Round 23 [16-17.03.2019]
KF Llapi - KF Ballkani 1-1
FC Drita Gjilan - KF Liria 2-0
KF Drenica - KF Ferizaj 0-0
KF Feronikeli - KF Trepça'89 5-0
KF Gjilani - KF KEK-u Obilić 2-0
FC Prishtinë - KF Flamurtari 3-0 [27.03.]

Round 24 [29-31.03.2019]
KF Liria - KF Llapi 0-4
KF Ferizaj - FC Drita Gjilan 1-2
KF KEK-u Obilić - KF Drenica 1-5
KF Gjilani - KF Trepça'89 1-1
KF Ballkani - FC Prishtinë 0-2
KF Flamurtari - KF Feronikeli 0-0

Round 25 [03-04.04.2019]
KF Drenica - KF Gjilani 0-0
FC Drita Gjilan - KF KEK-u Obilić 4-0
KF Llapi - KF Ferizaj 2-0
KF Trepça'89 - KF Flamurtari 1-0
KF Feronikeli - KF Ballkani 1-0
FC Prishtinë - KF Liria 3-0

Round 26 [06-08.04.2019]
KF Drenica - KF Trepça'89 2-0
KF KEK-u Obilić - KF Llapi 0-1
KF Ballkani - KF Flamurtari 2-0
KF Gjilani - FC Drita Gjilan 0-0
KF Liria - KF Feronikeli 0-4
KF Ferizaj - FC Prishtinë 0-2

Round 27 [12-14.04.2019]
KF Trepça'89 - KF Ballkani 2-1
KF Llapi - KF Gjilani 2-1
FC Prishtinë - KF KEK-u Obilić 1-0
KF Feronikeli - KF Ferizaj 1-2
FC Drita Gjilan - KF Drenica 2-2
KF Flamurtari - KF Liria 1-0

Round 28 [20-22.04.2019]
KF Gjilani - FC Prishtinë 0-1
KF Drenica - KF Llapi 0-2
KF KEK-u Obilić - KF Feronikeli 0-4
FC Drita Gjilan - KF Trepça'89 1-1
KF Ferizaj - KF Flamurtari 3-1
KF Liria - KF Ballkani 0-0

Round 29 [27-29.04.2019]
KF Llapi - FC Drita Gjilan 1-0
KF Feronikeli - KF Gjilani 2-0
KF Ballkani - KF Ferizaj 2-4
KF Trepça'89 - KF Liria 2-1
FC Prishtinë - KF Drenica 2-1
KF Flamurtari - KF KEK-u Obilić 2-1

Round 30 [04-05.05.2019]
KF Drenica - KF Feronikeli 0-1
FC Drita Gjilan - FC Prishtinë 1-1
KF Ferizaj - KF Liria 3-1
KF KEK-u Obilić - KF Ballkani 0-3
KF Gjilani - KF Flamurtari 0-1
KF Llapi - KF Trepça'89 4-1

Round 31 [10-11.05.2019]
KF Flamurtari - KF Drenica 0-0
KF Ballkani - KF Gjilani 1-0
KF Trepça'89 - KF Ferizaj 1-2
FC Prishtinë - KF Llapi 1-0
KF Feronikeli - FC Drita Gjilan 4-1
KF Liria - KF KEK-u Obilić 3-1

Round 32 [15-16.05.2019]
KF Drenica - KF Ballkani 1-1
FC Drita Gjilan - KF Flamurtari 1-2
KF Llapi - KF Feronikeli 1-3
FC Prishtinë - KF Trepça'89 3-0
KF KEK-u Obilić - KF Ferizaj 2-5
KF Gjilani - KF Liria 4-0

Round 33 [19.05.2019]
KF Ferizaj - KF Gjilani 2-1
KF Trepça'89 - KF KEK-u Obilić 4-0
KF Feronikeli - FC Prishtinë 1-0
KF Flamurtari - KF Llapi 3-2
KF Ballkani - FC Drita Gjilan 2-0
KF Liria - KF Drenica 1-3

Final Standings

1.	**KF Feronikeli Glogovac**	33	25	5	3	64	-	14	80
2.	FC Prishtinë	33	23	6	4	49	-	12	75
3.	KF Llapi Podujevë	33	22	3	8	54	-	24	69
4.	FC Drita Gjilan	33	14	6	13	47	-	39	48
5.	KF Ferizaj	33	14	4	15	39	-	41	46
6.	KF Flamurtari Prishtinë	33	12	9	12	33	-	39	45
7.	KF Drenica Skenderaj	33	11	10	12	41	-	34	43
8.	KF Ballkani Suva Reka	33	12	7	14	35	-	36	43
9.	KF Trepça'89 Mitrovicë (*Relegation Play-offs*)	33	11	9	13	40	-	45	42
10.	SC Gjilani (*Relegation Play-offs*)	33	10	8	15	28	-	37	38
11.	KF Liria Prizren (*Relegated*)	33	8	4	21	31	-	60	28
12.	KF KEK-u Obilić (*Relegated*)	33	0	1	32	24	-	104	1

Top goalscorers:

21	Kastriot Rexha *KF Feronikeli Glogovac*
13	Ahmed Januzi *KF Llapi Podujevë*
12	Festim Alidema *KF Llapi Podujevë*
11	Meriton Korenica *FC Prishtinë*

Relegation Play-offs 1st / 2nd Level [30.05.-01.06.2019]

SC Gjilani - KF Besa Pejë Peć	1-0(1-0)
KF Trepça'89 Mitrovicë - KF Vëllaznimi Gjakovë	4-2(1-2)

NATIONAL CUP
Kosovo Cup / Kupa e Kosovës 2018/2019

Fourth Round [08-09.12.2018]

KF Liria Prizren - FC Prishtinë	0-4
KF Fushë Kosova - KF Ferizaj	1-2
FC Drita Gjilan - KF Minatori	5-3
KF Besa Pejë Peć - KF Vëllaznimi Gjakovë	0-0 aet; 2-3 pen
KF Trepça'89 Mitrovicë - KF Flamurtari Prishtinë	3-0 aet
KF Kika Kamenica - KF Istogu	2-2 aet; 3-1 pen
KF Ballkani Suva Reka - SC Gjilani	3-0
KF Dukagjini Klinë - KF Feronikeli Glogovac	0-4

Quarter-Finals [09.02.2019]

FC Prishtinë - KF Trepça'89 Mitrovicë	0-0 aet; 4-5 pen
KF Ferizaj - KF Feronikeli Glogovac	0-1
KF Kika Kamenica - KF Ballkani Suva Reka	0-1 aet
KF Vëllaznimi Gjakovë - FC Drita Gjilan	1-0

Semi-Finals [17.04./01.05.2019]

KF Vëllaznimi Gjakovë - KF Trepça'89 Mitrovicë	0-4 / 1-0
KF Ballkani Suva Reka - KF Feronikeli Glogovac	1-2 / 0-2

Final

24.05.2019; Stadiumi "Fadil Vokrri", Prishtinë; Referee: Genc Nuza; Attendance: n/a
KF Feronikeli Glogovac - KF Trepça'89 Mitrovicë **5-1(1-0)**

Goals: 1-0 Astrit Fazliu (16), 2-0 Mendurim Hoti (27), 3-0 Albutrint Morina (66), 4-0 Kastriot Rexha (70), 4-1 Ardian Muja (73), 5-1 Kastriot Rexha (90+2).

THE CLUBS 2018/2019

Please note: only squads, number of matches and goals not available!

Klubi Futbollistik Ballkani Suva Reka

Founded: 1947
Stadium: Stadiumi i Qytetit të Suharekës, Suva Reka (1,500)

Goalkeepers:	DOB
Besnik Beqiraj	
Bledar Hajdini	16.06.1995
Endrit Kuqi	
Armend Rugji	30.12.1985
Defenders:	**DOB**
Visar Berisha	07.12.1986
Ramiz Bytyqi	10.01.1999
Elbasan Gashi	
Ilir Gegaj	
Dardan Jashari	28.03.1990
Besnik Krasniqi	01.02.1990
Liridon Kukaj	22.06.1983
Valentin Lezi	
Arber Potoku	19.04.1994
Victor Sevcenco (MDA)	08.09.1991
Uran Shala	
Midfielders:	**DOB**
Aldin Adžović (MNE)	18.04.1994
Almir Ajzeraj	05.10.1997
Endrit Asllanaj	
Blend Baftiu	17.02.1998
Fajton Bushati	06.05.1998
Tarik Čmajčanin (SRB)	18.06.1994
Gentian Elezaj (ALB)	18.02.1997
Caner Gëzimi	
Edvin Kuč (MNE)	27.10.1993
Ledion Muçaj (ALB)	04.09.1992
Visar Sahiti	
Qendrim Sejdiu	03.10.1987
Egzon Shabani	27.08.1989
Forwards:	**DOB**
Leart Emini	24.11.1992
Durim Gashi	14.06.1992
Leutrim Gashi	
Berat Hyseni	26.10.1986
Edi Maksutaj	
Borče Manevski (MKD)	05.07.1985
Bajram Nebihi	05.08.1988
Dionis Sopa	
Jetmir Topalli	07.02.1998
Trainer:	**DOB**
Sami Sermaxhaj	

Klubi Futbollistik Drenica Skenderaj

Founded: 1958
Stadium: Stadiumi"Bajram Aliu", Skenderaj (3,000)

Goalkeepers:	DOB
Drin Hodaj	27.02.1997
Besnik Shehu	13.06.1992
Arion Ymeri	30.03.1995
Defenders:	**DOB**
Prince Balde (LBR)	23.03.1998
Azem Bejta	03.08.1990
Shkelzen Lushtaku	22.06.1990
Muharrem Musa	
Edon Pasoma	21.08.1992
Arsen Sykaj (ALB)	16.04.1990
Midfielders:	**DOB**
Armend Abazi	17.08.1994
Nicholas Andrews (LBR)	04.08.1998
Argjend Bardhi	28.04.1993
Taulant Dajaku	09.01.1987
Besfort Dervishaj	24.09.1998
Qemail Elshani	
Atdhe Grajqevci	22.11.1998
Besart Islamaj	22.01.1993
Dijar Mustafa	07.11.1993
Rrahim Nimani	17.03.1999
Vigan Rexhaj	06.05.1993
Arbios Thaçi	13.10.1993
Ermal Veliqi	
Forwards:	**DOB**
Isa Eminhaziri	09.09.1987
Osman Mëziu	05.09.1999
Denis Peposhi (ALB)	01.02.1995
Diar Prokshi	27.08.1998
Hysen Tahiri	28.09.1992
Kreshnik Uka	07.01.1995
Trainer:	**DOB**
Tahir Lushtaku	

Football Club Drita Gjilan

Founded: 1947
Stadium: Stadiumi i Qytetit, Gjilan (15,000)

Goalkeepers:	DOB
Edvan Bakaj	09.10.1987
Mario Kirev (BUL)	15.08.1989
Dorart Ramadani	02.10.1998
Leutrim Rexhepi	16.04.1994
Defenders:	**DOB**
Sedat Berisha (MKD)	03.09.1989
Fidan Gërbeshi	19.05.1985
Denis Haliti	31.01.1997
Ervis Kaja (ALB)	29.07.1987
Viktor Kuka	25.06.1990
Liridon Leci	11.02.1985
Ardian Limani	18.11.1993
Drilon Musaj	11.09.1994
Përparim Osmani	27.03.1988
Adonis Ruhani (GER)	11.05.1994
Arbër Shala	23.12.1991
Midfielders:	**DOB**
Edenilson Bergonsi (BRA)	13.09.1987
Albin Krasniqi (ALB)	28.09.1988
Albin Krasniqi	03.06.2001
Endrit Krasniqi	26.10.1994
Përparim Livoreka	28.06.1987
Zgjim Mustafa	22.11.1994
Haxhi Neziraj (ALB)	16.03.1993
Bujar Shabani	11.10.1990
Filonit Shaqiri	29.05.1993
Erjon Vucaj (ALB)	25.12.1990
Forwards:	**DOB**
Klajdi Burba (ALB)	15.02.1999
Betim Haxhimusa	14.04.1992
Festim Krasniqi	12.07.1991
Leutrim Kryeziu	25.01.1999
Eri Lamçja (ALB)	10.03.1994
Ardit Mustafa	06.10.2001
Kyrian Nwabueze (NGA)	12.11.1992
Xhevdet Shabani	10.10.1986
Trainer:	**DOB**
Shpëtim Duro (ALB)	24.12.1959
Ardijan Nuhiji (MKD) [14.02.2019]	12.07.1978

Klubi Futbollistik Ferizaj

Founded: 1923
Stadium: Stadiumi "Ismet Shabani", Ferizaj (2,000)

Goalkeepers:	**DOB**
Armend Blakqori	06.08.1990
Kenan Haxhihamza	28.12.1996
Stefan Istatov (MKD)	27.12.1992
Burhan Mustafa (MKD)	22.07.1990
Defenders:	**DOB**
Bujamin Asani (MKD)	10.08.1988
Dardan Cerkini	27.09.1991
Hajradin Cuculi (MKD)	
Adnan Haxhaj	16.09.1987
Ervin Kacar (SRB)	25.10.1991
Albert Kaqiku	21.01.1995
Viktor Kuka	25.06.1990
Kristi Marku (ALB)	13.04.1995
Arbër Mone (ALB)	08.06.1988
Burim Shabani	02.03.1986
Veton Shabani	05.05.1990
Maringlen Shosha (ALB)	29.01.1987
Midfielders:	**DOB**
Armend Aliu (MKD)	26.04.1996
Florim Berisha	
Qendrim Dautaj	26.09.1998
Genc Hamiti	21.09.1993
Mirsad Idrizi	07.05.1985
Granit Jashari	20.08.1998
Rinor Jashari	
Fuad Karabegu	01.02.1991
Ylber Luma (MKD)	
Blerton Mustafa	
Egzon Shabani	27.08.1989
Bashkim Shala	05.04.1991
Forwards:	**DOB**
Florim Berbatovci	29.08.1989
Erli Çupi (ALB)	03.02.1997
Husein Demiri (MKD)	06.09.1995
Dren Gashi	25.01.1994
Durim Gashi	14.06.1992
Avdyl Haliti	24.04.1986
Mensur Idrizi (MKD)	08.03.1983
Ermal Krasniqi	07.09.1998
Mentor Mazrekaj	08.02.1989
Nazim Mulaku	01.05.1997
Qerim Tershanaj	
Trainer:	**DOB**
Afrim Tovërlani	17.01.1967

Klubi Futbollistik Feronikeli Glogovac

Founded: 1974
Stadium: Stadiumi "Rexhep Rexhepi", Glogovac (2,000)

Goalkeepers:	**DOB**
Gentrit Hasi	24.04.1997
Florjan Smakiqi	10.08.1998
Jacek Troshupa (POL)	04.10.1993
Defenders:	**DOB**
Prince Balde (LBR)	23.03.1998
Yll Hoxha	26.12.1987
Perparim Islami	01.05.1995
Drilon Lladrovci	27.07.1994
Drin Lladrovci	01.01.1997
Lapidar Lladrovci	15.12.1990
Arbër Prekazi	21.10.1989
Lorent Shala	20.08.2000
Astrit Thaqi	20.04.1993
Midfielders:	**DOB**
Berat Ahmeti	26.01.1995
Nicholas Andrews (LBR)	04.08.1998
Argjend Bardhi	28.04.1993
Albert Dabiqaj	10.07.1996
Lulzim Doshlaku	28.01.1991
Astrit Fazliu	28.10.1987
Alush Gavazaj	24.03.1995
Dorent Hajdari	28.01.2001
Jean Agostinho da Silva "Jean Carioca" (BRA)	01.06.1988
Hamed Koné (CIV)	02.11.1987
Met Millaku	15.11.1997
Albutrint Morina	20.02.1993
Riza Zhdrella	22.02.2000
Forwards:	**DOB**
Mendurim Hoti	23.02.1996
Rizon Hoti	
Lauren Ismailaj (ALB)	30.09.1995
Artur Magani (ALB)	08.07.1994
Diar Prokshi	27.08.1998
Kastriot Rexha	27.09.1988
Adonis Shala	23.10.1998
Mevlan Zeka	28.05.1994
Trainer:	**DOB**
Sulejman Starova (ALB)	12.12.1955
Zekirija Ramadani (MKD) [03.09.2018]	21.01.1978

Klubi Futbollistik Flamurtari Prishtinë

Founded: 1968
Stadium: Stadiumi "Xhemail Ibishi", Prishtinë (5,000)

Goalkeepers:	**DOB**
Ardit Nika	17.02.1998
Flamur Neziri	22.05.1987
Besnik Shehu	13.06.1992
Defenders:	**DOB**
Endrit Demolli	04.05.2001
Gentrit Dumani	13.07.1993
Angel Granchov (BUL)	16.10.1992
Veton Kabashi	
Lorik Maxhuni	02.07.1992
Ben Quansah (GHA)	20.07.1996
Veton Shabani	05.05.1990
Melos Zenunaj	
Midfielders:	**DOB**
Shqipdon Ademi	
Granit Ahmeti	19.02.1984
Mërgim Boshnjaku	
Agron Bruqi	
Getoar Dragusha	19.03.1993
Albinot Kozmaqi	12.01.2000
Adem Maliqi	
Vigan Rexhaj	06.05.1993
Liridon Voca	
Arbnor Zeqiri	02.08.1996
Edon Zeqiri	04.06.1988
Forwards:	**DOB**
Florim Berbatovci	29.08.1989
Nasir Ibrahim (CIV)	
Adamou Moussa Issa (NIG)	01.01.1995
Shend Kelmendi	21.09.1994
Egzon Krasniqi	17.07.1997
Ardit Shehaj (ALB)	23.09.1990
Alban Shillova	13.08.1992
Ilaz Zylfiu (SRB)	27.03.1998
Trainer:	**DOB**
Arsim Thaqi	25.05.1971

Soccer Club Gjilani

Founded: 1945
Stadium: Gjilan City Stadium, Gjilan (15,000)

Goalkeepers:	**DOB**
Kenan Haxhihamza	28.12.1996
Donat Kaqiu	20.09.1993
Petrit Terziu	03.12.2001
Defenders:	**DOB**
Erlis Frashëri (ALB)	13.05.1988
Armend Halili	
Premton Isufi	
Ylber Kastrati	09.04.1987
Edison Kqiku	16.01.1999
Vilson Lila (ALB)	06.10.1989
Endrien Magani (ALB)	06.06.1991
Mauricio José Marinho (BRA)	09.09.1993
Fisnik Papuqi	01.07.1983
Midfielders:	**DOB**
Keita Lanzeni Aziz (CIV)	28.12.1996
Ergon Hyseni	
Semir Hadžibulić (SRB)	16.08.1986
Jefferson Francisco Marques Lopes (BRA)	27.10.1989
Kledi Koçi (ALB)	16.02.1999
Salih Kosumi	22.09.1992
Ledion Muçaj (ALB)	04.09.1992
Arbër Mustafa	
Ansi Nika (ALB)	22.08.1990
Brunild Pepa (ALB)	22.11.1990
Edon Sadriu	20.05.1995
Kushtrim Shabani	08.02.1997
Forwards:	**DOB**
Alitin Aliu	11.11.1999
Shpend Asani (MKD)	14.11.1996
Trevin Caesar (TRI)	26.04.1989
Fiton Hajdari	19.09.1991
Vilfor Hysa (ALB)	09.09.1989
Wilber Mauricio Pérez Medrano (GUA)	26.09.1988
Keita Alassane Razak (CIV)	28.09.1996
Trainer:	**DOB**
Alban Hyseni	
Gentian Mezani (ALB) [20.03.2019]	13.10.1975

Klubi Futbollistik KEK-u Obilić

Founded: 1928
Stadium: Stadiumi "Agron Rama", Obilić (10,000)

Goalkeepers:	**DOB**
Habib Gllareva	19.01.2000
Drin Hodaj	27.02.1997
Ardit Nika	17.02.1998
Defenders:	**DOB**
Genc Bytyci	28.10.1984
Altin Govori	
Endrit Hashani	
Shkelzen Jashanica	07.09.1989
Ensar Krasniqi	
Liridon Kukaj	22.06.1983
Valmir Kutllovci	
Ardian Musliu	05.07.1997
Amir Prishtina	
Muhamet Rakovica	
Leonat Vitija	22.08.2000
Midfielders:	**DOB**
Gezim Berisha	
Adonis Dodolli	
Besart Dushi	01.02.1993
Ardit Gashi	
Atdhe Grajqevci	22.11.1998
Visar Hashani (CAN)	07.10.1999
Gentrit Krasniqi	
Rilind Nimani	11.01.1999
Ardit Preniqi	
Egzon Qerimi	
Drilon Tejeci	26.12.1997
Eris Thaqi	08.08.1999
Forwards:	**DOB**
Isa Eminhaziri	09.09.1987
Ehat Gjoka	
Pleurat Hajdini	21.01.1994
Fatlum Lleshi	
Shpëtim Preniqi	
Torvioll Stullqaku	
Vigan Veliu	02.03.1998
Trainer:	**DOB**
Enis Nasufi	

Klubi Futbollistik Liria Prizren

Founded: 1930
Stadium: Stadiumi "Përparim Thaçi", Prizren (15,000)

Goalkeepers:	**DOB**
Flamur Gashi	06.06.2000
Drilon Hodaj	
Defenders:	**DOB**
Valon Bytyqi	23.06.1990
Florian Daci (ALB)	02.04.1991
Behar Dina	
Robert Gjeraj	12.04.1985
Rilind Kastrati	
Jenuz Kolloni	
Armando José Nieves Vargas (COL)	14.11.1989
Jhonny Riascos (COL)	08.12.1988
Adrijan Rudović (MNE)	10.06.1995
Ibrahim Walidjo (CMR)	02.04.1989
Midfielders:	**DOB**
Diellor Beseni (ALB)	31.05.2002
Gentian Binishi	01.06.1997
Shpresim Fazlija (SUI)	08.03.1997
Liridon Fetahaj	21.09.1991
Luis Manuel Jiménez Vívas (VEN)	28.12.1995
Deji Mayowa Joel (NGA)	23.11.1992
Ramadan Kryeziu	25.07.1990
Maickol Pio Martins Aristegui (URU)	29.04.1993
Blendi Memaj	02.01.1995
Ilir Mustafa	07.08.1996
Granit Osmanollaj (ALB)	31.01.1997
Guillermo Abel Ramírez (VEN)	10.11.1989
Fitim Susuri	
Ragip Thaçi	
Gerald Tushe (ALB)	02.05.1991
Forwards:	**DOB**
Qendrim Gashi	27.03.1995
Fatih Karahoda	07.04.1987
Albin Memaj	
Aldo Mitraj (ALB)	12.01.1987
Roby Alberto Norales Núñez (HON)	25.01.1991
Trainer:	**DOB**
Vincenzo Alberto Annese (ITA)	22.09.1984

Klubi Futbollistik Llapi Podujevë

Founded: 1932
Stadium: Stadiumi "Zahir Pajaziti", Podujevë (10,000)

Goalkeepers:	**DOB**
Afrim Ademi	19.05.1989
Bledar Hajdini	16.06.1995
Eglant Haxho (ALB)	11.11.1988
Apollon Tara	16.05.2000
Defenders:	**DOB**
Ilir Blakçori	01.02.1993
Benjamin Emini	20.07.1992
Ardian Gjata	18.12.1997
Ardian Hoti	14.09.1996
Bujar Idrizi	11.12.1991
Dardan Jashari	28.03.1990
Armin Mujkić (BIH)	10.03.1994
Elvis Prençi (ALB)	26.06.1993
Egzon Sinani	07.06.1994
Rron Statovci	18.01.1997
Midfielders:	**DOB**
Lorik Aliu (ALB)	07.05.1996
Flamur Bajrami	10.02.1997
Bruno Arrabal Passamani (BRA)	22.02.1992
Behar Maliqi	22.09.1986
Hamdi Namani	16.10.1995
Klodian Nuri (ALB)	23.07.1995
Arbnor Ramadani	03.06.1994
Kushtrim Shabani	08.02.1997
Edon Zeqiri	04.06.1988
Mentor Zhdrella	06.10.1990
Forwards:	**DOB**
Festim Alidema	05.10.1997
Gentrit Begolli	21.02.1992
Fiton Hajdari	19.09.1991
Muhamet Hyseni	06.02.2001
Ahmed Januzi (ALB)	08.07.1988
Shend Kelmendi	21.09.1994
Ermal Krasniqi	07.09.1998
Miran Maksuti (MKD)	15.07.1993
Labinot Osmani	15.07.1985
Alban Rexhepi	15.12.1995
Remzifaik Selmani (MKD)	05.05.1997
Valmir Veliu	04.06.2000
Enis Zabërgja	22.06.1985
Trainer:	**DOB**
Bylbyl Sokoli	19.12.1958
Bekim Shotani [19.10.2018]	06.12.1974
Xhengiz Rexhepi (MKD) [19.12.2019]	

Football Club Prishtinë

Founded: 1922
Stadium: Stadiumi "Fadil Vokrri", Prishtinë (13,500)

Goalkeepers:	**DOB**
Laurit Behluli	17.05.2000
Visar Bekaj	24.05.1997
Alban Muqiqi	10.11.1995
Defenders:	**DOB**
Jamal Arago (GHA)	28.08.1993
Tun Bardhoku	12.09.1993
Abdul Bashiru (GHA)	17.04.1992
Leotrim Bekteshi	21.04.1992
Debatik Curri (ALB)	28.12.1983
Armend Dallku (ALB)	16.06.1983
Ahmet Haliti	01.10.1988
Lorik Maxhuni	02.07.1992
Përparim Osmani	27.03.1988
Armend Thaçi	10.10.1992
Leonat Vitija	22.08.2000
Agon Xhaka	09.06.1997
Midfielders:	**DOB**
Ergyn Ahmeti	21.12.1998
Lorik Boshnjaku	07.07.1995
Liridon Fetahaj	21.09.1991
Armend Gashi	29.01.2001
Donat Hasanaj	18.09.1998
Gauthier Mankenda (COD)	20.07.1997
Diar Miftaraj	20.10.1990
Argjend Mustafa	22.10.1993
Mergim Pefqeli	25.11.1993
Kastriot Selmani	08.07.1999
Qëndrim Zyba	03.02.2001
Forwards:	**DOB**
Arbër Hoxha	06.10.1998
Ahmed Januzi (ALB)	08.07.1988
Alen Jasaroski (MKD)	06.11.1991
Basit Khalid (GHA)	10.08.1996
Meriton Korenica	15.12.1997
Mario Morina (ALB)	16.10.1992
Bleon Sekiraqa	17.10.2000
Trainer:	**DOB**
Mirel Josa (ALB)	01.06.1963

Klubi Futbollistik Trepça'89 Mitrovicë

Founded: 1992
Stadium: Stadiumi "Riza Lushta", Mitrovicë (12,000)

Goalkeepers:	**DOB**
Arben Beqiri	02.06.1988
Enes Citaku	05.07.1997
Victor Hugo Golas (BRA)	27.12.1990
Ardit Hyseni	
Auron Loxha	15.11.2001
Defenders:	**DOB**
Richard Asare (GHA)	08.03.1995
Aleksandar Bagašovski (MKD)	15.11.1993
Elton Basriu (ALB)	03.08.1987
Dardan Cerkini	27.09.1991
Milot Kamberi	05.08.1997
Albert Kaqiku	21.01.1995
Ylber Maloku	04.01.1996
Rexhep Memini (ALB)	10.04.1994
Ergis Mersini (ALB)	30.09.1989
Edon Pasoma	21.08.1992
Arbër Pira	
Albion Pllana	20.08.2000
Robert Rrahmani	28.01.2001
Maringlen Shosha (ALB)	29.01.1987
Midfielders:	**DOB**
Taulant Avdyli	22.10.1998
Orgest Gava (ALB)	29.03.1990
Blagoj Gucev (MKD)	22.03.1990
Engjëll Hoti (GER)	26.02.1997
Hasan Hyseni	14.04.1997
Renato Hyshmeri (ALB)	04.03.1989
Muharrem Jashari	21.02.1998
Arb Manaj (ALB)	01.01.1997
Martin Mirčevski (MKD)	11.02.1997
Ardian Neziri	
Gzim Rusi	29.11.1994
Lassine Traoré (FRA)	
Forwards:	**DOB**
Ardian Berisha (SWE)	07.05.1998
Franck Betra (FRA)	18.12.1996
Antonio Bujčevski (MKD)	24.01.1990
Odi Henry Chibueze (NGA)	15.11.1992
Djibril Diawara (NGA)	
Ardian Muja	09.12.1997
Stojanco Velinov (MKD)	03.09.1989
Trainer:	**DOB**
Gugash Magani (ALB)	14.03.1965

SECOND LEVEL
First Football of Kosovo - Liga e Parë 2018/2019

1.	KF Vushtrria (*Promoted*)	30	23	3	4	45	-	19	72
2.	KF Dukagjini Klinë (*Promoted*)	30	18	5	7	51	-	26	59
3.	KF Besa Pejë Peć (*Promotion Play-offs*)	30	17	8	5	50	-	26	59
4.	KF Vëllaznimi Gjakovë (*Promotion Play-offs*)	30	15	9	6	40	-	18	54
5.	KF Vitia	30	14	5	11	31	-	36	47
6.	KF Trepça Mitrovicë	30	11	5	14	30	-	35	38
7.	KF Istogu	30	12	2	16	51	-	58	38
8.	KF Onix-Banjë	30	10	7	13	32	-	36	37
9.	KF Arbëria Lipljan	30	11	4	15	37	-	48	37
10.	KF Drenasi Glogovac	30	9	8	13	28	-	29	35
11.	KF 2 Korriku Prishtinë	30	10	5	15	34	-	42	35
12.	KF Vllaznia Požaranje	30	10	4	16	28	-	42	34
13.	KF Ramiz Sadiku Prishtinë (*Relegation Play-offs*)	30	11	0	19	35	-	46	33
14.	KF Bashkimi (*Relegation Play-offs*)	30	9	5	16	31	-	51	32
15.	KF Fushë Kosova (*Relegated*)	30	10	7	13	27	-	29	31
16.	KF Kika Kamenica (*Relegated*)	30	7	9	14	33	-	42	30

Relegation Play-offs 2nd / 3rd Level

KF Dardana - KF Bashkimi	3-0
KF Ramiz Sadiku Prishtinë - KF Rahoveci	4-0

NATIONAL TEAM

INTERNATIONAL MATCHES
(16.07.2018 – 15.07.2019)

07.09.2018	Bakı	Azerbaijan - Kosovo	0-0	(UNL)
10.09.2018	Prishtinë	Kosovo - Faroe Islands	2-0(0-0)	(UNL)
11.10.2018	Prishtinë	Kosovo - Malta	3-1(1-0)	(UNL)
14.10.2018	Tórshavn	Faroe Islands - Kosovo	1-1(0-1)	(UNL)
17.11.2018	Attard	Malta - Kosovo	0-5(0-1)	(UNL)
20.11.2018	Prishtinë	Azerbaijan - Kosovo	4-0(1-0)	(UNL)
21.03.2019	Prishtinë	Kosovo - Denmark	2-2(1-0)	(F)
25.03.2019	Prishtinë	Kosovo - Bulgaria	1-1(0-1)	(ECQ)
07.06.2019	Podgorica	Montenegro - Kosovo	1-1(0-1)	(ECQ)
10.06.2019	Sofia	Bulgaria - Kosovo	2-3(1-1)	(ECQ)

07.09.2018 AZERBAIJAN - KOSOVO 0-0 UEFA Nations League D, Group 3
Olimpiya Stadionu, Bakı; Referee: Ola Hobber Nilsen (Norway); Attendance: 19,500
KVX: Samir Ujkani (Cap), Fidan Aliti, Leart Paqarada, Amir Kadri Rrahmani, Mërgim Vojvoda, Herolind Shala, Hekuran Kryeziu, Arbër Zeneli (84.Idriz Voca), Bersant Celina (70.Donis Avdijaj), Vedat Muriqi, Edon Zhegrova (63.Milot Rashica). Trainer: Bernard Challandes (Switzerland).

10.09.2018 KOSOVO - FAROE ISLANDS 2-0(0-0) UEFA Nations League D, Group 3
Stadiumi „Fadil Vokrri“, Prishtinë; Referee: Bart Vertenten (Belgium); Attendance: 12,677
KVX: Samir Ujkani (Cap), Fidan Aliti, Amir Kadri Rrahmani, Mërgim Vojvoda, Herolind Shala, Hekuran Kryeziu, Benjamin Kololli, Donis Avdijaj (68.Besar Halimi), Milot Rashica (79.Edon Zhegrova), Atdhe Nuhiu (84.Vedat Muriqi), Arbër Zeneli. Trainer: Bernard Challandes (Switzerland).
Goals: Arbër Zeneli (50), Atdhe Nuhiu (55).

11.10.2018 KOSOVO - MALTA 3-1(1-0) UEFA Nations League D, Group 3
Stadiumi "Fadil Vokrri", Prishtinë; Referee: Tamás Bognár (Hungary); Attendance: 12,420
KVX: Samir Ujkani (Cap), Fidan Aliti, Amir Kadri Rrahmani, Mërgim Vojvoda, Herolind Shala, Valon Berisha (74.Besar Halimi), Hekuran Kryeziu, Benjamin Kololli, Arbër Zeneli (77.Milot Rashica), Vedat Muriqi (83.Lirim Kastrati), Edon Zhegrova. Trainer: Bernard Challandes (Switzerland).
Goals: Benjamin Kololli (30), Vedat Muriqi (68), Benjamin Kololli (81).

14.10.2018 FAROE ISLANDS - KOSOVO 1-1(0-1) UEFA Nations League D, Group 3
Tórsvøllur, Tórshavn; Referee: Miroslav Zelinka (Czech Republic); Attendance: 2,300
KVX: Samir Ujkani (Cap), Fidan Aliti, Amir Kadri Rrahmani, Mërgim Vojvoda, Ardin Dallku, Idriz Voca (54.Besar Halimi), Herolind Shala, Valon Berisha, Milot Rashica (90+1.Vedat Muriqi), Atdhe Nuhiu, Edon Zhegrova (74.Arbër Zeneli). Trainer: Bernard Challandes (Switzerland).
Goal: Milot Rashica (9).

17.11.2018 MALTA - KOSOVO 0-5(0-1) UEFA Nations League D, Group 3
Ta'Qali National Stadium, Attard; Referee: Bartosz Frankowski (Poland); Attendance: 2,115
KVX: Samir Ujkani (Cap), Fidan Aliti, Amir Kadri Rrahmani, Mërgim Vojvoda, Herolind Shala, Valon Berisha (61.Besar Halimi), Hekuran Kryeziu, Benjamin Kololli, Milot Rashica, Arbër Zeneli (71.Donis Avdijaj), Vedat Muriqi (84.Shkelqim Demhasaj). Trainer: Bernard Challandes (Switzerland).
Goals: Vedat Muriqi (15), Benjamin Kololli (70), Donis Avdijaj (78, 80), Milot Rashica (86).

20.11.2018 AZERBAIJAN - KOSOVO 4-0(1-0) UEFA Nations League D, Group 3
Stadiumi "Fadil Vokrri", Prishtinë; Referee: Benoît Millot (France); Attendance: 12,532
KVX: Arijanet Anan Muric, Fidan Aliti, Amir Kadri Rrahmani, Mërgim Vojvoda, Herolind Shala, Valon Berisha (Cap) (85.Besar Halimi), Hekuran Kryeziu, Benjamin Kololli, Milot Rashica (74.Edon Zhegrova), Arbër Zeneli, Vedat Muriqi (69.Atdhe Nuhiu). Trainer: Bernard Challandes (Switzerland).
Goals: Arbër Zeneli (2, 50), Amir Kadri Rrahmani (61), Arbër Zeneli (76).

21.03.2019 KOSOVO - DENMARK 2-2(1-0) Friendly International
Stadiumi „Fadil Vokrri", Prishtinë; Referee: Ali Palabiyik (Turkey); Attendance: 13,000
KVX: Arijanet Anan Muric (46.Samir Ujkani), Fidan Aliti, Leart Paqarada, Amir Kadri Rrahmani, Mërgim Vojvoda, Herolind Shala (Cap), Besar Halimi (81.Lirim Kastrati), Milot Rashica (46.Edon Zhegrova), Arbër Zeneli (70.Bernard Berisha), Bersant Celina (71.Idriz Voca), Vedat Muriqi (81.Atdhe Nuhiu). Trainer: Bernard Challandes (Switzerland).
Goals: Amir Kadri Rrahmani (42), Bersant Celina (66).

25.03.2019 KOSOVO - BULGARIA 1-1(0-1) 16th EC. Qualifiers
Stadiumi "Fadil Vokrri", Prishtinë; Referee: Gediminas Mažeika (Lithuania); Attendance: 12,580
KVX: Arijanet Anan Muric, Fidan Aliti, Amir Kadri Rrahmani, Mërgim Vojvoda, Herolind Shala (59.Edon Zhegrova), Hekuran Kryeziu (Cap), Benjamin Kololli (78.Leart Paqarada), Milot Rashica, Arbër Zeneli, Bersant Celina (58.Besar Halimi), Vedat Muriqi. Trainer: Bernard Challandes (Switzerland).
Goal: Arbër Zeneli (61).

07.06.2019 MONTENEGRO - KOSOVO 1-1(0-1) 16th EC. Qualifiers
Stadion pod Goricom, Gorica; Referee: Daniele Orsato (Italy); Attendance: *played behind closed doors*
KVX: Arijanet Anan Muric, Fidan Aliti, Leart Paqarada (69.Benjamin Kololli), Amir Kadri Rrahmani (Cap), Mërgim Vojvoda, Idriz Voca, Besar Halimi, Milot Rashica, Arbër Zeneli (39.Edon Zhegrova), Bersant Celina (78.Elbasan Rashani), Vedat Muriqi. Trainer: Bernard Challandes (Switzerland).
Goal: Milot Rashica (24).

10.06.2019 BULGARIA - KOSOVO 2-3(1-1) 16th EC. Qualifiers
Nationalen Stadion "Vasil Levski", Sofia; Referee: Mads-Kristoffer Kristoffersen (Denmark); Attendance: 4,994
KVX: Arijanet Anan Muric, Fidan Aliti, Amir Kadri Rrahmani (Cap), Mërgim Vojvoda (62.Florent Hadergjonaj), Idriz Voca (62.Anel Rashkaj), Besar Halimi, Benjamin Kololli, Milot Rashica, Bersant Celina, Vedat Muriqi, Edon Zhegrova (76.Elbasan Rashani). Trainer: Bernard Challandes (Switzerland).
Goals: Milot Rashica (14), Vedat Muriqi (64), Elbasan Rashani (90+3).

NATIONAL TEAM PLAYERS
(16.07.2018 – 15.07.2019)

Name	DOB	Caps	Goals	2018/2019:	*Club*
Goalkeepers					
Arijanet Anan MURIC	07.11.1998	**5**	**0**	2018/2019:	*Manchester City FC (HUN)*
Samir UJKANI	05.07.1988	**25**	**0**	2018/2019:	*Çaykur Rizespor (TUR)*
Defenders					
Fidan ALITI	03.10.1993	**15**	**0**	2018: 03.02.2019->	*KF Skënderbeu Korçë (ALB)* *Kalmar FF (SWE)*
Ardin DALLKU	01.11.1994	**2**	**0**	2018:	*FK Vorskla Poltava (UKR)*
Florent HADERGJONAJ	31.07.1994	**2**	**0**	2019:	*Huddersfield Town FC (ENG)*
Lirim KASTRATI	16.01.1999	**2**	**0**	2018/2019:	*NK Lokomotiva Zagreb (CRO)*
Leart PAQARADA	10.08.1994	**17**	**1**	2018/2019:	*SV Sandhausen (GER)*
Amir Kadri RRAHMANI	24.02.1994	**24**	**4**	2018/2019:	*GNK Dinamo Zagreb (CRO)*
Mërgim VOJVODA	01.02.1995	**19**	**0**	2018/2019:	*Royal Excelsior Mouscron (BEL)*
Midfielders					
Bernard BERISHA	21.10.1991	**14**	**0**	2019:	*FK Akhmat Grozny (RUS)*
Valon BERISHA	07.02.1993	**14**	**1**	2018:	*SS Lazio Roma (ITA)*
Bersant CELINA	09.09.1996	**15**	**2**	2018/2019:	*Swansea City AFC (WAL)*
Besar HALIMI	12.12.1994	**19**	**1**	2018/2019:	*Brøndby IF (DEN)*
Benjamin KOLOLLI	15.05.1992	**12**	**3**	2018/2019:	*FC Zürich (SUI)*
Hekuran KRYEZIU	12.12.1992	**19**	**1**	2018/2019:	*FC Zürich (SUI)*
Milot RASHICA	28.06.1996	**24**	**4**	2018/2019:	*SV Werder Bremen (GER)*
Anel RASHKAJ	19.08.1989	**4**	**0**	2019:	*IFK Eskilstuna (SWE)*
Herolind SHALA	02.01.1992	**15**	**0**	2018: 11.02.2019->	*IK Start Kristiansand (NOR)* *Vålerenga Fotball Oslo (NOR)*
Idriz VOCA	15.05.1997	**7**	**0**	2018/2019:	*FC Luzern (SUI)*
Arbër ZENELI	25.02.1995	**18**	**7**	2018: 26.01.2019->	*SC Heerenveen (NED)* *Stade de Reims (FRA)*
Edon ZHEGROVA	31.03.1999	**3**	**2**	2018: 04.02.2019->	*KRC Genk (BEL)* *FC Basel (SUI)*
Forwards					
Donis AVDIJAJ	25.08.1996	**6**	**2**	2018:	*Willem II Tilburg (NED)*
Shkelqim DEMHASAJ	19.04.1996	**1**	**0**	2018:	*FC Luzern (SUI)*
Vedat MURIQI	24.04.1994	**20**	**5**	2018/2019:	*Çaykur Rizespor (TUR)*
Atdhe NUHIU	29.07.1989	**14**	**2**	2018/2019:	*Sheffield Wednesday FC (ENG)*
Elbasan RASHANI	09.05.1993	**7**	**4**	2019:	*Odds BK Skien (NOR)*

National team coach

Bernard CHALLANDES (Switzerland) [from 02.03.2018]	26.07.1951	13 M; 8 W; 5 D; 0 L; 28-8

LATVIA

The Country:

Latvijas Republika (Republic of Latvia)
Capital: Rīga
Surface: 64,589 km²
Inhabitants: 1,919,968 [2018]
Time: UTC+2

The FA:

Latvijas Futbola federācija
Olympic Sports Centre, Grostonas Street 6b, 1013 Rīga
Tel: +371 6729 2988
Foundation date: 19.06.1921
Member of FIFA since: 1922
Member of UEFA since: 1992
Website: www.lff.lv

NATIONAL TEAM RECORDS

First international match:	24.09.1922, Rīga:	Latvia – Estonia 1-1
Most international caps:	Vitālijs Astafjevs	- 167 caps (1992-2010)
Most international goals:	Māris Verpakovskis	- 29 goals / 104 caps (1999-2014)

UEFA EUROPEAN CHAMPIONSHIP	
1960	-
1964	-
1968	-
1972	-
1976	-
1980	-
1984	-
1988	-
1992	-
1996	Qualifiers
2000	Qualifiers
2004	Final Tournament (Group Stage)
2008	Qualifiers
2012	Qualifiers
2016	Qualifiers

FIFA WORLD CUP	
1930	Did not enter
1934	Did not enter
1938	Entry not accepted by FIFA
1950	-
1954	-
1958	-
1962	-
1966	-
1970	-
1974	-
1978	-
1982	-
1986	-
1990	-
1994	Qualifiers
1998	Qualifiers
2002	Qualifiers
2006	Qualifiers
2010	Qualifiers
2014	Qualifiers
2018	Qualifiers

UEFA NATIONS LEAGUE
2018/2019 – League D

OLYMPIC FOOTBALL TOURNAMENTS 1908-2016							
1908	-	**1948**	-	**1972**	-	**1996**	Qualifiers
1912	-	**1952**	-	**1976**	-	**2000**	Qualifiers
1920	-	**1956**	-	**1980**	-	**2004**	Qualifiers
1924	-	**1960**	-	**1984**	-	**2008**	Qualifiers
1928	1/8 - Finals	**1964**	-	**1988**	-	**2012**	Qualifiers
1936	Did not enter	**1968**	-	**1992**	-	**2016**	Qualifiers

FIFA CONFEDERATIONS CUP 1992-2017
None

LATVIAN CLUB HONOURS IN EUROPEAN CLUB COMPETITIONS:

European Champion Clubs' Cup (1956-1992) / UEFA Champions League (1993-2019)
None
Fairs Cup (1858-1971) / UEFA Cup (1972-2009) / UEFA Europa League (2010-2019)
None
UEFA Super Cup (1972-2018)
None
European Cup Winners' Cup 1961-1999*
None

**defunct competition*

NATIONAL COMPETITIONS
TABLE OF HONOURS

LATVIAN SSR (SOVIET ERA) CHAMPIONS

1941	*Championship Cancelled*
1942/1944	*Championship Interrupted*
1945	FK Dinamo Rīga
1946	Daugava Liepāja
1947	Daugava Liepāja
1948	Žmiļova Komanda
1949	Sarkanais Metalurgs Liepāja
1950	AVN Rīga
1951	Sarkanais Metalurgs Liepāja
1952	AVN Rīga
1953	Sarkanais Metalurgs Liepāja
1954	Sarkanais Metalurgs Liepāja
1955	Darba Rezerves Rīga
1956	Sarkanais Metalurgs Liepāja
1957	Sarkanais Metalurgs Liepāja
1958	Sarkanais Metalurgs Liepāja

1959	RER Rīga
1960	ASK Rīga
1961	ASK Rīga
1962	ASK Rīga
1963	ASK Rīga
1964	ASK Rīga
1965	ASK Rīga
1966	ESR Rīga
1967	ESR Rīga
1968	Starts Brocēni
1969	FK Venta Ventspils
1970	VEF Rīga
1971	VEF Rīga
1972	FK Jūrnieks
1973	VEF Rīga
1974	VEF Rīga

1975	VEF Rīga
1976	Enerģija Rīga
1977	Enerģija Rīga
1978	Ķīmiķis Daugavpils
1979	Elektrons Rīga
1980	Ķīmiķis Daugavpils
1981	Elektrons Rīga
1982	Elektrons Rīga
1983	VEF Rīga
1984	Torpedo Rīga
1985	FK Alfa
1986	Torpedo Rīga
1987	Torpedo Rīga
1988	RAF Jelgava
1989	RAF Jelgava
1990	Gauja Valmiera

	CHAMPIONS*	CUP WINNERS	BEST GOALSCORERS	
1910	RV Union Rīga	-	-	
1911	Britannia FC Rīga	-	-	
1912	RV Union Rīga	-	-	
1913	SV Kaiserwald Rīga	-	-	
1914	Britannia FC Rīga	-	-	
1915	Britannia FC Rīga	-	-	
	--	--	--	
1922	Kaiserwald Rīga	-	-	
1923	Kaiserwald Rīga	-	-	
1924	RFK Rīga	-	-	
1925	RFK Rīga	-	-	
1926	RFK Rīga	-	-	
1927	Olimpia Liepaja	-	-	
1928	Olimpia Liepaja	-	-	
1929	Olimpia Liepaja	-	-	
1930	RFK Rīga	-	-	
1931	RFK Rīga	-	-	
1932	ASK Rīga	-	-	
1933	Olimpia Liepaja	-	-	
1934	RFK Rīga	-	-	
1935	RFK Rīga	-	-	
1936	Olimpia Liepaja	-	-	
1937	*No competition*	RFK Rīga	-	
1938	Olimpia Liepaja	Rīgas Vilki	-	
1939	Olimpia Liepaja	RFK Rīga	-	
1940	RFK Rīga	*No competition*	-	
	--	--	--	
1991	Skonto FC Rīga	Celtnieks Daugavpils	Vjačeslavs Ževnerovičs (Celtnieks Daugavpils)	27
1992	Skonto FC Rīga	Skonto FC Rīga	Vjačeslavs Ževnerovičs (VEF Riga)	19
1993	Skonto FC Rīga	RAF Jelgava	Aleksandrs Jeļisejevs (Skonto FC Rīga)	20
1994	Skonto FC Rīga	Olimpija Rīga	Vladimirs Babičevs (Skonto FC Rīga)	14
1995	Skonto FC Rīga	Skonto FC Rīga	Vitālijs Astafjevs (Skonto FC Rīga)	19
1996	Skonto FC Rīga	RAF Jelgava	Mihails Miholaps (FK Daugava Rīga)	33
1997	Skonto FC Rīga	Skonto FC Rīga	David Chaladze (GEO, Skonto FC Rīga)	25
1998	Skonto FC Rīga	Skonto FC Rīga	Viktors Dobrecovs (FK Liepājas Metalurgs)	23
1999	Skonto FC Rīga	FK Rīga	Viktors Dobrecovs (FK Liepājas Metalurgs)	22
2000	Skonto FC Rīga	Skonto FC Rīga	Vladimirs Koļesņičenko (Skonto FC Rīga)	17
2001	Skonto FC Rīga	Skonto FC Rīga	Mihails Miholaps (Skonto FC Rīga)	24
2002	Skonto FC Rīga	Skonto FC Rīga	Mihails Miholaps (Skonto FC Rīga)	23
2003	Skonto FC Rīga	FK Ventspils	Viktors Dobrecovs (FK Liepājas Metalurgs)	36
2004	Skonto FC Rīga	FK Ventspils	Aleksandr Katasonov (RUS, FK Liepājas Metalurgs)	21
2005	FK Liepājas Metalurgs	FK Ventspils	Viktors Dobrecovs (FK Liepājas Metalurgs) Igors Sļesarčuks (FK Venta/FK Ventspils)	18
2006	FK Ventspils	FK Liepājas Metalurgs	Mihails Miholaps (Skonto FC Rīga)	15
2007	FK Ventspils	FK Ventspils	Vits Rimkus (FK Ventspils)	20
2008	FK Ventspils	FK Daugava Daugavpils	Vits Rimkus (FK Ventspils)	14
2009	FK Liepājas Metalurgs	*No competition*	Kristaps Grebis (FK Liepājas Metalurgs)	30
2010	Skonto FC Rīga	FK Jelgava	Deniss Rakeļs (FK Liepājas Metalurgs) Nathan Júnior Soares de Carvalho (BRA, Skonto FC Rīga)	18
2011	FK Ventspils	FK Ventspils	Nathan Júnior Soares de Carvalho (BRA, Skonto FC Rīga)	22

2012	FC Daugava Daugavpils	Skonto FC Rīga	Mamuka Ghonghadze (GEO, FC Daugava Daugavpils)	18
2013	FK Ventspils	FK Ventspils	Artūrs Karašausks (Skonto FC Rīga) Andrejs Kovaļovs (FC Daugava Daugavpils)	16
2014	FK Ventspils	FK Jelgava	Vladislavs Gutkovskis (Skonto FC Rīga)	28
2015	FK Liepāja	FK Jelgava	Dāvis Ikaunieks (FK Liepaja)	15
2016	JPFS/FK Spartaks Jūrmala	FK Jelgava FK Ventspils (2016/2017)	Ģirts Karlsons (FK Ventspils)	17
2017	JPFS/FK Spartaks Jūrmala	FK Liepāja	Yevgeniy Kozlov (RUS, JPFS/FK Spartaks Jūrmala) Artūrs Karašausks (FK Liepāja)	12
2018	Rīga FC	Rīga FC	Darko Lemajić (SRB, Rīga FC)	15

*Please note: Champions of the Riga Football League (1910-1915) and Latvian Championship (1922–1940 and since 1991);
RAF Jelgava was called later FK Jelgava.

NATIONAL CHAMPIONSHIP
Virsliga 2018
(31.03.2018 – 10.11.2018)

Results

Round 1 [31.03.-01.04.2018]
FK Liepāja - Rīga FC 1-0(0-0)
FK Ventspils - Valmiera Glass 3-1(2-0)
FK Rīgas F. s. - FS Metta/LU 3-1(2-0)
FK Jelgava - Spartaks Jūrmala 1-0(0-0)

Round 2 [06-08.04.2018]
FK Jelgava - FK Ventspils 0-2(0-0)
Spartaks Jūrmala - FS Metta/LU 3-0(0-0)
Rīga FC - FK Rīgas F. s. 1-2(1-0)
FK Liepāja - Valmiera Glass 4-0(1-0)

Round 3 [13-15.04.2018]
FS Metta/LU - Rīga FC 0-1(0-1)
Valmiera Glass - Spartaks Jūrmala 2-4(1-4)
FK Rīgas F. s. - FK Jelgava 3-0(1-0)
FK Ventspils - FK Liepāja 1-1(0-0)

Round 4 [21-23.04.2018]
FK Jelgava - Rīga FC 0-1(0-1)
Valmiera Glass - FK Rīgas F. s. 0-6(0-1)
Spartaks Jūrmala - FK Ventspils 1-2(1-1)
FS Metta/LU - FK Liepāja 0-3(0-1)

Round 5 [28-30.04.2018]
FK Rīgas F. s. - Spartaks Jūrmala 0-2(0-1)
FS Metta/LU - Valmiera Glass 2-2(0-0)
FK Ventspils - Rīga FC 1-0(1-0)
FK Liepāja - FK Jelgava 3-1(1-0)

Round 6 [04-06.05.2018]
Spartaks Jūrmala - FK Liepāja 2-2(2-1)
Rīga FC - Valmiera Glass 6-1(2-0)
FK Ventspils - FK Rīgas F. s. 1-1(0-0)
FK Jelgava - FS Metta/LU 1-1(1-1)

Round 7 [11-12.05.2018]
FK Jelgava - Valmiera Glass 5-1(3-0)
FK Liepāja - FK Rīgas F. s. 3-5(1-2)
Spartaks Jūrmala - Rīga FC 0-1(0-0)
FS Metta/LU - FK Ventspils 2-2(2-0)

Round 8 [16.05.2018]
Spartaks Jūrmala - FK Jelgava 1-0(0-0)
Rīga FC - FK Liepāja 2-2(1-0)
Valmiera Glass - FK Ventspils 1-3(0-0)
FS Metta/LU - FK Rīgas F. s. 0-1(0-1)

Round 9 [20-21.05.2018]
FS Metta/LU - Spartaks Jūrmala 1-3(1-1)
Valmiera Glass - FK Liepāja 0-2(0-1)
FK Ventspils - FK Jelgava 0-0
FK Rīgas F. s. - Rīga FC 2-1(0-1)

Round 10 [26-27.05.2018]
Spartaks Jūrmala - Valmiera Glass 3-0(2-0)
FK Liepāja - FK Ventspils 1-4(1-1)
FK Jelgava - FK Rīgas F. s. 0-2(0-1)
Rīga FC - FS Metta/LU 1-0(0-0)

Round 11 [15-16.06.2018]
FK Ventspils - Spartaks Jūrmala 1-2(1-2)
Rīga FC - FK Jelgava 1-0(0-0)
FK Rīgas F. s. - Valmiera Glass 4-0(1-0)
FS Metta/LU - FK Liepāja 0-2(0-1)

Round 12 [21-22.06.2018]
FK Liepāja - FK Jelgava 2-0(1-0)
Rīga FC - FK Ventspils 1-0(0-0)
Spartaks Jūrmala - FK Rīgas F. s. 0-2(0-0)
Valmiera Glass - FS Metta/LU 1-1(0-1)

Round 13 [29.06.-01.07.2018]
FK Rīgas F. s. - FK Ventspils 3-1(0-0)
Valmiera Glass - Rīga FC 0-2(0-1)
FK Liepāja - Spartaks Jūrmala 1-1(0-0)
FK Jelgava - FS Metta/LU 1-0(0-0)

Round 14 [15.07.2018]
Rīga FC - Spartaks Jūrmala 1-0(1-0) [26.06.]
FK Jelgava - Valmiera Glass 3-2(1-1)
FK Ventspils - FS Metta/LU 3-1(0-1)
FK Rīgas F. s. - FK Liepāja 0-1(0-0) [03.10.]

Round 15 [22.07.2018]
FK Ventspils - Valmiera Glass 4-1(3-1)
Spartaks Jūrmala - FK Jelgava 4-1(1-0)
FS Metta/LU - FK Rīgas F. s. 0-2(0-0)
Rīga FC - FK Liepāja 1-0(1-0) [28.08.]

Round 16 [29-30.07.2018]
FK Liepāja - Valmiera Glass 6-2(4-1)
FK Jelgava - FK Ventspils 0-3(0-2)
Spartaks Jūrmala - FS Metta/LU 4-3(1-0)
Rīga FC - FK Rīgas F. s. 1-0(0-0)

Round 17 [12-13.08.2018]
FS Metta/LU - Rīga FC 0-2(0-2)
FK Ventspils - FK Liepāja 1-0(0-0)
FK Rīgas F. s. - FK Jelgava 1-0(1-0)
Valmiera - Spartaks Jūrmala 2-1(1-1) [03.10.]

Round 18 [18-19.08.2018]
FK Jelgava - Rīga FC 0-3(0-1)
FK Liepāja - FS Metta/LU 0-1(0-1)
Valmiera Glass - FK Rīgas F. s. 2-4(0-2)
Spartaks Jūrmala - FK Ventspils 1-2(0-1)

Round 19 [24-25.08.2018]
FK Ventspils - Rīga FC 0-1(0-1)
FK Jelgava - FK Liepāja 0-2(0-1)
FK Rīgas F. s. - Spartaks Jūrmala 0-1(0-1)
FS Metta/LU - Valmiera Glass 2-1(1-1)

Round 20 [01.09.2018]
FK Ventspils - FK Rīgas F. s. 2-0(1-0)
Spartaks Jūrmala - FK Liepāja 2-2(1-1)
Rīga FC - Valmiera Glass 3-0(0-0)
FS Metta/LU - FK Jelgava 3-0(1-0)

Round 21 [15.09.2018]
Spartaks Jūrmala - Rīga FC 1-3(0-1)
Valmiera Glass - FK Jelgava 1-4(1-2)
FK Liepāja - FK Rīgas F. s. 1-0(0-0)
FS Metta/LU - FK Ventspils 0-2(0-2)

Round 22 [23-24.09.2018]
FK Jelgava - Spartaks Jūrmala 0-0
Valmiera Glass - FK Ventspils 1-6(0-3)
FK Liepāja - Rīga FC 0-0
FK Rīgas F. s. - FS Metta/LU 3-0(2-0)

Round 23 [28-29.09.2018]
FS Metta/LU - Spartaks Jūrmala 0-3(0-0)
Valmiera Glass - FK Liepāja 0-3(0-1)
FK Ventspils - FK Jelgava 2-0(0-0)
FK Rīgas F. s. - Rīga FC 1-2(1-0)

Round 24 [06-07.10.2018]
Rīga FC - FS Metta/LU 2-1(0-1)
FK Jelgava - FK Rīgas F. s. 0-4(0-3)
Spartaks Jūrmala - Valmiera Glass 4-0(1-0)
FK Liepāja - FK Ventspils 0-1(0-1)

Round 25 [19-20.10.2018]
FK Rīgas F. s. - Valmiera Glass 3-0(1-0)
Rīga FC - FK Jelgava 2-0(0-0)
FK Ventspils - Spartaks Jūrmala 1-1(1-0)
FK Liepāja - FS Metta/LU 0-1(0-0)

Round 26 [28.10.2018]
Spartaks Jūrmala - FK Rīgas F. s. 0-4(0-0)
FK Jelgava - FK Liepāja 0-2(0-2)
Valmiera Glass - FS Metta/LU 0-2(0-0)
Rīga FC - FK Ventspils 0-0

Round 27 [04.11.2018]
FK Rīgas F. s. - FK Ventspils 1-2(0-2)
FK Liepāja - Spartaks Jūrmala 1-0(1-0)
Valmiera Glass - Rīga FC 0-2(0-2)
FS Metta/LU - FK Jelgava 1-2(0-1)

Round 28 [10.11.2018]
Valmiera Glass - FK Jelgava 1-0(0-0)
Rīga FC - Spartaks Jūrmala 4-4(1-1)
FK Rīgas F. s. - FK Liepāja 0-1(0-0)
FK Ventspils - FS Metta/LU 4-1(3-1)

Final Standings

1.	**Rīga FC**	28	20	4	4	45	-	16	64
2.	FK Ventspils	28	18	6	4	54	-	22	60
3.	FK Rīgas Futbola Skola	28	18	1	9	57	-	23	55
4.	FK Liepāja	28	15	6	7	46	-	25	51
5.	JPFS/FK Spartaks Jūrmala	28	12	6	10	48	-	37	42
6.	FK Jelgava	28	6	3	19	19	-	48	21
7.	FS Metta/Latvijas Universitāte Rīga (*Play-offs*)	28	5	4	19	24	-	52	19
8.	Valmiera Glass ViA FK	28	2	2	24	22	-	92	8

Please note: Valmiera Glass ViA FK were reprieved from relegation as the top level was extended to 9 clubs for 2019.

Top goalscorers:

15 Darko Lemajić (SRB,) *Rīga FC*

14 Maksym Marusych (UKR) *FK Rīgas Futbola Skola*

14 Oluwatosin Aiyegun (NGA) *FK Ventspils*

13 Adeleke Akinola Akinyemi (NGA) *FK Ventspils*

Relegation Play-offs [14-17.11.2018]

FS Metta/Latvijas Universitāte Rīga - SK Super Nova Olaine	7-2	3-0

NATIONAL CUP
Latvijas Kauss 2018

1/8-Finals [06-07.07.2018]

Ghetto FC/Gvatar - JPFS/FK Spartaks Jūrmala	1-8
SK Super Nova Olaine - Rīga FC	0-2
Preiļu BJSS - Valmiera Glass ViA FK	0-3
FS Metta/Latvijas Universitāte - FK Jelgava	2-1
Grobiņas SC - BFC Daugavpils/Progress	2-6
FK Limbaži - FK Rīgas Futbola Skola	0-15
RTU FC/Skonto Academy Rīga - FK Liepāja	0-5
FC BetLanes - FK Ventspils	1-2

Quarter-Finals [04-06.08.2018]

Valmiera Glass ViA FK - FK Rīgas Futbola Skola	0-3
Rīga FC - JPFS/FK Spartaks Jūrmala	3-1
BFC Daugavpils/Progress - FS Metta/ Lat.Univ.	3-3 aet; 1-4 pen
FK Liepāja - FK Ventspils	0-1 aet

Semi-Finals [19.09.2018]

FS Metta/Latvijas Universitāte - Rīga FC	1-2
FK Ventspils - FK Rīgas Futbola Skola	2-1

Final

24.10.2018; Daugava Stadions, Rīga; Referee: Dmitrijs Naļivaiko; Attendance: 1,000
Rīga FC - FK Ventspils **0-0; 5-4 on penalties**

Rīga FC: Roberts Ozols, Antons Kurakins, Vladislavs Gabovs, Volodymyr Baenko, Elvis Stuglis, Armands Pētersons (62.Ivan Lukjanovs), Tomislav Šarić, Stefan Panić, Ivan Enin (61.Felipe Bezerra Brisola), Deniss Rakeļs, Kamil Biliński. Trainer: Viktor Skripnik (Ukraine).

FK Ventspils: Vitālijs Meļņičenko, Vadims Žuļevs, Abdoul Mamah, Nauris Bulvītis, Hélio Monteiro Batista, Ritvars Rugins, Eduards Tīdenbergs, Abdullahi Alfa (120.Medzit Neziri), Sename Dové Womé Dobe (53.Vasili Pavlov; 110.Amâncio José Pinto Fortes), Oluwatosin Aiyegun, Anastasijs Mordatenko. Trainer: Dejan Vukičević (Montenegro).

Penalties: Ivan Lukjanovs 1-0; Oluwatosin Aiyegun 1-1; Deniss Rakeļs (missed); Amâncio José Pinto Fortes 1-2; Kamil Biliński (missed); Ritvars Rugins (missed); Felipe Bezerra Brisola 2-2; Eduards Tīdenbergs (missed); Stefan Panić 3-2; Medzit Neziri 3-3; Volodymyr Baenko 4-3; Vadims Žuļevs 4-4; Tomislav Šarić 5-4; Nauris Bulvītis (saved).

THE CLUBS 2018

Futbola klubs Jelgava

Founded: 2004
Stadium: Olympic Sports Center of Zemgale, Jelgava (1,560)

Goalkeepers:	**DOB**	**M**	**(s)**	**G**
Jānis Krūmiņš	09.01.1992	13		
Vladislavs Kurakins	09.07.1996	12		
Mārcis Melecis	23.09.1991	3		
Defenders:	**DOB**	**M**	**(s)**	**G**
Vyacheslav Emeljanenko (RUS)	01.05.1995	15	(1)	
El Hadj Sady Guèye (SEN)	16.01.1990	2	(1)	
Viktors Litvinskis	07.02.1996		(1)	
Ivo Minkevičs	28.06.1999	17	(3)	1
Sigitas Olberkis (LTU)	19.04.1997	20	(2)	
Valērijs Redjko	10.03.1983	4	(3)	
Makhmadnaim Sharifi (RUS)	03.06.1992	12		
Maksim Shiryaev (RUS)	13.07.1995	17	(1)	
Midfielders:	**DOB**	**M**	**(s)**	**G**
Yaël Eisden (CUW)	11.01.1994	7	(1)	1
Mindaugas Grigaravičius (LTU)	15.07.1992	24	(3)	2
Edgars Jermolaevs	16.06.1992	1	(4)	
Andrejs Kiriļins	03.11.1995	11	(5)	
Andris Krušatins	01.09.1996	19	(5)	1
Artis Lazdiņš	03.05.1986	15	(1)	
Guram Lukava (GEO)	14.04.1995	14	(1)	2
Ryotaro Nakano (JPN)	13.06.1988	13	(6)	
Maksims Rafaļskis	14.05.1984	15	(3)	
Alans Siņeļnikovs	14.05.1990	16	(2)	2
Helvijs Staļģis	14.04.1999	6		
Daniils Ulimbaševs	12.03.1992	7	(5)	1
Forwards:	**DOB**	**M**	**(s)**	**G**
Daņiils Hvoiņickis	08.04.1998	8	(2)	1
Nikita Kolyaev (RUS)	23.07.1989	3	(3)	3
Vladislavs Kozlovs	30.11.1987	16	(3)	4
Marks Kurtišs	26.01.1998	18	(8)	1
Aleksandr Nekrasov (RUS)	20.08.1998		(3)	
Leo Salmiņš	24.02.1997		(2)	
Germans Saveļjevs	20.05.1999		(1)	
Trainer:	**DOB**	**M**		
Ravil Sabitov (RUS)	08.03.1968	10		
Marians Pahars [05.06.2018]	05.08.1976	18		

Futbola klubs Liepāja

Founded: 2014
Stadium: Daugava Stadium, Liepāja (5,008)

Goalkeepers:	DOB	M	(s)	G
Arsen Beglaryan (ARM)	18.02.1993	15		
Valentīns Raļkevičs	08.03.1991	1		
Krišjānis Zviedris	25.01.1997	12		
Defenders:	**DOB**	**M**	**(s)**	**G**
El Hadj Sady Guèye (SEN)	16.01.1990	12		
Deniss Ivanovs	11.01.1984	5	(6)	
Antons Jemeļins	19.02.1984	5	(2)	
Seydina Keita (SEN)	28.12.1992	27		4
Gonzalo Negro (ARG)	26.09.1994	17		1
Endijs Šlampe	24.07.1994	1	(1)	
Kristers Tobers	13.12.2000	23	(1)	2
Alexis Joel Zárate Maldonado (ARG)	08.05.1994	3		
Midfielders:	**DOB**	**M**	**(s)**	**G**
Deivids Dobrecovs	26.02.1997		(1)	
Toms Gucs	28.04.1992		(1)	
Dmitrijs Hmizs	31.07.1992	18	(6)	
Jānis Ikaunieks	16.02.1995	17		9
Raivis Jurkovskis	09.12.1996	18	(3)	1
Mārtiņš Ķigurs	31.03.1997	9	(8)	3
Igors Kozlovs	26.03.1987	19	(6)	1
Jānis Krautmanis	22.04.1997		(1)	
Khassim Soumaré (SEN)	23.12.1991	5		
Leonel Strumia (ARG)	29.09.1992	25	(2)	1
Benjamin Opeyemi Teidi (NGA)	07.05.1994	2	(3)	
Cristián Damián Torres	18.06.1985	19	(5)	
Forwards:	**DOB**	**M**	**(s)**	**G**
Verners Apiņš	14.04.1992	19	(3)	5
Kristaps Grebis	13.12.1980		(9)	1
Dame Guèye (SEN)	12.08.1995	2	(1)	
Vladimir Kamešs	28.10.1988	7		2
Artūrs Karašausks	29.01.1992	12		4
Ģirts Karlsons	07.06.1981	6	(11)	11
Ēriks Punculs	18.01.1994	9	(1)	1
Trainer:	**DOB**	**M**		
Tamaz Pertia	23.12.1974	14		
Mareks Zuntners [31.07.2018]	13.02.1983	5		
Gordon Young (SCO) [14.09.2018]	29.04.1964	9		

Futbola klubs Metta / Latvijas Universitāte Rīga

Founded: 02.05.2006
Stadium: Hanzas vidusskolas laukums, Rīga (2,000)

Goalkeepers:	DOB	M	(s)	G
Dāvis Ošs	03.12.1994	28		
Defenders:	**DOB**	**M**	**(s)**	**G**
Usman Abbas (NGA)	10.07.1998	21	(2)	
Emīls Birka	25.04.2000	8	(5)	
Krists Gulbis	15.01.1997	21		
Kabelo Seriba (RSA)	12.05.1997	26	(1)	1
Kirils Ševeļovs	02.06.1990	28		
Rendijs Šibass	01.05.1997	9	(15)	2
Dāvis Strods	24.02.1996	11	(6)	
Normunds Uldriķis	29.01.2001	5		
Midfielders:	**DOB**	**M**	**(s)**	**G**
Tamirlan Dzhamalutdinov (RUS)	28.07.1996	26	(1)	7
Eduards Emsis	23.02.1996	15	(1)	1
Benson Fazili (CAN)	12.01.2000	9	(2)	
Jēkabs Lagūns	16.01.2002	1	(8)	
Kristaps Liepa	14.03.1998	13	(1)	
Rihards Ozoliņš	31.05.2001	17	(7)	
Forwards:	**DOB**	**M**	**(s)**	**G**
Sunnyboy Sandi Dolo (LBR)	28.09.1996		(2)	
Vladislavs Fjodorovs	27.09.1996	26	(1)	5
Van-Dave Gbowea Harmon (LBR)	22.09.1995	9	(3)	2
Ņikita Ivanovs	25.03.1996	22	(1)	4
Ņikita Kovaļonoks	02.07.1995	7	(11)	1
Renārs Varslavāns	23.08.2001	6	(13)	
Matīss Zēģele	24.09.2000		(1)	
Trainer:	**DOB**	**M**		
Andris Riherts	31.05.1981	28		

Futbola klubs Rīgas Futbola Skola

Founded: 2011
Stadium: Stadions Arkādija, Rīga (1,000)

Goalkeepers:	DOB	M	(s)	G
Dmitrijs Grigorjevs	13.05.1992	1		
Kaspars Ikstens	05.06.1988	27		
Defenders:	**DOB**	**M**	**(s)**	**G**
Daniels Balodis	10.06.1998	2		
Kaspars Dubra	20.12.1990	23		4
Vjačeslavs Isajevs	27.08.1993	23		
Michael Ofosu-Appiah (GHA)	29.12.1989		(2)	
Nika Sandokhadze (GEO)	20.02.1994	8		
Milan Savić (SRB)	04.04.1994	16	(1)	
Lasha Shergelashvili (GEO)	17.01.1992	25	(2)	2
Aleksandrs Solovjovs	25.02.1988	17	(2)	1
Vladislavs Sorokins	10.05.1997	15	(6)	
Midfielders:	**DOB**	**M**	**(s)**	**G**
Elivelto Ribeiro Dantas (BRA)	02.01.1992	8	(5)	4
Aleksandrs Fertovs	16.06.1987	26		
Dāvis Indrāns	06.06.1995	7	(9)	2
Jevgēņijs Kazačoks	12.08.1995	4	(6)	
Gļebs Kļuškins	01.10.1992	16	(4)	5
Roberts Savaļnieks	04.02.1993	22	(6)	6
Beka Vachiberadze (GEO)	05.03.1996	24	(2)	5
Forwards:	**DOB**	**M**	**(s)**	**G**
Artis Jaudzems	04.04.1995		(12)	2
Maksim Marusych (UKR)	17.07.1993	27		14
Dmitry Platonov (BLR)	07.02.1986	7	(5)	1
Marko Regža	20.01.1999	1	(2)	1
Irakli Sikharulidze (GEO)	18.07.1990	5	(6)	1
Maksims Toņiševs	12.05.2000		(1)	
Roberts Uldriķis	03.04.1998	4	(6)	7
Trainer:	**DOB**	**M**		
Valdas Dambrauskas	07.01.1977	28		

Rīga Football Club

Founded: 2014 (*as merger of FC Caramba Riga and Dinamo Rīga*)
Stadium: Skonto Stadions, Rīga (8,207)

Goalkeepers:	DOB	M	(s)	G
Germans Māliņš	12.10.1987	4		
Roberts Ozols	10.09.1995	24		
Defenders:	**DOB**	**M**	**(s)**	**G**
Volodymyr Baenko (UKR)	09.02.1990	22	(1)	5
Antonijs Černomordijs	26.09.1996	16	(2)	
Vladislavs Gabovs	13.07.1987	13		1
Antons Kurakins	01.01.1990	21	(3)	1
Viktors Litvinskis	07.02.1996	1		
Mario Maslać (SRB)	09.09.1990	3		
Elvis Stuglis	04.07.1993	18	(1)	5
Midfielders:	**DOB**	**M**	**(s)**	**G**
Boriss Bogdaškins	21.02.1990	12	(2)	
Kristers Čudars	03.09.1999	1	(7)	
George Davies (SLE)	16.11.1996	15	(3)	
Ivan Enin (RUS)	06.02.1994	16	(5)	
Valeriy Fedorchuk (UKR)	05.10.1988	5	(2)	1
Felipe Bezerra Brisola (BRA)	06.06.1990	5	(2)	1
Krišs Kārkliņš	31.01.1996	12	(8)	1
Oļegs Laizāns	28.03.1987	6	(2)	
Romāns Mickevičs	29.03.1993	5	(4)	
Stefan Panić (SRB)	20.09.1992	12		
Armands Pētersons	05.12.1990	12	(6)	2
Tomislav Šarić (SVN)	24.06.1990	13	(1)	
Thiago De Almeida Primão (BRA)	11.02.1993	3	(3)	2
Bogdan Vaštšuk (EST)	04.10.1995	7	(2)	
Milan Vušurović (MNE)	18.04.1995	6	(2)	
Forwards:	**DOB**	**M**	**(s)**	**G**
Kamil Biliński (POL)	23.01.1988	3	(5)	2
Gaël Junior Etock (CMR)	05.07.1993		(6)	
Bohdan Kovalenko (UKR)	24.04.1997	5	(3)	
Darko Lemajić (SRB)	20.08.1993	21	(3)	15
Ivan Lukjanovs	24.01.1987	10	(1)	4
Ēriks Punculs	18.01.1994	2	(3)	
Deniss Rakeļs	20.08.1992	11	(1)	2
Sergiy Zagynaylov (UKR)	03.01.1991	4	(1)	2
Trainer:	**DOB**	**M**		
Goce Sedloski (MKD)	10.04.1974	9		
Mihails Koņevs [25.05.2018]	01.07.1963	5		
Viktor Skripnik (UKR) [05.07.2018]	19.11.1969	14		

Jūrmalas Futbola un Peldēšanas skola/ Futbola klubs Spartaks Jūrmala

Founded: 2007
Stadium: Slokas Stadium, Jūrmala (2,800)

Goalkeepers:	DOB	M	(s)	G
Mārcis Melecis	23.09.1991	2		
Jevģēnijs Nerugals	26.02.1989	25	(1)	
Andrejs Pavlovs	22.02.1979	1		
Defenders:	**DOB**	**M**	**(s)**	**G**
Gints Freimanis	09.05.1985	21	(2)	
Aleksandar Kosorić (BIH)	30.01.1987	27		1
Pāvels Mihadjuks	27.05.1980	13	(4)	1
Tomas Mikuckis (LTU)	13.01.1983	5	(1)	
Mārcis Ošs	25.07.1991	16		3
Ingus Šlampe	31.01.1989	24	(1)	1
Midfielders:	**DOB**	**M**	**(s)**	**G**
Oleg Dmitriev (RUS)	18.11.1995	11	(4)	2
Nikola Kovačević (SRB)	14.04.1994	2	(1)	
Andrejs Kovaļjovs	23.03.1989	8	(3)	2
Artemiy Maleev (RUS)	04.05.1991	25	(1)	5
Ingars Stuglis	12.02.1996	12	(5)	
Edgars Vardanjans	09.05.1993	5	(1)	
Aleksejs Višņakovs	03.02.1984	26	(1)	12
Vitor Silva Honorato „Vitor Faísca" (BRA)	16.04.1989	9	(1)	
Jurijs Žigajevs	14.11.1985	3	(4)	
Forwards:	**DOB**	**M**	**(s)**	**G**
Gadzhi Adzhiev (RUS)	01.06.1994		(1)	
Diego Ezequiel Aguirre (ARG)	11.01.1993	3	(6)	
Denis Davydov (RUS)	22.03.1995	7	(5)	2
Edgars Gauračs	10.03.1988		(7)	2
Evgeni Kobzar (RUS)	09.08.1992	23	(3)	6
Ričards Korzāns	03.05.1997	10	(10)	
Ariagner Steven Smith Medina (NCA)	13.12.1998	5	(7)	1
Aleksandr Prudnikov (RUS)	26.02.1989	9		4
Kaspars Svārups	28.01.1994	12	(11)	4
Rolands Vagančuks	05.01.1998	4		
Trainer:	**DOB**	**M**		
Samvel Babayan (UZB)	19.05.1971	3		
Aleksandr Grishin [21.04.2018]	18.11.1971	13		
Tomas Ražanauskas (LTU) [13.08.2018]	07.01.1976	12		

Valmieras Glass / Vidzemes Augstskola Futbola klubs

Founded: 1996
Stadium: „Jānis Daliņš" Stadions, Valmiera (2,000)

Goalkeepers:	DOB	M	(s)	G
Elvis Arnavs	08.04.1994	12		
Marks Bogdanovs	02.12.1986	13		
Kaspars Ribaks	02.08.1990	3		
Defenders:	**DOB**	**M**	**(s)**	**G**
Anthony Bakmaz (AUS)	07.03.1992	6		
Alexandru Belevschi (MDA)	21.03.1995	2	(3)	
Roberts Cipe	27.07.1997	17	(4)	1
Ivan Knyazev (RUS)	05.11.1992	2		
Klāvs Kramēns	07.07.2000	10	(2)	
Madis Miķelsons	18.01.1994	26		
Camrom William Junior Nguesseu (SWE)	30.11.1995	2		
Niks Rubežis	30.09.1998		(1)	
Massamba Sambou (SEN)	17.09.1986	3		1
Elmārs Sietinsons	01.11.1996	16	(4)	1
Artūrs Talcis	15.10.2001		(1)	
Midfielders:	**DOB**	**M**	**(s)**	**G**
Artūrs Bankavs	05.08.1994	16		1
Māris Barkovskis	12.02.2002	2	(2)	1
Mārcis Ērglis	17.01.1992	23	(1)	3
Alvis Jaunzems	16.06.1999	25	(1)	3
Valts Jaunzems	18.09.1995	17	(6)	1
Thierry Mukuta Kiesse (COD)	05.01.1989	5		
Egils Arturs Nazarovs	14.05.2000		(7)	
Artūrs Pallo	27.02.1989	16		1
Eduards Stīpnieks	28.11.1998	7	(8)	
Jānis Taulavičus	14.04.1999	7	(5)	
Valdis Veinbergs	12.01.1982	5	(1)	
Kārlis Zvirbulis	16.03.2001		(1)	
Forwards:	**DOB**	**M**	**(s)**	**G**
Ulvis Bērziņš	17.06.1997	13	(5)	1
Konstantīns Fjodorovs	28.04.1996	3	(3)	
Rashid Hesus Grigorio Browne (NED)	28.09.1993	4	(6)	
Gatis Kalniņš	12.08.1981	18	(4)	3
Kristers Lūsiņš	09.05.2000	13	(7)	2
Erik Ricardo Persson Gray (SWE)	01.09.1993	9	(4)	3
Ingars Pūlis	24.01.2001		(1)	
Niks Savaļnieks	06.05.1987	11	(4)	
Rolands Vagančuks	05.01.1998	2	(2)	
Trainer:	**DOB**	**M**		
Gatis Erglis	24.04.1969	10		
Nikolay Trubachov (UKR) [30.05.1997]	20.05.1957	18		

Futbola klubs Ventspils

Founded: 1997
Stadium: Ventspils Olimpiskais Stadions, Ventspils (3,044)

Goalkeepers:	DOB	M	(s)	G
Ivans Baturins	25.06.1997	2		
Vitālijs Meļņičenko	11.11.1987	19		
Maksims Uvarenko	17.01.1987	7		
Defenders:	**DOB**	**M**	**(s)**	**G**
Nauris Bulvītis	15.03.1987	26		2
Hélio Monteiro Batista (BRA)	28.01.1990	6	(5)	2
Vitālijs Jagodinskis	28.02.1992	13		
Dmitrijs Klimaševičs	16.04.1995	1	(2)	
Ņikita Koļesovs	25.09.1996	13		
Dmitrijs Litvinskis	17.08.1999	2	(1)	
Abdoul Mamah (TOG)	24.08.1985	15	(3)	
Medzit Neziri (MKD)	02.09.1990	1	(7)	
Rashid Abdul Obuobi (GHA)	18.12.1994	7	(1)	
Artjoms Solomatovs	09.08.1994			
Vadims Žuļevs	01.03.1988	19	(3)	1
Midfielders:	**DOB**	**M**	**(s)**	**G**
Abdullahi Alfa (NGA)	29.07.1996	10	(3)	1
Mariss Bite	08.11.1999		(2)	
Maxim Cojocaru (MDA)	13.01.1998		(6)	
Artem Filimonov (UKR)	21.02.1994	2	(2)	
Giuly Mandzhgaladze (UKR)	09.09.1992	4	(4)	2
Pedro Rafael Amado Mendes (POR)	06.12.1993	7		1
Vitālijs Rečickis	08.09.1986	12		
Ritvars Rugins	17.10.1989	22	(2)	1
Sténio Nivaldo Matos dos Santos (CPV)	06.05.1988	9	(2)	3
Raens Tālbergs	14.09.2000	2	(7)	
Eduards Tīdenbergs	18.12.1994	20	(6)	1
Sename Dové Womé Dobe (TOG)	08.06.1991	10	(1)	2
Forwards:	**DOB**	**M**	**(s)**	**G**
Oluwatosin Aiyegun (NGA)	26.06.1998	27		14
Adeleke Akinola Akinyemi (NGA)	11.08.1998	17		13
Aleksey Alekseev (RUS)	12.06.1988	1	(4)	
Kirill Burykin (RUS)	06.08.1998	1	(3)	
Amâncio José Pinto Fortes (ANG)	18.04.1990	8	(1)	5
Oleksiy Antonov (UKR)	08.05.1986	7	(4)	3
Kaspars Kokins	26.04.2000	1	(6)	
Anastasijs Mordatenko	24.08.1996	10	(1)	3
Vasili Pavlov (RUS)	24.07.1990	7	(5)	
Trainer:	**DOB**	**M**		
Dejan Vukičević (MNE)	27.04.1968	28		

SECOND LEVEL
komanda.lv Pirmā līga 2018

Regular Season

1.	BFC Daugavpils/Progress*	22	19	1	2	120	-	14	58
2.	SK Super Nova Olaine	22	17	2	3	81	-	20	53
3.	FK Tukums 2000/TSS	22	16	0	6	53	-	21	48
4.	Rēzeknes FA/BJSS	22	12	3	7	71	-	33	39
5.	FK Auda Rīga	22	12	1	9	45	-	48	37
6.	RTU FC/Skonto Academy Rīga	22	10	5	7	70	-	33	35
7.	FK Smiltene/BJSS	22	10	3	9	54	-	63	33
8.	JDFS Alberts Rīga	22	8	4	10	39	-	48	28
9.	Grobiņas SC	22	6	2	14	40	-	75	20
10.	Balvu Sporta centrs	22	3	3	16	19	-	115	12
11.	FK Staiceles Bebri (*Relegated*)	22	2	4	16	15	-	78	10
12.	Preiļu BJSS (*Relegated*)	22	3	0	19	24	-	83	9

*merger between BFC Daugavpils and FK Progress Olaine.
Top-4 teams qualified for the Promotion Round.

Promotion Round

1.	BFC Daugavpils/Progress (*Promoted*)	25	22	1	2	131	-	16	67
2.	SK Super Nova Olaine (*Promotion Play-offs*)	25	19	2	4	90	-	27	59
3.	FK Tukums 2000/TSS	25	17	0	8	57	-	27	51
4.	Rēzeknes FA/BJSS	25	12	3	10	76	-	47	39

NATIONAL TEAM

INTERNATIONAL MATCHES
(16.07.2018 – 15.07.2019)

06.09.2018	Rīga	Latvia - Andorra	0-0	(UNL)
09.09.2018	Tbilisi	Georgia - Latvia	1-0(0-0)	(UNL)
13.10.2018	Rīga	Latvia - Kazakhstan	1-1(1-1)	(UNL)
16.10.2018	Rīga	Latvia - Georgia	0-3(0-2)	(UNL)
15.11.2018	Astana	Kazakhstan - Latvia	1-1(1-0)	(UNL)
19.11.2018	Andorra la Vella	Andorra - Latvia	0-0	(UNL)
21.03.2019	Skopje	North Macedonia - Latvia	3-1(2-0)	(ECQ)
24.03.2019	Warszawa	Poland - Latvia	2-0(0-0)	(ECQ)
07.06.2019	Rīga	Latvia - Israel	0-3(0-1)	(ECQ)
10.06.2019	Rīga	Latvia - Slovenia	0-5(0-4)	(ECQ)

06.09.2018 LATVIA - ANDORRA 0-0 UEFA Nations League D, Group 1
Daugavas Stadions, Rīga; Referee: Keith Kennedy (Northern Ireland); Attendance: 4,803
LVA: Andris Vaņins (Cap), Vladislavs Gabovs, Aleksandrs Solovjovs (76.Artūrs Karašausks), Kaspars Dubra, Vitālijs Jagodinskis, Ivans Lukjanovs, Aleksandrs Fertovs, Glebs Kļuškins, Dāvis Ikaunieks (61.Roberts Uldrikis), Deniss Rakeļs, Valerijs Šabala (84.Vladislavs Gutkovskis). Trainer: Mika-Matti Petteri Paatelainen (Finland).

09.09.2018 GEORGIA - LATVIA 1-0(0-0) UEFA Nations League D, Group 1
"Boris Paichadze" Dinamo Arena, Tbilisi; Referee: Referee: Anastasios Papapetrou (Greece); Attendance: 45,716
LVA: Andris Vaņins (Cap), Vladislavs Gabovs, Kaspars Dubra, Vitālijs Maksimenko, Vitālijs Jagodinskis, Vjačeslavs Isajevs, Ivans Lukjanovs (81.Deniss Rakeļs), Aleksandrs Fertovs, Ritvars Rugins (78.Roberts Savaļnieks), Artūrs Karašausks, Vladislavs Gutkovskis (72.Valerijs Šabala). Trainer: Mika-Matti Petteri Paatelainen (Finland).

13.10.2018 LATVIA - KAZAKHSTAN 1-1(1-1) UEFA Nations League D, Group 1
Daugava stadions, Rīga; Referee: Harald Lechner (Austria); Attendance: 4,878
LVA: Andris Vaņins (Cap), Kaspars Dubra, Vitālijs Maksimenko, Vitālijs Jagodinskis, Vjačeslavs Isajevs (27.Aleksandrs Fertovs), Ivans Lukjanovs, Ritvars Rugins (67.Andrejs Cigaņiks), Deniss Rakeļs, Valerijs Šabala, Roberts Savaļnieks, Artūrs Karašausks (73.Vladislavs Gutkovskis). Trainer: Mika-Matti Petteri Paatelainen (Finland).
Goal: Artūrs Karašausks (40).

16.10.2018 LATVIA - GEORGIA 0-3(0-2) UEFA Nations League D, Group 1
Daugavas Stadions, Rīga; Referee: Petr Ardeleanu (Czech Republic); Attendance: 3,185
LVA: Andris Vaņins (Cap), Vadims Žuļevs, Igors Tarasovs, Kaspars Dubra, Vitālijs Maksimenko, Vitālijs Jagodinskis, Aleksandrs Fertovs (46.Vjačeslavs Isajevs), Andrejs Cigaņiks, Deniss Rakeļs, Artūrs Karašausks (70.Dāvis Ikaunieks), Vladislavs Gutkovskis (71.Valerijs Šabala). Trainer: Mika-Matti Petteri Paatelainen (Finland).

15.11.2018 KAZAKHSTAN - LATVIA 1-1(1-0) UEFA Nations League D, Group 1
Astana Arena, Astana; Referee: Jens Maae (Denmark); Attendance: 21,463
LVA: Andris Vaņins (Cap), Vladislavs Gabovs, Igors Tarasovs, Kaspars Dubra, Vitālijs Maksimenko, Vitālijs Jagodinskis, Vjačeslavs Isajevs, Andrejs Cigaņiks (46.Roberts Savaļnieks), Deniss Rakeļs, Valerijs Šabala (72.Dāvis Ikaunieks), Artūrs Karašausks (62.Ritvars Rugins). Trainer: Mika-Matti Petteri Paatelainen (Finland).
Goal: Deniss Rakeļs (48).

19.11.2018 ANDORRA - LATVIA 0-0 UEFA Nations League D, Group 1
Estadi Nacional, Andorra la Vella; Referee: Halil Umut Meler (Turkey); Attendance: 1,021
LVA: Andris Vaņins (Cap), Vladislavs Gabovs, Igors Tarasovs, Kaspars Dubra, Vitālijs Maksimenko, Vitālijs Jagodinskis, Vjačeslavs Isajevs, Andrejs Cigaņiks (46.Roberts Savaļnieks), Deniss Rakeļs, Valerijs Šabala (72.Dāvis Ikaunieks), Artūrs Karašausks (62.Ritvars Rugins). Trainer: Mika-Matti Petteri Paatelainen (Finland).

21.03.2019 NORTH MACEDONIA - LATVIA 3-1(2-0) 16th EC. Qualifiers
"Toše Proeski" National Arena, Skopje; Referee: Halis Özkahya (Turkey); Attendance: 7,043
LVA: Andris Vaņins (Cap) (33.Pāvels Šteinbors), Vladislavs Gabovs, Igors Tarasovs, Kaspars Dubra, Vitālijs Maksimenko, Vjačeslavs Isajevs, Mārcis Ošs, Andrejs Cigaņiks [*sent off 90+1*], Deniss Rakeļs, Valerijs Šabala (79.Roberts Uldrikis), Artūrs Karašausks (68.Kristers Tobers). Trainer: Slaviša Stojanovič (Slovenia).
Goal: Darko Velkovski (87 own goal).

24.03.2019 POLAND - LATVIA 2-0(0-0) 16th EC. Qualifiers
Stadion PGE Narodowy, Warszawa; Referee: Aliyar Aghayev (Azerbaijan); Attendance: 51,112
LVA: Pāvels Šteinbors, Kaspars Dubra (Cap), Vitālijs Maksimenko, Vjačeslavs Isajevs, Mārcis Ošs, Oļegs Laizāns, Dāvis Ikaunieks, Deniss Rakeļs, Roberts Savaļnieks (80.Vladislavs Gabovs), Vladislavs Gutkovskis (70.Roberts Uldrikis), Artūrs Karašausks (85.Kristers Tobers). Trainer: Slaviša Stojanovič (Slovenia).

07.06.2019 LATVIA - ISRAEL 0-3(0-1) 16th EC. Qualifiers
Daugava Stadions, Rīga; Referee: Sergei Ivanov (Russia); Attendance: 5,508
LVA: Pāvels Šteinbors, Kaspars Dubra (Cap), Vitālijs Maksimenko, Mārcis Ošs, Oļegs Laizāns (79.Ritvars Rugins), Jānis Ikaunieks (57.Andrejs Cigaņiks), Kristers Tobers, Deniss Rakeļs, Roberts Savaļnieks, Artūrs Karašausks (67.Vladimirs Kamešs), Vladislavs Gutkovskis. Trainer: Slaviša Stojanovič (Slovenia).

10.06.2019 LATVIA - SLOVENIA 0-5(0-4) 16th EC. Qualifiers
Daugava Stadions, Rīga; Referee: Kevin Clancy (Scotland); Attendance: 4,011
LVA: Pāvels Šteinbors, Aleksandrs Solovjovs, Kaspars Dubra (Cap), Vitālijs Maksimenko (16.Vitālijs Jagodinskis), Mārcis Ošs, Vladimirs Kamešs, Oļegs Laizāns, Kristers Tobers (69.Ritvars Rugins), Deniss Rakeļs (78.Daniels Ontužāns), Roberts Savaļnieks, Vladislavs Gutkovskis. Trainer: Slaviša Stojanovič (Slovenia).

NATIONAL TEAM PLAYERS
(16.07.2018 – 15.07.2019)

Name	DOB	Caps	Goals	2018/2019:	*Club*
Goalkeepers					
Pāvels ŠTEINBORS	21.09.1985	**8**	**0**	2019:	*MKS Arka Gdynia (POL)*
Andris VAŅINS	30.04.1980	**97**	**0**	2018/2019:	*FC Zürich (SUI)*
Defenders					
Kaspars DUBRA	20.12.1990	**32**	**2**	2018: 04.01.2019->	*FK Rīgas Futbola Skola* *FC Irtysh Pavlodar (KAZ)*
Vladislavs GABOVS	13.07.1987	**41**	**0**	2018/2019:	*Rīga FC*
Vitālijs JAGODINSKIS	28.02.1992	**29**	**0**	2018: 21.01.2019->	*FK Ventspils* *FK Rīgas Futbola Skola*
Vitālijs MAKSIMENKO	08.12.1990	**46**	**1**	2018/2019:	*NK Olimpija Ljubljana (SVN)*
Mārcis OŠS	25.07.1991	**7**	**0**	2019:	*Neuchâtel Xamax FCS (SUI)*
Aleksandrs SOLOVJOVS	25.02.1988	**9**	**0**	2018/2019:	*FK Rīgas Futbola Skola*
Igors TARASOVS	16.10.1988	**30**	**1**	2018/2019:	*WKS Śląsk Wrocław (POL)*
Vadims ŽUĻEVS	01.03.1988	**1**	**0**	2018:	*FK Ventspils*
Midfielders					
Andrejs CIGAŅIKS	12.04.1997	**6**	**0**	2018/2019:	*SC Cambuur Leeuwarden (NED)*
Aleksandrs FERTOVS	16.06.1987	**42**	**0**	2018:	*FK Rīgas Futbola Skola*
Jānis IKAUNIEKS	16.02.1995	**21**	**3**	2019:	*FK Liepāja*
Vjačeslavs ISAJEVS	27.08.1993	**7**	**0**	2018/2019:	*FK Rīgas Futbola Skola*
Vladimirs KAMEŠS	28.10.1988	**19**	**1**	2019:	*FK SKA-Khabarovsk (RUS)*
Gļebs KĻUŠKINS	01.10.1992	**18**	**1**	2018:	*FK Rīgas Futbola Skola*
Oļegs LAIZĀNS	28.03.1987	**49**	**0**	2019:	*Rīga FC*
Ivans LUKJANOVS	24.01.1987	**20**	**0**	2018:	*Rīga FC*
Daniels ONTUŽĀNS	07.03.2000	**1**	**0**	2019:	*FC Bayern München II (GER)*
Ritvars RUGINS	17.10.1989	**32**	**0**	2018: 07.01.2019->	*FK Ventspils* *Rīga FC*
Roberts SAVAĻNIEKS	04.02.1993	**14**	**0**	2018/2019:	*FK Rīgas Futbola Skola*
Kristers TOBERS	13.12.2000	**4**	**0**	2019:	*FK Liepāja*
Forwards					
Vladislavs GUTKOVSKIS	02.04.1995	**12**	**0**	2018/2019:	*Bruk-Bet Termalica Nieciecza KS (POL)*
Dāvis IKAUNIEKS	07.01.1994	**21**	**4**	2018/2019:	*FK Jablonec (CZE)*
Artūrs KARAŠAUSKS	29.01.1992	**24**	**1**	2018: 08.02.2019->	*FC Akzhayik Oral (KAZ)* *Rīga FC*
Deniss RAKEĻS	20.08.1992	**30**	**1**	2018: 01.01.2019->	*Rīga FC* *Pafos FC Paphos (CYP)*
Valērijs ŠABALA	12.10.1994	**51**	**12**	2018/2019:	*TS Podbeskidzie Bielsko-Biała (POL)*
Roberts ULDRIĶIS	03.04.1998	**10**	**1**	2018/2019:	*FC Sion (SUI)*

National team coach

Mika-Matti Petteri PAATELAINEN (Finland) [10.05.2018 – 04.12.2018]	03.02.1967	9 M; 1 W; 5 D; 3 L; 5-10
Slaviša STOJANOVIČ (Slovenia) [from 01.03.2019]	06.12.1969	4 M; 0 W; 0 D; 4 L; 1-13

LIECHTENSTEIN

The Country:

Fürstentum Liechtenstein (Principality of Liechtenstein)
Capital: Vaduz
Surface: 160 km²
Inhabitants: 38,547 [2017]
Time: UTC+1

The FA:

Liechtensteiner Fussballverband
Landstrasse 149, 9494 Schaan
Tel: +423 237 4747
Foundation date: 1934
Member of FIFA since: 1974
Member of UEFA since: 1974
Website: www.lfv.li

NATIONAL TEAM RECORDS

First international match:	09.03.1982, Balzers:	Liechtenstein – Switzerland 0-1
Most international caps:	Peter Karl Jehle	- 132 caps (1998-2018)
Most international goals:	Mario Frick	- 16 goals / 125 caps (1993-2015)

UEFA EUROPEAN CHAMPIONSHIP	
1960	Did not enter
1964	Did not enter
1968	Did not enter
1972	Did not enter
1976	Did not enter
1980	Did not enter
1984	Did not enter
1988	Did not enter
1992	Did not enter
1996	Qualifiers
2000	Qualifiers
2004	Qualifiers
2008	Qualifiers
2012	Qualifiers
2016	Qualifiers

FIFA WORLD CUP	
1930	Did not enter
1934	Did not enter
1938	Did not enter
1950	Did not enter
1954	Did not enter
1958	Did not enter
1962	Did not enter
1966	Did not enter
1970	Did not enter
1974	Did not enter
1978	Did not enter
1982	Did not enter
1986	Did not enter
1990	Did not enter
1994	Did not enter
1998	Qualifiers
2002	Qualifiers
2006	Qualifiers
2010	Qualifiers
2014	Qualifiers
2018	Qualifiers

UEFA NATIONS LEAGUE

2018/2019 – League D

OLYMPIC FOOTBALL TOURNAMENTS 1908-2016

1988, 2008, 2012, 2016 (Qualifiers)

FIFA CONFEDERATIONS CUP 1992-2017

None

LIECHTENSTEIN CLUB HONOURS IN EUROPEAN CLUB COMPETITIONS:

European Champion Clubs' Cup (1956-1992) / UEFA Champions League (1993-2019)

None

Fairs Cup (1858-1971) / UEFA Cup (1972-2009) / UEFA Europa League (2010-2019)

None

UEFA Super Cup (1972-2018)

None

European Cup Winners' Cup 1961-1999*

None

**defunct competition*

NATIONAL COMPETITIONS
TABLE OF HONOURS

	CHAMPIONS
1932	FC Vaduz (*unofficial*)
1934	FC Triesen
1935	FC Triesen
1936	FC Vaduz
1937	FC Triesen

CUP WINNERS

1945/1946	FC Triesen	1970/1971	FC Vaduz	1995/1996	FC Vaduz
1946/1947	FC Triesen	1971/1972	FC Triesen	1996/1997	FC Balzers
1947/1948	FC Triesen	1972/1973	FC Balzers	1997/1998	FC Vaduz
1948/1949	FC Vaduz	1973/1974	FC Vaduz	1998/1999	FC Vaduz
1949/1950	FC Triesen	1974/1975	FC Triesen	1999/2000	FC Vaduz
1950/1951	FC Triesen	1975/1976	USV Eschen/Mauren	2000/2001	FC Vaduz
1951/1952	FC Vaduz	1976/1977	USV Eschen/Mauren	2001/2002	FC Vaduz
1952/1953	FC Vaduz	1977/1978	USV Eschen/Mauren	2002/2003	FC Vaduz
1953/1954	FC Vaduz	1978/1979	FC Balzers	2003/2004	FC Vaduz
1954/1955	FC Schaan	1979/1980	FC Vaduz	2004/2005	FC Vaduz
1955/1956	FC Vaduz	1980/1981	FC Balzers	2005/2006	FC Vaduz
1956/1957	FC Vaduz	1981/1982	FC Balzers	2006/2007	FC Vaduz
1957/1958	FC Vaduz	1982/1983	FC Balzers	2007/2008	FC Vaduz
1958/1959	FC Vaduz	1983/1984	FC Balzers	2008/2009	FC Vaduz
1959/1960	FC Vaduz	1984/1985	FC Vaduz	2009/2010	FC Vaduz
1960/1961	FC Vaduz	1985/1986	FC Vaduz	2010/2011	FC Vaduz
1961/1962	FC Vaduz	1986/1987	USV Eschen/Mauren	2011/2012	USV Eschen/Mauren
1962/1963	FC Schaan	1987/1988	FC Vaduz	2012/2013	FC Vaduz
1963/1964	FC Balzers	1988/1989	FC Balzers	2013/2014	FC Vaduz
1964/1965	FC Triesen	1989/1990	FC Vaduz	2014/2015	FC Vaduz
1965/1966	FC Vaduz	1990/1991	FC Balzers	2015/2016	FC Vaduz
1966/1967	FC Vaduz	1991/1992	FC Vaduz	2016/2017	FC Vaduz
1967/1968	FC Vaduz	1992/1993	FC Balzers	2017/2018	FC Vaduz
1968/1969	FC Vaduz	1993/1994	FC Schaan	2018/2019	FC Vaduz
1969/1970	FC Vaduz	1994/1995	FC Vaduz		

NATIONAL CUP
Liechtensteiner Cup 2018/2019

First Round [21-28.08.2018]	
FC Triesenberg - FC Balzers II	4-1
FC Schaan II - FC Ruggell II	0-3
FC Triesenberg II - USV Eschen/Mauren II	1-2

Secoond Round [12-25.09.2018]	
FC Triesen - USV Eschen/Mauren II	0-1
FC Triesen II - FC Schaan	1-5
USV Eschen/Mauren III - FC Triesenberg	0-4
FC Ruggell II - FC Balzers III	4-1

Quarter-Finals [23/24.10.-07.11.2018]			
FC Triesenberg - USV Eschen/Mauren	1-5	USV Eschen/Mauren II - FC Ruggell	1-5
FC Ruggell II - FC Schaan	0-3	FC Balzers - FC Vaduz	1-2

Semi-Finals [09.04.2019]			
USV Eschen/Mauren - FC Vaduz	0-1	FC Schaan - FC Ruggell	0-1

Final

01.05.2019; Rheinpark Stadion, Vaduz; Referee: Alessandro Dudic (Switzerland); Attendance: 1,122

FC Vaduz - FC Rugell **3-2(1-1)**

FC Vaduz: Andreas Hirzel, Maximilian Göppel (27.Nils Von Niderhäusern), Tomislav Puljic, Berkay Sülüngöz, Sandro Wieser (46.Milan Gajic), Gianni Antoniazzi, Boris Prokopic (78.Aron Sele), Philipp Muntwiler, Maurice Brunner, Mohamed Coulibaly (66.Manuel Sutter), Igor Tadic. Trainer: Mario Frick.

FC Rugell: Pirmin Marxer, Philipp Seemann, Manuel Ritter, Alexander Marxer, Stefan Maag (51.Johannes Hirschbühl), Nicola Kollmann (72.Stefan Bischof), Shkelqim Mamuti, Luca Ritter, Menderes Caglar (77.Leoran Amzi), Alessandro Crescenti (59.Agan Amzi), Agim Zeciri. Trainer: Vito Troisio.

Goals: 1-0 Sandro Wieser (36), 1-1 Nicola Kollmann (45), 2-1 Mohamed Coulibaly (52), 3-1 Berkay Sülüngöz (77), 3-2 Agim Zeciri (86 penalty).

NATIONAL TEAM

INTERNATIONAL MATCHES
(16.07.2018 – 15.07.2019)

06.09.2018	Yerevan	Armenia - Liechtenstein	2-1(1-1)	(UNL)
09.09.2018	Vaduz	Liechtenstein - Gibraltar	2-0(1-0)	(UNL)
13.10.2018	Skopje	North Macedonia - Liechtenstein	4-1(3-1)	(UNL)
16.10.2018	Gibraltar	Gibraltar - Liechtenstein	2-1(0-1)	(UNL)
16.11.2018	Vaduz	Liechtenstein - North Macedonia	0-2(0-0)	(UNL)
19.11.2018	Vaduz	Liechtenstein - Armenia	2-2(1-1)	(UNL)
23.03.2019	Vaduz	Liechtenstein - Greece	0-2(0-1)	(ECQ)
26.03.2019	Parma	Italy - Liechtenstein	6-0(4-0)	(ECQ)
08.06.2019	Yerevan	Armenia - Liechtenstein	3-0(2-0)	(ECQ)
11.06.2019	Vaduz	Liechtenstein - Finland	0-2(0-1)	(ECQ)

06.09.2018 ARMENIA - LIECHTENSTEIN 2-1(1-1) UEFA Nations League D, Group 4
„Vazgen Sargsyan" Hanrapetakan Stadium, Yerevan; Referee: Enea Jorgji (Albania); Attendance: 5,132
LIE: Benjamin Büchel, Martin Rechsteiner (80.Seyhan Yildiz), Daniel Kaufmann, Nicolas Hasler, Maximilian Göppel, Michele Polverino (Cap) [*sent off 74*], Sandro Wieser, Sandro Wolfinger (81.Livio Meier), Aron Sele, Dennis Salanović, Philippe Erne (48.Simon Kühne). Trainer: René Pauritsch (Austria).
Goal: Sandro Wolfinger (33).

09.09.2018 LIECHTENSTEIN - GIBRALTAR 2-0(1-0) UEFA Nations League D, Group 4
Rheinpark Stadion, Vaduz; Referee: Alan Mario Sant (Malta); Attendance: 1,110
LIE: Benjamin Büchel, Daniel Kaufmann, Nicolas Hasler (Cap), Ivan Quintans, Maximilian Göppel, Sandro Wieser, Sandro Wolfinger (74.Simon Kühne), Aron Sele, Dennis Salanović, Livio Meier (89.Niklas Kieber), Robin Gubser (82.Seyhan Yildiz). Trainer: René Pauritsch (Austria).
Goals: Dennis Salanović (32), Sandro Wieser (72).

13.10.2018 NORTH MACEDONIA - LIECHTENSTEIN 4-1(3-1) UEFA Nations League D, Group 4
"Toše Proeski" National Arena, Skopje; Referee: Roi Reinshreiber (Israel); Attendance: 8,100
LIE: Benjamin Büchel, Martin Rechsteiner, Daniel Kaufmann, Nicolas Hasler, Seyhan Yildiz, Maximilian Göppel, Michele Polverino (Cap), Sandro Wieser, Marcel Büchel (72.Philippe Erne), Sandro Wolfinger (79.Niklas Kieber), Aron Sele (29.Robin Gubser). Trainer: René Pauritsch (Austria).
Goal: Seyhan Yildiz (37).

16.10.2018 GIBRALTAR - LIECHTENSTEIN 2-1(0-1) UEFA Nations League D, Group 4
Victoria Stadium, Gibraltar; Referee: Vasilis Dimitriou (Cyprus); Attendance: 2,000
LIE: Benjamin Büchel, Daniel Kaufmann, Nicolas Hasler, Fabian Eberle, Maximilian Göppel, Michele Polverino (Cap) (83.Philippe Erne), Sandro Wieser (46.Andreas Malin), Marcel Büchel (68.Marco Wolfinger), Dennis Salanović, Livio Meier, Robin Gubser. Trainer: René Pauritsch (Austria).
Goal: Dennis Salanović (15).

16.11.2018 LIECHTENSTEIN - NORTH MACEDONIA 0-2(0-0) UEFA Nations League D, Group 4
Rheinpark Stadion, Vaduz; Referee: Petr Ardeleanu (Czech Republic); Attendance: 2,116
LIE: Benjamin Büchel, Martin Rechsteiner, Nicolas Hasler, Ivan Quintans (76.Fabian Eberle), Maximilian Göppel, Michele Polverino (Cap), Sandro Wieser [*sent off 50*], Daniel Matthias Brändle (75.Philippe Erne), Aron Sele (76.Marcel Büchel), Dennis Salanović, Livio Meier. Trainer: René Pauritsch (Austria).

19.11.2018 LIECHTENSTEIN - ARMENIA 2-2(1-1) UEFA Nations League D, Group 4
Rheinpark Stadion, Vaduz; Referee: Alain Durieux (Luxembourg); Attendance: 1,166
LIE: Benjamin Büchel, Martin Rechsteiner, Nicolas Hasler, Ivan Quintans (83.Fabian Eberle), Maximilian Göppel, Jens Hofer, Michele Polverino (Cap), Marcel Büchel (62.Daniel Matthias Brändle), Aron Sele (57.Martin Büchel), Dennis Salanović, Livio Meier. Trainer: René Pauritsch (Austria).
Goals: Marcel Büchel (44), Nicolas Hasler (47).

23.03.2019 LIECHTENSTEIN - GREECE 0-2(0-1) 16th EC. Qualifiers
Rheinpark Stadion, Vaduz; Referee: Alexandre Boucaut (Belgium); Attendance: 2,711
LIE: Benjamin Büchel, Martin Rechsteiner, Daniel Kaufmann, Nicolas Hasler (86.Noah Frick), Maximilian Göppel, Martin Büchel (67.Aron Sele), Michele Polverino (Cap), Sandro Wieser, Sandro Wolfinger, Dennis Salanović, Robin Gubser (76.Seyhan Yildiz). Trainer: Helgi Kolviðsson (Iceland).

26.03.2019 ITALY - LIECHTENSTEIN 6-0(4-0) 16th EC. Qualifiers
Stadio "Ennio Tardini", Parma; Referee: Kirill Levnikov (Russia); Attendance: 19,834
LIE: Benjamin Büchel, Daniel Kaufmann [*sent off 45+2*], Nicolas Hasler, Maximilian Göppel, Jens Hofer, Michele Polverino (Cap), Sandro Wieser, Sandro Wolfinger, Aron Sele (46.Andreas Malin), Dennis Salanović (82.Martin Büchel), Simon Kühne (68.Livio Meier). Trainer: Helgi Kolviðsson (Iceland).

08.06.2019 ARMENIA - LIECHTENSTEIN 3-0(2-0) 16th EC. Qualifiers
„Vazgen Sargsyan" Hanrapetakan Stadium, Yerevan; Referee: Nikola Popov (Bulgaria); Attendance: 10,000
LIE: Thomas Hobi, Maximilian Göppel, Nicolas Hasler, Andreas Malin, Jens Hofer, Michele Polverino (Cap), Marcel Büchel, Sandro Wolfinger (85.Daniel Matthias Brändle), Aron Sele (81.Livio Meier), Dennis Salanović, Yanik Frick (46.Simon Kühne). Trainer: Helgi Kolviðsson (Iceland).

11.06.2019 LIECHTENSTEIN - FINLAND 0-2(0-1) 16th EC. Qualifiers
Rheinpark Stadion, Vaduz; Referee: Jens Maae (Denmark); Attendance: 2,160
LIE: Thomas Hobi, Martin Rechsteiner, Daniel Kaufmann, Nicolas Hasler (Cap), Jens Hofer, Sandro Wieser (46.Michele Polverino), Marcel Büchel (54.Martin Büchel), Sandro Wolfinger (77.Daniel Matthias Brändle), Aron Sele, Dennis Salanović, Simon Kühne. Trainer: Helgi Kolviðsson (Iceland).

NATIONAL TEAM PLAYERS (16.07.2018 – 15.07.2019)					
Name	**DOB**	**Caps**	**Goals**	**2018/2019:**	***Club***
Goalkeepers					
Benjamin BÜCHEL	04.07.1989	**23**	**0**	2018/2019:	*FC Thalwil Ochsenrain (SUI)*
Thomas HOBI	20.06.1993	**2**	**0**	2019:	*VfB Hohenems (AUT)*
Defenders					
Daniel Matthias BRÄNDLE	23.01.1992	**23**	**0**	2018/2019:	*SV Pullach (GER)*
Fabian EBERLE	27.07.1992	**7**	**0**	2018:	*FC Konolfingen (SUI)*
Maximilian GÖPPEL	31.08.1997	**24**	**1**	2018/2019:	*FC Vaduz*
Jens HOFER	01.10.1997	**4**	**0**	2018/2019:	*FC Münsingen (SUI)*
Daniel KAUFMANN	22.12.1990	**53**	**1**	2018/2019:	*FC Balzers*
Andreas MALIN	31.01.1994	**14**	**0**	2018/2019:	*FC Dornbirn (AUT)*
Michele POLVERINO	26.09.1984	**75**	**6**	2018/2019:	*FC Balzers*
Ivan QUINTANS	15.10.1989	**31**	**0**	2018:	*USV Eschen/Mauren*
Martin RECHSTEINER	15.02.1989	**41**	**0**	2018/2019:	*FC Balzers*
Seyhan YILDIZ	30.04.1989	**32**	**1**	2018/2019:	*FC Balzers*
Midfielders					
Marcel BÜCHEL	18.03.1991	**17**	**1**	2018/2019:	*Empoli FC (ITA)*
Martin BÜCHEL	19.02.1987	**76**	**2**	2018/2019:	*FC Zürich U21 (SUI)*
Philippe ERNE	14.12.1986	**35**	**1**	2018:	*FC Balzers*
Robin GUBSER	17.04.1991	**32**	**1**	2018/2019:	*USV Eschen/Mauren*
Nicolas HASLER	04.05.1991	**61**	**3**	2018/2019:	*Chicago Fire SC (USA)*
Livio MEIER	10.01.1998	**8**	**0**	2018/2019:	*USV Eschen/Mauren*
Aron SELE	02.09.1996	**16**	**0**	2018/2019:	*FC Vaduz*
Sandro WIESER	03.02.1993	**51**	**2**	2018/2019:	*FC Vaduz*
Marco WOLFINGER	18.04.1989	**1**	**0**	2018:	*FC Balzers*
Sandro WOLFINGER	24.08.1991	**29**	**2**	2018/2019:	*USV Eschen/Mauren*
Forwards					
Noah FRICK	26.10.2001	**1**	**0**	2019:	*FC Vaduz*
Yanik FRICK	27.05.1998	**7**	**0**	2019:	*FC Rapperswil-Jona (SUI)*
Niklas KIEBER	04.03.1993	**11**	**0**	2018:	*USV Eschen/Mauren*
Simon KÜHNE	30.04.1994	**22**	**0**	2018/2019:	*USV Eschen/Mauren*
Dennis SALANOVIĆ	26.02.1996	**35**	**3**	2018/2019:	*FC Thun (SUI)*

National team coach		
René PAURITSCH (Austria) [29.10.2012 – 20.11.2018]	04.02.1964	49 M; 4 W; 7 D; 38 L; 22-128
Helgi KOLVIÐSSON (Iceland) [from 01.01.2019]	13.09.1971	4 M; 0 W; 0 D; 4 L; 0-13

LITHUANIA

The Country:
Lietuvos Respublika (Republic of Lithuania)
Capital: Vilnius
Surface: 65,300 km²
Inhabitants: 2,790,842 [2019]
Time: UTC+2

The FA:
Lietuvos futbolo federacija
Stadiono g. 2, 02106 Vilnius
Tel: +370 5263 8741
Foundation date: 1922
Member of FIFA since: 1923
Member of UEFA since: 1992
Website: www.lff.lt

NATIONAL TEAM RECORDS

First international match:	24.06.1923, Kaunas:	Lithuania – Estonia 0-5	
Most international caps:	Andrius Skerla		- 84 caps (1998-2012)
Most international goals:	Tomas Danilevičius		- 19 goals / 71 caps (1998-2014)

UEFA EUROPEAN CHAMPIONSHIP	
1960	-
1964	-
1968	-
1972	-
1976	-
1980	-
1984	-
1988	-
1992	-
1996	Qualifiers
2000	Qualifiers
2004	Qualifiers
2008	Qualifiers
2012	Qualifiers
2016	Qualifiers

FIFA WORLD CUP	
1930	Did Not Enter
1934	Qualifiers
1938	Qualifiers
1950	-
1954	-
1958	-
1962	-
1966	-
1970	-
1974	-
1978	-
1982	-
1986	-
1990	-
1994	Qualifiers
1998	Qualifiers
2002	Qualifiers
2006	Qualifiers
2010	Qualifiers
2014	Qualifiers
2018	Qualifiers

UEFA NATIONS LEAGUE
2018/2019 – League C

OLYMPIC FOOTBALL TOURNAMENTS 1908-2016							
1908	-	**1948**	-	**1972**	-	**1996**	Qualifiers
1912	-	**1952**	-	**1976**	-	**2000**	Qualifiers
1920	-	**1956**	-	**1980**	-	**2004**	Qualifiers
1924	FT/Preliminary Round	**1960**	-	**1984**	-	**2008**	Qualifiers
1928	-	**1964**	-	**1988**	-	**2012**	Qualifiers
1936	-	**1968**	-	**1992**	-	**2016**	Qualifiers

FIFA CONFEDERATIONS CUP 1992-2017
None

LITHUANIAN CLUB HONOURS IN EUROPEAN CLUB COMPETITIONS:

European Champion Clubs' Cup (1956-1992) / UEFA Champions League (1993-2019)
None
Fairs Cup (1858-1971) / UEFA Cup (1972-2009) / UEFA Europa League (2010-2019)
None
UEFA Super Cup (1972-2019)
None
European Cup Winners' Cup 1961-1999*
None

**defunct competition*

NATIONAL COMPETITIONS
TABLE OF HONOURS

LITHUANIAN SSR (SOVIET ERA) CHAMPIONS

1945	Spartakas Kaunas
1946	Dinamo Kaunas
1947	Lokomotyvas Kaunas
1948	Elnias Šiauliai
1949	Elnias Šiauliai
1950	Inkaras Kaunas
1951	Inkaras Kaunas
1952	Karininkų Namai Vilnius
1953	Elnias Šiauliai
1954	Inkaras Kaunas
1955	Lima Kaunas
1956	Linų Audiniai Plungė
1957	Elnias Šiauliai
1958	Elnias Šiauliai
1958/1959	Raudonoji Žvaigždė Vilnius
1959/1960	Elnias Šiauliai
1960/1961	Elnias Šiauliai
1961/1962	FK Atletas Kaunas
1962/1963	Statyba Panevėžys
1964	Inkaras Kaunas
1965	Inkaras Kaunas
1966	Nevėžis Kėdainiai
1967	Saliutas Vilnius
1968	Statyba Panevėžys
1969	Statybininkas Šiauliai
1970	FK Atletas Kaunas
1971	Pažanga Vilnius
1972	Nevėžis Kėdainiai
1973	Nevėžis Kėdainiai
1974	Tauras Šiauliai
1975	Dainava Alytus
1976	Atmosfera Mažeikiai
1977	Statybininkas Šiauliai
1978	Atlantas Klaipėda
1979	Atmosfera Mažeikiai
1980	Atlantas Klaipėda
1981	Atlantas Klaipėda
1982	Pažanga Vilnius
1983	Pažanga Vilnius
1984	Atlantas Klaipėda
1985	Ekranas Panevėžys
1986	Banga Kaunas
1987	Tauras Tauragė
1988	SRT Vilnius
1989	Banga Kaunas

	CHAMPIONS	CUP WINNERS	BEST GOALSCORERS	
1922	LFLS Kaunas	-	-	
1923	LFLS Kaunas	-	-	
1924	Kovas Kaunas	-	-	
1925	Kovas Kaunas	-	-	
1926	Kovas Kaunas	-	-	
1927	LFLS Kaunas	-	-	
1928	KSS Klaipėda	-	-	
1929	KSS Klaipėda	-	-	
1930	KSS Klaipėda	-	-	
1931	KSS Klaipėda	-	-	
1932	LFLS Kaunas	-	-	
1933	Kovas Kaunas	-	-	
1934	MSK Kaunas	-	-	
1935	Kovas Kaunas	-	-	
1936	Kovas Kaunas	-	-	
1937	KSS Klaipėda	-	-	
1937/1938	KSS Klaipėda	-	-	
1938/1939	LGSF Kaunas	-	-	
1939/1940	*Competition abandoned*	-	-	
1941	*Competition not finished*	-	-	
1942	LFLS Kaunas	-	-	
1942/1943	Tauras Kaunas	-	-	
1943/1944	*Competition not finished*	-	-	
	--	--	--	
1990	FK Sirijus Klaipėda	FK Sirijus Klaipėda	Dalius Bajorūnas (FK Tauras Šiauliai)	22
1991	FK Žalgiris Vilnius	FK Žalgiris Vilnius	Egidijus Meidus (Vilija Kaunas)	13
1991/1992	FK Žalgiris Vilnius	FK Makabi Vilnius	Remigijus Pocius (FK Granitas Klaipėda / FK Sakalas Šiauliai) Vaidotas Šlekys (FK Ekranas Panevėžys)	14
1992/1993	FK Ekranas Panevėžys	FK Žalgiris Vilnius	Vaidotas Šlekys (FK Ekranas Panevėžys)	16
1993/1994	ROMAR Mažeikiai	FK Žalgiris Vilnius	Vaidotas Šlekys (FK Ekranas Panevėžys) Robertas Žalys (FBK Kaunas)	16
1994/1995	FK Inkaras-Grifas Kaunas	FK Inkaras-Grifas Kaunas	Eimantas Poderis (FK Žalgiris Vilnius / FK Inkaras-Grifas Kaunas)	24
1995/1996	FK Inkaras-Grifas Kaunas	FK Kareda-Sakalas Šiauliai	Edgaras Jankauskas (FK Žalgiris Vilnius)	25
1996/1997	FK Kareda Šiauliai	FK Žalgiris Vilnius	Remigijus Pocius (FK Kareda Šiauliai)	14
1997/1998	FK Kareda Šiauliai	FK Ekranas Panevėžys	Vidas Dančenka (FK Kareda Šiauliai)	26
1998/1999	FK Žalgiris Vilnius	FK Kareda Šiauliai	Artūras Fomenka (FK Kareda Šiauliai)	14
1999	FBK Kaunas	*No competition*	Nerijus Vasiliauskas (FK Žalgiris Vilnius)	10
2000	FBK Kaunas	FK Ekranas Panevėžys (1999/2000)	Andrius Velička (FBK Kaunas)	26
2001	FBK Kaunas	FK Atlantas Klaipėda (2000/01)	Remigijus Pocius (FBK Kaunas)	22
2002	FBK Kaunas	FBK Kaunas (2001/02)	Audrius Šlekys (FBK Kaunas)	19
2003	FBK Kaunas	FK Sūduva Marijampolė (2002/03) FK Žalgiris Vilnius (2003)	Ričardas Beniušis (FK Atlantas Klaipėda / FBK Kaunas)	16
2004	FBK Kaunas	FBK Kaunas	Povilas Lukšys (FK Ekranas Panevėžys)	19
2005	FK Ekranas Panevėžys	FBK Kaunas	Mantas Savėnas (FK Ekranas Panevėžys)	27
2006	FBK Kaunas	FK Sūduva Marijampolė	Serhiy Kuznetsov (UKR, FK Vėtra Vilnius)	18
2007	FBK Kaunas	*No competition*	Povilas Lukšys (FK Ekranas Panevėžys)	26
2008	FK Ekranas Panevėžys	FBK Kaunas (2007/08)	Rafael Pompeo Rodrigues Ledesma (BRA, FBK Kaunas)	14
2009	FK Ekranas Panevėžys	FK Sūduva Marijampolė (2008/09)	Valdas Trakys (FK Ekranas Panevėžys)	20
2010	FK Ekranas Panevėžys	FK Ekranas Panevėžys (2009/10)	Povilas Lukšys (FK Sūduva Marijampolė)	16
2011	FK Ekranas Panevėžys	FK Ekranas Panevėžys (2010/11)	Deivydas Matulevičius (FK Žalgiris Vilnius)	19

2012	FK Ekranas Panevėžys	FK Žalgiris Vilnius (2011/12)	Artūras Rimkevičius (FK Šiauliai)	35
2013	FK Žalgiris Vilnius	FK Žalgiris Vilnius (2012/13)	Nerijus Valskis (FK Sūduva Marijampolė)	27
2014	FK Žalgiris Vilnius	FK Žalgiris Vilnius (2013/14)	Niko Tokić (CRO, FK Šiauliai)	19
2015	FK Žalgiris Vilnius	FK Žalgiris Vilnius (2014/15)	Tomas Radzinevičius (FK Sūduva Marijampolė)	28
2016	FK Žalgiris Vilnius	FK Žalgiris Vilnius (2015/16) FK Žalgiris Vilnius (2016)	Andrija Kaluđerović (SRB, FK Žalgiris Vilnius)	20
2017	FK Sūduva Marijampolė	FC Stumbras Kaunas	Darvydas Šernas (FK Žalgiris Vilnius)	18
2018	FK Sūduva Marijampolė	FK Žalgiris Vilnius	Liviu Ion Antal (ROU, FK Žalgiris Vilnius)	23

NATIONAL CHAMPIONSHIP

A Lyga 2018

(24.02.2018 – 11.11.2018)

Regular Season - Results

Round 1 [24-25.02.2018]
FK Sūduva - FC Stumbras 2-0(0-0)
FK Trakai - FK Atlantas 0-1(0-0)
FK Palanga - FK Jonava 1-1(1-0)
FK Žalgiris - FK Kauno Žalgiris 2-0(1-0)

Round 2 [03-04.03.2018]
FK Kauno Žalgiris - FK Trakai 1-4(0-1)
FK Sūduva - FK Palanga 2-0(0-0)
FK Jonava - FK Atlantas 1-1(0-0)
FC Stumbras - FK Žalgiris 0-0

Round 3 [07-08.03.2018]
FK Atlantas - FK Kauno Žalgiris 0-1(0-1)
FK Trakai - FC Stumbras 1-1(1-0)
FK Sūduva - FK Jonava 4-2(4-1)
FK Žalgiris - FK Palanga 4-0(2-0)

Round 4 [13-17.03.2018]
FK Palanga - FK Trakai 1-1(1-0)
FC Stumbras - FK Atlantas 0-2(0-1)
FK Sūduva - FK Žalgiris 0-0
FK Jonava - FK Kauno Žalgiris 0-1(0-1)

Round 5 [30-31.03.2018]
FK Atlantas - FK Palanga 1-1(1-1)
FK Žalgiris - FK Jonava 1-2(1-0)
FK Kauno Žalgiris - FC Stumbras 0-1(0-0)
FK Trakai - FK Sūduva 1-4(1-1)

Round 6 [04-07.04.2018]
FC Stumbras - FK Jonava 4-0(3-0)
FK Palanga - FK Kauno Žalgiris 1-0(0-0)
FK Sūduva - FK Atlantas 2-1(1-0)
FK Žalgiris - FK Trakai 3-2(0-2)

Round 7 [11-12.04.2018]
FK Atlantas - FK Žalgiris 2-5(2-2)
FC Stumbras - FK Palanga 0-1(0-0)
FK Sūduva - FK Kauno Žalgiris 4-1(1-0)
FK Trakai - FK Jonava 1-1(0-1)

Round 8 [17-18.04.2018]
FK Jonava - FK Palanga 4-0(2-0)
FC Stumbras - FK Sūduva 0-1(0-1)
FK Atlantas - FK Trakai 0-2(0-1)
FK Kauno Žalgiris - FK Žalgiris 0-0

Round 9 [22-25.04.2018]
FK Žalgiris - FC Stumbras 1-1(0-1)
FK Palanga - FK Sūduva 0-2(0-0)
FK Trakai - FK Kauno Žalgiris 2-0(0-0)
FK Atlantas - FK Jonava 1-0(1-0)

Round 10 [28-29.04.2018]
FK Jonava - FK Sūduva 0-0
FK Palanga - FK Žalgiris 1-2(1-2)
FK Kauno Žalgiris - FK Atlantas 2-3(1-1)
FC Stumbras - FK Trakai 0-2(0-1)

Round 11 [02-03.05.2018]
FK Palanga - FK Trakai 1-0(1-0)
FK Žalgiris - FK Sūduva 2-3(2-2)
FK Kauno Žalgiris - FK Jonava 1-0(0-0)
FK Atlantas - FC Stumbras 0-0

Round 12 [06-09.05.2018]
FK Sūduva - FK Trakai 0-0
FC Stumbras - FK Kauno Žalgiris 0-2(0-1)
FK Jonava - FK Žalgiris 1-2(0-1)
FK Palanga - FK Atlantas 0-2(0-1)

Round 13 [12-13.05.2018]
FK Trakai - FK Žalgiris 0-1(0-1)
FK Atlantas - FK Sūduva 0-3(0-0)
FK Jonava - FC Stumbras 0-2(0-1)
FK Kauno Žalgiris - FK Palanga 0-0

Round 14 [16-19.05.2018]
FK Palanga - FC Stumbras 0-2(0-0)
FK Jonava - FK Trakai 0-0
FK Žalgiris - FK Atlantas 3-1(1-0)
FK Kauno Žalg.- FK Sūduva 0-3(0-1) [01.07.]

Round 15 [22-24.05.2018]
FK Sūduva - FC Stumbras 3-0(0-0)
FK Kauno Žalgiris - FK Žalgiris 0-1(0-0)
FK Trakai - FK Atlantas 1-2(0-1)
FK Palanga - FK Jonava 3-1(2-0)

Round 16 [14-16.06.2018]
FK Kauno Žalgiris - FK Trakai 1-1(0-1)
FK Jonava - FK Atlantas 2-1(1-1)
FK Žalgiris - FC Stumbras 0-1(0-0)
FK Palanga - FK Sūduva 1-4(0-1)

Round 17 [19-20.06.2018]
FC Stumbras - FK Trakai 1-0(1-0)
FK Žalgiris - FK Palanga 2-0(1-0)
FK Sūduva - FK Jonava 2-0(1-0)
FK Atlantas - FK Kauno Žal. 0-1(0-1) [15.08.]

Round 18 [27.06.2018]
FK Trakai - FK Palanga 3-1(2-1) [18.03.]
FK Jonava - FK Kauno Žalgiris 0-2(0-2)
FK Sūduva - FK Žalgiris 0-1(0-0)
FC Stumbras - FK Atlantas 2-1(1-0) [25.08.]

Round 19 [03-04.07.2018]
FK Trakai - FK Jonava 1-0(0-0) [20.05.]
FC Stumbras - FK Palanga 2-0(0-0)
FK Kauno Žalgiris - FK Sūduva 1-0(0-0)
FK Atlantas - FK Žalgiris 1-5(1-3) [07.10.]

Round 20 [04-07.08.2018]
FK Jonava - FC Stumbras 1-3(1-2)
FK Sūduva - FK Atlantas 3-0(1-0)
FK Palanga - FK Kauno Žalgiris 0-1(0-1)
FK Žalgiris - FK Trakai 2-2(0-1) [21.10.]

Round 21 [11.08.2018]
FK Palanga - FK Atlantas 2-0(1-0)
FK Kauno Žalgiris - FC Stumbras 0-2(0-0)
FK Trakai - FK Sūduva 0-0 [26.09.]
FK Žalgiris - FK Jonava 2-1(2-0) [17.10.]

Round 22 [18-19.08.2018]
FK Jonava - FK Palanga 3-1(0-0)
FK Atlantas - FK Trakai 0-2(0-1)
FK Žalgiris - FK Kauno Žalgiris 4-0(2-0)
FC Stumbras - FK Sūduva 1-2(1-1) [07.10.]

Round 23 [22-23.08.2018]
FC Stumbras - FK Žalgiris 0-2(0-2)
FK Atlantas - FK Jonava 1-1(1-0)
FK Trakai - FK Kauno Žalgiris 1-0(0-0)
FK Sūduva - FK Palanga 5-0(2-0) [15.09.]

Round 24 [28-29.08.2018]
FK Kauno Žalgiris - FK Atlantas 4-0(2-0)
FK Palanga - FK Žalgiris 0-5(0-2)
FK Trakai - FC Stumbras 2-2(0-0)
FK Jonava - FK Sūduva 1-2(0-1) [21.10.]

Round 25 [19-22.09.2018]
FK Kauno Žalgiris - FK Jonava 1-1(0-0)
FK Atlantas - FC Stumbras 1-3(0-2)
FK Trakai - FK Palanga 3-0(1-0)
FC Stumbras - FK Kauno Žalgiris 0-0

Round 26 [21-29.09.2018]
FK Žalgiris - FK Sūduva 1-0(0-0)
FK Atlantas - FK Palanga 1-1(0-0)
FK Jonava - FK Žalgiris 0-6(0-3)
FK Sūduva - FK Trakai 2-1(2-0)

Round 27 [04-05.10.2018]
FC Stumbras - FK Jonava 3-0(1-0)
FK Atlantas - FK Sūduva 2-5(1-2)
FK Trakai - FK Žalgiris 1-0(1-0)
FK Kauno Žalgiris - FK Palanga 2-0(1-0)

Round 28 [24.10.2018]
FK Jonava - FK Trakai 1-3(0-1) [12.08.]
FK Palanga - FC Stumbras 1-5(0-2)
FK Žalgiris - FK Atlantas 3-1(2-1)
FK Sūduva - FK Kauno Žalgiris 1-0(1-0)

Final Standings

1.	FK Sūduva Marijampolė	28	21	4	3	59 - 16	67
2.	FK Žalgiris Vilnius	28	19	5	4	60 - 20	62
3.	FC Stumbras Kaunas	28	13	6	9	36 - 25	45
4.	FK Trakai	28	11	9	8	37 - 26	42
5.	FK Kauno Žalgiris Kaunas	28	10	5	13	22 - 31	35
6.	FK Atlantas Klaipėda	28	6	5	17	26 - 55	23
7.	FK Palanga (*Relegation Play-offs*)	28	5	5	18	17 - 58	20
8.	FK Jonava (*Relegated*)	28	4	7	17	24 - 50	19

Teams ranked 1-6 were qualified for the Championship Round.

Championship Round

Results

Round 29 [28.10.2018]
FK Trakai - FK Žalgiris 0-1(0-1)
FK Kauno Žalgiris - FK Sūduva 1-1(0-0)
FC Stumbras - FK Atlantas 6-0(1-0)

Round 30 [31.10.2018]
FK Atlantas - FK Kauno Žalgiris 1-3(1-2)
FK Sūduva - FK Trakai 1-0(0-0)
FK Žalgiris - FC Stumbras 2-0(1-0)

Round 31 [03.11.2018]
FC Stumbras - FK Sūduva 1-4(0-3)
FK Trakai - FK Kauno Žalgiris 1-0(0-0)
FK Žalgiris - FK Atlantas 0-0

Round 32 [07.11.2018]
FK Žalgiris - FK Kauno Žalgiris 5-2(1-1)
FC Stumbras - FK Trakai 0-3(0-1)
FK Sūduva - FK Atlantas 6-0(1-0)

Round 33 [11.11.2018]
FK Atlantas - FK Trakai 1-5(0-4)
FK Sūduva - FK Žalgiris 1-2(0-1)
FK Kauno Žalgiris - FC Stumbras 1-2(0-0)

Final Standings

1.	**FK Sūduva Marijampolė**	33	24	5	4	72 - 20	77
2.	FK Žalgiris Vilnius	33	23	6	4	70 - 23	75
3.	FK Trakai	33	14	9	10	46 - 29	51
4.	FC Stumbras Kaunas	33	15	6	12	45 - 35	51
5.	FK Kauno Žalgiris Kaunas	33	11	6	16	29 - 41	39
6.	FK Atlantas Klaipėda	33	6	6	21	28 - 75	24

Top goalscorers:

23 Liviu Ion Antal (ROU)
FK Žalgiris Vilnius

17 Marcos Soares Elias Junior (BRA)
FC Stumbras Kaunas

13 Donatas Kazlauskas
FK Atlantas Klaipėda / FK Trakai

Relegation Play-offs [28.10.-03.11.2018]

DFK Dainava Alytus - FK Palanga	0-3(0-2)	0-2(0-0)

FK Palanga remains at highest level.

NATIONAL CUP
Lietuvos futbolo taurė 2018

First Round [25-28.04.2018]

Akmenės Cementas - Mažeikiai Šiauliai FA	3-6	FK Panerys Vilnius - FK Koralas Klaipėda	4-1
Merkys - DFK Dainava Alytus	0-7	Geležinis Vilkas - Sveikata Kybartai	0-8
FK Banga Gargždai - FC Džiugas Telšiai	0-0; 4-3pen	FK Šilas Kazlų Rūda - FM Ateitis	4-3

Byes: FK Nevėžis Kėdainiai, FC Pakruojis (I Lyga), FK Babrungas Plungė, FC Hegelmann Litauen Kaunas, Gargždų Pramogos SC, FK SANED Joniškis (II Lyga), FK Elektrėnų Versmė (III Lyga), Top Kickers Vilnius (IV Lyga).

Second Round [24-28.05.2018]

FK Šiauliai - FK Sūduva Marijampolė	0-7	FK Vilniaus Vytis - FK Atlantas Klaipėda	1-7
FK Šilas Kazlų Rūda - FK Kruoja Pakruojis	1-2 aet	Pramogos-SC Gargždai - FK Banga Gargždai	1-2
FK Elektrėnų Versmė - TERA Vilnius	3-1	FK Panevėžys - FK Palanga	0-1
FK Sakuona-Rugpienių - FK Nevėžis	1-5	FC Hegelmann Litauen Kaunas - FC Kupiškis	0-1
FK Babrungas Plungė - Sveikata Kybartai	5-3	FK Panerys Vilnius - FK Trakai	0-1
Minija Kretinga - FK Žalgiris Vilnius	0-3	TOP Kickers Vilnius - FK Kauno Žalgiris Kaunas	2-7
FC Viltis Vilnius - FK Utenis Utena	1-0	FK SANED Joniškis - FK Dainava Alytus	0-9
FK Kėdainiai - FC Stumbras Kaunas	0-6	SK Saulininkas Šiauliai - FK Jonava	2-11

Third Round [23.06.-01.07.2018]

FK Trakai - FK Sūduva Marijampolė	0-3	FK Jonava - FK Žalgiris Vilnius	0-5
FC Kupiškis - FK Kauno Žalgiris Kaunas	1-7	FK Babrungas Plungė – FC Viltis Vilnius	2-3
FK Nevėžis - FK Palanga	0-4	FK Elektrėnų Versmė - FK Dainava Alytus	0-10
FK Banga Gargždai - FK Kruoja Pakruojis	1-0	FK Atlantas Klaipėda - FC Stumbras Kaunas [07.08.]	1-3

Quarter-Finals [31.08.-02.09.2018]			
FK Banga Gargzdai - FK Dainava Alytus	1-2	FK Sūduva Marijampolė - FK Žalgiris Vilnius	1-4
Viltis Vilnius - FC Stumbras Kaunas	0-3	FK Kauno Žalgiris Kaunas - FK Palanga	2-0

Semi-Finals [15-16.09.2018]			
FK Kauno Žalgiris Kaunas - FK Žalgiris Vilnius	0-3	FK Dainava Alytus - FC Stumbras Kaunas	0-4

Final

30.09.2018; Alytus stadionas, Alytus; Referee: Jurij Paškovskij; Attendance: 1,782

FK Žalgiris Vilnius - FC Stumbras Kaunas 3-0(2-0)

Žalgiris: Rodrigo Martins Josviaki, Lukas Čerkauskas, Marcos Soares Elias Junior (73.Miguel Ângelo Ferreira Pires), André Filipe Lopes Almeida, Rimvydas Sadauskas, Rafael da Silva Floro, Matheus Bissi da Silva, Dominykas Galkevičius (67.Alsény Bah), Levan Matcharashvili (54.António João Belo Andrade), Lucas Villela Rezende, Nasro Bouchareb. Trainer: Mariano Barreto (Portugal).

Stumbras: Armantas Vitkauskas, Donovan Carlos Saverio Slijngard, Mamadou Mbodj, Rolandas Baravykas, Slavko Blagojević, Saulius Mikoliūnas (64.Domantas Šimkus), Jérémy Manzorro (82.Marcus Vinícius Vidal Cunha „Marquinhos Carioca“), Marko Tomić, Liviu Ion Antal (71.Tomáš Malec), Tomáš Šimkovič, Ugochukwu Louis Ogana. Trainer: Valdas Urbonas.

Goals: 1-0 Tomáš Šimkovič (34), 2-0 Marko Tomić (43), 3-0 Marcus Vinícius Vidal Cunha „Marquinhos Carioca“ (88).

THE CLUBS 2018

Please note: matches and goals includes statistics of both Regular Season and Championship Round.

Futbolo Klubas Atlantas Klaipėda

Founded: 1962
Stadium: Klaipėdos centrinis stadionas, Klaipėda (4,428)

Goalkeepers:	**DOB**	**M**	**(s)**	**G**
Pāvels Doroševs (LVA)	09.10.1980	14		
Eimantas Graželis	04.02.2000	1		
Denis Khvalytskiy (UKR)	30.05.1997	1		
Lukas Paukštė	25.09.1998	2		
Dawid Smug (POL)	14.01.1994	15		
Defenders:	**DOB**	**M**	**(s)**	**G**
Martun Abovyan (RUS)	14.01.1994	13		
Lukas Artimavičius	12.08.1994	12		
Benas Babenskas	25.04.2001	1		
Andrius Bartkus	21.01.1986	18	(1)	1
Danilo Beskorovayniy (UKR)	07.02.1999	5		
Abdoulaye Diallo (SEN)	21.10.1992	6	(2)	1
Mantas Fridrikas	13.09.1988	7		
Tomas Gvazdinskas	03.04.2000	3	(1)	
Jonas Latakas	14.01.2000	1	(2)	
Ruslan Marushka (UKR)	23.08.1998	7	(5)	
Bogdan Mytsyk (UKR)	08.03.1998	5	(2)	
Ivan Pecha (SVK)	23.01.1986	7	(2)	
Deividas Šiuša	08.08.1999	15	(3)	
Dovydas Švambaris	20.06.2000		(1)	
Midfielders:	**DOB**	**M**	**(s)**	**G**
Martynas Bačko	25.03.2000		(1)	
Bruno Vieira de Souza „Bruninho“ (BRA)	12.08.1997		(1)	
Dominykas Čiesna	19.06.2000		(2)	
Omar Diarra (BEL)	15.08.1994	4	(3)	
Rokas Filipavicius	22.12.1999	6	(4)	1
Gustas Gumbaravičius	21.02.2000	13	(2)	
Donatas Kazlauskas	31.03.1994	7	(4)	3
Mikhail Kolyadko (BLR)	21.11.1988	16		1
Igor Krmar (SRB)	14.05.1991	2		
Vladislav Kučerovas	06.07.2000		(1)	
Leandro da Silva (BRA)	26.06.1985	16	(2)	
Aleksandr Levšinas	14.08.1999	12		
Dovydas Norvilas	05.04.1993	9	(2)	
Mindaugas Panka	01.05.1984	9		1
Marius Papšys	13.05.1989	22	(7)	4
Juro Pejić (CRO)	25.11.1991	7	(3)	
Skirmantas Rakauskas	07.01.1996	1	(6)	
Glebas Sonas	10.02.2000		(1)	
Domantas Šimkus	10.02.1996	15		2
Yuri Teterenko (UKR)	22.01.1997	10	(2)	1
Justas Vainikaitis	24.06.2000	1	(2)	
Gerardas Žukauskas	07.07.1994	5	(1)	
Forwards:	**DOB**	**M**	**(s)**	**G**
Edvinas Baniulis	03.01.1997	12	(2)	5
Vice Kendeš (CRO)	09.05.1994	4	(7)	
Anıl Koç (TUR)	29.01.1995	10	(5)	2
Tadas Labukas	10.01.1984	17	(3)	2
Bruno Mauricio Lemiechevsky Melessi (URU)	03.03.1994	10	(3)	3
Deividas Lukošius	24.01.1991	16	(2)	1
Yurii Zakharkiv (UKR)	21.03.1996	6	(2)	
Trainer:	**DOB**	**M**		
Algimantas Briaunys	03.11.1964	33		

Futbolo klubas Jonava

Founded: 1991
Stadium: Jonavos centrinis stadionas, Jonava (1,008)

Goalkeepers:	**DOB**	**M**	**(s)**	**G**
Nemanja Bjelan (SRB)	16.11.1993	3		
Guilherme Cioletti Ferreira da Silva (BRA)	30.03.1994	21		
Lukas Paukštė	25.09.1998	4		
Defenders:	**DOB**	**M**	**(s)**	**G**
Lukas Artimavičius	12.08.1994	9		
Marius Činikas	17.05.1986	17	(1)	
Martynas Dapkus	16.02.1993	21		
Gilberto Ferreira Gomes Filho (BRA)	11.03.1994	11	(2)	
Jeon Yong-Il (KOR)	27.03.1999	5	(5)	1
Arūnas Klimavičius	05.10.1982	6		2
Ronicel Fortes Andrade Santos „Rony" (CPV)	10.01.1995	10	(2)	
Karolis Šilkaitis	02.06.1996	12	(4)	
Aurimas Tručinskas	25.10.1994	22	(1)	
Midfielders:	**DOB**	**M**	**(s)**	**G**
Vilius Armanavičius	08.05.1995	7	(1)	1
Joseph William Anthony Di Chiara (CAN)	30.01.1992	6		
Mohamed-Emi Djabrailov (RUS)	24.03.1993	8	(2)	3
Tadas Eliošius	01.03.1990	13	(2)	3
Tautvydas Eliošius	03.11.1991	13	(10)	
Kamran Guliyev (AZE)	11.03.2000		(4)	
Fahad Ishmail (ENG)	02.09.1996	7	(4)	
Arnas Paškevičius	28.06.1996		(1)	
Tomas Salamanavičius	31.03.1993	4	(6)	
Gytis Vasylius	12.08.1999	4	(4)	
Ernestas Veliulis	22.08.1992	22	(1)	4
Eugen Zasavițchi (MDA)	24.11.1992	18		
Forwards:	**DOB**	**M**	**(s)**	**G**
Kler Low Eh Hmoo Heh (ENG)	21.10.1996	4	(4)	
Vytautas Lukša	14.08.1984	12	(6)	
Michael Thuíque Dias Santos (BRA)	21.03.1993	8		2
Artjoms Osipovs (LVA)	08.01.1989	10	(3)	
Tural Elkhan Rzayev (AZE)	26.08.1993	6	(1)	
Laurynas Stonkus	18.01.1992	22	(4)	8
Klaudijus Upstas	30.10.1994	3	(2)	
Trainer:	**DOB**	**M**		
Filipe Alves Ribeiro (POR)	04.05.1975	13		
Darius Gvildys [15.05.2018]	26.05.1970	5		
Artūras Ramoška [12.07.2018]	09.08.1963	10		

Futbolo klubas Kauno Žalgiris Kaunas

Founded: 2004
Stadium: „Stepono Dariaus ir Stasio Girėno" stadionas, Kaunas (9,180)

Goalkeepers:	**DOB**	**M**	**(s)**	**G**
Martynas Matuzas	28.08.1989	20		
Deividas Mikelionis	08.05.1995	13		
Defenders:	**DOB**	**M**	**(s)**	**G**
Ante Bakmaz (CRO)	07.03.1992	13	(1)	
Markas Beneta	08.07.1993	29	(1)	1
Ignas Dedura	01.06.1978	13	(2)	
Matas Dedura	17.05.2002		(2)	
Arūnas Klimavičius	05.10.1982	14		
Illya Kolpachuk (BLR)	09.10.1990	8	(2)	1
Ernestas Mockus	05.08.2000	5	(3)	
Pijus Širvys	01.04.1998	17	(8)	2
Tomas Snapkauskas	12.06.1992	26	(1)	
Gabrielius Zagurskas	13.05.1992	15	(1)	
Midfielders:	**DOB**	**M**	**(s)**	**G**
Karolis Gvildys	13.04.1994	3		
Edvinas Kloniūnas	28.06.1998	27		3
Mikhail Kolyadko (BLR)	21.11.1988	8		
Povilas Malakas	08.10.1998	4	(1)	1
Yuriy Mamaev (RUS)	03.02.1984	14	(7)	
Simonas Paulius	12.05.1991	18		1
Linas Pilibaitis	05.04.1985	28		6
Matas Popiera	26.08.1999		(11)	
Aurimas Raginis	18.08.1991	21	(11)	1
Gratas Sirgėdas	17.12.1994	20	(4)	5
Forwards:	**DOB**	**M**	**(s)**	**G**
Andrei Bursuc (MDA)	23.05.1997		(5)	
João Vitor Brandão Figueiredo (BRA)	27.05.1996	20	(2)	4
Rokas Krušnauskas	04.11.1995	10	(4)	2
Ernestas Mickevičius	11.11.1996	17	(15)	2
Trainer:	**DOB**	**M**		
Mindaugas Čepas	06.06.1978	33		

Palangos Futbolo Klubas

Founded: 2011
Stadium: Palanga stadionas, Palanga (1,212)

Goalkeepers:	**DOB**	**M**	**(s)**	**G**
Tadas Norbutas	25.02.1994	10		
Anton Tsvetkov	15.01.1994	18		
Defenders:	**DOB**	**M**	**(s)**	**G**
Mindaugas Bagužis	11.04.1983	19		
Waly Diouf (SEN)	05.05.1997	21		
Rokas Gecevicius	04.07.1997	1	(10)	
Brice Goupy (FRA)	12.10.1995	15	(3)	1
Aurimas Jurgelevičius	09.01.1997		(8)	
Simonas Juška	28.03.1994	1	(1)	
Vladislav Kaborda (BLR)	24.07.1995	17	(1)	
Vilius Kazlauskas	26.02.1999		(1)	
Justas Raziūnas	23.01.1995	22		
Aurimas Skurdelis	06.03.1994	8	(1)	
Ricardas Šveikauskas	09.04.1997	25		
Sigitas Urbys	07.11.1995	16	(5)	
Midfielders:	**DOB**	**M**	**(s)**	**G**
Godspower Tower Aniefiok (NGA)	27.01.1997	4	(1)	
Tomas Dombrauskis	24.09.1996	14	(6)	4
Valentin Furdui (MDA)	01.09.1987	18		1
Edvardas Gaurilovas	10.05.1985	3		
Lukman Haruna Abdulkarim (NGA)	04.12.1990	4	(4)	
Akinjide Elijah Idowu (NGA)	09.09.1996	3		
Gvidas Juška	17.08.1982	15	(11)	4
Yven Rochild Victor Moyo (CGO)	15.03.1992	10		
Dovydas Norvilas	05.04.1993	13	(2)	
Matas Radžiukynas	05.04.1999		(12)	
Gerardas Žukauskas	07.07.1994	9	(1)	
Forwards:	**DOB**	**M**	**(s)**	**G**
Mohamed Malela Bangoura (GUI)	22.10.1998		(2)	
Donatas Konikas	21.04.1998	6	(7)	
Lucky Omerou (NGA)	15.09.1995	9		
Ransford Osei (GHA)	05.12.1990		(3)	
Simonas Urbys	07.11.1995	27		6
Benny Younaev (RUS)	07.05.1996		(5)	
Trainer:	**DOB**	**M**		
Valdas Trakys	20.0.1979	28		

Football Club Stumbras Kaunas

Founded: 2013
Stadium: „Stepono Dariaus ir Stasio Girėno“ stadionas, Kaunas (9,180)

Goalkeepers:	**DOB**	**M**	**(s)**	**G**
Giedrius Kvedaras	09.07.1991	3	(1)	
Rodrigo Martins Josviaki (BRA)	16.02.1995	30		
Defenders:	**DOB**	**M**	**(s)**	**G**
André Filipe Lopes Almeida (POR)	16.05.1995	31		2
Domantas Antanavičius	18.11.1998	4	(2)	
Lukas Čerkauskas	12.03.1994	31		
Jardel Rodrigues Afonso Nazaré (POR)	16.05.1995	19		
David Sebastião Bondo Kuagika (ANG)	10.08.1990	9		
Marcos Soares Elias Junior (BRA)	31.05.1994	25	(3)	17
Dmytro Nagiev (AZE)	27.11.1995	1		
Rokas Rasimavičius	21.09.2001		(2)	
Rimvydas Sadauskas	21.07.1996	29		
Midfielders:	**DOB**	**M**	**(s)**	**G**
Odiquir Agostinho Cá (POR)	24.07.1993	14		
Amran Al Jassasi (OMA)	11.03.1996		(5)	
Vilius Armalas	21.07.2000	7	(1)	
Vilius Armanavičius	08.05.1995	7	(3)	
António João Belo Andrade	18.08.1994	9	(6)	5
Lukas Čepkauskas	15.03.1997		(2)	
Fábio Miguel Rico Lopes (POR)	10.01.1993	11		2
Dominykas Galkevičius	16.10.1986	23	(2)	2
Renato Gomes (POR)	08.10.1998		(1)	
Matheus Bissi da Silva (BRA)	19.03.1991	13	(1)	
Miguel Ângelo Ferreira Pires (POR)	28.10.1996	3	(11)	
Denys Pidruchnyi (UKR)	10.07.2001	1	(1)	
Rafael da Silva Floro (POR)	19.01.1994	10		2
Kgaogelo Rathete Sekgota (RSA)	22.06.1997	13	(5)	1
Ibrahima Sory Elisa Soumah (GUI)	01.01.1998		(1)	
Gavi Thompson (NGA)	02.02.2000		(1)	
Forwards:	**DOB**	**M**	**(s)**	**G**
Alsény Bah (GUI)	26.12.1994	6	(11)	3
Nasro Bouchareb (FRA)	29.01.1994	23	(5)	6
Jaisen Jaren Clifford (RSA)	04.02.1996		(4)	
Lucas Villela Rezende (BRA)	24.03.1993	27	(5)	1
Levan Matcharashvili (GEO)	24.03.1997	9	(19)	3
Tayeb Meziani (ALG)	27.02.1996	3	(1)	
Tiago Filipe Gonçalves Soares Luís (POR)	01.12.1999		(3)	
Yuhao Liu (CHN)	14.05.1994	2		
Trainer:	**DOB**	**M**		
Mariano Barreto (POR)	18.01.1957	33		

Futbolo Klubas Sūduva Marijampolė

Founded: 1921
Stadium: ARVI Football Arena, Marijampolė (6,250)

Goalkeepers:	**DOB**	**M**	**(s)**	**G**
Ivan Kardum (CRO)	18.07.1987	33		
Defenders:	**DOB**	**M**	**(s)**	**G**
Marius Činikas	17.05.1986	4	(1)	
Vitaly Gayduchik (BLR)	12.07.1989	20	(2)	
Marko Iharoš (CRO)	23.06.1996		(1)	
Algis Jankauskas	27.09.1982	31		1
Semir Kerla (BIH)	26.09.1987	16		1
Aleksandar Živanović (SRB)	08.04.1987	29		2
Midfielders:	**DOB**	**M**	**(s)**	**G**
Gerson Elias Acevedo Rojas (CHI)	05.04.1988	20	(5)	10
Domantas Antanavičius	18.11.1998		(1)	
Jovan Čađenović (MNE)	13.01.1995	13		
Bruno de Araújo Dybal (BRA)	03.03.1994		(7)	
Guilherme Ozelame Finkler „Gui“ (BRA)	24.09.1985	8	(2)	2
Povilas Leimonas	16.11.1987	18	(10)	
Giedrius Matulevičius	05.03.1997	11	(12)	3
Alassane N'Diaye (FRA)	25.02.1990	14	(2)	2
Daniel Offenbacher (AUT)	18.02.1992	13		3
Vaidas Slavickas	26.02.1986	19		1
Andro Švrljuga (CRO)	24.10.1985	31		6
Ovidijus Verbickas	04.07.1993	21	(1)	9
Forwards:	**DOB**	**M**	**(s)**	**G**
Segei Amirzian	26.12.1999		(3)	
Rigino Cicilia (NED)	23.09.1994	19	(10)	8
Sandro Gotal (AUT)	09.09.1991	7	(6)	8
Julius Kasparavičius	03.04.1995	5	(12)	3
Karolis Laukžemis	11.03.1992	10	(1)	6
Josip Tadić (CRO)	22.08.1987	13	(1)	6
Mihret Topčagić (AUT)	21.06.1988	2	(3)	
Robertas Vėževičius	05.01.1986	6	(10)	
Trainer:	**DOB**	**M**		
Vladimir Cheburin (KAZ)	07.06.1965	33		

Futbolo Klubas Trakai

Founded: 2005
Stadium: LFF stadionas, Vilnius (5,067)

Goalkeepers:	**DOB**	**M**	**(s)**	**G**
Tymofey Sheremeta (UKR)	06.10.1995	10		
Tomas Švedkauskas	22.06.1994	23		
Defenders:	**DOB**	**M**	**(s)**	**G**
Valdemars Borovskis	05.02.1984	31		2
Justinas Januševskis	26.03.1994	28		2
Andrius Kazakevičius	23.01.1995		(4)	
Rokas Masenzovas	02.08.1994	1	(2)	
Etienne Mukanya (BEL)	04.01.1995	17	(3)	5
Alon Netzer (ISR)	02.06.1993	5	(1)	
Kevin Ntika Bondombe (BEL)	24.07.1995	4	(2)	
Evgeniy Osipov (RUS)	29.10.1986	29		3
Mychailo Shyshka (UKR)	05.07.1994	17		
Ernestas Stočkūnas	11.05.1998	2	(3)	
Midfielders:	**DOB**	**M**	**(s)**	**G**
Elvinas Ališauskas	22.02.1999		(4)	
Diniyar Bilyaletdinov (RUS)	27.02.1985	23	(2)	5
Deividas Česnauskis	30.06.1981	9	(3)	2
Svajūnas Čyžas	26.01.1998	12	(11)	
Rokas Filipavicius	22.12.1999	1		
Klaidas Janonis	13.05.1997		(5)	
Valentin Jeriomenko	19.02.1989	24	(1)	2
Donatas Kazlauskas	31.03.1994	13		10
Aleksandr Levšinas	14.08.1999	6	(1)	
Vytautas Lukša	14.08.1984	6	(3)	
Justinas Marazas	23.02.2000	22	(8)	8
Vaidas Šilėnas	16.07.1985	18	(3)	
Lajo Traore (CIV)	20.12.1993	12	(5)	
Modestas Vorobjovas	30.12.1995	22	(2)	2
Forwards:	**DOB**	**M**	**(s)**	**G**
Edvinas Baniulis	03.01.1997	2	(5)	
Rokas Gedminas	13.04.1993	12	(3)	1
Vadim Manzon (RUS)	05.12.1994	7	(6)	3
Dovydas Virkšas	01.07.1997	7	(5)	1
Trainer:	**DOB**	**M**		
Oleg Vasilenko (RUS)	06.10.1973	15		
Virmantas Lemežis [18.05.2018]	07.06.1980	3		
José Antonio Vicuña Ochandorena „Kibu Vicuña“ (ESP) [18.06.2018]	20.11.1971	9		
Albert Rybak (BLR) [11.10.2018]	16.05.1973	6		

Futbolo klubas Žalgiris Vilnius

Founded: 1947
Stadium: LFF stadionas, Vilnius (5,067)

Goalkeepers:	**DOB**	**M**	**(s)**	**G**
Džiugas Bartkus	07.11.1989	21		
Armantas Vitkauskas	23.03.1989	12		
Defenders:	**DOB**	**M**	**(s)**	**G**
Dominykas Barauskas	18.04.1997	2	(1)	
Rolandas Baravykas	23.08.1995	29	(2)	
Venelin Filipov (BUL)	20.08.1990	5	(4)	
Georgas Freidgeimas	10.08.1987	2		
Linas Klimavičius	10.04.1989	16	(4)	
Mamadou Mbodj (SEN)	12.03.1993	28		
Diego Alejandro Oyarzún Carrasco (CHI)	19.01.1993	5	(2)	
Donovan Carlos Saverio Slijngard (SUR)	28.08.1987	25	(2)	
Midfielders:	**DOB**	**M**	**(s)**	**G**
Slavko Blagojević (CRO)	21.03.1987	23	(1)	
Dominyk Kodz	25.04.2000		(2)	
Jérémy Manzorro (FRA)	11.11.1991	20	(4)	2
Marcus Vinícius Vidal Cunha „Marquinhos Carioca“ (BRA)	28.05.1992	14	(12)	4
Daniel Romanovskij	19.06.1996	3	(2)	
Tomáš Šimkovič (AUT)	16.04.1987	30	(1)	7
Domantas Šimkus	10.02.1996	6	(8)	2
Marko Tomić (SRB)	28.10.1991	27	(2)	6
Karolis Uzéla	11.03.2000	1	(4)	
Forwards:	**DOB**	**M**	**(s)**	**G**
Liviu Ion Antal (ROU)	02.06.1989	23	(4)	23
Tomáš Malec (SVK)	05.01.1993	17	(9)	8
Saulius Mikoliūnas	02.05.1984	19	(6)	2
Komla Serge Nyuiadzi (TOG)	17.09.1991	19	(4)	2
Ugochukwu Louis Ogana (NGA)	29.12.1995	16	(12)	10
Trainer:	**DOB**	**M**		
Aurelijus Skarbalius	12.05.1973	17		
Valdas Urbonas [23.06.2018]	29.11.1967	16		

SECOND LEVEL
LFF I Lyga 2018

1.	FK Panevėžys (*Promoted*)	26	18	4	4	77 - 26	58
2.	DFK Dainava Alytus (*Promotion Play-offs*)	26	17	6	3	59 - 22	57
3.	FK Banga Gargždai	26	18	0	8	51 - 24	54
4.	FK Nevėžis Kėdainiai	26	16	5	5	63 - 31	53
5.	FC Džiugas Telšiai	26	14	3	9	49 - 34	45
6.	FC Vytis Vilnius	26	13	5	8	67 - 44	44
7.	FC Pakruojis	26	13	3	10	44 - 44	42
8.	FK Utenis Utena	26	12	5	9	46 - 33	41
9.	FC Stumbras Kaunas „B“	26	10	6	10	42 - 37	36
10.	Nacionalinė Futbolo Akademija	26	8	3	15	44 - 45	27
11.	FK Trakai „B“	26	7	5	14	39 - 59	26
12.	FK Žalgiris Vilnius "B"	26	6	3	17	26 - 57	21
13.	FC Kupiškis (*Relegated*)	26	4	2	20	46 - 91	14
14.	FK Koralas Klaipėda (*Relegated*)	26	1	0	25	5 - 111	3

*Please note: FK Koralas Klaipėda failed to appear twice for league matches and was subsequently disqualified from the league on 19 September 2018.

NATIONAL TEAM

INTERNATIONAL MATCHES
(16.07.2018 – 15.07.2019)

07.09.2018	Vilnius	Lithuania - Serbia	0-1(0-1)	(UNL)
10.09.2018	Podgorica	Montenegro - Lithuania	2-0(2-0)	(UNL)
11.10.2018	Vilnius	Lithuania - Romania	1-2(0-1)	(UNL)
14.10.2018	Vilnius	Lithuania - Montenegro	1-4(0-3)	(UNL)
17.11.2018	Ploieşti	Romania - Lithuania	3-0(1-0)	(UNL)
20.11.2018	Beograd	Serbia - Lithuania	4-1(0-0)	(UNL)
22.03.2019	Lëtzebuerg	Luxembourg - Lithuania	2-1(1-1)	(ECQ)
25.03.2019	Bakı	Azerbaijan - Lithuania	0-0	(F)
07.06.2019	Vilnius	Lithuania - Luxembourg	1-1(0-1)	(ECQ)
10.06.2019	Beograd	Serbia - Lithuania	4-1(3-0)	(ECQ)

07.09.2018 LITHUANIA - SERBIA 0-1(0-1) UEFA Nations League C, Group 2
LFF Stadionas, Vilnius; Referee: Robert Adam Madden (Scotland); Attendance: 4,378
LTU: Ernestas Šetkus, Algis Jankauskas, Linas Klimavičius, Egidijus Vaitkūnas, Rolandas Baravykas, Mantas Kuklys (46.Modestas Vorobjovas), Artūras Žulpa, Arvydas Novikovas, Fedor Černych (Cap), Vykintas Slivka, Ovidijus Verbickas (72.Darvydas Šernas). Trainer: Edgaras Jankauskas.

10.09.2018 MONTENEGRO - LITHUANIA 2-0(2-0) UEFA Nations League C, Group 2
Stadion Pod Goricom, Podgorica; Referee: Jakob Kehlet (Denmark); Attendance: 5,239
LTU: Ernestas Šetkus, Linas Klimavičius, Egidijus Vaitkūnas, Povilas Leimonas (46.Valdemar Borovskij), Artūras Žulpa, Arvydas Novikovas, Fedor Černych (Cap), Vykintas Slivka, Ovidijus Verbickas (46.Mantas Kuklys), Modestas Vorobjovas, Justas Lasickas (62.Darvydas Šernas). Trainer: Edgaras Jankauskas.

11.10.2018 LITHUANIA - ROMANIA 1-2(0-1) UEFA Nations League C, Group 2
LFF Stadionas, Vilnius; Referee: François Letexier (France); Attendance: 2,279
LTU: Ernestas Šetkus, Vaidas Slavickas, Algis Jankauskas, Linas Klimavičius, Rolandas Baravykas, Artūras Žulpa, Arvydas Novikovas, Fedor Černych (Cap) (87.Deimantas Petravičius), Vykintas Slivka, Modestas Vorobjovas (63.Mantas Kuklys), Darvydas Šernas (63.Nerijus Valskis). Trainer: Edgaras Jankauskas.
Goal: Artūras Žulpa (90).

14.10.2018 LITHUANIA - MONTENEGRO 1-4(0-3) UEFA Nations League C, Group 2
LFF Stadionas, Vilnius; Referee: Robert Schörgenhofer (Austria); Attendance: 1,515
LTU: Ernestas Šetkus, Linas Klimavičius, Valdemar Borovskij, Rolandas Baravykas, Justinas Januševskij, Artūras Žulpa, Arvydas Novikovas, Vykintas Slivka, Fedor Černych (Cap) (50.Deimantas Petravičius), Modestas Vorobjovas (46.Mantas Kuklys), Nerijus Valskis (79.Donatas Kazlauskas). Trainer: Edgaras Jankauskas.
Goal: Rolandas Baravykas (88).

17.11.2018 ROMANIA - LITHUANIA 3-0(1-0) UEFA Nations League C, Group 2
Stadionul „Ilie Oană", Ploieşti; Referee: Marco Guida (Italy); Attendance: *behind closed doors.*
LTU: Ernestas Šetkus, Egidijus Vaitkūnas, Edvinas Girdvainis, Rolandas Baravykas, Artūras Žulpa, Arvydas Novikovas [*sent off 88*], Fedor Černych (Cap) (74.Darvydas Šernas), Deimantas Petravičius (80.Donatas Kazlauskas), Domantas Šimkus (65.Vykintas Slivka), Modestas Vorobjovas, Gratas Sirgėdas. Trainer: Edgaras Jankauskas.

20.11.2018 SERBIA - LITHUANIA 4-1(0-0) UEFA Nations League C, Group 2
Stadion Partizan, Beograd; Referee: Kristo Tohver (Estonia); Attendance: 2,088
LTU: Ernestas Šetkus, Vaidas Slavickas, Edvinas Girdvainis, Rolandas Baravykas, Justinas Januševskij, Artūras Žulpa (87.Algis Jankauskas), Fedor Černych (Cap), Deimantas Petravičius, Donatas Kazlauskas (59.Darvydas Šernas), Modestas Vorobjovas (69.Giedrius Matulevičius), Gratas Sirgėdas. Trainer: Edgaras Jankauskas.
Goal: Deimantas Petravičius (64).

22.03.2019 LUXEMBOURG - LITHUANIA 2-1(1-1) 16th EC. Qualifiers
Stade „Josy Barthel", Lëtzebuerg; Referee: Roey Reinshreiber (Israel); Attendance: 3,353
LTU: Ernestas Šetkus, Vaidas Slavickas, Algis Jankauskas, Linas Klimavičius, Mantas Kuklys, Rolandas Baravykas, Saulius Mikoliūnas (76.Justinas Marazas), Arvydas Novikovas (56.Artūras Žulpa), Fedor Černych (Cap), Deimantas Petravičius (61.Nerijus Valskis), Vykintas Slivka. Trainer: Valdas Urbonas.
Goal: Fedor Černych (14).

25.03.2019 AZERBAIJAN - LITHUANIA 0-0 Friendly International
Bakcell Arena, Bakı; Referee: Horaţiu Feşnic (Romania); Attendance: 3,122
LTU: Emilijus Zubas (46.Džiugas Bartkus), Linas Klimavičius, Markus Palionis, Egidijus Vaitkūnas (88.Vytautas Andriuškevičius), Rolandas Baravykas, Arvydas Novikovas (82.Mantas Kuklys), Modestas Vorobjovas, Fedor Černych (Cap) (66.Saulius Mikoliūnas), Vykintas Slivka, Nerijus Valskis (46.Deimantas Petravičius), Paulius Golubickas (62.Justinas Marazas). Trainer: Valdas Urbonas.

07.06.2019 LITHUANIA - LUXEMBOURG 1-1(0-1) 16th EC. Qualifiers
LFF Stadionas, Vilnius; Referee: Ádam Farkas (Hungary); Attendance: 3,263
LTU: Džiugas Bartkus, Linas Klimavičius, Markus Palionis, Vytautas Andriuškevičius, Saulius Mikoliūnas [*sent off 42*], Arvydas Novikovas, Fedor Černych (Cap) (89.Donatas Kazlauskas), Vykintas Slivka, Modestas Vorobjovas [*sent off 90+4*], Nerijus Valskis (55.Karolis Laukžemis), Paulius Golubickas (52.Domantas Šimkus). Trainer: Valdas Urbonas.
Goal: Arvydas Novikovas (74).

10.06.2019 SERBIA - LITHUANIA 4-1(3-0) 16th EC. Qualifiers

Stadion "Rajko Mitić", Beograd; Referee: Adrien Jaccotet (Switzerland); Attendance: *played behind closed doors*

LTU: Džiugas Bartkus, Algis Jankauskas (46.Karolis Chvedukas), Linas Klimavičius, Markus Palionis, Vytautas Andriuškevičius, Rolandas Baravykas, Arvydas Novikovas, Fedor Černych (Cap) (69.Deimantas Petravičius), Vykintas Slivka, Domantas Šimkus, Karolis Laukžemis (77.Nerijus Valskis). Trainer: Valdas Urbonas.

Goal: Arvydas Novikovas (71 penalty).

NATIONAL TEAM PLAYERS
(16.07.2018 – 15.07.2019)

Name	DOB	Caps	Goals	2018/2019:	Club
Goalkeepers					
Džiugas BARTKUS	07.11.1989	**5**	**0**	2018/2019:	*Hapoel Ironi Kiryat Shmona FC (ISR)*
Ernestas ŠETKUS	25.05.1985	**27**	**0**	2018/2019:	*Hapoel Haifa FC (ISR)*
Emilijus ZUBAS	10.07.1990	**13**	**0**	2019:	*Bnei Yehuda Tel Aviv FC (ISR)*
Defenders					
Vytautas ANDRIUŠKEVIČIUS	08.10.1990	**31**	**0**	2019:	*FK Sūduva Marijampolė*
Rolandas BARAVYKAS	23.08.1995	**17**	**1**	2018/2019:	*FK Žalgiris Vilnius*
Valdemar BOROVSKIJ	02.05.1984	**27**	**0**	2018:	*FK Trakai*
Edvinas GIRDVAINIS	17.01.1993	**16**	**0**	2018:	*Keşlə FK Bakı (AZE)*
Algis JANKAUSKAS	27.09.1982	**13**	**0**	2018/2019:	*FK Sūduva Marijampolė*
Justinas JANUŠEVSKIJ	26.03.1994	**3**	**0**	2018:	*FK Trakai*
Linas KLIMAVIČIUS	10.04.1989	**24**	**0**	2018: 23.01.2019->	*FK Žalgiris Vilnius* *FC Dinamo Bucureşti (ROU)*
Saulius MIKOLIŪNAS	02.05.1984	**78**	**5**	2019:	*FK Žalgiris Vilnius*
Markus PALIONIS	12.05.1987	**5**	**0**	2019:	*SSV Jahn Regensburg (GER)*
Vaidas SLAVICKAS	26.02.1986	**19**	**0**	2018/2019:	*FK Sūduva Marijampolė*
Egidijus VAITKŪNAS	08.08.1988	**43**	**0**	2018: 21.01.2019->	*FC Minsk (BLR)* *FK Kauno Žalgiris Kaunas*
Artūras ŽULPA	10.06.1990	**35**	**1**	2018/2019:	*FC Tobol Kostanay (KAZ)*
Midfielders					
Karolis CHVEDUKAS	21.04.1991	**20**	**0**	2019:	*Waterford FC (IRL)*
Paulius GOLUBICKAS	19.08.1999	**2**	**0**	2019:	*FK Sūduva Marijampolė*
Donatas KAZLAUSKAS	31.03.1994	**9**	**0**	2018:	*FK Trakai*
Mantas KUKLYS	10.06.1987	**35**	**0**	2018/2019:	*FC Zhetisu Taldiqorghan (KAZ)*
Justas LASICKAS	06.10.1997	**7**	**0**	2018:	*Jagiellonia Białystok (POL)*
Povilas LEIMONAS	16.11.1987	**5**	**0**	2018:	*FK Sūduva Marijampolė*
Justinas MARAZAS	23.02.2000	**2**	**0**	2019:	*Wisła Płock (POL)*
Giedrius MATULEVIČIUS	05.03.1997	**1**	**0**	2018:	*FK Sūduva Marijampolė*
Arvydas NOVIKOVAS	18.12.1990	**55**	**7**	2018/2019:	*Jagiellonia Białystok (POL)*
Deimantas PETRAVIČIUS	02.09.1995	**14**	**1**	2018/2019:	*Falkirk FC (SCO)*
Gratas SIRGĖDAS	17.12.1994	**7**	**0**	2018:	*FK Kauno Žalgiris Kaunas*
Vykintas SLIVKA	29.04.1995	**36**	**2**	2018/2019:	*Hibernian FC Edinburgh (SCO)*
Domantas ŠIMKUS	10.02.1996	**3**	**0**	2018/2019:	*FK Žalgiris Vilnius*
Ovidijus VERBICKAS	04.07.1993	**12**	**1**	2018:	*FK Sūduva Marijampolė*
Modestas VOROBJOVAS	30.12.1995	**13**	**0**	2018: 23.01.2019->	*FK Trakai* *FK Žalgiris Vilnius*
Forwards					
Fedor ČERNYCH	21.05.1991	**52**	**9**	2018/2019:	*FK Dinamo Moskva (RUS)*
Karolis LAUKŽEMIS	11.03.1992	**8**	**1**	2019:	*NK Istra 1961 Pula (CRO)*
Darvydas ŠERNAS	22.07.1984	**47**	**5**	2018:	*FC Sogdiana Jizzakh (UZB)*
Nerijus VALSKIS	04.08.1987	**25**	**1**	2018: 01.01.2019->	*Ratchaburi Mitr Phol FC (THA)* *Hapoel Tel Aviv FC (ISR)*

National team coach

Edgaras JANKAUSKAS [12.01.2016 – 04.12.2018]	12.03.1975	28 M; 3 W; 5 D; 20 L; 15-57
Valdas URBONAS [from 02.02.2019]	29.11.1967	4 M; 0 W; 2 D; 2 L; 3-7

LUXEMBOURG

The Country:

Groussherzogtum Lëtzebuerg (Grand Duchy of Lëtzebuerg)
Capital: Lëtzebuerg
Surface: 2,586.4 km²
Inhabitants: 613,894 [2019]
Time: UTC+1

The FA:

Fédération Luxembourgeoise de Football / Lëtzebuerger Foussballfederatioun
BP, 5 Rue de Limpach, 3901 Mondercange
Tel: +352 488 665 1
Foundation date: 1908
Member of FIFA since: 1910
Member of UEFA since: 1954
Website: www.flf.lu

NATIONAL TEAM RECORDS

First international match:	29.10.1911, Lëtzebuerg:	Luxembourg – France 1-4
Most international caps:	Mario Mutsch	- 102 caps (2005-2019)
Most international goals:	Léon Mart	- 16 goals / 24 caps (1933-1946)

UEFA EUROPEAN CHAMPIONSHIP	
1960	Did not enter
1964	Qualifiers
1968	Qualifiers
1972	Qualifiers
1976	Qualifiers
1980	Qualifiers
1984	Qualifiers
1988	Qualifiers
1992	Qualifiers
1996	Qualifiers
2000	Qualifiers
2004	Qualifiers
2008	Qualifiers
2012	Qualifiers
2016	Qualifiers

FIFA WORLD CUP	
1930	Did not enter
1934	Qualifiers
1938	Qualifiers
1950	Qualifiers
1954	Qualifiers
1958	Qualifiers
1962	Qualifiers
1966	Qualifiers
1970	Qualifiers
1974	Qualifiers
1978	Qualifiers
1982	Qualifiers
1986	Qualifiers
1990	Qualifiers
1994	Qualifiers
1998	Qualifiers
2002	Qualifiers
2006	Qualifiers
2010	Qualifiers
2014	Qualifiers
2018	Qualifiers

UEFA NATIONS LEAGUE
2018/2019 – League D (promoted to League C)

OLYMPIC FOOTBALL TOURNAMENTS 1908-2016							
1908	-	**1948**	1/8 - Finals	**1972**	Qualifiers	**1996**	Qualifiers
1912	-	**1952**	Round 1	**1976**	Qualifiers	**2000**	Qualifiers
1920	Round 1	**1956**	-	**1980**	Did not enter	**2004**	Qualifiers
1924	1/8 - Finals	**1960**	Qualifiers	**1984**	Did not enter	**2008**	Qualifiers
1928	1/8 - Finals	**1964**	Did not enter	**1988**	Did not enter	**2012**	Qualifiers
1936	1/8 - Finals	**1968**	Did not enter	**1992**	Qualifiers	**2016**	Qualifiers

FIFA CONFEDERATIONS CUP 1992-2017
None

LUXEMBOURGIAN CLUB HONOURS IN EUROPEAN CLUB COMPETITIONS:

European Champion Clubs.Cup (1956-1992) / UEFA Champions League (1993-2019)
None
Fairs Cup (1858-1971) / UEFA Cup (1972-2009) / UEFA Europa League (2010-2019)
None
UEFA Super Cup (1972-2018)
None
European Cup Winners.Cup 1961-1999*
None

*defunct competition

NATIONAL COMPETITIONS
TABLE OF HONOURS

	CHAMPIONS	CUP WINNERS	BEST GOALSCORERS	
1909/1910	Racing Club Lëtzebuerg	-	-	
1910/1911	Sporting Club Lëtzebuerg	-	-	
1911/1912	US Hollerich Bonnevoie	-	-	
1912/1913	*No competition*	-	-	
1913/1914	US Hollerich Bonnevoie	-	-	
1914/1915	US Hollerich Bonnevoie	-	-	
1915/1916	US Hollerich Bonnevoie	-	-	
1916/1917	US Hollerich Bonnevoie	-	-	
1917/1918	CS Fola Esch	-	-	
1918/1919	Sporting Club Lëtzebuerg	-	-	
1919/1920	CS Fola Esch	-	-	
1920/1921	AS la Jeunesse d'Esch/Alzette	-	-	
1921/1922	CS Fola Esch	Racing Club Lëtzebuerg	-	
1922/1923	FA Red Boys Differdange	CS Fola Esch	-	
1923/1924	CS Fola Esch	CS Fola Esch	-	
1924/1925	CA Spora Lëtzebuerg	FA Red Boys Differdange	-	
1925/1926	FA Red Boys Differdange	FA Red Boys Differdange	-	
1926/1927	Union Sportive Lëtzebuerg	FA Red Boys Differdange	-	
1927/1928	CA Spora Lëtzebuerg	CA Spora Lëtzebuerg	-	
1928/1929	CA Spora Lëtzebuerg	FA Red Boys Differdange	-	
1929/1930	CS Fola Esch	FA Red Boys Differdange	-	
1930/1931	FA Red Boys Differdange	FA Red Boys Differdange	-	
1931/1932	FA Red Boys Differdange	CA Spora Lëtzebuerg	-	
1932/1933	FA Red Boys Differdange	FC Progrès Niederkorn	-	
1933/1934	CA Spora Lëtzebuerg	FA Red Boys Differdange	-	
1934/1935	CA Spora Lëtzebuerg	AS la Jeunesse d'Esch/Alzette	-	
1935/1936	CA Spora Lëtzebuerg	FA Red Boys Differdange	-	
1936/1937	AS la Jeunesse d'Esch/Alzette	AS la Jeunesse d'Esch/Alzette	-	
1937/1938	CA Spora Lëtzebuerg	Stade Dudelange	-	
1938/1939	Stade Dudelange	Union Sportive Dudelange	-	
1939/1940	Stade Dudelange	CA Spora Lëtzebuerg	-	
1940-1944	*No competition*	*No competition*	-	
1944/1945	Stade Dudelange	FC Progrès Niederkorn	-	
1945/1946	Stade Dudelange	AS la Jeunesse d'Esch/Alzette	Camille Libar (Stade Dudelange) Paul Feller (Stade Dudelange)	17
1946/1947	Stade Dudelange	Union Sportive Lëtzebuerg	Camille Libar (Stade Dudelange)	22
1947/1948	Stade Dudelange	Stade Dudelange	Nic Kettel (Stade Dudelange) René Conrad (Union Sportive Dudelange) Charles Wagner (SC Tétange)	18
1948/1949	CA Spora Lëtzebuerg	Stade Dudelange	Jules Gales (CA Spora Lëtzebuerg)	19
1949/1950	Stade Dudelange	CA Spora Lëtzebuerg	Jules Gales (CA Spora Lëtzebuerg)	18
1950/1951	AS la Jeunesse d'Esch/Alzette	SC Tétange	Jules Gales (CA Spora Lëtzebuerg)	27
1951/1952	The National Schifflange	FA Red Boys Differdange	Alphonse Schumacher (The National Schifflange)	16
1952/1953	FC Progrès Niederkorn	FA Red Boys Differdange	Henri Fickinger (FC Progrès Niederkorn) François Muller (Red Star Merl-Belair) Roger Weydert (Union Sportive Lëtzebuerg)	18
1953/1954	AS la Jeunesse d'Esch/Alzette	AS la Jeunesse d'Esch/Alzette	Alphonse Schumacher (CS Fola Esch)	29
1954/1955	Stade Dudelange	CS Fola Esch	Alphonse Schumacher (CS Fola Esch)	20
1955/1956	CA Spora Lëtzebuerg	Stade Dudelange	Jean Halsdorf (Stade Dudelange)	23
1956/1957	Stade Dudelange	CA Spora Lëtzebuerg	François Muller (CS Grevenmacher)	36
1957/1958	AS la Jeunesse d'Esch/Alzette	FA Red Boys Differdange	François Jadin (Alliance Dudelange)	17
1958/1959	AS la Jeunesse d'Esch/Alzette	Union Sportive Lëtzebuerg	Marcel Scheer (CA Spora Lëtzebuerg)	19
1959/1960	AS la Jeunesse d'Esch/Alzette	The National Schifflange	Louis Pilot (CS Fola Esch)	18
1960/1961	CA Spora Lëtzebuerg	Alliance Dudelange	Paul May (AS la Jeunesse d'Esch/Alzette)	24
1961/1962	Union Sportive Lëtzebuerg	Alliance Dudelange	Henri Cirelli (Alliance Dudelange)	23
1962/1963	AS la Jeunesse d'Esch/Alzette	Union Sportive Lëtzebuerg	Bert Heger (Stade Dudelange)	20
1963/1964	FC Aris Bonnevoie	Union Sportive Lëtzebuerg	Johny Leonard (Union Sportive Lëtzebuerg)	22
1964/1965	Stade Dudelange	CA Spora Lëtzebuerg	Johny Leonard (Union Sportive Lëtzebuerg)	18
1965/1966	FC Aris Bonnevoie	CA Spora Lëtzebuerg	Bert Heger (FC Aris Bonnevoie) Johny Leonard (Union Sportive Lëtzebuerg)	23
1966/1967	AS la Jeunesse d'Esch/Alzette	FC Aris Bonnevoie	Jemp Mertl (Union Sportive Lëtzebuerg)	22
1967/1968	AS la Jeunesse d'Esch/Alzette	Union Sportive Rumelange	Rainer Schönwälder (Union Sportive Lëtzebuerg)	28
1968/1969	FC Avenir Beggen	Union Sportive Lëtzebuerg	Bert Heger (FC Avenir Beggen)	30
1969/1970	AS la Jeunesse d'Esch/Alzette	Union Sportive Lëtzebuerg	Carlo Devillet (CA Spora Lëtzebuerg)	31
1970/1971	Union Sportive Lëtzebuerg	Jeunesse Hautcharage	Nico Braun (Union Sportive Lëtzebuerg)	25
1971/1972	FC Aris Bonnevoie	FA Red Boys Differdange	Furio Cardoni (Union Sportive Rumelange) Carlo Devillet (FC Aris Bonnevoie)	21
1972/1973	AS la Jeunesse d'Esch/Alzette	AS la Jeunesse d'Esch/Alzette	Johny Grettnich (FC Etzella Ettelbruck) Jean-Pierre Hoffmann (AS la Jeunesse Esch/Alzette)	27
1973/1974	AS la Jeunesse d'Esch/Alzette	AS la Jeunesse d'Esch/Alzette	Carlo Devillet (CA Spora Lëtzebuerg)	23
1974/1975	AS la Jeunesse d'Esch/Alzette	Union Sportive Rumelange	Jean-Paul Lehnen (FC Etzella Ettelbruck)	16

1975/1976	AS la Jeunesse d'Esch/Alzette	AS la Jeunesse d'Esch/Alzette	René Muller (FA Red Boys Differdange) Albert Pissinger (FC Aris Bonnevoie)	20
1976/1977	AS la Jeunesse d'Esch/Alzette	FC Progrès Niederkorn	Johny Hopp (FC Progrès Niederkorn)	19
1977/1978	FC Progrès Niederkorn	FC Progrès Niederkorn	René Muller (FA Red Boys Differdange)	18
1978/1979	FA Red Boys Differdange	FA Red Boys Differdange	Aly May (FC Progrès Niederkorn)	18
1979/1980	AS la Jeunesse d'Esch/Alzette	CA Spora Lëtzebuerg	Roby Langers (Union Sportive Lëtzebuerg)	26
1980/1981	FC Progrès Niederkorn	AS la Jeunesse d'Esch/Alzette	Aly May (FC Progrès Niederkorn)	18
1981/1982	FC Avenir Beggen	FA Red Boys Differdange	Armin Krings (FC Avenir Beggen)	25
1982/1983	AS la Jeunesse d'Esch/Alzette	FC Avenir Beggen	Gérard Simon (AS la Jeunesse d'Esch/Alzette)	23
1983/1984	FC Avenir Beggen	FC Avenir Beggen	Armin Krings (FC Avenir Beggen) Manou Scheitler (AS la Jeunesse d'Esch/Alzette)	26
1984/1985	AS la Jeunesse d'Esch/Alzette	FA Red Boys Differdange	Armin Krings (FC Avenir Beggen) Jean-Luc Guillot (AS la Jeunesse d'Esch/Alzette)	16
1985/1986	FC Avenir Beggen	Union Sportive Lëtzebuerg	Armin Krings (FC Avenir Beggen)	25
1986/1987	AS la Jeunesse d'Esch/Alzette	FC Avenir Beggen	Armin Krings (FC Avenir Beggen)	24
1987/1988	AS la Jeunesse d'Esch/Alzette	AS la Jeunesse d'Esch/Alzette	Patrick Morocutti (Union Sportive Lëtzebuerg)	26
1988/1989	CA Spora Lëtzebuerg	Union Sportive Lëtzebuerg	Theo Scholten (AS la Jeunesse d'Esch/Alzette) Markus Krahen (GER, FC Avenir Beggen) Armin Krings (FC Avenir Beggen)	21
1989/1990	Union Sportive Lëtzebuerg	FC Swift Hesperange	Markus Krahen (GER, FC Avenir Beggen)	30
1990/1991	Union Sportive Lëtzebuerg	Union Sportive Lëtzebuerg	Patrick Morocutti (Union Sportive Lëtzebuerg)	23
1991/1992	Union Sportive Lëtzebuerg	FC Avenir Beggen	Markus Krahen (GER, FC Avenir Beggen)	19
1992/1993	FC Avenir Beggen	FC Avenir Beggen	Armin Krings (FC Avenir Beggen)	23
1993/1994	FC Avenir Beggen	FC Avenir Beggen	Stefano Fanelli (F91 Dudelange)	19
1994/1995	AS la Jeunesse d'Esch/Alzette	CS Grevenmacher	Yves Heinen (FC Differdange 03)	22
1995/1996	AS la Jeunesse d'Esch/Alzette	Union Sportive Lëtzebuerg	Mikhail Zaritski (FC Avenir Beggen)	18
1996/1997	AS la Jeunesse d'Esch/Alzette	AS la Jeunesse d'Esch/Alzette	Mikhail Zaritski (FC Sporting Mertzig) Franco Iovino (FC Wiltz 71)	19
1997/1998	AS la Jeunesse d'Esch/Alzette	CS Grevenmacher	Mikhail Zaritski (FC Sporting Mertzig)	29
1998/1999	AS la Jeunesse d'Esch/Alzette	AS la Jeunesse d'Esch/Alzette	Frédéric Cicchirillo (FRA, FC Sporting Mertzig)	25
1999/2000	F91 Dudelange	AS la Jeunesse d'Esch/Alzette	Marcel Christophe (FC Mondercange)	26
2000/2001	F91 Dudelange	FC Etzella Ettelbruck	Mikhail Zaritski (FC Sporting Mertzig)	23
2001/2002	F91 Dudelange	FC Avenir Beggen	Frédéric Cicchirillo (FRA, F91 Dudelange)	24
2002/2003	CS Grevenmacher	CS Grevenmacher	Daniel Huss (CS Grevenmacher)	22
2003/2004	AS la Jeunesse d'Esch/Alzette	F91 Dudelange	José Manuel Gomes de Andrade (POR, CA Spora Lëtzebuerg)	24
2004/2005	F91 Dudelange	CS Pétange	Sergio Pupovac (CS Alliance 01 Lëtzebuerg)	24
2005/2006	F91 Dudelange	F91 Dudelange	Fatih Sözen (TUR, CS Grevenmacher)	23
2006/2007	F91 Dudelange	F91 Dudelange	Daniel da Mota Alves (FC Etzella Ettelbruck)	24
2007/2008	F91 Dudelange	CS Grevenmacher	Emmanuel Coquelet (FRA, F91 Dudelange)	20
2008/2009	F91 Dudelange	F91 Dudelange	Pierre Piskor (FRA, FC Differdange 03)	30
2009/2010	AS la Jeunesse d'Esch/Alzette	FC Differdange 03	Daniel Huss (CS Grevenmacher)	22
2010/2011	F91 Dudelange	FC Differdange 03	Sanel Ibrahimović (BIH, FC Wiltz 71)	18
2011/2012	F91 Dudelange	F91 Dudelange	Omar Er Rafik (MAR, FC Differdange 03)	23
2012/2013	CS Fola Esch	AS la Jeunesse d'Esch/Alzette	Edis Osmanović (BIH, FC Wiltz 71)	21
2013/2014	F91 Dudelange	FC Differdange 03	Sanel Ibrahimović (BIH, AS la Jeunesse d'Esch/Alzette)	22
2014/2015	CS Fola Esch	FC Differdange 03	Sanel Ibrahimović (BIH, AS la Jeunesse d'Esch/Alzette)	21
2015/2016	F91 Dudelange	F91 Dudelange	Julien Jahier (FRA, RFCU Lëtzebuerg)	18
2016/2017	F91 Dudelange	F91 Dudelange	Omar Er Rafik (MAR, FC Differdange 03)	26
2017/2018	F91 Dudelange	Racing FC	David Turpel (F91 Dudelange)	33
2018/2019	F91 Dudelange	F91 Dudelange	Samir Ali Hadji (FRA, CS Fola Esch)	23

NATIONAL CHAMPIONSHIP
BGL Ligue 2018/2019
(05.08.2018 – 19.05.2019)

Results

Round 1 [05-06.08.2018]
Jeunesse d'Esch - Fola Esch 3-1
Etzella Ettelbruck - Racing FCU 1-1
US Rumelange - Progrès Niederkorn 2-1
US Hostert - UNA Strassen 1-6
Victoria Rosport - Union Titus Pétange 0-1
FC Differdange 03 - US Mondorf 2-0
RM Hamm Benfica - F91 Dudelange 1-3

Round 2 [11-13.08.2018]
Union Titus Pétange - US Hostert 2-1
Jeunesse d'Esch - US Rumelange 3-1
Racing FCU - Victoria Rosport 2-2
UNA Strassen - RM Hamm Benfica 0-3
US Mondorf - Fola Esch 2-0
F91 Dudelange - FC Differdange 03 0-2
Pr. Niederkorn - Etzella Ett. 4-3 [22.08.2018]

Round 3 [17-19.08.2018]
US Hostert - Racing FCU 0-4
US Mondorf - Jeunesse d'Esch 0-2
RM Hamm Benfica - Union Titus Pétange 2-2
Etzella Ettelbruck - US Rumelange 2-1
FC Differdange 03 - UNA Strassen 1-3
Victoria Rosport - Progrès Niederkorn 2-1
Fola Esch - F91 Dudelange 1-2 [26.09.2018]

Round 4 [26.08.2018]
Jeunesse d'Esch - Etzella Ettelbruck 1-0
US Rumelange - Victoria Rosport 3-2
Progrès Niederkorn - US Hostert 1-1
Racing FCU - RM Hamm Benfica 1-0
Union Titus Pétange - FC Differdange 03 0-1
UNA Strassen - Fola Esch 0-2
F91 Dudelange - US Mondorf 1-4

Round 5 [31.08.-02.09.2018]
FC Differdange 03 - Racing FCU 1-0
RM Hamm Benfica - Progrès Niederkorn 1-2
US Hostert - US Rumelange 4-2
US Mondorf - UNA Strassen 2-2
Victoria Rosport - Etzella Ettelbruck 0-3
Fola Esch - Union Titus Pétange 3-0
F91 Dudelange - Jeunesse Esch 1-3 [31.10.18]

Round 6 [15-16.09.2018]
Progrès Niederkorn - FC Differdange 03 2-0
UNA Strassen - F91 Dudelange 0-2
Jeunesse d'Esch - Victoria Rosport 1-1
Etzella Ettelbruck - US Hostert 0-1
US Rumelange - RM Hamm Benfica 1-3
Racing FCU - Fola Esch 2-1
Union Titus Pétange - US Mondorf 1-0

Round 7 [30.09.-01.10.2018]
F91 Dudelange - Union Titus Pétange 6-1
FC Differdange 03 - US Rumelange 3-2
RM Hamm Benfica - Etzella Ettelbruck 1-1
US Hostert - Victoria Rosport 0-3
US Mondorf - Racing FCU 0-3
UNA Strassen - Jeunesse d'Esch 0-4
Fola Esch - Progrès Niederkorn 2-1

Round 8 [06-07.10.2018]
Union Titus Pétange - UNA Strassen 3-1
Etzella Ettelbruck - FC Differdange 03 1-0
Progrès Niederkorn - US Mondorf 2-1
Jeunesse d'Esch - US Hostert 3-0
Victoria Rosport - RM Hamm Benfica 3-1
US Rumelange - Fola Esch 0-3
Racing FCU - F91 Dudelange 1-1

Round 9 [20-21.10.2018]
F91 Dudelange - Progrès Niederkorn 4-1
Union Titus Pétange - Jeunesse d'Esch 3-2
UNA Strassen - Racing FCU 1-2
US Mondorf - US Rumelange 4-3
Fola Esch - Etzella Ettelbruck 6-0
FC Differdange 03 - Victoria Rosport 3-0
RM Hamm Benfica - US Hostert 1-2

Round 10 [03-04.11.2018]
Progrès Niederkorn - UNA Strassen 2-0
Victoria Rosport - Fola Esch 1-4
Jeunesse d'Esch - RM Hamm Benfica 4-0
US Hostert - FC Differdange 03 1-1
Etzella Ettelbruck - US Mondorf 2-0
US Rumelange - F91 Dudelange 2-9
Racing FCU - Union Titus Pétange 4-1

Round 11 [10-11.11.2018]
Fola Esch - US Hostert 4-1
FC Differdange 03 - RM Hamm Benfica 4-0
Racing FCU - Jeunesse d'Esch 0-1
Union Titus Pétange - Progrès Niederkorn 1-5
UNA Strassen - US Rumelange 4-1
F91 Dudelange - Etzella Ettelbruck 4-2
US Mondorf - Victoria Rosport 4-0

Round 12 [25.11.2018]
RM Hamm Benfica - Fola Esch 1-2
Jeunesse d'Esch - FC Differdange 03 0-0
US Hostert - US Mondorf 1-1
Victoria Rosport - F91 Dudelange 2-2
Etzella Ettelbruck - UNA Strassen 0-2
US Rumelange - Union Titus Pétange 0-0
Progrès Niederkorn - Racing FCU 2-0

Round 13 [02.12.2018]
Fola Esch - FC Differdange 03 3-0
UNA Strassen - Victoria Rosport 4-0
Progrès Niederkorn - Jeunesse d'Esch 5-0
Racing FCU - US Rumelange 2-2
Union Titus Pétange - Etzella Ettelbruck 1-1
F91 Dudelange - US Hostert 4-1
US Mondorf - RM Hamm Benfica 2-2

Round 14 [23-24.02.2019]
US Rumelange - Jeunesse d'Esch 1-1
Etzella Ettelbruck - Progrès Niederkorn 1-1
Victoria Rosport - Racing FCU 1-1
US Hostert - Union Titus Pétange 0-3
RM Hamm Benfica - UNA Strassen 1-3
FC Differdange 03 - F91 Dudelange 0-4
Fola Esch - US Mondorf 5-0

Round 15 [01-03.03.2019]
UNA Strassen - FC Differdange 03 2-0
Progrès Niederkorn - Victoria Rosport 3-3
Jeunesse d'Esch - US Mondorf 1-2
F91 Dudelange - Fola Esch 1-1
Union Titus Pétange - RM Hamm Benfica 3-0
Racing FCU - US Hostert 2-0
US Rumelange - Etzella Ettelbruck 3-5

Round 16 [10.03.2019]
RM Hamm Benfica - Racing FCU 2-0
Etzella Ettelbruck - Jeunesse d'Esch 1-1
Victoria Rosport - US Rumelange 4-2
US Hostert - Progrès Niederkorn 0-1
FC Differdange 03 - Union Titus Pétange 1-5
Fola Esch - UNA Strassen 1-1
US Mondorf - F91 Dudelange 1-2

Round 17 [15-17.03.2019]
Jeunesse d'Esch - F91 Dudelange 0-3
Union Titus Pétange - Fola Esch 2-1
Racing FCU - FC Differdange 03 3-3
Progrès Niederkorn - RM Hamm Benfica 1-0
US Rumelange - US Hostert 0-4
UNA Strassen - US Mondorf 1-0
Etzella Ettelbruck - Victoria Rosport 0-0

Round 18 [30-31.03.2019]
F91 Dudelange - UNA Strassen 1-1
US Mondorf - Union Titus Pétange 4-1
FC Differdange 03 - Progrès Niederkorn 2-0
Victoria Rosport - Jeunesse d'Esch 1-2
US Hostert - Etzella Ettelbruck 4-0
RM Hamm Benfica - US Rumelange 0-1
Fola Esch - Racing FCU 3-0

Round 19 [07.04.2019]
Progrès Niederkorn - Fola Esch 1-1
Jeunesse d'Esch - UNA Strassen 1-2
Union Titus Pétange - F91 Dudelange 1-3
Racing FCU - US Mondorf 3-0
US Rumelange - FC Differdange 03 1-2
Etzella Ettelbruck - RM Hamm Benfica 0-3
Victoria Rosport - US Hostert 2-0

Round 20 [14.04.2019]
US Hostert - Jeunesse d'Esch 2-3
RM Hamm Benfica - Victoria Rosport 1-3
FC Differdange 03 - Etzella Ettelbruck 2-0
Fola Esch - US Rumelange 7-0
US Mondorf - Progrès Niederkorn 1-0
F91 Dudelange - Racing FCU 2-0
UNA Strassen - Union Titus Pétange 2-1

Round 21 [20.04.2019]
Jeunesse d'Esch - Union Titus Pétange 1-1
Racing FCU - UNA Strassen 4-1
Progrès Niederkorn - F91 Dudelange 0-2
US Rumelange - US Mondorf 1-3
Victoria Rosport - FC Differdange 03 0-1
US Hostert - RM Hamm Benfica 1-0
Etzella Ettelbruck - Fola Esch 2-2

Round 22 [26-28.04.2019]
Union Titus Pétange - Racing FCU 0-1
Fola Esch - Victoria Rosport 1-1
RM Hamm Benfica - Jeunesse d'Esch 0-2
US Mondorf - Etzella Ettelbruck 1-0
F91 Dudelange - US Rumelange 2-2
FC Differdange 03 - US Hostert 3-1
UNA Strassen - Progrès Niederkorn 2-4

Round 23 [01.05.2019]
US Hostert - Fola Esch 2-3
US Rumelange - UNA Strassen 0-2
Victoria Rosport - US Mondorf 0-4
Etzella Ettelbruck - F91 Dudelange 0-2
RM Hamm Benfica - FC Differdange 03 1-1
Jeunesse d'Esch - Racing FCU 1-0
Progrès Niederkorn - Union Titus Pétange 1-0

Round 24 [05.05.2019]
Fola Esch - RM Hamm Benfica 2-0
US Mondorf - US Hostert 2-2
UNA Strassen - Etzella Ettelbruck 2-1
Union Titus Pétange - US Rumelange 2-1
Racing FCU - Progrès Niederkorn 5-0
FC Differdange 03 - Jeunesse d'Esch 2-0
F91 Dudelange - Victoria Rosport 2-0

Round 25 [12.05.2019]
Jeunesse d'Esch - Progrès Niederkorn 1-1
US Rumelange - Racing FCU 2-1
Etzella Ettelbruck - Union Titus Pétange 2-1
Victoria Rosport - UNA Strassen 2-1
US Hostert - F91 Dudelange 3-4
RM Hamm Benfica - US Mondorf 2-1
FC Differdange 03 - Fola Esch 0-4

Round 26 [19.05.2019]
US Mondorf - FC Differdange 03 0-0
F91 Dudelange - RM Hamm Benfica 5-3
UNA Strassen - US Hostert 2-4
Union Titus Pétange - Victoria Rosport 2-0
Racing FCU - Etzella Ettelbruck 0-3
Progrès Niederkorn - US Rumelange 3-0
Fola Esch - Jeunesse d'Esch 2-5

Final Standings

1.	**F91 Dudelange**	26	18	5	3	72	-	33	59
2.	CS Fola Esch	26	15	5	6	65	-	28	50
3.	AS La Jeunesse d'Esch/Alzette	26	14	6	6	46	-	30	48
4.	FC Progrès Niederkorn	26	13	5	8	45	-	35	44
5.	FC Differdange 03	26	13	5	8	35	-	33	44
6.	Racing FC Union Lëtzebuerg	26	11	6	9	42	-	31	39
7.	FC UNA Strassen	26	12	3	11	46	-	43	39
8.	Union Titus Pétange	26	11	4	11	38	-	43	37
9.	US Mondorf-les-Bains	26	10	5	11	39	-	39	35
10.	FC Etzella Ettelbrück	26	7	7	12	31	-	44	28
11.	FC Victoria Rosport	26	7	7	12	33	-	49	28
12.	US Hostert (*Relegation Play-offs*)	26	7	4	15	37	-	58	25
13.	FC RM Hamm Benfica (*Relegated*)	26	5	4	17	29	-	50	19
14.	US Rumelange (*Relegated*)	26	4	4	18	34	-	76	16

Top goalscorers:

23 Samir Ali Hadji (FRA)
CS Fola Esch

14 Mickaël Jager (FRA)
FC UNA Strassen

14 David Turpel
F91 Düdelingen

13 Bertino João Cabral Barbosa (POR)
RM Hamm Benfica

Relegation Play-offs

US Hostert - FC Swift Hesperange	2-0(2-0)

US Hostert remains at first level.

NATIONAL CUP
Coupe du Luxembourg 2018/2019

First Round [07/09/12.09.2018]

Alliance Aischdall - CS Grevenmacher	2-1
Luna Oberkorn - Union 05 FC Kayl-Tétange	1-3
AS Colmarberg - Rupensia Lusitanos Larochette	3-1
SC Ell - Jeunesse Biwer	0-5
Tricolore Gasperich - US Moutfort	1-3
FC Brouch - FC 47 Bastendorf	1-9
CS Bourscheid - FC Noertzange HF	5-4
Red Star Merl - FC Mondercange	0-4
Résidence Walferdange - Jeunesse Useldange	2-4
FC Biekerech - Blo-Weiss Medernach	0-11
Minière Lasauvage - ES Schouweiler	2-3
Claravallis Clervaux - Berdenia Berburg	1-6
FC Munsbach - FC CeBra 01 Cessange	0-6
AS Hosingen - FC Koerich/Simmern	2-3
Racing Heiderscheid - Orania Vianden	3-4
Racing Troisvierges - AS Wincrange	0-2
FC Kopstal - Sporting Bertrange	0-7
CS Obercorn - US Berdorf	5-3
Blo Weiss Itzig - US Boevange	3-0 (awarded)
US Reisdorf - Excelsior Grevels	0-4
US Folschette - Young Boys Diekirch	0-3
Les Ardoisiers Perlé - FC Avenir Beggen	1-0
FC Minerva Lintgen - Sporting Mertzig	5-1
ES Clemency - SC Bettembourg	2-5
FC Ehlerange - Union Remich/Bous	0-2
CS Sanem - Marisca Mersch	6-4
Red Boys Aspelt - Syra Mensdorf	0-3
Daring Club Echternach - FC Pratzerthal/Rédange	5-0
AS Luxembourg-Porto - Sporting Steinfort	0-1
FC Green Boys 77 - FF Norden 02	1-3
US Feulen - US Rambrouch	3-0
FC Red-Black/Egalite 07 - Jeunesse Schieren	1-2
Olympia Christnach - Yellow Boys Weiler	1-9
Jeunesse Gilsdorf - FC Kehlen	2-4
FC Schifflange 95 - FC Lorentzweiler	2-1
The Belval Belvaux - Alisontia Steinsel	0-4

Second Round [21-23.09.2018]

Syra Mensdorf - FC 72 Erpeldange	2-3
Berdenia Berburg - AS La Jeunesse d'Esch/Alzette	0-3
Sporting Steinfort - FC Victoria Rosport	0-1
FC Koerich/Simmern - FC Atert Bissen	2-7
Jeunesse Biwer - Blue Boys Muhlenbach	0-4
AS Colmarberg - Union Titus Pétange	0-4
FC Minerva Lintgen - US Hostert	0-4
Jeunesse Useldange - FC UNA Strassen	1-6
Blo-Weiss Medernach - Koeppchen Wormeldange	2-4 aet
CS Obercorn - US Mertert/Wasserbillig	1-5
ES Schouweiler - FC Wiltz 71	0-6
Jeunesse Schieren - FC Swift Hesperange	3-6
FC Mondercange - US Esch	0-1
AS Wincrange - UN Käerjéng	0-6
FC 47 Bastendorf - FC Etzella Ettelbruck	1-10
Blo Weiss Itzig - CS Fola Esch	1-7
FC Schifflange 95 - FC Mamer 32	1-4
FF Norden 02 - FC Differdange 03	1-2
Young Boys Diekirch - FC Jeunesse Canach	2-4
Les Ardoisiers Perlé - US Sandweiler	1-4 aet
Orania Vianden - US Mondorf	0-7
SC Bettembourg - Racing FC Union Lëtzebuerg	0-7
Alliance Aischdall - Jeunesse Junglinster	4-3
Union Remich/Bous - US Rumelange	0-1
Alisontia Steinsel - FC Rodange 91	0-1
Daring Club Echternach - FC RM Hamm Benfica	0-4
US Moutfort - Sporting Bertrange	2-3
CS Sanem - Union 05 FC Kayl-Tétange	1-3
FC CeBra 01 Cessange - Yellow Boys Weiler	3-0
CS Bourscheid - Excelsior Grevels	2-0
FC Kehlen - F91 Dudelange	1-7
US Feulen - FC Progrès Niederkorn	1-4

Third Round [27-28.10.2018]			
CS Bourscheid - CS Fola Esch	1-16	FC Mamer 32 - Blue Boys Muhlenbach	0-1
UN Käerjéng - AS La Jeunesse d'Esch/Alzette	0-5	FC CeBra 01 Cessange - FC Etzella Ettelbruck	0-2
US Mertert/Wasserbillig - Koeppchen Wormeldange	5-1	Sporting Bertrange - Alliance Aischdall	3-2
FC Progrès Niederkorn - US Hostert	1-0	FC Swift Hesperange - US Mondorf	1-3
US Sandweiler - F91 Dudelange	0-6	Racing FC Union Lëtzebuerg - FC Differdange 03	4-5 pen
US Esch - Union Titus Pétange	2-1 aet	FC Rodange 91 - FC Victoria Rosport	8-9 pen
FC 72 Erpeldange - FC RM Hamm Benfica	2-6 aet	Union 05 FC Kayl-Tétange - FC Wiltz 71	3-4 pen
FC Jeunesse Canach - FC Atert Bissen	0-2	US Rumelange - FC UNA Strassen	1-4

1/8-Finals [09/17.12.2018]			
F91 Dudelange - CS Fola Esch	2-1	Sporting Bertrange - US Mertert/Wasserbillig	1-3 aet
FC Wiltz 71 - FC Victoria Rosport	0-2	FC RM Hamm Benfica - FC Progrès Niederkorn	2-4
US Esch - FC UNA Strassen	1-2 aet	FC Etzella Ettelbruck - La Jeunesse d'Esch/Alzette	1-0
US Mondorf - FC Differdange 03	2-1 aet	Blue Boys Muhlenbach - FC Atert Bissen	1-0

Quarter-Finals [03.04.2019]			
US Mertert/Wasserbillig - FC Victoria Rosport	2-0	F91 Dudelange - US Mondorf	3-2 aet
FC Etzella Ettelbruck - FC UNA Strassen	7-6 pen	Blue Boys Muhlenbach - FC Progrès Niederkorn	0-3

Semi-Finals [24.04.2019]			
F91 Dudelange - FC Progrès Niederkorn	3-1	US Mertert/Wasserbillig - FC Etzella Ettelbruck	0-3

Final

26.05.2019; Stade „Josy Barthel", Lëtzebuerg; Referee: Sergio Rodrigues; Attendance: 2,866

F91 Dudelange - FC Etzella Ettelbrück **5-0(0-0)**

F91 Dudelange: Jonathan Joubert (Cap), Kevin Malget (46.Aniss El Hriti), Jerry Prempeh, Tom Schnell, Edisson Jordanov, Clément Couturier (70.Danel Sinani), Stélvio Rosa da Cruz, Mario Pokar, Dominik Stolz, Sanel Ibrahimović (74.Nicolas Perez), David Turpel. Trainer: Dino Toppmöller (Germany).

Etzella Ettelbrück: Sebastian Grub, Pol Schlesser, Dominik Zwick, Losseni Keita [*sent off 65*], Jader Soares, Joël Magalhaes (62.Jakub Jarecki), Kevin Holtz (Cap), Diogo Miguel Zambujo Pimentel, Lex Nicolay (46.Sven Kalisa), Mefail Kadrija (73.Adam Bouzid), Julian Bidon. Trainer: Claude Ottelé.

Goals: 1-0 Clément Couturier (55), 2-0 David Turpel (59), 3-0 Edisson Jordanov (66), 4-0 Dominik Stolz (69), 5-0 Nicolas Perez (88).

THE CLUBS 2018/2019

Foussballclub Déifferdeng 03

Founded: 2003 (*as merger of FA Red Boys Differdange and AS Differdange*)
Stadium: Stade Parc des Sports, Differdange (2,400)

Goalkeepers:	**DOB**	**M**	**(s)**	**G**
Julien Weber	12.10.1985	26		
Defenders:	**DOB**	**M**	**(s)**	**G**
Geoffrey Franzoni	18.02.1991	25		1
Mathias Jänisch	27.08.1990	20		1
André Rodrigues	06.12.1987	12	(7)	
Alexandre Semedo	22.08.1989	2		
Henrique Ferreira Serrano	22.02.1999	1	(1)	
Tom Siebenaler	28.09.1990	23		2
David Vandenbroeck (BEL)	12.07.1985	26		1
Midfielders:	**DOB**	**M**	**(s)**	**G**
Gonçalo Almeida da Silva (POR)	26.11.1990	10	(1)	3
Gilles Bettmer	31.03.1989	18	(5)	
Mickael Garos	10.05.1988	23		3
Ndriqim Halili	29.01.1993	6	(3)	
Ryan Lohei	11.04.2001	1	(15)	
Ricardo Couto Pinto	14.01.1996	7	(8)	3
Pedro Ribeiro	17.11.1989	2	(11)	1
Ilhan Skenderović	15.05.1999		(2)	
Jordan Swistek (FRA)	25.08.1991	12	(8)	1
Forwards:	**DOB**	**M**	**(s)**	**G**
Gauthier Caron (FRA)	27.12.1989	21	(1)	4
Maxime Deruffe (FRA)	13.05.1988	21		6
Edvin Muratovic	15.02.1997	14	(7)	7
Jordan Oukache (FRA)	09.06.1995	16	(4)	1
Thibault Sponar (FRA)	19.09.2000		(1)	
Trainer:	**DOB**	**M**		
Arno Bonvini	14.10.1975	17		
Paolo Amodio [18.03.2019]	28.05.1973	9		

F91 Dudelange

Founded: 1991
Stadium: Stade „Jos Nosbaum", Dudelange (2,558)

Goalkeepers:	DOB	M	(s)	G
Enzo Esposito	06.10.1998	4		
Joé Frising	13.01.1994	3		
Jonathan Joubert	12.09.1979	24		
Defenders:	**DOB**	**M**	**(s)**	**G**
Milan Biševac (SRB)	31.08.1983	3		1
Salif Dramé (SEN)	03.01.1997	1		
Aniss El Hriti (FRA)	28.07.1989	12		
Edisson Jordanov (BUL)	08.06.1993	21		3
Kevin Malget	15.01.1991	14	(3)	3
Bryan Mélisse (FRA)	25.03.1989	13		1
Clayton De Sousa Moreira	24.02.1988	4	(6)	
Jerry Prempeh (GHA)	29.12.1988	23		
Tom Schnell	08.10.1985	17	(3)	
Midfielders:	**DOB**	**M**	**(s)**	**G**
Clément Couturier (FRA)	13.09.1993	16	(1)	6
Leon Jensen (GER)	19.05.1997	6	(2)	
Yannick Kakoko (GER)	26.01.1990	3		
Levan Kenia (GEO)	18.10.1990	4	(7)	1
Marc-André Kruska (GER)	29.06.1987	12	(1)	2
Mario Pokar (GER)	18.01.1990	18	(7)	5
Danel Sinani	05.04.1997	22	(3)	7
Delvin Skenderović	23.01.1994		(3)	
Stélvio Rosa da Cruz (ANG)	24.01.1989	15	(4)	4
Dominik Stolz (GER)	04.05.1990	11	(3)	3
Jordann Yéyé (FRA)	02.11.1988	4		
Forwards:	**DOB**	**M**	**(s)**	**G**
Edis Agović	12.07.1993	1	(8)	1
Sofian Benzouien (MAR)	11.08.1986		(2)	1
Sanel Ibrahimović (BIH)	24.11.1987	9	(8)	11
Nicolas Perez (FRA)	26.10.1990	9	(7)	7
Patrick Stumpf (GER)	11.04.1988		(4)	1
David Turpel	19.10.1992	22	(4)	14
Trainer:	**DOB**	**M**		
Dino Toppmöller (GER)	23.11.1980	26		

Cercle sportif Fola Esch

Founded: 1906
Stadium: Stade „Émile Mayrisch", Esch-sur-Alzette (3,826)

Goalkeepers:	DOB	M	(s)	G
Emmanuel Tomas Cabral (POR)	02.08.1996	1		
Thomas Hym (FRA)	29.08.1987	25		
Defenders:	**DOB**	**M**	**(s)**	**G**
Billy Bernard	29.04.1991	17		1
Peter Chrappan (SVK)	21.12.1984	1		
Mehdi Kirch (FRA)	27.01.1990	18	(1)	1
Julien Klein (FRA)	07.04.1988	26		1
Tom Laterza	09.05.1992	14	(2)	1
Guillaume Mura (FRA)	09.01.1986	3	(1)	
Roman Pierrard (FRA)	11.09.1997	10	(5)	
Cédric Sacras	28.09.1996	12	(6)	
Midfielders:	**DOB**	**M**	**(s)**	**G**
Lucas Correia	18.04.2002		(1)	
Jakob Dallevedove (GER)	21.11.1987		(5)	
Rodrigue Dikaba (COD)	28.10.1985	26		2
Bruno Freire	27.03.1999	2	(6)	
Ryan Klapp	10.01.1993	16	(5)	6
Corentin Koçur (BEL)	17.10.1995	8		1
Gérard Mersch	08.09.1996	2	(4)	
Veldin Muharemović (BIH)	06.12.1984	17	(3)	
Enis Saiti (MKD)	25.12.1989	1	(9)	1
Dejvid Sinani	02.04.1993	21	(4)	6
Forwards:	**DOB**	**M**	**(s)**	**G**
Stefano Bensi	11.08.1988	22	(3)	10
Ken Corral	08.05.1992	5	(12)	3
Achraf Drif (FRA)	22.03.1992	3	(4)	
Samir Ali Hadji (MAR)	12.09.1989	26		23
Zachary Hadji (FRA)	08.10.1996		(1)	
Dritro Kelmendi	18.11.2000		(1)	
Moussa Seydi (SEN)	21.08.1996	10	(4)	9
Trainer:	**DOB**	**M**		
Thomas Klasen (GER)	16.09.1983	2		
Jeff Strasser [16.08.2018]	05.10.1974	24		

Foussballclub Etzella Ettelbruck

Founded: 21.05.1917
Stadium: Stade Am Deich, Ettelbruck (2,020)

Goalkeepers:	DOB	M	(s)	G
André Leite Barrela	22.01.2001	4		
Sebastian Grub	18.10.1987	22		
Defenders:	**DOB**	**M**	**(s)**	**G**
Losseni Keita (GUI)	01.04.1984	25		
Joël Magalhaes	22.04.1991	6	(8)	
Yanis N'Gbin	22.10.1999	4	(3)	
Lex Nicolay	27.03.1997	6	(9)	
Pol Schlesser	12.06.1996	14	(4)	
Jader Soares	19.08.1996	25		
Dominik Zwick (GER)	26.01.1989	24	(1)	3
Midfielders:	**DOB**	**M**	**(s)**	**G**
Adam Bouzid (FRA)	30.11.1987	10	(1)	
Diogo Miguel Zambujo Pimentel (POR)	16.07.1997	23		2
Miguel Teixeira Fernandes	17.06.2001	1		
Kevin Holtz	06.03.1993	23	(2)	10
Jakub Jarecki (POL)	15.09.1995	15	(8)	3
Mefail Kadrija (GER)	22.09.1991	23	(1)	4
Sven Kalisa	14.03.1997	13	(9)	2
Gianni Medina da Mata	22.12.2001	3		1
Bruno Correia Mendes (POR)	10.12.1994	9	(12)	2
Forwards:	**DOB**	**M**	**(s)**	**G**
Benjamin Arnold (GER)	25.09.1995	15	(5)	1
Julian Bidon (GER)	22.10.1990	19	(2)	2
Ridwane Bouchibti (BEL)	29.12.1993	2	(9)	1
Trainer:	**DOB**	**M**		
Claude Ottelé	01.04.1967	26		

Football Club Union Sportive Hostert

Founded: 1946
Stadium: Stade „Jos Becker“, Hostert (1,500)

Goalkeepers:	DOB	M	(s)	G
Marc Pleimling	11.06.1989	20		
Valentin Roulez	12.12.1996	6		
Defenders:	**DOB**	**M**	**(s)**	**G**
Gianluca Bei	17.05.1995	8		
Julien Bertoux (FRA)	24.01.1993	5		
Aldin Derviševič	19.08.1989	16	(4)	1
João Paulo de Sousa Pacheco	25.02.1999		(1)	
Eric Hoffmann	21.06.1984	24	(1)	1
Alexandre Sacras	14.12.2000	6	(9)	
Cedric Steinmetz	27.09.1999	17		
Chris Stumpf	28.08.1994	23	(1)	1
Midfielders:	**DOB**	**M**	**(s)**	**G**
Din Derviševič	19.05.1991	4	(4)	1
Rasheed Eichhorn (GER)	19.09.1997	25		3
Jun Cai Wang	05.04.1990	17	(9)	2
Khalid Lahyani (GER)	24.02.1993	25		3
Corenthyn Lavie (FRA)	04.12.1996	12	(1)	10
René Peters	15.06.1981	21	(3)	3
Léon Schmit	28.09.2001	3	(6)	
Denis Stumpf	09.09.1997	13	(4)	3
Taïmo Vaz Djassi (POR)	09.03.1988	1	(3)	
Bigen Yala Lusala (BEL)	20.10.1992	1	(4)	
Forwards:	**DOB**	**M**	**(s)**	**G**
Admir Desević (MNE)	08.05.1992	20	(4)	2
Dine Dango-Hendrix (BEL)	31.05.1994	8	(8)	5
Pascal Hurth (GER)	24.01.1995	2	(6)	1
Jérémy Serwy (BEL)	04.06.1991	9	(3)	1
Trainer:	**DOB**	**M**		
Henri Bossi (FRA)	20.02.1958	26		

Association Sportive la Jeunesse d'Esch/Alzette

Founded: 1907
Stadium: Stade de la Frontière, Esch-sur-Alzette (5,400)

Goalkeepers:	DOB	M	(s)	G
Luca Ivesic	07.04.1995		(1)	
Lazare Kupatadze (GEO)	08.02.1996	3		
Kévin Sommer (FRA)	08.11.1989	23		
Defenders:	**DOB**	**M**	**(s)**	**G**
Ricardo Delgado	22.02.1994	26		3
Alessandro Fiorani	19.02.1989	22	(1)	
Emmanuel Lapierre (FRA)	05.08.1993	23		
Arsène Menèssou (BEN)	03.12.1987	17	(2)	3
David Mendes Merces	08.11.2000	1		
Adrien Portier (FRA)	02.02.1988	4		
Brandon Soares Rosa	15.08.1998	3	(1)	
Johannes Steinbach (GER)	02.07.1992	25		1
Midfielders:	**DOB**	**M**	**(s)**	**G**
Joël Pedro de Almeida	10.04.1992	17	(4)	3
David Soares de Sousa	15.07.1995	8	(7)	2
Luca Duriatti	11.02.1998	7	(3)	1
Miloš Todorović	18.08.1995	24	(2)	2
Forwards:	**DOB**	**M**	**(s)**	**G**
Andrea Deidda	15.12.1993	6	(5)	1
Omar Er Rafik (MAR)	07.01.1986	12	(13)	5
Almir Klica (MNE)	10.11.1998	5	(6)	2
Frederick Kyereh (GER)	18.10.1993	15	(3)	4
Antonio Luisi	07.10.1994	10	(1)	9
Hakim Menaï (FRA)	27.03.1986	11	(13)	1
Momar N'Diaye (SEN)	13.07.1987	12	(9)	5
Omar Natami (ITA)	15.12.1998	12	(5)	2
Trainer:	**DOB**	**M**		
Marc Thomé	04.11.1963	19		
Sébastien Grandjean (BEL) [09.04.2019]	16.06.1970	7		

Union sportive de Mondorf-les-Bains

Founded: 1915
Stadium: Stade "Jeannot Mayrisch", Mondorf-les-Bains (3,600)

Goalkeepers:	DOB	M	(s)	G
Glenn Marques da Costa	10.06.1994	9		
Koray Ozcan (FRA)	01.02.1995	17		
Ricardo Jorge Aguiar de Brito (POR)	30.04.1993		(1)	
Defenders:	**DOB**	**M**	**(s)**	**G**
Ahmed Benhemine (FRA)	15.01.1987	24	(1)	
Christophe de Sousa	16.01.1992		(2)	
Fatih Eren (TUR)	17.01.1995	18		
Michael Monteiro	11.12.1991	19	(1)	1
Bosson Romaric (CIV)	12.04.1988	18	(2)	
Midfielders:	**DOB**	**M**	**(s)**	**G**
Marwane Benamra (ALG)	09.04.1995	18	(1)	12
João Carlos Amaral Marques Coimbra (POR)	24.05.1986	21	(1)	
Bruno Da Rocha	13.02.1998	5	(11)	
David Mendes da Silva	10.11.1986	11	(2)	
Olivier Marques	21.03.1992	19		3
Andy May	02.09.1989	22		
Amine Nabli (TUN)	27.05.1985	25		1
Fahret Selimović	26.09.1993	2	(1)	
Cedric Soares dos Santos	19.10.1995	4	(14)	1
Faraji Taarimte (FRA)	17.08.1994	7	(2)	
Fabrice Yao (CIV)	29.12.1995	21	(4)	2
Cedric Zimmer	28.10.1999		(1)	
Forwards:	**DOB**	**M**	**(s)**	**G**
Benjamin Hégué (FRA)	16.03.1989	1	(5)	2
Ezequiel Cabral Barbosa "Keu" (POR)	30.09.1987	4	(4)	2
João Pedro Pinto Martins (ANG)	20.06.1982	8	(8)	6
Stefan Lopes Rocha	24.09.1998	1	(9)	
Brian da Silva Santos	10.03.1999		(1)	
Alessandro Scanzano	14.03.1996	12	(7)	9
Trainer:	**DOB**	**M**		
Carlos Paulo Cardoso Gomes Caçote (POR)	31.03.1975	21		
Arno Bonvini [24.04.2019]	14.10.1975	5		

Football Club Progrès Niederkorn

Founded: 1919
Stadium: Stade „Jos Haupert", Niederkorn (2,800)

Goalkeepers:	**DOB**	**M**	**(s)**	**G**
Sebastien Flauss	19.08.1989	21		
Charly Schinker	05.11.1987	5	(1)	
Defenders:	**DOB**	**M**	**(s)**	**G**
Adrien Ferino (FRA)	16.06.1992	14	(1)	1
Jordan Gobron (FRA)	04.06.1992	16		
Tim Hall	15.04.1997	10	(1)	2
Metin Karayer (FRA)	18.05.1992	21	(1)	1
Kevin Kerger	17.11.1994	9	(7)	
Yann Matias Marques	12.11.1996	14	(2)	
Marvin Martins	17.02.1995	22	(2)	3
Mario Mutsch	03.09.1984	9	(2)	
David Soares Marques	20.02.1991	8	(2)	
Ben Vogel	22.12.1994	16	(5)	
Midfielders:	**DOB**	**M**	**(s)**	**G**
Yannick Bastos	30.05.1993	11	(4)	1
Farid Ikene	15.12.2000	1	(6)	
Belmin Muratović (MNE)	27.03.1998	6	(5)	
Dzenid Ramdedović	25.02.1992	6	(5)	1
Igor Teles Santos	27.04.2000		(6)	
Mike Schneider	01.02.1995	3	(3)	1
Olivier Thill	17.12.1996	1	(1)	
Sebastien Thill	29.12.1993	25	(1)	5
Forwards:	**DOB**	**M**	**(s)**	**G**
Mayron de Almeida (BEL)	22.11.1995	23	(1)	6
Patrick Etshimi Kindenge (CGO)	26.02.1989	5	(7)	3
Emmanuel Françoise (FRA)	08.06.1987	16	(3)	6
Aleksandre Karapetian (ARM)	23.12.1987	19	(5)	11
Romeu Freitas Torres (POR)	07.08.1986	5	(4)	3
Trainer:	**DOB**	**M**		
Paolo Amodio	28.05.1973	7		
Cyril Serredszum [04.10.2018]	02.10.1971	17		
Mario Mutsch [10.05.2019]	03.09.1984	2		

Racing Football Club Union Lëtzebuerg

Founded: 12.05.2005 (as merger of Spora, Union and CS Alliance 01 Lëtzebuerg)
Stadium: Stade "Achille Hammerel", Lëtzebuerg (5,814)

Goalkeepers:	**DOB**	**M**	**(s)**	**G**
Romain Ruffier (FRA)	04.10.1989	26		
Defenders:	**DOB**	**M**	**(s)**	**G**
Thomas Birk (GER)	05.07.1988	22		3
Ricardo Da Silva Diomisio	23.01.1998		(8)	1
Henrique da Silva Gomes (BRA)	20.08.1982	23	(1)	1
Joscelino Silva Dos Santos (POR)	29.08.1989	8	(7)	
Dylan Meireles	24.12.1997		(1)	
Benoit Nyssen (BEL)	12.09.1997	9		
Jordi Oliveira González	15.07.1998	1	(1)	
Alexandre Semedo Borges	22.08.1989		(1)	
Pit Simon	17.02.1998	23		2
Midfielders:	**DOB**	**M**	**(s)**	**G**
Laurent Karim Agouazi (ALG)	16.03.1984	11		4
Arthur Ataide Barros Rocha	28.02.1999	2	(5)	
Julien Humbert (FRA)	23.06.1984	17	(2)	1
Matteo Lamarra	14.07.2000		(1)	
Pape Ibra M'Boup (SEN)	19.08.1987	14	(1)	2
Kevin Nakache (FRA)	05.04.1989	22		5
Tarek Nouidra (FRA)	09.05.1987	19	(1)	1
Florik Shala	19.07.1997	21	(3)	8
Jérôme Simon (FRA)	12.09.1993	5		1
Forwards:	**DOB**	**M**	**(s)**	**G**
Amar Čatić	07.08.1995	1	(8)	
Daniel da Mota Alves	11.09.1985	22	(2)	4
Jonathan Hennetier (FRA)	06.11.1991	25		3
Edis Osmanović (BIH)	30.06.1988	3	(4)	1
Benssad Sulejmani	12.08.1999	1	(5)	
Sebastian Szimayer (GER)	15.05.1990	11	(10)	4
Trainer:	**DOB**	**M**		
Patrick Grettnich	03.03.1972	12		
Frank Defays (BEL) [01.01.2019]	23.02.1974	14		

Union Sportive Rumelange

Founded: 1908
Stadium: Stade Municipal, Rumelange (2,950)

Goalkeepers:	**DOB**	**M**	**(s)**	**G**
Yan Heil	05.09.1990	13		
Jérôme Winckel	20.12.1985	13		
Defenders:	**DOB**	**M**	**(s)**	**G**
Luca Borbiconi	22.07.1999	5	(8)	
Ricardo Borges Alves	20.06.1999	6	(4)	
Bryan Maison	04.07.1997	23		2
Marcos Martins	12.05.2000	7	(1)	
José Raphael Rodrigues dos Santos Silva	16.02.1989	9	(3)	
Eric Schmit	29.10.1999	5	(4)	
Mateusz Siebert (POL)	04.04.1989	18		
François Thior (FRA)	11.02.1985	23	(2)	
Midfielders:	**DOB**	**M**	**(s)**	**G**
Ajdin Bjelić	07.03.1999	12	(7)	
Bryan Gomes da Silva (POR)	05.12.1993	15	(5)	5
Jeremiah Dabrowski (POL)	26.09.1995		(4)	1
Etienne Donval (FRA)	04.04.1995	19	(1)	1
Nenad Dragović	04.06.1994	22		
Julien Fostier (FRA)	27.08.1990	19	(5)	2
Tom Ivesić	17.07.1999	12	(3)	
Omar Muhović	14.11.1997	1	(1)	
Eduardo Mendes Silva	28.01.2001	1	(1)	
Forwards:	**DOB**	**M**	**(s)**	**G**
Christophe Cunha da Fonseca	08.01.1995	7	(2)	
Jules Diallo (FRA)	08.03.1993	19		8
Yann Hoffmann	02.02.2002	1	(4)	
Olivier Cristophe Lusamba (COD)	16.03.1993	17	(6)	6
Kerim Skenderović (MNE)	26.06.1997		(1)	
Fatih Şahin (TUR)	18.01.1985	19	(3)	9
Trainer:	**DOB**	**M**		
Sven Loscheider		20		
Gerard Jeitz [16.04.2019]	10.03.1961	6		

Football Club Rapid Mansfeldia Hamm Benfica Lëtzebuerg

Founded: 26.03.2004
Stadium: Terrain de Football Cents, Hamm, Lëtzebuerg (2,800)

Goalkeepers:	**DOB**	**M**	**(s)**	**G**
Dany Rodrigues da Silva (POR)	10.02.1994	9		
Tiago Alves Gil (POR)	15.05.1985	17		
Defenders:	**DOB**	**M**	**(s)**	**G**
Samuel Correia	29.09.1997	11	(4)	
Pedro Miguel Neves da Costa "Costinha" (POR)	11.03.1994	23		
José Inácio Cabral Barbosa (POR)	15.11.1983	2		
Mehdi Martin (FRA)	11.01.1990	12		
Alexandros Papadopoulos (GRE)	02.03.1997	6	(1)	
Paulo Ricardo Pereira Arantes (POR)	15.11.1986	25		3
Emanuel Valentin Gomes de Sousa	21.02.2000		(1)	
William Alberto Lima Andrade (CPV)	04.05.1992	8	(3)	
Midfielders:	**DOB**	**M**	**(s)**	**G**
Assim Alomerović	25.01.1983	2	(9)	
Yannic Borges Sanches	19.05.2000		(1)	
Raphael de Sousa	05.03.1003	4	(3)	
Emanuel Valentin Gomes de Sousa	21.02.2000	13	(2)	1
Fabien Heinz	30.07.1998	15	(3)	
Rafael Monteiro Machado (BRA)	15.05.1995	15	(3)	
Ronny Walder Alves Souto Amado (CPV)	07.12.1978	23		1
Denilson Santos Lopes	12.09.1998	7	(4)	
Ashot Sardaryan (ARM)	23.03.1992	2		
Forwards:	**DOB**	**M**	**(s)**	**G**
Alessandro Alunni	19.12.1991	20	(5)	1
Issa Bah (GUI)	05.07.2002		(10)	1
Claudio Borges Furtado (POR)	06.08.1991	4	(3)	1
Pedro Miguel Ferro Bernardo (BRA)	21.07.1987	4	(2)	
Gonçalo Manuel Costa Pessoa (POR)	15.01.1996	9	(2)	
Alexio Alexandre dos Santos Mendes "Lélé Mendes" (POR)	08.10.1993	13	(5)	1
Eddire Mokrani (ALG)	23.01.1991	20	(3)	7
Bertino João Cabral Barbosa "Tino Barbosa" (POR)	06.05.1992	22	(1)	13
Trainer:	**DOB**	**M**		
Daniel Santos	14.09.1981	15		
Gonçalo Francisco Santos Cruz (POR) [04.03.2019]	25.10.1987	4		
Pedro Miguel Resende dos Reis Morais (POR) [08.04.2019]	19.04.1977	7		

Football Club UNA Strassen

Founded: 1922
Stadium: Complexe Sportif „Jean Wirtz", Strassen (2,000)

Goalkeepers:	**DOB**	**M**	**(s)**	**G**
Jason Gonçalves Martins	01.11.1995	1		
Ralph Schon	20.01.1990	25		
Defenders:	**DOB**	**M**	**(s)**	**G**
Gauthier Bernardelli (FRA)	21.08.1992	13	(1)	3
Stéphane d'Angelo (FRA)	02.06.1999		(2)	
Gilson Delgado (CPV)	19.10.1992	10	(7)	
Antoine Goulard (FRA)	18.12.1985	10	(1)	
Patrice Mondon-Konan (FRA)	17.03.1983	10	(2)	1
Quentin Zilli (FRA)	16.02.1999	13	(2)	
Midfielders:	**DOB**	**M**	**(s)**	**G**
Grégory Adler (FRA)	27.04.1989	9		
Alen Agović	28.11.1997	18	(4)	
Denis Agović	13.07.1993	25		
Sam Alverdi	23.08.1997		(1)	
Valerio Barbaro	16.02.1998	3	(9)	1
Ben Payal	08.09.1988	21		1
Alexis Lafon	26.01.1986	15	(2)	2
Kevin Lourenço Joaquim	12.05.1992	21	(1)	9
Tony Mastrangelo	01.09.1994	23	(2)	
Bob Simon	17.01.1996	4	(9)	1
Théo Sully (FRA)	13.02.1996	6	(3)	1
Forwards:	**DOB**	**M**	**(s)**	**G**
Mickaël Jager	13.01.1989	15	(9)	14
Pedro Andre dos Santos Ribeiro	21.11.1990	8	(4)	1
Benjamin Runser (FRA)	04.09.1991	14	(8)	5
Kevin Ruppert	16.08.1991	5	(9)	5
Yuki Tsuchihashi (JPN)	20.04.1995	17	(1)	1
Trainer:	**DOB**	**M**		
Manuel Correia (POR)	28.03.1976	26		

Union Titus Pétange

Founded: 2015
Stadium: Stade Municipal de Pétange, Pétange (2,400)

Goalkeepers:	**DOB**	**M**	**(s)**	**G**
Andrea Amodio	13.07.1997	10		
Jean Chopin (FRA)	09.10.1994	16		
Defenders:	**DOB**	**M**	**(s)**	**G**
Jules Diouf (FRA)	05.03.1992	12		
Joel Armando da Mata dos Santos	04.09.1995	12	(2)	
Tun Held	11.01.2001	12		1
Dylan Martins Teixeira	27.01.2001	1	(1)	
William Vale Marques	03.01.2001	2		
Glodi Zingha Casemiro (ANG)	04.11.1993	12	(6)	
Midfielders:	**DOB**	**M**	**(s)**	**G**
Artur Abreu Pereira	11.08.1994	24		8
Kenan Avdusinović	03.03.1998	3	(15)	
Adnan Bašić (BIH)	13.12.1996	7	(10)	3
Lucas Lima Carnevalli (BRA)	29.03.1995	22		3
Diego Alves Esch Miranda (BRA)	07.08.1998	10	(2)	3
Dani Gaspar	16.06.2000	1	(1)	
Mounir Hamzaoui (MAR)	09.12.1987	19	(2)	
Michel Kettenmeyer	07.02.1989	11	(2)	
Goncalo Peixoto Rodrigues	24.07.2000	4	(1)	
Gianluigi Pitisci (BEL)	22.10.2002	2		
Kai Schwitz	23.05.1997		(3)	
Nicola Schreiner	01.09.1995	2	(2)	
Marco Schuhmann (GER)	15.09.1994		(1)	
Christian Silaj (GER)	07.04.1992	21		1
Forwards:	**DOB**	**M**	**(s)**	**G**
Filip Bojić (CRO)	05.10.1992	22		7
Semsudin Dzanic (BIH)	12.07.1992	17	(9)	3
Eliot Gashi	15.04.1995	5	(10)	2
Luís Filipe de Castro Ribeiro (POR)	27.04.1986	12		
Ebrahima Ibou Sawaneh (GAM)	07.09.1986	12	(1)	7
Patrik Teixeira	10.05.1996	15	(6)	
Trainer:	**DOB**	**M**		
Baltemar José de Oliveira Brito	04.06.1951			
Carlos Manuel Fangueiro Soares "Fangueiro" [01.01.2019]	19.12.1976			

Football Club Victoria Rosport

Founded: 01.10.1928
Stadium: VictoriArena, Rosport (1,000)

Goalkeepers:	**DOB**	**M**	**(s)**	**G**
Noé Bouche	12.04.2001	1		
Niklas Bürger (GER)	07.10.1992	25		
Defenders:	**DOB**	**M**	**(s)**	**G**
Daniel Bartsch (GER)	07.05.1987	25		
Eric Brandenburger	08.09.1998	17	(3)	
Nicolas Dücker (GER)	05.02.1990	2	(1)	
Gilles Feltes	06.12.1995	25		1
Fabian Fisch (GER)	27.05.1999	21		1
Philippe Werdel	12.05.1990	16	(1)	
Midfielders:	**DOB**	**M**	**(s)**	**G**
Michel Bechtold	01.07.1995	21	(4)	1
Jakob Dallevedove (GER)	21.11.1987	13		1
Gabriel Gaspar Pereira	20.07.1990	5	(5)	
Tim Hartmann (GER)	08.12.1989	15	(10)	1
Timo Heinz (GER)	06.03.1991	26		2
Maximilian Koch (GER)	07.01.2000	1		
Kevin Marques	16.01.1998	7	(13)	
Ramiro Soares Valente	26.01.1989	10	(9)	
Florian Weirich (GER)	23.09.1990	23	(3)	7
Devann Yao (USA)	05.04.1990	2	(2)	2
Forwards:	**DOB**	**M**	**(s)**	**G**
Alexander Biedermann (GER)	03.01.1995	24	(2)	12
Patrik Kasel (GER)	04.04.1986	3	(4)	1
Daniel Kurz (GER)	06.02.1997	2	(4)	
Jeff Lascak	13.02.1994	2	(11)	1
Trainer:	**DOB**	**M**		
Pedro Miguel Resende dos Reis Morais (POR)	19.04.1977			
René Roller [08.04.2019]	02.08.1959			

SECOND LEVEL
Éierepromotioun / Promotion d'Honneur 2018/2019

1.	FC Rodange 91 (*Promoted*)	26	19	4	3	58 - 18	61
2.	Blue Boys Mühlenbach (*Promoted*)	26	18	5	3	55 - 25	59
3.	FC Swift Hesperange (*Promotion Play-offs*)	26	18	1	7	73 - 27	55
4.	US Esch/Alzette	26	16	4	6	47 - 28	52
5.	UN Käerjéng 97	26	12	8	6	47 - 31	44
6.	FC Wiltz 71	26	11	6	9	45 - 34	39
7.	Union Mertert/Wasserbillig	26	9	8	9	41 - 41	35
8.	FC Mamer 32	26	9	3	14	41 - 59	30
9.	FC Jeunesse Junglinster	26	7	6	13	25 - 42	27
10.	FC Jeunesse Canach	26	5	11	10	42 - 45	26
11.	FC 72 Erpeldange (*Relegation Play-offs*)	26	7	5	14	42 - 63	26
12.	FC Atert Bissen (*Relegation Play-offs*)	26	6	7	13	31 - 52	25
13.	FC Koeppchen Wormeldange (*Relegated*)	26	3	6	17	24 - 65	15
14.	US Sandweiler (*Relegated*)	26	4	2	20	31 - 72	14

Relegation Play-offs (2nd / 3rd Level)

FC 72 Erpeldange - FC Blô-Weiss Medernach	1-3 aet
FC Atert Bissen - FC Yellow Boys Weiler	1-3 aet

NATIONAL TEAM

INTERNATIONAL MATCHES
(16.07.2018 – 15.07.2019)

08.09.2018	Lëtzebuerg	Luxembourg - Moldova	4-0(1-0)	(UNL)
11.09.2018	Serravalle	San Marino - Luxembourg	0-3(0-2)	(UNL)
12.10.2018	Minsk	Belarus - Luxembourg	1-0(1-0)	(UNL)
15.10.2018	Lëtzebuerg	Luxembourg - San Marino	3-0(1-0)	(UNL)
15.11.2018	Lëtzebuerg	Luxembourg - Belarus	0-2(0-1)	(UNL)
18.11.2018	Chişinău	Moldova - Luxembourg	1-1(0-0)	(UNL)
22.03.2019	Lëtzebuerg	Luxembourg - Lithuania	2-1(1-1)	(ECQ)
25.03.2019	Lëtzebuerg	Luxembourg - Ukraine	1-2(1-1)	(ECQ)
02.06.2019	Lëtzebuerg	Luxembourg - Madagascar	3-3(1-2)	(F)
07.06.2019	Vilnius	Lithuania - Luxembourg	1-1(0-1)	(ECQ)
10.06.2019	Lviv	Ukraine - Luxembourg	1-0(1-0)	(ECQ)

08.09.2018 LUXEMBOURG - MOLDOVA 4-0(1-0) UEFA Nations League D, Group 2
Stade "Josy Barthel", Lëtzebuerg; Referee: Robert Harvey (Republic of Ireland); Attendance: 2,956
LUX: Anthony Moris, Lars Christian Krogh Gerson, Kevin Malget, Maxime Chanot, Laurent Jans (Cap), Dirk Carlson, Christopher Martins Pereira, Olivier Thill (78.Mario Mutsch), Danel Sinani, David Turpel (59.Aurélien Joachim), Gerson Rodrigues Correia Leal (55.Daniel da Mota Alves). Trainer: Luc Holtz.
Goals: Kevin Malget (39), Olivier Thill (60), Danel Sinani (75), Christopher Martins Pereira (83).

11.09.2018 SAN MARINO - LUXEMBOURG 0-3(0-2) UEFA Nations League D, Group 2
San Marino Stadium, Serravalle; Referee: Filip Glova (Slovakia); Attendance: 794
LUX: Anthony Moris, Maxime Chanot (70.Mathias Jänisch), Laurent Jans (Cap), Dirk Carlson, Chris Philipps, Christopher Martins Pereira, Olivier Thill (46.Vincent Thill), Danel Sinani, Leandro Barreiro Martins (46.Mario Mutsch), Daniel da Mota Alves, Aurélien Joachim. Trainer: Luc Holtz.
Goals: Maxime Chanot (9), Aurélien Joachim (45+1), Danel Sinani (52).

12.10.2018 BELARUS - LUXEMBOURG 1-0(1-0) UEFA Nations League D, Group 2
Stadion Dynama, Minsk; Referee: Ali Palabıyık (Turkey); Attendance: 14,122
LUX: Anthony Moris, Kevin Malget (46.Enes Mahmutovic), Maxime Chanot, Laurent Jans (Cap), Dirk Carlson, Chris Philipps, Christopher Martins Pereira, Olivier Thill (57.Gerson Rodrigues Correia Leal), Danel Sinani, David Turpel (72.Daniel da Mota Alves), Aurélien Joachim. Trainer: Luc Holtz.

15.10.2018 LUXEMBOURG - SAN MARINO 3-0(1-0) UEFA Nations League D, Group 2
Stade "Josy Barthel", Lëtzebuerg; Referee: Aleksandrs Golubevs (Latvia); Attendance: 2,876
LUX: Ralph Schon, Mathias Jänisch, Maxime Chanot, Laurent Jans (Cap) (69.Florian Bohnert), Chris Philipps, Christopher Martins Pereira, Olivier Thill, Danel Sinani, Vincent Thill, Leandro Barreiro Martins (67.Daniel da Mota Alves), David Turpel (76.Maurice John Deville). Trainer: Luc Holtz.
Goals: David Turpel (4), Danel Sinani (65), Vincent Thill (73).

15.11.2018 LUXEMBOURG - BELARUS 0-2(0-1) UEFA Nations League D, Group 2
Stade "Josy Barthel", Letzëbuerg; Referee: Serdar Gözübüyük (Netherlands); Attendance: 4,533
LUX: Anthony Moris, Lars Christian Krogh Gerson (46.Stefano Bensi), Mathias Jänisch, Maxime Chanot, Laurent Jans (Cap), Chris Philipps, Christopher Martins Pereira, Olivier Thill, Danel Sinani, Aurélien Joachim, David Turpel (67.Daniel da Mota Alves). Trainer: Luc Holtz.

18.11.2018 MOLDOVA - LUXEMBOURG 1-1(0-0) UEFA Nations League D, Group 2
Stadionul Zimbru, Chişinău; Referee: Adrien Jaccottet (Switzerland); Attendance: 4,642
LUX: Anthony Moris, Maxime Chanot, Laurent Jans (Cap), Enes Mahmutovic, Dirk Carlson, Chris Philipps (31.Olivier Thill), Leandro Barreiro Martins, Daniel da Mota Alves, Stefano Bensi (81.David Turpel), Florian Bohnert (59.Danel Sinani), Aurélien Joachim. Trainer: Luc Holtz.
Goal: Stefano Bensi (70).

22.03.2019 LUXEMBOURG - LITHUANIA 2-1(1-1) 16th EC. Qualifiers
Stade „Josy Barthel", Lëtzebuerg; Referee: Roey Reinshreiber (Israel); Attendance: 3,353
LUX: Anthony Moris, Lars Christian Krogh Gerson, Maxime Chanot, Laurent Jans (Cap), Dirk Carlson, Christopher Martins Pereira, Olivier Thill, Vincent Thill (78.David Turpel), Leandro Barreiro Martins (67.Danel Sinani), Daniel da Mota Alves (58.Stefano Bensi), Gerson Rodrigues Correia Leal. Trainer: Luc Holtz.
Goals: Leandro Barreiro Martins (45), Gerson Rodrigues Correia Leal (55).

25.03.2019 LUXEMBOURG - UKRAINE 1-2(1-1) 16th EC. Qualifiers
Stade "Josy Barthel", Lëtzebuerg; Referee: Mattias Gestranius (Finland); Attendance: 4,653
LUX: Anthony Moris, Kevin Malget, Maxime Chanot, Laurent Jans (Cap), Dirk Carlson, Christopher Martins Pereira, Olivier Thill (90+1.Mario Mutsch), Vincent Thill (74.Stefano Bensi), Leandro Barreiro Martins, David Turpel, Gerson Rodrigues Correia Leal. Trainer: Luc Holtz.
Goal: David Turpel (34).

02.06.2019 LUXEMBOURG - MADAGASCAR 3-3(1-2) Friendly International
Stade "Josy Barthel", Lëtzebuerg; Referee: Neil Doyle (Republic of Ireland); Attendance: 1,831
LUX: Anthony Moris (46.Ralph Schon), Laurent Jans (Cap), Enes Mahmutovic (46.Kevin Malget), Dirk Carlson, Vahid Selimović, Danel Sinani (83.Marvin Martins Santos da Graça), Christopher Martins Pereira (63.Mario Mutsch), Vincent Thill, Leandro Barreiro Martins (78.Aldin Skenderovic), Daniel da Mota Alves, David Turpel (63.Kevin Holtz). Trainer: Luc Holtz.
Goals: Vincent Thill (2), Vahid Selimović (90+1), Laurent Jans (90+2).

07.06.2019 LITHUANIA - LUXEMBOURG 1-1(0-1) 16th EC. Qualifiers
LFF Stadionas, Vilnius; Referee: Ádám Farkas (Hungary); Attendance: 3,263
LUX: Anthony Moris, Lars Christian Krogh Gerson, Laurent Jans (Cap), Dirk Carlson (61.Kevin Malget), Vahid Selimović, Christopher Martins Pereira, Olivier Thill (80.Danel Sinani), Vincent Thill, Leandro Barreiro Martins, David Turpel (67.Stefano Bensi), Gerson Rodrigues Correia Leal. Trainer: Luc Holtz.
Goal: Gerson Rodrigues Correia Leal (21).

10.06.2019 UKRAINE - LUXEMBOURG 1-0(1-0) 16th EC. Qualifiers

Arena Lviv, Lviv; Referee: Peter Kralović (Slovakia); Attendance: 34,700

LUX: Anthony Moris, Lars Christian Krogh Gerson, Maxime Chanot, Laurent Jans (Cap), Marvin Martins Santos da Graça, Christopher Martins Pereira, Olivier Thill (77.David Turpel), Vincent Thill, Leandro Barreiro Martins, Daniel da Mota Alves (52.Stefano Bensi), Gerson Rodrigues Correia Leal. Trainer: Luc Holtz.

NATIONAL TEAM PLAYERS
(16.07.2018 – 15.07.2019)

Name	DOB	Caps	Goals	2018/2019:	*Club*
Goalkeepers					
Anthony MORIS	29.04.1990	**22**	**0**	2018/2019:	*Royal Excelsior Virton (BEL)*
Ralph SCHON	20.01.1990	**9**	**0**	2018/2019:	*FC UNA Strassen*
Defenders					
Dirk CARLSON	01.04.1998	**17**	**0**	2018/2019:	*Grasshopper Club Zürich (SUI)*
Maxime CHANOT	21.11.1989	**34**	**2**	2018/2019:	*New York City FC (USA)*
Marvin Martins Santos DA GRAÇA	17.02.1995	**6**	**1**	2019:	*FC Progrès Niederkorn*
Enes MAHMUTOVIC	22.05.1997	**11**	**0**	2018: 01.01.2019->	*Yeovil Town FC (ENG, on loan)* *Middlesbrough FC (ENG)*
Kevin MALGET	15.01.1991	**33**	**2**	2018/2019:	*F91 Dudelange*
Mario MUTSCH	03.09.1984	**102**	**4**	2018/2019:	*FC Progrès Niederkorn*
Chris PHILIPPS	08.03.1994	**52**	**0**	2018:	*Legia Warszawa (POL)*
Vahid SELIMOVIĆ	03.04.1997	**2**	**1**	2018/2019:	*Apollon FC Limassol (CYP)*
Aldin SKENDEROVIC	28.06.1997	**10**	**0**	2019:	*SV Elversberg (GER)*
Midfielders					
Leandro BARREIRO Martins	03.01.2000	**11**	**1**	2018/2019:	*1.FSV Mainz 05 (GER)*
Lars Christian Krogh GERSON	05.02.1990	**69**	**4**	2018/2019:	*IFK Norrköping (SWE)*
Kevin HOLTZ	06.03.1993	**1**	**0**	2018/2019:	*FC Etzella Ettelbrück*
Laurent JANS	05.08.1992	**58**	**1**	2018/2019:	*FC Metz (FRA)*
Mathias JÄNISCH	27.08.1990	**59**	**1**	2018:	*FC Differdange 03*
Christopher MARTINS Pereira	19.02.1997	**38**	**1**	2018/2019:	*ES Troyes AC (FRA)*
Gerson RODRIGUES Correia Leal	20.06.1995	**18**	**2**	2018: 16.01.2019->	*FC Sheriff Tiraspol (MDA)* *Júbilo Iwata (JPN)*
Danel SINANI	05.04.1997	**15**	**3**	2018/2019:	*F91 Dudelange*
Olivier THILL	17.12.1997	**16**	**2**	2018/2019:	*FK Ufa (GER)*
Vincent THILL	04.02.2000	**23**	**3**	2018/2019:	*Pau FC (FRA)*
Forwards					
Stefano BENSI	11.08.1988	**48**	**5**	2018/2019:	*CS Fola Esch*
Florian BOHNERT	09.11.1997	**13**	**1**	2018:	*FK Pirmasens (GER)*
Daniel DA MOTA Alves	11.09.1985	**95**	**7**	2018/2019:	*Racing FC Union Lëtzebuerg*
Maurice John DEVILLE	31.07.1992	**37**	**3**	2018/2019:	*SV Waldhof Mannheim (GER)*
Aurélien JOACHIM	10.08.1986	**78**	**15**	2018:	*K Lierse SK (BEL)*
David TURPEL	19.10.1992	**47**	**4**	2018/2019:	*F91 Dudelange*

National team coach

Luc HOLTZ [from 03.08.2010]	14.06.1969	83 M; 16 W; 17 D; 50 L; 65-170

MALTA

The Country:

Republic of Malta (Repubblika ta' Malta)
Capital: Valletta
Surface: 316 km²
Inhabitants: 493,559 [2019]
Time: UTC+1

The FA:

Assoċjazzjoni tal-Futbol ta' Malta
Millennium Stand, Floor 2 National Stadium, Ta'Qali, ATD4000 Malta
Tel: +356 21 232 581
Foundation date: 1900
Member of FIFA since: 1959
Member of UEFA since: 1960
Website: www.mfa.com.mt

NATIONAL TEAM RECORDS

First international match:	24.02.1957, Gzira:	Malta – Austria 2-3
Most international caps:	Michael Mifsud	- 139 caps (2000-2019)
Most international goals:	Michael Mifsud	- 41 goals / 139 caps (2000-2019)

UEFA EUROPEAN CHAMPIONSHIP	
1960	Did Not Enter
1964	Qualifiers
1968	Did Not Enter
1972	Qualifiers
1976	Qualifiers
1980	Qualifiers
1984	Qualifiers
1988	Qualifiers
1992	Qualifiers
1996	Qualifiers
2000	Qualifiers
2004	Qualifiers
2008	Qualifiers
2012	Qualifiers
2016	Qualifiers

FIFA WORLD CUP	
1930	Did Not Enter
1934	Did Not Enter
1938	Did Not Enter
1950	Did Not Enter
1954	Did Not Enter
1958	Did Not Enter
1962	Did Not Enter
1966	Did Not Enter
1970	Did Not Enter
1974	Qualifiers
1978	Qualifiers
1982	Qualifiers
1986	Qualifiers
1990	Qualifiers
1994	Qualifiers
1998	Qualifiers
2002	Qualifiers
2006	Qualifiers
2010	Qualifiers
2014	Qualifiers
2018	Qualifiers

UEFA NATIONS LEAGUE
2018/2019 – League D

OLYMPIC FOOTBALL TOURNAMENTS 1908-2016							
1908	-	**1948**	-	**1972**	*Withdrew*	**1996**	Qualifiers
1912	-	**1952**	-	**1976**	Did Not Enter	**2000**	Qualifiers
1920	-	**1956**	-	**1980**	Did Not Enter	**2004**	Qualifiers
1924	-	**1960**	Did Not Enter	**1984**	Did Not Enter	**2008**	Qualifiers
1928	-	**1964**	Did Not Enter	**1988**	Did Not Enter	**2012**	Qualifiers
1936	-	**1968**	Did Not Enter	**1992**	Qualifiers	**2016**	Qualifiers

FIFA CONFEDERATIONS CUP 1992-2017
None

MALTESE CLUB HONOURS IN EUROPEAN CLUB COMPETITIONS:

European Champion Clubs' Cup (1956-1992) / UEFA Champions League (1993-2019)
None
Fairs Cup (1858-1971) / UEFA Cup (1972-2009) / UEFA Europa League (2010-2019)
None
UEFA Super Cup (1972-2018)
None
European Cup Winners' Cup 1961-1999*
None

**defunct competition*

NATIONAL COMPETITIONS
TABLE OF HONOURS

	CHAMPIONS	CUP WINNERS	BEST GOALSCORERS	
1909/1910	Floriana FC	-	Salvu Samuele (Floriana FC)	4
1910/1911	*No championship*	-	-	
1911/1912	Floriana FC	-	*not known*	
1912/1913	Floriana FC	-	*not known*	
1913/1914	Ħamrun Spartans FC	-	*not known*	
1914/1915	Valletta United FC	-	*not known*	
1915/1916	*No championship*	-	-	
1916/1917	St. George's FC	-	*not known*	
1917/1918	Ħamrun Spartans FC	-	*not known*	
1918/1919	The King's Own Malta Regiment	-	*not known*	
1919/1920	Sliema Wanderers FC	-	*not known*	
1920/1921	Floriana FC	-	*not known*	
1921/1922	Floriana FC	-	*not known*	
1922/1923	Sliema Wanderers FC	-	*not known*	
1923/1924	Sliema Wanderers FC	-	*not known*	
1924/1925	Floriana FC	-	*not known*	
1925/1926	Sliema Wanderers FC	-	*not known*	
1926/1927	Floriana FC	-	*not known*	
1927/1928	Floriana FC	-	*not known*	
1928/1929	Floriana FC	-	P. Friggieri (Floriana FC)	4
1929/1930	Sliema Wanderers FC	-	*not known*	
1930/1931	Floriana FC	-	C. Cauchi (Floriana FC)	4
1931/1932	Valletta United FC	-	*not known*	
1932/1933	Sliema Wanderers FC	-	*not known*	
1933/1934	Sliema Wanderers FC	-	A. Brincat (Sliema Wanderers FC)	2
1934/1935	Floriana FC	Sliema Wanderers FC	Tony Nicholl (Sliema Wanderers FC)	11
1935/1936	Sliema Wanderers FC	Sliema Wanderers FC	Anton Mayerhoffer (AUT, Floriana FC)	3
1936/1937	Floriana FC	Sliema Wanderers FC	George Albert Bond (ENG, Floriana FC)	4
1937/1938	Sliema Wanderers FC	Floriana FC	Tony Nicholl (Sliema Wanderers FC) C. Cauchi (Floriana FC)	5
1938/1939	Sliema Wanderers FC	Melita FC St. Julian's	Tony Nicholl (Sliema Wanderers FC)	8
1939/1940	Sliema Wanderers FC	Sliema Wanderers FC	Tony Nicholl (Sliema Wanderers FC)	18
1940-1944	*No championship*	-	-	
1944/1945	Valletta FC	Floriana FC	Tony Nicholl (Sliema Athletics FC)	6
1945/1946	Valletta FC	Sliema Wanderers FC	*not known*	
1946/1947	Ħamrun Spartans FC	Floriana FC	Maurice Decesare (Melita FC St. Julian's) C. Galea (Floriana FC)	11
1947/1948	Valletta FC	Sliema Wanderers FC	Freddie Landolina (Ħamrun Spartans FC)	16
1948/1949	Sliema Wanderers FC	Floriana FC	Salvinu Schembri (Valletta FC) Tony Nicholl (Sliema Wanderers FC)	11
1949/1950	Floriana FC	Floriana FC	Pace (Valletta FC)	16
1950/1951	Floriana FC	Sliema Wanderers FC	Pullu Demanuele (Valletta FC)	14
1951/1952	Floriana FC	Sliema Wanderers FC	Lolly Borg (Floriana FC)	17
1952/1953	Floriana FC	Floriana FC	Pace (Valletta FC)	9
1953/1954	Sliema Wanderers FC	Floriana FC	Tony Nicholl (Sliema Wanderers FC)	12
1954/1955	Floriana FC	Floriana FC	Lolly Borg (Floriana FC) Tony Cauchi (Floriana FC)	13
1955/1956	Sliema Wanderers FC	Sliema Wanderers FC	Sammy Nicholl (Sliema Wanderers FC)	15
1956/1957	Sliema Wanderers FC	Floriana FC	Sammy Nicholl (Sliema Wanderers FC)	14
1957/1958	Floriana FC	Floriana FC	Pullu Demanuele (Floriana FC)	14
1958/1959	Valletta FC	Sliema Wanderers FC	A. Cassar (Ħamrun Spartans FC)	11
1959/1960	Valletta FC	Valletta FC	F. Zammit (Valletta FC) M. Azzopardi (Valletta FC)	12
1960/1961	Hibernians FC Paola	Floriana FC	Tony Cauchi (Floriana FC)	12
1961/1962	Floriana FC	Hibernians FC Paola	Tony Cauchi (Floriana FC)	17
1962/1963	Valletta FC	Sliema Wanderers FC	M. Azzopardi (Valletta FC)	20
1963/1964	Sliema Wanderers FC	Valletta FC	A. Borg (Valletta FC)	11
1964/1965	Sliema Wanderers FC	Sliema Wanderers FC	Joseph Cini (Sliema Wanderers FC)	12
1965/1966	Sliema Wanderers FC	Floriana FC	John Bonnett (Sliema Wanderers FC) Ronald Cocks (Sliema Wanderers FC)	6
1966/1967	Hibernians FC Paola	Floriana FC	A. Delia (Hibernians FC Paola)	8
1967/1968	Floriana FC	Sliema Wanderers FC	Joseph Cini (Sliema Wanderers FC)	10
1968/1969	Hibernians FC Paola	Sliema Wanderers FC	C. Cassar (Hibernians FC Paola)	9
1969/1970	Floriana FC	Hibernians FC Paola	Joseph Cini (Sliema Wanderers FC) Ronald Cocks (Sliema Wanderers FC)	7
1970/1971	Sliema Wanderers FC	Hibernians FC Paola	Raymond Xuereb (Floriana FC)	5
1971/1972	Sliema Wanderers FC	Floriana FC	Tony Giglio (Valletta FC)	9
1972/1973	Floriana FC	Għira United FC	C. Borg (Ħamrun Spartans FC)	10
1973/1974	Valletta FC	Sliema Wanderers FC	T. Camilleri (Sliema Wanderers FC)	9
1974/1975	Floriana FC	Valletta FC	Raymond Xuereb (Floriana FC)	17
1975/1976	Sliema Wanderers FC	Floriana FC	Richard Aquilina (Sliema Wanderers FC)	9

1976/1977	Floriana FC	Valletta FC	Raymond Xuereb (Floriana FC)	16
1977/1978	Valletta FC	Valletta FC	Leonard Farrugia (Valletta FC)	16
1978/1979	Hibernians FC Paola	Sliema Wanderers FC	C. Brincat (Marsa FC)	11
1979/1980	Valletta FC	Hibernians FC Paola	Emanuel Fabri (Sliema Wanderers FC) Leonard Farrugia (Valletta FC) F. Cristiano (Valletta FC)	15
1980/1981	Hibernians FC Paola	Floriana FC	Ernest Spiteri-Gonzi (Hibernians FC Paola)	13
1981/1982	Hibernians FC Paola	Hibernians FC Paola	Ernest Spiteri-Gonzi (Hibernians FC Paola)	12
1982/1983	Ħamrun Spartans FC	Ħamrun Spartans FC	Leo Refalo (Ħamrun Spartans FC)	7
1983/1984	Valletta FC	Ħamrun Spartans FC	Georgi Ivanov (BUL, Ħamrun Spartans FC) Charles Muscat (Żurrieq FC)	7
1984/1985	Rabat Ajax FC	Żurrieq FC	Leonard Farrugia (Valletta FC)	9
1985/1986	Rabat Ajax FC	Rabat Ajax FC	Gianluca De Ponti (ITA, Żurrieq FC)	8
1986/1987	Ħamrun Spartans FC	Ħamrun Spartans FC	Carmel Busuttil (Rabat Ajax FC)	10
1987/1988	Ħamrun Spartans FC	Ħamrun Spartans FC	Barry Gallagher (ENG, Ħamrun Spartans FC)	7
1988/1989	Sliema Wanderers FC	Ħamrun Spartans FC	Joseph Zarb (Valletta FC)	11
1989/1990	Valletta FC	Sliema Wanderers FC	Joseph Zarb (Valletta FC)	17
1990/1991	Ħamrun Spartans FC	Valletta FC	Joseph Zarb (Valletta FC)	12
1991/1992	Valletta FC	Ħamrun Spartans FC	Stefan Sultana (Ħamrun Spartans FC)	22
1992/1993	Floriana FC	Floriana FC	Carl Zachhau (DEN, Hibernians FC Paola)	22
1993/1994	Hibernians FC Paola	Floriana FC	Carl Zachhau (DEN, Hibernians FC Paola) Joseph Zarb (Valletta FC)	17
1994/1995	Hibernians FC Paola	Valletta FC	Carl Saunders (ENG, Sliema Wanderers FC)	18
1995/1996	Sliema Wanderers FC	Valletta FC	Aldrin Muscat (Sliema Wanderers FC)	18
1996/1997	Valletta FC	Valletta FC	Danilo Dončić (SRB, Valletta FC)	32
1997/1998	Valletta FC	Hibernians FC Paola	Joseph Brincat (Birkirkara FC/Floriana FC)	19
1998/1999	Valletta FC	Valletta FC	Gilbert Agius (Valletta FC)	20
1999/2000	Birkirkara FC	Sliema Wanderers FC	Michael Mifsud (Sliema Wanderers FC)	21
2000/2001	Valletta FC	Valletta FC	Michael Mifsud (Sliema Wanderers FC)	30
2001/2002	Hibernians FC Paola	Birkirkara FC	Danilo Dončić (SRB, Sliema Wanderers FC)	32
2002/2003	Sliema Wanderers FC	Birkirkara FC	Adrian Mifsud (Hibernians FC Paola) Danilo Dončić (SRB, Sliema Wanderers FC) Michael Galea (Birkirkara FC)	18
2003/2004	Sliema Wanderers FC	Sliema Wanderers FC	Danilo Dončić (SRB, Sliema Wanderers FC)	19
2004/2005	Sliema Wanderers FC	Birkirkara FC	Andrew Cohen (Hibernians FC Paola)	21
2005/2006	Birkirkara FC	Hibernians FC Paola	Michael Galea (Birkirkara FC)	19
2006/2007	Marsaxlokk FC	Hibernians FC Paola	Daniel Bogdanović (Marsaxlokk FC)	31
2007/2008	Valletta FC	Birkirkara FC	Omar Sebastián Monesterolo (ARG, Valletta FC)	19
2008/2009	Hibernians FC Paola	Sliema Wanderers FC	Terence Scerri (Hibernians FC Paola)	26
2009/2010	Birkirkara FC	Valletta FC	Camilo Sanvezzo (BRA, Qormi FC)	24
2010/2011	Valletta FC	Floriana FC	Alfred Effiong (NGA, Marsaxlokk FC)	17
2011/2012	Valletta FC	Hibernians FC Paola	Obinna Obiefule (NGA, Marsaxlokk FC/Mosta FC)	34
2012/2013	Birkirkara FC	Hibernians FC Paola	José Luis Negrín (ESP, Melita FC St. Julian's/Rabat Ajax FC)	22
2013/2014	Valletta FC	Valletta FC	Jhonnattann Benites da Conceiçao (BRA, Birkirkara FC) Edison Luiz dos Santos "Tarabai" (BRA, Hibernians FC Paola)	21
2014/2015	Hibernians FC Paola	Birkirkara FC	Jorginho (BRA, Hibernians FC Paola) Edison Luiz dos Santos "Tarabai" (BRA, Hibernians FC Paola)	25
2015/2016	Valletta FC	Sliema Wanderers FC	Mario Fontanella (ITA, Floriana FC)	20
2016/2017	Hibernians FC Paola	Floriana FC	Bojan Kaljević (MNE, Balzan FC)	23
2017/2018	Valletta FC	Valletta FC	Amadou Samb (SEN, Gżira United FC)	21
2018/2019	Valletta FC	Balzan FC	Taylon Nicolas Correa Marcolino (BRA, Hibernians FC Paola)	19

NATIONAL CHAMPIONSHIP

Maltese Premier League 2018/2019
(17.08.2018 – 27.04.2019)

Results

Round 1 [17-18.08.2018]
Qormi FC - Senglea Athletic 1-0(0-0)
Birkirkara FC - Balzan FC 1-0(1-0)
Hibernians FC - Pietà Hotspurs 2-1(1-0)
Mosta FC - St. Andrews FC 1-3(1-1)
Hamrun Spartans - Floriana FC 2-0(0-0)
Sliema Wanderers - Valletta FC 3-0(1-0)
Tarxien Rainbows - Gżira United 1-4(0-2)

Round 2 [24-25.08.2018]
Senglea Athletic - Mosta FC 0-2(0-2)
Floriana FC - Sliema Wanderers 0-1(0-1)
St. Andrews FC - Tarxien Rainbows 1-5(0-2)
Gżira United - Hamrun Spartans 0-0
Pietà Hotspurs - Birkirkara FC 1-2(1-0)
Valletta FC - Hibernians FC 1-2(0-0)
Balzan FC - Qormi FC 4-2(1-0)

Round 3 [14-16.09.2018]
Hibernians FC - Floriana FC 0-2(0-1)
Qormi FC - Pietà Hotspurs 2-2(1-1)
Senglea Athletic - Balzan FC 0-5(0-2)
Hamrun Spartans - St. Andrews FC 1-0(0-0)
Mosta FC - Tarxien Rainbows 3-1(2-1)
Birkirkara FC - Valletta FC 0-3(0-0)
Sliema Wanderers - Gżira United 0-2(0-1)

Round 4 [21-23.09.2018]
Pietà Hotspurs - Senglea Athletic 1-1(1-0)
Valletta FC - Qormi FC 6-0(1-0)
Balzan FC - Mosta FC 3-1(2-1)
St. Andrews FC - Sliema Wanderers 0-2(0-1)
Tarxien Rainbows - Hamrun Spartans 2-1(1-1)
Gżira United - Hibernians FC 3-2(2-1)
Floriana FC - Birkirkara FC 0-2(0-0)

Round 5 [28-30.09.2018]
Hibernians FC - St. Andrews FC 2-0(0-0)
Qormi FC - Floriana FC 1-3(0-2)
Senglea Athletic - Valletta FC 1-5(0-4)
Balzan FC - Pietà Hotspurs 1-0(0-0)
Mosta FC - Hamrun Spartans 0-0
Sliema Wanderers - Tarxien Rainbo. 3-1(1-0)
Birkirkara FC - Gżira United 1-2(1-0)

Round 6 [05-06.10.2018]
Pietà Hotspurs - Mosta FC 3-1(2-0)
Valletta FC - Balzan FC 4-1(1-1)
Hamrun Spartans - Sliema Wanderers 0-0
Gżira United - Qormi FC 1-0(0-0)
Floriana FC - Senglea Athletic 4-1(2-1)
Tarxien Rainbows - Hibernians FC 2-4(1-1)
St. Andrews FC - Birkirkara FC 2-0(0-0)

Round 7 [19-22.10.2018]
Senglea Athletic - Gżira United 0-1(0-0)
Qormi FC - St. Andrews FC 0-2(0-1)
Pietà Hotspurs - Valletta FC 0-4(0-4)
Birkirkara FC - Tarxien Rainbows 2-0(1-0)
Mosta FC - Sliema Wanderers 1-2(1-1)
Hibernians FC - Hamrun Spartans 2-1(1-1)
Balzan FC - Floriana FC 2-0(0-0)

Round 8 [26-29.10.2018]
Hamrun Spartans - Birkirkara FC 2-1(1-1)
Floriana FC - Pietà Hotspurs 1-2(1-0)
Tarxien Rainbows - Qormi FC 1-0(0-0)
Valletta FC - Mosta FC 5-0(2-0)
Gżira United - Balzan FC 3-0(0-0)
St. Andrews FC - Senglea Athletic 1-2(0-1)
Sliema Wanderers - Hibernians FC 0-1(0-0)

Round 9 [02-04.11.2018]
Birkirkara FC - Sliema Wanderers 2-0(1-0)
Pietà Hotspurs - Gżira United 1-1(0-0)
Senglea Athletic - Tarxien Rainbows 1-2(0-2)
Balzan FC - St. Andrews FC 0-2(0-2)
Mosta FC - Hibernians FC 0-4(0-2)
Qormi FC - Hamrun Spartans 0-2(0-1)
Valletta FC - Floriana FC 1-0(0-0)

Round 10 [09-11.11.2018]
Gżira United - Valletta FC 0-0
Hamrun Spartans - Senglea Athletic 1-0(0-0)
St. Andrews FC - Pietà Hotspurs 3-3(2-1)
Sliema Wanderers - Qormi FC 2-0(1-0)
Tarxien Rainbows - Balzan FC 1-3(0-2)
Floriana FC - Mosta FC 1-0(1-0)
Hibernians FC - Birkirkara FC 2-1(1-0)

Round 11 [23-25.11.2018]
Balzan FC - Hamrun Spartans 2-2(2-2)
Mosta FC - Birkirkara FC 0-3(0-0)
Senglea Athletic - Sliema Wanderers 0-2(0-1)
Floriana FC - Gżira United 0-1(0-0)
Valletta FC - St. Andrews FC 1-0(0-0)
Pietà Hotspurs - Tarxien Rainbows 0-3(0-1)
Qormi FC - Hibernians FC 1-2(0-1)

Round 12 [07-09.12.2018]
Birkirkara FC - Qormi FC 2-1(1-1)
Hamrun Spartans - Pietà Hotspurs 3-2(3-2)
St. Andrews FC - Floriana FC 3-0(awarded)
Sliema Wanderers - Balzan FC 1-3(0-0)
Tarxien Rainbows - Valletta FC 0-7(0-5)
Gżira United - Mosta FC 3-3(0-1)
Hibernians FC - Senglea Athletic 2-0(2-0)

Round 13 [14-17.12.2018]
Gżira United - St. Andrews FC 2-1(1-0)
Mosta FC - Qormi FC 2-0(1-0)
Pietà Hotspurs - Sliema Wanderers 0-3(0-0)
Senglea Athletic - Birkirkara FC 0-2(0-1)
Floriana FC - Tarxien Rainbows 4-0(2-0)
Balzan FC - Hibernians FC 2-2(1-1)
Valletta FC - Hamrun Spartans 0-1(0-0)

Round 14 [11-13.01.2019]
Floriana FC - Hamrun Spartans 1-1(1-0)
Pietà Hotspurs - Hibernians FC 0-2(0-2)
Gżira United - Tarxien Rainbows 1-1(0-0)
St. Andrews FC - Mosta FC 1-1(1-0)
Balzan FC - Birkirkara FC 0-0
Senglea Athletic - Qormi FC 4-0(1-0)
Valletta FC - Sliema Wanderers 2-0(1-0)

Round 15 [18-20.01.2019]
Birkirkara FC - Pietà Hotspurs 3-0(1-0)
Hamrun Spartans - Gżira United 1-1(1-0)
Sliema Wanderers - Floriana FC 1-1(0-1)
Mosta FC - Senglea Athletic 0-3(0-1)
Tarxien Rainbows - St. Andrews FC 2-1(1-0)
Qormi FC - Balzan FC 1-3(0-2)
Hibernians FC - Valletta FC 1-2(1-0)

Round 16 [01-03.02.2019]
Balzan FC - Senglea Athletic 1-2(1-0)
Pietà Hotspurs - Qormi FC 0-2(0-0)
St. Andrews FC - Hamrun Spartans 0-3(0-1)
Floriana FC - Hibernians FC 0-1(0-0)
Tarxien Rainbows - Mosta FC 0-2(0-0)
Gżira United - Sliema Wanderers 1-1(1-1)
Valletta FC - Birkirkara FC 2-0(0-0)

Round 17 [08-10.02.2019]
Qormi FC - Valletta FC 1-2(1-2)
Mosta FC - Balzan FC 0-0
Senglea Athletic - Pietà Hotspurs 2-1(1-1)
Hamrun Spartans - Tarxien Rainbows 3-0(1-0)
Sliema Wanderers - St. Andrews FC 1-1(1-0)
Hibernians FC - Gżira United 1-0(1-0)
Birkirkara FC - Floriana FC 0-0

Round 18 [15-17.02.2019]
Tarxien Rainbo. - Sliema Wanderers 1-2(0-1)
Valletta FC - Senglea Athletic 3-3(2-1)
St. Andrews FC - Hibernians FC 1-2(1-0)
Hamrun Spartans - Mosta FC 0-1(0-0)
Floriana FC - Qormi FC 0-1(0-1)
Pietà Hotspurs - Balzan FC 0-3(0-1)
Gżira United - Birkirkara FC 1-1(0-0)

Round 19 [01-02.03.2019]
Senglea Athletic - Floriana FC 0-1(0-1)
Balzan FC - Valletta FC 1-2(1-0)
Hibernians FC - Tarxien Rainbows 5-0(2-0)
Birkirkara FC - St. Andrews FC 2-0(0-0)
Mosta FC - Pietà Hotspurs 3-2(2-1)
Sliema Wanderers - Hamrun Spartans 2-1(0-0)
Qormi FC - Gżira United 1-4(0-3)

Round 20 [08-09.03.2019]
Tarxien Rainbows - Birkirkara FC 0-2(0-0)
Hamrun Spartans - Hibernians FC 1-1(1-0)
Sliema Wanderers - Mosta FC 3-1(2-0)
St. Andrews FC - Qormi FC 0-2(0-0)
Valletta FC - Pietà Hotspurs 3-0(3-0)
Gżira United - Senglea Athletic 3-1(1-1)
Floriana FC - Balzan FC 0-0

Round 21 [12-14.03.2019]
Hibernians FC - Sliema Wanderers 2-2(0-2)
Pietà Hotspurs - Floriana FC 0-2(0-0)
Birkirkara FC - Hamrun Spartans 0-1(0-0)
Balzan FC - Gżira United 0-0
Mosta FC - Valletta FC 0-1(0-1)
Senglea Athletic - St. Andrews FC 5-0(2-0)
Qormi FC - Tarxien Rainbows 1-2(1-1)

Round 22 [29-31.03.2019]
Hamrun Spartans - Qormi FC 2-1(1-0)
Gżira United - Pietà Hotspurs 5-2(3-1)
Tarxien Rainbows - Senglea Athletic 2-2(1-1)
St. Andrews FC - Balzan FC 0-1(0-0)
Hibernians FC - Mosta FC 1-1(1-0)
Sliema Wanderers - Birkirkara FC 0-1(0-0)
Floriana FC - Valletta FC 2-0(1-0)

Round 23 [05-07.04.2019]
Qormi FC - Sliema Wanderers 2-3(2-2)
Birkirkara FC - Hibernians FC 2-3(1-1)
Balzan FC - Tarxien Rainbows 2-0(0-0)
Senglea Athletic - Hamrun Spartans 2-2(1-0)
Mosta FC - Floriana FC 3-3(2-1)
Pietà Hotspurs - St. Andrews FC 3-1(0-0)
Valletta FC - Gżira United 1-1(1-0)

Round 24 [13-15.04.2019]
Tarxien Rainbows - Pietà Hotspurs 2-0(1-0)
Birkirkara FC - Mosta FC 1-2(1-0)
Hamrun Spartans - Balzan FC 1-1(0-0)
St. Andrews FC - Valletta FC 0-4(0-0)
Sliema Wanderers - Senglea Athletic 0-0
Gżira United - Floriana FC 1-0(1-0)
Hibernians FC - Qormi FC 1-3(1-2)

Round 25 [20-22.04.2019]
Mosta FC - Gżira United 1-1(1-0)
Pietà Hotspurs - Hamrun Spartans 0-2(0-1)
Balzan FC - Sliema Wanderers 2-1(2-1)
Valletta FC - Tarxien Rainbows 1-0(1-0)
Floriana FC - St. Andrews FC 0-1(0-0)
Qormi FC - Birkirkara FC 1-0(0-0)
Senglea Athletic - Hibernians FC 0-2(0-2)

Round 26 [26-27.04.2019]
Tarxien Rainbows - Floriana FC 0-3(0-2)
Birkirkara FC - Senglea Athletic 2-3(1-0)
Qormi FC - Mosta FC 1-1(0-0)
St. Andrews FC - Gżira United 1-0(1-0)
Hamrun Spartans - Valletta FC 1-1(0-1)
Hibernians FC - Balzan FC 5-1(1-0)
Sliema Wanderers - Pietà Hotspurs 2-1(1-0)

Championship Play-off (04.05.2019)

At the end of the season, Valletta FC and Hibernians FC Paola finished off equal on 58 points. As result a championship decider was played on 04.05.2019.

Valletta FC - Hibernians FC Paola 2-2(0-1,1-1,2-2); 4-2 on penalties
Goals: 0-1 Taylon Nicolas Correa Marcolino (19), 1-1 Jonathan Caruana (59), 2-1 Mario Fontanella (98), 2-2 Marco Sahanek (118).
Penalties: Miguel Ángel Alba, Santiago Malano, Bogdan Cătălin Gavrilă, Mario Fontanella / Marco Sahanek (missed), Jake Grech, Tiago Fonseca, Taylon Nicolas Correa Marcolino (saved).

Final Standings

1.	**Valletta FC**	26	18	4	4	61	-	18	58
2.	Hibernians FC Paola	26	18	4	4	54	-	27	58
3.	Gżira United FC	26	13	11	2	42	-	21	50
4.	Hamrun Spartans FC	26	12	10	4	35	-	20	46
5.	Sliema Wanderers FC	26	13	6	7	37	-	26	45
6.	Balzan FC	26	12	7	7	41	-	31	43
7.	Birkirkara FC	26	12	3	11	33	-	26	39
8.	Floriana FC	26	9	5	12	28	-	25	32
9.	Mosta FC	26	7	8	11	30	-	45	29
10.	Tarxien Rainbows FC	26	8	2	16	29	-	58	26
11.	Senglea Athletic FC	26	7	5	14	33	-	46	26
12.	St. Andrews FC (*Relegation Play-off*)	26	7	3	16	25	-	45	24
13.	Qormi FC (*Relegated*)	26	6	2	18	25	-	51	20
14.	Pietà Hotspurs FC (*Relegated*)	26	3	4	19	25	-	59	13

Top goalscorers:

19 Taylon Nicolas Correa Marcolino (BRA)
Hibernians FC Paola

17 Mario Fontanella (ITA)
Valletta FC

12 Haruna Zambuk Garba (NGA)
Gżira United FC

Relegation Play-offs (05.05.2019)

St. Andrews FC - Santa Lućija FC 1-4(1-2)

St. Andrews FC relegated, Santa Lućija FC promoted to the Premier League 2019/2010.

NATIONAL CUP
Maltese FA Trophy 2018/2019

Preliminary Round [31.08.-02.09.2018]

Oratory Youths FC - Għajnsielem FC	0-8	Sannat Lions FC - Ta' Xbiex SC	2-0
Munxar Falcons FC - Nadur Youngsters FC	0-4	Qala Saints FC - Għargħur FC	1-3
St. Lawrence Spurs FC - Għaxaq FC	0-2	SK Victoria Wanderers FC - Mtarfa FC	10-0
Marsa FCskala FC - Dingli Swallows FC	0-4	Victoria Hotspurs FC - Msida St. Joseph FC	8-0

First Round [06-09.09.2018]

Għarb Rangers FC - Xgħajra Tornadoes FC	2-1	SK Victoria Wanderers FC - Għaxaq FC	0-0 aet; 1-4 pen
Għajnsielem FC - Xewkija Tigers FC	0-2	Victoria Hotspurs FC - Attard FC	4-1
Żurrieq FC - Nadur Youngsters FC	0-4	Żebbuġ Rovers FC - Mdina Knights FC	0-1
Kirkop United FC - Kerċem Ajax FC	2-1	Għargħur FC - Xagħra United FC	3-1
Dingli Swallows FC - Sannat Lions FC	1-2		

Second Round [26-28.10.2018]

Mellieħa SC - Kalkara FC	2-0	Sannat Lions FC - Qrendi FC	0-3
Kirkop United FC - Vittoriosa Stars FC Birgu	1-2 aet	Żebbuġ Rangers FC - Marsaxlokk FC	1-0
Gudja United FC - Sirens FC San Pawl il-Baħar	2-1	Naxxar Lions FC - Żejtun Corinthians FC	1-2
St. George's FC Cospicua - Lija Athletic FC	0-4	Victoria Hotspurs FC - Siġġiewi FC	1-1 aet; 5-6 pen
St. Venera Lightnings FC - Pembroke Athleta FC	0-3	Mdina Knights FC - Għarb Rangers FC	2-1 aet
Mġarr United FC - San Ġwann FC	1-2	Luqa St. Andrew's FC - Rabat Ajax FC	0-5
Xewkija Tigers FC - Mqabba FC	6-1	Fgura United FC - Għaxaq FC	4-1 aet
Marsa FC - Għargħur FC	5-1	Santa Lucia FC - Birżebbuġa St. Peter's FC	2-2 aet; 2-4 pen
Melita FC - Swieqi United FC	1-0	Żabbar St. Patrick FC - Nadur Youngsters FC	0-7

Third Round [30.11.-03.12.2018]			
Birżebbuġa St. Peter's FC - Żebbuġ Rangers FC	0-5	Nadur Youngsters FC - Birkirkara FC	0-4
Qormi FC - Hibernians FC Paola	1-5	Marsa FC - Valletta FC	0-3
Mdina Knights FC - Pietà Hotspurs FC	1-4	Mellieħa SC - Lija Athletic FC	0-5
Gżira United FC - Rabat Ajax FC	4-0	Gudja United FC - Xewkija Tigers FC	1-2 aet
San Ġwann FC - Fgura United FC	0-1	Pembroke Athleta FC - Żejtun Corinthians FC	0-2
Balzan FC - Qrendi FC	5-1	Sliema Wanderers FC - St. Andrews FC	2-0
Siġġiewi FC - Melita FC	1-3	Vittoriosa Stars FC Birgu - Tarxien Rainbows FC	0-3
Floriana FC - Ħamrun Spartans FC	0-1	Senglea Athletic FC - Mosta FC	2-3 aet

1/8-Finals [26.01.2019]			
Hibernians FC Paola - Fgura United FC	4-0	Balzan FC - Xewkija Tigers FC	6-1
Pietà Hotspurs FC - Żejtun Corinthians FC	2-0	Gżira United FC - Melita FC	4-2
Mosta FC - Sliema Wanderers FC	2-1	Birkirkara FC - Ħamrun Spartans FC	2-1
Tarxien Rainbows FC - Żebbuġ Rangers FC	5-0	Lija Athletic FC - Valletta FC	1-7

Quarter-Finals [23.02./03-08.05.2019]			
Pietà Hotspurs FC - Gżira United FC	1-2 aet	Tarxien Rainbows FC - Balzan FC	0-2
Mosta FC - Birkirkara FC	1-2	Hibernians FC Paola - Valletta FC	2-3 aet

Semi-Finals [11-12.05.2019]			
Balzan FC - Birkirkara FC	3-2	Gżira United FC - Valletta FC	0-2

Final

18.05.2019; Ta' Qali National Stadium, Attard; Referee: Mario Apap; Attendance: 4,024
Balzan FC - Valletta FC **4-4(2-1,2-2,4-4); 5-4 on penalties**

Balzan: Sean Mintoff, Steven Bezzina (77.Andrija Majdevac), Aleksandar Kosorić, Ivan Božović, Uroš Ljubomirac, Paul Fenech, Carlos Eduardo de Fiori Mendes „Kadú" (34.Dale Camilleri; 105.Justin Grioli), Nenad Šljivić, Ricardo Calixto Correa Duarte, Alfred Effiong, Stephan Pisani (103.Sean Cipriott). Trainer: Jacques Scerri.

Valletta: Henry Bonello, Jonathan Caruana, Steve Borg (72.Joseph Zerafa), Jean Borg, Rowen Muscat, Raed Ibrahim Saleh (81.Nicolas Pulis), Kyrian Nwoko, Enmy Manuel Peña Beltré (120.Shaun Dimech), Santiago Malano, Bojan Kaljević (63.Bogdan Cătălin Gavrilă [*sent off 118*]), Mario Fontanella. Trainer: Darren Abdilla.

Goals: 1-0 Alfred Effiong (8), 1-1 Enmy Manuel Peña Beltré (40), 2-1 Alfred Effiong (44), 2-2 Enmy Manuel Peña Beltré (72), 3-2 Alfred Effiong (95), 4-2 Alfred Effiong (104), 4-3 Mario Fontanella (115 penalty), 4-4 Rowen Muscat (119).

Penalties: Santiago Malano 0-1; Aleksandar Kosorić 1-1; Mario Fontanella (saved); Nenad Šljivić 2-1; Rowen Muscat 2-2; Uroš Ljubomirac 3-2; Jean Borg 3-3; Andrija Majdevac 4-3; Nicolas Pulis 4-4; Alfred Effiong 5-4.

THE CLUBS 2018/2019

Please note: number of matches and goals by Valletta FC and Hibernians FC Paola contain Championship Play-off included!

Balzan Football Club

Founded: 1937
Stadium: St. Aloysius Sports and Recreational Complex, Birkirkara (100)

Goalkeepers:	DOB	M	(s)	G
Steve Sultana	07.09.1990	16		
Sean Mintoff	13.10.1985	10		
Defenders:	**DOB**	**M**	**(s)**	**G**
Harry Ascroft (AUS)	01.07.1995	2		
Steven Bezzina	05.01.1987	17	(2)	
Ivan Božović (SRB)	29.05.1990	18		1
Gary Camilleri	05.08.1999		(2)	
Justin Grioli	20.09.1987	13	(7)	
Michael Johnson	11.05.1994	10	(1)	2
Aleksandar Kosorić (BIH)	30.01.1987	9		1
Elkin Orlando Serrano Valero (COL)	17.03.1984	21	(1)	2
Midfielders:	**DOB**	**M**	**(s)**	**G**
Dale Camilleri	17.10.1992	7	(7)	1
Sean Cipriott	10.09.1997	1	(14)	
Ricardo Calixto Correa Duarte (URU)	20.07.1994	15	(1)	2
Paul Fenech	20.12.1986	12		
Neil Frendo	04.01.1999		(1)	
Carlos Eduardo de Fiori Mendes „Kadú" (BRA)	31.08.1986	10	(3)	1
Miloš Lepović (SRB)	03.10.1987	17		1
Uroš Ljubomirac (SRB)	12.04.1990	24		6
Yudai Miyamoto (JPN)	10.03.1997		(1)	
Nenad Šljivić (SRB)	08.06.1985	21		
Forwards:	**DOB**	**M**	**(s)**	**G**
Siraj Arab	25.03.1994	1	(9)	
Alfred Effiong	29.11.1984	21	(5)	9
Bojan Kaljević (MNE)	25.01.1986	1		
Alex da Paixão Alves "Lecão" (BRA)	17.01.1993	12		5
Andrija Majdevac (SRB)	07.08.1997	17	(6)	10
Lydon Micallef	16.05.1992		(10)	
Stephan Pisani	07.08.1992	11		
Trainer:	**DOB**	**M**		
Marko Mićović (SRB)	13.10.1974	16		
Jacques Scerri [05.02.2019]		10		

Birkirkara Football Club

Founded: 1950
Stadium: Mġarr Ground, Imgarr (300)

Goalkeepers:	DOB	M	(s)	G
Andrew James Hogg	02.03.1985	5		
Kristijan Naumovski (MKD)	17.09.1988	21		
Defenders:	**DOB**	**M**	**(s)**	**G**
Cain Attard	10.09.1994	21	(3)	2
Myles Beerman	13.03.1999	1	(7)	
Gianluca Bugeja	05.09.1999	1		
Danilo Augusto Chapoval de Azevedo "Danilo Quipapá" (BRA)	21.02.1994	21		1
Eduardo Ferreira dos Santos „Eduardo Mancha" (BRA)	24.11.1995	25	(1)	
Edward Herrera	14.11.1986		(8)	
Arian Mršulja (CRO)	11.02.1998	1		
Nikola Vukanac (SRB)	14.01.1986	9		1
Midfielders:	**DOB**	**M**	**(s)**	**G**
Terence Agius	15.01.1994	8	(7)	
Mislav Anđelković (CRO)	22.04.1988	22	(1)	1
Johan Bezzina	30.05.1994	11	(1)	
Clayton Failla	08.01.1986	5	(5)	1
Paul Fenech	20.12.1986	10	(2)	
Jake Grech	18.11.1997	11	(4)	5
Matthew Guillaumier	09.04.1998	14	(2)	1
Neil Micallef	13.01.1999		(1)	
Jordan Sciberras	23.03.1999		(1)	
Uchenna Calistus Umeh (NGA)	10.10.1991	1	(3)	
Kurt Zammit	26.02.1996	20	(1)	
Forwards:	**DOB**	**M**	**(s)**	**G**
Ahmed Abdulrahman Al Sherooqi (BHR)	22.05.2000		(1)	
Ayrton Attard	05.11.2000		(1)	
Milan Basrak (SRB)	24.12.1994	3	(2)	
Carlos Alberto Chavarria Rodríguez (NCA)	02.05.1994	4	(1)	1
Jorge Pereira da Silva "Jorginho" (BRA)	04.12.1985	6	(4)	2
Carlo Zammit Lonardelli	29.04.2001		(1)	
Marcelo Henrique França de Siqueira "Marcelinho" (BRA)	23.05.1994	18	(2)	3
Paul Mbong	02.09.2001	1	(2)	
Michael Mifsud	17.04.1981	15	(5)	7
Luke Montebello	13.08.1995	9	(2)	5
Petar Orlandić (MNE)	06.08.1990	5		2
Thiago Esmerindo de Souza de Brito (BRA)	20.08.1992	8	(5)	
Maurizio Vella (ITA)	10.05.1991	10		
Gianluca Zammit	19.08.1999		(3)	
Trainer:	**DOB**	**M**		
Paul Zammit	21.08.1969	21		
Mark Buttigieg [28.03.2019]		3		
John Buttigieg [18.04.2019]	05.10.1963	2		

Floriana Football Club

Founded: 1894
Stadium: Independence Arena, Floriana (3,000)

Goalkeepers:	DOB	M	(s)	G
Ini Etim Akpan (NGA)	03.08.1984	24		
Matthew Grech	19.02.1996	2		
Justin Spiteri	27.07.1985		(1)	
Defenders:	**DOB**	**M**	**(s)**	**G**
Arthur Henrique Ricciardi Oyama (BRA)	14.01.1987	23	(2)	5
Alex Cini	28.10.1991	21	(1)	
Isaac Galea	06.01.2002		(1)	
Edward Herrera	14.07.1986	6	(2)	1
Jurgen Pisani	03.09.1992	20	(2)	
Enzo Adrián Ruiz (ARG)	20.06.1989	24		
Mohammed Saleh (PLE)	18.07.1993	6		
Midfielders:	**DOB**	**M**	**(s)**	**G**
Ulises Jesús Arias (ARG)	05.08.1996	13		
Clyde Borg	20.03.1992	8	(12)	1
Brandon Bray	01.10.2001		(1)	
Gaston Cesani (ARG)	05.09.1995	9	(2)	
Marcelina Emerson (BRA)	24.02.1991	24		2
Clayton Failla	08.01.1986	11	(1)	2
Goran Galešić (BIH)	11.03.1989	2	(1)	
Dylan Grima	18.07.1990		(6)	
Ivica Guberac (SVN)	05.07.1988	1	(1)	
Kristian Keqi (ALB)	28.07.1996	8	(1)	3
Brandon Diego Paiber	05.06.1995	12		2
Bradley Sciberras	02.02.2001		(1)	
Thiago Galvão da Silva (BRA)	24.08.1989	15	(1)	2
Mattia Zarb	15.03.2000		(1)	
Forwards:	**DOB**	**M**	**(s)**	**G**
Daniel Agius	15.11.1996	1	(18)	1
Jacinto Júnior Conceição Cabral "Juninho" (BRA)	10.03.1992	11		3
Stephen Pisani	07.08.1992	14		
Ignacio Varela	20.07.1990	12	(1)	3
Maurizio Vella (ITA)	10.05.1991	8	(1)	1
Terence Vella	20.04.1990	3	(9)	1
Lucas Vieira da Silva (BRA)	04.03.1993	6	(1)	1
Patrick Wleh (LBR)	17.06.1991	2	(3)	
Trainer:	**DOB**	**M**		
Nicolas Hernan Chiesa (ARG)	13.05.1972	2		
Luís Carlos Bertolo Oliveira (BEL) [29.08.2018]	24.03.1969	8		
Guido Ugolotti (ITA) [14.11.2018]	28.09.1958	16		

Gżira United Football Club

Founded: 1947
Stadium: Ta' Qali National Stadium, Attard (17,797)

Goalkeepers:	DOB	M	(s)	G
Anthony Curmi	20.11.1982	3		
Justin Haber	09.06.1981	23		
Defenders:	**DOB**	**M**	**(s)**	**G**
Clifford Gatt Baldacchino	09.02.1988	10	(5)	
Myles Beerman	13.03.1999	3	(4)	
Sacha Borg	26.04.1993	17	(3)	
Fernando Barbosa	04.12.1992	18	(2)	1
Prince Loïc Destin Mambouana (FRA)	10.09.1990	5		1
Rodolfo dos Santos Soares (BRA)	20.05.1985	23		
Christian Sammut	25.02.1998		(1)	
Jaron Schembri	18.10.1998		(2)	
Thomas Veronese (ITA)	02.11.1986	6	(5)	
Midfielders:	**DOB**	**M**	**(s)**	**G**
Édison David Bilbao Zárate (CHI)	06.03.1987	22	(3)	4
Roderick Briffa	24.08.1981	21	(1)	
Andrew Cohen	13.05.1981	22	(2)	5
Gianmarco Conti (ITA)	01.02.1992	11	(1)	1
Juan Corbalan	03.03.1997	22		
Nicky Muscat	13.07.1996	17	(8)	2
Zachary Scerri	08.03.1996	16	(8)	
Forwards:	**DOB**	**M**	**(s)**	**G**
Luca Brincat	04.07.1997		(7)	
Sofian Domoraud Operi (FRA)	13.05.1996	1	(7)	
Haruna Garba	17.01.1994	22		12
Jorghino (BRA)	04.12.1985	5	(3)	1
Moad Lamlun	16.05.1998	1	(2)	
Justin Junior Mengolo (CMR)	24.06.1993	9	(1)	6
Amadou Samb (SEN)	22.04.1988	9		6
Trainer:	**DOB**	**M**		
Darren Abdilla		9		
Jesmond Zerafa [12.02.2019]	03.08.1965	17		

Ħamrun Spartans Football Club

Founded: 1907
Stadium: "Victor Tedesco" Stadium, Ħamrun (6,000)

Goalkeepers:	**DOB**	**M**	**(s)**	**G**
Manuel Bartolo	26.08.1983	21		
Sean Cini	27.07.1982	5	(1)	
Defenders:	**DOB**	**M**	**(s)**	**G**
Jeremy Busuttil	09.04.1999	1		
Karl Micallef	08.09.1996	24		1
Orestis Nikolopoulos (GRE)	26.08.1991	20		
Jorge Nicolás Pandiani Quaglia (URU)	10.04.1994	1		
Enrico Pepe (ITA)	12.11.1989	26		
Karl Schembri	03.11.1999		(1)	
Midfielders:	**DOB**	**M**	**(s)**	**G**
Conor Borg	13.05.1997	2	(8)	
Tristan Caruana	15.09.1991	24		2
Marco Criaco (ITA)	22.05.1989	14		4
Cain Cutajar	20.07.2000		(4)	
Matthew Gauci	02.09.1991	20	(3)	
Misael Miranda Gómez (MEX)	23.04.1996	1		
Antonio Monticelli (ITA)	25.05.1989	11		
Sebastián Ricardo Nayar (ARG)	10.05.1988	16	(1)	1
Njongo Lobe Priso Doding (CMR)	24.12.1988	8		
Andre Scicluna	22.09.1988	6	(2)	
Kevin Tulimieri (ITA)	15.03.1992	20		8
Russell Vella	06.04.2001		(2)	
Forwards:	**DOB**	**M**	**(s)**	**G**
Caetano Prósperi Calil (BRA)	20.05.1984	23		4
Ryan Darmanin	12.12.1985	1	(20)	2
Wilfried Domoraud (FRA)	18.08.1988	17		7
Massimo Ganci (ITA)	17.11.1981	4		2
Carlos Hernán Henneberg (ARG)	07.06.1990	12		1
Francesco Marra (ITA)	19.10.1999	2		
Donneil Alain Moukanza (FRA)	27.02.1991	6		1
Bradley Schembri	10.08.1998	1	(5)	1
Trainer:	**DOB**	**M**		
Giovanni Tedesco (ITA)	13.05.1972	26		

Hibernians Football Club Paola

Founded: 1922
Stadium: Hibernians Ground, Paola (2,968)

Goalkeepers:	**DOB**	**M**	**(s)**	**G**
Rudi Briffa	21.08.1996		(1)	
Andrew James Hogg	02.03.1985	15		
Marko Jovičić (SRB)	02.02.1995	12		
Defenders:	**DOB**	**M**	**(s)**	**G**
Andrei Agius	12.08.1986	27		4
Igor Bubnjić (CRO)	17.07.1992		(2)	
Timothy Tabone Desira	15.07.1995	2	(12)	
Márcio Leandro Barbosa de Silveira (BRA)	13.07.1988	12		
Isaac Ntow (GHA)	26.05.1994	18		
Nemanja Radojević (SRB)	05.02.1992	24		
Andreas Vella	27.01.2001		(1)	
Connor Zammit	26.09.1998	2	(8)	
Midfielders:	**DOB**	**M**	**(s)**	**G**
Johan Bezzina	30.05.1994	6	(6)	1
Ivan Blažević (CRO)	25.07.1992	4	(2)	
Jake Grech	18.11.1997	11		6
Guttiner Heider Fernando Costa Tenorio (BRA)	06.10.1994		(7)	1
Bjorn Kristensen	05.04.1993	21	(4)	2
Marco Sahanek (AUT)	27.01.1990	7	(6)	2
Dunstan Vella	27.04.1996	23	(3)	
David Xuereb	30.03.1998		(9)	
Forwards:	**DOB**	**M**	**(s)**	**G**
Daneel Abela	08.01.1999		(3)	
Jurgen Degabriele	10.10.1996	18		5
Marcelo Mariano Dias (BRA)	29.09.1985	21	(1)	
Joseph Essien Mbong	15.07.1997	26		3
Rafael Tardini Monteiro (BRA)	25.01.1992		(2)	
Tiago Adan Fonseca (BRA)	14.03.1988	26		11
Andrei Spiteri	18.04.2000		(1)	
Taylon Nicolas Correa Marcolino (BRA)	16.03.1995	22	(4)	19
Trainer:	**DOB**	**M**		
Stefano Sanderra (ITA)	21.06.1967	27		

Mosta Football Club

Founded: 1935
Stadium: "Charles Abela" Memorial Stadium, Mosta (600)

Goalkeepers:	**DOB**	**M**	**(s)**	**G**
Yves Stéphane Bitseki Moto (GAB)	23.04.1983	2		
Andreas Vella	14.10.1998	24		
Defenders:	**DOB**	**M**	**(s)**	**G**
Steve Bonnici	02.02.1989	9	(2)	
Gianluca Cuomo (USA)	02.04.1993	12		
Emmanuel Edet (NGA)	22.08.1989	1		
Jonas Rodriguez Ekani (CMR)	13.10.1992	8	(1)	
Tyron Farrugia	22.02.1989	22	(2)	3
Jurgen Grech	28.04.1999	1	(3)	
Tobi Jnohope (USA)	04.10.1997	3		
Francesco Mazzavillani (ITA)	04.08.1998	7	(1)	
Rafael Morisco da Silva (BRA)	04.08.1986	15		3
Massimo Sammartino (ITA)	08.09.1995	20		1
Dexter Xuereb	21.09.1997	18	(5)	1
Midfielders:	**DOB**	**M**	**(s)**	**G**
Duane Bonnici	10.10.1995	8	(4)	
Alessio De Cerchio (ITA)	24.07.1997	9		2
Federico Franchini (ITA)	23.01.1994	7		
Kyle Frendo	30.06.1995	7	(9)	
Misael Miranda Gómez (MEX)	23.04.1996	10		1
Kei Hirose (JPN)	20.11.1995	10		
Demir Imeri (MKD)	27.10.1995	6		3
Maycon Wesley dos Santos Gonçalves (BRA)	21.01.1999	1		
Liam Portelli	21.11.2000		(1)	
Romeu Péricles Romão (BRA)	10.04.1990	11		
Forwards:	**DOB**	**M**	**(s)**	**G**
Davy Claude Angan (CIV)	20.09.1987	8		4
Mohamed Aoudou (BEN)	19.02.1990	2		
James Brincat	03.12.1996	4	(17)	4
Zachary Brincat	24.06.1998	13	(9)	2
Juri Cisotti (ITA)	05.05.1993	18		1
Alex Darlington (WAL)	26.12.1988	3		
Renan Abner do Carmo de Oliveira (BRA)	08.05.1997	8	(1)	2
Akeem Roach (TRI)	10.10.1995	13		3
Falou Samb (SEN)	17.01.1997	3		
Mattia Vicaroni (ITA)	08.09.1998	1	(1)	
Kurt Zammit	01.12.1995	2	(9)	
Trainer:	**DOB**	**M**		
Enrico Piccioni (ITA)	23.11.1961	10		
Mark Miller (ENG) [22.11.2018]	22.09.1962	16		

Pietà Hotspurs Football Club

Founded: 1968
Stadium: Trinity Stadium, Pietà (1,000)

Goalkeepers:	DOB	M	(s)	G
Jacob Chircop St. John	11.06.1998	3		
Nicholas Vella	27.08.1989	23		
Defenders:	**DOB**	**M**	**(s)**	**G**
Juan Manuel Artiaga Roa (CHI)	29.01.1993	18	(3)	
Travis Bartolo	05.04.1995	9	(3)	
Quincy Bregman	21.07.1992		(1)	
Christian Degabriele	07.03.1997	9	(6)	
Christian Grech	20.02.1993	23		
Liam Mckay	22.05.2001		(2)	
Kyle Mercieca	30.04.1999		(1)	
Takasi Ose (JPN)	19.10.1995	19	(1)	
Nicolas Pisani	02.05.1998	6	(13)	3
Stefan Radovanović (SRB)	19.02.1992	7		
Harry Singh (ENG)	04.02.1996	1	(2)	
Antônio Orlando Queiroz Macedo Neto "Tony" (BRA)	11.05.1990	20		3
Midfielders:	**DOB**	**M**	**(s)**	**G**
Dylan Agius	26.12.1996	21	(2)	3
Clyde Bouvet	07.03.2001		(4)	
Jan Busuttil	06.03.1999	23	(1)	1
Jeremy Delmar	27.07.2001		(1)	
Jake Ghio	08.09.2001		(8)	
Jalo Ishaya Irimiya (NGA)	26.07.1997	22	(1)	
Gegi Kekua (GEO)	23.12.1995	2	(4)	
Ayrton Mizzi	21.02.1996	1	(2)	
Shunsuke Nakamura (JPN)	16.05.1994	7	(5)	2
Samuel Okoh (NGA)	18.09.2001		(2)	
Neil Pace Cocks	26.04.1996	20	(1)	
Sheldon Pisani	06.06.2001		(2)	
Uchenna Calistus Umeh (NGA)	10.10.1991	9		
Forwards:	**DOB**	**M**	**(s)**	**G**
Paul Chimezie (NGA)	10.06.1987	21	(1)	6
Gabriel Mensah (GHA)	05.10.1995	21		4
James Scicluna	04.03.1998	1	(10)	1
Trainer:	**DOB**	**M**		
Ramon Zammit		26		

Qormi Football Club

Founded: 1961
Stadium: Thomaso Ground, Qormi (500)

Goalkeepers:	DOB	M	(s)	G
Jamie Azzopardi	01.09.1997	16		
David Cassar	24.11.1987	10		
Defenders:	**DOB**	**M**	**(s)**	**G**
Alan Abela	01.11.1992	19	(3)	
Luboš Adamec (CZE)	27.04.1994	5		
Luke Busuttil	30.01.1994	3	(5)	1
Nathan Gauci	15.10.1999		(1)	
Joseph Gaetano Gesualdi	15.02.1992	6	(1)	
Nick Ghio	18.06.1998		(6)	
Danny Kabeya	22.03.1995	2		
Lucas Santana Dos Santos (BRA)	23.04.1998	11		
Davide Mansi (ITA)	18.01.1996	25		1
Iven Zammit	17.05.1997	8	(10)	1
Midfielders:	**DOB**	**M**	**(s)**	**G**
Mario Andrés Arrieta Suárez (MEX)	28.08.1992	4	(3)	
Alessio Cassar	27.02.1992	11	(7)	2
Luke Farrugia	12.11.1998		(2)	
Tensior Gusman	24.01.1997	12	(9)	7
Amos Kabeya (ENG)	26.08.1992		(1)	
Kim Seo-In (USA)	18.04.1995	10	(1)	
Kassiano Soares Mendonça (BRA)	24.04.1995	13		
Mboyo Jordy Lokando (BEL)	28.04.1997	11		
Manolito Micallef	16.11.1983	19	(4)	1
Mateus Regis da Silva (BRA)	27.07.1994	5		
Romeu Péricles Romão (BRA)	10.04.1990	10		
Yannick Yankam	12.12.1997	26		3
Forwards:	**DOB**	**M**	**(s)**	**G**
Alexsandro Ferreira dos Santos (BRA)	03.04.1997	7	(4)	
Mohamed Malela Bangoura (GUI)	22.10.1998	10	(1)	3
Michael Borg	18.10.1992	6	(9)	
Michael Camilleri	23.03.1993	4	(6)	
Freud Codjo Gnindokponou (FRA)	01.02.1994	11	(1)	1
Antonio Rozzi (ITA)	28.05.1994	11		4
Nedo Turković (BIH)	23.10.1989	3		
Wellington Oliveira Vieira "Wellington Petinha" (BRA)	20.01.1993	8		1
Trainer:	**DOB**	**M**		
Brian Spiteri		10		
Mario Muscat [16.11.2018]	18.08.1976	16		

Senglea Athletic Football Club

Founded: 22.03.1943
Stadium: Ta' Qali National Stadium, Attard (17,000)

Goalkeepers:	DOB	M	(s)	G
Matthew Farrugia	17.03.1985	22		
Bence Perger (HUN)	20.01.1996	2		
Philip Schranz	14.07.1996	2	(2)	
Defenders:	**DOB**	**M**	**(s)**	**G**
Matthew Bartolo	14.06.1986	3	(9)	
Daniel Buckle	29.07.1997	1	(1)	
Gary Camilleri	05.08.1999	2	(9)	
Zachary Cassar	02.11.1998	23	(1)	
Gonzalo Julian Gamarra Leyton (ARG)	02.07.1999	10		
Imanol González Benac (ARG)	06.01.1998	13		1
Marko Ivanović (MNE)	30.06.1995	2	(1)	
Arion Mršulja (CRO)	11.02.1998	7		1
Fernando Salvati (ITA)	15.08.1981	11		1
Christian Sammut	25.02.1998	8		
El Mehdi Sidqy (MAR)	06.01.1984	10		1
Rayson Vella	18.01.1991	1	(2)	
Andre White	01.01.1991	7	(1)	
Midfielders:	**DOB**	**M**	**(s)**	**G**
Salvatore Amabile (ITA)	12.07.1998		(1)	
Fabrizio Bramati (ITA)	12.06.1993	6	(1)	
Cézar Rocha Robortella „Cezinha" (BRA)	26.01.1989		(1)	
Mahamadou Cissé (FRA)	01.05.1992	1		
Karl Cutajar	30.05.1992	9	(13)	
Carsten Dimech	21.07.1991		(1)	
Matías Nicolás García (ARG)	22.07.1996	22		4
Noureddine Lachrah (BEL)	17.04.1998	2		
Dylan Micallef	30.06.1994	4	(3)	
Larson Mallia	16.04.1993	3	(5)	
Taisei Marukawa (JPN)	30.01.1997	10		1
Nikola Mitić (SRB)	27.12.1995	2		
Yudai Miyamoto (JPN)	10.03.1997	1		
Brandon Muscat	03.11.1994	10		
Gonzalo Nicolas Virano (ARG)	22.07.1999	3		
Braian Alexis Volpini (ARG)	16.06.1998	12		3
Kieran Xuereb	22.07.1998	2	(4)	
Forwards:	**DOB**	**M**	**(s)**	**G**
Augusto René Cáseres (ARG)	21.11.1997	19		8
Francisco Diego Venancio da Silva (BRA)	27.06.1993	13		6
Leighton Grech	23.03.1990	23	(1)	4
Manuel Guillari (ITA)	16.08.1997	4	(2)	
Salvatore Moccia (ITA)	03.06.1997	1	(1)	
Rômulo Silva Santos (BRA)	01.11.1992	8		2
Bradley Schembri	10.08.1998		(6)	
Luke Scorfna	24.07.1993		(1)	
Roman Chanturia (GEO)	09.02.1996	7	(1)	1
Trainer:	**DOB**	**M**		
Bruno Russo (ITA)	27.04.1966			
Enzo Potenza (ITA) [20.09.2018]		23		

Sliema Wanderers Football Club

Founded: 1909
Stadium: Tigne Sports Complex, Sliema (1,000)

Goalkeepers:	**DOB**	**M**	**(s)**	**G**
Timothy Aquilina	12.06.1998	7	(1)	
Jake Galea	15.04.1996	19		
Defenders:	**DOB**	**M**	**(s)**	**G**
Goran Adamović (SRB)	24.04.1987	11		
Nii Nortey Ashong (GHA)	17.11.1994	21		1
Stefano Bianciardi	15.03.1985	25		
Alex Muscat	14.12.1984	3	(1)	1
Jonathan Pearson	13.01.1987	7	(3)	2
Midfielders:	**DOB**	**M**	**(s)**	**G**
Edmond Agius	23.02.1987	3	(3)	
Ayrton Azzopardi	12.09.1993		(2)	
Gareth Barone	04.07.2001		(2)	
Stefan Cassar	29.10.1997	3	(5)	
Ryan Fenech	20.04.1986	15	(4)	2
John Mintoff	23.08.1988	11	(8)	
Matias Roberto Muchardi (ARG)	09.02.1988	23		4
Claudio Pani (ITA)	11.03.1986	17		1
Michele Sansone	02.07.1998	19	(6)	1
Mark Scerri	16.01.1990	14	(2)	2
Kurt Shaw	01.04.1999	19	(6)	3
Peter Xuereb	07.05.1992	3	(2)	
Forwards:	**DOB**	**M**	**(s)**	**G**
Kilian Amehi (FRA)	14.11.1997	5	(6)	1
Younes Bnou Marzouk (MAR)	02.03.1996	19	(2)	8
Omar Elouni	16.03.1999		(2)	
Jean Paul Farrugia	21.03.1992	3	(3)	1
Jefferson Mateus de Assis Estácio (BRA)	21.10.1994	15		5
Carlos Eduardo Alba Olivares (MEX)	14.04.1995		(3)	
Frank Temile (NGA)	15.07.1990	13	(4)	1
Ignacio Lucas Varela (ARG)	20.07.1990	11		3
Trainer:	**DOB**	**M**		
John Buttigieg	05.10.1963	17		
Stefano Maccoppi(ITA)[11.02.2019]	21.04.1962	9		

St. Andrews Football Club

Founded: 1968 (*as Luxol St. Andrews*)
Stadium: Luxol Stadium, St. Andrew's (800)

Goalkeepers:	**DOB**	**M**	**(s)**	**G**
Matthew Cremona Calleja	14.09.1994	25		
Elməddin Məmmədov (AZE)	09.10.1995	1		
Defenders:	**DOB**	**M**	**(s)**	**G**
Adrian Borg	20.05.1989	22	(1)	3
Dejan Debono	20.11.2000	2	(6)	
Stewart Malik O'Shea (USA)	30.04.1997	1		
Karl Pulo	30.07.1989	1	(2)	
Jason Vandelannoite (BEL)	06.11.1986	2		
Matteja Veselji	14.03.2002		(2)	
Midfielders:	**DOB**	**M**	**(s)**	**G**
Travis Blagrove (JAM)	12.10.1993	22		
Kyle Brandon Butler (JAM)	16.01.1998	1		
Miguel D'Alessandro	09.04.1999	1	(1)	
Martin George Edward Davis (JAM)	11.10.1996	26		6
Joseph Farrugia	26.07.1981	19	(6)	
Marcus Grima	22.07.2000	1	(2)	
Kemmu Degran Jackson (JAM)	11.07.1995	9	(3)	
Matthew Woo Ling (TRI)	15.09.1996	15	(4)	3
Kurt Magro	04.06.1986	16	(6)	
Ricardo Adrián Martín (JAM)	04.06.1988	19	(1)	1
Kevyn McFarlane (JAM)	27.11.1994	16	(1)	
Chevaughn Nicolas Mclaren (JAM)	04.05.1994	1		
Adam Magri Overend	03.05.2000		(1)	
Kemar David Reid (JAM)	15.08.1994	16	(4)	1
Luke Sciberras	15.09.1989	4	(11)	
Forwards:	**DOB**	**M**	**(s)**	**G**
Kevaughn Atkinson (JAM)	11.11.1995	13		6
Amoy Brown (JAM)	31.08.1996	13		
Aidan Friggieri	28.04.1998	7	(13)	
Alexander Satariano	25.10.2001	22	(1)	1
Jacob Walker	31.07.1997	11	(6)	
Trainer:	**DOB**	**M**		
Michael Woods	23.03.1962	26		

Tarxien Rainbows Football Club

Founded: 1934 (*as Rainbows Tarxien*)
Stadium: "Tony Cassar" Sports Ground, Tarxien (1,000)

Goalkeepers:	**DOB**	**M**	**(s)**	**G**
Dorian Bugeja	24.01.1998	2	(1)	
Maverick Buhagiar	28.07.1998	6		
Andrea Cassar	19.12.1992	18		
Defenders:	**DOB**	**M**	**(s)**	**G**
Andrew Agius	01.06.1991	6	(6)	
Gabriel Aquilina	07.12.1995	21	(2)	3
Marco Botta (ITA)	20.02.1997	8	(2)	
Juan Cruz Gill (ARG)	18.07.1983	10		
Luke Grech	06.01.1994	8	(5)	
Prince Loïc Destin Mambouana (FRA)	10.09.1990	10		
Stefan Radovanović (SRB)	19.02.1992	13		
Radu Rogac (MDA)	07.06.1995	7	(1)	
Thomas Veronese (ITA)	02.11.1986	1		
Jens Wemmer (GER)	31.10.1985	18		5
Daniel Zerafa	08.04.1994	18	(3)	1
Midfielders:	**DOB**	**M**	**(s)**	**G**
Matthew Brincat	07.01.1997	5	(8)	
Anderson Francisco de Barros "Dê" (BRA)	09.04.1986	24		
Owen Francalanza	17.11.1998		(1)	
Andre Scicluna	22.09.1988	11		1
Matthew Spiteri	06.10.1998	10	(11)	1
Matthew Tabone	29.04.1992	4		
Daniel Vassallo	03.12.1996		(4)	
Forwards:	**DOB**	**M**	**(s)**	**G**
Siraj Arab	25.03.1994	8	(2)	
Miguel Ciantar	17.10.1990	4	(7)	
Daren Falzon	08.05.1992	13	(4)	3
Jacson da Paixão Nepunoceno (BRA)	16.12.1989	6	(4)	
Alexander Nilsson (SWE)	23.10.1992	17	(4)	2
Michele Paolucci (ITA)	06.02.1986	18	(2)	7
Ricardo da Silva Faria "Ricardinho" (BRA)	09.02.1992	20	(3)	4
Trainer:	**DOB**	**M**		
Jose Borg		26		

Valletta Football Club
Founded: 1943
Stadium: Centenary Stadium, Valletta / Sirens Stadium, San Pawl il-Baħar (2,000 / 600)

Goalkeepers:	**DOB**	**M**	**(s)**	**G**
Henry Bonello	13.10.1988	25		
Yenez Cini	04.01.1994	2	(1)	
Defenders:	**DOB**	**M**	**(s)**	**G**
Jean Borg	08.01.1998	10	(12)	
Steve Borg	15.05.1988	22	(2)	2
Ryan Camilleri	22.05.1988	20	(2)	
Jonathan Caruana	24.07.1986	14	(9)	2
Juan Cruz Gill (ARG)	18.07.1983	1		
Joseph Zerafa	31.05.1988	21	(1)	
Midfielders:	**DOB**	**M**	**(s)**	**G**
Shaun Dimech	08.08.2001		(1)	
Bogdan Cătălin Gavrilă (ROU)	06.02.1992	6	(13)	5
Antonio Monticelli (ITA)	25.05.1989	1	(4)	
Rowen Muscat	05.06.1991	20		
Kyrian Nwoko	04.07.1997	8	(13)	2
Enmy Manuel Peña Beltré (DOM)	17.09.1992	24	(1)	2
Raed Ibrahim Saleh (OMA)	09.06.1992	14	(2)	1
Forwards:	**DOB**	**M**	**(s)**	**G**
Miguel Ángel Alba (ARG)	14.08.1988	24	(1)	10
Mario Fontanella (ITA)	28.06.1989	27		18
Bojan Kaljević	25.01.1986	17	(2)	11
Santiago Malano (ARG)	29.01.1987	26		3
Matteo Piciollo (ITA)	15.10.1992	15	(3)	4
Nicolas Pulis	29.01.1998		(8)	
Zied Soussi (TUN)	02.07.1993		(1)	
Trainer:	**DOB**	**M**		
Danilo Dončić (SRB)	20.08.1969	23		
Gilbert Agius [13.04.2019]	21.02.1974	4		

SECOND LEVEL
Maltese First Division 2018/2019

1.	Sirens FC San Pawl il-Baħar (*Promoted*)	26	18	5	3	60	-	19	59
2.	Gudja United FC (*Promoted*)	26	15	7	4	44	-	28	52
3.	Santa Luċija FC (*Promotion Play-off*)	26	13	9	4	68	-	32	48
4.	Naxxar Lions FC	26	13	6	7	47	-	35	45
5.	Pembroke Athleta FC	26	10	10	6	34	-	22	40
6.	Żebbuġ Rangers FC	26	10	7	9	35	-	30	37
7.	Lija Athletic FC	26	9	8	9	49	-	50	35
8.	Swieqi United FC	26	10	4	12	38	-	39	34
9.	Mqabba FC	26	9	5	12	25	-	39	32
10.	Żejtun Corinthians FC	26	8	8	10	35	-	32	32
11.	Qrendi FC	26	10	2	14	41	-	50	32
12.	Vittoriosa Stars FC Birgu (*Relegation Play-off*)	26	6	11	9	27	-	36	29
13.	Żabbar St. Patrick FC (*Relegated*)	26	7	2	17	30	-	52	23
14.	Marsa FC (*Relegated*)	26	1	2	23	17	-	86	5

Relegation Play-offs (2nd / 3rd Level)

Vittoriosa Stars FC Birgu - Mgarr United FC 2-2 aet; 3-2 pen

NATIONAL TEAM

INTERNATIONAL MATCHES
(16.07.2018 – 15.07.2019)

07.09.2018	Tórshavn	Faroe Islands - Malta	3-1(2-1)	(UNL)
10.09.2018	Attard	Malta - Azerbaijan	1-1(1-1)	(UNL)
11.10.2018	Pristina	Kosovo - Malta	3-1(1-0)	(UNL)
14.10.2018	Bakı	Azerbaijan - Malta	1-1(0-1)	(UNL)
17.11.2018	Attard	Malta - Kosovo	0-5(0-1)	(UNL)
20.11.2018	Attard	Malta - Faroe Islands	1-1(1-1)	(UNL)
23.03.2019	Attard	Malta - Faroe Islands	2-1(1-0)	(ECQ)
26.03.2019	Attard	Malta - Spain	0-2(0-1)	(ECQ)
07.06.2019	Stockholm	Sweden - Malta	3-0(1-0)	(ECQ)
10.06.2019	Attard	Malta - Romania	0-4(0-3)	(ECQ)

07.09.2018 FAROE ISLANDS - MALTA 3-1(2-1) UEFA Nations League D, Group 3
Tórsvøllur, Tórshavn; Referee: Ville Nevalainen (Finland); Attendance: 3,234
MLT: Andrew James Hogg, Joseph Zerafa, Andrei Agius, Steve Borg, Zach Muscat (73.Jean Paul Farrugia), André Schembri, Paul Fenech, Rowen Muscat (60.Stephen Pisani), Michael Mifsud (Cap), Alfred Effiong (84.Andrew Cohen), Joseph Mbong. Trainer: Raymond Farrugia.
Goal: Michael Mifsud (42).

10.09.2018 MALTA - AZERBAIJAN 1-1(1-1) UEFA Nations League D, Group 3
Ta'Qali National Stadium, Attard; Referee: Referee: Nikola Dabanović (Montenegro); Attendance: 4,500
MLT: Andrew James Hogg, Joseph Zerafa, Andrei Agius (51.Ferdinando Apap), Ryan Camilleri, Steve Borg, André Schembri, Paul Fenech, Ryan Fenech (64.Roderick Briffa), Michael Mifsud (Cap), Jean Paul Farrugia (78.Alfred Effiong), Joseph Mbong. Trainer: Raymond Farrugia.
Goal: Andrei Agius (10 penalty).

11.10.2018 KOSOVO - MALTA 3-1(1-0) UEFA Nations League D, Group 3
Stadiumi "Fadil Vokrri", Prishtinë; Referee: Tamás Bognár (Hungary); Attendance: 12,420
MLT: Andrew James Hogg, Andrei Agius, Steve Borg, Ferdinando Apap, Clayton Failla, André Schembri (64.Alfred Effiong), Paul Fenech (60.Roderick Briffa), Rowen Muscat (84.Stephen Pisani), Juan Carlos Corbalan, Michael Mifsud (Cap) [*sent off 70*], Joseph Mbong. Trainer: Raymond Farrugia.
Goal: Andrei Agius (51).

14.10.2018 AZERBAIJAN - MALTA 1-1(0-1) UEFA Nations League D, Group 3
Olimpiya Stadionu, Bakı; Referee: Referee: Ivan Bebek (Croatia); Attendance: 16,200
MLT: Andrew James Hogg, Joseph Zerafa, Andrei Agius, Ryan Camilleri, Steve Borg, André Schembri (Cap) (86.Jean Paul Farrugia), Paul Fenech, Rowen Muscat (70.Roderick Briffa), Juan Carlos Corbalan, Alfred Effiong (82.Jake Grech), Joseph Mbong. Trainer: Raymond Farrugia.
Goal: Rowen Muscat (37).

17.11.2018 MALTA - KOSOVO 0-5(0-1) UEFA Nations League D, Group 3
Ta'Qali National Stadium, Attard; Referee: Bartosz Frankowski (Poland); Attendance: 2,115
MLT: Andrew James Hogg, Jonathan Caruana, Joseph Zerafa, Ryan Camilleri, Zach Muscat, André Schembri, Roderick Briffa (Cap)(75.Paul Fenech), Rowen Muscat (64.Michael Mifsud), Luke Gambin, Juan Carlos Corbalan (65.Alfred Effiong), Joseph Mbong. Trainer: Raymond Farrugia.

20.11.2018 MALTA - FAROE ISLANDS 1-1(1-1) UEFA Nations League D, Group 3
National Stadium, Ta'Qali; Referee: Vitali Meshkov (Russia); Attendance: 2,152
MLT: Andrew James Hogg, Andrei Agius, Steve Borg, Zach Muscat (66.Jonathan Caruana), Clayton Failla (80.Kyrian Nwoko), André Schembri (Cap), Paul Fenech, Rowen Muscat, Juan Carlos Corbalan (78.Joseph Zerafa), Michael Mifsud, Joseph Mbong. Trainer: Raymond Farrugia.
Goal: Juan Carlos Corbalan (4).

23.03.2019 MALTA - FAROE ISLANDS 2-1(1-0) 16th EC. Qualifiers
National Stadium, Ta'Qali; Referee: Vilhjálmur Þórarinsson (Iceland); Attendance: 7,531
MLT: Henry Bonello, Jonathan Caruana, Andrei Agius [*sent off 62*], Steve Borg, Paul Fenech, Rowen Muscat (84.John Mintoff), Juan Carlos Corbalan (63.Zach Muscat), Kyrian Nwoko, Matthew Guillaumier, Michael Mifsud (Cap) (71.Joseph Zerafa), Joseph Mbong. Trainer: Raymond Farrugia.
Goals: Kyrian Nwoko (13), Steve Borg (77 penalty).

26.03.2019 MALTA - SPAIN 0-2(0-1) 16th EC. Qualifiers
Ta'Qali National Stadium, Attard; Referee: Andrew Dallas (Scotland); Attendance: 16,542
MLT: Henry Bonello, Jonathan Caruana (85.Karl Micallef), Joseph Zerafa, Steve Borg, Zach Muscat, Paul Fenech (Cap), John Mintoff (69.Michael Mifsud), Juan Carlos Corbalan, Kyrian Nwoko, Matthew Guillaumier, Joseph Mbong (65.Rowen Muscat). Trainer: Raymond Farrugia.

07.06.2019 SWEDEN - MALTA 3-0(1-0) 16th EC. Qualifiers
Friends Arena, Stockholm; Referee: Robert Harvey (Republic of Ireland); Attendance: 26,421
MLT: Henry Bonello, Andrei Agius (Cap), Steve Borg (80.Ferdinando Apap), Zach Muscat, Rowen Muscat, Luke Gambin, Jake Grech (64.Paul Fenech), Juan Carlos Corbalan, Alfred Effiong, Luke Montebello (71.Kyrian Nwoko), Joseph Mbong. Trainer: Raymond Farrugia.

10.06.2019 MALTA - ROMANIA 0-4(0-3) 16th EC. Qualifiers
Ta'Qali National Stadium, Attard; Referee: Dennis Higler (Netherlands); Attendance: 6,471
MLT: Henry Bonello, Joseph Zerafa, Andrei Agius (Cap), Steve Borg, Zach Muscat, Paul Fenech (59.Jake Grech), Rowen Muscat, Luke Gambin (67.Michael Mifsud), Juan Carlos Corbalan (84.Luke Montebello), Alfred Effiong, Joseph Mbong. Trainer: Raymond Farrugia.

NATIONAL TEAM PLAYERS
(16.07.2018 – 15.07.2019)

Name	DOB	Caps	Goals	2018/2019:	Club
Goalkeepers					
Henry BONELLO	13.10.1988	**11**	**0**	2019:	*Valletta FC*
Andrew James HOGG	02.03.1985	**67**	**0**	2018:	*Hibernians Paola FC*
Defenders					
Andrei AGIUS	12.08.1986	**84**	**5**	2018/2019:	*Hibernians FC Paola*
Ferdinando APAP	29.07.1992	**4**	**0**	2018/2019:	*Victoria Hotspurs FC*
Steve BORG	15.05.1988	**45**	**1**	2018/2019:	*Valletta FC*
Ryan CAMILLERI	22.05.1988	**42**	**0**	2018:	*Valletta FC*
Jonathan CARUANA	24.07.1986	**44**	**2**	2018/2019:	*Valletta FC*
Karl MICALLEF	08.09.1996	**1**	**0**	2019:	*Hamrun Spartans FC*
Zach MUSCAT	22.08.1993	**34**	**1**	2018: 31.01.2019->	*US Pistoiese 1921 (ITA)* *SC Olhanense (POR)*
Joseph ZERAFA	31.05.1988	**32**	**0**	2018/2019:	*Valletta FC*
Midfielders					
Roderick BRIFFA	24.08.1981	**100**	**1**	2018/2019:	*Gżira United FC*
Juan Carlos CORBALAN	13.03.1997	**8**	**1**	2018/2019:	*Gżira United FC*
Clayton FAILLA	08.01.1986	**58**	**2**	2018:	*Floriana FC*
Paul FENECH	20.12.1986	**57**	**1**	2018: 05.01.2019->	*Birkirkara FC* *Balzan FC*
Ryan FENECH	20.04.1986	**48**	**1**	2018:	*Sliema Wanderers FC*
Luke GAMBIN	16.03.1993	**19**	**0**	2018/2019:	*Crawley Town FC (ENG)*
Jake GRECH	18.11.1997	**5**	**0**	2018: 29.01.2019->	*Birkirkara FC* *Hibernians FC Paola*
Matthew GUILLAUMIER	09.04.1998	**2**	**0**	2019:	*Birkirkara FC*
John MINTOFF	23.08.1988	**10**	**0**	2019:	*Sliema Wanderers FC*
Rowen MUSCAT	05.06.1991	**41**	**1**	2018/2019:	*Valletta FC*
Stephen PISANI	07.08.1992	**18**	**0**	2018:	*Floriana FC*
Forwards					
Andrew COHEN	13.05.1981	**68**	**1**	2018:	*Gżira United FC*
Alfred EFFIONG	29.11.1984	**32**	**4**	2018/2019:	*Balzan FC*
Jean Paul FARRUGIA	21.03.1992	**14**	**1**	2018:	*Sliema Wanderers FC*
Joseph MBONG	15.07.1997	**12**	**0**	2018/2019:	*Hibernians FC Paola*
Michael MIFSUD	17.04.1981	**139**	**41**	2018/2019:	*Birkirkara FC*
Luke MONTEBELLO	13.08.1995	**3**	**0**	2019:	*Birkirkara FC*
Kyrian NWOKO	04.07.1997	**7**	**1**	2018/2019:	*Valletta FC*
André SCHEMBRI	27.05.1986	**94**	**3**	2018:	*Apollon Limassol FC (CYP)*

National team coach

Raymond FARRUGIA (from 02.05.2018)	01.10.1955	12 M; 1 W; 4 D; 7 L; 8-26

MOLDOVA

The Country:
Republica Moldova (Republic of Moldova)
Capital: Chişinău
Surface: 33,846 km²
Inhabitants: 2,681,735 [2019]
Time: UTC+2

The FA:
Federaţia Moldovenească de Fotbal
Strada Tricolorului 39, 2012 Chişinău
Tel: +373 22 210 413
Foundation date: 1990
Member of FIFA since: 1994
Member of UEFA since: 1993
Website: www.fmf.md

NATIONAL TEAM RECORDS

First international match:	02.07.1991, Chişinău:	Moldova – Georgia 2-4
Most international caps:	Alexandru Ion Epureanu	- 91 caps (2006-2018)
Most international goals:	Serghei Cleşcenco	- 11 goals / 69 caps (1991-2006)

UEFA EUROPEAN CHAMPIONSHIP	
1960	-
1964	-
1968	-
1972	-
1976	-
1980	-
1984	-
1988	-
1992	-
1996	Qualifiers
2000	Qualifiers
2004	Qualifiers
2008	Qualifiers
2012	Qualifiers
2016	Qualifiers

FIFA WORLD CUP	
1930	-
1934	-
1938	-
1950	-
1954	-
1958	-
1962	-
1966	-
1970	-
1974	-
1978	-
1982	-
1986	-
1990	-
1994	Did Not Enter
1998	Qualifiers
2002	Qualifiers
2006	Qualifiers
2010	Qualifiers
2014	Qualifiers
2018	Qualifiers

UEFA NATIONS LEAGUE
2018/2019 – League D (promoted to League C)

OLYMPIC FOOTBALL TOURNAMENTS 1908-2016							
1908	-	**1948**	-	**1972**	-	**1996**	Qualifiers
1912	-	**1952**	-	**1976**	-	**2000**	Qualifiers
1920	-	**1956**	-	**1980**	-	**2004**	Qualifiers
1924	-	**1960**	-	**1984**	-	**2008**	Qualifiers
1928	-	**1964**	-	**1988**	-	**2012**	Qualifiers
1936	-	**1968**	-	**1992**	Did Not Enter	**2016**	Qualifiers

FIFA CONFEDERATIONS CUP 1992-2017
None

MOLDOVAN CLUB HONOURS IN EUROPEAN CLUB COMPETITIONS:

European Champion Clubs' Cup (1956-1992) / UEFA Champions League (1993-2019)
None
Fairs Cup (1858-1971) / UEFA Cup (1972-2009) / UEFA Europa League (2010-2019)
None
UEFA Super Cup (1972-2018)
None
European Cup Winners' Cup 1961-1999*
None

**defunct competition*

NATIONAL COMPETITIONS
TABLE OF HONOURS

MOLDOVAN SSR (SOVIET ERA) CHAMPIONS

1945	Dinamo Chişinău
1946	Dinamo Chişinău
1947	Dinamo Chişinău
1948	Dinamo Chişinău
1949	Burevestnik Bender
1950	Krasnoe Znamia Chişinău
1951	Krasnoe Znamia Chişinău
1952	Dinamo Chişinău
1953	Dinamo Chişinău
1954	KSKhI Chişinău
1955	Burevestnik Bender
1956	Spartak Tiraspol
1957	KSKhI Chişinău
1958	Moldavkabel' Bender
1959	NIISVIV Chişinău
1960	Tiraspol
1961	KSKhI Chişinău
1962	Universitet Chişinău
1963	Temp Tiraspol
1964	Temp Tiraspol'
1965	Energhia Tiraspol
1966	Stroindustria Bălţi
1967	Nistrul Bender
1968	Temp Tiraspol
1969	Politehnik Chişinău
1970	Politehnik Chişinău
1971	Pişcevik Bender
1972	Kolhoz im. Lenina Edineţ
1973	Pişcevik Bender
1974	Dinamo Chişinău
1975	Dinamo Chişinău
1976	Stroitel Tiraspol
1977	Stroitel Tiraspol
1978	Nistru Tiraspol
1979	Nistru Ciobruciu
1980	Nistru Ciobruciu
1981	Grănicerul Glodeni
1982	Grănicerul Glodeni
1983	Grănicerul Glodeni
1984	Grănicerul Glodeni
1985	Iskra-Stal
1986	Avangard Lazovsk
1987	Tekstilshchik Tiraspol
1988	Tighina Bender
1989	Tekstilshchik Tiraspol
1990	Moldovgidromaş Chişinău
1991	Speranţa Nisporeni

	CHAMPIONS	CUP WINNERS	BEST GOALSCORERS	
1992	FC Zimbru Chişinău	FC Bugeac Comrat	Serghei Alexandrov (FC Bugeac Comrat) Oleg Flentea (FC Constructorul Chişinău)	13
1992/1993	FC Zimbru Chişinău	FC Tiligul-Tiras Tiraspol	Vladimir Kosse (FC Tiligul-Tiras Tiraspol)	30
1993/1994	FC Zimbru Chişinău	FC Tiligul-Tiras Tiraspol	Vladimir Kosse (FC Tiligul-Tiras Tiraspol)	24
1994/1995	FC Zimbru Chişinău	FC Tiligul-Tiras Tiraspol	Vladislav Gavriliuc (FC Nistru Otaci / FC Zimbru Chişinău)	20
1995/1996	FC Zimbru Chişinău	FC Constructorul Chişinău	Vladislav Gavriliuc (FC Zimbru Chişinău)	34
1996/1997	FC Constructorul Chişinău	FC Zimbru Chişinău	Serghei Rogaciov (FC Constructorul Chişinău / FC Olimpia Bălţi)	35
1997/1998	FC Zimbru Chişinău	FC Zimbru Chişinău	Serghei Clescenco (FC Zimbru Chişinău)	25
1998/1999	FC Zimbru Chişinău	FC Sheriff Tiraspol	Serghei Rogaciov (FC Sheriff Tiraspol)	21
1999/2000	FC Zimbru Chişinău	FC Constructorul Chişinău	Serghei Rogaciov (FC Sheriff Tiraspol)	20
2000/2001	FC Sheriff Tiraspol	FC Sheriff Tiraspol	Ruslan Barburoş (Haiducul Sporting Hânceşti / FC Agro Chişinău / FC Sheriff Tiraspol) David Mujiri (GEO, FC Sheriff Tiraspol)	17
2001/2002	FC Sheriff Tiraspol	FC Sheriff Tiraspol	Ruslan Barburoş (FC Sheriff Tiraspol)	17
2002/2003	FC Sheriff Tiraspol	FC Zimbru Chişinău	Serghei Dadu (FC Tiraspol / FC Sheriff Tiraspol)	19
2003/2004	FC Sheriff Tiraspol	FC Zimbru Chişinău	Vladimir Shishelov (UZB, FC Zimbru Chişinău)	15
2004/2005	FC Sheriff Tiraspol	FC Nistru Otaci	Cătălin Sergiu Lichioiu (ROU, FC Nistru Otaci)	16
2005/2006	FC Sheriff Tiraspol	FC Sheriff Tiraspol	Aliaksei Kuchuk (BLR, FC Sheriff Tiraspol)	13
2006/2007	FC Sheriff Tiraspol	FC Zimbru Chişinău	Aliaksei Kuchuk (BLR, FC Sheriff Tiraspol)	17
2007/2008	FC Sheriff Tiraspol	FC Sheriff Tiraspol	Igor Picuşceac (FC Tiraspol / FC Sheriff Tiraspol)	14
2008/2009	FC Sheriff Tiraspol	FC Sheriff Tiraspol	Oleg Andronic (FC Zimbru Chişinău)	16
2009/2010	FC Sheriff Tiraspol	FC Sheriff Tiraspol	Alexandru Maximov (FC Viitorul Orhei) Jymmy Dougllas França (BRA, FC Sheriff Tiraspol)	13
2010/2011	FC Dacia Chişinău	FC Iskra-Stal Rîbniţa	Gheorghe Boghiu (FC Milsami Orhei)	26
2011/2012	FC Sheriff Tiraspol	FC Milsami Orhei	Wilfried Bendjamin Balima (BFA, FC Sheriff Tiraspol)	18
2012/2013	FC Sheriff Tiraspol	FC Tiraspol	Gheorghe Boghiu (FC Milsami Orhei)	16
2013/2014	FC Sheriff Tiraspol	FC Zimbru Chişinău	Luvannor Henrique de Sousa Silva (BRA, FC Sheriff Tiraspol)	26
2014/2015	FC Milsami Orhei	FC Sheriff Tiraspol	Ricardo Cavalcante Mendes "Ricardinho" (BRA, FC Sheriff Tiraspol)	19
2015/2016	FC Sheriff Tiraspol	FC Zaria Bălţi	Danijel Subotić (SUI, FC Sheriff Tiraspol)	12
2016/2017	FC Sheriff Tiraspol	FC Sheriff Tiraspol	Ricardo Cavalcante Mendes "Ricardinho" (BRA, FC Sheriff Tiraspol)	15
2017	FC Sheriff Tiraspol	FC Milsami Orhei (2017/18)	Vitalie Damaşcan (FC Sheriff Tiraspol)	13
2018	FC Sheriff Tiraspol	FC Sheriff Tiraspol (2018/19)	Vladimir Ambros (CS Petrocub Hînceşti)	12

NATIONAL CHAMPIONSHIP

Divizia Naţională 2018

(01.04.2018 – 24.11.2018)

Results

Round 1 [01.04.2018]
FC Sheriff - Petrocub Hînceşti 3-0(1-0)
Milsami Orhei - FC Zimbru 1-0(0-0)
FC Sfântul Gheorghe - Dinamo-Auto 0-1(0-1)
Speranţa Nisporeni - Zaria Bălţi 0-0

Round 2 [07.04.2018]
FC Sheriff - Speranţa Nisporeni 3-0(2-0)
FC Zimbru - FC Sfântul Gheorghe 1-1(0-0)
Dinamo-Auto - Zaria Bălţi 0-0
Petrocub Hînceşti - Milsami Orhei 1-2(1-2)

Round 3 [14.04.2018]
Milsami Orhei - FC Sheriff 0-1(0-0)
Sfântul Gheorghe - Petrocub Hînceşti 3-6(1-3)
Zaria Bălţi - FC Zimbru 1-1(0-0)
Speranţa Nisporeni - Dinamo-Auto 0-0

Round 4 [22.04.2018]
Petrocub Hînceşti - Zaria Bălţi 3-0(1-0)
Milsami Orhei - FC Sfântul Gheorghe 1-0(0-0)
FC Sheriff - Dinamo-Auto 5-2(1-1)
FC Zimbru - Speranţa Nisporeni 1-1(0-0)

Round 5 [28-29.04.2018]
Speranţa Nisporeni - Petrocub Hînceşti 0-0
Zaria Bălţi - Milsami Orhei 2-2(2-2)
FC Sfântul Gheorghe - FC Sheriff 2-2(2-2)
Dinamo-Auto - FC Zimbru 1-3(1-2)

Round 6 [05.05.2018]
Petrocub Hînceşti - Dinamo-Auto 0-3(0-1)
Milsami Orhei - Speranţa Nisporeni 0-1(0-0)
FC Sfântul Gheorghe - Zaria Bălţi 1-0(0-0)
FC Sheriff - FC Zimbru 3-1(1-0)

Round 7 [13.05.2018]
Zaria Bălţi - FC Sheriff 0-1(0-1)
Speranţa Nispor. - Sfântul Gheorghe 1-1(1-1)
Dinamo-Auto - Milsami Orhei 0-2(0-2)
FC Zimbru - Petrocub Hînceşti 2-2(1-0)

Round 8 [18-20.05.2018]
FC Zimbru - Milsami Orhei 0-0
Petrocub Hînceşti - FC Sheriff 1-0(0-0)
Dinamo-Auto - FC Sfântul Gheorghe 0-0
Zaria Bălţi - Speranţa Nisporeni 2-1(0-0)

Round 9 [27.05.2018]
Speranţa Nisporeni - FC Sheriff 0-0
Zaria Bălţi - Dinamo-Auto 1-1(1-0)
FC Sfântul Gheorghe - FC Zimbru 1-0(1-0)
Milsami Orhei - Petrocub Hînceşti 2-1(0-1)

Round 10 [27.06.2018]
Dinamo-Auto - Speranţa Nisporeni 1-2(1-0)
FC Sheriff - Milsami Orhei 0-0
FC Zimbru - Zaria Bălţi 0-3(awarded)
Petrocub Hînceşti - Sfântul Gheorghe 3-1(1-0)

Round 11 [09-10.06.2018]
Zaria Bălţi - Petrocub Hînceşti 1-2(1-1)
Speranţa Nisporeni - FC Zimbru 1-1(0-1)
Dinamo-Auto - FC Sheriff 0-5(0-2)
FC Sfântul Gheorghe - Milsami Orhei 0-1(0-1)

Round 12 [16.06.2018]
FC Sheriff - FC Sfântul Gheorghe 4-0(3-0)
FC Zimbru - Dinamo-Auto 2-2(1-2)
Milsami Orhei - Zaria Bălţi 3-1(2-0)
Petrocub Hînceşti - Speranţa Nispor. 1-1(1-1)

Round 13 [24.06.2018]
Dinamo-Auto - Petrocub Hînceşti 2-2(1-0)
Speranţa Nisporeni - Milsami Orhei 1-2(1-1)
Zaria Bălţi - FC Sfântul Gheorghe 1-1(1-0)
FC Zimbru - FC Sheriff 0-1(0-1)

Round 14 [01.07.2018]
Sfântul Gheorghe - Speranţa Nispor. 2-2(0-0)
FC Sheriff - Zaria Bălţi 5-1(3-1)
Milsami Orhei - Dinamo-Auto 4-0(0-0)
Petrocub Hînceşti - FC Zimbru 3-0(awarded)

Round 15 [04-05.08.2018]
FC Sfântul Gheorghe - Dinamo-Auto 5-2(1-1)
Zaria Bălţi - Speranţa Nisporeni 0-0
Petrocub Hînceşti - FC Sheriff 1-0(1-0)
Milsami Orhei - FC Zimbru 1-1(1-0)

Round 16 [11-12.08.2018]
Dinamo-Auto - Zaria Bălţi 0-1(0-0)
FC Zimbru - FC Sfântul Gheorghe 2-1(0-0)
Petrocub Hînceşti - Milsami Orhei 1-1(1-0)
FC Sheriff - Speranţa Nisporeni 2-0(1-0)

Round 17 [19-20.08.2018]
Zaria Bălţi - FC Zimbru 0-1(0-0)
Sfântul Gheorghe - Petrocub Hînceşti 1-0(0-0)
Speranţa Nisporeni - Dinamo-Auto 1-0(1-0)
Milsami Orhei - FC Sheriff 0-2(0-1)

Round 18 [25-26.08.2018]
Petrocub Hînceşti - Zaria Bălţi 1-1(1-1)
FC Zimbru - Speranţa Nisporeni 0-3(awarded)
FC Sheriff - Dinamo-Auto 2-0(2-0)
Milsami Orhei - FC Sfântul Gheorghe 3-0(2-0)

Round 19 [01-02.09.2018]
Speranţa Nispor. - Petrocub Hînceşti 1-2(1-2)
Zaria Bălţi - Milsami Orhei 3-4(2-2)
Dinamo-Auto - FC Zimbru 3-0(awarded)
FC Sfântul Gheorghe - FC Sheriff 1-3(0-0)

Round 20 [15-16.09.2018]
FC Sfântul Gheorghe - Zaria Bălţi 1-0(0-0)
Petrocub Hînceşti - Dinamo-Auto 3-0(1-0)
FC Sheriff - FC Zimbru 3-0(awarded)
Milsami Orhei - Speranţa Nisporeni 0-1(0-0)

Round 21 [22.09.2018]
Speranţa Nispor. - Sfântul Gheorghe 4-1(2-1)
Dinamo-Auto - Milsami Orhei 1-0(1-0)
FC Sheriff - Zaria Bălţi 5-2(1-2)
FC Zimbru - Petrocub Hînceşti 0-0

Round 22 [30.09.2018]
FC Zimbru - Milsami Orhei 2-0(1-0)
Dinamo-Auto - FC Sfântul Gheorghe 3-1(2-1)
Speranţa Nisporeni - Zaria Bălţi 1-2(0-1)
FC Sheriff - Petrocub Hînceşti 0-0

Round 23 [06.10.2018]
Speranţa Nisporeni - FC Sheriff 0-0
Zaria Bălţi - Dinamo-Auto 1-1(1-0)
FC Sfântul Gheorghe - FC Zimbru 3-1(1-1)
Milsami Orhei - Petrocub Hînceşti 1-2(1-2)

Round 24 [20-21.10.2018]
Dinamo-Auto - Speranţa Nisporeni 0-1(0-0)
FC Zimbru - Zaria Bălţi 3-1(1-1)
Petrocub Hînceşti - FC Sfântul Gheorghe 0-0
FC Sheriff - Milsami Orhei 1-1(0-0)

Round 25 [27.10.2018]
Zaria Bălţi - Petrocub Hînceşti 1-2(0-1)
Speranţa Nisporeni - FC Zimbru 1-3(0-2)
Dinamo-Auto - FC Sheriff 0-1(0-1)
FC Sfântul Gheorghe - Milsami Orhei 0-2(0-0)

Round 26 [04.11.2018]
Milsami Orhei - Zaria Bălţi 3-0(0-0)
FC Zimbru - Dinamo-Auto 1-0(0-0)
FC Sheriff - FC Sfântul Gheorghe 4-1(1-0)
Petrocub Hînceşti - Speranţa Nispor. 1-0(1-0)

Round 27 [10.11.2018]
FC Zimbru - FC Sheriff 1-0(1-0)
Dinamo-Auto - Petrocub Hînceşti 1-0(1-0)
Speranţa Nisporeni - Milsami Orhei 1-0(1-0)
Zaria Bălţi - FC Sfântul Gheorghe 1-1(1-0)

Round 28 [24.11.2018]
Zaria Bălţi - FC Sheriff 0-2(0-1)
Sfântul Gheorghe - Speranţa Nispor. 1-2(1-1)
Milsami Orhei - Dinamo-Auto 0-1(0-0)
Petrocub Hînceşti - FC Zimbru 0-1(0-1)

Final Standings

1.	**FC Sheriff Tiraspol**	28	19	6	3	58	-	14	63
2.	FC Milsami Orhei	28	13	6	9	36	-	24	45
3.	CS Petrocub Hînceşti	28	12	9	7	38	-	28	45
4.	CSF Speranţa Nisporeni	28	9	11	8	27	-	26	38
5.	FC Zimbru Chişinău	28	9	9	10	28	-	37	36
6.	FC Dinamo-Auto Tiraspol	28	7	7	14	25	-	43	28
7.	FC Sfântul Gheorghe Suruceni	28	6	8	14	30	-	50	26
8.	FC Zaria Bălţi (*Relegated*)	28	4	10	14	26	-	46	22

Top goalscorers:

12 Vladimir Ambros
CS Petrocub Hînceşti
9 Alhaji Kamara (SLE)
FC Sheriff Tiraspol
8 Ziguy Badibanga (BEL)
FC Sheriff Tiraspol
8 Gerson Leal Rodrigues Gouveia (LUX)
FC Sheriff Tiraspol

NATIONAL CUP
Cupa Moldovei 2018/2019

Second Round [09.06.2018]

CF Soroca - FC Grănicerul Glodeni	3-5	FC Tighina - CSF Sparta Chişinău	0-3
FC Edineţ - FC Floreşti	0-1	FC Flacăra Mingir - FC Cahul-2005	0-2
FC Bogzeşti - FC Iskra Rîbniţa	w/o	CSF Sparta Chişinău II - FC Maiak Chirsova	3-0
FC Speranţa Drochia - FC Codru Lozova	0-2	CS Fulger Ialoveni - FC Victoria Bardar	2-3

1/8 - Finals [20.06.-05/06/07.07.2018]

FC Grănicerul Glodeni - FC Milsami Orhei	0-2 / 2-4	CSF Speranţa Nisporeni - FC Codru Lozova	0-1 / 2-1
FC Sfîntul Gheorghe - CSF Sparta Chişinău	7-2 / 3-3	FC Sheriff Tiraspol - FC Iskra Rîbniţa	7-0 / 9-1
FC Cahul-2005 - FC Dinamo-Auto Tiraspol	1-0 / 0-5	FC Zimbru Chişinău - CSF Sparta Chişinău II	0-0 / 4-1
FC Victoria Bardar - FC Zaria Bălţi	1-4 / 1-4	CS Petrocub Hînceşti - FC Floreşti	10-2 / 6-1

Quarter-Finals [26.09.-31.10.2018]

FC Dinamo-Auto Tiraspol - FC Sfîntul Gheorghe	0-3 / 2-1	FC Sheriff Tiraspol - CSF Speranţa Nisporeni	3-0 / 3-0
FC Zaria Bălţi - FC Zimbru Chişinău	3-2 / 1-7	CS Petrocub Hînceşti - FC Milsami Orhei	0-2 / 1-0

Semi-Finals [16/17.04.-07/08.05.2019]

FC Sheriff Tiraspol - FC Milsami Orhei	2-0 / 0-0	FC Zimbru Chişinău - FC Sfîntul Gheorghe	0-1 / 1-3

Final

22.05.2019; Stadionul Zimbru, Chişinău; Referee: István Kovács (Romania); Attendance: 5,250

FC Sheriff Tiraspol - FC Sfântul Gheorghe Suruceni **1-0(0-0,0-0)**

FC Sheriff: Zvonimir Mikulić, Cristiano da Silva Leite, Vladimir Kovačević, Evghenii Berco (46.Antun Palić), Mateo Sušić, Veaceslav Posmac, Mihail Ghecev, José Ángel Jurado de la Torre (70.Yuri Kendysh), Alexandru Belousov, Gheorghe Anton, Evgheni Oancea (46.Leandro Joaquim Ribeiro; 117.Jarosław Jach). Trainer: Zoran Zekić (Croatia).

FC Sfântul Gheorghe: Nicolae Cebotari, Maxim Focşa, Andrey Novicov, Serghei Svinarenco (90.Vladimir Ghinaitis), Alexandru Suvorov, Sergiu Istrati (97.Dimitrii Mandrîcenco), Garegin Kirakosyan (81.Artiom Carastoian), Petru Ojog, Eugeniu Slivca (53.Vitalie Plămădeală), Artiom Razgoniuc, Alexandru Boiciuc. Trainer: Sergiu Cebotari.

Goal: 1-0 Leandro Joaquim Ribeiro (92).

THE CLUBS 2018

Football Club Dinamo-Auto Tiraspol

Founded: 24.07.2009
Stadium: Stadionul Dinamo-Auto, Tiraspol (1,300)

Goalkeepers:	**DOB**	**M**	**(s)**	**G**
Cristian Avram	27.07.1994	26		
Alexandru Zveaghinţev	26.07.1987	2	(1)	
Defenders:	**DOB**	**M**	**(s)**	**G**
Vitali Bordian	11.08.1984	25		
Bogdan Boychuk (UKR)	30.05.1996	20		2
Serghei Diulgher	21.03.1991	24	(1)	2
Oleksandr Lapin (UKR)	21.05.1996	2	(2)	
Sandu Mateescu	20.12.1998	15	(1)	
Alexandru Scripcenco	13.01.1991	6	(1)	
Iaser Ţurcan	07.01.1998	21	(3)	1
Midfielders:	**DOB**	**M**	**(s)**	**G**
Valentin Bîrdan	13.05.1995		(2)	
Serghei Bobrov	07.09.1991	7	(8)	
Anatoli Cheptine	20.05.1990	19	(2)	1
Nichita Ciumacenko	23.01.2000	1		
Andrey Eliseev (RUS)	22.05.1991	8	(2)	
Serghei Gheorghiev	20.10.1991	6	(1)	
Cristian Jalbă	02.02.1997	13		1
Denis Janu	18.05.1995	18	(4)	5
Vladyslav Kraev (UKR)	05.02.1995	11	(1)	
Maxim Mihaliov	22.08.1986	14		
Aleksandru Paşcenco	28.05.1989	8	(2)	
Vladimir Rassulov	11.11.1992	9	(5)	
Roman Şumchin	11.03.1993	1	(3)	
Corneliu Ţîbuleac	23.08.1996	9	(1)	
Victor Truhanov	30.01.1991	8	(2)	
Forwards:	**DOB**	**M**	**(s)**	**G**
Alexandru Bejan	07.05.1996	8	(1)	2
Octavian Onofrei	16.05.1991	7	(4)	1
Eugeniu Rebenja	05.03.1995	20	(4)	7
Trainer:	**DOB**	**M**		
Igor Dobrovolski (RUS)	27.08.1967	28		

Football Club Milsami Orhei

Founded: 2005
Stadium: Complexul Sportiv Raional, Orhei (2,539)

Goalkeepers:	**DOB**	**M**	**(s)**	**G**
Anatolii Chririnciuc	04.02.1989	3		
Radu Mîţu	04.11.1994	25		
Defenders:	**DOB**	**M**	**(s)**	**G**
Constantin Bogdan	29.12.1993	17	(2)	2
Vadim Bolohan	15.08.1986	17	(2)	
Artur Crăciun	29.06.1998	23	(2)	1
Dinu Graur	27.12.1994	26		
Vasile Jardan	20.07.1993	6	(4)	1
Andrei Novicov	24.04.1986	6	(1)	
Midfielders:	**DOB**	**M**	**(s)**	**G**
Gheorghe Andronic	25.09.1991	7	(7)	1
Alexandru Antoniuc	23.05.1989	24	(3)	7
Andrei Cojocari	21.01.1987	25	(1)	1
Vergiliu Olaru	07.06.1997		(3)	
Mihai Plătică	15.03.1990	24	(1)	7
Vadim Raţă	05.05.1993	24	(3)	3
Andrei Rusnac	22.09.1996	21	(2)	
Forwards:	**DOB**	**M**	**(s)**	**G**
Oleg Andronic	06.02.1989	2	(4)	
Maxim Antoniuc	15.01.1991	8	(9)	2
Igor Bugaev	26.06.1984	8	(7)	4
Aleksandr Butenko (RUS)	20.07.1998	11	(3)	5
Ion Ibrean	21.03.1998	2	(9)	
Sergiu Plătică	05.06.1991	21	(3)	1
Romeo Constantin Surdu (ROU)	12.01.1984	6	(13)	1
Veaceslav Zagaevschii	04.04.1996	2	(4)	
Trainer:	**DOB**	**M**		
Veaceslav Rusnac	27.08.1975	28		

Club Sportiv Petrocub Hînceşti

Founded: 1994
Stadium: Stadionul Orăşenesc, Hînceşti (1,500)

Goalkeepers:	**DOB**	**M**	**(s)**	**G**
Dumitru Celeadnic	23.04.1992	27		
Victor Străistari	21.06.1999	1		
Defenders:	**DOB**	**M**	**(s)**	**G**
Valerii Macriţchii	13.02.1996	6	(1)	1
Maxim Potîrniche	13.06.1989	27		1
Radu Rogac	07.06.1995	6	(2)	1
Arcadie Rusu	28.06.1993	7	(7)	
Ion Sandu	09.03.1993	9		
Vlad Slivca	10.09.1998	14	(6)	2
Midfielders:	**DOB**	**M**	**(s)**	**G**
Alexandru Ambros	26.04.1999		(1)	
Vladimir Ambros	30.12.1993	21	(2)	12
Eduard Ciornîi	09.05.2000		(1)	
Maxim Cojocaru	13.01.1998	11	(1)	
Jessie Guera Djou (CMR)	03.05.1997	21	(1)	
Donalio Melachio Douanla (CMR)	24.09.1997	20	(3)	
Mihail Ghecev	05.11.1997	1	(8)	1
Vladislav Ivanov	07.05.1990	14	(4)	3
Jacques Ghislain Onana Ndzomo	23.08.1993	10	(5)	
Vadim Paireli	08.11.1995	5	(1)	1
Artur Pătraş	01.10.1988	18	(8)	3
Daniel Pîslă	14.06.1986	1	(6)	
Christi Taras	26.09.1998	3	(1)	
Dan Taras	13.02.1994	21	(1)	3
Alexandru Vremea	03.11.1991	13	(9)	
Forwards:	**DOB**	**M**	**(s)**	**G**
Serghei Alexeev	31.05.1986		(1)	
Alexandru Bejan	07.05.1996	14		3
Andrei Macriţchii	13.02.1996	9		1
Sergiu Matei	23.04.1992		(6)	
Victor Mudrac	03.03.1994	25	(1)	3
Marin Popescu	24.09.1999		(1)	
Artiom Puntus	31.05.1995	4	(3)	2
Trainer:	**DOB**	**M**		
Lilian Popescu	15.11.1973	28		

Fotbal Club Sfântul Gheorghe Suruceni

Founded: 2003
Stadium: Stadionul Suruceni, Suruceni (1,500)

Goalkeepers:	**DOB**	**M**	**(s)**	**G**
Dmitrii Burac	20.03.1997	1		
Dorian Răilean	13.10.1993	24		
Maxim Railean	27.03.2000	3		
Defenders:	**DOB**	**M**	**(s)**	**G**
Iulian Erhan	01.07.1986	23		1
Vladimir Ghinaitis	30.03.1995	14	(1)	
Valerii Macriţchii	13.02.1996	9	(1)	
Denis Rassulov	02.01.1990	6		
Artiom Razgoniuc	01.10.1995	8		1
Serghei Svinarenco	18.09.1996	5		
Mihail Tîşcul	25.02.1997	6		
Midfielders:	**DOB**	**M**	**(s)**	**G**
Mohammed Ahmed Hassan Al Hardan (BHR)	06.10.1997	4		
Ştefan Burghiu	28.03.1991	20		
Vadim Călugher	07.09.1995	8	(2)	2
Iurie Cebotari	23.03.1997		(2)	
Mihail Ghecev	05.11.1997	9	(3)	
Sergiu Istrati	07.08.1988	11	(17)	6
Teodor Lungu	12.06.1995	4		
Dimitrii Mandrîcenco	13.05.1997	7	(2)	
Petru Ojog	17.07.1990	19	(2)	1
Vadim Paireli	08.11.1995	9	(4)	3
Aleksandru Paşcenco	28.05.1989	5	(6)	
Vitalie Plămădeală	21.01.1985	25	(2)	1
Dmitri Semirov	27.12.1995	1	(3)	1
Eugeniu Slivca	13.07.1989	7	(1)	
Alexandru Suvorov	02.02.1987	23	(2)	5
Aleksandru Tofan	19.08.1987	7		
Ivan Urvanţev	02.05.1997	3	(2)	
Forwards:	**DOB**	**M**	**(s)**	**G**
Juvenal Agnero (CIV)	29.12.1998	3	(4)	
Artiom Carastoian	10.10.1999		(2)	
Alexandru Curteian	27.09.1996		(2)	
Igor Dima	11.02.1993	3	(2)	
Andrei Macriţchii	13.02.1996	7	(1)	1
Victor Martin	12.03.1997	7	(3)	1
Alexandru Maxim	19.01.1986	6	(6)	1
Oleg Molla	22.02.1986	7	(3)	1
Sergiu Nazar	02.07.1997	5	(2)	2
Artiom Puntus	31.05.1995	9	(3)	3
Trainer:	**DOB**	**M**		
Sergiu Secu	28.11.1972	4		
Sergiu Cebotari [15.04.2018]	21.02.1981	24		

Fotbal Club Sheriff Tiraspol

Founded: 04.04.1997
Stadium: Stadionul Sheriff, Tiraspol (12,746)

Goalkeepers:	**DOB**	**M**	**(s)**	**G**
Nicolae Cebotari	24.05.1997	1		
Zvonimir Mikulić (CRO)	05.02.1990	10	(1)	
Serghei Paşcenco	18.12.1982	17		
Defenders:	**DOB**	**M**	**(s)**	**G**
Cristiano da Silva Leite (BRA)	29.08.1993	22	(1)	1
Vladimir Kovačević (SRB)	11.11.1992	5	(3)	
Ante Kulušić (CRO)	06.06.1986	20	(3)	2
Veaceslav Posmac	07.11.1990	25		1
Petru Racu	17.07.1987	17	(5)	
Mateo Sušić (BIH)	18.11.1990	22	(1)	2
Ivan Voropai	21.04.1998	1		
Midfielders:	**DOB**	**M**	**(s)**	**G**
Gheorghe Anton	27.01.1993	16	(1)	1
Wilfried Balima (BFA)	20.03.1985	10	(5)	
Alexandru Belousov	14.05.1998	6	(4)	1
Artiom Bilinschii	19.11.1996	1	(1)	
Andrei Cobeţ	03.01.1997	5	(6)	2
Jeremy de Nooijer (CUW)	15.03.1992	7	(3)	1
Rifet Kapič (BIH)	03.07.1995	9	(5)	4
Yuri Kendysh (BLR)	10.06.1990	14	(4)	2
Dominik Kovačić (CRO)	05.01.1994	1	(2)	
Vsevolod Nihaev	04.05.1999		(2)	
Evgheni Oancea	05.01.1996	18	(5)	5
Antun Palić (CRO)	25.06.1988	10		2
Artiom Razgoniuc	01.10.1995	1	(2)	
Forwards:	**DOB**	**M**	**(s)**	**G**
Ziguy Badibanga (BEL)	26.11.1991	18	(1)	8
Alexandru Boiciuc	21.08.1997	6	(3)	2
Vitalie Damaşcan	24.01.1999	5	(5)	4
Abdoul Gafar (BFA)	30.12.1998	4	(9)	1
Aras Özbiliz (ARM)	09.03.1990	2	(2)	
Gerson Leal Rodrigues Gouveia (LUX)	20.06.1995	17	(5)	8
Jairo De Macedo Da Silva (BRA)	06.05.1992	2		
Joalisson Santos Oliveira „Jô“ (BRA)	31.03.1991	3		1
Alhaji Kamara (SLE)	16.04.1994	13	(1)	9
Trainer:	**DOB**	**M**		
Roberto Bordin (ITA)	10.01.1965	4		
Goran Sablić (SRB)	07.06.2018	24		

Clubul Sportiv de Fotbal Speranţa Nisporeni

Founded: 1991
Stadium: Complexul Sportiv Raional, Orhei (2,539)

Goalkeepers:	**DOB**	**M**	**(s)**	**G**
Daniil Avdyushkin (RUS)	01.10.1993	20		
Mihail Paiuş	06.02.1983	4		
Nicolae Ţurcan	09.12.1989	2		
Defenders:	**DOB**	**M**	**(s)**	**G**
Ion Arabadji	31.07.1984	24	(2)	
Narcisse Bambara (BFA)	23.06.1989	7		
Mihail Bolun	16.05.1989	27		1
Horia Crişan	27.06.1991	8	(2)	
Ion Digori	13.01.1987	5	(4)	2
Ştefan Efros	08.05.1990	27		1
Vitalie Negru	15.01.1987	3	(3)	
Ichaka Tiehi (CIV)	01.01.1996	11		
Andrei Trifan	11.02.1996	1		
Midfielders:	**DOB**	**M**	**(s)**	**G**
Said-Ali Akhmaev (RUS)	30.05.1996	2	(2)	
Vladimir Bogdanović (SRB)	05.10.1986	23		
Georgiy Bugulov (RUS)	17.03.1993	11	(1)	
Fabrice Eloundou (CMR)	30.08.1994	18		4
Valerii Kutsenko (UKR)	02.11.1986	7	(2)	1
Constantin Mandricenco	19.02.1991	2		
Alisher Mirzoev (TJK)	01.01.1999	7	(7)	1
Valeriu Osipenco	27.07.1996	7	(3)	
Viorel Primac	23.01.1985	8	(2)	1
Constantin Sandu	15.09.1993	11	(3)	3
Stanislav Sinkovsky	16.04.1994	3	(7)	
Valeriu Tiron	08.04.1993	6	(5)	1
Vladimir Titievschii	18.06.1998	5	(1)	
Forwards:	**DOB**	**M**	**(s)**	**G**
Ion Drăgan	14.06.1996	16	(8)	4
Constantin Iavorschi	16.03.1990	5	(9)	1
Maxim Iurcu	01.02.1993	28		4
Alexandru Maxim	19.01.1986		(4)	
Marin Popescu	24.09.1999	2	(1)	
Nicolai Porojniuc	12.08.1995	8	(2)	
Trainer:	**DOB**	**M**		
Cristian Efros	06.01.1992	28		

Fotbal Club Zaria Bălţi

Founded: 1984 (*known as FC Olimpia Bălţi between 1992-2014*)
Stadium: Stadionul Orăşenesc, Bălţi (5,953)

Goalkeepers:	**DOB**	**M**	**(s)**	**G**
Vladimir Livşiţ	23.03.1984	28		
Defenders:	**DOB**	**M**	**(s)**	**G**
David Cemschi	12.05.1995	20	(3)	1
Daniel Dumbravanu	22.07.2001	5		
Maxim Focşa	21.04.1992	6		
Diogo Santos Rangel (TLS)	19.08.1991	8	(1)	
Vasile Rusu	28.07.1985	14		2
Serghei Svinarenco	18.09.1996	1	(2)	
Aleksandru Tofan	19.08.1987	7		
Midfielders:	**DOB**	**M**	**(s)**	**G**
Mihai Apostol	21.01.1997	10	(1)	2
Rodrigo Bostan	25.07.1997	23	(2)	
Ion Burlacu	03.02.1995	11		
Cristian Dros	15.04.1998	19	(3)	
Oleg Ermak (UKR)	09.03.1986	18	(2)	1
Rubén Marcelo Gómez García (ARG)	26.01.1984	24	(2)	
Vladimir Grigorişin	11.12.1999		(1)	
Alexandru Grosu	18.04.1988	5	(2)	
Lucas Rodrigues Ramos da Silva (BRA)	20.04.1992	14		2
Dmitri Semirov	27.12.1995	6	(1)	
Ivan Urvanţev	02.05.1997	2	(5)	
Forwards:	**DOB**	**M**	**(s)**	**G**
Serghei Alexeev	31.05.1986	2	(8)	
Paulo Conrado do Carmo Sardin (BRA)	18.07.1991	5		4
Daniel Danu	26.08.2002		(4)	
Guilherme Silva de Oliveira (BRA)	07.08.1992	7	(1)	
Vadim Gulceac	06.08.1998	24	(3)	5
Jean Patric Lima dos Reis (BRA)	14.05.1997	10	(2)	2
Ion Lăcustă	24.02.1995		(2)	
Maxim Mihaliov	22.08.1986	10	(3)	
Georgi Ovsyannikov	12.10.1985	22	(5)	4
Dumitru Rogac	07.11.1998	7	(3)	1
Trainer:	**DOB**	**M**		
Vlad Goian (ROU)	14.11.1970	28		

Fotbal Club Zimbru Chişinău

Founded: 1947
Stadium: Stadionul Zimbru, Chişinău (10,400)

Goalkeepers:	**DOB**	**M**	**(s)**	**G**
Victor Buga	29.06.1994	7		
Mickaël Meira (POR)	25.01.1994	8		
Emil Tîmbur	21.07.1997	13		
Defenders:	**DOB**	**M**	**(s)**	**G**
Igor Arhirii	17.02.1997		(1)	
Narcisse Bambara (BFA)	23.06.1989	3	(5)	
Victor Bogaciuc	17.10.1999	1		
Cassius Vinicius Coelho (BRA)	15.06.1995	5	(1)	
Valentin Chişca	14.08.1999	1		
Alexei Ciopa	27.10.1998	5	(1)	1
Denis Furtuna	13.10.1999	5	(1)	
Victor Golovatenco	28.04.1984	9		1
Ion Jardan	10.01.1990	26		2
Anatolie Prepeliţă	06.08.1997	14		
Alexandru Starîş	04.01.1995	13	(1)	
Dmitriy Telegin (RUS)	02.02.1992	15	(2)	
Midfielders:	**DOB**	**M**	**(s)**	**G**
João Tiago Almeida Teixeira (POR)	07.05.1996	12	(1)	3
Cristian Nagornîi	17.06.1998	7		
Marius Obekop Bedzigui (CMR)	19.12.1994	9	(3)	4
Alexandru Onica	25.07.1984	21		2
Daniel Pîslă	14.06.1986	5	(5)	
Sandro Emanuel Gonçalves Reis Pires Semedo (POR)	03.12.1996	6	(1)	
Radu Scoarţă	03.07.1999	8	(5)	2
Eugeniu Sidorenco	19.03.1989	4	(7)	1
Victor Stînă	20.03.1998	8	(6)	3
Igor Ţîgîrlaş	24.02.1984	14	(9)	
Veaceslav Zagaevschii	04.04.1996	1	(2)	
Eugen Zasaviţchi	24.11.1992	12	(2)	1
Forwards:	**DOB**	**M**	**(s)**	**G**
Ilie Damaşcan	12.10.1995	26	(2)	5
Ion Donţu	09.09.1999	1	(4)	
Nichita Iuraşco	17.05.1999	11	(4)	
Petru Neagu	13.08.1999	5	(2)	
Ion Nicolăescu	07.09.1998	10	(2)	5
Willian Pozo-Venta (NOR)	27.08.1997	11	(7)	2
Blaise Yaméogo (BFA)	28.12.1993	12	(6)	3
Trainer:	**DOB**	**M**		
Emil Pisarenco	30.07.1992	14		
Sorin Colceag (ROU) [01.08.2018]	11.03.1972	14		

SECOND LEVEL
Divizia A 2018

1.	FC Codru Lozova (*Promoted*)	22	14	6	2	53	-	20	48
2.	FC Floreşti	22	12	4	6	40	-	27	40
3.	FC Sîngerei	22	10	6	6	47	-	42	36
4.	FC Victoria Bardar	22	10	5	7	51	-	43	35
5.	FC Grănicerul Glodeni	22	10	4	8	43	-	35	34
6.	FC Saxan Gagauz Yeri*	22	9	3	10	41	-	31	30
7.	FC Ungheni	22	7	7	8	50	-	65	28
8.	FC Cahul-2005	22	7	6	9	38	-	31	27
9.	FC Sireţi	22	6	5	11	36	-	47	23
10.	FC Real Succes Chişinău	22	6	4	12	49	-	75	22
11.	CSF Sparta Chişinău	22	5	6	11	34	-	51	21
12.	FC Iskra Rîbniţa	22	4	8	10	27	-	42	20

Please note: FC Saxan Gagauz Yeri failed to get the license for the 2019 season and were expelled from the league.

NATIONAL TEAM

INTERNATIONAL MATCHES
(16.07.2018 – 15.07.2019)

08.09.2018	Lëtzebuerg	Luxembourg - Moldova	4-0(1-0)	(UNL)
11.09.2018	Chişinău	Moldova - Belarus	0-0	(UNL)
12.10.2018	Chişinău	Moldova - San Marino	2-0(1-0)	(UNL)
15.10.2018	Minsk	Belarus - Moldova	0-0	(UNL)
15.11.2018	Serravalle	San Marino - Moldova	0-1(0-0)	(UNL)
18.11.2018	Chişinău	Moldova - Luxembourg	1-1(0-0)	(UNL)
21.02.2019	Kumköy	Kazakhstan - Moldova	1-0(0-0)	(F)
22.03.2019	Chişinău	Moldova - France	1-4(0-3)	(ECQ)
25.03.2019	Eskişehir	Turkey - Moldova	4-0(2-0)	(ECQ)
08.06.2019	Chişinău	Moldova - Andorra	1-0(1-0)	(ECQ)
11.06.2019	Elbasan	Albania - Moldova	2-0(0-0)	(ECQ)

08.09.2018 LUXEMBOURG - MOLDOVA 4-0(1-0) UEFA Nations League D, Group 2
Stade "Josy Barthel", Lëtzebuerg; Referee: Robert Harvey (Republic of Ireland); Attendance: 2,956
MDA: Alexei Coşelev, Alexandru Epureanu (Cap), Veaceslav Posmac, Dinu Graur, Oleg Reabciuk, Alexandru Antoniuc, Radu Gînsari (62.Ion Nicolăescu), Alexandru Gaţcan, Cătălin Carp (77.Andrei Cojocari), Eugeniu Cociuc, Alexandru Dedov (63.Sergiu Plătică). Trainer: Alexandru Spiridon.

11.09.2018 MOLDOVA - BELARUS 0-0 UEFA Nations League D, Group 2
Stadionul Zimbru, Chişinău; Referee: Mario Zebec (Croatia); Attendance: 4,942
MDA: Alexei Coşelev, Alexandru Epureanu (Cap), Veaceslav Posmac, Dinu Graur, Oleg Reabciuk, Artur Ioniţă, Alexandru Antoniuc (86.Sergiu Plătică), Radu Gînsari, Cătălin Carp (63.Eugeniu Cociuc), Alexandru Gaţcan, Ion Nicolăescu (68.Vitalie Damaşcan). Trainer: Alexandru Spiridon.

12.10.2018 MOLDOVA - SAN MARINO 2-0(1-0) UEFA Nations League D, Group 2
Stadionul Zimbru, Chişinău; Referee: Bryn Markham-Jones (Wales); Attendance: 5,242
MDA: Alexei Coşelev, Alexandru Epureanu (Cap), Veaceslav Posmac, Oleg Reabciuk (46.Alexandru Dedov), Artur Ioniţă, Alexandru Antoniuc, Radu Gînsari (79.Constantin Sandu), Alexandru Gaţcan, Cătălin Carp, Eugeniu Cociuc, Vitalie Damaşcan (54.Alexandru Boiciuc). Trainer: Alexandru Spiridon.
Goals: Radu Gînsari (31, 67).

15.10.2018 BELARUS - MOLDOVA 0-0 UEFA Nations League D, Group 2
Stadion Dynama, Minsk; Referee: Kevin John Clancy (Scotland); Attendance: 10,870
MDA: Alexei Coşelev, Alexandru Epureanu (Cap), Ion Jardan, Veaceslav Posmac, Oleg Reabciuk, Artur Ioniţă, Alexandru Antoniuc (65.Constantin Sandu), Radu Gînsari (78.Alexandru Dedov), Cătălin Carp, Alexandru Gaţcan, Vitalie Damaşcan (72.Alexandru Boiciuc). Trainer: Alexandru Spiridon.

15.11.2018 SAN MARINO - MOLDOVA 0-1(0-0) UEFA Nations League D, Group 2
San Marino Stadium, Serravalle; Referee: Georgios Kominis (Greece); Attendance: 747
MDA: Alexei Coşelev, Alexandru Epureanu (Cap), Veaceslav Posmac, Oleg Reabciuk, Artur Ioniţă, Alexandru Antoniuc (66.Alexandru Dedov), Radu Gînsari, Cătălin Carp, Alexandru Gaţcan, Eugeniu Cociuc (60.Constantin Sandu), Ion Nicolăescu (46.Vitalie Damaşcan). Trainer: Alexandru Spiridon.
Goal: Vitalie Damaşcan (78).

18.11.2018 MOLDOVA - LUXEMBOURG 1-1(0-0) UEFA Nations League D, Group 2
Stadionul Zimbru, Chişinău; Referee: Adrien Jaccottet (Switzerland); Attendance: 4,642
MDA: Alexei Coşelev, Alexandru Epureanu, Ion Jardan, Veaceslav Posmac, Oleg Reabciuk, Artur Ioniţă, Alexandru Antoniuc, Radu Gînsari (82.Alexandru Dedov), Cătălin Carp, Alexandru Gaţcan (Cap) (83.Eugeniu Cebotaru), Vitalie Damaşcan (71.Ion Nicolăescu). Trainer: Alexandru Spiridon.
Goal: Radu Gînsari (58 penalty).

21.02.2019 KAZAKHSTAN - MOLDOVA 1-0(0-0) Friendly International
Titanic Deluxe Belek Futbol Sahası, Kumköy; Referee: Manfredas Lukjančukas (Lithuania); Attendance: 500
MDA: Dumitru Celeadnic (88.Dorian Răilean), Ion Jardan, Dinu Graur, Iaser Ţurcan (88.Valerii Macriţchii), Alexandru Antoniuc, Artiom Rozgoniuc, Gheorghe Anton (74.Dan Taras), Veaceslav Posmac (Cap) (62.Andrei Macriţchii), Vladimir Ambros, Constantin Sandu (88.Sergiu Plătică), Nicolae Milinceanu (62.Ion Nicolăescu). Trainer: Alexandru Spiridon.

22.03.2019 MOLDOVA - FRANCE 1-4(0-3) 16th EC. Qualifiers
Stadionul Zimbru, Chişinău; Referee: Aleksandar Stavrev (Macedonia); Attendance: 10,042
MDA: Alexei Coşelev, Ion Jardan, Veaceslav Posmac, Oleg Reabciuk, Eugeniu Cebotaru, Artur Ioniţă (Cap), Alexandru Antoniuc (73.Vladimir Ambros), Radu Gînsari, Cătălin Carp, Eugeniu Cociuc (46.Artiom Rozgoniuc), Ion Nicolăescu (59.Vitalie Damaşcan). Trainer: Alexandru Spiridon.
Goal: Vladimir Ambros (89).

25.03.2019 TURKEY - MOLDOVA 4-0(2-0) 16th EC. Qualifiers
"Yeni Atatürk" Stadyumu, Eskişehir; Referee: Serhiy Boyko (Ukraine); Attendance: 29,456
MDA: Alexei Coşelev, Ion Jardan, Veaceslav Posmac, Dinu Graur, Oleg Reabciuk, Eugeniu Cebotaru, Artur Ioniţă (Cap), Radu Gînsari (73.Alexandru Antoniuc), Artiom Rozgoniuc, Cătălin Carp (46.Iaser Ţurcan), Vladimir Ambros (57.Ion Nicolăescu). Trainer: Alexandru Spiridon.

08.06.2019 MOLDOVA - ANDORRA 1-0(1-0) 16th EC. Qualifiers
Stadionul Zimbru, Chişinău; Referee: Bojan Pandžić (Sweden); Attendance: 5,000
MDA: Alexei Coşelev, Igor Armaş, Ion Jardan, Ştefan Efros, Oleg Reabciuk, Alexandru Suvorov (50.Eugeniu Cebotaru), Artur Ioniţă (Cap) [*sent off 47*], Alexandru Antoniuc (64.Eugeniu Cociuc), Cătălin Carp, Radu Gînsari, Vitalie Damaşcan (80.Alexandru Boiciuc). Trainer: Alexandru Spiridon.
Goal: Igor Armaş (8).

11.06.2019 ALBANIA - MOLDOVA 2-0(0-0) 16th EC. Qualifiers
Elbasan Arena, Elbasan; Referee: Ville Nevalainen (Finland); Attendance: 5,004
MDA: Alexei Coşelev, Igor Armaş (Cap), Ion Jardan (76.Dinu Graur), Ştefan Efros, Oleg Reabciuk, Eugeniu Cebotaru, Alexandru Suvorov (74.Eugeniu Cociuc), Alexandru Antoniuc, Radu Gînsari, Cătălin Carp, Vitalie Damaşcan (70.Alexandru Boiciuc). Trainer: Alexandru Spiridon.

NATIONAL TEAM PLAYERS
(16.07.2018 – 15.07.2019)

Name	DOB	Caps	Goals	2018/2019:	*Club*
			Goalkeepers		
Dumitru CELEADNIC	23.04.1992	**1**	**0**	2019:	*FC Sheriff Tiraspol*
Alexei COŞELEV	19.11.1993	**15**	**0**	2018/2019:	*Fortuna Sittard (NED)*
Dorian RĂILEAN	13.10.1993	**1**	**0**	2018/2019:	*CS Petrocub Hînceşti*
			Defenders		
Igor ARMAŞ	14.07.1987	**54**	**5**	2019:	*FC Voluntari (ROU)*
Ştefan EFROS	08.05.1990	**2**	**0**	2019:	*CSF Speranţa Nisporeni*
Alexandru EPUREANU	27.09.1986	**91**	**8**	2018:	*İstanbul Başakşehir FK (TUR)*
Dinu GRAUR	27.12.1994	**9**	**0**	2018/2019:	*FC Milsami Orhei*
Ion JARDAN	10.01.1990	**29**	**0**	2018: 29.01.2019->	*FC Zimbru Chişinău* *CS Petrocub Hînceşti*
Andrei MACRIŢCHII	13.02.1996	**2**	**0**	2019:	*FC Sheriff Tiraspol*
Valerii MACRIŢCHII	13.02.1996	**2**	**0**	2019:	*FC Sheriff Tiraspol*
Sergiu PLĂTICĂ	09.06.1991	**11**	**0**	2018/2019:	*FC Milsami Orhei*
Veaceslav POSMAC	07.11.1990	**34**	**2**	2018/2019:	*FC Sheriff Tiraspol*
Oleg REABCIUK	16.01.1998	**12**	**0**	2018/2019:	*FC do Porto "B" (POR)*
Artiom ROZGONIUC	01.10.1995	**9**	**0**	2018/2019:	*FC Sheriff Tiraspol*
			Midfielders		
Gheorghe ANTON	27.01.1993	**6**	**0**	2019:	*FC Sheriff Tiraspol*
Alexandru ANTONIUC	23.05.1989	**44**	**3**	2018/2019:	*FC Milsami Orhei*
Cătălin CARP	20.10.1993	**26**	**1**	2018/2019:	*FK Ufa (RUS)*
Eugeniu CEBOTARU	16.10.1984	**61**	**1**	2018/2019:	*FK Sibir Novosibirsk (RUS)*
Eugeniu COCIUC	11.05.1993	**16**	**0**	2018/2019:	*Səbail FK Bakı (AZE)*
Andrei COJOCARI	21.01.1987	**38**	**2**	2018:	*FC Milsami Orhei*
Alexandru DEDOV	26.07.1989	**54**	**3**	2018:	*Zirə FK Bakı (AZE)*
Alexandru GAŢCAN	27.03.1984	**63**	**5**	2018:	*FK Rostov (RUS)*
Radu GÎNSARI	10.12.1991	**34**	**7**	2018/2019:	*Hapoel Haifa FC (ISR)*
Artur IONIŢĂ	17.08.1990	**39**	**3**	2018/2019:	*Cagliari Calcio (ITA)*
Constantin SANDU	15.09.1993	**4**	**0**	2018/2019:	*CSF Speranţa Nisporeni*
Alexandru SUVOROV	02.02.1987	**52**	**5**	2019:	*FC Sfântul Gheorghe Suruceni*
Dan TARAS	13.02.1994	**3**	**0**	2019:	*CS Petrocub Hînceşti*
Iaser ŢURCAN	07.01.1998	**2**	**0**	2018/2019:	*CS Petrocub Hînceşti*
			Forwards		
Vladimir AMBROS	30.12.1993	**11**	**0**	2019:	*CS Petrocub Hînceşti*
Alexandru BOICIUC	21.08.1997	**6**	**0**	2018: 23.02.2019->	*FC Sheriff Tiraspol* *FC Sfântul Gheorghe Suruceni*
Vitalie DAMAŞCAN	24.01.1999	**12**	**1**	2018/2019:	*Torino FC (ITA)*
Nicolae MILINCEANU	01.08.1992	**8**	**0**	2019:	*FC Chiasso (SUI)*
Ion NICOLĂESCU	07.09.1998	**7**	**0**	2018/2019:	*FC Shakhtyor Solihorsk (BLR)*

National team coach

Alexandru SPIRIDON [from 12.01.2018]	20.07.1960	16 M; 3 W; 5 D; 8 L; 7-22 Complete record as trainer of Moldova: 20 M; 4 W; 5 D; 11 L; 11-32 (15.08.2001 – 06.10.2001) & (from 12.01.2018)

MONTENEGRO

The Country:
Crna Gora (Montenegro)
Capital: Podgorica
Surface: 13,812 km²
Inhabitants: 622,359 [2018]
Time: UTC+1

The FA:
Fudbalski savez Crne Gore
Bulevar Veljka Vlahovica bb ME, 81000 Podgorica
Tel: +382 20 445 609
Foundation date: 1931
Member of FIFA since: 2007
Member of UEFA since: 2007
Website: www.fscg.co.me

NATIONAL TEAM RECORDS

First international match:	24.03.2007, Podgorica:	Montenegro – Hungary 2-1
Most international caps:	Fatos Bećiraj	- 63 caps (since 2009)
Most international goals:	Stevan Jovetić	- 24 goals / 51 caps (2007-2018)

UEFA EUROPEAN CHAMPIONSHIP	
1960	-
1964	-
1968	-
1972	-
1976	-
1980	-
1984	-
1988	-
1992	-
1996	-
2000	-
2004	-
2008	-
2012	Qualifiers
2016	Qualifiers

FIFA WORLD CUP	
1930	-
1934	-
1938	-
1950	-
1954	-
1958	-
1962	-
1966	-
1970	-
1974	-
1978	-
1982	-
1986	-
1990	-
1994	-
1998	-
2002	-
2006	-
2010	Qualifiers
2014	Qualifiers
2018	Qualifiers

UEFA NATIONS LEAGUE
2018/2019 – League C

OLYMPIC FOOTBALL TOURNAMENTS 1908-2016							
1908	-	**1948**	-	**1972**	-	**1996**	-
1912	-	**1952**	-	**1976**	-	**2000**	-
1920	-	**1956**	-	**1980**	-	**2004**	-
1924	-	**1960**	-	**1984**	-	**2008**	-
1928	-	**1964**	-	**1988**	-	**2012**	Qualifiers
1936	-	**1968**	-	**1992**	-	**2016**	Qualifiers

FIFA CONFEDERATIONS CUP 1992-2017
None

MONTENEGRIN CLUB HONOURS IN EUROPEAN CLUB COMPETITIONS:

European Champion Clubs.Cup (1956-1992) / UEFA Champions League (1993-2019)
None
Fairs Cup (1858-1971) / UEFA Cup (1972-2009) / UEFA Europa League (2010-2019)
None
UEFA Super Cup (1972-2018)
None
European Cup Winners.Cup 1961-1999*
None

**defunct competition*

NATIONAL COMPETITIONS
TABLE OF HONOURS

	CHAMPIONS	CUP WINNERS	BEST GOALSCORERS	
2006/2007	FK Zeta Golubovci	FK Rudar Pljevlja	Damir Čakar (FK Rudar Pljevlja) Žarko Korać (FK Zeta Golubovci)	16
2007/2008	FK Budućnost Podgorica	FK Mogren Budva	Ivan Jablan (FK Lovćen Cetinje)	13
2008/2009	FK Mogren Budva	OFK Petrovac	Fatos Bećiraj (FK Budućnost Podgorica)	18
2009/2010	FK Rudar Pljevlja	FK Rudar Pljevlja	Ivan Bošković (OFK Grbalj)	28
2010/2011	FK Mogren Budva	FK Rudar Pljevlja	Ivan Vuković (FK Budućnost Podgorica)	20
2011/2012	FK Budućnost Podgorica	FK Čelik Nikšić	Admir Adrović (FK Budućnost Podgorica)	22
2012/2013	FK Sutjeska Nikšić	FK Budućnost Podgorica	Admir Adrović (FK Budućnost Podgorica) Žarko Korać (FK Zeta Golubovci)	15
2013/2014	FK Sutjeska Nikšić	FK Lovćen Cetinje	Stefan Mugoša (OFK Titograd Podgorica)	15
2014/2015	FK Rudar Pljevlja	FK Mladost Podgorica	Goran Vujović (FK Sutjeska Nikšić)	21
2015/2016	FK Mladost Podgorica	FK Rudar Pljevlja	Marko Šćepanović (FK Mladost Podgorica)	19
2016/2017	FK Budućnost Podgorica	FK Sutjeska Nikšić	Zoran Petrović (OFK Titograd Podgorica)	14
2017/2018	FK Sutjeska Nikšić	FK Mladost Podgorica	Igor Ivanović (FK Sutjeska Nikšić)	14
2018/2019	FK Sutjeska Nikšić	FK Budućnost Podgorica	Nikola Krstović (FK Zeta Golubovci)	17

NATIONAL CHAMPIONSHIP
Prva Crnogorska Fudbal Liga 2018/2019
(03.08.2018 – 25.05.2019)

Results

Round 1 [03-05.08.2018]
Iskra Danilovgrad - FK Budućnost 0-1(0-0)
OFK Titograd - Rudar Pljevlja 0-0
FK Zeta - OFK Petrovac 0-0
OFK Grbalj - FK Lovćen 0-1(0-0)
Sutjeska Nikšić - FK Mornar 1-1(1-1)

Round 2 [11-12.08.2018]
Rudar Pljevlja - FK Zeta 0-0
FK Lovćen - Sutjeska Nikšić 1-1(1-0)
Iskra Danilovgrad - OFK Titograd 0-1(0-0)
OFK Petrovac - OFK Grbalj 0-1(0-0)
FK Budućnost - FK Mornar 3-0(2-0)

Round 3 [15.08.2018]
OFK Titograd - FK Budućnost 1-0(0-0)
FK Zeta - Iskra Danilovgrad 1-3(0-2)
OFK Grbalj - Rudar Pljevlja 0-1(0-1)
FK Mornar - FK Lovćen 2-4(1-2)
Sutjeska Nikšić - OFK Petrovac 2-1(0-0)

Round 4 [18-19.08.2018]
Rudar Pljevlja - Sutjeska Nikšić 1-2(1-1)
Iskra Danilovgrad - OFK Grbalj 0-0
OFK Titograd - FK Zeta 2-1(1-1)
OFK Petrovac - FK Mornar 1-0(0-0)
FK Budućnost - FK Lovćen 0-0

Round 5 [25.08.2018]
FK Zeta - FK Budućnost 0-1(0-1)
OFK Grbalj - OFK Titograd 0-1(0-0)
FK Mornar - Rudar Pljevlja 1-1(0-0)
FK Lovćen - OFK Petrovac 1-3(0-1)
Sutjeska Nikšić - Iskra Danilovgrad 1-2(0-0)

Round 6 [01-02.09.2018]
Rudar Pljevlja - FK Lovćen 0-0
Iskra Danilovgrad - FK Mornar 2-0(0-0)
FK Zeta - OFK Grbalj 0-0
FK Budućnost - OFK Petrovac 1-1(1-1)
OFK Titograd - Sutjeska Nikšić 0-0

Round 7 [15.09.2018]
OFK Grbalj - FK Budućnost 0-1(0-0)
Sutjeska Nikšić - FK Zeta 0-1(0-0)
FK Mornar - OFK Titograd 0-1(0-1)
FK Lovćen - Iskra Danilovgrad 0-2(0-0)
OFK Petrovac - Rudar Pljevlja 3-1(1-0)

Round 8 [19.09.2018]
Iskra Danilovgrad - OFK Petrovac 0-1(0-0)
OFK Titograd - FK Lovćen 0-0
FK Zeta - FK Mornar 2-0(0-0)
OFK Grbalj - Sutjeska Nikšić 0-1(0-1)
FK Budućnost - Rudar Pljevlja 0-0

Round 9 [22-23.09.2018]
Rudar Pljevlja - Iskra Danilovgrad 0-0
FK Lovćen - FK Zeta 0-2(0-2)
OFK Petrovac - OFK Titograd 1-2(0-2)
Sutjeska Nikšić - FK Budućnost 2-1(0-0)
FK Mornar - OFK Grbalj 1-1(1-0)

Round 10 [29.09.2018]
FK Budućnost - Iskra Danilovgrad 1-0(1-0)
Rudar Pljevlja - OFK Titograd 3-1(1-0)
FK Lovćen - OFK Grbalj 0-5(0-2)
FK Mornar - Sutjeska Nikšić 0-1(0-1)
OFK Petrovac - FK Zeta 0-1(0-0)

Round 11 [06.10.2018]
FK Mornar - FK Budućnost 0-1(0-0)
Sutjeska Nikšić - FK Lovćen 1-1(0-0)
OFK Grbalj - OFK Petrovac 4-0(1-0)
FK Zeta - Rudar Pljevlja 0-0
OFK Titograd - Iskra Danilovgrad 1-1(1-1)

Round 12 [20.10.2018]
Iskra Danilovgrad - FK Zeta 1-2(0-1)
Rudar Pljevlja - OFK Grbalj 0-0
OFK Petrovac - Sutjeska Nikšić 1-0(0-0)
FK Lovćen - FK Mornar 0-1(0-0)
FK Budućnost - OFK Titograd 2-1(1-1)

Round 13 [27.10.2018]
FK Lovćen - FK Budućnost 0-0
FK Mornar - OFK Petrovac 0-1(0-0)
Sutjeska Nikšić - Rudar Pljevlja 2-0(0-0)
OFK Grbalj - Iskra Danilovgrad 0-0
FK Zeta - OFK Titograd 1-0(1-0)

Round 14 [03.11.2018]
FK Budućnost - FK Zeta 0-2(0-1)
OFK Titograd - OFK Grbalj 0-2(0-1)
Iskra Danilovgrad - Sutjeska Nikšić 0-4(0-3)
Rudar Pljevlja - FK Mornar 1-1(1-1)
OFK Petrovac - FK Lovćen 1-0(0-0)

Round 15 [10.11.2018]
OFK Petrovac - FK Budućnost 1-1(0-1)
FK Lovćen - Rudar Pljevlja 1-3(0-1)
FK Mornar - Iskra Danilovgrad 1-1(0-1)
Sutjeska Nikšić - OFK Titograd 3-0(1-0)
OFK Grbalj - FK Zeta 1-1(0-0)

Round 16 [24.11.2018]
FK Budućnost - OFK Grbalj 1-1(1-0)
FK Zeta - Sutjeska Nikšić 0-0
OFK Titograd - FK Mornar 1-0(0-0)
Iskra Danilovgrad - FK Lovćen 1-3(1-1)
Rudar Pljevlja - OFK Petrovac 0-4(0-1)

Round 17 [01.12.2018]
Rudar Pljevlja - FK Budućnost 2-1(0-1)
FK Lovćen - OFK Titograd 2-2(0-1)
FK Mornar - FK Zeta 0-0
Sutjeska Nikšić - OFK Grbalj 3-0(2-0)
OFK Petrovac - Iskra Danilovgrad 1-2(1-2)

Round 18 [05.12.2018]
OFK Grbalj - FK Mornar 2-0(1-0)
FK Zeta - FK Lovćen 3-0(1-0)
OFK Titograd - OFK Petrovac 3-0(1-0)
Iskra Danilovgrad - Rudar Pljevlja 1-1(0-1)
FK Budućnost - Sutjeska Nikšić 1-1(0-1)

Round 19 [08-09.12.2018]
OFK Titograd - Rudar Pljevlja 1-0(1-0)
FK Zeta - OFK Petrovac 0-0
OFK Grbalj - FK Lovćen 3-2(0-1)
Sutjeska Nikšić - FK Mornar 2-1(1-0)
Iskra Danilovgrad - FK Budućnost 0-0

Round 20 [19.02.2019]
FK Budućnost - FK Mornar 5-0(3-0)
Iskra Danilovgrad - OFK Titograd 2-3(1-2)
FK Lovćen - Sutjeska Nikšić 1-3(0-0)
OFK Petrovac - OFK Grbalj 3-3(2-1)
Rudar Pljevlja - FK Zeta 1-1(0-0)

Round 21 [26.02.2019]
FK Mornar - FK Lovćen 0-0
Sutjeska Nikšić - OFK Petrovac 2-1(1-1)
FK Zeta - Iskra Danilovgrad 0-2(0-0)
OFK Grbalj - Rudar Pljevlja 1-1(1-1)
OFK Titograd - FK Budućnost 1-2(0-2)

Round 22 [02.03.2019]
FK Budućnost - FK Lovćen 7-0(5-0)
Iskra Danilovgrad - OFK Grbalj 1-1(1-0)
OFK Petrovac - FK Mornar 2-1(1-0)
Rudar Pljevlja - Sutjeska Nikšić 1-1(0-1)
OFK Titograd - FK Zeta 0-2(0-1)

Round 23 [08-09.03.2019]
FK Mornar - Rudar Pljevlja 0-0
FK Zeta - FK Budućnost 0-3(0-2)
OFK Grbalj - OFK Titograd 1-0(1-0)
FK Lovćen - OFK Petrovac 1-3(0-1)
Sutjeska Nikšić - Iskra Danilovgrad 2-0(1-0)

Round 24 [13.03.2019]
FK Budućnost - OFK Petrovac 3-0(1-0)
FK Zeta - OFK Grbalj 1-0(0-0)
Iskra Danilovgrad - FK Mornar 1-1(1-1)
Rudar Pljevlja - FK Lovćen 2-1(0-0)
OFK Titograd - Sutjeska Nikšić 0-1(0-1)

Round 25 [17.03.2019]
Sutjeska Nikšić - FK Zeta 1-0(0-0)
OFK Grbalj - FK Budućnost 1-1(1-0)
FK Lovćen - Iskra Danilovgrad 1-2(1-0)
FK Mornar - OFK Titograd 0-3(0-2)
OFK Petrovac - Rudar Pljevlja 3-2(2-0)

Round 26 [30.03.2019]
FK Budućnost - Rudar Pljevlja 1-0(1-0)
FK Zeta - FK Mornar 2-0(0-0)
OFK Grbalj - Sutjeska Nikšić 0-0
Iskra Danilovgrad - OFK Petrovac 2-1(0-0)
OFK Titograd - FK Lovćen 3-2(1-2)

Round 27 [03.04.2019]
FK Lovćen - FK Zeta 1-0(0-0)
FK Mornar - OFK Grbalj 2-4(0-3)
OFK Petrovac - OFK Titograd 0-1(0-1)
Rudar Pljevlja - Iskra Danilovgrad 1-1(0-0)
Sutjeska Nikšić - FK Budućnost 2-2(1-2)

Round 28 [06-07.04.2019]
Rudar Pljevlja - OFK Titograd 2-2(2-2)
FK Budućnost - Iskra Danilovgrad 3-1(1-0)
FK Lovćen - OFK Grbalj 1-1(0-0)
FK Mornar - Sutjeska Nikšić 0-3(0-2)
OFK Petrovac - FK Zeta 0-2(0-1)

Round 29 [13.04.2019]
Sutjeska Nikšić - FK Lovćen 4-0(1-0)
FK Zeta - Rudar Pljevlja 2-1(1-1)
OFK Grbalj - OFK Petrovac 2-0(1-0)
FK Mornar - FK Budućnost 0-1(0-1)
OFK Titograd - Iskra Danilovgrad 1-2(1-1)

Round 30 [20-21.04.2019]
Iskra Danilovgrad - FK Zeta 0-1(0-0)
FK Lovćen - FK Mornar 1-0(0-0)
Rudar Pljevlja - OFK Grbalj 3-0(1-0)
FK Budućnost - OFK Titograd 4-0(2-0)
OFK Petrovac - Sutjeska Nikšić 0-1(0-0)

Round 31 [27.04.2019]
Sutjeska Nikšić - Rudar Pljevlja 4-0(3-0)
FK Zeta - OFK Titograd 1-1(0-1)
OFK Grbalj - Iskra Danilovgrad 2-1(1-0)
FK Lovćen - FK Budućnost 1-1(0-1)
FK Mornar - OFK Petrovac 1-5(1-2)

Round 32 [04.05.2019]
FK Budućnost - FK Zeta 0-0
Iskra Danilovgrad - Sutjeska Nikšić 1-1(1-0)
OFK Petrovac - FK Lovćen 0-0
Rudar Pljevlja - FK Mornar 3-1(3-1)
OFK Titograd - OFK Grbalj 2-2(0-2)

Round 33 [11.05.2019]
Sutjeska Nikšić - OFK Titograd 1-2(1-1)
OFK Grbalj - FK Zeta 0-0
FK Lovćen - Rudar Pljevlja 0-1(0-0)
FK Mornar - Iskra Danilovgrad 1-3(1-0)
OFK Petrovac - FK Budućnost 0-0

Round 34 [15.05.2019]
FK Budućnost - OFK Grbalj 5-3(1-2)
FK Zeta - Sutjeska Nikšić 1-1(1-0)
Iskra Danilovgrad - FK Lovćen 2-0(2-0)
Rudar Pljevlja - OFK Petrovac 0-1(0-0)
OFK Titograd - FK Mornar 6-1(4-0)

Round 35 [19.05.2019]
Sutjeska Nikšić - OFK Grbalj 2-0(1-0)
FK Lovćen - OFK Titograd 1-3(0-1)
FK Mornar - FK Zeta 0-3(0-2)
OFK Petrovac - Iskra Danilovgrad 0-4(0-0)
Rudar Pljevlja - FK Budućnost 2-2(0-1)

Round 36 [25.05.2019]
FK Budućnost - Sutjeska Nikšić 0-2(0-1)
FK Zeta - FK Lovćen 3-2(0-1)
OFK Grbalj - FK Mornar 4-0(1-0)
Iskra Danilovgrad - Rudar Pljevlja 5-1(4-0)
OFK Titograd - OFK Petrovac 1-1(0-0)

Final Standings

1.	**FK Sutjeska Nikšić**	36	21	11	4	58	-	21	74
2.	FK Budućnost Podgorica	36	17	14	5	56	-	25	65
3.	FK Zeta Golubovci	36	16	13	7	36	-	21	61
4.	OFK Titograd Podgorica	36	16	9	11	47	-	41	57
5.	FK Iskra Danilovgrad	36	13	11	12	46	-	39	50
6.	OFK Grbalj Radanovići	36	11	15	10	45	-	36	48
7.	OFK Petrovac	36	13	8	15	40	-	45	47
8.	FK Rudar Pljevlja (*Relegation Play-offs*)	36	8	17	11	35	-	44	41
9.	FK Lovćen Cetinje (*Relegation Play-offs*)	36	5	11	20	29	-	65	26
10.	FK Mornar Bar (*Relegated*)	36	1	9	26	17	-	72	12

Top goalscorers:

17 Nikola Krstović *FK Zeta Golubovci*

12 Vladan Kordić *FK Grbalj Radanovići*
12 Božo Marković *FK Sutjeska Nikšić*
12 Darko Nikač *FK Iskra Danilovgrad*
12 Aleksandar Vujačić *FK Budućnost Podgorica / OFK Petrovac*

Promotion / Relegation Play-offs [29.05.-10.06.2019]

FK Bokelj Kotor - **FK Rudar Pljevlja**	0-2(0-1)	1-2(1-1)
FK Lovćen Cetinje - **FK Kom Zlatica**	0-1(0-1)	0-1(0-0)

NATIONAL CUP
Kup Crne Gore 2018/2019

First Round [28-30.08.2018]

FK Hajduk Bar - FK Mornar Bar	0-13
FK Sloga Bar - FK Iskra Danilovgrad	0-3 (awarded)
FK Berane - FK Rudar Pljevlja	0-3 (awarded)
FK Komovi Andrijevica - FK Zeta Golubovci	0-6
FK Crvena Stijena Tološi - FK Sutjeska Nikšić	0-7
FK Jedinstvo Bijelo Polje - FK Lovćen Cetinje	0-2
FK Bokelj Kotor - OFK Petrovac	0-1
FK Ribnica Konik - FK KOM Podgorica	0-7
OFK Borac Bijelo Polje - FK Dečić Tuzi	0-5
FK Arsenal Tivat – FK Jezero Plav	3-0
FK Otrant Ulcinj - OFK Mladost Lješkopolje	0-1

1/8-Finals [03/24.10.2018]

FK Lovćen Cetinje - FK Dečić Tuzi	2-1 / 1-1
FK Rudar Pljevlja - FK Budućnost Podgorica	0-0 / 0-1
OFK Petrovac - OFK Titograd Podgorica	0-1 / 3-1 pen
OFK Mladost Lješkopolje - FK KOM Podgorica	1-0 / 3-0
FK Zeta Golubovci - FK Grbalj Radanovići	1-0 / 2-1
FK Sutjeska Nikšić - FK Iskra Danilovgrad	3-0 / 4-1
FK Arsenal Tivat - FK Mornar Bar	0-1 / 0-3
Bye: FK Igalo	

Quarter-Finals [07/28.11.2018]

FK Budućnost Podgorica - OFK Mladost Lješkopolje	1-1 / 1-0
FK Mornar Bar - FK Lovćen Cetinje	0-1 / 0-3
OFK Petrovac - FK Zeta Golubovci	1-1 / 1-0
FK Sutjeska Nikšić - FK Igalo	2-0 / 2-1

Semi-Finals [17-18.04./01.05.2019]			
FK Lovćen Cetinje - OFK Petrovac	1-1 / 4-0	FK Budućnost Podgorica - FK Sutjeska	0-0 / 1-1

Final

30.05.2019; Stadion pod Goricom, Podgorica; Referee: Milovan Milačić; Attendance: 7,500

FK Budućnost Podgorica - FK Lovćen Cetinje **2-0(1-0)**

Budućnost Podgorica: Miloš Dragojević, Periša Pešukić, Ilija Tučević, Dejan Boljević, Stefan Filipović, Draško Božović, Luka Mirković, Miloš Mijić, Miloš Krkotić (39.Milivoje Raičević), Mihailo Perović (82.Bojan Roganović), Igor Ivanović (73.Dejan Zarubica). Trainer: Branko Brnović.

Lovćen Cetinje: Ivan Janjušević, Mirko Radišić, Blažo Rajović, Marko Draganić, Ivan Pejaković (72.Željko Marković), Matija Pejović, Luka Petričević (70.Jovan Vujović), Novica Eraković (46.Marko Đurović), Andrija Kaluđerović, Driton Camaj, Goran Vujović. Trainer: Aleksandar Miljenović.

Goals: 1-0 Mihailo Perović (8), 2-0 Mihailo Perović (23 penalty), 3-0 Mihailo Perović (68), 4-0 Dejan Zarubica (90).

THE CLUBS 2018/2019

Fudbalski Klub Budućnost Podgorica

Founded: 1925
Stadium: Stadion pod Goricom, Podgorica (15,230)

Goalkeepers:	**DOB**	**M**	**(s)**	**G**
Miloš Dragojević	03.02.1989	3		
Milan Mijatović (SRB)	26.07.1987	33		
Defenders:	**DOB**	**M**	**(s)**	**G**
Vladan Adžić	05.07.1987	13		
Dejan Boljević	30.05.1990	9	(4)	1
Dominique Correia (SEN)	04.09.1992	12		
Slavko Damjanović	02.11.1992	24		1
Stefan Filipović (SRB)	21.06.1994	3	(2)	
Stefan Milić	06.07.2000	27	(2)	3
Periša Pešukić	07.12.1997	16		
Bojan Roganović	28.09.2000	7	(6)	
Ilija Tučević	18.10.1995	25	(4)	1
Midfielders:	**DOB**	**M**	**(s)**	**G**
Dušan Bakić	23.02.1999	6	(10)	1
Balša Boričić	07.01.1997	1	(3)	
Draško Božović	30.06.1988	27	(2)	4
Ivan Delić	15.02.1986	1	(5)	
Milan Đurišić	11.04.1987	11	(3)	
Miloš Krkotić	29.09.1987	5	(5)	1
Miloš Mijić (SRB)	22.11.1989	30		7
Luka Mirković	01.11.1990	28	(1)	4
Balša Sekulić	10.06.1998	3	(7)	
Vasilije Terzić	12.05.1999	6	(13)	
Petar Vukčević	02.03.2001	4	(3)	
Forwards:	**DOB**	**M**	**(s)**	**G**
Igor Ivanović	09.09.1990	28	(2)	7
Mihailo Perović	23.01.1997	22	(10)	7
Milivoje Raičević	21.07.1993	11	(8)	1
Dušan Stoiljkovič (SRB)	05.09.1994	12	(4)	7
Miljan Vlaisavljević	16.04.1991	13	(5)	1
Aleksandar Vujačić	19.03.1990	13		8
Dejan Zarubica	11.04.1993	3	(7)	1
Trainer:	**DOB**	**M**		
Zoran Govedarica (SRB)	14.04.1968	6		
Radislav Dragičević (SRB) [15.09.2018]	13.09.1971	5		
Branko Brnović [07.10.2018]	08.08.1967	25		

Omladinski fudbalski klub Grbalj Radanovići

Founded: 1995
Stadium: Stadion Donja Sutvara, Radanovići (1,500)

Goalkeepers:	**DOB**	**M**	**(s)**	**G**
Marko Kordić	22.02.1995	34		
Balša Popović	10.06.2000	2		
Defenders:	**DOB**	**M**	**(s)**	**G**
Predrag Jović (SRB)	29.05.1987	33		
Ćetko Manojlović	03.01.1991	9	(1)	
Ivan Mićunović	22.02.2000		(4)	
Aleksandar Milić	24.08.1998	4		
Ivan Racković	13.09.1994	1	(5)	
Miloš Radulović	23.02.1990	5	(1)	
Đorđije Vučićević	13.03.1999		(1)	
José Marcos Alves Luis „Zé Marcos“ (BRA)	01.02.1998	13		1
Midfielders:	**DOB**	**M**	**(s)**	**G**
Srđan Bošković	24.12.1994	2	(10)	
Marko Đukanović	22.10.1996	12		1
Andrija Kaluđerović	29.10.1993	2	(3)	
Vladan Kordić	22.06.1998	19	(7)	12
Dejan Kotorac	31.05.1996	30	(3)	5
Aleksandar Macanović	16.04.1993	9	(1)	
Marko Merdović	17.11.1998	24	(1)	
Ivan Mijušković	17.02.1988	31	(1)	1
Julián Montenegro (ARG)	23.03.1989	19	(3)	
Lazar Pajović	10.11.1995		(7)	
Nikola Stanišić	22.03.2000	1	(6)	
Đorđe Šteševć	02.06.2002	1	(2)	
Nedeljko Vlahović	15.01.1984	3	(6)	1
Petar Vukčević	15.08.1987	30	(2)	4
Forwards:	**DOB**	**M**	**(s)**	**G**
Zdravko Dragićević	17.06.1986	25	(7)	1
Miloš Džugurdić (SRB)	02.12.1992	20	(4)	5
Stefan Đorđević	16.11.1990	19	(8)	7
Predrag Kašćelan	30.06.1990	27	(4)	1
Drago Milović	23.05.1994		(1)	
Dejan Perović	19.08.2002		(1)	
Miloš Perović (BIH)	12.02.1994		(2)	
Nikola Popović (SRB)	31.05.1994	8	(3)	1
Ivan Vuković	09.02.1987	13	(2)	3
Trainer:	**DOB**	**M**		
Veselin Stešević	18.12.1965	36		

Fudbalski Klub Iskra Danilovgrad

Founded: 1919
Stadium: Stadion „Braće Velašević“, Danilovgrad (2,000)

Goalkeepers:	**DOB**	**M**	**(s)**	**G**
Srđan Blažić	26.11.1982	27		
Igor Mrvaljević	02.05.1998	9		
Defenders:	**DOB**	**M**	**(s)**	**G**
Miloš Drinčić	14.02.1999	33		1
Andrija Kaluđerović	14.06.1990		(1)	
Nikola Karaklajić (SRB)	05.02.1995	27	(3)	2
Nikola Kumburović	13.11.1999	9	(1)	
Miloš Lakić	21.12.1985	30		1
Luka Malešević	01.08.1998	27		
Luka Pejović	31.07.1985	27	(1)	1
Midfielders:	**DOB**	**M**	**(s)**	**G**
Balša Boričić	07.01.1997	13	(1)	3
Igor Burzanović	25.08.1985	13	(2)	1
Goran Burzanović	04.08.1984	10	(13)	3
Miomir Đuričković	26.07.1997	20	(8)	1
Milan Đurišić	11.04.1987	16		4
Miroje Jovanović	10.03.1987	30	(3)	
Danilo Marković	15.07.1998	9	(6)	
Luka Pavićević	02.02.1999		(2)	
Vladislav Rogošić	21.09.1994	15	(13)	3
Irfan Šahman	05.10.1993	25	(2)	1
Danilo Tomić	23.06.1986	1	(3)	
Forwards:	**DOB**	**M**	**(s)**	**G**
Danko Kovačević (SRB)	10.07.1991		(3)	
Vuk Milačić	09.08.1999	1	(5)	
Bogdan Milič	24.11.1987	5	(7)	1
Stefan Milošević	23.06.1996	18		9
Darko Nikač	15.09.1990	16	(1)	12
Deni Piranić	16.02.1999	1	(4)	1
Dejan Račić	15.07.1998	1	(1)	
Đorđe Šaletić	06.01.2002		(2)	
Filip Vorotović	08.03.1998	4	(7)	
Nikola Zvrko	07.03.1995	9	(8)	1
Trainer:	**DOB**	**M**		
Aleksandar Nedović	05.09.1978	36		

Fudbalski klub Lovćen Cetinje

Founded: 1913
Stadium: Stadion Obilića Poljana, Cetinje (2,000)

Goalkeepers:	**DOB**	**M**	**(s)**	**G**
Ivan Janjušević	11.07.1986	9		
Jovan Perović	28.12.1989	1		
Mico Perović	04.07.1993	26	(1)	
Defenders:	**DOB**	**M**	**(s)**	**G**
Danilo Bracanović	09.04.2000	4	(1)	
Marko Draganić	19.09.1994	22	(3)	1
Aleksa Latković	30.10.2000		(2)	
Igor Marković	05.11.1995	7	(5)	
Mirko Radišić	01.09.1990	30		1
Miloš Radunović	07.07.1990	26	(4)	
Blažo Rajović	26.03.1986	15		
Vladan Tatar	28.01.1984	2		
Midfielders:	**DOB**	**M**	**(s)**	**G**
Božidar Bujiša	15.05.1999		(13)	
Driton Camaj	07.03.1997	34		5
Nikola Draganić	19.09.1994	6	(12)	
Novica Eraković	12.11.1999	29	(1)	
Blažo Igumanović	19.01.1986	23	(1)	1
Andrija Kaluđerović	29.10.1993	15		
Željko Marković	25.01.1996	13	(5)	1
Nikola Mudreša	22.04.2001		(3)	
Ivan Pejaković	22.08.1992	13		2
Miloš Pejaković	16.08.1995		(1)	
Matija Pejović	04.10.2000	11	(2)	1
Luka Petričević	06.07.1992	21	(4)	
Petar Roganović	16.09.2000	4	(6)	
Miloš Stevović	14.09.1989	3	(11)	1
Filip Vujović	18.10.1997	6	(2)	
Jovan Vujović (BIH)	20.01.1996	16	(2)	
Forwards:	**DOB**	**M**	**(s)**	**G**
Petar Čavor	05.12.1997	2	(4)	2
Marko Đurović	08.05.1988	10	(13)	3
Ivan Jablan	18.07.1979	2	(6)	2
Goran Vujović	03.05.1987	29		8
Ilija Vujović	15.02.2001		(1)	
Dejan Zarubica	11.04.1993	17	(2)	1
Trainer:	**DOB**	**M**		
Dejan Roganović	28.10.1972	9		
Aleksandar Miljenović [25.09.2018]	31.10.1963	27		

Fudbalski klub Mornar Bar

Founded: 1923
Stadium: Stadion Topolica, Bar (2,500)

Goalkeepers:	**DOB**	**M**	**(s)**	**G**
Amir Begzić	05.12.2002	1		
Ljubomir Đurović	19.06.1989	9		
Marko Novović	24.11.1996	21		
Luka Raičević	02.12.1994	5	(2)	
Defenders:	**DOB**	**M**	**(s)**	**G**
Dušan Bigović	07.05.1998	3	(3)	
Vasilije Kovacevic	30.04.2000		(1)	
Stevan Marković	31.01.1988	26		1
Vuk Martinović	19.09.1989	29	(2)	
Malić Mucević			(1)	
Jovan Pajović	28.08.1996	18		
Nikola Popović	13.09.1997	13	(1)	
Ronaldo Rudović (USA)	12.06.1996	4		
Velimir Vlahović	20.01.2000	10		
Đorđe Vojvodić	31.05.1986	11	(1)	
Midfielders:	**DOB**	**M**	**(s)**	**G**
Radovan Barjaktarović	10.07.1999	8	(8)	
Balša Božović	01.05.1987	9	(3)	
Predrag Brnović	22.10.1986	29	(1)	
Balša Bušković	07.03.1998	6	(9)	
Denis Džanović	03.06.1993	15	(3)	4
Janko Giljen			(1)	
Filip Kalačević	12.03.1994	19	(5)	2
Danilo Leković	15.01.1999	2	(1)	
Nemanja Leverda	07.06.1992	8	(8)	
Boris Merdović	08.12.1989	9	(6)	
Luka Merdović	06.10.1997	21	(9)	
Fatmir Molabećirović	06.01.1988	5	(1)	
Marko Puljiz		6	(3)	
Benjamin Redžović	12.07.1995	1		
Kristijan Škrelja	11.10.1997	14	(9)	1
Nikola Vujošević	07.03.1996	24	(4)	
Forwards:	**DOB**	**M**	**(s)**	**G**
Ivan Ivanović	14.09.1989	11	(6)	
Dejan Jovančov (SRB)	28.09.1987	5	(1)	1
Luka Klikovac	01.06.1993	11	(2)	1
Lazar Lalošević	07.05.1995	7	(5)	1
Belmin Mehović	08.10.1998	4		
Dejan Račić	15.07.1998	9	(6)	4
Nino Vukmarković	17.12.1994	23	(6)	
Trainer:	**DOB**	**M**		
Aleksandar Madzar	21.08.1978	6		
Goran Milojević (SRB) [06.09.2018]	06.12.1964	13		
Dervis Hadžiosmanović (BIH) [13.02.2019]	09.08.1959	17		

Omladinski fudbalski klub Petrovac

Founded: 1969
Stadium: Stadion pod Malim brdom, Petrovac (1,630)

Goalkeepers:	DOB	M	(s)	G
Ognjen Bogićević	14.09.1993	4		
Sava Mugoša	10.07.1993	2		
Stefan Popović	11.01.1993	30		
Defenders:	**DOB**	**M**	**(s)**	**G**
Zoran Mikijelj	13.12.1991	27		1
Martin Prenkočević	17.02.1999	2	(8)	1
Milos Sofranac	05.04.2000		(1)	
Ryoya Tachibana (JPN)	04.04.1996	19	(3)	
Nenad Vujović	02.01.1989	21	(1)	2
Midfielders:	**DOB**	**M**	**(s)**	**G**
Mirza Đurđević		4	(4)	
Velizar Janketić	15.11.1996	2	(8)	
Demir Kajević	20.04.1989	34		
Miloš Kalezić	09.08.1993	33		7
Marko Kažić	16.11.1995	11	(10)	3
Pjeter Ljuljđuraj	29.06.1992	14	(1)	
Marko Marković	05.09.1987	28	(3)	
Luka Medigović	03.04.1995	7	(4)	
Halil Muharemović	06.11.1997	23	(6)	2
Lazar Pajović (SRB)	26.08.1991	29	(1)	
Nikola Savović	30.09.1994	3	(2)	
Slaven Stjepanović	02.11.1987	3	(2)	
Danilo Tomić	23.06.1986	8		
Kristijan Vulaj	25.06.1998	17	(10)	2
Forwards:	**DOB**	**M**	**(s)**	**G**
Benjamin Kacić	28.06.1991	13	(11)	4
Boris Kopitović	27.04.1995	9	(17)	4
Jovan Vučinić	20.01.1992	7	(12)	3
Aleksandar Vujačić	19.03.1990	18		4
Sho Yamamoto (JPN)	12.11.1996	28	(2)	7
Trainer:	**DOB**	**M**		
Rudolf Marčić	21.08.1974	36		

Fudbalski Klub Rudar Pljevlja

Founded: 1920
Stadium: Stadion pod Golubinjom, Pljevlja (10,000)

Goalkeepers:	DOB	M	(s)	G
Zoran Aković	26.12.1985	12		
Adis Kuč	30.11.1998	8		
Bogoslav Lučić	30.11.2001		(1)	
Vidoje Popović	28.06.1997	9		
Vuk Radović	28.02.1993	7	(1)	
Defenders:	**DOB**	**M**	**(s)**	**G**
Armin Bošnjak	20.04.1994	12	(2)	1
Stefan Drašković (SRB)	27.07.1989	7		
Milija Golubović	25.04.1996	28	(1)	2
Nemanja Kartal	17.07.1994	21	(2)	
Jasmin Mecinović (MKD)	22.10.1990	13		
Periša Pešukić	07.12.1997	17		
Andrija Raznatović	24.12.2000	14	(2)	
Nemanja Sekulić	29.03.1994	17		
Janko Simović	02.04.1987	6	(2)	
Željko Tomašević	05.04.1988	18	(3)	
Midfielders:	**DOB**	**M**	**(s)**	**G**
Janko Gogić	22.02.2000	1	(8)	1
Velizar Janketić	15.11.1996	2	(9)	
Aleksandar Macanović	16.04.1993	13	(4)	2
Danilo Marković	15.07.1998	16		
Elom Nya-Vedji (TOG)	24.11.1997	17		3
Patrick Felipe Justino Alves (BRA)	29.06.1994	14	(1)	2
Ivan Racković	13.09.1994	6	(11)	3
Alphonse Denis Soppo (CMR)	15.05.1985	25	(1)	2
Berin Tahirović	19.11.1999	2	(3)	
Danin Talović	08.03.1995	1	(4)	
Lazar Vujošević	20.03.1998	1		
Miloš Vukić	08.10.1994	1	(2)	
Miloš Zečević	28.01.1999	24	(9)	3
Forwards:	**DOB**	**M**	**(s)**	**G**
Radomir Đalović	29.10.1982	34		10
Eniks Kriještorac	17.01.1999	1	(6)	
Edvin Kuč	27.10.1993	15	(2)	3
Taku Morinaga (JPN)	18.05.1995	1	(6)	
Milivoje Mrdak	17.02.1993		(9)	
Ivan Pejaković	22.08.1992	15	(3)	1
Marko Vuković	20.03.1996	18	(8)	2
Trainer:	**DOB**	**M**		
Edis Mulalić (BIH)	23.10.1975	19		
Nenad Vukčević [10.01.2019]	25.11.1974	17		

Fudbalski Klub Sutjeska Nikšić

Founded: 1927
Stadium: Stadion kraj Bistrice, Nikšić (6,180)

Goalkeepers:	DOB	M	(s)	G
Vladan Giljen	07.12.1989	34		
Suad Ličina	08.02.1995	2	(1)	
Defenders:	**DOB**	**M**	**(s)**	**G**
Darko Bulatović	05.09.1989	34		1
Stefan Cicmil	16.08.1990	25	(1)	3
Bojan Ciger (SRB)	18.06.1994	14	(1)	1
Dragan Grivić	12.02.1996	13	(1)	
Nemanja Nedić	06.04.1995	31		3
Marko Vučić	30.12.1996	32	(2)	5
Midfielders:	**DOB**	**M**	**(s)**	**G**
Vladan Bubanja	21.02.1999	23	(8)	2
Marko Ćetković	10.07.1986	27	(3)	5
Branislav Janković	08.02.1992	15		
Stefan Lončar	19.02.1996	17	(1)	4
Aleksa Marušić	08.06.1999	6	(4)	2
Luka Merdović	14.03.1989	14	(7)	5
Milutin Osmajić	25.07.1999	12	(11)	2
Stefan Stefanović (SRB)	22.08.1991	22	(3)	1
Miljan Vlaisavljević	16.04.1991	4	(5)	2
Miloš Vučić	26.08.1995	10		
Forwards:	**DOB**	**M**	**(s)**	**G**
Zakaria Almabrouk Al Harish (LBY)	23.10.1998	15	(8)	3
Bojan Božović	03.02.1985	14	(18)	5
Stefan Denković	16.06.1991	4		1
Žarko Grbović	20.05.1995	8	(6)	
Šaleta Kordić	19.04.1993	4	(4)	
Božo Marković	26.10.1989	15	(9)	12
Veljko Vuković (SRB)	14.07.1989	1	(3)	1
Trainer:	**DOB**	**M**		
Nikola Rakojević	15.01.1958	36		

Omladinski fudbalski klub Titograd Podgorica

Founded: 1951
Stadium: Stadion FK Mladost, Podgorica (2,000)

Goalkeepers:	**DOB**	**M**	**(s)**	**G**
Saša Ivanović	26.06.1984	4		
Damir Ljuljanović	23.02.1992	32		
Defenders:	**DOB**	**M**	**(s)**	**G**
Miloš Bakrač	25.02.1992	13		
Balša Banović	26.01.1998	15		
Hrvoje Bukvić (CRO)	26.01.1995	1		
Radoš Dedić	17.05.1993	1		
Jovan Nikolić	21.07.1991	33		
Ivan Novović	26.04.1989	31	(1)	
Branko Ojdanić (BIH)	21.06.1990	19	(1)	
Slobodan Perišić	04.10.2000	3	(3)	
Miloš Radulović	06.08.1990	15	(4)	
Marko Roganović	21.06.1996	25	(2)	
Radule Živković (SRB)	20.10.1990	25		
Midfielders:	**DOB**	**M**	**(s)**	**G**
Miloš Brnović	26.04.2000		(9)	1
Zaim Divanović	09.12.2000	4	(8)	
Vasko Kalezić	14.03.1994	12	(1)	3
Pjeter Ljuljđuraj	29.06.1992	6	(4)	
Marko Miličković	31.03.1998	21	(13)	4
Zvonko Pamić (CRO)	04.02.1991	9	(2)	2
Vojin Pavlović	09.11.1993	34	(1)	9
Mirko Raičević	22.03.1982	13	(16)	2
Balša Sekulić	10.06.1998	6	(7)	2
Danilo Vukićević	14.12.1998		(1)	
Forwards:	**DOB**	**M**	**(s)**	**G**
Egzon Dinosha	18.01.2001		(3)	
Ognjen Gašević	02.04.2002	1	(9)	1
Mendy Mamadou (SEN)	04.10.1998	20	(4)	5
Elie Matouke (CMR)	03.01.1993		(2)	
Marko Pavićević (SRB)	03.09.1986	34		11
Zoran Petrović	14.07.1997	19	(3)	5
Alden Škrijelj	18.10.2000		(2)	
Trainer:	**DOB**	**M**		
Igor Pamić (CRO)	19.11.1969	19		
Edis Mulalić (BIH) [31.01.2019]	23.10.1975	3		
Peter Pacult (AUT) [08.03.2019]	28.10.1959	14		

Fudbalski Klub Zeta Golubovci

Founded: 1927
Stadium: Stadion Trešnjica, Golubovci (5,000)

Goalkeepers:	**DOB**	**M**	**(s)**	**G**
Stanislav Namaşco (MDA)	10.11.1986	36		
Defenders:	**DOB**	**M**	**(s)**	**G**
Jovan Baošić	07.07.1995	22	(2)	
Armin Bošnjak	20.04.1994	14	(1)	1
Zvonko Ceklić	11.04.1999	11	(8)	
Balša Goranović	06.02.1998	16	(10)	
Stefan Knežević	07.05.1997	3	(6)	
Goran Milojko	05.01.1994	34		1
Igor Vujačić	08.08.1994	32		1
Midfielders:	**DOB**	**M**	**(s)**	**G**
Aldin Adžović	18.06.1994	19		4
Davor Kontić	30.10.1999	1	(6)	
Srdjan Krstović	05.08.2000	17	(7)	
Lazar Lambulić	12.03.2000	6	(18)	1
Matija Lambulić	12.03.2003		(3)	
Mijat Lambulić	14.11.2001		(1)	
Nemanja Sekulić	29.03.1994	16		2
Amel Tuzović	31.03.1995	33		
Đorđije Vukčević	18.08.1996	34	(1)	
Stefan Vukčević	11.04.1997	16	(4)	
Alex Yamoah (GHA)	10.01.1995	19	(5)	3
Forwards:	**DOB**	**M**	**(s)**	**G**
Vasilije Klikovac	25.05.1999		(2)	
Nikola Krstović	05.04.2000	32	(1)	17
Pavle Krstović	18.04.1999	1	(7)	
Danilo Pešukić	20.09.2000	25	(2)	3
Ivan Vukčević	04.12.2001	9	(16)	3
Trainer:	**DOB**	**M**		
Dragoljub Đuretić	07.06.1955	19		
Dejan Roganović [04.02.2019]	28.10.1972	17		

SECOND LEVEL
Druga Liga 2018/2019

1.	OFK Mladost Lješkopolje (*Promoted*)	36	20	7	9	59	-	34	67
2.	FK Kom Zlatica (*Promotion Play-offs*)	36	17	9	10	40	-	30	60
3.	FK Bokelj Kotor (*Promotion Play-offs*)	36	16	10	10	51	-	25	58
4.	FK Otrant-Olympic Ulcinj	36	14	9	13	40	-	39	51
5.	FK Arsenal Tivat	36	13	10	13	34	-	29	49
6.	FK Jedinstvo Bijelo Polje	36	11	15	10	26	-	25	48
7.	FK Jezero Plav	36	13	9	14	32	-	43	48
8.	FK Dečić Tuzi*	36	13	10	13	40	-	39	46
9.	FK Igalo (*Relegated*)	36	11	10	15	28	-	34	43
10.	FK Berane* (*Relegated*)	36	6	3	27	26	-	78	18

**3 points deducted*

NATIONAL TEAM

INTERNATIONAL MATCHES
(16.07.2018 – 15.07.2019)

07.09.2018	Ploieşti	Romania - Montenegro	0-0	(UNL)
10.09.2018	Podgorica	Montenegro - Lithuania	2-0(2-0)	(UNL)
11.10.2018	Podgorica	Montenegro - Serbia	0-2(0-1)	(UNL)
14.10.2018	Vilnius	Lithuania - Montenegro	1-4(0-3)	(UNL)
17.11.2018	Beograd	Serbia - Montenegro	2-1(2-0)	(UNL)
20.11.2018	Podgorica	Montenegro - Romania	0-1(0-1)	(UNL)
22.03.2019	Sofia	Bulgaria - Montenegro	1-1(0-0)	(ECQ)
25.03.2019	Podgorica	Montenegro - England	1-5(1-2)	(ECQ)
07.06.2019	Podgorica	Montenegro - Kosovo	1-1(0-1)	(ECQ)
10.06.2019	Olomouc	Czech Republic - Montenegro	3-0(1-0)	(ECQ)

07.09.2018 ROMANIA - MONTENEGRO 0-0 UEFA Nations League C, Group 4
Stadionul "Ilie Oană", Ploieşti; Referee: Ivan Kružliak (Slovakia); Attendance: *played behind closed doors*
MNE: Danijel Petković, Žarko Tomašević, Stefan Savić (Cap), Marko Simić, Filip Stojković, Aleksandar Šćekić (74.Nebojša Kosović), Nikola Vukčević, Mirko Ivanić, Stefan Mugoša [*sent off 77*], Aleksandar Boljević (81.Fatos Bećiraj), Vladimir Jovović.Trainer: Ljubiša Tumbaković (Serbia).

10.09.2018 MONTENEGRO - LITHUANIA 2-0(2-0) UEFA Nations League C, Group 4
Stadion Pod Goricom, Podgorica; Referee: Jakob Kehlet (Denmark); Attendance: 5,239
MNE: Danijel Petković, Žarko Tomašević, Stefan Savić (Cap) (80.Boris Kopitović), Marko Simić, Filip Stojković, Nebojša Kosović, Nikola Vukčević (72.Aleksandar Šćekić), Marko Janković (87.Aleksandar Boljević), Mirko Ivanić, Fatos Bećiraj, Vladimir Jovović. Trainer: Ljubiša Tumbaković (Serbia).
Goals: Stefan Savić (34 penalty), Marko Janković (35).

11.10.2018 MONTENEGRO - SERBIA 0-2(0-1) UEFA Nations League C, Group 4
Stadion pod Goricom, Podgorica; Referee: Gianluca Rocchi (Italy); Attendance: 9,394
MNE: Danijel Petković, Žarko Tomašević, Marko Simić, Filip Stojković(46.Marko Janković), Adam Marušić, Marko Vešović, Aleksandar Šćekić (73.Mirko Ivanić), Nikola Vukčević, Fatos Bećiraj (80.Stefan Mugoša), Stevan Jovetić (Cap), Vladimir Jovović. Trainer: Ljubiša Tumbaković (Serbia).

14.10.2018 LITHUANIA - MONTENEGRO 1-4(0-3) UEFA Nations League C, Group 4
LFF Stadionas, Vilnius; Referee: Robert Schörgenhofer (Austria); Attendance: 1,515
MNE: Danijel Petković, Žarko Tomašević, Marko Simić (Cap), Boris Kopitović, Filip Stojković (87.Risto Radunović), Marko Vešović (56.Darko Zorić), Aleksandar Šćekić, Nebojša Kosović, Mirko Ivanić, Stefan Mugoša, Vladimir Jovović (72.Fatos Bećiraj). Trainer: Ljubiša Tumbaković (Serbia).
Goals: Stefan Mugoša (10), Boris Kopitović (35), Stefan Mugoša (45+1 penalty), Darko Zorić (86).

17.11.2018 SERBIA - MONTENEGRO 2-1(2-0) UEFA Nations League C, Group 4
Stadion "Rajko Mitić", Beograd; Referee: Alberto Undiano Mallenco (Spain); Attendance: 15,416
MNE: Danijel Petković, Marko Simić (Cap), Boris Kopitović, Adam Marušić, Marko Vešović, Aleksandar Šćekić (46.Aleksandar Boljević), Nebojša Kosović, Marko Janković (82.Luka Đorđević), Mirko Ivanić, Stefan Mugoša, Vladimir Jovović. Trainer: Ljubiša Tumbaković (Serbia).
Goal: Stefan Mugoša (70).

20.11.2018 MONTENEGRO - ROMANIA 0-1(0-1) UEFA Nations League C, Group 4
Stadion pod Goricom, Podgorica; Referee: Felix Zwayer (Germany); Attendance: 3,574
MNE: Danijel Petković, Marko Simić, Boris Kopitović, Adam Marušić (87.Emrah Klimenta), Marko Vešović, Nebojša Kosović, Marko Janković (81.Luka Đorđević), Mirko Ivanić, Fatos Bećiraj (Cap) (64.Aleksandar Boljević), Stefan Mugoša, Vladimir Jovović. Trainer: Ljubiša Tumbaković (Serbia).

22.03.2019 BULGARIA - MONTENEGRO 1-1(0-0) 16th EC. Qualifiers
Nationalen Stadion "Vasil Levski", Sofia; Referee: Ruddy Buquet (France); Attendance: 5,652
MNE: Danijel Petković, Žarko Tomašević, Marko Simić, Filip Stojković, Adam Marušić, Marko Vešović (78.Vladimir Jovović), Nikola Vukčević, Marko Janković (64.Aleksandar Boljević), Mirko Ivanić, Fatos Bećiraj (Cap), Stefan Mugoša (89.Nebojša Kosović). Trainer: Ljubiša Tumbaković (Serbia).
Goal: Stefan Mugoša (50).

25.03.2019 MONTENEGRO - ENGLAND 1-5(1-2) 16th EC. Qualifiers
Stadion pod Goricom, Podgorica; Referee: Aleksei Kulbakov (Belarus); Attendance: 8,329
MNE: Danijel Petković, Žarko Tomašević, Stefan Savić (Cap), Marko Simić (74.Vladimir Jovović), Filip Stojković, Adam Marušić, Marko Vešović (70.Aleksandar Boljević), Nikola Vukčević, Mirko Ivanić, Fatos Bećiraj (61.Marko Janković), Stefan Mugoša. Trainer: Ljubiša Tumbaković (Serbia).
Goal: Marko Vešović (17).

07.06.2019 MONTENEGRO - KOSOVO 1-1(0-1) 16th EC. Qualifiers
Stadion pod Goricom, Gorica; Referee: Daniele Orsato (Italy); Attendance: *played behind closed doors*
MNE: Milan Mijatović, Žarko Tomašević (71.Aleksandar Boljević), Marko Simić, Igor Vujačić, Adam Marušić, Marko Vešović, Aleksandar Šćekić (59.Marko Bakić), Nebojša Kosović, Marko Janković (85.Vladimir Jovović), Fatos Bećiraj (Cap), Stefan Mugoša. Trainer: Miodrag Džudović.
Goal: Stefan Mugoša (69).

10.06.2019 CZECH REPUBLIC - MONTENEGRO 3-0(1-0) 16th EC. Qualifiers
Stadion Andrův, Olomouc; Referee: Vladislav Bezborodov (Russia); Attendance: 11,565
MNE: Milan Mijatović, Risto Radunović, Boris Kopitović, Igor Vujačić, Adam Marušić (60.Marko Janković), Marko Vešović, Nebojša Kosović, Nikola Vukčević (Cap) (67.Vukan Savićević), Marko Bakić, Stefan Mugoša (85.Fatos Bećiraj), Vladimir Jovović. Trainer: Miodrag Džudović.

NATIONAL TEAM PLAYERS
(16.07.2018 – 15.07.2019)

Name	DOB	Caps	Goals	2018/2019:	*Club*
				Goalkeepers	
Milan MIJATOVIĆ	26.07.1987	**6**	**0**	2019:	*FK Budućnost Podgorica*
Danijel PETKOVIĆ	25.05.1993	**17**	**0**	2018/2019:	*FC Lorient-Bretagne Sud (FRA)*
				Defenders	
Emrah KLIMENTA	13.02.1991	**7**	**0**	2018:	*Sacramento Republic FC (USA)*
Boris KOPITOVIĆ	17.09.1994	**6**	**1**	2018/2019:	*FK Čukarički (SRB)*
Adam MARUŠIĆ	17.10.1992	**29**	**0**	2018/2019:	*SS Lazio Roma (ITA)*
Risto RADUNOVIĆ	04.05.1992	**2**	**0**	2018/2019:	*AFC Astra Giurgiu (ROU)*
Stefan SAVIĆ	08.01.1991	**51**	**5**	2018/2019:	*Club Atlético de Madrid (ESP)*
Marko SIMIĆ	16.06.1987	**36**	**1**	2018/2019:	*FC Pakhtakor Tashkent (UZB)*
Filip STOJKOVIĆ	22.01.1993	**15**	**0**	2018/2019:	*FK Crvena zvezda Beograd (SRB)*
Žarko TOMAŠEVIĆ	22.02.1990	**36**	**4**	2018/2019: 28.04.2019->	*KV Oostende (BEL)* *Unattached*
Igor VUJAČIĆ	08.08.1994	**2**	**0**	2019:	*FK Zeta Golubovci*
				Midfielders	
Marko BAKIĆ	01.11.1993	**14**	**0**	2019:	*Royal Excel Mouscron (BEL)*
Aleksandar BOLJEVIĆ	12.12.1995	**11**	**0**	2018/2019:	*KVRS Waasland-Beveren (BEL)*
Mirko IVANIĆ	13.09.1993	**15**	**1**	2018: 08.02.2019->	*FC BATE Borisov (BLR)* *FK Crvena zvezda Beograd (SRB)*
Marko JANKOVIĆ	09.07.1995	**18**	**1**	2018: 31.01.2019->	*FK Partizan Beograd (SRB)* *SPAL Ferrara (ITA)*
Vladimir JOVOVIĆ	26.10.1994	**27**	**0**	2018/2019:	*FK Jablonec (CZE)*
Vukan SAVIĆEVIĆ	29.01.1994	**2**	**0**	2019:	*Wisła Kraków (POL)*
Aleksandar ŠĆEKIĆ	12.12.1991	**16**	**0**	2018/2019:	*FK Partizan Beograd (SRB)*
Marko VEŠOVIĆ	28.08.1991	**27**	**2**	2018/2019:	*Legia Warszawa (POL)*
Nikola VUKČEVIĆ	13.12.1991	**34**	**1**	2018/2019:	*Levante UD Valencia (ESP)*
Darko ZORIĆ	12.09.1993	**4**	**1**	2018/2019:	*FK Čukarički (SRB)*
				Forwards	
Fatos BEĆIRAJ	22.05.1988	**63**	**9**	2018/2019:	*Maccabi Netanya FC (ISR)*
Luka ĐORĐEVIĆ	09.07.1994	**11**	**1**	2018/2019:	*FK Zenit St. Petersburg (RUS)*
Stevan JOVETIĆ	02.11.1989	**51**	**24**	2018:	*AS Monaco FC (FRA)*
Stefan MUGOŠA	23.02.1992	**31**	**8**	2018/2019:	*Incheon United FC (KOR)*

National team coach

Ljubiša TUMBAKOVIĆ (Serbia) [19.01.2016 – 07.06.2019]	02.09.1952	26 M; 7 W; 7 D; 12 L; 33-33
Miodrag DŽUDOVIĆ [07-10.06.2019]	06.09.1979	2 M; 0 W; 1 D; 1 L; 1-4

NETHERLANDS

The Country:
Nederland (Netherlands)
Capital: Amsterdam
Surface: 41,543 km²
Inhabitants: 17,336,891 [2019]
Time: UTC+1

The FA:
Koninklijke Nederlandse Voetbalbond
Woudenbergseweg 56-58 Postbus 515 3700, Am Zeist
Tel: +31 343 499 201
Foundation date: 1889
Member of FIFA since: 1904
Member of UEFA since: 1954
Website: www.knvb.nl

NATIONAL TEAM RECORDS

First international match:	30.04.1905, Antwerpen:	Belgium – Netherlands 1-4
Most international caps:	Wesley Benjamin Sneijder	- 134 caps (2003-2018)
Most international goals:	Robin van Persie	- 50 goals / 102 caps (2005-2017)

UEFA EUROPEAN CHAMPIONSHIP	
1960	Did not enter
1964	Qualifiers
1968	Qualifiers
1972	Qualifiers
1976	Final Tournament (3rd Place)
1980	Final Tournament (Group Stage)
1984	Qualifiers
1988	**Final Tournament (Winners)**
1992	Final Tournament (Semi-Finals)
1996	Final Tournament (Quarter-Finals)
2000	Final Tournament (Semi-Finals)
2004	Final Tournament (Semi-Finals)
2008	Final Tournament (Quarter-Finals)
2012	Final Tournament (Group Stage)
2016	Qualifiers

FIFA WORLD CUP	
1930	Did not enter
1934	Final Tournament (1st Round)
1938	Final Tournament (1st Round)
1950	Did not enter
1954	Did not enter
1958	Qualifiers
1962	Qualifiers
1966	Qualifiers
1970	Qualifiers
1974	Final Tournament (Runners-up)
1978	Final Tournament (Runners-up)
1982	Qualifiers
1986	Qualifiers
1990	Final Tournament (2nd Round of 16)
1994	Final Tournament (Quarter-Finals)
1998	Final Tournament (4th Place)
2002	Qualifiers
2006	Final Tournament (2nd Round of 16)
2010	Final Tournament (Runners-up)
2014	Final Tournament (3rd Place)
2018	Qualifiers

UEFA NATIONS LEAGUE
2018/2019 – League A; Final Tournament – Runners-up

OLYMPIC FOOTBALL TOURNAMENTS 1908-2016							
1908	3rd Place	**1948**	1/8 - Finals	**1972**	Qualifiers	**1996**	Qualifiers
1912	3rd Place	**1952**	Qualifiers	**1976**	Qualifiers	**2000**	Qualifiers
1920	3rd Place	**1956**	Did not enter	**1980**	Qualifiers	**2004**	Qualifiers
1924	4th Place	**1960**	Qualifiers	**1984**	Qualifiers	**2008**	Quarter-Finals
1928	1/8 - Finals	**1964**	Qualifiers	**1988**	Qualifiers	**2012**	Qualifiers
1936	Did not enter	**1968**	Qualifiers	**1992**	Qualifiers	**2016**	Qualifiers

FIFA CONFEDERATIONS CUP 1992-2017
None

NETHERLANDIAN CLUB HONOURS IN EUROPEAN CLUB COMPETITIONS:

European Champion Clubs' Cup (1956-1992) / UEFA Champions League (1993-2019)		
AFC Ajax Amsterdam	**4**	1970/1971, 1971/1972, 1972/1973, 1994/1995
Feyenoord Rotterdam	**1**	1969/1970
PSV Eindhoven	**1**	1987/1988
Fairs Cup (1858-1971) / UEFA Cup (1972-2009) / UEFA Europa League (2010-2019)		
Feyenoord Rotterdam	**2**	1973/1974, 2001/2002
PSV Eindhoven	**1**	1977/1978
AFC Ajax Amsterdam	**1**	1991/1992
UEFA Super Cup (1972-2018)		
AFC Ajax Amsterdam	**2**	1973, 1995

*European Cup Winners' Cup 1961-1999**		
AFC Ajax Amsterdam	**1**	1986/1987

**defunct competition*

NATIONAL COMPETITIONS
TABLE OF HONOURS

	CHAMPIONS*	CUP WINNERS	BEST GOALSCORERS
1888/1889	VV Concordia Rotterdam	-	-
1889/1890	HFC Haarlem	-	-
1890/1891	HVV Den Haag	-	-
1891/1892	RAP Amsterdam	-	-
1892/1893	HFC Haarlem	-	-
1893/1894	RAP Amsterdam	-	-
1894/1895	HFC Haarlem	-	-
1895/1896	HVV Den Haag	-	-
1896/1897	RAP Amsterdam	-	-
1897/1898	RAP Amsterdam	-	-
1898/1899	RAP Amsterdam	RAP Amsterdam	-
1899/1900	HVV Den Haag	Velocitas Breda	-
1900/1901	HVV Den Haag	HBS Craeyenhout	-
1901/1902	HVV Den Haag	Haarlem	-
1902/1903	HVV Den Haag	HVV Den Haag	-
1903/1904	HBS Craeyenhout	HFC Haarlem	-
1904/1905	HVV Den Haag	VOC Rotterdam	-
1905/1906	HBS Craeyenhout	VV Concordia Rotterdam	-
1906/1907	HVV Den Haag	VOC Rotterdam	-
1907/1908	Quick Den Haag	HBS Craeyenhout 2	-
1908/1909	Sparta Rotterdam	Quick Den Haag 2	-
1909/1910	HVV Den Haag	Quick Den Haag 2	-
1910/1911	Sparta Rotterdam	Quick Den Haag	-
1911/1912	Sparta Rotterdam	HFC Haarlem	-
1912/1913	Sparta Rotterdam	Koninklijke HFC Haarlem	-
1913/1914	HVV Den Haag	Dordrechtsche FC	-
1914/1915	Sparta Rotterdam	Koninklijke HFC Haarlem	-
1915/1916	Willem II Tilburg	Quick Den Haag	-
1916/1917	Go Ahead Eagles Deventer	AFC Ajax Amsterdam	-
1917/1918	AFC Ajax Amsterdam	Racing Club Heemstede	-
1918/1919	AFC Ajax Amsterdam	*No competition*	-
1919/1920	Be Quick 1887 Groningen	CVV Rotterdam	-
1920/1921	NAC Breda	Schoten Harlem	-
1921/1922	Go Ahead Eagles Deventer	*No competition*	-
1922/1923	Racing Club Heemstede	*No competition*	-
1923/1924	SC Feijenoord Rotterdam	*No competition*	-
1924/1925	HBS Craeyenhout	Zaanlandsche FC	-
1925/1926	SC Enschede	LONGA Lichtenvoorde	-
1926/1927	Heracles Almelo	VUC Den Haag	-
1927/1928	SC Feijenoord Rotterdam	Racing Club Heemstede	-
1928/1929	PSV Eindhoven	*No competition*	-
1929/1930	Go Ahead Eagles Deventer	SC Feijenoord Rotterdam	-
1930/1931	AFC Ajax Amsterdam	*No competition*	-
1931/1932	AFC Ajax Amsterdam	DFC	-
1932/1933	Go Ahead Eagles Deventer	*No competition*	-
1933/1934	AFC Ajax Amsterdam	Velocitas Groningen	-
1934/1935	PSV Eindhoven	SC Feijenoord Rotterdam	-
1935/1936	SC Feijenoord Rotterdam	Roermond FC	-
1936/1937	AFC Ajax Amsterdam	FC Eindhoven	-
1937/1938	SC Feijenoord Rotterdam	VSV Velsen	-
1938/1939	AFC Ajax Amsterdam	FC Wageningen	-
1939/1940	SC Feijenoord Rotterdam	*No competition*	-
1940/1941	Heracles Almelo	*No competition*	-
1941/1942	ADO Den Haag	*No competition*	-
1942/1943	ADO Den Haag	AFC Ajax Amsterdam	-
1943/1944	AVV De Volewijckers Amsterdam	Willem II Tilburg	-
1944/1945	*No competition*	*No competition*	-
1945/1946	HFC Haarlem	*No competition*	-
1946/1947	AFC Ajax Amsterdam	*No competition*	-
1947/1948	BVV Den Bosch	FC Wageningen	-
1948/1949	Schiedamse VV	Quick 1888 Nijmegen	-
1949/1950	SV Limburgia Brunssum	PSV Eindhoven	-
1950/1951	PSV Eindhoven	*No competition*	-
1951/1952	Willem II Tilburg	*No competition*	-
1952/1953	Racing Club Heemstede	*No competition*	-
1953/1954	FC Eindhoven	*No competition*	-
1954/1955	Willem II Tilburg	*No competition*	-

1955/1956	Rapid JC Kerkrade	*No competition*	-	
1956/1957	AFC Ajax Amsterdam	Fortuna '54 Geleen	Coenraad Henrik Dillen (PSV Eindhoven)	43
1957/1958	VV DOS Utrecht	Sparta Rotterdam	Leonard Canjels (NAC Breda)	32
1958/1959	Sparta Rotterdam	VVV	Leonard Canjels (NAC Breda)	34
1959/1960	AFC Ajax Amsterdam	*No competition*	Hendrik Groot (AFC Ajax Amsterdam)	38
1960/1961	SC Feijenoord Rotterdam	AFC Ajax Amsterdam	Hendrik Groot (AFC Ajax Amsterdam)	41
1961/1962	SC Feijenoord Rotterdam	Sparta Rotterdam	Dick Tol (FC Volendam)	27
1962/1963	PSV Eindhoven	Willem II Tilburg	Pierre Kerkhofs (PSV Eindhoven)	22
1963/1964	DWS Amsterdam	Fortuna '54 Geleen	Frans Geurtsen (DWS Amsterdam)	28
1964/1965	SC Feijenoord Rotterdam	SC Feijenoord Rotterdam	Frans Geurtsen (DWS Amsterdam)	23
1965/1966	AFC Ajax Amsterdam	Sparta Rotterdam	Wilhelmus Martinus Leonardus Johannes van der Kuijlen (PSV Eindhoven) Piet Kruiver (SC Feijenoord Rotterdam)	23
1966/1967	AFC Ajax Amsterdam	AFC Ajax Amsterdam	Hendrik Johannes Cruijff (AFC Ajax Amsterdam)	33
1967/1968	AFC Ajax Amsterdam	ADO Den Haag	Ove Kindvall (SWE, SC Feijenoord Rotterdam)	28
1968/1969	SC Feijenoord Rotterdam	SC Feijenoord Rotterdam	Dirk Wouter Johannes van Dijk (FC Twente Enschede) Bengt Ove Kindvall (SWE, SC Feijenoord Rotterdam)	30
1969/1970	AFC Ajax Amsterdam	AFC Ajax Amsterdam	Wilhelmus Martinus Leonardus Johannes van der Kuijlen (PSV Eindhoven)	26
1970/1971	SC Feijenoord Rotterdam	AFC Ajax Amsterdam	Bengt Ove Kindvall (SWE, SC Feijenoord Rotterdam)	24
1971/1972	AFC Ajax Amsterdam	AFC Ajax Amsterdam	Hendrik Johannes Cruijff (AFC Ajax Amsterdam)	25
1972/1973	AFC Ajax Amsterdam	NAC Breda	Franciscus Janssens (NEC Nijmegen) Willy Brokamp (MVV Maastricht)	18
1973/1974	SC Feyenoord Rotterdam	PSV Eindhoven	Wilhelmus Martinus Leonardus Johannes van der Kuijlen (PSV Eindhoven)	27
1974/1975	PSV Eindhoven	FC Den Haag	Geertruida Maria Geels (AFC Ajax Amsterdam)	30
1975/1976	PSV Eindhoven	PSV Eindhoven	Geertruida Maria Geels (AFC Ajax Amsterdam)	29
1976/1977	AFC Ajax Amsterdam	FC Twente Enschede	Geertruida Maria Geels (AFC Ajax Amsterdam)	34
1977/1978	PSV Eindhoven	AZ'67 Alkmaar	Geertruida Maria Geels (AFC Ajax Amsterdam)	30
1978/1979	AFC Ajax Amsterdam	AFC Ajax Amsterdam	Cornelis Kist (AZ'67 Alkmaar)	34
1979/1980	AFC Ajax Amsterdam	SC Feyenoord Rotterdam	Cornelis Kist (AZ'67 Alkmaar)	27
1980/1981	AZ'67 Alkmaar '67	AZ'67 Alkmaar	Geertruida Maria Geels (Sparta Rotterdam)	22
1981/1982	AFC Ajax Amsterdam	AZ'67 Alkmaar	Willem Cornelis Nicolaas Kieft (AFC Ajax Amsterdam)	32
1982/1983	AFC Ajax Amsterdam	AFC Ajax Amsterdam	Peter Houtman (SC Feyenoord Rotterdam)	30
1983/1984	SC Feyenoord Rotterdam	SC Feyenoord Rotterdam	Marcel van Basten (AFC Ajax Amsterdam)	28
1984/1985	AFC Ajax Amsterdam	FC Utrecht	Marcel van Basten (AFC Ajax Amsterdam)	22
1985/1986	PSV Eindhoven	AFC Ajax Amsterdam	Marcel van Basten (AFC Ajax Amsterdam)	37
1986/1987	PSV Eindhoven	AFC Ajax Amsterdam	Marcel van Basten (AFC Ajax Amsterdam)	31
1987/1988	PSV Eindhoven	PSV Eindhoven	Willem Cornelis Nicolaas Kieft (PSV Eindhoven)	29
1988/1989	PSV Eindhoven	PSV Eindhoven	Romário de Souza Faria (BRA, PSV Eindhoven)	19
1989/1990	AFC Ajax Amsterdam	PSV Eindhoven	Romário de Souza Faria (BRA, PSV Eindhoven)	23
1990/1991	PSV Eindhoven	SC Feyenoord Rotterdam	Romário de Souza Faria (BRA, PSV Eindhoven) Dennis Nicolaas Maria Bergkamp (AFC Ajax Amsterdam)	25
1991/1992	PSV Eindhoven	SC Feyenoord Rotterdam	Dennis Nicolaas Maria Bergkamp (AFC Ajax Amsterdam)	24
1992/1993	SC Feyenoord Rotterdam	AFC Ajax Amsterdam	Dennis Nicolaas Maria Bergkamp (AFC Ajax Amsterdam)	26
1993/1994	AFC Ajax Amsterdam	SC Feyenoord Rotterdam	Jari Olavi Litmanen (FIN, AFC Ajax Amsterdam)	26
1994/1995	AFC Ajax Amsterdam	SC Feyenoord Rotterdam	Ronaldo Luís Nazário de Lima (BRA, PSV Eindhoven)	30
1995/1996	AFC Ajax Amsterdam	PSV Eindhoven	Luc Gilbert Cyrille Nilis (BEL, PSV Eindhoven)	21
1996/1997	PSV Eindhoven	Roda JC Kerkrade	Luc Gilbert Cyrille Nilis (BEL, PSV Eindhoven)	21
1997/1998	AFC Ajax Amsterdam	AFC Ajax Amsterdam	Nikolaos Machlas (GRE, SBV Vitesse Arnhem)	34
1998/1999	SC Feyenoord Rotterdam	AFC Ajax Amsterdam	Rutgerus Johannes Martinus van Nistelrooy (PSV Eindhoven)	31
1999/2000	PSV Eindhoven	Roda JC Kerkrade	Rutgerus Johannes Martinus van Nistelrooy (PSV Eindhoven)	29
2000/2001	PSV Eindhoven	FC Twente Enschede	Mateja Kežman (SRB, PSV Eindhoven)	24
2001/2002	AFC Ajax Amsterdam	AFC Ajax Amsterdam	Petrus Ferdinandus Johannes van Hooijdonk (SC Feyenoord Rotterdam)	24
2002/2003	PSV Eindhoven	FC Utrecht	Mateja Kežman (SRB, PSV Eindhoven)	35
2003/2004	AFC Ajax Amsterdam	FC Utrecht	Mateja Kežman (SRB, PSV Eindhoven)	31
2004/2005	PSV Eindhoven	PSV Eindhoven	Dirk Kuyt (SC Feyenoord Rotterdam)	29
2005/2006	PSV Eindhoven	AFC Ajax Amsterdam	Dirk Jan Klaas Huntelaar (SC Heerenveen/AFC Ajax Amsterdam)	33
2006/2007	PSV Eindhoven	AFC Ajax Amsterdam	Afonso Alves Martins Júnior (BRA, SC Heerenveen)	34
2007/2008	PSV Eindhoven	SC Feyenoord Rotterdam	Dirk Jan Klaas Huntelaar (AFC Ajax Amsterdam)	33
2008/2009	AZ Alkmaar	SC Heerenveen	Mounir El Hamdaoui (MAR, AZ Alkmaar)	23
2009/2010	FC Twente Enschede	AFC Ajax Amsterdam	Luis Alberto Suárez Díaz (URU, AFC Ajax Amsterdam)	35
2010/2011	AFC Ajax Amsterdam	FC Twente Enschede	Björn Vleminckx (BEL, NEC Nijmegen)	23
2011/2012	AFC Ajax Amsterdam	PSV Eindhoven	Bas Dost (SC Heerenveen)	32

2012/2013	AFC Ajax Amsterdam	AZ Alkmaar	Wilfried Guemiand Bony (CIV, SBV Vitesse Arnhem)	31
2013/2014	AFC Ajax Amsterdam	PEC Zwolle	Alfreð Finnbogason (ISL, SC Heerenveen)	29
2014/2015	PSV Eindhoven	FC Groningen	Memphis Depay (PSV Eindhoven)	22
2015/2016	PSV Eindhoven	Feyenoord Rotterdam	Vincent Janssen (AZ Alkmaar)	27
2016/2017	Feyenoord Rotterdam	SBV Vitesse Arnhem	Nicolai Mick Jørgensen (DEN, Feyenoord Rotterdam)	21
2017/2018	PSV Eindhoven	Feyenoord Rotterdam	Alireza Jahanbakhsh (IRN, AZ Alkmaar)	21
2018/2019	AFC Ajax Amsterdam	AFC Ajax Amsterdam	Luuk de Jong (PSV Eindhoven) Dušan Tadić (SRB, AFC Ajax Amsterdam)	28

*National Champions (1888–1956), Eredivisie (since 1956)

NATIONAL CHAMPIONSHIP
Eredivisie 2018/2019
(10.08.2018 – 12.05.2019)

Results

Round 1 [10-12.08.2018]
PEC Zwolle - SC Heerenveen 2-3(1-3)
Willem II - VVV-Venlo 0-1(0-1)
AFC Ajax - Heracles Almelo 1-1(0-0)
PSV Eindhoven - FC Utrecht 4-0(1-0)
SBV Excelsior - Fortuna Sittard 1-1(1-0)
ADO Den Haag - FC Emmen 1-2(0-2)
De Graafschap - Feyenoord 2-0(1-0)
SBV Vitesse - FC Groningen 5-1(2-1)
AZ Alkmaar - NAC Breda 5-0(3-0)

Round 2 [17-19.08.2018]
FC Groningen - Willem II 0-1(0-1)
NAC Breda - De Graafschap 3-0(1-0)
VVV-Venlo - AFC Ajax 0-1(0-0)
Fortuna Sittard - PSV Eindhoven 1-2(0-1)
Heracles Almelo - ADO Den Haag 4-2(3-2)
FC Utrecht - PEC Zwolle 2-0(2-0)
Feyenoord - SBV Excelsior 3-0(1-0)
FC Emmen - AZ Alkmaar 1-4(1-3)
SC Heerenveen - SBV Vitesse 1-1(1-0)

Round 3 [24-26.08.2018]
ADO Den Haag - Fortuna Sittard 3-1(2-0)
AFC Ajax - FC Emmen 5-0(2-0)
De Graafschap - FC Groningen 0-1(0-1)
NAC Breda - SBV Excelsior 0-2(0-1)
PEC Zwolle - PSV Eindhoven 1-2(0-1)
Willem II - Heracles Almelo 5-0(3-0)
SC Heerenveen - Feyenoord 3-5(0-3)
FC Utrecht - VVV-Venlo 1-1(1-0)
AZ Alkmaar - SBV Vitesse 0-0

Round 4 [31.08.-02.09.2018]
FC Emmen - De Graafschap 1-1(0-0)
VVV-Venlo - SC Heerenveen 1-1(0-1)
PSV Eindhoven - Willem II 6-1(4-0)
SBV Excelsior - ADO Den Haag 2-4(0-2)
Fortuna Sittard - FC Utrecht 1-1(0-0)
FC Groningen - PEC Zwolle 0-1(0-0)
Heracles Almelo - AZ Alkmaar 3-2(1-1)
SBV Vitesse - AFC Ajax 0-4(0-3)
Feyenoord - NAC Breda 4-2(1-1)

Round 5 [15-16.09.2018]
De Graafschap - VVV-Venlo 1-2(0-2)
ADO Den Haag - PSV Eindhoven 0-7(0-2)
Willem II - SBV Excelsior 2-2(0-1)
AFC Ajax - FC Groningen 3-0(1-0)
AZ Alkmaar - Feyenoord 1-1(1-1)
SC Heerenveen - Heracles Almelo 3-5(1-1)
FC Utrecht - FC Emmen 1-2(1-0)
NAC Breda - Fortuna Sittard 2-3(1-1)
PEC Zwolle - SBV Vitesse 0-2(0-2)

Round 6 [21-23.09.2018]
Heracles Almelo - De Graafschap 4-0(1-0)
Fortuna Sittard - Willem II 4-4(2-2)
SBV Excelsior - SC Heerenveen 3-3(2-0)
VVV-Venlo - NAC Breda 3-0(2-0)
SBV Vitesse - ADO Den Haag 1-1(1-0)
Feyenoord - FC Utrecht 1-0(0-0)
FC Emmen - PEC Zwolle 0-1(0-1)
FC Groningen - AZ Alkmaar 1-3(1-1)
PSV Eindhoven - AFC Ajax 3-0(3-0)

Round 7 [29-30.09.2018]
SC Heerenveen - ADO Den Haag 1-1(1-1)
NAC Breda - PSV Eindhoven 0-2(0-0)
Fortuna Sittard - AFC Ajax 0-2(0-0)
SBV Excelsior - VVV-Venlo 1-0(1-0)
Heracles Almelo - FC Emmen 2-1(2-0)
De Graafschap - Willem II 2-1(1-0)
AZ Alkmaar - PEC Zwolle 2-2(1-1)
FC Groningen - FC Utrecht 1-1(0-1)
Feyenoord - SBV Vitesse 2-1(0-1)

Round 8 [05-07.10.2018]
FC Utrecht - NAC Breda 2-1(1-0)
ADO Den Haag - FC Groningen 1-0(1-0)
PEC Zwolle - SBV Excelsior 2-0(1-0)
PSV Eindhoven - VVV-Venlo 4-0(1-0)
De Graafschap - SC Heerenveen 0-5(0-4)
FC Emmen - Fortuna Sittard 3-3(1-0)
Willem II - Feyenoord 1-1(0-0)
SBV Vitesse - Heracles Almelo 4-0(2-0)
AFC Ajax - AZ Alkmaar 5-0(1-0)

Round 9 [20-21.10.2018]
PSV Eindhoven - FC Emmen 6-0(4-0)
SBV Excelsior - SBV Vitesse 2-0(1-0)
SC Heerenveen - AFC Ajax 0-4(0-2)
FC Utrecht - AZ Alkmaar 2-1(1-1)
NAC Breda - Willem II 2-2(1-2)
Heracles Almelo - FC Groningen 4-1(1-1)
Feyenoord - PEC Zwolle 3-0(2-0)
VVV-Venlo - ADO Den Haag 2-0(1-0)
Fortuna Sittard - De Graafschap 3-1(1-0)

Round 10 [26-28.10.2018]
FC Emmen - VVV-Venlo 1-1(0-1)
ADO Den Haag - NAC Breda 1-1(1-1)
De Graafschap - SBV Excelsior 4-1(1-1)
FC Groningen - PSV Eindhoven 1-2(1-1)
PEC Zwolle - Heracles Almelo 1-1(0-1)
SBV Vitesse - Fortuna Sittard 2-1(1-1)
Willem II - FC Utrecht 0-1(0-0)
AFC Ajax - Feyenoord 3-0(2-0)
AZ Alkmaar - SC Heerenveen 2-3(1-1)

Round 11 [02-04.11.2018]
SBV Excelsior - FC Groningen 2-4(1-2)
NAC Breda - Heracles Almelo 2-1(1-0)
PSV Eindhoven - SBV Vitesse 1-0(0-0)
AFC Ajax - Willem II 2-0(2-0)
AZ Alkmaar - De Graafschap 1-0(0-0)
SC Heerenveen - FC Emmen 1-1(1-0)
FC Utrecht - ADO Den Haag 3-0(1-0)
Fortuna Sittard - PEC Zwolle 3-0(1-0)
Feyenoord - VVV-Venlo 4-1(2-0) [06.12.18]

Round 12 [09-11.11.2018]
PEC Zwolle - Willem II 2-3(0-2)
FC Emmen - NAC Breda 2-0(0-0)
De Graafschap - PSV Eindhoven 1-4(1-2)
SBV Vitesse - FC Utrecht 2-1(0-0)
VVV-Venlo - Fortuna Sittard 3-2(2-1)
FC Groningen - SC Heerenveen 2-0(2-0)
SBV Excelsior - AFC Ajax 1-7(0-2)
ADO Den Haag - AZ Alkmaar 0-1(0-0)
Heracles Almelo - Feyenoord 0-2(0-0)

Round 13 [24-25.11.2018]
PEC Zwolle - ADO Den Haag 2-3(2-2)
NAC Breda - AFC Ajax 0-3(0-1)
PSV Eindhoven - SC Heerenveen 3-0(1-0)
Fortuna Sittard - Heracles Almelo 3-0(2-0)
FC Emmen - SBV Excelsior 1-2(0-0)
FC Utrecht - De Graafschap 5-0(3-0)
Feyenoord - FC Groningen 1-0(1-0)
Willem II - SBV Vitesse 1-3(0-3)
VVV-Venlo - AZ Alkmaar 2-2(1-2)

Round 14 [30.11.-02.12.2018]
SBV Excelsior - FC Utrecht 3-3(3-0)
SBV Vitesse - FC Emmen 1-1(1-0)
AZ Alkmaar - Willem II 0-2(0-2)
De Graafschap - PEC Zwolle 0-2(0-1)
SC Heerenveen - Fortuna Sittard 3-1(1-0)
AFC Ajax - ADO Den Haag 5-1(3-1)
Feyenoord - PSV Eindhoven 2-1(2-0)
Heracles Almelo - VVV-Venlo 4-1(1-0)
FC Groningen - NAC Breda 5-2(1-1)

Round 15 [07-09.12.2018]
Fortuna Sittard - AZ Alkmaar 0-3(0-1)
PSV Eindhoven - SBV Excelsior 6-0(2-0)
Willem II - SC Heerenveen 1-5(1-2)
PEC Zwolle - AFC Ajax 1-4(1-2)
ADO Den Haag - De Graafschap 0-0
FC Utrecht - Heracles Almelo 3-1(3-0)
VVV-Venlo - FC Groningen 0-0
FC Emmen - Feyenoord 1-4(0-0)
NAC Breda - SBV Vitesse 2-1(1-0)

Round 16 [14-16.12.2018]
Willem II - ADO Den Haag 0-3(0-1)
PEC Zwolle - NAC Breda 0-0
AZ Alkmaar - SBV Excelsior 2-1(1-1)
Heracles Almelo - PSV Eindhoven 0-4(0-2)
SBV Vitesse - VVV-Venlo 2-1(1-0)
SC Heerenveen - FC Utrecht 2-3(0-3)
AFC Ajax - De Graafschap 8-0(3-0)
FC Groningen - FC Emmen 1-2(0-0)
Feyenoord - Fortuna Sittard 0-2(0-0)

Round 17 [21-23.12.2018]
VVV-Venlo - PEC Zwolle 2-0(1-0)
Fortuna Sittard - FC Groningen 0-0
NAC Breda - SC Heerenveen 4-2(1-2)
PSV Eindhoven - AZ Alkmaar 3-1(1-1)
SBV Excelsior - Heracles Almelo 0-3(0-2)
FC Utrecht - AFC Ajax 1-3(0-1)
De Graafschap - SBV Vitesse 2-2(1-1)
ADO Den Haag - Feyenoord 2-2(1-1)
FC Emmen - Willem II 0-2(0-1)

Round 18 [18-20.01.2019]
SBV Vitesse - SBV Excelsior 3-2(2-0)
AZ Alkmaar - FC Utrecht 3-0(2-0)
PEC Zwolle - Feyenoord 3-1(1-1)
ADO Den Haag - VVV-Venlo 2-4(1-1)
FC Groningen - Heracles Almelo 3-0(1-0)
Willem II - NAC Breda 2-0(1-0)
De Graafschap - Fortuna Sittard 5-1(3-0)
FC Emmen - PSV Eindhoven 2-2(0-1)
AFC Ajax - SC Heerenveen 4-4(3-1)

Round 19 [25-27.01.2019]
NAC Breda - ADO Den Haag 1-1(0-1)
Heracles Almelo - PEC Zwolle 0-2(0-1)
SBV Excelsior - De Graafschap 2-0(0-0)
PSV Eindhoven - FC Groningen 2-1(2-1)
VVV-Venlo - FC Emmen 2-3(1-1)
Fortuna Sittard - SBV Vitesse 2-1(0-1)
FC Utrecht - Willem II 0-1(0-0)
Feyenoord - AFC Ajax 6-2(3-2)
SC Heerenveen - AZ Alkmaar 0-2(0-0)

Round 20 [01-03.02.2019]
De Graafschap - NAC Breda 3-0(1-0)
SBV Vitesse - SC Heerenveen 2-2(1-1)
Willem II - FC Groningen 1-2(0-2)
AFC Ajax - VVV-Venlo 6-0(1-0)
AZ Alkmaar - FC Emmen 5-0(3-0)
SBV Excelsior - Feyenoord 2-1(0-0)
PEC Zwolle - FC Utrecht 4-3(1-1)
PSV Eindhoven - Fortuna Sittard 5-0(1-0)
ADO Den Haag - Heracles Almelo 2-0(0-0)

Round 21 [08-10.02.2019]
NAC Breda - AZ Alkmaar 0-3(0-1)
Heracles Almelo - AFC Ajax 1-0(1-0)
SC Heerenveen - PEC Zwolle 1-1(1-1)
VVV-Venlo - Willem II 2-1(1-0)
Feyenoord - De Graafschap 4-0(1-0)
Fortuna Sittard - SBV Excelsior 4-1(2-0)
FC Groningen - SBV Vitesse 2-1(1-1)
FC Emmen - ADO Den Haag 3-2(2-0)
FC Utrecht - PSV Eindhoven 2-2(2-0)

Round 22 [15-17.02.2019]
ADO Den Haag - PEC Zwolle 1-0(1-0)
AZ Alkmaar - VVV-Venlo 3-0(2-0)
SC Heerenveen - PSV Eindhoven 2-2(2-0)
Heracles Almelo - Fortuna Sittard 6-0(1-0)
SBV Vitesse - Willem II 3-2(1-0)
AFC Ajax - NAC Breda 5-0(1-0)
SBV Excelsior - FC Emmen 2-1(0-0)
FC Groningen - Feyenoord 1-0(1-0)
De Graafschap - FC Utrecht 0-1(0-0)

Round 23 [22-24.02.2019]
VVV-Venlo - Heracles Almelo 0-1(0-0)
FC Utrecht - SBV Excelsior 0-0
PEC Zwolle - De Graafschap 0-3(0-1)
Fortuna Sittard - SC Heerenveen 2-4(2-1)
NAC Breda - FC Groningen 0-0
ADO Den Haag - AFC Ajax 1-5(1-2)
PSV Eindhoven - Feyenoord 1-1(0-0)
FC Emmen - SBV Vitesse 0-3(0-1)
Willem II - AZ Alkmaar 2-1(2-0)

Round 24 [01-03.03.2019]
De Graafschap - ADO Den Haag 1-1(0-1)
Heracles Almelo - FC Utrecht 1-5(0-1)
SBV Excelsior - PSV Eindhoven 0-2(0-1)
SBV Vitesse - NAC Breda 4-1(0-1)
SC Heerenveen - Willem II 4-2(3-0)
FC Groningen - VVV-Venlo 3-2(2-1)
AZ Alkmaar - Fortuna Sittard 4-2(1-2)
Feyenoord - FC Emmen 4-0(1-0)
AFC Ajax - PEC Zwolle 2-1(1-0) [13.03.19]

Round 25 [08-10.03.2019]
FC Utrecht - FC Groningen 0-0
VVV-Venlo - SBV Excelsior 1-0(1-0)
PSV Eindhoven - NAC Breda 2-0(1-0)
ADO Den Haag - SC Heerenveen 2-3(0-1)
Willem II - De Graafschap 3-2(2-1)
PEC Zwolle - AZ Alkmaar 0-0
SBV Vitesse - Feyenoord 1-1(0-1)
FC Emmen - Heracles Almelo 1-1(0-1)
AFC Ajax - Fortuna Sittard 4-0(2-0)

Round 26 [15-17.03.2019]
Fortuna Sittard - FC Emmen 3-1(3-0)
SC Heerenveen - De Graafschap 0-3(0-1)
Feyenoord - Willem II 2-3(1-1)
NAC Breda - FC Utrecht 0-4(0-2)
Heracles Almelo - SBV Vitesse 3-2(2-2)
VVV-Venlo - PSV Eindhoven 0-1(0-0)
AZ Alkmaar - AFC Ajax 1-0(0-0)
FC Groningen - ADO Den Haag 1-0(1-0)
SBV Excelsior - PEC Zwolle 0-2(0-0)

Round 27 [30-31.03.2019]
Willem II - Fortuna Sittard 3-2(1-1)
ADO Den Haag - SBV Vitesse 3-3(2-3)
De Graafschap - Heracles Almelo 1-2(1-0)
SC Heerenveen - SBV Excelsior 1-0(0-0)
AZ Alkmaar - FC Groningen 1-0(0-0)
NAC Breda - VVV-Venlo 1-1(0-1)
FC Utrecht - Feyenoord 3-2(1-0)
PEC Zwolle - FC Emmen 3-0(2-0)
AFC Ajax - PSV Eindhoven 3-1(1-0)

Round 28 [02-04.04.2019]
SBV Vitesse - AZ Alkmaar 2-2(0-2)
Heracles Almelo - Willem II 3-4(0-1)
FC Groningen - De Graafschap 1-0(0-0)
VVV-Venlo - FC Utrecht 2-6(2-1)
SBV Excelsior - NAC Breda 1-2(1-0)
Fortuna Sittard - ADO Den Haag 0-0
FC Emmen - AFC Ajax 2-5(0-2)
PSV Eindhoven - PEC Zwolle 4-0(1-0)
Feyenoord - SC Heerenveen 3-0(1-0)

Round 29 [06-07.04.2019]
Willem II - AFC Ajax 1-4(1-2)
ADO Den Haag - FC Utrecht 5-0(3-0)
FC Groningen - SBV Excelsior 1-0(0-0)
De Graafschap - AZ Alkmaar 1-1(0-0)
Heracles Almelo - NAC Breda 1-0(0-0)
FC Emmen - SC Heerenveen 2-0(1-0)
PEC Zwolle - Fortuna Sittard 5-0(1-0)
VVV-Venlo - Feyenoord 0-3(0-1)
SBV Vitesse - PSV Eindhoven 3-3(1-1)

Round 30 [12-14.04.2019]
NAC Breda - FC Emmen 1-1(0-1)
AZ Alkmaar - ADO Den Haag 2-3(0-1)
AFC Ajax - SBV Excelsior 6-2(3-1)
Feyenoord - Heracles Almelo 2-1(1-0)
Fortuna Sittard - VVV-Venlo 1-1(1-0)
PSV Eindhoven - De Graafschap 2-1(0-1)
Willem II - PEC Zwolle 2-0(1-0)
SC Heerenveen - FC Groningen 1-1(1-0)
FC Utrecht - SBV Vitesse 0-0

Round 31 [19-21.04.2019]
Heracles Almelo - SC Heerenveen 2-1(1-1)
FC Emmen - FC Utrecht 2-0(2-0)
FC Groningen - AFC Ajax 0-1(0-0)
SBV Vitesse - PEC Zwolle 4-1(1-1)
Feyenoord - AZ Alkmaar 2-1(0-1)
VVV-Venlo - De Graafschap 4-1(1-1)
SBV Excelsior - Willem II 1-1(0-1)
Fortuna Sittard - NAC Breda 2-1(1-0)
PSV Eindhoven - ADO Den Haag 3-1(1-0)

Round 32 [23-25.04.2019]
De Graafschap - FC Emmen 1-0(1-0)
SC Heerenveen - VVV-Venlo 2-2(1-0)
AZ Alkmaar - Heracles Almelo 2-1(1-1)
AFC Ajax - SBV Vitesse 4-2(1-0)
FC Utrecht - Fortuna Sittard 2-1(1-1)
NAC Breda - Feyenoord 0-4(0-2)
ADO Den Haag - SBV Excelsior 3-1(2-1)
Willem II - PSV Eindhoven 0-3(0-2)
PEC Zwolle - Groningen 3-2(0-1) [29.04.19]

Round 33 [15.05.2019]
FC Utrecht - SC Heerenveen 3-1(1-1)
NAC Breda - PEC Zwolle 0-0
PSV Eindhoven - Heracles Almelo 3-1(1-1)
Fortuna Sittard - Feyenoord 1-4(1-1)
SBV Excelsior - AZ Alkmaar 4-2(1-1)
De Graafschap - AFC Ajax 1-4(1-2)
VVV-Venlo - SBV Vitesse 1-3(0-2)
ADO Den Haag - Willem II 6-2(1-1)
FC Emmen - FC Groningen 1-0(1-0)

Round 34 [12.05.2019]
SC Heerenveen - NAC Breda 2-1(0-0)
Feyenoord - ADO Den Haag 0-2(0-1)
AZ Alkmaar - PSV Eindhoven 1-0(0-0)
Willem II - FC Emmen 2-3(2-1)
PEC Zwolle - VVV-Venlo 2-4(1-0)
AFC Ajax - FC Utrecht 4-1(2-1)
Heracles Almelo - SBV Excelsior 4-5(1-2)
SBV Vitesse - De Graafschap 6-1(2-0)
FC Groningen - Fortuna Sittard 3-0(1-0)

Final Standings							
1. **AFC Ajax Amsterdam**	34	28	2	4	119	- 32	86
2. PSV Eindhoven	34	26	5	3	98	- 26	83
3. Feyenoord Rotterdam	34	20	5	9	75	- 41	65
4. AZ Alkmaar	34	17	7	10	64	- 43	58
5. SBV Vitesse Arnhem	34	14	11	9	70	- 51	53
6. FC Utrecht	34	15	8	11	60	- 51	53
7. Heracles Almelo	34	15	3	16	61	- 68	48
8. FC Groningen	34	13	6	15	39	- 41	45
9. ADO Den Haag	34	12	9	13	58	- 63	45
10. Willem II Tilburg	34	13	5	16	58	- 72	44
11. SC Heerenveen	34	10	11	13	64	- 73	41
12. VVV-Venlo	34	11	8	15	47	- 63	41
13. PEC Zwolle	34	11	6	17	44	- 57	39
14. FC Emmen	34	10	8	16	41	- 72	38
15. Fortuna Sittard	34	9	7	18	50	- 80	34
16. SBV Excelsior Rotterdam (*Relegation Play-offs*)	34	9	6	19	46	- 79	33
17. VBV De Graafschap Doetinchem (*Rel Play-offs*)	34	8	5	21	38	- 75	29
18. NAC Breda (*Relegated*)	34	5	8	21	29	- 74	23

Top goalscorers:

28 Luuk de Jong
PSV Eindhoven

28 Dušan Tadić (SRB)
AFC Ajax Amsterdam

19 Adrián Dalmau Vaquer (ESP)
Heracles Almelo

17 Nasser el Khayati
ADO Den Haag

17 Hirving Rodrigo Lozano Bahena (MEX)
PSV Eindhoven

Please note: teams ranked 5-8 were qualified for the European competition play-offs.

European competition play-offs

Semi-Finals [18-21.05.2019]	Heracles Almelo - FC Utrecht	0-2	0-3
	FC Groningen - SBV Vitesse Arnhem	2-1	1-3
Final [24-28.05.2019]	**FC Utrecht** - SBV Vitesse Arnhem	1-1	2-0

NATIONAL CUP
KNVB Beker 2018/2019

First Round [25-27.09.2018]

Amsterdamsche FC - SC Telstar IJmuiden	5-0(1-0)
RKC Waalwijk - NAC Breda	2-0(1-0)
VV Noordwijk - Sparta Rotterdam	3-2(1-2)
FC Den Bosch - Heracles Almelo	1-2(1-1)
DVS'33 Ermelo - SV Roda JC Kerkrade	0-6(0-3)
VV Sint Bavo - VBV De Graafschap Doetinchem	3-3 aet; 3-5 pen
SVV Scheveningen - SC Cambuur Leeuwarden	2-3(2-1,2-2)
Koninklijke HFC Haarlem - Harkemase Boys	4-0(1-0)
Helmond Sport - Fortuna Sittard	0-5(0-1)
Go Ahead Eagles Deventer - FC Eindhoven	2-0(0-0)
Almere City FC - FC Dordrecht	1-0(1-0)
ODIN '59 Heemskerk - FC Lisse	1-0(1-0)
FC Volendam - Willem II Tilburg	1-2(1-1)
RKVV Westlandia - VVV-Venlo	0-3(0-1)
Rijnsburgse Boys - Tot Ons Plezier Oss	1-1 aet; 4-5 pen
SV Spakenburg - SV DFS Opheusden	3-0(1-0)
Kozakken Boys Werkendam - ONS Sneek	3-1(3-1)
SBV Excelsior Rotterdam - NEC Nijmegen	2-3(2-1,2-2)
VV OJC Rosmalen - ADO Den Haag	0-6(0-3)
VV Excelsior Maassluis - PSV Eindhoven	0-4(0-2)
RKAV Volendam - SBV Vitesse Arnhem	1-2(0-2)
VV Eemdijk - ASWH Ido-Ambacht	1-4(0-2)
VV DOVO Veenendaal - SV Urk	2-2 aet; 4-5 pen
VV Katwijk - SC Heerenveen	0-1(0-0,0-0)
RKSV Groene Ster – SV TEC Tiel	2-1(1-0)
VV Staphorst - PEC Zwolle	0-1(0-1)
HVV Te Werve - AFC Ajax Amsterdam	0-7(0-4)
MVV Alcides - AZ Alkmaar	0-6(0-4)
OFC Oostzaan - FC Emmen	1-3(0-1)
FC Groningen - FC Twente Enschede	0-2(0-1)
FC Utrecht - MVV Maastricht	2-0(0-0)
VV Gemert - Feyenoord Rotterdam	0-4(0-2)

Second Round [30.10.-01.11.2018]

PSV Eindhoven - RKC Waalwijk	2-3(1-1,2-2)
Amsterdamsche FC - Tot Ons Plezier Oss	1-0(0-0)
Kozakken Boys Werkendam - Almere City FC	2-1(1-0)
FC Twente Enschede - VV Noordwijk	4-2(3-1)
SC Cambuur Leeuw. - Koninklijke HFC Haarlem	2-1(1-0)
SV Urk - SV Roda JC Kerkrade	0-1(0-0)
VBV De Graafschap Doetinchem - PEC Zwolle	2-5(0-3)
Heracles Almelo - SBV Vitesse Arnhem	0-2(0-1)
Willem II Tilburg - SV Spakenburg	5-0(2-0)
FC Utrecht - ASWH Ido-Ambacht	5-1(2-1)
FC Emmen - ODIN '59 Heemskerk	1-3(1-1)
AZ Alkmaar - VVV-Venlo	2-0(0-0)
RKSV Groene Ster - SC Heerenveen	1-3(1-0)
AFC Ajax Amsterdam - Go Ahead Eagles Deventer	3-0(2-0)
NEC Nijmegen - Fortuna Sittard	2-3(2-1)
Feyenoord Rotterdam - ADO Den Haag	5-1(2-1)

1/8-Finals [18-20.12.2018]

Willem II Tilburg - Amsterdamsche FC	3-0(3-0)
FC Twente Enschede - RKC Waalwijk	2-0(1-0)
AZ Alkmaar - PEC Zwolle	5-0(3-0)
ODIN '59 Heemskerk - SC Heerenveen	1-3(1-1)
Fortuna Sittard - SC Cambuur Leeuwarden	2-1(1-0)
SV Roda JC Kerkrade - AFC Ajax Amsterdam	1-1 aet; 2-4 pen
Kozakken Boys Werkendam - SBV Vitesse Arnhem	1-2(0-1)
Feyenoord Rotterdam - FC Utrecht	1-0(1-0)

Quarter-Finals [22-24.01.2019]

AZ Alkmaar - SBV Vitesse Arnhem	2-0(1-0)
FC Twente Enschede - Willem II Tilburg	2-3(0-0)
Feyenoord Rotterdam - Fortuna Sittard	4-1(1-0)
AFC Ajax Amsterdam - SC Heerenveen	3-1(3-0)

Semi-Finals [27-28.02.2019]

Feyenoord Rotterdam - AFC Ajax Amsterdam	0-3(0-1)
Willem II Tilburg - AZ Alkmaar	1-1 aet; 2-1 pen

Final

05.05.2019; Stadion Feijenoord, Rotterdam; Referee: Serdar Gözübüyük; Attendance: 45,709

AFC Ajax Amsterdam - Willem II Tilburg **4-0(2-0)**

Ajax: André Onana, Rasmus Nissen Kristensen, Matthijs de Ligt (Cap), Daley Blind, Nicolás Alejandro Tagliafico, Noussair Mazraoui, Donny van de Beek, Frenkie de Jong (79.Lasse Schöne), Hakim Ziyech (58.David Neres Campos), Dirk Jan Klaas Huntelaar, Dušan Tadić (73.Zakaria Labyad). Trainer: Erik ten Hag.

Willem II: Timon Wellenreuther, Fernando Lewis, Thomas Meißner, Jordens Peters (Cap) (62.Daniel Crowley), Freek Heerkens, Damil Dankerlui (62.Marios Vrousai), Renato Fabrizio Tapia Cortijo, Pol Llonch Puyaltó, Diego José Palacios Espinoza, Alexander Isak, Evangelos Pavlidis. Trainer: Adrianus Cornelis Koster.

Goals: 1-0 Daley Blind (38), 2-0 Dirk Jan Klaas Huntelaar (39), 3-0 Dirk Jan Klaas Huntelaar (67), 4-0 Rasmus Nissen Kristensen (76).

THE CLUBS 2018/2019

Alles Door Oefening Den Haag

Founded: 01.02.1905
Stadium: Stadion "Cars Jeans", Den Haag (15,000)

Goalkeepers:	DOB	M	(s)	G
Indy Groothuizen	22.07.1996	12		
Mike Havekotte	12.09.1995		(1)	
Robert Zwinkels	04.05.1983	22		
Defenders:	**DOB**	**M**	**(s)**	**G**
Tom Beugelsdijk	07.08.1990	25	(1)	
Wilfried Kanon (CIV)	06.07.1993	29	(1)	1
Bas Kuipers	17.08.1994	2	(1)	
Nick Kuipers	08.10.1992	5	(3)	1
Aaron Meijers	28.10.1987	31		2
Shaquille Pinas	19.03.1998	8	(11)	
Giovanni Troupée	20.03.1998	21		1
Midfielders:	**DOB**	**M**	**(s)**	**G**
Danny Bakker	16.01.1995	24		2
Kyle Ebecilio	17.02.1994		(1)	
Nasser el Khayati	07.02.1989	33		17
Erik Falkenburg	05.05.1988	14	(10)	5
John Goossens	25.07.1988	15	(6)	1
Donny Gorter	15.06.1988	1	(1)	
Lex Immers	08.06.1986	34		7
Dion Malone	13.02.1989	24	(5)	1
Forwards:	**DOB**	**M**	**(s)**	**G**
Sheraldo Becker	09.02.1995	33		7
Yahya Boussakou	04.03.2000		(1)	
Thijmen Goppel	16.02.1997		(22)	
Elson Quincy Hooi (CUW)	01.10.1991	14	(7)	1
Melvyn Lorenzen (UGA)	26.11.1994	11	(11)	2
Tomáš Necid (CZE)	13.08.1989	16	(10)	9
Zhang Yuning (CHN)	05.01.1997		(6)	
Trainer:	**DOB**	**M**		
Alfons Groenendijk	17.05.1964	34		

Amsterdamsche Football Club Ajax

Founded: 18.03.1900
Stadium: "Johan Cruyff" Arena, Amsterdam (54,033)

Goalkeepers:	DOB	M	(s)	G
Kostas Lamprou (GRE)	18.09.1991	1	(1)	
André Onana (CMR)	02.04.1996	33		
Defenders:	**DOB**	**M**	**(s)**	**G**
Daley Blind	09.03.1990	34		5
Matthijs de Ligt	12.08.1999	33		3
Rasmus Nissen Kristensen (DEN)	11.07.1997	5	(7)	
Lisandro Magallán (ARG)	27.09.1993	1	(1)	
Noussair Mazraoui (MAR)	14.11.1997	26	(2)	1
Perr Schuurs	26.11.1999		(1)	
Daley Sinkgraven	04.07.1995	1	(8)	
Nicolás Alejandro Tagliafico (ARG)	31.08.1992	29		2
Joël Veltman	15.01.1992	4	(5)	1
Max Wöber (AUT)	04.02.1998	4	(4)	
Midfielders:	**DOB**	**M**	**(s)**	**G**
Frenkie de Jong	12.05.1997	30	(1)	3
Dani de Wit	28.01.1998		(4)	
Carel Eiting	11.02.1998	4	(3)	
Jurgen Ekkelenkamp	05.04.2000		(3)	
Ryan Gravenberch	15.06.2002		(1)	
Zakaria Labyad (MAR)	09.03.1993	2	(10)	1
Lasse Schöne (DEN)	27.05.1986	27	(3)	5
Donny van de Beek	18.04.1997	28	(6)	9
Hakim Ziyech (MAR)	19.03.1993	29		16
Forwards:	**DOB**	**M**	**(s)**	**G**
David Neres Campos (BRA)	03.03.1997	20	(9)	8
Kasper Dolberg (DEN)	06.10.1997	15	(10)	11
Dirk Jan Klaas Huntelaar	12.08.1983	13	(15)	16
Dennis Johnsen (NOR)	17.02.1998		(1)	
Noa Lang	17.06.1999		(3)	
Kaj Sierhuis	27.04.1998	1	(1)	
Dušan Tadić (SRB)	20.11.1988	34		28
Lassina Traoré (BFA)	12.01.2001		(1)	
Trainer:	**DOB**	**M**		
Erik ten Hag	02.02.1970	34		

Alkmaar Zaanstreek Alkmaar

Founded: 10.05.1967
Stadium: Stadion AFAS, Alkmaar (17,023)

Goalkeepers:	DOB	M	(s)	G
Marco Bizot	10.03.1991	34		
Defenders:	**DOB**	**M**	**(s)**	**G**
Léon Bergsma	25.01.1997		(2)	
Pantelis Hatzidiakos (GRE)	18.01.1997	13	(4)	1
Teun Koopmeiners	28.02.1998	32		8
Thomas Ouwejan	30.09.1996	31		2
Jonas Svensson (NOR)	06.03.1993	32		1
Ricardo van Rhijn	13.06.1991	7	(7)	1
Ron Vlaar	16.02.1985	28		2
Owen Wijndal	28.11.1999	3	(5)	
Stijn Wuytens (BEL)	08.10.1989	2	(6)	
Midfielders:	**DOB**	**M**	**(s)**	**G**
Kenzo Goudmijn	18.12.2001		(1)	
Jeremy Helmer	03.07.1997		(1)	
Adam Maher	20.07.1993	21	(4)	1
Fredrik Midtsjø (NOR)	11.08.1993	33		1
Guus Til	22.12.1997	33		12
Marko Vejinović	03.02.1990	1	(3)	
Forwards:	**DOB**	**M**	**(s)**	**G**
Myron Boadu	14.01.2001	5	(3)	3
Ferdy Druijf	12.02.1998		(2)	
Albert Guðmundsson (ISL)	15.06.1997	14	(11)	6
Oussama Idrissi (MAR)	26.02.1996	31	(1)	8
Bjørn Johnsen (NOR)	06.11.1991	7	(15)	6
Dorin Rotariu (ROU)	29.07.1995		(8)	
Mats Seuntjens	17.04.1992	27	(5)	6
Calvin Stengs	18.12.1998	20	(1)	3
Trainer:	**DOB**	**M**		
John van den Brom	04.10.1966	34		

Vereniging Betaald Voetbal De Graafschap Doetinchem

Founded: 01.02.1954
Stadium: Stadion De Vijverberg, Doetinchem (12,600)

Goalkeepers:	DOB	M	(s)	G
Nigel Bertrams	08.01.1993	10	(1)	
Agil Etemadi (IRN)	23.04.1987	2	(1)	
Hidde Jurjus	09.02.1994	22		
Defenders:	**DOB**	**M**	**(s)**	**G**
Myenty Abena	12.12.1994	10	(2)	
Ruben Ligeon	24.05.1992	1	(1)	
Lars Nieuwpoort	29.10.1994	6	(4)	
Sven Nieuwpoort	13.04.1993	18	(1)	
Leeroy Owusu	13.08.1996	34		1
Bart Straalman	22.08.1996	25	(1)	1
Jordy Tutuarima	28.04.1993	31	(1)	
Ted van de Pavert	06.01.1992	20	(1)	
Midfielders:	**DOB**	**M**	**(s)**	**G**
Erik Bakker	21.03.1990	13	(6)	
Youssef el Jebli	27.12.1992	30	(2)	10
Robert Klaasen	06.09.1993	6	(4)	
Azor Matusiwa	28.04.1998	16		
Stef Nijland	10.08.1988	10	(4)	2
Frank Olijve	07.03.1989	12	(6)	1
Javier Vet	09.09.1993	17	(4)	1
Forwards:	**DOB**	**M**	**(s)**	**G**
Nabil Bahoui (SWE)	05.02.1991	3	(4)	
Charlison Benschop (CUW)	21.08.1989	12	(2)	3
Delano Burgzorg	07.11.1998	15	(11)	5
Mohamed Hamdaoui	10.06.1993	1	(3)	
Furdjel Narsingh	13.03.1988	21	(7)	3
Fabian Serrarens	09.02.1991	20	(7)	7
Jordy Thomassen	15.04.1993	3	(9)	
Daryl van Mieghem	05.12.1989	16	(17)	1
Trainer:	**DOB**	**M**		
Henk de Jong	27.08.1964	34		

Football Club Emmen

Founded: 21.08.1925
Stadium: De Oude Meerdijk, Emmen (8,600)

Goalkeepers:	DOB	M	(s)	G
Kjell Scherpen	23.01.2000	34		
Dennis Telgenkamp	09.05.1987		(1)	
Defenders:	**DOB**	**M**	**(s)**	**G**
Nick Bakker	21.07.1992	33		1
Caner Çavlan	05.02.1992	33	(1)	4
Kjelt Engbers	14.09.1999		(1)	
Stef Gronsveld	11.01.1996	9	(3)	1
Gersom Klok	07.10.1990	16	(1)	
Nick Kuipers	08.10.1992	8	(2)	
Andrej Lukić (CRO)	02.04.1994	6	(1)	
Nico Neidhart (GER)	27.09.1994	2	(4)	
Tim Siekman	25.05.1990	8	(5)	
Easah Suliman (ENG)	26.01.1998		(3)	
Keziah Veendorp	17.02.1997	25	(3)	1
Midfielders:	**DOB**	**M**	**(s)**	**G**
Alexander Bannink	20.02.1990	20	(4)	4
Hilal Ben Moussa	22.05.1992	17	(1)	1
Glenn Bijl	13.07.1995	32		2
Henk Bos	12.11.1992		(8)	
Michael Chacón	11.04.1994	29	(2)	2
Robbert de Vos	26.05.1996		(3)	
Wouter Marinus	18.02.1995	3	(8)	
Reuven Niemeijer	27.03.1995	9	(10)	2
Forwards:	**DOB**	**M**	**(s)**	**G**
Jafar Arias (CUW)	16.06.1995	19	(14)	4
Sven Braken	12.06.1993	6	(6)	2
Michael de Leeuw	07.10.1986	16		3
Anco Jansen	09.03.1989	28	(1)	5
Nicklas Pedersen (DEN)	10.10.1987	7	(5)	4
Cas Peters	13.05.1993		(1)	
Luciano Slagveer	05.10.1993	14	(10)	3
Trainer:	**DOB**	**M**		
Dick Lukkien	28.03.1972	34		

Stichting Betaald Voetbal Excelsior Rotterdam

Founded: 23.07.1902
Stadium: Stadion "Van Donge & De Roo", Rotterdam (4,500)

Goalkeepers:	**DOB**	**M**	**(s)**	**G**
Alessandro Damen	17.05.1990	20	(3)	
Sonny Stevens	22.06.1992	14		
Defenders:	**DOB**	**M**	**(s)**	**G**
Lorenzo Burnet	11.01.1991	28	(1)	
Jeffry Fortes (CPV)	22.03.1989	31	(1)	4
Siebe Horemans (BEL)	02.06.1998	9		
Jurgen Mattheij	01.04.1993	32		3
Hervé Matthys (BEL)	19.01.1996	22		
Thomas Oude Kotte	20.03.1996	18	(3)	
Robin van der Meer	21.02.1995	3	(13)	1
Midfielders:	**DOB**	**M**	**(s)**	**G**
Redouan el Hankouri	03.02.2001		(1)	
Anouar Hadouir	14.09.1982	2	(9)	
Doğucan Haspolat	11.02.2000	4	(10)	
Ryan Koolwijk	08.08.1985	32		3
Ali Messaoud	13.04.1991	28	(2)	7
Jerdy Schouten	12.01.1997	31		1
Forwards:	**DOB**	**M**	**(s)**	**G**
Mikael Anderson (ISL)	01.07.1998	7	(10)	1
Luigi Bruins	09.03.1987	28	(1)	6
Jinty Caenepeel (BEL)	18.07.1996		(1)	
Dennis Eckert Ayensa (GER)	09.01.1997	3	(9)	2
Marcus Edwards (ENG)	03.12.1998	19	(6)	2
Mounir El Hamdaoui (MAR)	14.07.1984	16	(10)	4
Carlito Fermina	06.02.2000		(2)	
Denis Mahmudov (MKD)	11.06.1989	6	(12)	3
Elías Már Ómarsson (ISL)	18.01.1995	21	(2)	7
Trainer:	**DOB**	**M**		
Adrie Poldervaart	20.12.1970	28		
André Hoekstra [08.04.2019]	05.04.1962	1		
Ricardo Moniz [08.04.2019]	17.06.1964	5		

Feyenoord Rotterdam

Founded: 19.07.1908
Stadium: Stadion Feijenoord, Rotterdam (51,177)

Goalkeepers:	**DOB**	**M**	**(s)**	**G**
Justin Bijlow	22.01.1998	16		
Joris Delle (FRA)	29.03.1990	1	(1)	
Kenneth Vermeer	10.01.1986	17	(1)	
Defenders:	**DOB**	**M**	**(s)**	**G**
Eric Fernando Botteghin (BRA)	31.08.1987	20	(2)	2
Lutsharel Geertruida	18.07.2000		(2)	
Ridgeciano Haps	12.06.1993	6	(3)	
Tyrell Malacia	17.08.1999	16	(1)	3
Rhu-Endly Aurelio Jean-Carlo "Cuco" Martina (CUW)	25.09.1989	11		
Bart Nieuwkoop	07.03.1996	6	(7)	
Jerry St. Juste	19.10.1996	21	(2)	3
Renato Fabrizio Tapia Cortijo (PER)	28.07.1995	1	(3)	
Sven van Beek	28.07.1994	21	(1)	
Jan-Arie van der Heijden	03.03.1988	23	(1)	2
Calvin Verdonk	26.04.1997	12		1
Midfielders:	**DOB**	**M**	**(s)**	**G**
Yassin Ayoub (MAR)	06.03.1994		(16)	2
Wouter Burger	16.02.2001		(1)	
Jordy Clasie	27.06.1991	33		1
Orkun Kökçü (TUR)	29.12.2000	5	(6)	3
Jens Toornstra	04.04.1989	28	(4)	8
Tonny Emilio Trindade de Vilhena	03.01.1995	32	(1)	6
Forwards:	**DOB**	**M**	**(s)**	**G**
Steven Berghuis	19.12.1991	32	(1)	12
Jean-Paul Boëtius	22.03.1994	1		
Mohammed el Hankouri (MAR)	01.07.1997		(5)	
Nicolai Jørgensen (DEN)	15.01.1991	15	(9)	7
Sam Larsson (SWE)	10.04.1993	29	(3)	6
Luis Sinisterra (COL)	17.06.1999		(5)	
Robin van Persie	06.08.1983	23	(2)	16
Dylan Vente	09.05.1999	5	(8)	1
Trainer:	**DOB**	**M**		
Giovanni Christiaan van Bronckhorst	05.02.1975	34		

Fortuna Sittard

Founded: 01.07.1968
Stadium: Fortuna Sittard Stadion, Sittard (10,300)

Goalkeepers:	**DOB**	**M**	**(s)**	**G**
Alexei Koşelev (MDA)	19.11.1993	34		
Defenders:	**DOB**	**M**	**(s)**	**G**
Alessandro Ciranni (BEL)	28.06.1996	13	(4)	
Wessel Dammers	01.03.1995	17		1
Mahamadou Dembélé (FRA)	10.04.1999	1	(2)	
Clint Essers	21.01.1997	7	(8)	
Kai Heerings	12.01.1990	21		
Calvin Mac-Intosch	09.08.1989	12		
Michael Gonçalves Pinto „Mica" (POR)	04.06.1993	27	(1)	
Branislav Niňaj (SVK)	17.05.1994	21		3
Marco Ospitalieri (BEL)	06.04.1992	7	(3)	
Rubén Alejandro Ramírez Dos Ramos (VEN)	18.10.1995	3	(4)	
Midfielders:	**DOB**	**M**	**(s)**	**G**
André Filipe Cunha Vidigal (POR)	17.08.1998	3	(7)	2
Andrija Balić (CRO)	11.08.1997	10	(3)	1
Amadou Ciss (SEN)	07.09.1999		(10)	
Mark Diemers	11.10.1993	34		7
Ahmed El Messaoudi (MAR)	03.08.1995	22	(7)	5
Lars Hutten	18.03.1990	10	(15)	2
José Rodríguez Martínez (ESP)	16.12.1994	23	(1)	2
Jorrit Smeets	25.03.1995	28	(4)	2
Anthony Syhre (GER)	18.03.1995	1		
Forwards:	**DOB**	**M**	**(s)**	**G**
Djibril Dianessy (FRA)	29.03.1996		(2)	
Áron Dobos (HUN)	08.06.2000		(2)	
Lazaros Lamprou (GRE)	19.12.1997	19	(5)	7
Lisandro Semedo (POR)	12.03.1996	23	(5)	3
Andrija Novakovich (USA)	21.09.1996	27	(2)	9
Finn Stokkers	18.04.1996	10	(8)	5
Gavin Vlijter	12.02.1997	1	(2)	
Agim Zeka (ALB)	06.09.1998		(1)	
Trainer:	**DOB**	**M**		
René Eijer	01.01.1963	34		

Football Club Groningen

Founded: 16.06.1971
Stadium: Stadion Noordlease, Groningen (22,550)

Goalkeepers:	DOB	M	(s)	G
Sergio Padt	06.06.1990	34		
Defenders:	**DOB**	**M**	**(s)**	**G**
Amir Absalem	19.06.1997	2	(1)	
Julian Chabot (GER)	12.02.1998	26	(2)	1
Tim Handwerker (GER)	19.05.1998	31		
Mike te Wierik	08.06.1992	33		
Deyovaisio Zeefuik	11.03.1998	30		1
Midfielders:	**DOB**	**M**	**(s)**	**G**
Iliass Bel Hassani	16.09.1992	12	(2)	1
Thomas Bruns	07.01.1992	12	(3)	2
Ritsu Doan (JPN)	16.06.1998	30		5
Jesper Drost	11.01.1993	2		
Ajdin Hrustić (AUS)	05.07.1996	10	(8)	
Samir Memišević (BIH)	13.08.1993	33		4
Ludovit Reis	01.06.2000	26	(3)	1
Tom van de Looi	02.07.1999	7	(10)	
Daniël van Kaam	23.06.2000		(1)	
Django Warmerdam	02.09.1995	21	(3)	2
Forwards:	**DOB**	**M**	**(s)**	**G**
Carlos Uriel Antuna Romero (MEX)	21.08.1997	2	(7)	
Michael Breij	15.01.1997	5	(4)	1
Zander Mateo Cassierra Cabezas (COL)	13.04.1997	7	(3)	1
Mohammed el Hankouri (MAR)	01.07.1997	3	(13)	1
Tim Freriks	02.10.1998		(6)	
Paul Gladon	18.03.1992	4	(10)	5
Mimoun Mahi (MAR)	13.03.1994	23	(3)	7
Ahmad Mendes Moreira	27.06.1995	1	(12)	1
Jannik Pohl (DEN)	06.04.1996	3	(4)	1
Kaj Sierhuis	27.04.1998	15	(2)	3
Tom van Weert	07.06.1990	2		
Trainer:	**DOB**	**M**		
Danny Buijs	21.06.1982	34		

Sportclub Heerenveen

Founded: 20.07.1920
Stadium: Stadion "Abe Lenstra", Heerenveen (26,100)

Goalkeepers:	DOB	M	(s)	G
Warner Hahn	15.06.1992	34		
Defenders:	**DOB**	**M**	**(s)**	**G**
Dave Bulthuis	28.06.1990	13		2
Ibrahim Drešević (KVX)	24.01.1997	2	(4)	
Sherel Floranus	23.08.1998	16	(1)	
Jizz Hornkamp	07.03.1998	8	(10)	2
Daniel Høegh (DEN)	06.01.1991	31		2
Nicolai Næss (NOR)	18.01.1993		(1)	
Kik Pierie	20.07.2000	31		2
Doke Schmidt	07.04.1992	10	(3)	
Lucas Woudenberg	25.04.1994	24	(2)	
Midfielders:	**DOB**	**M**	**(s)**	**G**
Jordy Bruijn	23.07.1997		(8)	
Yuki Kobayashi (JPN)	24.04.1992	25	(4)	
Rodney Kongolo	09.01.1998	2	(7)	
Ben Rienstra	05.06.1990	30	(2)	4
Stijn Schaars	11.01.1984	7	(2)	
Morten Thorsby (NOR)	05.05.1996	13	(7)	5
Pelle van Amersfoort	01.04.1996	11	(17)	4
Michel Vlap	02.06.1997	33	(1)	16
Forwards:	**DOB**	**M**	**(s)**	**G**
Dennis Johnsen (NOR)	17.02.1998	6	(7)	
Sam Lammers	30.04.1997	30	(1)	16
Nemanja Mihajlović (SRB)	19.01.1996	8	(7)	1
Marco Rodrigo Rojas (NZL)	05.11.1991		(3)	
Mitchell van Bergen	27.08.1999	23	(7)	7
Arber Zeneli (KVX)	25.02.1995	17		3
Trainer:	**DOB**	**M**		
Jan Olde Riekerink	22.02.1963	29		
Johnny Jansen [10.04.2019]	02.03.1975	5		

Heracles Almelo

Founded: 1903
Stadium: Stadion Polman, Almelo (12,080)

Goalkeepers:	DOB	M	(s)	G
Janis Blaswich (GER)	02.05.1991	33		
Michael Brouwer	21.01.1993	1	(1)	
Defenders:	**DOB**	**M**	**(s)**	**G**
Tim Breukers	04.11.1987	24	(2)	
Lennart Czyborra (GER)	03.05.1999	16	(4)	
Wout Droste	20.05.1989	10	(2)	
Mats Knoester	19.11.1998	1	(2)	
Robin Pröpper	23.09.1993	5		
Maximilian Rossmann (GER)	06.05.1995	29		1
Stephen Sama (GER)	05.03.1993	4	(4)	
Tim van de Berg	23.11.1997		(2)	
Dario Van Den Buijs (BEL)	12.09.1995	27	(1)	1
Bart van Hintum	16.01.1987	21	(3)	1
Midfielders:	**DOB**	**M**	**(s)**	**G**
Jesper Drost	11.01.1993	13	(8)	2
Lerin Duarte	11.08.1990	20	(9)	6
Alexander Merkel (KAZ)	22.02.1992	30	(2)	
Mohammed Osman (SYR)	01.01.1994	28	(3)	5
Yoëll van Nieff	17.06.1993	10	(5)	
Forwards:	**DOB**	**M**	**(s)**	**G**
Adrián Dalmau Vaquer (ESP)	27.03.1994	27	(4)	19
Dabney dos Santos	31.07.1996	5	(12)	
Zeki Erkılınç	22.01.1998		(1)	
Joey Konings	21.04.1998	5	(10)	2
Brandley Kuwas (CUW)	19.09.1992	31	(2)	10
Kristoffer Peterson (SWE)	28.11.1994	31	(2)	12
Silvester van der Water	30.09.1995	3	(9)	
Vincent Vermeij	09.08.1994		(8)	1
Trainer:	**DOB**	**M**		
Frank Wormuth (GER)	13.09.1960	34		

NOAD ADVENDO Combinatie Breda

Founded: 19.09.1992
Stadium: Stadion „Rat Verlegh", Breda (19,000)

Goalkeepers:	DOB	M	(s)	G
Mark Romano Birighitti (AUS)	17.04.1991	1		
Arijanet Murić (KVX)	07.11.1998	1		
Karol Niemczycki (POL)	05.07.1999	1		
Benjamin van Leer	09.04.1992	31		
Defenders:	**DOB**	**M**	**(s)**	**G**
Dorian Dervite (FRA)	25.07.1988	5		
Alex Gersbach (AUS)	08.05.1997	7		
Khalid Karami	29.12.1989	9	(1)	
Daan Klomp	10.08.1998	8	(1)	
Menno Koch	02.07.1994	33		2
Greg Leigh (ENG)	30.09.1994	14	(2)	1
Jethro Mashart	08.05.2000	2		
Karol Mets (EST)	16.05.1993	15		1
Erik Palmer-Brown (USA)	24.04.1997	18		1
Fabian Sporkslede	03.08.1993	11	(2)	
Pele van Anholt	23.04.1991	14	(2)	
Midfielders:	**DOB**	**M**	**(s)**	**G**
Yassine Azzagari	24.07.2001		(1)	
Jurich Carolina (CUW)	15.07.1998	6		
Grad Damen	14.08.1997	3	(1)	
Mounir el Allouchi	27.09.1994	21	(7)	
Luka Ilić (SRB)	02.07.1999	8	(8)	2
Anouar Kali	03.06.1991	20	(1)	
Ramon Lundqvist (SWE)	10.05.1997	16	(1)	
Gianluca Nijholt	14.02.1990	22		2
Marwin Reuvers	04.03.1999	2	(3)	
Jordan van der Gaag	03.01.1999		(2)	
Arno Verschueren (BEL)	08.04.1997	14	(4)	1
Forwards:	**DOB**	**M**	**(s)**	**G**
Sullay Kaikai (ENG)	26.08.1995	1	(5)	
Gervane Kastaneer (CUW)	09.06.1996	10	(11)	2
Giovanni Korte	01.08.1993	19	(7)	2
Robert Mühren	18.05.1989	3	(11)	
Paolo Fernandes Cantin (ESP)	19.08.1998	4	(4)	
Mikhail Rosheuvel	10.08.1990	27	(6)	5
Mitchell te Vrede	07.08.1991	28	(2)	10
Sydney van Hooijdonk	06.02.2000		(12)	
Trainer:	**DOB**	**M**		
Mitchell van der Gaag	22.11.1971	26		
Ruud Brood [22.03.2019]	19.10.1962	8		

Prins Hendrik Ende Desespereert Nimmer Combinatie Zwolle

Founded: 12.06.1910
Stadium: Stadion MAC³PARK, Zwolle (12,500)

Goalkeepers:	DOB	M	(s)	G
Diederik Boer	24.09.1980	6	(1)	
Mickey van der Hart	13.06.1994	28	(1)	
Defenders:	**DOB**	**M**	**(s)**	**G**
Kingsley Ehizibue	25.05.1995	32		1
Darryl Lachman (CUW)	11.11.1989	18	(2)	
Thomas Lam (FIN)	18.12.1993	25		4
Ruben Ligeon	24.05.1992	1		
Dirk Marcellis	13.04.1988	2		
Yuta Nakayama (JPN)	16.02.1997	2	(2)	
Kenneth Paal	24.06.1997	28	(1)	
Alessandro Tripaldelli (ITA)	09.02.1999	1	(1)	
Sepp van den Berg	20.12.2001	10	(5)	
Bram van Polen	11.10.1985	22		2
Midfielders:	**DOB**	**M**	**(s)**	**G**
Ouasim Bouy (MAR)	11.06.1993	12	(6)	
Pelle Clement	19.05.1996	17		
Rick Dekker	15.03.1995	12	(3)	1
Zian Flemming	01.08.1998	12	(13)	2
Denis Genreau (AUS)	21.05.1999	6	(4)	
Gustavo Hamer	24.06.1997	20	(3)	
Clint Leemans	15.09.1995	11	(10)	2
Younes Namli (DEN)	20.06.1994	32	(1)	4
Forwards:	**DOB**	**M**	**(s)**	**G**
Stanley Elbers	14.05.1992	3	(20)	1
Terell Ondaan	09.09.1993		(1)	
Gianluca Scamacca (ITA)	01.01.1999	1	(7)	
Lennart Thy (GER)	25.02.1992	15	(2)	9
Vito van Crooy	29.01.1996	27	(3)	9
Mike van Duinen	06.11.1991	31	(2)	8
Trainer:	**DOB**	**M**		
Johannes Nicolaas van't Schip	30.12.1963	16		
Gert-Peter de Gunst [19.12.2018]	23.11.1968	1		
Jaap Stam [28.12.2018]	17.07.1972	17		

Philips Sport Vereniging Eindhoven

Founded: 31.08.1913
Stadium: Stadion Philips, Eindhoven (36,500)

Goalkeepers:	DOB	M	(s)	G
Jeroen Zoet	06.01.1991	34		
Defenders:	**DOB**	**M**	**(s)**	**G**
Aziz Behich (AUS)	16.12.1990		(4)	
Denzel Dumfries	18.04.1996	34		4
Nicolas Isimat-Mirin (FRA)	15.11.1991	1		
José Ángel Esmoris Tasende „José Angeliño" (ESP)	04.01.1997	34		1
Trent Lucas Sainsbury (AUS)	05.01.1992	2	(3)	
Daniel Schwaab (GER)	23.08.1988	31		1
Jordan Teze	30.09.1999		(1)	
Nick Viergever	03.08.1989	34		3
Midfielders:	**DOB**	**M**	**(s)**	**G**
Érick Gabriel Gutiérrez Galaviz (MEX)	15.06.1995	5	(11)	3
Jorrit Hendrix	06.02.1995	27	(2)	1
Mohamed Ihattaren	12.02.2002	4	(8)	
Mauro Jaqueson Júnior Ferreira Dos Santos (BRA)	06.05.1999		(4)	
Gastón Rodrigo Pereiro López (URU)	11.06.1995	23	(4)	10
Bart Ramselaar	29.06.1996		(4)	
Dante Rigo (BEL)	11.12.1998	1	(4)	1
Pablo Paulino Rosario	07.01.1997	32		
Michal Sadílek (CZE)	31.05.1999	7	(4)	1
Forwards:	**DOB**	**M**	**(s)**	**G**
Zakaria Aboukhlal	18.02.2000		(1)	
Steven Charles Bergwijn	08.10.1997	33		14
Luuk de Jong	27.08.1990	34		28
Cody Gakpo	07.05.1999	2	(14)	1
Hirving Rodrigo Lozano Bahena (MEX)	30.07.1995	30		17
Donyell Malen	19.01.1999	6	(25)	10
Maximiliano Samuel Romero (ARG)	09.01.1999		(1)	
Matthias Verreth (BEL)	20.02.1998		(1)	
Trainer:	**DOB**	**M**		
Mark Peter Gertruda Andreas van Bommel	22.04.1977	34		

Football Club Utrecht

Founded: 01.07.1970
Stadium: Stadion Galgenwaard, Utrecht (23,750)

Goalkeepers:	DOB	M	(s)	G
David Jensen (DEN)	25.03.1992	33		
Maarten Paes	14.05.1998	1		
Defenders:	**DOB**	**M**	**(s)**	**G**
Emil Bergström (SWE)	19.05.1993	6	(3)	1
Nicolas Gavory (FRA)	16.02.1995	30	(1)	1
Leon Guwara (GER)	28.06.1996	9	(3)	
Willem Janssen	04.07.1986	32		6
Sean Klaiber	13.07.1994	33		2
Ramon Leeuwin	01.09.1987	1		
Timo Letschert	25.05.1993	29	(2)	2
Giovanni Troupée	20.03.1998	1		
Mark van der Maarel	12.08.1989	7	(9)	
Midfielders:	**DOB**	**M**	**(s)**	**G**
Riechedly Bazoer	12.10.1996	11	(1)	3
Urby Emanuelson	16.06.1986	21	(3)	4
Simon Gustafson (SWE)	11.01.1995	33		8
Rico Strieder (GER)	06.07.1992	2	(4)	
Sander van de Streek	24.03.1993	26	(7)	8
Joris van Overeem	01.06.1994	30	(1)	2
Forwards:	**DOB**	**M**	**(s)**	**G**
Jean-Christophe Bahebeck (FRA)	01.05.1993	8	(4)	3
Othman Boussaid (BEL)	07.03.2000	7	(10)	1
Cyriel Dessers (BEL)	08.12.1994	3	(8)	3
Lukas Görtler (GER)	15.06.1994	1	(13)	
Gyrano Kerk	02.12.1995	30	(3)	8
Michiel Kramer	03.12.1988	4	(4)	1
Simon Makienok (DEN)	21.11.1990		(3)	
Oussama Tannane (MAR)	23.03.1994	13	(2)	1
Nick Venema	09.04.1999	3	(12)	4
Trainer:	**DOB**	**M**		
Jean-Paul de Jong	17.10.1970	4		
Marinus Dijkhuizen [04.09.2018]	04.01.1972	-		
Dick Advocaat [12.09.2018]	27.09.1947	30		

Stichting Betaald Voetbal Vitesse Arnhem

Founded: 14.05.1892
Stadium: GelreDome, Arnhem (25,500)

Goalkeepers:	DOB	M	(s)	G
Eduardo dos Reis Carvalho (POR)	19.09.1982	27		
Remko Pasveer	08.11.1983	7		
Defenders:	**DOB**	**M**	**(s)**	**G**
Alexander Büttner	11.02.1989	26	(2)	2
Max Oliver Clark (ENG)	19.01.1996	18	(5)	1
Jake Clarke-Salter (ENG)	22.09.1997	28		1
Danilho Doekhi	30.06.1998	15	(5)	
Vyacheslav Karavaev (RUS)	20.05.1995	33		1
Rasmus Thelander (DEN)	09.07.1991	5	(4)	
Maikel van der Werff	22.04.1989	21	(1)	3
Midfielders:	**DOB**	**M**	**(s)**	**G**
Mukhtar Abdullahi Ali (KSA)	30.10.1997	2	(4)	1
Matúš Bero (SVK)	06.09.1995	29	(1)	9
Thomas Bruns	07.01.1992	1	(7)	
Navarone Foor	04.02.1992	27	(3)	5
Richie Musaba	06.12.2000		(1)	1
Martin Ødegaard (NOR)	17.12.1998	29	(2)	8
Thulani Caleeb Serero (RSA)	11.04.1990	30	(1)	1
Forwards:	**DOB**	**M**	**(s)**	**G**
Roy Beerens	22.12.1987	12	(4)	1
Thomas Buitink	14.01.2000	8	(9)	7
Oussama Darfalou (ALG)	29.09.1993	14	(11)	7
Mohammed Dauda (GHA)	20.02.1998	6	(6)	3
Hilary Chukwah Gong (NGA)	10.10.1998		(6)	
Bryan Linssen	08.10.1990	28	(2)	12
Richonell Margaret	07.07.2000		(4)	
Tim Matavž (SVN)	13.01.1989	8	(6)	6
Charly Musonda (BEL)	15.10.1996		(1)	
Mitchell van Bergen	27.08.1999		(3)	
Trainer:	**DOB**	**M**		
Leonid Slutski (RUS)	04.05.1971	34		

Venlose Voetbal Vereniging Venlo

Founded: 07.02.1903
Stadium: Stadion Seacon, Venlo (8,000)

Goalkeepers:	DOB	M	(s)	G
Lars Unnerstall (GER)	20.07.1990	33		
Delano van Crooy	05.06.1991	1	(1)	
Defenders:	**DOB**	**M**	**(s)**	**G**
Axel Borgmann (GER)	08.07.1994	3	(4)	
Tristan Dekker	27.03.1998	3	(7)	
Roel Janssen	16.06.1990	21	(2)	
Josimar Do Sameiro Spencer Silva Lima (CPV)	02.08.1989	2		
Evren Korkmaz (TUR)	27.04.1997		(2)	
Chris Kum	13.09.1985	18	(6)	
Jerold Promes	09.03.1984	22		
Nils Röseler (GER)	10.02.1992	34		1
Moreno Rutten	28.04.1993	32		1
Damian van Bruggen	18.03.1996	6	(12)	
Midfielders:	**DOB**	**M**	**(s)**	**G**
Simon Janssen	25.09.2000		(1)	
Evert Linthorst	03.03.2000	7	(6)	
Danny Post	07.04.1989	28		3
Ralf Seuntjens	17.04.1989	24	(5)	2
Sem Steijn	12.11.2001		(2)	1
Tino-Sven Sušić (BIH)	13.02.1992	25	(2)	5
Peter van Ooijen	16.02.1992	18	(7)	2
Forwards:	**DOB**	**M**	**(s)**	**G**
Jay-Roy Grot	13.03.1998	19	(14)	6
Patrick Joosten	14.04.1996	21	(9)	6
Peniel Mlapa (TOG)	20.02.1991	29	(1)	15
Johnathan Opoku	18.04.1990	23	(6)	5
Martin Samuelsen (NOR)	17.04.1997	5	(5)	
Trainer:	**DOB**	**M**		
Maurice Steijn	20.11.1973	34		

Willem II Tilburg

Founded: 12.08.1896
Stadium: Stadion „Koning Willem II", Tilburg (14,500)

Goalkeepers:	**DOB**	**M**	**(s)**	**G**
Mattijs Branderhorst	31.12.1993	1		
Timon Wellenreuther (GER)	03.12.1995	29		
Michael Woud (NZL)	16.01.1999	4		
Defenders:	**DOB**	**M**	**(s)**	**G**
Damil Dankerlui	24.08.1996	29	(3)	3
Freek Heerkens	13.09.1989	27	(1)	1
Fernando Lewis	31.01.1993	26		2
James McGarry (NZL)	09.04.1998	2	(3)	
Thomas Meißner (GER)	26.03.1991	22	(3)	1
Diego José Palacios Espinoza (ECU)	12.07.1999	27		
Jordens Peters	03.05.1987	17	(2)	
Victor van den Bogert	12.08.1999	1		
Midfielders:	**DOB**	**M**	**(s)**	**G**
Atakan Akkaynak (GER)	05.01.1999	5	(3)	1
Vurnon Anita	04.04.1989	14	(13)	
Daniel Crowley (ENG)	03.08.1997	34		5
Elmo Lieftink	03.02.1994	5	(3)	
Pol Llonch Puyaltó (ESP)	07.10.1992	29	(1)	1
Dries Saddiki	09.08.1996	4	(17)	1
Renato Fabrizio Tapia Cortijo (PER)	28.07.1995	15	(1)	1
Forwards:	**DOB**	**M**	**(s)**	**G**
Donis Avdijaj (KVX)	25.08.1996	14	(1)	4
Karim Coulibaly (FRA)	03.06.1993		(4)	
Jordy Croux (BEL)	15.01.1994	4	(4)	
Francisco Sol Ortiz „Fran Sol" (ESP)	13.03.1992	17		13
Alexander Isak (SWE)	21.09.1999	15	(1)	13
Dimitrios Kolovos (GRE)	27.04.1993		(3)	
Kristófer Kristinsson (ISL)	07.04.1999	1	(10)	1
Aras Özbiliz (ARM)	09.03.1990	10	(4)	1
Evangelos Pavlidis (GRE)	21.11.1998	9	(5)	5
Marios Vrousai (GRE)	02.07.1998	13	(3)	4
Trainer:	**DOB**	**M**		
Adrianus Cornelis Koster	18.11.1954	34		

SECOND LEVEL
Eerste Divisie 2018/2019

1.	FC Twente Enschede (*Promoted*)	38	25	5	8	72	-	39	80
2.	Sparta Rotterdam (*Promotion Play-offs*)	38	19	12	7	78	-	47	69
3.	Jong PSV Eindhoven*	38	18	9	11	77	-	59	63
4.	FC Den Bosch (*Promotion Play-offs*)	38	18	9	11	64	-	49	63
5.	Go Ahead Eagles Deventer (*Promotion Play-offs*)	38	19	6	13	63	-	57	63
6.	Tot Ons Plezier Oss (*Promotion Play-offs*)	38	18	8	12	48	-	40	62
7.	Almere City FC (*Promotion Play-offs*)	38	19	5	14	60	-	63	62
8.	RKC Waalwijk (*Promotion Play-offs*)	38	18	5	15	69	-	57	59
9.	NEC Nijmegen (*Promotion Play-offs*)	38	16	10	12	73	-	60	58
10.	SC Cambuur Leeuwarden (*Promotion Play-offs*)	38	16	10	12	61	-	48	58
11.	Jong Ajax Amsterdam*	38	16	8	14	81	-	67	56
12.	MVV Maastricht	38	14	12	12	49	-	53	54
13.	SV Roda JC Kerkrade	38	14	11	13	57	-	59	53
14.	FC Eindhoven	38	13	9	16	52	-	48	48
15.	SC Telstar Velsen	38	14	6	18	45	-	58	48
16.	FC Volendam	38	9	14	15	46	-	62	41
17.	FC Dordrecht	38	9	9	20	54	-	84	36
18.	Jong AZ Alkmaar*	38	7	12	19	46	-	67	33
19.	Jong FC Utrecht*	38	5	8	25	47	-	90	23
20.	Helmond Sport	38	4	10	24	37	-	72	22

*Please note: Reserves teams aren't eligible to be promoted to the Eredivisie!

Promotion Play-offs (1st / 2nd Level)

First Round	NEC Nijmegen - RKC Waalwijk	2-0(2-0)	0-3(0-1)
	SC Cambuur Leeuwarden - Almere City FC	2-2(1-1)	2-1(2-0)
Second Round	Go Ahead Eagles Deventer - FC Den Bosch	2-2(1-1)	1-0(0-0)
	RKC Waalwijk - SBV Excelsior Rotterdam	2-1(0-0)	1-1(1-0)
	Tot Ons Plezier Oss - Sparta Rotterdam	0-2(0-0)	0-3(0-1)
	SC Cambuur Leeuwarden - VBV De Graafschap Doetinchem	1-1(1-1)	0-2(0-2)
Third Round	RKC Waalwijk - Go Ahead Eagles Deventer	0-0	5-4(2-1)
	Sparta Rotterdam - VBV De Graafschap Doetinchem	1-2(1-0)	2-0(0-0)

RKC Waalwijk and **Sparta Rotterdam** were promoted to the 2019/2020 Eredivisie.

NATIONAL TEAM

INTERNATIONAL MATCHES
(16.07.2018 – 15.07.2019)

06.09.2018	Amsterdam	Netherlands - Peru	2-1(0-1)	(F)
09.09.2018	Paris	France - Netherlands	2-1(1-0)	(UNL)
13.10.2018	Amsterdam	Netherlands - Germany	3-0(1-0)	(UNL)
16.10.2018	Bruxelles	Belgium - Netherlands	1-1(1-1)	(F)
16.11.2018	Rotterdam	Netherlands - France	2-0(1-0)	(UNL)
19.11.2018	Gelsenkirchen	Germany - Netherlands	2-2(2-0)	(UNL)
21.03.2019	Rotterdam	Netherlands - Belarus	4-0(2-0)	(ECQ)
24.03.2019	Amsterdam	Netherlands - Germany	2-3(0-2)	(ECQ)
06.06.2019	Guimarães	Netherlands - England	3-1(0-1,1-1)	(UNL)
09.06.2019	Porto	Portugal - Netherlands	1-0(0-0)	(UNL)

06.09.2018 NETHERLANDS - PERU 2-1(0-1) Friendly International
"Johan Cruyff" Arena, Amsterdam; Referee: Tobias Stieler (Germany); Attendance: 40,127
NED: Jacobus Antonius Peter Cillessen, Kenny Tete (72.Daryl Janmaat), Virgil van Dijk, Matthijs de Ligt, Daley Blind, Wesley Sneijder (Cap) (62.Quincy Anton Promes), Ruud Willem Vormer (85.Justin Dean Kluivert), Georginio Gregion Emile Wijnaldum (46.Frenkie de Jong), Kevin Johannes Willem Strootman (46.David Petrus Wenceslaus Henri Pröpper), Ryan Guno Babel (86.Tonny Emilio Trindade de Vilhena), Memphis Depay. Trainer: Ronald Koeman.
Goals: Memphis Depay (60, 83).

09.09.2018 FRANCE - NETHERLANDS 2-1(1-0) UEFA Nations League A, Group 1
Stade de France, Saint-Denis, Paris; Referee: Alberto Undiano Mallenco (Spain); Attendance: 76,452
NED: Jacobus Antonius Peter Cillessen, Kenny Tete (82.Daryl Janmaat), Virgil van Dijk (Cap), Matthijs de Ligt, Daley Blind, David Petrus Wenceslaus Henri Pröpper, Frenkie de Jong, Georginio Gregion Emile Wijnaldum, Ryan Guno Babel (88.Luuk de Jong), Memphis Depay, Quincy Anton Promes (76.Ruud Willem Vormer). Trainer: Ronald Koeman.
Goal: Ryan Guno Babel (67).

13.10.2018 NETHERLANDS - GERMANY 3-0(1-0) UEFA Nations League A, Group 1
"Johan Cruyff" Arena, Amsterdam; Referee: Cüneyt Çakır (Turkey); Attendance: 52,536
NED: Jacobus Antonius Peter Cillessen, Denzel Dumfries, Virgil van Dijk (Cap), Matthijs de Ligt, Daley Blind, Marten Elco de Roon, Frenkie de Jong (77.Nathan Aké), Georginio Gregion Emile Wijnaldum, Ryan Guno Babel (68.Arnaut Danjuma Groeneveld), Memphis Depay, Steven Charles Bergwijn (68.Quincy Anton Promes). Trainer: Ronald Koeman.
Goals: Virgil van Dijk (30), Memphis Depay (87), Georginio Gregion Emile Wijnaldum (90+3).

16.10.2018 BELGIUM - NETHERLANDS 1-1(1-1) Friendly International
Stade "Roi Baudouin", Bruxelles; Referee: Artur Manuel Soares Dias (Portugal); Attendance: 34,747
NED: Jacobus Antonius Peter Cillessen, Denzel Dumfries (46.Hans Hateboer), Stefan de Vrij, Nathan Aké, Daley Blind (Cap), Donny van de Beek (61.Patrick van Aanholt), Matthijs de Ligt (46.Pablo Paulino Rosario), Kevin Johannes Willem Strootman (73.Luuk de Jong), Memphis Depay, Arnaut Danjuma Groeneveld (61.Tonny Emilio Trindade de Vilhena), Quincy Anton Promes (73.Steven Charles Bergwijn). Trainer: Ronald Koeman.
Goal: Arnaut Danjuma Groeneveld (27).

16.11.2018 NETHERLANDS - FRANCE 2-0(1-0) UEFA Nations League A, Group 1
Stadion Feijenoord, Rotterdam; Referee: Anthony Taylor (England); Attendance: 44,366
NED: Jacobus Antonius Peter Cillessen, Denzel Dumfries, Virgil van Dijk (Cap), Matthijs de Ligt, Daley Blind, Marten Elco de Roon, Frenkie de Jong, Georginio Gregion Emile Wijnaldum (89.Tonny Emilio Trindade de Vilhena), Ryan Guno Babel (90+2.Nathan Aké), Memphis Depay, Steven Charles Bergwijn (86.Quincy Anton Promes). Trainer: Ronald Koeman.
Goals: Georginio Gregion Emile Wijnaldum (44), Memphis Depay (90+6 penalty).

19.11.2018 GERMANY - NETHERLANDS 2-2(2-0) UEFA Nations League A, Group 1
Veltins-Arena, Gelsenkirchen; Referee: Ovidiu Alin Haţegan (Romania); Attendance: 42,186
NED: Jacobus Antonius Peter Cillessen, Kenny Tete, Virgil van Dijk (Cap), Matthijs de Ligt, Daley Blind, Marten Elco de Roon, Frenkie de Jong, Georginio Gregion Emile Wijnaldum (60.Tonny Emilio Trindade de Vilhena), Ryan Guno Babel (46.Javairô Joreno Faustino Dilrosun; 66.Luuk de Jong), Memphis Depay, Quincy Anton Promes. Trainer: Ronald Koeman.
Goals: Quincy Anton Promes (85), Virgil van Dijk (90+1).

21.03.2019 NETHERLANDS - BELARUS 4-0(2-0) 16th EC. Qualifiers
Stadion Feijenoord, Rotterdam; Referee: Davide Massa (Italy); Attendance: 38,604
NED: Jacobus Antonius Peter Cillessen, Denzel Dumfries (68.Kenny Tete), Virgil van Dijk (Cap), Matthijs de Ligt, Daley Blind, Marten Elco de Roon (46.David Petrus Wenceslaus Henri Pröpper), Frenkie de Jong, Georginio Gregion Emile Wijnaldum, Ryan Guno Babel (59.Quincy Anton Promes), Memphis Depay, Steven Charles Bergwijn. Trainer: Ronald Koeman.
Goals: Memphis Depay (1), Georginio Gregion Emile Wijnaldum (21), Memphis Depay (55 penalty), Virgil van Dijk (86).

24.03.2019 NETHERLANDS - GERMANY 2-3(0-2) 16th EC. Qualifiers
"Johan Cruyff" Arena, Amsterdam; Referee: Jesús Gil Manzano (Spain); Attendance: 51,694
NED: Jacobus Antonius Peter Cillessen, Denzel Dumfries, Virgil van Dijk (Cap), Matthijs de Ligt, Daley Blind, Marten Elco de Roon (90+1.Luuk de Jong), Frenkie de Jong, Georginio Gregion Emile Wijnaldum, Ryan Guno Babel (46.Steven Charles Bergwijn), Memphis Depay, Quincy Anton Promes. Trainer: Ronald Koeman.
Goals: Matthijs de Ligt (48), Memphis Depay (63).

06.06.2019 NETHERLANDS - ENGLAND 3-1(0-1,1-1) UEFA Nations League, Semi-Finals
Estádio „D. Afonso Henriques", Guimarães (Portugal); Referee: Clément Turpin (France); Attendance: 25,711
NED: Jacobus Antonius Peter Cillessen, Denzel Dumfries, Virgil van Dijk (Cap), Matthijs de Ligt, Daley Blind, Marten Elco de Roon (68.Donny van de Beek), Frenkie de Jong (114.Kevin Johannes Willem Strootman), Georginio Gregion Emile Wijnaldum, Ryan Guno Babel (68.Quincy Anton Promes), Memphis Depay, Steven Charles Bergwijn (90.David Petrus Wenceslaus Henri Pröpper). Trainer: Ronald Koeman.
Goals: Matthijs de Ligt (73), Kyle Andrew Walker (97 own goal), Quincy Anton Promes (114).

09.06.2019 **PORTUGAL - NETHERLANDS** **1-0(0-0)** UEFA Nations League, Final

Estádio do Dragão, Porto; Referee: Alberto Undiano Mallenco (Spain); Attendance: 43,199

NED: Jacobus Antonius Peter Cillessen, Denzel Dumfries, Virgil van Dijk (Cap), Matthijs de Ligt, Daley Blind, Marten Elco de Roon (81.Luuk de Jong), Frenkie de Jong, Georginio Gregion Emile Wijnaldum, Ryan Guno Babel (46.Quincy Anton Promes), Memphis Depay, Steven Charles Bergwijn (60.Donny van de Beek). Trainer: Ronald Koeman.

NATIONAL TEAM PLAYERS
(16.07.2018 – 15.07.2019)

Name	DOB	Caps	Goals	2018/2019:	Club
Goalkeepers					
Jacobus Antonius Peter CILLESSEN	22.04.1989	**50**	**0**	2018/2019:	*FC Barcelona (ESP)*
Defenders					
Nathan Benjamin AKÉ	18.02.1995	**10**	**1**	2018:	*AFC Bournemouth (ENG)*
Daley BLIND	09.03.1990	**64**	**2**	2018/2019:	*AFC Ajax Amsterdam*
Matthijs DE LIGT	12.08.1999	**17**	**2**	2018/2019:	*AFC Ajax Amsterdam*
Stefan DE VRIJ	05.02.1992	**37**	**3**	2018:	*FC Internazionale Milano (ITA)*
Denzel DUMFRIES	18.04.1996	**7**	**0**	2018/2019:	*PSV Eindhoven*
Hans HATEBOER	09.01.1994	**3**	**0**	2018:	*Atalanta Bergamasca Calcio (ITA)*
Daryl JANMAAT	22.07.1989	**34**	**0**	2018:	*Watford FC (ENG)*
Kenny TETE	09.10.1995	**13**	**0**	2018/2019:	*Olympique Lyonnais (FRA)*
Patrick John Miguel VAN AANHOLT	29.08.1990	**9**	**0**	2018:	*Crystal Palace FC London (ENG)*
Virgil VAN DIJK	08.07.1991	**28**	**4**	2018/2019:	*Liverpool FC (ENG)*
Midfielders					
Frenkie DE JONG	12.05.1997	**9**	**0**	2018/2019:	*AFC Ajax Amsterdam*
Marten Elco DE ROON	29.03.1991	**12**	**0**	2018/2019:	*Atalanta Bergamasca Calcio (ITA)*
David Petrus Wenceslaus Henri PRÖPPER	02.09.1991	**15**	**3**	2018/2019:	*Brighton & Hove Albion FC (ENG)*
Pablo Paulino ROSARIO	07.01.1997	**1**	**0**	2018:	*PSV Eindhoven*
Wesley Benjamin SNEIJDER	09.06.1984	**134**	**31**	2018/2019:	*Al-Gharafa SC Al Rayyan (QATZ)*
Kevin Johannes Willem STROOTMAN	13.02.1990	**44**	**3**	2018/2019:	*Olympique de Marseille (FRA)*
Donny VAN DE BEEK	18.04.1997	**7**	**0**	2018/2019:	*AFC Ajax Amsterdam*
Tonny Emilio Trindade de VILHENA	03.01.1995	**15**	**0**	2018:	*Feyenoord Rotterdam*
Rudy Willem VORMER	11.05.1988	**4**	**0**	2018:	*Club Brugge KV (BEL)*
Georginio Gregion Emile WIJNALDUM	11.11.1990	**57**	**11**	2018/2019:	*Liverpool FC (ENG)*
Forwards					
Ryan Guno BABEL	19.12.1986	**58**	**8**	2018: 15.01.2019->	*Beşiktaş JK İstanbul (TUR)* *Fulham FC London (ENG)*
Steven Charles BERGWIJN	08.10.1997	**7**	**0**	2018/2019:	*PSV Eindhoven*
Luuk DE JONG	27.08.1990	**19**	**4**	2018/2019:	*PSV Eindhoven*
Memphis DEPAY	13.02.1994	**48**	**16**	2018/2019:	*Olympique Lyonnais (FRA)*
Javairô Joreno Faustino DILROSUN	22.06.1998	**1**	**0**	2018:	*Hertha BSC Berlin (GER)*
Arnaut Danjuma GROENEVELD	31.01.1997	**2**	**1**	2018:	*Club Brugge KV (BEL)*
Justin Dean KLUIVERT	05.05.1999	**2**	**0**	2018:	*AS Roma (ITA)*
Quincy Anton PROMES	04.01.1992	**38**	**7**	2018/2019:	*Sevilla FC (ESP)*

National team coach

Ronald KOEMAN [from 06.02.2018]	21.03.1963	14 M; 6 W; 4 D; 4 L; 25-14

NORTH MACEDONIA

The Country:

Република Северна Македонија (Republic of North Macedonia)
Capital: Skopje
Surface: 25,713 km²
Inhabitants: 2,103,721 [2017]
Time: UTC+1

The FA:

Fudbalska Federacija na Severna Makedonija
bul. Asnom bb, 1000 Skopje
Tel: +389 23 129291
Foundation date: 1926
Member of FIFA since: 1926/1994
Member of UEFA since: 1954/1994
Website: www.ffm.com.mk

NATIONAL TEAM RECORDS

First international match:	13.10.1993, Kranj:	Slovenia – Macedonia 1-4
Most international caps:	Goran Pandev	- 103 caps (since 2001)
Most international goals:	Goran Pandev	- 33 goals / 103 caps (since 2001)

UEFA EUROPEAN CHAMPIONSHIP	
1960	-
1964	-
1968	-
1972	-
1976	-
1980	-
1984	-
1988	-
1992	-
1996	Qualifiers
2000	Qualifiers
2004	Qualifiers
2008	Qualifiers
2012	Qualifiers
2016	Qualifiers

FIFA WORLD CUP	
1930	-
1934	-
1938	-
1950	-
1954	-
1958	-
1962	-
1966	-
1970	-
1974	-
1978	-
1982	-
1986	-
1990	-
1994	Did not enter
1998	Qualifiers
2002	Qualifiers
2006	Qualifiers
2010	Qualifiers
2014	Qualifiers
2018	Qualifiers

UEFA NATIONS LEAGUE

2018/2019 – League D (promoted to League C)

OLYMPIC FOOTBALL TOURNAMENTS 1908-2016

1908	-	**1948**	-	**1972**	-	**1996**	Qualifiers
1912	-	**1952**	-	**1976**	-	**2000**	Qualifiers
1920	-	**1956**	-	**1980**	-	**2004**	Qualifiers
1924	-	**1960**	-	**1984**	-	**2008**	Qualifiers
1928	-	**1964**	-	**1988**	-	**2012**	Qualifiers
1936	-	**1968**	-	**1992**	Did not enter	**2016**	Qualifiers

FIFA CONFEDERATIONS CUP 1992-2017

None

MACEDONIAN CLUB HONOURS IN EUROPEAN CLUB COMPETITIONS:

European Champion Clubs' Cup (1956-1992) / UEFA Champions League (1993-2019)

None

Fairs Cup (1858-1971) / UEFA Cup (1972-2009) / UEFA Europa League (2010-2019)

None

UEFA Super Cup (1972-2018)

None

European Cup Winners' Cup 1961-1999*

None

**defunct competition*

NATIONAL COMPETITIONS
TABLE OF HONOURS

Royal League
(territory of Vardarska Banovina belonging to the Kingdom of Yugoslavia)

	CHAMPIONS
1929	Pobeda Skopje
1930	Jug Skopje, SSK Skopje, Sparta Skopje*
1931	*Championship not finished*
1932	SSK Skopje
1933	SSK Skopje
1934	SSK Skopje
1935	*Championship not finished*
1936	Gragjanski Skopje
1937	*Championship not finished*
1938	Gragjanski Skopje
1939	Gragjanski Skopje
1940	SSK Skopje
1941	SSK Skopje

As part of Bulgaria

	CHAMPIONS
1942	Makedonija Skopje
1943	ZhSK Skopje
1944	ZhSK Skopje

All 3 teams finished with equal number of points

Republic League (within F.R. Yugoslavia)

1944/1945	Makedonija Skopje
1945/1946	Pobeda Skopje
1946/1947	Makedonija Skopje
1947/1948	Dinamo Skopje
1948/1949	11 Oktomvri Kumanovo
1949/1950	Rabotnik Bitola
1950/1951	Rabotnik Bitola
1951/1952	Rabotnichki Skopje
1952/1953	Pobeda Prilep
1953/1954	Rabotnichki Skopje
1954/1955	Rabotnichki Skopje
1955/1956	Vardar Skopje
1956/1957	Rabotnichki Skopje
1957/1958	Rabotnichki Skopje
1958/1959	Pobeda Prilep
1959/1960	Pelister Bitola
1960/1961	Pelister Bitola
1961/1962	Pobeda Prilep
1962/1963	Pobeda Prilep
1963/1964	Bregalnica Shtip
1964/1965	Teteks Tetovo
1965/1966	Rabotnichki Skopje
1966/1967	Bregalnica Shtip
1967/1968	Rabotnichki Skopje
1968/1969	Teteks Tetovo
1969/1970	MIK Skopje
1970/1971	Kumanovo
1971/1972	Tikvesh Kavadarci
1972/1973	Rabotnichki Skopje
1973/1974	Teteks Tetovo
1974/1975	Pelister Bitola
1975/1976	Bregalnica Shtip
1976/1977	Rabotnichki Skopje
1977/1978	Tikvesh Kavadarci
1978/1979	Pobeda Prilep
1979/1980	Rabotnichki Skopje
1980/1981	Pobeda Prilep
1981/1982	Pelister Bitola
1982/1983	Belasica Strumica
1983/1984	Bregalnica Shtip
1984/1985	Teteks Tetovo
1985/1986	Pobeda Prilep
1986/1987	Metalurg Skopje
1987/1988	Belasica Strumica
1988/1989	Borec-Titov Veles
1989/1990	Balkan Skopje
1990/1991	Makedonija Skopje
1991/1992	Sasa Makedonska Kamenica

After proclamation of independence - Macedonian First League

	CHAMPIONS	CUP WINNERS	BEST GOALSCORERS	
1992/1993	FK Vardar Skopje	FK Vardar Skopje	Saša Ćirić (FK Vardar Skopje)	36
1993/1994	FK Vardar Skopje	FK Sileks Kratovo	Zoran Boshkovski (FK Sileks Kratovo)	21
1994/1995	FK Vardar Skopje	FK Vardar Skopje	Saša Ćirić (FK Vardar Skopje)	35
1995/1996	FK Sileks Kratovo	FK Sloga Jugomagnat Skopje	Zoran Boshkovski (FK Sileks Kratovo)	20
1996/1997	FK Sileks Kratovo	FK Sileks Kratovo	Vancho Micevski (FK Sileks Kratovo) Miroslav Gjokić (FK Sileks Kratovo)	16
1997/1998	FK Sileks Kratovo	FK Vardar Skopje	Vancho Atanasov (FK Belasica Stremica)	12
1998/1999	FK Sloga Jugomagnat Skopje	FK Vardar Skopje	Rogério Oliveira da Costa (FK Pobeda Prilep)	22
1999/2000	FK Sloga Jugomagnat Skopje	FK Sloga Jugomagnat Skopje	Argjend Beqiri (FK Sloga Jugomagnat Skopje)	19
2000/2001	FK Sloga Jugomagnat Skopje	FK Pelister Bitola	Argjend Beqiri (FK Sloga Jugomagnat Skopje)	27
2001/2002	FK Vardar Skopje	FK Pobeda Prilep	Miroslav Gjokić (FK Pobeda Prilep)	22
2002/2003	FK Vardar Skopje	FK Cementarnica 55 Skopje	Ljubiša Savić (FK Bregalnica Štip / FK Sloga Jugomagnat Skopje)	25
2003/2004	FK Pobeda Prilep	FK Sloga Jugomagnat Skopje	Dragan Dimitrovski (FK Pobeda Prilep)	25
2004/2005	FK Rabotnički Skopje	KF Bashkimi Kumanovo	Aleksandar Stojanovski (FK Belasica Stremica) Stevica Ristić (FK Sileks Kratovo)	26
2005/2006	FK Rabotnički Skopje	FK Makedonija Gjorče Petrov	Stevica Ristić (FK Sileks Kratovo)	27
2006/2007	FK Pobeda Prilep	FK Vardar Skopje	Boban Janchevski (KF Bashkimi Kumanovo / KF Renova Džepčište)	26
2007/2008	FK Rabotnički Skopje	FK Rabotnički Skopje	Ivica Gligorovski (FK Milano Kumanovo)	15
2008/2009	FK Makedonija Gjorče Petrov	FK Rabotnički Skopje	Ivica Gligorovski (FK Milano Kumanovo)	14
2009/2010	KF Renova Džepčište	FK Teteks Tetovo	Bobi Bozhinovski (FK Rabotnički Skopje)	15
2010/2011	KF Shkëndija Tetovo	FK Metalurg Skopje	Hristijan Kirovski (FK Skopje)	20
2011/2012	FK Vardar Skopje	KF Renova Džepčište	Filip Ivanovski (FK Vardar Skopje)	24
2012/2013	FK Vardar Skopje	FK Teteks Tetovo	Jovan Kostovski (FK Vardar Skopje)	22
2013/2014	FK Rabotnički Skopje	FK Rabotnički Skopje	Dejan Blazhevski (FK Horizont Turnovo)	19
2014/2015	FK Vardar Skopje	FK Rabotnički Skopje	Izair Emini (KF Renova Džepčište)	20
2015/2016	FK Vardar Skopje	KF Shkëndija Tetovo	Besart Ibraimi (KF Shkëndija Tetovo)	26
2016/2017	FK Vardar Skopje	FK Pelister Bitola	Besart Ibraimi (KF Shkëndija Tetovo)	20

2017/2018	KF Shkëndija Tetovo	KF Shkëndija Tetovo	Ferhan Hasani (KF Shkëndija Tetovo) Besart Ibraimi (KF Shkëndija Tetovo)	22
2018/2019	KF Shkëndija Tetovo	Fudb. Akademija Pandev Strumica	Vlatko Stojanovski (KF Renova Džepčište)	18

NATIONAL CHAMPIONSHIP

Macedonian First Football League – Prva Liga 2018/2019

(11.08.2017 – 26.05.2018)

Results

Round 1 [11-12.08.2018]
FK Rabotnički - KF Renova 3-4(1-2)
KF Shkëndija - Vardar Skopje 2-2(0-1)
Sileks Kratovo - FC Shkupi 1-1(1-0)
FK Pobeda Prilep - FK Belasica 1-0(0-0)
Akademija Pandev - FK Makedonija 2-1(1-0)

Round 2 [18-19.08.2018]
FK Rabotnički - Sileks Kratovo 2-1(2-0)
FK Makedonija - KF Shkëndija 0-0
KF Renova - Vardar Skopje 0-1(0-0)
FK Belasica - Akademija Pandev 0-2(0-0)
FC Shkupi - FK Pobeda Prilep 0-0

Round 3 [26-27.08.2018]
Sileks Kratovo - KF Renova 1-0(0-0)
Akademija Pandev - FC Shkupi 1-0(1-0)
FK Pobeda Prilep - FK Rabotnički 0-2(0-1)
Vardar Skopje - FK Makedonija 1-0(1-0)
KF Shkëndija - FK Belasica 4-1(2-1)

Round 4 [01-02.09.2018]
FK Belasica - Vardar Skopje 1-1(0-0)
KF Renova - FK Makedonija 1-1(1-1)
Sileks Kratovo - FK Pobeda Prilep 0-0
FK Rabotnički - Akademija Pandev 1-0(1-0)
FC Shkupi - KF Shkëndija 1-2(1-2)

Round 5 [16.09.2018]
Akademija Pandev - Sileks Kratovo 3-0(0-0)
KF Shkëndija - FK Rabotnički 6-2(3-1)
Vardar Skopje - FC Shkupi 2-1(0-1)
FK Makedonija - FK Belasica 0-0
FK Pobeda Prilep - KF Renova 1-0(1-0)

Round 6 [22-23.09.2018]
FK Rabotnički - Vardar Skopje 0-2(0-1)
FC Shkupi - FK Makedonija 2-1(1-0)
KF Renova - FK Belasica 0-2(0-0)
Sileks Kratovo - KF Shkëndija 1-2(0-1)
Pobeda Prilep - Akademija Pandev 2-4(1-2)

Round 7 [26.09.2018]
KF Shkëndija - FK Pobeda Prilep 0-2(0-0)
Akademija Pandev - KF Renova 0-2(0-1)
Vardar Skopje - Sileks Kratovo 1-0(0-0)
FK Makedonija - FK Rabotnički 3-0(2-0)
FK Belasica - FC Shkupi 1-0(1-0)

Round 8 [29.09.2018]
FK Rabotnički - FK Belasica 1-1(1-1)
Sileks Kratovo - FK Makedonija 1-1(0-1)
KF Renova - FC Shkupi 2-0(1-0)
FK Pobeda Prilep - Vardar Skopje 0-1(0-0)
Akademija Pandev - KF Shkëndija 0-0

Round 9 [06.10.2018]
Vardar Skopje - Akademija Pandev 3-0(1-0)
FK Makedonija - FK Pobeda Prilep 1-0(1-0)
FK Belasica - Sileks Kratovo 1-1(0-0)
KF Shkëndija - KF Renova 2-2(1-0)
FC Shkupi - FK Rabotnički 1-1(1-0)

Round 10 [21.10.2018]
KF Renova - FK Rabotnički 0-2(0-1)
FC Shkupi - Sileks Kratovo 2-0(0-0)
FK Belasica - FK Pobeda Prilep 2-1(1-0)
FK Makedonija - Akademija Pandev 1-0(0-0)
Vardar Skopje - KF Shkëndija 0-2(0-1)

Round 11 [28.10.2018]
KF Shkëndija - FK Makedonija 5-1(2-0)
Vardar Skopje - KF Renova 0-0
Akademija Pandev - FK Belasica 3-0(2-0)
FK Pobeda Prilep - FC Shkupi 2-0(1-0)
Sileks Kratovo - FK Rabotnički 2-0(1-0)

Round 12 [31.10.2018]
KF Renova - Sileks Kratovo 1-1(0-0)
FC Shkupi - Akademija Pandev 1-0(0-0)
FK Rabotnički - FK Pobeda Prilep 3-1(0-0)
FK Belasica - KF Shkëndija 0-2(0-1)
FK Makedonija - Vardar Skopje 1-3(0-1)

Round 13 [04.11.2018]
Vardar Skopje - FK Belasica 1-1(1-0)
KF Shkëndija - FC Shkupi 3-0(2-0)
Akademija Pandev - FK Rabotnički 1-0(0-0)
FK Makedonija - KF Renova 1-2(1-0)
FK Pobeda Prilep - Sileks Kratovo 2-0(0-0)

Round 14 [10.11.2018]
Sileks Kratovo - Akademija Pandev 1-0(1-0)
FK Rabotnički - KF Shkëndija 1-2(1-1)
FC Shkupi - Vardar Skopje 1-0(0-0)
FK Belasica - FK Makedonija 1-4(1-2)
KF Renova - FK Pobeda Prilep 2-1(1-1)

Round 15 [22.11.2018]
FK Makedonija - FC Shkupi 2-2(1-2)
FK Belasica - KF Renova 3-1(1-1)
Vardar Skopje - FK Rabotnički 0-1(0-0)
KF Shkëndija - Sileks Kratovo 5-0(2-0)
Akademija Pandev - Pobeda Prilep 2-1(1-1)

Round 16 [25.11.2018]
FK Pobeda Prilep - KF Shkëndija 0-2(0-0)
KF Renova - Akademija Pandev 1-1(1-1)
Sileks Kratovo - Vardar Skopje 0-1(0-1)
FK Rabotnički - FK Makedonija 5-1(2-0)
FC Shkupi - FK Belasica 1-0(0-0)

Round 17 [28.11.2018]
FK Belasica - FK Rabotnički 1-2(0-2)
FK Makedonija - Sileks Kratovo 1-1(1-0)
FC Shkupi - KF Renova 1-1(0-1)
Vardar Skopje - FK Pobeda Prilep 3-0(1-0)
KF Shkëndija - Akademija Pandev 0-1(0-1)

Round 18 [02.12.2018]
Akademija Pandev - Vardar Skopje 0-0
FK Pobeda Prilep - FK Makedonija 0-2(0-2)
Sileks Kratovo - FK Belasica 1-0(1-0)
KF Renova - KF Shkëndija 0-3(0-1)
FK Rabotnički - FC Shkupi 0-2(0-1)

Round 19 [17.02.2019]
FK Rabotnički - KF Renova 1-1(1-0)
Sileks Kratovo - FC Shkupi 2-2(2-0)
FK Pobeda Prilep - FK Belasica 1-1(1-1)
Akademija Pandev - FK Makedonija 3-0(1-0)
KF Shkëndija - Vardar Skopje 1-0(1-0)

Round 20 [24.02.2019]
KF Shkëndija - FK Makedonija 1-1(0-1)
KF Renova - Vardar Skopje 4-0(2-0)
FK Belasica - Akademija Pandev 0-1(0-1)
FC Shkupi - FK Pobeda Prilep 3-0(1-0)
FK Rabotnički - Sileks Kratovo 1-1(0-1)

Round 21 [03.03.2019]
Sileks Kratovo - KF Renova 0-0
Akademija Pandev - FC Shkupi 0-2(0-1)
FK Pobeda Prilep - FK Rabotnički 0-1(0-1)
KF Shkëndija - FK Belasica 3-0(0-0)
Vardar Skopje - FK Makedonija 3-1(2-0)

Round 22 [10.03.2019]
FK Belasica - Vardar Skopje 0-0
FC Shkupi - KF Shkëndija 1-0(1-0)
FK Rabotnički - Akademija Pandev 1-2(0-1)
KF Renova - FK Makedonija 0-0
Sileks Kratovo - FK Pobeda Prilep 1-0(0-0)

Round 23 [16.03.2019]
Akademija Pandev - Sileks Kratovo 2-0(1-0)
KF Shkëndija - FK Rabotnički 1-0(0-0)
Vardar Skopje - FC Shkupi 1-0(1-0)
FK Makedonija - FK Belasica 2-1(1-0)
FK Pobeda Prilep - KF Renova 2-3(0-2)

Round 24 [28.03.2019]
FC Shkupi - FK Makedonija 0-1(0-0)
KF Renova - FK Belasica 3-2(2-1)
FK Rabotnički - Vardar Skopje 0-2(0-1)
Sileks Kratovo - KF Shkëndija 0-3(0-1)
Pobeda Prilep - Akademija Pandev 1-3(0-0)

Round 25 [31.03.2019]
KF Shkëndija - FK Pobeda Prilep 5-2(3-0)
Akademija Pandev - KF Renova 2-1(1-0)
Vardar Skopje - Sileks Kratovo 1-0(0-0)
FK Makedonija - FK Rabotnički 1-1(0-0)
FK Belasica - FC Shkupi 2-0(1-0)

Round 26 [03.04.2019]
FK Rabotnički - FK Belasica 1-1(0-0)
Sileks Kratovo - FK Makedonija 1-1(0-1)
KF Renova - FC Shkupi 1-0(1-0)
FK Pobeda Prilep - Vardar Skopje 0-0
Akademija Pandev - KF Shkëndija 0-1(0-1)

Round 27 [07.04.2019]
Vardar Skopje - Akademija Pandev 1-1(1-0)
FK Makedonija - FK Pobeda Prilep 3-0(1-0)
FK Belasica - Sileks Kratovo 0-1(0-0)
KF Shkëndija - KF Renova 2-1(1-1)
FC Shkupi - FK Rabotnički 1-2(1-0)

Round 28 [14.04.2019]
KF Renova - FK Rabotnički 1-2(0-0)
FC Shkupi - Sileks Kratovo 2-1(2-0)
FK Belasica - FK Pobeda Prilep 1-1(0-0)
FK Makedonija - Akademija Pandev 1-1(0-1)
Vardar Skopje - KF Shkëndija 0-0

Round 29 [20.04.2019]
KF Shkëndija - FK Makedonija 4-2(3-0)
Vardar Skopje - KF Renova 2-0(1-0)
Akademija Pandev - FK Belasica 0-2(0-2)
FK Pobeda Prilep - FC Shkupi 0-3(0-0)
Sileks Kratovo - FK Rabotnički 1-0(0-0)

Round 30 [24.04.2019]
KF Renova - Sileks Kratovo 1-0(1-0)
FC Shkupi - Akademija Pandev 1-0(0-0)
FK Rabotnički - FK Pobeda Prilep 1-2(1-0)
FK Belasica - KF Shkëndija 2-1(1-0)
FK Makedonija - Vardar Skopje 0-2(0-1)

Round 31 [27.04.2019]
Vardar Skopje - FK Belasica 1-1(0-1)
KF Shkëndija - FC Shkupi 5-1(3-0)
Akademija Pandev - FK Rabotnički 3-1(1-0)
FK Makedonija - KF Renova 3-1(2-1)
FK Pobeda Prilep - Sileks Kratovo 0-1(0-1)

Round 32 [04.05.2019]
Sileks Kratovo - Akademija Pandev 3-0(1-0)
FK Rabotnički - KF Shkëndija 0-1(0-0)
FC Shkupi - Vardar Skopje 2-2(1-1)
FK Belasica - FK Makedonija 3-1(1-0)
KF Renova - FK Pobeda Prilep 9-1(5-1)

Round 33 [08.05.2019]
FK Makedonija - FC Shkupi 1-0(1-0)
FK Belasica - KF Renova 3-2(1-1)
Vardar Skopje - FK Rabotnički 1-1(0-1)
KF Shkëndija - Sileks Kratovo 0-0
Akademija Pandev - Pobeda Prilep 4-0(1-0)

Round 34 [12.05.2019]
FK Pobeda Prilep - KF Shkëndija 1-4(1-3)
KF Renova - Akademija Pandev 1-1(1-1)
Sileks Kratovo - Vardar Skopje 1-0(1-0)
FK Rabotnički - FK Makedonija 2-0(2-0)
FC Shkupi - FK Belasica 2-2(1-1)

Round 35 [19.05.2019]
FK Belasica - FK Rabotnički 0-1(0-1)
FK Makedonija - Sileks Kratovo 2-0(2-0)
FC Shkupi - KF Renova 2-2(1-0)
Vardar Skopje - FK Pobeda Prilep 6-0(4-0)
KF Shkëndija - Akademija Pandev 4-1(1-0)

Round 36 [26.05.2019]
Akademija Pandev - Vardar Skopje 1-1(0-0)
FK Pobeda Prilep - FK Makedonija 1-3(0-1)
Sileks Kratovo - FK Belasica 2-1(1-0)
KF Renova - KF Shkëndija 3-2(2-1)
FK Rabotnički - FC Shkupi 1-2(0-0)

Final Standings

1.	**KF Shkëndija Tetovo**	36	24	7	5	80	-	29	79
2.	FK Vardar Skopje	36	17	13	6	45	-	23	64
3.	Fudbalska Akademija Pandev Strumica	36	17	7	12	45	-	35	58
4.	FC Shkupi Čair	36	13	9	14	40	-	42	48
5.	FK Makedonija Gjorče Petrov Skopje	36	12	11	13	45	-	50	47
6.	KF Renova Džepčište	36	12	11	13	53	-	49	47
7.	FK Rabotnički Skopje	36	13	7	16	43	-	49	46
8.	FK Sileks Kratovo (*Relegation Play-off*)	36	11	11	14	27	-	39	44
9.	FK Belasica Strumica (*Relegated*)	36	9	11	16	37	-	49	38
10.	FK Pobeda AD Prilep (*Relegated*)	36	6	5	25	26	-	76	23

Top goalscorers:

18 Vlatko Stojanovski *KF Renova Džepčište*
16 Ljupco Doriev *Fudbalska Akademija Pandev Strumica*
11 Izair Emini *KF Shkëndija Tetovo*
11 Besart Ibraimi *KF Shkëndija Tetovo*
11 Hristijan Kirovski *FK Makedonija*
11 Petar Petkovski *FK Rabotnički Skopje*
11 Emran Ramadani *KF Renova Džepčište*

Relegation Play-offs [05.06.2019]

FK Sileks Kratovo - GFK Tikveš 1930 Kavadarci 3-2(3-1)

NATIONAL CUP
Kup na Makedonija 2018/2019

First Round [22/29.08./12.09.2018]

KF Korabi Debar - FK Borec 1919 Veles	1-0
KF Vëllazërimi 77 Kičevo - FK Belasica Strumica	0-4
FK Vardar Negotino - FK Skopje	1-3
KF Fortuna Skopje - FK Rabotnički Skopje	0-6
FK Labunishta - Fudb. Akademija Pandev Strumica	1-3
FK Kit-Go Pehčevo - FC Shkupi Čair	2-0
FK Poeševo - FK Bregalnica 2008 Štip	0-4
KF Vardari Forinë - FK Vardar Skopje	0-4
GFK Osogovo Kočani - FK Pelister Bitola	0-1
FK Teteks Tetovo - KF Gostivari	0-1
FK Bratstvo-Vlaznimi Sredno Konjari - FK Sileks K.	0-7
GFK Tikveš 1930 Kavadarci - KF Renova Džepčište	2-1
FK Prevalec Veles - FK Makedonija Gjorče Petrov	0-2
FC Struga Trim-Lum - FK Pobeda AD Prilep	1-2
FK Kožuf Gevgelija - KF Shkëndija Tetovo	0-2

Second Round [19.09.-03.10.2018]

GFK Tikveš 1930 Kavadarci - FK Rabotnički Skopje	0-1 / 1-1
KF Gostivari - FK Pobeda AD Prilep	1-2 / 1-4
FK Vardar Skopje - FK Makedonija Gjorče Petrov	1-1 / 1-2
FK Skopje - FK Sileks Kratovo	0-2 / 1-2
KF Shkëndija Tetovo - FK Kit-Go Pehčevo	2-0 / 5-0
FK Bregalnica 2008 Štip - FA Pandev Strumica	2-6 / 1-0
FK Pelister Bitola - FK Belasica Strumica	0-2 / 1-3

KF Korabi Debar got a bye to the quarter-finals.

Quarter-Finals [07.11.-05.12.2018]

KF Shkëndija Tetovo - FK Pobeda AD Prilep	0-1 / 0-2
FK Sileks Kratovo - FK Belasica Strumica	0-2 / 0-2
Fud. Akademija Pandev Strumica - KF Korabi Debar	3-1 / 6-1
FK Makedonija Gjorče Petrov - FK Rabotnički Skop.	1-0 / 1-0

Semi-Finals [27.02./06.03.-10.04.2019]

FK Belasica Strumica - FK Makedonija G. Petrov	0-1 / 0-1
Fud. Akademija Pandev Strumica - FK Pobeda Prilep	3-1 / 3-1

Final

22.05.2019; "Toše Proeski" National Arena, Skopje; Referee: Marjan Eckoski; Attendance: 3,000
Fudbalska Akademija Pandev Strumica - FK Makedonija Gjorče Petrov Skopje **2-2(1-1,2-2,2-2); 4-2 on penalties**

Akademija Pandev: Dušan Čubraković, David Atanasovski, Dime Dimov, Tomislav Iliev, Stefan Kostov, Georgi Stoilov, Ljupco Doriev, Kristijan Stojkovski (69.Kristijan Ivanov), Daniel Milovanovikj (89.Ačo Stojkov), Saško Pandev (79.Mario Krstovski), Stojanco Velinov. Trainer: Jugoslav Trencovski.

Makedonija: Marko Jovanovski, Izaldo Braz da Silva Junior (110.Filip Stojanovski), Bianor das Graças Lima da Silva, Hristijan Pecov (120.Filip Misevski), André Lucas Matos Gama „André Penalva", Bobi Božinovski, Kristijan Filipovski (72.Paulo Eduardo Carvalho „Padú"), Sabit Bilalli, Dejan Tanturovski, Robson da Silva, Hristijan Kirovski (101.Benjamin Demir). Trainer: Aleksandar Tanevski.

Goals: 1-0 Saško Pandev (10), 1-1 Robson da Silva (21), 1-2 Dejan Tanturovski (84), 2-2 Ljupco Doriev (86 penalty).

Penalties: Robson da Silva (saved); Georgi Stoilov 1-0; Paulo Eduardo Carvalho „Padú" 1-1; Ljupco Doriev 2-1; André Lucas Matos Gama „André Penalva" 2-2; Tomislav Iliev 3-2; Dejan Tanturovski (saved); Stojanco Velinov 4-2.

Fudbalska Akademija Pandev Strumica

Founded: 2010
Stadium: Stadion Kukuš, Strumica (1,500)

Goalkeepers:	DOB	M	(s)	G
Marko Alchevski	16.04.2002		(1)	
Dušan Čubraković (SRB)	21.07.1995	34		
David Denkovski	17.08.2000	2		
Defenders:	**DOB**	**M**	**(s)**	**G**
David Atanasovski	21.10.1996	25	(1)	
Dime Dimov	25.07.1994	30	(2)	2
Tomislav Iliev	02.12.1993	31		2
Zoran Ivanovski	07.05.2000		(3)	
Vane Jovanov	28.12.1998	8	(7)	
Stefan Kostov	31.10.1996	20		1
Mihail Manevski	25.02.1999	14	(5)	
Stojan Stojčevski	30.10.1992	6	(1)	
Vanče Šikov	19.07.1985	9	(3)	1
Riste Temelkov	02.10.1997	17	(4)	
Filip Trajanovski	21.03.1999	6	(1)	
Midfielders:	**DOB**	**M**	**(s)**	**G**
Ljupco Doriev	13.09.1995	28	(3)	16
Kristijan Ivanov	21.05.1995	24	(6)	1
Filip Mihailov	10.07.1998	6	(3)	
Georgi Stoilov	25.08.1995	29	(2)	2
Kristijan Stojkovski	17.09.1991	12	(2)	1
Goran Tomovski	21.07.1998	10		1
Forwards:	**DOB**	**M**	**(s)**	**G**
Vasko Ivanov	12.02.2002		(1)	
Mario Krstovski	03.04.1998	19	(14)	5
Daniel Milovanovikj	10.08.1998	24	(6)	6
Aleksandar Mishov	21.07.1998	5	(5)	2
Saško Pandev	01.05.1987	19	(12)	2
Ačo Stojkov	29.04.1983	8	(20)	2
Stojanco Velinov	03.09.1989	10	(4)	
Trainer:	**DOB**	**M**		
Jugoslav Trencovski	29.11.1976	36		

Fudbalski klub Belasica Strumica

Founded: 22.04.1922
Stadium: Stadion Mladost, Strumica (9,200)

Goalkeepers:	DOB	M	(s)	G
Mite Arabadjiev	11.02.2000	3		
Dimitar Gjorgiev	23.01.1997	1		
Goran Pašovski	15.02.1980	2	(1)	
Nikola Vujanac (SRB)	22.06.1991	30	(3)	
Defenders:	**DOB**	**M**	**(s)**	**G**
Vlatko Drobarov	02.11.1992	29	(1)	1
Gjorgje Dzhonov	20.09.1991	15	(2)	1
Tome Janev	02.04.1990	5		
David Kalpacki	01.06.2000	19		
Mario Maslać (SRB)	09.09.1990	16		1
Aleksandar Milusev	05.04.1988	27	(2)	1
Zoran Mitevski	03.02.1995	27	(2)	1
Filip Naumchevski	26.10.1992		(1)	
Jordan Serafimovski	13.05.1991	22	(10)	1
Midfielders:	**DOB**	**M**	**(s)**	**G**
Nikola Božinov	15.03.1996	4	(3)	
Hristijan Denkovski	15.04.1994	4	(7)	2
Blagoj Istatov	14.10.1999	2	(1)	
Stojan Jankov	11.04.2000	4		
Martin Mircevski	11.02.1997	9	(7)	3
Viktor Serafimovski	24.10.1995	10	(3)	
Dragan Stojkov	23.02.1988	26	(5)	
Stefan Sulev	24.08.1989	11	(17)	
Krste Todorov	24.12.1987	3	(3)	
Marjan Tasev	02.05.1985	9	(4)	
Stephan Vujčić (GER)	03.01.1986	19	(3)	
Irfan Vušljanin (SRB)	07.01.1986	14	(2)	2
Forwards:	**DOB**	**M**	**(s)**	**G**
Zoran Baldovaliev	04.03.1983	22	(8)	4
Pepi Gorgiev	04.10.1994	21	(7)	9
Filip Ivanovski	01.05.1985	11	(1)	4
Nemanja Petrov (SRB)	22.08.1995	10	(2)	
Dušan Savić	01.10.1985	11	(5)	5
Blagoj Stojanov	09.06.1999	10		
Trainer:	**DOB**	**M**		
Marjan Živković (SRB)	21.05.1973	18		
Rade Cicmilovikj [04.12.2018]	22.12.1978	5		
Gjoko Hadzievski [23.03.2019]	31.03.1955	5		
Aleksandar Stojanov [18.04.2019]	14.11.1984	8		

Fudbalski klub Makedonija Gjorče Petrov Skopje

Founded: 1932
Stadium: Stadion „Gjorče Petrov", Skopje (3,000)

Goalkeepers:	DOB	M	(s)	G
Stojan Dimovski	19.09.1982	3		
Marko Jovanovski	24.07.1988	33		
Defenders:	**DOB**	**M**	**(s)**	**G**
Bianor das Graças Lima da Silva (BRA)	28.06.1994	23		
Izaldo Braz da Silva Junior (BRA)	03.06.1993	16		
Leovigildo Júnior Reis Rodrigues „Juninho" (BRA)	26.12.1995	18		
Filip Misevski	01.11.1991	21		
Hristijan Pecov	30.04.1994	26	(2)	
André Lucas Matos Gama „André Penalva" (BRA)	01.12.1994	10	(2)	
Filip Stojanovski	01.12.1996	14	(2)	
Trajce Stojkovski	23.02.1989	1		
Midfielders:	**DOB**	**M**	**(s)**	**G**
Ilirid Ademi	04.03.1995	9	(14)	2
Filip Aleksovski	25.03.2000			
Sabit Bilalli	15.08.1997	34		
David Blaževski	30.04.2001			
Martin Blaževski	13.05.1992	2	(5)	
Bobi Božinovski	24.02.1981	36		8
Sefer Emini	15.07.2000		(1)	
Kristijan Filipovski	02.10.1996	17	(9)	1
Robson da Silva (BRA)	14.07.1995	32	(1)	7
Metin Rushiti	23.03.2001		(1)	
Ostoja Stjepanović	17.02.1985	11	(5)	1
Filip Stojchevski	04.02.1999	8	(6)	1
Dejan Tanturovski	12.08.1992	33	(1)	9
Forwards:	**DOB**	**M**	**(s)**	**G**
Benjamin Demir	16.05.1996	2	(10)	1
Luiz Felipe Santos de Souza „Felipe Paulista" (BRA)	21.01.1994	3	(7)	
Mihajlo Jakimoski	16.04.1996		(3)	
Jeferson Damasceno da Silva (BRA)	14.06.1994	3	(4)	
Hristijan Kirovski	12.10.1985	31	(2)	11
Filip Koleceski	10.06.1988		(4)	
Kristijan Kostovski	15.12.1995	3	(9)	1
Bojan Miovski	24.06.1999		(5)	1
Ivan Nastevski	30.07.1991		(1)	
Paulo Eduardo Carvalho „Padú" (BRA)	31.10.1997	7	(6)	2
Arbin Vosha	04.08.2001		(3)	
Trainer:	**DOB**	**M**		
Aleksandar Tanevski	24.07.1983	36		

Fudbalski klub Pobeda Prilep

Founded: 2010
Stadium: Stadion „Goce Delchev", Prilep (15,000)

Goalkeepers:	DOB	M	(s)	G
Daniel Kotevski	16.08.1999	8	(2)	
Antonio Stolevski	09.05.2002	1		
Darko Tofiloski	13.01.1986	27		
Defenders:	**DOB**	**M**	**(s)**	**G**
Bunjamin Asani	10.08.1988	9	(3)	
Hristijan Dragarski	16.04.1992	17		
Aleksandar Isaevski	19.05.1995	14	(2)	
Nikola Jaćimović	03.03.1991	24		
Aleksandar Krstevski	03.09.1983	1		
Igor Panoski	18.03.1999	14		
Aleksandar Ristevski	21.08.1989	9		1
Angelce Timovski	13.11.1994	21	(10)	1
Viktor Velkoski	14.11.1995	5		
Midfielders:	**DOB**	**M**	**(s)**	**G**
Nove Aceski	26.05.1987		(1)	
Filip Beshovski	14.02.2000	1		
David Josheski	04.10.2002		(2)	
Martin Josifoski	24.09.2000		(1)	
Borce Makeshoski	24.11.2001		(1)	
Riste Markoski	30.04.1986	16		
Burhan Mustafov	02.03.1994	12	(3)	2
Jordancho Naumovski	15.02.1995	21	(5)	
Kiril Nedelkov	28.10.2000		(2)	
Sašo Shoposki	18.06.1997		(1)	
Petar Simonoski	31.01.2002		(1)	
Blagoja Spirkoski	13.07.1996	25	(5)	
Dino Spirkoski	08.01.1999	6	(4)	
Filip Spirkoski	08.06.2000		(2)	
Gjorgji Tanušev	07.01.1991	23		6
Luka Trajkoski	08.02.2000	12	(4)	1
Hristijan Veceski	07.05.1999	6	(2)	
Forwards:	**DOB**	**M**	**(s)**	**G**
Trajce Efremov	10.11.1997	17	(4)	4
Blagoja Gesoski	28.04.1981	1	(12)	
Antonio Kalanoski	25.04.1994	6	(12)	
Daniel Karceski	07.03.1992	24		
Yannick Makota (CMR)	20.01.1992	26	(4)	5
Bogdan Mandić	01.09.1998	8	(13)	
Mario Naumoski	31.08.2000	19	(4)	
Kyrian Chinazorm Nwabueze (NGA)	12.11.1992	14		6
Blagojce Ristevski	28.07.2001	1		
Filip Risteski	18.01.1999	7	(1)	
Hristijan Svrtinovski	14.02.2000	1	(1)	
Trainer:	**DOB**	**M**		
Toni Meglenski	22.05.1981	17		
Jane Nikoloski [30.11.2018]	12.12.1973	6		
Toni Meglenski [22.03.2019]	22.05.1981	13		

Fudbalski klub Rabotnički Skopje

Founded: 04.10.1937
Stadium: "Toše Proeski" National Arena, Skopje (36,460)

Goalkeepers:	DOB	M	(s)	G
Daniel Božinovski	08.07.1989	16		
Risto Jankov	05.09.1998	20	(1)	
Defenders:	**DOB**	**M**	**(s)**	**G**
Joël Bopesu (COD)	25.01.1995	14	(4)	
Alexander Borja Córdoba (COL)	25.10.1998	17	(1)	
Vladimir Dimitrovski	30.11.1988	24		1
Bojan Gjorgievski	25.01.1992	12	(3)	
Sebastián Herrera Cardona (COL)	23.01.1995	28	(1)	3
Dejan Mitrev	20.07.1988	11	(3)	
Leon Najdovski	17.10.1994	2	(1)	
Stefan Simonovski	29.08.2000		(2)	
Dušan Stević (SRB)	25.07.1995	8	(3)	1
Oliver Stoimenovski	26.03.1999	2		
Stojan Stojčevski	30.10.1992	4	(1)	
Blagoja Todorovski	11.06.1985	12		
Emil Viyachki (BUL)	18.05.1990	17		2
Midfielders:	**DOB**	**M**	**(s)**	**G**
Kristijan Ackovski	15.02.1998	9	(9)	2
Dejan Blaževski	06.12.1985	11	(2)	1
Nikolay Dyulgerov (BUL)	10.03.1988	2	(1)	
Davit Manoyan (ARM)	05.07.1990	11	(5)	
Oliver Peev	08.06.1987	33		5
Milovan Petrovikj	23.01.1990	15		
Ljubomir Stevanović (SRB)	08.08.1986	13		
Ostoja Stjepanović	17.02.1985	14		5
Forwards:	**DOB**	**M**	**(s)**	**G**
Geoffrey Charles Chinedu (NGA)	01.10.1997	9	(21)	1
Lavdrim Fazliu	06.10.1999	5	(15)	
Blaže Ilijoski	09.07.1984	15		2
Jacinto Júnior Conceição Cabral „Júninho" (BRA)	10.03.1992	4	(1)	1
Andrej Lazarov	08.09.1999		(1)	
Igor Nedeljković (SRB)	24.09.1991	10	(1)	
Filip Petkovski	24.05.1990	4	(8)	2
Petar Petkovski	03.01.1997	31	(2)	11
Martin Petrovski	16.03.1999		(2)	
Nikolce Sarkoski	08.03.1994	22	(7)	3
Mario Stankovski	06.09.1999	1	(3)	
Trainer:	**DOB**	**M**		
Đorđe Jovanovski	22.03.1956	9		
Zikica Tasevski [09.10.2018]	15.02.1978	15		
Blaze Lazarevski [30.03.2019]	03.02.1956	12		

Klubi Futbollit Renova Džepčište

Founded: 2003
Stadium: Ecolog Arena, Tetovo (15,000)

Goalkeepers:	DOB	M	(s)	G
Uroš Đurić (SRB)	01.12.1993	16	(2)	
Arian Iseni	19.04.2000	4		
Matija Kobetić (CRO)	08.11.1984	16	(2)	
Defenders:	**DOB**	**M**	**(s)**	**G**
Xhelil Abdulla	25.09.1991	30	(2)	
Saimir Fetai	04.04.1989	18	(5)	
Nenad Miškovski	26.12.1986	33		2
Aleksandar Ristevski	11.05.1992		(3)	
Nehar Sadiki	16.03.1998	8	(2)	1
Bashkim Velija	01.08.1993	34		1
Fisnik Zuka	03.09.1995	26	(5)	
Midfielders:	**DOB**	**M**	**(s)**	**G**
Ermadin Adem	07.07.1990	8	(3)	1
Ersin Fetahi	01.08.1996		(1)	
Argjent Gafuri	30.03.1988	18	(10)	2
Fatjon Jusufi	06.03.1997	13	(1)	2
Florian Kadriu	29.08.1996	10	(17)	1
Burhan Mustafov	02.03.1994	12	(5)	5
Fisnik Nuhiu	26.01.1983	28	(6)	1
Emran Ramadani	29.01.1992	26	(5)	11
Burim Sadiki	05.08.1989	10	(6)	
Muhamed Useini	21.11.1988	13		3
Forwards:	**DOB**	**M**	**(s)**	**G**
Lutfi Bilali	14.04.1992	3	(7)	
Fernando Silva dos Santos (BRA)	18.05.1991	6	(5)	
Miran Maksuti	15.07.1993	1	(5)	
Emmanuel Mbella (FRA)	18.06.1992	7	(6)	1
Bojan Miovski	24.06.1999	7		3
Nikola Pantović (SRB)	19.03.1994		(4)	
Vlatko Stojanovski	23.04.1997	31	(1)	18
Alban Sulejmani	14.04.1998	18	(4)	1
Trainer:	**DOB**	**M**		
Jeton Bekiri	18.06.1982	9		
Nikola Ilievski [09.10.2018]	16.12.1954	27		

Klubi Futbollistik Shkendija Tetovo

Founded: 27.08.1979
Stadium: Ecolog Arena, Tetovo (15,000)

Goalkeepers:	**DOB**	**M**	**(s)**	**G**
Artan Iljazi	24.02.1999	2		
Bekim Redjepi	27.10.1996	9		
Kostadin Zahov	08.11.1987	25		
Defenders:	**DOB**	**M**	**(s)**	**G**
Mevlan Adili	30.03.1994	4	(5)	
Egzon Bejtulai	07.01.1994	29		4
Konstantin Cheshmedijev	29.01.1996	8	(3)	
Zija Merdjani	22.10.1995	5	(2)	
Gledi Mici (ALB)	06.02.1991	31	(1)	1
Mevlan Murati	05.03.1994	26		
Visar Musliu	13.11.1994	29		4
Almir Redjepi	04.04.2001		(2)	
Leard Sadriu (KVX)	22.04.2001	7		
Blagoja Todorovski	11.06.1985	6		
Midfielders:	**DOB**	**M**	**(s)**	**G**
Armend Alimi	11.12.1987	27		3
Berat Beqiri (ALB)	03.06.1996	3	(2)	
Jakup Berisha	20.02.2000	4	(2)	1
Besmir Bojku	03.01.1995	13	(15)	5
Izair Emini	04.10.1985	19	(6)	11
Florent Ramadani	27.08.2000	1	(1)	
Jeton Shahini	15.06.2000		(1)	
Šćiprim Taipi (KVX)	19.02.1997	1	(4)	
Ennur Totre	29.10.1996	30	(2)	4
Arbin Zejnullai (ALB)	15.02.1999	4	(9)	3
Forwards:	**DOB**	**M**	**(s)**	**G**
Samir Fazli	22.04.1991	13	(7)	2
Agim Ibraimi	29.08.1988	13	(2)	3
Besart Ibraimi	17.12.1986	11		11
Omar Imeri (ALB)	13.12.1999	24	(1)	8
Ensar Ljuma	17.06.2000	1	(1)	1
Valmir Nafiu	23.04.1994	15	(14)	4
Marjan Radeski	10.02.1995	6	(5)	4
Aljbin Ramadani	20.10.2000		(1)	
Besart Redjepi	09.02.2000	2	(1)	
Remzifaik Selmani	05.05.1997	1	(5)	
Shefit Shefiti (ALB)	19.02.1998	8	(10)	4
Stênio Marcos da Fonseca Salazar Júnior (BRA)	10.06.1991	19	(4)	4
Trainer:	**DOB**	**M**		
Qatip Osmani	29.06.1969	36		

Futboll Club Shkupi Čair

Founded: 1927
Stadium: Stadion Čair, Skopje (6,000)

Goalkeepers:	**DOB**	**M**	**(s)**	**G**
Igor Aleksovski	24.02.1995	13		
Enes Azizi (SUI)	09.02.1994	16		
Saljadin Mustafi	13.04.1993	2	(1)	
Suat Zendeli	24.02.1981	5		
Defenders:	**DOB**	**M**	**(s)**	**G**
Basilio Ndong Owono Nchama (EQG)	17.01.1999	22	(2)	
Amir Bilali (ALB)	15.05.1994	33		1
Onyebuchi Emmanuel Ifeanyi (NGA)	04.04.2000		(2)	
Besart Krivanjeva	28.02.1996	15	(8)	
Blagojče Ljamčevski	07.04.1987	7	(7)	
Besir Ramadani (ALB)	09.06.2000	4	(2)	
Filip Ristovski	03.01.1995	17	(1)	
Toni Tipurić (AUT)	10.09.1990	18		1
Abdulkadir Zango (NGA)	19.06.1996	11	(4)	
Midfielders:	**DOB**	**M**	**(s)**	**G**
Ergin Abdul	03.02.1993		(2)	
Ermadin Adem	07.07.1990	3	(1)	
Muharem Bajrami	29.11.1985	24	(4)	5
Ron Broja (KVX)	09.04.1996	28	(3)	1
Bradhi Dakouri (CIV)	13.12.1992	25	(3)	
Besar Iseni	18.01.1997	10	(3)	1
Hamza Ramani	17.09.2002		(1)	
Berat Ustabaşı (TUR)	24.03.1994	15	(3)	5
Stephan Vujčić (GER)	03.01.1986	3		
Forwards:	**DOB**	**M**	**(s)**	**G**
Jusuf Aliu	21.08.2000	1	(5)	
Viktor Angelov	27.03.1994	25	(4)	6
Blaže Ilijoski	09.07.1984	7	(2)	2
Fatih Ismaili	29.08.1997	17		
Abdulhadi Jahja	03.06.1999		(2)	
Omer Jashari	13.11.2000	2	(2)	
Musli Lika	28.02.2000		(4)	
Suhejlj Muharem	25.08.2001	20	(14)	3
Sérgio Antonio Da Luiz Junior „Serginho" (BRA)	06.04.1995	31	(1)	7
Kristijan Stojkovski	17.09.1991	15	(2)	3
Maharafa Tandina (MLI)	18.08.1997	4	(2)	
Artan Veliu	09.12.1997	3	(17)	2
Trainer:	**DOB**	**M**		
Zekirija Ramadani	21.01.1978	3		
Hayati Soydas [01.09.2018]	01.05.1966	5		
Ümit Karan (TUR) [04.10.2018]	01.10.1976	28		

Fudbalski klub Sileks Kratovo

Founded: 1965
Stadium: Stadion Sileks, Kratovo (1,800)

Goalkeepers:	**DOB**	**M**	**(s)**	**G**
Andreja Efremov	02.09.1992	17	(1)	
Blagojce Ivanov	03.06.1999	2		
Hristijan Petkovski	17.08.1999	1		
Spasoje Stefanović (SRB)	12.10.1992	16		
Defenders:	**DOB**	**M**	**(s)**	**G**
Dejan Blagojević (SRB)	18.01.1990	28	(1)	1
Srđan Drasković (SRB)	08.01.1991	32	(1)	
Hristijan Grozdanoski	05.06.1993	26	(3)	1
Stefan Kocev	23.02.1994	26	(3)	
Filip Milenkovski	07.01.1990	23	(2)	
Filip Ristovski	03.01.1995	9	(4)	
Midfielders:	**DOB**	**M**	**(s)**	**G**
Charles Acolatsè (TOG)	05.05.1995	5	(4)	
Darko Aleksovski	23.12.1990	14	(12)	4
Dimitri Blagoevski	21.12.2000		(1)	
Filip Duranski	17.07.1991	34		3
Dimitar Ivanov	19.01.1995	2	(10)	1
Ivo Janakievski	09.06.1993	3	(3)	
Alpaj Jusuf	26.03.1998	7	(4)	
Petar Ljamčevski	08.08.1991	3	(4)	
Stefan Milosavljević	09.05.1992	2		
Louise Essengue Eloumou Parfait (CMR)	06.07.1990	16		3
Denis Ristov (SRB)	24.06.1990	8	(8)	
Viktor Serafimovski	24.10.1995	16		
Forwards:	**DOB**	**M**	**(s)**	**G**
Andrian Chavoli	15.09.1996	1	(9)	
Dario Desnikj	13.05.1994	4	(9)	
Darko Dodev	16.01.1998	28	(2)	1
Boban Georgiev	26.01.1997	29	(5)	8
Petar Ikić (SRB)	19.04.1991	3	(11)	
Emmanuel Mbella (FRA)	18.06.1992	14	(2)	1
Aleksandar Panovski	30.06.1988	10	(4)	
Marko Rajkovic (SRB)	13.11.1992	17	(1)	4
Trainer:	**DOB**	**M**		
Zikica Tasevski	15.02.1978	8		
Momcilo Mitevski [01.10.2018]		20		
Goran Simov (SRB) [16.04.2019]	31.03.1975	8		

Fudbalski Klub Vardar Skopje

Founded: 22.07.1947
Stadium: "Toše Proeski" National Arena, Skopje (36,460)

Goalkeepers:	DOB	M	(s)	G
Filip Gačevski	17.08.1990	35		
Filip Ilikj	26.01.1997	1		
Defenders:	**DOB**	**M**	**(s)**	**G**
Filip Antovski	24.11.2000	2	(1)	
Vladica Brdarovski	07.02.1990	28	(3)	4
Nicolás José Herranz (ARG)	17.06.1994	4		
Leovigildo Júnior Reis Rodrigues „Juninho" (BRA)	26.12.1995	15	(1)	3
Kosta Manev (FIN)	07.04.1993	27		
Stefan Naumceski	07.08.2000	1		
Evgen Novak (UKR)	01.02.1989	28		2
Goran Popov	02.10.1984	8		1
Jovan Popzlatanov	06.07.1996	11	(18)	5
Todor Todoroski	26.02.1999	13	(1)	
Kristijan Toševski	06.05.1994	19	(5)	
Midfielders:	**DOB**	**M**	**(s)**	**G**
Ali Adem	01.06.2000	7	(8)	
Daniel Avramovski	20.02.1995	14	(2)	1
Tigran Barseghyan (ARM)	22.09.1993	7		4
Jakup Berisha	20.02.2000	1	(5)	
Clarence Junior Bitang (CMR)	02.09.1992	22	(4)	
Matej Cvetanoski	18.08.1997	21	(7)	2
Bojan Dimoski	23.11.2001	3	(2)	
Besar Iseni	18.01.1997		(3)	1
Juan Felipe Alves Ribeiro (BRA)	05.12.1987	16	(2)	4
Darko Micevski	12.04.1992	33	(1)	8
Filip Najdovski	13.09.1992	24	(4)	2
Fitor Rexhepi	20.03.2000		(1)	
Aleks Taleski	17.06.2000		(6)	
Nildo Victor Juffo (BRA)	24.02.1993	12	(2)	1
Forwards:	**DOB**	**M**	**(s)**	**G**
Dzemal Ibishi	18.01.2001	8	(10)	1
Bojan Kolevski	20.06.2000	8	(7)	3
Maksim Maksimov (RUS)	04.11.1995	2	(2)	
David Velkovski	15.12.2000		(1)	
Willian Lira Sousa (BRA)	09.12.1993	26	(5)	3
Trainer:	**DOB**	**M**		
Aleksandar Vasoski	21.11.1979	36		

SECOND LEVEL
Vtora Liga 2018/2019

2. MFL Istok (Group East)

1.	FK Borec 1919 Veles (*Promoted*)	27	21	3	3	63 - 17	66
2.	GFK Tikveš 1930 Kavadarci (*Promotion Play-off*)	27	16	9	2	47 - 16	57
3.	FK Bregalnica 2008 Štip	27	15	7	5	54 - 26	52
4.	FK Kožuf Gevgelija	27	15	7	5	39 - 18	52
5.	FK Kit-Go Pehčevo	27	14	8	5	55 - 18	50
6.	FK Plačkovica Radoviš	27	7	7	13	27 - 39	28
7.	FK Detonit Junior Radoviš (*Relegated*)	27	8	3	16	31 - 53	27
8.	FK Sasa Makedonska Kamenica (*Relegated*)	27	5	5	17	24 - 55	20
9.	FK Vardar Negotino (*Relegated*)	27	4	2	21	19 - 60	14
10.	FK Partizan Obršani (*Relegated*)	27	4	1	22	10 - 67	13

2. MFL Zapad (Group West)

1.	FC Struga Trim-Lum (*Promoted*)	27	15	9	3	42 - 17	54
2.	FK Labunishta (*Promotion Play-off*)	27	11	10	6	23 - 27	43
3.	FK Pelister Bitola	27	11	8	8	27 - 20	41
4.	KF Vëllazërimi 77 Kičevo	27	11	6	10	34 - 32	39
5.	KF Gostivari	27	10	8	9	40 - 34	38
6.	FK Skopje	27	10	7	10	32 - 24	37
7.	KF Korabi Debar	27	10	6	11	32 - 30	36
8.	FK Teteks Tetovo (*Relegated*)	27	9	5	13	28 - 34	32
9.	FC Genç Kalemler Donla Banjica (*Relegated*)	27	6	8	13	25 - 35	26
10.	FK Goblen Kumanovo (*Relegated*)	27	4	9	14	15 - 45	21

Promotion Play-off [02.06.2019]

GFK Tikveš 1930 Kavadarci - FK Labunishta 6-3(3-1)

NATIONAL TEAM

INTERNATIONAL MATCHES
(16.07.2018 – 15.07.2019)

06.09.2018	Gibraltar	Gibraltar - North Macedonia	0-2(0-2)	(UNL)
09.09.2018	Skopje	North Macedonia - Armenia	2-0(1-0)	(UNL)
13.10.2018	Skopje	North Macedonia - Liechtenstein	4-1(3-1)	(UNL)
16.10.2018	Yerevan	Armenia - North Macedonia	4-0(1-0)	(UNL)
16.11.2018	Vaduz	Liechtenstein - North Macedonia	0-2(0-0)	(UNL)
19.11.2018	Skopje	North Macedonia - Gibraltar	4-0(1-0)	(UNL)
21.03.2019	Skopje	North Macedonia - Latvia	3-1(2-0)	(ECQ)
24.03.2019	Ljubljana	Slovenia - North Macedonia	1-1(1-0)	(ECQ)
07.06.2019	Skopje	North Macedonia - Poland	0-1(0-0)	(ECQ)
10.06.2019	Skopje	North Macedonia - Austria	1-4(1-1)	(ECQ)

06.09.2018 GIBRALTAR - NORTH MACEDONIA 0-2(0-2) UEFA Nations League D, Group 4
Victoria Stadium, Gibraltar; Referee: Jens Maae (Denmark); Attendance: 1,850
MKD: Stole Dimitrievski, Stefan Ristovski, Kire Ristevski, Visar Musliu, Stefan Spirovski, Ivan Tričkovski, Boban Nikolov, Enis Bardi (85.Egzon Bejtulai), Goran Pandev (Cap) (46.Ilija Nestorovski), Aleksandar Trajkovski (69.Eljif Elmas), Ezgjan Alioski. Trainer: Igor Angelovski.
Goals: Ivan Tričkovski (19), Ezgjan Alioski (35).

09.09.2018 NORTH MACEDONIA - ARMENIA 2-0(1-0) UEFA Nations League D, Group 4
"Toše Proeski" National Arena; Referee: Manuel Schüttengruber (Austria); Attendance: 4,730
MKD: Stole Dimitrievski, Stefan Ristovski, Kire Ristevski, Visar Musliu, Eljif Elmas, Egzon Bejtulai, Stefan Spirovski, Ivan Tričkovski (57.Aleksandar Trajkovski), Enis Bardi (74.Boban Nikolov), Goran Pandev (Cap) (69.Ilija Nestorovski), Ezgjan Alioski. Trainer: Igor Angelovski.
Goals: Ezgjan Alioski (14 penalty), Goran Pandev (59).

13.10.2018 NORTH MACEDONIA - LIECHTENSTEIN 4-1(3-1) UEFA Nations League D, Group 4
"Toše Proeski" National Arena, Skopje; Referee: Roi Reinshreiber (Israel); Attendance: 8,100
MKD: Stole Dimitrievski, Visar Musliu, Gjoko Zajkov, Egzon Bejtulai (77.Stefan Ristovski), Enis Bardi, Eljif Elmas, Goran Pandev (Cap) (69.Boban Nikolov), Ilija Nestorovski (83.Stefan Spirovski), Aleksandar Trajkovski, Ferhan Hasani, Ezgjan Alioski. Trainer: Igor Angelovski.
Goals: Aleksandar Trajkovski (10, 30), Goran Pandev (36), Ezgjan Alioski (67).

16.10.2018 ARMENIA - NORTH MACEDONIA 4-0(1-0) UEFA Nations League D, Group 4
„Vazgen Sargsyan" Hanrapetakan Stadium, Yerevan; Referee: Martin Strömbergsson (Sweden); Attendance: 8,300
MKD: Stole Dimitrievski, Stefan Ristovski, Kire Ristevski, Visar Musliu, Gjoko Zajkov (76.Ferhan Hasani), Arijan Ademi, Stefan Spirovski (58.Eljif Elmas [*sent off 90+3*]), Enis Bardi (65.Ilija Nestorovski), Goran Pandev (Cap), Aleksandar Trajkovski, Ezgjan Alioski. Trainer: Igor Angelovski.

16.11.2018 LIECHTENSTEIN - NORTH MACEDONIA 0-2(0-0) UEFA Nations League D, Group 4
Rheinpark Stadion, Vaduz; Referee: Petr Ardeleanu (Czech Republic); Attendance: 2,116
MKD: Stole Dimitrievski, Kire Ristevski, Visar Musliu, Egzon Bejtulai, Ivan Tričkovski (77.Stefan Spirovski; 85.Kristijan Toševski), Enis Bardi, Boban Nikolov, Goran Pandev (Cap), Ilija Nestorovski, Aleksandar Trajkovski, Ferhan Hasani (77.Krste Velkoski). Trainer: Igor Angelovski.
Goals: Enis Bardi (53), Ilija Nestorovski (90+1).

19.11.2018 NORTH MACEDONIA - GIBRALTAR 4-0(1-0) UEFA Nations League D, Group 4
"Toše Proeski" National Arena, Skopje; Referee: Daniyar Sakhi (Kazakhstan); Attendance: 2,152
MKD: Stole Dimitrievski, Kire Ristevski, Visar Musliu, Egzon Bejtulai, Ivan Tričkovski (Cap) (59.Ferhan Hasani), Boban Nikolov, Enis Bardi, Eljif Elmas (73.Arijan Ademi), Ilija Nestorovski (82.Krste Velkoski), Aleksandar Trajkovski, Ezgjan Alioski. Trainer: Igor Angelovski.
Goals: Enis Bardi (27), Ilija Nestorovski (67, 80), Aleksandar Trajkovski (90+2).

21.03.2019 NORTH MACEDONIA - LATVIA 3-1(2-0) 16th EC. Qualifiers
"Toše Proeski" National Arena, Skopje; Referee: Halis Özkahya (Turkey); Attendance: 7,043
MKD: Stole Dimitrievski, Stefan Ristovski, Visar Musliu, Darko Velkovski, Boban Nikolov, Enis Bardi, Goran Pandev (Cap) (71.Kire Ristevski), Ilija Nestorovski, Aleksandar Trajkovski (83.Kire Markoski), Ferhan Hasani (23.Eljif Elmas), Ezgjan Alioski. Trainer: Igor Angelovski.
Goals: Ezgjan Alioski (11), Eljif Elmas (29, 90+3).

24.03.2019 SLOVENIA - NORTH MACEDONIA 1-1(1-0) 16th EC. Qualifiers
Stadion Stožice, Ljubljana; Referee: Xavier Estrada Fernández (Spain); Attendance: 9,872
MKD: Stole Dimitrievski, Stefan Ristovski, Visar Musliu, Darko Velkovski, Egzon Bejtulai, Boban Nikolov, Enis Bardi, Eljif Elmas, Goran Pandev (Cap) (76.Aleksandar Trajkovski), Ilija Nestorovski (88.Kire Markoski), Ezgjan Alioski (90+3.Kire Ristevski). Trainer: Igor Angelovski.
Goal: Enis Bardi (47).

07.06.2019 NORTH MACEDONIA - POLAND 0-1(0-0) 16th EC. Qualifiers
"Toše Proeski" National Arena, Skopje; Referee: Referee: Gianluca Rocchi (Italy); Attendance: 25,000
MKD: Stole Dimitrievski, Stefan Ristovski (76.Arijan Ademi), Visar Musliu [*sent off 85*], Darko Velkovski, Egzon Bejtulai, Boban Nikolov (62.Aleksandar Trajkovski), Enis Bardi, Eljif Elmas, Goran Pandev (Cap) (84.Ferhan Hasani), Ilija Nestorovski, Ezgjan Alioski. Trainer: Igor Angelovski.

10.06.2019 NORTH MACEDONIA - AUSTRIA 1-4(1-1) 16th EC. Qualifiers
"Toše Proeski" National Arena, Skopje; Referee: Aleksei Eskov (Russia); Attendance: 10,501
MKD: Stole Dimitrievski, Stefan Ristovski, Darko Velkovski, Egzon Bejtulai, Arijan Ademi, Boban Nikolov (67.Ferhan Hasani), Enis Bardi, Eljif Elmas (55.Kire Ristevski), Goran Pandev (Cap), Ilija Nestorovski (56.Marjan Radeski), Ezgjan Alioski. Trainer: Igor Angelovski.
Goal: Martin Hinteregger (18, own goal).

NATIONAL TEAM PLAYERS
(16.07.2018 – 15.07.2019)

Name	DOB	Caps	Goals	2018/2019:	*Club*
Goalkeepers					
Stole DIMITRIEVSKI	25.12.1993	**28**	**0**	2018/2019:	*Rayo Vallecano de Madrid (ESP)*
Defenders					
Egzon BEJTULAI	07.01.1994	**8**	**0**	2018/2019:	*KF Shkëndija Tetovo*
Visar MUSLIU	13.11.1994	**15**	**1**	2018/2019:	*KF Shkëndija Tetovo*
Kire RISTEVSKI	22.10.1990	**33**	**0**	2018: 21.09.2018->	*Vasas SC Budapest (HUN)* *Újpest FC (HUN)*
Stefan RISTOVSKI	12.02.1992	**48**	**1**	2018/2019:	*Sporting Clube de Portugal Lisboa (POR)*
Kristijan TOŠEVSKI	06.05.1994	**6**	**0**	2018:	*FK Vardar Skopje*
Darko VELKOVSKI	21.06.1995	**15**	**0**	2018/2019:	*HNK Rijeka (CRO)*
Gjoko ZAJKOV	10.02.1995	**9**	**0**	2018:	*SC Charleroi (BEL)*
Midfielders					
Arijan ADEMI	29.05.1991	**11**	**2**	2018/2019:	*GNK Dinamo Zagreb (CRO)*
Ezgjan ALIOSKI	12.02.1992	**29**	**5**	2018/2019:	*Leeds United FC (ENG)*
Enis BARDI	02.07.1995	**23**	**4**	2018/2019:	*Levante UD Valencia (ESP)*
Eljif ELMAS	27.09.1999	**12**	**2**	2018/2019:	*Fenerbahçe SK İstanbul (TUR)*
Ferhan HASANI	18.06.1990	**38**	**2**	2018/2019:	*Al-Ra'ed FC Buraidah (KSA)*
Kire MARKOSKI	20.05.1995	**5**	**1**	2018/2019:	*FC Spartak Trnava (SVK)*
Boban NIKOLOV	28.07.1994	**17**	**1**	2018/2019:	*MOL Vidi FC Székesfehérvár (HUN)*
Marjan RADESKI	10.02.1995	**14**	**1**	2019:	*KF Shkëndija Tetovo*
Stefan SPIROVSKI	23.08.1990	**27**	**1**	2018:	*Ferencvárosi TC (HUN)*
Forwards					
Ilija NESTOROVSKI	12.03.1990	**31**	**8**	2018/2019:	*US Città di Palermo (ITA)*
Goran PANDEV	27.07.1983	**103**	**33**	2018/2019:	*Genoa C&FC (ITA)*
Aleksandar TRAJKOVSKI	05.09.1992	**50**	**15**	2018/2019:	*US Città di Palermo (ITA)*
Ivan TRIČKOVSKI	18.04.1987	**54**	**5**	2018:	*AEK Larnaca FC (CYP)*
Krste VELKOSKI	20.02.1988	**12**	**0**	2018:	*FK Sarajevo (BIH)*

National team coach

Igor ANGELOVSKI [from 16.10.2015]	02.06.1976	31 M; 13 W; 6 D; 12 L; 28-22

NORTHERN IRELAND

The Country:
Tuaisceart Éireann (Northern Ireland)
Capital: Belfast
Surface: 14,130 km²
Inhabitants: 1,876,695 [2017]
Time: UTC

The FA:
Irish Football Association
National Football Stadium Donegal Avenue BT12 5LW, Belfast
Tel: +44 28 9066 9458
Foundation date: 1880
Member of FIFA since: 1911
Member of UEFA since: 1954
Website: www.irishfa.com

NATIONAL TEAM RECORDS

First international match:	18.02.1882, Belfast:	Ireland – England 0-13
Most international caps:	Patrick Anthony Jennings	- 119 caps (1964-1986)
Most international goals:	David Jonathan Healy	- 36 goals / 95 caps (2000-2013)

UEFA EUROPEAN CHAMPIONSHIP	
1960	Did not enter
1964	Qualifiers
1968	Qualifiers
1972	Qualifiers
1976	Qualifiers
1980	Qualifiers
1984	Qualifiers
1988	Qualifiers
1992	Qualifiers
1996	Qualifiers
2000	Qualifiers
2004	Qualifiers
2008	Qualifiers
2012	Qualifiers
2016	Final Tournament (2nd Round of 16)

FIFA WORLD CUP	
1930	Did not enter
1934	Did not enter
1938	Did not enter
1950	Qualifiers
1954	Qualifiers
1958	Final Tournament (Quarter-Finals)
1962	Qualifiers
1966	Qualifiers
1970	Qualifiers
1974	Qualifiers
1978	Qualifiers
1982	Final Tournament (2nd Round)
1986	Final Tournament (Group Stage)
1990	Qualifiers
1994	Qualifiers
1998	Qualifiers
2002	Qualifiers
2006	Qualifiers
2010	Qualifiers
2014	Qualifiers
2018	Qualifiers

UEFA NATIONS LEAGUE
2018/2019 – League B

FIFA CONFEDERATIONS CUP 1992-2017
None

NORTHERN IRISH CLUB HONOURS IN EUROPEAN CLUB COMPETITIONS:

European Champion Clubs.Cup (1956-1992) / UEFA Champions League (1993-2019)
None
Fairs Cup (1858-1971) / UEFA Cup (1972-2009) / UEFA Europa League (2010-2019)
None
UEFA Super Cup (1972-2018)
None
European Cup Winners.Cup 1961-1999*
None

**defunct competition*

NATIONAL COMPETITIONS
TABLE OF HONOURS

	CHAMPIONS	CUP WINNERS	BEST GOALSCORERS	
1880/1881	-	Moyola Park AFC	-	
1881/1882	-	Queen's Island FC Belfast	-	
1882/1883	-	Cliftonville FAC	-	
1883/1884	-	Distillery FC Ballyskeagh	-	
1884/1885	-	Distillery FC Ballyskeagh	-	
1885/1886	-	Distillery FC Ballyskeagh	-	
1886/1887	-	Ulster FC Ballynafeigh	-	
1887/1888	-	Cliftonville FAC	-	
1888/1889	-	Distillery FC Ballyskeagh	-	
1889/1890	-	Gordon Highlanders	-	
1890/1891	Linfield FC Belfast	Linfield FC Belfast	Robert Hill (Linfield FC Belfast)	20
1891/1892	Linfield FC Belfast	Linfield FC Belfast	Tim Morrison (Linfield FC Belfast)	21
1892/1893	Linfield FC Belfast	Linfield FC Belfast	Robert Hill (Linfield FC Belfast) James Percy (Cliftonville FAC)	9
1893/1894	Glentoran FC Belfast	Distillery FC Ballyskeagh	Michael McErlean (Linfield FC Belfast)	9
1894/1895	Linfield FC Belfast	Linfield FC Belfast	George Gaukrodger (Linfield FC Belfast) Joe McAllen (Linfield FC Belfast)	4
1895/1896	Distillery FC Ballyskeagh	Distillery FC Ballyskeagh	-	
1896/1897	Glentoran FC Belfast	Cliftonville FAC	Johnny Darling (Linfield FC Belfast) Richard Peden (Linfield FC Belfast)	6
1897/1898	Linfield FC Belfast	Linfield FC Belfast	-	
1898/1899	Distillery FC Ballyskeagh	Linfield FC Belfast	-	
1899/1900	Belfast Celtic FC	Cliftonville FAC	-	
1900/1901	Distillery FC Ballyskeagh	Cliftonville FAC	-	
1901/1902	Linfield FC Belfast	Linfield FC Belfast	-	
1902/1903	Distillery FC Ballyskeagh	Distillery FC Ballyskeagh	-	
1903/1904	Linfield FC Belfast	Linfield FC Belfast	-	
1904/1905	Glentoran FC Belfast	Distillery FC Ballyskeagh	-	
1905/1906	Cliftonville FAC Distillery FC Ballyskeagh (shared)	Shelbourne FC Dublin	-	
1906/1907	Linfield FC Belfast	Cliftonville FAC	-	
1907/1908	Linfield FC Belfast	Bohemians FC Dublin	-	
1908/1909	Linfield FC Belfast	Cliftonville FAC	-	
1909/1910	Cliftonville FAC	Distillery FC Ballyskeagh	-	
1910/1911	Linfield FC Belfast	Shelbourne FC Dublin	-	
1911/1912	Glentoran FC Belfast	Linfield FC Belfast	-	
1912/1913	Glentoran FC Belfast	Linfield FC Belfast	-	
1913/1914	Linfield FC Belfast	Glentoran FC Belfast	-	
1914/1915	Belfast Celtic FC	Linfield FC Belfast	-	
1915/1916	*No competition*	Linfield FC Belfast	-	
1916/1917	*No competition*	Glentoran FC Belfast	-	
1917/1918	*No competition*	Belfast Celtic FC	-	
1918/1919	*No competition*	Linfield FC Belfast	-	
1919/1920	Belfast Celtic FC	Shelbourne FC Dublin	-	
1920/1921	Glentoran FC Belfast	Glentoran FC Belfast	-	
1921/1922	Linfield FC Belfast	Linfield FC Belfast	-	
1922/1923	Linfield FC Belfast	Linfield FC Belfast	-	
1923/1924	Queen's Island FC Belfast	Queen's Island FC Belfast	-	
1924/1925	Glentoran FC Belfast	Distillery FC Ballyskeagh	-	
1925/1926	Belfast Celtic FC	Belfast Celtic FC	-	
1926/1927	Belfast Celtic FC	Ards FC Newtownards	Joseph Gardiner Absolom Bambrick (Glentoran FC Belfast)	28
1927/1928	Belfast Celtic FC	Willowfield FC	-	
1928/1929	Belfast Celtic FC	Ballymena FC	Joseph Gardiner Absolom Bambrick (Linfield FC Belfast)	43
1929/1930	Linfield FC Belfast	Linfield FC Belfast	Joseph Gardiner Absolom Bambrick (Linfield FC Belfast)	50
1930/1931	Glentoran FC Belfast	Linfield FC Belfast	Fred Roberts (Glentoran FC Belfast)	55
1931/1932	Linfield FC Belfast	Glentoran FC Belfast	-	
1932/1933	Belfast Celtic FC	Glentoran FC Belfast	Joseph Gardiner Absolom Bambrick (Linfield FC Belfast)	40
1933/1934	Linfield FC Belfast	Linfield FC Belfast	-	
1934/1935	Linfield FC Belfast	Glentoran FC Belfast	-	
1935/1936	Belfast Celtic FC	Linfield FC Belfast	-	
1936/1937	Belfast Celtic FC	Belfast Celtic FC	-	
1937/1938	Belfast Celtic FC	Belfast Celtic FC	-	
1938/1939	Belfast Celtic FC	Linfield FC Belfast	-	
1939/1940	Belfast Celtic FC	Ballymena United FC	-	
1940/1941	*No competition*	Belfast Celtic FC	-	
1941/1942	*No competition*	Linfield FC Belfast	-	
1942/1943	*No competition*	Belfast Celtic FC	-	

1943/1944	*No competition*	Belfast Celtic FC	-	
1944/1945	*No competition*	Linfield FC Belfast	-	
1945/1946	*No competition*	Linfield FC Belfast	-	
1946/1947	*No competition*	Belfast Celtic FC	-	
1947/1948	Belfast Celtic FC	Linfield FC Belfast	James Jones (Belfast Celtic FC)	28
1948/1949	Linfield FC Belfast	Derry City FC	William Simpson (Linfield FC Belfast)	19
1949/1950	Linfield FC Belfast	Linfield FC Belfast	Sammy Hughes (Glentoran FC Belfast)	23
1950/1951	Glentoran FC Belfast	Glentoran FC Belfast	Sammy Hughes (Glentoran FC Belfast) Walter Allen (Portadown FC)	23
1951/1952	Glenavon FC Lurgan	Ards FC Newtownards	James Jones (Glenavon FC Lurgan)	27
1952/1953	Glentoran FC Belfast	Linfield FC Belfast	Sammy Hughes (Glentoran FC Belfast)	28
1953/1954	Linfield FC Belfast	Derry City FC	James Jones (Glenavon FC Lurgan)	32
1954/1955	Linfield FC Belfast	Dundela FC Belfast	Francis Coyle (Coleraine FC)	20
1955/1956	Linfield FC Belfast	Distillery FC Ballyskeagh	James Jones (Glenavon FC Lurgan)	26
1956/1957	Glenavon FC Lurgan	Glenavon FC Lurgan	James Jones (Glenavon FC Lurgan)	33
1957/1958	Ards FC Newtownards	Ballymena United FC	John Edward Thompson Milburn (Linfield FC Belfast)	29
1958/1959	Linfield FC Belfast	Glenavon FC Lurgan	John Edward Thompson Milburn (Linfield FC Belfast)	26
1959/1960	Glenavon FC Lurgan	Linfield FC Belfast	James Jones (Glenavon FC Lurgan)	29
1960/1961	Linfield FC Belfast	Glenavon FC Lurgan	Trevor Thompson (Glentoran FC Belfast)	22
1961/1962	Linfield FC Belfast	Linfield FC Belfast	Mick Lynch (Ards FC Newtownards)	20
1962/1963	Distillery FC Ballyskeagh	Linfield FC Belfast	Joe Meldrum (Distillery FC Ballyskeagh)	27
1963/1964	Glentoran FC Belfast	Derry City FC	Trevor Thompson (Linfield FC Belfast)	21
1964/1965	Derry City FC	Coleraine FC	Kenny Halliday (Coleraine FC) Dennis Guy (Glenavon FC Lurgan)	19
1965/1966	Linfield FC Belfast	Glentoran FC Belfast	Sammy Pavis (Linfield FC Belfast)	28
1966/1967	Glentoran FC Belfast	Crusaders FC Belfast	Sammy Pavis (Linfield FC Belfast)	25
1967/1968	Glentoran FC Belfast	Crusaders FC Belfast	Sammy Pavis (Linfield FC Belfast)	30
1968/1969	Linfield FC Belfast	Ards FC Newtownards	Danny Hale (Derry City FC)	21
1969/1970	Glentoran FC Belfast	Linfield FC Belfast	Des Dickson (Coleraine FC)	21
1970/1971	Linfield FC Belfast	Distillery FC Ballyskeagh	Bryan Hamilton (Linfield FC Belfast)	18
1971/1972	Glentoran FC Belfast	Coleraine FC	Peter Watson (Distillery FC Ballyskeagh) Des Dickson (Coleraine FC)	15
1972/1973	Crusaders FC Belfast	Glentoran FC Belfast	Des Dickson (Coleraine FC)	23
1973/1974	Coleraine FC	Ards FC Newtownards	Des Dickson (Coleraine FC)	24
1974/1975	Linfield FC Belfast	Coleraine FC	Martin Malone (Portadown FC)	15
1975/1976	Crusaders FC Belfast	Carrick Rangers FC	Des Dickson (Coleraine FC)	23
1976/1977	Glentoran FC Belfast	Coleraine FC	Ronnie McAteer (Crusaders FC Belfast)	20
1977/1978	Linfield FC Belfast	Linfield FC Belfast	Warren Feeney (Glentoran FC Belfast)	17
1978/1979	Linfield FC Belfast	Cliftonville FAC	Tommy Armstrong (Ards FC Newtownards)	21
1979/1980	Linfield FC Belfast	Linfield FC Belfast	James Martin (Glentoran FC Belfast)	17
1980/1981	Glentoran FC Belfast	Ballymena United FC	Des Dickson (Coleraine FC) Paul Malone (Ballymena United FC)	18
1981/1982	Linfield FC Belfast	Linfield FC Belfast	Gary Blackledge (Glentoran FC Belfast)	18
1982/1983	Linfield FC Belfast	Glentoran FC Belfast	James Campbell (Ards FC Newtownards)	15
1983/1984	Linfield FC Belfast	Ballymena United FC	Martin McGaughey (Linfield FC Belfast) Trevor Anderson (Linfield FC Belfast)	15
1984/1985	Linfield FC Belfast	Glentoran FC Belfast	Martin McGaughey (Linfield FC Belfast)	34
1985/1986	Linfield FC Belfast	Glentoran FC Belfast	Trevor Anderson (Linfield FC Belfast)	14
1986/1987	Linfield FC Belfast	Glentoran FC Belfast	Ray McCoy (Coleraine FC) Gary Macartney (Glentoran FC Belfast)	14
1987/1988	Glentoran FC Belfast	Glentoran FC Belfast	Martin McGaughey (Linfield FC Belfast)	18
1988/1989	Linfield FC Belfast	Ballymena United FC	Stephen Baxter (Linfield FC Belfast)	17
1989/1990	Portadown FC	Glentoran FC Belfast	Martin McGaughey (Linfield FC Belfast)	19
1990/1991	Portadown FC	Portadown FC	Stephen Derek McBride (Glenavon FC Lurgan)	22
1991/1992	Glentoran FC Belfast	Glenavon FC Lurgan	Harry McCourt (Omagh Town FAC) Stephen Derek McBride (Glenavon FC Lurgan)	18
1992/1993	Linfield FC Belfast	Bangor FC	Steve Cowan (Portadown FC)	23
1993/1994	Linfield FC Belfast	Linfield FC Belfast	Darren Erskine (Ards FC Newtownards) Stephen Derek McBride (Glenavon FC Lurgan)	22
1994/1995	Crusaders FC Belfast	Linfield FC Belfast	Glenn Ferguson (Glenavon FC Lurgan)	27
1995/1996	Portadown FC	Glentoran FC Belfast	Garry Andrew Haylock (Portadown FC)	19
1996/1997	Crusaders FC Belfast	Glenavon FC Lurgan	Garry Andrew Haylock (Portadown FC)	16
1997/1998	Cliftonville FAC	Glentoran FC Belfast	Vincent Thomas Arkins (Portadown FC)	22
1998/1999	Glentoran FC Belfast	Portadown FC	Vincent Thomas Arkins (Portadown FC)	19
1999/2000	Linfield FC Belfast	Glentoran FC Belfast	Vincent Thomas Arkins (Portadown FC)	29
2000/2001	Linfield FC Belfast	Glentoran FC Belfast	David James Larmour (Linfield FC Belfast)	17
2001/2002	Portadown FC	Linfield FC Belfast	Vincent Thomas Arkins (Portadown FC)	30
2002/2003	Glentoran FC Belfast	Coleraine FC	Vincent Thomas Arkins (Portadown FC)	29
2003/2004	Linfield FC Belfast	Glentoran FC Belfast	Glenn Ferguson (Linfield FC Belfast)	25
2004/2005	Glentoran FC Belfast	Portadown FC	Christopher Morgan (Glentoran FC Belfast)	19
2005/2006	Linfield FC Belfast	Linfield FC Belfast	Peter Thompson (Linfield FC Belfast)	25
2006/2007	Linfield FC Belfast	Linfield FC Belfast	Gary Hamilton (Glentoran FC Belfast)	27
2007/2008	Linfield FC Belfast	Linfield FC Belfast	Peter Thompson (Linfield FC Belfast)	29
2008/2009	Glentoran FC Belfast	Crusaders FC Belfast	Curtis Allen (Lisburn Distillery FC Ballyskeagh)	19
2009/2010	Linfield FC Belfast	Linfield FC Belfast	Rory Christopher Patterson (Coleraine FC)	30
2010/2011	Linfield FC Belfast	Linfield FC Belfast	Peter Thompson (Linfield FC Belfast)	23

2011/2012	Linfield FC Belfast	Linfield FC Belfast	Gary Kyle McCutcheon (Ballymena United FC)	27
2012/2013	Cliftonville FAC	Glentoran FC Belfast	Liam Boyce (Cliftonville FAC)	29
2013/2014	Cliftonville FAC	Glenavon FC Lurgan	Joseph Anthony Gormley (Cliftonville FAC)	27
2014/2015	Crusaders FC Belfast	Glentoran FC Belfast	Joseph Anthony Gormley (Cliftonville FAC)	31
2015/2016	Crusaders FC Belfast	Glenavon FC Lurgan	Paul Heatley (Crusaders FC Belfast) Andrew Waterworth (Linfield FC Belfast)	22
2016/2017	Linfield FC Belfast	Linfield FC Belfast	Andrew Mitchell (Dungannon Swifts)	25
2017/2018	Crusaders FC Belfast	Coleraine FC	Joseph Anthony Gormley (Cliftonville FAC)	22
2018/2019	Linfield FC Belfast	Crusaders FC Belfast	Joseph Anthony Gormley (Cliftonville FAC)	20

NATIONAL CHAMPIONSHIP
NIFL Premiership 2018/2019
(04.08.2018 – 27.04.2019)

Results

Round 1 [04-06.08.2018]
Coleraine FC - Warrenpoint Town 3-0(2-0)
Dungannon Swifts - Ballymena Unit. 0-2(0-1)
Glenavon FC - Linfield FC 0-1(0-1)
Glentoran FC - Cliftonville FAC 1-2(1-0)
Institute FC - Newry City AFC 1-0(1-0)
Crusaders FC - Ards FC 4-2(2-1)

Round 2 [10-11.08.2018]
Linfield FC - Institute FC 3-0(1-0)
Newry City AFC - Dungannon Swifts 2-1(0-0)
Ards FC - Glentoran FC 0-2(0-2)
Crusaders FC - Ballymena United 2-2(0-1)
Cliftonville FAC - Coleraine FC 1-2(0-0)
Warrenpoint Town - Glenavon FC 2-4(1-3)

Round 3 [17-18.08.2018]
Newry City AFC - Glenavon FC 1-2(1-2)
Ards FC - Ballymena United 1-2(1-0)
Crusaders FC - Linfield FC 0-2(0-1)
Dungannon Swifts - Cliftonville FAC 1-1(0-0)
Glentoran FC - Coleraine FC 2-2(0-1)
Institute FC - Warrenpoint Town 2-0(1-0)

Round 4 [24-25.08.2018]
Ards FC - Newry City AFC 4-0(3-0)
Coleraine FC - Institute FC 2-2(0-1)
Glenavon FC - Ballymena United 4-0(0-0)
Cliftonville FAC - Linfield FC 1-1(0-0)
Glentoran FC - Dungannon Swifts 2-1(2-0)
Warrenpoint Town - Crusaders FC 1-2(1-1)

Round 5 [01-03.09.2018]
Warrenpoint Town - Ballymena Unit. 1-6(0-4)
Glenavon FC - Glentoran FC 1-1(0-0)
Institute FC - Dungannon Swifts 0-0
Linfield FC - Ards FC 0-0
Newry City AFC - Cliftonville FAC 1-0(0-0)
Crusaders FC - Coleraine FC 0-3(0-1)

Round 6 [07.09.2018]
Cliftonville FAC - Institute FC 3-0(2-0)
Glentoran FC - Newry City AFC 4-1(2-0)
Warrenpoint Town - Linfield FC 0-5(0-2)
Ards FC - Glenavon FC 0-2(0-1) [25.09.18]
Coleraine FC - Ballymena 2-2(1-2) [25.09.18]
Dungannon S. - Crusaders 3-2(1-0) [25.09.18]

Round 7 [15.09.2018]
Ards FC - Coleraine FC 0-0
Crusaders FC - Newry City AFC 1-0(0-0)
Institute FC - Glenavon FC 1-4(1-3)
Linfield FC - Dungannon Swifts 3-0(2-0)
Warrenpoint T. - Cliftonville FAC 2-1(0-0)
Ballymena - Glentoran FC 2-1(1-0) [20.11.18]

Round 8 [21-22.09.2018]
Newry City AFC - Warrenpoint T. 1-1(0-0)
Cliftonville FAC - Ballymena United 3-2(2-1)
Coleraine FC - Linfield FC 0-0
Dungannon Swifts - Ards FC 0-0
Glenavon FC - Crusaders FC 3-2(1-1)
Glentoran FC - Institute FC 2-1(1-1)

Round 9 [29.09.2018]
Cliftonville FAC - Ards FC 3-1(0-1)
Glenavon FC - Dungannon Swifts 2-1(1-0)
Institute FC - Crusaders FC 1-4(1-1)
Linfield FC - Ballymena United 2-1(1-1)
Newry City AFC - Coleraine FC 1-1(1-0)
Warrenpoint Town - Glentoran FC 1-1(0-1)

Round 10 [05-08.10.2018]
Ards FC - Institute FC 0-1(0-0)
Crusaders FC - Cliftonville FAC 3-2(1-1)
Ballymena United - Newry City AFC 3-0(1-0)
Coleraine FC - Glenavon FC 1-4(1-2)
Dungannon Swifts - Warrenpoint T. 0-2(0-1)
Glentoran FC - Linfield FC 0-1(0-1)

Round 11 [13.10.2018]
Crusaders FC - Glentoran FC 3-0(2-0)
Institute FC - Ballymena United 1-2(0-0)
Linfield FC - Newry City AFC 3-1(2-0)
Warrenpoint Town - Ards FC 1-0(0-0)
Dungannon - Coleraine 0-2(0-2) [05.02.2019]
Glenavon - Cliftonville 0-2(0-1) [02.03.2019]

Round 12 [19-20.10.2018]
Newry City AFC - Institute FC 0-2(0-2)
Ards FC - Linfield FC 2-1(1-0)
Ballymena Unit. - Dungannon Swifts 1-1(1-1)
Cliftonville FAC - Warrenpoint T. 3-1(2-0)
Coleraine FC - Crusaders FC 1-0(0-0)
Glentoran FC - Glenavon FC 1-2(1-0)

Round 13 [27.10.2018]
Coleraine FC - Cliftonville FAC 1-2(1-2)
Ballymena United - Crusaders FC 3-0(1-0)
Dungannon Swifts - Linfield FC 1-2(1-0)
Glentoran FC - Ards FC 4-0(2-0)
Warrenpoint Town - Institute FC 0-1(0-0)
Glenavon FC - Newry City AFC 2-0(0-0)

Round 14 [02-03.11.2018]
Ballymena United - Glenavon FC 2-1(1-0)
Newry City AFC - Crusaders FC 0-3(0-0)
Institute FC - Coleraine FC 1-2(0-2)
Ards FC - Dungannon Swifts 2-2(1-1)
Cliftonville FAC - Glentoran FC 1-0(0-0)
Linfield FC - Warrenpoint Town 1-1(0-1)

Round 15 [10-12.11.2018]
Ards FC - Crusaders FC 0-1(0-0)
Dungannon Swifts - Institute FC 2-1(0-1)
Glenavon FC - Warrenpoint Town 1-1(1-1)
Glentoran FC - Ballymena United 0-1(0-1)
Linfield FC - Coleraine FC 1-2(0-1)
Cliftonville FAC - Newry City AFC 3-1(3-1)

Round 16 [17.11.2018]
Institute FC - Linfield FC 1-4(1-1)
Ballymena United - Cliftonville FAC 2-1(0-0)
Coleraine FC - Glentoran FC 1-1(0-1)
Crusaders FC - Glenavon FC 3-0(2-0)
Newry City AFC - Ards FC 2-0(0-0)
Warrenpoint T. - Dungannon Swifts 1-1(1-1)

Round 17 [23-24.11.2018]
Newry City AFC - Ballymena United 1-2(0-2)
Crusaders FC - Institute FC 3-2(1-0)
Dungannon Swifts - Glentoran FC 1-0(0-0)
Glenavon FC - Ards FC 3-1(1-0)
Linfield FC - Cliftonville FAC 4-2(2-1)
Warrenpoint Town - Coleraine FC 2-1(1-0)

Round 18 [30.11.-01.12.2018]
Coleraine FC - Newry City AFC 0-1(0-1)
Ards FC - Warrenpoint Town 1-1(0-0)
Ballymena United - Linfield FC 2-1(0-1)
Cliftonville FAC - Dungannon Swifts 5-1(3-1)
Glenavon FC - Institute FC 3-3(2-2)
Glentoran FC - Crusaders FC 2-2(2-2)

Round 19 [08.12.2018]
Cliftonville FAC - Glenavon FC 4-2(1-1)
Coleraine FC - Ards FC 1-0(0-0)
Dungannon Swifts - Newry City AFC 1-1(0-0)
Institute FC - Glentoran FC 3-3(1-2)
Linfield FC - Crusaders FC 4-1(2-0)
Warrenpoint Town - Ballymena Unit. 2-4(1-2)

Round 20 [14-15.12.2018]
Glenavon FC - Coleraine FC 4-0(2-0)
Ards FC - Cliftonville FAC 1-3(1-2)
Crusaders FC - Dungannon Swifts 1-0(1-0)
Newry City - Linfield 0-2(0-1) [22.01.2019]
Glentoran - Warrenpoint 3-1(2-0) [26.02.19]
Ballymena - Institute FC 6-1(4-0) [19.03.19]

Round 21 [22.12.2018]
Ballymena United - Ards FC 2-0(2-0)
Coleraine FC - Dungannon Swifts 2-1(1-0)
Crusaders FC - Warrenpoint Town 3-1(0-0)
Institute FC - Cliftonville FAC 6-4(3-1)
Linfield FC - Glenavon FC 0-0
Newry City - Glentoran 1-1(1-1) [05.02.2019]

Round 22 [26.12.2018]
Ballymena United - Coleraine FC 3-3(1-2)
Cliftonville FAC - Crusaders FC 1-5(0-2)
Dungannon Swifts - Glenavon FC 1-1(0-0)
Institute FC - Ards FC 1-0(1-0)
Linfield FC - Glentoran FC 4-0(1-0)
Warrenpoint T. - Newry City AFC 2-2(1-1)

Round 23 [29.12.2018]
Ballymena United - Newry City AFC 3-1(0-0)
Cliftonville FAC - Linfield FC 0-2(0-1)
Dungannon Swifts - Ards FC 0-3(0-1)
Glenavon FC - Institute FC 3-3(2-0)
Glentoran FC - Crusaders FC 0-1(0-0)
Warrenpoint Town - Coleraine FC 0-1(0-0)

Round 24 [01.01.2019]
Ards FC - Linfield FC 0-2(0-0)
Coleraine FC - Cliftonville FAC 4-1(2-0)
Crusaders FC - Ballymena United 3-2(2-1)
Glenavon FC - Warrenpoint Town 1-3(0-1)
Glentoran FC - Dungannon Swifts 2-4(1-1)
Newry City AFC - Institute FC 1-2(0-2)

Round 25 [11-12.01.2019]
Newry City AFC - Crusaders FC 0-1(0-1)
Ballymena Unit. - Dungannon Swifts 2-2(1-0)
Cliftonville FAC - Ards FC 4-1(1-1)
Coleraine FC - Glenavon FC 1-1(1-0)
Institute FC - Glentoran FC 0-2(0-1)
Linfield FC - Warrenpoint Town 4-0(1-0)

Round 26 [18-19.01.2019]
Ards FC - Coleraine FC 1-2(1-1)
Crusaders FC - Linfield FC 0-1(0-1)
Dungannon Swifts - Cliftonville FAC 3-1(1-0)
Glenavon FC - Ballymena United 0-2(0-2)
Glentoran FC - Newry City AFC 2-1(0-1)
Warrenpoint Town - Institute FC 4-0(3-0)

Round 27 [26-28.01.2019]
Ballymena United - Ards FC 4-1(2-1)
Cliftonville FAC - Glenavon FC 1-1(1-0)
Coleraine FC - Dungannon Swifts 1-2(1-1)
Institute FC - Crusaders FC 1-3(0-3)
Newry City AFC - Warrenpoint T. 0-2(0-2)
Linfield FC - Glentoran FC 4-2(2-0)

Round 28 [09.02.2019]
Cliftonville FAC - Newry City AFC 1-0(1-0)
Dungannon Swifts - Crusaders FC 1-0(0-0)
Glenavon FC - Ards FC 2-0(0-0)
Institute FC - Ballymena United 1-2(0-1)
Linfield FC - Coleraine FC 3-2(0-1)
Warrenpoint Town - Glentoran FC 0-5(0-4)

Round 29 [15-18.02.2019]
Ards FC - Institute FC 0-3(0-1)
Crusaders FC - Coleraine FC 4-2(3-1)
Dungannon Swifts - Warrenpoint T. 4-3(1-2)
Glentoran FC - Glenavon FC 1-2(1-0)
Ballymena - Cliftonville 2-1(2-0) [26.02.2019]
Newry City - Linfield 0-1(0-0) [26.02.2019]

Round 30 [22-23.02.2019]
Crusaders FC - Glenavon FC 1-1(1-0)
Ards FC - Newry City AFC 3-1(2-0)
Coleraine FC - Glentoran FC 2-0(0-0)
Institute FC - Dungannon Swifts 2-0(1-0)
Linfield FC - Ballymena United 1-0(0-0)
Warrenpoint T. - Cliftonville FAC 0-2(0-0)

Round 31 [ ]
Glenavon FC - Linfield FC 2-0(0-0)
Cliftonville FAC - Institute FC 1-0(0-0)
Coleraine FC - Ballymena United 0-4(0-2)
Dungannon Swifts - Newry City AFC 2-1(0-0)
Glentoran FC - Ards FC 1-1(0-1)
Warrenpoint - Crusaders 1-3(1-0) [19.03.19]

Round 32 [ ]
Newry City AFC - Coleraine FC 1-4(0-1)
Ards FC - Warrenpoint Town 0-1(0-1)
Ballymena United - Glentoran FC 0-2(0-1)
Crusaders FC - Cliftonville FAC 2-0(2-0)
Glenavon FC - Dungannon Swifts 1-0(0-0)
Linfield FC - Institute FC 2-0(0-0)

Round 33 [ ]
Dungannon Swifts - Linfield FC 0-5(0-3)
Institute FC - Coleraine FC 1-0(0-0)
Ards FC - Crusaders FC 2-2(1-0)
Ballymena Unit. - Warrenpoint Town 1-2(1-1)
Newry City AFC - Glenavon FC 0-1(0-0)
Cliftonville - Glentoran 2-1(0-1) [30.03.2019]

Final Standings

1.	Linfield FC Belfast	33	24	5	4	70 - 21	77
2.	Ballymena United FC	33	21	5	7	74 - 42	68
3.	Crusaders FC Belfast	33	20	4	9	65 - 44	64
4.	Glenavon FC Lurgan	33	17	9	7	60 - 40	60
5.	Cliftonville FAC	33	17	3	13	62 - 54	54
6.	Coleraine FC	33	14	9	10	51 - 46	51
7.	Glentoran FC Belfast	33	10	8	15	49 - 49	38
8.	Institute FC Derry	33	11	5	17	45 - 65	38
9.	Dungannon Swifts FC	33	9	9	15	37 - 56	36
10.	Warrenpoint Town FC	33	9	7	17	40 - 67	34
11.	Ards FC Newtownards	33	4	7	22	27 - 58	19
12.	Newry City AFC	33	4	5	24	23 - 61	17

Teams ranked 1-6 were qualified for the Championship Round, while teams ranked 7-12 were qualified for the Relegation Round.

Championship Round

Results

Round 34 [05-06.04.2019]
Ballymena United - Linfield FC 0-1(0-0)
Cliftonville FAC - Coleraine FC 4-2(3-2)
Glenavon FC - Crusaders FC 2-1(0-0)

Round 35 [13.04.2019]
Cliftonville FAC - Ballymena United 1-1(1-1)
Glenavon FC - Coleraine FC 1-1(0-0)
Linfield FC - Crusaders FC 0-0

Round 36 [20.04.2019]
Ballymena United - Coleraine FC 1-0(1-0)
Cliftonville FAC - Crusaders FC 2-0(2-0)
Linfield FC - Glenavon FC 0-4(0-2)

Round 37 [23.04.2019]
Ballymena United - Glenavon FC 4-3(2-1)
Coleraine FC - Crusaders FC 4-2(2-1)
Linfield FC - Cliftonville FAC 5-1(3-0)

Round 38 [27.04.2019]
Ballymena United - Crusaders FC 0-3(0-2)
Coleraine FC - Linfield FC 1-1(1-0)
Glenavon FC - Cliftonville FAC 4-0(3-0)

Final Standings

1.	**Linfield FC Belfast**	38	26	7	5	77 - 27	85
2.	Ballymena United FC	38	24	6	8	83 - 47	78
3.	Glenavon FC Lurgan	38	20	10	8	74 - 46	70
4.	Crusaders FC Belfast	38	20	5	13	68 - 55	65
5.	Cliftonville FAC	38	19	4	15	70 - 66	61
6.	Coleraine FC	38	15	11	12	59 - 55	56

Teams ranked third and 5-6 were qualified for the Europa League Play-offs.
Crusaders FC Belfast, as Irish Cup winners were qualified directly for the UEFA Europa League.

Top goalscorers:

20 Joseph Anthony Gormley *Cliftonville FAC*

19 Michael McCrudden *Institute FC Derry*
16 Andrew Waterworth *Linfield FC Belfast*
14 Rory Donnelly *Cliftonville FAC*
14 Paul Heatley *Crusaders FC Belfast*

Relegation Round

Results

Round 34 [05-06.04.2019]
Newry City AFC - Ards FC 3-0(2-0)
Dungannon Swifts - Glentoran FC 1-2(1-1)
Institute FC - Warrenpoint Town 2-1(0-0)

Round 35 [13.04.2019]
Ards FC - Glentoran FC 1-1(0-0)
Dungannon Swifts - Institute FC 2-1(0-0)
Warrenpoint T. - Newry City AFC 2-4(0-4)

Round 36 [19-20.04.2019]
Newry City AFC - Glentoran FC 0-2(0-2)
Institute FC - Ards FC 0-1(0-0)
Warrenpoint T. - Dungannon Swifts 5-3(2-3)

Round 37 [23.04.2019]
Ards FC - Dungannon Swifts 1-0(1-0)
Glentoran FC - Warrenpoint Town 2-2(0-1)
Institute FC - Newry City AFC 2-1(1-0)

Round 38 [27.04.2019]
Glentoran FC - Institute FC 2-0(0-0)
Newry City AFC - Dungannon Swifts 0-1(0-0)
Warrenpoint Town - Ards FC 1-1(1-1)

Final Standings

7.	Glentoran FC Belfast	38	13	10	15	58	-	53	49
8.	Institute FC Derry	38	13	5	20	50	-	72	44
9.	Dungannon Swifts FC	38	11	9	18	44	-	65	42
10.	Warrenpoint Town FC	38	10	9	19	51	-	79	39
11.	Ards FC Newtownards (*Relegation Play-offs*)	38	6	9	23	31	-	63	27
12.	Newry City AFC (*Relegated*)	38	6	5	27	31	-	68	23

Glentoran FC Belfast qualified for the Europa League Play-offs.

Europa League Play-offs [03-06.05.2019]

Glenavon FC Lurgan - Glentoran FC Belfast	2-4(1-0)
Cliftonville FAC - Coleraine FC	5-3(1-2,3-3)
Cliftonville FAC - Glentoran FC Belfast	2-0(0-0,0-0)

Relegation Play-offs (1st Level / 2nd Level) [03-06.05.2019]

Carrick Rangers FC - Ards FC Newtownards	1-0(1-0)	2-1(2-1)

Carrick Rangers FC promoted to the 2019/2010 NIFL Premiership.

NATIONAL CUP
Irish Cup 2018/2019

Fifth Round [05.01.2019]

Knockbreda FC Belfast - Strabane Athletic FC	1-2
Queen's Univ. AFC Belfast - Lisburn Distillery FC	6-0
Ards FC Newtownards - Carrick Rangers FC	0-1
Ballinamallard Unit. - Police Service of NI FC	5-1
Cliftonville FAC - Dungannon Swifts FC	0-1
Coleraine FC - Harland & Wolff Welders FC Belfast	2-0
Crusaders FC Belfast - Glentoran FC Belfast	4-1
Dergview FC Castlederg - Maiden City FC Derry	3-2
Dundela FC Belfast - Ballymena United FC	1-3
Glenavon FC Lurgan - Rosemount Recreation FC	5-0
Institute FC Derry - Warrenpoint Town FC	0-2
Larne FC - Newry City AFC	2-1
Limavady United - Larne Technical College O. Boys	0-2
Linfield FC Belfast - Ballyclare Comrades FC	1-0
Loughgall FC - Crumlin Star FC Belfast	1-4
Portadown FC - Abbey Villa FC Millisle	5-1

1/8-Finals [02/11.02.2019]

Larne Technical College O. Boys - Strabane Athletic	3-1
Coleraine FC - Dergview FC Castlederg	3-0
Larne FC - Crumlin Star FC Belfast	3-1
Linfield FC Belfast - Crusaders FC Belfast	1-2
Ballinamallard United FC - Carrick Rangers FC	1-0
Ballymena United FC - Portadown FC	4-1
Glenavon FC Lurgan - Dungannon Swifts FC	0-1
Warrenpoint Town FC - Queen's University AFC	2-0

Quarter-Finals [01-02.03.2019]

Larne FC - Coleraine FC	3-5 pen
Crusaders FC Belfast - Ballymena United FC	3-0
Dungannon Swifts FC - Ballinamallard United FC	2-2 aet; 2-3 pen
Warrenpoint Town - Larne Technical College OB	3-1

Semi-Finals [30.03.2019]

Ballinamallard United FC - Warrenpoint Town FC	5-4 pen
Coleraine FC - Crusaders FC Belfast	0-2

Final

04.05.2019; Windsor Park (Belfast; Referee: Ian McNabb; Attendance: n/a
Crusaders FC Belfast - Ballinamallard United FC **3-0(1-0)**

Crusaders FC: Harry Doherty, Billy Joe Burns, Colin Coates, Sean Ward, Declan Caddell, Michael Ruddy, Philip Lowry, Jordan Forsythe, David Cushley (52.Ross Clarke), Jordan Owens (87.Rory Patterson), Paul Heatley. Trainer: Stephen Baxter.

Ballinamallard United: John Connolly, Ross Taheny, Matthew Smyth, Ryan O'Reilly, Nathan Cashel, Aaron Arkinson, Chris Kelly (80.Simon Warrington), Richard Clarke, Jason McCartney (68.Robbie Hume), Darragh McBrien (59.Duwayne McManus), Ryan Campbell. Trainer: Harry McConkey.

Goals: 1-0 Jordan Owens (6), 2-0 Philip Lowry (47), 3-0 Ross Clarke (53).

THE CLUBS 2018/2019

Please note: matches and goals includes statistics of both regular season and play-offs (Championship or Relegation).

Ards Football Club Newtownards

Founded: 1900
Stadium: Clandeboye Park, Bangor (1,895)

Goalkeepers:	DOB	M	(s)	G
Samuel Johnston	26.03.1996	38		
Defenders:	**DOB**	**M**	**(s)**	**G**
Callum Byers	28.07.1997	31	(3)	
David Elebert (IRL)	21.03.1986	12		
Daryl Evans	01.10.1994	3		
Michael Kerr	06.03.1998	23	(2)	
Adam John McAleenan	13.07.2000	15	(4)	
Craig McClean	06.07.1985	34		1
Damien McNulty	10.02.1991	9		1
Reece Neale	14.05.1998	1		
Jonathan Taylor	30.06.1988	22		
Midfielders:	**DOB**	**M**	**(s)**	**G**
Kyle Cherry	13.05.1993	20	(9)	1
Jonah Heron	14.01.2003	1		1
Joshua Kelly	08.03.1999	31	(2)	
Eamon McAllister	19.11.1987	22	(7)	2
Eoghan McCawl	31.01.1996	5		
Kym Nelson	18.07.1995	26	(2)	1
Seán Noble (IRL)	20.03.1996	2		
Steven Shearer	19.07.2002		(3)	
Gareth Tommons	18.05.1989	27	(2)	3
Forwards:	**DOB**	**M**	**(s)**	**G**
Brendan Bennet	07.07.1994	1	(6)	
Aaron Boyd	12.02.1991		(3)	
Jonathan Frazer	30.05.1996	12		3
Darren Henderson	25.01.1986	6	(3)	2
Mark Kelly	23.02.1990	22	(10)	8
David McAllister	01.09.1994	25	(5)	
Scott McArthur	09.08.1999		(6)	
Marc Patrick McKenna	26.04.2000		(2)	
Michael McLellan	22.01.1993	14	(18)	7
Jonah Mitchell	23.06.1999	9	(5)	
Jonathan Smith	12.07.1997	2	(1)	
Ryan Strain	12.02.2000	5	(4)	
Trainer:	**DOB**	**M**		
Colin Nixon	08.09.1978	29		
Warren James Feeney [19.02.2019]	17.01.1981	9		

Ballymena United Football Club

Founded: 07.04.1928
Stadium: The Showgrounds, Ballymena (3,050)

Goalkeepers:	DOB	M	(s)	G
Ross Glendinning	18.05.1993	30		
Thomas McDermott	30.01.1998	7		
Jordan Williamson	23.05.1995	1		
Defenders:	**DOB**	**M**	**(s)**	**G**
Kofi Balmer	19.09.2000	22	(2)	1
Andrew Burns (ENG)	29.05.1992	7	(2)	1
Jim Ervin	05.06.1985	32		
Reece Glendinning	09.06.1995	5	(1)	1
Tony Kane (IRL)	29.08.1987	15	(13)	3
Steven McCullough	30.08.1994	35	(1)	4
Conor Quigley	04.12.1997	6		1
Albert Watson	08.09.1985	8		1
Scot Whiteside	16.06.1997	22	(2)	
Midfielders:	**DOB**	**M**	**(s)**	**G**
Jonathan Addis	27.09.1992	32		3
Spencer Beatti	16.01.2002		(1)	
William Faulkner	18.01.1990	7	(6)	2
Ryan Harpur (IRL)	01.12.1988		(4)	
James Knowles	06.04.1993	20	(3)	4
Adam Lecky	03.05.1991	31	(3)	11
Ryan Mayse	07.12.1993	13	(9)	6
Shane McGinty (IRL)	14.04.1994	6	(9)	2
Andy McGrory	15.12.1991	29	(1)	10
Leroy Millar	01.09.1995	26	(4)	6
Matthew Shevlin	07.12.1998	2	(4)	
Jude Winchester	13.04.1993	25	(4)	4
Forwards:	**DOB**	**M**	**(s)**	**G**
Cathair Friel	25.05.1993	23	(1)	13
Joe McKinney	02.01.1994	1		
Jonathan McMurray	19.09.1994	13	(11)	5
Francis Nolan	05.12.1999	1	(2)	
Trainer:	**DOB**	**M**		
David Jeffrey	28.10.1962	38		

Cliftonville Football & Athletic Club

Founded: 1879
Stadium: Solitude Stadium, Belfast (2,530)

Goalkeepers:	DOB	M	(s)	G
Richard Brush (ENG)	26.11.1984	31		
Brian Neeson	28.06.1989	7		
Defenders:	**DOB**	**M**	**(s)**	**G**
Liam Bagnall	17.05.1992	18	(3)	1
Garry Breen (IRL)	17.03.1989	24	(2)	1
Odhran Casey	09.04.2002		(1)	
Joe Gorman (IRL)	01.09.1994	13		
Jamie Harney	04.03.1996	22	(3)	3
Levi Ives	28.07.1997	28	(2)	3
Jamie McGovern	29.05.1989	26	(2)	
Damien McNulty	10.02.1991	3	(1)	
Midfielders:	**DOB**	**M**	**(s)**	**G**
Ryan Catney	17.02.1987	25	(6)	
Chris Curran	05.01.1991	37		2
Niall Grace	08.01.1993	7	(2)	
Aaron Harkin	03.03.1993	7		
Ruairí Harkin	11.10.1989	5	(3)	
Caoimhin McConnell	18.09.2000	8	(6)	
Conor McDonald (IRL)	14.06.1995	8	(5)	2
Daniel White	16.06.1996		(1)	
Forwards:	**DOB**	**M**	**(s)**	**G**
Ryan Curran	13.10.1993	25	(10)	13
Aaron Donnelly	27.03.2000	10	(2)	
Jay Donnelly	10.04.1995	15		4
Rory Donnelly	18.02.1992	24	(2)	15
Stephen Garrett	13.04.1987	10	(14)	1
Joe Gormley	26.11.1989	37		20
Ross Lavery	29.07.1996	7	(3)	
Thomas Maguire	09.09.1999	5	(13)	
Conor McMenamin	24.08.1995	16	(4)	5
Donal Rocks	13.07.2000		(2)	
Dylan Whiteway	03.01.1999		(1)	
Trainer:	**DOB**	**M**		
Barry Gray		26		
Michael Press [20.01.2019]		1		
Paddy McLaughlin [04.02.2019]	10.10.1979	11		

Coleraine Football Club

Founded: 1927
Stadium: The Showgrounds, Coleraine (2,496)

Goalkeepers:	**DOB**	**M**	**(s)**	**G**
Christopher Johns	13.05.1995	38		
Defenders:	**DOB**	**M**	**(s)**	**G**
Aaron Burns	29.05.1992	14	(2)	4
Aaron Canning	07.03.1992	27		1
Graham Crown	02.03.1992	9	(4)	
Ben Doherty	24.03.1997	15		3
Steven Douglas	27.09.1977	11	(6)	
Mark Edgar	17.02.1997	12	(1)	
Lyndon Kane	15.02.1997	5		
Dylan King	27.08.1998	8	(1)	1
Gareth McConaghie	05.04.1988	27	(2)	2
Ben Moore	12.03.2002	1		
Adam Mullan	24.10.1995	21	(4)	
Stephen O'Donnell	01.09.1992	22		1
Midfielders:	**DOB**	**M**	**(s)**	**G**
Jack Bradley	18.09.2001		(1)	
Cormac Burke	11.08.1993	5	(4)	1
Josh Carson	03.06.1993	25	(1)	2
Jamie Glackin	16.02.1995	12	(1)	1
Ciaron Harkin	15.01.1996	22	(1)	
Stephen Lowry	14.10.1986	31		4
Darren McCauley	21.02.1991	23		7
Jamie McGonigle	05.03.1996	28	(5)	11
Paul Owens	11.11.1982		(1)	
Ian Parkhill	07.04.1990	16	(10)	2
Dean Shiels	01.02.1985	8	(1)	2
Aaron Traynor	24.07.1990	8		
Andrew Whiteside	08.05.2001		(1)	
Forwards:	**DOB**	**M**	**(s)**	**G**
Eoin Bradley	31.12.1983	18	(14)	6
Caiolan Brennan	23.11.2001		(1)	
Dylan Davidson	20.03.1999	1	(6)	1
Alex Gawne	22.05.2001	1	(8)	
Bradley Lyons	26.05.1997	2	(1)	2
James McLaughlin	06.03.1990	8	(12)	6
Caleb Wan	06.11.2001		(1)	
Trainer:	**DOB**	**M**		
Oran Kearney	29.07.1978	5		
Rodney McAree [14.09.2018]	19.08.1974	33		

Crusaders Football Club Belfast

Founded: 1898
Stadium: Seaview Stadium, Belfast (3,383)

Goalkeepers:	**DOB**	**M**	**(s)**	**G**
Gerard Doherty (IRL)	24.08.1981	6		
Harry Doherty (IRL)	29.03.1996	9	(1)	
Sean O'Neill	11.04.1988	23	(1)	
Defenders:	**DOB**	**M**	**(s)**	**G**
Howard Beverland	30.03.1990	20	(2)	
Rodney Brown	13.08.1995	5	(4)	
Billy Joe Burns	28.04.1989	23	(4)	1
Declan Caddell	13.04.1988	20	(6)	2
Colin Coates	26.10.1985	24		3
Mark McChrystal	26.06.1984	19		
Kyle Owens	09.07.1992	20	(2)	2
Michael Ruddy	05.08.1993	15	(4)	1
Sean Ward	12.01.1984	22	(1)	
Midfielders:	**DOB**	**M**	**(s)**	**G**
Ross Clarke	17.05.1993	27	(4)	7
Jordan Forsythe	11.02.1991	28	(2)	3
Jamie Glackin	16.02.1995	3	(2)	
Rory Hale (IRL)	27.11.1996	11		
Philip Lowry	15.07.1989	19	(8)	3
Tom Mathieson	09.01.2000		(1)	
Matthew Snoddy	02.06.1993	16	(12)	3
Forwards:	**DOB**	**M**	**(s)**	**G**
Michael Carvill	03.04.1988	12	(5)	1
David Cushley	22.07.1989	15	(12)	9
Ronan Hale (IRL)	08.09.1998	7	(6)	3
Paul Heatley	30.06.1987	29	(1)	14
Reece McGinley	01.03.2000	5	(1)	
Jordan Owens	09.07.1989	17	(9)	7
Rory Patterson	16.07.1984	18	(11)	10
Gary Thompson	26.05.1990	5	(2)	
Trainer:	**DOB**	**M**		
Stephen Baxter	01.10.1965	38		

Dungannon Swifts Football Club

Founded: 1949
Stadium: Stangmore Park, Dungannon (5,000)

Goalkeepers:	**DOB**	**M**	**(s)**	**G**
Stuart Addis	05.07.1979	2		
Alex Moore	27.08.1998	27		
Evan Moran (IRL)	22.04.1997	5		
Niall Morgan	17.07.1991	4		
Defenders:	**DOB**	**M**	**(s)**	**G**
David Armstrong	23.01.1987	21	(4)	
Caolin Coyle	23.04.2000	2	(2)	
Jake Dykes (IRL)	30.06.1995	15	(1)	
James Ferrin	23.09.1989	4	(2)	
Chris Hegarty	13.08.1992	33		1
Cahal McGinty	29.09.2000		(1)	
Midfielders:	**DOB**	**M**	**(s)**	**G**
Cormac Burke	11.08.1993	6	(5)	
Seanan Clucas	08.11.1992	26	(2)	1
Shea Conway	30.09.2002		(1)	
Ben Gallagher	30.03.2002	1	(2)	
Ryan Harpur (IRL)	01.12.1988	11	(2)	2
Grant Hutchinson	11.11.1989	19	(8)	
Johnny Lafferty	02.01.1987	10	(16)	2
Kris Lowe	06.01.1996	29	(4)	1
Jarlath O'Rourke	13.02.1995	34	(1)	1
Mark Patton	08.07.1990	23	(7)	4
Alan Teggart	24.11.1986	26	(6)	1
Douglas Wilson	03.03.1994	24	(2)	2
Forwards:	**DOB**	**M**	**(s)**	**G**
Rhyss Campbell	30.11.1998	10	(14)	1
Michael Carvill	03.04.1988	6	(1)	1
Daniel Hughes	03.05.1992	22		9
Marcio Soares (POR)	07.04.1996		(2)	
Paul McElroy	07.07.1994	32	(3)	12
Corey McMullan	03.05.1996	13	(2)	1
Diarmuid O'Carroll (IRL)	16.03.1987	1	(3)	
Oisin Smyth	05.05.2000	12	(3)	2
Trainer:	**DOB**	**M**		
Rodney McAree	19.08.1974	5		
Dixie Robinson [14.09.2018]		3		
Kris Lindsay [26.09.2018]	05.02.1984	30		

Glenavon Football Club Lurgan

Founded: 1889
Stadium: Mourneview Park, Lurgan (4,160)

Goalkeepers:	DOB	M	(s)	G
James Taylor	12.05.1984	1		
Jonny Tuffey	20.01.1987	37		
Defenders:	**DOB**	**M**	**(s)**	**G**
Andrew Doyle	28.10.1990	3	(1)	
Leighton Jameson	21.01.2002		(1)	
Dylan King	27.08.1998	17	(1)	
Caolan Marron	04.07.1998	33		
Rhys Marshall	16.01.1995	33		4
Seamus Sharkey (ENG)	11.05.1990	12		1
James Singleton	22.08.1995	36		1
Cameron Stewart	11.03.1997	4	(1)	1
Midfielders:	**DOB**	**M**	**(s)**	**G**
Sammy Clingan	13.01.1984	9	(1)	3
Joshua Daniels	22.02.1996	33		7
Ben Doherty	24.03.1997	15	(4)	2
Robert Garrett	05.05.1988	10	(1)	1
Niall Grace	08.01.1993	7	(5)	1
Andrew Hall	19.09.1989	30	(4)	6
Aaron Harmon	05.11.1989	15	(9)	2
Conor McCloskey	29.01.1992	16	(10)	5
Gary Muir (SCO)	15.12.1985	5	(4)	1
Stephen Murray	29.12.1988	25	(7)	15
Mark Sykes	04.08.1997	22		4
Owen Taylor	03.10.2002		(1)	
Eoin Wearen (IRL)	02.10.1992	10	(1)	1
Forwards:	**DOB**	**M**	**(s)**	**G**
Oisin Barr	22.07.2002		(2)	
Stephen Donnelly (IRL)	18.01.1993	5	(6)	3
Gary Hamilton	06.10.1980	1	(10)	1
Ross Hunter	07.07.2002		(1)	1
Jordan Jenkins	28.02.2000	2	(24)	2
Daniel Larmour	03.09.1998	3	(3)	
Andrew Mitchell	25.01.1994	31		12
Robbie Norton	16.04.1998	3	(6)	
Trainer:	**DOB**	**M**		
Gary Hamilton	06.10.1980	38		

Glentoran Football Club Belfast

Founded: 1882
Stadium: The Oval, Belfast (6,054)

Goalkeepers:	DOB	M	(s)	G
Paul McLaughlin	30.03.2001		(1)	
Elliott Morris	04.05.1981	31		1
Dwayne Nelson	05.09.1984	7		
Defenders:	**DOB**	**M**	**(s)**	**G**
Calum Birney	19.04.1993	25	(1)	1
Lee Chapman	09.11.1994		(1)	
Joe Crowe	20.04.1998	16	(2)	
William Garrett	31.08.1991	23	(4)	1
Jamie Glover	22.01.2001	1	(1)	
Lukasz Gwiazda (POL)	18.10.1994	10	(1)	2
Daniel Kelly	06.01.1993		(1)	
Nathan Kerr	20.01.1998	31	(1)	
James McCarthy	19.10.2000	3	(6)	
Gavin Peers (IRL)	10.11.1985	10	(2)	
Ross Redman	23.11.1989	23		1
Malachy Smith	08.04.2001		(2)	
Midfielders:	**DOB**	**M**	**(s)**	**G**
James Ferrin	23.09.1989	5	(2)	
Chris Gallagher	30.03.1999	20	(6)	
Steven Gordon	27.07.1993	14	(5)	1
Jack Henderson	17.10.2000		(1)	
John Herron (SCO)	01.02.1994	29	(1)	5
Marcus Kane	08.12.1991	32	(2)	3
John McGuigan	28.08.1993	11	(2)	2
Peter McMahon (IRL)	20.04.1989	9	(7)	1
Darren Murray	24.10.1991	13	(1)	10
Conor Pepper (IRL)	04.05.1994	31	(1)	
Forwards:	**DOB**	**M**	**(s)**	**G**
Curtis Allen	22.02.1988	31	(4)	11
Sam Byrne (IRL)	23.07.1995	1	(6)	
Dylan Davidson	20.03.1999	11	(8)	1
Robbie McDaid	23.10.1996	27	(3)	12
Paul O'Neill	07.01.2000	4	(12)	3
Trainer:	**DOB**	**M**		
Ronald Joseph McFall	18.07.1945	22		
Gary Smyth [03.01.2019]	20.12.1969	11		
Michael McDermott [31.03.2019]	07.02.1974	5		

Institute Football Club Derry

Founded: 1905
Stadium: Brandywell Stadium, Derry (7,700)

Goalkeepers:	DOB	M	(s)	G
Conan Doherty	11.12.1999	1		
Martin Gallagher	26.10.1990	37		
Defenders:	**DOB**	**M**	**(s)**	**G**
Caoimhin Bonner	15.01.1993	29		
Dean Curry	11.11.1994	37		2
Shaun Leppard	19.07.2000	1		
Colm McLaughlin (IRL)	01.08.1993	36		1
Mark Scoltock	26.03.1985	7	(1)	1
Midfielders:	**DOB**	**M**	**(s)**	**G**
Gareth Brown	11.03.1992	11	(12)	1
Ronan Doherty	20.01.1996	30	(1)	2
Aaron Jarvis	10.05.1997	31	(2)	2
Thomas McBride	30.05.1992	8	(2)	
Caoimhin McCallion	02.06.1998		(1)	
Eamon McLaughlin	21.04.2000		(3)	
Jake Morrow	11.11.1999	9	(11)	1
Ryan Morrow	12.03.1995	21		
Forwards:	**DOB**	**M**	**(s)**	**G**
Stephen Curry	05.11.1990	16	(11)	3
Jamie Dunne (IRL)	02.07.1997	16	(9)	1
Aaron Harkin	13.12.1999	19	(2)	1
Nathan Harkin	13.12.1999	2		
Darren Henderson	25.01.1986	1	(9)	1
Joe McCready	24.07.1990	25	(3)	9
Michael McCrudden	31.07.1991	25		19
Jamie McIntyre	01.12.1996	14	(9)	1
Callum Moorehead	24.07.1998	8	(19)	1
Paul Smith	09.05.1996	5	(8)	2
Ronan Wilson	01.09.1998	29	(3)	1
Trainer:	**DOB**	**M**		
Paddy McLaughlin	10.10.1979	26		
Kevin Doherty (IRL) [05.02.2019]	02.07.1970	10		
John Quigg [22.04.2019]	23.12.1966	2		

Linfield Football Club Belfast

Founded: 1886
Stadium: Windsor Park, Belfast (18,167)

Goalkeepers:	DOB	M	(s)	G
Roy Carroll	30.09.1977	25		
Gareth Deane	14.06.1994	11		
Conor Mitchell	09.05.1996	2		
Defenders:	**DOB**	**M**	**(s)**	**G**
Jimmy Callacher	11.06.1991	36		9
Chris Casement	12.01.1988	31		3
Matthew Clarke	03.03.1994	18	(6)	
Trai Hume	18.03.2002	1	(1)	
Ryan McGivern	08.01.1990	5		
Caomhan McGuinness	14.01.2000	1	(1)	
Niall Quinn	02.08.1993	29	(7)	4
Joshua Robinson	30.06.1993	31	(1)	4
Mark Stafford	20.08.1987	6	(3)	1
Midfielders:	**DOB**	**M**	**(s)**	**G**
Joel Cooper	29.02.1996	30	(3)	7
Jake Corbett	28.07.2001		(1)	
Stephen Fallon	03.03.1997	13	(4)	
Robert Garrett	05.05.1988	6	(4)	
Daniel Kearns (IRL)	26.08.1991	21	(6)	3
Andy Mitchell	06.04.1992	19	(4)	1
Benjamin Möller (DEN)	11.12.1995	1	(1)	
Jamie Mulgrew	05.06.1986	30	(2)	1
Jordan Stewart	31.03.1995	19	(11)	10
Forwards:	**DOB**	**M**	**(s)**	**G**
Charlie Allen	22.11.2003		(1)	
Marek Červenka (CZE)	17.12.1992	5	(5)	
Brandon Doyle	20.08.1998	1	(1)	
Lorcan Forde	07.11.1999	1	(3)	
Kyle McClean	03.10.1998	7	(1)	1
Kirk Millar	07.08.1992	28	(7)	3
Michael O'Connor (IRL)	31.07.1998	12	(17)	9
Daniels Reynolds	24.03.1999	1	(4)	1
Andrew Waterworth	11.04.1986	28	(6)	17
Trainer:	**DOB**	**M**		
David Jonathan Healy	05.08.1979	38		

Newry City Athletic Football Club

Founded: 2013
Stadium: The Showgrounds, Newry (7,949)

Goalkeepers:	DOB	M	(s)	G
Andrew Coleman	13.06.1985	28		
Steven Maguire	14.12.1984	10	(1)	
Defenders:	**DOB**	**M**	**(s)**	**G**
John Boyle	01.03.1986	35		4
Noel Healy	27.07.1997	10	(2)	
Darren King	16.10.1985	34		
Kevin McArdle (IRL)	10.02.1988	4	(6)	1
Conor McCaul	27.09.1991	3	(1)	
Mark McCullough	14.07.1999		(1)	
Dale Montgomery	19.04.1991	28	(1)	3
Neil Mullen	02.07.1984		(7)	
Darragh Noonan	17.09.1994	26	(2)	2
Midfielders:	**DOB**	**M**	**(s)**	**G**
Declan Carville	13.12.1989	30	(1)	3
Pablo Cavalcante (BRA)	21.03.2000		(6)	
Conall Delaney	08.02.1998	3	(12)	1
Joshua Durnin	05.08.1997	4	(2)	
Mark Hughes	23.03.1985	31	(1)	1
Thomas McCann	12.03.1987	37		
Patrick Mooney	02.05.1991	13		
Stephen Teggart	19.01.1998	23	(7)	1
James Walker	24.01.1991	11	(9)	2
Forwards:	**DOB**	**M**	**(s)**	**G**
Stephen Hughes	18.11.1986	30	(2)	4
Keith Johnston	16.11.1986	1	(4)	
Stefan Lavery	20.07.1993	14	(8)	
Mark McCabe	27.05.1997	25	(5)	4
Karl Moody (IRL)	15.02.1993	3	(8)	1
Gerald Pender (IRL)	22.05.1994	6	(5)	1
Tiarnan Rushe	12.07.1997	9	(6)	3
Trainer:	**DOB**	**M**		
Darren Mullen		38		

Warrenpoint Town Football Club

Founded: 1987
Stadium: Milltown Stadium, Warrenpoint (1,280)

Goalkeepers:	DOB	M	(s)	G
Mark Byrne	15.09.2000	1		
Aaron McCarey (IRL)	14.01.1992	16		
Jonathan Parr	26.11.1985	2		
Jared Thompson	23.02.1999	8		
Berat Türker (GER)	04.10.1991	11	(1)	
Defenders:	**DOB**	**M**	**(s)**	**G**
Emmet Bennett (IRL)	08.07.1999	22	(6)	
Seanan Foster	29.01.1997	22	(5)	1
Simon Kelly (IRL)	04.07.1984	19	(9)	2
Maxim Kouogun (IRL)	14.03.1997	6		1
Hernany Macedo Marques (BRA)	15.02.1987	10	(2)	1
Stephen Moan	04.09.1990	14	(4)	
Anton Reilly (IRL)	09.10.1997	19	(4)	1
Daniel Wallace	21.10.1994	33	(1)	5
Conall Young	19.02.1999	4	(5)	
Midfielders:	**DOB**	**M**	**(s)**	**G**
Gavin Brennan (IRL)	23.01.1988	1	(1)	
Kris Cowan	14.01.2002		(1)	
Philip Donnelly (IRL)	29.04.1992	25	(8)	8
Andrew Fox	03.01.2000		(1)	
Lewis Houston	12.02.1998	1	(1)	
Joshua Lynch	06.04.1997	6	(8)	2
Matthew Lynch	07.03.1999	22	(4)	
James Magowan	04.07.2000	3	(3)	
Francis McCaffrey	22.04.1993	28	(4)	1
Connall McGrandless	12.01.1994	15	(5)	1
Robbie Norton	16.04.1998	16	(3)	2
Dean Watters (IRL)	20.06.1998	14	(6)	2
Forwards:	**DOB**	**M**	**(s)**	**G**
Ethan Copes	14.07.2001	1	(1)	
Lee Duffy (IRL)	07.10.1991	6	(6)	6
Mark Griffin (AUS)	16.06.1991	14	(4)	3
Ciarán O'Connor (IRL)	04.07.1996	25	(4)	3
Alan O'Sullivan (IRL)	24.03.1995	25	(4)	9
Eamon Scannell	10.01.1999	29	(2)	1
Trainer:	**DOB**	**M**		
Stephen McDonnell (IRL)	23.03.1992	38		

SECOND LEVEL
NIFL Championship 2018/2019

Regular Season

1.	Larne FC	22	17	3	2	58	-	16	54
2.	Carrick Rangers FC	22	12	3	7	34	-	28	39
3.	Portadown FC	22	11	5	6	42	-	37	38
4.	Dundela FC Belfast	22	10	6	6	50	-	39	36
5.	Harland & Wolff Welders FC Belfast	22	10	1	11	35	-	36	31
6.	Ballinamallard United FC	22	9	3	10	29	-	31	30
7.	Loughgall FC	22	8	5	9	43	-	39	29
8.	Ballyclare Comrades FC	22	8	5	9	40	-	47	29
9.	Police Service of Northern Ireland FC Belfast	22	7	5	10	36	-	46	26
10.	Knockbreda FC Belfast	22	7	4	11	32	-	45	25
11.	Limavady United FC	22	4	6	12	29	-	47	18
12.	Dergview FC Castlederg	22	5	2	15	29	-	46	17

Teams ranked 1-6 were qualified for the Promotion Round, while teams ranked 7-12 were qualified for the Relegation Round.

Promotion Round

1.	Larne FC (*Promoted*)	32	26	3	3	87	-	19	81
2.	Carrick Rangers FC (*Promotion Play-offs*)	32	20	4	8	59	-	42	64
3.	Portadown FC (*Promotion Play-offs*)	32	15	6	11	59	-	55	51
4.	Dundela FC Belfast	32	13	7	12	67	-	60	46
5.	Ballinamallard United FC	32	12	3	17	39	-	51	39
6.	Harland & Wolff Welders FC Belfast	32	11	2	19	45	-	68	35

Relegation Round

7.	Loughgall FC	32	11	9	12	60	-	52	42
8.	Dergview FC Castlederg	32	13	3	16	51	-	51	42
9.	Ballyclare Comrades FC	32	11	7	14	58	-	68	40
10.	Knockbreda FC Belfast	32	10	7	15	45	-	63	37
11.	Police Service of Northern Ireland FC Belfast (*Relegation Play-offs*)	32	9	7	16	48	-	72	34
12.	Limavady United FC (*Relegated*)	32	8	8	16	45	-	62	32

Promotion Play-offs [30.04.2019]

Carrick Rangers FC - Portadown FC 2-0(0-0)

Relegation Play-offs (2nd / 3rd Level) [30.04.-03.05.2019]

Annagh United FC - **Police Service of Northern Ireland FC Belfast** 1-4 2-1

NATIONAL TEAM

INTERNATIONAL MATCHES
(16.07.2018 – 15.07.2019)

08.09.2018	Belfast	Northern Ireland - Bosnia and Herzegovina	1-2(0-1)	(UNL)
11.09.2018	Belfast	Northern Ireland - Israel	3-0(2-0)	(F)
12.10.2018	Wien	Austria - Northern Ireland	1-0(0-0)	(UNL)
15.10.2018	Sarajevo	Bosnia and Herzegovina - Northern Ireland	2-0(1-0)	(UNL)
15.11.2018	Dublin	Republic of Ireland - Northern Ireland	0-0	(F)
18.11.2018	Belfast	Northern Ireland - Austria	1-2(0-0)	(UNL)
21.03.2019	Belfast	Northern Ireland - Estonia	2-0(0-0)	(ECQ)
24.03.2019	Belfast	Northern Ireland - Belarus	2-1(1-1)	(ECQ)
08.06.2019	Tallinn	Estonia - Northern Ireland	1-2(1-0)	(ECQ)
11.06.2019	Borisov	Belarus - Northern Ireland	0-1(0-0)	(ECQ)

08.09.2018 NORTHERN IRELAND - BOSNIA AND HERZEGOVINA 1-2(0-1) UEFA Nations League B, Group 3
Windsor Park, Belfast; Referee: Pavel Královec (Czech Republic); Attendance: 16,942
NIR: Bailey Peacock-Farrell, Jonathan Grant Evans, Craig George Cathcart, Conor Gerard McLaughlin (70.Liam Boyce), Jamal Lewis, Steven Davis (Cap), Oliver Norwood, Stuart Dallas, George Saville, Kyle Joseph George Lafferty (69.William Donald Grigg), Niall McGinn (76.Jamie John Ward). Trainer: Michael Andrew Martin O'Neill.
Goal: William Donald Grigg (90+3).

11.09.2018 NORTHERN IRELAND - ISRAEL 3-0(2-0) Friendly International
Windsor Park, Belfast; Referee: Hendrikus Sebastiaan Hermanus "Bas" Nijhuis (Netherlands); Attendance: 12,913
NIR: Trevor Carson (46.Michael McGovern), Jonathan Grant Evans, Craig George Cathcart, Jamal Lewis, Steven Davis (Cap), Corry John Evans (46.Oliver Norwood), Patrick James Coleman McNair, Stuart Dallas (77.Shane Kevin Ferguson), George Saville (71.Michael Smith), William Donald Grigg (65.Conor James Washington), Jordan Lewis Jones (65.Gavin Whyte). Trainer: Michael Andrew Martin O'Neill.
Goals: Steven Davis (13), Stuart Dallas (41), Gavin Whyte (67).

12.10.2018 AUSTRIA - NORTHERN IRELAND 1-0(0-0) UEFA Nations League B, Group 3
"Ernst Happel" Stadion, Wien; Referee: Referee: Georgi Kabakov (Bulgaria); Attendance: 22,300
NIR: Bailey Peacock-Farrell, Jonathan Grant Evans, Craig George Cathcart, Jamal Lewis, Steven Davis (Cap), Shane Kevin Ferguson (56.Corry John Evans), Oliver Norwood, Stuart Dallas, Patrick James Coleman McNair, George Saville (77.Kyle Thomas Vassell), Joshua Brendan David Magennis (79.William Donald Grigg). Trainer: Michael Andrew Martin O'Neill.

15.10.2018 BOSNIA AND HERZEGOVINA - NORTHERN IRELAND 2-0(1-0) UEFA Nations League B, Group 3
Stadion Grbavica, Sarajevo; Referee: Mattias Gestranius (Finland); Attendance: 11,050
NIR: Bailey Peacock-Farrell, Jonathan Grant Evans, Craig George Cathcart, Jamal Lewis, Steven Davis, Corry John Evans (Cap), Oliver Norwood (58.Gavin Whyte), Stuart Dallas, Patrick James Coleman McNair (71.Kyle Thomas Vassell), George Saville, Liam Boyce (80.Joshua Brendan David Magennis). Trainer: Michael Andrew Martin O'Neill.

15.11.2018 REPUBLIC OF IRELAND - NORTHERN IRELAND 0-0 Friendly International
Aviva Stadium, Dublin; Referee: Slavko Vinčić (Slovenia); Attendance: 31,241
NIR: Bailey Peacock-Farrell, Jonathan Grant Evans, Craig George Cathcart, Michael Smith (74.Jamie John Ward), Jamal Lewis, Steven Davis (Cap), Corry John Evans (65.Patrick James Coleman McNair), George Saville, Stuart Dallas, Liam Boyce (71.Kyle Joseph George Lafferty), Gavin Whyte (61.Jordan Lewis Jones). Trainer: Michael Andrew Martin O'Neill.

18.11.2018 NORTHERN IRELAND - AUSTRIA 1-2(0-0) UEFA Nations League B, Group 3
Windsor Park, Belfast; Referee: Jonathan Lardot (Belgium); Attendance: 17,895
NIR: Trevor Carson, Gareth McAuley, Jonathan Grant Evans, Michael Smith, Steven Davis (Cap), Stuart Dallas, George Saville, Niall McGinn (74.Gavin Whyte), Corry John Evans (88.Patrick James Coleman McNair), Liam Boyce (74.Kyle Joseph George Lafferty), Jordan Lewis Jones. Trainer: Michael Andrew Martin O'Neill.
Goal: Corry John Evans (59).

21.03.2019 NORTHERN IRELAND - ESTONIA 2-0(0-0) 16th EC. Qualifiers
Windsor Park, Belfast; Referee: Ivan Bebek (Croatia); Attendance: 18,176
NIR: Bailey Peacock-Farrell, Jonathan Grant Evans, Craig George Cathcart, Jamal Lewis, Steven Davis (Cap), Stuart Dallas, Patrick James Coleman McNair, George Saville, Kyle Joseph George Lafferty (76.Joshua Brendan David Magennis), Niall McGinn (85.Conor Gerard McLaughlin), Jordan Lewis Jones (81.Shane Kevin Ferguson). Trainer: Michael Andrew Martin O'Neill.
Goals: Niall McGinn (56), Steven Davis (75 penalty).

24.03.2019 NORTHERN IRELAND - BELARUS 2-1(1-1) 16th EC. Qualifiers
Windsor Park, Belfast; Referee: Paweł Raczkowski (Poland); Attendance: 18,188
NIR: Bailey Peacock-Farrell, Jonathan Grant Evans, Craig George Cathcart, Jamal Lewis, Steven Davis (Cap), Stuart Dallas, Patrick James Coleman McNair, George Saville, Kyle Joseph George Lafferty (79.Liam Boyce), Niall McGinn (68.Joshua Brendan David Magennis), Jordan Lewis Jones (85.Shane Kevin Ferguson). Trainer: Michael Andrew Martin O'Neill.
Goals: Jonathan Grant Evans (30), Joshua Brendan David Magennis (87).

08.06.2019 ESTONIA - NORTHERN IRELAND 1-2(1-0) 16th EC. Qualifiers
A. Le Coq Arena, Tallinn; Referee: Fabio Verissimo (Portugal); Attendance: 8,378
NIR: Bailey Peacock-Farrell, Jonathan Grant Evans, Craig George Cathcart, Michael Smith (64.Jordan Lewis Jones), Jamal Lewis, Steven Davis (Cap), Stuart Dallas, Patrick James Coleman McNair, George Saville (69.Joshua Brendan David Magennis, Liam Boyce (46.Conor James Washington), Gavin Whyte. Trainer: Michael Andrew Martin O'Neill.
Goals: Conor James Washington (77), Joshua Brendan David Magennis (80).

11.06.2019 BELARUS - NORTHERN IRELAND 0-1(0-0) 16th EC. Qualifiers

Borisov Arena, Borisov; Referee: Harald Lechner (Austria); Attendance: 5,350

NIR: Bailey Peacock-Farrell, Jonathan Grant Evans, Craig George Cathcart, Michael Smith, Jamal Lewis, Steven Davis (Cap), Corry John Evans (69.George Saville), Patrick James Coleman McNair, Joshua Brendan David Magennis (56.Stuart Dallas), Conor James Washington (72.Kyle Joseph George Lafferty), Jordan Lewis Jones. Trainer: Michael Andrew Martin O'Neill.

Goal: Patrick James Coleman McNair (86).

NATIONAL TEAM PLAYERS
(16.07.2018 – 15.07.2019)

Name	DOB	Caps	Goals	2018/2019:	*Club*
Goalkeepers					
Trevor CARSON	05.03.1988	**5**	**0**	2018:	*Motherwell FC (SCO)*
Michael McGOVERN	12.07.1984	**29**	**0**	2018:	*Norwich City FC (ENG)*
Bailey PEACOCK-FARRELL	29.10.1996	**9**	**0**	2018/2019:	*Leeds United FC (ENG)*
Defenders					
Craig George CATHCART	06.02.1989	**45**	**2**	2018/2019:	*Watford FC (ENG)*
Jonathan Grant EVANS	03.01.1988	**80**	**3**	2018/2019:	*Leicester City FC (ENG)*
Jamal Piaras LEWIS	25.01.1998	**10**	**0**	2018/2019:	*Norwich City FC*
Gareth Gerald McAULEY	05.12.1979	**80**	**9**	2018:	*Rangers FC Glasgow (SCO)*
Conor Gerard McLAUGHLIN	26.07.1991	**35**	**1**	2018/2019:	*Millwall FC London (ENG)*
Patrick James Coleman McNAIR	27.04.1995	**29**	**1**	2018/2019:	*Middlesbrough FC (ENG)*
Michael SMITH	04.09.1988	**6**	**0**	2018/2019:	*Heart of Midlothian FC Edinburgh (SCO)*
Midfielders					
Stuart Alan DALLAS	19.04.1991	**40**	**3**	2018/2019:	*Leeds United FC (ENG)*
Steven DAVIS	01.01.1985	**111**	**12**	2018: 06.01.2019->	*Southampton FC (ENG)* *Rangers FC Glasgow (SCO)*
Corry John EVANS	17.07.1990	**53**	**2**	2018/2019:	*Blackburn Rovers FC (ENG)*
Shane Kevin FERGUSON	12.07.1991	**39**	**1**	2018/2019:	*Millwall FC London (ENG)*
Jordan Lewis JONES	24.10.1994	**9**	**0**	2018/2019:	*Kilmarnock FC (SCO)*
Niall McGINN	20.07.1987	**57**	**4**	2018/2019:	*Aberdeen FC (SCO)*
Oliver James NORWOOD	12.04.1991	**57**	**0**	2018:	*Sheffield United FC (ENG)*
George Alan SAVILLE	01.06.1993	**15**	**0**	2018/2019:	*Middlesbrough FC (ENG)*
Gavin Whyte	31.01.1996	**5**	**1**	2018/2019:	*Oxford Uited FC (ENG)*
Forwards					
Liam BOYCE	08.04.1991	**19**	**1**	2018/2019:	*Burton Albion FC (ENG)*
William Donald GRIGG	03.07.1991	**13**	**2**	2018:	*Wigan Athletic FC (ENG)*
Kyle Joseph George LAFFERTY	16.09.1987	**73**	**20**	2018/2019:	*Rangers FC Glasgow (SCO)*
Joshua Brendan David MAGENNIS	15.05.1990	**44**	**6**	2018/2019:	*Bolton Wanderers FC (ENG)*
Kyle Thomas VASSELL	07.02.1993	**2**	**0**	2018:	*Rotherham United FC (ENG)*
Jamie John WARD	12.05.1986	**35**	**4**	2018:	*Charlton Athletic FC London (ENG)*
Conor James WASHINGTON	18.05.1992	**20**	**4**	2018/2019:	*Sheffield Wednesday FC (ENG)*

National team coach

Michael Andrew Martin O`NEILL [from 18.12.2011]	05.07.1969	66 M; 24 W; 17 D; 25 L; 69-70

NORWAY

The Country:
Kongeriket Norge (Kingdom of Norway)
Capital: Oslo
Surface: 385,203 km²
Inhabitants: 5,328,212 [2019]
Time: UTC+1

The FA:
Norges Fotballforbund
Servicebok 1 Ullevål Stadium, 0840 Oslo
Tel: +47 2102 9300
Founded: 1902
Member of FIFA since: 1908
Member of UEFA since: 1954
Website: www.fotball.no

NATIONAL TEAM RECORDS

First international match:	12.07.1908, Göteborg:	Sweden – Norway 11-3
Most international caps:	John Arne Semundseth Riise	- 110 caps (2000-2013)
Most international goals:	Jørgen Juve	- 33 goals / 45 caps (1928-1937)

UEFA EUROPEAN CHAMPIONSHIP	
1960	Qualifiers
1964	Qualifiers
1968	Qualifiers
1972	Qualifiers
1976	Qualifiers
1980	Qualifiers
1984	Qualifiers
1988	Qualifiers
1992	Qualifiers
1996	Qualifiers
2000	Final Tournament (Group Stage)
2004	Qualifiers
2008	Qualifiers
2012	Qualifiers
2016	Qualifiers

FIFA WORLD CUP	
1930	Did not enter
1934	Did not enter
1938	Final Tournament (1st Round)
1950	Did not enter
1954	Qualifiers
1958	Qualifiers
1962	Qualifiers
1966	Qualifiers
1970	Qualifiers
1974	Qualifiers
1978	Qualifiers
1982	Qualifiers
1986	Qualifiers
1990	Qualifiers
1994	Final Tournament (Group Stage)
1998	Final Tournament (2nd Round of 16)
2002	Qualifiers
2006	Qualifiers
2010	Qualifiers
2014	Qualifiers
2018	Qualifiers

UEFA NATIONS LEAGUE
2018/2019 – League C (promoted to League B)

OLYMPIC FOOTBALL TOURNAMENTS 1908-2016							
1908	-	**1948**	Did not enter	**1972**	Did not enter	**1996**	Qualifiers
1912	Quarter-Finals	**1952**	Round 1	**1976**	Qualifiers	**2000**	Qualifiers
1920	Quarter-Finals	**1956**	Did not enter	**1980**	Qualifiers	**2004**	Qualifiers
1924	Did not enter	**1960**	Qualifiers	**1984**	Group Stage	**2008**	Qualifiers
1928	Did not enter	**1964**	Did not enter	**1988**	Qualifiers	**2012**	Qualifiers
1936	3rd Place	**1968**	Did not enter	**1992**	Qualifiers	**2016**	Qualifiers

FIFA CONFEDERATIONS CUP 1992-2017
None

NORWEGIAN CLUB HONOURS IN EUROPEAN CLUB COMPETITIONS:

European Champion Clubs.Cup (1956-1992) / UEFA Champions League (1993-2019)
None
Fairs Cup (1858-1971) / UEFA Cup (1972-2009) / UEFA Europa League (2010-2019)
None
UEFA Super Cup (1972-2018)
None
European Cup Winners.Cup 1961-1999*
None

**defunct competition*

NATIONAL COMPETITIONS
TABLE OF HONOURS

	CHAMPIONS	CUP WINNERS	BEST GOALSCORERS	
1902	-	Sportsklubben Grane	-	
1903	-	Odds BK Skien	-	
1904	-	Odds BK Skien	-	
1905	-	Odds BK Skien	-	
1906	-	Odds BK Skien	-	
1907	-	Mercantile FK	-	
1908	-	Lyn 1896 FK Oslo	-	
1909	-	Lyn 1896 FK Oslo	-	
1910	-	Lyn 1896 FK Oslo	-	
1911	-	Lyn 1896 FK Oslo	-	
1912	-	Mercantile FK	-	
1913	-	Odds BK Skien	-	
1914	-	Frigg Oslo FK	-	
1915	-	Odds BK Skien	-	
1916	-	Frigg Oslo FK	-	
1917	-	Sarpsborg FK	-	
1918	-	Kvik FK Fredrikshald	-	
1919	-	Odds BK Skien	-	
1920	-	FK Ørn-Horten	-	
1921	-	Frigg Oslo FK Oslo	-	
1922	-	Odds BK Skien	-	
1923	-	SK Brann Bergen	-	
1924	-	Odds BK Skien	-	
1925	-	SK Brann Bergen	-	
1926	-	Odds BK Skien	-	
1927	-	FK Ørn-Horten	-	
1928	-	FK Ørn-Horten	-	
1929	-	Sarpsborg FK	-	
1930	-	FK Ørn-Horten	-	
1931	-	Odds BK Skien	-	
1932	-	Fredrikstad FK	-	
1933	-	Mjøndalen IF	-	
1934	-	Mjøndalen IF	-	
1935	-	Fredrikstad FK	-	
1936	-	Fredrikstad FK	-	
1937	-	Mjøndalen IF	-	
1937/1938	Fredrikstad FK	Fredrikstad FK	-	
1938/1939	Fredrikstad FK	Sarpsborg FK	-	
1939/1940	*Championship abandoned*	Fredrikstad FK	-	
1940/1941	*No competition*	*No competition*	-	
1941/1942	*No competition*	*No competition*	-	
1942/1943	*No competition*	*No competition*	-	
1943/1944	*No competition*	*No competition*	-	
1944/1945	*No competition*	Lyn 1896 FK Oslo	-	
1945/1946	*No competition*	Lyn 1896 FK Oslo	-	
1946/1947	*No competition*	Skeid Fotball Oslo	-	
1947/1948	SK Freidig Trondheim	Sarpsborg FK	-	
1948/1949	Fredrikstad FK	Sarpsborg FK	Arvid Havnås (Sandefjord BK)	12
1949/1950	IF Fram Larvik	Fredrikstad FK	Reidar Dørum (FK Ørn-Horten)	13
1950/1951	Fredrikstad FK	Sarpsborg FK	John Sveinsson (Lyn 1896 FK Oslo)	19
1951/1952	Fredrikstad FK	IL Sparta Sparsborg	Jan Tangen (Strømmen IF)	15
1952/1953	Larvik Turn & Idrettsforening	Viking FK Stavanger	Gunnar Thoresen (Larvik Turn & Idrettsforening) Per Jacobsen (Odds BK Skien)	15
1953/1954	Fredrikstad FK	Skeid Fotball Oslo	Gunnar Thoresen (Larvik Turn & Idrettsforening)	15
1954/1955	Larvik Turn & Idrettsforening	Skeid Fotball Oslo	Harald Hennum (Skeid Fotball Oslo)	13
1955/1956	Larvik Turn & Idrettsforening	Skeid Fotball Oslo	Willy Fossli (Asker Fotball)	17
1956/1957	Fredrikstad FK	Fredrikstad FK	Per Kristoffersen (Fredrikstad FK)	15
1957/1958	Viking FK Stavanger	Skeid Fotball Oslo	Harald Hennum (Skeid Fotball Oslo)	17
1958/1959	Lillestrøm SK	Viking FK Stavanger	Reidar Sundby (Larvik Turn & Idrettsforening)	13
1959/1960	Fredrikstad FK	Rosenborg BK Trondheim	Per Kristoffersen (Fredrikstad FK)	13
1960/1961	Fredrikstad FK	Fredrikstad FK	Per Kristoffersen (Fredrikstad FK)	15
1961/1962	SK Brann Bergen	SK Gjøvik-Lyn	Rolf Birger Pedersen (SK Brann Bergen)	26
1963	SK Brann Bergen	Skeid Fotball Oslo	Leif Eriksen (Vålerenga Fotball Oslo)	16
1964	Lyn 1896 FK Oslo	Rosenborg BK Trondheim	Ole Stavrum (Lyn 1896 FK Oslo)	18
1965	Vålerenga Fotball Oslo	Skeid Fotball Oslo	Harald Berg (Lyn 1896 FK Oslo)	19
1966	Skeid Fotball Oslo	Fredrikstad FK	Per Kristoffersen (Fredrikstad FK)	20
1967	Rosenborg BK Trondheim	Lyn 1896 FK Oslo	Odd Iversen (Rosenborg BK Trondheim)	17
1968	Lyn 1896 FK Oslo	Lyn 1896 FK Oslo	Odd Iversen (Rosenborg BK Trondheim)	30
1969	Rosenborg BK Trondheim	Strømsgodset IF Drammen	Odd Iversen (Rosenborg BK Trondheim)	26
1970	Strømsgodset IF Drammen	Strømsgodset IF Drammen	Steinar Pettersen (Strømsgodset IF Drammen)	16
1971	Rosenborg BK Trondheim	Rosenborg BK Trondheim	Jan Fuglset (Fredrikstad FK)	17
1972	Viking FK Stavanger	SK Brann Bergen	Egil Solberg (Mjøndalen IF)	

			Johannes Vold (Viking FK Stavanger)	16
1973	Viking FK Stavanger	Strømsgodset IF Drammen	Stein Karlsen (Hamarkameratene)	17
1974	Viking FK Stavanger	Skeid Fotball Oslo	Odd Berg (Molde FK)	13
1975	Viking FK Stavanger	FK Bodø/Glimt	Arne Dokken (Lillestrøm SK)	18
1976	Lillestrøm SK	SK Brann Bergen	Jan Fuglset (Molde FK)	17
1977	Lillestrøm SK	Lillestrøm SK	Trygve Johannessen (Viking FK Stavanger)	17
1978	IK Start Kristiansand	Lillestrøm SK	Tom Lund (Lillestrøm SK)	17
1979	Viking FK Stavanger	Viking FK Stavanger	Odd Iversen (Vålerenga Fotball Oslo)	16
1980	IK Start Kristiansand	Vålerenga Fotball Oslo	Arne Dokken (Lillestrøm SK)	14
1981	Vålerenga Fotball Oslo	Lillestrøm SK	Pål Jacobsen (Vålerenga Fotball Oslo)	16
1982	Viking FK Stavanger	SK Brann Bergen	Tor Arne Granerud (Hamarkameratene) Trygve Johannessen (Viking FK Stavanger)	11
1983	Vålerenga Fotball Oslo	Moss FK	Olav Nysæter (Kongsvinger IL)	14
1984	Vålerenga Fotball Oslo	Fredrikstad FK	Sverre Brandhaug (Rosenborg BK Trondheim)	13
1985	Rosenborg BK Trondheim	Lillestrøm SK	Jørn Andersen (Vålerenga Fotball Oslo)	23
1986	Lillestrøm SK	Tromsø IL	Arve Seland (IK Start Kristiansand)	12
1987	Moss FK	Bryne FK	Jan Kristian Fjærestad (Moss FK)	18
1988	Rosenborg BK Trondheim	Rosenborg BK Trondheim	Jan Åge Fjørtoft (Lillestrøm SK)	14
1989	Lillestrøm SK	Viking FK Stavanger	Jahn Ivar Jakobsen (Rosenborg BK Trondheim)	18
1990	Rosenborg BK Trondheim	Rosenborg BK Trondheim	Tore André Dahlum (IK Start Kristiansand)	20
1991	Viking FK Stavanger	Strømsgodset IF Drammen	Karl Petter Løken (Rosenborg BK Trondheim)	12
1992	Rosenborg BK Trondheim	Rosenborg BK Trondheim	Kjell Roar Kaasa (Kongsvinger IL)	17
1993	Rosenborg BK Trondheim	FK Bodø/Glimt	Mons Ivar Mjelde (Lillestrøm SK)	19
1994	Rosenborg BK Trondheim	Molde FK	Harald Martin Brattbakk (Rosenborg BK Trondheim)	17
1995	Rosenborg BK Trondheim	Rosenborg BK Trondheim	Harald Martin Brattbakk (Rosenborg BK Trondheim)	26
1996	Rosenborg BK Trondheim	Tromsø IL	Harald Martin Brattbakk (Rosenborg BK Trondheim)	28
1997	Rosenborg BK Trondheim	Vålerenga Fotball Oslo	Sigurd Rushfeldt (Rosenborg BK Trondheim)	27
1998	Rosenborg BK Trondheim	Stabæk Fotball Bærum	Sigurd Rushfeldt (Rosenborg BK Trondheim)	25
1999	Rosenborg BK Trondheim	Rosenborg BK Trondheim	Rune Lange (Tromsø IL)	23
2000	Rosenborg BK Trondheim	Odd Grenland Skien	Thorstein Helstad (SK Brann Bergen)	18
2001	Rosenborg BK Trondheim	Viking FK Stavanger	Frode Johnsen (Rosenborg BK Trondheim) Thorstein Helstad (SK Brann Bergen) Clayton Zane (AUS, Lillestrøm SK)	17
2002	Rosenborg BK Trondheim	Vålerenga Fotball Oslo	Harald Martin Brattbakk (Rosenborg BK Trondheim)	17
2003	Rosenborg BK Trondheim	Rosenborg BK Trondheim	Harald Martin Brattbakk (Rosenborg BK Trondheim)	17
2004	Rosenborg BK Trondheim	SK Brann Bergen	Frode Johnsen (Rosenborg BK Trondheim)	19
2005	Vålerenga Fotball Oslo	Molde FK	Ole Martin Årst (Tromsø IL)	16
2006	Rosenborg BK Trondheim	Fredrikstad FK	Daniel Nannskog (SWE, Stabæk Fotball Bærum)	19
2007	SK Brann Bergen	Lillestrøm SK	Thorstein Helstad (SK Brann Bergen)	22
2008	Stabæk Fotball Bærum	Vålerenga Fotball Oslo	Daniel Nannskog (SWE, Stabæk Fotball Bærum)	16
2009	Rosenborg BK Trondheim	Aalesunds FK	Rade Prica (SWE, Rosenborg BK Trondheim)	17
2010	Rosenborg BK Trondheim	Strømsgodset IF Drammen	Baye Djiby Fall (SEN, Molde FK)	16
2011	Molde FK	Aalesunds FK	Mustafa Abdellaoue (Tromsø IL)	17
2012	Molde FK	IL Hødd Ulsteinvik	Péter Kovács (HUN, Strømsgodset IF Drammen) Zdeněk Ondrášek (CZE, Tromsø IL)	14
2013	Strømsgodset IF Drammen	Molde FK	Frode Johnsen (Odds BK Skien)	16
2014	Molde FK	Molde FK	Viðar Örn Kjartansson (ISL, Vålerenga Fotball Oslo)	25
2015	Rosenborg BK Trondheim	Rosenborg BK Trondheim	Alexander Toft Søderlund (Rosenborg BK Trondheim)	22
2016	Rosenborg BK Trondheim	Rosenborg BK Trondheim	Christian Gytkjær (DEN, Rosenborg BK Trondheim)	19
2017	Rosenborg BK Trondheim	Lillestrøm SK	Nicklas Bendtner (DEN, Rosenborg BK Trondheim)	19
2018	Rosenborg BK Trondheim	Rosenborg BK Trondheim	Bi Sylvestre Franck Fortune Boli (CIV, Stabæk Fotball Bærum)	17

Please note: the Norwegian Championship was called Norgesserien (1937–1948), Hovedserien (1948–1962), 1. divisjon (1963–1989), Tippeligaen (1990–2016) and Eliteserien (since 2017).

NATIONAL CHAMPIONSHIP

Eliteserien 2018

(11.03.2018 – 24.11.2018)

Results

Round 1 [11-12.03.2018]
FK Bodø/Glimt - Lillestrøm SK 3-1(1-0)
IK Start - Tromsø IL 4-1(2-0)
Molde FK - Sandefjord 5-0(2-0)
Odds BK - FK Haugesund 1-2(0-0)
Strømsgodset - Stabæk 2-2(1-2)
Sarpsborg 08 - Rosenborg BK 1-0(0-0)
Kristiansund BK - Vålerenga 0-1(0-0)
Ranheim - SK Brann 0-2(0-1) [25.04.]

Round 2 [17-18.03.2018]
Lillestrøm SK - Sarpsborg 08 2-2(1-1)
Rosenborg BK - Kristiansund BK 2-2(0-1)
FK Haugesund - Molde FK 0-1(0-1)
SK Brann - FK Bodø/Glimt 2-0(2-0)
Vålerenga - Odds BK 2-1(0-0)
Sandefjord - Ranheim 1-2(1-0) [11.04.]
Tromsø IL - Strømsgodset 3-1(2-0) [11.04.]
Stabæk - IK Start 1-1(0-0) [25.04.]

Round 3 [02.04.2018]
FK Bodø/Glimt - FK Haugesund 0-3(0-2)
IK Start - Sandefjord 1-4(1-1)
Kristiansund BK - Lillestrøm SK 2-1(0-1)
Molde FK - Tromsø IL 2-1(2-1)
Ranheim - Stabæk 4-1(2-0)
Sarpsborg 08 - Vålerenga 3-0(1-0)
Strømsgodset - SK Brann 1-1(0-0)
Odds BK - Rosenborg BK 1-1(0-0)

Round 4 [07-09.04.2018]
Vålerenga - Strømsgodset 1-4(1-1)
FK Haugesund - Sarpsborg 08 1-1(1-0)
Odds BK - FK Bodø/Glimt 1-0(0-0)
Sandefjord - Stabæk 1-1(1-1)
SK Brann - Kristiansund BK 1-0(0-0)
Tromsø IL - Ranheim 4-0(0-0)
Rosenborg BK - Molde FK 4-0(2-0)
Lillestrøm SK - IK Start 1-0(1-0)

Round 5 [14-16.04.2018]
IK Start - Vålerenga 1-6(1-2)
Molde FK - Lillestrøm SK 2-1(1-1)
Ranheim - FK Haugesund 4-2(2-1)
Sandefjord - Kristiansund BK 3-3(1-1)
Stabæk - Tromsø IL 1-1(1-1)
Strømsgodset - Odds BK 3-0(0-0)
Sarpsborg 08 - SK Brann 1-2(0-1)
FK Bodø/Glimt - Rosenborg BK 0-1(0-0)

Round 6 [21-23.04.2018]
SK Brann - Stabæk 3-0(2-0)
FK Haugesund - Strømsgodset 1-0(1-0)
Kristiansund BK - FK Bodø/Glimt 1-1(1-1)
Lillestrøm SK - Ranheim 0-1(0-0)
Rosenborg BK - IK Start 2-0(0-0)
Tromsø IL - Sandefjord 4-1(4-1)
Vålerenga - Molde FK 0-0
Odds BK - Sarpsborg 08 3-1(1-1)

Round 7 [28-30.04.2018]
Ranheim - Vålerenga 2-2(1-1)
IK Start - FK Haugesund 0-1(0-0)
Molde FK - Odds BK 0-1(0-1)
Sandefjord - SK Brann 0-1(0-0)
Sarpsborg 08 - FK Bodø/Glimt 0-0
Tromsø IL - Kristiansund BK 0-0
Strømsgodset - Rosenborg BK 0-1(0-1)
Stabæk - Lillestrøm SK 3-2(1-1)

Round 8 [05-07.05.2018]
Rosenborg BK - Ranheim 1-1(0-0)
FK Bodø/Glimt - Strømsgodset 2-2(1-1)
Kristiansund BK - Stabæk 1-0(0-0)
Lillestrøm SK - Sandefjord 1-0(1-0)
Odds BK - IK Start 3-0(2-0)
Vålerenga - FK Haugesund 2-2(1-1)
SK Brann - Tromsø IL 3-0(2-0)
Sarpsborg 08 - Molde FK 2-2(2-2)

Round 9 [12-13.05.2018]
Sandefjord - Vålerenga 0-1(0-0)
IK Start - SK Brann 0-1(0-0)
FK Haugesund - Kristiansund BK 3-2(1-1)
Molde FK - FK Bodø/Glimt 1-2(1-0)
Ranheim - Odds BK 3-1(2-1)
Strømsgodset - Sarpsborg 08 1-2(1-0)
Tromsø IL - Lillestrøm SK 1-2(1-2)
Stabæk - Rosenborg BK 0-1(0-0)

Round 10 [16.05.2018]
FK Bodø/Glimt - Tromsø IL 0-1(0-1)
Kristiansund BK - Ranheim 1-3(0-1)
Molde FK - Strømsgodset 2-0(0-0)
Odds BK - Sandefjord 5-0(3-0)
Rosenborg BK - Lillestrøm SK 3-0(1-0)
Sarpsborg 08 - IK Start 4-0(2-0)
SK Brann - FK Haugesund 1-1(0-0)
Vålerenga - Stabæk 1-0(1-0)

Round 11 [21.05.2018]
FK Haugesund - Rosenborg BK 1-2(0-2)
IK Start - FK Bodø/Glimt 1-0(1-0)
Kristiansund BK - Strømsgodset 4-0(3-0)
Ranheim - Molde FK 3-1(0-1)
Sandefjord - Sarpsborg 08 0-1(0-1)
Stabæk - Odds BK 2-1(0-0)
Tromsø IL - Vålerenga 3-0(2-0)
Lillestrøm SK - SK Brann 1-1(1-0)

Round 12 [26-28.05.2018]
Vålerenga - Lillestrøm SK 1-0(0-0)
FK Bodø/Glimt - Ranheim 4-0(1-0)
FK Haugesund - Tromsø IL 1-0(1-0)
Molde FK - IK Start 3-1(1-1)
Odds BK - Kristiansund BK 1-2(0-0)
Strømsgodset - Sandefjord 2-0(1-0)
Rosenborg BK - SK Brann 1-2(0-0)
Sarpsborg 08 - Stabæk 4-2(1-1)

Round 13 [09-11.06.2018]
Kristiansund BK - Molde FK 1-0(0-0)
IK Start - Strømsgodset 1-1(1-0)
Lillestrøm SK - Odds BK 0-0
Ranheim - Sarpsborg 08 2-1(0-1)
Sandefjord - FK Haugesund 0-2(0-2)
Stabæk - FK Bodø/Glimt 0-0
SK Brann - Vålerenga 0-0
Tromsø IL - Rosenborg BK 2-1(1-0)

Round 14 [23-25.06.2018]
Molde FK - Stabæk 3-0(2-0)
FK Bodø/Glimt - Sandefjord 1-1(1-1)
FK Haugesund - Lillestrøm SK 2-2(1-1)
IK Start - Kristiansund BK 2-0(0-0)
Sarpsborg 08 - Tromsø IL 2-3(1-0)
Strømsgodset - Ranheim 3-0(2-0)
Rosenborg BK - Vålerenga 3-0(2-0)
Odds BK - SK Brann 0-1(0-0)

Round 15 [30.06.-02.07.2018]
Vålerenga - FK Bodø/Glimt 2-2(1-1)
Kristiansund BK - Sarpsborg 08 1-1(1-0)
Ranheim - IK Start 2-0(1-0)
Sandefjord - Rosenborg BK 0-1(0-0)
SK Brann - Molde FK 0-4(0-4)
Tromsø IL - Odds BK 2-1(1-1)
Stabæk - FK Haugesund 2-1(1-0)
Lillestrøm SK - Strømsgodset 1-1(0-1)

Round 16 [07-09.07.2018]
Rosenborg BK - Tromsø IL 2-1(1-0)
FK Bodø/Glimt - SK Brann 2-2(1-1)
FK Haugesund - Sandefjord 4-2(0-2)
IK Start - Stabæk 2-1(0-0)
Odds BK - Lillestrøm SK 3-1(1-0)
Sarpsborg 08 - Ranheim 4-1(3-0)
Molde FK - Vålerenga 5-1(3-1)
Strømsgodset - Kristiansund BK 2-3(1-3)

Round 17 [04-06.08.2018]
Ranheim - Rosenborg BK 1-3(1-2)
Kristiansund BK - Odds BK 1-1(0-1)
Stabæk - Sarpsborg 08 1-3(1-3)
Strømsgodset - FK Bodø/Glimt 4-0(1-0)
Tromsø IL - FK Haugesund 1-2(0-1)
Vålerenga - Sandefjord 2-2(0-1)
Lillestrøm SK - Molde FK 2-2(1-1)
SK Brann - IK Start 4-1(2-0)

Round 18 [10-13.08.2018]
Sandefjord - Tromsø IL 1-0(0-0)
FK Bodø/Glimt - Kristiansund BK 3-0(2-0)
IK Start - Ranheim 0-0
Molde FK - SK Brann 5-1(3-1)
Rosenborg BK - Stabæk 1-1(0-0)
Sarpsborg 08 - Lillestrøm SK 2-0(0-0)
Odds BK - Strømsgodset 2-2(2-0)
FK Haugesund - Vålerenga 1-0(0-0)

Round 19 [19-20.08.2018]
Kristiansund BK - Rosenborg BK 0-2(0-0)
Lillestrøm SK - FK Haugesund 1-1(1-1)
Ranheim - Sandefjord 1-1(0-1)
SK Brann - Sarpsborg 08 2-0(1-0)
Stabæk - Molde FK 3-1(2-0)
Strømsgodset - IK Start 1-1(0-1)
Vålerenga - Tromsø IL 3-0(1-0)
FK Bodø/Glimt - Odds BK 1-1(1-1)

Round 20 [25-27.08.2018]
Tromsø IL - FK Bodø/Glimt 1-2(0-0)
FK Haugesund - Stabæk 2-0(2-0)
Molde FK - Ranheim 2-3(0-0)
Rosenborg BK - Strømsgodset 4-3(2-1)
Sandefjord - Lillestrøm SK 1-3(0-1)
Sarpsborg 08 - Kristiansund BK 1-2(0-1)
Vålerenga - SK Brann 2-0(0-0)
IK Start - Odds BK 0-1(0-1)

Round 21 [01-02.09.2018]
Strømsgodset - Tromsø IL 2-4(1-2)
Stabæk - Sandefjord 3-3(1-1)
FK Bodø/Glimt - Sarpsborg 08 3-1(2-1)
Kristiansund BK - IK Start 1-1(0-1)
Odds BK - Molde FK 1-1(0-1)
Rosenborg BK - FK Haugesund 1-0(1-0)
SK Brann - Ranheim 1-0(0-0)
Lillestrøm SK - Vålerenga 0-1(0-1)

Round 22 [15-17.09.2018]
FK Haugesund - SK Brann 1-3(0-2)
IK Start - Lillestrøm SK 3-0(2-0)
Ranheim - Strømsgodset 1-1(1-0)
Sandefjord - FK Bodø/Glimt 1-1(0-0)
Sarpsborg 08 - Odds BK 1-2(0-1)
Tromsø IL - Stabæk 0-0
Vålerenga - Rosenborg BK 2-3(1-1)
Molde FK - Kristiansund BK 3-2(1-1)

Round 23 [22-24.09.2018]
Odds BK - Vålerenga 3-2(1-0)
FK Bodø/Glimt - IK Start 1-2(0-0)
Kristiansund BK - FK Haugesund 2-1(0-1)
SK Brann - Sandefjord 1-1(0-0)
Stabæk - Ranheim 3-2(1-1)
Strømsgodset - Molde FK 1-2(1-2)
Rosenborg BK - Sarpsborg 08 3-1(0-1)
Lillestrøm SK - Tromsø IL 1-0(0-0)

Round 24 [29.09.-01.10.2018]
Sandefjord - Odds BK 1-1(1-0)
FK Haugesund - FK Bodø/Glimt 1-0(0-0)
Lillestrøm SK - Stabæk 3-2(0-0)
Ranheim - Kristiansund BK 2-1(0-1)
Sarpsborg 08 - Strømsgodset 0-1(0-1)
Vålerenga - IK Start 3-2(1-0)
Molde FK - Rosenborg BK 1-0(1-0)
Tromsø IL - SK Brann 2-1(1-1)

Round 25 [06-07.10.2018]
Stabæk - Vålerenga 1-1(1-0)
Strømsgodset - FK Haugesund 0-1(0-0)
FK Bodø/Glimt - Molde FK 0-1(0-0)
IK Start - Sarpsborg 08 1-0(0-0)
Kristiansund BK - Tromsø IL 5-1(1-0)
Odds BK - Ranheim 2-0(0-0)
Rosenborg BK - Sandefjord 1-1(0-1)
SK Brann - Lillestrøm SK 1-1(0-0)

Round 26 [20-21.10.2018]
Molde FK - Sarpsborg 08 2-2(1-2)
Sandefjord - Strømsgodset 2-1(1-0)
FK Haugesund - Odds BK 2-0(1-0)
Lillestrøm SK - Rosenborg BK 0-0
Ranheim - FK Bodø/Glimt 0-0
Tromsø IL - IK Start 1-2(0-1)
Vålerenga - Kristiansund BK 0-2(0-0)
Stabæk - SK Brann 1-2(0-0)

Round 27 [27-29.10.2018]
Strømsgodset - Vålerenga 2-0(0-0)
FK Bodø/Glimt - Stabæk 1-1(0-0)
Kristiansund BK - Sandefjord 3-2(2-1)
Odds BK - Tromsø IL 1-0(0-0)
Ranheim - Lillestrøm SK 3-2(2-1)
Sarpsborg 08 - FK Haugesund 2-1(2-0)
SK Brann - Rosenborg BK 1-2(0-2)
IK Start - Molde FK 1-3(1-0)

Round 28 [03-05.11.2018]
Stabæk - Kristiansund BK 0-1(0-0)
FK Haugesund - Ranheim 2-0(1-0)
Rosenborg BK - Odds BK 3-1(1-0)
Sandefjord - IK Start 4-1(3-1)
Tromsø IL - Molde FK 2-4(1-2)
Vålerenga - Sarpsborg 08 0-0
SK Brann - Strømsgodset 3-1(1-0)
Lillestrøm SK - FK Bodø/Glimt 1-1(1-1)

Round 29 [11.11.2018]
FK Bodø/Glimt - Vålerenga 1-1(1-1)
IK Start - Rosenborg BK 0-1(0-1)
Kristiansund BK - SK Brann 3-1(1-0)
Molde FK - FK Haugesund 2-0(1-0)
Odds BK - Stabæk 0-3(0-1)
Ranheim - Tromsø IL 1-2(0-2)
Sarpsborg 08 - Sandefjord 1-1(0-0)
Strømsgodset - Lillestrøm SK 2-2(1-1)

Round 30 [24.11.2018]
FK Haugesund - IK Start 3-1(0-1)
Lillestrøm SK - Kristiansund BK 2-0(1-0)
Rosenborg BK - FK Bodø/Glimt 1-1(0-0)
Sandefjord - Molde FK 1-3(1-0)
SK Brann - Odds BK 1-0(1-0)
Stabæk - Strømsgodset 2-2(1-1)
Tromsø IL - Sarpsborg 08 0-2(0-2)
Vålerenga - Ranheim 2-1(0-0)

Final Standings

1.	**Rosenborg BK Trondheim**	30	19	7	4	51	-	24	64
2.	Molde FK	30	18	5	7	63	-	36	59
3.	SK Brann Bergen	30	17	7	6	45	-	31	58
4.	FK Haugesund	30	16	5	9	45	-	33	53
5.	Kristiansund BK	30	13	7	10	46	-	41	46
6.	Vålerenga Fotball Oslo	30	11	9	10	39	-	44	42
7.	Ranheim IL Trondheim	30	12	6	12	43	-	50	42
8.	Sarpsborg 08 FF	30	11	8	11	46	-	39	41
9.	Odds BK Skien	30	11	7	12	39	-	38	40
10.	Tromsø IL	30	11	3	16	41	-	48	36
11.	FK Bodø/Glimt	30	6	14	10	32	-	35	32
12.	Lillestrøm SK	30	7	11	12	34	-	44	32
13.	Strømsgodset IF Drammen	30	7	10	13	46	-	48	31
14.	Stabæk Fotball Bærum (*Releg./Promo Play-offs*)	30	6	11	13	37	-	50	29
15.	IK Start Kristiansand (*Relegated*)	30	8	5	17	30	-	54	29
16.	Sandefjord Fotball (*Relegated*)	30	4	11	15	35	-	57	23

Top goalscorers:

17 Bi Sylvestre Franck Fortune Boli (CIV)
Stabæk Fotball Bærum

14 Marcus Pedersen
Strømsgodset IF Drammen

12 Erling Braut Håland
Molde FK

12 Patrick Mortensen (DEN)
Sarpsborg 08 FF

12 Thomas Lehne Olsen
Lillestrøm SK

Relegation / Promotion Play-offs

Stabæk Fotball Bærum - Aalesunds FK 1-0(1-0) 1-1(0-1)

Stabæk Fotball Bærum remains at first level for 2019.

NATIONAL CUP
Norgesmesterskapet 2018

First Round [17-19.04.2018]

Moss FK - Kråkerøy IL	4-0(2-0)	Madla - Viking FK Stavanger	0-2(0-2)
Bjørnevatn IL - Alta IF	0-3(0-0)	Nybergsund IL-Trysil - Elverum Fotball	0-1(0-0)
Harstad IL - Mosjøen IL	5-3(0-0,2-2)	Oppsal IF - Kongsvinger IL	0-4(0-2)
Arna-Bjørnar - Lyseklostér IL	1-1 aet; 0-1 pen	Orkla FK - Nardo FK	2-1(0-0)
Årvoll IL - Vålerenga Fotball Oslo	0-8(0-5)	Os TF - Åsane Fotball	1-6(0-5)
Asker SK - Follo FK	5-0(2-0)	Østsiden IL - Sarpsborg 08 FF	2-9(1-7)
Bærum SK - Drøbak-Frogn IL	2-1(1-0)	Øystese IL - Sogndal Fotball	1-4(1-0)
Bergsøy IL - Aalesunds FK	2-1(0-1)	Pors Grenland - Notodden FK	1-2(0-0,1-1)
Byåsen Toppfotball - Levanger FK	0-3(0-1)	Raufoss IL - Skjetten SK	6-0(3-0)
Eidsvold TF - Kjelsås Fotball	1-3(0-1)	IL Skarphedin - Odds BK Skien	0-9(0-3)
Eiger FK - Egersunds IK	0-1(0-1)	Skjervøy IK - Tromsø IL	1-3(0-1)
Eik Tønsberg - Sandefjord Fotball	1-6(1-3)	Skjold IL - FK Haugesund	0-3(0-3)
Fana IL - Nest-Sotra Fotball	0-1(0-1)	Sola Fotball - Sandnes Ulf	2-3(1-0)
Fjøra FK - Florø SK	2-3(0-0,2-2)	Sortland IL - FK Mjølner	1-2(0-0,1-1)
FK Arendal - Flekkerøy IL	2-0(1-0)	Sotra SK - SK Vard	1-1 aet; 4-3 pen
FK Ørn-Horten - Lyn 1896 Fotballklubb	3-1(1-0)	Staal Jørpeland - Bryne FK	0-1(0-0)
FK Senja - Finnsnes IL	2-1(1-0)	Steinkjer IFK - Strindheim IL	4-2(1-1)
FK Vidar - Vardeneset BK	5-1(2-1)	Sunndal Fotball - Kristiansund BK	0-4(0-1)
IL Flint - Mjøndalen IF	2-4(0-1,2-2)	Tertnes - FK Fyllingsdalen	0-1(0-0)
IF Fløya - Tromsdalen UIL	1-3(0-1,1-1)	SK Træff - Molde FK	1-6(0-4)
Frigg Oslo FK - Strømmen IF	0-3(0-1)	Ullern IF - Stabæk Fotball Bærum	3-5(2-0,2-2)
Gjelleråsen IF - Ullensaker/Kisa IL	0-3(0-2)	Vestfossen IF - Strømsgodset IF Drammen	1-4(0-1)
Grorud IL - FK Tønsberg	2-0(0-0)	FK Vigør - IK Start Kristiansand	1-8(0-5)
Halsen IF - Fram Larvik	0-4(0-2)	Vindbjart FK - FK Jerv	1-2(1-0)
SK Herd - Brattvåg IL	1-4(1-2)	Volda TI - IL Hødd	0-1(0-0)
IL Stjørdals-Blink - Kolstad IL	6-0(3-0)	IL Sandviken - SK Brann Bergen	1-6(0-4)
Kløfta IL - Lillestrøm SK	0-3(0-2)	IK Junkeren - Mo IL	1-0(1-0)
Korsvoll IL - Lørenskog IF	0-1(0-0)	Tynset IF - Hamarkameratene	0-3(0-2)
Kvik Halden - Fredrikstad FK	0-4(0-2)	Valdres FK - Brumunddal	2-1(1-0,1-1)
Fotballklubben Kvik Trondheim - Ranheim IL Trond.	0-1(0-0)	Melbo IL - FK Bodø/Glimt	1-4(0-2)
Lillehammer FK - Hønefoss BK	0-2(0-0)	Lokomotiv Oslo - KFUM-Kameratene Oslo	0-3(0-0)
Lommedalen IL - Skeid Fotball Oslo	0-2(0-1)	Trygg/Lade - Rosenborg BK Trondheim	2-4(2-1)

Second Round [01-03.05.2018]

Orkla FK - Ranheim IL Trondheim	1-3(0-2)	IL Hødd - Florø SK	1-0(0-0,0-0)
Grorud IL - Vålerenga Fotball Oslo	0-1(0-1)	Brattvåg IL - Molde FK	1-0(0-0,0-0)
Kongsvinger IL - Raufoss IL	4-2(1-2)	Bergsøy IL - Kristiansund BK	0-6(0-3)
FK Mjølner - IL Stjørdals-Blink	2-1(1-0)	Sandnes Ulf - FK Vidar	1-0(1-0)
IK Junkeren - Levanger FK	0-3(0-1)	Harstad IL - FK Bodø/Glimt	2-5(1-1)
Lysekloster IL - FK Haugesund	1-2(0-1)	FK Fyllingsdalen - Sogndal Fotball	2-1(1-0,1-1)
Sotra SK - SK Brann Bergen	0-4(0-3)	Valdres FK - Strømsgodset IF Drammen	1-3(0-1)
Strømmen IF - Bærum SK	1-2(0-0)	Hamarkameratene - Hønefoss BK	4-0(0-0,0-0)
FK Ørn-Horten - Sarpsborg 08 FF	0-6(0-4)	Alta IF - Tromsdalen UIL	3-1(0-0,1-1)
FK Arendal - IK Start Kristiansand	0-3(0-0)	Nest-Sotra Fotball - Åsane Fotball	3-3 aet; 6-5 pen
Fredrikstad FK - Odds BK Skien	1-3(0-2)	Fram Larvik - Mjøndalen IF	2-3(1-1,1-1)
Elverum Fotball - KFUM-Kameratene Oslo	2-3(1-1,1-1)	Kjelsås Fotball - Ullensaker/Kisa IL	0-3(0-1)
Skeid Fotball Oslo - Sandefjord Fotball	3-0(1-0)	FK Senja - Tromsø IL	0-1(0-0,0-0)
Steinkjer IFK - Rosenborg BK Trondheim	0-5(0-3)	Bryne FK - Viking FK Stavanger	1-0(0-0)
Egersunds IK - FK Jerv	2-1(1-1)	Moss FK - Stabæk Fotball Bærum	0-1(0-0,0-0)
Notodden FK - Asker SK	3-0(0-0)	Lørenskog IF - Lillestrøm SK	1-5(1-1)

Third Round [09-10.05.2018]

Bærum SK - Strømsgodset IF Drammen	0-3(0-0)	Egersunds IK - IK Start Kristiansand	0-1(0-0)
Notodden FK - Odds BK Skien	1-1 aet; 1-3 pen	FK Fyllingsdalen - SK Brann Bergen	0-1(0-0)
Ullensaker/Kisa IL - Kongsvinger IL	3-2(2-2,2-2)	Alta IF - Tromsø IL	0-1(0-0,0-0)
Brattvåg IL - Rosenborg BK Trondheim	0-1(0-0)	Levanger FK - Ranheim IL Trondheim	2-4(1-0)
FK Mjølner - FK Bodø/Glimt	1-2(0-0)	Bryne FK - Sandnes Ulf	1-0(0-0)
KFUM-Kameratene Oslo - Lillestrøm SK	1-3(0-2)	Skeid Fotball Oslo - Vålerenga Fotball Oslo	1-2(0-1)
Nest-Sotra Fotball - FK Haugesund	1-2(1-0)	IL Hødd - Kristiansund BK	2-0(2-0)
Mjøndalen IF - Stabæk Fotball Bærum	2-0(0-0)	Hamarkameratene - Sarpsborg 08 FF	1-0(0-0)

1/8-Finals [30.05./13-14.06.2018]

Rosenborg BK Trondheim - Odds BK Skien	2-2 aet; 7-6 pen	Mjøndalen IF - FK Haugesund	2-2 aet; 6-7 pen
Lillestrøm SK - SK Brann Bergen	4-1(0-0)	Ullensaker/Kisa IL - Bryne FK	0-0 aet; 3-4 pen
IK Start Kristiansand - Hamarkameratene	1-1 aet; 5-3 pen	Tromsø IL - Vålerenga Fotball Oslo	3-3 aet; 4-5 pen
FK Bodø/Glimt - IL Hødd	1-1 aet; 5-4 pen	Strømsgodset IF Drammen - Ranheim IL Trondheim	2-0(0-0)

Quarter-Finals [26-27.09.2018]

IK Start Kristiansand - FK Bodø/Glimt	2-1(1-1)	Lillestrøm SK - Bryne FK	2-0(0-0)
Rosenborg BK Trondheim - Vålerenga Fotball Oslo	2-0(1-0)	FK Haugesund - Strømsgodset IF Drammen	0-1(0-1)

Semi-Finals [31.10.-01.11.2018]

Strømsgodset IF Drammen - Lillestrøm SK	3-0(0-0)	Rosenborg BK Trondheim - IK Start Kristiansand	2-1(0-1)

Final

02.12.2018; Ullevaal Stadion, Oslo; Referee: Trond Døvle; Attendance: 22,182

Rosenborg BK Trondheim - Strømsgodset IF Drammen **4-1(2-1)**

Rosenborg: André Hansen, Vegar Eggen Hedenstad (75.Jonathan Levi), Tore Reginiussen, Even Hovland, Birger Solberg Meling, Mike Jensen (Cap), Anders Konradsen, Anders Trondsen, Pål André Helland (81.Alexander Søderlund), Nicklas Bendtner, Samuel Adeniyi Adegbenro (56.Yann-Erik De Lanlay). Trainer: Rini Coolen (Netherlands).

Strømsgodset: Morten Sætra, Mounir Hamoud, Jacob Glesnes (Cap), Jonathan Parr, Henning Hauger, Lars-Christopher Vilsvik (82.Kristoffer Tokstad), Herman Stengel (82.Martin Rønning Ovenstad), Amahl Pellegrino (76.Lars Sætra), Tokmac Nguen, Eirik Ulland Andersen, Mustafa Abdellaoue. Trainer: Björn Petter Ingebretsen.

Goals: 0-1 Mustafa Abdellaoue (13), 1-1 Mike Jensen (18), 2-1 Anders Konradsen (32), 3-1 Nicklas Bendtner (52), 4-1 Nicklas Bendtner (90).

THE CLUBS 2018

Fotballklubben Bodø/Glimt

Founded: 19.09.2016
Stadium: Aspmyra Stadion, Bodø (7,354)

Goalkeepers:	**DOB**	**M**	**(s)**	**G**
Zoran Popović (SRB)	28.05.1988	7		
Ricardo Henrique Schuck Friedrich (BRA)	18.02.1993	23		
Defenders:	**DOB**	**M**	**(s)**	**G**
Fredrik Bjørkan	21.08.1998	13		
Martin Bjørnbak	22.03.1992	29		4
José Isidoro Gómez Torres (ESP)	01.08.1986	20	(1)	
Thomas Jacobsen	16.09.1983	13	(3)	
Emil Jonassen	17.02.1993	8	(4)	
Marius Lode	11.03.1993	16		
Brede Moe	15.12.1991	20		1
Eirik Steen	03.10.1993	1	(3)	
Midfielders:	**DOB**	**M**	**(s)**	**G**
Patrick Berg	24.11.1997	6	(13)	
Thomas Drage	20.02.1992	1	(11)	
Håkon Evjen	14.02.2000	8	(7)	1
Runar Hauge	01.09.2001			
José Ángel Jurado de la Torre (ESP)	21.06.1992	28		1
Morten Ågnes Konradsen	03.05.1996		(4)	
Vegard Moberg	23.01.1991	20	(4)	
Ulrik Saltnes	10.11.1992	28		4
Forwards:	**DOB**	**M**	**(s)**	**G**
Jens Hauge	12.10.1999	3	(8)	
Geir Herrem	28.01.1988		(16)	1
Amor Layouni (TUN)	03.10.1992	29	(1)	3
Trond Olsen	05.02.1984	5	(5)	
Kristian Opseth	06.01.1990	30		10
Marco Tagbajumi (NGA)	01.07.1988		(4)	
Philip Zinckernagel (DEN)	16.12.1994	22	(2)	6
Trainer:	**DOB**	**M**		
Kjetil Knutsen	02.10.1968	30		

Sportsklubben Brann Bergen

Founded: 26.09.1908
Stadium: Brann Stadion, Bergen (17,686)

Goalkeepers:	**DOB**	**M**	**(s)**	**G**
Markus Pettersen	12.02.1999	8		
Samuel Şahin-Radlinger (AUT)	07.11.1992	22		
Defenders:	**DOB**	**M**	**(s)**	**G**
Bismar Gilberto Acosta Evans (CRC)	19.12.1986	25	(2)	2
Thomas Grøgaard	08.02.1994	12		
Ruben Kristiansen	20.02.1988	12	(1)	
Christian Eggen Rismark	01.08.1991	6		1
Gilli Sørensen (FRO)	11.08.1992	27	(1)	3
Taijo Teniste (EST)	31.01.1988	23		1
Vito Wormgoor (NED)	16.11.1988	29		4
Midfielders:	**DOB**	**M**	**(s)**	**G**
Daouda Karamoko Bamba (CIV)	05.03.1995	7	(4)	4
Kristoffer Barmen	19.08.1993	23		3
Daniel Braaten	25.05.1982	3	(8)	
Fredrik Haugen	13.06.1992	27		4
Ruben Yttergård Jenssen	04.05.1988	10	(2)	
Gilbert Koomson (GHA)	09.09.1994	30		1
Peter Larsen	25.02.1989	10	(12)	5
Sivert Nilsen	02.10.1991	15		2
Amer Ordagić (BIH)	05.05.1993	5	(3)	1
Kasper Skaanes	19.03.1995		(2)	
Forwards:	**DOB**	**M**	**(s)**	**G**
Marius Bildøy	29.03.2000		(1)	
Henrik Johansen	22.03.1993	1	(17)	1
Azar Karadaş	09.08.1981		(15)	
Ludcinio Marengo (NED)	14.09.1991	12	(4)	2
Steffen Skålevik	31.01.1993	23	(5)	9
Deyver Antonio Vega Álvarez (CRC)	19.09.1992		(12)	1
Trainer:	**DOB**	**M**		
Lars Arne Nilsen	06.04.1964	30		

Fotballklubben Haugesund

Founded: 28.10.1993
Stadium: Haugesund Stadion, Haugesund (8,754)

Goalkeepers:	**DOB**	**M**	**(s)**	**G**
Per Bråtveit	15.02.1996	24		
Helge Sandvik	15.02.1990	6		
Defenders:	**DOB**	**M**	**(s)**	**G**
Kristoffer Haraldseid	17.01.1994	29		
Ben Karamoko (CIV)	17.05.1995	19	(1)	2
Fredrik Knudsen	30.08.1996	20	(3)	2
Joakim Nilsen	24.04.1991	30		1
Vegard Skjerve	22.05.1988	22		3
Midfielders:	**DOB**	**M**	**(s)**	**G**
David Babajide Akintola (NGA)	13.01.1996	30		9
Bruno Miguel Santos Leite (POR)	26.03.1995	11	(13)	1
Christian Grindheim	17.07.1983	26	(2)	4
Frederik Gytkjær (DEN)	16.03.1993	15	(2)	5
Ikenna Anthony Ikedi (NGA)	19.09.1998		(9)	
Torbjørn Kallevåg	21.08.1993	19	(7)	2
Aleksandar Kovačević (SRB)	09.01.1992		(2)	
Tobias Hammer Svendsen	31.08.1999	1	(7)	
Alexander Stølås	30.04.1989	29		4
Sondre Tronstad	26.08.1995	28	(1)	1
Kristoffer Velde	09.09.1999		(9)	2
Forwards:	**DOB**	**M**	**(s)**	**G**
Shuaibu Lalle Ibrahim (NGA)	19.12.1996		(1)	
Ibrahima Koné (MLI)	16.06.1999	10	(12)	1
Kevin Krygård	17.05.2000			
Ibrahima Wadji (SEN)	05.05.1995	11	(1)	6
Trainer:	**DOB**	**M**		
Eirik Horneland	14.03.1975	30		

Kristiansund Ballklubb

Founded: 02.09.2003
Stadium: Kristiansund Stadion, Kristiansund (4,000)

Goalkeepers:	**DOB**	**M**	**(s)**	**G**
Sean McDermott (IRL)	30.05.1993	29		
Andreas Vaikla (CAN)	19.02.1997	1		
Defenders:	**DOB**	**M**	**(s)**	**G**
Christoffer Aasbak	22.07.1993	25	(1)	1
Nikita Baranov (EST)	19.08.1992	5	(2)	
Joakim Bjerkås	15.01.1993		(1)	
Henrik Gjesdal	19.07.1993		(2)	
Christophe Charles Steven René Psyché (FRA)	28.07.1988	9	(4)	
Erlend Sivertsen	28.01.1991	5	(4)	
Sondre Sørli	30.10.1995	5	(18)	1
Bent Sørmo	22.09.1996	23	(3)	
Dan Peter Ulvestad	04.04.1989	27		4
Midfielders:	**DOB**	**M**	**(s)**	**G**
Stian Aasmundsen	02.11.1989	25	(2)	5
Daouda Bamba (CIV)	05.03.1995	18		7
Amidou Diop (SEN)	25.02.1992	21	(3)	1
Andreas Hopmark	06.07.1991	19	(1)	1
Jesper Isaksen	13.10.1999		(1)	
Liridon Kalludra (SWE)	05.11.1991	22	(4)	6
Brent Lepistu (EST)	26.03.1993	3	(12)	
Jonas Rønningen	27.11.1990	1	(3)	
Pål Erik Ulvestad	08.09.1990	11	(1)	
Forwards:	**DOB**	**M**	**(s)**	**G**
Karl Simon Alexandersson (SWE)	23.11.1992	2	(9)	
Bendik Bye	09.03.1990	19	(11)	9
Aliou Coly (SEN)	10.12.1992	21	(2)	2
Torgil Øwre Gjertsen	12.03.1992	23	(1)	3
Flamur Kastrati	14.11.1991	8		4
Benjamin Stokke	20.08.1990	8	(4)	1
Trainer:	**DOB**	**M**		
Christian Michelsen	14.03.1976	30		

Lillestrøm Sportsklubb

Founded: 02.04.1917
Stadium: Åråsen Stadion, Lillestrøm (12,250)

Goalkeepers:	**DOB**	**M**	**(s)**	**G**
Matvei Igonen (EST)	02.10.1996	6		
Marko Marić (CRO)	03.01.1996	24		
Defenders:	**DOB**	**M**	**(s)**	**G**
Marius Amundsen	22.09.1992	24	(1)	
Stefan Antonijević (USA)	24.01.1989	7	(6)	
Mats Haakenstad	14.11.1993	22	(5)	2
Frode Kippe	17.01.1978	26		
Simen Rafn	16.02.1992	26	(2)	1
Erik Sandberg	27.02.2000	3	(1)	
Midfielders:	**DOB**	**M**	**(s)**	**G**
Raphael Ayagwa (NGA)	13.02.1998		(2)	
Erik Brenden	07.01.1994	14	(10)	
Charles Ezeh (NGA)	18.11.1997	2	(5)	
Matthew Ifeanyi (NGA)	20.01.1997	30		4
Fredrik Krogstad	06.06.1995	22	(6)	1
Aleksander Melgalvis	10.08.1989	16	(8)	1
Simen Mikalsen	04.05.1993	20	(5)	
Kristoffer Ødemarksbakken	05.12.1995	7	(9)	2
Daniel Alexander Pedersen (DEN)	27.07.1992	12	(1)	
Forwards:	**DOB**	**M**	**(s)**	**G**
Moses Ebiye (NGA)	28.04.1997		(7)	
Erling Knudtzon	15.12.1988	20	(3)	1
Gary Martin (ENG)	10.10.1990	7	(12)	2
Thomas Olsen	29.06.1991	29		12
Arnór Smárason (ISL)	07.09.1988	13		7
Trainer:	**DOB**	**M**		
Arne Erlandsen	20.12.1959	14		
Arild Sundgot [27.06.2018]	17.04.1978	2		
Jörgen Lennartsson (SWE) [13.07.2018]	10.04.1965	14		

Molde Fotballklubb

Founded: 19.06.1911
Stadium: Aker Stadion, Molde (11,800)

Goalkeepers:	**DOB**	**M**	**(s)**	**G**
Andreas Linde (SWE)	24.07.1993	29		
Mathias Ranmark	16.10.1995	1		
Defenders:	**DOB**	**M**	**(s)**	**G**
Vegard Forren	16.02.1988	26		1
Ruben Gabrielsen	10.03.1992	24	(1)	2
Kristoffer Haugen	21.02.1994	26		2
Christopher Nilsson Telo (SWE)	04.11.1989	2		
Christoffer Remmer (DEN)	16.01.1993	22	(2)	
Isak Ssewankambo (SWE)	27.02.1996		(4)	
Midfielders:	**DOB**	**M**	**(s)**	**G**
Fredrik Aursnes	10.12.1995	23	(6)	8
Fredrik Brustad	22.06.1989	11	(5)	1
Magnus Wolff Eikrem	08.08.1990	12	(2)	4
Stian Gregersen	17.05.1995	9	(5)	
Eirik Hestad	26.06.1995	29	(1)	8
Etzaz Hussain	27.01.1993	21	(2)	5
Mathias Normann	28.05.1996	8	(2)	1
Babacar Sarr (SEN)	15.02.1991	22	(5)	4
Petter Strand	24.08.1994	14	(12)	1
Tobias Svendsen	31.08.1999	1	(6)	
Forwards:	**DOB**	**M**	**(s)**	**G**
Thomas Olivier Amang A Kegueni (CMR)	09.02.1998	5	(2)	1
Paweł Cibicki (SWE)	09.01.1994	11	(2)	3
Daniel Chima Chukwu (NGA)	04.04.1991	4	(7)	3
Erling Håland	21.07.2000	17	(8)	12
Leke Samson James (NGA)	01.11.1992	5	(4)	3
Mattias Moström (SWE)	25.02.1983	8	(10)	2
Ibrahima Wadji (SEN)	05.05.1995		(4)	1
Trainer:	**DOB**	**M**		
Ole Gunnar Solskjær	26.02.1973	30		

Odds Ballklubb Skien

Founded: 31.03.1894
Stadium: Skagerak Arena, Skien (12,500)

Goalkeepers:	**DOB**	**M**	**(s)**	**G**
Viljar Myhra	21.07.1996	2		
Sondre Rossbach	07.02.1996	28		
Defenders:	**DOB**	**M**	**(s)**	**G**
Vegard Bergan	20.02.1995	27	(3)	1
Fredrik Berge	06.02.1990	5		
Odin Lurås Bjørtuft	19.12.1998		(2)	
Thomas Grøgaard	08.02.1994	12	(2)	
Steffen Hagen	08.03.1986	28	(1)	1
John Kitolano	18.10.1999	6		
Andreas Kristoffer Nordvik	18.03.1987		(2)	
Espen Ruud	26.02.1984	29		8
Midfielders:	**DOB**	**M**	**(s)**	**G**
Martin Broberg (SWE)	24.09.1990	17	(7)	4
Vebjørn Hoff	13.02.1996	27		
Markus Kaasa	15.07.1997	14	(4)	1
Joshua Kitolano	03.08.2001	8	(8)	
Stefan Mladenović	03.04.1994	4	(13)	1
Fredrik Nordkvelle	13.09.1985	14	(10)	2
Birk Risa	13.02.1998	26		1
Jone Samuelsen	06.07.1984	21	(2)	1
André Sødlund	22.12.1996	2	(3)	
Forwards:	**DOB**	**M**	**(s)**	**G**
Torgeir Børven	03.12.1991	16	(5)	5
Filip Møller Delaveris	10.12.2000		(1)	
Marius Larsen	14.05.2000		(1)	
Tobias Lauritsen	30.08.1997	4	(14)	1
Bilal Njie	13.06.1998	14	(8)	3
Elbasan Rashani (KVX)	09.05.1993	26	(1)	7
Trainer:	**DOB**	**M**		
Dag-Eilev Fagermo	28.01.1967	30		

Ranheim Fotball Trondheim

Founded: 17.02.1901
Stadium: EXTRA Arena, Trondheim (3,000)

Goalkeepers:	**DOB**	**M**	**(s)**	**G**
Even Barli	24.07.1991	30		
Defenders:	**DOB**	**M**	**(s)**	**G**
Øyvind Alseth	13.08.1994	6	(9)	
Karl Eek	25.06.1988		(1)	
Aleksander Foosnæs	05.06.1994	29		1
Ivar Furu	07.05.1994	11	(8)	
Daniel Kvande	08.04.1995	30		
Christian Rismark	01.08.1991	18		1
Glenn Walker	17.06.1998		(1)	
Aslak Witry	10.03.1996	26		2
Midfielders:	**DOB**	**M**	**(s)**	**G**
Eirik Dønnem	21.07.1990	29		1
Kristoffer Løkberg	22.01.1992	28		6
Mads Reginiussen	02.01.1988	26		9
Simen Sandmæl	04.08.1990	2	(4)	1
Sondre Sørløkk	08.05.1997	5	(11)	
Magnus Stamnestrø	18.04.1992		(2)	
Jakob Tromsdal	08.10.1997		(4)	
Forwards:	**DOB**	**M**	**(s)**	**G**
Andreas Helmersen	15.03.1998	11	(12)	3
Michael Karlsen	03.02.1990	17	(5)	8
Mats Lillebo	29.07.1994	3	(4)	
Joachim Olufsen	14.07.1995	3	(4)	
Kim Riksvold	26.10.1993	5	(1)	1
Ola Solbakken	07.09.1998	6	(5)	
Sivert Solli	25.07.1997	2	(6)	
Øyvind Storflor	18.12.1979	13	(10)	3
Erik Tønne	03.07.1991	30		7
Trainer:	**DOB**	**M**		
Svein Maalen	25.02.1978	30		

Rosenborg Ballklub Trondheim

Founded: 19.05.1917
Stadium: Lerkendal Stadion, Trondheim (21,405)

Goalkeepers:	**DOB**	**M**	**(s)**	**G**
André Hansen	17.12.1989	29		
Arild Østbø	19.04.1991	1	(2)	
Defenders:	**DOB**	**M**	**(s)**	**G**
Alexander Joseph Gersbach (AUS)	08.05.1997	3		
Vegar Eggen Hedenstad	26.06.1991	27		
Even Hovland	14.02.1989	27		
Birger Solberg Meling	17.12.1994	28		1
Jacob Rasmussen (DEN)	28.05.1997	7	(3)	
Tore Reginiussen	10.04.1986	29		2
Erlend Reitan	11.09.1997	5	(4)	
Besim Šerbečić (BIH)	01.05.1998	1	(3)	
Midfielders:	**DOB**	**M**	**(s)**	**G**
Đorđe Denić (SRB)	01.04.1996	5	(3)	
Issam Jebali (TUN)	25.12.1991	7		3
Mike Jensen (DEN)	19.02.1988	28		6
Anders Konradsen	18.07.1990	17	(1)	5
Morten Ågnes Konradsen	03.05.1996		(1)	
Jonathan Levi (SWE)	23.01.1996	10	(9)	4
Marius Lundemo	11.04.1994	7	(9)	2
Anders Trondsen	30.03.1995	24		2
Forwards:	**DOB**	**M**	**(s)**	**G**
Samuel Adeniyi Adegbenro (NGA)	03.12.1995	5	(2)	3
Nicklas Bendtner (DEN)	16.01.1988	22	(1)	5
Erik Botheim	10.01.2000	1	(5)	1
Emil Konradsen Ceide	03.09.2001		(2)	
Yann-Erik De Lanlay	14.05.1992	9	(8)	3
Pål André Helland	04.01.1990	19	(1)	5
Alexander Søderlund	03.08.1987	17	(10)	8
Matthías Vilhjálmsson (ISL)	30.01.1987	2	(5)	
Rafik Zekhnini	12.01.1998		(6)	
Trainer:	**DOB**	**M**		
Kåre Ingebrigtsen	11.11.1965	16		
Rini Coolen (NED) [19.07.2018]	10.02.1967	14		

Sandefjord Fotball

Founded: 10.09.1998
Stadium: Komplett Arena, Sandefjord (6,582)

Goalkeepers:	**DOB**	**M**	**(s)**	**G**
Eirik Johansen	12.07.1992	29		
Ingvar Jónsson (ISL)	18.10.1989	1		
Defenders:	**DOB**	**M**	**(s)**	**G**
Victor Bindia (SEN)	06.08.1989	13	(3)	
Andrew Eleftheriou (ENG)	08.11.1997	3	(1)	
Lars Grorud	02.07.1983	20	(4)	1
Marius Christopher Høibråten	23.01.1995	12		
El-Hadji Kane (SEN)	11.04.1995	8		
Stian Lunder Ringstad	29.08.1991	14		1
Abdoulaye Seck (SEN)	04.06.1992	2	(4)	
Joackim Solberg	11.04.1989	13	(2)	1
Midfielders:	**DOB**	**M**	**(s)**	**G**
Ole Breistøl	11.07.1998		(5)	
Mohammed Fellah	24.05.1989	4		2
William Kurtović (SWE)	22.06.1996	6	(5)	1
Erik Mjelde	06.03.1984	9	(7)	
Sander Risan Mørk	06.12.2000		(1)	
Emil Pálsson (ISL)	10.06.1993	18		
Pau Morer Vicente (ESP)	10.10.1995	14	(8)	2
Christer Reppesgård Hansen	29.03.1993	28	(1)	
André Sødlund	22.12.1996	10	(3)	
Håvard Storbæk	25.05.1986	22	(5)	4
Marc Vales González (AND)	04.04.1990	11	(1)	
Enric Vallès (NED)	01.03.1990	25		2
Forwards:	**DOB**	**M**	**(s)**	**G**
Fitim Azemi	25.06.1992	3	(2)	
Pontus Engblom (SWE)	03.11.1991	22	(7)	6
George Gibson	29.08.2000		(11)	
Flamur Kastrati	14.11.1991	15	(1)	4
Herman Nilsen	30.04.1999	4	(3)	
Mohamed Ofkir	04.08.1996	14	(7)	3
Rubén Herráiz Alcaraz „Rufo" (ESP)	13.01.1993	10	(2)	7
Sabawon Shamohammad	10.12.1998		(3)	
Trainer:	**DOB**	**M**		
Magnus Powell (SWE)	28.10.1974	6		
Geir Ludvig Fevang [26.04.2018]	17.11.1980	6		
Martí Cifuentes Corvillo (ESP) [31.05.2018]	07.07.1982	18		

Sarpsborg 08 Fotballforening

Founded: 15.01.2008
Stadium: Sarpsborg Stadion, Sarpsborg (4,700)

Goalkeepers:	**DOB**	**M**	**(s)**	**G**
Aslak Falch	25.05.1992	18		
Aleksandr Vasyutin (RUS)	04.03.1995	12		
Defenders:	**DOB**	**M**	**(s)**	**G**
Sulayman Bojang	03.09.1997	1		
Jørgen Horn	07.06.1987	7	(1)	1
Joonas Tamm (EST)	02.02.1992	22	(2)	2
Joachim Thomassen	04.05.1988	27		2
Bjørn Utvik	28.02.1996	7	(2)	
Midfielders:	**DOB**	**M**	**(s)**	**G**
Amin Askar	01.10.1985	23	(1)	4
Ole Halvorsen	02.10.1987	23	(1)	5
Tobias Heintz	13.07.1998	13	(10)	2
Joackim Jørgensen	20.09.1988	24		
Matti Lund Nielsen (DEN)	08.05.1988	25	(3)	1
Usman Muhammed (NGA)	04.03.1994	1	(5)	
Orri Sigurður Ómarsson (ISL)	18.02.1995		(2)	
Harmeet Singh	12.11.1990	18	(10)	1
Jon-Helge Tveita	27.01.1992	23	(2)	1
Gaute Vetti	02.09.1998	2	(5)	
Kristoffer Zachariassen	27.10.1994	25	(1)	4
Forwards:	**DOB**	**M**	**(s)**	**G**
Mikkel Agger (DEN)	01.11.1992	10	(12)	3
Jørgen Larsen	06.02.2000	2	(4)	
Kristoffer Larsen	19.01.1992	4	(12)	1
Patrick Mortensen (DEN)	13.07.1989	28		12
Rashad Muhammed (FRA)	25.09.1993	9	(4)	1
Ronnie Schwartz (DEN)	29.08.1989	6	(8)	5
Trainer:	**DOB**	**M**		
Geir Bakke	23.10.1969	30		

Stabæk Fotball Bærum

Founded: 16.03.1912
Stadium: Nadderud Stadion, Bærum (7,000)

Goalkeepers:	**DOB**	**M**	**(s)**	**G**
Simen Kjellevold	07.11.1994	1	(1)	
Robert Marcus Sandberg (SWE)	07.11.1990	12		
Mandé Sayouba (CIV)	15.06.1993	17		
Defenders:	**DOB**	**M**	**(s)**	**G**
Vadim Demidov	10.10.1986	25		1
Andreas Hanche-Olsen	17.01.1997	18	(5)	
Ronald José Hernández Pimentel (VEN)	04.10.1997	18	(3)	
Jeppe Moe	03.08.1995	29		
Steinar Strømnes	19.03.1987	4	(1)	
Midfielders:	**DOB**	**M**	**(s)**	**G**
Kristoffer Askildsen	09.01.2001	1		
Emil Bohinen	12.03.1999	3	(8)	
Tobias Børkeeiet	18.04.1999	20	(7)	
Tonny Brochmann (DEN)	11.08.1989	15	(1)	3
Ola Brynhildsen	27.04.1999	13	(10)	4
Daniel Granli	01.05.1994	28	(1)	
Aboubakar Keita (CIV)	05.11.1997	10		2
Martin Ovenstad	18.04.1994	5	(3)	
John Hou Sæter	13.01.1998	19	(4)	
Filip Valenčič (SVN)	07.01.1992	1	(5)	
Hugo Vetlesen	29.02.2000	20	(4)	1
Forwards:	**DOB**	**M**	**(s)**	**G**
Oscar Aga	06.01.2001		(7)	
Franck Boli (CIV)	07.12.1993	29		17
Moussa Njie	02.10.1995	13	(2)	1
Ohi Omoijuanfo	10.01.1994	29	(1)	8
Trainer:	**DOB**	**M**		
Antonio Ordinas Pou (ESP)	19.08.1974	14		
Jan Peder Jalland [27.06.2018]	02.05.1980	1		
Henning Stille Berg [04.07.2018]	01.09.1969	15		

Idrettsklubben Start Kristiansand

Founded: 19.09.1905
Stadium: Sør Arena, Kristiansand (14,563)

Goalkeepers:	DOB	M	(s)	G
Benjamin Boujar	30.11.1993		(1)	
Jonas Deumeland (GER)	09.02.1988	26		
Håkon Opdal	11.06.1982	4	(1)	
Defenders:	**DOB**	**M**	**(s)**	**G**
Espen Berger	09.03.1994	16	(3)	
Elliot Käck (SWE)	18.09.1989	28		2
Simon Larsen	01.06.1988	25		
Damion Lowe (JAM)	05.05.1993	23		1
Henrik Robstad	12.05.1991	14	(7)	
Eirik Wichne	12.05.1997	23		
Midfielders:	**DOB**	**M**	**(s)**	**G**
Afeez Aremu Olalekan (NGA)	03.10.1999	23	(3)	3
Espen Børufsen	04.03.1988	8	(1)	2
Tobias Christensen	11.05.2000	15	(10)	1
Kristján Finnbogason (ISL)	12.01.1995	11	(2)	2
Adnan Hadžić	08.03.1999	9	(7)	
Niklas Sandberg	18.05.1995	7	(8)	
Erlend Segberg	12.04.1997	16		
Herolind Xhavit Shala (KVX)	01.02.1992	13	(1)	3
Aron Sigurðarson (ISL)	08.10.1993	12	(5)	1
Kasper Skaanes	19.03.1995	14	(2)	
Isaac Twum (GHA)	14.02.1998	10	(3)	
Forwards:	**DOB**	**M**	**(s)**	**G**
Adeleke Akinola Akinyemi (NGA)	11.08.1998	12		3
Mathias Bringaker	30.01.1997	1	(20)	5
Kevin Kabran (SWE)	22.11.1993	19	(3)	6
Ibrahim Mensah Arafat (GHA)	11.01.1995		(2)	
Lars-Jørgen Salvesen	19.02.1996	1	(3)	
Trainer:	**DOB**	**M**		
Mark James Dempsey (ENG)	14.01.1964	10		
Mick Priest (ENG) [19.05.2018]	28.07.1976	2		
Kjetil André Rekdal [01.06.2018]	06.11.1968	18		

Strømsgodset Toppfotball Drammen

Founded: 10.02.1907
Stadium: Marienlyst Stadion, Drammen (8,935)

Goalkeepers:	DOB	M	(s)	G
Pål Heigre	15.03.1995	1		
Espen Pettersen	10.05.1980	22		
Morten Sætra	18.06.1997	7		
Defenders:	**DOB**	**M**	**(s)**	**G**
Jacob Glesnes	25.03.1994	30		1
Mounir Hamoud	01.02.1985	6	(2)	
Marius Høibråten	23.01.1995	11	(2)	
Christopher Lindquist	30.10.1995	7		
Kim Madsen	12.03.1989	2		
Jonathan Parr	21.10.1988	27		1
Stian Ringstad	29.08.1991	3		
Lars Sætra	24.07.1991	12	(6)	1
Midfielders:	**DOB**	**M**	**(s)**	**G**
Hasan Duman	12.04.1999		(3)	
Francisco Santos Silva Júnior (POR)	18.01.1992	14	(4)	
Mathias Gjerstrøm	30.06.1997		(1)	
Henning Hauger	17.07.1985	24	(2)	
Johan Hove	07.09.2000	1	(4)	
Bassel Jradi (DEN)	06.07.1993	15	(1)	2
Tokmac Nguen	20.10.1993	25	(3)	7
Martin Rønning Ovenstad	18.04.1994	2	(3)	
Amahl Pellegrino	18.06.1990	11	(14)	2
Herman Stengel	26.08.1995	18	(7)	1
Kristoffer Tokstad	05.07.1991	10	(4)	1
Lars-Christopher Vilsvik	18.10.1988	22		
Forwards:	**DOB**	**M**	**(s)**	**G**
Mustafa Abdellaoue	01.08.1988	10	(14)	7
Eirik Ulland Andersen	21.09.1992	28		6
Andreas Hoven	20.02.1998		(2)	
Marcus Pedersen	08.06.1990	22	(1)	14
Trainer:	**DOB**	**M**		
Tor Olle Skullerud	10.12.1970	12		
Björn Petter Ingebretsen [07.06.2018]	26.05.1967	18		

Tromsø Idrettslag

Founded: 15.09.1920
Stadium: Alfheim Stadion, Tromsø (6,859)

Goalkeepers:	DOB	M	(s)	G
Jacob Karlstrøm	09.01.1997	6	(1)	
Gudmund Kongshavn	23.01.1991	24	(1)	
Defenders:	**DOB**	**M**	**(s)**	**G**
Kent-Are Antonsen	12.02.1995	27	(2)	5
Jostein Gundersen	02.04.1996	24		3
Tom Høgli	24.02.1984	13		
Lasse Nilsen	21.02.1995	25	(1)	3
Hans Norbye	16.01.1987		(3)	
Magnar Ødegaard	11.05.1993	28		1
Simen Wangberg	06.05.1991	25		2
Midfielders:	**DOB**	**M**	**(s)**	**G**
Magnus Andersen	28.05.1986	5	(4)	1
Gjermund Åsen	22.05.1991	21		2
Daniel Berntsen	04.04.1993	25	(3)	5
Mikael Ingebrigtsen	21.07.1996	11	(1)	2
Oliver Kjærgaard (DEN)	11.07.1998		(2)	
Christian Landu	25.01.1992	3	(9)	
Marcus Pedersen	16.06.2000		(3)	
Morten Gamst Pedersen	08.09.1981	27		1
Robert Taylor (FIN)	21.10.1994	27		4
Onni Valakari (FIN)	18.08.1999	8	(5)	2
Forwards:	**DOB**	**M**	**(s)**	**G**
Mushagalusa Bakenga Joar Bahati Namugunga	08.08.1992	11	(14)	2
Runar Espejord	26.02.1996	18	(1)	6
Sigurd Grønli	17.10.2000		(7)	
El Hadj Mour Samb (SEN)	08.01.1994	1	(8)	
Slobodan Vuk (SVN)	15.09.1989	1	(9)	2
Trainer:	**DOB**	**M**		
Simo Valakari (FIN)	28.04.1973	30		

Vålerenga Fotball Oslo

Founded: 29.07.1913
Stadium: Intility Arena, Oslo (17,233)

Goalkeepers:	**DOB**	**M**	**(s)**	**G**
Adambathia Larsen Kwarasey (GHA)	12.12.1987	30		
Defenders:	**DOB**	**M**	**(s)**	**G**
Sam Adekugbe (CAN)	16.01.1995	26	(1)	
Christian Borchgrevink	11.05.1999	1	(1)	
Luis Felipe Carvalho da Silva (URU)	18.09.1993	20	(2)	1
Enar Jääger (EST)	18.11.1984	1	(2)	
João Diogo Serpa Meira (POR)	30.04.1987	1	(1)	
Ivan Näsberg	22.04.1996	14		
Jonatan Nation	01.07.1990	28		2
Amin Nouri	10.01.1990	29	(1)	2
Midfielders:	**DOB**	**M**	**(s)**	**G**
Mohammed Abu (GHA)	14.11.1991	10		
Ernest Agyiri (GHA)	06.03.1998		(5)	
Aron Dønnum	20.04.1998		(8)	
Samúel Kári Friðjónsson (ISL)	22.02.1996	11	(6)	1
Magnus Grødem	14.08.1998	7	(14)	1
Abdisalam Ibrahim	01.05.1991	12	(5)	
Erik Gustav Roger Israelsson (SWE)	25.02.1989	10		
Simen Juklerød	18.05.1994	7	(4)	
Magnus Lekven	13.01.1988	19	(1)	1
Felix Myhre	04.03.1999	6	(13)	3
Forwards:	**DOB**	**M**	**(s)**	**G**
Fitim Azemi	25.06.1992		(3)	
Chidera Ejuke (NGA)	02.01.1998	26	(3)	3
Bård Finne	13.02.1995	21	(4)	10
Daniel Holm	30.07.1985	23	(1)	1
Sam Johnson (LBR)	06.05.1993	24		11
Peter Michael (NGA)	10.05.1998	4	(9)	3
Trainer:	**DOB**	**M**		
Ronny Deila	21.09.1975	30		

SECOND LEVEL
OBOS-ligaen 2018

1.	Viking FK Stavanger (*Promoted*)	30	20	1	9	68	-	44	61
2.	Mjøndalen IF (*Promoted*)	30	17	9	4	49	-	24	60
3.	Aalesunds FK (*Promotion Play-offs*)	30	18	5	7	58	-	31	59
4.	Sogndal Fotball (*Promotion Play-offs*)	30	15	6	9	47	-	31	51
5.	Ullensaker/Kisa IL (*Promotion Play-offs*)	30	11	10	9	59	-	49	43
6.	Nest-Sotra Fotball (*Promotion Play-offs*)	30	12	7	11	43	-	41	43
7.	Tromsdalen UIL Tromsø	30	12	7	11	43	-	47	43
8.	Kongsvinger IL	30	12	6	12	59	-	49	42
9.	Hamarkameratene	30	12	6	12	46	-	44	42
10.	Sandnes Ulf	30	11	9	10	43	-	47	42
11.	Strømmen IF	30	12	2	16	49	-	53	38
12.	Notodden Fotballklubb	30	10	6	14	36	-	40	36
13.	FK Jerv Grimstad	30	8	11	11	31	-	41	35
14.	Åsane Fotball (*Relegation Play-offs*)	30	9	6	15	38	-	57	33
15.	Florø SK (*Relegated*)	30	8	3	19	27	-	59	27
16.	Levanger FK (*Relegated*)	30	3	6	21	32	-	71	15

Promotion Play-offs

Aalesunds FK - Nest-Sotra Fotball 1-0(0-0)
Sogndal Fotball - Ullensaker/Kisa IL 1-0(0-0)

Aalesunds FK - Sogndal Fotball 3-1(0-0)

Aalesunds FK qualified for the First Level Relegation/Promotion Play-offs .

Relegation Play-offs (2nd / 3rd Level)

KFUM-Kameratene Oslo - Åsane Fotball 1-2(0-0) 3-1(0-1)

NATIONAL TEAM

INTERNATIONAL MATCHES
(16.07.2018 – 15.07.2019)

06.09.2018	Oslo	Norway - Cyprus	2-0(2-0)	(UNL)
09.09.2018	Sofia	Bulgaria - Norway	1-0(0-0)	(UNL)
13.10.2018	Oslo	Norway - Slovenia	1-0(1-0)	(UNL)
16.10.2018	Oslo	Norway - Bulgaria	1-0(1-0)	(UNL)
16.11.2018	Ljubljana	Slovenia - Norway	1-1(1-0)	(UNL)
19.11.2018	Nicosia	Cyprus - Norway	0-2(0-1)	(UNL)
23.03.2019	Valencia	Spain - Norway	2-1(1-0)	(ECQ)
26.03.2019	Oslo	Norway - Sweden	3-3(1-0)	(ECQ)
07.06.2019	Oslo	Norway - Romania	2-2(0-0)	(ECQ)
10.06.2019	Tórshavn	Faroe Islands - Norway	0-2(0-0)	(ECQ)

06.09.2018 NORWAY - CYPRUS 2-0(2-0) UEFA Nations League C, Group 3
Ullevaal Stadion, Oslo; Referee: István Kovács (Romania); Attendance: 6,572
NOR: Rune Almenning Jarstein, Håvard Nordtveit, Omar Elabdellaoui, Birger Solberg Meling, Kristoffer Vassbakk Ajer, Stefan Marius Johansen (Cap) (72.Iver Tobias Rørvik Fossum), Markus Henriksen, Mohamed Amine Elyounoussi, Sander Gard Bolin Berge (69.Ole Kristian Selnæs), Joshua Christian Kojo King (90.Tarik Elyounoussi), Bjørn Maars Johnsen. Trainer: Lars Edvin Lagerbäck (Sweden).
Goals: Stefan Marius Johansen (21, 42).

09.09.2018 BULGARIA - NORWAY 1-0(0-0) UEFA Nations League C, Group 3
Nationalen Stadion "Vasil Levski", Sofia; Referee: Daniel Stefański (Poland); Attendance: 7,100
NOR: Rune Almenning Jarstein, Håvard Nordtveit [*sent off 88*], Omar Elabdellaoui, Birger Solberg Meling, Kristoffer Vassbakk Ajer, Stefan Marius Johansen (Cap) (62.Iver Tobias Rørvik Fossum), Markus Henriksen, Mohamed Amine Elyounoussi, Sander Gard Bolin Berge (78.Ole Kristian Selnæs), Joshua Christian Kojo King, Bjørn Maars Johnsen (46.Alexander Sørloth). Trainer: Lars Edvin Lagerbäck (Sweden).

13.10.2018 NORWAY - SLOVENIA 1-0(1-0) UEFA Nations League C, Group 3
Ullevaal Stadion, Oslo; Referee: Daniel Siebert (Germany); Attendance: 14,712
NOR: Rune Almenning Jarstein, Even Hovland, Omar Elabdellaoui, Haitam Aleesami, Sigurd Rosted, Stefan Marius Johansen (Cap) (80.Iver Tobias Rørvik Fossum), Markus Henriksen, Ole Kristian Selnæs, Tarik Elyounoussi (75.Bjørn Maars Johnsen, Mohamed Amine Elyounoussi (90+3.Martin Linnes), Joshua Christian Kojo King. Trainer: Lars Edvin Lagerbäck (Sweden).
Goal: Ole Kristian Selnæs (45+5).

16.10.2018 NORWAY - BULGARIA 1-0(1-0) UEFA Nations League C, Group 3
Ullevaal Stadion, Oslo; Referee: John Beaton (Scotland); Attendance: 9,523
NOR: Rune Almenning Jarstein, Håvard Nordtveit, Omar Elabdellaoui, Haitam Aleesami, Sigurd Rosted, Stefan Marius Johansen (Cap) (78.Iver Tobias Rørvik Fossum), Markus Henriksen, Ole Kristian Selnæs, Mohamed Amine Elyounoussi, Tarik Elyounoussi, Joshua Christian Kojo King. Trainer: Lars Edvin Lagerbäck (Sweden).
Goal: Mohamed Amine Elyounoussi (31).

16.11.2018 SLOVENIA - NORWAY 1-1(1-0) UEFA Nations League C, Group 3
Stadion Stožice, Ljubljana; Referee: Ruddy Buquet (France); Attendance: 10,254
NOR: Rune Almenning Jarstein, Håvard Nordtveit, Omar Elabdellaoui, Haitam Aleesami, Sigurd Rosted, Stefan Marius Johansen (Cap) (57.Martin Ødegaard), Markus Henriksen, Ole Kristian Selnæs, Mohamed Amine Elyounoussi, Ola Williams Kamara (75.Alexander Sørloth), Tarik Elyounoussi (63.Bjørn Maars Johnsen). Trainer: Lars Edvin Lagerbäck (Sweden).
Goal: Bjørn Maars Johnsen (85).

19.11.2018 CYPRUS - NORWAY 0-2(0-1) UEFA Nations League C, Group 3
Stádio GSP, Nicosia; Referee: István Vad (Hungary); Attendance: 1,513
NOR: Rune Almenning Jarstein, Håvard Nordtveit, Omar Elabdellaoui (Cap), Sigurd Rosted, Birger Solberg Meling, Markus Henriksen, Ole Kristian Selnæs, Mohamed Amine Elyounoussi [*sent off 90*], Iver Tobias Rørvik Fossum (46.Martin Ødegaard), Ola Williams Kamara (90+2.Sander Gard Bolin Berge), Tarik Elyounoussi (71.Alexander Sørloth). Trainer: Lars Edvin Lagerbäck (Sweden).
Goals: Ola Williams Kamara (36, 48).

23.03.2019 SPAIN - NORWAY 2-1(1-0) 16th EC. Qualifiers
Estadio Mestalla, Valencia; Referee: Andris Treimanis (Latvia); Attendance: 39,752
NOR: Rune Almenning Jarstein, Håvard Nordtveit, Omar Elabdellaoui, Haitam Aleesami, Kristoffer Vassbakk Ajer, Stefan Marius Johansen (Cap) (77.Ola Williams Kamara), Markus Henriksen, Ole Kristian Selnæs, Martin Ødegaard (56.Mohamed Amine Elyounoussi), Tarik Elyounoussi (55.Bjørn Maars Johnsen), Joshua Christian Kojo King. Trainer: Lars Edvin Lagerbäck (Sweden).
Goal: Joshua Christian Kojo King (65 penalty).

26.03.2019 NORWAY - SWEDEN 3-3(1-0) 16th EC. Qualifiers
Ullevaal Stadion, Oslo; Referee: Gianluca Rocchi (Italy); Attendance: 23,459
NOR: Rune Almenning Jarstein, Håvard Nordtveit, Omar Elabdellaoui (Cap), Haitam Aleesami, Kristoffer Vassbakk Ajer, Markus Henriksen, Ole Kristian Selnæs, Mohamed Amine Elyounoussi (72.Ola Williams Kamara), Martin Ødegaard, Joshua Christian Kojo King, Bjørn Maars Johnsen (87.Alexander Sørloth). Trainer: Lars Edvin Lagerbäck (Sweden).
Goals: Bjørn Maars Johnsen (41), Joshua Christian Kojo King (59), Ola Williams Kamara (90+7).

07.06.2019 NORWAY - ROMANIA 2-2(0-0) 16th EC. Qualifiers
Ullevaal Stadion, Oslo; Referee: Sergei Karasev (Russia); Attendance: 17,664
NOR: Sten Michael Grytebust, Håvard Nordtveit, Omar Elabdellaoui (Cap), Haitam Aleesami, Kristoffer Vassbakk Ajer, Markus Henriksen, Ole Kristian Selnæs, Martin Ødegaard, Sander Gard Bolin Berge, Tarik Elyounoussi (84.Ola Williams Kamara), Joshua Christian Kojo King. Trainer: Lars Edvin Lagerbäck (Sweden).
Goals: Tarik Elyounoussi (56), Martin Ødegaard (70).

10.06.2019 **FAROE ISLANDS - NORWAY** **0-2(0-0)** 16th EC. Qualifiers

Tórsvøllur, Tórshavn; Referee: Donatas Rumšas (Lithuania); Attendance: 3,083

NOR: André Hansen, Håvard Nordtveit, Omar Elabdellaoui (Cap), Haitam Aleesami, Martin Ødegaard, Kristoffer Vassbakk Ajer, Markus Henriksen (72.Stefan Marius Johansen), Ole Kristian Selnæs (81.Fredrik Midtsjø), Sander Gard Bolin Berge, Tarik Elyounoussi (58.Ola Williams Kamara), Bjørn Maars Johnsen. Trainer: Lars Edvin Lagerbäck (Sweden).

Goals: Bjørn Maars Johnsen (49, 83).

NATIONAL TEAM PLAYERS
(16.07.2018 – 15.07.2019)

Name	DOB	Caps	Goals	2018/2019:	*Club*
Goalkeepers					
Sten Michael GRYTEBUST	25.10.1989	**5**	**0**	2019:	*Odense BK (DEN)*
André HANSEN	17.12.1989	**4**	**0**	2019:	*Rosenborg BK Trondheim*
Rune Almenning JARSTEIN	29.09.1984	**60**	**0**	2018/2019:	*Hertha BSC Berlin (GER)*
Defenders					
Kristoffer Vassbakk AJER	17.04.1998	**10**	**0**	2018/2019:	*Celtic FC Glasgow (SCO)*
Haitam ALEESAMI	31.07.1991	**23**	**0**	2018/2019:	*US Città di Palermo (ITA)*
Omar ELABDELLAOUI	05.12.1991	**38**	**0**	2018/2019:	*Olympiacos SFP Peiraiás (GRE)*
Even HOVLAND	14.02.1989	**25**	**0**	2018:	*Rosenborg BK Trondheim*
Martin LINNES	20.09.1991	**23**	**1**	31.01.2019	*Galatasaray SK İstanbul (TUR)*
Birger Solberg MELING	17.12.1994	**10**	**0**	2018:	*Rosenborg BK Trondheim*
Håvard NORDTVEIT	21.06.1990	**49**	**2**	2019:	*TSG 1899 Hoffenheim (GER)*
				31.01.2019->	*Fulham FC London (ENG, on loan)*
Tore REGINIUSSEN	10.04.1986	**27**	**3**	2018:	*Rosenborg BK Trondheim*
Sigurd ROSTED	22.07.1994	**5**	**1**	2018:	*KAA Gent (BEL)*
Midfielders					
Sander Gard Bolin BERGE	14.02.1998	**14**	**0**	2018/2019:	*KRC Genk (BEL)*
Mohamed Amine ELYOUNOUSSI	02.03.1994	**24**	**5**	2018/2019:	*Southampton FC (ENG)*
Iver Tobias Rørvik FOSSUM	15.07.1996	**12**	**0**	2018:	*SV Hannover'96 (GER)*
Markus HENRIKSEN	25.07.1992	**49**	**3**	2018/2019:	*Hull City AFC (ENG)*
Stefan Marius JOHANSEN	08.01.1991	**48**	**5**	2018/2019:	*Fulham FC London (ENG)*
				31.01.2019->	*West Bromwich Albion FC (ENG)*
				31.05.2019->	*Fulham FC London (ENG)*
Fredrik MIDTSJØ	11.08.1993	**4**	**0**	2019:	*AZ Alkmaar (NED)*
Ole Kristian SELNÆS	07.07.1994	**27**	**2**	2018:	*AS Saint-Étienne (FRA)*
				09.02.2019->	*Shenzhen FC (CHN)*
Martin ØDEGAARD	17.12.1998	**18**	**1**	2018/2019:	*SC Heerenveen (NED)*
Forwards					
Tarik ELYOUNOUSSI	23.02.1988	**56**	**10**	2018/2019:	*AIK Stockholm (SWE)*
Bjørn Maars JOHNSEN	06.11.1991	**13**	**5**	2018/2019:	*AZ Alkmaar (NED)*
Ola Williams KAMARA	15.10.1989	**17**	**7**	2018/2019:	*Los Angeles Galaxy (USA)*
				28.02.2019->	*Shenzhen FC (CHN)*
Joshua Christian Kojo KING	15.01.1992	**40**	**14**	2018/2019:	*AFC Bournemouth (ENG)*
Alexander SØRLOTH	05.12.1995	**18**	**2**	2018:	*Crystal Palace FC London (ENG)*
				08.01.2019->	*KAA Gent (BEL, on loan)*

National team coach

Lars Edvin LAGERBÄCK (*Sweden*) [from 01.02.2017]	16.07.1948	23 M; 12 W; 5 D; 6 L; 37-25

POLAND

The Country:
Rzeczpospolita Polska (Republic of Poland)
Capital: Warszawa
Surface: 312,679 km²
Inhabitants: 38,433,600 [2017]
Time: UTC+1

The FA:
Polski Związek Piłki Nożnej
Bitwy Warszawskiej 1920r. 7 02-366, Warszawa
Tel: +48 22 551 2300
Founded: 1919
Member of FIFA since: 1923
Member of UEFA since: 1954
Website: www.pzpn.pl

NATIONAL TEAM RECORDS

First international match:	18.12.1921, Budapest:	Hungary – Poland 1-0
Most international caps:	Jakub Błaszczykowski	- 106 caps (since 2006)
	Robert Lewandowski	- 106 caps (since 2008)
Most international goals:	Robert Lewandowski	- 57 goals / 106 caps (since 2008)

UEFA EUROPEAN CHAMPIONSHIP	
1960	Qualifiers
1964	Qualifiers
1968	Qualifiers
1972	Qualifiers
1976	Qualifiers
1980	Qualifiers
1984	Qualifiers
1988	Qualifiers
1992	Qualifiers
1996	Qualifiers
2000	Qualifiers
2004	Qualifiers
2008	Final Tournament (Group Stage)
2012	Final Tournament (Group Stage)
2016	Final Tournament (Quarter-Finals)

FIFA WORLD CUP	
1930	Did not enter
1934	Qualifiers
1938	Final Tournament (1st Round)
1950	Did not enter
1954	*Withdrew*
1958	Qualifiers
1962	Qualifiers
1966	Qualifiers
1970	Qualifiers
1974	Final Tournament (3rd Place)
1978	Final Tournament (Round 2)
1982	Final Tournament (3rd Place)
1986	Final Tournament (2nd Round of 16)
1990	Qualifiers
1994	Qualifiers
1998	Qualifiers
2002	Final Tournament (Group Stage)
2006	Final Tournament (Group Stage)
2010	Qualifiers
2014	Qualifiers
2018	Final Tournament (Group Stage)

UEFA NATIONS LEAGUE
2018/2019 – League A

OLYMPIC FOOTBALL TOURNAMENTS 1908-2016							
1908	-	**1948**	Did not enter	**1972**	**Winners**	**1996**	Qualifiers
1912	-	**1952**	Round 1	**1976**	Runners-up	**2000**	Qualifiers
1920	-	**1956**	Did not enter	**1980**	Qualifiers	**2004**	Qualifiers
1924	Preliminary Round	**1960**	Group Stage	**1984**	Qualifiers	**2008**	Qualifiers
1928	Did not enter	**1964**	Qualifiers	**1988**	Qualifiers	**2012**	Qualifiers
1936	4th Place	**1968**	Qualifiers	**1992**	Runners-up	**2016**	Qualifiers

FIFA CONFEDERATIONS CUP 1992-2017
None

POLISH CLUB HONOURS IN EUROPEAN CLUB COMPETITIONS:

European Champion Clubs' Cup (1956-1992) / UEFA Champions League (1993-2019)
None
Fairs Cup (1858-1971) / UEFA Cup (1972-2009) / UEFA Europa League (2010-2019)
None
UEFA Super Cup (1972-2018)
None
European Cup Winners' Cup 1961-1999*
None

**defunct competition*

NATIONAL COMPETITIONS
TABLE OF HONOURS

	CHAMPIONS	CUP WINNERS	BEST GOALSCORERS	
1920	*Championship abandoned*	-	-	
1921	KS Cracovia Kraków	-	-	
1922	LKS Pogoń Lwów	-	-	
1923	LKS Pogoń Lwów	-	-	
1924	*No competition*	-	-	
1925	LKS Pogoń Lwów	-	-	
1926	LKS Pogoń Lwów	Wisła Kraków	-	
1927	Wisła Kraków	-	Henryk Reyman (Wisła Kraków)	37
1928	Wisła Kraków	-	Ludwik Gintel (KS Cracovia Kraków)	28
1929	KS Warta Poznań	-	Rochus Nastula (Czarni Lwów)	25
1930	KS Cracovia Kraków	-	Karol Kossok (KS Cracovia Kraków)	24
1931	RKS Garbarnia Kraków	-	Walerian Kisieliński (Wisła Kraków)	24
1932	KS Cracovia Kraków	-	Kajetan Kryszkiewicz (KS Warta Poznań)	16
1933	KS Ruch Wielkie Hajduki Chorzów	-	Artur Woźniak (Wisła Kraków)	19
1934	KS Ruch Wielkie Hajduki Chorzów	-	Ernst Wilimowski (KS Ruch Wielkie Hajduki Chorzów)	33
1935	KS Ruch Wielkie Hajduki Chorzów	-	Michał Matyas (LKS Pogoń Lwów)	22
1936	KS Ruch Wielkie Hajduki Chorzów	-	Teodor Peterek (KS Ruch Wielkie Hajduki Chorzów) Ernst Wilimowski (KS Ruch Wielkie Hajduki Chorzów)	18
1937	KS Cracovia Kraków	-	Artur Woźniak (Wisła Kraków)	12
1938	KS Ruch Wielkie Hajduki Chorzów	-	Teodor Peterek (KS Ruch Wielkie Hajduki Chorzów)	21
1939	*Championship abandoned*	-	Ernst Wilimowski (KS Ruch Wielkie Hajduki Chorzów)	12
1940	*No competition*	-	-	
1941	*No competition*	-	-	
1942	*No competition*	-	-	
1943	*No competition*	-	-	
1944	*No competition*	-	-	
1945	*No competition*	-	-	
1946	Polonia Warszawa	-	-	
1947	KS Warta Poznań	-	-	
1948	KS Cracovia Kraków	-	Józef Kohut (Wisła Kraków)	31
1949	Wisła Kraków	-	Teodor Anioła (KKS Lech Poznań)	20
1950	Wisła Kraków	-	Teodor Anioła (KKS Lech Poznań)	21
1951	Unia Chorzów	Unia Chorzów	Teodor Anioła (KKS Lech Poznań)	20
1952	Unia Chorzów	Kolejarz Warszawa	Gerard Cieślik (Unia Chorzów)	11
1953	Unia Chorzów	WKS Gwardia Warszawa (1953/54)	Gerard Cieślik (Unia Chorzów)	24
1954	KS Polonia Bytom	WKS Gwardia Warszawa	Henryk Kempny (KS Polonia Bytom) Ernst Pohl (Legia Warszawa)	13
1955	CWKS Warszawa	CWKS Warszawa	Stanisław Hachorek (WKS Gwardia Warszawa)	16
1956	CWKS Warszawa	CWKS Warszawa	Henryk Kempny (Legia Warszawa)	21
1957	KS Górnik Zabrze	ŁKS Łódź	Lucjan Brychczy (Legia Warszawa)	19
1958	ŁKS Łódź	*No competition*	Władysław Soporek (ŁKS Łódź)	19
1959	KS Górnik Zabrze	*No competition*	Jan Liberda (KS Polonia Bytom) Ernst Pohl (KS Górnik Zabrze)	21
1960	Ruch Chorzów	*No competition*	Marian Norkowski (Polonia Bydgoszcz)	17
1961	KS Górnik Zabrze	*No competition*	Ernst Pohl (KS Górnik Zabrze)	24
1962	KS Polonia Bytom	Zagłębie Sosnowiec	Jan Liberda (KS Polonia Bytom)	16
1962/1963	KS Górnik Zabrze	Zagłębie Sosnowiec	Marian Kielec (MKS Pogoń Szczecin)	18
1963/1964	KS Górnik Zabrze	CWKS Warszawa	Lucjan Brychczy (Legia Warszawa) Józef Gałeczka (Zagłębie Sosnowiec) Jerzy Wilim (TS Szombierki Bytom)	18
1964/1965	KS Górnik Zabrze	KS Górnik Zabrze	Lucjan Brychczy (Legia Warszawa)	18
1965/1966	KS Górnik Zabrze	CWKS Warszawa	Włodzimierz Lubański (KS Górnik Zabrze)	23
1966/1967	KS Górnik Zabrze	Wisła Kraków	Włodzimierz Lubański (KS Górnik Zabrze)	18
1967/1968	Ruch Chorzów	KS Górnik Zabrze	Włodzimierz Lubański (KS Górnik Zabrze)	24
1968/1969	CWKS Legia Warszawa	KS Górnik Zabrze	Włodzimierz Lubański (KS Górnik Zabrze)	22
1969/1970	CWKS Legia Warszawa	KS Górnik Zabrze	Andrzej Jarosik (Zagłębie Sosnowiec)	18
1970/1971	KS Górnik Zabrze	KS Górnik Zabrze	Andrzej Jarosik (Zagłębie Sosnowiec)	13
1971/1972	KS Górnik Zabrze	KS Górnik Zabrze	Ryszard Szymczak (WKS Gwardia Warszawa)	16
1972/1973	FKS Stal Mielec	CWKS Legia Warszawa	Grzegorz Lato (FKS Stal Mielec)	13
1973/1974	Ruch Chorzów	Ruch Chorzów	Zdzisław Kapka (Wisła Kraków)	15
1974/1975	Ruch Chorzów	Stal Rzeszów	Grzegorz Lato (FKS Stal Mielec)	19
1975/1976	FKS Stal Mielec	KS Śląsk Wrocław	Kazimierz Kmiecik (Wisła Kraków)	20
1976/1977	KS Śląsk Wrocław	Zagłębie Sosnowiec	Włodzimierz Mazur (Zagłębie Sosnowiec)	17
1977/1978	Wisła Kraków	Zagłębie Sosnowiec	Kazimierz Kmiecik (Wisła Kraków)	15
1978/1979	Ruch Chorzów	MZKS Arka Gdynia	Kazimierz Kmiecik (Wisła Kraków)	17
1979/1980	TS Szombierki Bytom	CWKS Legia Warszawa	Kazimierz Kmiecik (Wisła Kraków)	24
1980/1981	RTS Widzew Łódź	CWKS Legia Warszawa	Krzysztof Adamczyk (Legia Warszawa)	18
1981/1982	RTS Widzew Łódź	KKS Lech Poznań	Grzegorz Kapica (TS Szombierki Bytom)	15

1982/1983	KKS Lech Poznań	KS Lechia Gdańsk	Mirosław Okoński (KKS Lech Poznań) Mirosław Tłokiński (RTS Widzew Łódź)	15
1983/1984	KKS Lech Poznań	KKS Lech Poznań	Włodzimierz Ciołek (Górnik Wałbrzych)	14
1984/1985	KS Górnik Zabrze	RTS Widzew Łódź	Leszek Iwanicki (LKP Motor Lublin)	14
1985/1986	KS Górnik Zabrze	GKS Katowice	Andrzej Zgutczyński (KS Górnik Zabrze)	20
1986/1987	KS Górnik Zabrze	KS Śląsk Wrocław	Marek Leśniak (MKS Pogoń Szczecin)	24
1987/1988	KS Górnik Zabrze	KKS Lech Poznań	Dariusz Dziekanowski (Legia Warszawa)	20
1988/1989	Ruch Chorzów	CWKS Legia Warszawa	Krzysztof Warzycha (Ruch Chorzów)	24
1989/1990	KKS Lech Poznań	CWKS Legia Warszawa	Andrzej Juskowiak (KKS Lech Poznań)	18
1990/1991	Zagłębie Lubin	GKS Katowice	Tomasz Dziubiński (Wisła Kraków)	21
1991/1992	KKS Lech Poznań	MKS Miedź Legnica	Jerzy Podbrożny (KKS Lech Poznań) Mirosław Waligóra (KS Hutnik Kraków)	20
1992/1993	KKS Lech Poznań	GKS Katowice	Jerzy Podbrożny (KKS Lech Poznań)	25
1993/1994	Legia Warszawa	Legia Warszawa	Zenon Burzawa (Sokół Pniewy)	21
1994/1995	Legia Warszawa	Legia Warszawa	Bogusław Cygan (FKS Stal Mielec)	16
1995/1996	RTS Widzew Łódź	Ruch Chorzów	Marek Koniarek (RTS Widzew Łódź)	29
1996/1997	RTS Widzew Łódź	Legia Warszawa	Mirosław Trzeciak (ŁKS Łódź)	18
1997/1998	ŁKS Łódź	KS Amica Wronki	Arkadiusz Bąk (Polonia Warszawa) Sylwester Czereszewski (Legia Warszawa) Mariusz Śrutwa (Ruch Chorzów)	14
1998/1999	Wisła Kraków	KS Amica Wronki	Tomasz Frankowski (Wisła Kraków)	21
1999/2000	Polonia Warszawa	KS Amica Wronki	Adam Kompała (KS Górnik Zabrze)	19
2000/2001	Wisła Kraków	Polonia Warszawa	Tomasz Frankowski (Wisła Kraków)	18
2001/2002	Legia Warszawa	Wisła Kraków	Maciej Żurawski (Wisła Kraków)	21
2002/2003	Wisła Kraków	Wisła Kraków	Stanko Svitlica (SRB, Legia Warszawa)	24
2003/2004	Wisła Kraków	KKS Lech Poznań	Maciej Żurawski (Wisła Kraków)	20
2004/2005	Wisła Kraków	KS Dyskobolia Grodzisk Wielkopolski	Tomasz Frankowski (Wisła Kraków)	25
2005/2006	Legia Warszawa	Wisła Płock	Grzegorz Piechna (Korona Kielce)	21
2006/2007	Zagłębie Lubin	KS Dyskobolia Grodzisk Wielkopolski	Piotr Reiss (KKS Lech Poznań)	15
2007/2008	Wisła Kraków	Legia Warszawa	Paweł Brożek (Wisła Kraków)	23
2008/2009	Wisła Kraków	KKS Lech Poznań	Paweł Brożek (Wisła Kraków) Takesure Chinyama (ZIM, Legia Warszawa)	19
2009/2010	KKS Lech Poznań	Jagiellonia Białystok	Robert Lewandowski (KKS Lech Poznań)	18
2010/2011	Wisła Kraków	Legia Warszawa	Tomasz Frankowski (Jagiellonia Białystok)	14
2011/2012	KS Śląsk Wrocław	Legia Warszawa	Artjoms Rudņevs (LVA, KKS Lech Poznań)	22
2012/2013	Legia Warszawa	Legia Warszawa	Róbert Demjan (SVK, TS Podbeskidzie Bielsko-Biała)	14
2013/2014	Legia Warszawa	SP Zawisza Bydgoszcz	Marcin Robak (GKS Piast Gliwice / MKS Pogoń Szczecin)	22
2014/2015	KKS Lech Poznań	Legia Warszawa	Kamil Wilczek (GKS Piast Gliwice)	20
2015/2016	Legia Warszawa	Legia Warszawa	Nemanja Nikolić (HUN, Legia Warszawa)	28
2016/2017	Legia Warszawa	MZKS Arka Gdynia	Marco Filipe Lopes Paixão (POR, KS Lechia Gdańsk) Marcin Robak (KKS Lech Poznań)	18
2017/2018	Legia Warszawa	Legia Warszawa	Carlos Daniel López Huesca "Carlitos" (ESP, Wisła Kraków)	24
2018/2019	GKS Piast Gliwice	KS Lechia Gdańsk	Igor Angulo Alboniga (ESP, KS Górnik Zabrze)	24

Ruch Chorzów = KS Ruch Wielkie Hajduki Chorzów (1927-1939), Unia Chorzów (1949-1954), Unia-Ruch Chorzów (1955).
Legia Warszawa = CWKS Warszawa (1950-1967), CWKS Legia Warszawa (1967-1990).

NATIONAL CHAMPIONSHIP

Ekstraklasa 2018/2019

(20.07.2018 – 19.05.2019)

Results

Round 1 [20-23.07.2018]
Miedź Legnica - Pogoń Szczecin 1-0(0-0)
Jagiellonia Białyst. - Lechia Gdańsk 0-1(0-1)
Śląsk Wrocław - Cracovia Kraków 3-1(1-1)
Wisła Kraków - Arka Gdynia 0-0
Legia Warszawa - Zagłębie Lubin 1-3(1-2)
Górnik Zabrze - Korona Kielce 1-1(0-0)
Wisła Płock - Lech Poznań 1-2(0-1)
Zagłębie Sosnowiec - Piast Gliwice 1-2(1-0)

Round 2 [27-30.07.2018]
Lechia Gdańsk - Śląsk Wrocław 1-1(1-0)
Wisła Kraków - Miedź Legnica 2-1(1-0)
Zagłębie Lubin - Zagłębie Sosnowiec 2-1(0-0)
Korona Kielce - Legia Warszawa 1-2(1-0)
Górnik Zabrze - Wisła Płock 1-1(0-0)
Arka Gdynia - Jagiellonia Białystok 0-2(0-1)
Lech Poznań - Cracovia Kraków 2-0(1-0)
Pogoń Szczecin - Piast Gliwice 0-2(0-2)

Round 3 [03-06.08.2018]
Wisła Płock - Korona Kielce 1-2(0-0)
Zagłębie Sosnowiec - Pogoń Szczec. 3-0(1-0)
Piast Gliwice - Zagłębie Lubin 2-1(1-1)
Legia Warszawa - Lechia Gdańsk 0-0
Śląsk Wrocław - Lech Poznań 0-1(0-0)
Jagiellonia Białystok - Wisła Kraków 1-0(0-0)
Miedź Legnica - Górnik Zabrze 1-3(1-0)
Cracovia Kraków - Arka Gdynia 0-0

Round 4 [10-13.08.2018]
Lechia Gdańsk - Miedź Legnica 2-0(1-0)
Wisła Kraków - Wisła Płock 1-1(1-0)
Pogoń Szczecin - Cracovia Kraków 1-1(1-0)
Arka Gdynia - Górnik Zabrze 1-1(0-1)
Piast Gliwice - Legia Warszawa 1-3(0-1)
Lech Poznań - Zagłębie Sosnowiec 4-0(3-0)
Zagłębie Lubin - Jagiellonia Białyst. 0-2(0-1)
Korona Kielce - Śląsk Wrocław 2-1(1-1)

Round 5 [17-20.08.2018]
Cracovia Kraków - Zagłębie Lubin 0-1(0-1)
Miedź Legnica - Korona Kielce 1-1(0-0)
Wisła Płock - Arka Gdynia 1-3(0-0)
Górnik Zabrze - Lechia Gdańsk 0-2(0-2)
Legia Warszawa - Zagłębie Sosnow. 2-1(1-0)
Jagiellonia Białystok - Piast Gliwice 2-1(1-0)
Lech Poznań - Wisła Kraków 2-5(2-1)
Śląsk Wrocław - Pogoń Szczecin 0-0

Round 6 [24-27.08.2018]
Piast Gliwice - Cracovia Kraków 3-1(2-0)
Korona Kielce - Arka Gdynia 2-1(1-0)
Pogoń Szczecin - Lechia Gdańsk 2-3(1-0)
Wisła Kraków - Górnik Zabrze 3-0(2-0)
Jagiellonia Białyst. - Miedź Legnica 2-3(0-0)
Legia Warszawa - Wisła Płock 1-4(0-2)
Zagłębie Lubin - Lech Poznań 2-1(1-0)
Zagłębie Sosnowiec - Śląsk Wrocław 3-3(0-2)

Round 7 [31.08.-02.09.2018]
Górnik Zabrze - Pogoń Szczecin 1-1(0-0)
Lechia Gdańsk - Korona Kielce 2-0(1-0)
Arka Gdynia - Zagłębie Sosnowiec 2-2(1-1)
Śląsk Wrocław - Wisła Kraków 0-1(0-0)
Lech Poznań - Piast Gliwice 1-1(1-0)
Miedź Legnica - Zagłębie Lubin 2-0(1-0)
Wisła Płock - Jagiellonia Białystok 1-1(1-0)
Cracovia Kraków - Legia Warszawa 0-0

Round 8 [14-17.09.2018]
Zagłębie Lubin - Śląsk Wrocław 4-0(2-0)
Jagiellonia Biał. - Cracovia Kraków 3-1(1-0)
Wisła Płock - Miedź Legnica 2-2(1-2)
Piast Gliwice - Arka Gdynia 1-0(0-0)
Wisła Kraków - Lechia Gdańsk 5-2(2-2)
Pogoń Szczecin - Korona Kielce 1-1(1-0)
Legia Warszawa - Lech Poznań 1-0(1-0)
Zagłębie Sosnowiec - Górnik Zabrze 1-1(1-0)

Round 9 [21-24.09.2018]
Pogoń Szczecin - Wisła Kraków 2-1(1-0)
Arka Gdynia - Lech Poznań 1-0(0-0)
Cracovia Kraków - Wisła Płock 3-1(2-0)
Lechia Gdańsk - Zagłębie Lubin 3-3(3-0)
Miedź Legnica - Legia Warszawa 1-4(1-1)
Śląsk Wrocław - Piast Gliwice 4-1(1-0)
Górnik Zabrze - Jagiellonia Białystok 1-3(1-0)
Korona Kielce - Zagłębie Sosnowiec 3-1(0-0)

Round 10 [28.09.-01.10.2018]
Wisła Płock - Lechia Gdańsk 1-0(0-0)
Legia Warszawa - Arka Gdynia 1-1(1-1)
Piast Gliwice - Górnik Zabrze 1-0(0-0)
Zagłębie Lubin - Pogoń Szczecin 0-2(0-1)
Wisła Kraków - Korona Kielce 0-1(0-0)
Zagłębie Sosnow. - Cracovia Kraków 1-1(1-0)
Lech Poznań - Miedź Legnica 2-1(1-0)
Jagiellonia Białyst. - Śląsk Wrocław 0-4(0-0)

Round 11 [05-07.10.2018]
Miedź Legnica - Piast Gliwice 2-2(2-2)
Górnik Zabrze - Lech Poznań 2-2(1-0)
Pogoń Szczecin - Wisła Płock 4-0(1-0)
Lechia Gdańsk - Zagłębie Sosnowiec 4-1(2-1)
Śląsk Wrocław - Legia Warszawa 0-1(0-1)
Arka Gdynia - Zagłębie Lubin 3-1(0-1)
Korona Kielce - Jagiellonia Białystok 1-1(0-1)
Cracovia Kraków - Wisła Kraków 0-2(0-2)

Round 12 [19-22.10.2018]
Piast Gliwice - Lechia Gdańsk 1-1(1-0)
Jagiellonia Białyst. - Pogoń Szczecin 2-1(0-0)
Zagłębie Sosnowiec - Miedź Legnica 3-1(2-1)
Śląsk Wrocław - Arka Gdynia 1-2(1-1)
Lech Poznań - Korona Kielce 2-1(1-0)
Zagłębie Lubin - Wisła Płock 3-3(1-2)
Legia Warszawa - Wisła Kraków 3-3(2-0)
Cracovia Kraków - Górnik Zabrze 2-0(0-0)

Round 13 [26-29.10.2018]
Miedź Legnica - Śląsk Wrocław 0-5(0-4)
Jagiellonia Białyst. - Legia Warszawa 1-1(1-0)
Wisła Płock - Piast Gliwice 1-1(0-0)
Lechia Gdańsk - Arka Gdynia 2-1(1-1)
Pogoń Szczecin - Lech Poznań 3-0(2-0)
Korona Kielce - Cracovia Kraków 0-1(0-1)
Górnik Zabrze - Zagłębie Lubin 2-0(1-0)
Wisła Kraków - Zagłębie Sosnowiec 2-2(1-0)

Round 14 [02-05.11.2018]
Arka Gdynia - Pogoń Szczecin 2-3(2-1)
Piast Gliwice - Wisła Kraków 2-0(1-0)
Cracovia Kraków - Miedź Legnica 0-0
Śląsk Wrocław - Wisła Płock 0-3(0-0)
Legia Warszawa - Górnik Zabrze 4-0(3-0)
Zagłębie Lubin - Korona Kielce 0-1(0-0)
Lech Poznań - Lechia Gdańsk 0-1(0-1)
Zagłębie Sosnowiec - Jagiellonia B. 1-4(0-1)

Round 15 [09-11.11.2018]
Górnik Zabrze - Śląsk Wrocław 2-2(2-1)
Pogoń Szczecin - Legia Warszawa 2-1(1-0)
Wisła Płock - Zagłębie Sosnowiec 2-0(1-0)
Lechia Gdańsk - Cracovia Kraków 1-0(0-0)
Wisła Kraków - Zagłębie Lubin 3-2(2-0)
Korona Kielce - Piast Gliwice 1-0(1-0)
Miedź Legnica - Arka Gdynia 0-4(0-1)
Jagiellonia Białystok - Lech Poznań 2-2(1-2)

Round 16 [23-26.11.2018]
Piast Gliwice - Zagłębie Sosnowiec 0-0
Korona Kielce - Górnik Zabrze 4-2(4-1)
Lech Poznań - Wisła Płock 2-1(2-1)
Cracovia Kraków - Śląsk Wrocław 1-1(0-1)
Pogoń Szczecin - Miedź Legnica 2-0(0-0)
Zagłębie Lubin - Legia Warszawa 0-1(0-1)
Lechia Gdańsk - Jagiellonia Białyst. 3-2(2-1)
Arka Gdynia - Wisła Kraków 4-1(2-1)

Round 17 [30.11.-03.12.2018]
Śląsk Wrocław - Lechia Gdańsk 0-2(0-2)
Jagiellonia Białystok - Arka Gdynia 3-1(0-0)
Wisła Płock - Górnik Zabrze 0-4(0-1)
Miedź Legnica - Wisła Kraków 2-0(2-0)
Legia Warszawa - Korona Kielce 3-0(2-0)
Zagłębie Sosnowiec - Zagłębie Lubin 1-2(1-2)
Cracovia Kraków - Lech Poznań 1-0(0-0)
Piast Gliwice - Pogoń Szczecin 3-0(2-0)

Round 18 [07-10.12.2018]
Zagłębie Lubin - Piast Gliwice 2-2(1-1)
Lech Poznań - Śląsk Wrocław 2-0(0-0)
Pogoń Szczecin - Zagłębie Sosnow. 1-0(0-0)
Korona Kielce - Wisła Płock 2-2(2-1)
Wisła Kraków - Jagiellonia Białystok 2-2(2-0)
Górnik Zabrze - Miedź Legnica 1-3(0-1)
Lechia Gdańsk - Legia Warszawa 0-0
Arka Gdynia - Cracovia Kraków 0-3(0-2)

Round 19 [14-17.12.2018]
Wisła Płock - Wisła Kraków 1-2(0-1)
Jagiellonia Białyst. - Zagłębie Lubin 0-4(0-3)
Cracovia Kraków - Pogoń Szczecin 2-1(0-1)
Górnik Zabrze - Arka Gdynia 1-1(1-0)
Legia Warszawa - Piast Gliwice 2-0(1-0)
Śląsk Wrocław - Korona Kielce 1-1(1-0)
Zagłębie Sosnowiec - Lech Poznań 0-6(0-2)
Miedź Legnica - Lechia Gdańsk 0-0

Round 20 [20-22.12.2018]
Pogoń Szczecin - Śląsk Wrocław 2-1(0-1)
Zagłębie Sosnow. - Legia Warszawa 2-3(1-0)
Arka Gdynia - Wisła Płock 3-3(0-2)
Piast Gliwice - Jagiellonia Białystok 1-1(1-1)
Wisła Kraków - Lech Poznań 0-1(0-0)
Korona Kielce - Miedź Legnica 0-0
Lechia Gdańsk - Górnik Zabrze 4-0(1-0)
Zagłębie Lubin - Cracovia Kraków 1-2(1-0)

Round 21 [08-11.02.2019]
Miedź Legnica - Jagiellonia Białyst. 0-3(0-2)
Lech Poznań - Zagłębie Lubin 1-2(0-0)
Śląsk Wrocław - Zagłębie Sosnowiec 2-0(1-0)
Cracovia Kraków - Piast Gliwice 2-1(1-1)
Lechia Gdańsk - Pogoń Szczecin 2-1(1-0)
Arka Gdynia - Korona Kielce 1-2(0-2)
Wisła Płock - Legia Warszawa 0-1(0-0)
Górnik Zabrze - Wisła Kraków 2-0(2-0)

Round 22 [15-18.02.2019]
Pogoń Szczecin - Górnik Zabrze 3-1(2-1)
Piast Gliwice - Lech Poznań 4-0(1-0)
Jagiellonia Białystok - Wisła Płock 1-0(0-0)
Zagłębie Sosnowiec - Arka Gdynia 3-2(1-2)
Korona Kielce - Lechia Gdańsk 0-0
Zagłębie Lubin - Miedź Legnica 3-0(2-0)
Legia Warszawa - Cracovia Kraków 0-2(0-2)
Wisła Kraków - Śląsk Wrocław 1-0(1-0)

Round 23 [22-25.02.2019]
Arka Gdynia - Piast Gliwice 1-2(0-2)
Korona Kielce - Pogoń Szczecin 1-1(0-1)
Górnik Zabrze - Zagłębie Sosnowiec 2-1(1-0)
Lech Poznań - Legia Warszawa 2-0(1-0)
Lechia Gdańsk - Wisła Kraków 1-0(1-0)
Miedź Legnica - Wisła Płock 2-1(1-1)
Cracovia Kraków - Jagiellonia Biał. 1-0(0-0)
Śląsk Wrocław - Zagłębie Lubin 2-0(1-0)

Round 24 [01-04.03.2019]
Piast Gliwice - Śląsk Wrocław 2-0(1-0)
Legia Warszawa - Miedź Legnica 2-0(1-0)
Zagłębie Sosnowiec - Korona Kielce 4-1(1-1)
Jagiellonia Białystok - Górnik Zabrze 2-2(1-1)
Wisła Płock - Cracovia Kraków 3-2(1-0)
Wisła Kraków - Pogoń Szczecin 2-3(0-2)
Lech Poznań - Arka Gdynia 1-0(1-0)
Zagłębie Lubin - Lechia Gdańsk 2-1(1-1)

Round 25 [08-11.03.2019]
Górnik Zabrze - Piast Gliwice 0-2(0-1)
Śląsk Wrocław - Jagiellonia Białyst. 2-0(2-0)
Cracovia Kraków - Zagłębie Sosnow. 2-1(1-0)
Korona Kielce - Wisła Kraków 2-6(2-2)
Arka Gdynia - Legia Warszawa 1-2(0-0)
Pogoń Szczecin - Zagłębie Lubin 0-3(0-1)
Miedź Legnica - Lech Poznań 3-2(2-0)
Lechia Gdańsk - Wisła Płock 1-1(0-0)

Round 26 [15-17.03.2019]
Wisła Płock - Pogoń Szczecin 0-2(0-1)
Lech Poznań - Górnik Zabrze 0-3(0-1)
Jagiellonia Białystok - Korona Kielce 1-3(0-2)
Zagłębie Sosnowiec - Lechia Gdańsk 0-1(0-1)
Legia Warszawa - Śląsk Wrocław 1-0(0-0)
Piast Gliwice - Miedź Legnica 2-1(1-0)
Zagłębie Lubin - Arka Gdynia 0-0
Wisła Kraków - Cracovia Kraków 3-2(2-0)

Round 27 [29-31.03.2019]
Wisła Płock - Zagłębie Lubin 0-1(0-0)
Górnik Zabrze - Cracovia Kraków 0-1(0-1)
Lechia Gdańsk - Piast Gliwice 2-0(2-0)
Miedź Legnica - Zagłębie Sosnowiec 0-2(0-1)
Arka Gdynia - Śląsk Wrocław 0-2(0-0)
Korona Kielce - Lech Poznań 0-0
Pogoń Szczecin - Jagiellonia Białystok 0-0
Wisła Kraków - Legia Warszawa 4-0(2-0)

Round 28 [02-03.04.2019]
Cracovia Kraków - Korona Kielce 2-1(1-0)
Śląsk Wrocław - Miedź Legnica 0-0
Arka Gdynia - Lechia Gdańsk 0-0
Zagłębie Lubin - Górnik Zabrze 1-1(0-0)
Lech Poznań - Pogoń Szczecin 3-2(2-0)
Piast Gliwice - Wisła Płock 1-0(1-0)
Legia Warszawa - Jagiellonia Białyst. 3-0(2-0)
Zagłębie Sosnowiec - Wisła Kraków 4-3(2-1)

Round 29 [05-08.04.2019]
Korona Kielce - Zagłębie Lubin 0-2(0-0)
Miedź Legnica - Cracovia Kraków 2-1(2-0)
Jagiellonia Białyst. - Zagłębie Sosn. 2-1(2-0)
Wisła Kraków - Piast Gliwice 2-2(1-1)
Lechia Gdańsk - Lech Poznań 1-0(1-0)
Pogoń Szczecin - Arka Gdynia 3-3(1-1)
Górnik Zabrze - Legia Warszawa 1-2(1-0)
Wisła Płock - Śląsk Wrocław 2-0(0-0)

Round 30 [13.04.2019]
Arka Gdynia - Miedź Legnica 1-1(0-0)
Cracovia Kraków - Lechia Gdańsk 4-2(1-1)
Lech Poznań - Jagiellonia Białystok 0-2(0-1)
Legia Warszawa - Pogoń Szczecin 3-1(0-1)
Piast Gliwice - Korona Kielce 4-0(2-0)
Śląsk Wrocław - Górnik Zabrze 0-1(0-0)
Zagłębie Lubin - Wisła Kraków 3-1(2-0)
Zagłębie Sosnowiec - Wisła Płock 1-3(1-2)

Final Standings

1.	KS Lechia Gdańsk	30	17	9	4	45	-	25	60
2.	Legia Warszawa	30	18	6	6	48	-	31	60
3.	GKS Piast Gliwice	30	15	8	7	47	-	31	53
4.	KS Cracovia Kraków	30	14	6	10	39	-	34	48
5.	Zagłębie Lubin	30	14	5	11	48	-	38	47
6.	Jagiellonia Białystok	30	13	8	9	45	-	41	47
7.	MKS Pogoń Szczecin	30	12	7	11	44	-	42	43
8.	KKS Lech Poznań	30	13	4	13	41	-	40	43
9.	Wisła Kraków	30	12	6	12	55	-	48	42
10.	Korona Kielce	30	10	10	10	35	-	44	40
11.	MKS Miedź Legnica	30	8	8	14	30	-	52	32
12.	KS Górnik Zabrze	30	7	10	13	36	-	49	31
13.	WKS Śląsk Wrocław	30	8	7	15	35	-	37	31
14.	Wisła Płock	30	7	9	14	40	-	49	30
15.	MZKS Arka Gdynia	30	6	11	13	39	-	44	29
16.	Zagłębie Sosnowiec	30	6	6	18	41	-	63	24

Teams ranked 1-8 were qualified for the Championship Round, while teams ranked 9-16 were qualified for the Relegation Round.

Championship Round

Results

Round 31 [20.04.2019]
Lechia Gdańsk - Piast Gliwice 0-2(0-1)
Zagłębie Lubin - Pogoń Szczecin 2-3(2-2)
Jagiellonia Białystok - Lech Poznań 3-3(1-2)
Legia Warszawa - Cracovia Kraków 1-0(0-0)

Round 32 [23-24.04.2019]
Piast Gliwice - Zagłębie Lubin 1-0(1-0)
Cracovia Kraków - Jagiellonia Biał. 0-1(0-1)
Pogoń Szczecin - Lechia Gdańsk 3-4(0-0)
Lech Poznań - Legia Warszawa 1-0(0-0)

Round 33 [26-27.04.2019]
Zagłębie Lubin - Jagiellonia Białyst. 2-0(2-0)
Piast Gliwice - Cracovia Kraków 3-1(1-1)
Pogoń Szczecin - Lech Poznań 1-1(1-0)
Lechia Gdańsk - Legia Warszawa 1-3(1-0)

Round 34 [04-06.05.2019]
Lech Poznań - Zagłębie Lubin 1-1(0-0)
Legia Warszawa - Piast Gliwice 0-1(0-1)
Cracovia Kraków - Lechia Gdańsk 2-0(0-0)
Jagiellonia Białyst. - Pogoń Szczecin 4-2(2-1)

Round 35 [11-12.05.2019]
Cracovia Kraków - Lech Poznań 1-0(1-0)
Piast Gliwice - Jagiellonia Białystok 2-1(1-0)
Legia Warszawa - Pogoń Szczecin 1-1(0-1)
Lechia Gdańsk - Zagłębie Lubin 1-1(0-1)

Round 36 [15.05.2019]
Jagiellonia Białyst. - Legia Warszawa 1-0(1-0)
Pogoń Szczecin - Piast Gliwice 0-0
Lech Poznań - Lechia Gdańsk 2-1(0-0)
Zagłębie Lubin - Cracovia Kraków 1-2(0-0)

Round 37 [19.05.2019]
Legia Warszawa - Zagłębie Lubin 2-2(1-1)
Piast Gliwice - Lech Poznań 1-0(1-0)
Cracovia Kraków - Pogoń Szczecin 0-3(0-1)
Lechia Gdańsk - Jagiellonia Białyst. 2-0(1-0)

Final Standings

1.	**GKS Piast Gliwice**	37	21	9	7	57 - 33	72
2.	Legia Warszawa	37	20	8	9	55 - 38	68
3.	KS Lechia Gdańsk	37	19	10	8	54 - 38	67
4.	KS Cracovia Kraków	37	17	6	14	45 - 43	57
5.	Jagiellonia Białystok	37	16	9	12	55 - 52	57
6.	Zagłębie Lubin	37	15	8	14	57 - 48	53
7.	MKS Pogoń Szczecin	37	14	10	13	57 - 54	52
8.	KKS Lech Poznań	37	15	7	15	49 - 48	52

Top goalscorers:

24 Igor Angulo Alboniga (ESP) *KS Górnik Zabrze*

18 Marcin Robak *WKS Śląsk Wrocław*

16 Carlos Daniel López Huesca "Carlitos" (ESP) *Legia Warszawa*

16 Jesús Imaz Ballesté (ESP) *Wisła Kraków / Jagiellonia Białystok*

Relegation Round

Results

Round 31 [22.04.2019]
Wisła Kraków - Wisła Płock 2-3(2-1)
Miedź Legnica - Zagłębie Sosnowiec 2-2(2-1)
Korona Kielce - Śląsk Wrocław 2-0(1-0)
Górnik Zabrze - Arka Gdynia 1-0(0-0)

Round 32 [25.04.2019]
Arka Gdynia - Miedź Legnica 2-0(1-0)
Wisła Płock - Korona Kielce 2-1(2-1)
Zagłębie Sosnowiec - Wisła Kraków 2-1(0-1)
Śląsk Wrocław - Górnik Zabrze 1-2(1-0)

Round 33 [28-29.04.2019]
Miedź Legnica - Wisła Płock 3-2(3-1)
Korona Kielce - Arka Gdynia 0-2(0-1)
Wisła Kraków - Śląsk Wrocław 1-1(1-1)
Górnik Zabrze - Zagłębie Sosnowiec 4-0(3-0)

Round 34 [03-05.05.2019]
Wisła Płock - Arka Gdynia 1-1(0-0)
Górnik Zabrze - Wisła Kraków 1-2(1-1)
Korona Kielce - Miedź Legnica 0-0
Zagłębie Sosnowiec - Śląsk Wrocław 2-4(0-1)

Round 35 [10-11.05.2019]
Arka Gdynia - Zagłębie Sosnowiec 2-0(0-0)
Wisła Kraków - Korona Kielce 1-0(0-0)
Śląsk Wrocław - Wisła Płock 2-1(1-1)
Miedź Legnica - Górnik Zabrze 0-1(0-0)

Round 36 [13-14.05.2019]
Arka Gdynia - Wisła Kraków 3-1(1-1)
Miedź Legnica - Śląsk Wrocław 0-2(0-0)
Zagłębie Sosnowiec - Korona Kielce 2-4(1-2)
Górnik Zabrze - Wisła Płock 0-1(0-1)

Round 37 [18.05.2019]
Śląsk Wrocław - Arka Gdynia 4-0(2-0)
Korona Kielce - Górnik Zabrze 0-3(0-0)
Wisła Płock - Zagłębie Sosnowiec 0-0
Wisła Kraków - Miedź Legnica 4-5(1-1)

Final Standings

9.	Wisła Kraków	37	14	7	16	67 - 63	49
10.	Korona Kielce	37	12	11	14	42 - 54	47
11.	KS Górnik Zabrze	37	12	10	15	48 - 53	46
12.	WKS Śląsk Wrocław	37	12	8	17	49 - 45	44
13.	MZKS Arka Gdynia	37	10	12	15	49 - 51	42
14.	Wisła Płock	37	10	11	16	50 - 58	41
15.	MKS Miedź Legnica (*Relegated*)	37	10	10	17	40 - 65	40
16.	Zagłębie Sosnowiec (*Relegated*)	37	7	8	22	49 - 80	29

NATIONAL CUP
Puchar Polski 2018/2019

First Round [25-27.09./02-03.10.2018]

ŁKS Łódź - KKS Lech Poznań	0-1(0-0,0-0)
MKS Śląsk Świętochłowice - MZKS Arka Gdynia	0-3(0-3)
KS Siarka Tarnobrzeg - Wisła Płock	1-4(0-1)
WKS Gryf Wejherowo - OKS Stomil Olsztyn	1-3(0-3)
Polonia Głubczyce - MKS Chrobry Głogów	0-8(0-4)
MKS Chojniczanka Chojnice - Legia Warszawa	0-1(0-1)
MKP Pogoń Siedlce - FKS Stal Mielec	2-1(0-1)
Ruch Chorzów - OKS Odra Opole	1-5(1-2)
Wisła Kraków - KS Lechia Gdańsk	1-1 aet; 4-5 pen
KS Olimpia Elbląg - WKS Śląsk Wrocław	0-3(0-2)
CWKS Resovia Rzeszów – KS Warta Poznań	2-0(2-0)
KP Starogard Gdanski – GKS Górnik Łęczna	1-0(1-0)
Elana Toruń - MKS Bytovia Bytów	1-3(0-2)
Lechia Dzierżoniów - Jagiellonia Białystok	0-1(0-0)
GKS Drwinia - KS Wisła Puławy	0-1(0-1)
Polonia Środa Wielkopol. - RKS Radomiak Radom	4-3(0-0)
Tur Bielsk Podlaski - Bruk-Bet Termalica Nieciecza	1-4(0-1)
KS ROW 1964 Rybnik - KS Cracovia Kraków	1-3(1-0)
KS Paradyz - MKS Puszcza Niepołomice	0-7(0-4)
KS Falubaz Zielona Góra - SKS Wigry Suwałki	0-1(0-1)
Huragan Morąg - Zagłębie Lubin	3-2(0-1)
Legionovia Legionowo - GKS Tychy '71	2-1(1-1)
KKPN Bałtyk Koszalin - KS Rozwój Katowice	1-3(1-1,1-1)
GKS Jastrzębie - GKS Piast Gliwice	1-2(0-2)
MKS Kluczbork - TS Podbeskidzie Bielsko-Biała	0-2(0-2)
MKS Sandecja Nowy Sącz - MKS Miedź Legnica	0-3(0-2)
GKS Bełchatów - RKS Garbarnia Kraków	1-1 aet; 6-5 pen
GKS Katowice - MKS Pogoń Szczecin	1-1 aet; 4-3 pen
GKS Olimpia Grudziądz - Zagłębie Sosnowiec	0-0 aet; 5-3 pen
Unia Hrubieszów - KS Górnik Zabrze	0-9(0-4)
Wisła Sandomierz - Korona Kielce	3-2(1-2)
Victoria Sulejówek - RKS Raków Częstochowa	0-4

Second Round [30-31.10./07.11.2018]

Huragan Morąg - MZKS Arka Gdynia	0-1(0-0)
MKS Bytovia Bytów - WKS Śląsk Wrocław	0-3(0-2)
RKS Raków Częstochowa - KKS Lech Poznań	1-0(1-0)
MKP Pogoń Siedlce - MKS Chrobry Głogów	1-2(0-2)
GKS Piast Gliwice - Legia Warszawa	1-1 aet; 2-4 pen
Polonia Środa Wielkopolska - OKS Odra Opole	0-1(0-0)
Wisła Sandomierz - TS Podbeskidzie Bielsko-Biała	3-2(1-0,2-2)
Legionovia Legionowo - KS Górnik Zabrze	0-1(0-1)
Bruk-Bet Termalica Nieciecza - KS Cracovia Kraków	2-0(0-0)
GKS Olimpia Grudziądz - Wisła Płock	2-7(1-4)
KS Wisła Puławy - KS Rozwój Katowice	0-1(0-1)
GKS Bełchatów - MKS Miedź Legnica	0-1(0-0)
GKS Katowice - Jagiellonia Białystok	0-1(0-0,0-0)
CWKS Resovia Rzeszów - KS Lechia Gdańsk	1-3(1-0)
KP Starogard Gdanski - MKS Puszcza Niepołomice	1-3(0-1)
SKS Wigry Suwałki - OKS Stomil Olsztyn	3-2(1-1)

1/8-Finals [04-06.12.2018]			
MKS Puszcza Niepołomice - Wisła Płock	3-1(1-0)	Bruk-Bet Termalica Nieciecza - KS Lechia Gdańsk	1-3(0-1)
WKS Śląsk Wrocław - MKS Miedź Legnica	0-1(0-1)	MKS Chrobry Głogów - Legia Warszawa	0-3(0-2)
MZKS Arka Gdynia - Jagiellonia Białystok	0-2(0-0)	KS Rozwój Katowice - KS Górnik Zabrze	1-4(1-1,1-1)
Wisła Sandomierz - OKS Odra Opole	0-1(0-1)	SKS Wigry Suwałki - RKS Raków Częstochowa	0-3(0-2)

Quarter-Finals [27.02./12-14.03.2019]			
KS Górnik Zabrze - KS Lechia Gdańsk	1-2(0-1)	RKS Raków Częstochowa - Legia Warszawa	2-1(1-1,1-1)
OKS Odra Opole - Jagiellonia Białystok	0-2(0-0)	MKS Puszcza Niepołomice - MKS Miedź Legnica	0-1(0-1)

Semi-Finals [09-10.04.2019]			
Jagiellonia Białystok - MKS Miedź Legnica	2-1(0-0)	RKS Raków Częstochowa - KS Lechia Gdańsk	0-1(0-1)

Final

02.05.2019; Stadion Narodowy, Warszawa; Referee: Bartosz Frankowski; Attendance: 44,158
KS Lechia Gdańsk - Jagiellonia Białystok **1-0(0-0)**

Lechia Gdańsk: Zlatan Alomerović, João Aniceto Grandela Nunes, Filip Mladenović, Michał Nalepa, Błażej Augustyn, Jarosław Kubicki, Daniel Łukasik (90.Steven Vitória), Tomasz Makowski, Konrad Michalak (69.Artur Sobiech), Lukáš Haraslín (90.Patryk Lipski), Flávio Emanuel Lopes Paixão. Trainer: Piotr Stokowiec.

Jagiellonia: Marián Kelemen, Andrej Kadlec (90.Jakub Wójcicki), Guilherme Haubert Sityá, Zoran Arsenić, Ivan Runje, Böðvar Böðvarsson, Taras Romanczuk, Marko Poletanović (90.Bartosz Kwiecień), Arvydas Novikovas, Patryk Klimala, Jesús Imaz Ballesté. Trainer: Ireneusz Mamrot.

Goal: 1-0 Artur Sobiech (90).

THE CLUBS 2018/2019

Please note: matches and goals includes statistics of both regular season and play-offs (Championship or Europa League).

Morski Klub Sportowy Arka Gdynia

Founded: 1929
Stadium: Stadion Miejski, Gdynia (15,139)

Goalkeepers:	DOB	M	(s)	G
Pāvels Šteinbors (LVA)	21.09.1985	37		
Defenders:	**DOB**	**M**	**(s)**	**G**
Adam Danch	15.12.1987	10	(14)	1
Frederik Helstrup (DEN)	16.03.1993	29		1
Adrian Klimczak	26.07.1997		(1)	
Christian Maghoma (COD)	08.11.1997	15		
Adam Marciniak	28.09.1988	34		1
Luka Marić (CRO)	25.04.1987	23		
Michael Olczyk	08.03.1997	4	(1)	
Tadeusz Socha	15.02.1988	4	(6)	
Dawid Sołdecki	29.04.1987	4	(3)	
Robert Sulewski	07.02.1994	1	(1)	
Damian Zbozień	25.04.1989	33	(1)	5
Midfielders:	**DOB**	**M**	**(s)**	**G**
Nabil Aankour (MAR)	09.08.1993	16	(10)	2
Andriy Bogdanov (UKR)	21.01.1990	6	(2)	
Goran Cvijanovič (SVN)	09.09.1986	4	(12)	
Karol Danielak	29.09.1991		(4)	
Adam Deja	24.06.1993	26	(1)	2
Michał Janota	29.07.1990	32		10
Michał Nalepa	24.03.1995	29		2
Mateusz Stepien	12.02.2002		(1)	
Marko Vejinović (NED)	03.02.1990	14		5
Forwards:	**DOB**	**M**	**(s)**	**G**
Maksymilian Banaszewski	22.03.1995	4	(4)	
Maciej Jankowski	04.01.1990	28	(4)	10
Aleksandar Kolev (BUL)	08.12.1992	17		1
Jan Łoś	20.07.2000		(2)	
Marcus Vinícius da Silva de Oliveira (BRA)	29.03.1984	3	(8)	1
Mateusz Młyński	02.01.2001	4	(8)	1
Rafał Siemaszko	11.09.1986	7	(19)	2
Luka Zarandia (GEO)	17.02.1996	23	(5)	5
Trainer:	**DOB**	**M**		
Zbigniew Smółka	12.05.1972	28		
Grzegorz Witt [03.04.2019]	03.05.1969	1		
Jacek Zielinski [12.04.2019]	22.03.1961	8		

Miejski Klub Sportowy Cracovia Kraków

Founded: 13.06.1906
Stadium: Stadion "Marszałek Józef Piłsudski", Kraków (15,016)

Goalkeepers:	DOB	M	(s)	G
Maciej Gostomski	27.09.1988	11		
Michal Peškovič (SVK)	08.02.1982	26		
Defenders:	**DOB**	**M**	**(s)**	**G**
Niko Datković (CRO)	21.04.1993	20	(2)	1
Diego Gustavo Ferraresso Scheda (BRA)	21.05.1992	19	(5)	
Oleksiy Dytyatev (UKR)	07.11.1988	25	(2)	1
Michał Helik	09.09.1995	28	(4)	
Kamil Pestka	22.08.1998	2	(1)	
Cornel Emilian Râpă (ROU)	16.01.1990	30	(3)	1
Michal Sipľak (SVK)	02.02.1996	28	(2)	1
Midfielders:	**DOB**	**M**	**(s)**	**G**
Marcin Budziński	06.07.1990	11	(3)	
Miroslav Čovilo (SRB)	06.05.1986	1		
Damian Dąbrowski	27.08.1992	20	(4)	
Milan Dimun (SVK)	19.09.1996	23	(9)	1
Janusz Gol	11.11.1985	30		
Sergiu Cătălin Hanca (ROU)	04.04.1992	13	(3)	2
Radosław Kanach	03.04.1999		(1)	
Francisco Javier Hernández González"Javi Hernández" (ESP)	06.06.1989	27	(6)	10
Jakub Serafin	25.05.1996	3	(3)	
Forwards:	**DOB**	**M**	**(s)**	**G**
Airam López Cabrera (ESP)	21.10.1987	24	(3)	14
Bojan Čečarić (SRB)	10.10.1993	3	(4)	
Antonini Čulina (CRO)	27.01.1992	1	(1)	
Adrian Danek	01.08.1994	1		
Eladio Zorrilla Jiménez (ESP)	13.07.1990	1	(1)	
Gerard Oliva Gorgori (ESP)	07.10.1989	3		1
Daniel Pik	20.07.2000		(4)	
Filip Piszczek	26.05.1995	11	(17)	6
Serder Serderov (RUS)	10.03.1994	2	(4)	
Sebastian Strózik	15.05.1999	4	(16)	1
Mateusz Szczepaniak	23.01.1991		(2)	
Vinícius Ferreira Dias (BRA)	31.01.1999		(1)	
Mateusz Wdowiak	28.08.1996	30	(4)	3
Sergei Zenjov (EST)	20.04.1989	10	(2)	1
Trainer:	**DOB**	**M**		
Michał Probierz	24.09.1972	37		

Klub Sportowy Górnik Zabrze

Founded: 14.12.1948
Stadium: Stadion „Ernest Pohl“, Zabrze (24,413)

Goalkeepers:	**DOB**	**M**	**(s)**	**G**
Daniel Bielica	30.04.1999	1		
Martin Chudý (SVK)	23.04.1989	17		
Tomasz Loska	26.01.1996	19		
Defenders:	**DOB**	**M**	**(s)**	**G**
Adam Arnarson (ISL)	27.08.1995	5	(7)	
Paweł Bochniewicz	30.01.1996	31	(1)	1
Daniel Suárez García-Osorio „Dani Suárez“ (ESP)	07.05.1990	26	(5)	4
Adrian Gryszkiewicz	13.12.1999	20	(2)	
Michał Koj	28.07.1993	12	(2)	
Kacper Michalski	03.01.2000	10	(1)	
Boris Sekulić (SRB)	21.10.1991	13		2
Przemysław Wiśniewski	27.07.1998	23	(2)	
Adam Wolniewicz	18.03.1993	4	(4)	
Midfielders:	**DOB**	**M**	**(s)**	**G**
Maciej Ambrosiewicz	24.05.1998	11	(10)	
Wiktor Biedrzycki	31.07.1997	2	(1)	
Valeriane Gvilia (GEO)	24.05.1994	17		1
Jesús Jiménez Núñez (ESP)	05.11.1993	32	(4)	5
Daniel Liszka	17.02.2000	8	(2)	
Mateusz Matras	23.01.1991	16		3
Szymon Matuszek	07.01.1989	18	(11)	
Konrad Nowak	07.11.1994	2	(10)	
Daniel Smuga	18.01.1997	9	(6)	1
Szymon Żurkowski	25.09.1997	30	(1)	3
Forwards:	**DOB**	**M**	**(s)**	**G**
Igor Angulo Alboniga (ESP)	26.01.1984	34	(3)	24
Ishmael Baidoo (GHA)	01.12.1998	2	(3)	
Ioannis Mystakidis (GRE)	07.12.1994	6	(3)	
Adam Ryczkowski	30.04.1997	6	(4)	
Marcin Urynowicz	16.03.1996	4	(4)	1
Łukasz Wolsztyński	08.12.1994	10	(12)	1
Rafał Wolsztyński	08.12.1994		(6)	
Kamil Zapolnik	09.09.1992	19	(5)	2
Trainer:	**DOB**	**M**		
Marcin Brosz	11.04.1973	37		

Jagiellonia Białystok Sportowa Spółka Akcyjna

Founded: 30.05.1920
Stadium: Stadion Miejski, Białystok (22,432)

Goalkeepers:	**DOB**	**M**	**(s)**	**G**
Marián Kelemen (SVK)	07.12.1979	28		
Grzegorz Sandomierski	05.09.1989	9	(1)	
Defenders:	**DOB**	**M**	**(s)**	**G**
Zoran Arsenić (CRO)	02.06.1994	13		
Böðvar Böðvarsson (ISL)	09.04.1995	15	(1)	
Łukasz Burliga	10.05.1988	10	(1)	1
Guilherme Haubert Sityá (BRA)	01.04.1990	31	(3)	2
Andrej Kadlec (SVK)	02.02.1996	8	(1)	1
Łukasz Klemenz	24.09.1995	6	(1)	1
Nemanja Mitrovič (SVN)	15.10.1992	30		1
Michal Ozga	23.06.2000	1		
Ivan Runje (CRO)	09.10.1990	30		3
Midfielders:	**DOB**	**M**	**(s)**	**G**
Martin Adamec (SVK)	14.08.1998	2	(6)	
Rafał Grzyb	16.01.1983	2	(2)	
Martin Košťál (SVK)	23.02.1996	9	(6)	
Bartosz Kwiecień	07.05.1994	12	(15)	1
Mateusz Machaj	28.06.1989	6	(7)	
Marko Poletanović (SRB)	20.07.1993	20	(5)	2
Martin Pospíšil (CZE)	26.06.1991	29	(5)	1
Taras Romanczuk (UKR)	14.11.1991	32	(1)	1
Mile Savković (SRB)	11.03.1992	3	(8)	1
Piotr Wlazło	03.06.1989	1		
Forwards:	**DOB**	**M**	**(s)**	**G**
Roman Bezjak (SVN)	21.02.1989	10	(6)	3
Jesús Imaz Ballesté (ESP)	26.09.1990	12	(2)	10
Przemysław Frankowski	12.04.1995	13	(2)	3
Patryk Klimala	05.08.1998	8	(14)	1
Justas Lasickas (LTU)	06.10.1997		(1)	
Arvydas Novikovas (LTU)	18.12.1990	30	(1)	9
Cillian Sheridan (IRL)	23.02.1989	7	(3)	3
Stefan Šćepović (SRB)	10.01.1990	3	(3)	
Karol Świderski	23.01.1997	11	(6)	8
Maciej Twarowski	13.03.2001		(3)	
Jakub Wójcicki	09.07.1988	16	(7)	1
Trainer:	**DOB**	**M**		
Ireneusz Mamrot	13.12.1970	37		

Korona Kielce

Founded: 10.07.1973
Stadium: Kolporter Arena, Kielce (15,550)

Goalkeepers:	**DOB**	**M**	**(s)**	**G**
Matthias Hamrol (GER)	31.12.1993	27		
Michał Miśkiewicz	20.01.1989	8		
Paweł Sokół	02.03.2000	2		
Defenders:	**DOB**	**M**	**(s)**	**G**
Aleksandar Bjelica (SRB)	07.01.1994	2	(1)	
Elhadji Pape Djibril Diaw (SEN)	31.12.1994	19	(1)	2
Iván Márquez Álvarez (ESP)	09.06.1994	24		
Ken Kallaste (EST)	31.08.1988	6	(6)	1
Łukasz Kosakiewicz	19.09.1990	16	(9)	
Adnan Kovačević (BIH)	09.09.1993	30	(1)	2
Piotr Malarczyk	01.08.1991	7	(9)	
Piotr Pierzchala	29.06.1999	1		
Bartosz Rymaniak	13.11.1989	31		
Joonas Tamm (EST)	02.02.1992	5	(1)	
Midfielders:	**DOB**	**M**	**(s)**	**G**
Marcin Cebula	06.12.1995	13	(8)	3
Michael Gardawski (GER)	25.09.1990	32		1
Ognjen Gnjatić (BIH)	16.10.1991	11	(2)	
Zlatko Janjić (BIH)	07.05.1986	10	(7)	1
Ivan Jukić (BIH)	21.06.1996	15	(6)	3
Mateusz Możdżeń	14.03.1991	9	(5)	1
Oliver Petrak (CRO)	06.02.1991	28	(3)	
Oskar Sewerzynski	12.08.2001	1	(4)	
Oktawian Skrzecz	30.05.1997	2	(3)	
Daniel Szelągowski	02.09.2002		(1)	
Jakub Żubrowski	21.03.1992	28	(4)	
Forwards:	**DOB**	**M**	**(s)**	**G**
Vato Arveladze (GEO)	04.03.1998	13	(10)	4
Felicio Anando Brown Forbes (CRC)	28.08.1991	13	(6)	3
Maciej Górski	01.03.1990	5	(10)	2
Matej Pučko (SVN)	06.10.1993	22	(7)	5
Elia Soriano (ITA)	26.06.1989	27	(6)	14
Trainer:	**DOB**	**M**		
Gino Lettieri (ITA)	23.12.1966	37		

Kolejowy Klub Sportowy Lech Poznań

Founded: 19.03.1922
Stadium: INEA Stadion, Poznań (43,269)

Goalkeepers:	**DOB**	**M**	**(s)**	**G**
Jasmin Burić (BIH)	18.02.1987	27		
Matúš Putnocký (SVK)	01.11.1984	10	(1)	
Defenders:	**DOB**	**M**	**(s)**	**G**
Dimitrios Goutas (GRE)	04.04.1994	8	(1)	
Robert Gumny	04.06.1998	19		1
Rafał Janicki	05.07.1992	21		
Volodymyr Kostevych (UKR)	23.10.1992	24	(2)	1
Maciej Orłowski	07.01.1994	2		
Thomas Rogne (NOR)	29.06.1990	22	(1)	1
Piotr Tomasik	31.10.1987	9	(7)	
Vernon De Marco Morlacchi (ARG)	18.11.1992	12	(3)	
Nikola Vujadinović (MNE)	31.07.1986	22	(1)	3
Marcin Wasielewski	23.08.1994	13	(4)	1
Midfielders:	**DOB**	**M**	**(s)**	**G**
Tomasz Cywka	27.06.1988	7	(2)	1
Maciej Gajos	19.03.1991	14	(12)	2
Darko Jevtić (SUI)	08.02.1993	20	(6)	3
Krzysztof Kołodziej	14.02.1993	1	(2)	
Filip Marchwiński	10.01.2002	3	(8)	2
Pedro Miguel Amorim Pereira Silva „Pedro Tiba“ (POR)	31.08.1988	33		4
Mihai Cosmin Răduţ (ROU)	18.03.1990	4	(5)	
Mateusz Skrzypczak	22.08.2000	2	(1)	
Łukasz Trałka	11.05.1984	25	(2)	1
Forwards:	**DOB**	**M**	**(s)**	**G**
Dionisio Emanuel Villalba Rojano „Dioni“ (ESP)	21.12.1989		(7)	
Christian Gytkjær (DEN)	06.05.1990	29	(2)	12
João Pedro Reis Amaral (POR)	07.09.1991	20	(5)	8
Kamil Jóźwiak	22.04.1998	25	(6)	3
Tymoteusz Klupś	26.02.2000	10	(10)	1
Maciej Makuszewski	29.09.1989	22	(7)	
Hubert Sobol	25.06.2000		(1)	
Paweł Tomczyk	04.05.1998	2	(8)	2
Timur Zhamaletdinov (RUS)	21.05.1997	1	(6)	1
Trainer:	**DOB**	**M**		
Ivan Đurđević (SRB)	05.02.1977	14		
Dariusz Zuraw [04.11.2018]	14.11.1972	2		
Adam Nawalka [25.11.2018]	23.10.1957	11		
Dariusz Zuraw [31.03.2019]	14.11.1972	10		

Klub Sportowy Lechia Gdańsk Spółka Akcyjna

Founded: 1945
Stadium: Stadion Energa Gdańsk, Gdańsk (43,615)

Goalkeepers:	**DOB**	**M**	**(s)**	**G**
Zlatan Alomerović (GER)	15.06.1991	9		
Dušan Kuciak (SVK)	21.05.1985	28		
Defenders:	**DOB**	**M**	**(s)**	**G**
Błażej Augustyn	26.01.1988	30		2
Adam Chrzanowski	31.03.1999	1	(2)	1
Filip Dymerski	05.04.2002		(1)	
Karol Fila	13.06.1998	17	(12)	1
João Aniceto Grandela Nunes (POR)	19.11.1995	17	(6)	
Mateusz Lewandowski	18.03.1993	1	(1)	
Filip Mladenović (SRB)	15.08.1991	35		3
Michał Nalepa	22.01.1993	35		3
Paweł Stolarski	28.01.1996	3	(1)	
Steven Vitória (CAN)	11.01.1987	8	(7)	1
Midfielders:	**DOB**	**M**	**(s)**	**G**
Ariel Borysiuk	29.07.1991		(5)	
Jarosław Kubicki	07.08.1995	35		4
Patryk Lipski	12.06.1994	19	(2)	5
Daniel Łukasik	28.04.1991	33	(1)	1
Tomasz Makowski	19.07.1999	17	(5)	
Mateusz Sopoćko	26.06.1999	1	(4)	
Egy Maulana Vikri (IDN)	07.07.2000		(2)	
Rafał Wolski	10.11.1992	7	(2)	1
Forwards:	**DOB**	**M**	**(s)**	**G**
Jakub Arak	02.04.1995	6	(18)	1
Flávio Emanuel Lopes Paixão (POR)	19.09.1984	35	(2)	15
Lukáš Haraslín (SVK)	26.05.1996	27	(6)	4
Michał Mak	14.11.1991	12	(7)	2
Konrad Michalak	19.09.1997	15	(7)	1
Sławomir Peszko	19.02.1985		(1)	
Artur Sobiech	12.06.1990	14	(12)	8
Mateusz Żukowski	23.11.2001	2	(6)	
Trainer:	**DOB**	**M**		
Piotr Stokowiec	25.05.1972			

Legia Warszawa

Founded: 1916
Stadium: Stadion “Marszałek Józef Piłsudski”, Warszawa (31,800)

Goalkeepers:	**DOB**	**M**	**(s)**	**G**
Radosław Cierzniak	24.04.1983	15		
Radosław Majecki	16.11.1999	14		
Arkadiusz Malarz	19.06.1980	8		
Defenders:	**DOB**	**M**	**(s)**	**G**
Iñaki Astiz Ventura (ESP)	05.11.1983	6	(4)	
Adam Hloušek (CZE)	20.12.1988	23	(2)	3
Mateusz Hołownia	06.05.1998	3		
Artur Jędrzejczyk	04.11.1987	31		3
Luís Augusto Martins Rocha (POR)	27.06.1993	11		
Michał Pazdan	21.09.1987	2		
William Rémy (FRA)	04.04.1991	16		2
Paweł Stolarski	28.01.1996	12	(2)	1
Marko Vešović (MNE)	28.08.1991	25		
Mateusz Wieteska	11.02.1997	22	(5)	
Mateusz Żyro	28.10.1998	3		
Midfielders:	**DOB**	**M**	**(s)**	**G**
André Renato Soares Martins (POR)	21.01.1990	23	(3)	2
Domagoj Antolić (CRO)	30.06.1990	21	(4)	
Carlos Miguel Ribeiro Dias „Cafú“ (POR)	26.02.1993	27	(4)	4
Kasper Hämäläinen (FIN)	08.08.1986	11	(6)	2
Krzysztof Mączyński	23.05.1987	3	(1)	1
Christian Pasquato (ITA)	20.07.1989		(7)	
Chris Philipps (LUX)	08.03.1994	2	(3)	
Miroslav Radović (SRB)	16.01.1984	2	(6)	
Sebastian Szymański	10.05.1999	31	(3)	2
Forwards:	**DOB**	**M**	**(s)**	**G**
Carlos Daniel López Huesca „Carlitos“ (ESP)	12.06.1990	29	(7)	16
Eduardo Alves da Silva (CRO)	25.02.1983		(1)	
Iuri José Picanço Medeiros (POR)	10.07.1994	8	(6)	3
José Kanté Martínez (GUI)	27.09.1990	5	(11)	2
Michał Kucharczyk	20.03.1991	24	(4)	4
Sandro Kulenović (CRO)	04.12.1999	5	(16)	4
Konrad Michalak	19.09.1997	1		
Dominik Adrián Nagy (HUN)	08.05.1995	22	(8)	5
Jarosław Niezgoda	15.03.1995		(5)	
Salvador José Milhazes Agra (POR)	11.11.1991	2	(2)	
Trainer:	**DOB**	**M**		
Dean Klafurić (CRO)	26.07.1972	2		
Aleksandar Vuković (SRB) [01.08.2018]	25.08.1979	2		
Ricardo Manuel Andrade e Silva Sá Pinto (POR) [13.08.2018]	10.10.1972	23		
Aleksandar Vuković (SRB) [02.04.2019]	25.08.1979	10		

Miejski Klub Sportowy Miedź Legnica Spółka Akcyjna

Founded: 1971
Stadium: Stadion im. Orła Białego, Legnica (6,244)

Goalkeepers:	DOB	M	(s)	G
Soslan Dzhanaev (RUS)	13.03.1987	7		
Anton Kanibolotskiy (UKR)	16.05.1988	20		
Łukasz Sapela	21.09.1982	10		
Defenders:	**DOB**	**M**	**(s)**	**G**
Frank Adu Kwame (GHA)	16.05.1985	6		
Grzegorz Bartczak	21.06.1985	22	(2)	
Tomislav Božić (CRO)	01.11.1987	18	(1)	
Jonathan de Amo Pérez (ESP)	13.01.1990	3	(1)	
Francisco Pablo Cruz Torres „Fran Cruz" (ESP)	22.06.1991	7	(1)	
Aleksandar Miljković (SRB)	26.02.1990	16	(1)	
Elton Monteiro (SUI)	22.02.1994	3	(1)	
Božo Musa (CRO)	15.09.1988	11	(1)	1
Kornel Osyra	07.02.1993	20		
Artur Pikk (EST)	05.03.1993	18	(4)	1
Paweł Zieliński	17.07.1990	28	(3)	3
Mateusz Żyro	28.10.1998	2	(4)	
Midfielders:	**DOB**	**M**	**(s)**	**G**
Rafał Augustyniak	14.10.1993	21	(1)	2
Borja Fernández Fernández (ESP)	16.08.1995	26	(4)	
Petteri Forsell (FIN)	16.10.1990	33	(4)	13
Łukasz Garguła	25.02.1981	2	(9)	
Juan del Carmen Cámara Mesa (ESP)	13.02.1994	23	(4)	3
Patryk Makuch	11.04.1999		(3)	
Omar Santana Cabrera (ESP)	14.04.1991	21	(3)	1
Adrian Purzycki	02.08.1997	12	(5)	
Forwards:	**DOB**	**M**	**(s)**	**G**
Joan Ángel Román Ollé (ESP)	18.05.1993	9	(3)	5
Wojciech Łobodziński	20.10.1982	7	(9)	
Marcos García Barreno „Marquitos" (ESP)	21.03.1987	9	(1)	2
Henrik Ojamaa (EST)	20.05.1991	24	(11)	3
Fabian Piasecki	04.05.1995	13	(15)	1
Mateusz Piątkowski	22.11.1984	5	(9)	1
Mateusz Szczepaniak	23.01.1991	11	(7)	3
Trainer:	**DOB**	**M**		
Dominik Nowak	07.02.1972	37		

Gliwicki Klub Sportowy Piast Gliwice

Founded: 18.06.1945
Stadium: Stadion Miejski, Gliwice (10,037)

Goalkeepers:	DOB	M	(s)	G
František Plach (SVK)	08.03.1992	25		
Jakub Szmatuła	22.03.1981	12		
Defenders:	**DOB**	**M**	**(s)**	**G**
Jakub Czerwiński	06.08.1991	36		3
Mikkel Kirkeskov (DEN)	05.09.1991	36		2
Martin Konczkowski	14.09.1993	28	(4)	
Uroš Korun (SVN)	25.05.1987	9		
Tomasz Mokwa	10.02.1993	4	(1)	
Marcin Pietrowski	01.03.1988	23	(2)	1
Aleksandar Sedlar (SRB)	13.12.1991	30		6
Midfielders:	**DOB**	**M**	**(s)**	**G**
Patryk Dziczek	25.03.1998	32	(1)	3
Tom Hateley (ENG)	12.09.1989	29	(5)	4
Tomasz Jodłowiec	08.09.1985	17	(8)	4
Patryk Sokołowski	25.09.1994		(12)	1
Forwards:	**DOB**	**M**	**(s)**	**G**
Karsten Ayong (CZE)	20.01.1998		(1)	
Gerard Badía Cortés (ESP)	18.10.1989	7	(14)	2
Denis Gojko	16.02.1998	1	(4)	
Aleksander Jagiełło	02.02.1995	6	(10)	
Jorge Félix Muñoz García (ESP)	22.08.1991	31	(3)	6
Mateusz Mak	14.11.1991	11	(9)	1
Michal Papadopulos (CZE)	14.04.1985	17	(15)	5
Piotr Parzyszek	08.09.1993	20	(13)	9
Karol Stanek	03.10.1999		(1)	
Paweł Tomczyk	04.05.1998		(4)	2
César Joel Valencia Castillo (ECU)	16.11.1994	33		6
Trainer:	**DOB**	**M**		
Waldemar Fornalik	11.04.1963	37		

Morski Klub Sportowy Pogoń Szczecin

Founded: 21.04.1948
Stadium: Stadion „Florian Krygier", Szczecin (18,027)

Goalkeepers:	DOB	M	(s)	G
Łukasz Budziłek	19.03.1991	1		
Jakub Bursztyn	25.03.1998	10		
Łukasz Załuska	16.06.1982	26		
Defenders:	**DOB**	**M**	**(s)**	**G**
Jakub Bartkowski	07.11.1991	11	(2)	
Lasha Dvali (GEO)	14.05.1995	13		1
Jarosław Fojut	17.10.1987	8	(2)	
Mariusz Malec	04.04.1995	21	(1)	1
Hubert Matynia	04.11.1995	22	(7)	
David Niepsuj	16.08.1995	10		
Ricardo Nuno Dos Santos Nunes (RSA)	18.06.1986	19	(1)	
David Steć (AUT)	10.05.1994	21	(5)	
Sebastian Walukiewicz	05.04.2000	28	(1)	1
Midfielders:				
Dawid Błanik	15.04.1997	1	(7)	
Kamil Drygas	07.09.1991	34	(1)	10
Tomasz Hołota	27.01.1991	5	(3)	
Jin Izumisawa (JPN)	17.12.1991		(1)	1
Kacper Kozłowski	16.10.2003		(1)	
Zvonimir Kožulj (BIH)	15.11.1993	31	(3)	9
Radosław Majewski	15.12.1986	32	(4)	8
Tomás Podstawski (POR)	30.01.1995	30		1
Sebastian Rudol	21.02.1995	4	(6)	
Maciej Żurawski	22.12.2000		(1)	
Forwards:	**DOB**	**M**	**(s)**	**G**
Adrian Benedyczak	24.11.2000	3	(9)	
Soufian Benyamina (GER)	02.03.1990	3	(12)	2
Adam Buksa	12.07.1996	22		11
Spas Delev (BUL)	22.09.1989	6	(8)	2
Adam Frączczak	07.08.1987	7	(1)	1
Iker Guarrotxena Vallejo (ESP)	06.12.1992	16	(8)	5
Santeri Hostikka (FIN)	30.09.1997	2	(6)	
Sebastian Kowalczyk	22.08.1998	19	(9)	2
Marcin Listkowski	10.02.1998		(2)	
Michał Żyro	20.09.1992	2	(9)	1
Trainer:	**DOB**	**M**		
Kosta Runjaić (GER)	04.06.1971	37		

Wrocławski Klub Sportowy Śląsk Wrocław Spółka Akcyjna

Founded: 18.03.1946
Stadium: Stadion Miejski, Wrocław (42,771)

Goalkeepers:	**DOB**	**M**	**(s)**	**G**
Jakub Słowik	31.08.1991	35		
Dariusz Szczerbal	02.11.1995		(1)	
Jakub Wrąbel	08.06.1996	2		
Defenders:	**DOB**	**M**	**(s)**	**G**
Augusto Pereira Loureiro (POR)	30.08.1987	13	(4)	2
Łukasz Broź	17.12.1985	22		
Piotr Celeban	25.06.1985	30		3
Đorđe Čotra (SRB)	13.09.1984	14	(1)	1
Kamil Dankowski	22.07.1996	10	(1)	
Wojciech Golla	12.01.1992	35		1
Mateusz Hołownia	06.05.1998	7	(1)	
Paweł Kucharczyk	04.05.1997	1		
Mariusz Pawelec	14.04.1986	10		
Igors Tarasovs (LVA)	16.10.1988	14	(3)	1
Midfielders:	**DOB**	**M**	**(s)**	**G**
Michał Chrapek	03.04.1992	27	(5)	3
Damian Gąska	24.11.1996	12	(17)	
Jakub Łabojko	03.10.1997	17	(4)	1
Krzysztof Mączyński	23.05.1987	15		
Maciej Pałaszewski	07.04.1998	9	(3)	
Mateusz Radecki	02.04.1993	10	(19)	4
Forwards:	**DOB**	**M**	**(s)**	**G**
Farshad Ahmadzadeh (IRN)	23.09.1992	12	(13)	1
Mateusz Cholewiak	05.02.1990	24	(5)	4
Jakub Kosecki	29.08.1990	1		1
Daniel Łuczak	12.07.1996	2	(2)	
Lubambo Musonda (ZAM)	01.03.1995	9	(3)	
Róbert Pich (SVK)	12.11.1988	31	(2)	6
Arkadiusz Piech	07.06.1985	15	(9)	2
Marcin Robak	29.11.1982	30	(5)	18
Piotr Samiec-Talar	02.11.2001		(1)	
Daniel Szczepan	05.06.1995		(7)	
Trainer:	**DOB**	**M**		
Tadeusz Pawłowski	14.10.1953	18		
Pawel Barylski [11.12.2018]	20.09.1975	2		
Vitezslav Lavicka (CZE) [03.01.2019]	30.04.1963	17		

Wisła Kraków Spółka Akcyjna

Founded: 1906
Stadium: Stadion „Henryk Reyman", Kraków (33,326)

Goalkeepers:	**DOB**	**M**	**(s)**	**G**
Michał Buchalik	03.02.1989	4		
Mateusz Lis	27.02.1997	33	(2)	
Defenders:	**DOB**	**M**	**(s)**	**G**
Zoran Arsenić (CRO)	02.06.1994	9	(3)	
Jakub Bartkowski	07.11.1991	17	(1)	1
Łukasz Burliga	10.05.1988	7	(4)	2
Marcin Grabowski	21.05.2000	5	(3)	
Daniel Hoyo-Kowalski	12.07.2003	4		
Łukasz Klemenz	24.09.1995	8	(2)	
Matej Palčič (SVN)	21.06.1993	9	(3)	2
Rafał Pietrzak	30.01.1992	35	(1)	3
Maciej Sadlok	29.06.1989	27		
Dawid Szot	29.04.2001	2		
Marcin Wasilewski	09.06.1980	28		
Midfielders:	**DOB**	**M**	**(s)**	**G**
Jakub Bartosz	13.08.1996	1	(7)	
Vullnet Basha (ALB)	11.07.1990	30		3
Jakub Błaszczykowski	14.12.1985	8		5
Tibor Halilović (CRO)	18.03.1995	4	(7)	
Dawid Kort	29.04.1995	18	(2)	3
Martin Košťál (SVK)	23.02.1996	15	(4)	2
Emmanuel Kumah (GHA)	09.02.2000		(4)	
Daniel Morys	26.12.2000	1		
Patryk Plewka	02.01.2000	8	(10)	
Vukan Savičevič (MNE)	29.01.1994	11	(1)	2
Maciej Śliwa	22.05.2001	1	(4)	1
Wojciech Słomka	04.11.1998		(5)	
Kamil Wojtkowski	26.02.1998	6	(18)	1
Forwards:	**DOB**	**M**	**(s)**	**G**
Jesús Imaz Ballesté (ESP)	26.09.1990	16	(1)	6
Artur Balicki	11.10.1999		(2)	
Rafał Boguski	09.06.1984	23	(4)	2
Paweł Brożek	21.04.1983	5	(9)	2
Aleksander Buksa	15.01.2003		(4)	
Krzysztof Drzazga	20.06.1995	16	(1)	5
Marko Kolar (CRO)	31.05.1995	20	(6)	12
Patryk Małecki	01.08.1988	4	(1)	
Zdeněk Ondrášek (CZE)	22.12.1988	18	(1)	11
Sławomir Peszko	19.02.1985	14		3
Trainer:	**DOB**	**M**		
Maciej Stolarczyk	15.01.1972	37		

Wisła Płock Spółka Akcyjna

Founded: 1947
Stadium: Stadion „Kazimierza Górski", Płock (12,800)

Goalkeepers:	**DOB**	**M**	**(s)**	**G**
Thomas Dähne (GER)	04.01.1994	30		
Marcel Zapytowski	08.01.2001	1	(1)	
Bartłomiej Żynel	09.04.1998	6	(1)	
Defenders:	**DOB**	**M**	**(s)**	**G**
Ángel García Cabezali (ESP)	03.02.1993	16		
Adam Dźwigała	25.09.1995	20	(1)	
Igor Łasicki	26.06.1995	25	(2)	1
Jake McGing (AUS)	22.05.1994	12		
Bartłomiej Sielewski	09.08.1984	4	(6)	1
Cezary Stefańczyk	21.02.1984	17	(3)	
Patryk Stępiński	16.01.1995	9	(3)	
Alan Uryga	19.02.1994	35		3
Marcin Warcholak	08.08.1989	13		
Midfielders:	**DOB**	**M**	**(s)**	**G**
Ariel Borysiuk	29.07.1991	9	(3)	2
Dominik Furman	06.07.1992	36		6
Jakub Łukowski	25.05.1996	7	(10)	2
Justinas Marazas (LTU)	23.02.2000	5	(1)	
Damian Rasak	08.02.1996	28	(3)	
Semir Štilić (BIH)	08.10.1987	4	(8)	
Damian Szymański	16.06.1995	20		2
Mateusz Szwoch	19.03.1993	13	(3)	1
Nicolás Varela Batista (URU)	19.01.1991	20	(4)	1
Forwards:	**DOB**	**M**	**(s)**	**G**
Karol Angielski	20.03.1996	4	(13)	2
Carlos Miguel Tavares de Oliveira "Carlitos" (POR)	09.03.1993	2	(6)	1
Grzegorz Kuświk	23.05.1987	7	(8)	3
Giorgi Merebashvili (GEO)	15.08.1986	24	(7)	6
Ricardo Cavalcante Mendes „Ricardinho" (BRA)	04.09.1989	27	(8)	10
Alen Stevanović (SRB)	07.01.1991	4	(5)	1
Oskar Zawada	01.02.1996	9	(14)	6
Trainer:	**DOB**	**M**		
Dariusz Dzwigala	22.03.1969	11		
José Antonio Vicuña Ochandorena "Kibu" (ESP) [10.10.2018]	20.11.1971	17		
Leszek Ojrzynski [04.04.2019]	31.05.1972	9		

Zagłębie Lubin Spółka Akcyjna

Founded: 10.09.1945
Stadium: Stadion KGHM Zagłębia, Lubin (16,068)

Goalkeepers:	DOB	M	(s)	G
Konrad Forenc	17.07.1992	14		
Dominik Hładun	17.09.1995	23		
Piotr Leciejewski	23.03.1985		(1)	
Defenders:	**DOB**	**M**	**(s)**	**G**
Saša Balić (MNE)	29.01.1990	28	(1)	1
Alan Czerwiński	02.02.1993	11	(5)	
Maciej Dąbrowski	20.04.1987	19	(5)	
Daniel Dziwniel (GER)	19.08.1992	11	(4)	
Lubomír Guldan (SVK)	30.01.1983	34		1
Bartosz Kopacz	21.05.1992	23	(3)	1
Damian Oko	22.01.1997	16	(1)	
Jakub Tosik	21.05.1987	15	(7)	
Midfielders:	**DOB**	**M**	**(s)**	**G**
Filip Jagiełło	08.08.1997	31	(1)	2
Jakub Mareš (CZE)	26.01.1987	4	(21)	2
Mateusz Matras	23.01.1991	1	(6)	
Adam Matuszczyk	14.02.1989	13	(2)	
Patryk Mucha	11.09.1997		(1)	
Dawid Pakulski	23.07.1998	5	(11)	1
Łukasz Poręba	13.03.2000	3	(4)	1
Bartosz Slisz	29.03.1999	21	(1)	
Filip Starzyński	27.05.1991	33		13
Forwards:	**DOB**	**M**	**(s)**	**G**
Damjan Bohar (SVN)	18.10.1991	30	(5)	10
Łukasz Janoszka	18.03.1987	6	(5)	1
Łukasz Moneta	13.05.1994		(3)	
Bartłomiej Pawłowski	13.11.1992	33	(1)	8
Vladislav Sirotov (RUS)	27.10.1991	1	(9)	
Patryk Szysz	01.04.1998	1	(4)	1
Patryk Tuszyński	13.12.1989	30	(4)	10
Paweł Żyra	07.04.1998	1		
Trainer:	**DOB**	**M**		
Mariusz Lewandowski	18.05.1979	13		
Ben van Dael (NED) [29.10.2018]	03.03.1965	24		

Zagłębie Sosnowiec Spółka Akcyjna

Founded: 1906
Stadium: Stadion Ludowy, Sosnowiec (7,500)

Goalkeepers:	DOB	M	(s)	G
Lukáš Hroššo (SVK)	19.04.1987	12		
Dawid Kudła	21.03.1992	24		
Matko Perdijić (CRO)	26.05.1982	1	(1)	
Defenders:	**DOB**	**M**	**(s)**	**G**
Mateusz Cichocki	31.01.1992	20	(2)	
Lukáš Greššák (SVK)	23.01.1989	9	(3)	
Michael Heinloth (GER)	09.02.1992	24	(5)	
Roman Janicki	24.12.2000	1		
Arkadiusz Jędrych	27.05.1992	14	(3)	
Adam Kokoszka	06.10.1986	3	(1)	
Konrad Kumor	11.04.2000		(2)	
Patrik Mráz (SVK)	01.02.1987	24	(1)	1
Georgios Mygas (GRE)	07.04.1994	15		2
Nuno Jorge Nobre Barbosa Malheiro (POR)	01.02.1994	3		
Piotr Polczak	25.09.1986	25	(3)	2
Tymoteusz Puchacz	23.01.1999	2		
Martin Tóth (SVK)	13.10.1986	11		
Žarko Udovičić (SRB)	31.08.1987	30	(3)	9
Midfielders:	**DOB**	**M**	**(s)**	**G**
Bartlomiej Babiarz	03.02.1989	8	(4)	
Adam Banasiak	07.12.1989	9	(5)	
George Ivanishvili (SUI)	18.10.1989	3	(6)	
Giácomo Mello Corbellini (BRA)	08.11.1992	1	(4)	
Sebastian Milewski	30.04.1998	17	(6)	
Mateusz Możdżeń	14.03.1991	14		3
Tomasz Nowak	30.10.1985	11	(4)	
Tomasz Pietrzak	10.03.2000	1		
Kacper Radkowski	27.03.2001	1	(1)	
Dawid Ryndak	12.03.1989	3	(4)	
Callum Rzonca (ENG)	07.01.1997	1	(4)	
Dejan Vokič (SVN)	12.06.1996	7	(8)	
Forwards:	**DOB**	**M**	**(s)**	**G**
Alexander Domingos Christovão M'Futila (ANG)	14.03.1993	10	(5)	2
Giorgi Gabedava (GEO)	03.10.1989	8	(6)	3
Tomasz Nawotka	14.02.1997	12	(4)	1
Olaf Nowak	24.02.1998	5	(9)	4
Szymon Pawłowski	04.11.1986	31	(1)	5
Vamara Sanogo (FRA)	22.04.1995	25	(4)	11
Junior Torunarigha (GER)	18.04.1990	2	(8)	
Konrad Wrzesiński	10.09.1993	20		3
Trainer:	**DOB**	**M**		
Dariusz Banasik	16.07.1973	5		
Dariusz Dudek [21.08.2018]	08.04.1975	6		
Valdas Ivanauskas (LTU) [15.10.2018]	31.07.1966	26		

SECOND LEVEL
I liga 2018/2019

1.	RKS Raków Częstochowa (*Promoted*)	34	20	10	4	54	-	22	70
2.	ŁKS Łódź (*Promoted*)	34	20	9	5	58	-	23	69
3.	FKS Stal Mielec	34	18	10	6	59	-	28	64
4.	MKS Sandecja Nowy Sącz	34	14	13	7	35	-	29	55
5.	GKS Jastrzębie-Zdrój	34	12	12	10	43	-	38	48
6.	TS Podbeskidzie Bielsko-Biała	34	13	9	12	52	-	46	48
7.	GKS Tychy	34	12	11	11	48	-	41	47
8.	Bruk-Bet Termalica Nieciecza KS	34	12	10	12	45	-	46	46
9.	MKS Puszcza Niepołomice	34	12	8	14	37	-	45	44
10.	MKS Chojniczanka Chojnice	34	10	12	12	49	-	49	42
11.	OKS Stomil Olsztyn	34	11	10	13	38	-	43	40
12.	OKS Odra Opole	34	10	10	14	47	-	58	40
13.	KS Warta Poznań	34	10	9	15	31	-	43	39
14.	MKS Chrobry Głogów	34	10	9	15	29	-	39	39
15.	SKS Wigry Suwałki	34	9	10	15	40	-	56	37
16.	MKS Bytovia Bytów (*Relegated*)	34	7	16	11	45	-	50	37
17.	GKS Katowice (*Relegated*)	34	9	10	15	34	-	45	37
18.	RKS Garbarnia Kraków (*Relegated*)	34	5	6	23	21	-	64	21

NATIONAL TEAM

INTERNATIONAL MATCHES
(16.07.2018 – 15.07.2019)

07.09.2018	Bologna	Italy - Poland	1-1(0-1)	(UNL)
11.09.2018	Wrocław	Poland - Republic of Ireland	1-1(0-0)	(F)
11.10.2018	Chorzów	Poland - Portugal	2-3(1-2)	(UNL)
14.10.2018	Chorzów	Poland - Italy	0-1(0-0)	(UNL)
15.11.2018	Gdańsk	Poland - Czech Republic	0-1(0-0)	(F)
20.11.2018	Guimarães	Portugal - Poland	1-1(1-0)	(UNL)
21.03.2019	Wien	Austria - Poland	0-1(0-0)	(ECQ)
24.03.2019	Warszawa	Poland - Latvia	2-0(0-0)	(ECQ)
07.06.2019	Skopje	North Macedonia - Poland	0-1(0-0)	(ECQ)
10.06.2019	Warszawa	Poland - Israel	4-0(1-0)	(ECQ)

07.09.2018 ITALY - POLAND 1-1(0-1) UEFA Nations League A, Group 3
Stadio "Renato Dall'Ara", Bologna; Referee: Felix Zwayer (Germany); Attendance: 24,000
POL: Łukasz Fabiański, Kamil Jacek Glik, Bartosz Bereszyński, Jan Kacper Bednarek, Jakub Błaszczykowski (80.Rafał Pietrzak), Mateusz Andrzej Klich (56.Damian Szymański), Grzegorz Krychowiak, Piotr Sebastian Zieliński (66.Karol Linetty), Arkadiusz Reca, Rafał Kurzawa, Robert Lewandowski (Cap). Trainer: Jerzy Józef Brzęczek.
Goal: Piotr Sebastian Zieliński (40).

11.09.2018 POLAND - REPUBLIC OF IRELAND 1-1(0-0) Friendly International
Stadion Miejski, Wrocław; Referee: Boris Marhefka (Slovakia); Attendance: 25,455
POL: Wojciech Tomasz Szczęsny, Kamil Jacek Glik (Cap) (61.Jan Kacper Bednarek), Marcin Kamiński, Tomasz Kędziora, Jakub Błaszczykowski (81.Przemysław Frankowski), Grzegorz Krychowiak (73.Damian Szymański), Karol Linetty, Arkadiusz Reca (72.Rafał Pietrzak), Rafał Kurzawa (46.Damian Kądzior), Arkadiusz Krystian Milik, Krzysztof Piątek (61.Mateusz Andrzej Klich). Trainer: Jerzy Józef Brzęczek.
Goal: Mateusz Andrzej Klich (87).

11.10.2018 POLAND - PORTUGAL 2-3(1-2) UEFA Nations League A, Group 3
Stadion Śląski, Chorzów; Referee: Carlos del Cerro Grande (Spain); Attendance: 48,783
POL: Łukasz Fabiański, Artur Jędrzejczyk, Kamil Jacek Glik, Bartosz Bereszyński (46.Tomasz Kędziora), Jan Kacper Bednarek, Mateusz Andrzej Klich (63.Jakub Błaszczykowski), Grzegorz Krychowiak, Piotr Sebastian Zieliński, Rafał Kurzawa (64.Kamil Grosicki), Robert Lewandowski (Cap), Krzysztof Piątek. Trainer: Jerzy Józef Brzęczek.
Goals: Krzysztof Piątek (18), Jakub Błaszczykowski (77).

14.10.2018 POLAND - ITALY 0-1(0-0) UEFA Nations League A, Group 3
Stadion Śląski, Chorzów; Referee: Damir Skomina (Slovenia); Attendance: 41,692
POL: Wojciech Tomasz Szczęsny, Kamil Jacek Glik, Bartosz Bereszyński, Jan Kacper Bednarek, Piotr Sebastian Zieliński, Jacek Góralski, Karol Linetty (46.Jakub Błaszczykowski), Arkadiusz Reca (87.Artur Jędrzejczyk), Damian Szymański (46.Kamil Grosicki), Arkadiusz Krystian Milik, Robert Lewandowski (Cap). Trainer: Jerzy Józef Brzęczek.

15.11.2018 POLAND - CZECH REPUBLIC 0-1(0-0) Friendly International
Stadion Energa, Gdańsk; Referee: Stephan Klossner (Switzerland); Attendance: 34,783
POL: Łukasz Skorupski, Marcin Kamiński, Bartosz Bereszyński, Tomasz Kędziora, Jan Kacper Bednarek, Mateusz Andrzej Klich, Grzegorz Krychowiak, Piotr Sebastian Zieliński (69.Damian Kądzior), Przemysław Frankowski (63.Jakub Błaszczykowski), Kamil Grosicki (78.Arkadiusz Krystian Milik), Robert Lewandowski (Cap). Trainer: Jerzy Józef Brzęczek.

20.11.2018 PORTUGAL - POLAND 1-1(1-0) UEFA Nations League A, Group 3
Estádio "D. Afonso Henriques", Guimarães; Referee: Sergei Karasev (Russia); Attendance: 29,917
POL: Wojciech Tomasz Szczęsny, Thiago Rangel Cionek, Bartosz Bereszyński, Tomasz Kędziora, Jan Kacper Bednarek, Mateusz Andrzej Klich (75.Jacek Góralski), Grzegorz Krychowiak, Piotr Sebastian Zieliński (90+5.Damian Szymański), Przemysław Frankowski, Kamil Grosicki (Cap) (79.Damian Kądzior), Arkadiusz Krystian Milik. Trainer: Jerzy Józef Brzęczek.
Goal: Arkadiusz Krystian Milik (66 penalty).

21.03.2019 AUSTRIA - POLAND 0-1(0-0) 16th EC. Qualifiers
"Ernst Happel" Stadion, Wien; Referee: Anastasios Sidiropoulos (Greece); Attendance: 40,400
POL: Wojciech Tomasz Szczęsny, Kamil Jacek Glik, Bartosz Bereszyński, Tomasz Kędziora, Jan Kacper Bednarek, Mateusz Andrzej Klich, Grzegorz Krychowiak, Piotr Sebastian Zieliński (59.Krzysztof Piątek), Kamil Grosicki (90+1.Michał Pazdan), Arkadiusz Krystian Milik (46.Przemysław Frankowski), Robert Lewandowski (Cap). Trainer: Jerzy Józef Brzęczek.
Goal: Krzysztof Piątek (69).

24.03.2019 POLAND - LATVIA 2-0(0-0) 16th EC. Qualifiers
Stadion Narodowy, Warszawa; Referee: Aliyar Aghayev (Azerbaijan); Attendance: 51,112
POL: Wojciech Tomasz Szczęsny, Michał Pazdan, Kamil Jacek Glik, Tomasz Kędziora, Mateusz Andrzej Klich (62.Jakub Błaszczykowski), Grzegorz Krychowiak, Piotr Sebastian Zieliński, Arkadiusz Reca, Kamil Grosicki (83.Przemysław Frankowski), Robert Lewandowski (Cap), Krzysztof Piątek (87.Arkadiusz Krystian Milik). Trainer: Jerzy Józef Brzęczek.
Goals: Robert Lewandowski (76), Kamil Jacek Glik (84).

07.06.2019 NORTH MACEDONIA - POLAND 0-1(0-0) 16th EC. Qualifiers
"Toše Proeski" National Arena, Skopje; Referee: Referee: Gianluca Rocchi (Italy); Attendance: 25,000
POL: Łukasz Fabiański, Kamil Jacek Glik, Bartosz Bereszyński, Tomasz Kędziora, Jan Kacper Bednarek, Mateusz Andrzej Klich (90.Jacek Góralski), Grzegorz Krychowiak, Piotr Sebastian Zieliński, Przemysław Frankowski (46.Krzysztof Piątek), Kamil Grosicki (69.Maciej Rybus), Robert Lewandowski (Cap). Trainer: Jerzy Józef Brzęczek.
Goal: Krzysztof Piątek (47).

10.06.2019 POLAND - ISRAEL 4-0(1-0) 16th EC. Qualifiers

Stadion Narodowy, Warszawa; Referee: Tobias Stieler (Germany); Attendance: 57,229

POL: Łukasz Fabiański, Kamil Jacek Glik, Bartosz Bereszyński, Tomasz Kędziora, Jan Kacper Bednarek, Mateusz Andrzej Klich (75.Jacek Góralski), Grzegorz Krychowiak, Piotr Sebastian Zieliński, Kamil Grosicki (77.Damian Kądzior), Robert Lewandowski (Cap), Krzysztof Piątek (73.Arkadiusz Krystian Milik). Trainer: Jerzy Józef Brzęczek.

Goals: Krzysztof Piątek (35), Robert Lewandowski (56 penalty), Kamil Grosicki (59), Damian Kądzior (84).

NATIONAL TEAM PLAYERS
(16.07.2018 – 15.07.2019)

Name	DOB	Caps	Goals	2018/2019:	*Club*
Goalkeepers					
Łukasz FABIAŃSKI	18.04.1985	**50**	**0**	2018/2019:	*West Ham United FC London (ENG)*
Łukasz SKORUPSKI	05.05.1991	**3**	**0**	2018:	*Bologna FC 1909 (ITA)*
Wojciech Tomasz SZCZĘSNY	18.04.1990	**42**	**0**	2018/2019:	*Juventus FC Torino (ITA)*
Defenders					
Jan Kacper BEDNAREK	12.04.1996	**15**	**1**	2018/2019:	*Southampton FC (ENG)*
Bartosz BERESZYŃSKI	12.07.1992	**19**	**0**	2018/2019:	*UC Sampdoria Genova (ITA)*
Thiago Rangel CIONEK	21.04.1986	**21**	**0**	2018:	*SPAL Ferrara (ITA)*
Kamil Jacel GLIK	03.02.1988	**68**	**5**	2018/2019:	*AS Monaco FC (FRA)*
Artur JĘDRZEJCZYK	04.11.1987	**39**	**3**	2018:	*Legia Warszawa*
Marcin KAMIŃSKI	15.01.1992	**7**	**0**	2018:	*TSV Fortuna Düsseldorf (GER)*
Tomasz KĘDZIORA	11.06.1994	**11**	**0**	2018/2019:	*FK Dynamo Kyiv (UKR)*
Michał PAZDAN	21.09.1987	**38**	**0**	2019:	*MKE Ankaragücü SK (TUR)*
Rafał PIETRZAK	30.01.1992	**2**	**0**	2018:	*Wisła Kraków*
Arkadiusz RECA	17.06.1995	**4**	**0**	2018:	*Atalanta Bergamasca Calcio (ITA)*
Maciej RYBUS	19.08.1989	**54**	**2**	2019:	*FK Lokomotiv Moscow (RUS)*
Midfielders					
Jakub BŁASZCZYKOWSKI	14.12.1985	**106**	**21**	2018: 07.02.2019->	*VfL Wolfsburg (GER)* *Wisła Kraków*
Przemysław FRANKOWSKI	12.04.1995	**7**	**0**	2018: 22.01.2019->	*Jagiellonia Białystok* *Chicago Fire SC (USA)*
Jacek GÓRALSKI	21.09.1992	**11**	**0**	2018/2019:	*PFC Ludogorets Razgrad (BUL)*
Kamil GROSICKI	08.06.1988	**68**	**13**	2018/2019:	*Hull City AFC (ENG)*
Damian KĄDZIOR	16.06.1992	**4**	**0**	2018/2019:	*GNK Dinamo Zagreb (CRO)*
Mateusz Andrzej KLICH	13.06.1990	**19**	**2**	2018/2019:	*Leeds United FC (ENG)*
Grzegorz KRYCHOWIAK	29.01.1990	**63**	**3**	2018/2019:	*FK Lokomotiv Moskva (RUS)*
Rafał KURZAWA	29.01.1993	**7**	**0**	2018:	*Amiens SC (FRA)*
Karol LINETTY	02.02.1995	**23**	**1**	2018:	*UC Sampdoria Genova (ITA)*
Damian SZYMAŃSKI	16.06.1995	**4**	**0**	2018:	*Wisła Płock*
Piotr Sebastian ZIELIŃSKI	20.05.1994	**45**	**6**	2018/2019:	*SSC Napoli (ITA)*
Forwards					
Robert LEWANDOWSKI	21.08.1988	**106**	**57**	2018/2019:	*FC Bayern München (GER)*
Arkadiusz Krystian MILIK	28.02.1994	**48**	**13**	2018/2019:	*SSC Napoli (ITA)*
Krzysztof PIĄTEK	01.07.1995	**6**	**4**	2018: 23.01.2019->	*Genoa C&FC* *AC Milan (ITA)*

National team coach

Jerzy Józef BRZĘCZEK [from 12.07.2018]	18.03.1971	10 M; 4 W; 3 D; 3 L; 13-8

PORTUGAL

The Country:
República Portuguesa (Portuguese Republic)
Capital: Lisboa
Surface: 92,212 km²
Inhabitants: 10,276,617 [2018]
Time: UTC

The FA:
Federação Portuguesa de Futebol
Avenida das Seleções 1495-433 Cruz Quebrada - Dafundo
Tel: +351 21 325 2700
Founded: 31.03.1914
Member of FIFA since: 1923
Member of UEFA since: 1954
Website: www.fpf.pt

NATIONAL TEAM RECORDS

First international match:	18.12.1921, Madrid: Spain – Portugal 3-1(2-0)	
Most international caps:	Cristiano Ronaldo dos Santos Aveiro	- 158 caps (since 2003)
Most international goals:	Cristiano Ronaldo dos Santos Aveiro	- 88 goals / 158 caps (since 2003)

UEFA EUROPEAN CHAMPIONSHIP	
1960	Qualifiers
1964	Qualifiers
1968	Qualifiers
1972	Qualifiers
1976	Qualifiers
1980	Qualifiers
1984	Final Tournament (Semi-Finals)
1988	Qualifiers
1992	Qualifiers
1996	Final Tournament (Quarter-Finals)
2000	Final Tournament (Semi-Finals)
2004	Final Tournament (Runners-up)
2008	Final Tournament (Quarter-Finals)
2012	Final Tournament (Semi-Finals)
2016	**Final Tournament (Winners)**

FIFA WORLD CUP	
1930	Did not enter
1934	Qualifiers
1938	Qualifiers
1950	Qualifiers
1954	Qualifiers
1958	Qualifiers
1962	Qualifiers
1966	Final Tournament (3rd Place)
1970	Qualifiers
1974	Qualifiers
1978	Qualifiers
1982	Qualifiers
1986	Final Tournament (Group Stage)
1990	Qualifiers
1994	Qualifiers
1998	Qualifiers
2002	Final Tournament (Group Stage)
2006	Final Tournament (4th Place)
2010	Final Tournament (2nd Round of 16)
2014	Final Tournament (Group Stage)
2018	Final Tournament (2nd Round of 16)

UEFA NATIONS LEAGUE
2018/2019 – League A; Final Tournament – **Winners**

OLYMPIC FOOTBALL TOURNAMENTS 1908-2016							
1908	-	**1948**	Did not enter	**1972**	Did not enter	**1996**	4th Place
1912	-	**1952**	Did not enter	**1976**	Did not enter	**2000**	Qualifiers
1920	-	**1956**	Did not enter	**1980**	Did not enter	**2004**	Group Stage
1924	-	**1960**	Did not enter	**1984**	Qualifiers	**2008**	Qualifiers
1928	Quarter-Finals	**1964**	Did not enter	**1988**	Qualifiers	**2012**	Qualifiers
1936	Did not enter	**1968**	Did not enter	**1992**	Qualifiers	**2016**	Quarter-Finals

FIFA CONFEDERATIONS CUP 1992-2017
2017 (3rd Place)

PORTUGUESE CLUB HONOURS IN EUROPEAN CLUB COMPETITIONS:

European Champion Clubs.Cup (1956-1992) / UEFA Champions League (1993-2019)		
Sport Lisboa e Benfica	**2**	1960/1961, 1961/1962
FC do Porto	**2**	1986/1987, 2003/2004
Fairs Cup (1858-1971) / UEFA Cup (1972-2009) / UEFA Europa League (2010-2019)		
FC do Porto	**2**	2002/2003, 2010/2011
UEFA Super Cup (1972-2018)		
FC do Porto	**1**	1987
European Cup Winners.Cup 1961-1999*		
Sporting Clube de Portugal Lisboa	**1**	1963/1964

**defunct competition*

NATIONAL COMPETITIONS
TABLE OF HONOURS

Campeonato de Portugal (1922–1938)*

*created in 1922 and played in cup system, with all the clubs participating in elimination rounds, the winners were named Champions of Portugal. The league sytem started in 1934.

	CHAMPIONS
1922	FC do Porto
1922/1923	Sporting Clube de Portugal Lisboa
1923/1924	SC Olhanense
1924/1925	FC do Porto
1925/1926	CS Marítimo Funchal
1926/1927	CF Os Belenenses Lisboa
1927/1928	Carcavelinhos FC
1928/1929	CF Os Belenenses Lisboa
1929/1930	Sport Lisboa e Benfica
1930/1931	Sport Lisboa e Benfica
1931/1932	FC do Porto
1932/1933	CF Os Belenenses Lisboa
1933/1934	Sporting Clube de Portugal Lisboa
1934/1935	Sport Lisboa e Benfica
1935/1936	Sporting Clube de Portugal Lisboa
1936/1937	FC do Porto
1937/1938	Sporting Clube de Portugal Lisboa

	CHAMPIONS*	CUP WINNERS	BEST GOALSCORERS	
1934/1935	FC do Porto	-	Manuel Esteves Soeiro Vasques (Sporting Clube de Portugal Lisboa)	14
1935/1936	Sport Lisboa e Benfica	-	Artur de Sousa "Pinga" (FC do Porto)	21
1936/1937	Sport Lisboa e Benfica	-	Manuel Esteves Soeiro Vasques (Sporting Clube de Portugal Lisboa)	24
1937/1938	Sport Lisboa e Benfica	-	Fernando Baptista de Seixas Peyroteo de Vasconcelos (Sporting Clube de Portugal Lisboa)	34
1938/1939	FC do Porto	Associação Académica de Coimbra	José Monteiro "Costuras" (FC do Porto)	18
1939/1940	FC do Porto	Sport Lisboa e Benfica	Fernando Baptista de Seixas Peyroteo de Vasconcelos (Sporting Clube de Portugal Lisboa) Slavko Kodrnja (CRO, FC do Porto)	29
1940/1941	Sporting Clube de Portugal Lisboa	Sporting Clube de Portugal Lisboa	Fernando Baptista de Seixas Peyroteo de Vasconcelos (Sporting Clube de Portugal Lisboa)	29
1941/1942	Sport Lisboa e Benfica	CF Os Belenenses Lisboa	Manuel BeloCorreia Dias (FC do Porto)	36
1942/1943	Sport Lisboa e Benfica	Sport Lisboa e Benfica	Júlio Correia da Silva "Julinho" (Sport Lisboa e Benfica)	24
1943/1944	Sporting Clube de Portugal Lisboa	Sport Lisboa e Benfica	Francisco Rodrigues (Vitória FC Setúbal)	28
1944/1945	Sport Lisboa e Benfica	Sporting Clube de Portugal Lisboa	Francisco Rodrigues (Vitória FC Setúbal)	21
1945/1946	CF Os Belenenses Lisboa	Sporting Clube de Portugal Lisboa	Fernando Baptista de Seixas Peyroteo de Vasconcelos (Sporting Clube de Portugal Lisboa)	37
1946/1947	Sporting Clube de Portugal Lisboa	*No competition*	Fernando Baptista de Seixas Peyroteo de Vasconcelos (Sporting Clube de Portugal Lisboa)	43
1947/1948	Sporting Clube de Portugal Lisboa	Sporting Clube de Portugal Lisboa	António Araújo (FC do Porto)	36
1948/1949	Sporting Clube de Portugal Lisboa	Sport Lisboa e Benfica	Fernando Baptista de Seixas Peyroteo de Vasconcelos (Sporting Clube de Portugal Lisboa)	40
1949/1950	Sport Lisboa e Benfica	*No competition*	Júlio Correia da Silva "Julinho" (Sport Lisboa e Benfica)	29
1950/1951	Sporting Clube de Portugal Lisboa	Sport Lisboa e Benfica	Manuel Soeiro Vasques (Sporting Clube de Portugal Lisboa)	29
1951/1952	Sporting Clube de Portugal Lisboa	Sport Lisboa e Benfica	José Pinto de Carvalho Santos Águas (Sport Lisboa e Benfica)	28
1952/1953	Sporting Clube de Portugal Lisboa	Sport Lisboa e Benfica	Sebastião Lucas da Fonseca „Matateu" (CF Os Belenenses Lisboa)	29
1953/1954	Sporting Clube de Portugal Lisboa	Sporting Clube de Portugal Lisboa	João Baptista Martins (Sporting Clube de Portugal Lisboa)	31
1954/1955	Sport Lisboa e Benfica	Sport Lisboa e Benfica	Sebastião Lucas da Fonseca „Matateu" (CF Os Belenenses Lisboa)	32
1955/1956	FC do Porto	FC do Porto	José Pinto de Carvalho Santos Águas (Sport Lisboa e Benfica)	28
1956/1957	Sport Lisboa e Benfica	Sport Lisboa e Benfica	José Pinto de Carvalho Santos Águas (Sport Lisboa e Benfica)	30
1957/1958	Sporting Clube de Portugal Lisboa	FC do Porto	Arsénio Trindade Duarte (GD CUF do Barreiro)	23
1958/1959	FC do Porto	Sport Lisboa e Benfica	José Pinto de Carvalho Santos Águas (Sport Lisboa e Benfica)	26
1959/1960	Sport Lisboa e Benfica	CF Os Belenenses Lisboa	Edmur Pinto Ribeiro (Vitória SC Guimarães)	25

1960/1961	Sport Lisboa e Benfica	Leixões SC Porto	José Pinto de Carvalho Santos Águas (Sport Lisboa e Benfica)	27
1961/1962	Sporting Clube de Portugal Lisboa	Sport Lisboa e Benfica	Azumir Luis Casimiro Veríssimo (BRA, FC do Porto)	23
1962/1963	Sport Lisboa e Benfica	Sporting Clube de Portugal Lisboa	José Augusto Costa Sénica Torres (Sport Lisboa e Benfica)	26
1963/1964	Sport Lisboa e Benfica	Sport Lisboa e Benfica	Eusébio da Silva Ferreira (Sport Lisboa e Benfica)	28
1964/1965	Sport Lisboa e Benfica	Vitória FC Setúbal	Eusébio da Silva Ferreira (Sport Lisboa e Benfica)	28
1965/1966	Sporting Clube de Portugal Lisboa	Sporting Clube de Braga	Eusébio da Silva Ferreira (Sport Lisboa e Benfica) Ernesto de Figueiredo (Sporting Clube de Portugal Lisboa)	25
1966/1967	Sport Lisboa e Benfica	Vitória FC Setúbal	Eusébio da Silva Ferreira (Sport Lisboa e Benfica)	31
1967/1968	Sport Lisboa e Benfica	FC do Porto	Eusébio da Silva Ferreira (Sport Lisboa e Benfica)	43
1968/1969	Sport Lisboa e Benfica	Sport Lisboa e Benfica	Manuel António Leitão da Silva (Associação Académica de Coimbra)	19
1969/1970	Sporting Clube de Portugal Lisboa	Sport Lisboa e Benfica	Eusébio da Silva Ferreira (Sport Lisboa e Benfica)	20
1970/1971	Sport Lisboa e Benfica	Sporting Clube de Portugal Lisboa	Artur Jorge Braga Melo Teixeira (Sport Lisboa e Benfica)	23
1971/1972	Sport Lisboa e Benfica	Sport Lisboa e Benfica	Artur Jorge Braga Melo Teixeira (Sport Lisboa e Benfica)	27
1972/1973	Sport Lisboa e Benfica	Sporting Clube de Portugal Lisboa	Eusébio da Silva Ferreira (Sport Lisboa e Benfica)	40
1973/1974	Sporting Clube de Portugal Lisboa	Sporting Clube de Portugal Lisboa	Héctor Casimiro Yazalde (ARG, Sporting Clube de Portugal Lisboa)	46
1974/1975	Sport Lisboa e Benfica	Boavista FC do Porto	Héctor Casimiro Yazalde (ARG, Sporting Clube de Portugal Lisboa)	30
1975/1976	Sport Lisboa e Benfica	Boavista FC do Porto	Rui Manuel Trindade Jordão (Sport Lisboa e Benfica)	30
1976/1977	Sport Lisboa e Benfica	FC do Porto	Fernando Mendes Soares Gomes (FC do Porto)	26
1977/1978	FC do Porto	Sporting Clube de Portugal Lisboa	Fernando Mendes Soares Gomes (FC do Porto)	25
1978/1979	FC do Porto	Boavista FC do Porto	Fernando Mendes Soares Gomes (FC do Porto)	27
1979/1980	Sporting Clube de Portugal Lisboa	Sport Lisboa e Benfica	Rui Manuel Trindade Jordão (Sporting Clube de Portugal Lisboa)	31
1980/1981	Sport Lisboa e Benfica	Sport Lisboa e Benfica	Tamagnini Manuel Gomes Batista "Nené" (Sport Lisboa e Benfica)	20
1981/1982	Sporting Clube de Portugal Lisboa	Sporting Clube de Portugal Lisboa	Jacques Pereira (FC do Porto)	27
1982/1983	Sport Lisboa e Benfica	Sport Lisboa e Benfica	Fernando Mendes Soares Gomes (FC do Porto)	36
1983/1984	Sport Lisboa e Benfica	FC do Porto	Fernando Mendes Soares Gomes (FC do Porto) Tamagnini Manuel Gomes Batista "Nené" (Sport Lisboa e Benfica)	21
1984/1985	FC do Porto	Sport Lisboa e Benfica	Fernando Mendes Soares Gomes (FC do Porto)	39
1985/1986	FC do Porto	Sport Lisboa e Benfica	Manuel José Tavares Fernandes (Sporting Clube de Portugal Lisboa)	30
1986/1987	Sport Lisboa e Benfica	Sport Lisboa e Benfica	Paulo Roberto Bacinello "Paulinho Cascavel" (BRA, Vitória SC Guimarães)	22
1987/1988	FC do Porto	FC do Porto	Paulo Roberto Bacinello "Paulinho Cascavel" (BRA, Sporting Clube de Portugal Lisboa)	23
1988/1989	Sport Lisboa e Benfica	CF Os Belenenses Lisboa	Vata Matanu Garcia (ANG, Sport Lisboa e Benfica)	16
1989/1990	FC do Porto	CF Estrela da Amadora	Mats Magnusson (SWE, Sport Lisboa e Benfica)	33
1990/1991	Sport Lisboa e Benfica	FC do Porto	José Rui Lopes Águas (Sport Lisboa e Benfica)	25
1991/1992	FC do Porto	Boavista FC do Porto	Richard Daddy Owubokiri (NGA, Boavista FC do Porto)	30
1992/1993	FC do Porto	Sport Lisboa e Benfica	Jorge Paulo Cadete Santos Reis (Sporting Clube de Portugal Lisboa)	18
1993/1994	Sport Lisboa e Benfica	FC do Porto	Rashidi Yekini (NGA, Vitória FC Setúbal)	21
1994/1995	FC do Porto	Sporting Clube de Portugal Lisboa	Hassan Nader (MAR, SC Farense)	21
1995/1996	FC do Porto	Sport Lisboa e Benfica	Domingos José Paciência Oliveira (FC do Porto)	25
1996/1997	FC do Porto	Boavista FC do Porto	Mário Jardel de Almeida Ribeiro (BRA, FC do Porto)	30
1997/1998	FC do Porto	FC do Porto	Mário Jardel de Almeida Ribeiro (BRA, FC do Porto)	26
1998/1999	FC do Porto	SC Beira-Mar Aveiro	Mário Jardel de Almeida Ribeiro (BRA, FC do Porto)	36
1999/2000	Sporting Clube de Portugal Lisboa	FC do Porto	Mário Jardel de Almeida Ribeiro (BRA, FC do Porto)	37
2000/2001	Boavista FC do Porto	FC do Porto	Renivaldo Pereira de Jesus "Pena" (BRA, FC do Porto)	22
2001/2002	Sporting Clube de Portugal Lisboa	Sporting Clube de Portugal Lisboa	Mário Jardel de Almeida Ribeiro (BRA, Sporting Clube de Portugal Lisboa)	42
2002/2003	FC do Porto	FC do Porto	Fary Faye (SEN, SC Beira-Mar Aveiro)	18
2003/2004	FC do Porto	Sport Lisboa e Benfica	Benedict Saul McCarthy (RSA, FC do Porto)	20
2004/2005	Sport Lisboa e Benfica	Vitória FC Setúbal	Liédson da Silva Muniz (BRA, Sporting Clube de Portugal Lisboa)	25
2005/2006	FC do Porto	FC do Porto	Albert Meyong Zé (CMR, CF Os Belenenses Lisboa)	17
2006/2007	FC do Porto	Sporting Clube de Portugal Lisboa	Liédson da Silva Muniz (BRA, Sporting Clube de Portugal Lisboa)	15
2007/2008	FC do Porto	Sporting Clube de Portugal Lisboa	Lisandro López (ARG, FC do Porto)	24
2008/2009	FC do Porto	FC do Porto	Ânderson Miguel da Silva "Nenê" (BRA, CD Nacional Funchal)	20

2009/2010	Sport Lisboa e Benfica	FC do Porto	Óscar René Cardozo Marín (PAR, Sport Lisboa e Benfica)	26
2010/2011	FC do Porto	FC do Porto	Givanildo Vieira de Sousa "Hulk" (BRA, FC do Porto)	23
2011/2012	FC do Porto	Associação Académica de Coimbra	Óscar René Cardozo Marín (PAR, Sport Lisboa e Benfica)	20
2012/2013	FC do Porto	Vitória SC Guimarães	Jackson Arley Martínez Valencia (COL, FC do Porto)	26
2013/2014	Sport Lisboa e Benfica	Sport Lisboa e Benfica	Jackson Arley Martínez Valencia (COL, FC do Porto)	20
2014/2015	Sport Lisboa e Benfica	Sporting Clube de Portugal Lisboa	Jackson Arley Martínez Valencia (COL, FC do Porto)	21
2015/2016	Sport Lisboa e Benfica	Sporting Clube de Braga	Jonas Gonçalves Oliveira (BRA, Sport Lisboa e Benfica)	32
2016/2017	Sport Lisboa e Benfica	Sport Lisboa e Benfica	Bas Dost (NED, Sporting Clube de Portugal Lisboa)	34
2017/2018	FC do Porto	Desportivo das Aves	Jonas Gonçalves Oliveira (BRA, Sport Lisboa e Benfica)	34
2018/2019	Sport Lisboa e Benfica	Sporting Clube de Portugal Lisboa	Haris Seferović (SUI, Sport Lisboa e Benfica)	23

*Please note: Campeonato da Liga da Primeira Divisão (1934-1938), Campeonato Nacional da Primeira Divisão (1938-1999), Primeira Liga (since 1999).

NATIONAL CHAMPIONSHIP

Primeira Liga 2018/2019

(10.08.2018 – 19.05.2019)

Results

Round 1 [10-13.08.2018]
Benfica - Vitória Guimarães 3-2(3-0)
Vitória Setúbal - CD Aves 2-0(1-0)
CD Tondela - Belenenses 0-1(0-0)
FC Porto - GD Chaves 5-0(3-0)
CS Marítimo - Santa Clara 1-0(0-0)
CD Feirense - Rio Ave FC 2-0(2-0)
Moreirense FC - Sporting 1-3(1-1)
Sporting Braga - Nacional Funchal 4-2(2-2)
Portimonense SC - Boavista 0-2(0-0)

Round 2 [17-20.08.2018]
CD Aves - CD Tondela 2-2(1-1)
GD Chaves - Portimonense SC 2-0(2-0)
Boavista - Benfica 0-2(0-1)
Sporting - Vitória Setúbal 2-1(1-1)
Rio Ave FC - CS Marítimo 3-1(2-0)
Nacional Funchal - Moreirense FC 1-2(0-1)
Belenenses - FC Porto 2-3(0-1)
Santa Clara - Sporting Braga 3-3(0-3)
Vitória Guimarães - CD Feirense 0-1(0-0)

Round 3 [24-27.08.2018]
CS Marítimo - GD Chaves 2-1(0-1)
Portimonense SC - Santa Clara 2-2(0-1)
Benfica - Sporting 1-1(0-0)
FC Porto - Vitória Guimarães 2-3(2-0)
Vitória Setúbal - Nacional Funchal 1-2(0-1)
CD Feirense - Boavista 1-1(0-1)
CD Tondela - Rio Ave FC 1-1(0-1)
Sporting Braga - CD Aves 3-1(0-0)
Moreirense FC - Belenenses 1-1(0-0)

Round 4 [31.08.-02.09.2018]
GD Chaves - Sporting Braga 0-1(0-1)
Vitória Guimarães - CD Tondela 1-0(1-0)
Belenenses - Vitória Setúbal 0-0
Santa Clara - Boavista 4-2(1-1)
Sporting - CD Feirense 1-0(0-0)
Rio Ave FC - Portimonense SC 2-1(0-1)
CD Aves - CS Marítimo 0-1(0-1)
Nacional Funchal - Benfica 0-4(0-2)
FC Porto - Moreirense FC 3-0(2-0)

Round 5 [21-24.09.2018]
Boavista - GD Chaves 1-2(0-1)
Santa Clara - Rio Ave FC 1-3(0-0)
CS Marítimo - Belenenses 0-0
Vitória Setúbal - FC Porto 0-2(0-1)
CD Tondela - Moreirense FC 2-0(1-0)
CD Feirense - Nacional Funchal 0-0
Benfica - CD Aves 2-0(1-0)
Portimonense SC - Vitória Guimarães 3-2(1-0)
Sporting Braga - Sporting 1-0(0-0)

Round 6 [27.09.-01.10.2018]
GD Chaves - Benfica 2-2(0-1)
FC Porto - CD Tondela 1-0(0-0)
Moreirense FC - CD Feirense 1-0(0-0)
Rio Ave FC - Boavista 2-1(2-0)
Sporting - CS Marítimo 2-0(2-0)
Nacional Funchal - Santa Clara 0-3(0-1)
Vitória Guimarães - Vitória Setúbal 1-1(0-0)
Belenenses - Sporting Braga 0-3(0-2)
CD Aves - Portimonense SC 3-0(1-0)

Round 7 [05-07.10.2018]
CD Tondela - Nacional Funchal 1-1(0-0)
Santa Clara - GD Chaves 1-0(0-0)
CD Feirense - Belenenses 0-0
Vitória Setúbal - Moreirense FC 3-0(1-0)
CS Marítimo - Vitória Guimarães 1-3(0-1)
Sporting Braga - Rio Ave FC 1-1(1-1)
Boavista - CD Aves 1-0(0-0)
Benfica - FC Porto 1-0(0-0)
Portimonense SC - Sporting 4-2(2-0)

Round 8 [26-28.10.2018]
Nacional Funchal - Portimonense SC 0-1(0-1)
Vitória Guimarães - Sporting Braga 1-1(1-1)
CD Aves - Santa Clara 1-2(0-2)
Rio Ave FC - GD Chaves 1-0(0-0)
Belenenses - Benfica 2-0(2-0)
Moreirense FC - CS Marítimo 1-0(0-0)
CD Tondela - Vitória Setúbal 1-2(0-1)
FC Porto - CD Feirense 2-0(1-0)
Sporting - Boavista 3-0(1-0)

Round 9 [02-05.11.2018]
Benfica - Moreirense FC 1-3(1-3)
Portimonense SC - Belenenses 1-1(0-0)
CS Marítimo - FC Porto 0-2(0-0)
Boavista - Vitória Guimarães 0-0
CD Feirense - CD Tondela 2-4(1-1)
Santa Clara - Sporting 1-2(1-0)
Sporting Braga - Vitória Setúbal 2-1(2-1)
Rio Ave FC - Nacional Funchal 3-3(2-1)
GD Chaves - CD Aves 1-2(0-1)

Round 10 [09-11.11.2018]
Moreirense FC - Portimonense SC 2-0(1-0)
Vitória Setúbal - CD Feirense 2-1(1-1)
Belenenses - Boavista 0-0
CD Aves - Rio Ave FC 2-1(2-0)
Nacional Funchal - CS Marítimo 1-0(0-0)
FC Porto - Sporting Braga 1-0(0-0)
Vitória Guimarães - Santa Clara 2-0(1-0)
CD Tondela - Benfica 1-3(1-1)
Sporting - GD Chaves 2-1(1-0)

Round 11 [30.11.-03.12.2018]
Santa Clara - Belenenses 2-3(1-1)
CS Marítimo - Vitória Setúbal 0-1(0-0)
Benfica - CD Feirense 4-0(0-0)
Sporting Braga - Moreirense FC 2-0(2-0)
Portimonense SC - CD Tondela 3-2(3-1)
CD Aves - Nacional Funchal 2-3(1-1)
GD Chaves - Vitória Guimarães 0-1(0-1)
Boavista - FC Porto 0-1(0-0)
Rio Ave FC - Sporting 1-3(1-2)

Round 12 [07-10.12.2018]
FC Porto - Portimonense SC 4-1(1-1)
Belenenses - GD Chaves 1-0(1-0)
CD Tondela - Sporting Braga 0-1(0-1)
Vitória Setúbal - Benfica 0-1(0-1)
Nacional Funchal - Boavista 0-0
Moreirense FC - Santa Clara 0-1(0-0)
Vitória Guimarães - Rio Ave FC 3-2(2-1)
Sporting - CD Aves 4-1(2-1)
CD Feirense - CS Marítimo 1-1(0-0)

Round 13 [14-16.12.2018]
Portimonense SC - Vitória Setúbal 3-1(2-0)
Sporting Braga - CD Feirense 4-0(2-0)
GD Chaves - Moreirense FC 1-2(0-0)
Boavista - CD Tondela 2-0(2-0)
CD Aves - Vitória Guimarães 1-1(1-1)
Santa Clara - FC Porto 1-2(1-1)
Rio Ave FC - Belenenses 2-2(1-0)
CS Marítimo - Benfica 0-1(0-1)
Sporting - Nacional Funchal 5-2(1-2)

Round 14 [22-23.12.2018]
Vitória Setúbal - Santa Clara 0-2(0-1)
CD Tondela - CS Marítimo 2-1(1-1)
CD Feirense - Portimonense SC 0-1(0-0)
Belenenses - CD Aves 5-2(2-2)
Moreirense FC - Boavista 2-1(2-1)
Nacional Funchal - GD Chaves 2-0(1-0)
FC Porto - Rio Ave FC 2-1(2-1)
Benfica - Sporting Braga 6-2(2-0)
Vitória Guimarães - Sporting 1-0(1-0)

Round 15 [02-03.01.2019]
Santa Clara - CD Tondela 1-2(0-0)
Nacion. Funchal - Vitória Guimarães 1-0(1-0)
Boavista - Vitória Setúbal 1-0(0-0)
Sporting Braga - CS Marítimo 2-0(2-0)
Portimonense SC - Benfica 2-0(2-0)
Rio Ave FC - Moreirense FC 1-2(1-0)
GD Chaves - CD Feirense 0-0
Sporting - Belenenses 2-1(0-0)
CD Aves - FC Porto 0-1(0-1)

Round 16 [05-07.01.2019]
CS Marítimo - Portimonense SC 2-1(1-0)
Vitória Setúbal - GD Chaves 0-0
CD Feirense - Santa Clara 2-2(0-1)
Belenenses - Vitória Guimarães 1-0(1-0)
Benfica - Rio Ave FC 4-2(2-2)
Sporting Braga - Boavista 1-0(1-0)
Moreirense FC - CD Aves 1-0(0-0)
CD Tondela - Sporting 2-1(1-0)
FC Porto - Nacional Funchal 3-1(2-1)

Round 17 [10-13.01.2019]
Portimonense SC - Sporting Braga 1-1(1-0)
Santa Clara - Benfica 0-2(0-1)
CD Aves - CD Feirense 1-1(1-0)
Vitória Guimarães - Moreirense FC 1-0(0-0)
Sporting - FC Porto 0-0
Boavista - CS Marítimo 0-1(0-0)
Nacional Funchal - Belenenses 0-1(0-0)
GD Chaves - CD Tondela 2-1(1-0)
Rio Ave FC - Vitória Setúbal 1-1(1-0)

Round 18 [18-20.01.2019]
Nacional Funchal - Sporting Braga 0-3(0-0)
GD Chaves - FC Porto 1-4(0-2)
Vitória Guimarães - Benfica 0-1(0-0)
Belenenses - CD Tondela 2-2(1-2)
Sporting - Moreirense FC 2-1(2-1)
Santa Clara - CS Marítimo 0-1(0-1)
CD Aves - Vitória Setúbal 2-1(1-0)
Boavista - Portimonense SC 0-2(0-1)
Rio Ave FC - CD Feirense 0-0

Round 19 [28-30.01.2019]
CS Marítimo - Rio Ave FC 0-2(0-0)
Moreirense FC - Nacional Funchal 2-1(1-0)
CD Tondela - CD Aves 0-2(0-0)
CD Feirense - Vitória Guimarães 1-2(1-2)
Portimonense SC - GD Chaves 0-1(0-1)
Benfica - Boavista 5-1(2-1)
Sporting Braga - Santa Clara 1-0(0-0)
Vitória Setúbal - Sporting 1-1(1-0)
FC Porto - Belenenses 3-0(2-0)

Round 20 [01-04.02.2019]
Rio Ave FC - CD Tondela 2-2(1-1)
GD Chaves - CS Marítimo 1-0(0-0)
Boavista - CD Feirense 2-0(0-0)
CD Aves - Sporting Braga 0-2(0-0)
Santa Clara - Portimonense SC 2-1(1-1)
Nacional Funchal - Vitória Setúbal 0-0
Sporting - Benfica 2-4(1-2)
Vitória Guimarães - FC Porto 0-0
Belenenses - Moreirense FC 0-1(0-0)

Round 21 [08-11.02.2019]
Moreirense FC - FC Porto 1-1(0-0)
CS Marítimo - CD Aves 0-1(0-1)
Portimonense SC - Rio Ave FC 0-1(0-1)
CD Tondela - Vitória Guimarães 1-0(0-0)
Sporting Braga - GD Chaves 2-1(0-0)
Boavista - Santa Clara 1-0(0-0)
Benfica - Nacional Funchal 10-0(3-0)
CD Feirense - Sporting 1-3(0-1)
Vitória Setúbal - Belenenses 0-0

Round 22 [15-18.02.2019]
Rio Ave FC - Santa Clara 1-2(1-1)
Nacional Funchal - CD Feirense 4-0(1-0)
Vitória Guimarães - Portimonense SC 2-0(1-0)
FC Porto - Vitória Setúbal 2-0(1-0)
Moreirense FC - CD Tondela 2-0(1-0)
Belenenses - CS Marítimo 0-1(0-0)
GD Chaves - Boavista 1-1(1-0)
Sporting - Sporting Braga 3-0(1-0)
CD Aves - Benfica 0-3(0-2)

Round 23 [22-25.02.2019]
Sporting Braga - Belenenses 0-2(0-1)
CD Tondela - FC Porto 0-3(0-1)
CD Feirense - Moreirense FC 1-3(0-2)
Portimonense SC - CD Aves 1-1(0-1)
Vitória Setúbal - Vitória Guimarães 1-1(0-1)
Santa Clara - Nacional Funchal 2-0(0-0)
Boavista - Rio Ave FC 1-0(1-0)
CS Marítimo - Sporting 0-0
Benfica - GD Chaves 4-0(3-0)

Round 24 [01-04.03.2019]
CD Aves - Boavista 2-0(0-0)
Nacional Funchal - CD Tondela 3-2(1-1)
Moreirense FC - Vitória Setúbal 1-1(1-1)
FC Porto - Benfica 1-2(1-1)
GD Chaves - Santa Clara 0-0
Belenenses - CD Feirense 4-0(2-0)
Rio Ave FC - Sporting Braga 1-2(0-0)
Sporting - Portimonense SC 3-1(2-1)
Vitória Guimarães - CS Marítimo 1-0(0-0)

Round 25 [08-11.03.2019]
GD Chaves - Rio Ave FC 1-1(0-1)
CS Marítimo - Moreirense FC 3-2(1-2)
Sporting Braga - Vitória Guimarães 1-0(1-0)
Boavista - Sporting 1-2(1-1)
Santa Clara - CD Aves 0-0
Portimonense SC - Nacional Funchal 5-1(3-0)
Vitória Setúbal - CD Tondela 0-0
CD Feirense - FC Porto 1-2(1-2)
Benfica - Belenenses 2-2(0-0)

Round 26 [15-17.03.2019]
Sporting - Santa Clara 1-0(0-0)
Belenenses - Portimonense SC 2-2(0-2)
Vitória Setúbal - Sporting Braga 0-1(0-1)
Vitória Guimarães - Boavista 3-1(1-0)
FC Porto - CS Marítimo 3-0(0-0)
CD Aves - GD Chaves 0-1(0-1)
Nacional Funchal - Rio Ave FC 0-1(0-1)
Moreirense FC - Benfica 0-4(0-2)
CD Tondela - CD Feirense 1-1(0-1)

Round 27 [29.03.-01.04.2019]
Portimonense SC - Moreirense FC 0-2(0-1)
Sporting Braga - FC Porto 2-3(1-1)
GD Chaves - Sporting 1-3(0-1)
Santa Clara - Vitória Guimarães 1-0(1-0)
Benfica - CD Tondela 1-0(0-0)
CS Marítimo - Nacional Funchal 3-2(3-1)
Rio Ave FC - CD Aves 0-2(0-1)
Boavista - Belenenses 2-0(0-0)
CD Feirense - Vitória Setúbal 0-1(0-0)

Round 28 [05-08.04.2019]
FC Porto - Boavista 2-0(1-0)
Belenenses - Santa Clara 1-1(1-1)
Nacional Funchal - CD Aves 0-0
Vitória Guimarães - GD Chaves 4-0(3-0)
Moreirense FC - Sporting Braga 1-0(0-0)
Vitória Setúbal - CS Marítimo 1-0(1-0)
CD Feirense - Benfica 1-4(1-2)
Sporting - Rio Ave FC 3-0(2-0)
CD Tondela - Portimonense SC 3-2(0-2)

Round 29 [12-14.04.2019]
GD Chaves - Belenenses 2-2(1-1)
Santa Clara - Moreirense FC 1-1(1-1)
Portimonense SC - FC Porto 0-3(0-1)
CD Aves - Sporting 1-3(1-2)
Rio Ave FC - Vitória Guimarães 2-1(1-0)
CS Marítimo - CD Feirense 2-0(2-0)
Boavista - Nacional Funchal 1-0(1-0)
Sporting Braga - CD Tondela 3-0(1-0)
Benfica - Vitória Setúbal 4-2(2-1)

Round 30 [19-22.04.2019]
Vitória Setúbal - Portimonense SC 1-1(0-0)
CD Tondela - Boavista 1-0(1-0)
Nacional Funchal - Sporting 0-1(0-0)
Vitória Guimarães - CD Aves 0-2(0-1)
Belenenses - Rio Ave FC 1-3(0-2)
Moreirense FC - GD Chaves 0-1(0-0)
CD Feirense - Sporting Braga 0-2(0-0)
FC Porto - Santa Clara 1-0(1-0)
Benfica - CS Marítimo 6-0(1-0)

Round 31 [26-28.04.2019]
Rio Ave FC - FC Porto 2-2(0-2)
Santa Clara - Vitória Setúbal 0-0
Portimonense SC - CD Feirense 1-0(1-0)
Sporting - Vitória Guimarães 2-0(1-0)
CD Aves - Belenenses 3-0(0-0)
GD Chaves - Nacional Funchal 4-1(2-1)
CS Marítimo - CD Tondela 2-0(1-0)
Sporting Braga - Benfica 1-4(1-0)
Boavista - Moreirense FC 3-1(1-0)

Round 32 [03-06.05.2019]
Moreirense FC - Rio Ave FC 1-2(1-1)
CD Feirense - GD Chaves 4-4(2-1)
CS Marítimo - Sporting Braga 1-0(0-0)
Benfica - Portimonense SC 5-1(0-0)
FC Porto - CD Aves 4-0(2-0)
CD Tondela - Santa Clara 1-3(0-1)
Belenenses - Sporting 1-8(0-2)
Vitória Guimarães - Nacion. Funchal 2-2(1-0)
Vitória Setúbal - Boavista 0-3(0-0)

Round 33 [10-12.05.2019]
CD Aves - Moreirense FC 0-1(0-0)
Santa Clara - CD Feirense 4-4(2-3)
Portimonense SC - CS Marítimo 3-2(1-2)
Boavista - Sporting Braga 4-2(3-2)
Sporting - CD Tondela 1-1(1-0)
GD Chaves - Vitória Setúbal 1-2(0-2)
Vitória Guimarães - Belenenses 5-1(0-0)
Nacional Funchal - FC Porto 0-4(0-2)
Rio Ave FC - Benfica 2-3(0-2)

Round 34 [16-19.05.2019]
Belenenses - Nacional Funchal 3-0(1-0)
Sporting Braga - Portimonense SC 2-0(1-0)
CD Feirense - CD Aves 2-1(0-1)
CS Marítimo - Boavista 0-1(0-1)
Vitória Setúbal - Rio Ave FC 1-3(0-0)
Benfica - Santa Clara 4-1(3-0)
FC Porto - Sporting 2-1(0-0)
CD Tondela - GD Chaves 5-2(4-2)
Moreirense FC - Vitória Guimarães 1-3(1-1)

Final Standings

1.	**Sport Lisboa e Benfica**	34	28	3	3	103	-	31	87
2.	Sporting Clube de Portugal Lisboa	34	27	4	3	74	-	20	85
3.	FC do Porto	34	23	5	6	72	-	33	74
4.	Sporting Clube de Braga	34	21	4	9	56	-	37	67
5.	Vitória SC Guimarães	34	15	7	12	46	-	34	52
6.	Moreirense FC Moreira de Cónegos	34	16	4	14	39	-	44	52
7.	Rio Ave FC Vila do Conde	34	12	9	13	50	-	52	45
8.	Boavista FC Porto	34	13	5	16	34	-	40	44
9.	CF Os Belenenses Lisboa	34	10	13	11	42	-	51	43
10.	CD Santa Clara Açores	34	11	9	14	43	-	45	42
11.	CS Marítimo Funchal	34	12	3	19	26	-	44	39
12.	Portimonense SC Portimão	34	11	6	17	44	-	59	39
13.	Vitória FC Setúbal	34	8	12	14	28	-	39	36
14.	CD das Aves	34	10	6	18	35	-	49	36
15.	CD Tondela	34	9	8	17	40	-	54	35
16.	GD Chaves (*Relegated*)	34	8	8	18	34	-	57	32
17.	CD Nacional Funchal (*Relegated*)	34	7	7	20	33	-	73	28
18.	CD Feirense Santa Maria da Feira (*Relegated*)	34	3	11	20	27	-	64	20

Top goalscorers:

23	Haris Seferović (SUI) *Sport Lisboa e Benfica*
20	Bruno Miguel Borges Fernandes *Sporting Clube de Portugal Lisboa*
17	Rafael Alexandre Fernandes Ferreira da Silva *Sport Lisboa e Benfica*
15	Bas Dost (NED) *Sporting Clube de Portugal Lisboa*
15	Dyego Wilverson Ferreira Sousa *Sporting Clube de Braga*
15	João Félix Sequeira *Sport Lisboa e Benfica*
15	Francisco das Chagas Soares dos Santos "Tiquinho Soares" (BRA) *FC do Porto*

NATIONAL CUP
Taça de Portugal 2018/2019

Second Round [29-30.09.2018]

Gondomar SC - CD Cova Piedade	1-2
Leça FC - Leixões SC Porto	0-3
SC Praiense - CD Pinhalnovense	5-1
Juvent. de Pedras Salgadas - Académica de Coimbra	1-0
Portalegrense 1925 - SC Farense Faro	0-3
Clube Caçadores das Taipas - FC Arouca	0-1
FC Alverca - Académico de Viseu FC	0-3
Recreio Desportivo de Águeda - FC Famalicão	1-0
SG Sacavenense - Varzim SC	2-1
CD Condeixa - FC Paços de Ferreira	1-3
FC Cesarense - Sporting da Covilhã	1-2
CD Trofense - FC Penafiel	2-3
AD Os Limianos - CD Mafra	2-1
CD Fátima - AD Oliveirense	1-0
CF Vasco da Gama Vidigueira - GD Estoril Praia	0-1
GD Vitória Sernache - Sertanense FC	1-3
União FCI Tomar - UD Vilafranquense	0-3
SC Vila Real - AD Sanjoanense	5-4 pen
AD Fafe - Sporting Club Ideal	1-0
Caldas SC - GD Gafanha	0-3
Vila Flor SC - Amarante FC	0-5
Beneditense CD - CF Os Armacenenses	0-3
SC Rio Tinto - Moura AC	1-4
Silves FC – União SC Paredes	2-1
CF Santa Iria – SC Lourinhanense	3-1
CD Praia de Milfontes - SC Valenciano	2-5
FC Oliveira do Hospital - Lusitano FC Vildemoinhos	3-5 pen
GD Peniche - CDC Montalegre	1-3
Casa Pia AC – Clube Olimpico de Montijo	2-0
Anadia FC – SC Mineiro Aljustrelense	3-1
Merelinense FC - CF União da Madeira	0-3
UD Eirense - SC União Torreense	0-3
Lusitano Ginásio Clube - Clube Oriental de Lisboa	1-2
Gil Vicente FC - GD Chaves	0-1
GR Amigos da Paz - União SC Santiago	2-4
SC Espinho – Sport União Sintrense	0-0 aet; 6-5 pen
CD Torres Novas - SC Maria da Fonte	0-4
GD CRS Vila de Silgueiros - SC Angrense	0-1
Real SC Queluz - SC Mirandela	0-0 aet; 4-5 pen
Amora FC - SC Lamego	8-0
GD Mirandês - SC Coimbrões	2-3
FC Felgueiras 1932 - GD Joane	2-0
GS Loures - ARC Oleiros	1-0
Valadares Gaia FC - Louletano DC	0-1
SC Beira-Mar Aveiro - AR São Martinho	0-1
FC Vale Formoso - UD Leiria	0-3

Third Round [18-21.10.2018]

Sertanense FC - Sport Lisboa e Benfica	0-3
SC Vila Real - FC do Porto	0-6
SC Valenciano - Vitória SC Guimarães	0-7
CD Cova Piedade - Portimonense SC	2-1
Amora FC - CF Os Belenenses Lisboa	3-4 aet
SC Espinho - Académico de Viseu FC	3-3 aet; 11-10p
GS Loures - Sporting Clube de Portugal Lisboa	1-2
FC Vale Formoso - SC Coimbrões	4-3 aet
Moura AC - CS Marítimo Funchal	0-0 aet; 3-4 pen
CD Fátima - Boavista FC Porto	1-4
CF Os Armacenenses - Vitória FC Setúbal	1-2
SC União Torreense - Rio Ave FC	1-5
AR São Martinho - Moreirense FC	0-1
Lusitano FC de Vildemoinhos - CD Nacional Funchal	4-3 aet
SC Mirandela - CD Feirense	1-2 aet
SC Maria da Fonte - CD Santa Clara	1-2
GD Estoril Praia - CD Tondela	1-1 aet; 3-4 pen
JP Salgadas - GD Chaves	1-4
Casa Pia AC - SC Angrense	2-1
AD Os Limianos - Sporting da Covilhã	0-2
SC Farense Faro - FC Arouca	1-3
CDC Montalegre - Clube Oriental de Lisboa	2-1 aet
AD Fafe - FC Penafiel	0-0 aet; 0-1 pen
FC Paços de Ferreira - GD Gafanha	2-0
CF Santa Iria - SC Praiense	0-2
Recreio Desportivo de Águeda - Louletano DC	1-0
UD Vilafranquense - Anadia FC	0-4
Leixões SC Porto - Amarante FC	3-1
Silves FC - GD Chaves "B"	2-1
CF União da Madeira - União SC Santiago	2-0
SG Sacavenense - CD Aves	1-3
FC Felgueiras 1932 - Sporting Clube de Braga	0-1

Fourth Round [22/24-25.11.2018]			
Sport Lisboa e Benfica - FC Arouca	2-1	FC Paços de Ferreira - Casa Pia AC	3-1
CD Cova Piedade - CD Aves	0-3 aet	FC Penafiel - Vitória FC Setúbal	1-4
Lusitano FC Vildemoinhos - Sporting CP Lisboa	1-4	SC Espinho - Boavista FC Porto	0-4
FC do Porto - CF Os Belenenses Lisboa	2-0	CF União da Madeira - Vitória SC Guimarães	0-2
Sporting da Covilhã - Moreirense FC	0-3	CD Tondela - FC Vale Formoso	7-0
CDC Montalegre - Recreio Desportivo de Águeda	1-0	CS Marítimo Funchal - CD Feirense	0-3
Rio Ave FC - Silves FC	7-0	CD Santa Clara - GD Chaves	1-2
Leixões SC Porto - Anadia FC	1-0	Sporting Clube de Braga - SC Praiense	2-1

1/8-Finals [18-19.12.2018]			
Vitória FC Setúbal - Sporting Clube de Braga	0-1 aet	CD Aves - GD Chaves	2-0
Leixões SC Porto - CD Tondela	2-2 aet; 4-2 pen	Boavista FC Porto - Vitória SC Guimarães	0-1
FC do Porto - Moreirense FC	4-3	Sporting Clube de Portugal Lisboa - Rio Ave FC	5-2
CD Feirense - FC Paços de Ferreira	1-1 aet; 4-2 pen	CDC Montalegre - Sport Lisboa e Benfica	0-1

Quarter-Finals [15-16.01.2019]			
CD Aves - Sporting Clube de Braga	1-2	Vitória SC Guimarães - Sport Lisboa e Benfica	0-1
Leixões SC Porto - FC do Porto	1-2 aet	CD Feirense - Sporting Clube de Portugal Lisboa	0-2

Semi-Finals [06/26.02.-02/03.04.2019]			
Sport Lisboa e Benfica - Sporting CP Lisboa	2-1 / 0-1	FC do Porto - Sporting Clube de Braga	3-0 / 1-1

Final

25.05.2019; Estádio Nacional, Oeiras; Referee: Manuel Jorge Neves Moreira de Sousa; Attendance: 30,000

Sporting Clube de Portugal Lisboa - FC do Porto **2-2(1-1,1-1,1-2); 5-4 on penalties**

Sporting: Renan Ribeiro, Bruno Gaspar (65.Tiago Ilori), Sebastián Coates Nion, Jérémy Mathieu, Marcos Javier Acuña, Nemanja Gudelj (90+3.Idrissa Doumbia), Wendel (106.Jefferson), Raphinha, Bruno Fernandes (Cap), Abdoulay Diaby (74.Bas Dost), Luiz Phellype. Trainer: Marcel Keizer (Netherlands).

FC Porto: Vaná, Eder Militão (102.Hernâni), Felipe Monteiro, Pepe, Alex Telles (106.Fernando Andrade), Héctor Miguel Herrera López (Cap), Danilo, Otávio (77.Wilson Manafá), Moussa Marega (99.Adrián López Álvarez), Tiquinho Soares, Yacine Brahimi. Trainer: Sérgio Paulo Merceiro Da Conceição.

Goals: 0-1 Tiquinho Soares ((40), 1-1 Bruno Fernandes (45), 2-1 Bas Dost (101), 2-2 Felipe Monteiro (120).

Penalties: Tiquinho Soares (0-1; Bas Dost (missed); Danilo 0-2; Bruno Fernandes 1-2; Pepe (missed); Jérémy Mathieu 2-2; Adrián López Álvarez 2-3; Raphinha 3-3; Hernâni 3-4; Sebastián Coates Nion 4-4; Fernando Andrade (saved); Luiz Phellype 5-4.

THE CLUBS 2018/2019

Clube Desportivo das Aves

Founded: 12.11.1930
Stadium: Estádio do CD Aves, Aves (5,896)

Goalkeepers:	**DOB**	**M**	**(s)**	**G**
André Ferreira	29.05.1996	8		
Quentin Beunardeau (FRA)	27.02.1994	26		
Fabio (BRA)	11.05.1990		(1)	
Defenders:	**DOB**	**M**	**(s)**	**G**
Diego Galo (BRA)	14.01.1984	22		1
Issam El Adoua (MAR)	09.12.1986	13		
Jorge Fellipe (BRA)	27.10.1988	19		2
Mato Miloš (CRO)	30.06.1993	2	(4)	
Nélson Lenho	22.03.1984	8		
Carlos dos Santos Rodrigues „Ponck“ (CPV)	13.01.1995	31	(1)	2
Rodrigo (BRA)	26.12.1992	33		4
Rodrigo Defendi (BRA)	16.06.1986	11		2
Vitor Costa (BRA)	01.07.1994	24	(1)	1
Midfielders:	**DOB**	**M**	**(s)**	**G**
Mama Baldé (GNB)	06.11.1995	26	(2)	8
Braga	17.06.1983	7	(9)	
Bruno Lourenço	02.02.1998		(1)	
Claudio Falcão (BRA)	03.07.1994	16	(5)	2
Luis Carlos Olivera Fariña (ARG)	12.03.1991	15	(8)	1
Ablaye Faye (SEN)	10.04.1994	1	(1)	
Nildo Petrolina (BRA)	01.05.1986	9	(3)	2
Rúben Oliveira	14.12.1994	9	(11)	1
Tong Le (CHN)	29.04.1993		(1)	
Vítor Gomes	25.12.1987	28	(1)	3
Forwards:	**DOB**	**M**	**(s)**	**G**
Amilton (BRA)	12.08.1989	13	(2)	2
Bruno Gomes (BRA)	19.07.1996	3	(8)	
Caíque Lemes (BRA)	12.07.1993		(1)	
Abdoulaye Diallo (SEN)	15.01.1996		(3)	
Derley	29.12.1987	25	(5)	4
Hamdou Mohamed Elhouni (LBY)	12.02.1994	6	(6)	
Erik (BRA)	02.02.1995		(2)	
José Carlos Moreira Varela (CPV)	15.09.1997	1	(3)	
Luquinhas (BRA)	28.09.1996	16	(1)	
Michel Douglas (BRA)	16.01.1992		(5)	
Miguel Tavares	29.08.1998	1	(8)	
Ricardo Rodrigues	28.06.1995	1	(7)	
Trainer:	**DOB**	**M**		
José Albano Ferreira da Mota	25.02.1964	17		
Augusto Soares Inácio [16.01.2019]	01.02.1955	17		

Clube de Futebol Os Belenenses Lisboa

Founded: 23.09.1919
Stadium: Complexo Desportivo do Estádio Nacional, Oeiras (37,593)

Goalkeepers:	**DOB**	**M**	**(s)**	**G**
Guilherme Oliveira	12.04.1995		(1)	
Mika	08.03.1991	2		
Muriel Becker (BRA)	14.02.1987	32		
Defenders:	**DOB**	**M**	**(s)**	**G**
Cleylton (BRA)	19.03.1993	12	(3)	1
Diogo Calila	10.10.1998		(4)	
Gonçalo Silva	04.06.1991	31	(1)	
Gonçalo Tavares	16.05.1997	1		
Luís Silva	18.02.1999	1	(1)	
Reinildo Isnard Mandava (MOZ)	21.01.1994	14	(2)	
Nuno Tomás	15.09.1995	1	(2)	
Pierre Sagna (SEN)	21.08.1990	7	(6)	
Vincent Sasso (FRA)	16.02.1991	29		3
Midfielders:	**DOB**	**M**	**(s)**	**G**
André Santos	02.03.1989	26	(1)	1
Zakarya Bergdich (MAR)	07.01.1989	19	(6)	
Ousmane Dramé (FRA)	25.08.1992		(6)	
Eduardo Henrique (BRA)	17.05.1995	19	(5)	1
Filipe Chaby	22.01.1994		(1)	
Jonatan Lucca (BRA)	02.06.1994	25	(5)	3
Kiki	10.12.1994	3	(1)	
Matija Ljujić (SRB)	28.10.1993	8	(17)	
Nuno Coelho	23.11.1987	23	(1)	1
Nicolás Leandro Vélez (ARG)	04.07.1990	3	(3)	
Forwards:	**DOB**	**M**	**(s)**	**G**
Dálcio	22.05.1996	13	(10)	
Diogo Viana	22.02.1990	26	(4)	1
Douglas Aurélio (BRA)	27.03.1999		(1)	
Alfredo Gomes Ribeiro „Fredy"(ANG)	27.03.1990	17	(1)	6
Henrique Almeida (BRA)	27.05.1991	10	(5)	5
Alhassane Keita (GUI)	16.04.1992	12	(3)	3
Kikas	17.09.1998	7	(8)	5
Licá	08.09.1988	33	(1)	11
Tarzan	26.10.1994		(2)	
Trainer:	**DOB**	**M**		
Jorge Manuel Rebelo Fernandes"Silas"	01.09.1976	34		

Sport Lisboa e Benfica

Founded: 28.02.1904
Stadium: Estádio da Luz, Lisboa (64,642)

Goalkeepers:	**DOB**	**M**	**(s)**	**G**
Mile Svilar (BEL)	27.08.1999		(1)	
Odisseas Vlachodimos (GRE)	26.04.1994	34		
Defenders:	**DOB**	**M**	**(s)**	**G**
Álex Grimaldo (ESP)	20.09.1995	34		4
André Almeida	10.09.1990	33		2
Germán Andrés Conti (ARG)	03.06.1994	2	(2)	
Sébastien Corchia (FRA)	01.11.1990	1	(1)	
Ferro	26.03.1997	13		2
Jardel (BRA)	29.03.1986	19		2
Cristian Franco Lema (ARG)	24.03.1990	1		
Rúben Dias	14.05.1997	32		3
Midfielders:	**DOB**	**M**	**(s)**	**G**
Ljubomir Fejsa (SRB)	14.08.1988	17	(1)	
Florentino Luís	19.08.1999	9	(2)	1
Gabriel (BRA)	18.09.1993	14	(3)	
Gedson Fernandes	09.01.1999	11	(11)	
Filip Krovinović (CRO)	29.08.1995		(4)	
Eduardo Antonio Salvio (ARG)	13.07.1990	7	(7)	2
Andreas Samaris (GRE)	13.06.1989	17	(2)	2
Alfa Semedo Esteves (GNB)	30.08.1997		(5)	
Adel Taarabt (MAR)	24.05.1989	1	(5)	
Andrija Živković (SRB)	11.07.1996	6	(10)	
Forwards:	**DOB**	**M**	**(s)**	**G**
Nicolás Ignacio Castillo Mora (CHI)	14.02.1993	1	(3)	
Franco Emanuel Cervi (ARG)	26.05.1994	13	(7)	4
Facundo Ferreyra	14.03.1991	3	(2)	1
João Félix	10.11.1999	21	(5)	15
Jonas (BRA)	01.04.1984	10	(12)	11
Jota	30.03.1999		(4)	
Pizzi	06.10.1989	34		13
Rafa Silva	17.05.1993	21	(5)	17
Haris Seferović (SUI)	22.02.1992	20	(9)	23
Trainer:	**DOB**	**M**		
Rui Carlos Pinho da Vitória	16.04.1970	17		
Bruno Miguel Silva do Nascimento [04.01.2019]	12.05.1976	17		

Boavista Futebol Clube Porto

Founded: 01.08.1903
Stadium: Estádio do Bessa, Porto (27,363)

Goalkeepers:	**DOB**	**M**	**(s)**	**G**
Assis Giovanaz (BRA)	04.10.1989	1		
Helton Leite (BRA)	02.11.1990	21		
Rafael Bracalli (BRA)	05.05.1981	12		
Defenders:	**DOB**	**M**	**(s)**	**G**
Carraça	01.03.1993	18	(6)	
Edu Machado	26.04.1990	18	(1)	
Gonçalo Cardoso	21.10.2000	15		
Jubal Júnior (BRA)	29.08.1993	9	(4)	
Neris (BRA)	17.06.1992	32		1
Raphael Silva	20.04.1992	11	(2)	
Stéphane Sparagna (FRA)	17.02.1995	4		
João Talocha	30.08.1989	31		2
Midfielders:	**DOB**	**M**	**(s)**	**G**
Yaw Ackah (GHA)	01.06.1999		(2)	
David Simão	15.05.1990	13		1
Fábio Espinho	18.08.1985	19	(4)	2
Gabriel Nunes (BRA)	11.07.1994		(2)	
Idrissa Mandiang (SEN)	27.12.1984	16	(2)	
Matheus Índio (BRA)	28.02.1996	15	(2)	1
Nwankwo Obiora (NGA)	12.07.1991	14	(1)	3
Rafael Costa (BRA)	19.01.1991	21	(9)	2
Rochinha	03.05.1995	13	(3)	1
Samu	21.04.1996		(1)	
Aymen Tahar (ALG)	02.10.1989	2	(2)	
Forwards:	**DOB**	**M**	**(s)**	**G**
André Claro	31.03.1991	8	(8)	1
Alberto Bueno Calvo (ESP)	20.03.1988	10	(5)	2
Federico Matías Falcone (ARG)	21.02.1990	9	(14)	4
Gustavo Sauer (BRA)	30.04.1993	10		1
Ibrahim Koneh (CMR)	09.09.1994		(6)	
Mateus Galiano da Costa (ANG)	19.06.1984	22	(8)	5
Yusupha Njie (GAM)	03.01.1994	8	(3)	4
Perdigão (BRA)	17.07.1991	4	(8)	1
Rafa	28.07.1991	18	(7)	2
Trainer:	**DOB**	**M**		
António Jorge Rocha Simão	12.08.1976	18		
José Carlos Fernandes „Lito" Vidigal (ANG) [26.01.2019]	11.07.1969	16		

Sporting Clube de Braga

Founded: 19.01.1921
Stadium: Estádio Municipal de Braga, Braga (30,287)

Goalkeepers:	DOB	M	(s)	G
Matheus Magalhães (BRA)	19.07.1992	3		
Tiago Sá	11.01.1995	31		
Defenders:	**DOB**	**M**	**(s)**	**G**
Ailton (BRA)	16.03.1995	2		
Bruno Viana (BRA)	05.02.1995	32		
Diogo	07.01.1991	2	(1)	
Marcelo Goiano (BRA)	13.10.1987	29		1
Nuno Sequeira	19.08.1990	28	(1)	
Pablo Santos (BRA)	18.03.1992	19	(1)	2
Raul Silva (BRA)	04.11.1989	15		1
Midfielders:	**DOB**	**M**	**(s)**	**G**
Bruno Xadas	02.12.1997	2	(6)	1
Claudemir (BRA)	27.03.1988	27	(3)	2
Fransérgio (BRA)	18.10.1990	20	(6)	2

João Novais	10.07.1993	12	(12)	1
João Palhinha	09.07.1995	17	(6)	2
Ricardo Esgaio	16.05.1993	23	(2)	
Ricardo Ryller (BRA)	27.02.1994	3	(8)	
Forwards:	**DOB**	**M**	**(s)**	**G**
Dyego Sousa	14.09.1989	28	(5)	15
Eduardo (BRA)	07.06.1993	2	(4)	
Fábio Martins	24.07.1993	2	(9)	
Murilo (BRA)	31.10.1994	8	(5)	3
Paulinho	09.11.1992	18	(11)	5
Ricardo Horta	15.09.1994	27	(7)	8
Trincão	29.12.1999		(6)	
Wilson Eduardo	08.07.1990	24	(8)	12
Trainer:	**DOB**	**M**		
Abel Fernando Moreira Ferreira	22.12.1978	34		

Grupo Desportivo de Chaves

Founded: 27.09.1949
Stadium: Estádio Municipal "Eng. Manuel Branco Teixeira", Chaves (8,870)

Goalkeepers:	DOB	M	(s)	G
Antonio Filipe	14.04.1985	19		
Ricardo Nunes	06.07.1982	15	(1)	
Defenders:	**DOB**	**M**	**(s)**	**G**
Nemanja Ćalasan (SRB)	17.03.1996		(3)	
Gastón Matías Campi (ARG)	06.04.1991	16		2
Djavan (BRA)	31.12.1987	22	(1)	
Hugo Basto	14.05.1993	4		
Lionn (BRA)	29.01.1989	12		
Marcão (BRA)	05.06.1996	17		2
Luís Martins	10.06.1992	12	(3)	1
Nikola Maraš (SRB)	19.12.1995	28		4
Marlon (BRA)	22.05.1996		(1)	
Nuno André Coelho	07.01.1986	3	(1)	
Paulinho	13.07.1991	20	(2)	
Midfielders:	**DOB**	**M**	**(s)**	**G**
Bruno Gallo (BRA)	07.05.1988	30		3
Costinha	25.08.1992	9	(5)	1
Stephen Eustáquio (CAN)	21.12.1996	16		
Filipe Brigues	24.07.1990	2		
Filipe Melo	03.11.1989	2	(3)	

Jefferson (BRA)	14.04.1993	18	(2)	
João Teixeira	06.02.1994	1	(10)	
Renan Bressan Bardini (BLR)	03.11.1988	17	(7)	1
Erdem Şen (TUR)	05.01.1989	2	(4)	
Abdoul Zangre (BFA)	05.05.1997	1	(1)	
Forwards:	**DOB**	**M**	**(s)**	**G**
André Luis (BRA)	03.09.1994	9	(7)	3
Avtandil Ebralidze (GEO)	03.10.1991	8	(4)	
Gevorg Ghazaryan (ARM)	05.04.1988	11	(8)	2
Higor Platiny (BRA)	02.10.1990	4	(11)	3
Mika Borges	27.06.1997		(2)	
Niltinho (BRA)	11.09.1993	12	(14)	3
Perdigão (BRA)	17.07.1991	11	(1)	1
Rúben Macedo	09.03.1996	10	(2)	
Luther Singh (RSA)	05.08.1997	15	(2)	2
Willian Oliveira (BRA)	07.12.1991	28	(5)	5
Trainer:	**DOB**	**M**		
Daniel António Lopes Ramos	25.12.1970	12		
Tiago Fernandes [10.12.2018]	17.08.1981	13		
José Albano Ferreira da Mota [10.03.2019]	25.02.1964	9		

Clube Desportivo Feirense Santa Maria da Feira

Founded: 18.03.1918
Stadium: Estádio "Marcolino de Castro", Santa Maria da Feira (5,450)

Goalkeepers:	DOB	M	(s)	G
Dele Sunday Alampasu (NGA)	24.12.1996	1		
André Moreira	02.12.1995	5		
Bruno Brigido (BRA)	09.03.1991	4	(1)	
Caio Secco (BRA)	22.12.1990	24		
Defenders:	**DOB**	**M**	**(s)**	**G**
Antonio Briseño Vázquez (MEX)	05.02.1994	34		2
Bruno Nascimento (BRA)	30.05.1991	14	(1)	
Diga	30.03.1998	9	(1)	
Flávio (BRA)	12.05.1994	12		1
Mesquita	23.11.1990	10		
Roderick Alonso Miller Molina (PAN)	03.04.1992		(1)	
Philipe Sampaio (BRA)	11.11.1994	8	(2)	1
Tiago	29.07.1986	10	(1)	
Vítor Bruno	13.01.1990	27	(1)	1
Midfielders:	**DOB**	**M**	**(s)**	**G**
Afonso Brito	05.05.1999		(1)	
Kódjo Kassé Alphonse (CIV)	28.05.1993	3	(1)	
Elvis Macedo Babanco (CPV)	27.07.1985	21	(2)	2
Cris	17.01.1984	16	(1)	1
Fábio Sturgeon	04.02.1994	25	(3)	2

Aly Ghazal (EGY)	01.02.1992	10	(1)	
Jaílton Alves Miranda „Kuca" (CPV)	02.08.1989	2	(2)	
João Tavares	12.12.1998		(7)	
Marco Paulo Silva Soares (CPV)	16.06.1984	7	(9)	
Mateus Anderson (BRA)	06.03.1994	4	(3)	1
Lawrence Ofori (GHA)	28.06.1998	2	(6)	
Steven Petkov (BUL)	07.05.1995	5	(7)	1
Rafael Crivellaro (BRA)	18.02.1989	14	(6)	
Tiago Silva	02.06.1993	29		3
Forwards:	**DOB**	**M**	**(s)**	**G**
Edinho	07.07.1982	14	(10)	5
Edson Farias (BRA)	12.01.1992	23	(1)	
Brian Gómez (ARG)	15.02.1994	1	(5)	
João Silva	21.05.1990	10	(15)	2
Luís Machado	04.11.1992	20	(5)	1
José Adolfo Valencia Arrechea (COL)	18.12.1991	10	(5)	2
Trainer:	**DOB**	**M**		
Nuno Miguel Mata Ribeiro dos Santos	25.07.1978	20		
Filipe Gonçalo Pinto Martins [04.02.2019]	29.05.1978	14		

Club Sport Marítimo Funchal

Founded: 20.09.1910
Stadium: Estádio do Marítimo, Funchal (10,566)

Goalkeepers:	**DOB**	**M**	**(s)**	**G**
Amir Abedzadeh (IRN)	26.04.1993	13		
Charles (BRA)	04.02.1994	21		
Defenders:	**DOB**	**M**	**(s)**	**G**
Aloisio (BRA)	16.08.1997	1	(1)	
Bebeto (BRA)	01.01.1990	20	(2)	
Douglas Grolli (BRA)	05.10.1989	13		
Fábio China	07.07.1992	23		
Lucas África (BRA)	05.02.1995	19	(1)	
Marcão (BRA)	17.08.1995	4	(1)	
Nanu	17.05.1994	14	(1)	
Renê (BRA)	21.04.1992	12		
Rúben	17.02.1990	11		
Zainadine Abdula Mulungo Chavango Júnior (MOZ)	24.06.1988	31		1
Midfielders:	**DOB**	**M**	**(s)**	**G**
Jorge Iván Correa (ARG)	04.05.1993	24	(9)	3
Danny	07.08.1983	13		
Fabricio Baiano (BRA)	13.06.1992	19	(5)	
Jean Cleber (BRA)	29.04.1990	8	(12)	
João Gamboa	31.08.1996	11	(5)	
Pedro Pelágio	21.04.2000	8	(4)	
Josip Vuković (CRO)	02.05.1992	24	(1)	
Forwards:	**DOB**	**M**	**(s)**	**G**
Leandro Iván Barrera (ARG)	28.02.1991	15	(11)	2
Francisco Gonçalves Sacalumbo „Chico Banza“ (ANG)	17.12.1998		(1)	
Edgar Costa	14.04.1987	18	(8)	4
Everton (BRA)	03.07.1993		(2)	
Getterson (BRA)	16.05.1991	11	(3)	2
Ibson (BRA)	08.10.1989		(1)	
Diederrick Joel Tagueu Tadjo(CMR)	06.12.1993	24	(6)	8
Leandro Cardoso	11.05.1999		(3)	
Ricardo Valente	03.04.1991	3	(9)	1
Rodrigo Pinho (BRA)	30.05.1991	14	(11)	4
Ruan Teles (BRA)	23.10.1997		(1)	
Trainer:	**DOB**	**M**		
Cláudio José Ferreira Braga	23.11.1974	10		
Armando Gonçalves Teixeira „Petit“ [27.11.2018]	25.09.1976	24		

Moreirense Futebol Clube Moreira de Cónegos

Founded: 01.11.1938
Stadium: Parque de Jogos "Comendador Joaquim de Almeida Freitas", Moreira de Cónegos (6,152)

Goalkeepers:	**DOB**	**M**	**(s)**	**G**
Jhonatan (BRA)	08.05.1991	25		
Nuno Macedo	29.05.1999	2	(1)	
Pedro Trigueira	04.01.1988	7	(1)	
Defenders:	**DOB**	**M**	**(s)**	**G**
Mohamed Aberhoune (MAR)	03.05.1989	13	(1)	
Bruno Silva (BRA)	14.09.1992	6	(6)	
Anthony D'Alberto (BEL)	13.10.1994	16	(2)	
Fernandes	26.03.1996	21	(3)	1
Rafik Halliche (ALG)	02.09.1986	21	(1)	1
Iago Santos (BRA)	22.05.1992	15	(1)	
João Aurélio	17.08.1988	21		2
Rúben Lima	03.10.1989	20		
Midfielders:	**DOB**	**M**	**(s)**	**G**
Alan Schons (BRA)	24.05.1993	2	(6)	
Ângelo Neto (BRA)	02.09.1991	22	(7)	
Arsénio	30.08.1989	27	(3)	4
Ibrahima Camará (GUI)	25.01.1999	4	(3)	
Chiquinho	19.07.1995	32	(2)	8
Fábio Pacheco	26.05.1988	24	(3)	
Mamadou Loum (SEN)	30.12.1996	17		3
Pedro Nuno	13.01.1995	21	(7)	5
Forwards:	**DOB**	**M**	**(s)**	**G**
Bilel Aouacheria (FRA)	02.04.1994	9	(12)	1
Heriberto	19.02.1997	26	(6)	6
Lucas Rodrigues (BRA)	27.08.1999	1	(3)	
Nenê (BRA)	28.07.1983	13	(13)	3
Ricardo Almeida	09.05.1997		(1)	
Patricio Rodriguez (ARG)	04.05.1990	2	(10)	
César David Texeira Torres (URU)	27.02.1991	7	(10)	4
Trainer:	**DOB**	**M**		
Ivo Ricardo Abreu Vieira	10.01.1976	34		

Clube Desportivo Nacional Funchal

Founded: 08.12.1910
Stadium: Estádio da Madeira, Funchal (5,200)

Goalkeepers:	**DOB**	**M**	**(s)**	**G**
Daniel (BRA)	18.04.1987	28		
Ohoulo Framelin (CMR)	21.11.1996	1		
Lucas França (BRA)	19.01.1996	5	(2)	
Defenders:	**DOB**	**M**	**(s)**	**G**
Arthur Henrique (BRA)	17.06.1999	2		
Wesly Roberto Decas (HON)	11.08.1999	2		
Diogo Coelho	14.09.1993	12	(2)	1
Felipe (BRA)	07.08.1987	13	(1)	
Filipe Ferreira	27.09.1990	5		
Júlio César (BRA)	21.03.1995	27	(1)	
Kalindi (BRA)	29.08.1993	27	(1)	1
Mauro Cerqueira	20.08.1992	10		
Nuno Campos	13.06.1993	24	(1)	
Lazar Rosić (SRB)	29.06.1993	14		
Witiness Chimoio João Quembo „Witi“ (MOZ)	26.08.1996	21	(10)	2
Midfielders:	**DOB**	**M**	**(s)**	**G**
Ibrahim Alhassan (NGA)	03.11.1996	10	(2)	1
Kenji Joel Gorré (CPV)	29.09.1994	8	(3)	1
Jota	07.03.1993	18	(4)	
Kaká (BRA)	20.05.1991	2	(2)	
Sérgio Marakis (RSA)	11.11.1991	14	(2)	
Aleksandar Paločević (SRB)	22.08.1993	14	(10)	1
Sardor Rashidov (UZB)	14.06.1991	6	(1)	3
Fernando Damián Tissone Rodrigues (ARG)	24.07.1986	10	(2)	1
Vítor Gonçalves	29.03.1992	33		2
Forwards:	**DOB**	**M**	**(s)**	**G**
Giorgi Arabidze (GEO)	04.03.1998	4	(6)	
Camacho	23.06.1994	24	(2)	7
Diego Barcellos (BRA)	05.04.1985	1	(5)	
Avtandil Ebralidze (GEO)	03.10.1991	2	(1)	
Okacha Hamzaoui (ALG)	12.11.1990	11	(10)	2
José Brayan Riascos Valencia (COL)	10.10.1994	7	(18)	1
Bryan Giovanni Róchez Mejía (HON)	01.01.1995	19	(11)	10
Trainer:	**DOB**	**M**		
Francisco José Rodrigues Da Costa "Costinha"	01.12.1974	34		

Portimonense Sporting Clube Portimão

Founded: 14.08.1914
Stadium: Estádio Municipal, Portimão (5,870)

Goalkeepers:	DOB	M	(s)	G
Shuichi Gonda (JPN)	03.03.1989	1		
Leonardo (BRA)	28.12.1992	7		
Ricardo Ferreira	03.12.1989	26		
Defenders:	**DOB**	**M**	**(s)**	**G**
Felipe Macedo (BRA)	27.03.1994	1	(3)	
Emmanuel Hackman (GHA)	14.05.1995	10	(5)	
Henrique Gelain (BRA)	05.01.1995	11	(2)	1
Jadson Morais (BRA)	05.11.1991	21		2
Lucas Possignolo (BRA)	11.05.1994	27	(1)	
Rúben Fernandes	06.05.1986	32	(1)	
Vítor Tormena (BRA)	04.01.1996	25	(1)	1
Wilson Manafá	23.07.1994	15		2
Midfielders:	**DOB**	**M**	**(s)**	**G**
Bruno Reis	20.07.1999		(3)	
Bruno Tabata (BRA)	30.03.1997	25	(6)	3
Dener Clemente (BRA)	13.03.1992	19	(6)	3
Ewerton Pereira (BRA)	01.12.1992	13	(2)	1
Chidera Ezeh (NGA)	02.10.1997		(3)	
Guilherme Lazaroni (BRA)	18.11.1992	2	(1)	
Lucas Fernandes (BRA)	20.09.1997	21	(8)	1
Marcel Pereira (BRA)	16.10.1992		(3)	
Matheus Jesus (BRA)	10.04.1997		(1)	
Shoya Nakajima (JPN)	23.08.1994	13		5
Paulinho (BRA)	10.07.1994	24	(4)	6
Pedro Sá	01.12.1993	32		
Pepê (BRA)	06.01.1998		(1)	
Rafael Barbosa	29.03.1996		(4)	
Forwards:	**DOB**	**M**	**(s)**	**G**
Aylton Boa Morte	23.09.1993	7	(6)	2
Taofiq Jibril (NGA)	23.04.1998		(2)	
João Carlos (BRA)	01.03.1995	3	(11)	1
Jackson Arley Martínez Valencia (COL)	03.10.1986	25	(2)	9
Paulo Bóia (BRA)	26.06.1998		(5)	
Ruster (BRA)	24.08.1996		(9)	1
Wellington Carvalho (BRA)	21.11.1992	14	(9)	3
Trainer:	**DOB**	**M**		
António José dos Santos Folha	21.05.1971	34		

Futebol Clube do Porto

Founded: 28.09.1893
Stadium: Estádio do Dragão, Porto (50,034)

Goalkeepers:	DOB	M	(s)	G
Iker Casillas Fernández (ESP)	20.05.1981	31		
Vaná (BRA)	25.04.1991	3		
Defenders:	**DOB**	**M**	**(s)**	**G**
Alex Telles (BRA)	15.12.1992	33		4
Diogo Leite	23.01.1999	3		1
Eder Militão (BRA)	18.01.1998	29		3
Felipe Monteiro (BRA)	16.05.1989	31		1
Chancel Mbemba (COD)	08.08.1994	1	(2)	
Pepe	26.02.1983	13		2
Victorio Maximiliano Pereira Páez (URU)	08.06.1984	14	(4)	
Wilson Manafá	23.07.1994	8	(6)	1
Midfielders:	**DOB**	**M**	**(s)**	**G**
Danilo	09.09.1991	24	(2)	2
Héctor Miguel Herrera López(MEX)	19.04.1990	29	(4)	6
Mamadou Loum (SEN)	30.12.1996		(2)	
Óliver Torres Muñoz (ESP)	10.11.1994	13	(12)	2
Otávio (BRA)	09.02.1995	19	(9)	3
Sérgio Oliveira	02.06.1992	5	(3)	1
Forwards:	**DOB**	**M**	**(s)**	**G**
Vincent Aboubakar (CMR)	22.01.1992	6	(2)	4
Adrián López Álvarez (ESP)	08.01.1988	3	(8)	1
André Pereira	05.05.1995	3	(6)	1
Yacine Brahimi (ALG)	08.02.1990	27	(5)	10
Bruno Costa	19.04.1997		(2)	
Jesús Manuel Corona Ruiz (MEX)	06.01.1993	26	(8)	3
Fernando Andrade (BRA)	08.01.1993	1	(11)	
Hernâni	20.08.1991		(10)	1
Moussa Marega (MLI)	14.04.1991	28	(1)	11
Marius Mouandilmadji (CHA)	22.01.1998		(1)	1
Tiquinho Soares (BRA)	17.01.1991	24	(4)	15
Trainer:	**DOB**	**M**		
Sérgio Paulo Merceiro Da Conceição	15.11.1974	34		

Rio Ave Futebol Clube Vila do Conde

Founded: 10.05.1939
Stadium: Estádio dos Arcos, Vila do Conde (8,957)

Goalkeepers:	DOB	M	(s)	G
Léo Jardim (BRA)	20.03.1995	33		
Paulo Vítor (BRA)	21.11.1988	1		
Defenders:	**DOB**	**M**	**(s)**	**G**
Afonso Figueiredo	06.01.1993	8	(2)	
Toni Borevković (CRO)	18.06.1997	19		1
Fábio Coentrão	11.03.1988	20	(1)	
Junio Rocha (BRA)	27.02.1997	10		
Messias (BRA)	03.11.1994	5	(2)	
Miguel Rodrigues	16.03.1993		(2)	
Eliseu Mendja Nadjack Soares Cassamá (GNB)	06.02.1994	24		
Nélson Monte	30.07.1995	11	(2)	
Rúben Semedo	04.04.1994	14		2
Midfielders:	**DOB**	**M**	**(s)**	**G**
André (BRA)	03.06.1997		(2)	
Jonathan Buatu (ANG)	27.09.1993	19	(2)	
Diego Lopes (BRA)	03.05.1994	17	(2)	2
Filipe Augusto (BRA)	12.08.1993	12		1
Nikola Jambor (CRO)	25.09.1995	13	(11)	
João Schmidt (BRA)	19.05.1993	17	(2)	3
Joca	30.01.1996	1	(2)	
Leandrinho (BRA)	25.09.1993	7	(4)	
Matheus Reis (BRA)	18.02.1995	18	(4)	
Tarantini	07.10.1983	22	(2)	1
Vitó	18.09.1997		(3)	
Forwards:	**DOB**	**M**	**(s)**	**G**
Bruno Moreira	06.09.1987	19	(11)	9
Carlos (BRA)	15.08.1995	3	(4)	1
Carlos Vinícius (BRA)	22.03.1995	13	(1)	8
Damien Furtado (FRA)	08.03.1997		(5)	1
Gabrielzinho (BRA)	29.09.1996	17	(10)	3
Galeno (BRA)	22.10.1997	23	(4)	5
Gelson Dala (ANG)	13.07.1996	13	(6)	5
José Postiga	03.05.1996	1		
Murilo Freitas (BRA)	12.05.1996	5	(4)	
Nuno Santos	13.02.1995	6	(2)	3
Ronan (BRA)	22.04.1995	3	(6)	3
Ahmed Said (GHA)	20.04.1993	1	(3)	1
Trainer:	**DOB**	**M**		
José Manuel Martins Teixeira Gomes	28.08.1970	13		
Augusto Vilela Gama [23.12.2018]	26.01.1970	2		
Daniel António Lopes Ramos [03.01.2019]	25.12.1970	19		

Clube Desportivo Santa Clara Ponta Delgada

Founded: 31.01.1921
Stadium: Estádio de São Miguel, Ponta Delgada (10,000)

Goalkeepers:	**DOB**	**M**	**(s)**	**G**
João Lopes (BRA)	16.01.1996	3		
Marco Rocha	12.01.1987	25		
Serginho	06.12.1982	6	(1)	
Defenders:	**DOB**	**M**	**(s)**	**G**
Accioly (BRA)	30.03.1981	10	(2)	
César (BRA)	28.12.1992	28	(2)	2
Fábio Cardoso	19.04.1994	30		5
João Lucas	15.01.1996	19		
Mamadú Candé (GNB)	28.08.1991	18	(2)	1
Patrick (BRA)	22.01.1991	32		
Rui Silva	05.06.1996	1	(1)	
Midfielders:	**DOB**	**M**	**(s)**	**G**
Anderson Carvalho (BRA)	20.05.1990	15	(1)	
Bruno Lamas (BRA)	13.04.1994	28	(5)	2
Chico Ramos	10.04.1995	11	(1)	
Martin Chrien (SVK)	08.09.1995	14	(4)	1
Diogo Santos	13.11.1984		(2)	
Kaio Pantaleão (BRA)	18.09.1995	15	(7)	
Lucas Marques (BRA)	24.05.1995	2	(3)	
Minhoca	29.04.1988		(6)	
Pedro Pacheco (CAN)	27.06.1984	4	(4)	
Denis Omar Pineda Torres (SLV)	10.08.1995	11	(3)	1
Osama Rashid (IRQ)	17.01.1992	23	(2)	7
Forwards:	**DOB**	**M**	**(s)**	**G**
Clemente	14.10.1983	1	(2)	
Malick Evouna (GAB)	28.11.1992	1	(5)	
Fernando Andrade (BRA)	08.01.1993	12	(1)	4
Guilherme Schettine (BRA)	10.10.1995	14	(4)	7
Abdiel Arroyo Molinar (PAN)	13.12.1993		(5)	
Pablo Diogo (BRA)	18.12.1992	1	(11)	
Alfredo Horacio Stephens Francis (PAN)	25.12.1994	10	(6)	
Thiago Santana (BRA)	04.02.1993	4	(6)	2
Ukra	16.03.1988	11	(12)	
Zé Manuel	23.10.1990	25	(3)	8
Trainer:	**DOB**	**M**		
João Alexandre Oliveira Nunes Henriques	31.10.1972	34		

Sporting Clube de Portugal Lisboa

Founded: 01.07.1906
Stadium: Estádio "José Alvalade", Lisboa (50,049)

Goalkeepers:	**DOB**	**M**	**(s)**	**G**
Renan Ribeiro (BRA)	23.03.1990	26	(1)	
Romain Salin (FRA)	29.07.1984	8	(1)	
Defenders:	**DOB**	**M**	**(s)**	**G**
Lumor Agbenyenu (GHA)	15.08.1996	1		
André Pinto	05.10.1989	8	(3)	
Cristian Alexis Borja González (COL)	18.02.1993	10	(1)	
Bruno Gaspar	21.04.1993	12	(4)	1
Sebastián Coates Nion (URU)	07.10.1990	31		1
Jefferson (BRA)	05.07.1988	8	(3)	
Jérémy Mathieu (FRA)	29.10.1983	24		3
Stefan Ristovski (MKD)	12.02.1992	22	(1)	
Tiago Ilori	26.02.1993	4	(2)	
Midfielders:	**DOB**	**M**	**(s)**	**G**
Marcos Javier Acuña (ARG)	28.10.1991	30		1
Rodrigo Andrés Battaglia (ARG)	12.07.1991	8		
Bruno César (BRA)	03.11.1988	1	(3)	
Bruno Fernandes	08.09.1994	33		20
Chico Geraldes	18.04.1995		(3)	
Idrissa Doumbia (CIV)	14.04.1998	4	(8)	1
Nemanja Gudelj (SRB)	16.11.1991	26	(1)	1
Miguel Luís	27.02.1999	3	(5)	1
Josip Mišić (CRO)	28.06.1994	1	(2)	
Radosav Petrović (SRB)	08.03.1989	4	(7)	
Wendel (BRA)	28.08.1997	20	(1)	1
Forwards:	**DOB**	**M**	**(s)**	**G**
Carlos Mané	11.03.1994		(2)	
Luc Castaignos (NED)	27.09.1992		(3)	
Abdoulay Diaby (MLI)	21.05.1991	19	(10)	2
Bas Dost (NED)	31.05.1989	18	(4)	15
Jovane Eduardo Borges Cabral (CPV)	14.06.1998	6	(12)	2
Luiz Phellype (BRA)	27.09.1993	9	(5)	8
Fredy Henkyer Montero Muñoz (COL)	26.07.1987	6	(3)	2
Nani	17.11.1986	16	(2)	7
Raphinha (BRA)	14.12.1996	16	(8)	4
Trainer:	**DOB**	**M**		
José Vitor dos Santos Peseiro	04.04.1960	8		
Tiago Fernandes [02.11.2018]	17.08.1981	2		
Marcel Keizer (NED) [12.11.2018]	15.01.1969	24		

Clube Desportivo de Tondela

Founded: 06.06.1933
Stadium: Estádio "João Cardoso", Tondela (5,000)

Goalkeepers:	**DOB**	**M**	**(s)**	**G**
Cláudio Ramos	16.11.1991	34		
Defenders:	**DOB**	**M**	**(s)**	**G**
David Bruno	14.02.1992	22	(1)	1
Ícaro Silva (BRA)	16.04.1989	13	(2)	1
Joãozinho	02.07.1989	34		
Jorge Fernandes	02.04.1997	16	(3)	
Fahd Moufi (MAR)	05.05.1996	11	(2)	1
Ricardo Alves	09.05.1991	10	(1)	
Ricardo Costa	16.05.1981	27		1
Midfielders:	**DOB**	**M**	**(s)**	**G**
Bruno Monteiro	05.10.1984	31		2
Hélder Tavares	26.12.1989	15		
João Lamine Jaquité (GNB)	22.02.1996	12	(2)	
João Mendes	21.10.1994	1	(2)	
João Pedro	03.04.1993	11	(3)	1
João Reis	24.06.1992		(3)	
Sergio Peña Flores (PER)	28.09.1995	20	(12)	1
Pité	22.08.1994	2	(17)	3
Azongha Tembeng Abenego (CMR)	13.09.1991	2	(6)	
Forwards:	**DOB**	**M**	**(s)**	**G**
António Xavier	06.07.1992	29	(3)	3
Cristian Daniel Arango Duque(COL)	09.03.1995	7	(9)	1
Juan Antonio Delgado Baeza (CHI)	05.03.1993	21	(12)	6
Jhon Eduard Murillo Romaña (VEN)	04.06.1995	19	(13)	3
Miguel Cardoso	19.06.1994	2		
Fábio Patrick dos Reis dos Santos Fernandes (CPV)	13.12.1993	5	(4)	1
Pablo David Sabbag Daccarett(COL)	11.06.1997		(5)	1
Tó Mané	23.10.1992	30	(1)	12
Trainer:	**DOB**	**M**		
Pedro Miguel Marques da Costa Filipe "Pêpa"	14.12.1980	34		

Vitória Sport Clube de Guimarães

Founded: 22.09.1922
Stadium: Estádio "D. Afonso Henriques", Guimarães (30,007)

Goalkeepers:	DOB	M	(s)	G
Douglas Jesus (BRA)	09.03.1983	23		
Miguel Silva	07.04.1995	11		
Defenders:	**DOB**	**M**	**(s)**	**G**
Dodô (BRA)	17.11.1998	8	(1)	1
Frederico Venâncio	04.02.1993	4	(1)	
Florent Hanin (FRA)	04.02.1990	6	(3)	1
João Afonso	28.05.1990	5		
Pedro Henrique (BRA)	18.12.1992	32		2
Rafa Soares	09.05.1995	27		
Falaye Sacko (MLI)	01.05.1995	27	(1)	
Midfielders:	**DOB**	**M**	**(s)**	**G**
Joseph Amoah (GHA)	26.06.1994	11	(3)	
André André	26.08.1989	16		6
Guillermo León Celis Montiel(COL)	08.05.1993	2	(2)	1
João Carlos Teixeira	18.01.1993	5	(15)	
Mattheus Oliveira (BRA)	07.07.1994	19	(4)	3
Yordan Hernando Osorio Paredes (VEN)	10.05.1994	27		2
Pêpê	20.05.1997	9	(9)	
Rochinha	03.05.1995	6	(7)	2
Tózé	14.01.1993	30	(1)	9
Alhassan Wakaso (GHA)	07.01.1992	30		2
Forwards:	**DOB**	**M**	**(s)**	**G**
Alexandre Guedes	11.02.1994	25	(4)	6
Tyler Boyd (USA)	30.12.1994	4	(6)	
Davidson (BRA)	05.03.1991	30	(4)	8
Oscar Eduardo Estupiñán Vallesilla (COL)	29.12.1996		(4)	
Hélder Ferreira	05.04.1997		(3)	
Ola John (NED)	19.05.1992	10	(16)	1
Sebastián Rincón Lucumí (COL)	14.01.1994		(2)	
Gadji Celi Carmel Junior Tallo(CIV)	21.12.1992	2	(1)	
Welthon (BRA)	21.06.1992	4	(13)	1
Abdul-Aziz Yakubu (GHA)	10.11.1998	1		
Trainer:	**DOB**	**M**		
Luís Manuel Ribeiro Castro	03.09.1961	34		

Vitória Futebol Clube de Setúbal

Founded: 20.11.1910
Stadium: Estádio do Bonfim, Setúbal (14,274)

Goalkeepers:	DOB	M	(s)	G
Cristiano	29.11.1990	14		
Joel Pereira	28.06.1996	9		
Giorgi Makaridze (GEO)	31.03.1990	11		
Defenders:	**DOB**	**M**	**(s)**	**G**
André Sousa	26.02.1998	11	(6)	
Artur Jorge	14.08.1994	20	(1)	
Bruno Pires (BRA)	12.05.1992	1		
Cascardo (BRA)	24.03.1997	6	(1)	
Dankler (BRA)	24.01.1992	17		
Mano	09.04.1987	28	(3)	
Nuno Reis	31.01.1991	3		
Sílvio	28.09.1987	7	(1)	
Vasco Fernandes	12.11.1986	33		1
Midfielders:	**DOB**	**M**	**(s)**	**G**
Mikel Agu (NGA)	27.05.1993	17	(1)	1
André Pedrosa	12.04.1997		(3)	
Costinha	25.08.1992	5	(3)	1
Éber Bessa (BRA)	21.03.1992	27	(4)	2
Luís Cortez	18.04.1994		(1)	
Nuno Pinto	06.08.1986	10	(1)	
Nuno Valente	22.11.1991	18	(5)	2
Rúben Micael	19.08.1986	20	(6)	
Sávio Roberto (BRA)	30.04.1996	1	(3)	
Semedo	11.01.1985	29	(1)	2
Tiago Castro	31.01.1996	3	(2)	
Forwards:	**DOB**	**M**	**(s)**	**G**
Alex	27.08.1991	5	(6)	
Allef (BRA)	04.11.1994	2	(7)	1
Jhonder Leonel Cádiz Fernández(VEN)	29.07.1995	23	(8)	9
Hildeberto	02.03.1996	19	(7)	4
Frédéric Mendy (GNB)	18.09.1988	23	(5)	4
Kgaogelo Rathete Sekgota (RSA)	22.06.1997	1	(5)	
Valdumar Augusto Té (GNB)	14.08.1997	1	(7)	
Zéquinha	07.01.1987	10	(13)	1
Trainer:	**DOB**	**M**		
José Carlos Fernandes „Lito"Vidigal (ANG)	11.07.1969	18		
Sandro Miguel Laranjeira Mendes [28.01.2019]	04.02.1977	16		

SECOND LEVEL
LigaPro 2018/2019

1.	FC Paços de Ferreira (*Promoted*)	34	23	5	6	50 - 21	74
2.	FC Famalicão (*Promoted*)	34	21	6	7	57 - 34	69
3.	GD Estoril Praia	34	16	6	12	49 - 42	54
4.	Sport Lisboa e Benfica "B"	34	15	7	12	47 - 42	52
5.	Associação Académica de Coimbra	34	15	6	13	36 - 37	51
6.	Sporting da Covilhã	34	13	10	11	42 - 37	49
7.	Leixões SC Porto	34	12	9	13	35 - 36	45
8.	FC Penafiel	34	13	6	15	49 - 48	45
9.	FC do Porto "B"	34	11	11	12	41 - 42	44
10.	SC Farense Faro	34	11	10	13	39 - 35	43
11.	Académico de Viseu FC	34	12	7	15	49 - 54	43
12.	UD Oliveirense	34	11	10	13	44 - 49	43
13.	CD Cova da Piedade	34	11	9	14	25 - 42	42
14.	CD Mafra	34	10	11	13	40 - 44	41
15.	Varzim SC	34	11	8	15	25 - 37	41
16.	FC Arouca (*Relegated*)	34	10	10	14	40 - 45	40
17.	Sporting Clube de Braga "B" (*Relegated*)	34	11	4	19	38 - 45	37
18.	Vitória SC Guimarães "B" (*Relegated*)	34	6	13	15	41 - 57	31

NATIONAL TEAM

INTERNATIONAL MATCHES
(16.07.2018 – 15.07.2019)

06.09.2018	Faro/Loulé	Portugal - Croatia	1-1(1-1)	(F)
10.09.2018	Lisboa	Portugal - Italy	1-0(0-0)	(UNL)
11.10.2018	Chorzów	Poland - Portugal	2-3(1-2)	(UNL)
14.10.2018	Glasgow	Scotland - Portugal	1-3(0-1)	(F)
17.11.2018	Milano	Italy - Portugal	0-0	(UNL)
20.11.2018	Guimarães	Portugal - Poland	1-1(1-0)	(UNL)
22.03.2019	Lisboa	Portugal - Ukraine	0-0	(ECQ)
25.03.2019	Lisboa	Portugal - Serbia	1-1(1-1)	(ECQ)
05.06.2019	Porto	Portugal - Switzerland	3-1(1-0)	(UNL)
09.06.2019	Porto	Portugal - Netherlands	1-0(0-0)	(UNL)

06.09.2018 PORTUGAL - CROATIA 1-1(1-1) Friendly International
Estádio Algarve, Faro/Loulé; Referee: Xavier Estrada Fernández (Spain); Attendance: 26,355
POR: Rui Patrício, João Cancelo, Pepe (Cap), Mário Rui, Rúben Dias, Pizzi (61.Bruno Fernandes), Bruma (68.Rony Lopes), Bernardo Silva (46.Gelson Martins), William Carvalho (81.Sérgio Oliveira), Rúben Neves (86.Renato Sanches), André Silva (89.Gedson Fernandes). Trainer: Fernando Manuel Fernandes da Costa Santos.
Goal: Pepe (32).

10.09.2018 PORTUGAL - ITALY 1-0(0-0) UEFA Nations League A, Group 3
Estádio da Luz, Lisboa; Referee: William Collum (Scotland); Attendance: 52,635
POR: Rui Patrício, João Cancelo, Pepe (Cap), Mário Rui, Rúben Dias, Pizzi (74.Renato Sanches), William Carvalho (86.Sérgio Oliveira), Rúben Neves, Bernardo Silva, Bruma (77.Gelson Martins), André Silva. Trainer: Fernando Manuel Fernandes da Costa Santos.
Goal: André Silva (48).

11.10.2018 POLAND - PORTUGAL 2-3(1-2) UEFA Nations League A, Group 3
Stadion Śląski, Chorzów; Referee: Carlos del Cerro Grande (Spain); Attendance: 48,783
POR: Rui Patrício, João Cancelo, Pepe (Cap), Mário Rui, Rúben Dias, Pizzi (75.Renato Sanches), William Carvalho, Rafa Silva (85.Danilo Pereira), Bernardo Silva (90+1.Bruno Fernandes), Rúben Neves, André Silva. Trainer: Fernando Manuel Fernandes da Costa Santos.
Goals: André Silva (32), Kamil Jacek Glik (43 own goal), Bernardo Silva (52).

14.10.2018 SCOTLAND - PORTUGAL 1-3(0-1) Friendly International
Hampden Park, Glasgow; Referee: Ruddy Buquet (France); Attendance: 19,684
POR: Beto (Cap) (86.Cláudio Ramos), Luís Neto, Cédric Soares, Kévin Rodrigues, Rúben Dias (57.Pedro Mendes), Sérgio Oliveira (56.Renato Sanches), Danilo Pereira (90+1.William Carvalho), Bruno Fernandes (68.Gedson Fernandes), Éder, Bruma (90+1.Rafa Silva), Hélder Costa. Trainer: Fernando Manuel Fernandes da Costa Santos.
Goals: Hélder Costa (43), Éder (74), Bruma (84).

17.11.2018 ITALY - PORTUGAL 0-0 UEFA Nations League A, Group 3
Stadio "Giuseppe Meazza", Milano; Referee: Danny Desmond Makkelie (Netherlands); Attendance: 73,000
POR: Rui Patrício (Cap), João Cancelo, José Fonte, Mário Rui, Rúben Dias, Pizzi (68.João Mário), Bruma (85.Raphaël Guerreiro), Rúben Neves, Bernardo Silva, William Carvalho, André Silva (90.Danilo Pereira). Trainer: Fernando Manuel Fernandes da Costa Santos.

20.11.2018 PORTUGAL - POLAND 1-1(1-0) UEFA Nations League A, Group 3
Estádio "D. Afonso Henriques", Guimarães; Referee: Sergei Karasev (Russia); Attendance: 29,917
POR: Beto, João Cancelo, Pepe (Cap), Raphaël Guerreiro (61.João Mário), Kévin Rodrigues, Rúben Dias, Danilo Pereira [*sent off 63*], William Carvalho, Rafa Silva (70.Bruma), Renato Sanches, André Silva (87.Éder). Trainer: Fernando Manuel Fernandes da Costa Santos.
Goal: André Silva (34).

22.03.2019 PORTUGAL - UKRAINE 0-0 16th EC. Qualifiers
Estádio da Luz, Lisboa; Referee: Clément Turpin (France); Attendance: 58,355
POR: Rui Patrício, João Cancelo, Pepe, Raphaël Guerreiro, William Carvalho, Rúben Dias, João Moutinho (87.João Mário), Rúben Neves (62.Rafa Silva), Bernardo Silva, Cristiano Ronaldo (Cap), André Silva (73.Dyego Sousa). Trainer: Fernando Manuel Fernandes da Costa Santos.

25.03.2019 PORTUGAL - SERBIA 1-1(1-1) 16th EC. Qualifiers
Estádio da Luz, Lisboa; Referee: Szymon Marciniak (Poland); Attendance: 50,342
POR: Rui Patrício, João Cancelo, Pepe, Raphaël Guerreiro, Rúben Dias, Danilo Pereira, William Carvalho, Rafa Silva (84.Gonçalo Guedes), Bernardo Silva, Cristiano Ronaldo (Cap) (31.Pizzi), Dyego Sousa (57.André Silva). Trainer: Fernando Manuel Fernandes da Costa Santos.
Goal: Danilo Pereira (42).

05.06.2019 PORTUGAL - SWITZERLAND 3-1(1-0) UEFA Nations League, Semi-Finals
Estádio do Dragão, Porto; Referee: Dr. Felix Brych (Germany); Attendance: 42,415
POR: Rui Patrício, Nélson Semedo, Pepe (63.José Fonte), Raphaël Guerreiro, Rúben Dias, William Carvalho, Rúben Neves, Bruno Fernandes (90+1.João Moutinho), Bernardo Silva, Cristiano Ronaldo (Cap), João Félix (70.Gonçalo Guedes). Trainer: Fernando Manuel Fernandes da Costa Santos.
Goals: Cristiano Ronaldo (25, 88, 90).

09.06.2019 PORTUGAL - NETHERLANDS 1-0(0-0) UEFA Nations League, Final
Estádio do Dragão, Porto; Referee: Alberto Undiano Mallenco (Spain); Attendance: 43,199
POR: Rui Patrício, Nélson Semedo, José Fonte, Raphaël Guerreiro, Danilo Pereira, Rúben Dias, William Carvalho (90+3.Rúben Neves), Bruno Fernandes (81.João Moutinho), Bernardo Silva, Gonçalo Guedes (75.Rafa Silva), Cristiano Ronaldo (Cap). Trainer: Fernando Manuel Fernandes da Costa Santos.
Goal: Gonçalo Guedes (60).

NATIONAL TEAM PLAYERS
(16.07.2018 – 15.07.2019)

Name	DOB	Caps	Goals	2018/2019:	*Club*
Goalkeepers					
António Alberto Bastos Pimparel "BETO"	01.06.1982	**16**	**0**	2018:	*Göztepe SK İzmir (TUR)*
CLÁUDIO Pires Morais RAMOS	16.11.1991	**1**	**0**	2018:	*CD Tondela*
RUI Pedro dos Santos PATRÍCIO	15.02.1988	**81**	**0**	2018/2019:	*Wolverhampton Wanderers FC (ENG)*
Defenders					
CÉDRIC Ricardo Alves Soares	31.08.1991	**33**	**1**	2018:	*Southampton FC (ENG)*
JOÃO Pedro Cavaco CANCELO	27.05.1994	**14**	**3**	2018/2019:	*Juventus FC Torino (ITA)*
JOSÉ Miguel da Rocha FONTE	22.12.1983	**38**	**0**	2018/2019:	*Lille OSC (FRA)*
KÉVIN Manuel RODRIGUES	05.03.1994	**3**	**0**	2018:	*Real Sociedad de Fútbol San Sebastián (ESP)*
LUÍS Carlos Novo NETO	26.05.1988	**19**	**0**	2018:	*FK Zenit Saint Petersburg (RUS)*
MÁRIO RUI Silva Duarte	27.05.1991	**8**	**0**	2018:	*SSC Napoli (ITA)*
NÉLSON Cabral SEMEDO "Nelsinho"	16.11.1993	**10**	**0**	2019:	*FC Barcelona (ESP)*
PEDRO Filipe Teodósio MENDES	01.10.1990	**1**	**0**	2018:	*Montpellier-Hérault SC (FRA)*
Képler Laveran Lima Ferreira "PEPE"	26.02.1983	**106**	**7**	2018: 08.01.2019->	*Beşiktaş JK İstanbul (TUR)* *FC do Porto*
RAPHAËL Adelino José GUERREIRO	22.12.1993	**34**	**2**	2018/2019:	*BV Borussia Dortmund (GER)*
RÚBEN Santos Gato Alves DIAS	14.05.1997	**11**	**0**	2018/2019:	*Sport Lisboa e Benfica*
Midfielders					
BRUNO Miguel Borges FERNANDES	08.09.1994	**13**	**1**	2018/2019:	*Sporting Clube de Portugal Lisboa*
DANILO Luís Hélio PEREIRA	09.09.1991	**33**	**2**	2018/2019:	*FC do Porto*
GEDSON Carvalho FERNANDES	09.01.1999	**2**	**0**	2018:	*Sport Lisboa e Benfica*
JOÃO MÁRIO Naval da Costa Eduardo	19.01.1993	**43**	**2**	2018/2019:	*FC Internazionale Milano (ITA)*
JOÃO Filipe Iria Santos MOUTINHO	08.09.1986	**116**	**7**	2019:	*Wolverhampton Wanderers FC (ENG)*
Luís Miguel Afonso Fernandes "PIZZI"	06.10.1989	**14**	**2**	2018/2019:	*Sport Lisboa e Benfica*
Rafael Alexandre "RAFA" Fernandes Ferreira da SILVA	17.05.1993	**16**	**0**	2018/2019:	*Sport Lisboa e Benfica*
RENATO Júnior Luz SANCHES	18.08.1997	**18**	**1**	2018:	*FC Bayern München (GER)*
RÚBEN Diogo da Silva NEVES	13.03.1997	**12**	**0**	2018/2019:	*Wolverhampton Wanderers FC (ENG)*
SÉRGIO Miguel Relvas de OLIVEIRA	02.06.1992	**3**	**0**	2018:	*FC do Porto*
WILLIAM Silva de CARVALHO	07.04.1992	**57**	**2**	2018/2019:	*Real Betis Balompié Sevilla (ESP)*
Forwards					
ANDRÉ Miguel Valente SILVA	06.11.1995	**33**	**15**	2018/2019:	*Sevilla FC (ESP)*
BERNARDO Mota Veiga de Carvalho e SILVA	10.08.1994	**37**	**3**	2018/2019:	*Manchester City FC (ENG)*
Armindo Tué Na Bangna "BRUMA"	24.10.1994	**7**	**1**	2018:	*RasenBallsport Leipzig (GER)*
CRISTIANO RONALDO dos Santos Aveiro	05.02.1985	**158**	**88**	2019:	*Juventus FC Torino (ITA)*
DYEGO Wilverson Ferreira SOUSA	14.09.1989	**2**	**0**	2018/2019:	*Sporting Clube de Braga*
Éderzito António Macedo Lopes "ÉDER"	22.12.1987	**35**	**5**	2018:	*FK Lokomotiv Moskva (RUS)*
GELSON Dany Batalha MARTINS	11.05.1995	**21**	**0**	2018:	*Club Atlético de Madrid (ESP)*
GONÇALO Manuel Ganchinho GUEDES	29.11.1996	**17**	**4**	2018/2019:	*Valencia CF (ESP)*
HÉLDER Wander Sousa de Azevedo e COSTA	12.02.1994	**1**	**0**	2018:	*Wolverhampton Wanderers FC (ENG)*
JOÃO FÉLIX Sequeira	10.11.1999	**1**	**0**	2019:	*Sport Lisboa e Benfica*
Marcos Paulo Mesquita Lopes "RONY LOPES"	28.12.1995	**2**	**0**	2018:	*AS Monaco FC (FRA)*

National team coach

FERNANDO Manuel Fernandes da Costa SANTOS [from 23.09.2014]	10.10.1954	65 M; 39 W; 16 D; 10 L; 120-48

REPUBLIC OF IRELAND

The Country:

Éire (Republic of Ireland)
Capital: Dublin
Surface: 70,273 km²
Inhabitants: 4,921,500 [2019]
Time: UTC

The FA:

Football Association of Ireland
National Sports Campus Abbotstown, Dublin 15
Tel: +353 1 8999 500
Founded: 1921
Member of FIFA since: 1923
Member of UEFA since: 1954
Website: www.fai.ie

NATIONAL TEAM RECORDS

First international match:	21.03.1926, Torino:	Italy – Republic of Ireland 3-0
Most international caps:	Robert David Keane	- 146 caps (1998-2016)
Most international goals:	Robert David Keane	- 68 goals / 146 caps (1998-2016)

UEFA EUROPEAN CHAMPIONSHIP	
1960	Qualifiers
1964	Qualifiers
1968	Qualifiers
1972	Qualifiers
1976	Qualifiers
1980	Qualifiers
1984	Qualifiers
1988	Final Tournament (Group Stage)
1992	Qualifiers
1996	Qualifiers
2000	Qualifiers
2004	Qualifiers
2008	Qualifiers
2012	Final Tournament (Group Stage)
2016	Final Tournament (2nd Round of 16)

FIFA WORLD CUP	
1930	Did not enter
1934	Qualifiers
1938	Qualifiers
1950	Qualifiers
1954	Qualifiers
1958	Qualifiers
1962	Qualifiers
1966	Qualifiers
1970	Qualifiers
1974	Qualifiers
1978	Qualifiers
1982	Qualifiers
1986	Qualifiers
1990	Final Tournament (Quarter-Finals)
1994	Final Tournament (2nd Round of 16)
1998	Qualifiers
2002	Final Tournament (2nd Round of 16)
2006	Qualifiers
2010	Qualifiers
2014	Qualifiers
2018	Qualifiers

UEFA NATIONS LEAGUE
2018/2019 – League B

OLYMPIC FOOTBALL TOURNAMENTS 1908-2016							
1908	-	**1948**	Preliminary Round	**1972**	Qualifiers	**1996**	Qualifiers
1912	-	**1952**	Did not enter	**1976**	Qualifiers	**2000**	Qualifiers
1920	-	**1956**	Did not enter	**1980**	Qualifiers	**2004**	Qualifiers
1924	Quarter-Finals	**1960**	Qualifiers	**1984**	Did not enter	**2008**	Qualifiers
1928	-	**1964**	Did not enter	**1988**	Qualifiers	**2012**	Qualifiers
1936	-	**1968**	Did not enter	**1992**	Qualifiers	**2016**	Qualifiers

FIFA CONFEDERATIONS CUP 1992-2017
None

IRISH CLUB HONOURS IN EUROPEAN CLUB COMPETITIONS:

European Champion Clubs.Cup (1956-1992) / UEFA Champions League (1993-2019)
None
Fairs Cup (1858-1971) / UEFA Cup (1972-2009) / UEFA Europa League (2010-2019)
None
UEFA Super Cup (1972-2018)
None
European Cup Winners.Cup 1961-1999*
None

**defunct competition*

NATIONAL COMPETITIONS
TABLE OF HONOURS

	CHAMPIONS	CUP WINNERS	BEST GOALSCORERS	
1921/1922	St. James' Gate	St. James' Gate FC Dublin	Jack Kelly (St. James' Gate FC Dublin)	11
1922/1923	Shamrock Rovers FC Dublin	Alton United	Bob Fullam (Shamrock Rovers FC Dublin)	27
1923/1924	Bohemian FC Dublin	Athlone Town FC	Dave Roberts (Bohemian FC Dublin)	20
1924/1925	Shamrock Rovers FC Dublin	Shamrock Rovers FC Dublin	Billy Farrell (Shamrock Rovers FC Dublin)	25
1925/1926	Shelbourne FC Dublin	Fordsons FC Cork	Billy Farrell (Shamrock Rovers FC Dublin)	24
1926/1927	Shamrock Rovers FC Dublin	Drumcondra	David Byrne (Shamrock Rovers FC Dublin) John McMillan (Shelbourne FC Dublin)	17
1927/1928	Bohemian FC Dublin	Bohemian FC Dublin	Charlie Heinemann (Fordsons FC Cork)	24
1928/1929	Shelbourne FC Dublin	Shamrock Rovers FC Dublin	Eddie Carroll (Dundalk FC)	17
1929/1930	Bohemian FC Dublin	Shamrock Rovers FC Dublin	Johnny Ledwidge (Shelbourne FC Dublin)	16
1930/1931	Shelbourne FC Dublin	Shamrock Rovers FC Dublin	Alec Hair (Shelbourne FC Dublin)	29
1931/1932	Shamrock Rovers FC Dublin	Shamrock Rovers FC Dublin	Pearson Ferguson (Cork FC) Jack Forster (Waterford FC)	21
1932/1933	Dundalk FC	Shamrock Rovers FC Dublin	George Ebbs (St. James' Gate FC Dublin)	20
1933/1934	Bohemian FC Dublin	Cork FC	Alf Rigby (St. James' Gate FC Dublin)	13
1934/1935	Dolphin	Bohemian FC Dublin	Alf Rigby (St. James' Gate FC Dublin)	17
1935/1936	Bohemian FC Dublin	Shamrock Rovers FC Dublin	Jimmy Turnbull (Cork FC)	37
1936/1937	Sligo Rovers FC	Waterford FC	Bob Slater (Shelbourne FC Dublin, Waterford FC)	20
1937/1938	Shamrock Rovers FC Dublin	St. James' Gate FC Dublin	Willie Byrne (St. James' Gate FC Dublin)	25
1938/1939	Shamrock Rovers FC Dublin	Shelbourne FC Dublin	Paddy Bradshaw (St. James' Gate FC Dublin)	22
1939/1940	St. James' Gate	Shamrock Rovers FC Dublin	Paddy Bradshaw (St. James' Gate FC Dublin)	29
1940/1941	Cork United FC	Cork United FC	Mick O'Flanagan (Bohemian FC Dublin)	19
1941/1942	Cork United FC	Dundalk FC	Tommy Byrne (Limerick FC)	20
1942/1943	Cork United FC	Drumcondra	Sean McCarthy (Cork United FC)	16
1943/1944	Shelbourne FC Dublin	Shamrock Rovers FC Dublin	Sean McCarthy (Cork United FC)	16
1944/1945	Cork United FC	Shamrock Rovers FC Dublin	Sean McCarthy (Cork United FC)	26
1945/1946	Cork United FC	Drumcondra FC Dublin	Paddy O'Leary (Cork United FC)	15
1946/1947	Shelbourne FC Dublin	Cork United FC	Paddy Coad (Shamrock Rovers FC Dublin) Alf Hanson (Shelbourne FC Dublin)	11
1947/1948	Drumcondra FC Dublin	Shamrock Rovers FC Dublin	Sean McCarthy (Cork United FC)	13
1948/1949	Drumcondra FC Dublin	Dundalk FC	Bernard Lester (Transport FC Dublin) Eugene Noonan (Waterford FC) Paddy O'Leary (Cork Athletic FC)	12
1949/1950	Cork Athletic FC	Transport FC Dublin	Dave McCulloch (Waterford FC)	19
1950/1951	Cork Athletic FC	Cork Athletic FC	Dessie Glynn (Drumcondra FC Dublin)	20
1951/1952	St. Patrick's Athletic FC Dublin	Dundalk FC	Shay Gibbons (St. Patrick's Athletic FC Dublin)	26
1952/1953	Shelbourne FC Dublin	Cork Athletic FC	Shay Gibbons (St. Patrick's Athletic FC Dublin)	22
1953/1954	Shamrock Rovers FC Dublin	Drumcondra FC Dublin	Danny Jordan (Bohemian FC Dublin)	14
1954/1955	St. Patrick's Athletic FC Dublin	Shamrock Rovers FC Dublin	Jimmy Gauld (Waterford FC)	30
1955/1956	St. Patrick's Athletic FC Dublin	Shamrock Rovers FC Dublin	Shay Gibbons (St. Patrick's Athletic FC Dublin)	21
1956/1957	Shamrock Rovers FC Dublin	Drumcondra FC Dublin	Tommy Hamilton (Shamrock Rovers FC Dublin) Donal Leahy (Evergreen United FC Cork)	15
1957/1958	Drumcondra FC Dublin	Dundalk FC	Donal Leahy (Evergreen United FC Cork)	16
1958/1959	Shamrock Rovers FC Dublin	St. Patrick's Athletic FC Dublin	Donal Leahy (Evergreen United FC Cork)	22
1959/1960	Limerick FC	Shelbourne FC Dublin	Austin Noonan (Cork Celtic FC)	27
1960/1961	Drumcondra FC Dublin	St. Patrick's Athletic FC Dublin	Dan McCaffrey (Drumcondra FC Dublin)	29
1961/1962	Shelbourne FC Dublin	Shamrock Rovers FC Dublin	Eddie Bailham (Shamrock Rovers FC Dublin)	21
1962/1963	Dundalk FC	Shelbourne FC Dublin	Mick Lynch (Waterford FC)	12
1963/1964	Shamrock Rovers FC Dublin	Shamrock Rovers FC Dublin	Eddie Bailham (Shamrock Rovers FC Dublin) Jimmy Hasty (Dundalk FC) Johnny Kingston (Cork Hibernians FC)	18
1964/1965	Drumcondra FC Dublin	Shamrock Rovers FC Dublin	Jackie Mooney (Shamrock Rovers FC Dublin)	16
1965/1966	Waterford FC	Shamrock Rovers FC Dublin	Mick Lynch (Waterford FC)	17
1966/1967	Dundalk FC	Shamrock Rovers FC Dublin	Johnny Brooks (Sligo Rovers FC) Danny Hale (Dundalk FC)	15
1967/1968	Waterford FC	Shamrock Rovers FC Dublin	Carl Davenport (Cork Celtic FC) Ben Hannigan (Dundalk FC)	15
1968/1969	Waterford FC	Shamrock Rovers FC Dublin	Mick Leech (Shamrock Rovers FC Dublin)	19
1969/1970	Waterford FC	Bohemian FC Dublin	Brendan Bradley (Finn Harps FC Ballybofey)	18
1970/1971	Cork Hibernians FC	Limerick FC	Brendan Bradley (Finn Harps FC Ballybofey)	20
1971/1972	Waterford FC	Cork Hibernians FC	Alfie Hale (Waterford FC) Tony Marsden (Cork Hibernians FC)	22
1972/1973	Waterford FC	Cork Hibernians FC	Alfie Hale (Waterford FC) Terry Harkin (Finn Harps FC Ballybofey)	20
1973/1974	Cork Celtic FC	Finn Harps FC Ballybofey	Terry Flanagan (Bohemian FC Dublin) Turlough O'Connor (Bohemian FC Dublin)	18
1974/1975	Bohemian FC Dublin	Home Farm FC Dublin	Brendan Bradley (Finn Harps FC Ballybofey)	21
1975/1976	Dundalk FC	Bohemian FC Dublin	Brendan Bradley (Finn Harps FC Ballybofey)	29
1976/1977	Sligo Rovers FC	Dundalk FC	Syd Wallace (Waterford FC)	16
1977/1978	Bohemian FC Dublin	Shamrock Rovers FC Dublin	Turlough O'Connor (Bohemian FC Dublin)	24
1978/1979	Dundalk FC	Dundalk FC	John Delamere (Sligo Rovers FC, Shelbourne FC Dublin)	17

1979/1980	Limerick United FC	Waterford FC	Alan Campbell (Shamrock Rovers FC Dublin)	22
1980/1981	Athlone Town FC	Dundalk FC	Eugene Davis (Athlone Town FC)	23
1981/1982	Dundalk FC	Limerick United FC	Michael O'Connor (Athlone Town FC)	22
1982/1983	Athlone Town FC	Sligo Rovers FC	Noel Larkin (Athlone Town FC)	18
1983/1984	Shamrock Rovers FC Dublin	UCD	Alan Campbell (Shamrock Rovers FC Dublin)	24
1984/1985	Shamrock Rovers FC Dublin	Shamrock Rovers FC Dublin	Thomas Gaynor (Limerick City FC) Michael O'Connor (Athlone Town FC)	17
1985/1986	Shamrock Rovers FC Dublin	Shamrock Rovers FC Dublin	Tommy Gaynor (Limerick City FC)	15
1986/1987	Shamrock Rovers FC Dublin	Shamrock Rovers FC Dublin	Michael Byrne (Shamrock Rovers FC Dublin)	12
1987/1988	Dundalk FC	Dundalk FC	Jonathan Speak (Derry City FC)	24
1988/1989	Derry City FC	Derry City FC	William Robert Hamilton (NIR, Limerick City FC)	21
1989/1990	St. Patrick's Athletic FC Dublin	Bray Wanderers FC	Mark Ennis (St. Patrick's Athletic FC Dublin)	19
1990/1991	Dundalk FC	Galway United FC	Peter Hanrahan (Dundalk FC)	18
1991/1992	Shelbourne FC Dublin	Bohemian FC Dublin	John Caulfield (Cork City FC)	16
1992/1993	Cork City FC	Shelbourne FC Dublin	Pat Morley (Cork City FC)	20
1993/1994	Shamrock Rovers FC Dublin	Sligo Rovers FC	Stephen Geoghegan (Shamrock Rovers FC Dublin)	23
1994/1995	Dundalk FC	Derry City FC	John Caulfield (Cork City FC)	16
1995/1996	St. Patrick's Athletic FC Dublin	Shelbourne FC Dublin	Stephen Geoghegan (Shelbourne FC Dublin)	19
1996/1997	Derry City FC	Shelbourne FC Dublin	Anthony Cousins (Shamrock Rovers FC Dublin) Stephen Geoghegan (Shelbourne FC Dublin)	16
1997/1998	St. Patrick's Athletic FC Dublin	Cork City FC	Stephen Geoghegan (Shelbourne FC Dublin)	17
1998/1999	St. Patrick's Athletic FC Dublin	Bray Wanderers FC	Trevor Molloy (St. Patrick's Athletic FC Dublin)	15
1999/2000	Shelbourne FC Dublin	Shelbourne FC Dublin	Patrick Morley (Cork City FC)	20
2000/2001	Bohemian FC Dublin	Bohemian FC Dublin	Glen Crowe (Bohemian FC Dublin)	25
2001/2002	Shelbourne FC Dublin	Dundalk FC	Glen Crowe (Bohemian FC Dublin)	21
2002/2003	Bohemian FC Dublin	Derry City FC (2000)	Glen Crowe (Bohemian FC Dublin)	18
2003	Shelbourne FC Dublin	Longford Town FC	Jason Byrne (Shelbourne FC Dublin)	21
2004	Shelbourne FC Dublin	Longford Town FC	Jason Byrne (Shelbourne FC Dublin)	25
2005	Cork City FC	Drogheda United FC	Jason Byrne (Shelbourne FC Dublin)	22
2006	Shelbourne FC Dublin	Derry City FC	Jason Byrne (Shelbourne FC Dublin)	15
2007	Drogheda United FC	Cork City FC	Dave Mooney (Longford Town FC)	19
2008	Bohemian FC Dublin	Bohemian FC Dublin	Dave Mooney (Cork City FC) Mark Quigley (St. Patrick's Athletic FC Dublin) Mark Farren (Derry City FC)	15
2009	Bohemian FC Dublin	Sporting Fingal	Gary Michael Nolan Twigg (SCO, Shamrock Rovers FC Dublin)	24
2010	Shamrock Rovers FC Dublin	Sligo Rovers FC	Gary Michael Nolan Twigg (SCO, Shamrock Rovers FC Dublin)	20
2011	Shamrock Rovers FC Dublin	Sligo Rovers FC	Eamon Zayed (LBY, Derry City FC)	22
2012	Sligo Rovers FC	Derry City FC	Gary Michael Nolan Twigg (SCO, Shamrock Rovers FC Dublin)	22
2013	St. Patrick's Athletic FC Dublin	Sligo Rovers FC	Rory Christopher Patterson (NIR, Derry City FC)	18
2014	Dundalk FC	St. Patrick's Athletic FC Dublin	Patrick James Hoban (Dundalk FC) Christopher Joseph Fagan (St. Patrick's Athletic FC Dublin)	20
2015	Dundalk FC	Dundalk FC	Richard Patrick Towell (Dundalk FC)	25
2016	Dundalk FC	Cork City FC	Seán Patrick Maguire (Cork City FC)	18
2017	Cork City FC	Cork City FC	Seán Patrick Maguire (Cork City FC)	20
2018	Dundalk FC	Dundalk FC	Patrick James Hoban (Dundalk FC)	29

NATIONAL CHAMPIONSHIP

League of Ireland Premier Division 2018

(16.02.2018 – 26.10.2018)

Results

Round 1 [16-17.02.2018]
Bohemian - Shamrock Rovers 3-1(0-1)
Dundalk FC - Bray Wanderers 0-0
St Patrick's Athletic - Cork City 2-3(1-2)
Waterford FC - Derry City 2-1(1-1)
Sligo Rovers - Limerick FC 0-1(0-0)

Round 2 [23-24.02.2018]
Bray Wanderers - St Patrick's Athl. 1-2(1-2)
Cork City - Waterford FC 2-0(0-0)
Sligo Rovers - Derry City 2-1(0-0)
Shamrock Rovers - Dundalk FC 0-0
Limerick FC - Bohemian 1-1(0-0)

Round 3 [26-27.02.2018]
Waterford FC - St Patrick's Athletic 2-0(1-0)
Sligo Rovers - Cork City 1-4(0-2)
Shamrock Rovers - Bray Wanderers 6-0(1-0)
Bohemian - Derry City 0-1(0-0)
Dundalk FC - Limerick FC 8-0(4-0)

Round 4 [19.03.2018]
Cork City - Bohemian 3-0(2-0)
Limerick FC - Shamrock Rovers 0-1(0-0)
Bray Wanderers - Waterford 2-2(1-1) [14.05.]
Derry City - Dundalk FC 1-4(1-2) [14.05.]
St Patrick's A. - Sligo Rovers 2-0(0-0) [15.05.]

Round 5 [09.03.2018]
Bohemian - St Patrick's Athletic 0-1(0-1)
Limerick FC - Bray Wanderers 1-0(0-0)
Sligo Rovers - Waterford FC 1-2(0-1)
Dundalk FC - Cork City 1-0(1-0)
Shamrock Rovers - Derry City 6-1(1-0)

Round 6 [12.03.2018]
Bray Wanderers - Sligo Rovers 1-2(0-2)
Cork City - Shamrock Rovers 1-0(1-0)
Derry City - Limerick FC 5-0(1-0)
St Patrick's Athletic - Dundalk FC 0-0
Waterford FC - Bohemian 1-0(0-0)

Round 7 [16.03.2018]
Bohemian - Sligo Rovers 2-2(1-1)
Derry City - Bray Wanderers 5-1(1-0)
Dundalk FC - Waterford FC 1-0(0-0)
Limerick FC - Cork City 1-1(1-1)
Shamrock Rovers - St Patrick's Athl. 1-0(0-0)

Round 8 [23-24.03.2018]
Bohemian - Bray Wanderers 2-1(1-1)
St Patrick's Athletic - Limerick FC 1-0(0-0)
Waterford FC - Shamrock Rovers 2-1(2-1)
Sligo Rovers - Dundalk FC 0-2(0-1)
Cork City - Derry City 4-2(1-0) [04.06.]

Round 9 [30.03.2018]
Derry City - St Patrick's Athletic 2-1(1-0)
Bray Wanderers - Cork City 0-4(0-1)
Dundalk FC - Bohemian 3-0(2-0)
Limerick FC - Waterford FC 0-2(0-1)
Shamrock Rovers - Sligo Rovers 1-0(0-0)

Round 10 [06-07.04.2018]
Dundalk FC - Shamrock Rovers 2-1(0-0)
Bohemian - Limerick FC 0-0
St Patrick's Athl. - Bray Wanderers 5-0(3-0)
Waterford FC - Cork City 2-1(0-1)
Sligo Rovers - Derry City 0-2(0-1)

Round 11 [13-14.04.2018]
Bray Wanderers - Dundalk FC 0-2(0-1)
Cork City - St Patrick's Athletic 1-0(0-0)
Derry City - Waterford FC 1-0(0-0)
Shamrock Rovers - Bohemian 1-2(1-0)
Limerick FC - Sligo Rovers 1-2(0-0)

Round 12 [16-17.04.2018]
Bray Wanderers - Shamrock Rovers 1-0(0-0)
Derry City - Bohemian 3-1(1-1)
St Patrick's Athletic - Waterford FC 1-0(1-0)
Cork City - Sligo Rovers 1-0(0-0)
Limerick FC - Dundalk FC 0-3(0-2)

Round 13 [20-21.04.2018]
Dundalk FC - Derry City 2-2(2-1)
Waterford FC - Bray Wanderers 3-0(0-0)
Bohemian - Cork City 0-2(0-1)
Shamrock Rovers - Limerick FC 1-1(1-0)
Sligo Rovers - St Patrick's Athletic 0-0

Round 14 [27.04.2018]
Cork City - Dundalk FC 1-0(0-0)
Bray Wanderers - Limerick FC 0-1(0-0)
Derry City - Shamrock Rovers 0-0
St Patrick's Athletic - Bohemian 2-2(1-0)
Waterford FC - Sligo Rovers 1-1(1-1)

Round 15 [30.04.2018]
Bohemian - Waterford FC 0-1(0-1)
Dundalk FC - St Patrick's Athletic 5-0(0-0)
Limerick FC - Derry City 0-3(0-1)
Sligo Rovers - Bray Wanderers 2-1(2-0)
Shamrock Rovers - Cork City 3-0(2-0)

Round 16 [04-05.05.2018]
Bray Wanderers - Derry City 2-1(0-0)
St Patrick's Athl. - Shamrock Rovers 2-0(0-0)
Waterford FC - Dundalk FC 2-1(2-1)
Cork City - Limerick FC 2-1(1-1)
Sligo Rovers - Bohemian 0-2(0-0)

Round 17 [11.05.2018]
Bray Wanderers - Bohemian 1-3(1-2)
Derry City - Cork City 0-0
Dundalk FC - Sligo Rovers 2-1(1-1)
Limerick FC - St Patrick's Athletic 0-1(0-0)
Shamrock Rovers - Waterford FC 1-1(0-1)

Round 18 [18-19.05.2018]
Bohemian - Dundalk FC 0-2(0-1)
Cork City - Bray Wanderers 4-0(2-0)
St Patrick's Athletic - Derry City 5-2(3-2)
Waterford FC - Limerick FC 3-6(1-3)
Sligo Rovers - Shamrock Rovers 0-0

Round 19 [21-22.05.2018]
Limerick FC - Cork City 0-2(0-0)
Derry City - Bray Wanderers 2-0(1-0)
Dundalk FC - Waterford FC 2-0(1-0)
Shamrock Rovers - St Patrick's Athl. 3-0(2-0)
Bohemian - Sligo Rovers 0-3(0-2) [13.07.]

Round 20 [25.05.2018]
Bohemian - Shamrock Rovers 1-1(0-0)
Dundalk FC - Bray Wanderers 5-0(3-0)
St Patrick's Athletic - Cork City 1-3(0-1)
Sligo Rovers - Limerick FC 0-0
Waterford FC - Derry City 4-0(3-0)

Round 21 [01.06.2018]
Bray Wanderers - St Patrick's Athl. 3-1(0-0)
Cork City - Waterford FC 3-0(1-0)
Derry City - Sligo Rovers 0-2(0-1)
Limerick FC - Bohemian 1-1(1-0)
Shamrock Rovers - Dundalk FC 2-5(1-1)

Round 22 [08-09.06.2018]
Bohemian - Derry City 1-2(0-2)
Dundalk FC - Limerick FC 4-0(1-0)
Waterford FC - St Patrick's Athletic 2-0(0-0)
Shamrock Rovers - Bray Wanderers 5-0(1-0)
Sligo Rovers - Cork City 0-2(0-1)

Round 23 [15.06.2018]
Bray Wanderers - Waterford FC 0-0
Cork City - Bohemian 1-0(0-0)
Derry City - Dundalk FC 0-4(0-1)
Limerick FC - Shamrock Rovers 0-2(0-1)
St Patrick's Athletic - Sligo Rovers 0-3(0-2)

Round 24 [29-30.06.2018]
Dundalk FC - Cork City 2-1(0-0)
Bohemian - St Patrick's Athletic 1-0(1-0)
Limerick FC - Bray Wanderers 2-1(2-1)
Shamrock Rovers - Derry City 2-0(1-0)
Sligo Rovers - Waterford FC 2-3(2-3)

Round 25 [06-08.07.2018]
Cork City - Shamrock Rovers 0-0
Derry City - Limerick FC 2-1(1-1)
St Patrick's Athletic - Dundalk FC 1-3(1-0)
Waterford FC - Bohemian 1-1(0-1)
Bray Wanderers - Sligo Rovers 2-1(1-0)

Round 26 [20-23.07.2018]
Bohemian - Bray Wanderers 6-0(4-0)
St Patrick's Athletic - Limerick FC 2-1(0-1)
Waterford FC - Shamrock Rovers 0-1(0-0)
Cork City - Derry City 5-0(2-0)
Sligo Rovers - Dundalk FC 0-2(0-1) [20.08.]

Round 27 [27-29.07.2018]
Bray Wanderers - Cork City 1-3(0-3)
Derry City - St Patrick's Athletic 2-1(1-1)
Limerick FC - Waterford FC 2-1(1-0)
Shamrock Rovers - Sligo Rovers 2-0(0-0)
Dundalk FC - Bohemian 2-0(1-0)

Round 28 [03.08.2018]
Bohemian - Limerick FC 5-0(2-0)
St Patrick's Athl. - Bray Wanderers 3-0(1-0)
Derry City - Sligo Rovers 1-2(1-0)
Waterford FC - Cork City 1-2(1-1)
Dundalk FC - Shamrock Ro. 1-2(0-1) [28.08.]

Round 29 [17-19.08.2018]
Bray Wanderers - Dundalk FC 1-3(0-2)
Derry City - Waterford FC 1-2(1-2)
Limerick FC - Sligo Rovers 1-3(0-1)
Shamrock Rovers - Bohemian 0-1(0-0)
Cork City - St Patrick's Athletic 1-1(0-0)

Round 30 [31.08.2018]
Bray Wanderers - Shamrock Rovers 0-3(0-1)
Cork City - Sligo Rovers 1-2(1-0)
Derry City - Bohemian 0-2(0-1)
St Patrick's Athletic - Waterford FC 3-0(0-0)
Limerick FC - Dundalk FC 0-1(0-0)

Round 31 [14-15.09.2018]
Bohemian - Cork City 4-2(4-1)
Waterford FC - Bray Wanderers 2-0(1-0)
Shamrock Rovers - Limerick FC 5-0(4-0)
Sligo Rovers - St Patrick's Athletic 1-2(1-1)
Dundalk FC - Derry City 3-2(3-0) [25.09.]

Round 32 [21-22.09.2018]
Cork City - Dundalk FC 0-1(0-1)
Bray Wanderers - Limerick FC 0-2(0-2)
Waterford FC - Sligo Rovers 1-0(1-0)
Derry City - Shamrock Rovers 0-1(0-0)
St Patrick's Athletic - Bohemian 1-3(1-1)

Round 33 [05-06.10.2018]
Bohemian - Waterford FC 1-3(1-2)
Dundalk FC - St Patrick's Athletic 1-1(0-0)
Shamrock Rovers - Cork City 0-0
Limerick FC - Derry City 0-1(0-1)
Sligo Rovers - Bray Wanderers 2-1(0-0)

Round 34 [12.10.2018]
Cork City - Limerick FC 3-0(1-0)
St Patrick's Athl. - Shamrock Rovers 0-1(0-0)
Waterford FC - Dundalk FC 1-2(0-0)
Bray Wanderers - Derry City 2-1(1-1) [22.10.]
Sligo Rovers - Bohemian 1-1(1-1) [22.10.]

Round 35 [19.10.2018]
Limerick FC - St Patrick's Athletic 0-4(0-2)
Bray Wanderers - Bohemian 0-5(0-4)
Derry City - Cork City 0-3(0-1)
Dundalk FC - Sligo Rovers 5-0(3-0)
Shamrock Rovers - Waterford FC 3-1(2-0)

Round 36 [26.10.2018]
Bohemian - Dundalk FC 1-1(1-0)
Cork City - Bray Wanderers 5-1(4-0)
St Patrick's Athletic - Derry City 5-0(3-0)
Sligo Rovers - Shamrock Rovers 2-0(1-0)
Waterford FC - Limerick FC 4-1(2-1)

Final Standings

1.	**Dundalk FC**	36	27	6	3	85	-	20	87
2.	Cork City FC	36	24	5	7	71	-	27	77
3.	Shamrock Rovers FC	36	18	8	10	57	-	27	62
4.	Waterford FC	36	18	5	13	52	-	44	59
5.	St. Patrick's Athletic FC Dublin	36	15	5	16	51	-	47	50
6.	Bohemian FC Dublin	36	13	9	14	52	-	45	48
7.	Sligo Rovers FC	36	12	6	18	38	-	50	42
8.	Derry City FC	36	13	3	20	47	-	70	42
9.	Limerick FC (*Relegation Play-offs*)	36	7	6	23	25	-	75	27
10.	Bray Wanderers FC (*Relegated*)	36	5	3	28	23	-	96	18

Top goalscorers:

29 Patrick James Hoban
Dundalk FC

16 Kieran Sadlier
Cork City FC

14 Graham Cummins
Cork City FC

Relegation Play-offs [29.10.-02.11.2018]

Finn Harps FC Ballybofey - Limerick FC	1-0(1-0)	2-0(1-0)

Finn Harps FC Ballybofey promoted to the 2019 League of Ireland Premier Division.

NATIONAL CUP
FAI Cup 2018

First Round [10-12.08.2018]

Drogheda United FC - Shamrock Rovers FC	1-0(1-0)
University College Dublin AFC - Pike Rovers FC	2-0(1-0)
Dundalk FC - Cobh Ramblers FC	3-0(1-0)
Bray Wanderers FC - Finn Harps FC Ballybofey	1-3(1-0,1-1)
Inchicore Athletic FC - St. Patrick's Athletic FC	0-5(0-0)
Shelbourne FC Dublin - Athlone Town FC	4-0(1-0)
Wexford FC - Bohemian FC Dublin	0-7(0-4)
Skerries Town FC - Waterford FC	1-4(0-2)
Dublin Bus FC - CIE Ranch FC	0-1(0-0)
Blarney United FC - Derry City FC	2-12(0-7)
Maynooth University Town FC – Leeds FC	2-0(0-0)
Newmarket Celtic FC - Cabinteely FC	1-2(0-0)
North End United FC - Galway United FC	0-4(0-4)
Sligo Rovers FC - Longford Town FC	0-1(0-0)
Home Farm FC Dublin - Cork City FC	1-5(1-5)
Cockhill Celtic FC Buncrana - Limerick FC	0-2(0-0)

1/8-Finals [24-25.08.2018]

CIE Ranch FC - University College Dublin AFC	2-6(2-1,2-2)
Galway United FC - Bohemian FC Dublin	0-2(0-1)
Derry City FC - St. Patrick's Athletic FC Dublin	1-0(0-0)
Dundalk FC - Finn Harps FC Ballybofey	2-0(1-0)
Cork City FC - Maynooth University Town FC	4-0(1-0)
Drogheda United FC - Waterford FC	0-1(0-1)
Limerick FC - Cabinteely FC	2-1(1-0)
Longford Town - Shelbourne FC Dublin	2-0(1-0)

Quarter-Finals [07/19.09.2018]

Longford Town - Cork City FC	0-7(0-2)
University College Dublin AFC - Waterford FC	2-1(2-0)
Limerick FC - Dundalk FC	0-4(0-3)
Derry City FC - Bohemian FC Dublin	1-3(0-1)

Semi-Finals [28/30.09.-08.10.2018]

Dundalk FC - University College Dublin AFC	1-0(1-0)
Bohemian FC Dublin - Cork City FC	1-1 / 1-2

Final

04.11.2018; Aviva Stadium, Dublin; Referee: Neil Doyle; Attendance: 30,412
Dundalk FC - Cork City FC **2-1(1-1)**

Dundalk FC: Gary Rogers, Sean Gannon (86.Daniel Cleary), Brian Gartland, Sean Hoare, Dane Massey, Chris Shields, John Mountney (58.Jamie McGrath), Michael Duffy, Patrick James Hoban, Robbie Benson (90.Dean Jarvis), Patrick McEleney. Trainer: Stephen Kenny.

Cork City: Mark McNulty, Alan Bennett, Shane Griffin, Conor McCarthy, Sean McLoughlin, Gearóid Morrissey (67.Barry McNamee), Conor McCormack (85.Cian Murphy), Kieran Sadlier, Garry Buckley, Jimmy Keohane (76.Graham Cummins), Karl Sheppard. Trainer: Johnathan Caulfield (United States).

Goals: 1-0 Sean Hoare (18), 1-1 Kieran Sadlier (21 penalty), 2-1 Patrick McEleney (74).

THE CLUBS 2018

Bohemian Football Club Dublin

Founded: 06.09.1890
Stadium: Dalymount Park, Dublin (7,955)

Goalkeepers:	**DOB**	**M**	**(s)**	**G**
Colin McCabe	06.01.1997	3		
Shane Supple	04.05.1987	33		
Defenders:	**DOB**	**M**	**(s)**	**G**
Daniel Byrne	07.05.1993	12	(11)	1
Dan Casey	29.10.1997	31		3
Robert Cornwall	16.10.1994	24	(2)	2
Patrick Kirk	02.06.1998	9	(1)	
Darragh Leahy	15.04.1998	23	(1)	1
Jonathan Lunney	02.02.1998	17	(4)	2
Robert McCourt	06.04.1998	3		1
Ian Morris	27.02.1987	22	(6)	2
Derek Pender	02.10.1983	19		1
Midfielders:	**DOB**	**M**	**(s)**	**G**
Oscar Brennan	17.03.1996	22	(3)	
Keith Buckley	17.06.1992	29		1
Kevin Devaney	26.09.1990	19	(7)	5
Philip Gannon	11.10.1996	3	(6)	
Jamie Hamilton	19.01.1999	1	(1)	
Patrick Kavanagh	29.12.1985	11	(5)	1
Andy Lyons	02.08.2000	4	(1)	
Robert Manley	24.08.1997	1	(2)	
Karl Moore	09.11.1988	7	(4)	
Keith Ward	12.10.1990	25	(6)	2
Dylan Watts	11.04.1997	16	(4)	1
Forwards:	**DOB**	**M**	**(s)**	**G**
Dinny Corcoran	13.02.1989	24	(7)	11
Daniel Grant	23.10.2000	8	(11)	3
Ryan Graydon	11.04.1999	1		
Daniel Kelly	21.05.1996	9	(1)	5
Cristian Măgeruşan (ROU)	16.09.1999	1	(3)	2
Ryan Masterson	23.10.1996		(1)	
Promise Omochere	18.10.2000		(2)	
Ali Reghba	14.01.2000	1		2
Eoghan Stokes	17.05.1996	18	(13)	5
Trainer:	**DOB**	**M**		
Keith Long	14.11.1973	36		

Bray Wanderers Football Club

Founded: 1942
Stadium: Carlisle Grounds, Bray (7,000)

Goalkeepers:	**DOB**	**M**	**(s)**	**G**
Aaron Dillon	05.12.1996	13		
Enda Minogue	12.01.2002	1		
Evan Moran	22.04.1997	19		
Mark O'Connor	01.07.1996	3	(1)	
Defenders:	**DOB**	**M**	**(s)**	**G**
Jamie Crilly	28.12.2001	1	(2)	
Hugh Douglas	22.06.1993	14		
Darragh Gibbons	15.05.1998	8	(2)	1
Séan Harding	17.09.1988	12	(1)	
Dylan Hayes	09.04.1995	9	(1)	
Sean Heaney	27.01.1996	29	(3)	3
Conor Kenna	21.08.1984	29	(2)	
Kevin Lynch	21.03.1992	32		
Cian Maher	27.04.2001		(1)	
Daniel McKenna	12.12.1999	19	(2)	1
Alex Rafferty	05.02.2002		(1)	
Calvin Rogers	16.12.1999		(4)	
Cian Walsh	23.01.2001	3	(2)	
Midfielders:	**DOB**	**M**	**(s)**	**G**
Shane Flynn	14.10.2001		(1)	
Cory Galvin	10.01.1996	19	(3)	2
Rhys Gorman (ENG)	24.01.1994	18	(4)	
Jake Kelly	18.06.1990	10	(11)	1
Dragos Mamaliga	22.10.2000	2	(4)	
Gary McCabe	01.08.1988	24		4
Andrew McGovern	02.12.1998	3	(3)	
Darragh Noone	28.04.1997	13	(6)	
Paul O'Conor	10.08.1987	32	(2)	1
Byron O'Gorman	15.10.2001	1	(3)	
John Sullivan	06.01.1991	10	(5)	1
Craig Walsh	27.01.1992	3		
Forwards:	**DOB**	**M**	**(s)**	**G**
Ronan Coughlan	02.10.1995	19	(1)	4
Jake Ellis (ENG)	14.03.2001	8	(4)	2
Aaron Greene	02.01.1990	11		
Glen Hollywood	17.07.2001		(1)	
Daniel Kelly	21.05.1996	17	(6)	2
Gerald Pender	22.05.1994	14	(14)	1
Trainer:	**DOB**	**M**		
David Mackey	04.06.1960	9		
Graham Kelly [09.04.2018]		13		
Martin Russell [09.06.2018]	27.04.1967	3		
Graham Kelly [19.07.2018]		3		
Gary Cronin [07.08.2018]	16.03.1979	8		

Cork City Football Club

Founded: 1984
Stadium: Turners Cross, Cork (7,485)

Goalkeepers:	**DOB**	**M**	**(s)**	**G**
Peter Cherrie (SCO)	01.10.1983	6	(1)	
Mark McNulty	13.10.1980	30		
Defenders:	**DOB**	**M**	**(s)**	**G**
Tobi Adebayo-Rowling (ENG)	16.11.1996		(1)	
Aaron Barry	24.11.1992	14	(6)	1
Alan Bennett	04.10.1981	11	(1)	
Damien Delaney	20.07.1981	9	(1)	1
John Dunleavy	03.07.1991	1	(2)	
Shane Griffin	08.09.1994	29	(2)	
Colm Horgan	02.07.1994	15	(4)	1
Ronan Hurley	11.09.1999	3		
Danny Kane	23.04.1997	3	(2)	
Conor McCarthy	11.04.1998	19	(3)	1
Sean McLoughlin	13.11.1996	27		2
Pierce Phillips	28.09.1998	1	(1)	
Midfielders:	**DOB**	**M**	**(s)**	**G**
Steven Beattie	20.08.1988	13	(6)	
Garry Buckley	19.08.1993	23	(4)	9
Shane Daly-Butz	06.06.1996	2	(4)	1
Dale Holland	07.01.2000		(1)	
Conor McCormack	18.05.1990	32		
Barry McNamee (NIR)	17.02.1992	30	(3)	4
Gearóid Morrissey	17.11.1991	19	(5)	4
Kieran Sadlier	14.09.1994	27	(8)	16
Forwards:	**DOB**	**M**	**(s)**	**G**
Ronan Coughlan	02.10.1995	2	(2)	1
Graham Cummins	29.12.1987	33	(1)	14
Michael Howard (ENG)	17.10.1999		(3)	
Jimmy Keohane	22.01.1991	23	(10)	6
Cian Murphy	08.06.2000	1	(3)	
Josh O'Hanlon	25.09.1995		(20)	3
Karl Sheppard	14.02.1991	23	(8)	6
Trainer:	**DOB**	**M**		
Johnathan Caulfield (USA)	11.10.1964	36		

Derry City Football Club

Founded: 1928
Stadium: "Ryan McBride" Brandywell Stadium, Derry (3,700)

Goalkeepers:	**DOB**	**M**	**(s)**	**G**
Gerard Doherty	24.08.1981	34		
Eric Grimes	04.02.1995	2		
Defenders:	**DOB**	**M**	**(s)**	**G**
Armin Aganovic (SWE)	06.04.1994	2		1
Darren Cole (SCO)	03.01.1992	31	(1)	2
Ben Doherty (NIR)	24.03.1997	9	(7)	
Jack Doyle (ENG)	02.02.1997	20		1
Dapo Kayode (NGA)	30.09.1992		(2)	
Niall Logue (NIR)	07.08.1995	2	(2)	
Conor McDermott (NIR)	18.09.1997	19	(4)	
Gavin Peers	10.11.1985	17	(2)	
Danny Seaborne (ENG)	05.03.1987	8		
Eoin Toal (NIR)	15.02.1999	27	(3)	1
Scot Whiteside (NIR)	16.06.1997		(1)	
Midfielders:	**DOB**	**M**	**(s)**	**G**
Adrian Delap	30.11.1998	3	(8)	
Ben Fisk (CAN)	04.02.1993	8	(4)	1
Rory Hale	27.11.1996	31	(1)	5
Nicky Low (SCO)	06.01.1992	20	(3)	2
Jamie McDonagh (NIR)	08.05.1996	24	(8)	1
Aaron McEneff	09.07.1995	34	(1)	10
Kevin McHattie (SCO)	15.07.1993	8		
Dean Shiels (NIR)	01.02.1985	7	(3)	2
Aaron Splaine (SCO)	13.10.1996	10	(1)	1
Forwards:	**DOB**	**M**	**(s)**	**G**
Nathan Boyle (NIR)	14.04.1994		(5)	
John Cofie (ENG)	21.01.1993	1	(3)	
Ronan Curtis	29.03.1996	19	(3)	5
Cathal Farren	02.07.1998		(4)	
Ronan Hale	08.09.1998	26	(5)	4
David Hopkirk (SCO)	17.01.1993		(3)	1
Shane McNamee	01.06.1999	1	(4)	
Rory Patterson (NIR)	16.07.1984	22	(2)	6
Ally Roy (NIR)	26.07.1997	11		2
Trainer:	**DOB**	**M**		
Kenny Shiels (NIR)	27.04.1956	36		

Dundalk Football Club

Founded: 1903
Stadium: Oriel Park, Dundalk (4,500)

Goalkeepers:	**DOB**	**M**	**(s)**	**G**
Gary Rogers	25.09.1981	34		
Gabriel Sava (ITA)	15.10.1986	2	(1)	
Defenders:	**DOB**	**M**	**(s)**	**G**
Daniel Cleary	09.03.1996	26		3
Stephen Folan	14.01.1992	8	(1)	1
Sean Gannon	11.07.1991	23	(3)	1
Brian Gartland	04.11.1986	22		1
Sean Hoare	15.03.1994	27		2
Dean Jarvis (NIR)	01.06.1992	11	(8)	
Dane Massey	17.04.1988	27	(2)	1
Midfielders:	**DOB**	**M**	**(s)**	**G**
Karolis Chvedukas (LTU)	21.04.1991	2	(5)	1
Dylan Connolly	02.05.1995	17	(11)	4
Jamie McGrath	30.09.1996	25	(5)	2
John Mountney	22.02.1993	10	(8)	4
Stephen O'Donnell	15.01.1986	4	(6)	
Georgie Poynton	28.08.1997	1	(3)	
Chris Shields	27.12.1990	30	(3)	3
Forwards:	**DOB**	**M**	**(s)**	**G**
Krisztián Adorján (HUN)	19.01.1993	5	(11)	3
Robbie Benson	07.05.1992	32		9
Sam Byrne	23.07.1995		(2)	
Michael Duffy (NIR)	28.07.1994	36		13
Patrick James Hoban	28.07.1991	35	(1)	29
Georgie Kelly (NIR)	12.11.1996		(7)	
Patrick McEleney (NIR)	26.09.1992	8	(3)	1
Ronan Murray	12.09.1991	11	(12)	3
Marco Tagbajumi (NGA)	01.07.1988		(16)	2
Trainer:	**DOB**	**M**		
Stephen Kenny	30.10.1971	36		

Limerick Football Club

Founded: 1937
Stadium: Markets Field, Limerick (5,000)

Goalkeepers:	**DOB**	**M**	**(s)**	**G**
Jack Brady	17.12.1996	3		
Brendan Clarke	17.09.1985	24		
Tommy Holland	01.04.1998	9		
Defenders:	**DOB**	**M**	**(s)**	**G**
Killian Brouder	20.08.1998	19	(1)	
Killian Cantwell	24.05.1995	28	(4)	
Darren Dennehy	21.09.1988	11	(1)	1
Shaun Kelly	09.03.1989	23	(3)	
Colman Kennedy	11.02.1994	5	(1)	
Alan Murphy	13.02.1998	1		
Thomas O'Connor	31.03.2001	2		
Karl O'Sullivan	31.10.1999	12	(13)	1
Tony Whitehead	22.12.1995	17	(4)	
Midfielders:	**DOB**	**M**	**(s)**	**G**
Henry Cameron (NZL)	28.06.1997	2		
Connor Clifford	01.10.1991	11		
Cian Coleman	01.01.1997	28	(2)	2
Billy Dennehy	17.02.1987	28	(2)	4
Shane Duggan	03.01.1989	34		3
Connor Ellis	12.05.1997	17	(5)	2
Aaron Fitzgerald		1	(1)	
William Fitzgerald	19.05.1999	25	(7)	
Coleman Hennessy			(1)	
Daniel Kearns	26.08.1991	10	(3)	1
Barry Maguire (NED)	27.10.1989	17	(8)	3
Darren Murphy	04.04.1995	10	(2)	
Mark O'Sullivan	01.02.1983	9	(5)	1
Shane Tracy	14.09.1988	14	(3)	
Eoin Wearen	02.10.1992	19	(2)	
Forwards:	**DOB**	**M**	**(s)**	**G**
Ger Barry	31.07.1999	1		
Adam Foley	20.09.1999	1	(2)	
Jeff McGowan	07.02.1998		(4)	
Danny Morrissey	13.12.1993	12	(14)	5
Colm Walsh-O'Loghlen	12.04.1999	3	(7)	1
Trainer:	**DOB**	**M**		
Tommy Barrett	20.05.1979	36		

Shamrock Rovers Football Club Dublin

Founded: 1899
Stadium: Tallaght Stadium, Dublin (6,000)

Goalkeepers:	DOB	M	(s)	G
Gavin Bazunu	20.02.2002	4		
Tomer Chencinski (CAN)	01.12.1984	8		
Kevin Horgan	26.04.1997	13		
Alan Mannus (NIR)	19.05.1982	11		
Defenders:	**DOB**	**M**	**(s)**	**G**
Sam Bone (ENG)	06.02.1998	12	(8)	2
Ethan Boyle	04.01.1997	32		1
Luke Byrne	08.07.1993	9	(4)	
Ally Gilchrist (SCO)	03.03.1995	12		
Lee Grace	01.12.1992	35		1
Roberto Lopes	17.06.1992	25	(3)	4
Midfielders:	**DOB**	**M**	**(s)**	**G**
Aaron Bolger	02.02.2000	8	(6)	
Greg Bolger	09.09.1988	30	(1)	1
Trevor Clarke	26.03.1998	5	(1)	
Joel Coustrain	22.01.1996	19	(9)	2
Dean Dillon	08.06.1999		(2)	
Ronan Finn	21.12.1987	33		6
Brandon Kavanagh	21.09.2000	6	(10)	
Sean Kavanagh	20.01.1994	28	(2)	2
David McAllister	29.12.1988	4	(10)	2
Brandon Miele	28.08.1994	15	(11)	3
Joey O'Brien	17.02.1986	12	(1)	
Dylan Watts	11.04.1997	11		4
Forwards:	**DOB**	**M**	**(s)**	**G**
Sean Boyd	20.06.1998		(6)	1
Graham Dylan Burke	21.09.1993	22		13
Daniel Carr (TRI)	30.11.1993	28	(6)	11
Aaron Greene	02.01.1990	5	(3)	
Gary Shaw	10.05.1992	9	(14)	2
Dean Williams	09.02.2000		(1)	
Trainer:	**DOB**	**M**		
Stephen Bradley	19.11.1984	36		

Sligo Rovers Football Club

Founded: 1928
Stadium: The Showgrounds, Sligo (5,500)

Goalkeepers:	DOB	M	(s)	G
Mitchell Beeney (ENG)	03.10.1995	26		
Edward McGinty (SCO)	05.08.1999	4		
Micheál Schlingermann	23.06.1991	6		
Defenders:	**DOB**	**M**	**(s)**	**G**
Gary Boylan	24.04.1996	17		
Kyle Callan-McFadden	20.04.1995	27		
Regan Donelon	17.04.1996	17	(2)	
John Mahon	26.11.1999	24		1
Patrick McClean (NIR)	22.11.1996	26	(1)	1
Niall Morahan	30.05.2000	1	(2)	
Seamus Sharkey (ENG)	11.05.1990	19	(2)	1
Calum Waters (SCO)	10.03.1996	14	(2)	
Midfielders:	**DOB**	**M**	**(s)**	**G**
David Cawley	19.09.1991	29	(1)	5
Darren Collins	29.09.2000		(5)	
Raffaele Cretaro	15.10.1981	9	(16)	3
Eduardo Pincelli (BRA)	23.04.1983	9	(4)	1
Jack Keaney	18.01.1999	21	(4)	3
Liam Kerrigan	09.05.2000	3	(8)	
Lee Lynch	27.11.1991	11		
Caolan McAleer (NIR)	19.08.1993	22	(9)	4
Rhys McCabe (SCO)	24.07.1992	32		2
Lewis Morrison (SCO)	12.03.1999	9	(13)	1
Craig Roddan (ENG)	22.04.1993	4	(1)	
Kris Twardek (CAN)	08.03.1997	7	(4)	
Adam Wixted	02.04.1995	14	(12)	2
Forwards:	**DOB**	**M**	**(s)**	**G**
Michael Drennan	02.02.1994	13		6
Gregory Moorhouse	10.07.1994	9	(9)	1
Adam Morgan (ENG)	21.04.1994	13	(3)	4
Ally Roy (NIR)	26.07.1997	10	(8)	2
Trainer:	**DOB**	**M**		
Gerry Lyttle (NIR)	27.11.1977	36		

St. Patrick's Athletic Football Club Dublin

Founded: 1929
Stadium: Richmond Park, Dublin (2,800)

Goalkeepers:	DOB	M	(s)	G
Brendan Clarke	17.09.1985	12		1
Tyson Farago (CAN)	01.05.1991	2	(1)	
Barry Murphy	08.06.1985	22		
Defenders:	**DOB**	**M**	**(s)**	**G**
Michael Barker	16.08.1993	3	(3)	
Ian Bermingham	08.01.1989	33	(1)	2
Neill Byrne	02.03.1999		(1)	
Lee Desmond	22.01.1995	36		
Luke Heeney	06.02.1999		(1)	
Mick Leahy	30.04.1989	9	(1)	2
Simon Madden	01.05.1988	36		1
Joseph Manley	26.06.1999	1	(1)	
Kevin Toner	18.07.1996	30		4
Ian Turner	19.04.1989	2	(9)	1
Midfielders:	**DOB**	**M**	**(s)**	**G**
Killian Brennan	31.01.1984	7	(8)	1
Ryan Brennan	11.11.1991	32	(2)	4
Conan Byrne	10.07.1985	28	(5)	7
Connor Clifford	01.10.1991	7	(2)	2
James Doona	15.01.1998	7	(10)	2
Owen Garvan	29.01.1988	9	(1)	
Graham Kelly	31.10.1991	6	(8)	1
Jamie Lennon	09.05.1998	27	(2)	
Darragh Markey	23.05.1997	20	(10)	1
Forwards:	**DOB**	**M**	**(s)**	**G**
Thomas Byrne	26.01.1999	6	(8)	3
Achille Campion (FRA)	10.03.1990	4	(1)	2
Dean Clarke	29.03.1993	28	(2)	5
Chris Fagan	11.05.1989	6	(9)	1
Jake Keegan (USA)	21.04.1991	23	(9)	9
Trainer:	**DOB**	**M**		
Liam Buckley	14.04.1970	32		
Gerard O'Brien [26.09.2018]	02.07.1984	3		
Harry Kenny [25.10.2018]	13.04.1962	1		

Waterford Football Club Dublin

Founded: 1930
Stadium: Waterford Regional Sports Centre, Waterford (5,500)

Goalkeepers:	**DOB**	**M**	**(s)**	**G**
Matthew Connor	08.04.1997	10		
Niall Corbert	13.11.1994	7		
Lawrence Vigouroux (CHI)	19.11.1993	19		
Defenders:	**DOB**	**M**	**(s)**	**G**
Dylan Barnett	05.12.1996	29	(4)	
Kenny Browne	07.08.1986	27		1
Rory Feely	03.01.1997	26	(4)	2
John Kavanagh	19.07.1994	5	(3)	
Darryl Walsh	14.06.2000		(1)	
David Webster	07.04.1990	28		
Midfielders:	**DOB**	**M**	**(s)**	**G**
Stanley Aborah (BEL)	23.06.1987	23	(1)	3
Noe Baba	08.08.1996	5	(2)	
Garry Comerford	29.10.1993	19	(2)	1
Derek Daly	25.08.1997	8	(8)	1
Courtney Duffus	24.10.1995	23	(2)	10
Cory Galvin	10.01.1996	5	(1)	
Shane Griffin	31.12.1999		(1)	
Bastien Héry (FRA)	23.03.1992	30	(1)	4
Gavan Holohan	15.12.1991	26	(4)	5
Dessie Hutchinson	05.12.1996	6	(4)	4
Faysel Kasmi (BEL)	31.10.1995	9	(3)	2
Paul Keegan	05.07.1984	25	(5)	1
John Martin	05.01.1999	7	(7)	2
Dean O'Halloran	02.01.1996	8	(12)	1
Sander Puri (EST)	07.05.1988	16	(12)	5
Carlos Wilson Cachicote Rocha „Rudy" (POR)	05.01.1989	1	(2)	
Forwards:	**DOB**	**M**	**(s)**	**G**
Ismahil Akinade (NGA)	11.02.1994	26	(6)	5
Noel Hunt	26.12.1982	7	(1)	3
Dean Walsh	23.04.1997	1	(8)	
Trainer:	**DOB**	**M**		
Derek Browne		36		

SECOND LEVEL
League of Ireland First Division 2018

1.	University College Dublin AFC (*Promoted*)	27	17	6	4	59	-	29	57
2.	Finn Harps FC Ballybofey (*Promotion Play-offs*)	27	16	6	5	46	-	22	54
3.	Shelbourne FC Dublin (*Promotion Play-offs*)	27	13	11	3	52	-	21	50
4.	Drogheda United FC (*Promotion Play-offs*)	27	14	7	6	50	-	27	49
5.	Longford Town FC	27	13	6	8	54	-	36	45
6.	Galway United FC	27	10	7	10	41	-	36	37
7.	Cabinteely FC	27	9	3	15	32	-	45	30
8.	Cobh Ramblers FC	27	8	5	14	24	-	41	29
9.	Wexford FC Crossabeg	27	4	5	18	23	-	59	17
10.	Athlone Town FC	27	1	4	22	16	-	81	7

Promotion Play-offs (1st / 2nd Level)

Semi-Finals [05-08.10.2018]	Drogheda United FC - Shelbourne FC Dublin	0-1(0-1)	2-1 aet; 4-2 pen
Finals [05-08.10.2018]	Drogheda United FC - **Finn Harps FC Ballybofey**	1-1(1-0)	0-2(0-1)

NATIONAL TEAM

INTERNATIONAL MATCHES
(16.07.2018 – 15.07.2019)

06.09.2018	Cardiff	Wales - Republic of Ireland	4-1(3-0)	(UNL)
11.09.2018	Wrocław	Poland - Republic of Ireland	1-1(0-0)	(F)
13.10.2018	Dublin	Republic of Ireland - Denmark	0-0	(UNL)
16.10.2018	Dublin	Republic of Ireland - Wales	0-1(0-0)	(UNL)
15.11.2018	Dublin	Republic of Ireland - Northern Ireland	0-0	(F)
19.11.2018	Aarhus	Denmark - Republic of Ireland	0-0	(UNL)
23.03.2019	Gibraltar	Gibraltar - Republic of Ireland	0-1(0-0)	(ECQ)
26.03.2019	Dublin	Republic of Ireland - Georgia	1-0(1-0)	(ECQ)
07.06.2019	København	Denmark - Republic of Ireland	1-1(0-0)	(ECQ)
10.06.2019	Dublin	Republic of Ireland - Gibraltar	2-0(1-0)	(ECQ)

06.09.2018 WALES - REPUBLIC OF IRELAND 4-1(3-0) UEFA Nations League B, Group 4
Cardiff City Stadium, Cardiff; Referee: Clément Turpin (France); Attendance: 25,657
IRL: Darren Edward Andrew Randolph, Séamus Coleman (Cap), Stephen Ward (61.Enda John Stevens), Ciaran Clark, Shane Patrick Michael Duffy, Cyrus Sylvester Frederick Christie, Conor Hourihane (57.Shaun Williams), Jeffrey Patrick Hendrick, Callum Joshua Ryan O'Dowda, Jonathan Ronald Walters, Callum Jack Robinson (77.Daryl Jeremiah Horgan). Trainer: Martin Hugh Michael O'Neill (Northern Ireland).
Goal: Shaun Williams (66).

11.09.2018 POLAND - REPUBLIC OF IRELAND 1-1(0-0) Friendly International
Stadion Miejski, Wrocław; Referee: Boris Marhefka (Slovakia); Attendance: 25,455
IRL: Darren Edward Andrew Randolph, Richard John Keogh (Cap), Enda John Stevens, Kevin Finbarr Long, John Egan, Cyrus Sylvester Frederick Christie (54.Matthew James Doherty), Shaun Williams (73.Conor Hourihane), Jeffrey Patrick Hendrick (54.David Meyler), Callum Joshua Ryan O'Dowda (90.Alan Christopher Judge), Aiden Antony O'Brien (81.Daryl Jeremiah Horgan), Callum Jack Robinson (63.Graham Dylan Burke). Trainer: Martin Hugh Michael O'Neill (Northern Ireland).
Goal: Aiden Antony O'Brien (53).

13.10.2018 REPUBLIC OF IRELAND - DENMARK 0-0 UEFA Nations League B, Group 4
Aviva Stadium, Dublin; Referee: Xavier Estrada Fernández (Spain); Attendance: 41,220
IRL: Darren Edward Andrew Randolph, Richard John Keogh (Cap), Kevin Finbarr Long, Shane Patrick Michael Duffy, Cyrus Sylvester Frederick Christie, Matthew James Doherty, Harry Nicholas Arter (65.Callum Jack Robinson), James McClean, Jeffrey Patrick Hendrick, Callum Joshua Ryan O'Dowda (46.Enda John Stevens), Shane Long (83.Aiden Antony O'Brien). Trainer: Martin Hugh Michael O'Neill (Northern Ireland).

16.10.2018 REPUBLIC OF IRELAND - WALES 0-1(0-0) UEFA Nations League B, Group 4
Aviva Stadium, Dublin; Referee: Björn Kuipers (Netherlands); Attendance: 38,321
IRL: Darren Edward Andrew Randolph, Richard John Keogh (Cap), Kevin Finbarr Long (75.Scott Andrew Hogan), Shane Patrick Michael Duffy, Cyrus Sylvester Frederick Christie, Matthew James Doherty, Harry Nicholas Arter, James McClean, Jeffrey Patrick Hendrick, Aiden Antony O'Brien (56.Shane Long), Callum Jack Robinson (60.Seán Maguire). Trainer: Martin Hugh Michael O'Neill (Northern Ireland).

15.11.2018 REPUBLIC OF IRELAND - NORTHERN IRELAND 0-0 Friendly International
Aviva Stadium, Dublin; Referee: Slavko Vinčić (Slovenia); Attendance: 31,241
IRL: Darren Edward Andrew Randolph, Séamus Coleman, Shane Patrick Michael Duffy, John Egan, Darragh Patrick Lenihan (84.Cyrus Sylvester Frederick Christie), Glenn Whelan (Cap) (36.Conor Hourihane), James McClean (66.Enda John Stevens), Robert Brady, Jeffrey Patrick Hendrick, Callum Joshua Ryan O'Dowda (46.Ronan Curtis), Callum Jack Robinson (66.Seán Maguire; 80.Scott Andrew Hogan). Trainer: Martin Hugh Michael O'Neill (Northern Ireland).

19.11.2018 DENMARK - REPUBLIC OF IRELAND 0-0 UEFA Nations League B, Group 4
Ceres Park & Arena, Aarhus; Referee: Aliyar Aghayev (Azerbaijan); Attendance: 11,130
IRL: Darren Edward Andrew Randolph, Séamus Coleman (Cap), Richard John Keogh, Enda John Stevens, Kevin Finbarr Long, Shane Patrick Michael Duffy, Cyrus Sylvester Frederick Christie, Robert Brady (66.Callum Jack Robinson), Jeffrey Patrick Hendrick, Callum Joshua Ryan O'Dowda (80.Michael Oluwadurotimi Obafemi), Aiden Antony O'Brien (65.Ronan Curtis). Trainer: Martin Hugh Michael O'Neill (Northern Ireland).

23.03.2019 GIBRALTAR - REPUBLIC OF IRELAND 0-1(0-0) 16th EC. Qualifiers
Victoria Stadium, Gibraltar; Referee: Anastasios Papapetrou (Greece); Attendance: 2,000
IRL: Darren Edward Andrew Randolph, Séamus Coleman (Cap), Richard John Keogh, Enda John Stevens, Shane Patrick Michael Duffy, Matthew James Doherty (56.Robert Brady), Conor Hourihane, James McClean, Jeffrey Patrick Hendrick, David McGoldrick, Seán Maguire (72.Harry Nicholas Arter). Trainer: Michael Joseph McCarthy.
Goal: Jeffrey Patrick Hendrick (49).

26.03.2019 REPUBLIC OF IRELAND - GEORGIA 1-0(1-0) 16th EC. Qualifiers
Aviva Stadium, Dublin; Referee: Serdar Gözübüyük (Netherlands); Attendance: 40,317
IRL: Darren Edward Andrew Randolph, Séamus Coleman (Cap), Richard John Keogh, Enda John Stevens, Shane Patrick Michael Duffy, Glenn Whelan, Conor Hourihane, James McClean, Robert Brady (74.Aiden Antony O'Brien), Jeffrey Patrick Hendrick, David McGoldrick (81.Matthew James Doherty). Trainer: Michael Joseph McCarthy.
Goal: Conor Hourihane (36).

07.06.2019 DENMARK - REPUBLIC OF IRELAND 1-1(0-0) 16th EC. Qualifiers
Parken Stadium, København; Referee: Cüneyt Çakır (Turkey); Attendance: 34,610
IRL: Darren Edward Andrew Randolph, Séamus Coleman (Cap), Richard John Keogh, Enda John Stevens, Shane Patrick Michael Duffy, Glenn Whelan, Conor Hourihane (82.Scott Andrew Hogan), James McClean, Robert Brady (66.Alan Christopher Judge), Jeffrey Patrick Hendrick, David McGoldrick (88.Callum Jack Robinson). Trainer: Michael Joseph McCarthy.
Goal: Shane Patrick Michael Duffy (85).

10.06.2019 REPUBLIC OF IRELAND - GIBRALTAR 2-0(1-0) 16th EC. Qualifiers

Aviva Stadium, Dublin; Referee: Radu Petrescu (Romania); Attendance: 36,281

IRL: Darren Edward Andrew Randolph, Séamus Coleman (Cap), Richard John Keogh, Enda John Stevens, Shane Patrick Michael Duffy, Conor Hourihane, James McClean, Jeffrey Patrick Hendrick, David McGoldrick, Scott Andrew Hogan (66.Seán Maguire), Callum Jack Robinson (73.Robert Brady). Trainer: Michael Joseph McCarthy.

Goals: Joseph Luis Chipolina (29 own goal), Robert Brady (90+3).

NATIONAL TEAM PLAYERS
(16.07.2018 – 15.07.2019)

Name	DOB	Caps	Goals	2018/2019:	*Club*
Goalkeepers					
Darren Edward Andrew RANDOLPH	12.05.1987	**38**	**0**	2018/2019:	*Middlesbrough FC (ENG)*
Defenders					
Cyrus Sylvester Frederick CHRISTIE	30.09.1992	**23**	**2**	2018:	*Fulham FC London (ENG)*
Ciaran CLARK	26.09.1989	**32**	**2**	2018:	*Newcastle United FC (ENG)*
Séamus COLEMAN	11.10.1988	**53**	**1**	2018/2019:	*Everton FC Liverpool (ENG)*
Matthew James DOHERTY	16.01.1992	**7**	**0**	2018/2019:	*Wolverhampton Wanderers FC (ENG)*
Shane Patrick Michael DUFFY	01.01.1992	**29**	**3**	2018/2019:	*Brighton & Hove Albion FC (ENG)*
John EGAN	20.10.1992	**4**	**0**	2018:	*Sheffield United FC (ENG)*
Richard John KEOGH	11.08.1986	**25**	**1**	2018/2019:	*Derby County FC (ENG)*
Darragh Patrick LENIHAN	16.03.1994	**2**	**0**	2018:	*Blackburn Rovers FC (ENG)*
Kevin Finbarr LONG	18.08.1990	**11**	**0**	2018:	*Burnley FC (ENG)*
Enda John STEVENS	09.07.1990	**10**	**0**	2018/2019:	*Sheffield United FC (ENG)*
Stephen Robert WARD	20.08.1985	**50**	**3**	2018:	*Burnley FC (ENG)*
Midfielders					
Harry Nicholas ARTER	28.12.1989	**16**	**0**	2018/2019:	*AFC Bournemouth (ENG)*
Robert BRADY	14.01.1992	**45**	**8**	2018/2019:	*Burnley FC (ENG)*
Ronan CURTIS	29.03.1996	**2**	**0**	2018:	*Portsmouth FC (ENG)*
Jeffrey Patrick HENDRICK	31.01.1992	**49**	**2**	2018/2019:	*Burnley FC (ENG)*
Daryl Jeremiah HORGAN	10.08.1992	**6**	**0**	2018:	*Hibernian FC Edinburgh (SCO)*
Conor HOURIHANE	02.02.1991	**12**	**1**	2018/2019:	*Aston Villa FC Birmingham (ENG)*
Alan Christopher JUDGE	11.11.1988	**6**	**1**	2018: 14.01.2019->	*Brentford FC (ENG)* *Ipswich Town FC (ENG)*
James Joseph McCLEAN	22.04.1989	**67**	**10**	2018/2019:	*Stoke City FC (ENG)*
Callum Joshua Ryan O'DOWDA	23.04.1995	**15**	**0**	2018:	*Bristol City FC (ENG)*
Glenn David WHELAN	13.01.1984	**87**	**2**	2018/2019:	*Aston Villa FC Birmingham (ENG)*
Shaun WILLIAMS	19.10.1986	**3**	**0**	2018:	*Millwall FC London (ENG)*
Forwards					
Graham Dylan BURKE	21.09.1993	**3**	**1**	2018:	*Preston North End FC (ENG)*
Scott Andrew HOGAN	13.04.1992	**5**	**0**	2018: 31.01.2019->	*Aston Villa Birmingham FC (ENG)* *Sheffield United FC (ENG)*
Shane Patrick LONG	22.01.1987	**82**	**17**	2018:	*Southampton FC (ENG)*
Seán Patrick MAGUIRE	01.05.1994	**6**	**0**	2018/2019:	*Preston North End FC (ENG)*
David McGOLDRICK	29.11.1987	**10**	**0**	2019:	*Sheffield United FC (ENG)*
Aiden Antony O'BRIEN	04.10.1993	**5**	**0**	2018/2019:	*Millwall FC London (ENG)*
Michael Oluwadurotimi OBAFEMI	06.07.2000	**1**	**0**	2018:	*Southampton FC (ENG)*
Callum Jack ROBINSON	02.02.1995	**8**	**0**	2018/2019:	*Preston North End FC (ENG)*
Jonathan Ronald WALTERS	20.09.1983	**54**	**14**	2018/2019:	*Burnley FC (ENG)*

National team coach

Martin Hugh Michael O'NEILL (Northern Ireland) [05.03.2013 – 21.11.2018]	01.03.1956	55 M; 19 W; 20 D; 16 L; 68-56
Michael Joseph "Mick" McCARTHY [from 25.11.2018]	07.02.1959	4 M; 3 W; 1 D; 0 L; 5-1 Complete record as trainer of Republic of Ireland: 72 M; 32 W; 21 D; 19 L; 117-68 (27.03.1996 – 16.10.2002) & (from 25.11.2018)

ROMANIA

The Country:
România (Romania)
Capital: Bucureşti
Surface: 238,397 km²
Inhabitants: 19,401,658 [2019]
Time: UTC+2

The FA:
Federaţia Română de Fotbal
Casa Fotbalului, Str. Serg. Şerbanică Vasile 12, 22186 Bucureşti
Tel: +40 21 325 0678
Founded: 00.00.1909
Member of FIFA since: 1923
Member of UEFA since: 1954
Website: www.frf.ro

NATIONAL TEAM RECORDS

First international match:	08.06.1922, Beograd:	Yugoslavia – Romania 1-2
Most international caps:	Dorinel Ionel Munteanu	- 134 caps (1991-2007)
Most international goals:	Gheorghe Hagi	- 35 goals / 125 caps (1983-2000)
	Adrian Mutu	- 35 goals / 77 caps (2000-2013)

UEFA EUROPEAN CHAMPIONSHIP	
1960	Qualifiers
1964	Qualifiers
1968	Qualifiers
1972	Qualifiers
1976	Qualifiers
1980	Qualifiers
1984	Final Tournament (Group Stage)
1988	Qualifiers
1992	Qualifiers
1996	Final Tournament (Group Stage)
2000	Final Tournament (Quarter-Finals)
2004	Qualifiers
2008	Final Tournament (Group Stage)
2012	Qualifiers
2016	Final Tournament (Group Stage)

FIFA WORLD CUP	
1930	Final Tournament (Group Stage)
1934	Final Tournament (1st Round)
1938	Final Tournament (1st Round)
1950	Did not enter
1954	Qualifiers
1958	Qualifiers
1962	*Withdrew*
1966	Qualifiers
1970	Final Tournament (Group Stage)
1974	Qualifiers
1978	Qualifiers
1982	Qualifiers
1986	Qualifiers
1990	Final Tournament (2nd Round of 16)
1994	Final Tournament (Quarter-Finals)
1998	Final Tournament (2nd Round of 16)
2002	Qualifiers
2006	Qualifiers
2010	Qualifiers
2014	Qualifiers
2018	Qualifiers

UEFA NATIONS LEAGUE
2018/2019 – League C (promoted to League B)

OLYMPIC FOOTBALL TOURNAMENTS 1908-2016							
1908	-	**1948**	Did not enter	**1972**	Qualifiers	**1996**	Qualifiers
1912	-	**1952**	Preliminary Round	**1976**	Qualifiers	**2000**	Qualifiers
1920	-	**1956**	Did not enter	**1980**	Qualifiers	**2004**	Qualifiers
1924	-	**1960**	Qualifiers	**1984**	Qualifiers	**2008**	Qualifiers
1928	1/8 - Finals	**1964**	Quarter-Finals	**1988**	Qualifiers	**2012**	Qualifiers
1936	Did not enter	**1968**	Qualifiers	**1992**	Qualifiers	**2016**	Qualifiers

FIFA CONFEDERATIONS CUP 1992-2017
None

ROMANIAN CLUB HONOURS IN EUROPEAN CLUB COMPETITIONS:

European Champion Clubs.Cup (1956-1992) / UEFA Champions League (1993-2019)		
FC Steaua Bucureşti	1	1985/1986
Fairs Cup (1858-1971) / UEFA Cup (1972-2009) / UEFA Europa League (2010-2019)		
None		
UEFA Super Cup (1972-2018)		
FC Steaua Bucureşti	1	1986
European Cup Winners.Cup 1961-1999*		
None		

**defunct competition*

NATIONAL COMPETITIONS
TABLE OF HONOURS

	CHAMPIONS*	CUP WINNERS	BEST GOALSCORERS	
1909/1910	Olympia Bucureşti	-	-	
1910/1911	Olympia Bucureşti	-	-	
1911/1912	United Ploieşti	-	-	
1912/1913	Colentina AC Bucureşti	-	-	
1913/1914	Colentina AC Bucureşti	-	-	
1914/1915	Româno-Americană Bucureşti	-	-	
1915/1916	Prahova Ploieşti	-	-	
1916/1917	*No competition*	-	-	
1917/1918	*No competition*	-	-	
1918/1919	*No competition*	-	-	
1919/1920	AS Venus Bucureşti	-	-	
1920/1921	AS Venus Bucureşti	-	-	
1921/1922	Chinezul Timişoara	-	-	
1922/1923	Chinezul Timişoara	-	-	
1923/1924	Chinezul Timişoara	-	-	
1924/1925	Chinezul Timişoara	-	-	
1925/1926	Chinezul Timişoara	-	-	
1926/1927	Chinezul Timişoara	-	-	
1927/1928	CS Colţea Braşov	-	-	
1928/1929	AS Venus Bucureşti	-	-	
1929/1930	FC Juventus Bucureşti	-	-	
1930/1931	UD Reşiţa	-	-	
1931/1932	AS Venus Bucureşti	-	-	
1932/1933	FC Ripensia Timişoara	-	-	
1933/1934	AS Venus Bucureşti	FC Ripensia Timişoara	Ştefan Dobay (FC Ripensia Timişoara)	25
1934/1935	FC Ripensia Timişoara	ACS CFR Bucureşti	Ştefan Dobay (FC Ripensia Timişoara)	24
1935/1936	FC Ripensia Timişoara	FC Ripensia Timişoara	Ştefan Barbu (ACS CFR Bucureşti)	23
1936/1937	AS Venus Bucureşti	FC Rapid Bucureşti	Ştefan Dobay (FC Ripensia Timişoara) Traian Iordache (Unirea Tricolor Bucureşti)	21
1937/1938	FC Ripensia Timişoara	FC Rapid Bucureşti	Árpád Thierjung (Chinezul Timişoara)	22
1938/1939	AS Venus Bucureşti	FC Rapid Bucureşti	Adalbert Marksteiner [Béla Marosvári] (FC Ripensia Timişoara)	21
1939/1940	AS Venus Bucureşti	FC Rapid Bucureşti	Ştefan Auer II [István Avar] (FC Rapid Bucureşti)	21
1940/1941	Unirea Tricolor Bucureşti	FC Rapid Bucureşti	Ion Bogdan (FC Rapid Bucureşti) Valeriu Niculescu (Unirea Tricolor Bucureşti)	21
1941/1942	*No competition*	FC Rapid Bucureşti	-	
1942/1943	*No competition*	CFR Turnu Severin	-	
1943/1944	*No competition*	*No competition*	-	
1944/1945	*No competition*	*No competition*	-	
1945/1946	*No competition*	*No competition*	-	
1946/1947	IT Arad	*No competition*	Ladislau Bonyhádi (IT Arad)	26
1947/1948	IT Arad	IT Arad	Ladislau Bonyhádi (IT Arad)	49
1948/1949	IC Oradea	CSCA Bucureşti	Gheorghe Váczi (IC Oradea)	24
1950	Flamura Roşie Arad	CCA Bucureşti	Andrei Rădulescu (Locomotiva Bucureşti)	18
1951	CCA Bucureşti	CCA Bucureşti	Gheorghe Váczi (Progresul Oradea)	23
1952	CCA Bucureşti	CCA Bucureşti	Titus Ozon (CS Dinamo Bucureşti)	17
1953	CCA Bucureşti	Flamura Roşie Arad	Titus Ozon (CS Dinamo Bucureşti)	12
1954	Flamura Roşie Arad	Metalul Reşiţa	Alexandru Ene I (CS Dinamo Bucureşti)	20
1955	CS Dinamo Bucureşti	CCA Bucureşti	Ion Ciosescu (Ştiinţa Timişoara)	18
1956	CCA Bucureşti	Progresul Oradea	Ion Alecsandrescu (CCA Bucureşti)	18
1957/1958	FC Petrolul Ploieşti	CS Ştiinţa Timişoara	Ion Ciosescu (CS Ştiinţa Timişoara)	21
1958/1959	FC Petrolul Ploieşti	CS Dinamo Bucureşti	Gheorghe Ene (CS Rapid Bucureşti)	17
1959/1960	CCA Bucureşti	Progresul Bucureşti	Gheorghe Constantin (CCA Bucureşti)	20
1960/1961	CCA Bucureşti	Arieşul Turda	Gheorghe Constantin (CCA Bucureşti)	22
1961/1962	CS Dinamo Bucureşti	CSA Steaua Bucureşti	Gheorghe Constantin (CSA Steaua Bucureşti)	24
1962/1963	CS Dinamo Bucureşti	FC Petrolul Ploieşti	Ion Gheorghe Ionescu (CS Rapid Bucureşti)	20
1963/1964	CS Dinamo Bucureşti	CS Dinamo Bucureşti	Constantin Frăţilă (CS Dinamo Bucureşti) Cornel Pavlovici (CSA Steaua Bucureşti)	19
1964/1965	CS Dinamo Bucureşti	Ştiinţa Cluj	Mihai Adam (Ştiinţa Cluj)	18
1965/1966	FC Petrolul Ploieşti	CSA Steaua Bucureşti	Ion Gheorghe Ionescu (CS Rapid Bucureşti)	24
1966/1967	CS Rapid Bucureşti	CSA Steaua Bucureşti	Ion Oblemenco (Universitatea Craiova)	17
1967/1968	CSA Steaua Bucureşti	CS Dinamo Bucureşti	Mihai Adam (CS Universitatea Cluj)	15
1968/1969	UT Arad	CSA Steaua Bucureşti	Florea Dumitrache (CS Dinamo Bucureşti)	22
1969/1970	UT Arad	CSA Steaua Bucureşti	Ion Oblemenco (CS Universitatea Craiova)	19
1970/1971	CS Dinamo Bucureşti	CSA Steaua Bucureşti	Constantin Moldoveanu (Politehnica Iaşi) Florea Dumitrache (CS Dinamo Bucureşti) Gheorghe Tătaru (CSA Steaua Bucureşti)	15
1971/1972	FC Argeş Piteşti	CS Rapid Bucureşti	Ion Oblemenco (CS Universitatea Craiova)	20
1972/1973	CS Dinamo Bucureşti	CS Chimia Râmnicu Vâlcea	Ion Oblemenco (CS Universitatea Craiova)	21
1973/1974	CS Universitatea Craiova	CSM Jiul Petroşani	Mihai Adam (CFR Cluj-Napoca)	23
1974/1975	CS Dinamo Bucureşti	CS Rapid Bucureşti	Dudu Georgescu (CS Dinamo Bucureşti)	33
1975/1976	CSA Steaua Bucureşti	CSA Steaua Bucureşti	Dudu Georgescu (CS Dinamo Bucureşti)	31

1976/1977	CS Dinamo Bucureşti	CS Universitatea Craiova	Dudu Georgescu (CS Dinamo Bucureşti)	47
1977/1978	CSA Steaua Bucureşti	CS Universitatea Craiova	Dudu Georgescu (CS Dinamo Bucureşti)	24
1978/1979	FC Argeş Piteşti	CSA Steaua Bucureşti	Marin Radu II (FC Argeş Piteşti)	22
1979/1980	CS Universitatea Craiova	CS Politehnica Timişoara	Septimiu Câmpeanu II (CS Universitatea Cluj)	24
1980/1981	CS Universitatea Craiova	CS Universitatea Craiova	Marin Radu II (FC Argeş Piteşti)	28
1981/1982	CS Dinamo Bucureşti	CS Dinamo Bucureşti	Anghel Iordănescu (CSA Steaua Bucureşti)	20
1982/1983	CS Dinamo Bucureşti	CS Universitatea Craiova	Petre Grosu (FC Bihor Oradea)	20
1983/1984	CS Dinamo Bucureşti	CS Dinamo Bucureşti	Marcel Coraş (CF Sportul Studenţesc Bucureşti)	20
1984/1985	CSA Steaua Bucureşti	CSA Steaua Bucureşti	Gheorghe Hagi (CF Sportul Studenţesc Bucureşti)	20
1985/1986	CSA Steaua Bucureşti	CS Dinamo Bucureşti	Gheorghe Hagi (CF Sportul Studenţesc Bucureşti)	31
1986/1987	CSA Steaua Bucureşti	CSA Steaua Bucureşti	Rodion Gorun Cămătaru (CS Dinamo Bucureşti)	44
1987/1988	CSA Steaua Bucureşti	CSA Steaua Bucureşti	Victor Piţurcă (CSA Steaua Bucureşti)	34
1988/1989	CSA Steaua Bucureşti	CSA Steaua Bucureşti	Dorin Mateuţ (CS Dinamo Bucureşti)	43
1989/1990	CS Dinamo Bucureşti	CS Dinamo Bucureşti	Gavril Balint (CSA Steaua Bucureşti)	19
1990/1991	CS Universitatea Craiova	CS Universitatea Craiova	Ovidiu Cornel Hanganu (FC Corvinul Hunedoara)	24
1991/1992	CS Dinamo Bucureşti	CSA Steaua Bucureşti	Gábor Gerstenmájer (CS Dinamo Bucureşti)	21
1992/1993	CSA Steaua Bucureşti	FC Universitatea Craiova	Ilie Dumitrescu (CSA Steaua Bucureşti)	24
1993/1994	CSA Steaua Bucureşti	ACF Gloria Bistriţa	Gheorghe Craioveanu (FC Universitatea Craiova)	21
1994/1995	CSA Steaua Bucureşti	FC Petrolul Ploieşti	Gheorghe Craioveanu (FC Universitatea Craiova)	27
1995/1996	CSA Steaua Bucureşti	CSA Steaua Bucureşti	Ion Vlădoiu (CSA Steaua Bucureşti)	25
1996/1997	CSA Steaua Bucureşti	CSA Steaua Bucureşti	Sabin Ilie (CSA Steaua Bucureşti)	31
1997/1998	CSA Steaua Bucureşti	UFC Rapid Bucureşti	Constantin Barbu (FC Argeş Piteşti) Ion Vasile Oană (ACF Gloria Bistriţa)	22
1998/1999	UFC Rapid Bucureşti	FC Steaua Bucureşti	Ioan Viorel Ganea (ACF Gloria Bistriţa)	28
1999/2000	FC Dinamo Bucureşti	FC Dinamo Bucureşti	Marian Savu (FC Naţional Bucureşti)	20
2000/2001	FC Steaua Bucureşti	FC Dinamo Bucureşti	Marius Constantin Niculae (FC Dinamo Bucureşti)	20
2001/2002	FC Dinamo Bucureşti	UFC Rapid Bucureşti	Cătălin Cursaru (FCM Bacău)	17
2002/2003	UFC Rapid Bucureşti	FC Dinamo Bucureşti	Claudiu Nicu Răducanu (FC Steaua Bucureşti)	21
2003/2004	FC Dinamo Bucureşti	FC Dinamo Bucureşti	Ionel Daniel Dănciulescu (FC Dinamo Bucureşti)	21
2004/2005	FC Steaua Bucureşti	FC Dinamo Bucureşti	Gheorghe Bucur (CF Sportul Studenţesc Bucureşti) Claudiu Iulian Niculescu (FC Dinamo Bucureşti)	21
2005/2006	FC Steaua Bucureşti	UFC Rapid Bucureşti	Ionuţ Costinel Mazilu (CF Sportul Studenţesc Bucureşti)	22
2006/2007	FC Dinamo Bucureşti	UFC Rapid Bucureşti	Claudiu Iulian Niculescu (FC Dinamo Bucureşti)	18
2007/2008	FC CFR 1907 Cluj-Napoca	FC CFR 1907 Cluj-Napoca	Ionel Daniel Dănciulescu (FC Dinamo Bucureşti)	21
2008/2009	FC Unirea Urziceni	FC CFR 1907 Cluj-Napoca	Gheorghe Bucur (FC Timişoara) Florin Constantin Costea (FC Universitatea Craiova)	17
2009/2010	FC CFR 1907 Cluj-Napoca	FC CFR 1907 Cluj-Napoca	Andrei Cristea (FC Dinamo Bucureşti)	16
2010/2011	ASC Oţelul Galaţi	FC Steaua Bucureşti	Ianis Alin Zicu (FC Timişoara)	18
2011/2012	FC CFR 1907 Cluj-Napoca	FC Dinamo Bucureşti	Wesley Lopes da Silva (BRA, FC Vaslui)	27
2012/2013	FC Steaua Bucureşti	FC Petrolul Ploieşti	Raul Andrei Rusescu (FC Steaua Bucureşti)	21
2013/2014	FC Steaua Bucureşti	AFC Astra Giurgiu	Liviu Ion Antal (FC Vaslui)	14
2014/2015	FC Steaua Bucureşti	FC Steaua Bucureşti	Grégory Tadé (FRA, FC CFR 1907 Cluj-Napoca)	18
2015/2016	AFC Astra Giurgiu	FC CFR 1907 Cluj-Napoca	Adrian Ioan Hora (CS Pandurii Târgu Jiu)	19
2016/2017	FC Viitorul Constanţa	FC Voluntari	Azdren Llullaku (ALB, CS Gaz Metan Mediaş)	16
2017/2018	FC CFR 1907 Cluj-Napoca	CS Universitatea Craiova	Marius George Ţucudean (FC Viitorul Constanţa, FC CFR 1907 Cluj-Napoca) Harlem-Eddy Gnohéré (FRA, FCSB Bucureşti)	15
2018/2019	FC CFR 1907 Cluj-Napoca	FC Viitorul Constanţa	Marius George Ţucudean (FC CFR 1907 Cluj-Napoca)	18

* Romanian Football Championship (1909–1921), Divizia A (1921–2006), Liga I (since 2006).

Club name changements:

FC Rapid Bucureşti = ACS CFR Bucureşti (1923-1936), FC Rapid Bucureşti (1936-1945), CFR Bucureşti (1945-1949), Locomotiva Bucureşti (1949-1958), CS Rapid Bucureşti (1958-1992), UFC Rapid Bucureşti (1992-2016), Academia Rapid Bucureşti (2017), FC Rapid Bucureşti (since 2018).

UT Arad = IT Arad (1945–1949), Flamura Roşie Arad (1950–1957), UT Arad (1958–2014), UTA Bătrâna Doamnă Arad (2014–2017), UT Arad (since 2017).

ACS CAO Oradea = CA Oradea (1919-1940), Nagyváradi AC (1940-1944), Libertatea Oradea (1945-1948), IC Oradea (1948-1951), Progresul Oradea (1951-1958), CS Oradea (1958-1961), Crişana Oradea (1961-1963).

FCSB Bucureşti = ASA Bucureşti (1947-1948), CSCA Bucureşti (1948-1950), CCA Bucureşti (1950-1961), CSA Steaua Bucureşti (1961-1998), FC Steaua Bucureşti (1998-2017), FCSB Bucureşti (since 2017).

FC Dinamo Bucureşti = CS Dinamo Bucureşti (1945-1992), FC Dinamo Bucureşti (since 1992).

ACS Poli Timişoara = SS Politehnica Timişoara (1921-1948), CSU Timişoara (1948-1950), CS Ştiinţa Timişoara (1950-1966), CS Politehnica Timişoara (1966-1969), FC Ripensia Timişoata (1969), CS Politehnica Timişoara (1969-1992), FC Politehnica Timişoara (1992-2012), ACS Poli Timişoara (since 2012).

FC Universitatea Cluj-Napoca = Universitatea Cluj (1919-1948), CSU Cluj (1948-1949), Ştiinţa Cluj (1949-1966), CS Universitatea Cluj (1966-1974), CS Universitatea Cluj-Napoca (1974-1992), FC Universitatea Cluj-Napoca (since 1992).

CS Universitatea Craiova = CSU Craiova (1948-1950), Ştiinţa Craiova (1950-1966), CS Universitatea Craiova (1966-1992), FC Universitatea Craiova (1992-2011), CS Universitatea Craiova (since 2013).

NATIONAL CHAMPIONSHIP
Liga I 2018/2019
(20.07.2018 – 02.06.2019)

Results

Round 1 [20-23.07.2018]
CFR Cluj - FC Botoşani 1-1(1-0)
FC Hermannstadt - Sepsi OSK 1-0(1-0)
Astra Giurgiu - FCSB Bucureşti 1-0(1-0)
Viitorul Constanţa - Dunărea Călăraşi 0-1(0-1)
Dinamo Bucureşti - FC Voluntari 2-1(0-0)
Gaz Metan Mediaş - Concordia Ch. 2-1(1-1)
Universitatea Craiova - Politehnica Iaşi 0-0

Round 2 [27-30.07.2018]
FC Botoşani - FC Hermannstadt 2-0(1-0)
Dunărea Călăraşi - CFR Cluj 0-0
Politehnica Iaşi - Astra Giurgiu 1-1(0-0)
Sepsi OSK - Universitatea Craiova 1-0(0-0)
FCSB Bucureşti - Dinamo Bucureşti 3-3(1-1)
FC Voluntari - Gaz Metan Mediaş 1-1(1-1)
Concordia Ch. - Viitorul Constanţa 1-1(1-0)

Round 3 [03-06.08.2018]
Universitatea Craiova - FC Botoşani 2-2(2-1)
Astra Giurgiu - Sepsi OSK 1-1(1-0)
CFR Cluj - Concordia Chiajna 2-1(0-0)
FC Hermannstadt - Dunărea Călăraşi 1-1(1-0)
FCSB Bucureşti - Politehnica Iaşi 4-0(1-0)
Viitorul Constanţa - FC Voluntari 2-0(0-0)
Gaz Metan Med. - Dinamo Bucureşti 3-2(1-1)

Round 4 [10-13.08.2018]
FC Botoşani - Astra Giurgiu 1-1(1-1)
Concordia Ch. - FC Hermannstadt 2-0(1-0)
Sepsi OSK - Politehnica Iaşi 3-0(1-0)
Dunărea Călăraşi - Univers. Craiova 1-3(0-1)
FC Voluntari - CFR Cluj 1-2(1-1)
Gaz Metan Mediaş - FCSB Bucureşti 1-3(1-0)
Dinamo Bucureşti - Viitorul Const. 1-0(1-0)

Round 5 [17-20.08.2018]
Politehnica Iaşi - FC Botoşani 2-1(2-0)
Astra Giurgiu - Dunărea Călăraşi 1-1(1-1)
Viitorul Constanţa - Gaz Metan Med. 2-0(1-0)
FCSB Bucureşti - Sepsi OSK 2-0(0-0)
CFR Cluj - Dinamo Bucureşti 3-1(0-0)
FC Hermannstadt - FC Voluntari 4-0(3-0)
Universitatea Craiova - Concordia C. 0-1(0-0)

Round 6 [24-27.08.2018]
Concordia Chiajna - Astra Giurgiu 0-3(0-0)
Dunărea Călăraşi - Politehnica Iaşi 2-0(0-0)
Dinamo Bucureşti - FC Hermannstadt 2-1(1-0)
Gaz Metan Mediaş - CFR Cluj 0-0
Viitorul Constanţa - FCSB Bucureşti 1-4(0-1)
FC Botoşani - Sepsi OSK 0-0
FC Voluntari - Universitatea Craiova 1-5(0-4)

Round 7 [31.08.-03.09.2018]
Sepsi OSK - Dunărea Călăraşi 1-0(1-0)
FC Hermannstadt - Gaz Metan Med. 0-1(0-0)
Astra Giurgiu - FC Voluntari 0-0
Univers. Craiova - Dinamo Bucureşti 3-0(1-0)
CFR Cluj - Viitorul Constanţa 1-2(0-0)
FCSB Bucureşti - FC Botoşani 2-2(2-1)
Politehnica Iaşi - Concordia Chiajna 3-0(2-0)

Round 8 [14-17.09.2018]
Concordia Chiajna - Sepsi OSK 0-3(0-0)
Dinamo Bucureşti - Astra Giurgiu 1-2(0-1)
Dunărea Călăraşi - FC Botoşani 3-2(2-1)
Gaz Metan Mediaş - Univer. Craiova 3-2(2-1)
FC Voluntari - Politehnica Iaşi 2-3(0-2)
CFR Cluj - FCSB Bucureşti 1-1(0-1)
Viitorul Constanţa - Hermannstadt 1-0(1-0)

Round 9 [21-24.09.2018]
Sepsi OSK - FC Voluntari 1-1(0-1)
Politehnica Iaşi - Dinamo Bucureşti 1-0(1-0)
FC Hermannstadt - CFR Cluj 0-1(0-0)
FC Botoşani - Concordia Chiajna 0-2(0-2)
Univers. Craiova - Viitorul Constanţa 2-0(1-0)
FCSB Bucureşti - Dunărea Călăraşi 2-0(2-0)
Astra Giurgiu - Gaz Metan Mediaş 3-0(1-0)

Round 10 [28.09.-01.10.2018]
Dinamo Bucureşti - Sepsi OSK 0-0
FC Voluntari - FC Botoşani 1-1(1-0)
Gaz Metan Mediaş - Politehnica Iaşi 1-0(0-0)
Viitorul Constanţa - Astra Giurgiu 1-0(0-0)
FC Hermannstadt - FCSB Bucureşti 1-3(1-1)
Concordia Ch. - Dunărea Călăraşi 1-1(0-1)
CFR Cluj - Universitatea Craiova 0-0

Round 11 [05-08.10.2018]
Politehnica Iaşi - Viitorul Constanţa 1-2(1-2)
Universitatea Craiova - Hermannstadt 1-1(1-1)
Astra Giurgiu - CFR Cluj 1-2(0-1)
Dunărea Călăraşi - FC Voluntari 1-1(1-0)
Sepsi OSK - Gaz Metan Mediaş 1-2(1-1)
FCSB Bucureşti - Concordia Chiajna 0-1(0-0)
FC Botoşani - Dinamo Bucureşti 2-0(1-0)

Round 12 [19-22.10.2018]
FC Voluntari - Concordia Chiajna 4-0(2-0)
CFR Cluj - Politehnica Iaşi 1-0(1-0)
FC Hermannstadt - Astra Giurgiu 0-2(0-0)
Viitorul Constanţa - Sepsi OSK 2-3(1-1)
Gaz Metan Mediaş - FC Botoşani 1-2(1-0)
Universit. Craiova - FCSB Bucureşti 2-1(0-1)
Dinamo Bucureşti - Dunărea Călăraşi 1-1(0-1)

Round 13 [26-29.10.2018]
Politehnica Iaşi - FC Hermannstadt 0-2(0-2)
Astra Giurgiu - Universitatea Craiova 0-3(0-1)
FC Botoşani - Viitorul Constanţa 1-2(0-0)
FCSB Bucureşti - FC Voluntari 2-1(0-0)
Dunărea Călăraşi - Gaz Metan Mediaş 0-0
Sepsi OSK - CFR Cluj 1-2(0-1)
Concordia Chiajna - Dinamo Bucureşti 0-0

Round 14 [02-05.11.2018]
Politehnica Iaşi - Universit. Craiova 0-3(0-0)
Sepsi OSK - FC Hermannstadt 1-3(1-0)
FC Botoşani - CFR Cluj 1-5(0-2)
Dunărea Călăraşi - Viitorul Constanţa 0-1(0-0)
FCSB Bucureşti - Astra Giurgiu 1-0(0-0)
Concordia Chiajna - Gaz Metan Mediaş 0-0
FC Voluntari - Dinamo Bucureşti 0-1(0-0)

Round 15 [09-12.11.2018]
Universitatea Craiova - Sepsi OSK 1-1(0-1)
Astra Giurgiu - Politehnica Iaşi 1-2(1-0)
Viitorul Constanţa - Concordia Chiajna 0-0
CFR Cluj - Dunărea Călăraşi 0-0
Dinamo Bucureşti - FCSB Bucureşti 1-1(1-0)
FC Hermannstadt - FC Botoşani 1-1(0-0)
Gaz Metan Mediaş - FC Voluntari 2-0(2-0)

Round 16 [23-26.11.2018]
Dinamo Bucureşti - Gaz Metan Med. 1-1(0-0)
Sepsi OSK - Astra Giurgiu 1-0(0-0)
Concordia Chiajna - CFR Cluj 0-1(0-1)
Dunărea Călăraşi - FC Hermannstadt 0-1(0-0)
FC Voluntari - Viitorul Constanţa 1-2(0-1)
Politehnica Iaşi - FCSB Bucureşti 1-2(0-0)
FC Botoşani - Universitatea Craiova 2-1(2-0)

Round 17 [30.11.-03.12.2018]
Politehnica Iaşi - Sepsi OSK 1-1(1-1)
CFR Cluj - FC Voluntari 5-0(1-0)
FC Hermannstadt - Concordia Ch. 2-1(2-1)
Viitorul Constanţa - Dinamo Buc. 4-1(2-1)
Universit. Craiova - Dunărea Călăraşi 1-0(1-0)
FCSB Bucureşti - Gaz Metan Mediaş 2-1(1-0)
Astra Giurgiu - FC Botoşani 1-1(0-0)

Round 18 [04-06.12.2018]
FC Voluntari - FC Hermannstadt 2-0(0-0)
Dinamo Bucureşti - CFR Cluj 0-3(0-1)
Gaz Metan Med. - Viitorul Constanţa 2-2(1-1)
Sepsi OSK - FCSB Bucureşti 4-2(2-0)
Dunărea Călăraşi - Astra Giurgiu 1-2(0-2)
FC Botoşani - Politehnica Iaşi 1-2(1-2)
Concordia Ch. - Universit. Craiova 1-3(1-3)

Round 19 [08-10.12.2018]
FC Hermannstadt - Dinamo Bucureşti 1-1(1-1)
CFR Cluj - Gaz Metan Mediaş 2-2(1-2)
Politehnica Iaşi - Dunărea Călăraşi 1-0(1-0)
Astra Giurgiu - Concordia Chiajna 3-1(0-0)
Sepsi OSK - FC Botoşani 0-1(0-1)
Universitatea Craiova - FC Voluntari 3-1(2-1)
FCSB Bucureşti - Viitorul Constanţa 2-0(1-0)

Round 20 [14-17.12.2018]
Concordia Chiajna - Politehnica Iaşi 3-6(1-2)
FC Voluntari - Astra Giurgiu 1-1(0-0)
Gaz Metan Mediaş - Hermannstadt 0-2(0-1)
Dinamo Bucureşti - Univers. Craiova 3-0(1-0)
Dunărea Călăraşi - Sepsi OSK 0-3(0-1)
FC Botoşani - FCSB Bucureşti 1-3(1-2)
Viitorul Constanţa - CFR Cluj 0-1(0-1)

Round 21 [19-22.12.2018]
Universitatea Craiova - Gaz Metan 2-0(0-0)
FC Botoşani - Dunărea Călăraşi 1-0(1-0)
Astra Giurgiu - Dinamo Bucureşti 4-1(2-0)
Politehnica Iaşi - FC Voluntari 2-2(1-0)
Sepsi OSK - Concordia Chiajna 3-0(2-0)
Hermannstadt - Viitorul Constanţa 1-0(1-0)
FCSB Bucureşti - CFR Cluj 0-2(0-1)

Round 22 [01-04.02.2019]
Concordia Chiajna - FC Botoşani 0-1(0-0)
Gaz Metan Mediaş - Astra Giurgiu 1-1(1-0)
Dunărea Călăraşi - FCSB Bucureşti 1-1(1-1)
CFR Cluj - FC Hermannstadt 1-1(0-1)
FC Voluntari - Sepsi OSK 4-2(2-1)
Viitorul Constanţa - Universitatea Craiova 0-0
Dinamo Bucureşti - Politehnica Iaşi 3-0(1-0)

Round 23 [08-11.02.2019]
Astra Giurgiu - Viitorul Constanţa 3-0(1-0)
Sepsi OSK - Dinamo Bucureşti 0-1(0-0)
Dunărea Călăraşi - Concordia Ch. 2-1(1-1)
Politehnica Iaşi - Gaz Metan Mediaş 1-0(1-0)
Universitatea Craiova - CFR Cluj 2-0(1-0)
FC Botoşani - FC Voluntari 1-0(1-0)
FCSB Bucureşti - FC Hermannstadt 3-0(2-0)

Round 24 [15-18.02.2019]
Viitorul Constanţa - Politehnica Iaşi 0-1(0-0)
Hermannstadt - Universitatea Craiova 0-1(0-0)
CFR Cluj - Astra Giurgiu 1-1(0-0)
FC Voluntari - Dunărea Călăraşi 0-0
Gaz Metan Mediaş - Sepsi OSK 0-1(0-1)
Dinamo Bucureşti - FC Botoşani 1-2(1-1)
Concordia Chiajna - FCSB Bucureşti 0-0

Round 25 [22-25.02.2019]
Sepsi OSK - Viitorul Constanța 0-0
Astra Giurgiu - FC Hermannstadt 1-0(0-0)
Politehnica Iași - CFR Cluj 0-1(0-0)
Dunărea Călărași - Dinamo București 0-0
FC Botoșani - Gaz Metan Mediaș 1-1(1-1)
FCSB București - Universit. Craiova 3-2(1-1)
Concordia Chiajna - FC Voluntari 1-3(0-0)

Round 26 [01-04.03.2019]
Dinamo București - Concordia Ch. 2-1(1-0)
Gaz Metan Mediaș - Dunărea Călărași 0-0
FC Voluntari - FCSB București 2-2(2-1)
FC Hermannstadt - Politehnica Iași 2-0(0-0)
Viitorul Constanța - FC Botoșani 1-0(1-0)
CFR Cluj - Sepsi OSK 1-0(1-0)
Universitatea Craiova - Astra Giurgiu 1-2(0-0)

Final Standings

1.	FC CFR 1907 Cluj-Napoca	26	15	9	2	39	-	16	54
2.	FCSB București	26	14	7	5	49	-	29	49
3.	CS Universitatea Craiova	26	13	6	7	43	-	24	45
4.	AFC Astra Giurgiu	26	11	9	6	36	-	23	42
5.	FC Viitorul Constanța	26	11	5	10	26	-	27	38
6.	ACS Sepsi OSK Sfântu Gheorghe	26	10	7	9	32	-	25	37
7.	FC Botoșani	26	9	9	8	31	-	33	36
8.	ACS Municipal Politehnica Iași	26	10	4	12	28	-	38	34
9.	FC Dinamo București	26	8	8	10	29	-	37	32
10.	AFC Hermannstadt Sibiu	26	9	5	12	25	-	28	32
11.	CS Gaz Metan Mediaș	26	7	10	9	25	-	32	31
12.	AFC Dunărea Călărași	26	4	12	10	16	-	25	24
13.	FC Voluntari	26	4	9	13	30	-	46	21
14.	CS Concordia Chiajna	26	4	6	16	19	-	45	18

Teams ranked 1-6 were qualified for the Championship Round, while teams ranked 7-14 were qualified for the Relegation Round.

Championship Round

Results

Round 1 [09-11.03.2019]
CFR Cluj - Sepsi OSK 3-1(1-0)
Universitatea Craiova - Astra Giurgiu 1-0(1-0)
FCSB București - Viitorul Constanța 1-2(1-1)

Round 2 [15-17.03.2019]
Sepsi OSK - Universitatea Craiova 0-1(0-1)
Viitorul Constanța - CFR Cluj 0-1(0-0)
Astra Giurgiu - FCSB București 0-2(0-2)

Round 3 [30.03.-01.04.2019]
CFR Cluj - Astra Giurgiu 1-0(0-0)
FCSB București - Universit. Craiova 3-2(2-2)
Sepsi OSK - Viitorul Constanța 0-0

Round 4 [07-08.04.2019]
Universitatea Craiova - CFR Cluj 0-0
Astra Giurgiu - Viitorul Constanța 1-4(1-2)
FCSB București - Sepsi OSK 2-0(0-0)

Round 5 [13-15.04.2019]
Viitorul Constanța - Univers. Craiova 2-1(1-1)
CFR Cluj - FCSB București 0-0
Sepsi OSK - Astra Giurgiu 0-1(0-0)

Round 6 [19-21.04.2019]
Astra Giurgiu - Universitatea Craiova 0-1(0-0)
Sepsi OSK - CFR Cluj 0-1(0-1)
Viitorul Constanța - FCSB București 1-1(0-0)

Round 7 [28-29.04.2019]
FCSB București - Astra Giurgiu 1-0(0-0)
Universitatea Craiova - Sepsi OSK 1-0(0-0)
CFR Cluj - Viitorul Constanța 3-1(0-1)

Round 8 [04-06.05.2019]
Viitorul Constanța - Sepsi OSK 3-1(0-0)
Universit. Craiova - FCSB București 0-2(0-1)
Astra Giurgiu - CFR Cluj 1-5(0-1)

Round 9 [11-13.05.2019]
Sepsi OSK - FCSB București 1-5(0-2)
CFR Cluj - Universitatea Craiova 1-0(1-0)
Viitorul Constanța - Astra Giurgiu 3-0(1-0)

Round 10 [18-20.05.2019]
Univers. Craiova - Viitorul Constanța 1-2(1-0)
FCSB București - CFR Cluj 1-0(0-0)
Astra Giurgiu - Sepsi OSK 3-2(2-1)

Final Standings

1.	**FC CFR 1907 Cluj-Napoca**	10	7	2	1	15	-	4	50
2.	FCSB București	10	7	2	1	18	-	6	48
3.	FC Viitorul Constanța	10	6	2	2	18	-	10	39
4.	CS Universitatea Craiova	10	4	1	5	8	-	10	36
5.	AFC Astra Giurgiu	10	2	0	8	6	-	20	27
6.	ACS Sepsi OSK Sfântu Gheorghe	10	0	1	9	5	-	20	20

Top goalscorers:

18 Marius George Țucudean
FC CFR 1907 Cluj-Napoca
15 Harlem-Eddy Gnohéré (FRA)
FCSB București
13 Mattia Montini (ITA)
FC Dinamo București
13 Elvir Koljić (BIH)
CS Universitatea Craiova
13 Alexandru Ionuț Mitriță
CS Universitatea Craiova

Relegation Round

Results

Round 1 [08-11.03.2019]
Dinamo Bucureşti - Dunărea Călăraşi 2-0(1-0)
Hermannstadt - Gaz Metan Mediaş 0-2(0-1)
Politehnica Iaşi - FC Voluntari 0-2(0-1)
FC Botoşani - Concordia Chiajna 0-0

Round 2 [16-18.03.2019]
Dunărea Călăraşi - Politehnica Iaşi 1-2(0-0)
Gaz Metan Med. - Dinamo Bucureşti 2-1(1-1)
Concordia Ch. - FC Hermannstadt 2-2(2-2)
FC Voluntari - FC Botoşani 2-1(1-0)

Round 3 [29.03.-01.04.2019]
Dinamo Bucureşti - FC Hermannstadt 2-0(2-0)
Concordia Chiajna - FC Voluntari 1-2(0-1)
Politehnica Iaşi - Gaz Metan Mediaş 1-2(0-0)
FC Botoşani - Dunărea Călăraşi 1-2(1-1)

Round 4 [05-07.04.2019]
Dinamo Bucureşti - Concordia Ch. 3-2(1-0)
Dunărea Călăraşi - FC Voluntari 1-1(0-0)
FC Hermannstadt - Politehnica Iaşi 0-1(0-0)
Gaz Metan Mediaş - FC Botoşani 2-0(1-0)

Round 5 [12-14.04.2019]
Concordia Ch. - Dunărea Călăraşi 3-0(2-0)
Politehnica Iaşi - Dinamo Bucureşti 0-1(0-0)
FC Botoşani - FC Hermannstadt 1-0(0-0)
FC Voluntari - Gaz Metan Mediaş 1-2(1-1)

Round 6 [19-22.04.2019]
FC Hermannstadt - FC Voluntari 1-1(1-1)
Gaz Metan Mediaş - Dunărea Călăraşi 0-0
Politehnica Iaşi - Concordia Chiajna 1-1(0-1)
Dinamo Bucureşti - FC Botoşani 1-0(0-0)

Round 7 [26-28.04.2019]
Concordia Chiajna - Gaz Metan Med. 0-2(0-0)
Dunărea Călăraşi - FC Hermannstadt 0-0
FC Voluntari - Dinamo Bucureşti 1-2(0-0)
FC Botoşani - Politehnica Iaşi 3-0(2-0)

Round 8 [03-05.05.2019]
Concordia Chiajna - FC Botoşani 2-2(1-0)
Gaz Metan Mediaş - Hermannstadt 4-1(1-0)
Dunărea Călăraşi - Dinamo Bucureşti 1-0(0-0)
FC Voluntari - Politehnica Iaşi 0-0

Round 9 [10-11.05.2019]
FC Botoşani - FC Voluntari 2-0(2-0)
Dinamo Bucureşti - Gaz Metan Med. 2-0(0-0)
FC Hermannstadt - Concordia Ch. 1-0(1-0)
Politehnica Iaşi - Dunărea Călăraşi 4-0(1-0)

Round 10 [14-15.05.2019]
Dunărea Călăraşi - FC Botoşani 0-2(0-2)
Gaz Metan Mediaş - Politehnica Iaşi 1-1(0-0)
FC Hermannstadt - Dinamo Bucureşti 0-0
FC Voluntari - Concordia Chiajna 2-1(0-1)

Round 11 [17-19.05.2019]
FC Botoşani - Gaz Metan Mediaş 1-0(1-0)
Politehnica Iaşi - FC Hermannstadt 1-1(0-0)
Concordia Ch. - Dinamo Bucureşti 0-2(0-0)
FC Voluntari - Dunărea Călăraşi 0-0

Round 12 [21-23.05.2019]
FC Hermannstadt - FC Botoşani 0-2(0-0)
Dunărea Călăraşi - Concordia Ch. 2-0(0-0)
Dinamo Bucureşti - Politehnica Iaşi 0-0
Gaz Metan Mediaş - FC Voluntari 4-0(1-0)

Round 13 [26-27.05.2019]
Dunărea Călăraşi - Gaz Metan Med. 0-1(0-0)
Concordia Chiajna - Politehnica Iaşi 4-1(2-0)
FC Voluntari - FC Hermannstadt 2-1(1-0)
FC Botoşani - Dinamo Bucureşti 1-0(1-0)

Round 14 [31.05.-02.06.2019]
Politehnica Iaşi - FC Botoşani 0-2(0-0)
Dinamo Bucureşti - FC Voluntari 0-0
FC Hermannstadt - Dunărea Călăraşi 2-1(0-0)
Gaz Metan Mediaş - Concordia Ch. 3-1(3-1)

Final Standings

7.	CS Gaz Metan Mediaş	14	10	2	2	25	-	9	48
8.	FC Botoşani	14	8	2	4	18	-	9	44
9.	FC Dinamo Bucureşti	14	8	3	3	16	-	7	43
10.	ACS Municipal Politehnica Iaşi	14	3	5	6	12	-	18	31
11.	FC Voluntari	14	5	5	4	14	-	16	31
12.	AFC Hermannstadt Sibiu *(Relegation Play-offs)*	14	2	5	7	9	-	19	27
13.	AFC Dunărea Călăraşi *(Relegated)*	14	3	4	7	8	-	18	25
14.	CS Concordia Chiajna *(Relegated)*	14	2	4	8	17	-	23	19

Relegation Play-offs [09-12.06.2019]

AS FC Universitatea Cluj - **AFC Hermannstadt Sibiu**	0-2(0-0)	1-0(0-0)

AFC Hermannstadt Sibiu remains at first level.

NATIONAL CUP
Cupa României 2018/2019

Fifth Round [25-27.09.2018]

FC Voluntari - FC Botoşani	2-1(2-0)
FK Csikszereda - ACS Energeticianul	2-1(1-0)
CS Sportul Snagov - CS Universitatea Craiova	0-2(0-1)
ASU Poli Timişoara - ACS Sepsi OSK Sf. Gheorghe	1-1 aet; 2-4 pen
ACS Dacia Unirea Brăila - FC Dinamo Bucureşti	1-3(1-2)
FC UT Arad - ACS Municipal Politehnica Iaşi	3-3 aet; 3-5 pen
CS Sporting Lieşti - CS Mioveni	0-3(0-1)
CSM Slatina - FC Dunărea Călăraşi	0-2(0-2)
FC Academica Clinceni - FC Hermannstadt Sibiu	0-2(0-0)
AFC Progresul Spartac Buc. - FC Universitatea Cluj	0-1(0-1)
CS Concordia Chiajna - FC Viitorul Constanţa	0-3(0-1)
AFC Chindia Târgovişte - FC CFR 1907 Cluj-Nap.	0-1(0-1)
CS Luceafărul Oradea - AFC Astra Giurgiu	1-5(0-0)
CSM Bucovina Rădăuţi - CS Gaz Metan Mediaş	1-1 aet; 7-8 pen
FC Rapid Bucureşti - AFC Turris-Oltul Turnu Măgur.	0-2(0-0)
FC Unirea 1924 Alba Iulia - FCSB Bucureşti	0-1(0-0)

1/8-Finals [30.10.-01.11.2018]

FC Hermannstadt Sibiu - FC Voluntari	3-0(1-0)
AFC Turris-Oltul Turnu Măg. - CS Univers. Craiova	1-4(1-0)
ACS Mun. Politehnica Iaşi - FC Viitorul Constanţa	2-2 aet; 3-5 pen
CS Mioveni - ACS Sepsi OSK Sfântu Gheorghe	0-5(0-4)
FC Universitatea Cluj - AFC Astra Giurgiu	3-4(3-2,3-3)
CS Gaz Metan Mediaş - FC CFR 1907 Cluj-Napoca	0-1(0-0)
FK Csikszereda - FC Dinamo Bucureşti	3-3 aet; 6-5 pen
FC Dunărea Călăraşi - FCSB Bucureşti	2-1(0-0)

Quarter-Finals [26-28.02.2019]

FC Hermannstadt Sibiu - FC Viitorul Constanţa	2-3(0-2)
FC Dunărea Călăraşi - AFC Astra Giurgiu	1-2(0-2)
ACS Sepsi OSK Sf.Gh. - FC CFR 1907 Cluj-Napoca	0-1(0-0)
FK Csikszereda - CS Universitatea Craiova	0-3(0-1)

Semi-Finals [03/04.-24/25.04.2019]			
FC CFR 1907 Cluj-Napoca - AFC Astra Giurgiu	1-3 / 2-2	CS Universitatea Craiova - FC Viitorul Constanța	1-2 / 0-2

Final

25.05.2019; Stadionul "Ilie Oană", Ploiești; Referee: Radu Petrescu; Attendance: 12,500
FC Viitorul Constanța - AFC Astra Giurgiu **2-1(0-1,1-1)**

Viitorul: Valentin Cojocaru (46.Árpád Tordai), Sebastian Mladen, Bogdan Țîru, Virgil Ghiță, Bradley de Nooijer, Lyes Houri (94.Vlad Achim), Tudor Cristian Băluță, Ianis Hagi (Cap), Ionuț Vînă, Rivaldo Vítor Borba Ferreira Júnior „Rivaldinho" (63.Andreiaș Calcan), Denis Mihai Drăguș (70.Eric de Oliveira Pereira). Trainer: Gheorghe Hagi.

Astra: David Lazăr, Mike Cestor, Florin Bejan (106.Vahid Hambo), Risto Radunović, Filip Mrzljak (Cap), Mihai Butean, Romário Santos Pires [*sent off 81*], Romario Moise, Azdren Llullaku (86.Erico Constantino da Silva), Valentin Gheorghe (68.Julien Bègue), Denis Alibec (72.Silviu Balaure). Trainer: Marius Constantin Măldărășanu.

Goals: 0-1 Denis Alibec (41), 1-1 Virgil Ghiță (76), 2-1 Eric de Oliveira Pereira (105).

THE CLUBS 2018/2019

Please note: matches and goals includes statistics of both regular season and play-offs (Championship or Relegation).

Asociația Fotbal Club Astra Giurgiu

Founded: 18.09.1921 (*as Clubul Sportiv Astra-Română Giurgiu*)
Stadium: Stadionul "Marin Anastasovici", Giurgiu (8,500)

Goalkeepers:	**DOB**	**M**	**(s)**	**G**
Plamen Iliev (BUL)	30.11.1991	8		
David Lazăr	08.08.1991	26		
Miguel José Oliveira Silva Santos (POR)	21.10.1994	2		
Defenders:	**DOB**	**M**	**(s)**	**G**
Florin Bejan	28.03.1991	26	(2)	1
Claudiu Belu	07.11.1993	22	(1)	2
Mike Cestor (FRA)	30.04.1992	26	(2)	1
Radu Crișan	27.04.1996	4	(4)	
Constantin Dima	21.07.1999	2	(1)	
Erico Constantino da Silva (BRA)	20.07.1989	19	(2)	1
Risto Radunović (MNE)	04.05.1992	26	(1)	
Andrei Trușescu	27.05.1999	1		
Midfielders:	**DOB**	**M**	**(s)**	**G**
Dylan Bahamboula (CGO)	22.05.1995	1	(4)	1
Ciprian Biceanu	26.02.1994	18	(9)	
Robert Boboc	27.05.1995		(1)	
Laurențiu Buș	27.08.1987	5	(6)	2
Mihai Butean	14.09.1996	23	(1)	2
Radu Chiriac	04.01.2000		(1)	
Valentin Gheorghe	14.02.1997	12	(13)	2
Djiman Waidi Koukou (CGO)	14.11.1990	4		
Romario Moise	21.09.1996	11	(10)	2
Filip Mrzljak (CRO)	16.04.1993	26		2
Romário Santos Pires (BRA)	16.01.1989	10	(1)	
Neluț Roșu	05.07.1993	23	(9)	5
Alexandru Stan	07.02.1989	4		
Forwards:	**DOB**	**M**	**(s)**	**G**
Denis Alibec	05.01.1991	22	(4)	5
Silviu Balaure	06.02.1996	11	(7)	2
Julien Bègue (FRA)	08.08.1993	21	(10)	4
Raul Gavîrliță	18.08.1999		(1)	
Vahid Hambo (FIN)	03.02.1995	2	(3)	
Azdren Llullaku (ALB)	15.02.1988	29	(5)	7
Justin Junior Mengolo (CMR)	24.06.1993		(1)	
Jacques Zoua Daogari (CMR)	06.09.1991	12	(8)	1
Trainer:	**DOB**	**M**		
Marius Constantin Măldărășanu	19.04.1975	36		

Fotbal Club Botoșani

Founded: 2001
Stadium: Stadionul Municipal, Botoșani (12,000)

Goalkeepers:	**DOB**	**M**	**(s)**	**G**
Ianoș Brînză (MDA)	12.09.1998	2		
Martin Fraisl (AUT)	10.05.1993	15		
Eduard Pap	01.07.1994	23		
Defenders:	**DOB**	**M**	**(s)**	**G**
Andrei Burcă	15.04.1993	39		2
Andrei Chindriș	12.01.1999	5	(6)	
Andrei Dumitraș	23.01.1988	17	(2)	1
Marcel Holzmann (AUT)	03.09.1990	6	(2)	1
George Miron	28.05.1994	35	(1)	2
Andrei Patache	29.10.1987	29	(1)	
Andrei Pițian	16.11.1995	7		
Aristides Soiledis (GRE)	08.02.1991	20	(1)	
Midfielders:	**DOB**	**M**	**(s)**	**G**
Laurențiu Buș	27.08.1987	1	(11)	1
Alexandru Corban	29.01.1998		(2)	
Moussa Diakité (MLI)	17.12.1998		(1)	
Diego Fabbrini (ITA)	31.07.1990	29	(2)	5
Eduard Florescu	27.06.1997		(3)	
Lóránd Fülöp	24.07.1997	21	(4)	8
Lossémy Karaboué (CIV)	18.03.1988	16	(7)	
Răzvan Oaidă	02.03.1998	16	(9)	1
Hervin Ongenda (FRA)	24.06.1995	24	(13)	3
Enriko Papa (ALB)	12.03.1993	18	(15)	1
Dragoș Penescu	24.02.2000		(1)	
Alexandru Piftor	09.05.1999	1	(2)	
Jonathan Yoni Emanuel Rodríguez (ARG)	07.06.1990	34		5
Marian Târșă	16.04.1998	2	(7)	
Forwards:	**DOB**	**M**	**(s)**	**G**
Marko Brekalo (CRO)	24.11.1992	1	(4)	
Sebastian Chitoșcă	02.10.1992	7	(9)	1
Cătălin Golofca	21.04.1990	39		8
Mihai Roman I	16.10.1984	4		
Mihai Roman II	31.05.1992	27	(10)	8
Nikola Trujić (SRB)	14.04.1992	2	(5)	1
Trainer:	**DOB**	**M**		
Constantin Enache	11.03.1973	15		
Liviu Ciobotariu [16.11.2018]	26.03.1971	25		

Fotbal Club Căile Ferate Române 1907 Cluj-Napoca

Founded: 1907 (*as Kolozsvári Vasutas Sport Club*)
Stadium: Stadionul "Dr. Constantin Rădulescu", Cluj-Napoca (23,500)

Goalkeepers:	DOB	M	(s)	G
Giedrius Arlauskis (LTU)	01.12.1987	31		
Jesús Fernández Collado (ESP)	11.06.1988	3		
Cosmin Vâtcă	12.05.1982	2		
Defenders:	**DOB**	**M**	**(s)**	**G**
Kévin Boli (FRA)	21.06.1991	9	(1)	
Mário Jorge Melico Paulino „Camora" (POR)	21.09.1986	32		1
Ádám Lang (HUN)	17.01.1993	13	(5)	
Cristian Marian Manea	09.08.1997	33	(1)	1
Andrei Mureşan	01.08.1985	19	(3)	2
Paulo Vinícius de Souza Nascimento (BRA)	12.08.1984	31		2
Andrei Peteleu	20.08.1992	6	(2)	
Andrei Radu	21.06.1996	1		
Midfielders:	**DOB**	**M**	**(s)**	**G**
Mihai Bordeianu	18.11.1991	23	(3)	1
Valentin Costache	02.08.1998	5	(13)	1
Juan Emmanuel Culio (ARG)	30.08.1983	25		5
Ciprian Ioan Deac	16.02.1986	24	(2)	4
Damjan Đoković (CRO)	18.04.1990	31	(2)	4
Ovidiu Hoban	27.12.1982	5	(7)	1
Alexandru Ioniţă	14.12.1994	12	(11)	2
Cătălin Itu	26.10.1999		(1)	
Mate Maleš (CRO)	11.03.1989	7	(1)	
Thierry Rua Moutinho (SUI)	26.02.1991	6	(10)	1
Alexandru Păun	01.04.1995	19	(8)	3
Claudiu Petrila	07.11.2000		(5)	
Forwards:	**DOB**	**M**	**(s)**	**G**
Cristian Bud	26.06.1985	2	(2)	
Giuseppe De Luca	11.10.1991	1	(2)	
Júlio César Pereira Baptista (BRA)	01.10.1981		(2)	
Sebastian Mailat	01.01.1997	3	(7)	
Billel Omrani (FRA)	02.06.1993	28	(4)	6
Robert Ndip Tambe (CMR)	22.02.1994	1	(5)	
Marius George Ţucudean	30.04.1991	24	(3)	18
Urko Vera Mateos (ESP)	14.05.1987		(2)	
Trainer:	**DOB**	**M**		
Edward Iordănescu	16.06.1978	1		
António Conceição da Silva Oliveira [26.07.2018]	06.12.1961	23		
Alin Minteuan [19.02.2019]	12.11.1976	4		
Dan Vasile Petrescu [22.03.2019]	22.12.1967	8		

Clubul Sportiv Concordia Chiajna

Founded: 1957
Stadium: Stadionul Concordia, Chiajna (5,123)

Goalkeepers:	DOB	M	(s)	G
Alessandro Caparco (ITA)	07.09.1983	13	(4)	
Alexandru Costache	10.10.1999	2		
Alexandru Greab	26.05.1992	11		
Ionel Mişu	24.07.2001	1		
Victor Râmniceanu	30.11.1989	13		
Defenders:	**DOB**	**M**	**(s)**	**G**
Cristian Albu	17.08.1993	17	(8)	1
Ştefan Bărboianu	24.01.1988	17	(6)	
Liassine Cadamuro (FRA)	05.03.1988	14		1
Nicuşor Fota	01.12.1996	19	(2)	
João Meira (POR)	30.04.1987	13	(1)	
Georgios Koutroubis (GRE)	10.02.1991	9		
Mihai Leca	14.04.1992	14	(1)	1
Andrei Marc	29.04.1993	33		5
Gabriel Matei	26.02.1990	14		
Andrei Paliu	11.07.2000	1	(1)	
Dan Panait	16.02.1997	5	(3)	1
Andrei Radu	21.06.1996	8	(3)	
Alexandru Stănică	06.09.2000	2	(3)	
Midfielders:	**DOB**	**M**	**(s)**	**G**
Cristian Balgiu	03.08.1994		(1)	
Dan Bucşă	23.06.1988	4	(1)	
Ionuţ Constantin	27.07.2001		(1)	
Marian Cristescu	17.03.1985	13	(13)	1
Ronaldo Deaconu	13.05.1997	12	(4)	
Mişu Georgian	24.07.2001	1		
Guessan Ghislain (CIV)	15.09.1992	14	(9)	3
Nicolás Gorobsov (ARG)	25.11.1989	35	(1)	4
Răzvan Grădinaru	23.08.1995	31	(4)	1
Jules Iloki (FRA)	14.01.1992	2	(5)	
Petre Ivanovici	02.03.1990	19	(11)	2
Nivaldo Alves Freitas Santos (CPV)	10.07.1988	15	(6)	2
Marian Obedeanu	11.12.2000		(1)	
Andrei Prepeliţă	08.12.1985	18	(1)	1
Adrian Ropotan	08.05.1986	16	(3)	2
Forwards:	**DOB**	**M**	**(s)**	**G**
Thaer Fayed Al Bawab (JOR)	01.03.1985	18	(7)	4
Marius Alexe	22.02.1990	8		
Paul Batin	29.06.1987	12	(8)	4
Simon Măzărache	10.01.1993	6	(7)	
Sofien Moussa (TUN)	06.02.1988	11	(2)	3
Trainer:	**DOB**	**M**		
Ionuţ Badea	14.10.1975	8		
Dorinel Ionel Munteanu[18.09.2018]	25.06.1968	13		
Adrian Falub [08.01.2019]	08.09.1971	19		

Fotbal Club Dinamo Bucureşti

Founded: 14.05.1948
Stadium: Stadionul Dinamo, Bucureşti (15,032)

Goalkeepers:	**DOB**	**M**	**(s)**	**G**
Parfait Mandanda (COD)	10.11.1989	12		
Sean McDermott (IRL)	30.05.1993	3		
Vlad Muţiu	02.02.1995	7		
Jaime Manuel Penedo Cano (PAN)	26.09.1981	18		
Defenders:	**DOB**	**M**	**(s)**	**G**
Naser Aliji (SUI)	27.12.1993	16		
Denis Ciobotariu	10.06.1998	16		
Nicolae Corbu	10.05.1994	13		
Kino Delorge (BEL)	05.01.1998	2	(1)	
Damien Dussaut (FRA)	08.11.1994	9	(1)	
Ricardo Grigore	07.04.1999	22	(4)	1
Giorgios Katsikas (GRE)	14.06.1990	14		
Linas Klimavičius (LTU)	10.04.1989	17		1
Facundo Mallo Blanco (URU)	16.01.1995	2	(1)	
Teddy Mézague (FRA)	27.05.1990	4		
Jordan Mustoe (ENG)	28.01.1991	2	(1)	
Vlad Olteanu	21.03.1996	5	(1)	
Sergiu Popovici	23.03.1993	12	(1)	
Deian Sorescu	29.08.1997	30	(5)	2
Midfielders:	**DOB**	**M**	**(s)**	**G**
Rachid Aït-Atmane (ALG)	04.02.1993	11	(1)	
Armando Enrique Cooper Whitaker (PAN)	26.11.1987	10	(1)	
Geani Creţu	12.01.2000		(1)	
Ioan Filip	20.05.1989	13	(1)	
Tomislav Gomelt (CRO)	07.01.1995	10	(2)	
Sergiu Hanca	04.04.1992	16	(2)	2
Nabil Jaadi (BEL)	01.07.1996	2	(6)	
Reda Jaadi (BEL)	14.02.1995	11	(3)	1
Elvis Kabashi (ALB)	20.02.1994	2	(1)	
May Mahlangu (RSA)	01.05.1989	5		1
Mamoutou N'Diaye (MLI)	15.03.1990	7	(11)	1
Dan Nistor	05.06.1988	32		4
Mihai Popescu	07.05.1993	16		2
Ionuţ Şerban	07.08.1995	3	(3)	
Andrei Ţîrcoveanu	22.05.1997		(1)	
Forwards:	**DOB**	**M**	**(s)**	**G**
Alexander Domingos Christovão M'Futila (ANG)	14.03.1993	3	(6)	
Mircea Axente	14.03.1987	3	(7)	1
Diogo Ferreira Salomão (POR)	14.09.1988	19	(1)	6
Gheorghe Teodor Grozav	29.09.1990	2	(1)	
Robert Moldoveanu	08.03.1999	3	(12)	1
Mattia Montini (ITA)	28.02.1992	21	(2)	13
Mihai Alexandru Neicuţescu	29.09.1998	1	(6)	
Athanasios Papazoglou (GRE)	30.03.1988	10	(4)	4
Ivan Pešić (CRO)	06.04.1992	4	(6)	1
Daniel Popa	14.07.1994	15	(15)	2
Danijel Subotić (SUI)	31.01.1989	3	(2)	1
Simon Zenke (NGA)	24.12.1988	14	(7)	1
Trainer:	**DOB**	**M**		
Florin Bratu	02.01.1980	11		
Mircea Rednic [15.10.2018]	09.04.1962	7		
Ionel Dănciulescu [06.12.2018]	06.12.1976	22		

Asociaţia Fotbal Club Dunărea 2005 Călăraşi

Founded: 1962
Stadium: Stadionul Dinamo, Bucureşti (15,032)

Goalkeepers:	**DOB**	**M**	**(s)**	**G**
Nicolae Calancea (MDA)	29.08.1986	7		
Cezar Lungu	06.04.1988	4	(1)	
Gabriel Popa	27.08.1985	1		
Cătălin Straton	09.10.1989	28		
Defenders:	**DOB**	**M**	**(s)**	**G**
Ionuţ Balaur	06.06.1989	2		
Selim Ben Djemia (TUN)	29.01.1989	5	(4)	
Stelian Cucu	15.09.1989	6	(7)	
Alin Dobrosavlevici	21.10.1994	37		2
Filip Gligorov (MKD)	31.07.1993	24		
Denis Ispas	05.09.1993	11	(1)	
Srdjan Luchin	04.03.1986	18	(1)	1
Gabriel Simion	22.05.1998	20	(7)	
Cristian Sîrghi	23.11.1986	3	(1)	
Bogdan Şandru	04.07.1989	6	(1)	
Alin Şeroni	26.03.1987	6	(1)	
Ionuţ Ţenea	21.03.1996	5		
Ştefan Vlădoiu	28.12.1998	6		
Wallace Alves da Silva (BRA)	20.10.1989	9		
Midfielders:	**DOB**	**M**	**(s)**	**G**
Alexandru Bourceanu	24.04.1985	17	(5)	
Lucian Buzan	09.03.1999	1	(1)	
Marian Drăghiceanu	07.07.1999	1	(1)	
Gabriel Enache	18.08.1990	12		
Steliano Filip	15.05.1994	6	(1)	1
Conor Henderson (IRL)	08.09.1991	4	(7)	
Georgian Honciu	20.04.1989	21	(9)	2
Gabriel Iancu	15.04.1994	11	(1)	2
Laurenţiu Marinescu	25.08.1984		(1)	
Gaston Mendy (SEN)	22.11.1985	27	(2)	
Aitor Monroy Rueda (ESP)	18.10.1987	3	(1)	
Alexandru Munteanu	31.10.1987	6	(7)	
Valentin Munteanu	24.10.1989	5	(15)	
Abdelhakim Omrani (ALG)	18.02.1991		(1)	
Silviu Pană	24.09.1991	10		1
Cristian Puşcaş	29.01.1994	11	(1)	
Ianis Stoica	08.12.2002	1	(1)	
Forwards:	**DOB**	**M**	**(s)**	**G**
Valentin Alexandru	17.09.1991	5	(4)	1
Najib Ammari (ALG)	10.04.1992	18		4
Alin Babei	13.12.1997	1		
Daniel Dumitru Benzar	30.12.1997	9	(5)	1
Nicolae Cârnaţ	08.04.1998	8	(1)	
Sacha Clémence (FRA)	01.06.1988	3	(4)	
Baudoin Kanda	17.04.1993	13	(1)	2
Hamidou Keyta (FRA)	17.12.1994	8	(12)	1
Junior M'Pia Mapuku (CGO)	07.01.1990		(4)	
Gaëtan Missi Mezu Kouakou (GAB)	04.05.1996	3	(2)	
Mediop Ndiaye (SEN)	02.06.1991	23	(7)	6
Aymen Souda (FRA)	28.02.1993	15	(2)	
Trainer:	**DOB**	**M**		
Dan Alexa	28.10.1979	40		

Sport Club Fotbal Club FCSB Bucureşti

Founded: 07.06.1947 (*as AS Armata Bucureşti*)
Stadium: Arena Naţională, Bucureşti (55,634)

Goalkeepers:	DOB	M	(s)	G
Cristian Emanuel Bălgrădean	21.03.1988	34		
Andrei Vlad	15.04.1999	2	(1)	
Defenders:	**DOB**	**M**	**(s)**	**G**
Mihai Alexandru Bălaşa	14.01.1995	18	(2)	
Romario Sandu Benzar	26.03.1992	31		
Lucian Filip	25.09.1990	28	(3)	3
Iraneuton Sousa Morais Junior „Maranhão" (BRA)	22.07.1986	27	(1)	
Marko Momčilović (SRB)	11.06.1987	2	(1)	
Bogdan Planić (SRB)	19.01.1992	27	(1)	
Midfielders:	**DOB**	**M**	**(s)**	**G**
Daniel Dumitru Benzar	30.12.1997		(2)	1
Iulian Cristea	17.07.1994	10		1
Antonio Jakoliš (CRO)	28.02.1992	4	(4)	
Florentin Matei	15.04.1993	3	(3)	
Olimpiu Moruţan	25.04.1999	4	(23)	2
Dragoş Ionuţ Nedelcu	16.02.1997	22	(4)	
Mihai Doru Pintilii	09.11.1984	8	(1)	
Ovidiu Popescu	27.02.1994	8	(2)	
Kamer Qaka (ALB)	11.04.1995	3	(2)	
Alexandru Stan	07.02.1989	9	(1)	
Adrian Marius Stoian	11.02.1991	1	(1)	
Florin Lucian Tănase	30.12.1994	33	(1)	10
Hristo Zlatinski (BUL)	22.01.1985	2	(1)	
Forwards:	**DOB**	**M**	**(s)**	**G**
Florinel Teodor Coman	10.04.1998	29	(6)	11
Filipe Andrade Teixeira (POR)	02.10.1980	13	(14)	2
Harlem-Eddy Gnohéré (FRA)	21.02.1988	20	(9)	15
Ioan Hora	21.08.1988	9	(5)	6
Dennis Man	26.08.1998	33		9
Mihai Roman I	16.10.1984	9	(7)	1
Raul Andrei Rusescu	09.07.1988	7	(12)	4
Trainer:	**DOB**	**M**		
Nicolae Marius Dică	09.05.1980	21		
Mihai Teja [27.12.2018]	22.09.1978	15		

Clubul Sportiv Gaz Metan Mediaş

Founded: 1945 (*as Karres Mediaş*)
Stadium: Stadionul Gaz Metan, Mediaş (7,814)

Goalkeepers:	DOB	M	(s)	G
Andrei Cristea	09.01.2000	1		
Răzvan Pleşca	25.11.1982	37		
Ricardo Jorge Cecília Batista (POR)	19.11.1986	2		
Defenders:	**DOB**	**M**	**(s)**	**G**
André Micael Pereira (POR)	04.02.1989	10	(2)	
Sorin Busu	08.07.1989	22	(2)	
Nasser Chamed (COM)	04.10.1993	20	(11)	2
Mite Cikarski (MKD)	06.01.1993	3		
Marius Constantin	25.10.1984	31	(1)	2
Valentin Creţu	02.01.1989	33		1
Bradley Diallo (FRA)	20.07.1990	12	(4)	
Antoni Ivanov (BUL)	11.09.1995	23	(7)	1
Marian Pleaşcă	06.02.1990	2	(3)	
Midfielders:	**DOB**	**M**	**(s)**	**G**
Paul Costea	02.03.1999		(5)	
Iulian Cristea	17.07.1994	23		3
Boubacar Fofana (GUI)	06.11.1989	31		2
Ionuţ Larie	16.01.1987	13		3
Luís Miguel Coimbra Aurélio (POR)	17.08.1988	33	(3)	1
Darius Olaru	03.03.1998	32	(2)	4
Pedro Rafael Amado Mendes (POR)	06.12.1993		(2)	
Roberto Romeo (ITA)	27.04.1990	8	(8)	
Mihai Stancu	29.01.1996		(3)	
Răzvan Trif	09.10.1997	11	(6)	1
Forwards:	**DOB**	**M**	**(s)**	**G**
Alexandru Buziuc	15.03.1994	1	(10)	
Carlos Manuel dos Santos Fortes (POR)	09.11.1994	18	(1)	5
David Caiado Dias (POR)	02.05.1987	25	(2)	5
Ely Ernesto Lopes Fernandes (CPV)	04.11.1990	22	(11)	3
Sebastian Mailat	01.01.1997	5	(13)	
Mário Júnior Rondón Fernández(VEN)	26.03.1986	16	(2)	10
Yazalde Gomes Pinto (POR)	21.09.1988	6	(18)	5
Trainer:	**DOB**	**M**		
Mihai Teja	22.09.1978	21		
Edward Iordănescu [07.01.2019]	16.06.1978	19		

Fotbal Club Hermannstadt Sibiu

Founded: 29.07.2015
Stadium: Stadionul Municipal, Sibiu (14,200)

Goalkeepers:	DOB	M	(s)	G
Cătălin Căbuz	18.06.1996	38		
Toma Niga	15.08.1997	2		
Defenders:	**DOB**	**M**	**(s)**	**G**
Florin Acsinte	10.04.1987	2	(4)	
Alexandru Coman	16.10.1991	7		
Gabriel Company Vives (ESP)	16.02.1992	13	(1)	
Alexandru Dandea	23.01.1988	33		1
Alexandru Măţel	17.10.1989	16		
Nemanja Mijušković (MNE)	04.03.1992	23	(7)	
Claudiu Pamfile	14.01.1997	2	(5)	
Cătălin Pîrvulescu	11.06.1991	15		
Ionuţ Stoica	06.01.1988	29		2
Midfielders:	**DOB**	**M**	**(s)**	**G**
Ilja Antonov (EST)	05.12.1992	14	(3)	
Bruno Chalkiadakis (GRE)	07.04.1993	7	(1)	
Răzvan Dâlbea	08.10.1981	33	(1)	3
Lucian Dumitriu	21.09.1992	21	(6)	4
Filip Jazvić (CRO)	22.10.1990	10	(7)	2
Daniel Offenbacher (AUT)	18.02.1992	12	(1)	
Pedro Manuel da Silva Moreira (POR)	15.03.1989	5	(4)	
Ionut Petrescu	29.06.1993	22	(10)	3
Sergiu Popovici	23.03.1993	6	(6)	1
Tiberiu Serediuc	02.07.1992	14	(4)	
Daniel Tătar	21.10.1987	37		4
Forwards:	**DOB**	**M**	**(s)**	**G**
Besart Abdurahimi (MKD)	31.07.1990		(4)	
Luis Alberto Alí Vega (BOL)	17.04.1994		(5)	
Ştefan Blănaru	20.02.1989	30	(9)	4
Alexandru Curtean	27.03.1987	3	(1)	
Andrei Herghelegiu	21.03.1992	2	(4)	
Ivan Lendrić (CRO)	08.08.1991	5	(5)	2
Michaël Jordan N'Kololo (COD)	09.11.1992	8	(8)	1
Bogdan Rusu	09.04.1990	6	(11)	
Juvhel Tsoumou (CGO)	27.12.1990	25	(12)	7
Trainer:	**DOB**	**M**		
Alexandru Pelici	10.01.1974	11		
Vasile Miriuţă (HUN) [09.10.2018]	19.09.1968	29		

Asociaţia Club Sportiv Sepsi Oltul Sport Klub Sfântu Gheorghe

Founded: 2011
Stadium: Stadionul "Silviu Ploeşteanu", Braşov (8,800)

Goalkeepers:	DOB	M	(s)	G
Béla Fejér	11.10.1995	12		
Roland Niczuly	21.09.1995	24		
Defenders:	**DOB**	**M**	**(s)**	**G**
Gabriel Rodrigues de Moura (BRA)	18.06.1988	33	(1)	
Igor Jovanović (CRO)	03.05.1989	34		1
Aboud Omar Khamis (KEN)	09.09.1992	8		
Sebastian Rudol (POL)	21.02.1995	4	(2)	
Adrián Rus	18.03.1996	14		
Florin Ştefan	09.05.1996	21	(6)	3
Ionuţ Ursu	21.03.1989	1	(2)	
Ousmane Viera (CIV)	21.12.1986	31		1
Midfielders:	**DOB**	**M**	**(s)**	**G**
Balaska Etele	08.10.2002		(1)	
Dylan Armando Flores Knowles (CRC)	30.05.1993	8	(1)	
István Fülöp	18.05.1990	12	(3)	
Aleksandr Karnitskiy (BLR)	14.02.1989	15	(8)	1
Joseph Mensah (GHA)	29.09.1994	7	(19)	3
Călin Popescu	15.11.2001		(3)	
Daisuke Sato (PHI)	20.09.1994	24	(4)	
Gabriel Vaşvari	13.11.1986	28	(4)	3
Stefan Velev (BUL)	02.05.1989	33	(1)	1
Forwards:	**DOB**	**M**	**(s)**	**G**
Nicolae Cârnaţ	08.04.1998	1	(3)	
Gabriel Dodoi	27.09.1998		(1)	
Stephan Drăghici	30.01.1998	14	(6)	
Attila Hadnagy	08.09.1980		(7)	
Yasin Hamed	09.12.1999	7	(20)	4
Bryan Nouvier (FRA)	21.06.1995	19	(2)	3
Dániel Prosser (HUN)	15.06.1994	2		
Marko Simonovski (MKD)	02.01.1992	9	(11)	5
Andrei Sîntean	16.06.1999	1	(1)	
Ibrahima Tandia (FRA)	12.07.1993	34		11
Trainer:	**DOB**	**M**		
Eugen Neagoe	22.08.1967	33		
Marin Barbu [02.05.2019]	27.09.1958	3		

Asociaţia Club Sportiv Municipal Politehnica Iaşi

Founded: 16.08.2010 (*as ACSMU Politehnica Iaşi*)
Stadium: Stadionul "Emil Alexandrescu", Iaşi (12,500)

Goalkeepers:	DOB	M	(s)	G
Alberto Cobrea	01.11.1990	5		
Rubén Miño Peralta (ESP)	18.01.1989	10		
Denis Rusu (MDA)	02.08.1990	23		
Ştefan Târnovanu	09.05.2000	2		
Defenders:	**DOB**	**M**	**(s)**	**G**
Adrià Gallego Arias (ESP)	24.02.1990	21		
Gabriel Bosoi	11.08.1987	6	(4)	
Cosmin Frăsinescu	10.02.1985	36		1
Florin Gardoş	29.10.1988	12	(2)	1
Marius Mihalache	14.12.1984	27		
Ionut Panţîru	22.03.1996	16	(5)	
Paul Pârvulescu	11.08.1988	3	(1)	
Midfielders:	**DOB**	**M**	**(s)**	**G**
Narcis Bădic	15.07.1991	3	(6)	
Marius Chelaru	02.03.1997	8	(2)	
Ionuţ Cioinac	14.01.1991	32		2
Francisc Cristea	02.12.2002	2	(2)	
Dylan Armando Flores Knowles (CRC)	30.05.1993	22		7
João Tiago Almeida Teixeira (POR)	07.05.1996	7	(3)	3
Mădălin Mihăescu	21.10.1988	8	(6)	1
Martin Mimoun (FRA)	11.06.1992	1	(4)	
Filipe Guterres Nascimento (POR)	07.01.1995	9	(3)	1
Patrick Petre	09.05.1997	13	(11)	1
Mario Pipoş	02.02.2001		(3)	
Luís Carlos Almada Soares „Platini" (CPV)	16.04.1986	25	(3)	6
Kamer Qaka (ALB)	11.04.1995	21	(3)	
Laurenţiu Rus	07.05.1985	18	(3)	
Cătălin Ştefănescu	30.11.1994	2	(1)	
Alexandru Zaharia	25.05.1990	9	(13)	1
Forwards:	**DOB**	**M**	**(s)**	**G**
Aguinaldo Policarpo Mendes Veiga (ANG)	25.03.1989		(4)	
Lawson Bekui (GHA)	12.08.1994	2	(6)	1
Boris Garrós Torrent (ESP)	22.06.1988	7	(2)	1
Andrei Burlacu	12.01.1997	6	(2)	
Andrei Cristea	15.05.1984	19		6
Vlad Danale	28.01.1998		(1)	
Luwagga Kizito (UGA)	20.12.1993	3	(1)	
Lewis Mbah Enoh (CMR)	23.10.1992	6	(12)	2
Daudet N'Dongala (FRA)	16.09.1994		(5)	
Moussa Sanoh (NED)	20.07.1995	21	(5)	4
Willy Semedo (FRA)	27.04.1994	4	(6)	
Andrei Sin	26.10.1991	31	(1)	1
Alexandru Zaharia	09.09.2000	9	(13)	1
Trainer:	**DOB**	**M**		
Flavius Vladimir Stoican	24.11.1976	40		

Universitatea Craiova 1948 Club Sportiv

Founded: 1948; re-founded 2013
Stadium: Stadionul "Ion Oblemenco", Craiova (30,929)

Goalkeepers:	DOB	M	(s)	G
Mirko Pigliacelli (ITA)	30.06.1993	36		1
Defenders:	**DOB**	**M**	**(s)**	**G**
Stephane Acka (CIV)	11.10.1990	3	(1)	
Florin Borta	21.06.1999	3		
Marius Briceag	06.04.1992	12	(1)	
Radoslav Dimitrov (BUL)	12.08.1988	7	(3)	
Isaac Donkor (GHA)	15.08.1995	23	(4)	
Florin Gardoş	29.10.1988	4		
Renato Kelić (CRO)	31.03.1991	28	(3)	1
Ivan Martić (CRO)	02.10.1990	23	(1)	1
Răzvan Popa	04.01.1997	2	(1)	
Tiago Emanuel Canelas Almeida Ferreira (POR)	10.07.1993	22	(3)	
Midfielders:	**DOB**	**M**	**(s)**	**G**
Nicuşor Silviu Bancu	18.09.1992	32	(1)	4
Ovidiu Bic	23.02.1994		(7)	
Alexandru Cicâldău	08.07.1997	34	(1)	4
Matteo Fedele (SUI)	20.07.1992	16	(9)	2
Alexandru Mateiu	10.12.1989	32	(2)	4
Nuno Miguel Monteiro Rocha(CPV)	25.03.1992	5	(11)	2
Hristo Zlatinski (BUL)	22.01.1985		(1)	
Forwards:	**DOB**	**M**	**(s)**	**G**
Raoul Baicu	05.04.2000	2	(7)	
Cristian Bărbuţ	22.04.1995	25	(7)	3
Andrei Burlacu	12.01.1997	6	(6)	1
Carlos Manuel dos Santos Fortes (POR)	09.11.1994	4	(7)	
Andrei Cristea	15.05.1984	8	(2)	1
Stephan Drăghici	30.01.1998	2	(4)	
Dominik Glavina (CRO)	06.12.1992	1	(3)	
Elvir Koljič (BIH)	08.07.1995	19		13
Jovan Marković	23.03.2001		(4)	
César Daniel Meza Colli (PAR)	05.10.1991	4	(11)	
Valentin Mihăilă	02.02.2000	25	(4)	1
Alexandru Ionuţ Mitriţă	08.02.1995	18		13
Trainer:	**DOB**	**M**		
Devis Mangia (ITA)	06.06.1974	31		
Corneliu Papură [15.04.2019]	05.09.1973	5		

Fotbal Club Viitorul Constanța

Founded: 2009
Stadium: Stadionul Viitorul, Constanța (4,554)

Goalkeepers:	**DOB**	**M**	**(s)**	**G**
Alexandru Buzbuchi	31.10.1993	5	(1)	
Valentin Cojocaru	01.10.1995	27		
Árpád Tordai	11.03.1997	4		
Defenders:	**DOB**	**M**	**(s)**	**G**
Radu Boboc	24.04.1999	13	(9)	
Bradley de Nooijer (NED)	07.11.1997	31		1
Virgil Ghiță	04.06.1998	17	(3)	1
Robert Hodorogea	24.03.1995	1	(1)	
Bas Kuipers (NED)	17.08.1994	6		
Marius Leca	06.07.2000		(1)	
Srdjan Luchin	04.03.1986	11	(2)	1
Sebastian Mladen	11.12.1991	28	(2)	1
Bogdan Țîru	15.03.1994	25		
Midfielders:	**DOB**	**M**	**(s)**	**G**
Vlad Achim	07.04.1989	15	(13)	1
Andrei Artean	14.08.1993	18	(5)	
Tudor Cristian Băluță	27.03.1999	26	(1)	1
Carlos Casap	29.12.1998	5	(1)	1
Eric de Oliveira Pereira (BRA)	05.12.1985	4	(2)	3
Ianis Hagi	22.10.1998	30	(1)	10
Lyes Houri (FRA)	19.01.1996	13	(12)	3
Paul Iacob	21.06.1996	8	(2)	
Alexandru Mățan	29.08.1999	9	(4)	
Amir Natkho (RUS)	09.07.1996	1		
Andrei Tîrcoveanu	22.05.1997		(4)	
Forwards:	**DOB**	**M**	**(s)**	**G**
Andreiaș Calcan	09.04.1994	7	(2)	4
Andrei Ciobanu	18.01.1998	10	(13)	
Denis Mihai Drăguș	06.07.1999	27	(4)	7
George Ganea	26.05.1999	4	(3)	2
Mailson Lima Duarte Lopes (CPV)	29.05.1994	6	(2)	
Alexi Pitu	05.06.2002		(5)	
Rivaldo Vítor Borba Ferreira Júnior „Rivaldinho" (BRA)	29.04.1995	5	(6)	2
Alexandru Stoica	30.06.1997	1		
Ionuț Vînă	20.02.1995	30		2
Mihai Voduț	28.07.1994	9	(8)	2
Trainer:	**DOB**	**M**		
Gheorghe Hagi	05.02.1965	36		

Fotbal Club Voluntari

Founded: 2010 (*as Inter Voluntari*)
Stadium: Stadionul „Anghel Iordănescu", Voluntari (4,600)

Goalkeepers:	**DOB**	**M**	**(s)**	**G**
Virgil Drăghia	31.07.1990	6		
Bozhidar Mitrev (BUL)	31.03.1987	6		
Răzvan Petrariu	27.03.1995		(1)	
Cosmin Vâtcă	12.05.1982	28		
Defenders:	**DOB**	**M**	**(s)**	**G**
Cosmin Achim	19.09.1995		(1)	
Igor Armaș (MDA)	14.07.1987	23		3
Alfonso Artabe Meca (ESP)	18.08.1988	4		
Ionuț Balaur	06.06.1989	29	(2)	2
Bogdan Bucurică	11.02.1986	15		
Robert Hodorogea	24.03.1995	12	(4)	1
Sebastian Ignat	10.03.2000	2		
Jetmir Krasniqi (SUI)	01.01.1995	3		
Aïssa Laïdouni (FRA)	13.12.1996	29		6
Mircea Leasă	22.02.1999	3		
Adriano Russo (ITA)	06.06.1987	6		
Alexandru Vlad	06.12.1989	28	(1)	1
Ivan Zgrablić (CRO)	15.03.1991	6	(3)	
Wallace Alves da Silva (BRA)	20.10.1989	6		
Midfielders:	**DOB**	**M**	**(s)**	**G**
Florin Balan	02.01.2002		(1)	
Mihai Căpățînă	16.12.1995	33	(4)	3
Alexandru Ciucur	01.03.1990	6	(9)	
Gabriel Deac	26.04.1995	9	(20)	2
Ion Gheorghe	08.10.1999	31	(2)	
Costin Lazăr	24.04.1981	2	(3)	
Doru Popadiuc	18.02.1995	4	(3)	1
Alexandru Răuță	17.06.1992	30	(3)	
Ricardo José Veiga Varzim Miranda „Ricardinho" (POR)	24.03.1994	26	(2)	5
Ivan Sesar (BIH)	29.08.1989	5	(1)	
Franco Signorelli (VEN)	01.01.1991	9		
Bogdan Szijj	11.11.1998	1	(2)	
Forwards:	**DOB**	**M**	**(s)**	**G**
Adrian Bălan	14.03.1990	7	(10)	
Abdelhak Belahmeur (FRA)	26.07.1991	10	(5)	1
Richard Gadze (GHA)	23.08.1993	24	(4)	6
Gabriel Iancu	15.04.1994		(1)	
Nathan Kabasele (BEL)	14.01.1994		(8)	1
Geoffrey Malfleury (MTQ)	20.01.1988	7	(6)	2
Adelin Pîrcălabu	01.05.1996	3	(4)	
Alexandru Ionuț Stoica	23.01.2000	1		
Alexandru Tudorie	19.03.1996	26	(10)	10
Trainer:	**DOB**	**M**		
Daniel Opriță	10.08.1981	14		
Cristiano Bergodi (ITA)[08.11.2018]	14.10.1964	26		

SECOND LEVEL
Liga II 2018/2019

1.	AFC Chindia Târgoviște (*Promoted*)	38	27	7	4	79	-	33	88
2.	FC Academica Clinceni (*Promoted*)	38	28	3	7	77	-	24	87
3.	FC Universitatea Cluj (*Promotion Play-offs*)	38	25	7	6	85	-	26	82
4.	FC Petrolul Ploiești	38	24	5	9	77	-	38	77
5.	CS Sportul Snagov	38	21	7	10	56	-	37	70
6.	FC Argeș Pitești	38	20	8	10	54	-	33	68
7.	CS Mioveni	38	18	7	13	63	-	41	61
8.	CS Luceafărul Oradea* (*Relegated*)	38	14	10	14	57	-	59	52
9.	FC Metaloglobus București	38	14	7	17	43	-	56	49
10.	ASU Politehnica Timișoara	38	13	9	16	39	-	38	48
11.	ASC Daco-Getica București	38	11	14	13	54	-	55	47
12.	FC Ripensia Timișoara	38	12	11	15	44	-	54	47
13.	FC UT Arad	38	13	8	17	55	-	64	47
14.	FC Farul Constanța 1920	38	14	5	19	46	-	60	47
15.	CS Pandurii Târgu Jiu	38	12	8	18	57	-	65	44
16.	ACS Energeticianul Petroșani	38	9	12	17	46	-	55	39
17.	CS Aerostar Bacău (*Relegated*)	38	11	5	22	60	-	68	38
18.	ACS Poli Timișoara (*Relegated*)	38	7	8	23	31	-	67	29
19.	CS Balotești (*Relegated*)	38	6	6	26	31	-	88	24
20.	ACS Dacia Unirea Brăila (*Relegated*)	38	4	7	27	30	-	123	19

**CS Luceafărul Oradea withdrew at the end of the season and will continue at third level next season.*

NATIONAL TEAM

INTERNATIONAL MATCHES
(16.07.2018 – 15.07.2019)

07.09.2018	Ploieşti	Romania - Montenegro	0-0	(UNL)
10.09.2018	Beograd	Serbia - Romania	2-2(1-0)	(UNL)
11.10.2018	Vilnius	Lithuania - Romania	1-2(0-1)	(UNL)
14.10.2018	Bucureşti	Romania - Serbia	0-0	(UNL)
17.11.2018	Ploieşti	Romania - Lithuania	3-0(1-0)	(UNL)
20.11.2018	Podgorica	Montenegro - Romania	0-1(0-1)	(UNL)
23.03.2019	Stockholm	Sweden - Romania	2-1(2-0)	(ECQ)
26.03.2019	Cluj-Napoca	Romania - Faroe Islands	4-1(3-1)	(ECQ)
07.06.2019	Oslo	Norvegia - Romania	2-2(0-0)	(ECQ)
10.06.2019	Attard	Malta - Romania	0-4(0-3)	(ECQ)

07.09.2018 ROMANIA - MONTENEGRO 0-0 UEFA Nations League C, Group 4
Stadionul "Ilie Oană", Ploieşti; Referee: Ivan Kružliak (Slovakia); Attendance: *played behind closed doors.*
ROU: Anton Ciprian Tătăruşanu, Ionuţ Cristian Săpunaru, Vlad Iulian Chiricheş (Cap) (31.Mihai Alexandru Bălaşa), Romario Sandu Benzar, Nicuşor Silviu Bancu, Alexandru Mihăiţă Chipciu, Mihai Doru Pintilii (73.Paul Viorel Anton), Nicolae Claudiu Stanciu, Alexandru Iulian Maxim, Claudiu Andrei Keşerü, Alexandru Ionuţ Mitriţă (68.Constantin Valentin Budescu). Trainer: Cosmin Marius Contra.

10.09.2018 SERBIA - ROMANIA 2-2(1-0) UEFA Nations League C, Group 4
Stadion Partizan, Beograd; Referee: Vladislav Bezborodov (Russia); Attendance: 15,496
ROU: Anton Ciprian Tătăruşanu, Ionuţ Cristian Săpunaru (Cap), Nicuşor Silviu Bancu, Mihai Alexandru Bălaşa, Cristian Marian Manea, Alexandru Mihăiţă Chipciu (90+4.Dorin Rotariu), Paul Viorel Anton, Nicolae Claudiu Stanciu, Răzvan Gabriel Marin, Marius George Ţucudean (82.Claudiu Andrei Keşerü), Denis Mihai Drăguş (61.Alexandru Ionuţ Mitriţă). Trainer: Cosmin Marius Contra.
Goals: Nicolae Claudiu Stanciu (48 penalty), Marius George Ţucudean (68).

11.10.2018 LITHUANIA - ROMANIA 1-2(0-1) UEFA Nations League C, Group 4
LFF Stadionas, Vilnius; Referee: François Letexier (France); Attendance: 2,279
ROU: Anton Ciprian Tătăruşanu, Ionuţ Cristian Săpunaru (Cap), Gabriel Sebastian Tamaş, Nicuşor Silviu Bancu, Cristian Marian Manea, Alexandru Mihăiţă Chipciu, Paul Viorel Anton, Nicolae Claudiu Stanciu (87.Dorin Rotariu), Răzvan Gabriel Marin, Marius George Ţucudean (71.Claudiu Andrei Keşerü), Alexandru Ionuţ Mitriţă (78.Alexandru Iulian Maxim). Trainer: Cosmin Marius Contra.
Goals: Alexandru Mihăiţă Chipciu (13), Alexandru Iulian Maxim (90+4).

14.10.2018 ROMANIA - SERBIA 0-0 UEFA Nations League C, Group 4
Arena Naţională, Bucureşti; Referee: Bernie Raymond "Kevin" Blom (Netherlands); Attendance: 48,513
ROU: Anton Ciprian Tătăruşanu, Ionuţ Cristian Săpunaru (Cap), Gabriel Sebastian Tamaş [*sent off 44*], Alin Dorinel Toşca, Cristian Marian Manea, Tudor Cristian Băluţă, Nicolae Claudiu Stanciu, Alexandru Iulian Maxim (71.Dorin Rotariu), Răzvan Gabriel Marin, Marius George Ţucudean (80.Claudiu Andrei Keşerü), Denis Mihai Drăguş. Trainer: Cosmin Marius Contra.

17.11.2018 ROMANIA - LITHUANIA 3-0(1-0) UEFA Nations League C, Group 4
Stadionul „Ilie Oană", Ploieşti; Referee: Marco Guida (Italy); Attendance: *played behind closed doors.*
ROU: Anton Ciprian Tătăruşanu, Ionuţ Cristian Săpunaru (Cap), Cosmin Iosif Moţi, Romario Sandu Benzar, Nicuşor Silviu Bancu, Alexandru Mihăiţă Chipciu (65.Ciprian Ioan Deac), Paul Viorel Anton, Nicolae Claudiu Stanciu (72.Alexandru Cicâldău), Alexandru Iulian Maxim, George Alexandru Puşcaş, Claudiu Andrei Keşerü (68.Ianis Hagi). Trainer: Cosmin Marius Contra.
Goals: George Alexandru Puşcaş (7), Claudiu Andrei Keşerü (47), Nicolae Claudiu Stanciu (65).

20.11.2018 MONTENEGRO - ROMANIA 0-1(0-1) UEFA Nations League C, Group 4
Stadion pod Goricom, Podgorica; Referee: Felix Zwayer (Germany); Attendance: 3,574
ROU: Anton Ciprian Tătăruşanu, Ionuţ Cristian Săpunaru (Cap), Cosmin Iosif Moţi, Alin Dorinel Toşca, Cristian Marian Manea, Alexandru Mihăiţă Chipciu (82.Ciprian Ioan Deac), Paul Viorel Anton, Nicolae Claudiu Stanciu, Alexandru Iulian Maxim, Claudiu Andrei Keşerü (88.Tudor Cristian Băluţă), Marius George Ţucudean (74.George Alexandru Puşcaş). Trainer: Cosmin Marius Contra.
Goal: Marius George Ţucudean (44).

23.03.2019 SWEDEN - ROMANIA 2-1(2-0) 16th EC. Qualifiers
Friends Arena, Stockholm; Referee: Michael Oliver (England); Attendance: 30,115
ROU: Anton Ciprian Tătăruşanu, Ionuţ Cristian Săpunaru (Cap), Dragoş Grigore, Nicuşor Silviu Bancu, Cristian Marian Manea, Alexandru Mihăiţă Chipciu, Tudor Cristian Băluţă (78.Andrei Virgil Ivan), Nicolae Claudiu Stanciu, Răzvan Gabriel Marin, George Alexandru Puşcaş (64.Ianis Hagi), Alexandru Ionuţ Mitriţă (46.Claudiu Andrei Keşerü). Trainer: Cosmin Marius Contra.
Goal: Claudiu Andrei Keşerü (58).

26.03.2019 ROMANIA - FAROE ISLANDS 4-1(3-1) 16th EC. Qualifiers
Stadionul "Dr. Constantin Rădulescu", Cluj-Napoca; Referee: Halil Umut Meler (Turkey); Attendance: 10,502
ROU: Anton Ciprian Tătăruşanu (Cap), Cosmin Iosif Moţi, Dragoş Grigore, Romario Sandu Benzar (46.Ianis Hagi), Nicuşor Silviu Bancu, Alexandru Mihăiţă Chipciu, Ciprian Ioan Deac, Nicolae Claudiu Stanciu (78.Dennis Man), Răzvan Gabriel Marin, Claudiu Andrei Keşerü (69.Alexandru Cicâldău), George Alexandru Puşcaş. Trainer: Cosmin Marius Contra.
Goals: Ciprian Ioan Deac (26), Claudiu Andrei Keşerü (29, 33), George Alexandru Puşcaş (63).

07.06.2019 NORVEGIA - ROMANIA 2-2(0-0) 16th EC. Qualifiers
Ullevaal Stadion, Oslo; Referee: Sergei Karasev (Russia); Attendance: 17,664
ROU: Anton Ciprian Tătăruşanu, Ionuţ Cristian Săpunaru (Cap), Dragoş Grigore, Alin Dorinel Toşca, Alexandru Mihăiţă Chipciu, Ciprian Ioan Deac, Paul Viorel Anton, Nicolae Claudiu Stanciu (71.Alexandru Iulian Maxim), Claudiu Andrei Keşerü, Gheorghe Grozav (60.Ianis Hagi), George Alexandru Puşcaş (60.Marius George Ţucudean). Trainer: Cosmin Marius Contra.
Goals: Claudiu Andrei Keşerü (77, 90+2).

10.06.2019 MALTA - ROMANIA 0-4(0-3) 16th EC. Qualifiers

Ta'Qali National Stadium, Attard; Referee: Dennis Higler (Netherlands); Attendance: 6,471

ROU: Anton Ciprian Tătăruşanu (Cap), Ionuţ Nedelcearu (35.Ionuţ Cristian Săpunaru), Iulian Lucian Cristea, Nicuşor Silviu Bancu, Alexandru Mihăiţă Chipciu [*sent off 81*], Tudor Cristian Băluţă, Alexandru Iulian Maxim (74.Dorin Rotariu), Răzvan Gabriel Marin, Ianis Hagi, Claudiu Andrei Keşerü (65.Dennis Man), George Alexandru Puşcaş. Trainer: Cosmin Marius Contra.

Goals: George Alexandru Puşcaş (7, 29), Alexandru Mihăiţă Chipciu (34), Dennis Man (90+1).

NATIONAL TEAM PLAYERS
(16.07.2018 – 15.07.2019)

Name	DOB	Caps	Goals	2018/2019:	*Club*
Goalkeepers					
Anton Ciprian TĂTĂRUŞAN	09.02.1986	**62**	**0**	2018/2019:	*FC Nantes (FRA)*
Defenders					
Nicuşor Silviu BANCU	18.09.1992	**10**	**0**	2018/2019:	*CS Universitatea Craiova*
Mihai Alexandru BĂLAŞA	14.01.1995	**6**	**0**	2018:	*FCSB Bucureşti*
Romario Sandu BENZAR	26.03.1992	**15**	**0**	2018/2019:	*FCSB Bucureşti*
Vlad Iulian CHIRICHEŞ	14.11.1989	**55**	**0**	2018/2019:	*SSC Napoli (ITA)*
Iulian Lucian CRISTEA	17.07.1994	**1**	**0**	2018/2019:	*FCSB Bucureşti*
Dragoş GRIGORE	07.09.1986	**36**	**0**	2019:	*PFC Ludogorets Razgrad (BUL)*
Cristian Marian MANEA	09.08.1997	**8**	**1**	2018/2019:	*FC CFR 1907 Cluj-Napoca*
Cosmin Iosif MOŢI	03.12.1984	**15**	**0**	2018/2019:	*PFC Ludogorets Razgrad (BUL)*
Ionuţ NEDELCEARU	25.04.1996	**4**	**0**	2018/2019:	*FK Ufa (RUS)*
Ionuţ Cristian SĂPUNARU	05.04.1984	**36**	**0**	2018/2019:	*Kayserispor Kulübü (TUR)*
Gabriel Sebastian TAMAŞ	09.11.1983	**67**	**3**	2018:	*Hapoel Haifa FC (ISR)*
Alin Dorinel TOŞCA	14.03.1992	**16**	**0**	2018/2019:	*PAOK Thessaloníki (GRE)*
Midfielders					
Paul Viorel ANTON	10.05.1991	**9**	**0**	2018/2019:	*FK Krylia Sovetov Samara (RUS)*
Tudor Cristian BĂLUŢĂ	27.03.1999	**5**	**0**	2018/2019:	*FC Viitorul Constanţa*
Constantin Valentin BUDESCU	19.02.1989	**12**	**5**	2018:	*Al Shabab FC Riyadh (KSA)*
Alexandru Mihăiţă CHIPCIU	18.05.1989	**46**	**6**	2018/2019:	*AC Sparta Praha (CZE)*
Alexandru CICÂLDĂU	08.07.1997	**4**	**0**	2018/2019:	*CS Universitatea Craiova*
Ciprian Ioan DEAC	16.02.1986	**20**	**4**	2018/2019:	*FC CFR 1907 Cluj-Napoca*
Gheorghe Teodor GROZAV	29.09.1990	**29**	**5**	2019:	*Kisvárda FC (HUN)*
Ianis HAGI	22.10.1998	**5**	**0**	2018/2019:	*FC Viitorul Constanţa*
Dennis MAN	26.08.1998	**4**	**0**	2019:	*FCSB Bucureşti*
Răzvan Gabriel MARIN	23.05.1996	**17**	**1**	2018/2019:	*R Standard Liège (BEL)*
Alexandru Iulian MAXIM	08.07.1990	**37**	**5**	2018/2019:	*1.FSV Mainz 05 (GER)*
Alexandru Ionuţ MITRIŢĂ	08.02.1995	**7**	**0**	2018: 04.02.2019->	*CS Universitatea Craiova* *New York City FC (USA)*
Mihai Doru PINTILII	09.11.1984	**44**	**1**	2018:	*FCSB Bucureşti*
Dorin ROTARIU	29.07.1995	**10**	**1**	2018:	*AZ Alkmaar (NED)*
Nicolae Claudiu STANCIU	07.05.1993	**31**	**10**	2018: 28.01.2019->	*AC Sparta Praha (CZE)* *Al-Ahly SC Doha (QAT)*
Forwards					
Denis Mihai DRĂGUŞ	06.07.1999	**2**	**0**	2018:	*FC Viitorul Constanţa*
Andrei Virgil IVAN	04.01.1997	**7**	**0**	2019:	*SK Rapid Wien (AUT)*
Claudiu Andrei KEŞERÜ	02.12.1986	**33**	**12**	2018/2019:	*PFC Ludogorets Razgrad (BUL)*
George Alexandru PUŞCAŞ	08.04.1996	**8**	**4**	2018/2019:	*US Città di Palermo (ITA)*
Marius George ŢUCUDEAN	30.04.1991	**10**	**3**	2018/2019:	*FC CFR 1907 Cluj-Napoca*

National team coach

Cosmin Marius CONTRA [from 22.09.2017]	15.12.1975	18 M; 11 W; 5 D; 2 L; 33-16

RUSSIA

The Country:

Российская Федерация (Russian Federation)
Capital: Moskva
Surface: 17,098,246 km²
Inhabitants: 146,793,744 [2019]
Time: UTC+2 to +12

The FA:

Российский Футбольный Союз (Russian Football Union)
7 Narodnaya Street, 115172 Moskva
Tel: +7 495 926 1300
Founded: 19.01.1912
Member of FIFA since: 1912-1917 and since 1992
Member of UEFA since: 1954
Website: www.rfs.ru

NATIONAL TEAM RECORDS

First international match:	30.06.1912, Stockholm:	Finland – Russia 2-1	
Most international caps:	Sergey Ignashevich		- 127 caps (2002-2018)
Most international goals:	Aleksandr Kerzhakov		- 30 goals / 91 caps (2002-2016)

UEFA EUROPEAN CHAMPIONSHIP	
1960	-*
1964	-
1968	-
1972	-
1976	-
1980	-
1984	-
1988	-
1992	-
1996	Final Tournament (Group Stage)
2000	Qualifiers
2004	Final Tournament (Group Stage)
2008	Final Tournament (Semi-Finals)
2012	Final Tournament (Group Stage)
2016	Final Tournament (Group Stage)

**from 1960 to 1992 as Soviet Union/C.I.S.*

FIFA WORLD CUP	
1930	-**
1934	-
1938	-
1950	-
1954	-
1958	-
1962	-
1966	-
1970	-
1974	-
1978	-
1982	-
1986	-
1990	-
1994	Final Tournament (Group Stage)
1998	Qualifiers
2002	Final Tournament (Group Stage)
2006	Qualifiers
2010	Qualifiers
2014	Final Tournament (Group Stage)
2018	Final Tournament (Quarter-Finals)

***from 1930 to 1990 as Soviet Union*

UEFA NATIONS LEAGUE
2018/2019 – League B

OLYMPIC FOOTBALL TOURNAMENTS 1908-2016							
1908	-	**1948**	-	**1972**	-	**1996**	Qualifiers
1912	Quarter-Finals	**1952**	-	**1976**	-	**2000**	Qualifiers
1920	-	**1956**	-	**1980**	-	**2004**	Qualifiers
1924	-	**1960**	-	**1984**	-	**2008**	Qualifiers
1928	-	**1964**	-	**1988**	-	**2012**	Qualifiers
1936	-	**1968**	-	**1992**	-	**2016**	Qualifiers

FIFA CONFEDERATIONS CUP 1992-2017
2017 (Group Stage)

RUSSIAN CLUB HONOURS IN EUROPEAN CLUB COMPETITIONS:

European Champion Clubs.Cup (1956-1992) / UEFA Champions League (1993-2019)		
None		
Fairs Cup (1858-1971) / UEFA Cup (1972-2009) / UEFA Europa League (2010-2019)		
FK CSKA Moskva	**1**	2004/2005
FK Zenit Saint Petersburg	**1**	2007/2008
UEFA Super Cup (1972-2018)		
FK Zenit Saint Petersburg	**1**	2008
European Cup Winners.Cup 1961-1999*		
None		

**defunct competition*

NATIONAL COMPETITIONS
TABLE OF HONOURS

Football championship of Russian Empire

	CHAMPIONS
1912	Saint Petersburg
1913	Odessa
1914	*Championship cancelled*

Football championship of Russian SFSR among city teams

	CHAMPIONS
1920	Moskva
1921	*No competition*
1922	Moskva
1923	*No competition*
1924	Leningrad
1925	*No competition*
1926	*No competition*
1927	Moskva
1928	Moskva
1929	*No competition*
1930	*No competition*
1931	Moskva
1932	Leningrad
1933	*No competition*
1934	Voronezh
1935	*No competition*

Soviet League (1936–1991)

	CHAMPIONS	CUP WINNERS	BEST GOALSCORERS	
1936 (spring)	Dinamo Moskva	-	Mikhail Semichastny (Dinamo Moskva)	6
1936 (autumn)	Spartak Moskva	Lokomotiv Moskva	Georgy Glazkov (Spartak Moskva)	7
1937	Dinamo Moskva	Dinamo Moskva	Boris Paichadze (Dinamo Tbilisi) Leonid Rumyantsev (Spartak Moskva) Vasily Smirnov (Dinamo Moskva)	8
1938	Spartak Moskva	Spartak Moskva	Makar Goncharenko (Dinamo Kiev)	19
1939	Spartak Moskva	Spartak Moskva	Grigory Fedotov (CDKA Moskva)	21
1940	Dinamo Moskva	*No competition*	Grigory Fedotov (CDKA Moskva) Sergei Solovyov (Dinamo Moskva)	21
1941	*No competition*	*No competition*	-	
1942	*No competition*	*No competition*	-	
1943	*No competition*	*No competition*	-	
1944	*No competition*	Zenit Leningrad	-	
1945	Dinamo Moskva	CDKA Moskva	Vsevolod Bobrov (CDKA Moskva)	24
1946	CDKA Moskva	Spartak Moskva	Aleksandr Ponomaryov (Torpedo Moskva)	18
1947	CDKA Moskva	Spartak Moskva	Vsevolod Bobrov (CDKA Moskva) Valentin Nikolayev (CDKA Moskva) Sergei Solovyov (Dinamo Moskva)	14
1948	CDKA Moskva	CDKA Moskva	Sergei Solovyov (Dinamo Moskva)	25
1949	Dinamo Moskva	Torpedo Moskva	Nikita Simonyan (Spartak Moskva)	26
1950	CDKA Moskva	Spartak Moskva	Nikita Simonyan (Spartak Moskva)	34
1951	CDSA Moskva	CDSA Moskva	Avtandil Gogoberidze (Dinamo Tbilisi)	16
1952	Spartak Moskva	Torpedo Moskva	Andrey Zazroyev (Dinamo Kiev)	11
1953	Spartak Moskva	Dinamo Moskva	Nikita Simonyan (Spartak Moskva)	14
1954	Dinamo Moskva	Dynamo Kiev	Anatoli Ilyin (Spartak Moskva) Vladimir Ilyin (Dinamo Moskva) Antonin Sochnev (Trudovye Reservy Leningrad)	11
1955	Dinamo Moskva	CDSA Moskva	Eduard Streltsov (Torpedo Moskva)	15
1956	Spartak Moskva	*No competition*	Vasily Buzunov (ODO Sverdlovsk)	17
1957	Dinamo Moskva	Lokomotiv Moskva	Vasily Buzunov (CSK MO Moskva)	16
1958	Spartak Moskva	Spartak Moskva	Anatoli Ilyin (Spartak Moskva)	19
1959	Dinamo Moskva	-	Zaur Kaloyev (Dinamo Tbilisi)	16
1960	Torpedo Moskva	Torpedo Moskva (1959/60)	Zaur Kaloyev (Dinamo Tbilisi) Gennady Gusarov (Torpedo Moskva)	20
1961	Dinamo Kiev	Shakhtyor Stalino	Gennady Gusarov (Torpedo Moskva)	22
1962	Spartak Moskva	Shakhtyor Stalino	Mikhail Mustygin (Belarus Minsk)	17
1963	Dinamo Moskva	Spartak Moskva	Oleg Kopaev (SKA Rostov-na-Donu)	27
1964	Dinamo Tbilisi	Dynamo Kiev	Vladimir Fedotov (CSKA Moskva)	16
1965	Torpedo Moskva	Spartak Moskva	Oleg Kopaev (SKA Rostov-na-Donu)	18
1966	Dinamo Kiev	Dynamo Kiev (1965/66)	Ilya Datunashvili (Dinamo Tbilisi)	20

1967	Dinamo Kiev	Dinamo Moskva (1966/67)	Mikhail Mustygin (Dinamo Minsk)	19
1968	Dinamo Kiev	Torpedo Moskva (1967/68)	Georgi Gavasheli (Dinamo Tbilisi) Berador Abduraimov (Pakhtakor Tashkent)	22
1969	Spartak Moskva	Karpaty Lviv	Nikolai Osyanin (Spartak Moskva) Vladimir Proskurin (SKA Rostov-na-Donu) Dzhemal Kherhadze (Torpedo Kutaisi)	16
1970	CSKA Moskva	Dinamo Moskva	Givi Nodia (Dinamo Tbilisi)	17
1971	Dinamo Kiev	Spartak Moskva	Eduard Malofeev (Dinamo Minsk)	16
1972	Zarya Voroshilovgrad	Torpedo Moskva	Oleg Blokhin (Dinamo Kiev)	14
1973	Ararat Yerevan	Ararat Yerevan	Oleg Blokhin (Dinamo Kiev)	18
1974	Dinamo Kiev	Dynamo Kiev	Oleg Blokhin (Dinamo Kiev)	20
1975	Dinamo Kiev	Ararat Yerevan	Oleg Blokhin (Dinamo Kiev)	18
1976 (spring)	Dinamo Moskva	-	Arkady Andreasian (Ararat Yerevan)	8
1976 (autumn)	Torpedo Moskva	Dinamo Tbilisi	Aleksandr Markin (Zenit Leningrad)	13
1977	Dinamo Kiev	Dinamo Moskva	Oleg Blokhin (Dinamo Kiev)	17
1978	Dinamo Tbilisi	Dynamo Kiev	Georgi Yartsev (Spartak Moskva)	19
1979	Spartak Moskva	Dinamo Tbilisi	Vitali Starukhin (Shakhtar Donetsk)	26
1980	Dinamo Kiev	Shakhtar Donetsk	Sergey Andreev (SKA Rostov-na-Donu)	20
1981	Dinamo Kiev	SKA Rostov-on-Don	Ramaz Shengelia (Dinamo Tbilisi)	23
1982	Dinamo Minsk	Dynamo Kiev	Andrei Yakubik (Pakhtakor Tashkent)	23
1983	Dnipro Dnipropetrovsk	Shakhtar Donetsk	Yuriy Gavrilov (Spartak Moskva)	18
1984	Zenit Leningrad	Dinamo Moskva	Sergey Andreev (SKA Rostov-na-Donu)	20
1985	Dinamo Kiev	Dynamo Kiev	Oleg Protasov (Dnipro Dnipropetrovsk)	35
1986	Dinamo Kiev	Torpedo Moskva	Aleksandr Borodyuk (Dinamo Moskva)	21
1987	Spartak Moskva	Dynamo Kiev	Oleg Protasov (Dnipro Dnipropetrovsk)	18
1988	Dnipro Dnipropetrovsk	Metalist Kharkiv	Yevhen Shakhov (Dnipro Dnipropetrovsk) Aleksandr Borodyuk (Dinamo Moskva)	16
1989	Spartak Moskva	Dnipro Dnipropetrovsk	Sergey Rodionov (Spartak Moskva)	16
1990	Dinamo Kiev	Dynamo Kiev	Oleg Protasov (Dinamo Kiev) Valery Shmarov (Spartak Moskva)	12
1991	CSKA Moskva	CSKA Moskva	Igor Kolyvanov (Dinamo Moskva)	18

Russian League (1992–present)

	CHAMPIONS	CUP WINNERS	BEST GOALSCORERS	
1992	FK Spartak Moskva	FK Spartak Moskva	Vali Gasimov (AZE, FK Dinamo Moskva)	16
1993	FK Spartak Moskva	FK Torpedo Moskva	Viktor Panchenko (FK KamAZ Naberezhnye Chelny)	21
1994	FK Spartak Moskva	FK Spartak Moskva	Igor Simutenkov (FK Dinamo Moskva)	21
1995	FK Alania Vladikavkaz	FK Dinamo Moskva	Oleg Veretennikov (Rotor Volgograd)	25
1996	FK Spartak Moskva	FK Lokomotiv Moskva	Aleksandr Maslov (FK Rostselmash Rostov-na-Donu)	23
1997	FK Spartak Moskva	FK Lokomotiv Moskva	Oleg Veretennikov (FK Rotor Volgograd)	22
1998	FK Spartak Moskva	FK Spartak Moskva	Oleg Veretennikov (FK Rotor Volgograd)	22
1999	FK Spartak Moskva	FK Zenit Saint Petersburg	Georgi Demetradze (GEO, FK Alania Vladikavkaz)	21
2000	FK Spartak Moskva	FK Lokomotiv Moskva	Dmitri Loskov (FK Lokomotiv Moskva)	18
2001	FK Spartak Moskva	FK Lokomotiv Moskva	Dmitri Vyazmikin (FK Torpedo Moskva)	18
2002	FK Lokomotiv Moskva	FK CSKA Moskva	Rolan Gusev (FK CSKA Moskva) Dmitri Kirichenko (FK CSKA Moskva)	15
2003	FK CSKA Moskva	FK Spartak Moskva	Dmitri Loskov (FK Lokomotiv Moskva)	14
2004	FK Lokomotiv Moskva	FK Terek Grozny	Aleksandr Kerzhakov (FK Zenit Saint Petersburg)	18
2005	FK CSKA Moskva	FK CSKA Moskva	Dmitri Kirichenko (FK Moskva)	14
2006	FK CSKA Moskva	FK CSKA Moskva	Roman Pavlyuchenko (FK Spartak Moskva)	18
2007	FK Zenit Saint Petersburg	FK Lokomotiv Moskva	Roman Pavlyuchenko (FK Spartak Moskva) Roman Adamov (FK Moskva)	14
2008	FK Rubin Kazan	FK CSKA Moskva	Vágner Silva de Souza "Vágner Love" (BRA, FK CSKA Moskva)	20
2009	FK Rubin Kazan	FK CSKA Moskva	Welliton Soares de Morais (BRA, FK Spartak Moskva)	21
2010	FK Zenit Saint Petersburg	FK Zenit Saint Petersburg	Welliton Soares de Morais (BRA, FK Spartak Moskva)	19
2010/2011	-	FK CSKA Moskva	-	
2011/2012	FK Zenit Saint Petersburg	FK Rubin Kazan	Seydou Doumbia (CIV, FK CSKA Moskva)	28
2012/2013	FK CSKA Moskva	FK CSKA Moskva	Yura Movsisyan (ARM, FK Spartak Moskva) Francisco Wánderson do Carmo Carneiro (BRA, FK Krasnodar)	13
2013/2014	FK CSKA Moskva	FK Rostov	Seydou Doumbia (CIV, FK CSKA Moskva)	18
2014/2015	FK Zenit Saint Petersburg	FK Lokomotiv Moskva	Givanildo Vieira de Sousa "Hulk" (BRA, FK Zenit Saint Petersburg)	15
2015/2016	FK CSKA Moskva	FK Zenit Saint Petersburg	Fyodor Smolov (FK Krasnodar)	20
2016/2017	FK Spartak Moskva	FK Lokomotiv Moskva	Fyodor Smolov (FK Krasnodar)	18
2017/2018	FK Lokomotiv Moskva	FK Tosno	Quincy Anton Promes (NED, FK Spartak Moskva)	15
2018/2019	FK Zenit Saint Petersburg	FK Lokomotiv Moskva	Fedor Chalov (FK CSKA Moskva)	15

Club name changements: **FK CSKA Moskva** = OPPW Moskva (1924-1928), CDKA Moskva (1928-1951), CDSA Moskva (1951-1953), WWS Moskva (1953-1957), CSKMO Moskva (1957-1960), CSKA Moskva (1960-1988), FK CSKA Moskva (since 1988).

NATIONAL CHAMPIONSHIP

Premier League 2018/2019

(28.07.2018 – 26.05.2019)

Results

Round 1 [28-31.07.2018]
FK Ural - Anzhi Makhachkala 0-1(0-0)
Spartak Moskva - FK Orenburg 1-0(1-0)
FK Rostov - Akhmat Grozny 1-0(1-0)
Yenisey Krasnoyarsk - FK Zenit 0-2(0-0)
Arsenal Tula - Dinamo Moskva 0-0
Rubin Kazan - FK Krasnodar 2-1(2-1)
FK Ufa - Lokomotiv Moskva 0-0
Krylia Sovetov - CSKA Moskva 0-0

Round 2 [03-06.08.2018]
Dinamo Moskva - Rubin Kazan 1-1(1-0)
FK Ural - FK Krasnodar 1-2(1-0)
FK Zenit - Arsenal Tula 1-0(0-0)
Lokomotiv Moskva - Spartak Moskva 0-0
Krylia Sovetov - FK Orenburg 0-3(0-3)
CSKA Moskva - FK Rostov 0-1(0-1)
Akhmat Grozny - Yenisey Krasnoy. 1-0(0-0)
FK Ufa - Anzhi Makhachkala 3-0(1-0)

Round 3 [10-13.08.2018]
FK Ural - Dinamo Moskva 1-1(0-0)
Yenisey Krasnoy. - CSKA Moskva 1-1(0-0)
Spartak Moskva - Anzhi Makhachk. 1-0(0-0)
FK Rostov - Krylia Sovetov 0-1(0-1)
FK Orenburg - Lokomotiv Moskva 1-0(0-0)
Arsenal Tula - Akhmat Grozny 3-1(0-1)
FK Ufa - FK Krasnodar 0-1(0-0)
Rubin Kazan - FK Zenit 0-1(0-0)

Round 4 [17-20.08.2018]
Anzhi Makhachkala - FK Orenburg 1-3(1-0)
CSKA Moskva - Arsenal Tula 3-0(1-0)
FK Krasnodar - Spartak Moskva 0-1(0-0)
Akhmat Grozny - Rubin Kazan 1-1(0-0)
Krylia Sovetov - Lokomotiv Moskva 0-1(0-1)
FK Zenit - FK Ural 4-1(2-1)
FK Rostov - Yenisey Krasnoyarsk 4-0(2-0)
Dinamo Moskva - FK Ufa 3-0(0-0)

Round 5 [24-27.08.2018]
Arsenal Tula - FK Rostov 0-1(0-0)
FK Ural - Akhmat Grozny 2-1(0-1)
Rubin Kazan - CSKA Moskva 1-1(1-0)
Spartak Moskva - Dinamo Moskva 2-1(2-0)
FK Orenburg - FK Krasnodar 1-1(1-0)
FK Ufa - FK Zenit 0-2(0-2)
Lokomotiv Moskva - Anzhi Makhach 2-1(0-0)
Yenisey Krasnoy. - Krylia Sovetov 1-0(1-0)

Round 6 [31.08.-02.09.2018]
FK Rostov - Rubin Kazan 1-1(1-0)
Krylia Sovetov - Anzhi Makhachkala 1-0(0-0)
CSKA Moskva - FK Ural 4-0(2-0)
FK Krasnodar - Lokomotiv Moskva 2-1(1-1)
Yenisey Krasnoyarsk - Arsenal Tula 0-0
Dinamo Moskva - FK Orenburg 2-0(0-0)
FK Zenit - Spartak Moskva 0-0
Akhmat Grozny - FK Ufa 2-1(0-0)

Round 7 [14-17.09.2018]
Lokomotiv Moskva - Dinamo Mosk. 1-1(1-1)
Rubin Kazan - Yenisey Krasnoyarsk 1-0(1-0)
FK Ufa - CSKA Moskva 0-3(0-1)
Arsenal Tula - Krylia Sovetov 4-0(1-0)
FK Orenburg - FK Zenit 1-2(0-2)
Anzhi Makhachkala - FK Krasnodar 0-4(0-2)
Spartak Moskva - Akhmat Grozny 1-2(0-1)
FK Ural - FK Rostov 1-1(0-0)

Round 8 [22-24.09.2018]
Yenisey Krasnoyarsk - FK Ural 1-2(0-1)
Dinamo Moskva - Anzhi Makhachk. 0-1(0-0)
Arsenal Tula - Rubin Kazan 2-2(1-0)
FK Rostov - FK Ufa 0-0
Akhmat Grozny - FK Orenburg 1-1(1-0)
FK Zenit - Lokomotiv Moskva 5-3(1-1)
CSKA Moskva - Spartak Moskva 1-1(0-1)
Krylia Sovetov - FK Krasnodar 0-3(0-0)

Round 9 [28.09.-01.10.2018]
FK Orenburg - CSKA Moskva 0-1(0-1)
FK Ural - Arsenal Tula 2-1(0-1)
FK Ufa - Yenisey Krasnoyarsk 2-1(0-1)
Lokomotiv Moskva - Akhmat Grozny 2-0(0-0)
Anzhi Makhachkala - FK Zenit 2-1(0-0)
FK Krasnodar - Dinamo Moskva 3-0(2-0)
Spartak Moskva - FK Rostov 0-1(0-0)
Rubin Kazan - Krylia Sovetov 2-1(1-0)

Round 10 [05-07.10.2018]
Arsenal Tula - FK Ufa 1-1(0-1)
Krylia Sovetov - Dinamo Moskva 1-0(0-0)
FK Rostov - FK Orenburg 0-1(0-1)
Rubin Kazan - FK Ural 1-0(1-0)
Yenisey Krasnoy. - Spartak Moskva 2-3(0-0)
Akhmat Grozny - Anzhi Makhachkala 0-0
FK Zenit - FK Krasnodar 2-1(0-0)
CSKA Moskva - Lokomotiv Moskva 0-1(0-0)

Round 11 [19-21.10.2018]
Anzhi Makhachkala - CSKA Moskva 0-2(0-1)
Lokomotiv Moskva - FK Rostov 2-1(1-1)
FK Orenburg - Yenisey Krasnoyarsk 0-0
FK Ural - Krylia Sovetov 1-1(1-0)
FK Ufa - Rubin Kazan 0-0
Dinamo Moskva - FK Zenit 1-0(0-0)
Spartak Moskva - Arsenal Tula 2-3(2-1)
FK Krasnodar - Akhmat Grozny 0-1(0-0)

Round 12 [27-29.10.2018]
FK Ural - FK Ufa 1-1(0-1)
Arsenal Tula - FK Orenburg 2-2(1-0)
FK Rostov - Anzhi Makhachkala 1-0(1-0)
Yenisey Krasn. - Lokomotiv Moskva 0-3(0-1)
Akhmat Grozny - Dinamo Moskva 0-0
CSKA Moskva - FK Krasnodar 1-2(0-0)
Krylia Sovetov - FK Zenit 0-1(0-1)
Rubin Kazan - Spartak Moskva 1-1(0-0)

Round 13 [03-05.11.2018]
Lokomotiv Moskva - Arsenal Tula 3-1(1-1)
Dinamo Moskva - CSKA Moskva 0-0
FK Zenit - Akhmat Grozny 1-0(1-0)
FK Krasnodar - FK Rostov 2-2(1-1)
Spartak Moskva - FK Ural 1-2(0-1)
FK Orenburg - Rubin Kazan 1-0(0-0)
FK Ufa - Krylia Sovetov 1-2(0-1)
Anzhi Makhachk. - Yenisey Krasnoy. 2-1(1-0)

Round 14 [09-11.11.2018]
Arsenal Tula - Anzhi Makhachkala 2-0(1-0)
FK Ural - FK Orenburg 2-1(1-0)
Krylia Sovetov - Akhmat Grozny 1-2(0-0)
FK Rostov - Dinamo Moskva 0-0
FK Ufa - Spartak Moskva 2-0(0-0)
FK Krasnodar - Yenisey Krasnoyarsk 3-0(0-0)
Rubin Kazan - Lokomotiv Moskva 0-0
CSKA Moskva - FK Zenit 2-0(2-0)

Round 15 [23-25.11.2018]
Akhmat Grozny - CSKA Moskva 0-2(0-0)
Lokomotiv Moskva - FK Ural 1-2(1-1)
Dinamo Moskva - Yenisey Krasnoy. 1-2(0-1)
FK Orenburg - FK Ufa 1-0(0-0)
Anzhi Makhachkala - Rubin Kazan 1-1(1-1)
Spartak Moskva - Krylia Sovetov 3-1(0-0)
FK Krasnodar - Arsenal Tula 3-0(1-0)
FK Zenit - FK Rostov 2-0(1-0)

Round 16 [30.11.-03.12.2018]
Rubin Kazan - Dinamo Moskva 1-1(0-0)
Yenisey Krasnoy. - Akhmat Grozny 1-1(0-0)
Anzhi Makhachkala - FK Ufa 0-0
FK Krasnodar - FK Ural 2-0(0-0)
FK Rostov - CSKA Moskva 0-0
Spartak Moskva - Lokomotiv Mosk. 2-1(2-0)
Arsenal Tula - FK Zenit 4-2(2-1)
Orenburg - Krylia Sov. 3-1(2-1) [03.04.2019]

Round 17 [08-10.12.2018]
Krylia Sovetov - FK Rostov 1-0(1-0)
CSKA Moskva - Yenisey Krasnoy. 2-1(2-0)
Lokomotiv Moskva - FK Orenburg 2-1(0-1)
Anzhi Makhachk. - Spartak Moskva 0-3(0-1)
Dinamo Moskva - FK Ural 4-0(2-0)
FK Krasnodar - FK Ufa 1-1(1-1)
FK Zenit - Rubin Kazan 1-2(0-1)
Akhmat Grozny - Arsenal Tula 2-0(1-0)

Round 18 [01-03.03.2019]
FK Orenburg - Anzhi Makhachkala 0-1(0-0)
FK Ural - FK Zenit 0-1(0-1)
Arsenal Tula - CSKA Moskva 2-0(0-0)
Lokomotiv Moskva - Krylia Sovetov 2-2(1-1)
Rubin Kazan - Akhmat Grozny 1-0(0-0)
FK Ufa - Dinamo Moskva 1-2(1-0)
Yenisey Krasnoyarsk - FK Rostov 1-1(0-0)
Spartak Moskva - FK Krasnodar 1-1(1-1)

Round 19 [09-11.03.2019]
Krylia Sovetov - Yenisey Krasnoy. 4-0(1-0)
CSKA Moskva - Rubin Kazan 3-0(1-0)
FK Rostov - Arsenal Tula 0-0
FK Zenit - FK Ufa 2-1(2-1)
Dinamo Moskva - Spartak Moskva 0-1(0-1)
Anzhi Makh. - Lokomotiv Moskva 0-2(0-1)
Akhmat Grozny - FK Ural 1-1(0-1)
FK Krasnodar - FK Orenburg 2-2(0-1)

Round 20 [15-17.03.2019]
Anzhi Makhachkala - Krylia Sovetov 0-2(0-1)
FK Orenburg - Dinamo Moskva 1-0(0-0)
FK Ural - CSKA Moskva 0-1(0-0)
Rubin Kazan - FK Rostov 0-2(0-0)
Arsenal Tula - Yenisey Krasnoyarsk 2-0(1-0)
FK Ufa - Akhmat Grozny 0-1(0-0)
Lokomotiv Moskva - FK Krasnodar 1-0(0-0)
Spartak Moskva - FK Zenit 1-1(1-1)

Round 21 [29-31.03.2019]
Krylia Sovetov - Arsenal Tula 0-1(0-0)
Yenisey Krasnoyarsk - Rubin Kazan 1-1(0-0)
Dinamo Moskva - Lokomotiv Mosk. 0-1(0-0)
Akhmat Grozny - Spartak Moskva 1-3(1-1)
FK Rostov - FK Ural 2-1(1-0)
FK Zenit - FK Orenburg 3-1(0-1)
CSKA Moskva - FK Ufa 2-2(1-0)
FK Krasnodar - Anzhi Makhachkala 5-0(2-0)

Round 22 [06-08.04.2019]
Anzhi Makhachk. - Dinamo Moskva 1-1(1-0)
FK Krasnodar - Krylia Sovetov 1-0(0-0)
Spartak Moskva - CSKA Moskva 0-2(0-0)
FK Ufa - FK Rostov 1-0(1-0)
FK Ural - Yenisey Krasnoyarsk 3-2(0-1)
Rubin Kazan - Arsenal Tula 0-0
Lokomotiv Moskva - FK Zenit 1-1(0-0)
FK Orenburg - Akhmat Grozny 1-3(1-1)

Round 23 [12-14.04.2019]
Krylia Sovetov - Rubin Kazan 1-0(0-0)
Yenisey Krasnoyarsk - FK Ufa 0-0
Arsenal Tula - FK Ural 0-0
CSKA Moskva - FK Orenburg 2-3(2-2)
Akhmat Grozny - Lokomotiv Moskva 1-3(0-1)
Dinamo Moskva - FK Krasnodar 1-1(0-0)
FK Zenit - Anzhi Makhachkala 5-0(2-0)
FK Rostov - Spartak Moskva 2-1(1-1)

Round 24 [19-21.04.2019]
Anzhi Makhachk. - Akhmat Grozny 0-1(0-0)
FK Ufa - Arsenal Tula 1-2(1-2)
FK Orenburg - FK Rostov 3-0(1-0)
Dinamo Moskva - Krylia Sovetov 1-0(0-0)
Lokomotiv Moskva - CSKA Moskva 1-1(1-1)
FK Krasnodar - FK Zenit 2-3(1-1)
FK Ural - Rubin Kazan 2-1(1-1)
Spartak Moskva - Yenisey Krasnoy. 2-0(1-0)

Round 25 [24-25.04.2019]
FK Rostov - Lokomotiv Moskva 1-2(1-1)
Akhmat Grozny - FK Krasnodar 1-1(1-0)
Rubin Kazan - FK Ufa 1-1(0-1)
CSKA Moskva - Anzhi Makhachkala 2-0(1-0)
FK Zenit - Dinamo Moskva 2-0(0-0)
Yenisey Krasnoyarsk - FK Orenburg 2-1(1-0)
Krylia Sovetov - FK Ural 0-1(0-0)
Arsenal Tula - Spartak Moskva 3-0(3-0)

Round 26 [27-29.04.2019]
Anzhi Makhachkala - FK Rostov 1-1(0-1)
Dinamo Moskva - Akhmat Grozny 0-0
FK Ufa - FK Ural 4-1(1-1)
Lokomotiv Moskva - Yenisey Krasn. 2-1(0-0)
FK Zenit - Krylia Sovetov 4-2(3-2)
FK Krasnodar - CSKA Moskva 2-0(1-0)
FK Orenburg - Arsenal Tula 1-1(0-0)
Spartak Moskva - Rubin Kazan 1-1(1-0)

Round 27 [03-05.05.2019]
Yenisey Krasnoy. - Anzhi Makhachk. 3-1(0-1)
Rubin Kazan - FK Orenburg 2-0(1-0)
FK Ural - Spartak Moskva 0-1(0-0)
Akhmat Grozny - FK Zenit 1-1(0-0)
Arsenal Tula - Lokomotiv Moskva 2-0(1-0)
Krylia Sovetov - FK Ufa 1-1(1-0)
CSKA Moskva - Dinamo Moskva 2-2(1-2)
FK Rostov - FK Krasnodar 1-1(0-1)

Round 28 [10-12.05.2019]
FK Orenburg - FK Ural 2-2(0-0)
Dinamo Moskva - FK Rostov 0-0
Anzhi Makhachkala - Arsenal Tula 0-1(0-1)
Lokomotiv Moskva - Rubin Kazan 4-0(2-0)
Yenisey Krasnoyarsk - FK Krasnodar 0-4(0-2)
Akhmat Grozny - Krylia Sovetov 2-1(2-1)
Spartak Moskva - FK Ufa 1-0(1-0)
FK Zenit - CSKA Moskva 3-1(1-1)

Round 29 [18-20.05.2019]
FK Ufa - FK Orenburg 0-2(0-1)
CSKA Moskva - Akhmat Grozny 1-0(0-0)
Krylia Sovetov - Spartak Moskva 1-2(0-1)
FK Ural - Lokomotiv Moskva 2-2(1-1)
Yenisey Krasnoy. - Dinamo Moskva 2-2(1-1)
Arsenal Tula - FK Krasnodar 0-3(0-0)
FK Rostov - FK Zenit 1-0(0-0)
Rubin Kazan - Anzhi Makhachkala 0-0

Round 30 [26.05.2019]
CSKA Moskva - Krylia Sovetov 6-0(1-0)
Akhmat Grozny - FK Rostov 1-0(1-0)
FK Zenit - Yenisey Krasnoyarsk 4-1(1-0)
Dinamo Moskva - Arsenal Tula 3-3(2-1)
FK Krasnodar - Rubin Kazan 1-0(0-0)
Anzhi Makhachkala - FK Ural 0-2(0-0)
Lokomotiv Moskva - FK Ufa 1-0(1-0)
FK Orenburg - Spartak Moskva 2-0(1-0)

Final Standings

1.	**FK Zenit Saint Petersburg**	30	20	4	6	57	-	29	64
2.	FK Lokomotiv Moskva	30	16	8	6	45	-	28	56
3.	FK Krasnodar	30	16	8	6	55	-	23	56
4.	FK CSKA Moskva	30	14	9	7	46	-	23	51
5.	FK Spartak Moskva	30	14	7	9	36	-	31	49
6.	FK Arsenal Tula	30	12	10	8	40	-	33	46
7.	FK Orenburg	30	12	7	11	39	-	34	43
8.	FK Akhmat Grozny	30	11	9	10	29	-	30	42
9.	FK Rostov	30	10	11	9	25	-	23	41
10.	FK Ural Yekaterinburg	30	10	8	12	33	-	45	38
11.	FK Rubin Kazan	30	7	15	8	24	-	30	36
12.	FK Dinamo Moskva	30	6	15	9	28	-	28	33
13.	PFK Krylia Sovetov Samara (*Relegat. Play-offs*)	30	8	4	18	25	-	46	28
14.	FK Ufa (*Relegation Play-offs*)	30	5	11	14	24	-	34	26
15.	FK Anzhi Makhachkala (*Relegated*)	30	5	6	19	13	-	50	21
16.	FK Yenisey Krasnoyarsk (*Relegated*)	30	4	8	18	24	-	55	20

Top goalscorers:

15 Fedor Chalov
FK CSKA Moskva

13 Sardar Azmoun (IRN)
FK Rubin Kazan / FK Zenit St Petersburg

12 Viktor Johan Anton Claesson (SWE)
FK Krasnodar

11 Sebastián Driussi (ARG)
FK Zenit Saint Petersburg

11 Anton Miranchuk
FK Lokomotiv Moskva

Relegation Play-offs [30.05.-02.06.2019]

FK Ufa - FK Tom Tomsk	2-0(1-0)	0-1(0-1)
FK Nizhny Novgorod - **PFK Krylia Sovetov Samara**	1-3(1-0)	1-0(1-0)

Both FK Ufa and PFK Krylia Sovetov Samara retained their places at first level.

NATIONAL CUP
Kubok Rossii (Кубок России) 2018/2019

Fourth Round [22.08.2018]

FK Luch Vladivostok - FK SKA-Khabarovsk	0-2(0-1)
FK Sakhalin - FK Zenit Irkutsk	3-0(1-0)
FK Dinamo Barnaul - FK Tom Tomsk	0-0 aet; 5-4 pen
FK Chelyabinsk - FK Olimpiyets Nizhny Novgorod	0-1(0-0)
Znamya Truda Orekhovo-Zuevo - FK Baltika Kalin.	0-1(0-1)
FK Tyumen - FK Sibir Novosibirsk	2-1(1-1,1-1)
FK Volgar Astrakhan - FK Fakel Voronezh	0-0 aet; 4-2 pen
FK Syzran-2003 - FK Rotor Volgograd	1-1 aet; 4-3 pen
FK Neftekhimik Nizhnekamsk - FK Mordovia Saran.	1-0(0-0)
FK Luki-Energiya Velikiye Luki - FK Chertanovo M.	0-0 aet; 5-4 pen
Tekstilshchik Ivanovo - FK Khimki	2-3(0-2)
FK Dinamo Bryansk - FK Avangard Kursk	1-3(0-2)
FK Kaluga - FK Tambov	0-0 aet; 2-4 pen
FK Chernomorets Novorossisk - PFK Sochi	2-1(1-1)
Chayka Peschanokopskoye - FK Torpedo Armavir	2-0(0-0)
FK Torpedo Moskva - FK Shinnik Yaroslavl	2-0(1-0)

Fifth Round [25-27.09./10.10.2018]

FK Dinamo Barnaul - FK Orenburg	0-2(0-1)
FK Neftekhimik Nizhnekamsk - FK Ural	2-3(0-1)
FK Sakhalin - FK Arsenal Tula	1-2(0-2)
FK SKA-Khabarovsk - FK Akhmat Grozny	3-3 aet; 2-4 pen
FK Syzran-2003 - FK Rostov	0-4(0-2)
FK Luki-Energiya V. Luki - FK Yenisey Krasnoyarsk	1-2(1-1)
FK Volgar Astrakhan - FK Zenit Saint Petersburg	0-4(0-2)
FK Chernomorets Novorossisk - FK Spartak Moskva	0-1(0-1)
FK Khimki - FK Rubin Kazan	0-1(0-0,0-0)
FK Chayka Peschanokopskoye - FK Anzhi Makhach.	1-2(0-1)
FK Olimpiyets Nizhny Novgorod - FK Ufa	0-0 aet; 5-3 pen
FK Torpedo Moskva - FK Dinamo Moskva	0-1(0-1)
FK Baltika Kaliningrad - FK Lokomotiv Moskva	2-3(1-1,2-2)
FK Avangard Kursk - FK Krasnodar	0-2(0-1)
FK Tambov - PFK Krylia Sovetov Samara	1-2(1-0,1-1)
FK Tyumen - FK CSKA Moskva	1-1 aet; 3-0 pen

1/8-Finals [25/31.10./01.11.2018]			
FK Rubin Kazan - FK Dinamo Moskva	1-0(0-0)	FK Akhmat Grozny - FK Arsenal Tula	0-2(0-1)
FK Orenburg - FK Tyumen	1-0(1-0)	PFK Krylia Sovetov Samara - FK Krasnodar	1-2(0-0,1-1)
FK Ural - FK Olimpiyets Nizhny Novgorod	2-0(0-0,0-0)	FK Rostov - FK Zenit Saint Petersburg	3-1(1-1)
FK Lokomotiv Moskva - FK Yenisey Krasnoyarsk	4-1(2-0)	FK Spartak Moskva - FK Anzhi Makhachkala	1-0(1-0)

Quarter-Finals [28.11./05.12.2018-24.02./06-07.03.2019]			
FK Orenburg - FK Arsenal Tula	2-4 / 1-1	FK Krasnodar - FK Rostov	2-2 / 0-1
FK Lokomotiv Moskva - FK Rubin Kazan	1-0 / 1-0	FK Spartak Moskva - FK Ural	1-1 / 0-1

Semi-Finals [03.04.-15.05.2019]			
FK Ural - FK Arsenal Tula	1-0 / 2-2	FK Lokomotiv Moskva - FK Rostov	2-2 / 2-0

Final

22.05.2019; Cosmos Arena, Samara; Referee: Sergey Lapochkin; Attendance: 38,018
FK Lokomotiv Moskva - FK Ural Yekaterinburg **1-0(1-0)**

Lokomotiv Moskva: Guilherme Alvin Marinato, Brian Oladapo Idowu, Vedran Ćorluka, Mikhail Lysov, Manuel Henriques Tavares Fernandes, Dmitry Barinov, Grzegorz Krychowiak, Anton Miranchuk (67.Dmitriy Tarasov), Aleksey Miranchuk, Fedor Smolov (90.Khvicha Kvaratskhelia), Rifat Zhemaletdinov. Trainer: Yuriy Semin.

Ural Yekaterinburg: Yaroslav Godzyur, Stefan Strandberg, Denis Kulakov, Mikhail Merkulov, Petrus Boumal, Artem Fiedler (84.Yuriy Bavin), Othman El Kabir, Roman Emelyanov, Vladimir Ilyin, Andrey Panyukov (56.Marco Aratore), Pavel Pogrebnyak. Trainer: Dmitri Parfenov.

Goal: 1-0 Dmitry Barinov (27).

THE CLUBS 2018/2019

Fudbolnij Klub Akhmat Grozny

Founded: 1958
Stadium: Akhmat-Arena, Grozny (30,597)

Goalkeepers:	DOB	M	(s)	G
Evgeniy Gorodov	13.12.1985	29		
Vitaliy Gudiev	22.04.1995	1		
Defenders:	**DOB**	**M**	**(s)**	**G**
Wilker José Ángel Romero (VEN)	18.03.1993	18		1
Milad Mohammadi (IRN)	29.09.1993	28		1
Magomed Musalov	09.02.1994	4	(1)	
Zoran Nižić (CRO)	11.10.1989	9	(1)	
Zaurbek Pliev	27.09.1991	17	(2)	
Rodolfo Dantas Bispo (BRA)	23.10.1982	8	(3)	1
Andrei Semyonov	24.03.1989	27		1
Rizvan Utsiev	07.02.1988	26	(1)	
Midfielders:	**DOB**	**M**	**(s)**	**G**
Bernard Berisha (KVX)	24.10.1991	12	(9)	
Idrissa Doumbia (CIV)	14.04.1998	15	(1)	1
Mikhail Gashchenkov	19.06.1992	6	(4)	
Ismael Silva Lima (BRA)	01.12.1994	26	(3)	2
Oleg Ivanov	04.08.1986	24	(3)	5
Evgeny Kharin	11.06.1995		(2)	
Ravanelli Ferreira dos Santos (BRA)	29.08.1997	16	(1)	4
Odise Roshi (ALB)	22.05.1991	5	(8)	
Lechii Sadulaev	08.01.2000		(2)	
Anton Shvets	26.04.1993	19	(1)	2
Damian Szymański (POL)	16.06.1995	8	(1)	
Forwards:	**DOB**	**M**	**(s)**	**G**
Bekim Balaj (ALB)	11.01.1991	13	(9)	3
Ablaye Mbengue (SEN)	15.05.1992	10	(15)	5
Magomed Mitrishev	10.09.1992	8	(8)	2
Zaur Sadaev	06.11.1989	1	(3)	
Trainer:	**DOB**	**M**		
Igor Ledyakhov	22.05.1968	5		
Ruslan Idigov [02.09.2018]	29.03.1966	1		
Rashid Rakhimov [05.09.2018]	18.03.1965	24		

Fudbolnij Klub Anzhi Makhachkala

Founded: 1991
Stadium: Anzhi Arena, Kaspiysk (26,400)

Goalkeepers:	DOB	M	(s)	G
Yury Dyupin	17.03.1988	30		
Defenders:	**DOB**	**M**	**(s)**	**G**
Dmitriy Belorukov	24.03.1983	9		
Jhon Carlos Chancellor Cedeño (VEN)	02.01.1992	13	(1)	
Nikita Chistyakov	08.08.2000	3		
Magomed Elmurzaev	16.06.1997	1	(3)	
Evgeniy Gapon	20.04.1991	17		
Pavel Kaloshin	13.03.1998	12		
Ivan Novoseltsev	25.08.1991	11		1
Alikadi Saidov	02.04.1999	1		
Igor Udaly	08.12.1984	23	(2)	
Midfielders:	**DOB**	**M**	**(s)**	**G**
Nikita Andreev	02.11.1997		(1)	
Paul Viorel Anton (ROU)	10.05.1991		(2)	1
Anton Belov	02.05.1996	6		
Igor Chaykovskiy (UKR)	07.10.1991	11	(1)	
Shakhban Gaydarov	21.01.1997	6	(1)	
Roland Gigolaev	04.01.1990	25		
Danil Glebov	03.11.1999	5	(3)	
Adłan Katsaev	20.02.1988	10	(10)	
Dostonbek Khamdamov (UZB)	24.07.1996	1	(4)	
Vladislav Kulik	27.02.1985	24		3
Magomed Magomedov	22.07.1997		(1)	
Amir Mokhammad	23.02.1996	3	(3)	
Gaël Ondoua (CMR)	04.11.1995	19	(6)	
Mohammed Rabiu (GHA)	31.12.1989	11		
Konstantin Savichev	06.03.1994	14		
Guram Tetrashvili	02.08.1988	3	(1)	
Kamil Zakirov	15.11.1998	11	(2)	1
Forwards:	**DOB**	**M**	**(s)**	**G**
Gamid Agalarov	16.07.2000	2	(5)	
Apti Akhyadov	24.08.1993	12	(10)	
Pavel Dolgov	16.08.1996	16	(7)	2
Ivan Ivanchenko	07.09.1998	4	(5)	
Juan Eduardo Lescano (ARG)	29.10.1992		(4)	
Ivan Markelov	17.04.1988	3	(12)	
Andrés Fabián Ponce Núñez (VEN)	11.11.1996	24	(3)	5
Trainer:	**DOB**	**M**		
Magomed Adiev	30.06.1977	30		

Fudbolnij Klub Arsenal Tula

Founded: 1946
Stadium: Arsenal Stadium, Tula (20,048)

Goalkeepers:	**DOB**	**M**	**(s)**	**G**
Mikhail Levashov	04.10.1991	15		
Artur Nigmatullin	17.05.1991	15	(1)	
Defenders:	**DOB**	**M**	**(s)**	**G**
Maksim Belyaev	30.09.1991	28		1
Aleksandr Denisov	23.02.1989	4	(1)	
Gia Grigalava (GEO)	05.08.1989	26		1
Abdul Kadiri Mohammed (GHA)	07.03.1996	20	(2)	1
Anri Khagush	23.09.1986	16	(5)	
Kirill Kombarov	22.01.1987	21	(1)	
Bakary Koné (BFA)	27.04.1988	1		
Víctor Álvarez (ESP)	14.03.1993	22	(1)	
Maksim Volodko (BLR)	10.11.1992	1	(1)	
Midfielders:	**DOB**	**M**	**(s)**	**G**
Mihail Aleksandrov (BUL)	11.06.1989	1		
Kantemir Berkhamov	07.08.1988	12	(4)	
Goran Čaušić (SRB)	05.05.1992	4	(1)	
Igor Gorbatenko	13.02.1989	22	(6)	3
Georgi Kostadinov (BUL)	07.09.1990	19	(7)	1
Sergey Tkachev	19.05.1989	20	(6)	5
Forwards:	**DOB**	**M**	**(s)**	**G**
Guram Adzhoev	27.02.1995		(5)	
Zelimkhan Bakaev	01.07.1996	21	(4)	8
Luka Đorđević (MNE)	09.07.1994	23		7
Yaroslav Ivakin	22.07.1998		(2)	
Evans Kangwa (ZAM)	21.06.1992	15	(10)	4
Daniil Lesovoy (UKR)	12.01.1998	3	(10)	2
Reziuan Mirzov	22.06.1993	18	(5)	6
Ognjen Ožegović (SRB)	09.06.1994	3	(5)	1
Trainer:	**DOB**	**M**		
Oleg Kononov	23.03.1966	14		
Igor Cherevchenko [13.11.2018]	21.08.1974	16		

Profesionalniy Fudbolnij Klub CSKA [Central Sport Club of the Army] Moskva

Founded: 27.08.1911
Stadium: VEB Arena, Moskva (30,000)

Goalkeepers:	**DOB**	**M**	**(s)**	**G**
Igor Akinfeev	08.04.1986	30		
Defenders:	**DOB**	**M**	**(s)**	**G**
Nikita Chernov	14.01.1996	10	(1)	
Igor Diveev	27.09.1999	10		
Hörður Magnússon (ISL)	11.02.1993	22	(1)	2
Mário Fernandes	19.09.1990	28		1
Kirill Nababkin	08.09.1986	23	(2)	
Rodrigo Nascimento França „Rodrigo Becão“ (BRA)	19.01.1996	28		
Georgiy Shchennikov	27.04.1991	16	(4)	1
Viktor Vasin	06.10.1988	4	(2)	
Midfielders:	**DOB**	**M**	**(s)**	**G**
Ilzat Akhmetov	31.12.1997	21	(5)	
Jaka Bijol (SVN)	05.02.1999	12	(11)	4
Kristijan Bistrović (CRO)	09.04.1998	12	(8)	2
Alan Dzagoev	17.06.1990	6	(1)	
Dmitri Efremov	01.04.1995	6	(8)	
Astemir Gordyushenko	30.03.1997		(2)	
Khetag Khosonov	18.06.1998	1	(4)	
Konstantin Kuchaev	18.03.1998		(3)	
Ivan Oblyakov	05.07.1998	22	(1)	3
Arnór Sigurðsson (ISL)	15.05.1999	14	(7)	5
Nikola Vlašić (CRO)	04.10.1997	25		5
Forwards:	**DOB**	**M**	**(s)**	**G**
Fedor Chalov	10.04.1998	27	(3)	15
Abel Mathías Hernández Platero(URU)	08.08.1990	5	(9)	3
Takuma Nishimura (JPN)	22.10.1996	4	(8)	2
Timur Zhamaletdinov	21.05.1997	4	(8)	3
Vitali Zhironkin	10.03.2000			
Trainer:	**DOB**	**M**		
Viktor Goncharenko	10.09.1977	30		

Fudbolnij Klub Dinamo Moskva

Founded: 18.04.1923
Stadium: Arena Khimki, Khimki (18,636)

Goalkeepers:	**DOB**	**M**	**(s)**	**G**
Anton Shunin	27.01.1987	30		
Defenders:	**DOB**	**M**	**(s)**	**G**
Roman Evgenyev	23.02.1999	16	(2)	
Sebastian Holmén (SWE)	29.04.1992	17	(3)	
Aleksey Kozlov	25.12.1986	22	(1)	1
Grigori Morozov	06.06.1994	18	(4)	
Vladimir Moskvichev	02.03.2000	2	(3)	
Konstantin Rausch	15.03.1990	13	(3)	
Vladimir Rykov	13.11.1987	11	(3)	1
Toni Šunjić (BIH)	15.12.1988	29		1
Ivan Temnikov	28.01.1989		(5)	
Midfielders:	**DOB**	**M**	**(s)**	**G**
João Natailton Ramos dos Santos „Joãozinho“ (BRA)	25.12.1988	29	(1)	4
Danil Lipovoy	22.09.1999		(3)	
Anton Sosnin	27.01.1990	5	(7)	
Samba Sow (MLI)	29.04.1989	15	(2)	
Anton Terekhov	30.01.1998		(2)	
Abdul-Aziz Tetteh (GHA)	25.05.1990	25		1
Artur Yusupov	01.09.1989	12		1
Forwards:	**DOB**	**M**	**(s)**	**G**
Fiodor Černych (LTU)	21.05.1991	18	(4)	2
Vyacheslav Grulev	23.03.1999	1	(10)	2
Evgeniy Lutsenko	25.02.1987	26	(4)	4
Evgeni Markov	07.07.1994	8	(15)	3
Miguel Felipe Nunes Cardoso (POR)	19.06.1994	14	(2)	3
Kirill Panchenko	16.10.1989	19	(4)	5
Trainer:	**DOB**	**M**		
Dmitriy Khokhlov	22.12.1975	30		

Fudbolnij Klub Krasnodar

Founded: 22.02.2008
Stadium: Krasnodar Stadium, Krasnodar (34,291)

Goalkeepers:	DOB	M	(s)	G
Stanislav Kritsyuk	01.12.1990	12		
Matvei Safonov	25.02.1999	14		
Andrey Sinitsyn	23.06.1988	4	(1)	
Defenders:	**DOB**	**M**	**(s)**	**G**
Jón Fjóluson (ISL)	10.04.1989	5	(1)	
Nikolay Markov	20.04.1985	3		
Aleksandr Martinovich (BLR)	26.08.1987	28		
Sergey Petrov	02.01.1991	22		1
Cristian Leonel Ramírez Zambrano (ECU)	12.08.1994	17	(6)	
Roman Shishkin	27.01.1987	1	(2)	
Dmitriy Skopintsev	02.03.1997	5	(4)	1
Uroš Spajić (SRB)	13.02.1993	28		
Midfielders:	**DOB**	**M**	**(s)**	**G**
Viktor Johan Anton Claesson (SWE)	02.01.1992	28	(1)	12
Christian Alberto Cueva Bravo (PER)	23.11.1991	3	(12)	
Yuriy Gazinskiy	20.07.1989	27	(1)	2
Artem Golubev	21.01.1999		(2)	
Charles Kaboré (BFA)	09.02.1988	24		1
Pavel Mamaev	17.09.1988	8	(2)	3
Kristoffer Olsson (SWE)	30.06.1995	1	(5)	
Mauricio Ernesto Pereyra Antonini (URU)	15.03.1990	21	(5)	3
Dmitriy Stotskiy	01.12.1989	19	(6)	1
Daniil Utkin	12.10.1999	2	(5)	1
Ilya Zhigulev	01.02.1996	1	(1)	
Forwards:	**DOB**	**M**	**(s)**	**G**
Ariclenes da Silva Ferreira „Ari“	11.12.1985	13	(3)	8
Ivan Ignatyev	06.01.1999	13	(7)	7
Tornike Okriashvili (GEO)	12.02.1992		(2)	
Fedor Smolov	09.02.1990	2		1
Magomed Suleymanov	16.12.1999	3	(17)	8
Wanderson Maciel Sousa Campos (BRA)	07.10.1994	26	(4)	6
Trainer:	**DOB**	**M**		
Murad Musaev	10.11.1983	30		

Professionalnij Fudbolnij Klub Krylia Sovetov Samara

Founded: 1942
Stadium: Samara Arena, Samara (44,918)

Goalkeepers:	DOB	M	(s)	G
Evgeniy Konyukhov	21.11.1986	7		
Sergey Ryzhikov	19.09.1980	23		
Defenders:	**DOB**	**M**	**(s)**	**G**
Taras Burlak	22.02.1990	22	(1)	2
Nikita Chicherin	18.08.1990	15	(2)	
Vitaliy Denisov (UZB)	23.02.1987	15		
José Nadson Ferreira (BRA)	18.10.1984	7		
Vladimir Poluyakhtov	11.07.1989	11	(3)	
Agustín Maximiliano Rogel Paita (URU)	17.10.1997	14		
Miral Samardžič (SVN)	17.02.1987	21	(1)	1
Roman Shishkin	27.01.1987	12		
Midfielders:	**DOB**	**M**	**(s)**	**G**
Azer Aliev	12.05.1994		(1)	
Jano Ananidze (GEO)	10.10.1992	8		1
Paul Viorel Anton (ROU)	10.05.1991	15	(8)	2
Evgeniy Bashkirov	06.07.1991	11	(4)	
Alan Chochiev	07.09.1991	9		
Gennady Kiselev	03.01.1999		(1)	
Oleg Lanin	22.01.1996	6	(2)	
Srđan Mijailović (SRB)	10.11.1993	5	(1)	
Mohammed Rabiu (GHA)	31.12.1989	8	(1)	
Aleksandr Samedov	19.07.1984	8	(1)	
Georgi Tigiev	26.05.1995	1	(1)	
Mikhail Tikhonov	17.07.1998		(1)	
Artiom Timofeev	12.01.1994	9	(1)	1
Denis Tkachuk	02.07.1989	15	(6)	2
Georgii Zotov	12.01.1990	20	(6)	
Forwards:	**DOB**	**M**	**(s)**	**G**
Maksim Kanunnikov	14.07.1991	19	(1)	5
Sergey Kornilenko (BLR)	14.06.1983	12	(9)	4
Yohan Mollo (FRA)	18.07.1989	4	(3)	
Ramil Sheydaev (AZE)	15.03.1996	10	(8)	4
Aleksandr Sobolev	07.03.1997	5	(7)	1
Vanja Vučićević (SRB)	22.03.1998	1	(2)	
Pavel Yakovlev	07.04.1991	8	(9)	1
Anton Zinkovskiy	14.04.1996	9	(4)	1
Trainer:	**DOB**	**M**		
Andrey Tikhonov	16.10.1970	9		
Miodrag Božović (MNE) [05.10.2018]	22.06.1968	21		

Fudbolnij Klub Lokomotiv Moskva

Founded: 23.07.1922
Stadium: Lokomotiv Stadium, Moskva (28,800)

Goalkeepers:	DOB	M	(s)	G
Guilherme Alvin Marinato	12.12.1985	30		
Defenders:	**DOB**	**M**	**(s)**	**G**
Vedran Ćorluka (CRO)	05.02.1986	20	(1)	
Benedikt Höwedes (GER)	29.02.1988	15	(2)	3
Brian Oladapo Idowu (NGA)	18.05.1992	6	(7)	
Solomon Kverkvelia (GEO)	06.02.1992	30		1
Ivan Lapshov	01.05.1999		(1)	
Mikhail Lysov	29.01.1998	6	(2)	
Stanislav Magkeev	27.03.1999		(1)	
Boris Rotenberg (FIN)	19.05.1986		(1)	
Maciej Rybus (POL)	19.08.1989	16		1
Midfielders:	**DOB**	**M**	**(s)**	**G**
Dmitry Barinov	11.09.1996	17	(6)	1
Igor Denisov	17.05.1984	17		
Vladislav Ignatiev	20.01.1987	25	(1)	
Grzegorz Krychowiak (POL)	29.01.1990	27		2
Manuel Henriques Tavares Fernandes (POR)	05.02.1986	16	(4)	4
Aleksey Miranchuk	17.10.1995	30		3
Anton Miranchuk	17.10.1995	21	(4)	11
Dmitriy Tarasov	18.03.1987	4	(5)	
Forwards:	**DOB**	**M**	**(s)**	**G**
Éderzito António Macedo Lopes „Éder“ (POR)	22.12.1987	10	(12)	1
Jefferson Agustin Farfán Guadalupe (PER)	26.10.1984	17	(3)	8
Khvicha Kvaratskhelia (GEO)	12.02.2001	1	(6)	1
Fedor Smolov	09.02.1990	17	(5)	6
Roman Tugarev	22.07.1998	1	(4)	
Rifat Zhemaletdinov	20.09.1996	4	(9)	1
Trainer:	**DOB**	**M**		
Yuriy Semin	11.05.1947	30		

Fudbolnij Klub Orenburg

Founded: 1976
Stadium: Gazovik Stadium, Orenburg (7,500)

Goalkeepers:	DOB	M	(s)	G
Aleksandr Dovbnya	10.04.1987	8		
Evgeni Frolov	05.02.1988	22		
Defenders:	**DOB**	**M**	**(s)**	**G**
Dmitri Andreev	26.09.1980	11	(3)	
Silvije Begić (CRO)	03.06.1993	23		2
Saveliy Kozlov	19.01.1997	8		
Andrey Malykh	24.08.1988	22	(1)	
Adessoye Oyewole	18.09.1982	22		3
Vitaliy Shakov	09.01.1991	5	(1)	
Sergey Terekhov	27.06.1990	28		3
Midfielders:	**DOB**	**M**	**(s)**	**G**
Vadim Afonin (UZB)	29.09.1987	19	(7)	1
Sergey Breev	22.04.1987	12	(1)	1
Grigoriy Chirkin	26.02.1986	6	(9)	1
Artyom Kulishev	26.08.1993	1	(8)	1
Nikita Malyarov	23.10.1989	8	(2)	
Danijel Miškić (CRO)	11.10.1993	26	(1)	1
Denis Popovič (SVN)	15.10.1989	21	(3)	2
Ricardo Alves Coelho da Silva (POR)	25.03.1993	3	(7)	3
Mikhail Sivakov (BLR)	16.01.1988	19	(3)	1
Forwards:	**DOB**	**M**	**(s)**	**G**
Andrea Chukanov	18.12.1995	4	(15)	2
Đorđe Despotović (SRB)	04.03.1992	20	(3)	4
Artem Galadzhan	22.05.1998	4	(4)	2
Andrey Kozlov	23.02.1989	9	(12)	3
Aleksey Sutormin	10.01.1994	29		8
Trainer:	**DOB**	**M**		
Vladimir Fedotov	12.08.1966	30		

Fudbolnij Klub Rostov

Founded: 1930
Stadium: Rostov Arena, Rostov-na-Donu (37,868)

Goalkeepers:	DOB	M	(s)	G
Ilya Abaev	02.08.1981	11		
Sergey Pesyakov	16.12.1988	19		
Defenders:	**DOB**	**M**	**(s)**	**G**
Evgeniy Chernov	23.10.1992	12		
Dennis Hadžikadunić (SWE)	09.07.1998	8		
Sverrir Ingason (ISL)	05.08.1993	17		2
Arseniy Logashov	20.08.1991	10	(3)	
Miha Mevlja (SVN)	12.06.1990	7		
Ivan Novoseltsev	25.08.1991	8	(1)	
Sergey Parshivlyuk	18.03.1989	22	(2)	1
Ragnar Sigurðsson (ISL)	19.06.1986	27		
Dmitriy Skopintsev	02.03.1997	15		
Maciej Wilusz (POL)	25.09.1988	16		
Midfielders:	**DOB**	**M**	**(s)**	**G**
Roman Eremenko (FIN)	19.03.1987	9		3
Alexandru Gaţcan (MDA)	27.03.1984	23	(1)	1
Danil Glebov	03.11.1999	6	(2)	
Ayaz Guliev	27.11.1996	13	(1)	1
Aleksey Ionov	18.02.1989	20	(5)	6
Tsimafei Kalachev (BLR)	01.05.1981	5	(7)	
Mathias Normann (NOR)	28.05.1996	9		
Konstantin Pliev	26.10.1996	2	(2)	
Anton Salétros	12.04.1996	6		
Artem Shchadin	01.11.1992	2	(4)	
Artur Yusupov	01.09.1989	10	(3)	
Aleksandr Zuev	26.06.1996	9	(13)	1
Forwards:	**DOB**	**M**	**(s)**	**G**
Viðar Örn Kjartansson (ISL)	11.03.1990	1	(7)	
Reziuan Mirzov	22.06.1993		(3)	
Ivelin Popov (BUL)	26.10.1987	8	(4)	1
Eldor Shomurodov (UZB)	29.06.1995	10	(16)	3
Björn Sigurðarson (ISL)	26.02.1991	21	(5)	5
Baktiyor Zaynutdinov (KAZ)	02.04.1998	4	(6)	
Trainer:	**DOB**	**M**		
Valeriy Karpin	02.02.1969	30		

Fudbolnij Klub Rubin Kazan

Founded: 20.04.1958
Stadium: Kazan Arena, Kazan (45,379)

Goalkeepers:	DOB	M	(s)	G
Egor Baburin	09.08.1993	6		
Soslan Dzhanaev	13.03.1987	4		
Ivan Konovalov	18.08.1994	20		
Defenders:	**DOB**	**M**	**(s)**	**G**
Rail Abdullin	06.08.2000	1		
César González Navas (ESP)	14.02.1980	17		
José Manuel Flores Moreno „Chico" (ESP)	06.03.1987	8		
Vladimir Granat	22.05.1987	13	(1)	
Igor Kalinin (UKR)	11.11.1995	5	(1)	1
Ruslan Kambolov	01.01.1990	25	(2)	
Fedor Kudryashov	05.04.1987	8	(1)	
Egor Sorokin	04.11.1995	21	(6)	6
Danil Stepanov	25.01.2000	7	(3)	
Ibrahim Tsallagov	12.12.1990	16		
Filip Uremović (CRO)	11.02.1997	22	(1)	1
Vitali Ustinov	03.05.1991	17	(3)	
Midfielders:	**DOB**	**M**	**(s)**	**G**
Roman Akbashev	01.11.1991	2	(3)	
Khoren Bairamyan (ARM)	07.01.1992	20	(4)	2
Evgeniy Bashkirov	06.07.1991	9	(3)	1
Igor Konovalov	08.07.1996	27		1
Pavel Mogilevets	25.01.1993	18	(9)	
Vladislav Panteleev	15.08.1996		(4)	
Vyacheslav Podberezkin	21.06.1992	17	(4)	1
Reza Shekari (IRN)	31.05.1998		(3)	
Forwards:	**DOB**	**M**	**(s)**	**G**
Sardar Azmoun (IRN)	01.01.1995	14		4
Aleksandr Bukharov	12.03.1985	6	(15)	
Dmitriy Poloz	12.07.1991	23	(4)	5
Artur Sagitov	07.01.2000	4	(9)	1
Trainer:	**DOB**	**M**		
Kurban Berdiyev (TKM)	25.08.1952	30		

Fudbolnij Klub Spartak Moskva

Founded: 18.04.1922
Stadium: Otkrytiye Arena, Moskva (45,360)

Goalkeepers:	DOB	M	(s)	G
Aleksandr Maksimenko	19.03.1998	22	(1)	
Artem Rebrov	04.03.1984	3		
Aleksandr Selikhov	07.04.1994	5		
Defenders:	**DOB**	**M**	**(s)**	**G**
Ayrton Lucas Dantas de Medeiros (BRA)	19.06.1997	12	(1)	
Salvatore Bocchetti (ITA)	30.11.1986	14	(1)	
Georgi Dzhikiya	21.11.1993	25	(1)	2
Andrey Eshchenko	09.02.1984	9	(3)	
Samuel Gigot (FRA)	12.10.1993	9		1
Ilya Kutepov	29.07.1993	9		
Marko Petković (SRB)	03.09.1992	3	(2)	
Nikolai Rasskazov	04.01.1998	16		1
Midfielders:	**DOB**	**M**	**(s)**	**G**
Jano Ananidze (GEO)	10.10.1992		(1)	
Roman Eremenko (FIN)	19.03.1987	1	(3)	
Fernando Lucas Martins (BRA)	03.03.1992	19	(1)	3
Ilya Gaponov	25.10.1997	5		
Denis Glushakov	27.01.1987	15	(3)	3
Ayaz Guliev	27.11.1996	9	(1)	1
Sofiane Hanni (ALG)	29.12.1990	15	(3)	1
Mikhail Ignatov	04.05.2000	3	(5)	1
Dmitriy Kombarov	22.01.1987	13		1
Aleksandr Lomovitskiy	27.01.1998	9	(8)	
Lorenzo Antonio Melgarejo Sanabria (PAR)	10.08.1990	19	(4)	3
Georgi Melkadze	04.04.1997	3	(7)	
Vladislav Panteleev	15.08.1996		(1)	
Aleksandr Samedov	19.07.1984	4	(4)	
Aleksandr Tashaev	23.06.1994	10	(7)	
Artiom Timofeev	12.01.1994	1	(6)	1
Nail Umyarov	27.06.2000	2	(3)	
Roman Zobnin	11.02.1994	25	(1)	1
Forwards:	**DOB**	**M**	**(s)**	**G**
Maksim Glushenkov	28.07.1999		(5)	
Luiz Adriano de Souza da Silva (BRA)	12.04.1987	16	(7)	6
Sylvanus Nimely (LBR)	04.09.1998		(1)	
Pedro Rocha Neves (BRA)	01.10.1994	1		
Ivelin Popov (BUL)	26.10.1987	6	(7)	
Quincy Anton Promes (NED)	04.01.1992	5		1
José Luís Mendes Andrade „Zé Luís“ (CPV)	24.01.1991	22	(3)	10
Trainer:	**DOB**	**M**		
Massimo Carrera (ITA)	22.04.1964	11		
Raúl Ruiz González-Riancho (ESP) [22.10.2018]	13.02.1960	3		
Oleg Kononov [12.11.2018]	23.03.1966	16		

Fudbolnij Klub Ufa

Founded: 2009
Stadium: Neftyanik Stadium, Ufa (15,234)

Goalkeepers:	DOB	M	(s)	G
Aleksandr Belenov	13.09.1986	29		
Georgi Sheliya	11.12.1988	1		
Defenders:	**DOB**	**M**	**(s)**	**G**
Pavel Alikin	06.03.1984	20	(1)	1
Igor Diveev	27.09.1999	1	(1)	
Bojan Jokić (SVN)	17.05.1986	20		
Daniil Krugovoy	28.05.1998	8	(1)	
Ionuţ Nedelcearu (ROU)	25.04.1996	26		1
Aleksey Nikitin	27.01.1992	9	(1)	
Aleksandr Putsko	24.02.1993	16		
Aleksandr Sukhov	03.01.1986	12	(2)	
Jemal Tabidze (GEO)	18.03.1996	13		
Denis Tumasyan	24.04.1985	3	(1)	
Dmitri Zhivoglyadov	29.05.1994	20	(1)	
Midfielders:	**DOB**	**M**	**(s)**	**G**
Azer Aliev	12.05.1994		(13)	
Igor Bezdenezhnykh	08.08.1996	4	(2)	
Cătălin Carp (MDA)	20.10.1993	23	(1)	2
Ivan Oblyakov	05.07.1998	4	(1)	
Ivan Paurević (CRO)	01.07.1991	13	(9)	
Vero Salatić (SRB)	14.11.1985	10	(2)	
Oliver Thill (LUX)	17.12.1996	18	(4)	1
Ondřej Vaněk (CZE)	05.07.1990	11	(6)	4
Azamat Zaseev	29.04.1988	2	(3)	
Forwards:	**DOB**	**M**	**(s)**	**G**
Lovro Bizjak (SVN)	12.11.1993	8	(12)	2
Kehinde Abdul Feyi Fatai (NGA)	19.02.1990	1	(1)	
Sylvester Emeka Igboun (NGA)	08.09.1990	25	(2)	9
Vyacheslav Krotov	14.02.1993	8	(11)	1
Yerkebulan Seidakhmet (KAZ)	04.02.2000		(1)	
Dmitry Sysuyev	13.01.1988	20	(2)	2
Andrés Vombergar (ARG)	20.11.1994	5	(6)	1
Trainer:	**DOB**	**M**		
Sergey Tomarov	25.05.1982	13		
Dmitri Kirichenko [07.11.2018]	17.01.1977	7		
Vadim Evseev [28.03.2019]	08.01.1976	10		

Fudbolnij Klub Ural Yekaterinburg

Founded: 1930
Stadium: Central Stadium, Yekaterinburg (35,696)

Goalkeepers:	DOB	M	(s)	G
Yaroslav Godzyur (UKR)	06.03.1985	30		
Defenders:	**DOB**	**M**	**(s)**	**G**
Gregor Balažic (SVN)	12.02.1988	17		
Sergei Bryzgalov	15.11.1992	13	(3)	1
Aleksandr Dantsev	14.10.1984	1	(2)	
Dominik Dinga (SRB)	07.04.1998	1	(1)	
Varazdat Haroyan (ARM)	24.08.1992	12	(4)	1
Dzhamaldin Khodzhaniyazov	18.07.1996	1		
Denis Kulakov (UKR)	01.05.1986	28		1
Mikhail Merkulov	26.01.1994	27	(1)	
Denis Polyakov (BLR)	17.04.1991	10	(1)	
Stefan Strandberg (NOR)	25.07.1990	10		
Midfielders:	**DOB**	**M**	**(s)**	**G**
Marco Aratore (SUI)	04.06.1991	9	(10)	
Yuriy Bavin	05.02.1994	7	(3)	1
Eric Cosmin Bicfalvi (ROU)	05.02.1988	25	(1)	6
Petrus Boumal (CMR)	20.04.1993	22	(1)	
Andrey Egorychev	14.02.1993	12	(8)	1
Othman El Kabir (NED)	17.07.1991	24	(4)	4
Roman Emelyanov	08.05.1992	7	(5)	
Aleksey Evseev	30.03.1994	1	(4)	
Artem Fiedler	14.07.1983	9	(4)	
Anatoliy Katrich	09.07.1994		(1)	
Ilya Zhigulev	01.02.1996	2	(3)	
Forwards:	**DOB**	**M**	**(s)**	**G**
Nikolai Dimitrov (BUL)	15.10.1987	26	(1)	5
Vladimir Ilyin	20.05.1992	12	(8)	1
Andrey Panyukov	25.09.1994	15	(6)	6
Pavel Pogrebnyak	08.11.1983	9	(2)	3
Artem Yusupov	29.04.1997		(3)	
Trainer:	**DOB**	**M**		
Dmitri Parfenov	11.09.1974	30		

Fudbolnij Klub Yenisey Krasnoyarsk

Founded: 1937
Stadium: Central Stadium, Krasnoyarsk (22,500)

Goalkeepers:	DOB	M	(s)	G
Maksim Edapin	03.04.2000		(1)	
Mikhail Filippov	10.06.1992	3		
Yuriy Nesterenko	12.06.1991	10		
David Yurchenko	27.03.1986	17		
Defenders:	**DOB**	**M**	**(s)**	**G**
Rade Dugalić (SRB)	05.11.1992	14		1
Ali Gadzhibekov	06.08.1989	20		1
Shamil Gasanov	30.07.1993	3		
Aleksey Gritsaenko	25.05.1995	14	(2)	
Valerii Kiçin (KGZ)	12.10.1992	25	(1)	2
Petar Zanev (BUL)	18.10.1985	14	(1)	1
Dmitriy Yatchenko	25.08.1986	22		2
Midfielders:	**DOB**	**M**	**(s)**	**G**
Oleg Danchenko (UKR)	01.08.1994	11		
Azim Fatullaev	07.06.1986	7	(3)	
Aleksandr Kharitonov	04.04.1983		(1)	
Arsen Khubulov	13.12.1990	3	(5)	
Mikhail Komkov	01.10.1984	12	(7)	1
Pavel Komolov	10.03.1989	15	(7)	1
Mikhail Kostyukov	09.08.1991	8	(5)	4
Fegor Ogude (NGA)	29.07.1987	26		1
Pavel Rozhkov	31.12.1986	2	(2)	
Babacar Sarr (SEN)	15.02.1991	13		1
Maksim Semakin	26.10.1983	8	(3)	
Dmitriy Torbinskiy	28.04.1984	12	(2)	1
Aleksandr Zotov	27.08.1990	22	(3)	1
Forwards:	**DOB**	**M**	**(s)**	**G**
Darko Bodul (AUT)	11.01.1989	7	(3)	
Enis Gavazaj	21.03.1995	2	(5)	
Aleksandr Kutyin	13.02.1986	12	(6)	3
Marko Obradović (SRB)	30.06.1991	2	(11)	
Artur Sarkisov (ARM)	19.01.1987	14	(9)	1
Konstantin Savichev	06.03.1994	5	(3)	
Aleksandr Sobolev	07.03.1997	7	(3)	3
Trainer:	**DOB**	**M**		
Dmitri Alenichev	20.10.1972	30		

Fudbolnij Klub Zenit Saint Petersburg

Founded: 25.05.1925
Stadium: Krestovsky Stadium, Saint Petersburg (64,287)

Goalkeepers:	DOB	M	(s)	G
Mikhail Kerzhakov	28.01.1987	1		
Andrei Lunev	13.11.1991	29		
Defenders:	**DOB**	**M**	**(s)**	**G**
Aleksandr Anyukov	28.09.1982	7	(9)	
Branislav Ivanović (SRB)	22.02.1984	28		1
Emanuel Hernán Mammana (ARG)	10.02.1996	4	(2)	
Miha Mevlja (SVN)	12.06.1990	6		
Elmir Nabiullin	08.03.1995	10	(1)	
Luís Carlos Novo Neto (POR)	26.05.1988	13		
Yaroslav Rakitskiy (UKR)	03.08.1989	12		3
Evgeniy Chernov	23.10.1992	5		
Igor Smolnikov	08.08.1988	21	(2)	1
Denis Terentyev	13.08.1992		(1)	
Midfielders:	**DOB**	**M**	**(s)**	**G**
Wilmar Enrique Barrios Teherán (COL)	17.10.1993	10		1
Aleksandr Erokhin	13.10.1989	13	(3)	6
Hernani Azevedo Junior (BRA)	27.03.1994	5	(9)	1
Claudio Matías Kranevitter (ARG)	21.05.1993	2	(4)	
Daler Kuzyaev	15.01.1993	16	(2)	2
Claudio Marchisio (ITA)	19.01.1986	5	(4)	2
Leon Musaev	25.01.1999	1	(3)	
Christian Fernando Noboa Tello (ECU)	09.04.1985	8	(3)	
Magomed Ozdoev	05.11.1992	10	(6)	
Leandro Daniel Paredes (ARG)	29.06.1994	15		3
Emiliano Ariel Rigoni (ARG)	04.02.1993	8	(3)	3
Oleg Shatov	29.07.1990	11	(8)	3
Yuriy Zhirkov	20.08.1983	12		
Forwards:	**DOB**	**M**	**(s)**	**G**
Sardar Azmoun (IRN)	01.01.1995	12		9
Sebastián Driussi (ARG)	09.02.1996	21	(6)	11
Artyom Dzyuba	22.08.1988	27		8
Aleksandr Kokorin	19.03.1991		(3)	
Róbert Mak (SVK)	08.03.1991	17	(4)	1
Ilya Vorobyov	11.07.1999			
Anton Zabolotny	13.06.1991	1	(15)	
Trainer:	**DOB**	**M**		
Sergei Semak	27.02.1976	30		

SECOND LEVEL
Russian National Football League 2018/2019

1.	FK Tambov (*Promoted*)	38	21	10	7	55	-	35	73
2.	PFK Sochi (*Promoted*)	38	19	12	7	63	-	34	69
3.	FK Tom Tomsk (*Promotion Play-offs*)	38	17	13	8	40	-	25	64
4.	FK Nizhny Novgorod (*Promotion Play-offs*)	38	18	8	12	41	-	31	62
5.	FK Chertanovo Moskva	38	17	10	11	65	-	53	61
6.	FK Shinnik Yaroslavl	38	16	12	10	42	-	31	60
7.	FK SKA-Khabarovsk	38	15	13	10	46	-	41	58
8.	FK Avangard Kursk	38	16	8	14	48	-	42	56
9.	FK Khimki	38	14	11	13	47	-	49	53
10.	FK Krasnodar-2	38	12	15	11	45	-	52	51
11.	FK Rotor Volgograd	38	12	14	12	34	-	36	50
12.	FK Mordovia Saransk	38	12	11	15	37	-	46	47
13.	FK Luch Vladivostok	38	10	17	11	29	-	28	47
14.	FK Spartak-2 Moskva	38	12	10	16	45	-	47	46
15.	FK Armavir	38	10	14	14	32	-	44	44
16.	FK Baltika Kaliningrad	38	10	12	16	38	-	52	42
17.	FK Fakel Voronezh	38	9	14	15	36	-	40	41
18.	FK Sibir Novosibirsk (*Relegated*)	38	8	13	17	28	-	45	37
19.	FK Zenit-2 Saint Petersburg (*Relegated*)	38	7	7	24	33	-	57	28
20.	FK Tyumen (*Relegated*)	38	5	16	17	30	-	46	25

NATIONAL TEAM

INTERNATIONAL MATCHES
(16.07.2018 – 15.07.2019)

07.09.2018	Trabzon	Turkey - Russia	1-2(1-1)	(UNL)
10.09.2018	Rostov-na-Donu	Russia - Czech Republic	5-1(3-0)	(F)
11.10.2018	Kaliningrad	Russia - Sweden	0-0	(UNL)
14.10.2018	Sochi	Russia - Turkey	2-0(1-0)	(UNL)
15.11.2018	Leipzig	Germany - Russia	3-0(3-0)	(F)
20.11.2018	Stockholm	Sweden - Russia	2-0(1-0)	(UNL)
21.03.2019	Bruxelles	Belgium - Russia	3-1(2-1)	(ECQ)
24.03.2019	Nur-Sultan	Kazakhstan - Russia	0-4(0-2)	(ECQ)
08.06.2019	Saransk	Russia - San Marino	9-0(4-0)	(ECQ)
11.06.2019	Nizhny Novgorod	Russia - Cyprus	1-0(1-0)	(ECQ)

07.09.2018 TURKEY - RUSSIA 1-2(1-1) UEFA Nations League B, Group 2
Medical Park Stadyumu, Trabzon; Referee: Artur Manuel Soares Dias (Portugal); Attendance: 27,423
RUS: Andrey Lunyov, Mário Figueira Fernandes, Roman Neustädter, Fyodor Kudryashov (82.Konstantin Rausch), Georgiy Dzhikiya, Aleksandr Yerokhin, Yuriy Gazinskiy, Denis Cheryshev (73.Pavel Mogilevets), Roman Zobnin, Daler Kuzyayev (79.Aleksey Ionov), Artyom Dzyuba (Cap). Trainer: Stanislav Cherchesov.
Goals: Denis Cheryshev (13), Artyom Dzyuba (49).

10.09.2018 RUSSIA - CZECH REPUBLIC 5-1(3-0) Friendly International
Rostov Arena, Rostov-na-Donu; Referee: Äliyar Ağhayev (Azerbaijan); Attendance: 45,000
RUS: Andrey Lunyov, Mário Figueira Fernandes (64.Igor Smolnikov), Roman Neustädter, Konstantin Rausch (87.Yegor Sorokin), Andrey Semyonov, Aleksey Ionov (62.Roman Zobnin), Aleksandr Yerokhin, Yuriy Gazinskiy (Cap) (85.Ruslan Kambolov), Denis Cheryshev (80.Dmitriy Stotskiy), Daler Kuzyayev, Anton Zabolotny (73.Dmitriy Poloz). Trainer: Stanislav Cherchesov.
Goals: Aleksey Ionov (8), Anton Zabolotny (24), Aleksey Ionov (29 penalty), Aleksandr Yerokhin (78), Dmitriy Poloz (83).

11.10.2018 RUSSIA - SWEDEN 0-0 UEFA Nations League B, Group 2
Stadion Kaliningrad, Kaliningrad; Referee: Referee: Luca Banti (Italy); Attendance: 31,698
RUS: Guilherme Alvim Marinato, Mário Figueira Fernandes, Roman Neustädter, Konstantin Rausch, Georgiy Dzhikiya, Aleksey Ionov (76.Daler Kuzyayev), Yuriy Gazinskiy, Denis Cheryshev (87.Anton Zabolotny), Roman Zobnin, Aleksandr Golovin, Artyom Dzyuba (Cap). Trainer: Stanislav Cherchesov.

14.10.2018 RUSSIA - TURKEY 2-0(1-0) UEFA Nations League B, Group 2
Fisht Olympic Stadium, Sochi; Referee: Paweł Raczkowski (Poland); Attendance: 38,288
RUS: Guilherme Alvim Marinato, Fyodor Kudryashov, Mário Figueira Fernandes, Roman Neustädter, Georgiy Dzhikiya, Aleksey Ionov (82.Ruslan Kambolov), Yuriy Gazinskiy, Roman Zobnin, Daler Kuzyayev (71.Denis Cheryshev), Aleksandr Golovin (90+2.Dmitriy Poloz), Artyom Dzyuba (Cap). Trainer: Stanislav Cherchesov.
Goals: Roman Neustädter (20), Denis Cheryshev (78).

15.11.2018 GERMANY - RUSSIA 3-0(3-0) Friendly International
Red Bull Arena, Leipzig; Referee: Sandro Schärer (Switzerland); Attendance: 35,288
RUS: Andrey Lunyov, Kirill Nababkin (78.Andrey Semyonov), Roman Neustädter, Konstantin Rausch (73.Fyodor Kudryashov), Georgiy Dzhikiya, Aleksey Ionov (75.Dmitriy Poloz), Aleksandr Yerokhin, Yuriy Gazinskiy (Cap), Daler Kuzyayev (71.Ruslan Kambolov), Aleksey Miranchuk (61.Anton Miranchuk), Ari (55.Anton Zabolotny). Trainer: Stanislav Cherchesov.

20.11.2018 SWEDEN - RUSSIA 2-0(1-0) UEFA Nations League B, Group 2
Friends Arena, Stockholm; Referee: Benoît Bastien (France); Attendance: 20,223
RUS: Andrey Lunyov, Kirill Nababkin, Roman Neustädter, Georgiy Dzhikiya, Aleksey Ionov (69.Anton Zabolotny), Vladislav Ignatyev, Aleksandr Yerokhin (77.Ari), Yuriy Gazinskiy, Daler Kuzyayev, Artyom Dzyuba (Cap), Dmitriy Poloz (46.Ruslan Kambolov). Trainer: Stanislav Cherchesov.

21.03.2019 BELGIUM - RUSSIA 3-1(2-1) 16th EC. Qualifiers
Stade "Roi Baudouin", Bruxelles; Referee: Ovidiu Alin Haţegan (Romania); Attendance: 34,245
RUS: Guilherme Alvim Marinato, Mário Figueira Fernandes, Kirill Nababkin, Fyodor Kudryashov, Yuriy Zhirkov, Georgiy Dzhikiya, Denis Cheryshev (64.Fyodor Chalov), Daler Kuzyayev (26.Anton Miranchuk), Aleksandr Golovin [*sent off 90*], Ilzat Akhmetov, Artyom Dzyuba (Cap) (77.Fyodor Smolov). Trainer: Stanislav Cherchesov.
Goal: Denis Cheryshev (16).

24.03.2019 KAZAKHSTAN - RUSSIA 0-4(0-2) 16th EC. Qualifiers
Astana Arena, Nur-Sultan; Referee: Slavko Vinčić (Slovenia); Attendance: 29,582
RUS: Guilherme Alvim Marinato, Mário Figueira Fernandes, Fyodor Kudryashov, Andrey Semyonov, Georgiy Dzhikiya, Aleksey Ionov (61.Vladislav Ignatyev), Yuriy Gazinskiy, Magomed Ozdoyev, Denis Cheryshev, Ilzat Akhmetov (72.Aleksey Miranchuk), Artyom Dzyuba (Cap) (82.Fyodor Chalov). Trainer: Stanislav Cherchesov.
Goals: Denis Cheryshev (19, 45+2), Artyom Dzyuba (52), Abzal Beysebekov (62 own goal).

08.06.2019 RUSSIA - SAN MARINO 9-0(4-0) 16th EC. Qualifiers
Mordovia Arena, Saransk; Referee: Mohammed Al Hakim (Sweden); Attendance: 42,241
RUS: Guilherme Alvim Marinato, Mário Figueira Fernandes, Fyodor Kudryashov, Andrey Semyonov, Georgiy Dzhikiya, Magomed Ozdoyev, Roman Zobnin (72.Dmitriy Barinov), Aleksandr Golovin, Aleksey Miranchuk (60.Aleksey Ionov), Anton Miranchuk (60.Fyodor Smolov), Artyom Dzyuba (Cap). Trainer: Stanislav Cherchesov.
Goals: Michele Cevoli (25 own goal), Artyom Dzyuba (31 penalty), Fyodor Kudryashov (36), Anton Miranchuk (41), Artyom Dzyuba (73, 76), Fyodor Smolov (77, 83), Artyom Dzyuba (88).

11.06.2019 RUSSIA - CYPRUS 1-0(1-0) 16th EC. Qualifiers

Nizhny Novgorod Stadium, Nizhny Novgorod; Referee: Marco Di Bello (Italy); Attendance: 42,228

RUS: Guilherme Alvim Marinato, Mário Figueira Fernandes, Fyodor Kudryashov, Andrey Semyonov, Magomed Ozdoyev, Georgiy Dzhikiya, Aleksey Ionov (90+2.Ilzat Akhmetov), Roman Zobnin (78.Dmitriy Barinov), Aleksandr Golovin, Anton Miranchuk (63.Aleksey Miranchuk), Artyom Dzyuba (Cap). Trainer: Stanislav Cherchesov.

Goal: Aleksey Ionov (38).

NATIONAL TEAM PLAYERS
(16.07.2018 – 15.07.2019)

Name	DOB	Caps	Goals	2018/2019:	*Club*
					Goalkeepers
GUILHERME Alvim Marinato	12.12.1985	**8**	**0**	2018/2019:	*FK Lokomotiv Moskva*
Andrey LUNYOV	13.11.1991	**7**	**0**	2018:	*FK Zenit Saint Petersburg*
					Defenders
Georgiy DZHIKIYA	21.11.1993	**17**	**0**	2018/2019:	*FK Spartak Moskva*
Mário Figueira FERNANDES	19.09.1990	**18**	**1**	2018/2019:	*FK CSKA Moskva*
Vladislav IGNATYEV	20.01.1987	**5**	**0**	2018/2019:	*FK Lokomotiv Moskva*
Fyodor KUDRYASHOV	05.04.1987	**30**	**1**	2018: 31.01.2019->	*FK Rubin Kazan* *İstanbul Başakşehir FK (TUR)*
Kirill NABABKIN	08.09.1986	**5**	**0**	2018/2019:	*FK CSKA Moskva*
Roman NEUSTÄDTER	18.02.1988	**12**	**1**	2018:	*Fenerbahçe SK İstanbul (TUR)*
Konstantin RAUSCH	15.03.1990	**9**	**0**	2018:	*FK Dinamo Moskva*
Andrey SEMYONOV	24.03.1989	**11**	**0**	2018/2019:	*FK Akhmat Grozny*
Igor SMOLNIKOV	08.08.1988	**29**	**0**	2018:	*FK Zenit Saint Petersburg*
Yegor SOROKIN	04.11.1995	**1**	**0**	2018:	*FK Rubin Kazan*
					Midfielders
Ilzat AKHMETOV	31.12.1997	**4**	**0**	2019:	*FK CSKA Moskva*
Dmitriy BARINOV	11.09.1996	**2**	**0**	2019:	*FK Lokomotiv Moskva*
Denis CHERYSHEV	26.12.1990	**22**	**9**	2018/2019:	*Valencia CF (ESP)*
Yuriy GAZINSKIY	20.07.1989	**17**	**1**	2018/2019:	*FK Krasnodar*
Aleksandr GOLOVIN	30.05.1996	**28**	**3**	2018/2019:	*AS Monaco FC (FRA)*
Aleksey IONOV	18.02.1989	**20**	**3**	2018/2019:	*FK Rostov*
Ruslan KAMBOLOV	01.01.1990	**6**	**0**	2018:	*FK Rubin Kazan*
Daler KUZYAYEV	15.01.1993	**18**	**0**	2018/2019:	*FK Zenit Saint Petersburg*
Aleksey MIRANCHUK	17.10.1995	**23**	**4**	2018/2019:	*FK Lokomotiv Moskva*
Anton MIRANCHUK	17.10. 1995	**10**	**1**	2018/2019:	*FK Lokomotiv Moskva*
Pavel MOGILEVETS	25.01.1993	**4**	**0**	2018:	*FK Rubin Kazan*
Magomed OZDOYEV	05.11.1992	**16**	**1**	2019:	*FK Zenit Saint Petersburg*
Dmitriy STOTSKIY	01.12.1989	**1**	**0**	2018:	*FK Krasnodar*
Aleksandr YEROKHIN	13.10.1989	**23**	**1**	2018:	*FK Zenit Saint Petersburg*
Yuri ZHIRKOV	20.08.1983	**88**	**2**	2019:	*FK Zenit Saint Petersburg*
Roman ZOBNIN	11.02.1994	**23**	**0**	2018/2019:	*FK Spartak Moskva*
					Forwards
Ariclenes da Silva Ferreira "ARI"	11.12.1985	**2**	**0**	2018:	*FK Krasnodar*
Fyodor CHALOV	10.04.1998	**2**	**0**	2019:	*FK CSKA Moskva*
Artyom DZYUBA	22.08.1988	**36**	**20**	2018/2019:	*FK Zenit Saint Petersburg*
Dmitriy POLOZ	12.07.1991	**19**	**3**	2018:	*FK Rubin Kazan*
Fyodor SMOLOV	05.02.1990	**39**	**14**	2018/2019:	*FK Lokomotiv Moskva*
Anton ZABOLOTNY	13.06.1991	**9**	**1**	2018:	*FK Zenit Saint Petersburg*

National team coach

Stanislav Salamovich CHERCHESOV (from 11.08.2016)	02.09.1963	35 M; 13 W; 9 D; 13 L; 61-47

SAN MARINO

The Country:

Repubblica di San Marino (Republic of San Marino)
Capital: San Marino
Surface: 61,2 km²
Inhabitants: 33,344 [2018]
Time: UTC+1

The FA:

Federazione Sammarinese Giuoco Calcio
Strada di Montecchio, 17 47890 San Marino
Tel: +378 0549 990 515
Founded: 1931
Member of FIFA since: 1988
Member of UEFA since: 1988
Website: www.fsgc.sm

NATIONAL TEAM RECORDS

First international match:	23.08.1986, Serravalle:	San Marino – Canada Olympic Team 0-1
Most international caps:	Andy Selva	- 73 caps (1998-2016)
Most international goals:	Andy Selva	- 8 goals / 73 caps (1998-2016)

UEFA EUROPEAN CHAMPIONSHIP	
1960	*Did not enter*
1964	*Did not enter*
1968	*Did not enter*
1972	*Did not enter*
1976	*Did not enter*
1980	*Did not enter*
1984	*Did not enter*
1988	*Did not enter*
1992	Qualifiers
1996	Qualifiers
2000	Qualifiers
2004	Qualifiers
2008	Qualifiers
2012	Qualifiers
2016	Qualifiers

FIFA WORLD CUP	
1930	*Did not enter*
1934	*Did not enter*
1938	*Did not enter*
1950	*Did not enter*
1954	*Did not enter*
1958	*Did not enter*
1962	*Did not enter*
1966	*Did not enter*
1970	*Did not enter*
1974	*Did not enter*
1978	*Did not enter*
1982	*Did not enter*
1986	*Did not enter*
1990	*Did not enter*
1994	Qualifiers
1998	Qualifiers
2002	Qualifiers
2006	Qualifiers
2010	Qualifiers
2014	Qualifiers
2018	Qualifiers

UEFA NATIONS LEAGUE
2018/2019 – League D

OLYMPIC FOOTBALL TOURNAMENTS 1908-2016							
1908	-	**1948**	*Did not enter*	**1972**	*Did not enter*	**1996**	Qualifiers
1912	-	**1952**	*Did not enter*	**1976**	*Did not enter*	**2000**	*Did not enter*
1920	-	**1956**	*Did not enter*	**1980**	*Did not enter*	**2004**	Qualifiers
1924	-	**1960**	*Did not enter*	**1984**	*Did not enter*	**2008**	Qualifiers
1928	-	**1964**	*Did not enter*	**1988**	*Did not enter*	**2012**	Qualifiers
1936	*Did not enter*	**1968**	*Did not enter*	**1992**	*Did not enter*	**2016**	Qualifiers

FIFA CONFEDERATIONS CUP 1992-2017
None

SAN MARINESE CLUB HONOURS IN EUROPEAN CLUB COMPETITIONS:

European Champion Clubs' Cup (1956-1992) / UEFA Champions League (1993-2019)
None
Fairs Cup (1858-1971) / UEFA Cup (1972-2009) / UEFA Europa League (2010-2019)
None
UEFA Super Cup (1972-2018)
None
European Cup Winners' Cup 1961-1999*
None

*defunct competition

NATIONAL COMPETITIONS
TABLE OF HONOURS

Please note: until the introduction of a regular championship in 1985/86, the Coppa Titano was the only annual tournament for San Marinese clubs.

CUP WINNERS 1937-1985

1937	AC Libertas Borgo Maggiore
1938-1949	*No competition*
1950	AC Libertas Borgo Maggiore
1951-1953	*No competition*
1954	AC Libertas Borgo Maggiore
1955-1957	*No competition*
1958	AC Libertas Borgo Maggiore
1959	AC Libertas Borgo Maggiore
1960	*No competition*
1961	AC Libertas Borgo Maggiore
1962-1964	*No competition*
1965	SS Juvenes Serravalle
1966	SP Tre Fiori Fiorentino
1967	SP Tre Penne Città di San Marino
1968	SS Juvenes Serravalle
1969	*Competition abandoned*
1970	SP Tre Penne Città di San Marino
1971	SP Tre Fiori Fiorentino
1972	FC Domagnano
1973	*Competition abandoned*
1974	SP Tre Fiori Fiorentino
1975	SP Tre Fiori Fiorentino
1976	SS Juvenes Serravalle
1977	SS Juvenes Serravalle
1978	SS Juvenes Serravalle
1979	SS Juvenes Serravalle
1980	SS Cosmos Serravalle
1981	SS Cosmos Serravalle
1982	SP Tre Penne Città di San Marino
1983	SP Tre Penne Città di San Marino
1984	SS Juvenes Serravalle
1985	SP Tre Fiori Fiorentino

	CHAMPIONS	CUP WINNERS	BEST GOALSCORERS	
1985/1986	SC Faetano	SP La Fiorita Montegiardino	-	
1986/1987	SP La Fiorita Montegiardino	AC Libertas Borgo Maggiore	-	
1987/1988	SP Tre Fiori Fiorentino	FC Domagnano	-	
1988/1989	FC Domagnano	AC Libertas Borgo Maggiore	-	
1989/1990	SP La Fiorita Montegiardino	FC Domagnano	-	
1990/1991	SC Faetano	AC Libertas Borgo Maggiore	-	
1991/1992	SS Montevito Fiorentino	FC Domagnano	-	
1992/1993	SP Tre Fiori Fiorentino	SC Faetano	-	
1993/1994	SP Tre Fiori Fiorentino	SC Faetano	-	
1994/1995	SP Tre Fiori Fiorentino	SS Cosmos Serravalle	-	
1995/1996	AC Libertas Borgo Maggiore	FC Domagnano	-	
1996/1997	SS Folgore/Falciano Serravalle	SS Murata	-	
1997/1998	SS Folgore/Falciano Serravalle	SC Faetano	Damiano Vannucci (SS Virtus Acquaviva)	21
1998/1999	SC Faetano	SS Cosmos Serravalle	-	
1999/2000	SS Folgore/Falciano Serravalle	SP Tre Penne Città di San Marino	-	
2000/2001	SS Cosmos Serravalle	FC Domagnano	-	
2001/2002	FC Domagnano	FC Domagnano	-	
2002/2003	FC Domagnano	FC Domagnano	-	
2003/2004	SS Pennarossa Chiesanuova	SS Pennarossa Chiesanuova	Damiano Vannucci (SS Virtus Acquaviva)	15
2004/2005	FC Domagnano	SS Pennarossa Chiesanuova	Matteo Pazzaglia (SS Montevito Fiorentino)	19
2005/2006	SS Murata	AC Libertas Borgo Maggiore	-	
2006/2007	SS Murata	SS Murata	-	
2007/2008	SS Murata	SS Murata	-	
2008/2009	SP Tre Fiori Fiorentino	AC Juvenes/Dogana	-	
2009/2010	SP Tre Fiori Fiorentino	SP Tre Fiori Fiorentino	Simon Parma (SS Virtus Acquaviva)	13
2010/2011	SP Tre Fiori Fiorentino	AC Juvenes/Dogana	Jose Hirsch (SS Virtus Acquaviva) Marco Fantini (AC Juvenes/Dogana) Roberto Gatti (ITA, SS Murata) Alessandro Giunta (ITA, SP Tre Fiori Fiorentino) Francesco Viroli (ITA, SC Faetano)	13
2011/2012	SP Tre Penne Città di San Marino	SP La Fiorita Montegiardino	Cristian Rubén Menin (SS SS Cosmos Serravalle) Simon Parma (SP La Fiorita Montegiardino)	11
2012/2013	SP Tre Penne Città di San Marino	SP La Fiorita Montegiardino	Alberto Cannini (SP Tre Fiori Fiorentino) Denis Iencinella (FC Fiorentino)	17
2013/2014	SP La Fiorita Montegiardino	AC Libertas Borgo Maggiore	Valentin Grigore (ROU, SS Cosmos Serravalle) Giacomo Gualtieri (SP La Fiorita Montegiardino)	18
2014/2015	SS Folgore/Falciano Serravalle	SS Folgore/Falciano Serravalle	Daniele Friguglietti (ITA, San Giovanni)	16
2015/2016	SP Tre Penne Città di San Marino	SP La Fiorita Montegiardino	Marco Martini (ITA, SP La Fiorita Montegiardino)	20
2016/2017	SP La Fiorita Montegiardino	SP Tre Penne Città di San Marino	Marco Martini (ITA, SP La Fiorita Montegiardino)	27
2017/2018	SP La Fiorita Montegiardino	SP La Fiorita Montegiardino	Imre Badalassi (ITA, SP Tre Fiori Fiorentino)	18
2018/2019	SP Tre Penne Città di San Marino	SP Tre Fiori Fiorentino	Andrea Compagno (ITA, SP Tre Fiori Fiorentino)	22

NATIONAL CHAMPIONSHIP

Campionato Sammarinese di Calcio 2018/2019

(21.09.2018 – 25.05.2019)

Regular Season

Round 1 [21-23.09.2018]
SP Tre Fiori - AC Juvenes/Dogana 3-1
SC Faetano - SP La Fiorita 0-1
SS Virtus - SP Tre Penne 0-8
SP Cailungo - FC Fiorentino 0-1
SS San Giovanni - SS Pennarossa 0-1
FC Domagnano - AC Libertas 1-0
SS Murata - SS Folgore/Falciano 1-7

Round 2 [28-30.09.2018]
SS Pennarossa - SS Murata 2-0
SS Folgore/Falciano - SP Tre Penne 0-0
SS Cosmos - AC Libertas 3-3
SP Tre Fiori - SS Virtus 5-2
AC Juvenes/Dogana - SS San Giovanni 4-1
FC Fiorentino - SP La Fiorita 2-2
FC Domagnano - SC Faetano 1-0

Round 3 [05-07.10.2018]
SP La Fiorita - FC Domagnano 1-0
SC Faetano - SS Cosmos 0-4
SS Virtus - SS Pennarossa 0-2
AC Libertas - SP Cailungo 1-0
SP Tre Penne - SS Murata 0-1
SS San Giovanni - SP Tre Fiori 0-5
SS Folgore/Falciano - AC Juvenes/Dogana 2-1

Round 4 [20-21.10.2018]
FC Domagnano - FC Fiorentino 0-0
AC Juvenes/Dogana - SS Murata 2-2
SP Tre Fiori - SS Folgore/Falciano 2-0
SP Cailungo - SS Cosmos 2-1
AC Libertas - SC Faetano 1-0
SS Pennarossa - SP Tre Penne 3-2
SS Virtus - SS San Giovanni 1-1

Round 5 [27-28.10.2018]
SP La Fiorita - AC Libertas 4-1
SP Tre Penne - AC Juvenes/Dogana 3-0
SS Folgore/Falciano - SS San Giovanni 0-0
SC Faetano - SP Cailungo 1-3
FC Fiorentino - SS Cosmos 2-0
SS Murata - SS Virtus 4-0
SS Pennarossa - SP Tre Fiori 1-3

Round 6 [03-04.11.2018]
SS San Giovanni - SS Murata 0-0
SS Folgore/Falciano - SS Pennarossa 3-0
FC Fiorentino - SC Faetano 1-1
SS Cosmos - FC Domagnano 1-3
AC Juvenes/Dogana - SS Virtus 1-0
SP Tre Fiori - SP Tre Penne 2-1
SP La Fiorita - SP Cailungo 2-1

Round 7 [10-11.11.2018]
SP Tre Penne - SS San Giovanni 5-0
AC Juvenes/Dogana - SS Pennarossa 3-0
SS Murata - SP Tre Fiori 3-1
SS Virtus - SS Folgore/Falciano 1-3
AC Libertas - FC Fiorentino 3-3
SS Cosmos - SP La Fiorita 0-4
SP Cailungo - FC Domagnano 1-3

Final Standings – Gruppo A

1.	SP Tre Fiori Fiorentino	7	6	0	1	21 - 8	18
2.	SS Folgore Falciano Calcio Serravalle	7	5	1	1	18 - 5	16
3.	SS Pennarossa Chiesanuova	7	4	0	3	9 - 11	12
4.	SS Murata Città di San Marino	7	3	2	2	11 - 12	11
5.	AC Juvenes/Dogana Serravalle	7	3	1	3	12 - 11	10
6.	SP Tre Penne Città di San Marino	7	3	0	4	19 - 9	9
7.	SS San Giovanni Borgo Maggiore	7	0	3	4	2 - 16	3
8.	SS Virtus Acquaviva	7	0	1	6	4 - 24	1

Final Standings – Gruppo B

1.	SP La Fiorita Montegiardino	6	5	1	0	14 - 4	16
2.	FC Domagnano	6	4	1	1	8 - 3	13
3.	FC Fiorentino	6	3	3	0	11 - 6	12
4.	AC Libertas Borgo Maggiore	6	2	2	2	9 - 11	8
5.	SP Cailungo Borgo Maggiore	6	2	0	4	7 - 9	6
6.	SS Cosmos Serravalle	6	1	1	4	9 - 14	4
7.	SC Faetano	6	0	0	6	2 - 13	0

Please note: the top four clubs from each group advanced to group 1 of the second stage, while the other teams advanced to group 2 of the second stage.

Second Stage

Results

Round 1 [24-25.11.2018]
SS Folgore/Falciano - SP La Fiorita 1-2
AC Libertas - FC Fiorentino 1-1
SS Pennarossa - SP Tre Fiori 0-3
FC Domagnano - SS Murata 0-1
SS Cosmos - AC Juvenes/Dogana 0-2
SP Cailungo - SP Tre Penne 0-3
SS Virtus - SS San Giovanni 0-1

Round 2 [01-02.12.2018]
SC Faetano - SP Cailungo 3-2
SP Tre Penne - SS Virtus 4-1
AC Juvenes/Dogana - SS San Giovanni 2-0
SS Folgore/Falciano - AC Libertas 3-2
SS Murata - FC Fiorentino 0-2
SP Tre Fiori - FC Domagnano 5-0
SP La Fiorita - SS Pennarossa 7-1

Round 3 [08-09.12.2018]
AC Libertas - SP Tre Fiori 2-2
SS Murata - SP La Fiorita 0-9
SS Pennarossa - SS Folgore/Falciano 3-1
FC Fiorentino - FC Domagnano 2-0
SS Virtus - SC Faetano 1-3
SS San Giovanni - SP Tre Penne 0-3
SP Cailungo - SS Cosmos 0-0

Round 4 [12-13.01.2019]
SS Cosmos - SC Faetano 1-0
SP Tre Penne - AC Juvenes/Dogana 2-1
SP Cailungo - SS Virtus 3-2
AC Libertas - SS Pennarossa 3-0
SP Tre Fiori - FC Fiorentino 2-2
SS Folgore/Falciano - SS Murata 0-0
SP La Fiorita - FC Domagnano 4-0

Round 5 [19-20.01.2019]
SP Tre Fiori - SS Folgore/Falciano 0-3
FC Domagnano - AC Libertas 2-2
SS Murata - SS Pennarossa 1-0
FC Fiorentino - SP La Fiorita 0-2
SS Virtus - SS Cosmos 0-1
SS San Giovanni - SP Cailungo 1-1
AC Juvenes/Dogana - SC Faetano 2-2

Round 6 [26-27.01.2019]
SS Murata - SP Tre Fiori 0-3
SS Folgore/Falciano - FC Fiorentino 1-1
SP La Fiorita - AC Libertas 2-0
SS Pennarossa - FC Domagnano 2-0
SS San Giovanni - SS Cosmos 0-1
SC Faetano - SP Tre Penne 0-2
SS Virtus - AC Juvenes/Dogana 2-4

Round 7 [02-03.02.2019]
SP Cailungo - AC Juvenes/Dogana 2-2
SS Cosmos - SP Tre Penne 0-2
SC Faetano - SS San Giovanni 1-0
FC Domagnano - SS Folgore/Falciano 2-2
SP La Fiorita - SP Tre Fiori 4-1
FC Fiorentino - SS Pennarossa 1-1
AC Libertas - SS Murata 3-1

Round 8 [09-10.02.2019]
SP La Fiorita - SS Folgore/Falciano 2-1
FC Fiorentino - AC Libertas 2-2
SP Tre Fiori - SS Pennarossa 3-1
SS Murata - FC Domagnano 2-3
AC Juvenes/Dogana - SS Cosmos 3-1
SP Tre Penne - SP Cailungo 5-2
SS San Giovanni - SS Virtus 0-0

Round 9 [16-17.02.2019]
SP Cailungo - SC Faetano 2-1
SS Virtus - SP Tre Penne 0-4
SS San Giovanni - AC Juvenes/Dogana 1-0
FC Fiorentino - SS Murata 0-3
AC Libertas - SS Folgore/Falciano 0-1
FC Domagnano - SP Tre Fiori 2-2
SS Pennarossa - SP La Fiorita 1-0

Round 10 [23-24.02.2019]
SC Faetano - SS Virtus 5-0
SP Tre Penne - SS San Giovanni 3-1
SS Cosmos - SP Cailungo 1-1
SP Tre Fiori - AC Libertas 2-0
SP La Fiorita - SS Murata 3-0
SS Folgore/Falciano - SS Pennarossa 1-0
FC Domagnano - FC Fiorentino 2-1

Round 11 [02-03.03.2019]
SS Pennarossa - AC Libertas 1-3
FC Fiorentino - SP Tre Fiori 2-2
SS Murata - SS Folgore/Falciano 0-0
FC Domagnano - SP La Fiorita 2-4
SC Faetano - SS Cosmos 1-1
AC Juvenes/Dogana - SP Tre Penne 0-0
SS Virtus - SP Cailungo 2-3

Round 12 [09-10.03.2019]
SS Cosmos - SS Virtus 2-0
SP Cailungo - SS San Giovanni 1-0
SC Faetano - AC Juvenes/Dogana 1-2
SS Folgore/Falciano - SP Tre Fiori 3-2
AC Libertas - FC Domagnano 3-3
SS Pennarossa - SS Murata 1-1
SP La Fiorita - FC Fiorentino 5-2

Round 13 [16-17.03.2019]
SP Tre Fiori - SS Murata 5-1
FC Domagnano - SS Pennarossa 1-2
FC Fiorentino - SS Folgore/Falciano 2-3
AC Libertas - SP La Fiorita 1-1
SS Cosmos - SS San Giovanni 5-1
SP Tre Penne - SC Faetano 2-1
AC Juvenes/Dogana - SS Virtus 7-1

Round 14 [30-31.03.2019]
AC Juvenes/Dogana - SP Cailungo 1-1
SP Tre Penne - SS Cosmos 4-0
SS San Giovanni - SC Faetano 1-5
SS Folgore/Falciano - FC Domagnano 3-4
SP Tre Fiori - SP La Fiorita 0-3
SS Pennarossa - FC Fiorentino 0-2
SS Murata - AC Libertas 2-1

Final Standings – Gruppo 1

1.	SP La Fiorita Montegiardino	14	12	1	1	48	-	10	37
2.	SP Tre Fiori Fiorentino	14	6	4	4	32	-	23	22
3.	SS Folgore Falciano Calcio Serravalle	14	6	4	4	23	-	20	22
4.	AC Libertas Borgo Maggiore	14	3	6	5	23	-	23	15
5.	FC Fiorentino	14	3	6	5	20	-	24	15
6.	SS Murata Città di San Marino	14	4	3	7	12	-	30	15
7.	SS Pennarossa Chiesanuova	14	4	2	8	13	-	27	14
8.	FC Domagnano	14	3	4	7	21	-	35	13

Please note: the top six clubs advanced to the Championship Play-offs.

Final Standings – Gruppo 2

1.	SP Tre Penne Città di San Marino	12	11	1	0	34	-	6	34
2.	AC Juvenes/Dogana Serravalle	12	6	4	2	27	-	14	22
3.	SS Cosmos Serravalle	12	5	3	4	13	-	14	18
4.	SC Faetano	12	5	2	5	24	-	17	17
5.	SP Cailungo Borgo Maggiore	12	4	5	3	18	-	21	17
6.	SS San Giovanni Borgo Maggiore	12	2	2	8	6	-	22	8
7.	SS Virtus Acquaviva	12	0	1	11	9	-	37	1

Please note: the winner and runner-up advanced to the Championship Play-offs.

Qualifier for Play-offs [03.04.2019]	AC Juvenes/Dogana Serravalle - SS Cosmos Serravalle	3-1(1-0)

5th – 8th Place Play-offs

Semi-Finals [10.05.2019]	AC Juvenes/Dogana Serravalle - SS Murata Città di San Marino	4-0(3-0)
	FC Fiorentino - SS Folgore Falciano Calcio Serravalle	0-4(0-1)
7th Place Play-off [16.05.2019]	SS Murata Città di San Marino - FC Fiorentino	3-0(2-0)
5th Place Play-off [16.05.2019]	AC Juvenes/Dogana Serravalle - SS Folgore Falciano Calcio Serravalle	1-0(0-0)

Championship Play-offs

Quarter-Finals [25.04.-05.05.2019]	SP La Fiorita Montegiardino - AC Juvenes/Dogana Serravalle	1-0(0-0)	5-0(2-0)
	AC Libertas Borgo Maggiore - SS Murata Città di San Marino	1-0(1-0)	4-0(2-0)
	SP Tre Fiori Fiorentino - FC Fiorentino	2-1(2-1)	1-0(0-0)
	SP Tre Penne Città di San Marino - SS Folgore Falciano Calcio Serravalle	1-0(1-0)	1-1(1-1)
Semi-Finals [11-18.05.2019]	SP La Fiorita Montegiardino - AC Libertas Borgo Maggiore	1-0(1-0)	4-0(0-0)
	SP Tre Fiori Fiorentino - SP Tre Penne Città di San Marino	0-1(0-0)	1-2(0-0)
Third Place Play-off [24.05.2018]	AC Libertas Borgo Maggiore - SP Tre Fiori Fiorentino	1-3(0-2)	

Championship Final

25.05.2019; Campo sportivo di Fonte dell'Ovo, San Marino; Referee: Luca Barbeno; Attendance: n/a
SP La Fiorita Montegiardino - SP Tre Penne Città di San Marino **1-3(1-0,1-1)**
La Fiorita: Gianluca Vivan, Samuele Olivi, Carlo Valentini (66.Riccardo Michelotti), Roberto Di Maio, Marco Gasperoni, Riccardo Mezzadri, Adrián Ricchiuti (78.Luca Righini), Simone Loiodice, Armando Amati, Danilo Ezequiel Rinaldi, Alessandro Chiurato (74.Fabrizio Castellazzi). Trainer: Alberto Manca (Italy).
Tre Penne: Mattia Migani, Mirko Palazzi (76.Alex Gasperoni), Davide Cesarini, Christofer Genestreti, Dario Merendino, Nicola Chiaruzzi (76.Kevin Marigliano), Nicola Gai, Luca Patregnani, Stefano Fraternali, Michael Angelini [*sent off 101*], Raul Ura (85.Luca Ceccaroli). Trainer: Stefano Ceci.
Goals: 1-0 Alessandro Chiurato (43), 1-1 Stefano Fraternali (90+2), 1-2 Michael Angelini (100), 1-3 Kevin Marigliano (115).

Champions 2018/2019: **SP Tre Penne Città di San Marino**

Top goalscorer: Andrea Compagno (ITA, SP Tre Fiori Fiorentino) – 22 goals

NATIONAL CUP
Coppa Titano Final 2018/2019

1/8-Finals [23/24.10.-06/07.11.2018]

FC Fiorentino - SP Tre Fiori Fiorentino	0-4 / 2-0
FC Domagnano - SS Folgore Falciano Calcio	0-1 / 0-0
SS San Giovanni B.Maggiore - AC Libertas B.Magg.	1-0 / 9-10 pen
SS Murata Città di San Marino - SC Faetano	1-1 / 4-1
SP Tre Penne C.di San Marino - AC Juvenes/Dogana	3-2 / 5-1
SS Virtus Acquaviva - SP Cailungo Borgo Maggiore	0-1 / 0-3
SS Pennarossa Chiesanuova - SS Cosmos Serravalle	2-3 / 1-2

Quarter-Finals [04/05.-16.12.2018]

SP Tre Penne C.d.San Marino - SP Cailungo B.Magg.	3-1 / 3-0
SS Cosmos Serravalle - SS Folgore Falciano Calcio	2-0 / 0-4
SP La Fiorita Montegiardino - SP Tre Fiori Fiorent.	1-1 / 0-1
SS Murata C.San Marino - AC Libertas Borgo Magg.	0-1 / 1-3

Semi-Finals [06/07.-13/14.04.2019]

SP Tre Penne - SS Folgore Falciano Calcio Serravalle	0-0 / 1-2
SP Tre Fiori Fiorentino - AC Libertas B. Maggiore	2-0 / 2-1

Final

19.04.2019; Campo Sportivo di Falciano, Falciano; Referee: Gianluca Ceccarelli; Attendance: n/a
SP Tre Fiori Fiorentino - SS Folgore Falciano Calcio Serravalle **1-0(1-0)**

Tre Fiori: Aldo Simoncini, Cristian Zaccardo, Davide Bologna, Daniele Lusini, Matias Ramón Castro [*sent off 90+1*], Manolo Pestrin, Mattia Giardi (63.Davide Massaro), Andrea Tamagnini, Nicolás Leonel Castro, Joel Apezteguía Hijuelos (81.Davide Succi), Andrea Compagno. Trainer: Matteo Cecchetti (Italy).

Folgore Falciano: Simone Venturini, Cristian Brolli, Francesco Bossa (74.Luca Rossi), Francesco Sartori, Luca Bezzi, Marco Domeniconi, Stefano Sacco (78.Matteo Serafini), Andrea Nucci, Lorenzo Dormi, Marco Bernardi (82.William Innocenti), Imre Badalassi. Trainer: Oscar Lasagni (Italy).

Goal: 1-0 Nicolás Leonel Castro (20).

THE CLUBS 2018/2019

Please note: matches and goals includes statistics of regular season, second stage and Championship play-offs.

Società Polisportiva Cailungo Borgo Maggiore

Founded: 1974
Stadium: Stadio Fonte Dell'Ovo, Città di San Marino (500)

Goalkeepers:	DOB	M	(s)	G
Massimo Francioni	17.06.1993	7		
Alberto Gallinetta (ITA)	16.04.1992	8		
Pietro Magnani	18.12.1997	3		
Defenders:	**DOB**	**M**	**(s)**	**G**
Maicol Acquarelli (ITA)	21.09.1993	4	(2)	1
Daniele Angeli	27.09.1992	8	(3)	1
Mattia Gualandi	08.04.1994	7	(2)	
Manuel Iuzzolino (ITA)	05.05.1990	16		
Giovanni Padovani (ITA)	30.11.1995	1	(2)	
Roberto Peluso (ITA)	06.04.1989	6		
Nicolò Poli (ITA)	10.10.1989	10	(1)	
Michele Rossi	26.01.1995	12	(1)	
Amedeo Valentini (ITA)	06.05.1994	5	(1)	
Midfielders:	**DOB**	**M**	**(s)**	**G**
Simone Ciavatta	18.09.1991	8	(3)	
Luca Cicchetti (ITA)	04.09.1997	4		2
Michele Conti (ITA)	26.04.1991	16		4
Alberto Del Prete (ITA)	21.08.1995	10	(1)	1
Filippo Matteoni	27.05.1996		(2)	
Simone Matteoni	26.04.1992	1	(4)	
Marco Oliva (ITA)	25.06.1989	6		
Simone Santarini	17.10.1991	2		
Nicola Tamburini (ITA)	05.01.1986	9		
Davide Venerucci	08.06.1997	2	(7)	
Forwards:	**DOB**	**M**	**(s)**	**G**
Federico Bonavita (ITA)	23.07.1990	9		3
Andreas Bucci	07.06.1989		(11)	1
Filippo Del Prete (ITA)	03.07.1989	3	(4)	
Marco Gian Donati	27.08.1998		(1)	
Enrico Pellino (ITA)	24.05.1997	14	(1)	3
Jacopo Raschi	28.04.1998	15	(1)	5
Matteo Ricci Frabattista (ITA)	29.06.1998	7		1
Pietro Semprini	27.01.1993	5	(5)	2
Trainer:	**DOB**	**M**		
Claudio Bartoletti	09.06.1958	18		

Società Sportiva Cosmos Serravalle

Founded: 1979
Stadium: San Marino Stadium, Serravalle (7,000)

Goalkeepers:	**DOB**	**M**	**(s)**	**G**
Gabriele Giulianelli	09.09.1998	1		
Andrea Gregori	30.12.1987	18		
Defenders:	**DOB**	**M**	**(s)**	**G**
Francesco Baschetti (ITA)	08.01.1986	16		
Alex Cavalli	26.02.1992	11	(2)	
Matteo Colonna	10.05.1990	11	(1)	
Daniel Giulianelli	12.01.1995	4	(2)	
Marco Grossi (ITA)	10.02.1988	13		1
Manuel Molinari	20.08.1986	1	(1)	
Stefano Sartini	02.05.2000	6	(3)	1
Midfielders:	**DOB**	**M**	**(s)**	**G**
Michele Cervellini	14.04.1988	17		
Lorenzo Dormi (ITA)	11.02.1995	8		2
Fabiano Grassi (ITA)	06.05.1988	13		
Fabio Giovagnoli (ITA)	10.06.1992	6	(6)	1
Tommaso Guerra	22.08.1990		(4)	
Lorenzo Marcattili (ITA)	20.09.1993	2	(4)	
Marco Morri	11.06.1997		(2)	
Manuel Sanchini	20.03.1993	1	(1)	
Armando Senja (ALB)	26.07.1997	5	(4)	
Guido Zaghini (ITA)	06.12.1988	6	(1)	
Kevin Zonzini	11.08.1997	15	(3)	
Forwards:	**DOB**	**M**	**(s)**	**G**
Alessandro Bianchi	19.07.1989	11	(6)	3
Riccardo Bonfigli (ITA)	13.12.1997	4	(2)	
Kevin Caminero (ITA)	11.07.1993	11		6
Manuel Canini (ITA)	22.08.1993	9	(3)	1
Cristian Negri	16.01.1985		(2)	
Roberto Neri (ITA)	06.08.1983	17	(1)	8
Marco Rosti	21.10.1988	3	(2)	
Trainer:	**DOB**	**M**		
Giancarlo Carnevali (ITA)		8		
Ivo Crescentini (ITA) [19.12.2018]	14.09.1957	11		

Football Club Domagnano

Founded: 1966
Stadium: Campo sportivo, Domagnano (500)

Goalkeepers:	**DOB**	**M**	**(s)**	**G**
Santino Arena (ITA)	11.02.1987	6		
Giacomo Muraccini	15.09.1990	14		
Defenders:	**DOB**	**M**	**(s)**	**G**
Andrea Battistini (ITA)	26.05.1991	14	(1)	
Federico Buldrini (ITA)	19.08.1983	7	(6)	
Lorenzo Buscarini	27.05.1991	2	(10)	1
Davide Dolcini	30.01.1991	6	(5)	
Angelo Faetanini	17.01.1993	11	(1)	
Matteo Ferrari (ITA)	20.10.1994	18		1
Giovanni Rossi (ITA)	15.02.1989	19		1
Juri Tamburini (ITA)	07.07.1977	5		1
Mattia Valentini	10.12.1998	13		
Midfielders:	**DOB**	**M**	**(s)**	**G**
Luca Ceccaroli	05.07.1995	6	(2)	2
Marco Ceccaroli	09.03.1992	3	(2)	
Elia Donati (ITA)	07.08.2000	9	(1)	
Alessio Faetanini	01.01.1990	1		
Manuel Muccioli (ITA)	12.12.1996	4	(2)	
Paolo Rossi (ITA)	06.09.1983	14		1
Andrea Venerucci	21.11.1989	14	(1)	
Forwards:	**DOB**	**M**	**(s)**	**G**
Nicolò Angelini	15.03.1992	18	(2)	14
Alessandro Bianchini (ITA)	26.04.1994	14	(1)	3
Davide Capelli (ITA)	05.06.1999	1	(5)	
Filippo Burioni	20.05.1998	2	(4)	
Rivolino Gavoci (ITA)	14.07.1991	11		4
Jacopo Gualandi (ITA)	11.01.1996		(3)	
Ramiro Martín Lago (ARG)	14.10.1987	8	(11)	1
Trainer:	**DOB**	**M**		
Cristian Protti (ITA)	17.04.1973	20		

Società Calcio Faetano

Founded: 1962
Stadium: San Marino Stadium, Serravalle (7,000)

Goalkeepers:	**DOB**	**M**	**(s)**	**G**
Luca Bianchi	27.02.1990	1		
Marco Donati (ITA)	26.05.1983	1		
Manuel Ermeti (ITA)	11.08.1981	16		
Defenders:	**DOB**	**M**	**(s)**	**G**
Stefano Babbini (ITA)	18.07.1981	6		1
Mirko Bartolucci (ITA)	15.10.1999	11		
Alex Della Valle	13.06.1990	11		
Luca Filippi (ITA)	27.09.1988	8		
Manuel Marconi (ITA)	18.05.1987	6	(6)	
Roberto Peluso (ITA)	06.04.1989	6		
Luca Pianini (ITA)	08.10.1991	1	(1)	
Giacomo Rinaldi	23.03.1990	15	(2)	
Vittorio Valentini	09.10.1973	1	(4)	
Midfielders:	**DOB**	**M**	**(s)**	**G**
Aziz Diallo (SEN)	11.05.1997	2	(1)	
Mattia Giardi	15.12.1991	8		2
Leonardo Magnani (ITA)	08.10.1998	15		5
Alessandro Pioli (ITA)	20.01.1992	12		1
Giulio Strologo (ITA)	01.08.1991	14	(1)	
Nicola Tamburini (ITA)	05.01.1986	7	(2)	1
Luca Tomassoni (ITA)	21.11.1994	3	(7)	1
Simone Ugolini	28.02.1991	9	(3)	
Denis Veronesi	17.06.1988		(1)	
Forwards:	**DOB**	**M**	**(s)**	**G**
Pier Giuseppe Della Valle	18.05.2000	3	(1)	
Eric Fedeli (ITA)	13.01.1992	13	(2)	9
Daniele Friguglietti (ITA)	21.11.1979	12	(6)	3
Richard Amaechi Johnson (NED)	17.10.1996		(4)	
Nicholas Ronchi (ITA)	12.04.1989	4	(4)	
Marco Ugolini (ITA)	23.12.1986	14	(4)	2
Trainer:	**DOB**	**M**		
Not known				

Football Club Fiorentino

Founded: 1974
Stadium: Campo Sportivo, Fiorentino (700)

Goalkeepers:	DOB	M	(s)	G
Angelo Balsamini (ITA)	12.12.1989	4		
Michele Berardi	30.11.1991		(1)	
Luca Bianchi (ITA)	07.01.1990	20		
Defenders:	**DOB**	**M**	**(s)**	**G**
Andrea Bernardi	01.01.1987	6	(5)	
Juri Biordi	01.01.1995	23	(1)	3
Manuel Carlini	26.05.1993	8	(4)	
Nicolò Ferrari (ITA)	03.02.1991	17		1
Mirko Paglialonga (ITA)	19.09.1983	20	(3)	
Samuele Paoloni	18.01.1997	4	(5)	
Emiliano Martin Polanco (ITA)	05.07.1984	4	(5)	
Masimilliano Pratelli (ITA)	14.07.1983	19		1
Midfielders:	**DOB**	**M**	**(s)**	**G**
Andrea Borgagni	21.10.1996	3	(5)	
Matteo Camillini (ITA)	10.01.1984	14	(6)	
Andrea Cecolli	22.09.1993	8	(2)	1
Henrik Cekirri (ALB)	18.12.1994	4	(8)	1
Alessandro Giangrandi (ITA)	09.12.1996	15	(6)	
Emanuele Liotta (ITA)	04.09.1993		(1)	1
Lorenzo Liverani	13.05.1993	8	(11)	
Daniele Maiani	04.08.1993	19	(1)	
Alessandro Molinari	01.01.1994	17	(1)	
Forwards:	**DOB**	**M**	**(s)**	**G**
Enea Jaupi (ALB)	06.10.1993	19		10
Alvaro Musta (ALB)	10.11.1989	12	(3)	1
Simone Rossi (ITA)	13.06.1987	20	(1)	13
Trainer:	**DOB**	**M**		
Massimo Campo (ITA)	15.04.1975	24		

Società Sportiva Folgore Falciano Calcio Serravalle

Founded: 1972
Stadium: San Marino Stadium, Serravalle (7,000)

Goalkeepers:	DOB	M	(s)	G
Davide Bicchiarelli	19.05.1985	11		
Riccardo Raschi	29.09.1992	1		
Angelo Russo (ITA)	18.12.1987		(1)	
Simone Venturini (ITA)	27.05.1998	13		
Defenders:	**DOB**	**M**	**(s)**	**G**
Marco Berardi	12.02.1993	1	(5)	
Francesco Bossa (ITA)	26.05.1990	19		1
Cristian Brolli	28.02.1992	19		1
Stefano Lessi (ITA)	30.11.1990	7	(3)	
Luca Rossi (ITA)	14.04.1993	7	(2)	
Andrea Sabbadini (ITA)	21.05.1985	6	(2)	
Francesco Sartori (ITA)	07.03.1993	17	(4)	2
Midfielders:	**DOB**	**M**	**(s)**	**G**
Riccardo Aluigi	29.03.1994	3	(4)	
Luca Bezzi (ITA)	05.06.1989	21		1
Michele Casadei	24.01.1992	2	(4)	
Marco Domeniconi	29.01.1984	15	(2)	2
Lorenzo Dormi (ITA)	11.02.1995	12	(2)	3
Andrea Nucci (ITA)	06.09.1986	23		
Simone Perrino (ITA)	18.02.1997	2	(2)	
Stefano Sacco	10.02.1991	16	(5)	1
Umberto Semeraro (ITA)	09.02.1992	8	(5)	3
Matteo Serafini (ITA)	13.02.1994	8	(5)	
Forwards:	**DOB**	**M**	**(s)**	**G**
Pier Giorgio Altissimi (ITA)	09.04.1994		(3)	
Imre Badalassi (ITA)	08.02.1995	20	(2)	15
Paolo Basile (ITA)	08.06.1992	8	(2)	3
Marco Bernardi	02.01.1994	17	(4)	5
Achille Della Valle	31.01.1989	5	(3)	
Antonio Gravina (ITA)	22.02.1994	4		2
William Innocenti (ITA)	30.04.1987	6	(6)	3
Nicolò Venerucci	27.08.1995	4	(4)	
Trainer:	**DOB**	**M**		
Oscar Lasagni (ITA)	04.10.1971	25		

Associazione Calcio Juvenes/Dogana Serravalle

Founded: 2000 (*as merger of SS Juvenes Serravalle and GS Dogana*)
Stadium: San Marino Stadium, Serravalle (7,000)

Goalkeepers:	DOB	M	(s)	G
Eros Gobbi	16.10.1989	7		
Simone Guerra	31.10.1982	8		
Mattia Manzaroli	03.10.1991	9		
Defenders:	**DOB**	**M**	**(s)**	**G**
Matteo Cacchi (ITA)	04.07.1988	3	(2)	
Enrico Casadei	18.02.1996	12	(2)	
Nicola Canini	14.08.1988		(6)	
Alex Gattei Colonna (ITA)	16.07.1988	13		1
Enrico Mantovani (ITA)	14.11.1986	16	(4)	
Mirko Mantovani	14.11.1986	21		1
Mattia Merlini	23.12.1993	12	(2)	1
Michael Parma (ITA)	28.03.1998	12		
Filippo Quaranta	11.09.1998	6	(3)	
Thomas Raschi	11.07.1996	11	(9)	3
Luca Rossi (ITA)	14.04.1993	2	(1)	
Daniele Villa (ITA)	24.05.1982	8	(1)	1
Alessandro Zonzini	11.10.1994		(1)	
Midfielders:	**DOB**	**M**	**(s)**	**G**
Enrico Antonioni (ITA)	08.02.1982	6	(2)	1
Nicolò Bacchiocchi	26.02.1991	9		2
Fabio Cuomo (ITA)	03.03.1997	7	(2)	2
Alessandro D'Elia (ITA)	27.03.1995	17		8
Lorenzo Gasperoni	03.01.199	18	(3)	3
Cristian Gatti	06.05.1999	7	(8)	
Matteo Semprini (ITA)	30.03.1995	17	(1)	1
Nicola Zafferani	06.11.1991		(6)	1
Forwards:	**DOB**	**M**	**(s)**	**G**
Tommaso Angelelli (ITA)	30.08.1992	13		4
Lorenzo Cevoli	05.07.1997	6	(8)	2
Stefano Del Grande (ITA)	31.07.1984	1	(1)	
Hamed Sako (ITA)	24.08.1999	1	(7)	1
Luca Sorrentino (ITA)	08.05.1994	22		14
Trainer:	**DOB**	**M**		
Cristian Brigliadori (ITA)	07.04.1978	24		

Società Polisportiva La Fiorita Montegiardino

Founded: 1967
Stadium: Stadio "Igor Crescentini", Montegiardino (700)

Goalkeepers:	**DOB**	**M**	**(s)**	**G**
Alex Stimac (ITA)	22.06.1996	6	(2)	
Gianluca Vivan (ITA)	27.12.1983	19		
Defenders:	**DOB**	**M**	**(s)**	**G**
Roberto Di Maio (ITA)	21.09.1982	24		3
Marco Gasperoni (ITA)	18.02.1992	21		5
Thomas Manfredini (ITA)	27.05.1980	2		
Riccardo Mezzadri (ITA)	14.04.1986	21	(1)	2
Samuele Olivi (ITA)	01.08.1980	17	(1)	2
Carlo Valentini	15.03.1982	7	(1)	1
Michele Zanotti	25.11.1988		(2)	
Midfielders:	**DOB**	**M**	**(s)**	**G**
Armando Amati (ITA)	15.01.1995	19	(4)	2
Nicola Cavalli	15.12.1986		(3)	
Simone Loiodice (ITA)	16.03.1989	19	(2)	
Riccardo Michelotti	13.09.1999	5	(8)	2
Tiziano Mottola	06.07.1986	6	(8)	1
Samuel Pancotti	31.10.2000	1	(2)	
Adrián Ricchiuti (ARG)	30.06.1978	19	(1)	8
Luca Righini (ITA)	25.12.1990	18	(4)	3
Forwards:	**DOB**	**M**	**(s)**	**G**
Fabrizio Castellazzi (ITA)	29.07.1984	12	(5)	12
Alessandro Chiurato (ITA)	16.01.1983	15	(3)	12
Alessandro Guidi	14.12.1986	1	(12)	3
Adolfo Hirsch	31.01.1986	16	(3)	6
Danilo Ezequiel Rinaldi	18.04.1986	24	(1)	7
Moussa Souare (GUI)	01.07.1998	3	(9)	3
Vincent Paul Vultaggio	17.08.1998		(1)	
Trainer:	**DOB**	**M**		
Alberto Manca (ITA)		25		

Associazione Calcio Libertas Borgo Maggiore

Founded: 1928
Stadium: Campo sportivo, Borgo Maggiore (1,000)

Goalkeepers:	**DOB**	**M**	**(s)**	**G**
Matteo Delai (ITA)	11.08.1987	6		
Matteo Zavoli	06.07.1996	19	(1)	
Defenders:	**DOB**	**M**	**(s)**	**G**
Manuel Battistini	22.07.1994	23		1
Matteo Cacchi (ITA)	04.07.1988	9		
Francesco De Rosa	10.10.1983	5		
Patrik Giulianelli (ITA)	18.04.1998	9	(1)	1
Federico Pesaresi (ITA)	09.08.1996	22	(1)	1
Daniele Rocchi (ITA)	23.06.1982	4		
Davide Simoncini	03.08.1986	23		
Francesco Stacchini	18.01.1997		(4)	
Midfielders:	**DOB**	**M**	**(s)**	**G**
Amir Aissaoui (ITA)	03.12.1992	8	(6)	
Mariano Alvarez	05.02.1996	1	(1)	
Michael Battistini	08.10.1996	13	(9)	2
Maicol Berretti	01.05.1989	9	(8)	
Alberto Celli	24.06.1985	1	(1)	
Pasquale De Vita (ITA)	03.03.1994	6		
Vicent Eliott (FRA)	12.08.1998	3	(3)	
Matteo Gaiani (ITA)	02.01.1995	2	(1)	3
Enrico Golinucci	16.07.1991	16	(2)	3
Mattia Lualdi (ITA)	26.07.1992	17	(2)	4
Umberto Semeraro (ITA)	09.02.1992	5	(3)	3
Forwards:	**DOB**	**M**	**(s)**	**G**
Antonio Gravina (ITA)	22.02.1994	7	(2)	3
Riccardo Paganelli (ITA)	09.06.1987	16	(3)	7
Francesco Perrotta (ITA)	27.08.1981	3	(5)	
Giorgio Mariotti	06.05.1986	4	(9)	1
Gian Luca Morelli (ITA)	13.02.1985	19	(2)	9
Yao N'Guessan Wilfried Nacanibou (CIV)	14.05.1988	1	(1)	
Jacopo Ordonselli (ITA)	07.07.1994	6	(2)	
Trainer:	**DOB**	**M**		
Roberto Marcucci	09.05.1963	25		

Società Sportiva Murata Città di San Marino

Founded: 1966
Stadium: Campo sportivo, Montegiardino (1,000)

Goalkeepers:	**DOB**	**M**	**(s)**	**G**
Denis Broccoli (ITA)	10.08.1988	1		
Mauricio Gennari	26.06.1998	5		
Matteo Renzetti (ITA)	15.11.1997	19		
Defenders:	**DOB**	**M**	**(s)**	**G**
Nicola Albani	15.04.1981	20		
Thomas Cavalli (ITA)	17.01.1988	12	(4)	
Hervé Diedhiou (SEN)	05.01.1994	21		2
Luca Ortibaldi (ITA)	29.04.1988	17	(1)	1
Juan Gabriel Sosa (ARG)	17.08.1982	18	(5)	3
Massimo Vagnetti	25.06.1979	1	(3)	
Elia Venerucci	14.09.1996	2	(2)	
Midfielders:	**DOB**	**M**	**(s)**	**G**
Marco Cecchetti	03.02.1997	20	(3)	2
Manuel Cocco (ITA)	01.05.2000	9	(1)	1
Assane Fall (SEN)	26.02.1994	18	(1)	
Nicola Moroni	05.05.1997		(2)	
Matteo Nanni	07.03.1993	10	(9)	
Raffaele Seccia (ITA)	03.02.1993	19	(2)	1
Forwards:	**DOB**	**M**	**(s)**	**G**
Nicolas Cavalli (ITA)	22.04.1994	3	(4)	
Alessandro Di Filippo (ITA)	07.07.1996	17	(5)	4
Diego Alejandro Gómez López (COL)	11.09.1999	8	(8)	
Jacopo Muggeo (ITA)	19.08.1990	19	(1)	
Alvaro Musta (ALB)	10.11.1989	8	(1)	1
Nicolo Neri (ITA)	10.03.1997	11	(7)	
Michele Pieri (ITA)	16.06.1992	17	(5)	11
Trainer:	**DOB**	**M**		
Massimo Gori	01.01.1970	25		

Società Sportiva Pennarossa Chiesanuova

Founded: 1968
Stadium: Campo sportivo, Chiesanuova (300)

Goalkeepers:	DOB	M	(s)	G
Luca Giuliani (ITA)	15.02.1983	2		
Matteo Ugolini	27.01.1986	19		
Defenders:	**DOB**	**M**	**(s)**	**G**
Marco Baldani	05.12.1997	7	(2)	
Andrea Boschi (ITA)	19.05.1998	2	(4)	
Daniele Conti (ITA)	06.06.1990	20	(1)	1
Andrea Fratta	10.11.1984	18		1
Matteo Giannoni	25.03.1988	3	(3)	
Kevin Martin (ITA)	24.03.1995	10		
Gabriele Raffaelli (ITA)	28.05.1994	17		2
Midfielders:	**DOB**	**M**	**(s)**	**G**
Adam Adami Martins (BRA)	24.06.1992	8	(1)	2
Amir Aissaoui (ITA)	30.12.1992	5		
Mariano Alvarez	05.02.1996		(1)	
Maximiliano Baizan	23.03.1993	4	(9)	
Emanuele Bindi (ITA)	23.02.1999	2	(3)	
Alberto Celli	24.06.1985	6		1
Matias Colagiovanni	16.01.1993	10		1
Florin Cristian Grigore (ROU)	09.04.1984	7		
Christian Maccagno (ITA)	05.06.1983	11	(4)	
Alex Partisani (ITA)	25.01.1992	2	(2)	
Elia Pignani (ITA)	21.09.1992	3	(1)	
Francesco Rossi	08.02.1994	3	(5)	
Matteo Sebastiani (ITA)	12.12.1990	18		
Forwards:	**DOB**	**M**	**(s)**	**G**
Nicholas Capozzi (ITA)	12.12.1987	1	(2)	
Nicola Ciacci	07.07.1982	10	(5)	2
Francesko Halilaj (ITA)	09.05.1992	12	(1)	8
Nicolò Mariotti	28.01.2000	10	(2)	2
Alessandro Podeschi	05.04.1997	6	(4)	
Franklin Pierce Silva Bahiano	13.04.1984	10	(4)	1
Vincent Paul Vultaggio	17.08.1998	5	(1)	1
Trainer:	**DOB**	**M**		
Denis Guerra (ITA)	27.04.1974	21		

Società Sportiva San Giovanni Borgo Maggiore

Founded: 1948
Stadium: Stadio Borgo Maggiore, Borgo Maggiore (1,000)

Goalkeepers:	DOB	M	(s)	G
Alberto Caldari (ITA)	13.02.1986	3	(1)	
Andrea Manzaroli	12.02.1995	15		
Giuseppe Taddei	10.12.1992	1		
Defenders:	**DOB**	**M**	**(s)**	**G**
Filippo Maria Baffoni (ITA)	25.09.1991	17	(1)	
Marco Borgelli (ITA)	19.01.1981	4	(2)	
Edoardo Cecchetti	14.07.1993	16	(2)	
Lorenzo Fortunato	08.01.1988	1	(3)	
Nicola Grechi (ITA)	05.01.1989	14	(1)	
Luca Guidi (ITA)	17.05.1990	10	(4)	1
Alberto La Pia (ITA)	02.02.1981	9	(2)	
Stefano Lessi (ITA)	30.11.1990	8		
Francesco Matteucci (ITA)	30.08.1995	19		2
Matteo Matteucci (ITA)	30.01.1997	7	(6)	
Diego Pasquali (ARG)	15.11.1989	2	(2)	
Loris Zafferani	14.08.1983	3	(1)	
Midfielders:	**DOB**	**M**	**(s)**	**G**
Alessandro Caforio	06.08.1992	17		
Riccardo Dragoni (ITA)	24.05.1991	8	(1)	1
Alessandro Grilli	04.06.1989	8	(2)	
Giovanni Paduano (ITA)	28.01.1984	3	(5)	
Nicolo Tamagnini	07.02.1988	9		
Denis Veronesi	17.06.1988		(1)	
Andrea Zanotti	05.05.1992	7		
Forwards:	**DOB**	**M**	**(s)**	**G**
Sabri Bouguila (ITA)	21.09.1996	1	(4)	
Alberto Cannini (ITA)	13.01.1981	2	(4)	2
Espedito Marinaro (ITA)	10.09.1992	5	(4)	
Andrea Moroni	10.10.1985	14	(3)	
Giovanni Tani (ITA)	21.04.1973	6	(1)	2
Trainer:	**DOB**	**M**		
Daniele Baldi (ITA)	07.06.1960	19		

Società Polisportiva Tre Fiori Fiorentino

Founded: 1949
Stadium: Stadio di Fiorentino, Fiorentino (1,000)

Goalkeepers:	DOB	M	(s)	G
Nicolò Battistini (ITA)	03.07.1999	3	(1)	
Michele Ceccoli	04.12.1973	1		
Aldo Simoncini	30.08.1986	22		
Defenders:	**DOB**	**M**	**(s)**	**G**
Maicol Acquarelli (ITA)	21.09.1993	3	(5)	
Davide Bologna (ITA)	19.01.1988	18	(1)	1
Matias Ramón Castro (ARG)	29.04.1997	11		
Luca Filippi (ITA)	27.09.1988	7		
Daniele Lusini (ITA)	10.03.1982	14	(1)	
Roberto Miano (ITA)	26.10.1996	3	(1)	
Andrea Muccioli	13.02.2000	4	(2)	
Davide Succi (ITA)	07.06.1990	6	(3)	
Midfielders:	**DOB**	**M**	**(s)**	**G**
Nicolás Leonel Castro (ARG)	19.06.1993	10		
Marco De Angelis	17.05.1999	3	(6)	
Nicola Della Valle	19.05.1997	17	(3)	
Danny Gasperoni	09.06.1998	7	(1)	1
Mattia Giardi	15.12.1991	9	(1)	
Eduardo Marconi	22.10.1998	2	(8)	
Filippo Matteoni	27.05.1996	4	(5)	
Simone Matteoni	26.04.1992	2	(4)	
Manolo Pestrin (ITA)	30.10.1978	23		1
Giacomo Pracucci (ITA)	21.01.1997	14	(5)	
Andrea Tamagnini	27.09.1997	17	(3)	1
Marco Zannoni (ITA)	14.08.1982	8	(8)	
Forwards:	**DOB**	**M**	**(s)**	**G**
Joel Apezteguía Hijuelos (CUB)	17.12.1983	21	(3)	16
Andrea Compagno (ITA)	22.04.1996	24		22
Espedito Marinaro (ITA)	10.09.1992		(3)	
Davide Massaro (ITA)	10.02.1998	24		12
Mirco Vassallo (ITA)	28.02.1993	9	(6)	6
Trainer:	**DOB**	**M**		
Matteo Cecchetti (ITA)	01.01.1979	26		

Società Polisportiva Tre Penne Città di San Marino

Founded: 1956
Stadium: Stadio Fonte Dell'Ovo, Città di San Marino (500)

Goalkeepers:	**DOB**	**M**	**(s)**	**G**
Mauro Lanzoni (ITA)	20.09.1987	1		
Mattia Migani (ITA)	10.03.1992	23		
Defenders:	**DOB**	**M**	**(s)**	**G**
Davide Cesarini	16.02.1995	16		1
Christofer Genestreti (ITA)	30.05.1984	22	(1)	
Dario Merendino (ITA)	14.11.1983	21		
Mirko Palazzi	21.03.1987	18	(4)	5
Andrea Rossi	20.07.1987	7	(3)	1
Midfielders:	**DOB**	**M**	**(s)**	**G**
Daniele Amadei	15.01.1989		(2)	
Pietro Calzolari	28.10.1991	3	(6)	
Luca Ceccaroli	05.07.1995	10	(2)	7
Nicola Chiaruzzi	25.12.1987	8	(6)	2
Enrico Cibelli	14.07.1987	13	(6)	3
Thomas De Marini	02.11.1998		(3)	
Stefano Fraternali (ITA)	13.04.1986	20	(1)	3
Nicola Gai (ITA)	06.12.1987	23		14
Alex Gasperoni	30.06.1984	16	(5)	2
Luca Patregnani (ITA)	08.04.1985	19		2
Riccardo Santini	13.10.1986	3	(9)	1
Giacomo Zafferani	16.07.1996		(4)	
Forwards:	**DOB**	**M**	**(s)**	**G**
Luca Albani (ITA)	15.12.1993		(1)	
Marco Martini (ITA)	12.04.1979	19	(2)	12
Federico Ceccarini (ITA)	11.01.1997		(1)	
Kevin Marigliano (ITA)	10.05.1993	3	(11)	4
Michele Simoncelli (ITA)	03.03.1982	8		1
Raul Ura (ITA)	10.09.1998	11	(3)	3
Trainer:	**DOB**	**M**		
Luigi Bizzotto (ITA)	08.03.1970	9		
Stefano Ceci [03.12.2018]	16.10.1969	15		

Società Sportiva Virtus Acquaviva

Founded: 1964
Stadium: Stadio di Acquaviva, Acquaviva (2,000)

Goalkeepers:	**DOB**	**M**	**(s)**	**G**
Simone Guerra (ITA)	31.10.1982	1	(1)	
Luca Lelli	25.09.1979	15		
Erik Santini (ITA)	20.05.1992	3		
Defenders:	**DOB**	**M**	**(s)**	**G**
David Astolfi (ITA)	10.02.1998	18		
Francesco Bonfè	27.05.1994	13	(3)	
Andrea Boschi (ITA)	19.05.1998	5	(1)	
Federico Corbelli	16.01.1998	1	(1)	
Nicola Gavagnin (ITA)	04.01.1990	3	(1)	
Xhulio Gega (ALB)	17.02.1995	16	(1)	
Matteo Guiducci (ITA)	28.11.1980	12		
Marco Pazzaglia	14.02.1998	2	(5)	
Andrea Righi	16.09.1997	11	(1)	
Luca Righi	01.04.1995	16		2
Midfielders:	**DOB**	**M**	**(s)**	**G**
Riccardo Bettini (ITA)	07.07.1996	9	(5)	1
Nicholas Brilli (ITA)	05.02.1990	9		
Riccardo Colonna	10.04.1999	15		1
Luca Molari (ITA)	12.07.1990	6	(1)	
Nicola Moroni	05.05.1997		(1)	
Christian Pala	13.07.1996		(5)	
Simone Santarini	17.10.1991	5		
Luca Tomassoni (ITA)	21.11.1994	2		
Luca Tosi	23.07.1994	7	(4)	
Forwards:	**DOB**	**M**	**(s)**	**G**
Paolo Casadei	29.01.1995	7	(8)	
Federico Ceccarini (ITA)	11.01.1997	4	(2)	2
Matteo Giardi	14.04.1997	10	(6)	5
Tommaso Raffaelli (ITA)	06.09.1991	7	(6)	
Bajram Skender (ITA)	28.04.1996	3	(5)	1
Raul Ura (ITA)	10.09.1998	9		1
Trainer:	**DOB**	**M**		
Mirco Fratta (ITA)	19.04.1961	19		

NATIONAL TEAM

INTERNATIONAL MATCHES
(16.07.2018 – 15.07.2019)

08.09.2018	Minsk	Belarus - San Marino	5-0(2-0)	(UNL)
11.09.2018	Serravalle	San Marino - Luxembourg	0-3(0-2)	(UNL)
12.10.2018	Chişinău	Moldova - San Marino	2-0(1-0)	(UNL)
15.10.2018	Lëtzebuerg	Luxembourg - San Marino	3-0(1-0)	(UNL)
15.11.2018	Serravalle	San Marino - Moldova	0-1(0-0)	(UNL)
18.11.2018	Serravalle	San Marino - Belarus	0-2(0-1)	(UNL)
21.03.2019	Nicosia	Cyprus - San Marino	5-0(4-0)	(ECQ)
24.03.2019	Serravalle	San Marino - Scotland	0-2(0-1)	(ECQ)
08.06.2019	Saransk	Russia - San Marino	9-0(4-0)	(ECQ)
11.06.2019	Nur-Sultan	Kazakhstan - San Marino	4-0(1-0)	(ECQ)

08.09.2018 BELARUS - SAN MARINO 5-0(2-0) UEFA Nations League D, Group 2
Stadion Dynama, Minsk; Referee: Sandro Schärer (Switzerland); Attendance: 13,634
SMR: Elia Benedettini, Davide Simoncini (Cap), Mirko Palazzi, Juri Biordi, Manuel Battistini, Davide Cesarini (81.Danilo Ezequiel Rinaldi), Alex Gasperoni (63.José Adolfo Hirsch), Mattia Giardi, Filippo Berardi, Lorenzo Lunadei, Matteo Giampaolo Vitaioli (62.Fabio Tomassini). Trainer: Franco Varrella.

11.09.2018 SAN MARINO - LUXEMBOURG 0-3(0-2) UEFA Nations League D, Group 2
San Marino Stadium, Serravalle; Referee: Filip Glova (Slovakia); Attendance: 794
SMR: Elia Benedettini, Davide Simoncini (Cap), Mirko Palazzi, Cristian Brolli, Andrea Grandoni, Mattia Giardi, Enrico Golinucci (88.Lorenzo Lunadei), Manuel Battistini, Filippo Berardi (72.Fabio Tomassini), Matteo Giampaolo Vitaioli, Danilo Ezequiel Rinaldi. Trainer: Franco Varrella.

12.10.2018 MOLDOVA - SAN MARINO 2-0(1-0) UEFA Nations League D, Group 2
Stadionul Zimbru, Chişinău; Referee: Bryn Markham-Jones (Wales); Attendance: 5,242
SMR: Elia Benedettini, Fabio Vitaioli, Cristian Brolli, Manuel Battistini, Andrea Grandoni, Alex Gasperoni, Mattia Giardi (46.Mirko Palazzi), Enrico Golinucci (84.Alessandro Golinucci), José Adolfo Hirsch (71.Fabio Tomassini), Marcello Mularoni, Matteo Giampaolo Vitaioli (Cap). Trainer: Franco Varrella.

15.10.2018 LUXEMBOURG - SAN MARINO 3-0(1-0) UEFA Nations League D, Group 2
Stade "Josy Barthel", Lëtzebuerg; Referee: Aleksandrs Golubevs (Latvia); Attendance: 2,876
SMR: Elia Benedettini, Fabio Vitaioli, Davide Simoncini (Cap), Davide Cesarini, Andrea Grandoni (76.Mirko Palazzi), Alex Gasperoni [*sent off 54*], Mattia Giardi, Enrico Golinucci (85.Alessandro Golinucci), Marcello Mularoni, Matteo Giampaolo Vitaioli, Fabio Tomassini (61.Lorenzo Lunadei). Trainer: Franco Varrella.

15.11.2018 SAN MARINO - MOLDOVA 0-1(0-0) UEFA Nations League D, Group 2
San Marino Stadium, Serravalle; Referee: Georgios Kominis (Greece); Attendance: 747
SMR: Elia Benedettini, Fabio Vitaioli, Davide Simoncini (Cap), Mirko Palazzi, Manuel Battistini, Andrea Grandoni (87.José Adolfo Hirsch), Enrico Golinucci, Marcello Mularoni, Lorenzo Lunadei (76.Alessandro Golinucci), Matteo Giampaolo Vitaioli (81.Fabio Tomassini), Nicola Nanni. Trainer: Franco Varrella.

18.11.2018 SAN MARINO - BELARUS 0-2(0-1) UEFA Nations League D, Group 2
San Marino Stadium, Serravalle; Referee: Giorgi Kruashvili (Georgia); Attendance: 736
SMR: Elia Benedettini, Fabio Vitaioli, Davide Simoncini (Cap), Mirko Palazzi, Alex Gasperoni (62.Fabio Tomassini), Enrico Golinucci, José Adolfo Hirsch (90.Davide Cesarini), Alessandro Golinucci, Manuel Battistini, Danilo Ezequiel Rinaldi, Nicola Nanni (63.Mattia Giardi). Trainer: Franco Varrella.

21.03.2019 CYPRUS - SAN MARINO 5-0(4-0) 16th EC. Qualifiers
Stádio GSP, Nicosia; Referee: Juri Frischer (Estonia); Attendance: 3,175
SMR: Elia Benedettini, Davide Simoncini (Cap), Mirko Palazzi, Manuel Battistini, Michele Cevoli, Mattia Giardi (74.Lorenzo Lunadei), Enrico Golinucci, Marcello Mularoni, Filippo Berardi, Danilo Ezequiel Rinaldi (46.José Adolfo Hirsch), Nicola Nanni (46.Matteo Giampaolo Vitaioli). Trainer: Franco Varrella.

24.03.2019 SAN MARINO - SCOTLAND 0-2(0-1) 16th EC. Qualifiers
San Marino Stadium, Serravalle; Referee: Manuel Schüttengruber (Austria); Attendance: 4,077
SMR: Elia Benedettini, Davide Simoncini (Cap) (86.Lorenzo Lunadei), Mirko Palazzi, Manuel Battistini, Michele Cevoli, Enrico Golinucci, José Adolfo Hirsch (77.Andrea Grandoni), Alessandro Golinucci, Marcello Mularoni, Filippo Berardi, Matteo Giampaolo Vitaioli (60.Nicola Nanni). Trainer: Franco Varrella.

08.06.2019 RUSSIA - SAN MARINO 9-0(4-0) 16th EC. Qualifiers
Mordovia Arena, Saransk; Referee: Mohammed Al Hakim (Sweden); Attendance: 42,241
SMR: Elia Benedettini, Fabio Vitaioli, Mirko Palazzi (50.Luca Censoni), Manuel Battistini, Andrea Grandoni, Michele Cevoli, Enrico Golinucci, Alessandro Golinucci (64.Lorenzo Lunadei), Marcello Mularoni, Matteo Giampaolo Vitaioli (Cap), Danilo Ezequiel Rinaldi (56.Fabio Tomassini). Trainer: Franco Varrella.

11.06.2019 KAZAKHSTAN - SAN MARINO 4-0(1-0) 16th EC. Qualifiers
Astana Arena, Nur-Sultan; Referee: Bartosz Frankowski (Poland); Attendance: 18,652
SMR: Elia Benedettini, Fabio Vitaioli, Cristian Brolli, Davide Cesarini (77.Manuel Battistini), Andrea Grandoni, Luca Censoni, Michael Battistini (46.Enrico Golinucci), Marcello Mularoni, Lorenzo Lunadei, Matteo Giampaolo Vitaioli (Cap) (83.Marco Bernardi), Nicola Nanni. Trainer: Franco Varrella.

NATIONAL TEAM PLAYERS
(16.07.2018 – 15.07.2019)

Name	DOB	Caps	Goals	2018/2019:	Club
Goalkeepers					
Elia BENEDETTINI	22.06.1995	**17**	**0**	2018/2019:	*Novara Calcio (ITA)*
Defenders					
Manuel BATTISTINI	11.07.1994	**24**	**0**	2018/2019:	*AC Libertas Borgo Maggiore*
Juri BIORDI	01.01.1995	**6**	**0**	2018:	*FC Fiorentino*
Cristian BROLLI	28.02.1992	**25**	**0**	2018/2019:	*SS Folgore Falciano Calcio Serravalle*
Davide CESARINI	16.02.1995	**15**	**0**	2018/2019:	*SP Tre Penne Città di San Marino*
Michele CEVOLI	22.07.1998	**6**	**0**	2019:	*San Marino Calcio Serravalle*
Andrea GRANDONI	23.03.1997	**11**	**0**	2018: 12.12.2018->	*San Marino Calcio Serravalle* *ACD Marignanese Calcio (ITA)*
Mirko PALAZZI	21.03.1987	**46**	**1**	2018/2019:	*SP Tre Penne Città di San Marino*
Davide SIMONCINI	30.08.1986	**57**	**0**	2018/2019:	*AC Libertas Borgo Maggiore*
Fabio VITAIOLI	05.04.1984	**53**	**0**	2018/2019:	*ASD Tropical Coriano (ITA)*
Midfielders					
Michael BATTISTINI	08.10.1996	**4**	**0**	2019:	*AC Libertas Borgo Maggiore*
Luca CENSONI	18.07.1996	**2**	**0**	2019:	*SSD Fya Riccione (ITA)*
Alex GASPERONI	30.06.1984	**44**	**1**	2018:	*SP Tre Penne Città di San Marino*
Mattia GIARDI	15.12.1991	**6**	**0**	2018: 16.01.2019->	*SC Faetano* *SP Tre Fiori Fiorentino*
Alessandro GOLINUCCI	10.10.1994	**13**	**0**	2018: 01.2019->	*US Pietracuta San Leo (ITA)* *ASD Tropical Coriano (ITA)*
Enrico GOLINUCCI	16.07.1991	**15**	**0**	2018/2019:	*AC Libertas Borgo Maggiore*
Lorenzo LUNADEI	12.07.1997	**9**	**0**	2018/2019:	*SSD Fya Riccione (ITA)*
Marcello MULARONI	08.09.1998	**7**	**0**	2018/2019:	*US Pietracuta San Leo (ITA)*
Forwards					
Filippo BERARDI	18.05.1997	**8**	**0**	2018/2019:	*SS Monopoli 1966 (ITA)*
Marco BERNARDI	02.01.1994	**6**	**0**	2019:	*SS Folgore Falciano Calcio Serravalle*
José Adolfo HIRSCH	31.01.1986	**28**	**0**	2018/2019:	*SP La Fiorita Montegiardino*
Nicola NANNI	02.05.2000	**5**	**0**	2018/2019:	*FC Crotone (ITA)*
Danilo Ezequiel RINALDI	18.04.1986	**40**	**1**	2018/2019:	*SP La Fiorita Montegiardino*
Fabio TOMASSINI	05.02.1996	**13**	**0**	2018/2019:	*US Pietracuta San Leo (ITA)*
Matteo Giampaolo VITAIOLI	27.10.1989	**57**	**1**	2018/2019:	*ASD Tropical Coriano (ITA)*

National team coach

Franco VARRELLA [from 15.01.2018]	25.01.1953	10 M; 0 W; 0 D; 10 L; 0-36

SCOTLAND

The Country:
Scotland
Capital: Edinburgh
Surface: 77,933 km²
Inhabitants: 5,424,800 [2017]
Time: UTC

The FA:
Scottish Football Association
Hampden Park G42 9AY Glasgow
Tel: +44 141 616 6000
Founded: 1873
Member of FIFA since: 1910
Member of UEFA since: 1954
Website: www.scottishfa.co.uk

NATIONAL TEAM RECORDS

First international match:	30.11.1872, Glasgow:	Scotland – England 0-0
Most international caps:	Kenneth Mathieson Dalglish	- 102 caps (1971-1986)
Most international goals:	Denis Law	- 30 goals / 55 caps (1958-1974)

UEFA EUROPEAN CHAMPIONSHIP	
1960	Did not enter
1964	Did not enter
1968	Qualifiers
1972	Qualifiers
1976	Qualifiers
1980	Qualifiers
1984	Qualifiers
1988	Qualifiers
1992	Final Tournament (Group Stage)
1996	Final Tournament (Group Stage)
2000	Qualifiers
2004	Qualifiers
2008	Qualifiers
2012	Qualifiers
2016	Qualifiers

FIFA WORLD CUP	
1930	Did not enter
1934	Did not enter
1938	Did not enter
1950	*Withdrew after being qualified*
1954	Final Tournament (Group Stage)
1958	Final Tournament (Group Stage)
1962	Qualifiers
1966	Qualifiers
1970	Qualifiers
1974	Final Tournament (Group Stage)
1978	Final Tournament (Group Stage)
1982	Final Tournament (Group Stage)
1986	Final Tournament (Group Stage)
1990	Final Tournament (Group Stage)
1994	Qualifiers
1998	Final Tournament (Group Stage)
2002	Qualifiers
2006	Qualifiers
2010	Qualifiers
2014	Qualifiers
2018	Qualifiers

UEFA NATIONS LEAGUE

2018/2019 – League C (promoted to League B)

FIFA CONFEDERATIONS CUP 1992-2017

None

SCOTTISH CLUB HONOURS IN EUROPEAN CLUB COMPETITIONS:

European Champion Clubs.Cup (1956-1992) / UEFA Champions League (1993-2019)		
Celtic FC Glasgow	**1**	1966/1967
Fairs Cup (1858-1971) / UEFA Cup (1972-2009) / UEFA Europa League (2010-2019)		
None		
UEFA Super Cup (1972-2018)		
Aberdeen FC	**1**	1983
European Cup Winners.Cup 1961-1999*		
Rangers FC Glasgow	**1**	1971/1972
Aberdeen FC	**1**	1982/1983

**defunct competition*

NATIONAL COMPETITIONS
TABLE OF HONOURS

	CHAMPIONS	CUP WINNERS	BEST GOALSCORERS	
1873/1874	-	Queen's Park FC Glasgow	-	
1874/1875	-	Queen's Park FC Glasgow	-	
1875/1876	-	Queen's Park FC Glasgow	-	
1876/1877	-	Vale of Leven FC Alexandria	-	
1877/1878	-	Vale of Leven FC Alexandria	-	
1878/1879	-	Vale of Leven FC Alexandria	-	
1879/1880	-	Queen's Park FC Glasgow	-	
1880/1881	-	Queen's Park FC Glasgow	-	
1881/1882	-	Queen's Park FC Glasgow	-	
1882/1883	-	Dumbarton FC	-	
1883/1884	-	Queen's Park FC Glasgow	-	
1884/1885	-	Renton FC	-	
1885/1886	-	Queen's Park FC Glasgow	-	
1886/1887	-	Hibernian FC Edinburgh	-	
1887/1888	-	Renton FC	-	
1888/1889	-	Third Lanark AC Glasgow	-	
1889/1890	-	Queen's Park FC Glasgow	-	
1890/1891	Dumbarton FC Rangers FC Glasgow [joint winners]	Heart of Midlothian FC Edinburgh	Jack Bell (Dumbarton FC)	20
1891/1892	Dumbarton FC	Celtic FC Glasgow	Jack Bell (Dumbarton FC)	23
1892/1893	Celtic FC Glasgow	Queen's Park FC Glasgow	Sandy McMahon (Celtic FC Glasgow) John Campbell (Celtic FC Glasgow)	11
1893/1894	Celtic FC Glasgow	Rangers FC Glasgow	Sandy McMahon (Celtic FC Glasgow)	16
1894/1895	Heart of Midlothian FC Edinburgh	St. Bernard's FC Edinburgh	James Miller (Clyde FC Cumbernauld)	12
1895/1896	Celtic FC Glasgow	Heart of Midlothian FC Edinburgh	Allan Martin (Celtic FC Glasgow)	19
1896/1897	Heart of Midlothian FC Edinburgh	Rangers FC Glasgow	Willie Taylor (Heart of Midlothian FC Edinburgh)	12
1897/1898	Celtic FC Glasgow	Rangers FC Glasgow	Robert Hamilton (Rangers FC Glasgow)	18
1898/1899	Rangers FC Glasgow	Celtic FC Glasgow	Robert Hamilton (Rangers FC Glasgow)	25
1899/1900	Rangers FC Glasgow	Celtic FC Glasgow	Robert Hamilton (Rangers FC Glasgow) William Michael (Heart of Midlothian FC Edinburgh)	15
1900/1901	Rangers FC Glasgow	Heart of Midlothian FC Edinburgh	Robert Hamilton (Rangers FC Glasgow)	20
1901/1902	Rangers FC Glasgow	Hibernian FC Edinburgh	William Maxwell (Third Lanark AC Glasgow)	10
1902/1903	Hibernian FC Edinburgh	Rangers FC Glasgow	David Reid (Hibernian FC Edinburgh)	14
1903/1904	Third Lanark AC Glasgow	Celtic FC Glasgow	Robert Hamilton (Rangers FC Glasgow)	28
1904/1905	Celtic FC Glasgow	Third Lanark AC Glasgow	Robert Hamilton (Rangers FC Glasgow) James Quinn (Celtic FC Glasgow)	19
1905/1906	Celtic FC Glasgow	Heart of Midlothian FC Edinburgh	James Quinn (Celtic FC Glasgow)	20
1906/1907	Celtic FC Glasgow	Celtic FC Glasgow	James Quinn (Celtic FC Glasgow)	29
1907/1908	Celtic FC Glasgow	Celtic FC Glasgow	Jock Simpson (Falkirk FC)	32
1908/1909	Celtic FC Glasgow	*No competition*	John Hunter (Dundee FC)	29
1909/1910	Celtic FC Glasgow	Dundee FC	James Quinn (Celtic FC Glasgow) Jock Simpson (Falkirk FC)	24
1910/1911	Rangers FC Glasgow	Celtic FC Glasgow	William Reid (Rangers FC Glasgow)	38
1911/1912	Rangers FC Glasgow	Celtic FC Glasgow	William Reid (Rangers FC Glasgow)	33
1912/1913	Rangers FC Glasgow	Falkirk FC	James Reid (Airdrieonians FC)	30
1913/1914	Celtic FC Glasgow	Celtic FC Glasgow	James Reid (Airdrieonians FC)	27
1914/1915	Celtic FC Glasgow	*No competition*	Tom Gracie (Heart of Midlothian FC Edinburgh) James Richardson (Ayr United FC)	29
1915/1916	Celtic FC Glasgow	*No competition*	James McColl (Celtic FC Glasgow)	34
1916/1917	Celtic FC Glasgow	*No competition*	Herbert George Yarnall (ENG, Airdrieonians FC)	39
1917/1918	Rangers FC Glasgow	*No competition*	Hugh Ferguson (Motherwell FC)	35
1918/1919	Celtic FC Glasgow	*No competition*	David McLean (Rangers FC Glasgow)	29
1919/1920	Rangers FC Glasgow	Kilmarnock FC	Hugh Ferguson (Motherwell FC)	33
1920/1921	Rangers FC Glasgow	Partick Thistle FC Glasgow	Hugh Ferguson (Motherwell FC)	43
1921/1922	Celtic FC Glasgow	Greenock Morton FC	Duncan Walker (St. Mirren FC Paisley)	45
1922/1923	Rangers FC Glasgow	Celtic FC Glasgow	John White (Heart of Midlothian FC Edinburgh)	30
1923/1924	Rangers FC Glasgow	Airdrieonians FC	David Halliday (Dundee FC)	38
1924/1925	Rangers FC Glasgow	Celtic FC Glasgow	William Alexander Devlin (Cowdenbeath FC)	33
1925/1926	Celtic FC Glasgow	St. Mirren FC Paisley	William Alexander Devlin (Cowdenbeath FC)	40
1926/1927	Rangers FC Glasgow	Celtic FC Glasgow	James Edward McGrory (Celtic FC Glasgow)	49
1927/1928	Rangers FC Glasgow	Rangers FC Glasgow	James Edward McGrory (Celtic FC Glasgow)	47
1928/1929	Rangers FC Glasgow	Kilmarnock FC	Evelyn Morrison (Falkirk FC)	43
1929/1930	Rangers FC Glasgow	Rangers FC Glasgow	Benjamin Collard Yorston (Aberdeen FC)	38
1930/1931	Rangers FC Glasgow	Celtic FC Glasgow	Bernard Joseph Battles Jr. (Heart of Midlothian FC Edinburgh)	44
1931/1932	Motherwell FC	Rangers FC Glasgow	William MacFadyen (Motherwell FC)	52
1932/1933	Rangers FC Glasgow	Celtic FC Glasgow	William MacFadyen (Motherwell FC)	45
1933/1934	Rangers FC Glasgow	Rangers FC Glasgow	James Smith (Rangers FC Glasgow)	41
1934/1935	Rangers FC Glasgow	Rangers FC Glasgow	James Smith (Rangers FC Glasgow)	36

1935/1936	Celtic FC Glasgow	Rangers FC Glasgow	James Edward McGrory (Celtic FC Glasgow)	50
1936/1937	Rangers FC Glasgow	Celtic FC Glasgow	David Wilson (Hamilton Academical)	34
1937/1938	Celtic FC Glasgow	East Fife FC Methil	Andrew Black (Heart of Midlothian FC Edinburgh)	40
1938/1939	Rangers FC Glasgow	Clyde FC Cumbernauld	Alexander Venters (Rangers FC Glasgow)	35
1939/1940	*No competition*	*No competition*	-	
1940/1941	*No competition*	*No competition*	-	
1941/1942	*No competition*	*No competition*	-	
1942/1943	*No competition*	*No competition*	-	
1943/1944	*No competition*	*No competition*	-	
1944/1945	*No competition*	*No competition*	-	
1945/1946	*No competition*	*No competition*	-	
1946/1947	Rangers FC Glasgow	Aberdeen FC	Robert Carmichael Mitchell (Third Lanark AC Glasgow)	22
1947/1948	Hibernian FC Edinburgh	Rangers FC Glasgow	Archie Aikman (Falkirk FC)	20
1948/1949	Rangers FC Glasgow	Rangers FC Glasgow	Alexander Gair Stott (Dundee FC)	30
1949/1950	Rangers FC Glasgow	Rangers FC Glasgow	Willie Bauld (Heart of Midlothian FC Edinburgh)	30
1950/1951	Hibernian FC Edinburgh	Celtic FC Glasgow	Lawrance Reilly (Hibernian FC Edinburgh)	22
1951/1952	Hibernian FC Edinburgh	Motherwell FC	Lawrance Reilly (Hibernian FC Edinburgh)	27
1952/1953	Rangers FC Glasgow	Rangers FC Glasgow	Lawrance Reilly (Hibernian FC Edinburgh) Charlie Fleming (East Fife FC Methil)	30
1953/1954	Celtic FC Glasgow	Celtic FC Glasgow	James Wardhaugh (Heart of Midlothian FC Edinburgh)	27
1954/1955	Aberdeen FC	Clyde FC Cumbernauld	Willie Bauld (Heart of Midlothian FC Edinburgh)	21
1955/1956	Rangers FC Glasgow	Heart of Midlothian FC Edinburgh	James Wardhaugh (Heart of Midlothian FC Edinburgh)	28
1956/1957	Rangers FC Glasgow	Falkirk FC	Hugh Baird (Airdrieonians FC)	33
1957/1958	Heart of Midlothian FC Edinburgh	Clyde FC Cumbernauld	James Wardhaugh (Heart of Midlothian FC Edinburgh) James Murray (Heart of Midlothian FC Edinburgh)	28
1958/1959	Rangers FC Glasgow	St. Mirren FC Paisley	Joseph Henry Baker (Hibernian FC Edinburgh)	25
1959/1960	Heart of Midlothian FC Edinburgh	Rangers FC Glasgow	Joseph Henry Baker (Hibernian FC Edinburgh)	42
1960/1961	Rangers FC Glasgow	Dunfermline Athletic FC	Alexander Harley (Third Lanark AC Glasgow)	42
1961/1962	Dundee FC	Rangers FC Glasgow	Alan John Gilzean (Dundee FC)	24
1962/1963	Rangers FC Glasgow	Rangers FC Glasgow	James Millar (Rangers FC Glasgow)	27
1963/1964	Rangers FC Glasgow	Rangers FC Glasgow	Alan John Gilzean (Dundee FC)	32
1964/1965	Kilmarnock FC	Celtic FC Glasgow	Jim Forrest (Rangers FC Glasgow)	30
1965/1966	Celtic FC Glasgow	Rangers FC Glasgow	James McBride (Celtic FC Glasgow) Alexander Chapman Ferguson (Dunfermline Athletic FC)	31
1966/1967	Celtic FC Glasgow	Celtic FC Glasgow	Thomas Stephen Chalmers (Celtic FC Glasgow)	21
1967/1968	Celtic FC Glasgow	Dunfermline Athletic FC	Robert Lennox (Celtic FC Glasgow)	32
1968/1969	Celtic FC Glasgow	Celtic FC Glasgow	Kenneth Cameron (Dundee United FC)	26
1969/1970	Celtic FC Glasgow	Aberdeen FC	Colin Anderson Stein (Rangers FC Glasgow)	24
1970/1971	Celtic FC Glasgow	Celtic FC Glasgow	Henry Anthony Hood (Celtic FC Glasgow)	22
1971/1972	Celtic FC Glasgow	Celtic FC Glasgow	Joseph Montgomery Harper (Aberdeen FC)	33
1972/1973	Celtic FC Glasgow	Rangers FC Glasgow	Alan Fordyce Gordon (Hibernian FC Edinburgh)	27
1973/1974	Celtic FC Glasgow	Celtic FC Glasgow	John Kelly Deans (Celtic FC Glasgow)	26
1974/1975	Rangers FC Glasgow	Celtic FC Glasgow	Andrew Mullen Gray (Dundee United FC) William Pettigrew (Motherwell FC)	20
1975/1976	Rangers FC Glasgow	Rangers FC Glasgow	Kenneth Mathieson Dalglish (Celtic FC Glasgow)	24
1976/1977	Celtic FC Glasgow	Celtic FC Glasgow	William Pettigrew (Motherwell FC)	21
1977/1978	Rangers FC Glasgow	Rangers FC Glasgow	Derek Joseph Johnstone (Rangers FC Glasgow)	25
1978/1979	Celtic FC Glasgow	Rangers FC Glasgow	Andrew Ritchie (Greenock Morton FC)	22
1979/1980	Aberdeen FC	Celtic FC Glasgow	Douglas McKenzie Somner (St. Mirren FC Paisley)	25
1980/1981	Celtic FC Glasgow	Rangers FC Glasgow	Francis Peter McGarvey (Celtic FC Glasgow)	23
1981/1982	Celtic FC Glasgow	Aberdeen FC	George McKinley Cassidy McCluskey (Celtic FC Glasgow)	21
1982/1983	Dundee United FC	Aberdeen FC	Charles Nicholas (Celtic FC Glasgow)	29
1983/1984	Aberdeen FC	Aberdeen FC	Brian John McClair (Celtic FC Glasgow)	23
1984/1985	Aberdeen FC	Celtic FC Glasgow	Douglas Francis McDougall (Aberdeen FC)	22
1985/1986	Celtic FC Glasgow	Aberdeen FC	Alistair Murdoch McCoist (Rangers FC Glasgow)	24
1986/1987	Rangers FC Glasgow	St. Mirren FC Paisley	Brian John McClair (Celtic FC Glasgow)	35
1987/1988	Celtic FC Glasgow	Celtic FC Glasgow	Tommy Coyne (Dundee FC)	33
1988/1989	Rangers FC Glasgow	Celtic FC Glasgow	Mark EdwardMcGhee (Celtic FC Glasgow) Charles Nicholas (Aberdeen FC)	16
1989/1990	Rangers FC Glasgow	Aberdeen FC	John Grant Robertson (Heart of Midlothian FC Edinburgh)	17
1990/1991	Rangers FC Glasgow	Motherwell FC	Tommy Coyne (Celtic FC Glasgow)	18
1991/1992	Rangers FC Glasgow	Rangers FC Glasgow	Alistair Murdoch McCoist (Rangers FC Glasgow)	34
1992/1993	Rangers FC Glasgow	Rangers FC Glasgow	Alistair Murdoch McCoist (Rangers FC Glasgow)	34
1993/1994	Rangers FC Glasgow	Dundee United FC	Mark Wayne Hateley (ENG, Rangers FC Glasgow)	22
1994/1995	Rangers FC Glasgow	Celtic FC Glasgow	Tommy Coyne (Motherwell FC)	16
1995/1996	Rangers FC Glasgow	Rangers FC Glasgow	Petrus Ferdinandus Johannes van Hooijdonk (NED, Celtic FC Glasgow)	26
1996/1997	Rangers FC Glasgow	Kilmarnock FC	Jorge Paulo Cadete Santos Reis (POR, Celtic FC Glasgow)	25
1997/1998	Celtic FC Glasgow	Heart of Midlothian FC Edinburgh	Marco Negri (ITA, Rangers FC Glasgow)	32
1998/1999	Rangers FC Glasgow	Rangers FC Glasgow	Henrik Edward Larsson (SWE, Celtic FC Glasgow)	29

1999/2000	Rangers FC Glasgow	Rangers FC Glasgow	Mark Anthony Viduka (AUS, Celtic FC Glasgow)	25
2000/2001	Celtic FC Glasgow	Celtic FC Glasgow	Henrik Edward Larsson (SWE, Celtic FC Glasgow)	35
2001/2002	Celtic FC Glasgow	Rangers FC Glasgow	Henrik Edward Larsson (SWE, Celtic FC Glasgow)	29
2002/2003	Rangers FC Glasgow	Rangers FC Glasgow	Henrik Edward Larsson (SWE, Celtic FC Glasgow)	28
2003/2004	Celtic FC Glasgow	Celtic FC Glasgow	Henrik Edward Larsson (SWE, Celtic FC Glasgow)	30
2004/2005	Rangers FC Glasgow	Celtic FC Glasgow	John Hartson (WAL, Celtic FC Glasgow)	25
2005/2006	Celtic FC Glasgow	Heart of Midlothian FC Edinburgh	Kris Boyd (Kilmarnock FC / Rangers FC Glasgow)	32
2006/2007	Celtic FC Glasgow	Celtic FC Glasgow	Kris Boyd (Rangers FC Glasgow)	20
2007/2008	Celtic FC Glasgow	Rangers FC Glasgow	Scott Douglas McDonald (AUS, Celtic FC Glasgow)	25
2008/2009	Rangers FC Glasgow	Rangers FC Glasgow	Kris Boyd (Rangers FC Glasgow)	27
2009/2010	Rangers FC Glasgow	Dundee United FC	Kris Boyd (Rangers FC Glasgow)	23
2010/2011	Rangers FC Glasgow	Celtic FC Glasgow	Kenneth Miller (Rangers FC Glasgow)	21
2011/2012	Celtic FC Glasgow	Heart of Midlothian FC Edinburgh	Gary Hooper (ENG, Celtic FC Glasgow)	24
2012/2013	Celtic FC Glasgow	Celtic FC Glasgow	Michael Higdon (ENG, Motherwell FC)	26
2013/2014	Celtic FC Glasgow	St. Johnstone FC Perth	Kristian Arran Commons (Celtic FC Glasgow)	27
2014/2015	Celtic FC Glasgow	Inverness Caledonian Thistle FC	Adam Christopher Rooney (IRL, Aberdeen FC)	18
2015/2016	Celtic FC Glasgow	Hibernian FC Edinburgh	Leigh Griffiths (Celtic FC Glasgow)	31
2016/2017	Celtic FC Glasgow	Celtic FC Glasgow	Liam Boyce (NIR, Ross County FC Dingwall)	23
2017/2018	Celtic FC Glasgow	Celtic FC Glasgow	Kris Boyd (Kilmarnock FC)	18
2018/2019	Celtic FC Glasgow	Celtic FC Glasgow	Alfredo José Morelos Aviléz (COL, Rangers FC Glasgow)	18

NATIONAL CHAMPIONSHIP
Scottish Premiership 2018/2019
(04.08.2018 – 19.05.2019)

Regular Season - Results

Round 1 [04-05.08.2018]
Celtic FC - Livingston FC 3-1(2-0)
Hamilton - Heart of Midlothian 1-4(1-1)
St. Mirren FC - Dundee FC 2-1(1-1)
Kilmarnock FC - St. Johnstone FC 2-0(0-0)
Aberdeen FC - Rangers FC 1-1(0-1)
Hibernian FC - Motherwell FC 3-0(2-0)

Round 2 [11-12.08.2018]
Heart of Midlothian - Celtic FC 1-0(0-0)
Dundee FC - Aberdeen FC 0-1(0-0)
Livingston FC - Kilmarnock FC 0-0
Motherwell FC - Hamilton 0-1(0-0)
Rangers FC - St. Mirren FC 2-0(2-0)
St. Johnstone FC - Hibernian FC 1-1(1-0)

Round 3 [25-26.08.2018]
Hibernian FC - Aberdeen FC 1-1(0-1)
Kilmarnock FC - Heart of Midlothian 0-1(0-0)
St. Johnstone FC - Dundee FC 1-0(0-0)
St. Mirren FC - Livingston FC 0-2(0-2)
Motherwell FC - Rangers FC 3-3(2-3)
Celtic FC - Hamilton 1-0(0-0)

Round 4 [01-02.09.2018]
Aberdeen FC - Kilmarnock FC 0-2(0-1)
Dundee FC - Motherwell FC 1-3(0-0)
Hamilton - St. Johnstone FC 1-2(0-2)
Heart of Midlothian - St. Mirren FC 4-1(4-1)
Livingston FC - Hibernian FC 2-1(0-0)
Celtic FC - Rangers FC 1-0(0-0)

Round 5 [14-15.09.2018]
St. Mirren FC - Celtic FC 0-0
Hibernian FC - Kilmarnock FC 3-2(2-2)
Livingston FC - Hamilton 1-0(1-0)
Motherwell FC - Heart of Midlothian 0-1(0-1)
Rangers FC - Dundee FC 4-0(3-0)
St. Johnstone FC - Aberdeen FC 1-1(1-0)

Round 6 [22-23.09.2018]
Aberdeen FC - Motherwell FC 1-0(1-0)
Dundee FC - Hibernian FC 0-3(0-0)
Hamilton - St. Mirren FC 3-0(2-0)
Heart of Midlothian - Livingston FC 0-0
Kilmarnock FC - Celtic FC 2-1(0-1)
Rangers FC - St. Johnstone FC 5-1(2-0)

Round 7 [29-30.09.2018]
Celtic FC - Aberdeen FC 1-0(0-0)
Hamilton - Dundee FC 0-2(0-1)
Heart of Midlothian - St. Johnstone 2-1(1-0)
Kilmarnock FC - Motherwell FC 3-1(2-1)
St. Mirren FC - Hibernian FC 0-1(0-1)
Livingston FC - Rangers FC 1-0(1-0)

Round 8 [06-07.10.2018]
Aberdeen FC - St. Mirren FC 4-1(3-0)
Dundee FC - Kilmarnock FC 1-2(1-1)
Hibernian FC - Hamilton 6-0(3-0)
Motherwell FC - Livingston FC 1-1(1-0)
Rangers FC - Heart of Midlothian 3-1(3-0)
St. Johnstone FC - Celtic FC 0-6(0-5)

Round 9 [20-21.10.2018]
Celtic FC - Hibernian FC 4-2(2-0)
Heart of Midlothian - Aberdeen FC 2-1(2-0)
Livingston FC - Dundee FC 4-0(2-0)
Motherwell FC - St. Johnstone FC 0-1(0-0)
St. Mirren FC - Kilmarnock FC 1-2(1-0)
Hamilton - Rangers FC 1-4(0-1)

Round 10 [23-27.10.2018]
Dundee FC - Heart of Midlothian 0-3(0-2)
Kilmarnock FC - Hamilton 1-1(1-1)
St. Johnstone FC - St. Mirren FC 2-0(0-0)
Aberdeen - Livingston 3-2(1-2) [11.12.2018]
Celtic - Motherwell FC 3-0(3-0) [19.12.2018]
Hibernian FC - Rangers FC 0-0 [19.12.2018]

Round 11 [31.10.2018]
Aberdeen FC - Hamilton 3-0(2-0)
Dundee FC - Celtic FC 0-5(0-4)
Heart of Midlothian - Hibernian FC 0-0
Livingston FC - St. Johnstone FC 0-1(0-1)
Rangers FC - Kilmarnock FC 1-1(1-1)
St. Mirren FC - Motherwell FC 0-2(0-1)

Round 12 [03-04.11.2018]
St. Mirren FC - Rangers FC 0-2(0-0)
Celtic FC - Heart of Midlothian 5-0(3-0)
Hamilton - Livingston FC 1-0(0-0)
Hibernian FC - St. Johnstone FC 0-1(0-0)
Motherwell FC - Dundee FC 1-0(0-0)
Kilmarnock FC - Aberdeen FC 1-2(1-0)

Round 13 [09-11.11.2018]
Aberdeen FC - Hibernian FC 1-0(1-0)
Dundee FC - St. Mirren FC 1-1(1-1)
Heart of Midlothian - Kilmarnock FC 0-1(0-0)
St. Johnstone FC - Hamilton 4-0(2-0)
Livingston FC - Celtic FC 0-0
Rangers FC - Motherwell FC 7-1(3-1)

Round 14 [24.11.2018]
Hamilton - Celtic FC 0-3(0-1)
Hibernian FC - Dundee FC 2-2(2-1)
Motherwell FC - Aberdeen FC 3-0(2-0)
Rangers FC - Livingston FC 3-0(1-0)
St. Johnstone FC - Kilmarnock FC 0-0
St. Mirren FC - Heart of Midlothian 2-0(0-0)

Round 15 [01-02.12.2018]
Kilmarnock FC - Hibernian FC 3-0(2-0)
Livingston FC - Motherwell FC 2-0(1-0)
St. Mirren FC - Hamilton 1-3(1-2)
Heart of Midlothian - Rangers FC 1-2(1-2)
Aberdeen - Dundee FC 5-1(2-0) [18.12.2019]
Celtic - St. Johnstone 2-0(0-0) [20.01.2019]

Round 16 [05.12.2018]
Dundee FC - Hamilton 4-0(1-0)
Hibernian FC - St. Mirren FC 2-2(0-1)
Kilmarnock FC - Livingston FC 2-0(2-0)
Motherwell FC - Celtic FC 1-1(0-1)
Rangers FC - Aberdeen FC 0-1(0-1)
St. Johnstone - Heart of Midlothian 2-2(1-2)

Round 17 [08-09.12.2018]
Aberdeen FC - St. Johnstone FC 0-2(0-0)
Celtic FC - Kilmarnock FC 5-1(4-0)
Hamilton - Hibernian FC 0-1(0-0)
Heart of Midlothian - Motherwell FC 1-0(1-0)
Livingston FC - St. Mirren FC 3-1(0-1)
Dundee FC - Rangers FC 1-1(1-1)

Round 18 [14-16.12.2018]
Livingston FC - Heart of Midlothian 5-0(0-0)
Kilmarnock FC - Dundee FC 3-1(0-0)
St. Johnstone FC - Motherwell FC 1-2(0-2)
St. Mirren FC - Aberdeen FC 1-2(1-1)
Hibernian FC - Celtic FC 2-0(1-0)
Rangers FC - Hamilton 1-0(1-0)

Round 19 [22-23.12.2018]
Aberdeen FC - Heart of Midlothian 2-0(1-0)
Celtic FC - Dundee FC 3-0(1-0)
Hamilton - Kilmarnock FC 1-1(1-1)
Hibernian FC - Livingston FC 1-1(0-0)
Motherwell FC - St. Mirren FC 0-1(0-0)
St. Johnstone FC - Rangers FC 1-2(1-0)

Round 20 [26.12.2018]
Aberdeen FC - Celtic FC 3-4(1-1)
St. Mirren FC - St. Johnstone FC 0-1(0-0)
Dundee FC - Livingston FC 0-0
Heart of Midlothian - Hamilton 2-0(2-0)
Motherwell FC - Kilmarnock FC 0-1(0-1)
Rangers FC - Hibernian FC 1-1(1-0)

Round 21 [29.12.2018]
Rangers FC - Celtic FC 1-0(1-0)
Dundee FC - St. Johnstone FC 0-2(0-1)
Hamilton - Motherwell FC 1-2(1-1)
Kilmarnock FC - St. Mirren FC 2-1(2-1)
Livingston FC - Aberdeen FC 1-2(0-0)
Hibernian FC - Heart of Midlothian 0-1(0-1)

Round 22 [23.01.2019]
Celtic FC - St. Mirren FC 4-0(2-0)
Hamilton - Aberdeen FC 0-3(0-1)
Heart of Midlothian - Dundee FC 1-2(1-1)
Kilmarnock FC - Rangers FC 2-1(1-1)
Motherwell FC - Hibernian FC 1-0(1-0)
St. Johnstone FC - Livingston FC 1-0(0-0)

Round 23 [26-27.01.2019]
Aberdeen FC - Kilmarnock FC 0-0
Celtic FC - Hamilton 3-0(1-0)
Dundee FC - Motherwell FC 0-1(0-0)
Heart of Midlothian - St. Johnstone 2-0(0-0)
St. Mirren FC - Hibernian FC 1-3(1-0)
Livingston FC - Rangers FC 0-3(0-1)

Round 24 [01-03.02.2019]
Kilmarnock FC - Heart of Midlothian 1-2(1-2)
Hamilton - Dundee FC 1-1(0-0)
Hibernian FC - Aberdeen FC 1-2(1-2)
Motherwell FC - Livingston FC 3-0(3-0)
Rangers FC - St. Mirren FC 4-0(1-0)
St. Johnstone FC - Celtic FC 0-2(0-0)

Round 25 [06.02.2019]
Aberdeen FC - Rangers FC 2-4(1-3)
Celtic FC - Hibernian FC 2-0(1-0)
Dundee FC - Kilmarnock FC 2-2(2-1)
Hamilton - St. Johnstone FC 2-1(0-0)
Heart of Midlothian - Livingston FC 0-0
St. Mirren FC - Motherwell FC 1-2(0-1)

Round 26 [16-17.02.2019]
Aberdeen FC - St. Mirren FC 2-2(1-1)
Hibernian FC - Hamilton 2-0(2-0)
Livingston FC - Dundee FC 1-2(1-0)
Rangers FC - St. Johnstone FC 0-0
Motherwell FC - Heart of Midlothian 2-1(1-1)
Kilmarnock FC - Celtic FC 0-1(0-0)

Round 27 [22-24.02.2019]
Dundee FC - Hibernian FC 2-4(1-2)
Heart of Midlothian - St. Mirren FC 1-1(0-0)
Livingston FC - Kilmarnock FC 1-0(1-0)
St. Johnstone FC - Aberdeen FC 0-2(0-1)
Hamilton - Rangers FC 0-5(0-4)
Celtic FC - Motherwell FC 4-1(2-0)

Round 28 [27.02.-02.03.2019]
Aberdeen FC - Hamilton 0-2(0-1)
Heart of Midlothian - Celtic FC 1-2(0-1)
Rangers FC - Dundee FC 4-0(3-0)
St. Johnstone FC - Hibernian FC 1-2(1-0)
Kilmarnock FC - Motherwell FC 0-0
St. Mirren FC - Livingston FC 1-0(0-0)

Round 29 [08-11.03.2019]
Hibernian FC - Rangers FC 1-1(0-1)
Celtic FC - Aberdeen FC 0-0
Dundee FC - Heart of Midlothian 0-1(0-1)
Livingston FC - St. Johnstone FC 3-1(1-1)
Motherwell FC - Hamilton 3-0(3-0)
St. Mirren FC - Kilmarnock FC 0-1(0-0)

Round 30 [16-17.03.2019]
Aberdeen FC - Livingston FC 1-1(1-1)
Hamilton - Heart of Midlothian 1-0(1-0)
Hibernian FC - Motherwell FC 2-0(2-0)
Rangers FC - Kilmarnock FC 1-1(0-1)
Dundee FC - Celtic FC 0-1(0-0)
St. Johnstone - St. Mirren 1-0(1-0) [27.03.19]

Round 31 [29-31.03.2019]
Livingston FC - Hibernian FC 1-2(0-0)
Heart of Midlothian - Aberdeen FC 2-1(0-1)
Kilmarnock FC - Hamilton 5-0(1-0)
Motherwell FC - St. Johnstone FC 3-0(0-0)
St. Mirren FC - Dundee FC 2-1(1-1)
Celtic FC - Rangers FC 2-1(1-0)

Round 32 [03.04.2019]
Aberdeen FC - Motherwell FC 3-1(1-1)
Hibernian FC - Kilmarnock FC 0-0
Livingston FC - Hamilton 2-0(0-0)
Rangers FC - Heart of Midlothian 3-0(2-0)
St. Johnstone FC - Dundee FC 2-0(1-0)
St. Mirren FC - Celtic FC 0-2(0-1)

Round 33 [06-07.04.2019]
Heart of Midlothian - Hibernian FC 1-2(1-1)
Celtic FC - Livingston FC 0-0
Dundee FC - Aberdeen FC 0-2(0-0)
Hamilton - St. Mirren FC 1-1(0-0)
Kilmarnock FC - St. Johnstone FC 2-0(2-0)
Motherwell FC - Rangers FC 0-3(0-2)

Final Standings

1.	Celtic FC Glasgow	33	24	5	4	71	-	17	77
2.	Rangers FC Glasgow	33	19	9	5	73	-	24	66
3.	Kilmarnock FC	33	16	10	7	46	-	28	58
4.	Aberdeen FC	33	17	7	9	52	-	37	58
5.	Hibernian FC Edinburgh	33	14	10	9	49	-	34	52
6.	Heart of Midlothian FC Edinburgh	33	15	5	13	38	-	41	50
7.	St. Johnstone FC Perth	33	13	5	15	32	-	44	44
8.	Motherwell FC	33	13	4	16	37	-	47	43
9.	Livingston FC	33	11	9	13	35	-	33	42
10.	Hamilton Academical FC	33	7	4	22	21	-	69	25
11.	St. Mirren FC Paisley	33	5	6	22	24	-	61	21
12.	Dundee FC	33	4	6	23	25	-	68	18

Teams ranked 1-6 were qualified for the Championship Round, while teams ranked 7-12 were qualified for the Relegation Round.

Championship Round

Results

Round 34 [20-21.04.2019]
Heart of Midlothian - Rangers FC 1-3(0-2)
Kilmarnock FC - Aberdeen FC 0-1(0-0)
Hibernian FC - Celtic FC 0-0

Round 35 [27-28.04.2019]
Celtic FC - Kilmarnock FC 1-0(0-0)
Hibernian FC - Heart of Midlothian 1-1(0-0)
Rangers FC - Aberdeen FC 2-0(0-0)

Round 36 [04-05.05.2019]
Aberdeen FC - Celtic FC 0-3(0-1)
Heart of Midlothian - Kilmarnock FC 0-1(0-0)
Rangers FC - Hibernian FC 1-0(1-0)

Round 37 [10-12.05.2019]
Aberdeen FC - Heart of Midlothian 2-1(0-0)
Kilmarnock FC - Hibernian FC 1-0(1-0)
Rangers FC - Celtic FC 2-0(1-0)

Round 38 [19.05.2019]
Celtic FC - Heart of Midlothian 2-1(1-1)
Hibernian FC - Aberdeen FC 1-2(1-1)
Kilmarnock FC - Rangers FC 2-1(1-0)

Final Standings								
1. **Celtic FC Glasgow**	38	27	6	5	77	-	20	87
2. Rangers FC Glasgow	38	23	9	6	82	-	27	78
3. Kilmarnock FC	38	19	10	9	50	-	31	67
4. Aberdeen FC	38	20	7	11	57	-	44	67
5. Hibernian FC Edinburgh	38	14	12	12	51	-	39	54
6. Heart of Midlothian FC Edinburgh	38	15	6	17	42	-	50	51

Top goalscorers:

18 Alfredo José Morelos Aviléz (COL)
Rangers FC Glasgow

17 Sam Cosgrove (ENG)
Aberdeen FC

15 Odsonne Édouard (FRA) *Celtic FC*
15 David Turnbull *Motherwell FC*

Relegation Round

Round 34 [20.04.2019]
Hamilton - Motherwell FC 1-1(0-1)
Livingston FC - St. Mirren FC 1-3(1-1)
St. Johnstone FC - Dundee FC 2-0(0-0)

Round 35 [27.04.2019]
Hamilton - Livingston FC 3-3(1-0)
Motherwell FC - Dundee FC 4-3(2-2)
St. Mirren FC - St. Johnstone FC 1-1(0-0)

Round 36 [04.05.2019]
Dundee FC - Hamilton 0-1(0-0)
Motherwell FC - St. Mirren FC 1-1(0-0)
St. Johnstone FC - Livingston FC 1-1(1-0)

Round 37 [11-13.05.2019]
Livingston FC - Dundee FC 0-1(0-1)
St. Johnstone FC - Motherwell FC 2-0(1-0)
St. Mirren FC - Hamilton 2-0(0-0)

Round 38 [18.05.2019]
Dundee FC - St. Mirren FC 2-3(1-0)
Hamilton - St. Johnstone FC 2-0(1-0)
Motherwell FC - Livingston FC 3-2(3-0)

Final Standings								
7. St. Johnstone FC Perth	38	15	7	16	38	-	48	52
8. Motherwell FC	38	15	6	17	46	-	56	51
9. Livingston FC	38	11	11	16	42	-	44	44
10. Hamilton Academical FC	38	9	6	23	28	-	75	33
11. St. Mirren FC Paisley (*Relegation Play-offs*)	38	8	8	22	34	-	66	32
12. Dundee FC (*Relegated*)	38	5	6	27	31	-	78	21

Relegation Play-offs [23-26.05.2019]

Dundee United FC - St. Mirren FC Paisley	0-0	1-1 aet; 0-2 pen

St. Mirren FC Paisley remains at first level.

NATIONAL CUP
Scottish Cup 2018/2019

First Round [21-29.09.2018]

Inverurie Loco Works FC - Fraserburgh FC	3-4	Dalbeattie Star FC - Kelty Hearts FC	0-0 / 1-3
Brora Rangers FC Glasgow - Turriff United FC	4-3	Rothes FC - Clachnacuddin FC	4-0
Gala Fairydean Rovers FC - Lossiemouth FC	6-0	Whitehill Welfare FC - Edinburgh University AFC	1-0
Caledonian Braves FC - Buckie Thistle FC	3-1	Wick Academy FC - Auchinleck Talbot FC	1-2
Nairn County FC - Beith Juniors FC	1-3	Strathspey Thistle FC - Coldstream FC	0-2
Forres Mechanics FC - Civil Service Strollers	2-2 / 1-2	Deveronvale FC - Bonnyrigg Rose AFC	2-1
Burntisland Shipyard - Cumbernauld Colts	1-4	Huntly FC - East Stirlingshire FC Falkirk	1-4
Linlithgow RFC - Fort William FC	3-0	University of Stirling FC - Keith FC	2-1
Gretna FC 2008 - Vale of Leithen FC	3-2		

Second Round [20/27.10.2018]

Albion Rovers FC - Formartine United FC Pitmedden	0-2	East Kilbride FC - The Spartans FC Edinburgh	3-1
Beith Juniors FC - Linlithgow Rose FC	4-0	Edinburgh City FC - Civil Service Strollers FC	1-0
Berwick Rangers FC Glasgow - Gretna FC	3-1	Caledonian Braves FC - Fraserburgh FC	1-2
Brora Rangers FC Glasgow - Coldstream FC	6-0	Elgin City FC - Whitehill Welfare FC Rosewell	2-0
Cove Rangers - Auchinleck Talbot FC	1-1 / 1-2	Gala Fairydean Rovers FC - East Stirlingshire FC	2-0
Cowdenbeath FC - Clyde FC 2008	2-1	Peterhead FC - Kelty Hearts FC	3-2
Cumbernauld Colts FC - BSC Glasgow FC	1-4	Rothes FC - Annan Athletic FC	0-1
Deveronvale FC - University of Stirling FC	1-2	Stirling Albion FC - Queen's Park FC Glasgow	1-2

Third Round [24-27.11./04.12.2018]

Beith Juniors FC - Ayr United FC	0-3	Fraserburgh FC - Auchinleck Talbot FC	0-1
Airdrieonians FC - Dumbarton FC	3-0	Greenock Morton FC - Peterhead FC	1-1 / 3-0
Alloa Athletic FC - Brechin City FC	3-0	Montrose FC - Annan Athletic FC	0-0 / 4-3
Arbroath FC - Stranraer FC	0-1	Queen of the South FC Dum. - Formartine United FC	4-1
Berwick Rangers FC Glasgow - East Fife FC Methil	1-2	Queen's Park FC Glasgow - Raith Rovers FC	0-3
Cowdenbeath FC - Brora Rangers FC Glasgow	1-0	Stenhousemuir FC - Falkirk FC	4-2
East Kilbride FC - Gala Fairydean Rovers FC	1-0	University of Stirling FC - Elgin City FC	0-4
Forfar Athletic FC - BSC Glasgow FC	2-0	Edinburgh City FC - Inverness Caledonian Thistle FC	1-1 / 1-6

Fourth Round [19-20/29-30.01.2019]

Auchinleck Talbot FC - Ayr United FC	1-0	Motherwell FC - Ross County FC	1-2
East Fife FC Methil - Greenock Morton FC	2-1	Raith Rovers FC - Dunfermline Athletic FC	3-0
St. Mirren FC - Alloa Athletic FC	3-2	Montrose FC - Dundee United FC	0-4
Inverness Caledonian Thistle FC - East Kilbride FC	4-0	Kilmarnock FC - Forfar Athletic FC	2-0
Hibernian FC Edinburgh - Elgin City FC	4-0	Partick Thistle FC Glasgow - Stranraer FC	4-1
Aberdeen FC - Stenhousemuir FC	1-1 / 4-1	Celtic FC Glasgow - Airdrieonians FC	3-0
St. Johnstone FC - Hamilton Academical FC	2-0	Heart of Midlothian FC Edinburgh - Livingston FC	1-0
Dundee FC - Queen of the South FC Dumfries	1-1 / 0-3	Cowdenbeath FC - Rangers FC Glasgow	1-3

1/8-Finals [09-11./19-20.02.2019]

Hibernian FC Edinburgh - Raith Rovers FC	3-1	Celtic FC Glasgow - St. Johnstone FC	5-0
St. Mirren FC - Dundee United FC	1-2	Heart of Midlothian FC Edin - Auchinleck Talbot FC	4-0
East Fife FC Methil - Partick Thistle FC Glasgow	0-1	Aberdeen FC - Queen of the South FC Dumfries	4-1
Kilmarnock FC - Rangers FC Glasgow	0-0 / 0-5	Ross County FC - Inverness Caledonian Thistle FC	2-2 / 4-5 pen

Quarter-Finals [02-04./12.03.2019]

Hibernian FC Edinburgh - Celtic FC Glasgow	0-2	Dundee United FC - Inverness Caledon. Thistle FC	1-2
Aberdeen FC - Rangers FC Glasgow	1-1 / 2-0	Partick Thistle FC Glasgow - Heart of Midlothian FC	1-1 / 1-2

Semi-Finals [13-14.04.2019]

Heart of Midlothian FC - Inverness Caledonian Thistle FC	3-0	Aberdeen FC - Celtic FC Glasgow	0-3

Final

25.05.2019; Hampden Park, Glasgow; Referee: William Collum; Attendance: 49,434

Celtic FC Glasgow - Heart of Midlothian FC Edinburgh **2-1(0-0)**

Celtic: Scott Bain, Mikael Lustig, Jozo Šimunović, Kristoffer Ajer, Jonny Hayes (89.Nir Bitton), Scott Brown, Callum William McGregor, James Forrest, Tom Rogić (70.Olivier Ntcham), Michael Johnston (72.Scott Sinclair), Odsonne Édouard. Trainer: Neil Lennon (England).

Heart of Midlothian: Zdeněk Zlámal, Michael Smith, John Souttar, Christophe Didier Berra, Aaron Hickey, Ryan Edwards, Peter Haring (81.Oliver Bozanić), Arnaud Sutchuin-Djoum, Sean Clare (75.Craig Wighton), Steven MacLean (78.Uche Ikpeazu), Jake David Mulraney. Trainer: Craig Levein.

Goals: 0-1 Ryan Edwards (52), 1-1 Odsonne Édouard (62 penalty), 2-1 Odsonne Édouard (82).

THE CLUBS 2018/2019

Please note: matches and goals includes statistics of both regular season and play-offs (Championship or Relegation).

Aberdeen Football Club

Founded: 14.04.1903
Stadium: Pittodrie Stadium, Aberdeen (20,866)

Goalkeepers:	DOB	M	(s)	G
Tomáš Černý (CZE)	10.04.1985	1	(1)	
Joe Lewis (ENG)	06.10.1987	37		
Defenders:	**DOB**	**M**	**(s)**	**G**
Dominic Ball (NIR)	02.08.1995	24	(7)	
Andrew Considine	01.04.1987	33		3
Michael Devlin	03.10.1993	16	(6)	1
Greg Halford (ENG)	08.12.1984		(2)	
Tommie Hoban (IRL)	24.01.1994	4	(1)	1
Shay Logan (ENG)	29.01.1988	25	(1)	
Max Lowe (ENG)	11.05.1997	31	(2)	2
Jack MacKenzie	07.04.2000	1		
Scott McKenna	12.11.1996	29		2
Graeme Shinnie	04.08.1991	36		3
Midfielders:	**DOB**	**M**	**(s)**	**G**
Dean Campbell	19.03.2001	1	(6)	
Lewis Ferguson	24.08.1999	33		5
Chris Forrester (IRL)	17.12.1992	1	(4)	
Stephen Gleeson (IRL)	03.08.1988	7	(8)	
Gary Mackay-Steven	31.08.1990	19	(1)	4
Ethan Ross	15.08.2001		(4)	
Frank Ross	18.02.1998	1		
Miko Virtanen (FIN)	26.01.1999		(1)	
Forwards:	**DOB**	**M**	**(s)**	**G**
Bruce Anderson	23.09.1998	1	(13)	2
Sam Cosgrove (ENG)	02.12.1996	29	(6)	17
Stevie May	03.11.1992	21	(11)	2
Niall McGinn (NIR)	20.07.1987	22	(5)	5
Connor McLennan	05.10.1999	18	(3)	3
Greg Stewart	17.03.1990	12	(3)	2
James Wilson (ENG)	01.12.1995	12	(12)	4
Scott Wright	08.08.1997	4	(9)	
Trainer:	**DOB**	**M**		
Derek-John McInnes	05.07.1971	38		

Celtic Football Club Glasgow

Founded: 06.11.1887
Stadium: Celtic Park, Glasgow (60,411)

Goalkeepers:	DOB	M	(s)	G
Scott Bain	22.11.1991	20		
Craig Sinclair Gordon	31.12.1982	18		
Defenders:	**DOB**	**M**	**(s)**	**G**
Kristoffer Ajer (NOR)	17.04.1998	23	(5)	
Filip Benković (CRO)	13.07.1997	17	(3)	2
Dedryck Boyata (BEL)	28.11.1990	19		1
Cristian Esteban Gamboa Luna (CRC)	24.10.1989	1		
Jack Hendry	07.05.1995	3	(1)	
Emilio Arturo Izaguirre Girón(HON)	10.05.1986	13	(1)	
Mikael Lustig (SWE)	13.12.1986	26	(1)	2
Tony Ralston	16.11.1998	3	(1)	1
Jozo Šimunović (CRO)	04.08.1994	16	(2)	2
Kieran Tierney	05.06.1997	20	(1)	
Jeremy Toljan (GER)	08.08.1994	7	(3)	
Midfielders:	**DOB**	**M**	**(s)**	**G**
Nir Bitton (ISR)	30.10.1991	4	(3)	
Scott Brown	25.06.1985	29	(1)	1
Ryan Christie	22.02.1995	17	(6)	9
Jules Christ Kouassi Eboué (CIV)	13.12.1997	1	(1)	
James Forrest	07.07.1991	31	(2)	11
Jonny Hayes (IRL)	09.07.1987	7	(9)	
Ewan Henderson	27.03.2000	4	(1)	
Callum William McGregor	14.06.1993	33	(2)	3
Lewis Morgan	30.09.1996		(9)	
Youssuf Mulumbu (COD)	25.01.1987	1		
Olivier Ntcham (FRA)	09.02.1996	16	(4)	3
Tom Rogić (AUS)	16.12.1992	16	(5)	3
Scott Sinclair (ENG)	25.03.1989	24	(9)	9
Forwards:	**DOB**	**M**	**(s)**	**G**
Daniel Arzani (AUS)	04.01.1999		(1)	
Vakoun Bayo (CIV)	10.01.1997		(1)	
Oliver Jasen Burke	07.04.1997	9	(5)	4
Karamoko Dembélé (ENG)	22.02.2003		(1)	
Moussa Dembélé (FRA)	12.07.1996	1		
Odsonne Édouard (FRA)	16.01.1998	22	(10)	15
Leigh Griffiths	20.08.1990	6	(5)	2
Michael Johnston	19.04.1999	7	(7)	5
Timothy Weah (USA)	22.02.2000	4	(9)	3
Trainer:	**DOB**	**M**		
Brendan Rodgers (NIR)	26.01.1973	27		
Neil Lennon (ENG) [26.02.2019]	25.06.1971	11		

Dundee Football Club

Founded: 1893
Stadium: Dens Park, Dundee (11,506)

Goalkeepers:	DOB	M	(s)	G
Timothy Dieng (SUI)	23.11.1994	16		
Jack Hamilton	22.03.1994	17		
Elliot Parish (ENG)	20.05.1990	5		
Defenders:	**DOB**	**M**	**(s)**	**G**
Andy Boyle (IRL)	07.03.1991	11	(2)	
Steven Caulker (ENG)	29.12.1991	2		
Andreas Hadenius (SWE)	18.03.1991	3		
Ryan Inniss (ENG)	05.06.1995	9	(2)	
Cammy Kerr	10.09.1995	27	(1)	1
Genseric Pedro Kusunga (ANG)	12.03.1988	22	(2)	1
Ryan James McGowan (AUS)	15.08.1989	15		
Josh Meekings (ENG)	02.09.1992	4		
Calvin Miller	09.01.1998	15	(1)	1
Darren O'Dea (IRL)	04.02.1987	20	(1)	
Nathan Ralph (ENG)	14.02.1993	26		1
Midfielders:	**DOB**	**M**	**(s)**	**G**
Jesse Curran (AUS)	16.07.1996	24	(10)	1
Andy Dales (ENG)	13.11.1994	8	(2)	
Roarie Deacon (ENG)	12.10.1991	1	(4)	
Matthew Henvey	04.01.2000		(1)	
James Horsfield (ENG)	21.09.1995	10	(1)	
Glen Kamara (FIN)	28.10.1995	16	(1)	
Jack Lambert (ENG)	19.03.1999		(4)	
Kharl Madianga (FRA)	30.01.1994	9	(1)	2
Callum Moore	22.03.2000	1	(2)	
Josh Mulligan	12.01.2002		(1)	
Adil Nabi (ENG)	28.02.1994	6	(7)	1
Elton N'Gwatala (FRA)	23.05.1993	7	(2)	1
John O'Sullivan (IRL)	18.09.1993	6	(5)	
Finlay Robertson	12.11.2002	1		
Ethan Robson (ENG)	25.10.1996	12	(1)	2
Lewis Spence	28.01.1996	10	(3)	
Martin Woods	01.01.1986	22	(2)	2
Forwards:	**DOB**	**M**	**(s)**	**G**
Craig Curran (ENG)	23.08.1989	11	(3)	
Benjamin Källman (FIN)	17.06.1998	11	(7)	1
Paul McGowan	07.10.1987	23	(7)	2
Jean Alassane Mendy (NOR)	02.02.1990	3	(3)	
Kenny Miller	23.12.1979	21	(12)	8
Sofien Moussa (TUN)	06.02.1988	4	(5)	
Andrew Nelson (ENG)	16.09.1997	9	(3)	4
Craig Wighton	27.07.1997		(3)	
Scott Wright	08.08.1997	11	(2)	3
Trainer:	**DOB**	**M**		
Neil McCann	11.08.1974	8		
James McIntyre [17.10.2018]	24.05.1972	29		
James McPake (ENG) [13.05.2019]	24.06.1984	1		

Hamilton Academical Football Club

Founded: 1874
Stadium: New Douglas Park, Hamilton (6,018)

Goalkeepers:	DOB	M	(s)	G
Ryan Fulton (ENG)	23.05.1996	4		
Jacob Marsden (ENG)	14.10.1996		(1)	
Ján Mucha (SVK)	05.12.1982	2		
Gary Woods (ENG)	01.10.1990	32		
Defenders:	**DOB**	**M**	**(s)**	**G**
Alexandros Gogić (CYP)	13.04.1994	12	(4)	
Ziggy Gordon	23.04.1993	35	(1)	2
Matt Kilgallon (ENG)	08.01.1984	25		
Aaron McGowan (ENG)	24.07.1996	35		2
Scott McMann	09.07.1996	27	(1)	
Alex Penny (ENG)	16.02.1997	3	(5)	
Lennard Sowah (GER)	23.08.1992	14	(4)	
Delphin Dougie Jerk Tshiembe (DEN)	17.07.1991	15	(4)	
Shaun Want	09.02.1997	9	(1)	
Midfielders:	**DOB**	**M**	**(s)**	**G**
Tony Andreu (FRA)	22.05.1988	15	(2)	1
Sam Kelly (ENG)	21.10.1993	3	(3)	
Darren Lyon	08.06.1995	1		
Scott Martin	01.04.1997	26	(5)	
Reegan Mimnaugh	18.12.2001	5	(3)	
Lewis Smith	16.03.2000		(4)	
Tom Taiwo (ENG)	27.02.1990	12	(4)	
Forwards:	**DOB**	**M**	**(s)**	**G**
Rakish Bingham (ENG)	25.10.1993	11	(8)	1
Steven Boyd	12.04.1997	10	(13)	2
Fredrik Brustad (NOR)	22.06.1989	11	(4)	1
Ross Cunningham	23.05.1998		(3)	
Steve Davies (ENG)	29.12.1987	5	(4)	2
Mason Enigbokan-Bloomfield(ENG)	06.11.1996	1	(4)	1
Dougie Imrie	03.08.1983	22	(7)	4
James Keatings	20.02.1992	8	(9)	1
Darian MacKinnon	09.10.1986	29		1
David McMillan (IRL)	14.12.1988	4	(4)	
Mikel Miller (ENG)	01.01.1996	25	(6)	5
George Oakley (ENG)	18.11.1995	14	(1)	4
Marios Ogboe (GRE)	10.10.1994	3	(3)	1
Trainer:	**DOB**	**M**		
Martin Canning	03.12.1981	22		
Brian Rice [31.01.2019]	11.10.1963	16		

Heart of Midlothian Football Club Edinburgh

Founded: 1874
Stadium: Tynecastle Park, Edinburgh (20,099)

Goalkeepers:	DOB	M	(s)	G
Colin Doyle (IRL)	12.08.1985	9		
Zdeněk Zlámal (CZE)	05.11.1985	29		
Defenders:	**DOB**	**M**	**(s)**	**G**
Christophe Didier Berra	31.01.1985	25		
Bobby Burns (NIR)	07.10.1999	3	(2)	1
Clevid Dikamona (FRA)	23.06.1990	12	(9)	1
Jimmy Dunne (IRL)	19.10.1997	12		2
Marcus Godinho (CAN)	28.06.1997	11	(1)	1
Peter Haring (AUT)	02.06.1993	26		5
Aaron Hickey	10.06.2002	1	(1)	
Aaron Hughes (NIR)	08.11.1979	1	(4)	
Demetri Mitchell (ENG)	11.01.1997	14	(6)	
Michael Smith (NIR)	04.09.1988	28		
John Souttar	25.09.1996	23	(1)	
Midfielders:	**DOB**	**M**	**(s)**	**G**
Danny Amankwaa (DEN)	30.01.1994		(2)	
Oliver Bozanić (AUS)	08.01.1989	15	(10)	3
Jamie Brandon	05.02.1998	5	(2)	
Sean Clare (ENG)	18.09.1996	23	(5)	3
Harry Cochrane	25.04.2001	6	(2)	
Ryan Edwards (AUS)	17.11.1993	2	(2)	
Ben Garuccio (AUS)	15.06.1995	13	(4)	
Andy Irving	13.05.2000	1		
Oliver Lee (ENG)	11.07.1991	23	(8)	3
Callumn Morrison	05.07.1999	15	(10)	1
Jake David Mulraney (IRL)	05.04.1996	15	(6)	1
Conor Shaughnessy (IRL)	30.06.1996	10		
Connor Smith	01.02.2002	2	(1)	
Arnaud Sutchuin-Djoum (CMR)	02.05.1989	30	(2)	3
Forwards:	**DOB**	**M**	**(s)**	**G**
Uche Ikpeazu (ENG)	28.02.1995	15	(2)	3
Aidan Keena (IRL)	25.04.1999	1	(4)	
Kyle Lafferty (NIR)	16.09.1987	1	(1)	1
Steven MacLean	23.08.1982	17	(8)	3
Anthony McDonald	17.03.2001		(3)	
Steven John Naismith	14.09.1986	19		10
David Vaněček (CZE)	09.03.1991	3	(2)	
Craig Wighton	27.07.1997	8	(9)	
Trainer:	**DOB**	**M**		
Craig Levein	22.10.1964	38		

Hibernian Football Club Edinburgh

Founded: 06.08.1875
Stadium: Easter Road Stadium, Edinburgh (20,421)

Goalkeepers:	**DOB**	**M**	**(s)**	**G**
Ádám Bogdán (HUN)	27.09.1987	17	(1)	
Ross Laidlaw	12.07.1992	1		
Ofir Marciano (ISR)	07.10.1989	20		
Defenders:	**DOB**	**M**	**(s)**	**G**
Efe Eric Ambrose Emoubo (NGA)	18.10.1988	21		
David Gray	04.05.1988	22	(2)	3
Paul Hanlon	20.01.1990	26		1
Darnell Johnson (ENG)	03.09.1998		(1)	
Sean Mackie	04.11.1998	3	(7)	
Darren McGregor	07.08.1985	22	(2)	2
Mark Milligan (AUS)	04.08.1985	25	(3)	
Miquel Nelom (NED)	22.09.1990	2	(1)	
Ryan Porteous	25.03.1999	16		3
Jonathan Spector (USA)	01.03.1986		(1)	
Steven Whittaker	16.06.1984	12	(3)	
Midfielders:	**DOB**	**M**	**(s)**	**G**
Marvin Bartley (ENG)	04.07.1986	7	(6)	
Gaël Bigirimana (BDI)	22.10.1993		(1)	
Ryan Gauld	16.12.1995	4	(1)	
Daryl Horgan (IRL)	10.08.1992	26	(8)	3
Emerson Hyndman (USA)	07.04.1996	10	(5)	1
Stephen Mallan	25.03.1996	36	(1)	7
Charalampos Mavrias (GRE)	21.02.1994	2		
John McGinn	18.10.1994	1		
Fraser Murray	07.05.1999	2	(4)	
Stéphane Oméonga (BEL)	27.03.1996	11	(4)	
Vykintas Slivka (LTU)	29.04.1995	19	(10)	1
Lewis Stevenson	05.01.1988	33	(1)	
Danny Swanson	28.12.1986		(2)	
Forwards:	**DOB**	**M**	**(s)**	**G**
Thomas Agyepong (GHA)	10.10.1995	1	(8)	1
Lewis Allan	25.10.1996	2	(4)	
Martin Boyle (AUS)	25.04.1993	17	(1)	4
James Gullan	02.07.1999		(2)	
Florian Kamberi (SUI)	08.03.1995	30	(3)	8
Jamie Maclaren (AUS)	29.07.1993	6	(6)	1
Marc Graeme McNulty	14.09.1992	13	(2)	7
Oliver Shaw	12.09.1998	11	(15)	6
Trainer:	**DOB**	**M**		
Neil Lennon	25.06.1971	21		
Eddie May [22.01.2019]	30.08.1967	4		
Paul Heckingbottom (ENG) [13.02.2019]	17.07.1977	13		

Kilmarnock Football Club

Founded: 05.01.1869
Stadium: Rugby Park, Kilmarnock (17,889)

Goalkeepers:	**DOB**	**M**	**(s)**	**G**
Daniel Bachmann (AUT)	09.07.1994	25		
Jamie MacDonald	17.04.1986	13		
Devlin MacKay	23.01.1997		(1)	
Defenders:	**DOB**	**M**	**(s)**	**G**
Scott Boyd	04.06.1986	16	(1)	1
Kirk Broadfoot	08.08.1984	25	(2)	1
Alex Bruce (NIR)	28.09.1984	3	(1)	
Stuart Findlay	14.09.1995	31		3
Ross Millen	28.09.1994	2	(2)	1
Stephen Gerard O'Donnell	11.05.1992	36	(1)	
Calum Waters	10.03.1996	2		
Midfielders:	**DOB**	**M**	**(s)**	**G**
Eamonn Brophy	10.03.1996	23	(6)	11
Chris Burke	02.12.1983	30	(4)	5
Jack Byrne (IRL)	24.04.1996		(5)	
Gary Dicker (IRL)	31.07.1986	30	(5)	
Jordan Jones (NIR)	24.10.1994	25	(3)	4
Youssuf Mulumbu (COD)	25.01.1987	9	(1)	1
Alan Power (IRL)	23.01.1988	35	(1)	1
Greg Taylor	05.11.1997	36		1
Dominic Thomas	14.02.1996		(1)	
Aaron Tshibola (ENG)	02.01.1995	21	(6)	1
Iain Wilson	15.12.1998		(6)	
Forwards:	**DOB**	**M**	**(s)**	**G**
Kris Boyd	18.08.1983	10	(10)	2
Bright Enobakhare (NGA)	08.02.1998	2	(4)	
Lee Erwin	19.03.1994	1		
Greg Kiltie	18.01.1997		(3)	
Conor McAleny (ENG)	12.08.1992	6	(5)	3
Rory McKenzie	07.10.1993	14	(10)	1
Liam Millar (CAN)	27.09.1999	2	(11)	1
Mikael Ndjoli (ENG)	16.12.1998	5	(19)	2
Greg Stewart	17.03.1990	16		8
Trainer:	**DOB**	**M**		
Steve Clarke	29.08.1963	38		

Livingston Football Club

Founded: 1943
Stadium: Almondvale Stadium ["Tony Macaroni" Arena], Livingston (9,512)

Goalkeepers:	**DOB**	**M**	**(s)**	**G**
Liam Kelly	23.01.1996	36		
Ross Stewart	16.04.1995	2		
Defenders:	**DOB**	**M**	**(s)**	**G**
Ciaron Brown (ENG)	14.01.1998	4	(1)	
James Brown (ENG)	12.01.1998	1		
Bobby Burns (NIR)	07.10.1999	3	(5)	
Declan Gallagher	13.02.1991	38		1
Craig Halkett	29.05.1995	34		7
Ricki Lamie	20.06.1993	23	(2)	
Steve Lawson (FRA)	08.08.1994	16	(9)	1
Alan Lithgow	12.03.1988	35		2
Jack McMillan	18.12.1997	2	(5)	1
Hakeem Odofin (ENG)	13.04.1998	7	(6)	
Steven Saunders	30.03.1991	2	(1)	
Henk van Schaik (NED)	20.01.1998		(1)	
Midfielders:	**DOB**	**M**	**(s)**	**G**
Shaun Byrne	09.06.1993	29	(3)	2
Nicky Cadden	19.09.1996	4	(8)	
Chris Erskine	08.02.1987	8	(2)	1
Keaghan Jacobs (RSA)	09.09.1989	26	(5)	1
Steven Lawless	12.04.1991	29	(6)	3
Scott Robinson	12.03.1992	19	(7)	2
Craig Sibbald	18.05.1995	16	(10)	3
Gregg Wylde	23.03.1991		(2)	
Forwards:	**DOB**	**M**	**(s)**	**G**
Raffaele De Vita (ITA)	23.09.1987		(3)	
Jack Hamilton	30.06.2000	2	(11)	1
Ryan Hardie	17.03.1997	13	(8)	7
Egli Kaja (ALB)	26.07.1997	2	(4)	
Dolly Doningos Menga (ANG)	02.05.1993	20	(5)	2
Kenneth Miller	23.12.1979	2		
Lee Miller	18.03.1983	6	(3)	
Scott Pittman	09.07.1992	38		6
Scott Tiffoney	26.08.1998	1	(7)	2
Trainer:	**DOB**	**M**		
Kenneth Miller	23.12.1979	2		
Gary Holt [23.08.2018]	09.03.1973	36		

Motherwell Football Club

Founded: 17.05.1886
Stadium: Fir Park, Motherwell (13,677)

Goalkeepers:	DOB	M	(s)	G
Trevor Carson (NIR)	05.08.1988	12		
Rohan Ferguson	06.12.1997		(1)	
Mark Gillespie (ENG)	27.03.1992	26	(1)	
Defenders:	**DOB**	**M**	**(s)**	**G**
Tom Aldred	11.09.1990	37		3
David Devine	20.06.2001		(1)	
Liam Donnelly (NIR)	07.03.1996	6	(1)	1
Charles Dunne (IRL)	13.02.1993	23		
Peter Hartley (ENG)	03.04.1988	14		1
Adam Livingstone	22.02.1998		(3)	
Barry Maguire	27.04.1998	1	(1)	
Christian Mbulu (ENG)	06.08.1996	4	(2)	
Carl McHugh (IRL)	05.02.1993	20	(8)	1
Richard Tait	02.12.1989	37	(1)	1
Aaron Taylor-Sinclair	08.04.1991	5	(1)	
Midfielders:	**DOB**	**M**	**(s)**	**G**
Alejandro Rodríguez Gorrin (ESP)	01.08.1993	16	(4)	
Gregory Ariyibi (USA)	18.01.1995	17		2
Gaël Bigirimana (BDI)	22.10.1993	12	(7)	1
Chris Cadden	19.09.1996	15	(5)	1
Allan Campbell	04.07.1998	31	(4)	2
Dean Cornelius	11.04.2001		(1)	
Elliott Frear (ENG)	11.09.1990	4	(18)	1
Liam Grimshaw (ENG)	02.02.1995	30	(1)	
Andy Rose (AUS)	13.02.1990	10	(2)	
David Turnbull	10.07.1999	27	(3)	15
Forwards:	**DOB**	**M**	**(s)**	**G**
Ryan Bowman (ENG)	30.11.1991	7	(9)	1
Jake Hastie	18.03.1998	12	(2)	6
Danny Johnson (ENG)	28.02.1993	12	(10)	6
Curtis Main (ENG)	20.06.1992	28	(3)	3
Ross McCormack	18.08.1986		(3)	
Conor Sammon (IRL)	06.11.1986	6	(10)	
James Scott	30.08.2000	6	(6)	1
Jamie Semple	17.05.2001		(3)	
Trainer:	**DOB**	**M**		
Stephen Robinson (NIR)	10.12.1974	38		

Rangers Football Club Glasgow

Founded: 1872
Stadium: Ibrox Park Stadium, Glasgow (50,817)

Goalkeepers:	DOB	M	(s)	G
Andrew Firth (ENG)	26.09.1996		(1)	
Wesley Foderingham (ENG)	14.01.1991	4		
Allan McGregor	31.01.1982	34		
Defenders:	**DOB**	**M**	**(s)**	**G**
Borna Barišić (CRO)	10.11.1992	14	(2)	
Jon Flanagan (ENG)	01.01.1993	14	(2)	
Connor Goldson (ENG)	18.12.1992	34		3
Nikola Katić (CRO)	10.10.1996	16	(2)	1
Gareth McAuley (NIR)	05.12.1979	6	(1)	
Matt Polster (USA)	08.06.1993		(1)	
James Tavernier (ENG)	31.10.1991	36	(1)	14
Lee Wallace	21.08.1987		(3)	
Joe Worrall (ENG)	10.01.1997	20	(2)	
Midfielders:	**DOB**	**M**	**(s)**	**G**
Scott Arfield (CAN)	01.11.1988	28	(1)	11
Lassana Coulibaly (MLI)	10.04.1996	14	(5)	1
Steven Davis (NIR)	01.01.1985	10	(4)	
Graham Dorrans	05.05.1987		(1)	
Ovie Ejaria (ENG)	18.11.1997	11	(3)	1
Andy Halliday	11.10.1991	18	(5)	1
Ryan Jack	27.02.1992	26	(4)	4
Glen Kamara (FIN)	28.10.1995	12	(1)	1
Ryan Kent (ENG)	11.11.1996	25	(2)	6
Ross McCrorie	18.03.1998	11	(9)	
Glenn Middleton	01.01.2000	4	(11)	2
Jordan Rossiter (ENG)	24.03.1997	2	(2)	
Joshua Dean Windass (ENG)	29.01.1994	1		
Forwards:	**DOB**	**M**	**(s)**	**G**
Serge Atakayi (FIN)	30.01.1999		(1)	
Adedapo Awokoya-Mebude	29.07.2001		(1)	
Daniel João Santos Candeias (POR)	25.02.1988	26	(7)	5
Jermain Defoe (ENG)	07.10.1982	10	(7)	8
Eros Grezda (ALB)	15.04.1995	7	(6)	2
Kyle Lafferty (NIR)	16.09.1987	6	(15)	4
Alfredo José Morelos Aviléz (COL)	21.06.1996	27	(3)	18
Jamie Murphy	28.08.1989	2		
Umar Sadiq (NGA)	02.02.1997		(1)	
Trainer:	**DOB**	**M**		
Steven George Gerrard (ENG)	30.05.1980	38		

St. Johnstone Football Club Perth

Founded: 1884
Stadium: McDiarmid Park, Perth (10,696)

Goalkeepers:	DOB	M	(s)	G
Cammy Bell	18.09.1986	4		
Zander Clark	26.06.1992	34		
Defenders:	**DOB**	**M**	**(s)**	**G**
Steven Anderson	19.12.1985	2	(1)	
Aaron Comrie	03.02.1997	1		
Brian Easton	05.03.1988	1		
Ricky Foster	31.07.1985	37		
Liam Gordon	26.01.1996	10	(3)	
Jason Kerr	06.02.1997	37		2
Joe Shaughnessy (IRL)	06.07.1992	32	(1)	3
Scott Tanser (ENG)	23.10.1994	37		3
Midfielders:	**DOB**	**M**	**(s)**	**G**
Blair Alston	23.02.1992	10	(11)	4
Ross Callachan	04.09.1993	17	(7)	1
Liam Craig	27.12.1986	33	(3)	2
Murray Davidson	07.03.1988	26	(2)	3
Sean Goss (ENG)	01.10.1995	6		
Oliver Hamilton	13.12.2001		(1)	
Alistair McCann	04.12.1999		(1)	
Tristan Nydam (ENG)	06.11.1999	1	(4)	
Stefan Scougall	07.12.1992		(1)	
Danny Swanson	28.12.1986	6	(17)	
David Wotherspoon (CAN)	16.01.1990	20	(9)	2
Drey Wright (ENG)	30.04.1994	13	(1)	1
Forwards:	**DOB**	**M**	**(s)**	**G**
Callum Hendry	08.12.1997	5	(7)	2
Chris Kane	05.09.1994	14	(16)	3
Matthew Kennedy (NIR)	01.11.1994	34	(2)	6
David McMillan (IRL)	14.12.1988	7	(5)	2
Jordan Northcott	09.02.2002		(1)	
Michael O'Halloran	06.01.1991	9	(5)	1
Tony Watt	29.12.1993	22	(7)	2
Trainer:	**DOB**	**M**		
Thomas James Wright (NIR)	29.08.1963	38		

St. Mirren Football Club Paisley

Founded: 1877
Stadium: St. Mirren Park, St. Mirren (7,937)

Goalkeepers:	**DOB**	**M**	**(s)**	**G**
Václav Hladký (CZE)	14.11.1990	17		
Dean Lyness (ENG)	20.07.1991	4		
Danny Rogers (IRL)	23.03.1994	4		
Craig Samson	24.08.1984	13		
Defenders:	**DOB**	**M**	**(s)**	**G**
Jack Baird	07.02.1997	30	(3)	
Laurenţiu Nicolae Corbu (ROU)	10.05.1994	1	(2)	
Hayden Coulson (ENG)	17.06.1998	5	(1)	
Anton Ferdinand (ENG)	18.02.1985	18		
Lee Hodson (NIR)	02.10.1991	19	(1)	
Alfie Jones	07.10.1997	14		2
Cole Kpekawa (ENG)	20.05.1996	4		
Gary MacKenzie	15.10.1985	5		
Paul McGinn	22.10.1990	34	(1)	3
Mateo Mužek (CRO)	29.04.1995	13	(1)	
Mihai Cristian Popescu (ROU)	07.05.1993	17		
Midfielders:	**DOB**	**M**	**(s)**	**G**
Ryan Marc Edwards (AUS)	17.11.1993	11	(3)	
Ethan Erhahon	09.05.2001	19	(1)	
Ryan Flynn	04.09.1988	20	(6)	1
Adam Hammill (IRL)	25.01.1988	12	(1)	4
Jim Kellermann (ENG)	11.12.1995	1	(2)	
Jordan Kirkpatrick	06.03.1992		(2)	
Cameron MacPherson	29.12.1998	10	(3)	1
Kyle Magennis	26.08.1998	11	(3)	2
Brad Lyons (NIR)	26.05.1997	14	(1)	1
Stephen McGinn	02.12.1988	31	(3)	1
Ian McShane	20.12.1992	4	(4)	
Greg Tansey (ENG)	21.11.1988	4	(2)	
Matty Willock (ENG)	20.08.1996	7	(5)	
Forwards:	**DOB**	**M**	**(s)**	**G**
Cameron Breadner	13.10.2000		(2)	
Nicolai Brock-Madsen (DEN)	09.01.1993	3	(1)	
Cody Cooke (ENG)	02.03.1993	3	(8)	3
Anders Dreyer (DEN)	02.05.1998	8	(2)	1
Simeon Jackson (CAN)	28.03.1987	22	(8)	5
Samuel Jamieson	14.03.1999		(2)	
Kyle McAllister	21.01.1999	8	(6)	2
Danny Mullen	01.03.1995	16	(7)	5
Duckens Moses Nazon (HAI)	07.04.1994	6	(4)	1
Cammy Smith	24.08.1995	9	(10)	
Ross Stewart	01.09.1996	1		
Trainer:	**DOB**	**M**		
Alan Stubbs (ENG)	06.10.1971	4		
Brian Rice [03.09.2018]	11.10.1963	-		
Oran Kearney (NIR) [07.09.2018]	29.07.1978	34		

SECOND LEVEL
Scottish Championship 2018/2019

1.	Ross County FC Dingwall (*Promoted*)	36	21	8	7	63	-	34	71
2.	Dundee United FC (*Premiership Play-offs*)	36	19	8	9	49	-	40	65
3.	Inverness Caledonian Thistle FC (*Premiership Play-offs*)	36	14	14	8	48	-	40	56
4.	Ayr United FC (*Premiership Play-offs*)	36	15	9	12	50	-	38	54
5.	Greenock Morton FC	36	11	13	12	36	-	45	46
6.	Partick Thistle FC Glasgow	36	12	7	17	43	-	52	43
7.	Dunfermline Athletic FC	36	11	8	17	33	-	40	41
8.	Alloa Athletic FC	36	10	9	17	39	-	53	39
9.	Queen of the South FC Dumfries (*Relegation Play-offs*)	36	9	11	16	41	-	48	38
10.	Falkirk FC (*Relegated*)	36	9	11	16	37	-	49	38

Premiership Play-offs [07-11.05.2019]

Ayr United FC - Inverness Caledonian Thistle FC	1-3(0-1)	1-1(1-0)
Inverness Caledonian Thistle FC - **Dundee United FC**	0-1(0-0)	0-3(0-1)

Relegation Play-offs (2nd / 3rd Level) [07-18.05.2019]

Montrose FC - Queen of the South FC Dumfries	2-1(1-0)	0-5(0-5)
Raith Rovers FC Kirkcaldy - Forfar Athletic FC	2-1(1-1)	1-1(0-0)
Raith Rovers FC Kirkcaldy - **Queen of the South FC Dumfries**	1-3(0-2)	0-0

Queen of the South FC Dumfries remains at second level.

NATIONAL TEAM

INTERNATIONAL MATCHES
(16.07.2018 – 15.07.2019)

07.09.2018	Glasgow	Scotland - Belgium	0-4(0-1)	(F)
10.09.2018	Glasgow	Scotland - Albania	2-0(0-0)	(UNL)
11.10.2018	Haifa	Israel - Scotland	2-1(0-1)	(UNL)
14.10.2018	Glasgow	Scotland - Portugal	1-3(0-1)	(F)
17.11.2018	Shkodër	Albania - Scotland	0-4(0-2)	(UNL)
20.11.2018	Glasgow	Scotland - Israel	3-2(2-1)	(UNL)
21.03.2019	Nur-Sultan	Kazakhstan - Scotland	3-0(2-0)	(ECQ)
24.03.2019	Serravalle	San Marino - Scotland	0-2(0-1)	(ECQ)
08.06.2019	Glasgow	Scotland - Cyprus	2-1(0-0)	(ECQ)
11.06.2019	Bruxelles	Belgium - Scotland	3-0(1-0)	(ECQ)

07.09.2018 SCOTLAND - BELGIUM 0-4(0-1) Friendly International

Hampden Park, Glasgow; Referee: Luca Banti (Italy); Attendance: 20,196

SCO: Craig Sinclair Gordon, Charles Patrick Mulgrew (68.Stephen Gerard O'Donnell), Andrew Robertson (Cap), John Souttar, Kieran Tierney, Kevin David McDonald (53.Robert Snodgrass), Stuart Armstrong (53.Ryan Jack), Callum William McGregor (68.Johnathon Simpson Snedden Russell), Ryan Fraser, John McGinn (73.Graeme Shinnie), Leigh Griffiths (46.Steven John Naismith). Trainer: Alexander McLeish.

10.09.2018 SCOTLAND - ALBANIA 2-0(0-0) UEFA Nations League C, Group 1

Hampden Park, Glasgow; Referee: Matej Jug (Slovenia); Attendance: 17,455

SCO: Allan McGregor, Charles Patrick Mulgrew, Stephen Gerard O'Donnell, Andrew Robertson (Cap), John Souttar, Kieran Tierney, Kevin David McDonald (46.Stuart Armstrong), Callum William McGregor (79.Scott Francis McTominay), John McGinn, Steven John Naismith, Johnathon Simpson Snedden Russell (70.Leigh Griffiths). Trainer: Alexander McLeish.

Goals: Berat Gjimshiti (47 own goal), Steven John Naismith (68).

11.10.2018 ISRAEL - SCOTLAND 2-1(0-1) UEFA Nations League C, Group 1

"Sammy Ofer" Stadium, Haifa; Referee: Daniel Stefański (Poland); Attendance: 10,234

SCO: Allan McGregor, Charles Patrick Mulgrew (46.Scott McKenna), Stephen Gerard O'Donnell, Andrew Robertson (Cap), John Souttar [*sent off 61*], Kieran Tierney, Kevin David McDonald, Callum William McGregor, John McGinn, Steven John Naismith (76.Oliver Robert McBurnie), Johnathon Simpson Snedden Russell (67.James Forrest). Trainer: Alexander McLeish.

Goal: Charles Patrick Mulgrew (25 penalty).

14.10.2018 SCOTLAND - PORTUGAL 1-3(0-1) Friendly International

Hampden Park, Glasgow; Referee: Ruddy Buquet (France); Attendance: 19,684

SCO: Craig Sinclair Gordon, Stephen Gerard O'Donnell, Andrew Robertson (Cap), Scott McKenna, Jack Hendry, James Forrest, Stuart Armstrong (77.Kevin David McDonald), Callum William McGregor, John McGinn (67.Graeme Shinnie), Steven John Naismith, Oliver Robert McBurnie (76.Gary Mackay-Steven). Trainer: Alexander McLeish.

Goal: Steven John Naismith (90+3).

17.11.2018 ALBANIA - SCOTLAND 0-4(0-2) UEFA Nations League C, Group 1

Stadiumi "Loro Boriçi", Shkodër; Referee: Vladislav Bezborodov (Russia); Attendance: 8,632

SCO: Allan McGregor, Andrew Robertson (Cap), Callum Thomas Owen Paterson, David Bates, Scott McKenna, James Forrest, Stuart Armstrong (61.Scott Francis McTominay), Callum William McGregor, Ryan Fraser (73.Johnathon Simpson Snedden Russell), Ryan Christie, Steven Kenneth Fletcher (68.Matthew Phillips). Trainer: Alexander McLeish.

Goals: Ryan Fraser (14), Steven Kenneth Fletcher (45+2 penalty), James Forrest (55, 67).

20.11.2018 SCOTLAND - ISRAEL 3-2(2-1) UEFA Nations League C, Group 1

Hampden Park, Glasgow; Referee: Tobias Welz (Germany); Attendance: 21,281

SCO: Allan McGregor, Andrew Robertson (Cap), Callum Thomas Owen Paterson, David Bates, Scott McKenna, James Forrest, Stuart Armstrong (76.Matthew Phillips), Callum William McGregor, Ryan Fraser, Ryan Christie (76.Graeme Shinnie), Steven Kenneth Fletcher (87.Scott Francis McTominay). Trainer: Alexander McLeish.

Goals: James Forrest (34, 43, 64).

21.03.2019 KAZAKHSTAN - SCOTLAND 3-0(2-0) 16th EC. Qualifiers

Astana Arena, Nur-Sultan; Referee: Srđan Jovanović (Serbia); Attendance: 27,641

SCO: Scott Bain, Graeme Shinnie, David Bates, Scott McKenna, James Forrest (81.Marc Graeme McNulty), Liam Palmer, Stuart Armstrong, Callum William McGregor (Cap), John McGinn (69.Scott Francis McTominay), Oliver Jasen Burke, Oliver Robert McBurnie (61.Johnathon Simpson Snedden Russell). Trainer: Alexander McLeish.

24.03.2019 SAN MARINO - SCOTLAND 0-2(0-1) 16th EC. Qualifiers

San Marino Stadium, Serravalle; Referee: Manuel Schüttengruber (Austria); Attendance: 4,077

SCO: Scott Bain, Stephen Gerard O'Donnell, Andrew Robertson (Cap), Callum Thomas Owen Paterson (37.Marc Graeme McNulty), David Bates, Scott McKenna, Kenneth McLean, Stuart Armstrong (71.James Forrest), Callum William McGregor (56.Scott Francis McTominay), Ryan Fraser, Johnathon Simpson Snedden Russell. Trainer: Alexander McLeish.

Goals: Kenneth McLean (4), Johnathon Simpson Snedden Russell (74).

08.06.2019 SCOTLAND - CYPRUS 2-1(0-0) 16th EC. Qualifiers

Hampden Park, Glasgow; Referee: Ola Hobber Nilsen (Norway); Attendance: 31,277

SCO: David James Marshall, Charles Patrick Mulgrew, Stephen Gerard O'Donnell, Andrew Robertson (Cap), Scott McKenna, James Forrest, Kenneth McLean, Ryan Fraser, Callum William McGregor (88.Stuart Armstrong), John McGinn (79.Scott Francis McTominay), Eamonn Brophy (73.Oliver Jasen Burke). Trainer: Stephen Clarke.

Goals: Andrew Robertson (61), Oliver Jasen Burke (89).

11.06.2019 BELGIUM - SCOTLAND 3-0(1-0) 16th EC. Qualifiers

Stade "Roi Baudouin", Bruxelles; Referee: Petr Ardeleanu (Czech Republic); Attendance: 32,482

SCO: David James Marshall, Charles Patrick Mulgrew (Cap), Stephen Gerard O'Donnell, Scott McKenna, Greg Taylor, Kenneth McLean, Stuart Armstrong (32.Ryan Fraser), Callum William McGregor, Oliver Jasen Burke, Scott Francis McTominay, Johnathon Simpson Snedden Russell (67.James Forrest). Trainer: Stephen Clarke.

NATIONAL TEAM PLAYERS
(16.07.2018 – 15.07.2019)

Name	DOB	Caps	Goals	2018/2019:	*Club*
Goalkeepers					
Scott BAIN	22.11.1991	**3**	**0**	2019:	*Celtic FC Glasgow*
Craig Sinclair GORDON	31.12.1982	**54**	**0**	2018:	*Celtic FC Glasgow*
David James MARSHALL	05.03.1985	**29**	**0**	2019:	*Hull City AFC (ENG)*
Allan James McGREGOR	31.01.1982	**42**	**0**	2018:	*Rangers FC Glasgow*
Defenders					
David BATES	05.10.1996	**2**	**0**	2018/2019:	*Hamburger SV (GER)*
Jack HENDRY	07.05.1995	**3**	**0**	2018:	*Celtic FC Glasgow*
Scott McKENNA	12.11.1996	**12**	**0**	2018/2019:	*Aberdeen FC*
Charles Patrick MULGREW	06.03.1986	**41**	**3**	2018/2019:	*Blackburn Rovers FC (ENG)*
Stephen Gerard O'DONNELL	11.05.1992	**9**	**0**	2018/2019:	*Kilmarnock FC*
Liam PALMER	19.09.1991	**1**	**0**	2019:	*Sheffield Wednesday FC (ENG)*
Andrew ROBERTSON	11.03.1994	**30**	**3**	2018/2019:	*Liverpool FC (ENG)*
Graeme SHINNIE	04.08.1991	**6**	**0**	2018/2019:	*Aberdeen FC*
John SOUTTAR	25.09.1996	**3**	**0**	2018:	*Heart of Midlothian FC Edinburgh*
Greg TAYLOR	05.11.1997	**1**	**0**	2019:	*Kilmarnock FC*
Kieran TIERNEY	05.06.1997	**12**	**0**	2018:	*Celtic FC Glasgow*
Midfielders					
Stuart ARMSTRONG	30.03.1992	**15**	**1**	2018/2019:	*Southampton FC (ENG)*
James FORREST	07.07.1991	**30**	**5**	2018/2019:	*Celtic FC Glasgow*
Ryan JACK	27.02.1992	**2**	**0**	2018:	*Rangers FC Glasgow*
Gary MACKAY-STEVEN	31.08.1990	**2**	**0**	2018:	*Aberdeen FC*
Kevin David McDONALD	04.11.1988	**5**	**0**	2018:	*Fulham FC London (ENG)*
John McGINN	18.10.1994	**15**	**0**	2018/2019:	*Aston Villa FC Birmingham (ENG)*
Callum William McGREGOR	14.06.1993	**13**	**0**	2018/2019:	*Celtic FC Glasgow*
Kenneth McLEAN	08.01.1992	**8**	**1**	2019:	*Norwich City FC (ENG)*
Scott Francis McTOMINAY	08.12.1996	**9**	**0**	2018/2019:	*Manchester United FC (ENG)*
Callum Thomas Owen PATERSON	13.10.1994	**12**	**0**	2018/2019:	*Cardiff City FC (WAL)*
Robert SNODGRASS	07.09.1987	**26**	**7**	2018/2019:	*West Ham United FC London (ENG)*
Forwards					
Eamonn BROPHY	10.03.1996	**1**	**0**	2019:	*Kilmarnock FC*
Oliver Jasen BURKE	07.04.1997	**8**	**1**	2019:	*Celtic FC Glasgow*
Ryan CHRISTIE	22.02.1995	**6**	**0**	2018/2019:	*Celtic FC Glasgow*
Steven Kenneth FLETCHER	26.03.1987	**33**	**10**	2018:	*Sheffield Wednesday FC (ENG)*
Ryan FRASER	24.02.1994	**9**	**1**	2018/2019:	*AFC Bournemouth (ENG)*
Leigh GRIFFITHS	20.08.1990	**18**	**4**	2018:	*Celtic FC Glasgow*
Oliver Robert McBURNIE	04.06.1996	**7**	**0**	2018/2019:	*Swansea City AFC (WAL)*
Marc Graeme McNULTY	14.09.1992	**2**	**0**	2019:	*Hibernian FC Edinburgh*
Steven John NAISMITH	14.09.1986	**49**	**9**	2018:	*Heart of Midlothian FC Edinburgh*
Matthew PHILLIPS	13.03.1991	**14**	**1**	2018:	*West Bromwich Albion FC (ENG)*
Johnathon Simpson Snedden RUSSELL	08.04.1990	**12**	**1**	2018/2019:	*Sporting Kansas City (USA)*

National team coach

Alexander McLEISH [16.02.2018 – 18.04.2019]	21.01.1959	12 M; 5 W; 0 D; 7 L; 14-18 Complete record as trainer of Scotland: 22 M; 12 W; 0 D; 10 L; 27-27 (24.03.2007 – 17.11.2007) & (16.02.2018 – 18.04.2019)
Stephen "Steve" CLARKE [from 20.05.2019]	29.08.1963	2 M; 1 W; 0 D; 1 L; 2-4

SERBIA

The Country:

Република Србија (Republic of Serbia)
Capital: Beograd
Surface: 77,474 km²
Inhabitants: 6,963,764 [2019]
Time: UTC+1

The FA:

Fudbalski savez Srbije
35, Terazije CP 263, 11000 Beograd
Tel: +381 11 323 4253
Founded: 1919
Member of FIFA since: 1921
Member of UEFA since: 1954
Website: www.fss.org.rs

NATIONAL TEAM RECORDS

First international match:	28.08.1920, Antwerpen:	Czechoslovakia – Yugoslavia 7-0
Most international caps:	Branislav Ivanović	- 105 caps (2005-2018)
Most international goals:	Stjepan Bobek	- 38 goals / 63 caps (1946-1956)

UEFA EUROPEAN CHAMPIONSHIP*	
1960	Final Tournament (Runners-up)
1964	Qualifiers
1968	Final Tournament (Runners-up)
1972	Qualifiers
1976	Final Tournament (4th Place)
1980	Qualifiers
1984	Final Tournament (Group Stage)
1988	Qualifiers
1992	*Qualified / Suspended*
1996	*Suspended*
2000	Final Tournament (Quarter-Finals)
2004	Qualifiers
2008	Qualifiers
2012	Qualifiers
2016	Qualifiers

FIFA WORLD CUP*	
1930	Final Tournament (4th Place)
1934	Qualifiers
1938	Qualifiers
1950	Final Tournament (Group Stage)
1954	Final Tournament (Quarter-Finals)
1958	Final Tournament (Quarter-Finals)
1962	Final Tournament (4th Place)
1966	Qualifiers
1970	Qualifiers
1974	Final Tournament (2nd Round)
1978	Qualifiers
1982	Final Tournament (Group Stage)
1986	Qualifiers
1990	Final Tournament (Quarter-Finals)
1994	*Suspended*
1998	Final Tournament (2nd Round of 16)
2002	Qualifiers
2006	Final Tournament (Group Stage)
2010	Final Tournament (Group Stage)
2014	Qualifiers
2018	Final Tournament (Group Stage)

*as Yugoslavia (1930-2002), Serbia and Montenegro (2002-2006).

UEFA NATIONS LEAGUE
2018/2019 – League C (promoted to League B)

OLYMPIC FOOTBALL TOURNAMENTS 1908-2016

1908	-	**1948**	Runners-up	**1972**	Qualifiers	**1996**	*Suspended*
1912	-	**1952**	Runners-up	**1976**	Qualifiers	**2000**	Qualifiers
1920	Round 1	**1956**	Runners-up	**1980**	4th Place	**2004**	Group Stage
1924	Qualifiers	**1960**	**Winners**	**1984**	3rd Place	**2008**	Group Stage
1928	1/8 - Finals	**1964**	Quarter-Finals	**1988**	Group Stage	**2012**	Qualifiers
1936	Did not enter	**1968**	Did not enter	**1992**	Qualifiers	**2016**	Qualifiers

FIFA CONFEDERATIONS CUP 1992-2017
None

SERBIAN CLUB HONOURS IN EUROPEAN CLUB COMPETITIONS:

European Champion Clubs.Cup (1956-1992) / UEFA Champions League (1993-2019)		
FK Crvena Zvezda Beograd	**1**	1990/1991
Fairs Cup (1858-1971) / UEFA Cup (1972-2009) / UEFA Europa League (2010-2019)		
None		
UEFA Super Cup (1972-2018)		
None		
European Cup Winners.Cup 1961-1999*		
None		

**defunct competition*

NATIONAL COMPETITIONS
TABLE OF HONOURS

Kingdom of Yugoslavia (1923–1940)

	CHAMPIONS	CUP WINNERS	BEST GOALSCORERS	
1923	HŠK Građanski Zagreb	HAŠK Zagreb	Dragan Jovanović (SK Jugoslavija Beograd)	4
1924	SK Jugoslavija Beograd	Zagreb XI	Dragan Jovanović (SK Jugoslavija Beograd)	6
1925	SK Jugoslavija Beograd	Zagreb XI	Dragan Jovanović (SK Jugoslavija Beograd)	4
1926	HŠK Građanski Zagreb	Zagreb XI	Dušan Petković (SK Jugoslavija Beograd)	4
1927	NK Hajduk Split	Beograd XI	Kuzman Sotirović (BSK Beograd)	6
1928	HŠK Građanski Zagreb	*No competition*	Ljubo Benčić (NK Hajduk Split)	8
1929	NK Hajduk Split	*No competition*	Đorđe Vujadinović (BSK Beograd)	10
1930	HŠK Concordia Zagreb	*No competition*	Blagoje Marjanović (BSK Beograd)	10
1930/1931	BSK Beograd	*No competition*	Đorđe Vujadinović (BSK Beograd)	12
1931/1932	HŠK Concordia Zagreb	*No competition*	Svetislav Valjarević (HŠK Concordia Zagreb)	10
1932/1933	BSK Beograd	*No competition*	Vladimir Kragić (NK Hajduk Split)	21
1933/1934	*No competition*	BSK Beograd	-	
1934/1935	BSK Beograd	*No competition*	Leo Lemešić (NK Hajduk Split)	18
1935/1936	BSK Beograd	SK Jugoslavija	Blagoje Marjanović (BSK Beograd)	5
1936/1937	HŠK Građanski Zagreb	*No competition*	Blagoje Marjanović (BSK Beograd)	21
1937/1938	HAŠK Zagreb	*No competition*	August Lešnik (HŠK Građanski Zagreb)	17
1938/1939	BSK Beograd	*No competition*	August Lešnik (HŠK Građanski Zagreb)	22
1939/1940	HŠK Građanski Zagreb	HŠK Građanski Zagreb	Svetislav Glišović (BSK Beograd)	10

SFR Yugoslavia (1945–1992)

	CHAMPIONS	CUP WINNERS	BEST GOALSCORERS	
1945	S.R. Serbia	*No competition*	Stjepan Bobek (JNA)	8
1946/1947	FK Partizan Beograd	FK Partizan Beograd	Franjo Wölfl (NK Dinamo Zagreb)	28
1947/1948	NK Dinamo Zagreb	FK Crvena Zvezda Beograd	Franjo Wölfl (NK Dinamo Zagreb)	22
1948/1949	FK Partizan Beograd	FK Crvena Zvezda Beograd	Frane Matošić (NK Hajduk Split)	17
1950	NK Hajduk Split	FK Crvena Zvezda Beograd	Marko Valok (FK Partizan Beograd)	17
1951	FK Crvena Zvezda Beograd	NK Dinamo Zagreb	Kosta Tomašević (FK Crvena Zvezda Beograd)	16
1952	NK Hajduk Split	FK Partizan Beograd	Stanoje Jocić (BSK Beograd)	13
1952/1953	FK Crvena Zvezda Beograd	BSK Beograd	Todor Živanović (FK Crvena Zvezda Beograd)	17
1953/1954	NK Dinamo Zagreb	FK Partizan Beograd	Stjepan Bobek (FK Partizan Beograd)	21
1954/1955	NK Hajduk Split	BSK Beograd	Predrag Marković (BSK Beograd) Kosta Tomašević (FK Spartak Subotica) Bernard Vukas (NK Hajduk Split)	20
1955/1956	FK Crvena Zvezda Beograd	*No competition*	Muhamed Mujić (FK Velež Mostar) Tihomir Ognjanov (FK Spartak Subotica) Todor Veselinović (FK Vojvodina Novi Sad)	21
1956/1957	FK Crvena Zvezda Beograd	FK Partizan Beograd	Todor Veselinović (FK Vojvodina Novi Sad)	28
1957/1958	NK Dinamo Zagreb	FK Crvena Zvezda Beograd	Todor Veselinović (FK Vojvodina Novi Sad)	19
1958/1959	FK Crvena Zvezda Beograd	FK Crvena Zvezda Beograd	Bora Kostić (FK Crvena Zvezda Beograd)	25
1959/1960	FK Crvena Zvezda Beograd	NK Dinamo Zagreb	Bora Kostić (FK Crvena Zvezda Beograd)	19
1960/1961	FK Partizan Beograd	FK Vardar Skoplje	Zoran Prljinčević (FK Radnički Beograd) Todor Veselinović (FK Vojvodina Novi Sad)	16
1961/1962	FK Partizan Beograd	OFK Beograd	Dražan Jerković (NK Dinamo Zagreb)	16
1962/1963	FK Partizan Beograd	NK Dinamo Zagreb	Mišo Smajlović (FK Željezničar Sarajevo)	18
1963/1964	FK Crvena Zvezda Beograd	FK Crvena Zvezda Beograd	Asim Ferhatović (FK Sarajevo)	19
1964/1965	FK Partizan Beograd	NK Dinamo Zagreb	Zlatko Dračić (NK Zagreb)	23
1965/1966	FK Vojvodina Novi Sad	OFK Beograd	Petar Nadoveza (NK Hajduk Split)	21
1966/1967	FK Sarajevo	NK Hajduk Split	Mustafa Hasanagić (FK Partizan Beograd)	18
1967/1968	FK Crvena Zvezda Beograd	FK Crvena Zvezda Beograd	Slobodan Santrač (OFK Beograd)	22
1968/1969	FK Crvena Zvezda Beograd	NK Dinamo Zagreb	Vojin Lazarević (FK Crvena Zvezda Beograd)	22
1969/1970	FK Crvena Zvezda Beograd	FK Crvena Zvezda Beograd	Slobodan Santrač (OFK Beograd) Dušan Bajević (FK Velež Mostar)	20
1970/1971	NK Hajduk Split	FK Crvena Zvezda Beograd	Petar Nadoveza (NK Hajduk Split) Božo Janković (FK Željezničar Sarajevo)	20
1971/1972	FK Željezničar Sarajevo	NK Hajduk Split	Slobodan Santrač (OFK Beograd)	33
1972/1973	FK Crvena Zvezda Beograd	NK Hajduk Split	Slobodan Santrač (OFK Beograd) Vojin Lazarević (FK Crvena Zvezda Beograd)	25
1973/1974	NK Hajduk Split	NK Hajduk Split	Danilo Popivoda (Olimpija Ljubljana)	17
1974/1975	NK Hajduk Split	NK Hajduk Split	Dušan Savić (FK Crvena Zvezda Beograd) Boško Đorđević (FK Partizan Beograd)	20
1975/1976	FK Partizan Beograd	NK Hajduk Split	Nenad Bjeković (FK Partizan Beograd)	24
1976/1977	FK Crvena Zvezda Beograd	NK Rijeka	Zoran Filipović (FK Crvena Zvezda Beograd)	21
1977/1978	FK Partizan Beograd	NK Rijeka	Radomir Savić (FK Sarajevo)	21
1978/1979	NK Hajduk Split	NK Dinamo Zagreb	Dušan Savić (FK Crvena Zvezda Beograd)	24
1979/1980	FK Crvena Zvezda Beograd	FK Crvena Zvezda Beograd	Safet Sušić (FK Sarajevo) Dragoljub Kostić (FK Napredak Kruševac)	17
1980/1981	FK Crvena Zvezda Beograd	FK Velež Mostar	Milan Radović (NK Rijeka)	26
1981/1982	NK Dinamo Zagreb	FK Crvena Zvezda Beograd	Snješko Cerin (NK Dinamo Zagreb)	19

1982/1983	FK Partizan Beograd	NK Dinamo Zagreb	Sulejman Halilović (NK Dinamo Vinkovci)	18
1983/1984	FK Crvena Zvezda Beograd	NK Hajduk Split	Darko Pančev (FK Vardar Skoplje)	19
1984/1985	FK Sarajevo	FK Crvena Zvezda Beograd	Zlatko Vujović (NK Hajduk Split)	25
1985/1986	FK Partizan Beograd	FK Velež Mostar	Davor Čop (NK Dinamo Vinkovci)	20
1986/1987	FK Vardar Skoplje	NK Hajduk Split	Radmilo Mihajlović (FK Željezničar Sarajevo)	23
1987/1988	FK Crvena Zvezda Beograd	FK Borac Banja Luka	Duško Milinković (FK Rad Beograd)	16
1988/1989	FK Vojvodina Novi Sad	FK Partizan Beograd	Davor Šuker (NK Osijek)	18
1989/1990	FK Crvena Zvezda Beograd	FK Crvena Zvezda Beograd	Darko Pančev (FK Crvena Zvezda Beograd)	25
1990/1991	FK Crvena Zvezda Beograd	NK Hajduk Split	Darko Pančev (FK Crvena Zvezda Beograd)	34
1991/1992	FK Crvena Zvezda Beograd	*No competition*	Darko Pančev (FK Crvena Zvezda Beograd)	25

First League of Serbia and Montenegro (1992–2006)

	CHAMPIONS	CUP WINNERS	BEST GOALSCORERS	
1992/1993	FK Partizan Beograd	FK Crvena Zvezda Beograd	Anto Drobnjak (FK Crvena Zvezda Beograd) Vesko Mihajlović (FK Vojvodina Novi Sad)	22
1993/1994	FK Partizan Beograd	FK Partizan Beograd	Savo Milošević (FK Partizan Beograd)	21
1994/1995	FK Crvena Zvezda Beograd	FK Crvena Zvezda Beograd	Savo Milošević (FK Partizan Beograd)	30
1995/1996	FK Partizan Beograd	FK Crvena Zvezda Beograd	Vojislav Budimirović (FK Čukarički)	23
1996/1997	FK Partizan Beograd	FK Crvena Zvezda Beograd	Zoran Jovičić (FK Crvena Zvezda Beograd)	21
1997/1998	FK Obilić Beograd	FK Partizan Beograd	Saša Marković (FK Železnik Beograd/ FK Crvena Zvezda Beograd)	27
1998/1999	FK Partizan Beograd	FK Crvena Zvezda Beograd	Dejan Osmanović (FK Hajduk Kula)	16
1999/2000	FK Crvena Zvezda Beograd	FK Crvena Zvezda Beograd	Mateja Kežman (FK Partizan Beograd)	27
2000/2001	FK Crvena Zvezda Beograd	FK Partizan Beograd	Petar Divić (OFK Beograd)	27
2001/2002	FK Partizan Beograd	FK Crvena Zvezda Beograd	Zoran Đurašković (FK Mladost Lučani)	27
2002/2003	FK Partizan Beograd	FK Sartid Smederevo	Zvonimir Vukić (FK Partizan Beograd)	22
2003/2004	FK Crvena Zvezda Beograd	FK Crvena Zvezda Beograd	Nikola Žigić (FK Crvena Zvezda Beograd)	19
2004/2005	FK Partizan Beograd	FK Železnik Beograd	Marko Pantelić (FK Crvena Zvezda Beograd)	21
2005/2006	FK Crvena Zvezda Beograd	FK Crvena Zvezda Beograd	Srđan Radonjić (FK Partizan Beograd)	20

Serbian Superliga (since 2006)

	CHAMPIONS	CUP WINNERS	BEST GOALSCORERS	
2006/2007	FK Crvena Zvezda Beograd	FK Crvena Zvezda Beograd	Srđan Baljak (FK Banat Zrenjanin)	18
2007/2008	FK Partizan Beograd	FK Partizan Beograd	Nenad Jestrović (FK Crvena Zvezda Beograd)	13
2008/2009	FK Partizan Beograd	FK Partizan Beograd	Lamine Diarra (SEN, FK Partizan Beograd)	19
2009/2010	FK Partizan Beograd	FK Crvena Zvezda Beograd	Dragan Mrđa (FK Vojvodina Novi Sad)	22
2010/2011	FK Partizan Beograd	FK Partizan Beograd	Ivica Iliev (FK Partizan Beograd) Andrija Kaluđerović (FK Crvena Zvezda Beograd)	13
2011/2012	FK Partizan Beograd	FK Crvena Zvezda Beograd	Darko Spalević (FK Radnički Kragujevac)	19
2012/2013	FK Partizan Beograd	FK Jagodina	Miloš Stojanović (FK Jagodina)	19
2013/2014	FK Crvena Zvezda Beograd	FK Vojvodina Novi Sad	Dragan Mrđa (FK Crvena Zvezda Beograd)	19
2014/2015	FK Partizan Beograd	FK Čukarički	Patrick Friday Eze (NGA, FK Mladost Lučani)	15
2015/2016	FK Crvena Zvezda Beograd	FK Partizan Beograd	Aleksandar Katai (FK Crvena Zvezda Beograd)	21
2016/2017	FK Partizan Beograd	FK Partizan Beograd	Uroš Đurđević (FK Partizan Beograd) Leonardo da Silva Souza (BRA, FK Partizan Beograd)	24
2017/2018	FK Crvena Zvezda Beograd	FK Partizan Beograd	Aleksandar Pešić (FK Crvena Zvezda Beograd)	25
2018/2019	FK Crvena Zvezda Beograd	FK Partizan Beograd	Nermin Haskić (BIH, FK Radnički Niš)	24

NATIONAL CHAMPIONSHIP
Serbian SuperLiga 2018/2019
(20.07.2018 – 19.05.2019)

Regular Season - Results

Round 1 [20-23.07.2018]
Crvena Zvezda - Dinamo Vranje 3-0(1-0)
Vojvodina - Mladost Lučani 1-1(1-1)
FK Voždovac - OFK Bačka 1-0(1-0)
FK Napredak - Rad Beograd 1-0(1-0)
FK Čukarički - FK Zemun 1-1(1-0)
Radnik Surdulica - Partizan 1-0(0-0)
Radnički Niš - Proleter Novi Sad 3-1(2-0)
Spartak Subotica - FK Mačva Šabac 1-0(0-0)

Round 2 [28-29.07.2018]
FK Zemun - Vojvodina 1-1(0-0)
Mladost Lučani - Radnik Surdulica 1-0(0-0)
Rad Beograd - FK Čukarički 0-3(0-1)
FK Mačva Šabac - FK Napredak 1-0(1-0)
Proleter Novi Sad - FK Voždovac 2-1(0-0)
OFK Bačka - Spartak Subotica 2-1(0-1)
Dinamo Vranje - Partizan 0-1(0-0)
Crvena Zvezda - Radnički Niš 2-0(1-0)

Round 3 [03-06.08.2018]
FK Čukarički - FK Mačva Šabac 1-0(0-0)
FK Voždovac - Crvena Zvezda 1-2(0-2)
FK Napredak - OFK Bačka 1-1(0-1)
Radnik Surdulica - FK Zemun 2-1(2-0)
Partizan - Mladost Lučani 0-0
Radnički Niš - Dinamo Vranje 2-0(1-0)
Vojvodina - Rad Beograd 1-2(0-1)
Spartak Subotica - Proleter Novi Sad 0-4(0-2)

Round 4 [10-12.08.2018]
Radnički Niš - FK Voždovac 1-0(0-0)
Proleter Novi Sad - FK Napredak 1-1(1-0)
Dinamo Vranje - Mladost Lučani 1-3(0-1)
Rad Beograd - Radnik Surdulica 3-1(2-1)
FK Mačva Šabac - Vojvodina 0-0
OFK Bačka - FK Čukarički 1-1(0-0)
FK Zemun - Partizan 0-1(0-1)
Crvena Zvezda - Spartak Subotica 3-0(1-0)

Round 5 [18-19.08.2018]
FK Čukarički - Proleter Novi Sad 1-0(0-0)
FK Voždovac - Dinamo Vranje 2-0(0-0)
Vojvodina - OFK Bačka 2-0(0-0)
Mladost Lučani - FK Zemun 2-1(0-1)
Spartak Subotica - Radnički Niš 1-4(0-2)
Radnik Surdulica - FK Mačva Šabac 0-1(0-1)
Partizan - Rad Beograd 1-0(0-0) [19.09.]
Napredak - Crvena Zvezda 0-3(0-2) [26.09.]

Round 6 [24-26.08.2018]
Proleter Novi Sad - Vojvodina 0-1(0-0)
Rad Beograd - Mladost Lučani 1-1(1-1)
OFK Bačka - Radnik Surdulica 1-0(1-0)
Radnički Niš - FK Napredak 3-3(1-1)
Crvena Zvezda - FK Čukarički 2-1(0-0)
FK Mačva Šabac - Partizan 1-3(1-0)
Dinamo Vranje - FK Zemun 1-0(0-0)
FK Voždovac - Spartak Subotica 0-0

Round 7 [31.08.-02.09.2018]
Mladost Lučani - FK Mačva Šabac 1-2(1-1)
FK Zemun - Rad Beograd 1-0(0-0)
FK Čukarički - Radnički Niš 1-1(1-1)
FK Napredak - FK Voždovac 0-0
Radnik Surdulica - Proleter Novi Sad 0-0
Spartak Subotica - Dinamo Vranje 2-0(1-0)
Vojvodina - Crvena Zvezda 1-4(1-2)
Partizan - OFK Bačka 1-0(0-0)

Round 8 [14-16.09.2018]
Radnički Niš - Vojvodina 1-0(0-0)
Proleter Novi Sad - Partizan 0-1(0-1)
Dinamo Vranje - Rad Beograd 0-1(0-0)
FK Mačva Šabac - FK Zemun 0-2(0-1)
OFK Bačka - Mladost Lučani 0-2(0-0)
Crvena Zvezda - Radnik Surdulica 6-0(2-0)
Spartak Subotica - FK Napredak 0-1(0-1)
FK Voždovac - FK Čukarički 1-3(1-0)

Round 9 [21-23.09.2018]
FK Čukarički - Spartak Subotica 3-1(1-0)
FK Napredak - Dinamo Vranje 3-0(2-0)
FK Zemun - OFK Bačka 2-2(1-0)
Vojvodina - FK Voždovac 3-0(1-0)
Radnik Surdulica - Radnički Niš 1-2(1-0)
Mladost Lučani - Proleter Novi Sad 1-0(0-0)
Rad Beograd - FK Mačva Šabac 1-0(0-0)
Partizan - Crvena Zvezda 1-1(1-0)

Round 10 [29-30.09.2018]
Crvena Zvezda - Mladost Lučani 2-1(0-0)
Proleter Novi Sad - FK Zemun 4-1(3-0)
Spartak Subotica - Vojvodina 0-1(0-0)
Dinamo Vranje - FK Mačva Šabac 1-0(0-0)
OFK Bačka - Rad Beograd 1-0(1-0)
Radnički Niš - Partizan 2-2(1-0)
FK Voždovac - Radnik Surdulica 1-0(0-0)
FK Napredak - FK Čukarički 1-1(1-0)

Round 11 [05-07.10.2018]
Partizan - FK Voždovac 4-0(2-0)
Radnik Surdulica - Spartak Subotica 0-0
Mladost Lučani - Radnički Niš 0-1(0-0)
FK Mačva Šabac - OFK Bačka 2-0(0-0)
FK Čukarički - Dinamo Vranje 6-1(1-0)
Vojvodina - FK Napredak 0-1(0-1)
Rad Beograd - Proleter Novi Sad 1-3(1-1)
FK Zemun - Crvena Zvezda 1-2(1-1)

Round 12 [19-21.10.2018]
FK Čukarički - Vojvodina 1-0(0-0)
FK Voždovac - Mladost Lučani 1-1(0-0)
Proleter Novi Sad - FK Mačva Šabac 1-0(0-0)
Crvena Zvezda - Rad Beograd 3-1(2-0)
Radnički Niš - FK Zemun 2-0(2-0)
FK Napredak - Radnik Surdulica 1-1(1-0)
Spartak Subotica - Partizan 0-0
Dinamo Vranje - OFK Bačka 1-1(0-1)

Round 13 [27-28.10.2018]
FK Zemun - FK Voždovac 2-1(2-1)
Vojvodina - Dinamo Vranje 2-0(2-0)
Radnik Surdulica - FK Čukarički 1-0(0-0)
Partizan - FK Napredak 1-1(1-0)
Rad Beograd - Radnički Niš 0-0
OFK Bačka - Proleter Novi Sad 0-1(0-1)
FK Mačva Šabac - Crvena Zvezda 0-2(0-1)
Mladost Lučani - Spartak Subotica 2-1(1-0)

Round 14 [31.10.2018]
Dinamo Vranje - Proleter Novi Sad 2-4(1-1)
Spartak Subotica - FK Zemun 2-2(2-0)
Radnički Niš - FK Mačva Šabac 3-0(1-0)
FK Voždovac - Rad Beograd 2-0(1-0)
FK Napredak - Mladost Lučani 4-1(2-1)
Vojvodina - Radnik Surdulica 1-0(1-0)
FK Čukarički - Partizan 1-1(0-1)
Crvena Zvezda - OFK Bačka 3-1(2-0)

Round 15 [03-04.11.2018]
Proleter Novi Sad - Crvena Zvezda 0-2(0-1)
Radnik Surdulica - Dinamo Vranje 2-0(2-0)
Mladost Lučani - FK Čukarički 3-4(1-2)
OFK Bačka - Radnički Niš 0-2(0-2)
FK Zemun - FK Napredak 0-2(0-0)
Rad Beograd - Spartak Subotica 1-1(0-0)
FK Mačva Šabac - FK Voždovac 2-0(1-0)
Partizan - Vojvodina 2-0(1-0)

Round 16 [09-10.11.2018]
Proleter Novi Sad - Radnički Niš 1-2(1-0)
OFK Bačka - FK Voždovac 1-0(0-0)
FK Mačva Šabac - Spartak Subotica 0-0
FK Zemun - FK Čukarički 0-3(0-1)
Partizan - Radnik Surdulica 2-0(1-0)
Dinamo Vranje - Crvena Zvezda 0-3(0-1)
Mladost Lučani - Vojvodina 1-0(1-0)
Rad Beograd - FK Napredak 0-2(0-2)

Round 17 [23-25.11.2018]
FK Čukarički - Rad Beograd 2-1(0-1)
FK Napredak - FK Mačva Šabac 2-0(1-0)
Spartak Subotica - OFK Bačka 3-0(1-0)
Radnik Surdulica - Mladost Lučani 1-0(1-0)
Vojvodina - FK Zemun 0-0
FK Voždovac - Proleter Novi Sad 0-0
Radnički Niš - Crvena Zvezda 2-2(2-1)
Partizan - Dinamo Vranje 6-0(2-0)

Round 18 [30.11.-01.12.2018]
OFK Bačka - FK Napredak 3-3(1-1)
Rad Beograd - Vojvodina 0-1(0-1)
FK Zemun - Radnik Surdulica 0-0
FK Mačva Šabac - FK Čukarički 1-0(1-0)
Mladost Lučani - Partizan 1-1(0-0)
Dinamo Vranje - Radnički Niš 0-4(0-2)
Proleter Novi Sad - Spartak Subotica 2-2(0-1)
Crvena Zvezda - FK Voždovac 2-0(2-0)

Round 19 [05.12.2018]
Mladost Lučani - Dinamo Vranje 2-0(1-0)
Radnik Surdulica - Rad Beograd 1-0(1-0)
Vojvodina - FK Mačva Šabac 1-1(1-0)
FK Čukarički - OFK Bačka 3-0(1-0)
FK Napredak - Proleter Novi Sad 1-1(1-0)
Spartak Subotica - Crvena Zvezda 1-3(0-2)
FK Voždovac - Radnički Niš 0-1(0-0)
Partizan - FK Zemun 1-0(1-0)

Round 20 [08-09.12.2018]
Crvena Zvezda - FK Napredak 3-0(1-0)
Dinamo Vranje - FK Voždovac 1-2(0-1)
Radnički Niš - Spartak Subotica 3-0(1-0)
FK Mačva Šabac - Radnik Surdulica 1-2(1-2)
FK Zemun - Mladost Lučani 0-3(0-2)
Proleter Novi Sad - FK Čukarički 0-0
OFK Bačka - Vojvodina 0-0
Rad Beograd - Partizan 0-3(0-2)

Round 21 [14-17.12.2018]
Partizan - FK Mačva Šabac 0-0
Radnik Surdulica - OFK Bačka 3-2(2-1)
Spartak Subotica - FK Voždovac 3-2(0-2)
Vojvodina - Proleter Novi Sad 0-0
FK Čukarički - Crvena Zvezda 1-2(1-2)
FK Zemun - Dinamo Vranje 1-2(1-1)
Mladost Lučani - Rad Beograd 0-0
FK Napredak - Radnički Niš 1-2(1-2)

Round 22 [15-17.02.2019]
FK Voždovac - FK Napredak 4-0(3-0)
OFK Bačka - Partizan 0-3(0-1)
Proleter Novi Sad - Radnik Surdulica 0-0
FK Mačva Šabac - Mladost Lučani 0-1(0-1)
Radnički Niš - FK Čukarički 2-0(2-0)
Crvena Zvezda - Vojvodina 4-0(2-0)
Dinamo Vranje - Spartak Subotica 1-0(1-0)
Rad Beograd - FK Zemun 2-2(1-1)

Round 23 [22-24.02.2019]
Vojvodina - Radnički Niš 0-1(0-0)
FK Zemun - FK Mačva Šabac 0-0
Mladost Lučani - OFK Bačka 5-0(2-0)
FK Napredak - Spartak Subotica 0-0
Radnik Surdulica - Crvena Zvezda 0-1(0-1)
Partizan - Proleter Novi Sad 3-0(3-0)
FK Čukarički - FK Voždovac 3-0(2-0)
Rad Beograd - Dinamo Vranje 1-1(1-0)

Round 24 [01-03.03.2019]
FK Mačva Šabac - Rad Beograd 0-0
Dinamo Vranje - FK Napredak 4-0(1-0)
Spartak Subotica - FK Čukarički 1-2(0-2)
FK Voždovac - Vojvodina 1-0(0-0)
Radnički Niš - Radnik Surdulica 4-1(3-1)
Proleter Novi Sad - Mladost Lučani 2-0(1-0)
Crvena Zvezda - Partizan 1-1(0-1)
OFK Bačka - FK Zemun 2-0(0-0)

Round 25 [06.03.2019]
FK Zemun - Proleter Novi Sad 0-0
FK Mačva Šabac - Dinamo Vranje 0-0
Rad Beograd - OFK Bačka 1-1(1-0)
Mladost Lučani - Crvena Zvezda 1-3(0-2)
Radnik Surdulica - FK Voždovac 2-1(2-1)
FK Čukarički - FK Napredak 2-1(0-1)
Partizan - Radnički Niš 0-1(0-1)
Vojvodina - Spartak Subotica 1-2(1-0)

Round 26 [09-10.03.2019]
Radnički Niš - Mladost Lučani 1-0(1-0)
FK Napredak - Vojvodina 0-0
Crvena Zvezda - FK Zemun 4-0(2-0)
Dinamo Vranje - FK Čukarički 0-0
Spartak Subotica - Radnik Surdulica 3-2(1-1)
FK Voždovac - Partizan 1-0(0-0)
Proleter Novi Sad - Rad Beograd 0-0
OFK Bačka - FK Mačva Šabac 0-1(0-1)

Round 27 [15-17.03.2019]
OFK Bačka - Dinamo Vranje 5-1(4-0)
FK Zemun - Radnički Niš 0-1(0-0)
Partizan - Spartak Subotica 1-3(1-1)
Radnik Surdulica - FK Napredak 1-0(0-0)
FK Mačva Šabac - Proleter Novi Sad 2-1(1-1)
Rad Beograd - Crvena Zvezda 0-3(0-1)
Mladost Lučani - FK Voždovac 3-1(2-1)
Vojvodina - FK Čukarički 0-0

Round 28 [29-31.03.2019]
Proleter Novi Sad - OFK Bačka 3-0(1-0)
Dinamo Vranje - Vojvodina 1-3(1-1)
Spartak Subotica - Mladost Lučani 1-0(1-0)
FK Čukarički - Radnik Surdulica 2-0(2-0)
Radnički Niš - Rad Beograd 2-0(1-0)
Crvena Zvezda - FK Mačva Šabac 2-1(1-1)
FK Napredak - Partizan 1-0(1-0)
FK Voždovac - FK Zemun 3-1(0-1)

Round 29 [03.04.2019]
Rad Beograd - FK Voždovac 0-1(0-0)
FK Zemun - Spartak Subotica 0-2(0-0)
OFK Bačka - Crvena Zvezda 1-3(1-2)
Proleter Novi Sad - Dinamo Vranje 0-0
FK Mačva Šabac - Radnički Niš 0-0
Mladost Lučani - FK Napredak 2-0(1-0)
Radnik Surdulica - Vojvodina 0-1(0-1)
Partizan - FK Čukarički 3-2(1-1)

Round 30 [07.04.2019]
Dinamo Vranje - Radnik Surdulica 0-3(0-1)
Vojvodina - Partizan 3-2(1-1)
FK Čukarički - Mladost Lučani 0-0
FK Napredak - FK Zemun 1-0(1-0)
Spartak Subotica - Rad Beograd 1-0(0-0)
FK Voždovac - FK Mačva Šabac 1-0(1-0)
Radnički Niš - OFK Bačka 5-1(4-0)
Crvena Zvezda - Proleter Novi Sad 4-0(1-0)

Final Standings

1.	FK Crvena Zvezda Beograd	30	27	3	0	80	-	16	84
2.	FK Radnički Niš	30	23	6	1	58	-	17	75
3.	FK Partizan Beograd	30	15	9	6	45	-	20	54
4.	FK Čukarički Beograd	30	15	9	6	48	-	25	54
5.	FK Mladost Lučani	30	13	7	10	39	-	29	46
6.	FK Napredak Kruševac	30	10	11	9	32	-	35	41
7.	FK Vojvodina Novi Sad	30	10	9	11	24	-	26	39
8.	FK Proleter Novi Sad	30	9	11	10	31	-	29	38
9.	FK Spartak Subotica	30	10	8	12	32	-	40	38
10.	FK Radnik Surdulica	30	11	5	14	25	-	35	38
11.	FK Voždovac Beograd	30	11	4	15	28	-	37	37
12.	FK Mačva Šabac	30	8	8	14	16	-	26	32
13.	OFK Bačka Bačka Palanka	30	6	7	17	26	-	54	25
14.	FK Rad Beograd	30	4	9	17	16	-	39	21
15.	FK Dinamo Vranje	30	5	5	20	18	-	62	20
16.	FK Zemun Beograd	30	3	9	18	19	-	47	18

Teams ranked 1-8 were qualified for the Championship Round, while teams ranked 9-16 were qualified for the Relegation Round.
Points from the regular season are halved with half points rounded up.

Championship Round

Results

Round 31 [13.04.2019]
Crvena Zvezda - Radnički Niš 3-0(2-0)
Mladost Lučani - FK Napredak 2-1(1-1)
Partizan - FK Čukarički 3-0(1-0)
Vojvodina - Proleter Novi Sad 0-1(0-0)

Round 32 [20-21.04.2019]
FK Čukarički - Crvena Zvezda 3-2(2-2)
FK Napredak - Vojvodina 5-0(2-0)
Proleter Novi Sad - Mladost Lučani 0-1(0-0)
Radnički Niš - Partizan 3-1(1-1)

Round 33 [25.04.2019]
Radnički Niš - FK Čukarički 2-2(1-1)
Mladost Lučani - Vojvodina 3-1(1-0)
FK Napredak - Proleter Novi Sad 2-0(1-0)
Crvena Zvezda - Partizan 2-1(0-0)

Round 34 [30.04.-01.05.2019]
Proleter Novi Sad - Radnički Niš 2-3(1-0)
Vojvodina - Crvena Zvezda 0-5(0-2)
Partizan - Mladost Lučani 2-1(1-0)
FK Čukarički - FK Napredak 5-2(2-0)

Round 35 [05.05.2019]
Crvena Zvezda - Mladost Lučani 1-0(0-0)
FK Čukarički - Proleter Novi Sad 3-0(2-0)
Radnički Niš - Vojvodina 0-0
Partizan - FK Napredak 2-1(0-1)

Round 36 [10-11.05.2019]
Proleter Novi Sad - Crvena Zvezda 0-1(0-0)
Mladost Lučani - FK Čukarički 1-1(0-1)
FK Napredak - Radnički Niš 3-3(3-2)
Vojvodina - Partizan 1-2(1-1)

Round 37 [19.05.2019]
Crvena Zvezda - FK Napredak 3-0(1-0)
Radnički Niš - Mladost Lučani 2-2(1-0)
Partizan - Proleter Novi Sad 2-0(1-0)
FK Čukarički - Vojvodina 1-1(0-1)

Final Standings

1.	**FK Crvena Zvezda Beograd**	37	33	3	1	97	-	20	60
2.	FK Radnički Niš	37	25	10	2	71	-	30	48
3.	FK Partizan Beograd	37	20	9	8	58	-	28	42
4.	FK Čukarički Beograd	37	18	12	7	63	-	36	39
5.	FK Mladost Lučani	37	16	9	12	49	-	37	34
6.	FK Napredak Kruševac	37	12	12	13	46	-	50	28
7.	FK Vojvodina Novi Sad	37	10	11	16	27	-	43	22
8.	FK Proleter Novi Sad	37	10	11	16	34	-	41	22

Top goalscorers:

24 Nermin Haskić (BIH)
FK Radnički Niš

20 Ricardo Jorge Pires Gomes (CPV)
FK Partizan Beograd

18 Ognjen Mudrinski
FK Čukarički Beograd

Relegation Round

Results

Round 31 [12-13.04.2019]
Spartak Subotica - Rad Beograd 2-0(1-0)
Radnik Surdulica - OFK Bačka 1-1(1-0)
FK Voždovac - FK Zemun 2-2(2-1)
FK Mačva Šabac - Dinamo Vranje 2-0(1-0)

Round 32 [19-20.04.2019]
FK Zemun - Spartak Subotica 0-0
Dinamo Vranje - FK Voždovac 1-0(1-0)
OFK Bačka - FK Mačva Šabac 2-2(1-0)
Rad Beograd - Radnik Surdulica 1-0(0-0)

Round 33 [25.04.2019]
Spartak Subotica - OFK Bačka 0-1(0-0)
FK Mačva Šabac - FK Zemun 1-5(1-2)
Radnik Surdulica - Dinamo Vranje 1-1(1-0)
FK Voždovac - Rad Beograd 1-1(1-0)

Round 34 [01.05.2019]
Radnik Surdulica - FK Voždovac 4-2(1-0)
Rad Beograd - Dinamo Vranje 1-0(1-0)
FK Zemun - OFK Bačka 7-0(4-0)
FK Mačva Šabac - Spartak Subotica 2-1(1-1)

Round 35 [05.05.2019]
Spartak Subotica - Radnik Surdulica 3-3(2-2)
FK Voždovac - FK Mačva Šabac 1-1(1-1)
OFK Bačka - Rad Beograd 1-2(0-1)
Dinamo Vranje - FK Zemun 1-0(1-0)

Round 36 [11.05.2019]
Dinamo Vranje - Spartak Subotica 2-1(0-1)
FK Voždovac - OFK Bačka 1-0(0-0)
FK Zemun - Radnik Surdulica 2-1(0-1)
FK Mačva Šabac - Rad Beograd 0-0

Round 37 [19.05.2019]
Spartak Subotica - FK Voždovac 2-1(1-1)
OFK Bačka - Dinamo Vranje 0-1(0-0)
Radnik Surdulica - FK Mačva Šabac 3-0(2-0)
Rad Beograd - FK Zemun 1-1(0-1)

Final Standings

9.	FK Spartak Subotica	37	13	8	16	38	-	45	28
10.	FK Radnik Surdulica	37	12	10	15	41	-	49	27
11.	FK Voždovac Beograd	37	12	7	18	36	-	48	25
12.	FK Mačva Šabac	37	10	11	16	24	-	38	25
13.	FK Rad Beograd	37	7	12	18	22	-	44	23
14.	FK Dinamo Vranje (*Relegation Play-offs*)	37	9	6	22	24	-	67	23
15.	FK Zemun Beograd (*Relegated*)	37	6	12	19	36	-	53	21
16.	OFK Bačka Bačka Palanka (*Relegated*)	37	7	9	21	31	-	68	18

Relegation Play-offs [30.05.-02.06.2019]

FK Inđija - FK Dinamo Vranje	3-0(3-0)	0-2(0-1)

FK Inđija promoted for the Serbian SuperLiga 2019/2020.

NATIONAL CUP
Kup Srbije 2018/2019

Qualifiers [12.09.2018]

FK Mladost Bački Jarak – FK ČSK Pivara	3-0
FK Trayal Kruševac - FK Radnički Pirot	0-1
FK Mokra Gora Zubin Potok - FK Sloboda Užice	4-5 pen
FK Kolubara Lazarevac - FK Temnić 1924	2-0

Second Round [26.09/17.10.2018]

FK Kolubara Lazarevac - FK Partizan Beograd	1-2(0-1)
FK Inđija - FK Zemun	0-2(0-2)
FK Sinđelić Beograd - FK Voždovac Beograd	1-0(1-0)
FK Radnik Surdulica - FK Radnički Pirot	5-0(1-0)
FK Mladost Bački Jarak - FK Čukarički Beograd	0-2(0-0)
TSC Bačka Topola - FK Rad Beograd	2-0(1-0)
FK Javor Ivanjica - FK Novi Pazar	3-0(0-0)
FK Proleter Novi Sad - FK Mladost Lučani	1-1 aet; 3-4 pen
LFK Mladost Lučani - FK Spartak Subotica	0-2(0-1)
FK Mačva Šabac - FK Radnički 1923 Kragujevac	1-0(0-0)
FK Sloboda Užice - FK Borac Čačak	0-3(0-0)
OFK Bačka Bač. Palanka - FK Budućnost Dobanovci	1-1 aet; 3-4 pen
FK Vojvodina Novi Sad - FK Teleoptik Zemun	2-0(0-0)
FK Radnički Niš - FK Bežanija	4-1(1-0)
FK Napredak Kruš. - FK Metalac Gornji Milanovac	2-0(1-0)
FK Dinamo Vranje - FK Crvena Zvezda Beograd	0-2(0-1)

1/8-Finals [24.10./14.11./21.11.2018]

FK Zemun - FK Partizan Beograd	0-2(0-0)
FK Budućnost Dobanovci - FK Radnički Niš	1-4(1-4)
FK Spartak Subotica - FK Mačva Šabac	1-0(0-0)
FK Vojvodina Novi Sad - FK Sinđelić Beograd	4-0(0-0)
FK Borac Čačak - FK Napredak Kruševac	0-4(0-0)
FK Čukarički Beograd - FK Mladost Lučani	1-4(0-2)
FK Javor Ivanjica - FK Radnik Surdulica	1-1 aet; 4-5 pen
FK Crvena Zvezda Beograd - TSC Bačka Topola	4-1(1-0)

Quarter-Finals [13.03.2019]

FK Spartak Subotica - FK Mladost Lučani	1-2(1-0)
FK Napredak Kruševac - FK Partizan Beograd	0-4(0-2)
FK Radnički Niš - FK Vojvodina Novi Sad	2-1(1-0)
FK Crvena Zvezda Beograd - FK Radnik Surdulica	2-1(2-0)

Semi-Finals [16-17.04./15.05.2019]

FK Crvena Zvezda Beograd - FK Mladost Lučani	4-1 / 0-0
FK Partizan Beograd - FK Radnički Niš	1-0 / 1-1

Final

23.05.2019; Stadion "Rajko Mitić", Beograd; Referee: Novak Simović; Attendance: 20,000
FK Partizan Beograd - FK Crvena Zvezda Beograd **1-0(1-0)**

Partizan: Vladimir Stojković, Strahinja Pavlović, Bojan Ostojić, Slobodan Urošević (81.Zlatan Šehović), Nemanja Miletić, Zoran Tošić (90.Saša Ilić), Saša Zdjelar, Aleksandar Šćekić, Danilo Pantić, Ricardo Jorge Pires Gomes, Đorđe Ivanović (74.Lazar Pavlović). Trainer: Savo Milošević.

Crvena Zvezda: Milan Borjan, Nemanja Milunović, Milan Rodić, Filip Stojković (83.Marko Gobeljić), Vujadin Savić, Branko Jovićić (51.Aleksa Vukanović), Mirko Ivanić, Marko Marin, Dušan Jovančić, Mohamed Ben Nabouhane (69.Dejan Joveljić), Milan Pavkov. Trainer: Vladan Milojević.

Goal: 1-0 Bojan Ostojić (14).

THE CLUBS 2018/2019

Please note: matches and goals includes statistics of both regular season and play-offs (Championship or Relegation Round).

Omladinski Fudbalski Klub Bačka Bačka Palanka

Founded: 1945
Stadium: Stadion „Slavko Maletin Vava", Bačka Palanka (5,500)

Goalkeepers:	**DOB**	**M**	**(s)**	**G**
Aleksa Milojević	08.01.2000	1		
Rastko Šuljagić	27.01.1995	1		
Bojan Zogovič (MNE)	16.02.1989	35		
Defenders:	**DOB**	**M**	**(s)**	**G**
Nikola Đurić	06.11.1989	2	(2)	
Darko Gojković	26.09.1988	15		
Srđan Grabež	02.04.1991	23		2
Nemanja Ilić	27.08.1992	31		1
Stefan Jovanović	07.04.1994	25		
Aleksandar Kostić	24.01.2000	5	(2)	
Ivan Šubert	14.10.1993	2	(3)	
Dragan Žarković	16.04.1986	13	(1)	2
Miloš Živković	01.12.1984	6		
Midfielders:	**DOB**	**M**	**(s)**	**G**
Miroslav Bjeloš	29.10.1990	30		2
Ivan Đorić	07.07.1995	11	(7)	
Nebojša Gavrić	27.08.1991	27	(5)	2
Lazar Kojić	11.12.1999	3	(3)	
Milan Makarić	04.10.1995	30	(1)	5
Igor Pantić	19.06.1905		(1)	
Marko Pantić	18.06.1998	29	(3)	1
Uglješa Radinović	25.08.1993	28	(5)	3
Milan Spremo	27.04.1995	11	(10)	
Branislav Tomić	12.02.1995	16		1
Vesko Trivunović	13.01.1980		(6)	
Nikola Žakula	18.08.1992	4	(6)	
Forwards:	**DOB**	**M**	**(s)**	**G**
Zeljko Arsić	26.07.1997	3	(12)	
Filip Bajić	18.11.1993	9	(1)	2
Vojislav Balabanović	15.12.1995		(7)	
Damir Čeković	19.03.1990	6	(3)	1
Stefan Cvetković	12.01.1998		(2)	
Miloš Gordić	10.12.1992	1	(3)	
Aleksandar Katanić	15.08.1995		(5)	
Vido Marković	22.06.1905		(3)	
Luka Mićić	28.02.1995	18	(11)	5
Nemanja Mladenović	03.03.1993	12	(3)	1
Nikola Radović	10.07.1992	10	(5)	1
Trainer:	**DOB**	**M**		
Dejan Celar	30.05.1975	15		
Dragan Đorđević [05.11.2018]	19.03.1960	6		
Zoran Govedarica [09.01.2019]	14.04.1968	13		
Dalibor Škorić [03.05.2019]	09.09.1971	1		
Trivo Ilić [07.05.2019]	21.02.1966	2		

Fudbalski Klub Crvena Zvezda Beograd

Founded: 04.03.1945
Stadium: Stadion „Rajko Mitić", Beograd (55,538)

Goalkeepers:	**DOB**	**M**	**(s)**	**G**
Milan Borjan (CAN)	23.10.1987	28		
Zoran Popović	28.05.1988	9	(1)	
Defenders:	**DOB**	**M**	**(s)**	**G**
Srđan Babić	22.04.1996	21		3
Miloš Degenek (AUS)	28.04.1994	19	(1)	
Milan Gajić	28.01.1996	10	(1)	1
Stefan Hajdin	15.04.1994	5	(1)	
Nenad Krstičić	03.07.1990	11	(2)	1
Nemanja Milunović	31.05.1989	12		
Milan Rodić	02.04.1991	18		1
Vujadin Savić	01.07.1990	18	(1)	1
Filip Stojković (MNE)	22.01.1993	23		1
Rashid Sumaila (GHA)	18.12.1992	2	(1)	
Aleksa Terzić	17.08.1999	2		
Midfielders:	**DOB**	**M**	**(s)**	**G**
Mohamed Ben Nabouhane (COM)	10.06.1989	21	(3)	17
Goran Čaušić	05.05.1992	12	(9)	1
Lorenzo Ebecilio (NED)	24.09.1991	15	(4)	2
Marko Gobeljić	13.09.1992	19	(6)	5
Mirko Ivanić (MNE)	13.09.1993	10	(4)	1
Erik Jirka (SVK)	19.09.1997	1	(5)	
Dušan Jovančić	19.10.1990	25	(2)	2
Branko Jovičić	18.03.1993	19	(5)	1
Marko Marin (GER)	13.03.1989	18	(4)	6
Dejan Meleg	01.10.1994	3	(2)	
Nenad Milijaš	30.04.1983	2	(5)	
Veljko Simić	17.02.1995	18	(8)	6
Slavoljub Srnić	12.01.1992	6	(3)	1
Aleksa Vukanović	18.06.1992	6	(4)	2
Miloš Vulić	19.08.1996	1	(4)	
Forwards:	**DOB**	**M**	**(s)**	**G**
Richmond Boakye (GHA)	28.01.1993	10	(5)	13
Milan Jevtović	13.06.1993	4	(6)	4
Jonathan Renato Barbosa "Cafú" (BRA)	10.07.1991	4	(3)	2
Dejan Joveljić	07.08.1999	9	(8)	8
Nemanja Milić	25.05.1990	2	(3)	
Milan Pavkov	09.02.1994	20	(7)	12
Nikola Stojiljković	17.08.1992	4	(3)	3
Trainer:	**DOB**	**M**		
Vladan Milojević	09.03.1970	37		

Fudbalski Klub Čukarički Beograd

Founded: 04.07.1926 *(as Čukarički SK)*
Stadium: Stadion Čukarički, Beograd (4,070)

Goalkeepers:	**DOB**	**M**	**(s)**	**G**
Nemanja Belić	24.04.1987	4	(1)	
Nemanja Stevanović	08.05.1992	33		
Defenders:	**DOB**	**M**	**(s)**	**G**
Miroslav Bogosavac	14.10.1996	32		1
Đorđe Đurić	10.08.1991		(1)	
Dimitrije Kamenović	16.07.2000	3		
Boris Kopitović (MNE)	17.09.1994	29	(1)	4
Darko Puškarić	13.07.1985	23		1
Stefan Šapić	26.02.1997	25	(3)	2
Miladin Stevanović	11.02.1996	31		2
Stefan Veličković	17.01.1999	4	(4)	
Midfielders:	**DOB**	**M**	**(s)**	**G**
Kosta Aleksić	09.03.1998		(4)	
Veljko Birmančević	05.03.1998	14	(11)	
Marko Docić	21.04.1993	36		3
Nikola Drinčić (MNE)	07.09.1984	1		
Aleksandar Đorđević	20.12.1999	23		
Uroš Ignjatović	18.02.2001	1		
Asmir Kajević (MNE)	15.02.1990	16	(10)	6
Nenad Kiso	30.04.1989	3	(4)	
Stefan Kovač	14.01.1999	7	(2)	2
Luka Luković	16.10.1996	9	(6)	1
Samuel Owusu (GHA)	28.03.1996	32		7
Marko Šarić	28.11.1998		(7)	1
Luka Stojanović	04.01.1994	31	(3)	11
Darko Zorić (MNE)	12.09.1993	5	(7)	1
Forwards:	**DOB**	**M**	**(s)**	**G**
Nemanja Belaković	08.01.1997	3		
Petar Bojić	04.09.1991	4	(5)	
Ognjen Mudrinski	15.11.1991	28	(6)	18
Slobodan Tedić	13.04.2000	8	(23)	2
Milutin Vidosavljević	21.02.2001	2	(9)	1
Trainer:	**DOB**	**M**		
Simo Krunić (BIH)	03.01.1969	37		

Fudbalski Klub Dinamo Vranje

Founded: 24.01.1947
Stadium: Stadion Surdulica, Surdulica (3,312)

Goalkeepers:	**DOB**	**M**	**(s)**	**G**
Uroš Đurić	01.12.1993	15	(1)	
Nikola Lakić (BIH)	01.10.1995	13	(1)	
Nikola Perić	04.02.1992	8		
Ognjen Ristić	27.03.2002	1		
Defenders:	**DOB**	**M**	**(s)**	**G**
Nikola Đurić	06.11.1989	10		
Danijel Gašić	19.01.1987	25		2
Vladimir Ilić	24.02.1999	6		
Nikola Jovanović	12.06.1992	12	(1)	
Dušan Lalatović	29.11.1998	4	(3)	
Samuel Godwin Okon (NGA)	15.12.1996	2		
Filip Pavišić	15.01.1994	27	(1)	
Milan Stanković	18.10.1991	9	(3)	
Nikola Stevanović	13.09.1998	17	(5)	
Taigo De Araujo (BRA)	28.05.1997		(4)	
Aleksandar Tasić	06.04.1988	2		
Nikola Vukajlović	13.05.1996	18	(1)	
Jovan Zucović	17.04.1990	5		
Midfielders:	**DOB**	**M**	**(s)**	**G**
Nemanja Cvijanovic (SUI)	12.01.1997		(1)	
Marko Đurišić	17.07.1997	14	(11)	
Miloš Jokić	07.06.1987	4		
Ninoslav Karapandžić	11.02.1992	2	(4)	
Davor Nedeljković	04.02.1996	19	(5)	2
Miloš Ozegovič	11.05.1992	15		
Pavle Propadalo	24.11.1994		(2)	
Seydou Seck (SEN)	08.02.1991	1	(2)	
Okomayin Onimisi Segun (NGA)	29.11.1993	25	(1)	
Marko Stanojević	24.05.1997		(2)	
Aleksandar Stojković	15.08.1990	5	(3)	
Božidar Veškovac	10.01.1997	5	(5)	
Forwards:	**DOB**	**M**	**(s)**	**G**
Miloš Antić	03.07.1989	5	(6)	
Željko Dimitrov	19.02.1994	30	(5)	12
Lazar Đokić (MNE)	16.05.1996	5	(1)	1
Ferdinand Fru Fon (CMR)	30.05.1998		(1)	
Lefteris Matsoukas (GRE)	07.03.1990	10	(5)	2
Marko Mitrović (SWE)	27.06.1992	2	(5)	1
Nikola Popović	31.05.1994	14	(1)	1
Marko Radivojević	24.09.1995	3	(9)	
Luka Ratković	09.04.1997	22	(7)	
Milosav Sicović	12.11.1999	7	(5)	
Vasilije Spasić	23.10.1999		(5)	
Mlađan Stevanović	01.01.1995	25		2
Zakaria Suraka (GHA)	17.01.1996	20	(3)	1
Trainer:	**DOB**	**M**		
Dragan Antić	20.09.1963	15		
Radmilo Jovanović [09.11.2018]	08.07.1950	10		
Dragan Antić [09.03.2019]	20.09.1963	12		

Fudbalski Klub Mačva Šabac

Founded: 1919
Stadium: Stadion Gradski, Šabac (8,000)

Goalkeepers:	**DOB**	**M**	**(s)**	**G**
Dušan Puletić	05.01.1989	36		
Miloš Savić	19.06.1997	1		
Defenders:	**DOB**	**M**	**(s)**	**G**
Nenad Jovanović	12.05.1988	25	(6)	1
Mladen Lazarević	15.01.1984	10	(1)	1
Slavko Marić	07.03.1984	14	(7)	
Marko Mijailović	14.08.1997	14		
Filip Pejović	26.06.1982	36		1
Igor Ristivojević	08.08.1988	31		
Nemanja Tošić	23.01.1997	23	(2)	
Midfielders:	**DOB**	**M**	**(s)**	**G**
Miloš Adamović	19.06.1988	28	(1)	1
Dejan Babić	20.04.1989	4	(9)	
Đorđe Belić	18.12.1997		(1)	
Filip Božić (BIH)	09.03.1999	2	(1)	
Nenad Gavrić	12.12.1991	30	(1)	6
Lazar Ivić	24.10.1992	33	(2)	
Predrag Jeremić	22.11.1987	10	(5)	
Marko Jevtić	17.02.1996	6	(3)	
Nikola Kosanić (BIH)	06.03.1999		(1)	
Branislav Marković	17.03.1997	7	(13)	
Andrew Marveggio (AUS)	22.04.1992	1	(4)	
Stefan Milosavljević	09.05.1992	13	(8)	1
Ivan Obrovac	08.12.1986	18	(3)	1
Aleksandar Stevanović	14.07.1996	2	(3)	
Nikola Žakula	18.08.1992		(2)	
Forwards:	**DOB**	**M**	**(s)**	**G**
Aleksandar Đoković	16.12.1991	9	(9)	2
Miodrag Gemović	25.12.1994	18	(5)	
Petar Gigić	07.03.1997	21	(4)	7
Đorđe Šušnjar	18.02.1992	15	(12)	2
Lazar Vladisavljević	09.07.1992		(1)	
Trainer:	**DOB**	**M**		
Dragan Aničić	04.11.1970	12		
Darko Tešović [23.10.2018]	03.08.1970	25		

Fudbalski Klub Mladost Lučani

Founded: 1952
Stadium: Stadion Mladost, Lučani (8,000)

Goalkeepers:	**DOB**	**M**	**(s)**	**G**
Dragan Rosić	15.11.1996	36		
Zlatko Zečević	10.08.1983	1		
Defenders:	**DOB**	**M**	**(s)**	**G**
Nikola Andrić	23.05.1992	35		
Marko Jevremović	23.02.1996	4	(4)	1
Petar Jovanović (BIH)	12.07.1982	24	(9)	
Nikola Leković	19.12.1989	21	(2)	
Nemanja Micević	28.01.1999		(1)	
Ivan Milošević	03.11.1984	23	(1)	
Ivan Pešić	07.07.1989	22	(6)	
Miloš Ristić	06.04.1994	3	(8)	1
Miloš Šatara (BIH)	28.10.1995	14		
Uroš Sinđić	19.01.1986	18	(10)	
Midfielders:	**DOB**	**M**	**(s)**	**G**
Petar Bojić	04.09.1991	13		2
Stefan Dimić	01.05.1993	8	(11)	2
Lazar Jovanović	13.07.1993	22	(9)	3
Jovan Markoski	23.06.1980	9	(7)	
Predrag Pavlović	19.08.1986	29	(6)	4
Aleksandr Pejović	28.12.1990	32		13
Vladimir Radivojević	04.02.1986	34		10
Lazar Selenić	21.08.1999	1		
Janko Tumbasević (MNE)	14.01.1985	31		6
Forwards:	**DOB**	**M**	**(s)**	**G**
Viktor Amos (NGA)	05.03.1999		(1)	
Badara Badji (SEN)	24.02.1994		(1)	
Đorđe Babić	04.08.2000		(1)	
Milan Bojović	13.04.1987	12	(2)	3
Stefan Golubović	01.08.1996	3	(6)	
Obiora Odita (NGA)	14.05.1983	11	(14)	3
Stefan Tesić	18.06.1998	1	(2)	
Trainer:	**DOB**	**M**		
Nenad Milovanović	15.08.1969	37		

Fudbalski Klub Napredak Kruševac

Founded: 08.12.1946
Stadium: Stadion Mladost, Kruševac (10,331)

Goalkeepers:	**DOB**	**M**	**(s)**	**G**
Slobodan Janković	29.08.1981	1		
Nikola Petrović	10.04.1988	36		
Defenders:	**DOB**	**M**	**(s)**	**G**
Nikola Aksentijević	09.03.1993	15		
Nikola Boranijašević	19.05.1992	20		2
Stefan Deák	23.03.1991	4	(2)	
Marko Marinković	06.01.1994	20	(4)	1
Milan Obradović	27.12.1999	11	(1)	
Miloš Ostojić	03.08.1991	29	(1)	1
Nemanja Petrović	17.04.1992	34		
Josip Projić	23.08.1987	2	(2)	
Dušan Veškovac	16.03.1986	25		
Midfielders:	**DOB**	**M**	**(s)**	**G**
Krsta Bojić	09.07.1999		(3)	
Ivan Đorić	07.07.1995	14	(1)	3
Nikola Eskić (BIH)	19.12.1997	17	(11)	2
Igor Ivanović	28.07.1997	12	(7)	4
Filip Jović	06.08.1997	5	(10)	
Miroljub Kostić	05.06.1988	20		1
Jovan Markoski	23.06.1980		(2)	
Luka Stevanović	25.12.1998	1	(11)	
Aleksa Vukanović	18.06.1992	20		12
Miljan Vukadinović (CZE)	27.12.1992	1	(2)	
Miloš Vulić	19.08.1996	19		4
Đuro Zec	06.03.1990	13	(3)	1
Forwards:	**DOB**	**M**	**(s)**	**G**
Enver Alivodić	27.12.1984	22	(11)	3
Regis Samuel Baha (CMR)	21.10.1996	20	(3)	1
Andrej Ilić	03.04.2000	9	(4)	2
Ibrahima N'Diaye (SEN)	01.02.1994	32		7
Anes Rušević	02.12.1996	2	(16)	1
Miloš Zukanović	08.02.1996	3	(8)	1
Trainer:	**DOB**	**M**		
Milorad Kosanović	04.01.1951	37		

Fudbalski Klub Partizan Beograd

Founded: 04.10.1945
Stadium: Stadion Partizan, Beograd (32,710)

Goalkeepers:	**DOB**	**M**	**(s)**	**G**
Filip Kljajić	16.08.1990	8	(1)	
Vladimir Stojković	28.07.1983	29		
Defenders:	**DOB**	**M**	**(s)**	**G**
Marc Valiente Hernández (ESP)	29.03.1987	30	(1)	
Svetozar Marković	23.03.2000	24	(1)	1
Nemanja Miletić	16.01.1991	29		3
Nemanja G. Miletić	26.07.1991	13	(3)	
Bojan Ostojić	12.02.1984	6	(3)	
Strahinja Pavlović	24.05.2001	11		
Zlatan Šehović	08.08.2000	6	(3)	
Slobodan Urošević	15.04.1994	18	(5)	
Miroslav Vulićević	29.05.1985	8	(1)	
Midfielders:	**DOB**	**M**	**(s)**	**G**
Armin Đerlek	15.07.2000	9	(3)	
Gabriel Nicolae Enache (ROU)	18.08.1990	4	(4)	2
Saša Ilić	30.12.1977	1	(11)	
Nebojša Kosović (MNE)	24.02.1995	13	(6)	
Danilo Pantić	26.10.1996	29	(3)	6
Lazar Pavlović	02.11.2001		(1)	

Aleksandar Šćekić (MNE)	12.12.1991	20	(1)	1
Milan Smiljanić	19.11.1986	7	(6)	
Seydouba Soumah (GUI)	11.06.1991	2	(2)	
Zoran Tošić	28.04.1987	8	(8)	4
Goran Zakarić (BIH)	07.11.1992	25	(4)	4
Saša Zdjelar	20.03.1995	26	(6)	1
Forwards:	**DOB**	**M**	**(s)**	**G**
Dejan Georgijević	19.01.1994		(3)	
Đorđe Ivanović (CRO)	20.11.1995	8	(12)	7
Marko Janković (MNE)	09.07.1995	12	(1)	1
Nemanja Nikolić	19.10.1992	24	(5)	7
Moussa Njie (NOR)	02.10.1995		(2)	
Ognjen Ožegović	09.06.1994	2	(2)	1
Ricardo Jorge Pires Gomes (CPV)	18.12.1991	35	(1)	20
Filip Stevanović	25.09.2002		(4)	
Trainer:	**DOB**	**M**		
Miroslav Đukić	19.02.1966	2		
Zoran Mirković [04.08.2018]	21.09.1971	24		
Žarko Lazetić [11.03.2019]	22.02.1982	1		
Savo Milošević [28.03.2019]	01.09.1973	10		

Fudbalski Klub Proleter Novi Sad

Founded: 1951
Stadium: Stadion Karađorđe, Novi Sad (15,000)

Goalkeepers:	**DOB**	**M**	**(s)**	**G**
Vladan Elesin	12.12.1995	5		
Miloš Vesić	23.07.1989	32		
Defenders:	**DOB**	**M**	**(s)**	**G**
Aleksandar Andrejević	28.03.1992	20		1
Joseph Bempah (GHA)	05.09.1995	3	(7)	
Mitar Ćuković (MNE)	06.04.1995	20	(3)	
Miljan Jablan	30.01.1985	12	(1)	
Nenad Kočović	20.02.1995	4		
Zarija Lambulić	25.05.1998	29	(1)	
Leandro Climaco Pinto (BRA)	24.01.1994	13	(1)	
Danilo Nikolić	29.07.1983		(2)	
David Petrović	25.05.2000		(1)	
Vasilije Radenović (MNE)	10.05.1994	2	(3)	
Aleksandar Tanasin	15.11.1991	33		
Midfielders:	**DOB**	**M**	**(s)**	**G**
Stefan Bukorac	15.02.1991	17	(2)	
Predrag Govedarica	21.10.1984	12		1
Nikola Ilić	03.11.1995	5	(3)	
Miloš Janković	22.06.1905		(1)	

Miloš Jokić	07.06.1987	5	(6)	
Strahinja Jovanović	01.06.1999	3	(7)	
Ognjen Krasić	09.04.1988	8	(6)	1
Dušan Mićić	29.11.1984	11		
Ognjen Mitrović	30.06.1999	17	(4)	
Dušan Plavšić	23.05.1992	19	(10)	
Srđan Šćepanović	23.10.1998	5	(5)	
Dragomir Vukobratović	12.05.1988	3	(9)	
Forwards:	**DOB**	**M**	**(s)**	**G**
Stefan Čolović	16.04.1994	34		8
Nemanja Čović	18.06.1991	34		10
Strahinja Krstevski (MKD)	08.06.1997		(2)	1
Milan Mirosavljev	24.04.1995	13	(5)	5
Slobodan Novaković	15.10.1986	19	(14)	1
Branislav Pjošta	10.04.2001		(1)	
Uroš Stamenić	14.10.1996	5	(9)	
Srđan Vujaklija	23.03.1988	24	(4)	5
Trainer:	**DOB**	**M**		
Dragan Radojičić (MNE)	03.06.1970	37		

Fudbalski Klub Rad Beograd

Founded: 10.03.1958
Stadium: Stadion „Kralj Petar Prvi", Beograd (6,000)

Goalkeepers:	**DOB**	**M**	**(s)**	**G**
Dušan Marković	03.04.1998	36		
Mladen Živković	26.08.1989	1		
Defenders:	**DOB**	**M**	**(s)**	**G**
Đorđe Bašanović	31.07.1996	3	(1)	
Nikola Ignjatijević	12.12.1983	15		
Branislav Jovanović	21.09.1985	15		1
Miloš Marković	10.12.1986	5	(3)	
Milan Perendija	05.01.1986	33		1
Nikola Šipčić	17.05.1995	35		3
Goran Smiljanić	31.01.1990	10	(3)	2
Dušan Stević	25.07.1995	12		
Miloš Tanović	19.05.1996	7		
Nikola Tričković	15.11.1999	16	(3)	
Stefan Vico (MNE)	28.02.1995	15		
Vladimir Volkov (MNE)	06.06.1986	7		2
José Marcos Alves Luis „Zé Marcos" (BRA)	01.02.1998	1		
Midfielders:	**DOB**	**M**	**(s)**	**G**
Srđan Ajković (MNE)	15.10.1991	2		
Filip Bainović	23.06.1996	24	(8)	1
Milorad Balabanović	18.01.1990	7	(2)	1

Aleksandar Busnić	04.12.1997	10	(6)	
Đorđe Denić	01.04.1996	1		1
Vanja Ilić	03.01.1999	4	(7)	
Zoran Ljubinković	04.07.1982	2	(5)	
Marko Jović	23.04.1998	4	(3)	
Bogdan Mladenović	04.04.1996	25	(2)	2
Njegoš Petrović	18.07.1999	26	(2)	1
Branko Riznić	04.10.1999		(3)	
Veljko Roganović	10.01.1998		(1)	
Marko Stojanović	01.02.1998	3	(5)	
Dušan Zivković	31.07.1996	5	(13)	
Forwards:	**DOB**	**M**	**(s)**	**G**
Filip Kasalica (MNE)	17.12.1988	17	(8)	1
Aleksandar Lutovac	28.06.1997	17	(1)	1
Nenad Marinković	28.09.1988	12	(5)	2
Stefan Mihajlović	24.06.1994	15	(6)	1
Dejan Parađina	05.02.1999	2	(2)	
Miloš Trifunović	15.10.1984	9	(5)	2
Veljko Trifunović	04.08.1998	1	(6)	
Borko Veselinović	06.01.1986	10	(5)	
Trainer:	**DOB**	**M**		
Milorad Kosanović	04.01.1951	37		

Fudbalski Klub Radnički Niš

Founded: 24.04.1923
Stadium: Stadion Čair, Niš (18,151)

Goalkeepers:	DOB	M	(s)	G
Ivan Bulajić	29.03.1995	1	(1)	
Milorad Kojić	03.02.1999	2	(1)	
Mladen Živković	26.08.1989	3		
Borivoje Ristić	19.09.1983	31		
Defenders:	**DOB**	**M**	**(s)**	**G**
Nikola Aksentijević	09.03.1993	4		
Taras Bondarenko (UKR)	23.09.1992	31	(1)	2
Đorđe Crnomarković	10.09.1993	32		
Stefan Đorđević	13.03.1991	18		1
Andrija Mijailović	07.06.1995	1	(1)	
Radovan Pankov	05.08.1995	35		3
Nikola Stanković	18.12.1993	19		
Aleksandar Todorovski (MKD)	26.02.1984	31		
Marko Živković	17.05.1994	2	(1)	
Midfielders:	**DOB**	**M**	**(s)**	**G**
Andreja Apostolović	16.06.1996		(1)	
Siniša Babić	13.02.1991	5	(1)	2
Petar Ćirković	21.06.1905		(1)	
Uroš Damnjanović	08.02.1995	2	(2)	
Nikola Drinčić (MNE)	07.09.1984	30		4
Petar Grbić (MNE)	07.08.1988	29	(3)	3
Aleksa Jovanović	27.05.1999	4	(8)	
Aleksandar Jovanović	17.12.1985	2	(10)	1
Damir Kojašević (MNE)	03.06.1987	9	(1)	2
Dušan Mićić	29.11.1984	3		
Ryota Noma (JPN)	15.11.1991	17	(11)	2
Petar Petrović	15.09.1995	4	(7)	2
Lazar Ranđelović	05.08.1997	31	(5)	7
Petar Ristić	29.03.2000		(2)	
Saša Stojanović	21.01.1983	9	(8)	2
Forwards:	**DOB**	**M**	**(s)**	**G**
Nikola Čumić	20.11.1998	1	(7)	1
Nermin Haskić (BIH)	27.06.1989	33	(1)	24
Marko Mitrović (SWE)	27.06.1992		(3)	
Marko Mrkić	20.08.1996	3	(6)	1
Slađan Nikodijević	01.05.1990	4	(22)	4
Aleksandar Stanisavljević	11.06.1989	11	(6)	8
Trainer:	**DOB**	**M**		
Nenad Lalatović	22.12.1977	37		

Fudbalski Klub Radnik Surdulica

Founded: 1926
Stadium: Stadion Surdulica, Surdulica (3,312)

Goalkeepers:	DOB	M	(s)	G
Milovan Lekić	24.08.1993	2	(1)	
Nikola Vasiljević	24.06.1996	35		
Defenders:	**DOB**	**M**	**(s)**	**G**
Marko Čubrilo (BIH)	03.05.1998	6		
Faton Džemaili (ALB)	15.11.1998		(1)	
Predrag Đorđević	30.06.1990	21	(5)	
Ivan Kričak	19.07.1996	7	(3)	1
Miloš Milovanović	09.12.1987	20	(5)	3
Siniša Mladenović	05.01.1991	19		
Tomislav Pajović	15.03.1986	12		1
Vladan Pavlović	24.02.1984	9	(10)	1
Dušan Stevanović	22.06.1996	31		
Dragan Žarković	16.04.1986	17	(1)	
Midfielders:	**DOB**	**M**	**(s)**	**G**
Bojan Bojić	03.03.2000	3	(8)	
Uroš Damnjanović	08.02.1995	6	(4)	2
Lazar Kojić	11.12.1999	9	(3)	
Nikola Kovačević	14.04.1994	11	(5)	
Francis Kyeremeh (GHA)	23.06.1997	30	(5)	2
Dušan Pantelić	15.04.1993	19	(1)	3
Bratislav Pejčić	17.01.1983	17	(7)	
Risto Ristović	05.05.1988	27	(5)	2
Filip Stanisavljević	20.05.1987	29		1
Filip Stojanović	19.05.1988	17	(13)	2
Forwards:	**DOB**	**M**	**(s)**	**G**
Zoran Danoski (MKD)	20.10.1990	4	(7)	1
Krsta Đorđević	24.09.1993		(1)	
Aleksandar Miladinović	06.03.2000		(3)	1
Stefan Nikolić (MNE)	16.04.1990	10	(6)	
Bogdan Stamenković	19.01.1998	7	(5)	2
Milan Stojanović	23.06.1998	4	(9)	3
Igor Zlatanović	10.02.1998	35		13
Trainer:	**DOB**	**M**		
Mladen Dodić	20.08.1969	6		
Goran Jocić [31.08.2018]		1		
Milan Milanović [04.09.2018]	10.01.1963	30		

Fudbalski Klub Spartak Subotica

Founded: 21.04.1945
Stadium: Stadion Subotica, Subotica (13,000)

Goalkeepers:	DOB	M	(s)	G
Ivan Lučić	17.10.1996	3		
Miloš Ostojić	21.04.1996	28		
Nikola Perić	04.02.1992	6		
Defenders:	**DOB**	**M**	**(s)**	**G**
Luka Cucin	24.11.1998	2		
Nemanja Ćalasan	17.03.1996	18		1
Benjamin Demir (MKD)	16.05.1996	1		
David Dunđerski	28.10.1999	12	(15)	
Draško Đorđević	01.08.1993	4	(6)	
Filip Jović	27.02.2000		(1)	
Dejan Kerkez	20.01.1996	30	(1)	2
Sergiy Kulynych (UKR)	09.01.1995	1	(2)	
Stefan Milošević	07.04.1995	32	(1)	2
Vladimir Otašević	08.06.1986	13		1
Slavko Radovanović	18.10.2000	1	(1)	
Slađan Rakić	13.06.1999	5	(6)	
Nemanja Tekijaški	02.03.1997	30		
Andrija Vukčević (MNE)	11.10.1996	17	(8)	1
Midfielders:	**DOB**	**M**	**(s)**	**G**
Tim Chow (TPE)	18.01.1994	5	(1)	
Nemanja Glavčić	19.02.1997	30	(1)	1
Bassey Inyang Howells (NGA)	20.04.1996		(3)	
Branimir Jočić	10.07.1994	6	(2)	
Jovan Lazić	03.02.1999	1		
Milan Marčić	14.03.1996	22	(2)	3
Nemanja Matijević	27.06.1999	1		
Andrija Milić	15.07.2001	1	(2)	
Đorđe Radovanović	06.05.1993	3	(4)	
Mile Savković	11.03.1992	1	(1)	2
Noboru Shimura (JPN)	11.03.1993	16	(2)	1
Vladimir Torbica	20.09.1980	5	(10)	
Uros Vukićević	29.05.2000		(1)	
Forwards:	**DOB**	**M**	**(s)**	**G**
Samuel Afum (GHA)	24.12.1990	2	(1)	
Luka Bijelović	11.04.2001		(1)	
Bojan Čečarić	10.10.1993	18		3
Stefan Denković (MNE)	16.06.1991	25	(1)	9
Dejan Đenić	02.06.1986	16	(10)	3
Ognjen Đuričin	03.09.1995	3		
Milan Lučić	20.03.1999	1	(2)	
Nemanja Mladenović	03.03.1993	8	(4)	1
Nemanja Obradović	29.05.1989	22	(3)	6
Stefan Sormaz	10.08.1999	3	(5)	2
Nikola Tripković	28.01.1998	2	(3)	
Lazar Tufegdžić	22.02.1997	13	(2)	2
Trainer:	**DOB**	**M**		
Vladimir Gaćinović (BIH)	03.01.1966	10		
Predrag Rogan [02.10.2018]	02.08.1974	27		

Fudbalski Klub Vojvodina Novi Sad

Founded: 06.03.1914
Stadium: Stadion Karađorđe, Novi Sad (15,000)

Goalkeepers:	DOB	M	(s)	G
Emil Rockov	27.01.1995	35		
Nikola Simić	21.12.1996	2	(1)	
Defenders:	**DOB**	**M**	**(s)**	**G**
Nikola Antić	04.01.1994	14		
Marko Bjeković	21.09.2000		(1)	
Diamantis Chouchoumis (GRE)	17.07.1994	5	(1)	
Mladen Devetak	12.03.1999	12	(2)	
Lazar Đorđević	14.07.1992	7		
Daniel Graovac (BIH)	08.08.1993	31		
Milan Lazarević	10.01.1997	16	(4)	
Siniša Saničanin (BIH)	24.04.1995	28		
Aranđel Stojković	02.03.1995	24	(3)	
Ranko Veselinović	24.03.1999	16	(3)	
Midfielders:	**DOB**	**M**	**(s)**	**G**
Lazar Arsić	24.09.1991	13	(7)	2
Milan Đurić	03.10.1987	31	(3)	6
Damjan Gojkov	02.01.1998	14	(15)	1
Aleksandar Mesarović	27.09.1998	6	(9)	
Aleksandar Mirkov	08.01.1996		(3)	
Vuk Mitošević	12.02.1991	14		1
Mihajlo Nešković	09.02.2000	9	(4)	
Eze Okeuhie (NGA)	06.06.1993	19	(3)	4
Nikola Srećković	26.04.1996	6	(6)	1
Mirko Topić	05.02.2001	1	(1)	
Lazar Zličić	07.02.1997		(1)	
Damir Zlomislić (BIH)	20.07.1991	17		
Dejan Zukić	07.05.2001	6	(4)	1
Forwards:	**DOB**	**M**	**(s)**	**G**
Darko Bjedov	28.03.1989	2	(6)	
Seku Conneh (LBR)	10.11.1995	1	(2)	
Ognjen Đuričin	03.09.1995	15	(6)	1
Ismaël Fofana (CIV)	08.09.1988	12	(1)	2
Nikola Gajić	23.04.1998	7	(15)	1
Andrej Jakovljević	12.04.2000	1		
Bojan Matić	22.12.1991	13	(1)	4
Nemanja Milojević (GRE)	23.02.1998	30	(5)	2
Dragoljub Savić	25.04.2001		(1)	
Trainer:	**DOB**	**M**		
Aleksander Veselinović	23.05.1970	7		
Dragomir Okuka [08.09.2018]	02.04.1954	10		
Radovan Krivokapić (MNE)[26.11.2018]	14.08.1978	20		

Fudbalski Klub Voždovac Beograd

Founded: 1912
Stadium: Stadion Shopping Center, Beograd (5,200)

Goalkeepers:	DOB	M	(s)	G
Marko Ilić	03.02.1998	29		
Mihajlo Karadžić	15.06.2000		(1)	
Marko Knežević	29.03.1989	8		
Defenders:	**DOB**	**M**	**(s)**	**G**
Jovica Blagojević	27.08.1998	2		
Strahinja Bošnjak	18.02.1999	4	(2)	
Marko Jovanović	26.03.1988	29	(1)	1
Bojan Kovačević	28.04.1996	17	(2)	
Dušan Matović	08.07.1983	1	(1)	
Miloš Mihajlov	15.12.1982	33		1
Nikola Mikić	13.09.1985	20	(2)	1
Branko Ostojić	03.01.1984	1		
Božidar Veličković	07.01.1995	3	(1)	
Midfielders:	**DOB**	**M**	**(s)**	**G**
Lazar Arsić	24.09.1991	12	(3)	3
Nikola Ćirković	04.12.1991	35		
Aleksandar Ješić	13.09.1994	5	(2)	2
Andrija Luković	24.10.1994	28	(5)	7
Igor Maksimović	31.07.1999	3	(6)	
Zoran Milutinovič (BIH)	01.03.1988	8	(2)	
Jovan Nišić	03.03.1998	1	(6)	
Miloš Pavlović	27.11.1983	29	(2)	1
Todor Petrović	18.08.1994	6	(5)	
Stefan Purtić	06.08.1998	7	(7)	
Nikola Srećković	26.04.1996	2	(1)	
Dragoljub Srnić	12.01.1992	14	(1)	1
Lazar Zličić	07.02.1997	8	(5)	1
Marko Zoćević	19.05.1993	4	(5)	
Forwards:	**DOB**	**M**	**(s)**	**G**
Borko Duronjić	24.09.1997	23	(8)	2
Aleksandar Jevtić	30.03.1985	6	(5)	1
Alen Mašović	07.08.1994	23	(9)	4
Luka Milunović	21.12.1992	7	(4)	
Marko Pavićević	03.09.1986		(2)	
Predrag Sikimić	29.08.1982	10	(1)	3
Filip Stuparević	30.08.2000	20	(10)	8
Nikola Trujić	14.04.1992	9	(2)	
Trainer:	**DOB**	**M**		
Branko Vojinović	02.09.1961	9		
Jovan Damjanović [24.09.2018]	04.10.1982	2		
Dragan Aničić [14.10.2018]	04.11.1970	26		

Fudbalski Klub Zemun Beograd

Founded: 20.10.1946
Stadium: Stadion Zemun, Beograd (10,000)

Goalkeepers:	DOB	M	(s)	G
Milos Krunić	22.11.1996		(1)	
Marko Milošević	07.02.1991	37		
Defenders:	**DOB**	**M**	**(s)**	**G**
Emir Azemović (MNE)	06.01.1997	23	(3)	1
Strahinja Bošnjak	18.02.1999	3	(4)	
Nenad Cvetković	03.01.1996	16		1
Marko Đalović	19.05.1986	23	(5)	
Slavko Lukić	14.03.1989	8		1
Andrija Mijailović	07.06.1995	10	(1)	
Mihailo Milutinović	14.02.1995	8	(1)	
Siniša Mladenović	05.01.1991	14		
Nikola Petrović	01.01.2000		(1)	
Ivan Rogač	18.06.1992	2		
Milan Savić	04.04.1994	10		
Predrag Stanimirović	09.09.1995	6		
Borislav Terzić (BIH)	01.11.1991	2	(1)	
Branislav Trajković	29.08.1989	14		
Nemanja Vučić	11.06.1996	18		3
Stefan Živković	01.06.1990	9	(1)	
Miloš Zlatković	01.01.1997	1		
Midfielders:	**DOB**	**M**	**(s)**	**G**
Đorđe Bašanović	31.07.1996	4	(2)	
Nikola Cuckić	11.04.1997	1		
Ivan Ilić	17.03.2001	13	(3)	3
Nenad Kiso	30.04.1989	14		
Stevan Luković	16.03.1993	16		1
Dejan Maksimović (BIH)	11.10.1995	3		
Takuya Murayama (JPN)	08.08.1989	2	(3)	
Mateja Njamculović	02.10.2001		(1)	
Miloš Podunavac	11.06.1997	3	(7)	
Nikola Ristović	16.01.2001	6	(2)	1
Daniel Romanovskij (LTU)	19.06.1996	1	(3)	
Veljko Simić	17.02.1995	2		2
Luka Sinđić	13.02.1993	7		
Hendrik Somaeb (NAM)	29.09.1992	4	(7)	2
Andreja Stojanović	20.06.1905	3	(3)	
Nikola Stojković	02.02.1995	14	(1)	2
Nemanja Tomić	21.01.1988	8	(12)	4
Miloš Tošeski (MKD)	24.02.1998	14	(9)	
Miljan Vukadinović (CZE)	27.12.1992	18		
Forwards:	**DOB**	**M**	**(s)**	**G**
Vasilije Janjić	25.01.1995	2	(3)	
Ljubomir Kovacević (MNE)	23.02.2000		(2)	
Filip Kukuličić (MNE)	13.02.1996	23	(3)	6
Aleksa Marković (CAN)	27.02.1997	4	(3)	
Momčilo Mrkaić (BIH)	21.09.1990	20	(8)	6
Nikola Nešović	17.10.1993	7	(4)	1
Dušan Savić (MKD)	01.10.1985	9	(6)	1
Dejan Vidić	10.08.1993	5	(6)	
Trainer:	**DOB**	**M**		
Milan Milanović	10.01.1963	4		
Miloš Kruščić [13.08.2018]	03.10.1976	6		
Dejan Đurđević [04.07.1967]	15.11.2018	20		
Radomir Koković [11.04.2019]	06.01.1984	7		

SECOND LEVEL

Prva Liga Srbija 2018/2019

Regular Season – Final Standings

1.	TSC Bačka Topola	30	20	8	2	64	-	19	68
2.	FK Javor Ivanjica	30	19	6	5	61	-	27	63
3.	FK Inđija	30	17	6	7	48	-	21	57
4.	FK Zlatibor Čajetina	30	16	2	12	41	-	30	50
5.	FK Radnički 1923 Kragujevac	30	14	7	9	36	-	32	49
6.	FK Metalac Gornji Milanovac	30	13	9	8	45	-	32	48
7.	FK Bežanija	30	14	3	13	40	-	38	45
8.	FK Sinđelić Beograd	30	11	11	8	28	-	24	44
9.	OFK Žarkovo	30	11	8	11	37	-	38	41
10.	FK Trayal Kruševac	30	12	5	13	27	-	32	41
11.	OFK Bečej 1918	30	10	6	14	33	-	37	36
12.	FK Budućnost Dobanovci	30	8	9	13	26	-	35	33
13.	FK Teleoptik Zemun	30	6	9	15	26	-	44	27
14.	FK Borac Čačak	30	6	7	17	23	-	44	25
15.	FK Sloboda Užice	30	5	6	19	16	-	56	21
16.	FK Novi Pazar	30	3	8	19	13	-	55	17

Teams ranked 1-8 were qualified for the Promotion Round, while teams ranked 9-16 were qualified for the Relegation Round.
Points from the regular season are halved with half points rounded up.

Promotion Round

1.	TSC Bačka Topola (*Promoted*)	30	26	9	2	80	-	27	53
2.	FK Javor Ivanjica (*Promoted*)	30	23	8	6	78	-	37	46
3.	FK Inđija (*Promotion Play-offs*)	30	20	7	10	57	-	29	39
4.	FK Radnički 1923 Kragujevac	30	16	11	10	42	-	36	35
5.	FK Metalac Gornji Milanovac	30	15	12	10	51	-	35	33
6.	FK Zlatibor Čajetina	30	18	3	16	48	-	42	32
7.	FK Bežanija	30	15	5	17	48	-	50	28
8.	FK Sinđelić Beograd	30	11	13	13	35	-	43	24

Relegation Round

9.	FK Trayal Kruševac	30	15	7	15	38	-	40	32
10.	FK Budućnost Dobanovci	30	13	9	15	35	-	41	32
11.	OFK Žarkovo	30	14	9	14	42	-	44	31
12.	FK Borac Čačak	30	10	9	18	34	-	49	27
13.	OFK Bečej 1918 (*Relegated*)	30	12	8	17	39	-	44	26
14.	FK Novi Pazar (*Relegated*)	30	7	8	22	28	-	63	21
15.	FK Teleoptik Zemun (*Relegated*)	30	7	10	20	31	-	58	18
16.	FK Sloboda Užice (*Relegated*)	30	6	8	23	22	-	70	16

NATIONAL TEAM

INTERNATIONAL MATCHES
(16.07.2018 – 15.07.2019)

07.09.2018	Vilnius	Lithuania - Serbia	0-1(0-1)	(UNL)
10.09.2018	Beograd	Serbia - Romania	2-2(1-0)	(UNL)
11.10.2018	Podgorica	Montenegro - Serbia	0-2(0-1)	(UNL)
14.10.2018	Bucureşti	Romania - Serbia	0-0	(UNL)
17.11.2018	Beograd	Serbia - Montenegro	2-1(2-0)	(UNL)
20.11.2018	Beograd	Serbia - Lithuania	4-1(0-0)	(UNL)
20.03.2019	Wolfsburg	Germany - Serbia	1-1(0-1)	(F)
25.03.2019	Lisboa	Portugal - Serbia	1-1(1-1)	(ECQ)
07.06.2019	Lviv	Ukraine - Serbia	5-0(2-0)	(ECQ)
10.06.2019	Beograd	Serbia - Lithuania	4-1(3-0)	(ECQ)

07.09.2018 LITHUANIA - SERBIA 0-1(0-1) UEFA Nations League C, Group 4
LFF Stadionas, Vilnius; Referee: Robert Adam Madden (Scotland); Attendance: 4,378
SRB: Marko Dmitrović, Antonio Rukavina, Milan Rodić (77.Aleksandar Kolarov), Miloš Veljković, Nikola Milenković, Nemanja Maksimović, Nemanja Matić (Cap) (82.Saša Lukić), Filip Kostić (90.Nemanja Radonjić), Andrija Živković, Dušan Tadić, Aleksandar Mitrović. Trainer: Mladen Krstajić.
Goal: Dušan Tadić (38 penalty).

10.09.2018 SERBIA - ROMANIA 2-2(1-0) UEFA Nations League C, Group 4
Stadion Partizan, Beograd; Referee: Vladislav Bezborodov (Russia); Attendance: 15,496
SRB: Marko Dmitrović, Antonio Rukavina, Uroš Spajić, Miloš Veljković, Aleksandar Kolarov (Cap), Adem Ljajić (77.Aleksandar Prijović), Saša Lukić (71.Nemanja Matić), Sergej Milinković-Savić (64.Filip Kostić), Nemanja Maksimović, Dušan Tadić, Aleksandar Mitrović. Trainer: Mladen Krstajić.
Goals: Aleksandar Mitrović (26, 63).

11.10.2018 MONTENEGRO - SERBIA 0-2(0-1) UEFA Nations League C, Group 4
Stadion pod Goricom, Podgorica; Referee: Gianluca Rocchi (Italy); Attendance: 9,394
SRB: Marko Dmitrović, Antonio Rukavina, Milan Rodić, Miloš Veljković, Nikola Milenković, Andrija Živković, Mijat Gaćinović (79.Sergej Milinković-Savić), Saša Lukić (73.Branko Jovičić), Nemanja Maksimović, Dušan Tadić (Cap), Aleksandar Mitrović (90+3.Nemanja Radonjić). Trainer: Mladen Krstajić.
Goals: Aleksandar Mitrović (18 penalty, 81).

14.10.2018 ROMANIA - SERBIA 0-0 UEFA Nations League C, Group 4
Arena Naţională, Bucureşti; Referee: Bernie Raymond "Kevin" Blom (Netherlands); Attendance: 48,513
SRB: Predrag Rajković, Antonio Rukavina, Milan Rodić (77.Nemanja Miletić), Miloš Veljković, Nikola Milenković, Mijat Gaćinović (63.Sergej Milinković-Savić), Saša Lukić, Nemanja Radonjić, Nemanja Maksimović, Dušan Tadić (Cap), Aleksandar Mitrović. Trainer: Mladen Krstajić.

17.11.2018 SERBIA - MONTENEGRO 2-1(2-0) UEFA Nations League C, Group 4
Stadion "Rajko Mitić", Beograd; Referee: Alberto Undiano Mallenco (Spain); Attendance: 15,416
SRB: Predrag Rajković, Antonio Rukavina, Miloš Veljković, Nikola Milenković, Aleksandar Kolarov (Cap), Nemanja Matić, Adem Ljajić (90+2.Nemanja Radonjić), Mijat Gaćinović (71.Saša Lukić), Nemanja Maksimović, Dušan Tadić, Aleksandar Mitrović (83.Luka Jović). Trainer: Mladen Krstajić.
Goals: Adem Ljajić (30), Aleksandar Mitrović (32).

20.11.2018 SERBIA - LITHUANIA 4-1(0-0) UEFA Nations League C, Group 4
Stadion Partizan, Beograd; Referee: Kristo Tohver (Estonia); Attendance: 2,088
SRB: Predrag Rajković, Antonio Rukavina (Cap), Milan Rodić, Miloš Veljković, Nikola Milenković, Adem Ljajić (82.Danijel Aleksić), Andrija Živković, Mijat Gaćinović (46.Aleksandar Prijović), Saša Lukić (77.Ljubomir Fejsa), Nemanja Maksimović, Aleksandar Mitrović. Trainer: Mladen Krstajić.
Goals: Artūras Žulpa (51 own goal), Aleksandar Mitrović (58), Aleksandar Prijović (71), Adem Ljajić (74).

20.03.2019 GERMANY - SERBIA 1-1(0-1) Friendly International
Volkswagen Arena, Wolfsburg; Referee: Robert Madden (Scotland); Attendance: 26,101
SRB: Marko Dmitrović, Antonio Rukavina (Cap), Uroš Spajić, Miroslav Bogosavac (80.Stefan Mitrović), Nikola Milenković, Darko Lazović (79.Andrija Živković), Adem Ljajić, Mijat Gaćinović (62.Nemanja Radonjić), Sergej Milinković-Savić (62.Saša Lukić), Nemanja Maksimović (88.Branko Jovičić), Luka Jović (71.Milan Pavkov). Trainer: Mladen Krstajić.
Goal: Luka Jović (12).

25.03.2019 PORTUGAL - SERBIA 1-1(1-1) 16th EC. Qualifiers
Estádio da Luz, Lisboa; Referee: Szymon Marciniak (Poland); Attendance: 50,342
SRB: Marko Dmitrović, Antonio Rukavina, Filip Mladenović, Uroš Spajić, Nikola Milenković, Darko Lazović (69.Andrija Živković), Adem Ljajić (87.Sergej Milinković-Savić), Mijat Gaćinović (21.Nemanja Radonjić), Nemanja Maksimović, Dušan Tadić (Cap), Aleksandar Mitrović. Trainer: Mladen Krstajić.
Goal: Dušan Tadić (7 penalty).

07.06.2019 UKRAINE - SERBIA 5-0(2-0) 16th EC. Qualifiers
Olympiyskiy Stadium, Kyiv; Referee: Antonio Miguel Mateu Lahoz (Spain); Attendance: 34,915
SRB: Marko Dmitrović, Uroš Spajić, Nikola Milenković, Aleksandar Kolarov (Cap), Filip Kostić, Adem Ljajić (60.Ljubomir Fejsa), Mijat Gaćinović, Aleksandar Prijović (53.Aleksandar Mitrović), Nemanja Maksimović, Dušan Tadić, Luka Jović (72.Darko Lazović). Trainer: Mladen Krstajić.

10.06.2019 SERBIA - LITHUANIA 4-1(3-0) 16th EC. Qualifiers
Stadion "Rajko Mitić", Beograd; Referee: Adrien Jaccotet (Switzerland); Attendance: *played behind closed doors*
SRB: Marko Dmitrović, Antonio Rukavina, Uroš Spajić, Nikola Milenković, Aleksandar Kolarov (Cap), Filip Kostić (71.Andrija Živković), Saša Lukić, Nemanja Maksimović, Dušan Tadić (81.Adem Ljajić), Aleksandar Mitrović, Luka Jović (87.Aleksandar Katai). Trainer: Mladen Krstajić.
Goals: Aleksandar Mitrović (20, 34), Luka Jović (35), Adem Ljajić (90+2).

NATIONAL TEAM PLAYERS
(16.07.2018 – 15.07.2019)

Name	DOB	Caps	Goals	2018/2019:	Club
Goalkeepers					
Marko DMITROVIĆ	24.01.1992	**9**	**0**	2018/2019:	*SD Eibar (ESP)*
Predrag RAJKOVIĆ	31.10.1995	**11**	**0**	2018:	*Maccabi Tel Aviv FC (ISR)*
Defenders					
Miroslav BOGOSAVAC	14.10.1996	**1**	**0**	2019:	*FK Čukarički Beograd*
Aleksandar KOLAROV	10.11.1985	**84**	**11**	2018/2019:	*AS Roma (ITA)*
Nikola MILENKOVIĆ	12.10.1997	**15**	**0**	2018/2019:	*ACF Fiorentina (ITA)*
Nemanja MILETIĆ	16.01.1991	**1**	**0**	2018:	*FK Partizan Beograd*
Stefan MITROVIĆ	22.05.1990	**14**	**0**	2019:	*Racing Club Strasbourg (FRA)*
Filip MLADENOVIĆ	15.08.1991	**7**	**0**	2018/2019:	*KS Lechia Gdańsk (POL)*
Milan RODIĆ	02.04.1991	**5**	**0**	2018:	*FK Crvena Zvezda Beograd*
Antonio RUKAVINA	26.01.1984	**58**	**0**	2018/2019:	*Astana FC (KAZ)*
Uroš SPAJIĆ	13.02.1993	**10**	**0**	2018/2019:	*FK Krasnodar (RUS)*
Miloš VELJKOVIĆ	26.09.1995	**9**	**0**	2018:	*SV Werder Bremen (GER)*
Midfielders					
Ljubomir FEJSA	14.08.1988	**25**	**0**	2018/2019:	*Sport Lisboa e Benfica (POR)*
Mijat GAĆINOVIĆ	08.02.1995	**14**	**2**	2018/2019:	*Eintracht Frankfurt (GER)*
Branko JOVIČIĆ	18.03.1993	**2**	**0**	2018/2019:	*FK Crvena Zvezda Beograd*
Aleksandar KATAI	06.02.1991	**7**	**0**	2019:	*Chicago Fire SC (USA)*
Filip KOSTIĆ	01.11.1992	**30**	**2**	2018/2019:	*Eintracht Frankfurt (GER)*
Darko LAZOVIĆ	15.09.1990	**8**	**0**	2019:	*Genoa C&FC (ITA)*
Adem LJAJIĆ	29.09.1991	**39**	**9**	2018/2019:	*Beşiktaş JK İstanbul (TUR)*
Nemanja MAKSIMOVIĆ	26.01.1995	**15**	**0**	2018/2019:	*Getafe CF (ESP)*
Nemanja MATIĆ	01.08.1988	**46**	**2**	2018:	*Manchester United FC (ENG)*
Sergej MILINKOVIĆ-SAVIĆ	27.02.1995	**12**	**0**	2018/2019:	*SS Lazio Roma (ITA)*
Nemanja RADONJIĆ	15.02.1996	**11**	**0**	2018/2019:	*Olympique de Marseille (ITA)*
Dušan TADIĆ	20.11.1988	**64**	**15**	2018/2019:	*AFC Ajax Amsterdam (NED)*
Andrija ŽIVKOVIĆ	11.07.1996	**17**	**0**	2018/2019:	*Sport Lisboa e Benfica (POR)*
Forwards					
Danijel ALEKSIĆ	30.04.1991	**2**	**0**	2018:	*Yeni Malatyaspor Spor Kulübü (TUR)*
Luka JOVIĆ	23.12.1997	**6**	**2**	2018/2019:	*Eintracht Frankfurt (GER)*
Aleksandar MITROVIĆ	16.09.1994	**49**	**25**	2018/2019:	*Fulham FC London (ENG)*
Milan PAVKOV	09.02.1994	**1**	**0**	2019:	*FK Crvena Zvezda Beograd*
Aleksandar PRIJOVIĆ	21.04.1990	**13**	**2**	2018: 10.01.2019->	*PAOK Thessaloníki (GRE)* *Al-Ittihad FC Jeddah (KSA)*

National team coach

Mladen KRSTAJIĆ [30.10.2017 – 13.06.2019]	04.03.1974	19 M; 9 W; 5 D; 5 L; 30-21

SLOVAKIA

The Country:
Slovenská republika (Slovak Republic)
Capital: Bratislava
Surface: 49,035 km²
Inhabitants: 5,450,421 [2018]
Time: UTC+1

The FA:
Slovenský futbalový zväz
Tomášikova 30C, 821 01 Bratislava
Tel: +421 2 4820 6000
Founded: 04.11.1938
Member of FIFA since: 1994
Member of UEFA since: 1993
Website: www.futbalsfz.sk

NATIONAL TEAM RECORDS

First international match:	27.08.1939, Bratislava:	Slovakia – Germany 2-0
Most international caps:	Marek Hamšik	- 114 caps (since 2007)
Most international goals:	Marek Hamšik	- 24 goals / 114 caps (since 2007)

UEFA EUROPEAN CHAMPIONSHIP	
1960	-
1964	-
1968	-
1972	-
1976	-
1980	-
1984	-
1988	-
1992	-
1996	Qualifiers
2000	Qualifiers
2004	Qualifiers
2008	Qualifiers
2012	Qualifiers
2016	Final Tournament (2nd Round of 16)

FIFA WORLD CUP	
1930	-
1934	-
1938	-
1950	-
1954	-
1958	-
1962	-
1966	-
1970	-
1974	-
1978	-
1982	-
1986	-
1990	-
1994	-
1998	Qualifiers
2002	Qualifiers
2006	Qualifiers
2010	Final Tournament (2nd Round of 16)
2014	Qualifiers
2018	Qualifiers

UEFA NATIONS LEAGUE
2018/2019 – League B

OLYMPIC FOOTBALL TOURNAMENTS 1908-2016							
1908	-	**1948**	-	**1972**	-	**1996**	Qualifiers
1912	-	**1952**	-	**1976**	-	**2000**	Group Stage
1920	-	**1956**	-	**1980**	-	**2004**	Qualifiers
1924	-	**1960**	-	**1984**	-	**2008**	Qualifiers
1928	-	**1964**	-	**1988**	-	**2012**	Qualifiers
1936	-	**1968**	-	**1992**	-	**2016**	Qualifiers

FIFA CONFEDERATIONS CUP 1992-2017
None

SLOVAK CLUB HONOURS IN EUROPEAN CLUB COMPETITIONS:

European Champion Clubs.Cup (1956-1992) / UEFA Champions League (1993-2019)		
None		
Fairs Cup (1858-1971) / UEFA Cup (1972-2009) / UEFA Europa League (2010-2019)		
None		
UEFA Super Cup (1972-2018)		
None		
European Cup Winners.Cup 1961-1999*		
ŠK Slovan Bratislava*	**1**	1968/1969
**represented Czechoslovakia*		

**defunct competition*

NATIONAL COMPETITIONS
TABLE OF HONOURS

Please note: Slovakia was part of Czechoslovakia (1918–1993). First Slovak championship [Zväzové Majstrovstvá Slovenska] was played between Slovak teams (1925–1933).

Zväzové Majstrovstvá Slovenska (1925-1933)

	CHAMPIONS
1925	1. ČsŠK Bratislava
1925/1926	1. ČsŠK Bratislava
1926/1927	1. ČsŠK Bratislava
1927/1928	SK Žilina
1928/1929	SK Žilina
1929/1930	1. ČsŠK Bratislava
1930/1931	Ligeti SC Bratislava
1931/1932	1. ČsŠK Bratislava
1932/1933	SC Rusj Uzhorod

Slovenská liga (1939–1945)

	CHAMPIONS
1938/1939	Sparta Považská Bystrica
1939/1940	ŠK Bratislava
1940/1941	ŠK Bratislava
1941/1942	ŠK Bratislava
1942/1943	OAP Bratislava
1943/1944	ŠK Bratislava

	CHAMPIONS	CUP WINNERS	BEST GOALSCORERS	
1993/1994	ŠK Slovan Bratislava	ŠK Slovan Bratislava	Pavol Diňa (DAC Dunajska Streda)	19
1994/1995	ŠK Slovan Bratislava	FK Inter Bratislava	Robert Semenik (MFK Dukla Banská Bystrica)	18
1995/1996	ŠK Slovan Bratislava	FC Chemlon Humenné	Robert Semenik (1. FC Košice)	29
1996/1997	1. FC Košice	ŠK Slovan Bratislava	Jozef Kožlej (1. FC Košice)	22
1997/1998	1. FC Košice	FC Spartak Trnava	Ľubomír Luhový (FC Spartak Trnava)	17
1998/1999	ŠK Slovan Bratislava	ŠK Slovan Bratislava	Martin Fabuš (TJ Ozeta Dukla Trenčín)	19
1999/2000	FK Inter Bratislava	FK Inter Bratislava	Szilárd Németh (FK Inter Bratislava)	16
2000/2001	FK Inter Bratislava	FK Inter Bratislava	Szilárd Németh (FK Inter Bratislava)	23
2001/2002	MŠK Žilina	FK VTJ Koba Senec	Marek Mintál (MŠK Žilina)	21
2002/2003	MŠK Žilina	FK Matador Púchov	Marek Mintál (MŠK Žilina) Martin Fabuš (Laugaricio Trenčín / MŠK Žilina)	20
2003/2004	MŠK Žilina	FC Artmedia Petržalka	Roland Števko (MFK Ružomberok)	17
2004/2005	Artmedia Bratislava	MFK Dukla Banská Bystrica	Filip Šebo (FC Artmedia Petržalka)	22
2005/2006	MFK Ružomberok	MFK Ružomberok	Róbert Rák (FC Nitra) Erik Jendrišek (MFK Ružomberok)	21
2006/2007	MŠK Žilina	FC ViOn Zlaté Moravce	Tomáš Oravec (FC Artmedia Petržalka)	16
2007/2008	FC Artmedia Petržalka	FC Artmedia Petržalka	Ján Novák (MFK Košice)	17
2008/2009	ŠK Slovan Bratislava	MFK Košice	Pavol Masaryk (ŠK Slovan Bratislava)	15
2009/2010	MŠK Žilina	ŠK Slovan Bratislava	Róbert Rák (FC Nitra)	18
2010/2011	ŠK Slovan Bratislava	ŠK Slovan Bratislava	Filip Šebo (ŠK Slovan Bratislava)	22
2011/2012	MŠK Žilina	MŠK Žilina	Pavol Masaryk (MFK Ružomberok)	18
2012/2013	ŠK Slovan Bratislava	ŠK Slovan Bratislava	David Depetris (AS Trenčín)	16
2013/2014	ŠK Slovan Bratislava	MFK Košice	Tomáš Malec (AS Trenčín)	14
2014/2015	AS Trenčín	AS Trenčín	Matej Jelić (CRO, MŠK Žilina) Jan Kalabiška (CZE, FK Senica)	19
2015/2016	AS Trenčín	AS Trenčín	Gino Ronald van Kessel (CUW, AS Trenčín)	17
2016/2017	MŠK Žilina	ŠK Slovan Bratislava	Filip Hlohovský (MŠK Žilina) Seydouba Soumah (GUI, ŠK Slovan Bratislava)	20
2017/2018	FC Spartak Trnava	ŠK Slovan Bratislava	Samuel Mráz (MŠK Žilina)	21
2018/2019	ŠK Slovan Bratislava	FC Spartak Trnava	Andraž Šporar (SVN, ŠK Slovan Bratislava)	29

NATIONAL CHAMPIONSHIP

Slovak Fortuna Liga 2018/2019

(21.07.2018 – 24.05.2019)

Regular Season - Results

Round 1 [21-22.07.2018]
FK Senica - Spartak Trnava 1-0(1-0)
MFK Ružomberok - ŠKF Sereď 0-0
FK Železiarne - Dunajská Streda 1-2(0-1)
Zlaté Moravce - Slovan Bratislava 1-4(1-1)
MFK Zemplín - MŠK Žilina 0-1(0-1) [21.08.]
FC Nitra - AS Trenčín 2-1(1-0) [25.09.2018]

Round 2 [28-29.07.2018]
MŠK Žilina - FC Nitra 2-1(1-1)
Spartak Trnava - Zlaté Moravce 1-0(0-0)
ŠKF Sereď - FK Senica 2-1(0-1)
Dunajská Streda - MFK Zemplín 4-1(3-0)
Slovan Bratislava - FK Železiarne 3-0(1-0)
AS Trenčín - MFK Ružomberok 1-4(1-1)

Round 3 [04-05.08.2018]
FK Železiarne - Spartak Trnava 1-0(0-0)
MFK Ružomberok - MŠK Žilina 3-1(1-1)
Zlaté Moravce - FK Senica 4-0(1-0)
MFK Zemplín - Slovan Bratislava 1-2(0-2)
FC Nitra - Dunajská Streda 2-3(1-0)
AS Trenčín - ŠKF Sereď 5-1(2-0)

Round 4 [11-12.08.2018]
Dunajská Streda - MFK Ružomberok 2-2(1-1)
FK Senica - FK Železiarne 1-1(0-0)
Spartak Trnava - MFK Zemplín 3-0(1-0)
ŠKF Sereď - Zlaté Moravce 2-0(1-0)
MŠK Žilina - AS Trenčín 2-3(1-1)
Slovan Bratislava - FC Nitra 1-1(0-1)

Round 5 [18-19.08.2018]
FC Nitra - Spartak Trnava 0-0
MFK Zemplín - FK Senica 1-1(1-1)
FK Železiarne - Zlaté Moravce 3-0(1-0)
MŠK Žilina - ŠKF Sereď 2-1(0-0)
Ružomberok - Slovan Bratislava 0-2(0-0)
AS Trenčín - Dunajská Streda 3-3(0-1)

Round 6 [25-26.08.2018]
Dunajská Streda - MŠK Žilina 0-0
FK Senica - FC Nitra 1-1(0-0)
Zlaté Moravce - MFK Zemplín 2-0(1-0)
ŠKF Sereď - FK Železiarne 1-2(1-0)
Slovan Bratislava - AS Trenčín 3-3(3-1)
Spartak Trnava - MFK Ružomberok 0-0

Round 7 [01-02.09.2018]
MŠK Žilina - Slovan Bratislava 0-1(0-0)
MFK Zemplín - FK Železiarne 2-0(1-0)
FC Nitra - Zlaté Moravce 4-1(1-1)
MFK Ružomberok - FK Senica 4-0(2-0)
Dunajská Streda - ŠKF Sereď 5-0(3-0)
AS Trenčín - Spartak Trnava 1-0(0-0)

Round 8 [15.09.2018]
Slovan Bratislava - Dunajská Streda 3-2(2-0)
Spartak Trnava - MŠK Žilina 1-2(0-0)
FK Železiarne - FC Nitra 3-2(2-1)
FK Senica - AS Trenčín 0-2(0-0)
Zlaté Moravce - MFK Ružomberok 1-1(0-0)
ŠKF Sereď - MFK Zemplín 2-1(0-1)

Round 9 [22-23.09.2018]
FC Nitra - MFK Zemplín 2-1(1-1)
MFK Ružomberok - FK Železiarne 3-0(2-0)
AS Trenčín - Zlaté Moravce 1-0(1-0)
MŠK Žilina - FK Senica 5-0(1-0)
Slovan Bratislava - ŠKF Sereď 2-1(2-1)
Dunajská Streda - Spartak Trnava 3-2(1-1)

Round 10 [29.09.2018]
ŠKF Sereď - FC Nitra 2-1(1-1)
Spartak Trnava - Slovan Bratislava 1-2(1-1)
MFK Zemplín - MFK Ružomberok 2-2(0-2)
FK Železiarne - AS Trenčín 2-0(2-0)
FK Senica - Dunajská Streda 1-2(0-0)
Zlaté Moravce - MŠK Žilina 1-2(1-2)

Round 11 [06-07.10.2018]
MFK Ružomberok - FC Nitra 3-1(2-1)
Slovan Bratislava - FK Senica 2-2(0-1)
AS Trenčín - MFK Zemplín 1-2(0-0)
MŠK Žilina - FK Železiarne 2-0(1-0)
Dunajská Streda - Zlaté Moravce 3-1(2-1)
Spartak Trnava - ŠKF Sereď 2-1(1-1)

Round 12 [20.10.2018]
Spartak Trnava - FK Senica 4-1(2-1)
Dunajská Streda - FK Železiarne 3-2(1-2)
Slovan Bratislava - Zlaté Moravce 3-1(2-1)
AS Trenčín - FC Nitra 0-1(0-1)
MŠK Žilina - MFK Zemplín 2-2(1-0)
ŠKF Sereď - MFK Ružomberok 3-1(0-1)

Round 13 [27-28.10.2018]
MFK Ružomberok - AS Trenčín 1-0(0-0)
FK Železiarne - Slovan Bratislava 0-2(0-1)
MFK Zemplín - Dunajská Streda 2-1(0-0)
FC Nitra - MŠK Žilina 0-2(0-2)
FK Senica - ŠKF Sereď 0-0
Zlaté Moravce - Spartak Trnava 1-1(0-0)

Round 14 [03.11.2018]
MŠK Žilina - MFK Ružomberok 3-0(1-0)
Dunajská Streda - FC Nitra 1-0(1-0)
FK Senica - Zlaté Moravce 3-0(0-0)
Slovan Bratislava - MFK Zemplín 6-0(3-0)
Spartak Trnava - FK Železiarne 2-0(1-0)
ŠKF Sereď - AS Trenčín 3-1(2-0)

Round 15 [10-11.11.2018]
AS Trenčín - MŠK Žilina 0-2(0-2)
MFK Ružomberok - Dunajská Streda 0-1(0-0)
FK Železiarne - FK Senica 2-4(1-3)
MFK Zemplín - Spartak Trnava 1-0(1-0)
FC Nitra - Slovan Bratislava 1-2(0-2)
Zlaté Moravce - ŠKF Sereď 0-1(0-0)

Round 16 [24.11.2018]
ŠKF Sereď - MŠK Žilina 1-1(0-1)
FK Senica - MFK Zemplín 2-4(2-2)
Slovan Bratislava - Ružomberok 1-1(0-1)
Spartak Trnava - FC Nitra 2-3(0-1)
Zlaté Moravce - FK Železiarne 1-0(1-0)
Dunajská Streda - AS Trenčín 0-0

Round 17 [01-02.12.2018]
AS Trenčín - Slovan Bratislava 0-3(0-2)
MFK Zemplín - Zlaté Moravce 3-0(1-0)
FC Nitra - FK Senica 1-0(1-0)
FK Železiarne - ŠKF Sereď 1-1(1-1)
MŠK Žilina - Dunajská Streda 2-2(1-1)
MFK Ružomberok - Spartak Trnava 3-1(1-0)

Round 18 [08.12.2018]
Slovan Bratislava - MŠK Žilina 5-2(4-0)
FK Železiarne - MFK Zemplín 0-1(0-0)
FK Senica - MFK Ružomberok 1-1(1-1)
Zlaté Moravce - FC Nitra 0-3(0-0)
ŠKF Sereď - Dunajská Streda 0-1(0-0)
Spartak Trnava - AS Trenčín 3-1(2-1)

Round 19 [16.02.2019]
FC Nitra - FK Železiarne 1-3(1-1)
MFK Ružomberok - Zlaté Moravce 4-0(2-0)
AS Trenčín - FK Senica 3-0(1-0)
MŠK Žilina - Spartak Trnava 1-1(0-0)
MFK Zemplín - ŠKF Sereď 1-0(1-0)
Dunajská Streda - Slovan Bratislava 0-1(0-0)

Round 20 [23.02.2019]
FK Železiarne - MFK Ružomberok 0-1(0-0)
FK Senica - MŠK Žilina 0-1(0-1)
Spartak Trnava - Dunajská Streda 3-1(1-1)
Zlaté Moravce - AS Trenčín 3-1(1-0)
ŠKF Sereď - Slovan Bratislava 0-1(0-1)
MFK Zemplín - FC Nitra 0-0

Round 21 [02-03.03.2019]
Dunajská Streda - FK Senica 1-0(0-0)
MFK Ružomberok - MFK Zemplín 0-0
AS Trenčín - FK Železiarne 1-1(1-0)
MŠK Žilina - Zlaté Moravce 2-1(1-1)
FC Nitra - ŠKF Sereď 0-2(0-2)
Slovan Bratislava - Spartak Trnava 2-0(0-0)

Round 22 [09.03.2019]
MFK Zemplín - AS Trenčín 4-2(3-1)
FC Nitra - MFK Ružomberok 0-0
FK Železiarne - MŠK Žilina 0-2(0-1)
FK Senica - Slovan Bratislava 1-2(1-1)
Zlaté Moravce - Dunajská Streda 1-2(1-0)
ŠKF Sereď - Spartak Trnava 3-1(0-0)

Final Standings

1.	ŠK Slovan Bratislava	22	18	4	0	53 - 18	58
2.	MŠK Žilina	22	13	5	4	39 - 23	44
3.	FK DAC Dunajská Streda	22	13	5	4	42 - 27	44
4.	MFK Ružomberok	22	9	9	4	34 - 20	36
5.	MFK Zemplín Michalovce	22	9	5	8	29 - 33	32
6.	ŠKF Sereď	22	9	4	9	27 - 29	31
7.	FC Nitra	22	7	5	10	27 - 30	26
8.	FC Spartak Trnava	22	7	4	11	28 - 28	25
9.	AS Trenčín	22	6	4	12	30 - 40	22
10.	FK Železiarne Podbrezová	22	6	3	13	22 - 35	21
11.	FK Senica	22	3	6	13	20 - 43	15
12.	FC ViOn Zlaté Moravce	22	4	2	16	19 - 44	14

Teams ranked 1-6 were qualified for the Championship Round, while teams ranked 7-12 were qualified for the Relegation Round.

Championship Round

Round 23 [16-17.03.2019]
ŠKF Sereď - Slovan Bratislava 1-4(0-2)
MŠK Žilina - MFK Zemplín 4-0(1-0)
Dunajská Streda - MFK Ružomberok 1-1(0-1)

Round 24 [30-31.03.2019]
MFK Ružomberok - MŠK Žilina 1-1(0-1)
MFK Zemplín - ŠKF Sereď 2-0(2-0)
Slovan Bratislava - Dunajská Streda 3-1(0-0)

Round 25 [06-07.04.2019]
Dunajská Streda - MŠK Žilina 1-0(1-0)
ŠKF Sereď - MFK Ružomberok 0-1(0-0)
Slovan Bratislava - MFK Zemplín 4-1(1-0)

Round 26 [13-14.04.2019]
ŠKF Sereď - Dunajská Streda 0-5(0-3)
MFK Ružomberok - MFK Zemplín 1-0(0-0)
MŠK Žilina - Slovan Bratislava 0-3(0-2)

Round 27 [20-21.04.2019]
MŠK Žilina - ŠKF Sereď 1-2(0-1)
MFK Zemplín - Dunajská Streda 0-2(0-0)
Slovan Bratislava - Ružomberok 3-2(1-0)

Round 28 [27-28.04.2019]
Dunajská Streda - Slovan Bratislava 1-0(0-0)
MFK Zemplín - MŠK Žilina 2-1(2-0)
MFK Ružomberok - ŠKF Sereď 1-0(1-0)

Round 29 [04-05.05.2019]
ŠKF Sereď - MFK Zemplín 2-2(1-1)
Ružomberok - Slovan Bratislava 3-2(2-1)
MŠK Žilina - Dunajská Streda 1-2(0-1)

Round 30 [11.05.2019]
Slovan Bratislava - MŠK Žilina 6-2(3-0)
MFK Zemplín - MFK Ružomberok 0-3(0-1)
Dunajská Streda - ŠKF Sereď 3-4(1-3)

Round 31 [18.05.2019]
MFK Zemplín - Slovan Bratislava 3-3(2-1)
ŠKF Sereď - MŠK Žilina 2-3(1-3)
MFK Ružomberok - Dunajská Streda 1-0(1-0)

Round 32 [24.05.2019]
MŠK Žilina - MFK Ružomberok 4-2(1-1)
Dunajská Streda - MFK Zemplín 5-0(3-0)
Slovan Bratislava - ŠKF Sereď 3-1(1-0)

Final Standings

1.	**ŠK Slovan Bratislava**	32	25	5	2	84 - 33	80
2.	FK DAC Dunajská Streda	32	19	6	7	63 - 37	63
3.	MFK Ružomberok	32	15	11	6	50 - 31	56
4.	MŠK Žilina	32	16	6	10	56 - 44	54
5.	MFK Zemplín Michalovce	32	11	7	14	39 - 58	40
6.	ŠKF Sereď	32	11	5	16	39 - 54	38

Top goalscorers:

29 Andraž Šporar (SVN) *ŠK Slovan Bratislava*

13 Róbert Boženík *MŠK Žilina*

12 Mohammed Rharsalla Khadfi (MAR) *ŠK Slovan Bratislava*

12 Hamza Čataković (BIH) *AS Trenčín*

Relegation Round

Round 23 [16.03.2019]
FK Železiarne - FC Nitra 1-1(1-0)
Zlaté Moravce - FK Senica 3-2(2-1)
AS Trenčín - Spartak Trnava 0-1(0-1)

Round 24 [30.03.2019]
FC Nitra - AS Trenčín 2-2(1-1)
FK Senica - FK Železiarne 0-0
Spartak Trnava - Zlaté Moravce 0-1(0-0)

Round 25 [06.04.2019]
AS Trenčín - FK Senica 2-3(0-2)
Spartak Trnava - FC Nitra 1-1(0-0)
Zlaté Moravce - FK Železiarne 2-1(0-0)

Round 26 [13.04.2019]
FK Železiarne - Spartak Trnava 0-0
AS Trenčín - Zlaté Moravce 1-0(0-0)
FK Senica - FC Nitra 4-1(2-0)

Round 27 [20.04.2019]
Spartak Trnava - FK Senica 0-1(0-0)
FK Železiarne - AS Trenčín 0-0
FC Nitra - Zlaté Moravce 2-2(1-2)

Round 28 [26-27.04.2019]
FC Nitra - FK Železiarne 2-2(2-2)
FK Senica - AS Trenčín 4-0(1-0)
Zlaté Moravce - Spartak Trnava 1-1(0-0)

Round 29 [04.05.2019]
FK Senica - Spartak Trnava 2-0(0-0)
AS Trenčín - FC Nitra 1-4(1-1)
FK Železiarne - Zlaté Moravce 0-1(0-0)

Round 30 [11.05.2019]
Spartak Trnava - FK Železiarne 3-1(1-1)
Zlaté Moravce - AS Trenčín 2-1(0-0)
FC Nitra - FK Senica 2-3(1-2)

Round 31 [18.05.2019]
FK Senica - Zlaté Moravce 3-1(2-0)
FC Nitra - Spartak Trnava 0-1(0-0)
AS Trenčín - FK Železiarne 4-0(2-0)

Round 32 [24.05.2019]
FK Železiarne - FK Senica 1-0(0-0)
Zlaté Moravce - FC Nitra 1-0(1-0)
Spartak Trnava - AS Trenčín 0-0

Final Standings

7.	FC Spartak Trnava	32	10	8	14	35 - 35	38
8.	FK Senica	32	10	7	15	42 - 53	37
9.	FC Nitra	32	8	10	14	42 - 48	34
10.	FC ViOn Zlaté Moravce	32	10	4	18	33 - 55	34
11.	AS Trenčín (*Relegation Play-offs*)	32	8	7	17	41 - 56	31
12.	FK Železiarne Podbrezová (*Relegated*)	32	7	8	17	28 - 48	29

Relegation Play-offs

FK Poprad - AS Trenčín	2-0(1-0)	1-4(1-2)

AS Trenčín remains at first level.

NATIONAL CUP

Slovenský Pohár 2018/2019

Fourth Round [29.08./04-05.09./12.09./18-19.09/26.09.2018]

FC Pata - FK Raven Povazská Bystrica	0-2
TJ Prameň Kováčová - Tatran Liptovský Mikuláš	2-5
Oravské Veselé - 1. FC Tatran Prešov	3-4 pen
ŠK Sačurov - NFL Partizán Bardejov	1-3
AFC Nové Mesto - OFK Malženice	2-4 pen
OFK Dunajská Lužná - FK Šamorín	0-2
TJ Štart Hrabušice - FK Košice	6-7 pen
FK 09 Bacúch - KFC Komárno	7-6 pen
FK Humenné - MFK Vranov nad Topľou	1-4
FC Slovan Galanta - ŠKF Sereď	0-2
FK Gerlachov - MFK Ružomberok	2-6
Kysucké Nové Mesto - FC ViOn Zlaté Moravce	0-3
FK Kechnec - FK Železiarne Podbrezová	0-2
FK Kolárovo - MFK Dubnica	0-4
TJ Sokol Medzibrod - FTC Fiľakovo	0-3
TJ Mladosť Kalša - FK Slavoj Trebišov	5-4 pen
MŠK Spišské Podhradie - FK Poprad	0-3
MŠK Námestovo - MFK Zemplín Michalovce	4-5 pen
OŠK Pavlovce nad Uhom - SK Odeva Lipany	4-5 pen
Slovan Šimonovany - FC Rohožník	2-0
ŠK Čierne - FC Lokomotíva Košice	0-1
ŠK FC Vydrany - KFC Kalná nad Hronom	4-0
Slovan Hlohovec - FK Senica	1-2
MFK Lokomotíva Zvolen - FK Inter Bratislava	7-6 pen
Družstevník Dvory nad Žitavou - FC Nitra	0-7
TJ Iskra Horné Orešany - MFK Vrbové	5-3
Liptovská Štiavnica - AS Trenčín	0-6
Tatran Krásno - MŠK Žilina	0-6
TJ Tatran Chlebnice - FK Pohronie	0-2
MFK Rusovce - MFK Skalica	1-2
TJ Kovo Beluša - FK DAC Dunajská Streda	1-4
Slovan Most - FC Spartak Trnava	1-3

Fifth Round [02.10./09-11.10./16.10./23.10.2018]

MFK Vranov nad Topľou - FK DAC Dunajská Streda	2-5
FK Košice - MFK Dubnica	1-0
FC Lokomotíva Košice - AS Trenčín	1-5
OFK Malženice - FK Železiarne Podbrezová	1-2
MFK Lokomotíva Zvolen - FC ViOn Zlaté Moravce	1-2
TJ Mladosť Kalša - FK Poprad	1-3
FTC Fiľakovo - Tatran Liptovský Mikuláš	2-4
FK 09 Bacúch - SK Odeva Lipany	1-3
FK Raven Povazská Bystrica - FK Šamorín	0-1
ŠK FC Vydrany - FC Nitra	0-3
TJ Iskra Horné Orešany - FK Senica	0-11
Slovan Šimonovany - MFK Zemplín Michalovce	0-4
MFK Skalica - MFK Ružomberok	4-1
NFL Partizán Bardejov - FC Spartak Trnava	0-5
FK Pohronie - ŠKF Sereď	2-3
1. FC Tatran Prešov - MŠK Žilina	1-2

1/8-Finals [23-24.10./06.11./16.11.2018]

FK Šamorín - FK Poprad	1-1 aet; 7-8 pen
FC Nitra - Tatran Liptovský Mikuláš	2-2 aet; 3-1 pen
MFK Zemplín Michalovce - SK Odeva Lipany	4-2
FK Senica - FK DAC Dunajská Streda	5-1
FK Košice - FC ViOn Zlaté Moravce	3-1
MFK Skalica - AS Trenčín	2-1
MŠK Žilina - ŠKF Sereď	3-1
FK Železiarne Podbrezová - FC Spartak Trnava	0-2

Quarter-Finals [12-13.03.2019]

MŠK Žilina - MFK Skalica	4-1
FK Senica - FC Nitra	5-1
FK Košice - FC Spartak Trnava	0-0 aet; 3-4 pen
MFK Zemplín Michalovce - FK Poprad	2-1

Semi-Finals [02-03.04./16-17.04.2019]

MŠK Žilina - MFK Zemplín Michalovce	1-1 / 2-0
FC Spartak Trnava - FK Senica	1-0 / 0-0

Final

01.05.2019; Štadión pod Zoborom, Nitra; Referee: Jozef Pavlik; Attendance: 6,053

FC Spartak Trnava - MŠK Žilina **3-3(2-0,3-3,3-3); 4-1 on penalties**

Spartak Trnava: Petr Bolek (119.Dobrivoj Rusov), Matúš Turňa, Myenty Abena, Tomáš Košút, Matúš Čonka, Lucas Lovat, Marek Janečka (106.David Alberto Depetris), Anton Sloboda (Cap), Fabian Miesenböck (72.Štefan Pekár), Kire Markoski (75.Macario Hing-Glover), Kubilay Yilmaz. Trainer: Michal Ščasný (Czech Republic).

MŠK Žilina: Miloš Volešák, Benson Anang (106.Jan Minarik), Martin Králik, Filip Kaša, Branislav Sluka, Miroslav Káčer, Michal Škvarka (Cap), Iván Santiago Díaz (46.Jakub Holúbek), Jaroslav Mihalík (99.Ján Bernát), Filip Balaj (116.Viktor Pečovský), Róbert Boženík. Trainer: Jaroslav Kentoš.

Goals: 1-0 Fabian Miesenböck (20), 2-0 Kire Markoski (45), 3-0 Kire Markoski (48), 3-1 Filip Balaj (50), 3-2 Róbert Boženík (68), 3-3 Filip Balaj (71).

Penalties: Tomáš Košút 1-0; Jakub Holúbek 1-1; David Alberto Depetris 2-1; Miroslav Káčer (missed); Lucas Lovat 3-1; Róbert Boženík (missed); Myenty Abena 4-1.

THE CLUBS 2018/2019

Please note: matches and goals includes statistics of both regular season and play-offs (Championship or Relegation Round).

Asociácia športov Trenčín

Founded: 1992 *(as TJ Ozeta Dukla Trenčín)*
Stadium: Štadión Myjava, Myjava (2,709)

Goalkeepers:	DOB	M	(s)	G
Denis Chudý	01.02.2000	9		
Libor Hrdlička	02.01.1986	8		
Igor Šemrinec	22.11.1987	15		
Defenders:	**DOB**	**M**	**(s)**	**G**
Keston Julien (TRI)	26.10.1998	4	(1)	
Peter Kleščík	18.09.1988	13	(2)	1
Adam Laczkó	02.04.1997	4		
Jamie Lawrence (WAL)	22.08.1992	3		
Erhan Mašović (SRB)	22.11.1998	14		
Marián Pišoja	16.06.2000	1	(1)	
Lukáš Skovajsa	27.03.1994	25	(1)	
Adrián Slávik	12.04.1999	9	(3)	
Martin Šulek	15.01.1998	22	(2)	
Reuben Yem (NGA)	29.10.1997	24		
Midfielders:	**DOB**	**M**	**(s)**	**G**
Hamza Čataković (BIH)	15.01.1997	21	(8)	12
Milan Corryn (BEL)	04.04.1999	14	(8)	1
Aschraf el Mahdioui (NED)	24.05.1996	16		1
Jakub Kadák	14.12.2000		(4)	
Mohammed Lamine (GHA)	02.02.2002	10	(1)	1
Jakub Paur	04.07.1992	16	(5)	2
Ante Roguljić (CRO)	11.03.1996	7	(6)	1
Desley Ubbink (NED)	15.06.1993	15	(6)	2
Philippe van Arnhem (NED)	24.08.1996	15	(4)	
Abdul Zubairu (NGA)	03.10.1998	18	(6)	
Forwards:	**DOB**	**M**	**(s)**	**G**
Philip Azongo (NGA)	21.05.1997	4		
Osman Bukari (GHA)	13.12.1998	19	(3)	1
Milan Kvocera	01.01.1998	4	(8)	
Antonio Mance (CRO)	07.08.1995	12	(6)	7
Richard Kule Mbombo (COD)	10.05.1996		(1)	
Joey Sleegers (NED)	20.07.1994	22	(6)	8
Chukwuemeka Chukwugozie Umeh (NGA)	23.10.1999	8	(6)	2
Trainer:	**DOB**	**M**		
Ricardo Moniz (NED)	17.06.1964	13		
Vladimir Cifranič [29.10.2018]	01.10.1975	10		
Matthias Kohler (GER) [20.03.2019]	09.06.1991	5		
Vladimir Cifranič [03.05.2019]	01.10.1975	1		
Ivan Galad [07.05.2019]	10.04.1963	3		

Futbalový klub DAC 1904 Dunajská Streda

Founded: 1904 *(as Dunaszerdahelyi Atlétikai Club)*
Stadium: MOL Aréna, Dunajská Streda (9,901)

Goalkeepers:	DOB	M	(s)	G
Martin Jedlička (CZE)	24.01.1998	29		
Tomasz Kucz (POL)	06.07.1999	1		
Patrik Macej (CZE)	11.06.1994	2		
Defenders:	**DOB**	**M**	**(s)**	**G**
Éric Javier Davis Grajales (PAN)	31.03.1991	26		6
Tomáš Huk	22.12.1994	30		1
Souleymane Koné (CIV)	01.05.1996	18	(6)	2
Kristián Koštrna	15.12.1993	23	(2)	1
Marin Ljubičić (CRO)	15.06.1988	1	(1)	
Ľubomír Šatka	02.12.1995	25	(4)	2
Milan Šimčák	23.08.1995	4	(6)	
Dominik Špiriak	22.03.1999	1	(1)	
Timotej Zahumenský	17.07.1995	3	(5)	
Midfielders:	**DOB**	**M**	**(s)**	**G**
Denis Baumgartner	02.02.1998		(1)	
Martin Bednár	22.04.1999	4	(11)	
César Rodolfo Blackman Camarena (PAN)	02.04.1998	3	(3)	
Christián Herc	30.09.1998	25	(4)	3
Zsolt Kalmár (HUN)	09.06.1995	28	(1)	8
Ladislav Nagy	24.01.2001		(1)	
Connor Ronan (IRL)	06.03.1998	11	(3)	1
Maksym Tretyakov (UKR)	06.03.1996	9	(8)	1
Kristopher Vida (HUN)	23.06.1995	29		11
Máté Vida (HUN)	08.03.1996	25	(3)	
Forwards:	**DOB**	**M**	**(s)**	**G**
Ladislav Almási	06.03.1999		(1)	
Karsten Ayong (CZE)	20.01.1998		(1)	
Vakoun Bayo (CIV)	10.01.1997	16		11
Stanislav Bilenkyi (UKR)	22.08.1998		(8)	1
Lukáš Čmelík	13.04.1996	8	(5)	1
Marko Divković (CRO)	11.06.1999	20	(5)	5
Erik Pačinda	09.05.1989	7	(3)	4
Abdulrahman Taiwo (NGA)	05.08.1998	4	(5)	4
Trainer:	**DOB**	**M**		
Peter Hyballa (GER)	05.12.1975	32		

Football Club Nitra

Founded: 1909 *(as as Nyitrai ÖTTSO)*
Stadium: Štadión pod Zoborom, Nitra (5,500)

Goalkeepers:	DOB	M	(s)	G
Lukáš Hroššo	19.04.1987	18		
Branislav Pindroch	30.10.1991	10		
Dávid Šipoš	14.08.1998	4	(1)	
Defenders:	**DOB**	**M**	**(s)**	**G**
Marek Dubeň	11.07.1994	3		
Lukáš Fabiš	05.05.1998	3	(1)	1
Pavol Farkaš	27.03.1985	27	(1)	1
René Kotrík	14.03.1996	3	(4)	
Richard Križan	23.09.1997	16		1
MacDonald Ngwa Niba (CMR)	08.08.1994	16	(2)	
Ivan Zgrablić (CRO)	15.03.1991	4	(1)	
Midfielders:	**DOB**	**M**	**(s)**	**G**
Frederik Bilovský	03.03.1992	14		3
Márius Charizopulos	09.11.1990	24	(3)	1
Ilya Cherednychenko (UKR)	12.06.1995	3	(7)	
Ján Chovanec	22.03.1984	28	(1)	1
Andrej Fábry	01.03.1997	15	(1)	7
Tomáš Kóňa	01.03.1984	25	(2)	3
Martin Macho	23.01.1998		(5)	
Miloš Šimončič	27.05.1987	24	(2)	3
Šimon Štefanec	05.09.1998	2	(3)	
Christián Steinhübel	02.10.1994		(6)	
Patrik Šurnovský	13.11.1997	6	(4)	
Róbert Valenta	10.11.1990		(1)	
Ondrej Vrábel	23.04.1999		(4)	
Forwards:	**DOB**	**M**	**(s)**	**G**
Marián Chobot	31.08.1999	20	(2)	2
Marek Fábry	07.08.1998	5	(9)	1
Nikola Gatarić (CRO)	09.03.1992	9	(1)	1
Dominik Guláš	28.06.1999	1	(6)	
Matúš Kuník	14.05.1997	16	(2)	1
Jaroslav Machovec	05.09.1986	7	(11)	1
Nemanja Soković (SRB)	08.05.1996	7	(5)	1
Abdulrahman Taiwo (NGA)	05.08.1998	17	(1)	2
Tomáš Vestenický	06.04.1996	25	(5)	10
Trainer:	**DOB**	**M**		
Ivan Galád	10.04.1963	22		
Michal Kuruc [13.03.2019]	29.09.1981	10		

Mestský futbalový klub Ružomberok

Founded: 1906 (*as Rózsahegyi Sport Club*)
Stadium: Štadión pod Čebraťom, Ružomberok (4,817)

Goalkeepers:	DOB	M	(s)	G
Jan Čtvrtečka (CZE)	14.08.1998	2		
Matúš Macík	19.05.1993	30		
Defenders:	**DOB**	**M**	**(s)**	**G**
Matej Čurma	27.03.1996	19	(1)	
Michal Jonec	30.07.1996	18	(4)	
Dominik Kružliak	10.07.1996	21	(1)	1
Ján Maslo	05.02.1986	28		
Yani Urdinov (MKD)	28.03.1991	17	(1)	
Midfielders:	**DOB**	**M**	**(s)**	**G**
Adam Brenkus	08.01.1999	1	(3)	
Erik Daniel (CZE)	04.02.1992	16		1
Peter Gál-Andrezly	03.05.1990	30	(1)	6
Viktor Jedinák	08.02.1998		(10)	1
Matúš Kmeť	27.06.2000	7	(8)	
Matej Kochan	21.11.1992	12	(5)	1
Tihomir Kostadinov (MKD)	04.03.1996	22	(7)	6
Zinedin Mustedanagić (BIH)	01.08.1998	17	(8)	6
Kristi Qose (ALB)	10.06.1995	28	(1)	9
Dalibor Takáč	11.10.1997	25	(6)	2
Filip Twardzik (CZE)	10.02.1993	19		1
Marek Zsigmund	20.04.1997		(1)	
Forwards:	**DOB**	**M**	**(s)**	**G**
Tomáš Bobček	08.09.2001		(4)	
Štefan Gerec	10.11.1992	16	(9)	5
Rastislav Kružliak	11.07.1999		(8)	
Dominik Kunca	04.03.1992	1	(6)	
Matej Madlenak	07.02.1999	6	(2)	
Ismar Tandir (BIH)	19.08.1995	17	(2)	9
Trainer:	**DOB**	**M**		
David Holoubek	08.06.1980	32		

Futbalový klub Senica

Founded: 1921
Stadium: OMS Arena, Senica (5,070)

Goalkeepers:	DOB	M	(s)	G
Federico Taborda (ARG)	01.11.1988	30		
Vojtěch Vorel (CZE)	18.06.1996	2		
Defenders:	**DOB**	**M**	**(s)**	**G**
Patrick Asmah (GHA)	25.01.1996	18	(1)	2
Gabriel Dubois (FRA)	04.03.1996	3	(2)	
Carlos Daniel Silveira da Graça „Kay“ (CPV)	05.01.1988	20		4
Mihovil Klapan (CRO)	27.03.1995	12	(7)	
Juraj Kotula	30.09.1995	17		
Lukáš Kučera	18.04.2000	3	(1)	
Victor Nirennold (FRA)	05.04.1991	6	(3)	
Erik Otrísal	28.06.1996	17	(6)	
Roberto Dias Correia Filho (BRA)	08.08.1988	30		5
Stjepan Vuković (CRO)	20.01.1997	1		
Midfielders:	**DOB**	**M**	**(s)**	**G**
Frank Andersson Castañeda Vélez (COL)	17.07.1994	27	(3)	5
Diego Alejandro Cuadros Velázquez (COL)	28.05.1996	2	(3)	
Sofian El Moudane (FRA)	16.03.1994	12		1
Joan Sebastián Jaramillo Herrera (COL)	14.04.1994	9		
Jean Alexandre Deretti (BRA)	01.05.1993	19	(5)	5
Alan Kováč	22.05.1993		(6)	
Jakub Krč	02.09.1997	18	(8)	
Sacha Petshi (FRA)	21.06.1992	19	(3)	2
Julián Caro Sepulveda	07.02.2000	1	(1)	
Naren Stiven Solano Pereira (COL)	15.01.1996	3	(9)	1
Marko Tešija (CRO)	14.01.1992	26	(2)	3
Marko Totka	12.09.2000	1	(1)	
José Luís Mendes Lopes „Zézinho“ (GNB)	23.09.1992	19	(9)	
Forwards:	**DOB**	**M**	**(s)**	**G**
Edmund Addo (GHA)	17.05.2000		(2)	
Kevaughn Atkinson (JAM)	11.11.1995		(2)	
Désiré Azankpo (BEN)	06.05.1993	17	(8)	4
Richard Enríque Celis Sánchez (VEN)	23.04.1996	2	(6)	
Filip Dangubić (CRO)	05.05.1995	6	(3)	2
Dominik Martišiak	09.07.2000		(2)	
David Melis	18.09.2001		(1)	
Eric Kleybel Ramírez Matheus (VEN)	20.11.1998	12		5
Trainer:	**DOB**	**M**		
Ton Caanen (NED)	18.03.1966	2		
Frederico Ricardo Cordeiro Rodrigues (POR [03.08.2018]	18.02.1979	16		
Ricardo José Moutinho Chéu (POR) [09.01.2019]	14.05.1981	14		

Športový Klub Futbalu Sereď

Founded: 28.06.1914 (*as Sereďský športový klub*)
Stadium: Štadión pod Zoborom, Nitra (5,500)

Goalkeepers:	DOB	M	(s)	G
David Samuel Nwolokor (NGA)	10.01.1996	12		
Pavol Penksa	07.11.1985	20		
Defenders:	**DOB**	**M**	**(s)**	**G**
Djiby Ba (SEN)	21.03.1993	22		2
Matej Dybala	16.07.1999	1		
Tomáš Hučko	03.10.1985	23	(3)	1
Martin Mečiar	23.07.1993	6	(10)	
Jozef Menich	15.09.1994	24	(1)	1
Ľubomir Michalík	13.08.1983	28		
Martin Sus (CZE)	15.03.1990	23	(3)	1
Midfielders:	**DOB**	**M**	**(s)**	**G**
Banjole Olawale Adekuoroye(NGA)	16.02.1996	20	(2)	3
Aldo Omar Baéz (ARG)	05.09.1988	16	(6)	2
Rudolf Bilas	10.11.1992	6	(6)	
Alex Iván	11.10.1997	11	(2)	1
Marek Kuzma	22.06.1988	8	(4)	
Matej Loduha	28.05.1993	4	(5)	
Kristián Lukáčik	29.03.1998	1	(3)	
Adam Morong	16.06.1993	30		4
Filip Pankarićan (SRB)	28.03.1993	19	(8)	1
Róbert Richnák	03.05.1992	5	(8)	
Nemanja Subotić (SRB)	23.01.1992		(6)	
Denis Ventúra	01.08.1995	20		2
Forwards:	**DOB**	**M**	**(s)**	**G**
Nikola Gatarić (CRO)	09.03.1992	16	(1)	6
Miloš Lačný	08.03.1988	10	(2)	4
Vahagn Militosyan (ARM)	10.06.1993	2	(2)	
Chris Ondong Mba (FRA)	07.08.1993		(5)	1
Dino Špehar (CRO)	08.02.1994	6	(8)	4
Kathon St. Hillaire (TRI)	05.11.1997		(3)	
Ľubomír Ulrich	01.02.1989	19	(7)	2
Trainer:	**DOB**	**M**		
Marian Sarmir		7		
Karel Stromšík (CZE) [03.09.2018]	12.04.1958	25		

Športový klub Slovan Bratislava

Founded: 03.05.1919 *(as 1. ČsŠK Bratislava)*
Stadium: Štadión Tehelné pole, Bratislava (22,500)

Goalkeepers:	DOB	M	(s)	G
Dominik Greif	06.04.1997	28		
Michal Šulla	15.07.1991	4		
Defenders:	**DOB**	**M**	**(s)**	**G**
Mitch Apau (NED)	27.04.1990	24	(1)	3
Kenan Bajrič (SVN)	20.12.1994	31		1
Vasil Bozhikov (BUL)	02.06.1988	23	(1)	1
Richárd Guzmics (HUN)	16.04.1987	4	(6)	
Adam Laczkó	02.04.1997	1	(4)	
Marin Ljubičić (CRO)	15.06.1988	20	(1)	8
Jurij Medveděv (CZE)	18.06.1996	8	(2)	
Stefan Stangl (AUT)	20.10.1991	1		
Artem Sukhotsky (UKR)	06.12.1992	26		1
Kornél Šaláta	24.01.1985	10	(2)	2
Midfielders:	**DOB**	**M**	**(s)**	**G**
Joeri de Kamps (NED)	10.02.1992	22	(1)	
Dávid Holman (HUN)	17.03.1993	20	(4)	6
José Antonio Delgado Villar „Nono“ (ESP)	30.03.1993	8	(6)	
Denis Potoma	15.02.2000		(1)	
Ibrahim Rabiu (NGA)	15.03.1991	5	(3)	
Milan Rundić (SRB)	29.03.1992	1		
Vukan Savičevič (MNE)	29.01.1994	5	(11)	1
Ricky van Haaren (NED)	21.06.1991	1		1
Forwards:	**DOB**	**M**	**(s)**	**G**
Aleksandar Čavrić (SRB)	18.05.1994	24	(3)	4
Boris Cmiljanić (MNE)	17.03.1996	3	(9)	1
Dejan Drazič (SRB)	26.09.1995	21	(10)	7
Filip Hološko	17.01.1984	2	(7)	1
Dávid Hrnčár	10.12.1997		(1)	
Mohammed Rharsalla Khadfi(MAR)	15.09.1993	27	(2)	12
Rafael Rogério da Silva „Rafael Ratão“ (BRA)	30.11.1995	1	(4)	1
Andraž Šporar (SVN)	27.02.1994	30		29
Dávid Strelec	04.04.2001	2	(11)	2
Róbert Vittek	01.04.1982		(1)	
Trainer:	**DOB**	**M**		
Martin Ševela	20.11.1975	32		

Football Club Spartak Trnava

Founded: 30.05.1923 *(as TŠS Trnava)*
Stadium: Štadión "Antona Malatinského", Trnava (19,200)

Goalkeepers:	DOB	M	(s)	G
Petr Bolek (CZE)	13.06.1984	8		
Martin Chudý	23.04.1989	11		
Dobrivoj Rusov	13.01.1993	12		
Dominik Takáč	12.01.1999	1		
Defenders:	**DOB**	**M**	**(s)**	**G**
Myenty Abena (NED)	12.12.1994	14		
Matúš Čonka	15.10.1990	17	(3)	
Václav Dudl (CZE)	22.09.1999	3	(1)	
Boris Godál	27.05.1987	9	(1)	1
Lukáš Greššák	23.01.1989	11	(1)	
Ivan Hladík	30.01.1993	7	(2)	1
Denis Horník	13.07.1997		(1)	
Marek Janečka	09.06.1983	14		
Oliver Janso	08.10.1993	9	(1)	
Andrej Kadlec	02.02.1996	10		
Tomáš Košút	13.01.1990	8		
Lucas Lovat (BRA)	15.01.1997	8	(2)	
Lukáš Lupták	28.07.1990	7	(1)	
Matej Oravec	30.03.1998	12	(1)	
Martin Tóth	13.10.1986	16		
Matúš Turňa	11.05.1986	12	(1)	
Midfielders:	**DOB**	**M**	**(s)**	**G**
Musefiu Ashiru (NGA)	26.06.1994	2	(3)	
Tomáš Brigant	11.10.1994	1	(1)	
Vakhtang Chanturishvili (GEO)	05.08.1993	8	(2)	3
Erik Grendel	13.10.1988	19	(3)	4
Macario Hing-Glover (USA)	04.04.1995	4	(1)	
Alexander Horvat	25.09.2000		(2)	
Erik Jirka	19.09.1997	11	(4)	
Jiří Kulhánek (CZE)	08.03.1996	8	(2)	
Ivan Mesík	01.06.2001	1		
Fabian Miesenböck (AUT)	07.07.1993	12	(9)	4
Kristián Mihálek	10.03.2000	2		
Jakub Rada (CZE)	05.05.1987	8	(3)	1
Anton Sloboda	10.07.1987	10	(4)	2
Ján Vlasko	11.01.1990	2		1
Forwards:	**DOB**	**M**	**(s)**	**G**
Marek Bakoš	15.04.1983	6	(3)	2
Filip Dangubić (CRO)	05.05.1995	7	(3)	
David Alberto Depetris (ARG)	11.11.1988	9		2
Ali Ghorbani (IRN)	18.09.1990	6	(3)	2
Senad Jarović (BIH)	20.01.1998		(2)	
Andrej Lovás	28.05.1991		(4)	
Patryk Małecki (POL)	01.08.1988	5	(2)	1
Kire Markoski (MKD)	20.02.1995	9	(3)	1
Štefan Pekár	03.12.1988	7	(8)	
Davit Skhirtladze (GEO)	16.03.1993	5	(3)	
Rafael Tavares (BRA)	26.06.2000	5	(4)	
Tom Vantruba	07.02.1998	1	(1)	
Kubilay Yilmaz (AUT)	09.07.1996	15	(4)	9
Trainer:	**DOB**	**M**		
Radoslav Látal (CZE)	06.01.1970	18		
Michal Ščasný (CZE) [01.01.2019]	19.08.1978	14		

Mestský Futbalový klub Zemplín Michalovce

Founded: 1912 (*as NAC Michalovce*)
Stadium: Mestský futbalový štadión, Michalovce (4,440)

Goalkeepers:	DOB	M	(s)	G
Gerard Bieszczad (POL)	05.02.1993	2		
Matús Kira	10.10.1994	30		
Defenders:	**DOB**	**M**	**(s)**	**G**
Danilo Beskorovayniy (UKR)	07.02.1999	20	(2)	1
José Carrillo Mancilla (ESP)	04.05.1995	26		2
Peter Kavka	20.11.1990	9		
Martin Kolesár	10.12.1997	5	(4)	
Alejandro Mitrano (VEN)	04.04.1998	1	(1)	
Tomasz Nawotka (POL)	14.02.1997	6	(1)	1
Denis Petro	18.06.1999	4		
Dominik Špiriak	22.03.1999	7	(3)	
Matúš Vojtko	05.10.2000	21		1
Midfielders:	**DOB**	**M**	**(s)**	**G**
Martin Bednár	22.04.1999	3		1
Matúš Begala	07.04.2001		(1)	
Stanislav Danko	17.03.1994	11	(3)	
Jakub Grič	05.07.1996	18	(4)	
Hovhannes Harutyunyan (ARM)	25.05.1999	2	(3)	
Brian Iloski (USA)	04.09.1995	3	(3)	
Peter Kolesár	09.07.1998	25	(3)	5
Til Mavretic (SVN)	19.11.1997	2	(2)	
Lazaros Rota (ALB)	23.08.1997	25	(1)	1
Matej Trusa	29.11.2000	2	(6)	
Jozef-Šimon Turík	19.07.1995	21	(3)	4
Blažej Vaščák	23.11.1983	18		2
Igor Žofčák	10.04.1983	22		5
Forwards:	**DOB**	**M**	**(s)**	**G**
Cheick Alan Diarra (FRA)	23.06.1993	19	(5)	4
Armen Hovhannisyan (ARM)	07.03.2000		(1)	
José David Casado García (ESP)	14.01.1988	11		1
Christos Kountouriotis (GRE)	02.01.1998	8	(6)	
Dawid Kurminowski (POL)	24.02.1999	3	(13)	1
Martin Regáli	12.10.1993	4	(8)	2
Sadam Sulley (GHA)	16.10.1996	14	(13)	4
Mamadou Tounkara (SEN)	19.01.1996	6	(3)	2
Yuriy Zakharkiv (UKR)	21.03.1996	4	(2)	2
Trainer:	**DOB**	**M**		
Anton Šoltís	05.02.1976	32		

Football Club Viliam Ondrejka Zlaté Moravce

Founded: 1995
Stadium: Štadión FC ViOn, Zlaté Moravce (4,000)

Goalkeepers:	DOB	M	(s)	G
Adrián Chovan	08.10.1995	18		
Martin Krnáč	30.01.1985	14		
Defenders:	**DOB**	**M**	**(s)**	**G**
Antonio Asanović (CRO)	30.11.1991	14		1
Patrik Banovič	13.11.1991	17		
Martin Chren	02.01.1984	23	(2)	1
Peter Čögley	11.08.1988	27		1
Nikola Dimitrijević (SRB)	10.05.1991	10	(4)	1
Adam Jamrich	07.07.1998	1		
Krešimir Kelez (CRO)	14.03.1995	3	(4)	
Noé Achille Kwin Ambam (CMR)	14.01.1990	12		1
Oliver Práznovský	15.02.1991	10	(6)	1
Maduka Christopher Udeh (NGA)	03.09.1997	4	(3)	1
Midfielders:	**DOB**	**M**	**(s)**	**G**
Jakub Brašeň	02.05.1989	30		1
José David Casado García (ESP)	14.01.1988	7	(7)	1
Tomáš Ďubek	22.01.1987	23	(3)	9
Denis Duga	05.09.1994	10	(12)	
Tomce Grozdanovski (MKD)	14.03.2000	8	(1)	
Karol Karlik	29.06.1986	10	(10)	
Vladyslav Khomutov (UKR)	04.06.1998	2	(1)	
Branislav Ľupták	05.06.1991	22		1
Peter Orávik	18.12.1988	11	(6)	1
Dávid Richtárech	22.04.1996	13	(5)	2
Forwards:	**DOB**	**M**	**(s)**	**G**
Tomáš Dočekal (CZE)	24.05.1989	11	(1)	
Ewerton Paixao da Silva (BRA)	28.12.1996	16	(1)	2
Jakub Švec	03.12.2000	15	(11)	5
Vladimír Tkáč	09.01.1998	1	(5)	1
Ľubomír Urgela	29.01.1990	7	(10)	1
Martin Válovčan	14.05.1993	13		2
Trainer:	**DOB**	**M**		
Juraj Jarábek	03.10.1962	14		
Branislav Mráz [06.11.2018]	13.07.1973	4		
Karol Praženica [13.12.2018]	15.11.1970	14		

Futbalový klub Železiarne Podbrezová

Founded: 1920 (*as RTJ Podbrezová*)
Stadium: ZELPO Aréna, Podbrezová (4,061)

Goalkeepers:	DOB	M	(s)	G
Martin Kuciak	15.03.1982	18		
Richard Ludha	08.11.2000	1		
Martin Vantruba	07.02.1998	13		
Defenders:	**DOB**	**M**	**(s)**	**G**
Martin Baran	03.01.1988	14		
Marek Bartoš	13.10.1996	23	(2)	
Jakub Kiwior (POL)	15.02.2000	14		1
Jan Krivak	10.11.1993	3	(2)	
Daniel Magda	25.11.1997	9	(4)	
Alexander Mojžiš	02.01.1999	17		1
Matej Oravec	30.03.1998	14		1
Matej Podstavek	21.02.1991	8	(1)	
Matúš Turňa	11.05.1986	16		
Midfielders:	**DOB**	**M**	**(s)**	**G**
Michal Breznaník	16.12.1985	16	(3)	5
Samuel Datko	24.06.2001	4		1
David Adeniyi Fadairo	07.11.2000	1	(1)	
Roland Galčík	30.07.2001	1	(4)	
Filip Halgoš	09.03.1998	1	(5)	
Filip Hlohovský	16.06.1988	9		1
Adrián Kopičár	13.01.1997	1	(1)	
Filip Lepies	22.12.1999	1	(3)	
Dávid Leško	04.06.1988	26	(1)	8
Nicolas Mejri	27.05.2000	1	(3)	
Viktor Mojžiš	02.01.1999		(1)	
Stijepo Njire	14.03.1991	1	(3)	
Michal Obročník	04.06.1991	28		3
René Paraj	04.08.1992	11	(2)	
Jozef Pastorek	26.09.1998	1	(1)	
Jozef Špyrka	30.05.1999	13	(1)	1
Samuel Štefánik	16.11.1991	2	(1)	
Jesse Marshall Thompson Edge(NZL)	26.02.1995	6		
Lukaš Urbanič	15.12.1998	3		1
Miroslav Viazanko	27.10.1981	23	(3)	2
Forwards:	**DOB**	**M**	**(s)**	**G**
Matúš Mikuš	08.07.1991	15	(3)	1
Victor Olatunji (NGA)	05.09.1999	4	(5)	
Endy Opoku Bernadina (NED)	03.05.1995	11	(5)	
Daniel Pavúk	03.02.1998	4	(6)	1
Jakub Sedláček	09.03.1998	11	(1)	
Daniel Skiba (POL)	05.12.2000		(1)	
Iliya Tereshchenko (UKR)	27.05.1998		(2)	
Peter Voško	17.08.2000	1	(5)	
Jakub Więzik (POL)	15.07.1991	7	(11)	1
Trainer:	**DOB**	**M**		
Marek Fabula	05.08.1975	16		
Gergely Geri [28.11.2018]	19.01.1977	2		
Vladimír Veselý [07.01.2019]	08.07.1976	14		

Mestský Športový klub Žilina

Founded: 20.06.1908 (*as Zsolnai Testgyakorlók Köre*)
Stadium: Štadión pod Dubňom, Žilina (11,258)

Goalkeepers:	DOB	M	(s)	G
Dominik Holec	28.07.1994	30		
Miloš Volešák	20.04.1984	2		
Defenders:	**DOB**	**M**	**(s)**	**G**
Benson Anang (GHA)	01.05.2000	21	(1)	1
Jakub Holúbek	12.01.1991	12	(8)	4
Filip Kaša (CZE)	01.01.1994	29		3
Adam Kopas	16.08.1999	1	(1)	
Martin Králik	03.04.1995	19	(5)	1
Luka Lochoshvili (GEO)	29.05.1998	3		
Vladimír Majdan	07.04.1999	6		
Jan Minarik	25.07.1997	7		
Branislav Sluka	23.01.1999	27	(2)	3
Samuel Šuľa	12.04.2000		(1)	
Aleksandar Šušnjar (AUS)	19.08.1995	11	(1)	
Midfielders:	**DOB**	**M**	**(s)**	**G**
Ján Bernát	10.01.2001	4	(3)	
Eugeniu Cociuc (MDA)	11.05.1993	2		1
Iván Santiago Díaz (ARG)	23.01.1993	25	(1)	2
Enis Fazlagić (MKD)	27.03.2000	15		
Martin Gamboš	23.01.1998	3	(4)	1
Miroslav Káčer	02.02.1996	24	(1)	5
Jaroslav Mihalík	27.07.1994	23	(2)	5
Patrik Myslovič	28.05.2001	6		
Viktor Pečovský	24.05.1983	5	(9)	
Michal Škvarka	19.08.1992	23	(3)	9
Michal Tomič	30.03.1999	11	(11)	1
Kristián Vallo	02.06.1998	4	(8)	1
Forwards:	**DOB**	**M**	**(s)**	**G**
Filip Balaj	02.08.1997	7	(19)	4
Vahan Bichakhchyan (ARM)	09.07.1999		(1)	
Róbert Boženík	18.11.1999	26	(6)	13
Roland Gerebenits	07.05.2000		(6)	
Lukáš Jánošík	05.03.1994	6	(3)	1
Trainer:	**DOB**	**M**		
Jaroslav Kentoš	14.05.1974	32		

SECOND LEVEL

2. Liga 2018/2019

1.	FK Pohronie Žiar nad Hronom (*Promoted*)	30	18	7	5	48	- 25	61
2.	FK Poprad (*Promotion Play-offs*)	30	18	4	8	52	- 36	58
3.	MFK Skalica	30	16	5	9	47	- 32	53
4.	MFK Tatran Liptovský Mikuláš	30	15	5	10	56	- 41	50
5.	KFC Komárno	30	13	7	10	48	- 38	46
6.	MFK Dukla Banská Bystrica	30	12	10	8	49	- 35	46
7.	FK Dubnica nad Váhom	30	13	6	11	55	- 42	45
8.	FC Petržalka Bratislava	30	12	9	9	41	- 38	45
9.	MŠK Žilina „B“	30	12	5	13	54	- 59	41
10.	NFL Partizán Bardejov	30	10	9	11	41	- 46	39
11.	FC Lokomotíva Košice	30	10	8	12	38	- 44	38
12.	FC ŠTK Fluminense Šamorín 1914	30	10	7	13	46	- 48	37
13.	FK Slavoj Trebišov	30	8	6	16	24	- 44	30
14.	FK Inter Bratislava (*Relegated*)	30	8	5	17	37	- 56	29
15.	1. FC Tatran Prešov (*Relegated*)	30	7	6	17	30	- 41	27
16.	ŠK Odeva Lipany (*Relegated*)	30	7	3	20	23	- 64	24

NATIONAL TEAM

INTERNATIONAL MATCHES
(16.07.2018 – 15.07.2019)

05.09.2018	Trnava	Slovakia - Denmark	3-0(2-0)	(F)
09.09.2018	Lviv	Ukraine - Slovakia	1-0(0-0)	(UNL)
13.10.2018	Trnava	Slovakia - Czech Republic	1-2(0-0)	(UNL)
16.10.2018	Stockholm	Sweden - Slovakia	1-1(0-0)	(F)
16.11.2018	Trnava	Slovakia - Ukraine	4-1(2-0)	(UNL)
19.11.2018	Praha	Czech Republic - Slovakia	1-0(1-0)	(UNL)
21.03.2019	Trnava	Slovakia - Hungary	2-0(1-0)	(ECQ)
24.03.2019	Cardiff	Wales - Slovakia	1-0(1-0)	(ECQ)
07.06.2019	Trnava	Slovakia - Jordan	5-1(0-1)	(F)
11.06.2019	Bakı	Azerbaijan - Slovakia	1-5(1-3)	(ECQ)

05.09.2018 SLOVAKIA - DENMARK 3-0(2-0) Friendly International
Štadión "Antona Malatinského", Trnava; Referee: Julian Weinberger (Austria); Attendance: 6,432
SVK: Matúš Kozáčik, Martin Škrtel (Cap) (83.Norbert Gyömbér), Tomáš Hubočan, Róbert Mazáň, Ľubomír Šatka, Marek Hamšík (61.Ondrej Duda), Juraj Kucka (61.Ján Greguš), Albert Rusnák (46.Róbert Mak), Patrik Hrošovský, Adam Nemec (46.Michal Ďuriš), Vladimír Weiss (67.Erik Pačinda). Trainer: Ján Kozák.
Goals: Adam Nemec (11), Albert Rusnák (37), Adam Fogt (79 own goal).

09.09.2018 UKRAINE - SLOVAKIA 1-0(0-0) UEFA Nations League B, Group 1
Arena Lviv, Lviv; Referee: Anastasios Sidiropoulos (Greece); Attendance: *played behind closed doors*
SVK: Martin Dúbravka, Martin Škrtel (Cap), Tomáš Hubočan, Ľubomír Šatka, Milan Škriniar, Juraj Kucka (78.Ján Greguš), Róbert Mak, Marek Hamšík, Stanislav Lobotka, Adam Nemec (65.Ondrej Duda), Vladimír Weiss (70.Albert Rusnák). Trainer: Ján Kozák.

13.10.2018 SLOVAKIA - CZECH REPUBLIC 1-2(0-0) UEFA Nations League B, Group 1
Štadión "Antona Malatinského", Trnava; Referee: Slavko Vinčić (Slovenia); Attendance: 17,251
SVK: Martin Dúbravka, Martin Škrtel (Cap), Tomáš Hubočan (80.Dávid Hancko), Peter Pekarík (46.Erik Sabo), Milan Škriniar, Juraj Kucka (54.Vladimír Weiss), Róbert Mak, Marek Hamšík, Stanislav Lobotka, Ondrej Duda, Adam Nemec. Trainer: Ján Kozák.
Goal: Marek Hamšík (62).

16.10.2018 SWEDEN - SLOVAKIA 1-1(0-0) Friendly International
Friends Arena, Stockholm; Referee: Jakob Kehlet (Denmark); Attendance: 9,876
SVK: Martin Dúbravka, Milan Škriniar, Martin Škrtel (Cap) (83.Ľubomír Šatka), Dávid Hancko, Juraj Kucka (57.Patrik Hrošovský), Róbert Mak (66.Matúš Bero), Marek Hamšík (67.Ondrej Duda), Erik Sabo, Albert Rusnák, Stanislav Lobotka (56.Ján Greguš), Adam Nemec (71.Samuel Mráz). Trainer: Štefan Tarkovič.
Goal: Albert Rusnák (84).

16.11.2018 SLOVAKIA - UKRAINE 4-1(2-0) UEFA Nations League B, Group 1
Štadión "Antona Malatinského", Trnava; Referee: Nikola Dabanović (Montenegro); Attendance: 9,764
SVK: Martin Dúbravka, Martin Škrtel (Cap), Peter Pekarík, Milan Škriniar, Dávid Hancko, Juraj Kucka (30.Matúš Bero), Ján Greguš, Marek Hamšík, Róbert Mak (69.Miroslav Stoch), Albert Rusnák, Adam Zreľák (82.Michal Ďuriš). Trainer: Pavel Hapal (Czech Republic).
Goals: Albert Rusnák (6), Juraj Kucka (26), Adam Zreľák (52), Róbert Mak (61).

19.11.2018 CZECH REPUBLIC - SLOVAKIA 1-0(1-0) UEFA Nations League B, Group 1
Stadion Sinobo, Praha; Referee: Alejandro José Hernández Hernández (Spain); Attendance: 16,623
SVK: Martin Dúbravka, Martin Škrtel (Cap), Peter Pekarík, Milan Škriniar, Dávid Hancko, Miroslav Stoch, Ján Greguš (58.Ondrej Duda), Marek Hamšík, Albert Rusnák (58.Róbert Mak), Matúš Bero, Adam Zreľák (79.Adam Nemec). Trainer: Pavel Hapal (Czech Republic).

21.03.2019 SLOVAKIA - HUNGARY 2-0(1-0) 16th EC. Qualifiers
Štadión "Antona Malatinského", Trnava; Referee: Vladislav Bezborodov (Russia); Attendance: 14,235
SVK: Martin Dúbravka, Peter Pekarík, Milan Škriniar, Denis Vavro, Dávid Hancko, Juraj Kucka, Róbert Mak (79.Miroslav Stoch), Marek Hamšík (Cap), Albert Rusnák (90+2.Jaroslav Mihalík), Stanislav Lobotka, Ondrej Duda (87.Pavol Šafranko). Trainer: Pavel Hapal (Czech Republic).
Goals: Ondrej Duda (42), Albert Rusnák (85).

24.03.2019 WALES - SLOVAKIA 1-0(1-0) 16th EC. Qualifiers
Cardiff City Stadium, Cardiff; Referee: Felix Zwayer (Germany); Attendance: 31,617
SVK: Martin Dúbravka, Peter Pekarík (90.Pavol Šafranko), Milan Škriniar, Denis Vavro, Dávid Hancko, Juraj Kucka, Marek Hamšík (Cap), Róbert Mak (69.Miroslav Stoch), Albert Rusnák, Stanislav Lobotka, Ondrej Duda (65.Michal Ďuriš). Trainer: Pavel Hapal (Czech Republic).

07.06.2019 SLOVAKIA - JORDAN 5-1(0-1) Friendly International
Štadión "Antona Malatinského", Trnava; Referee: Tomasz Musial (Poland); Attendance: 3,454
SVK: Matúš Kozáčik (46.Dominik Greif), Lukáš Štetina, Róbert Mazáň, Ľubomír Šatka, Branislav Niňaj, Miroslav Stoch (46.Lukáš Haraslín), Jaroslav Mihalík, Matúš Bero (61.László Bénes), Patrik Hrošovský (Cap) (46.Ján Greguš), Martin Chrien (73.Samuel Mráz), Pavol Šafranko (46.Róbert Boženík). Trainer: Pavel Hapal (Czech Republic).
Goals: Lukáš Haraslín (50), Martin Chrien (55), Ján Greguš (71 penalty), Samuel Mráz (74), Jaroslav Mihalík (84).

11.06.2019 AZERBAIJAN - SLOVAKIA 1-5(1-3) 16th EC. Qualifiers
Bakcell Arena, Bakı; Referee: John Beaton (Scotland); Attendance: 8,200
SVK: Martin Dúbravka, Peter Pekarík, Milan Škriniar, Denis Vavro, Dávid Hancko, Juraj Kucka, Róbert Mak, Marek Hamšík (Cap) (86.Lukáš Haraslín), Albert Rusnák, Stanislav Lobotka (84.Ján Greguš), Róbert Boženík (71.Ondrej Duda). Trainer: Pavel Hapal (Czech Republic).
Goals: Stanislav Lobotka (8), Juraj Kucka (27), Marek Hamšík (30, 57), Dávid Hancko (85).

NATIONAL TEAM PLAYERS
(16.07.2018 – 15.07.2019)

Name	DOB	Caps	Goals	2018/2019:	Club
Goalkeepers					
Martin DÚBRAVKA	15.01.1989	**18**	**0**	2018/2019:	*Newcastle United FC (ENG)*
Dominik GREIF	06.04.1997	**1**	**0**	2019:	*ŠK Slovan Bratislava*
Matúš KOZÁČIK	27.12.1983	**29**	**0**	2018/2019:	*FC Viktoria Plzeň (CZE)*
Defenders					
Norbert GYÖMBÉR	03.07.1992	**21**	**0**	2018/2019:	*AC Perugia Calcio (ITA)*
Dávid HANCKO	13.12.1997	**7**	**1**	2018/2019:	*ACF Fiorentina (ITA)*
Tomáš HUBOČAN	17.09.1985	**64**	**0**	2018:	*Olympique de Marseille (FRA)*
Róbert MAZÁŇ	09.02.1994	**7**	**0**	2018: 28.01.2019->	*RC Celta de Vigo (ESP)* *Venezia FC (ITA)*
Branislav NIŇAJ	17.05.1994	**2**	**0**	2019:	*Fortuna Sittard (NED)*
Peter PEKARÍK	30.10.1986	**88**	**2**	2018/2019:	*Hertha BSC Berlin (GER)*
Ľubomír ŠATKA	02.12.1995	**7**	**0**	2018/2019:	*FK DAC Dunajská Streda*
Milan ŠKRINIAR	11.02.1995	**26**	**0**	2018/2019:	*FC Internazionale Milano (ITA)*
Martin ŠKRTEL	15.12.1984	**103**	**6**	2018:	*Fenerbahçe SK İstanbul (TUR)*
Lukáš ŠTETINA	28.07.1991	**3**	**1**	2019:	*AC Sparta Praha (CZE)*
Denis VAVRO	10.04.1996	**3**	**0**	2019:	*FC København (DEN)*
Midfielders					
Matúš BERO	06.09.1995	**9**	**0**	2018/2019:	*SBV Vitesse Arnhem (NED)*
László BÉNES	09.09.1997	**2**	**0**	2019:	*KSV Holstein Kiel (GER)*
Róbert BOŽENÍK	18.11.1999	**2**	**0**	2019:	*MŠK Žilina*
Martin CHRIEN	08.09.1995	**1**	**1**	2019:	*CD Santa Clara Açores (POR)*
Ondrej DUDA	05.12.1994	**33**	**5**	2018/2019:	*Hertha BSC Berlin (GER)*
Ján GREGUŠ	29.01.1991	**24**	**3**	2018: 01.01.2019->	*FC København (DEN)* *Minnesota United FC (USA)*
Marek HAMŠÍK	27.07.1987	**114**	**24**	2018: 14.02.2019->	*SSC Napoli (ITA)* *Dalian Yifamg FC (CHN)*
Lukáš HARASLÍN	26.05.1996	**2**	**1**	2019:	*KS Lechia Gdańsk (POL)*
Patrik HROŠOVSKÝ	22.04.1992	**23**	**0**	2018/2019:	*FC Viktoria Plzeň (CZE)*
Juraj KUCKA	26.02.1987	**67**	**8**	2018: 15.01.2019->	*Trabzonspor Kulübü (TUR)* *Parma FC (ITA)*
Stanislav LOBOTKA	25.11.1994	**17**	**3**	2018/2019:	*RC Celta de Vigo (ESP)*
Róbert MAK	08.03.1991	**54**	**11**	2018/2019:	*FK Zenit Saint Petersburg (RUS)*
Jaroslav MIHALÍK	02.07.1994	**6**	**1**	2019:	*MŠK Žilina*
Albert RUSNÁK	07.07.1994	**20**	**5**	2018/2019:	*Real Salt Lake (USA)*
Erik SABO	22.11.1991	**17**	**0**	2018:	*Hapoel Be'er Sheva FC (ISR)*
Miroslav STOCH	19.10.1989	**60**	**6**	2018/2019:	*SK Slavia Praha (CZE)*
Vladimír WEISS	30.11.1989	**67**	**7**	2018/2019:	*Al-Gharafa SC Al Rayyan (QAT)*
Forwards					
Michal ĎURIŠ	01.06.1988	**42**	**5**	2018/2019:	*Anorthosis Famagusta FC (CYP)*
Samuel MRÁZ	13.05.1997	**2**	**0**	2018: 30.01.2019->	*Empoli FC (ITA)* *FC Crotone (ITA)*
Adam NEMEC	02.09.1985	**42**	**13**	2018/2019:	*Pafos FC Paphos (CYP)*
Erik PAČINDA	09.09.1989	**4**	**1**	2018:	*FK DAC Dunajská Streda*
Pavol ŠAFRANKO	16.11.1994	**3**	**0**	2019:	*Dundee United FC (SCO)*
Adam ZREĽÁK	05.05.1994	**4**	**2**	2018:	*1. FC Nürnberg (GER)*

National team coach

Ján KOZÁK [01.07.2013 – 14.10.2018]	17.04.1954	54 M; 29 W; 10 D; 15 L; 80-48
Štefan TARKOVIČ [15.10. – 22.10.2018; Caretaker]	18.02.1973	1 M; 0 W; 1 D; 0 L; 1-1
Pavel HAPAL (Czech Republic) [from 22.10.2018]	27.07.1969	6 M; 4 W; 0 D; 2 L; 16-4

SLOVENIA

The Country:
Republika Slovenija (Republic of Slovenia)
Capital: Ljubljana
Surface: 20,273 km²
Inhabitants: 2,084,301 [2018]
Time: UTC+1

The FA:
Nogometna zveza Slovenije
Predoslje 40 a, p.p. 130, 4000 Kranj
Tel: +386 4 27 59 400
Founded: 23.04.1920
Member of FIFA since: 1992
Member of UEFA since: 1992
Website: www.nzs.si

NATIONAL TEAM RECORDS

First international match:	03.06.1992, Tallinn:	Estonia – Slovenia 1-1
Most international caps:	Boštjan Cesar	- 101 caps (2003-2018)
Most international goals:	Zlatko Zahovič	- 35 goals / 80 caps (1992-2004)

UEFA EUROPEAN CHAMPIONSHIP	
1960	-
1964	-
1968	-
1972	-
1976	-
1980	-
1984	-
1988	-
1992	-
1996	Qualifiers
2000	Final Tournament (Group Stage)
2004	Qualifiers
2008	Qualifiers
2012	Qualifiers
2016	Qualifiers

Please note: Part of Yugoslavia between 1930-1990.

FIFA WORLD CUP	
1930	-
1934	-
1938	-
1950	-
1954	-
1958	-
1962	-
1966	-
1970	-
1974	-
1978	-
1982	-
1986	-
1990	-
1994	Did not enter
1998	Qualifiers
2002	Final Tournament (Group Stage)
2006	Qualifiers
2010	Final Tournament (Group Stage)
2014	Qualifiers
2018	Qualifiers

UEFA NATIONS LEAGUE
2018/2019 – League C

OLYMPIC FOOTBALL TOURNAMENTS 1908-2016							
1908		**1948**		**1972**		**1996**	
1912		**1952**		**1976**		**2000**	
1920		**1956**		**1980**		**2004**	
1924		**1960**		**1984**		**2008**	
1928		**1964**		**1988**		**2012**	
1936		**1968**		**1992**		**2016**	

FIFA CONFEDERATIONS CUP 1992-2017
None

SLOVENIAN CLUB HONOURS IN EUROPEAN CLUB COMPETITIONS:

European Champion Clubs.Cup (1956-1992) / UEFA Champions League (1993-2019)
None
Fairs Cup (1858-1971) / UEFA Cup (1972-2009) / UEFA Europa League (2010-2019)
None
UEFA Super Cup (1972-2018)
None
European Cup Winners.Cup 1961-1999*
None

**defunct competition*

NATIONAL COMPETITIONS
TABLE OF HONOURS

	CHAMPIONS	CUP WINNERS	BEST GOALSCORERS	
1991/1992	NK Olimpija Ljubljana	NK Maribor	Zoran Ubavič (NK Olimpija Ljubljana)	29
1992/1993	NK Olimpija Ljubljana	NK Olimpija Ljubljana	Sašo Udovič (ND Slovan Ljubljana)	25
1993/1994	NK Olimpija Ljubljana	NK Maribor	Štefan Škaper (NK Beltinci)	23
1994/1995	NK Olimpija Ljubljana	NK Mura Murska Sobota	Štefan Škaper (NK Beltinci)	25
1995/1996	ND Gorica	NK Olimpija Ljubljana	Ermin Šiljak (NK Olimpija Ljubljana)	28
1996/1997	NK Maribor	NK Maribor	Faik Kamberović (BIH, NK Celje)	21
1997/1998	NK Maribor	NK Rudar Velenje	Ismet Ekmečić (NK Olimpija Ljubljana)	21
1998/1999	NK Maribor	NK Maribor	Novica Nikčević (SRB, ND Gorica)	17
1999/2000	NK Maribor	NK Olimpija Ljubljana	Kliton Bozgo (ALB, NK Maribor)	24
2000/2001	NK Maribor	ND Gorica	Damir Pekič (NK Celje)	23
2001/2002	NK Maribor	ND Gorica	Romano Obilinović (CRO, NK Primorje Ajdovščina)	16
2002/2003	NK Maribor	NK Olimpija Ljubljana	Marko Kmetec (NK Ljubljana / NK Olimpija Ljubljana)	21
2003/2004	ND Gorica	NK Maribor	Dražen Žeželj (NK Ljubljana / NK Primorje Ajdovščina)	19
2004/2005	ND Gorica	NK Celje	Kliton Bozgo (ALB, NK Maribor)	18
2005/2006	ND Gorica	FC Koper	Miran Burgič (ND Gorica)	24
2006/2007	NK Domžale	FC Koper	Nikola Nikezić (MNE, NK Domžale / ND Gorica)	22
2007/2008	NK Domžale	NK Interblock Ljubljana	Dario Zahora (CRO, NK Domžale)	22
2008/2009	NK Maribor	NK Interblock Ljubljana	Etien Velikonja (ND Gorica)	17
2009/2010	FC Koper	NK Maribor	Milan Osterc (FC Koper)	23
2010/2011	NK Maribor	NK Domžale	Marcos Magno Morales Tavares (BRA, NK Maribor)	16
2011/2012	NK Maribor	NK Maribor	Dare Vršič (NK Olimpija Ljubljana)	22
2012/2013	NK Maribor	NK Maribor	Marcos Magno Morales Tavares (BRA, NK Maribor)	17
2013/2014	NK Maribor	ND Gorica	Mate Eterović (CRO, NK Rudar Velenje)	19
2014/2015	NK Maribor	FC Koper	Marcos Magno Morales Tavares (BRA, NK Maribor)	17
2015/2016	NK Olimpija Ljubljana	NK Maribor	Rok Kronaveter (NK Olimpija Ljubljana) Jean-Philippe Mendy (FRA, NK Maribor) Andraž Šporar (NK Olimpija Ljubljana)	17
2016/2017	NK Maribor	NK Domžale	John Mary Honi Uzuegbunam (CMR, NK Rudar Velenje)	17
2017/2018	NK Olimpija Ljubljana	NK Olimpija Ljubljana	Luka Zahović (NK Maribor)	18
2018/2019	NK Maribor	NK Olimpija Ljubljana	Luka Zahović (NK Maribor)	18

NATIONAL CHAMPIONSHIP
Prva liga Telekom Slovenije 2018/2019
(20.07.2018 – 25.05.2019)

Results

Round 1 [20-22.07.2018]
NK Aluminij - NK Celje 2-1(1-1)
NŠ Mura - NK Triglav 1-1(1-1)
ND Gorica - Olimpija Ljubljana 2-0(1-0)
Rudar Velenje - NK Maribor 0-5(0-1)
NK Domžale - NK Krško 2-0(0-0)

Round 2 [27-29.07.2018]
NK Celje - ND Gorica 2-2(2-0)
NK Triglav - NK Aluminij 1-3(1-1)
NK Maribor - NŠ Mura 0-0
NK Domžale - Rudar Velenje 3-1(1-0)
NK Krško - Olimpija Ljubljana 0-0

Round 3 [05-06.08.2018]
NK Aluminij - NK Maribor 2-5(0-1)
NŠ Mura - NK Domžale 5-1(2-0)
Olimpija Ljubljana - NK Celje 2-2(2-1)
Rudar Velenje - NK Krško 1-1(0-1)
ND Gorica - NK Triglav 1-1(1-0)

Round 4 [11-13.08.2018]
NK Krško - NK Celje 1-1(1-0)
NK Triglav - Olimpija Ljubljana 0-4(0-1)
NK Maribor - ND Gorica 5-0(3-0)
NK Domžale - NK Aluminij 3-1(2-0)
Rudar Velenje - NŠ Mura 3-2(2-1)

Round 5 [18-19.08.2018]
NK Celje - NK Triglav 1-3(0-0)
NK Aluminij - Rudar Velenje 3-0(1-0)
NŠ Mura - NK Krško 0-1(0-0)
ND Gorica - NK Domžale 1-0(1-0)
Olimpija Ljubljana - NK Maribor 0-3(0-1)

Round 6 [25-29.08.2018]
NK Krško - NK Triglav 1-1(0-0)
NŠ Mura - NK Aluminij 3-2(2-0)
NK Domžale - Olimpija Ljubljana 1-2(0-2)
NK Maribor - NK Celje 1-1(0-0)
Rudar Velenje - ND Gorica 0-2(0-0)

Round 7 [31.08.-02.09.2018]
NK Aluminij - NK Krško 1-0(1-0)
NK Celje - NK Domžale 0-0
NK Triglav - NK Maribor 1-5(0-2)
ND Gorica - NŠ Mura 2-2(0-1)
Olimpija Ljubljana - Rudar Velenje 5-0(2-0)

Round 8 [15-16.09.2018]
NK Aluminij - ND Gorica 0-0
Rudar Velenje - NK Celje 0-1(0-1)
NK Krško - NK Maribor 0-2(0-0)
NŠ Mura - Olimpija Ljubljana 0-2(0-1)
NK Domžale - NK Triglav 1-2(0-1)

Round 9 [22-23.09.2018]
ND Gorica - NK Krško 1-0(0-0)
NK Maribor - NK Domžale 2-2(2-1)
NK Triglav - Rudar Velenje 1-2(0-1)
NK Celje - NŠ Mura 1-0(1-0)
Olimpija Ljubljana - NK Aluminij 3-1(0-0)

Round 10 [26-27.09.2018]
NK Krško - NK Domžale 0-4(0-2)
NK Triglav - NŠ Mura 3-0(1-0)
NK Maribor - Rudar Velenje 3-0(2-0)
NK Celje - NK Aluminij 1-1(0-0)
Olimpija Ljubljana - ND Gorica 2-2(0-0)

Round 11 [30.09.-01.10.2018]
NŠ Mura - NK Maribor 4-1(2-0)
Rudar Velenje - NK Domžale 2-1(0-1)
Olimpija Ljubljana - NK Krško 1-1(1-0)
ND Gorica - NK Celje 1-1(1-1)
NK Aluminij - NK Triglav 2-0(2-0)

Round 12 [05-07.10.2018]
NK Krško - Rudar Velenje 0-0
NK Domžale - NŠ Mura 2-2(1-0)
NK Maribor - NK Aluminij 2-1(1-0)
NK Celje - Olimpija Ljubljana 1-3(1-1)
NK Triglav - ND Gorica 2-4(1-1)

Round 13 [20-21.10.2018]
NŠ Mura - Rudar Velenje 2-1(1-1)
ND Gorica - NK Maribor 0-3(0-1)
NK Aluminij - NK Domžale 0-0
NK Celje - NK Krško 2-1(1-1)
Olimpija Ljubljana - NK Triglav 2-0(1-0)

Round 14 [27-28.10.2018]
NK Triglav - NK Celje 1-2(0-2)
NK Maribor - Olimpija Ljubljana 1-2(1-0)
NK Krško - NŠ Mura 2-0(0-0)
Rudar Velenje - NK Aluminij 3-2(1-1)
NK Domžale - ND Gorica 3-1(2-0) [07.11.18]

Round 15 [03-04.11.2018]
ND Gorica - Rudar Velenje 2-2(1-1)
NK Triglav - NK Krško 4-3(2-2)
NK Celje - NK Maribor 0-5(0-3)
Olimpija Ljubljana - NK Domžale 4-4(2-3)
NK Aluminij - NŠ Mura 0-2(0-1)

Round 16 [10-11.11.2018]
NŠ Mura - ND Gorica 1-0(1-0)
NK Maribor - NK Triglav 4-1(1-1)
NK Domžale - NK Celje 1-1(0-0)
Rudar Velenje - Olimpija Ljubljana 1-2(0-2)
NK Krško - NK Aluminij 1-3(0-1)

Round 17 [23-25.11.2018]
Olimpija Ljubljana - NŠ Mura 2-2(1-0)
NK Celje - Rudar Velenje 2-0(0-0)
NK Maribor - NK Krško 3-0(0-0)
NK Triglav - NK Domžale 1-4(0-2)
ND Gorica - NK Aluminij 0-1(0-0)

Round 18 [01-02.12.2018]
NK Aluminij - Olimpija Ljubljana 6-2(3-1)
NK Domžale - NK Maribor 1-2(1-1)
NK Krško - ND Gorica 1-0(0-0)
NŠ Mura - NK Celje 0-1(0-0)
Rudar Velenje - NK Triglav 3-1(0-1)

Round 19 [07-09.12.2018]
Rudar Velenje - NK Maribor 1-3(1-1)
ND Gorica - Olimpija Ljubljana 1-3(1-1)
NK Domžale - NK Krško 2-1(0-0)
NŠ Mura - NK Triglav 0-0
NK Aluminij - NK Celje 4-1(3-1)

Round 20 [23-24.02.2019]
NK Celje - ND Gorica 4-3(4-2)
NK Maribor - NŠ Mura 1-1(0-0)
NK Triglav - NK Aluminij 3-0(3-0)
NK Domžale - Rudar Velenje 6-2(1-0)
NK Krško - Olimpija Ljubljana 1-4(1-1)

Round 21 [02-03.03.2019]
NŠ Mura - NK Domžale 0-0
Olimpija Ljubljana - NK Celje 2-0(1-0)
NK Aluminij - NK Maribor 0-1(0-0)
Rudar Velenje - NK Krško 1-0(1-0)
ND Gorica - NK Triglav 1-2(1-1)

Round 22 [09-10.03.2019]
NK Triglav - Olimpija Ljubljana 2-1(0-1)
NK Maribor - ND Gorica 2-1(0-0)
NK Krško - NK Celje 1-1(0-0)
Rudar Velenje - NŠ Mura 1-0(0-0)
NK Domžale - NK Aluminij 3-0(1-0)

Round 23 [16-17.03.2019]
NK Celje - NK Triglav 4-0(1-0)
NŠ Mura - NK Krško 5-0(2-0)
Olimpija Ljubljana - NK Maribor 0-0
NK Aluminij - Rudar Velenje 4-0(1-0)
ND Gorica - NK Domžale 2-1(0-0)

Round 24 [30-31.03.2019]
NK Domžale - Olimpija Ljubljana 1-3(0-1)
NK Maribor - NK Celje 1-1(0-0)
Rudar Velenje - ND Gorica 2-2(0-1)
NK Krško - NK Triglav 1-3(1-0)
NŠ Mura - NK Aluminij 3-0(1-0)

Round 25 [06-07.04.2019]
NK Triglav - NK Maribor 1-2(0-1)
NK Celje - NK Domžale 2-3(1-2)
ND Gorica - NŠ Mura 0-1(0-0)
Olimpija Ljubljana - Rudar Velenje 3-3(2-0)
NK Aluminij - NK Krško 1-1(1-1)

Round 26 [10-11.04.2019]
Rudar Velenje - NK Celje 0-3(0-0)
NK Krško - NK Maribor 0-1(0-1)
NK Domžale - NK Triglav 6-1(2-0)
NK Aluminij - ND Gorica 3-1(1-0)
NŠ Mura - Olimpija Ljubljana 0-0

Round 27 [13-14.04.2019]
NK Triglav - Rudar Velenje 0-4(0-2)
NK Maribor - NK Domžale 1-0(0-0)
NK Celje - NŠ Mura 0-2(0-2)
Olimpija Ljubljana - NK Aluminij 2-0(0-0)
ND Gorica - NK Krško 1-2(1-1)

Round 28 [19-22.04.2019]
Olimpija Ljubljana - ND Gorica 3-1(1-0)
NK Celje - NK Aluminij 1-0(0-0)
NK Triglav - NŠ Mura 2-1(0-1)
NK Maribor - Rudar Velenje 3-1(1-0)
NK Krško - NK Domžale 1-2(0-2)

Round 29 [27-28.04.2019]
Rudar Velenje - NK Domžale 1-2(1-0)
NK Aluminij - NK Triglav 2-1(0-1)
ND Gorica - NK Celje 4-0(4-0)
NŠ Mura - NK Maribor 2-2(1-1)
Olimpija Ljubljana - NK Krško 3-2(2-0)

Round 30 [01-02.05.2019]
NK Domžale - NŠ Mura 1-1(1-1)
NK Maribor - NK Aluminij 1-1(0-1)
NK Triglav - ND Gorica 1-1(1-0)
NK Celje - Olimpija Ljubljana 1-0(1-0)
NK Krško - Rudar Velenje 1-2(0-0)

Round 31 [04-06.05.2019]
NK Aluminij - NK Domžale 0-3(0-1)
NŠ Mura - Rudar Velenje 3-3(1-1)
ND Gorica - NK Maribor 1-3(0-2)
Olimpija Ljubljana - NK Triglav 4-2(2-1)
NK Celje - NK Krško 0-0

Round 32 [10-12.05.2019]
NK Domžale - ND Gorica 2-1(0-1)
Rudar Velenje - NK Aluminij 3-0(0-0)
NK Krško - NŠ Mura 0-3(0-1)
NK Maribor - Olimpija Ljubljana 0-3(0-3)
NK Triglav - NK Celje 0-3(0-2)

Round 33 [14-15.05.2019]
ND Gorica - Rudar Velenje 1-2(0-2)
NK Triglav - NK Krško 3-1(2-0)
Olimpija Ljubljana - NK Domžale 1-4(0-2)
NK Aluminij - NŠ Mura 0-1(0-0)
NK Celje - NK Maribor 1-3(1-0)

Round 34 [18-19.05.2019]
Rudar Velenje - Olimpija Ljubljana 1-2(1-0)
NK Maribor - NK Triglav 3-3(1-1)
NŠ Mura - ND Gorica 3-0(2-0)
NK Domžale - NK Celje 1-1(0-1)
NK Krško - NK Aluminij 1-3(0-2)

Round 35 [22.05.2019]
NK Maribor - NK Krško 2-0(1-0)
NK Celje - Rudar Velenje 0-2(0-0)
Olimpija Ljubljana - NŠ Mura 1-0(0-0)
ND Gorica - NK Aluminij 0-0
NK Triglav - NK Domžale 1-4(1-1)

Round 36 [25.05.2019]
NK Domžale - NK Maribor 2-1(2-1)
NK Krško - ND Gorica 3-2(1-1)
NK Aluminij - Olimpija Ljubljana 1-0(1-0)
NŠ Mura - NK Celje 1-1(0-1)
Rudar Velenje - NK Triglav 2-2(1-0)

Final Standings

1.	**NK Maribor**	36	23	9	4	81	-	33	78
2.	NK Olimpija Ljubljana	36	20	9	7	73	-	47	69
3.	NK Domžale	36	18	9	9	76	-	47	63
4.	NŠ Mura Murska Sobota	36	13	13	10	52	-	36	52
5.	NK Celje	36	12	13	11	45	-	51	49
6.	NK Aluminij Kidričevo	36	14	6	16	50	-	53	48
7.	NK Rudar Velenje	36	12	7	17	50	-	73	43
8.	NK Triglav Kranj	36	10	7	19	51	-	83	37
9.	ND Gorica (*Relegation Play-offs*)	36	7	10	19	44	-	63	31
10.	NK Krško (*Relegated*)	36	5	9	22	29	-	65	24

Top goalscorers:

18 Luka Zahović *NK Maribor*

17 Rok Kronaveter *NK Olimpija Ljubljana*
17 Luka Majcen *NK Triglav Kranj*

15 Rok Sirk *NŠ Mura Murska Sobota*
15 Milan Tučić *NK Rudar Velenje*

Relegation Play-offs

NK Tabor Sežana - ND Gorica 2-1(2-1) 0-0
NK Tabor Sežana promoted to the 2019/2020 Prva liga Slovenije.

NATIONAL CUP
Pokal Nogometne zveze Slovenije 2018/2019

First Round [14-16.08.2018]

NK Turnišče - NK Krško	0-8
Akumulator Mežica - NK Brda	1-7
NK Grad - NK Aluminij Kidričevo	1-2
NK Drava Ptuj - AŠK Bravo Ljubljana	0-2
ŠD Videm - NK Triglav	1-2 aet
NK Jesenice - FC Koper	0-12
NK Plama Podgrad - ND Gorica	0-5
NK Šampion Celje - NK Ivančna Gorica	0-1 aet
NK Nafta Lendava 1903 - NK Ankaran Postojna	2-1
ND Bilje - NK Celje	0-2
DNŠ Prevalje - NK Kranj	5-1
NK Rogaška - NŠ Mura	1-3

1/8-Finals [12/19-20.09.2018]			
NŠ Mura Murska Sobota - NK Rudar Velenje	1-0	NK Brda - ND Gorica	0-2
AŠK Bravo Ljubljana - NK Maribor	2-3	DNŠ Prevalje - NK Aluminij Kidričevo	0-3
FC Koper - NK Nafta Lendava 1903	2-0	NK Celje - NK Krško	0-3
NK Ivančna Gorica - NK Domžale	0-3	NK Olimpija Ljubljana - NK Triglav	2-1

Quarter-Finals [17/23-24.10./31.10.2018]			
FC Koper - NK Olimpija Ljubljana	0-5 / 1-1	ND Gorica - NŠ Mura Murska Sobota	0-3 / 2-3
NK Maribor - NK Domžale	1-0 / 2-2	NK Krško - NK Aluminij Kidričevo	2-2 / 0-0

Semi-Finals [03-04.04./23-24.2019]			
NK Maribor - NŠ Mura Murska Sobota	1-0 / 1-1	NK Aluminij Kidričevo - NK Olimpija Ljubljana	1-2 / 0-4

Final

30.05.2019; Stadion Z'dežele, Celje; Referee: Matej Jug; Attendance: 8,623
NK Olimpija Ljubljana - NK Maribor **2-1(1-0)**

Olimpija Ljubljana: Nejc Vidmar, Vitālijs Maksimenko, Macky Frank Bagnack Mouegni, Dino Štiglec, Jan Andrejašič, Marko Putinčanin, Stefan Savić, Tomislav Tomić, Asmir Suljić (90.Mario Jurčevič), Endri Çekiçi (90.Vitja Valenčič), Haris Kadrić (86.Rok Kidrič). Trainer: Safet Hadžič.

NK Maribor: Kenan Pirić, Mitja Viler, Saša Ivković, Blaž Vrhovec (77.Jan Mlakar), Aleks Pihler, Alexandru Crețu, Dino Hotič, Amir Dervišević (67.Marcos Magno Morales Tavares), Martin Milec, Luka Zahovič, Jasmin Mešanović. Trainer: Darko Milanič.

Goals: 1-0 Stefan Savić (17), 2-0 Stefan Savić (75), 2-1 (90).

THE CLUBS 2018/2019

Nogometni klub Aluminij Kidričevo

Founded: 1946
Stadium: Aluminij Sports Park, Kidričevo (532)

Goalkeepers:	DOB	M	(s)	G
Luka Janžekovič	14.03.1997	34		
Matija Kovačić (CRO)	25.02.1994	2	(1)	
Defenders:	**DOB**	**M**	**(s)**	**G**
Stanley Amuzie (NGA)	28.02.1996	13	(2)	
Erik Gliha	13.02.1997	16		
Damir Grgić (CRO)	18.05.1992	14	(5)	2
Nemanja Jakšić (SRB)	11.07.1995	17		
Mihovil Klapan (CRO)	27.03.1995	2		
Luka Koblar	08.08.1999	9	(2)	
Ivan Kontek (CRO)	29.01.1997	30	(1)	
Ilija Martinović (MNE)	31.01.1994	23	(4)	
Sanin Muminovič (BIH)	02.11.1990	27		2
Luka Petek	13.10.1997	1		
Aljaž Ploj	30.08.1998	4	(4)	
Anton Rogina	05.02.1996	9	(2)	1
Midfielders:	**DOB**	**M**	**(s)**	**G**
Marcel Čermák (CZE)	25.11.1998	1	(3)	
Lucas Horvat	13.10.1985	30	(1)	2
Alen Krajnc	01.07.1995	19	(12)	4
Nikola Leko (BIH)	30.09.1996	8	(14)	3
Elvir Maloku (ALB)	14.05.1996	12	(4)	1
Jure Matjašič	31.05.1992	15	(1)	2
Dejan Petrovič	12.01.1998	33		3
Matic Vrbanec	28.10.1996	22	(3)	4
Forwards:	**DOB**	**M**	**(s)**	**G**
David Bosilj	01.02.2002		(3)	
Kruno Ivančić (CRO)	18.01.1994	1	(4)	
Marcel Kene	19.01.1998		(2)	1
Rok Kidrič	27.04.1995	18		6
Nik Marinšek	16.02.1999	4	(17)	1
Ibrahim Arafat Mensah (GHA)	11.01.1995	4		1
Luka Štor	05.07.1998	10	(4)	5
Francesco Tahiraj (ALB)	21.09.1996	17	(1)	9
Tadej Trdina	25.01.1988	1	(13)	2
Trainer:	**DOB**	**M**		
Oliver Bogatinov	26.09.1978	36		

Nogometni klub Celje

Founded: 28.12.1919 *(as SK Celje)*
Stadium: Stadion Z'dežele, Celje (13,059)

Goalkeepers:	DOB	M	(s)	G
Metod Jurhar	07.12.1997	19		
Matjaž Rozman	03.01.1987	17		
Defenders:	**DOB**	**M**	**(s)**	**G**
Jan Andrejašič	16.09.1995	15		
Amadej Brecl	06.04.1997	27	(1)	2
Elvedin Džinič	25.08.1985	11		2
Žan Flis	30.07.1997	1	(3)	
Dušan Stojinović	26.08.2000	19		
Deni Štraus	20.04.1996	14	(7)	
Lan Štravs	03.03.2000		(2)	
Jure Travner	28.09.1985	26	(1)	
Tadej Vidmajer	10.03.1992	20	(1)	1
Žan Zaletel	16.09.1999	27		1
Midfielders:	**DOB**	**M**	**(s)**	**G**
Žan Benedičič	03.10.1995	8	(9)	1
Lovro Cvek (CRO)	06.07.1995	30	(5)	
Jakob Novak	04.03.1998	16	(6)	
Janez Pišek	04.05.1998	28	(3)	
Nino Pungaršek	01.11.1995	21	(4)	3
Rok Štraus	03.03.1987	1	(19)	
Juš Štusej	20.04.2000		(1)	
Rudi Vancaš	15.03.1994	27		14
Forwards:	**DOB**	**M**	**(s)**	**G**
Elvir Ibišević (BIH)	10.02.1998	9	(13)	1
Joaquim Manuel Welo Lupeta „Jucie Lupeta“ (POR)	24.03.1993	3	(2)	2
Luka Kerin	23.03.1999	5	(7)	1
Gašper Koritnik	06.01.2001		(2)	
Mitja Lotrič	03.09.1994	26	(3)	8
Tilen Pečnik	16.05.1998	3	(7)	
Dario Vizinger (CRO)	06.06.1998	23	(5)	9
Trainer:	**DOB**	**M**		
Dušan Kosič	23.04.1971	36		

Nogometni klub Domžale

Founded: 07.11.1920 (*as SK Disk Domžale*)
Stadium: Športni park Domžale (3,100)

Goalkeepers:	**DOB**	**M**	**(s)**	**G**
Klemen Mihelak	31.12.2001	1		
Dejan Milič	24.01.1984	5		
Ajdin Mulalič	13.09.1994	14		
Krševan Santini (CRO)	11.04.1987	16		
Defenders:	**DOB**	**M**	**(s)**	**G**
Gaber Dobrovoljc	27.01.1993	33		2
Tilen Klemenčič	21.08.1995	32		3
Dario Melnjak (CRO)	31.10.1992	18		4
Darrick-Kobie Morris (CRO)	15.07.1995	4	(2)	
Matija Rom	01.11.1998	24	(1)	
Gregor Sikošek	13.02.1994	25	(1)	
Matija Širok	31.05.1991	2		
Blaž Urh	07.07.1999	1	(1)	
Midfielders:	**DOB**	**M**	**(s)**	**G**
Adam Gnezda Čerin	16.07.1999	33	(2)	7
Nermin Hodžić (BIH)	13.07.1994	15	(12)	
Zeni Husmani (MKD)	28.11.1990	6		1
Senijad Ibričić (BIH)	26.09.1985	30		10
Andraž Kirm	06.09.1984	9	(2)	
Jure Obšivač (CRO)	28.05.1990		(1)	
Žiga Repas	29.05.2001		(1)	
Tamar Svetlin	30.07.2001	1	(1)	
Jošt Urbančič	12.04.2001	1		
Amedej Vetrih	16.09.1990	16		5
Žan Žužek	26.01.1997	3	(18)	
Forwards:	**DOB**	**M**	**(s)**	**G**
Lovro Bizjak	12.11.1993	2	(1)	
Mark Čeh	20.08.2001	1		
Nermin Haljeta	07.06.1997		(2)	1
Agim Ibraimi (MKD)	29.08.1988	12	(4)	2
Dario Kolobarić	06.02.2000	1	(2)	2
Dejan Lazarevič	15.02.1990	6	(6)	1
Tonći Mujan (CRO)	19.07.1995	30	(5)	5
Shamar Nicholson (JAM)	16.03.1997	19	(10)	13
Tilen Pečnik	16.05.1998	4	(4)	1
Matej Podlogar	23.02.1991	17	(11)	5
Rubén Belima Rodríguez (ESP)	11.02.1992	1	(4)	
Slobodan Vuk	15.09.1989	14	(14)	7
Trainer:	**DOB**	**M**		
Simon Rožman	06.04.1983	36		

Nogometno društvo Gorica

Founded: 1947 (*as FD Gorica*)
Stadium: Športni park Nova Gorica (3,100)

Goalkeepers:	**DOB**	**M**	**(s)**	**G**
Uroš Likar	01.10.1999	1		
Grega Sorčan	05.03.1996	34		
Januš Štrukelj	08.04.1991	1	(1)	
Defenders:	**DOB**	**M**	**(s)**	**G**
Uroš Celcer	07.04.1989	28	(1)	2
Jani Curk	27.02.1994	16	(2)	
Adel Halilović (BIH)	17.03.1996	12		1
Adis Hodžić	16.01.1999	10	(11)	2
Alen Jogan	24.08.1985	1		
Matija Kavčič	11.07.1997	10	(10)	2
Tine Kavčič	16.02.1994	15	(1)	
Žiga Lipušček	05.01.1997	29		5
Vladimir Oršolić (BIH)	03.06.1997	6		
Matteo Tomiček (CRO)	24.01.1997	30	(1)	
Midfielders:	**DOB**	**M**	**(s)**	**G**
Rok Bužinel	28.03.1998	2	(3)	
Amel Džuzdanovič	26.08.1994	5	(9)	
Rok Grudina	24.12.1994	27	(1)	1
Jan Humar	24.03.1996	5	(6)	
Jaka Kolenc	23.02.1994	28	(5)	1
Basholli Kosovar	30.06.2001		(1)	
Andrej Kotnik	04.08.1995	19	(1)	1
Žan Luk Leban	15.12.2002	1	(1)	
Amadej Marinič	10.10.2000	1		
Leon Marinič	21.11.1997	6	(4)	
Goran Trivunovič	12.06.2000		(1)	
Forwards:	**DOB**	**M**	**(s)**	**G**
Kristjan Cvijanović	26.03.2000		(1)	
Andrija Filipović (CRO)	18.04.1997	27	(1)	8
Mark Gulič	15.08.1997	3	(15)	1
Nik Jermol	17.08.1999	2	(12)	1
Tim Matič	14.08.1998	1		
Bede Osuji (NGA)	21.01.1996	32		5
Kristijan Šipek	01.06.1995	13	(3)	
Semir Smailagić (BIH)	18.09.1998	15	(13)	6
Etien Velikonja	26.12.1988	16		8
Trainer:	**DOB**	**M**		
Miran Srebrnič	08.01.1970	19		
Nermin Bašić (BIH) [05.01.2019]	24.11.1983	6		
Saša Kolman [10.04.2019]	01.05.1984	11		

Nogometni klub Krško

Founded: 11.05.1922
Stadium: Stadion "Matije Gubca", Krško (1,470)

Goalkeepers:	**DOB**	**M**	**(s)**	**G**
Žiga Frelih	06.02.1998	11	(2)	
Marko Zalokar	18.06.1990	25		
Defenders:	**DOB**	**M**	**(s)**	**G**
Ivica Batarelo (CRO)	12.05.1998	5		
Slavko Brekalo (BIH)	25.02.1990	15		
Mario Cetina (CRO)	28.01.1995	16		1
Leo Ejup	09.09.1994	9		
Milan Ilić (SRB)	12.05.1987	10	(2)	1
Aleksandr Kulinitš (EST)	24.05.1992	12	(3)	
Mark Španring	13.06.2001		(1)	
Daniel Štefulj (CRO)	08.11.1999	23	(6)	
Dario Tomić (CRO)	23.06.1987	5	(1)	
Stephen Wiredu	05.06.1996		(1)	
Tomaž Zakrajšek	24.03.2000	15	(1)	
Midfielders:	**DOB**	**M**	**(s)**	**G**
Nemanja Ahčin (SRB)	07.04.1994	1		
Darijo Čavar (CRO)	02.04.1991		(1)	
Marco da Silva (FRA)	10.04.1992	30	(1)	5
Žan Florjanc	27.11.1997	1	(1)	
Macario Hing-Glover (USA)	04.04.1995	11		
David Kovačič	27.01.1999	5	(11)	
Marko Kuntarič	27.05.1994		(1)	
Sandi Ogrinec	05.06.1998	16	(4)	
Ivan Petrović (SRB)	03.07.1993	6	(2)	
Mario Vojković (AUT)	11.01.1995	4		
Luka Volarič	13.01.1991	31		
Forwards:	**DOB**	**M**	**(s)**	**G**
Ivan Božić (BIH)	19.11.1983	1	(2)	
Robert Jandrek (CRO)	30.08.1995	13	(3)	
Ante Kordić (CRO)	26.01.1992	21	(1)	3
Karlo Majić (CRO)	03.03.1998		(3)	
Nikola Mandić (CRO)	19.03.1995	5	(5)	1
Marin Perić (CRO)	17.10.1990	14	(2)	3
Milan Ristovski (MKD)	08.04.1998	11	(5)	2
Ester Sokler	04.06.1999	6	(18)	
Nenad Srećković (SRB)	11.04.1988	18		
Luka Vekič	10.04.1995	7	(16)	2
Dalibor Volaš	27.02.1987	25	(3)	6
Ante Vukušic (CRO)	04.06.1991	24	(3)	4
Trainer:	**DOB**	**M**		
Alen Ščulac	15.09.1971	16		
Radovan Karanović (BIH)[15.11.2018]	03.10.1968	3		
Milan Đjuričić (CRO) [01.02.2019]	03.08.1945	4		
Andrej Panadić [27.03.2019]	09.03.1969	13		

Nogometni klub Maribor

Founded: 12.12.1960
Stadium: Stadion Ljudski vrt, Maribor (12,702)

Goalkeepers:	DOB	M	(s)	G
Jasmin Handanovič	28.01.1978	16		
Kenan Pirić (BIH)	07.07.1994	20		
Defenders:	**DOB**	**M**	**(s)**	**G**
Saša Ivković (SRB)	13.05.1993	35		7
Žan Kolmanič	03.03.2000	13	(1)	
Aleksander Rajčevič	17.11.1986	18	(1)	
Marko Šuler	09.03.1983	11		1
Luka Uskoković (MNE)	10.04.1996	7		1
Mitja Viler	01.09.1986	24		
Midfielders:	**DOB**	**M**	**(s)**	**G**
Alexandru Crețu (ROU)	24.04.1992	14	(9)	
Amir Dervišević	04.07.1992	28	(4)	4
Dino Hotič (BIH)	26.07.1995	27	(2)	9
Denis Klinar	21.02.1992	20		
Martin Milec	20.09.1991	11		
Aleks Pihler	15.01.1994	20	(7)	2
Blaž Vrhovec	20.02.1992	23	(4)	3
Dare Vršič	26.09.1984	9	(16)	1
Nino Žugelj	23.05.2000	1	(2)	
Forwards:	**DOB**	**M**	**(s)**	**G**
Gregor Bajde	29.04.1994	4	(9)	2
Felipe Silva Correa dos Santos (BRA)	03.01.1997	5	(10)	2
Martin Kramarič	14.11.1997	5	(5)	
Marcos Magno Morales Tavares(BRA)	30.03.1984	10	(22)	9
Jasmin Mešanović (BIH)	06.01.1992	21	(7)	8
Jan Mlakar	23.10.1998	22	(4)	13
Nardin Mulahusejnović (BIH)	09.02.1998		(1)	
Luka Zahovič	15.11.1995	32		18
Trainer:	**DOB**	**M**		
Darko Milanič	18.12.1967	36		

Nogometna šola Mura Murska Sobota

Founded: 14.05.2012
Stadium: Mestni stadion Fazanerija, Murska Sobota (3,782)

Goalkeepers:	DOB	M	(s)	G
Matko Obradović (CRO)	11.05.1991	24		
Dean Šafarić (CRO)	02.01.1993	12		
Defenders:	**DOB**	**M**	**(s)**	**G**
Aleksandar Bošković (CRO)	01.04.1996	23	(1)	1
Žan Karničnik	18.09.1994	18	(17)	2
Žiga Kous	27.10.1992	28	(2)	1
Dejan Kurbus	16.01.1993	1		
Ziga Laci	20.07.2002		(2)	
Špiro Peričić (CRO)	08.10.1993	22		
Klemen Šturm	27.06.1994	30		
Midfielders:	**DOB**	**M**	**(s)**	**G**
Tomi Horvat	24.03.1999	12	(18)	2
Nino Kouter	19.12.1993	33	(2)	7
Alen Kozar	07.04.1995	31		2
Nik Lorbek	17.04.1996	33		3
Matic Maruško	30.11.1990	31	(4)	1
Klemen Pucko	27.01.1996	6	(2)	1
Jon Šporn	22.05.1997	2	(3)	1
Luka Šušnjara	04.04.1997	25	(7)	5
Forwards:	**DOB**	**M**	**(s)**	**G**
Luka Bobičanec (CRO)	23.05.1993	24	(6)	2
Armin Ćerimagić (BIH)	14.01.1994	3	(11)	1
Amadej Maroša	07.02.1994	13	(15)	7
Filip Perčić	17.06.2000		(2)	
Mihael Rebernik (CRO)	06.08.1996		(6)	
Rok Sirk	10.09.1993	25	(8)	15
Trainer:	**DOB**	**M**		
Ante Šimundža	28.09.1971	36		

Nogometni klub Olimpija Ljubljana

Founded: 02.03.2005 (*as NK Bežigrad Ljubljana*)
Stadium: Stadion Stožice, Ljubljana (16,038)

Goalkeepers:	DOB	M	(s)	G
Aljaž Ivačič	29.12.1993	18		
Nejc Vidmar	31.03.1989	18		
Defenders:	**DOB**	**M**	**(s)**	**G**
Jan Andrejašič	16.09.1995	9	(2)	
Macky Frank Bagnack Mouegni(CMR)	07.06.1995	23		1
Eric Boakye (GHA)	19.11.1999	16	(1)	
Matija Burin	25.03.2001	2		
Marko Gajić (SRB)	10.03.1992	4		
Ben Gasser	21.03.1995		(1)	
Branko Ilič	06.02.1983	10	(1)	
Adam Jakupovič	18.05.2000		(2)	
Mario Jurčević	01.06.1995	14	(5)	2
Vitālijs Maksimenko (LVA)	08.12.1990	27	(2)	2
Mirza Mujčić (SWE)	07.04.1994	4	(3)	
Dino Štiglec (CRO)	03.10.1990	23	(3)	1
Aris Zarifovič	02.06.1988	11	(2)	
Midfielders:	**DOB**	**M**	**(s)**	**G**
Goran Brkić (SRB)	28.04.1991	10	(2)	3
Nik Kapun	09.01.1994	4	(3)	1
Oliver Kregar	22.06.2000	1	(5)	
Rok Kronaveter	07.12.1986	24	(1)	17
Danijel Miškić (CRO)	11.10.1993	1		
Marko Putinčanin (SRB)	16.12.1987	25	(1)	4
Stefan Savić (AUT)	09.01.1994	27	(8)	7
Asmir Suljić (BIH)	11.09.1991	28	(4)	4
Tomislav Tomić (BIH)	16.11.1990	31		1
Vitja Valenčič	12.03.1999	6	(5)	
Forwards:	**DOB**	**M**	**(s)**	**G**
Issah Abass (GHA)	26.09.1998	3	(1)	
Kingsley Boateng (GHA)	07.04.1994	2	(7)	2
Matic Črnic	12.06.1992	11	(8)	3
Endri Çekiçi (ALB)	23.11.1996	8	(1)	6
Joaquim Manuel Welo Lupeta „Jucie Lupeta“ (POR)	24.03.1993	9	(11)	5
Haris Kadrić	16.03.2000	4	(6)	1
Rok Kidrič	27.04.1995	7	(7)	3
Ivan Lendrić (CRO)	08.08.1991		(5)	
Antonio Lukanović (CRO)	06.03.1998	1	(2)	
Andrés Vombergar (ARG)	20.11.1994	15	(1)	10
Trainer:	**DOB**	**M**		
Ilija Stolica (SRB)	07.07.1979	2		
Aleksandar Linta (SRB)[01.08.2018]	22.10.1975	3		
Safet Hadžič [26.08.2018]	08.11.1968	2		
Zoran Barišić (AUT) [04.09.2018]	22.05.1970	12		
Robert Pevnik [08.01.2019]	18.02.1969	7		
Safet Hadžič [13.04.2019]	08.11.1968	10		

Nogometni klub Rudar Velenje

Founded: 1948
Stadium: Mestni stadion ob jezeru, Velenje (2,341)

Goalkeepers:	DOB	M	(s)	G
Anže Malnar	17.09.1997	1		
Marko Pridigar	18.05.1985	25		
Matej Radan	13.05.1990	9		
Tomaž Stopajnik	14.01.2001	1		
Defenders:	**DOB**	**M**	**(s)**	**G**
Sandi Čoralič	12.02.1998	2		
Marko Ćosić (CRO)	02.03.1994	14		
David Hrubik (SRB)	19.06.1997	26	(1)	2
Gašper Jovan	25.02.2001		(2)	
David Kašnik	16.01.1987	19		2
Robert Pušaver	09.05.1995	27	(2)	
Josip Tomašević (CRO)	26.09.1993	33		
Ivan Vasiljević (SRB)	05.11.1998	11	(2)	
Midfielders:	**DOB**	**M**	**(s)**	**G**
David Arap (CRO)	09.03.1995	23	(2)	
Klemen Bolha	19.03.1993	27	(1)	1
Haris Dedič	06.07.1997	4		
Cene Kitek	09.04.2000	2		
Rijad Kobiljar (BIH)	08.04.1996	10	(7)	2
Aljaž Krefl	20.02.1994	9		1
Haoran Li (CHN)	12.01.1993		(4)	
Domagoj Muić (CRO)	05.09.1993	5	(1)	
Anže Pišek	06.10.1996	7	(11)	1
Nejc Pušnik	06.08.1998	12	(6)	1
Matej Šantek (CRO)	25.12.1999		(9)	
Žiga Škoflek	22.07.1994	17	(9)	12
Damjan Trifkovič	22.07.1987	27	(1)	3
Tim Vodeb	24.04.1990	1	(14)	1
Adam Vosnjak	26.07.2000	2		
Amadej Vošnjak	26.07.2000		(1)	
Forwards:	**DOB**	**M**	**(s)**	**G**
Leon Črnčič	02.03.1990	18	(6)	2
Abu Kamara (LBR)	01.04.1997	3	(2)	
Djair Parfitt-Williams (BER)	01.10.1996	4		
Dominik Radić (CRO)	26.08.1996	27	(8)	5
Ante Solomun (CRO)	06.03.1998	1	(6)	
Vlatko Šimunac (CRO)	01.02.1990		(4)	1
Milan Tučić	15.08.1996	29	(6)	15
Trainer:	**DOB**	**M**		
Marijan Pušnik	01.11.1960	23		
Almir Sulejmanović [29.03.2019]	26.01.1978	13		

Nogometni klub Triglav Kranj

Founded: 1920 (*as SK Korotan*); re-founded 1997
Stadium: Stadion Stanka Mlakarja, Kranj (2,060)

Goalkeepers:	DOB	M	(s)	G
Jalen Arko	09.09.1999	13		
Luka Čadež	01.03.2000	14		
Darjan Curanovič	05.04.1986	9		
Defenders:	**DOB**	**M**	**(s)**	**G**
Ermin Alić (MNE)	23.02.1992	14		
Momir Bojić	15.10.1993	8	(6)	
Kristjan Česen	17.07.1997	22	(3)	1
Tin Karamatić (CRO)	01.03.1993	5	(3)	1
Drilon Kryeziu	01.07.1999	14	(4)	
Ožbej Kuhar	21.04.1997	6		
Žan Kumer	16.05.1996	20		
Veron Salja	29.05.1998	9	(1)	
Midfielders:	**DOB**	**M**	**(s)**	**G**
Ivan Crnov (CRO)	01.02.1990	13	(4)	3
Rok Elsner	25.01.1986	18		
Marko Gajić	10.04.1997	8	(9)	3
Matic Kopač	23.11.1998		(8)	
Nejc Križaj	26.09.1989		(4)	
Egzon Kryeziu	25.04.2000	30	(2)	3
Aleš Mertelj	22.03.1987	16		1
Tilen Mlakar	26.04.1995	32		3
Joel Osikel (NGA)	17.06.1998		(2)	
Nejc Pušnik	06.08.1998		(2)	
Žan Rogelj	25.11.1999	19	(3)	
Muamer Svraka (BIH)	14.02.1988	7	(6)	2
David Tijanič	16.07.1997	31	(2)	7
Gašper Udovič	22.05.1995	26	(5)	2
Forwards:	**DOB**	**M**	**(s)**	**G**
Dickson Afoakwa (GHA)	26.04.1998	10	(4)	2
Qendrim Hasanaj	03.05.1999	1	(6)	
Deni Jurić (AUS)	03.09.1997	2	(5)	
Luka Majcen	25.07.1989	33		17
Tom Žurga	17.01.1998	16	(10)	5
Trainer:	**DOB**	**M**		
Dejan Dončić	21.10.1972	36		

SECOND LEVEL
Slovenian Second League 2018/2019

1.	AŠK Bravo Ljubljana (*Promoted*)	30	22	3	5	70	-	28	69
2.	NK Tabor Sežana (*Promotion Play-offs*)	30	19	6	5	59	-	22	63
3.	NK Radomlje	30	18	5	7	71	-	38	59
4.	NK Krka Novo Mesto	30	15	9	6	59	-	41	54
5.	NK Nafta Lendava 1903	30	14	8	8	52	-	35	50
6.	NK Fužinar Ravne na Koroškem	30	13	9	8	46	-	34	48
7.	NK Drava Ptuj	30	13	6	11	49	-	35	45
8.	NK Dob	30	10	10	10	46	-	42	40
9.	ND Bilje	30	10	6	14	33	-	54	36
10.	NK Rogaška Slatina	30	8	10	12	35	-	50	34
11.	ND Beltinci	30	9	4	17	35	-	57	31
12.	NK Brda Dobrovo	30	6	11	13	35	-	46	29
13.	NK Jadran Dekani	30	7	7	16	44	-	65	28
14.	NK Brežice 1919	30	6	8	16	32	-	52	26
15.	ND Ilirija 1911 (*Relegated*)	30	7	5	18	33	-	65	26
16.	NK Ankaran Postojna (*Relegated*)	30	6	7	17	27	-	62	22

NATIONAL TEAM

INTERNATIONAL MATCHES
(16.07.2018 – 15.07.2019)

06.09.2018	Ljubljana	Slovenia - Bulgaria	1-2(1-1)	(UNL)
09.09.2018	Nicosia	Cyprus - Slovenia	2-1(0-0)	(UNL)
13.10.2018	Oslo	Norway - Slovenia	1-0(1-0)	(UNL)
16.10.2018	Ljubljana	Slovenia - Cyprus	1-1(0-1)	(UNL)
16.11.2018	Ljubljana	Slovenia - Norway	1-1(1-0)	(UNL)
19.11.2018	Sofia	Bulgaria - Slovenia	1-1(0-0)	(UNL)
21.03.2019	Haifa	Israel - Slovenia	1-1(0-0)	(ECQ)
24.03.2019	Ljubljana	Slovenia - North Macedonia	1-1(1-0)	(ECQ)
07.06.2019	Klagenfurt	Austria - Slovenia	1-0(0-0)	(ECQ)
10.06.2019	Rīga	Latvia - Slovenia	0-5(0-4)	(ECQ)

06.09.2018 SLOVENIA - BULGARIA 1-2(1-1) UEFA Nations League C, Group 3
Stadion Stožice, Ljubljana; Referee: Davide Massa (Italy); Attendance: 5,100
SVN: Vid Belec, Bojan Jokić (Cap), Nejc Skubic, Aljaž Struna, Miha Mevlja, Kevin Kampl (83.Amir Derviševič), Rene Krhin (66.Roman Bezjak), Jasmin Kurtić, Miha Zajc, Benjamin Verbič, Andraž Šporar (73.Tim Matavž). Trainer: Tomaž Kavčič.
Goal: Miha Zajc (40).

09.09.2018 CYPRUS - SLOVENIA 2-1(0-0) UEFA Nations League C, Group 3
Stádio GSP, Nicosia; Referee: Andris Treimanis (Latvia); Attendance: 1,115
SVN: Vid Belec, Bojan Jokić (Cap), Miha Mevlja, Miha Blažič, Petar Stojanović, Jasmin Kurtić (77.Leo Štulac), Amir Derviševič, Miha Zajc, Benjamin Verbič (46.Roman Bezjak), Domen Črnigoj, Robert Berić (83.Andraž Šporar). Trainer: Tomaž Kavčič.
Goal: Robert Berić (54).

13.10.2018 NORWAY - SLOVENIA 1-0(1-0) UEFA Nations League C, Group 3
Ullevaal Stadion, Oslo; Referee: Daniel Siebert (Germany); Attendance: 14,712
SVN: Vid Belec, Bojan Jokić (Cap), Nejc Skubic, Miha Mevlja, Luka Krajnc (9.Nemanja Mitrovič), Rene Krhin, Miha Zajc, Leo Štulac (46.Jaka Bijol), Domen Črnigoj (61.Josip Iličić), Roman Bezjak, Andraž Šporar. Trainer: Tomaž Kavčič.

16.10.2018 SLOVENIA - CYPRUS 1-1(0-1) UEFA Nations League C, Group 3
Stadion Stožice, Ljubljana; Referee: Mads-Kristoffer Kristoffersen (Denmark); Attendance: 5,318
SVN: Vid Belec, Bojan Jokić (Cap) (58.Jure Balkovec), Nejc Skubic, Miha Mevlja, Nemanja Mitrovič, Josip Iličić [*sent off 90*], Rene Krhin (75.Luka Zahovič), Miha Zajc, Domen Črnigoj, Roman Bezjak (46.Amir Derviševič), Robert Berić. Trainer: Tomaž Kavčič.
Goal: Nejc Skubic (83).

16.11.2018 SLOVENIA - NORWAY 1-1(1-0) UEFA Nations League C, Group 3
Stadion Stožice, Ljubljana; Referee: Ruddy Buquet (France); Attendance: 10,254
SVN: Vid Belec, Andraž Struna, Nejc Skubic, Aljaž Struna, Miha Mevlja, Rajko Rotman, Amir Derviševič, Miha Zajc (69.Robert Berić), Benjamin Verbič (Cap), Domen Črnigoj (58.Roman Bezjak), Andraž Šporar (84.Jaka Bijol).Trainer: Igor Benedejčič.
Goal: Benjamin Verbič (9).

19.11.2018 BULGARIA - SLOVENIA 1-1(0-0) UEFA Nations League C, Group 3
Nationalen Stadion "Vasil Levski", Sofia; Referee: Hüseyin Göçek (Turkey); Attendance: 3,092
SVN: Vid Belec, Andraž Struna, Nejc Skubic, Miha Mevlja, Miha Blažič, Josip Iličić (Cap), Rajko Rotman, Amir Derviševič (58.Jaka Bijol), Miha Zajc (88.Leo Štulac), Benjamin Verbič (73.Rudi Požeg Vancaš), Roman Bezjak. Trainer: Igor Benedejčič.
Goal: Miha Zajc (75).

21.03.2019 ISRAEL - SLOVENIA 1-1(0-0) 16th EC. Qualifiers
"Sammy Ofer" Stadium, Haifa; Referee: Tiago Bruno Lopes Martins (Portugal); Attendance: 12,430
SVN: Jan Oblak, Bojan Jokić (Cap), Aljaž Struna, Miha Mevlja, Petar Stojanović, Josip Iličić, Rene Krhin, Jasmin Kurtić, Miha Zajc (62.Domen Črnigoj), Benjamin Verbič (90.Jaka Bijol), Andraž Šporar (85.Damjan Bohar). Trainer: Matjaž Kek.
Goal: Andraž Šporar (48).

24.03.2019 SLOVENIA - NORTH MACEDONIA 1-1(1-0) 16th EC. Qualifiers
Stadion Stožice, Ljubljana; Referee: Xavier Estrada Fernández (Spain); Attendance: 9,872
SVN: Jan Oblak, Bojan Jokić (Cap), Aljaž Struna, Miha Mevlja, Petar Stojanović, Josip Iličić, Rene Krhin, Jasmin Kurtić, Miha Zajc (90.Luka Zahovič), Benjamin Verbič (84.Domen Črnigoj), Andraž Šporar (71.Robert Berić). Trainer: Matjaž Kek.
Goal: Miha Zajc (34).

07.06.2019 AUSTRIA - SLOVENIA 1-0(0-0) 16th EC. Qualifiers
Wörthersee Stadion, Klagenfurt; Referee: Aleksei Kulbakov (Belarus); Attendance: 19,200
SVN: Jan Oblak, Bojan Jokić (Cap), Aljaž Struna, Miha Mevlja, Petar Stojanović, Josip Iličić, Jasmin Kurtić, Miha Zajc (69.Damjan Bohar), Domen Črnigoj (78.Robert Berić), Jaka Bijol (63.Denis Popovič), Andraž Šporar. Trainer: Matjaž Kek.

10.06.2019 LATVIA - SLOVENIA 0-5(0-4) 16th EC. Qualifiers
Daugava Stadions, Rīga; Referee: Kevin Clancy (Scotland); Attendance: 4,011
SVN: Jan Oblak, Bojan Jokić (Cap), Aljaž Struna, Miha Mevlja, Petar Stojanović, Josip Iličić, Denis Popovič (77.Luka Zahovič), Jasmin Kurtić, Miha Zajc (64.Jaka Bijol), Domen Črnigoj (83.Žan Majer), Robert Berić. Trainer: Matjaž Kek.
Goals: Domen Črnigoj (24, 27), Josip Iličić (29 penalty), Josip Iličić (44), Miha Zajc (47).

NATIONAL TEAM PLAYERS
(16.07.2018 – 15.07.2019)

Name	DOB	Caps	Goals	2018/2019:	*Club*
Goalkeepers					
Vid BELEC	06.06.1990	**13**	**0**	2018:	*UC Sampdoria Genova (ITA)*
Jan OBLAK	07.01.1993	**22**	**0**	2018/2019:	*Club Atlético de Madrid (ESP)*
Defenders					
Jure BALKOVEC	09.09.1994	**1**	**0**	2018:	*Hellas Verona FC (ITA)*
Miha BLAŽIČ	08.05.1993	**3**	**0**	2018:	*Ferencvárosi TC (HUN)*
Bojan JOKIĆ	17.05.1986	**98**	**1**	2018/2019:	*FK Ufa (RUS)*
Luka KRAJNC	19.09.1994	**4**	**0**	2018:	*Frosinone Calcio*
Miha MEVLJA	12.06.1990	**21**	**1**	2018: 21.02.2019->	*FK Zenit Saint Petersburg (RUS)* *FK Rostov (RUS)*
Nemanja MITROVIĆ	15.10.1992	**3**	**0**	2018:	*Jagiellonia Białystok (POL)*
Rudi POŽEG VANCAŠ	15.03.1994	**1**	**0**	2018:	*NK Celje*
Nejc SKUBIC	13.06.1989	**15**	**0**	2018:	*Konyaspor Kulübü (TUR)*
Petar STOJANOVIĆ	07.10.1995	**10**	**0**	2018/2019:	*GNK Dinamo Zagreb (CRO)*
Aljaž STRUNA	04.08.1990	**16**	**0**	2018: 01.01.2019->	*US Città di Palermo (ITA)* *Houston Dynamo (USA)*
Andraž STRUNA	23.04.1989	**27**	**0**	2018:	*Anorthosis FC Famagusta (CYP)*
Leo ŠTULAC	26.09.1994	**3**	**0**	2018:	*Parma FC (ITA)*
Midfielders					
Jaka BIJOL	05.02.1999	**6**	**0**	2018/2019:	*FK CSKA Moskva (RUS)*
Damjan BOHAR	18.10.1991	**3**	**0**	2019:	*Zagłębie Lubin*
Domen ČRNIGOJ	18.11.1995	**11**	**2**	2018/2019:	*FC Lugano (SUI)*
Amir DERVIŠEVIĆ	04.07.1992	**6**	**0**	2018:	*NK Maribor*
Josip ILIČIĆ	29.01.1988	**59**	**7**	2018/2019:	*Atalanta Bergamasca Calcio (ITA)*
Kevin KAMPL	09.10.1990	**28**	**2**	2018:	*RasenBallsport Leipzig (GER)*
Rene KRHIN	21.05.1990	**42**	**2**	2018/2019:	*FC Nantes (FRA)*
Jasmin KURTIĆ	10.01.1989	**52**	**1**	2018/2019:	*SPAL Ferrara (ITA)*
Žan MAJER	25.07.1992	**2**	**0**	2019:	*US Lecce (ITA)*
Denis POPOVIČ	15.10.1989	**2**	**0**	2019:	*FK Orenburg (RUS)*
Rajko ROTMAN	19.03.1989	**15**	**0**	2018:	*Kayserispor Kulübü (TUR)*
Benjamin VERBIČ	27.11.1993	**23**	**3**	2018/2019:	*FK Dinamo Kyiv (UKR)*
Miha ZAJC	01.07.1994	**15**	**5**	2018: 31.01.2019->	*Empoli FC (ITA)* *Fenerbahçe SK İstanbul (TUR)*
Forwards					
Robert BERIĆ	17.06.1991	**22**	**2**	2018/2019:	*AS Saint-Étienne (FRA)*
Roman BEZJAK	21.02.1989	**28**	**4**	2018/2019:	*Jagiellonia Białystok (POL)*
Tim MATAVŽ	13.01.1989	**37**	**10**	2018:	*SBV Vitesse Arnhem (NED)*
Andraž ŠPORAR	27.02.1994	**14**	**1**	2018/2019:	*ŠK Slovan Bratislava (SVK)*
Luka ZAHOVIČ	15.11.1995	**3**	**0**	2018/2019:	*NK Maribor*

National team coach

Tomaž KAVČIČ [04.12.2017 – 17.10.2018]	28.11.1953	7 M; 1 W; 1 D; 5 L; 5-11
Igor BENEDEJČIČ [03.11.-26.11.2018]	28.07.1969	2 M; 0 W; 2 D; 0 L; 2-2
Matjaž KEK [from 27.11.2018]	09.09.1961	4 M; 1 W; 2 D; 1 L; 7-3 Complete record as trainer of Slovenia: 53 M; 22 W; 10 D; 21 L; 68-44 (07.02.2007 – 11.10.2011) & (from 27.11.2018)

SPAIN

The Country:
Reino de España (Kingdom of Spain)
Capital: Madrid
Surface: 505,990 km²
Inhabitants: 46,733,038 [2018]
Time: UTC

The FA:
Real Federación Española de Fútbol
Ramón y Cajal, s/n Apartado postal 385, 28230 Las Rozas (Madrid)
Tel: +34 91 495 9800
Founded: 14.10.1909
Member of FIFA since: 1913
Member of UEFA since: 1954
Website: www.rfef.es

NATIONAL TEAM RECORDS

First international match:	28.08.1920, Bruxelles:	Spain – Denmark 1-0	
Most international caps:	Iker Casillas Fernández		- 167 caps (2000-2016)
Most international goals:	David Villa Sánchez		- 59 goals / 98 caps (2005-2017)

UEFA EUROPEAN CHAMPIONSHIP	
1960	Qualifiers
1964	**Final Tournament (Winners)**
1968	Qualifiers
1972	Qualifiers
1976	Qualifiers
1980	Final Tournament (Group Stage)
1984	Final Tournament (Runners-up)
1988	Final Tournament (Group Stage)
1992	Qualifiers
1996	Final Tournament (Quarter-Finals)
2000	Final Tournament (Quarter-Finals)
2004	Final Tournament (Group Stage)
2008	**Final Tournament (Winners)**
2012	**Final Tournament (Winners)**
2016	Final Tournament (2nd Round of 16)

FIFA WORLD CUP	
1930	Did not enter
1934	Final Tournament (Quarter-Finals)
1938	*Withdrew*
1950	Final Tournament (4th Place)
1954	Qualifiers
1958	Qualifiers
1962	Final Tournament (Group Stage)
1966	Final Tournament (Group Stage)
1970	Qualifiers
1974	Qualifiers
1978	Final Tournament (Group Stage)
1982	Final Tournament (2nd Round)
1986	Final Tournament (Quarter-Finals)
1990	Final Tournament (2nd Round of 16)
1994	Final Tournament (Quarter-Finals)
1998	Final Tournament (Group Stage)
2002	Final Tournament (Quarter-Finals)
2006	Final Tournament (2nd Round of 16)
2010	**Final Tournament (Winners)**
2014	Final Tournament (Group Stage)
2018	Final Tournament (2nd Round of 16)

UEFA NATIONS LEAGUE
2018/2019 – League A

OLYMPIC FOOTBALL TOURNAMENTS 1908-2016							
1908	-	**1948**	Did not enter	**1972**	Qualifiers	**1996**	Quarter-Finals
1912	-	**1952**	Did not enter	**1976**	Group Stage	**2000**	Runners-up
1920	Quarter-Finals	**1956**	Did not enter	**1980**	Group Stage	**2004**	Qualifiers
1924	Preliminary Round	**1960**	Did not enter	**1984**	Qualifiers	**2008**	Qualifiers
1928	Quarter-Finals	**1964**	Qualifiers	**1988**	Qualifiers	**2012**	Group Stage
1936	Did not enter	**1968**	Quarter-Finals	**1992**	**Winners**	**2016**	Qualifiers

FIFA CONFEDERATIONS CUP 1992-2017
2009 (3rd Place), 2013 (Runners-up)

SPANISH CLUB HONOURS IN EUROPEAN CLUB COMPETITIONS:

European Champion Clubs.Cup (1956-1992) / UEFA Champions League (1993-2019)		
Real Madrid CF	**13**	1955/1956, 1956/1957, 1957/1958, 1958/1959, 1959/1960, 1965/1966, 1997/1998, 1999/2000, 2001/2002, 2013/2014, 2015/2016, 2016/2017, 2017/2018
FC Barcelona	**5**	1991/1992, 2005/2006, 2008/2009, 2010/2011, 2014/2015
Fairs Cup (1858-1971) / UEFA Cup (1972-2009) / UEFA Europa League (2010-2019)		
Sevilla FC	**5**	2005/2006, 2006/2007, 2013/2014, 2014/2015, 2015/2016
FC Barcelona	**3**	1955-1958, 1958-1960, 1965/1966
Club Atlético de Madrid	**3**	2009/2010, 2011/2012, 2017/2018

Valencia CF	**3**	1961/1962, 1962/1963, 2003/2004
Real Madrid CF	**2**	1984/1985, 1985/1986
Real Zaragoza	**1**	1963/1964
UEFA Super Cup (1972-2018)		
FC Barcelona	**5**	1992, 1997, 2009, 2011, 2015
Real Madrid CF	**4**	2002, 2014, 2016, 2017
Club Atlético de Madrid	**3**	2010, 2012, 2018
Valencia CF	**2**	1980, 2004
Sevilla FC	**1**	2006
European Cup Winners.Cup 1961-1999*		
FC Barcelona	**4**	1978/1979, 1981/1982, 1988/1989, 1996/1997
Club Atlético de Madrid	**1**	1961/1962
Valencia CF	**1**	1979/1980
Real Zaragoza	**1**	1994/1995

**defunct competition*

NATIONAL COMPETITIONS TABLE OF HONOURS

	CHAMPIONS	CUP WINNERS	BEST GOALSCORERS	
1903	-	Athletic Club Bilbao	-	
1904	-	Athletic Club Bilbao	-	
1905	-	Madrid FC	-	
1906	-	Madrid FC	-	
1907	-	Madrid FC	-	
1908	-	Madrid FC	-	
1909	-	Real Sociedad de Fútbol San Sebastián	-	
1910	-	FC Barcelona (FEF)* Athletic Club Bilbao (UECF)**	-	
1911	-	Athletic Club Bilbao	-	
1912	-	FC Barcelona	-	
1913	-	Racing Club de Irún (FEF) FC Barcelona (UECF)	-	
1914	-	Athletic Club Bilbao	-	
1915	-	Athletic Club Bilbao	-	
1916	-	Athletic Club Bilbao	-	
1917	-	Madrid FC	-	
1918	-	Real Unión Club de Irún	-	
1919	-	Arenas Club de Getxo	-	
1920	-	FC Barcelona	-	
1921	-	Athletic Club Bilbao	-	
1922	-	FC Barcelona	-	
1923	-	Athletic Club Bilbao	-	
1924	-	Real Unión Club de Irún	-	
1925	-	FC Barcelona	-	
1926	-	FC Barcelona	-	
1927	-	Real Unión Club de Irún	-	
1928	-	FC Barcelona	-	
1929	FC Barcelona	RCD Español Barcelona	Francisco "Paco" Bienzobas Ocáriz (Real Sociedad de Fútbol San Sebastián)	14
1929/1930	Athletic Club Bilbao	Athletic Club Bilbao	Guillermo Gorostiza Paredes (Athletic Club Bilbao)	19
1930/1931	Athletic Club Bilbao	Athletic Club Bilbao	Agustín Sauto Arana "Bata" (Athletic Club Bilbao)	27
1931/1932	Real Madrid FC	Athletic Club Bilbao	Guillermo Gorostiza Paredes (Athletic Club Bilbao)	12
1932/1933	Real Madrid FC	Athletic Club Bilbao	Manuel Olivares Lapeña (Real Madrid FC)	16
1933/1934	Athletic Club Bilbao	Real Madrid FC	Isidro Lángara Galarraga (Real Oviedo CF)	27
1934/1935	Real Betis Balompié Sevilla	Sevilla FC	Isidro Lángara Galarraga (Real Oviedo CF)	26
1935/1936	Athletic Club Bilbao	Real Madrid FC	Isidro Lángara Galarraga (Real Oviedo CF)	27
1936/1937	*League Cancelled*	*No competition*	-	
1937/1938	*League Cancelled*	*No competition*	-	
1938/1939	*League Cancelled*	Sevilla FC	-	
1939/1940	Atlético Aviación Madrid	RCD Español Barcelona	Víctor Unamuno Ibarzabal (Athletic Club Bilbao)	22
1940/1941	Atlético Aviación Madrid	Valencia CF	Prudencio Sánchez Fernández "Pruden" (Atlético Aviación Madrid)	30
1941/1942	Valencia CF	CF Barcelona	Edmundo Suárez Trabanco "Mundo" (Valencia CF)	27
1942/1943	Atlético Club de Bilbao	Atlético Club de Bilbao	Mariano Martín Alonso (CF Barcelona)	32
1943/1944	Valencia CF	Atlético Club de Bilbao	Edmundo Suárez Trabanco "Mundo" (Valencia CF)	27
1944/1945	CF Barcelona	Atlético Club de Bilbao	Pedro Telmo Zarraonandía Montoya (Atlético Club de Bilbao)	19
1945/1946	Sevilla FC	Real Madrid CF	Pedro Telmo Zarraonandía Montoya (Atlético Club de Bilbao)	24
1946/1947	Valencia CF	Real Madrid CF	Pedro Telmo Zarraonandía Montoya (Atlético Club de Bilbao)	34
1947/1948	CF Barcelona	Sevilla FC	Manuel Fernández Fernández "Pahiño" (RC Celta de Vigo)	23

1948/1949	CF Barcelona	Valencia CF	César Rodríguez Álvarez (CF Barcelona)	28
1949/1950	Club Atlético de Madrid	Atlético Club de Bilbao	Pedro Telmo Zarraonandía Montoya (Atlético Club de Bilbao)	25
1950/1951	Club Atlético de Madrid	CF Barcelona	Pedro Telmo Zarraonandía Montoya (Atlético Club de Bilbao)	38
1951/1952	CF Barcelona	CF Barcelona	Manuel Fernández Fernández "Pahiño" (Real Madrid CF)	28
1952/1953	CF Barcelona	CF Barcelona	Pedro Telmo Zarraonandía Montoya (Atlético Club de Bilbao)	24
1953/1954	Real Madrid CF	Valencia CF	Alfredo Stéfano Di Stéfano Laulhé (Real Madrid CF)	27
1954/1955	Real Madrid CF	Atlético Club de Bilbao	Juan Arza Iñigo (Sevilla FC)	28
1955/1956	Atlético Club de Bilbao	Atlético Club de Bilbao	Alfredo Stéfano Di Stéfano Laulhé (Real Madrid CF)	24
1956/1957	Real Madrid CF	CF Barcelona	Alfredo Stéfano Di Stéfano Laulhé (Real Madrid CF)	31
1957/1958	Real Madrid CF	Atlético Club de Bilbao	Manuel Badenes Calduch (Real Valladolid CF) Alfredo Stéfano Di Stéfano Laulhé (Real Madrid CF) Ricardo de la Virgen (Valencia CF)	19
1958/1959	CF Barcelona	CF Barcelona	Alfredo Stéfano Di Stéfano Laulhé (Real Madrid CF	23
1959/1960	CF Barcelona	Club Atlético de Madrid	Ferenc Puskás (HUN, Real Madrid CF)	26
1960/1961	Real Madrid CF	Club Atlético de Madrid	Ferenc Puskás (HUN, Real Madrid CF)	27
1961/1962	Real Madrid CF	Real Madrid CF	Juan Roberto Seminario Rodríguez (PER, Real Zaragoza)	25
1962/1963	Real Madrid CF	CF Barcelona	Ferenc Puskás (HUN, Real Madrid CF)	26
1963/1964	Real Madrid CF	Real Zaragoza	Ferenc Puskás (HUN, Real Madrid CF)	20
1964/1965	Real Madrid CF	Club Atlético de Madrid	Cayetano Ré Ramírez (PAR, CF Barcelona)	25
1965/1966	Club Atlético de Madrid	Real Zaragoza	Luciano Sánchez Rodríguez "Vavá" (Elche CF)	19
1966/1967	Real Madrid CF	Valencia CF	Waldo Machado da Silva (BRA, Valencia CF)	24
1967/1968	Real Madrid CF	CF Barcelona	Fidel Uriarte Macho (Atlético Club de Bilbao)	22
1968/1969	Real Madrid CF	Atlético Club de Bilbao	Amancio Amaro Varela (Club Atlético de Madrid) José Eulogio Gárate Ormaechea (Real Madrid CF)	14
1969/1970	Club Atlético de Madrid	Real Madrid CF	Amancio Amaro Varela (Real Madrid CF) José Luis Aragonés Suárez (Club Atlético de Madrid) José Eulogio Gárate Ormaechea (Club Atlético de Madrid)	16
1970/1971	Valencia CF	CF Barcelona	José Eulogio Gárate Ormaechea (Club Atlético de Madrid) Carles Rexach i Cerdà (CF Barcelona)	17
1971/1972	Real Madrid CF	Club Atlético de Madrid	Enrique Porta Guíu (Granada CF)	20
1972/1973	Club Atlético de Madrid	Athletic Club Bilbao	Mariano Arias Chamorro "Marianín" (Real Oviedo CF)	19
1973/1974	CF Barcelona	Real Madrid CF	Enrique Castro González "Quini" (Real Sporting de Gijón)	20
1974/1975	Real Madrid CF	Real Madrid CF	Carlos Ruiz Herrero (Athletic Club Bilbao)	19
1975/1976	Real Madrid CF	Club Atlético de Madrid	Enrique Castro González "Quini" (Real Sporting de Gijón)	21
1976/1977	Club Atlético de Madrid	Real Betis Balompié Sevilla	Mario Alberto Kempes Chiodi (ARG, Valencia CF)	24
1977/1978	Real Madrid CF	FC Barcelona	Mario Alberto Kempes Chiodi (ARG, Valencia CF)	28
1978/1979	Real Madrid CF	Valencia CF	Johann Krankl (AUT, FC Barcelona)	29
1979/1980	Real Madrid CF	Real Madrid CF	Enrique Castro González "Quini" (Real Sporting de Gijón)	24
1980/1981	Real Sociedad de Fútbol San Sebastián	FC Barcelona	Enrique Castro González "Quini" (FC Barcelona)	20
1981/1982	Real Sociedad de Fútbol San Sebastián	Real Madrid CF	Enrique Castro González "Quini" (FC Barcelona)	26
1982/1983	Athletic Club Bilbao	FC Barcelona	Hipólito Rincón Povedano (Real Betis Balompié Sevilla)	20
1983/1984	Athletic Club Bilbao	Athletic Club Bilbao	Jorge Orosmán da Silva Echeverrito (URU, Real Valladolid CF) Juan Gómez González "Juanito" (Real Madrid CF)	17
1984/1985	FC Barcelona	Club Atlético de Madrid	Hugo Sánchez Márquez (MEX, Club Atlético de Madrid)	19
1985/1986	Real Madrid CF	Real Zaragoza	Hugo Sánchez Márquez (MEX, Real Madrid CF)	22
1986/1987	Real Madrid CF	Real Sociedad de Fútbol San Sebastián	Hugo Sánchez Márquez (MEX, Real Madrid CF)	34
1987/1988	Real Madrid CF	FC Barcelona	Hugo Sánchez Márquez (MEX, Real Madrid CF)	29
1988/1989	Real Madrid CF	Real Madrid CF	Baltazar Maria de Morais Júnior (BRA, Club Atlético de Madrid)	35
1989/1990	Real Madrid CF	FC Barcelona	Hugo Sánchez Márquez (MEX, Real Madrid CF)	38
1990/1991	FC Barcelona	Club Atlético de Madrid	Emilio Butragueño Santos (Real Madrid CF)	19
1991/1992	FC Barcelona	Club Atlético de Madrid	Manuel Sánchez Delgado "Manolo" (Club Atlético de Madrid)	27
1992/1993	FC Barcelona	Real Madrid CF	José Roberto Gama de Oliveira "Bebeto" (RC Deportivo La Coruña)	29
1993/1994	FC Barcelona	Real Zaragoza	Romário de Souza Faria (BRA, FC Barcelona)	30
1994/1995	Real Madrid CF	RC Deportivo La Coruña	Iván Luis Zamorano Zamora (CHI, Real Madrid CF)	28
1995/1996	Club Atlético de Madrid	Club Atlético de Madrid	Juan Antonio Pizzi Torroja (CD Tenerife)	31
1996/1997	Real Madrid CF	FC Barcelona	Ronaldo Luís Nazário de Lima (BRA, FC Barcelona)	34
1997/1998	FC Barcelona	FC Barcelona	Christian Vieri (Club Atlético de Madrid)	24
1998/1999	FC Barcelona	Valencia CF	Raúl González Blanco (Real Madrid CF)	25
1999/2000	RC Deportivo La Coruña	RCD Espanyol Barcelona	Salvador Ballesta Vialcho "Salva" (Real Racing Club de Santander)	27
2000/2001	Real Madrid CF	Real Zaragoza	Raúl González Blanco (Real Madrid CF)	24
2001/2002	Valencia CF	RC Deportivo La Coruña	Diego Tristán Herrera (RC Deportivo La Coruña)	21
2002/2003	Real Madrid CF	RCD Mallorca	Rudolphus Antonius "Roy" Makaay (NED, RC Deportivo La Coruña)	29
2003/2004	Valencia CF	Real Zaragoza	Ronaldo Luís Nazário de Lima (BRA, Real Madrid CF)	25
2004/2005	FC Barcelona	Real Betis Balompié Sevilla	Diego Forlán Corazzo (URU, Villarreal CF)	25

2005/2006	FC Barcelona	RCD Espanyol Barcelona	Samuel Eto'o Fils (CMR, FC Barcelona)	26
2006/2007	Real Madrid CF	Sevilla FC	Rutgerus Johannes Martinus "Ruud" van Nistelrooy (NED, Real Madrid CF)	25
2007/2008	Real Madrid CF	Valencia CF	Daniel González Güiza (RCD Mallorca)	27
2008/2009	FC Barcelona	FC Barcelona	Diego Forlán Corazzo (URU, Club Atlético de Madrid)	32
2009/2010	FC Barcelona	Sevilla FC	Lionel Andrés Messi Cuccittini (ARG, FC Barcelona)	34
2010/2011	FC Barcelona	Real Madrid CF	Cristiano Ronaldo dos Santos Aveiro (POR, Real Madrid CF)	40
2011/2012	Real Madrid CF	FC Barcelona	Lionel Andrés Messi Cuccittini (ARG, FC Barcelona)	50
2012/2013	FC Barcelona	Club Atlético de Madrid	Lionel Andrés Messi Cuccittini (ARG, FC Barcelona)	46
2013/2014	Club Atlético de Madrid	Real Madrid CF	Cristiano Ronaldo dos Santos Aveiro (POR, Real Madrid CF)	31
2014/2015	FC Barcelona	FC Barcelona	Cristiano Ronaldo dos Santos Aveiro (POR, Real Madrid CF)	48
2015/2016	FC Barcelona	FC Barcelona	Luis Alberto Suárez Díaz (URU, FC Barcelona)	40
2016/2017	Real Madrid CF	FC Barcelona	Lionel Andrés Messi Cuccittini (ARG, FC Barcelona)	37
2017/2018	FC Barcelona	FC Barcelona	Lionel Andrés Messi Cuccittini (ARG, FC Barcelona)	34
2018/2019	FC Barcelona	Valencia CF	Lionel Andrés Messi Cuccittini (ARG, FC Barcelona)	36

*FEF = Federación Española de Fútbol
**UECF = Unión Española de Clubes de Fútbol
Name changements:
Real Madrid CF = Madrid FC (1902-1920); Real Madrid FC (1920-1938), Real Madrid CF (since 1938).
Athletic Club Bilbao = Atlético Club de Bilbao (1940-1972)
FC FC Barcelona = CF FC Barcelona (1941-1974)
Real Unión Club de Irún = Racing Club de Irún (1901-1915)
RCD Espayol Barcelona = RCD Español Barcelona Barcelona (1910-1995)
Sevilla FC = Sevilla CF (1938-1986)
Club Atlético de Madrid = Athletic Club Madrid (1903-1926); Club Club Atlético de Madrid (1926-1939); Atlético Aviación Madrid (1939-1947); Club Atlético de Madrid (since 1947)
Valencia CF = Valencia FC (1919-1940)

NATIONAL CHAMPIONSHIP
La Liga 2018/2019
(17.08.2018 – 19.05.2019)

Results

Round 1 [17-20.08.2018]
Girona FC - Real Valladolid 0-0
Real Betis - Levante UD 0-3(0-1)
Celta Vigo - Espanyol Barcelona 1-1(0-1)
Villarreal CF - Real Sociedad 1-2(1-1)
FC Barcelona - CD Alavés 3-0(0-0)
SD Eibar - SD Huesca 1-2(0-2)
Rayo Vallecano - Sevilla FC 1-4(0-3)
Real Madrid - Getafe CF 2-0(1-0)
Valencia CF - Atlético Madrid 1-1(0-1)
Athletic Bilbao - CD Leganés 2-1(1-1)

Round 2 [24-27.08.2018]
Getafe CF - SD Eibar 2-0(1-0)
CD Leganés - Real Sociedad 2-2(0-2)
CD Alavés - Real Betis 0-0
Atlético Madrid - Rayo Vallecano 1-0(0-0)
Real Valladolid - FC Barcelona 0-1(0-0)
Espanyol Barcelona - Valencia CF 2-0(0-0)
Girona FC - Real Madrid 1-4(1-1)
Sevilla FC - Villarreal CF 0-0
Levante UD - Celta Vigo 1-2(0-2)
Athletic Bilbao - SD Huesca 2-2(0-0)

Round 3 [31.08.-02.09.2018]
Getafe CF - Real Valladolid 0-0
SD Eibar - Real Sociedad 2-1(1-1)
Villarreal CF - Girona FC 0-1(0-0)
Celta Vigo - Atlético Madrid 2-0(0-0)
Real Madrid - CD Leganés 4-1(1-1)
Levante UD - Valencia CF 2-2(2-1)
CD Alavés - Espanyol Barcelona 2-1(0-1)
FC Barcelona - SD Huesca 8-2(3-2)
Real Betis - Sevilla FC 1-0(0-0)
Rayo Vallecano - Athletic Bilbao 1-1(1-0)

Round 4 [14-17.09.2018]
SD Huesca - Rayo Vallecano 0-1(0-1)
Atlético Madrid - SD Eibar 1-1(0-0)
Real Sociedad - FC Barcelona 1-2(1-0)
Valencia CF - Real Betis 0-0
Athletic Bilbao - Real Madrid 1-1(1-0)
CD Leganés - Villarreal CF 0-1(0-0)
Espanyol Barcelona - Levante UD 1-0(0-0)
Real Valladolid - CD Alavés 0-1(0-0)
Sevilla FC - Getafe CF 0-2(0-2)
Girona FC - Celta Vigo 3-2(2-1)

Round 5 [21-23.09.2018]
SD Huesca - Real Sociedad 0-1(0-0)
Rayo Vallecano - CD Alavés 1-5(1-2)
Celta Vigo - Real Valladolid 3-3(2-1)
SD Eibar - CD Leganés 1-0(0-0)
Getafe CF - Atlético Madrid 0-2(0-1)
Real Madrid - Espanyol Barcelona 1-0(1-0)
Levante UD - Sevilla FC 2-6(1-4)
Villarreal CF - Valencia CF 0-0
Real Betis - Athletic Bilbao 2-2(0-2)
FC Barcelona - Girona FC 2-2(1-1)

Round 6 [25-27.09.2018]
Espanyol Barcelona - SD Eibar 1-0(0-0)
Real Sociedad - Rayo Vallecano 2-2(1-2)
Atlético Madrid - SD Huesca 3-0(3-0)
Athletic Bilbao - Villarreal CF 0-3(0-0)
CD Leganés - FC Barcelona 2-1(0-1)
Valencia CF - Celta Vigo 1-1(1-0)
Sevilla FC - Real Madrid 3-0(3-0)
CD Alavés - Getafe CF 1-1(0-0)
Real Valladolid - Levante UD 2-1(0-0)
Girona FC - Real Betis 0-1(0-0)

Round 7 [28.09.-01.10.2018]
Rayo Vallecano - Espanyol Barc. 2-2(1-2)
Real Sociedad - Valencia CF 0-1(0-1)
FC Barcelona - Athletic Bilbao 1-1(0-1)
SD Eibar - Sevilla FC 1-3(0-0)
Real Madrid - Atlético Madrid 0-0
SD Huesca - Girona FC 1-1(0-1)
Villarreal CF - Real Valladolid 0-1(0-0)
Levante UD - CD Alavés 2-1(2-1)
Real Betis - CD Leganés 1-0(0-0)
Celta Vigo - Getafe CF 1-1(1-0)

Round 8 [05-07.10.2018]
Athletic Bilbao - Real Sociedad 1-3(1-1)
Girona FC - SD Eibar 2-3(2-2)
Getafe CF - Levante UD 0-1(0-0)
CD Alavés - Real Madrid 1-0(0-0)
CD Leganés - Rayo Vallecano 1-0(1-0)
Real Valladolid - SD Huesca 1-0(1-0)
Atlético Madrid - Real Betis 1-0(0-0)
Espanyol Barcelona - Villarreal CF 3-1(1-1)
Sevilla FC - Celta Vigo 2-1(1-0)
Valencia CF - FC Barcelona 1-1(1-1)

Round 9 [19-22.10.2018]
Celta Vigo - CD Alavés 0-1(0-0)
Real Madrid - Levante UD 1-2(0-2)
Valencia CF - CD Leganés 1-1(0-0)
Villarreal CF - Atlético Madrid 1-1(0-0)
FC Barcelona - Sevilla FC 4-2(2-0)
Rayo Vallecano - Getafe CF 1-2(0-0)
SD Eibar - Athletic Bilbao 1-1(1-1)
SD Huesca - Espanyol Barcelona 0-2(0-1)
Real Betis - Real Valladolid 0-1(0-1)
Real Sociedad - Girona FC 0-0

Round 10 [26-28.10.2018]
Real Valladolid - Espanyol Barcelona 1-1(0-1)
Girona FC - Rayo Vallecano 2-1(2-0)
Athletic Bilbao - Valencia CF 0-0
Celta Vigo - SD Eibar 4-0(2-0)
Levante UD - CD Leganés 2-0(1-0)
Atlético Madrid - Real Sociedad 2-0(1-0)
Getafe CF - Real Betis 2-0(0-0)
FC Barcelona - Real Madrid 5-1(2-0)
CD Alavés - Villarreal CF 2-1(0-1)
Sevilla FC - SD Huesca 2-1(0-0)

Round 11 [03-05.11.2018]
CD Leganés - Atlético Madrid 1-1(0-0)
Real Madrid - Real Valladolid 2-0(0-0)
Valencia CF - Girona FC 0-1(0-0)
Rayo Vallecano - FC Barcelona 2-3(1-1)
SD Eibar - CD Alavés 2-1(0-1)
Villarreal CF - Levante UD 1-1(0-0)
Real Sociedad - Sevilla FC 0-0
SD Huesca - Getafe CF 1-1(0-0)
Real Betis - Celta Vigo 3-3(1-0)
Espanyol Barcelona - Athletic Bilbao 1-0(1-0)

Round 12 [09-11.11.2018]
Levante UD - Real Sociedad 1-3(1-0)
Real Valladolid - SD Eibar 0-0
Getafe CF - Valencia CF 0-1(0-0)
Atlético Madrid - Athletic Bilbao 3-2(0-1)
Girona FC - CD Leganés 0-0
CD Alavés - SD Huesca 2-1(1-1)
FC Barcelona - Real Betis 3-4(0-2)
Rayo Vallecano - Villarreal CF 2-2(1-1)
Sevilla FC - Espanyol Barcelona 2-1(0-1)
Celta Vigo - Real Madrid 2-4(0-1)

Round 13 [23-26.11.2018]
CD Leganés - CD Alavés 1-0(1-0)
SD Eibar - Real Madrid 3-0(1-0)
Valencia CF - Rayo Vallecano 3-0(1-0)
SD Huesca - Levante UD 2-2(1-1)
Atlético Madrid - FC Barcelona 1-1(0-0)
Athletic Bilbao - Getafe CF 1-1(0-0)
Sevilla FC - Real Valladolid 1-0(1-0)
Espanyol Barcelona - Girona FC 1-3(0-2)
Villarreal CF - Real Betis 2-1(0-0)
Real Sociedad - Celta Vigo 2-1(1-0)

Round 14 [30.11.-03.12.2018]
Rayo Vallecano - SD Eibar 1-0(0-0)
Celta Vigo - SD Huesca 2-0(1-0)
Real Valladolid - CD Leganés 2-4(0-2)
Getafe CF - Espanyol Barcelona 3-0(0-0)
Real Madrid - Valencia CF 2-0(1-0)
Real Betis - Real Sociedad 1-0(1-0)
Girona FC - Atlético Madrid 1-1(1-0)
FC Barcelona - Villarreal CF 2-0(1-0)
CD Alavés - Sevilla FC 1-1(1-0)
Levante UD - Athletic Bilbao 3-0(1-0)

Round 15 [07-10.12.2018]
CD Leganés - Getafe CF 1-1(0-1)
Atlético Madrid - CD Alavés 3-0(1-0)
Valencia CF - Sevilla FC 1-1(0-0)
Villarreal CF - Celta Vigo 2-3(0-1)
Espanyol Barcelona - FC Barcelona 0-4(0-3)
SD Eibar - Levante UD 4-4(1-2)
SD Huesca - Real Madrid 0-1(0-1)
Real Sociedad - Real Valladolid 1-2(0-1)
Real Betis - Rayo Vallecano 2-0(0-0)
Athletic Bilbao - Girona FC 1-0(0-0)

Round 16 [14-17.12.2018]
Celta Vigo - CD Leganés 0-0
Getafe CF - Real Sociedad 1-0(1-0)
Real Valladolid - Atlético Madrid 2-3(0-2)
Real Madrid - Rayo Vallecano 1-0(1-0)
SD Eibar - Valencia CF 1-1(0-1)
Sevilla FC - Girona FC 2-0(0-0)
Espanyol Barcelona - Real Betis 1-3(1-1)
SD Huesca - Villarreal CF 2-2(1-0)
Levante UD - FC Barcelona 0-5(0-2)
CD Alavés - Athletic Bilbao 0-0

Round 17 [21-23.12.2018]
Girona FC - Getafe CF 1-1(0-0)
Real Sociedad - CD Alavés 0-1(0-1)
Real Betis - SD Eibar 1-1(1-0)
Atlético Madrid - Espanyol Barcel. 1-0(0-0)
FC Barcelona - Celta Vigo 2-0(2-0)
Athletic Bilbao - Real Valladolid 1-1(1-0)
Valencia CF - SD Huesca 2-1(1-0)
CD Leganés - Sevilla FC 1-1(1-0)
Rayo Vallecano - Levante UD 2-1(1-0)
Villarreal - Real Madrid 2-2(1-2) [03.01.2019]

Round 18 [04-07.01.2019]
Levante UD - Girona FC 2-2(0-1)
Espanyol Barcelona - CD Leganés 1-0(1-0)
Real Valladolid - Rayo Vallecano 0-1(0-1)
CD Alavés - Valencia CF 2-1(2-1)
SD Huesca - Real Betis 2-1(0-0)
SD Eibar - Villarreal CF 0-0
Sevilla FC - Atlético Madrid 1-1(1-1)
Real Madrid - Real Sociedad 0-2(0-1)
Getafe CF - FC Barcelona 1-2(1-2)
Celta Vigo - Athletic Bilbao 1-2(1-1)

Round 19 [11-14.01.2019]
Rayo Vallecano - Celta Vigo 4-2(2-2)
CD Leganés - SD Huesca 1-0(0-0)
Valencia CF - Real Valladolid 1-1(0-0)
Girona FC - CD Alavés 1-1(1-0)
Villarreal CF - Getafe CF 1-2(0-0)
Atlético Madrid - Levante UD 1-0(0-0)
Athletic Bilbao - Sevilla FC 2-0(1-0)
FC Barcelona - SD Eibar 3-0(1-0)
Real Betis - Real Madrid 1-2(0-1)
Real Sociedad - Espanyol Barcelona 3-2(2-2)

Round 20 [18-21.01.2019]
Getafe CF - CD Alavés 4-0(1-0)
Real Madrid - Sevilla FC 2-0(0-0)
SD Huesca - Atlético Madrid 0-3(0-1)
Celta Vigo - Valencia CF 1-2(1-0)
Real Betis - Girona FC 3-2(1-2)
Villarreal CF - Athletic Bilbao 1-1(0-1)
Levante UD - Real Valladolid 2-0(1-0)
Rayo Vallecano - Real Sociedad 2-2(2-1)
FC Barcelona - CD Leganés 3-1(1-0)
SD Eibar - Espanyol Barcelona 3-0(1-0)

Round 21 [26-28.01.2019]
Sevilla FC - Levante UD 5-0(0-0)
Atlético Madrid - Getafe CF 2-0(2-0)
CD Leganés - SD Eibar 2-2(0-2)
Valencia CF - Villarreal CF 3-0(1-0)
Real Valladolid - Celta Vigo 2-1(0-1)
Girona FC - FC Barcelona 0-2(0-1)
Athletic Bilbao - Real Betis 1-0(1-0)
Real Sociedad - SD Huesca 0-0
Espanyol Barcelona - Real Madrid 2-4(1-3)
CD Alavés - Rayo Vallecano 0-1(0-0)

Round 22 [01-04.02.2019]
SD Huesca - Real Valladolid 4-0(1-0)
Levante UD - Getafe CF 0-0
Real Sociedad - Athletic Bilbao 2-1(2-0)
FC Barcelona - Valencia CF 2-2(1-2)
Celta Vigo - Sevilla FC 1-0(0-0)
Villarreal CF - Espanyol Barcelona 2-2(1-0)
Real Betis - Atlético Madrid 1-0(0-0)
SD Eibar - Girona FC 3-0(1-0)
Real Madrid - CD Alavés 3-0(1-0)
Rayo Vallecano - CD Leganés 1-2(0-1)

Round 23 [08-11.02.2019]
Real Valladolid - Villarreal CF 0-0
Getafe CF - Celta Vigo 3-1(1-1)
Atlético Madrid - Real Madrid 1-3(1-2)
Espanyol Barcel. - Rayo Vallecano 2-1(0-1)
Girona FC - SD Huesca 0-2(0-2)
CD Leganés - Real Betis 3-0(2-0)
Valencia CF - Real Sociedad 0-0
Sevilla FC - SD Eibar 2-2(0-1)
Athletic Bilbao - FC Barcelona 0-0
CD Alavés - Levante UD 2-0(1-0)

Round 24 [15-18.02.2019]
SD Eibar - Getafe CF 2-2(0-1)
Celta Vigo - Levante UD 1-4(0-2)
Rayo Vallecano - Atlético Madrid 0-1(0-0)
Real Sociedad - CD Leganés 3-0(0-0)
FC Barcelona - Real Valladolid 1-0(1-0)
Real Madrid - Girona FC 1-2(1-0)
Valencia CF - Espanyol Barcelona 0-0
Villarreal CF - Sevilla FC 3-0(2-0)
Real Betis - CD Alavés 1-1(1-1)
SD Huesca - Athletic Bilbao 0-1(0-1)

Round 25 [22-25.02.2019]
Espanyol Barcelona - SD Huesca 1-1(0-0)
Getafe CF - Rayo Vallecano 2-1(1-0)
Sevilla FC - FC Barcelona 2-4(2-1)
CD Alavés - Celta Vigo 0-0
Athletic Bilbao - SD Eibar 1-0(1-0)
CD Leganés - Valencia CF 1-1(0-1)
Atlético Madrid - Villarreal CF 2-0(1-0)
Real Valladolid - Real Betis 0-2(0-1)
Levante UD - Real Madrid 1-2(0-1)
Girona FC - Real Sociedad 0-0

Round 26 [01-04.03.2019]
Rayo Vallecano - Girona FC 0-2(0-1)
Espanyol Barcelona - Real Valladolid 3-1(1-1)
Villarreal CF - CD Alavés 1-2(0-0)
SD Huesca - Sevilla FC 2-1(1-0)
Real Madrid - FC Barcelona 0-1(0-1)
SD Eibar - Celta Vigo 1-0(0-0)
Real Betis - Getafe CF 1-2(0-2)
Real Sociedad - Atlético Madrid 0-2(0-2)
Valencia CF - Athletic Bilbao 2-0(0-0)
CD Leganés - Levante UD 1-0(1-0)

Round 27 [08-10.03.2019]
Athletic Bilbao - Espanyol Barcelona 1-1(0-1)
CD Alavés - SD Eibar 1-1(0-0)
Atlético Madrid - CD Leganés 1-0(0-0)
FC Barcelona - Rayo Vallecano 3-1(1-1)
Getafe CF - SD Huesca 2-1(0-1)
Celta Vigo - Real Betis 0-1(0-0)
Girona FC - Valencia CF 2-3(1-1)
Levante UD - Villarreal CF 0-2(0-0)
Sevilla FC - Real Sociedad 5-2(1-1)
Real Valladolid - Real Madrid 1-4(1-1)

Round 28 [15-17.03.2019]
Real Sociedad - Levante UD 1-1(1-0)
SD Huesca - CD Alavés 1-3(1-1)
Real Madrid - Celta Vigo 2-0(0-0)
Athletic Bilbao - Atlético Madrid 2-0(0-0)
CD Leganés - Girona FC 0-2(0-2)
SD Eibar - Real Valladolid 1-2(0-0)
Espanyol Barcelona - Sevilla FC 0-1(0-0)
Valencia CF - Getafe CF 0-0
Villarreal CF - Rayo Vallecano 3-1(0-1)
Real Betis - FC Barcelona 1-4(0-2)

Round 29 [29-31.03.2019]
Girona FC - Athletic Bilbao 1-2(1-0)
Getafe CF - CD Leganés 0-2(0-0)
FC Barcelona - Espanyol Barcelona 2-0(0-0)
Celta Vigo - Villarreal CF 3-2(0-2)
CD Alavés - Atlético Madrid 0-4(0-2)
Levante UD - SD Eibar 2-2(2-1)
Rayo Vallecano - Real Betis 1-1(1-0)
Sevilla FC - Valencia CF 0-1(0-1)
Real Valladolid - Real Sociedad 1-1(1-0)
Real Madrid - SD Huesca 3-2(1-1)

Round 30 [02-04.04.2019]
Atlético Madrid - Girona FC 2-0(0-0)
Espanyol Barcelona - Getafe CF 1-1(0-0)
Villarreal CF - FC Barcelona 4-4(1-2)
Athletic Bilbao - Levante UD 3-2(2-0)
SD Eibar - Rayo Vallecano 2-1(0-1)
SD Huesca - Celta Vigo 3-3(0-1)
Valencia CF - Real Madrid 2-1(1-0)
Sevilla FC - CD Alavés 2-0(1-0)
CD Leganés - Real Valladolid 1-0(0-0)
Real Sociedad - Real Betis 2-1(1-0)

Round 31 [06-07.04.2019]
Girona FC - Espanyol Barcelona 1-2(0-0)
Real Madrid - SD Eibar 2-1(0-1)
Rayo Vallecano - Valencia CF 2-0(1-0)
FC Barcelona - Atlético Madrid 2-0(0-0)
CD Alavés - CD Leganés 1-1(1-0)
Getafe CF - Athletic Bilbao 1-0(0-0)
Real Valladolid - Sevilla FC 0-2(0-0)
Celta Vigo - Real Sociedad 3-1(0-1)
Levante UD - SD Huesca 2-2(1-0)
Real Betis - Villarreal CF 2-1(1-1)

Round 32 [13-15.04.2019]
Espanyol Barcelona - CD Alavés 2-1(1-0)
SD Huesca - FC Barcelona 0-0
Atlético Madrid - Celta Vigo 2-0(1-0)
Sevilla FC - Real Betis 3-2(1-0)
Real Valladolid - Getafe CF 2-2(1-1)
Athletic Bilbao - Rayo Vallecano 3-2(1-1)
Real Sociedad - SD Eibar 1-1(1-0)
Girona FC - Villarreal CF 0-1(0-1)
Valencia CF - Levante UD 3-1(1-0)
CD Leganés - Real Madrid 1-1(1-0)

Round 33 [19-21.04.2019]
CD Alavés - Real Valladolid 2-2(2-1)
Celta Vigo - Girona FC 2-1(1-0)
SD Eibar - Atlético Madrid 0-1(0-0)
Rayo Vallecano - SD Huesca 0-0
FC Barcelona - Real Sociedad 2-1(1-0)
Levante UD - Espanyol Barcelona 2-2(0-1)
Getafe CF - Sevilla FC 3-0(2-0)
Real Madrid - Athletic Bilbao 3-0(0-0)
Villarreal CF - CD Leganés 2-1(0-0)
Real Betis - Valencia CF 1-2(0-1)

Round 34 [23-25.04.2019]
SD Huesca - SD Eibar 2-0(0-0)
Real Valladolid - Girona FC 1-0(0-0)
CD Alavés - FC Barcelona 0-2(0-0)
Atlético Madrid - Valencia CF 3-2(1-1)
CD Leganés - Athletic Bilbao 0-1(0-1)
Espanyol Barcelona - Celta Vigo 1-1(1-0)
Levante UD - Real Betis 4-0(2-0)
Sevilla FC - Rayo Vallecano 5-0(0-0)
Real Sociedad - Villarreal CF 0-1(0-0)
Getafe CF - Real Madrid 0-0

Round 35 [27-29.04.2019]
Athletic Bilbao - CD Alavés 1-1(1-1)
Atlético Madrid - Real Valladolid 1-0(0-0)
CD Leganés - Celta Vigo 0-0
FC Barcelona - Levante UD 1-0(0-0)
Valencia CF - SD Eibar 0-1(0-0)
Girona FC - Sevilla FC 1-0(0-0)
Real Sociedad - Getafe CF 2-1(1-0)
Villarreal CF - SD Huesca 1-1(1-0)
Rayo Vallecano - Real Madrid 1-0(1-0)
Real Betis - Espanyol Barcelona 1-1(0-1)

Round 36 [03-05.05.2019]
Sevilla FC - CD Leganés 0-3(0-2)
Levante UD - Rayo Vallecano 4-1(2-0)
Espanyol Barcel. - Atlético Madrid 3-0(1-0)
CD Alavés - Real Sociedad 0-1(0-1)
Celta Vigo - FC Barcelona 2-0(0-0)
Getafe CF - Girona FC 2-0(1-0)
SD Eibar - Real Betis 1-0(1-0)
Real Madrid - Villarreal CF 3-2(2-1)
Real Valladolid - Athletic Bilbao 1-0(1-0)
SD Huesca - Valencia CF 2-6(0-5)

Round 37 [12.05.2019]
Athletic Bilbao - Celta Vigo 3-1(3-0)
Atlético Madrid - Sevilla FC 1-1(1-0)
FC Barcelona - Getafe CF 2-0(1-0)
Real Betis - SD Huesca 2-1(1-0)
Girona FC - Levante UD 1-2(0-0)
Rayo Vallecano - Real Valladolid 1-2(0-1)
Valencia CF - CD Alavés 3-1(2-1)
Villarreal CF - SD Eibar 1-0(0-0)
CD Leganés - Espanyol Barcelona 0-2(0-1)
Real Sociedad - Real Madrid 3-1(1-1)

Round 38 [18-19.05.2019]
Levante UD - Atlético Madrid 2-2(2-0)
Espanyol Barcelona - Real Sociedad 2-0(0-0)
Getafe CF - Villarreal CF 2-2(1-1)
Sevilla FC - Athletic Bilbao 2-0(1-0)
Real Valladolid - Valencia CF 0-2(0-1)
CD Alavés - Girona FC 2-1(1-0)
Celta Vigo - Rayo Vallecano 2-2(0-1)
SD Huesca - CD Leganés 2-1(0-1)
Real Madrid - Real Betis 0-2(0-0)
SD Eibar - FC Barcelona 2-2(2-2)

Final Standings

1.	**FC Barcelona**	38	26	9	3	90	-	36	87
2.	Club Atlético de Madrid	38	22	10	6	55	-	29	76
3.	Real Madrid CF	38	21	5	12	63	-	46	68
4.	Valencia CF	38	15	16	7	51	-	35	61
5.	Getafe CF	38	15	14	9	48	-	35	59
6.	Sevilla FC	38	17	8	13	62	-	47	59
7.	RCD Espanyol Barcelona	38	14	11	13	48	-	50	53
8.	Athletic Club Bilbao	38	13	14	11	41	-	45	53
9.	Real Sociedad de Fútbol San Sebastián	38	13	11	14	45	-	46	50
10.	Real Betis Balompié Sevilla	38	14	8	16	44	-	52	50
11.	Deportivo Alavés Vitoria-Gasteiz	38	13	11	14	39	-	50	50
12.	SD Eibar	38	11	14	13	46	-	50	47
13.	CD Leganés	38	11	12	15	37	-	43	45
14.	Villarreal CF	38	10	14	14	49	-	52	44
15.	Levante UD Valencia	38	11	11	16	59	-	66	44
16.	Real Valladolid CF	38	10	11	17	32	-	51	41
17.	RC Celta de Vigo	38	10	11	17	53	-	62	41
18.	Girona FC (*Relegated*)	38	9	10	19	37	-	53	37
19.	SD Huesca (*Relegated*)	38	7	12	19	43	-	65	33
20.	Rayo Vallecano de Madrid (*Relegated*)	38	8	8	22	41	-	70	32

Top goalscorers:

36 Lionel Andrés Messi Cuccittini (ARG)
FC Barcelona

21 Karim Mostafa Benzema (FRA)
Real Madrid CF

21 Luis Alberto Suárez Díaz (URU)
FC Barcelona

20 Iago Aspas Juncal
RC Celta de Vigo

19 Cristhian Ricardo Stuani Curbelo (URU)
Girona FC

18 Wissam Ben Yedder (FRA)
Sevilla FC

NATIONAL CUP
Copa del Rey 2018/2019

First Round [05.09.2018]

CD Mensajero - SD Compostela	0-3	UCAM Murcia CF - AD Ceuta FC	2-0
UD Poblense - Ontinyent CF	1-4	Barakaldo CF - UD Mutilvera	3-4 pen
Club Rápido de Bouzas - Unionistas de Salamanca	0-4	CD Mirandés - Real Racing Club de Santander	0-1
CF Internacional de Madrid - CF Fuenlabrada	4-5 pen	CD Calahorra - RS Gimnástica Torrelavega	4-2 pen
CDA Navalcarnero - CD Leonesa	0-2	UE Cornellà - UE Sant Andreu	2-3 pen
UP Langreo - UD Logroñés	1-2	Yeclano Deportivo - UD Melilla	1-2 aet
Club Gernika - SCD Durango	1-0	Marbella FC - CD Ebro	0-1
CD Castellón - UB Conquense	1-0	CD Don Benito - FC Cartagena	0-1
Club Lleida Esportiu - CD Teruel	2-0	Talavera CF - Real Jaén CF	3-4 pen

Second Round [11-13.09.2018]

Málaga CF - UD Almería	1-2	CF Villanovense - CF Badalona	2-1
RCD Mallorca - Real Oviedo	1-0	UD Melilla - CD Tudelano	3-0
CD Ebro - Real Murcia CF	1-1 aet; 5-4 pen	Lorca FC - Unionistas de Salamanca CF	2-1 aet
Ontinyent CF - Real Jaén CF	1-1 aet; 6-5 pen	Real Zaragoza - RC Deportivo La Coruña	2-1
CA Osasuna Pamplona - CF Reus Deportiu	1-2	FC Cartagena - UD Logroñés	1-1 aet; 4-5 pen
AD Alcorcón - Extremadura UD Almendralejo	1-0	CD Tenerife - Cádiz CF	1-2
Club Lleida Esportiu - SD Compostela	1-0	Córdoba CF - Club Gimnàstic de Tarragona	2-0
UCAM Murcia CF - Real Racing Club de Santander	0-2	CD Numancia - Real Sporting de Gijón	1-2
CD Leonesa - CF Fuenlabrada	1-1 aet; 5-4 pen	Albacete Balompié - CD Lugo	2-3
UE Sant Andreu - Club Gernika	1-0 aet	UD Las Palmas - CF Rayo Majadahonda	1-2
CD Calahorra - CD Castellón	2-0	Elche CF - Granada CF	2-1

Third Round [16.-1810.2018]

Elche CF - Córdoba CF	1-4	UD Melilla - Ontinyent CF	2-0
CD Ebro - Club Lleida Esportiu	2-1	Lorca FC - CD Leonesa	0-3
CD Lugo - AD Alcorcón	1-0	Real Zaragoza - Cádiz CF	0-1
UD Mutilvera - CF Villanovense	1-3	CF Rayo Majadahonda - Real Sporting de Gijón	1-1 aet; 3-4 pen
UE Sant Andreu - CD Calahorra	1-0 aet	UD Almería - CF Reus Deportiu	3-1
Real Racing Club de Santander - UD Logroñés	1-0		

Fourth Round [30-31.10./01.11./28.11./04-06.12.2018]

CD Ebro - Valencia CF	1-2 / 0-1	CD Leonesa - FC Barcelona	0-1 / 1-4
CD Lugo - Levante UD Valencia	1-1 / 0-2	Real Sporting de Gijón - SD Eibar	2-0 / 2-2
CD Leganés - Rayo Vallecano de Madrid	2-2 / 1-0	CF Villanovense - Sevilla FC	0-0 / 0-1
UE Sant Andreu - Club Atlético de Madrid	0-1 / 0-4	RC Celta Vigo - Real Sociedad de Fút. San Sebastián	1-1 / 0-2
UD Melilla - Real Madrid CF	0-4 / 1-6	UD Almería - Villarreal CF	3-3 / 0-8
RCD Mallorca - Real Valladolid CF	1-2 / 1-2	Cádiz CF - RCD Espanyol Barcelona	2-1 / 0-1
Córdoba CF - Getafe CF	1-2 / 1-5	Real Racing Club de Santander - Real Betis	0-1 / 0-4
Deportivo Alavés - Girona FC	2-2 / 1-2	Athletic Bilbao - SD Huesca	4-0 / 4-0

1/8-Finals [08-10/15-17.01.2019]

Real Sporting de Gijón - Valencia CF	2-1 / 0-3	Real Madrid CF - CD Leganés	3-0 / 0-1
Girona FC - Club Atlético de Madrid	1-1 / 3-3	Athletic Bilbao - Sevilla FC	1-3 / 1-0
Getafe CF - Real Valladolid CF	1-0 / 1-1	Real Betis - Real Sociedad de Fútbol San Sebastián	0-0 / 2-2
Villarreal CF - RCD Espanyol Barcelona	2-2 / 1-3	Levante UD Valencia - FC Barcelona	2-1 / 0-3

Quarter-Finals [22-24/29-31.01.2019]

Getafe CF - Valencia CF	1-0 / 1-3	RCD Espanyol Barcelona - Real Betis	1-1 / 1-3 aet
Sevilla FC - FC Barcelona	2-0 / 1-6	Real Madrid CF - Girona FC	4-2 / 3-1

Semi-Finals [06-07/27-28.02.2019]

FC Barcelona - Real Madrid CF	1-1 / 3-0	Real Betis - Valencia CF	2-2 / 0-1

Final

25.05.2019; Estadio "Benito Villamarín", Sevilla; Referee: Alberto Undiano Mallenco; Attendance: 53,698
Valencia CF - FC Barcelona **2-1(1-0)**

Valencia CF: Jaume Doménech Sánchez, Ezequiel Marcelo Garay, Gabriel Armando de Abreu „Gabriel Paulista", José Luis Gayà Peña, Carlos Soler Barragán, Daniel Wass, Daniel Parejo Muñoz (Cap) (65.Geoffrey Kondogbia), Francis Coquelin, Gonçalo Manuel Ganchinho Guedes, Rodrigo Moreno Machado (88.Mouctar Diakhaby), Kevin Dominique Gameiro (72.Cristiano Piccini). Trainer: Marcelino García Toral.

FC Barcelona: Jacobus Antonius Peter Cillessen, Nélson Cabral Semedo (46.Malcom Filipe Silva de Oliveira), Clément Nicolas Laurent Lenglet, Gerard Piqué i Bernabéu, Jordi Alba Ramos, Arthur Henrique Ramos de Oliveira Melo (46.Arturo Erasmo Vidal Pardo), Sergio Busquets Burgos, Ivan Rakitić (76.Carles Aleñá Castillo), Sergi Roberto Carnicer, Lionel Andrés Messi Cuccitini, Philippe Coutinho Correia. Trainer: Ernesto Valverde Tejedor.

Goals: 1-0 Kevin Dominique Gameiro (22), 2-0 Rodrigo Moreno Machado (33), 2-1 Lionel Andrés Messi Cuccitini (73).

THE CLUBS 2018/2019

Deportivo Alavés Vitoria-Gasteiz

Founded: 23.01.1921
Stadium: Estadio Mendizorrotza, Vitoria-Gasteiz (19,840)

Goalkeepers:	DOB	M	(s)	G
Antonio Sivera Salvá	11.08.1996	3		
Fernando Pacheco Flores	18.05.1992	35		
Defenders:	**DOB**	**M**	**(s)**	**G**
Adrián Marín Gómez	09.01.1997	2	(4)	
Rubén Duarte Sánchez	18.10.1995	33		
Rodrigo Ely (ITA)	03.11.1993	5		
Victor Laguardia Cisneros	05.11.1989	36		1
Guillermo Alfonso Maripán Loayza (CHI)	06.05.1994	22	(1)	2
Martín Aguirregabiria Padilla	10.05.1996	23	(4)	
Carlos Martín Vigaray	07.09.1994	7	(1)	
Joaquín „Ximo“ Navarro Jiménez	23.01.1990	28	(3)	2
Midfielders:	**DOB**	**M**	**(s)**	**G**
Darko Brašanac (SRB)	12.02.1992	17	(7)	
Takashi Inui (JPN)	02.06.1988	10	(2)	2
Jonathan Rodríguez Menéndez „Jony“	09.07.1991	34	(2)	5
Manuel „Manu„ Alejandro García Sánchez	26.04.1986	25	(9)	1
Tomás Pina Isla	14.10.1987	27	(1)	2
Daniel Alejandro Torres Rojas (COL)	15.11.1989	1	(1)	
Mubarak Wakaso (GHA)	25.07.1990	18	(11)	1
Forwards:	**DOB**	**M**	**(s)**	**G**
Alejandro "Álex" Blanco Sánchez	16.12.1998		(2)	
Borja González Tomás	25.08.1992	18	(9)	5
Jorge Franco Alviz „Burgui“	29.10.1993	5	(11)	1
Jonathan Calleri (ARG)	23.09.1993	33	(1)	9
John Alberto Guidetti (SWE)	15.04.1992	6	(16)	2
Ibai Gómez Pérez	11.11.1989	17	(1)	3
Diego Alejandro Rolán Silva (URU)	24.03.1993	3	(6)	
Rubén Sobrino Pozuelo	16.02.1992	10	(10)	3
Patrick Twumasi (GHA)	09.05.1994		(11)	
Trainer:	**DOB**	**M**		
Abelardo Fernández Antuña	19.04.1970	38		

Athletic Club Bilbao

Founded: 1898
Stadium: Estadio San Mamés, Bilbao (53,289)

Goalkeepers:	DOB	M	(s)	G
Iago Herrerín Buisán	25.01.1988	31		
Unai Simón Mendibil	11.06.1997	7		
Defenders:	**DOB**	**M**	**(s)**	**G**
Mikel Balenziaga Oruesagasti	29.02.1988	6	(5)	
Ander Capa Rodríguez	14.05.1992	17	(8)	
Óscar de Marcos Arana	14.04.1989	28	(2)	1
Cristian George Ganea (ROU)	24.05.1992	1		
Iñigo Martínez Berridi	17.05.1991	33		
Iñigo Lekue Martínez	04.05.1993	2	(2)	
Peru Nolaskoain Esnal	25.10.1998	4	(4)	2
Unai Núñez Gestoso	30.01.1997	11	(1)	
Yeray Álvarez López	24.01.1995	30		
Yuri Berchiche Izeta	10.02.1990	35		2
Midfielders:	**DOB**	**M**	**(s)**	**G**
Beñat Etxebarria Urkiaga	19.02.1987	25	(2)	1
Iñigo Córdoba Querejeta	13.03.1997	15	(8)	
Daniel „Dani“ García Carrillo	24.05.1990	29		
Ander Iturraspe Derteano	08.03.1989	1	(2)	
Mikel Rico Moreno	04.11.1984	3	(1)	
Raúl García Escudero	11.07.1986	27	(6)	9
Mikel San José Domínguez	30.05.1989	16	(17)	
Markel Susaeta Laskurain	14.12.1987	15	(7)	1
Unai López Cabrera	30.10.1995	3	(4)	
Forwards:	**DOB**	**M**	**(s)**	**G**
Aritz Aduriz Zubeldia	11.02.1981	10	(10)	2
Gorka Guruzeta Rodríguez	12.09.1996		(6)	
Ibai Gómez Pérez	11.11.1989	6	(8)	
Kenan Kodro (BIH)	19.08.1993		(11)	1
Iker Muniain Goñi	19.12.1992	27	(7)	7
Iñaki Williams Dannis	15.06.1994	36	(2)	13
Trainer:	**DOB**	**M**		
Manolo Eduardo Berizzo (ARG)	13.11.1969	14		
Gaizka Garitano Agirre [05.12.2018]	09.07.1975	24		

Club Atlético de Madrid

Founded: 26.04.1903 (*as Athletic Club de Madrid*)
Stadium: Estadio Metropolitano, Madrid (67,703)

Goalkeepers:	DOB	M	(s)	G
Antonio Adán Garrido	13.05.1987	1		
Jan Oblak (SVN)	07.01.1993	37		
Defenders:	**DOB**	**M**	**(s)**	**G**
Santiago "Santi" Arias Naranjo (COL)	13.01.1992	20	(5)	1
Carlos Isaac Muñoz Obejero	30.04.1998	1		
Filipe Luís Kasmirski (BRA)	09.08.1985	24	(3)	2
José María Giménez de Vargas (URU)	20.01.1995	19	(2)	
Diego Roberto Godín Leal (URU)	16.02.1986	28	(2)	3
Lucas François Bernard Hernández (FRA)	14.02.1996	13	(1)	1
Juan Francisco Torres Belén „Juanfran"	09.01.1985	18	(4)	
Francisco Javier Montero Rubio	14.01.1999	4	(5)	
Stefan Savić (MNE)	08.01.1991	17	(1)	
Andrés Felipe Solano Dávila (COL)	24.02.1998	1		
Midfielders:	**DOB**	**M**	**(s)**	**G**
Gelson Dany Batalha Martins (POR)	11.05.1995	1	(7)	
Jorge Resurrección Merodio „Koke“	08.01.1992	29	(1)	3
Thomas Benoît Lemar (FRA)	12.11.1995	22	(9)	3
Thomas Partey (GHA)	13.06.1993	22	(10)	3
Rodrigo Hernández Cascante „Rodri“	22.06.1996	32	(2)	3
Saúl Ñíguez Esclapez	21.11.1994	32	(1)	4
Antonio Moya Vega „Toni Moya"	20.03.1998	1		
Forwards:	**DOB**	**M**	**(s)**	**G**
Borja Garcés Moreno	06.08.1999		(1)	1
Ángel Martín Correa Martínez (ARG)	09.03.1995	20	(16)	3
Diego da Silva Costa	07.10.1988	14	(2)	2
Antoine Griezmann (FRA)	21.03.1991	37		15
Joaquín Muñoz Benavides	10.03.1999		(1)	
Nikola Kalinić (CRO)	05.01.1988	7	(10)	2
Álvaro Borja Morata Martín	23.10.1992	13	(2)	6
Sergio Camello Pérez	10.02.2001		(1)	1
Víctor Mollejo Carpintero	21.01.2001		(4)	
Víctor Machín Pérez „Vitolo“	02.11.1989	5	(15)	
Trainer:	**DOB**	**M**		
Diego Pablo Simeone (ARG)	28.04.1970	38		

Futbol Club Barcelona

Founded: 29.11.1899 (*as Foot-Ball Club Barcelona*)
Stadium: Estadio Camp Nou, Barcelona (99,354)

Goalkeepers:	**DOB**	**M**	**(s)**	**G**
Jacobus Antonius Peter Cillessen (NED)	22.04.1989	3		
Marc-André ter Stegen (GER)	30.04.1992	35		
Defenders:	**DOB**	**M**	**(s)**	**G**
Jordi Alba Ramos	21.03.1989	32	(4)	2
Clément Nicolas Laurent Lenglet (FRA)	17.06.1995	22	(1)	1
Jeison Fabián Murillo Cerón (COL)	27.05.1992	1	(1)	
Nélson Cabral Semedo (POR)	16.11.1993	20	(6)	1
Gerard Piqué i Bernabéu	02.02.1987	35		4
Jean-Clair Todibo (FRA)	30.12.1999	2		
Samuel Yves Umtiti (FRA)	14.11.1993	13	(1)	
Thomas Vermaelen (BEL)	14.11.1985	7	(2)	
Moussa Wagué (SEN)	04.10.1998	2	(1)	
Midfielders:	**DOB**	**M**	**(s)**	**G**
Álex Collado Gutiérrez	22.04.1999		(1)	
Arthur Henrique Ramos de Oliveira Melo (BRA)	12.08.1996	19	(8)	
Kevin-Prince Boateng (GHA)	06.03.1987	3		
Sergio Busquets Burgos	16.07.1988	30	(5)	
Carles Aleñá Castillo	05.01.1998	6	(11)	2
Philippe Coutinho Correia (BRA)	12.06.1992	22	(12)	5
Denis Suárez Fernández	06.01.1994		(2)	
Rafael Alcântara do Nascimento „Rafinha" (BRA)	12.02.1993	3	(2)	
Ivan Rakitić (CRO)	10.03.1988	29	(5)	3
Ricard "Riqui" Puig Martí	13.08.1999	2		
Sergi Roberto Carnicer	07.02.1992	23	(6)	
Arturo Erasmo Vidal Pardo (CHI)	22.05.1987	22	(11)	3
Forwards:	**DOB**	**M**	**(s)**	**G**
Abel Ruiz Ortega	28.01.2000		(1)	
Carles Pérez Sayol	16.02.1998		(1)	
Ousmane Dembélé (FRA)	15.05.1997	20	(9)	8
Malcom Filipe Silva de Oliveira (BRA)	26.02.1997	6	(9)	1
Lionel Andrés Messi Cuccitini (ARG)	24.06.1987	29	(5)	36
Munir El Haddadi Mohamed		1	(6)	1
Luis Alberto Suárez Díaz (URU)	24.01.1987	31	(2)	21
Trainer:	**DOB**	**M**		
Ernesto Valverde Tejedor	09.02.1964	38		

Real Club Celta de Vigo

Founded: 23.08.1923
Stadium: Estadio Balaídos, Vigo (29,000)

Goalkeepers:	**DOB**	**M**	**(s)**	**G**
Rubén Blanco Veiga	25.07.1995	25		
Sergio Álvarez Conde	03.08.1986	13		
Defenders:	**DOB**	**M**	**(s)**	**G**
Júnior Osmar Ignacio Alonso Mujica (PAR)	09.02.1993	6	(3)	
Néstor Alejandro Araujo Razo (MEX)	29.08.1991	30	(2)	3
Gustavo Daniel Cabral (ARG)	14.10.1985	21	(3)	
David Costas Cordal	26.03.1995	13	(2)	
Wesley Theodorus Hoedt (NED)	06.03.1994	9	(1)	
Hugo Mallo Novegil	22.06.1991	35		1
David Juncà Reñe	16.11.1993	21		
Kevin Vázquez Comesaña	23.03.1993	2	(2)	
Róbert Mazáň (SVK)	09.02.1994	1		
Lucas René Olaza Catrofe (URU)	21.07.1994	10		
Facundo Sebastián Roncaglia (ARG)	10.02.1987	12		
Midfielders:	**DOB**	**M**	**(s)**	**G**
Ryad Boudebouz (ALG)	19.02.1990	8	(3)	1
Sofiane Boufal (MAR)	17.09.1993	25	(10)	3
Brais Méndez Portela	07.01.1997	27	(4)	6
Francisco José "Fran" Beltrán Peinado	03.02.1999	16	(14)	1
Andrew Hjulsager (DEN)	15.01.1995	2	(13)	
Mathias Jensen (DEN)	01.01.1996	3	(3)	
Jozabed Sánchez Ruiz	08.03.1991	14	(6)	
Stanislav Lobotka (SVK)	25.11.1994	27	(4)	
Okay Yokuşlu (TUR)	09.03.1994	26	(4)	2
Forwards:	**DOB**	**M**	**(s)**	**G**
Dennis Eckert (GER)	09.01.1997	1	(8)	
Maximiliano Gómez González (URU)	14.08.1996	33	(2)	13
Iago Aspas Juncal	01.08.1987	26	(1)	20
Emmanuel Apeh (NGA)	25.10.1996		(2)	
Emre Mor (TUR)	24.07.1997	4	(6)	
Pione Sisto Ifolo Emirmija (DEN)	04.02.1995	8	(17)	2
Trainer:	**DOB**	**M**		
Ricardo Antonio Mohamed Matijević (ARG)	02.04.1970	12		
José Miguel Azevedo Cardoso(POR)[12.11.18]	28.05.1972	13		
Francisco "Fran" Escribá Segura [03.03.2019]	03.05.1965	13		

Sociedad Deportiva Eibar

Founded: 30.11.1940
Stadium: Estadio Ipurua, Eibar (7,083)

Goalkeepers:	**DOB**	**M**	**(s)**	**G**
Marko Dmitrović (SRB)	24.01.1992	24		
Asier Riesgo Unamuno	06.10.1983	14		
Defenders:	**DOB**	**M**	**(s)**	**G**
Anaitz Arbilla Zabala	15.05.1987	22	(3)	1
Pedro Bigas Rigo	15.05.1990	7	(3)	
José Ángel Valdés Díaz „Cote"	05.09.1989	34	(1)	1
Marc Cucurella Saseta	22.07.1998	26	(5)	1
Iván Andrés Ramis Barrios	25.10.1984	20	(1)	
Jordi Calavera Espinach	02.08.1995		(1)	
Paulo André Rodrigues de Oliveira (POR)	08.01.1992	24	(4)	
Rubén Peña Jiménez	18.07.1991	30	(1)	1
Midfielders:	**DOB**	**M**	**(s)**	**G**
Pablo Ezequiel de Blasis (ARG)	04.02.1988	16	(8)	2
Pape Diop (SEN)	19.03.1986	27	(1)	1
Gonzalo Escalante (ARG)	27.03.1993	18	(14)	4
Pablo Hervías Ruiz	08.03.1993	2	(1)	
Joan Jordán Moreno	06.07.1994	32	(4)	4
Pedro León Sánchez Gil	24.11.1986	5	(4)	1
Sergio Álvarez Díaz	23.01.1992	12	(7)	
Forwards:	**DOB**	**M**	**(s)**	**G**
Tiago Manuel Dias Correia „Bebé" (POR)	12.07.1990	1	(1)	
Charles Días de Oliveira (BRA)	04.04.1984	17	(17)	14
Enrique García Martínez „Kike García"	25.11.1989	15	(15)	3
Marc Cardona Rovira	08.07.1995	6	(11)	3
Miguel Mari Sánchez	30.06.1997		(2)	
Fabián Ariel Orellana Valenzuela (CHI)	27.01.1986	31	(2)	3
Pere Milla Peña	23.09.1992	5		
Sergi Enrich Ametller	26.02.1990	30	(5)	7
Trainer:	**DOB**	**M**		
José Luis Mendilibar Etxebarria	14.03.1961	38		

Reial Club Deportiu Espanyol de Barcelona

Founded: 28.10.1900 (*as Sociedad Española de Football*)
Stadium: RCDE Stadium [Estadi Cornellà-El Prat], Barcelona (40,500)

Goalkeepers:	**DOB**	**M**	**(s)**	**G**
Diego López Rodríguez	03.11.1981	38		
Defenders:	**DOB**	**M**	**(s)**	**G**
Adrià Giner Pedrosa	13.05.1998	8	(4)	1
Dídac Vilà Rosselló	09.06.1989	27		
Óscar Esau Duarte Gaitan (CRC)	03.06.1989	7	(4)	
Javier López Rodriguez „Javi López"	21.01.1986	21	(2)	
Lluís López Mármol	05.03.1997	5	(1)	
Mario Hermoso Canseco	18.06.1995	31	(1)	3
Edinaldo Gomes Pereira „Naldo" (BRA)	25.08.1988	16		1
Roberto José Rosales Altuve (VEN)	20.11.1988	20	(1)	3
Midfielders:	**DOB**	**M**	**(s)**	**G**
Alejandro „Álex" López Moreno	02.06.1997	1	(3)	
Alfa Semedo Esteves (GNB)	30.08.1997		(3)	
David López Silva	09.10.1989	21		
Esteban Félix Granero Molina	02.07.1987	24	(4)	3
Marc Roca Junqué	26.11.1996	35		1
Óscar Melendo Jiménez	23.08.1997	22	(10)	
Hernán Arsenio Pérez González (PAR)	25.02.1989	10	(9)	1
Sergi Darder Moll	22.12.1993	32	(2)	4
Víctor Sánchez Mata	08.09.1987	13	(11)	
Forwards:	**DOB**	**M**	**(s)**	**G**
Borja Iglesias Quintás	17.01.1993	35	(2)	17
Facundo Ferreyra (ARG)	14.03.1991	1	(8)	1
Leonardo Carrilho Baptistão „Leo Baptistão" (BRA)	26.08.1992	14	(6)	2
Pablo Daniel Piatti (ARG)	31.03.1989	6	(14)	1
Javier „Javi" Puado Díaz	25.05.1998	2	(13)	
Sergio García de la Fuente	09.06.1983	17	(12)	2
Wu Lei (CHN)	19.11.1991	12	(4)	3
Trainer:	**DOB**	**M**		
Joan Francesc Ferrer Sicilia „Rubi"	05.07.1970	38		

Getafe Club de Fútbol

Founded: 08.07.1983
Stadium: Estadio Coliseum „Alfonso Pérez“, Getafe (17,000)

Goalkeepers:	**DOB**	**M**	**(s)**	**G**
Leandro Chichizola (ARG)	27.03.1990	1		
David Soria Solís	04.04.1993	37		
Defenders:	**DOB**	**M**	**(s)**	**G**
Vitorino Gabriel Pacheco Antunes (POR)	01.04.1987	25	(3)	1
Bruno González Cabrera	24.05.1990	18	(5)	
Leandro Daniel Cabrera Sasía (URU)	17.06.1991	31	(1)	2
Dakonam Djené (TOG)	31.12.1991	34		
Dimitri Foulquier (GLP)	23.03.1993	23	(2)	3
Ignasi Miquel Pons	28.09.1992	4	(3)	
Mathías Olivera Miramontes (URU)	31.10.1997	12	(2)	
Damián Nicolás Suárez Suárez (URU)	27.04.1988	36		
Midfielders:	**DOB**	**M**	**(s)**	**G**
Mauro Wilney Arambarri Rosa (URU)	30.09.1995	32	(1)	1
Sebastián Carlos Cristóforo Pepe (URU)	23.08.1993	4	(11)	
Mathieu Pierre Flamini (FRA)	07.03.1984	4	(6)	
Iván Alejo Peralta	10.02.1995	2	(2)	
Nemanja Maksimović (SRB)	26.01.1995	36		1
Markel Bergara Larrañaga	05.05.1986		(3)	
Francisco Portillo Soler	13.06.1990	19	(13)	1
Roberto Ibáñez Castro	22.03.1993		(7)	
Gaku Shibasaki (JPN)	28.05.1992	5	(2)	
Forwards:	**DOB**	**M**	**(s)**	**G**
Ángel Luís Rodríguez Díaz	26.04.1987	20	(17)	8
Amath Diedhiou (SEN)	16.07.1996	13	(2)	1
Hugo Duro Perales	10.11.1999	5	(6)	
Jaime Mata Arnaiz	24.10.1988	27	(7)	14
Jorge Molina Vidal	22.04.1982	28	(10)	14
Samuel Sáiz Alonso	22.01.1991	2	(8)	1
Sergio "Sergi" Guardiola Navarro	29.05.1991		(3)	
Trainer:	**DOB**	**M**		
José Bordalás Jiménez	05.03.1964	38		

Girona Futbol Club

Founded: 23.07.1930
Stadium: Estadio Montilivi, Girona (13,450)

Goalkeepers:	**DOB**	**M**	**(s)**	**G**
Yassine Bounou (MAR)	05.04.1991	32		
Gorka Iraizoz Moreno	06.03.1981	6	(1)	
Defenders:	**DOB**	**M**	**(s)**	**G**
Carles Planas Antolínez	04.03.1991	4	(3)	
Bernardo José Espinosa Zúñiga (COL)	11.07.1989	31		1
Juan Pedro López Ramírez	30.04.1991	31	(2)	
Marc Muniesa Martínez	27.03.1992	15	(4)	
Pedro Alcalá Guirado	19.03.1989	20	(5)	1
Jonás Ramalho Chimeno	10.06.1993	18	(4)	1
Raúl García Carnero	30.04.1989	10		
Midfielders:	**DOB**	**M**	**(s)**	**G**
Francesc Aday Benítez Caraballo	16.12.1987	8	(2)	
Aleix García Serrano	28.06.1997	20	(11)	2
Álex Granell Nogué	02.08.1988	26	(6)	
Borja García Freire	02.11.1990	30	(3)	1
David Timor Copoví	17.10.1989	2		
Douglas Luiz Soares de Paulo (BRA)	09.05.1998	16	(7)	
Paik Seung-ho (KOR)	17.03.1997		(3)	
Pere Pons Riera	20.02.1993	32	(2)	1
Cristián Portugués Manzanera „Portu“	21.05.1992	33	(1)	9
Valery Fernández Estrada	23.11.1999	10	(7)	
Forwards:	**DOB**	**M**	**(s)**	**G**
Seydou Doumbia (CIV)	31.12.1987	5	(12)	2
Anthony Rubén Lozano Colón (HON)	25.04.1993	7	(13)	
Johan Andrés Mojica Palacio (COL)	21.08.1992		(1)	
Pedro Antonio Porro Sauceda	13.09.1999	25	(7)	
Patrick Roberts (ENG)	05.02.1997	6	(13)	
Kévin Soni (CMR)	17.04.1998	1	(4)	
Cristhian Ricardo Stuani Curbelo (URU)	12.10.1986	30	(2)	19
Trainer:	**DOB**	**M**		
Eusebio Sacristán Mena	13.04.1964	38		

Sociedad Deportiva Huesca

Founded: 29.03.1960
Stadium: Estadio El Alcoraz, Huesca (7,638)

Goalkeepers:	**DOB**	**M**	**(s)**	**G**
Aleksandar Jovanović (SRB)	06.12.1992	12		
Roberto Santamaría Ciprián	27.02.1985	20		
Axel Wilfredo Werner (ARG)	28.02.1996	6		
Defenders:	**DOB**	**M**	**(s)**	**G**
Carlos Akapo Martínez (EQG)	12.03.1993	12	(1)	
Rajko Brežančić (SRB)	21.08.1989		(1)	
Adrián Diéguez Grande	04.02.1996	8	(1)	
Xabier Etxeita Gorritxategi	31.10.1987	30	(1)	4
Javier "Javi" Galán Gil	19.11.1994	16		
Martín Maximiliano Mantovani (ARG)	07.07.1984	6	(3)	2
Jorge Miramón Santagertrudis	02.06.1989	30		1
Pablo Insua Blanco	09.09.1993	10		
Jorge Pulido Mayoral	08.04.1991	32		3
Rúben Afonso Borges Semedo (POR)	04.04.1994	9	(2)	
Midfielders:	**DOB**	**M**	**(s)**	**G**
Juan Pablo Añor Acosta (VEN)	24.01.1994	8	(6)	2
Juan José Camacho Barnola	02.08.1980		(3)	
Christian Rivera Hernández	09.07.1997	19	(3)	2
David Ferreiro Quiroga	01.04.1988	23	(12)	1
Serdar Gürler (TUR)	14.09.1991	5	(8)	
Yangel Clemente Herrera Ravelo (VEN)	07.01.1998	14	(2)	
Juan Aguilera Núñez	13.09.1985	4	(2)	
Lluís Sastre Reus	26.03.1986	1	(3)	
Luís Carlos Correia Pinto „Luisinho“ (POR)	05.05.1985	6	(1)	
Gonzalo Julián Melero Manzanares	02.01.1994	14	(8)	2
Moisés „Moi“ Gómez Bordonado	23.06.1994	35	(1)	2
Damián Marcelo Musto (ARG)	09.06.1987	20	(4)	
Forwards:	**DOB**	**M**	**(s)**	**G**
Alejandro "Álex" Gallar Falguera	19.03.1992	10	(15)	4
Luis Ezequiel Ávila (ARG)	06.02.1994	20	(14)	10
Enric Gallego Puigsech	12.09.1986	17	(2)	5
Juan Camilo Hernández Suárez (COL)	22.04.1999	25	(9)	4
Samuele Longo (ITA)	12.01.1992	6	(9)	1
Trainer:	**DOB**	**M**		
Leonardo Neoren Franco (ARG)	20.05.1977	8		
Francisco Javier Rodríguez Vílchez [10.10.18]	17.09.1978	30		

Club Deportivo Leganés

Founded: 26.06.1928
Stadium: Estadio Butarque, Leganés (11,454)

Goalkeepers:	DOB	M	(s)	G
Iván Cuéllar Sacristán	27.05.1984	34		
Andriy Lunin (UKR)	11.02.1999	4	(1)	
Defenders:	**DOB**	**M**	**(s)**	**G**
Unai Bustinza Martínez	02.02.1992	24	(1)	
Juan Francisco Moreno Fuertes „Juanfran"	11.09.1988	17	(6)	1
Vasyl Kravets (UKR)	20.08.1997	6		
Ezequiel Matías Muñoz (ARG)	08.10.1990	2	(1)	
Allan-Roméo Nyom (CMR)	10.05.1988	20	(3)	1
Kenneth Josiah Omeruo (NGA)	17.10.1993	27	(1)	
Raúl García Carnero	30.04.1989	4	(1)	
Diego Antonio Reyes Rosales (MEX)	19.09.1992	4	(2)	
Rodrigo Tarín Higón	05.07.1996	15	(3)	
Jonathan Cristian Silva (ARG)	29.06.1994	30		3
Dimitrios Siovas (GRE)	16.09.1988	34		1
Midfielders:	**DOB**	**M**	**(s)**	**G**
Nabil El Zhar (MAR)	27.08.1986	9	(18)	4
Javier Eraso Goñi	22.03.1990	9	(4)	
Gerard Gumbau Garriga	18.12.1994	13	(3)	1
José Manuel Arnaiz Díaz	15.04.1995		(6)	
Mikel Vesga Arruti	08.04.1993	23	(3)	1
Óscar Rodríguez Arnaiz	28.06.1998	29	(2)	4
José Luis García del Pozo „Recio"	11.01.1991	15	(3)	
Rubén Pérez del Mármol	26.04.1989	27	(4)	
Alexander Szymanowski (ARG)	13.10.1988		(1)	
Forwards:	**DOB**	**M**	**(s)**	**G**
Martin Christensen Braithwaite (DEN)	05.06.1991	16	(3)	4
Daniel "Dani" Ojeda Saranova	03.12.1994	2	(3)	
Guido Marcelo Carrillo (ARG)	25.05.1991	23	(9)	6
Youssef En-Nesyri (MAR)	01.06.1997	22	(9)	9
Diego Alejandro Rolán Silva (URU)	24.03.1993	2	(4)	
Sabin Merino Zuloaga	04.01.1992	2	(10)	
Michael Nicolás Santos Rosadilla (URU)	13.03.1993	5	(11)	1
Trainer:	**DOB**	**M**		
Mauricio Andrés Pellegrino Luna (ARG)	05.10.1971	38		

Levante Unión Deportiva Valencia

Founded: 09.09.1909
Stadium: Estadio Ciutat de València, Valencia (26,354)

Goalkeepers:	DOB	M	(s)	G
Aitor Fernández Abarisketa	03.05.1991	16		
Jorge Ruiz Ojeada „Koke Vegas"	27.09.1995	1		
Oier Olazábal Paredes	14.09.1989	21		
Defenders:	**DOB**	**M**	**(s)**	**G**
Antonio Manuel Luna Rodríguez	17.03.1991	14	(2)	
Erick Cathriel Cabaco Almada (URU)	19.04.1995	20	(1)	2
José Manuel Rodríguez Benito „Chema"	03.03.1992	13	(6)	2
Jorge Andújar Moreno „Coke"	26.04.1987	19	(8)	4
Pedro López Muñoz	01.11.1983	4	(4)	
Roberto Suárez Pier „Róber"	16.02.1995	32	(1)	1
Rúben Miguel Nunes Vezo (POR)	25.04.1994	15		2
Sergio Postigo Redondo	04.11.1988	17	(4)	1
Antonio García Aranda „Toño García"	07.11.1989	21		2
Midfielders:	**DOB**	**M**	**(s)**	**G**
Enis Bardhi (MKD)	02.07.1995	31	(5)	3
José Ángel Gómez Campaña	31.05.1993	36		3
Cheick Doukouré (CIV)	11.09.1992	3	(6)	
Francisco Jesús López de la Manzanara Delgado	12.09.1996	1	(3)	
David Remeseiro Salgueiro „Jason"	06.07.1994	26	(4)	2
José Luis Morales Nogales	23.07.1987	35	(2)	12
Sanjin Prcić (BIH)	20.11.1993	6	(4)	
Nikola Vukčević (MNE)	13.12.1991	9	(7)	
Forwards:	**DOB**	**M**	**(s)**	**G**
Emmanuel Boateng (GHA)	23.05.1996	7	(9)	1
Borja Mayoral Moya	05.04.1997	16	(13)	3
Raphael Dwamena (GHA)	12.09.1995	1	(11)	
Roger Martí Salvador	03.01.1991	23	(8)	13
Rubén Rochina Naixes	23.03.1991	23	(4)	4
Moses Daddy Simon (NGA)	12.07.1995	8	(11)	1
Trainer:	**DOB**	**M**		
Francisco José López Fernández	19.09.1967	38		

Rayo Vallecano de Madrid

Founded: 29.05.1924
Stadium: Campo de Fútbol de Vallecas, Puente de Vallecas, Madrid (14,708)

Goalkeepers:	DOB	M	(s)	G
Alberto García Cabrera	09.02.1985	17		
Stole Dimitrievski (MKD)	25.12.1993	21		
Defenders:	**DOB**	**M**	**(s)**	**G**
Luis Jan Piers Advíncula Castrillón (PER)	02.03.1990	27	(1)	1
Sergio Akieme Rodríguez	16.12.1997	2		
Abdoulaye Ba (SEN)	01.01.1991	25	(1)	1
Alejandro Catena Marugán	28.10.1994	2		
José Antonio Dorado Ramírez	10.07.1982	1		
Alejandro Gálvez Jimena	06.06.1989	17		1
Jordi Amat Maas	21.03.1992	31		
Roberto Román Triguero „Tito"	11.07.1985	12	(3)	
Emiliano Daniel Velázquez Maldonado (URU)	30.04.1994	14	(4)	
Midfielders:	**DOB**	**M**	**(s)**	**G**
Uche Agbo (NGA)	04.12.1995	5	(1)	
Alexandre „Álex" Moreno Lopera	08.06.1993	36		1
Álvaro García Rivera	27.10.1992	17	(18)	4
Gorka Elustondo Urkola	18.03.1987	3	(2)	
Giannelli Imbula (FRA)	12.09.1992	21	(1)	1
Mario Suárez Mata	24.02.1987	11	(3)	2
Álvaro Medrán Just	15.03.1994	12	(9)	3
Santiago "Santi" Comesaña Veiga	05.10.1996	23	(2)	1
Forwards:	**DOB**	**M**	**(s)**	**G**
Alexander „Álex" Alegría Moreno	10.10.1992		(9)	
Tiago Manuel Dias Correia „Bebé" (POR)	12.07.1990	13	(14)	1
Franco Matías Di Santo (ARG)	07.04.1989	1	(5)	
Adrián Embarba Blazquez	05.07.1992	27	(9)	5
Javier "Javi" Guerra Rodríguez	15.03.1982	1	(7)	
José Ángel Pozo la Rosa	15.03.1996	16	(13)	3
Gaël Kakuta (COD)	21.06.1991	9	(3)	1
Raúl de Tomás Gómez	17.10.1994	32	(1)	14
Sergio Moreno Martínez	01.01.1999		(1)	
Óscar Guido Trejo (ARG)	26.04.1988	22	(4)	1
Trainer:	**DOB**	**M**		
Miguel Ángel Sánchez Muñoz „Míchel"	30.10.1975	27		
Francisco „Paco" Jémez Martín [19.03.2019]	18.04.1970	11		

Real Betis Balompié Sevilla

Founded: 12.09.1907
Stadium: Estadio "Benito Villamarín", Sevilla (60,720)

Goalkeepers:	**DOB**	**M**	**(s)**	**G**
Joel Robles Blázquez	17.06.1990	5		
Pau López Sabata	13.12.1994	33		
Defenders:	**DOB**	**M**	**(s)**	**G**
Antonio Barragán Fernández	12.06.1987	12	(2)	
Marc Bartra Aragall	15.01.1991	33		1
Emerson Aparecido Leite de Souza Junior (BRA)	14.01.1999	4	(2)	
Zouhair Feddal (MAR)	01.01.1989	19	(2)	1
Héctor Junior Firpo Adamés	22.08.1996	22	(2)	3
Francisco Javier Guerrero Martín	11.03.1996	22		
Aïssa Mandi (ALG)	22.10.1991	34	(1)	1
Sidnei Rechel da Silva Júnior (BRA)	23.08.1989	20	(4)	1
Midfielders:	**DOB**	**M**	**(s)**	**G**
Ryad Boudebouz (ALG)	19.02.1990	6	(3)	
Sergio Canales Madrazo	16.02.1991	30	(2)	7
José Andrés Guardado Hernández (MEX)	28.09.1986	27	(4)	
Takashi Inui (JPN)	02.06.1988	5	(3)	
Francisco Javier „Javi" García Fernández	08.02.1987	6	(7)	
Joaquín Sánchez Rodríguez	21.07.1981	17	(13)	6
Wilfrid Kaptoum (CMR)	07.07.1996	9	(1)	
Giovani Lo Celso (ARG)	09.04.1996	27	(5)	9
William Silva de Carvalho (POR)	07.04.1992	26	(4)	
Forwards:	**DOB**	**M**	**(s)**	**G**
Cristian Tello Herrera	11.08.1991	13	(16)	4
Jesé Rodríguez Ruiz	26.02.1993	9	(5)	2
Diego Lainez Leyva (MEX)	09.06.2000	3	(9)	
Lorenzo Morón García „Loren"	30.12.1993	22	(11)	6
Sergio León Limones	06.01.1989	6	(10)	
Arnaldo Antonio Sanabria Ayala (PAR)	04.03.1996	8	(7)	2
Trainer:	**DOB**	**M**		
Enrique Setién Solar	27.09.1958	38		

Real Madrid Club de Fútbol

Founded: 06.03.1902 (*as Madrid Football Club*)
Stadium: Estadio "Santiago Bernabéu", Madrid (81,044)

Goalkeepers:	**DOB**	**M**	**(s)**	**G**
Thibaut Nicolas Marc Courtois (BEL)	11.05.1992	27		
Keylor Antonio Navas Gamboa (CRC)	15.12.1986	10		
Luca Zidane Fernández (FRA)	13.05.1998	1		
Defenders:	**DOB**	**M**	**(s)**	**G**
Daniel Carvajal Ramos	11.01.1992	23	(1)	1
Javier „Javi" Sánchez de Felipe	14.03.1997		(1)	
Marcelo Vieira da Silva Júnior (BRA)	12.05.1988	21	(2)	2
José Ignacio Fernández Iglesias „Nacho"	18.01.1990	19	(1)	
Álvaro Odriozola Arzalluz	14.12.1995	14		
Sergio Reguilón Rodríguez	16.12.1996	13	(1)	
Sergio Ramos García	30.03.1986	28		6
Jesús Vallejo Lázaro	05.01.1997	4	(1)	1
Raphaël Varane (FRA)	25.04.1993	31	(1)	2
Midfielders:	**DOB**	**M**	**(s)**	**G**
Brahim Abdelkader Díaz	03.08.1999	5	(4)	1
Carlos Henrique Casemiro (BRA)	23.02.1992	27	(2)	3
Daniel „Dani" Ceballos Fernández	07.08.1996	13	(10)	3
Francisco Román Alarcón Suárez „Isco"	21.04.1992	11	(16)	3
Toni Kroos (GER)	04.01.1990	26	(2)	
Marco Asensio Willemsen	21.01.1996	19	(11)	1
Marcos Llorente Moreno	30.01.1995	6	(1)	
Luka Modrić (CRO)	09.09.1985	31	(3)	3
Federico Santiago Valverde Dipetta (URU)	22.07.1998	6	(10)	
Forwards:	**DOB**	**M**	**(s)**	**G**
Gareth Frank Bale (WAL)	16.07.1989	21	(8)	8
Karim Mostafa Benzema (FRA)	19.12.1987	35	(1)	21
Cristo Ramón González Pérez	24.10.1997		(1)	
Lucas Vázquez Iglesias	01.07.1991	15	(16)	1
Mariano Díaz Mejía (DOM)	01.08.1993	3	(10)	3
Vinícius José Paixão de Oliveira Júnior (BRA)	12.07.2000	9	(9)	2
Trainer:	**DOB**	**M**		
Julen Lopetegui Argote	28.09.1966	10		
Santiago Hernán Solari Poggio (ARG) [29.10.18]	07.10.1976	17		
Zinédine Zidane (FRA) [11.03.2019]	23.06.1972	11		

Real Sociedad de Fútbol San Sebastián

Founded: 07.09.1909
Stadium: Estadio Anoeta, San Sebastián (32,000)

Goalkeepers:	**DOB**	**M**	**(s)**	**G**
Miguel Ángel Moyá Rumbo	02.04.1984	11		
Gerónimo Rulli (ARG)	20.05.1992	27		
Defenders:	**DOB**	**M**	**(s)**	**G**
Aihen Muñoz Capellán	16.08.1997	11		
Álex Sola López Ocaña	09.06.1999	1		
Andoni Gorosabel Espinosa	04.08.1996	6	(1)	
Aritz Elustondo Irribaría	28.03.1994	24	(3)	1
Theo Bernard François Hernandez (FRA)	06.10.1997	22	(2)	1
Joseba Zaldúa Bengoetxea	24.06.1992	25	(1)	1
Robin Le Normand (FRA)	11.11.1996	3	(1)	
Diego Javier Llorente Ríos	16.08.1993	20	(1)	
Héctor Alfredo Moreno Herrera (MEX)	17.01.1988	21	(4)	1
Raúl Rodríguez Navas	11.05.1988	15	(1)	
Kévin Manuel Rodrigues (POR)	05.03.1994	5	(2)	
Midfielders:	**DOB**	**M**	**(s)**	**G**
Ander Guevara Lajo	07.07.1997	1		
Asier Illarramendi Andonegu	08.03.1990	20	(3)	1
Adnan Januzaj (BEL)	05.02.1995	13	(7)	1
Luca Sangalli Fuentes	10.02.1995	12	(6)	1
Martín Merquelanz Castellanos	12.06.1995		(1)	
Martín Zubimendi Ibáñez	02.02.1999		(1)	
Mikel Merino Zazón	22.06.1996	24	(5)	3
Rubén Pardo Gutiérrez	22.10.1992	16	(8)	1
Igor Zubeldía Elorza	30.03.1997	29	(3)	
David Zurutuza Veillet	19.07.1986	13	(8)	2
Forwards:	**DOB**	**M**	**(s)**	**G**
Ander Barrenetxea Muguruza	27.12.2001	5	(4)	1
Jon Bautista Orgilles	03.07.1995	4	(14)	1
Juan Miguel Jiménez López „Juanmi"	20.05.1993	16	(14)	5
Mikel Oyarzabal Ugarte	21.04.1997	36	(1)	13
Roberto López Alcaide	24.04.2000		(1)	
Sandro Ramírez Castillo	09.07.1995	10	(14)	
Willian José da Silva (BRA)	23.11.1991	28	(3)	11
Trainer:	**DOB**	**M**		
Asier Garitano Aguirrezabal	06.12.1969	17		
Imanol Alguacil Barrenetxea [27.12.2018]	04.07.1971	21		

Sevilla Fútbol Club

Founded: 25.01.1890
Stadium: Estadio "Ramón Sánchez Pizjuán", Sevilla (42,714)

Goalkeepers:	DOB	M	(s)	G
Javier "Javi" Díaz Sánchez	15.05.1997	1		
Juan Soriano Oropesa	23.08.1997	4		
Tomáš Vaclík (CZE)	29.03.1989	33		
Defenders:	**DOB**	**M**	**(s)**	**G**
Daniel Filipe Martins Carriço (POR)	04.08.1988	24		1
Sergio Escudero Palomo	02.09.1989	18	(3)	
Joris Gnagnon (FRA)	13.01.1997	4	(3)	
Guilherme Antonio Arana Lopes (BRA)	14.04.1997	8	(1)	
Simon Thorup Kjær (DEN)	26.03.1989	25	(1)	
Gabriel Iván Mercado (ARG)	18.03.1987	19	(4)	2
Sergi Gómez Solà	28.03.1992	31	(1)	
Maximilian Wöber (AUT)	04.02.1998	6	(1)	
Midfielders:	**DOB**	**M**	**(s)**	**G**
Aleix Vidal Parreu	21.08.1989	5	(6)	
Ibrahim Amadou (CMR)	06.04.1993	7	(10)	
Éver Maximiliano David Banega (ARG)	29.06.1988	32		3
Maxime Gonalons (FRA)	10.03.1989	5	(5)	
Jesús Navas González	21.11.1985	31	(1)	1
Pablo Sarabia García	11.05.1992	30	(3)	12
Marko Rog (CRO)	19.07.1995	4	(6)	
Roque Mesa Quevedo	07.06.1989	20	(11)	2
Franco Damian Vázquez (ITA)	22.02.1989	26	(8)	3
Forwards:	**DOB**	**M**	**(s)**	**G**
André Miguel Valente da Silva (POR)	06.11.1995	25	(2)	9
Wissam Ben Yedder (FRA)	12.08.1990	31	(4)	18
Bryan Gil Salvatierra	11.02.2001		(11)	1
Munir El Haddadi Mohamed	01.09.1995	12	(4)	5
Luis Fernando Muriel Fruito (COL)	16.04.1991	1	(5)	1
Manuel Agudo Durán „Nolito"	15.10.1986	1	(3)	
Quincy Anton Promes (NED)	04.01.1992	15	(18)	2
Trainer:	**DOB**	**M**		
Pablo Javier Machín Díez	07.04.1975	27		
Joaquín de Jesús Caparrós Camino[15.03.2019]	15.10.1955	11		

Valencia Club de Fútbol

Founded: 18.03.1909
Stadium: Estadio Mestalla, Valencia (49,500)

Goalkeepers:	DOB	M	(s)	G
Jaume Doménech Sánchez	05.11.1990	4		
Norberto Murara Neto (BRA)	19.07.1989	34		
Defenders:	**DOB**	**M**	**(s)**	**G**
Mouctar Diakhaby (FRA)	19.12.1996	16	(6)	2
Gabriel Armando de Abreu „Gabriel Paulista" (BRA)	26.11.1990	30		
Ezequiel Marcelo Garay (ARG)	10.10.1986	24		2
José Luis Gayà Peña	25.05.1995	35		1
Jeison Fabián Murillo Cerón (COL)	27.05.1992	1		
Cristiano Piccini (ITA)	26.09.1992	21	(2)	1
Facundo Sebastián Roncaglia (ARG)	10.02.1987	7		
Antonio Latorre Grueso „Toni Lato"	21.11.1997	3	(1)	
Rúben Miguel Nunes Vezo (POR)	25.04.1994	2	(2)	
Midfielders:	**DOB**	**M**	**(s)**	**G**
Carlos Soler Barragán	02.01.1997	27	(4)	2
Denis Cheryshev (RUS)	26.12.1990	19	(8)	2
Francis Coquelin (FRA)	13.05.1991	20	(6)	
Geoffrey Kondogbia (CTA)	15.02.1993	14	(5)	1
Lee Kang-In (KOR)	19.02.2001		(3)	
Daniel Parejo Muñoz	16.04.1989	35	(1)	9
Daniel Wass (DEN)	31.05.1989	26	(6)	1
Forwards:	**DOB**	**M**	**(s)**	**G**
Michy Batshuayi-Atunga (BEL)	02.10.1993	4	(11)	1
Ferrán Torres García	29.02.2000	8	(16)	2
Kevin Dominique Gameiro (FRA)	09.05.1987	16	(17)	6
Gonçalo Manuel Ganchinho Guedes (POR)	29.11.1996	18	(7)	5
Rodrigo Moreno Machado	06.03.1991	29	(4)	8
Rubén Sobrino Pozuelo	01.06.1992	2	(2)	
Santiago Mina Lorenzo „Santi Mina"	07.12.1995	23	(7)	7
Trainer:	**DOB**	**M**		
Marcelino García Toral	14.08.1965	38		

Real Valladolid Club de Fútbol

Founded: 20.06.1928
Stadium: Estadio "José Zorrilla", Valladolid (26,512)

Goalkeepers:	DOB	M	(s)	G
Jordi Masip López	03.01.1989	35		
Yoel Rodríguez Oterino	28.08.1988	3		
Defenders:	**DOB**	**M**	**(s)**	**G**
Fernando Calero Villa	14.09.1995	35	(1)	1
Javier „Javi" Moyano Lujano	23.02.1986	25	(2)	
Joaquín Fernández Moreno	31.05.1996	9	(4)	1
Francisco José „Kiko" Olivas Alba	21.08.1988	35		
Moisés Delgado López „Moi"	18.04.1994	3		
José Ignacio Martínez García „Nacho"	07.03.1989	35		1
Midfielders:	**DOB**	**M**	**(s)**	**G**
Rubén Alcaraz Jiménez	01.05.1991	34		3
Antonio Jesús Regal Angulo „Antoñito"	24.12.1987	18	(12)	2
Borja Fernández Fernández	14.01.1981	10	(9)	
Moctar El Hacen (MTN)	31.12.1997		(1)	
Sergio Gontán Gallardo „Keko"	28.12.1991	20	(6)	2
Miguel Alfonso Herrero Javaloyas „Míchel"	29.07.1988	27	(8)	1
Sergio "Sergi" Guardiola Navarro	29.05.1991	17		3
Leonardo Gabriel Suárez (ARG)	30.03.1996	7	(5)	2
Laureano Antonio „Toni" Villa Suárez	07.01.1995	21	(5)	2
Anuar Tuhami (MAR)	15.01.1995	12	(7)	1
Daniele Verde (ITA)	20.06.1996	4	(18)	2
Forwards:	**DOB**	**M**	**(s)**	**G**
Christopher "Cris" Ramos de la Flor	18.01.1997	1		
Duje Čop (CRO)	01.02.1990	6	(12)	
Miguel de la Fuente Escudero	03.09.1999		(2)	
Iván López Álvarez „Ivi"	29.06.1994		(3)	
Óscar Plano Pedreño	11.02.1991	30	(3)	3
Pablo Hervías Ruiz	08.03.1993	2	(1)	
Stiven Ricardo Plaza Castillo (ECU)	11.03.1999		(2)	
Enes Ünal (TUR)	10.05.1997	24	(9)	6
Waldo Rubio Marín	17.08.1995	5	(3)	1
Trainer:	**DOB**	**M**		
Sergio González Soriano	10.11.1976	38		

Villarreal Club de Fútbol

Founded: 10.03.1923
Stadium: Estadio de la Cerámica, Villarreal (24,890)

Goalkeepers:	DOB	M	(s)	G
Andrés Fernández Moreno	16.12.1986	6		
Sergio Asenjo Andrés	28.06.1989	32		
Defenders:	**DOB**	**M**	**(s)**	**G**
Álvaro González Soberón	08.01.1990	33		1
Daniele Bonera (ITA)	31.05.1981	4	(1)	
José Ramiro Funes Mori (ARG)	05.03.1991	29	(2)	2
Jaume Vincent Costa Jordá	18.03.1988	18	(3)	1
Miguel Arturo Layún Prado (MEX)	25.06.1988	5	(3)	
Mario Gaspar Pérez Martínez	24.11.1990	30	(1)	1
Miguel Juan Llambrich „Miguelón“	18.01.1996	5	(3)	
Víctor Ruiz Torre	25.01.1989	22		
Xavier "Xavi" Quintillà Guasch	23.08.1996	7		
Midfielders:	**DOB**	**M**	**(s)**	**G**
Santiago Cáseres (ARG)	25.02.1997	17	(6)	
Dani Raba Antolí	29.10.1995	2	(6)	
Vicente Iborra de la Fuente	16.01.1988	19		3
Manuel Rolando Iturra Urrutia (CHI)	23.06.1984	1	(2)	
Javier Fuego Martínez „Javi Fuego“	04.01.1984	3	(2)	
Manuel "Manu" Morlanes Ariño	12.01.1999	7	(3)	
Pablo Fornals Malla	22.02.1996	28	(7)	2
Alfonso Pedraza Sag	09.04.1996	22	(12)	3
Santiago "Santi" Cazorla González	13.12.1984	30	(5)	4
Manuel Trigueros Muñoz	17.10.1991	18	(6)	
Forwards:	**DOB**	**M**	**(s)**	**G**
Carlos Arturo Bacca Ahumada (COL)	08.09.1986	12	(21)	6
Samuel Chukwueze (NGA)	22.05.1999	19	(7)	5
Gerard Moreno Balagueró	07.04.1992	25	(10)	8
Nicola Sansone (ITA)	10.09.1991		(3)	1
Karl Toko Ekambi (CMR)	14.09.1992	24	(10)	10
Trainer:	**DOB**	**M**		
Javier Calleja Revilla	12.05.1978	**14**		
Luis García Plaza [10.12.2018]	01.12.1972	7		
Javier Calleja Revilla [29.01.2019]	12.05.1978	17		

SECOND LEVEL
Segunda División 2018/2019

1.	CA Osasuna (*Promoted*)	42	26	9	7	59 - 35	87
2.	Granada CF (*Promoted*)	42	22	13	7	52 - 28	79
3.	Málaga CF (*Promotion Play-offs*)	42	21	11	10	51 - 31	74
4.	Albacete Balompié (*Promotion Play-offs*)	42	19	14	9	54 - 38	71
5.	RCD Mallorca (*Promotion Play-offs*)	42	19	12	11	53 - 37	69
6.	RC Deportivo La Coruña (*Promot. Play-offs*)	42	17	17	8	49 - 31	68
7.	Cádiz CF	42	16	16	10	53 - 36	64
8.	Real Oviedo CF	42	17	12	13	48 - 48	63
9.	Real Sporting de Gijón	42	16	13	13	43 - 38	61
10.	Unión Deportiva Almería	42	15	15	12	51 - 39	60
11.	Elche CF	42	13	16	13	49 - 52	55
12.	UD Las Palmas	42	12	18	12	48 - 50	54
13.	Extremadura UD Almendralejo	42	14	11	17	43 - 47	53
14.	Agrupación Deportiva Alcorcón	42	14	10	18	35 - 41	52
15.	Real Zaragoza	42	13	12	17	49 - 51	51
16.	CD Tenerife	42	11	17	14	40 - 50	50
17.	CD Numancia de Soria	42	11	16	15	42 - 50	49
18.	CD Lugo	42	10	17	15	43 - 51	47
19.	CF Rayo Majadahonda (*Relegated*)	42	12	9	21	46 - 61	45
20.	Club Gimnàstic de Tarragona (*Relegated*)	42	9	9	24	30 - 63	36
21.	Córdoba CF (*Relegated*)	42	7	13	22	47 - 78	34
22.	CF Reus Deportiu* (*Relegated*)	42	5	6	31	16 - 48	0

*Please note: CF Reus Deportiu was disqualified by the Spanish FA for financial issues.

Promotion Play-offs [12-23.06.2019]

RC Deportivo La Coruña - Málaga CF	4-2(1-2)	1-0(0-0)
RCD Mallorca - Albacete Balompié	2-0(1-0)	0-1(0-1)
RC Deportivo La Coruña - RCD Mallorca	2-0(1-0)	0-3(0-1)

RCD Mallorca promoted to La Liga 2019/2020.

NATIONAL TEAM

INTERNATIONAL MATCHES
(16.07.2018 – 15.07.2019)

08.09.2018	London	England - Spain	1-2(1-2)	(UNL)
11.09.2018	Elche	Spain - Croatia	6-0(3-0)	(UNL)
11.10.2018	Cardiff	Wales - Spain	1-4(0-3)	(F)
15.10.2018	Sevilla	Spain - England	2-3(0-3)	(UNL)
15.11.2018	Zagreb	Croatia - Spain	3-2(0-0)	(UNL)
18.11.2018	Las Palmas de Gran Canaria	Spain - Bosnia and Herzegovina	1-0(0-0)	(F)
23.03.2019	Valencia	Spain - Norway	2-1(1-0)	(ECQ)
26.03.2019	Attard	Malta - Spain	0-2(0-1)	(ECQ)
07.06.2019	Tórshavn	Faroe Islands - Spain	1-4(1-3)	(ECQ)
10.06.2019	Madrid	Spain - Sweden	3-0(0-0)	(ECQ)

08.09.2018 ENGLAND - SPAIN 1-2(1-2) UEFA Nations League A, Group 4
Wembley Stadium, London; Referee: Danny Desmond Makkelie (Netherlands); Attendance: 81,392
ESP: David de Gea, Dani Carvajal, Nacho, Sergio Ramos (Cap), Marcos Alonso (87.Iñigo Martínez), Sergio Busquets, Thiago Alcântara (80.Sergi Roberto), Isco, Saúl, Rodrigo, Iago Aspas (68.Marco Asensio). Trainer: Luis Enrique Martínez García.
Goals: Saúl (13), Rodrigo (32).

11.09.2018 SPAIN - CROATIA 6-0(3-0) UEFA Nations League A, Group 4
Estadio "Manuel Martínez Valero", Elche; Referee: Benoît Bastien (France); Attendance: 26,900
ESP: David de Gea, Dani Carvajal (75.Azpilicueta), Nacho, Sergio Ramos (Cap), José Gayà, Sergio Busquets (59.Rodri Hernández), Isco, Marco Asensio, Dani Ceballos, Rodrigo, Saúl (65.Thiago Alcântara). Trainer: Luis Enrique Martínez García.
Goals: Saúl (24), Marco Asensio (33), Lovre Kalinić (35 own goal), Rodrigo (49), Sergio Ramos (57), Isco (70).

11.10.2018 WALES - SPAIN 1-4(0-3) Friendly International
Principality Stadium, Cardiff; Referee: Anthony Taylor (England); Attendance: 50,232
ESP: David de Gea (46.Kepa), Azpilicueta (63.Jonny Castro), Sergio Ramos (Cap) (46.Marc Bartra), José Gayà, Raúl Albiol, Dani Ceballos, Rodri Hernández, Saúl (46.Koke), Suso (81.Rodrigo), Álvaro Morata, Paco Alcácer (73.Iago Aspas). Trainer: Luis Enrique Martínez García.
Goals: Paco Alcácer (8), Sergio Ramos (19), Paco Alcácer (29), Marc Bartra (74).

15.10.2018 SPAIN - ENGLAND 2-3(0-3) UEFA Nations League A, Group 4
Estadio "Benito Villamarín", Sevilla; Referee: Szymon Marciniak (Poland); Attendance: 50,355
ESP: David de Gea, Nacho, Sergio Ramos (Cap), Jonny Castro, Marcos Alonso, Sergio Busquets, Thiago Alcântara, Saúl (57.Paco Alcácer), Marco Asensio, Rodrigo (72.Álvaro Morata), Iago Aspas (57.Dani Ceballos). Trainer: Luis Enrique Martínez García.
Goals: Paco Alcácer (58), Sergio Ramos (90+8).

15.11.2018 CROATIA - SPAIN 3-2(0-0) UEFA Nations League A, Group 4
Stadion Maksimir, Zagreb; Referee: Aleksei Kulbakov (Belarus); Attendance: 33,018
ESP: David de Gea, Iñigo Martínez, Sergio Ramos (Cap), Jordi Alba, Sergio Busquets, Sergi Roberto, Isco, Saúl (74.Suso), Dani Ceballos, Iago Aspas (64.Álvaro Morata), Rodrigo (61.Marco Asensio). Trainer: Luis Enrique Martínez García.
Goals: Dani Ceballos (56), Sergio Ramos (78 penalty).

18.11.2018 SPAIN - BOSNIA AND HERZEGOVINA 1-0(0-0) Friendly International
Estadio de Gran Canaria, Las Palmas; Referee: Carlos Miguel Taborda Xistra (Portugal); Attendance: 17,798
ESP: Kepa (75.Pau López), Jonny Castro (51.Azpilicueta), Diego Llorente, Mario Hermoso, José Gayà, Isco (Cap), Marco Asensio, Dani Ceballos (64.Pablo Fornals), Rodri Hernández, Suso (59.Brais Méndez), Álvaro Morata (64.Rodrigo). Trainer: Luis Enrique Martínez García.
Goal: Brais Méndez (78).

23.03.2019 SPAIN - NORWAY 2-1(1-0) 16th EC. Qualifiers
Estadio Mestalla, Valencia; Referee: Andris Treimanis (Latvia); Attendance: 39,752
ESP: David de Gea, Jesús Navas, Sergio Ramos (Cap), Jordi Alba, Iñigo Martínez, Dani Parejo (76.Rodri Hernández), Sergio Busquets, Marco Asensio, Dani Ceballos (74.Sergio Canales, Álvaro Morata (89.Jaime Mata), Rodrigo. Trainer: Luis Enrique Martínez García.
Goals: Rodrigo (16), Sergio Ramos (71 penalty).

26.03.2019 MALTA - SPAIN 0-2(0-1) 16th EC. Qualifiers
Ta'Qali National Stadium, Attard; Referee: Andrew Dallas (Scotland); Attendance: 16,542
ESP: Kepa, Mario Hermoso, Sergio Ramos (Cap), José Gayà, Juan Bernat (56.Iker Muniain), Sergi Roberto, Sergio Canales, Saúl (65.Jesús Navas), Marco Asensio, Rodri Hernández, Álvaro Morata (79.Rodrigo). Trainer: Luis Enrique Martínez García.
Goals: Álvaro Morata (31, 73).

07.06.2019 FAROE ISLANDS - SPAIN 1-4(1-3) 16th EC. Qualifiers
Tórsvøllur, Tórshavn; Referee: Enea Jorgji (Albania); Attendance: 4,800
ESP: Kepa, Mario Hermoso, Sergio Ramos (Cap) (46.Diego Llorente), José Gayà, Jesús Navas, Sergi Roberto, Santi Cazorla, Isco (74.Fabián Ruiz), Rodri Hernández, Iago Aspas (56.Marco Asensio), Álvaro Morata. Trainer: Luis Enrique Martínez García.
Goals: Sergio Ramos (6), Jesús Navas (19), Teitur Matras Gestsson (34 own goal), José Gayà (71).

10.06.2019 SPAIN - SWEDEN 3-0(0-0) 16th EC. Qualifiers
Estadio "Santiago Bernabéu", Madrid; Referee: William Collum (Scotland); Attendance: 72,205
ESP: Kepa, Dani Carvajal, Sergio Ramos (Cap), Jordi Alba, Iñigo Martínez (88.Diego Llorente), Dani Parejo, Sergio Busquets, Isco, Marco Asensio (65.Álvaro Morata), Fabián Ruiz, Rodrigo (71.Mikel Oyarzabal). Trainer: Luis Enrique Martínez García.
Goals: Sergio Ramos (64 penalty), Álvaro Morata (85 penalty), Mikel Oyarzabal (87).

NATIONAL TEAM PLAYERS
(16.07.2018 – 15.07.2019)

Name	DOB	Caps	Goals	2018/2019:	Club
Goalkeepers					
DAVID DE GEA Quintana	07.11.1990	**39**	**0**	2018/2019:	*Manchester United FC (ENG)*
KEPA Arrizabalaga Revuelta	03.10.1994	**6**	**0**	2018/2019:	*Chelsea FC London (ENG)*
PAU LÓPEZ Sabata	13.12.1994	**1**	**0**	2018:	*Real Betis Balompié Sevilla*
Defenders					
César AZPILICUETA Tanco	28.08.1989	**25**	**0**	2018:	*Chelsea FC London (ENG)*
Daniel "DANI" CARVAJAL Ramos	11.01.1992	**21**	**0**	2018/2019:	*Real Madrid CF*
DIEGO Javier LLORENTE Ríos	16.08.1993	**4**	**0**	2018/2019:	*Real Sociedad de Fútbol San Sebastián*
IÑIGO MARTÍNEZ Berridi	17.05.1991	**8**	**0**	2019:	*Athletic Club Bilbao*
JESÚS NAVAS González	21.11.1985	**38**	**4**	2019:	*Sevilla FC*
Johnathan "JONNY" CASTRO Otto	03.03.1994	**3**	**0**	2018:	*Wolverhampton Wanderers FC (ENG)*
JORDI ALBA Ramos	21.03.1989	**69**	**8**	2018/2019:	*FC Barcelona*
JOSÉ Luis GAYÀ Peña	25.03.1995	**5**	**1**	2018/2019:	*Valencia CF*
JUAN BERNAT Velasco	01.03.1993	**8**	**0**	2019:	*Paris Saint-Germain FC (FRA)*
MARC BARTRA Aregall	15.01.1991	**14**	**1**	2018:	*Real Betis Balompié Sevilla*
MARCOS ALONSO Mendoza	28.12.1990	**3**	**0**	2018:	*Chelsea FC London (ENG)*
MARIO HERMOSO Canseco	18.06.1995	**3**	**0**	2018/2019:	*RCD Espanyol Barcelona*
José Ignacio Fernández Iglesias "NACHO"	18.01.1990	**22**	**1**	2018:	*Real Madrid CF*
RAÚL ALBIOL Tortajada	04.09.1985	**52**	**0**	2018:	*SSC Napoli (ITA)*
SERGIO RAMOS García	30.03.1986	**165**	**20**	2018/2019:	*Real Madrid CF*
Midfielders					
BRAIS MÉNDEZ Portela	07.01.1997	**1**	**1**	2018:	*RC Celta de Vigo*
Daniel "DANI" CEBALLOS Fernández	07.08.1996	**6**	**1**	2018/2019:	*Real Madrid CF*
Daniel "DANI" PAREJO Muñoz	16.04.1989	**3**	**0**	2019:	*Valencia CF*
FABIÁN RUIZ Peña	03.04.1996	**2**	**0**	2019:	*SSC Napoli (ITA)*
Francisco Román Alarcón Suárez "ISCO"	21.04.1992	**38**	**12**	2018/2019:	*Real Madrid CF*
Jorge Resurrección Merodio "KOKE"	08.01.1992	**44**	**0**	2018:	*Club Atlético de Madrid*
MARCO ASENSIO Willemsen	21.01.1996	**24**	**1**	2018/2019:	*Real Madrid CF*
PABLO FORNALS Malla	22.02.1996	**2**	**0**	2018:	*Villarreal CF*
Rodrigo "RODRI" HERNÁNDEZ Cascante	22.06.1996	**7**	**0**	2018/2019:	*Club Atlético de Madrid*
Santiago "SANTI" CAZORLA González	13.12.1984	**78**	**14**	2018/2019:	*Villarreal CF*
SAÚL Ñíguez Esclápez	21.11.1994	**16**	**2**	2018/2019:	*Club Atlético de Madrid*
SERGI ROBERTO Carnicer	07.02.1992	**7**	**1**	2018/2019:	*FC Barcelona*
SERGIO BUSQUETS Burgos	16.07.1988	**113**	**2**	2018/2019:	*FC Barcelona*
SERGIO CANALES Madrazo	16.02.1991	**2**	**0**	2019:	*Real Betis Balompié Sevilla*
Jesús Joaquín Fernández Sáez de la Torre "SUSO"	19.11.1993	**4**	**0**	2018:	*AC Milan (ITA)*
THIAGO ALCÂNTARA do Nascimento	11.04.1991	**34**	**2**	2018:	*FC Bayern München (GER)*
Forwards					
ÁLVARO Borja MORATA Martín	23.10.1992	**31**	**16**	2018: 28.01.2019->	*Chelsea FC London (ENG)* *Club Atlético de Madrid*
IAGO ASPAS Juncal	01.08.1987	**18**	**6**	2018/2019:	*RC Celta de Vigo*
IKER MUNIAIN Goñi	19.12.1992	**2**	**0**	2019:	*Athletic Club Bilbao*
JAIME MATA Arnaiz	24.10.1988	**1**	**0**	2019:	*Getafe CF*
MIKEL OYARZABAL Ugarte	21.04.1997	**2**	**1**	2018/2019:	*Real Sociedad de Fútbol San Sebastián*
Francisco "PACO" ALCÁCER García	30.08.1993	**15**	**9**	2018:	*BV Borussia Dortmund (GER)*
RODRIGO Moreno Machado	06.03.1991	**18**	**5**	2018/2019:	*Valencia CF*

National team coach

LUIS ENRIQUE Martínez García [09.07.2018 – 19.06.2018]	08.05.1970	10 M; 8 W; 0 D; 2 L; 28-10

SWEDEN

The Country:

Konungariket Sverige (Kingdom of Sweden)
Capital: Stockholm
Surface: 450,295 km²
Inhabitants: 10,302,984 [2019]
Time: UTC+1

The FA:

Svenska Fotbollsförbundet
Evenemangsgatan 31, 171 23 Solna
Tel: +46 8 735 0900
Founded: 1904
Member of FIFA since: 1904
Member of UEFA since: 1954
Website: www.svenskfotboll.se

NATIONAL TEAM RECORDS

First international match:	12.07.1908, Göteborg:	Sweden – Norway 11-3	
Most international caps:	Anders Gunnar Svensson		- 148 caps (1999-2013)
Most international goals:	Zlatan Ibrahimović		- 62 goals / 116 caps (2001-2016)

UEFA EUROPEAN CHAMPIONSHIP	
1960	Did not enter
1964	Qualifiers
1968	Qualifiers
1972	Qualifiers
1976	Qualifiers
1980	Qualifiers
1984	Qualifiers
1988	Qualifiers
1992	Final Tournament (Semi-Finals)
1996	Qualifiers
2000	Final Tournament (Group Stage)
2004	Final Tournament (Quarter-Finals)
2008	Final Tournament (Group Stage)
2012	Final Tournament (Group Stage)
2016	Final Tournament (Group Stage)

FIFA WORLD CUP	
1930	Did not enter
1934	Final Tournament (Quarter-Finals)
1938	Final Tournament (4th Place)
1950	Final Tournament (3rd Place)
1954	Qualifiers
1958	Final Tournament (Runners-up)
1962	Qualifiers
1966	Qualifiers
1970	Final Tournament (Group Stage)
1974	Final Tournament (2nd Round)
1978	Final Tournament (Group Stage)
1982	Qualifiers
1986	Qualifiers
1990	Final Tournament (Group Stage)
1994	Final Tournament (3rd Place)
1998	Qualifiers
2002	Final Tournament (2nd Round of 16)
2006	Final Tournament (2nd Round of 16)
2010	Qualifiers
2014	Qualifiers
2018	Final Tournament (Quarter-Finals)

UEFA NATIONS LEAGUE
2018/2019 – League B (promoted to League A)

OLYMPIC FOOTBALL TOURNAMENTS 1908-2016							
1908	4th Place	**1948**	**Winners**	**1972**	Did not enter	**1996**	Qualifiers
1912	Round 1	**1952**	3rd Place	**1976**	Did not enter	**2000**	Qualifiers
1920	Quarter-Finals	**1956**	Did not enter	**1980**	Did not enter	**2004**	Qualifiers
1924	3rd Place	**1960**	Did not enter	**1984**	Did not enter	**2008**	Qualifiers
1928	Did not enter	**1964**	Qualifiers	**1988**	Quarter-Finals	**2012**	Qualifiers
1936	1/8 - Finals	**1968**	Did not enter	**1992**	Quarter-Finals	**2016**	Group Stage

FIFA CONFEDERATIONS CUP 1992-2017
None

SWEDISH CLUB HONOURS IN EUROPEAN CLUB COMPETITIONS:

European Champion Clubs.Cup (1956-1992) / UEFA Champions League (1993-2019)		
None		
Fairs Cup (1858-1971) / UEFA Cup (1972-2009) / UEFA Europa League (2010-2019)		
IFK Göteborg	**2**	10981/1982, 1986/1987
UEFA Super Cup (1972-2018)		
None		
European Cup Winners.Cup 1961-1999*		
None		

**defunct competition*

NATIONAL COMPETITIONS
TABLE OF HONOURS

	CHAMPIONS*	CUP WINNERS	BEST GOALSCORERS	
1896	Örgryte IS Göteborg	-	-	
1897	Örgryte IS Göteborg	-	-	
1898	Örgryte IS Göteborg	-	-	
1899	Örgryte IS Göteborg	-	-	
1900	AIK Stockholm	-	-	
1901	AIK Stockholm	-	-	
1902	Örgryte IS Göteborg	-	-	
1903	Göteborgs IF	-	-	
1904	Örgryte IS Göteborg	-	-	
1905	Örgryte IS Göteborg	-	-	
1906	Örgryte IS Göteborg	-	-	
1907	Örgryte IS Göteborg	-	-	
1908	IFK Göteborg	-	-	
1909	Örgryte IS Göteborg	-	-	
1910	IFK Göteborg	-	-	
1911	AIK Stockholm	-	-	
1912	Djurgårdens IF Stockholm	-	-	
1913	Örgryte IS Göteborg	-	-	
1914	AIK Stockholm	-	-	
1915	Djurgårdens IF Stockholm	-	-	
1916	AIK Stockholm	-	-	
1917	Djurgårdens IF Stockholm	-	-	
1918	IFK Göteborg	-	-	
1919	GAIS Göteborg	-	-	
1920	Djurgårdens IF Stockholm	-	-	
1921	IFK Eskilstuna	-	-	
1922	GAIS Göteborg	-	-	
1923	AIK Stockholm	-	-	
1924	Fässbergs IF Mölndal	-	-	
1925	Brynäs IF Gävle	-	-	
	--	--	--	
1930/1931	GAIS Göteborg	-	John Nilsson (GAIS Göteborg)	26
1931/1932	AIK Stockholm	-	Carl-Erik Holmberg (Örgryte IS Göteborg)	29
1932/1933	Helsingborgs IF	-	Torsten Bunke (Helsingborgs IF)	21
1933/1934	Helsingborgs IF	-	Sven Jonasson (IF Elfsborg Borås)	20
1934/1935	IFK Göteborg	-	Harry Andersson (IK Sleipner Norrköping)	23
1935/1936	IF Elfsborg Borås	-	Sven Jonasson (IF Elfsborg Borås)	24
1936/1937	AIK Stockholm	-	Olle Zethlerlund (AIK Stockholm)	23
1937/1938	IK Sleipner Norrköping	-	Curt Hjelm (IK Sleipner Norrköping)	13
1938/1939	IF Elfsborg Borås	-	Erik Persson (AIK Stockholm) Ove Andersson (Malmö FF) Yngve Lindgren (Örgryte IS Göteborg)	16
1939/1940	IF Elfsborg Borås	-	Anders Pålsson (Helsingborgs IF)	17
1940/1941	Helsingborgs IF	Helsingborgs IF	Stig Nyström (IK Brage Borlänge)	17
1941/1942	IFK Göteborg	GAIS Göteborg	Sven Jacobsson (GAIS Göteborg)	20
1942/1943	IFK Norrköping	IFK Norrköping	Gunnar Nordahl (Degerfors IF)	16
1943/1944	Malmö FF	Malmö FF	Leif Larsson (IFK Göteborg)	19
1944/1945	IFK Norrköping	IFK Norrköping	Gunnar Nordahl (IFK Norrköping)	27
1945/1946	IFK Norrköping	Malmö FF	Gunnar Nordahl (IFK Norrköping)	25
1946/1947	IFK Norrköping	Malmö FF	Gunnar Gren (IFK Göteborg)	18
1947/1948	IFK Norrköping	Råå IF	Gunnar Nordahl (IFK Norrköping)	18
1948/1949	Malmö FF	AIK Stockholm	Carl-Johan Franck (Helsingborgs IF)	19
1949/1950	Malmö FF	AIK Stockholm	Ingvar Rydell (Malmö FF)	22
1950/1951	Malmö FF	Malmö FF	Hasse Jeppson (Djurgårdens IF Stockholm)	17
1951/1952	IFK Norrköping	*No competition*	Karl-Alfred Jacobsson (GAIS Göteborg)	17
1952/1953	Malmö FF	Malmö FF	Karl-Alfred Jacobsson (GAIS Göteborg)	24
1953/1954	GAIS Göteborg	*No competition*	Karl-Alfred Jacobsson (GAIS Göteborg)	21
1954/1955	Djurgårdens IF Stockholm	*No competition*	Kurt Hamrin (AIK Stockholm)	22
1955/1956	IFK Norrköping	*No competition*	Sylve Bengtsson (Halmstads BK)	22
1956/1957	IFK Norrköping	*No competition*	Harry Bild (IFK Norrköping)	19
1957/1958	IFK Göteborg	*No competition*	Bertil Johansson (IFK Göteborg) Henry Källgren (IFK Norrköping)	27
1959	Djurgårdens IF Stockholm	*No competition*	Rune Börjesson (Örgryte IS Göteborg)	21
1960	IFK Norrköping	*No competition*	Rune Börjesson (Örgryte IS Göteborg)	24
1961	IF Elfsborg Borås	*No competition*	Bertil Johansson (IFK Göteborg)	20
1962	IFK Norrköping	*No competition*	Leif Skiöld (Djurgårdens IF Stockholm)	21
1963	IFK Norrköping	*No competition*	Lars Heinermann (Degerfors IF) Bo Larsson (Malmö FF)	17
1964	Djurgårdens IF Stockholm	*No competition*	Krister Granbom (Helsingborgs IF)	22
1965	Malmö FF	*No competition*	Bo Larsson (Malmö FF)	28
1966	Djurgårdens IF Stockholm	*No competition*	Ove Kindvall (IFK Norrköping)	20

1967	Malmö FF	Malmö FF	Dag Szepanski (Malmö FF)	22
1968	Östers IF Växjö	*No competition*	Ove Eklund (Åtvidabergs FF)	16
1969	IFK Göteborg	IFK Norrköping (1968/69)	Reine Almqvist (IFK Göteborg)	16
1970	Malmö FF	Åtvidabergs FF (1969/70)	Bo Larsson (Malmö FF)	16
1971	Malmö FF	Åtvidabergs FF (1970/71)	Roland Sandberg (Åtvidabergs FF)	17
1972	Åtvidabergs FF	Landskrona BoIS (1971/72)	Ralf Edström (Åtvidabergs FF) Roland Sandberg (Åtvidabergs FF)	16
1973	Åtvidabergs FF	Malmö FF (1972/73)	Jan Mattsson (Östers IF Växjö)	20
1974	Malmö FF	Malmö FF (1973/74)	Jan Mattsson (Östers IF Växjö)	22
1975	Malmö FF	Malmö FF (1974/75)	Jan Mattsson (Östers IF Växjö)	31
1976	Halmstads BK	AIK Stockholm (1975/76)	Rutger Backe (Halmstads BK)	21
1977	Malmö FF	Östers IF Växjö (1976/77)	Reine Almqvist (IFK Göteborg) Mats Aronsson (Landskrona BoIS)	15
1978	Östers IF Växjö	Malmö FF (1977/78)	Tommy Berggren (Djurgårdens IF Stockholm)	19
1979	Halmstads BK	IFK Göteborg (1978/79)	Mats Werner (Hammarby IF)	14
1980	Östers IF Växjö	Malmö FF (1979/80)	Billy Ohlsson (Hammarby IF)	19
1981	Östers IF Växjö	Kalmar FF (1980/81)	Torbjörn Nilsson (IFK Göteborg)	20
1982	IFK Göteborg	IFK Göteborg (1981/82)	Dan Corneliusson (IFK Göteborg)	12
1983	IFK Göteborg	IFK Göteborg (1982/83)	Thomas Ahlström (IF Elfsborg Borås)	16
1984	IFK Göteborg	Malmö FF (1983/84)	Billy Ohlsson (Hammarby IF)	14
1985	Örgryte IS Göteborg	AIK Stockholm (1984/85)	Sören Börjesson (Örgryte IS Göteborg) Peter Karlsson (Kalmar FF) William Lansdowne (ENG, Kalmar FF)	10
1986	Malmö FF	Malmö FF (1985/86)	Johnny Ekström (IFK Göteborg)	13
1987	IFK Göteborg	Kalmar FF (1986/87)	Lasse Larsson (Malmö FF)	19
1988	Malmö FF	IFK Norrköping (1987/88)	Dan Martin Nataniel Dahlin (Malmö FF)	17
1989	IFK Norrköping	Malmö FF (1988/89)	Jan Hellström (IFK Norrköping)	16
1990	IFK Göteborg	Djurgårdens IF Stockholm (1989/90)	Kaj Eskelinen (IFK Göteborg)	10
1991	IFK Göteborg	IFK Norrköping (1990/91) IFK Göteborg (1991)	Bernt Kennet Andersson (IFK Göteborg)	13
1992	AIK Stockholm	*No competition*	Hans Eklund (Östers IF Växjö)	16
1993	IFK Göteborg	Degerfors IF (1992/93)	Henrik Bertilsson (Halmstads BK) Mats Lilienberg (Trelleborgs FF)	18
1994	IFK Göteborg	IFK Norrköping (1993/94)	Niclas Kindvall (IFK Norrköping)	23
1995	IFK Göteborg	Halmstads BK (1994/95)	Niklas Skoog (Västra Frölunda IF)	17
1996	IFK Göteborg	AIK Stockholm (1995/96)	Andreas Andersson (IFK Göteborg)	19
1997	Halmstads BK	AIK Stockholm (1996/97)	Mats Lilienberg (Halmstads BK) Christer Mattiasson (IF Elfsborg Borås) Dan Sahlin (Örebro SK)	14
1998	AIK Stockholm	Helsingborgs IF (1997/98)	Arild Stavrum (Helsingborgs IF)	18
1999	Helsingborgs IF	AIK Stockholm (1998/99)	Marcus Allbäck (Örgryte IS Göteborg)	15
2000	Halmstads BK	Örgryte IS Göteborg (1999/2000)	Fredrik Berglund (IF Elfsborg Borås)	18
2001	Hammarby IF	IF Elfsborg Borås (2000/01)	Stefan Selaković (Halmstads BK)	15
2002	Djurgårdens IF Stockholm	Djurgårdens IF Stockholm	Peter Emeka Ijeh (NGA, Malmö FF)	24
2003	Djurgårdens IF Stockholm	IF Elfsborg Borås	Niklas Skoog (Malmö FF)	22
2004	Malmö FF	Djurgårdens IF Stockholm	Markus Rosenberg (Halmstads BK)	14
2005	Djurgårdens IF Stockholm	Djurgårdens IF Stockholm	Gunnar Heiðar Þorvaldsson (ISL, Halmstads BK)	16
2006	IF Elfsborg Borås	Helsingborgs IF	Ariclenes da Silva Ferreira "Ari" (BRA, Kalmar FF)	15
2007	IFK Göteborg	Kalmar FF	Marcus Berg (IFK Göteborg) Razak Omotoyossi (BEN, Helsingborgs IF)	14
2008	Kalmar FF	IFK Göteborg	Patrik Ingelsten (Kalmar FF)	19
2009	AIK Stockholm	AIK Stockholm	Tobias Hysén (IFK Göteborg) Francisco Wánderson do Carmo Carneiro (BRA, GAIS Göteborg)	18
2010	Malmö FF	Helsingborgs IF	Alexander Gerndt (Gefle IF / Helsingborgs IF)	20
2011	Helsingborgs IF	Helsingborgs IF	Mathias Ranégie (BK Häcken Göteborg / Malmö FF)	21
2012	IF Elfsborg Borås	*No competition*	Abdul Majeed Waris (GHA, BK Häcken Göteborg)	23
2013	Malmö FF	IFK Göteborg (2012/13)	Imad Khalili (IFK Norrköping / Helsingborgs IF)	15
2014	Malmö FF	IF Elfsborg Borås (2013/14)	Lasse Vibe (IFK Göteborg)	23
2015	IFK Norrköping	IFK Göteborg (2014/15)	Emir Kujović (IFK Norrköping)	21
2016	Malmö FF	BK Häcken Göteborg (2015/16)	John Owoeri (NGA, BK Häcken Göteborg)	17
2017	Malmö FF	Östersunds FK (2016/17)	Karl Albin Elis Holmberg (IFK Norrköping) Magnus Eriksson (Djurgårdens IF Stockholm)	14
2018	AIK Stockholm	Djurgårdens IF Stockholm (2017/18)	Paulo José de Oliveira „Paulinho" (BRA, BK Häcken Göteborg)	20

*Svenska Mästerskapet (1896–1925), Allsvenskan (1931–1981), Allsvenskan Play-offs (1982–1990), Mästerskapsserien (1991–1992), Allsvenskan (since 1993).

NATIONAL CHAMPIONSHIP

Allsvenskan 2018

(01.04.2018 – 11.11.2018)

Results

Round 1 [01-02.04.2018]
BK Häcken - Kalmar FF 1-0(0-0)
Hammarby IF - IK Sirius 3-1(1-0)
Östersunds FK - Djurgårdens IF 0-1(0-1)
Trelleborgs FF - IFK Göteborg 1-3(1-1)
AIK Stockholm - Dalkurd FF 2-0(1-0)
IFK Norrköping - Brommapojkarna 2-1(1-0)
IF Elfsborg - Malmö FF 1-2(1-2)
GIF Sundsvall - Örebro SK 0-0

Round 2 [07-10.04.2018]
Örebro SK - IFK Norrköping 1-1(0-0)
Djurgårdens IF - Trelleborgs FF 1-1(1-0)
Kalmar FF - IF Elfsborg 1-0(1-0)
Dalkurd FF - Östersunds FK 3-0(1-0)
IF Brommapojkarna - BK Häcken 2-0(1-0)
Malmö FF - AIK Stockholm 1-1(1-1)
IFK Göteborg - Hammarby IF 1-2(0-0)
IK Sirius - GIF Sundsvall 1-3(1-1) [03.07.]

Round 3 [13-16.04.2018]
GIF Sundsvall - Malmö FF 2-2(0-0)
Trelleborgs FF - Örebro SK 1-2(1-1)
IF Elfsborg - IK Sirius 0-1(0-0)
BK Häcken - Dalkurd FF 3-0(1-0)
AIK Stockholm - Djurgårdens IF 2-0(1-0)
IFK Norrköping - Kalmar FF 3-1(1-1)
Östersunds FK - IFK Göteborg 2-1(0-0)
Hammarby IF - IF Brommapojkarna 4-0(1-0)

Round 4 [17-19.04.2018]
GIF Sundsvall - Trelleborgs FF 1-0(0-0)
Djurgårdens IF - Malmö FF 3-0(0-0)
Kalmar FF - Östersunds FK 1-1(0-1)
Örebro SK - AIK Stockholm 1-1(1-0)
IK Sirius - BK Häcken 0-0
IF Brommapojkarna - IF Elfsborg 0-2(0-0)
IFK Göteborg - Dalkurd FF 1-0(1-0)
Hammarby IF - IFK Norrköping 2-1(2-0)

Round 5 [21-23.04.2018]
Östersunds FK - Örebro SK 0-2(0-1)
Dalkurd FF - GIF Sundsvall 2-2(2-1)
BK Häcken - Hammarby IF 2-2(1-2)
AIK Stockholm - IFK Göteborg 2-0(1-0)
Trelleborgs FF - Kalmar FF 0-1(0-0)
IF Elfsborg - Djurgårdens IF 2-2(1-2)
Malmö FF - IF Brommapojkarna 3-1(1-0)
IFK Norrköping - IK Sirius 1-0(0-0)

Round 6 [27-30.04.2018]
AIK Stockholm - IK Sirius 2-0(1-0)
IFK Göteborg - BK Häcken 2-1(1-0)
Djurgårdens IF - Hammarby IF 1-2(0-1)
GIF Sundsvall - IF Elfsborg 2-1(1-0)
Kalmar FF - Malmö FF 3-0(3-0)
IFK Norrköping - Trelleborgs FF 1-2(0-0)
IF Brommapojkarna - Östersunds FK 0-4(0-1)
Örebro SK - Dalkurd FF 3-2(0-0)

Round 7 [05-07.05.2018]
Hammarby IF - GIF Sundsvall 4-3(3-0)
Östersunds FK - IFK Norrköping 0-2(0-2)
IF Brommapojkarna - Djurgårdens IF 1-0(1-0)
Dalkurd FF - Kalmar FF 1-2(1-1)
IF Elfsborg - AIK Stockholm 0-0
Trelleborgs FF - BK Häcken 0-3(0-2)
Malmö FF - IFK Göteborg 1-2(0-1)
IK Sirius - Örebro SK 2-4(0-1)

Round 8 [12-14.05.2018]
GIF Sundsvall - IF Brommapojkarna 3-0(2-0)
Djurgårdens IF - Dalkurd FF 1-0(0-0)
IFK Göteborg - IFK Norrköping 0-2(0-0)
Örebro SK - Hammarby IF 1-2(1-0)
Trelleborgs FF - Malmö FF 1-0(0-0)
AIK Stockholm - Östersunds FK 1-1(1-0)
BK Häcken - IF Elfsborg 5-0(2-0)
Kalmar FF - IK Sirius 1-0(1-0)

Round 9 [17-21.05.2018]
Djurgårdens IF - Örebro SK 2-0(0-0)
IF Brommapojkarna - Kalmar FF 2-1(2-0)
IK Sirius - Trelleborgs FF 1-1(1-1)
GIF Sundsvall - Östersunds FK 2-3(1-2)
IFK Norrköping - Dalkurd FF 4-2(1-1)
Hammarby IF - AIK Stockholm 0-1(0-0)
Malmö FF - BK Häcken 2-0(0-0)
IF Elfsborg - IFK Göteborg 1-1(0-0)

Round 10 [22-24.05.2018]
Hammarby IF - Malmö FF 3-2(1-1) [16.05.]
Örebro SK - Kalmar FF 2-1(1-1)
BK Häcken - AIK Stockholm 1-1(1-0)
IFK Norrköping - GIF Sundsvall 1-0(0-0)
Östersunds FK - IK Sirius 5-2(1-1)
Dalkurd FF - IF Elfsborg 1-4(0-1)
IFK Göteborg - Djurgårdens IF 1-3(0-2)
Trelleborgs FF - IF Brommapojkarna 2-1(2-0)

Round 11 [26-27.05.2018]
AIK Stockholm - IFK Norrköping 3-3(2-0)
Östersunds FK - BK Häcken 2-0(1-0)
Kalmar FF - Hammarby IF 1-1(0-0)
Malmö FF - Dalkurd FF 1-1(0-1)
GIF Sundsvall - IFK Göteborg 2-0(1-0)
IF Brommapojkarna - Örebro SK 0-0
IF Elfsborg - Trelleborgs FF 2-1(2-1)
IK Sirius - Djurgårdens IF 1-5(0-1)

Round 12 [07-09.07.2018]
IK Sirius - Malmö FF 0-4(0-1)
Dalkurd FF - IF Brommapojkarna 3-0(3-0)
BK Häcken - GIF Sundsvall 3-0(1-0)
Trelleborgs FF - AIK Stockholm 1-4(0-0)
IFK Göteborg - Kalmar FF 1-3(0-1)
Djurgårdens IF - IFK Norrköping 1-1(1-0)
Örebro SK - IF Elfsborg 1-2(0-0)
Hammarby IF - Östersunds FK 1-2(1-0)

Round 13 [14-16.07.2018]
IF Brommapojkarna - IK Sirius 0-1(0-0)
Dalkurd FF - Trelleborgs FF 2-2(1-0)
Malmö FF - Östersunds FK 1-1(1-0)
IFK Göteborg - Örebro SK 2-0(1-0)
Kalmar FF - Djurgårdens IF 0-1(0-1)
IFK Norrköping - BK Häcken 2-1(1-1)
GIF Sundsvall - AIK Stockholm 0-1(0-0)
IF Elfsborg - Hammarby IF 0-0

Round 14 [21-23.07.2018]
Örebro SK - Malmö FF 1-2(0-0)
Östersunds FK - Trelleborgs FF 4-1(4-1)
Kalmar FF - GIF Sundsvall 0-2(0-1)
AIK Stockholm - Brommapojkarna 5-1(1-1)
Djurgårdens IF - BK Häcken 2-1(1-1)
IK Sirius - IFK Göteborg 3-2(1-2)
Hammarby IF - Dalkurd FF 4-1(4-0)
IFK Norrköping - IF Elfsborg 1-0(1-0)

Round 15 [28-30.07.2018]
IFK Göteborg - IF Brommapojkarna 3-0(1-0)
Östersunds FK - IF Elfsborg 1-0(1-0)
Dalkurd FF - IK Sirius 1-3(0-2)
Malmö FF - IFK Norrköping 2-1(1-0)
AIK Stockholm - Kalmar FF 1-0(0-0)
Djurgårdens IF - GIF Sundsvall 1-1(0-0)
BK Häcken - Örebro SK 1-1(0-0)
Trelleborgs FF - Hammarby IF 1-3(0-2)

Round 16 [04-06.08.2018]
IK Sirius - AIK Stockholm 2-3(2-1) [02.05.]
Malmö FF - Djurgårdens IF 1-0(0-0) [03.05.]
IF Brommapojkarna - Dalkurd FF 2-1(0-1)
Kalmar FF - IFK Göteborg 2-1(0-0)
Hammarby IF - Trelleborgs FF 1-0(0-0)
Örebro SK - BK Häcken 1-2(0-0)
IF Elfsborg - Östersunds FK 0-2(0-2)
GIF Sundsvall - IFK Norrköping 1-1(0-1)

Round 17 [10-13.08.2018]
Dalkurd FF - Malmö FF 0-1(0-1)
IFK Göteborg - IK Sirius 2-3(0-0)
Örebro SK - IF Brommapojkarna 0-1(0-0)
BK Häcken - Djurgårdens IF 5-0(2-0)
Östersunds FK - Kalmar FF 2-0(0-0)
AIK Stockholm - IF Elfsborg 1-0(0-0)
IFK Norrköping - Hammarby IF 0-0
Trelleborgs FF - GIF Sundsvall 1-6(1-3)

Round 18 [17-20.08.2018]
IK Sirius - Dalkurd FF 2-3(0-1)
Malmö FF - Trelleborgs FF 3-0(3-0)
IF Elfsborg - IFK Norrköping 0-1(0-0)
GIF Sundsvall - BK Häcken 0-2(0-1)
Brommapojkarna - AIK Stockholm 0-2(0-1)
Djurgårdens IF - Kalmar FF 0-2(0-1)
IFK Göteborg - Östersunds FK 2-1(2-1)
Hammarby IF - Örebro SK 2-0(1-0)

Round 19 [26-27.08.2018]
BK Häcken - IF Brommapojkarna 6-0(3-0)
Malmö FF - IK Sirius 5-0(0-0)
Östersunds FK - GIF Sundsvall 1-2(1-0)
AIK Stockholm - Trelleborgs FF 2-0(1-0)
Djurgårdens IF - IF Elfsborg 2-2(0-0)
Dalkurd FF - Hammarby IF 2-3(1-2)
Kalmar FF - Örebro SK 0-1(0-0)
IFK Norrköping - IFK Göteborg 2-1(0-0)

Round 20 [31.08.-02.09.2018]
Trelleborgs FF - IFK Norrköping 1-1(1-1)
AIK Stockholm - BK Häcken 3-0(3-0)
Örebro SK - Östersunds FK 2-1(1-0)
IF Brommapojkarna - Malmö FF 0-3(0-1)
Dalkurd FF - IFK Göteborg 1-1(1-0)
Hammarby IF - Djurgårdens IF 1-3(0-1)
IF Elfsborg - Kalmar FF 1-1(1-1)
GIF Sundsvall - IK Sirius 4-0(0-0)

Round 21 [15-17.09.2018]
Örebro SK - GIF Sundsvall 2-1(0-1)
Östersunds FK - Malmö FF 2-3(2-2)
IFK Norrköping - AIK Stockholm 2-0(0-0)
Djurgårdens IF - IF Brommapojkarna 0-1(0-0)
IFK Göteborg - IF Elfsborg 2-2(0-2)
BK Häcken - Trelleborgs FF 2-1(1-1)
Kalmar FF - Dalkurd FF 0-0
IK Sirius - Hammarby IF 1-1(1-0)

Round 22 [21-24.09.2018]
IF Brommapojkarna - GIF Sundsvall 1-3(0-1)
IF Elfsborg - Örebro SK 1-0(1-0)
IK Sirius - Östersunds FK 0-1(0-0)
Trelleborgs FF - Djurgårdens IF 0-3(0-2)
Dalkurd FF - IFK Norrköping 0-2(0-2)
AIK Stockholm - Hammarby IF 1-0(0-0)
Malmö FF - Kalmar FF 4-0(3-0)
BK Häcken - IFK Göteborg 4-1(2-0)

Round 23 [25-27.09.2018]
Örebro SK - IK Sirius 0-0
Hammarby IF - IF Elfsborg 0-1(0-1)
IFK Norrköping - Malmö FF 3-1(2-1)
Östersunds FK - IF Brommapojkarna 3-1(1-0)
GIF Sundsvall - Djurgårdens IF 1-1(0-1)
Trelleborgs FF - Dalkurd FF 0-1(0-0)
IFK Göteborg - AIK Stockholm 0-2(0-1)
Kalmar FF - BK Häcken 1-2(1-0)

Round 24 [29.09.-01.10.2018]
IK Sirius - IFK Norrköping 1-1(0-1)
Dalkurd FF - AIK Stockholm 0-4(0-2)
Kalmar FF - IF Brommapojkarna 1-1(0-0)
Djurgårdens IF - Östersunds FK 0-2(0-1)
Malmö FF - GIF Sundsvall 0-0
IF Elfsborg - BK Häcken 0-3(0-0)
Hammarby IF - IFK Göteborg 3-0(1-0)
Örebro SK - Trelleborgs FF 4-0(2-0)

Round 25 [05-08.10.2018]
Östersunds FK - Dalkurd FF 3-0(2-0)
IK Sirius - IF Elfsborg 4-2(2-2)
IFK Göteborg - Trelleborgs FF 2-2(1-1)
BK Häcken - Malmö FF 1-1(0-0)
AIK Stockholm - Örebro SK 1-1(1-0)
IF Brommapojkarna - Hammarby IF 2-4(1-1)
IFK Norrköping - Djurgårdens IF 1-1(1-0)
GIF Sundsvall - Kalmar FF 2-0(1-0)

Round 26 [20-22.10.2018]
Malmö FF - Hammarby IF 2-1(0-1)
Dalkurd FF - Örebro SK 1-0(0-0)
Djurgårdens IF - AIK Stockholm 0-0
BK Häcken - Östersunds FK 2-0(2-0)
IF Elfsborg - GIF Sundsvall 2-0(0-0)
Kalmar FF - IFK Norrköping 1-2(1-1)
Trelleborgs FF - IK Sirius 1-2(1-1)
IF Brommapojkarna - IFK Göteborg 0-2(0-1)

Round 27 [26-29.10.2018]
IFK Göteborg - GIF Sundsvall 1-2(0-2)
Trelleborgs FF - IF Elfsborg 2-2(0-2)
Dalkurd FF - BK Häcken 0-5(0-3)
Hammarby IF - Kalmar FF 0-0
Örebro SK - Djurgårdens IF 1-1(0-1)
IFK Norrköping - Östersunds FK 4-2(2-1)
IK Sirius - IF Brommapojkarna 4-2(1-1)
AIK Stockholm - Malmö FF 1-1(0-1)

Round 28 [30.10.-01.11.2018]
IF Elfsborg - Dalkurd FF 0-0
Brommapojkarna - IFK Norrköping 0-1(0-0)
Djurgårdens IF - IFK Göteborg 2-0(2-0)
BK Häcken - IK Sirius 2-1(1-1)
Kalmar FF - Trelleborgs FF 2-1(0-0)
GIF Sundsvall - Hammarby IF 2-3(0-2)
Malmö FF - Örebro SK 4-0(2-0)
Östersunds FK - AIK Stockholm 1-2(0-2)

Round 29 [04-05.11.2018]
IFK Göteborg - Malmö FF 0-3(0-0)
IFK Norrköping - Örebro SK 3-2(0-1)
AIK Stockholm - GIF Sundsvall 0-0
Hammarby IF - BK Häcken 1-0(0-0)
Dalkurd FF - Djurgårdens IF 1-2(1-1)
IF Elfsborg - IF Brommapojkarna 1-2(1-0)
IK Sirius - Kalmar FF 1-1(0-0)
Trelleborgs FF - Östersunds FK 0-1(0-1)

Round 30 [11.11.2018]
IF Brommapojkarna - Trelleborgs FF 3-0(2-0)
Djurgårdens IF - IK Sirius 1-0(1-0)
BK Häcken - IFK Norrköping 0-1(0-1)
Kalmar FF - AIK Stockholm 0-1(0-1)
Malmö FF - IF Elfsborg 2-0(0-0)
Örebro SK - IFK Göteborg 1-3(0-1)
Östersunds FK - Hammarby IF 3-3(2-0)
GIF Sundsvall - Dalkurd FF 0-1(0-1)

Final Standings

1.	**AIK Stockholm**	30	19	10	1	50	-	16	67
2.	IFK Norrköping	30	19	8	3	51	-	27	65
3.	Malmö FF	30	17	7	6	57	-	29	58
4.	Hammarby IF Stockholm	30	17	7	6	56	-	35	58
5.	BK Häcken Göteborg	30	16	5	9	58	-	27	53
6.	Östersunds FK	30	15	4	11	51	-	39	49
7.	Djurgårdens IF Stockholm	30	13	9	8	40	-	31	48
8.	GIF Sundsvall	30	12	8	10	47	-	35	44
9.	Örebro SK	30	9	8	13	34	-	40	35
10.	Kalmar FF	30	9	7	14	27	-	35	34
11.	IFK Göteborg	30	9	4	17	38	-	53	31
12.	IF Elfsborg Borås	30	7	9	14	29	-	41	30
13.	IK Sirius Uppsala	30	8	6	16	37	-	61	30
14.	IF Brommapojkarna (*Relegation Play-offs*)	30	8	2	20	25	-	64	26
15.	Dalkurd FF Uppsala (*Relegated*)	30	6	6	18	30	-	57	24
16.	Trelleborgs FF (*Relegated*)	30	3	6	21	24	-	64	15

Top goalscorers:

20 Paulo José de Oliveira „Paulinho" (BRA)
BK Häcken Göteborg

17 Linus Hallenius
GIF Sundsvall

13 Nikola Đurđić (SRB)
Hammarby IF Stockholm

13 Markus Rosenberg
Malmö FF

12 Romain Gall (USA)
GIF Sundsvall / Malmö FF

12 Henok Goitom (ERI)
AIK Stockholm

Relegation Play-offs

AFC Eskilstuna - IF Brommapojkarna	0-1(0-1)	2-1(0-1)

AFC Eskilstuna promoted to the Allsvenskan 2019.

NATIONAL CUP
Svenska Cupen 2018/2019

Second Round [15/21-23.08./22.11.2018]

Karlstad BK - Gefle IF	1-0(0-0)
Team ThorenGruppen FF - AFC Eskilstuna	0-3(0-1)
Strömsbergs IF - IK Sirius Uppsala	0-4(0-3)
Karlbergs BK - Dalkurd FF	1-2(0-0,1-1)
Skoftebyns IF - Falkenbergs FF	1-4(0-3)
Hässleholms IF - Trelleborgs FF	3-2(1-1,2-2)
Nyköpings BIS - GIF Sundsvall	3-2(0-0,1-1)
FC Rosengård 1917 - Landskrona BoIS	2-0(2-0)
Assyriska Turabdin IK - Kalmar FF	3-1(1-1)
Sävedalens IF - Halmstads BK	0-2(0-0)
Hudiksvalls FF - Jönköpings Södra IF	1-3(0-0)
IF Sylvia - Djurgårdens IF Stockholm	0-4(0-2)
Eskilsminne IF - Helsingborgs IF	1-0(0-0)
FK Karlskrona - Varbergs BoIS	0-6(0-2)
Motala AIF - IF Elfsborg Borås	0-4(0-4)
Växjö United FC - BK Häcken Göteborg	0-5(0-4)
Carlstad United BK - Hammarby IF Stockholm	0-3(0-2)
Brottby SK - IFK Norrköping	0-10(0-4)
Enskede IK - Degerfors IF	1-2(0-0,1-1)
Arameisk-Syrianska IF - IK Frej	1-2(0-1)
FC Gute - Östersunds FK	2-5(0-3)
Akropolis IF Spånga - Örebro SK	1-2(0-0)
Västerås SK - IK Brage Borlänge	1-3(0-3)
Sandvikens IF - AIK Stockholm	0-2(0-1)
Friska Viljor FC - IF Brommapojkarna	1-3(0-1,1-1)
Smedby AIS - GAIS Göteborg	0-3(0-1)
Assyriska BK - IFK Värnamo	0-5(0-3)
Lindome GIF - Norrby IF Borås	0-1(0-0)
Skövde AIK - Östers IF Växjö	0-3(0-1)
Hisingsbacka FC - Örgryte IS Göteborg	1-5(1-4)
Torns IF - IFK Göteborg	0-4(0-1)
Lunds BK - Malmö FF	0-2(0-0)

Third Round [16.02.-04.03.2019]

Group 1	
AIK Stockholm - Jönköpings Södra IF	1-0(1-0)
Örgryte IS Göteborg - Norrby IF Borås	2-0(1-0)
Norrby IF Borås - AIK Stockholm	1-1(1-1)
Örgryte IS Göteborg - Jönköpings Södra IF	1-2(1-0)
Jönköpings Södra IF - Norrby IF Borås	1-0(1-0)
AIK Stockholm - Örgryte IS Göteborg	1-0(0-0)
Qualified: AIK Stockholm	

Group 2	
Assyriska Turabdin IK - AFC Eskilstuna	0-4(0-3)
IFK Norrköping - IFK Värnamo	3-1(1-0)
Assyriska Turabdin IK - IFK Norrköping	0-2(0-1)
AFC Eskilstuna - IFK Värnamo	4-0(1-0)
IFK Värnamo - Assyriska Turabdin IK	3-4(2-1)
IFK Norrköping - AFC Eskilstuna	1-1(0-1)
Qualified: AFC Eskilstuna	

Group 3	
Malmö FF - Degerfors IF	3-2(1-1)
Falkenbergs FF - Östers IF Växjö	1-2(0-1)
Falkenbergs FF - Degerfors IF	2-1(0-1)
Östers IF Växjö - Malmö FF	2-1(0-0)
Degerfors IF - Östers IF Växjö	1-3(0-1)
Malmö FF - Falkenbergs FF	2-0(2-0)
Qualified: Östers IF Växjö	

Group 4	
Hammarby IF Stockholm - Varbergs BoIS	3-0(1-0)
Eskilsminne IF - Dalkurd FF	0-2(0-1)
Eskilsminne IF - Hammarby IF Stockholm	1-1(1-1)
Dalkurd FF - Varbergs BoIS	1-0(1-0)
Varbergs BoIS - Eskilsminne IF	1-1(1-0)
Hammarby IF Stockholm - Dalkurd FF	3-1(2-1)
Qualified: Hammarby IF Stockholm	

Group 5	
BK Häcken Göteborg - IK Brage Borlänge	6-1(4-0)
FC Rosengård 1917 - IF Brommapojkarna	1-3(0-1)
FC Rosengård 1917 - BK Häcken Göteborg	0-4(0-2)
IF Brommapojkarna - IK Brage Borlänge	4-2(0-1)
IK Brage Borlänge - FC Rosengård 1917	4-2(1-0)
BK Häcken Göteborg - IF Brommapojkarna	1-0(0-0)
Qualified: BK Häcken Göteborg	

Group 6	
Östersunds FK - Halmstads BK	0-0
Karlstad BK - IK Sirius Uppsala	1-2(0-1)
Karlstad BK - Östersunds FK	3-2(1-1)
IK Sirius Uppsala - Halmstads BK	1-2(1-2)
Halmstads BK - Karlstad BK	1-1(1-0)
Östersunds FK - IK Sirius Uppsala	3-0(1-0)
Qualified: Halmstads BK	

Group 7	
Djurgårdens IF Stockholm - IK Frej	2-1(1-0)
Hässleholms IF - IF Elfsborg Borås	1-5(1-1)
Hässleholms IF - Djurgårdens IF Stockholm	0-3(0-2)
IF Elfsborg Borås - IK Frej	1-1(0-1)
IK Frej - Hässleholms IF	7-0(2-0)
Djurgårdens IF Stockholm - IF Elfsborg Borås	3-2(0-1)
Qualified: Djurgårdens IF Stockholm	

Group 8	
Örebro SK - GAIS Göteborg	2-1
Nyköpings BIS - IFK Göteborg	0-2(0-1)
Nyköpings BIS - Örebro SK	1-0(0-0)
IFK Göteborg - GAIS Göteborg	0-3 (awarded)
GAIS Göteborg - Nyköpings BIS	4-3(1-2)
Örebro SK - IFK Göteborg	3-3(3-1)
Qualified: GAIS Göteborg	

Quarter-Finals [09-10.03.2019]

BK Häcken Göteborg - GAIS Göteborg	4-1(1-0)
Östers IF Växjö - AIK Stockholm	2-4(1-1,2-2)
Djurgårdens IF Stock. - Hammarby IF Stockholm	0-0 aet; 4-2 pen
AFC Eskilstuna - Halmstads BK	2-1(1-0,1-1)

Semi-Finals [16-17.03.2019]

Djurgårdens IF Stockholm - BK Häcken Göteborg	2-3(2-1,2-2)
AIK Stockholm - AFC Eskilstuna	1-1 aet; 5-6 pen

Final

30.05.2019; Bravida Arena, Göteborg; Referee: Kristoffer Karlsson; Attendance: 4,958

BK Häcken Göteborg - AFC Eskilstuna **3-0(1-0)**

BK Häcken: Peter Abrahamsson, Joona Toivio, Elohor Godswill Ekpolo, Rasmus Lindgren (Cap), Erik Friberg, Ahmed Yasin Ghani Mousa (90+2.Mervan Çelik), Alexander Faltsetas (80.Gustav Berggren), Adam Andersson, Daleho Irandust (88.Viktor Lundberg), Paulo José de Oliveira „Paulinho“, Alexander Thomas Jeremejeff. Trainer: Andreas Alm.

AFC Eskilstuna: Ole Petter Söderberg, Jesper Björkman, George Felix Michel Melki, José León Bernal, Adnan Kojić, Kadir Hodžić, Anel Raskaj (Cap), Ferid Ali (66.Wilhelm Loeper), Ivan Bobko (88.Jacob Lackell), Gustav Jarl (74.Daniel Miljanović), Samuel Onyedikachuwu Nnamani. Trainer: Nemanja Miljanović.

Goals: 1-0 Alexander Faltsetas (10), 2-0 Joona Toivio (76), 3-0 Viktor Lundberg (90).

Allmänna Idrottsklubben Stockholm

Founded: 15.02.1891
Stadium: Friends Arena, Stockholm (50,000)

Goalkeepers:	DOB	M	(s)	G
Budimir Janošević (SRB)	21.10.1989	9		
Oscar Carl Linnér	23.02.1997	21		
Defenders:	**DOB**	**M**	**(s)**	**G**
Panajotis Dimitriadis	12.08.1986	8	(4)	1
Joel Ekstrand	04.02.1989		(1)	
Haukur Hauksson (ISL)	01.09.1991	2	(2)	
Per Tony Robin Jansson	15.11.1991	25		2
Per Karlsson	02.01.1986	30		
Robert Lundström	01.11.1989	5		1
Goran Alexander Sjöström Milošević	30.01.1992	26	(1)	
Midfielders:	**DOB**	**M**	**(s)**	**G**
Enoch Adu (GHA)	14.09.1990	27		
Bilal Hussein	22.04.2000		(1)	
Sebastian Bengt Ulf Larsson	06.06.1985	12	(3)	2
Rasmus Lindkvist	16.05.1990	18	(7)	2
Mats Kristoffer Olsson	30.06.1995	29		5
Heradi Rashidi	24.07.1994	14	(2)	1
Anton Salétros	12.04.1996	7	(5)	3
Nicolás Marcelo Stefanelli (ARG)	22.11.1994	6	(12)	6
Daniel Sundgren	22.11.1990	22	(2)	1
Ahmed Yasin Ghani Mousa (IRQ)	22.04.1991	9	(5)	1
Forwards:	**DOB**	**M**	**(s)**	**G**
Denni Avdić	05.09.1988	1	(18)	
Nabil Bahoui	05.02.1991	8	(3)	3
Tarik Elyounoussi (NOR)	23.02.1988	22	(3)	8
Henok Goitom (ERI)	22.09.1984	28	(2)	12
Stefan Silva	11.03.1990	1	(5)	1
Trainer:	**DOB**	**M**		
Rikard Norling	04.06.1971	30		

Bollklubben Häcken Göteborg

Founded: 02.08.1940
Stadium: Bravida Arena, Göteborg (6,500)

Goalkeepers:	DOB	M	(s)	G
Peter Abrahamsson	18.07.1988	28		
Jonathan Rasheed	21.11.1991	2		
Defenders:	**DOB**	**M**	**(s)**	**G**
Eric Joel Andersson	11.11.1996	8		
Alexander Angelin	30.01.1990	1	(1)	
Kari Arkivuo (FIN)	23.06.1983	19	(3)	
Elohor Godswill Ekpolo (NGA)	14.05.1995	16		
Johan Hammar	22.02.1994	10	(5)	1
Rasmus Lindgren	29.11.1984	28		
Juhani Ojala (FIN)	19.06.1989	4	(2)	
Joona Toivio (FIN)	04.04.1988	12		
Emil Wahlström	02.03.1987	8	(5)	
Midfielders:	**DOB**	**M**	**(s)**	**G**
Kevin Ackermann	24.05.2001		(1)	
Adam Andersson	11.11.1996	17	(6)	
Gustav Berggren	07.09.1997	7	(10)	
Karl Bohm	24.08.1995	1	(5)	1
Mervan Çelik	26.05.1990	7	(14)	1
Alexander Faltsetas	04.07.1987	26		4
Erik Friberg	10.02.1986	25	(1)	1
Lucas Hedlund	18.08.1998		(1)	
Daleho Irandust	04.06.1998	27	(2)	4
Kevin Yakob	10.01.2000		(1)	1
Forwards:	**DOB**	**M**	**(s)**	**G**
Mostafa El Kabir (MAR)	05.10.1988	5	(4)	2
Alhassan Kamara (SLE)	16.03.1993	8	(6)	2
Alexander Thomas Jeremejeff	12.10.1993	15		9
Viktor Lundberg	04.03.1991	15	(10)	6
Mohammed Nasiru (GHA)	06.06.1994	14	(3)	4
Paulo José de Oliveira „Paulinho" (BRA)	09.04.1986	27		20
Trainer:	**DOB**	**M**		
Andreas Alm	19.06.1973	30		

Dalkurd Fotbollsförening

Founded: 26.09.2004
Stadium: Gavlevallen, Gävle (6,500)

Goalkeepers:	DOB	M	(s)	G
Abdulaziz Demircan (TUR)	05.02.1991	8		
Sixten Mohlin	17.01.1996	18	(1)	
Stefan van der Lei (NED)	05.03.1993	4		
Defenders:	**DOB**	**M**	**(s)**	**G**
Peshraw Azizi	19.01.1988		(3)	
Kebba Ceesay	14.11.1987	21	(3)	1
Alex De John (USA)	10.05.1991	15	(3)	2
Alexander Ekblad	07.08.1987	9		
Irfan Jašarević (BIH)	24.08.1995	7	(1)	
Henrik Löfkvist	05.05.1995	28		2
Malkolm Moënza	15.11.1993	21	(5)	1
Simon Strand	25.05.1993	29		1
Markus Thorbjörnsson	01.10.1987	11		
Robin Tranberg	06.02.1993	21	(3)	2
Midfielders:	**DOB**	**M**	**(s)**	**G**
Ammar Ahmed	03.07.1988	12	(8)	
Rewan Amin (IRQ)	08.01.1996	15		
Oliver Berg (NOR)	28.08.1993	11	(2)	1
Johan Bertilsson	15.02.1988	3	(2)	
Heradi Rashidi	24.07.1994	2	(3)	
Adam Ståhl	08.10.1994	11		
Yukiya Sugita (JPN)	07.04.1993	14		2
Smajl Suljević	15.07.1994		(2)	
Forwards:	**DOB**	**M**	**(s)**	**G**
Alibek Aliev	16.08.1996		(2)	
Ahmed Awad Mohammad (PLE)	01.06.1992	12	(10)	3
Ferhad Ayaz	10.10.1994	14	(7)	3
Younés Bnou Marzouk (FRA)	02.03.1996	4	(6)	1
Mohamed Buya (SLE)	10.01.1995	13		9
Rawez Lawan	04.10.1987	13	(8)	1
Eero Markkanen (FIN)	03.07.1991	8	(4)	1
Leonard Pllana (KVX)	26.08.1996	2	(3)	
Andrew Stadler (USA)	01.05.1988	4	(8)	
Trainer:	**DOB**	**M**		
Azrudin Valentić (BIH)	21.07.1971	10		
Adil Kizil [26.05.2018]	20.01.1984	1		
Johan Sandahl [11.06.2018]	20.02.1979	19		

Djurgårdens Idrottsförening Stockholm

Founded: 12.03.1891
Stadium: Tele2 Arena, Stockholm (30,000)

Goalkeepers:	**DOB**	**M**	**(s)**	**G**
Andreas Isaksson	03.10.1981	24		
Tommi Vaiho	13.09.1988	6	(1)	
Defenders:	**DOB**	**M**	**(s)**	**G**
Johan Andersson	15.06.1995		(1)	
Hans Oskar Jonathan Augustinsson	30.03.1996	26		1
Felix Beijmo	31.01.1998	11		1
Erik Berg	30.12.1988	9	(2)	
Marcus Danielsson	08.04.1989	25		2
Niklas Gunnarsson (NOR)	27.04.1991	12	(8)	
Jacob Larsson	08.04.1994	23	(1)	1
Jonas Olsson	10.03.1983	18	(1)	
Midfielders:	**DOB**	**M**	**(s)**	**G**
Nicklas Bärkroth	19.01.1992	12	(2)	
Jesper Karlström	21.06.1995	20	(5)	
Kerim Mrabti	20.05.1994	23	(1)	6
Haris Radetinac (SRB)	28.10.1985	20	(7)	2
Jonathan Ring	05.12.1991	21	(8)	4
Besard Šabović	05.01.1998		(2)	
Fredrik Ulvestad (NOR)	17.06.1992	22	(1)	1
Kevin Walker	03.08.1989	13	(8)	2
Forwards:	**DOB**	**M**	**(s)**	**G**
Aliou Badji (SEN)	10.10.1997	16	(12)	8
Edward Chilufya (ZAM)	17.09.1999		(8)	
Omar Eddahri	30.08.1990	4	(2)	
Tino Kadewere (ZIM)	05.01.1996	12		8
Dženis Kozica	28.04.1993	12	(16)	3
Yura Movsisyan (ARM)	02.08.1987	1	(3)	
Trainer:	**DOB**	**M**		
Özcan Melkemichel	21.02.1968	30		

Gymnastik- och Idrottsföreningen Sundsvall

Founded: 25.08.1903
Stadium: Idrottsparken, Sundsvall (7,700)

Goalkeepers:	**DOB**	**M**	**(s)**	**G**
William Eskelinen	03.09.1996	30		
Defenders:	**DOB**	**M**	**(s)**	**G**
Eric Björkander	11.06.1996	23	(3)	
Carlos Moros Gracia (ESP)	15.04.1993	29		1
Samuel de los Reyes Domínguez (ESP)	15.02.1992	1	(8)	
David Myrestam	04.04.1987	29		
Dennis Olsson	03.10.1994	24	(3)	
Juho Pirttijoki (FIN)	30.07.1996		(3)	
Pol Moreno Sánchez (ESP)	09.05.1994	8	(6)	
Jonathan Tamimi-Syberg (JOR)	12.10.1994	30		1
Midfielders:	**DOB**	**M**	**(s)**	**G**
Amaro Bahtijar	26.08.1998		(1)	
Oliver Berg (NOR)	28.08.1993	6	(7)	1
Juan José Ciércoles Sagra (ESP)	27.05.1988	27		
David Batanero Puigbó (ESP)	27.09.1988	27		5
Romain Gall (USA)	31.01.1995	13		6
Erik Granat	09.08.1995		(1)	
Jonathan Morsay	05.10.1997		(14)	
Christian Rubio Sivodedov	07.11.1997	4	(7)	
Maic Sema	02.12.1988	23	(1)	7
Kim Skoglund	28.08.1987	2	(14)	
Forwards:	**DOB**	**M**	**(s)**	**G**
Linus Hallenius	01.04.1989	29		17
David Haro Iniesta (ESP)	17.07.1990	4	(11)	2
Chidi Dauda Omeje (NGA)	05.05.1990	1		
Peter Wilson	09.10.1996	20	(5)	4
Trainer:	**DOB**	**M**		
Joel Cedergren	22.07.1974	30		

Hammarby Idrottsförening Fotbollförening Stockholm

Founded: 07.03.1897
Stadium: Tele2 Arena, Stockholm (30,000)

Goalkeepers:	**DOB**	**M**	**(s)**	**G**
Davor Blažević	07.02.1993	5		
Johan Sellberg-Wiland	24.01.1981	25		
Defenders:	**DOB**	**M**	**(s)**	**G**
Vivaldo Borges dos Santos Neto(BRA)	13.09.1996	24	(2)	
Marcus Degerlund	16.03.1998		(1)	
David Fällman	02.04.1990	26	(1)	
Mads Fenger (DEN)	10.09.1990	15	(4)	2
Oscar Krusnell	17.02.1999		(1)	
Bjørn Paulsen (DEN)	02.07.1991	28	(1)	5
Simon Sandberg	25.03.1994	20	(3)	
Mats Solheim (NOR)	03.12.1987	9	(6)	
Midfielders:	**DOB**	**M**	**(s)**	**G**
Jeppe Andersen (DEN)	06.12.1992	26		1
Junes Barny	04.11.1989	7	(6)	1
Leo Bengtsson	26.05.1998	1	(9)	
Jiloan Hamad	06.11.1990	27	(2)	11
Gershon Koffie (GHA)	25.08.1991		(1)	
Serge-Junior Martinsson Ngouali (GAB)	23.01.1992	26		1
Vladimir Rodić (MNE)	07.09.1993	10	(4)	3
Forwards:	**DOB**	**M**	**(s)**	**G**
Kennedy Bakırcıoğlu	02.11.1980		(12)	1
Pa Amat Dibba (GAM)	15.10.1987	5	(5)	7
Nikola Đurđić (SRB)	01.04.1986	26	(1)	13
Imad Khalili (PLE)	03.04.1987	15	(6)	3
Arnór Smárason (ISL)	07.09.1988		(4)	
Sander Svendsen (NOR)	06.08.1997	4	(15)	
Muamer Tanković	22.02.1995	30		7
Erkan Zengin	05.08.1985	1	(2)	
Trainer:	**DOB**	**M**		
Stefan Billborn	15.11.1972	30		

Idrottsföreningen Brommapojkarna

Founded: 13.04.1942
Stadium: Grimsta Idrottsplats, Stockholm (8,000)

Goalkeepers:	DOB	M	(s)	G
Nikola Petrić (SRB)	11.05.1991	30		
Defenders:	**DOB**	**M**	**(s)**	**G**
Fritiof Björkén	03.01.1991	29		2
Johan Falkmar	10.11.1993	12	(1)	
Erik Figueroa	04.01.1991	23	(3)	1
Mohanad Jeahze	10.04.1997	8	(2)	
David Ochieng (KEN)	07.10.1992	10	(3)	
Ludvig Öhman	09.10.1991	21	(1)	
Martin Rauschenberg Brorsen(DEN)	15.01.1992	16	(1)	1
Midfielders:	**DOB**	**M**	**(s)**	**G**
Rasmus Alm	17.08.1995	1	(7)	
Markus Gustafsson	06.03.1989	28		2
Antonio Nieves Martín „Maikel" (ESP)	02.12.1989	12	(8)	
Eric Omondi (KEN)	18.08.1994	17	(8)	2
Jacob Ortmark	29.08.1997	1	(4)	
Gustav Sandberg-Magnusson	03.02.1992	27		1
Moustafa Zeidan	07.06.1998	7	(8)	
Forwards:	**DOB**	**M**	**(s)**	**G**
Bajram Ajeti (ALB)	05.05.1989	7	(1)	2
Christopher Brandeborn	05.03.1991	12	(5)	
Kristján Flóki Finnbogason (ISL)	12.01.1995	9	(3)	2
Philip Hellquist	12.05.1991	17		5
Jack Lahne	24.10.2001	7	(12)	4
Marko Nikolić	17.09.1997	4	(6)	
Alexander Nilsson	02.09.1990	11	(4)	1
Petar Petrović (SRB)	15.09.1995	5	(8)	1
Tim Söderström	04.01.1994	16	(4)	
Trainer:	**DOB**	**M**		
Luis Berkemeier Pimenta (POR)	25.09.1981	19		
Gonçalo Pereira (POR) [01.09.2018]		1		
Roberth Björknesjö [10.09.2018]	30.04.1973	10		

Idrottsföreningen Elfsborg Borås

Founded: 26.06.1904 (*as Borås Fotbollslag*)
Stadium: Borås Arena, Borås (16,899)

Goalkeepers:	DOB	M	(s)	G
David Olsson	27.06.1997		(1)	
Kevin Stuhr-Ellegaard (DEN)	23.05.1983	30		
Defenders:	**DOB**	**M**	**(s)**	**G**
Ibrahim Drešević (KVX)	24.01.1997	22	(1)	
Gustav Henriksson	03.02.1998	2		
Frederik Holst (DEN)	24.09.1994	13		1
Jørgen Horn (NOR)	07.06.1987	3	(1)	
Jon Jönsson	08.07.1983	7	(2)	1
Rami Kaib	08.05.1997	22	(1)	
Adam Lundqvist	20.03.1994	5		
Jesper Manns	05.08.1995	4	(2)	
Christopher McVey	12.04.1997		(1)	
Joakim Nilsson	06.02.1994	26	(1)	1
Midfielders:	**DOB**	**M**	**(s)**	**G**
Alex James Dyer (MSR)	11.06.1990	13	(4)	2
Robert Gojani	19.10.1992	25	(1)	
Daniel Gustavsson	29.08.1990	19	(7)	2
Samuel Holmén	28.06.1984	23	(2)	
Stefan Ishizaki	15.05.1982	25	(1)	1
Issam Jebali (TUN)	25.12.1991	14	(1)	3
Jesper Karlsson	25.07.1998	4	(18)	
Simon Lundevall	23.09.1988	26	(3)	5
Simon Olsson	14.09.1997	17	(5)	
Forwards:	**DOB**	**M**	**(s)**	**G**
Emir Bajrami	07.03.1988		(7)	
David Boysen (DEN)	30.04.1991	1	(2)	
Per Frick	14.04.1992	13	(6)	3
Arian Kabashi	14.03.1997		(5)	
Chinedu Ogbuke Obasi (NGA)	01.06.1986	10		4
Viktor Prodell	29.02.1988	6	(17)	4
Trainer:	**DOB**	**M**		
Bo Jimmy Thelin	14.03.1978	30		

Idrottsföreningen Kamraterna Göteborg

Founded: 04.10.1904
Stadium: Ullevi Stadion, Göteborg (18,600)

Goalkeepers:	DOB	M	(s)	G
Tom Amos	06.02.1998	3		
Pontus Jacob Ragne Dahlberg	21.01.1999	10		
Erik Dahlin	28.04.1989	17		
Defenders:	**DOB**	**M**	**(s)**	**G**
André Calisir (ARM)	13.06.1990	23		
Kristopher Santos Da Graca	16.01.1998	3	(1)	
Marcus Degerlund	16.03.1998		(4)	
Billy Nordström	18.09.1995	6	(8)	
Sebastian Ohlsson	26.05.1993	25	(1)	3
Emil Salomonsson	28.04.1989	29		1
Carl Starfelt	01.06.1995	29	(1)	
Victor Wernersson	06.07.1995	26	(4)	2
Midfielders:	**DOB**	**M**	**(s)**	**G**
Amin Affane	21.01.1994	11	(9)	1
Mix Diskerud (USA)	02.10.1990	12		2
Sebastian Eriksson	31.01.1989	11		
August Erlingmark	22.04.1998	12	(9)	1
Mikael Ingebrigtsen (NOR)	21.07.1996		(4)	
Fredrik Jensen (NOR)	18.05.1993	10	(2)	
Giorgi Kharaishvili (GEO)	29.07.1996	22	(5)	9
Vajebah Kaliefah Sakor (NOR)	14.04.1996	17	(6)	3
David Wiklander	03.10.1984	15	(1)	
Alhassan Yusuf (NGA)	18.07.2000		(1)	
Forwards:	**DOB**	**M**	**(s)**	**G**
Sargon Abraham	07.02.1991	4	(9)	1
Gustav Engvall	29.04.1996	7	(3)	1
Tobias Hysén	09.03.1982	9	(12)	1
Patrik Karlsson-Lagemyr	18.12.1996	8	(7)	1
Benjamin Nygren	08.07.2001	2	(1)	2
Elías Már Ómarsson (ISL)	18.01.1995	10	(2)	8
Robin Söder	01.04.1991	9		2
Trainer:	**DOB**	**M**		
Poya Asbaghi	17.07.1985	30		

Idrottsföreningen Kamraterna Norrköping

Founded: 29.05.1897
Stadium: Nya Parken, Norrköping (15,734)

Goalkeepers:	DOB	M	(s)	G
Isak Pettersson	06.06.1997	30		
Defenders:	**DOB**	**M**	**(s)**	**G**
Henrik Castegren	28.03.1996	7	(2)	
Per Filip Dagerstål	01.02.1997	20	(4)	2
Jón Fjóluson (ISL)	10.04.1989	13		
Kasper Larsen (DEN)	25.01.1993	6	(2)	1
Ian Rey Smith Quirós (CRC)	06.03.1998	15	(5)	2
Linus Wahlqvist	11.11.1996	12		
Midfielders:	**DOB**	**M**	**(s)**	**G**
Andreas Blomqvist	05.05.1992		(2)	
Alexander Fransson	02.04.1994	18		2
Lars Gerson (LUX)	05.02.1990	16	(8)	1
Alexander Jakobsen (EGY)	18.03.1994	8	(13)	1
Andreas Johansson	10.03.1982	30		1
Arnór Sigurðsson (ISL)	15.05.1999	10	(7)	3
Daniel Sjölund (FIN)	22.04.1983	1	(7)	1
Eric Smith	08.01.1997	8	(1)	
Johan Simon Thern	18.09.1992	28		5
Guðmundur Þórarinsson (ISL)	15.04.1992	29		2
Forwards:	**DOB**	**M**	**(s)**	**G**
Karl Albin Elis Holmberg	03.03.1993	23	(5)	9
Jordan Larsson	20.06.1997	7	(19)	1
David Moberg-Karlsson	20.03.1994	29		10
Simon Skrabb (FIN)	19.01.1995	20	(9)	7
Johannes Vall	19.10.1992		(1)	
Trainer:	**DOB**	**M**		
Jens Gustafsson	15.10.1978	30		

Idrottsklubben Sirius Uppsala

Founded: 1907
Stadium: Studenternas IP, Uppsala (6,300)

Goalkeepers:	DOB	M	(s)	G
Karim Fegrouche (MAR)	14.02.1982	10	(1)	
Lukas Jonsson	21.10.1992	15		
Josh Wicks (USA)	01.11.1983	2		
Joakim Wulff	06.02.1979	3		
Defenders:	**DOB**	**M**	**(s)**	**G**
Jesper Arvidsson	01.01.1985	18	(2)	4
Tim Björkström	08.01.1991	24		
Axel Björnström	10.09.1995	6	(9)	
Daniel Jarl	13.04.1992	7	(1)	
Karl Larson	28.10.1991	18	(2)	
Linus Nygren	11.05.1998		(1)	
Oscar Pehrsson	10.04.1988	23	(2)	1
Midfielders:	**DOB**	**M**	**(s)**	**G**
Mauricio Albornoz	10.03.1988	4	(4)	
Robert Åhman-Persson	26.03.1987	12	(3)	1
Johan Eiswhold	21.06.1990	21	(2)	
Sherko Faiqi	18.07.1999	2	(3)	
Charbel Georges	28.09.1993	5	(6)	1
Christer Gustafsson	31.12.1987	22	(1)	3
Philip Haglund	22.03.1987	26	(1)	10
Oscar Kindlund	12.02.1997	2	(2)	
Okechukwu Henry Offia (NGA)	26.12.1999	1	(2)	
Abdul Razak (CIV)	11.11.1992	7	(5)	
Mohammed Saeid (ERI)	24.12.1990	9	(3)	1
Niklas Thor	21.02.1986	2	(3)	
Stefano Vecchia	23.01.1995	14	(5)	1
Forwards:	**DOB**	**M**	**(s)**	**G**
Omar Eddahri	30.08.1990	3	(3)	
Jonas Lindberg	24.03.1989	6	(5)	
Sam Lundholm	01.07.1994	18	(6)	4
Shkodran Maholi	10.04.1993	7	(6)	1
Moses Ogbu (NGA)	07.02.1991	24	(4)	7
Ian Sirelius	28.10.1987	19	(6)	3
Trainer:	**DOB**	**M**		
Kim Bergstrand	18.04.1968	30		

Kalmar Fotbollsförening

Founded: 15.06.1910 (*as IF Göta*)
Stadium: Guldfågeln Arena, Kalmar (12,000)

Goalkeepers:	DOB	M	(s)	G
Lucas Johansson	11.07.1994	30		
Defenders:	**DOB**	**M**	**(s)**	**G**
Viktor Agardius	23.10.1989	27		
Chima Akas Uche (NGA)	03.05.1994	25		
Gbenga Arokoyo (NGA)	01.11.1992	1	(4)	1
Mikael Bertil Dyrestam (GUI)	10.12.1991	17	(6)	1
Emin Nouri (AZE)	22.07.1985	3		
Johan Stenmark	26.02.1999	8		
Marcus Thorbjörnsson	01.10.1987	1		
Midfielders:	**DOB**	**M**	**(s)**	**G**
Rasmus Elm	17.03.1988	15	(4)	1
Viktor Elm	13.11.1985	28		4
Tobias Eriksson	19.03.1985	9	(4)	1
Herman Hallberg	22.05.1997	21	(2)	
Charles Melker Otto Hallberg	20.10.1995	12	(1)	
Adam Hellborg	30.07.1998	3	(6)	
Hugo Gomes dos Santos Silva „Jajá“ (BRA)	18.03.1995	1	(2)	
Romario Pereira Sipião (BRA)	10.08.1985	29		5
Filip Sachpekidis	03.07.1997	3	(6)	1
Forwards:	**DOB**	**M**	**(s)**	**G**
Papa Diouf (SEN)	22.06.1989	26	(2)	2
Adrian Edqvist	20.05.1999	3	(5)	
Erton Fejzullahu	09.04.1988	13	(5)	3
Nils Fröling	20.04.2000	7	(7)	2
Hiago de Oliveira Ramiro (BRA)	20.09.1991	12	(13)	4
Alexander Ahl Holmström	04.04.1999		(2)	
Isak Magnusson	16.06.1998	20	(6)	1
Nixon Darlanio Reis Cardoso (BRA)	20.07.1992		(7)	
Måns Söderqvist	08.02.1993	16	(3)	1
Trainer:	**DOB**	**M**		
Nanne Bergstrand	28.04.1956	15		
Henrik Rydström [31.07.2018]	16.02.1976	15		

Malmö Fotbollförening

Founded: 24.02.1910
Stadium: Swedbank Stadion, Malmö (22,500)

Goalkeepers:	**DOB**	**M**	**(s)**	**G**
Fredrik Andersson	25.10.1988	4		
Johan Dahlin	08.09.1986	25		
Walter Viitala (FIN)	09.01.1992	1	(1)	
Defenders:	**DOB**	**M**	**(s)**	**G**
Hugo Andersson	01.01.1999	1	(3)	1
Rasmus Bengtsson	26.06.1986	12	(1)	
Egzon Binaku	27.08.1995	12	(6)	
Franz Brorsson	30.01.1996	21	(2)	
Eric Larsson	15.07.1991	22	(3)	2
Lasse Nielsen (DEN)	08.01.1988	26	(1)	
Behrang Safari	09.02.1985	19	(2)	
Isak Ssewankambo	27.02.1996	1	(4)	
Andreas Vindheim (NOR)	04.08.1995	7	(3)	1
Midfielders:	**DOB**	**M**	**(s)**	**G**
Samuel Adrian	02.03.1998	1	(8)	
Fouad Bachirou (COM)	15.04.1990	19	(3)	
Anders Christiansen (DEN)	08.06.1990	9	(6)	2
Bonke Innocent (NGA)	20.01.1996	8	(7)	
Felix Konstandeliasz	26.03.1999		(3)	
Oscar Lewicki	14.07.1992	25	(3)	
Søren Rieks (DEN)	07.04.1987	25	(1)	10
Mattias Svanberg	05.01.1999	12		2
Arnór Ingvi Traustason (ISL)	30.04.1993	16	(6)	4
Pavle Vagić	24.01.2000		(1)	
Forwards:	**DOB**	**M**	**(s)**	**G**
Marcus Antonsson	08.05.1991	12	(3)	8
Romain Gall (USA)	31.01.1995	10	(2)	6
Alexander Thomas Jeremejeff	12.10.1993	8	(5)	1
Markus Rosenberg	27.09.1982	21	(6)	13
Carlos Strandberg	14.04.1996	13	(6)	7
Trainer:	**DOB**	**M**		
Magnus Pehrsson	25.05.1976	9		
Daniel Andersson [14.05.2018]	28.08.1977	3		
Uwe Rösler (GER) [12.06.2018]	15.11.1968	18		

Örebro Sportklubb

Founded: 28.10.1908
Stadium: Behrn Arena, Örebro (12,300)

Goalkeepers:	**DOB**	**M**	**(s)**	**G**
Oscar Jansson	23.12.1990	30		
Defenders:	**DOB**	**M**	**(s)**	**G**
Michael Almebäck	04.04.1988	28		
Daniel Björnkvist	08.01.1989	30		1
Arvid Brorsson	08.05.1999	3	(1)	
Fabio De Sousa Silva (BRA)	13.01.1996	2	(3)	
Albin Granlund (FIN)	01.09.1989	14	(6)	
Brendan Hines-Ike (USA)	07.04.1994	13		
Martin Lorentzson	21.07.1984	23		1
Sebastian Ring	18.04.1995	17	(8)	
Viktor Tranberg (DEN)	26.02.1997	13		
Midfielders:	**DOB**	**M**	**(s)**	**G**
Alfred Ajdarević (KVX)	20.06.1998		(2)	
Simon Amin	13.11.1997	1	(10)	
Johan Bertilsson	15.02.1988	7	(5)	2
Nahir Besara	25.02.1991	28	(2)	5
Nordin Gerzić	09.11.1983	21		2
Johan Mårtensson	16.02.1989	22	(1)	1
Filip Rogić	14.06.1993	28		7
Forwards:	**DOB**	**M**	**(s)**	**G**
Isaac Boye Edegware (NGA)	05.01.1997	4	(11)	1
Rodin Deprem	23.05.1998	1	(7)	
Chibuike Kennedy Igboananike (NGA)	08.02.1989	21	(3)	9
Michael Junior Omoh (NGA)	29.08.1991	16	(9)	1
Viktor Sköld	31.07.1989	8	(7)	2
Trainer:	**DOB**	**M**		
Axel Kjäll	01.06.1981	30		

Östersunds Fotbollsklubb

Founded: 31.10.1996
Stadium: Jämtkraft Arena, Östersund (8,466)

Goalkeepers:	**DOB**	**M**	**(s)**	**G**
Andreas Andersson	27.02.1991	8	(1)	
Aly Keita	08.12.1986	22		
Defenders:	**DOB**	**M**	**(s)**	**G**
Doug Bergqvist	29.03.1993	22	(1)	
Patrick Kpozo (GHA)	15.07.1997	5	(11)	1
Ronald Mukiibi	16.09.1991	18	(5)	2
Samuel Laryeal Mensah (GHA)	19.05.1989	10	(4)	1
Sotirios Papagiannopoulos	05.09.1990	11		1
Tom Pettersson	25.03.1990	28		2
Noah Sonko Sundberg	06.06.1996	17	(4)	1
Dennis Widgren	28.03.1994	20	(2)	2
Midfielders:	**DOB**	**M**	**(s)**	**G**
Rewan Amin (NED)	08.01.1996	11	(1)	
Frank Arhin (GHA)	16.02.1999	4	(6)	
Henrik Bellman	24.03.1999		(1)	
Curtis Edwards (ENG)	12.01.1994	28	(1)	7
Ludvig Fritzson	25.08.1995	13	(11)	1
Jamie Hopcutt (ENG)	23.06.1992	14	(9)	5
Simon Kroon	16.06.1993	4		1
Brwa Nouri (IRQ)	23.01.1987	13	(1)	2
Ken Nlata Sema	30.09.1993	11		
Smajl Suljević	15.07.1994		(4)	
Tesfaldet Simon Tekie	04.06.1997	12	(3)	1
Forwards:	**DOB**	**M**	**(s)**	**G**
Hosam Aiesh	14.04.1995	21	(2)	3
Alhaji Gero (NGA)	10.10.1993	6	(3)	1
Saman Ghoddos (IRN)	06.09.1993	14	(1)	9
Dino Islamović	17.01.1994	16	(6)	9
Jerell Sellars (ENG)	11.12.1995	2	(4)	1
Trainer:	**DOB**	**M**		
Graham Potter (ENG)	20.05.1975	11		
Ian Burchnall (ENG) [20.06.2018]	11.02.1983	19		

Trelleborgs Fotbollsförening

Founded: 06.12.1926
Stadium: Vångavallen, Trelleborg (7,000)

Goalkeepers:	DOB	M	(s)	G
Marko Johansson	25.08.1998	29		
Dennis Petersson	14.12.1994	1		
Defenders:	**DOB**	**M**	**(s)**	**G**
Alexander Blomqvist	03.08.1994	29		1
Dennis Hadžikadunić	09.07.1998	10		
Isak Jönsson	11.01.1999	12	(1)	1
Lasse Nielsen (DEN)	03.03.1987	17	(5)	2
Albin Nilsson	11.08.1993	2	(1)	
Victor Nilsson	14.07.1993	3	(1)	
Jacob Palander	04.05.1995	1		
Kofi Sarkodie (USA)	22.03.1991	11		
Jasmin Sudić	24.11.1990	10		
Anton Tideman	02.09.1992	23		
Midfielders:	**DOB**	**M**	**(s)**	**G**
Erik Andersson	03.05.1997	17	(2)	2
Magnus Andersson	27.04.1981	1	(2)	
Johan Brannefalk	09.12.1997	4	(13)	
Haris Brkić	17.09.1999		(1)	
Felix Hörberg	19.05.1999	27	(3)	4
Oscar Johansson	06.05.1995	9	(4)	
Zoran Jovanović	25.09.1986	22	(1)	1
Furkan Motori	18.08.1995		(5)	
Robin Nilsson	15.09.1988	22	(5)	1
Sebastian Ohlsson	31.12.1992	24	(4)	1
Forwards:	**DOB**	**M**	**(s)**	**G**
Freddie Brorsson	04.06.1997	12	(13)	1
Salif Camara-Jönsson	09.09.1983	9	(1)	2
Deniz Hümmet	13.09.1996	22	(6)	5
Óttar Karlsson (ISL)	21.02.1997	4	(10)	1
Marcus Pode	27.03.1986	9	(9)	1
Trainer:	**DOB**	**M**		
Lars Anders Patrick Winqvist	05.08.1976	30		

SECOND LEVEL
Superettan 2018

1.	Helsingborgs IF (*Promoted*)	30	18	9	3	59	-	30	63
2.	Falkenbergs FF (*Promoted*)	30	18	5	7	61	-	34	59
3.	AFC Eskilstuna (*Promotion Play-offs*)	30	13	15	2	40	-	16	54
4.	Örgryte IS Göteborg	30	15	7	8	56	-	37	52
5.	Halmstads BK	30	15	6	9	49	-	38	51
6.	IK Brage Borlänge	30	12	9	9	46	-	45	45
7.	Degerfors IF	30	11	9	10	45	-	46	42
8.	Östers IF Växjö	30	11	8	11	48	-	43	41
9.	IK Frej	30	10	7	13	46	-	56	37
10.	GAIS Göteborg	30	8	11	11	40	-	41	35
11.	Jönköpings Södra IF	30	9	8	13	31	-	38	35
12.	Norrby IF Borås	30	9	7	14	31	-	50	34
13.	IFK Värnamo (*Relegation Play-offs*)	30	9	5	16	31	-	48	32
14.	Varbergs BoIS (*Relegation Play-offs*)	30	7	8	15	43	-	54	29
15.	Gefle IF Gävle (*Relegated*)	30	6	7	17	31	-	60	25
16.	Landskrona BoIS (*Relegated*)	30	5	7	18	35	-	56	22

Relegation Play-offs (2nd / 3rd Level)

Syrianska FC Södertälje - IFK Värnamo	1-0(0-0)	2-2(1-0)
Oskarshamns AIK - **Varbergs BoIS**	4-2(2-0)	0-2(0-2)

NATIONAL TEAM

INTERNATIONAL MATCHES
(16.07.2018 – 15.07.2019)

06.09.2018	Wien	Austria - Sweden	2-0(1-0)	(F)
10.09.2018	Stockholm	Sweden - Turkey	2-3(1-0)	(UNL)
11.10.2018	Kaliningrad	Russia - Sweden	0-0	(UNL)
16.10.2018	Stockholm	Sweden - Slovakia	1-1(0-0)	(F)
17.11.2018	Konya	Turkey - Sweden	0-1(0-0)	(UNL)
20.11.2018	Stockholm	Sweden - Russia	2-0(1-0)	(UNL)
08.01.2019	Doha	Sweden - Finland	0-1(0-1)	(F)
11.01.2019	Doha	Iceland - Sweden	2-2(1-1)	(F)
23.03.2019	Stockholm	Sweden - Romania	2-1(2-0)	(ECQ)
26.03.2019	Oslo	Norway - Sweden	3-3(1-0)	(ECQ)
07.06.2019	Stockholm	Sweden - Malta	3-0(1-0)	(ECQ)
10.06.2019	Madrid	Spain - Sweden	3-0(0-0)	(ECQ)

06.09.2018 AUSTRIA - SWEDEN 2-0(1-0) Friendly International
Generali Arena, Wien; Referee: Paweł Gil (Poland); Attendance: 11,000
SWE: Kristoffer Nordfeldt (46.Karl-Johan Johnsson), Niklas Hult, Pontus Sven Gustav Jansson (Cap), Emil Henry Kristoffer Krafth, Filip Viktor Helander, Gustav Svensson (78.Sebastian Bengt Ulf Larsson), Oscar Hiljemark (62.Sam Andreas Larsson), Marcus Christer Rohdén, Ken Nlata Sema (67.Viktor Johan Anton Claesson), Isaac Thelin (46.John Olof Alberto Guidetti), Robin Kwamina Quaison. Trainer: Jan Olof Andersson.

10.09.2018 SWEDEN - TURKEY 2-3(1-0) UEFA Nations League B, Group 2
Friends Arena, Stockholm; Referee: Jesús Gil Manzano (Spain); Attendance: 21,832
SWE: Robin Patrick Olsen, Carl Mikael Lustig (79.Emil Henry Kristoffer Krafth), Pontus Sven Gustav Jansson, Victor Lindelöf, Ludwig Augustinsson, Sebastian Bengt Ulf Larsson (Cap), Albin Ekdal (56.Oscar Hiljemark), Jakup Jimmy Durmaz (71.Marcus Christer Rohdén), Viktor Johan Anton Claesson, Marcus Berg, Isaac Thelin. Trainer: Jan Olof Andersson.
Goals: Isaac Thelin (35), Viktor Johan Anton Claesson (49).

11.10.2018 RUSSIA - SWEDEN 0-0 UEFA Nations League B, Group 2
Stadion Kaliningrad, Kaliningrad; Referee: Referee: Luca Banti (Italy); Attendance: 31,698
SWE: Robin Patrick Olsen, Andreas Granqvist (Cap), Carl Mikael Lustig, Victor Lindelöf, Ludwig Augustinsson, Gustav Svensson, Sebastian Bengt Ulf Larsson, Emil Peter Forsberg, Viktor Johan Anton Claesson, Marcus Berg (83.Martin Sebastian Andersson), Isaac Thelin (71.John Olof Alberto Guidetti). Trainer: Jan Olof Andersson.

16.10.2018 SWEDEN - SLOVAKIA 1-1(0-0) Friendly International
Friends Arena, Stockholm; Referee: Jakob Kehlet (Denmark); Attendance: 9,876
SWE: Karl-Johan Johnsson (46.Kristoffer Nordfeldt), Martin Tony Waikwa Olsson, Andreas Granqvist (Cap) (81.Sotirios Papagiannopoulos), Pontus Sven Gustav Jansson, Emil Henry Kristoffer Krafth, Albin Ekdal (82.Marcus Christer Rohdén), Jakup Jimmy Durmaz (66.Viktor Johan Anton Claesson), Oscar Hiljemark (81.Kristoffer Peterson), Mats Kristoffer Olsson, John Olof Alberto Guidetti, Martin Sebastian Andersson (66.Marcus Berg). Trainer: Jan Olof Andersson.
Goal: John Olof Alberto Guidetti (52).

17.11.2018 TURKEY - SWEDEN 0-1(0-0) UEFA Nations League B, Group 2
Konya Büyükşehir Stadium, Konya; Referee: István Kovács (Romania); Attendance: 37,425
SWE: Robin Patrick Olsen, Martin Tony Waikwa Olsson, Andreas Granqvist (Cap), Carl Mikael Lustig, Victor Lindelöf (46.Filip Viktor Helander), Ludwig Augustinsson, Jakob Valdemar Olsson Johansson, Sebastian Bengt Ulf Larsson, Albin Ekdal (81.Gustav Svensson), Viktor Johan Anton Claesson (90.Isaac Thelin), Marcus Berg. Trainer: Jan Olof Andersson.
Goal: Andreas Granqvist (71 penalty).

20.11.2018 SWEDEN - RUSSIA 2-0(1-0) UEFA Nations League B, Group 2
Friends Arena, Stockholm; Referee: Benoît Bastien (France); Attendance: 20,223
SWE: Robin Patrick Olsen, Martin Tony Waikwa Olsson (71.Isaac Thelin), Andreas Granqvist (Cap), Carl Mikael Lustig, Victor Lindelöf, Ludwig Augustinsson, Jakob Valdemar Olsson Johansson, Sebastian Bengt Ulf Larsson, Viktor Johan Anton Claesson (80.Gustav Svensson), Mats Kristoffer Olsson (89.John Olof Alberto Guidetti), Marcus Berg. Trainer: Jan Olof Andersson.
Goals: Victor Lindelöf (41), Marcus Berg (72).

08.01.2019 SWEDEN - FINLAND 0-1(0-1) Friendly International
"Sheikh Jassim Bin Hamad" Stadium, Doha (Qatar); Referee: Abdulla Ali Al Athba Al Marri (Qatar); Attendance: 326
SWE: Jacob Karl Anders Rinne, Goran Alexander Sjöström Milošević (Cap), Per Tony Robin Jansson, Eric Joel Andersson, Hans Oskar Jonathan Augustinsson (63.Adam Andersson), Simon Hjalmar Friedel Tibbling (29.Johan Simon Thern), Alexander Fransson, Hosam Aiesh, Daleho Irandust, Karl Albin Elis Holmberg (63.Viktor Einar Gyökeres), Alexander Thomas Jeremejeff. Trainer: Jan Olof Andersson.

11.01.2019 ICELAND - SWEDEN 2-2(1-1) Friendly International
Khalifa International Stadium, Doha (Qatar); Referee: Mohammed Ahmed Al Shammari (Qatar); Attendance: 187
SWE: Oscar Carl Linnér (46.Isak Pettersson), Sotirios Papagiannopoulos (Cap), Eric Joel Andersson, Per Filip Dagerstål, Johan Simon Thern, Charles Melker Otto Hallberg (86.Goran Alexander Sjöström Milošević), Adam Andersson, Tesfaldet Simon Tekie (64.Alexander Fransson), Jonathan Levi (78.Daleho Irandust), Muamer Tanković (78.Karl Albin Elis Holmberg), Viktor Einar Gyökeres. Trainer: Jan Olof Andersson.
Goals: Viktor Einar Gyökeres (47), Johan Simon Thern (66).

23.03.2019 SWEDEN - ROMANIA 2-1(2-0) 16th EC. Qualifiers
Friends Arena, Stockholm; Referee: Michael Oliver (England); Attendance: 30,115
SWE: Robin Patrick Olsen, Andreas Granqvist (Cap), Carl Mikael Lustig (24.Emil Henry Kristoffer Krafth), Ludwig Augustinsson, Filip Viktor Helander, Sebastian Bengt Ulf Larsson, Emil Peter Forsberg (68.Gustav Svensson), Viktor Johan Anton Claesson, Mats Kristoffer Olsson, Marcus Berg, Robin Kwamina Quaison (88.Alexander Isak). Trainer: Jan Olof Andersson.
Goals: Robin Kwamina Quaison (33), Viktor Johan Anton Claesson (40).

26.03.2019 NORWAY - SWEDEN **3-3(1-0)** 16th EC. Qualifiers

Ullevaal Stadion, Oslo; Referee: Gianluca Rocchi (Italy); Attendance: 23,459

SWE: Robin Patrick Olsen, Andreas Granqvist (Cap), Ludwig Augustinsson, Emil Henry Kristoffer Krafth, Filip Viktor Helander, Sebastian Bengt Ulf Larsson (62.Alexander Isak), Albin Ekdal (66.Gustav Svensson), Mats Kristoffer Olsson (90+5.Martin Sebastian Andersson), Viktor Johan Anton Claesson, Marcus Berg, Robin Kwamina Quaison. Trainer: Jan Olof Andersson.

Goals: Viktor Johan Anton Claesson (70), Håvard Nordtveit (86 own goal), Robin Kwamina Quaison (90+1).

07.06.2019 SWEDEN - MALTA **3-0(1-0)** 16th EC. Qualifiers

Friends Arena, Stockholm; Referee: Robert Harvey (Republic of Ireland); Attendance: 26,421

SWE: Robin Patrick Olsen, Carl Mikael Lustig, Pontus Sven Gustav Jansson, Ludwig Augustinsson, Filip Viktor Helander, Albin Ekdal (Cap) (77.Sebastian Bengt Ulf Larsson), Emil Peter Forsberg, Viktor Johan Anton Claesson, Mats Kristoffer Olsson, Marcus Berg (68.Alexander Isak), Robin Kwamina Quaison (85.John Olof Alberto Guidetti). Trainer: Jan Olof Andersson.

Goals: Robin Kwamina Quaison (2), Viktor Johan Anton Claesson (50), Alexander Isak (81).

10.06.2019 SPAIN - SWEDEN **3-0(0-0)** 16th EC. Qualifiers

Estadio "Santiago Bernabéu", Madrid; Referee: William Collum (Scotland); Attendance: 72,205

SWE: Robin Patrick Olsen, Carl Mikael Lustig, Pontus Sven Gustav Jansson, Ludwig Augustinsson, Filip Viktor Helander, Sebastian Bengt Ulf Larsson (82.Alexander Isak), Albin Ekdal (Cap) (86.Mats Kristoffer Olsson), Emil Peter Forsberg, Viktor Johan Anton Claesson (27.Jakob Valdemar Olsson Johansson), Marcus Berg, Robin Kwamina Quaison. Trainer: Jan Olof Andersson.

NATIONAL TEAM PLAYERS
(16.07.2018 – 15.07.2019)

Name	DOB	Caps	Goals	2018/2019:	*Club*
Goalkeepers					
Karl-Johan JOHNSSON	28.01.1990	**7**	**0**	2018:	*En Avant de Guingamp (FRA)*
Oscar Carl LINNÉR	23.02.1997	**1**	**0**	2019:	*AIK Stockholm*
Kristoffer NORDFELDT	23.06.1989	**10**	**0**	2018:	*Swansea City AFC (WAL)*
Robin Patrick OLSEN	08.01.1990	**31**	**0**	2018/2019:	*AS Roma (ITA)*
Isak PETTERSSON	06.06.1997	**1**	**0**	2019:	*IFK Norrköping*
Jacob Karl Anders RINNE	20 06 1993	**3**	**0**	2018/2019:	*Aalborg BK (DEN)*
Defenders					
Adam ANDERSSON	11.11.1996	**2**	**0**	2019:	*BK Häcken Göteborg*
Eric Joel ANDERSSON	11.11.1996	**3**	**0**	2019:	*FC Midtjylland Herning*
Hans Carl Ludwig AUGUSTINSSON	21.04.1994	**28**	**1**	2018/2019:	*SV Werder Bremen (GER)*
Hans Oskar Jonathan AUGUSTINSSON	30.03.1996	**1**	**0**	2019:	*Djurgårdens IF Stockholm*
Per Filip DAGERSTÅL	01.02.1997	**2**	**0**	2019:	*IFK Norrköping*
Andreas GRANQVIST	16.04.1985	**83**	**9**	2018/2019:	*Helsingborgs IF*
Filip Viktor HELANDER	22.04.1993	**10**	**0**	2018/2019:	*Bologna FC 1909 (ITA)*
Niklas HULT	13.02.1990	**8**	**0**	2018:	*AEK Athína (GRE)*
Pontus Sven Gustav JANSSON	13.02.1991	**22**	**0**	2018/2019:	*Leeds United FC (ENG)*
Per Tony Robin JANSSON	15.11.1991	**1**	**0**	2019:	*AIK Stockholm*
Emil Henry Kristoffer KRAFTH	02.08.1994	**20**	**0**	2018/2019:	*Amiens SC (FRA)*
Victor Jörgen Nilsson LINDELÖF	17.07.1994	**29**	**2**	2018/2019:	*Manchester United FC (ENG)*
Carl Mikael LUSTIG	13.12.1986	**77**	**6**	2018/2019:	*Celtic FC Glasgow (SCO)*
Goran Alexander Sjöström MILOŠEVIĆ	30.01.1992	**7**	**0**	2019:	*AIK Stockholm*
Martin Tony Waikwa OLSSON	17.05.1988	**48**	**5**	2018:	*Swansea City AFC (WAL)*
Sotirios PAPAGIANNOPOULOS	05.09.1990	**4**	**0**	2018/2019:	*FC København (DEN)*
Midfielders					
Hosam AIESH	14.04.1995	**1**	**0**	2019:	*Östersunds FK*
Viktor Johan Anton CLAESSON	02.01.1992	**37**	**7**	2018/2019:	*FK Krasnodar (RUS)*
Jakup Jimmy DURMAZ	22.03.1989	**48**	**3**	2018:	*Toulouse FC (FRA)*
Albin EKDAL	28.07.1989	**45**	**0**	2018/2019:	*UC Sampdoria Genova (ITA)*
Emil Peter FORSBERG	23.10.1991	**45**	**7**	2018/2019:	*RasenBallsport Leipzig (GER)*
Alexander FRANSSON	02.04.1994	**8**	**0**	2018/2019:	*IFK Norrköping*
Charles Melker Otto HALLBERG	20.10.1995	**3**	**0**	2019:	*Vejle BK (DEN)*
Oscar HILJEMARK	28.06.1992	**27**	**2**	2018:	*Genoa CFC (ITA)*
Daleho IRANDUST	04.06.1998	**2**	**0**	2019:	*BK Häcken Göteborg*
Alexander ISAK	21.09.1999	**6**	**2**	2019:	*Willem II Tilburg (NED)*
Jakob Valdemar Olsson JOHANSSON	21.06.1990	**18**	**1**	2018/2019:	*Stade Rennais FC (FRA)*
Sam Andreas LARSSON	10.04.1993	**5**	**1**	2018:	*Feyenoord Rotterdam (NED)*
Sebastian Bengt Ulf LARSSON	06.06.1985	**113**	**6**	2018/2019:	*AIK Stockholm*
Jonathan LEVI	23.01.1996	**1**	**0**	2019:	*Rosenborg BK Trondheim (NOR)*

Mats Kristoffer OLSSON	30.06.1995	**9**	**0**	2018: 07.01.2019->	*AIK Stockholm* *FK Krasnodar (RUS)*
Marcus Christer ROHDÉN	11.05.1991	**15**	**1**	2018:	*FC Crotone (ITA)*
Ken Nlata SEMA	30.09.1993	**6**	**0**	2018:	*Watford FC (ENG)*
Karl Gustav Johan SVENSSON	07.02.1987	**22**	**0**	2018/2019:	*Seattle Sounders (USA)*
Muamer TANKOVIĆ	22.02.1995	**2**	**0**	2019:	*Hammarby IF Stockholm*
Tesfaldet Simon TEKIE	04.06.1997	**1**	**0**	2019:	*KAA Gent (BEL)*
Johan Simon THERN	18.09.1992	**4**	**2**	2018/2019:	*IFK Norrköping*
Simon Hjalmar Friedel TIBBLING	07.09.1994	**1**	**0**	2019:	*Brøndby IF (DEN)*

Forwards

Martin Sebastian ANDERSSON	15.07.1991	**5**	**2**	2018/2019:	*1. FC Union Berlin (GER)*
Marcus BERG	17.08.1986	**71**	**19**	2018/2019:	*Al Ain FC (UAE)*
John Olof Alberto GUIDETTI	15.04.1992	**27**	**2**	2018/2019:	*Deportivo Alavés Vitoria-Gasteiz (ESP)*
Viktor Einar GYÖKERES	04.06.1998	**2**	**1**	2019:	*Brighton & Hove Albion FC (ENG)*
Karl Albin Elis HOLMBERG	03.03.1993	**4**	**1**	2019:	*IFK Norrköping*
Alexander Thomas JEREMEJEFF	12.10.1993	**1**	**0**	2019:	*BK Häcken Göteborg*
Kristoffer PETERSON	28.11.1994	**1**	**0**	2018:	*Heracles Almelo (NED)*
Robin Kwamina QUAISON	09.10.1993	**10**	**5**	2018/2019:	*1. FSV Mainz 05 (GER)*
Isaac Kiese THELIN	24.06.1992	**29**	**3**	2018/2019:	*TSV Bayer 04 Leverkusen (GER)*

National team coach

Jan Olof "Janne" ANDERSSON [from 23.06.2016]	29.09.1962	40 M; 18 W; 10 D; 12 L; 65-38

SWITZERLAND

The Country:
Schweizerische Eidgenossenschaft (Swiss Confederation)
Capital: Bern
Surface: 41,285 km²
Inhabitants: 8,570,146 [2019]
Time: UTC+1

The FA:
Schweizerischer Fussballverband
Worbstrasse 48, Postfach 3000, Bern 15
Tel: +41 31 950 8111
Founded: 07.04.1895
Member of FIFA since: 1904
Member of UEFA since: 1954
Website: www.football.ch

NATIONAL TEAM RECORDS

First international match:	12.02.1905, Paris:	France – Switzerland 1-0
Most international caps:	Heinz Hermann	- 118 caps (1978-1991)
Most international goals:	Alexander Frei	- 42 goals / 84 caps (2001-2011)

UEFA EUROPEAN CHAMPIONSHIP	
1960	Did not enter
1964	Qualifiers
1968	Qualifiers
1972	Qualifiers
1976	Qualifiers
1980	Qualifiers
1984	Qualifiers
1988	Qualifiers
1992	Qualifiers
1996	Final Tournament (Group Stage)
2000	Qualifiers
2004	Final Tournament (Group Stage)
2008	Final Tournament (Group Stage)
2012	Qualifiers
2016	Final Tournament (2nd Round of 16)

FIFA WORLD CUP	
1930	Did not enter
1934	Final Tournament (Quarter-Finals)
1938	Final Tournament (Quarter-Finals)
1950	Final Tournament (Group Stage)
1954	Final Tournament (Quarter-Finals)
1958	Qualifiers
1962	Final Tournament (Group Stage)
1966	Final Tournament (Group Stage)
1970	Qualifiers
1974	Qualifiers
1978	Qualifiers
1982	Qualifiers
1986	Qualifiers
1990	Qualifiers
1994	Final Tournament (2nd Round of 16)
1998	Qualifiers
2002	Qualifiers
2006	Final Tournament (2nd Round of 16)
2010	Final Tournament (Group Stage)
2014	Final Tournament (2nd Round of 16)
2018	Final Tournament (2nd Round of 16)

UEFA NATIONS LEAGUE
2018/2019 – League A; Final Tournament – 4th Place

OLYMPIC FOOTBALL TOURNAMENTS 1908-2016							
1908	-	**1948**	Did not enter	**1972**	Qualifiers	**1996**	Qualifiers
1912	-	**1952**	Did not enter	**1976**	Did not enter	**2000**	Qualifiers
1920	-	**1956**	Did not enter	**1980**	Did not enter	**2004**	Qualifiers
1924	Runners-up	**1960**	Qualifiers	**1984**	Did not enter	**2008**	Qualifiers
1928	1/8 - Finals	**1964**	Qualifiers	**1988**	Qualifiers	**2012**	Group Stage
1936	Did not enter	**1968**	Qualifiers	**1992**	Qualifiers	**2016**	Qualifiers

FIFA CONFEDERATIONS CUP 1992-2017
None

SWISS CLUB HONOURS IN EUROPEAN CLUB COMPETITIONS:

European Champion Clubs' Cup (1956-1992) / UEFA Champions League (1993-2019)
None
Fairs Cup (1858-1971) / UEFA Cup (1972-2009) / UEFA Europa League (2010-2019)
None
UEFA Super Cup (1972-2018)
None
European Cup Winners' Cup 1961-1999*
None

**defunct competition*

NATIONAL COMPETITIONS
TABLE OF HONOURS

	CHAMPIONS	CUP WINNERS	BEST GOALSCORERS	
1898/1899	Anglo-American Club FC Zürich	-	-	
1899/1900	Grasshopper Club Zürich	-	-	
1900/1901	Grasshopper Club Zürich	-	-	
1901/1902	FC Zürich	-	-	
1902/1903	BSC Young Boys Bern	-	-	
1903/1904	FC St. Gallen	-	-	
1904/1905	Grasshopper Club Zürich	-	-	
1905/1906	FC Winterthur	-	-	
1906/1907	Servette FC Genève	-	-	
1907/1908	FC Winterthur	-	-	
1908/1909	BSC Young Boys Bern	-	-	
1909/1910	BSC Young Boys Bern	-	-	
1910/1911	BSC Young Boys Bern	-	-	
1911/1912	FC Aarau	-	-	
1912/1913	Montriond Lausanne	-	-	
1913/1914	FC Aarau	-	-	
1914/1915	SC Brühl St. Gallen	-	-	
1915/1916	Cantonal Neuchâtel	-	-	
1916/1917	FC Winterthur	-	-	
1917/1918	Servette FC Genève	-	-	
1918/1919	Étoile La Chaux-de-Fonds	-	-	
1919/1920	BSC Young Boys Bern	-	-	
1920/1921	Grasshopper Club Zürich	-	-	
1921/1922	Servette FC Genève	-	-	
1922/1923	*Title not awarded*	-	-	
1923/1924	FC Zürich	-	-	
1924/1925	Servette FC Genève	-	-	
1925/1926	Servette FC Genève	Grasshopper Club Zürich	-	
1926/1927	Grasshopper Club Zürich	Grasshopper Club Zürich	-	
1927/1928	Grasshopper Club Zürich	Servette FC Genève FC	-	
1928/1929	BSC Young Boys Bern	Urania Genève Sport	-	
1929/1930	Servette FC Genève	BSC Young Boys Bern	-	
1930/1931	Grasshopper Club Zürich	FC Lugano	-	
1931/1932	FC Lausanne-Sport	Grasshopper Club Zürich	-	
1932/1933	Servette FC Genève	FC Basel	-	
1933/1934	Servette FC Genève	Grasshopper Club Zürich	Leopold Kielholz (Servette FC Genève)	40
1934/1935	FC Lausanne-Sport	FC Lausanne-Sport	Engelbert Bösch (AUT, FC Bern)	27
1935/1936	FC Lausanne-Sport	Young Fellows FC Zürich	Willy Jäggi (FC Lausanne-Sport)	27
1936/1937	Grasshopper Club Zürich	Grasshopper Club Zürich	Alessandro Frigerio Payán (Young Fellows FC Zürich)	23
1937/1938	FC Lugano	Grasshopper Club Zürich	Numa Monnard (FC Basel)	20
1938/1939	Grasshopper Club Zürich	FC Lausanne-Sport	Josef Artimovics (AUT, FC Grenchen)	15
1939/1940	Servette FC Genève	Grasshopper Club Zürich	Georges Aeby (Servette FC Genève)	22
1940/1941	FC Lugano	Grasshopper Club Zürich	Alessandro Frigerio Payán (FC Lugano)	26
1941/1942	Grasshopper Club Zürich	Grasshopper Club Zürich	Alessandro Frigerio Payán (FC Lugano)	23
1942/1943	Grasshopper Club Zürich	Grasshopper Club Zürich	Lauro Amadò (Grasshopper Club Zürich)	31
1943/1944	FC Lausanne-Sport	FC Lausanne-Sport	Erich Andres (Young Fellows FC Zürich)	23
1944/1945	Grasshopper Club Zürich	BSC Young Boys Bern	Hans-Peter Friedländer (Grasshopper Club Zürich)	26
1945/1946	Servette FC Genève	Grasshopper Club Zürich	Hans-Peter Friedländer (Grasshopper Club Zürich)	25
1946/1947	FC Biel-Bienne	FC Basel	Lauro Amadò (Grasshopper Club Zürich) Hans Blaser (BSC Young Boys Bern)	19
1947/1948	AC Bellinzona	FC La Chaux-de-Fonds	Josef Righetti (FC Grenchen)	26
1948/1949	FC Lugano	Servette FC Genève FC	Jacques Fatton (Servette FC Genève)	21
1949/1950	Servette FC Genève	FC Lausanne-Sport	Jacques Fatton (Servette FC Genève)	32
1950/1951	FC Lausanne-Sport	FC La Chaux-de-Fonds	Hans-Peter Friedländer (FC Lausanne-Sport)	23
1951/1952	Grasshopper Club Zürich	Grasshopper Club Zürich	Josef Hügi (FC Basel)	24
1952/1953	FC Basel	BSC Young Boys Bern	Josef Hügi (FC Basel) Eugen Meier (BSC Young Boys Bern)	32
1953/1954	FC La Chaux-de-Fonds	FC La Chaux-de-Fonds	Josef Hügi (FC Basel)	29
1954/1955	FC La Chaux-de-Fonds	FC La Chaux-de-Fonds	Marcel Mauron (FC La Chaux-de-Fonds)	30
1955/1956	Grasshopper Club Zürich	Grasshopper Club Zürich	Branislav Vukosavljević (YUG, Grasshopper Club Zürich)	33
1956/1957	BSC Young Boys Bern	FC La Chaux-de-Fonds	Adrien Kauer (FC La Chaux-de-Fonds)	29
1957/1958	BSC Young Boys Bern	BSC Young Boys Bern	Ernst Wechselberger (GER, BSC Young Boys Bern)	22
1958/1959	BSC Young Boys Bern	FC Grenchen	Eugen Meier (BSC Young Boys Bern)	24
1959/1960	BSC Young Boys Bern	FC Luzern	Willy Schneider (BSC Young Boys Bern)	25
1960/1961	Servette FC Genève	FC La Chaux-de-Fonds	Giuliano Robbiani (Grasshopper Club Zürich)	27
1961/1962	Servette FC Genève	FC Lausanne-Sport	Jacques Fatton (Servette FC Genève)	25
1962/1963	FC Zürich	FC Basel	Peter von Burg (FC Zürich)	24
1963/1964	FC La Chaux-de-Fonds	FC Lausanne-Sport	Michel Desbiolles (Servette FC Genève)	23

1964/1965	FC Lausanne-Sport	FC Sion	Rolf Blättler (Grasshopper Club Zürich) Pierre Kerkhoffs (NED, FC Lausanne-Sport)	19
1965/1966	FC Zürich	FC Zürich	Rolf Blättler (Grasshopper Club Zürich)	28
1966/1967	FC Basel	FC Basel	Rolf Blättler (Grasshopper Club Zürich)	24
1967/1968	FC Zürich	FC Lugano	Friedrich Künzli (FC Zürich)	28
1968/1969	FC Basel	FC St. Gallen	Hans-Otto Peters (GER, FC Biel-Bienne)	24
1969/1970	FC Basel	FC Zürich	Friedrich Künzli (FC Zürich)	19
1970/1971	Grasshopper Club Zürich	Servette FC Genève FC	Walter Müller (BSC Young Boys Bern)	19
1971/1972	FC Basel	FC Zürich	Herbert Dimmeler (FC Winterthur) Bernd Dörfel (GER, Servette FC Genève)	17
1972/1973	FC Basel	FC Zürich	Ottmar Hitzfeld (FC Basel) Jan-Olof Grahn (FC Lausanne-Sport)	18
1973/1974	FC Zürich	FC Sion	Daniel Jeandupeux (FC Zürich)	22
1974/1975	FC Zürich	FC Basel	Ilija Katić (FC Zürich)	23
1975/1976	FC Zürich	FC Zürich	Peter Risi (FC Zürich)	33
1976/1977	FC Basel	BSC Young Boys Bern	Franco Cucinotta (ITA, FC Zürich)	28
1977/1978	Grasshopper Club Zürich	Servette FC Genève FC	Friedrich Künzli (FC Lausanne-Sport)	21
1978/1979	Servette FC Genève	Servette FC Genève FC	Peter Risi (FC Zürich)	16
1979/1980	FC Basel	FC Sion	Claudio Sulser (Grasshopper Club Zürich)	25
1980/1981	FC Zürich	FC Lausanne-Sport	Peter Risi (FC Luzern)	18
1981/1982	Grasshopper Club Zürich	FC Sion	Claudio Sulser (Grasshopper Club Zürich)	23
1982/1983	Grasshopper Club Zürich	Grasshopper Club Zürich	Jean-Paul Brigger (Servette FC Genève)	23
1983/1984	Grasshopper Club Zürich	Servette FC Genève FC	Georges Bregy (FC Sion)	21
1984/1985	Servette FC Genève	FC Aarau	Dominique Cina (FC Sion)	24
1985/1986	BSC Young Boys Bern	FC Sion	Steen Thychosen (DEN, FC Lausanne-Sport)	21
1986/1987	Neuchâtel Xamax FCS	BSC Young Boys Bern	John Hartmann Eriksen (DEN, Servette FC Genève)	28
1987/1988	Neuchâtel Xamax FCS	Grasshopper Club Zürich	John Hartmann Eriksen (DEN, Servette FC Genève)	36
1988/1989	FC Luzern	Grasshopper Club Zürich	Karl-Heinz Rummenigge (GER, Servette FC Genève)	24
1989/1990	Grasshopper Club Zürich	Grasshopper Club Zürich	Iván Luis Zamorano Zamora (CHI, FC St. Gallen)	23
1990/1991	Grasshopper Club Zürich	FC Sion	Dario Zuffi (BSC Young Boys Bern)	17
1991/1992	FC Sion	FC Luzern	Miklos Jon Molnar (DEN, Servette FC Genève)	18
1992/1993	FC Aarau	FC Lugano	„Sonny" Anderson da Silva (BRA, Servette FC Genève)	20
1993/1994	Servette FC Genève	Grasshopper Club Zürich	Élber de Souza (BRA, Grasshopper Club Zürich)	21
1994/1995	Grasshopper Club Zürich	FC Sion	Petar Aleksandrov (BUL, Neuchâtel Xamax FCS)	24
1995/1996	Grasshopper Club Zürich	FC Sion	Petar Aleksandrov (BUL, FC Luzern) Viorel Dinu Moldovan (ROU, Neuchâtel Xamax FCS)	19
1996/1997	FC Sion	FC Sion	Viorel Dinu Moldovan (ROU, Grasshopper Club Zürich)	27
1997/1998	Grasshopper Club Zürich	FC Lausanne-Sport	Shabani Christophe Nonda (COD, FC Zürich)	24
1998/1999	Servette FC Genève	FC Lausanne-Sport	Alexandre Rey (Servette FC Genève)	19
1999/2000	FC St. Gallen	FC Zürich	Charles Amoah (GHA, FC St. Gallen)	25
2000/2001	Grasshopper Club Zürich	Servette FC Genève FC	Stéphane Chapuisat (Grasshopper Club Zürich) Christian Eduardo Giménez (ARG, FC Lugano)	21
2001/2002	FC Basel	FC Basel	Christian Eduardo Giménez (ARG, FC Lugano) Richard Darío Núñez Pereyra (URU, Grasshopper Club Zürich)	28
2002/2003	Grasshopper Club Zürich	FC Basel	Richard Darío Núñez Pereyra (URU, Grasshopper Club Zürich)	27
2003/2004	FC Basel	FC Will 1900	Stéphane Chapuisat (BSC Young Boys Bern)	23
2004/2005	FC Basel	FC Zürich	Christian Eduardo Giménez (ARG, FC Basel)	27
2005/2006	FC Zürich	FC Sion	Alhassane Keita Otchico (GUI, FC Zürich)	20
2006/2007	FC Zürich	FC Basel	Mladen Petrić (CRO, FC Basel)	19
2007/2008	FC Basel	FC Basel	Hakan Yakin (BSC Young Boys Bern)	24
2008/2009	FC Zürich	FC Sion	Seydou Doumbia (CIV, BSC Young Boys Bern)	20
2009/2010	FC Basel	FC Basel	Seydou Doumbia (CIV, BSC Young Boys Bern)	30
2010/2011	FC Basel	FC Sion	Alexander Frei (FC Basel)	27
2011/2012	FC Basel	FC Basel	Alexander Frei (FC Basel)	24
2012/2013	FC Basel	Grasshopper Club Zürich	Ezequiel Óscar Scarione (ARG, FC St. Gallen)	21
2013/2014	FC Basel	FC Zürich	Shkëlzen Taib Gashi (ALB, Grasshopper Club Zürich)	19
2014/2015	FC Basel	FC Sion	Shkëlzen Taib Gashi (ALB, FC Basel)	21
2015/2016	FC Basel	FC Zürich	Moanes Daobur (ISR, Grasshopper Club Zürich)	19
2016/2017	FC Basel	FC Basel	Seydou Doumbia (CIV, FC Basel)	20
2017/2018	BSC Young Boys Bern	FC Zürich	Albian Afrim Ajeti (FC Basel)	17
2018/2019	BSC Young Boys Bern	FC Basel	Guillaume Hoarau (FRA, BSC Young Boys Bern)	24

Name changements of first level: Serie A (1898–1931), National League (1931–1944), National League A (1944–2003), Super League (since 2003).

NATIONAL CHAMPIONSHIP

Swiss Super League 2018/2019

(21.07.2018 – 25.05.2019)

Results

Round 1 [21-22.07.2018]
FC Basel - FC St.Gallen 1-2(0-0)
FC Luzern - Neuchâtel Xamax 0-2(0-1)
Young Boys - Grasshopper Club 2-0(0-0)
FC Sion - FC Lugano 1-2(0-2)
FC Zürich - FC Thun 2-1(1-0)

Round 2 [28-29.07.2018]
Grasshopper Club - FC Zürich 0-2(0-0)
Neuchâtel Xamax - FC Basel 1-1(0-0)
FC Lugano - Young Boys 0-2(0-1)
FC St.Gallen - FC Sion 2-4(0-2)
FC Thun - FC Luzern 2-1(0-1)

Round 3 [04-05.08.2018]
FC Basel - Grasshopper Club 4-2(2-0)
FC Luzern - FC Lugano 4-2(2-1)
Young Boys - FC Zürich 4-0(3-0)
FC Sion - Neuchâtel Xamax 3-0(2-0)
FC St.Gallen - FC Thun 3-2(3-0)

Round 4 [11-12.08.2018]
FC Lugano - Grasshopper Club 2-2(1-0)
Neuchâtel Xamax - FC Thun 1-5(1-3)
FC Basel - FC Sion 3-2(2-1)
FC Luzern - Young Boys 2-3(0-1)
FC Zürich - FC St.Gallen 0-0

Round 5 [25-26.08.2018]
Young Boys - Neuchâtel Xamax 5-2(2-1)
Grasshopper Club - FC Sion 2-1(0-0)
FC Zürich - FC Basel 1-1(0-1)
FC St.Gallen - FC Luzern 0-1(0-0)
FC Thun - FC Lugano 1-1(0-0)

Round 6 [01-02.09.2018]
FC Lugano - FC Zürich 1-0(1-0)
FC Sion - Young Boys 0-3(0-1)
FC Basel - FC Thun 1-1(1-1)
FC Luzern - Grasshopper Club 2-1(0-1)
Neuchâtel Xamax - FC St.Gallen 2-3(1-0)

Round 7 [22-23.09.2018]
Grasshopper Club - Neuchâtel Xam. 3-1(1-0)
FC Thun - FC Sion 4-1(0-0)
Young Boys - FC Basel 7-1(2-0)
FC St.Gallen - FC Lugano 2-2(2-0)
FC Zürich - FC Luzern 1-0(0-0)

Round 8 [25-27.09.2018]
Grasshopper Club - FC Thun 0-2(0-0)
Young Boys - FC St.Gallen 2-0(2-0)
FC Basel - FC Luzern 2-1(1-0)
Neuchâtel Xamax - FC Lugano 2-1(1-0)
FC Sion - FC Zürich 1-2(0-1)

Round 9 [29-30.09.2018]
FC St.Gallen - Grasshopper Club 2-1(0-1)
FC Thun - Young Boys 1-4(1-2)
FC Lugano - FC Basel 2-2(0-1)
FC Luzern - FC Sion 1-3(0-1)
FC Zürich - Neuchâtel Xamax 0-0

Round 10 [06-07.10.2018]
FC St.Gallen - FC Basel 1-3(1-1)
Young Boys - FC Luzern 2-3(0-1)
Grasshopper Club - FC Lugano 2-1(2-1)
Neuchâtel Xamax - FC Sion 1-1(1-1)
FC Thun - FC Zürich 2-2(0-1)

Round 11 [20-21.10.2018]
FC Luzern - FC Thun 0-2(0-0)
FC Zürich - Young Boys 3-3(2-0)
FC Basel - Neuchâtel Xamax 1-1(1-0)
FC Lugano - FC St.Gallen 3-1(2-0)
FC Sion - Grasshopper Club 0-0

Round 12 [27-28.10.2018]
Grasshopper Club - FC Basel 1-3(0-3)
Young Boys - FC Sion 3-2(0-2)
Neuchâtel Xamax - FC Luzern 1-2(1-1)
FC Lugano - FC Thun 2-1(2-1)
FC St.Gallen - FC Zürich 3-2(1-0)

Round 13 [03-04.11.2018]
Grasshopper Club - Young Boys 0-3(0-0)
FC Thun - Neuchâtel Xamax 2-2(1-0)
FC Basel - FC Lugano 3-2(2-0)
FC Luzern - FC Zürich 2-5(1-2)
FC Sion - FC St.Gallen 0-1(0-1)

Round 14 [10-11.11.2018]
FC Lugano - FC Luzern 1-4(0-1)
FC Thun - FC Basel 4-2(1-2)
Neuchâtel Xam. - Grasshopper Club 2-3(0-1)
FC St.Gallen - Young Boys 2-3(1-3)
FC Zürich - FC Sion 1-2(0-0)

Round 15 [24-25.11.2018]
Neuchâtel Xamax - FC Zürich 3-3(1-0)
Young Boys - FC Lugano 1-0(0-0)
Grasshopper Club - FC St.Gallen 2-1(2-0)
FC Luzern - FC Basel 1-1(1-0)
FC Sion - FC Thun 2-1(1-0)

Round 16 [01-02.12.2018]
FC Sion - FC Luzern 2-0(0-0)
FC Thun - FC St.Gallen 2-0(0-0)
FC Basel - Young Boys 1-3(1-0)
FC Lugano - Neuchâtel Xamax 2-2(1-0)
FC Zürich - Grasshopper Club 2-0(0-0)

Round 17 [08-09.12.2018]
FC St.Gallen - Neuchâtel Xamax 3-2(2-1)
Young Boys - FC Thun 3-2(0-1)
FC Basel - FC Zürich 2-0(1-0)
Grasshopper Club - FC Luzern 2-3(2-2)
FC Lugano - FC Sion 2-2(1-1)

Round 18 [15-16.12.2018]
FC Sion - FC Basel 1-2(1-0)
FC Thun - Grasshopper Club 1-0(0-0)
Neuchâtel Xamax - Young Boys 1-4(0-2)
FC Luzern - FC St.Gallen 2-1(2-0)
FC Zürich - FC Lugano 0-0

Round 19 [02-06.02.2019]
Young Boys - Neuchâtel Xamax 2-0(1-0)
Grasshopper Club - FC Basel 0-4(0-2)
FC Lugano - FC Thun 1-3(0-1)
FC St.Gallen - FC Zürich 3-1(1-0)
FC Luzern - FC Sion 1-3(1-1) [13.02.]

Round 20 [09-10.02.2019]
FC Basel - FC St.Gallen 1-1(0-0)
FC Zürich - Grasshopper Club 3-1(1-1)
Neuchâtel Xamax - FC Luzern 2-1(2-0)
FC Sion - FC Lugano 2-2(1-1)
FC Thun - Young Boys 1-1(0-1)

Round 21 [16-17.02.2019]
FC Luzern - FC Lugano 0-3(0-1)
FC St.Gallen - FC Thun 1-3(0-1)
FC Basel - FC Sion 1-0(1-0)
Grasshopper Club - Neuchâtel Xam. 0-1(0-1)
Young Boys - FC Zürich 2-0(0-0)

Round 22 [23-24.02.2019]
Neuchâtel Xamax - FC Basel 0-2(0-1)
FC Sion - FC St.Gallen 2-2(1-1)
FC Lugano - Young Boys 0-1(0-0)
FC Thun - Grasshopper Club 1-1(1-1)
FC Zürich - FC Luzern 1-1(1-0)

Round 23 [02-03.03.2019]
Grasshopper Club - FC Luzern 1-3(0-2)
Young Boys - FC Sion 1-0(0-0)
FC Basel - FC Thun 3-1(2-0)
FC St.Gallen - Neuchâtel Xamax 3-0(1-0)
FC Zürich - FC Lugano 0-1(0-1)

Round 24 [09-10.03.2019]
Grasshopper Club - Young Boys 0-1(0-0)
Neuchâtel Xamax - FC Sion 3-1(2-0)
FC Lugano - FC Basel 1-1(1-1)
FC Luzern - FC St.Gallen 3-0(1-0)
FC Thun - FC Zürich 2-2(2-1)

Round 25 [16-17.03.2019]
FC Sion - Grasshopper Club 3-0 (awarded)
FC St.Gallen - FC Lugano 0-2(0-1)
FC Basel - Young Boys 2-2(1-2)
FC Thun - FC Luzern 1-1(0-0)
FC Zürich - Neuchâtel Xamax 2-1(0-0)

Round 26 [30-31.03.2019]
FC Luzern - FC Basel 0-1(0-0)
FC Sion - FC Zürich 1-0(1-0)
Grasshopper Club - FC Lugano 1-1(1-1)
Neuchâtel Xamax - FC Thun 3-2(0-1)
Young Boys - FC St.Gallen 3-2(1-1)

Round 27 [03-04.04.2019]
FC Lugano - Neuchâtel Xamax 0-0
FC St.Gallen - Grasshopper Club 0-0
FC Zürich - FC Basel 0-2(0-0)
FC Thun - FC Sion 1-2(1-2)
FC Luzern - Young Boys 1-3(0-0) [10.04.]

Round 28 [06-07.04.2019]
Grasshopper Club - FC Zürich 1-1(0-1)
Neuchâtel Xamax - FC St.Gallen 0-1(0-0)
FC Basel - FC Lugano 1-1(0-0)
FC Sion - FC Luzern 2-2(1-1)
Young Boys - FC Thun 5-1(4-0)

Round 29 [13-14.04.2019]
FC Basel - Grasshopper Club 0-0
FC Luzern - Neuchâtel Xamax 0-1(0-0)
FC Lugano - FC Sion 1-1(0-0)
FC Thun - FC St.Gallen 0-0
FC Zürich - Young Boys 0-1(0-0)

Round 30 [19-22.04.2019]
FC Lugano - FC Zürich 3-0(1-0)
FC Sion - FC Basel 0-3(0-1)
Grasshopper Club - FC Thun 1-1(0-0)
FC St.Gallen - FC Luzern 1-2(0-1)
Neuchâtel Xamax - Young Boys 1-0(0-0)

Round 31 [27-28.04.2019]
Neuchâtel Xam. - Grasshopper Club 1-1(0-1)
FC Luzern - FC Thun 3-1(2-0)
FC St.Gallen - FC Basel 0-3(0-1)
Young Boys - FC Lugano 2-2(2-1)
FC Zürich - FC Sion 1-0(0-0)

Round 32 [04-05.05.2019]
FC Basel - FC Zürich 3-0(0-0)
Grasshopper Club - FC St.Gallen 0-1(0-0)
FC Lugano - FC Luzern 1-0(1-0)
FC Thun - Neuchâtel Xamax 0-2(0-0)
FC Sion - Young Boys 0-4(0-2)

Round 33 [11-12.05.2019]
Neuchâtel Xamax - FC Zürich 1-2(0-0)
FC Thun - FC Lugano 1-0(1-0)
FC Luzern - Grasshopper Club 4-0 (awarded)
FC St.Gallen - FC Sion 2-1(1-0)
Young Boys - FC Basel 3-1(0-1)

Round 34 [15-16.05.2019]
FC Basel - FC Luzern 3-2(2-0)
FC Sion - Neuchâtel Xamax 1-0(0-0)
FC Zürich - FC Thun 3-0(3-0)
FC Lugano - FC St.Gallen 1-0(1-0)
Young Boys - Grasshopper Club 6-1(3-0)

Round 35 [22.05.2019]
Grasshopper Club - FC Sion 0-3(0-2)
Neuchâtel Xamax - FC Lugano 1-1(0-1)
FC Luzern - FC Zürich 3-0(2-0)
FC St.Gallen - Young Boys 4-1(2-0)
FC Thun - FC Basel 1-2(0-0)

Round 36 [25.05.2019]
FC Basel - Neuchâtel Xamax 4-1(1-0)
FC Lugano - Grasshopper Club 3-3(1-1)
FC Sion - FC Thun 0-1(0-0)
Young Boys - FC Luzern 4-0(1-0)
FC Zürich - FC St.Gallen 1-1(0-1)

Final Standings

1.	**BSC Young Boys Bern**	36	29	4	3	99	-	36	91
2.	FC Basel	36	20	11	5	71	-	46	71
3.	FC Lugano	36	10	16	10	50	-	49	46
4.	FC Thun	36	12	10	14	57	-	58	46
5.	FC Luzern	36	14	4	18	56	-	61	46
6.	FC St. Gallen	36	13	7	16	49	-	58	46
7.	FC Zürich	36	11	11	14	43	-	52	44
8.	FC Sion	36	12	7	17	50	-	55	43
9.	Neuchâtel Xamax FCS (*Relegation Play-offs*)	36	9	10	17	44	-	65	37
10.	Grasshopper Club Zürich (*Relegated*)	36	5	10	21	32	-	71	25

Top goalscorers:

24 Guillaume Hoarau (FRA)
BSC Young Boys Bern

15 Jean-Pierre Nsame (CMR)
BSC Young Boys Bern

15 Dejan Sorgić (SRB)
FC Thun

14 Albian Afrim Ajeti
FC Basel

14 Raphaël Nuzzolo
Neuchâtel Xamax FCS

Relegation Play-offs [30.05.-02.06.2019]

Neuchâtel Xamax FCS - FC Aarau	0-4(0-3)	4-0(3-0); 5-4 pen

Neuchâtel Xamax FCS remains at first level.

NATIONAL CUP
Schweizer Cup 2018/2019

First Round [18-19.08.2018]

FC Willisau - FC Breitenrain Bern	1-3(0-2)
Zug 94 - FC Red Star Zürich	1-2(0-2)
FC Frauenfeld - FC Rapperswil-Jona	0-5(0-0)
FC Solothurn - FC Stade Nyonnais	0-2(0-1)
FC Amriswil - FC Aarau	1-2(0-1,1-1)
SC Goldau - FC Bavois	1-3(0-0)
FC Veyrier Sports - FC Thun	1-5(1-4)
AC Malcantone - FC Moutier	0-2(0-2)
FC Uzwil - FC Wil 1900	0-3(0-1)
FC Bellach - FC Chiasso	0-7(0-3)
AC Bellinzona - SC Young Fellows Juventus Zürich	4-0(3-0)
AS Novazzano - FC Echallens	0-4(0-1)
FC Meyrin - SC Cham	1-6(1-2)
FC Erde - FC Azzurri 90 LS Chavannes	1-5(0-3)
FC Langnau - SC Kriens	0-6(0-3)
FC Meilen - Servette FC Genève	0-6(0-2)
FC Kosova Zürich - FC Lausanne-Sport	0-4(0-2)
FC Greifensee - FC Winterthur	0-3(0-2)
FC Concordia Basel - FC Zürich	0-6(0-4)
FC Montlingen - FC Basel	0-3(0-1)
FC Grand-Saconnex - FC Muri	3-5(1-0,3-3)
FC Portalban/Gletterens - FC Wohlen	3-4(0-1,2-2)
FC Köniz - FC Sion	0-3(0-1)
FC Biel/Bienne - BSC Young Boys Bern	2-3(0-1,2-2)
SC Buochs - Grasshopper Club Zürich	0-2(0-1)
FC Freienbach - FC Schaffhausen	0-5(0-3)
FC Ueberstorf - FC St.Gallen	0-6(0-2)
FC Gland - FC Luzern	1-9(0-4)
FC Dietikon - FC Lugano	0-4(0-2)
FC Klingnau - FC Bramois	7-0(2-0)
FC Fleurier - FC Nidau	3-1(1-0)
Yverdon-Sport FC - Neuchâtel Xamax FCS	0-1(0-0)

Second Round [14-16.09.2018]

FC Bavois - FC Rapperswil-Jona	2-3(0-0,1-1)
FC Echallens - FC Basel	2-7(0-0)
FC Red Star Zürich - SC Cham	1-0(1-0)
Servette FC Genève - FC Luzern	3-3 aet; 4-5 pen
FC Wohlen - FC Wil 1900	0-1
AC Bellinzona - FC Winterthur	1-2(0-1)
FC Breitenrain Bern - FC Zürich	2-4(0-3)
FC Schaffhausen - BSC Young Boys Bern	2-3(0-0,2-2)
FC Azzurri 90 LS Chavannes - FC Lugano	0-1(0-1)
FC Moutier - FC Thun	1-3(1-2)
FC Stade Nyonnais - Grasshopper Club Zürich	3-1(1-1)
FC Aarau - Neuchâtel Xamax FCS	1-2(1-2)
FC Fleurier - SC Kriens	1-4(1-1)
FC Klingnau - FC Chiasso	0-2(0-0,0-0)
FC Muri - FC St.Gallen	0-7(0-5)
FC Lausanne-Sport - FC Sion	0-1(0-1)

1/8-Finals [31.10.-01.11.2018]

FC Stade Nyonnais - BSC Young Boys Bern	0-1(0-0)
FC Wil 1900 - FC Thun	1-1 aet; 3-5 pen
FC Winterthur - FC Basel	0-1(0-0)
FC Red Star Zürich - FC Zürich	2-3(1-3)
FC Lugano - Neuchâtel Xamax FCS	3-1(0-0,1-1)
FC Rapperswil-Jona - SC Kriens	1-4(0-1)
FC Chiasso - FC Luzern	0-2(0-0)
FC St.Gallen - FC Sion	1-2(0-0,1-1)

Quarter-Finals [27-28.02./06.03.2019]	
FC Sion - FC Basel	2-4(0-0,2-2)
FC Thun - FC Lugano	3-2(1-1)
FC Zürich - SC Kriens	2-1(1-1)
FC Luzern - BSC Young Boys Bern	4-0(1-0)

Semi-Finals [23-25.04.2019]	
FC Luzern - FC Thun	0-1(0-0)
FC Zürich - FC Basel	1-3(0-1)

Final

19.05.2019; Stade Suisse, Wankdorf, Bern; Referee: Fedayi San; Attendance: 20,500

FC Basel - FC Thun **2-1(1-0)**

FC Basel: Jonas Omlin, Blas Miguel Riveros Galeano, Marek Suchý, Éder Fabián Álvarez Balanta, Carlos Augusto Zambrano Ochandarte, Fabian Frei (90.Ricky van Wolfswinkel), Luca Zuffi (72.Zdravko Kuzmanović), Valentin Stocker (67.Kevin Bua), Taulant Xhaka, Noah Okafor, Albian Afrim Ajeti. Trainer: Marcel Koller.

FC Thun: Guillaume Faivre, Roy Gelmi, Chris Kablan, Sven Joss, Kenan Fatkić, Basil Stillhart, Matteo Tosetti (79.Dennis Salanović), Moreno Costanzo, Marvin Spielmann (90.Dominik Schwizer), Nicola Sutter (26.Gregory Karlen), Dejan Sorgić. Trainer: Marc Schneider.

Goals: 1-0 Albian Afrim Ajeti (23), 2-0 Fabian Frei (77), 2-1 Dejan Sorgić (82).

THE CLUBS 2018/2019

Fussball Club Basel 1893

Founded: 15.11.1893
Stadium: St. Jakob-Park, Basel (37,994)

Goalkeepers:	**DOB**	**M**	**(s)**	**G**
António Signori Dominique (ANG)	25.07.1994		(1)	
Martin Hansen (DEN)	15.06.1990	9		
Jonas Omlin	10.01.1994	27		
Defenders:	**DOB**	**M**	**(s)**	**G**
Éder Fabián Álvarez Balanta (COL)	28.02.1993	18	(2)	2
Eray Cömert	04.02.1998	24		1
Yves Kaiser	30.04.1998	6		
Raoul Petretta (ITA)	24.03.1997	20	(1)	1
Blas Miguel Riveros Galeano (PAR)	03.02.1998	16	(3)	2
Marek Suchý (CZE)	29.03.1988	17	(2)	2
Silvan Widmer	05.03.1993	31		1
Carlos Augusto Zambrano Ochandarte (PER)	10.07.1989	6	(1)	1
Midfielders:	**DOB**	**M**	**(s)**	**G**
Kevin Bua	11.08.1993	16	(5)	4
Samuele Campo	06.07.1995	8	(8)	7
Serey Dié (CIV)	07.11.1984	9	(3)	1
Fabian Frei	08.01.1989	29	(4)	4
Zdravko Kuzmanović (SRB)	22.09.1987	6	(7)	1
Yannick Marchand	09.02.2000		(1)	
Valentin Stocker	12.04.1989	11	(6)	2
Taulant Xhaka (ALB)	28.03.1991	25	(4)	
Luca Zuffi	27.03.1990	29	(5)	7
Forwards:	**DOB**	**M**	**(s)**	**G**
Albian Afrim Ajeti	26.02.1997	26	(6)	14
Aldo Kalulu (FRA)	21.01.1996	10	(7)	
Dimitri Joseph Oberlin Mfomo	27.09.1997	1	(13)	
Noah Okafor	24.05.2000	17	(7)	3
Afimico Pululu (FRA)	23.03.1999	2	(8)	
Tician Tushi	02.04.2001		(1)	
Ricky van Wolfswinkel (NED)	27.01.1989	29	(3)	13
Julian Vonmoos	01.04.2001		(1)	1
Edon Zhegrova (KVX)	31.03.1999	4	(4)	
Trainer:	**DOB**	**M**		
Raphaël Wicky	26.04.1977	1		
Alex Frei [26.07.2018]	15.07.1979	1		
Marcel Koller [02.08.2018]	11.11.1960	34		

Grasshopper Club Zürich

Founded: 01.09.1886
Stadium: Letzigrund Stadion, Zürich (26,104)

Goalkeepers:	**DOB**	**M**	**(s)**	**G**
Heinz Lindner (AUT)	17.07.1990	35		
Mateo Matic	07.01.1996	1		
Defenders:	**DOB**	**M**	**(s)**	**G**
Arlind Ajeti	25.09.1993	16		2
Allan Arigoni	04.11.1998	1		
Aleksandar Cvetković (SRB)	04.06.1995	20	(7)	1
Souleyman Doumbia (CIV)	24.09.1996	15		
Euclides da Silva Cabral (POR)	05.01.1999	3	(3)	
Anthony Goelzer (FRA)	12.09.1998	5	(1)	
Numa Lavanchy	25.08.1993	14		
Nathan Raphael Pelae Cardoso (BRA)	13.05.1995	7	(2)	1
Jean-Pierre Rhyner	16.03.1996	20		1
Cédric Zesiger	24.06.1998	15	(6)	1
Midfielders:	**DOB**	**M**	**(s)**	**G**
Lucas Andersen (DEN)	13.09.1994	1	(3)	
Mersim Asllani	07.06.1999	7		
Mergim Bajrami	02.05.2000	1	(2)	
Nedim Bajrami	28.02.1999	31	(2)	3
Marko Bašić (CRO)	25.05.1988	6	(1)	
Caiuby Francisco da Silva (BRA)	14.07.1988	9		
Djibril Diani (FRA)	11.02.1998	20	(2)	
Nikola Gjorgjev (MKD)	22.08.1997	4		
Raphael Holzhauser (AUT)	16.02.1993	21		3
Robin Kamber	15.02.1996	11	(4)	
Meriton Kastrati	05.03.1998	1		
Bujar Lika	11.08.1992	10	(3)	
Giotto Morandi	04.03.1999	1		
Charles Monginda Pickel	15.05.1997		(1)	
Petar Pusic	25.01.1999	13	(8)	1
Yoric Ravet (FRA)	12.09.1989	14		1
Rúnar Sigurjónsson (ISL)	18.06.1990	15	(1)	
Gjelbrim Taipi (KVX)	13.12.1992	4	(12)	
Forwards:	**DOB**	**M**	**(s)**	**G**
Nabil Bahoui (SWE)	05.02.1991	15	(2)	3
Marco Djuricin (AUT)	12.12.1992	19	(4)	6
Jeffrén Isaac Suárez Bermúdez(ESP)	20.01.1988	8	(2)	
Aly Mallé (MLI)	03.04.1998	1	(5)	
Ridge Munsy (COD)	09.07.1989		(1)	
Julien N'Goy (BEL)	02.11.1997	16	(6)	5
Aimery Pinga Maria	06.01.1998	13	(6)	2
Amel Rustemoski (MKD)	06.07.2000	2	(3)	
Nikola Sukacev	24.02.1998	1	(5)	
Shani Tarashaj	07.02.1995		(9)	
Trainer:	**DOB**	**M**		
Thorsten Fink (GER)	29.10.1967	23		
Tomislav Stipić (CRO) [06.03.2019]	01.08.1979	8		
Uli Forte (ITA) [09.04.2019]	30.04.1974	5		

Football Club Lugano

Founded: 1908; re-founded 2004 (*as AC Lugano*)
Stadium: Stadio Cornaredo, Lugano (6,390)

Goalkeepers:	**DOB**	**M**	**(s)**	**G**
Noam Baumann	10.04.1996	23	(1)	
David Da Costa	19.04.1986	13	(1)	
Defenders:	**DOB**	**M**	**(s)**	**G**
Stanley Amuzie (NGA)	28.02.1996	1	(2)	
Fabio Daprelà	19.02.1991	24		2
Ákos Kecskés (HUN)	04.01.1996	7		
Numa Lavanchy	25.08.1993	14		1
Mijat Marić	30.04.1984	26		
Edoardo Masciangelo (ITA)	08.07.1996	15		
Fulvio Sulmoni	04.01.1986	26		
Eloge Yao (CIV)	20.01.1996	12	(3)	1
Midfielders:	**DOB**	**M**	**(s)**	**G**
Eris Abedini	29.08.1998	3	(5)	
Mattia Bottani	24.05.1991	19	(11)	4
Petar Brlek (CRO)	29.01.1994	9	(16)	2
Miroslav Čovilo (SRB)	06.05.1986	13	(10)	3
Domen Črnigoj (SVN)	18.11.1995	19	(7)	
Valon Fazliu	02.02.1996	1	(5)	
Vladimir Golemić (SRB)	28.06.1991	2		
Roman Macek (CZE)	18.04.1997		(3)	
Dragan Mihajlović	22.08.1991	21	(7)	1
Mario Piccinocchi (ITA)	21.02.1995	15	(2)	
Jonathan Maximiliano Sabbatini Perfecto (URU)	31.03.1988	34		5
Bálint Vécsei (HUN)	13.07.1993	29	(1)	1
Forwards:	**DOB**	**M**	**(s)**	**G**
Salah Aziz Binous	04.08.2000		(1)	
Carlos Alberto de Souza Júnior „Carlinhos" (BRA)	08.08.1994	28	(3)	13
Assan Ceesay (GAM)	17.03.1994	3	(2)	2
Alexander Gerndt (SWE)	14.07.1986	30	(2)	9
Marc Janko (AUT)	25.06.1983	1	(7)	
Leutrim Kryeziu (KVX)	25.01.1999		(1)	
Armando Sadiku (ALB)	27.05.1991	8	(8)	3
Trainer:	**DOB**	**M**		
Guillermo Abascal Pérez (ESP)	13.04.1989	9		
Fabio Celestini [03.10.2018]	31.10.1975	27		

Fussball-Club Luzern

Founded: 12.08.1901
Stadium: Swissporarena, Luzern (16,490)

Goalkeepers:	**DOB**	**M**	**(s)**	**G**
Mirko Salvi	14.02.1994	10		
David Zibung	10.01.1984	26		
Defenders:	**DOB**	**M**	**(s)**	**G**
Lazar Ćirković (SRB)	22.08.1992	14	(2)	1
Simon Grether	20.05.1992	20	(3)	
Otar Kakabadze (GEO)	27.06.1995	9	(3)	
Stefan Knežević	30.10.1996	8		1
Lucas Alves de Araujo „Lucão"(BRA)	22.07.1992	30	(1)	1
Claudio Lustenberger	06.01.1987		(2)	
Yannick Schmid	11.05.1995	4	(5)	
Marvin Schulz (GER)	15.01.1995	33		5
Christian Schwegler	06.06.1984	26	(1)	
Silvan Sidler	07.07.1998	23	(1)	
Midfielders:	**DOB**	**M**	**(s)**	**G**
Olivier Custodio	10.02.1995	15	(11)	
Dren Feka (GER)	09.06.1997	2	(1)	
Valeriane Gvilia (GEO)	24.05.1994	7	(4)	1
Tsiy William Ndenge (GER)	13.06.1997	8	(6)	
Francisco Rodríguez	14.09.1995	1	(3)	1
Christian Schneuwly	07.02.1988	26	(9)	4
Pascal Schürpf	15.07.1989	32	(2)	9
Filip Ugrinić	05.01.1999	6	(8)	1
Idriz Voca (KVX)	15.05.1997	27	(3)	1
Forwards:	**DOB**	**M**	**(s)**	**G**
Shkelqim Demhasaj	19.04.1996	15	(16)	4
Blessing Chibukie Eleke (NGA)	05.03.1996	25	(7)	13
Tomi Jurić (AUS)	22.07.1991	4	(3)	
Eric Tia (CIV)	28.11.1996			
Ruben Vargas	05.08.1998	25	(6)	8
Trainer:	**DOB**	**M**		
René Weiler	13.09.1973	21		
Thomas Häberli [21.02.2019]	11.04.1974	15		

Football Club de Sion

Founded: 1909
Stadium: Stade Tourbillon, Sion (14,283)

Goalkeepers:	**DOB**	**M**	**(s)**	**G**
Timothy Fayulu	24.07.1999	2		
Kevin Fickentscher	06.07.1988	33		
Anthony Maisonnial (FRA)	23.03.1998	1		
Defenders:	**DOB**	**M**	**(s)**	**G**
Ayoub Abdellaoui (ALG)	16.02.1993	15	(4)	
André Luis Neitzke (BRA)	24.11.1986	28	(2)	1
Martin Angha	22.01.1994	4		
Jan Bamert	09.03.1998	12		
Ermir Lenjani (ALB)	05.08.1989	23	(2)	6
Quentin Maceiras	10.10.1995	28	(2)	1
Bruno Morgado	16.12.1997	18	(1)	1
Raphael Rossi Branco (BRA)	25.07.1990	9	(1)	1
Midfielders:	**DOB**	**M**	**(s)**	**G**
Adryan Oliveira Tavares (BRA)	10.08.1994	8	(12)	7
José Aguilar Martínez (ESP)	05.02.2001		(1)	
Baltazar Costa Rodrigues de Oliveira (BRA)	06.05.2000	1	(8)	
Carlos Alberto Alves Garcia „Carlitos" (POR)	06.09.1982	4	(3)	
Anto Grgic	28.11.1996	18	(2)	4
Pajtim Kasami	02.06.1992	30	(4)	8
Xavier Kouassi (CIV)	28.12.1989	25		
Burim Kukeli (ALB)	16.01.1984	2	(1)	
Freddy Mveng (CMR)	29.05.1992	12	(5)	1
Birama N'Doye (SEN)	27.03.1994	23	(6)	1
Alexandre Dimitri Song Billong(CMR)	09.09.1987	6	(3)	
Bastien Toma	24.06.1999	29	(3)	3
Guy Christian Zock A Bep (CMR)	06.05.1994	15	(1)	
Forwards:	**DOB**	**M**	**(s)**	**G**
Robert Acquafresca (ITA)	11.09.1987		(1)	
Noah Blasucci	19.06.1999	1		
Nasser Daoudou M'Sa (FRA)	26.02.1998	2	(1)	
Moussa Djitté (SEN)	04.10.1999	15	(8)	3
Yassin Fortune (FRA)	30.01.1999	11	(12)	2
Cleilton Monteiro da Costa „Itaitinga" (BRA)	04.10.1998	5	(4)	4
Jared Khasa (FRA)	04.11.1997	2	(4)	
Philippe Almeida Costa (BRA)	01.03.2000	2	(5)	1
Roberts Uldriķis (LVA)	03.04.1998	12	(9)	4
Trainer:	**DOB**	**M**		
Maurizio Jacobacci (ITA)	11.01.1963	6		
Murat Yakin [17.09.2018]	15.09.1974	26		
Christian Zermatten [07.05.2019]	21.06.1966	4		

Fussballclub St. Gallen 1879

Founded: 19.04.1879
Stadium: kybunpark, St. Gallen (19,456)

Goalkeepers:	DOB	M	(s)	G
Daniel Lopar	19.04.1985	2	(1)	
Dejan Stojanović (AUT)	19.07.1993	34		
Defenders:	**DOB**	**M**	**(s)**	**G**
Silvan Hefti	25.10.1997	35		1
Slimen Kchouk (TUN)	07.05.1994	3	(2)	
Philippe Koch	08.02.1991	1		
Nicolas Lüchinger	16.10.1994	20		
Leonel Mosevich (ARG)	04.02.1997	12	(1)	
Musah Nuhu (GHA)	17.01.1997	9	(4)	1
Leonidas Stergiou	03.03.2002	10	(1)	
Milan Vilotić (SRB)	21.10.1986	16		
Alain Wiss	21.08.1990	4	(1)	
Andreas Wittwer	05.10.1990	29	(3)	
Midfielders:	**DOB**	**M**	**(s)**	**G**
Marco Aratore	04.06.1991		(2)	
Majeed Ashimeru (GHA)	10.10.1997	31	(3)	4
Axel Bakayoko (FRA)	06.01.1998	20	(11)	4
Tranquillo Barnetta	22.05.1985	15	(10)	9
Jordi Quintillà Guasch (ESP)	25.10.1993	34		2
Alessandro Kräuchi	03.06.1998	3	(3)	
Stjepan Kukuruzović	07.06.1989	1	(1)	2
Dereck Kutesa	06.12.1997	24	(11)	4
Miro Muheim	24.03.1998		(1)	
Vincent Sierro	08.10.1995	32	(3)	11
Peter Tschernegg (AUT)	23.07.1992	4	(3)	
Forwards:	**DOB**	**M**	**(s)**	**G**
Roman Buess	21.09.1992	6	(9)	1
Angelo Campos	30.03.2000		(3)	
Nassim Ben Khalifa	13.01.1992	10	(1)	
Jérémy Guillemenot	06.01.1998	9	(2)	3
Cedric Itten	27.12.1996	7	(1)	4
Kekuta Manneh (USA)	30.12.1994	6	(1)	
Simone Rapp	01.10.1992	7	(9)	2
Yannis Tafer (FRA)	11.02.1991	11	(13)	
Víctor Ruiz Abril (ESP)	02.11.1993	1	(4)	
Trainer:	**DOB**	**M**		
Peter Zeidler (GER)	08.08.1962	36		

Fussballclub Thun 1898

Founded: 1898
Stadium: Stockhorn Arena, Thun (10,014)

Goalkeepers:	DOB	M	(s)	G
Guillaume Faivre	20.02.1987	36		
Defenders:	**DOB**	**M**	**(s)**	**G**
Kevin Bigler	05.10.1992	9	(3)	1
Mickaël Facchinetti	15.02.1991	7	(3)	1
Roy Gelmi	01.03.1995	27	(3)	
Stefan Glarner	21.11.1987	33		
Sven Joss	18.07.1994	11	(2)	
Chris Kablan	30.11.1994	20	(3)	1
Miguel Rodrigues	07.12.1996	23		1
Midfielders:	**DOB**	**M**	**(s)**	**G**
Moreno Costanzo	20.02.1988	7	(4)	2
Kenan Fatkić (SVN)	20.08.1997	9	(14)	1
Dennis Hediger	22.09.1986	19		2
Gregory Karlen	30.01.1995	21	(7)	3
Nelson Ferreira Coelho (POR)	26.05.1982	5	(9)	
Dennis Salanović (LIE)	26.02.1996	7	(23)	5
Dominik Schwizer	25.06.1996	8	(8)	
Marvin Spielmann	23.02.1996	31	(3)	12
Basil Stillhart	24.03.1994	33	(1)	5
Nicola Sutter	08.05.1995	32	(1)	4
Matteo Tosetti	15.02.1992	22	(3)	2
Forwards:	**DOB**	**M**	**(s)**	**G**
Nicolas Hunziker	23.02.1996	2	(12)	
Nuno Filipe da Silva (POR)	14.03.1994	3	(4)	
Dejan Sorgić (SRB)	15.09.1989	31	(2)	15
Trainer:	**DOB**	**M**		
Marc Schneider	23.07.1980	36		

Berner Sport Club Young Boys

Founded: 14.03.1898
Stadium: Stade de Suisse, Bern (31,789)

Goalkeepers:	DOB	M	(s)	G
David von Ballmoos	30.12.1994	34		
Marco Wölfli	22.08.1982	2	(2)	
Defenders:	**DOB**	**M**	**(s)**	**G**
Loris Benito Souto	07.01.1992	31		1
Mohamed Camara (GUI)	28.08.1997	14		2
Ulisses Garcia	11.01.1996	11	(12)	3
Jan Kronig	24.06.2000	2		
Jordan Lotomba	29.09.1998	1	(4)	
Melingo Kevin Mbabu	19.04.1995	23	(1)	
Léo Seydoux	16.03.1998	1	(2)	
Steve von Bergen	10.06.1983	28		1
Gregory Wüthrich	04.12.1994	11	(3)	
Midfielders:	**DOB**	**M**	**(s)**	**G**
Michel Aebischer	06.01.1997	19	(7)	3
Leonardo Bertone	14.03.1994	4	(4)	1
Gianluca Gaudino (GER)	11.11.1996	3	(8)	1
Sandro Lauper	25.10.1996	22	(6)	1
Sékou Sanogo (CIV)	05.05.1989	15		1
Thorsten Schick (AUT)	19.05.1990	14	(12)	1
Djibril Sow	06.02.1997	27	(1)	3
Miralem Sulejmani (SRB)	05.12.1988	11	(6)	7
Forwards:	**DOB**	**M**	**(s)**	**G**
Roger Assalé (CIV)	13.11.1993	27	(6)	9
Christian Fassnacht	11.11.1993	31	(4)	11
Guillaume Hoarau (FRA)	05.03.1984	21	(7)	24
Felix Mambimbi	18.01.2001		(2)	
Nicolas Ngamaleu (CMR)	09.07.1994	24	(8)	12
Jean-Pierre Nsamé (CMR)	01.05.1993	20	(11)	15
Trainer:	**DOB**	**M**		
Gerardo Seoane	30.10.1978	36		

Fussballclub Zürich

Founded: 01.08.1896
Stadium: Letzigrund Stadion, Zürich (26,104)

Goalkeepers:	DOB	M	(s)	G
Yanick Brecher	25.05.1993	35		
Andris Vaņins (LVA)	30.04.1980	1	(1)	
Defenders:	**DOB**	**M**	**(s)**	**G**
Umaru Bangura (SLE)	07.10.1987	25		
Fabio Dixon	21.06.1999	1	(2)	
Hakim Guenouche (FRA)	30.05.2000	1	(1)	
Maren Haile-Selassie	13.03.1999		(1)	
Pa Modou Jagne (GAM)	26.12.1989	18	(2)	1
Levan Kharabadze (GEO)	26.01.2000	14	(2)	1
Mirlind Kryeziu	26.01.1997	14	(5)	
Andreas Maxsø (DEN)	18.03.1994	26	(2)	1
Alain Nef	06.02.1982	13	(8)	
Becir Omeragic	20.01.2002	2	(3)	
Kevin Rüegg	05.08.1998	26		2
Grégory Sertić (FRA)	05.08.1989	11		
Joel Untersee	11.02.1994	6	(2)	
Midfielders:	**DOB**	**M**	**(s)**	**G**
Izer Aliu	15.11.1999	1	(1)	
Toni Domgjoni (CRO)	04.09.1998	27	(3)	1
Salim Khelifi	26.01.1994	18	(7)	4
Benjamin Kololli (KVX)	15.05.1992	22	(8)	10
Hekuran Kryeziu (KVX)	12.02.1993	26	(2)	2
Antonio Marchesano	18.01.1991	21	(6)	2
Victor Pálsson (ISL)	30.04.1991	13	(1)	
Roberto Rodríguez	28.07.1990	3	(4)	1
Marco Schönbächler	11.01.1990	12	(3)	1
Simon Sohm	11.04.2001	3	(3)	
Adrian Winter	08.07.1986	13	(10)	3
Lavdim Zumberi	27.11.1999	3	(2)	
Forwards:	**DOB**	**M**	**(s)**	**G**
Nicolás Andereggen (ARG)	22.09.1999		(1)	
Salah Binous	04.08.2000		(2)	
Assan Ceesay (GAM)	17.03.1994	12	(10)	3
Raphael Dwamena (GHA)	12.09.1995		(1)	
Michael Frey	19.07.1994	2	(1)	
Yann Kasai	14.04.1998		(4)	
Stephen Odey (NGA)	15.01.1998	27	(5)	10
Trainer:	**DOB**	**M**		
Ludovic Magnin	20.04.1979	36		

Neuchâtel Xamax FCS

Founded: 1916 / 2013 merger with FC Serrières)
Stadium: Stade de la Maladière, Neuchâtel (11,997)

Goalkeepers:	DOB	M	(s)	G
Matthias Minder	03.02.1993	1		
Laurent Walthert	30.03.1984	35		
Defenders:	**DOB**	**M**	**(s)**	**G**
Igor Đurić	30.08.1988	12		
Arbnor Fejzulahi (ALB)	08.04.1993	4	(2)	
Mike Gomes	19.09.1988	34		
Jérémy Huyghebaert (BEL)	07.01.1989	8		
William Le Pogam (FRA)	03.03.1993	3		
Miguel Santana Luna „Maikel" (ESP)	18.11.1991	3	(1)	
Mārcis Ošs (LVA)	25.07.1991	25		1
Mustafa Sejmenović (BIH)	03.01.1986	27		2
Arbenit Xhemajli	23.04.1998	14	(3)	
Midfielders:	**DOB**	**M**	**(s)**	**G**
Thibault Corbaz	07.01.1994	12	(12)	
Pietro Di Nardo	08.02.1990	18	(8)	2
Serey Dié (CIV)	07.11.1984	10		1
Charles-André Doudin	12.09.1986	26		4
Janick Kamber	26.02.1992	30		
Liridon Mulaj	04.01.1999		(2)	
Hamed Koné (CIV)	02.11.1987	3	(3)	
Charles Monginda Pickel	15.05.1997	21	(5)	2
Dilan Qela (KVX)	07.08.1998		(1)	
Geoffrey Tréand (FRA)	16.01.1986	13	(12)	2
Max Veloso	27.03.1992	18	(7)	2
Forwards:	**DOB**	**M**	**(s)**	**G**
Kemal Ademi	23.01.1996	13	(13)	8
Tunahan Çiçek	12.05.1992	2	(3)	
Gaëtan Karlen	07.06.1993	8	(6)	2
Frédéric Nimani N'Galou (CTA)	08.10.1988		(1)	
Raphaël Nuzzolo	05.07.1983	34	(1)	14
Afimico Pululu (FRA)	23.03.1999	10	(5)	2
Samir Ramizi (KVX)	24.07.1991	12	(17)	2
Trainer:	**DOB**	**M**		
Michel Decastel	22.10.1955	19		
Stéphane Henchoz [05.02.2019]	07.09.1974	17		

SECOND LEVEL

Swiss Challenge League 2018/2019

1.	Servette FC Genève (*Promoted*)	36	24	7	5	90	-	37	79
2.	FC Aarau (*Promotion Play-offs*)	36	19	7	10	63	-	46	64
3.	FC Lausanne-Sport	36	16	15	5	64	-	36	63
4.	FC Winterthur	36	16	8	12	57	-	51	56
5.	FC Wil 1900	36	10	12	14	33	-	47	42
6.	FC Vaduz	36	11	9	16	48	-	70	42
7.	FC Schaffhausen	36	10	9	17	43	-	62	39
8.	SC Kriens	36	7	15	14	46	-	58	36
9.	FC Chiasso	36	9	9	18	43	-	67	36
10.	FC Rapperswil-Jona (*Relegated*)	36	10	5	21	47	-	59	35

NATIONAL TEAM

INTERNATIONAL MATCHES
(16.07.2018 – 15.07.2019)

08.09.2018	St. Gallen	Switzerland - Iceland	6-0(2-0)	(UNL)
11.09.2018	Leicester	England - Switzerland	1-0(0-0)	(F)
12.10.2018	Bruxelles	Belgium - Switzerland	2-1(0-0)	(UNL)
15.10.2018	Reykjavík	Iceland - Switzerland	1-2(0-1)	(UNL)
14.11.2018	Lugano	Switzerland - Qatar	0-1(0-0)	(F)
18.11.2018	Luzern	Switzerland - Belgium	5-2(3-2)	(UNL)
23.03.2019	Tbilisi	Georgia - Switzerland	0-2(0-0)	(ECQ)
26.03.2019	Basel	Switzerland - Denmark	3-3(1-0)	(ECQ)
05.06.2019	Porto	Portugal - Switzerland	3-1(1-0)	(UNL)
09.06.2019	Guimarães	Switzerland - England	0-0; 5-6 on penalties	(UNL)

08.09.2018 SWITZERLAND - ICELAND 6-0(2-0) UEFA Nations League A, Group 2
Kybunpark, St. Gallen; Referee: Michael Oliver (England); Attendance: 14,912
SUI: Yann Sommer, Fabian Schär, Melingo Kevin Mbabu, Manuel Obafemi Akanji, Ricardo Iván Rodríguez Araya, Steven Zuber (79.Djibril Sow), Granit Xhaka (Cap), Denis Lemi Zakaria Lako Lado, Xherdan Shaqiri, Haris Seferovic (72.Admir Mehmedi), Breel Donald Embolo (65.Albian Afrim Ajeti). Trainer: Vladimir Petković (Bosnia and Herzegovina).
Goals: Steven Zuber (13), Denis Lemi Zakaria Lako Lado (23), Xherdan Shaqiri (53), Haris Seferovic (67), Albian Afrim Ajeti (71), Admir Mehmedi (82).

11.09.2018 ENGLAND - SWITZERLAND 1-0(0-0) Friendly International
King Power Stadium, Leicester; Referee: Clément Turpin (France); Attendance: 30,256
SUI: Yann Sommer, Stephan Lichtsteiner (Cap), Fabian Schär, Manuel Obafemi Akanji (46.Admir Mehmedi), Danon Issouf Johannes Djourou Gbadjere, Ricardo Iván Rodríguez Araya (46.Jacques François Moubandje), Granit Xhaka, Remo Marco Freuler (66.Steven Zuber), Denis Lemi Zakaria Lako Lado (66.Edimilson Fernandes Ribeiro), Xherdan Shaqiri (80.Haris Seferovic), Mario Gavranović (66.Albian Afrim Ajeti). Trainer: Vladimir Petković (Bosnia and Herzegovina).

12.10.2018 BELGIUM - SWITZERLAND 2-1(0-0) UEFA Nations League A, Group 2
Stade "Roi Baudouin", Bruxelles; Referee: Antonio Miguel Mateu Lahoz (Spain); Attendance: 39,049
SUI: Yann Sommer, Michael Rico Lang, Nico Elvedi, Fabian Schär, Ricardo Iván Rodríguez Araya, Steven Zuber, Granit Xhaka (Cap), Remo Marco Freuler (87.Christian Fassnacht), Xherdan Shaqiri, Denis Lemi Zakaria Lako Lado (83.Edimilson Fernandes Ribeiro), Haris Seferovic (69.Mario Gavranović). Trainer: Vladimir Petković (Bosnia and Herzegovina).
Goal: Mario Gavranović (76).

15.10.2018 ICELAND - SWITZERLAND 1-2(0-1) UEFA Nations League A, Group 2
Laugardalsvöllur, Reykjavík; Referee: Andreas Ekberg (Sweden); Attendance: 8,663
SUI: Yvon Landry Mvogo Nganoma, Michael Rico Lang, Nico Elvedi, Fabian Schär, Jacques François Moubandje, Steven Zuber (88.Christian Fassnacht), Granit Xhaka (Cap), Denis Lemi Zakaria Lako Lado, Xherdan Shaqiri, Haris Seferovic (90+1.Albian Afrim Ajeti), Mario Gavranović (69.Edimilson Fernandes Ribeiro). Trainer: Vladimir Petković (Bosnia and Herzegovina).
Goals: Haris Seferovic (52), Michael Rico Lang (67).

14.11.2018 SWITZERLAND - QATAR 0-1(0-0) Friendly International
Stadio di Cornaredo, Lugano; Referee: Bernie Raymond "Kevin" Blom (Netherlands); Attendance: 4,170
SUI: Yvon Landry Mvogo Nganoma, Michael Rico Lang (62.Melingo Kevin Mbabu), Loris Benito Souto, Fabian Schär, Léo Sébastien Lacroix, Granit Xhaka (Cap) (46.Edimilson Fernandes Ribeiro), Steven Zuber (46.Jacques François Moubandje), Remo Marco Freuler (46.Xherdan Shaqiri), Denis Lemi Zakaria Lako Lado (68.Djibril Sow), Christian Fassnacht, Mario Gavranović (46.Albian Afrim Ajeti). Trainer: Vladimir Petković (Bosnia and Herzegovina).

18.11.2018 SWITZERLAND - BELGIUM 5-2(3-2) UEFA Nations League A, Group 2
Swissporarena, Luzern; Referee: Daniele Orsato (Italy); Attendance: 15,000
SUI: Yann Sommer, Nico Elvedi, Timm Klose, Melingo Kevin Mbabu, Ricardo Iván Rodríguez Araya, Steven Zuber (87.Loris Benito Souto), Granit Xhaka (Cap), Remo Marco Freuler (79.Denis Lemi Zakaria Lako Lado), Edimilson Fernandes Ribeiro, Xherdan Shaqiri, Haris Seferovic (90+2.Albian Afrim Ajeti). Trainer: Vladimir Petković (Bosnia and Herzegovina).
Goals: Ricardo Iván Rodríguez Araya (26 penalty), Haris Seferovic (31, 44), Nico Elvedi (62), Haris Seferovic (84).

23.03.2019 GEORGIA - SWITZERLAND 0-2(0-0) 16th EC. Qualifiers
"Boris Paichadze" Dinamo Arena, Tbilisi; Referee: Craig Pawson (England); Attendance: 49,207
SUI: Yann Sommer, Stephan Lichtsteiner (Cap), Fabian Schär, Manuel Obafemi Akanji, Ricardo Iván Rodríguez Araya, Steven Zuber, Granit Xhaka, Remo Marco Freuler (89.Djibril Sow), Denis Lemi Zakaria Lako Lado, Mario Gavranović (61.Albian Afrim Ajeti), Breel Donald Embolo (84.Renato Steffen). Trainer: Vladimir Petković (Bosnia and Herzegovina).
Goals: Steven Zuber (56), Denis Lemi Zakaria Lako Lado (80).

26.03.2019 SWITZERLAND - DENMARK 3-3(1-0) 16th EC. Qualifiers
St. Jakob Park, Basel; Referee: Damir Skomina (Slovenia); Attendance: 18,352
SUI: Yann Sommer, Melingo Kevin Mbabu, Nico Elvedi, Manuel Obafemi Akanji, Ricardo Iván Rodríguez Araya (46.Loris Benito Souto), Steven Zuber, Granit Xhaka (Cap) (79.Djibril Sow), Remo Marco Freuler, Denis Lemi Zakaria Lako Lado, Albian Afrim Ajeti (71.Admir Mehmedi), Breel Donald Embolo. Trainer: Vladimir Petković (Bosnia and Herzegovina).
Goals: Remo Marco Freuler (19), Granit Xhaka (66), Breel Donald Embolo (76).

05.06.2019 PORTUGAL - SWITZERLAND 3-1(1-0) UEFA Nations League, Semi-Finals
Estádio do Dragão, Porto; Referee: Dr. Felix Brych (Germany); Attendance: 42,415
SUI: Yann Sommer, Fabian Schär, Melingo Kevin Mbabu, Manuel Obafemi Akanji, Ricardo Iván Rodríguez Araya, Steven Zuber (83.Renato Steffen), Granit Xhaka (Cap), Remo Marco Freuler (89.Josip Drmić), Denis Lemi Zakaria Lako Lado (71.Edimilson Fernandes Ribeiro), Xherdan Shaqiri, Haris Seferovic. Trainer: Vladimir Petković (Bosnia and Herzegovina).
Goal: Ricardo Iván Rodríguez Araya (57 penalty).

09.06.2019 SWITZERLAND - ENGLAND **0-0; 5-6 on penalties** UEFA Nations League, Third Place Play-off
Estádio „D. Afonso Henriques", Guimarães (Portugal); Referee: Ovidiu Alin Haţegan (Romania); Attendance: 15,742
SUI: Yann Sommer, Fabian Schär, Melingo Kevin Mbabu, Nico Elvedi, Ricardo Iván Rodríguez Araya (87.Josip Drmić), Manuel Obafemi Akanji, Granit Xhaka (Cap), Remo Marco Freuler, Edimilson Fernandes Ribeiro (61.Denis Lemi Zakaria Lako Lado), Xherdan Shaqiri (65.Steven Zuber), Haris Seferovic (113.Noah Okafor). Trainer: Vladimir Petković (Bosnia and Herzegovina).
Penalties: Steven Zuber, Granit Xhaka, Manuel Obafemi Akanji, Melingo Kevin Mbabu, Fabian Schär, Josip Drmić (saved).

NATIONAL TEAM PLAYERS
(16.07.2018 – 15.07.2019)

Name	DOB	Caps	Goals	2018/2019:	*Club*
Goalkeepers					
Yvon Landry MVOGO Nganoma	06.06.1994	**2**	**0**	2018:	*RasenBallsport Leipzig (GER)*
Yann SOMMER	17.12.1988	**47**	**0**	2018/2019:	*Borussia VfL Mönchengladbach (GER)*
Defenders					
Manuel Obafemi AKANJI	19.07.1995	**17**	**0**	2018/2019:	*BV Borussia 09 Dortmund (GER)*
Loris BENITO Souto	07.01.1992	**3**	**0**	2018/2019:	*BSC Young Boys Bern*
Danon Issouf Johannes DJOUROU Gbadjere	18.01.1987	**76**	**2**	2018:	*SPAL Ferrara (ITA)*
Nico ELVEDI	30.09.1996	**11**	**1**	2018/2019:	*Borussia VfL Mönchengladbach (GER)*
Timm KLOSE	09.05.1988	**17**	**0**	2018:	*Norwich City FC (ENG)*
Léo Sébastien LACROIX	27.02.1992	**1**	**0**	2018:	*Hamburger SV (GER)*
Michael Rico LANG	08.02.1991	**30**	**3**	2018:	*Borussia VfL Mönchengladbach (GER)*
Stephan LICHTSTEINER	16.01.1984	**105**	**8**	2018/2019:	*Arsenal FC London (ENG)*
Melingo Kevin MBABU	19.04.1995	**6**	**0**	2018/2019:	*BSC Young Boys Bern*
Jacques François MOUBANDJE	21.06.1990	**21**	**0**	2018:	*Toulouse FC (FRA)*
Ricardo Iván RODRÍGUEZ Araya	25.08.1992	**65**	**7**	2018/2019:	*AC Milan (ITA)*
Fabian Lukas SCHÄR	20.12.1991	**50**	**7**	2018/2019:	*Newcastle United FC (ENG)*
Midfielders					
Christian FASSNACHT	11.11.1993	**3**	**0**	2018:	*BSC Young Boys Bern*
Edimilson FERNANDES Ribeiro	15.04.1996	**10**	**0**	2018/2019:	*ACF Fiorentina (ENG)*
Remo Marco FREULER	15.04.1992	**18**	**1**	2018/2019:	*Atalanta Bergamasca Calcio (ITA)*
Xherdan SHAQIRI	10.10.1991	**82**	**22**	2018/2019:	*Liverpool FC (ENG)*
Djibril SOW	06.02.1997	**4**	**0**	2018/2019:	*BSC Young Boys Bern*
Renato STEFFEN	03.11.1991	**7**	**0**	2019:	*VfL Wolfsburg (GER)*
Granit XHAKA	27.09.1992	**76**	**11**	2018/2019:	*Arsenal FC London (ENG)*
Denis Lemi ZAKARIA Lako Lado	20.11.1996	**22**	**2**	2018/2019:	*Borussia VfL Mönchengladbach (GER)*
Steven ZUBER	17.08.1991	**25**	**6**	2018: 09.01.2019->	*TSG 1899 Hoffenheim (GER)* *VfB Stuttgart (GER)*
Forwards					
Albian Afrim AJETI	26.02.1997	**7**	**1**	2018/2019:	*FC Basel*
Josip DRMIĆ	08.08.1992	**34**	**10**	2018/2019:	*Borussia VfL Mönchengladbach (GER)*
Breel Donald EMBOLO	14.02.1997	**32**	**4**	2018/2019:	*FC Schalke 04 Gelsenkirchen (GER)*
Mario GAVRANOVIĆ	24.11.1989	**21**	**6**	2018/2019:	*GNK Dinamo Zagreb (CRO)*
Admir MEHMEDI	16.03.1991	**61**	**8**	2018/2019:	*VfL Wolfsburg (GER)*
Noah OKAFOR	24.05.2000	**1**	**0**	2019:	*FC Basel*
Haris SEFEROVIC	22.02.1992	**61**	**17**	2018/2019:	*Sport Lisboa e Benfica (POR)*

National team coach

Vladimir PETKOVIĆ (Bosnia and Herzegovina) [from 01.08.2014]	15.08.1963	54 M; 31 W; 10 D; 13 L; 100-47

TURKEY

The Country:

Türkiye Cumhuriyeti (Republic of Turkey)
Capital: Ankara
Surface: 783,356 km²
Inhabitants: 82,003,882 [2018]
Time: UTC+3

The FA:

Türkiye Futbol Federasyonu
Hasan Dogan Milli Takimlar Kamp ve Egitim Tesisleri Riva Beykoz, İstanbul
Tel: +90 216 554 51 00
Founded: 1923
Member of FIFA since: 1923
Member of UEFA since: 1962
Website: www.tff.org

NATIONAL TEAM RECORDS

First international match:	26.10.1923, İstanbul:	Turkey – Romania 2-2
Most international caps:	Rüştü Reçber	- 120 caps (1994-2012)
Most international goals:	Hakan Şükür	- 51 goals / 112 caps (1992-2007)

UEFA EUROPEAN CHAMPIONSHIP	
1960	Qualifiers
1964	Qualifiers
1968	Qualifiers
1972	Qualifiers
1976	Qualifiers
1980	Qualifiers
1984	Qualifiers
1988	Qualifiers
1992	Qualifiers
1996	Final Tournament (Group Stage)
2000	Final Tournament (Quarter-Finals)
2004	Qualifiers
2008	Final Tournament (Semi-Finals)
2012	Qualifiers
2016	Final Tournament (Group Stage)

FIFA WORLD CUP	
1930	Did not enter
1934	*Withdrew*
1938	Did not enter
1950	*Qualified but withdrew*
1954	Final Tournament (Group Stage)
1958	*Withdrew*
1962	Qualifiers
1966	Qualifiers
1970	Qualifiers
1974	Qualifiers
1978	Qualifiers
1982	Qualifiers
1986	Qualifiers
1990	Qualifiers
1994	Qualifiers
1998	Qualifiers
2002	Final Tournament (3rd Place)
2006	Qualifiers
2010	Qualifiers
2014	Qualifiers
2018	Qualifiers

UEFA NATIONS LEAGUE
2018/2019 – League B

OLYMPIC FOOTBALL TOURNAMENTS 1908-2016							
1908	-	**1948**	Quarter-Finals	**1972**	Qualifiers	**1996**	Qualifiers
1912	-	**1952**	Quarter-Finals	**1976**	Qualifiers	**2000**	Qualifiers
1920	-	**1956**	*Withdrew*	**1980**	Group Stage	**2004**	Qualifiers
1924	Preliminary Round	**1960**	Group Stage	**1984**	*Withdrew*	**2008**	Qualifiers
1928	1/8 - Finals	**1964**	Qualifiers	**1988**	Qualifiers	**2012**	Qualifiers
1936	1/8 - Finals	**1968**	Qualifiers	**1992**	Qualifiers	**2016**	Qualifiers

FIFA CONFEDERATIONS CUP 1992-2017
2003 (3rd Place)

TURKISH CLUB HONOURS IN EUROPEAN CLUB COMPETITIONS:

European Champion Clubs.Cup (1956-1992) / UEFA Champions League (1993-2019)		
None		
Fairs Cup (1858-1971) / UEFA Cup (1972-2009) / UEFA Europa League (2010-2019)		
Galatasaray SK İstanbul	**1**	1999/2000
UEFA Super Cup (1972-2018)		
Galatasaray SK İstanbul	**1**	2000
European Cup Winners.Cup 1961-1999*		
None		

**defunct competition*

NATIONAL COMPETITIONS
TABLE OF HONOURS

Turkish Football Championship (1924–1951)*

	CHAMPIONS
1924	Harbiye Ankara
1925-1926	*No competition*
1927	Muhafızgücü SK Ankara
1928 - 1931	*No competition*
1932	İstanbulspor
1933	Fenerbahçe SK İstanbul
1934	Beşiktaş JK İstanbul
1935	Fenerbahçe SK İstanbul
1936 - 1939	*No competition*
1940	Eskişehir Demirspor
1941	Gençlerbirliği Ankara SK Ankara
1942	Harp Okulu SK Ankara
1943	*No competition*
1944	Fenerbahçe SK İstanbul
1945	Harp Okulu SK Ankara
1946	Gençlerbirliği Ankara SK Ankara
1947	Ankara Demirspor
1948	*No competition*
1949	MKE Ankaragücü
1950	Göztepe SK İzmir
1951	Beşiktaş JK İstanbul

**Not recognized by Turkish FA.*

National Division (1937–1950)*

	CHAMPIONS
1937	Fenerbahçe SK İstanbul
1938	Güneş SK İstanbul
1939	Galatasaray SK İstanbul
1940	Fenerbahçe SK İstanbul
1941	Beşiktaş JK İstanbul
1942	*No competition*
1943	Fenerbahçe SK İstanbul
1944	Beşiktaş JK İstanbul
1945	Fenerbahçe SK İstanbul
1946	Fenerbahçe SK İstanbul
1947	Beşiktaş JK İstanbul
1948	*No competition*
1949	*No competition*
1950	Fenerbahçe SK İstanbul

	CHAMPIONS	CUP WINNERS	BEST GOALSCORERS	
1956/1957**	Beşiktaş JK İstanbul	-	Nazmi Bilge (Beşiktaş JK İstanbul)	8
1957/1958**	Beşiktaş JK İstanbul	-	Lefter Küçükandonyadis (Fenerbahçe SK İstanbul) Metin Oktay (Galatasaray SK İstanbul)	10
1958/1959	Fenerbahçe SK İstanbul	-	Metin Oktay (Galatasaray SK İstanbul)	11
1959/1960	Beşiktaş JK İstanbul	-	Metin Oktay (Galatasaray SK İstanbul)	33
1960/1961	Fenerbahçe SK İstanbul	-	Metin Oktay (Galatasaray SK İstanbul)	36
1961/1962	Galatasaray SK İstanbul	-	Fikri Elma (Ankara Demirspor)	21
1962/1963	Galatasaray SK İstanbul	Galatasaray SK İstanbul	Metin Oktay (Galatasaray SK İstanbul)	38
1963/1964	Fenerbahçe SK İstanbul	Galatasaray SK İstanbul	Güven Önüt (Beşiktaş JK İstanbul)	19
1964/1965	Fenerbahçe SK İstanbul	Galatasaray SK İstanbul	Metin Oktay (Galatasaray SK İstanbul)	17
1965/1966	Beşiktaş JK İstanbul	Galatasaray SK İstanbul	Ertan Adatepe (MKE Ankaragücü)	20
1966/1967	Beşiktaş JK İstanbul	Altay SK İzmir	Ertan Adatepe (MKE Ankaragücü)	18
1967/1968	Fenerbahçe SK İstanbul	Fenerbahçe SK İstanbul	Fevzi Zemzem (Göztepe SK İzmir)	19
1968/1969	Galatasaray SK İstanbul	Göztepe SK İzmir	Metin Oktay (Galatasaray SK İstanbul)	17
1969/1970	Fenerbahçe SK İstanbul	Göztepe SK İzmir	Fethi Heper (Eskişehirspor Kulübü)	13
1970/1971	Galatasaray SK İstanbul	Eskişehirspor Kulübü	Ogün Altıparmak (Fenerbahçe SK İstanbul)	16
1971/1972	Galatasaray SK İstanbul	MKE Ankaragücü	Fethi Heper (Eskişehirspor Kulübü)	20
1972/1973	Galatasaray SK İstanbul	Galatasaray SK İstanbul	Osman Arpacıoğlu (Fenerbahçe SK İstanbul)	16
1973/1974	Fenerbahçe SK İstanbul	Fenerbahçe SK İstanbul	Cemil Turan (Fenerbahçe SK İstanbul)	14
1974/1975	Fenerbahçe SK İstanbul	Beşiktaş JK İstanbul	Ömer Kaner (Eskişehirspor Kulübü)	14
1975/1976	Trabzonspor Kulübü	Galatasaray SK İstanbul	Cemil Turan (Fenerbahçe SK İstanbul) Ali Osman Renklibay (MKE Ankaragücü)	17
1976/1977	Trabzonspor Kulübü	Trabzonspor Kulübü	Necmi Perekli (Trabzonspor Kulübü)	18
1977/1978	Fenerbahçe SK İstanbul	Trabzonspor Kulübü	Cemil Turan (Fenerbahçe SK İstanbul)	17
1978/1979	Trabzonspor Kulübü	Fenerbahçe SK İstanbul	Özer Umdu (Adanaspor AŞ)	15
1979/1980	Trabzonspor Kulübü	Altay SK İzmir	Mustafa Denizli (Altay SK İzmir) Bahtiyar Yorulmaz (Bursaspor Kulübü)	12
1980/1981	Trabzonspor Kulübü	MKE Ankaragücü	Bora Öztürk (Adanaspor AŞ)	15
1981/1982	Beşiktaş JK İstanbul	Galatasaray SK İstanbul	Selçuk Yula (Fenerbahçe SK İstanbul)	16
1982/1983	Fenerbahçe SK İstanbul	Fenerbahçe SK İstanbul	Selçuk Yula (Fenerbahçe SK İstanbul)	19
1983/1984	Trabzonspor Kulübü	Trabzonspor Kulübü	Tarik Hodžić (YUG, Galatasaray SK İstanbul)	16
1984/1985	Fenerbahçe SK İstanbul	Galatasaray SK İstanbul	Aykut Yiğit (Sakaryaspor Kulübü)	20
1985/1986	Beşiktaş JK İstanbul	Bursaspor Kulübü	Tanju Çolak (Samsunspor Kulübü)	33
1986/1987	Galatasaray SK İstanbul	Gençlerbirliği Ankara	Tanju Çolak (Samsunspor Kulübü)	25
1987/1988	Galatasaray SK İstanbul	Sakaryaspor Kulübü	Tanju Çolak (Galatasaray SK İstanbul)	39
1988/1989	Fenerbahçe SK İstanbul	Beşiktaş JK İstanbul	Aykut Kocaman (Fenerbahçe SK İstanbul)	29
1989/1990	Beşiktaş JK İstanbul	Beşiktaş JK İstanbul	Feyyaz Uçar (Beşiktaş JK İstanbul)	28
1990/1991	Beşiktaş JK İstanbul	Galatasaray SK İstanbul	Tanju Çolak (Galatasaray SK İstanbul)	31
1991/1992	Beşiktaş JK İstanbul	Trabzonspor Kulübü	Aykut Kocaman (Fenerbahçe SK İstanbul)	25
1992/1993	Galatasaray SK İstanbul	Galatasaray SK İstanbul	Tanju Çolak (Fenerbahçe SK İstanbul)	27
1993/1994	Galatasaray SK İstanbul	Beşiktaş JK İstanbul	Bülent Uygun (Fenerbahçe SK İstanbul)	22
1994/1995	Beşiktaş JK İstanbul	Trabzonspor Kulübü	Aykut Kocaman (Fenerbahçe SK İstanbul)	27
1995/1996	Fenerbahçe SK İstanbul	Galatasaray SK İstanbul	Shota Arveladze (GEO, Trabzonspor Kulübü)	25
1996/1997	Galatasaray SK İstanbul	Kocaelispor Kulübü	Hakan Şükür (Galatasaray SK İstanbul)	38

1997/1998	Galatasaray SK İstanbul	Beşiktaş JK İstanbul	Hakan Şükür (Galatasaray SK İstanbul)	33
1998/1999	Galatasaray SK İstanbul	Galatasaray SK İstanbul	Hakan Şükür (Galatasaray SK İstanbul)	19
1999/2000	Galatasaray SK İstanbul	Galatasaray SK İstanbul	Serkan Aykut (Samsunspor Kulübü)	30
2000/2001	Fenerbahçe SK İstanbul	Gençlerbirliği Ankara	Okan Yılmaz (Bursaspor Kulübü)	23
2001/2002	Galatasaray SK İstanbul	Kocaelispor Kulübü	Arif Erdem (Galatasaray SK İstanbul) İlhan Mansız (Beşiktaş JK İstanbul)	21
2002/2003	Beşiktaş JK İstanbul	Trabzonspor Kulübü	Okan Yılmaz (Bursaspor Kulübü)	24
2003/2004	Fenerbahçe SK İstanbul	Trabzonspor Kulübü	Zafer Biryol (Atiker Konyaspor Kulübü)	25
2004/2005	Fenerbahçe SK İstanbul	Galatasaray SK İstanbul	Fatih Tekke (Trabzonspor Kulübü)	31
2005/2006	Galatasaray SK İstanbul	Beşiktaş JK İstanbul	Gökhan Ünal (Kayseri Erciyesspor Kulübü)	25
2006/2007	Fenerbahçe SK İstanbul	Beşiktaş JK İstanbul	Alexsandro de Souza "Alex" (BRA, Fenerbahçe SK İstanbul)	19
2007/2008	Galatasaray SK İstanbul	Kayseri Erciyesspor Kulübü	Semih Şentürk (Fenerbahçe SK İstanbul)	17
2008/2009	Beşiktaş JK İstanbul	Beşiktaş JK İstanbul	Milan Baroš (CZE, Galatasaray SK İstanbul)	20
2009/2010	Bursaspor Kulübü	Trabzonspor Kulübü	Ariza Makukula (POR, Kayseri Erciyesspor Kulübü)	21
2010/2011	Fenerbahçe SK İstanbul	Beşiktaş JK İstanbul	Alexsandro de Souza "Alex" (BRA, Fenerbahçe SK İstanbul)	28
2011/2012	Galatasaray SK İstanbul	Fenerbahçe SK İstanbul	Burak Yılmaz (Trabzonspor Kulübü)	33
2012/2013	Galatasaray SK İstanbul	Fenerbahçe SK İstanbul	Burak Yılmaz (Galatasaray SK İstanbul)	24
2013/2014	Fenerbahçe SK İstanbul	Galatasaray SK İstanbul	Aatif Chahechouhe (MAR, Sivasspor Kulübü)	17
2014/2015	Galatasaray SK İstanbul	Galatasaray SK İstanbul	José Fernando Viana de Santana "Fernandão" (BRA, Bursaspor Kulübü)	22
2015/2016	Beşiktaş JK İstanbul	Galatasaray SK İstanbul	Mario Gómez García (Beşiktaş JK İstanbul)	26
2016/2017	Beşiktaş JK İstanbul	Atiker Konyaspor Kulübü	Vágner Silva de Souza (BRA, Alanyaspor)	23
2017/2018	Galatasaray SK İstanbul	Akhisar Belediyespor Gençlik SK	Bafétimbi Gomis (FRA, Galatasaray SK İstanbul)	29
2018/2019	Galatasaray SK İstanbul	Galatasaray SK İstanbul	Mbaye Diagne (SEN, Kasımpaşa Spor Kulübü / Galatasaray SK İstanbul)	30

***recognized by Turkish FA only since 2002.*

NATIONAL CHAMPIONSHIP
Süper Lig 2018/2019
(10.08.2018 – 26.05.2019)

Results

Round 1 [10-13.08.2018]
MKE Ankaragücü - Galatasaray 1-3(1-2)
Çaykur Rizespor - Kasımpaşa 2-3(1-0)
Sivasspor - Alanyaspor 1-0(0-0)
Fenerbahçe - Bursaspor 2-1(2-1)
İstanbul Başakşehir - Trabzonspor 2-0(1-0)
Konyaspor - Erzurumspor 3-2(2-1)
Beşiktaş - Akhisar Belediye 2-1(2-0)
Göztepe - Malatyaspor 1-3(0-1)
Kayserispor - Antalyaspor 2-0(1-0)

Round 2 [17-20.08.2018]
Trabzonspor - Sivasspor 3-1(3-1)
Bursaspor - Kayserispor 0-0
Antalyaspor - Konyaspor 3-3(1-2)
Malatyaspor - Fenerbahçe 1-0(0-0)
Erzurumspor - Beşiktaş 1-3(1-0)
Akhisar Belediye - Çaykur Rizespor 1-1(0-1)
Alanyaspor - MKE Ankaragücü 0-2(0-0)
Galatasaray - Göztepe 1-0(1-0)
Kasımpaşa - İstanbul Başakşehir 2-1(0-0)

Round 3 [24-27.08.2018]
Çaykur Rizespor - Erzurumspor 0-0
MKE Ankaragücü - Trabzonspor 2-2(1-1)
Göztepe - Fenerbahçe 1-0(0-0)
Kayserispor - Malatyaspor 0-0
Sivasspor - Kasımpaşa 0-3(0-1)
Beşiktaş - Antalyaspor 2-3(1-3)
Konyaspor - Bursaspor 1-1(1-1)
İstanbul Başakş. - Akhisar Belediye 3-1(1-1)
Galatasaray - Alanyaspor 6-0(1-0)

Round 4 [31.08.-02.09.2018]
Malatyaspor - Konyaspor 0-1(0-1)
Fenerbahçe - Kayserispor 2-3(1-0)
Akhisar Belediye - Sivasspor 1-1(0-0)
Trabzonspor - Galatasaray 4-0(3-0)
Alanyaspor - Göztepe 1-0(0-0)
Erzurumspor - İstanbul Başakşehir 0-1(0-1)
Kasımpaşa - MKE Ankaragücü 2-1(1-0)
Antalyaspor - Çaykur Rizespor 2-1(0-1)
Bursaspor - Beşiktaş 1-1(0-0)

Round 5 [14-17.09.2018]
Galatasaray - Kasımpaşa 4-1(0-0)
MKE Ankaragücü - Akhisar Belediye 1-0(1-0)
Göztepe - Kayserispor 2-0(2-0)
Beşiktaş - Malatyaspor 2-1(0-0)
Sivasspor - Erzurumspor 2-2(1-1)
İstanbul Başakşehir - Antalyaspor 4-0(1-0)
Çaykur Rizespor - Bursaspor 1-1(0-1)
Konyaspor - Fenerbahçe 0-1(0-0)
Alanyaspor - Trabzonspor 1-0(1-0)

Round 6 [21-24.09.2018]
Erzurumspor - MKE Ankaragücü 0-1(0-0)
Bursaspor - İstanbul Başakşehir 0-0
Malatyaspor - Çaykur Rizespor 1-0(1-0)
Kayserispor - Konyaspor 0-2(0-2)
Trabzonspor - Göztepe 1-2(0-2)
Kasımpaşa - Alanyaspor 1-2(0-1)
Antalyaspor - Sivasspor 2-1(2-1)
Akhisar Belediye - Galatasaray 3-0(0-0)
Fenerbahçe - Beşiktaş 1-1(0-1)

Round 7 [28.09.-01.10.2018]
Galatasaray - Erzurumspor 1-0(0-0)
Trabzonspor - Kasımpaşa 4-2(1-2)
Alanyaspor - Akhisar Belediye 2-1(1-0)
Beşiktaş - Kayserispor 2-0(1-0)
Sivasspor - Bursaspor 2-0(1-0)
Göztepe - Konyaspor 3-2(2-0)
Çaykur Rizespor - Fenerbahçe 3-0(3-0)
MKE Ankaragücü - Antalyaspor 0-1(0-1)
İstanbul Başakşehir - Malatyaspor 1-1(0-1)

Round 8 [05-07.10.2018]
Kasımpaşa - Göztepe 3-1(1-0)
Kayserispor - Çaykur Rizespor 2-2(0-1)
Erzurumspor - Alanyaspor 1-0(0-0)
Bursaspor - MKE Ankaragücü 1-0(1-0)
Antalyaspor - Galatasaray 0-1(0-0)
Malatyaspor - Sivasspor 4-4(1-3)
Fenerbahçe - İstanbul Başakşehir 0-0
Akhisar Belediye - Trabzonspor 1-3(0-2)
Konyaspor - Beşiktaş 2-2(1-0)

Round 9 [19-22.10.2018]
Galatasaray - Bursaspor 1-1(0-0)
Kasımpaşa - Akhisar Belediye 5-0(0-0)
İstanbul Başakşehir - Kayserispor 1-0(1-0)
Sivasspor - Fenerbahçe 0-0
Çaykur Rizespor - Konyaspor 1-1(1-0)
MKE Ankaragücü - Malatyaspor 1-0(1-0)
Alanyaspor - Antalyaspor 0-1(0-1)
Göztepe - Beşiktaş 2-0(0-0)
Trabzonspor - Erzurumspor 0-0

Round 10 [26-29.10.2018]
Bursaspor - Alanyaspor 2-0(2-0)
Erzurumspor - Kasımpaşa 1-1(1-0)
Konyaspor - İstanbul Başakşehir 0-1(0-0)
Antalyaspor - Trabzonspor 1-1(1-1)
Kayserispor - Sivasspor 2-0(0-0)
Malatyaspor - Galatasaray 2-0(1-0)
Fenerbahçe - MKE Ankaragücü 1-3(0-1)
Akhisar Belediye - Göztepe 1-0(1-0)
Beşiktaş - Çaykur Rizespor 4-1(2-0)

Round 11 [02-05.11.2018]
Galatasaray - Fenerbahçe 2-2(1-0)
Kasımpaşa - Antalyaspor 1-2(1-1)
Akhisar Belediye - Erzurumspor 1-1(1-1)
İstanbul Başakşehir - Beşiktaş 1-0(1-0)
MKE Ankaragücü - Kayserispor 3-1(2-0)
Alanyaspor - Malatyaspor 0-1(0-1)
Trabzonspor - Bursaspor 1-1(1-0)
Göztepe - Çaykur Rizespor 2-0(1-0)
Sivasspor - Konyaspor 0-0

Round 12 [09-11.11.2018]
Malatyaspor - Trabzonspor 5-0(2-0)
Erzurumspor - Göztepe 2-1(1-0)
Konyaspor - MKE Ankaragücü 2-0(0-0)
Çaykur Rizespor - İstanbul Başakş. 1-2(0-0)
Kayserispor - Galatasaray 0-3(0-1)
Bursaspor - Kasımpaşa 1-2(1-1)
Fenerbahçe - Alanyaspor 2-0(2-0)
Antalyaspor - Akhisar Belediye 1-2(0-0)
Beşiktaş - Sivasspor 1-2(1-1)

Round 13 [23-26.11.2018]
Galatasaray - Konyaspor 1-1(0-0)
Erzurumspor - Antalyaspor 1-0(0-0)
Alanyaspor - Kayserispor 5-0(1-0)
MKE Ankaragücü - Beşiktaş 1-4(0-3)
Sivasspor - Çaykur Rizespor 1-1(0-0)
Akhisar Belediye - Bursaspor 2-4(2-1)
Trabzonspor - Fenerbahçe 2-1(0-0)
Kasımpaşa - Malatyaspor 3-0(1-0)
Göztepe - İstanbul Başakşehir 0-2(0-1)

Round 14 [30.11.-03.12.2018]
Çaykur Rizespor - MKE Ankaragücü 1-1(0-1)
Konyaspor - Alanyaspor 2-0(0-0)
İstanbul Başakşehir - Sivasspor 0-1(0-1)
Antalyaspor - Göztepe 1-0(1-0)
Kayserispor - Trabzonspor 0-2(0-0)
Bursaspor - Erzurumspor 2-1(1-1)
Beşiktaş - Galatasaray 1-0(1-0)
Malatyaspor - Akhisar Belediye 1-1(1-0)
Fenerbahçe - Kasımpaşa 2-2(2-1)

Round 15 [07-10.12.2018]
Alanyaspor - Beşiktaş 0-0
Sivasspor - Göztepe 2-0(0-0)
Trabzonspor - Konyaspor 3-0(0-0)
Galatasaray - Çaykur Rizespor 2-2(1-0)
Erzurumspor - Malatyaspor 1-3(1-0)
Bursaspor - Antalyaspor 0-2(0-2)
Akhisar Belediye - Fenerbahçe 3-0(1-0)
MKE Ankaragücü - İstanbul Başakş. 0-1(0-1)
Kasımpaşa - Kayserispor 0-3(0-1)

Round 16 [14-17.12.2018]
Göztepe - Bursaspor 0-0
Çaykur Rizespor - Alanyaspor 1-1(0-1)
Sivasspor - MKE Ankaragücü 4-0(2-0)
Konyaspor - Kasımpaşa 3-2(0-0)
İstanbul Başakşehir - Galatasaray 1-1(1-1)
Malatyaspor - Antalyaspor 2-0(2-0)
Kayserispor - Akhisar Belediye 1-0(0-0)
Beşiktaş - Trabzonspor 2-2(0-1)
Fenerbahçe - Erzurumspor 2-2(2-0)

Round 17 [22-24.12.2018]
MKE Ankaragücü - Göztepe 0-3(0-0)
Alanyaspor - İstanbul Başakşehir 1-1(0-1)
Kasımpaşa - Beşiktaş 4-1(2-0)
Erzurumspor - Kayserispor 1-1(1-1)
Trabzonspor - Çaykur Rizespor 4-1(1-0)
Bursaspor - Malatyaspor 1-1(1-0)
Galatasaray - Sivasspor 4-2(2-2)
Antalyaspor - Fenerbahçe 0-0
Akhisar Belediye - Konyaspor 0-0

Round 18 [18-21.01.2019]
Akhisar Belediye - Beşiktaş 0-3(0-1)
Erzurumspor - Konyaspor 1-2(0-1)
Malatyaspor - Göztepe 3-2(2-2)
Antalyaspor - Kayserispor 0-0
Galatasaray - MKE Ankaragücü 6-0(3-0)
Alanyaspor - Sivasspor 2-0(2-0)
Trabzonspor - İstanbul Başakşehir 2-4(0-2)
Kasımpaşa - Çaykur Rizespor 0-1(0-1)
Bursaspor - Fenerbahçe 1-1(0-1)

Round 19 [25-28.01.2019]
Beşiktaş - Erzurumspor 1-1(0-0)
Kayserispor - Bursaspor 1-1(0-1)
Göztepe - Galatasaray 0-1(0-0)
Çaykur Rizespor - Akhisar Belediye 3-1(0-1)
Konyaspor - Antalyaspor 2-0(1-0)
Sivasspor - Trabzonspor 1-1(0-0)
İstanbul Başakşehir - Kasımpaşa 2-0(1-0)
MKE Ankaragücü - Alanyaspor 0-2(0-1)
Fenerbahçe - Malatyaspor 3-2(2-2)

Round 20 [01-04.02.2019]
Fenerbahçe - Göztepe 2-0(1-0)
Malatyaspor - Kayserispor 1-1(1-1)
Kasımpaşa - Sivasspor 1-3(1-1)
Trabzonspor - MKE Ankaragücü 1-0(1-0)
Alanyaspor - Galatasaray 1-1(1-0)
Erzurumspor - Çaykur Rizespor 0-1(0-0)
Akhisar Belediye - İstanbul Başakş. 0-3(0-2)
Antalyaspor - Beşiktaş 2-6(0-3)
Bursaspor - Konyaspor 0-0

Round 21 [08-11.02.2019]
Kayserispor - Fenerbahçe 1-0(0-0)
İstanbul Başakşehir - Erzurumspor 1-1(1-0)
Çaykur Rizespor - Antalyaspor 1-1(1-0)
Beşiktaş - Bursaspor 2-0(1-0)
Konyaspor - Malatyaspor 1-1(0-0)
Göztepe - Alanyaspor 3-2(2-1)
Galatasaray - Trabzonspor 3-1(2-1)
MKE Ankaragücü - Kasımpaşa 3-0(1-0)
Sivasspor - Akhisar Belediye 2-1(1-0)

Round 22 [15-18.02.2019]
Malatyaspor - Beşiktaş 1-2(0-0)
Akhisar Belediye - MKE Ankaragücü 0-0
Bursaspor - Çaykur Rizespor 0-2(0-1)
Fenerbahçe - Konyaspor 1-1(1-1)
Erzurumspor - Sivasspor 4-2(2-1)
Trabzonspor - Alanyaspor 0-2(0-0)
Kayserispor - Göztepe 2-1(1-0)
Kasımpaşa - Galatasaray 1-4(1-2)
Antalyaspor - İstanbul Başakşehir 0-1(0-1)

Round 23 [22-25.02.2019]
Göztepe - Trabzonspor 1-3(0-1)
Çaykur Rizespor - Malatyaspor 3-0(1-0)
Sivasspor - Antalyaspor 1-2(0-2)
Alanyaspor - Kasımpaşa 3-0(1-0)
MKE Ankaragücü - Erzurumspor 2-1(1-0)
Konyaspor - Kayserispor 0-1(0-0)
Galatasaray - Akhisar Belediye 1-0(0-0)
İstanbul Başakşehir - Bursaspor 3-0(2-0)
Beşiktaş - Fenerbahçe 3-3(3-0)

Round 24 [01-04.03.2019]
Antalyaspor - MKE Ankaragücü 2-4(2-3)
Bursaspor - Sivasspor 3-2(1-1)
Kayserispor - Beşiktaş 2-2(0-1)
Fenerbahçe - Çaykur Rizespor 3-2(2-1)
Konyaspor - Göztepe 1-1(1-0)
Malatyaspor - İstanbul Başakşehir 0-2(0-1)
Erzurumspor - Galatasaray 1-1(1-0)
Kasımpaşa - Trabzonspor 2-2(0-2)
Akhisar Belediye - Alanyaspor 3-1(0-0)

Round 25 [08-11.03.2019]
Sivasspor - Malatyaspor 2-0(2-0)
Trabzonspor - Akhisar Belediye 2-1(0-0)
İstanbul Başakşehir - Fenerbahçe 2-1(1-0)
MKE Ankaragücü - Bursaspor 0-0
Alanyaspor - Erzurumspor 2-1(1-0)
Göztepe - Kasımpaşa 0-0
Çaykur Rizespor - Kayserispor 3-0(1-0)
Beşiktaş - Konyaspor 3-2(2-1)
Galatasaray - Antalyaspor 5-0(1-0)

Round 26 [15-17.03.2019]
Fenerbahçe - Sivasspor 2-1(0-0)
Konyaspor - Çaykur Rizespor 0-2(0-1)
Akhisar Belediye - Kasımpaşa 2-3(1-1)
Erzurumspor - Trabzonspor 0-1(0-0)
Antalyaspor - Alanyaspor 3-0(2-0)
Beşiktaş - Göztepe 1-0(0-0)
Malatyaspor - MKE Ankaragücü 3-1(0-0)
Kayserispor - İstanbul Başakşehir 1-1(1-0)
Bursaspor - Galatasaray 2-3(2-1)

Round 27 [05-08.04.2019]
Trabzonspor - Antalyaspor 4-1(1-1)
Sivasspor - Kayserispor 1-3(0-3)
Alanyaspor - Bursaspor 1-0(0-0)
Galatasaray - Malatyaspor 3-0(1-0)
Kasımpaşa - Erzurumspor 2-1(1-0)
Göztepe - Akhisar Belediye 0-1(0-0)
MKE Ankaragücü - Fenerbahçe 1-1(1-0)
İstanbul Başakşehir - Konyaspor 2-0(0-0)
Çaykur Rizespor - Beşiktaş 2-7(1-2)

Round 28 [12-15.04.2019]
Bursaspor - Trabzonspor 0-1(0-0)
Çaykur Rizespor - Göztepe 1-0(0-0)
Konyaspor - Sivasspor 1-1(1-1)
Beşiktaş - İstanbul Başakşehir 2-1(1-1)
Kayserispor - MKE Ankaragücü 0-2(0-0)
Antalyaspor - Kasımpaşa 1-0(1-0)
Malatyaspor - Alanyaspor 1-1(1-1)
Fenerbahçe - Galatasaray 1-1(0-0)
Erzurumspor - Akhisar Belediye 2-1(0-0)

Round 29 [19-22.04.2019]
Kasımpaşa - Bursaspor 1-1(0-0)
Trabzonspor - Malatyaspor 2-1(1-1)
Akhisar Belediye - Antalyaspor 1-2(0-2)
Galatasaray - Kayserispor 3-1(3-1)
Göztepe - Erzurumspor 0-1(0-1)
MKE Ankaragücü - Konyaspor 0-0
İstanbul Başakş. - Çaykur Rizespor 1-1(0-0)
Alanyaspor - Fenerbahçe 1-0(0-0)
Sivasspor - Beşiktaş 1-2(1-1)

Round 30 [26-29.04.2019]
İstanbul Başakşehir - Göztepe 0-2(0-1)
Çaykur Rizespor - Sivasspor 0-0
Antalyaspor - Erzurumspor 1-1(1-0)
Fenerbahçe - Trabzonspor 1-1(0-1)
Kayserispor - Alanyaspor 1-1(1-1)
Bursaspor - Akhisar Belediye 0-0
Beşiktaş - MKE Ankaragücü 4-1(1-0)
Malatyaspor - Kasımpaşa 2-1(1-0)
Konyaspor - Galatasaray 0-0

Round 31 [03-06.05.2019]
Sivasspor - İstanbul Başakşehir 0-0
MKE Ankaragücü - Çaykur Rizespor 2-2(0-1)
Erzurumspor - Bursaspor 2-0(0-0)
Kasımpaşa - Fenerbahçe 1-3(1-1)
Akhisar Belediye - Malatyaspor 0-2(0-0)
Göztepe - Antalyaspor 4-1(2-1)
Galatasaray - Beşiktaş 2-0(1-0)
Alanyaspor - Konyaspor 2-4(1-2)
Trabzonspor - Kayserispor 4-2(2-1)

Round 32 [10-13.05.2019]
Antalyaspor - Bursaspor 0-1(0-1)
Çaykur Rizespor - Galatasaray 2-3(1-1)
Fenerbahçe - Akhisar Belediye 2-1(2-1)
Göztepe - Sivasspor 3-3(1-2)
Kayserispor - Kasımpaşa 2-1(0-1)
Konyaspor - Trabzonspor 2-2(2-1)
İstanbul Başakş. - MKE Ankaragücü 2-1(0-1)
Malatyaspor - Erzurumspor 3-1(0-0)
Beşiktaş - Alanyaspor 2-1(1-1)

Round 33 [17-20.05.2019]
Kasımpaşa - Konyaspor 1-1(0-1)
Antalyaspor - Malatyaspor 3-0(1-0)
Trabzonspor - Beşiktaş 2-1(0-0)
Akhisar Belediye - Kayserispor 2-2(1-0)
Bursaspor - Göztepe 0-0
Alanyaspor - Çaykur Rizespor 1-1(1-0)
Galatasaray - İstanbul Başakşehir 2-1(0-1)
MKE Ankaragücü - Sivasspor 3-1(2-0)
Erzurumspor - Fenerbahçe 0-1(0-0)

Round 34 [24-26.05.2019]
İstanbul Başakşehir - Alanyaspor 1-1(1-1)
Beşiktaş - Kasımpaşa 3-2(3-1)
Sivasspor - Galatasaray 4-3(2-2)
Çaykur Rizespor - Trabzonspor 2-3(1-3)
Konyaspor - Akhisar Belediye 0-0
Göztepe - MKE Ankaragücü 2-1(1-0)
Fenerbahçe - Antalyaspor 3-1(1-1)
Kayserispor - Erzurumspor 0-2(0-2)
Malatyaspor - Bursaspor 1-2(0-2)

Final Standings

1.	**Galatasaray SK İstanbul**	34	20	9	5	72	-	36	69
2.	İstanbul Başakşehir FK	34	19	10	5	49	-	22	67
3.	Beşiktaş JK İstanbul	34	19	8	7	72	-	46	65
4.	Trabzonspor Kulübü	34	18	9	7	64	-	46	63
5.	Yeni Malatya Spor Kulübü	34	13	8	13	47	-	46	47
6.	Fenerbahçe SK İstanbul	34	11	13	10	44	-	44	46
7.	Antalyaspor Kulübü	34	13	6	15	39	-	55	45
8.	Konyaspor Kulübü	34	9	17	8	40	-	38	44
9.	Alanyaspor	34	12	8	14	37	-	43	44
10.	Kayserispor Kulübü	34	10	11	13	35	-	50	41
11.	Çaykur Rizespor Kulübü	34	9	14	11	48	-	50	41
12.	Sivasspor Kulübü	34	10	11	13	49	-	54	41
13.	MKE Ankaragücü	34	11	7	16	38	-	53	40
14.	Kasımpaşa Spor Kulübü	34	11	6	17	53	-	62	39
15.	Göztepe SK İzmir	34	11	5	18	37	-	42	38
16.	Bursaspor Kulübü (*Relegated*)	34	7	16	11	28	-	37	37
17.	Büyükşehir Belediye Erzurumspor (*Relegated*)	34	8	11	15	36	-	43	35
18.	Akhisar Belediye Gençlik ve SK (*Relegated*)	34	6	9	19	33	-	54	27

Top goalscorers:

30 Mbaye Diagne (SEN)
Kasımpaşa SK / Galatasaray SK İstanbul

17 Vedat Muriqi (KVX)
Çaykur Rizespor Kulübü

16 Papiss Demba Cissé (SEN)
Alanyaspor

16 Burak Yılmaz
Trabzonspor / Beşiktaş JK İstanbul

15 Hugo Andrés Rodallega Camacho (COL)
Trabzonspor Kulübü

14 Henry Chukwuemeka Onyekuru (NGA)
Galatasaray SK İstanbul

NATIONAL CUP
Türkiye Kupasi 2018/2019

Fourth Round [30/31.10./01.11.2018]

Batman Petrolspor - Kasımpaşa SK	2-3
Sivas Belediyespor - Denizlispor Kulübü	3-2 aet
Kastamonuspor - Altay SK İzmir	2-3 aet
Fatih Karagümrük SK - Afjet Afyonspor	4-0
Büyükşehir Belediye Erzurumspor - Keçiörengücü	2-2 aet; 4-5 pen
Antalyaspor Kulübü - Yomraspor	1-1 aet; 3-0 pen
Bursaspor Kulübü - 1461 Trabzon	1-2 aet
Bugsaşspor - Trabzonspor Kulübü	0-2
Altındağ Belediyespor - Alanyaspor	1-3
Hatayspor Antakya - Fethiyespor	3-1
Bodrum Belediye - Sivasspor	2-1
Bandırmaspor - Vanspor FK	0-0 aet; 2-4 pen
Darıca Gençlerbirliği SK Ankara - Karabükspor	6-1
Aydın Nazilli Belediyespor - Osmanlıspor FK	3-2
Şile Yıldızspor - Boluspor Kulübü	2-5
Ümraniyespor - 24 Erzincanspor	5-1
MKE Ankaragücü - Erbaaspor	1-0
Kayserispor Kulübü - Pazarspor	6-1
Yeni Malatya Spor Kulübü - Kırklarelispor	1-0
Kahramanmarasspor - Atiker Konyaspor	3-0
Sarıyer SK - Çaykur Rizespor Kulübü	1-2
Gümüşhanespor - Giresunspor	2-2 aet; 3-5 pen
Etimesgut Belediyespor - Istanbulspor	2-1
Adana Demirspor Kulübü - Dersim Spor	3-1 aet
Menemen Belediyespor - Zonguldak Kömürspor	2-0
Balıkesirspor - Pendikspor	3-1
Göztepe SK İzmir - Çengelköyspor	4-0
Gençlerbirliği SK Ankara - Diyarbekirspor	1-0

Fifth Round [04-06.12./18-20.12.2018]

Sivas Belediyespor - Trabzonspor Kulübü	2-2 / 0-5
Aydın Nazilli Belediyespor - Göztepe SK İzmir	0-3 / 1-2
Gençlerbirliği SK Ankara - Hatayspor Antakya	2-1 / 0-2
Antalyaspor Kulübü - Darıca Gençlerbirliği	2-2 / 1-0
Alanyaspor - Kahramanmarasspor	7-2 / 1-2
Çaykur Rizespor Kulübü - Balıkesirspor	0-2 / 1-1
Keçiörengücü - Galatasaray SK İstanbul	1-2 / 1-1
Ümraniyespor - 1461 Trabzon	4-1 / 1-3
Boluspor Kulübü - Vanspor FK	5-1 / 2-2
Altay SK İzmir - Kayserispor Kulübü	1-2 / 1-4
Adana Demirspor Kulübü - İstanbul Başakşehir FK	1-1 / 0-2
Bodrum Belediye - MKE Ankaragücü	4-2 / 2-3
Fatih Karagümrük SK - Akhisar Belediye Gençlik SK	1-4 / 0-2
Menemen Belediyespor - Kasımpaşa SK	1-2 / 1-4
Yeni Malatya Spor Kulübü - Etimesgut Belediyespor	2-0 / 2-0
Fenerbahçe SK İstanbul - Giresunspor	1-0 / 5-2

1/8-Finals [15-22.01./23-29/01.2019]

Kayserispor Kulübü - Akhisar Belediye Gençlik SK	1-2 / 0-0
Antalyaspor Kulübü - Göztepe SK İzmir	3-3 / 0-3
Yeni Malatya Spor Kulübü - Bodrum Belediye	3-2 / 2-1
İstanbul Başakşehir FK - Hatayspor Antakya	1-0 / 1-4
Trabzonspor Kulübü - Balıkesirspor	2-1 / 3-1
Alanyaspor - Kasımpaşa SK	0-0 / 0-1 aet
Ümraniyespor - Fenerbahçe SK İstanbul	1-0 / 1-0
Boluspor Kulübü - Galatasaray SK İstanbul	0-1 / 1-4

Quarter-Finals [05-07.02.26-28.02.2019]

Trabzonspor Kulübü - Ümraniyespor	0-0 / 1-3
Yeni Malatya Spor Kulübü - Göztepe SK İzmir	1-0 / 5-3 pen
Galatasaray SK İstanbul - Hatayspor Antakya	2-0 / 2-4
Akhisar Belediye Gençlik SK - Kasımpaşa SK	3-1 / 2-1

Semi-Finals [02-03./24-25.042019]

Galatasaray SK İstanbul - Yeni Malatya Spor Kulübü	0-0 / 5-2
Ümraniyespor - Akhisar Belediye Gençlik SK	0-1 / 0-1

Final

15.05.2019; Yeni 4 Eylül Stadyumu, Sivas; Referee: Suat Arslanboğa; Attendance: n/a
Galatasaray SK İstanbul - Akhisar Belediye Gençlik ve Spor Kulübü **3-1(0-0)**

Galatasaray: Néstor Fernando Muslera Micol, Mariano Ferreira Filho, Martin Linnes, Christian Luyindama Nekadio, Marcos do Nascimento Teixeira „Marcão",Selçuk İnan (74.Ryan Donk), Younès Belhanda, Papa Alioune N'Diaye (67.Sinan Gümüş), Sofiane Féghouli (90.Fernando Francisco Reges), Henry Chukwuemeka Onyekuru, Mbaye Diagne. Trainer: Fatih Terim.

Akhisar Belediye Gençlik: Fatih Öztürk, Avdija Vršajević (60.Aykut Çeviker), Hugo Miguel de Almeida Costa Lopes [*sent off 78*], Zeki Yavru (90.Sokol Çikalleshi), Caner Osmanpaşa, Kadir Keleş, Rajko Rotman, Hélder Jorge Leal Rodrigues Barbosa, Güray Vural (87.Jeremy Loteteka Bokila), Abdoulwhaid Sissoko, Elvis Manu. Trainer: Cem Kavçak.

Goals: 0-1 Elvis Manu (57), 1-1 Sinan Gümüş (80), 2-1 Sofiane Féghouli (88), 3-1 Mbaye Diagne (90).

THE CLUBS 2018/2019

Akhisar Belediye Gençlik ve Spor Kulübü

Founded: 08.04.1970
Stadium: Spor Toto Akhisar Stadyumu, Akhisar (12,139)

Goalkeepers:	**DOB**	**M**	**(s)**	**G**
Milan Lukač (SRB)	04.10.1985	7	(1)	
Fatih Öztürk (FRA)	22.12.1986	26		
Halil Yeral	01.01.2000	1		
Defenders:	**DOB**	**M**	**(s)**	**G**
Gökmen Aydoğdu	27.08.2000		(1)	
Ömer Bayram	27.07.1991	3		
Edin Cocalić (BIH)	05.12.1987	9		1
Kadir Keleş	01.01.1988	18	(1)	
Hugo Miguel de Almeida Costa Lopes (POR)	19.12.1986	19	(2)	1
Dogukan Nelik	05.12.2000		(1)	
Dany Nounkeu (CMR)	11.04.1986	1	(3)	
Caner Osmanpaşa	15.01.1988	30	(1)	
Avdija Vršajević (BIH)	06.03.1986	16	(4)	
Zeki Yavru	05.09.1991	12		2
Mustafa Yumlu	25.09.1987	10		2
Midfielders:	**DOB**	**M**	**(s)**	**G**
Eray Ataseven	29.06.1993	6	(5)	
Aykut Çeviker	03.01.1990	17	(2)	
Onurcan Güler	24.03.1995		(4)	
Ali Güneren	08.04.2000		(1)	
Hélder Jorge Leal Rodrigues Barbosa (POR)	25.05.1987	22	(6)	4
Josué Filipe Soares Pesqueira (POR)	17.09.1990	17	(3)	2
Bilal Kisa	22.06.1983	6	(10)	1
Musa Nizam	08.09.1990	3	(1)	
Adrien Regattin (MAR)	22.08.1991	13	(10)	3
Rajko Rotman (SVN)	19.03.1989	9	(2)	
Sergio Antonio Borges Junior „Serginho" (BRA)	04.08.1986	18	(6)	
Abdoulwhaid Sissoko (FRA)	20.03.1990	31	(1)	
Güray Vural	11.06.1988	24	(2)	2
Forwards:	**DOB**	**M**	**(s)**	**G**
Onur Ayik	28.01.1990	11	(12)	1
Jeremy Loteteka Bokila (COD)	14.11.1988	9	(7)	4
Sokol Çikalleshi (ALB)	27.07.1990	8	(5)	
Daniel Larsson (SWE)	25.01.1987	2	(1)	
Elvis Manu (GHA)	13.08.1993	20	(8)	7
Yevhen Seleznyov (UKR)	20.07.1985	6	(1)	3
Trainer:	**DOB**	**M**		
Safet Sušić (BIH)	13.04.1955	6		
Cihat Arslan [25.09.2018]	09.02.1970	15		
Cem Kavçak [13.02.2019]	03.07.1978	13		

Alanyaspor

Founded: 1948
Stadium: Alanya Oba Stadyumu, Alanya (10,842)

Goalkeepers:	**DOB**	**M**	**(s)**	**G**
Ufuk Ceylan	23.06.1986	8		
Haydar Yilmaz	19.01.1984	26	(1)	
Defenders:	**DOB**	**M**	**(s)**	**G**
Cenk Alkılıç	09.12.1987	11	(6)	
Wanderson Sousa Carneiro „Baiano" (BRA)	23.02.1987	24	(2)	
Barış Başdaş	17.01.1990	3	(1)	
Emre Bekir	17.08.1998		(1)	
Steven Caulker (ENG)	29.12.1991	9	(1)	1
Merih Demiral	05.03.1998	16		1
Fabrice N'Sakala (COD)	21.07.1990	32		
Giorgos Tzavellas (GRE)	26.11.1987	27		1
Welinton Souza Silva (BRA)	10.04.1989	15	(5)	1
Midfielders:	**DOB**	**M**	**(s)**	**G**
Emre Akbaba	04.10.1992		(1)	
Hasan Ayaroğlu	22.03.1995		(12)	
Ceyhun Gülselam	25.12.1987	25	(1)	
Efecan Karaca	16.11.1989	33	(1)	2
Filipe Augusto Carvalho Souza (BRA)	12.08.1993	2	(3)	
Ioannis Maniatis (GRE)	12.10.1986	12	(3)	1
Joel Chukwuma Obi (NGA)	22.05.1991		(2)	
Isaac Sackey (GHA)	04.04.1994	17	(4)	
Ozan Tufan	23.03.1995	14	(3)	
Taha Yalçıner	12.01.1987	3	(11)	
Forwards:	**DOB**	**M**	**(s)**	**G**
Deyvison Rogério da Silva „Bobô" (BRA)	09.01.1985	7	(4)	
Papiss Demba Cissé (SEN)	03.06.1985	25	(1)	16
Djalma Braume Manuel Abel Campos (ANG)	30.05.1987	24	(4)	4
Serges Flavier Mbilla Etame (CMR)	22.06.1988		(1)	
Antenor Junior Fernandes da Silva Vitoria (CHI)	10.04.1988	14	(11)	7
Emre Güral	05.04.1989		(2)	
Josef Šural (CZE)	30.05.1990	3	(6)	1
Lucas Martín Villafáñez (ARG)	04.10.1991	24	(8)	
Trainer:	**DOB**	**M**		
Mesut Bakkal	19.03.1964	12		
Sergen Yalcin [12.11.2018]	05.10.1972	22		

Makina ve Kimya Endüstrisi Ankaragücü

Founded: 31.08.1910
Stadium: Eryaman Stadyumu, Ankara (20,071)

Goalkeepers:	DOB	M	(s)	G
Altay Bayındır	14.04.1998	17		
Korcan Çelikay	31.12.1987	9		
Johannes Hopf (SWE)	16.06.1987	8		
Defenders:	**DOB**	**M**	**(s)**	**G**
Yalçın Ayhan	01.05.1982	16	(1)	
Thomas Heurtaux (FRA)	03.07.1988	2	(2)	
Cebrail Karayel	15.08.1994	3		
Stelios Kitsiou (GRE)	28.09.1993	14		
Bakary Koné (BFA)	27.04.1988	11	(3)	
Alihan Kubalas	26.10.1991	13	(3)	
Ante Kulušić (CRO)	06.06.1986	13		
Michał Pazdan (POL)	21.09.1987	14		2
Łukasz Szukała (POL)	26.05.1984		(1)	
Tiago Miguel Baía Pinto (POR)	01.02.1988	26		1
Midfielders:	**DOB**	**M**	**(s)**	**G**
Sedat Ağçay	22.09.1981	16	(8)	
Héctor Miguel Canteros (ARG)	15.03.1989	12		1
Brice Dja Djedjé (CIV)	23.12.1990	18	(1)	
Ricardo Faty (SEN)	04.08.1986	18	(1)	3
Aydin Karabulut	25.01.1988		(3)	
Wilfred Moke (COD)	12.02.1988	10	(3)	
Arif Morkaya	30.05.1989	3		
Thibault Moulin (FRA)	13.01.1990	10	(10)	

Nduka Morrisson Ozokwo (NGA)	25.12.1988		(2)	
Erdem Özgenç	05.01.1989	15		1
Anton Putsila (BLR)	10.06.1987	4	(5)	
Mehmet Sak	04.04.1990	5	(4)	
Ezequiel Óscar Scarione (ARG)	14.07.1985	2	(3)	
Forwards:	**DOB**	**M**	**(s)**	**G**
Thievy Guivane Bifouma Koulossa (CGO)	13.05.1992	13		1
Tyler Boyd (NZL)	30.12.1994	14		6
Alessio Cerci (ITA)	23.07.1987	3	(9)	1
Mostafa El Kabir (MAR)	05.10.1988	14		6
Youness Mokhtar	29.08.1991	10	(2)	1
Kubilay Kanatsızkuş	28.03.1997	8	(2)	1
Olanrewaju Muhammed Kehinde (NGA)	07.05.1994		(8)	
Dever Akeem Orgill (JAM)	08.03.1990	14		6
Kenan Özer	16.08.1987	8	(6)	1
İlhan Parlak	18.01.1987	16	(15)	4
Hadi Sacko (FRA)	24.03.1994	14	(1)	3
Zaur Sadaev (RUS)	06.11.1989	1	(6)	
Trainer:	**DOB**	**M**		
Ismail Kartal	15.06.1961	16		
Bayram Kadir Bektaş [19.12.2018]	10.02.1974	1		
Mustafa Kaplan [09.01.2019]	02.09.1967	17		

Antalyaspor Kulübü

Founded: 02.07.1966
Stadium: Antalya Stadyumu, Antalya (33,032)

Goalkeepers:	DOB	M	(s)	G
Ruud Boffin (BEL)	05.11.1987	31		
Ferhat Kaplan	07.01.1989	3		
Defenders:	**DOB**	**M**	**(s)**	**G**
Tarik Çamdal	24.03.1991	1	(1)	
Osman Çelik	27.11.1991		(1)	
Ondřej Čelůstka (CZE)	18.06.1989	24		
Luis Francisco Grando „Chico"(BRA)	02.02.1987	26	(1)	2
Aly Cissokho (FRA)	15.09.1987	20	(2)	
Diego Ângelo de Oliveira (BRA)	12.02.1986	29		3
Salih Dursun	12.07.1991	12	(1)	
Birkan Öksüz	19.03.1996	1		
Bahadir Öztürk	10.01.1995	10	(1)	
Nazim Sangaré (GER)	30.05.1994	32		2
Midfielders:	**DOB**	**M**	**(s)**	**G**
Harun Alpsoy (SUI)	03.03.1997	5	(7)	1
Abdelaziz Barrada (MAR)	19.06.1989		(5)	
Charles Fernando Basílio da Silva (BRA)	14.02.1985	13	(1)	

Richard Danilo Maciel Sousa Campos (BEL)	13.01.1990	3	(5)	
Yekta Kurtuluş	11.12.1985	14	(7)	1
Serdar Özkan	01.01.1987	11	(12)	2
Hakan Özmert	03.06.1985	30	(1)	4
Doğukan Sinik	21.01.1999	22	(11)	
William Vainqueur (FRA)	19.11.1988	3	(4)	
Sergen Yatağan	17.05.1999		(1)	
Zeki Yildirim	15.01.1991	5	(5)	
Forwards:	**DOB**	**M**	**(s)**	**G**
Amilton Minervino da Silva (BRA)	12.08.1989	13	(1)	1
Souleymane Doukara (FRA)	29.09.1991	21	(5)	10
Jean Armel Drolé (CIV)	18.08.1997	3	(17)	
Mevlüt Erdinç	25.02.1987	17	(7)	12
Alfredo Gomes Ribeiro „Fredy"(ANG)	27.03.1990	12	(1)	
Fehmi Koç	28.08.2003		(1)	
Maicón Marques Bitencourt (BRA)	18.02.1990	13	(1)	1
Erman Vardar	14.12.2001		(1)	
Trainer:	**DOB**	**M**		
Bülent Korkmaz	24.11.1968	34		

Beşiktaş Jimnastik Kulübü İstanbul

Founded: 04.03.1903
Stadium: Vodafone Park, Istanbul (43,500)

Goalkeepers:	DOB	M	(s)	G
Loris Karius (GER)	22.06.1993	30		
Utku Yuvakuran	02.11.1997	1		
Tolga Zengin	10.10.1983	3		
Defenders:	**DOB**	**M**	**(s)**	**G**
Adriano Correia Claro (BRA)	26.10.1984	18	(4)	
Fatih Aksoy	06.11.1997		(2)	
Caner Erkin	04.10.1988	20	(8)	1
Gökhan Gönül	04.01.1985	27	(2)	3
Nicolas Isimat-Mirin (FRA)	15.11.1991	14		
Képler Laveran Lima Ferreira „Pepe" (POR)	26.02.1983	10		3
Enzo Pablo Roco Roco (CHI)	16.08.1992	2	(4)	
Domagoj Vida (CRO)	29.04.1989	31		3
Rıdvan Yılmaz	21.05.2001		(1)	
Midfielders:	**DOB**	**M**	**(s)**	**G**
Tolgay Arslan (GER)	16.08.1990	5	(3)	
Atiba Hutchinson (CAN)	08.02.1983	25	(2)	4
Shinji Kagawa (JPN)	17.03.1989	4	(10)	4
Gary Alexis Medel Soto (CHI)	03.08.1987	22	(2)	

Oğuzhan Özyakup	23.09.1992	10	(9)	1
Dorukhan Toköz	21.05.1996	19	(1)	3
Gökhan Töre	20.01.1992	1	(1)	
Necip Uysal	24.01.1991	11	(7)	
Forwards:	**DOB**	**M**	**(s)**	**G**
Álvaro Negredo Sánchez (ESP)	20.08.1985	4		2
Ryan Guno Babel (NED)	19.12.1986	10	(2)	4
Cyle Christopher Larin (CAN)	17.04.1995	2	(10)	1
Jeremain Marciano Lens (NED)	24.11.1987	19	(9)	1
Adem Ljajić (SRB)	29.09.1991	25	(2)	9
Mustafa Pektemek	11.08.1988	6	(7)	5
Ricardo Andrade Quaresma Bernardo (POR)	26.09.1983	21	(5)	3
Vágner Silva Nascimento „Vágner Love" (BRA)	11.06.1984	5	(3)	3
Güven Yalçın	18.01.1999	14	(8)	8
Burak Yılmaz	15.07.1985	15		11
Trainer:	**DOB**	**M**		
Şenol Güneş	01.06.1952	34		

Bursaspor Kulübü Derneği

Founded: 01.06.1963
Stadium: Timsah Arena, Bursa (43,877)

Goalkeepers:	**DOB**	**M**	**(s)**	**G**
Okan Koçuk	27.07.1995	22		
Muhammed Şengezer	05.01.1997	9		
Harun Tekin	17.06.1989	3		
Defenders:	**DOB**	**M**	**(s)**	**G**
Onur Atasayar	01.01.1995	4	(1)	
Aziz Eraltay Behich (AUS)	16.12.1990	3		
Aurélien Bayard Chedjou Fongang (CMR)	20.06.1985	26		1
Ertuğrul Ersoy	13.02.1997	30		1
Burak Kapacak	08.12.1999	9	(7)	
Iasmin Latovlevici (ROU)	11.05.1986	20	(5)	3
Cengiz Meraş	20.12.1995	27		2
Emre Taşdemir	08.08.1995		(1)	
William Troost-Ekong (NGA)	01.09.1993	1		1
Santiago Vergini (ARG)	03.08.1988	8		
Barış Yardımcı	14.08.1992	26		
Midfielders:	**DOB**	**M**	**(s)**	**G**
Jani Atanasov (MKD)	31.10.1999		(3)	
Stéphane Badji (SEN)	18.01.1990	28	(1)	
Yusuf Erdoğan	07.08.1992	18	(8)	1
Aytaç Kara	23.03.1993	32		6
Ramazan Keskin	04.01.1999	3	(4)	1
Henri Saivet (SEN)	26.10.1990	24	(5)	2
Abdullahi Shehu (NGA)	12.03.1993	8	(5)	1
Furkan Soyalp	12.06.1995	6	(7)	
Forwards:	**DOB**	**M**	**(s)**	**G**
Allano Brendon de Souza Lima (BRA)	24.04.1995	17	(14)	1
Kubilay Kanatsızkuş	28.03.1997		(5)	
Jirès Kembo Ekoko (COD)	08.01.1988		(2)	
Mehmet Nayir	28.06.1993	13	(12)	4
Tomáš Necid (CZE)	13.08.1989	1	(1)	
Diafra Sakho (SEN)	24.12.1989	15	(5)	3
Bogdan Stancu (ROU)	28.06.1987	5	(2)	
Tunay Torun	21.04.1990	16	(9)	
Çağatay Yılmaz	01.01.2000		(1)	
Trainer:	**DOB**	**M**		
Samet Aybaba	03.09.1955	27		
Mesut Bakkal [11.04.2019]	19.03.1964	7		

Çaykur Rizespor Kulübü

Founded: 19.05.1953
Stadium: "Rize Şehir" Stadyumu, Rize (15,332)

Goalkeepers:	**DOB**	**M**	**(s)**	**G**
Gökhan Akkan	01.01.1995	34		
Samir Ujkani (KVX)	05.07.1988		(1)	
Defenders:	**DOB**	**M**	**(s)**	**G**
Mohamed Aberhoune (MAR)	03.05.1989	14	(2)	1
Koray Altınay	11.10.1991	6	(3)	
Chidozie Collins Awaziem (NGA)	01.01.1997	15	(1)	
Jakub Brabec	06.08.1992	17		
Matic Fink (SVN)	27.02.1990	4	(4)	
Jarosław Jach (POL)	17.02.1994	3	(2)	
Dario Melnjak (CRO)	31.10.1992	15	(1)	4
Orhan Ovacıklı	23.11.1988	13	(3)	
Montassar Talbi (TUN)	26.05.1998	1		
Mehmet Uslu	25.02.1988	17	(2)	
Midfielders:	**DOB**	**M**	**(s)**	**G**
Okechukwu Godson Azubuike (NGA)	19.04.1997	14		1
Aatif Chahechouhe (FRA)	02.07.1986	11	(1)	3
Musa Çağıran	17.11.1992	14	(3)	
Ali Çamdalı	22.02.1984	10	(1)	1
Abdullah Durak	01.04.1987	12	(7)	
Mikola Morozyuk (UKR)	17.01.1988	13	(1)	
Davide Petrucci (ITA)	05.10.1991	8	(2)	
Fernando Henrique Boldrin „Rick" (BRA)	23.02.1989	30		4
Merouane Saâdane (MAR)	17.01.1992	23	(7)	2
Mustafa Saymak (NED)	11.02.1993	2	(13)	
Çınar Tarhan	20.05.1997		(1)	
Aminu Umar (NGA)	06.03.1995	26	(5)	6
Robin Yalcin (GER)	25.01.1994	10	(5)	1
Forwards:	**DOB**	**M**	**(s)**	**G**
Oğulcan Çağlayan	22.03.1996		(1)	
Oleksandr Hladkyi (UKR)	24.08.1987	1	(7)	
Süleyman Koç (GER)	09.06.1989	3	(10)	
Vedat Muriqi (KVX)	24.04.1994	34		17
Préjuce Nakoulma (BFA)	21.04.1987	1	(11)	2
Braian José Samudio Segovia (PAR)	23.12.1995	23	(6)	5
Trainer:	**DOB**	**M**		
Ibrahim Üzülmez	10.03.1974	6		
Okan Buruk [24.09.2018]	19.10.1973	28		

Büyükşehir Belediye Erzurumspor

Founded: 2005
Stadium: "Kazım Karabekir" Stadyumu, Erzurum (23,277)

Goalkeepers:	**DOB**	**M**	**(s)**	**G**
Hakan Canbazoğlu	28.11.1987	2		
Ibrahim Šehić (BIH)	02.09.1988	32		
Defenders:	**DOB**	**M**	**(s)**	**G**
Stephane Acka (CIV)	11.10.1990	3	(2)	
Hakan Arslan	12.03.1989	8	(1)	1
Auremir Evangelista dos Santos (BRA)	10.09.1991	13	(1)	1
Lokman Gör	15.12.1990	27	(1)	2
Pierre Kanstrup (DEN)	21.02.1989	13	(1)	
Egemen Korkmaz	03.11.1982	19	(1)	1
Serkan Kurtuluş	01.01.1990	3	(3)	
Léo Schwechlen (FRA)	05.06.1989	34		1
Tolga Ünlü	10.09.1989	17	(1)	
Midfielders:	**DOB**	**M**	**(s)**	**G**
Ibrahim Akdağ	21.07.1991	21	(8)	3
Sefa Akgün	30.06.2000		(1)	
Taylan Antalyalı	08.01.1995	27	(4)	6
Emrah Başsan	17.04.1992	25	(6)	1
Erhan Çelenk	16.03.1989	3	(7)	
Özer Hurmacı	20.11.1986	15	(1)	
Moussa Koné (CIV)	12.02.1990	9	(11)	
Osman Şahin	13.01.1998		(2)	
Jasmin Šćuk (BIH)	14.07.1990	27	(4)	4
Siphiwe Tshabalala (RSA)	25.09.1984	5	(12)	
Forwards:	**DOB**	**M**	**(s)**	**G**
Samuel Eduok (NGA)	31.01.1994	15		4
Samed Kaya	10.09.1995		(3)	
Arsen Khubulov (RUS)	13.12.1990	1	(2)	
Rashad Muhammed (FRA)	25.09.1993	4	(5)	2
Ridge Munsy (SUI)	09.07.1989	7	(5)	
Gabriel Obertan (FRA)	26.02.1989	9	(1)	1
Kristian Opseth (NOR)	06.01.1990	8	(4)	1
Gilles Sunu (TOG)	30.03.1991	24	(4)	4
Lennart Thy (GER)	25.02.1992	3	(9)	1
Trainer:	**DOB**	**M**		
Mehmet Altiparmak [15.11.2017]	01.05.1969	6		
Mehmet Özdilek [27.09.2018]	01.04.1966	18		
Hamza Hamzaoglu [07.03.2019]	01.07.1970	10		

Fenerbahçe Spor Kulübü

Founded: 03.05.1907 (*as Fenerbahçe Futbol Kulübü*)
Stadium: Ülker Stadyumu, Istanbul (50,509)

Goalkeepers:	**DOB**	**M**	**(s)**	**G**
Volkan Demirel	27.10.1981	12		
Harun Tekin	17.06.1989	22		
Defenders:	**DOB**	**M**	**(s)**	**G**
Serdar Aziz	23.10.1990	10		1
Sadık Çiftpinar	01.01.1993	8	(1)	1
Nabil Dirar (MAR)	25.02.1986	15	(1)	1
Yiğithan Güveli	16.05.1998		(1)	
Hasan-Ali Kaldırım	09.12.1989	31		2
Ismail Köybaşı	10.07.1989	5	(4)	
Şener Özbayraklı	23.01.1990	8	(1)	
Diego Antonio Reyes Rosales(MEX)	19.09.1992	4	(4)	
Martin Škrtel (SVK)	15.12.1984	27		1
Midfielders:	**DOB**	**M**	**(s)**	**G**
Barış Alıcı	24.06.1997	4	(4)	
Tolgay Arslan (GER)	16.08.1990	9	(2)	
Aatif Chahechouhe (FRA)	02.07.1986	3		
Mehmet Ekici	25.03.1990	12	(9)	3
Eljif Elmas (MKD)	24.09.1999	17	(12)	4
Oğuz Güçtekin	06.04.1999	1	(1)	
Mauricio Anibal Isla Isla (CHI)	12.06.1988	26	(2)	
Jailson Marques Siqueira (BRA)	07.09.1995	16	(3)	2
Roman Neustädter (RUS)	18.02.1988	21		1
Alper Potuk	08.04.1991	1	(7)	
Josef de Souza Dias (BRA)	11.02.1989	2		1
Mehmet Topal	03.03.1986	24	(4)	1
Mathieu Valbuena (FRA)	28.09.1984	13	(9)	3
Miha Zajc (SVN)	01.07.1994	8	(2)	2
Forwards:	**DOB**	**M**	**(s)**	**G**
André Morgan Rami Ayew (GHA)	17.12.1989	22	(7)	5
Yassine Benzia (ALG)	08.09.1994	8	(5)	
Michael Frey (SUI)	19.07.1994	5	(9)	3
Giuliano Victor de Paula (BRA)	31.05.1990	1		1
Victor Moses (NGA)	12.12.1990	8	(6)	4
Islam Slimani (ALG)	18.06.1988	14	(1)	1
Roberto Soldado Rillo (ESP)	27.05.1985	17	(4)	6
Yusuf Tunç	18.09.2000			
Trainer:	**DOB**	**M**		
Phillip John William Cocu (NED)	29.10.1970	10		
Erwin Koeman (NED) [28.10.2018]	20.09.1961	5		
Ersun Yanal [14.12.2018]	17.12.1961	19		

Galatasaray Spor Kulübü İstanbul

Founded: 30.10.1905 (*as Galata-Serai Football Club*)
Stadium: Türk Telekom Stadyumu, Istanbul (52,652)

Goalkeepers:	**DOB**	**M**	**(s)**	**G**
İsmail Çipe	05.01.1995	1	(1)	
Néstor Fernando Muslera Micol (URU)	16.06.1986	33		
Defenders:	**DOB**	**M**	**(s)**	**G**
Serdar Aziz	23.10.1990	10		2
Ömer Bayram	27.07.1991	7	(5)	1
Ahmet Çalık	26.02.1994	5	(2)	
Ozan Kabak	25.03.2000	12	(1)	
Semih Kaya	24.02.1991	3	(2)	
Martin Linnes (NOR)	20.09.1991	11	(8)	2
Christian Luyindama Nekadio(COD)	08.01.1994	11		
Maicon Pereira Roque (BRA)	14.09.1988	11	(4)	1
Marcos do Nascimento Teixeira „Marcão“ (BRA)	05.06.1996	15		
Mariano Ferreira Filho (BRA)	23.06.1986	28	(2)	
Yuto Nagatomo (JPN)	12.09.1986	17		1
Emre Taşdemir	08.08.1995	5	(2)	
Midfielders:	**DOB**	**M**	**(s)**	**G**
Emre Akbaba	04.10.1992	9	(7)	2
Younès Belhanda (MAR)	25.02.1990	23	(1)	4
Ryan Donk (NED)	30.03.1986	17	(5)	2
Sofiane Féghouli (ALG)	26.12.1989	24	(5)	9
Fernando Francisco Reges (BRA)	25.07.1987	21	(1)	2
Gökay Güney	19.05.1999		(1)	
Selçuk İnan	10.02.1985	9	(13)	
Mustafa Kapı	08.08.2002		(1)	
Papa Alioune N'Diaye (SEN)	27.10.1990	22	(1)	3
Garry Mendes Rodrigues (CPV)	27.11.1990	10	(2)	3
Celil Yüksel	01.01.1998		(2)	
Forwards:	**DOB**	**M**	**(s)**	**G**
Yunus Akgün	07.07.2000	1	(10)	
Muğdat Çelik	03.01.1990	2	(8)	2
Eren Derdiyok (SUI)	12.06.1988	11	(2)	7
Mbaye Diagne (SEN)	28.10.1991	11	(1)	10
Bafétimbi Gomis (FRA)	06.08.1985		(1)	
Sinan Gümüş (GER)	15.01.1994	14	(5)	4
Konstantinos Mitroglou (GRE)	12.03.1988	3	(4)	1
Henry Chukwuemeka Onyekuru(NGA)	05.06.1997	28	(3)	14
Trainer:	**DOB**	**M**		
Fatih Terim	04.09.1953	34		

Göztepe Spor Kulübü İzmir

Founded: 14.06.1925 (*as Göztepe Gençlik Kulübü*)
Stadium: Bornova Stadyumu, İzmir (12,500)

Goalkeepers:	**DOB**	**M**	**(s)**	**G**
Mehmet Bakırbaş	01.06.1996	1	(1)	
António Alberto Bastos Pimparel „Beto“ (POR)	01.05.1982	33		
Defenders:	**DOB**	**M**	**(s)**	**G**
Lumor Agbenyenu (GHA)	15.08.1996	8	(1)	
Hakan Çinemre	13.02.1994		(1)	
Berkan Emir	06.02.1988	19	(4)	
Lamine Gassama (SEN)	20.10.1989	27	(1)	
Ricardo Martins de Araújo „Kadu“ (BRA)	20.07.1986	6	(1)	
Cristian Chagas Tarouco „Titi“ (BRA)	12.03.1988	32		
Adama Traoré (CIV)	03.02.1990	8		
Wallace Reis da Silva (BRA)	26.12.1987	27	(1)	1
Midfielders:	**DOB**	**M**	**(s)**	**G**
Halil Akbunar	09.10.1993	25	(3)	3
Tayfur Bingöl	11.01.1993	11	(10)	
André Biyogo Poko (GAB)	07.03.1993	22	(5)	1
Celso Borges Mora (CRC)	27.05.1988	27	(5)	1
André Castro Pereira (POR)	02.04.1988	30	(1)	1
Serdar Gürler	14.09.1991	12	(3)	2
Yalçın Kayan	30.01.1999		(2)	
Axel Ngando (FRA)	13.07.1993	1	(13)	1
Yasin Öztekin	19.03.1987	21	(5)	8
Alpaslan Öztürk	16.07.1993	17	(8)	3
Forwards:	**DOB**	**M**	**(s)**	**G**
Sokol Çikalleshi (ALB)	27.07.1990		(7)	
Nabil Ghilas (ALG)	20.04.1990	3	(5)	1
Yoan Gouffran (FRA)	25.05.1986	6	(10)	1
Cameron Jerome (ENG)	14.08.1986	23	(5)	5
Deniz Kadah	02.03.1986	15	(7)	7
Samed Kaya	10.09.1995		(3)	
Trainer:	**DOB**	**M**		
Bayram Kadir Bektaş	10.02.1974	15		
Kemal Özdeş [10.12.2018]	10.05.1970	7		
Tamer Tuna [26.02.2019]	01.07.1976	12		

İstanbul Başakşehir Futbol Kulübü

Founded: 1990 (*as İstanbul Büyükşehir Belediyespor*); re-founded 05.06.2004
Stadium: Başakşehir „Fatih Terim“ Stadyumu, Istanbul (17,801)

Goalkeepers:	DOB	M	(s)	G
Volkan Babacan	11.08.1988		(1)	
Mert Günok	01.03.1989	34		
Defenders:	**DOB**	**M**	**(s)**	**G**
Gaël Clichy (FRA)	26.07.1985	25		1
Manuel Da Costa (MAR)	06.05.1986	12		3
Alexandru Epureanu (MDA)	27.09.1986	22		2
Uilson de Souza Paula Junior „Junior Caiçara“ (BRA)	27.04.1989	33		
Fedor Kudryashov (RUS)	05.04.1987	8		1
Serdar Taşçı (GER)	24.04.1987	4		
Uğur Uçar	05.04.1987	5		
Midfielders:	**DOB**	**M**	**(s)**	**G**
Joseph Attamah (GHA)	22.05.1994	7	(4)	
Soner Aydoğdu	05.01.1991	5	(13)	
Emre Belözoğlu	07.09.1980	19	(5)	1
Kerim Frei	19.11.1993	4	(4)	
Gökhan Inler (SUI)	27.06.1984	7	(5)	
Miloš Jojić (SRB)	19.03.1992	2	(6)	
İrfan Kahveci	15.07.1995	31	(1)	4
José Márcio da Costa „Márcio Mossoró“ (BRA)	04.07.1983	24	(5)	3
Mahmut Tekdemir	20.01.1988	32		
Arda Turan	30.01.1987	8	(6)	
Edin Višća (BIH)	17.02.1990	34		13
Forwards:	**DOB**	**M**	**(s)**	**G**
Emmanuel Adebayor (TOG)	26.02.1984	8	(11)	3
Demba Ba (SEN)	25.05.1985		(5)	2
Rijad Bajić (BIH)	06.05.1994	11	(11)	6
Eljero George Rinaldo Elia (NED)	13.02.1987	12	(9)	1
Stefano Napoleoni (ITA)	26.06.1986	13	(13)	3
Róbson de Souza „Robinho“ (BRA)	25.01.1984	14	(3)	4
Trainer:	**DOB**	**M**		
Abdullah Avcı	31.07.1963	34		

Kasımpaşa Spor Kulübü

Founded: 15.01.1921
Stadium: „Recep Tayyip Erdoğan“ Stadyumu, Istanbul (14,234)

Goalkeepers:	DOB	M	(s)	G
Ramazan Köse	12.05.1988	25		
Simone Scuffet (ITA)	31.05.1996	9	(1)	
Defenders:	**DOB**	**M**	**(s)**	**G**
Syam Ben Youssef (TUN)	31.03.1989	32		2
Özgür Çek	03.01.1991	5	(16)	
Karim Hafez Ramadan Seif Eldin (EGY)	12.03.1996	7	(6)	
Josué Humberto Gonçalves de Sá (POR)	17.06.1992	13	(4)	1
Loret Sadiku (ALB)	28.07.1991	28	(1)	1
Olivier Veigneau (FRA)	16.07.1985	24	(3)	
Midfielders:	**DOB**	**M**	**(s)**	**G**
Hakan Demir	08.05.1998		(7)	
İlhan Depe	10.09.1992	12	(8)	
Haris Hajradinović (BIH)	18.02.1994	11	(5)	1
Tobias Heintz (NOR)	13.07.1998		(8)	
Abdul Khalili (SWE)	07.06.1992	6	(2)	2
David Pavelka (CZE)	18.05.1991	26	(2)	1
Strahil Popov (BUL)	31.08.1990	33		
Veysel Sarı	25.07.1988	26	(2)	1
Tarkan Serbest	02.05.1994	27	(6)	2
Azad Toptik	12.02.1999		(1)	
Mahmoud Ahmed Ibrahim Hassan „Trezeguet“ (EGY)	01.10.1994	34		9
Onur Ural	22.02.1997	1	(1)	
Uğurcan Yazğılı	09.04.1999		(1)	
Forwards:	**DOB**	**M**	**(s)**	**G**
Hasan Bilal	12.03.1998		(4)	
Mbaye Diagne (SEN)	28.10.1991	17		20
Samuel Eduok (NGA)	31.01.1994	16	(2)	5
Mustafa Ethem Erboğa	11.01.1999		(2)	
Bengali-Fodé Koita (FRA)	21.10.1990	15	(10)	5
Stipe Perica (CRO)	07.07.1995	7	(5)	2
Trainer:	**DOB**	**M**		
Kemal Özdeş	10.05.1970	7		
Mustafa Denizli [04.10.2018]	10.11.1949	25		
Ilyas Öztürk [15.05.2019]	20.01.1969	2		

Kayseri Spor Kulübü

Founded: 1966
Stadium: „Kadir Has“ Stadyumu, Kayseri (32,864)

Goalkeepers:	DOB	M	(s)	G
Silviu Lung jr. (ROU)	04.06.1989	29		
Muammer Yıldırım	14.09.1990	5	(2)	
Defenders:	**DOB**	**M**	**(s)**	**G**
Sakıb Aytaç	24.11.1991	3		
Adem Doğan	05.10.2001		(1)	
Levent Gülen (SUI)	24.02.1994	13	(13)	
Jean-Armel Kana-Biyik (CMR)	03.07.1989	29		
Oleksandr Kucher (UKR)	22.10.1982	12	(8)	
Mert Özyildirim	28.02.1995	1	(7)	
Cristian Ionuț Săpunaru (ROU)	05.04.1984	30	(1)	2
Tiago Jorge Oliveira Lopes (POR)	04.01.1989	30		
Atila Turan (FRA)	10.04.1992	24	(3)	
Midfielders:	**DOB**	**M**	**(s)**	**G**
Hasan Acar	16.12.1994	11	(6)	3
Tjaronn Chery (NED)	04.06.1988	33		9
Samil Çinaz (GER)	08.03.1986	22	(3)	2
Hakan Çıtak	02.03.1999		(2)	
Emre Demir	15.01.2004		(1)	
Nurettin Korkmaz	27.06.2002	1		
Bernard Mensah (GHA)	17.10.1994	22	(2)	3
Rajko Rotman (SVN)	19.03.1989	10		
Deniz Türüç	29.01.1993	26		3
Forwards:	**DOB**	**M**	**(s)**	**G**
Bilal Başaçıkoğlu	26.03.1995	14	(8)	
Umut Bulut	15.03.1983	28		2
Kazim Çelik	06.01.2000		(1)	
Asamoah Gyan (GHA)	22.11.1985		(14)	4
Artem Kravets (UKR)	03.06.1989	15	(8)	5
Silvestre Manuel Gonçalves Varela (POR)	02.02.1985	16	(16)	1
Trainer:	**DOB**	**M**		
Ertuğrul Sağlam	19.11.1969	14		
Hikmet Karaman [06.12.2018]	09.03.1960	20		

Konyaspor Kulübü

Founded: 22.06.1922
Stadium: Konya Büyükşehir Stadyumu, Konya (42,276)

Goalkeepers:	**DOB**	**M**	**(s)**	**G**
Serkan Kırıntılı	15.02.1985	33		
Ertuğrul Taşkıran	05.11.1989	1		
Defenders:	**DOB**	**M**	**(s)**	**G**
Selim Ay	31.07.1991	6	(1)	
Uğur Demirok	08.07.1988	24	(1)	1
Fallou Diagné (SEN)	14.08.1989	11	(2)	
Petar Filipović (CRO)	14.09.1990	11	(1)	1
Volkan Fındıklı	13.10.1990	19	(3)	1
Jens Jønsson (DEN)	10.01.1993	21	(1)	4
Evgeniy Opanasenko (UKR)	25.08.1990	6	(3)	
Ferhat Öztorun	08.05.1987	18	(1)	
Nejc Skubic (SVN)	13.06.1989	31		2
Ali Turan	06.09.1983	14	(1)	
Leonard Zuta (MKD)	09.08.1992	12		
Midfielders:	**DOB**	**M**	**(s)**	**G**
Vedat Bora	17.01.1995	1	(4)	
Ali Çamdalı	22.02.1984		(3)	
Amir Hadžiahmetović (BIH)	08.03.1997	6	(8)	
Marko Jevtović (SRB)	24.07.1993	27	(2)	2
Deni Milošević (BIH)	09.03.1995	28	(5)	1
Wilfred Moke (COD)	12.02.1988	3	(3)	
Ömer Şahiner	02.01.1992	26	(1)	8
Abdou Traoré (BFA)	28.12.1988	14	(7)	
Forwards:	**DOB**	**M**	**(s)**	**G**
Mücahit Akçay	13.04.1998	3	(5)	
Moryké Fofana (CIV)	23.11.1991	21	(11)	6
Cristopher Paolo César Hurtado Huertas (PER)	27.07.1990	2	(13)	2
Adis Jahović (MKD)	18.03.1987	19	(9)	6
Mustapha Yatabaré (MLI)	26.01.1986	17	(12)	5
Trainer:	**DOB**	**M**		
Rıza Çalımbay	02.02.1963	12		
Aykut Kocaman [19.11.2018]	05.04.1965	22		

Sivasspor Kulübü

Founded: 09.05.1967
Stadium: Sivas Arena, Sivas (27,532)

Goalkeepers:	**DOB**	**M**	**(s)**	**G**
Tolgahan Acar	04.06.1986	26		
Ali Vural	10.07.1990	8		
Defenders:	**DOB**	**M**	**(s)**	**G**
Fatih Aksoy	06.11.1997	3	(5)	1
Mattias Bjärsmyr (SWE)	03.01.1986	27	(1)	
Uğur Çiftçi	04.05.1992	18	(3)	
David Braz Oliveira Filho (BRA)	21.05.1987	30	(1)	3
Douglas Pereira dos Santos (BRA)	06.08.1990	32		3
Ziya Erdal	05.01.1988	23	(4)	
Carl Medjani (FRA)	15.05.1985	13	(2)	
Paul Papp (ROU)	11.11.1989	9	(7)	
Midfielders:	**DOB**	**M**	**(s)**	**G**
Hakan Arslan	18.07.1988	33		3
Özer Hurmacı	20.11.1986	8	(4)	1
Emre Kılınç	23.08.1994	31		7
Delvin N'Dinga (CGO)	14.03.1988	21	(1)	1
Serhiy Rybalka (UKR)	01.04.1990	23	(5)	4
İlker Sayan	04.05.1993		(2)	
Gabriel Andrei Torje (ROU)	22.11.1989	7	(12)	
Mert Hakan Yandaş	19.08.1994	2	(7)	
Erdoğan Yeşilyurt	06.11.1993	1	(17)	1
Forwards:	**DOB**	**M**	**(s)**	**G**
Cyriac Gohi Bi Zoro Sede (CIV)	15.08.1990		(6)	
Muhammed Demir	10.01.1992	12	(10)	4
Fousséni Diabaté (MLI)	18.10.1995	16	(1)	2
Aydin Karabulut	25.01.1988		(1)	
Arouna Koné (CIV)	11.11.1983	15	(11)	10
Robson de Souza „Robinho“ (BRA)	25.01.1984	16		8
Trainer:	**DOB**	**M**		
Tamer Tuna	01.07.1976	12		
Hakan Keleş [19.11.2018]	08.01.1972	22		

Trabzonspor Kulübü

Founded: 02.08.1967
Stadium: „Şenol Güneş“ Stadyumu, Trabzon (41,513)

Goalkeepers:	**DOB**	**M**	**(s)**	**G**
Arda Akbulut	01.01.2001	2		
Uğurcan Çakir	05.04.1996	20		
Onur Kıvrak	01.01.1988	12		
Defenders:	**DOB**	**M**	**(s)**	**G**
Mustafa Akbaş	30.05.1990	4		
Majid Hosseini (IRN)	20.06.1996	23	(2)	
Luis Ezequiel Ibáñez (ARG)	15.07.1988	3	(2)	
João Pedro da Silva Pereira (POR)	25.02.1984	21	(1)	
Ali Karnapoğlu	30.04.1999		(1)	
Filip Novák (CZE)	26.06.1990	29		5
Zargo Touré (SEN)	11.11.1989	22	(5)	
Hüseyin Türkmen	01.01.1998	22	(1)	
Midfielders:	**DOB**	**M**	**(s)**	**G**
Murat Akpinar	24.01.1999		(6)	1
Batuhan Artarslan	25.05.1994		(9)	
Kâmil Çörekçi	01.02.1992	11		
Berkay Kara	27.03.1999		(1)	
Juraj Kucka (SVK)	26.02.1987	2	(6)	
Abdülkadir Ömür	25.06.1999	25	(4)	5
Ogenyi Onazi (NGA)	25.12.1992	16		2
Abdülkadir Parmak	28.12.1994	13	(5)	2
Olcay Şahan	26.05.1987	10	(9)	2
José Ernesto Sosa (ARG)	19.06.1985	29		5
Zeki Yavru	05.09.1991	1		
Yusuf Yazıcı	29.01.1997	28	(2)	4
Forwards:	**DOB**	**M**	**(s)**	**G**
Vahid Amiri (IRN)	02.04.1988	8	(14)	1
Caleb Ekuban (GHA)	23.03.1994	12	(17)	5
Anthony Nnaduzor Nwakaeme (NGA)	21.03.1989	25	(2)	10
Hugo Rodallega Martínez (COL)	25.07.1985	30	(3)	15
Burak Yılmaz	15.07.1985	6	(1)	5
Trainer:	**DOB**	**M**		
Ünal Karaman	29.06.1966	34		

Yeni Malatya Spor Kulübü

Founded: 1986
Stadium: Malatya Arena, Malatya (27,044)

Goalkeepers:	DOB	M	(s)	G
Fabien Farnolle (BEN)	21.09.1984	20		
Ertaç Özbir	25.10.1989	14		
Defenders:	**DOB**	**M**	**(s)**	**G**
Mustafa Akbaş	30.05.1990	11	(1)	
Murat Akça	13.07.1990	14		
Gökhan Akkan	30.08.1998		(1)	
Bülent Cevahir	13.02.1992	12	(1)	
Issam Chebake (MAR)	12.10.1989	26	(3)	
Sadık Çiftpinar	01.01.1993	16		
Arturo Rafael Mina Meza (ECU)	08.10.1990	24	(2)	3
Muenfuh Sincere Seth (NGA)	28.04.1998	10		
Midfielders:	**DOB**	**M**	**(s)**	**G**
Barış Alıcı	24.06.1997	1	(5)	
Buğra Çağıran	01.01.1995	8	(7)	
Mitchell Donald (NED)	10.12.1988	23	(3)	5
Mustafa Eskihellac	05.05.1997		(5)	
Guilherme Costa Marques (BRA)	21.05.1991	26	(4)	5
Ahmed Ildız	29.11.1996	12	(11)	1
Erkan Kaş	10.09.1991	14	(3)	
Sulley Muniru (GHA)	25.10.1992	1	(4)	
Mickaël Pereira (FRA)	08.12.1987	12	(11)	
Robin Yalcin (GER)	25.01.1994	7	(4)	1
Murat Yıldırım	18.05.1987	26	(2)	
Forwards:	**DOB**	**M**	**(s)**	**G**
Danijel Aleksić (SRB)	30.04.1991	28	(4)	10
Thievy Bifouma (CGO)	13.05.1992	7	(3)	2
Khalid Boutaïb (MAR)	24.04.1987	13	(3)	4
Adem Büyük	30.08.1987	27		6
Issiar Dia (FRA)	08.06.1987	1	(1)	
Aboubakar Kamara (FRA)	07.03.1995	7	(3)	1
Ömer Şişmanoğlu	01.08.1989	6	(10)	5
Eren Tozlu	27.12.1990	8	(11)	3
Trainer:	**DOB**	**M**		
Erol Bulut	30.01.1975	30		
Ali Ravcı [30.04.2019]	01.01.1973	4		

SECOND LEVEL
TFF First League 2018/2019

1.	Denizlispor Kulübü (*Promoted*)	34	21	9	4	67	-	32	72
2.	Gençlerbirliği SK Ankara (*Promoted*)	34	22	4	8	50	-	28	70
3.	Hatayspor Antakya (*Promotion Play-offs*)	34	19	10	5	57	-	22	67
4.	Osmanlıspor FK Ankara (*Promotion Play-offs*)	34	19	5	10	49	-	26	62
5.	Gazişehir Gaziantep FK (*Promotion Play-offs*)	34	17	8	9	60	-	31	59
6.	Adana Demirspor Kulübü (*Promotion Play-offs*)	34	17	7	10	50	-	36	58
7.	Altınordu FK İzmir	34	16	9	9	50	-	33	57
8.	Ümraniyespor Kulübü	34	14	11	9	44	-	37	53
9.	Boluspor Kulübü	34	14	7	13	41	-	41	49
10.	Altay SK İzmir	34	12	11	11	52	-	40	47
11.	İstanbulspor	34	10	13	11	45	-	46	43
12.	Adanaspor AŞ	34	9	10	15	41	-	49	37
13.	Giresunspor Kulübü	34	8	12	14	32	-	41	36
14.	Eskişehirspor Kulübü	34	9	8	17	44	-	66	35
15.	Balıkesirspor Kulübü Derneği(1)	34	11	7	16	36	-	45	34
16.	Afjet Afyonspor Kulübü (*Relegated*)	34	7	9	18	38	-	55	30
17.	Elazığspor Kulübü Derneği (*Relegated*)	34	6	7	21	38	-	64	25
18.	Kardemir Demir Çelik Karabükspor(2) (*Relegated*)	34	0	3	31	10	-	112	0

(1) *6 points deducted*
(2) *3 points deducted*

Relegation Play-offs

Adana Demirspor Kulübü - Hatayspor Antakya	0-0	2-3
Gazişehir Gaziantep FK - Osmanlıspor FK Ankara	2-0	0-2; 9-8 pen
Hatayspor Antakya - Gazişehir Gaziantep FK	1-1; 3-5 pen	

Gazişehir Gaziantep FK promoted to the 2019/2020 Süper Lig.

NATIONAL TEAM

INTERNATIONAL MATCHES
(16.07.2018 – 15.07.2019)

07.09.2018	Trabzon	Turkey - Russia	1-2(1-1)	(UNL)
10.09.2018	Stockholm	Sweden - Turkey	2-3(1-0)	(UNL)
11.10.2018	Rize	Turkey - Bosnia and Herzegovina	0-0	(F)
14.10.2018	Sochi	Russia - Turkey	2-0(1-0)	(UNL)
17.11.2018	Konya	Turkey - Sweden	0-1(0-0)	(UNL)
20.11.2018	Antalya	Turkey - Ukraine	0-0	(F)
22.03.2019	Shkodër	Albania - Turkey	0-2(0-1)	(ECQ)
25.03.2019	Eskişehir	Turkey - Moldova	4-0(2-0)	(ECQ)
30.05.2019	Antalya	Turkey - Greece	2-1(2-0)	(F)
02.06.2019	Alanya	Turkey - Uzbekistan	2-0(1-0)	(F)
08.06.2019	Konya	Turkey - France	2-0(2-0)	(ECQ)
11.06.2019	Reykjavík	Iceland - Turkey	2-1(2-1)	(ECQ)

07.09.2018 TURKEY - RUSSIA 1-2(1-1) UEFA Nations League B, Group 2
Medical Park Stadyumu, Trabzon; Referee: Artur Manuel Soares Dias (Portugal); Attendance: 27,423
TUR: Serkan Kırıntılı, Serdar Aziz (46.Kaan Ayhan), Hasan Ali Kaldırım, Şener Özbayraklı, Çağlar Söyüncü, Mehmet Topal (Cap) (71.Yunus Mallı), Okay Yokuşlu, Hakan Çalhanoğlu, Cengiz Ünder, Yusuf Yazıcı (57.Oğuzhan Özyakup), Cenk Tosun. Trainer: Mircea Lucescu (Romania).
Goal: Serdar Aziz (41).

10.09.2018 SWEDEN - TURKEY 2-3(1-0) UEFA Nations League B, Group 2
Friends Arena, Stockholm; Referee: Jesús Gil Manzano (Spain); Attendance: 21,832
TUR: Sinan Bolat, Ömer Bayram , Kaan Ayhan, Zeki Çelik, Çağlar Söyüncü, Oğuzhan Özyakup, Mehmet Topal (Cap) (62.Emre Akbaba), Okay Yokuşlu, Hakan Çalhanoğlu (86.Yunus Mallı), Cengiz Ünder (77.Serdar Gürler), Cenk Tosun. Trainer: Mircea Lucescu (Romania).
Goals: Hakan Çalhanoğlu (51), Emre Akbaba (88, 90+2).

11.10.2018 TURKEY - BOSNIA AND HERZEGOVINA 0-0 Friendly International
"Yeni Rize Şehir" Stadyumu, Rize; Referee: Sergei Karasev (Russia); Attendance: 15,196
TUR: Sinan Bolat, Ömer Bayram, Şener Özbayraklı (86.Mert Müldür), Kaan Ayhan (82.Ertugrul Ersoy), Çağlar Söyüncü, Mahmut Tekdemir (65.Yunus Mallı), Oğuzhan Özyakup (Cap) (86.Berkay Özcan), Okay Yokuşlu, Hakan Çalhanoğlu, Cengiz Ünder (80.Serdar Gürler), Enes Ünal (46.Cenk Tosun). Trainer: Mircea Lucescu (Romania).

14.10.2018 RUSSIA - TURKEY 2-0(1-0) UEFA Nations League B, Group 2
Fisht Olympic Stadium, Sochi; Referee: Paweł Raczkowski (Poland); Attendance: 38,288
TUR: Sinan Bolat, Serdar Aziz, Hasan Ali Kaldırım (75.Ömer Bayram), Zeki Çelik, Çağlar Söyüncü, Mahmut Tekdemir (63.Berkay Özcan), Oğuzhan Özyakup (Cap) (84.Yunus Mallı), Okay Yokuşlu, Hakan Çalhanoğlu, Cengiz Ünder, Cenk Tosun. Trainer: Mircea Lucescu (Romania).

17.11.2018 TURKEY - SWEDEN 0-1(0-0) UEFA Nations League B, Group 2
Büyükşehir Stadium, Konya; Referee: István Kovács (Romania); Attendance: 37,425
TUR: Sinan Bolat, Kaan Ayhan, Hasan Ali Kaldırım (87.Ömer Bayram), Zeki Çelik, Çağlar Söyüncü, Mahmut Tekdemir (72.İrfan Can Kahveci), Yunus Mallı (83.Oğuzhan Özyakup), Hakan Çalhanoğlu (Cap), Okay Yokuşlu, Cengiz Ünder, Cenk Tosun. Trainer: Mircea Lucescu (Romania).

20.11.2018 TURKEY - UKRAINE 0-0 Friendly International
Antalya Stadyumu, Antalya; Referee: Genc Nuza (Kosovo); Attendance: 25,000
TUR: Sinan Bolat, Kaan Ayhan (54.Ertugrul Ersoy), Ömer Bayram, Çağlar Söyüncü, Mert Müldür (85.Merih Demiral), Yunus Mallı (74.Mehmet Topal), Oğuzhan Özyakup (Cap) (46.Serdar Gürler), Okay Yokuşlu, İrfan Can Kahveci (89.Aytaç Kara), Cengiz Ünder, Enes Ünal (46.Cenk Tosun). Trainer: Mircea Lucescu (Romania).

22.03.2019 ALBANIA - TURKEY 0-2(0-1) 16th EC. Qualifiers
Stadiumi "Loro Boriçi", Shkodër; Referee: Tobias Stieler (Germany); Attendance: 11,730
TUR: Fehmi Mert Günok, Gökhan Gönül (46.Zeki Çelik), Hasan Ali Kaldırım, Kaan Ayhan, Merih Demiral, Emre Belözoğlu (Cap) (65.Dorukhan Toköz), Mahmut Tekdemir, Okay Yokuşlu, Hakan Çalhanoğlu, Burak Yılmaz (88.Deniz Türüç), Cenk Tosun. Trainer: Şenol Güneş.
Goals: Burak Yılmaz (21), Hakan Çalhanoğlu (55).

25.03.2019 TURKEY - MOLDOVA 4-0(2-0) 16th EC. Qualifiers
"Yeni Atatürk" Stadyumu, Eskişehir; Referee: Serhiy Boyko (Ukraine); Attendance: 29,456
TUR: Fehmi Mert Günok, Hasan Ali Kaldırım, Kaan Ayhan, Zeki Çelik, Mahmut Tekdemir, Merih Demiral, Dorukhan Toköz (84.Emre Belözoğlu), Hakan Çalhanoğlu (66.Yusuf Yazıcı), Burak Yılmaz (Cap), Deniz Türüç (78.Efecan Karaca), Cenk Tosun. Trainer: Şenol Güneş.
Goals: Hasan Ali Kaldırım (24), Cenk Tosun (26, 53), Kaan Ayhan (70).

30.05.2019 TURKEY - GREECE 2-1(2-0) Friendly International
Antalya Stadyumu, Antalya; Referee: Radu Petrescu (Romania); Attendance: n/a
TUR: Uğurcan Çakır, Kaan Ayhan, Nazim Sangaré, Çağlar Söyüncü, Cengiz Umut Meraş, Okay Yokuşlu (61.Mahmut Tekdemir), Ozan Tufan (46.Oğuzhan Özyakup), Yusuf Yazıcı (46.İrfan Can Kahveci), Cengiz Ünder (80.Emre Belözoğlu), Kenan Karaman (46.Abdülkadir Ömür), Cenk Tosun (Cap) (55.Güven Yalçın). Trainer: Şenol Güneş.
Goals: Cengiz Ünder (11), Kenan Karaman (17).

02.06.2019 TURKEY - UZBEKISTAN 2-0(1-0) Friendly International
"Bahçeşehir Okulları" Arena, Alanya; Referee: Srđan Jovanović (Serbia); Attendance: 9,000
TUR: Sinan Bolat, Emre Taşdemir, Zeki Çelik, Çağlar Söyüncü, Merih Demiral, Efecan Karaca (46.Ömer Ali Şahiner), Yunus Mallı (46.Kenan Karaman), Oğuzhan Özyakup (Cap) (65.Abdülkadir Ömür), İrfan Can Kahveci (90+1.Emre Belözoğlu), Dorukhan Toköz (83.Deniz Türüç), Enes Ünal (66.Ozan Tufan). Trainer: Şenol Güneş.
Goals: Zeki Çelik (17, 57).

08.06.2019 **TURKEY - FRANCE** **2-0(2-0)** 16th EC. Qualifiers
Büyükşehir Stadium, Konya; Referee: Damir Skomina (Slovenia); Attendance: 36,783
TUR: Fehmi Mert Günok, Kaan Ayhan, Hasan Ali Kaldırım, Zeki Çelik, Merih Demiral, Mahmut Tekdemir, Dorukhan Toköz (90.Abdülkadir Ömür), Cengiz Ünder (85.Yusuf Yazıcı), İrfan Can Kahveci (80.Ozan Tufan), Burak Yılmaz (Cap), Kenan Karaman. Trainer: Şenol Güneş.
Goals: Kaan Ayhan (30), Cengiz Ünder (40).

11.06.2019 **ICELAND - TURKEY** **2-1(2-1)** 16th EC. Qualifiers
Laugardalsvöllur, Reykjavík; Referee: Szymon Marciniak (Poland); Attendance: 9,680
TUR: Fehmi Mert Günok, Hasan Ali Kaldırım, Kaan Ayhan, Zeki Çelik, Merih Demiral, Hakan Çalhanoğlu, İrfan Can Kahveci (63.Abdülkadir Ömür), Dorukhan Toköz (85.Güven Yalçın), Ozan Tufan, Burak Yılmaz (Cap), Kenan Karaman (46.Yusuf Yazıcı). Trainer: Şenol Güneş.
Goal: Dorukhan Toköz (40).

NATIONAL TEAM PLAYERS
(16.07.2018 – 15.07.2019)

Name	DOB	Caps	Goals	2018/2019:	*Club*
Goalkeepers					
FEHMI Mert Günok	01.03.1989	**10**	**0**	2019:	*İstanbul Başakşehir FK*
SERKAN Kırıntılı	15.02.1985	**4**	**0**	2018:	*Konyaspor Kulübü*
SINAN Bolat	03.09.1988	**12**	**0**	2018/2019:	*Antwerp FC (BEL)*
UĞURCAN Çakır	05.04.1996	**1**	**0**	2018/2019:	*Trabzonspor Kulübü*
Defenders					
ÇAĞLAR Söyüncü	23.05.1996	**24**	**1**	2018/2019:	*Leicester City FC (ENG)*
EMRE Taşdemir	08.08.1995	**5**	**0**	2019:	*Galatasaray SK İstanbul*
ERTUGRUL Ersoy	13.02.1997	**2**	**0**	2018:	*Bursaspor Kulübü*
GÖKHAN Gönül	04.01.1985	**66**	**1**	2019:	*Beşiktaş JK İstanbul*
HASAN Ali Kaldırım	09.12.1989	**32**	**1**	2018/2019:	*Fenerbahçe SK İstanbul*
KAAN Ayhan	10.11.1994	**23**	**2**	2018/2019:	*TSV Fortuna Düsseldorf (GER)*
MERIH Demiral	05.03.1998	**6**	**0**	2018:	*Alanyaspor*
				30.01.2019->	*US Sassuolo Calcio (ITA)*
MERT Müldür	03.04.1999	**2**	**0**	2018:	*SK Rapid Wien (AUT)*
NAZIM Sangaré	30.05.1994	**1**	**0**	2019:	*Antalyaspor Kulübü*
ÖMER Bayram	27.07.1991	**7**	**0**	2018:	*Galatasaray SK İstanbul*
ŞENER Özbayraklı	23.01.1990	**17**	**0**	2018:	*Fenerbahçe SK İstanbul*
SERDAR Aziz	23.10.1990	**17**	**1**	2018:	*Galatasaray SK İstanbul*
Cengiz UMUT Meraş	20.12.1995	**1**	**0**	2019:	*Bursaspor Kulübü*
ZEKI Çelik	17.02.1997	**9**	**2**	2018/2019:	*Lille OSC (FRA)*
Midfielders					
ABDÜLKADIR Ömür	25.06.1999	**4**	**0**	2019:	*Trabzonspor Kulübü*
AYTAÇ Kara	23.03.1993	**2**	**0**	2018:	*Bursaspor Kulübü*
BERKAY Özcan	15.02.1998	**3**	**0**	2018:	*VfB Stuttgart (GER)*
CENGIZ Ünder	14.07.1997	**19**	**6**	2018/2019:	*AS Roma (ITA)*
DENIZ Türüç	29.01.1993	**5**	**0**	2019:	*Kayserispor Kulübü*
DORUKHAN Toköz	21.05.1996	**5**	**1**	2019:	*Beşiktaş JK İstanbul*
EFECAN Karaca	16.11.1989	**2**	**0**	2019:	*Alanyaspor*
EMRE Akbaba	04.10.1992	**6**	**3**	2018:	*Galatasaray SK İstanbul*
EMRE Belözoğlu	07.09.1980	**99**	**9**	2018/2019:	*İstanbul Başakşehir FK*
HAKAN Çalhanoğlu	08.02.1994	**41**	**10**	2018/2019:	*AC Milan (ITA)*
İRFAN Can Kahveci	15.06.1995	**10**	**0**	2018/2019:	*İstanbul Başakşehir FK*
KENAN Karaman	05.03.1994	**7**	**1**	2018/2019:	*SV Hannover 96 (GER)*
MAHMUT Tekdemir	20.01.1988	**12**	**0**	2018/2019:	*İstanbul Başakşehir FK*
MEHMET Topal	03.03.1986	**81**	**2**	2018:	*Fenerbahçe SK İstanbul*
OĞUZHAN Özyakup	23.09.1992	**43**	**1**	2018/2019:	*Beşiktaş JK İstanbul*
OKAY Yokuşlu	09.03.1994	**22**	**1**	2018/2019:	*RC Celta de Vigo (ESP)*
OZAN Tufan	23.03.1995	**43**	**4**	2019:	*Alanyaspor*
ÖMER Ali Şahiner	02.01.1992	**1**	**0**	2019:	*Konyaspor Kulübü*
SERDAR Gürler	14.09.1991	**7**	**0**	2018:	*SD Huesca (ESP)*
YUNUS Mallı	24.02.1992	**25**	**1**	2018/2019:	*VfL Wolfsburg (GER)*
YUSUF Yazıcı	29.01.1997	**14**	**0**	2018/2019:	*Trabzonspor Kulübü*

Forwards

BURAK Yılmaz	15.07.1985	**56**	**24**	2019:	*Beşiktaş JK İstanbul*
CENK Tosun	07.06.1991	**38**	**13**	2018/2019:	*Everton FC Liverpool (ENG)*
ENES Ünal	10.05.1997	**12**	**0**	2018/2019:	*Real Valladolid CF (ESP)*
GÜVEN Yalçın	18.01.1999	**2**	**0**	2018/2019:	*Beşiktaş JK İstanbul*

National team coach

Mircea LUCESCU (Romania) [from 04.08.2017]	29.07.1945	11 M; 3 W; 4 D; 4 L; 13-18
ŞENOL Güneş [from 18.03.2019]	01.06.1952	6 M; 5 W; 0 D; 1 L; 13-3 Complete record as trainer of Turkey: 56 M; 28 W; 13 D; 15 L; 84-53 (16.08.2000 – 19.11.2003) & (from 18.03.2019)

UKRAINE

The Country:
Україна (Ukraine)
Capital: Kyiv
Surface: 603,628 km²
Inhabitants: 42,030,832 [2019]
Time: UTC+2

The FA:
Федерація Футболу України [Football Federation of Ukraine]
Provulok Laboratornyi, 7-A P.O. Box 55, 01133 Kyiv
Tel: +380 44 521 0535
Founded: 1991
Member of FIFA since: 1992
Member of UEFA since: 1992
Website: ffu.ua

NATIONAL TEAM RECORDS

First international match:	29.04.1992, Uzhgorod:	Ukraine – Hungary 1-3
Most international caps:	Anatoliy Tymoshchuk	- 144 caps (2000-2016)
Most international goals:	Andriy Shevchenko	- 48 goals / 111 caps (1995-2012)

UEFA EUROPEAN CHAMPIONSHIP	
1960	-
1964	-
1968	-
1972	-
1976	-
1980	-
1984	-
1988	-
1992	-
1996	Qualifiers
2000	Qualifiers
2004	Qualifiers
2008	Qualifiers
2012	Final Tournament (Group Stage)
2016	Final Tournament (Group Stage)

**was part of Soviet Union between 1930-1990*

FIFA WORLD CUP	
1930	-
1934	-
1938	-
1950	-
1954	-
1958	-
1962	-
1966	-
1970	-
1974	-
1978	-
1982	-
1986	-
1990	-
1994	Did not enter
1998	Qualifiers
2002	Qualifiers
2006	Final Tournament (Quarter-Finals)
2010	Qualifiers
2014	Qualifiers
2018	Qualifiers

UEFA NATIONS LEAGUE
2018/2019 – League B (promoted to League A)

OLYMPIC FOOTBALL TOURNAMENTS 1908-2016							
1908	-	**1948**	-	**1972**	-	**1996**	Qualifiers
1912	-	**1952**	-	**1976**	-	**2000**	Qualifiers
1920	-	**1956**	-	**1980**	-	**2004**	Qualifiers
1924	-	**1960**	-	**1984**	-	**2008**	Qualifiers
1928	-	**1964**	-	**1988**	-	**2012**	Qualifiers
1936	-	**1968**	-	**1992**	-	**2016**	Qualifiers

FIFA CONFEDERATIONS CUP 1992-2017
None

UKRAINIAN CLUB HONOURS IN EUROPEAN CLUB COMPETITIONS:

European Champion Clubs' Cup (1956-1992) / UEFA Champions League (1993-2019)		
None		
Fairs Cup (1858-1971) / UEFA Cup (1972-2009) / UEFA Europa League (2010-2019)		
FK Shakhtar Donetsk	**1**	2008/2009
UEFA Super Cup (1972-2018)		
FK Dinamo Kyiv*	**1**	1975
European Cup Winners' Cup 1961-1999*		
FK Dinamo Kyiv*	**2**	1974/1975, 1985/1986
**represented the Soviet Union*		

**defunct competition*

NATIONAL COMPETITIONS
TABLE OF HONOURS

Championship of cities

	CHAMPIONS
1921	Kharkiv
1922	Kharkiv
1923	Kharkiv
1924	Kharkiv
1925	*No competition*
1926	*No competition*
1927	Kharkiv
1928	Kharkiv
1929	*No competition*
1930	*No competition*
1931	Kyiv
1932	Kharkiv
1933	*No competition*
1934	Kharkiv
1935	Dnipropetrovsk

Championship of the Proletarian Sports Society Dinamo

	CHAMPIONS
1929	Dinamo Kharkiv
1931	Dinamo Kyiv
1932	Dinamo Kharkiv
1933	Dinamo Kyiv
1934	Dinamo Kharkiv
1935	Dinamo Kyiv

UKRAINIAN SSR (SOVIET ERA) CHAMPIONS

1936	Zavod Ordzhonikidze Kramators'k
1937	Spartak Dnipropetrovs'k
1938	Dzerzhynec Voroshylovgrad
1939	Lokomotyv Zaporizhzhya
1940	Lokomotyv Zaporizhzhya
1941-1945	*No competition*
1946	Spartak Uzhgorod
1947	Bil'shovyk Mukacheve
1948	Torpedo Odesa
1949	Pishevik Odesa
1950	Spartak Uzhgorod
1951	Budinok ofitseriv Kyiv
1952	Metalurg Zaporizhzhya
1953	Spartak Uzhgorod
1954	Mashinobudivnik Kyiv
1955	Spartak Stanislav
1956	Shakhtar Stakhanov
1957	SKVO Odesa
1958	Arsenal Kyiv
1959	Avangard Zhovti Vody
1960	Metalurg Zaporizhzhya
1961	Chornomorets Odesa
1962	Trudovi Rezervy Voroshylovgrad
1963	SKA Odesa
1964	Lokomotyv Vinnytsa
1965	SKA L'viv
1966	Avangard Zhovti Vody
1967	Avtomobilist Zhytomyr
1968	Avangard Ternopil
1969	Spartak Ivano-Frankivs'k
1970	Metalurg Zaporizhzhya
1971	Krivbas Kryvyi Rih
1972	Spartak Ivano-Frankivs'k
1973	Tavria Simferopil
1974	Sudostroitel Nikolaev
1975	Krivbas Kryvyi Rih
1976	Krivbas Kryvyi Rih
1977	SKA Odesa
1978	Metalist Kharkiv
1979	Kolos Nikopil
1980	SKA Kyiv
1981	Krivbas Kryvyi Rih
1982	Bukovyna Chernivtsi
1983	SKA Kyiv
1984	Nyva Vinnytsa
1985	Tavrya Simferopil
1986	Zarya Voroshylovgrad
1987	Tavrya Simferopil
1988	Bukovyna Chernivtsi
1989	Volyn Lutsk
1990	Bukovyna Chernivtsi
1991	Karpaty Lviv

	CHAMPIONS	CUP WINNERS	BEST GOALSCORERS	
1992	SC Tavriya Simferopol	FK Chornomorets Odesa	Yuriy Hudymenko (SC Tavriya Simferopol)	12
1992/1993	FK Dinamo Kyiv	FK Dinamo Kyiv	Serhiy Husyev (FK Chornomorets Odesa)	17
1993/1994	FK Dinamo Kyiv	FK Chornomorets Odesa	Tymerlan Huseinov (FK Chornomorets Odesa)	18
1994/1995	FK Dinamo Kyiv	FK Shakhtar Donetsk	Arsen Avakov (TJK, FK Metalurh Zaporizhya)	21
1995/1996	FK Dinamo Kyiv	FK Dinamo Kyiv	Tymerlan Huseinov (FK Chornomorets Odesa)	20
1996/1997	FK Dinamo Kyiv	FK Shakhtar Donetsk	Oleh Matveyev (FK Shakhtar Donetsk)	21
1997/1998	FK Dinamo Kyiv	FK Dinamo Kyiv	Serhiy Rebrov (FK Dinamo Kyiv)	22
1998/1999	FK Dinamo Kyiv	FK Dinamo Kyiv	Andriy Shevchenko (FK Dinamo Kyiv)	18
1999/2000	FK Dinamo Kyiv	FK Dinamo Kyiv	Maksim Shatskikh (UZB, FK Dinamo Kyiv)	20
2000/2001	FK Dinamo Kyiv	FK Shakhtar Donetsk	Andrij Vorobej (FK Shakhtar Donetsk)	21
2001/2002	FK Shakhtar Donetsk	FK Shakhtar Donetsk	Serhiy Shyshchenko (FK Metalurh Donetsk)	12
2002/2003	FK Dinamo Kyiv	FK Dinamo Kyiv	Maksim Shatskikh (UZB, FK Dinamo Kyiv)	22
2003/2004	FK Dinamo Kyiv	FK Shakhtar Donetsk	Giorgi Demetradze (GEO, FK Metalurh Donetsk)	18
2004/2005	FK Shakhtar Donetsk	FK Dinamo Kyiv	Olexandr Kosyrin (FK Chornomorets Odesa)	14
2005/2006	FK Shakhtar Donetsk	FK Dinamo Kyiv	Evaeverson Lemos da Silva "Brandão" (FK Shakhtar Donetsk) Emmanuel Osei Okoduwa (NGA, FK Arsenal Kyiv)	15
2006/2007	FK Dinamo Kyiv	FK Dinamo Kyiv	Oleksandr Hladkyi (FK Kharkhiv)	13
2007/2008	FK Shakhtar Donetsk	FK Shakhtar Donetsk	Marko Dević (FK Metalist Kharkhiv)	19
2008/2009	FK Dinamo Kyiv	FK Vorskla Poltava	Olexander Kowpak (SC Tavriya Simferopol)	17
2009/2010	FK Shakhtar Donetsk	SC Tavriya Simferopol	Artem Milevsky (FK Dinamo Kyiv)	17
2010/2011	FK Shakhtar Donetsk	FK Shakhtar Donetsk	Yevhen Seleznyov (FC Dnipro Dnipropetrovsk)	17
2011/2012	FK Shakhtar Donetsk	FK Shakhtar Donetsk	Yevhen Seleznyov (FK Shakhtar Donetsk) Maicon Pereira de Oliveira (VRA, FK Volyn Lutsk)	14
2012/2013	FK Shakhtar Donetsk	FK Shakhtar Donetsk	Henrikh Mkhitaryan (ARM, FK Shakhtar Donetsk)	25
2013/2014	FK Shakhtar Donetsk	FK Dinamo Kyiv	Luiz Adriano de Souza da Silva (FK Shakhtar Donetsk)	20
2014/2015	FK Dinamo Kyiv	FK Dinamo Kyiv	Alex Teixeira Santos (BRA, FK Shakhtar Donetsk) Eric Cosmin Bicfalvi (ROU, FK Volyn Lutsk)	17
2015/2016	FK Dinamo Kyiv	FK Shakhtar Donetsk	Alex Teixeira Santos (BRA, FK Shakhtar Donetsk)	22
2016/2017	FK Shakhtar Donetsk	FK Shakhtar Donetsk	Andriy Yarmolenko (FK Dinamo Kyiv)	15

2017/2018	FK Shakhtar Donetsk	FK Shakhtar Donetsk	Facundo Ferreyra (ARG, FK Shakhtar Donetsk)	21
2018/2019	FK Shakhtar Donetsk	FK Shakhtar Donetsk	Aluísio Chaves Ribeiro Moraes Júnior (FK Shakhtar Donetsk)	19

NATIONAL CHAMPIONSHIP
Ukrainian Premier League 2018/2019
(22.07.2018 – 30.05.2019)

Regular Season - Results

Round 1 [22-25.07.2018]
Zorya Luhansk - FK Mariupol 2-1(0-1)
Karpaty Lviv - FC Oleksandriya 0-2(0-0)
Arsenal Kyiv - FK Lviv 0-2(0-1)
Chornomorets - Olimpik Donetsk 2-1(1-0)
Desna Chernihiv - Shakhtar Donetsk 0-2(0-1)
Dinamo Kyiv - Vorskla Poltava 1-0(1-0)

Round 2 [28-29.07.2018]
FC Oleksandriya - Zorya Luhansk 1-0(0-0)
FK Lviv - Dinamo Kyiv 0-1(0-0)
Karpaty Lviv - Chornomorets Odesa 1-0(1-0)
Olimpik Donetsk - Vorskla Poltava 1-0(0-0)
FK Mariupol - Desna Chernihiv 1-4(0-2)
Shakhtar Donetsk - Arsenal Kyiv 3-0(3-0)

Round 3 [03-05.08.2018]
Dinamo Kyiv - Shakhtar Donetsk 1-0(0-0)
Vorskla Poltava - FK Lviv 1-0(0-0)
Zorya Luhansk - Chornomorets 1-1(1-0)
Karpaty Lviv - Olimpik Donetsk 2-2(2-0)
Arsenal Kyiv - FK Mariupol 1-2(1-2)
Desna Chernihiv - FC Oleksandriya 0-2(0-1)

Round 4 [10-12.08.2018]
Olimpik Donetsk - FK Lviv 1-1(0-0)
Shakhtar Donetsk - Vorskla Poltava 4-1(0-1)
Karpaty Lviv - Zorya Luhansk 0-1(0-0)
FC Oleksandriya - Arsenal Kyiv 1-0(0-0)
Chornomorets - Desna Chernihiv 1-0(0-0)
FK Mariupol - Dinamo Kyiv 0-2(0-2) [26.09.]

Round 5 [17-19.08.2018]
Arsenal Kyiv - Chornomorets Odesa 1-1(1-1)
FK Lviv - Shakhtar Donetsk 0-2(0-1)
Dinamo Kyiv - FC Oleksandriya 1-0(0-0)
Desna Chernihiv - Karpaty Lviv 2-2(2-0)
Zorya Luhansk - Olimpik Donetsk 0-0
Vorskla Poltava - FK Mariupol 2-1(1-1)

Round 6 [24-26.08.2018]
Olimpik Donetsk - Shakhtar Donetsk 2-5(1-4)
FC Oleksandriya - Vorskla Poltava 2-0(2-0)
Chornomorets Odesa - Dinamo Kyiv 1-1(0-0)
Karpaty Lviv - Arsenal Kyiv 1-2(0-2)
FK Mariupol - FK Lviv 2-2(0-1)
Zorya Luhansk - Desna Chernihiv 0-2(0-1)

Round 7 [31.08.-02.09.2018]
Vorskla Poltava - Chornomorets 2-1(0-0)
Shakhtar Donetsk - FK Mariupol 2-0(1-0)
Desna Chernihiv - Olimpik Donetsk 0-1(0-0)
FK Lviv - FC Oleksandriya 2-2(2-0)
Arsenal Kyiv - Zorya Luhansk 0-5(0-3)
Dinamo Kyiv - Karpaty Lviv 0-2(0-2)

Round 8 [14-16.09.2018]
Desna Chernihiv - Arsenal Kyiv 1-0(1-0)
FC Oleksandriya - Shakhtar Donetsk 0-2(0-1)
Karpaty Lviv - Vorskla Poltava 0-1(0-0)
Olimpik Donetsk - FK Mariupol 1-3(1-1)
Zorya Luhansk - Dinamo Kyiv 1-1(1-0)
Chornomorets Odesa - FK Lviv 0-1(0-1)

Round 9 [22-23.09.2018]
FK Mariupol - FC Oleksandriya 1-0(1-0)
FK Lviv - Karpaty Lviv 1-1(0-0)
Arsenal Kyiv - Olimpik Donetsk 1-3(0-1)
Dinamo Kyiv - Desna Chernihiv 4-0(1-0)
Shakhtar Donetsk - Chornomorets 3-0(0-0)
Vorskla Poltava - Zorya Luhansk 2-1(0-0)

Round 10 [28-30.09.2018]
Karpaty Lviv - Shakhtar Donetsk 1-6(0-5)
Olimpik Donetsk - FC Oleksandriya 2-3(2-1)
Desna Chernihiv - Vorskla Poltava 0-2(0-1)
Chornomorets Odesa - FK Mariupol 0-1(0-0)
Zorya Luhansk - FK Lviv 0-0
Arsenal Kyiv - Dinamo Kyiv 0-1(0-1)

Round 11 [06-07.10.2018]
FK Mariupol - Karpaty Lviv 1-1(0-1)
FC Oleksandriya - Chornomorets 3-2(1-1)
FK Lviv - Desna Chernihiv 1-3(0-2)
Dinamo Kyiv - Olimpik Donetsk 1-0(1-0)
Shakhtar Donetsk - Zorya Luhansk 1-1(1-0)
Vorskla Poltava - Arsenal Kyiv 0-2(0-0)

Round 12 [19-21.10.2018]
Shakhtar Donetsk - Desna Chernihiv 1-0(0-0)
FK Mariupol - Zorya Luhansk 3-2(2-0)
Vorskla Poltava - Dinamo Kyiv 0-1(0-1)
FK Lviv - Arsenal Kyiv 1-0(1-0)
Olimpik Donetsk - Chornomorets 1-0(0-0)
FC Oleksandriya - Karpaty Lviv 2-1(2-0)

Round 13 [27-28.10.2018]
Desna Chernihiv - FK Mariupol 2-0(1-0)
Arsenal Kyiv - Shakhtar Donetsk 0-3(0-1)
Zorya Luhansk - FC Oleksandriya 0-0
Chornomorets Odesa - Karpaty Lviv 0-5(0-1)
Dinamo Kyiv - FK Lviv 0-1(0-1)
Vorskla Poltava - Olimpik Donetsk 2-1(1-1)

Round 14 [03-04.11.2018]
FK Mariupol - Arsenal Kyiv 1-0(0-0)
Shakhtar Donetsk - Dinamo Kyiv 2-1(0-1)
Olimpik Donetsk - Karpaty Lviv 1-2(0-1)
FC Oleksandriya - Desna Chernihiv 1-1(0-0)
FK Lviv - Vorskla Poltava 0-2(0-2)
Chornomorets - Zorya Luhansk 0-3(0-1)

Round 15 [10-11.11.2018]
FK Lviv - Olimpik Donetsk 1-1(1-0)
Desna Chernihiv - Chornomorets 2-0(0-0)
Zorya Luhansk - Karpaty Lviv 2-1(1-1)
Arsenal Kyiv - FC Oleksandriya 0-3(0-1)
Dinamo Kyiv - FK Mariupol 4-0(1-0)
Vorskla Poltava - Shakhtar Donetsk 0-2(0-2)

Round 16 [23-25.11.2018]
Shakhtar Donetsk - FK Lviv 0-0
Karpaty Lviv - Desna Chernihiv 0-2(0-2)
FK Mariupol - Vorskla Poltava 1-0(0-0)
Olimpik Donetsk - Zorya Luhansk 1-1(0-0)
Chornomorets Odesa - Arsenal Kyiv 2-1(0-0)
FC Oleksandriya - Dinamo Kyiv 2-1(1-1)

Round 17 [01-03.12.2018]
Desna Chernihiv - Zorya Luhansk 0-2(0-1)
Arsenal Kyiv - Karpaty Lviv 1-1(1-0)
FK Lviv - FK Mariupol 2-2(2-1)
Shakhtar Donetsk - Olimpik Donetsk 2-2(1-0)
Vorskla Poltava - FC Oleksandriya 0-1(0-1)
Dinamo Kyiv - Chornomorets Odesa 2-0(1-0)

Round 18 [07-09.12.2018]
FK Mariupol - Shakhtar Donetsk 0-3(0-0)
Karpaty Lviv - Dinamo Kyiv 0-4(0-1)
Zorya Luhansk - Arsenal Kyiv 3-0(1-0)
Chornomorets - Vorskla Poltava 0-1(0-1)
Olimpik Donetsk - Desna Chernihiv 1-1(0-0)
FC Oleksandriya - FK Lviv 1-2(0-2)

Round 19 23-25.02.2019 [ ]
FK Mariupol - Olimpik Donetsk 2-1(1-1)
FK Lviv - Chornomorets Odesa 0-1(0-1)
Arsenal Kyiv - Desna Chernihiv 0-2(0-1)
Vorskla Poltava - Karpaty Lviv 0-4(0-1)
Dinamo Kyiv - Zorya Luhansk 5-0(3-0)
Shakhtar Donetsk - FC Oleksandriya 2-0(2-0)

Round 20 [02-03.03.2019]
Desna Chernihiv - Dinamo Kyiv 1-2(0-1)
Chornomorets - Shakhtar Donetsk 0-1(0-0)
Olimpik Donetsk - Arsenal Kyiv 0-1(0-1)
Zorya Luhansk - Vorskla Poltava 3-0(1-0)
Karpaty Lviv - FK Lviv 0-1(0-1)
FC Oleksandriya - FK Mariupol 1-1(0-1)

Round 21 [09-10.03.2019]
FK Mariupol - Chornomorets Odesa 0-0
Vorskla Poltava - Desna Chernihiv 0-0
FK Lviv - Zorya Luhansk 0-0
Dinamo Kyiv - Arsenal Kyiv 4-0(4-0)
Shakhtar Donetsk - Karpaty Lviv 5-0(3-0)
FC Oleksandriya - Olimpik Donetsk 1-1(0-0)

Round 22 [16-18.03.2019]
Chornomorets - FC Oleksandriya 0-3(0-3)
Zorya Luhansk - Shakhtar Donetsk 0-1(0-1)
Desna Chernihiv - FK Lviv 0-1(0-0)
Karpaty Lviv - FK Mariupol 1-1(1-1)
Olimpik Donetsk - Dinamo Kyiv 1-2(1-2)
Arsenal Kyiv - Vorskla Poltava 2-2(1-1)

Final Standings

1.	FK Shakhtar Donetsk	22	18	3	1	52 - 9	57
2.	FK Dinamo Kyiv	22	16	2	4	40 - 11	50
3.	FC Oleksandriya	22	12	5	5	31 - 19	41
4.	FK Zorya Luhansk	22	8	8	6	28 - 20	32
5.	FK Lviv	22	7	9	6	19 - 20	30
6.	FK Mariupol	22	8	6	8	24 - 33	30
7.	FK Vorskla Poltava	22	9	2	11	18 - 28	29
8.	FK Desna Chernihiv	22	8	4	10	23 - 24	28
9.	FK Karpaty Lviv	22	5	6	11	26 - 37	21
10.	FK Olimpik Donetsk	22	4	8	10	25 - 33	20
11.	FK Chornomorets Odesa	22	4	4	14	12 - 34	16
12.	FK Arsenal Kyiv	22	3	3	16	12 - 42	12

Teams ranked 1-6 were qualified for the Championship Round, while teams ranked 7-12 were qualified for the Relegation Round.
Please note: FK Lviv merged with NK Veres Rivne in May 2018 and played as FK Lviv in the Ukrainian Premier League 2018/2019.

Championship Round

Round 23 [03.04.2019]
FC Oleksandriya - Shakhtar Donetsk 0-1(0-1)
Zorya Luhansk - Dinamo Kyiv 2-3(1-0)
FK Lviv - FK Mariupol 2-3(1-0)

Round 24 [13.04.2019]
FK Mariupol - Dinamo Kyiv 0-1(0-0)
Shakhtar Donetsk - Zorya Luhansk 3-0(1-0)
FK Lviv - FC Oleksandriya 1-2(0-0)

Round 25 [24.04.2019]
Zorya Luhansk - FK Lviv 2-1(0-1)
FC Oleksandriya - FK Mariupol 2-1(2-1)
Dinamo Kyiv - Shakhtar Donetsk 0-0

Round 26 [28.04.2019]
FK Mariupol - Shakhtar Donetsk 0-1(0-1)
FC Oleksandriya - Zorya Luhansk 0-2(0-1)
FK Lviv - Dinamo Kyiv 0-1(0-1)

Round 27 [04.05.2019]
Zorya Luhansk - FK Mariupol 0-1(0-1)
Dinamo Kyiv - FC Oleksandriya 1-1(0-1)
Shakhtar Donetsk - FK Lviv 5-0(1-0)

Round 28 [11.05.2019]
FK Mariupol - FK Lviv 2-0(0-0)
Dinamo Kyiv - Zorya Luhansk 1-1(1-0)
Shakhtar Donetsk - FC Oleksandriya 2-1(1-1)

Round 29 [18-19.05.2019]
Dinamo Kyiv - FK Mariupol 2-1(1-0)
FC Oleksandriya - FK Lviv 0-1(0-0)
Zorya Luhansk - Shakhtar Donetsk 0-1(0-1)

Round 30 [22.05.2019]
FK Lviv - Zorya Luhansk 0-0
FK Mariupol - FC Oleksandriya 1-1(1-1)
Shakhtar Donetsk - Dinamo Kyiv 1-1(0-1)

Round 31 [26.05.2019]
Dinamo Kyiv - FK Lviv 2-1(0-1)
Zorya Luhansk - FC Oleksandriya 3-1(2-1)
Shakhtar Donetsk - FK Mariupol 4-0(0-0)

Round 32 [30.05.2019]
FK Mariupol - Zorya Luhansk 3-1(0-1)
FC Oleksandriya - Dinamo Kyiv 0-2(0-1)
FK Lviv - Shakhtar Donetsk 0-3(0-0)

Final Standings

1.	**FK Shakhtar Donetsk**	32	26	5	1	73 - 11	83
2.	FK Dinamo Kyiv	32	22	6	4	54 - 18	72
3.	FC Oleksandriya	32	14	7	11	39 - 34	49
4.	FK Mariupol	32	12	7	13	36 - 47	43
5.	FK Zorya Luhansk	32	11	10	11	39 - 34	43
6.	FK Lviv	32	8	10	14	25 - 40	34

Top goalscorers:

19 Aluísio Chaves Ribeiro Moraes Júnior
FK Shakhtar Donetsk

18 Viktor Tsyhankov
FK Dinamo Kyiv

14 Marian Shved
FK Karpaty Lviv

Relegation Round

Round 23 [02-06.04.2019]
Karpaty Lviv - Vorskla Poltava 4-0(2-0)
Olimpik Donetsk - Desna Chernihiv 0-2(0-1)
Chornomorets Odesa - Arsenal Kyiv 1-3(0-3)

Round 24 [14.04.2019]
Desna Chernihiv - Karpaty Lviv 2-1(1-1)
Arsenal Kyiv - Vorskla Poltava 1-0(0-0)
Chornomorets - Olimpik Donetsk 1-1(0-1)

Round 25 [23.04.2019]
Olimpik Donetsk - Arsenal Kyiv 2-0(2-0)
Karpaty Lviv - Chornomorets Odesa 0-0
Vorskla Poltava - Desna Chernihiv 3-3(0-3)

Round 26 [27-29.04.2019]
Chornomorets - Vorskla Poltava 1-2(1-0)
Olimpik Donetsk - Karpaty Lviv 3-2(1-1)
Arsenal Kyiv - Desna Chernihiv 2-0(2-0)

Round 27 [05.05.2019]
Olimpik Donetsk - Vorskla Poltava 1-1(0-1)
Desna Chernihiv - Chornomorets 2-4(2-1)
Karpaty Lviv - Arsenal Kyiv 1-2(0-1)

Round 28 [12.05.2019]
Desna Chernihiv - Olimpik Donetsk 2-1(1-0)
Arsenal Kyiv - Chornomorets Odesa 3-3(0-1)
Vorskla Poltava - Karpaty Lviv 1-1(1-0)

Round 29 [18.05.2019]
Vorskla Poltava - Arsenal Kyiv 2-0(1-0)
Karpaty Lviv - Desna Chernihiv 2-0(0-0)
Olimpik Donetsk - Chornomorets 2-1(1-0)

Round 30 [21.05.2019]
Desna Chernihiv - Vorskla Poltava 0-1(0-1)
Chornomorets Odesa - Karpaty Lviv 3-1(1-0)
Arsenal Kyiv - Olimpik Donetsk 1-1(1-1)

Round 31 [25.05.2019]
Karpaty Lviv - Olimpik Donetsk 3-3(1-1)
Vorskla Poltava - Chornomorets Odesa 1-2(0-1)
Desna Chernihiv - Arsenal Kyiv 1-0(1-0)

Round 32 [29.05.2019]
Arsenal Kyiv - Karpaty Lviv 2-3(1-3)
Vorskla Poltava - Olimpik Donetsk 2-2(2-0)
Chornomorets - Desna Chernihiv 3-0(0-0)

Final Standings

7.	FK Vorskla Poltava	32	12	6	14	31 - 43	42
8.	FK Desna Chernihiv	32	12	5	15	35 - 41	41
9.	FK Olimpik Donetsk	32	7	13	12	41 - 48	34
10.	FK Karpaty Lviv (*Relegation Play-offs*)	32	8	9	15	44 - 53	33
11.	FK Chornomorets Odesa (*Relegation Play-offs*)	32	8	7	17	31 - 49	31
12.	FK Arsenal Kyiv (*Relegated*)	32	7	5	20	26 - 56	26

Relegation Play-offs [04-08.06.2019]

FK Chornomorets Odesa - **FK Kolos Kovalivka**	0-0	0-2(0-0)
FK Karpaty Lviv - FK Volyn Lutsk	0-0	3-1(1-1)*

*3-0 awarded.

FK Kolos Kovalivka were promoted to the Ukrainian Premier League 2019/2020 while FK Karpaty Lviv retains its place at first level.

NATIONAL CUP
Ukrainian Cup 2018/2019

First Round [17-18.07.2018]

SC Tavriya Simferopol – SC Chaika Petropavlivska	1-0	FK Real Pharma Odessa - FK Nyva Vinnytsia	0-2
FK Naftovik-Ukrnafta – FK Hirnik Kriviy Rih	0-3 (awarded)	FK Enerhiya Nova Kakhovka - FK Kristal Kherson	0-1
FK Viktoriya Mykolaivka - PFK Ternopil	2-1	FK Nikopol-NPHU - FK Myr Hornostayivka	1-4
FK LNZ-Lebedyn – FK Polissya Zhytomyr	4-2 pen	FK Podillya-Khmelnitskiy - FK Metalurg Zaporizhya	0-2
FK Kalush - FSK Bukovina	4-3 pen	NK Veres Rivne- FC Mynai	9-10 pen

Second Round [22.08./20.09.2018]

PFK Sumy - FK Kobra Kharkiv	w/o	FK Kremin - FK Zirka Kropyvnytskyi	1-2(1-0)
FK Nyva Vinnytsia - FK Hirnik Kriviy Rih	2-1(0-0)	FK Balkany Zorya - MFK Mykolaiv	0-1(0-1)
FC Mynai - FK Prykarpattia Ivano-Frankivsk	3-1(3-1)	FK Kristal Kherson - FK Ahrobiznes Volochysk	1-1 aet; 4-2 pen
FK Viktoriya Mykolaivka - FK Myr Hornostayivka	1-1 aet; 1-3 pen	FK LNZ-Lebedyn – FK Hirnik Kriviy Rih	1-1 aet; 2-4 pen
FK Cherkashchyna - FK Rukh Vynnyky	3-1(3-1)	FK Inhulets Petrove - FK Kolos Kovalivka	1-0(0-0)
FK Kalush – FK Avangard Kramatorsk	2-1(1-1,1-1)	FK Metalist 1925 Kharkov - FK Obolon-Brovar Kyiv	2-0(0-0)
SC Tavriya Simferopol - FK Volyn Lutsk	2-3(1-1,1-1)	FK Metalurg Zaporizhya - SC Dnipro-1	0-2(0-0)

Third Round [25-26.09.2018]

PFK Sumy - FK Karpaty Lviv	0-3(0-1)	FK Zirka Kropyvnytskyi - FK Olimpik Donetsk	1-1 aet; 4-5 pen
FK Kristal Kherson - FK Desna Chernihiv	2-3(0-0)	FK Cherkashchyna – FK Arsenal Kyiv	3-2(0-1,2-2)
FK Myr Hornostayivka - FK Inhulets Petrove	0-3(0-1)	FC Mynai - MFK Mykolaiv	3-1(1-0)
FK Nyva Vinnytsia - FK Hirnik Kriviy Rih	0-0 aet; 3-4 pen	SC Dnipro-1 - FK Volyn Lutsk	2-1(1-0)
FK Kalush - FK Metalist 1925 Kharkov	1-0(0-0,0-0)	FK Chernomorets Odessa - FC Oleksandriya	3-0(1-0)

1/8-Finals [31.10.2018]

FK Kalush - SC Dnipro-1	0-3(0-3)	FK Chernomorets Odessa - FK Vorskla Poltava	1-2(0-0)
FC Mynai - FK Dinamo Kyiv	1-3(1-0)	FK Cherkashchyna - FK Karpaty Lviv	0-1(0-0)
FK Hirnik Kriviy Rih - FK Lviv	0-1(0-0)	FK Shakhtar Donetsk - FK Olimpik Donetsk	3-2(0-0)
FK Inhulets Petrove - FK Mariupol	3-1(2-0)	FK Desna Chernihiv - FK Zorya Lugansk	1-1 aet; 4-5 pen

Quarter-Finals [07.04.2019]

FK Lviv - FK Zorya Lugansk	0-1(0-0)	Shakhtar Donetsk - FK Dinamo Kyiv	1-1 aet; 4-3 pen
FK Inhulets Petrove - FK Karpaty Lviv	1-1 aet; 5-4 pen	SC Dnipro-1 - FK Vorskla Poltava	2-0(0-0)

Semi-Finals [17.04.2019]

FK Inhulets Petrove - FK Zorya Lugansk	2-1(2-1)	SC Dnipro-1 - FK Shakhtar Donetsk	0-2(0-0)

Final

19.05.2019; Slavutych Arena, Zaporizhia; Referee: Yevhen Aranovskyi; Attendance: 11,100

FK Shakhtar Donetsk – FC Inhulets Petrove **4-0(1-0)**

Shakhtar Donetsk: Oleksiy Shevchenko, Serhiy Krivtsov, Mykola Matvienko, Ismaily Gonçalves dos Santos, Serhiy Bolbat, Alan Patrick Lourenço, Marcos Antônio Silva Santos, Mateus Cardoso Lemos Martins „Tetê" (72.Wellington „Nem" Silva Sanches Aguiar), Viktor Kovalenko (61.Manor Solomon), Taison Barcellos Freda (Cap), Aluísio Chaves Ribeiro Moraes Júnior (62.Olarenwaju Kayode). Trainer: Paulo Alexandre Rodrigues Fonseca (Portugal).

Inhulets Petrove: Anton Sytnykov, Denys Balan, Maksym Kovalyov, Vitaliy Pavlov, Oleh Synyohub, Vladyslav Lupashko (Cap), Illya Kovalenko, Vladyslav Klymenko (67.Oleksandr Kucherenko), Yevhen Zaporozhets, Artem Schedryi (83.Oleksandr Kozak), Oleksandr Mishurenko (34.Nika Sichinava). Trainer: Serhiy Lavrynenko.

Goals: 1-0 Mateus Cardoso Lemos Martins „Tetê" (27), 2-0 Mateus Cardoso Lemos Martins „Tetê" (39), 3-0 Aluísio Chaves Ribeiro Moraes Júnior (45+1), 4-0 Manor Solomon (64).

THE CLUBS 2018/2019

Please note: matches and goals includes statistics of both regular season and play-offs (Championship or Relegation).

Futbolnij Klub Arsenal Kyiv

Founded: 1925
Stadium: "Lobanovsky" Dinamo Stadium, Kyiv (16,873)

Goalkeepers:	DOB	M	(s)	G
Orest Budyuk	23.08.1995	2		
Roman Pidkivka	09.05.1995	14		
Serhiy Sitalo	20.12.1986	16		
Defenders:	**DOB**	**M**	**(s)**	**G**
Serge Akakpo (TOG)	15.10.1987	5		
Serhiy Datsenko	06.09.1987	1	(1)	
Vladyslav Dubinchak	01.07.1998	28		
Ivan Jelić Balta (CRO)	17.09.1992	4		
Danylo Karas	02.01.1997	6	(2)	
Oleksyi Maydanevych	18.07.1991	12	(1)	1
Oleksandr Nasonov	28.04.1992	6	(3)	
Marko Nikolić (SRB)	31.03.1998	3	(1)	
Oleksandr Osman	18.04.1996	2	(3)	
Oscar Piris (ARG)	06.06.1989	7		
Danylo Sagutkin	19.04.1996	13	(5)	
Sergey Semeniuk (BLR)	27.01.1991	5	(8)	1
Maksim Zhichikov	07.11.1992	14		
Dmytro Zozulya	09.06.1988	4	(1)	
Midfielders:	**DOB**	**M**	**(s)**	**G**
Artur Avagimian	16.01.1997	7	(1)	2
Dmytro Bashlay	25.04.1990	12		
Yuriy Bushman	14.05.1990	8	(2)	
Ruslan Chernenko	29.09.1992		(1)	
Andriy Dombrovskyi	12.08.1995	27	(2)	
Volodomyr Doronin	15.01.1993	2	(3)	
Serhiy Hryn	06.06.1994	6	(2)	4
Stefan Jevtoski (MKD)	02.09.1997	10	(1)	
Vladislav Kalitvintsev	04.01.1993	10	(1)	1
Artem Kozak	28.05.1998	2	(2)	
Aurélien Ngeyitala Lola (COD)	29.05.1994	13	(2)	1
Mykhailo Mudryk	05.01.2001	6	(4)	
Pavel Orekhovskiy	13.05.1996	22	(2)	3
Andriy Stryzhak	22.10.1999	2	(3)	
Vyacheslav Tankovski	16.08.1995	12		1
Serhiy Vakulenko	07.09.1993	12		7
Yury Vakulko	10.11.1997	6	(3)	
Curtis Yebli (FRA)	30.03.1997	2	(2)	
Forwards:	**DOB**	**M**	**(s)**	**G**
Leonid Akulinin	07.03.1993	6		
Vladyslav Alekseyev	29.04.1998	8	(1)	
Denis Balanyuk	16.01.1997	6	(2)	
Maksim Feshchuk	25.11.1985	4	(2)	
Gegam Kadimyan (ARM)	19.10.1992	7	(4)	
Oleksandr Kovpak	02.02.1983	4	(9)	3
Jaba Lipartia (GEO)	16.11.1987	2	(9)	
Gaëtan Missi Mezu (GAB)	04.05.1996	8	(1)	1
Vadym Semchuk	24.11.1993	1		
Vladyslav Semotyuk	14.11.2000	1		
Daniil Sukhoruchko	21.02.2000		(1)	
Denys Yanakov	01.01.1999	2	(2)	
Oleksandr Yermachenko	29.01.1993	2	(3)	
Trainer:	**DOB**	**M**		
Fabrizio Ravanelli (ITA)	11.12.1968	10		
Viacheslav Hroznyi [01.10.2018]	12.07.1956	8		
Ihor Leonov [16.01.2019]	14.09.1967	14		

Futbolnij Klub Chornomorets Odesa

Founded: 26.03.1936
Stadium: Chornomorets Stadium, Odesa (34,164)

Goalkeepers:	DOB	M	(s)	G
Andriy Kozhukhar	20.07.1999	8		
Serhiy Litovchenko	04.10.1987	24		
Defenders:	**DOB**	**M**	**(s)**	**G**
Oleksandr Golikov	13.11.1991	7		
Vitali Goshkoderia	08.01.1988	10		1
Glib Grachov	15.05.1997	28		2
Andriy Myshchenko	07.04.1991	11	(1)	
Denys Norenkov	25.07.1996	13	(2)	
Oleh Ostapenko	11.06.1997	5	(4)	
Yuri Romaniuk	06.05.1997	9		
Dmytro Ryzhuk	05.04.1992	29		2
Ivan Trubochkin	17.03.1993	24	(1)	
Artem Yarmolenko	18.01.1998	1	(1)	
Midfielders:	**DOB**	**M**	**(s)**	**G**
Volodimir Arzhanov	29.11.1985	10		
Ruslan Babenko	08.07.1992	27	(1)	2
Artem Chorniy	23.10.1989	23	(6)	2
Artur Karnoza	02.08.1990		(9)	
Vladislav Khamelyuk	05.04.1998	3	(5)	
Dmytro Leonov	06.11.1988	8	(3)	
Yevhen Morozenko	16.12.1991	9		
Mykola Musolitin	21.01.1999	14	(10)	2
Robert Mutzers (NED)	06.04.1993	1	(4)	
Oleksiy Savchenko	27.09.1993	14		1
Yevhen Smirnov	16.04.1993	12		1
Volodymyr Tanchyk	17.10.1991	14		3
Mykyta Tatarkov	04.01.1995	8	(6)	2
Forwards:	**DOB**	**M**	**(s)**	**G**
Anatoliy Didenko	09.06.1982	6	(1)	
Volodymir Koval	06.03.1992	18	(5)	2
Vasili Pavlov (RUS)	24.07.1990	1	(12)	3
Dmytro Semeniv	24.06.1998	4	(7)	1
Andriy Shtohrin	14.12.1998	1	(10)	
Árni Vilhjálmsson (ISL)	09.05.1994	10	(2)	7
Trainer:	**DOB**	**M**		
Angel Chervenkov (BUL)	10.06.1964	32		

Futbolnij Klub Desna Chernihiv

Founded: 1960
Stadium: Chernihiv Stadium, Chernihiv (12,060)

Goalkeepers:	**DOB**	**M**	**(s)**	**G**
Ihor Litovka	05.06.1988	11		
Evgen Past	16.03.1988	21		
Defenders:	**DOB**	**M**	**(s)**	**G**
Anton Bratkov	14.05.1993	14	(2)	
Denis Favorov	01.04.1991	31		7
Andriy Gitchenko	02.10.1984	24		2
Maksym Imerekov	23.01.1991	21		
Serhiy Lyulka	22.03.1990	7	(6)	
Dmytro Nemchaninov	27.01.1990	5		
Temur Partsvaniya	06.07.1991	3	(5)	
Andriy Slinkin	19.02.1991	7	(1)	
Vitaliy Yermakov	07.06.1992	3	(4)	
Midfielders:	**DOB**	**M**	**(s)**	**G**
Maxym Banasevich	31.01.1995	2	(9)	
Yevhenii Belych	09.01.2001		(1)	
Andriy Bogdanov	21.01.1990	11	(2)	1
Artem Favorov	19.03.1994	26	(2)	5
Egor Kartushov	05.01.1991	22	(4)	2
Luka Koberidze (GEO)	09.09.1994	7	(4)	
Rienat Mochuliak	15.02.1998		(1)	
Andriy Mostoviy	24.01.1988	24		
Vladislav Ohirya	03.04.1990	28		
Sergey Starenkiy	20.09.1984	10	(12)	3
Oleksandr Volkov	07.02.1989	16	(3)	
Andriy Yakimov	15.06.1997	2	(2)	
Forwards:	**DOB**	**M**	**(s)**	**G**
Denys Bezborodko	31.05.1994	16	(7)	5
Aleksandr Filipov	23.10.1992	24	(4)	5
Dmytro Khlyobas	09.05.1994	11	(10)	3
Ruslan Kisil	23.10.1991	1		
Oleksandr Kovpak	02.02.1983		(7)	
Mykhaylo Kozak	20.01.1991	1	(3)	
Mykhaylo Sergiychuk	29.07.1991	4	(7)	2
Trainer:	**DOB**	**M**		
Oleksandr Riabokon	21.02.1964	32		

Futbolnij Klub Dinamo Kyiv

Founded: 13.05.1927
Stadium: NSC Olimpiyskiy, Kyiv (70,050) / "Lobanovsky" Dinamo Stadium, Kyiv (16,873)

Goalkeepers:	**DOB**	**M**	**(s)**	**G**
Denys Boyko	29.01.1988	25	(1)	
Georgiy Bushchan	31.05.1994	7		
Defenders:	**DOB**	**M**	**(s)**	**G**
Mykyta Burda	24.03.1995	26		2
Tamás Kádár (HUN)	14.03.1990	20	(2)	
Tomasz Kędziora (POL)	11.06.1994	27		2
Vitaliy Mykolenko	29.05.1999	22	(1)	
Josip Pivarić (CRO)	30.01.1989	6		
Denys Popov	17.02.1999	1		
Artem Shabanov	07.03.1992	15	(2)	
Sidcley Ferreira Pereira (BRA)	13.05.1993	12	(5)	1
Midfielders:	**DOB**	**M**	**(s)**	**G**
Akhmed Alibekov	29.05.1998	2	(2)	
Oleksandr Andrievsky	25.06.1994	8	(4)	
Vitaliy Buyalskyi	06.01.1993	22		3
Carlos María de Pena Bonino (URU)	11.03.1992	8		1
Mikkel Duelund (DEN)	29.06.1997	2	(7)	1
Denys Garmash	19.04.1990	7	(6)	2
Vladislav Kalitvintsev	04.01.1993		(1)	
Mykyta Kravchenko	14.06.1997	1	(1)	
Mikola Morozyuk	17.01.1988	11	(1)	1
Mykola Shaparenko	04.10.1998	12	(10)	5
Volodymyr Shepelev	01.06.1997	24		
Yevhenii Smyrnyi	18.08.1998	1	(2)	
Serhiy Sydorchuk	02.05.1991	15	(8)	1
Danilo das Neves Pinheiro „Tchê Tchê" (BRA)	30.08.1992	6	(3)	
Viktor Tsyhankov	15.11.1997	30	(1)	18
Vitor Frerazin Bueno (BRA)	05.09.1994		(2)	
Forwards:	**DOB**	**M**	**(s)**	**G**
Artem Besedin	31.03.1996	9	(3)	2
Francisco Sol Ortíz (ESP)	13.03.1992	2		1
Ievgenii Isaienko	07.08.2000		(2)	
Nazariy Rusyn	25.10.1998	9	(10)	5
Vladyslav Supriaha	15.02.2000	2	(4)	
Heorhii Tsitaishvili	18.11.2000	1	(4)	
Benjamin Verbič (SVN)	27.11.1993	19	(2)	7
Trainer:	**DOB**	**M**		
Alyaksandr Khatskevich (BLR)	19.10.1973	32		

Futbolnij Klub Karpaty Lviv

Founded: 18.01.1963
Stadium: Ukraina Stadium, Lviv (28,051)

Goalkeepers:	**DOB**	**M**	**(s)**	**G**
Maksim Kuchinskiy	28.06.1988	22		
German Penkov	26.05.1994	2		
Mykyta Shevchenko	26.01.1993	8		
Defenders:	**DOB**	**M**	**(s)**	**G**
Oleh Borodai	07.01.1993	9	(3)	
Artem Fedetskiy	26.04.1985	12	(2)	
Papa Gueye (SEN)	07.06.1984	12	(2)	
Oleksiy Kovtun	05.02.1995	16		
Orest Lebedenko	23.09.1998	12	(1)	
Ivan Lobay	21.05.1996	1		
Adi Mehremić (BIH)	26.04.1992	22	(1)	1
Denis Miroshnichenko	11.10.1994	18	(3)	2
Serhiy Myakushko	15.04.1993	26	(6)	8
Andriy Nesterov	02.07.1990	5	(1)	1
Nika Sandokhadze (GEO)	20.02.1994	9		
Roman Slyva	23.09.2000	2	(1)	
Midfielders:	**DOB**	**M**	**(s)**	**G**
Andriy Busko	20.05.1997	5	(4)	
Cristian Damián Erbes (ARG)	06.01.1990	13	(2)	1
Oleh Golodyuk	02.01.1988	4	(1)	
Martin Hongla (CMR)	16.03.1998	13		2
Petro Kharzhevskyi	03.01.2000		(1)	
Dmytro Klyots	15.04.1996	19	(2)	
Roman Tolochko	25.10.1998	4	(3)	
Nazar Verbnyi	26.07.1997	5	(3)	
Abdoul Yoda (FRA)	25.10.1988	8	(2)	1
Forwards:	**DOB**	**M**	**(s)**	**G**
Jorge Andrés Carrascal Guardo (COL)	25.05.1998	14	(2)	
Roman Debelko	08.08.1993	3	(9)	1
Francisco Di Franco (ARG)	28.01.1995	26	(3)	3
Oleksiy Gutsulyak	25.12.1997	20	(8)	4
Alán Kevin Méndez Olivera (URU)	10.01.1996	2	(11)	
Cristian Ioan Ponde (POR)	26.01.1995	14	(7)	6
Catriel Ignacio Sánchez (ARG)	17.07.1998		(1)	
Maryan Shved	16.07.1997	24		14
Danylo Sikan	16.04.2001		(1)	
Rodrigo Mauricio Vargas Castillo (BOL)	19.10.1994	2	(11)	
William Camargo (BRA)	01.06.1999		(1)	
Trainer:	**DOB**	**M**		
Oleg Boychyshyn	12.08.1973	18		
Fabriciano González Penelas (ESP) [13.01.2019]	25.04.1955	13		
Oleksandr Chyzhevskyi[27.05.2019]	27.05.1971	1		

Futbolnij Klub Lviv

Founded: 2006
Stadium: Arena Lviv, Lviv (34,915)

Goalkeepers:	**DOB**	**M**	**(s)**	**G**
Aleksandr Bandura	30.05.1986	24		
Bogdan Sarnavskiy	29.01.1995	8		
Defenders:	**DOB**	**M**	**(s)**	**G**
Volodymyr Adamyuk	17.07.1991	32		3
Vasyl Bilyi	13.03.1990	1	(1)	
Serhiy Borzenko	22.06.1986	17	(1)	
Maksym Brama	01.02.2002		(1)	
Oleksandr Holikov	13.11.1991	12	(4)	
Lucas Taylor Maia Reis (BRA)	10.04.1995	14	(2)	3
Oleksandr Nasonov	28.04.1992	9	(3)	
Vadym Paramonov	18.03.1991	23	(2)	1
Vladyslav Pryimak	30.08.1996	17	(6)	1
Yuriy Putrash	29.01.1990	5	(1)	
Vicente de Paula Mercedes (BRA)	02.03.1996	6	(5)	
Serhiy Voronin	24.03.1987	15		2
Midfielders:	**DOB**	**M**	**(s)**	**G**
Augusto Bruno da Silva (BRA)	22.02.1992	11		
Murilo Vinicius Leite Cadina (BRA)	27.01.1997	1	(6)	
Jonatan da Silva Lima (BRA)	04.01.1992	11	(5)	
Maksim Kalenchuk	05.12.1989	10	(1)	
Maxim Khimchak	13.02.2000		(1)	
Luiz Felipe Veloso Santos (BRA)	07.04.1997	11	(1)	1
Martan Fernando Gonsalves Pimenta „Marthã“ (BRA)	20.06.1997	20	(4)	
Dmitro Penteleychuk	09.08.2000	1	(1)	
Rafael Sabino dos Santos (BRA)	17.06.1996	17	(6)	
Vadym Yanchak	07.02.1999		(5)	
Artur Zapadnya	04.06.1990	15	(2)	1
Forwards:	**DOB**	**M**	**(s)**	**G**
Alvaro Luis Tavares Vieira (BRA)	10.03.1995	11	(1)	1
Rogerio Alves dos Santos „China“ (BRA)	02.08.1996	3	(6)	
Henrique Araujo de Oliveira (BRA)	07.08.1998	2	(3)	
Bruno Duarte da Silva (BRA)	24.03.1996	28		9
Yuri Ivanochko	04.04.1998		(1)	
Julio Cesar Moreira Ribeiro (BRA)	18.04.1995	2	(8)	
Kauê da Silva (BRA)	04.01.1997	1	(2)	
Sergey Kyslenko	30.06.1998		(1)	
Guilherme Giovan Sanchudo da Silva „Panambi“ (BRA)	11.03.1995	1	(3)	
Pedro Vitor Ferreira da Silva (BRA)	20.03.1998	12	(1)	2
José Vitor Rodrigues da Silva dos Santos „Pernambuco“ (BRA)	28.04.1998	8	(4)	
Serhiy Petrov	21.05.1997	1	(1)	
Rostyslav Voloshynovych	23.05.1991	3	(2)	
Trainer:	**DOB**	**M**		
Yuriy Bakalov	16.01.1966	24		
Bohdan Blavatskyi [17.04.2019]	07.06.1963	8		

Futbolnij Klub Mariupol

Founded: 1963
Stadium: Illichivets Stadium, Mariupol (12,680)

Goalkeepers:	**DOB**	**M**	**(s)**	**G**
Evgen Galchuk	05.03.1992	18		
Rustam Khudzhamov	05.10.1982	14		
Defenders:	**DOB**	**M**	**(s)**	**G**
Maksym Bilyi	21.06.1990	4	(2)	
Oleksii Bykov	29.03.1998	20		
Serhiy Chobotenko	16.01.1997	18	(4)	
Joyskim Dawa (CMR)	09.04.1996	7		
Besir Demiri (MKD)	01.08.1994	19	(2)	
Ihor Kiryukhantsev	29.01.1996	11	(2)	
Mikita Peterman	12.06.1999		(1)	
Ihor Tishchenko	11.05.1989	16	(9)	
Serhiy Yavorskiy	05.07.1989	28		
Midfielders:	**DOB**	**M**	**(s)**	**G**
Evgeniy Bilokin	16.06.1998	1	(3)	
Valeriy Fedorchuk	05.10.1988	20	(2)	3
Serhiy Gorbunov	14.03.1994	5	(5)	
Danylo Ignatenko	13.03.1997	15	(5)	
Andriy Korobenko	28.05.1997	1		
Danylo Litovchenko	21.07.2000		(1)	
Dmytro Myshnov	26.01.1994	29	(2)	
Oleksandr Pikhalonok	07.05.1997	21	(5)	5
Pavel Polegenko	06.01.1995	17	(4)	
Yevhen Prodanov	24.01.1998		(1)	
Illia Putria	15.05.1998	2	(2)	
Oleksandr Zubkov	03.08.1996	19	(3)	8
Forwards:	**DOB**	**M**	**(s)**	**G**
Andriy Boryachuk	23.04.1996	15	(11)	7
Vladyslav Buhai	27.10.1997		(4)	
Ihor Bykovsky	05.09.1996		(1)	
Vyacheslav Churko	10.05.1993	17	(6)	2
Ruslan Fomin	02.03.1986	15	(3)	5
Danylo Sikan	16.04.2001	2	(4)	
Vladislav Vakula	29.04.1999	18	(12)	6
Trainer:	**DOB**	**M**		
Oleksandr Babich	15.02.1979	32		

Futbolnij Klub Oleksandriya

Founded: 1948
Stadium: CSC Nika Stadium, Oleksandriya (7,000)

Goalkeepers:	**DOB**	**M**	**(s)**	**G**
Yuri Pankiv	03.11.1984	31		
Dmytro Rudyk	26.08.1992	1		
Defenders:	**DOB**	**M**	**(s)**	**G**
Vladislav Baboglo	14.11.1998	12		1
Andriy Batsula	06.02.1992	1		
Valeriy Bondarenko	03.02.1994	18		1
Glib Bukhal	12.11.1995	5		
Oleksiy Dovgiy	02.11.1989	6	(8)	1
Stanislav Mikitsey	07.09.1989	11	(4)	
Pavlo Pashaev (AZE)	04.01.1988	21	(1)	
Anton Shendrik	26.05.1986	26		1
Timur Stetskov	27.01.1998	5	(2)	
Andriy Tsurikov	05.10.1992	22	(2)	3
Midfielders:	**DOB**	**M**	**(s)**	**G**
Eugene Banada	29.02.1992	27	(3)	9
Denis Dedechko	02.07.1987	4	(4)	
Dmytro Grechyshkin	22.09.1991	15	(4)	1
Vasili Gritsuk	21.11.1987	3	(4)	2
Kirilo Kovalets	02.07.1993	22	(4)	5
Valeri Luchkevych	11.01.1996	13		2
Artem Polyarus	05.07.1992	19	(3)	1
Yevhen Protasov	23.07.1997	10	(10)	
Maksym Zaderaka	07.09.1994	16	(10)	
Andriy Zaporozhan	21.03.1983	23	(1)	3
Forwards:	**DOB**	**M**	**(s)**	**G**
Vitali Ponomar	31.05.1990	8	(16)	1
Dmytro Shastal	30.12.1995	11	(11)	4
Artem Sitalo	01.08.1989	22	(7)	4
Denys Ustymenko	12.04.1999		(2)	
Trainer:	**DOB**	**M**		
Volodymyr Sharan	18.09.1971	32		

Futbolnij Klub Olimpik Donetsk

Founded: 2001
Stadium: "Lobanovsky" Dinamo Stadium, Kyiv (16,873)

Goalkeepers:	DOB	M	(s)	G
Betim Halimi (KVX)	28.02.1996	4		
Vladimir Krynsky	14.01.1997	17		
Konstantin Machnovskiy	01.01.1989	11		
Defenders:	**DOB**	**M**	**(s)**	**G**
Dmitro Grishko	02.12.1985	27		1
Yegor Klymenchuk	11.11.1997	5		
Serhii Melinyshyn	26.05.1997	1		
Dmytro Nemchaninov	27.01.1990	6	(2)	
Ihor Snurnitsyn	07.03.2000	12	(2)	
Evgeniy Tsymbalyuk	19.06.1996	15	(3)	
Evgeniy Zubeyko	30.09.1989	16		
Midfielders:	**DOB**	**M**	**(s)**	**G**
Oleksiy Gay	06.11.1982	21		3
Vitaliy Koltsov	20.03.1994	18	(3)	1
Anton Kravchenko	23.03.1991	12	(2)	1
Andriy Kravchuk	26.02.1999	5	(3)	
Pavlo Ksonz	02.01.1987	30		
Yevhen Morozenko	16.12.1991	1	(1)	
Evgeny Pasich	13.07.1993	15	(8)	4
Gennady Pasich	13.07.1993	14	(6)	4
Serhiy Politylo	09.01.1989	20	(1)	2
Ivan Sondey	15.01.1994	8	(11)	
Yevhen Troyanovskiy	02.07.1993		(5)	
Rinar Valeev	22.08.1987	2	(7)	
Roman Vantukh	04.07.1998	11	(1)	1
Forwards:	**DOB**	**M**	**(s)**	**G**
Vitaliy Balashov	15.01.1991	17	(5)	3
Stanislav Bilenkyi	22.08.1998		(2)	
Dmytro Bilonoh	26.05.1995	3	(2)	1
Maksym Degtyarev	30.05.1993	19	(10)	8
Matar Dièye (SEN)	10.01.1998	11	(2)	7
Maxime Do Couto Teixeira (FRA)	13.12.1996	17	(8)	1
Anton Shynder	13.06.1987	2	(7)	1
Serhiy Vakulenko	07.09.1993	11		2
Artur Zagorulko	13.02.1993	1		
Trainer:	**DOB**	**M**		
Roman Sanzhar	28.05.1979	10		
Viacheslav Shevchuk [03.10.2018]	13.05.1979	14		
Ihor Klymovskiy [17.04.2019]	17.12.1972	8		

Futbolnij Klub Shakhtar Donetsk

Founded: 24.05.1936
Stadium: OSC Metalist Stadium, Kharkiv (40,003)

Goalkeepers:	DOB	M	(s)	G
Oleh Kudryk	17.10.1996	1		
Andriy Pyatov	28.06.1984	27		
Oleksiy Shevchenko	24.02.1992	3		
Anatolii Trubin	01.08.2001	1		
Defenders:	**DOB**	**M**	**(s)**	**G**
Valeriy Bondar	27.02.1999		(1)	
Valeriy Bondarenko	03.02.1994	1		
Bohdan Butko	13.01.1991	12	(2)	
Oleh Danchenko	01.08.1994	8	(1)	
Ismaily Gonçalves dos Santos(BRA)	11.01.1990	27		
Davit Khotcholava (GEO)	08.02.1993	25		2
Serhiy Kryvtsov	15.03.1991	20	(1)	
Maksym Malyshev	24.12.1992		(3)	
Mykola Matviyenko	02.05.1996	12	(6)	3
Ivan Ordets	08.07.1992	1	(1)	
Yaroslav Rakitskyi	03.08.1989	11		1
Midfielders:	**DOB**	**M**	**(s)**	**G**
Alan Patrick Lourenço (BRA)	13.05.1991	23	(4)	2
Serhiy Bolbat	13.06.1993	17	(3)	3
Bruno Ferreira Bonfim „Dentinho" (BRA)	19.01.1989	4	(8)	4
Viktor Kovalenko	14.02.1996	16	(9)	7
Marcos Antônio Silva Santos (BRA)	13.06.2000	7	(1)	
Marlos Romero Bonfim	07.06.1988	16	(3)	9
Maycon de Andrade Barberan(BRA)	15.07.1997	11	(10)	4
Taras Stepanenko	08.08.1989	22	(4)	4
Andriy Totovytskyy	20.01.1993	1	(5)	
Forwards:	**DOB**	**M**	**(s)**	**G**
Fernando dos Santos Pedro (BRA)	01.03.1999	8	(10)	2
Olarenwaju Kayode (NGA)	08.05.1993	3	(7)	1
Marcos Robson Cipriano (BRA)	27.02.1999	1	(4)	
Manor Solomon (ISR)	24.07.1999	6	(5)	
Aluísio Chaves Ribeiro Moraes Júnior	04.04.1987	27		19
Taison Barcellos Freda (BRA)	13.01.1988	23	(2)	3
Mateus Cardoso Lemos Martins „Tetê" (BRA)	15.02.2000	4	(4)	2
Wellington „Nem" Silva Sanches Aguiar (BRA)	06.02.1992	14	(1)	3
Trainer:	**DOB**	**M**		
Paulo Alexandre Rodrigues Fonseca (POR)	05.03.1973	32		

Futbolnij Klub Vorskla Poltava

Founded: 1955
Stadium: Vorskla Stadium, Poltava (24,795)

Goalkeepers:	DOB	M	(s)	G
Bogdan Shust	04.03.1986	22		
Oleksandr Tkachenko	19.02.1993	10		
Defenders:	**DOB**	**M**	**(s)**	**G**
Oleksandr Chizhov	10.08.1986	15		1
Ardin Dallku (KVX)	01.11.1994	14	(4)	1
Andro Giorgadze (GEO)	03.05.1996	6	(2)	
Ibrahiim Kané (MLI)	23.06.2000	7	(3)	
Evgeny Martynenko	25.06.1993	12		
Ihor Perduta	15.11.1990	27		
Taras Sakiv	19.11.1997	7	(3)	
Vadim Sapay	07.02.1986	16	(1)	
Denis Taraduda	17.08.2000	1		
Najeeb Yakubu (GHA)	01.05.2000	4	(1)	1
Midfielders:	**DOB**	**M**	**(s)**	**G**
Artur Sérgio Batista de Souza (BRA)	05.08.1994	17	(3)	
Volodimir Chesnakov	12.02.1988	24	(1)	1
Artem Gabelyuk	02.01.1995	14	(7)	2
Aleksandr Kobakhidze (GEO)	11.02.1987	13	(3)	
Dmitro Kravchenko	25.02.1995	8	(1)	
Marian Mysyk	02.10.1996	3	(10)	
Todor Petrović (SRB)	18.08.1994	8	(1)	1
Pavlo Rebenok	23.07.1985	24	(6)	3
Vyacheslav Sharpar	02.06.1987	27		6
Aleksandr Sklyar	26.02.1991	14	(9)	
Forwards:	**DOB**	**M**	**(s)**	**G**
Gegam Kadimyan (ARM)	19.10.1992	1	(3)	
Yuriy Kolomoyets	22.03.1990	20	(6)	2
Vladyslav Kulach	07.05.1993	13	(1)	4
Nicolas Mores da Cruz „Nicolas Careca" (BRA)	18.05.1997	14	(10)	2
Volodymyr Odariuk	13.02.1994		(3)	
Mykhaylo Serhiychuk	29.07.1991	1	(9)	
Edin Šehić (BIH)	03.02.1995	3	(5)	
Denis Vasin	04.03.1989	7	(1)	3
Trainer:	**DOB**	**M**		
Vasil Sachko	03.05.1975	22		
Vitaliy Kosovskyi [28.03.2019]	11.08.1973	10		

Futbolnij Klub Zorya Luhansk

Founded: 1923
Stadium: Slavutych-Arena, Zaporizhia (12,000)

Goalkeepers:	DOB	M	(s)	G
Luiz Felipe da Silva Nunes (BRA)	24.04.1997	12		
Zauri Makharadze (GEO)	24.03.1993	12		
Nikita Shevchenko	26.01.1993	8		
Defenders:	**DOB**	**M**	**(s)**	**G**
Maksym Bilyi	21.06.1990	4		1
Vyacheslav Checher	15.12.1980	3	(1)	
Nikita Kamenyuka	03.06.1985	4	(1)	1
Dmytro Lytvyn	21.11.1996	8	(3)	
Bogdan Mykhaylychenko	21.03.1997	19	(2)	
Vasyl Pryima	10.06.1991	4	(1)	
Oleksandr Svatok	27.09.1994	16		
Oleksandr Tymchyk	20.01.1997	20	(1)	1
Vitaliy Vernidub	17.10.1987	26		1
Midfielders:	**DOB**	**M**	**(s)**	**G**
Levan Arveladze	06.04.1993	14	(8)	
Ihor Chaykovskiy	07.10.1991	7	(2)	
Yevhen Cheberko	23.01.1998	16		
Artem Gordienko	04.03.1991	8	(2)	2
Vladyslav Kabayev	01.09.1995	11	(11)	1
Oleksandr Karavayev	02.06.1992	30	(1)	8
Maksym Kazakov	06.02.1996	2	(1)	
Ihor Kharatin	02.02.1995	12	(4)	2
Dmytro Khomchenovsky	16.04.1990	23	(1)	4
Vladyslav Kochergin	30.04.1996	8	(10)	1
Bohdan Lednev	04.07.1998	12	(10)	1
Mateus Norton Gomes Chaves (BRA)	19.07.1996		(1)	
Serhiy Mayboroda	21.11.1997	3	(1)	1
Silas Araujo Da Silva (BRA)	30.05.1996	22	(4)	3
Forwards:	**DOB**	**M**	**(s)**	**G**
Pylyp Budkovsky	10.03.1992	11	(2)	1
Artem Gromov	14.01.1990	15	(9)	7
Nemanja Ivanović (SRB)	14.05.1997	1	(5)	
Maksym Lunyov	22.05.1998	8	(5)	1
Rafael Rogério da Silva „Rafael Ratão" (BRA)	30.11.1995	10	(1)	2
Leonardo Acevedo Ruíz (COL)	18.04.1996	3	(7)	
Trainer:	**DOB**	**M**		
Yuriy Vernydub	22.01.1966	32		

SECOND LEVEL
Ukrainian First League 2018/2019

1.	SC Dnipro-1 (*Promoted*)	28	21	4	3	72	-	21	67
2.	FK Kolos Kovalivka (*Promotion Play-offs*)	28	15	9	4	45	-	18	54
3.	FK Volyn Lutsk (*Promotion Play-offs*)	28	17	7	4	55	-	30	52
4.	FC Metalist 1925 Kharkiv	28	15	6	7	35	-	20	51
5.	FK Avanhard Kramatorsk	28	14	6	8	44	-	26	48
6.	FK Obolon-Brovar Kyiv	28	13	8	7	35	-	28	47
7.	FK Inhulets Petrove	28	11	9	8	35	-	32	42
8.	FK Balkany Zorya	28	10	8	10	28	-	31	38
9.	MFK Mykolaiv	28	10	7	11	34	-	32	37
10.	FK Prykarpattia Ivano-Frankivsk	28	10	4	14	41	-	39	34
11.	FK Rukh Vynnyky	28	8	10	10	35	-	35	34
12.	FK Hirnyk-Sport Horishni Plavni	28	5	12	11	24	-	43	27
13.	FK Ahrobiznes Volochysk (*Relegation Play-offs*)	28	3	10	15	17	-	36	19
14.	PFK Sumy (*Relegation Play-offs*)	28	3	7	18	21	-	91	16
15.	FK Zirka Kropyvnytskyi*	28	1	1	26	10	-	49	4
16.	FK Kobra Kharkiv**	-	-	-	-	-	-	-	-

* FK Zirka Kropyvnytskyi withdrew in February 2019.
** FK Kobra Kharkiv (called earlier FK Helios Kharkiv) withdrew and all results were annulled.

Relegation Play-offs [29.05.-02.06.2019]

MFK Metalurh Zaporizhya - **FK Ahrobiznes Volochysk**	0-4(0-3)	1-0(0-0)
PFK Sumy - **FK Cherkashchyna-Akademiya**	0-4(0-0)	1-3(1-2)

FK Cherkashchyna-Akademiya were promoted for the Ukrainian First League 2019/2020 while FK Ahrobiznes Volochysk retains its place at second level.

NATIONAL TEAM

INTERNATIONAL MATCHES
(16.07.2018 – 15.07.2019)

06.09.2018	Uherské Hradiště	Czech Republic - Ukraine	1-2(1-1)	(UNL)
09.09.2018	Lviv	Ukraine - Slovakia	1-0(0-0)	(UNL)
10.10.2018	Genova	Italy - Ukraine	1-1(0-0)	(F)
16.10.2018	Kharkiv	Ukraine - Czech Republic	1-0(1-0)	(UNL)
16.11.2018	Trnava	Slovakia - Ukraine	4-1(2-0)	(UNL)
20.11.2018	Antalya	Turkey - Ukraine	0-0	(F)
22.03.2019	Lisboa	Portugal - Ukraine	0-0	(ECQ)
25.03.2019	Lëtzebuerg	Luxemburg - Ukraine	1-2(1-0)	(ECQ)
07.06.2019	Lviv	Ukraine - Serbia	5-0(2-0)	(ECQ)
10.06.2019	Lviv	Ukraine - Luxembourg	1-0(1-0)	(ECQ)

06.09.2018 CZECH REPUBLIC - UKRAINE 1-2(1-1) UEFA Nations League B, Group 1
Městský Fotbalový Stadion Miroslava Valenty, Uherské Hradiště; Referee: Anthony Taylor (England); Attendance: 7,974
UKR: Andriy Pyatov (Cap), Serhiy Kryvtsov, Yaroslav Rakytskyi, Mykola Matviyenko, Marlos Romero Bonfim, Taras Stepanenko, Yevhen Konoplyanka (77.Viktor Tsyhankov), Ruslan Malinovskyi, Oleksandr Karavaev, Andriy Yarmolenko (66.Oleksandr Zinchenko), Roman Yaremchuk (85.Yevhen Seleznyov). Trainer: Andriy Shevchenko.
Goals: Yevhen Konoplyanka (45+1), Oleksandr Zinchenko (90+3).

09.09.2018 UKRAINE - SLOVAKIA 1-0(0-0) UEFA Nations League B, Group 1
Arena Lviv, Lviv; Referee: Anastasios Sidiropoulos (Greece); Attendance: *played behind closed doors*
UKR: Andriy Pyatov (Cap), Yaroslav Rakytskyi, Mykyta Burda, Mykola Matviyenko, Marlos Romero Bonfim, Taras Stepanenko (86.Serhiy Sydorchuk), Yevhen Konoplyanka (78.Viktor Tsyhankov), Ruslan Malinovskyi (71.Oleksandr Zinchenko), Oleksandr Karavaev, Andriy Yarmolenko, Roman Yaremchuk. Trainer: Andriy Shevchenko.
Goal: Andriy Yarmolenko (80 penalty).

10.10.2018 ITALY - UKRAINE 1-1(0-0) Friendly International
Stadio "Luigi Ferraris", Genova; Referee: Rade Obrenović(Slovenia); Attendance: 12,000
UKR: Andriy Pyatov (Cap), Yaroslav Rakytskyi (88.Serhiy Kryvtsov), Mykyta Burda, Oleksandr Zinchenko, Mykola Matviyenko, Marlos Romero Bonfim (46.Viktor Tsyhankov), Yevhen Konoplyanka (73.Ivan Petryak), Serhiy Sydorchuk (56.Taras Stepanenko), Ruslan Malinovskyi, Oleksandr Karavaev, Roman Yaremchuk (76.Artem Kravets; 90.Bohdan Butko). Trainer: Andriy Shevchenko.
Goal: Ruslan Malinovskyi (62).

16.10.2018 UKRAINE - CZECH REPUBLIC 1-0(1-0) UEFA Nations League B, Group 1
Regional Sport Complex Metalist, Kharkiv; Referee: Gediminas Mažeika (Lithuania); Attendance: 35,330
UKR: Andriy Pyatov (Cap), Yaroslav Rakytskyi, Mykyta Burda, Mykola Matviyenko, Marlos Romero Bonfim, Taras Stepanenko, Yevhen Konoplyanka (70.Viktor Tsyhankov), Ruslan Malinovskyi (86.Oleksandr Zinchenko), Andriy Yarmolenko, Oleksandr Karavaev, Roman Yaremchuk. Trainer: Andriy Shevchenko.
Goal: Ruslan Malinovskyi (43).

16.11.2018 SLOVAKIA - UKRAINE 4-1(2-0) UEFA Nations League B, Group 1
Štadión "Antona Malatinského", Trnava; Referee: Nikola Dabanović (Montenegro); Attendance: 9,764
UKR: Denys Boyko, Serhiy Kryvtsov (14.Ihor Plastun), Mykyta Burda, Oleksandr Zinchenko, Mykola Matviyenko, Taras Stepanenko, Yevhen Konoplyanka (Cap) (65.Mykola Shaparenko), Ruslan Malinovskyi, Oleksandr Karavaev, Viktor Tsyhankov, Andriy Boryachuk (62.Viktor Kovalenko). Trainer: Andriy Shevchenko.
Goal: Yevhen Konoplyanka (47).

20.11.2018 TURKEY - UKRAINE 0-0 Friendly International
Antalya Stadyumu, Antalya; Referee: Genc Nuza (Kosovo); Attendance: 25,000
UKR: Andriy Lunin, Ihor Plastun, Oleksandr Zinchenko, Mykola Matviyenko, Vitaliy Mykolenko, Yevhen Konoplyanka (Cap) (64.Serhiy Bolbat), Yevhen Makarenko (83.Vitaliy Buyalskyi), Oleksandr Karavaev, Viktor Kovalenko (85.Andriy Boryachuk), Viktor Tsyhankov (77.Maryan Shved), Mykola Shaparenko (46.Ruslan Malinovskyi). Trainer: Andriy Shevchenko.

22.03.2019 PORTUGAL - UKRAINE 0-0 16th EC. Qualifiers
Estadio da Luz, Lisboa; Referee: Clément Turpin(France); Attendance: 58,355
UKR: Andriy Pyatov (Cap), Serhiy Kryvtsov, Oleksandr Zinchenko, Mykola Matviyenko, Vitaliy Mykolenko, Marlos Romero Bonfim (67.Viktor Tsyhankov), Taras Stepanenko, Yevhen Konoplyanka (87.Vitaliy Buyalskyi), Ruslan Malinovskyi, Oleksandr Karavaev, Roman Yaremchuk (76.Aluísio Chaves Ribeiro Moraes Júnior). Trainer: Andriy Shevchenko.

25.03.2019 LUXEMBOURG - UKRAINE 1-2(1-0) 16th EC. Qualifiers
Stade "Josy Barthel", Lëtzebuerg; Referee: Mattias Gestranius (Finland); Attendance: 4,653
UKR: Andriy Pyatov (Cap), Bohdan Butko (79.Oleksandr Karavaev; 87.Vitaliy Buyalskyi), Mykyta Burda, Oleksandr Zinchenko, Mykola Matviyenko, Vitaliy Mykolenko, Yevhen Konoplyanka, Roman Bezus (64.Roman Yaremchuk), Ruslan Malinovskyi, Viktor Tsyhankov, Aluísio Chaves Ribeiro Moraes Júnior. Trainer: Andriy Shevchenko.
Goals: Viktor Tsyhankov (49), Gerson Leal Rodrigues Gouveia (90+3 own goal).

07.06.2019 UKRAINE - SERBIA 5-0(2-0) 16th EC. Qualifiers
Olympiyskiy Stadium, Kyiv; Referee: Antonio Miguel Mateu Lahoz (Spain); Attendance: 34,915
UKR: Andriy Pyatov (Cap), Serhiy Kryvtsov, Oleksandr Zinchenko, Mykola Matviyenko, Vitaliy Mykolenko, Taras Stepanenko (72.Volodymyr Shepelev), Yevhen Konoplyanka (76.Viktor Kovalenko), Ruslan Malinovskyi, Oleksandr Karavaev, Viktor Tsyhankov, Roman Yaremchuk (67.Artem Kravets). Trainer: Andriy Shevchenko.
Goals: Viktor Tsyhankov (26, 27), Yevhen Konoplyanka (46), Roman Yaremchuk (58), Yevhen Konoplyanka (75).

10.06.2019 **UKRAINE - LUXEMBOURG** **1-0(1-0)** 16th EC. Qualifiers

Arena Lviv, Lviv; Referee: Peter Kralović (Slovakia); Attendance: 34,423

UKR: Andriy Pyatov (Cap), Serhiy Kryvtsov, Oleksandr Zinchenko, Mykola Matviyenko, Vitaliy Mykolenko, Taras Stepanenko, Yevhen Konoplyanka (80.Viktor Kovalenko), Ruslan Malinovskyi, Oleksandr Karavaev, Viktor Tsyhankov (88.Eduard Sobol), Roman Yaremchuk. Trainer: Andriy Shevchenko.

Goal: Roman Yaremchuk (6).

NATIONAL TEAM PLAYERS
(16.07.2018 – 15.07.2019)

Name	DOB	Caps	Goals	2018/2019:	*Club*
Goalkeepers					
Denys BOYKO	29.01.1988	**6**	**0**	2018:	*FK Dinamo Kyiv*
Andriy LUNIN	11.02.1999	**3**	**0**	2018:	*CD Leganés (ESP)*
Andriy PYATOV	28.06.1984	**89**	**0**	2018/2019:	*FK Shakhtar Donetsk*
Defenders					
Serhiy BOLBAT	13.06.1993	**2**	**0**	2018:	*FK Shakhtar Donetsk*
Mykyta BURDA	24.04.1995	**7**	**0**	2018/2019:	*FK Dinamo Kyiv*
Bohdan BUTKO	13.01.1991	**33**	**0**	2018/2019:	*FK Shakhtar Donetsk*
Oleksandr KARAVAYEV	02.06.1992	**22**	**1**	2018/2019:	*FK Zorya Luhansk*
Serhiy KRYVTSOV	15.03.1991	**12**	**0**	2018/2019:	*FK Shakhtar Donetsk*
Mykola MATVIYENKO	02.05.1996	**20**	**0**	2018/2019:	*FK Shakhtar Donetsk*
Vitaliy MYKOLENKO	29.05.1999	**5**	**0**	2018/2019:	*FK Dinamo Kyiv*
Ihor PLASTUN	20.08.1990	**2**	**0**	2018:	*KAA Gent (BEL)*
Yaroslav RAKITSKYI	03.08.1989	**54**	**4**	2018/2019:	*FK Shakhtar Donetsk*
Eduard SOBOL	20.04.1995	**11**	**0**	2019:	*FK Jablonec (CZE)*
Oleksandr ZINCHENKO	15.12.1996	**27**	**2**	2018/2019:	*Manchester City FC (ENG)*
Midfielders					
Roman BEZUS	26.09.1990	**20**	**4**	2019:	*KAA Gent (BEL)*
Vitaliy BUYALSKYI	06.01.1993	**6**	**0**	2018/2019:	*FK Dinamo Kyiv*
Yevhen KONOPLYANKA	29.09.1989	**82**	**21**	2018/2019:	*FC Schalke 04 Gelsenkirchen (GER)*
Viktor KOVALENKO	14.02.1996	**22**	**0**	2018/2019:	*FK Shakhtar Donetsk*
Yevhen MAKARENKO	21.05.1991	**4**	**0**	2018:	*RSC Anderlecht Bruxelles (BEL)*
Ruslan MALINOVSKYI	04.05.1993	**22**	**2**	2018/2019:	*KRC Genk (BEL)*
MARLOS Romero Bonfim	07.06.1988	**12**	**0**	2018/2019:	*FK Shakhtar Donetsk*
Ivan PETRYAK	13.03.1994	**5**	**0**	2018:	*Ferencvárosi TC (HUN)*
Mykola SHAPARENKO	04.10.1998	**4**	**0**	2018:	*FK Dinamo Kyiv*
Volodymyr SHEPELEV	01.06.1997	**3**	**0**	2019:	*FK Dinamo Kyiv*
Maryan SHVED	16.07.1997	**1**	**0**	2018:	*FK Karpaty Lviv*
Taras STEPANENKO	08.08.1989	**54**	**3**	2018/2019:	*FK Shakhtar Donetsk*
Serhiy SYDORCHUK	02.05.1991	**25**	**2**	2018:	*FK Dinamo Kyiv*
Viktor TSYHANKOV	15.11.1997	**15**	**3**	2018/2019:	*FK Dinamo Kyiv*
Andriy YARMOLENKO	23.10.1989	**80**	**36**	2018:	*West Ham United FC London (ENG)*
Forwards					
Andriy BORYACHUK	23.04.1996	**2**	**0**	2018:	*FK Mariupol*
Aluísio Chaves Ribeiro Moraes JÚNIOR	04.04.1987	**2**	**0**	2019:	*FK Shakhtar Donetsk*
Artem KRAVETS	03.06.1989	**23**	**8**	2018/2019:	*Kayserispor Kulübü (TUR)*
Yevhen SELEZNYOV	20.07.1985	**58**	**11**	2018:	*Akhisar Belediye Gençlik SK (TUR)*
Roman YAREMCHUK	27.11.1995	**8**	**2**	2018/2019:	*KAA Gent (BEL)*

National team coach

Andriy SHEVCHENKO [from 15.07.2016]	29.09.1976	27 M; 15 W; 7 D; 5 L; 38-21

WALES

The Country:
Cymru (Wales)
Capital: Cardiff
Surface: 20,779 km²
Inhabitants: 3,125,000 [2017]
Time: UTC

The FA:
Football Association of Wales
11/12 Neptune Court Vanguard Way, CF24 5PJ Cardiff
Tel: +44 29 2043 5830
Founded: 1876
Member of FIFA: 1910-1920; 1924-1928; since 1946
Member of UEFA since: 1954
Website: www.faw.org.uk

NATIONAL TEAM RECORDS

First international match:	25.03.1876, Glasgow:	Scotland – Wales 4-0
Most international caps:	Christopher Ross Gunter	- 95 caps (since 2007)
Most international goals:	Gareth Frank Bale	- 31 goals / 77 caps (since 2006)

UEFA EUROPEAN CHAMPIONSHIP	
1960	Did not enter
1964	Qualifiers
1968	Qualifiers
1972	Qualifiers
1976	Qualifiers
1980	Qualifiers
1984	Qualifiers
1988	Qualifiers
1992	Qualifiers
1996	Qualifiers
2000	Qualifiers
2004	Qualifiers
2008	Qualifiers
2012	Qualifiers
2016	Final Tournament (Semi-Finals)

FIFA WORLD CUP	
1930	*Not a FIFA member*
1934	*Not a FIFA member*
1938	*Not a FIFA member*
1950	Qualifiers
1954	Qualifiers
1958	Final Tournament (Quarter-Finals)
1962	Qualifiers
1966	Qualifiers
1970	Qualifiers
1974	Qualifiers
1978	Qualifiers
1982	Qualifiers
1986	Qualifiers
1990	Qualifiers
1994	Qualifiers
1998	Qualifiers
2002	Qualifiers
2006	Qualifiers
2010	Qualifiers
2014	Qualifiers
2018	Qualifiers

UEFA NATIONS LEAGUE

2018/2019 – League B

FIFA CONFEDERATIONS CUP 1992-2017

None

WELSH CLUB HONOURS IN EUROPEAN CLUB COMPETITIONS:

European Champion Clubs.Cup (1956-1992) / UEFA Champions League (1993-2019)

None

Fairs Cup (1858-1971) / UEFA Cup (1972-2009) / UEFA Europa League (2010-2019)

None

UEFA Super Cup (1972-2018)

None

European Cup Winners.Cup 1961-1999*

None

**defunct competition*

NATIONAL COMPETITIONS
TABLE OF HONOURS

	CHAMPIONS*	CUP WINNERS	BEST GOALSCORERS
1877/1878	-	Wrexham AFC	-
1878/1879	-	Newtown White Stars FC	-
1879/1880	-	Ruabon Druids FC	-
1880/1881	-	Ruabon Druids FC	-
1881/1882	-	Ruabon Druids FC	-
1882/1883	-	Wrexham AFC	-
1883/1884	-	Oswestry Town FC Shropshire(ENG)	-
1884/1885	-	Ruabon Druids FC	-
1885/1886	-	Ruabon Druids FC	-
1886/1887	-	Chirk AAA FC	-
1887/1888	-	Chirk AAA FC	-
1888/1889	-	Bangor City FC	-
1889/1890	-	Chirk AAA FC	-
1890/1891	-	Shrewsbury Town FC (ENG)	-
1891/1892	-	Chirk AAA FC	-
1892/1893	-	Wrexham AFC	-
1893/1894	-	Chirk AAA FC	-
1894/1895	-	Newtown AFC	-
1895/1896	-	Bangor City FC	-
1896/1897	-	Wrexham AFC	-
1897/1898	-	Ruabon Druids FC	-
1898/1899	-	Ruabon Druids FC	-
1899/1900	-	Aberystwyth Town FC	-
1900/1901	-	Oswestry Town FC Shropshire(ENG)	-
1901/1902	-	Wellington Town FC (ENG)	-
1902/1903	-	Wrexham AFC	-
1903/1904	-	Ruabon Druids FC	-
1904/1905	-	Wrexham AFC	-
1905/1906	-	Wellington Town FC (ENG)	-
1906/1907	-	Oswestry Town FC Shropshire(ENG)	-
1907/1908	-	Chester City FC (ENG)	-
1908/1909	-	Wrexham AFC	-
1909/1910	-	Wrexham AFC	-
1910/1911	-	Wrexham AFC	-
1911/1912	-	Cardiff City	-
1912/1913	-	Swansea Town AFC	-
1913/1914	-	Wrexham AFC	-
1914/1915	-	Wrexham AFC	-
1915/1916	-	*No competition*	-
1916/1917	-	*No competition*	-
1917/1918	-	*No competition*	-
1918/1919	-	*No competition*	-
1919/1920	-	Cardiff City FC	-
1920/1921	-	Wrexham AFC	-
1921/1922	-	Cardiff City FC	-
1922/1923	-	Cardiff City FC	-
1923/1924	-	Wrexham AFC	-
1924/1925	-	Wrexham AFC	-
1925/1926	-	Ebbw Vale FC	-
1926/1927	-	Cardiff City FC	-
1927/1928	-	Cardiff City FC	-
1928/1929	-	Connah's Quay & Shotton FC	-
1929/1930	-	Cardiff City FC	-
1930/1931	-	Wrexham AFC	-
1931/1932	-	Swansea Town AFC	-
1932/1933	-	Chester City FC (ENG)	-
1933/1934	-	Bristol City FC (ENG)	-
1934/1935	-	Tranmere Rovers FC (ENG)	-
1935/1936	-	Crewe Alexandra FC (ENG)	-
1936/1937	-	Crewe Alexandra FC (ENG)	-
1937/1938	-	Shrewsbury Town FC (ENG)	-
1938/1939	-	South Liverpool FC (ENG)	-
1939/1940	-	Wellington Town FC (ENG)	-
1940/1941	-	*No competition*	-
1941/1942	-	*No competition*	-
1942/1943	-	*No competition*	-
1943/1944	-	*No competition*	-
1944/1945	-	*No competition*	-
1945/1946	-	*No competition*	-
1946/1947	-	Chester City FC (ENG)	-
1947/1948	-	Lovell's Athletic FC	-
1948/1949	-	Merthyr Tydfil FC	-

1949/1950	-	Swansea Town AFC	-	
1950/1951	-	Merthyr Tydfil FC	-	
1951/1952	-	Rhyl FC	-	
1952/1953	-	Rhyl FC	-	
1953/1954	-	Flint Town United FC	-	
1954/1955	-	Barry Town United FC	-	
1955/1956	-	Cardiff City FC	-	
1956/1957	-	Wrexham AFC	-	
1957/1958	-	Wrexham AFC	-	
1958/1959	-	Cardiff City FC	-	
1959/1960	-	Wrexham AFC	-	
1960/1961	-	Swansea Town AFC	-	
1961/1962	-	Bangor City FC	-	
1962/1963	-	Borough United FC	-	
1963/1964	-	Cardiff City FC	-	
1964/1965	-	Cardiff City FC	-	
1965/1966	-	Swansea Town AFC	-	
1966/1967	-	Cardiff City FC	-	
1967/1968	-	Cardiff City FC	-	
1968/1969	-	Cardiff City FC	-	
1969/1970	-	Cardiff City FC	-	
1970/1971	-	Cardiff City FC	-	
1971/1972	-	Wrexham AFC	-	
1972/1973	-	Cardiff City FC	-	
1973/1974	-	Cardiff City FC	-	
1974/1975	-	Wrexham AFC	-	
1975/1976	-	Cardiff City FC	-	
1976/1977	-	Shrewsbury Town FC (ENG)	-	
1977/1978	-	Wrexham AFC	-	
1978/1979	-	Shrewsbury Town FC (ENG)	-	
1979/1980	-	Newport County AFC	-	
1980/1981	-	Swansea City FC	-	
1981/1982	-	Swansea City FC	-	
1982/1983	-	Swansea City FC	-	
1983/1984	-	Shrewsbury Town FC (ENG)	-	
1984/1985	-	Shrewsbury Town FC (ENG)	-	
1985/1986	-	Wrexham AFC	-	
1986/1987	-	Merthyr Tydfil FC	-	
1987/1988	-	Cardiff City FC	-	
1988/1989	-	Swansea City FC	-	
1989/1990	-	Hereford United FC (ENG)	-	
1990/1991	-	Swansea City FC	-	
1991/1992	-	Cardiff City FC	-	
1992/1993	Cwmbrân Town AFC	Cardiff City FC	Steve Woods (Ebbw Vale FC)	29
1993/1994	Bangor City FC	Barry Town United FC	Dave Taylor (Porthmadog FC)	43
1994/1995	Bangor City FC	Wrexham AFC	Frank Mottram (Bangor City FC)	31
1995/1996	Barry Town United FC	Llansantffraid FC	Ken McKenna (Conwy United FC)	38
1996/1997	Barry Town United FC	Barry Town United FC	Anthony Bird (Barry Town United FC)	42
1997/1998	Barry Town United FC	Bangor City FC	Eifion Wyn Williams (Barry Town United FC)	40
1998/1999	Barry Town United FC	Inter CableTel Cardiff	Eifion Wyn Williams (Barry Town United FC)	28
1999/2000	Total Network Solutions	Bangor City FC	Chris Summers (Cwmbrân Town AFC)	28
2000/2001	Barry Town United FC	Barry Town United FC	Graham Evans (Caersws FC)	25
2001/2002	Barry Town United FC	Barry Town United FC	Marc Lloyd-Williams (Bangor City FC)	47
2002/2003	Barry Town United FC	Barry Town United FC	Graham Evans (Caersws FC)	24
2003/2004	Rhyl FC	Rhyl FC	Graham Evans (Caersws FC)	24
2004/2005	Total Network Solutions	Total Network Solutions	Marc Lloyd-Williams (Total Network Solutions)	31
2005/2006	Total Network Solutions	Rhyl FC	Rhys Griffiths (Port Talbot Town FC)	28
2006/2007	The New Saints FC	Carmarthen Town FC	Rhys Griffiths (Llanelli Town AFC)	30
2007/2008	Llanelli Town AFC	Bangor City FC	Rhys Griffiths (Llanelli Town AFC)	40
2008/2009	Rhyl FC	Bangor City FC	Rhys Griffiths (Llanelli Town AFC)	31
2009/2010	The New Saints FC	Bangor City FC	Rhys Griffiths (Llanelli Town AFC)	30
2010/2011	Bangor City FC	Llanelli Town AFC	Rhys Griffiths (Llanelli Town AFC)	25
2011/2012	The New Saints FC	The New Saints FC	Rhys Griffiths (Llanelli Town AFC)	24
2012/2013	The New Saints FC	Prestatyn Town FC	Michael Wilde (The New Saints FC)	25
2013/2014	The New Saints FC	The New Saints FC	Chris Venables (Aberystwyth Town FC)	20
2014/2015	The New Saints FC	The New Saints FC	Chris Venables (Aberystwyth Town FC)	28
2015/2016	The New Saints FC	The New Saints FC	Chris Venables (Bala Town FC)	20
2016/2017	The New Saints FC	Bala Town FC	Jason Oswell (ENG, Newtown AFC)	22
2017/2018	The New Saints FC	Connah's Quay Nomads FC	Gregory Alexander Draper (NZL, The New Saints FC)	11
2018/2019	The New Saints FC	The New Saints FC	Steven Anthony Tames (ENG, Bala Town FC)	17

Please note: Championship called League of Wales (1992–2002) and Welsh Premier League (since 2002)

NATIONAL CHAMPIONSHIP
Welsh Premier League 2018/2019
(10.08.2018 – 26.04.2019)

Regular Season - Results

Round 1 [10-12.08.2018]
Aberystwyth Town - Llandudno FC 1-0(1-0)
Bala Town - Carmarthen Town 2-1(1-0)
Metropolitan - Newtown AFC 2-1(2-0)
The New Saints - Barry Town 5-1(3-1)
Llanelli Town - Connah's Quay 0-7(0-3)
Caernarfon Town - Cefn Druids 1-0(1-0)

Round 2 [17-19.08.2018]
Aberystwyth Town - Metropolitan 1-4(0-3)
Newtown AFC - Caernarfon Town 2-0(1-0)
Carmarthen Town - Llandudno FC 0-0
Cefn Druids - Llanelli Town 2-3(2-0)
Barry Town - Bala Town 3-2(2-1)
Connah's Quay - The New Saints 1-0(0-0)

Round 3 [24-26.08.2018]
Llanelli Town - Barry Town 1-1(1-0)
Bala Town - Cefn Druids 2-1(1-0)
Connah's Quay - Aberystwyth Town 2-1(2-0)
Llandudno FC - Newtown AFC 0-0
The New Saints - Carmarthen Town 6-0(3-0)
Metropolitan - Caernarfon Town 0-1(0-1)

Round 4 [31.08.-01.09.2018]
Aberystwyth Town - Llanelli Town 3-1(0-1)
Caernarfon Town - The New Saints 0-3(0-1)
Carmarthen Town - Metropolitan 2-0(1-0)
Newtown AFC - Bala Town 2-0(1-0)
Barry Town - Connah's Quay 2-0(1-0)
Cefn Druids - Llandudno FC 2-1(1-1)

Round 5 [08-11.09.2018]
Bala Town - Llanelli Town 3-1(2-0)
Carmarthen Town - Newtown AFC 3-0(1-0)
Llandudno FC - Barry Town 2-0(2-0)
Metropolitan - Cefn Druids 1-0(0-0)
Connah's Quay - Caernarfon Town 0-1(0-1)
The New Saints - Aberystwyth Town 6-0(4-0)

Round 6 [14-16.09.2018]
Connah's Quay - Newtown AFC 3-1(1-0)
Llanelli Town - The New Saints 0-2(0-2)
Caernarfon Town - Barry Town 0-1(0-0)
Cefn Druids - Carmarthen Town 4-0(2-0)
Aberystwyth Town - Bala Town 3-2(1-0)
Metropolitan - Llandudno FC 0-1(0-0)

Round 7 [21-22.09.2018]
The New Saints - Bala Town 0-0
Barry Town - Cefn Druids 2-1(0-1)
Caernarfon Town - Llanelli Town 3-0(0-0)
Carmarthen Town - Aberystwyth T. 2-2(2-0)
Newtown AFC - Metropolitan 2-1(2-1)
Llandudno FC - Connah's Quay 0-4(0-2)

Round 8 [28-30.09.2018]
Bala Town - Llandudno FC 2-1(1-0)
Cefn Druids - Caernarfon Town 1-1(1-0)
Llanelli Town - Newtown AFC 1-3(1-1)
Aberystwyth Town - Barry Town 0-1(0-1)
Connah's Quay - Carmarthen Town 3-1(1-0)
Metropolitan - The New Saints 4-1(2-0)

Round 9 [05-07.10.2018]
Caernarfon Town - Bala Town 2-2(1-1)
Cefn Druids - Aberystwyth Town 1-0(0-0)
Carmarthen Town - The New Saints 0-3(0-0)
Llandudno FC - Llanelli Town 1-2(1-1)
Newtown AFC - Barry Town 2-0(1-0)
Metropolitan - Connah's Quay 1-3(1-2)

Round 10 [12-17.10.2018]
Aberystwyth Town - Caernarfon Town 0-0
Bala Town - Newtown AFC 3-2(1-0)
Llanelli Town - Metropolitan 0-2(0-0)
Barry Town - Carmarthen Town 1-0(0-0)
Connah's Quay - Cefn Druids 3-1(0-1)
The New Saints - Llandudno FC 6-1(4-0)

Round 11 [19-20.10.2018]
Barry Town - Llanelli Town 5-2(2-1)
Caernarfon Town - Newtown AFC 0-3(0-0)
Carmarthen Town - Bala Town 1-2(1-1)
Cefn Druids - Metropolitan 1-1(0-1)
Llandudno FC - Aberystwyth Town 0-1(0-0)
The New Saints - Connah's Quay 3-0(1-0)

Round 12 [26-28.10.2018]
Caernarfon Town - Connah's Quay 0-0
Llandudno FC - Cefn Druids 0-0
Llanelli Town - Aberystwyth Town 1-3(1-2)
Bala Town - Barry Town 0-1(0-1)
Newtown AFC - The New Saints 1-1(1-0)
Metropolitan - Carmarthen Town 1-1(0-1)

Round 13 [02-04.11.2018]
Aberystwyth Town - The New Saints 1-0(0-0)
Cefn Druids - Newtown AFC 1-1(1-0)
Carmarthen Town - Caernarfon Town 4-3(2-1)
Connah's Quay - Llanelli Town 6-0(4-0)
Bala Town - Metropolitan 3-0(1-0)
Barry Town - Llandudno FC 2-1(1-1)

Round 14 [09-11.11.2018]
Llandudno FC - Bala Town 2-4(0-1)
The New Saints - Caernarfon Town 0-1(0-0)
Carmarthen Town - Cefn Druids 2-3(2-0)
Connah's Quay - Barry Town 2-2(1-2)
Newtown AFC - Llanelli Town 7-1(5-0)
Metropolitan - Aberystwyth Town 2-3(2-0)

Round 15 [17-21.11.2018]
Bala Town - Aberystwyth Town 2-3(1-0)
Llandudno FC - Carmarthen Town 1-2(1-1)
Llanelli Town - Cefn Druids 2-0(1-0)
Barry Town - The New Saints 0-2(0-0)
Caernarfon Town - Metropolitan 2-0(2-0)
Newtown AFC - Connah's Quay 1-1(0-1)

Round 16 [30.11.-01.12.2018]
Aberystwyth Town - Carmarthen T. 1-1(1-0)
Cefn Druids - Bala Town 2-2(0-2)
Connah's Quay - Llandudno FC 3-0(1-0)
Llanelli Town - Caernarfon Town 2-2(0-0)
The New Saints - Metropolitan 1-1(0-0)
Barry Town - Newtown AFC 4-1(0-0)

Round 17 [14-15.12.2018]
Bala Town - The New Saints 1-1(0-1)
Caernarfon Town - Aberystwyth T. 4-0(1-0)
Metropolitan - Llanelli Town 4-0(1-0)
Carmarthen Town - Barry Town 2-3(0-0)
Cefn Druids - Connah's Quay 1-2(0-0)
Newtown AFC - Llandudno FC 3-1(1-1)

Round 18 [21-22.12.2018]
Aberystwyth Town - Cefn Druids 0-2(0-1)
Connah's Quay - Metropolitan 6-1(4-1)
Llandudno FC - The New Saints 0-4(0-2)
Llanelli Town - Bala Town 1-7(1-3)
Newtown AFC - Carmarthen Town 1-1(1-1)
Barry Town - Caernarfon Town 2-1(1-1)

Round 19 [26-29.12.2018]
Llanelli Town - Carmarthen Town 1-1(0-0)
Barry Town - Metropolitan 2-1(2-1)
Aberystwyth Town - Newtown AFC 0-2(0-1)
Bala Town - Connah's Quay 2-1(2-1)
The New Saints - Cefn Druids 7-0(3-0)
Caernarfon Town - Llandudno FC 3-3(2-3)

Round 20 [30.12.2018-01.01.2019]
Newtown AFC - Aberystwyth Town 2-1(1-0)
Metropolitan - Barry Town 3-0(1-0)
Cefn Druids - The New Saints 0-3(0-2)
Connah's Quay - Bala Town 4-1(2-1)
Llandudno FC - Caernarfon Town 1-1(0-0)
Carmarthen Town - Llanelli Town 2-0(1-0)

Round 21 [04-05.01.2019]
Aberystwyth Town - Connah's Quay 1-6(1-2)
The New Saints - Newtown AFC 4-0(2-0)
Caernarfon Town - Carmarthen Town 3-1(1-1)
Metropolitan - Bala Town 3-0(1-0)
Cefn Druids - Barry Town 2-5(2-1)
Llanelli Town - Llandudno FC 2-1(2-1)

Round 22 [12.01.2019]
Bala Town - Caernarfon Town 1-3(1-0)
Barry Town - Aberystwyth Town 2-1(2-0)
Carmarthen Town - Connah's Quay 3-2(0-1)
Llandudno FC - Metropolitan 0-3(0-2)
Newtown AFC - Cefn Druids 1-1(0-1)
The New Saints - Llanelli Town 5-0(2-0)

Final Standings

1.	Barry Town United FC	22	15	2	5	40 - 31	47
2.	The New Saints FC	22	14	4	4	63 - 12	46
3.	Connah's Quay Nomads FC	22	14	3	5	59 - 23	45
4.	Newtown AFC	22	10	6	6	38 - 29	36
5.	Caernarfon Town FC	22	9	7	6	32 - 26	34
6.	Bala Town FC	22	10	4	8	43 - 38	34
7.	Cardiff Metropolitan University FC	22	9	3	10	35 - 31	30
8.	Aberystwyth Town FC	22	8	3	11	26 - 43	27
9.	Carmarthen Town AFC	22	6	6	10	30 - 42	24
10.	Cefn Druids AFC	22	5	6	11	26 - 40	21
11.	Llanelli Town AFC	22	4	3	15	21 - 70	15
12.	Llandudno FC	22	2	5	15	17 - 45	11

Teams ranked 1-6 were qualified for the Championship Round, while teams ranked 7-12 were qualified for the Relegation Round.

Championship Round

Round 23 [02.02.2019]
Caernarfon Town - Barry Town 2-0(0-0)
Newtown AFC - Connah's Quay 1-2(1-0)
Bala Town - The New Saints 0-7(0-2) [03.04.]

Round 24 [08.02.2019]
Connah's Quay - Caernarfon Town 6-2(3-1)
The New Saints - Newtown AFC 5-0(2-0)
Barry Town - Bala Town 0-2(0-1) [16.03.]

Round 25 [16.02.2019]
Newtown AFC - Caernarfon Town 3-2(1-0)
The New Saints - Barry Town 2-2(2-1)
Connah's Quay - Bala Town 1-0(0-0) [26.02.]

Round 26 [22-25.02.2019]
Bala Town - Newtown AFC 2-2(1-2)
Barry Town - Connah's Quay 1-1(1-1)
Caernarfon Town - The New Saints 0-3(0-2)

Round 27 [08-09.03.2019]
Caernarfon Town - Bala Town 1-0(1-0)
Newtown AFC - Barry Town 3-0(3-0)
Connah's Quay - The New Saints 0-2(0-1)

Round 28 [15/22-23.03.2019]
Connah's Quay - Newtown AFC 2-0(1-0)
The New Saints - Bala Town 3-1(0-0)
Barry Town - Caernarfon Town 4-0(2-0)

Round 29 [05-06.04.2019]
Caernarfon Town - Connah's Quay 1-0(1-0)
Bala Town - Barry Town 2-5(0-0)
Newtown AFC - The New Saints 0-6(0-2)

Round 30 [12-13.04.2019]
Bala Town - Connah's Quay 1-4(1-2)
Caernarfon Town - Newtown AFC 4-1(2-0)
Barry Town - The New Saints 0-4(0-1)

Round 31 [19-20.04.2019]
Newtown AFC - Bala Town 2-3(2-2)
Connah's Quay - Barry Town 1-1(1-0)
The New Saints - Caernarfon Town 3-1(1-1)

Round 32 [26.04.2019]
Bala Town - Caernarfon Town 1-0(1-0)
Barry Town - Newtown AFC 1-3(0-1)
The New Saints - Connah's Quay 1-0(1-0)

Final Standings

1.	**The New Saints FC**	32	23	5	4	99 - 16	74
2.	Connah's Quay Nomads FC	32	19	5	8	76 - 33	62
3.	Barry Town United FC	32	17	5	10	54 - 51	56
4.	Caernarfon Town FC	32	13	7	12	45 - 47	46
5.	Newtown AFC	32	13	7	12	53 - 56	46
6.	Bala Town FC	32	13	5	14	55 - 63	44

Please note: teams ranked 4-5-6-7 (Relegation Round) were qualified for the Europa League Play-offs.

Top goalscorers:

17 Steven Anthony Tames (ENG)
Bala Town FC

15 Gregory Alexander Draper (NZL)
The New Saints FC

12 Liam Thomas
Caernarfon Town FC

Relegation Round

Round 23 [01-02.02.2019]
Aberystwyth Town - Llandudno FC 1-1(0-1)
Carmarthen Town - Metropolitan 1-0(0-0)
Cefn Druids - Llanelli Town 0-0

Round 24 [08-10.02.2019]
Llanelli Town - Aberystwyth Town 2-4(0-3)
Llandudno FC - Carmarthen Town 3-1(2-0)
Metropolitan - Cefn Druids 3-0(0-0)

Round 25 [15-16.02.2019]
Cefn Druids - Aberystwyth Town 3-1(2-1)
Llanelli Town - Carmarthen Town 0-3(0-2)
Metropolitan - Llandudno FC 3-0(1-0)

Round 26 [23.02.2019]
Aberystwyth Town - Metropolitan 2-0(1-0)
Carmarthen Town - Cefn Druids 0-1(0-0)
Llandudno FC - Llanelli Town 4-2(0-0)

Round 27 [08.03.2019]
Aberystwyth Town - Carmarthen T. 3-2(2-1)
Cefn Druids - Llandudno FC 2-2(1-1)
Llanelli Town - Metropolitan 0-4(0-1)

Round 28 [22-23.03.2019]
Llandudno FC - Aberystwyth Town 1-2(1-0)
Metropolitan - Carmarthen Town 1-0(0-0)
Llanelli Town - Cefn Druids 1-3(0-1)

Round 29 [05-06.04.2019]
Aberystwyth Town - Llanelli Town 3-2(1-0)
Carmarthen Town - Llandudno FC 2-0(2-0)
Cefn Druids - Metropolitan 3-1(2-0)

Round 30 [12-13.04.2019]
Aberystwyth Town - Cefn Druids 0-0
Carmarthen Town - Llanelli Town 3-1(2-1)
Llandudno FC - Metropolitan 1-2(0-1)

Round 31 [20.04.2019]
Metropolitan - Aberystwyth Town 1-0(1-0)
Cefn Druids - Carmarthen Town 0-1(0-0)
Llanelli Town - Llandudno FC 0-4(0-2)

Round 32 [26.04.2019]
Metropolitan - Llanelli Town 3-2(1-1)
Carmarthen Town - Aberystwyth T. 6-2(1-1)
Llandudno FC - Cefn Druids 0-5(0-3)

Final Standings

7.	Cardiff Metropolitan University FC	32	16	3	13	53 - 40		51
8.	Aberystwyth Town FC	32	13	5	14	44 - 61		44
9.	Carmarthen Town AFC(1)	32	12	6	14	49 - 53		39
10.	Cefn Druids AFC	32	10	9	13	43 - 49		39
11.	Llandudno FC (*Relegated*)	32	5	7	20	33 - 65		22
12.	Llanelli Town AFC (*Relegated*)	32	4	4	24	31 - 101		16

(1)3 points deducted;

Europa League Play-offs

Semi-Finals (10-11.05.2019)	Newtown AFC - Bala Town FC	1-2(0-1)
	Caernarfon Town FC - Cardiff Metropolitan University FC	2-3(1-1)
Final (19.05.2019)	Bala Town FC - **Cardiff Metropolitan University FC**	1-1(1-1,1-1,1-1); 1-3 pen

NATIONAL CUP
Welsh Cup 2018/2019

First Round [19-20.10.2018]

Penlan Club - Goytre United FC	0-1
Cefn Albion FC - Dolgellau Athletic Amateur	7-1
Llandudno Albion FC - St. Asaph City FC	3-4 aet
Briton Ferry Llansawel AFC - Caerau Ely AFC	1-0
Cambrian & Clydach Vale - Port Talbot Town FC	5-0
Cwmamman United FC Glanaman - Dinas Powys FC	4-0
Cwmbran Celtic FC - Ammanford AFC	3-0
Cwmbrân Town FC - Afan Lido FC Port Talbot	3-2
Garden Village AFC Swansea - Blaenrhondda AFC	1-2
Llandrindod Wells FC - Aberbargoed Buds	3-4 pen
Llanidloes Town FC - Pontypridd Town AFC Cardiff	1-2
Panteg AFC Griffithstown - Pen-y-Bont FC Bridgent	1-3
Pontyclun FC - Llantwit Major FC	3-1
Radnor Valley - Goytre AFC Penperlleni	1-2
STM Sports St. Mellons - Haverfordwest County	1-2
Sully Sports - Brecon Corries AFC	3-1
Ton Pentre FC - Pencoed Athletic AFC	3-1
Trefelin BGC - Swansea University FC	1-2
Treharris Athletic Western FC - Cornelly United FC	3-2
Undy Athletic FC - Monmouth Town FC	3-4
West End FC Mayhill - Caldicot Town AFC	0-6
Ynysddu Welfare - Taffs Well AFC	2-1
Bangor City FC - Mold Alexandra FC	4-2
Berriew FC - Penrhyncoch FC	5-4 pen
Buckley Town FC - Brymbo FC Tanyfron	3-1
Caersws FC - Holywell Town FC	3-2 aet
Coedpoeth United FC - Ruthin Town FC	2-3
Conwy Borough FC - Rhyl FC	1-2
Pwllheli FC - Porthmadog FC	0-3
Denbigh Town FC - Holyhead Town FC	9-3
Gresford Athletic FC - Brickfield Rangers FC	4-3 aet
Guilsfield FC - Rhostyllen FC	2-0
Hawarden Rangers FC - Llanfair United	2-3
Holyhead Hotspur FC - Corwen FC	4-2
Llangefni Town FC - Borth United	2-0
Llanrhaeadr-ym-Mochnant - Flint Town United FC	1-2
Llay Welfare FC - Rhydymwyn FC	2-0
Penycae FC - Airbus UK Broughton FC	0-4
Prestatyn Town FC - New Brighton Villa	5-1
Llandudno Amateurs FC - Dyffryn Nanttle Vale FC	2-4 aet

Second Round [09-10/17.11.2018]

Caldicot Town AFC - Cambrian & Clydach Vale	2-3
Sully Sports - Cwmbran Celtic FC	1-3
Airbus UK Broughton FC - Llay Welfare FC	9-1
Bangor City FC - Cefn Albion FC	6-1
Buckley Town FC - Denbigh Town FC	1-3
Flint Town United FC - Gresford Athletic FC	3-2
Guilsfield FC - Dyffryn Nanttle Vale FC	4-3
Holyhead Hotspur FC - Ruthin Town FC	3-1
Llanfair United - Porthmadog FC	1-4
Llangefni Town FC - St. Asaph City FC	5-1
Prestatyn Town FC - Berriew FC	6-3
Rhyl FC - Caersws FC	3-1
Cwmbrân Town FC - Ton Pentre FC	1-2
Goytre United FC - Pontyclun FC	1-0
Haverfordwest County AFC - Swansea University FC	4-3
Monmouth Town FC - Ynysddu Welfare	1-3
Pontypridd Town AFC Cardiff - Goytre AFC	6-3
Aberbargoed Buds - Pen-y-Bont FC Bridgent	0-2
Cwmamman United FC - Blaenrhondda AFC	2-1
Treharris Athletic Western FC - Briton Ferry AFC	3-4

Third Round [07-08/11.12.2018]

Barry Town United FC - Pen-y-Bont FC Bridgent	4-1 aet
Bangor City FC - Holyhead Hotspur FC	4-1
Prestatyn Town FC - Caernarfon Town FC	0-3
Cwmbran Celtic FC - The New Saints FC	0-3
Cwmamman United FC - Aberystwyth Town FC	3-4
Airbus UK Broughton FC - Porthmadog FC	4-2 pen
Goytre United FC - Carmarthen Town AFC	0-3
Denbigh Town FC - Cambrian & Clydach Vale	1-2
Guilsfield FC - Connah's Quay Nomads FC	2-4
Llangefni Town FC - Llanelli Town AFC	1-0
Newtown AFC - Rhyl FC	1-2
Ton Pentre FC - Cardiff Metropolitan University FC	1-4
Briton Ferry Llansawel AFC - Llandudno FC	2-3
Haverfordwest County AFC - Pontypridd Town AFC	3-0
Ynysddu Welfare - Cefn Druids AFC	1-3
Flint Town United FC - Bala Town FC	0-3

1/8-Finals [26.01.2019]

Carmarthen Town AFC - Connah's Quay Nomads FC	1-3
Haverfordwest County AFC - Bala Town FC	0-4 aet
Barry Town United FC - Cefn Druids AFC	3-2
Airbus UK Broughton FC - The New Saints FC	2-5
Cambrian & Clydach Vale BG Club - Rhyl FC	3-1 pen
Aberystwyth Town FC - Cardiff Metropolitan U. FC	1-3
Llangefni Town FC - Llandudno FC	1-3
Bangor City FC - Caernarfon Town FC	1-2

Quarter-Finals [01-02.03.2019]

Caernarfon Town FC - Connah's Quay Nomads FC	1-2
Bala Town FC - Cardiff Metropolitan University FC	0-1 aet
Llandudno FC - The New Saints FC	1-8
Barry Town United FC - Cambrian & Clydach Vale	3-2

Semi-Finals [30-31.03.2019]			
The New Saints FC - Barry Town United FC	2-0	Cardiff Metropolitan - Connah's Quay Nomads FC	0-3

Final

05.05.2019; Rhosymedre Stadium, Rhosymedre; Referee: David Howard Morgan; Attendance: 1,256
The New Saints FC - Connah's Quay Nomads FC **3-0(2-0)**

The New Saints: Paul Harrison, Jack Bodenham, Chris Marriott (60.Joash Nembhard), Blaine Hudson, Kane Lewis (74.Simon Spender), Jon Routledge, Ryan Brobbel, Daniel Redmond, Jamie Mullan, Gregory Alexander Draper (81.Dean Ebbe), Adrian Cieślewicz. Trainer: Scott Ruscoe (England).

Connah's Quay Nomad: John Danby, John Disney, George Horan, Danny Harrison, Danny Holmes, Callum Morris, Declan Poole, Jay Owen (87.Adam Barton), Michael Wilde, Jamie Insall (69.Andrew Owens), Michael Bakare (46.Ryan Wignall). Trainer: Andrew Morrison (Scotland).

Goals: 1-0 Gregory Alexander Draper (7), 2-0 Ryan Brobbel (33), 3-0 Ryan Brobbel (62).

THE CLUBS 2018/2019

Please note: matches and goals includes statistics of both regular season and play-offs (Championship, Relegation and Europa League Play-offs).

Aberystwyth Town Football Club

Founded: 1884
Stadium: Park Avenue, Aberystwyth (5,000)

Goalkeepers:	**DOB**	**M**	**(s)**	**G**
Leigh Jenkins	16.10.1991	5		
Terry McCormick	25.09.1983	26		
Adam Walters	21.09.1995	1		
Defenders:	**DOB**	**M**	**(s)**	**G**
Wes Baynes	12.10.1988	30		4
Steffan Edwards	10.10.1989	28	(1)	
Alan Goodall	02.12.1981	15	(2)	
Lee Jenkins	28.06.1979	11	(5)	1
Carwyn Jones		3		
Carwyn Morgan		1		
Declan Walker (IRL)	01.03.1992	30		6
Ryan Wollacott (ENG)	01.12.1994	31		3
Midfielders:	**DOB**	**M**	**(s)**	**G**
Niall Coleridge		1	(4)	
Harry Cottam		1		
Ryan Edwards	25.05.1994	28	(1)	
Matthew Jones	14.07.1999	30		
Geoff Kellaway (ENG)	07.04.1986	19	(11)	9
Jamie McDaid	29.03.1994		(9)	1
Joe Phillips	20.10.1994	12	(13)	1
Jack Rimmer	29.03.1999	4	(8)	
Alec Williams	19.05.1987		(1)	
Forwards:	**DOB**	**M**	**(s)**	**G**
Porya Ahmadi (IRN)	08.01.1993	16	(5)	5
Nashawn Blake	14.12.1996		(7)	
Paulo Mendes	08.07.1993	26	(3)	3
Ashley Ruane (ENG)	25.06.1985	24	(4)	6
Marc Williams	27.07.1988	10		4
Trainer:	**DOB**	**M**		
Seamus Heath (NIR)	06.12.1961	4		
Gavin Allen [03.09.2018]	17.06.1976	24		
Matthew Bishop [24.03.2019]	15.09.1973	4		

Bala Town Football Club

Founded: 1880
Stadium: Maes Tegid Stadium, Bala (3,000)

Goalkeepers:	**DOB**	**M**	**(s)**	**G**
Keighan Jones	04.04.1997	4		
Ashley Morris	31.07.1984	30		
Defenders:	**DOB**	**M**	**(s)**	**G**
Andrew Burns (IRL)	02.07.1993	33	(1)	1
Evan Horwood (ENG)	10.03.1986	10	(15)	1
Stuart Jones (ENG)	28.08.1986	21	(2)	1
Stuart J. Jones	14.03.1984	20		
Shaun Kelly (ENG)	11.12.1988	3	(2)	
Anthony Miley	30.08.1992	24		
Sean Smith (ENG)	12.12.1994	33		2
Anthony Stephens	21.01.1994	8	(2)	1
Midfielders:	**DOB**	**M**	**(s)**	**G**
Nathan Burke (ENG)	15.09.1995	32	(2)	1
Danny Gosset	30.09.1994	15	(7)	
Henry Jones	18.09.1993	32	(1)	14
Rob Pearson (ENG)	16.11.1990	7	(5)	
Christian Seargeant	13.09.1986	4		
Ryan Valentine	19.08.1982		(1)	
Forwards:	**DOB**	**M**	**(s)**	**G**
Joe Edwards			(1)	
Mike Hayes (ENG)	21.11.1987	12	(11)	3
Ian Sheridan (ENG)	12.03.1989	8	(17)	1
Kieran Smith (ENG)	03.06.1992	23	(4)	4
Steven Tames (ENG)	19.01.1992	24		17
Chris Venables	23.07.1985	29		12
Trainer:	**DOB**	**M**		
Colin Caton	22.08.1970	34		

Barry Town United Football Club

Founded: 1912 (*as Barry AFC*)
Stadium: Jenner Park, Barry (3,500)

Goalkeepers:	**DOB**	**M**	**(s)**	**G**
Oliver Davies	31.12.1994	1		
Mike Lewis	04.04.1989	31		
Defenders:	**DOB**	**M**	**(s)**	**G**
Rhys Abbruzzese	23.03.1998	3	(1)	
Luke Cooper	02.04.1993	31		1
Lewis Cosslett	03.10.1989	8		
Chris Hugh	22.01.1992	30		3
Paul Morgan	28.06.1994	9	(2)	
Curtis Watkins	11.09.1995	25	(1)	1
Midfielders:	**DOB**	**M**	**(s)**	**G**
Tom Fry	31.05.1997	9	(14)	1
Michael George			(1)	
Louis Gerrard	04.09.1992	2	(16)	
Clayton Green	27.02.1994	23	(5)	2
Troy Greening (ENG)	17.04.1993	27	(5)	
Marcus Jones	24.06.1974	2	(4)	1
Robbie Patten	29.11.1996	27	(1)	1
Evan Press	26.06.2000		(5)	
Macauley Southam-Hales	02.02.1996	21		1
Forwards:	**DOB**	**M**	**(s)**	**G**
Jordan Cotterill	20.10.1988	16	(5)	7
Drew Fahiya	17.04.1988	5	(16)	2
Jonathan Hood	07.02.1991	24	(1)	7
Kayne McLaggon	21.09.1990	30	(2)	14
Samuel Snaith	05.05.2000		(3)	
Momodou Touray	30.07.1999	28	(3)	13
Trainer:	**DOB**	**M**		
Gavin Chesterfield		32		

Caernarfon Town Football Club

Founded: 1937
Stadium: The Oval, Caernarfon (3,000)

Goalkeepers:	**DOB**	**M**	**(s)**	**G**
Nick Bould	07.09.1995	2	(1)	
Alex Ramsay	15.07.1993	31		
Defenders:	**DOB**	**M**	**(s)**	**G**
Gareth Edwards	20.07.1983	26	(1)	1
Noah Edwards	30.05.1996	20	(3)	2
Ben Maher (ENG)	28.09.1995	8	(6)	
Rhys Roberts	17.07.1985	22	(3)	
Clive Williams	01.01.1991	4	(3)	
Joe Williams	17.02.1989	24	(3)	
Midfielders:	**DOB**	**M**	**(s)**	**G**
Sion Bradley	20.02.1998	17	(13)	5
Jamie Crowther	10.02.1992	27	(2)	
Gareth Evans	29.04.1987	30	(2)	1
Dion Owen	23.05.2001		(1)	
Kevin Roberts	29.12.1982	2	(10)	
Ross Stephens	28.05.1985	4	(4)	
Leo Smith	15.05.1998	7	(1)	
Ryan Williams	10.05.1998	29		
Forwards:	**DOB**	**M**	**(s)**	**G**
Jamie Breeze	10.01.1992	26	(6)	5
Danny Brookwell	09.03.1993	16	(11)	6
Nathan Craig	25.10.1991	28	(2)	14
Cai Jones	03.10.1992	14	(14)	5
Darren Thomas	20.01.1987	26	(4)	7
Trainer:	**DOB**	**M**		
Sean Eardley		33		

Cardiff Metropolitan University Football Club

Founded: 2000 (*as UWIC Inter Cardiff*)
Stadium: Cyncoed Campus, Cardiff (1,620)

Goalkeepers:	**DOB**	**M**	**(s)**	**G**
Esa Aalto (FIN)	08.02.1994	4	(1)	
Daniel Evans	08.02.1997	1	(1)	
Will Fuller	07.07.1993	6		
Alex Lang	10.10.1999	20		
Max Manson		3		
Defenders:	**DOB**	**M**	**(s)**	**G**
Liam Black	02.07.1994	6	(2)	1
Matt Clubb		1		
Louis Hadergjonaj		1		
Emlyn Lewis	14.06.1996	33		
Kyle McCarthy	12.04.1993	33		3
Dylan Rees	17.09.1996	30		
Matt Swindlehurst	01.02.1997	2	(1)	
Guto Williams	10.05.2000	14	(6)	
Bradley Woolridge	16.12.1992	21		
Midfielders:	**DOB**	**M**	**(s)**	**G**
Chris Baker	29.11.1993	30	(1)	4
Ben Bowler	12.03.1995	6	(3)	
Charlie Corsby	14.10.1991	5		2
Joel Edwards (ENG)	18.08.1991	19	(1)	
Ioan Evans	30.05.1997		(1)	
Will Evans	01.07.1997	26	(3)	6
Rhydian Morgan	19.06.1999	13	(4)	
Matt Neale	10.11.1997	8	(8)	
Dion Phillips	12.09.1998	1	(8)	
Sam Pashen		1		
Gruff Stead			(1)	
Rhys Thomas	20.12.1997	3	(7)	2
Forwards:	**DOB**	**M**	**(s)**	**G**
Eliot Evans	26.11.1991	31		10
Brad Flay	29.01.1997	1	(2)	
Gwion Howell	12.02.1997	1	(2)	
Harry Owen (ENG)	15.02.1996	9	(14)	4
Tim Parker	19.03.1996	1	(3)	2
Adam Roscrow	17.02.1995	23	(2)	15
Samuel Snaith	05.05.2000	15	(3)	6
Dan Spencer	19.05.1993	6	(3)	1
Liam Warman	01.05.1999		(4)	
Trainer:	**DOB**	**M**		
Christian Edwards	25.11.1975			

Carmarthen Town Association Football Club

Founded: 1950
Stadium: Richmond Park, Carmarthen (3,000)

Goalkeepers:	**DOB**	**M**	**(s)**	**G**
Lee Idzi	08.02.1988	32		
Defenders:	**DOB**	**M**	**(s)**	**G**
Lewis Baldwin		7	(2)	
Declan Carroll	04.07.1993	16	(9)	3
Luke Cummings	25.10.1991	21	(5)	1
Mael Davies	10.10.1998	29		2
Craig Hanford	08.07.1984	4	(12)	
Jordan Knott	13.09.1993	21		1
Lee Surman	03.04.1986	28	(1)	
Dave Vincent	17.06.1990	24	(3)	
Midfielders:	**DOB**	**M**	**(s)**	**G**
Dwayne Coultress	25.05.1994	2	(2)	
Lewis Harling	11.06.1992	8	(1)	
Ceri Morgan	22.01.1991	27	(1)	2
Aidan O'Kelly (ENG)	13.08.1997	10	(2)	
Liam Thomas	06.11.1991	32		23
Jordan Vickers		15	(13)	
Greg Walters	10.01.1995	27	(1)	2
Forwards:	**DOB**	**M**	**(s)**	**G**
Luke Bowen	07.03.1988	27		11
Sean Hanbury	05.08.1999	13	(10)	2
Tyrrell Webbe	27.12.1989	9		
Jay Woodford			(11)	
Trainer:	**DOB**	**M**		
Neil Smothers	08.12.1977	32		

Cefn Druids Association Football Club Cefn Mawr

Founded: 1872
Stadium: The Rock Stadium, Wrexham (3,000)

Goalkeepers:	**DOB**	**M**	**(s)**	**G**
Michael Jones (ENG)	03.12.1987	30		
Joel Thompson	16.05.1997	2		
Defenders:	**DOB**	**M**	**(s)**	**G**
Naim Arsan	14.12.1993	28	(2)	2
Neil Ashton (ENG)	15.01.1985	25		2
Jordan Evans	23.09.1995	17	(7)	4
Adam Hesp	30.08.1991		(1)	
Alun Morris	13.04.1989	3	(1)	
Nathan Peate	02.05.1991	28		4
Moussa Samassa (FRA)	07.08.1996	1	(1)	
Aaron Simpson	19.10.1995	19		1
Midfielders:	**DOB**	**M**	**(s)**	**G**
Ben Burrows	06.10.1998	1		
Iwan Cartwright	09.08.1996	24	(4)	
Ilan ap Gareth (ENG)	11.05.1999		(8)	
Danny Gosset	30.09.1994	9		
Fisnik Hajdari	16.03.1997	9	(6)	2
Ryan Kershaw	21.09.1995	27	(1)	2
Virgil Moutaud (FRA)	06.11.1992		(1)	
Alec Mudimu (ZIM)	08.04.1995	19	(5)	1
Matty Owen	23.07.1994	23	(1)	1
Forwards:	**DOB**	**M**	**(s)**	**G**
James Davies	02.10.1993	23	(2)	8
Jack Kenny	14.10.1991	10		6
John Owen	18.08.1992	9	(1)	1
Arkadiusz Piskorski (POL)	24.04.1990	14	(9)	2
Dean Rittenberg	13.05.1996	31		8
Jonathon Taylor	12.05.1989		(1)	
Trainer:	**DOB**	**M**		
Huw Griffiths	09.02.1977	32		

Connah's Quay Nomads Football Club

Founded: 1946
Stadium: Deeside Stadium, Connah's Quay (1,500)

Goalkeepers:	**DOB**	**M**	**(s)**	**G**
Lewis Brass	26.08.1996	3		
John Danby (ENG)	20.09.1981	27		
John Rushton	17.05.1990	2		
Defenders:	**DOB**	**M**	**(s)**	**G**
John Disney	15.05.1992	30	(1)	
Priestley Farquharson	15.03.1997	6	(1)	
Danny Holmes	06.01.1989	27		
George Horan (ENG)	18.02.1982	22		1
Jake Phillips	31.01.1997	4	(3)	
Jonny Spittle (ENG)	13.08.1994	2	(7)	
Laurence Wilson	10.10.1986	13	(3)	1
Midfielders:	**DOB**	**M**	**(s)**	**G**
Adam Barton (NIR)	07.01.1991	8		2
Danny Harrison (ENG)	04.11.1982	19	(2)	1
Robert Hughes	22.04.1992	11	(14)	3
Craig Jones	12.12.1989	2	(2)	
Callum Morris (ENG)	01.09.1992	27	(3)	14
Jay Owen	14.01.1991	2	(5)	2
Michael Parker	31.10.1987	16	(4)	3
Declan Poole (ENG)	05.09.1995	17	(6)	3
Ryan Wignall (ENG)	12.03.1989	21	(2)	5
Forwards:	**DOB**	**M**	**(s)**	**G**
Michael Bakare (ENG)	01.12.1986	24	(6)	14
Connor Harwood	02.02.2000		(3)	1
Jamie Insall (ENG)	01.03.1992	2	(1)	
Jack Kenny	14.10.1991	2	(4)	
Andrew Owens (ENG)	15.10.1989	21	(6)	9
Michael Wilde	27.08.1983	24	(2)	13
Nathan Woolfe (ENG)	06.10.1988	2	(10)	3
Trainer:	**DOB**	**M**		
Andrew Morrison (SCO)	30.07.1970	32		

Llandudno Football Club

Founded: 1988
Stadium: Park MBi Maesdu Stadium, Llandudno (1,013)

Goalkeepers:	**DOB**	**M**	**(s)**	**G**
Dave Guinn			(1)	
Connor Roberts	08.12.1992	4		
Shaun Pearson	16.08.1990	28		
Defenders:	**DOB**	**M**	**(s)**	**G**
Kai Edwards	29.01.1991	30		
Mike Pearson	19.01.1988	26		2
Ieuan Hewitt		5	(3)	
Dafydd Thomas		2	(3)	
Steve Thomas		26	(1)	1
Midfielders:	**DOB**	**M**	**(s)**	**G**
Yalany Baio (GNB)	10.10.1994	10		2
Ben Clark	14.10.2000	10	(2)	1
Mark Connolly (ENG)	02.07.1984	20	(8)	2
Sameron Dool (ENG)	07.06.1999	7	(1)	2
Zebb Edwards	08.05.1999	2	(1)	
Zyaac Edwards	25.04.1994	20		
Jay Gibbs	19.10.1992	1		
Danny Hughes	28.05.1988	31		1
Adam Montgomery		2		
Tom Owens	25.09.1991	2	(2)	
Leo Smith	15.05.1998	15	(4)	1
Gary Taylor-Fletcher (ENG)	04.06.1981	2		3
Telor Williams		2	(8)	
Forwards:	**DOB**	**M**	**(s)**	**G**
Les Davies	29.10.1984	10	(2)	1
Alfons Fosu-Mensah (NED)	04.03.1994	1	(3)	1
George Harry	07.06.1999	24	(7)	6
Aron Hughes	15.02.2000		(1)	
Osian Jones			(1)	
Toby Jones	25.08.1992	25	(3)	1
John Owen	18.08.1992	13	(3)	2
Ryan Wade (ENG)	22.01.1988	2		
Alun Webb	28.12.1993	22	(7)	6
Matthew Williams	05.11.1982	10	(2)	1
Trainer:	**DOB**	**M**		
Iwan Williams	28.03.1985	32		

Llanelli Town Association Football Club

Founded: 1896
Stadium: Stebonheath Park, Llanelli (3,700)

Goalkeepers:	**DOB**	**M**	**(s)**	**G**
Scott Coughlan	10.02.1999	12		
Oliver Davies	31.12.1994	20		
Kai Rees			(2)	
Defenders:	**DOB**	**M**	**(s)**	**G**
Daniel Alfei	23.02.1992	18		
Lee Bevan	10.07.1987	12		1
Carlos Indja		5		
Jordan Davies	05.07.1990	22	(1)	
Joe Hunt	18.11.1999	9		1
Callum Howard		1		
Kurtis March	30.03.1993	17	(1)	2
James Parry	27.05.1995	1		
Cai Smith	03.09.1998	2	(1)	
Scott Tancock	29.12.1993	24		
Chris Thomas	16.01.1983	18	(1)	
Midfielders:	**DOB**	**M**	**(s)**	**G**
Leon Britton	16.09.1982	2		
Joe Clarke	13.09.1991	27		3
Joe Dyer		3	(3)	
Lenny Evans		5	(3)	1
Anthony Finselbach	05.09.1991	15	(2)	
Michael George		18	(1)	3
Kyle Graves	01.04.1989	2		
Chris Jones	14.02.1990	31	(1)	7
Jordan Jones	04.09.1998	4	(1)	
Ross Jones	17.02.1990	11	(5)	
Reasat Khaton (BAN)	01.08.1989	1	(9)	
Luke Morgan	10.10.1991	1	(2)	
Anthony Nelson	31.07.1997	7	(9)	
Jamie Owen		6	(4)	
Robbie Thomas		1	(1)	
Forwards:	**DOB**	**M**	**(s)**	**G**
Jordan Follows	23.03.1990	13	(4)	1
Tristan Jenkins		5	(12)	1
Mark Jones	01.05.1989	5	(2)	
James Loveridge	16.05.1994	27	(1)	9
Emile Ngoy (COD)	02.02.1997	6	(3)	
Billie-Jay Wright			(1)	
Trainer:	**DOB**	**M**		
Andy Hill	18.10.1978	32		

Newtown Association Football Club

Founded: 1875
Stadium: Latham Park, Newtown (5,000)

Goalkeepers:	**DOB**	**M**	**(s)**	**G**
David Jones	03.02.1990	30		
Jack Perry (ENG)	31.10.1997	3	(2)	
Defenders:	**DOB**	**M**	**(s)**	**G**
Ben Bailey (ENG)	03.02.1991	16		1
Sam Barnes (ENG)	16.10.1991	9		
Jake Cook (ENG)	06.10.1995	2	(3)	
Kieran Mills-Evans	11.10.1992	31		1
Callum Roberts	16.10.1998	31		2
Craig T. Williams	21.12.1987	23	(3)	2
Midfielders:	**DOB**	**M**	**(s)**	**G**
Jay Denny (USA)	06.01.1986	32	(1)	
Alex Fletcher (ENG)	17.11.1996	33		3
Tom Goodwin	12.01.1990	1	(7)	
George Hughes (ENG)	23.03.1999	11	(2)	1
Joe Kenton	19.05.1998	25	(7)	5
Steven Leslie (SCO)	05.11.1987	20	(10)	7
Sam Phillips	24.02.1999	9	(14)	1
Forwards:	**DOB**	**M**	**(s)**	**G**
Porya Ahmadi (IRN)	08.01.1993	8	(3)	4
Luke Boundford	30.01.1988	14	(16)	6
Ethan Jones (ENG)	03.04.1998	6	(11)	1
Neil Mitchell (ENG)	01.04.1988	28	(1)	8
Nicky Rushton	03.02.1992	31		11
Trainer:	**DOB**	**M**		
Chris Hughes (SCO)	21.04.1979	33		

The New Saints of Oswestry Town & Llansantffraid Football Club

Founded: 1959
Stadium: Park Hall Stadium, Oswestry (2,000)

Goalkeepers:	**DOB**	**M**	**(s)**	**G**
Paul Harrison (ENG)	18.12.1984	32		
Defenders:	**DOB**	**M**	**(s)**	**G**
Jack Bodenham	29.09.1999	9	(1)	1
Ben Cabango	30.05.2000	16		
Kane Lewis	17.03.1998	9	(4)	1
Blaine Hudson (ENG)	28.10.1991	25		3
Chris Marriott (ENG)	24.09.1989	28		
Joash Nembhard (ENG)	13.03.1998	8	(2)	1
Simon Spender	15.11.1985	26		1
Midfielders:	**DOB**	**M**	**(s)**	**G**
Ryan Brobbel (NIR)	05.03.1993	22	(1)	15
Ben Clark	14.10.2000		(1)	
Aeron Edwards	16.02.1988	24		12
Josh Hmami (ENG)	22.03.2000		(3)	
Tom Holland (IRL)	22.04.1997	28	(1)	
Jon Routledge (ENG)	23.11.1989	25	(1)	2
Daniel Redmond (ENG)	02.03.1991	23	(1)	2
Christian Seargeant (ENG)	13.09.1986	3	(4)	2
Billy Whitehouse (ENG)	13.06.1996	1	(3)	
Forwards:	**DOB**	**M**	**(s)**	**G**
Kurtis Byrne (IRL)	09.04.1990	15	(15)	12
Adrian Cieslewicz (POL)	16.11.1990	12	(13)	4
Gregory Alexander Draper (NZL)	13.08.1989	10	(19)	27
Dean Ebbe (IRL)	16.07.1994	8	(13)	5
Jamie Mullan (ENG)	10.02.1988	28	(1)	10
Trainer:	**DOB**	**M**		
Scott Ruscoe (ENG)	15.12.1977	32		

SECOND LEVEL

Welsh Football League Division One 2018/2019

Cymru Alliance League

1.	Airbus UK Broughton FC (*Promoted*)	30	24	4	2	75	-	20	76
2.	Flint Town United FC	30	17	7	6	52	-	31	58
3.	Porthmadog FC	30	17	6	7	60	-	32	57
4.	Bangor City FC	30	16	3	11	68	-	48	51
5.	Rhyl FC	30	16	3	11	55	-	44	51
6.	Guilsfield FC	30	13	6	11	43	-	45	45
7.	Ruthin Town FC	30	13	4	13	46	-	47	43
8.	Buckley Town FC	30	12	6	12	51	-	50	42
9.	Prestatyn Town FC	30	11	6	13	52	-	49	39
10.	Gresford Athletic FC	30	10	9	11	42	-	46	39
11.	Conwy Borough FC	30	9	9	12	46	-	42	36
12.	Llanrhaeadr FC	30	10	2	18	34	-	71	32
13.	Penrhyncoch FC	30	7	9	14	35	-	44	30
14.	Holywell Town FC (*Relegated*)	30	8	6	16	38	-	58	30
15.	Denbigh Town FC (*Relegated*)	30	9	2	19	37	-	65	29
16.	Holyhead Hotspur FC (*Relegated*)	30	5	4	21	29	-	71	19

Welsh Football League Division One

1.	Pen-y-Bont FC Bridgent (*Promoted*)	30	25	5	0	81	-	22	80
2.	Cambrian & Clydach Vale Boys & Girls Club	30	18	6	6	58	-	32	60
3.	Haverfordwest County AFC	30	16	6	8	69	-	34	54
4.	Afan Lido FC Port Talbot	30	15	6	9	68	-	59	51
5.	Goytre United FC	30	15	5	10	52	-	39	50
6.	Cwmamman United FC Glanaman	30	14	8	8	55	-	55	50
7.	Llantwit Major FC	30	14	6	10	46	-	37	48
8.	Briton Ferry Llansawel AFC	30	12	6	12	44	-	50	42
9.	Ammanford AFC	30	10	6	14	51	-	57	36
10.	Cwmbran Celtic FC	30	10	6	14	49	-	57	36
11.	Pontypridd Town AFC Cardiff	30	9	6	15	52	-	66	33
12.	Undy Athletic FC	30	8	7	15	51	-	64	31
13.	Port Talbot Town FC (*Relegated*)	30	6	11	13	39	-	50	29
14.	Taff's Well AFC	30	7	4	19	33	-	62	25
15.	Goytre AFC Penperlleni (*Relegated*)	30	6	6	18	39	-	65	24
16.	Ton Pentre FC (*Relegated*)	30	6	4	20	38	-	76	22

NATIONAL TEAM

INTERNATIONAL MATCHES
(16.07.2018 – 15.07.2019)

06.09.2018	Cardiff	Wales - Republic of Ireland	4-1(3-0)	(UNL)
09.09.2018	Aarhus	Denmark - Wales	2-0(1-0)	(UNL)
11.10.2018	Cardiff	Wales - Spain	1-4(0-3)	(F)
16.10.2018	Dublin	Republic of Ireland - Wales	0-1(0-0)	(UNL)
16.11.2018	Cardiff	Wales - Denmark	1-2(0-1)	(UNL)
20.11.2018	Elbasan	Albania - Wales	1-0(0-0)	(F)
20.03.2019	Wrexham	Wales - Trinidad and Tobago	1-0(0-0)	(F)
24.03.2019	Cardiff	Wales - Slovakia	1-0(1-0)	(ECQ)
08.06.2019	Osijek	Croatia - Wales	2-1(1-0)	(ECQ)
11.06.2019	Budapest	Hungary - Wales	1-0(0-0)	(ECQ)

06.09.2018 WALES - REPUBLIC OF IRELAND 4-1(3-0) UEFA Nations League B, Group 4
Cardiff City Stadium, Cardiff; Referee: Clément Turpin (France); Attendance: 25,657
WAL: Wayne Robert Hennessey, Ashley Errol Williams (Cap), Benjamin Thomas Davies (81.Paul Dummett), Ethan Kwame Colm Raymond Ampadu (67.Matthew Robert Smith), Christopher James Mepham, Joseph Michael Allen, Aaron James Ramsey, Thomas Morris Lawrence, David Robert Brooks, Connor Richard John Roberts, Gareth Frank Bale (75.Tyler D'Whyte Roberts). Trainer: Ryan Joseph Giggs.
Goals: Thomas Morris Lawrence (6), Gareth Frank Bale (18), Aaron James Ramsey (37), Connor Richard John Roberts (55).

09.09.2018 DENMARK - WALES 2-0(1-0) UEFA Nations League B, Group 4
Ceres Park & Arena, Aarhus; Referee: Deniz Aytekin (Germany); Attendance: 17,506
WAL: Wayne Robert Hennessey, Christopher Ross Gunter, James Grant Chester, Benjamin Thomas Davies, Ethan Kwame Colm Raymond Ampadu (72.Tyler D'Whyte Roberts), Christopher James Mepham, Joseph Michael Allen, Aaron James Ramsey, Thomas Morris Lawrence (79.Benjamin Woodburn), Connor Richard John Roberts (59.David Robert Brooks), Gareth Frank Bale (Cap). Trainer: Ryan Joseph Giggs.

11.10.2018 WALES - SPAIN 1-4(0-3) Friendly International
Principality Stadium, Cardiff; Referee: Anthony Taylor (England); Attendance: 50,232
WAL: Wayne Robert Hennessey, Christopher Ross Gunter, Ashley Errol Williams (Cap) (46.James Grant Chester), Declan Christopher John (62.Thomas Morris Lawrence), Benjamin Thomas Davies (62.Ashley Darel Jazz Richards), Ethan Kwame Colm Raymond Ampadu (50.Andrew Philip King), Joseph Michael Allen (62.Matthew Robert Smith), Aaron James Ramsey, Harry Wilson (46.David Robert Brooks), Connor Richard John Roberts, Samuel Michael Vokes. Trainer: Ryan Joseph Giggs.
Goal: Samuel Michael Vokes (89).

16.10.2018 REPUBLIC OF IRELAND - WALES 0-1(0-0) UEFA Nations League B, Group 4
Aviva Stadium, Dublin; Referee: Björn Kuipers (Netherlands); Attendance: 38,321
WAL: Wayne Robert Hennessey, Ashley Errol Williams (Cap), James Grant Chester, Benjamin Thomas Davies, Joseph Michael Allen, Thomas Morris Lawrence, Harry Wilson (85.Christopher Ross Gunter), David Robert Brooks (87.Andrew Philip King), Matthew Robert Smith (75.George Stanley Thomas), Connor Richard John Roberts, Tyler D'Whyte Roberts. Trainer: Ryan Joseph Giggs.
Goal: Harry Wilson (58).

16.11.2018 WALES - DENMARK 1-2(0-1) UEFA Nations League B, Group 4
Cardiff City Stadium, Cardiff; Referee: Ivan Kružliak (Slovakia); Attendance: 32,354
WAL: Wayne Robert Hennessey, Ashley Errol Williams (Cap), James Grant Chester (50.Ethan Kwame Colm Raymond Ampadu), Paul Dummett (39.Christopher Ross Gunter), Joseph Michael Allen, Aaron James Ramsey, Thomas Morris Lawrence, David Robert Brooks, Tyler D'Whyte Roberts (68.Harry Wilson),
Connor Richard John Roberts, Gareth Frank Bale. Trainer: Ryan Joseph Giggs.
Goal: Gareth Frank Bale (89).

20.11.2018 ALBANIA - WALES 1-0(0-0) Friendly International
Elbasan Arena, Elbasan; Referee: Dejan Jakimovski (Macedonia); Attendance: 3,000
WAL: Daniel Ward, Christopher Ross Gunter (Cap), James Alexander Lawrence, Thomas Alun Lockyer, Andrew Philip King, Joseph Michael Allen (56.Aaron James Ramsey), Daniel Owen James (56.Benjamin Woodburn), Harry Wilson, David Robert Brooks (59.Gareth Frank Bale), Connor Richard John Roberts (78.Kieron Samuel Freeman), Samuel Michael Vokes (78.Rabbi Matondo). Trainer: Ryan Joseph Giggs.

20.03.2019 WALES - TRINIDAD AND TOBAGO 1-0(0-0) Friendly International
The Racecourse, Wrexham; Referee: Timothy Marshall (Northern Ireland); Attendance: 10,326
WAL: Daniel Ward (46.Adam Rhys Davies), Christopher Ross Gunter, Neil John Taylor, Ashley Errol Williams (Cap) (61.James Alexander Lawrence), Paul Dummett (61.Declan Christopher John), Lee Evans, William Robert Vaulks, Benjamin Woodburn, Ryan Peter Hedges, George Stanley Thomas, Tyler D'Whyte Roberts (71.Rabbi Matondo). Trainer: Ryan Joseph Giggs.
Goal: Benjamin Woodburn (90+2).

24.03.2019 WALES - SLOVAKIA 1-0(1-0) 16th EC. Qualifiers
Cardiff City Stadium, Cardiff; Referee: Felix Zwayer (Germany); Attendance: 31,617
WAL: Wayne Robert Hennessey, Benjamin Thomas Davies, James Alexander Lawrence, Christopher James Mepham, Joseph Michael Allen, Matthew Robert Smith, Harry Wilson (87.William Robert Vaulks), Daniel Owen James (72.Ashley Errol Williams), David Robert Brooks (60.Tyler D'Whyte Roberts), Connor Richard John Roberts, Gareth Frank Bale (Cap). Trainer: Ryan Joseph Giggs.
Goal: Daniel Owen James (5).

08.06.2019 CROATIA - WALES 2-1(1-0) 16th EC. Qualifiers
Stadion Gradski Vrt, Osijek; Referee: István Kovács (Romania); Attendance: 17,061
WAL: Wayne Robert Hennessey, Benjamin Thomas Davies, James Alexander Lawrence, Christopher James Mepham, Joseph Michael Allen, William Robert Vaulks (66.Ethan Kwame Colm Raymond Ampadu), Daniel Owen James (79.Rabbi Matondo), Harry Wilson, Matthew Robert Smith (65.David Robert Brooks), Connor Richard John Roberts, Gareth Frank Bale (Cap). Trainer: Ryan Joseph Giggs.
Goal: David Robert Brooks (77).

11.06.2019 **HUNGARY - WALES** **1-0(0-0)** 16th EC. Qualifiers

Groupama Aréna, Budapest; Referee: Matej Jug (Slovenia); Attendance: 18,350

WAL: Wayne Robert Hennessey, Christopher Ross Gunter, Ashley Errol Williams (Cap), Benjamin Thomas Davies, James Alexander Lawrence, Ethan Kwame Colm Raymond Ampadu (54.Matthew Robert Smith), Joseph Michael Allen, Thomas Morris Lawrence (79.Samuel Michael Vokes), Daniel Owen James, David Robert Brooks (73.Harry Wilson), Gareth Frank Bale. Trainer: Ryan Joseph Giggs.

NATIONAL TEAM PLAYERS
(16.07.2018 – 15.07.2019)

Name	DOB	Caps	Goals	2018/2019:	*Club*
Goalkeepers					
Adam Rhys DAVIES	17.07.1992	**1**	**0**	2019:	*Barnsley FC (ENG)*
Wayne Robert HENNESSEY	24.01.1987	**84**	**0**	2018/2019:	*Crystal Palace FC London (ENG)*
Daniel WARD	22.06.1993	**6**	**0**	2018/2019:	*Leicester City FC (ENG)*
Defenders					
James Grant CHESTER	23.01.1989	**35**	**0**	2018/2019:	*Aston Villa FC Birmingham (ENG)*
Benjamin Thomas DAVIES	24.04.1993	**46**	**0**	2018/2019:	*Tottenham Hotspur FC London (ENG)*
Paul DUMMETT	26.09.1991	**5**	**0**	2018/2019:	*Newcastle United FC (ENG)*
Kieron Samuel FREEMAN	21.03.1992	**1**	**0**	2018:	*Sheffield United FC (ENG)*
Christopher Ross GUNTER	21.07.1989	**95**	**0**	2018/2019:	*Reading FC (ENG)*
Declan Christopher JOHN	30.06.1995	**7**	**0**	2018/2019:	*Swansea City AFC*
James Alexander LAWRENCE	22.08.1992	**5**	**0**	2018/2019:	*RSC Anderlecht Bruxelles (BEL)*
Thomas Alun LOCKYER	03.12.1994	**5**	**0**	2018:	*Bristol Rovers FC (ENG)*
Christopher James MEPHAM	05.10.1997	**2**	**0**	2018: 22.01.2019->	*Brentford FC (ENG)* *AFC Bournemouth (ENG)*
Ashley Darel Jazz RICHARDS	12.04.1991	**14**	**0**	2018:	*Cardiff City FC*
Connor Richard John ROBERTS	23.09.1995	**10**	**1**	2018/2019:	*Swansea City AFC*
Neil John TAYLOR	07.02.1989	**42**	**1**	2019:	*Aston Villa FC Birmingham (ENG)*
Ashley Errol WILLIAMS	23.08.1984	**86**	**2**	2018/2019:	*Stoke City FC (ENG)*
Midfielders					
Joseph Michael ALLEN	14.03.1990	**51**	**2**	2018/2019:	*Stoke City FC (ENG)*
Ethan Kwame Colm Raymond AMPADU	14.09.2000	**8**	**0**	2018/2019:	*Chelsea FC London (ENG)*
David Robert BROOKS	08.07.1997	**12**	**1**	2018/2019:	*AFC Bournemouth (ENG)*
Lee EVANS	24.07.1994	**4**	**0**	2018/2019:	*Wigan Athletic FC (ENG)*
Ryan Peter HEDGES	08.07.1995	**3**	**0**	2019:	*Barnsley FC (ENG)*
Daniel Owen JAMES	10.11.1997	**4**	**1**	2018/2019:	*Swansea City AFC*
Andrew Philip KING	29.10.1988	**50**	**2**	2018/2019:	*Leicester City FC (ENG)*
Aaron James RAMSEY	26.12.1990	**58**	**14**	2018:	*Arsenal FC London (ENG)*
Matthew Robert SMITH	22.11.1999	**7**	**0**	2018/2019:	*FC Twente Enschede (NED)*
William Robert VAULKS	13.09.1993	**3**	**0**	2019:	*Rotherham United FC (ENG)*
Harry WILSON	22.03.1997	**11**	**2**	2018/2019:	*Derby County FC (ENG)*
Forwards					
Gareth Frank BALE	16.07.1989	**77**	**31**	2018/2019:	*Real Madrid CF (ESP)*
Thomas Morris LAWRENCE	13.01.1994	**19**	**3**	2018/2019:	*Derby County FC (ENG)*
Rabbi MATONDO	09.09.2000	**3**	**0**	2018: 30.01.2019->	*Manchester City FC (ENG)* *FC Schalke 04 Gelsenkirchen 04 (GER)*
Tyler D'Whyte ROBERTS	12.01.1999	**6**	**0**	2018/2019:	*Leeds United FC (ENG)*
George Stanley THOMAS	24.03.1997	**3**	**0**	2018/2019:	*Scunthorpe United FC (ENG)*
Samuel Michael VOKES	21.10.1989	**62**	**11**	2018: 31.01.2019->	*Burnley FC (ENG)* *Stoke City FC (ENG)*
Benjamin WOODBURN	15.10.1999	**7**	**1**	2018: 09.01.2019->	*Sheffield United FC (ENG)* *Liverpool FC (ENG)*

National team coach

Ryan Joseph GIGGS [from 15.01.2018]	29.11.1973	13 M; 5 W; 1 D; 7 L; 16-14